HOLT McDOUGAL

Literature

Grade 12

WILLIAM SHAKESPEARE'S
MACBETH
DIRECTED BY MILES POTTER

NOVEMBER 25 - DECEMBER 2, 8:00 PM
DECEMBER 3, 2:00 PM & 8:00 PM
SIR JAMES DUNN THEATRE
DALHOUSIE ARTS CENTRE
BOX OFFICE: 494.3820
TICKETS: $12/$6 STUDENT/SENIOR
DALHOUSIE UNIVERSITY

COMMON
CORE

EDITION

Typeset in *The Sans* from LucasFonts.

Acknowledgments appear at the back of the book, following the Index of Titles and Authors.

ART CREDITS

COVER, TITLE PAGE

Front Cover, Title Page: (tc) © Dalhousie University Department of Theatre. Halifax, Nova Scotia; (tr) Image Asset Management Ltd./Superstock; (bc) Hulton Archive/Getty Images; (bkgd) Patrick Ingrand/Getty Images; (bl) Ken Kinzie/HMH Publishers.

Back Cover: (tl) Bettmann/Corbis; (br) Portrait of William Shakespeare (1907), Max Bihn. © Blue Lantern Studios/Corbis; (c) Elizabeth I. After oil by Zucchero. © Lebrecht Music and Arts Photo Library/Alamy; (bl) Science Museum/Science and Society Picture Library.

FM9: © Getty Images

FM39: © Age Fotostock America, Inc.

Art Credits are continued at the back of the book, following the Acknowledgments.

Printed in the U.S.A.

ISBN 978-0-547-61842-5

4 5 6 7 8 9 10   0868   20 19 18 17 16 15 14 13 12 11

4500312018   B C D E F G

HOLT McDOUGAL

Literature

Grade 12

Janet Allen

Arthur N. Applebee

Jim Burke

Douglas Carnine

Yvette Jackson

Carol Jago

Robert T. Jiménez

Judith A. Langer

Robert J. Marzano

Mary Lou McCloskey

Donna M. Ogle

Carol Booth Olson

Lydia Stack

Carol Ann Tomlinson

Special Contributor: Kylene Beers

SENIOR PROGRAM CONSULTANTS

JANET ALLEN Reading and Literacy Specialist; creator of the popular "It's Never Too Late"/"Reading for Life" Institutes. Dr. Allen is an internationally known consultant who specializes in literacy work with at-risk students. Her publications include *Tools for Content Literacy; It's Never Too Late: Leading Adolescents to Lifelong Learning; Yellow Brick Roads: Shared and Guided Paths to Independent Reading; Words, Words, Words: Teaching Vocabulary in Grades 4–12;* and *Testing 1, 2, 3 . . . Bridging Best Practice and High-Stakes Assessments.* Dr. Allen was a high school reading and English teacher for more than 20 years.

ARTHUR N. APPLEBEE Leading Professor, School of Education at the University at Albany, State University of New York; Director of the Center on English Learning and Achievement. During his varied career, Dr. Applebee has been both a researcher and a teacher, working in institutional settings with children with severe learning problems, in public schools, as a staff member of the National Council of Teachers of English, and in professional education. He was elected to the International Reading Hall of Fame and has received, among other honors, the David H. Russell Award for Distinguished Research in the Teaching of English.

JIM BURKE Lecturer and Author; Teacher of English at Burlingame High School, Burlingame, California. Mr. Burke is a popular presenter at educational conferences across the country and is the author of numerous books for teachers, including *School Smarts: The Four Cs of Academic Success; The English Teacher's Companion; Reading Reminders; Writing Reminders;* and *ACCESSing School: Teaching Struggling Readers to Achieve Academic and Personal Success.* He is the recipient of NCTE's Exemplary English Leadership Award and was inducted into the California Reading Association's Hall of Fame.

DOUGLAS CARNINE Professor of Education at the University of Oregon; Director of the Western Region Reading First Technical Assistance Center. Dr. Carnine is nationally known for his focus on research-based practices in education, especially curriculum designs that prepare instructors of K–12 students. He has received the Lifetime Achievement Award from the Council for Exceptional Children and the Ersted Award for outstanding teaching at the University of Oregon. Dr. Carnine frequently consults on educational policy with government groups, businesses, communities, and teacher unions.

YVETTE JACKSON Executive Director of the National Urban Alliance for Effective Education. Nationally recognized for her work in assessing the learning potential of underachieving urban students, Dr. Jackson is also a presenter for the Harvard Principal Center and is a member of the Differentiation Faculty of the Association for Supervision and Curriculum Development. Dr. Jackson's research focuses on literacy, gifted education, and cognitive mediation theory. She designed the Comprehensive Education Plan for the New York City Public Schools and has served as their Director of Gifted Programs.

CAROL JAGO Teacher of English with thirty-two years of experience at Santa Monica High School in California; Author and nationally known Lecturer; and Past President of the National Council of Teachers of English. With varied experience in standards assessment and secondary education, Ms. Jago is the author of numerous books on education and is active with the California Association of Teachers of English, editing its scholarly journal *California English* since 1996. Ms. Jago also served on the planning committee for the 2009 NAEP Framework and the 2011 NAEP Writing Framework.

ROBERT T. JIMÉNEZ Professor of Language, Literacy, and Culture at Vanderbilt University. Dr. Jiménez's research focuses on the language and literacy practices of Latino students. A former bilingual education teacher, he is now conducting research on how written language is thought about and used in contemporary Mexico. Dr. Jiménez has received several research and teaching honors, including two Fulbright awards from the Council for the International Exchange of Scholars and the Albert J. Harris Award from the International Reading Association.

JUDITH A. LANGER Distinguished Professor at the University at Albany, State University of New York; Director of the Center on English Learning and Achievement; Director of the Albany Institute for Research in Education. An internationally known scholar in English language arts education, Dr. Langer specializes in developing teaching approaches that can enrich and improve what gets done on a daily basis in classrooms. Her publications include *Getting to Excellent: How to Create Better Schools* and *Effective Literacy Instruction: Building Successful Reading and Writing Programs.*

ROBERT J. MARZANO Senior Scholar at Mid-Continent Research for Education and Learning (McREL); Associate Professor at Cardinal Stritch University in Milwaukee, Wisconsin; President of Marzano & Associates. An internationally known researcher, trainer, and speaker, Dr. Marzano has developed programs that translate research and theory into practical tools for K–12 teachers and administrators. He has written extensively on such topics as reading and writing instruction, thinking skills, school effectiveness, assessment, and standards implementation.

DONNA M. OGLE Professor of Reading and Language at National-Louis University in Chicago, Illinois; Past President of the International Reading Association. Creator of the well-known KWL strategy, Dr. Ogle has directed many staff development projects translating theory and research into school practice in middle and secondary schools throughout the United States and has served as a consultant on literacy projects worldwide. Her extensive international experience includes coordinating the Reading and Writing for Critical Thinking Project in Eastern Europe, developing integrated curriculum for a USAID Afghan Education Project, and speaking and consulting on projects in several Latin American countries and in Asia.

CAROL BOOTH OLSON Senior Lecturer in the Department of Education at the University of California, Irvine; Director of the UCI site of the National Writing Project. Dr. Olson writes and lectures extensively on the reading/writing connection, critical thinking through writing, interactive strategies for teaching writing, and the use of multicultural literature with students of culturally diverse backgrounds. She has received many awards, including the California Association of Teachers of English Award of Merit, the Outstanding California Education Research Award, and the UC Irvine Excellence in Teaching Award.

CAROL ANN TOMLINSON Professor of Educational Research, Foundations, and Policy at the University of Virginia; Co-Director of the University's Institutes on Academic Diversity. An internationally known expert on differentiated instruction, Dr. Tomlinson helps teachers and administrators develop effective methods of teaching academically diverse learners. She was a teacher of middle and high school English for 22 years prior to teaching at the University of Virginia. Her books on differentiated instruction have been translated into eight languages.

SPECIAL CONTRIBUTOR:
KYLENE BEERS Special Consultant; Former Middle School Teacher; nationally known Lecturer and Author on reading and literacy; and former President of the National Council of Teachers of English. Dr. Beers is the nationally known author of *When Kids Can't Read: What Teachers Can Do* and co-editor of *Adolescent Literacy: Turning Promise into Practice,* as well as articles in the *Journal of Adolescent and Adult Literacy.* Former editor of *Voices from the Middle,* she is the 2001 recipient of NCTE's Richard W. Halley Award, given for outstanding contributions to middle-school literacy.

ENGLISH LEARNER SPECIALISTS

MARY LOU McCLOSKEY Past President of Teachers of English to Speakers of Other Languages (TESOL); Director of Teacher Development and Curriculum Design for Educo in Atlanta, Georgia. Dr. McCloskey is a former teacher in multilingual and multicultural classrooms. She has worked with teachers, teacher educators, and departments of education around the world on teaching English as a second and foreign language. She is author of *On Our Way to English, Voices in Literature, Integrating English,* and *Visions: Language, Literature, Content.* Her awards include the Le Moyne College Ignatian Award for Professional Achievement and the TESOL D. Scott Enright Service Award.

LYDIA STACK International ESL consultant. Her areas of expertise are English language teaching strategies, ESL standards for students and teachers, and curriculum writing. Her teaching experience includes 25 years as an elementary and high school ESL teacher. She is a past president of TESOL. Her awards include the James E. Alatis Award for Service to TESOL (2003) and the San Francisco STAR Teacher Award (1989). Her publications include *On Our Way to English; Wordways: Games for Language Learning;* and *Visions: Language, Literature, Content.*

CURRICULUM SPECIALIST

WILLIAM L. McBRIDE Curriculum Specialist. Dr. McBride is a nationally known speaker, educator, and author who now trains teachers in instructional methodologies. A former reading specialist, English teacher, and social studies teacher, he holds a Masters in Reading and a Ph.D. in Curriculum and Instruction from the University of North Carolina at Chapel Hill. Dr. McBride has contributed to the development of textbook series in language arts, social studies, science, and vocabulary. He is also known for his novel *Entertaining an Elephant,* which tells the story of a burned-out teacher who becomes re-inspired with both his profession and his life.

MEDIA SPECIALISTS

DAVID M. CONSIDINE Professor of Instructional Technology and Media Studies at Appalachian State University in North Carolina. Dr. Considine has served as a media literacy consultant to the U.S. government and to the media industry, including Discovery Communications and Cable in the Classroom. He has also conducted media literacy workshops and training for county and state health departments across the United States. Among his many publications are *Visual Messages: Integrating Imagery into Instruction,* and *Imagine That: Developing Critical Viewing and Thinking Through Children's Literature.*

LARKIN PAULUZZI Teacher and Media Specialist; trainer for the New Jersey Writing Project. Ms. Pauluzzi puts her extensive classroom experience to use in developing teacher-friendly curriculum materials and workshops in many different areas, including media literacy. She has led media literacy training workshops in several districts throughout Texas, guiding teachers in the meaningful and practical uses of media in the classroom. Ms. Pauluzzi has taught students at all levels, from Title I Reading to AP English IV. She also spearheads a technology club at her school, working with students to produce media and technology to serve both the school and the community.

LISA K. SCHEFFLER Teacher and Media Specialist. Ms. Scheffler has designed and taught media literacy and video production curriculum, in addition to teaching language arts and speech. Using her knowledge of mass communication theory, coupled with real classroom experience, she has developed ready-to-use materials that help teachers incorporate media literacy into their curricula. She has taught film and television studies at the University of North Texas and has served as a contributing writer for the Texas Education Agency's statewide viewing and representing curriculum.

TEACHER ADVISORS

These are some of the many educators from across the country who played a crucial role in the development of the tables of contents, the lesson design, and other key components of this program:

Virginia L. Alford, MacArthur High School, San Antonio, Texas

Yvonne L. Allen, Shaker Heights High School, Shaker Heights, Ohio

Dave T. Anderson, Hinsdale South High School, Darien, Illinois

Kacy Colleen Anglim, Portland Public Schools District, Portland, Oregon

Jordana Benone, North High School, Torrance, California

Patricia Blood, Howell High School, Farmingdale, New Jersey

Marjorie Bloom, Eau Gallie High School, Melbourne, Florida

Edward J. Blotzer, Wilkinsburg Junior/Senior High School, Wilkinsburg, Pennsylvania

Stephen D. Bournes, Evanston Township High School, Evanston, Illinois

Barbara M. Bowling, Mt. Tabor High School, Winston-Salem, North Carolina

Kiala Boykin-Givehand, Duval County Public Schools, Jacksonville, Florida

Laura L. Brown, Adlai Stevenson High School, Lincolnshire, Illinois

Cynthia Burke, Yavneh Academy, Dallas, Texas

Hoppy Chandler, San Diego City Schools, San Diego, California

Gary Chmielewski, St. Benedict High School, Chicago, Illinois

Delorse Cole-Stewart, Milwaukee Public Schools, Milwaukee, Wisconsin

Kathy Dahlgren, Skokie, Illinois

Diana Dilger, Rosa Parks Middle School, Dixmoor, Illinois

L. Calvin Dillon, Gaither High School, Tampa, Florida

Dori Dolata, Rufus King High School, Milwaukee, Wisconsin

Jon Epstein, Marietta High School, Marietta, Georgia

Helen Ervin, Fort Bend Independent School District, Sugar Land, Texas

Sue Friedman, Buffalo Grove High School, Buffalo Grove, Illinois

Chris Gee, Bel Air High School, El Paso, Texas

Paula Grasel, The Horizon Center, Gainesville, Georgia

Rochelle L. Greene-Brady, Kenwood Academy, Chicago, Illinois

Christopher Guarraia, Centreville High School, Clifton, Virginia

Michele M. Hettinger, Niles West High School, Skokie, Illinois

Elizabeth Holcomb, Forest Hill High School, Jackson, Mississippi

Jim Horan, Hinsdale Central High School, Hinsdale, Illinois

James Paul Hunter, Oak Park-River Forest High School, Oak Park, Illinois

Susan P. Kelly, Director of Curriculum, Island Trees School District, Levittown, New York

Beverley A. Lanier, Varina High School, Richmond, Virginia

Pat Laws, Charlotte-Mecklenburg Schools, Charlotte, North Carolina

Diana R. Martinez, Treviño School of Communications & Fine Arts, Laredo, Texas

Natalie Martinez, Stephen F. Austin High School, Houston, Texas

Elizabeth Matarazzo, Ysleta High School, El Paso, Texas

Carol M. McDonald, J. Frank Dobie High School, Houston, Texas

Amy Millikan, Consultant, Chicago, Illinois

Eileen Murphy, Walter Payton Preparatory High School, Chicago, Illinois

Lisa Omark, New Haven Public Schools, New Haven, Connecticut

Kaine Osburn, Wheeling High School, Wheeling, Illinois

Andrea J. Phillips, Terry Sanford High School, Fayetteville, North Carolina

Cathy Reilly, Sayreville Public Schools, Sayreville, New Jersey

Mark D. Simon, Neuqua Valley High School, Naperville, Illinois

Scott Snow, Seguin High School, Arlington, Texas

Jane W. Speidel, Brevard County Schools, Viera, Florida

Cheryl E. Sullivan, Lisle Community School District, Lisle, Illinois

Anita Usmiani, Hamilton Township Public Schools, Hamilton Square, New Jersey

Linda Valdez, Oxnard Union High School District, Oxnard, California

Nancy Walker, Longview High School, Longview, Texas

Kurt Weiler, New Trier High School, Winnetka, Illinois

Elizabeth Whittaker, Larkin High School, Elgin, Illinois

Linda S. Williams, Woodlawn High School, Baltimore, Maryland

John R. Williamson, Fort Thomas Independent Schools, Fort Thomas, Kentucky

Anna N. Winters, Simeon High School, Chicago, Illinois

Tonora D. Wyckoff, North Shore Senior High School, Houston, Texas

Karen Zajac, Glenbard South High School, Glen Ellyn, Illinois

Cynthia Zimmerman, Mose Vines Preparatory High School, Chicago, Illinois

Lynda Zimmerman, El Camino High School, South San Francisco, California

Ruth E. Zurich, Brown Deer High School, Brown Deer, Wisconsin

COMMON CORE

OVERVIEW
Student Edition

- Understanding the English Language Arts Common Core State Standards
- English Language Arts Common Core State Standards
- Spotlight on Common Core State Standards

LESSONS WITH EMBEDDED COMMON CORE INSTRUCTION

COMMON
CORE
   Look for the Common Core symbol throughout the book. It highlights targeted objectives to help you succeed in mastering the knowledge and skills you will need for college or for a career.

© Getty Images

COMMON CORE CONTENTS

COMMON CORE

CONTENTS IN BRIEF

Online at

Log in to learn more at **thinkcentral.com,** *where you can access most program resources in one convenient location.*

LITERATURE AND READING CENTER

- Author Biographies
- *PowerNotes* Presentations
- Professional Audio Recordings of Selections
- Graphic Organizers
- Analysis Frames
- NovelWise

WRITING AND GRAMMAR CENTER

- Interactive Student Models*
- Interactive Graphic Organizers*
- Interactive Revision Lessons*
- *GrammarNotes* Presentations and Practice

also available on WriteSmart CD-ROM

VOCABULARY CENTER

- *WordSharp* Interactive Vocabulary Tutor
- Vocabulary Practice Copy Masters

MEDIA AND TECHNOLOGY CENTER

- MediaScope: Media Literacy Instruction
- Digital Storytelling
- Speaking and Listening Support

RESEARCH CENTER

- Writing and Research in a Digital Age
- Citation Guide

Assessment Center

- Program Assessments
- Level Up Online Tutorials
- Online Essay Scoring

MORE TECHNOLOGY

Student One Stop

Access an electronic version of your textbook, complete with selection audio and worksheets.

Media Smart DVD-ROM

Sharpen your critical viewing and analysis skills with these in-depth interactive media studies.

The Origins of a Nation
THE ANGLO-SAXON AND MEDIEVAL PERIODS

449–1485

The Anglo-Saxon Epic

STANDARDS FOCUS
Characteristics of an Epic

Vocabulary Strategies

The Anglo-Saxon suffix *-some, p. 72*
Dictionary etymologies, *p. 94*
Words from French, *p. 168*
The Latin prefix *mal-, p. 182*

The Latin root *temp, p. 198*
Nuanced meanings in a thesaurus, *p. 215*
Multiple-meaning words, *p. 264*

COMMON CORE
UNIT 2

A Celebration of Human Achievement
THE ENGLISH RENAISSANCE
1485–1660

Vocabulary Strategies

Analogies and connotations, *p. 450*
Using context clues, *p. 460*
The Latin prefix *trans-*, *p. 512*

COMMON CORE

UNIT 3

Tradition and Reason
THE RESTORATION AND THE 18TH CENTURY

1660–1798

The Rise of Women Writers

Vocabulary Strategies

Language references, *p. 633*
Analogies, *p. 656*
Synonyms as context clues, *p. 668*

Using a dictionary, *p. 678*
Specialized dictionaries, *p. 689*
Analogies, *p. 728*

Emotion and Experimentation
THE FLOWERING OF ROMANTICISM

1798–1832

Revolt Against Neoclassicism

An Era of Rapid Change
THE VICTORIANS
1832–1901

The Influence of Romanticism

> **Vocabulary Strategies**
>
> Using context clues, *p. 992*
> The development of English, *p. 1008*
> Contrasts as context clues, *p. 1028*
> Using a dictionary, *p. 1042*

COMMON CORE
UNIT 6

New Ideas, New Voices
MODERN AND CONTEMPORARY LITERATURE

1901–PRESENT

Responses to War and Colonialism

Postwar Writers

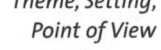

Investigation and Discovery
THE POWER OF RESEARCH

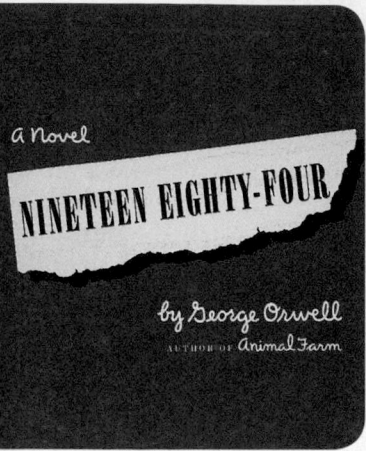

A Novel

NINETEEN EIGHTY-FOUR

by George Orwell
AUTHOR OF *Animal Farm*

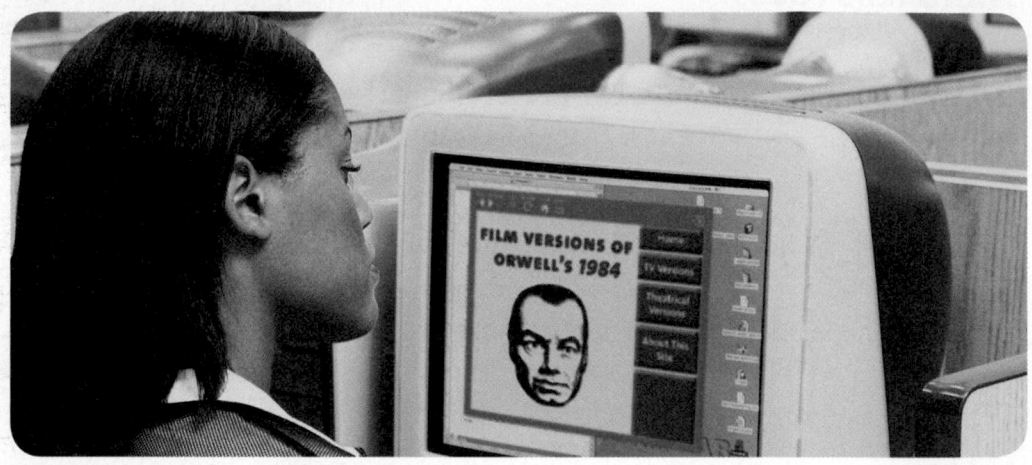

STANDARDS FOCUS
Use Reference Materials and Technology, Evaluate Sources

Use Reference Materials and Technology, Evaluate Sources

Selections by Genre

DRAMA

Features

STUDENT GUIDE TO ACADEMIC SUCCESS

STUDENT GUIDE

© Age Fotostock America, Inc.

The Common Core for Uncommon Achievement

Carol Jago

*"If you don't know where you are going,
any road will get you there." – Lewis Carroll*

The Common Core State Standards make clear where students are going. They describe what today's children need to know and be able to do to thrive in post-secondary education and the workplace. By focusing on results — the destination — rather than on the how — the means of transportation — the Common Core allows for a variety of teaching methods and many different classroom approaches. The challenge for teachers is to turn the daily journey towards this destination into an intellectual adventure.

One way to think about the Common Core is as a kind of GPS device to situate curriculum. While some students may choose the road less traveled, the objective is fixed. When students become lost through a wrong turn, teachers recalculate the route, providing a calm and confident voice that guides all students to academic achievement and deep literacy.

Shared Responsibility for Students' Literacy Development

The Common Core State Standards insist that the responsibility for helping students achieve literacy is not the sole responsibility of the English teacher. The introduction states clearly that, "instruction in reading, writing, speaking, listening, and language (should) be a shared responsibility within the school" (4). Citing NAEP Reading assessment test specification guidelines, the Common Core recommends that 55% of what students read in grade 8 and 70% in grade 12 should be informational text. These percentages are not meant to reflect the balance of reading materials in English class alone but rather the totality of what students should be reading across the curriculum in history/social studies, science, and technical subjects as well as in English. Given the type of reading that will be required of students in college and of graduates in the workplace, this distribution is both relevant and practical.

Understanding of Other Perspectives and Cultures

The Common Core also makes clear the importance of literature in the education of America's children. "Through reading great classic and contemporary works of literature representative of a variety of periods, cultures, and worldviews, students can vicariously inhabit worlds and have experiences much different from their own" (7). Reading literature demands that readers look inward, examine their beliefs in light of new information, consider the world through different eyes, take time for reflection. Such reading is a key to student learning.

The Purpose of Exemplar Texts

To describe the quality and complexity of the works students should read at each grade level, the Common Core offers lists of "exemplar texts." While some may choose to treat the texts on these lists as required reading, such usage would represent a misunderstanding of their purpose. "The choices should serve as useful guideposts in helping educators select texts of similar complexity, quality, and range for their own classrooms. They expressly do not represent a partial or complete reading list" (Appendix B, 2). The poems, stories, novels, and nonfiction that appear on the Common Core lists are intended as models for guiding — not dictating — text selection.

The Difference Between Persuasion and Argument

The Common Core writing standards describe the types and purposes for writing that students need to master. You will find extended definitions of argument, informative/explanatory writing, and narrative writing in Appendix A. Of particular note is the distinction the Common Core draws between persuasion and argument. "When writing to persuade, writers employ a variety of persuasive strategies. One common strategy is an appeal to the credibility, character, or authority of the writer (or speaker). A logical argument, on the other hand, convinces the audience because of the perceived merit and reasonableness of the claims and proofs offered rather than either the emotions the writing evokes in the audience or the character or credentials of the writer" (24). Because of its importance for college and workplace readiness, argument holds a special place in the Common Core writing standards.

> *One way to think about the Common Core is as a kind of GPS device ...*

Complex Literary and Informational Texts

Throughout the Common Core document you will notice the anchor standard, "Read and comprehend complex literary and informational texts independently and proficiently." It isn't enough for students to read with a teacher by their side. They need to be able, often with a little help from their friends or from the habits of mind they learned from their teachers, to read for themselves. They need to be able, like Huck Finn, to head out for the territory on their own. Such a journey requires confidence in one's ability to navigate uncharted waters and to overcome challenges their teachers can't foresee or even imagine. As we guide students on the academic adventure that is high school, let us never forget that the path we tread is the path to intellectual freedom.

WORKS CITED

Common Core State Standards for English Language Arts and History/Social Studies, Science, & Technical Subjects. 2010.

Appendix B. Common Core State Standards for English Language Arts and History/Social Studies, Science, & Technical Subjects. 2010.

Carol Jago has taught middle and high school for over 30 years and was a member of the Common Core Initiative feedback team. She serves as president of the National Council of Teachers of English.

Understanding the Common Core State Standards

What are the English Language Arts Common Core State Standards?

The Common Core State Standards for English Language Arts indicate what you should know and be able to do by the end of your grade level. These understandings and skills will help you be better prepared for future classes, college courses, and a career. For this reason, the standards for each strand in English Language Arts (such as reading informational text or writing) directly relate to the College and Career Readiness Anchor Standards for each strand. The Anchor Standards broadly outline the understandings and skills you should learn by the end of high school so that you are well-prepared for college or for a career.

How do I learn the English Language Arts Common Core State Standards?

Your textbook is closely aligned to the English Language Arts Common Core State Standards. Every time you learn a concept or practice a skill, you are working on mastery of one of the standards. Each unit, each selection, and each workshop in your textbook connects to one or more of the standards for English Language Arts listed on the following pages.

The English Language Arts Common Core State Standards are divided into five strands: Reading Literature, Reading Informational Text, Writing, Speaking and Listening, and Language.

Reading Literature (RL)

This strand concerns the literary texts you will read at this grade level: stories, drama, and poetry. The Common Core State Standards stress that you should read a range of texts of increasing complexity as you progress through high school.

Reading Informational Text (RI)

Informational text includes a broad range of literary nonfiction, including exposition, argument, and functional text, such as personal essays, speeches, opinion pieces, memoirs, and historical and technical accounts. The Common Core State Standards stress that you will also read a range of informational texts of increasing complexity as you progress from grade to grade.

Writing (W)

The Writing strand focuses on your generating three types of texts: arguments, informative or explanatory texts, and narratives, as well as using the writing process and technology to develop and share your writing. The Common Core State Standards also emphasize research and specify that you should write routinely for both short and extended time frames.

Speaking and Listening (SL)

The Common Core State Standards focus on comprehending information presented in a variety of media and formats, on participating in collaborative discussions, and on presenting knowledge and ideas clearly.

Language (L)

The standards in the Language strand address the conventions of Standard English grammar, usage, and mechanics; knowledge of language; and vocabulary acquisition and use.

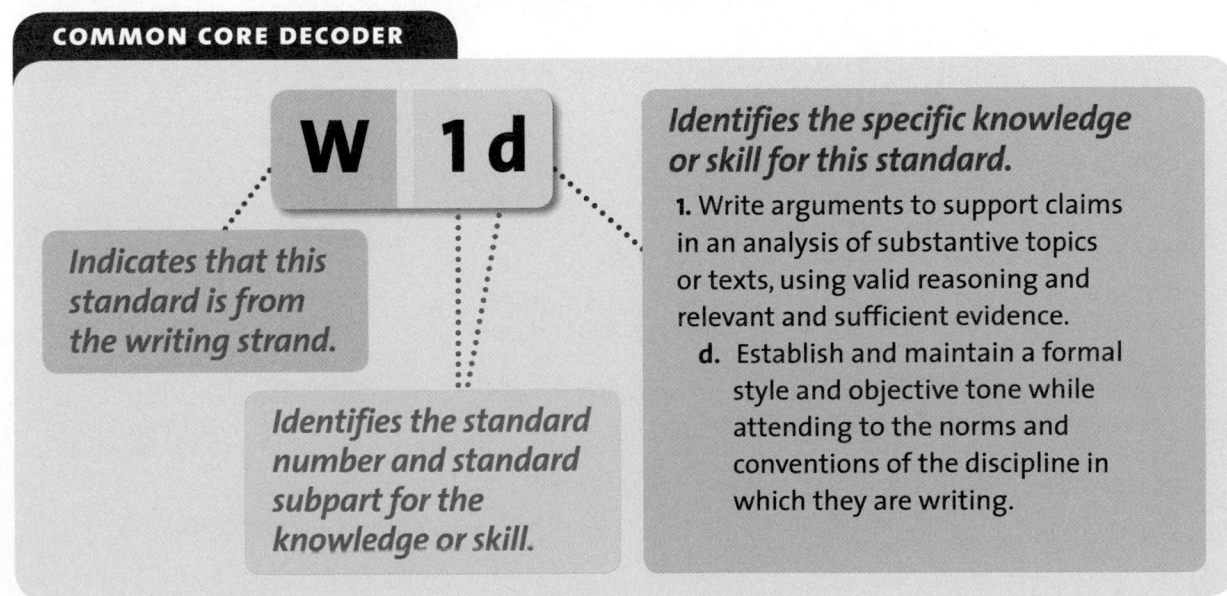

COMMON CORE DECODER

W 1 d

Indicates that this standard is from the writing strand.

Identifies the standard number and standard subpart for the knowledge or skill.

Identifies the specific knowledge or skill for this standard.

1. Write arguments to support claims in an analysis of substantive topics or texts, using valid reasoning and relevant and sufficient evidence.

   d. Establish and maintain a formal style and objective tone while attending to the norms and conventions of the discipline in which they are writing.

English Language Arts Common Core State Standards

Listed below are the English Language Arts Common Core State Standards that you are required to master by the end of grade 12. We have provided a summary of the concepts you will learn on your way to mastering each standard. The CCR anchor standards and high school grade-specific standards for each strand work together to define college and career readiness expectations—the former providing broad standards, the latter providing additional specificity.

College and Career Readiness Anchor Standards for Reading

COMMON CORE STATE STANDARDS

KEY IDEAS AND DETAILS

1. Read closely to determine what the text says explicitly and to make logical inferences from it; cite specific textual evidence when writing or speaking to support conclusions drawn from the text.

2. Determine central ideas or themes of a text and analyze their development; summarize the key supporting details and ideas.

3. Analyze how and why individuals, events, and ideas develop and interact over the course of a text.

CRAFT AND STRUCTURE

4. Interpret words and phrases as they are used in a text, including determining technical, connotative, and figurative meanings, and analyze how specific word choices shape meaning or tone.

5. Analyze the structure of texts, including how specific sentences, paragraphs, and larger portions of the text (e.g., a section, chapter, scene, or stanza) relate to each other and the whole.

6. Assess how point of view or purpose shapes the content and style of a text.

INTEGRATION OF KNOWLEDGE AND IDEAS

7. Integrate and evaluate content presented in diverse formats and media, including visually and quantitatively, as well as in words.

8. Delineate and evaluate the argument and specific claims in a text, including the validity of the reasoning as well as the relevance and sufficiency of the evidence.

9. Analyze how two or more texts address similar themes or topics in order to build knowledge or to compare the approaches the authors take.

RANGE OF READING AND LEVEL OF TEXT COMPLEXITY

10. Read and comprehend complex literary and informational texts independently and proficiently.

Reading Standards for Literature, Grades 11–12 Students

The College and Career Readiness Anchor Standards for Reading apply to both literature and informational text.

COMMON CORE STATE STANDARD	WHAT IT MEANS TO YOU
KEY IDEAS AND DETAILS	
1. Cite strong and thorough textual evidence to support analysis of what the text says explicitly as well as inferences drawn from the text, including determining where the text leaves matters uncertain.	You will use strong evidence from a text to support your analysis of its central ideas—both those that are stated directly and those that are suggested—and to show where the text leaves matters uncertain.
2. Determine two or more themes or central ideas of a text and analyze their development over the course of the text, including how they interact and build on one another to produce a complex account; provide an objective summary of the text.	You will analyze the development of at least two of a text's key ideas and themes by showing how they progress and interact throughout the text. You will also summarize the text as a whole without adding your own ideas or opinions.
3. Analyze the impact of the author's choices regarding how to develop and relate elements of a story or drama (e.g., where a story is set, how the action is ordered, how the characters are introduced and developed).	You will analyze the author's choices related to setting, plot structure, and characterization in a story or drama.
CRAFT AND STRUCTURE	
4. Determine the meaning of words and phrases as they are used in the text, including figurative and connotative meanings; analyze the impact of specific word choices on meaning and tone, including words with multiple meanings or language that is particularly fresh, engaging, or beautiful. (Include Shakespeare as well as other authors.)	You will analyze specific words and phrases in the text to determine both their figurative and connotative meanings, as well as how they contribute to the text's tone and meaning as a whole. You will also consider multiple-meaning words and vivid language.
5. Analyze how an author's choices concerning how to structure specific parts of a text (e.g., the choice of where to begin or end a story, the choice to provide a comedic or tragic resolution) contribute to its overall structure and meaning as well as its aesthetic impact.	You will analyze the ways in which the author has chosen to structure and order the text and determine how those choices shape the text's meaning and affect the reader.
6. Analyze a case in which grasping a point of view requires distinguishing what is directly stated in a text from what is really meant (e.g., satire, sarcasm, irony, or understatement).	You will understand a point of view in which what is really meant is different from what is said or stated.
INTEGRATION OF KNOWLEDGE AND IDEAS	
7. Analyze multiple interpretations of a story, drama, or poem (e.g., recorded or live production of a play or recorded novel or poetry), evaluating how each version interprets the source text. (Include at least one play by Shakespeare and one play by an American dramatist.)	You will compare and contrast multiple interpretations of a story, drama, or poem, and analyze how each draws from and uses the source text.
8. (Not applicable to literature)	

Reading Standards for Literature, Grades 11–12 Students, continued

COMMON CORE STATE STANDARD	WHAT IT MEANS TO YOU
9. Demonstrate knowledge of eighteenth-, nineteenth- and early-twentieth-century foundational works of American literature, including how two or more texts from the same period treat similar themes or topics.	You will analyze, compare, and contrast important eighteenth-, nineteenth-, and early-twentieth-century works of American literature.
RANGE OF READING AND LEVEL OF TEXT COMPLEXITY 10. By the end of grade 12, read and comprehend literature, including stories, dramas, and poems, at the high end of the grades 11–12 CCR text complexity band independently and proficiently.	You will read and understand grade-level appropriate literary texts by the end of grade 12.

Spotlight on Common Core

COMMON CORE **RL 1** Cite strong and thorough textual evidence to support analysis of what the text says explicitly as well as inferences drawn from the text.

Literature: Citing Textual Evidence

The Common Core State Standards stress the importance of providing strong and thorough support for your analysis of any text that you read, from short stories, to dramas, to epic poems. To support your analysis you need to provide **textual evidence**, which means using ideas and details from the text. You can do this in two ways:

1. identify the ideas and details that enable you to analyze what the text clearly states

2. identify the ideas and details that enable you to draw inferences, or make logical assumptions, about the text

Throughout this book, in questions about individual texts and in writing about texts, you will be asked to support your ideas with text evidence. Study the following example:

Read the following poem, "Ozymandias" by Percy Bysshe Shelley, a Romantic poet. *Ozymandias* is the Greek name for the Egyptian pharaoh Rameses II, who reigned from 1279 to 1213 BC. Then answer the two questions that follow the poem.

> I met a traveller from an antique land
> Who said: Two vast and trunkless legs[1] of stone
> Stand in the desert. . . Near them, on the sand,
> Half sunk, a shattered visage[2] lies, whose frown,
> 5 And wrinkled lip, and sneer of cold command,
> Tell that its sculptor well those passions read
> Which yet survive, stamped on these lifeless things,
> The hand that mocked them and the heart that fed;[3]
>
> ――――――
> 1. **trunkless legs:** legs separated from the rest of the body.
> 2. **visage:** face.
> 3. **lines 6–8:** The passions outlast the sculptor whose hand mocked those passions and the king whose heart fed those passions.

> And on the pedestal these words appear:
> 10 "My name is Ozymandias, king of kings:
> Look on my works, ye Mighty, and despair!"
> Nothing beside remains. Round the decay
> Of that colossal wreck, boundless and bare
> The lone and level sands stretch far away.

1. What imagery does the poet use to characterize the statue of Ozymandias? Support your response with text evidence.

2. What can you infer about Ozymandias's position in the world from the poem? Support your response with text evidence.

LEARN HOW Citing Textual Evidence The questions that follow "Ozymandias" ask you to cite text evidence, but for different reasons. The first question directs you to probe what the poem says explicitly; the second question relates to the inferences you make in reading the poem.

To support your analysis, you need to identify specific ideas and details in the poem that will support your response to either type of question. These ideas and details can be specific words or **quotations** from the text, **paraphrases** of the text, or a **summary** of the text or of a relevant part of the text. Remember that to paraphrase, you use your own words instead of the exact words in the text. To summarize, you briefly retell what the text says, again in your own words.

Here are two examples of how to respond to the questions. Notice how the writer uses the types of text evidence to support each analysis.

1. What imagery does the poet use to characterize the statue of Ozymandias? Support your response with text evidence.

In the poem "Ozymandias" by Percy Bysshe Shelley, the speaker describes the disintegrating statue of a once-powerful king in the desert. The statue is in fragments: "Two vast and trunkless legs of stone" (line 3) stand on one part of the sand. The statue's face, a "shattered visage," (line 4) lies nearby. Nevertheless, the king's "sneer of cold command" (line 5) is still evident, as is the inscription in which he declares his great power (lines 10–11). The king's words strongly contrast with the statue's decayed state.

- summary of the poem
- quotation marks and line numbers indicate direct citations
- paraphrase: statue's inscription

2. What can you infer about Ozymandias's position in the world from the poem? Support your response with text evidence.

Ozymandias was a powerful enough ruler to be represented by a statue of himself inscribed as "king of kings" (line 10). His "sneer of cold command" (line 5) implies that he was a ruthless, demanding king. However, the disintegration of his statue also implies that his power was ultimately vain and arrogant. The poem's final lines describe the isolated, seemingly endless desert that surrounds the statue and suggest how empty, insignificant, and transient Ozymandias's power finally is.

- direct quotations support the writer's inferences
- inferences supported with a paraphrase

Spotlight on Common Core

COMMON CORE

RL 2 Determine two or more themes or central ideas of a text and analyze their development over the course of the text, including how they interact and build on one another to produce a complex account; provide an objective summary of the text.

Literature: Analyzing Two or More Themes

The **theme** of a text is the underlying message it conveys. Many literary works have more than one theme, and those themes often build on one another to produce an even more complex theme. To analyze a text with one or more themes, you can follow these steps:

1. Summarize the poem briefly and objectively to help you identify its major themes.

2. Determine the central themes of the text by paying close attention to the author's use of language, including literary devices (such as imagery and figurative language). Support your conclusions with evidence from the text, such as quotations or paraphrases.

3. Analyze the relationship between the two themes. How do they combine, or build upon each other, to form an even more complex theme?

Throughout this book, you will be asked to identify the themes of a variety of works from a variety of literary genres and to determine how they interact. Study the following example:

Read the following poem, "Sonnet 18" by William Shakespeare, the great Elizabethan poet and dramatist. Then answer the questions that follow the poem.

> Shall I compare thee to a summer's day?
> Thou art more lovely and more temperate:
> Rough winds do shake the darling buds of May,
> And summer's lease hath all too short a date:
> 5 Sometime too hot the eye of heaven shines,
> And often is his gold complexion dimmed;
> And every fair from fair sometime declines,
> By chance or nature's changing course untrimmed;[1]
> But thy eternal summer shall not fade,
> 10 Nor lose possession of that fair thou owest;[2]
> Nor shall Death brag thou wander'st in his shade,
> When in eternal lines to time thou growest:
>   So long as men can breathe or eyes can see,
>   So long lives this, and this gives life to thee.[3]

---

1. **lines 7–8, fair from. . . untrimmed:** beauty eventually fades, due to misfortune or natural aging.
2. **line 10, thou owest:** you own; you possess.
3. **line 12, when. . . growest:** when in immortal poetry you become a part of time.

---

1. Briefly summarize the poem in your own words.

2. What are the two central themes of the poem? Support your conclusion with evidence from the text.

3. How do these two themes combine, or build upon each other, to form a third theme?

LEARN HOW Analyzing Two or More Themes You can analyze a complex text by following a few steps. First, **summarize** the poem by briefly restating what happens in it in your own words. Summarizing the poem helps you identify the poem's major themes and how they interact. An effective summary is objective, meaning it does not include your thoughts or feelings about the work.

Next, in order to discuss how two or more themes in a text build upon one another, you must first identify those themes. What are the primary ideas or messages portrayed in the work? If you are unsure, ask yourself these questions.

- Who is the speaker and what is his or her main subject?
- How does the speaker feel about this subject? To what or whom does the speaker compare or contrast the subject?
- What kind of language, imagery, and devices does the speaker use to describe the subject?

Finally, ask yourself how the themes combine to form a third theme. Notice how the following example uses this three-step approach.

1. Briefly summarize the poem in your own words.

> In Shakespeare's "Sonnet 18," the speaker compares a person he or she loves to a summer's day. Summer fades quickly, but the beloved's beauty is "eternal" because the poem immortalizes it.

brief, objective summary

2. What are the two central themes of the poem? Support your conclusion with evidence from the text.

> In the first lines, the speaker compares his beloved to a summer's day. Summer is described as turbulent, featuring "rough winds" and unpleasant changes in temperature ("Sometimes too hot the eye of heaven shines"). Summer also fades too fast ("summer's lease hath all too short a date"). One theme of this poem is the inevitable, turbulent passage of time.
>
> In contrast, the beauty of the beloved is stable ("thy eternal summer shall not fade") because the poem preserves it for eternity. The poem makes the beloved's beauty live forever: "So long lives this, and this gives life to thee." The second theme is the power of art to portray beauty.

text evidence

first theme

text evidence

second theme

3. How do these two themes combine, or build upon each other, to form a third theme?

> The two themes of the inevitable passage of time and the power of art build upon one another in the poem. In the end, art is more powerful than nature because it can preserve beauty for all time.

interaction of two themes

In your reading of complex texts throughout this book, determine whether the author includes more than one theme, as well as how those themes interact to create yet another theme. The richness of British literature ensures that you will encounter multiple themes in many texts.

Reading Standards for Informational Text, Grades 11–12 Students

COMMON CORE STATE STANDARD	WHAT IT MEANS TO YOU
KEY IDEAS AND DETAILS	
1. Cite strong and thorough textual evidence to support analysis of what the text says explicitly as well as inferences drawn from the text, including determining where the text leaves matters uncertain.	You will use details and information from the text to support your analysis of its central ideas—both those that are stated directly and those that are suggested—and to show where the text leaves matters uncertain.
2. Determine two or more central ideas of a text and analyze their development over the course of the text, including how they interact and build on one another to provide a complex analysis; provide an objective summary of the text.	You will analyze the development of at least two of a text's key ideas by showing how they progress and interact throughout the text. You will also summarize the text as a whole without adding your own ideas or opinions.
3. Analyze a complex set of ideas or sequence of events and explain how specific individuals, ideas, or events interact and develop over the course of the text.	You will analyze the specific interactions among a set of ideas, individuals, or a sequence of events in a text.
CRAFT AND STRUCTURE	
4. Determine the meaning of words and phrases as they are used in a text, including figurative, connotative, and technical meanings; analyze how an author uses and refines the meaning of a key term or terms over the course of a text (e.g., how Madison defines *faction* in *Federalist* No. 10).	You will analyze specific words and phrases in the text to determine their figurative, connotative, and technical meanings, as well as to uncover how an author uses them throughout a text.
5. Analyze and evaluate the effectiveness of the structure an author uses in his or her exposition or argument, including whether the structure makes points clear, convincing, and engaging.	You will examine a text's structure and evaluate whether it makes the author's claims clear, convincing, and interesting.
6. Determine an author's point of view or purpose in a text in which the rhetoric is particularly effective, analyzing how style and content contribute to the power, persuasiveness or beauty of the text.	You will understand the author's purpose and perspective on a topic and analyze how the author uses language to affect the reader.
INTEGRATION OF KNOWLEDGE AND IDEAS	
7. Integrate and evaluate multiple sources of information presented in different media or formats (e.g., visually, quantitatively) as well as in words in order to address a question or solve a problem.	You will integrate multiple and varied sources of information to address a question or solve a problem.
8. Delineate and evaluate the reasoning in seminal U.S. texts, including the application of constitutional principles and use of legal reasoning (e.g., in U.S. Supreme Court majority opinions and dissents) and the premises, purposes, and arguments in works of public advocacy (e.g., *The Federalist*, presidential addresses).	You will analyze the reasoning and underlying principles of important and influential U.S. texts for their support of the principles of democracy.

Reading Standards for Informational Text, Grades 11–12 Students, continued

COMMON CORE STATE STANDARD	WHAT IT MEANS TO YOU
9. Analyze seventeenth-, eighteenth-, and nineteenth-century foundational U.S. documents of historical and literary significance (including The Declaration of Independence, the Preamble to the Constitution, the Bill of Rights, and Lincoln's Second Inaugural Address) for their themes, purposes, and rhetorical features.	You will read and analyze important eighteenth-, nineteenth-, and early-twentieth-century documents pertaining to American history to determine their themes, purposes, and use of language.
RANGE OF READING AND LEVEL OF TEXT COMPLEXITY **10.** By the end of grade 12, read and comprehend literary nonfiction at the high end of the grades 11–12 CCR text complexity band independently and proficiently.	You will demonstrate the ability to read and understand grade-level appropriate literary nonfiction texts by the end of grade 12.

Spotlight on Common Core

COMMON CORE

RI 5 Analyze and evaluate the effectiveness of the structure an author uses in his or her exposition or argument, including whether the structure makes the points clear, convincing, and engaging.

Informational Texts: Analyzing Structure

To evaluate the effectiveness of an argument, you need to analyze its structure, or the order in which the writer presents the components of the argument, such as claims, reasons, and rhetorical devices. You can do this by:

1. identifying the order in which the writer presents his or her major points
2. evaluating to what extent the argument's structure helps convey its points clearly, convincingly, and engagingly to the reader

Throughout this book, you will be asked to consider the structure of a variety of informational texts, including arguments and expository texts. Study the following example:

> Read this excerpt from "Female Orations," a text written in the seventeenth century by Margaret Cavendish, the Duchess of Newcastle. At a time when women could not own property or vote and often received little formal education, a group of women gather to discuss the limitations in their lives. In Part I, one of the women starts the discussion by sharing her views on men and women. Answer the questions that follow the excerpt.

> **Ladies, gentlewomen, and other inferior women, but not less worthy:** I have been industrious to assemble you together, and wish I were so fortunate as to persuade you to make frequent assemblies, associations, and combinations amongst our sex, that we may unite in prudent counsels, to make ourselves as free, happy, and famous as men; whereas now we live and die as if we were produced from beasts, rather than from men; for men are happy, and we women are miserable; they possess all the ease, rest, pleasure, wealth, power, and fame; whereas women are restless with labor, easeless with pain, melancholy for want of[1] pleasures, helpless for want of power, and die in oblivion, for want of fame. Nevertheless,
>
> ---
> 1. **for want of:** due to the lack of.

men are so unconscionable[2] and cruel against us that they endeavor to bar us of all sorts of liberty, and will not suffer[3] us freely to associate amongst our own sex; but would fain[4] bury us in their houses or beds, as in a grave. The truth is, we live like bats or owls, labor like beasts, and die like worms.

---

2. **unconscionable:** not led by conscience.
3. **suffer:** allow.
4. **fain:** gladly.

1. What is the structure, or organization, of this argument?
2. How effective is this structure in making the points clear, convincing, and engaging?

LEARN HOW Analyzing Structure   The first question following the excerpt asks you to identify the structure of the argument; the second asks you to evaluate the effectiveness of this structure. To support your analysis, you need specific support in the form of quotations from the text. You may also **paraphrase**, restating each point briefly in your own words in the order in which it appears.

A writer usually begins with a **claim**, his or her position on an issue or problem. The writer then builds the argument, adding increasingly strong **reasons** and **evidence** (such as examples and opinions) to support the claim. The writer may include literary devices, such as similes, metaphors, and imagery to engage the reader with colorful language to make his or her point. Above all, it is important that the writer make the points clearly and convincingly in a way that engages the reader enough to consider the writer's argument.

1. What is the structure, or organization, of this argument?

> The speaker claims that women are drastically unequal to men. She begins by wishing that women could gather more often to discuss how to be as "free, happy, and famous as men." She then provides two parallel lists contrasting examples of the power men have ("all the ease, rest, pleasure, wealth, power, and fame") with examples of the deprivation women suffer ("restless with labor, easeless with pain..."). Next, she intensifies this argument by comparing how men deprive women of their liberty and humanity, treating women as if "in a grave." Finally, the speaker closes her argument with three striking similes that sum up women's subhuman existence: "...we live like bats or owls, labor like beasts, and die like worms."

argument based on more and more vivid comparisons

2. How effective is this structure in making the points clear, convincing, and engaging?

> The structure conveys the speaker's position clearly. The argument becomes increasingly intense as it goes on, making the opinions the writer presents memorable and potentially convincing. The increasingly

analysis of effectiveness

lively, if horrifying, imagery keeps the reader engaged. The final sentence is a strong reminder of the speaker's main point that women are not treated as equal human beings. By offering solutions for the problem described, the speaker might have made an even stronger conclusion, thus strengthening the argument.

one weakness of the argument

As you analyze other arguments and expository texts throughout this book, be sure to consider how effectively a text's structure conveys the writer's points and strengthens his or her argument.

College and Career Readiness Anchor Standards for Writing

COMMON CORE STATE STANDARDS

TEXT TYPES AND PURPOSES

1. Write arguments to support claims in an analysis of substantive topics or texts, using valid reasoning and relevant and sufficient evidence.

2. Write informative/explanatory texts to examine and convey complex ideas and information clearly and accurately through the effective selection, organization, and analysis of content.

3. Write narratives to develop real or imagined experiences or events using effective technique, well-chosen details, and well-structured event sequences.

PRODUCTION AND DISTRIBUTION OF WRITING

4. Produce clear and coherent writing in which the development, organization, and style are appropriate to task, purpose, and audience.

5. Develop and strengthen writing as needed by planning, revising, editing, rewriting, or trying a new approach.

6. Use technology, including the Internet, to produce and publish writing and to interact and collaborate with others.

RESEARCH TO BUILD AND PRESENT KNOWLEDGE

7. Conduct short as well as more sustained research projects based on focused questions, demonstrating understanding of the subject under investigation.

8. Gather relevant information from multiple print and digital sources, assess the credibility and accuracy of each source, and integrate the information while avoiding plagiarism.

9. Draw evidence from literary or informational texts to support analysis, reflection, and research.

RANGE OF WRITING

10. Write routinely over extended time frames (time for research, reflection, and revision) and shorter time frames (a single sitting or a day or two) for a range of tasks, purposes, and audiences.

Writing Standards, Grades 11–12 Students

COMMON CORE STATE STANDARD	WHAT IT MEANS TO YOU
TEXT TYPES AND PURPOSES	
1. Write arguments to support claims in an analysis of substantive topics or texts, using valid reasoning and relevant and sufficient evidence.	You will write and develop arguments with strong evidence and valid reasoning that include
a. Introduce precise, knowledgeable claim(s), establish the significance of the claim(s), distinguish the claim(s) from alternate or opposing claims, and create an organization that logically sequences claim(s), counterclaims, reasons, and evidence.	**a.** a clear organization of precise claims and counterclaims
b. Develop claim(s) and counterclaims fairly and thoroughly, supplying the most relevant evidence for each while pointing out the strengths and limitations of both in a manner that anticipates the audience's knowledge level, concerns, values, and possible biases.	**b.** relevant and unbiased support for claims that incorporates audience considerations
c. Use words, phrases, and clauses as well as varied syntax to link the major sections of the text, create cohesion, and clarify the relationships between claim(s) and reasons, between reasons and evidence, and between claim(s) and counterclaims.	**c.** use of transitional words, phrases, and clauses and varied sentence structures to link information and clarify relationships
d. Establish and maintain a formal style and objective tone while attending to the norms and conventions of the discipline in which they are writing.	**d.** a tone and style that is appropriate and that adheres to the conventions, or expectations, of the discipline
e. Provide a concluding statement or section that follows from and supports the argument presented.	**e.** a strong concluding statement or section that summarizes the evidence presented
2. Write informative/explanatory texts to examine and convey complex ideas, concepts, and information clearly and accurately through the effective selection, organization, and analysis of content.	You will write clear, well-organized, and thoughtful informative and explanatory texts with
a. Introduce a topic; organize complex ideas, concepts, and information so that each new element builds on that which precedes it to create a unified whole; include formatting (e.g., headings), graphics (e.g., figures, tables), and multimedia when useful to aiding comprehension.	**a.** a clear introduction and an organization that builds on each successive idea, including formats, headings, graphic organizers (when appropriate), and multimedia
b. Develop the topic thoroughly by selecting the most significant and relevant facts, extended definitions, concrete details, quotations, or other information and examples appropriate to the audience's knowledge of the topic.	**b.** a sufficient variety of support and background information
c. Use appropriate and varied transitions and syntax to link the major sections of the text, create cohesion, and clarify the relationships among complex ideas and concepts.	**c.** appropriate and varied transitions and sentence structures

COMMON CORE STATE STANDARD	WHAT IT MEANS TO YOU
TEXT TYPES AND PURPOSES	
d. Use precise language, domain-specific vocabulary, and techniques such as metaphor, simile, and analogy to manage the complexity of the topic.	d. precise language, relevant vocabulary, and the use of comparisons to express complex ideas
e. Establish and maintain a formal style and objective tone while attending to the norms and conventions of the discipline in which they are writing.	e. an appropriate tone and style that adheres to the conventions, or expectations, of the discipline
f. Provide a concluding statement or section that follows from and supports the information or explanation presented (e.g., articulating implications or the significance of the topic).	f. a strong concluding statement or section that logically relates to the information presented in the text and that restates the importance or relevance of the topic
3. Write narratives to develop real or imagined experiences or events using effective technique, well-chosen details, and well-structured event sequences.	You will write clear, well-structured, detailed narrative texts that
a. Engage and orient the reader by setting out a problem, situation, or observation and its significance, establishing one or multiple point(s) of view, and introducing a narrator and/or characters; create a smooth progression of experiences or events.	a. draw your readers in with a clear topic, well-developed point(s) of view, a well-developed narrator and characters, and an interesting progression of events or ideas
b. Use narrative techniques, such as dialogue, pacing, description, reflection, and multiple plot lines, to develop experiences, events, and/or characters.	b. use a range of literary techniques to develop and expand on events and/or characters
c. Use a variety of techniques to sequence events so that they build on one another to create a coherent whole and build toward a particular tone and outcome (e.g., a sense of mystery, suspense, growth, or resolution).	c. have a coherent sequence and structure that create the appropriate tone and ending for readers
d. Use precise words and phrases, telling details, and sensory language to convey a vivid picture of the experiences, events, setting, and/or characters.	d. use precise words, sensory details, and language in order to keep readers interested
e. Provide a conclusion that follows from and reflects on what is experienced, observed, or resolved over the course of the narrative.	e. have a strong and logical conclusion that reflects on the topic
PRODUCTION AND DISTRIBUTION OF WRITING	
4. Produce clear and coherent writing in which the development, organization, and style are appropriate to task, purpose, and audience.	You will produce writing that is appropriate to the task, purpose, and audience for whom you are writing.
5. Develop and strengthen writing as needed by planning, revising, editing, rewriting, or trying a new approach, focusing on addressing what is most significant for a specific purpose and audience.	You will revise and refine your writing, using a variety of strategies, to address what is most important for your purpose and audience.
6. Use technology, including the Internet, to produce, publish, and update individual or shared writing products in response to ongoing feedback, including new arguments or information.	You will use technology to share your writing, provide links to other relevant information, and to update your information as needed.

Writing Standards, Grades 11–12 Students, continued

COMMON CORE STATE STANDARD	WHAT IT MEANS TO YOU
RESEARCH TO BUILD AND PRESENT KNOWLEDGE	
7. Conduct short as well as more sustained research projects to answer a question (including a self-generated question) or solve a problem; narrow or broaden the inquiry when appropriate; synthesize multiple sources on the subject, demonstrating understanding of the subject under investigation.	You will engage in short and more complex research tasks that include answering a question or solving a problem by using multiple sources. Your understanding of the subject will be evident in the product you develop.
8. Gather relevant information from multiple authoritative print and digital sources, using advanced searches effectively; assess the strengths and limitations of each source in terms of the task, purpose, and audience; integrate information into the text selectively to maintain the flow of ideas, avoiding plagiarism and overreliance on any one source and following a standard format for citation.	You will effectively conduct searches to gather information from a variety of print and digital sources and will evaluate each source in terms of the goal of your research. You will appropriately cite your sources of information and will follow a standard format for citation, such as the MLA or APA guidelines.
9. Draw evidence from literary or informational texts to support analysis, reflection, and research. **a.** Apply *grades 11–12 Reading standards* to literature (e.g., "Demonstrate knowledge of eighteenth-, nineteenth- and early-twentieth-century foundational works of American literature, including how two or more texts from the same period treat similar themes or topics"). **b.** Apply *grades 11–12 Reading standards* to literary nonfiction (e.g., "Delineate and evaluate the reasoning in seminal U.S. texts, including the application of constitutional principles and use of legal reasoning [e.g., in U.S. Supreme Court Case majority opinions and dissents] and the premises, purposes, and arguments in works of public advocacy [e.g., *The Federalist*, presidential addresses]").	You will paraphrase, summarize, quote, and cite primary and secondary sources, using both literary and informational texts, to support your analysis, reflection, and research, for purposes including **a.** written analysis of themes, author's choices, or point of view in works of literature **b.** written analysis of central ideas, text structure, word choice, point of view, or reasoning in works of literary nonfiction
RANGE OF WRITING	
10. Write routinely over extended time frames (time for research, reflection, and revision) and shorter time frames (a single sitting or a day or two) for a range of tasks, purposes, and audiences.	You will write a variety of texts for different purposes and audiences over both short and extended periods of time.

Spotlight on Common Core

Writing: Maintaining Clarity and Coherence

The Common Core State Standards stress the need to communicate clearly and coherently with your readers, so they can follow and understand what you have written.

Pre-planning helps you define your project and establish a realistic timeframe. Having insufficient time to draft, revise, and proofread will compromise the clarity and coherence of your writing.

COMMON CORE

W 4 Produce clear and coherent writing in which the development, organization, and style are appropriate to task, purpose, and audience.
W 10 Write routinely over extended time frames (time for research, reflection, and revision) and shorter time frames (a single sitting or a day or two) for a range of tasks, purposes, and audiences.

For example, what are you writing? A letter to a newspaper takes less time to write than a research paper. You also need plenty of time to research, draft, revise, and proofread what you have written, especially if you have a specific deadline. Give yourself more time than you need in case you have unexpected scheduling conflicts, need to start over and try a new approach to your topic, or must do extra research.

LEARN HOW **Planning Your Writing Process** Study the chart below. It provides some additional questions that you can ask yourself to help you plan your writing process and produce your best work.

Planning Your Writing Process	
Question	Examples
What is my final product?	• *A research paper for history class* • *A proposal to launch a school literary magazine* • *A letter to a newspaper*
What is my topic?	• *Queen Elizabeth I in Renaissance England* • *The benefits of a school literary magazine* • *The unfair portrayal of teenagers in an editorial*
What is my purpose, or reason, for writing?	• *To research and explain the rise to power of Queen Elizabeth I* • *To obtain permission and funding for a new school publication* • *To write an opposing argument to the opinions expressed in an editorial*
Who is my audience?	• *Other students in class* • *A committee of school board members and the school principal* • *The newspaper's editors and readers*
How much time do I have? Am I writing over a short or extended period of time?	• *One month* • *Two weeks* • *Two days*

You can plan your writing process once you understand your task, purpose, audience, and timeframe. For example, you can decide how much time you should spend researching your topic based on your purpose and due date. You might try drafting a schedule, using a calendar and your prior knowledge to decide how much time to allow for each step in the writing process.

LEARN HOW **Using Writing Strategies** With a writing plan, you can concentrate on producing clear and coherent writing. The **Writing Workshops** in this book provide several strategies to help you write effectively. Study the chart below. The highlighted text in the right column reflects the boldfaced points in the left column.

Writing Strategies	
DEVELOPMENT	**WHAT DOES IT LOOK LIKE?**
• Include a memorable introduction and concluding statement or section. • Utilize a **controlling idea or thesis statement.** • Introduce sufficient facts, definitions, **concrete details,** quotations, and other examples that are appropriate to the audience's knowledge of the topic.	*Female monarchs were the exception, not the rule, in Renaissance Europe. King Henry VIII (1491–1547) was displeased when his wife gave birth to a girl, rather than the male heir he wanted. Ironically, the daughter Henry did not want ultimately surpassed her father, becoming one of England's most powerful and beloved monarchs as well as an accomplished military commander. This paper will establish how Queen Elizabeth I (1533–1603) rose from disfavor to be loved by England and feared by other nations.*

Writing Strategies	*continued*
ORGANIZATION	**WHAT DOES IT LOOK LIKE?**
• Establish a **logical organization** that makes sense for the purpose and audience. • Provide graphics, use formatting, or other text features to help aid comprehension, if necessary. • Use organizational patterns, such as **cause-and-effect,** definitions, or compare-contrast to help readers understand the relationship between ideas. • Include words, phrases, and clauses that link sections of text and **create cohesion,** or flow. • Organize complex ideas, concepts, and information to **make important connections and distinctions.**	*There are three major ways the school would benefit from establishing and funding an online literary magazine.* *First, an online literary magazine will provide students with an in-house, professional publication. This will make their work available to the school community, increase student writers' self-respect and productivity, and enhance school pride.* *Second, students who work on the magazine will develop skills in editing, graphics, and desktop publishing. This, in turn, will help students gain valuable job skills.* *Third, this publication would contribute to student literacy by encouraging all students to participate personally in the reading and writing process. Many students keep journals or write poems and short stories. A student literary magazine provides a forum for sharing their work*
LANGUAGE AND STYLE	**WHAT DOES IT LOOK LIKE?**
• Maintain an **appropriate style and tone,** such as formal and objective for academic writing. • Use **precise language and telling details.** • Exhibit a strong command of grammar, usage, capitalization, and punctuation.	*I appreciate Mr. Swanson's argument that teenagers need to be more hardworking and responsible, but his conclusions are biased. Like some adults, he assumes most teenagers are lazy and unfocused. Mr. Swanson fails to account for the responsibilities many teenagers successfully face each day. These include working at part-time jobs to save for college and caring for younger siblings while parents work. These tasks are often in addition to demanding class schedules and participation in extracurricular school activities and volunteering.*

Authors combine different strategies to maintain clarity and coherence in their writing. They apply these strategies to texts of varied lengths, purposes, and complexity. Be sure to notice these strategies as you analyze texts throughout this book, and be sure to use them to improve your own writing.

College and Career Readiness Anchor Standards for Speaking and Listening

COMMON CORE STATE STANDARDS

COMPREHENSION AND COLLABORATION

1. Prepare for and participate effectively in a range of conversations and collaborations with diverse partners, building on others' ideas and expressing their own clearly and persuasively.

2. Integrate and evaluate information presented in diverse media and formats, including visually, quantitatively, and orally.

3. Evaluate a speaker's point of view, reasoning, and use of evidence and rhetoric.

PRESENTATION OF KNOWLEDGE AND IDEAS

4. Present information, findings, and supporting evidence such that listeners can follow the line of reasoning and the organization, development, and style are appropriate to task, purpose, and audience.

College and Career Readiness Anchor Standards for Speaking and Listening, continued

COMMON CORE STATE STANDARDS

5. Make strategic use of digital media and visual displays of data to express information and enhance understanding of presentations.

6. Adapt speech to a variety of contexts and communicative tasks, demonstrating command of formal English when indicated or appropriate.

Speaking and Listening Standards, Grades 11–12 Students

COMMON CORE STATE STANDARD	WHAT IT MEANS TO YOU
COMPREHENSION AND COLLABORATION **1.** Initiate and participate effectively in a range of collaborative discussions (one-on-one, in groups, and teacher-led) with diverse partners on grades 11–12 topics, texts, and issues, building on others' ideas and expressing their own clearly and persuasively.	You will actively participate in a variety of discussions in which you
a. Come to discussions prepared, having read and researched material under study; explicitly draw on that preparation by referring to evidence from texts and other research on the topic or issue to stimulate a thoughtful, well-reasoned exchange of ideas.	**a.** have read any relevant material beforehand and have come to the discussion prepared with background research
b. Work with peers to promote civil, democratic discussions and decision-making, set clear goals and deadlines, and establish individual roles as needed.	**b.** work with others to establish goals, processes, and roles within the group in order to have reasonable discussions
c. Propel conversations by posing and responding to questions that probe reasoning and evidence; ensure a hearing for a full range of positions on a topic or issue; clarify, verify, or challenge ideas and conclusions; and promote divergent and creative perspectives.	**c.** ask and respond to questions, encourage a range of positions, and relate the current topic to other relevant information and perspectives
d. Respond thoughtfully to diverse perspectives; synthesize comments, claims, and evidence made on all sides of an issue; resolve contradictions when possible; and determine what additional information or research is required to deepen the investigation or complete the task.	**d.** respond to different perspectives, summarize points of agreement or disagreement when needed, help to resolve unclear points, and set out a plan for additional research as needed
2. Integrate multiple sources of information presented in diverse formats and media (e.g., visually, quantitatively, orally) in order to make informed decisions and solve problems, evaluating the credibility and accuracy of each source and noting any discrepancies among the data.	You will integrate multiple and varied sources of information, assessing the credibility and accuracy of each source to aid the group-discussion process.

Speaking and Listening Standards, Grades 11–12 Students, continued

COMMON CORE STATE STANDARD		WHAT IT MEANS TO YOU
3. Evaluate a speaker's point of view, reasoning, and use of evidence and rhetoric, assessing the stance, premises, links among ideas, word choice, points of emphasis, and tone used.	▶	You will evaluate a speaker's argument and analyze the nature of the speaker's reasoning or evidence.
PRESENTATION OF KNOWLEDGE AND IDEAS		
4. Present information, findings, and supporting evidence, conveying a clear and distinct perspective, such that listeners can follow the line of reasoning, alternative or opposing perspectives are addressed, and the organization, development, substance, and style are appropriate to purpose, audience, and a range of formal and informal tasks.	▶	You will organize and present information, evidence, and your perspective to your listeners in a logical sequence and style that are appropriate to your task, purpose, and audience.
5. Make strategic use of digital media (e.g., textual, graphical, audio, visual, and interactive elements) in presentations to enhance understanding of findings, reasoning, and evidence and to add interest.	▶	You will use digital media to enhance understanding and to add interest to your presentations.
6. Adapt speech to a variety of contexts and tasks, demonstrating command of formal English when indicated or appropriate.	▶	You will adapt the formality of your speech appropriately, depending on its context and purpose.

Spotlight on Common Core

Speaking and Listening: Interacting Constructively in Discussions

COMMON CORE

SL 1b Work with peers to promote civil, democratic discussions and decision-making, set clear goals and deadlines, and establish individual roles as needed.

The Common Core State Standards note the importance of working constructively with your peers in group discussions. These discussions provide an opportunity to share opinions and ideas in order to answer a question, solve a problem, or reach consensus. A productive group discussion follows a democratic model. All participants should feel that they have ample opportunity to share their opinions and ideas, while also making an effort to acknowledge those that may be different from their own.

Before you begin your group discussion, assign roles to group members to keep the discussion moving in a smooth, organized fashion. You will need:

1. a **chairperson** who keeps the group focused on its goal or purpose, participates in the discussion and keeps it on track, and helps resolve conflicts
2. a **recorder** who takes notes on the discussion and summarizes suggestions and decisions
3. a **timekeeper** who keeps the discussion on schedule

Then, answer these questions:

1. What is the goal or purpose of the discussion? In other words, what should this discussion accomplish?
2. How much time does the group have for the discussion?
3. What rules will guide the discussion?

Then, establish rules to ensure a productive, open, energetic discussion in which participants may establish their opinions while remaining open-minded.

- Interrupting another speaker is rude and wastes time. Each participant needs sufficient time to convey his or her thoughts. If time is short, consider establishing a reasonable limit on how long each participant may speak to be monitored by the timekeeper.
- It is natural, and often helpful, for members of the group to have divergent points of view. A participant who stubbornly or aggressively dominates a discussion will block the free flow of ideas. Some participants may not get a chance to speak or may not feel that they should. Before the situation gets out of hand, the chairperson should quickly take action by politely reminding participants to treat each other with respect and allow everyone an equal opportunity to speak.

Active listening is the process of receiving, interpreting, evaluating, and responding to a message. In addition to showing your respect for your peers' opinions, even if they differ from your own, you may gain a fresh perspective that expands your own point of view about the issue under discussion.

- Fully focus your attention on what your peers say. Even if you disagree with what is being said, continue to listen respectfully. The chairperson should remind members of the group to do this if the discussion becomes too impassioned.
- When it's your turn, first summarize, or restate, the previous speaker's position briefly in your own words to verify that you have understood it. Ask the previous speaker clarifying questions if needed or refer to the recorder for further verification.
- State your own views as clearly, carefully, and concisely as you can.
- Respond diplomatically if another participant questions or disagrees with your opinion.
- Be willing to defend your point of view, but be open to changing your mind about it as well. You can profit from looking at an issue from an angle you might not have considered before.

Do not fear disagreement. A constructive disagreement helps participants to sharpen their minds. A lively discussion may help you clarify your opinion, provide additional evidence to support it, and sharpen your mind overall. You may learn something new and exciting from your opponent that causes you to see the world with fresh eyes.

When a difference of opinion arises, speak calmly, ask questions respectfully, and remain open-minded. Remember, you do not have to resolve all disagreements. Participants can respectfully agree to disagree. When disagreements arise:

- You should not aggressively interrupt or talk over one another.
- You and your opponent must present reasons or evidence to support your positions. If you say you like or dislike an idea, you must explain why. It is not enough to simply say you agree or disagree.
- See if you and your opponent can compromise or agree on part of the issue.
- Watch the time. You may not be able to come to a full agreement, but disagreements can spiral out of control. If it does not look as if agreement or compromise can be reached, participants need to agree to disagree and move on.

LEARN HOW **Interacting in Discussions** The following chart presents examples of effective discussion behaviors. The students are discussing the contemporary relevance of Shakespeare's plays.

Effective Behavior	What It Looks Like	
Support others' contributions.	Jason believes that literary works are a product of their historical time period. He says that there are limits to how much they apply to the present day because western culture has radically changed over time. Raj listens carefully to Jason's comments to ensure that he fully understands them and waits for his turn to speak	Jason states his views and Raj listens respectfully.
State your own views thoughtfully.	Raj summarizes Jason's opinion and asks Jason if his summary is accurate. Jason nods. Raj agrees that while some aspects of western culture have indeed radically changed, most aspects of human nature remain the same; therefore, Shakespeare's themes are still relevant.	Raj offers an alternative perspective, after summarizing Jason's points.

Summarize agreements and disagreements.	*Latoya is the chairperson of the group. She asks the recorder to summarize Jason and Raj's comments so far. It is then her turn to respond. She notes that neither one of them has offered concrete examples to back up their opinions. She asks if of they can do so. Jason goes first.*	As chairperson, Latoya points out that both speakers must offer evidence for their views.
Justify your views or consider new ones.	*Jason pauses to think and then answers Latoya. He notes that Shakespeare's plays cannot possibly apply to a dramatic historical shift, such as the change in women's roles over the last century. For example, women now have options, such as work opportunities, that people in Shakespeare's time could never have imagined. Raj had not considered this possibility. He was ready to defend his position, but now he realizes he may have to adjust it.*	Jason offers a concrete example, which prompts Raj to reconsider his position.

Throughout this book you will have opportunities to contribute to a variety of group discussions. Be sure to contribute effectively by understanding and modeling effective attitudes and behaviors. When you learn how to contribute effectively to group discussions, other participants will be more likely to listen to you and to grasp your views or perspectives on a topic or issue. Moreover, the discussion will bear fruit for everyone.

College and Career Readiness Anchor Standards for Language

COMMON CORE STATE STANDARDS

CONVENTIONS OF STANDARD ENGLISH

1. Demonstrate command of the conventions of standard English grammar and usage when writing or speaking.

2. Demonstrate command of the conventions of standard English capitalization, punctuation, and spelling when writing.

KNOWLEDGE OF LANGUAGE

3. Apply knowledge of language to understand how language functions in different contexts, to make effective choices for meaning or style, and to comprehend more fully when reading or listening.

VOCABULARY ACQUISITION AND USE

4. Determine or clarify the meaning of unknown and multiple-meaning words and phrases by using context clues, analyzing meaningful word parts, and consulting general and specialized reference materials, as appropriate.

5. Demonstrate understanding of word relationships and nuances in word meanings.

6. Acquire and use accurately a range of general academic and domain-specific words and phrases sufficient for reading, writing, speaking, and listening at the college and career readiness level; demonstrate independence in gathering vocabulary knowledge when considering a word or phrase important to comprehension or expression.

Language Standards, Grades 11–12 Students

COMMON CORE STATE STANDARD	WHAT IT MEANS TO YOU
CONVENTIONS OF STANDARD ENGLISH	
1. Demonstrate command of the conventions of standard English grammar and usage when writing or speaking.	You will correctly use the conventions of English grammar and usage, including
a. Apply the understanding that usage is a matter of convention, can change over time, and is sometimes contested.	**a.** demonstrating that usage follows accepted standards and can change or be contested
b. Resolve issues of complex or contested usage, consulting references (e.g., *Merriam-Webster's Dictionary of English Usage, Garner's Modern American Usage*) as needed.	**b.** using references to resolve disagreements or uncertainty about usage
2. Demonstrate command of the conventions of standard English capitalization, punctuation, and spelling when writing.	You will correctly use the conventions of standard English capitalization, punctuation, and spelling, including
a. Observe hyphenation conventions.	**a.** hyphens
b. Spell correctly.	**b.** spelling
KNOWLEDGE OF LANGUAGE	
3. Apply knowledge of language to understand how language functions in different contexts, to make effective choices for meaning or style, and to comprehend more fully when reading or listening.	You will apply your knowledge of language in different contexts to guide choices in your own writing and speaking by
a. Vary syntax for effect, consulting references (e.g., Tufte's *Artful Sentences*) for guidance as needed; apply an understanding of syntax to the study of complex texts when reading.	**a.** using appropriate references for guidance to vary your syntax and to understand syntax in complex texts
VOCABULARY ACQUISITION AND USE	
4. Determine or clarify the meaning of unknown and multiple-meaning words and phrases based on grades 11–12 reading and content, choosing flexibly from a range of strategies.	You will understand the meaning of grade-level appropriate words and phrases by
a. Use context (e.g., the overall meaning of a sentence, paragraph, or text; a word's position or function in a sentence) as a clue to the meaning of a word or phrase.	**a.** using context clues
b. Identify and correctly use patterns of word changes that indicate different meanings or parts of speech (e.g., *conceive, conception, conceivable*).	**b.** applying various forms of words according to meaning or part of speech
c. Consult general and specialized reference materials (e.g., dictionaries, glossaries, thesauruses), both print and digital, to find the pronunciation of a word or determine or clarify its precise meaning, its part of speech, its etymology, or its standard usage.	**c.** using reference materials to determine and clarify word meaning, part of speech, etymology, and standard usage
d. Verify the preliminary determination of the meaning of a word or phrase (e.g., by checking the inferred meaning in context or in a dictionary).	**d.** inferring and verifying the meanings of words in context

COMMON CORE STATE STANDARD	WHAT IT MEANS TO YOU

5. Demonstrate understanding of figurative language, word relationships, and nuances in word meanings.
   a. Interpret figures of speech (e.g., hyperbole, paradox) in context and analyze their role in the text.
   b. Analyze nuances in the meaning of words with similar denotations.
	You will understand figurative language, word relationships, and slight differences in word meanings by
	   a. interpreting figures of speech in context
	
	   b. analyzing slight differences in the meanings of similar words

6. Acquire and use accurately general academic and domain-specific words and phrases, sufficient for reading, writing, speaking, and listening at the college and career readiness level; demonstrate independence in gathering vocabulary knowledge when considering a word or phrase important to comprehension or expression.	You will develop and use a range of vocabulary at the college and career readiness level and will demonstrate that you can successfully acquire new vocabulary independently.

Spotlight on Common Core

 COMMON CORE

L 1a Apply the understanding that usage is a matter of convention, can change over time, and is sometimes contested. **L 1b** Resolve issues of complex or contested usage, consulting references (e.g., *Merriam-Webster's Dictionary of English Usage, Garner's Modern American Usage*) as needed.

Language: Understanding Usage

The English language is centuries old but ever-changing. For example, the words *text* and *message* have existed in English since the fourteenth century, but the term *text message,* meaning a form of electronic communication, is only a few decades old. Nonetheless, the rules of English usage that govern how and when to use words still apply. A handwritten letter qualifies as a *text* and a *message,* but it would be incorrect to refer to it as a *text message.*

Other words fall out of use generally, or become archaic, but live on in literature. "Thee" and "thou" no longer stand for "you" and "yours" in English today, but you will still encounter them in older texts.

LEARN HOW Understanding Usage English usage, like language, changes over time, and sometimes inspires controversy or confusion. For example, read these sentences. Should a sentence end with a preposition?

> *A word's meaning is often based on the language it derives <u>from</u>.*

> *A word's meaning is often based on the language <u>from</u> which it derives.*

Correct usage has long dictated that ending a sentence with a preposition (such as *from* or *with*) is incorrect. However, some writers have complained that ending sentences with a preposition sounds more natural.

Language experts no longer agree about this rule. Because it is controversial, you are safer applying the original rule to formal writing; the second sentence above is the better choice. Consulting a reference book that focuses on English usage is the best way to find the most authoritative information about current rules and practices.

Many words are often confused, misused, or nonstandard (not considered part of standard English). What is the difference between *every one* and *everyone? awfully* or *very? could have* or *could of?*

Confused Words *fewer* or *less?*	**Incorrect:** I made *less* cookies than last time. **Correct:** I made *fewer* cookies than last time. **Incorrect:** Please put *fewer* sugar in the lemonade. **Correct:** Please put *less* sugar in the lemonade.	Correct usage depends on the context in which each word is used. *Less* refers to general amounts when individual items cannot be counted. *Fewer* refers to items you can count.
Misused Words *awfully* or *very?*	**Incorrect:** I was *awfully* happy to see Paul. **Correct:** I was *very* happy to see Paul.	*Awfully* is colloquial, meaning it is not appropriate to use in formal speaking and writing.
Nonstandard Words *could of* or *could have?*	**Incorrect:** I *could of* left home earlier. **Correct:** I *could have* left home earlier.	*Could of* is nonstandard, so avoid using it in favor of *could have.*

See page R79, **Commonly Confused Words,** for additional examples.

LEARN HOW Using References to Resolve Usage Informal language is colloquial, or everyday, language you might use with friends or family: "Hector and Kevin want to *hang out* after school."

Likewise, substituting "u" instead of *you* or the number 4 for the word *for* is common in text-messaging. However, while you may use these abbreviations in casual text messages and e-mails, avoid them in formal contexts like school reports or job applications.

Formal language is more appropriate for business, legal, and academic contexts. It is important to make this distinction. For example, if you use informal language in a résumé or cover letter, you will appear unprofessional and a potential employer will not take you seriously. Read the following example of how to exchange informal for formal language in this sentence from a cover letter.

> **Informal Usage:** I can do an **awesome job 4 u.** My **boss really likes** me, so you can **phone him up** and he will **let you know** how I **helped him out.**

> **Formal Usage:** I **have excellent qualifications for the position.** If you wish to **contact** him, my **former employer, Mr. DeLuca,** will be **happy to recommend me** and **discuss my skills.**

When in doubt about whether a word is appropriate for its context, consult a dictionary of English usage such as *Merriam-Webster's Dictionary of English Usage, Garner's Modern American Usage,* or *The American Heritage Book of English Usage.*

Like the language itself, the rules that govern it change over time. Experts may even argue about, or contest, the correct usage of a word. The word *data* comes from the Latin *datum.* In Latin, *data* is considered plural, so it has been treated as a plural noun in English, too, and takes a plural verb: *The data the scientists collected **are** irreplaceable.*

However, over time, data has come to mean a "singular mass of information" and some newspapers and magazines now treat it as a singular noun that takes a singular verb: *The **data,** which the scientists gathered for months, **is** no longer valid.* According to *Merriam-Webster* and *American Heritage,* both the singular and plural forms of *data* are acceptable, although the plural form still dominates scientific and academic writing. In other words, in formal contexts, it is still safer to treat *data* as a plural noun.

Particularly as you write and speak in your classes and in your endeavors after high school, be aware of correct usage. Remember that you can add to your knowledge by consulting appropriate reference sources.

Spotlight on Common Core

COMMON CORE L3a Vary syntax for effect, consulting references (e.g., Tufte's *Artful Sentences*) for guidance as needed; apply an understanding of syntax to the study of complex texts when reading.

Language: Varying Syntax for Effect

Syntax comes from the Greek word for arrangement, or ordering together. It refers to the way a writer arranges words, phrases, clauses, and sentences to create an effect on the reader. If a writer's prose is needlessly repetitive or lacks verbal rhythm, or flow, it sounds lifeless and loses its effectiveness.

In order to avoid this problem, you should vary the syntax in your writing. This benefits your writing in several ways. Instead of sounding dull, your prose will come alive and engage your reader. Varying syntax also allows you to add information or emphasize specific words or ideas to dramatic effect so they convey your message better. In order to vary syntax:

1. Vary sentence lengths for emphasis within paragraphs by alternating long and short sentences.

2. Vary sentence structure by rearranging or adding words, phrases, or clauses to individual sentences or by combining multiple sentences.

LEARN HOW Varying Syntax When you vary syntax, remember that your writing must remain appropriate to your task, purpose, and audience. Each sentence must be clear and coherent. For additional options about how to vary syntax, you may consult a reference (such as Virginia Tufte's *Artful Sentences: Syntax as Style*).

You can vary syntax for emphasis by varying sentence length. Read the concluding paragraph below from "Evidence of Progress," a political commentary about England written in 1830 by the Victorian writer Thomas Babington Macaulay (see pages 1032–1035).

> . . . Our rulers will best promote the improvement of the nation by strictly confining themselves to their own legitimate duties, by leaving capital to find its most lucrative course, commodities their fair price, industry and intelligence their natural reward, idleness and folly their natural punishment, by maintaining peace, by defending property, by diminishing the price of law, and by observing strict economy in every department of the State. Let the Government do this: the People will assuredly do the rest.

Macaulay offers a long list of duties the government should perform. He effectively uses parallel structure to indicate how British rulers can improve the country ("by strictly confining themselves," "by leaving capital," "by maintaining peace," and so on). To great effect, he follows this list with a much shorter, blunter sentence: "Let the Government do this: the People will assuredly do the rest." The sentence's brevity makes it sound definitive and resolute. It is memorable and solidifies his argument because it has the ring of conviction. The rhetorical balance between the two halves of the sentence suggests that the actions of the people are as important as the duties of the government for Macaulay.

Here are some examples of how to revise sentences to vary syntax. These sentences come from an argument about the British monarchy. Note how each revision changes the effect of these sentences on the reader.

> The British monarchy should end. The royal family costs too much. They do not contribute to society. They are planning an expensive royal wedding. British people are losing their jobs.

Desired Effect	Revision
To improve rhythm	The royal family costs too much and does not contribute to society enough. To make matters worse, as they plan an expensive royal wedding, British people are losing their jobs. The British monarchy should end.
To create emphasis	People are losing their jobs, but the royal family is still planning an expensive wedding. The British monarchy should end. The royal family costs too much and contributes too little.
To create emphasis and drama	Why is the royal family planning an expensive wedding when British people are losing their jobs? Abolish the British monarchy now! They cost too much and contribute too little.
To create emphasis and drama and to add important information	As the royal family plans a multi-million dollar wedding, thousands of British people are losing their jobs. It is time to end a monarchy that spends extravagant sums, but won't use them to help their own people.

In your own writing, be sure to vary syntax to affect your readers. As you read the texts in this book, notice how authors vary syntax to affect you as a reader.

Exploring British Literature

INTRODUCING
THE ESSENTIALS

- Text Analysis Workshop
- Academic Vocabulary Workshop
- Writing Process Workshop

NUMB. I

The SPECTATOR.

Non fumum ex fulgore, sed ex fumo dare lucem
Cogitat; ut speciosa dehinc miracula promat. Hor.

To be Continued every Day.

Thursday, March 1. 1711.

I Have observed, that a Reader seldom peruses a Book with Pleasure 'till he knows whether the Writer of it be a black or a fair Man, of a mild or cholerick Disposition, Married or a ſtinguished my ſelf by a moſt profound Silence: For, during the Space of eight Years, excepting in the publick Exerciſes of the College, I ſcarce uttered the Quantity of an hundred Words; and in-

Insights and Perspectives

The study of British literature is a remarkable journey that begins with an Anglo-Saxon epic set in a land plagued by monsters and continues through works in which modern writers tackle contemporary issues. Along the way, you'll encounter Robin Hood, King Arthur, and other legendary characters who remain a vital part of popular culture because they still have the power to captivate. You'll explore masterpieces—such as *The Canterbury Tales* and *Macbeth*—that have changed the way we view society and ourselves. You'll also learn how British literature has influenced American traditions. The literature in this book can help you . . .

Connect HISTORY and Literature

British literature spans about 1,500 years—from Old English poems to modern bestsellers. As you read, you'll be asked to make connections between individual works and the real-life conditions that inspired them. In this way, you'll gain a greater understanding of the people and events that shaped Britain over the centuries.

Explore BIG IDEAS

Can love bring more suffering than joy? What makes an effective leader? People of all time periods and cultures have grappled with questions about love and politics. Some ideas are universal, as you'll discover when you read sonnets by lovestruck poets and speeches by such leaders as Elizabeth I and Winston Churchill.

Build CULTURAL LITERACY

Who was the Bard of Avon? Where does the phrase "Big Brother" come from? There are certain people, events, phrases, and ideas so embedded in today's culture that everyone should be familiar with them. Studying British literature helps you develop an awareness of the authors, literary works, and historical milestones that still matter.

Appreciate a LEGACY

Why read an Anglo-Saxon epic about a fierce warrior or a medieval legend about heroic knights? Some characters and themes in early works of British literature live on in today's stories and movies. In this book, you'll find out why such tales as *Beowulf* and *Le Morte d'Arthur* continue to be reimagined by cultures around the globe.

Literature and Nonfiction in Context

To best appreciate works of British literature and nonfiction, you should have some sense of their **historical context,** or the social conditions that gave rise to them. Geoffrey Chaucer's *The Canterbury Tales,* for example, is unmistakably a product of its time. The rich stories in Chaucer's work strongly reflect the customs and people of his medieval world. Similarly, the early 20th-century fiction of James Joyce is forever linked with his boyhood experiences in Dublin, Ireland's bustling capital. As you read this book, you will become more familiar with Britain's long, fabled history and the circumstances that influenced the thoughts and words of its finest writers.

COMMON CORE

Included in this workshop:
RL 3, RL 4, RL 10, RI 7, L 3a, L 4a, L 4c

BRITISH LITERATURE AND NONFICTION IN CONTEXT

THE ANGLO SAXON PERIOD 449–1066	THE MEDIEVAL PERIOD 1066–1485	THE ENGLISH RENAISSANCE 1485–1660	THE RESTORATION AND THE EIGHTEENTH CENTURY 1660–1798
• The Beowulf Poet • The Venerable Bede	• Geoffrey Chaucer • The Gawain Poet • Sir Thomas Malory	• Christopher Marlowe • William Shakespeare • John Milton • John Donne	• Daniel Defoe • Alexander Pope • Jonathan Swift • Samuel Johnson • Mary Wollstonecraft

| **449** The Anglo-Saxon invasion of Britain begins.

793 Vikings begin raids on England, eventually conquering northern and eastern regions.

871 Alfred the Great becomes king of Wessex. | **1066** Norman Conquest—William the Conquerer becomes king of England.

1215 King John signs the Magna Carta, limiting royal authority.

1337 The Hundred Years' War with France begins (to 1453).

1347 The bubonic plague reaches Europe, killing millions. | **1517** Martin Luther begins the Protestant Reformation.

1558 The reign of Elizabeth I begins (to 1603).

1609 Galileo Galilei studies the heavens with a telescope.

1642 The English Civil War erupts (to 1651). | **1665** The Great Plague of London kills thousands.

1760 The reign of George III begins (to 1820).

1775 War with colonies in North America erupts (to 1783).

1789 The French Revolution rises in Paris (to 1799). |

Literary Movements

Like music and art, literature can be organized into historical periods. Within each period, there are groups of writers who play a key role in the development of literary movements, or noteworthy trends in literature. Some movements are so important that historical periods are named after them. While grunge and hip hop are examples of trends in music history, British literature counts romanticism and modernism among its important trends. Studying these literary movements in context will allow you to better grasp how, when, and why various works of British literature came into being.

ROMANTICISM 1798–1832	THE VICTORIAN AGE 1832–1901	MODERNISM 1901–1950	POSTMODERNISM 1950–PRESENT
• William Wordsworth • Samuel Taylor Coleridge • George Gordon, Lord Byron • Percy Bysshe Shelley • John Keats	• Alfred, Lord Tennyson • The Brontë Sisters • Anthony Trollope • Charles Dickens • George Eliot	• T. S. Eliot • Virginia Woolf • James Joyce • George Orwell • W. H. Auden	• Samuel Beckett • Ted Hughes • Seamus Heaney • William Trevor • Nadine Gordimer

1811 George III is declared insane; Prince of Wales is named regent. **1815** Britain and Prussia conquer Napoleon Bonaparte at Waterloo. **1817** Ludwig van Beethoven begins composing Ninth Symphony (to 1824).	**1837** At age 19, Victoria I begins her reign (to 1901). **1859** Charles Darwin publishes *On the Origin of Species*. **1861** Civil War erupts in the United States (to 1865). **1879** Ireland pressures for home rule.	**1918** British military deaths total about 750,000 at the end of World War I. **1921** Irish Free State is established (becomes the Republic of Ireland in 1949). **1936** The reign of George VI begins (to 1952). **1939** Britain joins France in battling Germany in World War II (to 1945).	**1952** Elizabeth II becomes Britain's monarch. **1997** Britain returns Hong Kong to China, ending 155 years of colonial rule. **2003** Britain joins the Iraq War. **2007** Protestants and Catholics in northern Ireland agree to a historic power-sharing plan.

Using Critical Lenses

Think about what you see when you look through a camera's lens. What do you consider before you snap a photograph? Do you want your subject to be brightly lit or cast in shadow? Should you focus on objects in the center or something off to the side? Believe it or not, you can ask similar questions when you're reading literature. Using critical lenses can help shed light on the works you read and bring overlooked elements into focus. For example, how did the author's life influence his or her writing? What social tensions affected the author? Looking through different lenses, you may discover more to literature than meets the eye.

THE LENSES	QUESTIONS TO ASK	
LITERARY LENS When you look through a literary lens, you focus on such elements as plot, theme, and author's style in various forms of literature, including poetry.	• What is the specific form of poetry or prose, and what are its characteristics? • What is distinctive about this author's style? • How is imagery used to establish the setting and mood?	
HISTORICAL AND CULTURAL LENSES Historical and cultural lenses help you consider how elements of history and culture may have influenced the author and the writing.	• What was going on in the country at the time this work was written? • What questions, issues, and concerns were people of the time grappling with? • How are those events and issues, as well as the author's attitude toward them, reflected in the writing?	
BIOGRAPHICAL LENS The biographical lens focuses your attention on the author's background. It prompts you to consider how factors such as heritage, personal experiences, and economic circumstances may have shaped him or her.	• What were the defining events or experiences in the author's life? • What people—other writers, friends, family members—were known influences on him or her? • What role did culture or heritage play in shaping the author's attitude toward his or her subject?	
OTHER LENSES • psychological • social • political • philosophical/moral	• What motivations might be influencing a character's behavior? (psychological) • Do you agree with the character's choices and decisions? Are they ethical and honest? (moral)	

MODEL: CRITICAL LENSES

David Copperfield is considered one of Charles Dickens's most autobiographical works. It is set in early 19th-century London, when the Industrial Revolution first began. Cities became crowded, and the working class struggled to survive. In this excerpt, an orphaned Copperfield takes a job for his own survival. Read the entire passage first. Then read it again, using critical lenses to answer the **Close Read** questions.

from David Copperfield

Novel by **Charles Dickens**

I know enough of the world now, to have almost lost the capacity of being much surprised by anything; but it is matter of some surprise to me, even now, that I can have been so easily thrown away at such an age. A child of excellent abilities, and with strong powers of observation, quick, eager, delicate, and
5 soon hurt bodily and mentally, it seems wonderful to me that nobody should have made any sign in my behalf. But none was made; and I became, at ten years old, a little labouring hind[1] in the service of Murdstone and Grinby.

Murdstone and Grinby's warehouse was at the water-side. It was down in Blackfriars.[2] Modern improvements have altered the place; but it was the last
10 house at the bottom of a narrow street, curving down hill to the river, with some stairs at the end, where people took boat. It was a crazy old house with a wharf of its own, abutting on the water when the tide was in, and on the mud when the tide was out, and literally overrun with rats. Its panelled rooms, discoloured with the dirt and smoke of a hundred years, I dare say; its decaying
15 floors and staircase; the squeaking and scuffling of the old grey rats down in the cellars; and the dirt and rottenness of the place; are things, not of many years ago, in my mind, but of the present instant. They are all before me, just as they were in the evil hour when I went among them for the first time, with my trembling hand in Mr. Quinion's.
20 Murdstone and Grinby's trade was among a good many kinds of people but an important branch of it was the supply of wines and spirits to certain packet ships. I forget now where they chiefly went, but I think there were some among them that made voyages both to the East and West Indies. I know that a great many empty bottles were one of the consequences of this traffic, and that certain
25 men and boys were employed to examine them against the light, and reject those that were flawed, and to rinse and wash them. When the empty bottles ran short, there were labels to be pasted on full ones, or corks to be fitted to them, or seals to be put upon the corks, or finished bottles to be packed in casks. All this work was my work, and of the boys employed upon it I was one.

---

1. **hind:** a farm laborer or skilled worker.

2. **Blackfriars:** a small district in Central London.

Close Read

1. **Cultural Lens** David feels he was "thrown away" to become a worker at a young age. What can you infer about his society's attitude toward both work and the education and welfare of children?

2. **Literary/Historical Lenses** Reread the boxed text. What imagery does Dickens use to describe the setting? Consider what this suggests about the working conditions of the time.

3. **Historical Lens** How might the process described in lines 23–28 be handled today? How has the need for human labor changed since the Industrial Revolution?

30   There were three or four of us, counting me. My working place was established in a corner of the warehouse, where Mr. Quinion could see me, when he chose to stand up on the bottom rail of his stool in the counting-house, and look at me through a window above the desk. Hither, on the first morning of my so auspiciously beginning life on my own account, the oldest of the regular boys

35   was summoned to show me my business. His name was Mick Walker, and he wore a ragged apron and a paper cap. He informed me that his father was a bargeman, and walked, in a black velvet head-dress, in the Lord Mayor's Show.[3] He also informed me that our principal associate would be another boy whom he introduced by the—to me—extraordinary name of Mealy Potatoes. I discovered,

40   however, that this youth had not been christened by that name, but that it had been bestowed upon him in the warehouse, on account of his complexion, which was pale or mealy. . . .

No words can express the secret agony of my soul as I sunk into this companionship; compared these henceforth everyday associates with those of my

45   happier childhood—not to say with Steerforth, Traddles, and the rest of those boys; and felt my hopes of growing up to be a learned and distinguished man crushed in my bosom. The deep remembrance of the sense I had, of being utterly without hope now; of the shame I felt in my position; of the misery it was to my young heart to believe that day by day what I had learned, and thought, and

50   delighted in, and raised my fancy and my emulation up by, would pass away from me, little by little, never to be brought back anymore; cannot be written.

---

3. **Lord Mayor's Show:** the parade in which the newly elected mayor proceeds through London, pledging allegiance to the crown.

You may find the following information about Charles Dickens interesting in light of the passage you just read. Refer back to the excerpt from *David Copperfield* as needed to answer the **Close Read** questions.

Charles Dickens

Charles Dickens was born in 1812 in Portsmouth, England, during the height of the Industrial Revolution. The Dickens family, like many others, moved to overcrowded London to find work. Two years later, Charles'

5   father was imprisoned for unpaid debts. To help support his family of ten, twelve-year-old Charles withdrew from school and went to work labeling bottles in a warehouse. It was common for factory owners of this era to demand that child laborers work 14-hour days, 6 days a week, in dirty and unsafe conditions. Dickens eventually returned

10   to school and became a law clerk, then a journalist, and finally a novelist. *David Copperfield* and his other popular novels made Dickens a champion of the working class. He died in 1870, having become one of the most beloved authors of his day.

Close Read

4. **Psychological Lens** Why might Mick Walker have chosen to share these specific details about his father so quickly?

5. **Cultural Lens** What do you learn about David's values in the boxed lines? Decide whether you think the author shares these values.

6. **Literary Lens** Why do you think Dickens chose a first-person narrator to tell the story of David Copperfield?

Close Read

1. **Biographical Lens** How does your knowledge of Dickens's childhood affect your understanding of the *David Copperfield* excerpt?

2. **Biographical Lens** What might Dickens's purpose have been in describing David Copperfield's experience at Murdstone and Grinby's warehouse?

Literature and Nonfiction Strategies

 Record your observations in your **Reader/Writer Notebook.**

❶ Understand Form

British literature includes not only short stories, novels, and dramas but also a wide range of poetic forms, such as the sonnet, ballad, epic, and ode. When you approach new forms that are unfamiliar, you can rely on strategies such as those below.

FORM	STRATEGIES
Epic: a long, narrative poem celebrating the adventures of a great hero.	• Read in complete sentences. Don't stop at the ends of lines. • Take notes to keep track of the events in the hero's journey. • Decide what virtues the epic hero embodies. They probably reflect important cultural values at that time.
Sonnet: a lyric poem of 14 lines.	• Read the poem aloud, noting the rhyming pattern, rhythm, and other sound devices. • Identify the shift in the speaker's mood or message. • Use a chart to record sensory images—words or phrases that appeal to the five senses.

❷ Clarify Meaning

When you read British literature and nonfiction, you will encounter unfamiliar language and difficult sentence structures. Use these strategies and tips to help unlock the meaning of challenging texts.

• **Break Down Sentences** Break down complicated sentences by first locating the sentence's main subject and verb. Then, identify objects, modifiers, and phrases. Try restating the sentences more simply, rearranging word order if necessary.

• **Use Context Clues** A word's context—the words and sentences that surround it—often gives clues to the word's meaning. Dialects, for example, have their own rules of grammar and pronunciation, which you can figure out from context clues.

• **Consult References** When you encounter an unfamiliar word or allusion, check the vocabulary definitions and footnotes provided in this book or look the word up in a print or digital reference source.

❸ Ask Your Own Questions

An important part of analyzing texts is knowing what questions to ask as you read. What should you look for when you read a story, drama, or news article? To make your reading more meaningful, it's also important to ask the questions *you* wonder about so that you connect what you read to yourself and the world around you. The following features of your textbook will help you ask the right questions and read with your own questions in mind.

Where to Look	What You'll Find
Text Analysis Workshops (throughout every unit)	Interactive practice models and **Close Read** questions
Side notes and discussion questions	Questions (throughout and following each selection) that focus on text analysis
Analysis Frames THINK central Go to **thinkcentral.com**. KEYWORD: HML12-9	Guided questions for analyzing different types of texts

What Is Academic Vocabulary?

COMMON CORE

Included in this workshop:
L 3, L 4, L 4a–b, L 6

Answer, first, watch—these are everyday words that you hear and use in conversations with family and friends. In school, however, you are just as likely to hear or read *respond, primary,* and *monitor.* Each of these words is a synonym for one of the earlier three words; but unlike the earlier words, they are part of a special vocabulary called **academic vocabulary,** the language used to talk and write about school subject matter.

Why use academic vocabulary? In some cases, academic vocabulary doesn't have an exact equivalent in everyday language. It may be a label for a very big idea—as *culture* includes all products of human work and thought. On the other hand, it may have a very precise meaning—as *consent* means not just "agreement" but "agreement to a proposal." Even when an exact synonym exists, however, using academic vocabulary sends a signal to your audience: that you want to be taken seriously. Understanding and using academic vocabulary will help you to be successful in school and on assessments. This web shows examples of academic vocabulary words in different subject areas.

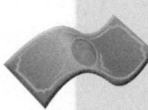

ECONOMICS
Analyze how scarcity leads nations to make choices about the use of **resources**.

LANGUAGE ARTS
How does Lady Macbeth **respond** to her husband's reluctance to commit murder?

GOVERNMENT
It is important to understand the role of **culture,** geography, and history in government.

ACADEMIC VOCABULARY
The language that you use to think, talk, and write about different subject areas you are studying

PHYSIOLOGY
What are the **phases** of cell division?

PRE-CALCULUS
Use the properties of the function to **analyze** and solve the problem.

PHYSICS
The molecular **structure** of rocks on the ocean floor aligns with the earth's magnetic poles.

Use the following chart to become familiar with some of the academic vocabulary terms in this book. As you read, look for the activities labeled "Academic Vocabulary in Writing" and "Academic Vocabulary in Speaking." These activities provide opportunities to use academic language in your writing and discussions.

Word	Definition	Example
affect	to influence	How does the poem's imagery **affect** its mood?
analyze	to take something apart in order to see how it works	Describe and **analyze** the motion represented in the velocity-time graph.
consent	to agree to someone's proposal	Individuals **consent** to join the labor market for a variety of reasons.
culture	all products of human work and thought, including behavior patterns, arts, beliefs, and institutions	How does our **culture** influence the way children are educated in our society?
draft	any of the stages of development of a plan, document, or picture	Include a Works Cited list in the final **draft** of your research report.
hypothesis	a tentative idea or explanation that can be tested by further investigation	Developing a testable **hypothesis** is a critical step in any scientific experiment.
monitor	to keep close watch over	You can **monitor** your understanding of a difficult text as you read by pausing to summarize mentally each paragraph.
phase	a stage of development	A traditional economy is usually the first **phase** of a civilization's economic development.
primary	first (in sequence, rank, or importance)	The **primary** role of government is to provide society with institutions and processes through which binding decisions are made.
resources	something that can be used for support or help, such as land, labor, or minerals.	The Internet is a useful **resource** for research material, but be careful to evaluate the reliability of each source.
respond	to answer, reply, or react	Most patients **respond** favorably to a combination of surgery and physical therapy.
structure	arrangement or organization; to give order or form	The speaker was able to **structure** his argument in a logical and persuasive way.

Academic Vocabulary in Action

The terms below are examples of commonly used academic vocabulary. Knowing the meaning of these terms is essential for completing the activities and lessons in this book as well as mastering test items.

structure *(noun and verb)*

Defining the Word

The noun *structure* means "arrangement or organization." It can also refer to something constructed, such as a building. As a verb *structure* means "to give form or order to." In a science class, you may learn about the structure of the human body. In a language arts class, you may be asked to structure a report by creating an outline.

Using the Word

Once you understand the meaning of a word root, you will be able to understand the meanings of other words built on the same root. The word root *stru,* from the Latin word *struere,* means "to arrange."

- In a chart like this one, make a list of other words you know formed from the root *stru.*

- Look up each word in a dictionary and write down its meaning.

- Write a sentence using each word.

Word	Definition	Sentence
construe	to build in one's mind; interpret	It would be a mistake to construe her silence as a lack of intelligence.

respond *(verb)*

Defining the Word

To *respond* is to answer or to react. You learn how prices respond to demand in economics. In a physics class, you may be asked to predict how two objects in collision respond in zero gravity. When reading literature, you will often respond by looking for the main concept or idea the author is trying to communicate.

Using the Word

Practice using words related to *respond.*

- Use a chart like the one shown to identify subject areas in which you have seen the words related to *respond* used.

- Write a brief definition of the word, using a dictionary if necessary.

- Write a sentence using the word in the context of that specific subject area.

Related Word: Definition	Subject Area	Sentence
Response: answer or reaction	economics	Price inflation is a response to excessive money supply.

Strategies That Work: Vocabulary

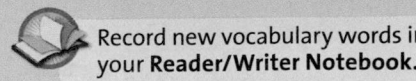
Record new vocabulary words in your **Reader/Writer Notebook.**

❶ Analyze Prefixes and Suffixes

Technical or specialized vocabulary—the language of specific content areas, like science, mathematics, or social studies—often contains Greek or Latin affixes. Recognizing these word parts can help you figure out a word's meaning.

Prefixes	Examples
auto- (self)	autocrat, autodidact, autoimmune, automation
proto- (first)	protohistory, protoplasm, prototype, protozoan
sub- (under)	subaltern, subatomic, subculture, sub rosa, subsistence

Suffixes	Examples
-ate (become, cause, or form)	decimate, enervate, saturate, triangulate, invalidate
-escent (in the process of)	incandescent, putrescent, quiescent, senescent
-ic (relating to)	acidic, anaerobic, historic, iambic, metric

❷ Use Context Clues

Using **context**—the words, phrases, or sentences that surround a word—is another effective way to understand unfamiliar words as you read. When you come across an unfamiliar word, look not only for familiar affixes but also for context clues. They will often give you important information about the word's meaning, as in the following example:

> Many governing bodies have open-meeting standards to avoid *sub rosa* conferences between legislators and special interest groups.

You can tell that *sub rosa* means "secret." The words *to avoid* contrast *sub rosa* conferences with open meetings.

❸ Keep a Word List

Unlocking the meaning of unfamiliar words as you read is one way to develop your vocabulary. Another way is to keep a list of those new words so that you remember them the next time you see them. Try classifying the words in different ways so that you have a variety of mental "hooks" to help spur your memory.

Interactive Vocabulary **THINK** central
Go to **thinkcentral.com.**
KEYWORD: HML12-13

*For a complete list of terms in this book, see the **Glossary of Academic Vocabulary in English & Spanish** on pages R131–R132.*

Words from Physiology
respond: to react
scheme: a diagram of a system

Words from Economics
resource: anything used for economic development
structure: arrangement or organization

Words from Language Arts
resource: something that helps
respond: to reply
scheme: a secret plan

Words with re- ("go back")
resource: anything used for economic development
respond: to reply or react

Expressing Ideas in Writing

Russian author Vladimir Nabokov once commented on the challenge of writing, "The pages are still blank, but there is a miraculous feeling of the words being there, written in invisible ink and clamoring to become visible." Writing is a powerful way to explore opinions, share insights, and evaluate information. The challenge lies in making your ideas "visible" to readers, whether you're writing on paper or on screen.

⬤ COMMON CORE

Included in this workshop:
W 4, W 5, SL 1a–b, L 1, L 2, L 3

Consider Your Options

Are you contributing to a wiki about your favorite hobby, posting an editorial on a class blog about a controversial school issue, or writing a research paper for your English class? Start by clarifying three fundamental considerations—your **purpose,** your **audience,** and the **format** of your writing.

PURPOSE

Why am I writing?
- to entertain
- to inform or explain
- to argue or persuade
- to describe
- to reflect
- to inspire or motivate

AUDIENCE

Who are my readers?
- classmates
- teacher
- friends
- online community
- college admissions office
- potential employer
- community members

FORMAT

Which format will best suit my purpose and audience?
- analytical essay
- short story
- wiki
- research paper
- news article
- speech
- summary
- letter
- poem
- proposal
- blog entry
- critique
- podcast

Continue with the Process

As you complete the **Writing Workshops** in this book, you'll discover the process that works best for you. Use this model as a guide.

THE WRITING PROCESS

PLANNING/PREWRITING

At this stage, decide what you want to write about. Start by generating ideas using one of the prewriting strategies listed on page 17. Keep your **purpose** and **audience** in mind as you narrow and refine your topic.

Depending on your **format,** you also might formulate your **thesis,** or **opinion, statement** and collect evidence to support your main points.

WHAT DOES IT LOOK LIKE?

T. S. Eliot's "Preludes"
- gritty images of urban life
- speaker despairs over society's cruel indifference

Both
- individuals suffering
- society indifferent

W. H. Auden's "Musée des Beaux Arts"
- images of peaceful scene; boy drowns, and others carry on
- speaker employs a matter-of-fact, ironic tone

DRAFTING

Give shape to your ideas by writing a first draft. If you're writing an informal piece, such as a blog or a journal entry, you might start writing with no set plan. If you're doing a more formal assignment, such as an analytical essay or a research paper, draft from an outline. Either way, don't expect perfection in your first draft; you may need to do several drafts before hitting your stride.

WHAT DOES IT LOOK LIKE?

I. Imagery
   A. Negative imagery in "Preludes"
   B. Peaceful imagery in "Musée des Beaux Arts"
II. Speaker's attitude
   A. Speaker's despairing tone in "Preludes"
   B. Speaker's ironic tone in "Musée des Beaux Arts"
III. Historical influences on poet

REVISING

Do a critical review of your draft, evaluating its development, organization, and style.
- Check your draft against a rubric such as the one on the following page.
- Ask a peer reader for feedback.
- Consider trying a new approach if something is not working.

ASK A PEER READER

- What is my main idea or thesis? Have I communicated it effectively?
- Where should I add more details or evidence?
- Do my ideas flow smoothly? If not, where do I need to reorganize my points or add transitions?

EDITING AND PUBLISHING

Proofread your draft for errors in grammar, spelling, and mechanics. Then get your writing out where others can read it. Where you publish, of course, depends on your purpose, audience, and format.

WHAT DOES IT LOOK LIKE?

In "Preludes," T. S. Eliot describes the alienating affects of the industrial age, especially on those laboring in crowded cities.

Scoring Rubric

Score	COMMON CORE TRAITS
6	• **Development** Includes a meaningful, engaging introduction; thoroughly develops the topic with well-chosen, relevant, and sufficient evidence; ends powerfully • **Organization** Logically organizes complex ideas, concepts, and information; uses appropriate and varied transitions to create cohesion and clarify relationships among ideas • **Language** Uses precise language in imaginative ways; maintains an appropriate style and tone for the audience and purpose; shows a strong command of conventions
5	• **Development** Has an engaging introduction; develops the topic with relevant, well-chosen evidence; has an effective concluding section • **Organization** Logically organizes ideas, concepts, and information; uses appropriate transitions to create cohesion and clarify relationships • **Language** Effectively uses precise language; maintains an appropriate style and tone for the audience and purpose; has a few errors in conventions
4	• **Development** Has an introduction, but it could be more engaging; lacks sufficient support for one or two ideas; has an adequate, though routine, concluding section • **Organization** Is logically organized, with one or two exceptions; could use a few more transitions to clarify the relationships among ideas • **Language** Includes some vague word choices; has one or two lapses in style and tone; includes a few distracting errors in conventions
3	• **Development** Has both an introduction and conclusion, but they are superficial or uninteresting; includes some unsupported ideas or irrelevant evidence • **Organization** Has some flaws in organization; needs more transitions • **Language** Uses words correctly, though language is unimaginative; has frequent lapses in style and tone; has some critical errors in conventions
2	• **Development** Has an unfocused, uninteresting introduction; does not develop most ideas; ends abruptly • **Organization** Has an illogical organization; lacks transitions throughout • **Language** Uses vague language and misuses some words; lapses into an inappropriate style and tone in many places; contains many distracting errors in conventions
1	• **Development** Lacks an introduction, development, and a concluding section • **Organization** Has no discernible organization; lacks transitions or uses inappropriate ones • **Language** Uses many words incorrectly; employs an inappropriate style and tone for the audience and purpose; has major problems with conventions

Strategies That Work: Writing

Record your writing ideas, plans, and notes in your **Reader/Writer Notebook.**

❶ Use Prewriting Strategies

Use any of the following strategies to get beyond the blank page:

- **Rely on current events.** Keep abreast of scientific discoveries, controversial issues, and newsworthy events. They can be great sources for topic ideas.

- **Confer with others.** Generate topic ideas by brainstorming with classmates or friends.

- **Get visual.** Nudge your ideas to flow by creating a graphic organizer, such as a Venn diagram or a story board.

- **Freewrite.** Write continuously for several minutes, recording any ideas without judging them.

- **Write from a prompt.** Consult the prompts featured in the **Writing Workshops.**

Writing Online
THINK central
Go to thinkcentral.com.
KEYWORD: HML12N-17

❷ Partner with a Peer Reader

Peer readers can help you determine where to strengthen your writing to better reach your purpose for your audience. Consider the following guidelines:

When You're the Writer	When You're the Reader
• Identify the kind of feedback you would like to receive. Should your reader evaluate your argument, your style, or both?	• Start by reading the piece carefully. Then, read it a second time to critically evaluate it.
• Inform your reader about your intended purpose and audience.	• Focus on specific recommendations for strengthening the work, not just on its weaknesses.
• Listen to your reader's criticisms calmly and respectfully. Remember that *you* will decide how to use these comments.	• Be respectful.
	• Point out effective parts of the writing. Remember that constructive criticism is the best kind of feedback.
• Be willing to consider new approaches to your writing.	• Don't rewrite the work yourself.

❸ Think About Purpose and Audience

Your purpose and audience should guide every decision you make about your writing, from the **tone**, or attitude, you communicate to the development of your argument. Ask yourself questions like the ones to the right as you plan, draft, and revise.

Questions To Ask

- What is my purpose? What do I want my audience to know, do, or act upon as a result of my writing?

- What does my audience know about this topic? What information should I include to help them understand it?

- What level of language should I use for this particular audience? Formal? Conversational? Technical?

- How might my audience's perspective on the topic influence my treatment of the topic?

UNIT 1

Preview Unit Goals

TEXT ANALYSIS
- Understand historical context and cultural influences of the Anglo-Saxon and medieval periods
- Analyze characteristics of epics, medieval romances, and ballads
- Identify and analyze elements of Old English poetry
- Analyze imagery and figurative language
- Analyze methods authors use to introduce and develop characters
- Analyze story structure including cause and effect
- Analyze plot complications
- Analyze characteristics of historical writing and primary sources
- Identify and analyze an author's purpose

READING
- Paraphrase and summarize
- Make inferences; draw conclusions
- Synthesize ideas on a topic from a variety of sources and genres

WRITING AND LANGUAGE
- Write an analysis of a poem
- Use adjectives and verbs to create imagery
- Use subordinate clauses, participial phrases, and prepositional phrases

SPEAKING AND LISTENING
- Prepare and deliver an analysis

VOCABULARY
- Understand that the English language changes over time
- Use knowledge of roots and affixes to help determine word meaning
- Use context to determine meaning of multiple-meaning words
- Consult references to research word origins to determine word meaning

ACADEMIC VOCABULARY
- concept
- culture
- parallel
- structure
- section

MEDIA AND VIEWING
- Analyze multiple interpretations of a story, evaluating how each version interprets the source text
- Integrate ideas on similar topics presented in a variety of media

Find It Online!

Go to thinkcentral.com for the interactive version of this unit.

The Anglo-Saxon and Medieval Periods 449–1485

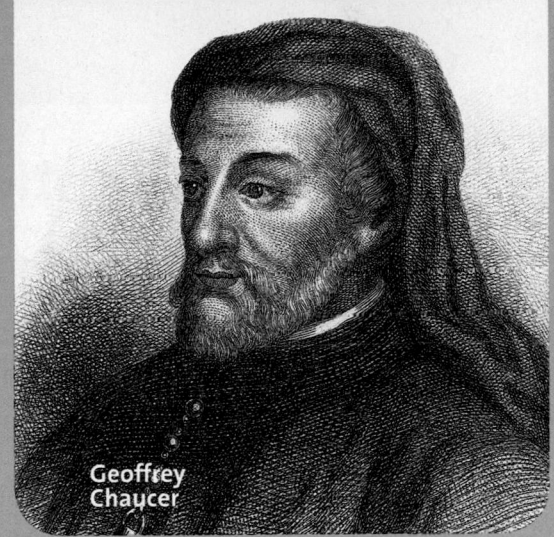

Geoffrey Chaucer

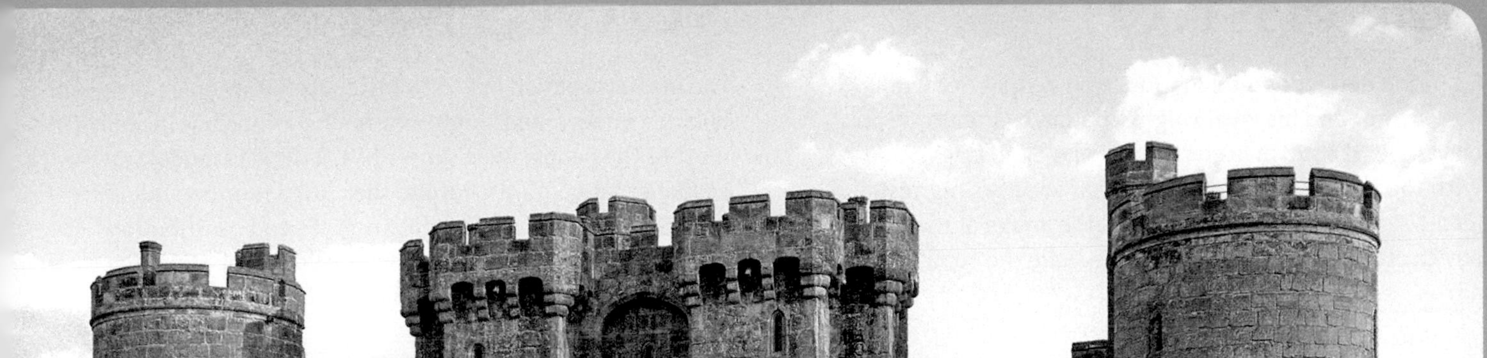

THE ORIGINS OF A NATION

- The Anglo-Saxon Epic
- Reflections of Common Life
- The Age of Chaucer
- Medieval Romance

Media Smart DVD-ROM

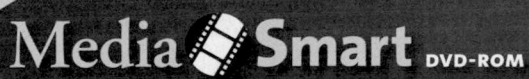

Great Stories on Film

Discover how a movie captures the imagination of viewers in a scene from *King Arthur.* Page 266

Questions of the Times

DISCUSS Read and discuss these questions with a partner, and share your thoughts with the class. Then read on to explore the ways in which these issues affected the literature of the Anglo-Saxon and medieval periods.

What makes a true HERO?

From the fierce, doomed Anglo-Saxon warrior Beowulf to King Arthur and his loyal knights, bound by their code of chivalry, early British literature shows a deep fascination with the hero as the embodiment of society's highest ideals. As these ideals have shifted, the image of the hero has changed too. What do you believe are the qualities of a true hero?

Who really shapes SOCIETY?

The medieval period in British history conjures up images of kings, queens, and knights in shining armor, but in reality most of the people were simple peasants. The feudal system ensured that peasants, despite their large numbers, had very little political power. Yet their struggles and contributions helped build a great nation. What do you think truly shapes society? Is it the power of the few or the struggles of many?

COMMON CORE

RL 9 Demonstrate knowledge of foundational works of literature, including how two or more texts from the same period treat similar themes or topics.
RI 9 Analyze documents of historical and literary significance for their themes, purposes, and rhetorical features.

Does FATE control our lives?

The seafaring Anglo-Saxons led harsh, brutal lives, often cut short by violence, disease, or the unpredictable tempests of the icy North Sea. They admired strength and courage but ultimately saw humans as helpless victims of a grim, implacable fate they called *wyrd*. Do you believe people can determine their own futures, or does chance or fate play a part?

Can people live up to high IDEALS?

During the medieval period, there were elaborate rules of conduct to guide behavior in battle as well as in romance. This code of chivalry assumed that knights were uniformly gallant and loyal, ladies fair and devout, manners impeccable, and jousting the way to prove bravery and win favor. Is it possible to live up to such high ideals? Is it worth trying?

The Anglo-Saxon and Medieval Periods
449–1485
The Origins of a Nation

A towering circle of ancient stones, draped in the mist of centuries. The clatter of horses' hooves, the clash of swords and spears. A tiny island whose motley tongue would become the language of the world, and whose laws, customs, and literature would help form Western civilization. This is England, and the story begins here.

The Anglo-Saxon Period: Historical Context

Britain's early years were dominated by successive waves of invaders. Among them were the Anglo-Saxons—a people who gave us the first masterpieces of English literature.

Centuries of Invasion

The Dark Ages, as the Anglo-Saxon period is often called, was a time of bloody conflicts, ignorance, violence, and barbarism. Life was difficult, and the literature of the period reflects that reality. Little imagery of the brief English summers appears in this literature; winter prevails, and spring comes slowly, if at all. The people were serious minded, and the reader finds scarce humor in their literature. Indeed, many of the stories and poems present heroic struggles in which only the strong survive. And no wonder.

EARLY BRITAIN The first person ever to write about England may have been the Roman general **Julius Caesar,** who in 55 B.C. attempted to conquer the British Isles. Put off by fierce Celtic warriors, Caesar hastily claimed victory for Rome and returned to Europe, leaving the **Britons** (as the people were known) and their neighbors to the north and west, the **Picts** and **Gaels,** in peace.

A century later, however, the Roman army returned in force and made good Caesar's claim. Britain became a province of the great Roman Empire, and the Romans introduced cities, roads, written scholarship, and eventually Christianity to the island. Their rule lasted more than three hundred years. "Romanized" Britons adapted to an urban lifestyle, living in villas and frequenting public baths, and came to depend on the Roman military for protection. Then, early in the fifth century, the Romans pulled out of Britain, called home to help defend their beleaguered empire against hordes of invaders. With no central government or army, it was not long before Britain, too, became a target for invasion.

ANGLO-SAXONS The **Angles** and **Saxons,** along with other Germanic tribes, began arriving from northern Europe around A.D. 449. The Britons—perhaps led by a Celtic chieftain named **Arthur** (likely the genesis of the legendary **King Arthur** of myth and folklore)—fought a series of battles against the invaders. Eventually, however, the Britons were driven to the west (Cornwall and Wales), the north (Scotland), and across the English Channel to an area of France that became known as Brittany.

Settled by the Anglo-Saxons, the main part of Britain took on a new name: **Angle-land,** or **England.** Anglo-Saxon culture became the basis for English culture, and their gutteral, vigorous language became the spoken language of the people, the language now known as **Old English.**

COMMON CORE

RL 9 Demonstrate knowledge of foundational works of literature, including how two or more texts from the same period treat similar themes or topics. **RI 9** Analyze documents of historical and literary significance for their themes, purposes, and rhetorical features. **L 1a** Apply the understanding that usage is a matter of convention, can change over time, and is sometimes contested.

▶ **TAKING NOTES**

Outlining As you read this introduction, use an outline to record main ideas about the historical events and literature of each period. You can use headings, boldfaced terms, and the information in boxes like this one as starting points. (See page R49 in the **Research Handbook** for more help with outlining.)

I. *Historical Context*
  A. Centuries of Invasion
    1. Early Britain
    2. Anglo-Saxons
    3. Vikings
  B. The Norman Conquest

Stonehenge, an ancient monument located in Wiltshire, England

VIKINGS The 790s brought the next wave of invaders, a fearsome group of seafaring marauders from the rocky, windswept coasts of Denmark and Norway: the **Vikings.** Shrieking wildly and waving giant battle-axes, Viking raiders looted, killed, and burned down entire villages. At first, they hit and ran; later, finding England a more pleasant spot to spend the winter than their icy homeland, the Danish invaders set up camps and gradually gained control of much of the north and east of the country.

In the south, the Danes finally met defeat at the hands of a powerful Anglo-Saxon king known as **Alfred the Great.** Alfred unified the English, and under his rule, learning and culture flourished. The *Anglo-Saxon Chronicle,* a record of English history, was initiated at his bidding.

The Norman Conquest

In 1042, a descendant of Alfred's took the throne, the deeply religious **Edward the Confessor.** Edward, who had no children, had once sworn an oath making his French cousin William, duke of Normandy, his heir—or so William claimed. When Edward died, however, a council of nobles and church officials chose an English earl named Harold to succeed him. Incensed, William led his Norman army in what was to be the last successful invasion of the island of Britain: the **Norman Conquest.** Harold was killed at the Battle of Hastings in 1066, and on Christmas Day of that year, **William the Conqueror** was crowned king of England.

The Norman Conquest ended Anglo-Saxon dominance in England. Losing their land to the conquerors, noble families sank into the peasantry, and a new class of privileged Normans took their place.

> **A Voice from the Times**
>
> *William returned to Hastings, and waited there to know whether the people would submit to him. But when he found that they would not come to him, he went up with all his force that was left and that came since to him from over sea, and ravaged all the country. . . .*
>
> **—Anglo-Saxon Chronicle**

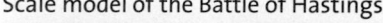
Scale model of the Battle of Hastings

Cultural Influences

Early Anglo-Saxon literature reflected a fatalistic worldview, while later works were influenced by rapidly spreading Christianity.

The Spread of Christianity

Like all cultures, that of the Anglo-Saxons changed over time. The early invaders were seafaring wanderers whose lives were bleak, violent, and short. Their pagan religion was marked by a strong belief in *wyrd,* or fate, and they saved their admiration for heroic warriors whose fate it was to prevail in battle. As the Anglo-Saxons settled into their new land, however, they became an agricultural people— less violent, more secure, more civilized.

The bleak fatalism of the Anglo-Saxons' early beliefs may have reflected the reality of their lives, but it offered little hope. Life was harsh, it taught, and the only certainty was that it would end in death. **Christianity** opened up a bright new possibility: that the suffering of this world was merely a prelude to the eternal happiness of heaven.

CHRISTIANITY TAKES HOLD No one knows exactly when the first Christian missionaries arrived in Britain, but by A.D. 300 the number of Christians on the island was significant. Over the next two centuries, Christianity spread to Ireland and Scotland, including the Picts and Angles in the north. In 597, a Roman missionary named **Augustine** arrived in the kingdom of Kent, where he established a monastery at **Canterbury.** From there, Christianity spread so rapidly that by 690 all of Britain was at least nominally Christian, though many held on to some pagan traditions and beliefs.

Monasteries became centers of intellectual, literary, artistic, and social activity. At a time when schools and libraries were completely unknown, monasteries offered the only opportunity for education. Monastic scholars imported books from the Continent, which were then painstakingly copied. In addition, original works were written, mostly in scholarly Latin, but later in Old English. The earliest recorded history of the English people came from the clergy at the monasteries. The greatest of these monks was the **Venerable Bede** (c. 673–735), author of *A History of the English Church and People.*

When Vikings invaded in the late eighth and ninth centuries, they plundered monasteries and threatened to obliterate all traces of cultural refinement. Yet Christianity continued as a dominant cultural force for more than a thousand years to come.

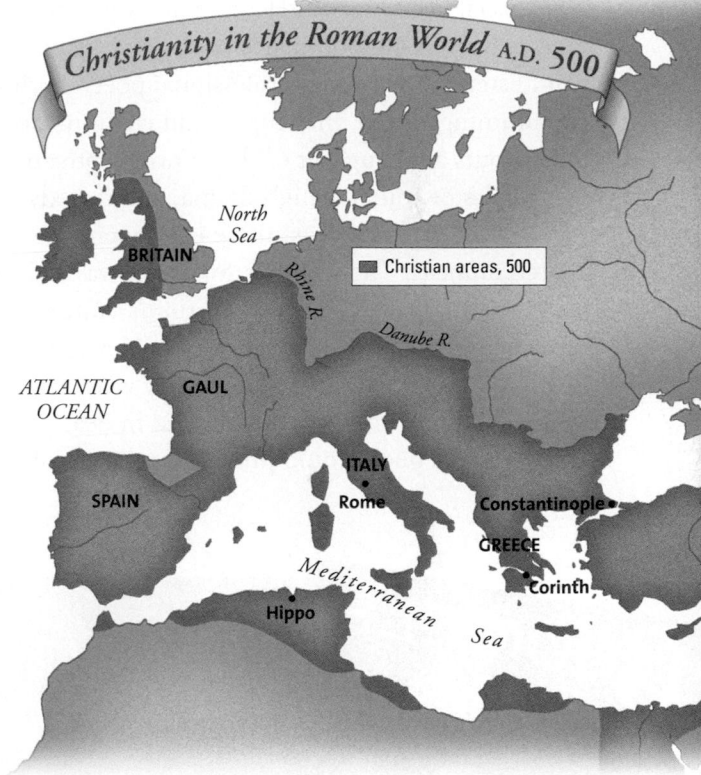

Christianity in the Roman World A.D. 500

North Sea

BRITAIN

Christian areas, 500

Rhine R.

Danube R.

ATLANTIC OCEAN

GAUL

SPAIN

ITALY
Rome

Constantinople

GREECE

Mediterranean Sea

Corinth

Hippo

Literature of the Times

Anglo-Saxon literature often focused on great heroes such as Beowulf, though sometimes it addressed everyday concerns.

The Epic Tradition

The early literature of the Anglo-Saxon period mostly took the form of lengthy **epic poems** praising the deeds of heroic warriors. These poems reflected the reality of life at this time, which was often brutal. However, the context in which these poems were delivered was certainly not grim. In the great **mead halls** of kings and nobles, Anglo-Saxons would gather on special occasions to celebrate in style. They feasted on pies and roasted meats heaped high on platters, warmed themselves before a roaring fire, and listened to **scops**—professional poets—bring the epic poems to life. Strumming a harp, the scop would chant in a clear voice that carried over the shouts and laughter of the crowd, captivating them for hours on end with tales of courage, high drama, and tragedy.

To the Anglo-Saxons, these epic poems were far more than simple entertainment. The scop's performance was a history lesson, moral sermon, and pep talk rolled into one, instilling cultural pride and teaching how a true hero should behave. At the same time, in true Anglo-Saxon fashion, the scop reminded his listeners that they were helpless in the hands of fate and that all human ambition would end in death. With no hope for an afterlife, only an epic poem could provide a measure of immortality.

▶ *For Your Outline*

THE EPIC TRADITION

- Epic poems praised deeds of heroic warriors.
- Poems were recited by scops in mead halls.
- Poems instilled cultural pride.

COMMON LIFE

- Lyric poems reflected everyday reality.
- *Exeter Book* contains surviving lyrics.
- Writing moved from Latin to English.
- Medieval literature also explored everyday concerns.

Cover and illustration from a contemporary graphic work by Gareth Hinds, based on the epic poem *Beowulf*

These epic poems were an **oral art form:** memorized and performed, not written down. Later, as Christianity spread through Britain, literacy spread too, and poems were more likely to be recorded. In this age before printing presses, however, manuscripts had to be written out by hand, copied slowly and laboriously by scribes. Thus, only a fraction of Anglo-Saxon poetry has survived, in manuscripts produced centuries after the poems were originally composed. The most famous survivor is the epic *Beowulf,* about a legendary hero of the northern European past. In more than 3,000 lines, *Beowulf* relates the tale of a heroic warrior who battles monsters and dragons to protect the people. Yet Beowulf, while performing superhuman deeds, is not immortal. His death comes from wounds incurred in his final, great fight.

Reflections of Common Life

While epics such as *Beowulf* gave Anglo-Saxons a taste of glory, scops also sang shorter, **lyric poems,** such as **"The Seafarer,"** that reflected a more everyday reality: the wretchedness of a cold, wet sailor clinging to his storm-tossed boat; the misery and resentment of his wife, left alone for months or years, not knowing if her husband would ever return.

Some of these poems mourn loss and death in the mood of grim fatalism typical of early Anglo-Saxon times; others, written after the advent of Christianity, express religious faith or offer moral instruction. A manuscript known as the *Exeter Book* contains many of the surviving Anglo-Saxon lyrics, including more than 90 riddles, such as this one: *Wonder was on the wave, when water became bone.* Answer: *an iceberg.*

EARLY AUTHORS Most Old English poems are anonymous. One of the few poets known by name was a monk called **Caedmon,** described by the **Venerable Bede** in his famous history of England. Like most scholars of his day, Bede wrote in Latin, the language of the church. It was not until the reign of Alfred the Great that writing in English began to be widespread; in addition to the *Anglo-Saxon Chronicle,* which was written in the language of the people, Alfred encouraged English translations of the Bible and other Latin works.

As England moved into the Middle Ages, its literature continued to capture the rhythms of everyday life. The medieval period was one of social turbulence and unrest, and several works give modern readers a glimpse of the individual hopes and fears of people of the time. **Margery Kempe,** for example, describes a crisis of faith brought on by childbirth; the letters of **Margaret Paston** and her family mainly deal with issues of marriage and managing the family estate.

A CHANGING LANGUAGE

Old English

Just as Britain's fifth-century invaders eventually united into a nation called England, their closely related Germanic dialects evolved over time into a distinct language called English— today called Old English to distinguish it from later forms of the language.

A Different Language Old English was very different from the language we know today. Though about half of our basic vocabulary comes from the Anglo-Saxon language, a modern English speaker would find the harsh sounds impossible to understand.

Some words can still be recognized in writing, though the spelling is a little unfamiliar: for instance, *scōh* (shoe), *hunig* (honey), *milc* (milk), and *faeder* (father). Other words have disappeared entirely, such as *hathearl* (angry) and *gleowian* (joke).

Grammatically, the language was more complex than modern English, with words changing form to indicate different functions, so that word order was more flexible than it is now.

The Growth of English The most valuable characteristic of Old English, however, was its ability to change and grow, to adopt new words as the need arose. While Christianity brought Latin words such as *cloister, priest,* and *candle* into the Anglo-Saxon vocabulary, encounters with the Vikings brought *skull, die, crawl,* and *rotten.* The arrival of the Normans in 1066 would stretch the language even farther, with thousands of words from the French.

The Medieval Period:
Historical Context

With the Norman Conquest, England entered the medieval period, a time of innovation in the midst of war.

The Monarchy

After his victory at Hastings, William the Conqueror lost no time taking full control of England. He was a new kind of king—powerful, well-organized, determined to exert his authority down to the smallest detail. Many people resented innovations such as the *Domesday Book,* an extraordinary tax record of every bit of property owned, from fish ponds to litters of pigs. Still, no one could deny that William brought law and order to the land, "so that," as one scribe wrote shortly after William's death, "any honest man could travel over his kingdom without injury with his bosom full of gold."

Power struggles in the decades after William's death left England in a state of near-anarchy until 1154, when his great-grandson Henry Plantagenet took

▶ **For Your Outline**
The Medieval Period
I. Historical Context
 A. The Monarchy
   1. William the Conqueror

View of London with London Bridge in far distance, Royal Manuscript. From *The Poems of Charles, Duke of Orleans.* © British Museum/Harper Collins Publishers/The Art Archive.

◀ **Analyze Visuals**
This illustration from an illuminated manuscript of his poems depicts Charles, the French Duke of Orleans, imprisoned in the Tower of London. Charles was captured at the Battle of Agincourt during the Hundred Years' War and imprisoned for the next 25 years. Yet like most captured nobles, his confinement was not strict: he was allowed to live in a style similar to that which he had known as a free man. What details show how Charles lived? Does the Tower look as you imagined it? Explain.

the throne as **Henry II.** One of medieval England's most memorable rulers, Henry reformed the judicial system by setting up royal courts throughout the country, establishing a system of juries, and beginning to form English common law out of a patchwork of centuries-old practices.

Henry's son Richard I, known as **Richard the Lion-Hearted,** spent most of his ten-year reign fighting wars abroad. During his absence, his younger brother, John, plotted against him. The villain of **Robin Hood** legends, **King John** was treacherous and bad-tempered, quarreling with nobles and raising their taxes until they threatened to rebel. In 1215 he was forced to sign the **Magna Carta** ("Great Charter"), which limited royal authority by granting more power to the barons—an early step on the road to democracy.

War and Plague

As the medieval period drew to a close, war was a near-constant fact of life. The **Hundred Years' War** between England and France began in 1337, during the reign of Edward III. As the war continued on and off for more than a century, England also had to weather several domestic crises, including a terrible plague known as the **Black Death,** which killed a third of England's population.

When the war finally ended in 1453, England had lost nearly all of its French possessions. Two rival families claimed the throne—the house of York, whose symbol was a white rose, and the house of Lancaster, whose symbol was a red rose. The fighting that ensued, known as the **Wars of the Roses,** ended in 1485 when the Lancastrian **Henry Tudor** killed the Yorkist king Richard III at Bosworth Field and took the throne as Henry VII. This event marked the end of the Middle Ages in England.

> ### A Voice from the Times
>
> *No freeman shall be taken, or imprisoned, or outlawed, or exiled, or in any way harmed, nor will we go upon him nor will we send upon him, except by the legal judgment of his peers or by the law of the land.*
>
> **—Magna Carta**

Cultural Influences

Medieval literature is best understood in the context of three powerful influences on medieval society: feudalism, the church, and a code of conduct called chivalry.

Three Social Forces

THE FEUDAL SYSTEM Feudalism was a political and economic system that William the Conquerer introduced into England after the Norman Conquest. Based on the premise that the king owns all the land in the kingdom, William kept a fourth of the land for himself, granted a fourth to the church, and parceled out the rest to loyal barons, who, in return, either paid him or supplied him with warriors called knights. The barons swore allegiance to the king, the knights to the barons, and so on down the social ladder. At the bottom of the ladder were the conquered Anglo-Saxons, many of whom were serfs—peasants bound to land they could not own.

THE POWER OF THE CHURCH There was one grand exception to the feudal system's hierarchy: the church. Led by the pope in Rome, the medieval church wielded tremendous power—levying taxes, making its own laws, running its own courts, and keeping kings and noblemen in line with the threat of excommunication. The church owned more land than anyone in Europe, and its soaring stone cathedrals and great abbeys were as impressive as any castle. The church's power did lead to conflicts with the monarchy. When Henry II's archbishop and friend Thomas à Becket began favoring church interests over those of the crown, four knights loyal to the king murdered him. Becket was declared a saint, and his shrine at Canterbury became a popular destination for pilgrims, such as those described in **Geoffrey Chaucer's *The Canterbury Tales*.**

CHIVALRY AND COURTLY LOVE Medieval literature, including the famous stories of **King Arthur,** was influenced by another social force as well—the ideals of chivalry and courtly love made popular during Henry II's reign. Henry's wife, Eleanor of Aquitaine, brought from French court circles the concept of **chivalry,** a code of honor intended to govern knightly behavior. The code encouraged knights to be generous, brave, honest, pious, and honorable, to defend the weak and to battle evil and uphold good. It also encouraged knights to go on holy quests such as the Crusades, the military expeditions in which European Christians attempted to wrest the holy city of Jerusalem from Muslim control.

Eleanor and her daughter Marie applied chivalric ideals to the relationships between men and women as well. They presided over a "court of love," where lords and ladies would come to be entertained by music and tales of King Arthur and other romantic heroes and argue about the proper conduct of a love affair. **Courtly love** and the concept of chivalry represented ideals rarely met in real life. Yet they served as inspiration for some of the finest literature of the time.

> ### A Voice from the Times
>
> - *Marriage is no real excuse for not loving.*
> - *He who is jealous cannot love.*
> - *When made public, love rarely endures.*
> - *A new love puts an old one to flight.*
> - *Every lover regularly turns pale in the presence of his beloved.*
>
> —"rules" from the 12th-century book *The Art of Courtly Love*

La Belle Dame Sans Merci, Walter Crane. Private collection. © Bridgeman Art Library.

Literature of the Times

Medieval works, such as _The Canterbury Tales_ and Arthurian romances, drew from many sources, historical and contemporary, while reflecting the society and ideals of their time.

The Age of Chaucer

The most famous writer of medieval times, "the father of English literature," was **Geoffrey Chaucer,** a poet who demonstrated the potential of English as a literary language. Drawing on sources as diverse as French poetry, English songs, Greek classics, contemporary Italian tales, and Aesop's fables, Chaucer masterfully blended old with new, all in the natural rhythms of Middle English, the spoken language of the time.

AN ENGLISH MASTERPIECE _The Canterbury Tales,_ Chaucer's best-known work, displays his ability as a storyteller, his keen sense of humor, and his sharp eye for detail. A collection of tales ranging from irreverent to inspirational, it is held together by a **frame story** about a group of pilgrims who pass time on their journey to the shrine of Thomas à Becket by telling stories. The pilgrims' characters are revealed through the stories they tell and their reactions to one another's tales. Though Chaucer apparently intended to have each of the 30 pilgrims tell 4 stories apiece, he died having completed only 24 of the tales.

Chaucer lived during a time of change and turmoil in England. He was born just a few years after the outbreak of the Hundred Years' War and was still a small child when the bubonic plague hit Europe. The Black Death, as it was known, greatly reduced the population, which led to a shortage of laborers. In turn, serfs realized their new value and left the land to work in towns and on neighboring estates. This shift led to the decline of feudalism and the growth of a new middle class, to which Chaucer's family belonged. In addition, the war with France had spurred the re-emergence of the English language among the ruling class. With its cast of characters ranging across British society, from the "perfect gentle Knight" to a common miller, and its use of everyday English rather than elevated Latin or French, _The Canterbury Tales_ reflected all of these developments.

OTHER WORKS Chaucer was not the only poet of his time to compose in English or to write about ordinary people; **William Langland** did both in his masterpiece _Piers Plowman_ (see page 124), as did writers of the popular **ballads** of the day—narrative songs telling of the lives of common folks

Detail of _Lydgate and the Canterbury Pilgrims leaving Canterbury_ (1520). From John Lydgate's _Troy Book and Story of Thebes._ (Roy.18.D.II. Folio No: 148). British Library, London. © HIP/Art Resource, New York.

▶ **For Your Outline**

THE AGE OF CHAUCER

- Geoffrey Chaucer is "the father of English literature."

- Chaucer's _The Canterbury Tales_ reflected his society and led to an appreciation for English as a literary language.

- Ballads are narrative songs relating the lives of common folk.

or of characters and events from folklore (see page 216). The combination of Chaucer's literary gifts and social status, however, led to a new appreciation of English as a language that, while useful in everyday life, was elegant and poetic as well.

CHAUCER'S LEGACY *The Canterbury Tales* and Chaucer's other works were wildly popular in his own time and inspired a generation of English poets. One admirer sent him a ballad, addressed to "noble Geoffrey Chaucer," that described him as the ancient thinkers Socrates, Seneca, and Ovid all rolled into one. Another poet, John Lydgate, wrote after Chaucer's death, "We may try to counterfeit his style, but it will not be; the well is dry." Three-quarters of a century later, *The Canterbury Tales* was still so widely enjoyed that it was among the earliest books chosen to be published by William Caxton, the first English printer.

Medieval Romance

Medieval **romances,** stories of adventure, gallant love, chivalry, and heroism, represent for many readers the social order and ideals of the Middle Ages. Yet tales such as those of the good **King Arthur** and his sword Excalibur, Merlin the magician, Queen Guinevere, and Sir Lancelot and the Knights of the Round Table were set in an idealized world quite unlike the real medieval England, with its plagues, political battles, and civil unrest. In fact, while it is true that **chivalry** and **courtly love** were ideals made popular during the medieval period, the real Arthur was not of this age.

A LEGENDARY HERO From what little is known of him, Arthur was a Briton, a Romanized descendant of the long-haired, blue-dyed warriors who fought Caesar's army. A Latin history written around A.D. 800, two hundred years or more after Arthur's death, first mentions "Artorius" as a leader in the sixth-century battles against Anglo-Saxon invaders.

For centuries, oral poets in Wales celebrated their legendary hero Arthur just as Anglo-Saxon scops celebrated Beowulf. Then, about 1135, the monk **Geoffrey of Monmouth** produced a Latin "history" based on old Welsh legends. Geoffrey's book caught the fancy of French, German, and English writers, who soon created their own versions of the legends, updating them to reflect then-current notions of chivalry. While the traditional tales focused on Arthur himself and on his courage and success in battle, these new romances used Arthur and his court as a backdrop for stories about knights who go through trials and perform great feats—often (influenced by the idea of courtly love) in the service of a lady.

A CHANGING LANGUAGE

Middle English

Along with political and cultural upheaval, the Norman Conquest led to great changes in the English language. Despite their Viking origins, by 1066 the Normans spoke a dialect of Old French, which they brought to England.

Status Talk Norman French became the language of the English court, of government business, of the new nobility, and of the scholars, cooks, and craftspeople that the Norman barons brought with them to serve their more "refined" needs. The use of English became confined to the conquered, mostly peasant population.

Hints of this class division still survive in modern English. For instance, Anglo-Saxons tending cattle in the field called the animal a *cŭ*, or cow, while the Norman aristocrats who dined on the product of their labors used the Old French word *buef,* or beef.

Ever adaptable, English soon incorporated thousands of words and many grammatical conventions from Norman French. These changes led to the development of Middle English, a form much closer than Old English to the language we speak today.

English Makes a Comeback During the long war with France, it came to seem unpatriotic among the upper class to use the language of the nation's number-one enemy, especially since Anglo-Norman French was ridiculed by the "real" French speakers across the English Channel. By the end of the Hundred Years' War, English had once again become the first language of most of the English nobility.

Morte d'Arthur (1862), John Mulcaster Carrick. Private collection. © Fine Art Photographic Library, London/Art Resource, New York.

TWO FAVORITES About 1375, an anonymous English poet wrote *Sir Gawain and the Green Knight,* recounting the marvelous adventures of a knight of Arthur's court who faces a series of extraordinary challenges. Exciting, suspenseful, and peopled by an array of memorable characters, from the mysterious green giant who survives beheading to the all-too-human Sir Gawain, the 2,500-line poem is easy to imagine as a favorite of troubadors and their audiences.

A century later, in *Le Morte d'Arthur,* **Sir Thomas Malory** retold a number of the French Arthurian tales in Middle English. Despite its title, which means "The Death of Arthur," Malory's book includes many episodes in the life of the legendary king and is considered a precursor to the modern novel. Oddly enough, it was printed just weeks before the final battle in the **Wars of the Roses,** the last English battle ever fought by knights in armor. Fittingly then, the literary fall of Camelot coincided with the real-life end of chivalry—and the end of the Middle Ages as well.

> ▶ *For Your Outline*
> **MEDIEVAL ROMANCE**
> - Romances are stories of adventure, love, heroism, and chivalry.
> - They are set in an idealized world unlike medieval England.
> - The real Arthur was a 6th-century warrior.
> - *Sir Gawain and the Green Knight* and *Le Morte d'Arthur* are two medieval romances.

Connecting Literature, History, and Culture

Use this timeline and the questions on the next page to gain insight into the Anglo-Saxon and medieval periods.

BRITISH LITERARY MILESTONES

400	600	800
	CIRCA 673 The Venerable Bede is born. ▶ 	**892** Authors begin compiling data for the *Anglo-Saxon Chronicle,* a year-by-year diary of important world events.
	CIRCA 750 The surviving version of *Beowulf* is likely composed.	**CIRCA 975** Anglo-Saxon verse is collected in the *Exeter Book.*

HISTORICAL CONTEXT

400	600	800
449 The Anglo-Saxon invasion of Britain begins.	**664** The British Christian Church unites with the Roman Catholic Church.	**871** Alfred the Great becomes king of Wessex (to 899).
597 Christian missionaries land in Kent; Christianity begins to spread among Anglo-Saxons. ▼	**793** Vikings begin the first of many raids on the Anglo-Saxon kingdom.	**886** Alfred wins important victory over Danes; Danes accept Christianity. ▼

WORLD CULTURE AND EVENTS

400	600	800
500 A mathematician in India calculates the value of pi.		**800** Charlemagne, who unites much of Europe, is crowned emperor of the Holy Roman Empire. ▶
527 Justinian I becomes Byzantine emperor.		**CIRCA 800** The Chinese invent gunpowder.
		CIRCA 880 Mayan culture begins decline.

600s Block printing is developed in China and Korea. ▲

630 The prophet Muhammad conquers Mecca, which becomes the holiest city of Islam.

- Though William Caxton established the first British printing press, in what countries was printing first developed? When?
- Based on what you've learned in the introductory essay, why are there so few literary milestones recorded for the early years in Britain?

COMMON CORE

RI 7 Integrate and evaluate multiple sources of information presented in different media or formats as well as in words in order to address a question or solve a problem.

1000

CIRCA 1000 The surviving version of *Beowulf* is recorded by monks.

1086 The *Domesday Book* records results of a property survey ordered by William the Conquerer.

1200

CIRCA 1375 *Sir Gawain and the Green Knight* is composed.

CIRCA 1387 Chaucer begins *The Canterbury Tales.* ▶

1400

CIRCA 1420 The earliest surviving Paston letter is written.

1485 William Caxton prints Sir Thomas Malory's *Le Morte d'Arthur.*

1000

1016 Canute, a Dane, becomes king of England (to 1035).

1066 In what will become known as the Norman Conquest, William the Conqueror defeats Harold and becomes king of England.

1170 Thomas à Becket is murdered.

1171 Henry II declares himself lord of Ireland, beginning centuries of English-Irish conflict.

1200

1215 King John signs the Magna Carta. ▲

1282 England conquers Wales.

1295 A model Parliament is assembled under Edward I.

1337 The Hundred Years' War with France begins (to 1453).

1400

CIRCA 1430 Modern English develops from Middle English.

CIRCA 1476 Wiliam Caxton establishes first printing press in Britain; prints first dated book in the English language (1477). ▼

1000

1054 The Christian Church divides into east and west branches.

1095 The first of centuries of "holy wars" called Crusades begins (to 1272).

1192 The Japanese emperor takes the title of shogun.

1200

1206 Genghis Khan begins Mongol conquest of much of Asia (to 1227). ▶

CIRCA 1300 The Renaissance begins in northern Italy.

1347 Bubonic plague reaches Europe, killing millions.

1400

1431 Joan of Arc is burned at the stake.

1453 Ottomans conquer Constantinople.

CIRCA 1455 In Germany, the Gutenberg Bible is produced on a printing press.

The Legacy of the Era

Arthur Lives

Stories of King Arthur and his loyal knights have never lost their appeal. From Alfred, Lord Tennyson's 19th-century epic *Idylls of the King,* to Mark Twain's satiric novel *A Connecticut Yankee in King Arthur's Court,* to the *Star Wars* movies, in which Jedi knights battle evil in outer space, each generation continues to create its own interpretations of the Arthurian romance.

CREATE With a partner, search online for other incarnations of the Arthurian legend. Use keywords such as *"King Arthur," Camelot, "Knights of the Round Table," Guinevere,* and *Lancelot* to begin your search. From your results, create a collage of images and words to show the prevalence of the Arthurian legend over the years.

Keira Knightley and Clive Owen in the 2004 film *King Arthur*

Modern Monarchy

In the early days of England, kings ruled the land with absolute authority. In 1215, the Magna Carta transferred some of that power to the noblemen. Today, the monarchy plays a less active role in government, yet to many the royal family is still the public face of Great Britain and the embodiment of a beloved and romantic tradition.

RESEARCH Go online to research today's royal family. How involved in creating legislation is today's monarch? What role does the royalty play in international affairs? What philanthropies or organizations have members of the royal family founded? Report your findings to the class in a brief oral report.

Princes William and Harry supporting the charity Sport Relief

Stories in Song

Though clubs, music channels, and MP3 players have taken the place of banquet halls, the spirit of the scops and troubadors survives in modern ballads—popular songs that tell a story. Like the original oral literature, these contemporary verses combine words and music in an appealing, memorable way. They also reveal the values of our modern culture as surely as the ancient ballads did theirs.

DISCUSS With a small group, brainstorm examples of current songs that tell a story. Choose one or two and discuss what they reveal about the worldviews of those who sing and listen to them.

Musician and singer Tori Amos

The Epic

What do you do to celebrate the heroes of your day? Hold a parade? Have a party? Attend a banquet where speakers chronicle the hero's deeds? As far back as the third millenium B.C., heroes have been celebrated in a variety of ways. One type of celebration common to many cultures throughout history is to honor the hero's story in an epic.

The Epic Tradition

COMMON CORE

Included in this workshop:
RL 2 Provide an objective summary of the text. **RL 3** Analyze the impact of the author's choices regarding how to develop and relate elements of a story. **RL 4** Determine the meaning of words and phrases as they are used in the text, including figurative meanings.

An **epic** is a long narrative poem that celebrates a hero's deeds. The earliest epic tales survived for centuries as oral traditions before they were finally written down. They came into existence as spoken words and were retold by poets from one generation to the next. Most orally composed epics date back to preliterate periods—before the cultures that produced them had developed written forms.

Detail of Bayeux Tapestry (11th century)

Since many epics were based on historical fact, their public performance provided both entertainment and education for the audience. The oral poets (known in different cultures as *scops* or *bards*) drew upon existing songs and legends, which they embellished or combined with original material. The poets had to be master improvisers, able to compose verse in their heads while simultaneously singing or chanting it. One characteristic feature of oral poetry is the repetition of certain words, phrases, or even lines. Two of the most notable examples of repeated elements are stock epithets and kennings.

- **Stock epithets** are adjectives that point out special traits of particular persons or things. In Homer, stock epithets are often compound adjectives, such as the "swift-footed" used to describe Achilles in the *Iliad* (page 78).

- **Kennings** are poetic synonyms found in Germanic poems, such as the Anglo-Saxon epic *Beowulf* (page 42). Rather than being an adjective, like an epithet, a kenning is a descriptive phrase or compound word that substitutes for a noun. For example, in *Beowulf* "the Almighty's enemy" and "sin-stained demon" are two kennings that are used in place of Grendel's name.

Stock epithets and kennings were building blocks that a poet could recite while mentally preparing for the next line or stanza. Epithets had an added advantage—they were designed to fit metrically into specific parts of the lines of verse. In skillful hands, these "formulas" helped to establish tone and reinforce character traits and setting.

Epic Proportions

Epics from different languages and time periods do not always have the same characteristics. Kennings, for example, are not found in Homer's epics. All epics, however, concern the actions of a **hero,** who can be described as

- being of noble birth or high position, and often of great historical or legendary importance

- exhibiting **character traits,** or qualities, that reflect important ideals of society

- performing courageous, sometimes superhuman, deeds that reflect the values of the era

- performing actions that often determine the fate of a nation or group of people

In addition, most epics share certain **conventions,** which reflect the larger-than-life events that a hero might experience.

- The **setting** is vast in scope, often involving more than one nation.

- The **plot** is complicated by supernatural beings or events and may involve a long and dangerous journey through foreign lands.

- **Dialogue** often includes long, formal speeches delivered by the major characters.

- The **theme** reflects timeless values, such as courage and honor, and encompasses universal ideas, such as good and evil or life and death.

- The **style** includes formal **diction** (the writer's choice of words and sentence structure) and a serious **tone** (the expression of the writer's attitude toward the subject).

STRATEGIES FOR READING AN EPIC

When reading an epic, use the following strategies:

- Decide what virtues the hero embodies.

- Determine the hero's role in bringing about any changes in fortune for the characters, the nation, or the group of people depicted in the story.

- If a passage confuses you, go back and summarize the main idea of the passage.

> A powerful monster, living down
> In the darkness, growled in pain, impatient
> As day after day the music rang
> Loud in that hall, the harp's rejoicing
> Call and the poet's clear songs, sung
> Of the ancient beginnings of us all, recalling
> The Almighty making the earth, shaping
> These beautiful plains marked off by oceans,
> Then proudly setting the sun and moon
> To glow across the land and light it;
>
> —*from* Beowulf

Close Read

What characteristics of the epic do you recognize in this passage?

from **Beowulf**

Epic Poem by the Beowulf Poet Translated by Burton Raffel

VIDEO TRAILER THINK central KEYWORD: HML12-40A

DID YOU KNOW?

The original *Beowulf* manuscript . . .

- exists in only one copy.
- was damaged and nearly destroyed in a fire in the 18th century.
- has now been preserved through digitization.

Meet the Author

The Beowulf Poet about 750?

"Hear me!" So begins *Beowulf,* the oldest surviving epic poem in English. The command was intended to capture the listening audience's attention, for *Beowulf* was originally chanted or sung aloud. Centuries of poet-singers, called scops (shōps), recited the adventures of Beowulf. It is our great fortune that eventually a gifted poet unified the heroic accounts and produced an enduring work of art.

By Anonymous Unfortunately, we don't know who that poet was or when *Beowulf* was composed. Scholars contend that the poet may have lived anytime between the middle of the seventh century A.D. and the end of the tenth century. However, we do know where the poem was written. In the fifth century, bloody warfare in northern Europe had driven many Germanic-speaking tribes, including groups of Angles, Saxons, and Jutes, to abandon their homes. Many of these groups settled in England, where they established what is now called Anglo-Saxon civilization.

The people of the Anglo-Saxon period spoke a language known as Old English, the language in which *Beowulf* was composed.

Old English bears little resemblance to Modern English and so must be translated for readers today. By the time *Beowulf* was written, the Anglo-Saxons had also converted to Christianity. This Christian influence is evident in the poem.

Long Ago and Far Away Although *Beowulf* was composed in England, the poem describes events that take place in Scandinavia around the 500s among two groups: the Danes of what is now Denmark and the Geats (gēts) of what is now Sweden. Beowulf is a Geat warrior who crosses the sea to defeat Grendel, a monster who is terrorizing the Danes. He later returns to his homeland to succeed his uncle as king of the Geats.

Beowulf celebrates warrior culture and deeds requiring great strength and courage. Scops recited the poem and other tales in mead halls, large wooden buildings that provided a safe haven for warriors returning from battle. During the performances, audiences feasted and drank mead, an alcoholic beverage.

Survivor The sole surviving copy of *Beowulf* dates from about the year 1000. It is the work of Christian monks who preserved the literature of the past by copying manuscripts. After suffering mistreatment and several near-disasters, the *Beowulf* manuscript is now safely housed in the British Library in London.

THINK central

Author Online

Go to **thinkcentral.com.** KEYWORD: HML12-40B

● TEXT ANALYSIS: CHARACTERISTICS OF AN EPIC

An **epic,** a long narrative poem that traces the adventures of a great hero, has the power to transport you to another time and place. *Beowulf* takes you to the Anglo-Saxon period and the land of the Danes and the Geats, where a mighty warrior battles fantastic monsters. As you read the poem, note some of the following characteristics of epic poetry:

- The **hero** is a legendary figure who performs deeds requiring incredible courage and strength.
- The hero embodies **character traits** that reflect lofty ideals.
- The poet uses formal **diction** and a serious **tone.**
- The poem reflects timeless values and **universal themes.**

▨ READING STRATEGY: READING OLD ENGLISH POETRY

Old English poetry is marked by a strong rhythm that is easy to chant or sing. Here are some of the techniques used in an Old English poem:

- **alliteration,** or the repetition of consonant sounds at the beginning of words, which helps unify the lines

  So mankind's enemy <u>c</u>ontinued his <u>c</u>rimes

- **caesura** (sĭ-zhŏŏr'ə), or a pause dividing each line, with each part having two accented syllables to help maintain the rhythm of the lines

  Hĕ tóok whăt hĕ wántĕd, // áll thĕ tréasŭres

- **kenning,** a metaphorical compound word or phrase substituted for a noun or name, which enhances meaning— for example, "mankind's enemy" used in place of "Grendel"

As you read *Beowulf,* note examples of these techniques and consider their effect on rhythm and meaning in the poem.

▲ VOCABULARY IN CONTEXT

The words shown here help convey the monstrous forces Beowulf faces in the epic. Choose a word from the list that has the same definition as each numbered item.

WORD LIST		
affliction	lair	purge
gorge	livid	talon
infamous	loathsome	

1. claw   **2.** burden   **3.** notorious   **4.** cram

 Complete the activities in your **Reader/Writer Notebook**.

Where do MONSTERS *lurk?*

Unlike the monsters in *Beowulf,* those in our world are not always easy to identify. Evil can hide in the most unexpected places: behind a smiling face, between the lines of a law, in otherwise noble-sounding words. Even when evil is clearly exposed, people may disagree on how to confront it.

QUICKWRITE What does *evil* mean to you? Write your own definition of the word, and provide some examples of real-life monsters.

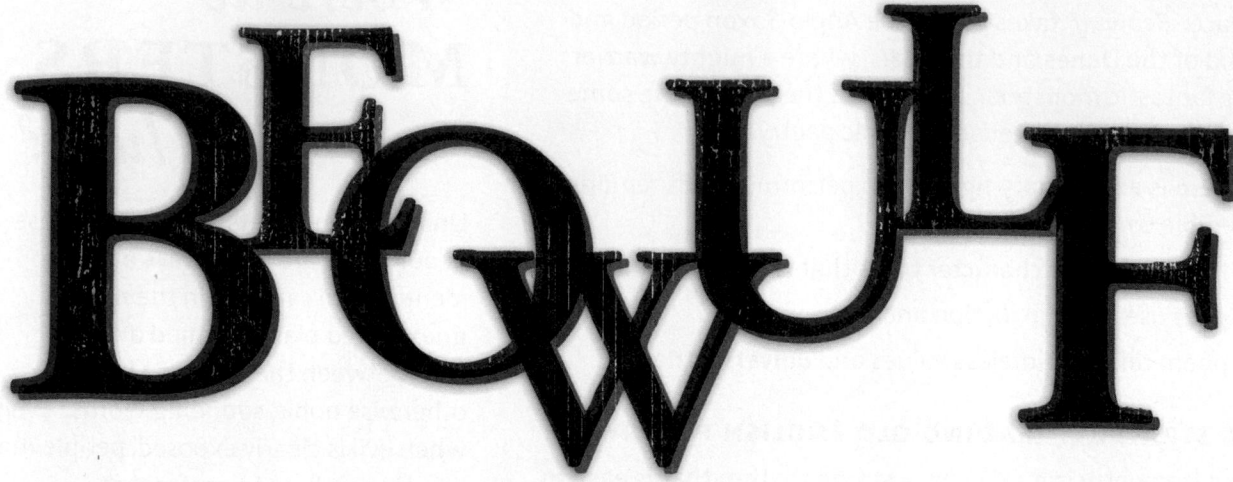

Hrothgar (hrôth'gär'), *king of the Danes, has built a wonderful mead hall called Herot* (hĕr'ət), *where his subjects congregate and make merry. As this selection opens, a fierce and powerful monster named Grendel invades the mead hall, bringing death and destruction.*

GRENDEL

A powerful monster, living down
In the darkness, growled in pain, impatient
As day after day the music rang
Loud in that hall, the harp's rejoicing
5 Call and the poet's clear songs, sung
Of the ancient beginnings of us all, recalling
The Almighty making the earth, shaping
These beautiful plains marked off by oceans,
Then proudly setting the sun and moon
10 To glow across the land and light it;
The corners of the earth were made lovely with trees
And leaves, made quick with life, with each
Of the nations who now move on its face. And then
As now warriors sang of their pleasure:

Ⓐ OLD ENGLISH POETRY
Reread lines 1–2 aloud. Notice the use of **alliteration** with the repetition of the letters *p* and *d*. What **mood, or feeling,** does the alliteration convey?

Analyze Visuals ▶
Examine the composition, or arrangement of shapes, in this photograph. How does the angle of the photo contribute to its impact?

15 So Hrothgar's men lived happy in his hall
   Till the monster stirred, that demon, that fiend,
   Grendel, who haunted the moors, the wild
   Marshes, and made his home in a hell
   Not hell but earth. He was spawned in that slime,
20 Conceived by a pair of those monsters born
   Of Cain, murderous creatures banished
   By God, punished forever for the crime
   Of Abel's death. The Almighty drove
   Those demons out, and their exile was bitter,
25 Shut away from men; they split
   Into a thousand forms of evil—spirits
   And fiends, goblins, monsters, giants,
   A brood forever opposing the Lord's
   Will, and again and again defeated. **B**

30   Then, when darkness had dropped, Grendel
   Went up to Herot, wondering what the warriors
   Would do in that hall when their drinking was done.
   He found them sprawled in sleep, suspecting
   Nothing, their dreams undisturbed. The monster's
35 Thoughts were as quick as his greed or his claws:
   He slipped through the door and there in the silence
   Snatched up thirty men, smashed them
   Unknowing in their beds and ran out with their bodies,
   The blood dripping behind him, back
40 To his **lair**, delighted with his night's slaughter.
       At daybreak, with the sun's first light, they saw
   How well he had worked, and in that gray morning
   Broke their long feast with tears and laments
   For the dead. Hrothgar, their lord, sat joyless
45 In Herot, a mighty prince mourning
   The fate of his lost friends and companions,
   Knowing by its tracks that some demon had torn
   His followers apart. He wept, fearing
   The beginning might not be the end. And that night **C**
50 Grendel came again, so set
   On murder that no crime could ever be enough,
   No savage assault quench his lust
   For evil. Then each warrior tried
   To escape him, searched for rest in different
55 Beds, as far from Herot as they could find,
   Seeing how Grendel hunted when they slept.
   Distance was safety; the only survivors
   Were those who fled him. Hate had triumphed.

17 moors (mŏŏrz): broad, open regions with patches of bog.

19 spawned: given birth to.

21 Cain: the eldest son of Adam and Eve. According to the Bible (Genesis 4), he murdered his younger brother Abel.

B EPIC
Note the description in lines 23–29 of supernatural creatures that are "again and again defeated." What **universal theme** might these lines suggest?

lair (lâr) *n.* the den or resting place of a wild animal

C EPIC
What is the **tone** of lines 44–49? What words and details convey this tone?

So Grendel ruled, fought with the righteous,
60 One against many, and won; so Herot
Stood empty, and stayed deserted for years,
Twelve winters of grief for Hrothgar, king
Of the Danes, sorrow heaped at his door
By hell-forged hands. His misery leaped **D**
65 The seas, was told and sung in all
Men's ears: how Grendel's hatred began,
How the monster relished his savage war
On the Danes, keeping the bloody feud
Alive, seeking no peace, offering
70 No truce, accepting no settlement, no price
In gold or land, and paying the living
For one crime only with another. No one
Waited for reparation from his plundering claws:
That shadow of death hunted in the darkness,
75 Stalked Hrothgar's warriors, old
And young, lying in waiting, hidden
In mist, invisibly following them from the edge
Of the marsh, always there, unseen.
    So mankind's enemy continued his crimes,
80 Killing as often as he could, coming
Alone, bloodthirsty and horrible. Though he lived
In Herot, when the night hid him, he never
Dared to touch king Hrothgar's glorious
Throne, protected by God—God,
85 Whose love Grendel could not know. But Hrothgar's
Heart was bent. The best and most noble
Of his council debated remedies, sat
In secret sessions, talking of terror
And wondering what the bravest of warriors could do.
90 And sometimes they sacrificed to the old stone gods,
Made heathen vows, hoping for Hell's
Support, the Devil's guidance in driving
Their **affliction** off. That was their way,
And the heathen's only hope, Hell
95 Always in their hearts, knowing neither God
Nor His passing as He walks through our world, the Lord
Of Heaven and earth; their ears could not hear
His praise nor know His glory. Let them
Beware, those who are thrust into danger,
100 Clutched at by trouble, yet can carry no solace
In their hearts, cannot hope to be better! Hail
To those who will rise to God, drop off
Their dead bodies and seek our Father's peace!

D OLD ENGLISH POETRY
What does the **kenning** "hell-forged hands" in line 64 suggest about Grendel?

73 reparation: something done to make amends for loss or suffering. In Germanic society, someone who killed another person was generally expected to make a payment to the victim's family as a way of restoring peace.

84 The reference to God shows the influence of Christianity on the Beowulf Poet.

91 heathen (hē′thən): pagan; non-Christian. Though the Beowulf Poet was a Christian, he recognized that the characters in the poem lived before the Germanic tribes were converted to Christianity, when they still worshiped "the old stone gods."

affliction (ə-flĭk′shən) *n.* a force that oppresses or causes suffering

BEOWULF

The Oseberg Ship (850), Viking. Viking Ship Museum, Bygdoy, Norway. © Werner Forman/Art Resource, New York.

So the living sorrow of Healfdane's son
105 Simmered, bitter and fresh, and no wisdom
Or strength could break it: that agony hung
On king and people alike, harsh
And unending, violent and cruel, and evil.
In his far-off home Beowulf, Higlac's
110 Follower and the strongest of the Geats—greater
And stronger than anyone anywhere in this world—
Heard how Grendel filled nights with horror
And quickly commanded a boat fitted out,
Proclaiming that he'd go to that famous king,
115 Would sail across the sea to Hrothgar,
Now when help was needed. None
Of the wise ones regretted his going, much
As he was loved by the Geats: the omens were good,
And they urged the adventure on. So Beowulf
120 Chose the mightiest men he could find,
The bravest and best of the Geats, fourteen
In all, and led them down to their boat;

104 Healfdane's son: Hrothgar.

109–110 Higlac's follower: a warrior loyal to Higlac (hĭg′lăk′), king of the Geats (and Beowulf's uncle).

He knew the sea, would point the prow
Straight to that distant Danish shore. . . .**E**

Beowulf and his men sail over the sea to the land of the Danes to offer
help to Hrothgar. They are escorted by a Danish guard to Herot, where
Wulfgar, one of Hrothgar's soldiers, tells the king of their arrival. Hrothgar
knows of Beowulf and is ready to welcome the young prince and his men.

125   Then Wulfgar went to the door and addressed
The waiting seafarers with soldier's words:
        "My lord, the great king of the Danes, commands me
To tell you that he knows of your noble birth
And that having come to him from over the open
130 Sea you have come bravely and are welcome.
Now go to him as you are, in your armor and helmets,
But leave your battle-shields here, and your spears,
Let them lie waiting for the promises your words
May make."
                Beowulf arose, with his men
135 Around him, ordering a few to remain
With their weapons, leading the others quickly
Along under Herot's steep roof into Hrothgar's
Presence. Standing on that prince's own hearth,
Helmeted, the silvery metal of his mail shirt
140 Gleaming with a smith's high art, he greeted
The Danes' great lord:
                        "Hail, Hrothgar!
Higlac is my cousin and my king; the days
Of my youth have been filled with glory. Now Grendel's
Name has echoed in our land: sailors
145 Have brought us stories of Herot, the best
Of all mead-halls, deserted and useless when the moon
Hangs in skies the sun had lit,
Light and life fleeing together.
My people have said, the wisest, most knowing
150 And best of them, that my duty was to go to the Danes'
Great king. They have seen my strength for themselves,
Have watched me rise from the darkness of war,
Dripping with my enemies' blood. I drove
Five great giants into chains, chased
155 All of that race from the earth. I swam
In the blackness of night, hunting monsters
Out of the ocean, and killing them one

E **EPIC**
An **epic** is a long narrative poem that traces the adventures of a great hero. Almost all national cultures have their own epics, whose stories and heroes play a role in defining the national character. An epic may describe how a nation was established or highlight specific **traits** associated with its people. Read lines 109–124. At what point in the story is Beowulf introduced? What traits of an epic hero does he appear to possess? Which traits of Beowulf's might also be used to describe the British people and their origins?

139 mail shirt: flexible body armor made of metal links or overlapping metal scales.

140 smith's high art: the skilled craft of a blacksmith (a person who fashions objects from iron).

142 cousin: here, a general term for a relative. Beowulf is actually Higlac's nephew.

By one; death was my errand and the fate
They had earned. Now Grendel and I are called **F**
160 Together, and I've come. Grant me, then,
Lord and protector of this noble place,
A single request! I have come so far,
Oh shelterer of warriors and your people's loved friend,
That this one favor you should not refuse me—
165 That I, alone and with the help of my men,
May **purge** all evil from this hall. I have heard,
Too, that the monster's scorn of men
Is so great that he needs no weapons and fears none.
Nor will I. My lord Higlac
170 Might think less of me if I let my sword
Go where my feet were afraid to, if I hid
Behind some broad linden shield: my hands
Alone shall fight for me, struggle for life
Against the monster. God must decide
175 Who will be given to death's cold grip.
Grendel's plan, I think, will be
What it has been before, to invade this hall
And **gorge** his belly with our bodies. If he can,
If he can. And I think, if my time will have come,
180 There'll be nothing to mourn over, no corpse to prepare
For its grave: Grendel will carry our bloody
Flesh to the moors, crunch on our bones
And smear torn scraps of our skin on the walls
Of his den. No, I expect no Danes
185 Will fret about sewing our shrouds, if he wins.
And if death does take me, send the hammered
Mail of my armor to Higlac, return
The inheritance I had from Hrethel, and he
From Wayland. Fate will unwind as it must!"

190   Hrothgar replied, protector of the Danes:
         "Beowulf, you've come to us in friendship, and because
Of the reception your father found at our court.
Edgetho had begun a bitter feud,
Killing Hathlaf, a Wulfing warrior:
195 Your father's countrymen were afraid of war,
If he returned to his home, and they turned him away.
Then he traveled across the curving waves
To the land of the Danes. I was new to the throne,
Then, a young man ruling this wide

F EPIC
Notice that in lines 153–159, Beowulf boasts about past victories that required superhuman strength and courage. Why might the people of Beowulf's time have valued such **traits?**

purge (pûrj) *v.* to cleanse or rid of something undesirable

172 linden shield: a shield made from the wood of a linden tree.

172–174 Beowulf insists on fighting Grendel without weapons.

gorge (gôrj) *v.* to stuff with food; glut

185 shrouds: cloths in which dead bodies are wrapped.

188 Hrethel (hrĕth′əl): a former king of the Geats—Higlac's father and Beowulf's grandfather.

189 Wayland: a famous blacksmith and magician.

193 Edgetho (ĕj′thō): Beowulf's father.

194 Wulfing: a member of another Germanic tribe.

200 Kingdom and its golden city: Hergar,
My older brother, a far better man
Than I, had died and dying made me,
Second among Healfdane's sons, first
In this nation. I bought the end of Edgetho's
205 Quarrel, sent ancient treasures through the ocean's
Furrows to the Wulfings; your father swore
He'd keep that peace. My tongue grows heavy,
And my heart, when I try to tell you what Grendel
Has brought us, the damage he's done, here
210 In this hall. You see for yourself how much smaller **G**
Our ranks have become, and can guess what we've lost
To his terror. Surely the Lord Almighty
Could stop his madness, smother his lust!
How many times have my men, glowing
215 With courage drawn from too many cups
Of ale, sworn to stay after dark
And stem that horror with a sweep of their swords.
And then, in the morning, this mead-hall glittering
With new light would be drenched with blood, the benches
220 Stained red, the floors, all wet from that fiend's
Savage assault—and my soldiers would be fewer
Still, death taking more and more.
But to table, Beowulf, a banquet in your honor:
Let us toast your victories, and talk of the future." **H**
225   Then Hrothgar's men gave places to the Geats,
Yielded benches to the brave visitors
And led them to the feast. The keeper of the mead
Came carrying out the carved flasks,
And poured that bright sweetness. A poet
230 Sang, from time to time, in a clear
Pure voice. Danes and visiting Geats
Celebrated as one, drank and rejoiced. . . .

G OLD ENGLISH POETRY
Observe that as Hrothgar begins
to speak about Grendel in lines
207–210, his **tone**, or his attitude
toward his subject, becomes
bleak and despairing. What
repeated sounds does the poet
use to suggest this tone?

H EPIC
Note that Hrothgar delivers
a long speech to Beowulf in
lines 190–224. What values are
reflected in the speech?

THE BATTLE WITH GRENDEL

After the banquet, Hrothgar and his followers leave Herot, and Beowulf and his warriors remain to spend the night. Beowulf reiterates his intent to fight Grendel without a sword and, while his followers sleep, lies waiting, eager for Grendel to appear.

Out from the marsh, from the foot of misty
Hills and bogs, bearing God's hatred,
235 Grendel came, hoping to kill 🔲
Anyone he could trap on this trip to high Herot.
He moved quickly through the cloudy night,
Up from his swampland, sliding silently
Toward that gold-shining hall. He had visited Hrothgar's
240 Home before, knew the way—
But never, before nor after that night,
Found Herot defended so firmly, his reception
So harsh. He journeyed, forever joyless,
Straight to the door, then snapped it open,
245 Tore its iron fasteners with a touch

🔲 **OLD ENGLISH POETRY**
Reread lines 233–235. Notice that the translator uses punctuation to convey the effect of the midline pauses, or **caesuras,** in the lines. In what way does the rhythm created by the pauses reinforce the action recounted here?

And rushed angrily over the threshold.
He strode quickly across the inlaid
Floor, snarling and fierce: his eyes
Gleamed in the darkness, burned with a gruesome
250 Light. Then he stopped, seeing the hall
Crowded with sleeping warriors, stuffed
With rows of young soldiers resting together.
And his heart laughed, he relished the sight,
Intended to tear the life from those bodies
255 By morning; the monster's mind was hot
With the thought of food and the feasting his belly
Would soon know. But fate, that night, intended
Grendel to gnaw the broken bones
Of his last human supper. Human
260 Eyes were watching his evil steps,
Waiting to see his swift hard claws.
Grendel snatched at the first Geat
He came to, ripped him apart, cut
His body to bits with powerful jaws,
265 Drank the blood from his veins and bolted
Him down, hands and feet; death
And Grendel's great teeth came together,
Snapping life shut. Then he stepped to another
Still body, clutched at Beowulf with his claws,
270 Grasped at a strong-hearted wakeful sleeper
—And was instantly seized himself, claws
Bent back as Beowulf leaned up on one arm.
     That shepherd of evil, guardian of crime,
Knew at once that nowhere on earth
275 Had he met a man whose hands were harder;
His mind was flooded with fear—but nothing
Could take his **talons** and himself from that tight
Hard grip. Grendel's one thought was to run
From Beowulf, flee back to his marsh and hide there:
280 This was a different Herot than the hall he had emptied.
But Higlac's follower remembered his final
Boast and, standing erect, stopped
The monster's flight, fastened those claws
In his fists till they cracked, clutched Grendel
285 Closer. The **infamous** killer fought
For his freedom, wanting no flesh but retreat,
Desiring nothing but escape; his claws
Had been caught, he was trapped. That trip to Herot
Was a miserable journey for the writhing monster!

246 threshold: the strip of wood or stone at the bottom of a doorway.

talon (tăl'ən) *n.* a claw

278–289 Up to this point Grendel has killed his human victims easily.

infamous (ĭn'fə-məs) *adj.* having a very bad reputation

290   The high hall rang, its roof boards swayed,
     And Danes shook with terror. Down
     The aisles the battle swept, angry
     And wild. Herot trembled, wonderfully
     Built to withstand the blows, the struggling
295   Great bodies beating at its beautiful walls;
     Shaped and fastened with iron, inside
     And out, artfully worked, the building
     Stood firm. Its benches rattled, fell
     To the floor, gold-covered boards grating
300   As Grendel and Beowulf battled across them. **J**
     Hrothgar's wise men had fashioned Herot
     To stand forever; only fire,
     They had planned, could shatter what such skill had put
     Together, swallow in hot flames such splendor
305   Of ivory and iron and wood. Suddenly
     The sounds changed, the Danes started
     In new terror, cowering in their beds as the terrible
     Screams of the Almighty's enemy sang
     In the darkness, the horrible shrieks of pain
310   And defeat, the tears torn out of Grendel's
     Taut throat, hell's captive caught in the arms
     Of him who of all the men on earth
     Was the strongest.

               That mighty protector of men
     Meant to hold the monster till its life
315   Leaped out, knowing the fiend was no use
     To anyone in Denmark. All of Beowulf's
     Band had jumped from their beds, ancestral
     Swords raised and ready, determined
     To protect their prince if they could. Their courage
320   Was great but all wasted: they could hack at Grendel
     From every side, trying to open
     A path for his evil soul, but their points
     Could not hurt him, the sharpest and hardest iron
     Could not scratch at his skin, for that sin-stained demon
325   Had bewitched all men's weapons, laid spells
     That blunted every mortal man's blade. And yet his time had come, his days
     And yet his time had come, his days
     Were over, his death near; down
     To hell he would go, swept groaning and helpless
330 To the waiting hands of still worse fiends.

J OLD ENGLISH POETRY
Reread lines 293–300. What impression of the battle does the **alliteration** help convey?

COMMON CORE L 4a

Language Coach

Homophones Many word pairs sound alike but have different spellings and meanings. For example, *taught* is the past tense of *teach*. Which word in line 311 is a homophone for *taught*? Guess the word's meaning using the surrounding text.

Now he discovered—once the afflictor
Of men, tormentor of their days—what it meant
To feud with Almighty God: Grendel
Saw that his strength was deserting him, his claws
335 Bound fast, Higlac's brave follower tearing at
His hands. The monster's hatred rose higher,
But his power had gone. He twisted in pain,
And the bleeding sinews deep in his shoulder
Snapped, muscle and bone split
340 And broke. The battle was over, Beowulf
Had been granted new glory: Grendel escaped,
But wounded as he was could flee to his den,
His miserable hole at the bottom of the marsh,
Only to die, to wait for the end
345 Of all his days. And after that bloody
Combat the Danes laughed with delight.
He who had come to them from across the sea,
Bold and strong-minded, had driven affliction
Off, purged Herot clean. He was happy,
350 Now, with that night's fierce work; the Danes
Had been served as he'd boasted he'd serve them; Beowulf,
A prince of the Geats, had killed Grendel,
Ended the grief, the sorrow, the suffering
Forced on Hrothgar's helpless people
355 By a bloodthirsty fiend. No Dane doubted
The victory, for the proof, hanging high
From the rafters where Beowulf had hung it, was the monster's
Arm, claw and shoulder and all.

　　　　And then, in the morning, crowds surrounded
360 Herot, warriors coming to that hall
From faraway lands, princes and leaders
Of men hurrying to behold the monster's
Great staggering tracks. They gaped with no sense
Of sorrow, felt no regret for his suffering,
365 Went tracing his bloody footprints, his beaten
And lonely flight, to the edge of the lake
Where he'd dragged his corpselike way, doomed
And already weary of his vanishing life.
The water was bloody, steaming and boiling
370 In horrible pounding waves, heat
Sucked from his magic veins; but the swirling
Surf had covered his death, hidden

338 sinews (sĭn′yo͞oz): the tendons that connect muscles to bones.

Deep in murky darkness his miserable
End, as hell opened to receive him. **K**
375   Then old and young rejoiced, turned back
From that happy pilgrimage, mounted their hard-hooved
Horses, high-spirited stallions, and rode them
Slowly toward Herot again, retelling
Beowulf's bravery as they jogged along.
380 And over and over they swore that nowhere
On earth or under the spreading sky
Or between the seas, neither south nor north,
Was there a warrior worthier to rule over men.
(But no one meant Beowulf's praise to belittle
385 Hrothgar, their kind and gracious king!)
        And sometimes, when the path ran straight and clear,
They would let their horses race, red
And brown and pale yellow backs streaming
Down the road. And sometimes a proud old soldier
390 Who had heard songs of the ancient heroes
And could sing them all through, story after story,
Would weave a net of words for Beowulf's
Victory, tying the knot of his verses
Smoothly, swiftly, into place with a poet's
395 Quick skill, singing his new song aloud
While he shaped it, and the old songs as well. . . . **L**

K GRAMMAR AND STYLE
To capture a scene, the poet often uses vivid **imagery.** Notice the use in lines 369–374, for example, of **adjectives** such as *bloody, steaming, pounding,* and *swirling* to help readers see and feel the violent, churning water.

L OLD ENGLISH POETRY
Reread lines 389–396. In what ways does this description reflect the techniques used by Anglo-Saxon poets? Cite details.

Text Analysis

1. **Clarify** Why does Beowulf journey across the sea to the land of the Danes?

2. **Summarize** How does Beowulf trap and kill Grendel?

3. **Analyze Motivation** What drives Grendel to attack so many men at Herot, the mead hall?

4. **Make Inferences** Why does Beowulf hang Grendel's arm from the rafters of Herot?

GRENDEL'S MOTHER

Although one monster has died, another still lives. From her lair in a
cold and murky lake, where she has been brooding over her loss, Grendel's
mother emerges, bent on revenge.

    So she reached Herot,
Where the Danes slept as though already dead;
Her visit ended their good fortune, reversed
400 The bright vane of their luck. No female, no matter
How fierce, could have come with a man's strength,
Fought with the power and courage men fight with,
Smashing their shining swords, their bloody,
Hammer-forged blades onto boar-headed helmets,
405 Slashing and stabbing with the sharpest of points.
The soldiers raised their shields and drew
Those gleaming swords, swung them above
The piled-up benches, leaving their mail shirts
And their helmets where they'd lain when the terror took hold of them.
410 To save her life she moved still faster,
Took a single victim and fled from the hall,
Running to the moors, discovered, but her supper
Assured, sheltered in her dripping claws.
She'd taken Hrothgar's closest friend,
415 The man he most loved of all men on earth;
She'd killed a glorious soldier, cut
A noble life short. No Geat could have stopped her:
Beowulf and his band had been given better

What mood is conveyed by this photograph? Which elements help create that mood?

400 vane: a device that turns to show the direction the wind is blowing—here associated metaphorically with luck, which is as changeable as the wind.

404 boar-headed helmets: Germanic warriors often wore helmets bearing the images of wild pigs or other fierce creatures in the hope that the images would increase their ferocity and protect them against their enemies.

Beds; sleep had come to them in a different
420 Hall. Then all Herot burst into shouts:
She had carried off Grendel's claw. Sorrow
Had returned to Denmark. They'd traded deaths,
Danes and monsters, and no one had won,
Both had lost! . . .

Devastated by the loss of his friend, Hrothgar sends for Beowulf and
recounts what Grendel's mother has done. Then Hrothgar describes
the dark lake where Grendel's mother has dwelt with her son.

425 "They live in secret places, windy
Cliffs, wolf-dens where water pours
From the rocks, then runs underground, where mist
Steams like black clouds, and the groves of trees
Growing out over their lake are all covered
430 With frozen spray, and wind down snakelike
Roots that reach as far as the water
And help keep it dark. At night that lake
Burns like a torch. No one knows its bottom,
No wisdom reaches such depths. A deer,
435 Hunted through the woods by packs of hounds,
A stag with great horns, though driven through the forest
From faraway places, prefers to die
On those shores, refuses to save its life
In that water. It isn't far, nor is it
440 A pleasant spot! When the wind stirs
And storms, waves splash toward the sky,
As dark as the air, as black as the rain
That the heavens weep. Our only help,
Again, lies with you. Grendel's mother
445 Is hidden in her terrible home, in a place
You've not seen. Seek it, if you dare! Save us,
Once more, and again twisted gold,
Heaped-up ancient treasure, will reward you
For the battle you win!" . . .

447–449 Germanic warriors placed great importance on amassing treasure as a way of acquiring fame and temporarily defeating fate.

THE BATTLE WITH GRENDEL'S MOTHER

Beowulf accepts Hrothgar's challenge, and the king and his men accompany the hero to the dreadful lair of Grendel's mother. Fearlessly, Beowulf prepares to battle the terrible creature.

450   He leaped into the lake, would not wait for anyone's
Answer; the heaving water covered him
Over. For hours he sank through the waves;
At last he saw the mud of the bottom.
And all at once the greedy she-wolf
455 Who'd ruled those waters for half a hundred
Years discovered him, saw that a creature
From above had come to explore the bottom
Of her wet world. She welcomed him in her claws,
Clutched at him savagely but could not harm him,
460 Tried to work her fingers through the tight
Ring-woven mail on his breast, but tore

And scratched in vain. Then she carried him, armor
And sword and all, to her home; he struggled
To free his weapon, and failed. The fight
465 Brought other monsters swimming to see
Her catch, a host of sea beasts who beat at
His mail shirt, stabbing with tusks and teeth
As they followed along. Then he realized, suddenly,
That she'd brought him into someone's battle-hall,
470 And there the water's heat could not hurt him,
Nor anything in the lake attack him through
The building's high-arching roof. A brilliant
Light burned all around him, the lake
Itself like a fiery flame. **Ⓜ**

                      Then he saw
475 The mighty water witch, and swung his sword,
His ring-marked blade, straight at her head;
The iron sang its fierce song,
Sang Beowulf's strength. But her guest
Discovered that no sword could slice her evil
480 Skin, that Hrunting could not hurt her, was useless
Now when he needed it. They wrestled, she ripped
And tore and clawed at him, bit holes in his helmet,
And that too failed him; for the first time in years
Of being worn to war it would earn no glory;
485 It was the last time anyone would wear it. But Beowulf
Longed only for fame, leaped back
Into battle. He tossed his sword aside,
Angry; the steel-edged blade lay where
He'd dropped it. If weapons were useless he'd use
490 His hands, the strength in his fingers. So fame
Comes to the men who mean to win it
And care about nothing else! He raised
His arms and seized her by the shoulder; anger
Doubled his strength, he threw her to the floor.
495 She fell, Grendel's fierce mother, and the Geats'
Proud prince was ready to leap on her. But she rose
At once and repaid him with her clutching claws,
Wildly tearing at him. He was weary, that best
And strongest of soldiers; his feet stumbled
500 And in an instant she had him down, held helpless.
Squatting with her weight on his stomach, she drew
A dagger, brown with dried blood, and prepared
To avenge her only son. But he was stretched

Ⓜ EPIC
Reread lines 464–474. What
details of the battle and its
setting are characteristic of
an epic?

476 his ring-marked blade: For the
battle with Grendel's mother, Beowulf
has been given an heirloom sword
with an intricately etched blade.

480 Hrunting (hrŭn'tĭng): the name
of Beowulf's sword. (Germanic
warriors' swords were possessions
of such value that they were often
given names.)

On his back, and her stabbing blade was blunted
505 By the woven mail shirt he wore on his chest.
The hammered links held; the point
Could not touch him. He'd have traveled to the bottom of the earth,
Edgetho's son, and died there, if that shining
Woven metal had not helped—and Holy
510 God, who sent him victory, gave judgment
For truth and right, Ruler of the Heavens,
Once Beowulf was back on his feet and fighting.

Then he saw, hanging on the wall, a heavy
Sword, hammered by giants, strong
515 And blessed with their magic, the best of all weapons
But so massive that no ordinary man could lift
Its carved and decorated length. He drew it
From its scabbard, broke the chain on its hilt,
And then, savage, now, angry
520 And desperate, lifted it high over his head
And struck with all the strength he had left,
Caught her in the neck and cut it through,
Broke bones and all. Her body fell
To the floor, lifeless, the sword was wet
525 With her blood, and Beowulf rejoiced at the sight.
The brilliant light shone, suddenly,
As though burning in that hall, and as bright as Heaven's
Own candle, lit in the sky. He looked **N**
At her home, then following along the wall
530 Went walking, his hands tight on the sword,
His heart still angry. He was hunting another
Dead monster, and took his weapon with him
For final revenge against Grendel's vicious
Attacks, his nighttime raids, over
535 And over, coming to Herot when Hrothgar's
Men slept, killing them in their beds,
Eating some on the spot, fifteen
Or more, and running to his **loathsome** moor
With another such sickening meal waiting
540 In his pouch. But Beowulf repaid him for those visits,
Found him lying dead in his corner,
Armless, exactly as that fierce fighter
Had sent him out from Herot, then struck off
His head with a single swift blow. The body
545 Jerked for the last time, then lay still.

N EPIC
What does the light described in lines 526–528 suggest about Beowulf's victory?

loathsome (lōth′səm) *adj.*
disgusting

The wise old warriors who surrounded Hrothgar,
Like him staring into the monsters' lake,
Saw the waves surging and blood
Spurting through. They spoke about Beowulf,
550 All the graybeards, whispered together
And said that hope was gone, that the hero
Had lost fame and his life at once, and would never
Return to the living, come back as triumphant
As he had left; almost all agreed that Grendel's
555 Mighty mother, the she-wolf, had killed him. ◎
The sun slid over past noon, went further
Down. The Danes gave up, left
The lake and went home, Hrothgar with them.
The Geats stayed, sat sadly, watching,
560 Imagining they saw their lord but not believing
They would ever see him again.
                —Then the sword
Melted, blood-soaked, dripping down
Like water, disappearing like ice when the world's
Eternal Lord loosens invisible
565 Fetters and unwinds icicles and frost
As only He can, He who rules
Time and seasons, He who is truly
God. The monsters' hall was full of
Rich treasures, but all that Beowulf took
570 Was Grendel's head and the hilt of the giants'
Jeweled sword; the rest of that ring-marked
Blade had dissolved in Grendel's steaming
Blood, boiling even after his death.
And then the battle's only survivor
575 Swam up and away from those silent corpses;
The water was calm and clean, the whole
Huge lake peaceful once the demons who'd lived in it
Were dead.
          Then that noble protector of all seamen
Swam to land, rejoicing in the heavy
580 Burdens he was bringing with him. He
And all his glorious band of Geats
Thanked God that their leader had come back unharmed;
They left the lake together. The Geats
Carried Beowulf's helmet, and his mail shirt.
585 Behind them the water slowly thickened
As the monsters' blood came seeping up.

550 graybeards: old men.

◎ **EPIC**
What do lines 549–555 suggest about attitudes toward fame in the Anglo-Saxon period?

578 that noble protector of all seamen: Beowulf, who will be buried in a tower that will serve as a navigational aid to sailors.

They walked quickly, happily, across
Roads all of them remembered, left
The lake and the cliffs alongside it, brave men
590 Staggering under the weight of Grendel's skull,
Too heavy for fewer than four of them to handle—
Two on each side of the spear jammed through it—
Yet proud of their ugly load and determined
That the Danes, seated in Herot, should see it. **P**
595 Soon, fourteen Geats arrived
At the hall, bold and warlike, and with Beowulf,
Their lord and leader, they walked on the mead-hall
Green. Then the Geats' brave prince entered
Herot, covered with glory for the daring
600 Battles he had fought; he sought Hrothgar
To salute him and show Grendel's head.
He carried that terrible trophy by the hair,
Brought it straight to where the Danes sat,
Drinking, the queen among them. It was a weird
605 And wonderful sight, and the warriors stared. . . .

P **EPIC**
Reread lines 587–594. Why do you think the Geats want the Danes to see Grendel's skull?

604 queen: Welthow, wife of Hrothgar.

Text Analysis

1. **Clarify** Why does Hrothgar ask Beowulf to battle Grendel's mother?

2. **Summarize** What does Beowulf do after he kills Grendel's mother?

3. **Compare and Contrast** Compare the two monsters. Does the behavior of Grendel's mother seem as wicked or unreasonable as Grendel's behavior? Support your opinion with evidence from the text.

BEOWULF'S LAST BATTLE

*With Grendel's mother destroyed, peace is restored to the land of the Danes, and
Beowulf, laden with Hrothgar's gifts, returns to the land of his own people, the
Geats. After his uncle and cousin die, Beowulf becomes king of the Geats and rules
in peace and prosperity for 50 years. One day, however, a fire-breathing dragon
that has been guarding a treasure for hundreds of years is disturbed by a thief,
who enters the treasure tower and steals a cup. The dragon begins terrorizing the
Geats, and Beowulf, now an old man, takes on the challenge of fighting it.*

    And Beowulf uttered his final boast:
    "I've never known fear, as a youth I fought
In endless battles. I am old, now,
But I will fight again, seek fame still,
610 If the dragon hiding in his tower dares
    To face me."

Then he said farewell to his followers, **Q**
Each in his turn, for the last time:
    "I'd use no sword, no weapon, if this beast
Could be killed without it, crushed to death
615 Like Grendel, gripped in my hands and torn
Limb from limb. But his breath will be burning
Hot, poison will pour from his tongue.
I feel no shame, with shield and sword
And armor, against this monster: when he comes to me
620 I mean to stand, not run from his shooting
Flames, stand till fate decides
Which of us wins. My heart is firm,
My hands calm: I need no hot
Words. Wait for me close by, my friends.
625 We shall see, soon, who will survive
This bloody battle, stand when the fighting
Is done. No one else could do
What I mean to, here, no man but me
Could hope to defeat this monster. No one
630 Could try. And this dragon's treasure, his gold
And everything hidden in that tower, will be mine
Or war will sweep me to a bitter death!"
    Then Beowulf rose, still brave, still strong,
And with his shield at his side, and a mail shirt on his breast,
635 Strode calmly, confidently, toward the tower, under
The rocky cliffs: no coward could have walked there!
And then he who'd endured dozens of desperate
Battles, who'd stood boldly while swords and shields
Clashed, the best of kings, saw
640 Huge stone arches and felt the heat
Of the dragon's breath, flooding down
Through the hidden entrance, too hot for anyone
To stand, a streaming current of fire
And smoke that blocked all passage. And the Geats'
645 Lord and leader, angry, lowered
His sword and roared out a battle cry,
A call so loud and clear that it reached through
The hoary rock, hung in the dragon's
Ear. The beast rose, angry,
650 Knowing a man had come—and then nothing
But war could have followed. Its breath came first,
A steaming cloud pouring from the stone,
Then the earth itself shook. Beowulf

Q OLD ENGLISH POETRY
Notice the repeated use of the letter *f* in lines 606–611. What **tone** does the **alliteration** help convey?

648 hoary (hôr′ē): gray with age.

Swung his shield into place, held it
655   In front of him, facing the entrance. The dragon
Coiled and uncoiled, its heart urging it
Into battle. Beowulf's ancient sword
Was waiting, unsheathed, his sharp and gleaming
Blade. The beast came closer; both of them
660   Were ready, each set on slaughter. The Geats'
Great prince stood firm, unmoving, prepared
Behind his high shield, waiting in his shining
Armor. The monster came quickly toward him,
Pouring out fire and smoke, hurrying
665   To its fate. Flames beat at the iron
Shield, and for a time it held, protected
Beowulf as he'd planned; then it began to melt,
And for the first time in his life that famous prince
Fought with fate against him, with glory
670   Denied him. He knew it, but he raised his sword
And struck at the dragon's scaly hide. **R**
The ancient blade broke, bit into
The monster's skin, drew blood, but cracked
And failed him before it went deep enough, helped him
675   Less than he needed. The dragon leaped
With pain, thrashed and beat at him, spouting
Murderous flames, spreading them everywhere.
And the Geats' ring-giver did not boast of glorious
Victories in other wars: his weapon
680   Had failed him, deserted him, now when he needed it
Most, that excellent sword. Edgetho's
Famous son stared at death,
Unwilling to leave this world, to exchange it
For a dwelling in some distant place—a journey
685   Into darkness that all men must make, as death
Ends their few brief hours on earth.
        Quickly, the dragon came at him, encouraged
As Beowulf fell back; its breath flared,
And he suffered, wrapped around in swirling
690   Flames—a king, before, but now
A beaten warrior. None of his comrades
Came to him, helped him, his brave and noble
Followers; they ran for their lives, fled
Deep in a wood. And only one of them
695   Remained, stood there, miserable, remembering,
As a good man must, what kinship should mean. **S**

R EPIC
Reread lines 668–671. What
do these lines reveal about the
qualities of an **epic hero?**

678 ring-giver: king; lord. When a
man swore allegiance to a Germanic
lord in return for his protection, the
lord typically bestowed a ring on his
follower to symbolize the bond.

S EPIC
What values are implied in lines
691–696? What message about
these values do the lines convey?

His name was Wiglaf, he was Wexstan's son
And a good soldier; his family had been Swedish,
Once. Watching Beowulf, he could see
700 How his king was suffering, burning. Remembering
Everything his lord and cousin had given him,
Armor and gold and the great estates
Wexstan's family enjoyed, Wiglaf's
Mind was made up; he raised his yellow
705 Shield and drew his sword. . . .
     And Wiglaf, his heart heavy, uttered
The kind of words his comrades deserved:
     "I remember how we sat in the mead-hall, drinking
And boasting of how brave we'd be when Beowulf
710 Needed us, he who gave us these swords
And armor: all of us swore to repay him,
When the time came, kindness for kindness
—With our lives, if he needed them. He allowed us to join him,
Chose us from all his great army, thinking
715 Our boasting words had some weight, believing
Our promises, trusting our swords. He took us
For soldiers, for men. He meant to kill
This monster himself, our mighty king,
Fight this battle alone and unaided,
720 As in the days when his strength and daring dazzled
Men's eyes. But those days are over and gone
And now our lord must lean on younger
Arms. And we must go to him, while angry
Flames burn at his flesh, help
725 Our glorious king! By almighty God,
I'd rather burn myself than see
Flames swirling around my lord.
And who are we to carry home
Our shields before we've slain his enemy
730 And ours, to run back to our homes with Beowulf
So hard-pressed here? I swear that nothing
He ever did deserved an end
Like this, dying miserably and alone,
Butchered by this savage beast: we swore
735 That these swords and armor were each for us all!" . . .

COMMON CORE L 5b

Language Coach

Connotation The images or feelings connected to a word are its **connotations.** *Killed* has many synonyms with different connotations. *Slain* (line 729) means "killed violently or in large numbers." *Butchered* (line 734) means "killed viciously." Why are these connotations important in lines 728–735?

Iron helmet covered with decorative panels of tinned bronze (early 600s). Anglo-Saxon. From Mound 1, Sutton Hoo, Suffolk, England. © The British Museum.

THE DEATH OF BEOWULF

Wiglaf joins Beowulf, who again attacks the dragon single-handed; but the remnant of his sword shatters, and the monster wounds him in the neck. Wiglaf then strikes the dragon, and he and Beowulf together finally succeed in killing the beast. Their triumph is short-lived, however, because Beowulf's wound proves to be mortal.

Beowulf spoke, in spite of the swollen,
Livid wound, knowing he'd unwound
His string of days on earth, seen
As much as God would grant him; all worldly

740 Pleasure was gone, as life would go,
Soon:
    "I'd leave my armor to my son,
Now, if God had given me an heir,
A child born of my body, his life
Created from mine. I've worn this crown

745 For fifty winters: no neighboring people
Have tried to threaten the Geats, sent soldiers

livid (lĭv′ĭd) *adj.* discolored from being bruised

Against us or talked of terror. My days
Have gone by as fate willed, waiting
For its word to be spoken, ruling as well
750 As I knew how, swearing no unholy oaths,
Seeking no lying wars. I can leave
This life happy; I can die, here,
Knowing the Lord of all life has never
Watched me wash my sword in blood
755 Born of my own family. Belovèd **T**
Wiglaf, go, quickly, find
The dragon's treasure: we've taken its life,
But its gold is ours, too. Hurry,
Bring me ancient silver, precious
760 Jewels, shining armor and gems,
Before I die. Death will be softer,
Leaving life and this people I've ruled
So long, if I look at this last of all prizes."

Then Wexstan's son went in, as quickly
765 As he could, did as the dying Beowulf
Asked, entered the inner darkness
Of the tower, went with his mail shirt and his sword.
Flushed with victory he groped his way,
A brave young warrior, and suddenly saw
770 Piles of gleaming gold, precious
Gems, scattered on the floor, cups
And bracelets, rusty old helmets, beautifully
Made but rotting with no hands to rub
And polish them. They lay where the dragon left them;
775 It had flown in the darkness, once, before fighting
Its final battle. (So gold can easily
Triumph, defeat the strongest of men,
No matter how deep it is hidden!) And he saw, **U**
Hanging high above, a golden
780 Banner, woven by the best of weavers
And beautiful. And over everything he saw
A strange light, shining everywhere,
On walls and floor and treasure. Nothing
Moved, no other monsters appeared;
785 He took what he wanted, all the treasures
That pleased his eye, heavy plates
And golden cups and the glorious banner,
Loaded his arms with all they could hold.

T EPIC
Note that Beowulf summarizes his 50-year reign in lines 744–755. What ideals are reflected in Beowulf's speech?

U EPIC
Reread lines 768–778. What **theme** do the lines suggest?

Beowulf's dagger, his iron blade,
790 Had finished the fire-spitting terror
That once protected tower and treasures
Alike; the gray-bearded lord of the Geats
Had ended those flying, burning raids
Forever. **V**

          Then Wiglaf went back, anxious
795 To return while Beowulf was alive, to bring him
Treasure they'd won together. He ran,
Hoping his wounded king, weak
And dying, had not left the world too soon.
Then he brought their treasure to Beowulf, and found
800 His famous king bloody, gasping
For breath. But Wiglaf sprinkled water
Over his lord, until the words
Deep in his breast broke through and were heard.
Beholding the treasure he spoke, haltingly:
805   "For this, this gold, these jewels, I thank
Our Father in Heaven, Ruler of the Earth—
For all of this, that His grace has given me,
Allowed me to bring to my people while breath
Still came to my lips. I sold my life
810 For this treasure, and I sold it well. Take
What I leave, Wiglaf, lead my people,
Help them; my time is gone. Have
The brave Geats build me a tomb,
When the funeral flames have burned me, and build it
815 Here, at the water's edge, high
On this spit of land, so sailors can see
This tower, and remember my name, and call it
Beowulf's tower, and boats in the darkness
And mist, crossing the sea, will know it." **W**
820   Then that brave king gave the golden
Necklace from around his throat to Wiglaf,
Gave him his gold-covered helmet, and his rings,
And his mail shirt, and ordered him to use them well:
    "You're the last of all our far-flung family.
825 Fate has swept our race away,
Taken warriors in their strength and led them
To the death that was waiting. And now I follow them."
    The old man's mouth was silent, spoke
No more, had said as much as it could;
830 He would sleep in the fire, soon. His soul

V OLD ENGLISH POETRY
Identify the **kennings** used in lines 789–794 to refer to the dragon and to Beowulf. What does the phrase used to describe Beowulf emphasize about the warrior?

816 spit: a narrow point of land extending into a body of water.

W EPIC
Reread lines 812–819. Why is it important to Beowulf that he leave a legacy behind?

Left his flesh, flew to glory. . . .
        And when the battle was over Beowulf's followers
Came out of the wood, cowards and traitors,
Knowing the dragon was dead. Afraid,
835 While it spit its fires, to fight in their lord's
Defense, to throw their javelins and spears,
They came like shamefaced jackals, their shields
In their hands, to the place where the prince lay dead,
And waited for Wiglaf to speak. He was sitting
840 Near Beowulf's body, wearily sprinkling
Water in the dead man's face, trying
To stir him. He could not. No one could have kept
Life in their lord's body, or turned
Aside the Lord's will: world
845 And men and all move as He orders,
And always have, and always will.
        Then Wiglaf turned and angrily told them
What men without courage must hear.
Wexstan's brave son stared at the traitors,
850 His heart sorrowful, and said what he had to:
        "I say what anyone who speaks the truth
Must say. . . .
          Too few of his warriors remembered
To come, when our lord faced death, alone.
855 And now the giving of swords, of golden
Rings and rich estates, is over,
Ended for you and everyone who shares
Your blood: when the brave Geats hear
How you bolted and ran none of your race
860 Will have anything left but their lives. And death
Would be better for them all, and for you, than the kind
Of life you can lead, branded with disgrace!". . . ⊗
        Then the warriors rose,
Walked slowly down from the cliff, stared
865 At those wonderful sights, stood weeping as they saw
Beowulf dead on the sand, their bold
Ring-giver resting in his last bed;
He'd reached the end of his days, their mighty
War-king, the great lord of the Geats,
870 Gone to a glorious death. . . .

836 javelins (jăv′lĭnz): light spears used as weapons.

837 jackals (jăk′əlz): doglike animals that sometimes feed on the flesh of dead beasts.

859 bolted: ran away; fled.

⊗ **EPIC**
What does Wiglaf's speech in lines 851–862 tell you about the importance of honor and the consequences of dishonorable behavior in Beowulf's time?

MOURNING BEOWULF

Then the Geats built the tower, as Beowulf
Had asked, strong and tall, so sailors
Could find it from far and wide; working
For ten long days they made his monument,
875 Sealed his ashes in walls as straight
And high as wise and willing hands
Could raise them. And the riches he and Wiglaf
Had won from the dragon, rings, necklaces,
Ancient, hammered armor—all
880 The treasures they'd taken were left there, too,
Silver and jewels buried in the sandy
Ground, back in the earth, again
And forever hidden and useless to men.
And then twelve of the bravest Geats
885 Rode their horses around the tower,
Telling their sorrow, telling stories
Of their dead king and his greatness, his glory,
Praising him for heroic deeds, for a life
As noble as his name. So should all men
890 Raise up words for their lords, warm
With love, when their shield and protector leaves
His body behind, sends his soul
On high. And so Beowulf's followers **Y**
Rode, mourning their belovèd leader,
895 Crying that no better king had ever
Lived, no prince so mild, no man
So open to his people, so deserving of praise.

▲ **Analyze Visuals**
What details in this photograph
suggest the mourning for
Beowulf? Explain.

Y **OLD ENGLISH POETRY**
Reread lines 889–893 aloud.
Notice the **alliteration** in the
phrases "words for their lords"
and "warm with love." How
would you describe the **tone** of
these lines?

896 mild: gentle or kindly.

Comprehension

1. **Recall** In what way does Beowulf's sword fail him?

2. **Summarize** How do the Geats honor Beowulf after he dies?

Text Analysis

● 3. **Examine Epic Characteristics** Review the discussion of the characteristics of an epic in the Text Analysis Workshop on pages 38–39. Then use a chart like the one shown to list Beowulf's traits as an **epic hero** and the deeds that reveal these traits. Is he a typical epic hero?

● 4. **Analyze Old English Poetry** Review the list you created as you read. In what ways might the **alliteration, caesuras,** and **kennings** in *Beowulf* have helped Anglo-Saxon poets chant or sing the poem and convey its meaning?

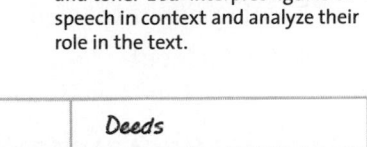

Traits	Deeds

5. **Analyze Theme** Beowulf is able to defeat Grendel and Grendel's mother, yet he loses his life when he battles the dragon. What themes does this suggest about the struggle between good and evil?

6. **Compare and Contrast** Compare and contrast the portrayals of Beowulf as a young and old man. Also compare Hrothgar's recollections of his early deeds with his limitations as an aged king. What view of youth and age do these comparisons convey? Support your conclusions with specific evidence.

7. **Draw Conclusions** Describe Beowulf's attitude toward death or mortality in each of the following passages: lines 179–189, lines 481–492, and lines 665–691. How does his attitude change over time?

8. **Evaluate Author's Purpose** Reread lines 81–85, which reveal the influence of Christianity on the Beowulf Poet. Why might the poet have chosen to describe Hrothgar and Grendel in terms of their relationship to God?

Text Criticism

9. **Different Perspectives** In his 20th-century novel *Grendel*, writer John Gardner tells the story of Grendel's attacks against the Danes from the monster's point of view. Consider the selection you have read from the perspectives of Grendel, Grendel's mother, and the dragon. What reasons might each of them have to hate Beowulf and other men?

Where do **MONSTERS** *lurk?*

Monsters like Grendel often combine human and animal features. Think of other monsters from literature, television, or film that combine these features. Why are such monsters particularly disturbing?

COMMON CORE

RL 2 Determine two or more themes or central ideas of a text. **RL 3** Analyze the impact of the author's choices regarding how to develop and relate elements of a story. **RL 4** Analyze the impact of specific word choices on meaning and tone. **L 5a** Interpret figures of speech in context and analyze their role in the text.

Vocabulary in Context

▲ **VOCABULARY PRACTICE**

Decide whether the words in each pair are synonyms or antonyms.

1. affliction/blessing
2. gorge/starve
3. infamous/respected
4. lair/hideout

5. livid/bruised
6. loathsome/delightful
7. purge/remove
8. talon/claw

WORD LIST

affliction
gorge
infamous
lair
livid
loathsome
purge
talon

ACADEMIC VOCABULARY IN WRITING

• concept • culture • parallel • section • structure

How has the **concept** of a hero changed since Beowulf's time? Write a paragraph about how the hero is represented in movies or TV in today's culture. Refer to at least one **section** of *Beowulf* for comparison. Use at least one additional Academic Vocabulary word in your response.

VOCABULARY STRATEGY: THE ANGLO-SAXON SUFFIX *-some*

Many English words with Anglo-Saxon word parts were born whole into Old English, changing slightly over time. Others developed from the combination of Old English word parts during the time when people spoke Middle English. The adjective-forming suffix *-some,* which means "like" or "tending to cause," appears in both types of words. In Old English, *-sum* occurred in the word *wynsum* (today's *winsome*). Later, the Middle English word *loth* ("to feel disgust") combined with the Old English *-sum* to make *lothsum:* "tending to cause disgust." Though the spelling has changed over time, *loathsome* has the same meaning today.

PRACTICE Use an adjective ending in the suffix *-some* to describe each person, place, or thing listed. Form the adjective by adding *-some* to a word shown in the equation.

1. a load of books to carry
2. a city skyline sparkling in the sun
3. a person who always argues
4. a smile that charms people
5. a cockroach

awe
burden
loathe   **+ -some**
quarrel
win

COMMON CORE

L 1a Apply the understanding that usage is a matter of convention and can change over time.
L 4b Identify and correctly use patterns of word changes that indicate different meanings or parts of speech.

Interactive Vocabulary THINK central

Go to **thinkcentral.com**.
KEYWORD: HML12-72

Language

◆ **GRAMMAR AND STYLE: Create Imagery**

Review the **Grammar and Style** note on page 54. To describe a scene or convey a mood, the Beowulf Poet uses **imagery**—words and phrases that create vivid sensory experiences for the audience. The poet frequently creates this imagery through an effective use of **adjectives** and **verbs**. Here is an example from the epic:

> The dragon *leaped*
> With pain, *thrashed* and *beat* at him, spouting
> *Murderous* flames, spreading them everywhere. (lines 675–677)

Notice that the verbs *leaped, thrashed,* and *beat* suggest a sense of movement and that the adjective *murderous* conveys the feeling of the flames' heat. The imagery in the sentence helps you envision the scene and experience its intensity.

PRACTICE Write down each of the following lines from *Beowulf*. Identify the adjectives and verbs in each sentence that create imagery and then write your own sentence with similar elements.

EXAMPLE

He *moved* quickly through the cloudy night, / Up from his swampland, *sliding silently* / Toward that *gold-shining* hall.

She drifted slowly down the leaf-strewn street, away from the city lights, winding sadly toward the deserted house.

---

1. . . . Grendel will carry our bloody / Flesh to the moors, crunch on our bones / And smear torn scraps of our skin on the walls / Of his den.

2. He strode quickly across the inlaid / Floor, snarling and fierce: his eyes / Gleamed in the darkness, burned with a gruesome / Light.

READING-WRITING CONNECTION

Expand your understanding of *Beowulf* by responding to this prompt. Then use the **revising tips** to improve your analysis.

WRITING PROMPT	REVISING TIPS
WRITE AN ANALYSIS The review on page 74 describes the experience of listening to an oral performance of *Beowulf*. Write a **three-to-five-paragraph analysis** of *Beowulf* in which you describe what features of the poem bring it to life for you. You might focus on its characters, its vivid descriptions, or its use of elements of Old English poetry.	• Clearly identify the features of the poem that make *Beowulf* a distinctive and powerful work of literature. • Include details from the poem to show how each of these features makes the poem come to life for you.

COMMON CORE

L 3 Apply knowledge of language to make effective choices for meaning or style. **W 2** Write informative/explanatory texts to examine and convey complex ideas, concepts, and information clearly and accurately through the effective selection, organization, and analysis of content. **W 9a (RL 4)** Analyze the impact of specific word choices on meaning and tone.

Interactive Revision

Go to **thinkcentral.com**.
KEYWORD: HML12-73

REVIEW Listening to the story of *Beowulf* sung by a scop playing a harp is not an experience confined to the past. American musician and medieval scholar Benjamin Bagby performs *Beowulf* in the original Anglo-Saxon to enthusiastic audiences. The following review captures the excitement of Bagby's *Beowulf*.

A Collaboration Across 1,200 Years

Review By
D. J. R. BRUCKNER

European noblemen of a thousand years ago had much more exciting and intelligent entertainment than anything to be found now. Anyone who doubts that need only look in on Benjamin Bagby's astonishing performance of the first quarter of the epic poem *Beowulf*—in Anglo-Saxon, no less—tonight at the Stanley H. Kaplan Penthouse at Lincoln Center. It will be the last of his three appearances in the Lincoln Center Festival.

From the moment he strode on stage on Sunday for the opening night, silencing the audience with that famous first word, "Hwaet!" ("Pay attention!"), until hell swallowed the "pagan soul" of the monster Grendel 80 minutes later,

Mr. Bagby came as close to holding hundreds of people in a spell as ever a man has. As the epic's warriors argued, boasted, fought or fell into the monster's maw, there were bursts of laughter, mutters and sighs, and when Mr. Bagby's voice stopped at the end, as abruptly as it had begun, there was an audible rippling gasp before a thunderclap of applause from cheering people who called him back again and again, unwilling to let him go.

Mr. Bagby—a Midwesterner who fell in love with *Beowulf* at 12 and who now is co-director of a medieval music ensemble, Sequentia, in Cologne, Germany—accompanies himself on a six-string lyre modeled on one found in a seventh-century tomb near Stuttgart. This surprisingly facile instrument underscores the meter of the epic

verses and is counterpoint to Mr. Bagby's voice as he recites, chants and occasionally sings the lines.

On the whole, this is a restrained presentation. The performer captures listeners at once simply by letting us feel his conviction that he has a tale to tell that is more captivating than any other story in the world. He avoids histrionic gestures, letting the majestic rhythms of the epic seize our emotions and guide them through the action. Gradually the many voices that fill the great poem emerge and

the listener always knows who is speaking: a warrior, a watchman, a king, a sarcastic drunk. A translation is handed out to the audience, but after a while one notices people are following it less and just letting the sound of this strange and beautiful language wash over them. Perhaps not so strange, after all—enough phrases begin to penetrate the understanding that one finally knows deep down that, yes, this is where English came from.

How authentic is all this? Well, we know from many historical sources that in the first millennium at royal or noble houses a performer called a scop would present epics. Mr. Bagby has lived with this epic for many years, as well as with ancient music, and his performance *is* his argument that *Beowulf* was meant to be heard, not read, and that this is the way we ought to hear it. It is a powerful argument, indeed. The test of it is that when he has finished, you leave with the overwhelming impression that you know the anonymous poet who created *Beowulf* more than a dozen centuries ago, that you have felt the man's personality touch you. That is a much too rare experience in theater.

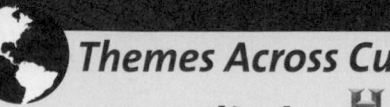
Epic Poem by Homer Translated by Robert Fitzgerald

DID YOU KNOW?

Homer . . .

- was probably illiterate.
- inspired Alexander the Great, who carried the *Iliad* with him on all of his military campaigns.
- is quoted more often than any other Western poet, with the possible exception of Shakespeare.

Meet the Author

Homer about 700 B.C.

Roughly a thousand years before the Beowulf Poet composed his epic poem, another oral poet, Homer, created two great epics. The *Iliad* and the *Odyssey* were an essential part of the ancient Greek world. Schoolchildren memorized verses from the poems, and scholars discussed their meaning. Alexander the Great slept with a gold-encrusted copy of the *Iliad* under his pillow. But little or nothing was known about the poet himself.

Man of Mystery Nothing much has changed today. Legend and mystery abound in the life of Homer. According to one of the most persistent legends, Homer was blind. However, some scholars have pointed out that the ancient Greeks typically depicted a sage or philosopher as a blind man to emphasize his exceptional inner vision.

The poet's birthplace and date of birth are also matters for speculation. For centuries, scholars even debated about whether Homer ever really existed. Today most agree that the author of the *Iliad* and the *Odyssey* was indeed a man named Homer who lived sometime between 800 and 600 B.C. and was born either in western Asia Minor or on one of the nearby Aegean islands. Evidence of his life has been gathered

indirectly from writings of ancient Greece and from Homer's poems.

Clash of Titans The *Iliad* relates events of the Trojan War, a conflict between Greeks and Trojans in the ancient city of Troy in Asia Minor. Most historians believe that some sort of war really did take place between Greece and Troy around 1200 B.C.

According to Homer's poem, the Trojan War began when Paris, a prince of Troy, kidnapped Helen, the world's most beautiful woman, from her husband, King Menelaus (mĕn´ə-lā´əs) of Greece. In retaliation, the king's brother, Agamemnon (ăg´ə-mĕm´nŏn), led the Greek army in an invasion of Troy. The Greeks laid siege to the city for ten years before finally achieving victory. The *Iliad* describes the final year of that siege.

Unlettered Genius Homer was able to draw on a rich oral tradition of stories about heroes and gods. Many scholars believe that he composed his epics orally, despite their great length and complexity. Homer probably could not read or write, but he may have recited his epics for someone else to record, thereby preserving the poems that became the foundation of Western literature.

Author Online

Go to **thinkcentral.com**. KEYWORD: HML12-76

THINKcentral

● TEXT ANALYSIS: SIMILE AND EPIC SIMILE

Homer often helps readers visualize the action in his epics with a **simile,** a figure of speech that uses the word *like* or *as* to make a comparison between two unlike things. A long simile, often continuing for a number of lines, is called an **epic simile.** In the following epic simile, Achilles compares his hatred for Hector to the hatred between enemies in nature:

> *As between men and lions there are none,*
> *no concord between wolves and sheep, but all*
> *hold one another hateful through and through,*
> *so there can be no courtesy between us ...*

As you read the selection from the *Iliad,* look for examples of similes and epic similes.

Review: **Epic**

● READING SKILL: CLASSIFY CHARACTERS

The *Iliad* is a complex poem involving many characters— both human and divine. To help you keep track of the epic's various characters as you read the *Iliad,* use a chart like the one shown to **classify** each character as a Greek, a Trojan, or a god. For each god, indicate whether he or she is helping the Greeks or the Trojans. Then note the important actions and characteristics of each character.

Character	Greek, Trojan, or God?	Actions/Characteristics
Thetis	• a sea goddess • helps the Greeks	• tries to console Achilles • loving toward son

▲ VOCABULARY IN CONTEXT

These words in the poem help convey the passions and exploits of war. Substitute the boldfaced word in each of the following sentences with a word from the list.

WORD LIST	abstain	havoc	scourge
	defile	ponderous	vulnerable
	felicity	rancor	

1. The feuding families viewed each other with **hatred.**
2. The elephant's **weighty** leg broke the trainer's stool.
3. The monster left behind a terrible trail of **devastation.**

 Complete the activities in your **Reader/Writer Notebook.**

What inspires COURAGE?

Running into a burning building to rescue a child. Standing up against gangs. Saving a drowning swimmer. These are all acts of courage. But what motivates people to perform them? After all, the logical thing to do when faced with danger is to run away. The three main characters in this epic draw on different types of strength when they confront their adversaries. What helps you find the courage to face your enemies and everyday dangers?

DISCUSS With a partner, discuss acts of courage you have witnessed or heard about. Talk about why these heroes did what they did. Are they different from other people? Is everyone capable of courageous acts? If your partner has a different perspective on courage or heroism, give those ideas thoughtful consideration before responding.

The ILIAD
HOMER

*While the Greeks are laying siege to Troy, a quarrel breaks out
between Agamemnon and his greatest warrior, Achilles (ə-kĭl'ēz). As
a result, the angry Achilles decides to remain in his tent and let the
Greeks fight without him. The Trojans, under the leadership of
Hector, are able to drive the Greeks back to the sea. During the
battle, Hector kills Achilles' best friend, Patroclus (pə-trō'kləs).
While grieving for his friend, Achilles is visited by his mother,
Thetis (thē'tĭs), a goddess of the sea.*

from Book 18 THE IMMORTAL SHIELD

>   Bending near
> her groaning son, the gentle goddess wailed
> and took his head between her hands in pity,
> saying softly:
>
>   "Child, why are you weeping?
> 5 What great sorrow came to you? Speak out,
> do not conceal it. Zeus
> did all you asked: Achaean troops,
> for want of you, were all forced back again
> upon the ship sterns, taking heavy losses
> 10 none of them could wish."
>
>   The great runner
> groaned and answered:
>
>   "Mother, yes, the master
> of high Olympus brought it all about,
> but how have I benefited? My greatest friend
> is gone: Patroclus, comrade in arms, whom I
> 15 held dear above all others—dear as myself—

Analyze Visuals ▶
What traits and emotions are
suggested by this painting of
Achilles? Which details help
convey them?

6–7 Previously Achilles asked Thetis
to persuade Zeus (zōōs), ruler of the
gods, to turn the tide of battle against
the Greeks so that they would see
how much they needed him.

7 Achaean (ə-kē'ən): Greek.

12 Olympus (ə-lĭm'pəs): the highest
mountain in Greece, on whose peak
the Greek gods and goddesses were
thought to dwell.

Achilles Contemplating the Body of Patroclus, Giovanni
Antonio Pellegrini. Musée Municipal, Soissons, France.
© Giraudon/Art Resource, New York.

now gone, lost; Hector cut him down, despoiled him
of my own arms, massive and fine, a wonder
in all men's eyes. The gods gave them to Peleus
that day they put you in a mortal's bed—
20 how I wish the immortals of the sea
had been your only consorts! How I wish
Peleus had taken a mortal queen! Sorrow
immeasurable is in store for you as well,
when your own child is lost: never again
25 on his homecoming day will you embrace him!
I must reject this life, my heart tells me,
reject the world of men,
if Hector does not feel my battering spear
tear the life out of him, making him pay
30 in his own blood for the slaughter of Patroclus!" **A**

Letting a tear fall, Thetis said:

                                            "You'll be
swift to meet your end, child, as you say:
your doom comes close on the heels of Hector's own."

Achilles the great runner ground his teeth
35 and said:

                        "May it come quickly. As things were,
I could not help my friend in his extremity.
Far from his home he died; he needed me
to shield him or to parry the death stroke.
For me there's no return to my own country.
40 Not the slightest gleam of hope did I
afford Patroclus or the other men
whom Hector overpowered. Here I sat,
my weight a useless burden to the earth,
and I am one who has no peer in war
45 among Achaean captains—
                                            though in council
there are wiser. Ai! let strife and **rancor**
perish from the lives of gods and men,
with anger that envenoms even the wise
and is far sweeter than slow-dripping honey,
50 clouding the hearts of men like smoke: just so
the marshal of the army, Agamemnon,
moved me to anger. But we'll let that go,

16–17 Patroclus wore Achilles' armor to frighten the Trojans. "Despoiled him of my own arms" refers to Hector's taking the armor from Patroclus' corpse.

18 Peleus (pē′lē-əs): Achilles' human father.

A **CLASSIFY CHARACTERS**
Reread lines 26–30. Notice that Achilles suggests that his heart is guiding him rather than his head. What characteristics does Achilles reveal in these lines?

38 parry: to turn aside; deflect.

rancor (răng′kər) *n.* bitter, long-lasting anger; ill will

48 envenoms (ĕn-vĕn′əmz): fills with poison.

though I'm still sore at heart; it is all past,
and I have quelled my passion as I must.

55 Now I must go to look for the destroyer
of my great friend. I shall confront the dark
drear spirit of death at any hour Zeus
and the other gods may wish to make an end.
Not even Heracles escaped that terror
60 though cherished by the Lord Zeus. Destiny
and Hera's bitter anger mastered him.
Likewise with me, if destiny like his
awaits me, I shall rest when I have fallen!
Now, though, may I win my perfect glory
65 and make some wife of Troy break down,
or some deep-breasted Dardan woman sob
and wipe tears from her soft cheeks. They'll know then
how long they had been spared the deaths of men,
while I **abstained** from war!
70 Do not attempt to keep me from the fight,
though you love me; you cannot make me listen."

*Achilles seeks to avenge Patroclus by slaughtering Trojans. Apollo, a
god who protects Troy, opens the gates of the city so the Trojans can
rush to safety inside the walls. Only Hector is left outside. Achilles
chases him around the walls three times. Finally the goddess Pallas
Athena, disguised as Hector's brother Deiphobus (dē-ĭf'ə-bəs), appears
to Hector and persuades him to fight Achilles.*

from Book 22 DESOLATION BEFORE TROY

And when at last the two men faced each other,
Hector was the first to speak. He said:

"I will no longer fear you as before,
75 son of Peleus, though I ran from you
round Priam's town three times and could not face you.
Now my soul would have me stand and fight,
whether I kill you or am killed. So come,
we'll summon gods here as our witnesses,
80 none higher, arbiters of a pact: I swear
that, terrible as you are,
I'll not insult your corpse should Zeus allow me
victory in the end, your life as prize.
Once I have your gear, I'll give your body
85 back to Achaeans. Grant me, too, this grace." **B**

59–61 Heracles (hĕr'ə-klēz'): another name for Hercules, the greatest legendary hero of ancient Greece, son of Zeus and a mortal woman named Alcmena (ălk-mē'nə). Zeus' wife, the goddess Hera (hîr'ə), hated and persecuted Heracles until his death.

66 Dardan (där'dn): Trojan.

abstain (ăb-stān') *v.* to hold oneself back from doing something

76 Priam's (prī'əmz) **town**: Troy. Priam is the Trojan King.

80 arbiters (är'bĭ-tərz): judges; referees.

B CLASSIFY CHARACTERS
In lines 82–85, Hector refers to the Greek and Trojan custom of returning the bodies of slain warriors to their people. What does this speech reveal about Hector?

Achilles Dragging the Body of Hector Around the Walls of Troy, Donato Creti. Oil on canvas, 142.5 cm. × 241.5 cm. Musée Massey, Tarbes, France. © Bridgeman Art Library.

But swift Achilles frowned at him and said:

"Hector, I'll have no talk of pacts with you,
forever unforgiven as you are.
As between men and lions there are none,
90 no concord between wolves and sheep, but all
hold one another hateful through and through,
so there can be no courtesy between us,
no sworn truce, till one of us is down
and glutting with his blood the wargod Ares.
95 Summon up what skills you have. By god,
you'd better be a spearman and a fighter!
Now there is no way out. Pallas Athena
will have the upper hand of you. The weapon
belongs to me. You'll pay the reckoning
100 in full for all the pain my men have borne,
who met death by your spear."

　　　　　　　　　He twirled and cast
his shaft with its long shadow. Splendid Hector,
keeping his eye upon the point, eluded it
by ducking at the instant of the cast,
105 so shaft and bronze shank passed him overhead
and punched into the earth. But unperceived
by Hector, Pallas Athena plucked it out
and gave it back to Achilles. Hector said: **C**

90 concord (kŏn'kôrd'): peace or harmony.

94 glutting with his blood the wargod Ares (âr'ēz): satisfying Ares, the god of war, by bleeding to death.

97–98 Pallas Athena, the goddess of wisdom, favors the Greeks.

C EPIC
Reread lines 102–108. What characteristic of an epic is revealed in these lines?

"A clean miss. Godlike as you are,
110 you have not yet known doom for me from Zeus.
You thought you had, by heaven. Then you turned
into a word-thrower, hoping to make me lose
my fighting heart and head in fear of you.
You cannot plant your spear between my shoulders
115 while I am running. If you have the gift,
just put it through my chest as I come forward.
Now it's for you to dodge my own. Would god
you'd give the whole shaft lodging in your body!
War for the Trojans would be eased
120 if you were blotted out, bane that you are."

With this he twirled his long spearshaft and cast it,
hitting his enemy mid-shield, but off
and away the spear rebounded. Furious
that he had lost it, made his throw for nothing,
125 Hector stood bemused. He had no other.
Then he gave a great shout to Deiphobus
to ask for a long spear. But there was no one
near him, not a soul. Now in his heart
the Trojan realized the truth and said:

130 "This is the end. The gods are calling deathward.
I had thought
a good soldier, Deiphobus, was with me.
He is inside the walls. Athena tricked me.
Death is near, and black, not at a distance,
135 not to be evaded. Long ago
this hour must have been to Zeus's liking
and to the liking of his archer son.
They have been well disposed before, but now
the appointed time's upon me. Still, I would not
140 die without delivering a stroke,
or die ingloriously, but in some action
memorable to men in days to come."

With this he drew the whetted blade that hung
upon his left flank, **ponderous** and long,
145 collecting all his might the way an eagle
narrows himself to dive through shady cloud
and strike a lamb or cowering hare: so Hector
lanced ahead and swung his whetted blade.
Achilles with wild fury in his heart

Language Coach

Fixed Expressions Words that, combined, have a special meaning are called **fixed expressions**. When Hector says, "by heaven" (line 111), he means, "as the gods are my witnesses." What similar expressions do we use today?

120 **bane:** a cause of distress, death, or ruin.

125 **bemused** (bĭ-myo͞ozd´): dazed; confused.

135–139 Zeus' "archer son" is Apollo, god of the sun, whose arrows may represent the sun's rays. Apollo typically favored the Trojans, while Zeus helped individuals on both sides.

ponderous (pŏn´dər-əs) *adj.* very heavy

150 pulled in upon his chest his beautiful shield—
his helmet with four burnished metal ridges
nodding above it, and the golden crest
Hephaestus locked there tossing in the wind.
Conspicuous as the evening star that comes,
155 amid the first in heaven, at fall of night,
and stands most lovely in the west, so shone
in sunlight the fine-pointed spear
Achilles poised in his right hand, with deadly
aim at Hector, at the skin where most
160 it lay exposed. But nearly all was covered **D**
by the bronze gear he took from slain Patroclus,
showing only, where his collarbones
divided neck and shoulders, the bare throat
where the destruction of a life is quickest.
165 Here, then, as the Trojan charged, Achilles
drove his point straight through the tender neck,
but did not cut the windpipe, leaving Hector
able to speak and to respond. He fell
aside into the dust. And Prince Achilles
170 now exulted:

                    "Hector, had you thought
that you could kill Patroclus and be safe?
Nothing to dread from me; I was not there.
All childishness. Though distant then, Patroclus'
comrade in arms was greater far than he—
175 and it is I who had been left behind
that day beside the deepsea ships who now
have made your knees give way. The dogs and kites
will rip your body. His will lie in honor
when the Achaeans give him funeral."

180 Hector, barely whispering, replied:

"I beg you by your soul and by your parents,
do not let the dogs feed on me
in your encampment by the ships. Accept
the bronze and gold my father will provide
185 as gifts, my father and her ladyship
my mother. Let them have my body back,
so that our men and women may accord me
decency of fire when I am dead."

153 Hephaestus (hĭ-fĕs′təs): the god of fire and blacksmith of the gods, who made Achilles' new armor.

D EPIC SIMILE
Note the epic simile in lines 154–160. What two things are being compared? What does the comparison suggest about the power of Achilles' spear?

177 kites: hawklike birds of prey.
178 "His [body]" refers to that of Patroclus.

185–186 Hector's father is Priam, and his mother is Hecuba (hĕk′yə-bə).
188 Burning the bodies of the dead was customary. Truces were often arranged for this purpose.

Achilles the great runner scowled and said:

190 "Beg me no beggary by soul or parents,
whining dog! Would god my passion drove me
to slaughter you and eat you raw, you've caused
such agony to me! No man exists
who could defend you from the carrion pack—
195 not if they spread for me ten times your ransom,
twenty times, and promise more as well;
aye, not if Priam, son of Dardanus,
tells them to buy you for your weight in gold!
You'll have no bed of death, nor will you be
200 laid out and mourned by her who gave you birth.
Dogs and birds will have you, every scrap."

Then at the point of death Lord Hector said:

"I see you now for what you are. No chance
to win you over. Iron in your breast
205 your heart is. Think a bit, though: this may be
a thing the gods in anger hold against you
on that day when Paris and Apollo
destroy you at the Gates, great as you are."

Even as he spoke, the end came, and death hid him;
210 spirit from body fluttered to undergloom,
bewailing fate that made him leave his youth
and manhood in the world. And as he died
Achilles spoke again. He said:

"Die, make an end. I shall accept my own
215 whenever Zeus and the other gods desire."

At this he pulled his spearhead from the body,
laying it aside, and stripped
the bloodstained shield and cuirass from his shoulders.
Other Achaeans hastened round to see
220 Hector's fine body and his comely face,
and no one came who did not stab the body.
Glancing at one another they would say:

"Now Hector has turned **vulnerable,** softer
than when he put the torches to the ships!"

---

194 carrion (kăr′ē-ən) **pack:** the wild animals that feed on dead flesh.

197 Dardanus (där′dn-əs): the founder of the line of Trojan kings. Here *son* means "descendant."

205–208 Although Achilles is still alive as the *Iliad* ends, other tales of the Trojan War tell how he is eventually killed by Hector's brother Paris, with the aid of Apollo.

218 cuirass (kwĭ-răs′): an armored breastplate. Hector is wearing the armor of Achilles that he took from Patroclus' body.

vulnerable (vŭl′nər-ə-bəl) *adj.* open to attack; easily hurt

224 Hector's torching of the ships occurred when the Trojans forced the Greeks (fighting without Achilles) back to the sea.

225 And he who said this would inflict a wound.
When the great master of pursuit, Achilles,
had the body stripped, he stood among them,
saying swiftly:

          "Friends, my lords and captains

228–229 captains of Argives (är′jīvz′): Greek officers.

of Argives, now that the gods at last have let me
230 bring to earth this man who wrought
havoc among us—more than all the rest—
come, we'll offer battle around the city,
to learn the intentions of the Trojans now.
Will they give up their strongpoint at this loss?
235 Can they fight on, though Hector's dead?

havoc (hăv′ək) *n.* widespread destruction

                     But wait:

why do I ponder, why take up these questions?
Down by the ships Patroclus' body lies
unwept, unburied. I shall not forget him
while I can keep my feet among the living.
240 If in the dead world they forget the dead,
I say there, too, I shall remember him,
my friend. Men of Achaea, lift a song!
Down to the ships we go, and take this body,
our glory. We have beaten Hector down,
245 to whom as to a god the Trojans prayed."

240 The "dead world" is the house of Hades, or the underworld, where the Greeks believed the shades of the dead to reside.

Indeed, he had in mind for Hector's body
outrage and shame. Behind both feet he pierced
the tendons, heel to ankle. Rawhide cords
he drew through both and lashed them to his chariot,
250 letting the man's head trail. Stepping aboard,
bearing the great trophy of the arms,
he shook the reins, and whipped the team ahead
into a willing run. A dustcloud rose
above the furrowing body; the dark tresses
255 flowed behind, and the head so princely once
lay back in dust. Zeus gave him to his enemies **E**
to be **defiled** in his own fatherland.
So his whole head was blackened. Looking down,
his mother tore her braids, threw off her veil,
260 and wailed, heartbroken to behold her son.
Piteously his father groaned, and round him
lamentation spread throughout the town,
most like the clamor to be heard if Ilion's

E **CLASSIFY CHARACTERS**
Reread lines 246–256. Why do you think Achilles mistreats Hector's body in this manner?

defile (dĭ-fīl′) *v.* to make filthy or impure; to violate the honor of

263 **Ilion's** (ĭl′ē-ənz): Troy's.

towers, top to bottom, seethed in flames.
265 They barely stayed the old man, mad with grief,
from passing through the gates. Then in the mire
he rolled, and begged them all, each man by name:

"Relent, friends. It is hard; but let me go
out of the city to the Achaean ships.
270 I'll make my plea to that demonic heart.
He may feel shame before his peers, or pity
my old age. His father, too, is old.
Peleus, who brought him up to be a **scourge**
to Trojans, cruel to all, but most to me,
275 so many of my sons in flower of youth
he cut away. And, though I grieve, I cannot
mourn them all as much as I do one,
for whom my grief will take me to the grave—
and that is Hector. Why could he not have died
280 where I might hold him? In our weeping, then,
his mother, now so destitute, and I
might have had surfeit and relief of tears."

scourge (skûrj) *n.* a source of great suffering or destruction

282 **surfeit** (sûr'fĭt): more than enough for satisfaction.

Achilles and his warriors return to their camp and carry out the burial rites for Patroclus. Three times, Achilles drags Hector's body behind his chariot around Patroclus' grave. Afterwards, the gods cleanse and restore the body, and Zeus asks Thetis to tell Achilles to return the body to the Trojans. Priam sets out for the Greek camp to ask Achilles to return the body. He is not aware that the god Hermes (hûr'mēz) helps him by putting the sentries to sleep and opening the gates. Hermes leads Priam to Achilles' tent and then vanishes.

from Book 24 A GRACE GIVEN IN SORROW

Priam,
the great king of Troy, passed by the others,
285 knelt down, took in his arms Achilles' knees,
and kissed the hands of wrath that killed his sons.

When, taken with mad Folly in his own land,
a man does murder and in exile finds
refuge in some rich house, then all who see him
290 stand in awe.
So these men stood. **F**

Achilles
gazed in wonder at the splendid king,

F **EPIC SIMILE**
Note the epic simile in lines 287–291. What does the simile emphasize about Priam's action?

and his companions marveled too, all silent,
with glances to and fro. Now Priam prayed
295 to the man before him:

                          "Remember your own father,
Achilles, in your godlike youth: his years
like mine are many, and he stands upon
the fearful doorstep of old age. He, too,
is hard pressed, it may be, by those around him,
300 there being no one able to defend him
from bane of war and ruin. Ah, but he
may nonetheless hear news of you alive,
and so with glad heart hope through all his days
for sight of his dear son, come back from Troy,
305 while I have deathly fortune. **G**

                                   Noble sons
I fathered here, but scarce one man is left me.
Fifty I had when the Achaeans came,
nineteen out of a single belly, others
born of attendant women. Most are gone.
310 Raging Ares cut their knees from under them.
And he who stood alone among them all,
their champion, and Troy's, ten days ago

Achilles Besought by Priam for the Body of his Son Hector (1776), Giovanni Battista
Cipriani. Oil on canvas, 42¹/₁₆″ × 41³/₄″. The Philadelphia Museum of Art.

G CLASSIFY CHARACTERS
Reread Priam's speech in lines
295–305. What tactic is Priam
using to persuade Achilles to
return Hector's body?

◄ **Analyze Visuals**
How do the gestures and facial
expressions in this painting
convey what happens in the
scene between Priam and
Achilles? Explain.

you killed him, fighting for his land, my prince,
Hector.

315   It is for him that I have come
among these ships, to beg him back from you,
and I bring ransom without stint.

316 stint: limitation.

                             Achilles,
be reverent toward the great gods! And take
pity on me, remember your own father.
Think me more pitiful by far, since I
320 have brought myself to do what no man else
has done before—to lift to my lips the hand
of one who killed my son."

                       Now in Achilles
the evocation of his father stirred
new longing, and an ache of grief. He lifted
325 the old man's hand and gently put him by.
Then both were overborne as they remembered:
the old king huddled at Achilles' feet
wept, and wept for Hector, killer of men,
while great Achilles wept for his own father
330 as for Patroclus once again; and sobbing
filled the room. **H**

326 overborne: overcome;
overwhelmed.

H **CLASSIFY CHARACTERS**
Notice the change in Achilles'
attitude in lines 322–331. What
qualities of Achilles do these
lines reveal?

                    But when Achilles' heart
had known the luxury of tears, and pain
within his breast and bones had passed away,
he stood then, raised the old king up, in pity
335 for his grey head and greybeard cheek, and spoke
in a warm rush of words:

                    "Ah, sad and old!
Trouble and pain you've borne, and bear, aplenty.
Only a great will could have brought you here
among the Achaean ships, and here alone
340 before the eyes of one who stripped your sons,
your many sons, in battle. Iron must be
the heart within you. Come, then, and sit down.
We'll probe our wounds no more but let them rest,
though grief lies heavy on us. Tears heal nothing,
345 drying so stiff and cold. This is the way
the gods ordained the destiny of men,

COMMON CORE L 4

Language Coach

Word Definitions You often
have to consider several
definitions to find the one
that fits. The word *ordained*
can mean 1) made a priest, 2)
designed, or 3) destined. Which
meaning fits the use of the word
in line 346? How can you tell?

to bear such burdens in our lives, while they
feel no affliction. At the door of Zeus **①**
are those two urns of good and evil gifts
350 that he may choose for us; and one for whom
the lightning's joyous king dips in both urns
will have by turns bad luck and good. But one
to whom he sends all evil—that man goes
contemptible by the will of Zeus; ravenous
355 hunger drives him over the wondrous earth,
unresting, without honor from gods or men.
Mixed fortune came to Peleus. Shining gifts
at the gods' hands he had from birth: **felicity,**
wealth overflowing, rule of the Myrmidons,
360 a bride immortal at his mortal side.
But then Zeus gave afflictions too—no family
of powerful sons grew up for him at home,
but one child, of all seasons and of none.
Can I stand by him in his age? Far from my country
365 I sit at Troy to grieve you and your children.
You, too, sir, in time past were fortunate,
we hear men say. From Macar's isle of Lesbos
northward, and south of Phrygia and the Straits,
no one had wealth like yours, or sons like yours.
370 Then gods out of the sky sent you this bitterness:
the years of siege, the battles and the losses.
Endure it, then. And do not mourn forever
for your dead son. There is no remedy.
You will not make him stand again. Rather
375 await some new misfortune to be suffered."

The old king in his majesty replied:

"Never give me a chair, my lord, while Hector
lies in your camp uncared for. Yield him to me
now. Allow me sight of him. Accept
380 the many gifts I bring. May they reward you,
and may you see your home again.
You spared my life at once and let me live."

Achilles, the great runner, frowned and eyed him **①**
under his brows:

　　　　　　　"Do not vex me, sir," he said.
385 "I have intended, in my own good time,

① CLASSIFY CHARACTERS
Reread lines 345–348. What is
Achilles' attitude toward fate?

felicity (fĭ-lĭs′ĭ-tē) *n.* happiness;
good fortune

359 Myrmidons (mûr′mə-dŏnz′):
a people of Thessaly in Greece,
subjects of Achilles' father, Peleus.

363 "Of all seasons and of none"
suggests that Achilles expects an
early death for himself.

367–368 Lesbos (lĕz′bŏs) ... **Phrygia**
(frĭj′ē-ə) ... **the Straits:** Lesbos is
an island off the western coast of
Asia Minor; Phrygia was an ancient
kingdom in western Asia Minor; the
Straits are the Dardanelles.

① EPIC
Note the use in line 383 of a
stock epithet, a brief phrase
(similar to a kenning) that points
out traits associated with a
character. What epithet is used
to describe Achilles in this line?
What traits does it underscore?

to yield up Hector to you. She who bore me,
the daughter of the Ancient of the sea,
has come with word to me from Zeus. I know
in your case, too—though you say nothing, Priam—

387 "The Ancient of the sea" is the sea god Nereus (nîr´ē-əs), father of Thetis.

390 that some god guided you to the shipways here.
No strong man in his best days could make entry
into this camp. How could he pass the guard,
or force our gateway?
                              Therefore, *let me be.*
Sting my sore heart again, and even here,

395 under my own roof, suppliant though you are,
I may not spare you, sir, but trample on
the express command of Zeus!"

395 suppliant (sŭp´lē-ənt): one who begs or pleads earnestly.

                              When he heard this,
the old man feared him and obeyed with silence.
Now like a lion at one bound Achilles

400 left the room. Close at his back the officers
Automedon and Alcimus went out—
comrades in arms whom he esteemed the most
after the dead Patroclus. They unharnessed
mules and horses, led the old king's crier

401 Automedon (ô-tŏm´ə-dn) ... **Alcimus** (ăl´sə-məs).

405 to a low bench and sat him down.
Then from the polished wagon
they took the piled-up price of Hector's body.
One chiton and two capes they left aside
as dress and shrouding for the homeward journey.

408 chiton (kī´t'n): a shirtlike garment; tunic.

410 Then, calling to the women slaves, Achilles
ordered the body bathed and rubbed with oil—
but lifted, too, and placed apart, where Priam
could not see his son—for seeing Hector
he might in his great pain give way to rage,

415 and fury then might rise up in Achilles
to slay the old king, flouting Zeus's word. **K**
So after bathing and anointing Hector
they drew the shirt and beautiful shrouding over him.
Then with his own hands lifting him, Achilles

K CLASSIFY CHARACTERS
Reread lines 410–416, which reveal Achilles' thoughts. What do the lines suggest about Achilles' temperament?

420 laid him upon a couch, and with his two
companions aiding, placed him in the wagon.
Now a bitter groan burst from Achilles,
who stood and prayed to his own dead friend:

                              "Patroclus,
do not be angry with me, if somehow

425 even in the world of Death you learn of this—
that I released Prince Hector to his father.
The gifts he gave were not unworthy. Aye,
and you shall have your share, this time as well."
The Prince Achilles turned back to his quarters.
430 He took again the splendid chair that stood
against the farther wall, then looked at Priam
and made his declaration:

                              "As you wished, sir,
the body of your son is now set free.
He lies in state. At the first sight of Dawn
435 you shall take charge of him yourself and see him.
Now let us think of supper. We are told
that even Niobe in her extremity
took thought for bread—though all her brood had
     perished,
her six young girls and six tall sons. Apollo,
440 making his silver longbow whip and sing,
shot the lads down, and Artemis with raining
arrows killed the daughters—all this after
Niobe had compared herself with Leto,
the smooth-cheeked goddess.
                              She has borne two children,
445 Niobe said, How many have I borne!
But soon those two destroyed the twelve.
                                        Besides,
nine days the dead lay stark, no one could bury them,
for Zeus had turned all folk of theirs to stone.
The gods made graves for them on the tenth day,
450 and then at last, being weak and spent with weeping,
Niobe thought of food. Among the rocks
of Sipylus' lonely mountainside, where nymphs
who race Achelous river go to rest,
she, too, long turned to stone, somewhere broods on
455 the gall immortal gods gave her to drink.

Like her we'll think of supper, noble sir.
Weep for your son again when you have borne him
back to Troy; there he'll be mourned indeed."

*Priam and Achilles agree to an 11-day truce. During that
time, the Trojans will mourn Hector's body before its burial.*

436–455 The mortal woman Niobe
(nī′ə-bē) claimed that having so
many children made her superior
to the goddess Leto (lē′tō), who had
only two. Leto's son and daughter,
Apollo and Artemis (är′tə-mĭs),
punished Niobe by killing all her
children. After many days of
grieving, Niobe asked the gods to
relieve her by turning her to stone.

452 Sipylus (sĭp′ə-ləs): a mountain
in west-central Asia Minor.

453 Achelous (ăk′ə-lō′əs): a river
near Mount Sipylus.

455 gall: bitterness; bile.

After Reading

Comprehension

1. **Recall** Why does Achilles vow to kill Hector?

2. **Recall** What does Achilles do with Hector after he kills him?

3. **Summarize** What happens when Priam confronts Achilles?

Text Analysis

● 4. **Analyze Epic Similes** Reread the following passages, which contain epic similes. Explain what is being compared in each simile, and identify the quality or qualities emphasized in the comparison.

   • "As between men . . . Ares." (lines 89–94)
   • "With this he . . . whetted blade." (lines 143–148)
   • "Conspicuous as . . . exposed." (lines 154–160)

● 5. **Classify Characters** Review the chart in which you classified the characters from the *Iliad*. Are the gods responsible for what happens to the mortals in the epic? Support your answer with specific details from the *Iliad*.

6. **Interpret Characters' Actions** Characters in the *Iliad* show courage in different ways. What courageous actions do Achilles, Hector, and Priam perform?

7. **Draw Conclusions** Reread lines 31–33. In these lines and in others, it is apparent that Achilles and other characters in the epic know that he is fated to die soon. What do you think prevents Achilles from attempting to change his fate?

8. **Make Judgments** In your opinion, do Achilles' feelings about his friend Patroclus justify the way he treats Hector? Cite evidence from the epic to explain your answer.

9. **Compare Epic Heroes** Compare and contrast Achilles and Beowulf as epic heroes. Use a diagram like the one shown to list and compare their traits and their actions. Which character do you think is more heroic?

Achilles   *Both*   *Beowulf*

Text Criticism

10. **Critical Interpretations** Critic John Scott has said that although the *Iliad* is set during wartime, "the real greatness of that poem is in the portrayal of powerful human emotions rather than in military exploits." Do you agree or disagree? Cite evidence to support your response.

What inspires COURAGE?

Which character in the *Iliad* would you define as most courageous? Which do you consider the least courageous? Why?

COMMON CORE

RL 1 Cite strong and thorough textual evidence to support analysis of what the text says explicitly as well as inferences drawn from the text. **RL 3** Analyze the impact of the author's choices regarding how to develop and relate elements of a story. **RL 4** Determine the meaning of words and phrases as they are used in the text, including figurative meanings. **RL 10** Read and comprehend literature.

Vocabulary in Context

▲ **VOCABULARY PRACTICE**

Identify the word that is not related in meaning to the other words in each numbered set.

1. (a) ponderous, (b) swift, (c) weighty

2. (a) cleanse, (b) defile, (c) corrupt

3. (a) strong, (b) vulnerable, (c) defenseless

4. (a) destruction, (b) havoc, (c) protection

5. (a) guardian, (b) protector, (c) scourge

6. (a) abstain, (b) proceed, (c) perform

7. (a) bitterness, (b) rancor, (c) felicity

WORD LIST
abstain
defile
felicity
havoc
ponderous
rancor
scourge
vulnerable

ACADEMIC VOCABULARY IN SPEAKING

- concept   - culture   - parallel   - section   - structure

Discuss the **concept** of revenge as it applies to this **section** of the *Iliad*. How does revenge act as a **parallel** motivation for Hector and Achilles? Use at least one additional Academic Vocabulary word in your discussion.

VOCABULARY STRATEGY: DICTIONARY ETYMOLOGIES

Learning to decode a word's **etymology,** or history, deepens your understanding of its connotations and derivations. Here is a typical dictionary's etymology:

scourge (skûrj) *n.* [ME < OFr *escorgie* < L *ex,* off, from + *corrigia,* a strap, whip]

The etymology is usually in brackets after the pronunciation and part of speech. The < symbol means "derived from." The etymology for *scourge* reads, "a Middle English (ME) word, from the Old French (OFr) *escorgie,* which comes from the Latin (L) prefix *ex-* ('off' or 'from') and *corrigia,* ('a strap' or 'whip')."

PRACTICE Consult a dictionary to answer the following questions about these vocabulary words. (Your dictionary's introduction will likely have information about the abbreviations and symbols used in its etymologies.)

1. What Middle English word does *havoc* come from?

2. Which word above comes from an Old French word meaning "to trample"?

3. Look up *excoriate.* Which word above is related to *excoriate?*

4. Which word above derives from the Latin word *tenere,* to hold back?

5. What Latin word or words are *vulnerable* and *revulsion* both related to?

> **COMMON CORE**
>
> **L 4c** Consult general and specialized reference materials to determine or clarify a word's etymology. **L 6** Acquire and use accurately general academic and domain-specific words and phrases.

The Epic in Translation

The following versions of *Beowulf* prove the power of the translator. Although both describe the same passage (Grendel's murderous raid on Herot), they are stunningly dissimilar.

> *"Then, when darkness had dropped, Grendel*
> *Went up to Herot, wondering what the warriors*
> *Would do in that hall when their drinking was done.*
> *He found them sprawled in sleep, suspecting*
> *Nothing, their dreams undisturbed.*
>
> **—Translated by Burton Raffel**

> *"So, after nightfall, Grendel set out*
> *for the lofty house, to see how the Ring-Danes*
> *were settling into it after their drink,*
> *and there he came upon them, a company of the best*
> *asleep from their feasting, insensible to pain*
> *and human sorrow.*
>
> **—Translated by Seamus Heaney**

Writing to Compare and Contrast

Write a short essay comparing and contrasting Raffel's and Heaney's translations. Which do you prefer? Why? Examine each translator's word choice, style, and the rhetorical devices they use. How does each translator portray the qualities of an epic?

Since you are writing a comparison-contrast essay, apply the Point-by-Point method. Use at least one body paragraph to show how the translations are similar. Then continue with additional similarities or move to differences between the two passages.

Point-by-Point Method

  Topic Sentence/Paragraph
- Translation 1
- Translation 2
  Topic Sentence/Paragraph
- Translation 1
- Translation 2

Extension Online

INQUIRY & RESEARCH With a partner, use the Internet to compile a list of literary and cinematic epics. Starting with a primary search engine, you may also want to integrate information from online movie databases and literary reference sites. Consider using advanced search terms such as *"epic hero"* (enclosed in quotation marks) to narrow your results. Of the works you find, which feature heroes closest in spirit and deeds to Beowulf?

The character Aragorn, a hero from the modern-day epic *The Lord of the Rings*

COMMON CORE

W 2a–b Organize complex ideas; develop the topic by selecting details, quotations, or other information. **W 7** Conduct short research projects; narrow the inquiry; synthesize multiple sources. **W 8** Gather relevant information from multiple sources, using advanced searches effectively.

from A History of the English Church and People

Historical Writing by the Venerable Bede

DID YOU KNOW?

The Venerable Bede . . .

- invented the footnote.
- popularized the dating of events from the birth of Christ—the B.C./A.D. system.

Meet the Author

The Venerable Bede c. 673–735

The Venerable Bede (bēd), regarded as the father of English history, lived and worked in a monastery in northern Britain during the late seventh and early eighth centuries. His most famous work, *A History of the English Church and People,* is a major source of information about life in Britain from the first successful Roman invasion (about A.D. 46) to A.D. 731. The book contains many stories about the spread of Christianity among the English.

Raised By Monks At the age of seven, Bede was taken by his parents to a monastery at Wearmouth, on the northeast coast of Britain, where he was left in the care of the abbot, Benedict Biscop. It is not known why the boy's parents left him or whether he ever saw them again. When he was nine, Bede moved a short distance to a new monastery at Jarrow, where he spent the rest of his life.

A Bookish Boy Bede seems to have been a naturally devout and studious child. He read widely in the monastery libraries and participated fully in the religious life of the monastery. He was exposed to the art and learning of Europe through the paintings, books, and religious objects brought from Rome by Abbot Biscop. Bede became a deacon of the church at the age of 19—six years earlier than was usual—and was ordained to the priesthood when he was 30.

Multitalented Scholar Bede was a brilliant scholar and a gifted writer and teacher. He was also a careful and thorough historian. He sought out original documents and reliable eyewitness accounts on which to base his writing. Working in a chilly, damp, poorly lit cell in the monastery, Bede managed to write about 40 books, including works on spelling, grammar, science, history, and religion.

Still Venerable Today Bede's reputation as a scholar and a devout monk spread throughout Europe during his lifetime and in the centuries following. (The honorific title "Venerable" was probably first applied to him during the century after his death, as an acknowledgment of his achievements.) Although Bede was influenced by the outlook of his time—as is evident in the miracle stories he included in his *History*—his carefulness and integrity are still respected and valued by scholars today, almost 1,300 years later.

Author Online

Go to **thinkcentral.com**. KEYWORD: HML12-96

THINK central

● TEXT ANALYSIS: HISTORICAL WRITING

Bede was one of the first to write about English history. **Historical writing** is a systematic account, often in narrative form, of the past of a nation or a group of people. Historical writing generally has the following characteristics:

- It is concerned with real events in the relatively distant past.
- The events are treated in chronological order.
- It is usually an objective retelling of facts rather than a personal interpretation. However, the author may have a specific purpose in mind, such as teaching a moral lesson.
- The author may incorporate literary devices, such as **anecdotes**, or brief stories that focus on an episode or event in a person's life to illustrate a point.

As you read the selection about the poet Caedmon (kăd′mən), consider Bede's use of narrative to tell Caedmon's story and what it tells you about life in Caedmon's time.

● READING SKILL: ANALYZE AUTHOR'S PURPOSE

The excerpt that you will read is an early **biography;** one of Bede's purposes is to inform readers about Caedmon's life. But there is a second purpose. In the Preface to Bede's *History,* he explains to King Ceolwulf (chāl′wŏŏlf′) his reason for writing about important Englishmen of the past. He believes that they serve as good role models to imitate or examples of bad behavior to avoid. As you read, take notes about Caedmon on a web diagram. Determine which details of Caedmon's life Bede emphasizes to present him as a positive role model.

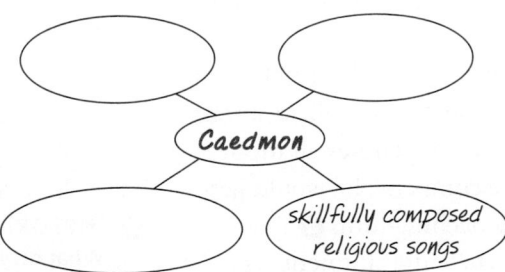

Caedmon

skillfully composed religious songs

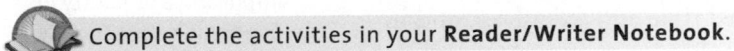

Complete the activities in your **Reader/Writer Notebook.**

How do dreams INSPIRE *you?*

History is full of stories of people who received a flash of inspiration during a dream. For example, the 19th-century German chemist Friedrich August Kekulé (kā′kōō-lā) said that the ringlike structure of the molecule benzene presented itself to him when he dozed off and dreamed of a snake holding its tail in its mouth. In the following selection, the Venerable Bede recounts a tale of a humble man who fell asleep one night and woke up the next morning an accomplished poet.

QUICKWRITE Write a description of a memorable dream that helped you discover something about yourself, solve a problem, or unlock a hidden talent. If no dream has ever inspired you in this way, describe something else that has, such as a conversation or a daydream.

A HISTORY OF THE ENGLISH CHURCH AND PEOPLE

The Venerable Bede

BACKGROUND Caedmon is the earliest English poet known to us by name, and Bede's *History* is the only source of information about him. According to Bede, Caedmon composed many poems written in English, his native tongue. However, only his first poem, a hymn to God the Creator, has survived. Caedmon lived at Whitby Abbey, a religious community on the coast of England. It was founded in 657 by St. Hilda, who in Caedmon's day was still the abbess in charge.

In this monastery of Whitby there lived a brother[1] whom God's grace made remarkable. So skillful was he in composing religious and devotional songs, that he could quickly turn whatever passages of Scripture were explained to him into delightful and moving poetry in his own English tongue. These verses of his stirred the hearts of many folk to despise the world and aspire to heavenly things. Others after him tried to compose religious poems in English, but none could compare with him, for he received this gift of poetry as a gift from God and did not acquire it through any human teacher. For this reason he could never compose any frivolous or profane verses, but only such as had a religious theme fell fittingly from
10 his devout lips. And although he followed a secular occupation until well advanced in years, he had never learned anything about poetry: indeed, whenever all those present at a feast took it in turns to sing and entertain the company, he would get up from table and go home directly he saw the harp[2] approaching him. **A**

On one such occasion he had left the house in which the entertainment was being held and went out to the stable, where it was his duty to look after the beasts that night. He lay down there at the appointed time and fell asleep, and in a dream he saw a man standing beside him who called him by name. "Caedmon,"

Analyze Visuals ▶
What ideas about Caedmon are conveyed through this image?

A HISTORICAL WRITING
What do you learn from this paragraph about the importance of poetry in Caedmon's time?

---

1. **brother:** a man who lives in or works for a religious community but is not a priest or monk.

2. **directly he saw the harp:** as soon as he saw the harp. In Anglo-Saxon times, poetry was often recited to the accompaniment of a small harp.

St. Caedmon. Detail of stained glass in Kirkby Malham Church. Yorkshire.
© Charles Walker/Topfoto/The Image Works, Inc.

he said, "sing me a song." "I don't know how to sing," he replied. "It is because I
cannot sing that I left the feast and came here." The man who addressed him then
20 said: "But you shall sing to me." "What should I sing about?" he replied. "Sing
about the Creation of all things," the other answered. And Caedmon immediately
began to sing verses in praise of God the Creator that he had never heard before,
and their theme ran thus: "Let us praise the Maker of the kingdom of heaven,
the power and purpose of our Creator, and the acts of the Father of glory. Let
us sing how the eternal God, the Author of all marvels, first created the heavens
for the sons of men as a roof to cover them, and how their almighty Protector
gave them the earth for their dwelling place." This is the general sense, but not
the actual words that Caedmon sang in his dream; for however excellent the
verses, it is impossible to translate them from one language into another[3] without
30 losing much of their beauty and dignity. When Caedmon awoke, he remembered
everything that he had sung in his dream, and soon added more verses in the same
style to the glory of God. **B**

Early in the morning he went to his superior the reeve,[4] and told him about
this gift that he had received. The reeve took him before the abbess, who ordered
him to give an account of his dream and repeat the verses in the presence of many
learned men, so that they might decide their quality and origin. All of them agreed
that Caedmon's gift had been given him by our Lord, and when they had explained
to him a passage of scriptural history or doctrine, they asked him to render it into
verse if he could. He promised to do this, and returned next morning with excellent
40 verses as they had ordered him. The abbess was delighted that God had given such
grace to the man, and advised him to abandon secular life and adopt the monastic
state. And when she had admitted him into the Community as a brother, she
ordered him to be instructed in the events of sacred history.[5] So Caedmon stored
up in his memory all that he learned, and like an animal chewing the cud, turned it
into such melodious verse that his delightful renderings turned his instructors into
his audience. He sang of the creation of the world, the origin of the human **C**
race, and the whole story of Genesis.[6] He sang of Israel's departure from Egypt,
their entry into the land of promise, and many other events of scriptural history. He
sang of the Lord's Incarnation, Passion, Resurrection, and Ascension into heaven,
50 the coming of the Holy Spirit, and the teaching of the Apostles. He also made
many poems on the terrors of the Last Judgment, the horrible pains of Hell, and the
joys of the kingdom of heaven. In addition to these, he composed several others on
the blessings and judgments of God, by which he sought to turn his hearers from
delight in wickedness, and to inspire them to love and do good. For Caedmon was
a deeply religious man, who humbly submitted to regular discipline,[7] and firmly
resisted all who tried to do evil, thus winning a happy death. **D**

---

3. **impossible ... another:** Caedmon's verses were composed in Old English, but Bede wrote his history in Latin.

4. **reeve:** the officer who oversaw the monastery's farms.

5. **sacred history:** the narratives of the Christian Bible.

6. **Genesis** (jĕn'ĭ-sĭs): the opening book of the Bible, which tells of God's creation of the universe and the first human beings.

7. **regular discipline:** the rules of monastic life.

COMMON CORE L 5b

Language Coach

Synonyms Identify the five words Caedmon uses to name God in his song (lines 23–27). Why does he use so many? Starting with *Creator*, rank the words on a numbered scale showing how closely related they are as synonyms (words with the same meaning).

B **HISTORICAL WRITING**
Reread lines 14–32. In this **anecdote**, to what does Bede attribute Caedmon's ability to compose poetry?

C **HISTORICAL WRITING**
Reread lines 33–46. According to this passage, what role did dreams play in real life during Caedmon's time?

D **AUTHOR'S PURPOSE**
What does Bede want readers to learn in lines 52–56 about how Caedmon's life changed?

Comprehension

1. **Recall** What was Caedmon's gift?

2. **Recall** How did Caedmon receive his gift?

3. **Clarify** How did Caedmon's life change because of his gift?

Text Analysis

4. **Draw Conclusions** What would be the reason for including Caedmon's story in a history of the English church?

● 5. **Analyze Author's Purpose** Review the notes you took about Caedmon as you read. What is the moral message that can be taken from his story? Does presenting Caedmon's story as a narrative of personal transformation help or hinder Bede's purpose?

● 6. **Analyze Historical Writing** What do you learn from Bede about life in seventh-century England? Discuss facts about each of the following:

   • religious life
   • language and literacy

7. **Apply Themes** What does Caedmon's story suggest about how creativity was viewed during his time?

Text Criticism

8. **Historical Context** Discuss ways in which Bede's purpose and worldview shape the way he presents information. How might a modern historian present information differently?

> *How do dreams* **INSPIRE** *you?*
>
> A dream inspires Caedmon to change the way he lives. What other factors might inspire a dramatic shift in the way someone lives?

COMMON CORE

RI 2 Determine two or more central ideas of a text and analyze their development over the course of the text. **RI 6** Determine an author's point of view or purpose in a text, analyzing how style and content contribute to the power, persuasiveness, or beauty of the text. **RI 9** Analyze documents of historical and literary significance for their themes, purposes, and rhetorical features.

The Seafarer
The Wanderer
The Wife's Lament

Poetry from the *Exeter Book*

COMMON CORE

RL 4 Analyze the impact of specific word choices on meaning and tone, including words with multiple meanings or language that is fresh, engaging, or beautiful. **RL 10** Read and comprehend literature, including poems. **L 4** Determine or clarify the meaning of unknown and multiple-meaning words and phrases. **L 4b** Identify and correctly use patterns of word changes that indicate different meanings or parts of speech. **L 5b** Analyze nuances in the meaning of words with similar denotations.

DID YOU KNOW?

The *Exeter Book* . . .

- consists of 131 leaves of parchment, each slightly bigger than a standard sheet of paper.

- has knife cuts on some of its pages, which suggests that at one point it was used as a cutting board.

- inspired the building of a 19-foot-high stainless-steel statue imprinted with riddles in the city of Exeter.

Meet the Author

The Exeter Book   c. 950

Nothing is known about the authors of "The Seafarer," "The Wanderer," and "The Wife's Lament." All three poems survive in the *Exeter Book,* a manuscript of Anglo-Saxon poems produced by a single scribe around A.D. 950. In addition to these and other secular poems, the *Exeter Book* contains religious verse, nearly 100 riddles, and a heroic narrative. It is the largest collection of Old English poetry in existence.

Neglected Treasure Originally, the *Exeter Book* belonged to Leofric (lā′ə-frĭk), the first bishop of Exeter. He donated it to the Exeter Cathedral library sometime between 1050 and 1072. For several centuries the book was neglected and abused; few people were able to read the Old English language in which it was written and thus had little use for it. Some pages are badly stained or scorched. The original binding and an unknown number of pages are lost.

Rediscovery With the rise of Anglo-Saxon studies in the 19th century, scholars began to take an interest in the *Exeter Book.* Benjamin Thorpe published the first complete translation in 1842. He assigned titles to "The Seafarer" and "The Wanderer," as none of the poems in the manuscript had titles. A photographic facsimile was published in 1933; it became the basis for later scholarly editions. A CD version, with facsimile pages and audio readings, was released in 2006.

The original manuscript still resides at the library at Exeter Cathedral, where it is cherished as one of the few surviving collections of Anglo-Saxon poetry.

TEXT ANALYSIS: IMAGERY

Poets communicate through **imagery,** words and phrases that re-create sensory experiences for the reader by appealing to one or more of the five senses. Notice how the imagery in this passage from "The Seafarer" appeals to the senses of sight, touch, and hearing:

> My feet were cast
> In icy bands, bound with frost,
> With frozen chains, and hardship groaned
> Around my heart.

The images bring to mind coldness and confinement and suggest the speaker's lonely, painful emotional state. As you read the following three poems, pay attention to the imagery, allowing it to evoke ideas and feelings in you.

Review: **Old English Poetry**

READING STRATEGY: MONITOR YOUR UNDERSTANDING

These poems have been translated from Old English into Modern English, but sections of the texts may still be hard to understand. Use the following strategies to understand them:

- **Visualize** the many images layered in the poems.
- **Question** as you read. Ask who the speaker is, for example.
- **Reread** passages that are confusing.
- **Paraphrase** difficult lines, restating them in your own words.
- **Clarify** events. The speakers remember past experiences and reflect on their present experiences. Let indentations and stanza breaks alert you that the speaker is turning to a new thought.

For each poem, create a chart to record what the speaker remembers or ponders in each section of the poem to help clarify events the speaker describes.

"The Seafarer"	
Section	Speaker Remembers or Ponders
Section 1 (lines 1–26)	being cold, hungry, and lonely on the sea
Section 2	

 Complete the activities in your **Reader/Writer Notebook.**

When are people most ALONE?

When people find themselves cut off from contact with others, the sense of isolation can be all consuming. It is not surprising that loneliness is a frequent topic in poetry written during the Anglo-Saxon era—an era during which disease, war, and other perils often wrenched people away from their loved ones. In many Anglo-Saxon poems, images of freezing seas and jagged cliffs mirror this sense of isolation and the challenge of living in a harsh, unpredictable world.

QUICKWRITE Imagine that you are making a five-minute silent film about isolation and loneliness. What would you show onscreen? Where would you set the film? Who would the main character be, and what would he or she be doing? List some visual images that come to mind.

> ### Film Images
>
> - single robed traveler, trudging across the Sahara Desert
>
> - endless sand dunes

The Seafarer

BACKGROUND The poems in the *Exeter Book* reflect the hardship and uncertainty of life in Anglo-Saxon times. Men who made their living on the sea had to leave behind their families and sail long distances in primitive, poorly equipped boats. The women and children left behind endured months and even years without knowing whether their menfolk would return. In addition, frequent outbreaks of disease and war scattered communities and brought untimely death to many people.

This tale is true, and mine. It tells
How the sea took me, swept me back
And forth in sorrow and fear and pain,
Showed me suffering in a hundred ships,
5 In a thousand ports, and in me. It tells
Of smashing surf when I sweated in the cold
Of an anxious watch, perched in the bow
As it dashed under cliffs. My feet were cast
In icy bands, bound with frost,
10 With frozen chains, and hardship groaned
Around my heart. Hunger tore
At my sea-weary soul. No man sheltered
On the quiet fairness of earth can feel
How wretched I was, drifting through winter
15 On an ice-cold sea, whirled in sorrow,
Alone in a world blown clear of love,
Hung with icicles. The hailstorms flew.
The only sound was the roaring sea,
The freezing waves. The song of the swan
20 Might serve for pleasure, the cry of the sea-fowl,
The death-noise of birds instead of laughter,
The mewing of gulls instead of mead.
Storms beat on the rocky cliffs and were echoed

COMMON CORE L 5b

Language Coach

Etymology A word's **etymology,** or origin, can help you understand its **connotations**—the images or feelings connected with a word. *Wretched,* which comes from the Old English *wrecca* ("outcast or exile"), means "miserable." Why is *wretched* a better word than *miserable* in lines 12–17?

22 mead (mēd): an alcoholic beverage drunk at Anglo-Saxon gatherings.

◀ **Analyze Visuals**
Describe the **mood** of this photograph as well as those on pages 109 and 113. What features of each landscape determine its mood?

By icy-feathered terns and the eagle's screams;
25 No kinsman could offer comfort there,
To a soul left drowning in desolation. Ⓐ
    And who could believe, knowing but
The passion of cities, swelled proud with wine
And no taste of misfortune, how often, how wearily,
30 I put myself back on the paths of the sea.
Night would blacken; it would snow from the north;
Frost bound the earth and hail would fall,
The coldest seeds. And how my heart
Would begin to beat, knowing once more
35 The salt waves tossing and the towering sea!
The time for journeys would come and my soul
Called me eagerly out, sent me over
The horizon, seeking foreigners' homes.
    But there isn't a man on earth so proud,
40 So born to greatness, so bold with his youth,
Grown so brave, or so graced by God,
That he feels no fear as the sails unfurl,
Wondering what Fate has willed and will do.
No harps ring in his heart, no rewards,

24 **terns:** sea birds similar to gulls.

Ⓐ **IMAGERY**
In lines 12–26, what senses does the imagery appeal to? Describe the **mood** created by the imagery.

45 No passion for women, no worldly pleasures,
Nothing, only the ocean's heave;
But longing wraps itself around him.
Orchards blossom, the towns bloom,
Fields grow lovely as the world springs fresh,
50 And all these admonish that willing mind
Leaping to journeys, always set
In thoughts traveling on a quickening tide.
So summer's sentinel, the cuckoo, sings
In his murmuring voice, and our hearts mourn
55 As he urges. Who could understand,
In ignorant ease, what we others suffer
As the paths of exile stretch endlessly on? **B**
      And yet my heart wanders away,
My soul roams with the sea, the whales'
60 Home, wandering to the widest corners
Of the world, returning ravenous with desire,
Flying solitary, screaming, exciting me
To the open ocean, breaking oaths
On the curve of a wave.
          Thus the joys of God **C**
65 Are fervent with life, where life itself
Fades quickly into the earth. The wealth
Of the world neither reaches to Heaven nor remains.
No man has ever faced the dawn
Certain which of Fate's three threats
70 Would fall: illness, or age, or an enemy's
Sword, snatching the life from his soul.
The praise the living pour on the dead
Flowers from reputation: plant
An earthly life of profit reaped
75 Even from hatred and rancor, of bravery
Flung in the devil's face, and death
Can only bring you earthly praise
And a song to celebrate a place
With the angels, life eternally blessed
80 In the hosts of Heaven.
          The days are gone
When the kingdoms of earth flourished in glory;
Now there are no rulers, no emperors,
No givers of gold, as once there were,
When wonderful things were worked among them
85 And they lived in lordly magnificence.
Those powers have vanished, those pleasures are dead,
The weakest survives and the world continues,
Kept spinning by toil. All glory is tarnished,

50 admonish (ăd-mŏn′ĭsh): criticize or caution.

53 summer's sentinel (sĕn′tə-nəl), **the cuckoo:** summer's guard or watchman. The cries of cuckoos are common in Europe in summer, but in autumn the birds migrate south.

B IMAGERY
Note how the images in lines 44–57 contrast with the images of the sea. How is the speaker affected by thoughts of life on land?

C MONITOR
Notice the break at line 64. Here the speaker turns to a new idea. How do you interpret the sentence beginning "Thus the joys of God …"?

80 hosts of Heaven: bands of angels.

The world's honor ages and shrinks,
90 Bent like the men who mold it. Their faces
Blanch as time advances, their beards
Wither and they mourn the memory of friends,
The sons of princes, sown in the dust.
The soul stripped of its flesh knows nothing
95 Of sweetness or sour, feels no pain,
Bends neither its hand nor its brain. A brother
Opens his palms and pours down gold
On his kinsman's grave, strewing his coffin
With treasures intended for Heaven, but nothing
100 Golden shakes the wrath of God
For a soul overflowing with sin, and nothing
Hidden on earth rises to Heaven. **D**
  We all fear God. He turns the earth,
He set it swinging firmly in space,
105 Gave life to the world and light to the sky.
Death leaps at the fools who forget their God.
He who lives humbly has angels from Heaven
To carry him courage and strength and belief.
A man must conquer pride, not kill it,
110 Be firm with his fellows, chaste for himself,
Treat all the world as the world deserves,
With love or with hate but never with harm,
Though an enemy seek to scorch him in hell,
Or set the flames of a funeral pyre
115 Under his lord. Fate is stronger
And God mightier than any man's mind.
Our thoughts should turn to where our home is,
Consider the ways of coming there,
Then strive for sure permission for us
120 To rise to that eternal joy,
That life born in the love of God
And the hope of Heaven. Praise the Holy **E**
Grace of Him who honored us,
Eternal, unchanging creator of earth. Amen.

Translated by Burton Raffel

D MONITOR
Visualize the images of the world in lines 80–102. What main idea do they convey?

110 chaste (chāst): pure in thought and deed.

114 funeral pyre (pīr): a bonfire for burning a corpse.

E MONITOR
Paraphrase the advice the speaker gives in lines 117–122. Where is "our home"?

Text Analysis

1. **Paraphrase** What views does the speaker express about earthly life and God in lines 64–124 ?

2. **Compare** How does the last half of the poem (from line 64 on) relate to the first half of the poem?

The Wanderer

This lonely traveler longs for grace,
For the mercy of God; grief hangs on
His heart and follows the frost-cold foam
He cuts in the sea, sailing endlessly,
5 Aimlessly, in exile. Fate has opened
A single port: memory. He sees
His kinsmen slaughtered again, and cries:
    "I've drunk too many lonely dawns,
Grey with mourning. Once there were men
10 To whom my heart could hurry, hot
With open longing. They're long since dead.
My heart has closed on itself, quietly
Learning that silence is noble and sorrow
Nothing that speech can cure. Sadness
15 Has never driven sadness off;
Fate blows hardest on a bleeding heart.
So those who thirst for glory smother
Secret weakness and longing, neither
Weep nor sigh nor listen to the sickness
20 In their souls. So I, lost and homeless,
Forced to flee the darkness that fell
On the earth and my lord. **F**
                              Leaving everything,
Weary with winter I wandered out
On the frozen waves, hoping to find
25 A place, a people, a lord to replace
My lost ones. No one knew me, now,
No one offered comfort, allowed
Me feasting or joy. How cruel a journey
I've traveled, sharing my bread with sorrow
30 Alone, an exile in every land,
Could only be told by telling my footsteps.
For who can hear: "friendless and poor,"
And know what I've known since the long cheerful nights
When, young and yearning, with my lord I yet feasted
35 Most welcome of all. That warmth is dead.
He only knows who needs his lord
As I do, eager for long-missing aid;
He only knows who never sleeps

COMMON CORE L 4b

Language Coach

Roots and Affixes Added to an adjective, the suffix *-ly* forms an adverb (like *endlessly* or *aimlessly*, lines 4–5). Added to a noun, *-ly* means "relating to" and forms an adjective. How is the suffix used in *ghostly* and *worldly* (lines 71–72)?

F MONITOR
What has happened to the speaker, and what is his state of mind?

31 **telling:** counting.

Without the deepest dreams of longing.
40 Sometimes it seems I see my lord,
Kiss and embrace him, bend my hands
And head to his knee, kneeling as though
He still sat enthroned, ruling his thanes.
And I open my eyes, embracing the air,
45 And see the brown sea-billows heave,
See the sea-birds bathe, spreading
Their white-feathered wings, watch the frost
And the hail and the snow. And heavy in heart
I long for my lord, alone and unloved.
50 Sometimes it seems I see my kin
And greet them gladly, give them welcome,
The best of friends. They fade away,
Swimming soundlessly out of sight,
Leaving nothing. **G**

    How loathsome become
55 The frozen waves to a weary heart.
  In this brief world I cannot wonder
That my mind is set on melancholy,
Because I never forget the fate
Of men, robbed of their riches, suddenly
60 Looted by death—the doom of earth,
Sent to us all by every rising
Sun. Wisdom is slow, and comes
But late. He who has it is patient;
He cannot be hasty to hate or speak,
65 He must be bold and yet not blind,
Nor ever too craven, complacent, or covetous,
Nor ready to gloat before he wins glory.
The man's a fool who flings his boasts
Hotly to the heavens, heeding his spleen
70 And not the better boldness of knowledge.
What knowing man knows not the ghostly,
Waste-like end of worldly wealth:
See, already the wreckage is there,
The wind-swept walls stand far and wide,
75 The storm-beaten blocks besmeared with frost,
The mead-halls crumbled, the monarchs thrown down
And stripped of their pleasures. The proudest of warriors
Now lie by the wall: some of them war
Destroyed; some the monstrous sea-bird
80 Bore over the ocean; to some the old wolf
Dealt out death; and for some dejected
Followers fashioned an earth-cave coffin.
Thus the Maker of men lays waste

43 thanes (thānz): followers of a lord.

G IMAGERY
In what way do the images from the speaker's past contrast with the images of the present?

69 spleen: bad temper. The spleen is a body organ that was formerly thought to be the seat of strong emotions.

This earth, crushing our callow mirth.
85 And the work of old giants stands withered and still." **H**

He who these ruins rightly sees,
And deeply considers this dark twisted life,
Who sagely remembers the endless slaughters
Of a bloody past, is bound to proclaim:
90   "Where is the war-steed? Where is the warrior?
       Where is his war-lord?
Where now the feasting-places? Where now the mead-hall
   pleasures?
Alas, bright cup! Alas, brave knight!
Alas, you glorious princes! All gone,
Lost in the night, as you never had lived.
95 And all that survives you a serpentine wall,
Wondrously high, worked in strange ways.
Mighty spears have slain these men,
Greedy weapons have framed their fate.
       These rocky slopes are beaten by storms,
100 This earth pinned down by driving snow,
By the horror of winter, smothering warmth
In the shadows of night. And the north angrily
Hurls its hailstorms at our helpless heads.
Everything earthly is evilly born,
105 Firmly clutched by a fickle Fate.
Fortune vanishes, friendship vanishes,
Man is fleeting, woman is fleeting,
And all this earth rolls into emptiness."

       So says the sage in his heart, sitting alone with His
          thought.
110 It's good to guard your faith, nor let your grief come forth
Until it cannot call for help, nor help but heed
The path you've placed before it. It's good to find your grace
In God, the heavenly rock where rests our every hope. **I**

Translated by Burton Raffel

84 callow (kăl′ō) **mirth:** childish joy.

H IMAGERY
What ideas about earthly life do you
get from the images in lines 74–85?
Note that "work of old giants" refers
to old ruins and burial mounds.

95 serpentine (sûr′pən-tēn′): winding or
twisting, like a snake.

I MONITOR
Reread lines 110–113. Is the wanderer
speaking, or is someone else? What
advice is offered in these lines?

Text Analysis

1. **Compare** How does the wanderer's present life
   compare with his former life?

2. **Summarize** What does a wise man understand,
   according to the wanderer?

The Wife's Lament

I make this song   about me full sadly **J**
my own wayfaring.   I a woman tell
what griefs I had   since I grew up
new or old   never more than now.
5 Ever I know   the dark of my exile.

First my lord went out   away from his people
over the wave-tumult.   I grieved each dawn
wondered where my lord   my first on earth might be.
Then I went forth   a friendless exile
10 to seek service   in my sorrow's need.
My man's kinsmen   began to plot
by darkened thought   to divide us two
so we most widely   in the world's kingdom
lived wretchedly   and I suffered longing.

15 My lord commanded me   to move my dwelling here.
I had few loved ones   in this land
or faithful friends.   For this my heart grieves:
that I should find the man   well matched to me
hard of fortune   mournful of mind
20 hiding his mood   thinking of murder. **K**

Blithe was our bearing   often we vowed
that but death alone   would part us two
naught else.   But this is turned round
now . . .   as if it never were
25 our friendship.   I must far and near
bear the anger   of my beloved.
The man sent me out   to live in the woods

J **OLD ENGLISH POETRY**
The translator has divided each line with a **caesura**, or pause, which helps maintain the rhythm of the line. What do the pauses emphasize?

6 my lord: the speaker's husband.

7 wave-tumult: a kenning, or compound metaphoric expression, for the sea.

COMMON CORE L 4
Language Coach

Multiple Meanings *Service* (line 10) can mean "help" or "the job of a servant," among other things. One obsolete meaning is "a pledge of love." How do these different meanings affect your interpretation of the events in lines 11–14?

K **MONITOR**
Why is the wife in exile?

under an oak tree   in this den in the earth.
Ancient this earth hall.   I am all longing.

30 The valleys are dark   the hills high
the yard overgrown   bitter with briars
a joyless dwelling.   Full oft the lack of my lord
seizes me cruelly here.   Friends there are on earth
living beloved   lying in bed
35 while I at dawn   am walking alone
under the oak tree   through these earth halls.
There I may sit   the summerlong day
there I can weep   over my exile
my many hardships.   Hence I may not rest
40 from this care of heart   which belongs to me ever
nor all this longing   that has caught me in this life. **L**

May that young man   be sad-minded always
hard his heart's thought   while he must wear
a blithe bearing   with care in the breast
45 a crowd of sorrows.   May on himself depend
all his world's joy.   Be he outlawed far
in a strange folk-land—   that my beloved sits
under a rocky cliff   rimed with frost
a lord dreary in spirit   drenched with water
50 in a ruined hall.   My lord endures
much care of mind.   He remembers too often
a happier dwelling.   Woe be to them
that for a loved one   must wait in longing. **M**

Translated by Ann Stanford

28–29 den . . . earth hall: In describing her living quarters, the speaker uses an expression something like the modern "hole in the ground."

L IMAGERY
What does the speaker's description of her surroundings express about her emotional state?

42 that young man: the speaker's husband. In these final lines, the speaker seems to wish for her husband to lead the same sort of life that he has forced her to endure.

M IMAGERY
What sad images does the speaker imagine in lines 42–50?

Comprehension

1. **Recall** How does the speaker in "The Seafarer" feel about life at sea?

2. **Clarify** Why is the title character in "The Wanderer" in exile?

3. **Clarify** In "The Wife's Lament," what does the wife wish for her husband?

Text Analysis

4. **Monitor Understanding** Review the charts you made as you read. What is the speaker remembering or pondering in each poem? What elements in each poem helped you reach these conclusions?

5. **Compare Texts** Compare these three poems, noting similarities you see in each of the following elements:

   • subject   • mood   • imagery   • theme

6. **Synthesize Ideas** What ideas about Anglo-Saxon life and religious attitudes do you get from the poems?

7. **Evaluate Imagery** How does the imagery in these poems reflect the passage of time? Support your answer with details from the poems.

8. **Apply Themes** What advice might the speakers of "The Seafarer" and "The Wanderer" give the speaker of "The Wife's Lament"? In what circumstances could modern people benefit from this advice?

Text Criticism

9. **Critical Interpretations** There has been much debate over the number of speakers in "The Seafarer." Some critics believe that a second person begins to speak at line 64, and others believe that there is only one speaker throughout the poem. Which interpretation do you believe is more accurate, and why?

> ### When are people most ALONE?
>
> A cold, stony landscape mirrors the harsh, unpredictable lives of the Anglo–Saxons. What other kinds of landscapes might evoke a feeling of isolation or loneliness?

COMMON CORE

RL 2 Determine two or more themes or central ideas of a text and analyze their development over the course of the text, including how they interact and build on one another to produce a complex account. **RL 4** Analyze the impact of specific word choices on meaning and tone, including words with multiple meanings or language that is fresh, engaging, or beautiful. **RL 9** Demonstrate knowledge of how two or more texts from the same period treat similar themes or topics. **RL 10** Read and comprehend literature, including poems.

from The Book of Margery Kempe

Autobiography by Margery Kempe

DID YOU KNOW?

Margery Kempe . . .

- gave birth to 14 children.
- was ridiculed for dressing all in white when married women customarily wore dark clothing.
- so annoyed the archbishop of York that he paid a man five shillings to escort her out of town.

Meet the Author

Margery Kempe c. 1373–1439

The Book of Margery Kempe (kĕmp), a religious mystic's story of her spiritual life, is thought to be the earliest surviving autobiography in the English language.

Ordinary Wife and Mother Margery Kempe was born about 1373 in Lynn—a town in the county of Norfolk, England—where her father served five terms as mayor. Although born to a prominent family, Kempe, like most women of her time, received little education. Around the age of 20, she married John Kempe, a tax collector, and raised a family.

Forsaking Secular Life At around the age of 40, Margery Kempe decided to become a "bride of Christ"—to live in chastity and preach to the world. As a vocal, outgoing speaker, she was quite an oddity at a time when most aspects of society, including the religious hierarchy, were controlled by men. Most women remained at home as wives and mothers. Any woman who wished to pursue a spiritual calling was expected to join a convent or to live as a recluse. Margery Kempe did neither.

Once Kempe had made her commitment to God, she began a series of religious pilgrimages to Jerusalem, Spain, Italy, and Germany. Although many men and women she

met considered her a model of human compassion and devotion, many others disapproved of her lifestyle.

A Gift of "Holy Tears" It was in Jerusalem that Kempe received her gift of "holy tears." She would fall into violent fits of crying at unpredictable times throughout the rest of her life, often during church services. Both the clergy and the common people found her hysterical crying at best annoying, at worst heretical. As a result, Kempe encountered a good deal of persecution and ridicule, although she maintained that her tears were a special gift from God, a physical token of her special worth in his eyes.

Her Life Story In the 1430s, Kempe began dictating her life story to scribes (like most women of her class, she was illiterate). She began her narrative by describing a deeply troubling experience following the birth of her first child, which eventually led to her devotion to a spiritual life. Her memoir is important for several reasons. It serves as a sort of time capsule of life in the 1400s, preserving for the reader the social customs, speech, and attitudes of the day. It also reveals the singular character of Kempe herself, a woman of strong faith who lived by her convictions despite intense social criticism and opposition.

View of Jerusalem

Author Online

THINK central

Go to **thinkcentral.com**. KEYWORD: HML12-116

TEXT ANALYSIS: AUTOBIOGRAPHY

The Book of Margery Kempe is an **autobiography,** a writer's account of his or her own life. An autobiography, as opposed to a diary or a memoir, is a sustained narrative that attempts to make sense of a person's life. Most autobiographies are written in the first person, with a narrator who uses the pronoun *I*. Kempe's autobiography is instead written in the third person, and Kempe is referred to as "she" or "this creature."

> *When this creature was twenty years of age, or somewhat more, she was married to a worshipful burgess [of Lynn] and was with child within a short time, as nature would have it.*

This third-person narration may reflect the fact that Kempe dictated her story to a scribe, who did the actual writing, or it may reflect her desire to be humble. As you read her autobiography, notice what her thoughts and experiences suggest about life in medieval times.

READING SKILL: DRAW CONCLUSIONS

To **draw a conclusion** is to reach a judgment based on text evidence, experience, and reasoning. For example, if a person answered a question hesitatingly and could not meet the questioner's eyes, you might conclude that the person was lying, based on these clues and your own knowledge of human behavior. As you read Kempe's autobiography, use a chart to note details from the text about her personality and beliefs, her illness, and the society she lives in. Note any additional thoughts you have about these subjects based on your own knowledge. Also note where the text leaves matters uncertain, requiring the reader to infer key information. Then after reading, draw conclusions about Kempe's life.

	Evidence from Text	My Own Thoughts / Knowledge	Conclusions
Personality			
Beliefs			
Illness			
Society			

 Complete the activities in your **Reader/Writer Notebook**.

Where do you find STRENGTH?

Margery Kempe didn't take the easy path in life. By living as a "bride of Christ" despite being a married woman, she challenged traditional women's roles and risked being branded as a heretic who could be burned at the stake. Her religious faith gave her the strength she needed to adhere to her convictions.

DISCUSS People have proved time and again that it is possible to overcome challenges, such as illness, poverty, physical disabilities, and oppression. With a group, discuss what gives people the strength to tackle a challenge or to keep going despite obstacles or setbacks. Draw evidence for your perspective from your own experiences or those of someone you know.

THE BOOK OF MARGERY KEMPE

Margery Kempe

CHAPTER ONE: ILLNESS AND RECOVERY

When this creature was twenty years of age, or somewhat more, she was married
to a worshipful burgess[1] [of Lynn] and was with child within a short time, as
nature would have it. And after she had conceived, she was troubled with severe
attacks of sickness until the child was born. And then, what with the labor-pains
she had in childbirth and the sickness that had gone before, she despaired of her
life, believing she might not live. Then she sent for her confessor,[2] for she had a
thing on her conscience which she had never revealed before that time in all her
life. For she was continually hindered by her enemy—the devil—always saying to
her while she was in good health that she didn't need to confess but to do penance
10 by herself alone, and all should be forgiven, for God is merciful enough. And
therefore this creature often did great penance in fasting on bread and water, and
performed other acts of charity with devout prayers, but she would not reveal that
one thing in confession. **A**

And when she was at any time sick or troubled, the devil said in her mind that
she should be damned, for she was not shriven[3] of that fault. Therefore, after her
child was born, and not believing she would live, she sent for her confessor, as said
before, fully wishing to be shriven of her whole lifetime, as near as she could.
And when she came to the point of saying that thing which she had so long
concealed, her confessor was a little too hasty and began sharply to reprove her
20 before she had fully said what she meant, and so she would say no more in spite of

---

1. **burgess** (bûr′jĭs): a citizen of an English town.
2. **confessor:** spiritual advisor; the priest to whom Margery confessed her sins.
3. **shriven:** absolved; forgiven for a sin or flaw.

Analyze Visuals ▶
What details suggest that
the woman pictured is
convalescent?

A AUTOBIOGRAPHY
Notice what Kempe tells
you about her life in lines
1–13. How does she view
herself and her actions?

Convalescent (Emma) (1872), Ford Madox Brown.
Colored chalks on paper. © Birmingham Museums
and Art Gallery/Bridgeman Art Library.

anything he might do. And soon after, because of the dread she had of damnation on the one hand, and his sharp reproving of her on the other, this creature went out of her mind and was amazingly disturbed and tormented with spirits for half a year, eight weeks and odd days.

And in this time she saw, as she thought, devils opening their mouths all alight with burning flames of fire, as if they would have swallowed her in, sometimes pawing at her, sometimes threatening her, sometimes pulling her and hauling her about both night and day during the said time. And also the devils called out to her with great threats, and bade her that she should forsake her Christian faith and belief, and deny her God, his mother, and all the saints in heaven, her good works and all good virtues, her father, her mother, and all her friends. And so she did. She slandered her husband, her friends, and her own self. She spoke many sharp and reproving words; she recognized no virtue nor goodness; she desired all wickedness; just as the spirits tempted her to say and do, so she said and did. She would have killed herself many a time as they stirred her to, and would have been

COMMON CORE L 3

Language Coach

Formal Language The translator of Kempe's autobiography uses **formal language** different from our everyday speech. Reread lines 28–31, which include the words "the devils . . . bade her that she should forsake her Christian faith. . . ." How could you say this informally?

Light Entering Empty Room (1995). Tempera on panel. © James Lynch/Getty Images.

damned with them in hell, and in witness of this she bit her own hand so violently that the mark could be seen for the rest of her life. And also she pitilessly tore the skin on her body near her heart with her nails, for she had no other implement, and she would have done something worse, except that she was tied up and
40 forcibly restrained both day and night so that she could not do as she wanted. **B**

And when she had long been troubled by these and many other temptations, so that people thought she should never have escaped from them alive, then one time as she lay by herself and her keepers were not with her, our merciful Lord Christ Jesus—ever to be trusted, worshiped be his name, never forsaking his servant in time of need—appeared to his creature who had forsaken him, in the likeness of a man, the most seemly, most beauteous, and most amiable that ever might be seen with man's eye, clad in a mantle of purple silk, sitting upon her bedside, looking upon her with so blessed a countenance that she was strengthened in all her spirits, and he said to her these words: "Daughter, why have you forsaken me, and
50 I never forsook you?" **C**

And as soon as he had said these words, she saw truly how the air opened as bright as any lightning, and he ascended up into the air, not hastily and quickly, but beautifully and gradually, so that she could clearly behold him in the air until it closed up again.

And presently the creature grew as calm in her wits and her reason as she ever was before, and asked her husband, as soon as he came to her, if she could have the keys of the buttery[4] to get her food and drink as she had done before. Her maids and her keepers advised him that he should not deliver up any keys to her, for they said she would only give away such goods as there were, because she did
60 not know what she was saying, as they believed.

Nevertheless, her husband, who always had tenderness and compassion for her, ordered that they should give her the keys. And she took food and drink as her bodily strength would allow her, and she once again recognized her friends and her household, and everybody else who came to her in order to see how our Lord Jesus Christ had worked his grace in her—blessed may he be, who is ever near in tribulation.[5] When people think he is far away from them he is very near through his grace. Afterwards this creature performed all her responsibilities wisely and soberly enough, except that she did not truly know our Lord's power to draw us to him.[6] ∿ **D**

B DRAW CONCLUSIONS
Reread lines 25–40. What conclusions do you draw about the nature of Kempe's illness? What details help you draw this conclusion?

C GRAMMAR AND STYLE
Notice how Kempe layers **subordinate clauses, participial phrases,** and **prepositional phrases** in a single-sentence paragraph to fully describe her vision of Jesus.

D AUTOBIOGRAPHY
How does Kempe conclude this first episode? How does she view herself at this point in her story?

---

4. **buttery:** pantry, where food provisions were stored.

5. **tribulation** (trĭb´yo lā´shon): suffering; distress.

6. **she did not . . . to him:** She still was not giving her complete devotion to God, as she would later.

Comprehension

1. **Recall** Why did Kempe send for a priest?

2. **Summarize** How did Kempe behave in the months after seeing the priest?

3. **Clarify** What changed her behavior?

Text Analysis

● 4. **Examine Autobiography** What kind of person does Kempe present herself to be, and for what purpose? Support your answer with details from the text. Be sure to note the key piece of information she leaves out of her autobiography.

● 5. **Draw Conclusions** Review the chart you made as you read. What conclusions did you draw about each of the following?

   • Kempe's personality
   • Kempe's religious beliefs
   • Kempe's illness
   • English society in Kempe's time

6. **Interpret Theme** Kempe undergoes a transformation during her illness. What does this transformation symbolize?

7. **Compare Texts** What does this selection have in common with Bede's account of Caedmon (page 98)? What do the two selections suggest about Christian beliefs in England during early times?

Text Criticism

8. **Compare Texts** Readers are often divided in their reactions to *The Book of Margery Kempe*. Some feel that Kempe was mentally unstable and should not be taken seriously. Others see her as a strong-minded woman who insisted on the validity of her own spiritual life. Do you agree with either of these opinions, or do you see Kempe differently? Why?

> ## *Where do you find* STRENGTH?
>
> Kempe drew upon her faith to find strength. Favorite activities, people, or places can also serve as sources of strength in difficult times. What activity, person, or place serves as such a source of strength during difficult times for you or someone you know?

COMMON CORE

RI 1 Cite evidence to support inferences, including determining where the text leaves matters uncertain. **RI 6** Determine an author's point of view or purpose in a text. **RI 9** Analyze documents of historical and literary significance for their themes and purposes.

Language

◆ **GRAMMAR AND STYLE: Craft Effective Sentences**

Review the **Grammar and Style** note on page 121. Margery Kempe uses a series of **subordinate clauses, prepositional phrases,** and **participial phrases** to chronicle the harrowing experience of her illness and recovery. The single, lengthy sentence below vividly portrays Kempe's visions:

> *And in this time she saw, as she thought, devils opening their mouths all alight with burning flames of fire, as if they would have swallowed her in, sometimes pawing at her, sometimes threatening her, sometimes pulling her and hauling her about both night and day during the said time.* (lines 25–28)

Kempe interjects the subordinate clause "as she thought" to alert readers that she was hallucinating, without unduly interrupting the flow of her description. Two prepositional phrases—"with burning flames" and "of fire"—provide vivid sensory details of Kempe's torment, as do the participial phrases she includes, such as "sometimes pawing at her" and "sometimes threatening her."

PRACTICE Rewrite the following paragraph by incorporating subordinate clauses, prepositional phrases, and participial phrases that mimic Kempe's style.

> The doctor told me the bad news and handed me a pair of crutches. I was going to have to use them for six weeks. It would take that long for my knee to heal. The first day on crutches was agony. It took me 20 minutes to travel one block. I had to stop every few steps to catch my breath.

> **EXAMPLE**
>
> *As the doctor told me the bad news, he put a pair of crutches in my hands.*

READING-WRITING CONNECTION

YOUR TURN Expand your understanding of the excerpt from *The Book of Margery Kempe* by responding to this prompt. Then, use the **revising tips** to improve your personal narrative.

WRITING PROMPT	REVISING TIPS
WRITE A SURVIVAL TALE Think about a time when you or someone you know recovered from an injury, illness, or some other difficult experience. Draft a **one-page personal narrative** in which you describe the attitudes and strategies that made it survivable. Conclude by reflecting on the importance of the experience.	• Ensure the story has a clear beginning, middle, and end. • Add descriptive details and sensory language to vividly portray the experience. • Use subordinate clauses, prepositional phrases, and participial phrases to create a smooth progression of events.

Interactive Revision

THINK central

Go to **thinkcentral.com**.
KEYWORD: HML12-123

Sidebar:

COMMON CORE

L 3 Apply knowledge of language to make effective choices for meaning or style. **W 3a, d–e** Set out a problem, situation, or observation and its significance; create a smooth progression of experiences or events; use precise words and phrases, telling details, and sensory language to convey a vivid picture of the experiences; provide a conclusion that reflects on what is experienced, observed, or resolved.

from **Piers Plowman**

Allegory by William Langland

COMMON CORE

RL 9 Demonstrate knowledge
of foundational works of
literature. **W 3b, d** Use narrative
techniques, such as dialogue
and description, to develop
experiences, events, and/or
characters; use telling details
to convey a vivid picture of the
experiences, events, setting, and/
or characters.

BACKGROUND *Piers Plowman* is a 14th-century narrative poem that combines deep religious faith with biting social satire. Its authorship is uncertain, but evidence points to William Langland, about whom little is known. The poem's large number of surviving manuscripts suggests its popularity in its day, and it influenced the works of later writers such as Edmund Spenser, John Milton, and John Bunyan. *Piers Plowman,* like much medieval literature, is written in Middle English alliterative verse, in which several words in each line repeat the same initial sound. For modern readers, the poem provides valuable insights into medieval life. This excerpt is a modern translation of the so-called B text, the second and best known of the poem's three surviving versions.

TEXT ANALYSIS *Piers Plowman* is an **allegory,** or work in which characters, settings, and events represent abstract concepts to convey a message, such as the need to lead a more moral life. Like the Venerable Bede (page 96) and Margery Kempe (page 116), Langland uses the device of a dream vision to portray a powerful spiritual struggle and transformation to his audience. Through a series of dreams, Will, the hero of *Piers Plowman,* travels to a strange, alternative world where Conscience, Reason, and Truth have human characteristics that allow them to walk, talk, and debate important religious issues. Each encounter with these characters represents another step in Will's quest to achieve greater spiritual understanding.

Allegories often incorporate **personification,** a figure of speech in which the author attributes human qualities to ideas. In *Piers Plowman* each of the Seven Deadly Sins has a distinct appearance, personality, and point of view. In the following excerpt, for example, Envy, characteristically dissatisfied, carries a knife, shakes his fists in frustration, and admits he deliberately causes trouble wherever he goes. In an effort to redeem himself, Envy begs Repentance to hear his confession in hopes of doing shrift, or penance, for his dreadful deeds.

WRITE After you read the excerpt, write a short allegory in which you convey a message about an abstract concept, such as love, anger, or fear, by personifying it as a character with human traits. If you saw this character walking down the street, what would he or she look like? How would he or she speak? What would this character say about him- or herself?

*E*nvy with heavy heart asked for shrift
And grieving for his guilt began his confession.
He was pale as a sheep's pelt, appeared to have the palsy.
He was clothed in a coarse cloth—I couldn't describe it—
A tabard and a tunic, a knife tied to his side,
Like those of a friar's frock were the foresleeves.
Like a leek that had lain long in the sun
So he looked with lean cheeks, louring foully.
His body was so blown up for anger that he bit his lips
10 And shook his fist fiercely, he wanted to avenge himself
With acts or with words when he saw his chance.
Every syllable he spat out was of a serpent's tongue;
From chiding and bringing charges was his chief livelihood,
With backbiting and bitter scorn and bearing false witness.
This was all his courtesy wherever he showed himself.
"I'd like to be shriven," said this scoundrel, "if shame would let me.
By God, I'd be gladder that Gib had bad luck
Than if I'd won this week a wey of Essex cheese.
I've a neighbor dwelling next door, I've done him harm often
20 And blamed him behind his back to blacken his name.
I've done my best to damage him day after day
And lied to lords about him to make him lose money,
And turned his friends into foes with my false tongue.
His good luck and his glad lot grieve me greatly.
Between household and household I often start disputes
So that both life and limb are lost for my speech. . . .
I condemn men when they do evil, yet I do much worse;
Whoever upbraids me for that, I hate him deadly after.
I wish that every one were my servant,
30 And if any man has more than I, that angers my heart.
So I live loveless like a loathsome dog
So that my breast is blown up for bitterness of spirit.
For many years I might not eat as a man ought
For envy and ill will are hard to digest.
Is there any sugar or sweet thing to assuage my swelling
Or any *diapenidion* that will drive it from my heart,
Or any shrift or shame, unless I have my stomach scraped?"
 "Yes, readily," said Repentance, directing him to live better;
"Sorrow for sins is salvation for souls."

from **The Paston Letters**

Letters by the Paston Family

COMMON CORE

RI 1 Cite evidence to support inferences drawn from the text. **RI 6** Determine an author's purpose in a text, analyzing how content contributes to the power, persuasiveness, or beauty of the text. **RI 9** Analyze documents of historical and literary significance for their themes, purposes, and rhetorical features. **SL 1a** Come to discussions prepared, having read and researched material under study. **L 4a** Use context as a clue to the meaning of a word.

DID YOU KNOW?

The Paston family . . .

- is immortalized in the old Norfolk saying "There never was a Paston poor, a Heydon a coward, or a Cornwallis a fool."
- claimed that they were willed the property of Sir John Fastolf, who inspired Falstaff, a comic character in three of Shakespeare's plays.

Meet the Author

The Paston Family

John Paston I (1421–1466) *married* (1440) Margaret Mautby (1422?–1484)

John II (1442–1479)   John III (1444–1504)   Margery (1447?–1479?) married (1469) Richard Calle

The 15th century in England was a period of great unrest and lawlessness. Landowners often attacked their neighbors' estates and betrayed their political allies. The Wars of the Roses, a conflict between two royal families for control of the kingdom, ravaged England between 1455 and 1485. In addition, several outbreaks of the plague devastated many English families during the century.

The Saga Begins A firsthand record of this turbulent era survives in more than 1,000 documents and letters written by the Pastons, an English landowning family. During the early 1400s, William Paston, a lawyer, began accumulating property in Norfolk, a county in eastern England, both through purchases and through his acquisition of estates inherited by his wife, Agnes Berry. William's extensive landholdings and growing prosperity earned him a number of enemies. Some even challenged his claim to certain properties and brought grief to William's descendants for many years.

Endless Legal Wrangling William Paston and Agnes Berry had five children. The oldest, John I, inherited much of the family property when his father died in 1444, and his marriage to Margaret Mautby led to the acquisition of even more property from his wife's family. Like his father, John I was a lawyer, possessed of skills that were much needed in his constant legal battles over claims to various properties. His many legal disputes required him to stay in London for long periods of time, leaving Margaret to manage the Paston estates. John I and Margaret's seven children included two sons named John—John II and John III—and a daughter named Margery. The letters you will read concern John I, Margaret, and these three children.

Anxiously Awaited Letters In their letters, the Pastons exchanged detailed information about their legal disputes and other problems. Although writing letters had become an important means of communication by the 15th century, sending the letters was not easy. They had to be delivered by hand, often by a servant or even a total stranger. Weeks might pass before a letter reached its destination, and many never arrived. Despite these limitations, the Pastons wrote hundreds of letters over the course of 90 years, leaving an invaluable source of information about the social and political conditions of the times.

Author Online

Go to **thinkcentral.com**. KEYWORD: HML12-126

THINK central

TEXT ANALYSIS: PRIMARY SOURCES

Primary sources, such as diaries and letters, are materials created by people who took part in or witnessed the events portrayed. These documents can help you synthesize ideas and make logical connections based on evidence from the text to draw conclusions about the people who wrote them and the period in which they lived. Consider this excerpt from a letter written by Margaret Paston to her husband:

> *They let me know that various of Lord Moleyns' men said that if they could get their hands on me they would keep me in the castle. They wanted you to get me out again, and said that it would not cause you much heart-ache.*

The excerpt shows that participants in land disputes of the time would sometimes resort to kidnapping for ransom. As you read these letters, determine what they reveal about their writers and life in the 15th century.

READING SKILL: UNDERSTAND WRITER'S PURPOSE

To understand a writer's purpose, you must make subtle **inferences,** or reasonable assumptions based on clues in the text. The writer may wish to accomplish a goal, such as explaining a situation or eliciting a desired response. For example, you can infer how much danger the Pastons face when Margaret urges her husband to "please take care when you eat or drink in any other men's company, for no one can be trusted." Clues to the writer's purpose may include

- significant details the writer includes about events or ideas
- the writer's opinions or observations
- attempts by the writer to influence the recipient's thoughts or actions

As you read each letter, note significant details the writer provides. Record your thoughts on a chart like the one shown to help you conclude what each writer's purpose is.

Writer/ Recipient/Date	Significant Details	Your Inferences	Writer's Purpose
Margaret to John I, 28 February 1449			

 Complete the activities in your **Reader/Writer Notebook**.

What disturbs your sense of SECURITY?

Imagine living with the fear of being struck down by the plague or learning that parts of your home and property had been destroyed—and feeling powerless to prevent further destruction. For the Paston family, such horrors were a reality. Although they were relatively wealthy and privileged, a sense of security was not something their money could buy.

DISCUSS Life in 21st-century America is radically different from life in 15th-century England, but events can still intrude upon our security. Working with a partner, think of a global, national, or local event that shook your sense of security. Prepare for a thoughtful discussion by researching details of the event that you might not have previously known. Discuss why you found the event disturbing and what you did to attempt to regain your peace of mind.

> Event
> Terrorist Attacks, 9-11-01
> **Aspects That Shook My Sense of Security**
> 1.
> 2.
> 3.
> **What I Did to Regain My Sense of Security**

The Paston Letters
The Paston Family

Margaret Paston, in the absence of her husband, John I, was able to deal equally well with small housekeeping problems and with family disasters, including attacks against the Paston manors. While she was living at the Paston estate of Gresham, it was attacked by a Lord Moleyns, who claimed rights to the property and ejected Margaret from her home. Margaret first escaped to a friend's house about a mile away; but later, fearing that Moleyns's band of men might kidnap her, she fled to the city of Norwich, where she wrote the following letter to her husband.

Margaret to John I
28 FEBRUARY 1449

Right worshipful husband, I commend myself to you, wishing with all my heart to hear that you are well, and begging that you will not be angry at my leaving the place where you left me. On my word, such news was brought to me by various people who are sympathetic to you and me that I did not dare stay there any longer. I will tell you who the people were when you come home. They let me know that various of Lord Moleyns' men said that if they could get their hands on me they would carry me off and keep me in the castle. They wanted you to get me out again, and said that it would not cause you much heart-ache. After I heard this news, I could not rest easy until I was here, and I did not dare go out of
10 the place where I was until I was ready to ride away. Nobody in the place knew **(A)** that I was leaving except the lady of the house, until an hour before I went. And I told her that I would come here to have clothes made for myself and the children, which I wanted made, and said I thought I would be here a fortnight[1] or three

Analyze Visuals ▶
What is the economic status of the family pictured? How can you tell?

(A) WRITER'S PURPOSE
What is Margaret explaining to John I in lines 1–10? Speculate about how she wants him to react.

---

1. **fortnight:** 14 nights, or two weeks.

The Four Conditions of Society: Nobility, Jean Bourdichon. Vellum. École Nationale Supérieure des Beaux-Arts, Paris. © Bridgeman Art Library.

weeks. Please keep the reason for my departure a secret until I talk to you, for those who warned me do not on any account want it known.

I spoke to your mother as I came this way, and she offered to let me stay in this town, if you agree. She would very much like us to stay at her place, and will send me such things as she can spare so that I can set up house until you can get a place and things of your own to set up a household. Please let me know by the man
20 who brings this what you would like me to do. I would be very unhappy to live so close to Gresham as I was until this matter is completely settled between you and Lord Moleyns.

Barow[2] told me that there was no better evidence in England than that Lord Moleyns has for [his title to] the manor of Gresham. I told him that I supposed the evidence was of the kind that William Hasard said yours was, and that the seals were not yet cold.[3] That, I said, was what I expected his lord's evidence to be like. I said I knew that your evidence was such that no one could have better evidence, and the seals on it were two hundred years older than he was. Then Barow said to me that if he came to London while you were there he would have
30 a drink with you, to quell any anger there was between you. He said that he only acted as a servant, and as he was ordered to do. Purry[4] will tell you about the conversation between Barow and me when I came from Walsingham.[5] I beg you with all my heart, for reverence of God, beware of Lord Moleyns and his men, however pleasantly they speak to you, and do not eat or drink with them; for they are so false that they cannot be trusted. And please take care when you eat or drink in any other men's company, for no one can be trusted. **B**

I beg you with all my heart that you will be kind enough to send me word how you are, and how your affairs are going, by the man who brings this. I am very surprised that you do not send me more news than you have done. . . .

In 1465, in still another property dispute, the Paston estate of Hellesdon was attacked by the duke of Suffolk, who had gained the support of several local officials. Although Margaret and John were not living at Hellesdon at the time, many of their servants and tenants suffered from the extensive damage. In the following two letters, Margaret tells her husband about the devastation.

Margaret to John I
17 OCTOBER 1465
40 . . . On Tuesday morning John Botillere, also John Palmer, Darcy Arnald your cook and William Malthouse of Aylsham were seized at Hellesdon by the bailiff

B **PRIMARY SOURCES**
From Margaret's statements in lines 23–36, what can you **infer** that a claimant might do to gain property in these times?

---

2. **Barow:** one of Lord Moleyns's men.

3. **the seals . . . cold:** A seal, often made by impressing a family emblem on hot wax, was placed on a document to show its authenticity. Margaret is suggesting that Lord Moleyns's documents are recent forgeries.

4. **Purry:** perhaps a servant or tenant of the Pastons'.

5. **Walsingham** (wôl′sĭng-əm): a town near Lynn in the English county of Norfolk.

of Eye,[6] called Bottisforth, and taken to Costessey,[7] and they are being kept there still without any warrant or authority from a justice of the peace; and they say they will carry them off to Eye prison and as many others of your men and tenants as they can get who are friendly towards you or have supported you, and they threaten to kill or imprison them.

The duke came to Norwich at 10 o'clock on Tuesday with five hundred men and he sent for the mayor, aldermen and sheriffs, asking them in the king's name that they should inquire of the constables of every ward within the city which men

50 had been on your side or had helped or supported your men at the time of any of these gatherings and if they could find any they should take them and arrest them and punish them; which the mayor did, and will do anything he can for him and his men. At this the mayor has arrested a man who was with me, called Robert Lovegold, a brazier,[8] and threatened him that he shall be hanged by the neck. So I would be glad if you could get a writ sent down for his release, if you think it can be done. He was only with me when Harlesdon and others attacked me at Lammas.[9] He is very true and faithful to you, so I would like him to be helped. I have no one attending me who dares to be known, except Little John. William Naunton is here with me, but he dares not be known because he is much threatened. I am told that

60 the old lady and the duke have been frequently set against us by what Harlesdon, the bailiff of Costessey, Andrews and Doget the bailiff's son and other false villains have told them, who want this affair pursued for their own pleasure; there are evil rumors about it in this part of the world and other places. **Ⓒ**

As for Sir John Heveningham, Sir John Wyndefeld and other respectable men, they have been made into their catspaws,[10] which will not do their reputation any good after this, I think. . . .

The lodge and remainder of your place was demolished on Tuesday and Wednesday, and the duke rode on Wednesday to Drayton and then to Costessey while the lodge at Hellesdon was being demolished. Last night at midnight

70 Thomas Slyford, Green, Porter and John Bottisforth the bailiff of Eye and others got a cart and took away the featherbeds and all the stuff of ours that was left at the parson's and Thomas Water's house for safe-keeping. I will send you lists later, as accurately as I can, of the things we have lost. Please let me know what you want me to do, whether you want me to stay at Caister[11] or come to you in London.

I have no time to write any more. God have you in his keeping. Written at Norwich on St. Luke's eve.[12]

M.P.

Ⓒ PRIMARY SOURCES
Reread lines 47–63. What methods of intimidation does the duke of Suffolk use against the Pastons? What is the Pastons' recourse?

---

6. **bailiff of Eye:** an administrative official of Eye, a town in the English county of Suffolk.

7. **Costessey:** an estate owned by the duke of Suffolk.

8. **brazier** (brā′zhər): a person who makes articles of brass.

9. **when Harlesdon ... Lammas** (lăm′əs): when Harlesdon and others of the duke of Suffolk's men attacked on Lammas, a religious feast celebrated on August 1.

10. **catspaws:** people who are deceived and used as tools by others; dupes.

11. **Caister:** one of the Paston estates.

12. **St. Luke's eve:** the eve of St. Luke's Day, a religious feast. The feasts of different saints were celebrated on different days throughout the year, and writers often dated letters with the name of a saint's day or eve instead of using days and months.

Margaret to John I
27 OCTOBER 1465

. . . I was at Hellesdon last Thursday and saw the place there, and indeed no one can imagine what a horrible mess it is unless they see it. Many people come out
80 each day, both from Norwich and elsewhere, to look at it, and they talk of it as a great shame. The duke would have done better to lose £1000[13] than to have caused this to be done, and you have all the more goodwill from people because it has been done so foully. And they made your tenants at Hellesdon and Drayton, and others, help them to break down the walls of both the house and the lodge: God knows, it was against their will, but they did not dare do otherwise for fear. I have spoken with your tenants both at Hellesdon and Drayton, and encouraged them as best I can.

The duke's men ransacked the church, and carried off all the goods that were left there, both ours and the tenants, and left little behind; they stood on the
90 high altar and ransacked the images, and took away everything they could find. They shut the parson out of the church until they had finished, and ransacked everyone's house in the town five or six times. The ringleaders in the thefts were the bailiff of Eye and the bailiff of Stradbroke, Thomas Slyford. And Slyford was the leader in robbing the church and, after the bailiff of Eye, it is he who has most of the proceeds of the robbery. As for the lead, brass, pewter, iron, doors, gates, and other household stuff, men from Costessey and Cawston have got it, and what they could not carry they hacked up in the most spiteful fashion. If possible, I would like some reputable men to be sent for from the king, to see how things are both there and at the lodge, before any snows come, so that they can report
100 the truth, because otherwise it will not be so plain as it is now. For reverence of God, finish your business now, for the expense and trouble we have each day is horrible, and it will be like this until you have finished; and your men dare not go around collecting your rents, while we keep here every day more than twenty people to save ourselves and the place; for indeed, if the place had not been strongly defended, the duke would have come here. . . . **D**

For the reverence of God, if any respectable and profitable method can be used to settle your business, do not neglect it, so that we can get out of these troubles and the great costs and expenses we have and may have in future. It is thought here that if my lord of Norfolk would act on your behalf, and got a commission to
110 inquire into the riots and robberies committed on you and others in this part of the world, then the whole county will wait on him and do as you wish, for people love and respect him more than any other lord, except the king and my lord of Warwick.[14] . . .

---

13. **£1000:** a thousand pounds (British money).

14. **the king . . . Warwick** (wŏr′ĭk): King Edward IV and the earl of Warwick, a figure so influential that he was known as Warwick the Kingmaker. Warwick put his friend, the Yorkist King Edward IV, on the throne but later turned against him and fought with the Lancastrian faction, who opposed the Yorkists in the War of the Roses.

COMMON CORE L 4a

Language Coach

Oral Fluency Part of reading fluently is correct pronunciation. As a plural noun meaning "profits," *proceeds* has a stress on the first syllable. As a form of the verb *proceed* ("go forward"), *proceeds* has a stress on its final syllable. Which pronunciation should you use in line 95?

D WRITER'S PURPOSE
In lines 97–105, what does Margaret ask John to do, and why?

Please do let me know quickly how you are and how your affairs are going, and let me know how your sons are. I came home late last night, and will be here until I hear from you again. Wykes came home on Saturday, but he did not meet your sons.

God have you in his keeping and send us good news from you. Written in haste on the eve of St. Simon and St. Jude.

By yours, M.P.

During the 15th century, most marriages among the upper classes were arranged by families, usually to strengthen economic or political ties. The Paston family was greatly alarmed, therefore, when they learned that Margery, a daughter of Margaret and John I, had secretly become engaged to the Paston bailiff Richard Calle. Eventually, the two were married, in spite of bitter opposition from Margery's family. In the following letter to Margery—the only piece of their correspondence to survive—Richard expresses his feelings about their predicament. The next letter is the response of Margery's mother, Margaret, to the situation, written to her son John II.

Richard Calle to Margery Paston
SPRING–SUMMER 1469

120 **My own lady and mistress,** and indeed my true wife before God,[15] I commend myself to you with a very sad heart as a man who cannot be cheerful and will not be until things stand otherwise with us than they do now. This life that we lead now pleases neither God nor the world, considering the great bond of matrimony that is made between us, and also the great love that has been, and I trust still is, between us, and which for my part was never greater. So I pray that Almighty God will comfort us as soon as it pleases him, for we who ought by rights to be most together are most apart; it seems a thousand years since I last spoke to you. I would rather be with you than all the wealth in the world. Alas, also, good lady, those who keep us apart like this, scarcely realize what they are doing: those who

130 hinder matrimony are cursed in church four times a year. It makes many men think that they can stretch a point of conscience in other matters as well as this one. But whatever happens, lady, bear it as you have done and be as cheerful as you can, for be sure, lady, that God in the long run will of his righteousness help his servants who mean to be true and want to live according to his laws. **E**

I realize, lady, that you have had as much sorrow on my account as any gentlewoman has ever had in this world; I wish to God that all the sorrow you have had had fallen on me, so that you were freed of it; for indeed, lady, it kills me to hear that you are being treated otherwise than you should be. This is a painful life we lead; I cannot imagine that we live like this without God being

140 displeased by it.

E WRITER'S PURPOSE
According to Richard, how do he and Margery stand in relation to God? How might his words affect Margery, and Margery's parents, were they to read them?

---

15. **my true wife before God:** In the 1400s, the vow of a man and woman spoken before God, even without a witness, was regarded as an official marriage.

Epistres en Vers François, dedicated to Anne de Bretagne (1500s). Parchment, 29.5 cm × 19.5 cm. 112 pages. Anne de Bretagne replies to her husband, fol.40 verso. Russian National Library, St. Petersburg, Russia.

◀ **Analyze Visuals**
In this picture, a noblewoman writes a letter to her husband. What indicates the formality of this activity?

You will want to know that I sent you a letter from London by my lad, and he told me he could not speak to you, because so great a watch was kept on both you and him. He told me that John Thresher came to him in your name, and said that you had sent him to my lad for a letter or token which you thought I had sent you; but he did not trust him and would not deliver anything to him. After that he brought a ring, saying that you sent it to him, commanding him to deliver the letter or token to him, which I gather since then from my lad was not sent by you, but was a plot of my mistress [i.e., Margaret Paston] and James Gloys.[16] Alas, what do they intend? I suppose they think we are not engaged; and if this is the case I am very surprised, for they are not being sensible, remembering how plainly I told my mistress about everything at the beginning, and I think you have told her so too, if you have done as you should. And if you have denied it, as I have been told

150

16. **James Gloys:** the Paston family chaplain.

you have done, it was done neither with a good conscience nor to the pleasure of God, unless you did it for fear and to please those who were with you at the time. If this was the reason you did it, it was justified, considering how insistently you were called on to deny it; and you were told many untrue stories about me, which, God knows, I was never guilty of.

My lad told me that your mother asked him if he had brought any letter to you, and she accused him falsely of many other things; among other things, she said to him in the end that I would not tell her about it at the beginning, but she expected that I would at the ending. As for that, God knows that she knew about it first from me and no one else. I do not know what my mistress means, for in truth there is no other gentlewoman alive who I respect more than her and whom I would be more sorry to displease, saving only yourself who by right I ought to cherish and love best, for I am bound to do so by God's law and will do so while I live, whatever may come of it. I expect that if you tell them the sober truth, they will not damn their souls for our sake. Even if I tell them the truth they will not believe me as much as they would you. And so, good lady, for reverence of God be plain with them and tell the truth, and if they will not agree, let it be between them, God and the devil; and as for the peril we should be in, I pray God it may lie on them and not on us. I am very sad and sorry when I think of their attitude. God guide them and send them rest and peace. **F**

I am very surprised that they are as concerned about this affair as I gather that they are, in view of the fact that nothing can be done about it, and that I deserve better; from any point of view there should be no obstacles to it. Also their honor does not depend on your marriage, but in their own marriage [i.e., John II's]; I pray God send them a marriage which will be to their honor, to God's pleasure and to their heart's ease, for otherwise it would be a great pity.

Mistress, I am frightened of writing to you, for I understand that you have showed the letters that I have sent you before to others, but I beg you, let no one see this letter. As soon as you have read it, burn it, for I would not want anyone to see it. You have had nothing in writing from me for two years, and I will not send you any more: so I leave everything to your wisdom.

Almighty Jesu preserve, keep and give you your heart's desire, which I am sure will please God. This letter was written with as great difficulty as I ever wrote anything in my life, for I have been very ill, and am not yet really recovered, may God amend it.

Margaret to her oldest son, John II
10 September 1469

. . . When I heard how she [Margery] had behaved, I ordered my servants that she was not to be allowed in my house. I had warned her, and she might have taken heed if she had been well-disposed. I sent messages to one or two others that they

COMMON CORE RI 1, RI 6

F **WRITER'S PURPOSE**
In order to reach conclusions about a writer's purpose, you must make **inferences,** or reasonable assumptions based on evidence from the text. These inferences can help clarify complicated relationships and events portrayed in the text. Based on this paragraph, what can you infer about the state of Richard and Margery's relationship? What is Margaret Paston's reaction to it? What does Richard hope to accomplish by writing this letter to Margery? Explain how you reached your conclusions.

should not let her in if she came. She was brought back to my house to be let in, and James Gloys told those who brought her that I had ordered them all that she should not be allowed in. So my lord of Norwich has lodged her at Roger Best's, to stay there until the day in question; God knows it is much against his will and his wife's, but they dare not do otherwise. I am sorry that they are burdened with her, but I am better off with her there than somewhere else, because he and his wife are sober and well-disposed to us, and she will not be allowed to play the good-for-nothing there. **G**

200   Please do not take all this too hard, because I know that it is a matter close to your heart, as it is to mine and other people's; but remember, as I do, that we have only lost a good-for-nothing in her, and take it less to heart: if she had been any good, whatever might have happened, things would not have been as they are, for even if he[17] were dead now, she would never be as close to me as she was. . . . You can be sure that she will regret her foolishness afterwards, and I pray to God that she does. Please, for my sake, be cheerful about all this. I trust that God will help us; may he do so in all our affairs.

Although the Pastons were considered wealthy, they faced continual struggles. They even experienced occasional financial difficulties, particularly after the death of John I in 1466. John II, though frequently in London to deal with family legal matters, seems at times to have paid more attention to his own interests. The Pastons were also affected by the ravages of warfare and disease. The following three letters deal with some of their hardships.

Margaret to John II
28 October 1470

. . . Unless you pay more attention to your expenses, you will bring great shame on yourself and your friends, and impoverish them so that none of us will be able to help each other, to the great encouragement of our enemies.

210   Those who claim to be your friends in this part of the world realize in what great danger and need you stand, both from various of your friends and from your enemies. It is rumored that I have parted with so much to you that I cannot help either you or any of my friends, which is no honor to us and causes people to esteem us less. At the moment it means that I must disperse my household and lodge somewhere, which I would be very loath to do if I were free to choose. It has caused a great deal of talk in this town and I would not have needed to do it if I had held back when I could. So for God's sake pay attention and be careful from now on, for I have handed over to you both my own property and your father's, and have held nothing back, either for myself or for his sake. . . . **H**

G **PRIMARY SOURCES**
Reread lines 188–198. What behavior seems expected of a daughter? How is disobedience punished?

H **WRITER'S PURPOSE**
Infer Margaret's reasons for writing this letter. What rumors does she hope to dispel and why?

---

17. **he:** Richard Calle.

John II to Margaret
APRIL 1471

220 *Mother,* I commend myself to you and let you know, blessed be God, my brother
John is alive and well, and in no danger of dying. Nevertheless he is badly hurt
by an arrow in his right arm below the elbow, and I have sent a surgeon to him,
who has dressed the wound; and he tells me that he hopes he will be healed within
a very short time. John Mylsent is dead. God have mercy on his soul; William
Mylsent is alive and all his other servants seem to have escaped.[18] . . .

John II to John III
15 SEPTEMBER 1471

. . . Please send me word if any of our friends or well-wishers are dead, for I
fear that there is great mortality in Norwich and in other boroughs and towns
in Norfolk: I assure you that it is the most widespread plague I ever knew of in
England, for by my faith I cannot hear of pilgrims going through the country
230 nor of any other man who rides or goes anywhere, that any town or borough in
England is free from the sickness. May God put an end to it, when it please him.
So, for God's sake, get my mother to take care of my younger brothers and see that
they are not anywhere where the sickness is prevalent, and that they do not amuse
themselves with other young people who go where the sickness is. If anyone has
died of the sickness, or is infected with it, in Norwich, for God's sake let her send
them to some friend of hers in the country; I would advise you to do the same. I
would rather my mother moved her household into the country. . . .

PRIMARY SOURCES
In this letter, what do you
learn about the plague
and what people do to
avoid being stricken?

---

18. **my brother John . . . escaped:** John II is describing the Battle of Barnet in the War of the Roses. The
Pastons fought with the Lancastrian faction, which King Edward IV's Yorkist faction defeated.

Comprehension

1. **Recall** What occurred at the Paston family estate of Hellesdon in October 1465?

2. **Clarify** Why does Margaret Paston consider her daughter Margery a "good-for-nothing"?

3. **Summarize** Briefly summarize Margaret's message to John II in her letter of 28 October 1470.

Text Analysis

● 4. **Understand Writer's Purpose** Review the chart you made as you read. Describe each letter writer's purpose on the basis of your inferences. Defend your conclusions with evidence from the text.

5. **Draw Conclusions** What conclusions did you draw about each letter writer's personality? In a chart, provide an appropriate adjective to describe each person. Support your descriptions with evidence from the letters.

Family Member	Description	Evidence
Margaret		
Richard Calle		
John II		

● 6. **Analyze Primary Sources** What do you learn from these letters about life in 15th-century England? Comment on what they tell you about the role property and family played in people's lives at that time.

7. **Analyze Style** These letters have been translated from Middle English into Modern English, but care was taken to preserve features of their original style. What do you notice about the language used in the letters? Does the language seem suited to the context? Explain.

Text Criticism

8. **Critical Interpretations** Critics have commented that the Paston letters should be read for their historical value, not their literary value. Do you agree? Explain why the letters are or are not "literature."

What disturbs your sense of **SECURITY?**

What are some of the negative results that might occur if you become overly concerned with losing your sense of security? Include specific examples to illustrate your point.

COMMON CORE

RI 1 Cite evidence to support inferences drawn from the text. **RI 6** Determine an author's purpose in a text, analyzing how content contributes to the power, persuasiveness, or beauty of the text. **RI 9** Analyze documents of historical and literary significance for their themes, purposes, and rhetorical features. **L 3** Apply knowledge of language to understand how language functions in different contexts.

Literature and the Common Life

By reading autobiographies, such as Margery Kempe's, and letters, such as Margaret Paston's, a reader can learn more intimately about what life was like during the writer's time: in this case, the Middle Ages. Nonfiction writing brings the lives of its authors to life in the reader's imagination.

Writing to Compare

Comparing two people, places, or things can help you reach a greater understanding about both of them. Write a comparison of two of the major figures in the nonfiction selections in the "Reflections of Common Life" section, using a chart like the one below to help you organize your thoughts. Then, select three of the categories from your chart. What major similarities or differences do you notice about the two figures based on these categories? What generalizations can you make about what their lives might have been like in the Middle Ages based on these similarities or differences? Include evidence from the two texts to support your analysis. Organize your essay by category to build toward your generalization.

	Name #1	Name #2
Occupation/Role		
Socioeconomic Status		
Family Relationships		
Hardships/Concerns		
Joys/Rewards		
Role of Religion in Life		

Extension

SPEAKING & LISTENING

Imagine a meeting between Margery Kempe and Margaret Paston. What might the two women discuss? With a partner, brainstorm some of the topics you think would come up in a conversation between the two. Then choose roles and role-play their conversation for the class. You might focus on one topic, such as family relationships, for your performance.

COMMON CORE

W 2a–b Organize ideas and information so that each element builds on that which precedes it; develop the topic by selecting facts, concrete details, quotations, or other information and examples. **W 9** Draw evidence from texts to support analysis. **SL 1a–b** Draw on preparation by referring to evidence from texts to stimulate a thoughtful exchange of ideas; work with peers to set clear goals and establish individual roles.

Medieval Narratives

Imagine you are living in London, England, in the year 1398, and you are similar to the type of person you are now: a student reading and learning about literature. What would you be reading? As an educated person in the 14th century, what might be of interest to you?

COMMON CORE

Included in this workshop:
RL 3 Analyze the impact of the author's choices regarding how to develop and relate elements of a story. **RL 6** Analyze a case in which grasping a point of view requires distinguishing what is directly stated in a text from what is really meant (e.g., irony). **RL 9** Demonstrate knowledge of foundational works of literature, including how two or more texts from the same period treat similar themes or topics.

The Medieval Reader

By the end of the 14th century, a typical Londoner who could read would have been interested in **narratives**—a type of writing that relates a series of events— written in verse. Typical **medieval narratives** included ballads, romances, allegories, and moral tales. Most of them were religious in theme, but many others were concerned with love, exemplary life and behavior, and political and societal issues. Although comedy and humor are not something we often associate with the Middle Ages, the medieval mind had a sophisticated sense of irony and a taste for comic narratives, which were, in fact, common.

Detail of *Lydgate and the Canterbury Pilgrims leaving Canterbury* (1520)

Between 1350 and 1400, a large body of narrative works was produced in England. These were written in Middle English, a language that had developed and replaced the use of French, which had been the predominant language of educated people in Britain. Literacy had become more common, and books were more widely available, although they were still copied by hand; thus, educated citizens had access to more literary works. Popular narratives of the time included *Sir Gawain and the Green Knight* (page 230) and the King Arthur romance (page 248), with their themes of chivalry, love, and religious devotion; William Langland's *Piers Plowman* (page 124), an allegory that exposed the corruption of church, state, and society; and Geoffrey Chaucer's groundbreaking work, *The Canterbury Tales* (page 144). It was Chaucer, with his sense of humor, style, and realistic characterizations, who overshadowed his peers and became known to subsequent generations as one of the greatest poets in the history of English literature.

Characteristics of Chaucer's Style

Chaucer had no illusions about humanity, and yet his works show a compassion and fondness for human nature with all its faults and idiosyncrasies. Though *The Canterbury Tales* went unfinished, it is the work that best exhibits his unique style, which encompasses a variety of traits.

- **Imagery and Figurative Language** Chaucer uses sparse but vivid imagery and figurative language to describe his characters' physical appearance, as in his depiction of the Summoner: "His face on fire, like a cherubin, / For he had carbuncles."

- **Irony** The contrast between expectation and reality is known as irony. The ironist seems to be writing with tongue in cheek, and Chaucer is a master of it. While calling attention to his characters' faults, he also emphasizes their essential humanity. This gives his writing a tone of detachment and compassion. Note the irony he uses in his description of the Doctor, one of the pilgrims described in "The Prologue" to *The Canterbury Tales*.

> Yet he was rather close as to expenses
> And kept the gold he won in pestilences.
> Gold stimulates the heart, or so we're told.
> He therefore had a special love of gold.
>
> —*from* "The Prologue"

- **Characterization** A writer develops characters by describing their physical appearance, making direct statements about them, and allowing them to express their personalities through dialogue. In *The Canterbury Tales*, each of Chaucer's characters is also clearly differentiated by the type of story he or she tells and the voice in which each tale is told. Compare these two passages, the first narrated by the Pardoner, and the second narrated by the Wife of Bath.

> It's of three rioters I have to tell
> Who, long before the morning service bell,
> Were sitting in a tavern for a drink.
>
> —*from* "The Pardoner's Tale"

> Others assert we women find it sweet
> When we are thought dependable, discreet
> And secret, firm of purpose and controlled,
> Never betraying things that we are told.
>
> —*from* "The Wife of Bath's Tale"

CHAUCER'S FRAME STORY

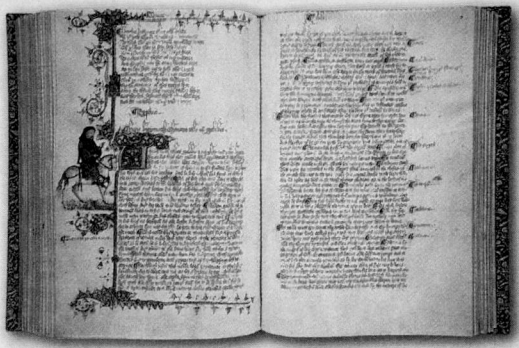

The **frame story** is a literary device that joins together one or more stories within a larger story, or frame. Frame stories have been used throughout the world and date back to antiquity. The *Panchatantra*, a collection of Sanskrit fables gathered around 200 B.C., is an ancient Indian example of a frame story. Giovanni Boccaccio's *Decameron* (page 208) is a well-known Italian frame story in which a collection of stories are told by different characters.

The Canterbury Tales is one of the most famous examples of the frame story. In his innovative use of the device, Chaucer interwove the frame with the tales. The plot of the frame involves pilgrims on a pilgrimage who are challenged to compete in telling the best tale. Chaucer reveals the pilgrims' personalities not only through their interactions between tales but also by the tales they tell. As a result, the frame itself acts as a long and engaging narrative whole.

Close Read

On the basis of these excerpts, how would you characterize the narrator of each tale?

The Prologue
from The Canterbury Tales
Poem by Geoffrey Chaucer Translated by Nevill Coghill

COMMON CORE

RL 1 Cite textual evidence to support analysis of what the text says explicitly. **RL 3** Analyze the impact of the author's choices regarding how to develop and relate elements of a story. **RL 4** Analyze the impact of specific word choices on tone. **RL 10** Read and comprehend literature.

DID YOU KNOW?

Geoffrey Chaucer . . .

- was captured and held for ransom while fighting for England in the Hundred Years' War.
- held various jobs, including royal messenger, justice of the peace, and forester.
- portrayed himself as a foolish character in a number of works.

Meet the Author

Geoffrey Chaucer 1340?–1400

Geoffrey Chaucer made an enormous mark on the language and literature of England. Writing in an age when French was widely spoken in educated circles, Chaucer was among the first writers to show that English could be a respectable literary language. Today, his work is considered a cornerstone of English literature.

Befriended by Royalty Chaucer was born sometime between 1340 and 1343, probably in London, in an era when expanding commerce was helping to bring about growth in villages and cities. His family, though not noble, was well off, and his parents were able to place him in the household of the wife of Prince Lionel, a son of King Edward III, where he served as an attendant. Such a position was a vital means of advancement; the young Chaucer learned the customs of upper-class life and came into contact with influential people. It may have been during this period that Chaucer met Lionel's younger brother, John of Gaunt, who would become Chaucer's lifelong patron and a leading political figure of the day.

A Knight and a Writer Although Chaucer wrote his first important work around 1370, writing was always a sideline; his primary career was in diplomacy. During Richard II's troubled reign (1377 to 1399), Chaucer was appointed a member of Parliament and knight of the shire. When Richard II was overthrown in 1399 by Henry Bolingbroke (who became King Henry IV), Chaucer managed to retain his political position, as Henry was the son of John of Gaunt.

Despite the turmoil of the 1380s and 1390s, the last two decades of Chaucer's life saw his finest literary achievements—the brilliant verse romance *Troilus and Criseyde* and his masterpiece, *The Canterbury Tales,* a collection of verse and prose tales of many different kinds. At the time of his death, Chaucer had penned nearly 20,000 lines of *The Canterbury Tales,* but many more tales were planned.

Uncommon Honor When he died in 1400, Chaucer was accorded a rare honor for a commoner—burial in London's Westminster Abbey. In 1556, an admirer erected an elaborate marble monument to his memory. This was the beginning of the Abbey's famous Poets' Corner, where many of England's most distinguished writers have since been buried.

● TEXT ANALYSIS: CHARACTERIZATION

Characterization refers to the techniques a writer uses to develop characters. In "The Prologue," the introduction to *The Canterbury Tales,* Chaucer offers a vivid portrait of English society during the Middle Ages. Among his 30 characters are clergy, aristocrats, and commoners. Chaucer employs a dramatic structure similar to Boccaccio's *The Decameron*—each pilgrim tells a tale. Some of the ways Chaucer characterizes the pilgrims include

- description of a character's appearance
- examples of a character's speech, thoughts, and actions
- the responses of others to a character
- the narrator's direct, or explicit, comments about a character

As you read, look for details that reveal the **character traits,** or consistent qualities, of each pilgrim.

▇ READING STRATEGY: PARAPHRASE

Reading medieval texts, such as *The Canterbury Tales,* can be challenging because they often contain unfamiliar words and complex sentences. One way that you can make sense of Chaucer's work is to **paraphrase,** or restate information in your own words. A paraphrase is usually the same length as the original text but contains simpler language. As you read, paraphrase difficult passages. Here is an example.

Chaucer's Words	Paraphrase
"When in April the sweet showers fall/And pierce the drought of March to the root, . . ." (lines 1–2)	When the April rains come and end the dryness of March, . . .

▲ VOCABULARY IN CONTEXT

The following boldfaced words are critical to understanding Chaucer's literary masterpiece. Try to figure out the meaning of each word from its context.

1. The refined gentleman always behaved with **courtliness.**
2. She remained calm and **sedately** finished her meal.
3. The popular politician was charming and **personable.**
4. When you save money in a bank, interest will **accrue.**
5. Does she suffer from heart disease or another **malady?**
6. She made an **entreaty** to the king, asking for a pardon.

 Complete the activities in your **Reader/Writer Notebook.**

What makes a great CHARACTER?

Creating a great character requires a sharp eye for detail, a keen understanding of people, and a brilliant imagination—all of which Chaucer possessed. Chaucer populated *The Canterbury Tales* with a colorful cast of characters whose virtues and flaws ring true even today, hundreds of years later.

QUICKWRITE Work with a partner to invent a character. Start with an intriguing name. Then come up with questions that will reveal basic information about the character, such as his or her age, physical appearance, family and friends, job, home, and personal tastes. Brainstorm possible answers for the questions. Then circle the responses that have the best potential for making a lively character.

Name: Bartholomew
　　　Throckmorton
1. What is his occupation?
　　duke
　　squire to a knight
　　sea captain
　　(town doctor)
　　grave digger
2. Where does he live?
3.
4.
5.

The CANTERBURY TALES

Geoffrey Chaucer

The PROLOGUE

> **BACKGROUND** In "The Prologue" of *The Canterbury Tales,* a group gathers at the Tabard Inn in Southwark, a town just south of London, to make a pilgrimage to the shrine of Saint Thomas à Becket at Canterbury. At the suggestion of the innkeeper, the group decides to hold a storytelling competition to pass the time as they travel. "The Prologue" introduces the "sundry folk" who will tell the stories and is followed by the tales themselves—24 in all.

When in April the sweet showers fall
And pierce the drought of March to the root, and all
The veins are bathed in liquor of such power
As brings about the engendering of the flower,
5 When also Zephyrus with his sweet breath
Exhales an air in every grove and heath
Upon the tender shoots, and the young sun
His half-course in the sign of the *Ram* has run,
And the small fowl are making melody
10 That sleep away the night with open eye
(So nature pricks them and their heart engages)
Then people long to go on pilgrimages
And palmers long to seek the stranger strands
Of far-off saints, hallowed in sundry lands,
15 And specially, from every shire's end
Of England, down to Canterbury they wend
To seek the holy blissful martyr, quick
To give his help to them when they were sick. **A**

It happened in that season that one day
20 In Southwark, at *The Tabard*, as I lay

5 Zephyrus (zĕf′ər-əs): the Greek god of the west wind.

8 the Ram: Aries—the first sign of the zodiac. The time is mid-April.

13 palmers: people journeying to religious shrines; pilgrims; **strands:** shores.

14 sundry (sŭn′drē): various.

15 shire's: county's.

17 martyr: St. Thomas à Becket.

A PARAPHRASE
Restate lines 1–18. Why does the group make its pilgrimage in April?

Illustrations by Teresa Fasolino.

Ready to go on pilgrimage and start
For Canterbury, most devout at heart,
At night there came into that hostelry
Some nine and twenty in a company
25 Of sundry folk happening then to fall
In fellowship, and they were pilgrims all
That towards Canterbury meant to ride.
The rooms and stables of the inn were wide;
They made us easy, all was of the best.
30 And, briefly, when the sun had gone to rest,
I'd spoken to them all upon the trip
And was soon one with them in fellowship,
Pledged to rise early and to take the way
To Canterbury, as you heard me say.

35 But none the less, while I have time and space,
Before my story takes a further pace,
It seems a reasonable thing to say
What their condition was, the full array
Of each of them, as it appeared to me,
40 According to profession and degree,
And what apparel they were riding in;
And at a Knight I therefore will begin. **B**
There was a *Knight,* a most distinguished man,
Who from the day on which he first began
45 To ride abroad had followed chivalry,
Truth, honor, generousness and courtesy.
He had done nobly in his sovereign's war
And ridden into battle, no man more,
As well in Christian as in heathen places,
50 And ever honored for his noble graces.

When we took Alexandria, he was there.
He often sat at table in the chair
Of honor, above all nations, when in Prussia.
In Lithuania he had ridden, and Russia,
55 No Christian man so often, of his rank.
When, in Granada, Algeciras sank
Under assault, he had been there, and in
North Africa, raiding Benamarin;
In Anatolia he had been as well
60 And fought when Ayas and Attalia fell,
For all along the Mediterranean coast
He had embarked with many a noble host.
In fifteen mortal battles he had been
And jousted for our faith at Tramissene

23 **hostelry** (hŏs′təl-rē): inn.

Language Coach

Roots and Affixes The suffix -*ship* can mean "someone entitled to a specific rank of" (*lordship*), "art or skill of" (*craftsmanship*), or "state of" (*friendship*). Which meaning applies to *fellowship*? Give another example of each use of -*ship*.

B **PARAPHRASE**
Paraphrase lines 35–42. What does the narrator set out to accomplish in "The Prologue"?

45 **chivalry** (shĭv′əl-rē): the code of behavior of medieval knights, which stressed the values listed in line 46.

51 **Alexandria:** a city in Egypt, captured by European Christians in 1365. All the places named in lines 51–64 were scenes of conflicts in which medieval Christians battled Muslims and other non-Christian peoples.

64 **jousted:** fought with a lance in an arranged battle against another knight.

65 Thrice in the lists, and always killed his man.
This same distinguished knight had led the van
Once with the Bey of Balat, doing work
For him against another heathen Turk;
He was of sovereign value in all eyes.
70 And though so much distinguished, he was wise
And in his bearing modest as a maid.
He never yet a boorish thing had said
In all his life to any, come what might;
He was a true, a perfect gentle-knight. **C**

75 Speaking of his equipment, he possessed
Fine horses, but he was not gaily dressed.
He wore a fustian tunic stained and dark
With smudges where his armor had left mark;
Just home from service, he had joined our ranks
80 To do his pilgrimage and render thanks.

He had his son with him, a fine young *Squire*,
A lover and cadet, a lad of fire
With locks as curly as if they had been pressed.
He was some twenty years of age, I guessed.
85 In stature he was of a moderate length,
With wonderful agility and strength.
He'd seen some service with the cavalry
In Flanders and Artois and Picardy
And had done valiantly in little space
90 Of time, in hope to win his lady's grace.
He was embroidered like a meadow bright
And full of freshest flowers, red and white.
Singing he was, or fluting all the day;
He was as fresh as is the month of May.
95 Short was his gown, the sleeves were long and wide;
He knew the way to sit a horse and ride.
He could make songs and poems and recite,
Knew how to joust and dance, to draw and write.
He loved so hotly that till dawn grew pale
100 He slept as little as a nightingale.
Courteous he was, lowly and serviceable,
And carved to serve his father at the table.

There was a *Yeoman* with him at his side,
No other servant; so he chose to ride.
105 This Yeoman wore a coat and hood of green,
And peacock-feathered arrows, bright and keen
And neatly sheathed, hung at his belt the while

65 **thrice:** three times; **lists:** fenced areas for jousting.

66 **van:** vanguard—the troops foremost in an attack.

67 **Bey of Balat:** a Turkish ruler.

C **CHARACTERIZATION**
Reread lines 43–74. What do the Knight's actions on and off the battlefield reveal about his character? Cite details to support your answer.

77 **fustian** (fŭs′chən): a strong cloth made of linen and cotton.

81 **Squire:** a young man attending on and receiving training from a knight.
82 **cadet:** soldier in training.

88 **Flanders and Artois** (är-twä′) **and Picardy** (pĭk′ər-dē): areas in what is now Belgium and northern France.

93 **fluting:** whistling.

103 **Yeoman** (yō′mən): an attendant in a noble household; **him:** the Knight.

—For he could dress his gear in yeoman style,
His arrows never drooped their feathers low—
110 And in his hand he bore a mighty bow.
His head was like a nut, his face was brown.
He knew the whole of woodcraft up and down.
A saucy brace was on his arm to ward
It from the bow-string, and a shield and sword
115 Hung at one side, and at the other slipped
A jaunty dirk, spear-sharp and well-equipped.
A medal of St. Christopher he wore
Of shining silver on his breast, and bore
A hunting-horn, well slung and burnished clean,
120 That dangled from a baldrick of bright green.
He was a proper forester, I guess.

There also was a *Nun,* a Prioress,
Her way of smiling very simple and coy.
Her greatest oath was only "By St. Loy!"
125 And she was known as Madam Eglantyne.
And well she sang a service, with a fine
Intoning through her nose, as was most seemly,
And she spoke daintily in French, extremely,
After the school of Stratford-atte-Bowe;
130 French in the Paris style she did not know.
At meat her manners were well taught withal;
No morsel from her lips did she let fall,
Nor dipped her fingers in the sauce too deep;
But she could carry a morsel up and keep
135 The smallest drop from falling on her breast.
For **courtliness** she had a special zest,
And she would wipe her upper lip so clean
That not a trace of grease was to be seen
Upon the cup when she had drunk; to eat,
140 She reached a hand **sedately** for the meat.
She certainly was very entertaining,
Pleasant and friendly in her ways, and straining
To counterfeit a courtly kind of grace,
A stately bearing fitting to her place,
145 And to seem dignified in all her dealings. **D**
As for her sympathies and tender feelings,
She was so charitably solicitous
She used to weep if she but saw a mouse
Caught in a trap, if it were dead or bleeding.
150 And she had little dogs she would be feeding
With roasted flesh, or milk, or fine white bread.
And bitterly she wept if one were dead

113 **saucy:** jaunty; stylish; **brace:** a leather arm-guard worn by archers.

116 **dirk:** small dagger.
117 **St. Christopher:** patron saint of travelers.

120 **baldrick:** shoulder strap.

122 **Prioress:** a nun ranking just below the abbess (head) of a convent.

124 **St. Loy:** St. Eligius (known as St. Éloi in France).

129 **Stratford-atte-Bowe:** a town (now part of London) near the Prioress's convent.
131 **at meat:** when dining; **withal:** moreover.

courtliness (kôrt′lē-nĭs) *n.* polite, elegant manners; refined behavior

sedately (sĭ-dāt′lē) *adv.* in a composed, dignified manner; calmly

143 **counterfeit:** imitate.

D **CHARACTERIZATION**
Reread lines 122–145. Which details suggest that the Prioress may be trying to appear more sophisticated than she really is?

Or someone took a stick and made it smart;
She was all sentiment and tender heart.
155 Her veil was gathered in a seemly way,
Her nose was elegant, her eyes glass-grey;
Her mouth was very small, but soft and red,
Her forehead, certainly, was fair of spread,
Almost a span across the brows, I own;
160 She was indeed by no means undergrown.
Her cloak, I noticed, had a graceful charm.
She wore a coral trinket on her arm,
A set of beads, the gaudies tricked in green,
Whence hung a golden brooch of brightest sheen
165 On which there first was graven a crowned A,
And lower, *Amor vincit omnia.*

Another *Nun,* the secretary at her cell,
Was riding with her, and *three Priests* as well.

A *Monk* there was, one of the finest sort
170 Who rode the country; hunting was his sport.
A manly man, to be an Abbot able;
Many a dainty horse he had in stable.
His bridle, when he rode, a man might hear
Jingling in a whistling wind as clear,
175 Aye, and as loud as does the chapel bell
Where my lord Monk was Prior of the cell.
The Rule of good St. Benet or St. Maur
As old and strict he tended to ignore;
He let go by the things of yesterday
180 And took the modern world's more spacious way.
He did not rate that text at a plucked hen
Which says that hunters are not holy men
And that a monk uncloistered is a mere
Fish out of water, flapping on the pier,
185 That is to say a monk out of his cloister.
That was a text he held not worth an oyster;
And I agreed and said his views were sound;
Was he to study till his head went round
Poring over books in cloisters? Must he toil
190 As Austin bade and till the very soil?
Was he to leave the world upon the shelf?
Let Austin have his labor to himself.

This Monk was therefore a good man to horse;
Greyhounds he had, as swift as birds, to course.
195 Hunting a hare or riding at a fence

159 span: a unit of length equal to nine inches. A broad forehead was considered a sign of beauty in Chaucer's day.

163 gaudies: the larger beads in a set of prayer beads.

166 *Amor vincit omnia* (ä′môr wĭn′kĭt ôm′nē-ə)**:** Latin for "Love conquers all things."

171 Abbot: the head of a monastery.
172 dainty: excellent.

176 Prior of the cell: head of a subsidiary group of monks.

177 St. Benet . . . St. Maur: St. Benedict, who established a strict set of rules for monks' behavior, and his follower, St. Maurus, who introduced those rules into France.

190 Austin: St. Augustine of Hippo, who recommended that monks engage in hard agricultural labor.

194 to course: for hunting.

Was all his fun, he spared for no expense.
I saw his sleeves were garnished at the hand
With fine grey fur, the finest in the land,
And on his hood, to fasten it at his chin
200 He had a wrought-gold cunningly fashioned pin;
Into a lover's knot it seemed to pass.
His head was bald and shone like looking-glass;
So did his face, as if it had been greased.
He was a fat and **personable** priest;
205 His prominent eyeballs never seemed to settle. **E**
They glittered like the flames beneath a kettle;
Supple his boots, his horse in fine condition.
He was a prelate fit for exhibition,
He was not pale like a tormented soul.
210 He liked a fat swan best, and roasted whole.
His palfrey was as brown as is a berry.

There was a *Friar*, a wanton one and merry,
A Limiter, a very festive fellow.
In all Four Orders there was none so mellow,
215 So glib with gallant phrase and well-turned speech.
He'd fixed up many a marriage, giving each
Of his young women what he could afford her.
He was a noble pillar to his Order.
Highly beloved and intimate was he
220 With County folk within his boundary,
And city dames of honor and possessions;
For he was qualified to hear confessions,

personable (pûr′sə-nə-bəl)
adj. pleasing in behavior and appearance

E **CHARACTERIZATION**
List three **character traits** of the Monk. In what ways does the narrator appear to poke fun at him?

211 palfrey (pôl′frē): saddle horse.

212 Friar: a member of a religious group sworn to poverty and living on charitable donations; **wanton** (wŏn′tən): playful; jolly.

213 Limiter: a friar licensed to beg for donations in a limited area.

214 Four Orders: the four groups of friars—Dominican, Franciscan, Carmelite, and Augustinian.

222 confessions: church rites in which people confess their sins to clergy members. Only certain friars were licensed to hear confessions.

Or so he said, with more than priestly scope;
He had a special license from the Pope.
225 Sweetly he heard his penitents at shrift
With pleasant absolution, for a gift.
He was an easy man in penance-giving
Where he could hope to make a decent living;
It's a sure sign whenever gifts are given
230 To a poor Order that a man's well shriven,
And should he give enough he knew in verity
The penitent repented in sincerity.
For many a fellow is so hard of heart
He cannot weep, for all his inward smart.
235 Therefore instead of weeping and of prayer
One should give silver for a poor Friar's care.
He kept his tippet stuffed with pins for curls,
And pocket-knives, to give to pretty girls.
And certainly his voice was gay and sturdy,
240 For he sang well and played the hurdy-gurdy.
At sing-songs he was champion of the hour.
His neck was whiter than a lily-flower
But strong enough to butt a bruiser down.
He knew the taverns well in every town
245 And every innkeeper and barmaid too
Better than lepers, beggars and that crew, **F**
For in so *eminent* a man as he
It was not fitting with the dignity
Of his position, dealing with a scum
250 Of wretched lepers; nothing good can come
Of commerce with such slum-and-gutter dwellers,
But only with the rich and victual-sellers.
But anywhere a profit might **accrue**
Courteous he was and lowly of service too.
255 Natural gifts like his were hard to match.
He was the finest beggar of his batch,
And, for his begging-district, paid a rent;
His brethren did no poaching where he went.
For though a widow mightn't have a shoe,
260 So pleasant was his holy how-d'ye-do
He got his farthing from her just the same
Before he left, and so his income came
To more than he laid out. And how he romped,
Just like a puppy! He was ever prompt
265 To arbitrate disputes on settling days
(For a small fee) in many helpful ways,
Not then appearing as your cloistered scholar
With threadbare habit hardly worth a dollar,

225 shrift: confession.

230 well shriven: completely forgiven through the rite of confession.
231 verity: truth.

237 tippet: an extension of a hood or sleeve, used as a pocket.

240 hurdy-gurdy: a stringed musical instrument, similar to a lute, played by turning a crank while pressing down keys.

F PARAPHRASE
Restate lines 237–246. How does the Friar spend the money he earns through hearing confessions?

252 victual (vĭt′l): food.

accrue (ə-krōō′) *v.* to be added or gained; to accumulate

261 farthing: a coin of small value used in England until recent times.

265 settling days: days on which disputes were settled out of court. Friars often acted as arbiters in the disputes and charged for their services, though forbidden by the church to do so.

But much more like a Doctor or a Pope.
270 Of double-worsted was the semi-cope
Upon his shoulders, and the swelling fold
About him, like a bell about its mold
When it is casting, rounded out his dress.
He lisped a little out of wantonness
275 To make his English sweet upon his tongue.
When he had played his harp, or having sung,
His eyes would twinkle in his head as bright
As any star upon a frosty night.
This worthy's name was Hubert, it appeared.

280 There was a *Merchant* with a forking beard
And motley dress; high on his horse he sat,
Upon his head a Flemish beaver hat
And on his feet daintily buckled boots.
He told of his opinions and pursuits
285 In solemn tones, he harped on his increase
Of capital; there should be sea-police
(He thought) upon the Harwich-Holland ranges;
He was expert at dabbling in exchanges.
This estimable Merchant so had set
290 His wits to work, none knew he was in debt,
He was so stately in administration,
In loans and bargains and negotiation.
He was an excellent fellow all the same;
To tell the truth I do not know his name. **G**

295 An *Oxford Cleric,* still a student though,
One who had taken logic long ago,
Was there; his horse was thinner than a rake,
And he was not too fat, I undertake,
But had a hollow look, a sober stare;
300 The thread upon his overcoat was bare.
He had found no preferment in the church
And he was too unworldly to make search
For secular employment. By his bed
He preferred having twenty books in red
305 And black, of Aristotle's philosophy,
Than costly clothes, fiddle or psaltery.
Though a philosopher, as I have told,
He had not found the stone for making gold.
Whatever money from his friends he took
310 He spent on learning or another book
And prayed for them most earnestly, returning
Thanks to them thus for paying for his learning.

270 double-worsted (wŏŏs'tĭd): a strong, fairly costly fabric made from tightly twisted woolen yarn; **semi-cope:** a short cloak.

281 motley: multicolored.

282 Flemish: from Flanders, an area in what is now Belgium and northern France.

287 Harwich-Holland ranges: shipping routes between Harwich (hăr'ĭj), a port on England's east coast, and the country of Holland.

288 exchanges: selling foreign currency at a profit.

G PARAPHRASE
Paraphrase lines 284–294. Is the Merchant a successful businessman? Why or why not?

295 Cleric: a student preparing for the priesthood.

301 preferment: advancement.

305 Aristotle's philosophy: the writings of Aristotle, a famous Greek philosopher of the fourth century B.C.

306 psaltery (sôl'tə-rē): a stringed instrument.

307–308 Though a philosopher ... gold: The "philosopher's stone" supposedly turned metals into gold.

His only care was study, and indeed
He never spoke a word more than was need,
315 Formal at that, respectful in the extreme,
Short, to the point, and lofty in his theme.
A tone of moral virtue filled his speech
And gladly would he learn, and gladly teach. **H**

A *Sergeant at the Law* who paid his calls,
320 Wary and wise, for clients at St. Paul's
There also was, of noted excellence.
Discreet he was, a man to reverence,
Or so he seemed, his sayings were so wise.
He often had been Justice of Assize
325 By letters patent, and in full commission.
His fame and learning and his high position
Had won him many a robe and many a fee.
There was no such conveyancer as he;
All was fee-simple to his strong digestion,
330 Not one conveyance could be called in question.
Though there was nowhere one so busy as he,
He was less busy than he seemed to be.
He knew of every judgment, case and crime
Ever recorded since King William's time.
335 He could dictate defenses or draft deeds;
No one could pinch a comma from his screeds
And he knew every statute off by rote.
He wore a homely parti-colored coat,
Girt with a silken belt of pin-stripe stuff;
340 Of his appearance I have said enough.

There was a *Franklin* with him, it appeared;
White as a daisy-petal was his beard.
A sanguine man, high-colored and benign,
He loved a morning sop of cake in wine.
345 He lived for pleasure and had always done,
For he was Epicurus' very son,
In whose opinion sensual delight
Was the one true felicity in sight.
As noted as St. Julian was for bounty
350 He made his household free to all the County.
His bread, his ale were finest of the fine
And no one had a better stock of wine.
His house was never short of bake-meat pies,
Of fish and flesh, and these in such supplies
355 It positively snowed with meat and drink
And all the dainties that a man could think. **I**

H CHARACTERIZATION
Reread lines 295–318. In what ways does the Oxford Cleric differ from the Monk and the Friar? Cite details.

319 Sergeant at the Law: a lawyer appointed by the monarch to serve as a judge.

320 St. Paul's: the cathedral of London, outside which lawyers met clients when the courts were closed.

324 Justice of Assize: a judge who traveled about the country to hear cases.

325 letters patent: royal documents commissioning a judge.

328 conveyancer: a lawyer specializing in conveyances (deeds) and property disputes.

329 fee-simple: property owned without restrictions.

334 King William's time: the reign of William the Conqueror.

336 screeds: documents.

341 Franklin: a wealthy landowner.

343 sanguine (săng'gwĭn): cheerful and good-natured.

346 Epicurus' very son: someone who pursues pleasure as the chief goal in life, as the ancient Greek philosopher Epicurus was supposed to have recommended.

349 St. Julian: the patron saint of hospitality; **bounty:** generosity.

I CHARACTERIZATION
What does the narrator state directly about the Franklin in lines 341–356?

According to the seasons of the year
Changes of dish were ordered to appear.
He kept fat partridges in coops, beyond,
360 Many a bream and pike were in his pond.
Woe to the cook unless the sauce was hot
And sharp, or if he wasn't on the spot!
And in his hall a table stood arrayed
And ready all day long, with places laid.
365 As Justice at the Sessions none stood higher;
He often had been Member for the Shire.
A dagger and a little purse of silk
Hung at his girdle, white as morning milk.
As Sheriff he checked audit, every entry.
370 He was a model among landed gentry.

A *Haberdasher,* a *Dyer,* a *Carpenter,*
A *Weaver* and a *Carpet-maker* were
Among our ranks, all in the livery
Of one impressive guild-fraternity.
375 They were so trim and fresh their gear would pass
For new. Their knives were not tricked out with brass
But wrought with purest silver, which avouches
A like display on girdles and on pouches.
Each seemed a worthy burgess, fit to grace
380 A guild-hall with a seat upon the dais.
Their wisdom would have justified a plan
To make each one of them an alderman;
They had the capital and revenue,
Besides their wives declared it was their due.
385 And if they did not think so, then they ought;
To be called *"Madam"* is a glorious thought,
And so is going to church and being seen
Having your mantle carried, like a queen.

They had a *Cook* with them who stood alone
390 For boiling chicken with a marrow-bone,
Sharp flavoring-powder and a spice for savor.
He could distinguish London ale by flavor,
And he could roast and seethe and broil and fry,
Make good thick soup and bake a tasty pie.
395 But what a pity—so it seemed to me,
That he should have an ulcer on his knee.
As for blancmange, he made it with the best.

There was a *Skipper* hailing from far west;
He came from Dartmouth, so I understood.

365 Sessions: local court proceedings.

366 Member for the Shire: his county's representative in Parliament.

368 girdle: belt.

369 Sheriff: a royal tax collector.

370 landed gentry (jĕn′trē): well-born, wealthy landowners.

371 Haberdasher: a seller of hats and other clothing accessories.

373–374 livery . . . guild-fraternity: uniform of a social or religious organization.

379 burgess (bûr′jĭs): citizen of a town.

382 alderman: town councilor.

388 mantle: cloak.

397 blancmange (blə-mänj′): a thick chicken stew with almonds.

399 Dartmouth (därt′məth): a port in southwestern England.

400 He rode a farmer's horse as best he could,
In a woolen gown that reached his knee.
A dagger on a lanyard falling free
Hung from his neck under his arm and down.
The summer heat had tanned his color brown,
405 And certainly he was an excellent fellow.
Many a draft of vintage, red and yellow,
He'd drawn at Bordeaux, while the trader snored.
The nicer rules of conscience he ignored.
If, when he fought, the enemy vessel sank,
410 He sent his prisoners home; they walked the plank.
As for his skill in reckoning his tides,
Currents and many another risk besides,
Moons, harbors, pilots, he had such dispatch
That none from Hull to Carthage was his match.
415 Hardy he was, prudent in undertaking;
His beard in many a tempest had its shaking,
And he knew all the havens as they were
From Gottland to the Cape of Finisterre,
And every creek in Brittany and Spain;
420 The barge he owned was called *The Maudelayne*.

A *Doctor* too emerged as we proceeded;
No one alive could talk as well as he did
On points of medicine and of surgery,
For, being grounded in astronomy,
425 He watched his patient closely for the hours
When, by his horoscope, he knew the powers
Of favorable planets, then ascendant,
Worked on the images for his dependent.
The cause of every **malady** you'd got
430 He knew, and whether dry, cold, moist or hot;
He knew their seat, their humor and condition.
He was a perfect practicing physician.
These causes being known for what they were,
He gave the man his medicine then and there.
435 All his apothecaries in a tribe
Were ready with the drugs he would prescribe
And each made money from the other's guile;
They had been friendly for a goodish while.
He was well-versed in Aesculapius too
440 And what Hippocrates and Rufus knew
And Dioscorides, now dead and gone,
Galen and Rhazes, Hali, Serapion,
Averroes, Avicenna, Constantine,
Scotch Bernard, John of Gaddesden, Gilbertine.

402 lanyard (lăn'yərd): a cord worn as a necklace.

406 vintage: wine.

407 Bordeaux (bôr-dō'): a region of France famous for its wine.

414 Hull ... Carthage: ports in England and in Spain. The places named in lines 414–419 show that the Skipper is familiar with all the western coast of Europe.

416 tempest: violent storm.

424 astronomy: astrology.

malady (măl'ə-dē) *n.* a disease or disorder; an ailment

430 dry, cold, moist ... hot: in medieval science, the four basic qualities that were thought to combine to form both the four elements of the world (fire, air, water, and earth) and the four humors of the human body.

435 apothecaries (ə-pŏth'ĭ-kĕr'ēz): druggists.

439–444 Aesculapius (ĕs'kyə-lā'pē-əs) ... **Gilbertine:** famous ancient and medieval medical experts.

◀ **Analyze Visuals**
What does this image
reveal about the ways in
which a medieval doctor's
practice differed from
that of a modern doctor?

445 In his own diet he observed some measure;
There were no superfluities for pleasure,
Only digestives, nutritives and such.
He did not read the Bible very much.
In blood-red garments, slashed with bluish grey
450 And lined with taffeta, he rode his way;
Yet he was rather close as to expenses
And kept the gold he won in pestilences.
Gold stimulates the heart, or so we're told.
He therefore had a special love of gold.

455 A worthy *woman* from beside *Bath* city
Was with us, somewhat deaf, which was a pity.
In making cloth she showed so great a bent
She bettered those of Ypres and of Ghent.
In all the parish not a dame dared stir
460 Towards the altar steps in front of her,
And if indeed they did, so wrath was she
As to be quite put out of charity.
Her kerchiefs were of finely woven ground;
I dared have sworn they weighed a good ten pound,
465 The ones she wore on Sunday, on her head.
Her hose were of the finest scarlet red
And gartered tight; her shoes were soft and new.
Bold was her face, handsome, and red in hue.
A worthy woman all her life, what's more
470 She'd had five husbands, all at the church door,
Apart from other company in youth;
No need just now to speak of that, forsooth.

446 superfluities (sōō'pər-flōō'ĭ-tēz):
excesses.

450 taffeta (tăf'ĭ-tə): a stiff, smooth
fabric.

452 pestilences: plagues.

455 Bath: a city in southwestern
England.

458 Ypres (ē'prə) **...Ghent** (gĕnt):
Flemish cities famous in the Middle
Ages for manufacturing fine wool
fabrics.
461 wrath (răth): angry.

463 ground: a textured fabric.

466 hose: stockings.

470 all at the church door: In
medieval times, a marriage was
performed outside or just within the
doors of a church; afterwards, the
marriage party went inside for mass.
472 forsooth: in truth; indeed.

And she had thrice been to Jerusalem,
Seen many strange rivers and passed over them;
475 She'd been to Rome and also to Boulogne,
St. James of Compostella and Cologne,
And she was skilled in wandering by the way.
She had gap-teeth, set widely, truth to say.
Easily on an ambling horse she sat
480 Well wimpled up, and on her head a hat
As broad as is a buckler or a shield;
She had a flowing mantle that concealed
Large hips, her heels spurred sharply under that.
In company she liked to laugh and chat
485 And knew the remedies for love's mischances,
An art in which she knew the oldest dances. **J**

A holy-minded man of good renown
There was, and poor, the *Parson* to a town,
Yet he was rich in holy thought and work.
490 He also was a learned man, a clerk,
Who truly knew Christ's gospel and would preach it
Devoutly to parishioners, and teach it.
Benign and wonderfully diligent,
And patient when adversity was sent
495 (For so he proved in much adversity)
He hated cursing to extort a fee,
Nay rather he preferred beyond a doubt
Giving to poor parishioners round about
Both from church offerings and his property;
500 He could in little find sufficiency.
Wide was his parish, with houses far asunder,
Yet he neglected not in rain or thunder,
In sickness or in grief, to pay a call
On the remotest, whether great or small,
505 Upon his feet, and in his hand a stave.
This noble example to his sheep he gave
That first he wrought, and afterwards he taught;
And it was from the Gospel he had caught
Those words, and he would add this figure too,
510 That if gold rust, what then will iron do?
For if a priest be foul in whom we trust
No wonder that a common man should rust;
And shame it is to see—let priests take stock—
A shitten shepherd and a snowy flock.
515 The true example that a priest should give
Is one of cleanness, how the sheep should live.

**473–476 Jerusalem . . . Rome . . .
Boulogne** (bōō-lōn'), **St. James of
Compostella and Cologne** (kə-lōn'):
popular destinations of religious
pilgrimages in the Middle Ages.

480 wimpled: with her hair and
neck covered by a cloth headdress.
481 buckler: small round shield.

J CHARACTERIZATION
Reread lines 455–486. Which
details help define the Wife of
Bath as a worldly woman?

490 clerk: scholar.

500 sufficiency: enough to get by on.
501 asunder: apart.

505 stave: staff.

507 wrought (rôt): worked.

509 figure: figure of speech.

He did not set his benefice to hire
And leave his sheep encumbered in the mire
Or run to London to earn easy bread
520 By singing masses for the wealthy dead,
Or find some Brotherhood and get enrolled.
He stayed at home and watched over his fold
So that no wolf should make the sheep miscarry.
He was a shepherd and no mercenary. **K**
525 Holy and virtuous he was, but then
Never contemptuous of sinful men,
Never disdainful, never too proud or fine,
But was discreet in teaching and benign.
His business was to show a fair behavior
530 And draw men thus to Heaven and their Savior,
Unless indeed a man were obstinate;
And such, whether of high or low estate,
He put to sharp rebuke, to say the least.
I think there never was a better priest.
535 He sought no pomp or glory in his dealings,
No scrupulosity had spiced his feelings.
Christ and His Twelve Apostles and their lore
He taught, but followed it himself before.

There was a *Plowman* with him there, his brother;
540 Many a load of dung one time or other
He must have carted through the morning dew.
He was an honest worker, good and true,
Living in peace and perfect charity,
And, as the gospel bade him, so did he,
545 Loving God best with all his heart and mind
And then his neighbor as himself, repined
At no misfortune, slacked for no content,
For steadily about his work he went
To thrash his corn, to dig or to manure
550 Or make a ditch; and he would help the poor **L**
For love of Christ and never take a penny
If he could help it, and, as prompt as any,
He paid his tithes in full when they were due
On what he owned, and on his earnings too.
555 He wore a tabard smock and rode a mare.

There was a *Reeve*, also a *Miller*, there,
A College *Manciple* from the Inns of Court,
A papal *Pardoner* and, in close consort,

K **PARAPHRASE**
Restate lines 515–524. In what ways does the Parson serve the members of his parish?

536 scrupulosity (skrŏō′pyə-lŏs′ĭ-tē): excessive concern with fine points of behavior.

L **CHARACTERIZATION**
Compare the Plowman with his brother, the Parson. What character traits do they seem to share?

555 tabard smock: a short loose jacket made of a heavy material.
556 Reeve: an estate manager;
557 Manciple: a servant in charge of purchasing food; **Inns of Court:** London institutions for training law students; **558 Pardoner:** a church official authorized to sell people pardons for their sins.

517 set his benefice (bĕn′ə-fĭs) **to hire:** pay someone to perform his parish duties for him.

A Church-Court *Summoner,* riding at a trot,
560 And finally myself—that was the lot.

The *Miller* was a chap of sixteen stone,
A great stout fellow big in brawn and bone.
He did well out of them, for he could go
And win the ram at any wrestling show.
565 Broad, knotty and short-shouldered, he would boast
He could heave any door off hinge and post,
Or take a run and break it with his head.
His beard, like any sow or fox, was red
And broad as well, as though it were a spade;
570 And, at its very tip, his nose displayed
A wart on which there stood a tuft of hair
Red as the bristles in an old sow's ear.
His nostrils were as black as they were wide.
He had a sword and buckler at his side,
575 His mighty mouth was like a furnace door. Ⓜ
A wrangler and buffoon, he had a store
Of tavern stories, filthy in the main.
His was a master-hand at stealing grain.
He felt it with his thumb and thus he knew
580 Its quality and took three times his due—
A thumb of gold, by God, to gauge an oat!
He wore a hood of blue and a white coat.
He liked to play his bagpipes up and down
And that was how he brought us out of town.

585 The *Manciple* came from the Inner Temple;
All caterers might follow his example
In buying victuals; he was never rash
Whether he bought on credit or paid cash.
He used to watch the market most precisely
590 And got in first, and so he did quite nicely.
Now isn't it a marvel of God's grace
That an illiterate fellow can outpace
The wisdom of a heap of learned men?
His masters—he had more than thirty then—
595 All versed in the abstrusest legal knowledge,
Could have produced a dozen from their College
Fit to be stewards in land and rents and game
To any Peer in England you could name,
And show him how to live on what he had
600 Debt-free (unless of course the Peer were mad)
Or be as frugal as he might desire,
And make them fit to help about the Shire

559 Summoner: a layman with the job of summoning sinners to church courts.

561 stone: a unit of weight equal to 14 pounds.

Ⓜ **GRAMMAR AND STYLE**
Review lines 570–575. Notice how Chaucer uses **similes,** or comparisons, to create a remarkably vivid—and unflattering—portrait of the Miller.

576 wrangler (răng′glər): a loud, argumentative person; **buffoon** (bə-foon′): a fool.

577 in the main: for the most part.

581 thumb of gold: a reference to a proverb, "An honest miller has a golden thumb"—perhaps meaning that there is no such thing as an honest miller.

585 Inner Temple: one of the Inns of Court.

594 his masters: the lawyers that the Manciple feeds.

595 abstrusest: most scholarly and difficult to understand.

597–598 stewards . . . Peer: estate managers for any nobleman.

In any legal case there was to try;
And yet this Manciple could wipe their eye.

605 The *Reeve* was old and choleric and thin;
His beard was shaven closely to the skin,
His shorn hair came abruptly to a stop
Above his ears, and he was docked on top
Just like a priest in front; his legs were lean,
610 Like sticks they were, no calf was to be seen.
He kept his bins and garners very trim;
No auditor could gain a point on him.
And he could judge by watching drought and rain
The yield he might expect from seed and grain.
615 His master's sheep, his animals and hens,
Pigs, horses, dairies, stores and cattle-pens
Were wholly trusted to his government.
He had been under contract to present
The accounts, right from his master's earliest years.
620 No one had ever caught him in arrears.
No bailiff, serf or herdsman dared to kick,
He knew their dodges, knew their every trick;
Feared like the plague he was, by those beneath.
He had a lovely dwelling on a heath,
625 Shadowed in green by trees above the sward.
A better hand at bargains than his lord,

604 wipe their eye: outdo them.

605 choleric (kŏl′ə-rĭk): having a temperament in which yellow bile predominates, and therefore prone to outbursts of anger.
608 docked: clipped short.

611 garners: buildings for storing grain.

617 government: authority.

620 in arrears: with unpaid debts.
621 bailiff: farm manager; **serf:** farm laborer.

625 sward: grassy plot.

He had grown rich and had a store of treasure
Well tucked away, yet out it came to pleasure
His lord with subtle loans or gifts of goods,
630 To earn his thanks and even coats and hoods.
When young he'd learnt a useful trade and still
He was a carpenter of first-rate skill.
The stallion-cob he rode at a slow trot
Was dapple-grey and bore the name of Scot.
635 He wore an overcoat of bluish shade
And rather long; he had a rusty blade
Slung at his side. He came, as I heard tell,
From Norfolk, near a place called Baldeswell.
His coat was tucked under his belt and splayed.
640 He rode the hindmost of our cavalcade.

There was a *Summoner* with us at that Inn,
His face on fire, like a cherubin,
For he had carbuncles. His eyes were narrow,
He was as hot and lecherous as a sparrow.
645 Black scabby brows he had, and a thin beard.
Children were afraid when he appeared.
No quicksilver, lead ointment, tartar creams,
No brimstone, no boracic, so it seems,
Could make a salve that had the power to bite,
650 Clean up or cure his whelks of knobby white
Or purge the pimples sitting on his cheeks.
Garlic he loved, and onions too, and leeks,
And drinking strong red wine till all was hazy.
Then he would shout and jabber as if crazy,
655 And wouldn't speak a word except in Latin
When he was drunk, such tags as he was pat in;
He only had a few, say two or three,
That he had mugged up out of some decree;
No wonder, for he heard them every day.
660 And, as you know, a man can teach a jay
To call out "Walter" better than the Pope.
But had you tried to test his wits and grope
For more, you'd have found nothing in the bag.
Then *"Questio quid juris"* was his tag.
665 He was a noble varlet and a kind one,
You'd meet none better if you went to find one.
Why, he'd allow—just for a quart of wine—
Any good lad to keep a concubine
A twelvemonth and dispense him altogether!
670 And he had finches of his own to feather:
And if he found some rascal with a maid

633 stallion-cob: a thickset, short-legged male horse.

638 Norfolk (nôr′fŏk): a county in eastern England.

642 cherubin (chĕr′ə-bĭn′): a type of angel—in the Middle Ages often depicted with a fiery red face.

643 carbuncles (kär′bŭng′kəlz): big pimples, considered a sign of lechery and drunkenness in the Middle Ages.

647–648 quicksilver . . . boracic (bə-răs′ĭk): substances used as skin medicines in medieval times.

650 whelks (hwĕlks): swellings.

656 tags: brief quotations.

658 mugged up: memorized.

660 jay: a bird that can be taught to mimic human speech without understanding it.

664 Questio quid juris (kwĕs′tē-ō kwĭd yŏŏr′ĭs): Latin for "The question is, What part of the law (is applicable)?"—a statement often heard in medieval courts.

He would instruct him not to be afraid
In such a case of the Archdeacon's curse
(Unless the rascal's soul were in his purse)
675 For in his purse the punishment should be.
"Purse is the good Archdeacon's Hell," said he.
But well I know he lied in what he said;
A curse should put a guilty man in dread,
For curses kill, as shriving brings, salvation.
680 We should beware of excommunication.
Thus, as he pleased, the man could bring duress
On any young fellow in the diocese.
He knew their secrets, they did what he said.
He wore a garland set upon his head
685 Large as the holly-bush upon a stake
Outside an ale-house, and he had a cake,
A round one, which it was his joke to wield
As if it were intended for a shield.

He and a gentle *Pardoner* rode together,
690 A bird from Charing Cross of the same feather,
Just back from visiting the Court of Rome.
He loudly sang, *"Come hither, love, come home!"*
The Summoner sang deep seconds to this song,
No trumpet ever sounded half so strong.
695 This Pardoner had hair as yellow as wax,
Hanging down smoothly like a hank of flax.
In driblets fell his locks behind his head
Down to his shoulders which they overspread;
Thinly they fell, like rat-tails, one by one.
700 He wore no hood upon his head, for fun;
The hood inside his wallet had been stowed,
He aimed at riding in the latest mode;
But for a little cap his head was bare
And he had bulging eye-balls, like a hare.
705 He'd sewed a holy relic on his cap;
His wallet lay before him on his lap,
Brimful of pardons come from Rome, all hot.
He had the same small voice a goat has got.
His chin no beard had harbored, nor would harbor,
710 Smoother than ever chin was left by barber.
I judge he was a gelding, or a mare.
As to his trade, from Berwick down to Ware
There was no pardoner of equal grace,
For in his trunk he had a pillow-case
715 Which he asserted was Our Lady's veil.

673 Archdeacon's curse: excommunication—an official exclusion of a person from participating in the rites of the church. (An archdeacon is a high church official.)

681 duress (dŏŏ-rĕs'): compulsion by means of threats.

682 diocese (dī'ə-sĭs): the district under a bishop's supervision.

685–686 the holly-bush ... ale-house: Since few people could read in the Middle Ages, many businesses identified themselves with symbols. Outside many taverns could be found wreaths of holly on stakes.

690 Charing Cross: a section of London.

696 flax: a pale grayish yellow fiber used for making linen cloth.

701 wallet: knapsack.

705 holy relic: an object revered because of its association with a holy person.

711 gelding (gĕl'dĭng): a castrated horse—here, a eunuch.

712 Berwick (bĕr'ĭk) ... **Ware:** towns in the north and the south of England.

715 Our Lady's veil: the kerchief of the Virgin Mary.

He said he had a gobbet of the sail
Saint Peter had the time when he made bold
To walk the waves, till Jesu Christ took hold.
He had a cross of metal set with stones
720 And, in a glass, a rubble of pigs' bones.
And with these relics, any time he found
Some poor up-country parson to astound,
In one short day, in money down, he drew
More than the parson in a month or two,
725 And by his flatteries and prevarication
Made monkeys of the priest and congregation. **N**
But still to do him justice first and last
In church he was a noble ecclesiast.
How well he read a lesson or told a story!
730 But best of all he sang an Offertory,
For well he knew that when that song was sung
He'd have to preach and tune his honey-tongue
And (well he could) win silver from the crowd.
That's why he sang so merrily and loud.

735 Now I have told you shortly, in a clause,
The rank, the array, the number and the cause
Of our assembly in this company
In Southwark, at that high-class hostelry
Known as *The Tabard,* close beside *The Bell.*
740 And now the time has come for me to tell
How we behaved that evening; I'll begin
After we had alighted at the Inn,
Then I'll report our journey, stage by stage,
All the remainder of our pilgrimage.
745 But first I beg of you, in courtesy,
Not to condemn me as unmannerly
If I speak plainly and with no concealings
And give account of all their words and dealings,
Using their very phrases as they fell.
750 For certainly, as you all know so well,
He who repeats a tale after a man
Is bound to say, as nearly as he can,
Each single word, if he remembers it,
However rudely spoken or unfit,
755 Or else the tale he tells will be untrue,
The things pretended and the phrases new.
He may not flinch although it were his brother,
He may as well say one word as another.
And Christ Himself spoke broad in Holy Writ,
760 Yet there is no scurrility in it,

716 gobbet: piece.

717–718 when he ... took hold: a reference to an incident in which Jesus extended a helping hand to Peter as he tried to walk on water (Matthew 14:29–31).

N PARAPHRASE
Paraphrase the description of the Pardoner in lines 712–726. How exactly does he earn a living?

739 The Bell: another inn.

745–756 The narrator apologizes in advance for using the exact words of his companions.

759 broad: bluntly; plainly.

760 scurrility (skə-rĭl′ĭ-tē): vulgarity; coarseness.

And Plato says, for those with power to read,
"The word should be as cousin to the deed."
Further I beg you to forgive it me
If I neglect the order and degree
765 And what is due to rank in what I've planned.
I'm short of wit as you will understand.

Our *Host* gave us great welcome; everyone
Was given a place and supper was begun.
He served the finest victuals you could think,
770 The wine was strong and we were glad to drink.
A very striking man our Host withal,
And fit to be a marshal in a hall.
His eyes were bright, his girth a little wide;
There is no finer burgess in Cheapside.
775 Bold in his speech, yet wise and full of tact,
There was no manly attribute he lacked,
What's more he was a merry-hearted man.
After our meal he jokingly began
To talk of sport, and, among other things
780 After we'd settled up our reckonings,
He said as follows: "Truly, gentlemen,
You're very welcome and I can't think when
—Upon my word I'm telling you no lie—
I've seen a gathering here that looked so spry,
785 No, not this year, as in this tavern now.
I'd think you up some fun if I knew how.
And, as it happens, a thought has just occurred

761 Plato (plā′tō): a famous philosopher of ancient Greece.

767 Host: the innkeeper of the Tabard.

772 marshal in a hall: an official in charge of arranging a nobleman's banquet.

774 Cheapside: the main business district of London in Chaucer's day.

780 settled up our reckonings: paid our bills.

To please you, costing nothing, on my word.
You're off to Canterbury—well, God speed!
790 Blessed St. Thomas answer to your need!
And I don't doubt, before the journey's done
You mean to while the time in tales and fun.
Indeed, there's little pleasure for your bones
Riding along and all as dumb as stones.
795 So let me then propose for your enjoyment,
Just as I said, a suitable employment.
And if my notion suits and you agree
And promise to submit yourselves to me
Playing your parts exactly as I say
800 Tomorrow as you ride along the way,
Then by my father's soul (and he is dead)
If you don't like it you can have my head!
Hold up your hands, and not another word."

Well, our opinion was not long deferred,
805 It seemed not worth a serious debate;
We all agreed to it at any rate
And bade him issue what commands he would.
"My lords," he said, "now listen for your good,
And please don't treat my notion with disdain.
810 This is the point. I'll make it short and plain.
Each one of you shall help to make things slip
By telling two stories on the outward trip
To Canterbury, that's what I intend,
And, on the homeward way to journey's end
815 Another two, tales from the days of old;
And then the man whose story is best told,
That is to say who gives the fullest measure
Of good morality and general pleasure,
He shall be given a supper, paid by all,
820 Here in this tavern, in this very hall,
When we come back again from Canterbury. ⊙
And in the hope to keep you bright and merry
I'll go along with you myself and ride
All at my own expense and serve as guide.
825 I'll be the judge, and those who won't obey
Shall pay for what we spend upon the way.
Now if you all agree to what you've heard
Tell me at once without another word,
And I will make arrangements early for it."

790 **St. Thomas:** St. Thomas à Becket, to whose shrine the pilgrims are traveling.

794 **dumb:** silent.

Language Coach

Multiple Meanings *Submit* has several meanings: (1) to yield to someone else's power, (2) to present for review, (3) to present as an opinion. Which meaning applies in line 798? Which meaning applies in this sentence? *I will submit my article to the school newspaper.*

807 **bade him:** asked him to.

COMMON CORE RL 4

⊙ **TONE**
In literature, **tone** refers to the attitude a writer takes toward a subject or character. A writer can communicate tone through diction, choice of details, and direct statements of his or her opinion. Tone can be serious, playful, admiring, mocking, or objective. How would you describe Chaucer's tone toward his characters throughout "The Prologue"? Why do you think he portrays his characters this way?

830 Of course we all agreed, in fact we swore it
Delightedly, and made **entreaty** too
That he should act as he proposed to do,
Become our Governor in short, and be
Judge of our tales and general referee,
835 And set the supper at a certain price.
We promised to be ruled by his advice
Come high, come low; unanimously thus
We set him up in judgment over us.
More wine was fetched, the business being done;
840 We drank it off and up went everyone
To bed without a moment of delay. ❿

Early next morning at the spring of day
Up rose our Host and roused us like a cock,
Gathering us together in a flock,
845 And off we rode at slightly faster pace
Than walking to St. Thomas' watering-place;
And there our Host drew up, began to ease
His horse, and said, "Now, listen if you please,
My lords! Remember what you promised me.
850 If evensong and matins will agree
Let's see who shall be first to tell a tale.
And as I hope to drink good wine and ale
I'll be your judge. The rebel who disobeys,
However much the journey costs, he pays.
855 Now draw for cut and then we can depart;
The man who draws the shortest cut shall start."

entreaty (ĕn-trē′tē) *n.* a serious request or plea

❿ **CHARACTERIZATION**
Examine the way the pilgrims respond to the Host in lines 830–841. What type of person do you think would appeal to so many?

843 cock: rooster (whose cry rouses people from sleep).

846 St. Thomas' watering-place: a brook about two miles from London.

850 If evensong and matins (măt′nz) **will agree:** if what you said last night is what you will do this morning. (Evensong and matins are evening and morning prayer services.)

855 draw for cut: draw lots.

Comprehension

1. **Recall** When and where does "The Prologue" take place?

2. **Recall** What event or circumstance causes the characters to gather?

3. **Summarize** What plan does the Host propose to the characters?

Text Analysis

● 4. **Analyze Characterization** Throughout the selection, Chaucer uses physical details—eyes, hair, clothing—to help develop his **characters.** Choose three pilgrims and describe how their outward appearances reflect their personalities.

5. **Identify Irony** Much of the humor of "The Prologue" is based on irony, the discrepancy between what appears to be true and what actually is true. Explain the irony in each of the following character portraits:

   - the Nun Prioress
   - the Merchant
   - the Skipper
   - the Doctor

● 6. **Draw Conclusions** Review what you **paraphrased** as you read the selection. Describe the narrator's personality and values.

7. **Examine Satire** A writer who pokes fun at behaviors and customs with the intent of improving society is creating **satire.** Review the descriptions of the Monk and the Friar in lines 169–279. What aspects of the medieval church does Chaucer satirize through these characters?

8. **Interpret Tone** In literature, **tone** refers to the attitude a writer takes toward a subject or character. Tone can be serious, playful, admiring, mocking, or objective. Review lines 455–486. What is Chaucer's tone toward the Wife of Bath? Cite specific words and phrases to support your answer.

Text Criticism

9. **Critical Interpretations** In 1809, the English poet and artist William Blake made the following observation: "Chaucer's pilgrims are the characters which compose all ages and nations. . . . Some of the names or titles are altered by time, but the characters themselves forever remain unaltered." Do you agree or disagree that Chaucer's characters seem timeless and universal? Support your opinion with details from the text and your own experiences.

> *What makes a great* **CHARACTER?**
>
> Which of Chaucer's characters do you like best? Which character traits make this character appealing to you?

COMMON CORE

RL 1 Cite textual evidence to support analysis of what the text says explicitly. **RL 3** Analyze the impact of the author's choices regarding how to develop and relate elements of a story. **RL 4** Analyze the impact of specific word choices on tone. **RL 6** Analyze a case in which grasping a point of view requires distinguishing what is directly stated in a text from what is really meant (e.g., irony). **RL 10** Read and comprehend literature.

Vocabulary in Context

▲ VOCABULARY PRACTICE

Use the details from "The Prologue" and your understanding of the boldfaced words to help you choose the answer to each question.

1. Which of these characters shows the most **courtliness?**
2. Which of these characters seems the most **personable?**
3. What does the Doctor believe can cause a **malady?**
4. Which of these characters tries the most to behave **sedately?**
5. Which character has seen money **accrue** in his savings?
6. To whom do the pilgrims make an **entreaty** about judging the story contest?

WORD LIST

accrue

courtliness

entreaty

malady

personable

sedately

ACADEMIC VOCABULARY IN WRITING

> • concept • culture • parallel • section • structure

Chaucer characters embody abstract **concepts** like greed and vanity, yet remain fully-realized, three-dimesional characters. Using at least two additional Academic Vocabulary words, write about how the **structure** of "The Prologue" allows Chaucer to give such a complete picture of the pilgrims.

VOCABULARY STRATEGY: WORDS FROM FRENCH

French has contributed words to English since the French-speaking Normans invaded England in 1066. A huge number of our "Latin" words actually come from Latin by way of Old French. Knowing the French origins of a word can help you understand its meanings. For example, knowing that *parley* comes from the French *parler,* which means "to speak," will tell you that a *parley* is a conference.

PRACTICE Based on the word list to the right and the following word bank, respond each item below:

> • malady • personable • entreaty • court • accrue

1. The words *accretion* and _____ both contain the core meaning of the Old French word *acreu.* What is that core meaning? _____

2. The core meaning of the English word _____ can be found in the Old French word for "sick." What is that word? _____

3. If the Normans had not invaded England in 1066, we might not say a friendly individual is _____.

4. Although it did not survive into Modern French, the Old French word *entraiter* survives in English in the form of _____.

Old French Root	Original Meaning
acreu	increased
entraiter	to deal with, beseech
malade	sick
persone	person

COMMON CORE

L 4 Determine or clarify the meaning of unknown words. **L 6** Acquire and use accurately general academic and domain-specific words.

Interactive Vocabulary **THINK** central

Go to **thinkcentral.com.**
KEYWORD: HML12-168

The Age of Chaucer

from The Pardoner's Tale
from The Canterbury Tales

Poem by Geoffrey Chaucer
Translated by Nevill Coghill

COMMON CORE

RL 3, RL 4, RL 6, RL 10

● **TEXT ANALYSIS: EXEMPLUM**

An **exemplum** is a short anecdote or story that illustrates a particular moral point. Developed in the late Middle Ages, this literary form was often used in sermons and other didactic literature. One famous example is Chaucer's "The Pardoner's Tale," which focuses on the subject of greed. As you read the selection, pay attention to the actions of the characters and to the narrator's description of his own practices.

Review: **Irony**

● **READING SKILL: PREDICT**

When you **predict,** you make guesses about what will happen next in a story based on text clues and your own prior knowledge. Predicting helps you become engaged in the story and motivates you to read on. To make predictions about "The Pardoner's Tale," use the following strategies:

• Note **foreshadowing,** or hints about future plot events.
• Think about the words, actions, and personalities of the three rioters to predict their behavior throughout the story.

As you read, record your predictions and any helpful text clues in a chart like the one shown. Later, complete the chart by explaining the actual outcomes of the story's events.

Predictions	Text Clues	Outcomes
The rioters will experience trouble.	The tavern boy warns them about the plague.	

▲ **VOCABULARY IN CONTEXT**

To see how many vocabulary words you already know, substitute a different word for each boldfaced term.

1. The miser demonstrated his **avarice** by amassing coins.
2. She used harsh words to **castigate** his awful behavior.
3. The two enemies came together for a secret **parley.**

 Complete the activities in your **Reader/Writer Notebook.**

What has the power to CORRUPT?

In the introduction to his tale, the Pardoner states, *"Radix malorum est cupiditas,"* which is Latin for "The love of money is the root of all evil"—a passage from the Bible. The expression suggests that the desire for riches often seduces people into abandoning their moral principles. Today, as in Chaucer's time, greed and other elements of human weakness often trigger grave acts of corruption.

DISCUSS With a small group of classmates, list several examples of corruption. Discuss the factors that you think prompted people to commit corrupt acts. Compare your conclusions with those of other groups.

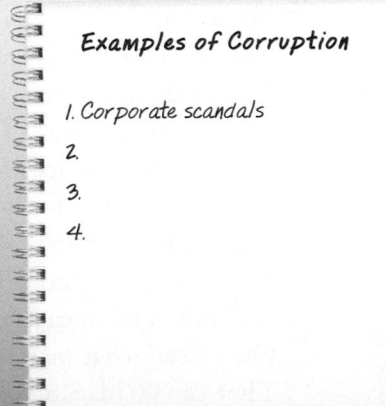

Examples of Corruption

1. Corporate scandals
2.
3.
4.

The PARDONER'S PROLOGUE

Geoffrey Chaucer

> **BACKGROUND** In the medieval church, a pardoner was a clergy member who had authority from the pope to grant indulgences—certificates of forgiveness—to people who showed great charity. In practice, however, many pardoners—such as Chaucer's pilgrim—were unethical and sold their certificates to make money for the church or themselves.

"My lords," he said, "in churches where I preach
I cultivate a haughty kind of speech
And ring it out as roundly as a bell;
I've got it all by heart, the tale I tell.
5 I have a text, it always is the same
And always has been, since I learnt the game,
Old as the hills and fresher than the grass,
Radix malorum est cupiditas. . . .

"I preach, as you have heard me say before,
10 And tell a hundred lying mockeries more.
I take great pains, and stretching out my neck
To east and west I crane about and peck
Just like a pigeon sitting on a barn.
My hands and tongue together spin the yarn
15 And all my antics are a joy to see.
The curse of **avarice** and cupidity
Is all my sermon, for it frees the pelf.
Out come the pence, and specially for myself,
For my exclusive purpose is to win
20 And not at all to **castigate** their sin.
Once dead what matter how their souls may fare?
They can go blackberrying, for all I care! . . .

"And thus I preach against the very vice
I make my living out of—avarice. **A**
25 And yet however guilty of that sin
Myself, with others I have power to win
Them from it, I can bring them to repent;
But that is not my principal intent.

Analyze Visuals ▶
What details in this image reflect the Pardoner's description of his preaching?

8 *Radix malorum est cupiditas* (rä′dĭks mä-lôr′əm ĕst′ kōō-pĭd′ĭ-täs′): Latin for "The love of money is the root of all evil" (1 Timothy 6:10).
10 mockeries: false tales.

avarice (ăv′ə-rĭs) *n.* greed

17 pelf: riches.
18 pence: pennies.

castigate (kăs′tĭ-gāt′) *v.* to criticize

A PREDICT
The Pardoner convinces people to buy certificates of forgiveness by reciting his moral stories. What can you predict about the characters and events of the tale he will tell?

Covetousness is both the root and stuff
30 Of all I preach. That ought to be enough.

"Well, then I give examples thick and fast
From bygone times, old stories from the past.
A yokel mind loves stories from of old,
Being the kind it can repeat and hold.
35 What! Do you think, as long as I can preach
And get their silver for the things I teach,
That I will live in poverty, from choice?
That's not the counsel of my inner voice!
No! Let me preach and beg from kirk to kirk
40 And never do an honest job of work,
No, nor make baskets, like St. Paul, to gain
A livelihood. I do not preach in vain.
There's no apostle I would counterfeit;
I mean to have money, wool and cheese and wheat
45 Though it were given me by the poorest lad
Or poorest village widow, though she had
A string of starving children, all agape. **B**
No, let me drink the liquor of the grape
And keep a jolly wench in every town!

50 "But listen, gentlemen; to bring things down
To a conclusion, would you like a tale?
Now as I've drunk a draft of corn-ripe ale,
By God it stands to reason I can strike
On some good story that you all will like.
55 For though I am a wholly vicious man
Don't think I can't tell moral tales. I can!
Here's one I often preach when out for winning. . . ."

33 yokel: rustic.

39 kirk: church.

41 St. Paul: a follower of Jesus Christ who made baskets and tents.

43 counterfeit: imitate.

B IRONY
Review lines 39–47. Why does the Pardoner tell his moral stories? Explain how his motive is ironic, or different from what you might have expected.

55 vicious: immoral; depraved.

The PARDONER'S TALE

It's of three rioters I have to tell
Who, long before the morning service bell,
60 Were sitting in a tavern for a drink.
And as they sat, they heard the hand-bell clink
Before a coffin going to the grave;
One of them called the little tavern-knave
And said "Go and find out at once—look spry!—
65 Whose corpse is in that coffin passing by;
And see you get the name correctly too."

"Sir," said the boy, "no need, I promise you;
Two hours before you came here I was told.
He was a friend of yours in days of old,
70 And suddenly, last night, the man was slain,
Upon his bench, face up, dead drunk again.
There came a privy thief, they call him Death,
Who kills us all round here, and in a breath
He speared him through the heart, he never stirred.
75 And then Death went his way without a word.
He's killed a thousand in the present plague,
And, sir, it doesn't do to be too vague
If you should meet him; you had best be wary.
Be on your guard with such an adversary,
80 Be primed to meet him everywhere you go,
That's what my mother said. It's all I know."

The publican joined in with, "By St. Mary,
What the child says is right; you'd best be wary,
This very year he killed, in a large village
85 A mile away, man, woman, serf at tillage,
Page in the household, children—all there were.
Yes, I imagine that he lives round there.
It's well to be prepared in these alarms,
He might do you dishonor." "Huh, God's arms!" **C**
90 The rioter said, "Is he so fierce to meet?
I'll search for him, by Jesus, street by street.
God's blessed bones! I'll register a vow!

---

58 rioters: rowdy people; revelers.

61–62 hand-bell . . . grave: In Chaucer's time, a bell was carried beside the coffin in a funeral procession.

63 tavern-knave (nāv): a serving boy in an inn.

72 privy (prĭv′ē): hidden; secretive.

76 Bubonic plague killed at least a quarter of the population of Europe in the mid-14th century.

82 publican: innkeeper; tavern owner.

86 page: boy servant.

C EXEMPLUM
Many characters in moral stories are **allegorical**— that is, they stand for abstract ideas, such as virtue and beauty. Identify the allegorical character presented in lines 72–89. Who fears him? Why?

Here, chaps! The three of us together now,
Hold up your hands, like me, and we'll be brothers
95 In this affair, and each defend the others,
And we will kill this traitor Death, I say!
Away with him as he has made away
With all our friends. God's dignity! Tonight!"

They made their bargain, swore with appetite,
100 These three, to live and die for one another
As brother-born might swear to his born brother.
And up they started in their drunken rage
And made towards this village which the page
And publican had spoken of before.
105 Many and grisly were the oaths they swore,
Tearing Christ's blessed body to a shred;
"If we can only catch him, Death is dead!" **D**

When they had gone not fully half a mile,
Just as they were about to cross a stile,
110 They came upon a very poor old man
Who humbly greeted them and thus began,
"God look to you, my lords, and give you quiet!"
To which the proudest of these men of riot
Gave back the answer, "What, old fool? Give place!
115 Why are you all wrapped up except your face?
Why live so long? Isn't it time to die?"

The old, old fellow looked him in the eye
And said, "Because I never yet have found,
Though I have walked to India, searching round
120 Village and city on my pilgrimage,
One who would change his youth to have my age.
And so my age is mine and must be still
Upon me, for such time as God may will.

"Not even Death, alas, will take my life;
125 So, like a wretched prisoner at strife
Within himself, I walk alone and wait
About the earth, which is my mother's gate,
Knock-knocking with my staff from night to noon
And crying, 'Mother, open to me soon!
130 Look at me, mother, won't you let me in?
See how I wither, flesh and blood and skin!
Alas! When will these bones be laid to rest?
Mother, I would exchange—for that were best—
The wardrobe in my chamber, standing there

D **PREDICT**
What qualities of the three men
does Chaucer emphasize in
lines 93–107? Predict what will
happen to them based on these
text clues.

109 stile: a stairway used to climb
over a fence or wall.

129 The old man addresses the earth
as his mother (recall the familiar
expressions "Mother Earth" and
"Mother Nature").

135 So long, for yours! Aye, for a shirt of hair
    To wrap me in!' She has refused her grace,
    Whence comes the pallor of my withered face.

        "But it dishonored you when you began
    To speak so roughly, sir, to an old man,
140 Unless he had injured you in word or deed.
    It says in holy writ, as you may read,
    'Thou shalt rise up before the hoary head
    And honor it.' And therefore be it said
    'Do no more harm to an old man than you,
145 Being now young, would have another do
    When you are old'—if you should live till then.
    And so may God be with you, gentlemen,
    For I must go whither I have to go."

135 **shirt of hair:** a rough shirt made
of animal hair, worn to punish
oneself for one's sins.

142 **hoary:** gray or white with age.

"By God," the gambler said, "you shan't do so,
150 You don't get off so easy, by St. John!
I heard you mention, just a moment gone,
A certain traitor Death who singles out
And kills the fine young fellows hereabout.
And you're his spy, by God! You wait a bit.
155 Say where he is or you shall pay for it,
By God and by the Holy Sacrament!
I say you've joined together by consent
To kill us younger folk, you thieving swine!" **E**

"Well, sirs," he said, "if it be your design
160 To find out Death, turn up this crooked way
Towards that grove, I left him there today
Under a tree, and there you'll find him waiting.
He isn't one to hide for all your prating.
You see that oak? He won't be far to find.
165 And God protect you that redeemed mankind,
Aye, and amend you!" Thus that ancient man.

At once the three young rioters began
To run, and reached the tree, and there they found
A pile of golden florins on the ground,
170 New-coined, eight bushels of them as they thought.
No longer was it Death those fellows sought,
For they were all so thrilled to see the sight,
The florins were so beautiful and bright,
That down they sat beside the precious pile.
175 The wickedest spoke first after a while.
"Brothers," he said, "you listen to what I say.
I'm pretty sharp although I joke away.
It's clear that Fortune has bestowed this treasure
To let us live in jollity and pleasure.
180 Light come, light go! We'll spend it as we ought.
God's precious dignity! Who would have thought
This morning was to be our lucky day?" **F**

"If one could only get the gold away,
Back to my house, or else to yours, perhaps—
185 For as you know, the gold is ours, chaps—
We'd all be at the top of fortune, hey?
But certainly it can't be done by day.
People would call us robbers—a strong gang,
So our own property would make us hang.
190 No, we must bring this treasure back by night
Some prudent way, and keep it out of sight.

E EXEMPLUM
To best illustrate a moral point, characters in an exemplum are usually good or evil. To which category does the gambler seem to belong? Cite evidence from lines 149–158 to support your response.

169 **florins:** coins.

178 "Fortune" here means "fate."

F IRONY
Reread lines 167–182. In what way is the discovery the rioters make ironic, or different from what you had anticipated?

And so as a solution I propose
We draw for lots and see the way it goes;
The one who draws the longest, lucky man,
195 Shall run to town as quickly as he can
To fetch us bread and wine—but keep things dark—
While two remain in hiding here to mark
Our heap of treasure. If there's no delay,
When night comes down we'll carry it away,
200 All three of us, wherever we have planned." **G**

He gathered lots and hid them in his hand
Bidding them draw for where the luck should fall.
It fell upon the youngest of them all,
And off he ran at once towards the town.

205   As soon as he had gone the first sat down
And thus began a **parley** with the other:
"You know that you can trust me as a brother;
Now let me tell you where your profit lies;
You know our friend has gone to get supplies
210 And here's a lot of gold that is to be
Divided equally amongst us three.
Nevertheless, if I could shape things thus
So that we shared it out—the two of us—
Wouldn't you take it as a friendly act?"

215   "But how?" the other said. "He knows the fact
That all the gold was left with me and you;
What can we tell him? What are we to do?"

"Is it a bargain," said the first, "or no?
For I can tell you in a word or so
220 What's to be done to bring the thing about."
"Trust me," the other said, "you needn't doubt
My word. I won't betray you, I'll be true."

"Well," said his friend, "you see that we are two,
And two are twice as powerful as one.
225 Now look; when he comes back, get up in fun
To have a wrestle; then, as you attack,
I'll up and put my dagger through his back
While you and he are struggling, as in game;
Then draw your dagger too and do the same.
230 Then all this money will be ours to spend,
Divided equally of course, dear friend.
Then we can **gratify** our lusts and fill

196 **keep things dark:** act in secret, without giving away what has happened.

G PREDICT
Reread lines 183–200. How do you think the three men will react to the challenge of sharing their treasure?

parley (pär′lē) *n.* a discussion or a conference

Language Coach

Fixed Expressions Many verbs take on a special meaning when followed by a particular preposition. An example of this type of fixed expression is *bring about*. Reread lines 219–220: "to bring the thing about" means "to cause the thing." Use *bring about* in another sentence.

The day with dicing at our own sweet will."
Thus these two miscreants agreed to slay
235 The third and youngest, as you heard me say.

The youngest, as he ran towards the town,
Kept turning over, rolling up and down
Within his heart the beauty of those bright
New florins, saying, "Lord, to think I might
240 Have all that treasure to myself alone!
Could there be anyone beneath the throne
Of God so happy as I then should be?" **H**

And so the Fiend, our common enemy,
Was given power to put it in his thought
245 That there was always poison to be bought,
And that with poison he could kill his friends.
To men in such a state the Devil sends
Thoughts of this kind, and has a full permission
To lure them on to sorrow and perdition;
250 For this young man was utterly content
To kill them both and never to repent.

And on he ran, he had no thought to tarry,
Came to the town, found an apothecary
And said, "Sell me some poison if you will,
255 I have a lot of rats I want to kill
And there's a polecat too about my yard
That takes my chickens and it hits me hard;
But I'll get even, as is only right,
With vermin that destroy a man by night."

260 The chemist answered, "I've a preparation
Which you shall have, and by my soul's salvation
If any living creature eat or drink
A mouthful, ere he has the time to think,
Though he took less than makes a grain of wheat,
265 You'll see him fall down dying at your feet;
Yes, die he must, and in so short a while
You'd hardly have the time to walk a mile,
The poison is so strong, you understand."

This cursed fellow grabbed into his hand
270 The box of poison and away he ran
Into a neighboring street, and found a man
Who lent him three large bottles. He withdrew
And deftly poured the poison into two.

233 dicing: gambling with dice.
234 miscreants (mĭs′krē-ənts): evildoers; villains.

H EXEMPLUM
Which details in lines 236–242 tell you that greed is the subject of this moral story?

243 Fiend: the Devil; Satan.

249 perdition: damnation; hell.

COMMON CORE RL 4
Language Coach

Multiple Meanings Usually, the suffix -ion turns a verb into a noun meaning "act or state of (verb + -ing)." But many -ion words also have special meanings. *Preparation* (line 260) means "something prepared" (like medicine). Give a more general meaning of *preparation*.

He kept the third one clean, as well he might,
275 For his own drink, meaning to work all night
Stacking the gold and carrying it away.
And when this rioter, this devil's clay,
Had filled his bottles up with wine, all three,
Back to rejoin his comrades sauntered he. **❶**

280   Why make a sermon of it? Why waste breath?
Exactly in the way they'd planned his death
They fell on him and slew him, two to one.
Then said the first of them when this was done,
"Now for a drink. Sit down and let's be merry,
285 For later on there'll be the corpse to bury."
And, as it happened, reaching for a sup,
He took a bottle full of poison up
And drank; and his companion, nothing loth,
Drank from it also, and they perished both.

290   There is, in Avicenna's long relation
Concerning poison and its operation,
Trust me, no ghastlier section to transcend
What these two wretches suffered at their end.
Thus these two murderers received their due,
295 So did the treacherous young poisoner too. **❶**

    O cursed sin! O blackguardly excess!
O treacherous homicide! O wickedness!
O gluttony that lusted on and diced! . . .
    Dearly beloved, God forgive your sin
300 And keep you from the vice of avarice!
My holy pardon frees you all of this,
Provided that you make the right approaches,
That is with sterling, rings, or silver brooches.
Bow down your heads under this holy bull!
305 Come on, you women, offer up your wool!
I'll write your name into my ledger; so!
Into the bliss of Heaven you shall go.
For I'll absolve you by my holy power,
You that make offering, clean as at the hour
310 When you were born. . . . That, sirs, is how I preach.
And Jesu Christ, soul's healer, aye, the leech
Of every soul, grant pardon and relieve you
Of sin, for that is best, I won't deceive you.

    One thing I should have mentioned in my tale,
315 Dear people. I've some relics in my bale

❶ PREDICT
What do you think will happen to the three men? Support your response with clues from the text.

288 nothing loth: not at all unwilling.

290 Avicenna's (ăv'ĭ-sĕn'əz) **long relation:** a medical text written by an 11th-century Islamic physician; it includes descriptions of various poisons and their effects.

❶ EXEMPLUM
Moral stories usually have straightforward plots, where events happen in quick succession. In what way does the story's conclusion fit this pattern?

299 The Pardoner is now addressing his fellow pilgrims.

304 bull: an official document from the pope.

311 leech: physician.

315 relics in my bale: Relics are the remains of a saint—bones, hair, or clothing. In medieval times, many relics were counterfeit.

And pardons too, as full and fine, I hope,
As any in England, given me by the Pope.
If there be one among you that is willing
To have my absolution for a shilling

320 Devoutly given, come! and do not harden
Your hearts but kneel in humbleness for pardon;
Or else, receive my pardon as we go.
You can renew it every town or so
Always provided that you still renew

325 Each time, and in good money, what is due.
It is an honor to you to have found
A pardoner with his credentials sound
Who can absolve you as you ply the spur
In any accident that may occur.

330 For instance—we are all at Fortune's beck—
Your horse may throw you down and break your neck.
What a security it is to all
To have me here among you and at call
With pardon for the lowly and the great

335 When soul leaves body for the future state!
And I advise our Host here to begin,
The most enveloped of you all in sin.
Come forward, Host, you shall be the first to pay,
And kiss my holy relics right away.

340 Only a groat. Come on, unbuckle your purse!

319 shilling: a coin worth twelve pence.

330–331 The Pardoner reminds the other pilgrims that death may come to them at any time.

340 groat: a silver coin worth four pence.

Comprehension

1. **Recall** What event prompts the three rioters to seek Death?

2. **Clarify** In what way is their discovery at the old tree unexpected?

3. **Summarize** Describe the events that directly lead to their deaths.

COMMON CORE

RL 3 Analyze the impact of the author's choices regarding how to develop and relate elements of a story. **RL 6** Analyze a case in which grasping a point of view requires distinguishing what is directly stated in a text from what is really meant (e.g., irony). **RL 10** Read and comprehend literature.

Text Analysis

4. **Examine Predictions** Look back at your list of predictions and text clues. Were you able to correctly anticipate everything that happened, or were you surprised by how some events developed?

5. **Compare and Contrast Characters** A **foil** is a character who provides a striking contrast to other characters. In what way does the old man serve as a foil to the three rioters?

6. **Analyze Exemplum** For each convention of medieval exemplum listed in the chart shown, provide an example from "The Pardoner's Tale." In what way is this literary form in keeping with the Pardoner's occupation?

Conventions of Medieval Exemplum	Examples
virtuous or evil characters	
tightly structured plot events	
allegorical or symbolic figures	
a distinct moral or lesson	

7. **Make Judgments About Irony** Chaucer is widely admired for his skillful use of irony—the discrepancy between what appears to be true and what actually is true. There are three main types of irony. **Verbal irony** occurs when a character says one thing but means another. **Situational irony** occurs when a character or reader expects one thing to happen but something else actually happens. **Dramatic irony** occurs when the reader or audience knows something that a character does not know. For each type of irony, provide an example from "The Pardoner's Tale." How essential is irony to the meaning of the story?

Text Criticism

8. **Historical Context** During the mid-14th century, the Black Death—a massive epidemic of the bubonic plague—swept through Asia and Europe. In Europe alone, one-quarter of the population died. In what ways might these circumstances have made people vulnerable to the tricks of the Pardoner and other unscrupulous clergymen?

What has the power to **CORRUPT?**

What theme, or central message, about corruption do you think Chaucer conveys in this story? How does it still hold true today?

Vocabulary in Context

▲ VOCABULARY PRACTICE

Indicate why each statement below is true or false. Use your knowledge of the boldfaced words and the context in which they appear to help you answer.

1. Counting your money all the time may be a sign of **avarice.**
2. Wise teachers **castigate** good behavior.
3. A **parley** might lead to peace between warring factions.

ACADEMIC VOCABULARY IN WRITING

> • concept • culture • parallel • section • structure

Would people today be taken in by the Pardoner's performance? Examine the **structure** of "The Pardoner's Tale" in this **section.** Then, write a description of a similar cautionary tale in today's **culture.** Use at least one Academic Vocabulary word in your response.

VOCABULARY STRATEGY: THE PREFIX *mal-*

In line 8 of "The Pardoner's Prologue" (page 170), the Pardoner quotes a Biblical verse in Latin: "*Radix malorum est cupiditas. . . .*" ("The love of money is the root of all evil . . .") You may recognize the word *malorum*. It gives us a prefix to many English words across many content areas: the prefix *mal-*, meaning "bad" or "wrong." To understand the meaning of words that start with *mal-*, use context clues as well as your knowledge of the prefix.

PRACTICE Answer each question in a complete sentence that uses a word from the word web. Then tell in what discipline (medical or legal, for example) each word is more likely to be used. Use your knowledge of the prefix *mal-* to help you, and consult a dictionary if necessary.

1. What might a bad doctor be guilty of?
2. What might happen if a person does not get enough food?
3. What disease might a mosquito carry?
4. What physical condition might develop from chronic pain?
5. What act might result in imprisonment?

Find a technical definition for one or more of the terms above using a **specialized dictionary,** such as a medical or legal dictionary. These can be found in libraries' reference shelves or online databases. Share your definition with the class.

COMMON CORE

L 4d Verify the preliminary determination of the meaning of a word. **L 6** Acquire and use accurately general academic and domain-specific words.

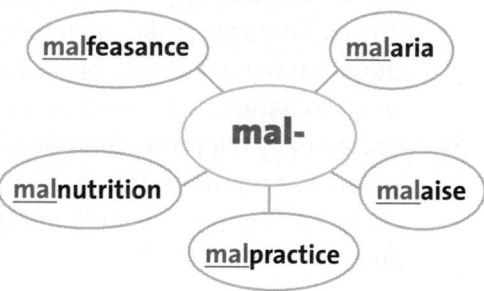

Interactive Vocabulary THINK central

Go to **thinkcentral.com.**
KEYWORD: HML12-182

The Wife of Bath's Tale
from The Canterbury Tales

Poem by Geoffrey Chaucer
Translated by Nevill Coghill

COMMON CORE

RL 3, RL 5

● **TEXT ANALYSIS: NARRATOR**

The **narrator** of a story is the character or voice that relates the story's events to the reader. Many narrators have distinct personalities that are revealed through the subject matter, tone, and language of their stories. In this selection, the narrator is the Wife of Bath, one of the most charismatic characters in *The Canterbury Tales*—and, arguably, in all of English literature. As you read, notice what she reveals about herself and medieval society in her lively tale.

■ **READING SKILL: ANALYZE STRUCTURE**

The Canterbury Tales has a sophisticated **structure,** or organization. The collection features a **frame story**—a story that surrounds and binds together one or more different narratives in a single work. The main story about the pilgrimage serves this purpose. It unifies 24 unrelated tales and provides a rationale for the entire collection.

In the interludes between the pilgrims' tales, the characters often argue with one another. Within the tales, narrators sometimes digress in their storytelling. Both types of interruptions contribute to the poem's overall meaning and its aesthetic impact. Use a chart like the one shown to keep track of these breaks in narration.

Interruptions	Reasons
The Pardoner interrupts the Wife of Bath (lines 1–6).	The previous discussion has made him afraid to marry.

▲ **VOCABULARY IN CONTEXT**

The boldfaced words help convey the wit and charm of the Wife of Bath. Use context clues to guess the meaning of each.

1. **implore** someone for a favor
2. cackle like a **crone**
3. the king's **sovereignty**
4. **bequeath** a legacy
5. everyday **temporal** concerns
6. **rebuke** someone for a mistake

 Complete the activities in your **Reader/Writer Notebook**.

Do men UNDERSTAND *women?*

Many jokes suggest that when it comes to emotional responses and attitudes toward relationships, men and women might as well be from different planets. But is there really such a gulf between the sexes? In "The Wife of Bath's Tale," a man becomes motivated to gain understanding of women when his life is at stake.

QUICKWRITE Are the differences between the sexes fundamental or superficial? Write one or two paragraphs in response to this question. Include examples to support your opinion.

The WIFE OF BATH'S PROLOGUE

Geoffrey Chaucer

The Pardoner started up, and thereupon
"Madam," he said, "by God and by St. John,
That's noble preaching no one could surpass!
I was about to take a wife; alas!
5 Am I to buy it on my flesh so dear?
There'll be no marrying for me this year!"

 "You wait," she said, "my story's not begun.
You'll taste another brew before I've done;
You'll find it doesn't taste as good as ale;
10 And when I've finished telling you my tale
Of tribulation in the married life
In which I've been an expert as a wife,
That is to say, myself have been the whip.
So please yourself whether you want to sip
15 At that same cask of marriage I shall broach.
Be cautious before making the approach,
For I'll give instances, and more than ten.
And those who won't be warned by other men,
By other men shall suffer their correction,
20 So Ptolemy has said, in this connection.
You read his *Almagest;* you'll find it there." **Ⓐ**

 "Madam, I put it to you as a prayer,"
The Pardoner said, "go on as you began!
Tell us your tale, spare not for any man.
25 Instruct us younger men in your technique."
"Gladly," she said, "if you will let me speak,
But still I hope the company won't reprove me
Though I should speak as fantasy may move me,
And please don't be offended at my views;
30 They're really only offered to amuse. . . ."

3 noble preaching: In the passage preceding this excerpt, the Wife of Bath has spoken at length about her view of marriage.

15 cask: barrel; **broach:** tap into.

20 Ptolemy (tŏl'ə-mē): a famous astronomer, mathematician, and geographer of ancient Egypt.

Ⓐ NARRATOR
In lines 7–21, the narrator introduces the subject of her tale—marriage and its many difficulties. What personal opinions and experiences does she also reveal?

The WIFE OF BATH'S TALE

When good King Arthur ruled in ancient days
(A king that every Briton loves to praise)
This was a land brim-full of fairy folk.
The Elf-Queen and her courtiers joined and broke
35 Their elfin dance on many a green mead,
Or so was the opinion once, I read,
Hundreds of years ago, in days of yore.
But no one now sees fairies any more.
For now the saintly charity and prayer
40 Of holy friars seem to have purged the air;
They search the countryside through field and stream
As thick as motes that speckle a sun-beam,
Blessing the halls, the chambers, kitchens, bowers,
Cities and boroughs, castles, courts and towers,
45 Thorpes, barns and stables, outhouses and dairies,
And that's the reason why there are no fairies.
Wherever there was wont to walk an elf
Today there walks the holy friar himself
As evening falls or when the daylight springs,
50 Saying his matins and his holy things,
Walking his limit round from town to town.
Women can now go safely up and down
By every bush or under every tree;
There is no other incubus but he,
55 So there is really no one else to hurt you
And he will do no more than take your virtue. **B**

Now it so happened, I began to say,
Long, long ago in good King Arthur's day,
There was a knight who was a lusty liver.
60 One day as he came riding from the river
He saw a maiden walking all forlorn
Ahead of him, alone as she was born.
And of that maiden, spite of all she said,
By very force he took her maidenhead.
65 This act of violence made such a stir,
So much petitioning to the king for her,
That he condemned the knight to lose his head
By course of law. He was as good as dead
(It seems that then the statutes took that view)
70 But that the queen, and other ladies too,

---

35 mead: meadow.

42 motes: specks of dust.

43 bowers: bedrooms.

45 thorpes: villages; **outhouses:** sheds.

47 wherever . . . elf: wherever an elf was accustomed to walk.

51 limit: the area to which a friar was restricted in his begging for donations.

54 incubus (ĭn′kyə-bəs): an evil spirit believed to descend on women.

B **ANALYZE STRUCTURE**
In the **frame story** of *The Canterbury Tales,* the Wife of Bath and the Friar have an ongoing quarrel. In what way does the Wife of Bath's digression in lines 39–56 reflect this dispute?

63–64 of that maiden . . . maidenhead: in spite of the maiden's protests, he robbed her of her virginity.

Implored the king to exercise his grace
So ceaselessly, he gave the queen the case
And granted her his life, and she could choose
Whether to show him mercy or refuse.

implore (ĭm-plôr') *v.* to plead; to beg

75 The queen returned him thanks with all her might,
And then she sent a summons to the knight
At her convenience, and expressed her will:
"You stand, for such is the position still,
In no way certain of your life," said she,
80 "Yet you shall live if you can answer me:
What is the thing that women most desire?
Beware the axe and say as I require.

     "If you can't answer on the moment, though,
I will concede you this: you are to go
85 A twelvemonth and a day to seek and learn
.   Sufficient answer, then you shall return.
I shall take gages from you to extort
Surrender of your body to the court." **C**

87 gages: pledges.

C NARRATOR
Review lines 57–88. What characteristics of the Wife's narrative style appear in the story's introduction?

     Sad was the knight and sorrowfully sighed,
90 But there! All other choices were denied,

And in the end he chose to go away
And to return after a year and day
Armed with such answer as there might be sent
To him by God. He took his leave and went.

95   He knocked at every house, searched every place,
Yes, anywhere that offered hope of grace.
What could it be that women wanted most?
But all the same he never touched a coast,
Country or town in which there seemed to be
100 Any two people willing to agree.

Some said that women wanted wealth and treasure,
"Honor," said some, some "Jollity and pleasure,"
Some "Gorgeous clothes" and others "Fun in bed,"
"To be oft widowed and remarried," said
105 Others again, and some that what most mattered
Was that we should be cosseted and flattered.
That's very near the truth, it seems to me;
A man can win us best with flattery.
To dance attendance on us, make a fuss,
110 Ensnares us all, the best and worst of us. **D**

Some say the things we most desire are these:
Freedom to do exactly as we please,
With no one to reprove our faults and lies,
Rather to have one call us good and wise.
115 Truly there's not a woman in ten score
Who has a fault, and someone rubs the sore,
But she will kick if what he says is true;
You try it out and you will find so too.
However vicious we may be within
120 We like to be thought wise and void of sin.
Others assert we women find it sweet
When we are thought dependable, discreet
And secret, firm of purpose and controlled,
Never betraying things that we are told.
125 But that's not worth the handle of a rake;
Women conceal a thing? For Heaven's sake!
Remember Midas? Will you hear the tale?

Among some other little things, now stale,
Ovid relates that under his long hair
130 The unhappy Midas grew a splendid pair
Of ass's ears; as subtly as he might,
He kept his foul deformity from sight;

106 cosseted (kŏs′ĭ-tĭd): pampered.

D NARRATOR
What is the narrator's opinion of flattery in lines 101–110? Consider what this view suggests about her personality.

115 ten score: 200.

117 but she will: who will not.

120 void of sin: sinless.

127 Midas: a legendary king of Phrygia, in Asia Minor.

129 Ovid (ŏv′ĭd): an ancient Roman poet whose *Metamorphoses* is a storehouse of Greek and Roman legends. According to Ovid, it was a barber, not Midas's wife, who told the secret of his donkey's ears.

Save for his wife, there was not one that knew.
He loved her best, and trusted in her too.
135 He begged her not to tell a living creature
That he possessed so horrible a feature.
And she—she swore, were all the world to win,
She would not do such villainy and sin
As saddle her husband with so foul a name;
140 Besides to speak would be to share the shame.
Nevertheless she thought she would have died
Keeping this secret bottled up inside;
It seemed to swell her heart and she, no doubt,
Thought it was on the point of bursting out.

145   Fearing to speak of it to woman or man,
Down to a reedy marsh she quickly ran
And reached the sedge. Her heart was all on fire
And, as a bittern bumbles in the mire,
She whispered to the water, near the ground,
150 "Betray me not, O water, with thy sound!
To thee alone I tell it: it appears
My husband has a pair of ass's ears!
Ah! My heart's well again, the secret's out!
I could no longer keep it, not a doubt."
155 And so you see, although we may hold fast
A little while, it must come out at last,
We can't keep secrets; as for Midas, well,
Read Ovid for his story; he will tell. **E**

    This knight that I am telling you about
160 Perceived at last he never would find out
What it could be that women loved the best.
Faint was the soul within his sorrowful breast,
As home he went, he dared no longer stay;
His year was up and now it was the day.

165   As he rode home in a dejected mood
Suddenly, at the margin of a wood,
He saw a dance upon the leafy floor
Of four and twenty ladies, nay, and more.
Eagerly he approached, in hope to learn
170 Some words of wisdom ere he should return;
But lo! Before he came to where they were,
Dancers and dance all vanished into air!
There wasn't a living creature to be seen
Save one old woman crouched upon the green.
175 A fouler-looking creature I suppose

133 **save:** except.

147 **sedge:** marsh grasses.

148 **bumbles in the mire:** booms in the swamp. (The bittern, a wading bird, is famous for its loud call.)

E **ANALYZE STRUCTURE**
Reread lines 128–158. In what way does the Wife of Bath digress, or wander, from her story about the knight? Explain what purpose this interruption might serve.

Could scarcely be imagined. She arose
And said, "Sir knight, there's no way on from here.
Tell me what you are looking for, my dear,
For peradventure that were best for you;
180 We old, old women know a thing or two."

    "Dear Mother," said the knight, "alack the day!
I am as good as dead if I can't say
What thing it is that women most desire;
If you could tell me I would pay your hire."
185 "Give me your hand," she said, "and swear to do
Whatever I shall next require of you
—If so to do should lie within your might—
And you shall know the answer before night."
"Upon my honor," he answered, "I agree."
190 "Then," said the **crone,** "I dare to guarantee
Your life is safe; I shall make good my claim.
Upon my life the queen will say the same.
Show me the very proudest of them all
In costly coverchief or jewelled caul
195 That dare say no to what I have to teach.
Let us go forward without further speech."
And then she crooned her gospel in his ear
And told him to be glad and not to fear.

    They came to court. This knight, in full array,
200 Stood forth and said, "O Queen, I've kept my day
And kept my word and have my answer ready."

    There sat the noble matrons and the heady
Young girls, and widows too, that have the grace
Of wisdom, all assembled in that place,
205 And there the queen herself was throned to hear
And judge his answer. Then the knight drew near
And silence was commanded through the hall.

    The queen gave order he should tell them all
What thing it was that women wanted most.
210 He stood not silent like a beast or post,
But gave his answer with the ringing word
Of a man's voice and the assembly heard:

    "My liege and lady, in general," said he,
"A woman wants the self-same **sovereignty**
215 Over her husband as over her lover,
And master him; he must not be above her.

179 peradventure: perhaps.

181 alack the day: an exclamation of sorrow, roughly equivalent to "Woe is me!"

crone (krōn) *n.* an ugly old woman

194 coverchief: kerchief; **caul** (kaul): an ornamental hairnet.

197 gospel: message.

199 in full array: in all his finery.

202 heady: giddy; impetuous.
203 grace: gift.

213 liege (lēj): lord.

sovereignty (sŏv′ər-ĭn-tē) *n.* rule; power

That is your greatest wish, whether you kill
Or spare me; please yourself. I wait your will."

In all the court not one that shook her head
220 Or contradicted what the knight had said;
Maid, wife and widow cried, "He's saved his life!"

And on the word up started the old wife,
The one the knight saw sitting on the green,
And cried, "Your mercy, sovereign lady queen!
225 Before the court disperses, do me right!
'Twas I who taught this answer to the knight,
For which he swore, and pledged his honor to it,
That the first thing I asked of him he'd do it,
So far as it should lie within his might.
230 Before this court I ask you then, sir knight,
To keep your word and take me for your wife;
For well you know that I have saved your life.
If this be false, deny it on your sword!"

"Alas!" he said, "Old lady, by the Lord
235 I know indeed that such was my behest,
But for God's love think of a new request,
Take all my goods, but leave my body free."
"A curse on us," she said, "if I agree!
I may be foul, I may be poor and old,
240 Yet will not choose to be, for all the gold
That's bedded in the earth or lies above,
Less than your wife, nay, than your very love!"

"My love?" said he. "By heaven, my damnation!
Alas that any of my race and station
245 Should ever make so foul a misalliance!"
Yet in the end his pleading and defiance
All went for nothing, he was forced to wed.
He takes his ancient wife and goes to bed.

Now peradventure some may well suspect
250 A lack of care in me since I neglect
To tell of the rejoicing and display
Made at the feast upon their wedding-day.
I have but a short answer to let fall;
I say there was no joy or feast at all,

255   Nothing but heaviness of heart and sorrow.
He married her in private on the morrow

235 behest (bĭ-hĕst′): promise.

244 race and station: family and rank.

245 misalliance (mĭs′ə-lī′əns): an unsuitable marriage.

And all day long stayed hidden like an owl,
It was such torture that his wife looked foul. **F**

      Great was the anguish churning in his head
260 When he and she were piloted to bed;
He wallowed back and forth in desperate style.
His ancient wife lay smiling all the while;
At last she said, "Bless us! Is this, my dear,
How knights and wives get on together here?
265 Are these the laws of good King Arthur's house?
Are knights of his all so contemptuous?
I am your own beloved and your wife,
And I am she, indeed, that saved your life;
And certainly I never did you wrong.
270 Then why, this first of nights, so sad a song?
You're carrying on as if you were half-witted.
Say, for God's love, what sin have I committed?
I'll put things right if you will tell me how."

      "Put right?" he cried. "That never can be now!
275 Nothing can ever be put right again!
You're old, and so abominably plain,
So poor to start with, so low-bred to follow;
It's little wonder if I twist and wallow!
God, that my heart would burst within my breast!"

280   "Is that," said she, "the cause of your unrest?"

      "Yes, certainly," he said, "and can you wonder?"

      "I could set right what you suppose a blunder,
That's if I cared to, in a day or two,
If I were shown more courtesy by you.
285 Just now," she said, "you spoke of gentle birth,
Such as descends from ancient wealth and worth.
If that's the claim you make for gentlemen
Such arrogance is hardly worth a hen.
Whoever loves to work for virtuous ends,
290 Public and private, and who most intends
To do what deeds of gentleness he can,
Take him to be the greatest gentleman.
Christ wills we take our gentleness from Him,
Not from a wealth of ancestry long dim,
295 Though they **bequeath** their whole establishment
By which we claim to be of high descent.

F **ANALYZE STRUCTURE**
Consider why the Wife of Bath speaks directly to the other pilgrims in lines 249–258. What effect might this digression have on her audience?

260 piloted: led. (In the Middle Ages, the wedding party typically escorted the bride and groom to their bedchamber.).

261 wallowed (wŏl'ōd): rolled around; thrashed about.

Language Coach

Roots A word's root contains its core meaning. The root of *abomination, -omin,* means "omen," or "sign." *Abominable* means "disgusting," like a bad omen. How does this information help you understand the meaning of *abominably* (line 276) and *ominous?*

bequeath (bĭ-kwēth') *v.* to leave in a will; to pass down as an inheritance

Our fathers cannot make us a bequest
Of all those virtues that became them best
And earned for them the name of gentlemen,
300 But bade us follow them as best we can.

    "Thus the wise poet of the Florentines,
Dante by name, has written in these lines,
For such is the opinion Dante launches:
'Seldom arises by these slender branches
305 Prowess of men, for it is God, no less,
Wills us to claim of Him our gentleness.'
For of our parents nothing can we claim
Save **temporal** things, and these may hurt and maim.

    "But everyone knows this as well as I;
310 For if gentility were implanted by
The natural course of lineage down the line,
Public or private, could it cease to shine
In doing the fair work of gentle deed?
No vice or villainy could then bear seed.

315   "Take fire and carry it to the darkest house
Between this kingdom and the Caucasus,

301 Florentines: the people of Florence, Italy.

302 Dante (dän'tā): a famous medieval Italian poet. Lines 304–306 refer to a passage in Dante's most famous work, *The Divine Comedy.*

temporal (tĕm'pər-əl) *adj.* of the material world; not eternal

310 gentility (jĕn-tĭl'ĭ-tē): the quality possessed by a gentle, or noble, person.

316 Caucasus (kô'kə-səs): a region of western Asia, between the Black and Caspian seas.

And shut the doors on it and leave it there,
It will burn on, and it will burn as fair
As if ten thousand men were there to see,
320 For fire will keep its nature and degree,
I can assure you, sir, until it dies.

"But gentleness, as you will recognize,
Is not annexed in nature to possessions.
Men fail in living up to their professions;
325 But fire never ceases to be fire.
God knows you'll often find, if you enquire,
Some lording full of villainy and shame.
If you would be esteemed for the mere name
Of having been by birth a gentleman
330 And stemming from some virtuous, noble clan,
And do not live yourself by gentle deed
Or take your father's noble code and creed,
You are no gentleman, though duke or earl.
Vice and bad manners are what make a churl.

335 "Gentility is only the renown
For bounty that your fathers handed down,
Quite foreign to your person, not your own;
Gentility must come from God alone.
That we are gentle comes to us by grace
340 And by no means is it bequeathed with place.

"Reflect how noble (says Valerius)
Was Tullius surnamed Hostilius,
Who rose from poverty to nobleness.
And read Boethius, Seneca no less,
345 Thus they express themselves and are agreed:
'Gentle is he that does a gentle deed.'
And therefore, my dear husband, I conclude
That even if my ancestors were rude,
Yet God on high—and so I hope He will—
350 Can grant me grace to live in virtue still,
A gentlewoman only when beginning
To live in virtue and to shrink from sinning.

"As for my poverty which you reprove,
Almighty God Himself in whom we move,
355 Believe and have our being, chose a life
Of poverty, and every man or wife,
Nay, every child can see our Heavenly King
Would never stoop to choose a shameful thing.

324 professions: beliefs; ideals.

327 lording: lord; nobleman.

334 churl (chûrl): low-class person; boor.

341 Valerius (və-lîr′ē-əs): Valerius Maximus, a Roman writer who compiled a collection of historical anecdotes.

342 Tullius (tŭl′ē-əs) **surnamed Hostilius** (hŏ-stĭl′ē-əs): the third king of the Romans.

344 Boethius (bō-ē′thē-əs): a Christian philosopher of the Dark Ages; **Seneca** (sĕn′ĭ-kə): an ancient Roman philosopher, writer, teacher, and politician.

No shame in poverty if the heart is gay,
360 As Seneca and all the learned say.
He who accepts his poverty unhurt
I'd say is rich although he lacked a shirt.
But truly poor are they who whine and fret
And covet what they cannot hope to get.
365 And he that, having nothing, covets not,
Is rich, though you may think he is a sot.

    "True poverty can find a song to sing.
Juvenal says a pleasant little thing:
'The poor can dance and sing in the relief
370 Of having nothing that will tempt a thief.'
Though it be hateful, poverty is good,
A great incentive to a livelihood,
And a great help to our capacity
For wisdom, if accepted patiently.
375 Poverty is, though wanting in estate,
A kind of wealth that none calumniate.
Poverty often, when the heart is lowly,
Brings one to God and teaches what is holy,
Gives knowledge of oneself and even lends
380 A glass by which to see one's truest friends.
And since it's no offense, let me be plain;
Do not **rebuke** my poverty again.

    "Lastly you taxed me, sir, with being old.
Yet even if you never had been told
385 By ancient books, you gentlemen engage,
Yourselves in honor to respect old age.
To call an old man 'father' shows good breeding,
And this could be supported from my reading.

    "You say I'm old and fouler than a fen.
390 You need not fear to be a cuckold, then.
Filth and old age, I'm sure you will agree,
Are powerful wardens over chastity.
Nevertheless, well knowing your delights,
I shall fulfil your worldly appetites. **G**

395   "You have two choices; which one will you try?
To have me old and ugly till I die,
But still a loyal, true, and humble wife
That never will displease you all her life,
Or would you rather I were young and pretty

366 sot: fool.

368 Juvenal (jōō′və-nəl): an ancient Roman satirist.

375 wanting in estate: lacking in grandeur.

376 calumniate (kə-lŭm′nē-āt′): criticize with false statements; slander.

rebuke (rĭ-byōōk′) *v.* to criticize

389 fen: marsh.

390 cuckold (kŭk′əld): a husband whose wife is unfaithful.

G NARRATOR
In lines 285–394, the old woman offers a lengthy rebuttal to the knight's complaints. Why might the narrator place her focus on the old woman and not the knight at this point in the story?

400 And chance your arm what happens in a city
　　Where friends will visit you because of me,
　　Yes, and in other places too, maybe.
　　Which would you have? The choice is all your own."

　　　　The knight thought long, and with a piteous groan
405 At last he said, with all the care in life,
　　"My lady and my love, my dearest wife,
　　I leave the matter to your wise decision.
　　You make the choice yourself, for the provision
　　Of what may be agreeable and rich
410 In honor to us both, I don't care which;
　　Whatever pleases you suffices me."

　　　　"And have I won the mastery?" said she,
　　"Since I'm to choose and rule as I think fit?"
　　"Certainly, wife," he answered her, "that's it."
415 "Kiss me," she cried. "No quarrels! On my oath
　　And word of honor, you shall find me both,
　　That is, both fair and faithful as a wife;
　　May I go howling mad and take my life
　　Unless I prove to be as good and true
420 As ever wife was since the world was new!
　　And if tomorrow when the sun's above
　　I seem less fair than any lady-love,
　　Than any queen or empress east or west,
　　Do with my life and death as you think best.
425 Cast up the curtain, husband. Look at me!"

　　　　And when indeed the knight had looked to see,
　　Lo, she was young and lovely, rich in charms.
　　In ecstasy he caught her in his arms,
　　His heart went bathing in a bath of blisses
430 And melted in a hundred thousand kisses,
　　And she responded in the fullest measure
　　With all that could delight or give him pleasure.

　　　　So they lived ever after to the end
　　In perfect bliss; and may Christ Jesus send
435 Us husbands meek and young and fresh in bed,
　　And grace to overbid them when we wed.
　　And—Jesu hear my prayer!—cut short the lives
　　Of those who won't be governed by their wives;
　　And all old, angry niggards of their pence,
440 God send them soon a very pestilence! ⓗ

400 **chance your arm:** take your chance on.

Language Coach

Derivations The word *pity* ("sympathetic sorrow") has several derivations, or related words, including *pitiful, pitying,* and *piteous* (line 404). Two derivations mean "causing pity," one sometimes means "causing disgust," and one means "having pity." Match each derivation of *pity* to its definition.

ⓗ **NARRATOR**
Reread the last paragraph. What is the Wife of Bath's attitude toward husbands who are controlling or misers ("niggards")? Cite the details that helped you draw this conclusion.

Comprehension

COMMON CORE

RL 3 Analyze the impact of the author's choices regarding how to develop and relate elements of a story. RL 5 Analyze how an author's choices concerning how to structure specific parts of a text contribute to its overall structure and meaning as well as its aesthetic impact.

1. **Recall** Describe the knight's original sentence and his revised punishment.

2. **Recall** What agreement does the knight make with the old woman?

3. **Recall** What information does the old woman share with the knight?

4. **Summarize** In what ways does the relationship between the knight and the old woman change during the course of the story?

Text Analysis

5. **Examine Narrator** In her tale, the Wife of Bath offers direct statements on friars (lines 39–56), women's desires (lines 101–126), and marriage (lines 433–440). Summarize each statement and then explain what each reveals about the Wife's personality.

6. **Analyze Structure** Review the chart you created as you read. Unlike other pilgrims, the Wife of Bath interrupts her story with various personal comments, anecdotes, and illustrative stories. What might she be trying to convey about herself with this additional information?

7. **Evaluate Plot** Review lines 404–432. Is the conclusion of the story satisfying? In your response, consider the knight's crime and the outcome of his actions.

8. **Make Judgments** The enduring appeal of *The Canterbury Tales* stems in part from Chaucer's remarkable ability to match stories and storytellers. In what way is the Wife of Bath's unusual tale well-suited to her personality? Cite evidence from the text to support your answer.

9. **Compare Texts** Compare the tales of the Pardoner and the Wife of Bath. Which character tells a better, more entertaining story? Cite evidence from both tales to support your opinion.

Text Criticism

10. **Social Context** Around 1185, Andreas Capellanus wrote *The Art of Courtly Love*. In this influential work, Capellanus states, "Love makes an ugly and rude person shine with all beauty, knows how to endow with nobility even one of humble birth, can even lend humility to the proud." In what ways does "The Wife of Bath's Tale" reflect Capellanus's understanding of love and its transforming power?

> *Do men* **UNDERSTAND** *women?*
>
> Are male writers capable of portraying realistic female characters? How well do you think Chaucer portrayed the Wife of Bath? What would you change about his characterization of women?

Vocabulary in Context

▲ VOCABULARY PRACTICE

Indicate whether the following pairs of words are synonyms or antonyms. Check your answers in a dictionary.

1. bequeath/inherit
2. crone/maiden
3. implore/beseech
4. rebuke/praise
5. sovereignty/rule
6. temporal/eternal

ACADEMIC VOCABULARY IN WRITING

> • concept   • culture   • parallel   • section   • structure

How do the two **parallel** stories—the knight searching for love and the Wife of Bath's role in the pilgrimage—share some of the same **concepts** about love and fidelity? Write a paragraph explaining how stories of those seeking love extend across cultures.

VOCABULARY STRATEGY: THE LATIN ROOT *temp*

The word *temporal* contains the root *temp*, from the Latin *tempus*, which means "time" or "a fixed period." Something *temporal* exists in time and is not eternal. The same root is found in several other English words.

PRACTICE In each sentence below, choose the word from the pair in parentheses that correctly completes each sentence. Use your knowledge of word parts and the context in which the word appears to help you make the correct choice.

1. The scientist explained that the age of the dinosaurs was not (*extemporaneous, contemporaneous*) with human existence.
2. The band conductor suddenly increased the march's (*tempo, temper*).
3. The senator (*contemporized, temporized*), hoping to delay the bill's passage.
4. The brightly colored chart helped us (*temporalize, extemporize*) the different geological areas we were studying.
5. President Lyndon B. Johnson was both respected and feared by many of his (*contemporaries, templates*).

COMMON CORE

L 4 Determine or clarify the meaning of unknown words. **L 6** Acquire and use accurately general academic and domain-specific words.

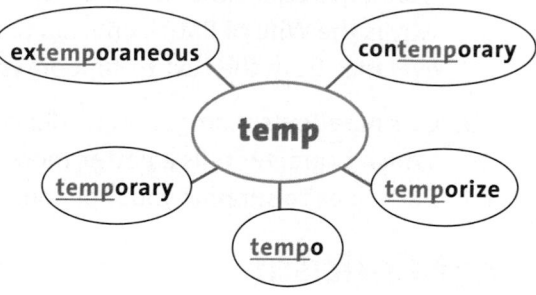

Interactive Vocabulary **THiNK** central

Go to **thinkcentral.com**.
KEYWORD: HML12-198

Language

◆ **GRAMMAR AND STYLE: Add Descriptive Details**

Review the **Grammar and Style** note on page 159. Chaucer was a keen observer who conveyed memorable details about characters through his use of **similes.**

Similes are figures of speech that use *like* or *as* to make a comparison. In the passage below, Chaucer conjures up a striking, if not complimentary, image of the balding Pardoner.

> *This Pardoner had hair as yellow as wax,*
> *Hanging down smoothly like a hank of flax.*
> *In driblets fell his locks behind his head*
> *Down to his shoulders which they overspread;*
> *Thinly they fell, like rat-tails, one by one.* (lines 695–699)

Notice how each of the highlighted prepositions is followed by a concrete visual image. These similes greatly enrich Chaucer's descriptions because they allow readers to form a vivid mental picture of a character.

PRACTICE Write sentences modeled on Chaucer's work.

> **EXAMPLE**
>
> There was a *Franklin* with him, it appeared;
> White as a daisy-petal was his beard.
>
> *There was a puppy with him, it appeared;*
> *Striped like a skunk, which seemed very weird.*

1. His eyes would twinkle in his head as bright
   As any star upon a frosty night.

2. His prominent eyeballs never seemed to settle.
   They glittered like the flames beneath a kettle.

READING-WRITING CONNECTION

YOUR TURN Expand your understanding of Chaucer's characters by responding to this prompt. Then, use the **revising tips** to improve your dialogue.

WRITING PROMPT	REVISING TIPS
CREATE A DIALOGUE How might the other pilgrims have reacted to "The Wife of Bath's Tale"? Write a dialogue in which at least two pilgrims, as well as the Wife of Bath herself, comment on the story and its message about men's and women's roles.	• Add stage directions to describe each pilgrim's tone of voice or body movements. • Clearly identify each pilgrim's opinion about men's and women's roles.

L 5 Demonstrate understanding of figurative language. **W 3b** Use dialogue to develop experiences, events, and/or characters.

Interactive Revision

THINK central

Go to **thinkcentral.com**.
KEYWORD: HML12-199

Pilgrimages: Journeys of the Spirit

- Book Excerpt, page 201
- Magazine Article, page 202
- Map and Illustrations, page 204

Use with selections from
The Canterbury Tales,
page 142.

COMMON CORE

RI 2 Provide an objective summary of a text. **RI 7** Integrate and evaluate multiple sources of information presented in different formats in order to address a question.

The Canterbury Tales is a collection of stories written as if they were told by pilgrims on their way to a holy site. The following selections describe what it was like to travel on a pilgrimage in Chaucer's time and also reveal why this ancient tradition still thrives today. As you read, consider how the information in these selections enhances your understanding of the characters in *The Canterbury Tales*.

Standards Focus: Synthesize

Whenever you put together facts, ideas, and details from different sources to form your own understanding of a topic, you are **synthesizing**, or integrating, information. You can usually gain deeper insight into a topic by synthesizing from several sources than by just reading one source.

Use a chart like the one below to synthesize details about pilgrims. Skim through "The Prologue" of *The Canterbury Tales,* looking for information about pilgrims and pilgrimages. Add to the chart any information that would help you answer the questions provided. Then, read the selections that follow, and add more details about pilgrims to your chart.

When your chart is complete, **summarize**, or briefly encapsulate, in no more than a few sentences, the purpose of taking a pilgrimage and what such a journey is like based on the information you collected about each work. Your purpose is not to form an opinion, but simply to sum up each author's viewpoint about pilgrimages and their importance.

Source	*The Canterbury Tales*	*A Distant Mirror*	"In the Footsteps of the Faithful"	"Pilgrimage Sites" Map
What kinds of people go on pilgrimages?				
Why do they go?				
What is the journey like?				
How does the pilgrimage affect them?				

In *A Distant Mirror*, historian Barbara Tuchman describes the hardships, including the difficulties of travel, faced by people of all classes in 14th-century Europe.

A Distant Mirror

Barbara Tuchman

Travel, "the mother of tidings," brought news of the world to castle and village, town and countryside. The rutted roads, always either too dusty or too muddy, carried an endless flow of pilgrims and peddlers, merchants with their packtrains, bishops making visitations, tax-collectors and royal officials, friars and pardoners, wandering scholars, jongleurs and preachers, messengers and couriers who wove the network of communications from city to city. Great nobles like the Coucys, bankers, prelates, abbeys, courts of justice, town governments, kings and their councils employed their own messengers. The King of England at mid-century kept twelve on hand who accompanied him at all times, ready to start, and were paid 3d. a day when on the
10 road and 4s. 8d. a year for shoes. . . .

The voyage from London to Lyon took about 18 days and from Canterbury to Rome about 30 days depending on the Channel crossing, which was unpredictable, often dangerous, sometimes fatal, and could take anywhere from three days to a month. One knight, Sir Hervé de Léon, was kept 15 days at sea by a storm and, besides having lost his horse overboard, arrived so battered and weakened "that he never had health thereafter." It was no wonder that, according to a ballad, when pilgrims took to sea for the voyage to Compostella or beyond, "Theyr hertes begin to fayle." . . . **A**

Travelers stopped before nightfall, those of the nobility taking shelter in some
20 nearby castle or monastery where they would be admitted indoors, while the mass of ordinary travelers on foot, including pilgrims, were housed and fed in a guest house outside the gate. They were entitled to one night's lodging at any monastery and could not be turned away unless they asked for a second night. Inns were available to merchants and others, though they were likely to be crowded, squalid, and flea-ridden, with several beds to a room and two travelers to a bed—or three to a bed in Germany, according to the disgusted report of the poet Deschamps, who was sent there on a mission for the French King. Moreover, he complained, neither bed nor table had clean linen, the innkeeper offered no choice of foods, a traveler in the Empire could find nothing to drink but beer; fleas, rats, and mice were unavoidable,
30 and the people of Bohemia lived like pigs. **B**

Given the hardships and the length of time consumed, people journeyed over long distances to an astonishing degree—from Paris to Florence, from Flanders to Hungary, London to Prague, Bohemia to Castile, crossing seas, alps, and rivers, walking to China like Marco Polo or three times to Jerusalem like the Wife of Bath.

A SYNTHESIZE
Reread lines 1–18. What were the hardships of traveling in the Middle Ages?

B SYNTHESIZE
What was it like for a pilgrim to stay at an inn?

Many people today still go on pilgrimages, often walking for long distances along ancient routes. Canadian writer Taras Grescoe writes about his journey to one of the most famous European pilgrimage sites.

In the Footsteps of the Faithful

Taras Grescoe

Little by little, the road to Santiago de Compostela was changing me. When I started off on the Camino Francés—a 1,200-year-old route across northern Spain to one of Catholicism's holiest shrines—I was unprepared for the camaraderie this pilgrimage fosters. Since A.D. 813, when the bones of St. James the Apostle were
10 discovered in a cave at the western tip of Galicia, devout pilgrims from all over Europe have tramped hundreds of miles across the snow-streaked Pyrenees and the sun-baked plains of Castile in a quest for absolution and spiritual growth. Beginning the walk in the French town of St. Jean-Pied-de-Port, I was part of this rare band of travelers for three weeks. **C**

20   In the shade of eucalyptus forests and olive groves, over tuna sandwiches and chocolate bars, I heard stories by turns touching and inspiring. A young mother—a Danish athlete—was alternately carrying and pushing her two blond-haired infants over the mountain trails and switchbacks, a feat of almost superhuman endurance. A 60-year-old man in disintegrating sandals and with
30 a long white beard paused just long enough to tell me he'd walked all the way from Rome, 40 miles a day. Next to a purling stream, I came across a pilgrim who'd lost his right leg and was being borne to Santiago on his trusty mare Lorena—named after his daughter, herself only recently recovered from leukemia.

C SYNTHESIZE
Reread lines 8–16. What are some reasons why people go on pilgrimages today?

The Camino Francés, which wends past storks on the chimney stacks of Rioja and seagulls on the moss-covered church spires of Galicia, is a crash course in medieval European history, with daily seminars in Romanesque architecture and the arcane iconography of the Knights Templar. I found myself walking on the original paving stones of Roman roads, staining my shoes on the red earth of the vineyards of Rioja, and losing my way in the fog of the Pyrenees. In a little town outside Logroño, I joined the queue at an unattended tap at a stone wall, from which Navarran red wine flowed free of charge, a local winery's gift to passing pilgrims.

As I walked, materialism and concern about self-image fell by the wayside; I divested myself of guidebooks and excess clothing, and sought only to fill my belly with nourishing food and to find simple lodgings each evening. I learned to expect the warm westerly wind that crosses the land just before sunset, the cool *tramontana* from the north, and the afternoon breeze that sends iridescent ripples through the fields. I realized I'd never truly seen the world go by at this human pace, three miles an hour, hour after hour, day in, day out—nor understood that the quality of one's travel experience is inversely proportional to the speed at which one travels. **D**

I finally walked into Santiago in the midst of a record spring heat wave. Sweaty and unshaven, I approached the wildflower- and lichen-covered cathedral where the bones of St. James the Apostle rested—a fantastic barnacle-encrusted reef looming over waves of stone houses. As I strode up the last set of stairs before my goal, I was overwhelmed by a connection with all those who, over the ages, had risked losing home, family, and life to follow their faith to some marvelous shrine at the edge of the earth.

Step by step, the Camino had made me one of its own: a pilgrim.

D SYNTHESIZE
Reread lines 57–75. How has the author been affected by his pilgrimage?

Pilgrims stop to kneel along the main pilgrimage route from southwest France to Santiago de Compostela.

Medieval pilgrims visited holy sites throughout Europe and in parts of Asia. These sites continue to serve as important spiritual centers as well as popular tourist attractions.

E **INFORMATIONAL TEXTS**

A map represents a portion of the earth's surface and a map scale shows the relationship between distance on a map and the distance on the earth's surface. Use the scale on the map to measure the distances between London and the pilgrimage sites, and notice the geographic features a pilgrim would have to cross to reach these sites. What does this add to your understanding of what it was like to make a pilgrimage in Chaucer's day?

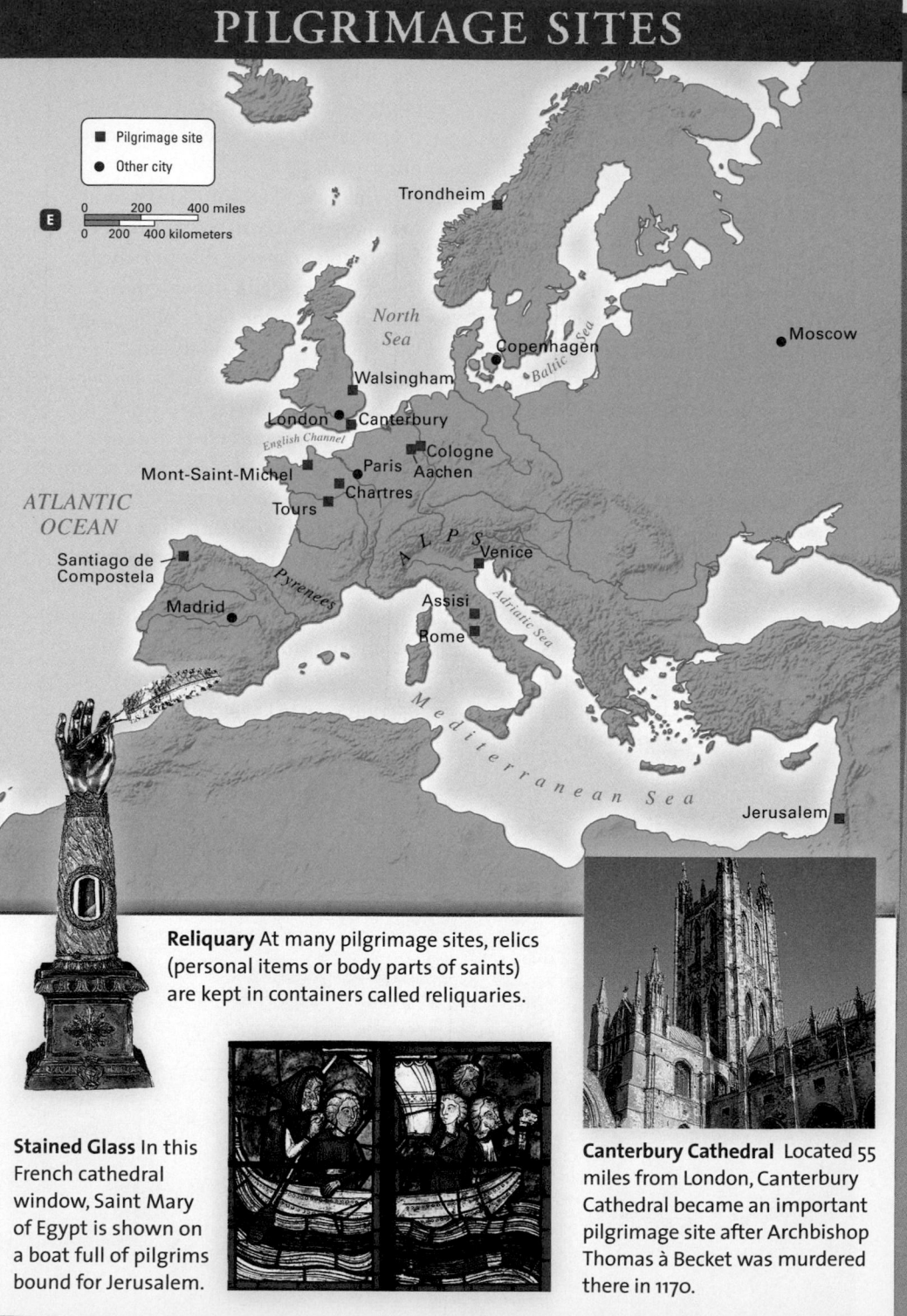

PILGRIMAGE SITES

- ■ Pilgrimage site
- ● Other city

E 0   200   400 miles
  0   200   400 kilometers

Trondheim
Moscow
North Sea
Copenhagen
Baltic Sea
Walsingham
London Canterbury
English Channel Cologne
Mont-Saint-Michel Paris Aachen
Chartres
ATLANTIC OCEAN
Tours
A L P S
Santiago de Compostela Venice
Pyrenees Adriatic Sea
Madrid Assisi
Rome
Mediterranean Sea
Jerusalem
North Sea

Reliquary At many pilgrimage sites, relics (personal items or body parts of saints) are kept in containers called reliquaries.

Stained Glass In this French cathedral window, Saint Mary of Egypt is shown on a boat full of pilgrims bound for Jerusalem.

Canterbury Cathedral Located 55 miles from London, Canterbury Cathedral became an important pilgrimage site after Archbishop Thomas à Becket was murdered there in 1170.

Comprehension

1. **Recall** According to Barbara Tuchman, what was sea travel like in Chaucer's day?

2. **Recall** During medieval times, how did the lodging offered to the nobility differ from the lodging available to members of other social classes?

3. **Clarify** How does Taras Grescoe feel about the slow pace of travel on a pilgrimage?

Text Analysis

4. **Analyze Author's Message** Reread lines 83–89 of "In the Footsteps of the Faithful." What experiences have allowed Grescoe to form the connection he describes? Use details from the selection to support your answer.

5. **Synthesize Information from Graphic Aids** Examine the photographs on page 204. How do these images help you understand the appeal of going on a pilgrimage?

COMMON CORE

RI 2 Provide an objective summary of a text. **RI 7** Integrate and evaluate multiple sources of information presented in different formats in order to address a question. **W 9** Draw evidence from literary or informational texts to support analysis and reflection.

Read for Information: Draw Conclusions

WRITING PROMPT

According to Chaucer, the other authors, and the map in this section, what is the purpose of a pilgrimage? What are the benefits and difficulties of a making a pilgrimage?

To answer this prompt, you will need to follow these steps:

1. Gather information about the purpose of a pilgrimage from the three selections as well as from "The Prologue" of *The Canterbury Tales*.

2. Consider the main ideas and information you have collected and the summary you created of each work. Ask yourself what conclusion you can draw from them about making a pilgrimage.

3. Present your conclusion in a topic sentence, and support it with ideas and information from the texts.

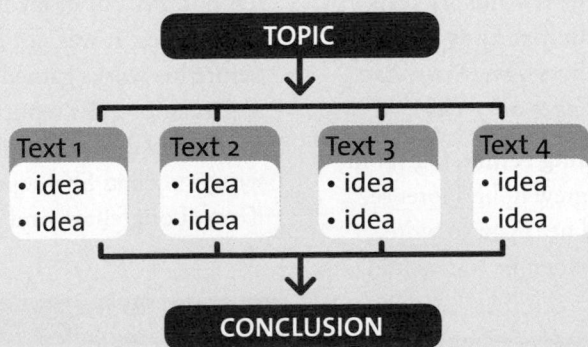

TOPIC

Text 1	Text 2	Text 3	Text 4
• idea • idea	• idea • idea	• idea • idea	• idea • idea

CONCLUSION

Federigo's Falcon: Fifth Day, Ninth Story
from **The Decameron**

Tale by Giovanni Boccaccio

COMMON CORE

RL 3 Analyze the impact of the author's choices regarding how to develop and relate elements of a story. **RL 10** Read and comprehend literature, including stories. **SL 1** Initiate and participate effectively in a range of collaborative discussions.

Meet the Author

Giovanni Boccaccio 1313–1375

Writing at the end of the medieval period, Giovanni Boccaccio helped set a new direction for literature, focusing on the human condition rather than on spiritual matters. His masterpiece, *The Decameron,* a strikingly modern work, established the contemporary language of his day as a legitimate mode of literary expression. The work signaled a sharp break from medieval literary traditions and helped define the literary sensibilities that held sway throughout the Renaissance.

Some scholars speculate that Boccaccio's *Decameron* influenced Geoffrey Chaucer in his writing of *The Canterbury Tales.* Although no direct evidence exists to support this view, there are notable similarities between the two collections. Both feature a frame story construction, a treasury of tales, and various sharply drawn characters. Moreover, both works contain adaptations of age-old narratives and literary forms that strongly appealed to their educated audiences. Most significantly, few literary texts celebrate humanity as freely and completely as *The Decameron* and *The Canterbury Tales.*

An Overbearing Father Giovanni Boccaccio grew up in Florence, Italy, and he began to write poetry when he was a child.

His father frowned upon his son's literary leanings, demanding that he forget about writing and learn business. While still a teenager, Boccaccio was sent to Naples, where he was apprenticed to a banker. When he failed at banking, his father arranged for him to study religious law. Boccaccio was unsuccessful at law, too, and after about 12 years in Naples, he returned home to seek other employment.

Fame Without Funds Because his father "strove to bend" his talent, Boccaccio complained that he was never able to reach his potential as a poet. Yet upon publication of *The Decameron,* he became something of a celebrity. In later years, he applied himself to more scholarly pursuits, producing a number of biographical and moralistic works. His literary and scholarly efforts never brought in much money, and he was nearly always in perilous financial straits. Eventually, he was reduced to earning a meager living by working as a scribe, painstakingly copying his own works and those of others. He died in 1375, temporarily out of favor in both Florence and Naples. It was not long, however, before his works gained renewed appreciation. His reputation has endured over many centuries, influencing later writers such as Shakespeare, Dryden, Keats, Longfellow, and Tennyson.

DID YOU KNOW?

Giovanni Boccaccio . . .

- survived the Black Death when it struck Florence, Italy, in 1348.
- fell in love with a woman whom he called "Fiammetta," or "little flame," who inspired his early writing.

Author Online

Go to **thinkcentral.com**. KEYWORD: HML12-206

THINK central

TEXT ANALYSIS: PLOT ELEMENTS

Many stories in *The Decameron* are adaptations of medieval folk tales, fables, and anecdotes, from which Boccaccio borrows a basic **plot,** or series of related events. He then transforms it by adding plot devices such as **complications**—problems that create moral dilemmas that motivate his characters' behavior. In "Federigo's Falcon," for example, Boccaccio introduces his main character, Federigo, in the following way:

As often happens to most men of gentle breeding, he fell in love, with a noble lady named Monna Giovanna. . . . [Yet] he lost his wealth and was reduced to poverty, . . .

Boccaccio presents Federigo as a traditional romantic hero who seeks the love of Monna Giovanna, a well-born woman. However, he quickly adds a complication to this situation— Federigo's loss of wealth. How can he win her love if he has no money? As you read the selection, notice how Boccaccio builds toward a surprising and powerful **climax,** or turning point, through complications in the story's plot.

READING SKILL: ANALYZE CAUSE AND EFFECT

In a well-crafted story, events are often related by cause and effect. The **cause** is an event that directly results in another event, which is the **effect.** Analyzing cause-and-effect relationships can help you better comprehend the complications of the story's plot and how they affect characters' actions. As you read "Federigo's Falcon," keep track of examples of cause and effect by making a diagram like the one shown.

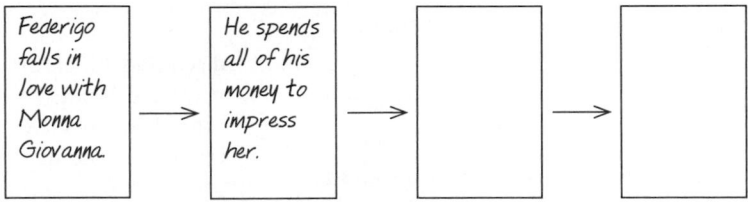

| Federigo falls in love with Monna Giovanna. | He spends all of his money to impress her. | | |

▲ VOCABULARY IN CONTEXT

These boldfaced vocabulary words are key to understanding Boccaccio's tale about love and its sacrifices. Restate each phrase, substituting a different word for the boldfaced term.

1. act with tact and **discretion**
2. **deign** to help a lowly peasant
3. behave with **presumption**
4. **compel** me to do my duty
5. offer **consolation** for your loss

What would you SACRIFICE for love?

Love is a powerful emotion—one for which some people are prepared to make a great sacrifice. "Federigo's Falcon" is a tale of a nobleman's idealized love for a woman and the lengths to which he goes to win her affection.

DISCUSS With a partner, list examples of sacrifices for love that you have heard of, read about, or seen in television shows or movies. Discuss the results of these sacrifices. Which examples do you find reasonable? Which examples seem extreme? Compare your conclusions with those of other students.

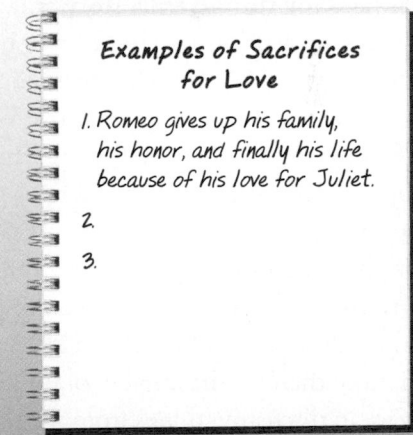

Examples of Sacrifices for Love

1. Romeo gives up his family, his honor, and finally his life because of his love for Juliet.

2.

3.

Complete the activities in your **Reader/Writer Notebook.**

Federigo's Falcon

Fifth Day, Ninth Story

Giovanni Boccaccio

> **BACKGROUND** Like Chaucer's *Canterbury Tales*, *The Decameron* is a collection of stories within a story. The frame, or outer story, involves ten characters who flee to the country to escape a plague that is ravaging Florence, Italy. For ten days they amuse themselves by telling stories, each day selecting a "king" or "queen" who presides over the storytelling. Their 100 tales make up the bulk of *The Decameron*. As this selection begins, the queen of the day decides that it is time to tell her own story.

Filomena had already finished speaking, and when the Queen saw there was no one left to speak except for Dioneo,[1] who was exempted because of his special privilege, she herself with a cheerful face said:

It is now my turn to tell a story and, dearest ladies, I shall do so most willingly with a tale similar in some respects to the preceding one, its purpose being not only to show you how much power your beauty has over the gentle heart, but also so that you yourselves may learn, whenever it is fitting, to be the donors of your favors instead of always leaving this act to the whim of Fortune,[2] who, as it happens, on most occasions bestows such favors with more abundance than

10 <u>discretion.</u>

You should know, then, that Coppo di Borghese Domenichi,[3] who once lived in our city and perhaps still does, a man of great and respected authority in our times, one most illustrious and worthy of eternal fame both for his way of life and his ability much more than for the nobility of his blood, often took delight, when he was an old man, in discussing things from the past with his neighbors and with others. He knew how to do this well, for he was more logical and had a better memory and a more eloquent style of speaking than any other man. Among the many beautiful tales he told, there was one he would often tell about a young man who once lived in Florence named Federigo, the son of Messer Filippo Alberighi,[4] renowned above all

20 other men in Tuscany for his prowess in arms and for his courtliness. **A**

Analyze Visuals ▶
What details in this painting suggest that the woman is wealthy?

discretion (dĭ-skrĕsh'ən) *n.* wise restraint; carefulness in one's actions and words

A PLOT
The **exposition** of a story introduces the characters and setting. What do you learn about these elements in lines 17–20?

---

1. **Dioneo** (dē'ô-nā'ō).
2. **Fortune:** a personification of the power that supposedly distributes good and bad luck to people.
3. **Coppo di Borghese Domenichi** (kôp'pō dē bôr-gā'zě dō-mě'nē-kē).
4. **Messer Filippo Alberighi** (mās'sĕr fē-lēp'pō äl'bě-rē'gē).

Portrait of a Lady (1522), Bernardino Luini. Andrew W. Mellon Collection 1937.1.37 © 2005 National Portrait Gallery, Washington, D.C.

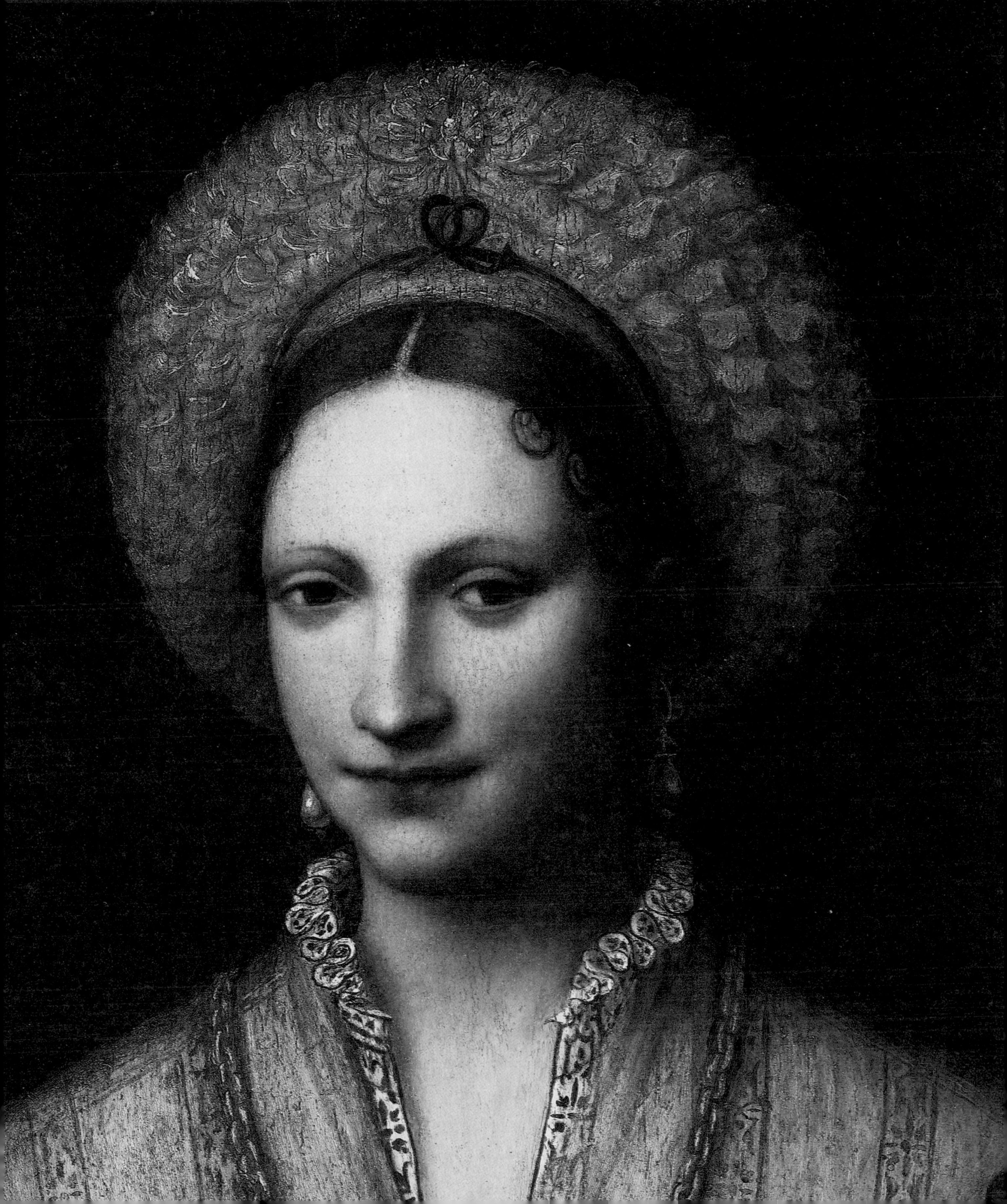

As often happens to most men of gentle breeding, he fell in love, with a noble lady named Monna Giovanna, in her day considered to be one of the most beautiful and most charming ladies that ever there was in Florence; and in order to win her love, he participated in jousts and tournaments,[5] organized and gave banquets, spending his money without restraint; but she, no less virtuous than beautiful, cared little for these things he did on her behalf, nor did she care for the one who did them. Now, as Federigo was spending far beyond his means and getting nowhere, as can easily happen, he lost his wealth and was reduced to poverty, and was left with nothing to his name but his little farm (from whose
30 revenues he lived very meagerly) and one falcon, which was among the finest of its kind in the world. **B**

More in love than ever, but knowing that he would never be able to live the way he wished to in the city, he went to live at Campi, where his farm was. There he passed his time hawking[6] whenever he could, imposing on no one, and enduring his poverty patiently. Now one day, during the time that Federigo was reduced to these extremes, it happened that the husband of Monna Giovanna fell ill, and realizing death was near, he made his last will: he was very rich, and he left everything to his son, who was just growing up, and since he had also loved Monna Giovanna very much, he made her his heir should his son die without any
40 legitimate children; and then he died. **C**

Monna Giovanna was now a widow, and every summer, as our women usually do, she would go to the country with her son to one of their estates very close by to Federigo's farm. Now this young boy of hers happened to become more and more friendly with Federigo and he began to enjoy birds and dogs; and after seeing Federigo's falcon fly many times, it made him so happy that he very much wished it were his own, but he did not dare to ask for it, for he could see how precious it was to Federigo. During this time, it happened that the young boy took ill, and his mother was much grieved, for he was her only child and she loved him dearly; she would spend the entire day by his side, never ceasing to comfort
50 him, asking him time and again if there was anything he wished, begging him to tell her what it might be, for if it was possible to obtain it, she would certainly do everything in her power to get it. After the young boy had heard her make this offer many times, he said:

"Mother, if you can arrange for me to have Federigo's falcon, I think I would get well quickly."

When the lady heard this, she was taken aback for a moment, and then she began thinking what she could do about it. She knew that Federigo had been in love with her for some time now, but she had never **deigned** to give him a second look; so, she said to herself:

B PLOT
Reread lines 21–31. What is the main **conflict,** or struggle, between Federigo and Monna Giovanna?

C CAUSE AND EFFECT
What effects does Federigo's love for Monna Giovanna cause? Cite specific details in your response.

deign (dān) *v.* to consider worthy of one's dignity; to condescend

---

5. **jousts and tournaments:** competitions in which knights displayed their skill in combat.
6. **he went . . . hawking:** He went to live in a town called Campi (käm'pē) in Tuscany, where he passed his time hunting with falcons, birds of prey trained to capture and retrieve small animals.

60   "How can I go to him, or even send someone, and ask for this falcon of his, which is, as I have heard tell, the finest that ever flew, and furthermore, his only means of support? And how can I be so insensitive as to wish to take away from this nobleman the only pleasure which is left to him?"

   And involved in these thoughts, knowing that she was certain to have the bird if she asked for it, but not knowing what to say to her son, she stood there without answering him. Finally the love she bore her son persuaded her that she should make him happy, and no matter what the consequences might be, she would not send for the bird, but rather go herself to fetch it and bring it back to him; so she answered her son:

70   "My son, cheer up and think only of getting well, for I promise you that first thing tomorrow morning I shall go and fetch it for you." **D**

   The child was so happy that he showed some improvement that very day. The following morning, the lady, accompanied by another woman, as if they were out for a stroll, went to Federigo's modest little house and asked for him. Since the weather for the past few days had not been right for hawking, Federigo happened to be in his orchard attending to certain tasks, and when he heard that Monna Giovanna was asking for him at the door, he was so surprised and happy that he rushed there; as she saw him coming, she rose to greet him with womanly grace, and once Federigo had welcomed her most courteously, she said:

80   "How do you do, Federigo?" Then she continued, "I have come to make amends for the harm you have suffered on my account by loving me more than you should have, and in token of this, I intend to have a simple meal with you and this companion of mine this very day."

   To this Federigo humbly replied: "Madonna,[7] I have no recollection of ever suffering any harm because of you; on the contrary: so much good have I received from you that if ever I was worth anything, it was because of your worth and the love I bore for you; and your generous visit is certainly so very dear to me that I would spend all over again all that I spent in the past, but you have come to a poor host."

   And having said this, he humbly led her through the house and into his garden,
90 and because he had no one there to keep her company, he said:

   "My lady, since there is no one else, this good woman, who is the wife of the farmer here, will keep you company while I see to the table."

   Though he was very poor, Federigo until now had never realized to what extent he had wasted his wealth; but this morning, the fact that he had nothing in the house with which he could honor the lady for the love of whom he had in the past entertained countless people, gave him cause to reflect: in great anguish, he cursed himself and his fortune, and like someone out of his senses he started running here and there throughout the house, but unable to find either money or anything he might be able to pawn, and since it was getting late and he was still very much
100 set on serving this noble lady some sort of meal, but unwilling to turn for help to

---

D PLOT
What important **complication** is introduced into the plot in lines 47–71? Explain the moral dilemma this complication in the **plot** creates. How does it affect Monna's behavior?

Language Coach

Fixed Expressions Some verbs have a special meaning when followed by a certain preposition. Reread lines 91–92. Here, *see to* means "attend to" or "take charge of." What does Federigo mean when he says he will "see to the table"?

---

7. **Madonna:** Italian for "my lady," a polite form of address used in speaking to a married woman. "Monna" is a contraction of this term.

even his own farmer (not to mention anyone else), he set his eyes upon his good falcon, which was sitting on its perch in a small room, and since he had nowhere else to turn, he took the bird, and finding it plump, he decided that it would be a worthy food for such a lady. So, without giving the matter a second thought, he wrung its neck and quickly gave it to his servant girl to pluck, prepare, and place on a spit to be roasted with care; and when he had set the table with the whitest of tablecloths (a few of which he still had left), he returned, with a cheerful face, to the lady in his garden and announced that the meal, such as he was able to prepare, was ready. **E**

110   The lady and her companion rose and went to the table together with Federigo, who waited upon them with the greatest devotion, and they ate the good falcon without knowing what it was they were eating. Then, having left the table and spent some time in pleasant conversation, the lady thought it time now to say what she had come to say, and so she spoke these kind words to Federigo:

"Federigo, if you recall your former way of life and my virtue, which you perhaps mistook for harshness and cruelty, I have no doubt at all that you will be amazed by my **presumption** when you hear what my main reason for coming here is; but if you had children, through whom you might have experienced the power of parental love, I feel certain that you would, at least in part, forgive 120 me. But, just as you have no child, I do have one, and I cannot escape the laws common to all mothers; the force of such laws **compels** me to follow them, against my own will and against good manners and duty, and to ask of you a gift which I know is most precious to you; and it is naturally so, since your extreme condition has left you no other delight, no other pleasure, no other **consolation;** and this gift is your falcon, which my son is so taken by that if I do not bring it to him, I fear his sickness will grow so much worse that I may lose him. And therefore I beg you, not because of the love that you bear for me, which does not oblige you in the least, but because of your own nobleness, which you have shown to be greater than that of all others in practicing courtliness, that you be pleased 130 to give it to me, so that I may say that I have saved the life of my son by means of this gift, and because of it I have placed him in your debt forever."

When he heard what the lady requested and knew that he could not oblige her because he had given her the falcon to eat, Federigo began to weep in her presence, for he could not utter a word in reply. The lady at first thought his tears were caused more by the sorrow of having to part with the good falcon than by anything else, and she was on the verge of telling him she no longer wished it, but she held back and waited for Federigo's reply once he stopped weeping. And he said:

"My lady, ever since it pleased God for me to place my love in you, I have felt that Fortune has been hostile to me in many ways, and I have complained of 140 her, but all this is nothing compared to what she has just done to me, and I shall never be at peace with her again, when I think how you have come here to my poor home, where, when it was rich, you never deigned to come, and how you requested but a small gift, and Fortune worked to make it impossible for me to give it to you; and why this is so I shall tell you in a few words. When I heard that

E CAUSE AND EFFECT
Reread lines 93–109. What specific circumstances cause Federigo to kill his beloved falcon?

presumption
(prĭ-zŭmp'shən) *n.* bold or outrageous behavior

compel (kəm-pĕl') *v.* to force or be forced to act in a certain way

consolation
(kŏn'sə-lā'shən) *n.* something that makes someone feel less sad or disappointed; comfort

you, out of your kindness, wished to dine with me, I considered it only fitting and proper, taking into account your excellence and your worthiness, that I should honor you, according to my possibilities, with a more precious food than that which I usually serve to other people. So I thought of the falcon for which you have just asked me and of its value and I judged it a food worthy of you, and this
150 very day I had it roasted and served to you as best I could. But seeing now that you desired it another way, my sorrow in not being able to serve you is so great that never shall I be able to console myself again." **F**

And after he had said this, he laid the feathers, the feet, and the beak of the bird before her as proof. When the lady heard and saw this, she first reproached him for having killed a falcon such as this to serve as a meal to a woman. But then to herself she commended the greatness of his spirit, which no poverty was able, or would be able, to diminish; then, having lost all hope of getting the falcon and thus, perhaps, of improving the health of her son, she thanked Federigo both for the honor paid to her and for his good intentions, and then left in grief to return
160 to her son. To his mother's extreme sorrow, whether in disappointment in not having the falcon or because his illness inevitably led to it, the boy passed from this life only a few days later. **G**

After the period of her mourning and her bitterness had passed, the lady was repeatedly urged by her brothers to remarry, since she was very rich and still young; and although she did not wish to do so, they became so insistent that remembering the worthiness of Federigo and his last act of generosity—that is, to have killed such a falcon to do her honor—she said to her brothers:

"I would prefer to remain a widow, if only that would be pleasing to you, but since you wish me to take a husband, you may be sure that I shall take no man
170 other than Federigo degli[8] Alberighi." **H**

In answer to this, her brothers, making fun of her, replied:

"You foolish woman, what are you saying? How can you want him? He hasn't a penny to his name."

To this she replied: "My brothers, I am well aware of what you say, but I would much rather have a man who lacks money than money that lacks a man."

Her brothers, seeing that she was determined and knowing Federigo to be of noble birth, no matter how poor he was, accepted her wishes and gave her with all her riches in marriage to him; when he found himself the husband of such a great lady, whom he had loved so much and who was so wealthy besides, he managed
180 his financial affairs with more prudence than in the past and lived with her happily the rest of his days. ∾

Translated by Mark Musa and Peter Bondanella

F PLOT
The **climax,** or turning point, is the moment of greatest intensity in a story. What shocking discovery does Federigo make in lines 115–152?

G PLOT
The **resolution** reveals the final outcome of events and ties up any loose ends of the story. How is the plot **complication** involving Monna's son resolved?

H CAUSE AND EFFECT
Why, exactly, does Monna Giovanna decide to marry Federigo? Explain the connection between her decision and Federigo's earlier behavior toward her.

---

8. **degli** (dĕl'yē): Italian for "of the"; used in names as a sign of noble birth.

Comprehension

1. **Recall** How does Federigo lose his fortune?

2. **Clarify** Why does Monna Giovanna want Federigo's falcon?

3. **Summarize** Describe the events that take place during Monna Giovanna's visit to Federigo.

Text Analysis

4. **Analyze Cause and Effect** Review the cause-and-effect diagram you created as you read the selection. What does the story's sequence of events suggest about the relationship between Federigo and Monna Giovanna? Cite details from the text to support your answer.

5. **Understand Plot Elements** What specific **moral dilemmas** arise from love in Boccaccio's tale and complicate its plot?

6. **Draw Conclusions About Character** When Monna visits Federigo's house, is her behavior virtuous or manipulative? Explain why you think so.

7. **Analyze Situational Irony** In literature, **situational irony** occurs when a reader or character expects one thing to happen but something entirely different occurs. Explain the situational irony in lines 153–162.

8. **Compare Texts** Money plays an important role in both "Federigo's Falcon" and Chaucer's "The Pardoner's Tale" (page 169). Compare Federigo's attitude toward money with that of the "three rioters" in Chaucer's tale. What do the characters' reactions reveal about their personalities?

Text Criticism

9. **Critical Interpretations** Author Walter Raleigh says of Boccaccio's tales, "The scene in which they are laid is as wide and well-ventilated as the world. The spirit which inspires them is an absolute humanity, unashamed and unafraid." How does this opinion apply to "Federigo's Falcon"? Cite evidence from the text to support your response.

> *What would you* **SACRIFICE** *for love?*
>
> Federigo eventually marries Monna after making great sacrifices for her love. What if you make a great sacrifice for love, but it does not produce the happy ending you expect? Would it still be worth having made this sacrifice? Why or why not?

COMMON CORE

RL 3 Analyze the impact of the author's choices regarding how to develop and relate elements of a story. **RL 10** Read and comprehend literature, including stories.

Vocabulary in Context

▲ VOCABULARY PRACTICE

Identify the antonym of the boldfaced vocabulary word.

1. **compel:** (a) instigate, (b) fascinate, (c) prevent
2. **consolation:** (a) irritation, (b) derivation, (c) comfort
3. **deign:** (a) esteem, (b) intrude, (c) condescend
4. **discretion:** (a) tactfulness, (b) recklessness, (c) strength
5. **presumption:** (a) assumption, (b) impudence, (c) timidity

ACADEMIC VOCABULARY IN SPEAKING

- concept • culture • parallel • section • structure

Were Federigo's sacrifices for love reasonable? Using Academic Vocabulary words, discuss with a classmate Federigo's **concept** of love as sacrifice.

VOCABULARY STRATEGY: NUANCED MEANINGS IN A THESAURUS

The word **thesaurus** comes from the Greek word for *treasure*. If you are having trouble finding just the right word to express an idea, a thesaurus will provide a treasury of synonyms. Printed and online thesauri are arranged either alphabetically or by subject with an alphabetical index. The example below is based on the best-known thesaurus, *Roget's*. If you looked up *compel*, you would find a short entry with a cross-reference to a longer entry that shows the nuanced meanings of synonyms. For example, *compel's* synonym *force* has two shades of meaning, marked by the boldfaced numbers.

> **compel** *v.* coerce, constrain, make, obligate, oblige, pressure. *See* FORCE.
>
> **force** *v.* **1.** To compel by pressure or threats: blackjack, coerce, dragoon. *Informal:* hijack, strong-arm. *See* PERSUASION. **2.** To cause to act in spite of resistance: coerce, compel, make, obligate, pressure. *See* ATTACK.

PRACTICE The boldfaced word in each sentence below is slightly wrong for the context of the sentence. Look up its synonym (in parentheses) in a thesaurus to find another word with the correct nuance, or shade of meaning. Then use each boldfaced word correctly in a new sentence.

1. He hated being **compelled** but couldn't ignore the villain's threats. (*forced*)
2. The citizens of the peaceful region enjoyed a life of **consolation**. (*comfort*)
3. Each campaign had **deigned** to a new low in negative advertising. (*stooped*)
4. Juan removed the bandage with **discretion**. (*caution*)
5. The counselor tried to instill a sense of **presumption** in her students. (*pride*)

COMMON CORE

L 4c Consult general and specialized reference materials (e.g., thesauruses). L 5b Analyze nuances in the meaning of words with similar denotations.

Interactive Vocabulary THINK central

Go to **thinkcentral.com**.
KEYWORD: HML12-215

Barbara Allan
Robin Hood and the Three Squires
Get Up and Bar the Door
Anonymous Ballads

DID YOU KNOW?

• In early English ballads, Robin Hood was not a champion of the poor but a hardened criminal.

• A sermon dating from 1405 reprimands those who would rather listen to a Robin Hood ballad than attend church services.

Introduction

Ballads

Throughout history, life's tragedies and comedies—real and fictional—have been depicted in song. Narrative songs called **ballads** were popular in England and Scotland during the medieval period, particularly among the common people, many of whom could not read or write. The best of the early ballads were transferred orally from one generation to the next. Stories often changed in the retelling, sometimes resulting in dozens of versions of the same ballad.

Popular Entertainment In the Middle Ages, just as today, audiences craved dramatic—even sensational—stories. Typical subjects of ballads included tragic love, domestic conflicts, disastrous wars and shipwrecks, sensational crimes, and the exploits of enterprising outlaws. Later ballads celebrated historical events and romantic heroes of an earlier chivalrous age. Revenge, rebellion, envy, betrayal, and superstition all found thematic expression in the ballad.

Unknown Authorship The ballad genre is thought to be nearly 1,000 years old, with the earliest known ballad dating from about 1300. Because ballads were not written down until the 18th century, early ballads are all anonymous—the names of

their composers lost forever in the mists of time.

The Legacy of "Barbara Allan" When waves of English, Irish, and Scottish immigrants settled in the New World during the 18th and 19th centuries, they brought many traditions, including their beloved ballads. Over time, some examples have proven consistently popular, becoming part of the American folk heritage. Among these enduring ballads is "Barbara Allan." In the 19th century, a young Abraham Lincoln reportedly knew and sang this tale of unrequited love. Much later, during the 1920s and 1930s, famed country singer Bradley Kincaid featured it on his radio broadcasts from Chicago and Boston. In the 1960s, there was a great resurgence of interest in folk music, particularly in ballads. Singers and political activists Bob Dylan and Joan Baez both recorded the legendary song to wide acclaim. Over the years, countless variations of "Barbara Allan" have been discovered in the United States, with roughly 100 variations observed in Virginia alone. Indeed, scholars believe that "Barbara Allan" is the most widespread folk song in the English language.

● POETIC FORM: BALLAD

Early English and Scottish **ballads** are dramatic stories told in song, using the language of common people. These ballads were composed orally and passed on to subsequent generations through numerous retellings. The three ballads in this lesson are written versions of folk songs that date back centuries.

Like works of fiction, ballads have characters and settings. Most examples also include certain conventions, such as

- tragic or sensational subject matter
- a simple plot involving a single incident
- dialogue

Additionally, ballads usually feature four-line stanzas, or **quatrains,** with rhyming second and fourth lines. The lines are heavily accented, and the stanzas contain repetition of words, phrases, and ideas. In the following example from "Barbara Allan," observe how the patterns of rhyme and repetition help make the lines musically appealing and easy to remember:

Ŏ slówlў, slówlў rắse shĕ úp,

Tŏ thĕ plắce whĕre hĕ wăs lýĭn',

Ănd whĕn shĕ drĕw thĕ cúrtaĭn bý,

"Yŏŭng mán, Ĭ thínk yŏu're dýĭn'."

● READING STRATEGY: UNDERSTAND DIALECT

Dialect is a distinct language spoken by a specific group of people from a particular region. In the ballads you are about to read, certain words from Scottish dialect appear—*twa*, for example, meaning *two*. To help you understand other examples of dialect in the poems, follow these steps:

- Read each ballad through once, using the notes to help you identify the meaning of each word in dialect, then reread the line in which it appears.

- Paraphrase the events in the section of the poem you are reading to make sure you understand what is happening at that point in the story. Understanding these events can provide a context to help you decipher dialect used in that section of the poem.

 Complete the activities in your **Reader/Writer Notebook**.

Why tell stories in SONG?

From time to time, you've probably been infected by an "earworm"—a song that gets stuck in your head and plays over and over and over until you want to scream. Although a nuisance, earworms illustrate what a potent combination rhyme, melody, and lyrics can be— something that no doubt helped ensure the survival of ballads over the centuries.

QUICKWRITE Think of a popular song, radio commercial jingle, or song you remember from your childhood for which you know all or most of the words. Write it down and analyze the elements that make the song so memorable.

BARBARA ALLAN

BARBARA ALLAN
BARBARA ALLAN

It was in and about the Martinmas time,   **1 Martinmas:** November 11 (St.
    When the green leaves were a-fallin';   Martin's Day).
That Sir John Graeme in the West Country
    Fell in love with Barbara Allan.

5 He sent his man down through the town
    To the place where she was dwellin':
"O haste and come to my master dear,
    Gin ye be Barbara Allan."   **8 Gin** (gĭn): if.

O slowly, slowly rase she up,   **9 rase** (rāz): rose.
10   To the place where he was lyin',
And when she drew the curtain by:
    "Young man, I think you're dyin'."

"O it's I'm sick, and very, very sick,
    And 'tis a' for Barbara Allan."
15 "O the better for me ye sal never be,   **15 sal:** shall.
    Though your heart's blood were a-spillin'.

"O dinna ye mind, young man," said she,   **17 dinna ye mind:** don't you
    "When ye the cups were fillin',   remember.
That ye made the healths gae round and round,   **19–20 made ... Allan:** made toasts
20   And slighted Barbara Allan?"   (drinking to people's health) but
                                  failed to toast Barbara Allan.

◀ **Analyze Visuals**
Notice the lighting and colors in this photograph. What mood do they help convey? Explain.

He turned his face unto the wall,
    And death with him was dealin':
"Adieu, adieu, my dear friends all,
    And be kind to Barbara Allan."

25 And slowly, slowly, rase she up,
    And slowly, slowly left him;
And sighing said she could not stay,
    Since death of life had reft him.

She had not gane a mile but twa,
30   When she heard the dead-bell knellin',
And every jow that the dead-bell ga'ed
    It cried, "Woe to Barbara Allan!" **A**

"O mother, mother, make my bed,
    O make it soft and narrow:
35 Since my love died for me today,
    I'll die for him tomorrow."

23 **Adieu:** goodbye.

28 **reft:** deprived.

29 **gane** (gān): gone; **twa:** two.
30 **dead-bell:** a church bell rung to announce a person's death.
31 **jow** (jou): stroke; **ga'ed:** gave.

A **UNDERSTAND DIALECT**
Reread lines 25–32. Which words capture the Scottish **dialect,** or regional language? Explain the strategies you used to understand these words.

ROBIN HOOD
AND THE
THREE SQUIRES

There are twelve months in all the year,
    As I hear many men say,
But the merriest month in all the year
    Is the merry month of May.

5 Now Robin Hood is to Nottingham gone,
    With a link-a-down and a-day,
And there he met a silly old woman,
    Was weeping on the way.

    "What news? what news, thou silly old woman?
10   What news hast thou for me?"
Said she, "There's three squires in Nottingham town,
    Today is condemned to dee."

    "O have they parishes burnt?" he said,
    "Or have they ministers slain?
15 Or have they robbed any virgin,
    Or with other men's wives have lain?"

    "They have no parishes burnt, good sir,"
    Nor yet have ministers slain,
Nor have they robbed any virgin,
20   Nor with other men's wives have lain."

    "O what have they done?" said bold Robin Hood,
    "I pray thee tell to me."
"It's for slaying of the king's fallow deer,
    Bearing their longbows with thee." **B**

---

7 silly: poor; innocent.

11 squires: well-born young men who served as knights' attendants.
12 dee: die.

23 fallow: yellowish red.

B UNDERSTAND DIALECT
Paraphrase lines 21–24. Why have the three squires been condemned to die?

25 "Dost thou not mind, old woman," he said,
    "Since thou made me sup and dine?
By the truth of my body," quoth bold Robin Hood,
    "You could not tell it in better time."

Now Robin Hood is to Nottingham gone,
30   *With a link-a-down and a-day,*
And there he met with a silly old palmer,
    Was walking along the highway.

"What news? what news, thou silly old man?
    What news, I do thee pray?"
35 Said he, "Three squires in Nottingham town
    Are condemned to die this day."

"Come change thine apparel with me, old man,
    Come change thine apparel for mine.
Here is forty shillings in good silver,
40   Go drink it in beer or wine."

"O thine apparel is good," he said,
    "And mine is ragged and torn.
Wherever you go, wherever you ride,
    Laugh ne'er an old man to scorn."

31 palmer: someone who carried a palm leaf to signify that he or she had made a pilgrimage to the Holy Land.

39 shillings: former English silver coins, each worth 1/20 of a pound.

45 "Come change thine apparel with me, old churl,
       Come change thine apparel with mine:
   Here are twenty pieces of good broad gold,
       Go feast thy brethren with wine." **C**

   Then he put on the old man's hat,
50   It stood full high on the crown:
   "The first bold bargain that I come at,
       It shall make thee come down."

   Then he put on the old man's cloak,
       Was patched black, blue, and red:
55 He thought it no shame all the day long
       To wear the bags of bread.

   Then he put on the old man's breeks,
       Was patched from ballup to side:
   "By the truth of my body," bold Robin can say,
60   "This man loved little pride."

   Then he put on the old man's hose,
       Were patched from knee to wrist:
   "By the truth of my body," said bold Robin Hood,
       "I'd laugh if I had any list."

65 Then he put on the old man's shoes,
       Were patched both beneath and aboon:
   Then Robin Hood swore a solemn oath,
       "It's good habit that makes a man."

   Now Robin Hood is to Nottingham gone,
70   *With a link-a-down and a-down,*
   And there he met with the proud sheriff,
       Was walking along the town.

   "O Christ you save, O sheriff," he said,
       "O Christ you save and see:
75 And what will you give to a silly old man
       Today will your hangman be?"

   "Some suits, some suits," the sheriff he said,
       "Some suits I'll give to thee;
   Some suits, some suits, and pence thirteen,
80   Today's a hangman's fee."

C BALLAD
Identify patterns of **repetition** and **rhyme** in lines 33–48. In what ways do these sound devices help you understand Robin's exchange with the old man?

57–58 **breeks . . . side:** trousers reaching to just below the knees, patched from the center to the side.

61 **hose:** tight-fitting outer garment.

64 **list:** wish to do so.

66 **aboon:** above.

68 **habit:** clothing.

73 **O Christ you save:** A respectful greeting meaning "God save you" or "God be with you."

79 **pence thirteen:** thirteen pennies.

Then Robin he turns him round about,
     And jumps from stock to stone:
"By the truth of my body," the sheriff he said,
     "That's well jumped, thou nimble old man."

85 "I was ne'er a hangman in all my life,
     Nor yet intends to trade.
But cursed be he," said bold Robin,
     "That first a hangman was made.

"I've a bag for meal, and a bag for malt,
90   And a bag for barley and corn,
A bag for bread, and a bag for beef,
     And a bag for my little small horn.

"I have a horn in my pocket:
     I got it from Robin Hood;
95 And still when I set it to my mouth,
     For thee it blows little good."

"O wind thy horn, thou proud fellow:
     Of thee I have no doubt;
I wish that thou give such a blast
100   Till both thy eyes fall out."

The first loud blast that he did blow,
     He blew both loud and shrill,
A hundred and fifty of Robin Hood's men
     Came riding over the hill.

105 The next loud blast that he did give,
     He blew both loud and amain,
And quickly sixty of Robin Hood's men
     Came shining over the plain.

"O who are those," the sheriff he said,
110   "Come tripping over the lea?"
"They're my attendants," brave Robin did say,
     "They'll pay a visit to thee."

They took the gallows from the slack,
     They set it in the glen;
115 They hanged the proud sheriff on that,
     Released their own three men. **D**

82 **stock:** a tree stump.

97 **wind:** blow.
98 **doubt:** fear.

106 **amain:** with full force.

108 **shining:** riding courageously.

110 **tripping over the lea** (lē): running over the meadow.
113 **slack:** a very small valley or hollow.

D **BALLAD**
Describe the **subject matter** of this ballad. Which aspects of the ballad would most likely appeal to an audience of common people? Explain your opinion.

GET UP AND BAR THE DOOR

It fell about the Martinmas time,
    And a gay time it was then,
When our goodwife got puddings to make,
    And she's boild them in the pan.

5 The wind sae cauld blew south and north,
    And blew into the floor;
Quoth our goodman to our goodwife,
    "Gae out and bar the door."

"My hand is in my hussyfskap,
10   Goodman, as ye may see;
An it should nae be barrd this hundred year,
    It's no be barrd for me."

They made a paction tween them twa,
    They made it firm and sure,
15 That the first word whae'er should speak,
    Should rise and bar the door. **E**

Then by there came two gentlemen,
    At twelve o'clock at night,
And they could neither see house nor hall,
20   Nor coal nor candle-light.

"Now whether is this a rich man's house,
    Or whether is it a poor?"

1 fell . . . time: happened around St. Martin's Day, November 11.

3 goodwife . . . make: mistress of the household had sausages to make.

5 sae cauld: so cold.

7 Quoth (kwōth) **. . . goodwife:** This husband said to his wife.

8 Gae . . . door: Go out and use the bar to fasten the door shut.

9 hussyfskap: household chores.

11–12 An . . . me: If it should not be barred for a hundred years, it shall still not be barred by me.

13 paction . . . twa: agreement between the two of them.

15 whae'er shoud: whoever should.

E UNDERSTAND DIALECT
Reread and **paraphrase** lines 1–16. What do the husband and wife agree to do? Why?

But ne'er a word wad ane o' them speak,
    For barring of the door.
25 And first they ate the white puddings,
    And then they ate the black;
Tho muckle thought the goodwife to hersel,
    Yet ne'er a word she spake.

Then said the one unto the other,
30   "Here, man, tak ye my knife;
Do ye tak aff the auld man's beard,
    And I'll kiss the goodwife."

"But there's nae water in the house,
    And what shall we do than?"
35 "What ails ye at the pudding-broo,
    That boils into the pan?"

O up then started our goodman,
    An angry man was he:
"Will ye kiss my wife before my een,
40   And scad me wi' pudding-bree?"

Then up and started our goodwife,
    Gied three skips on the floor:
"Goodman, you've spoken the foremost word,
    Get up and bar the door." **F**

27 muckle: a great deal.
28 spake: spoke.

31 tak … beard: take off the old man's beard.

35–36 What … pan?: What's wrong with using the broth the puddings are boiling in?

40 scad: scald; **bree:** broth.

F BALLAD
What might account for the enduring popularity of "Get Up and Bar the Door"? Consider the ballad's subject matter, dialogue, and musical qualities in your response.

Comprehension

1. **Recall** Why does Barbara Allan want to die?

2. **Summarize** What specific steps does Robin Hood take to rescue the three squires from execution?

3. **Clarify** In "Get Up and Bar the Door," what do the couple argue about?

Text Analysis

4. **Draw Conclusions About Characters** What does each of the following events suggest about the relationship between Barbara Allan and Sir John Graeme?

   • his request to see her (lines 1–8)

   • the reason for his illness (lines 13–14)

   • her statement "I'll die for him tomorrow" (line 36)

5. **Make Inferences** Poaching, the killing of a king's game, was punishable by death, even though poaching was often the only way common people could get meat. In "Robin Hood and the Three Squires," what can you infer is Robin's motive for helping the men accused of this crime?

6. **Understand Dialect** Dialect often provides clues about a poem's setting, or location and era. How does dialect help establish the setting of "Get Up and Bar the Door"? Cite evidence to support your ideas.

7. **Analyze Ballad Form** Provide an example from one ballad of repetition and regular rhyme and meter. How do these elements help make its story memorable and entertaining?

Text Criticism

8. **Historical Context** What general impressions of medieval society do you get from reading the ballads? Support your response with details.

> *Why tell stories in* **SONG?**
>
> What are some modern examples of stories told in song? Why do you think telling stories through song remains popular today?

COMMON CORE

RL 5 Analyze how an author's choices concerning how to structure specific parts of a text contribute to its aesthetic impact. **L 3** Apply knowledge of language to understand how language functions in different contexts and to comprehend more fully when reading.

Medieval Life and Times

Centuries after they were written, the colorful, dramatic tales of Chaucer and the lilting medieval ballads continue to entertain modern readers. These lively stories also provide insight into the culture of the Middle Ages. Medieval Europeans lived in a world vastly different from the secular, scientifically ordered world we know today. Consider Chaucer's description of a doctor.

> "A Doctor *too emerged as we proceeded;*
> *No one alive could talk as well as he did*
> *On points of medicine and of surgery,*
> *For, being grounded in astronomy,*
> *He watched his patient closely for the hours*
> *When, by his horoscope, he knew the powers*
> *of favorable planets, then ascendent,*
> *Work on the images for his dependant.*"

Can you imagine a trip to the hospital in which your doctor analyzed your horoscope? It was not only in matters of science but also in courtship, communities, religion, and daily life that the Middle Ages differed so wildly from our own contemporary age.

Writing to Analyze

Of the selections found on pages 144–225, choose three and analyze what they reveal about medieval life—not just how people looked and acted but what they believed and valued.

Consider

- the conflicts faced by the characters, as well as their goals and motivations
- the physical descriptions of the characters, their professions, their behavior, and any direct commentary on their values
- details about the communities in which they lived
- the tone displayed in the selections, and in particular the sense of humor

View of London, Jan Griffier, the Elder. Galleria Sabauda, Turin, Italy. © Alinari/Art Resource, New York.

Extension

VIEWING & REPRESENTING On the basis of Chaucer's descriptive details and your own impressions, select one pilgrim and visually represent that character in a drawing or computer-generated design. Be prepared to explain why you have represented the pilgrim as you have.

COMMON CORE

W 2 Write explanatory texts to examine and convey complex ideas and information through the analysis of content. **W 2b** Develop the topic thoroughly by selecting concrete details.

from Sir Gawain and the Green Knight

Romance by the Gawain Poet Translated by John Gardner

VIDEO TRAILER THINKcentral KEYWORD: HML12-228

Meet the Author

COMMON CORE

RL1 Cite textual evidence to support inferences drawn from the text. RL3 Analyze the impact of the author's choices regarding how to develop and relate elements of a story. RL5 Analyze how an author's choices concerning how to structure specific parts of a text contribute to its overall structure. SL1c Propel conversations by responding to questions that probe reasoning and evidence. L2b Spell correctly.

DID YOU KNOW?

- The first modern edition of *Sir Gawain and the Green Knight* was translated by J. R. R. Tolkien, a respected scholar of Old and Middle English as well as the author of *The Lord of the Rings*.

The Gawain Poet's rich imagination and skill with language have earned him recognition as one of the greatest medieval English poets. Yet his identity remains unknown. Scholars can only speculate on what the background of the Gawain Poet (as he is known) may have been.

Provincial Genius The Gawain Poet's descriptions and language suggest that he wrote the poem during the second half of the 14th century, which would have made him a contemporary of Chaucer's. His dialect, however, indicates that, unlike Chaucer, he was not a Londoner but probably lived somewhere in the northwestern part of England.

The only surviving early manuscript of *Sir Gawain and the Green Knight,* produced by an anonymous copyist around 1400, also contains three religious poems—*Pearl, Purity,* and *Patience*—that are believed to be the work of the Gawain Poet. The manuscript also includes a dozen rough illustrations of the four poems, though it is impossible to verify who created the images for this manuscript. Because *Pearl* is the most technically brilliant of the four poems, the Gawain Poet is sometimes also called the Pearl Poet.

A Man for All Seasons The Gawain Poet's works reveal that he was widely read in French and Latin and had some knowledge of law and theology. Although he was familiar with many details of medieval aristocratic life, his descriptions and metaphors also show a love of the countryside and rural life.

The Ideal Knight In the person of Sir Gawain—a nephew of the legendary King Arthur—the Gawain Poet portrays the ideals medieval knights would have striven to meet. Although real knights were far from perfect, legendary knights such as Sir Gawain dutifully obeyed a code of chivalry that represented a combination of Christian and military ideals, including faith, modesty, loyalty, courtesy, bravery, and honor.

Perhaps the most important virtue for a knight in the age of chivalry was what the Gawain Poet calls *trawthe,* a Middle English word translated variously as "truth," "devotion," and "fidelity." *Trawthe* meant not only keeping one's word but also remaining faithful to the vows taken at the ceremony of knighthood, which included both secular and religious chivalric responsibilities.

● TEXT ANALYSIS: MEDIEVAL ROMANCE

A **medieval romance** is a dramatic verse or prose narrative that usually involves adventurous heroes, idealized love, exotic places, and supernatural events. This genre first appeared in France during the 12th century and soon spread to England. Many of the best-known romances celebrate the legendary King Arthur and his knights, who often risk their lives for the love of a noble lady or to uphold the code of behavior known as chivalry. *Sir Gawain and the Green Knight* is considered one of the finest Arthurian romances. As you read, look for these characteristics of romance:

- idealized or larger-than-life characters
- a hero who faces a challenge or test
- exotic settings and supernatural or magical elements
- hidden or mistaken identity

Review: **Character Traits**

● READING SKILL: MAKE INFERENCES

When you **make inferences,** you are making logical guesses about a text or character based on your own experience and the evidence or clues you find in the text. Making inferences is sometimes called "reading between the lines" because you come to understand something in the text that the author has not explicitly stated. For example, we can infer from the following lines that Arthur and his knights may be frightened by the Green Knight's challenge:

If they were like stone before, they were stiller now,
Every last lord in the hall, both the high and the low;

As you read the excerpt from *Sir Gawain and the Green Knight,* pay close attention to the Gawain Poet's descriptions of the characters and settings. Record your inferences about the story in a chart like the one shown.

Details from the Text	Inferences
"And over his breast hung a beard as big as a bush" (line 4)	There's something wild and uncivilized about the Green Knight.

 Complete the activities in your **Reader/Writer Notebook**.

Is **HONOR** *worth dying for?*

Whether honor is worth dying for is a question a good medieval knight would have no trouble answering. The code of chivalry made it plain that it was his duty to defend—if necessary, with his life—his church, king, and country. Today, blind obedience is often looked upon with suspicion. Many people cannot accept the belief that an abstract concept is worth dying for.

DISCUSS Get together with several classmates to make a Venn diagram that compares and contrasts what it means to be honorable today with what it meant to a medieval knight. Are there similarities in the way we define *honor* today to a medieval knight's definition of it? Discuss how the idea of honor has changed and whether there are leaders today who might be thought of as modern-day knights.

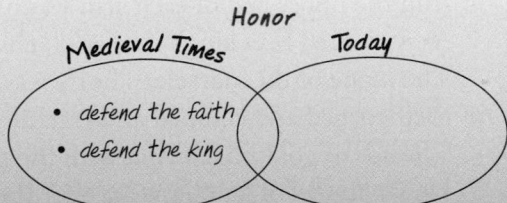

Honor
Medieval Times   Today
- defend the faith
- defend the king

Sir Gawain
AND THE
Green Knight

As the poem begins, Arthur and his knights are gathered to celebrate Christmas and the new year with feasting and revelry. In the midst of their festivities, an enormous man—who is entirely green—bounds through the door.

Splendid that knight errant stood in a splay of green,
And green, too, was the mane of his mighty destrier;
Fair fanning tresses enveloped the fighting man's shoulders,
And over his breast hung a beard as big as a bush;

5 The beard and the huge mane burgeoning forth from his head
Were clipped off clean in a straight line over his elbows,
And the upper half of each arm was hidden underneath
As if covered by a king's chaperon, closed round the neck.
The mane of the marvelous horse was much the same,

10 Well crisped and combed and carefully pranked with knots,
Threads of gold interwoven with the glorious green,
Now a thread of hair, now another thread of gold;
The tail of the horse and the forelock were tricked the same way,
And both were bound up with a band of brilliant green

15 Adorned with glittering jewels the length of the dock,
Then caught up tight with a thong in a criss-cross knot
Where many a bell tinkled brightly, all burnished gold.
So monstrous a mount, so mighty a man in the saddle
Was never once encountered on all this earth
                                    till then;

Analyze Visuals ▶

Which details in this image correspond with the Gawain Poet's description of the Green Knight?

Illustration by Herbert Cole in
English Fairy Tales by Ernest and Grace Rhys.

20 His eyes, like lightning, flashed,
And it seemed to many a man,
That any man who clashed
With him would not long stand. **(A)**

But the huge man came unarmed, without helmet or hauberk,
25 No breastplate or gorget or iron cleats on his arms;
He brought neither shield nor spearshaft to shove or to smite,
But instead he held in one hand a bough of the holly
That grows most green when all the groves are bare
And held in the other an ax, immense and unwieldy,
30 A pitiless battleblade terrible to tell of. . . .

(A) ROMANCE
What details in lines 1–23 make the Green Knight a larger-than-life figure?

24 hauberk (hô′bərk): a coat of chain mail (a type of armor).

25 breastplate or gorget (gôr′jĭt) **or iron cleats:** armor for the chest, the throat, or the shoulders and elbows.

Detail of *The Holy Grail Appears to the Knights of the Round Table* (1927–1932), by Morris & Company, Merton Abbey Tapestry Works, after design about 1891 by Edward Burne-Jones. 250 cm × 530 cm. Münchner Stadtmuseum, Munich.

King Arthur stared down at the stranger before the high dais
And greeted him nobly, for nothing on earth frightened him.
And he said to him, "Sir, you are welcome in this place;
I am the head of this court. They call me Arthur.
35 Get down from your horse, I beg you, and join us for dinner,
And then whatever you seek we will gladly see to."
But the stranger said, "No, so help me God on high,
My errand is hardly to sit at my ease in your castle!
But friend, since your praises are sung so far and wide,
40 Your castle the best ever built, people say, and your barons
The stoutest men in steel armor that ever rode steeds,
Most mighty and most worthy of all mortal men
And tough devils to toy with in tournament games,
And since courtesy is in flower in this court, they say,
45 All these tales, in truth, have drawn me to you at this time.
You may be assured by this holly branch I bear
That I come to you in peace, not spoiling for battle.
If I'd wanted to come in finery, fixed up for fighting,
I have back at home both a helmet and a hauberk,
50 A shield and a sharp spear that shines like fire,
And other weapons that I know pretty well how to use.
But since I don't come here for battle, my clothes are mere cloth.
Now if you are truly as bold as the people all say,
You will grant me gladly the little game that I ask
                              as my right."
55   Arthur gave him answer
                And said, "Sir noble knight,
                If it's a duel you're after,
                We'll furnish you your fight."

"Good heavens, I want no such thing! I assure you, Sire,
60 You've nothing but beardless babes about this bench!
If I were hasped in my armor and high on my horse,
You haven't a man that could match me, your might is so feeble.

And so all I ask of this court is a Christmas game,
For the Yule is here, and New Year's, and here sit young men;
65 If any man holds himself, here in this house, so hardy,
So bold in his blood—and so brainless in his head—
That he dares to stoutly exchange one stroke for another,
I shall let him have as my present this lovely gisarme,
This ax, as heavy as he'll need, to handle as he likes,
70 And I will abide the first blow, bare-necked as I sit.

31 dais (dā´ĭs): a raised platform where honored guests are seated.
33 this place: Camelot, Arthur's favorite castle and the site of his court of the Round Table.

43 In medieval tournaments, knights on horseback fought one another for sport.
44 courtesy is in flower: the high standards of behavior expected in a king's court are currently flourishing.
47 spoiling for: eager for.

61 hasped: fastened.

68 gisarme (gĭ-zärm´): a battle-ax with a long shaft and a two-edged blade.

If anyone here has the daring to try what I've offered,
Leap to me lightly, lad; lift up this weapon;
I give you the thing forever—you may think it your own;
And I will stand still for your stroke, steady on the floor,
75 Provided you honor my right, when my inning comes,
                  to repay.
          But let the respite be
          A twelvemonth and a day;
          Come now, my boys, let's see
          What any here can say."

76–77 let the respite . . . day: let the period of delay be a year and a day.

80 If they were like stone before, they were stiller now,
Every last lord in the hall, both the high and the low;
The stranger on his destrier stirred in the saddle
And ferociously his red eyes rolled around;
He lowered his grisly eyebrows, glistening green,
85 And waved his beard and waited for someone to rise;
When no one answered, he coughed, as if embarrassed,
And drew himself up straight and spoke again:
"What! Can this be King Arthur's court?" said the stranger,
"Whose renown runs through many a realm, flung far and wide?
90 What has become of your chivalry and your conquest,
Your greatness-of-heart and your grimness and grand words?
Behold the radiance and renown of the mighty Round Table
Overwhelmed by a word out of one man's mouth!
You shiver and blanch before a blow's been shown!" **B**
95 And with that he laughed so loud that the lord was distressed;
In chagrin, his blood shot up in his face and limbs
                  so fair;
          More angry he was than the wind,
          And likewise each man there;
          And Arthur, bravest of men,
100   Decided now to draw near.

And he said, "By heaven, sir, your request is strange;
But since you have come here for folly, you may as well find it.
I know no one here who's aghast of your great words.
Give me your gisarme, then, for the love of God,
105 And gladly I'll grant you the gift you have asked to be given."
Lightly the King leaped down and clutched it in his hand;
Then quickly that other lord alighted on his feet.
Arthur lay hold of the ax, he gripped it by the handle,
And he swung it up over him sternly, as if to strike.
110 The stranger stood before him, in stature higher

B MAKE INFERENCES
Why does the Green Knight taunt Arthur and his knights in lines 88–94?

102 folly: dangerous and foolish activity.

By a head or more than any man here in the house;
Sober and thoughtful he stood there and stroked his beard,
And with patience like a priest's he pulled down his collar,
No more unmanned or dismayed by Arthur's might

115 Than he'd be if some baron on the bench had brought him a glass
          of wine.
        Then Gawain, at Guinevere's side,
        Made to the King a sign:
        "I beseech you, Sire," he said,
        "Let this game be mine.

120 "Now if you, my worthy lord," said Gawain to the King,
  "Would command me to step from the dais and stand with you
    there,
  That I might without bad manners move down from my place
  (Though I couldn't, of course, if my liege lady disliked it)
  I'd be deeply honored to advise you before all the court;
125 For I think it unseemly, if I understand the matter,
  That challenges such as this churl has chosen to offer
  Be met by Your Majesty—much as it may amuse you—
  When so many bold-hearted barons sit about the bench:
  No men under Heaven, I am sure, are more hardy in will
130 Or better in body on the fields where battles are fought;
  I myself am the weakest, of course, and in wit the most feeble;
  My life would be least missed, if we let out the truth.
  Only as you are my uncle have I any honor,
  For excepting your blood, I bear in my body slight virtue. **C**
135 And since this affair that's befallen us here is so foolish,
  And since I have asked for it first, let it fall to me.
  If I've reasoned incorrectly, let all the court say,
             without blame."
        The nobles gather round
        And all advise the same:
140   "Let the King step down
        And give Sir Gawain the game!" . . .

Arthur grants Gawain's request to take on the Green Knight's challenge. The Green Knight asks Gawain to identify himself, and the two agree on their pact. Gawain then prepares to strike his blow against the Green Knight.

On the ground, the Green Knight got himself into position,
  His head bent forward a little, the bare flesh showing,
His long and lovely locks laid over his crown

114 unmanned: deprived of manly courage.

116 Guinevere: King Arthur's wife.

123 liege (lēj) **lady:** a lady to whom one owes loyalty and service; here used by Gawain to refer to Queen Guinevere.

126 churl: rude, uncouth person.

C CHARACTER TRAITS
What traits does Gawain reveal about himself in lines 120–134?

145 So that any man there might note the naked neck.
Sir Gawain laid hold of the ax and he hefted it high,
His pivot foot thrown forward before him on the floor,
And then, swiftly, he slashed at the naked neck;
The sharp of the battleblade shattered asunder the bones

150 And sank through the shining fat and slit it in two,
And the bit of the bright steel buried itself in the ground.
The fair head fell from the neck to the floor of the hall
And the people all kicked it away as it came near their feet.
The blood splashed up from the body and glistened on the green,
155 But he never faltered or fell for all of that,
But swiftly he started forth upon stout shanks

And rushed to reach out, where the King's retainers stood,
Caught hold of the lovely head, and lifted it up,
And leaped to his steed and snatched up the reins of the bridle,
160 Stepped into stirrups of steel and, striding aloft,
He held his head by the hair, high, in his hand;
And the stranger sat there as steadily in his saddle
As a man entirely unharmed, although he was headless
                    on his steed.
        He turned his trunk about,
165   That baleful body that bled,
        And many were faint with fright
        When all his say was said.

He held his head in his hand up high before him,
Addressing the face to the dearest of all on the dais;
170 And the eyelids lifted wide, and the eyes looked out,
And the mouth said just this much, as you may now hear:
"Look that you go, Sir Gawain, as good as your word,
And seek till you find me, as loyally, my friend,
As you've sworn in this hall to do, in the hearing of the knights. **D**

D ROMANCE
Which characteristics of
medieval romance are
reflected in lines 161–174?

175 Come to the Green Chapel, I charge you, and take
A stroke the same as you've given, for well you deserve
To be readily requited on New Year's morn.
Many men know me, the Knight of the Green Chapel;
Therefore if you seek to find me, you shall not fail.
180 Come or be counted a coward, as is fitting."
Then with a rough jerk he turned the reins
And haled away through the hall-door, his head in his hand,
And fire of the flint flew out from the hooves of the foal.
To what kingdom he was carried no man there knew,

185　No more than they knew what country it was he came from.

What then?
The King and Gawain there
Laugh at the thing and grin;
And yet, it was an affair
Most marvelous to men. **E**

As the end of the year approaches, Gawain leaves on his quest to find the Green Chapel and fulfill his pledge. After riding through wild country and encountering many dangers, he comes upon a splendid castle. The lord of the castle welcomes Gawain and invites him to stay with him and his lady for a few days.

The lord proposes that he will go out to hunt each day while Gawain stays at the castle. At the end of the day, they will exchange what they have won. While the lord is out hunting, the lady attempts to seduce Gawain. Gawain resists her, however, and on the first two days accepts only kisses, which he gives to the lord at the end of each day in exchange for what the lord has gained in the hunt. On the third day Gawain continues to resist the lady, but she presses him to accept another gift.

190　She held toward him a ring of the yellowest gold
And, standing aloft on the band, a stone like a star
From which flew splendid beams like the light of the sun;
And mark you well, it was worth a rich king's ransom.
But right away he refused it, replying in haste,
195　"My lady gay, I can hardly take gifts at the moment;
Having nothing to give, I'd be wrong to take gifts in turn."
She implored him again, still more earnestly, but again
He refused it and swore on his knighthood that he could take
　　nothing.
Grieved that he still would not take it, she told him then:
200　"If taking my ring would be wrong on account of its worth,
And being so much in my debt would be bothersome to you,
I'll give you merely this sash that's of slighter value."
She swiftly unfastened the sash that encircled her waist,
Tied around her fair tunic, inside her bright mantle;
205　It was made of green silk and was marked of gleaming gold **F**
Embroidered along the edges, ingeniously stitched.
This too she held out to the knight, and she earnestly begged him
To take it, trifling as it was, to remember her by.

E MAKE INFERENCES
Reread lines 185–189. What can you infer about Arthur and Gawain's feelings about their encounter with the Green Knight?

197 implored: begged.

204 tunic...mantle: shirtlike garment worn under a sleeveless cloak.

F GRAMMAR AND STYLE
The Gawain Poet uses alliterative **participial phrases** throughout the poem, which creates a rhythmic or "musical" effect in the selection. "Gleaming gold" in line 205 is a good example.

Queen Guinevere (1858), William Morris. Oil on canvas.

But again he said no, there was nothing at all he could take,
210 Neither treasure nor token, until such time as the Lord
Had granted him some end to his adventure.
"And therefore, I pray you, do not be displeased,
But give up, for I cannot grant it, however fair
                              or right.
               I know your worth and price,
215   And my debt's by no means slight;
               I swear through fire and ice
               To be your humble knight." **G**

"Do you lay aside this silk," said the lady then,
"Because it seems unworthy—as well it may?
220 Listen. Little as it is, it seems less in value,
But he who knew what charms are woven within it
Might place a better price on it, perchance.
For the man who goes to battle in this green lace,
As long as he keeps it looped around him,
225 No man under Heaven can hurt him, whoever may try,
For nothing on earth, however uncanny, can kill him."
The knight cast about in distress, and it came to his heart
This might be a treasure indeed when the time came to take
The blow he had bargained to suffer beside the Green Chapel.
230 If the gift meant remaining alive, it might well be worth it;
So he listened in silence and suffered the lady to speak,
And she pressed the sash upon him and begged him to take it,
And Gawain did, and she gave him the gift with great pleasure
And begged him, for her sake, to say not a word,
235 And to keep it hidden from her lord. And he said he would,
That except for themselves, this business would never be known
                              to a man. **H**
               He thanked her earnestly,
               And boldly his heart now ran;
               And now a third time she
240   Leaned down and kissed her man.

*When the lord returns at the end of the third day, Gawain gives him a
kiss but does not reveal the gift of the sash.*

G CHARACTER TRAITS
In lines 209–217, what does
Gawain's refusal of gifts suggest
about his character?

H MAKE INFERENCES
Reread lines 227–236. Why is
Gawain distressed when he
learns about the sash's magical
powers?

On New Year's Day Gawain must go to meet the Green Knight.
Wearing the green sash, he sets out before dawn. Gawain arrives at
a wild, rugged place, where he sees no chapel but hears the sound
of a blade being sharpened. Gawain calls out, and the Green Knight
appears with a huge ax. The Green Knight greets Gawain, who,
with pounding heart, bows his head to take his blow.

Quickly then the man in the green made ready,
    Grabbed up his keen-ground ax to strike Sir Gawain;
With all the might in his body he bore it aloft
And sharply brought it down as if to slay him;
245 Had he made it fall with the force he first intended
He would have stretched out the strongest man on earth.
But Sir Gawain cast a side glance at the ax
As it glided down to give him his Kingdom Come,
And his shoulders jerked away from the iron a little,
250 And the Green Knight caught the handle, holding it back,
And mocked the prince with many a proud reproof:
"*You* can't be Gawain," he said, "who's thought so good,
A man who's never been daunted on hill or dale!
For look how you flinch for fear before anything's felt!
255 I never heard tell that Sir Gawain was ever a coward!
I never moved a muscle when *you* came down;
In Arthur's hall I never so much as winced.
My head fell off at my feet, yet I never flickered;
But you! You tremble at heart before you're touched!
260 I'm bound to be called a better man than you, then,
                    my lord."
            Said Gawain, "I shied once:
            No more. You have my word.
            But if my head falls to the stones
            It cannot be restored.

265 "But be brisk, man, by your faith, and come to the point!
Deal out my doom if you can, and do it at once,
For I'll stand for one good stroke, and I'll start no more
Until your ax has hit—and that I swear."
"Here goes, then," said the other, and heaves it aloft
270 And stands there waiting, scowling like a madman;
He swings down sharp, then suddenly stops again,
Holds back the ax with his hand before it can hurt,
And Gawain stands there stirring not even a nerve;
He stood there still as a stone or the stock of a tree
275 That's wedged in rocky ground by a hundred roots. ◧
O, merrily then he spoke, the man in green:

248 his Kingdom Come: his death
and entry into the afterlife; a
reference to the sentence "Thy
kingdom come" in the Lord's Prayer.

259–260 The Green Knight has
proclaimed himself a better man
than Gawain.

◧ **MAKE INFERENCES**
Reread lines 271–275. Why does
the Green Knight stop his axe
from falling a second time?

"Good! You've got your heart back! Now I can hit you.
May all that glory the good King Arthur gave you
Prove efficacious now—if it ever can—
280 And save your neck." In rage Sir Gawain shouted,
"*Hit* me, hero! I'm right up to here with your threats!
Is it *you* that's the cringing coward after all?"
"Whoo!" said the man in green, "he's wrathful, too!
No pauses, then; I'll pay up my pledge at once,
                              I vow!"
285   He takes his stride to strike
                       And lifts his lip and brow;
                       It's not a thing Gawain can like,
                       For nothing can save him now!

He raises that ax up lightly and flashes it down,
290 And that blinding bit bites in at the knight's bare neck—
But hard as he hammered it down, it hurt him no more
Than to nick the nape of his neck, so it split the skin;
The sharp blade slit to the flesh through the shiny hide,
And red blood shot to his shoulders and spattered the ground.
295 And when Gawain saw his blood where it blinked in the snow
He sprang from the man with a leap to the length of a spear;
He snatched up his helmet swiftly and slapped it on,
Shifted his shield into place with a jerk of his shoulders,
And snapped his sword out faster than sight; said boldly—
300 And, mortal born of his mother that he was,
There was never on earth a man so happy by half—
"No more strokes, my friend; you've had your swing!
I've stood one swipe of your ax without resistance;
If you offer me any more, I'll repay you at once
305 With all the force and fire I've got—as you
                              will see.
                       I take one stroke, that's all,
                       For that was the compact we
                       Arranged in Arthur's hall;
                       But now, no more for me!"

310 The Green Knight remained where he stood, relaxing on his ax—
Settled the shaft on the rocks and leaned on the sharp end—
And studied the young man standing there, shoulders hunched,
And considered that staunch and doughty stance he took,
Undaunted yet, and in his heart he liked it;
315 And then he said merrily, with a mighty voice—
With a roar like rushing wind he reproved the knight—
"Here, don't be such an ogre on your ground!
Nobody here has behaved with bad manners toward you

Language Coach

Frequently Misused Words
Reread lines 278-280. *Efficacious* can be a synonym for *effective*, but only when applied to things. Both words mean "producing the desired effect." Is *efficacious* used correctly in this sentence? *King Arthur was an efficacious leader.* Why or why not?

307 **compact:** binding agreement.

313 **staunch:** firm; **doughty** (dou'tē): brave.

Or done a thing except as the contract said.

320 I owed you a stroke, and I've struck; consider yourself
Well paid. And now I release you from all further duties.
If I'd cared to hustle, it may be, perchance, that I might
Have hit somewhat harder, and then you might well be cross!
The first time I lifted my ax it was lighthearted sport,

325 I merely feinted and made no mark, as was right,
For you kept our pact of the first night with honor
And abided by your word and held yourself true to me,
Giving me all you owed as a good man should.
I feinted a second time, friend, for the morning

330 You kissed my pretty wife twice and returned me the kisses;
And so for the first two days, mere feints, nothing more
                    severe.
            A man who's true to his word,
            There's nothing he needs to fear;
            You failed me, though, on the third
335   Exchange, so I've tapped you here.

    "That sash you wear by your scabbard belongs to me;
    My own wife gave it to you, as I ought to know.
    I know, too, of your kisses and all your words
    And my wife's advances, for I myself arranged them.

340 It was I who sent her to test you. I'm convinced
    You're the finest man that ever walked this earth.
    As a pearl is of greater price than dry white peas,
    So Gawain indeed stands out above all other knights.
    But you lacked a little, sir; you were less than loyal;

345 But since it was not for the sash itself or for lust
    But because you loved your life, I blame you less."
    Sir Gawain stood in a study a long, long while,
    So miserable with disgrace that he wept within,
    And all the blood of his chest went up to his face

350 And he shrank away in shame from the man's gentle words.
    The first words Gawain could find to say were these:
    "Cursed be cowardice and covetousness both,
    Villainy and vice that destroy all virtue!"
    He caught at the knots of the girdle and loosened them

355 And fiercely flung the sash at the Green Knight.
    "There, there's my fault! The foul fiend vex it!
    Foolish cowardice taught me, from fear of your stroke,
    To bargain, covetous, and abandon my kind,

325 feinted (fān′tĭd): pretended to attack.

336 scabbard (skăb′ərd): a sheath for a dagger or sword.

354 girdle: sash.

356 vex: harass; torment.

The selflessness and loyalty suitable in knights;
360 Here I stand, faulty and false, much as I've feared them,
Both of them, untruth and treachery; may they see sorrow
                  and care!
        I can't deny my guilt;
        My works shine none too fair!
        Give me your good will
365   And henceforth I'll beware." **J**

*A*t that, the Green Knight laughed, saying graciously,
"Whatever harm I've had, I hold it amended
Since now you're confessed so clean, acknowledging sins
And bearing the plain penance of my point;
370 I consider you polished as white and as perfectly clean
As if you had never fallen since first you were born.
And I give you, sir, this gold-embroidered girdle,
For the cloth is as green as my gown. Sir Gawain, think
On this when you go forth among great princes;
375 Remember our struggle here; recall to your mind
This rich token. Remember the Green Chapel.
And now, come on, let's both go back to my castle
And finish the New Year's revels with feasting and joy,
                not strife,
        I beg you," said the lord,
380   And said, "As for my wife,
        She'll be your friend, no more
        A threat against your life."

"No, sir," said the knight, and seized his helmet
And quickly removed it, thanking the Green Knight,
385 "I've reveled too well already; but fortune be with you;
May He who gives all honors honor you well." . . .

And so they embraced and kissed and commended each other
To the Prince of Paradise, and parted then
                in the cold;
        Sir Gawain turned again
390   To Camelot and his lord;
        And as for the man of green,
        He went wherever he would. **K**

J ROMANCE
Paraphrase lines 357–365. What ideals of chivalry does Gawain believe he has betrayed?

367–371 The Green Knight is saying that Gawain has paid for his fault by admitting it and offering his head to the ax.

369 penance: punishment accepted by a person to show sorrow for wrongdoing; **point:** blade.

COMMON CORE L 2b

Language Coach

Roots and Affixes For words that end in a vowel and consonant, normal spelling rules require doubling the final consonant when adding a suffix that begins with a vowel. Reread line 385. Does *revel* follow this rule? What other words are like *revel*?

COMMON CORE RL 5

K PLOT
Sir Gawain and the Green Knight is a narrative: it has a clear beginning, middle and end, and focuses on a conflict and its eventual resolution. These elements of story-telling contribute to its **plot**, the sequence of actions and events that unfold in a narrative. Like most stories, this one builds to a **climax** as Gawain realizes he has betrayed his chivalric ideals, and the Green Knight passes judgment on him. Reread lines 366–392. What judgment does the Green Knight pass on Gawain? How does Gawain react? What is the resolution that results from this final scene?

Comprehension

1. **Recall** What challenge does the Green Knight make to King Arthur and his knights?

2. **Summarize** What happens when Sir Gawain meets the Green Knight on New Year's Day?

3. **Clarify** At the end of the poem, what is the Green Knight's opinion of Gawain?

Text Analysis

● 4. **Examine Medieval Romance** In medieval romances, there is often a character whose identity is hidden or mistaken. Explain how this characteristic affects the outcome of *Sir Gawain and the Green Knight*.

5. **Identify Situational Irony** Situational irony is a contrast between what is expected and what actually occurs. What is ironic about Sir Gawain's acceptance of the sash from the lady of the castle?

6. **Analyze Character's Motives** Why does Gawain decline the Green Knight's invitation to celebrate the new year together at the end of the poem?

● 7. **Make Inferences** Review the inference chart you created as you read. Which character shows greater courage, Sir Gawain or the Green Knight? Support your answer with evidence from the text.

8. **Compare Texts** Both *Sir Gawain and the Green Knight* and Chaucer's "The Wife of Bath's Tale" portray knights who undergo a test. Compare the **tone,** or writer's attitude toward a subject, in these two selections. Identify words and details that help convey the tone in each poem.

Text Criticism

9. **Social Context** It is believed that *Sir Gawain and the Green Knight* was written in the late 1300s, as the age of chivalry began to wane. Though legend has it that Gawain was one of Arthur's finest and most loyal knights, the Gawain Poet depicts him as flawed. Why might the Gawain poet have portrayed Gawain this way?

> *Is* **HONOR** *worth dying for?*
>
> King Arthur's knights devote themselves to following the code of chivalry. Trying to live up to such high ideals can be a double-edged sword. What are the advantages and disadvantages of having such high ideals?

COMMON CORE

RL 1 Cite textual evidence to support inferences drawn from the text. **RL 3** Analyze the impact of the author's choices regarding how to develop and relate elements of a story. **RL 5** Analyze how an author's choices concerning how to structure specific parts of a text contribute to its overall structure.

Language

◆ **GRAMMAR AND STYLE: Use Alliteration**

Review the **Grammar and Style** note on page 237. The lilting quality of the Gawain Poet's verse owes much to his use of **alliteration,** the repetition of consonant sounds at the beginning of words—a technique that can add emphasis, heighten mood, or create a musical effect in a line or passage. Many of the alliterative elements in the poem consist of **participles,** verb forms that function as adjectives, and **participial phrases,** participles plus their modifiers and complements.

> *Fair fanning tresses enveloped the fighting man's shoulders,*
> *And over his breast hung a beard as big as a bush;* (lines 3–4)

Notice how the writer uses the alliterative participles *fanning* and *fighting*, repeating the consonant *f* to emphasize the Green Knight's appearance.

PRACTICE Identify the participles in the following lines from the poem, then write your own passages by similarly using participles to create alliteration.

EXAMPLE

He lowered his grisly eyebrows, glistening green,
And waved his beard and waited for someone to rise;

He held a large ax, blinding bright,
But seemed friendly enough as he sized up the knights.

---

1. The sharp of the battleblade shattered asunder the bones
   And sank through the shining fat and slit it in two,

2. And then he said merrily, with a mighty voice—
   With a roar like rushing wind he reproved the knight—

READING-WRITING CONNECTION

YOUR TURN Expand your understanding of *Sir Gawain and the Green Knight* by responding to this prompt. Then, use the **revising tips** to improve your eyewitness account.

WRITING PROMPT	REVISING TIPS
CREATE AN EYEWITNESS ACCOUNT Imagine that you are a guest at King Arthur's court. Write a **three-to-five-paragraph eyewitness account** about the Green Knight's first appearance. Include a description of the event and excerpts from "interviews" with Knights of the Round Table who watched the event unfold.	• Organize your eyewitness account in chronological order and include quotations from various knights. • Add participial phrases and alliteration to at least one sentence to enliven your description.

◌ **COMMON CORE**

L 1 Demonstrate command of the conventions of standard English grammar when writing. **W 3** Write narratives to develop imagined events. **W 3a–b, d** Engage and orient the reader by introducing a narrator; create a smooth progression of events; use dialogue and description to develop events and characters; use precise words and phrases to convey a vivid picture of events and characters.

Interactive Revision **THINK** central

Go to **thinkcentral.com**.
KEYWORD: HML12-245

from Le Morte d'Arthur

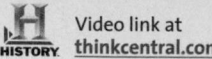 Video link at thinkcentral.com

Romance by Sir Thomas Malory Retold by Keith Baines

DID YOU KNOW?

Sir Thomas Malory . . .

- completed *Le Morte d'Arthur* while in Newgate Prison in London.
- spent more than ten years in prison, accused of violent acts.

Meet the Author

Sir Thomas Malory early 1400s–1471

The legend of King Arthur is one of the most popular and enduring legends in Western culture. Most English-speaking readers have been introduced to the Arthurian legend through *Le Morte d'Arthur,* a work consisting of a number of interwoven tales that chronicle the rise and fall of King Arthur and his court.

Adventurous Life Although his identity is not certain, most scholars believe that the author of *Le Morte d'Arthur* was born into a fairly prosperous family in Warwickshire, England. As a young man, Thomas Malory fought in the Hundred Years' War. He was knighted in about 1442 and was later elected to Parliament. Malory then became embroiled in the violent political conflicts that preceded the outbreak of the Wars of the Roses.

A staunch supporter of the house of Lancaster and its claim to the throne, Malory was imprisoned repeatedly by the Yorkist government on a variety of charges, including rape, robbery, cattle rustling, bribery, and attempted murder.

He pleaded innocent to all the charges, and his guilt was never proven. It is possible that his outspoken opposition to the ruling family provoked enemies to accuse him falsely in some instances.

Writing from Behind Bars Malory wrote *Le Morte d'Arthur* while serving a series of prison terms that began in 1451. He finished the work in prison in 1469. At the end of the book, he asks that readers "pray . . . that God send me good deliverance. And when I am dead, I pray you all pray for my soul."

The Arthurian Legends The first edition of *Le Morte d'Arthur* was published in 1485, fourteen years after Malory's death. *Le Morte d'Arthur* remains the most complete English version of the Arthurian legends, which are believed to have existed since the sixth century as part of the oral tradition in France and England. Some historians believe that the fictional Arthur was modeled on a real fifth- or sixth-century Celtic military leader, although the historical Arthur was undoubtedly very different from Malory's Arthur, who ruled an idealized world of romance, chivalry, and magic.

As the first prose epic written in English, *Le Morte d'Arthur* is an important milestone in English literature. It has proved to be an astonishingly popular work, having not once gone out of print since it was first published in 1485—a testament to Malory's singular talent as a writer.

THiNK central

Author Online

Go to **thinkcentral.com**. KEYWORD: HML12-246

TEXT ANALYSIS: CONFLICT

The plot of a medieval romance is typically driven by **conflict,** a struggle between opposing forces. The conflict can be **external,** between a character and an outside force, or it can be **internal,** taking place within the mind of a character. Sometimes a single event contains both types of conflict; for example, in a battle, a knight may externally struggle against an enemy warrior and internally struggle to be courageous and live up to the ideals of chivalry. In addition, conflicts often reveal a character's **motivations,** or reasons for acting in a certain way. As you read *Le Morte d'Arthur*, look for examples of both types of conflict faced by King Arthur, Sir Launcelot, and the other knights, and for how these conflicts shed light on each character's motivations.

Review: **Medieval Romance**

READING SKILL: SUMMARIZE

Summarizing can help you keep track of events in an action-filled narrative, such as a romance. When you **summarize** a narrative, you briefly describe its plot developments. An effective summary should describe events in the same order in which they appear in the narrative and leave out details that are not essential to the plot. As you read, use a chart like the one shown to help you summarize the main plot developments.

Passage	Summary
lines 1–6	Arthur sails to France, where Launcelot has settled, and attacks Launcelot's lands.

VOCABULARY IN CONTEXT

Knowing the following boldfaced words will help you read *Le Morte d'Arthur.* To show that you understand the terms, try to replace each one with a word or phrase that has the same meaning.

1. The king established **dominion** over the nation.
2. It is **incumbent** upon the captain to try to save his ship.
3. Having been robbed and injured, we seek **redress.**
4. The leader of the rebellion was able to **usurp** the throne.
5. Some people are open and frank, while others use **guile.**

 Complete the activities in your **Reader/Writer Notebook**.

What is your ultimate LOYALTY?

One of the most important components of the medieval code of chivalry was the requirement that a knight be loyal to his king and country. In *Le Morte d'Arthur,* Sir Launcelot, King Arthur's most exemplary knight, falls in love with the king's wife and faces a crisis of loyalty of epic proportions.

QUICKWRITE Loyalty is still a highly valued human quality, one that sometimes requires personal sacrifice. Make a list of individuals or groups to whom you owe some loyalty. Review your list, then write a paragraph to explain which person or group is the one you would not abandon under any circumstances.

Le Morte d'Arthur

Sir Thomas Malory

BACKGROUND King Arthur's favorite knight, Sir Launcelot, has fallen in love with the king's wife, Gwynevere. The secret love affair is exposed by Sir Modred, Arthur's son by another woman, and Gwynevere is sentenced to burn at the stake. While rescuing the imprisoned Gwynevere, Launcelot slays two knights who, unknown to him at the time, are the brothers of Sir Gawain, a favorite nephew of Arthur's. After a reconciliation, Launcelot returns Gwynevere to Arthur to be reinstated as queen. At the urging of Sir Gawain, who still wants revenge on Launcelot, the king banishes Launcelot to France, where the following excerpt begins.

Analyze Visuals ▶
What details in this image suggest the size and power of the opposing armies?

The Siege of Benwick

When Sir Launcelot had established **dominion** over France, he garrisoned the towns and settled with his army in the fortified city of Benwick, where his father King Ban had held court.

King Arthur, after appointing Sir Modred ruler in his absence, and instructing Queen Gwynevere to obey him, sailed to France with an army of sixty thousand men, and, on the advice of Sir Gawain, started laying waste[1] all before him. **Ⓐ**

News of the invasion reached Sir Launcelot, and his counselors advised him. Sir Bors[2] spoke first:

"My lord Sir Launcelot, is it wise to allow King Arthur to lay your lands waste
10 when sooner or later he will oblige you to offer him battle?"

dominion (də-mĭn′yən) *n.* rule or power to rule; mastery

Ⓐ CONFLICT
Reread lines 1–6 and the background note. How have Launcelot's past actions set the stage for his current conflict with King Arthur?

---

1. **laying waste:** destroying.
2. **Sir Bors:** Sir Bors de Ganis, Launcelot's cousin and the son of King Bors.

Arthur Uses Excalibur, Arthur Rackham.
Illustration from *The Romance of King Arthur*.

Sir Lyonel[3] spoke next: "My lord, I would recommend that we remain within the walls of our city until the invaders are weakened by cold and hunger, and then let us sally forth[4] and destroy them."

Next, King Bagdemagus: "Sir Launcelot, I understand that it is out of courtesy that you permit the king to ravage your lands, but where will this courtesy end? If you remain within the city, soon everything will be destroyed."

Then Sir Galyhud: "Sir, you command knights of royal blood; you cannot expect them to remain meekly within the city walls. I pray you, let us encounter the enemy on the open field, and they will soon repent of their expedition." **B**

20   And to this the seven knights of West Britain all muttered their assent. Then Sir Launcelot spoke:

"My lords, I am reluctant to shed Christian blood in a war against my own liege;[5] and yet I do know that these lands have already suffered depredation[6] in the wars between King Claudas and my father and uncle, King Ban and King Bors. Therefore I will next send a messenger to King Arthur and sue[7] for peace, for peace is always preferable to war."

Accordingly a young noblewoman accompanied by a dwarf was sent to King Arthur. They were received by the gentle knight Sir Lucas the Butler.

"My lady, you bring a message from Sir Launcelot?" he asked.

30   "My lord, I do. It is for the king."

"Alas! King Arthur would readily be reconciled to Sir Launcelot, but Sir Gawain forbids it; and it is a shame, because Sir Launcelot is certainly the greatest knight living."

The young noblewoman was brought before the king, and when he had heard Sir Launcelot's entreaties for peace he wept, and would readily have accepted them had not Sir Gawain spoken up:

"My liege, if we retreat now we will become a laughingstock, in this land and in our own. Surely our honor demands that we pursue this war to its proper conclusion."

40   "Sir Gawain, I will do as you advise, although reluctantly, for Sir Launcelot's terms are generous and he is still dear to me. I beg you make a reply to him on my behalf." **C**

Sir Gawain addressed the young noblewoman:

"Tell Sir Launcelot that we will not bandy words with him, and it is too late now to sue for peace. Further that I, Sir Gawain, shall not cease to strive against him until one of us is killed."

The young noblewoman was escorted back to Sir Launcelot, and when she had delivered Sir Gawain's message they both wept. Then Sir Bors spoke:

B SUMMARIZE
Summarize in one sentence the advice Launcelot receives from his counselors in lines 9–19.

C CONFLICT
What **internal conflict** does Arthur reveal in lines 34–42? How does it motivate his decision?

---

3. **Sir Lyonel** (lī′ən-əl): another of Launcelot's cousins.

4. **sally forth:** rush out suddenly in an attack.

5. **liege** (lēj): a lord or ruler to whom one owes loyalty and service.

6. **depredation** (dĕp′rĭ-dā′shən) n. destruction caused by robbery or looting

7. **sue:** appeal; beg.

"My lord, we beseech you, do not look so dismayed! You have many
50 trustworthy knights behind you; lead us onto the field and we will put an end to
this quarrel."

"My lords, I do not doubt you, but I pray you, be ruled by me: I will not
lead you against our liege until we ourselves are endangered; only then can we
honorably sally forth and defeat him."

Sir Launcelot's nobles submitted; but the next day it was seen that King Arthur
had laid siege to the city of Benwick. Then Sir Gawain rode before the city walls
and shouted a challenge:

"My lord Sir Launcelot: have you no knight who will dare to ride forth and
break spears with me? It is I, Sir Gawain."

60 Sir Bors accepted the challenge. He rode out of the castle gate, they
encountered, and he was wounded and flung from his horse. His comrades
helped him back to the castle, and then Sir Lyonel offered to joust. He too was
overthrown and helped back to the castle.

Thereafter, every day for six months Sir Gawain rode before the city and
overthrew whoever accepted his challenge. Meanwhile, as a result of skirmishes,
numbers on both sides were beginning to dwindle. Then one day Sir Gawain
challenged Sir Launcelot:

"My lord Sir Launcelot: traitor to the king and to me, come forth if you dare
and meet your mortal foe, instead of lurking like a coward in your castle!"

70 Sir Launcelot heard the challenge, and one of his kinsmen spoke to him:
"My lord, you must accept the challenge, or be shamed forever."

"Alas, that I should have to fight Sir Gawain!" said Sir Launcelot. "But now I
am obliged to."

Sir Launcelot gave orders for his most powerful courser[8] to be harnessed, and
when he had armed, rode to the tower and addressed King Arthur:

"My lord King Arthur, it is with a heavy heart that I set forth to do battle with
one of your own blood; but now it is **incumbent** upon my honor to do so. For six
months I have suffered your majesty to lay my lands waste and to besiege me in
my own city. My courtesy is repaid with insults, so deadly and shameful that now
80 I must by force of arms seek **redress**."

"Have done, Sir Launcelot, and let us to battle!" shouted Sir Gawain.

Sir Launcelot rode from the city at the head of his entire army. King Arthur was
astonished at his strength and realized that Sir Launcelot had not been boasting
when he claimed to have acted with forbearance[9]. "Alas, that I should ever have
come to war with him!" he said to himself.

It was agreed that the two combatants should fight to the death, with
interference from none. Sir Launcelot and Sir Gawain then drew apart and

---

COMMON CORE RL 4

Language Coach

Etymology A word's
etymology, or origin, can
help you understand its
connotations. In line 61,
encountered means "met
in battle." It comes from
the Old French *encontre*
("against"). How does
the etymology help you
understand the more
current meaning of
encountered?

incumbent (ĭn-kŭm′bənt)
adj. required as a duty or
an obligation

redress (rĭ-drĕs′) *n.*
repayment for a wrong
or an injury

---

8. **courser:** a horse trained for battle.

9. **forbearance** (fôr-bâr′əns) n. self-control; patient restraint

galloped furiously together, and so great was their strength that their horses crashed to the ground and both riders were overthrown.

90   A terrible sword fight commenced, and each felt the might of the other as fresh wounds were inflicted with every blow. For three hours they fought with scarcely a pause, and the blood seeped out from their armor and trickled to the ground. Sir Launcelot found to his dismay that Sir Gawain, instead of weakening, seemed to increase in strength as they proceeded, and he began to fear that he was battling not with a knight but with a fiend incarnate.[10] He decided to fight defensively and to conserve his strength.

It was a secret known only to King Arthur and to Sir Gawain himself that his strength increased for three hours in the morning, reaching its zenith[11] at noon, and waning again. This was due to an enchantment that had been cast over him
100 by a hermit[12] when he was still a youth. Often in the past, as now, he had taken advantage of this.

Thus when the hour of noon had passed, Sir Launcelot felt Sir Gawain's strength return to normal, and knew that he could defeat him.

"Sir Gawain, I have endured many hard blows from you these last three hours, but now beware, for I see that you have weakened, and it is I who am the stronger."

Thereupon Sir Launcelot redoubled his blows, and with one, catching Sir Gawain sidelong on the helmet, sent him reeling to the ground. Then he courteously stood back. **D**

110 "Sir Launcelot, I still defy you!" said Sir Gawain from the ground. "Why do you not kill me now? for I warn you that if ever I recover I shall challenge you again."

"Sir Gawain, by the grace of God I shall endure you again," Sir Launcelot replied, and then turned to the king:

"My liege, your expedition can find no honorable conclusion at these walls, so I pray you withdraw and spare your noble knights. Remember me with kindness and be guided, as ever, by the love of God."

"Alas!" said the king, "Sir Launcelot scruples[13] to fight against me or those of my blood, and once more I am beholden to him."

120 Sir Launcelot withdrew to the city and Sir Gawain was taken to his pavilion, where his wounds were dressed. King Arthur was doubly grieved, by his quarrel with Sir Launcelot and by the seriousness of Sir Gawain's wounds.

For three weeks, while Sir Gawain was recovering, the siege was relaxed and both sides skirmished only halfheartedly. But once recovered, Sir Gawain rode up to the castle walls and challenged Sir Launcelot again:

"Sir Launcelot, traitor! Come forth, it is Sir Gawain who challenges you."

D SUMMARIZE
Describe the battle between Launcelot and Gawain. What tactic does Launcelot use to overcome Gawain's secret advantage?

---

10. **fiend incarnate:** devil in human form.

11. **zenith:** highest point; peak.

12. **hermit:** a person living in solitude for religious reasons.

13. **scruples:** hesitates for reasons of principle.

"Sir Gawain, why these insults? I have the measure of your strength and you can do me but little harm."

"Come forth, traitor, and this time I shall make good my revenge!" Sir Gawain
130 shouted.

"Sir Gawain, I have once spared your life; should you not beware of meddling with me again?"

Sir Launcelot armed and rode out to meet him. They jousted and Sir Gawain broke his spear and was flung from his horse. He leaped up immediately, and putting his shield before him, called on Sir Launcelot to fight on foot.

"The issue[14] of a mare has failed me; but I am the issue of a king and a queen and I shall not fail!" he exclaimed.

As before, Sir Launcelot felt Sir Gawain's strength increase until noon, during which period he defended himself, and then weaken again.

140 "Sir Gawain, you are a proved knight, and with the increase of your strength until noon you must have overcome many of your opponents, but now your strength has gone, and once more you are at my mercy."

Sir Launcelot struck out lustily and by chance reopened the wound he had made before. Sir Gawain fell to the ground in a faint, but when he came to he said weakly:

"Sir Launcelot, I still defy you. Make an end of me, or I shall fight you again!"

"Sir Gawain, while you stand on your two feet I will not gainsay[15] you; but I will never strike a knight who has fallen. God defend me from such dishonor!" **E**

Sir Launcelot walked away and Sir Gawain continued to call after him:
150 "Traitor! Until one of us is dead I shall never give in!"

For a month Sir Gawain lay recovering from his wounds, and the siege remained; but then, as Sir Gawain was preparing to fight Sir Launcelot once more, King Arthur received news which caused him to strike camp and lead his army on a forced march to the coast, and thence to embark for Britain.

The Day of Destiny

During the absence of King Arthur from Britain, Sir Modred, already vested with sovereign powers,[16] had decided to **usurp** the throne. Accordingly, he had false letters written—announcing the death of King Arthur in battle—and delivered to himself. Then, calling a parliament, he ordered the letters to be read and persuaded the nobility to elect him king. The coronation took place at Canterbury
160 and was celebrated with a fifteen-day feast.

Sir Modred then settled in Camelot and made overtures to Queen Gwynevere to marry him. The queen seemingly acquiesced, but as soon as she had won his confidence, begged leave to make a journey to London in order to prepare her

E MEDIEVAL ROMANCE
In what ways does Launcelot exemplify the ideals of chivalry in lines 138–148?

usurp (yōō-sûrp′) v. to seize unlawfully by force

---

14. **issue:** offspring.

15. **gainsay:** deny.

16. **vested with sovereign powers:** given the authority of a king.

trousseau.[17] Sir Modred consented, and the queen rode straight to the Tower which, with the aid of her loyal nobles, she manned and provisioned for her defense. **F**

Sir Modred, outraged, at once marched against her, and laid siege to the Tower, but despite his large army, siege engines, and guns, was unable to effect a breach. He then tried to entice the queen from the Tower, first by **guile** and then by threats, but she would listen to neither. Finally the Archbishop of Canterbury
170 came forward to protest:

"Sir Modred, do you not fear God's displeasure? First you have falsely made yourself king; now you, who were begotten by King Arthur on his aunt,[18] try to marry your father's wife! If you do not revoke your evil deeds I shall curse you with bell, book, and candle."[19]

"Fie on you! Do your worst!" Sir Modred replied.

"Sir Modred, I warn you take heed! or the wrath of the Lord will descend upon you."

"Away, false priest, or I shall behead you!" **G**

The Archbishop withdrew, and after excommunicating Sir Modred, abandoned
180 his office and fled to Glastonbury. There he took up his abode as a simple hermit, and by fasting and prayer sought divine intercession[20] in the troubled affairs of his country.

Sir Modred tried to assassinate the Archbishop, but was too late. He continued to assail the queen with entreaties and threats, both of which failed, and then the news reached him that King Arthur was returning with his army from France in order to seek revenge.

Sir Modred now appealed to the barony to support him, and it has to be told that they came forward in large numbers to do so. Why? it will be asked. Was not King Arthur, the noblest sovereign Christendom had seen, now leading his armies
190 in a righteous cause? The answer lies in the people of Britain, who, then as now, were fickle. Those who so readily transferred their allegiance to Sir Modred did so with the excuse that whereas King Arthur's reign had led them into war and strife, Sir Modred promised them peace and festivity. **H**

Hence it was with an army of a hundred thousand that Sir Modred marched to Dover to battle against his own father, and to withhold from him his rightful crown.

As King Arthur with his fleet drew into the harbor, Sir Modred and his army launched forth in every available craft, and a bloody battle ensued in the ships and on the beach. If King Arthur's army were the smaller, their courage was the
200 higher, confident as they were of the righteousness of their cause. Without stint[21] they battled through the burning ships, the screaming wounded, and the corpses

---

17. **trousseau** (trōō'sō): clothes and linens that a bride brings to her marriage.

18. **begotten . . . aunt:** Modred is the son of Arthur and Queen Margawse, the sister of Arthur's mother, Queen Igraine.

19. **I shall curse you with bell, book, and candle:** The archbishop is threatening to excommunicate Modred— that is, to deny him participation in the rites of the church. In the medieval ritual of excommunication, a bell was rung, a book was shut, and a candle was extinguished.

20. **divine intercession:** assistance from God.

21. **stint:** holding back.

F SUMMARIZE
Reread lines 155–165 and summarize the events that open this section of the selection.

guile (gīl) *n.* clever trickery; deceit

G CONFLICT
Describe the **external conflict** in lines 166–178. What motivates Mordred's behavior?

Analyze Visuals ▶
William Morris was a designer and artist who was heavily influenced by medieval arts and crafts. What details in this image suggest Gwynevere's emotional state?

H SUMMARIZE
Summarize lines 187–193. Why do many people in Britain support Modred?

Guinevere (1858), William Morris. Watercolor and drawing on paper, 1,264 mm × 552 mm. Tate Gallery, London.

floating on the bloodstained waters. Once ashore they put Sir Modred's entire army to flight.

The battle over, King Arthur began a search for his casualties, and on peering into one of the ships found Sir Gawain, mortally wounded. Sir Gawain fainted when King Arthur lifted him in his arms; and when he came to, the king spoke:

"Alas! dear nephew, that you lie here thus, mortally wounded! What joy is now left to me on this earth? You must know it was you and Sir Launcelot I loved above all others, and it seems that I have lost you both."

210 "My good uncle, it was my pride and my stubbornness that brought all this about, for had I not urged you to war with Sir Launcelot your subjects would not now be in revolt. Alas, that Sir Launcelot is not here, for he would soon drive them out! And it is at Sir Launcelot's hands that I suffer my own death: the wound which he dealt me has reopened. I would not wish it otherwise, because is he not the greatest and gentlest of knights?

"I know that by noon I shall be dead, and I repent bitterly that I may not be reconciled to Sir Launcelot; therefore I pray you, good uncle, give me pen, paper, and ink so that I may write to him."

A priest was summoned and Sir Gawain confessed; then a clerk brought ink, 220 pen, and paper, and Sir Gawain wrote to Sir Launcelot as follows:

"Sir Launcelot, flower of the knighthood: I, Sir Gawain, son of King Lot of Orkney and of King Arthur's sister, send you my greetings!

"I am about to die; the cause of my death is the wound I received from you outside the city of Benwick; and I would make it known that my death was of my own seeking, that I was moved by the spirit of revenge and spite to provoke you to battle.

"Therefore, Sir Launcelot, I beseech you to visit my tomb and offer what prayers you will on my behalf; and for myself, I am content to die at the hands of the noblest knight living.

230 "One more request: that you hasten with your armies across the sea and give succor[22] to our noble king. Sir Modred, his bastard son, has usurped the throne and now holds against him with an army of a hundred thousand. He would have won the queen, too, but she fled to the Tower of London and there charged her loyal supporters with her defense.

"Today is the tenth of May, and at noon I shall give up the ghost; this letter is written partly with my blood. This morning we fought our way ashore, against the armies of Sir Modred, and that is how my wound came to be reopened. We won the day, but my lord King Arthur needs you, and I too, that on my tomb you may bestow your blessing." ❶

240 Sir Gawain fainted when he had finished, and the king wept. When he came to he was given extreme unction,[23] and died, as he had anticipated, at the hour of noon. The king buried him in the chapel at Dover Castle, and there many came to see him, and all noticed the wound on his head which he had received from Sir Launcelot.

---

22. **succor** (sŭk′ər) n. aid in a time of need; relief

23. **extreme unction:** a ritual in which a priest anoints and prays for a dying person.

❶ **SUMMARIZE**
Reread lines 221–239. Briefly summarize Gawain's letter to Sir Launcelot.

Then the news reached Arthur that Sir Modred offered him battle on the field at Baron Down. Arthur hastened there with his army, they fought, and Sir Modred fled once more, this time to Canterbury.

When King Arthur had begun the search for his wounded and dead, many volunteers from all parts of the country came to fight under his flag, convinced
250 now of the rightness of his cause. Arthur marched westward, and Sir Modred once more offered him battle. It was assigned for the Monday following Trinity Sunday, on Salisbury Down.

Sir Modred levied fresh troops from East Anglia and the places about London, and fresh volunteers came forward to help Arthur. Then, on the night of Trinity Sunday, Arthur was vouchsafed[24] a strange dream:

He was appareled in gold cloth and seated in a chair which stood on a pivoted scaffold. Below him, many fathoms deep, was a dark well, and in the water swam serpents, dragons, and wild beasts. Suddenly the scaffold tilted and Arthur was flung into the water, where all the creatures struggled toward him and began
260 tearing him limb from limb.

Arthur cried out in his sleep and his squires hastened to waken him. Later, as he lay between waking and sleeping, he thought he saw Sir Gawain, and with him a host of beautiful noblewomen. Arthur spoke:

"My sister's son! I thought you had died; but now I see you live, and I thank the lord Jesu! I pray you, tell me, who are these ladies?"

"My lord, these are the ladies I championed[25] in righteous quarrels when I was on earth. Our lord God has vouchsafed that we visit you and plead with you not to give battle to Sir Modred tomorrow, for if you do, not only will you yourself be killed, but all your noble followers too. We beg you to be warned, and to make a treaty
270 with Sir Modred, calling a truce for a month, and granting him whatever terms he may demand. In a month Sir Launcelot will be here, and he will defeat Sir Modred."

Thereupon Sir Gawain and the ladies vanished, and King Arthur once more summoned his squires and his counselors and told them his vision. Sir Lucas and Sir Bedivere were commissioned to make a treaty with Sir Modred. They were to be accompanied by two bishops and to grant, within reason, whatever terms he demanded.

The ambassadors found Sir Modred in command of an army of a hundred thousand and unwilling to listen to overtures of peace. However, the ambassadors eventually prevailed on him, and in return for the truce granted him suzerainty[26]
280 of Cornwall and Kent, and succession to the British throne when King Arthur died. The treaty was to be signed by King Arthur and Sir Modred the next day. They were to meet between the two armies, and each was to be accompanied by no more than fourteen knights.

Both King Arthur and Sir Modred suspected the other of treachery, and gave orders for their armies to attack at the sight of a naked sword. When they met at the appointed place the treaty was signed and both drank a glass of wine.

Language Coach

Roots and Affixes Two examples of **suffixes** (affixes at the end of a word) are –*ness* ("state of") and –*eous* ("full of"). Each suffix appears on this page, in lines 250 and 266. What is the base word in both cases? What does each word mean?

24. **vouchsafed:** granted.

25. **championed:** defended or fought for.

26. **suzerainty** (sōō′zər-ən-tē): the position of feudal lord.

Then, by chance, one of the soldiers was bitten in the foot by an adder[27] which had lain concealed in the brush. The soldier unthinkingly drew his sword to kill it, and at once, as the sword flashed in the light, the alarums[28] were given, trumpets
290 sounded, and both armies galloped into the attack. **J**

"Alas for this fateful day!" exclaimed King Arthur, as both he and Sir Modred hastily mounted and galloped back to their armies. There followed one of those rare and heartless battles in which both armies fought until they were destroyed. King Arthur, with his customary valor, led squadron after squadron of cavalry into the attack, and Sir Modred encountered him unflinchingly. As the number of dead and wounded mounted on both sides, the active combatants continued dauntless until nightfall, when four men alone survived.

King Arthur wept with dismay to see his beloved followers fallen; then, struggling toward him, unhorsed and badly wounded, he saw Sir Lucas the Butler
300 and his brother, Sir Bedivere.[29]

"Alas!" said the king, "that the day should come when I see all my noble knights destroyed! I would prefer that I myself had fallen. But what has become of the traitor Sir Modred, whose evil ambition was responsible for this carnage?"

Looking about him King Arthur then noticed Sir Modred leaning with his sword on a heap of the dead.

"Sir Lucas, I pray you give me my spear, for I have seen Sir Modred."

"Sire, I entreat you, remember your vision—how Sir Gawain appeared with a heaven-sent message to dissuade you from fighting Sir Modred. Allow this fateful day to pass; it is ours, for we three hold the field, while the enemy is broken."

310 "My lords, I care nothing for my life now! And while Sir Modred is at large I must kill him: there may not be another chance." **K**

"God speed you, then!" said Sir Bedivere.

When Sir Modred saw King Arthur advance with his spear, he rushed to meet him with drawn sword. Arthur caught Sir Modred below the shield and drove his spear through his body; Sir Modred, knowing that the wound was mortal, thrust himself up to the handle of the spear, and then, brandishing his sword in both hands, struck Arthur on the side of the helmet, cutting through it and into the skull beneath; then he crashed to the ground, gruesome and dead.

King Arthur fainted many times as Sir Lucas and Sir Bedivere struggled with
320 him to a small chapel nearby, where they managed to ease his wounds a little. When Arthur came to, he thought he heard cries coming from the battlefield.

"Sir Lucas, I pray you, find out who cries on the battlefield," he said.

Wounded as he was, Sir Lucas hobbled painfully to the field, and there in the moonlight saw the camp followers stealing gold and jewels from the dead, and murdering the wounded. He returned to the king and reported to him what he had seen, and then added:

J SUMMARIZE
Summarize lines 277–290. What leads to the breaking of the treaty between King Arthur and Modred?

K CONFLICT
What **motivates** Arthur's decision to fight Modred despite Sir Bedivere's advice?

---

27. **adder:** a poisonous snake.

28. **alarums:** calls to arms.

29. **Sir Lucas . . . Bedivere:** brothers who are members of King Arthur's court.

Arthur Versus Modred, Arthur Rackham. Illustration from *The Romance of King Arthur*.

"My lord, it surely would be better to move you to the nearest town?"

"My wounds forbid it. But alas for the good Sir Launcelot! How sadly I have missed him today! And now I must die—as Sir Gawain warned me I would—
330 repenting our quarrel with my last breath."

Sir Lucas and Sir Bedivere made one further attempt to lift the king. He fainted as they did so. Then Sir Lucas fainted as part of his intestines broke through a wound in the stomach. When the king came to, he saw Sir Lucas lying dead with foam at his mouth.

"Sweet Jesu, give him succor!" he said. "This noble knight has died trying to save my life—alas that this was so!"

▲ **Analyze Visuals**
What elements of this image help convey the ferocity of the battle between Arthur and Modred?

Sir Bedivere wept for his brother.

"Sir Bedivere, weep no more," said King Arthur, "for you can save neither your
340 brother nor me; and I would ask you to take my sword Excalibur[30] to the shore of
the lake and throw it in the water. Then return to me and tell me what you have
seen."

"My lord, as you command, it shall be done."

Sir Bedivere took the sword, but when he came to the water's edge, it appeared
so beautiful that he could not bring himself to throw it in, so instead he hid it by
a tree, and then returned to the king.

"Sir Bedivere, what did you see?"

"My lord, I saw nothing but the wind upon the waves."

"Then you did not obey me; I pray you, go swiftly again, and this time fulfill
350 my command."

Sir Bedivere went and returned again, but this time too he had failed to fulfill
the king's command.

"Sir Bedivere, what did you see?"

"My lord, nothing but the lapping of the waves."

"Sir Bedivere, twice you have betrayed me! And for the sake only of my sword: it
is unworthy of you! Now I pray you, do as I command, for I have not long to live."

This time Sir Bedivere wrapped the girdle around the sheath and hurled it as
far as he could into the water. A hand appeared from below the surface, took the
sword, waved it thrice, and disappeared again. Sir Bedivere returned to the king
360 and told him what he had seen. **Ⓛ**

"Sir Bedivere, I pray you now help me hence, or I fear it will be too late."

Sir Bedivere carried the king to the water's edge, and there found a barge in
which sat many beautiful ladies with their queen. All were wearing black hoods,
and when they saw the king, they raised their voices in a piteous lament.

"I pray you, set me in the barge," said the king.

Sir Bedivere did so, and one of the ladies laid the king's head in her lap; then
the queen spoke to him:

"My dear brother, you have stayed too long: I fear that the wound on your head
is already cold."

370 Thereupon they rowed away from the land and Sir Bedivere wept to see them go.

"My lord King Arthur, you have deserted me! I am alone now, and among
enemies."

"Sir Bedivere, take what comfort you may, for my time is passed, and now I
must be taken to Avalon[31] for my wound to be healed. If you hear of me no more,
I beg you pray for my soul."

The barge slowly crossed the water and out of sight while the ladies wept. Sir
Bedivere walked alone into the forest and there remained for the night.

In the morning he saw beyond the trees of a copse[32] a small hermitage.
He entered and found a hermit kneeling down by a fresh tomb. The hermit was

Ⓛ CONFLICT
What **internal conflict**
does Sir Bedivere
experience in lines
343–360? How does he
ultimately resolve it?

---

30. **Excalibur** (ĕk-skăl′ə-bər): Arthur's remarkable sword, which originally came from the Lady of the Lake.

31. **Avalon:** an island paradise of Celtic legend, where heroes are taken after death.

32. **copse** (kŏps): a grove of small trees.

380 weeping as he prayed, and then Sir Bedivere recognized him as the Archbishop of Canterbury, who had been banished by Sir Modred.

"Father, I pray you, tell me, whose tomb is this?"

"My son, I do not know. At midnight the body was brought here by a company of ladies. We buried it, they lit a hundred candles for the service, and rewarded me with a thousand bezants."[33]

"Father, King Arthur lies buried in this tomb."

Sir Bedivere fainted when he had spoken, and when he came to he begged the Archbishop to allow him to remain at the hermitage and end his days in fasting and prayer.

390 "Father, I wish only to be near to my true liege."

"My son, you are welcome; and do I not recognize you as Sir Bedivere the Bold, brother to Sir Lucas the Butler?"

Thus the Archbishop and Sir Bedivere remained at the hermitage, wearing the habits of hermits and devoting themselves to the tomb with fasting and prayers of contrition.[34]

Such was the death of King Arthur as written down by Sir Bedivere. By some it is told that there were three queens on the barge: Queen Morgan le Fay, the Queen of North Galys, and the Queen of the Waste Lands; and others include the name of Nyneve, the Lady of the Lake who had served King Arthur well in the 400 past, and had married the good knight Sir Pelleas.

In many parts of Britain it is believed that King Arthur did not die and that he will return to us and win fresh glory and the Holy Cross of our Lord Jesu Christ; but for myself I do not believe this, and would leave him buried peacefully in his tomb at Glastonbury, where the Archbishop of Canterbury and Sir Bedivere humbled themselves, and with prayers and fasting honored his memory. And inscribed on his tomb, men say, is this legend:

HIC IACET ARTHURUS,
REX QUONDAM REXQUE FUTURUS.[35]

---

33. **bezants** (bĕz′ənts): gold coins.

34. **contrition** (kən-trĭsh′ən): sincere regret for wrongdoing.

35. ***Hic iacet Arthurus, rex quondam rexque futurus*** (hĭk yä′kĕt är-tōō′rŏŏs rāks kwôn′dăm rāk′skwĕ fōō-tōō′rŏŏs) *Latin:* Here lies Arthur, the once and future king.

William Caxton, the first English printer, had a significant impact on the literature of his day. In his preface to the first edition of Malory's *Le Morte d'Arthur* (1485), Caxton describes his anticipated audience and reveals his purpose in publishing the work.

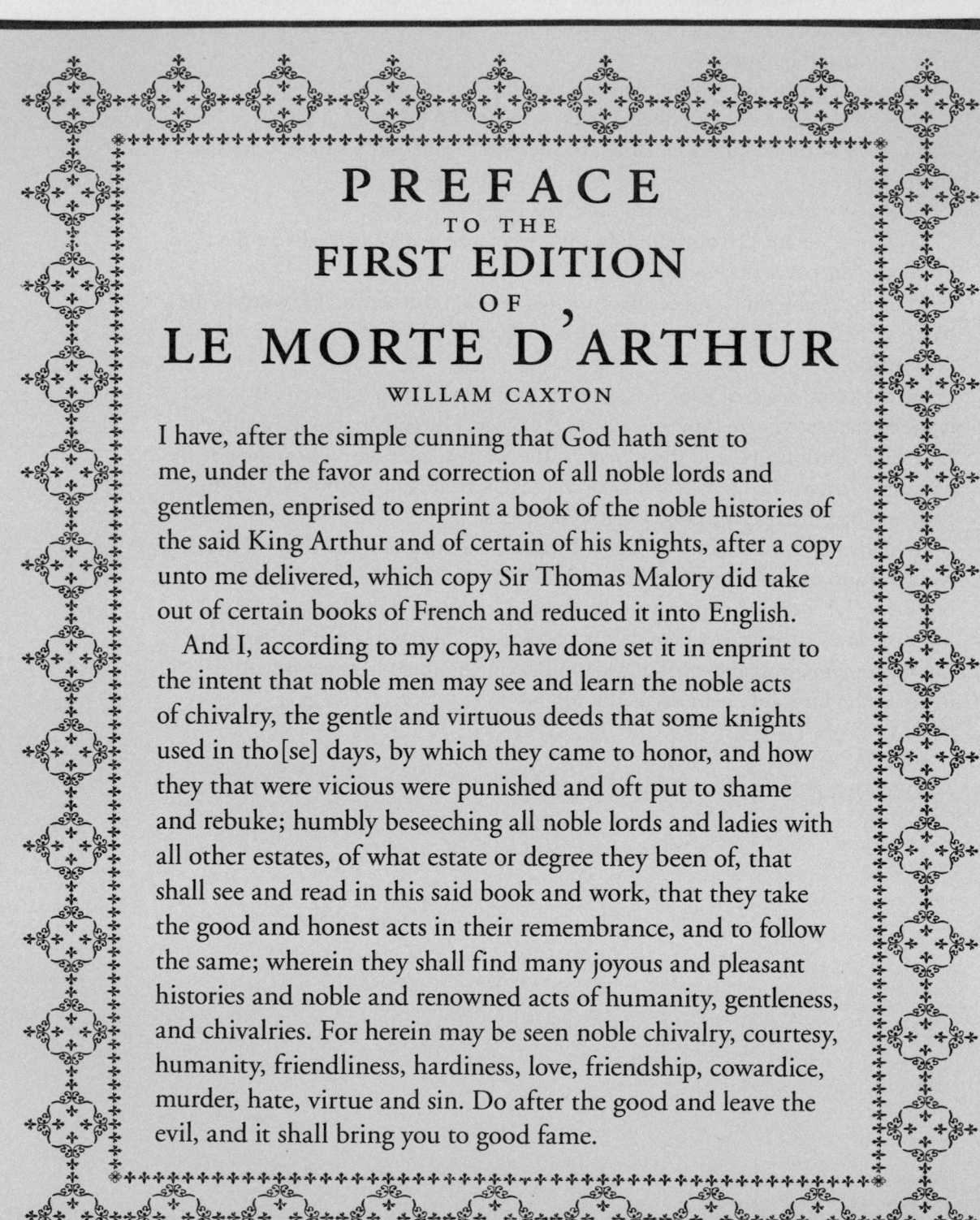

PREFACE
TO THE
FIRST EDITION
OF
LE MORTE D'ARTHUR

WILLAM CAXTON

I have, after the simple cunning that God hath sent to me, under the favor and correction of all noble lords and gentlemen, enprised to enprint a book of the noble histories of the said King Arthur and of certain of his knights, after a copy unto me delivered, which copy Sir Thomas Malory did take out of certain books of French and reduced it into English.

And I, according to my copy, have done set it in enprint to the intent that noble men may see and learn the noble acts of chivalry, the gentle and virtuous deeds that some knights used in tho[se] days, by which they came to honor, and how they that were vicious were punished and oft put to shame and rebuke; humbly beseeching all noble lords and ladies with all other estates, of what estate or degree they been of, that shall see and read in this said book and work, that they take the good and honest acts in their remembrance, and to follow the same; wherein they shall find many joyous and pleasant histories and noble and renowned acts of humanity, gentleness, and chivalries. For herein may be seen noble chivalry, courtesy, humanity, friendliness, hardiness, love, friendship, cowardice, murder, hate, virtue and sin. Do after the good and leave the evil, and it shall bring you to good fame.

Comprehension

1. **Recall** What prevents Arthur from accepting Launcelot's peace offers?

2. **Recall** Why does Arthur call off the siege of Benwick and return to Britain?

3. **Clarify** What happens when Arthur fights Modred?

Text Analysis

4. **Summarize** Review the chart you created as you read. Then summarize the ways in which Gawain's hostility toward Launcelot contributes to Arthur's downfall.

5. **Analyze Conflict** To what extent are Arthur's **internal** and **external conflicts** with Launcelot similar to his conflicts with Modred? In what ways are they different?

6. **Examine Medieval Romance** Review the Text Analysis instruction on page 229. *Le Morte d'Arthur* is one of the most influential medieval romances. What characteristics of medieval romance appear in this work?

7. **Compare and Contrast Characters** Make a Venn diagram like the one shown to help you compare and contrast Gawain's and Launcelot's character traits. Which knight's failure to exemplify the ideals of chivalry is greater? Support your answer with evidence from the text.

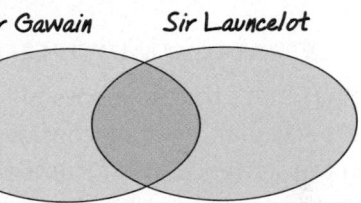

Sir Gawain   *Sir Launcelot*

8. **Evaluate Texts** In his preface on page 262, William Caxton explains that he has published *Le Morte d'Arthur* to provide a model for good behavior. How well does this selection from Malory's romance fulfill Caxton's purpose?

Text Criticism

9. **Critical Interpretations** One critic has suggested that when "confronted by a need to make a decision in a moment of crisis," Arthur "invariably chooses the wrong course of action" because he is unable or unwilling to see the situation as it really is. Think about the various conflicts, both internal and external, that Arthur struggles with in the selection, and consider the important decisions he makes. Do you agree or disagree that he "invariably chooses the wrong course of action"? Cite evidence from the text to support your opinion.

> *What is your ultimate* **LOYALTY?**
>
> Should Arthur have forgiven Launcelot for his disloyalty? Why or why not? Can loyalty, once lost, ever be restored? Explain your response.

COMMON CORE

RL 2 Provide an objective summary of the text.
RL 3 Analyze the impact of the author's choices regarding how to develop and relate elements of a story. **RL 5** Analyze how an author's choices concerning how to structure specific parts of a text contribute to its overall structure and meaning.

Vocabulary in Context

▲ VOCABULARY PRACTICE

Choose the vocabulary word that best completes each sentence. Use the context clues in the sentence to help you decide.

1. It is _____ on you to work hard if you want to succeed.
2. The queen had _____ over six new colonies.
3. The king's nephew tried to _____ power for himself.
4. He demanded that someone offer _____ for his grievances.
5. Clever but dishonest, she often used _____ to trick others.

WORD LIST
dominion
guile
incumbent
redress
usurp

ACADEMIC VOCABULARY IN SPEAKING

• concept • culture • parallel • section • structure

How do the internal conflicts of Gawain and Arthur **parallel** each other? Which of them changes most dramatically in response to his internal conflict and why? Discuss these questions with a partner, using at least two additional Academic Vocabulary words in your discussion.

VOCABULARY STRATEGY: MULTIPLE-MEANING WORDS

Incumbent has more than one possible meaning. To determine which meaning applies in a particular instance, consider the context, or surroundings. For instance, in the sentence "It is incumbent on my honor to do so," the context suggests that *incumbent* means "required as a duty or obligation."

COMMON CORE

L 4 Determine or clarify the meaning of multiple-meaning words. **L 4d** Verify the preliminary determination of the meaning of a word by checking the inferred meaning in context.

PRACTICE In the passage below, use context to determine the likely meaning of each boldfaced word. Then explain which context clues in the paragraph helped you determine the correct meaning of the word.

The legend of Arthur has captured the imagination of writers since at least 1136, with the appearance of Geoffrey of Monmouth's *History of the Kings of Britain*. From this text, later writers would **adopt** some of the essential **elements** of Arthurian lore: Merlin, Excalibur, and Arthur's final **repose** at Avalon. A few decades later, the French poet Chrétien de Troyes introduced the character of Launcelot to the growing **body** of Arthurian literature. *Le Morte d'Arthur* (1469), one of the earliest books printed in English, would eventually become the **ultimate** source for writers of Arthurian literature.

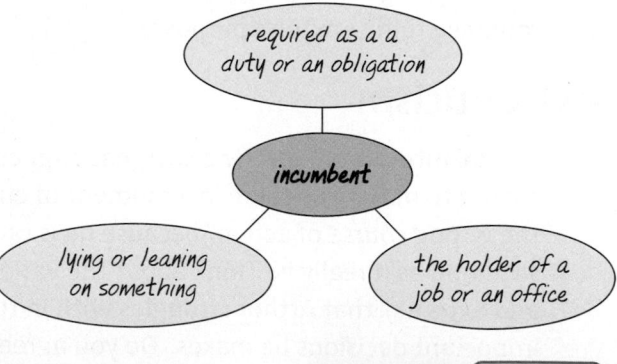

Interactive Vocabulary **THINK** central

Go to **thinkcentral.com**.
KEYWORD: HML12-264

The Legacy of Medieval Romance

Firmly embedded in the tradition of Arthurian romance is the code of chivalry prescribed for all knights. Along with the traits of bravery, courtesy, and personal honor, this code of conduct required that men behave gallantly toward women. It is this treatment of women that, even today, is most often associated with mention of the chivalric code.

Writing to Persuade

Re-examine the selections on pages 230–261 for examples of chivalric behavior, but look for more than just gallantry toward women. Find examples of knights displaying the other ideals of chivalry you've learned about: loyalty, modesty, faith, honor, bravery, and courtesy. Use these examples to write an essay persuading a contemporary audience—your peers, parents, and teachers—that chivalry is or is not an outmoded virtue in the 21st century.

Consider

- which details from the selections will provide you with the best support for your argument
- what language will best persuade your audience
- how to organize your writing to prove your argument clearly and logically

Extension

SPEAKING & LISTENING

Divide into teams to debate this statement: *Chivalry is dead.* You may use your persuasive essays as a jumping-off point, but with your team members find additional examples from today's world to prove that chivalry is alive and well or has withered and died in the face of our modern sensibilities and values.

COMMON CORE

W 1 Write arguments to support claims in an analysis of substantive topics or texts. **W 1a** Create an organization that logically sequences claim(s), reasons, and evidence. **W 9** Draw evidence from literary or informational texts to support analysis. **SL 1a** Come to discussions having read and researched material under study.

The Holy Grail Appears to the Knights of the Round Table (1450).

Legends in Film: King Arthur

Film Clips on Media Smart DVD-ROM

How do movies portray LEGENDS?

A **legend** is an unverified story passed down from earlier times. Legends often change over time as storytellers embellish some details and diminish others to appeal to different audiences or achieve different purposes. In addition, each society may impose its own values on a legendary figure. In examining two very different film versions of King Arthur, one of the Western world's oldest legends, you'll see how the era in which the films were created determined how the legendary king was portrayed.

Background

A Tale of Two Arthurs Some historians believe the Arthurian legend is based on the exploits of a real 5th- or 6th-century British military leader who defended Britain against invading Anglo-Saxons. In the 15th century, Sir Thomas Malory's *Le Morte d'Arthur* combined various versions of the legend to include supernatural elements, love stories, and detailed adventures of the Knights of the Round Table. Malory's interpretation of the Arthurian legend is the most widely read English language version in history.

Nearly 500 years after Malory's version, in December of 1960, Alan Jay Lerner and Frederick Loewe debuted *Camelot,* their musical retelling of the Arthurian legend. The tenor of the time was upbeat: the United States was a world superpower and had experienced eight years of unprecedented economic growth. Lerner and Loewe's Arthur reflects that time. Eschewing the brutal battle tales and death-defying adventures of Arthur and his brave knights, the musical focuses on the love triangle between Arthur, Guinevere, and Sir Lancelot. The first clip you'll view is from the film version of *Camelot,* which was released in 1967.

The second clip you'll view is from *King Arthur,* the 2004 film version of the Arthurian legend. It reflects its time as well. Filmed in the aftermath of the 2001 terrorist attacks on the United States and during the U.S. war in Iraq, *King Arthur* reflects the earliest known sources of Arthur's history, presenting him as a valiant but brutal defender of the failing Roman Empire and the British people under its rule. You'll view a clip from each film. As you analyze these very different interpretations of the King Arthur legend, consider the time in which each film was made and how it may have impacted the filmmakers' choices.

Media Literacy: Legends Over Time

Filmmakers adapting an old tale may go beyond a simple retelling. They can weave their own interpretations and beliefs into a film through **mise en scène,** a term that refers to the staging of a scene's action and the way in which it is photographed. The elements of mise en scène include **setting, props, lighting, composition, facial expressions, body language, costumes,** and **makeup.** Filmmakers carefully choose and combine each detail to form their overall vision. As you watch a legend adapted to film, think about how the filmmakers used mise en scène to reflect the issues of their time.

from Camelot

from King Arthur

ANALYZING MISE EN SCÈNE	OPTIMISTIC TIMES	PESSIMISTIC TIMES
Notice how the **setting** and **props** establish the world of the film.	An upbeat time may be reflected in lavish studio sets.	Less innocent times call for films shot on grim, realistic locations.
Lighting helps create mood and guide the audience's attention.	To reflect a positive time, soft lighting may bathe a scene in a tranquil glow.	The shadows and glares of harder, direct lighting can create a harsh mood of bleak reality.
Notice the **composition**—camera angles and movement, and the placement of characters and objects within the frame.	Characters moving closer together within the frame can convey a growing feeling of good will.	Choppy cuts and distance between two characters in an argument can imply conflict and create a disjointed feeling.
Watch the actors' **facial expressions** and **body language.**	In an era of idealism, an actor may portray a legendary hero as friendly and unguarded, even playful.	In more cynical times, a hero might be more closed-off, displaying the tense posture and set jaw of grim determination.
Consider the actors' **costumes** and **makeup.**	Idealized characters of traditional legends may display a surprising ability to remain clean and neat.	On the other hand, heroes in cynical times may be dirty and rumpled under the best of circumstances.

Viewing Guide for

King Arthur in Film

To critically analyze these clips, you may need to view them more than once. Both scenes depict Arthur and Guinevere's first meeting. Notice how the directors stage the scenes and how the actors portray their characters. Look for ways you think the *Camelot* clip might reflect the hopeful idealism of the 1960s and how the *King Arthur* clip might reflect a post-9/11 United States at war in 2004. Consider the following questions to help you examine the clips.

NOW VIEW

FIRST VIEWING: Comprehension

1. **Recall** In *Camelot*, what does Guinevere ask Arthur to do for her before she learns his identity?
2. **Recall** In *King Arthur*, how does Guinevere describe the impression she has of Arthur based on his reputation?

CLOSE VIEWING: Media Literacy

3. **Compare Performances** Guinevere is prominent in both of these clips. Compare the two actresses' portrayals of the queen-to-be. Describe the portrayals and cite details that create your impression of each. Consider
   - facial expressions
   - body language
   - costumes and makeup
4. **Make Judgments** Consider your own perceptions of how a king should act—especially a legendary king like Arthur. Of the two very different portrayals in these clips, which Arthur seems more like a truly legendary king? Cite examples from the clips to support your answer.
5. **Analyze Film Technique** Think about each element of **mise en scène** in the scenes you viewed. For each clip, describe the decisions the director made and the effect they had on the look and mood of the scene.

Write or Discuss

Analyze Historical Context Think about the eras in which these films were released. The musical that the film *Camelot* was based on came out in 1960, a time when many Americans were optimistic about the future. *King Arthur* was released in 2004, three years after the United States had been attacked by terrorists and during the U.S. war in Iraq. Write a paragraph describing whether you think these films reflect their times. Cite evidence from the clips to explain your answer. Consider

- the look of the films
- the way the characters are portrayed
- your knowledge of the eras in which the movies were released
- how the audiences of the day might have reacted to or interpreted the films

Create a Film Treatment

Create a Film Treatment A film treatment is a brief written description of a proposed film. It covers the basic plot lines and conflicts, the characters, and even location ideas. The purpose of a treatment is twofold: to interest financial backers, directors, and actors, and to provide those same people with a fully conceived and visualized sense of what the movie will be.

Choose a famous myth or legend on which to base a movie treatment. What message do you want to convey with your interpretation? What might the story offer today's society? How do you want audiences to perceive this legend? Your treatment should be as detailed as possible about the story you're going to tell, as well as how you're going to tell it.

HERE'S HOW Keep the following in mind as you write your treatment:

- Include details of the major plot lines.
- Describe the events in a detailed manner so readers can visualize them.
- Include information on costuming, setting, lighting, and composition.
- Include some representative dialogue from a key moment in the film.

Further Exploration

Many More Arthurs There have been many different film adaptations of the Arthurian legend, some that treat the legend respectfully and others that poke fun at the ancient story. While many movies concentrate on the romantic entanglements between King Arthur, Guinevere, and Sir Lancelot, others highlight the adventures of the Knights of the Round Table. Research some of the adaptations that have been filmed over the years, and choose a few that were made at different time periods. Watch them in a small group. Analyze the films to see how Arthur and the other main characters are presented. Are they heroic? comical? romantic? tragic? Present your findings to the class.

COMMON CORE

RL 7 Analyze multiple interpretations of a story, evaluating how each version interprets the source text. **W 1** Write arguments to support claims in an analysis of substantive topics. **W 7** Conduct short research projects to answer a question. **W 10** Write routinely over shorter time frames for a range of tasks, purposes, and audiences.

Media Tools

THINK central

Go to thinkcentral.com.
KEYWORD: HML12-269

Analysis of a Poem

You have seen how the literary elements of a poem work together to contribute to the poem's meaning. In this workshop, you will examine a poem of your choice and will present your findings in an analysis.

 Complete the workshop activities in your **Reader/Writer Notebook**.

WRITE WITH A PURPOSE

WRITING TASK

Write an essay in which you **analyze a poem.** Help your audience understand the poet's use of stylistic elements.

Idea Starters
- a poem in this book
- a poem by a local poet
- regional poetry from a favorite state or country
- poetry sites on the Internet

THE ESSENTIALS

Here are some common purposes, audiences, and formats for a literary analysis.

PURPOSES	AUDIENCES	FORMATS
• to share your analysis of a poem • to offer insight into the theme and literary techniques of a poem	• classmates and teacher • parents • literary club members • blog readers	• essay for class • blog • message board posting • literary review in school newspaper • podcast script

COMMON CORE TRAITS

1. DEVELOPMENT OF IDEAS
- presents an **engaging introduction**
- develops a **controlling idea** that offers an **analysis** of the author's style
- supports main points of analysis with **relevant details** and **quotations from the text**
- concludes with a **summary of main points** and insights

2. ORGANIZATION OF IDEAS
- **organizes** ideas in a logical way
- uses varied **transitions** and **syntax** to create cohesion and connect ideas

3. LANGUAGE FACILITY AND CONVENTIONS
- establishes and maintains a **formal style** and **objective tone**
- uses **precise language** and defines **domain-specific vocabulary**
- punctuates **quotations** correctly
- employs correct **grammar, usage,** and **spelling**

Writing Online

THINK central

Go to **thinkcentral.com**.
KEYWORD: HML12N-270

Planning/Prewriting

COMMON CORE   **W 2a–f** Write informative/explanatory texts to examine complex ideas clearly and accurately through the effective selection, organization, and analysis of content. **W 5** Develop and strengthen writing as needed by planning.

Getting Started

CHOOSE A POEM

To find a suitable poem, reread poems you have enjoyed in the past, page through this book, or ask others for a recommendation. Choose a poem of twelve to twenty-five lines that is complex and rich in meaning.

▶ **ASK YOURSELF:**

- What is my initial reaction to the poem?
- What is interesting about the poem?
- What makes this poem rich or complex?

THINK ABOUT AUDIENCE AND PURPOSE

In selecting a poem, keep in mind that your **purpose** is to analyze and share insights about the poem. Your analysis should enhance your **audience's** appreciation of the poem, so consider your audience's prior knowledge when writing your analysis.

▶ **ASK YOURSELF:**

- Who is my audience?
- What do I want my audience to know or think about the work?
- How can I convey my own analysis of the text to my audience?
- How might others analyze the poem?

GATHER IDEAS

Read your poem several times, including a few times out loud, to discover its unique aspects. Each reading will provide you with new insights and a better understanding of the poem's literary elements. Look for the following literary elements as you consider the focus of your analysis:

- **Speaker:** the voice that addresses the reader
- **Stylistic elements:** the techniques a writer uses to control language and create effects, such as **diction** (word choice), **sound effects** (rhyme, rhythm, alliteration, and repetition), **figurative language** (metaphor, simile, and personification), and imagery
- **Theme:** an insight about the human experience
- **Tone:** the poet's attitude toward the subject, the audience, or a character in the poem

▶ **TIP**

Each time you read the poem, look for a different literary element. The chart below identifies elements and useful questions.

Element	Analysis Questions
Speaker	* Who is the speaker? * Does the speaker narrate a story or describe a scene or emotion?
Style	* How does diction affect the poem? * What sound effects does the poet use? * What figurative language does the poet use?
Theme	* What is the poem's main idea? * Does the main idea reveal something about human nature?
Tone	* What attitude does the poet express?

Planning/Prewriting *continued*

Getting Started

NARROW YOUR FOCUS

Once you have an understanding of the significant ideas in the poem and how the literary elements help communicate those ideas, you can decide which of those elements are most significant.

▶ **ASK YOURSELF:**

- What elements dominate the poem?
- How do these elements help to communicate the poem's meaning?
- What **domain-specific vocabulary,** such as specialized literary terms, will I need to define for readers so that they can understand my analysis?

WRITE A CONTROLLING IDEA

Write a **controlling idea**—one or two sentences that identify the poem's key elements and sum up your insights about how they work together to create meaning.

▶ **WHAT DOES IT LOOK LIKE?**

Important elements: imagery, figurative language

Major points: Imagery and figurative language are used to reflect the emotions of the speaker.

Controlling idea: In "Missing the Sea," poet Derek Walcott uses images of absence and loss to express the agony of a shore-bound sailor.

GATHER SUPPORTING EVIDENCE

Your analysis should include the most significant and relevant **textual evidence,** in the form of direct quotations or concrete details from the poem, to support each of your main points.

You must **elaborate,** or explain thoroughly, how each piece of evidence supports your points. Add depth to your analysis by elaborating on the **ambiguities, complexities,** and **nuances** that make good poetry rich and meaningful.

▶ **WHAT DOES IT LOOK LIKE?**

- **Ambiguities** are words or lines that may be interpreted in different ways.

  The house in the poem may be a symbol of the living.

- **Complexities** are elements of the poem that may be more difficult to analyze.

  By comparing the absence of the wind to the death of a loved one, Walcott emphasizes a deep longing for the sea.

- **Nuances** are changes in the tone or meaning of the poem.

  The tone shifts from harsh images to the lonely, quiet ones of the unused clothes of the dead.

PEER REVIEW Share your controlling idea with a peer. Ask: What words or lines from the poem will help support my analysis?

YOUR TURN In your *Reader/Writer Notebook,* develop your writing plan and controlling idea. Consider these tips as you gather evidence:

- Reread the poem to find lines that contain key imagery.
- Think about how your evidence supports your controlling idea. Be prepared to adjust or revise your controlling idea as you analyze the evidence.

Drafting

The following chart shows a structure for organizing an effective analysis.

COMMON CORE

W 4 Produce clear and coherent writing appropriate to task, purpose, and audience. **W 9a (RL 1, 4)** Draw evidence from literary texts to support analysis; analyze the impact of specific word choices on meaning and tone. **L 1** Demonstrate command of the conventions of standard English grammar and usage.

Organizing Your Literary Analysis

INTRODUCTION
- Start with an **attention-grabbing quotation** or **bold statement.**
- Introduce the poem's **author** and **title.** State your **controlling idea** and key literary elements you will discuss.

▼

BODY
- Organize ideas so that each **new element** builds on the preceding ones to create a **unified whole.**
- Cite **concrete details, quotations,** and other **evidence** from the text to support your analysis.
- Use **varied transitions**—such as *in addition, although,* and *too*—to link related ideas and create cohesion.
- Maintain a **formal style** and **objective tone** by avoiding contractions and slang, choosing precise language, and discussing the poem in a neutral, unbiased way.

▼

CONCLUDING SECTION
- **Restate** your controlling idea, and **summarize** your main points.
- Show how the poem relates to **broader themes** or **experiences** in life.

GRAMMAR IN CONTEXT: EXCERPTING POETRY

You will want to use excerpts from the poem as supporting evidence in your analysis. For help excerpting poetry, study these guidelines and examples.

Quoting words, phrases, or clauses (up to one line in length): Integrate the word, phrase, or clause smoothly into your sentence, setting off the quotation in quotation marks. ▶

> The poem's speaker describes the wind as "something removed."

Quoting more than one line: Use a solidus, a slash mark (/), with a space on both sides to show line breaks. ▶

> The silence is said to "sound like the gnashing of windmills ground / To a dead halt."

Quoting more than two lines: An excerpt of more than two lines is usually set off from the text, either centered or indented. The excerpt should use the same spacing as the original. No quotation marks are used when excerpts are set off in this way. ▶

> Walcott uses abstract imagery to express the speaker's feeling of numb isolation.
>
> > It hoops this valley, weighs this mountain,
> > Estranges gesture, pushes this pencil
> > Through a thick nothing now,

YOUR TURN Develop a first draft of your analysis, following the structure outlined in the chart above. As you write, be sure to follow the rules for excerpting poetry.

Revising

As you revise, evaluate the controlling idea, evidence, and organization of your essay. Your goal is to determine if you have achieved your purpose and effectively communicated your ideas to your intended audience. The questions, tips, and strategies in the following chart will help you revise and improve your draft.

LITERARY ANALYSIS

Ask Yourself	Tips	Revision Strategies
1. **Does the introduction engage the audience and introduce the poem?**	▶ **Put parentheses around** the engaging opening. **Circle** the title of the poem and the name of the author.	▶ If necessary, **add** an engaging opening, such as a provocative quotation or a bold statement. **Add** the name of the poem and its author.
2. **Does the introduction identify the literary elements and state a controlling idea?**	▶ **Highlight** the controlling idea. **Bracket** the literary elements.	▶ If needed, **add** a controlling idea and identify the poem's literary elements.
3. **Is each point supported by well-chosen and relevant textual evidence, such as concrete details and quotations?**	▶ **Circle** each piece of evidence. **Draw an arrow** to the point it supports.	▶ **Add** concrete details or quotations from the poem to bolster any unsupported points.
4. **Does the writing establish and maintain a formal style and objective tone?**	▶ **Bracket** contractions, slang, and biased language.	▶ **Replace** informal or biased language with precise, objective text.
5. **Are varied transitions and syntax used to link ideas?**	▶ **Place a check mark** next to each transitional word or phrase. **Draw a star** next to any consecutive sentences that have the same structures.	▶ **Add** transitions where needed, or **replace** transitions to create variety. **Vary** the structures of starred sentences.
6. **Does the concluding section restate the controlling idea and make a connection between the poem and life?**	▶ **Highlight** the sentence restating the controlling idea. **Double-underline** the sentence or sentences connecting the poem to life.	▶ **Add** a sentence that restates the controlling idea, or **add** a sentence that connects the poem to life.

YOUR TURN **PEER REVIEW** Exchange your analysis with a classmate. As you read and comment on your classmate's essay, focus on the strength of the controlling idea and evidence. Give concrete suggestions for improvement, using the revision strategies in the chart.

 **COMMON CORE** **W 5** Develop and strengthen writing as needed by revising, editing, rewriting, or trying a new approach.

ANALYZE A STUDENT DRAFT

As you read this student draft, notice the comments on its strengths as well as suggestions for improvement.

Life and Death
by Robert Scott, Sea View High School

❶ Born in 1930 on the island of Saint Lucia, and later living in Jamaica and Trinidad, the poet Derek Walcott reveals the influence of countless sailors in his poem "Missing the Sea." The speaker laments the terrible emptiness of a house when occupied by a person who loves the freedom of the sea.

❷ The poem's speaker expresses his loss in images of sound or absence of the sound of the wind. The wind is an effective synecdoche (using parts to represent the whole) because it represents attributes associated with the sea: water, salt, and vastness. Although absent from the house, this wind becomes "something removed [that] roars in the ears of this house." Strong verbs ("roars," "hangs," "stuns") describe a wind so strong it "weighs this mountain." Every image is harsh. Even those that emphasize the silence at the same time create a grating noise, "sound like the gnashing of windmills ground / To a dead halt." An oxymoron is also used to illustrate its power: "a deafening absence, a blow." It is this absent force that propels the sailor-poet to write his lament: "pushes this pencil." The present state of the housebound speaker is "thick nothing now", emphasizing the negative and empty conditions through alliteration.

> Robert's introduction identifies the **poet** and **poem** but does not include a clear controlling idea.

> Robert cites examples of figurative language and defines **domain-specific vocabulary.**

LEARN HOW **Add a Controlling Idea** Although Robert's essay introduces the poet and title of the poem, it does not include a clear controlling idea. His controlling idea should connect the stylistic elements (imagery of absence and loss) to the meaning of the poem (the expression of the agony of the land-bound sailor).

ROBERT'S REVISION TO PARAGRAPH ❶

The speaker laments the terrible emptiness of a house when occupied by a person who loves the freedom of the sea.

In "Missing the Sea," Walcott uses imagery of absence and loss to express the agony of a shore-bound sailor.

3   In the last full stanza, Walcott uses the images of objects found in the house (silent cupboards and "sour laundry"), again using synecdoche. The lack of sound is emphasized with the cupboard, and the negative sensory images continue with the laundry.

4   These domestic images grow even stronger through the simile of the clothes of the dead. The deceased person's clothes are left exactly as in life. So too, the memory of the sea occupies the mind of the speaker, exactly as it did when he lived on the sea. He expects the sound of the wind but is left bereft and incredulous at its absence, just as one would feel looking at the clothes of a loved one who has passed away; the living, remaining person expresses his grief at the sight, just as the poem's speaker expresses his loss. By comparing the absence of the wind to the death of a loved one, Walcott emphasizes the depth of his passion and longing for the sea.

> The essay is arranged **sequentially,** moving from the poem's beginning to its end.

> Instead of providing a direct quotation, Robert **paraphrases** and **elaborates** on the content of the last stanza.

> Robert's analysis could be improved by a more effective **concluding section.**

LEARN HOW **Strengthen Your Concluding Section** Robert's analysis ends abruptly after his examination of the poem's last stanza. For his essay to be effective, he must restate his controlling idea, summarize the main points of the analysis, and articulate a related insight about life or human nature. Notice how he strengthened his analysis by adding a more effective concluding paragraph.

ROBERT'S REVISION TO THE CONCLUDING SECTION

By comparing the absence of the wind to the death of a loved one, Walcott emphasizes the depth of his passion and longing for the sea.

    ∧Even if readers have not experienced a sailor's life, most have suffered the loss of something or someone cherished. In "Missing the Sea," Walcott uses vivid imagery and strong figurative language to express the universal feeling of losing what you love most.

YOUR TURN Use the feedback from your peers and teacher as well as the two "Learn How" lessons to revise, rewrite, or try a new approach to your essay as needed. Evaluate how well you conveyed your controlling idea and addressed what is most significant for your specific purpose and audience.

COMMON CORE   **W 5** Develop and strengthen writing as needed by editing.
L 2 Demonstrate command of the conventions of standard English capitalization, punctuation, and spelling.

Editing and Publishing

In the editing stage, you review your analysis to make sure that it is free of grammar, spelling, usage, syntax, and punctuation errors. Mistakes can distract your audience from focusing on your ideas.

GRAMMAR IN CONTEXT: PUNCTUATING QUOTATIONS

Many of the quotations in your analysis may be fragments, or parts of a line or sentence. As noted earlier, poetry excerpts of two lines or fewer are set off by quotation marks.

> In the last full stanza, Walcott uses the images of objects found in the house (silent cupboards and **"sour laundry"**), again using synecdoche.
>
> [The quotation fragment is integrated into the sentence and set off by **quotation marks.**]

- Commas and periods are set inside the closing quotation mark.
- Question marks and exclamation points are set inside the quotation mark only if the quotation itself is a question or exclamation; if the question mark or exclamation point applies to the overall sentence rather than the quotation, the punctuation is set outside the end quotation mark.
- Semicolons, colons, and dashes are always placed outside the closing quotation mark.

As Robert edited his essay, he realized he had incorrectly punctuated a quotation. The comma should be set inside the closing quotation mark.

> The present state of the housebound speaker is "thick nothing now", emphasizing the negative and empty conditions through alliteration.

PUBLISH YOUR WRITING

Share your analysis with an audience.
- Share your analysis with members of a literary circle who enjoy poetry.
- Publish your analysis on a Web site devoted to the poet whose work you analyzed.
- Turn your analysis into an oral presentation and deliver it to your classmates.

YOUR TURN   Correct any errors in your analysis. Make sure that you connect your evidence to your controlling idea. Edit carefully and make sure you have punctuated quotations correctly. Then, publish your final essay where your audience is likely to see it.

Scoring Rubric

Use the rubric below to evaluate your analysis from the Writing Workshop or your response to the on-demand task on the next page.

LITERARY ANALYSIS

SCORE	COMMON CORE TRAITS
6	• **Development** Has an engaging introduction; includes a controlling idea with an insightful analysis of the poem; supports main points with significant, relevant evidence; ends powerfully • **Organization** Arranges ideas in an effective, logical order; uses varied transitions and syntax to create cohesion and link ideas • **Language** Consistently maintains a formal style; effectively uses precise language; shows a strong command of conventions
5	• **Development** Has an effective introduction; provides a controlling idea that offers an original analysis of the poem; supports main points with evidence; has a strong concluding section • **Organization** Arranges ideas logically; uses transitions and syntax to link ideas • **Language** Maintains a formal style; uses precise language; has a few errors in conventions
4	• **Development** Has an introduction that could be more engaging; includes a controlling idea that states an analysis of the poem; could use some more evidence; has an adequate concluding section • **Organization** Arranges ideas logically; could vary transitions more • **Language** Mostly maintains a formal style; needs more precise language at times; has a few distracting errors in conventions
3	• **Development** Has an adequate, though not memorable, introduction; has a controlling idea that makes an obvious statement about the poem's meaning; lacks sufficient support; has a routine concluding section • **Organization** Has some flaws in organization; needs more transitions to link ideas • **Language** Frequently lapses into an informal style; uses some vague word choices; has some significant errors in conventions
2	• **Development** Has a weak introduction and a controlling idea that does not relate to the writing task; lacks specific evidence; has a weak concluding section • **Organization** Has organizational flaws; lacks transitions throughout • **Language** Uses an informal style and vague language; has many errors in conventions
1	• **Development** Has no introduction or controlling idea; offers unrelated points as evidence; ends abruptly • **Organization** Includes a string of disconnected ideas with no overall organization • **Language** Uses an inappropriate style and language; has major problems with conventions

Preparing for Timed Writing

COMMON CORE

W 10 Write routinely over shorter time frames for a range of tasks, purposes, and audiences.

1. ANALYZE THE TASK   5 MIN

Read the task carefully. Then, read it again, noting the words that tell the topic, the audience, and the purpose.

> **WRITING TASK**
>
> The plots of most stories and novels are set into motion by the conflict, or problem,
>
> *Topic* ↘
>
> experienced by the main character. Think of a <u>conflict from a story or novel</u> you have
>
> *Audience* ↘
>
> read. Then, write an analysis <u>explaining to ⟨classmates⟩ whether the conflict is internal or
>
> <u>external and how it affects the plot and theme of the work.</u>   ← *Purpose*

2. PLAN YOUR RESPONSE   10 MIN

Once you have decided on a work of fiction and identified its main conflict, ask yourself these questions:

- Is the conflict external (caused by outside forces, events, or characters) or internal (caused by the character's opposing needs, emotions, or desires)?
- How does the conflict move the action forward?
- How is the conflict resolved?
- What theme does the author suggest through the resolution of the conflict?

3. RESPOND TO THE TASK   20 MIN

Begin your draft by writing your controlling idea—a statement about the conflict and its effect on the plot and theme of the fictional work. Then, do the following:

- Organize your response in sequential order, discussing the events as they occur in the work.
- Provide evidence—details from the text—to support your controlling idea.
- Elaborate on how each piece of evidence supports your controlling idea.
- Conclude your essay with a discussion of how the resolution affects the theme.

4. IMPROVE YOUR RESPONSE   5–10 MIN

Revising Check your draft against the task. Does your draft clearly state a controlling idea about the conflict and its effect on the fictional work as a whole? Does it provide sufficient evidence? Do you end with an insight into the fictional work and its theme?

Proofreading Find and correct any errors in grammar, usage, syntax, and spelling. Make sure that your paper and any edits are neatly written and legible.

Checking Your Final Copy Before you submit your paper, examine it once more to make sure that you are presenting your best work.

Presenting an Analysis

Writing an analysis about a poem probably helped you gain new insight into the poem. Now you can share your understanding with your classmates by adapting your essay for an oral presentation. In presenting your ideas to listeners rather than readers, you can use your voice as well as your body language to make your points.

 Complete the workshop activities in your **Reader/Writer Notebook.**

SPEAK WITH A PURPOSE

TASK

Adapt your essay into a **formal speech,** demonstrating an appropriate command of formal English grammar and usage when speaking. Practice your speech, and then present it to your class.

COMMON CORE TRAITS

A STRONG ORAL ANALYSIS . . .

- conveys a clear perspective and supports it with sufficient, relevant evidence
- is appropriate to the purpose and audience
- uses an effective blend of verbal and nonverbal techniques to communicate key points

COMMON CORE

SL 3 Evaluate a speaker's point of view, reasoning, and use of evidence. **SL 4** Present information, findings, and evidence, conveying a clear perspective. **SL 6** Adapt speech to a variety of tasks. **L 1** Demonstrate command of the conventions of standard English.

Adapt Your Essay

You will need to reorganize your material to make your analysis clear to listeners. Focus your oral presentation on the most important points about the literary elements you analyzed in your essay. Use these suggestions as you develop your presentation.

Introduction	Add an element of drama by
	• beginning with an **interesting quotation** from the work
	• stating an **anecdote** about the work or its author
	• making a **provocative comment** about the work
Body	Keep your listeners' attention by
	• **reading aloud** many lines from the poem
	• **focusing** on only the most important points of your original analysis
Concluding Section	Make a lasting impression on listeners by
	• framing a **final observation** in the context of a universal theme
	• ending with a **dynamic quotation** from the poem

THINK central
Speaking &
Listening Online
Go to **thinkcentral.com.**
KEYWORD: HML12-280

Deliver Your Speech

PREPARE NOTE CARDS

To speak effectively, you need to sound as natural and relaxed as possible. Rather than memorizing your presentation, use the following steps to help you prepare for your speech.

Step 1 Make concise notes on note cards.

Step 2 In your notes, write down key words and phrases about the main points in your analysis.

Step 3 Write down the quotations, details, and other evidence from the work that you will be presenting to support your analysis, and make sure you can read them.

Step 4 Arrange your note cards in the right order for a smooth presentation.

USE VERBAL AND NONVERBAL TECHNIQUES

Verbal and nonverbal techniques can make your presentation more effective. Use the following techniques to deliver an engaging presentation.

- **Pronunciation and Enunciation** It is natural to be nervous when speaking to a group, so focus on pronouncing words correctly. Speak clearly (enunciate) and speak at a natural pace so each word is understandable.

- **Emphasis** To get your main points across to your audience, change your tone and volume for emphasis. Pausing is also an effective way to emphasize something you have just said. It allows your listeners time to digest a point you made and lends suspense to a point you are about to make.

- **Facial Expressions and Gestures** Change your facial expressions as you deliver your presentation. A blank face is the physical equivalent of a monotone speaking voice; it almost guarantees that your audience will tune out. Although you may not use hand gestures when speaking casually, relaxed gestures can help emphasize your words and make the presentation seem more natural.

- **Eye Contact** Remember to make eye contact with members of your audience. Eye contact will engage your listeners and convey the message that you *want* them to understand what you are saying.

 **YOUR TURN**

As a Speaker Deliver your speech to a friend, making sure to incorporate the verbal and nonverbal techniques described on this page. Use your friend's feedback to make adjustments to your presentation and to improve your speaking skills.

As a Listener Evaluate a classmate's delivery of his or her analytical speech. Consider the speaker's point of view and whether it is well-supported with evidence from the poem. Listen carefully to see if you can follow the line of reasoning among the speaker's ideas, and note any places you feel lost. Consider whether the speaker emphasizes his or her points with an appropriate tone and word choices.

Assessment Practice

DIRECTIONS Read the following selections and then answer the questions.

from Beowulf

"My people have said, the wisest, most knowing
And best of them, that my duty was to go to the Danes'
Great king. They have seen my strength for themselves,
Have watched me rise from the darkness of war,
5   Dripping with my enemies' blood. I drove
Five great giants into chains, chased
All of that race from the earth. I swam
In the blackness of night, hunting monsters
Out of the ocean, and killing them one
10 By one; death was my errand and the fate
They had earned. Now Grendel and I are called
Together, and I've come. Grant me, then,
Lord and protector of this noble place,
A single request! I have come so far,
15 Oh shelterer of warriors and your people's loved friend,
That this one favor you should not refuse me—
That I, alone and with the help of my men,
May purge all evil from this hall. I have heard,
Too, that the monster's scorn of men
20 Is so great that he needs no weapons and fears none.
Nor will I. My lord Higlac
Might think less of me if I let my sword
Go where my feet were afraid to, if I hid
Behind some broad linden shield: my hands
25 Alone shall fight for me, struggle for life
Against the monster. God must decide
Who will be given to death's cold grip.
Grendel's plan, I think, will be
What it has been before, to invade this hall
30 And gorge his belly with our bodies. If he can,
If he can. And I think, if my time will have come,
There'll be nothing to mourn over, no corpse to prepare
For its grave: Grendel will carry our bloody
Flesh to the moors, crunch on our bones
35 And smear torn scraps of our skin on the walls

Of his den. No, I expect no Danes
Will fret about sewing our shrouds, if he wins.
And if death does take me, send the hammered
Mail of my armor to Higlac, return
40   The inheritance I had from Hrethel, and he
From Wayland. Fate will unwind as it must!"

Hrothgar replied, protector of the Danes:
"Beowulf, you've come to us in friendship, and because
Of the reception your father found at our court.
45   Edgetho had begun a bitter fcud,
Killing Hathlaf, a Wulfing warrior:
Your father's countrymen were afraid of war,
If he returned to his home, and they turned him away.
Then he traveled across the curving waves
50   To the land of the Danes."

from The Canterbury Tales
by Geoffrey Chaucer

He had his son with him, a fine young Squire,
A lover and cadet, a lad of fire
With locks as curly as if they had been pressed.
He was some twenty years of age, I guessed.
5   In stature he was of a moderate length,
With wonderful agility and strength.
He'd seen some service with the cavalry
In Flanders and Artois and Picardy
And had done valiantly in little space
10   Of time, in hope to win his lady's grace.
He was embroidered like a meadow bright
And full of freshest flowers, red and white.
Singing he was, or fluting all the day;
He was as fresh as is the month of May.
15   Short was his gown, the sleeves were long and wide;

GO ON

He knew the way to sit a horse and ride.
He could make songs and poems and recite,
Knew how to joust and dance, to draw and write.
He loved so hotly that till dawn grew pale
20   He slept as little as a nightingale.
Courteous he was, lowly and serviceable,
And carved to serve his father at the table.

Reading Comprehension

Use *Beowulf* (pp. 282–283) to answer questions 1–6.

1. In lines 1–3, which lofty ideal do Beowulf's people expect him to uphold?

   A. Honesty in all situations

   B. Mercy toward his enemies

   C. Charity for the less fortunate

   D. Responsibility toward those in need

2. Which phrase is a kenning for the word *sea*?

   A. *blackness of night*   **C.** *hammered / Mail*

   B. *this noble place*   **D.** *curving waves*

3. In lines 5–11, Beowulf boasts of his legendary —

   A. fear and need to overcome it

   B. pride and tendency to exaggerate

   C. kindness and desire to do good deeds

   D. hunting skills and belief in fate

4. In lines 11–18, Beowulf identifies the battle with Grendel as one between —

   A. humans and monsters

   B. intellect and emotion

   C. life and death

   D. good and evil

5. Beowulf's statement in lines 36–37 is ironic because —

   A. the Danes will not mourn Beowulf

   B. Beowulf and his men will survive

   C. there will be no corpses if Grendel wins

   D. Beowulf does not trust the Danes

6. In line 45, the alliteration in "begun a bitter feud" helps to —

   A. clarify the meaning of words

   B. create rhythm and unify ideas

   C. convey a sensory experience

   D. explain metaphors and similes

Use *The Canterbury Tales* (pp. 283–284) to answer questions 7–12.

7. Chaucer develops the Squire's character by —

   A. describing his appearance and talents

   B. comparing him to other young nobles

   C. showing other characters' reactions to him

   D. relating conversations between characters

8. In lines 7–14, it is ironic that the Squire is described as "singing he was, or fluting all the day" because —

   A. the reader assumes that all cadets receive musical instruction as part of their training

   B. Chaucer suggests that the Squire is more interested in traveling than in pleasing his lady

   C. the reader expects the Squire to be training for battle rather than playing music

   D. Chaucer depicts the Squire first as a wild horseman and then as a polite cadet

9. In lines 11–15, the Squire's style of dress suggests that he is —

   A. youthful and vain

   B. timid and scholarly

   C. rugged and unkempt

   D. strange and mysterious

10. Which one of the Squire's character traits emerges in lines 21–22?

   A. Bravery

   B. Innocence

   C. Leadership

   D. Respectfulness

11. Chaucer's gently ironic depiction of the Squire comes from the contrast between the young man's —

   A. artistic talents and his well-groomed appearance

   B. occupation as a knight in training and his personal interests

   C. average height and his impressive athletic abilities

   D. love of family and his loyalty to his country

12. Which lines in the excerpt characterize the Squire as a well-educated nobleman?

   A. Lines 1–3

   B. Lines 4–6

   C. Lines 7–10

   D. Lines 16–18

SHORT CONSTRUCTED RESPONSE
Write three or four sentences to answer each question.

13. In line 41, Beowulf exclaims, "Fate will unwind as it must!" What can you infer about his beliefs from this statement?

14. List three character traits of the Squire. Cite line references from the excerpt to support your choices.

Write two to three paragraphs to answer each question.

15. In lines 19–27, Beowulf says that he, like Grendel, needs no weapons to fight. What can you infer about Beowulf's character from these lines?

16. Chaucer compares the Squire to different things in nature. Identify two of these comparisons and explain what they reveal about the Squire.

GO ON ➡

Vocabulary

Use context clues and the Latin word definitions to answer the following questions.

1. The Latin word *statura* means "an upright posture." What is the most likely meaning of the word *stature* as it is used in line 5 of the excerpt from *The Canterbury Tales*?

A. Physical endurance

B. General intelligence

C. Height when standing

D. Professional reputation

2. The Latin word *moderari* means "to keep within measure." What is the most likely meaning of the word *moderate* as it is used in line 5 of the excerpt from *The Canterbury Tales*?

A. Average

B. Changeable

C. Ideal

D. Unusual

3. The Latin word *valere* means "to be strong." What is the most likely meaning of *valiantly* as it is used in line 9 of the excerpt from *The Canterbury Tales*?

A. Angrily

B. Bravely

C. Remarkably

D. Tirelessly

4. The Latin word *iuxta* means "nearby." The meaning of *joust* as it is used in line 18 of the excerpt from *The Canterbury Tales* is to —

A. tell amusing stories

B. engage in close combat

C. meet and merge with

D. travel over long distances

Use context clues and your knowledge of multiple-meaning words to answer the following questions.

5. The word *shield* in line 24 of the excerpt from *Beowulf* means —

A. decorative emblem

B. large lowland area

C. military officer's badge

D. piece of hand-held armor

6. Which meaning of *locks* is used in line 3 of the excerpt from *The Canterbury Tales*?

A. Lengths or curls of human hair

B. Devices operated by keys or combinations

C. Sections of a waterway closed off with gates

D. Holds used in wrestling and self-defense

7. Which meaning of *pressed* is used in line 3 of the excerpt from *The Canterbury Tales*?

A. Crowded closely

B. Urged to take action

C. Squeezed into shape

D. Forced into military service

8. Which meaning of *grace* is used in line 10 of the excerpt from *The Canterbury Tales*?

A. Approval

B. Charm

C. Exemption

D. Short prayer

Revising and Editing

DIRECTIONS Read this passage and answer the questions that follow.

(1) In the mid-14th century, the Black Death swept across Europe. (2) The plague had traveled along North African trade routes and over European trade routes. (3) Its victims suffered from symptoms such as a high fever and bad headaches and usually died. (4) In some cities, corpses were gathered in the streets. (5) The stench of bodies permeated the air. (6) By the year 1400, the awfully plague had killed approximately 25 million Europeans.

1. What is the most effective way to revise sentence 2?
   A. For a while, the plague had traveled along North African trade routes and European trade routes.
   B. The plague had traveled along North African trade routes and over European.
   C. The plague had traveled along North African and European trade routes.
   D. The plague had traveled along, over North African and European trade routes.

2. What change, if any, should be made in sentence 3?
   A. Insert an apostrophe in *Its*
   B. Insert a comma after *fever*
   C. Change *died* to **dead**
   D. Make no change

3. What is the most effective way to combine sentences 4 and 5?
   A. In some cities, corpses were gathered in the streets so that the stench of bodies permeated the air.
   B. In some cities, corpses were gathered in the streets where the stench of bodies permeated the air.
   C. In some cities, corpses were gathered in the streets, the stench of bodies permeated the air.
   D. In some cities, whose corpses were gathered in the streets where the stench of bodies permeated the air.

4. What change, if any, should be made in sentence 6?
   A. Change *had killed* to **has killed**
   B. Insert a comma after *killed*
   C. Change *awfully* to **awful**
   D. Make no change

5. Where is the best place to insert this sentence?

   Nearly two-thirds of the population of many European cities died within the first two years of the epidemic.

   A. At the beginning of the paragraph
   B. After sentence 2
   C. After sentence 3
   D. After sentence 6

287

Ideas for Independent Reading

Continue exploring the Questions of the Times on pages 20–21 with these additional works.

What makes a true HERO?

Beowulf
translated by Seamus Heaney

In this translation of *Beowulf*, Nobel-prize-winning poet Seamus Heaney uses direct, rich, and moving language to tell the tale of Beowulf's battles with the monster Grendel, Grendel's equally monstrous mother, and the dragon who brings about Beowulf's death. Heaney's translation is vivid and engaging, drawing new audiences into this ancient tale of honor and heroism.

Grendel
by John Gardner

In *Beowulf*, Grendel is a fearsome beast whose demise makes Beowulf a lauded hero. This modern retelling of the epic, however, views the whole story from a new perspective—namely, Grendel's. What is it like to be Grendel? What makes Grendel tick? When everyone thinks you're a monster, how does it change the way you look at yourself?

The Death of King Arthur
translated by James Cable

This story of Arthur begins with a sadly depleted Round Table as knight after knight heads to a strange land, searching for glory and the Holy Grail. Meanwhile, King Arthur is humiliated by the continuing romance between his queen, Guinevere, and his most famous knight, Lancelot. Weakened from within, Arthur's kingdom is attacked by the evil Mordred, and Arthur must rouse himself and his flawed yet loyal band to avert the worst.

Who really shapes SOCIETY?

Life in a Medieval Village
by Frances and Joseph Gies

Most people of the Middle Ages lived in villages, not castles or cities. This description of the medieval English village of Elton gives modern readers a sense of the everyday lives and concerns of the people who lived during this period. Many aspects of life are examined—dress, diet, housing, marriage, work, and the relationship between peasants and their lords.

The History of the Kings of Britain
by Geoffrey of Monmouth

By what right did the elite families of Britain come to rule over everyone else? In this influential volume written in the 12th century, Geoffrey of Monmouth shows that in many cases, becoming king was more the result of fast-talking and brute force than anything such as divine right. The author tears through the royal lines of Britain, touching upon such notables as Brutus of Rome, King Lear, and the legendary King Arthur. While unreliable as history, this chronicle's no-nonsense yet lyrical style makes it hard to put down.

COMMON CORE

RL 10 Read and comprehend literature. RI 10 Read and comprehend literary nonfiction.

Does FATE *control our lives?*

The Anglo-Saxon World: An Anthology
translated by Kevin Crossley-Holland

This anthology presents a wide selection of Anglo-Saxon poetry and prose, including chronicles, letters, and many of the greatest surviving poems printed in their entirety. Works such as *The Seafarer*, *The Wanderer*, the *Anglo-Saxon Chronicle*, and *Beowulf* give readers a fine sense of the values and lifestyles of the Anglo-Saxon people.

Everyman and Other Miracle and Morality Plays

In *Everyman*, an ordinary man faced with impending death gathers about him his friends, his family, and his best personal qualities. *Everyman* is an allegory, so these abstract qualities take bodily form in characters such as Good Deeds, Knowledge, and Beauty. Yet as his fate draws near, Everyman's friends and family—even his wife—desert him, leaving him with only his Good Deeds to accompany him to his reckoning.

Can people live up *to high* IDEALS?

The Once and Future King
by T. H. White

This retelling of the Arthurian legend follows Arthur from birth to death. Based largely on Sir Thomas Malory's *Le Morte d'Arthur*, this volume contains four full novels: *The Sword in the Stone*, *The Queen of Air and Darkness*, *The Ill-made Knight*, and *The Candle in the Wind*. Author T. H. White brings life, passion, and humor to a beloved legend.

The Letters of Abelard and Heloise
translated by Betty Radice

The most famous love story from medieval times is actually a true story told through the letters of two real-life lovers. Peter Abelard was a Parisian scholar and cleric who fell in love with his gifted pupil Heloise. Marrying in secret, Heloise bore Abelard's child. Yet the scandal associated with the marriage drove them apart. Abelard became a monk and Heloise the abbess of a convent, yet even as they tried to live according to their ideals, their feelings for one another remained strong.

Get Novel Wise THINK central

Go to **thinkcentral.com**.
KEYWORD: HML12-289

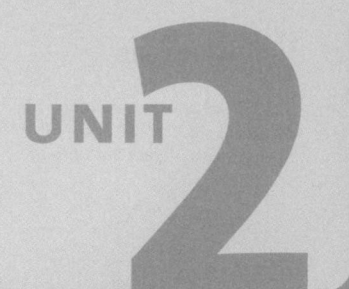

UNIT 2

Preview Unit Goals

TEXT ANALYSIS	• Understand the historical context and cultural influences of the Renaissance
	• Identify and analyze characteristics of Shakespearean tragedy
	• Interpret figurative language, including hyperbole, simile, metaphor
	• Analyze imagery
	• Identify and analyze sonnets, including Shakespearean, Petrarchan, and Spenserian
	• Identify and analyze rhyme, including rhyme scheme and end rhyme
	• Interpret metaphysical conceits
	• Analyze and evaluate an argument
READING	• Develop strategies for reading Shakespearean drama
	• Summarize key ideas in poetry
WRITING AND LANGUAGE	• Write an argument to support a claim in a critical review
	• Vary syntax for persuasive effect and cohesive flow
VOCABULARY	• Determine the connotative meanings of words as they are used in the text
	• Research word origins as an aid to understanding word meaning
ACADEMIC VOCABULARY	• attribute • monitor • primary
	• feature • phase
MEDIA AND VIEWING	• Analyze a film interpretation of a Shakespeare play, evaluating how it interprets the source text
	• Analyze visual techniques that create mood in film
	• Create a blog

THINK central

Find It Online!

Go to <u>thinkcentral.com</u> for the interactive version of this unit.

The English Renaissance

1485–1660

John Milton

A CELEBRATION OF HUMAN ACHIEVEMENT

- Pastoral Poems and Sonnets
- Shakespearean Drama
- The Rise of Humanism
- Spiritual and Devotional Writings
- The Metaphysical and Cavalier Poets

Media Smart DVD-ROM

Great Stories on Film

Discover how a movie captures the imagination of viewers in a scene from Macbeth. Page 440

Questions of the Times

DISCUSS Talk about the following questions with your classmates. Then turn the page to learn more about how these issues affected the lives of people during the English Renaissance.

Should religion be tied to POLITICS?

The Renaissance period in England was marked by religious conflict. Henry VIII and each successive monarch held a different view on the country's official religion. Leaders were assassinated, writers were imprisoned, and the country even endured a civil war over questions of religion. What is the proper role of religion in public life? How can societies reconcile religion and politics?

Why is love so COMPLICATED?

The Renaissance was a time of rapid change in the arts, literature, and learning. New ideas were embraced, and old ones—including the concept of love—were examined from fresh perspectives. Poets of the day put their pens to many different aspects of love: unrequited love, constant love, timeless love, fickle love. What is so fascinating about love? Why does it seem so complicated?

COMMON CORE

RL 9 Demonstrate knowledge of foundational works of literature, including how two or more texts from the same period treat similar themes or topics. RI 9 Analyze documents of historical and literary significance for their themes, purposes, and rhetorical features.

What is the IDEAL SOCIETY?

In certain respects, the Renaissance was a golden age—a time of relative peace and prosperity, a time of amazing advances in the arts and sciences. Yet people of the day began to question their society, examining its failings and asking themselves how it could be improved. Sir Thomas More even created a fictional "perfect world" that he called Utopia—a world ruled by reason. What do you think a perfect society might be like?

Why do people seek POWER?

During William Shakespeare's lifetime, there were frequent struggles for control in and around the court of Elizabeth I and her successor, James I. In turn, many of Shakespeare's plays dealt with themes of political conflict and the struggle to achieve balance between power, justice, and legitimate authority in society. What is so attractive about power? Is it a worthwhile objective, or does power inevitably corrupt people?

The English Renaissance

1485–1660

A Celebration of Human Achievement

"Be not afraid of greatness," wrote William Shakespeare, and indeed, the people of his time lived life on a grand scale—gazing deep into the heavens, sailing far beyond the edges of the map, filling their minds with the mystery and beauty of the world. Yet at the same time, the mysteries of religious faith brought intense conflict, both personal and political, to the citizens of Renaissance England.

The Renaissance: Historical Context

Writers, as well as kings, queens, and everyday citizens, could not help being affected by the religious conflict that defined their society during the Renaissance years.

The Monarchy and the Church

Writers during the English Renaissance often found their fates married to the shifting winds of political influence. As kings and queens rose to power and as varying forms of Christianity became the law of the land, writers found themselves either celebrated for their work or censured for it. Some writers, including **Sir Thomas More** and **Sir Walter Raleigh**, were even put to death for falling out of favor with the ruler of the day. As you will see, the kings and queens who ruled during this period held widely differing views on just about everything of importance, but especially religion.

THE TUDORS In 1485, **Henry Tudor** took the throne as Henry VII. A shrewd leader, Henry negotiated favorable commercial treaties abroad, built up the nation's merchant fleet, and financed expeditions that established English claims in the Americas. He also arranged for his son **Arthur** to marry the Spanish princess **Catherine of Aragon,** thereby creating a political alliance with Spain, England's greatest "New World" rival. When Arthur died unexpectedly, the pope granted a special dispensation, allowing Arthur's younger brother Henry, the new heir to the throne, to marry Catherine—a marriage that would have lasting consequences.

THE PROTESTANT REFORMATION During the reign of **Henry VIII,** dissatisfaction with the Roman Catholic Church was spreading in Europe. The great wealth and power of the church had led to corruption at many levels, from cardinals living in luxury to friars traveling the countryside selling "indulgences" to peasants in exchange for forgiveness of their sins.

In response, in 1517 a German monk named **Martin Luther** wrote out 95 theses, or arguments, against such practices and nailed them to the door of a church. Though the pope condemned him as a heretic, Luther's criticisms created a sensation, and printed copies were soon in circulation across Europe. Luther wanted the church to reform itself, but other protesters went farther, splitting off from Rome into reformed, **Protestant** churches.

THE CHURCH OF ENGLAND Henry VIII had at first remained loyal to Rome, yet he became obsessed with producing a male heir and so sought an annulment from his wife (who had given him only a daughter, Mary). When the pope refused, Henry broke with Rome and in 1534 declared himself head of the **Church of England.** He then divorced Catherine and married her court attendant, **Anne Boleyn.** In all, Henry went through six wives, but only one produced a son—the frail and sickly **Edward VI,** who succeeded at the age of 9 but died when he was just 15. During Edward's reign, a group of radical Protestants believed the church

COMMON CORE

RL 9 Demonstrate knowledge of foundational works of literature, including how two or more texts from the same period treat similar themes or topics. **RI 9** Analyze documents of historical and literary significance for their themes, purposes, and rhetorical features. **L 1a** Apply the understanding that usage is a matter of convention, can change over time, and is sometimes contested.

▶ **TAKING NOTES**

Outlining As you read this introduction, use an outline to record the main ideas about the history and literature of the period. You can use headings, boldfaced terms, and the information in these boxes as starting points. (See page R49 in the **Research Handbook** for more help with outlining.)

I. Historical Context
  A. The Monarchy and the Church
    1. the Tudors
    2. the Reformation
    3. the Church of England

Queen Elizabeth Watching The Merry Wives of Windsor *at the Globe Theatre,* David Scott. Oil on canvas. © Victoria & Albert Museum, London/Art Resource, New York.

needed even further reform and sought to "purify" it of all Roman practices. This group became known as **Puritans.** In coming years, Puritans would increasingly clash with the monarchy.

Following Edward, Catherine's daughter, Mary, took the throne. To avenge her mother, she brought back Roman Catholicism and persecuted Protestants, which earned her the nickname **Bloody Mary.** On her death in 1558, most citizens welcomed the succession of her half-sister, Elizabeth.

The Elizabethan Era

Elizabeth I, the unwanted daughter of Henry VIII and Anne Boleyn, proved to be one of the ablest monarchs in English history. During her long reign, England enjoyed a time of unprecedented prosperity and international prestige. Elizabeth was a consummate politician, exercising absolute authority while remaining sensitive to public opinion and respectful of Parliament. She kept England out of costly wars, ended the unpopular Spanish alliance, and encouraged overseas adventures, including **Sir Francis Drake's** circumnavigation of the globe and **Sir Walter Raleigh's** attempt to establish a colony in Virginia.

In religion, she steered a middle course, reestablishing the Church of England and using it as a buffer between Catholics and Puritans. Catholics, however, considered her cousin **Mary Stuart,** the queen of Scotland, to be the rightful heir to the English throne. After enduring years of conspiracies, Elizabeth ordered Mary beheaded in 1587. In response, Catholic Spain's Philip II sent a great Armada, or fleet of warships, to challenge the English navy. Aided by a violent storm, the smaller, more maneuverable English ships defeated the Spanish Armada, making Elizabeth the undisputed leader of a great military power.

> **A Voice from the Times**
>
> *I know I have the body but of a weak and feeble woman; but I have the heart and stomach of a king, and of a king of England too, and think foul scorn that Parma or Spain, or any prince of Europe, should dare to invade the borders of my realm.*
>
> **—Elizabeth I**

Elizabeth I, Armada portrait (c. 1588), English school. Oil on panel, 110.5 cm × 127 cm. © Bridgeman Art Library.

◄ Analyze Visuals
This portrait of Queen Elizabeth is rich with symbolism. The pearls adorning her hair and gown suggest purity, the imperial crown to her right suggests power, and the scenes of the defeat of the Spanish Armada behind her represent her greatest victory. In addition, Elizabeth's right hand is resting on a globe—specifically, her fingers rest upon the Americas. What might this last symbol suggest?

The Rise of the Stuarts

With Elizabeth's death in 1603, the powerful Tudor dynasty came to an end. Elizabeth was succeeded by her cousin James VI of Scotland (son of Mary Stuart), who ruled as **James I** of England.

James supported the Church of England, thus angering both Roman Catholic and Protestant extremists. Early in his reign, a Catholic group including Guy Fawkes plotted to kill him and blow up Parliament in the unsuccessful **Gunpowder Plot** of 1605. James and his son Charles both aroused opposition in the Puritan-dominated House of Commons with their extravagance, contempt for Parliament, and preference for Catholic-style "High-Church" rituals in the Anglican Church. Clashes with the Puritans only worsened when **Charles I** took the throne in 1625.

In 1629, Charles I dismissed **Parliament,** and he did not summon it again for 11 years. During this time, he took strong measures against his opponents. Thousands of English citizens—especially Puritans—emigrated to North America to escape persecution. Then, in 1637, Charles's attempt to introduce Anglican practices in Scotland's Presbyterian churches led to rebellion there. In need of funds to suppress the Scots, Charles, in 1640, was forced to reconvene Parliament, which promptly stripped many of his powers. He responded with a show of military force, and England was soon plunged into **civil war.**

The Defeat of the Monarchy

The English Civil War pitted the Royalists (mainly Catholics, Anglicans, and the nobility) against supporters of Parliament (Puritans, smaller landowners, and the middle class). Under the leadership of General **Oliver Cromwell,** the devout, disciplined Puritan army soundly defeated the Royalists in 1645, and the king surrendered a year later.

At first, Parliament established a **commonwealth** with Cromwell as head; later, they made him "lord protector" for life. The Puritan-dominated government proved no less autocratic than the Stuart reign, however. England's theaters were closed, most forms of recreation were suspended, and Sunday became a day of prayer, when even walking for pleasure was forbidden.

When Cromwell died in 1658, his son inherited his title but not his ability to handle the wrangling among political factions and an increasingly unruly public. In 1660, a new Parliament invited **Charles II,** son of Charles I, to return from exile and assume the throne. His reign ushered in a new chapter in English history, the **Restoration.**

THE ARTISTS' GALLERY

Self-Portrait, Nicholas Hilliard. © Victoria & Albert Museum, London/Art Resource, New York.

Renaissance Portraiture

During the Reformation, many Protestants objected to the practice of richly adorning churches with paintings and sculptures of biblical scenes and saints. Denied their traditional occupation, many English artists turned instead to painting the portraits of wealthy patrons.

Royal Portraits The most notable early portrait painter in England was actually a German, Hans Holbein the Younger. The son of a respected German painter, he came to England during the reign of Henry VIII, hoping to escape the turmoil of the Reformation. Soon, however, England broke with Rome, and Holbein had to give up painting religious subjects. Instead, he became the court painter for the royal family. One of his most striking paintings was his portrait of Henry VIII (see page 292).

Miniatures Unlike Holbein, who painted his subjects just the way he saw them—with their expressions revealing their personalities—later English portraitists painted in a refined, elegant style that flattered their noble patrons. During the reign of Elizabeth I, **miniatures** were in fashion—tiny portraits that could be set among precious stones and worn as jewelry or discreetly given as a token of romance at court. Nicholas Hilliard, whose *Self-Portrait* (1577) is shown here, was a master of the miniature.

Cultural Influences

Creativity flourished during the Renaissance, a time of invention, exploration, and appreciation for the arts.

The Renaissance

For writers, artists, scientists, and scholars—in fact, for anyone gripped by curiosity or the urge to create—the **Renaissance** was an amazing time to be alive. The Renaissance, which literally means "rebirth" or "revival," was marked by a surge of creative energy and the emergence of a worldview more modern than medieval. It began in Italy in the 14th century and rapidly spread north throughout Europe. In England, political instability delayed the advent of Renaissance ideas, but they began to take hold after 1485, when Henry VII took the throne, and reached full flower during the reign of Elizabeth I.

THE RENAISSANCE WORLDVIEW All through the Middle Ages, Europeans had focused their energy on religion and the afterlife, viewing this world primarily as preparation for the world to come. During the time of the Renaissance, people became much more interested in, and curious about, life on earth. A new emphasis was placed on the individual and on the development of human potential. The ideal "Renaissance man" was not a bold and dashing knight or a scholarly monk but a well-rounded person who cultivated his talents to the fullest.

CREATIVITY AND EXPLORATION Renaissance Europeans delighted in the arts and literature, the beauty of nature, human impulses, exploration, and a new sense of mastery over the world. This was the time of **Shakespeare, Galileo,** and **Columbus,** after all. Inventions and discoveries made possible things that had been previously unimaginable. The compass, for example, along with advances in astronomy, allowed ships to venture into uncharted seas, and subsequent exploration profoundly altered narrow medieval perceptions of the world. Gutenberg's **printing press** expanded horizons of a different sort. It meant that books no longer had to be copied out by hand. Once the rare and precious treasures of a privileged few, books were now widely available. In turn, by 1530 more than half of England's population could read.

The Renaissance flourished in Elizabethan times, when **theater** and literature reached new heights. Even Elizabeth's successor, James I, contributed to the period's literary legacy with his commissioning of a new translation of the **Bible.** With the reign of Puritan Oliver Cromwell and his closing of theaters, however, the period was near its end. The restoration of the monarchy in 1660 marked the official conclusion of the Renaissance period in English history.

Telescope, triangle, magnet compass, and pendulum clock belonging to Galileo Galilei (1564–1642)

Renaissance Literature

The English Renaissance nurtured the talents of such literary giants as Shakespeare, Milton, and Donne. Poetry, drama, humanist works, and religious writings defined the literature of the period.

Pastoral Poems and Sonnets

During the Renaissance, the creative energy of the English people burst forth into the greatest harvest of literature the Western world had yet known. Poets and playwrights, readers and listeners, all delighted in the vigor and beauty of the English language.

The glittering Elizabethan court was a focus of poetic creativity. Members of the court vied with one another to see who could create the most highly polished, technically perfect poems. The appreciative audience for these lyrics was the elite artistic and social circle that surrounded the queen. Elizabeth I herself wrote lyrics, and she patronized favorite poets and rewarded courtiers for eloquent poetic tributes. Among her protégés were **Sir Philip Sidney** and **Sir Walter Raleigh.** Raleigh, in turn, encouraged **Edmund Spenser,** who wrote the epic *The Faerie Queene* (1590) in honor of Elizabeth.

Sir Walter Raleigh and his contemporary **Christopher Marlowe** wrote excellent examples of a type of poetry popular with Elizabeth's court: the **pastoral.** A pastoral is a poem that portrays shepherds and rustic life, usually in an idealized manner. The poets did not attempt to write in the voice of a common shepherd, however. Their speakers used courtly language rather than the language of common speech. The pastoral's form was artificial as well, with meters and rhyme schemes characteristic of formal poetry.

IMPROVING NATURE The Elizabethans viewed nature as intricate, complex, and beautiful. To them, however, the natural world was a subject not for imitation but for improvement by creative minds. Nature provided raw material to be shaped into works of art. The greater the intricacy or "artificiality" of the result, the more admired the artistry of the poet. Elizabethan poets thus created ingenious metaphors, elaborate allegories, and complex analogies, often within the strictures of a popular verse form that came from Italy, the **sonnet** (see page 310).

Earlier poets, such as **Sir Thomas Wyatt** and **Henry Howard, Earl of Surrey,** had introduced into England the 14-line verse form, modifying it to better suit the English language. During Elizabethan times, the sonnet became the most popular form of love lyric. Sonnets were often published in sequences, such as **Edmund Spenser's** *Amoretti,* addressed to his future wife. **William Shakespeare's** sonnets do not form a clear sequence, but several address a mysterious dark lady some scholars think may have been the poet **Amelia Lanier.** The English sonnet eventually became known as the **Shakespearean sonnet,** in tribute to Shakespeare's mastery of the form.

Young Man Leaning Against a Tree Among Roses, Nicholas Hilliard. Miniature. © Victoria & Albert Museum, London/Art Resource, New York.

▶ *For Your Outline*

PASTORAL POEMS AND SONNETS

- Pastorals portray shepherds and rustic life, usually in an idealized manner.
- Elizabethans admired intricacy and artifice.
- The sonnet is a 14-line verse form, often published in sequences.

Shakespearean Drama

Although Shakespeare's contributions to poetry were great, he left an even clearer mark on drama, which came of age during the Elizabethan period. Elizabethan drama emerged from three sources: medieval plays, 16th-century interludes, and Latin and Greek classics.

The **mystery, miracle,** and **morality plays** of medieval times—simple plays performed in churches, inns, and marketplaces as a way of spreading religious knowledge—provided the opportunity for actors and writers to develop their craft within biblical story outlines already familiar to audiences. In the 16th century, another form of drama arose. Certain noble families of the time maintained their own companies of actors who, when they weren't doubling as household servants, amused their patrons with brief farcical **interludes** that ridiculed the manners and customs of commoners. These interludes had little to do with the Bible, paving the way for later Elizabethan dramatists to write plays with secular themes. The third source, **Latin and Greek dramas** that were revived during the Renaissance and studied at university centers such as Oxford and Cambridge, modeled for Elizabethan playwrights the characteristics of comedy and tragedy.

Renaissance dramatists borrowed devices from these earlier works but inserted their own elements consistent with the thinking of the age. As products of the Renaissance mindset, dramas dealt with the complexities of human life on earth rather than with the religious themes of earlier times. Plays were often staged at court, in the homes of wealthy nobles, and in inn yards where spectators could sit on the ground in front of the stage or in balconies overlooking it. A similar plan was used in England's first theaters, such as the famous **Globe Theater** in London.

SHAKESPEARE'S INFLUENCE By 1600, London had more playhouses than any other European capital. The Globe was the most successful, thanks to actor, poet, and playwright William Shakespeare. Tremendously versatile and prolific, Shakespeare contributed 37 plays to the theater's repertory: **tragedies,** such as *Othello;* **comedies,** such as *A Midsummer Night's Dream;* and **histories** about the kings of England. Shakespeare's clever wordplay, memorable characters, and complex plots appealed to everyone in his audience, from the uneducated "groundlings," who paid a penny to stand and watch, to the royal family, who received special private performances.

Being an actor himself, Shakespeare knew well the capabilities and limitations of the theater building and of the acting company for whom he wrote his plays. It wasn't easy putting on a crowd-pleasing performance in Elizabethan times. Besides having to memorize their lines, actors had to be able to sing and dance, wrestle and fence, clown and weep. Because the stage had no front curtain, the actors always walked on and off the stage in full view of the audience. Plays had to be written so that any character who died on stage could be unobtrusively hauled off.

> ▶ *For Your Outline*
>
> **SHAKESPEAREAN DRAMA**
>
> - Elizabethan drama came from three sources: medieval plays, 16th-century interludes, and Greek and Latin classics.
> - Plays focused on human complexities rather than religious themes.
> - The Globe was the most successful of many English theaters.
> - Shakespeare contributed 37 plays—comedies, tragedies, and histories.
> - Marlowe and Jonson were popular playwrights.
> - After 1649, Puritans closed theaters.

Laurence Fishburne and Kenneth Branagh in *Othello* (1995)

In retrospect, Shakespeare dominates the theater of the late 16th and early 17th centuries—in fact, his plays represent the height of the English dramatic tradition. At the time, however, others were equally admired. **Christopher Marlowe** was the first playwright to exploit the potential of the English language as a dramatic medium. His tragedies show the kind of psychological probing that is a hallmark of the finest Elizabethan and 17th-century dramas. Also popular were the comedies of a rugged, boisterous poet and playwright named **Ben Jonson.** His plays provided a satiric, somewhat cynical commentary on the lives of ordinary Londoners. Jonson's **masques,** especially, attracted aristocratic audiences, who flocked to the spectacular pageants with their elaborate scenery, costumes, music, and dance.

By the time of Elizabeth's death in 1603, the influence of the Puritans had begun to grow in England. Puritans, who believed that the Elizabethan dramas and the rowdy crowds they attracted were highly immoral, worked to close all the theaters. They were not immediately successful.

Shakespeare wrote some of his greatest tragedies, including *Macbeth* (see page 348), during the reign of Elizabeth's successor, James I. Shakespeare's interest in issues of power may have been sparked by the intense conflicts between the king and Parliament. When the Puritans overthrew James's son Charles in 1649, however, they finally closed all the playhouses. This act brought the final curtain down on the golden age of drama.

> **A Voice from the Times**
>
> *Soul of the age!*
> *The applause, delight, the*
> *   wonder of our stage!*
> *My Shakespeare, rise. . .*
> *Thou art a monument, without*
> *   a tomb,*
> *And art alive still, while thy*
> *   book doth live,*
> *And we have wits to read, and*
> *   praise to give.*
>
> **—Ben Jonson**

The Rise of Humanism

During the Renaissance, literature reflected another important influence: **humanism.** At this time, the universities of Europe buzzed with new ideas—about the worth and importance of the individual, about the spiritual value of beauty in nature and art, about the power of human reason to decide what was good and right. Those who taught these new ideas were called **humanists,** because they studied the **humanities** (art, history, philosophy, and literature; in other words, subjects that were human rather than sacred) and looked to the classics for wisdom and guidance.

Humanists were often devout Christians—one, in fact, became Pope Pius II—and they tried to reconcile the new ideas with their religious beliefs. In northern Europe, Christian humanists led by the Dutch monk **Erasmus** studied ancient Greek and Hebrew so they could read not just the classics but also the Bible and other sacred writings in the original. Naturally, reading the words of history's greatest thinkers gave Erasmus and his followers high ideals, and they sharply criticized European society, and especially the church, for falling short.

ENGLISH HUMANISTS Erasmus traveled widely throughout Europe, writing and teaching, and made many friends, among them the artist Hans Holbein the Younger and English writer and scholar **Sir Thomas More.** Like Erasmus, More saw much to criticize in the way the world was being run and believed humans could do better. In 1516, he published his book called ***Utopia*** (from the Greek for "no place"), about a perfect society on an imaginary island. In Utopia, there was no poverty or greed—not even private property; everything was shared, and everyone was equal. War and competition were unknown, and people were governed by reason.

Humanists were concerned with classical learning. One of their aims was to educate the sons of nobility to speak and write in Latin, the language of diplomacy and all higher learning. For humanist writers, however, reverence for the classics created a conflict: should they write their own works in Latin or English? Although many wrote in the classical Latin, others urged scholars to improve English by writing ambitious works in it. In any case, the humanist reverence for classics combined with a pride in the English language led to many distinguished **translations** throughout the period, including the **Earl of Surrey's** translation of Virgil's *Aeneid* and **George Chapman's** translations of Homer's *Iliad* and *Odyssey*.

Interestingly, the humanists reflected a fact of life during the Renaissance period—religion was a subject

▶ *For Your Outline*

HUMANISM

- Humanists were so called because they studied the humanities (art, history, philosophy, literature).

- Christian humanists criticized society.

- A reverence for the classics and pride in the English language led to distinguished translations.

- Humanists disagreed on religious issues.

Illustration of Sir Thomas More's island of Utopia

dear to most but agreed upon by few. From the outset, humanism was concerned with Christianity; but while early humanists, such as Sir Thomas More, a Catholic, primarily attacked Luther and the Protestants, later humanists, such as Roger Ascham, were earnest Protestants who attacked a more secular humanism coming out of Italy. These men went on to influence later Christian writers, such as the great John Milton.

Spiritual and Devotional Writings

Despite the religious turmoil that marked this period in English history, England remained a Christian nation, and its literature reflects the beliefs of its people. Spiritual and devotional writings became some of the most popular and influential works of the day. In fact, the **King James Bible** likely did more to mold English prose style than any other work.

For centuries, the church had resisted calls to translate the Latin Bible into languages the common people could understand, on the grounds that it would diminish church authority and lead to heresy. In fact, when the first English version of the Bible was translated by the 14th-century scholar **John Wycliffe,** he was attacked by a British archbishop as "that wretched and pestilent fellow . . . who crowned his wickedness by translating the Scriptures into the mother tongue." Another English translator, **William Tyndale,** fled to the continent during the early years of Henry VIII's reign, only to be condemned as a heretic and burned at the stake.

THE KING JAMES BIBLE Ironically, in the meantime Henry had broken with Rome, and in the following years English translations of the Bible proliferated. Finally, in 1604, James I commissioned 54 leading biblical scholars to create a new, "authorized" version, one based on the original Hebrew and Greek as well as on earlier translations from the Latin. Masterpieces of literature are not generally created by committee, but the King James Bible, completed in 1611, proved to be an exception. Its beautiful imagery, graceful simplicity, and measured cadences made it the principal Protestant Bible in English for more than 300 years, and it still remains the most important and influential of all the English translations.

TWO MASTERPIECES One of the earliest writers to be influenced by the King James Bible was the Puritan poet **John Milton.** In fact, it has been said that he knew the Bible by heart. His epic blank-verse poem *Paradise Lost* is based on the biblical story of the first humans, Adam and Eve, who are tempted by Satan to eat the forbidden fruit of the tree of knowledge. They eat and then are punished by being driven from the Garden of Eden out into the world, where they and all their descendants must suffer and die. A devout believer, Milton filled his work with energy and power, and none of the many "rebel" characters in literature since can equal his portrayal of Satan, the fallen angel. Dignified and elevated, even biblical, Milton's language is meant to evoke reverence for his religious

▶ *For Your Outline*

SPIRITUAL WRITING

- Early efforts to translate the Bible were censured by the church.
- The King James Bible was created by a committee of scholars; it became the most influential English translation.
- Milton's *Paradise Lost* is based on a biblical story.
- Bunyan's *The Pilgrim's Progress* is an allegory of the journey to the afterlife.

Detail of *Princess Elizabeth, Later Queen of Bohemia* (1606), Robert Peake the Elder. Oil on canvas, 60 3/4" x 31 1/4". Gift of Kate T. Davison, in memory of her husband, Henry Pomeroy Davison, 1951 (51.194.1). © Metropolitan Museum of Art, New York.

Demon Leaving Heaven from 1800s book illustration for *Paradise Lost* by John Milton. © Corbis.

◀ **Analyze Visuals**
Gustave Doré was a 19th-century artist known for his wood-engraved illustrations for famous works such as Dante's *Inferno*, Cervantes's *Don Quixote*, and Milton's *Paradise Lost*. According to the historian Millicent Rose, "Gigantic scale and limitless space had always fascinated Doré." How well does this Doré engraving from *Paradise Lost* capture the scale and space of the heavens?

themes. His rich and complex style, married with his devotion to religious themes, places Milton with other Renaissance Christian humanists, but his talent sets him apart as an artist.

Milton was a typical "Renaissance man"—a scholar who read widely, studying the classics as well as the Bible, and who was fluent in many languages. Fellow Puritan writer **John Bunyan,** on the other hand, was an uneducated tinker and preacher who spent many years in jail for his religious beliefs. While in jail, Bunyan wrote his greatest work, ***The Pilgrim's Progress***—an **allegory** in which a character named Christian undertakes a dangerous journey from this world to the next. Along the way, he encounters such obstacles as the Slough of Despond and meets characters with such names as Mr. Moneylove and Ignorance. Bunyan modeled his style on that of the English Bible, and he used concrete language and details familiar to most readers, enabling even the most basic of readers to share in Christian's experiences. Though *The Pilgrim's Progress* lacks the grandeur and complexity of *Paradise Lost,* its deeply felt simplicity made it one of the most widely read books in the English language.

The Metaphysical and Cavalier Poets

In the early 17th century, two new groups of poets emerged. The first was inspired by the literary man-of-all-trades **Ben Jonson.** Like Shakespeare, his friend and rival, Ben Jonson was not just a playwright but also an accomplished poet. Dissatisfied with the extravagant romance of Elizabethan lyrics, Jonson chose instead to imitate the graceful craftsmanship of classical forms. Far from the typical image of a refined poet, however, Jonson was a great bellowing bear of a man who loved an argument and didn't mind if it

▶ *For Your Outline*

METAPHYSICAL AND CAVALIER POETS

- Ben Jonson, a boisterous man and an accomplished poet, inspired later poets, called "sons of Ben."

- These poets were known as Cavaliers because they took the side of Charles I and his Royalist cavaliers.

- Cavalier poetry was charming and witty, dealing with themes of love, war, and *carpe diem*.

- John Donne wrote metaphysical poetry—poems characterized by themes of love, death, and religious devotion.

- Metaphysical poets used elaborate metaphors to explore life's complexities.

turned into a brawl, and his forceful personality won him as many admirers as his considerable talent did.

Jonson's followers, called "sons of Ben," were sophisticated young aristocrats, among them **Robert Herrick, Richard Lovelace,** and **Sir John Suckling.** These poets were known as the **Cavaliers,** because many of them took the side of Charles I in the civil war between Cromwell's "Roundheads" (so called for their closely cropped hair) and the long-haired Royalist cavaliers. Lighthearted, charming, witty, and sometimes cynical, Cavalier poetry dealt mainly with themes of love, war, chivalry, and loyalty to the throne and frequently advocated the philosophy of *carpe diem,* or living for the moment.

Jonson's contemporary, **John Donne,** is representative of a second group of poets, the **metaphysical poets**. These writers broke with convention, employing unusual imagery, elaborate metaphors, and irregular meter to produce intense poems characterized by themes of death, physical love, and religious devotion (see page 514). Whereas the Cavalier poets tended to treat limited, human-focused subjects, Donne and other metaphysical poets tried to encompass the vastness of the universe and to explore life's complexities and contradictions. Some ridiculed Donne for the philosophical tone of his love poems, saying that instead of winning over women he merely succeeded in perplexing them. However, Donne's unique blend of intellect and passion influenced many other poets, from his own time to the 21st century.

A CHANGING LANGUAGE

During the "great vowel shift" of the 1400s, the pronunciation of most English long vowels changed, and the final *e* in words like *take* was no longer pronounced. Yet early printers continued to use Middle English spellings—retaining, for example, the *k* and *e* in *knave,* even though the letters were no longer pronounced. This practice resulted in many of the inconsistent spellings for which modern English is known.

Renaissance English By 1500, Middle English had evolved into an early form of the modern English spoken today. Nevertheless, there are some differences. During the Renaissance, *thou, thee, thy,* and *thine* were used for familiar address, while *you, your,* and *yours* were reserved for more formal and impersonal situations. Speakers used the verb ending *–est* or *–st* with *thou* ("thou leadest") and *–eth* or *–th* with *she* and *he* ("he doth"). They also used fewer helping verbs, especially in questions ("Saw you the bird?").

Andrew Marvell Visiting His Friend John Milton, George Henry Boughton. Oil on canvas, 69.5 cm × 166 cm. Private collection. © Bridgeman Art Library.

Connecting Literature, History, and Culture

Use this timeline and the questions on the next page to gain insight into trends in England and other parts of the world during the Renaissance period.

BRITISH LITERARY MILESTONES

1485

CIRCA 1495 *Everyman,* the earliest morality play, is written anonymously.

1515

1516 Sir Thomas More publishes *Utopia* in Latin (published in English c. 1551).

1535 More is executed by order of Henry VIII after refusing to recognize the king as head of the church.

1545

1549 The *Book of Common Prayer* replaces Latin missals.

1557 Richard Tottel's anthology *Miscellany* is published, containing 97 poems attributed to Sir Thomas Wyatt.

1564 William Shakespeare is born.

HISTORICAL CONTEXT

1485

1485 The Wars of the Roses end as Henry Tudor defeats Richard III and takes the throne as Henry VII.

1509 The reign of Henry VIII begins (to 1547).

1515

1534 At insistence of Henry VIII, England breaks with Roman Catholic Church; Henry proclaims himself head of new Church of England. ▶

1536 Henry VIII unites England and Wales.

1545

1547 The reign of Edward VI begins.

1553 Mary Tudor, a Catholic, succeeds to the English throne.

1558 Protestant Elizabeth I begins her reign as queen of England (to 1603).

WORLD CULTURE AND EVENTS

1485

1492 Columbus sails to Bahamas in Western Hemisphere. ▼

1497 Vasco da Gama sails around Cape of Good Hope (Africa).

1503 Leonardo da Vinci paints the *Mona Lisa.*

1515

1517 Martin Luther inspires the Protestant Reformation.

1521 Cortés conquers the Aztecs in Mexico.

1522 Magellan's crew sails around the world.

1543 Polish astronomer Nicolaus Copernicus publishes his theory that the earth and other planets revolve around the sun.

1545

1547 Ivan the Terrible, after seizing power in Russia, becomes its first czar (to 1584).

1556 Emperor Akbar the Great begins rule over India at age 13.

MAKING CONNECTIONS

- What evidence do you see that the Renaissance was taking place in other European countries as well as in England?
- How important was religion to the politics of Europe? What influence did religion have on the literature of the period? Explain.

COMMON CORE

RI 7 Integrate and evaluate multiple sources of information presented in different media or formats as well as in words in order to address a question or solve a problem.

1575

CIRCA 1590 Shakespeare, settled in London, begins his career as playwright.

1597 The first edition of Francis Bacon's *Essays* is published.

1605

CIRCA 1606 Shakespeare's *Macbeth* is produced.

1610 Ben Jonson's popular play *The Alchemist* is produced.

1611 The King James Bible is published. It will become the standard English Bible for centuries to come.

1635

1642 Puritans close theaters in England (to 1660).

1644 John Milton's pamphlet *Areopagitica* attacks press censorship.

1658 Milton begins composing *Paradise Lost*.

1575

1580 Sir Francis Drake brings great treasures back to England after sailing around world.

1588 English navy defeats the Spanish Armada.

1603 James VI of Scotland becomes king of England as James I (to 1625).

1605

1607 English settlers establish Jamestown colony in Virginia.

1620 Pilgrims set sail on the *Mayflower*. ▲

1625 The reign of Charles I begins.

1635

1642 The English Civil War begins (to 1651).

1649 Charles I is beheaded; Oliver Cromwell takes power.

1660 The monarchy is restored with the accession of Charles II.

1575

1580 Michel de Montaigne publishes his *Essais* in France.

CIRCA 1586 Japanese kabuki theater is introduced. ▼

1605

1605 Miguel de Cervantes publishes *Don Quixote*.

1609 Italian scientist Galileo Galilei studies the heavens with a telescope.

1633 Galileo is condemned for supporting Copernicus's theory.

1635

1643 Louis XIV begins 72-year reign in France. ▶

1644 Ming Dynasty collapses and is replaced by the Qing Dynasty, China's last (to 1912).

The Legacy of the Renaissance

Renaissance People

COMMON CORE

W 7 Conduct short research projects to answer a question; narrow the inquiry; synthesize multiple sources, demonstrating understanding of the subject.
W 8 Gather relevant information from multiple digital sources.
SL 1 Initiate and participate effectively in collaborative discussions, building on others' ideas and expressing their own clearly and persuasively.

A "Renaissance man" was a person who encompassed a wide range of interests and abilities, such as Italy's Leonardo da Vinci, who was not only a painter and sculptor but also an architect, a scientist, and an engineer. England's Queen Elizabeth I could be considered the ultimate Renaissance woman. She was educated in Latin, Greek, French, Italian, history, and theology; she was an accomplished poet and speechwriter; and she was a consummate politician.

DISCUSS Who are today's "Renaissance people"? In our current world of increasing specialization, is there still value in being well-rounded?

Businessman and innovator Steven Jobs, media mogul Oprah Winfrey, and musician and activist Bono

A scene from Akira Kurosawa's 1985 movie *Ran*, the story of King Lear set in feudal Japan

The Play's the Thing

Shakespeare's plays have proven to have enormous staying power. They are still performed on stage all over the world as well as on film, with new movie versions coming out on a regular basis. Writers in all genres have used Shakespeare's plots as inspiration, transplanting *King Lear* to an Iowa cornfield or feudal Japan, and *Romeo and Juliet* to New York City streets or a Southern California shopping mall.

ONLINE RESEARCH With a partner, find a recent book or movie based on one of Shakespeare's plays. What changes make the story more relevant to today's concerns? What timeless issues remain?

Utopia and Dystopia

Since Sir Thomas More published *Utopia* in 1516, many other writers have tried to create their own vision of the ideal society, such as one run by women (as in *Herland*) or by the environmentally friendly (as in *Ecotopia*). Even more popular today are "dystopian" books and movies, nightmarish futuristic visions of the world gone bad (think *1984* and *The Matrix*).

QUICKWRITE Describe your own utopian or dystopian vision. What would have to change in our society to make your utopia possible— or to make sure your dystopia doesn't come true?

The Sonnet Form

How do you convey love for a person? For centuries, people have searched for just the right words to express how much they love someone, how long they have loved someone, or how uniquely they love someone. For many, poetry has been the vehicle for conveying love. Every form of poetry has been used to this end, but none more so than the sonnet.

Origins of the Sonnet

COMMON CORE

Included in this workshop:
RL 4 Determine the meaning of words and phrases as they are used in the text; analyze the impact of specific word choices on meaning and tone. **RL 5** Analyze how an author's choices concerning how to structure specific parts of a text contribute to its overall structure and meaning as well as its aesthetic impact. **RL 9** Demonstrate knowledge of foundational works of literature, including how two or more texts from the same period treat similar themes or topics.

In 13th-century Italy, poets introduced a poetic form called the sonnet, an Italian word meaning "little song." The **sonnet** is a 14-line lyric poem with a complicated rhyme scheme and a defined structure. Because of the technical skill required to write a sonnet, the form has challenged poets for centuries. The great Italian poet Francesco Petrarch (1304–1374) perfected the **Italian sonnet,** which is often called the **Petrarchan sonnet** in his honor. Petrarch felt that the

Henry Percy, 9th Earl of Northumberland (1595), Nicholas Hilliard.

sonnet, with its brevity and musical rhymes, was a perfect medium for the expression of emotion, especially love. Although Italian sonneteers did not restrict themselves to love as a subject, Petrarch wrote over 300 sonnets detailing his devotion to a beautiful but unobtainable woman whom he called Laura.

The English Sonnet

The English sonnet began with another lovelorn poet, Sir Thomas Wyatt (1503–1542). In the 1530s, Wyatt translated some of Petrarch's love sonnets and wrote a few of his own in a slight modification of the Italian form. Another English poet who deserves credit for popularizing the sonnet in England is Henry Howard, Earl of Surrey (1517–1547). Building on Wyatt's modifications to the form, Surrey changed the rhyme scheme of the sonnet to make it more suitable to the English language. Surrey's innovations distinguished the English sonnet from the Italian sonnet, and eventually became known as the **Shakespearean sonnet** because of Shakespeare's mastery of the form.

Edmund Spenser also introduced a variation on Wyatt's form based around an interlocking rhyme scheme (*abab bcbc cdcd ee*). Surrey's rhyme scheme allowed Shakespeare more freedom in his versification, and he used this freedom to expand on the typical sonnet subject matter. Instead of limiting himself to the subject of love, he introduced deep philosophical issues and perplexing ironies.

Sonnet Structure

The **Petrarchan form** has a two-part structure.

- The **octave** (the first 8 lines), usually rhyming *abbaabba*, establishes the speaker's situation.

- The **sestet** (the last 6 lines), usually with the rhyme scheme *cdcdcd* or *cdecde*, resolves, draws conclusions about, or expresses a reaction to the speaker's situation.

The Petrarchan sonnet has been called organic in its unity because the octave and sestet fit together naturally. Unity is also produced by the rhyme scheme, which involves only four or five different rhyming sounds.

The **Shakespearean form** also has 14 lines but is structured differently.

- Three **quatrains** (stanzas of 4 lines) are followed by a rhyming **couplet** (2 lines).

- The rhyme scheme is *abab cdcd efef gg*.

- The first quatrain introduces a situation, which is explored in the next two quatrains. The third quatrain (or sometimes the final couplet) usually includes a turn, or shift in thought. The couplet resolves the situation.

CHARACTERISTICS OF A SONNET

Length: 14 lines

Meter: iambic pentameter—lines containing five metrical units, each consisting of an unstressed syllable followed by a stressed syllable (‿ˊ‿ˊ‿ˊ‿ˊ‿ˊ)

Structure and rhyme scheme: a strict pattern; the three most common known as Petrarchan, Shakespearean, or Spenserian.

Subject: a focus on personal feelings and thoughts that are lyrical in nature

> The time of year thou mayst in me behold
> When yellow leaves, or none, or few, do hang
> Upon those boughs which shake against the cold,
> Bare ruined choirs, where late the sweet birds sang.
> In me thou see'st the twilight of such day
> As after sunset fadeth in the west;
> Which by and by black night doth take away,
> Death's second self, that seals up all in rest.
> In me thou see'st the glowing of such fire,
> That on the ashes of his youth doth lie,
> As the deathbed whereon it must expire,
> Consumed with that which it was nourished by.
>   This thou perceiv'st, which makes thy love more strong,
>   To love that well which thou must leave ere long.
>
> **—William Shakespeare, "Sonnet 73"**

Close Read

Explain the situation developed and explored in the three quatrains. How is it resolved in the couplet?

Notice that each quatrain elaborates on a particular image: autumn in the first quatrain, twilight in the second, and the embers of a fire in the third. The final couplet is a concise statement that pulls the sonnet together. Think of the closing couplet in a Shakespearean sonnet as a "punch line" that gives meaning to the whole.

The Passionate Shepherd to His Love

Poem by Christopher Marlowe

The Nymph's Reply to the Shepherd

Poem by Sir Walter Raleigh

VIDEO TRAILER **THINK** central KEYWORD: HML12-312A

Meet the Authors

Christopher Marlowe

1564–1593

Christopher Marlowe was the first great English playwright. In his brief career, he transformed theater by showing the potential power and beauty of blank verse dialogue.

Rise to Fame The son of a poor shoemaker, Marlowe attended Cambridge University on a scholarship. By age 23, he was the best-known playwright in England. His most famous play, *Dr. Faustus,* is about a scholar who sells his soul to the devil in return for knowledge, power, and pleasure. Marlowe also distinguished himself as a poet; his poem "The Passionate Shepherd to His Love" was so popular that it inspired responses in verse, including Raleigh's "The Nymph's Reply to the Shepherd." The two poems present sharply contrasting views on love.

Freethinker . . . and Criminal? Marlowe was a freethinker who questioned established authority and religious teaching, which gained him enemies in Elizabethan England. He was accused of being an atheist, a spy, a counterfeiter, a traitor, and a murderer. Although he spent time in prison, he was never convicted of any crime. He died from a stab wound in a tavern brawl at age 29. Some biographers speculate that he was murdered for political reasons.

Sir Walter Raleigh

1552?–1618

Like his friend Christopher Marlowe, Sir Walter Raleigh met a violent end. He was beheaded by an axe, which he called "sharp medicine." A soldier, explorer, and writer who enjoyed wealth and power under Queen Elizabeth I, Raleigh was imprisoned and executed by her successor, King James I.

The Queen's Favorite According to legend, Raleigh attracted Elizabeth's attention by taking off an expensive cloak and spreading it over the ground so she would not have to walk through mud. Raleigh became the queen's favorite, gaining a mansion and a monopoly on licensing wine. She also made him a knight and captain of her guard.

Losing It All When the queen found out that Raleigh had secretly married without her permission, she imprisoned him and his wife in the Tower of London. Raleigh bought his way out of prison and subsequently led several expeditions to the New World. But the queen's death in 1603 sealed his fate. King James distrusted Raleigh, who was imprisoned for 13 years on a charge of treason. The king released him to lead a gold-finding expedition to South America. But after that expedition ended in failure, Raleigh was executed.

Author Online

Go to thinkcentral.com. KEYWORD: HML12-312B

THINK central

POETIC FORM: PASTORAL

A **pastoral** is a poem that presents shepherds in idealized rural settings. Renaissance poets like Marlowe and Raleigh used the pastoral form to express their feelings and thoughts about love and other subjects. Shepherds in pastorals tend to use courtly speech. The poems usually have metrical patterns and rhyme schemes that help give them a musical or songlike quality. The imagery derives from commonplace country settings, as the following lines suggest:

And we will sit upon the rocks,
Seeing the shepherds feed their flocks.

As you read these poems, look for details of pastoral life and for the use of nature imagery to convey emotions and ideas.

READING SKILL: COMPARE SPEAKERS

The **speaker** in a poem is the voice that addresses the reader, much like the narrator in a work of fiction. Poets use the speakers they create to express ideas or tell a story from a specific point of view. The speaker and the poet are not necessarily identical, even when the words *I* and *me* are used.

The speakers in the following poems—the shepherd and the nymph—express very different attitudes about the topic of love. To identify the differences, consider

- whom the speaker is addressing
- the speaker's choice of words
- evidence of the speaker's attitude toward the poem's subject

As you read both poems, use a chart like the one shown to make notes on the speakers' differing attitudes toward love. Look for specific words and phrases that indicate their feelings.

Shepherd's Line	Nymph's Reply
"I will make thee beds of roses"	"flowers do fade"

 Complete the activities in your **Reader/Writer Notebook**.

Is PASSION *overrated?*

Throughout the ages, writers have composed poems and songs describing the ardor of new love. But have people placed too much emphasis on passion in romantic love? Are other aspects of love—such as friendship, respect, and trust—more important?

QUICKWRITE Make a list of qualities that you think are important in a romantic relationship. Rank the items, and then write a paragraph explaining the reasons for your ranking.

The Passionate Shepherd to His Love

Christopher Marlowe

Come live with me and be my love,
And we will all the pleasures prove
That valleys, groves, hills, and fields,
Woods, or steepy mountain yields.

5 And we will sit upon the rocks,
Seeing the shepherds feed their flocks,
By shallow rivers to whose falls
Melodious birds sing madrigals.

And I will make thee beds of roses
10 And a thousand fragrant posies,
A cap of flowers, and a kirtle
Embroidered all with leaves of myrtle;

A gown made of the finest wool
Which from our pretty lambs we pull; **Ⓐ**
15 Fair lined slippers for the cold,
With buckles of the purest gold;

A belt of straw and ivy buds,
With coral clasps and amber studs:
And if these pleasures may thee move,
20 Come live with me, and be my love.

The shepherds' swains shall dance and sing
For thy delight each May morning:
If these delights thy mind may move,
Then live with me and be my love.

2 prove: experience.

8 madrigals: songs of a type popular during the Renaissance.

11 kirtle: skirt or dress.

Ⓐ PASTORAL
What characteristics of **pastoral** poems do you find in lines 9–14?

21 swains: companions.

Working Wool (1500). From the series of *Noblemen in the Country.* Loire Valley workshops. Louvre, Paris. © Réunion des Musées Nationaux/Art Resource, New York.

The Nymph's Reply to the Shepherd

Sir Walter Raleigh

If all the world and love were young,
And truth in every shepherd's tongue,
These pretty pleasures might me move
To live with thee and be thy love.

5 Time drives the flocks from field to fold
When rivers rage and rocks grow cold,
And Philomel becometh dumb;
The rest complains of cares to come.

The flowers do fade, and wanton fields
10 To wayward winter reckoning yields;
A honey tongue, a heart of gall,
Is fancy's spring, but sorrow's fall.

Thy gowns, thy shoes, thy beds of roses,
Thy cap, thy kirtle, and thy posies
15 Soon break, soon wither, soon forgotten—
In folly ripe, in reason rotten. **B**

Thy belt of straw and ivy buds,
Thy coral clasps and amber studs,
All these in me no means can move
20 To come to thee and be thy love.

But could youth last and love still breed,
Had joys no date nor age no need,
Then these delights my mind might move
To live with thee and be thy love.

5 fold: a pen for animals, especially sheep.

7 Philomel: the nightingale; **dumb:** silent.

9 wanton: here, producing abundant crops; luxuriant.

B COMPARE SPEAKERS
Reread lines 13–16. How does the nymph directly refute the shepherd's promises?

22 date: ending.

Comprehension

1. **Recall** What gifts does the shepherd offer his beloved in Marlowe's poem?

2. **Recall** What does the shepherd ask from his love in return?

3. **Clarify** In Raleigh's poem, under what conditions might the nymph agree to live with the shepherd?

COMMON CORE

RL 4 Determine the meaning of words and phrases as they are used in the text; analyze the impact of specific word choices on meaning and tone.

Text Analysis

4. **Identify Pastoral Elements** What details does Marlowe use to create an idealized portrait of the rural life of shepherds?

5. **Make Inferences** Reread lines 1–4 of "The Nymph's Reply to the Shepherd." What does this statement suggest about the nymph's attitude toward the shepherd?

6. **Draw Conclusions** How would you describe the nymph's view of each of the following subjects? Cite evidence from Raleigh's poem.

   • lovers' words   • the value of love tokens   • planning for the future

7. **Analyze Imagery** In "The Nymph's Reply to the Shepherd," note Raleigh's use of imagery that reflects seasonal change. What idea is conveyed through this imagery?

8. **Compare Speakers** There are many lines in "The Nymph's Reply to the Shepherd" that parallel lines in "The Passionate Shepherd to His Love." Refer to the chart you made as you read these poems. What do the statements reveal about each poet's perspective on passion?

9. **Make Judgments** Raleigh was not the only Elizabethan poet who was inspired by "The Passionate Shepherd to His Love." What qualities do you think made Marlowe's poem so popular and intriguing? Support your opinion with evidence from the poem.

Text Criticism

10. **Critical Interpretations** One critic has suggested that Raleigh's "witty and sardonic" response to Marlowe's poem is a comment on "the human propensity for self-delusion." Do you agree or disagree? Consider the subject of both poems—idealized love—and what the speakers have to say about it.

Is **PASSION** *overrated?*

From your own perspective, how much emphasis should be placed on strong emotions or feelings? What role should logic play in love? What hints of logic or rational thought can you find in these poems?

Sonnet 30
Sonnet 75

Poetry by Edmund Spenser

COMMON CORE

RL 2 Determine two or more central ideas of a text and analyze their development over the course of the text, including how they interact and build on one another to produce a complex account; provide an objective summary of the text. **RL 5** Analyze how an author's choices concerning how to structure specific parts of a text contribute to its overall structure and meaning as well as its aesthetic impact.

DID YOU KNOW?

Edmund Spenser . . .

- worked as a servant to pay for his room and board at college.
- wrote a satire that was censored because it insulted Queen Elizabeth I and other English notables.

Meet the Author

Edmund Spenser 1552?–1599

Although Edmund Spenser was born in London and educated in England, he spent most of his life in Ireland. It was there that he wrote one of the greatest epic romances in English literature, *The Faerie Queene.* The poem tells the stories of six knights, each representing a particular moral virtue. Spenser was innovative in devising a new verse form, in mixing features of the Italian romance and the classical epic, and in using archaic English words.

Move to Ireland In 1576, Spenser earned a master's degree from Pembroke College at Cambridge University. Three years later, he published his first important work of poetry, *The Shepheardes Calender,* which was immediately popular. It consisted of 12 pastoral poems, one for each month of the year. In 1580, Spenser became secretary to the lord deputy of Ireland, who was charged with defending English settlers from native Irish opposed to England's colonization of Ireland. Spenser wrote the rest of his major poetry in Ireland, and that country's landscape and people greatly influenced his writing.

Spenser held various civil service posts during his years in Ireland. In 1589, he was granted a large estate surrounding Kilcolman Castle, which had been taken from an Irish rebel. Spenser's friend Sir Walter Raleigh owned a neighboring estate.

Second Marriage Spenser's courtship of his second wife, Elizabeth Boyle, inspired him to write a sonnet sequence (a series of related sonnets) called *Amoretti,* which means "little love poems." The details and emotions presented in the sonnets are thought to be partly autobiographical. "Sonnet 30" and "Sonnet 75" are part of this sonnet sequence. To celebrate his marriage to Boyle in 1594, Spenser wrote the lyric poem *Epithalamion.*

In 1598, just four years after Spenser's marriage, Irish rebels overran his estate and burned his home. Spenser and his family had to flee through an underground tunnel. They escaped to Cork, and a few months later, Spenser traveled to London to deliver documents reporting on the problems in Ireland. He died shortly after his arrival in London.

In honor of his great literary achievements, Spenser was buried near Geoffrey Chaucer—one of his favorite poets and a major influence—in what is now called the Poets' Corner of Westminster Abbey. An inscription on Spenser's monument calls him "the Prince of Poets in his time."

Author Online

Go to **thinkcentral.com**. KEYWORD: HML12-318

POETIC FORM: SPENSERIAN SONNET

The **Spenserian sonnet** is a variation on the English sonnet, which was introduced in Britain by Sir Thomas Wyatt in the 1530s. Like the English (or Shakespearean) sonnet, the Spenserian sonnet consists of three four-line units, called **quatrains,** followed by two rhymed lines, called a **couplet.** Each quatrain addresses the poem's central idea, thought, or question, and the couplet provides an answer or summation. What is unique to the Spenserian sonnet is the interlocking **rhyme scheme** (*abab bcbc cdcd ee*) that links the three quatrains.

As you read the following Spenserian sonnets, notice the rhymes that connect one quatrain to the next, and the way in which the sonnet's main idea is developed and resolved.

READING SKILL: SUMMARIZE CENTRAL IDEAS IN POETRY

When you **summarize** a poem, you briefly restate the central ideas or themes in your own words. Summarizing a sonnet's central ideas can help you understand and remember what you read, especially when the text or language is particularly complicated or difficult to understand. You can break down each quatrain and the couplet and use your own words to summarize the meaning of each part.

For each Spenser sonnet, use a chart like the one shown to help you summarize the central ideas in each part of the poem.

"Sonnet 75"	
Part of Poem	**Central Idea**
1st quatrain	Whenever I write my beloved's name in the sand, the waves wash it away.
2nd quatrain	
3rd quatrain	
couplet	

 Complete the activities in your **Reader/Writer Notebook**.

What makes your HEART *ache?*

Love can bring great joy— and great sorrow. Poets and songwriters probably lament the heartache of love as much as they extol its pleasures. Anyone who falls in love knows, or soon finds out, that the ride can be bumpy.

DISCUSS Think about all the things that can cause heartache in a loving relationship. Make a web of your ideas. Then share your web with a partner and compare your ideas.

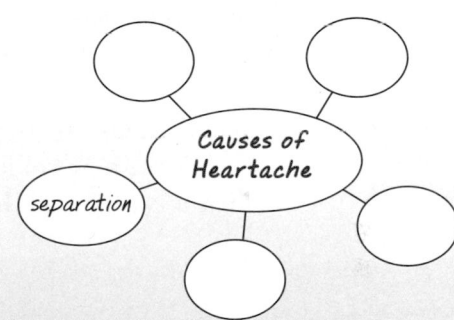

SONNET 30

Edmund Spenser

My love is like to ice, and I to fire;
How comes it then that this her cold so great
Is not dissolved through my so hot desire,
But harder grows the more I her entreat? **A**
5 Or how comes it that my exceeding heat
Is not delayed by her heart-frozen cold:
But that I burn much more in boiling sweat,
And feel my flames augmented manifold?
What more miraculous thing may be told
10 That fire which all things melts, should harden ice:
And ice which is congealed with senseless cold,
Should kindle fire by wonderful device.
Such is the pow'r of love in gentle mind,
That it can alter all the course of kind.

A SUMMARIZE
What is the central idea in lines 1–4?

8 augmented manifold: greatly increased.

11 congealed: solidified.

14 kind: nature.

SONNET 75

Edmund Spenser

One day I wrote her name upon the strand,
But came the waves and washéd it away:
Again I wrote it with a second hand,
But came the tide, and made my pains his prey.
5 "Vain man," said she, "that dost in vain assay,
A mortal thing so to immortalize.
For I myself shall like to this decay,
And eke my name be wipéd out likewise."
"Not so," quod I, "let baser things devise
10 To die in dust, but you shall live by fame:
My verse your virtues rare shall eternize,
And in the heavens write your glorious name,
Where whenas death shall all the world subdue,
Our love shall live, and later life renew." **B**

1 **strand:** beach.

5 **assay:** try.

8 **eke:** also.

9 **quod:** said.

B **SPENSERIAN SONNET**
Note the words Spenser uses in his end rhymes. In what ways are they related to the central ideas in this sonnet?

Comprehension

1. **Recall** In "Sonnet 30," to what does the speaker compare himself and his beloved?

2. **Recall** In "Sonnet 75," what happens when the speaker writes his lover's name in the sand?

3. **Paraphrase** In "Sonnet 75," how does the speaker's lover describe him and his actions (lines 5–6)?

Text Analysis

4. **Identify Paradox** A **paradox** is a statement that seems to contradict ordinary experience but actually reveals a hidden truth. What paradox does Spenser develop in "Sonnet 30"?

5. **Examine Spenserian Sonnet** Reread lines 13–14 of "Sonnet 30." Does this couplet suggest that the speaker has overcome the heartache expressed in the preceding quatrains? Support your answer.

6. **Summarize Central Ideas in Poetry** Look over the charts you created as you read. On the basis of the ideas you noted, what would you say is the **theme** or **themes** of each poem?

7. **Draw Conclusions** In these two sonnets, how would you characterize the speaker's views about the following?

   - a beloved woman ("Sonnet 75," lines 9–12)
   - romantic love ("Sonnet 30," lines 13–14; "Sonnet 75," lines 13–14)
   - the value of his poetry ("Sonnet 75," lines 11–14)

8. **Compare Texts** In "Sonnet 75," Spenser allows the speaker's lover to respond directly to the speaker. Compare her statements with those of the nymph in Raleigh's "The Nymph's Reply to the Shepherd" (page 316). In what ways are their responses similar?

Text Criticism

9. **Critical Interpretations** The poet John Hollander has written that some literary scholars have found **Spenserian sonnets** "somewhat syrupy beside Shakespeare." Do you think most contemporary readers would consider these sonnets by Spenser "syrupy"? Cite examples from the sonnets to support your answer.

COMMON CORE

RL 2 Determine two or more central ideas of a text and analyze their development over the course of the text, including how they interact and build on one another to produce a complex account; provide an objective summary of the text. **RL 5** Analyze how an author's choices concerning how to structure specific parts of a text contribute to its overall structure and meaning as well as its aesthetic impact. **L 5a** Interpret figures of speech (e.g., paradox) in context and analyze their role in the text.

> *What makes your* **HEART** *ache?*
>
> Heartache, or classic love sickness, is part of falling in love. Why does being "madly" in love have to involve the sadness of heartache?

Language

◆ **GRAMMAR IN CONTEXT:** Use Sensory Details

In "Sonnet 30," Spenser reinforces his images of fire and ice by using **adjectives** and **verbs** that appeal to the senses. Here is an example:

> *Or how comes it that my exceeding heat*
> *Is not delayed by her heart-frozen cold:*
> *But that I burn much more in boiling sweat,*
> *And feel my flames augmented manifold?* (lines 5–8)

Notice how the adjective *boiling* and the verb *burn* intensify the images. Such sensory details are especially effective when applied to subjects such as fire and ice, which have strong sensory associations. Spenser effectively uses these details to heighten the disparity between the two lovers' feelings.

PRACTICE Rewrite each of the following sentences, changing or adding adjectives and verbs to help create stronger sensory images.

EXAMPLE

As the director posted the final cast list on the board in the school theater, I waited in anticipation.

As the director posted the final cast list on the worn corkboard in the school theater, I stood as still as a stone, barely breathing in anticipation.

---

1. The room filled with applause each time the speaker made a good point.

2. When the movie ended, we walked to our favorite restaurant and discussed what we had just experienced.

3. I remained on the waiting-room couch while my grandfather met with his doctor.

READING-WRITING CONNECTION

 Expand your understanding of heartache by responding to this prompt. Then, use the **revising tips** to improve your letter.

WRITING PROMPT	REVISING TIPS
WRITE A LETTER We have all known someone who has suffered from **heartache.** Suppose that you are a friend of the speaker in "Sonnet 30." Would you console him or encourage him to move on? Using examples from the sonnet, write a **two-paragraph letter** with your advice to the speaker.	• Make sure some of the details you cite include sensory details. • Read your letter again. Did you answer all the questions in the prompt?

COMMON CORE

L 5 Demonstrate understanding of figurative language, word relationships, and nuances in word meanings. **W 1** Write arguments to support claims in an analysis of substantive topics or texts. **W 3d** Use precise words and phrases and sensory language to convey a vivid picture of the experiences, events, or characters.

Interactive Revision

Go to **thinkcentral.com.**
KEYWORD: HML12-323

Selected Poetry
by William Shakespeare

VIDEO TRAILER **THINK** central | KEYWORD: HML12-324A

COMMON CORE

RL 4 Analyze the impact of specific word choices on meaning, including words with multiple meanings or language that is fresh, engaging, or beautiful. **RL 5** Analyze how an author's choices concerning how to structure specific parts of a text contribute to its overall structure and meaning as well as its aesthetic impact.

Meet the Author

William Shakespeare 1564–1616

Shakespeare is the most influential writer in the English language. Four centuries after his death, he continues to occupy a central place in literary studies and in our culture at large. His plays are regularly performed around the world and have been made into numerous films.

Humble Beginnings Most of what is known about Shakespeare's life comes from court and church records. He was born in Stratford-upon-Avon, a small town in central England. His father was a successful businessman and town official, and his mother inherited farmland from her father. Shakespeare's family was initially prosperous but began having financial difficulties in the 1570s. Shakespeare probably attended Stratford's excellent grammar school, where he would have studied Latin and read classical authors.

No one knows what Shakespeare did immediately after he left school. In 1582, when he was 18 years old, he married Anne Hathaway, who was 26 years old. Six months later, they had a daughter. In 1585, they had twins, a boy and a girl. Shakespeare's son died at age 11.

Early Success as Actor and Playwright Sometime around 1590, Shakespeare moved to London and began working as an actor and playwright. He went on to become the most successful playwright of his time, earning enough to buy a large house in Stratford, where his wife and children lived. Although he retired to Stratford around 1612, he continued writing until his death at age 52.

Shakespeare the Poet In addition to his 37 plays, Shakespeare wrote an innovative collection of sonnets and two long narrative poems. In the 1590s, many English poets wrote sonnet sequences, which were usually addressed to an unattainable, idealized woman. Shakespeare expanded the conventions of the sonnet, making the form thematically more complex and less predictable. For example, the object of affection in some of his sonnets is not a divinely beautiful woman but a "dark lady" with all-too-human defects. He also wrote sonnets to an unidentified young man as well as to a rival poet. And while most sonnet writers focused primarily on love and beauty, Shakespeare addressed themes such as time, change, and death.

Because of his mastery of the sonnet's form and his broadening of its content, Shakespeare remains the undisputed master of the English sonnet. Today, the English sonnet is often referred to as the Shakespearean sonnet.

DID YOU KNOW?

William Shakespeare . . .

- never attended a university.
- was denounced early in his career by a jealous writer who called him an "upstart crow."

Church in Stratford-upon-Avon

Author Online

Go to **thinkcentral.com**. KEYWORD: HML12-324B

THINK central

● POETIC FORM: SHAKESPEAREAN SONNET

Shakespeare wrote very complex and sophisticated sonnets, moving beyond the traditional themes of love and beauty. The **Shakespearean sonnet** form, also known as the English sonnet, has the following characteristics:

- The sonnet contains three **quatrains** and a **couplet.**
- The **rhyme scheme** is *abab cdcd efef gg.*
- There is often a **turn,** or shift in thought, which occurs in the third quatrain or the couplet.

As you read these four sonnets, notice the way Shakespeare sets up his subjects in the early quatrains and employs the turn near the end.

● READING SKILL: ANALYZE IMAGERY

Among the many tools of poets, few are as important as **imagery**—words and phrases that re-create sensory experiences for the reader. Although Shakespeare often addresses philosophical themes in his sonnets, he breathes life into his ideas by evoking sights, sounds, smells, and textures. For example, in "Sonnet 116" Shakespeare uses the image "rosy lips and cheeks" to convey the idea of mortal flesh.

As you read the following sonnets, look for language that appeals to your senses. Use a chart like the one shown to identify ideas or emotions that are conveyed through this imagery.

Sonnet	Imagery	Idea or Emotion Conveyed
18	rough winds	Summer weather can be harsh.

 Complete the activities in your **Reader/Writer Notebook.**

Can LOVERS see clearly?

According to an old saying, "Love is blind," but to what extent is this true? The thrill of falling in love can cloud one's perceptions of a lover, but usually those clouds drift away over time. Is it possible to see a person's faults clearly and still love him or her?

PRESENT Working with a partner, list several fictional lovers from books, movies, or plays. For each couple, answer the question "Did they see each other clearly?" Discuss the reasons for your answers. What conclusions can you draw about the way love is portrayed in fiction? Present your conclusions to the class.

Sonnet
18

William Shakespeare

Shall I compare thee to a summer's day?
Thou art more lovely and more temperate:
Rough winds do shake the darling buds of May,
And summer's lease hath all too short a date:
5 Sometime too hot the eye of heaven shines,
And often is his gold complexion dimmed; **A**
And every fair from fair sometime declines,
By chance or nature's changing course untrimmed;
But thy eternal summer shall not fade,
10 Nor lose possession of that fair thou owest;
Nor shall Death brag thou wander'st in his shade,
When in eternal lines to time thou growest:
     So long as men can breathe, or eyes can see,
     So long lives this, and this gives life to thee.

A **ANALYZE IMAGERY**
What images does Shakespeare use in lines 1–6 to illustrate why summer is less temperate, or moderate, than the subject of the poem?

7–8 fair from ... untrimmed: beauty eventually fades, due to misfortune or natural aging.

10 thou owest: you own; you possess.

12 when ... growest: when in immortal poetry you become a part of time.

Analyze Visuals ▶
Compare this painting with the one on page 331. What can you discern about each subject?

Text Analysis

1. **Interpret** Reread lines 13–14 of "Sonnet 18." According to the speaker, what will allow the subject of the poem to become immortal?

2. **Make Inferences** Summer is the favorite time of year for many people. Why might Shakespeare have chosen to focus on the ways in which his subject is different from summer instead of describing how they are similar? Explain.

The Goddess Diana, Isaac Oliver. © Victoria & Albert Museum, London/Art Resource, New York.

Sonnet 29

William Shakespeare

When in disgrace with Fortune and men's eyes
I all alone beweep my outcast state,
And trouble deaf heaven with my bootless cries,
And look upon myself and curse my fate,
5 Wishing me like to one more rich in hope,
Featur'd like him, like him with friends possess'd,
Desiring this man's art, and that man's scope,
With what I most enjoy contented least;
Yet in these thoughts myself almost despising,
10 Haply I think on thee, and then my state,
Like to the lark at break of day arising
From sullen earth, sings hymns at heaven's gate,
    For thy sweet love rememb'red such wealth brings,
    That then I scorn to change my state with kings. **Ⓑ**

3 bootless: futile; useless.

6 featur'd like him: with his handsome features.

7 this man's art...scope: this man's skill and that man's intelligence.

10 haply: by chance.

11 lark: the English skylark, noted for its beautiful singing while soaring in flight.

Ⓑ SHAKESPEAREAN SONNET
Reread lines 13–14. In what way is this **couplet** related to the poem's second **quatrain?**

Text Analysis

1. **Summarize** What emotions does the speaker describe in the first two quatrains of "Sonnet 29"? What circumstances stir up these feelings?

2. **Analyze Tone** How does the speaker's tone change over the course of the poem?

Sonnet 116

William Shakespeare

Let me not to the marriage of true minds
Admit impediments; love is not love
Which alters when it alteration finds,
Or bends with the remover to remove.
5 O no, it is an ever-fixéd mark
That looks on tempests and is never shaken;
It is the star to every wand'ring bark,
Whose worth's unknown, although his height be taken.
Love's not Time's fool, though rosy lips and cheeks
10 Within his bending sickle's compass come,
Love alters not with his brief hours and weeks,
But bears it out even to the edge of doom.
    If this be error and upon me proved,
    I never writ, nor no man ever loved.

2 impediments: obstacles.

5 mark: a landmark seen from the sea and used by sailors as a guide in navigation.

7–8 the star . . . taken: the star—usually the North Star—whose altitude sailors measure in order to help guide their ships. A **bark** is a sailing ship.

10 within . . . come: come within range of Time's curving sickle.

12 bears . . . doom: endures even to Judgment Day, the time when, Christian teachings predict, the world will end and God will make his final judgment of all people.

Text Analysis

1. **Paraphrase** What does the speaker say about love in lines 9–12 of "Sonnet 116"?

2. **Analyze Metaphors** What metaphors does Shakespeare use in lines 5–8 to describe love? What do they suggest about the nature of love?

3. **Make Inferences** What view of love does the speaker react against in the poem?

Sonnet
130

William Shakespeare

My mistress' eyes are nothing like the sun;
Coral is far more red than her lips' red;
If snow be white, why then her breasts are dun;
If hairs be wires, black wires grow on her head.
5 I have seen roses damask'd, red and white,
But no such roses see I in her cheeks,
And in some perfumes is there more delight
Than in the breath that from my mistress reeks.
I love to hear her speak, yet well I know
10 That music hath a far more pleasing sound;
I grant I never saw a goddess go,
My mistress when she walks treads on the ground.
　　And yet, by heaven, I think my love as rare
　　As any she belied with false compare. **C**

3 dun: grayish brown.

5 damask'd: mottled; spotted or streaked with different colors.
8 reeks: is exhaled (used here without the word's present reference to offensive odors).

11 go: walk.

14 as any . . . compare: as any woman misrepresented by exaggerated comparisons.

COMMON CORE RL 4

C FIGURATIVE LANGUAGE
Shakespeare's sonnets are highly complex. While he does write about the traditional themes of love and beauty, he often uses new patterns of imagery, conceits, and allusions to reveal those themes. A **conceit** is an extended metaphor that compares two dissimilar things on several points. What are the elements of the conceit in this poem? What is being compared? How does the conceit reveal the theme of the poem?

Portrait of an Unknown Lady (1646), Cornelius Johnson. Oil on canvas, 794 cm × 641 cm.
Bequeathed by George Salting, 1910. © Tate Gallery, London/Art Resource, New York.

Comprehension

1. **Recall** What details does the speaker provide in "Sonnet 130" about his mistress's appearance?

2. **Clarify** What does the speaker suggest in lines 11–12 of "Sonnet 130"?

3. **Summarize** How does the speaker of "Sonnet 130" feel about his mistress?

Text Analysis

● 4. **Examine Shakespearean Sonnet** Where does the **turn** occur in "Sonnet 29"? What does this shift in thought reveal about the speaker?

5. **Analyze Simile** Reread lines 10–12 of "Sonnet 29." How does the comparison to the lark reflect the change that the speaker experiences?

● 6. **Analyze Imagery** Review the chart you created as you read. Which images does Shakespeare use in "Sonnet 130" to suggest the type of ideal woman glorified in traditional love sonnets?

7. **Interpret Themes** What ideas about the effects of time does Shakespeare convey in "Sonnet 18" and "Sonnet 116"?

8. **Make Judgments** Compare the views of beauty expressed in "Sonnet 18" and "Sonnet 130." Which sonnet do you consider more complimentary of the poem's subject? Explain why.

9. **Compare Texts** In what ways do the speakers of the following poems idealize love? Compare and contrast the themes, citing specific details.

   • Marlowe's "The Passionate Shepherd to His Love" (page 314)
   • Spenser's "Sonnet 30" (page 320)
   • Shakespeare's "Sonnet 116"

Text Criticism

10. **Historical Context** Shakespeare wrote his sonnets during the English Renaissance, a period of great social, religious, and political change. England was ruled at the time by a very powerful female monarch— Queen Elizabeth I—and though the changes were modest, women's role in society was evolving. In what ways does Shakespeare's "Sonnet 130" reflect this context?

Can LOVERS *see clearly?*

"Love is blind" can also mean that lovers cannot objectively see how they act when they are in love. Does Shakespeare suggest this is good, bad, or neither? What advice do you have for the poet in love?

COMMON CORE

RL 4 Analyze the impact of specific word choices on meaning, including words with multiple meanings or language that is particularly fresh, engaging, or beautiful. **RL 5** Analyze how an author's choices concerning how to structure specific parts of a text contribute to its overall structure and meaning as well as its aesthetic impact. **RL 9** Demonstrate knowledge of how two or more texts from the same period treat similar themes or topics.

Language

◆ **GRAMMAR IN CONTEXT: Create Rhythm**

While iambic pentameter serves as the main source of rhythm in Shakespeare's poetry, **parallelism**—the repetition of a particular grammatical structure—also adds a rhythmic quality to his writing. Here are two examples:

> *I all alone beweep my outcast state,*
> *And trouble deaf heaven with my bootless cries,*
> *And look upon myself and curse my fate,* ("Sonnet 29," lines 2–4)

> *If snow be white, why then her breasts are dun;*
> *If hairs be wires, black wires grow on her head.* ("Sonnet 130," lines 3–4)

In the example from "Sonnet 29," Shakespeare repeatedly uses the coordinating conjunction *and* followed by a predicate. In the example from "Sonnet 130," a subordinate clause introduced by *if* begins each line.

PRACTICE Rewrite the following pairs of sentences so that they are parallel.

EXAMPLE

He stands alone upon the riverbank.
Along the farther shore, she is walking unaware.

He stands alone upon the riverbank
She walks unaware along the farther shore.

---

1. No silly fool in love he'd ever be.
  She'd never see a crying idiot.

2. So gently she would brush his tangled hair.
  She would wipe away the tears so softly.

3. With just a word he took away her fear.
  He showed how much he cared with just a look.

READING-WRITING CONNECTION

YOUR TURN

Expand your understanding of the sonnet form by responding to this prompt. Then use the **revising tips** to improve your sonnet.

WRITING PROMPT	REVISING TIPS
WRITE A SONNET The best way to gain appreciation for the sonnet form is to write one. Choose someone you **love**—a friend, a family member, or even a pet—and write a **Shakespearean sonnet** expressing your feelings and thoughts for the loved one.	• Identify a problem in the quatrains that is solved in the couplet. • Add an instance of parallelism to your sonnet.

COMMON CORE

L 3a Apply an understanding of syntax to the study of complex texts when reading. **W 3d** Use precise words and phrases to convey a vivid picture of experiences, events, or characters.

Interactive Revision **THINK** central

Go to **thinkcentral.com**.
KEYWORD: HML12-333

Sonnet 90
Sonnet 292

Poetry by Francesco Petrarch

COMMON CORE

RL 4 Determine the meaning of words and phrases as they are used in the text, including figurative meanings. **RL 5** Analyze how an author's choices concerning how to structure specific parts of a text contribute to its overall structure and meaning as well as its aesthetic impact.

Meet the Author

Francesco Petrarch 1304–1374

Francesco Petrarch composed over 300 poems to a woman with whom he never had a relationship. But his innovation on the Italian sonnet form—usually referred to as the Petrarchan sonnet—immortalized both the poet and this mysterious woman.

Although Italian writers had written sonnets before Petrarch, he improved the 14-line poem's structure and wrote in the vernacular of the day, more closely reflecting the way people actually spoke. Petrarch's success established the sonnet as a major poetic form. Petrarch influenced poets throughout Europe, including Elizabethan poets like Spenser and Shakespeare.

DID YOU KNOW?

Francesco Petrarch . . .

- studied law at a university when he was only 12 years old.

- would spend his allowance on classical poetry, which so angered Petrarch's father that he burned most of the books.

(background)
Avignon, France

From Law Student to Clergyman Petrarch was born in Arezzo, Italy, where his father practiced law. Petrarch's father insisted that his sons study law, so the poet and his younger brother complied until their father died in 1326. By then, Petrarch had developed an interest in classical studies and, as he described it, "an unquenchable thirst for literature." After his father's death, Petrarch abandoned the study of law and became a Catholic clergyman. Living in Avignon, France, then the seat of the exiled papal court, Petrarch held a variety of church positions that provided him with a modest income as well as free time to devote to literature, classical studies, and extensive traveling.

The Love of His Life On Good Friday in 1327, when he was 22 years old, Petrarch saw a woman in the Church of Saint Clare in Avignon and immediately fell in love with her. For the rest of his life, he wrote and revised sonnets about his unrequited love for a woman he identified only as Laura. Like Petrarch's son and many of his friends, Laura died in the plague that devastated much of Europe in the mid-14th century. Petrarch recorded the date of her death—April 6, 1348—in a copy of a work by Virgil, a classical Roman poet whom he revered. After Laura's death, Petrarch continued to write sonnets reminiscing about her, including "Sonnet 292." The *Canzoniere,* his masterpiece, is a collection of 366 poems, most of them sonnets that focus on Laura and the themes of unrequited love, desperate love, eternal love, and tragic love.

Poet Laureate of Rome By the time Petrarch was in his mid-30s, his poetry was widely admired in Italy and France. He received invitations from both the University of Paris and the Senate in Rome to be poet laureate. In 1341, he became Rome's first poet laureate since ancient times.

Author Online

Go to thinkcentral.com. KEYWORD: HML12-334

THINK central

● POETIC FORM: PETRARCHAN SONNET

In reading sonnets by Spenser and Shakespeare, you've learned about two variations on the sonnet form. Two centuries earlier, Petrarch perfected his own form of the sonnet. The 14 lines of the **Petrarchan sonnet** are divided into two distinct parts.

- The **octave** (first 8 lines) introduces a situation, presents a problem, or raises a question. Its rhyme scheme is usually *abbaabba*.

- The **sestet** (the last 6 lines) is where the speaker comments on or resolves the problem or question. Its rhyme scheme is usually *cdcdcd* or *cdecde*.

Most of Petrarch's sonnets are about love, specifically unrequited love or love from afar. As you read the following sonnets, notice the relationship between the structure and the content of the poems.

● READING SKILL: ANALYZE METAPHOR

One element that makes Petrarch's sonnets so emotionally powerful is his use of metaphor. A **metaphor** is a figure of speech that makes a comparison between two unlike things. Unlike a simile, a metaphor does not use the word *like* or *as*. For example, the metaphor "in fragile bark on the tempestuous sea" compares the speaker's emotional state to a ship in stormy waters. Writers often use metaphors to help express emotions or convey abstract ideas.

As you read each of Petrarch's sonnets, use a chart like the one shown to record and analyze examples of metaphor.

"Sonnet 90"	
Metaphor	Comparison
"I had love's tinder in my breast unburned"	compares love that hasn't been aroused yet to unburned firewood

 Complete the activities in your **Reader/Writer Notebook**.

When does love become OBSESSION?

An obsession is an excessive preoccupation with a single idea or emotion. The theme of obsessive love appears in many movies, novels, and plays, as well as in real-life stories in newspapers and magazines. When exactly does love cross the line and become an obsession?

SURVEY Conduct a survey, asking several people you know to complete the statement "Love becomes an obsession when...." Put a star by the answers you agree with. Then share and discuss the results of your survey.

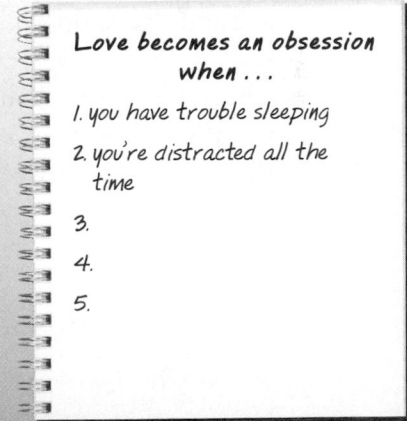

Love becomes an obsession when . . .
1. you have trouble sleeping
2. you're distracted all the time
3.
4.
5.

SONNET 90

Francesco Petrarch

Upon the breeze she spread her golden hair
that in a thousand gentle knots was turned,
and the sweet light beyond all measure burned
in eyes where now that radiance is rare;

5 and in her face there seemed to come an air
of pity, true or false, that I discerned:
I had love's tinder in my breast unburned,
was it a wonder if it kindled there? **A**

She moved not like a mortal, but as though
10 she bore an angel's form, her words had then
a sound that simple human voices lack;

a heavenly spirit, a living sun
was what I saw; now, if it is not so,
the wound's not healed because the bow grows slack.

Translated by Anthony Mortimer

Analyze Visuals ▶
In what ways does the drawing on page 337 resemble Petrarch's Laura?

A **PETRARCHAN SONNET**
Reread lines 1–8. What situation does Petrarch describe in this **octave**?

14 the wound's . . . slack: I still ache with love for her, even though her beauty has faded. Petrarch alludes to Cupid, Roman god of love, often portrayed as an archer whose arrows pierce the heart and cause someone to fall in love.

Head of a Woman (1472),
Leonardo da Vinci. Inv.: 428E.
Gabinetto dei Disegni e delle
Stampe, Uffizi, Florence.
© Scala/Art Resource, New York.

SONNET 292

Francesco Petrarch

The eyes I spoke of once in words that burn,
the arms and hands and feet and lovely face
that took me from myself for such a space
of time, and marked me out from other men;

5 the waving hair of unmixed gold that shone,
the smile that flashed with the angelic rays **B**
that used to make this earth a paradise,
are now a little dust, all feeling gone.

And yet I live, hence grief and rage for me,
10 left where the light I cherished never shows,
in fragile bark on the tempestuous sea.

Here let my loving song come to a close,
the vein of my accustomed art is dry,
and this, my lyre, turned at last to tears.

Translated by Anthony Mortimer

B ANALYZE METAPHOR
What idea or emotion does
Petrarch convey through the
use of metaphors in lines 5–6?

11 bark: sailing ship; **tempestuous:**
stormy.

14 lyre (līr): a stringed instrument
that poets traditionally plucked to
accompany the oral performance
of their poetry.

Comprehension

1. **Clarify** In "Sonnet 90," how has the speaker's beloved changed since he first fell in love with her?

2. **Clarify** What has happened to the speaker's beloved in "Sonnet 292"?

3. **Paraphrase** In your own words, what is the poet saying in lines 12–14 of "Sonnet 292"?

Text Analysis

● 4. **Examine Petrarchan Sonnet** In the **octave** of "Sonnet 90," the speaker describes the experience of falling in love. How does Petrarch use the **sestet** to develop a more complicated view of love? Cite details in your answer.

● 5. **Interpret Lines** Reread lines 10–11 of "Sonnet 292." What feeling does Petrarch express through the **metaphor** of being left "in fragile bark on the tempestuous sea"?

6. **Draw Conclusions** What ideas does Petrarch convey in these sonnets about the nature of beauty, poetic inspiration, and love at first sight?

● 7. **Analyze Metaphors** Review the chart you created as you read. What characteristics of love and the speaker's beloved are emphasized through the metaphors in these two sonnets?

8. **Make Judgments** Is each speaker truly in love with the woman he describes, or is he really just experiencing obsession? Support your opinion with examples from the sonnets.

9. **Compare Texts** Reread Shakespeare's "Sonnet 130" on page 330. Some of his imagery is intended as a parody of Petrarch's sonnets. Using a chart like the one shown, pick out examples of Petrarchan imagery from "Sonnet 90" and "Sonnet 292" that Shakespeare pokes fun at in "Sonnet 130."

Petrach's Image	Shakespeare's Parody
"the sweet light beyond all measure burned / in [her] eyes"	"My mistress' eyes are nothing like the sun"

Text Criticism

10. **Historical Context** A Petrarchan scholar said that Petrarch's expressions of love were nothing more than "a great fiction to compensate for a real state of affairs in which it was a man's world and a violent one at that." If Petrarch were writing today, how might he alter his portrayal of women?

> *When does love become* **OBSESSION?**
>
> Love is not always returned when given. Why do some people obsess over a person who does not love them?

COMMON CORE

RL 4 Determine the meaning of words and phrases as they are used in the text, including figurative meanings. **RL 5** Analyze how an author's choices concerning how to structure specific parts of a text contribute to its overall structure and meaning as well as its aesthetic impact.

Universal Themes in Love Poetry

> *"Come live with me and be my love,*
> *And we will all the pleasures prove*
> *That valleys, groves, hills, and fields,*
> *Woods, or steepy mountain yields."*
>
> —**Christopher Marlowe,**
> *from* **"The Passionate Shepherd to His Love"**

The speaker in "The Passionate Shepherd" does his best to convince his lover to return his affections. But love can be complicated, as becomes apparent when reading the rest of the poems in this section (pages 314–337). Each of these poems makes a point or comment about love that could be considered universal, yet none of the poems look at love from the same angle. What is the main message about love that each speaker conveys? Which speaker develops his ideas most fully?

Writing to Compare

Write a three-to-five paragraph essay comparing two or more of the poems you have read in this section, focusing on the theme of each poem and the literary devices used to develop the theme.

Consider

- how you would summarize the theme of each poem (Keep in mind that the final couplet in a sonnet often comments on the situation or question raised in the first 12 lines.)

- the use of literary devices such as symbolism, imagery, metaphor, and simile

- domain-specific words like quatrain, sestet, couplet, and octave

Extension

SPEAKING & LISTENING

Choose a poem from this section and rewrite it using modern language and modern imagery, but be sure to retain the poem's original theme. Deliver your poem to your class by reading it aloud in an expressive voice. Then, listen attentively while your classmates deliver their poems. Jot down key words and phrases, questions you have, and points you want to share with the speaker, such as things you liked about the poem. After listening to all of your classmates' poems, discuss which ones work best in their modern form and why.

COMMON CORE

W 2 Write informative texts to examine and convey complex ideas through the effective selection, organization, and analysis of content. **W 2b** Develop the topic by selecting information and examples appropriate to the audience's knowledge of the topic. **W 2d** Use domain-specific vocabulary to manage the complexity of the topic. **SL 6** Adapt speech to a variety of contexts and tasks.

Macbeth and Shakespeare's Theater

Scene from *Macbeth*, performed by the Pennsylvania Shakespeare Festival, 2004

The Scottish Play Say the name Macbeth backstage within earshot of actors taking part in a production of the play and you will probably be told to leave the theater, spin around three times, spit on the ground, and then ask for permission to return. Superstition holds that the play is cursed; even pronouncing its name backstage is supposed to bring bad luck. For that reason, cast and crew often refer to it as "the Scottish play" or "that play." Accidents and injuries (particularly sword wounds) have plagued productions of *Macbeth* throughout the play's 400-year history. The misfortunes seem to have begun with the very first performance in 1606, when the actor (a boy—more about that later) playing Lady Macbeth died backstage. Shakespeare himself had to step into the role.

The Globe Theater The first performance of *Macbeth* was held before King James at Hampton Court Palace. However, in Shakespeare's time most plays were performed in outdoor public theaters. These theaters resembled courtyards, with the stage surrounded on three sides by tall raised galleries. The best-known of these theaters in London was the Globe, where Shakespeare and his acting company performed.

The Globe was a three-story wooden structure that could hold as many as 3,000 people. Plays were performed on a platform stage in the theater's center. The poorer patrons, or "groundlings," stood around the stage to watch the performance. Wealthier patrons sat in the covered galleries.

Because the Globe was an open-air theater, performers had to depend on natural lighting for illumination. But Shakespeare found creative ways to work with the natural light. When *Macbeth* was performed at the Globe, audiences were probably struck by the sight in Act Five, Scene 1, of Lady Macbeth pacing around the stage with a candle. By that point in the play, the eerie scene would probably have been effective because the natural light may well have dimmed.

The Players Actors worked in close proximity to the groundlings, who stood around the stage, eating and drinking. If they disapproved of certain characters or lines, they would let the actors know by jeering or even throwing food. The large crowds also attracted pickpockets and other rough elements. The rowdiness of the audiences and the location of theaters near taverns and other unsavory establishments gave theaters, and actors, an immoral reputation. Because the theater was viewed as so disreputable, women were not allowed to perform. As with the ill-fated actor who was supposed to play Lady Macbeth in 1606, boys normally played all of the female roles.

The Fate of the Globe In 1613, the Globe's thatched roof caught fire during a performance of *Henry VIII,* and the theater was destroyed. It was quickly rebuilt at the same location, however, this time with a tiled gallery roof. Only 30 years later, Oliver Cromwell and the Puritans shut down the theater, suppressing what they considered a frivolous form of entertainment. But the Globe would rise again. In the 1990s, Shakespeare's theater was rebuilt to the same size and design of the old Globe. Since its official opening in 1997, the new Globe has become one of London's most popular tourist attractions.

THEATER STAGING

This drawing of the Swan theater, *left,* is one of the few historical sources of information about the design of Elizabethan public theaters. Because of their open-air design, performances could only take place in daylight and in warm weather. The drawing was used to reconstruct Shakespeare's Globe theater, *right,* in which a Zulu version of *Macbeth* was performed in 1997.

1 Though scenery was minimal, audiences still demanded a good show. A trapdoor in the stage led to a space below, from which ghosts— or the witches in *Macbeth*—could emerge.

2 The enclosed tower behind the stage offered a place to create sound effects, such as the thunder, drums, and bells heard in *Macbeth.*

3 Above the back of the stage and its small balcony was a painted ceiling called "the heavens." It contained trapdoors for the appearance of angels and spirits from the enclosed tower.

4 Props, such as swords and flags, and elaborate costumes added to the display.

Shakespearean Tragedy

Revenge, intrigue, murder, and insanity—these are just a few of the topics explored in William Shakespeare's tragedies. Basing his works on the Greek and Roman traditions of drama, Shakespeare created some of the most enduring tragedies, which continue to enthrall audiences to this day.

COMMON CORE

Included in this workshop:
RL 3 Analyze the impact of the author's choices regarding how to develop and relate elements of a drama. **RL 5** Analyze how an author's choices concerning how to structure specific parts of a text contribute to its overall structure and meaning. **L 3a** Apply an understanding of syntax to the study of complex texts when reading.

Renaissance Drama

During the Middle Ages, English drama focused mainly on religious themes, teaching moral lessons or retelling Bible stories to a populace that by and large could not read. With the Renaissance, however, came a rebirth of interest in the dramas of ancient Greece and Rome. First at England's universities and then among graduates of those universities, plays imitating classical models became increasingly popular. These plays fell into two main categories: comedies and tragedies.

Shakespeare's *King Lear*

In Renaissance England, **comedy** was broadly defined as a dramatic work with a happy ending; many comedies contained humor, but humor was not required. A **tragedy,** in contrast, was a work in which the main character, or **tragic hero,** came to an unhappy end. In addition to comedies and tragedies, Shakespeare wrote several plays classified as **histories,** which present stories about England's earlier monarchs. Of all Shakespeare's plays, however, his tragedies are the ones most often cited as his greatest.

The Greek Origins of Tragedy

In Western civilization, both comedies and tragedies arose in ancient Greece, where they were performed as part of elaborate outdoor festivals. According to the famous ancient Greek philosopher Aristotle, tragedy arouses pity and fear in the audience—pity for the hero and fear for all human beings, who are subject to character flaws and an unknown destiny. Seeing a tragedy unfold produces a **catharsis,** or cleansing, of these emotions in the audience.

In ancient Greek tragedies, the hero's tragic flaw is often **hubris**—excessive pride that leads the tragic hero to challenge the gods. Angered by such hubris, the gods unleash their retribution, or nemesis, on the hero. Ancient Greek tragedies also make use of a **chorus,** a group of performers who stand outside the action and comment on the events and characters in the play, often hinting at the doom to come and stressing the fatalistic aspect of the hero's downfall. By Shakespeare's day, the chorus consisted of only one person—a kind of narrator—or was dispensed with entirely.

Characteristics of Tragedy

The intention of tragedy is to exemplify the idea that human beings are doomed to suffer, fail, or die because of their own flaws, destiny, or fate. As part of this tradition, Shakespeare's tragedies share the following characteristics with the classic Greek tragedies.

CHARACTERISTICS OF TRAGEDY

THE TRAGIC HERO
- is the main character who comes to an unhappy or miserable end
- is generally a person of importance in society, such as a king or a queen
- ▶ exhibits extraordinary abilities but also a **tragic flaw**, a fatal error in judgment or weakness of character, that leads directly to his or her downfall

THE PLOT
- involves a **conflict** between the hero and a person or force, called the **antagonist**, which the hero must battle. Inevitably the conflict contributes to the hero's downfall.
- ▶ is built upon a series of causally related events that lead to the **catastrophe**, or tragic resolution. This final stage of the plot usually involves the death of the hero.
- is resolved when the tragic hero meets his or her doom with courage and dignity, reaffirming the grandeur of the human spirit.

THE THEME
- ▶ is the central idea conveyed by the work and usually focuses on an aspect of fate, ambition, loss, defeat, death, loyalty, impulse, or desire. Tragedies, such as Shakespeare's *Macbeth* (page 348), may contain several themes.

Shakespearean tragedy differs somewhat from classic Greek tragedy in that Shakespeare's works are not unrelentingly serious. For example, he often eased the intensity of the action by using the device of **comic relief**—a light, mildly humorous scene following a serious one.

In the following example from *Macbeth*, Act I, Scene 3, lines 143–147, Macbeth is expressing his thoughts, unheard by Banquo, about the witches' prophecy that he will be king of Scotland.

> **Macbeth.** [*Aside*] If chance will have me king, why, chance may crown me
> Without my stir.
> **Banquo.**　　　　　New honors come upon him,
> Like our strange garments, cleave not to their mold
> But with the aid of use.
> **Macbeth.** [*Aside*]　　　Come what come may,
> Time and the hour runs through the roughest day.

Close Read

In this short dialogue, what characteristics of a tragedy do you recognize?

Shakespeare's Conventions of Drama

The printed text of Shakespeare's plays, such as *Macbeth,* is like that of any drama. The play is divided into **acts,** which are divided into **scenes,** often marking a change in setting. The **dialogue** spoken by the characters is labeled to show who is speaking, and **stage directions,** written in italics and in parentheses, specify the setting (time and place) and how the characters should behave and speak. In addition, Shakespeare typically used the following literary devices in his dramas.

BLANK VERSE

Like many plays written before the 20th century, *Macbeth* is a **verse drama,** a play in which the dialogue consists almost entirely of poetry with a fixed pattern of rhythm, or meter. Many English verse dramas are written in **blank verse,** or unrhymed iambic pentameter, a meter in which the normal line contains five stressed syllables, each preceded by an unstressed syllable.

> So foul and fair a day I have not seen.

SOLILOQUY AND ASIDE

Playwrights rely on certain conventions to give the audience more information about the characters. Two such conventions are the soliloquy and the aside.

- A **soliloquy** is a speech that a character makes while alone on stage, to reveal his or her thoughts to the audience.

- An **aside** is a remark that a character makes in an undertone to the audience or another character but that others on stage are not supposed to hear. A stage direction clarifies that a remark is an aside; unless otherwise specified, the aside is to the audience. Here is an example from *Macbeth.*

> **Macbeth.** [*Aside*]   Glamis, and Thane of Cawdor!
> The greatest is behind.—[*To* Ross *and* Angus]   Thanks for your pains.
> [*Aside to* Banquo] Do you not hope your children shall be kings . . . ?

DRAMATIC IRONY

Irony is based on a contrast between appearance or expectation and reality. In **dramatic irony,** what appears true to one or more characters in a play is seen to be false by the audience, which has a more complete picture of the action. In Act One of *Macbeth,* dramatic irony can be found in Duncan's words to Lady Macbeth upon his arrival at the Macbeths' castle.

> Conduct me to mine host. We love him highly
> And shall continue our graces toward him.

Duncan is sure of Macbeth's loyalty and says that he will continue to honor Macbeth with marks of his favor. However, the audience knows that Macbeth is planning to murder Duncan to increase his own power. The audience recognizes the irony of Duncan's trusting remarks.

FORESHADOWING

Foreshadowing is a writer's use of hints or clues to suggest what events will occur later in a work. In Act One, Scene 1, the witches' dialogue opens the play with clues as to what is to come.

> **First Witch.** When shall we three meet again?
> In thunder, lightning, or in rain?
> **Second Witch.** When the hurly-burly's done,
> When the battle's lost and won.
> **Third Witch.** That will be ere the set of sun.
> **First Witch.** Where the place?
> **Second Witch.**   Upon the heath.
> **Third Witch.** There to meet with Macbeth.

Shakespearean Language

The English language in which Shakespeare wrote was quite different from today's. As you read a Shakespearean play, pay attention to the following.

SHAKESPEAREAN LANGUAGE

GRAMMATICAL FORMS	In Shakespeare's day, people still commonly used the pronouns *thou, thee, thy, thine,* and *thyself* in place of forms of *you.* Verb forms that are now outdated were also in use—*art* for *are* and *cometh* for *comes,* for example.
UNUSUAL WORD ORDER	Shakespeare often puts verbs before subjects, objects before verbs, and other sentence parts in positions that now seem unusual. For instance, Lady Macbeth says, "O, never shall sun that morrow see!" instead of "O, that morrow shall never see the sun!"
UNFAMILIAR VOCABULARY	Shakespeare's vocabulary included many words no longer in use (like *seeling,* meaning "blinding") or words with meanings different from their meanings today (like *choppy* meaning "chapped"). Shakespeare also coined new words, some of which (like *assassination*) have become a permanent part of the language.

STRATEGIES FOR READING DRAMA

1. Look over the opening cast of characters to familiarize yourself with the characters, their titles, and their relationships.
2. Study the plot summary and stage directions at the beginning of each scene. Try to develop a mental picture of the setting.
3. Pay attention to labels indicating who is speaking and to stage directions.
4. To get a better sense of what the dialogue might sound like, try reading some of it aloud.

Close Read

What do these lines of the witches' dialogue suggest about the conflict that will occur in the play? What might be the result, or **resolution,** of the conflict?

The Tragedy of Macbeth
Drama by William Shakespeare

VIDEO TRAILER THINKcentral KEYWORD: HML12-346A

DID YOU KNOW?

William Shakespeare . . .

- is often referred to as "the Bard"—an ancient Celtic term for a poet who composed songs about heroes.

- introduced more than 1,700 new words into the English language.

- has had his work translated into 118 languages, including sign language.

(background) Nash's House, a Shakespeare museum in Stratford-upon-Avon

Meet the Author

William Shakespeare 1564–1616

In 1592—the first time William Shakespeare was recognized as an actor, poet, and playwright—rival dramatist Robert Greene referred to him as an "upstart crow." Greene was probably jealous. Audiences had already begun to notice the young Shakespeare's promise. Of course, they couldn't have foreseen that in time he would be considered the greatest writer in the English language.

Stage-Struck Shakespeare probably arrived in London and began his career in the late 1580s. He left his wife, Anne Hathaway, and their three children behind in Stratford. Over the next 20 years, Shakespeare rarely returned home. (See the biography on page 324 for more about Shakespeare's early life in Stratford.)

Unlike most playwrights of his time, Shakespeare also worked as an actor. He even appeared in his own plays; among other roles, he played King Duncan in a stage production of *Macbeth*.

Public and critical acclaim for his work grew. His audiences craved variety, and Shakespeare responded by mastering all forms of drama. In the 1590s, he concentrated on comedies, such as *A Midsummer's Night Dream*, and histories, such as *Henry IV, Parts I* and *II*.

Toast of the Town In 1594, Shakespeare joined the Lord Chamberlain's Men, the most prestigious theater company in England. A measure of their success was that the theater company frequently performed before Queen Elizabeth I and her court. In 1599, they were also able to purchase and rebuild a theater across the Thames called the Globe.

The company's domination of the London theater scene continued after Elizabeth's Scottish cousin James succeeded her in 1603. James became the patron, or chief sponsor, of Shakespeare's company, thereafter known as the King's Men.

The Curtain Falls Between 1600 and 1607, Shakespeare wrote his greatest tragedies, including *Hamlet, Macbeth,* and *King Lear.* As he neared the end of his writing career and his life, even his comedies took on a darker tone. He wrote no more plays after 1613.

According to legend, Shakespeare died on April 23, 1616, the day of his 52nd birthday. In 1623, two theater colleagues published his plays in a volume called the First Folio. In an introduction to the volume, playwright Ben Jonson declared with great insight that Shakespeare "was not of an age, but for all time."

Author Online

Go to **thinkcentral.com**. KEYWORD: HML12-346B

TEXT ANALYSIS: SHAKESPEAREAN TRAGEDY

As you've learned, a Shakespearean **tragedy** presents a superior figure—the **tragic hero**—who comes to ruin because of an error in judgment or a weakness in character—a **tragic flaw.** One or more **antagonists,** or opposing characters, also work against the tragic hero, and the action builds to a **catastrophe,** a disastrous end involving deaths. As you read *Macbeth,* be aware of these dramatic conventions:

- The play is written in **blank verse,** or unrhymed **iambic pentameter,** in which the normal line has five stressed syllables, each preceded by an unstressed syllable.

- Characters often reveal their private thoughts through **soliloquies** and **asides,** which other characters cannot hear.

- Enjoyment of the play's action is sometimes enhanced through the use of **foreshadowing**—hints about what may happen later—and **dramatic irony**—the contrast created when the audience knows more about a situation than a character knows.

READING STRATEGY: READING SHAKESPEAREAN DRAMA

For centuries, Shakespeare has been celebrated for his powerful poetic language—what Shakespearean characters say defines them as much as what they do. However, the Bard's language can present a challenge for modern readers. Keep a chart like the one below to record the words and actions of Macbeth and Lady Macbeth to uncover their true personalities and motives. To help you understand Shakespearean language:

- Use stage directions, plot summaries, and sidenotes to establish the context, or circumstances, surrounding what characters say.

- Read important speeches aloud, such as soliloquies, focusing on clues they provide to each character's feelings and motivations.

- Shakespeare's unusual word order often puts verbs before subjects and objects before verbs. Find the subject, verb, and object in each line and rearrange them to clarify what the line means.

Character: Macbeth	
His Words or Actions	*What They Reveal About Him*
He defeats the enemy on the battlefield.	He's a brave and inspiring soldier and general.

 Complete the activities in your **Reader/Writer Notebook.**

Can you ever be too AMBITIOUS?

Ambition is a powerful motivating force. Often it is considered desirable, since it inspires people to realize their dreams. In fact, people without ambition are usually regarded as lazy. But is it possible to be overly ambitious? When might high aspirations lead to terrible consequences? Such questions are explored in the story of Macbeth, a general whose ambition is to become king.

QUICKWRITE With a partner, brainstorm a list of people—historical and contemporary— whose ambitions had tragic consequences. Beside their names, jot down what they hoped to achieve and the negative results of their ambitions.

THE TRAGEDY OF
MACBETH

William Shakespeare

BACKGROUND It is believed that Shakespeare wrote *Macbeth* largely to please King James. The Scottish king claimed to be descended from a historical figure named Banquo. In *Macbeth*, the witches predict that Banquo will be the first in a long line of kings. James's interest in witchcraft—he penned a book on the subject in 1597—may also account for the prominence of the witches themselves in the play. The play also spoke to James's fears of assassination; he had survived several attempts on his life.

Go Behind the Curtain

As you read the play, you will find photographs from the 2005 production of *Macbeth* by the Derby Playhouse in Derby, England. Photographs from other productions appear in the **Behind the Curtain** feature pages, which explore the stagecraft used to create exciting theatrical productions of this famous play.

CHARACTERS

Duncan, king of Scotland

HIS SONS
  Malcolm
  Donalbain

NOBLEMEN OF SCOTLAND
  Macbeth
  Banquo
  Macduff
  Lennox
  Ross
  Menteith (měn-tēth′)
  Angus
  Caithness (kāth′nĭs)

Fleance (flā′əns), son to Banquo
Siward (syōō′ərd), earl of Northumberland, general of the English forces
Young Siward, his son
Seyton (sā′tən), an officer attending on Macbeth
Son, to Macduff

An English Doctor
A Scottish Doctor
A Porter
An Old Man
Three Murderers
Lady Macbeth
Lady Macduff
A Gentlewoman attending on Lady Macbeth
Hecate (hěk′ĭt), goddess of witchcraft
Three Witches
Apparitions
Lords, Officers, Soldiers, Messengers, and Attendants

THE TIME
The 11th century

THE PLACE
Scotland and England

ACT 1

Scene 1 *An open place in Scotland.*
The play opens in a wild and lonely place in medieval Scotland. Three witches enter and speak of what they know will happen this day: the civil war will end, and they will meet Macbeth, one of the generals. Their meeting ends when their demon companions, in the form of a toad and a cat, call them away.

[*Thunder and lightning. Enter three* Witches.]

First Witch. When shall we three meet again?
In thunder, lightning, or in rain?

Second Witch. When the hurly-burly's done,
When the battle's lost and won.

5 **Third Witch.** That will be ere the set of sun.

First Witch. Where the place?

Second Witch.   Upon the heath.

Third Witch. There to meet with Macbeth.

First Witch. I come, Graymalkin.

Second Witch. Paddock calls.

Third Witch.   Anon.

10 **All.** Fair is foul, and foul is fair,
Hover through the fog and filthy air.

[*They exit.*]

3 hurly-burly: turmoil; uproar.

8–9 Graymalkin . . . Paddock: two demon helpers in the form of a cat and a toad; **Anon:** at once.

10 The witches delight in the confusion of good and bad, beauty and ugliness.

Scene 2 *King Duncan's camp near the battlefield.*
Duncan, the king of Scotland, waits in his camp for news of the battle. He learns that one of his generals, Macbeth, has been victorious in several battles. Not only has Macbeth defeated the rebellious Macdonwald, but he has also conquered the armies of the king of Norway and the Scottish traitor, the thane of Cawdor. Duncan orders the thane of Cawdor's execution and announces that Macbeth will receive the traitor's title.

[*Alarum within. Enter* King Duncan, Malcolm, Donalbain, Lennox, *with* Attendants, *meeting a bleeding* Captain.]

Duncan. What bloody man is that? He can report,
As seemeth by his plight, of the revolt
The newest state.

Malcolm.   This is the sergeant
Who, like a good and hardy soldier, fought
5 'Gainst my captivity.—Hail, brave friend!
Say to the King the knowledge of the broil
As thou didst leave it.

[Stage Direction] **Alarum within:** the sound of a trumpet offstage, a signal that soldiers should arm themselves.

5 'gainst my captivity: to save me from capture.
6 broil: battle.

The three witches, from the 2005 Derby
Playhouse production of *Macbeth*

Captain.   Doubtful it stood,
As two spent swimmers that do cling together
And choke their art. The merciless Macdonwald
10 (Worthy to be a rebel, for to that
The multiplying villainies of nature
Do swarm upon him) from the Western Isles
Of kerns and gallowglasses is supplied;
And Fortune, on his damnèd quarrel smiling,
15 Showed like a rebel's whore. But all's too weak;
For brave Macbeth (well he deserves that name),
Disdaining Fortune, with his brandished steel,
Which smoked with bloody execution,
Like valor's minion, carved out his passage
20 Till he faced the slave;
Which ne'er shook hands, nor bade farewell to him,
Till he unseamed him from the nave to th' chops,
And fixed his head upon our battlements.

Duncan. O valiant cousin, worthy gentleman!

25 **Captain.** As whence the sun 'gins his reflection
Shipwracking storms and direful thunders break,
So from that spring whence comfort seemed to come
Discomfort swells. Mark, King of Scotland, mark:
No sooner justice had, with valor armed,
30 Compelled these skipping kerns to trust their heels,
But the Norweyan lord, surveying vantage,
With furbished arms and new supplies of men,
Began a fresh assault.

Duncan. Dismayed not this our captains, Macbeth and Banquo?

35 **Captain.** Yes, as sparrows eagles, or the hare the lion.
If I say sooth, I must report they were
As cannons overcharged with double cracks,
So they doubly redoubled strokes upon the foe.
Except they meant to bathe in reeking wounds
40 Or memorize another Golgotha,
I cannot tell—
But I am faint. My gashes cry for help.

Duncan. So well thy words become thee as thy wounds:
They smack of honor both.—Go, get him surgeons.

[*The* Captain *is led off by* Attendants.]

[*Enter* Ross *and* Angus.]

45 Who comes here?

Malcolm.   The worthy Thane of Ross.

7–9 The two armies are compared to two exhausted swimmers who cling to each other and thus cannot swim.

9–13 The officer hates Macdonwald, whose evils (**multiplying villainies**) swarm like insects around him. His army consists of soldiers (**kerns and gallowglasses**) from the Hebrides (**Western Isles**).

19 valor's minion: the favorite of valor, meaning the bravest of all.

22 unseamed him ... chops: split him open from the navel to the jaw. *What does this act suggest about Macbeth?*

25–28 As the rising sun is sometimes followed by storms, a new assault on Macbeth began.

31–33 The king of Norway took an opportunity to attack.

36 sooth: the truth.

37 double cracks: a double load of ammunition.

39–40 The officer's admiration leads to exaggeration. He claims he cannot decide whether (**except**) Macbeth and Banquo wanted to bathe in blood or make the battlefield as famous as Golgotha, the site of Christ's crucifixion.

45 Thane: a Scottish noble, similar in rank to an English earl.

Lennox. What a haste looks through his eyes!
So should he look that seems to speak things strange.

Ross. God save the King.

Duncan. Whence cam'st thou, worthy thane?

50 **Ross.** From Fife, great king,
Where the Norweyan banners flout the sky
And fan our people cold.
Norway himself, with terrible numbers,
Assisted by that most disloyal traitor,
55 The Thane of Cawdor, began a dismal conflict,
Till that Bellona's bridegroom, lapped in proof,
Confronted him with self-comparisons,
Point against point, rebellious arm 'gainst arm,
Curbing his lavish spirit. And to conclude,
60 The victory fell on us.

Duncan.   Great happiness!

Ross. That now Sweno,
The Norways' king, craves composition.
Nor would we deign him burial of his men
Till he disbursèd at Saint Colme's Inch
65 Ten thousand dollars to our general use.

Duncan. No more that Thane of Cawdor shall deceive
Our bosom interest. Go, pronounce his present death,
And with his former title greet Macbeth.

Ross. I'll see it done.

70 **Duncan.** What he hath lost, noble Macbeth hath won.

[*They exit.*]

49–60 Ross has arrived from Fife, where Norway's troops had invaded and frightened the people. There the king of Norway, along with the thane of Cawdor, met Macbeth (described as the husband of **Bellona,** the goddess of war). Macbeth, in heavy armor (**proof**), challenged the enemy and achieved victory.

62 craves composition: wants a treaty.

63 deign: allow.

64 disbursèd at Saint Colme's Inch: paid at Saint Colme's Inch, an island in the North Sea.

66–67 deceive our bosom interest: betray our friendship; **present death:** immediate execution.

68 *What reward has the king decided to give to Macbeth?*

Scene 3 *A bleak place near the battlefield.*

While leaving the battlefield, Macbeth and Banquo meet the witches, who are gleefully discussing the trouble they have caused. The witches hail Macbeth by a title he already holds, thane of Glamis. Then they prophesy that he will become both thane of Cawdor and king. When Banquo asks about his future, they speak in riddles, saying that he will be the father of kings but not a king himself.

After the witches vanish, Ross and Angus arrive to announce that Macbeth has been named thane of Cawdor. The first part of the witches' prophecy has come true, and Macbeth is stunned. He immediately begins to consider the possibility of murdering King Duncan to fulfill the rest of the witches' prophecy to him. Shaken, he turns his thoughts away from this "horrid image."

[*Thunder. Enter the three* Witches.]

First Witch. Where hast thou been, sister?

Second Witch. Killing swine.

Third Witch. Sister, where thou?

First Witch. A sailor's wife had chestnuts in her lap
5   And munched and munched and munched. "Give me," quoth I.
"Aroint thee, witch," the rump-fed runnion cries.
Her husband's to Aleppo gone, master o' th' *Tiger;*
But in a sieve I'll thither sail
And, like a rat without a tail,
10 I'll do, I'll do, and I'll do.

Second Witch. I'll give thee a wind.

First Witch. Th' art kind.

Third Witch. And I another.

First Witch. I myself have all the other,
15 And the very ports they blow,
All the quarters that they know
I' th' shipman's card.
I'll drain him dry as hay.
Sleep shall neither night nor day
20 Hang upon his penthouse lid.
He shall live a man forbid.
Weary sev'nnights, nine times nine,
Shall he dwindle, peak, and pine.
Though his bark cannot be lost,
25 Yet it shall be tempest-tossed.
Look what I have.

Second Witch. Show me, show me.

First Witch. Here I have a pilot's thumb,
Wracked as homeward he did come.

[*Drum within*]

30 **Third Witch.** A drum, a drum!
Macbeth doth come.

All. [*Dancing in a circle*] The Weïrd Sisters, hand in hand,
Posters of the sea and land,
Thus do go about, about,
35 Thrice to thine, and thrice to mine
And thrice again, to make up nine.
Peace, the charm's wound up.

[*Enter* Macbeth *and* Banquo.]

Macbeth. So foul and fair a day I have not seen. **Ⓐ**

Banquo. How far is 't called to Forres?—What are these,
40 So withered, and so wild in their attire,
That look not like th' inhabitants o' th' earth
And yet are on 't?—Live you? Or are you aught
That man may question? You seem to understand me
By each at once her choppy finger laying
45 Upon her skinny lips. You should be women,
And yet your beards forbid me to interpret
That you are so.

Macbeth.   Speak, if you can. What are you?

First Witch. All hail, Macbeth! Hail to thee, Thane of Glamis!

Second Witch. All hail, Macbeth! Hail to thee, Thane of Cawdor!

50 **Third Witch.** All hail, Macbeth, that shalt be king hereafter!

Banquo. Good sir, why do you start and seem to fear
Things that do sound so fair? I' th' name of truth,
Are you fantastical, or that indeed
Which outwardly you show? My noble partner
55 You greet with present grace and great prediction
Of noble having and of royal hope,
That he seems rapt withal. To me you speak not.
If you can look into the seeds of time
And say which grain will grow and which will not,
60 Speak, then, to me, who neither beg nor fear
Your favors nor your hate.

First Witch. Hail!

Second Witch. Hail!

Third Witch. Hail!

65 **First Witch.** Lesser than Macbeth and greater.

Second Witch. Not so happy, yet much happier.

Third Witch. Thou shalt get kings, though thou be none.
So all hail, Macbeth and Banquo! **B**

First Witch. Banquo and Macbeth, all hail!

70 **Macbeth.** Stay, you imperfect speakers. Tell me more.
By Sinel's death I know I am Thane of Glamis.
But how of Cawdor? The Thane of Cawdor lives
A prosperous gentleman, and to be king
Stands not within the prospect of belief,
75 No more than to be Cawdor. Say from whence
You owe this strange intelligence or why
Upon this blasted heath you stop our way
With such prophetic greeting. Speak, I charge you.

[Witches *vanish*.]

42–46 aught: anything; **choppy:** chapped; **your beards:** Beards on women identified them as witches. Banquo vividly describes the witches. *What does he notice about them?*

48–50 *What is surprising about the three titles the witches use to greet Macbeth?*

53 are you fantastical: Are you (the witches) imaginary?

54–57 The witches' prophecies of noble possessions (**having**)—the lands and wealth of Cawdor—and kingship (**royal hope**) have left Macbeth dazed (**rapt withal**).

B FORESHADOWING
In lines 65–68, the witches compare Banquo to Macbeth and prophesy that Banquo will not be king but will father (**get**) future kings. What do you think their words predict for Macbeth?

75–76 whence: where. Macbeth wants to know where the witches received their knowledge (**strange intelligence**).

Banquo. The earth hath bubbles, as the water has,
80 And these are of them. Whither are they vanished?

Macbeth. Into the air, and what seemed corporal melted,
As breath into the wind. Would they had stayed!

Banquo. Were such things here as we do speak about?
Or have we eaten on the insane root
85 That takes the reason prisoner?

Macbeth. Your children shall be kings.

Banquo.   You shall be king.

Macbeth. And Thane of Cawdor too. Went it not so?

Banquo. To th' selfsame tune and words.—Who's here?

[*Enter* Ross *and* Angus.]

Ross. The King hath happily received, Macbeth,
90 The news of thy success, and, when he reads
Thy personal venture in the rebels' fight,
His wonders and his praises do contend
Which should be thine or his. Silenced with that,
In viewing o'er the rest o' th' selfsame day
95 He finds thee in the stout Norweyan ranks,
Nothing afeard of what thyself didst make,
Strange images of death. As thick as hail
Came post with post, and every one did bear
Thy praises in his kingdom's great defense,
100 And poured them down before him.

Angus.   We are sent
To give thee from our royal master thanks,
Only to herald thee into his sight,
Not pay thee.

Ross. And for an earnest of a greater honor,
105 He bade me, from him, call thee Thane of Cawdor,
In which addition, hail, most worthy thane,
For it is thine.

Banquo.   What, can the devil speak true?

Macbeth. The Thane of Cawdor lives. Why do you dress me
In borrowed robes?

Angus.   Who was the Thane lives yet,
110 But under heavy judgment bears that life
Which he deserves to lose. Whether he was combined
With those of Norway, or did line the rebel
With hidden help and vantage, or that with both
He labored in his country's wrack, I know not;
115 But treasons capital, confessed and proved,
Have overthrown him.

80 whither: where.

81 corporal: physical; real.

84 insane root: A number of plants were believed to cause insanity when eaten.

92–93 King Duncan hesitates between awe (**wonders**) and gratitude (**praises**) and is, as a result, speechless.

96–97 Although Macbeth left many dead (**strange images of death**), he obviously did not fear death himself.

104 earnest: partial payment.

106 addition: title.

111–116 The former thane of Cawdor may have been secretly allied (**combined**) with the king of Norway, or he may have supported the traitor Macdonwald (**did line the rebel**). But he is guilty of treasons that deserve the death penalty (**treasons capital**), having aimed at the country's ruin (**wrack**).

Macbeth. [*Aside*]   Glamis and Thane of Cawdor!
The greatest is behind. [*To Ross and* Angus] Thanks for your pains.
[*Aside to* Banquo] Do you not hope your children shall be kings
When those that gave the Thane of Cawdor to me
120 Promised no less to them?

Banquo.   That, trusted home,
Might yet enkindle you unto the crown,
Besides the Thane of Cawdor. But 'tis strange.
And oftentimes, to win us to our harm,
The instruments of darkness tell us truths,
125 Win us with honest trifles, to betray 's
In deepest consequence.—
Cousins, a word, I pray you.   [*They step aside.*]

Macbeth. [*Aside*]   Two truths are told
As happy prologues to the swelling act
Of the imperial theme.—I thank you, gentlemen.
130 [*Aside*] This supernatural soliciting
Cannot be ill, cannot be good. If ill,
Why hath it given me earnest of success
Commencing in a truth? I am Thane of Cawdor.
If good, why do I yield to that suggestion
135 Whose horrid image doth unfix my hair
And make my seated heart knock at my ribs
Against the use of nature? Present fears
Are less than horrible imaginings.
My thought, whose murder yet is but fantastical,
140 Shakes so my single state of man
That function is smothered in surmise,
And nothing is but what is not. **C**

Banquo.   Look how our partner's rapt.

Macbeth. [*Aside*] If chance will have me king, why, chance may
   crown me
Without my stir.

Banquo.   New honors come upon him,
145 Like our strange garments, cleave not to their mold
But with the aid of use.

Macbeth. [*Aside*]   Come what come may,
Time and the hour runs through the roughest day.

Banquo. Worthy Macbeth, we stay upon your leisure.

Macbeth. Give me your favor. My dull brain was wrought
150 With things forgotten. Kind gentlemen, your pains
Are registered where every day I turn
The leaf to read them. Let us toward the King.

---

116 Aside: a stage direction that means Macbeth is speaking to himself, beyond hearing.

120 home: fully; completely.

121 enkindle you unto: inflame your ambitions.

123–126 Banquo warns that evil powers often offer little truths to tempt people. The witches may be lying about what matters most (**in deepest consequence**).

C ASIDE
Reread Macbeth's aside in lines 130–142. What private thoughts does he reveal to the audience? Why might he want to keep these thoughts hidden from the other characters?

144 my stir: my doing anything.

146–147 Come what . . . roughest day: The future will arrive no matter what.

148 stay: wait.

150–152 your pains . . . read them: I will always remember your efforts. The metaphor refers to keeping a diary and reading it regularly.

[*Aside to* Banquo] Think upon what hath chanced, and at more time,
The interim having weighed it, let us speak
155 Our free hearts each to other.

Banquo.   Very gladly.

Macbeth. Till then, enough.—Come, friends.

[*They exit.*]

153–155 Macbeth wants to discuss the prophecies later, after he and Banquo have had time to think about them.

Scene 4 *A room in the king's palace at Forres.*

King Duncan receives news of the execution of the former thane of Cawdor.
As the king is admitting his bad judgment concerning the traitor, Macbeth
enters with Banquo, Ross, and Angus. Duncan expresses his gratitude to
them and then, in a most unusual action, officially names his own son
Malcolm as heir to the throne. To honor Macbeth, Duncan decides to visit
Macbeth's castle at Inverness. Macbeth, his thoughts full of dark ambition,
leaves to prepare for the king's visit.

[*Flourish. Enter* King Duncan, Lennox, Malcolm, Donalbain, *and*
Attendants.]

Duncan. Is execution done on Cawdor? Are not
Those in commission yet returned?

Malcolm.   My liege,
They are not yet come back. But I have spoke
With one that saw him die, who did report
5 That very frankly he confessed his treasons,
Implored your Highness' pardon, and set forth
A deep repentance. Nothing in his life
Became him like the leaving it. He died
As one that had been studied in his death
10 To throw away the dearest thing he owed
As 'twere a careless trifle.

Duncan.   There's no art
To find the mind's construction in the face.
He was a gentleman on whom I built
An absolute trust. **D**

[*Enter* Macbeth, Banquo, Ross, *and* Angus.]
                              O worthiest cousin,
15 The sin of my ingratitude even now
Was heavy on me. Thou art so far before
That swiftest wing of recompense is slow
To overtake thee. Would thou hadst less deserved,
That the proportion both of thanks and payment
20 Might have been mine! Only I have left to say,
More is thy due than more than all can pay.

2 those in commission: those who have the responsibility for Cawdor's execution.

6 set forth: showed.

8–11 He died as . . . trifle: He died as if he had rehearsed (**studied**) the moment. Though losing his life (**the dearest thing he owed**), he behaved with calm dignity.

D FORESHADOWING
Notice that in lines 11–14, Duncan admits he misjudged the thane of Cawdor, who proved a traitor. What might this admission foreshadow about the king?

14–21 The king feels that he cannot repay (**recompense**) Macbeth enough. Macbeth's qualities and accomplishments are of greater value than any thanks or payment Duncan can give.

Behind the Curtain

The 2004 Out of Joint Theatre Company production in London

COMMON CORE RL 7

Casting involves selecting actors to perform the roles in a play. Actors are chosen for their appearance (an actor playing Macbeth usually looks strong enough to be a soldier) and their ability to portray the psychological dimensions of a character through body language, such as gestures and expressions. In Shakespeare's time, only white male actors could be cast in plays, and boys played women's roles onstage because the theater was considered a corrupt environment unsuitable for women. In modern adaptations, casting incorporates actors from both genders and crosses racial lines.

Study the actors cast as Macbeth and Lady Macbeth in these photographs from modern productions of the play. How would you describe their physical appearance? What expressions or gestures does each actor use? What does the body language of the actors suggest about Macbeth and Lady Macbeth's relationship?

If you were staging this play, name two actors you would cast in these roles and explain why they would be intriguing and effective choices.

The 1999 Queen's Theatre production in London

The 2002 Albery Theatre production in London

Macbeth. The service and the loyalty I owe
In doing it pays itself. Your Highness' part
Is to receive our duties, and our duties
25 Are to your throne and state children and servants,
Which do but what they should by doing everything
Safe toward your love and honor.

Duncan.   Welcome hither.
I have begun to plant thee and will labor
To make thee full of growing.—Noble Banquo,
30 That hast no less deserved nor must be known
No less to have done so, let me enfold thee
And hold thee to my heart.

Banquo.   There, if I grow,
The harvest is your own.

Duncan.   My plenteous joys,
Wanton in fullness, seek to hide themselves
35 In drops of sorrow.—Sons, kinsmen, thanes,
And you whose places are the nearest, know
We will establish our estate upon
Our eldest, Malcolm, whom we name hereafter
The Prince of Cumberland; which honor must
40 Not unaccompanied invest him only,
But signs of nobleness, like stars, shall shine
On all deservers.—From hence to Inverness,
And bind us further to you.

Macbeth. The rest is labor which is not used for you.
45 I'll be myself the harbinger and make joyful
The hearing of my wife with your approach.
So humbly take my leave.

Duncan.   My worthy Cawdor.

Macbeth. [*Aside*] The Prince of Cumberland! That is a step
On which I must fall down or else o'erleap,
50 For in my way it lies. Stars, hide your fires;
Let not light see my black and deep desires.
The eye wink at the hand, yet let that be
Which the eye fears, when it is done, to see. **E**
[*He exits.*]

Duncan. True, worthy Banquo. He is full so valiant,
55 And in his commendations I am fed:
It is a banquet to me.—Let's after him,
Whose care is gone before to bid us welcome.
It is a peerless kinsman.
[*Flourish. They exit.*]

28–29 The king plans to give more honors to Macbeth. *What might Macbeth be thinking now?*

33–35 My plenteous . . . sorrow: The king is crying tears of joy.

39 Prince of Cumberland: the title given to the heir to the Scottish throne. *Now that Malcolm is heir, how might Macbeth react?*

42 Inverness: site of Macbeth's castle, where the king has just invited himself, giving another honor to Macbeth.

45 harbinger: a representative sent before a royal party to make proper arrangements for its arrival.

E TRAGEDY
Be aware that in Macbeth's aside in lines 48–53, he admits that he hopes the king will be murdered. Based on these lines, what do you think is Macbeth's **tragic flaw?**

Scene 5 *Macbeth's castle at Inverness.*

Lady Macbeth reads a letter from her husband that tells her of the witches'
prophecies, one of which has already come true. She is determined that
Macbeth will be king. However, she fears that he lacks the courage to kill
Duncan. After a messenger tells her the king is coming, she calls on the
powers of evil to help her do what must be done. When Macbeth arrives,
she tells him that the king must die that night but reminds him that he
must appear to be a good and loyal host.

[*Enter* Lady Macbeth, *alone, with a letter.*]

Lady Macbeth. [*Reading the letter*] "They met me in the day of success,
and I have learned by the perfect'st report they have more in them than
mortal knowledge. When I burned in desire to question them further,
they made themselves air, into which they vanished. Whiles I stood
5 rapt in the wonder of it came missives from the King, who all-hailed
me 'Thane of Cawdor,' by which title, before, these Weïrd Sisters
saluted me and referred me to the coming on of time with 'Hail, king
that shalt be.' This have I thought good to deliver thee, my ⬥**F**
dearest partner of greatness, that thou might'st not lose the dues of
10 rejoicing by being ignorant of what greatness is promised thee. Lay it
to thy heart, and farewell."

    Glamis thou art, and Cawdor, and shalt be
What thou art promised. Yet do I fear thy nature;
It is too full o' th' milk of human kindness
15 To catch the nearest way. Thou wouldst be great,
Art not without ambition, but without
The illness should attend it. What thou wouldst highly,
That wouldst thou holily; wouldst not play false
And yet wouldst wrongly win. Thou'd'st have, great Glamis,
20 That which cries "Thus thou must do," if thou have it,
And that which rather thou dost fear to do,
Than wishest should be undone. Hie thee hither,
That I may pour my spirits in thine ear
And chastise with the valor of my tongue
25 All that impedes thee from the golden round
Which fate and metaphysical aid doth seem
To have thee crowned withal. **G**

[*Enter* Messenger.]

                What is your tidings?

Messenger. The King comes here tonight.

Lady Macbeth.   Thou'rt mad to say it!
Is not thy master with him? who, were't so,
30 Would have informed for preparation.

Messenger. So please you, it is true. Our Thane is coming.
One of my fellows had the speed of him,

F GRAMMAR AND STYLE
Reread line 8. Shakespeare
frequently uses **inverted
sentences** and other types of
inverted word order to achieve
a poetic effect. Notice that in
this line, Shakespeare places
have, part of the verb phrase
have thought, before the subject
I to create a regular, pleasing
rhythm.

13–18 Lady Macbeth fears her
husband is too good (**too full o' th'
milk of human kindness**) to seize the
throne by murder (**the nearest way**).
Lacking the necessary wickedness
(**illness**), he wants to gain power
virtuously (**holily**).

G SOLILOQUY
Notice that in her soliloquy
in lines 12–27, Lady Macbeth
expresses her thoughts
about the prophecies. What
conclusions can you draw
about Lady Macbeth?

32 had the speed of him: rode faster
than he.

Who, almost dead for breath, had scarcely more
Than would make up his message.

Lady Macbeth.   Give him tending.
35 He brings great news.

[Messenger *exits*.]

                                        The raven himself is hoarse
That croaks the fatal entrance of Duncan
Under my battlements. Come, you spirits
That tend on mortal thoughts, unsex me here,
And fill me from the crown to the toe top-full
40 Of direst cruelty. Make thick my blood.
Stop up th' access and passage to remorse,
That no compunctious visitings of nature
Shake my fell purpose, nor keep peace between
Th' effect and it. Come to my woman's breasts
45 And take my milk for gall, you murd'ring ministers,
Wherever in your sightless substances
You wait on nature's mischief. Come, thick night,
And pall thee in the dunnest smoke of hell,
That my keen knife see not the wound it makes,
50 Nor heaven peep through the blanket of the dark
To cry "Hold, hold!"

[*Enter* Macbeth.]

                              Great Glamis, worthy Cawdor,
Greater than both by the all-hail hereafter!
Thy letters have transported me beyond
This ignorant present, and I feel now
55 The future in the instant.

Macbeth.   My dearest love,
Duncan comes here tonight.

Lady Macbeth.   And when goes hence?

Macbeth. Tomorrow, as he purposes.

Lady Macbeth.   O, never
Shall sun that morrow see!
Your face, my thane, is as a book where men
60 May read strange matters. To beguile the time,
Look like the time. Bear welcome in your eye,
Your hand, your tongue. Look like th' innocent flower,
But be the serpent under 't. He that's coming
Must be provided for; and you shall put
65 This night's great business into my dispatch,
Which shall to all our nights and days to come
Give solely sovereign sway and masterdom.

35 raven: The harsh cry of the raven, a bird symbolizing evil and misfortune, was supposed to indicate an approaching death.

37–51 Lady Macbeth calls on the spirits of evil to rid her of feminine weakness (**unsex me**) and to block out guilt. She wants no normal pangs of conscience (**compunctious visitings of nature**) to get in the way of her murderous plan. She asks that her mother's milk be turned to bile (**gall**) by the unseen evil forces (**murd'ring ministers, sightless substances**) that exist in nature. Furthermore, she asks that the night wrap (**pall**) itself in darkness as black as hell so that no one may see or stop the crime.

Language Coach

Roots and Affixes A word's root may contain its core meaning. The Latin root *ignorare*, meaning "to have no knowledge of," is the root of *ignore, ignoramus,* and *ignorant*. Reread lines 53–55. Why does Lady Macbeth call the present "ignorant"?

60–63 To beguile ... under 't: To fool (**beguile**) everyone, act as expected at such a time, that is, as a good host. *Who is more like a serpent, Lady Macbeth or her husband?*

65 my dispatch: my management.

67 give solely sovereign sway: bring absolute royal power.

Macbeth. We will speak further.

Lady Macbeth.   Only look up clear.
To alter favor ever is to fear.
70 Leave all the rest to me.

[*They exit.*]

Scene 6 *In front of Macbeth's castle.*
King Duncan and his party arrive, and Lady Macbeth welcomes them.
Duncan is generous in his praise of his hosts and eagerly awaits the arrival
of Macbeth.

[*Hautboys and Torches. Enter* King Duncan, Malcolm, Donalbain,
Banquo, Lennox, Macduff, Ross, Angus, *and* Attendants.]

Duncan. This castle hath a pleasant seat. The air
Nimbly and sweetly recommends itself
Unto our gentle senses.

Banquo.   This guest of summer,
The temple-haunting martlet, does approve,
5 By his loved mansionry, that the heaven's breath
Smells wooingly here. No jutty, frieze,
Buttress, nor coign of vantage, but this bird
Hath made his pendant bed and procreant cradle.
Where they most breed and haunt, I have observed,
10 The air is delicate.

[*Enter* Lady Macbeth.]

Duncan.   See, see, our honored hostess!—
The love that follows us sometime is our trouble,
Which still we thank as love. Herein I teach you
How you shall bid God 'ild us for your pains
And thank us for your trouble.

Lady Macbeth.   All our service,
15 In every point twice done and then done double,
Were poor and single business to contend
Against those honors deep and broad wherewith
Your Majesty loads our house. For those of old,
And the late dignities heaped up to them,
20 We rest your hermits.

Duncan.   Where's the Thane of Cawdor?
We coursed him at the heels and had a purpose
To be his purveyor; but he rides well,
And his great love (sharp as his spur) hath helped him
To his home before us. Fair and noble hostess,
25 We are your guest tonight.

69 **To alter . . . fear:** To change your expression (**favor**) is a sign of fear.

[Stage Direction] **hautboys:** oboes.

1 **seat:** location.

3–10 The martin (**martlet**) usually built its nest on a church (**temple**), where every projection (**jutty**), sculptured decoration (**frieze**), support (**buttress**), and convenient corner (**coign of vantage**) offered a good nesting site. Banquo sees the presence of the martin's hanging (**pendant**) nest, a breeding (**procreant**) place, as a sign of healthy air.

16 **single business:** weak service. Lady Macbeth claims that nothing she or her husband can do will match Duncan's generosity.

20 **we rest your hermits:** we can only repay you with prayers. The wealthy used to hire hermits to pray for the dead.

21 **coursed him at the heels:** followed him closely.

22 **purveyor:** one who makes advance arrangements for a royal visit.

Lady Macbeth greets King Duncan.

Lady Macbeth. Your servants ever
Have theirs, themselves, and what is theirs in compt
To make their audit at your Highness' pleasure,
Still to return your own.

Duncan. Give me your hand.
[*Taking her hand*]
Conduct me to mine host. We love him highly
30 And shall continue our graces towards him.
By your leave, hostess.

[*They exit.*]

Scene 7 *A room in Macbeth's castle.*

*Macbeth has left Duncan in the middle of dinner. Alone, he begins to
have second thoughts about his murderous plan. Lady Macbeth enters
and discovers that he has changed his mind. She scornfully accuses him
of cowardice and tells him that a true man would never back out of a
commitment. She reassures him of success and explains her plan. She will
make sure that the king's attendants drink too much. When they are fast
asleep, Macbeth will stab the king with the servants' weapons.*

[*Hautboys. Torches. Enter a* Sewer, *and divers* Servants *with dishes and
service over the stage. Then enter* Macbeth.]

Macbeth. If it were done when 'tis done, then 'twere well
It were done quickly. If th' assassination
Could trammel up the consequence and catch
With his surcease success, that but this blow
5 Might be the be-all and the end-all here,
But here, upon this bank and shoal of time,
We'd jump the life to come. But in these cases

25–28 Legally, Duncan owned everything in his kingdom. Lady Macbeth politely says that they hold his property in trust (**compt**), ready to return it (**make their audit**) whenever he wants.

H **DRAMATIC IRONY**
Why is the exchange between Lady Macbeth and Duncan in lines 25–31 ironic?

[Stage Direction] **Sewer:** the steward, the servant in charge of arranging the banquet and tasting the king's food; **divers:** various.

We still have judgment here, that we but teach
Bloody instructions, which, being taught, return
10 To plague th' inventor. This even-handed justice
Commends th' ingredience of our poisoned chalice
To our own lips. He's here in double trust:
First, as I am his kinsman and his subject,
Strong both against the deed; then, as his host,
15 Who should against his murderer shut the door,
Not bear the knife myself. Besides, this Duncan
Hath borne his faculties so meek, hath been
So clear in his great office, that his virtues
Will plead like angels, trumpet-tongued, against
20 The deep damnation of his taking-off;
And pity, like a naked newborn babe
Striding the blast, or heaven's cherubin horsed
Upon the sightless couriers of the air,
Shall blow the horrid deed in every eye,
25 That tears shall drown the wind. I have no spur
To prick the sides of my intent, but only
Vaulting ambition, which o'erleaps itself
And falls on th' other— ❶

[*Enter* Lady Macbeth.]

How now? What news?

Lady Macbeth. He has almost supped. Why have you left the chamber?

30 **Macbeth.** Hath he asked for me?

Lady Macbeth.   Know you not he has?

Macbeth. We will proceed no further in this business.
He hath honored me of late, and I have bought
Golden opinions from all sorts of people,
Which would be worn now in their newest gloss,
35 Not cast aside so soon.

Lady Macbeth.   Was the hope drunk
Wherein you dressed yourself? Hath it slept since?
And wakes it now, to look so green and pale
At what it did so freely? From this time
Such I account thy love. Art thou afeard
40 To be the same in thine own act and valor
As thou art in desire? Wouldst thou have that
Which thou esteem'st the ornament of life
And live a coward in thine own esteem,
Letting "I dare not" wait upon "I would,"
45 Like the poor cat i' th' adage?

Macbeth.   Prithee, peace.

1–10 Again, Macbeth argues with himself about murdering the king. If it could be done without causing problems later, then it would be good to do it soon. If Duncan's murder would have no negative consequences and be successfully completed with his death (**surcease**), then Macbeth would risk eternal damnation. He knows, however, that terrible deeds (**bloody instructions**) often backfire.

Language Coach

Homonyms Homonyms have different meanings but the same pronunciation. *Bear* can mean "shaggy, four-footed carnivore" or "carry." What does it mean in line 16? What form of *bear* in line 17 has a homonym meaning "come to life"? How is each homonym spelled?

❶ **SOLILOQUY**
Note that in lines 12–28 of his soliloquy, Macbeth lists the reasons why he shouldn't kill Duncan. How do you think other characters will react if Macbeth kills the king?

32–35 I have . . . so soon: The praises that Macbeth has received are, like new clothes, to be worn, not quickly thrown away. *What has Macbeth decided?*

35–38 Lady Macbeth sarcastically suggests that Macbeth's ambition must have been drunk, because it now seems to have a hangover (**to look so green and pale**).

39–45 Lady Macbeth criticizes Macbeth's weakened resolve to secure the crown (**ornament of life**) and calls him a coward. She compares him to a cat in a proverb (**adage**) who wouldn't catch fish because it feared wet feet.

I dare do all that may become a man.
Who dares do more is none.

Lady Macbeth.   What beast was't, then,
That made you break this enterprise to me?
When you durst do it, then you were a man;
50 And to be more than what you were, you would
Be so much more the man. Nor time nor place
Did then adhere, and yet you would make both.
They have made themselves, and that their fitness now
Does unmake you. I have given suck, and know
55 How tender 'tis to love the babe that milks me.
I would, while it was smiling in my face,
Have plucked my nipple from his boneless gums
And dashed the brains out, had I so sworn as you
Have done to this. ⓙ

Macbeth.   If we should fail—

Lady Macbeth.   We fail?
60 But screw your courage to the sticking place
And we'll not fail. When Duncan is asleep
(Whereto the rather shall his day's hard journey
Soundly invite him), his two chamberlains
Will I with wine and wassail so convince
65 That memory, the warder of the brain,
Shall be a fume, and the receipt of reason
A limbeck only. When in swinish sleep
Their drenchèd natures lie as in a death,
What cannot you and I perform upon
70 Th' unguarded Duncan? What not put upon
His spongy officers, who shall bear the guilt
Of our great quell?

Macbeth.   Bring forth men-children only,
For thy undaunted mettle should compose
Nothing but males. Will it not be received,
75 When we have marked with blood those sleepy two
Of his own chamber and used their very daggers,
That they have done 't?

Lady Macbeth.   Who dares receive it other,
As we shall make our griefs and clamor roar
Upon his death?

Macbeth.   I am settled and bend up
80 Each corporal agent to this terrible feat.
Away, and mock the time with fairest show.
False face must hide what the false heart doth know.

[*They exit.*]

54 **I have given suck:** I have nursed a baby.

ⓙ **TRAGEDY**
Reread lines 47–59. How does Lady Macbeth urge her husband to carry out his terrible plan?

60 When each string of a guitar or lute is tightened to the peg (**sticking place**), the instrument is ready to be played.

65–67 Memory was thought to be at the base of the brain, to guard against harmful vapors rising from the body. Lady Macbeth will get the guards so drunk that their reason will become like a still (**limbeck**), producing confused thoughts.

72 **quell:** murder.

72–74 **Bring forth ... males:** Your bold spirit (**undaunted mettle**) is better suited to raising males than females. *Do you think Macbeth's words express admiration?*

79–82 Now that Macbeth has made up his mind, every part of his body (**each corporal agent**) is tightened like a bow. He and Lady Macbeth will return to the banquet and deceive everyone (**mock the time**), hiding their evil intent with gracious faces.

Comprehension

1. **Recall** What predictions do the witches make about Macbeth and Banquo?

2. **Clarify** How does Macbeth react when Duncan declares his son Malcolm heir to the Scottish throne?

3. **Summarize** What do Macbeth and his wife plan to do to make the witches' predictions come true?

Text Analysis

4. **Identify Mood** Reread Scene 1, lines 1–11. What mood is created by the witches? Why do you think the drama opens with this scene?

5. **Make Inferences** What can you infer about Macbeth and Lady Macbeth's marriage from their interaction in Scene 7?

6. **Examine Shakespearean Drama** Review the actions you've recorded in your charts so far for Macbeth and Lady Macbeth. At this point in the play, which **character** do you think is more forceful? Cite evidence to explain your answer.

7. **Analyze Shakespearean Tragedy** Use a chart like the one shown to record the **soliloquies** and **asides** in Act One that provide insight into the characters who speak them. What do Macbeth's and Banquo's asides to each other after hearing the witches' prophecies (Scene 3, lines 118–126) reveal about each man?

Scene, Lines	Soliloquy or Aside?	Insight

8. **Make Judgments About a Character** What character traits do Macbeth's exploits on the battlefield demonstrate? Are these qualities consistent with the plot he devises? Explain why or why not.

Text Criticism

9. **Critical Interpretations** Some critics have pointed out that Macbeth clearly recognizes the immorality of his murderous plan and foresees its terrible consequences, yet still goes through with it. Why would Macbeth do this? Provide evidence from the text to support your explanation.

Can you ever be too AMBITIOUS?

Without the witches' predictions, do you think Macbeth and Lady Macbeth would have been satisfied with their place in life? Explain why.

COMMON CORE

RL 3 Analyze the impact of the author's choices regarding how to develop and relate elements of a drama. RL 4 Analyze the impact of specific word choices on meaning and tone. RL 5 Analyze how an author's choices concerning how to structure specific parts of a text contribute to its overall structure and meaning.

ACT 2

Scene 1 *The court of Macbeth's castle.*

It is past midnight, and Banquo and his son, Fleance, cannot sleep. When Macbeth appears, Banquo tells of his uneasy dreams about the witches. Macbeth promises that they will discuss the prophecies later, and Banquo goes to bed. Once alone, Macbeth imagines a dagger leading him toward the king's chamber. When he hears a bell, the signal from Lady Macbeth, he knows it is time to go to Duncan's room.

[*Enter* Banquo, *and* Fleance *with a torch before him.*]

Banquo. How goes the night, boy?

Fleance. The moon is down. I have not heard the clock.

Banquo. And she goes down at twelve.

Fleance.   I take 't, 'tis later, sir.

Banquo. Hold, take my sword. [*Giving his sword to* Fleance]
                              There's husbandry in heaven;
5 Their candles are all out. Take thee that too.
A heavy summons lies like lead upon me,
And yet I would not sleep. Merciful powers,
Restrain in me the cursèd thoughts that nature
Gives way to in repose.

[*Enter* Macbeth, *and a* Servant *with a torch.*]

                              Give me my sword.—Who's there?

10 **Macbeth.** A friend.

Banquo. What, sir, not yet at rest? The King's abed.
He hath been in unusual pleasure, and
Sent forth great largess to your offices.
This diamond he greets your wife withal,
15 By the name of most kind hostess, and shut up
In measureless content. [*He gives* Macbeth *a diamond.*]

Macbeth.   Being unprepared,
Our will became the servant to defect,
Which else should free have wrought. ⓐ

Banquo.   All's well.
I dreamt last night of the three Weïrd Sisters.
20 To you they have showed some truth.

Macbeth.   I think not of them.
Yet, when we can entreat an hour to serve,
We would spend it in some words upon that business,
If you would grant the time.

4–5 The heavens show economy (**husbandry**) by keeping the lights (**candles**) out—it is a starless night.

6 heavy summons: desire for sleep.

13 largess to your offices: gifts to the servants' quarters.

15 shut up: went to bed.

ⓐ **DRAMATIC IRONY**
Reread lines 16–18, in which Macbeth tells Banquo that he and his wife couldn't entertain the king as they would have liked. Why are these remarks ironic?

21 can entreat an hour: both have the time.

Macbeth and Lady Macbeth

Banquo.   At your kind'st leisure.

Macbeth. If you shall cleave to my consent, when 'tis,
25 It shall make honor for you.

Banquo.   So I lose none
In seeking to augment it, but still keep
My bosom franchised and allegiance clear,
I shall be counseled.

Macbeth.   Good repose the while.

Banquo. Thanks, sir. The like to you.

[Banquo *and* Fleance *exit*.]

30 **Macbeth.** Go bid thy mistress, when my drink is ready,
She strike upon the bell. Get thee to bed.

[Servant *exits*.]

Is this a dagger which I see before me,
The handle toward my hand? Come, let me clutch thee.
I have thee not, and yet I see thee still.
35 Art thou not, fatal vision, sensible
To feeling as to sight? or art thou but
A dagger of the mind, a false creation
Proceeding from the heat-oppressèd brain?
I see thee yet, in form as palpable
40 As this which now I draw. [*He draws his dagger.*]
Thou marshal'st me the way that I was going,
And such an instrument I was to use.
Mine eyes are made the fools o' th' other senses
Or else worth all the rest. I see thee still,
45 And, on thy blade and dudgeon, gouts of blood,
Which was not so before. There's no such thing.
It is the bloody business which informs
Thus to mine eyes. Now o'er the one-half world
Nature seems dead, and wicked dreams abuse
50 The curtained sleep. Witchcraft celebrates
Pale Hecate's off'rings, and withered murder,
Alarumed by his sentinel, the wolf,
Whose howl's his watch, thus with his stealthy pace,
With Tarquin's ravishing strides, towards his design
55 Moves like a ghost. Thou sure and firm-set earth,
Hear not my steps, which way they walk, for fear
Thy very stones prate of my whereabouts
And take the present horror from the time,
Which now suits with it. Whiles I threat, he lives.
60 Words to the heat of deeds too cold breath gives. **Ⓑ**

24–28 Macbeth asks Banquo for his support (**cleave to my consent**), promising honors in return. Banquo is willing to increase (**augment**) his honor provided he can keep a clear conscience and remain loyal to the king (**keep my bosom . . . clear**). *How do you think Macbeth feels about Banquo's virtuous stand?*

32–42 Macbeth sees a dagger hanging in midair before him and questions whether it is real (**palpable**) or the illusion of a disturbed (**heat-oppressèd**) mind. The floating, imaginary dagger, which leads (**marshal'st**) him to Duncan's room, prompts him to draw his own dagger.

43–44 Either his eyes are mistaken (**fools**) or his other senses are.

45 He sees drops of blood on the blade and handle.

Ⓑ SOLILOQUY
What does Macbeth's soliloquy in lines 32–60 reveal about his state of mind? Cite details that support your ideas.

[*A bell rings.*]

I go, and it is done. The bell invites me.
Hear it not, Duncan, for it is a knell
That summons thee to heaven or to hell.

[*He exits.*]

Scene 2 *Macbeth's castle.*

As Lady Macbeth waits for her husband, she explains how she drugged Duncan's servants. Suddenly a dazed and terrified Macbeth enters, carrying the bloody daggers that he used to murder Duncan. He imagines a voice that warns "Macbeth shall sleep no more" and is too afraid to return to the scene of the crime. Lady Macbeth takes the bloody daggers back so that the servants will be blamed. Startled by a knocking at the gate, she hurries back and tells Macbeth to wash off the blood and change into his nightclothes.

[*Enter* Lady Macbeth.]

Lady Macbeth. That which hath made them drunk hath made me bold.
What hath quenched them hath given me fire. Hark!—Peace.
It was the owl that shrieked, the fatal bellman,
Which gives the stern'st good-night. He is about it.
5 The doors are open, and the surfeited grooms
Do mock their charge with snores. I have drugged their possets,
That death and nature do contend about them
Whether they live or die.

Macbeth. [*Within*]   Who's there? what, ho!

Lady Macbeth. Alack, I am afraid they have awaked,
10 And 'tis not done. Th' attempt and not the deed
Confounds us. Hark!—I laid their daggers ready;
He could not miss 'em. Had he not resembled
My father as he slept, I had done 't.

[*Enter* Macbeth *with bloody daggers.*]

                              My husband?

Macbeth. I have done the deed. Didst thou not hear a noise?

15 **Lady Macbeth.** I heard the owl scream and the crickets cry.
Did not you speak?

Macbeth.   When?

Lady Macbeth.   Now.

Macbeth.   As I descended?

Lady Macbeth. Ay.

Macbeth.   Hark!—Who lies i' th' second chamber?

Lady Macbeth. Donalbain.

Macbeth.   This is a sorry sight.

62 knell: funeral bell.

3 fatal bellman: town crier.

5 surfeited grooms: drunken servants.

6 possets: drinks.

9–10 *Why does the sound of Macbeth's voice make his wife so afraid?*

11 confounds: destroys. If Duncan survives, they will be killed (as his attempted murderers).

Lady Macbeth. A foolish thought, to say a sorry sight.

20 **Macbeth.** There's one did laugh in 's sleep, and one cried "Murder!"
That they did wake each other. I stood and heard them.
But they did say their prayers and addressed them
Again to sleep.

Lady Macbeth. There are two lodged together.

Macbeth. One cried "God bless us" and "Amen" the other,
25 As they had seen me with these hangman's hands,
List'ning their fear. I could not say "Amen"
When they did say "God bless us."

Lady Macbeth. Consider it not so deeply.

Macbeth. But wherefore could not I pronounce "Amen"?
30 I had most need of blessing, and "Amen"
Stuck in my throat.

Lady Macbeth.　　　These deeds must not be thought
After these ways; so, it will make us mad.

Macbeth. Methought I heard a voice cry "Sleep no more!
Macbeth does murder sleep"—the innocent sleep,
35 Sleep that knits up the raveled sleave of care,
The death of each day's life, sore labor's bath,
Balm of hurt minds, great nature's second course,
Chief nourisher in life's feast.

Lady Macbeth.　　　　　What do you mean?

Macbeth. Still it cried "Sleep no more!" to all the house.
40 "Glamis hath murdered sleep, and therefore Cawdor
Shall sleep no more. Macbeth shall sleep no more." **C**

Lady Macbeth. Who was it that thus cried? Why, worthy thane,
You do unbend your noble strength to think
So brainsickly of things. Go get some water
45 And wash this filthy witness from your hand.—
Why did you bring these daggers from the place?
They must lie there. Go carry them and smear
The sleepy grooms with blood.

Macbeth.　　　　　　　I'll go no more.
I am afraid to think what I have done.
50 Look on 't again I dare not.

Lady Macbeth.　　　　Infirm of purpose!
Give me the daggers. The sleeping and the dead
Are but as pictures. 'Tis the eye of childhood
That fears a painted devil. If he do bleed,

25–26 He imagines that the sleepers could see him listening to their exclamations of fear, with his hands bloody like those of an executioner.

34–38 Sleep eases worries (**knits up the raveled sleave of care**), relieves the aches of physical work (**sore labor's bath**), soothes the anxious (**hurt minds**), and nourishes like food.

C FORESHADOWING
Reread lines 39–41. What mental state might the inability to sleep reflect? What do you suppose these lines foreshadow for Macbeth?

COMMON CORE L 4b

Language Coach

Roots and Affixes A **prefix** is an affix at the beginning of a word. The prefix *in-* can mean "in" or "not." What does it mean in *infirm* (line 50)? How can you tell? How would Lady Macbeth say this line?

I'll gild the faces of the grooms withal,
55 For it must seem their guilt.

[*She exits with the daggers. Knock within.*]

Macbeth.   Whence is that knocking?
How is 't with me when every noise appalls me?
What hands are here? Ha, they pluck out mine eyes.
Will all great Neptune's ocean wash this blood
Clean from my hand? No, this my hand will rather
60 The multitudinous seas incarnadine,
Making the green one red.

[*Enter Lady Macbeth.*]

Lady Macbeth. My hands are of your color, but I shame
To wear a heart so white.   [*Knock*]
                              I hear a knocking
At the south entry. Retire we to our chamber.
65 A little water clears us of this deed.
How easy is it, then! Your constancy
Hath left you unattended.   [*Knock*]
                              Hark, more knocking.
Get on your nightgown, lest occasion call us
And show us to be watchers. Be not lost
70 So poorly in your thoughts.

Macbeth. To know my deed 'twere best not know myself.
                              [*Knock*]
Wake Duncan with thy knocking. I would thou couldst.

[*They exit.*]

Scene 3 *Within Macbeth's castle, near the gate.*

The drunken porter staggers across the courtyard to answer the knocking.
After Lennox and Macduff are let in, Macbeth arrives to lead them to the
king's quarters. Macduff enters Duncan's room and discovers his murder.
Lennox and Macbeth then go to the scene, and Macbeth, pretending to be
enraged, kills the two servants. Amid all the commotion, Lady Macbeth
faints. Duncan's sons, Malcolm and Donalbain, fearing for their lives,
quietly leave, hoping to escape the country.

[*Knocking within. Enter a Porter.*]

Porter. Here's a knocking indeed! If a man were porter of hell gate, he **D**
should have old turning the key. [*Knock*] Knock, knock, knock! Who's
there, i' th' name of Beelzebub? Here's a farmer that hanged himself on
th' expectation of plenty. Come in time! Have napkins enough about
5 you; here you'll sweat for 't. [*Knock*] Knock, knock! Who's there, in th'

54–55 She'll cover (**gild**) the servants with blood, blaming them for the murder. *How is her attitude toward blood different from her husband's?*

59–61 this my hand . . . one red: The blood on my hand will redden (**incarnadine**) the seas.

66–67 Your constancy . . . unattended: Your courage has left you.

68–69 lest . . . watchers: in case we are called for and found awake (**watchers**), which would look suspicious.

71 To know . . . myself: To come to terms with what I have done, I must forget about my conscience.

D BLANK VERSE
Be aware that the porter's speech in lines 1–16 is written in prose rather than blank verse. Why do you think Shakespeare chose to have the porter speak in prose?

2 old turning the key: plenty of key turning. Hell's porter would be busy because so many people are ending up in hell these days.

3 Beelzebub: a devil.

other devil's name? Faith, here's an equivocator that could swear in both the scales against either scale, who committed treason enough for God's sake yet could not equivocate to heaven. O, come in, equivocator. [*Knock*] Knock, knock, knock! Who's there? Faith, here's an English
10 tailor come hither for stealing out of a French hose. Come in, tailor. Here you may roast your goose. [*Knock*] Knock, knock! Never at quiet. —What are you? —But this place is too cold for hell. I'll devilporter it no further. I had thought to have let in some of all professions that go the primrose way to th' everlasting bonfire. [*Knock*] Anon, anon! [*The*
15 Porter *opens the door to* Macduff *and* Lennox.]
I pray you, remember the porter. **E**

Macduff. Was it so late, friend, ere you went to bed
That you do lie so late?

Porter. Faith, sir, we were carousing till the second cock, and drink, sir,
20 is a great provoker of three things.

Macduff. What three things does drink especially provoke?

Porter. Marry, sir, nose-painting, sleep, and urine. Lechery, sir, it provokes and unprovokes. It provokes the desire, but it takes away the performance. Therefore much drink may be said to be an
25 equivocator with lechery. It makes him, and it mars him; it sets him on, and it takes him off; it persuades him and disheartens him; makes him stand to and not stand to; in conclusion, equivocates him in a sleep and, giving him the lie, leaves him.

Macduff. I believe drink gave thee the lie last night.

30 **Porter.** That it did, sir, i' th' very throat on me; but I requited him for his lie, and, I think, being too strong for him, though he took up my legs sometime, yet I made a shift to cast him.

Macduff. Is thy master stirring?

[*Enter* Macbeth.]

Our knocking has awaked him. Here he comes.
[*Porter exits.*]

35 **Lennox.** Good morrow, noble sir.

Macbeth.   Good morrow, both.

Macduff. Is the King stirring, worthy thane?

Macbeth.   Not yet.

Macduff. He did command me to call timely on him.
I have almost slipped the hour.

Macbeth.   I'll bring you to him.

Macduff. I know this is a joyful trouble to you,
40 But yet 'tis one.

3–10 The porter pretends he is welcoming a farmer who killed himself after his schemes to get rich (**expectation of plenty**) failed, a double talker (**equivocator**) who perjured himself yet couldn't talk his way into heaven, and a tailor who cheated his customers by skimping on material (**stealing out of a French hose**).

E TRAGEDY
Note that the porter's speech in lines 1–16 provides **comic relief**, which breaks the tension of the preceding scene. What is ironic about the porter's notion that he is opening hell's gate?

22–28 The porter jokes that alcohol stimulates lust (**lechery**) but makes the lover a failure.

29–32 More jokes about alcohol, this time described as a wrestler finally thrown off (**cast**) by the porter, who thus paid him back (**requited him**) for disappointment in love. *Cast* also means "to vomit" and "to urinate," two other ways of dealing with alcohol.

37 timely: early.
38 slipped the hour: missed the time.

Macbeth. The labor we delight in physics pain.
This is the door.

Macduff.   I'll make so bold to call,
For 'tis my limited service. [Macduff *exits.*]

Lennox. Goes the King hence today?

45 **Macbeth.** He does. He did appoint so.

Lennox. The night has been unruly. Where we lay,
Our chimneys were blown down and, as they say,
Lamentings heard i' th' air, strange screams of death,
And prophesying, with accents terrible,
50 Of dire combustion and confused events
New hatched to th' woeful time. The obscure bird
Clamored the livelong night. Some say the earth
Was feverous and did shake. **F**

Macbeth.   'Twas a rough night.

Lennox. My young remembrance cannot parallel
55 A fellow to it.

[*Enter* Macduff.]

Macduff.   O horror, horror, horror!
Tongue nor heart cannot conceive nor name thee!

Macbeth and Lennox. What's the matter?

Macduff. Confusion now hath made his masterpiece.
Most sacrilegious murder hath broke ope
60 The Lord's anointed temple and stole thence
The life o' th' building.

Macbeth.   What is 't you say? The life?

Lennox. Mean you his majesty?

Macduff. Approach the chamber and destroy your sight
With a new Gorgon. Do not bid me speak.
65 See and then speak yourselves.

[Macbeth *and* Lennox *exit.*]

                         Awake, awake!
Ring the alarum bell.—Murder and treason!
Banquo and Donalbain, Malcolm, awake!
Shake off this downy sleep, death's counterfeit,
And look on death itself. Up, up, and see
70 The great doom's image. Malcolm. Banquo.
As from your graves rise up and walk like sprites
To countenance this horror.—Ring the bell.

[*Bell rings.*]

41 physics: cures.

43 limited service: appointed duty.

F BLANK VERSE
In lines 46–53, Lennox discusses the strange events of the night and the confusion they foretell. Would prose have been as effective as blank verse in conveying the **mood** of the speech?

58–61 Macduff mourns Duncan's death as the destruction (**confusion**) of order and as sacrilegious, violating all that is holy. In Shakespeare's time the king was believed to be God's sacred representative on earth.

64 new Gorgon: Macduff compares the shocking sight of the corpse to a Gorgon, a monster of Greek mythology with snakes for hair. Anyone who saw a Gorgon turned to stone.

68 counterfeit: imitation.

70 great doom's image: a picture like the Last Judgment, the end of the world.

71 sprites: spirits. The spirits of the dead were supposed to rise on Judgment Day.

[*Enter* Lady Macbeth.]

Lady Macbeth. What's the business,
That such a hideous trumpet calls to parley
75 The sleepers of the house? Speak, speak!

Macduff.   O gentle lady,
'Tis not for you to hear what I can speak.
The repetition in a woman's ear
Would murder as it fell. **G**

[*Enter* Banquo.]

                              O Banquo, Banquo,
Our royal master's murdered.

Lady Macbeth.   Woe, alas!
80 What, in our house?

Banquo.   Too cruel anywhere.—
Dear Duff, I prithee, contradict thyself
And say it is not so.

[*Enter* Macbeth, Lennox, *and* Ross.]

Macbeth. Had I but died an hour before this chance,
I had lived a blessèd time; for from this instant
85 There's nothing serious in mortality.
All is but toys. Renown and grace is dead.
The wine of life is drawn, and the mere lees
Is left this vault to brag of.

[*Enter* Malcolm *and* Donalbain.]

Donalbain. What is amiss?

Macbeth.   You are, and do not know 't.
90 The spring, the head, the fountain of your blood
Is stopped; the very source of it is stopped.

Macduff. Your royal father's murdered.

Malcolm.   O, by whom?

Lennox. Those of his chamber, as it seemed, had done 't.
Their hands and faces were all badged with blood.
95 So were their daggers, which unwiped we found
Upon their pillows. They stared and were distracted.
No man's life was to be trusted with them.

Macbeth. O, yet I do repent me of my fury,
That I did kill them.

Macduff.   Wherefore did you so?

100 **Macbeth.** Who can be wise, amazed, temp'rate, and furious,
Loyal, and neutral, in a moment? No man.

G DRAMATIC IRONY
Recall Lady Macbeth's soliloquy in Act One, in which she calls on the spirits of evil to "unsex her." How do Macduff's words in lines 75–78 ironically echo Lady Macbeth's speech?

84–88 **for from . . . brag of:** From now on, nothing matters (**there's nothing serious**) in human life (**mortality**); even fame and grace have been made meaningless. The good wine of life has been removed (**drawn**), leaving only the dregs (**lees**). *Is Macbeth being completely insincere, or does he regret his crime?*

94 **badged:** marked.

Language Coach

Antonyms Words with opposite meanings are **antonyms**. Reread lines 100–101. *Temp'rate (temperate)* means "self-restrained." Which word in the same line is its antonym? Do other antonym pairs appear in these lines?

Th' expedition of my violent love
Outrun the pauser, reason. Here lay Duncan,
His silver skin laced with his golden blood,
105 And his gashed stabs looked like a breach in nature
For ruin's wasteful entrance; there the murderers,
Steeped in the colors of their trade, their daggers
Unmannerly breeched with gore. Who could refrain
That had a heart to love, and in that heart
110 Courage to make 's love known?

Lady Macbeth.   Help me hence, ho!

Macduff. Look to the lady.

Malcolm. [*Aside to* Donalbain] Why do we hold our tongues,
That most may claim this argument for ours?

Donalbain. [*Aside to* Malcolm]
What should be spoken here, where our fate,
Hid in an auger hole, may rush and seize us?
115 Let's away. Our tears are not yet brewed.

Malcolm. [*Aside to* Donalbain]
Nor our strong sorrow upon the foot of motion.

Banquo. Look to the lady.

[Lady Macbeth *is assisted to leave.*]

And when we have our naked frailties hid,
That suffer in exposure, let us meet
120 And question this most bloody piece of work
To know it further. Fears and scruples shake us.
In the great hand of God I stand, and thence
Against the undivulged pretense I fight
Of treasonous malice.

Macduff.   And so do I.

All.   So all.

125 **Macbeth.** Let's briefly put on manly readiness
And meet i' th' hall together.

All.   Well contented.

[*All but* Malcolm *and* Donalbain *exit.*]

Malcolm. What will you do? Let's not consort with them.
To show an unfelt sorrow is an office
Which the false man does easy. I'll to England.
130 **Donalbain.** To Ireland I. Our separated fortune
Shall keep us both the safer. Where we are,
There's daggers in men's smiles. The near in blood,
The nearer bloody.

102–103 He claims his emotions overpowered his reason, which would have made him pause to think before he killed Duncan's servants.

105 breach: a military term to describe a break in defenses, such as a hole in a castle wall.

110 Lady Macbeth faints.

111–112 Malcolm wonders why he and Donalbain are silent, since they have the most right to discuss the topic (**argument**) of their father's death.

118–121 Banquo suggests that they all meet to discuss the murder after they have dressed (**our naked frailties hid**), since people are shivering in their nightclothes (**suffer in exposure**).

121–124 Though shaken by fears and doubts (**scruples**), he will fight against the secret plans (**undivulged pretense**) of the traitor. *Do you think Banquo suspects Macbeth?*

127–129 Malcolm does not want to join (**consort with**) the others because one of them may have plotted the murder.

Behind the Curtain

The 1980 Old Vic Theatre production in London

The 2002 Albery Theatre production in London

The 2002 Shakespeare & Company production in Lenox, Massachusetts

COMMON CORE RL 7

There is no law that *Macbeth* must be staged in 11th-century Scotland for the sake of historical accuracy. Recent adaptations set the play in the late 20th century in such diverse places as a war-torn African state, the slums of Melbourne, Australia, and a Pennsylvania fast-food restaurant.

Because *Macbeth* is about the ruthless struggle for power, directors can adapt it surprisingly well to a variety of unexpected time periods and settings. Such innovative productions risk becoming gimmicks that may distract us from the play itself, but they also invite us to see it with fresh eyes. When an inventive adaptation works, it reminds us that Shakespeare's characters and themes remain relevant today.

Costumes reflect the production's time period and setting, as well as representing each character's personality or position. The production's costume designer carefully selects fabrics, colors, and details to create costumes for each character. In the top photograph, for example, the costume Macbeth wears tells us this is a traditional production of the play, set in medieval Scotland. Macbeth may parade publicly as king, but he has a bloody history to hide. His luxurious red robe may signify his power as king, but it is also the color of blood.

What time periods and settings do the two other photographs of Macbeth represent? What do these costumes suggest about his character? If you could stage *Macbeth* in any time or place, what would you choose? What costume would you have Macbeth wear to reflect his personality?

Malcolm.   This murderous shaft that's shot
Hath not yet lighted, and our safest way
135 Is to avoid the aim. Therefore to horse,
And let us not be dainty of leave-taking
But shift away. There's warrant in that theft
Which steals itself when there's no mercy left.

[*They exit.*]

Scene 4 *Outside Macbeth's castle.*
[*Enter* Ross *with an* Old Man.]

Old Man. Threescore and ten I can remember well,
Within the volume of which time I have seen
Hours dreadful and things strange, but this sore night
Hath trifled former knowings.

Ross.   Ha, good father,
5 Thou seest the heavens, as troubled with man's act,
Threaten his bloody stage. By th' clock 'tis day,
And yet dark night strangles the traveling lamp.
Is 't night's predominance or the day's shame
That darkness does the face of earth entomb
10 When living light should kiss it?

Old Man.   'Tis unnatural,
Even like the deed that's done. On Tuesday last
A falcon, tow'ring in her pride of place,
Was by a mousing owl hawked at and killed.

Ross. And Duncan's horses (a thing most strange and certain),
15 Beauteous and swift, the minions of their race,
Turned wild in nature, broke their stalls, flung out,
Contending 'gainst obedience, as they would
Make war with mankind.

Old Man.   'Tis said they eat each other.

Ross. They did so, to th' amazement of mine eyes
20 That looked upon 't.

[*Enter* Macduff.]

                    Here comes the good Macduff.—
How goes the world, sir, now?

Macduff.   Why, see you not?

Ross. Is 't known who did this more than bloody deed?

137–138 There's . . . left: There's good reason (**warrant**) to steal away from a situation that promises no mercy.

1–4 Nothing the old man has seen in 70 years (**threescore and ten**) has been as strange and terrible (**sore**) as this night. It has made other times seem trivial (**hath trifled**) by comparison.

6–10 By th' clock . . . kiss it: Though daytime, an unnatural darkness blots out the sun (**strangles the traveling lamp**).

12–13 The owl would never be expected to attack a high-flying (**tow'ring**) falcon, much less defeat one.

15 minions: best or favorites.

17 Contending 'gainst obedience: The well-trained horses rebelliously fought against all constraints.

Macduff. Those that Macbeth hath slain.

Ross.   Alas, the day,
What good could they pretend?

Macduff.   They were suborned.
25 Malcolm and Donalbain, the King's two sons,
Are stol'n away and fled, which puts upon them
Suspicion of the deed.

Ross.   'Gainst nature still!
Thriftless ambition, that will ravin up
Thine own lives' means. Then 'tis most like
30 The sovereignty will fall upon Macbeth.

Macduff. He is already named and gone to Scone
To be invested.

Ross.   Where is Duncan's body?

Macduff. Carried to Colmekill,
The sacred storehouse of his predecessors
35 And guardian of their bones.

Ross.   Will you to Scone?

Macduff. No, cousin, I'll to Fife.

Ross.   Well, I will thither.

Macduff. Well, may you see things well done there. Adieu,
Lest our old robes sit easier than our new.

Ross. Farewell, father.

40 **Old Man.** God's benison go with you and with those
That would make good of bad and friends of foes.

[*All exit.*]

24 **What . . . pretend:** Ross wonders what the servants could have hoped to achieve (**pretend**) by killing; **suborned:** hired or bribed.

27–29 He is horrified by the thought that the sons could act contrary to nature (**'gainst nature still**) because of wasteful (**thriftless**) ambition and greedily destroy (**ravin up**) their father, the source of their own life (**thine own lives' means**).

31–32 Macbeth went to the traditional site (**Scone**) where Scotland's kings were crowned.

40–41 The old man gives his blessing (**benison**) to Macduff and all those who would restore good and bring peace to the troubled land.

Comprehension

1. **Recall** Whom do Macbeth and his wife frame for Duncan's murder?

2. **Clarify** Why do Malcolm and Donalbain flee after their father's death?

3. **Summarize** How does the flight of Duncan's sons play into Macbeth's hands?

Text Analysis

4. **Identify Stage Directions** The stage directions in Act Two often contain instructions about **sound effects.** Find the important sound effects listed in the chart shown and note the action or events they signal. What purpose do you think these sound effects might play in the drama?

Sound Effects	Events They Signal
bell at the end of Scene 1	
knocking in Scene 2 and Scene 3	
alarum bell in Scene 3	

5. **Recognize Figurative Language** Reread Macbeth's dagger speech in Scene 1, lines 32–46. Note the use in these lines of **apostrophe,** a figure of speech in which an object is addressed directly. Why do you think Shakespeare chose to use apostrophe rather than have Macbeth describe a menacing dagger?

6. **Examine Shakespearean Drama** Review your notes about the actions of Macbeth and his wife in Act Two. What does each character do after Duncan's body is discovered? What do these actions reveal about them?

7. **Analyze Shakespearean Tragedy** Copy the following passages of **blank verse** from Act Two and mark the unstressed (˘) and stressed (´) syllables: Scene 1, line 32; Scene 2, lines 58–60; and Scene 3, lines 83–85. How does the rhythm of the lines help convey the meaning of each passage?

Text Criticism

8. **Author's Style** Shakespeare uses the drunken porter at the beginning of Scene 3 to provide **comic relief,** a humorous break from intense emotion. However, the porter's speech also ironically comments on Macbeth. Explain the connections that can be made between the porter's words and Macbeth's actions.

Can you ever be too **AMBITIOUS?**

Macbeth tries to hide his ambition and ignore its effects, but evidence of it seeps into the world around him. What are some of the symbols Shakespeare uses to represent the dangers of Macbeth's ambition?

COMMON CORE

RL 3 Analyze the impact of the author's choices regarding how to develop and relate elements of a drama. **RL 4** Analyze the impact of specific word choices on meaning and tone. **RL 5** Analyze how an author's choices concerning how to structure specific parts of a text contribute to its overall structure and meaning. **L 4b** Identify and correctly use patterns of word changes that indicate different meanings or parts of speech.

ACT 3

Scene 1 *Macbeth's palace at Forres.*

Banquo voices his suspicions of Macbeth but still hopes that the prophecy about his own children will prove true. Macbeth, as king, enters to request Banquo's presence at a state banquet. Banquo explains that he will be away during the day with his son, Fleance, but that they will return in time for the banquet. Alone, Macbeth expresses his fear of Banquo, because of the witches' promise that Banquo's sons will be kings. He persuades two murderers to kill Banquo and his son before the banquet.

[*Enter* Banquo.]

Banquo. Thou hast it now—King, Cawdor, Glamis, all
As the Weïrd Women promised, and I fear
Thou played'st most foully for 't. Yet it was said
It should not stand in thy posterity,
5 But that myself should be the root and father
Of many kings. If there come truth from them
(As upon thee, Macbeth, their speeches shine),
Why, by the verities on thee made good,
May they not be my oracles as well,
10 And set me up in hope? But hush, no more. **Ⓐ**

[*Sennet sounded. Enter* Macbeth *as King,* Lady Macbeth, Lennox, Ross,
Lords, *and* Attendants.]

Macbeth. Here's our chief guest.

Lady Macbeth.   If he had been forgotten,
It had been as a gap in our great feast
And all-thing unbecoming.

Macbeth. Tonight we hold a solemn supper, sir,
15 And I'll request your presence.

Banquo.   Let your Highness
Command upon me, to the which my duties
Are with a most indissoluble tie
Forever knit.

Macbeth.   Ride you this afternoon?

Banquo. Ay, my good lord.

20 **Macbeth.** We should have else desired your good advice
(Which still hath been both grave and prosperous)
In this day's council, but we'll take tomorrow.
Is 't far you ride?

Ⓐ SOLILOQUY
Reread lines 1–10, in which Banquo hopes the witches' predictions for him will come true as they have for Macbeth. Why might Banquo want to hide his thoughts from Macbeth?

[Stage Direction] **Sennet sounded:** A trumpet is sounded.

14–15 A king usually uses the royal pronoun *we.* Notice how Macbeth switches to *I,* keeping a personal tone with Banquo.

15–18 Banquo says he is duty bound to serve the king. *Do you think his tone is cold or warm here?*

21 grave and prosperous: thoughtful and profitable.

Banquo's murder

Banquo. As far, my lord, as will fill up the time
25 'Twixt this and supper. Go not my horse the better,
I must become a borrower of the night
For a dark hour or twain.

Macbeth.   Fail not our feast.

Banquo. My lord, I will not.

Macbeth. We hear our bloody cousins are bestowed
30 In England and in Ireland, not confessing
Their cruel parricide, filling their hearers
With strange invention. But of that tomorrow,
When therewithal we shall have cause of state
Craving us jointly. Hie you to horse. Adieu,
35 Till you return at night. Goes Fleance with you?

Banquo. Ay, my good lord. Our time does call upon 's.

Macbeth. I wish your horses swift and sure of foot,
And so I do commend you to their backs.
Farewell.

[Banquo *exits*.]

40 Let every man be master of his time
Till seven at night. To make society
The sweeter welcome, we will keep ourself
Till suppertime alone. While then, God be with you.

[Lords *and all but* Macbeth *and a* Servant *exit*.]

Sirrah, a word with you. Attend those men
45 Our pleasure?

Servant. They are, my lord, without the palace gate.

Macbeth. Bring them before us.

[Servant *exits*.]

                              To be thus is nothing,
But to be safely thus. Our fears in Banquo
Stick deep, and in his royalty of nature
50 Reigns that which would be feared. 'Tis much he dares,
And to that dauntless temper of his mind
He hath a wisdom that doth guide his valor
To act in safety. There is none but he
Whose being I do fear; and under him
55 My genius is rebuked, as it is said
Mark Antony's was by Caesar. He chid the sisters
When first they put the name of king upon me
And bade them speak to him. Then, prophet-like,
They hailed him father to a line of kings.

25–27 If his horse goes no faster than usual, he'll be back an hour or two (**twain**) after dark.

29 bloody cousins: murderous relatives (Malcolm and Donalbain); **bestowed:** settled.

32 strange invention: lies; stories they have invented. *What kinds of stories might they be telling?*

33–34 when . . . jointly: when matters of state will require the attention of us both.

40 be master of his time: do what he wants.

43 while: until.

44–45 sirrah: a term of address to an inferior; **Attend . . . pleasure:** Are they waiting for me?

47–48 To be thus . . . safely thus: To be king is worthless unless my position as king is safe.

51 dauntless temper: fearless temperament.

55–56 Banquo's mere presence forces back (**rebukes**) Macbeth's ruling spirit (**genius**). In ancient Rome, Octavius Caesar, who became emperor, had the same effect on his rival, Mark Antony.

60 Upon my head they placed a fruitless crown
   And put a barren scepter in my grip,
   Thence to be wrenched with an unlineal hand,
   No son of mine succeeding. If 't be so,
   For Banquo's issue have I filed my mind;
65 For them the gracious Duncan have I murdered,
   Put rancors in the vessel of my peace
   Only for them, and mine eternal jewel
   Given to the common enemy of man
   To make them kings, the seeds of Banquo kings.
70 Rather than so, come fate into the list,
   And champion me to th' utterance.—Who's there? **B**

[*Enter* Servant *and two* Murderers.]

[*To the* Servant] Now go to the door, and stay there till we call.
[Servant *exits.*]

Was it not yesterday we spoke together?
Murderers. It was, so please your Highness.

Macbeth.   Well then, now
75 Have you considered of my speeches? Know
   That it was he, in the times past, which held you
   So under fortune, which you thought had been
   Our innocent self. This I made good to you
   In our last conference, passed in probation with you
80 How you were borne in hand, how crossed, the instruments,
   Who wrought with them, and all things else that might
   To half a soul and to a notion crazed
   Say "Thus did Banquo."

First Murderer.   You made it known to us.

Macbeth. I did so, and went further, which is now
85 Our point of second meeting. Do you find
   Your patience so predominant in your nature
   That you can let this go? Are you so gospeled
   To pray for this good man and for his issue,
   Whose heavy hand hath bowed you to the grave
90 And beggared yours forever?

First Murderer.   We are men, my liege.

Macbeth. Ay, in the catalogue you go for men,
   As hounds and greyhounds, mongrels, spaniels, curs,
   Shoughs, water-rugs, and demi-wolves are clept
   All by the name of dogs. The valued file
95 Distinguishes the swift, the slow, the subtle,
   The housekeeper, the hunter, every one
   According to the gift which bounteous nature

60–69 They gave me a childless (**fruitless, barren**) crown and scepter, which will be taken away by someone outside my family (**unlineal**). It appears that I have committed murder, poisoned (**filed**) my mind, and destroyed my soul (**eternal jewel**) all for the benefit of Banquo's heirs.

B **TRAGEDY**
In lines 70–71, Macbeth challenges fate to enter the combat arena so that he can fight it to the death. What will be the likely result of Macbeth's efforts to fight fate?

75–83 Macbeth supposedly proved (**passed in probation**) Banquo's role, his deception (**how you were borne in hand**), his methods, and his allies. Even a half-wit (**half a soul**) or a crazed person would agree that Banquo caused their trouble.

87–90 He asks whether they are so influenced by the gospel's message of forgiveness (**so gospeled**) that they will pray for Banquo and his children despite his harshness, which will leave their own families beggars.

91–100 The true worth of a dog can be measured only by examining the record (**valued file**) of its special qualities (**particular addition**).

Hath in him closed; whereby he does receive
Particular addition, from the bill
100 That writes them all alike. And so of men.
Now, if you have a station in the file,
Not i' th' worst rank of manhood, say 't,
And I will put that business in your bosoms
Whose execution takes your enemy off,
105 Grapples you to the heart and love of us,
Who wear our health but sickly in his life,
Which in his death were perfect.

Second Murderer.   I am one, my liege,
Whom the vile blows and buffets of the world
Hath so incensed that I am reckless what
110 I do to spite the world.

First Murderer.   And I another
So weary with disasters, tugged with fortune,
That I would set my life on any chance,
To mend it or be rid on 't.

Macbeth.   Both of you
Know Banquo was your enemy.

Murderers.   True, my lord.

115 **Macbeth.** So is he mine, and in such bloody distance
That every minute of his being thrusts
Against my near'st of life. And though I could
With barefaced power sweep him from my sight
And bid my will avouch it, yet I must not,
120 For certain friends that are both his and mine,
Whose loves I may not drop, but wail his fall
Who I myself struck down. And thence it is
That I to your assistance do make love,
Masking the business from the common eye
125 For sundry weighty reasons.

Second Murderer.   We shall, my lord,
Perform what you command us.

First Murderer.   Though our lives—

Macbeth. Your spirits shine through you. Within this hour at most
I will advise you where to plant yourselves,
Acquaint you with the perfect spy o' th' time,
130 The moment on 't, for 't must be done tonight
And something from the palace; always thought
That I require a clearness. And with him
(To leave no rubs nor botches in the work)
Fleance, his son, that keeps him company,

103–107 Macbeth will give them a secret job (**business in your bosoms**) that will earn them his loyalty (**grapples you to the heart**) and love. Banquo's death will make this sick king healthy.

111 tugged with: knocked about by.

115–117 Banquo is near enough to draw blood, and like a menacing swordsman, his mere presence threatens (**thrusts against**) Macbeth's existence.

119 bid my will avouch it: justify it as my will.

Language Coach

Fixed Expressions What do you think the expression *the common eye* refers to in line 124? What is a similar **fixed**, or standard, **expression** in today's language?

127 Your spirits shine through you: Your courage is evident.

131–132 and something . . . clearness: The murder must be done away from the palace so that I remain blameless (**I require a clearness**).

135 Whose absence is no less material to me
Than is his father's, must embrace the fate
Of that dark hour. Resolve yourselves apart.
I'll come to you anon.

Murderers.   We are resolved, my lord.

Macbeth. I'll call upon you straight. Abide within.

[Murderers *exit*.]

140 It is concluded. Banquo, thy soul's flight,
If it find heaven, must find it out tonight.

[*He exits.*]

Scene 2 Macbeth's palace at Forres.
*Lady Macbeth and her husband discuss the troubled thoughts and bad
dreams they have had since Duncan's murder. However, they agree to hide
their dark emotions at the night's banquet. Lady Macbeth tries to comfort
the tormented Macbeth, but her words do no good. Instead, Macbeth hints
at some terrible event that will occur that night.*

[*Enter* Lady Macbeth *and a* Servant.]

Lady Macbeth. Is Banquo gone from court?

Servant. Ay, madam, but returns again tonight.

Lady Macbeth. Say to the King I would attend his leisure
For a few words.

Servant.   Madam, I will.

[*He exits.*]

Lady Macbeth.   Naught's had, all's spent,
5 Where our desire is got without content.
'Tis safer to be that which we destroy
Than by destruction dwell in doubtful joy. **C**

[*Enter* Macbeth.]

How now, my lord? Why do you keep alone,
Of sorriest fancies your companions making,
10 Using those thoughts which should indeed have died
With them they think on? Things without all remedy
Should be without regard. What's done is done.

Macbeth. We have scorched the snake, not killed it.
She'll close and be herself whilst our poor malice
15 Remains in danger of her former tooth.
But let the frame of things disjoint, both the worlds suffer,
Ere we will eat our meal in fear, and sleep
In the affliction of these terrible dreams
That shake us nightly. Better be with the dead,
20 Whom we, to gain our peace, have sent to peace,

135 absence: death. *Why is the death of Fleance so important?*

137 Resolve yourselves apart: Decide in private.

139 straight: soon.

4–7 Nothing (**naught**) has been gained; everything has been wasted (**spent**). It would be better to be dead like Duncan than to live in uncertain joy.

C SOLILOQUY
Compare Lady Macbeth's brief soliloquy in lines 4–7 with what she says to Macbeth in lines 8–12. Why do you think she wants to conceal her real feelings from her husband?

16–22 He would rather have the world fall apart (**the frame of things disjoint**) than be afflicted with such fears and nightmares. Death is preferable to life on the torture rack of mental anguish (**restless ecstasy**).

Than on the torture of the mind to lie
In restless ecstasy. Duncan is in his grave.
After life's fitful fever he sleeps well.
Treason has done his worst; nor steel nor poison,
25 Malice domestic, foreign levy, nothing
Can touch him further.

Lady Macbeth.   Come on, gentle my lord,
Sleek o'er your rugged looks. Be bright and jovial
Among your guests tonight.

Macbeth.   So shall I, love,
And so I pray be you. Let your remembrance
30 Apply to Banquo; present him eminence
Both with eye and tongue: unsafe the while that we
Must lave our honors in these flattering streams
And make our faces vizards to our hearts,
Disguising what they are.

Lady Macbeth.   You must leave this.

35 **Macbeth.** O, full of scorpions is my mind, dear wife!
Thou know'st that Banquo and his Fleance lives.

Lady Macbeth. But in them Nature's copy's not eterne.

Macbeth. There's comfort yet; they are assailable.
Then be thou jocund. Ere the bat hath flown
40 His cloistered flight, ere to black Hecate's summons
The shard-borne beetle with his drowsy hums
Hath rung night's yawning peal, there shall be done
A deed of dreadful note.

Lady Macbeth.   What's to be done?

Macbeth. Be innocent of the knowledge, dearest chuck,
45 Till thou applaud the deed.—Come, seeling night,
Scarf up the tender eye of pitiful day,
And with thy bloody and invisible hand
Cancel and tear to pieces that great bond
Which keeps me pale. Light thickens, and the crow
50 Makes wing to th' rooky wood.
Good things of day begin to droop and drowse,
Whiles night's black agents to their preys do rouse.—
Thou marvel'st at my words, but hold thee still.
Things bad begun make strong themselves by ill.
55 So prithee go with me.

[*They exit.*]

27 **sleek:** smooth.

30 **present him eminence:** pay special attention to him.

32 **lave ... streams:** wash (**lave**) our honor in streams of flattery—that is, falsify our feelings.
33 **vizards:** masks.

37 **in them ... not eterne:** Nature did not give them immortality.

39–43 **jocund:** cheerful; merry; **Ere the bat ... note:** Before nightfall, when the bats and beetles fly, something dreadful will happen.

44 **chuck:** chick (a term of affection).
45 **seeling:** blinding.

48 **great bond:** Banquo's life.

50 **rooky:** gloomy; also, filled with rooks, or crows.

54 Things brought about through evil need additional evil to make them strong.

Scene 3 *A park near the palace.*
The two murderers, joined by a third, ambush Banquo and Fleance,
killing Banquo. Fleance manages to escape in the darkness.

[*Enter three* Murderers.]

First Murderer. But who did bid thee join with us?

Third Murderer.   Macbeth.

Second Murderer. [*To the* First Murderer]
He needs not our mistrust, since he delivers
Our offices and what we have to do
To the direction just.

First Murderer.   Then stand with us.—
5 The west yet glimmers with some streaks of day.
Now spurs the lated traveler apace
To gain the timely inn, and near approaches
The subject of our watch.

Third Murderer.   Hark, I hear horses.

Banquo. [*Within*] Give us a light there, ho!

Second Murderer.   Then 'tis he. The rest
10 That are within the note of expectation
Already are i' th' court.

First Murderer.   His horses go about.

Third Murderer. Almost a mile; but he does usually
(So all men do) from hence to th' palace gate
Make it their walk.

[*Enter* Banquo *and* Fleance, *with a torch.*]

Second Murderer. A light, a light!

Third Murderer.   'Tis he.

15 **First Murderer.** Stand to 't.

Banquo. It will be rain tonight.

First Murderer.   Let it come down!

[*The three* Murderers *attack.*]

Banquo. O, treachery! Fly, good Fleance, fly, fly, fly!
Thou mayst revenge—O slave!

[*He dies.* Fleance *exits.*]

Third Murderer. Who did strike out the light?

First Murderer.   Was 't not the way?

20 **Third Murderer.** There's but one down. The son is fled.

Second Murderer. We have lost best half of our affair.

First Murderer. Well, let's away and say how much is done.

[*They exit.*]

2–4 He needs . . . just: Macbeth should not be distrustful, since he gave us the orders (**offices**) and we plan to follow his directions exactly.

6 lated: tardy; late.

9 Give us a light: Banquo, nearing the palace, calls for servants to bring a light.

9–11 Then 'tis . . . court: It must be Banquo, since all the other expected guests are already in the palace.

15 Stand to 't: Be prepared.

18 Thou mayst revenge: You might live to avenge my death.

19 Was 't not the way: Isn't that what we were supposed to do? Apparently, one of the murderers struck out the light, thus allowing Fleance to escape.

Scene 4 *The hall in the palace.*

As the banquet begins, one of the murderers reports on Banquo's death and Fleance's escape. Macbeth is disturbed by the news and even more shaken when he returns to the banquet table and sees the bloody ghost of Banquo. Only Macbeth sees the ghost, and his terrified reaction startles the guests. Lady Macbeth explains her husband's strange behavior as an illness from childhood that will soon pass. Once the ghost disappears, Macbeth calls for a toast to Banquo, whose ghost immediately reappears. Because Macbeth begins to rant and rave, Lady Macbeth dismisses the guests, fearful that her husband will reveal too much. Macbeth, alone with his wife, tells of his suspicions of Macduff, absent from the banquet. He also says he will visit the witches again and hints at bloody deeds yet to happen.

[*Banquet prepared. Enter* Macbeth, Lady Macbeth, Ross, Lennox, Lords, *and* Attendants.]

Macbeth. You know your own degrees; sit down. At first
And last, the hearty welcome.

1 your own degrees: where your rank entitles you to sit.

[*They sit.*]

Lords.   Thanks to your Majesty.

Macbeth. Ourself will mingle with society
And play the humble host.
5 Our hostess keeps her state, but in best time
We will require her welcome.

5 keeps her state: sits on her throne rather than at the banquet table.

Macbeth and one of the murderers

Lady Macbeth. Pronounce it for me, sir, to all our friends,
For my heart speaks they are welcome.

[*Enter* First Murderer *to the door.*]

Macbeth. See, they encounter thee with their hearts' thanks.
10 Both sides are even. Here I'll sit i' th' midst.
Be large in mirth. Anon we'll drink a measure
The table round. [*Approaching the* Murderer] There's blood upon thy
   face.

Murderer. 'Tis Banquo's then.

Macbeth. 'Tis better thee without than he within.
15 Is he dispatched?

Murderer. My lord, his throat is cut. That I did for him.

Macbeth. Thou art the best o' th' cutthroats,
Yet he's good that did the like for Fleance.
If thou didst it, thou art the nonpareil.

20 **Murderer.** Most royal sir, Fleance is 'scaped.

Macbeth. [*Aside*] Then comes my fit again. I had else been perfect,
Whole as the marble, founded as the rock,
As broad and general as the casing air.
But now I am cabined, cribbed, confined, bound in
25 To saucy doubts and fears.—But Banquo's safe? **D**

Murderer. Ay, my good lord. Safe in a ditch he bides,
With twenty trenchèd gashes on his head,
The least a death to nature.

Macbeth.   Thanks for that.
There the grown serpent lies. The worm that's fled
30 Hath nature that in time will venom breed,
No teeth for th' present. Get thee gone. Tomorrow
We'll hear ourselves again.

[Murderer *exits*.]

Lady Macbeth.   My royal lord,
You do not give the cheer. The feast is sold
That is not often vouched, while 'tis a-making,
35 'Tis given with welcome. To feed were best at home;
From thence, the sauce to meat is ceremony;
Meeting were bare without it.

[*Enter the Ghost of* Banquo, *and sits in* Macbeth's *place.*]

Macbeth. [*To* Lady Macbeth] Sweet remembrancer!—
Now, good digestion wait on appetite
And health on both!

Lennox.   May't please your Highness sit.

---

11 measure: toast. Macbeth keeps talking to his wife and guests as he casually edges toward the door to speak privately with the murderer.

15 dispatched: killed.

19 nonpareil: best.

23 casing: surrounding.

D ASIDE
Notice that Macbeth admits his fear in the aside in lines 21–25. What further actions might Macbeth take as a result of his fears?

29 worm: little serpent, that is, Fleance.

31 no teeth for th' present: too young to cause harm right now.

32 hear ourselves: talk together.

32–37 Macbeth must not forget his duties as host. A feast will be no different from a meal that one pays for unless the host gives his guests courteous attention (**ceremony**), the best part of any meal.

37 sweet remembrancer: a term of affection for his wife, who has reminded him of his duty.

40 Macbeth. Here had we now our country's honor roofed,
Were the graced person of our Banquo present,
Who may I rather challenge for unkindness
Than pity for mischance.

Ross. His absence, sir,
Lays blame upon his promise. Please 't your Highness
45 To grace us with your royal company?

Macbeth. The table's full.

Lennox. Here is a place reserved, sir.

Macbeth. Where?

Lennox. Here, my good lord. What is 't that moves your Highness?

Macbeth. Which of you have done this?

Lords. What, my good lord?

50 **Macbeth.** [*To the* Ghost] Thou canst not say I did it. Never shake
Thy gory locks at me.

Ross. Gentlemen, rise. His Highness is not well.

Lady Macbeth. Sit, worthy friends. My lord is often thus
And hath been from his youth. Pray you, keep seat.
55 The fit is momentary; upon a thought
He will again be well. If much you note him
You shall offend him and extend his passion.
Feed and regard him not. [*Drawing* Macbeth *aside*] Are you a man? **E**

Macbeth. Ay, and a bold one, that dare look on that
60 Which might appall the devil.

Lady Macbeth. O, proper stuff!
This is the very painting of your fear.
This is the air-drawn dagger which you said
Led you to Duncan. O, these flaws and starts,
Impostors to true fear, would well become
65 A woman's story at a winter's fire,
Authorized by her grandam. Shame itself!
Why do you make such faces? When all's done,
You look but on a stool.

Macbeth. Prithee see there. Behold, look! [*To the* Ghost] Lo, how say you?
70 Why, what care I? If thou canst nod, speak too.—
If charnel houses and our graves must send
Those that we bury back, our monuments
Shall be the maws of kites.

[Ghost *exits.*]

Lady Macbeth. What, quite unmanned in folly?

Macbeth. If I stand here, I saw him.

40–43 The best people of Scotland would all be under Macbeth's roof if Banquo were present too. He hopes Banquo's absence is due to rudeness rather than to some accident (**mischance**).

46 Macbeth finally notices that Banquo's ghost is present and sitting in the king's chair.

E DRAMATIC IRONY
In lines 53–58, Lady Macbeth tells her guests to pay no attention to her husband's fit. Why is the situation ironic?

60–68 She dismisses his hallucination as utter nonsense (**proper stuff**). His outbursts (**flaws and starts**) are the product of imaginary fears (**impostors to true fear**) and are unmanly, the kind of behavior described in a woman's story.

71–73 If burial vaults (**charnel houses**) give back the dead, then we may as well throw our bodies to the birds (**kites**), whose stomachs (**maws**) will become our tombs (**monuments**).

Lady Macbeth.   Fie, for shame!

75 **Macbeth.** Blood hath been shed ere now, i' th' olden time,
Ere humane statute purged the gentle weal;
Ay, and since too, murders have been performed
Too terrible for the ear. The time has been
That, when the brains were out, the man would die,
80 And there an end. But now they rise again
With twenty mortal murders on their crowns
And push us from our stools. This is more strange
Than such a murder is.

Lady Macbeth.   My worthy lord,
Your noble friends do lack you.

Macbeth.   I do forget.—
85 Do not muse at me, my most worthy friends.
I have a strange infirmity, which is nothing
To those that know me. Come, love and health to all.
Then I'll sit down.—Give me some wine. Fill full.

[*Enter* Ghost.]

I drink to the general joy o' th' whole table
90 And to our dear friend Banquo, whom we miss.
Would he were here! To all and him we thirst, **❶**
And all to all.

Lords.   Our duties, and the pledge.

[*They raise their drinking cups.*]

Macbeth. [*To the* Ghost] Avaunt, and quit my sight! Let the earth hide
   thee.
Thy bones are marrowless; thy blood is cold;
95 Thou hast no speculation in those eyes
Which thou dost glare with.

Lady Macbeth.   Think of this, good peers,
But as a thing of custom. 'Tis no other;
Only it spoils the pleasure of the time.

Macbeth. [*To the* Ghost] What man dare, I dare.
100 Approach thou like the rugged Russian bear,
The armed rhinoceros, or th' Hyrcan tiger;
Take any shape but that, and my firm nerves
Shall never tremble. Or be alive again
And dare me to the desert with thy sword.
105 If trembling I inhabit then, protest me
The baby of a girl. Hence, horrible shadow!
Unreal mock'ry, hence!

75–78 Macbeth desperately tries to justify his murder of Banquo. Murder has been common from ancient times to the present, though laws (**humane statute**) have tried to rid civilized society (**gentle weal**) of violence.

85 muse: wonder.

❶ DRAMATIC IRONY
Recognize the irony of Macbeth's remark about Banquo in line 91: "Would he were here!" How do you think an actor playing Macbeth should say this line?

93–96 avaunt: go away. Macbeth sees Banquo again. He tells Banquo that he is only a ghost, with unreal bones, cold blood, and no consciousness (**speculation**).

99–104 Macbeth would be willing to face Banquo in any other form, even his living self.

105–106 If trembling . . . girl: If I still tremble, call me a girl's doll.

[Ghost *exits*.]

                            Why, so, being gone,
I am a man again.—Pray you sit still.

Lady Macbeth. You have displaced the mirth, broke the good meeting
110 With most admired disorder.

    Macbeth.   Can such things be
And overcome us like a summer's cloud,
Without our special wonder? You make me strange
Even to the disposition that I owe,
When now I think you can behold such sights
115 And keep the natural ruby of your cheeks
When mine is blanched with fear.

    Ross.   What sights, my lord?

Lady Macbeth. I pray you speak not. He grows worse and worse.
Question enrages him. At once, good night.
Stand not upon the order of your going,
120 But go at once.

    Lennox.   Good night, and better health
Attend his Majesty.

    Lady Macbeth.   A kind good night to all.

[Lords *and all but* Macbeth *and* Lady Macbeth *exit*.]

Macbeth. It will have blood, they say; blood will have blood.
Stones have been known to move, and trees to speak;
Augurs and understood relations have
125 By maggot pies and choughs and rooks brought forth
The secret'st man of blood.—What is the night?

Lady Macbeth. Almost at odds with morning, which is which.

Macbeth. How say'st thou that Macduff denies his person
At our great bidding?

    Lady Macbeth.   Did you send to him, sir?

130 **Macbeth.** I hear it by the way; but I will send.
There's not a one of them but in his house
I keep a servant fee'd. I will tomorrow
(And betimes I will) to the Weïrd Sisters.
More shall they speak, for now I am bent to know
135 By the worst means the worst. For mine own good,
All causes shall give way. I am in blood
Stepped in so far that, should I wade no more,
Returning were as tedious as go o'er.
Strange things I have in head, that will to hand,
140 Which must be acted ere they may be scanned.

110 admired: astonishing.

110–116 Macbeth is bewildered by his wife's calm. Her reaction makes him seem a stranger to himself (**strange even to the disposition that I owe**): she seems to be the one with all the courage, since he is white (**blanched**) with fear.

119 Stand . . . going: Don't worry about the proper formalities of leaving.

122–126 Macbeth fears that Banquo's murder (**it**) will be revenged by his own murder. Stones, trees, or talking birds (**maggot pies and choughs and rooks**) may reveal the hidden knowledge (**augurs**) of his guilt.

128–129 How say'st . . . bidding: What do you think of Macduff's refusal to come? *Why do you think Macbeth is suddenly so concerned about Macduff?*

131–132 Macbeth has paid (**fee'd**) household servants to spy on every noble, including Macduff.

133 betimes: early.

134 bent: determined.

135–140 Macbeth will do anything to protect himself. He has stepped so far into a river of blood that it would make no sense to turn back. He will act upon his unnatural (**strange**) thoughts without having examined (**scanned**) them.

Promotion

Flyers and posters are among the materials used for **promotion,** in order to attract an audience for a play. What ideas do each of these posters for *Macbeth* communicate about the play? Which poster grabs your attention most, and why?

1985 poster for Verdi's opera *Macbeth*

Dalhousie University's 2005 production in Halifax, Nova Scotia

BY THE PRICKING
OF MY THUMBS
SOMETHING WICKED
THIS WAY COMES...

WILLIAM SHAKESPEARE'S
MACBETH
DIRECTED BY MILES POTTER

NOVEMBER 29 - DECEMBER 2, 8:00 PM
DECEMBER 3, 2:00 PM & 8:00 PM
SIR JAMES DUNN THEATRE
DALHOUSIE ARTS CENTRE
BOX OFFICE: 494.3820
TICKETS: $12/$6 STUDENT/SENIOR

DALHOUSIE
UNIVERSITY
Inspiring Minds

the large group presents:
michael hurst as william shakespeare's

MACBETH

The Large Group's 2004 production in Auckland, New Zealand

Lady Macbeth. You lack the season of all natures, sleep.

Macbeth. Come, we'll to sleep. My strange and self-abuse
Is the initiate fear that wants hard use.
We are yet but young in deed.

[*They exit.*]

Scene 5 *A heath.*

The goddess of witchcraft, Hecate, scolds the three witches for dealing independently with Macbeth. She outlines their next meeting with him, planning to cause his downfall by making him overconfident. (Experts believe this scene was not written by Shakespeare but rather was added later.)

[*Thunder. Enter the three* Witches, *meeting* Hecate.]

First Witch. Why, how now, Hecate? You look angerly.

Hecate. Have I not reason, beldams as you are, **G**
Saucy and overbold, how did you dare
To trade and traffic with Macbeth
5   In riddles and affairs of death,
And I, the mistress of your charms,
The close contriver of all harms,
Was never called to bear my part
Or show the glory of our art?
10 And which is worse, all you have done
Hath been but for a wayward son,
Spiteful and wrathful, who, as others do,
Loves for his own ends, not for you.
But make amends now. Get you gone,
15 And at the pit of Acheron
Meet me i' th' morning. Thither he
Will come to know his destiny.
Your vessels and your spells provide,
Your charms and everything beside.
20 I am for th' air. This night I'll spend
Unto a dismal and a fatal end.
Great business must be wrought ere noon.
Upon the corner of the moon
There hangs a vap'rous drop profound.
25 I'll catch it ere it come to ground,
And that, distilled by magic sleights,
Shall raise such artificial sprites
As by the strength of their illusion
Shall draw him on to his confusion.
30 He shall spurn fate, scorn death, and bear

141 season: preservative.

142–144 His vision of the ghost (**strange and self-abuse**) is only the result of a beginner's fear (**initiate fear**), to be cured with practice (**hard use**).

2 beldams: hags.

G BLANK VERSE
Read aloud a few lines from Hecate's speech (lines 2–33). Note that they are not written in blank verse. Why might the **rhyme** and **rhythm** of these lines be appropriate for a witch?

13 loves . . . you: cares only about his own goals, not about you.

15 Acheron: a river in hell, according to Greek mythology. Hecate plans to hold their meeting in a hellish place.

20–21 This . . . end: Tonight I'm working for a disastrous (**dismal**) and fatal end for Macbeth.

23–29 Hecate will obtain a magical drop from the moon, treat it with secret art, and so create spirits (**artificial sprites**) that will lead Macbeth to his destruction (**confusion**).

His hopes 'bove wisdom, grace, and fear.
And you all know, security
Is mortals' chiefest enemy. **H**

[*Music and a song*]

Hark! I am called. My little spirit, see,
35 Sits in a foggy cloud and stays for me.

[Hecate *exits.*]

[*Sing within "Come away, come away," etc.*]

First Witch. Come, let's make haste. She'll soon be back again.

[*They exit.*]

Scene 6 *The palace at Forres.*

Lennox and another Scottish lord review the events surrounding the murders of Duncan and Banquo, indirectly suggesting that Macbeth is both a murderer and a tyrant. It is reported that Macduff has gone to England, where Duncan's son Malcolm is staying with King Edward and raising an army to regain the Scottish throne. Macbeth, angered by Macduff's refusal to see him, is also preparing for war.

[*Enter* Lennox *and another* Lord.]

Lennox. My former speeches have but hit your thoughts,
Which can interpret farther. Only I say
Things have been strangely borne. The gracious Duncan
Was pitied of Macbeth; marry, he was dead.
5 And the right valiant Banquo walked too late,
Whom you may say, if 't please you, Fleance killed,
For Fleance fled. Men must not walk too late.
Who cannot want the thought how monstrous
It was for Malcolm and for Donalbain
10 To kill their gracious father? Damnèd fact,
How it did grieve Macbeth! Did he not straight
In pious rage the two delinquents tear
That were the slaves of drink and thralls of sleep?
Was not that nobly done? Ay, and wisely, too,
15 For 'twould have angered any heart alive
To hear the men deny 't. So that I say
He has borne all things well. And I do think
That had he Duncan's sons under his key
(As, an 't please heaven, he shall not) they should find
20 What 'twere to kill a father. So should Fleance.
But peace. For from broad words, and 'cause he failed
His presence at the tyrant's feast, I hear
Macduff lives in disgrace. Sir, can you tell
Where he bestows himself?

H TRAGEDY
Reread lines 23–33. How does Hecate reveal herself to be Macbeth's **antagonist**?

34–35 Like the other witches, Hecate has a demon helper (**my little spirit**). At the end of her speech, she is raised by pulley to "the heavens" of the stage.

1–3 Lennox and the other lord have shared suspicions of Macbeth.

6–7 Lennox is being ironic when he says that fleeing the scene of the crime must make Fleance guilty of his father's murder.

8–10 He says that everyone agrees on the horror of Duncan's murder by his sons. But Lennox has been consistently ironic, claiming to believe in what is obviously false. His words indirectly blame Macbeth.

12 pious: holy.

15–16 Again, he is being ironic. If the servants had lived, Macbeth might have been discovered.

21 from broad words: because of his frank talk.

24 bestows himself: is staying.

Lord.   The son of Duncan

25 (From whom this tyrant holds the due of birth)
Lives in the English court and is received
Of the most pious Edward with such grace
That the malevolence of fortune nothing
Takes from his high respect. Thither Macduff

30 Is gone to pray the holy king upon his aid
To wake Northumberland and warlike Siward
That, by the help of these (with Him above
To ratify the work), we may again
Give to our tables meat, sleep to our nights,

35 Free from our feasts and banquets bloody knives,
Do faithful homage, and receive free honors,
All which we pine for now. And this report
Hath so exasperate the King that he
Prepares for some attempt of war.

Lennox.   Sent he to Macduff?

40 **Lord.** He did, and with an absolute "Sir, not I,"
The cloudy messenger turns me his back
And hums, as who should say, "You'll rue the time
That clogs me with this answer."

Lennox.   And that well might

Advise him to a caution t' hold what distance

45 His wisdom can provide. Some holy angel
Fly to the court of England and unfold
His message ere he come, that a swift blessing
May soon return to this our suffering country
Under a hand accursed.

Lord.   I'll send my prayers with him.

[*They exit.*]

25 Macbeth keeps Malcolm from his birthright. As the eldest son of Duncan, Malcolm should be king.

27 Edward: Edward the Confessor, king of England from 1042 to 1066, a man known for his virtue and religion.

28–29 that . . . respect: Though Malcolm suffers from bad fortune (the loss of the throne), he is respectfully treated by Edward.

29–37 Macduff wants the king to persuade the people of Northumberland and their earl, Siward, to join Malcolm's cause.

40–43 The messenger, fearing Macbeth's anger, was unhappy (**cloudy**) with Macduff's refusal to cooperate. Because Macduff burdens (**clogs**) him with bad news, he will not hurry back.

Language Coach

Figures of Speech Shakespeare often uses a **figure of speech** in which a part stands for the whole. Reread lines 45–49. Who or what does *the hand accursed* (or "wicked hand") stand for?

Comprehension

1. **Recall** Whom does Macbeth command the two murderers to kill?

2. **Clarify** Why does Macbeth behave so strangely at the banquet?

3. **Summarize** In Scene 6, what does Lennox suggest about Macbeth?

Text Analysis

4. **Examine Shakespearean Drama** Review the notes you recorded on Macbeth and Lady Macbeth in Act Three. What do their actions reveal about how their relationship has changed since the death of Duncan? Be specific.

5. **Interpret Character Motives** Reread Scene 1, lines 47–56. Why does Macbeth fear Banquo and feel threatened by his "being"? Support your answer.

6. **Compare Actions** Compare and contrast Duncan's murder in Act Two with that of Banquo in Act Three. What does Banquo's murder suggest about how Macbeth has been affected by his first crime?

7. **Analyze Shakespearean Tragedy** Skim Act Three for remarks that create **dramatic irony.** In a chart like the one shown, explain why the remarks are ironic by jotting down what characters think or say and what the audience knows. How does the dramatic irony enhance your enjoyment of the play?

Scene, Lines	What Characters Think or Say	What Audience Knows

8. **Analyze Theme** In which moments of Act Three is manhood equated with a lack of fear? How valid is this view of manhood?

Text Criticism

9. **Critical Interpretations** In Scene 1, Macbeth meets with two murderers, but three murderers take part in Banquo's murder in Scene 3. Some people have speculated that the third murderer may be Macbeth himself. Is this plausible? Would that help explain his behavior at the banquet? Support your answer.

Can you ever be too AMBITIOUS?

Many characters pose a threat to Macbeth. Which characters in the play do you believe pose the greatest threat to him? Why?

COMMON CORE

RL 3 Analyze the impact of the author's choices regarding how to develop and relate elements of a drama. **RL 4** Analyze the impact of specific word choices on meaning and tone. **RL 5** Analyze how an author's choices concerning how to structure specific parts of a text contribute to its overall structure and meaning.

ACT 4

Scene 1 *A cave. In the middle, a boiling cauldron.*

The three witches prepare a potion in a boiling kettle. When Macbeth arrives, demanding to know his future, the witches raise three apparitions. The first, an armed (helmeted) head, tells him to beware of Macduff. Next, a bloody child assures Macbeth that he will never be harmed by anyone born of woman. The third apparition tells him that he will never be defeated until the trees of Birnam Wood move toward his castle at Dunsinane. Macbeth, now confident of his future, asks about Banquo's son. His confidence fades when the witches show him a line of kings who all resemble Banquo, suggesting that Banquo's sons will indeed be kings. Macbeth curses the witches as they disappear.

Lennox enters the cave and tells Macbeth that Macduff has gone to the English court. Hearing this, Macbeth swears to kill Macduff's family.

[*Thunder. Enter the three* Witches.]

First Witch. Thrice the brinded cat hath mewed.

Second Witch. Thrice, and once the hedge-pig whined.

Third Witch. Harpier cries "'Tis time, 'tis time!"

First Witch. Round about the cauldron go;
5 In the poisoned entrails throw.
Toad, that under cold stone
Days and nights has thirty-one
Sweltered venom sleeping got,
Boil thou first i' th' charmed pot.

[*The* Witches *circle the cauldron.*]

10 **All.** Double, double toil and trouble;
Fire burn, and cauldron bubble.

Second Witch. Fillet of a fenny snake
In the cauldron boil and bake.
Eye of newt and toe of frog,
15 Wool of bat and tongue of dog,
Adder's fork and blindworm's sting,
Lizard's leg and howlet's wing,
For a charm of powerful trouble,
Like a hell-broth boil and bubble.

20 **All.** Double, double toil and trouble;
Fire burn, and cauldron bubble.

Third Witch. Scale of dragon, tooth of wolf,
Witch's mummy, maw and gulf
Of the ravined salt-sea shark,

1–3 Magical signals and the call of the third witch's attending demon (**harpier**) tell the witches to begin.

4–34 The witches are stirring up a magical stew to bring trouble to humanity. Their recipe includes intestines (**entrails, chaudron**), a slice (**fillet**) of snake, eye of salamander (**newt**), snake tongue (**adder's fork**), a lizard (**blindworm**), a baby owl's (**howlet's**) wing, a shark's stomach and gullet (**maw and gulf**), the finger of a baby strangled by a prostitute (**drab**), and other gruesome ingredients. They stir their brew until it is thick and slimy (**slab**).

Macbeth and the three witches

25 Root of hemlock digged i' th' dark,
   Liver of blaspheming Jew,
   Gall of goat and slips of yew
   Slivered in the moon's eclipse,
   Nose of Turk and Tartar's lips,
30 Finger of birth-strangled babe
   Ditch-delivered by a drab,
   Make the gruel thick and slab.
   Add thereto a tiger's chaudron
   For th' ingredience of our cauldron.

35 **All.** Double, double toil and trouble;
   Fire burn, and cauldron bubble.

   Second Witch. Cool it with a baboon's blood.
   Then the charm is firm and good.

   [*Enter* Hecate *and the other three* Witches.]

   Hecate. O, well done! I commend your pains,
40 And everyone shall share i' th' gains.
   And now about the cauldron sing
   Like elves and fairies in a ring,
   Enchanting all that you put in.

   [*Music and a song: "Black Spirits," etc.* Hecate *exits.*]

   Second Witch. By the pricking of my thumbs,
45 Something wicked this way comes.
   Open, locks,
   Whoever knocks.

   [*Enter* Macbeth.]

   Macbeth. How now, you secret, black, and midnight hags?
   What is 't you do?

   All.   A deed without a name.

50 **Macbeth.** I conjure you by that which you profess
   (Howe'er you come to know it), answer me.
   Though you untie the winds and let them fight
   Against the churches, though the yeasty waves
   Confound and swallow navigation up,
55 Though bladed corn be lodged and trees blown down,
   Though castles topple on their warders' heads,
   Though palaces and pyramids do slope
   Their heads to their foundations, though the treasure
   Of nature's germens tumble all together
60 Even till destruction sicken, answer me
   To what I ask you.

Language Coach

Word Definitions Shakespeare (like other poets) invents many compound words by joining a noun and adjective with a hyphen. Reread lines 30–31. *Birth-strangled* is shorthand for "strangled at birth." Why do you think Shakespeare uses this short version? What does *ditch-delivered* mean?

[Stage Direction] **Enter Hecate . . . :** Most experts believe that the entrance of Hecate and three more witches was not written by Shakespeare. The characters were probably added later to expand the role of the witches, who were favorites of the audience.

50–61 Macbeth calls upon (**conjure**) the witches in the name of their dark magic (**that which you profess**). Though they unleash winds to topple churches and make foaming (**yeasty**) waves to destroy (**confound**) ships, though they flatten wheat (**corn**) fields, destroy buildings, and reduce nature's order to chaos by mixing all seeds (**germens**) together, he demands an answer to his question.

First Witch. Speak.

Second Witch.   Demand.

Third Witch.   We'll answer.

First Witch. Say if th' hadst rather hear it from our mouths
Or from our masters'.

Macbeth.   Call 'em. Let me see 'em.

First Witch. Pour in sow's blood that hath eaten
65 Her nine farrow; grease that's sweaten
From the murderers' gibbet throw
Into the flame.

All.   Come high or low;
Thyself and office deftly show.

[*Thunder.* First Apparition, *an Armed Head.*]

Macbeth. Tell me, thou unknown power—

First Witch.   He knows thy thought.
70 Hear his speech but say thou naught.

First Apparition. Macbeth! Macbeth! Macbeth! Beware Macduff!
Beware the Thane of Fife! Dismiss me. Enough.

[*He descends.*]

Macbeth. Whate'er thou art, for thy good caution, thanks.
Thou hast harped my fear aright. But one word more—

75 **First Witch.** He will not be commanded. Here's another
More potent than the first.

[*Thunder.* Second Apparition, *a Bloody Child.*]

Second Apparition. Macbeth! Macbeth! Macbeth!—

Macbeth. Had I three ears, I'd hear thee.

Second Apparition. Be bloody, bold, and resolute. Laugh to scorn
80 The power of man, for none of woman born
Shall harm Macbeth. **Ⓐ**

[*He descends.*]

Macbeth. Then live, Macduff; what need I fear of thee?
But yet I'll make assurance double sure
And take a bond of fate. Thou shalt not live,
85 That I may tell pale-hearted fear it lies,
And sleep in spite of thunder.

[*Thunder.* Third Apparition, *a Child Crowned, with a tree in his hand.*]
            What is this
That rises like the issue of a king
And wears upon his baby brow the round
And top of sovereignty?

63 masters: the demons whom the witches serve.

65–66 farrow: newborn pigs; **grease . . . gibbet:** grease from a gallows where murderers were hung.

[Stage Direction] Each of the three apparitions holds a clue to Macbeth's future. *What do you think is suggested by the armed head?*

74 harped: guessed. The apparition has confirmed Macbeth's fears of Macduff.

Ⓐ **FORESHADOWING**
Reread lines 79–81. Note the prophecy's apparent promise of safety. What effect do you think the prophecy will have on Macbeth?

84 The murder of Macduff will give Macbeth a guarantee (**bond**) of his fate and put his fears to rest.

87 issue: child.
88–89 the round and top: the crown.

All.   Listen, but speak not to 't.

90 **Third Apparition.** Be lion-mettled, proud, and take no care
Who chafes, who frets, or where conspirers are.
Macbeth shall never vanquished be until
Great Birnam Wood to high Dunsinane Hill
Shall come against him.   [*He descends.*]

Macbeth.   That will never be.
95 Who can impress the forest, bid the tree
Unfix his earthbound root? Sweet bodements, good!
Rebellious dead, rise never till the wood
Of Birnam rise, and our high-placed Macbeth
Shall live the lease of nature, pay his breath
100 To time and mortal custom. Yet my heart
Throbs to know one thing. Tell me, if your art
Can tell so much: shall Banquo's issue ever
Reign in this kingdom?

All.   Seek to know no more.

Macbeth. I will be satisfied. Deny me this,
105 And an eternal curse fall on you! Let me know!

                    [*Cauldron sinks. Hautboys.*]

Why sinks that cauldron? And what noise is this?

First Witch. Show.

Second Witch. Show.

Third Witch. Show.

110 **All.** Show his eyes, and grieve his heart.
Come like shadows; so depart.

[*A show of eight kings, the eighth king with a glass in his hand, and*
Banquo *last.*]

Macbeth. Thou art too like the spirit of Banquo. Down!
Thy crown does sear mine eyeballs. And thy hair,
Thou other gold-bound brow, is like the first.
115 A third is like the former.—Filthy hags,
Why do you show me this?—A fourth? Start, eyes!
What, will the line stretch out to th' crack of doom?
Another yet? A seventh? I'll see no more.
And yet the eighth appears who bears a glass
120 Which shows me many more, and some I see
That twofold balls and treble scepters carry.
Horrible sight! Now I see 'tis true,
For the blood-boltered Banquo smiles upon me
And points at them for his.

                    [*The* Apparitions *disappear.*]
                    What, is this so?

90–94 The third apparition tells Macbeth to take courage. He cannot be defeated unless Birnam Wood travels the 12-mile distance to Dunsinane Hill, where his castle is located.

95 impress: force into service.
96 bodements: prophecies.
97–100 Macbeth boasts that he will never again be troubled by ghosts (**rebellious dead**) and that he will live out his expected life span (**lease of nature**). He believes he will die (**pay his breath**) by natural causes (**mortal custom**).

106 The cauldron is sinking from sight to make room for the next apparition.

[Stage Direction] **A show . . . :** Macbeth next sees a procession (**show**) of eight kings, the last carrying a mirror (**glass**). According to legend, Fleance escaped to England, where he founded the Stuart family, to which King James belonged.

112–124 Macbeth is outraged that all eight kings in the procession look like Banquo. The mirror held by the last one shows a future with many more Banquo look-alikes as kings. The twofold balls and treble scepters pictured in the mirror foretell the union of Scotland and England in 1603, the year that James became king of both realms. Banquo, his hair matted (**boltered**) with blood, claims all the kings as his descendants. *What do you think is going through Macbeth's mind?*

Behind the Curtain

COMMON CORE RL 7

Blocking

The placement and movement of actors on the stage is called **blocking**. These photos from different productions of *Macbeth* show Act Four, Scene 1, in which Macbeth sees the apparitions. What different ideas about the scene do you get from the different positions of the actors? Which arrangement has the most visual impact? Explain.

The Royal Shakespeare Company's 1976 production

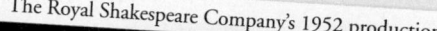

The Royal Shakespeare Company's 1952 production

The 2003 production by Utah's Pioneer Theatre Company

125 **First Witch.** Ay, sir, all this is so. But why
Stands Macbeth thus amazedly?
Come, sisters, cheer we up his sprites
And show the best of our delights.
I'll charm the air to give a sound
130 While you perform your antic round,
That this great king may kindly say
Our duties did his welcome pay.

[*Music. The* Witches *dance and vanish.*]

Macbeth. Where are they? Gone? Let this pernicious hour
Stand aye accursèd in the calendar!—
135 Come in, without there.

[*Enter* Lennox.]

Lennox.   What's your Grace's will?

Macbeth. Saw you the Weïrd Sisters?

Lennox.   No, my lord.

Macbeth. Came they not by you?

Lennox.   No, indeed, my lord.

Macbeth. Infected be the air whereon they ride,
And damned all those that trust them! I did hear
140 The galloping of horse. Who was 't came by?

Lennox. 'Tis two or three, my lord, that bring you word
Macduff is fled to England.

Macbeth.   Fled to England?

Lennox. Ay, my good lord.

Macbeth. [*Aside*] Time, thou anticipat'st my dread exploits.
145 The flighty purpose never is o'ertook
Unless the deed go with it. From this moment
The very firstlings of my heart shall be
The firstlings of my hand. And even now,
To crown my thoughts with acts, be it thought and done:
150 The castle of Macduff I will surprise,
Seize upon Fife, give to th' edge o' th' sword
His wife, his babes, and all unfortunate souls
That trace him in his line. No boasting like a fool;
This deed I'll do before this purpose cool.
155 But no more sights!—Where are these gentlemen?
Come bring me where they are.

[*They exit.*]

133 pernicious: evil.

134 aye: always.

135 After the witches vanish, Macbeth hears noises outside the cave and calls out.

144–156 Frustrated in his desire to kill Macduff, Macbeth blames his own hesitation, which gave his enemy time to flee. He concludes that one's plans (**flighty purpose**) are never achieved (**o'ertook**) unless carried out at once. From now on, Macbeth promises, he will act immediately on his impulses (**firstlings of my heart**) and complete (**crown**) his thoughts with acts. He will surprise Macduff's castle at Fife and kill his wife and children. *Why does Macbeth decide to kill Macduff's family?*

Scene 2 *Macduff's castle at Fife.*

Ross visits Lady Macduff to assure her of her husband's wisdom and courage. Lady Macduff cannot be comforted, believing that he left out of fear. After Ross leaves she tells her son, who is still loyal to his father, that Macduff was a traitor and is now dead. A messenger warns them to flee but is too late. Murderers sent by Macbeth burst in, killing both wife and son.

[*Enter* Lady Macduff, *her* Son, *and* Ross.]

Lady Macduff. What had he done to make him fly the land?

Ross. You must have patience, madam.

Lady Macduff.   He had none.
His flight was madness. When our actions do not,
Our fears do make us traitors.

Ross.   You know not
5   Whether it was his wisdom or his fear.

Lady Macduff. Wisdom? To leave his wife, to leave his babes,
His mansion and his titles in a place
From whence himself does fly? He loves us not;
He wants the natural touch; for the poor wren
10 (The most diminutive of birds) will fight,
Her young ones in her nest, against the owl.
All is the fear, and nothing is the love,
As little is the wisdom, where the flight
So runs against all reason.

Ross.   My dearest coz,
15 I pray you school yourself. But for your husband,
He is noble, wise, judicious, and best knows
The fits o' th' season. I dare not speak much further;
But cruel are the times when we are traitors
And do not know ourselves; when we hold rumor
20 From what we fear, yet know not what we fear,
But float upon a wild and violent sea
Each way and move—I take my leave of you.
Shall not be long but I'll be here again.
Things at the worst will cease or else climb upward
25 To what they were before.—My pretty cousin,
Blessing upon you.

Lady Macduff. Fathered he is, and yet he's fatherless.

Ross. I am so much a fool, should I stay longer
It would be my disgrace and your discomfort.
30 I take my leave at once.   [Ross *exits.*]

Lady Macduff.   Sirrah, your father's dead.
And what will you do now? How will you live?

3–4 Macduff's wife is worried that others will think her husband a traitor because his fears made him flee the country (**our fears do make us traitors**), though he was guilty of no wrongdoing.

9 wants the natural touch: lacks the instinct to protect his family.

12–14 Lady Macduff believes her husband is motivated entirely by fear, not by love of his family. His hasty flight is contrary to reason.

14 coz: cousin (a term used for any close relation).

15 school: control; **for:** as for.

17 fits o' th' season: disorders of the present time.

18–22 Ross laments the cruelty of the times that made Macduff flee. In such times, people are treated like traitors for no reason. Their fears make them believe (**hold**) rumors, though they do not know what to fear and drift aimlessly like ships tossed by a tempest.

28–30 Moved by pity for Macduff's family, Ross is near tears (**my disgrace**). He will leave before he embarrasses himself.

30–31 Why does Lady Macduff tell her son that his father is dead, though the boy heard her discussion with Ross?

Son. As birds do, mother.

Lady Macduff.   What, with worms and flies?

Son. With what I get, I mean; and so do they.

Lady Macduff. Poor bird, thou'dst never fear the net nor lime,
35 The pitfall nor the gin.

Son. Why should I, mother? Poor birds they are not set for.
My father is not dead, for all your saying.

Lady Macduff. Yes, he is dead. How wilt thou do for a father?

Son. Nay, how will you do for a husband?

40 **Lady Macduff.** Why, I can buy me twenty at any market.

Son. Then you'll buy 'em to sell again.

Lady Macduff. Thou speak'st with all thy wit,
And yet, i' faith, with wit enough for thee.

Son. Was my father a traitor, mother?

45 **Lady Macduff.** Ay, that he was.

Son. What is a traitor?

Lady Macduff. Why, one that swears and lies.

Son. And be all traitors that do so?

Lady Macduff. Every one that does so is a traitor and must be hanged.

50 **Son.** And must they all be hanged that swear and lie?

Lady Macduff. Every one.

Son. Who must hang them?

Lady Macduff. Why, the honest men.

Son. Then the liars and swearers are fools, for there are liars and
55 swearers enough to beat the honest men and hang up them.

Lady Macduff. Now God help thee, poor monkey! But how wilt thou
do for a father?

Son. If he were dead, you'd weep for him. If you would not, it were a
good sign that I should quickly have a new father.

60 **Lady Macduff.** Poor prattler, how thou talk'st!

[*Enter a* Messenger.]

Messenger. Bless you, fair dame. I am not to you known,
Though in your state of honor I am perfect.
I doubt some danger does approach you nearly.
If you will take a homely man's advice,
65 Be not found here. Hence with your little ones!
To fright you thus methinks I am too savage;
To do worse to you were fell cruelty,
Which is too nigh your person. Heaven preserve you!
I dare abide no longer.   [Messenger *exits.*]

32–35 The spirited son refuses to be defeated by their bleak situation. He will live as birds do, taking whatever comes his way. His mother responds in kind, calling attention to devices used to catch birds: nets, sticky birdlime (**lime**), snares (**pitfall**), and traps (**gin**).

40–43 Lady Macduff and her son affectionately joke about her ability to find a new husband. She expresses admiration for his intelligence (**with wit enough**).

44–53 Continuing his banter, the son asks if his father is a traitor. Lady Macduff, understandably hurt and confused by her husband's unexplained departure, answers yes.

54–60 Her son points out that traitors outnumber honest men in this troubled time. The mother's terms of affection, **monkey** and **prattler** (childish talker), suggest that his playfulness has won her over.

61–69 The messenger, who knows Lady Macduff is an honorable person (**in your state of honor I am perfect**), delivers a polite but desperate warning, urging her to flee immediately. While he apologizes for scaring her, he warns that she faces a deadly (**fell**) cruelty, one dangerously close (**too nigh**).

Lady Macduff, Ross, and children of Macduff

Lady Macduff.   Whither should I fly?
70 I have done no harm. But I remember now
I am in this earthly world, where to do harm
Is often laudable, to do good sometime
Accounted dangerous folly. Why then, alas,
Do I put up that womanly defense
75 To say I have done no harm?

[*Enter* Murderers.]

                              What are these faces? **B**

Murderer. Where is your husband?

Lady Macduff. I hope in no place so unsanctified
Where such as thou mayst find him.

Murderer.   He's a traitor.

Son. Thou liest, thou shag-eared villain!

Murderer.   What, you egg!

[*Stabbing him*]
80 Young fry of treachery!

Son.   He has killed me, mother.
Run away, I pray you,

[Lady Macduff *exits, crying "Murder!" followed by the* Murderers *bearing
the* Son's *body.*]

B SOLILOQUY
Reread Lady Macduff's speech
in lines 69–75. How have some
of the characters in the drama
reflected her conclusions about
"this earthly world"?

77 **unsanctified:** unholy.

79 **shag-eared:** long-haired. Note
how quickly the son reacts to the
word *traitor. How do you think he
feels about his father?*

80 **young fry:** small fish.

Scene 3 *England. Before King Edward's palace.*

Macduff urges Malcolm to join him in an invasion of Scotland, where the people suffer under Macbeth's harsh rule. Since Malcolm is uncertain of Macduff's motives, he tests him to see what kind of king Macduff would support. Once convinced of Macduff's honesty, Malcolm tells him that he has 10,000 soldiers ready to launch an attack. Ross arrives to tell them that some revolts against Macbeth have already begun. Reluctantly, Ross tells Macduff about the murder of his family. Wild with grief, Macduff vows to confront Macbeth and avenge the murders.

[*Enter* Malcolm *and* Macduff.]

Malcolm. Let us seek out some desolate shade and there
Weep our sad bosoms empty.

Macduff.   Let us rather
Hold fast the mortal sword and, like good men,
Bestride our downfall'n birthdom. Each new morn
5 New widows howl, new orphans cry, new sorrows
Strike heaven on the face, that it resounds
As if it felt with Scotland, and yelled out
Like syllable of dolor. **C**

Malcolm.   What I believe, I'll wail;
What know, believe; and what I can redress,
10 As I shall find the time to friend, I will.
What you have spoke, it may be so, perchance.
This tyrant, whose sole name blisters our tongues,
Was once thought honest. You have loved him well.
He hath not touched you yet. I am young, but something
15 You may deserve of him through me, and wisdom
To offer up a weak, poor, innocent lamb
T' appease an angry god.

Macduff. I am not treacherous.

Malcolm.   But Macbeth is.
A good and virtuous nature may recoil
20 In an imperial charge. But I shall crave your pardon.
That which you are, my thoughts cannot transpose.
Angels are bright still, though the brightest fell.
Though all things foul would wear the brows of grace,
Yet grace must still look so.

Macduff.   I have lost my hopes.

25 **Malcolm.** Perchance even there where I did find my doubts.
Why in that rawness left you wife and child,
Those precious motives, those strong knots of love,
Without leave-taking? I pray you,

1–8 In response to Malcolm's depression about Scotland, Macduff advises that they grab a deadly (**mortal**) sword and defend their homeland (**birthdom**). The anguished cries of Macbeth's victims strike heaven and make the skies echo with cries of sorrow (**syllable of dolor**).

C DRAMATIC IRONY
What is ironic about Macduff's speech in lines 2–8?

8–15 Malcolm will strike back only if the time is right (**as I shall find the time to friend**). Macduff may be sincere, but he may be deceiving Malcolm to gain a reward from Macbeth (**something you may deserve of him through me**).

18–24 Malcolm further explains the reasons for his suspicions. Even a good person may fall (**recoil**) into wickedness because of a king's command (**imperial charge**). If Macduff is innocent, he will not be harmed by these suspicions, which cannot change (**transpose**) his nature (**that which you are**). Virtue cannot be damaged even by those who fall into evil, like Lucifer (**the brightest angel**), and disguise themselves as virtuous (**wear the brows of grace**).

25–31 Malcolm cannot understand how Macduff could leave his family, a source of inspiration (**motives**) and love, in an unprotected state (**rawness**). He asks him not to be insulted by his suspicions (**jealousies**); Malcolm is guarding his own safety.

Let not my jealousies be your dishonors,
30 But mine own safeties. You may be rightly just,
Whatever I shall think.

Macduff.   Bleed, bleed, poor country!
Great tyranny, lay thou thy basis sure,
For goodness dare not check thee. Wear thou thy wrongs;
The title is affeered.—Fare thee well, lord.
35 I would not be the villain that thou think'st
For the whole space that's in the tyrant's grasp,
And the rich East to boot.

Malcolm.   Be not offended.
I speak not as in absolute fear of you.
I think our country sinks beneath the yoke.
40 It weeps, it bleeds, and each new day a gash
Is added to her wounds. I think withal
There would be hands uplifted in my right;
And here from gracious England have I offer
Of goodly thousands. But, for all this,
45 When I shall tread upon the tyrant's head
Or wear it on my sword, yet my poor country
Shall have more vices than it had before,
More suffer, and more sundry ways than ever,
By him that shall succeed.

Macduff.   What should he be?

50 **Malcolm.** It is myself I mean, in whom I know
All the particulars of vice so grafted
That, when they shall be opened, black Macbeth
Will seem as pure as snow, and the poor state
Esteem him as a lamb, being compared
55 With my confineless harms.

Macduff.   Not in the legions
Of horrid hell can come a devil more damned
In evils to top Macbeth.

Malcolm.   I grant him bloody,
Luxurious, avaricious, false, deceitful,
Sudden, malicious, smacking of every sin
60 That has a name. But there's no bottom, none,
In my voluptuousness. Your wives, your daughters,
Your matrons, and your maids could not fill up
The cistern of my lust, and my desire
All continent impediments would o'erbear
65 That did oppose my will. Better Macbeth
Than such an one to reign.

34 affeered: confirmed.

46–49 yet my . . . succeed: To test Macduff's honor and loyalty, Malcolm begins a lengthy description of his own fictitious vices. He suggests that Scotland may suffer more under his rule than under Macbeth's.

50–55 Malcolm says that his own vices are so plentiful and deeply planted (**grafted**) that Macbeth will seem innocent by comparison.

58 luxurious: lustful.

59 sudden: violent; **smacking:** tasting.

61 voluptuousness: lust.

63 cistern: large storage tank.

63–65 His lust is so great that it would overpower (**o'erbear**) all restraining obstacles (**continent impediments**).

Macduff.   Boundless intemperance
In nature is a tyranny. It hath been
Th' untimely emptying of the happy throne
And fall of many kings. But fear not yet
70 To take upon you what is yours. You may
Convey your pleasures in a spacious plenty
And yet seem cold—the time you may so hoodwink.
We have willing dames enough. There cannot be
That vulture in you to devour so many
75 As will to greatness dedicate themselves,
Finding it so inclined.

Malcolm.   With this there grows
In my most ill-composed affection such
A stanchless avarice that, were I king,
I should cut off the nobles for their lands,
80 Desire his jewels, and this other's house;
And my more-having would be as a sauce
To make me hunger more, that I should forge
Quarrels unjust against the good and loyal,
Destroying them for wealth.

Macduff.   This avarice
85 Sticks deeper, grows with more pernicious root
Than summer-seeming lust, and it hath been
The sword of our slain kings. Yet do not fear.
Scotland hath foisons to fill up your will
Of your mere own. All these are portable,
90 With other graces weighed.

Malcolm. But I have none. The king-becoming graces,
As justice, verity, temp'rance, stableness,
Bounty, perseverance, mercy, lowliness,
Devotion, patience, courage, fortitude,
95 I have no relish of them but abound
In the division of each several crime,
Acting it many ways. Nay, had I power, I should
Pour the sweet milk of concord into hell,
Uproar the universal peace, confound
100 All unity on earth.

Macduff.   O Scotland, Scotland!

Malcolm. If such a one be fit to govern, speak.
I am as I have spoken.

Macduff.   Fit to govern?
No, not to live.—O nation miserable,
With an untitled tyrant bloody-sceptered,
105 When shalt thou see thy wholesome days again,

66–76 Macduff describes uncontrolled desire (**boundless intemperance**) as a tyrant of human nature that has caused the early (**untimely**) downfall of many kings. When Malcolm is king, however, his lustful appetite (**vulture in you**) can be satisfied by the many women willing to give (**dedicate**) themselves to a king.

76–78 Malcolm adds insatiable greed (**stanchless avarice**) to the list of evils in his disposition (**affection**).

84–90 Macduff recognizes that greed is a deeper-rooted problem than lust, which passes as quickly as the summer (**summer-seeming**). But the king's property alone (**of your mere own**) offers plenty (**foisons**) to satisfy his desire. Malcolm's vices can be tolerated (**are portable**).

91–95 Malcolm claims that he lacks all the virtues appropriate to a king (**king-becoming graces**). His list of missing virtues includes truthfulness (**verity**), consistency (**stableness**), generosity (**bounty**), humility (**lowliness**), and religious devotion.

Since that the truest issue of thy throne
By his own interdiction stands accursed
And does blaspheme his breed?—Thy royal father
Was a most sainted king. The queen that bore thee,
110 Oft'ner upon her knees than on her feet,
Died every day she lived. Fare thee well.
These evils thou repeat'st upon thyself
Have banished me from Scotland.—O my breast,
Thy hope ends here!

Malcolm.   Macduff, this noble passion,
115 Child of integrity, hath from my soul
Wiped the black scruples, reconciled my thoughts
To thy good truth and honor. Devilish Macbeth
By many of these trains hath sought to win me
Into his power, and modest wisdom plucks me
120 From overcredulous haste. But God above
Deal between thee and me, for even now
I put myself to thy direction and
Unspeak mine own detraction, here abjure
The taints and blames I laid upon myself
125 For strangers to my nature. I am yet
Unknown to woman, never was forsworn,
Scarcely have coveted what was mine own,
At no time broke my faith, would not betray
The devil to his fellow, and delight
130 No less in truth than life. My first false speaking
Was this upon myself. What I am truly
Is thine and my poor country's to command—
Whither indeed, before thy here-approach,
Old Siward with ten thousand warlike men,
135 Already at a point, was setting forth.
Now we'll together, and the chance of goodness
Be like our warranted quarrel. Why are you silent?

Macduff. Such welcome and unwelcome things at once
'Tis hard to reconcile.

[*Enter a* Doctor.]

140 **Malcolm.** Well, more anon.—Comes the King forth, I pray you?

Doctor. Ay, sir. There are a crew of wretched souls
That stay his cure. Their malady convinces
The great assay of art, but at his touch
(Such sanctity hath heaven given his hand)
145 They presently amend.

Malcolm.   I thank you, doctor.

[Doctor *exits*.]

102–114 Macduff can see no relief for Scotland's suffering under a tyrant who has no right to the throne (**untitled**). The rightful heir (**truest issue**), Malcolm, bans himself from the throne (**by his own interdiction**) because of his evil. Malcolm's vices slander his parents (**blaspheme his breed**)—his saintly father and his mother who renounced the world (**died every day**) for her religion. Since Macduff will not help an evil man to become king, he will not be able to return to Scotland.

114–125 Macduff has finally convinced Malcolm of his honesty. Malcolm explains that his caution (**modest wisdom**) resulted from his fear of Macbeth's tricks. He takes back his accusations against himself (**unspeak mine own detraction**) and renounces (**abjure**) the evils he previously claimed.

133–137 Malcolm already has an army, 10,000 troops belonging to old Siward, the earl of Northumberland. Now that Macduff is an ally, he hopes the battle's result will match the justice of their cause (**warranted quarrel**).

Language Coach

Multiple Meanings Lines 142–143 contain three out-of-date usages. Here, *convinces* means "defeats"; *assay* means "efforts"; and *art* refers to medical practice. Rephrase the lines in modern language. With the help of a dictionary, use each word in a sentence with its modern meaning.

Macduff. What's the disease he means?

Malcolm.   'Tis called the evil:
A most miraculous work in this good king,
Which often since my here-remain in England
I have seen him do. How he solicits heaven
150 Himself best knows, but strangely visited people
All swoll'n and ulcerous, pitiful to the eye,
The mere despair of surgery, he cures,
Hanging a golden stamp about their necks
Put on with holy prayers; and, 'tis spoken,
155 To the succeeding royalty he leaves
The healing benediction. With this strange virtue,
He hath a heavenly gift of prophecy,
And sundry blessings hang about his throne
That speak him full of grace.

[*Enter* Ross.]

Macduff.   See who comes here.

160 **Malcolm.** My countryman, but yet I know him not.

Macduff. My ever-gentle cousin, welcome hither.

Malcolm. I know him now.—Good God betimes remove
The means that makes us strangers!

Ross.   Sir, amen.

Macduff. Stands Scotland where it did?

Ross.   Alas, poor country,
165 Almost afraid to know itself. It cannot
Be called our mother, but our grave, where nothing
But who knows nothing is once seen to smile;
Where sighs and groans and shrieks that rent the air
Are made, not marked; where violent sorrow seems
170 A modern ecstasy. The dead man's knell
Is there scarce asked for who, and good men's lives
Expire before the flowers in their caps,
Dying or ere they sicken. **D**

Macduff. O relation too nice and yet too true!

175 **Malcolm.** What's the newest grief?

Ross. That of an hour's age doth hiss the speaker.
Each minute teems a new one.

Macduff.   How does my wife?

Ross. Why, well.

Macduff.   And all my children?

Ross.   Well too.

141–159 Edward the Confessor, king of England, could reportedly heal the disease of scrofula (**the evil**) by his saintly touch. The doctor describes people who cannot be helped by medicine's best efforts (**the great assay of art**) waiting for the touch of the king's hand. Edward has cured many victims of this disease. Each time, he hangs a gold coin around their neck and offers prayers, a healing ritual that he will teach to his royal descendants (**succeeding royalty**).

162–163 Good God . . . strangers: May God remove Macbeth, who is the cause (**means**) of our being strangers.

D TRAGEDY
Reread lines 164–173, in which the audience learns that in Macbeth's bloody reign, screams go unnoticed (**are made, not marked**) and violent sorrow has become commonplace (**modern ecstasy**). What emotions does Macbeth inspire as a **tragic hero** at this point?

174 relation too nice: news that is too accurate.

176–177 If the news is more than an hour old, listeners hiss at the speaker for being outdated; every minute gives birth to a new grief.

Macduff. The tyrant has not battered at their peace?

180 **Ross.** No, they were well at peace when I did leave 'em.

Macduff. Be not a niggard of your speech. How goes 't?

Ross. When I came hither to transport the tidings
Which I have heavily borne, there ran a rumor
Of many worthy fellows that were out;
185 Which was to my belief witnessed the rather
For that I saw the tyrant's power afoot.
Now is the time of help. Your eye in Scotland
Would create soldiers, make our women fight
To doff their dire distresses.

Malcolm.   Be 't their comfort
190 We are coming thither. Gracious England hath
Lent us good Siward and ten thousand men;
An older and a better soldier none
That Christendom gives out.

Ross.   Would I could answer
This comfort with the like. But I have words
195 That would be howled out in the desert air,
Where hearing should not latch them.

Macduff.   What concern they—
The general cause, or is it a fee-grief
Due to some single breast?

Ross.   No mind that's honest
But in it shares some woe, though the main part
200 Pertains to you alone.

Macduff.   If it be mine,
Keep it not from me. Quickly let me have it.

Ross. Let not your ears despise my tongue forever,
Which shall possess them with the heaviest sound
That ever yet they heard.

Macduff.   Hum! I guess at it.

205 **Ross.** Your castle is surprised, your wife and babes
Savagely slaughtered. To relate the manner
Were on the quarry of these murdered deer
To add the death of you.

Malcolm.   Merciful heaven!
What, man, ne'er pull your hat upon your brows.
210 Give sorrow words. The grief that does not speak
Whispers the o'erfraught heart and bids it break.

Macduff. My children too?

Ross. Wife, children, servants, all that could be found.

180 well at peace: Ross knows about the murder of Macduff's wife and children, but the news is too terrible to report.

182–189 Notice how Ross avoids the subject of Macduff's family. He mentions the rumors of nobles who are rebelling (**out**) against Macbeth. Ross believes the rumors because he saw Macbeth's troops on the march (**tyrant's power afoot**). The presence (**eye**) of Malcolm and Macduff in Scotland would help raise soldiers and remove (**doff**) Macbeth's evil (**dire distresses**).

195 would: should.
196 latch: catch.

197 fee-grief: private sorrow.

198–199 No mind . . . woe: Every honorable (**honest**) person shares in this sorrow.

206–208 Ross won't add to Macduff's sorrow by telling him how his family was killed. He compares Macduff's dear ones to the piled bodies of killed deer (**quarry**).

210–211 The grief . . . break: Silence will only push an overburdened heart to the breaking point.

Macduff. And I must be from thence? My wife killed too?

215 **Ross.** I have said.

Malcolm. Be comforted.
Let's make us med'cines of our great revenge
To cure this deadly grief.

Macduff. He has no children. All my pretty ones?
220 Did you say "all"? O hell-kite! All?
What, all my pretty chickens and their dam
At one fell swoop?

Malcolm. Dispute it like a man.

Macduff.   I shall do so,
But I must also feel it as a man.
225 I cannot but remember such things were
That were most precious to me. Did heaven look on
And would not take their part? Sinful Macduff,
They were all struck for thee! Naught that I am,
Not for their own demerits, but for mine,
230 Fell slaughter on their souls. Heaven rest them now.

Malcolm. Be this the whetstone of your sword. Let grief
Convert to anger. Blunt not the heart; enrage it.

Macduff. O, I could play the woman with mine eyes
And braggart with my tongue! But, gentle heavens,
235 Cut short all intermission! Front to front
Bring thou this fiend of Scotland and myself.
Within my sword's length set him. If he scape,
Heaven forgive him too. **E**

Malcolm.   This tune goes manly.
Come, go we to the King. Our power is ready;
240 Our lack is nothing but our leave. Macbeth
Is ripe for shaking, and the powers above
Put on their instruments. Receive what cheer you may.
The night is long that never finds the day.

[*They exit.*]

214 Macduff laments his absence from the castle.

219–222 He has no children: possibly a reference to Macbeth, who has no children to be killed for revenge. Macduff compares Macbeth to a bird of prey (**hell-kite**) who kills defenseless chickens and their mother.

228 naught: nothing.

231 whetstone: grindstone used for sharpening.

E FORESHADOWING
What event does Macduff's speech in lines 233–238 foreshadow?

239–243 Our troops are ready to attack, needing only the king's permission (**our lack is nothing but our leave**). Like a ripe fruit, Macbeth is ready to fall, and heavenly powers are preparing to assist us. The long night of Macbeth's evil will be broken.

Comprehension

1. **Recall** What three messages does Macbeth receive from the three apparitions?

2. **Clarify** What happens to Lady Macduff and her children?

3. **Paraphrase** Reread Scene 3, lines 235–238. How would you paraphrase these lines?

Text Analysis

4. **Recognize Cause and Effect** What is the result—or effect—of each of the following events? Use specific details to explain your answers.

   - Macbeth's second visit to the Three Witches (Scene 1, lines 48–133)
   - Malcolm tests Macduff (Scene 3, lines 37–114)
   - Macduff's family is murdered (Scene 2, lines 76–81)

5. **Examine Shakespearean Drama** Review the notes you recorded about Macbeth's actions in Act Four. How does Macbeth react when he encounters the apparitions? What does his reaction reveal about how he has changed?

6. **Analyze Shakespearean Tragedy** What is **foreshadowed** by each of the apparitions that appear to Macbeth in Scene 1?

7. **Analyze Rhythm and Rhyme** Reread Scene 1, lines 4–38, in which the witches make their magical brew. What effect do you think the rhythm and rhyme in the lines would have on an audience?

8. **Compare Characters** Compare Lady Macbeth with Lady Macduff. How are the characters similar? How do they differ? Cite specific evidence from the play to support your ideas.

9. **Draw Conclusions** Lady Macduff and Malcolm both question Macduff's motives for fleeing Scotland. Think about the crimes Macbeth has already committed. Why might the nature and manner of these crimes have led Macduff to believe that his family would be safe at his castle?

Text Criticism

10. **Different Perspectives** In some productions of *Macbeth*, the director omits Malcolm's lengthy test of Macduff. Do you agree with this decision? What would be lost or gained by omitting the speech? Support your response.

Can you ever be too AMBITIOUS?

According to one definition, knowledge is power. When might this be true? When might it not be true? Provide concrete examples from the play that prove *and* disprove this definition of "knowledge."

COMMON CORE

RL 3 Analyze the impact of the author's choices regarding how to develop and relate elements of a drama. **RL 4** Analyze the impact of specific word choices on meaning and tone. **RL 5** Analyze how an author's choices concerning how to structure specific parts of a text contribute to its overall structure and meaning.

ACT 5

Scene 1 *Macbeth's castle at Dunsinane.*

A sleepwalking Lady Macbeth is observed by a concerned attendant, or gentlewoman, and a doctor. Lady Macbeth appears to be washing imagined blood from her hands. Her actions and confused speech greatly concern the doctor, and he warns the attendant to keep an eye on Lady Macbeth, fearing that she will harm herself.

[*Enter a* Doctor of Physic *and a* Waiting Gentlewoman.]

Doctor. I have two nights watched with you but can perceive no truth in your report. When was it she last walked?

Gentlewoman. Since his Majesty went into the field, I have seen her rise from her bed, throw her nightgown upon her, unlock her closet,
5 take forth paper, fold it, write upon' t, read it, afterwards seal it, and again return to bed; yet all this while in a most fast sleep.

Doctor. A great perturbation in nature, to receive at once the benefit of sleep and do the effects of watching. In this slumb'ry agitation, besides her walking and other actual performances, what at any time have you
10 heard her say?

Gentlewoman. That, sir, which I will not report after her.

Doctor. You may to me, and 'tis most meet you should.

Gentlewoman. Neither to you nor anyone, having no witness to confirm my speech.

[*Enter* Lady Macbeth *with a taper.*]

15 Lo you, here she comes. This is her very guise and, upon my life, fast asleep. Observe her; stand close.

Doctor. How came she by that light?

Gentlewoman. Why, it stood by her. She has light by her continually. 'Tis her command.

20 **Doctor.** You see her eyes are open.

Gentlewoman. Ay, but their sense are shut.

Doctor. What is it she does now? Look how she rubs her hands.

Gentlewoman. It is an accustomed action with her to seem thus washing her hands. I have known her continue in this a quarter of an hour.

25 **Lady Macbeth.** Yet here's a spot.

Doctor. Hark, she speaks. I will set down what comes from her, to satisfy my remembrance the more strongly.

Lady Macbeth. Out, damned spot, out, I say! One. Two. Why then, 'tis time to do 't. Hell is murky. Fie, my lord, fie, a soldier and afeard?

3 went into the field: went to battle.

7–8 A great . . . of watching: To behave as though awake (**watching**) while sleeping is a sign of a greatly troubled nature.

12 meet: appropriate.

13–14 The attendant won't repeat what Lady Macbeth has said, because there are no other witnesses to confirm her report. *What is she worried about?*

15 guise: usual manner.

16 stand close: hide yourself.

17 that light: her candle.

18–19 *Why might Lady Macbeth want a light by her at all times?*

Language Coach

Derivations Words formed from another word or base are **derivations.** For example, the word *custom,* meaning "habit," has many derivations, including *customary* and *customer.* Reread lines 23–24. What derivation of *custom* appears in these lines? What do you think it means?

Macduff and Macbeth

30 What need we fear who knows it, when none can call our power to
account? Yet who would have thought the old man to have had
so much blood in him? **A**

Doctor. Do you mark that?

Lady Macbeth. The Thane of Fife had a wife. Where is she now? What,
35 will these hands ne'er be clean? No more o' that, my lord, no more o'
that. You mar all with this starting.

Doctor. Go to, go to. You have known what you should not.

Gentlewoman. She has spoke what she should not, I am sure of that.
Heaven knows what she has known.

40 **Lady Macbeth.** Here's the smell of the blood still. All the perfumes of
Arabia will not sweeten this little hand. O, O, O!

Doctor. What a sigh is there! The heart is sorely charged.

Gentlewoman. I would not have such a heart in my bosom for the
dignity of the whole body.

45 **Doctor.** Well, well, well.

Gentlewoman. Pray God it be, sir.

Doctor. This disease is beyond my practice. Yet I have known those
which have walked in their sleep, who have died holily in their beds.

Lady Macbeth. Wash your hands. Put on your nightgown. Look not so
50 pale. I tell you yet again, Banquo's buried; he cannot come out on 's
grave.

Doctor. Even so?

Lady Macbeth. To bed, to bed. There's knocking at the gate. Come,
come, come, come. Give me your hand. What's done cannot be
55 undone. To bed, to bed, to bed.

[Lady Macbeth *exits.*]

Doctor. Will she go now to bed?

Gentlewoman. Directly.

Doctor. Foul whisp'rings are abroad. Unnatural deeds
Do breed unnatural troubles. Infected minds
60 To their deaf pillows will discharge their secrets.
More needs she the divine than the physician.
God, God forgive us all. Look after her.
Remove from her the means of all annoyance
And still keep eyes upon her. So good night.
65 My mind she has mated, and amazed my sight.
I think but dare not speak.

Gentlewoman.   Good night, good doctor.

[*They exit.*]

A **TRAGEDY**
Reread lines 28–32, in which
Lady Macbeth relives how she
persuaded her husband to
murder Duncan. What appears
to have happened to Lady
Macbeth as a result of their plot?

34–36 Lady Macbeth shows guilt
about Macduff's wife. Then she
addresses her husband, as if he were
having another ghostly fit (**starting**).

42 sorely charged: heavily burdened.

43–44 The gentlewoman says that
she would not want Lady Macbeth's
heavy heart in exchange for being
queen.

47 practice: skill.

50 on 's: of his.

52 *What has the doctor learned so far
from Lady Macbeth's ramblings?*

58 Foul whisp'rings are abroad:
Rumors of evil deeds are circulating.

61 She needs a priest more than a
doctor.

63 annoyance: injury. The doctor
may be worried about the possibility
of Lady Macbeth's committing
suicide.

65 mated: astonished.

Scene 2 *The country near Dunsinane.*

The Scottish rebels, led by Menteith, Caithness, Angus, and Lennox, have come to Birnam Wood to join Malcolm and his English army. They know that Dunsinane has been fortified by a furious and brave Macbeth. They also know that his men neither love nor respect him.

[*Drum and Colors. Enter* Menteith, Caithness, Angus, Lennox, *and* Soldiers.]

Menteith. The English power is near, led on by Malcolm,
His uncle Siward, and the good Macduff.
Revenges burn in them, for their dear causes
Would to the bleeding and the grim alarm
5 Excite the mortified man.

Angus.   Near Birnam Wood
Shall we well meet them. That way are they coming.

Caithness. Who knows if Donalbain be with his brother?

Lennox. For certain, sir, he is not. I have a file
Of all the gentry. There is Siward's son
10 And many unrough youths that even now
Protest their first of manhood.

Menteith.   What does the tyrant?

Caithness. Great Dunsinane he strongly fortifies.
Some say he's mad; others that lesser hate him
Do call it valiant fury. But for certain
15 He cannot buckle his distempered cause
Within the belt of rule.

Angus.   Now does he feel
His secret murders sticking on his hands.
Now minutely revolts upbraid his faith-breach.
Those he commands move only in command,
20 Nothing in love. Now does he feel his title
Hang loose about him, like a giant's robe
Upon a dwarfish thief.

Menteith.   Who, then, shall blame
His pestered senses to recoil and start
When all that is within him does condemn
25 Itself for being there?

Caithness.   Well, march we on
To give obedience where 'tis truly owed.
Meet we the med'cine of the sickly weal,
And with him pour we in our country's purge
Each drop of us.

3–5 for their dear . . . man: The cause of Malcolm and Macduff is so deeply felt that a dead (**mortified**) man would respond to their call to arms (**alarm**).

10–11 many . . . manhood: many soldiers who are too young to grow beards (**unrough**)—that is, who have hardly reached manhood.

15–16 Like a man so swollen with disease (**distempered**) that he cannot buckle his belt, Macbeth cannot control his evil actions.

18 Every minute, the revolts against Macbeth shame him for his treachery (**faith-breach**).

22–25 Macbeth's troubled nerves (**pestered senses**)—the product of his guilty conscience—have made him jumpy.

25–29 Caithness and the others will give their loyalty to the only help (**med'cine**) for the sick country (**weal**). They are willing to sacrifice their last drop of blood to cleanse (**purge**) Scotland.

Lennox.   Or so much as it needs
30 To dew the sovereign flower and drown the weeds.
Make we our march towards Birnam.

[*They exit marching.*]

Scene 3 *Dunsinane. A room in the castle.*

Macbeth awaits battle, confident of victory because of what he learned from the witches. After hearing that a huge army is ready to march upon his castle, he expresses bitter regrets about his life. While Macbeth prepares for battle, the doctor reports that he cannot cure Lady Macbeth, whose illness is mental, not physical.

[*Enter* Macbeth, *the* Doctor, *and* Attendants.]

Macbeth. Bring me no more reports. Let them fly all.
Till Birnam Wood remove to Dunsinane
I cannot taint with fear. What's the boy Malcolm?
Was he not born of woman? The spirits that know
5 All mortal consequences have pronounced me thus:
"Fear not, Macbeth. No man that's born of woman
Shall e'er have power upon thee." Then fly, false thanes,
And mingle with the English epicures.
The mind I sway by and the heart I bear
10 Shall never sag with doubt nor shake with fear.

[*Enter* Servant.]

The devil damn thee black, thou cream-faced loon!
Where got'st thou that goose-look?

Servant. There is ten thousand—

Macbeth.   Geese, villain?

Servant.   Soldiers, sir.

Macbeth. Go prick thy face and over-red thy fear,
15 Thou lily-livered boy. What soldiers, patch?
Death of thy soul! Those linen cheeks of thine
Are counselors to fear. What soldiers, whey-face?

Servant. The English force, so please you.

Macbeth. Take thy face hence.

[Servant *exits.*]

                    Seyton!—I am sick at heart
20 When I behold—Seyton, I say!—This push
Will cheer me ever or disseat me now.
I have lived long enough. My way of life
Is fall'n into the sere, the yellow leaf,
And that which should accompany old age,
25 As honor, love, obedience, troops of friends,

29–31 Lennox compares Malcolm to a flower that needs the blood of patriots to water (**dew**) it and drown out weeds like Macbeth.

1 Macbeth wants no more news of thanes who have gone to Malcolm's side.

2–10 Macbeth will not be infected (**taint**) with fear, because the witches (**spirits**), who know all human events (**mortal consequences**), have convinced him that he is invincible. He mocks the self-indulgent English (**English epicures**), then swears that he will never lack confidence.

11 loon: stupid rascal.

12 goose-look: look of fear.

14–17 Macbeth suggests that the servant cut his face so that blood will hide his cowardice. He repeatedly insults the servant, calling him a coward (**lily-livered**) and a clown (**patch**) and making fun of his white complexion (**linen cheeks, whey-face**).

20–28 This push . . . dare not: The upcoming battle will either make Macbeth secure (**cheer me ever**) or dethrone (**disseat**) him. He bitterly compares his life to a withered (**sere**) leaf. He cannot look forward to old age with friends and honor, but only to curses and empty flattery (**mouth-honor, breath**) from those too timid (**the poor heart**) to tell the truth.

I must not look to have, but in their stead
Curses, not loud but deep, mouth-honor, breath
Which the poor heart would fain deny and dare not.—
Seyton!

[*Enter* Seyton.]

30 **Seyton.** What's your gracious pleasure?

Macbeth.   What news more?

Seyton. All is confirmed, my lord, which was reported.

Macbeth. I'll fight till from my bones my flesh be hacked.
Give me my armor.

Seyton.   'Tis not needed yet.

Macbeth. I'll put it on.

35 Send out more horses. Skirr the country round.
Hang those that talk of fear. Give me mine armor.—
How does your patient, doctor?

Doctor.   Not so sick, my lord,
As she is troubled with thick-coming fancies
That keep her from her rest.

Macbeth.   Cure her of that.

40 Canst thou not minister to a mind diseased,
Pluck from the memory a rooted sorrow,
Raze out the written troubles of the brain,
And with some sweet oblivious antidote
Cleanse the stuffed bosom of that perilous stuff

45 Which weighs upon the heart? **B**

Doctor.   Therein the patient
Must minister to himself.

Macbeth. Throw physic to the dogs, I'll none of it.—
Come, put mine armor on. Give me my staff.

[Attendants *begin to arm him.*]

Seyton, send out.—Doctor, the thanes fly from me.—

50 Come, sir, dispatch.—If thou couldst, doctor, cast
The water of my land, find her disease,
And purge it to a sound and pristine health,
I would applaud thee to the very echo
That should applaud again.—Pull 't off, I say.—

55 What rhubarb, senna, or what purgative drug
Would scour these English hence? Hear'st thou of them?

Doctor. Ay, my good lord. Your royal preparation
Makes us hear something.

COMMON CORE L 5b

Language Coach

Denotation/Connotation The images or feelings associated with a word are its **connotations.** Reread line 32. The word *hacked* has several synonyms, including *chopped* and *sliced.* What connotations or feelings accompany *hacked* and its synonyms?

35 **skirr:** scour.

B **TRAGEDY**
In lines 39–45, Macbeth asks the doctor to remove the sorrow from Lady Macbeth's memory and relieve her overburdened heart. Why are these lines so moving?

47–54 Macbeth has lost his faith in the ability of medicine (**physic**) to help his wife. Then as he struggles into his armor, he says that if the doctor could diagnose Scotland's disease (**cast ... land**) and cure it, Macbeth would never stop praising him.

54 Pull 't off: Macbeth is referring to a piece of armor.

56 scour: purge; **them:** the English.

Macbeth.   Bring it after me.—
I will not be afraid of death and bane
60 Till Birnam Forest come to Dunsinane.

Doctor. [*Aside*] Were I from Dunsinane away and clear,
Profit again should hardly draw me here.

[*They exit.*]

Scene 4 *The country near Birnam Wood.*
The rebels and English forces have met in Birnam Wood. Malcolm orders each soldier to cut tree branches to camouflage himself. In this way Birnam Wood will march upon Dunsinane.

[*Drum and Colors. Enter* Malcolm, Siward, Macduff, Siward's son, Menteith, Caithness, Angus, *and* Soldiers, *marching.*]

Malcolm. Cousins, I hope the days are near at hand
That chambers will be safe.

Menteith.   We doubt it nothing.

Siward. What wood is this before us?

Menteith.   The wood of Birnam.

Malcolm. Let every soldier hew him down a bough
5 And bear 't before him. Thereby shall we shadow
The numbers of our host and make discovery
Err in report of us. **C**

Soldiers.   It shall be done.

Siward. We learn no other but the confident tyrant
Keeps still in Dunsinane and will endure
10 Our setting down before 't.

Malcolm.   'Tis his main hope;
For, where there is advantage to be given,
Both more and less have given him the revolt,
And none serve with him but constrainèd things
Whose hearts are absent too.

Macduff.   Let our just censures
15 Attend the true event, and put we on
Industrious soldiership.

Siward.   The time approaches
That will with due decision make us know
What we shall say we have and what we owe.
Thoughts speculative their unsure hopes relate,
20 But certain issue strokes must arbitrate;
Towards which, advance the war.

[*They exit marching.*]

C FORESHADOWING
In lines 4–7, Malcolm orders his men to cut down tree branches to camouflage themselves and confuse Macbeth's scouts. How will this affect the prophecy about Birnam Wood?

10 setting down: siege.

10–14 Malcolm says that men of all ranks (**both more and less**) have abandoned Macbeth. Only weak men who have been forced into service remain with him.

14–16 Macduff warns against overconfidence and advises that they attend to the business of fighting.

16–21 Siward says that the approaching battle will decide whether their claims will match what they actually possess (**owe**). Right now, their hopes and expectations are the product of guesswork (**thoughts speculative**); only fighting (**strokes**) can settle (**arbitrate**) the issue.

Cross-Cultural Adaptations

COMMON CORE RL 7

With its universal themes of ambition and guilt, *Macbeth* is often reimagined in other cultural settings. These photos show a Zulu version of the play, set in South Africa; a famous film adaptation, *Throne of Blood*, set in medieval Japan; and a version set among the Tlingit, an Alaskan native tribe. Notice how the settings and costumes, such as the Japanese statue and samurai dress in the middle photo, reflect these different cultural contexts.

Cross-cultural productions may even reinterpret the play to comment on broader political issues, such as in Tlingit adaptation of *Macbeth*. In Tlingit culture, one should always value the welfare of the tribe above one's own interests. Macbeth clearly favors his own desires at the expense of his countrymen's lives. In the Tlinglit *Macbeth*, when characters adhered to communal values, those cast members spoke in the language of the Tlingit; when they voiced individual concerns, they spoke Shakespearean English. According to the Tlingit adaptation of *Macbeth*, English is the language of selfish individuality and violence, while Tlingit is the language of tribal unity and peace.

If you could choose to set *Macbeth* in another cultural setting, what would it be? How would you adjust the set, costumes, or other aspects of the play to reflect this cultural setting?

Umabatha: The Zulu Macbeth, performed at Lincoln Center in 1997

Akira Kurosawa's 1957 film Throne of Blood

Macbeth, performed in 2004 by the Perseverance Theatre Company of Juneau, Alaska

Scene 5 Dunsinane. *Within the castle.*

Convinced of his powers, Macbeth mocks the enemy; his slaughters have left him fearless. News of Lady Macbeth's death stirs little emotion, only a comment on the emptiness of life. However, when a messenger reports that Birnam Wood seems to be moving toward the castle, Macbeth grows agitated. Fearing that the prophecies have deceived him, he decides to leave the castle to fight and die on the battlefield.

[*Enter* Macbeth, Seyton, *and* Soldiers, *with Drum and Colors.*]

Macbeth. Hang out our banners on the outward walls.
The cry is still "They come!" Our castle's strength
Will laugh a siege to scorn. Here let them lie
Till famine and the ague eat them up.
5 Were they not forced with those that should be ours,
We might have met them dareful, beard to beard,
And beat them backward home.

[*A cry within of women.*]

                              What is that noise?

Seyton. It is the cry of women, my good lord. [*He exits.*]

Macbeth. I have almost forgot the taste of fears.
10 The time has been my senses would have cooled
To hear a night-shriek, and my fell of hair
Would at a dismal treatise rouse and stir
As life were in 't. I have supped full with horrors.
Direness, familiar to my slaughterous thoughts,
15 Cannot once start me.

[*Enter* Seyton.]

                              Wherefore was that cry?

Seyton. The Queen, my lord, is dead.

Macbeth. She should have died hereafter.
There would have been a time for such a word.
Tomorrow and tomorrow and tomorrow
20 Creeps in this petty pace from day to day **D**
To the last syllable of recorded time,
And all our yesterdays have lighted fools
The way to dusty death. Out, out, brief candle!
Life's but a walking shadow, a poor player
25 That struts and frets his hour upon the stage
And then is heard no more. It is a tale
Told by an idiot, full of sound and fury,
Signifying nothing. **E**

[*Enter a* Messenger.]

Thou com'st to use thy tongue: thy story quickly.

4 ague: fever.

5–7 Macbeth complains that the attackers have been reinforced (**forced**) by deserters (**those that should be ours**), which has forced him to wait at Dunsinane instead of seeking victory on the battlefield.

9–15 There was a time when a scream in the night would have frozen Macbeth in fear and a terrifying tale (**dismal treatise**) would have made the hair on his skin (**fell of hair**) stand on end. But since he has fed on horror (**direness**), it cannot stir (**start**) him anymore.

17–18 Macbeth wishes that his wife had died later (**hereafter**), when he would have had time to mourn her.

D BLANK VERSE
Tap your foot to the **rhythm** as you read aloud lines 19–20. How does the rhythm of the lines mirror their meaning?

E TRAGEDY
Reread lines 24–28, in which Macbeth compares life to an actor with a small part to play. How does he probably view his ambitions now? Describe the emotions he inspires in you.

30 **Messenger.** Gracious my lord,
I should report that which I say I saw,
But know not how to do 't.

Macbeth.   Well, say, sir.

Messenger. As I did stand my watch upon the hill,
I looked toward Birnam, and anon methought
35 The wood began to move.

Macbeth.   Liar and slave!

Messenger. Let me endure your wrath, if 't be not so.
Within this three mile may you see it coming.
I say, a moving grove.

Macbeth.   If thou speak'st false,
Upon the next tree shall thou hang alive
40 Till famine cling thee. If thy speech be sooth,
I care not if thou dost for me as much.—
I pull in resolution and begin
To doubt th' equivocation of the fiend,
That lies like truth. "Fear not till Birnam Wood
45 Do come to Dunsinane," and now a wood
Comes toward Dunsinane. —Arm, arm, and out!—
If this which he avouches does appear,
There is nor flying hence nor tarrying here.
I 'gin to be aweary of the sun
50 And wish th' estate o' th' world were now undone.—
Ring the alarum bell! —Blow wind, come wrack,
At least we'll die with harness on our back. **F**

[*They exit.*]

Scene 6 *Dunsinane. Before the castle.*
*Malcolm and the combined forces reach the castle, throw away their
camouflage, and prepare for battle.*

[*Drum and Colors. Enter* Malcolm, Siward, Macduff, *and their army,
with boughs.*]

Malcolm. Now near enough. Your leafy screens throw down
And show like those you are. —You, worthy uncle,
Shall with my cousin, your right noble son,
Lead our first battle. Worthy Macduff and we
5 Shall take upon 's what else remains to do,
According to our order.

Siward.   Fare you well.
Do we but find the tyrant's power tonight,
Let us be beaten if we cannot fight.

38–52 The messenger's news has
dampened Macbeth's determination
(**resolution**); Macbeth begins to fear
that the witches have tricked him (**to
doubt th' equivocation of the fiend**).
His fear that the messenger tells the
truth (**avouches**) makes him decide
to confront the enemy instead of
staying in his castle. Weary of life, he
nevertheless decides to face death
and ruin (**wrack**) with his armor
(**harness**) on.

F **TRAGEDY**
Reread lines 47–52. Note that
Macbeth vows to take action,
which will probably lead to the
drama's **catastrophe,** or tragic
resolution. What is the likely
outcome of his action?

1–6 Malcolm commands the
troops to put down their branches
(**leafy screens**) and gives the battle
instructions.

7 power: forces.

Macduff. Make all our trumpets speak; give them all breath,
10 Those clamorous harbingers of blood and death.

[*They exit. Alarums continued.*]

Scene 7 *Another part of the battlefield.*
Macbeth kills young Siward, which restores his belief that he cannot be killed by any man born of a woman. Meanwhile, Macduff searches for the hated king. Young Siward's father reports that Macbeth's soldiers have surrendered and that many have even joined their attackers.

[*Enter* Macbeth.]

Macbeth. They have tied me to a stake. I cannot fly,
But, bear-like, I must fight the course. What's he
That was not born of woman? Such a one
Am I to fear, or none.

[*Enter* Young Siward.]

5 **Young Siward.** What is thy name?

Macbeth.   Thou'lt be afraid to hear it.

Young Siward. No, though thou call'st thyself a hotter name
Than any is in hell.

Macbeth.   My name's Macbeth.

Young Siward. The devil himself could not pronounce a title
More hateful to mine ear.

Macbeth.   No, nor more fearful.

10 **Young Siward.** Thou liest, abhorrèd tyrant. With my sword
I'll prove the lie thou speak'st.

[*They fight, and* Young Siward *is slain.*]

Macbeth.   Thou wast born of woman.
But swords I smile at, weapons laugh to scorn,
Brandished by man that's of a woman born. [*He exits.*] **G**

[*Alarums. Enter* Macduff.]

Macduff. That way the noise is. Tyrant, show thy face!
15 If thou beest slain, and with no stroke of mine,
My wife and children's ghosts will haunt me still.
I cannot strike at wretched kerns, whose arms
Are hired to bear their staves. Either thou, Macbeth,
Or else my sword with an unbattered edge
20 I sheathe again undeeded. There thou shouldst be;
By this great clatter, one of greatest note
Seems bruited. Let me find him, Fortune,
And more I beg not.

[*He exits. Alarums.*]

10 **harbingers:** announcers.

1–4 Macbeth compares himself to a bear tied to a post (a reference to the sport of bearbaiting, in which a bear was tied to a stake and attacked by dogs).

G **FORESHADOWING**
Be aware that in lines 11–13, Macbeth recalls the third prophecy. What conclusion might Macbeth draw from killing young Siward?

14–20 Macduff enters alone. He wants to avenge the murders of his wife and children and hopes to find Macbeth before someone else has the chance to kill him. Macduff does not want to fight the miserable hired soldiers (**kerns**), who are armed only with spears (**staves**). If he can't fight Macbeth, Macduff will leave his sword unused (**undeeded**).

20–23 After hearing sounds suggesting that a person of great distinction (**note**) is nearby, Macduff exits in pursuit of Macbeth.

[*Enter* Malcolm *and* Siward.]

Siward. This way, my lord. The castle's gently rendered.
25 The tyrant's people on both sides do fight,
The noble thanes do bravely in the war,
The day almost itself professes yours,
And little is to do.

Malcolm.   We have met with foes
That strike beside us.

Siward.   Enter, sir, the castle.

[*They exit. Alarum.*]

Scene 8 *Another part of the battlefield.*

*Macduff finally hunts down Macbeth, who is reluctant to fight because he
has already killed too many Macduffs. The still-proud Macbeth tells his
enemy that no man born of a woman can defeat him, only to learn that
Macduff was ripped from his mother's womb, thus not born naturally.
Rather than face humiliation, Macbeth decides to fight to the death.
After their fight takes them elsewhere, the Scottish lords, now in charge
of Macbeth's castle, discuss young Siward's noble death. Macduff returns
carrying Macbeth's bloody head, proclaiming final victory and declaring
Malcolm king of Scotland. The new king thanks his supporters and
promises rewards, while asking for God's help to restore order and harmony.*

[*Enter* Macbeth.]

Macbeth. Why should I play the Roman fool and die
On mine own sword? Whiles I see lives, the gashes
Do better upon them.

[*Enter* Macduff.]

Macduff.   Turn, hellhound, turn!

Macbeth. Of all men else I have avoided thee.
5 But get thee back. My soul is too much charged
With blood of thine already.

Macduff.   I have no words;
My voice is in my sword, thou bloodier villain
Than terms can give thee out.

[*Fight. Alarum.*]

Macbeth.   Thou losest labor.
As easy mayst thou the intrenchant air
10 With thy keen sword impress as make me bleed.
Let fall thy blade on vulnerable crests;
I bear a charmèd life, which must not yield
To one of woman born.

24 **gently rendered:** surrendered
without a fight.

27 You have almost won the day.

28–29 During the battle many
of Macbeth's men deserted to
Malcolm's army.

1–3 Macbeth vows to continue
fighting, refusing to commit suicide
in the style of a defeated Roman
general.

4–6 Macbeth does not want to fight
Macduff, having already killed so
many members of Macduff's family.

8–13 Macbeth says that Macduff
is wasting his effort. Trying to
wound Macbeth is as useless as
trying to wound the invulnerable
(**intrenchant**) air. Macduff should
attack other, more easily injured
foes, described in terms of helmets
(**crests**).

Macduff.   Despair thy charm,
And let the angel whom thou still hast served
15 Tell thee Macduff was from his mother's womb
Untimely ripped.

Macbeth. Accursèd be that tongue that tells me so,
For it hath cowed my better part of man!
And be these juggling fiends no more believed
20 That palter with us in a double sense,
That keep the word of promise to our ear
And break it to our hope. I'll not fight with thee.

Macduff. Then yield thee, coward,
And live to be the show and gaze o' th' time.
25 We'll have thee, as our rarer monsters are,
Painted upon a pole, and underwrit
"Here may you see the tyrant."

Macbeth.   I will not yield
To kiss the ground before young Malcolm's feet
And to be baited with the rabble's curse.
30 Though Birnam Wood be come to Dunsinane
And thou opposed, being of no woman born,
Yet I will try the last. Before my body
I throw my warlike shield. Lay on, Macduff,
And damned be him that first cries "Hold! Enough!" **Ⓗ**

[*They exit fighting. Alarums.*]

[*They enter fighting, and* Macbeth *is slain.* Macduff *exits carrying off*
Macbeth's *body. Retreat and flourish. Enter, with Drum and Colors,*
Malcolm, Siward, Ross, Thanes, *and* Soldiers.]

35 **Malcolm.** I would the friends we miss were safe arrived.

Siward. Some must go off; and yet by these I see
So great a day as this is cheaply bought.

Malcolm. Macduff is missing, and your noble son.

Ross. Your son, my lord, has paid a soldier's debt.
40 He only lived but till he was a man,
The which no sooner had his prowess confirmed
In the unshrinking station where he fought,
But like a man he died.

Siward.   Then he is dead?

Ross. Ay, and brought off the field. Your cause of sorrow
45 Must not be measured by his worth, for then
It hath no end.

Siward.   Had he his hurts before?

Ross. Ay, on the front.

15–16 Macduff...untimely ripped:
Macduff was a premature baby
delivered by cesarean section, an
operation that removes the child
directly from the mother's womb.

18 cowed my better part of man:
made my spirit, or soul, fearful.

19–22 The cheating witches
(**juggling fiends**) have tricked him
(**palter with us**) with words that
have double meanings.

23–27 Macduff scornfully tells
Macbeth to surrender so that he
can become a public spectacle
(**the show and gaze o' th' time**).
Macbeth's picture will be hung on a
pole (**painted upon a pole**) as if he
were part of a circus sideshow.

Ⓗ TRAGEDY
A **tragic hero** typically realizes
how he has contributed to his
own downfall and faces his end
with dignity. Notice that in lines
27–34, Macbeth realizes that he
is doomed. To what extent is he
redeemed by his determination
to fight to the death?

[Stage Direction] **Retreat...:** The
first trumpet call (**retreat**) signals the
battle's end. The next one (**flourish**)
announces Malcolm's entrance.

36–37 Though some must die (**go
off**) in battle, Siward can see that
their side does not have many
casualties.

44–46 Ross tells old Siward that if
he mourns his son according to the
boy's value, his sorrow will never end.

46 hurts before: wounds in the front
of his body, which indicate he died
facing his enemy.

Siward.   Why then, God's soldier be he!
Had I as many sons as I have hairs,
I would not wish them to a fairer death;
50 And so his knell is knolled.

Malcolm. He's worth more sorrow, and that I'll spend for him.

Siward. He's worth no more.
They say he parted well and paid his score,
And so, God be with him. Here comes newer comfort.

[*Enter* Macduff *with* Macbeth's *head.*]

55 **Macduff.** Hail, King! for so thou art. Behold where stands
Th' usurper's cursèd head. The time is free.
I see thee compassed with thy kingdom's pearl,
That speak my salutation in their minds,
Whose voices I desire aloud with mine.
60 Hail, King of Scotland!

All.   Hail, King of Scotland!

[*Flourish*]

Malcolm. We shall not spend a large expense of time
Before we reckon with your several loves
And make us even with you. My thanes and kinsmen,
Henceforth be earls, the first that ever Scotland
65 In such an honor named. What's more to do,
Which would be planted newly with the time,
As calling home our exiled friends abroad
That fled the snares of watchful tyranny,
Producing forth the cruel ministers
70 Of this dead butcher and his fiend-like queen
(Who, as 'tis thought, by self and violent hands,
Took off her life)—this, and what needful else
That calls upon us, by the grace of grace,
We will perform in measure, time, and place.
75 So thanks to all at once and to each one,
Whom we invite to see us crowned at Scone.

[*Flourish. All exit.*]

50 knell is knolled: Young Siward's death bell has already rung, meaning there is no need to mourn him further.

[Stage Direction] Macduff is probably carrying Macbeth's head on a pole.

56–57 The time . . . pearl: Macduff declares that the age (**time**) is now freed from tyranny. He sees Malcolm surrounded by Scotland's noblest men (**thy kingdom's pearl**).

61–76 Malcolm promises that he will quickly reward his nobles according to the devotion (**several loves**) they have shown. He gives the thanes new titles (**henceforth be earls**) and declares his intention, as a sign of the new age (**planted newly with the time**), to welcome back the exiles who fled Macbeth's tyranny and his cruel agents (**ministers**). Now that Scotland is free of the butcher Macbeth and his queen, who is reported to have killed herself, Malcolm asks for God's help to restore order and harmony. He concludes by inviting all present to his coronation.

Comprehension

1. **Recall** What happens to Lady Macbeth in Act Five?

2. **Clarify** Why does Macbeth have to face his enemies basically alone?

3. **Summarize** How do the apparitions' three predictions in Act Four come true?

Text Analysis

4. **Compare Scenes** Reread Scene 1, lines 28–55. Compare this scene, revealing Lady Macbeth's madness, with Scene 4 in Act Three, in which Macbeth believes he sees Banquo's ghost. What is ironic about Lady Macbeth's behavior in these scenes? (Recall that **situational irony** is a contrast between what is expected and what actually occurs.)

● 5. **Examine Shakespearean Drama** Review the notes you recorded as you read Act Five. How have both Macbeth and Lady Macbeth changed during the course of the play? Cite evidence to support your response.

6. **Interpret Figurative Language** Reread Macbeth's famous soliloquy in Scene 5, lines 19–28. In the **metaphors** in these lines, what does Shakespeare compare life to? What do the metaphors suggest about Macbeth's mental state?

● 7. **Analyze Shakespearean Tragedy** In a chart like the one shown, identify the characteristics of tragedy in *Macbeth*. To what extent is Macbeth redeemed in Act Five? In what ways could he be considered a **tragic hero** rather than a villain?

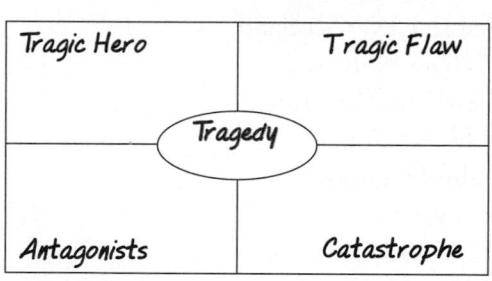

8. **Synthesize Themes** A theme is the central idea the writer wishes to share with the reader. Use specific details to explain the message *Macbeth* conveys about the following issues:

- appearance versus reality
- loyalty
- impulses and desires

Text Criticism

9. **Critical Interpretations** In a famous critique of Shakespeare's plays, the poet and critic Samuel Taylor Coleridge wrote, "The interest in the plot is always . . . on account of the characters, not vice versa." Do you agree, based on your reading of *Macbeth*? Support your answer.

> ### *Can you ever be too* **AMBITIOUS?**
> Do you think Macbeth's downfall is a result of fate, his own ambition, or other factors? Cite evidence from the play to support your argument.

COMMON CORE

RL 3 Analyze the impact of the author's choices regarding how to develop and relate elements of a drama. **RL 4** Analyze the impact of specific word choices on meaning and tone. **RL 5** Analyze how an author's choices concerning how to structure specific parts of a text contribute to its overall structure and meaning.

Language

◆ **GRAMMAR AND STYLE:** Vary Sentence Structure

Review the **Grammar and Style** note on page 361. A key aspect of Shakespeare's style is his use of **inverted sentences,** in which the subject follows the verb or part of the verb phrase. The Bard also often inverts word order by putting an object before a verb, an adjective after a noun, or a prepositional phrase before the noun or verb it modifies. Here are two examples from *Macbeth*:

> *Come, go we to the King.* (Act Four, Scene 3, line 239)

> *O, never / Shall sun that morrow see!* (Act One, Scene 5, lines 57–58)

Notice that in the first line, the verb *go* precedes the subject *we.* In the second sentence, the direct object *sun* appears before both the subject *morrow* and the verb *see.* Shakespeare used this kind of sentence structure primarily for poetic effect. You can use inverted sentences and other types of inverted word order to add variety to your writing or to emphasize a specific word or idea.

PRACTICE Write down each of the following lines from *Macbeth*. Identify the inverted parts of speech in each sentence and then write your own lines with a similar pattern.

> **EXAMPLE**
>
> Now does he feel / His secret murders sticking on his hands.
>
> *Now does she taste the sweet strawberries growing on the vines.*

1. My dull brain was wrought / With things forgotten.

2. O, full of scorpions is my mind, dear wife!

3. I'll fight, till from my bones my flesh be hacked.

READING-WRITING CONNECTION

YOUR TURN Expand your understanding of Shakespeare's language by responding to this prompt. Then use the **revising tips** to improve your speech.

WRITING PROMPT	REVISING TIPS
WRITE A SPEECH In a **persuasive speech,** you use the power of language to influence others. Imagine that you live in Scotland during the time of Macbeth. Write a **three-to-five-paragraph speech** in which you call for the overthrow of Macbeth. Be sure to use evidence that will support your argument and persuade your audience.	• Make sure you state your position clearly. • Vary sentence structure in the speech by adding one or two inverted sentences.

COMMON CORE

L 3a Vary syntax for effect; apply an understanding of syntax to the study of complex texts when reading. **W 1** Write arguments to support claims in an analysis, using valid reasoning and relevant and sufficient evidence. **W 1c** Use words, phrases, and clauses as well as varied syntax to create cohesion, and clarify the relationships between reasons and evidence. **W 9** Draw evidence from literary or informational texts to support analysis, reflection, and research.

Interactive Revision THINK central

Go to **thinkcentral.com**.
KEYWORD: HML12-433

The Real Macbeth

- Historical Account, page 435
- Newspaper Article, page 437

Use with *Macbeth*,
page 348.

COMMON CORE

RI 2 Provide an objective summary of the text. **RI 6** Determine an author's point of view or purpose in a text. **RI 7** Integrate and evaluate multiple sources of information presented in different media or formats in order to address a question or solve a problem.

When William Shakespeare wrote "the Scottish play," he based the plot, characters, and setting on details in Raphael Holinshed's historical account *Chronicles of England, Scotland, and Ireland*, published in 1587. Now you will read directly from this source of information and then look at a contemporary article by Julie Traves about the real Macbeth.

Standards Focus: Take Notes and Synthesize

When you synthesize, or integrate, ideas from different sources, you compare and combine the ideas to gain a better understanding of a subject. For example, Holinshed and Traves suggest very different things about who Macbeth really was. By synthesizing their ideas, we can begin to evaluate the accuracy of Shakespeare's portrayal of this Scottish king.

In order to compare these texts, it may be helpful to take notes about each work and then use those notes to summarize your findings. This process of gathering and organizing information can help you uncover the key relationships and patterns in each work. Use a chart like the one shown to take notes from each text, or create a different chart that works better for you.

Source	Important Details and Ideas About Macbeth
"Duncan's Murder" from <u>Holinshed's Chronicles</u>	
"Banquo's Murder" from <u>Holinshed's</u> <u>Chronicles</u>	
"Out, Damn Slander, Out" paragraphs 1 and 2	

First read *Holinshed's Chronicles*. Then, from each subsection, gather key details about Macbeth and list them in your chart. You will use these details to summarize the author's viewpoint. Organize the key details into brief summaries about how Macbeth is portrayed in each subsection. Use no more than a few sentences for each summary. Then combine these sentences to create a brief overall summary that describes the author's viewpoint about Macbeth. Follow the same process for Traves's newspaper article.

Finally, compare your summaries. What are the major similarities and differences in the way these authors view Macbeth?

from *Holinshed's Chronicles*

by Raphael Holinshed

Duncan's Murder

It fortuned, as Macbeth and Banquo journeyed toward Forres, where the King then lay, they went sporting by the way together without other company save only themselves, passing through the woods and fields, when suddenly, in midst of a laund,[1] there met them three women in strange and wild apparel, resembling creatures of elder[2] world; whom when they attentively beheld, wondering much at the sight, the first of them spoke and said, "All hail, Macbeth, Thane of Glamis!" (for he had lately entered into that dignity and office by the death of his father Sinel). The second of them said, "Hail, Macbeth, Thane of Cawdor!" But the third said, "All hail, Macbeth, that hereafter shalt be King of Scotland!" **A**

10   Then Banquo. "What manner of women," saith he, "are you, that seem so little favorable unto me, whereas to my fellow here, besides high offices, ye assign also the kingdom, appointing forth nothing for me at all?" "Yes," saith the first of them, "we promise greater benefits unto thee than unto him, for he shall reign indeed, but with an unlucky end; neither shall he leave any issue behind him to succeed in his place, where contrarily thou indeed shalt not reign at all, but of thee those shall be born which shall govern the Scottish kingdom by long order of continual descent." Herewith the foresaid women vanished immediately out of their sight. . . . Shortly after, the Thane of Cawdor being condemned at Forres of treason against the King committed, his lands, livings, and offices were given of the King's liberality to Macbeth. . . . **B**

20   Shortly after it chanced that King Duncan, having two sons by his wife (which was the daughter of Siward Earl of Northumberland), he made the elder of them (called Malcolm) Prince of Cumberland, as it were thereby to appoint him his successor in the kingdom immediately after his decease. Macbeth, sore troubled herewith, for that he saw by this means his hope sore hindered . . . he began to take counsel how he might

---

1. **laund:** glade.
2. **elder:** ancient.

A TAKE NOTES
According to Holinshed, whom did Macbeth and Banquo encounter on their way to Forres? What did the comments made to Macbeth suggest about his future?

B TAKE NOTES
Reread lines 17–19. Why was this event significant? Record the event and its significance in your notes.

usurp the kingdom by force, having a just quarrel[3] so to do (as he took the matter), for that Duncan did what in him lay to defraud him of all manner of title and claim which he might, in time to come, pretend[4] unto the crown.

The words of the three Weird Sisters also (of whom before ye have heard) greatly encouraged him hereunto; but specially his wife lay sore upon him[5] to attempt the thing,
30 as she that was very ambitious, burning in unquenchable desire to bear the name of a queen. At length, therefore, communicating his purposed intent with his trusty friends, amongst whom Banquo was the chiefest, upon confidence of their promised aid he slew the King at Inverness or (as some say) at Bothgowanan, in the sixth year of his reign. **C**

Banquo's Murder

This was but a counterfeit zeal of equity[6] showed by him, partly against his natural inclination, to purchase thereby the favor of the people. Shortly after, he began to show what he was, instead of equity practicing cruelty. For the prick of conscience (as it chanceth ever in tyrants and such as attain to any estate by unrighteous means) caused him ever to fear lest he should be served of the same cup as he had ministered to his predecessor. The words also of the three Weird Sisters would not out of his mind, which
40 as they promised him the kingdom, so likewise did they promise it at the same time unto the posterity of Banquo. He willed therefore the same Banquo, with his son named Fleance, to come to a supper that he had prepared for them; which was indeed, as he had devised, present death at the hands of certain murderers whom he hired to execute that deed, appointing them to meet with the same Banquo and his son without the palace, as they returned to their lodgings, and there to slay them, so that he would not have his house slandered but that in time to come he might clear himself if anything were laid to his charge upon any suspicion that might arise. **D**

It chanced by the benefit of the dark night that, though the father were slain, yet the son, by the help of almighty God reserving him to better fortune, escaped that danger;
50 and afterward, having some inkling (by the admonition of some friends which he had in the court) how his life was sought no less than his father's, who was slain not by chance-medley[7] (as by the handling of the matter Macbeth would have had it to appear) but even upon a prepensed[8] device, whereupon to avoid further peril he fled into Wales. **E**

---

3. **quarrel:** cause.

4. **pretend:** claim.

5. **lay sore upon him:** pressed him hard.

6. **equity:** fairness.

7. **chance-medley:** accidental homicide.

8. **prepensed:** premeditated.

C TAKE NOTES

Identify Macbeth's action in lines 31–33. What and/or who motivated him to commit this act? Explain.

Language Coach

Formal Language The formal language of historical and other academic texts is different from everyday language. Lines 34–35 contain two formal-sounding adverbs. The first, *but* (usually a conjunction, like *and*) means "only." The other, *thereby*, means "in that way." Say these lines more informally.

D TAKE NOTES

What did Macbeth hire men to do? Why? Reread lines 36–41 to identify his motives.

E TAKE NOTES

What did Fleance do? Why? Add this information to your notes.

Travel Section

Out, Damn Slander, Out

Julie Traves

On the 1,000th anniversary of Macbeth's birth, 20 members of the Scottish Parliament are trying to restore his honor—while at the same time boosting tourism. After all, the former king's influence, fictitious or otherwise, is widely felt across the landscape and landmarks of Scotland, from the castle he ruled in "the Scottish play" to the Iron Age hill fort where he reputedly met his demise.

A motion was put forward this year that "regrets the fact that Macbeth was misportrayed in the play by Shakespeare of that name," and notes the historical connections Macbeth had to locations all over Scotland. . . . Since the first performance of *Macbeth* nearly 500 years ago, the Scottish leader has been known as a faithless killer spurred on by witches and a "fiend-like queen." As scholar Frank Kermode writes in his introduction to *The Riverside Shakespeare,* "In no other play does Shakespeare show a nation so cruelly occupied by the powers of darkness."

(continued)

Language Coach

Frequently Misused Words *Fictitious* and *fictional* are so similar in sound and meaning that they are easily confused. *Fictional* means "relating to imaginative writing," as in "fictional hero." *Fictitious* (line 5) means "fake" or "imaginary." Which word has more negative associations, or connotations?

Glamis castle in Angus, Scotland—a famous Scottish castle, referred to by Shakespeare as Macbeth's home

In fact, the real Macbeth had a remarkably harmonious reign from 1040 to 1057. He is credited with spreading Christianity throughout Scotland, which prospered under his rule. In a recent interview with 30 the *Daily Telegraph,* historian Ted Cowan of Glasgow University said that "some of the ancient Highland clans looked to Macbeth as the last great Celtic ruler in Scotland." . . . **F**

The Bard based *Macbeth* on Raphael Holinshed's *Chronicles of England, Scotland and Ireland,* published in 1577. While this historical tract doesn't mention Macbeth's betrayal of Duncan, it does refer 40 to the killer of an earlier Scots king who was also urged on by his wife. This material was applied to *Macbeth,* in part, to comment on how ambition can go awry. The story of Macbeth was also altered as a way to pay tribute to—and legitimize— Scottish King James VI's rise to the English throne in 1603. **G**

These days, however, when people think of Macbeth, they don't think of royal 50 ancestry—or real history, for that matter. Most of the 120,000 visitors that go to Glamis Castle each year "make the link with Shakespeare," according to the castle's business manager Gill Crawford. And Glamis plays up that link: There was a performance of *Macbeth* on the grounds last year, and corporate groups can hire a Lady Macbeth to give the "out damn spot" speech (a message to striving 60 executives, perhaps?). . . .

Bill Jameson, a writer for the *Scotsman* newspaper, doubts whether tourists want to see monuments to a goody-goody king at all. He writes: "What draws visitors is the mystery of malevolence, and the wish to see the settings of great murders and misdemeanors."

And what do Scots themselves make of all this toil and trouble? Douglas Pattulo, a 70 parliamentary assistant, said that once the public learned that Macbeth was not "the baddie of history," they were mostly in favor of burnishing his image. . . .

F TAKE NOTES
So far, what new information about Macbeth has Julie Traves presented? Record this information in your notes.

G TAKE NOTES
Reread lines 35–47. According to the author, in what ways does Shakespeare manipulate Holinshed's details? Why did he change the story? Include these points in your notes.

Macbeth, Banquo, and the Three Witches. English School. Woodcut. Private collection. © Bridgeman Art Library.

Comprehension

1. **Recall** According to Holinshed, what were Macbeth's motives for killing Duncan? for attempting to have Banquo and Fleance killed?

2. **Recall** What were 20 members of the Scottish Parliament trying to do on the 1,000th anniversary of Macbeth's birth?

3. **Summarize** Describe the real Macbeth according to author Julie Traves.

Text Analysis

4. **Analyze Allusion** Consider the title "Out, Damn Slander, Out." What is Traves alluding to? What point is she making about Macbeth's reputation? Explain.

5. **Reflect on Your Notes** Suppose that Shakespeare had chosen to portray a more historically accurate Macbeth. Do you think he still would have managed to write an interesting play with a more virtuous protagonist? Explain.

COMMON CORE

RI 2 Provide an objective summary of the text. **RI 6** Determine an author's point of view or purpose in a text. **RI 7** Integrate and evaluate multiple sources of information presented in different media or formats in order to address a question or solve a problem. **W 2** Write informative/explanatory texts to examine and convey complex ideas. **W 2b** Develop the topic by selecting the most significant and relevant facts appropriate to the audience's knowledge of the topic. **W 9** Draw evidence from literary or informational texts to support analysis, reflection, and research.

Read for Information: Synthesize

WRITING PROMPT

Briefly discuss how Holinshed's negative portrayal of Macbeth differs from Traves's positive one. If Shakespeare had based his play on Traves's historically accurate, positive Macbeth instead of Holinshed's version, how would the play have changed? Do you think audiences would prefer to see a play about the positive Macbeth rather than the negative one? Why or why not? Include specific evidence from Holinshed, Traves, and Shakespeare's play in your essay.

To answer the prompt, you will synthesize information from the texts in this lesson and from Shakespeare's play. Follow these steps:

1. Gather specific information about the portrayal of Macbeth in Holinshed's and Traves's writings. Use this information to summarize each author's viewpoint so you can identify the essential differences between them.

2. Review the materials on Shakespeare's *Macbeth* (pages 340–341) and make notes about Macbeth as portrayed in the play.

3. Write down a few thoughts about why people take interest in a dramatic or historical character and how they might respond to the different portrayals of the Scottish king.

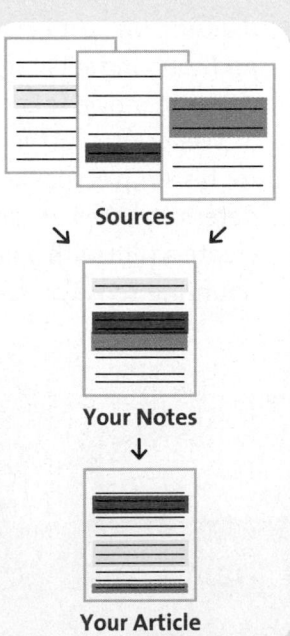

Sources

Your Notes

Your Article

From Page to Screen

COMMON CORE

RL 7 Analyze multiple interpretations of a drama, evaluating how each version interprets the source text.

In 1948 one of the world's greatest filmmakers took on the work of one of the world's greatest playwrights. Orson Welles produced, directed, starred in, and adapted the screenplay for Shakespeare's *Macbeth*. In this lesson, you'll view the opening scenes of Welles's expressionistic interpretation of the tragedy in order to explore how a director creates mood in a film.

The Filmmaker's Challenge

Orson Welles directed his first film, *Citizen Kane*, when he was only 25. Today it's considered by many critics to be among the best movies ever made. But by 1948, just seven years after *Citizen Kane*, Welles's reputation for being difficult and going over budget made it nearly impossible for him to get Hollywood backing.

Orson Welles edits *Macbeth*.

Welles's purpose, then, was to prove his critics wrong. To this end, he made *Macbeth* on a small budget and tight schedule, using many of the "guerrilla" filmmaking tactics of today's independent directors. He shot the film in just 21 days, dressing his cast in used costumes and cobbling sets together from old Western movie sets.

Welles was further challenged by the play itself. Shakespeare is notorious for his simple, sparse stage directions, so it is largely up to each director to determine the look and feel of a Shakespeare play or film. Welles chose to create a film with a dark, primitive tone, heavy with religious symbolism and a haunting sense of doom.

Comparing Texts: Creating Mood

Mood is the feeling or atmosphere that a work creates for the reader or viewer. The director of a play uses the sets, costumes, props, and lighting to develop this feeling. A film director uses these same elements, as well as the framing of each shot and the rhythm of the editing, to create the mood.

Before you view the clips from Welles's *Macbeth,* go back and skim Scenes 1 and 3 from Act One of the play. Think about the witches' dialogue in these scenes and the role the weird sisters play throughout the tragedy. What mood is created? How do lines such as "When the hurly-burly's done, / When the battle's lost and won," contribute to this mood?

Now consider *Macbeth's* brief opening stage direction.

Act One, Scene 1
An open place in Scotland.
[*Thunder and lightning. Enter three* Witches.]

Imagine you're a director. How would you stage or film this scene? What would your set look like? your costumes? When you view the film clips, consider how the details in Welles's adaptation establish the film's mood.

Viewing Guide

Media ❂ Smart DVD-ROM

- **Film:** *Macbeth*
- **Director:** Orson Welles
- **Genre:** Drama
- **Running Time:** 2 minutes

The two clips you'll view from *Macbeth* open the movie. They correspond to Act One, Scenes 1 and 3 of the play—the introduction to the witches, and Macbeth and Banquo's visit with the weird sisters. You may want to watch the clips more than once to subject them to close analysis.

NOW VIEW

CLOSE VIEWING: Media Analysis

1. **Compare Mood** Compare the clips you viewed with Act One, Scenes 1 and 3 from the play. How does the atmosphere Welles creates compare with that in the text?

2. **Analyze Shots** Identify two or three shots from the clips you viewed that would be impossible to re-create in a conventional stage performance. How do these shots contribute to the film's mood?

3. **Evaluate the Adaptation** How effective do you think Orson Welles was in adapting the opening of *Macbeth* to the big screen? Think about
   - the portrayal of the witches
   - the film's sets, props, and costumes
   - the types of shots Welles uses

FILM REVIEW This review of Orson Welles's film version of *Macbeth* appeared in the January 15, 1951, issue of the *New Republic*.

"BLOODY, BOLD, & RESOLUTE" ROBERT HATCH

WORD OF THE ORSON WELLES *Macbeth* has preceded it to New York and one takes a seat on the aisle, prepared for a quick escape if Glamis murders not only sleep but Shakespeare as well. The picture is by no means that bad; Welles's interpretation of the play is a perverse and limited one, but at least it *is* an interpretation, consistent and stated with conviction; perhaps for the screen it is even justifiable.

Taking his mood from the barbaric Holinshed chronicle rather than from the royal Elizabethan tragedy, Welles presents a *Macbeth* that looks at first glance as though it had been made in the Carlsbad Caverns by a company of Mongolian yak herders. Water seeps from every cave-like wall, and every performer is shaggy and shining with bear grease. The producer-editor has made a patchwork of Shakespeare's lines, and they are delivered with an uncouth savagery that deprives them of all their poetry and much of their sense. It is a performance in which the moral struggle—the tragedy—of *Macbeth* has been lost and violence is all.

The violence, however, is well stated; it is more than empty melodrama, having in it dark horror and a solemn recognition of the consequences of this brutish struggle. It is as though we watched our terrible ancestors in the dawn of history tearing at one another to establish the blood lines we now proudly call our heritage.

In this atmosphere, the witches appear to advantage; so do the murderers (of whom Macbeth is now one) and so does the spectacle of Birnam Wood moving upon Dunsinane. The soliloquies fare badly, the human relationships are reduced to surface struggles, and the moments of tenderness, remorse, and honor disappear entirely. Welles as Macbeth and Dan O'Herlihy and Edgar Barrier as Macduff and Banquo are striking primitive warriors; Alan Napier, in the invented role of an early church father, seems to have just given up painting himself blue and cutting the throats of human sacrifices in oak groves. On an animal level, these principal figures are impressive and even admirable. Jeanette Nolan is a ruthless, lustful, but curiously undangerous-looking Lady Macbeth. There is not enough intelligence in her villainy.

All in all, it seems fair to say of Welles's *Macbeth* that he has lost more of the play than he has preserved, but that what he does keep he presents with power and a conviction that will make it stick in the mind.

The Influence of Lady Macbeth

Literary critic Stephen Greenblatt discusses how Lady Macbeth influences her husband to put aside his natural unwillingness to murder.

> *"Macbeth and Lady Macbeth act on ambition, restless desire, and a will to power normally kept in check by the pragmatic, ethical, and religious considerations to which the wavering Macbeth initially gives voice. Lady Macbeth in effect works to liberate that will to power in her husband, freeing him from his 'sickly' fears of damnation so that he can act with a ruthless blend of murderous violence and cunning. In her radically disenchanted, coolly skeptical view, the murder of the king can be undertaken without fear of guilty conscience, vengeful ghosts, or divine judgment: 'The sleeping and the dead,' she tells her shaken husband, 'are but as pictures. 'Tis the eye of childhood / That fears a painted devil.'"*

Do you agree with this critic that Lady Macbeth sways her husband to commit murder? Or do you think Macbeth's own ambition would have pushed him to murder, even if Lady Macbeth had said or done nothing?

Writing to Analyze

Analyze the character of Lady Macbeth. Why does she want Macbeth to commit murder? How does she attempt to influence her husband? Is she successful in influencing him? What is the eventual outcome of her scheming?

Consider

- dialogue that reveals Lady Macbeth's motivation as well as her influence over her husband
- scenes between Lady Macbeth and Macbeth
- stage directions that add to your understanding of Lady Macbeth's character
- the resolution of the play

Extension Online

INQUIRY & RESEARCH Research a modern leader in politics, business, or religion who has fallen because of unbridled ambition. Analyze the factors that contributed to his or her downfall, and draw relevant comparisons to Macbeth. **Report** on your investigation to the class.

Ellen Terry as Lady Macbeth (1885-1886), John Singer Sargent.

(COMMON CORE)

W 2 Write informative texts to examine and convey complex ideas through the effective selection, organization, and analysis of content.
W 7 Conduct short research projects to answer a question or solve a problem.

from Utopia

Fiction by Sir Thomas More

Speech Before the Spanish Armada Invasion

Speech by Queen Elizabeth I

COMMON CORE

RL 4 Determine the meaning of words and phrases as they are used in the text; analyze the impact of specific word choices on meaning and tone. **RI 2** Determine two or more central ideas of a text and analyze their development. **RI 9** Analyze foundational documents of historical and literary significance for their themes, purposes, and rhetorical features.

Meet the Authors

Sir Thomas More   1478–1535

Sir Thomas More was uncommonly gifted. He became a powerful statesman and—400 years after his death—a saint. More was also considered one of the greatest lawyers and scholars of his day.

A Utopian Vision Born in London in 1478, More entered Parliament when he was 26. His experience in the political world convinced him that the time was ripe for change. In 1516, More wrote *Utopia,* a fictional work in which he enumerates the political, economic, and social problems afflicting 16th-century Europe. He also describes an ideal state ruled by reason.

A Fatal Falling Out The publication of *Utopia* thrust More into the spotlight, and in 1517 he joined King Henry VIII's council. Twelve years later, Henry appointed More lord chancellor.

However, a rift soon developed between More and Henry over the king's desire to break England's ties with the Roman Catholic Church. In 1534, More refused to approve legislation that would install Henry as head of the Church of England. More was tried and found guilty of treason. His final words as he stood before the executioner were, "The King's good servant, but God's first."

Queen Elizabeth I

1533–1603

On the day Elizabeth I was crowned, crowds cheered as she was carried through the streets. It was an auspicious beginning to her 45-year reign as queen of England.

Stark Beginning The daughter of King Henry VIII and Anne Boleyn, Elizabeth probably had a lonely childhood. Her father was deeply disappointed that his wife hadn't produced a male heir. Two years after Elizabeth's birth, he had her mother executed on charges of treason.

Despite his bitterness at not having a son, Henry provided Elizabeth with an excellent education normally given only to boys. This education would prove invaluable when she became queen.

Glorious Reign Elizabeth I ascended the throne in 1558. Her reign was a time of great prosperity and artistic achievement. Elizabeth also proved to be a shrewd politician and orator. In 1588, when a fleet of Spanish ships known as the Spanish Armada was preparing to invade England, Elizabeth delivered an inspiring speech to her soldiers. Despite having fewer ships and soldiers, the English fleet defeated the Armada.

TEXT ANALYSIS: RHETORICAL DEVICES

Both Sir Thomas More and Elizabeth I use **rhetorical devices**—techniques that communicate their ideas and support and strengthen their arguments. As you read, pay attention to their use of the following techniques:

- An **analogy** is a comparison made between two dissimilar things in order to explain an unfamiliar subject in terms of a familiar one. For example, More compares a bad ruler to an incompetent physician who cannot cure a disease except by creating another.
- **Repetition** is the repeated use of a word or phrase. For example, Elizabeth I repeats the phrase "I myself" to emphasize her personal involvement in England's defense.
- A **rhetorical question** is a question to which no answer is expected. (*Who is more eager for revolution than he who is discontented with his present state of life?*)
- **Antithesis** expresses contrasting ideas in parallel grammatical structures. (*I know I have the body but of a weak and feeble woman; but I have the heart and stomach of a king. . . .*)

READING SKILL: DRAW CONCLUSIONS

When you **draw conclusions** about a text, you make judgments about the author's meaning based on statements in the text. For example, if a writer consistently criticizes corruption in public officials, you might conclude that the writer values honesty and integrity. As you read the following selections, note ideas and supporting details that Thomas More and Queen Elizabeth consistently include that help you draw conclusions about their views of the proper role of a ruler.

▲ VOCABULARY IN CONTEXT

The words shown here help convey Elizabeth I's and Sir Thomas More's convictions about what constitutes a good ruler. Replace the boldfaced word in each of the following sentences with a word from the list.

WORD LIST	indolence	plundering
	lamentation	subjection

1. Loud **weeping** was heard at the good king's funeral.
2. The conquerors began **looting** the village after the battle.
3. As a result of his **idleness,** the bridge was never built.

 Complete the activities in your **Reader/Writer Notebook**.

What should we expect from our LEADERS?

During the Renaissance, a nation's leaders did not have to run for office. However, both Sir Thomas More and Elizabeth I suggest that even kings and queens must demonstrate effective leadership to win the support of their people.

SURVEY What qualities do you think are important in a leader? Rate each quality listed below by choosing a number from 1 (least important) to 5 (most important). Discuss your ratings with a classmate.

Leadership Qualities

Rate the importance of each quality by circling a number.

	least				most
Intelligence	1	2	3	4	5
Morality	1	2	3	4	5
Courage	1	2	3	4	5
Eloquence	1	2	3	4	5
Charisma	1	2	3	4	5

UTOPIA

Sir Thomas More

Suppose I should show that men choose a king for their own sake and not for his—to be plain, that by his labor and effort they may live well and safe from injustice and wrong. For this very reason, it belongs to the king to take more care for the welfare of his people than for his own, just as it is the duty of a shepherd, insofar as he is a shepherd, to feed his sheep rather than himself.[1] **A**

The blunt facts reveal that it is wrong to think that the poverty of the people is the safeguard of peace. Where will you find more quarreling than among beggars? Who is more eager for revolution than he who is discontented with his present state of life? Who is more reckless in the endeavor to upset everything, in the hope
10 of getting profit from some source or other, than he who has nothing to lose? Now if there were any king who was either so despicable or so hateful to his subjects that he could not keep them in **subjection** otherwise than by ill usage, **plundering,** and confiscation and by reducing them to beggary, it would surely be better for him to resign his throne than to keep it by such means—means by which, though he retain the name of authority, he loses its majesty. It is not consistent with the dignity of a king to exercise authority over beggars but over prosperous and happy subjects. This was certainly the sentiment of that noble and lofty spirit, Fabricus, who replied that he would rather be a ruler of rich people than be rich himself.[2]

To be sure, to have a single person enjoy a life of pleasure and self-indulgence
20 amid the groans and **lamentations** of all around him is to be the keeper, not of a kingdom, but of a jail. In fine,[3] as he is an incompetent physician who cannot cure one disease except by creating another, so he who cannot reform the lives of citizens in any other way than by depriving them of the good things of life must admit that he does not know how to rule free men.

Yea, the king had better amend his own **indolence** or arrogance, for these two vices generally cause his people to either despise him or to hate him. Let him live harmlessly on what is his own. Let him adjust his expenses to his revenues. Let him check mischief and crime, and, by training his subjects rightly, let him prevent rather than allow the spread of activities which he will have to punish afterwards.
30 Let him not be hasty in enforcing laws fallen into disuse, especially those which, long given up have never been missed. Let him never take in compensation for violation anything that a private person would be forbidden in court to appropriate for the reason that such would be an act of crooked craftiness.[4] **B**

---

1. **the duty of a shepherd . . . himself:** More's metaphor paraphrases the Bible (Ezekiel 34:2): "Woe be to the shepherds of Israel that do feed themselves: should not the shepherds feed the flocks?"

2. **Fabricus . . . himself:** Gaius Fabricius Luscinus was a Roman commander famous for his virtues. The statement attributed to him here was actually made by his associate M. Curius Dentatus.

3. **in fine:** in conclusion.

4. **an act of crooked craftiness:** sly, dishonest behavior.

A RHETORICAL DEVICES
Reread lines 1–5. What rhetorical device does More use? How does it strengthen his argument?

subjection (səb-jĕk′shən) *n.* the state of being under the authority or control of another

plundering (plŭn′dər-ĭng) *n.* taking property by force **plunder** *v.*

lamentation (lăm′ən-tā′shən) *n.* an expression of sorrow or regret

indolence (ĭn′də-ləns) *n.* the tendency to avoid work; laziness; idleness

B GRAMMAR AND STYLE
Reread lines 26–33. Note that More uses a succession of **imperative sentences** to convey his ideas about how a king should behave.

Bishop Sherbourne with Henry VIII (1800s), Louise Barnard. Chichester Cathedral, Sussex, United Kingdom. © Bridgeman Art Library.

SPEECH BEFORE THE
Spanish Armada Invasion

Queen Elizabeth I

MY LOVING PEOPLE,

We have been persuaded by some that are careful of our safety, to take heed how we commit our selves to armed multitudes, for fear of treachery; but I assure you I do not desire to live to distrust my faithful and loving people. Let tyrants fear, I have always so behaved myself that, under God, I have placed my chiefest strength and safeguard in the loyal hearts and good-will of my subjects; and therefore I am come amongst you, as you see, at this time, not for my recreation and disport,[1] but being resolved, in the midst and heat of the battle, to live or die amongst you all; to lay down for my God, and for my kingdom, and my people, my honor

10 and my blood, even in the dust. I know I have the body but of a weak and feeble woman; but I have the heart and stomach of a king, and of a king of England too, and think foul scorn that Parma or Spain, or any prince of Europe,[2] should dare to invade the borders of my realm; to which rather than any dishonor shall grow by me, I myself will take up arms, I myself will be your general, judge, and rewarder of every one of your virtues in the field. I know already, for your forwardness you have deserved rewards and crowns; and We do assure you in the word of a prince, they shall be duly paid you. In the mean time, my lieutenant general shall be in my stead,[3] than whom never prince commanded a more noble or worthy subject; not doubting but by your obedience to my general, by your concord[4] in the camp,

20 and your valor in the field, we shall shortly have a famous victory over those enemies of my God, of my kingdom, and of my people. **C D**

---

1. **disport:** entertainment.
2. **Parma or Spain . . . Europe:** the duke of Parma, the king of Spain, or any other monarch of Europe. Alessandro Farnese, duke of the Italian city of Parma, was a skillful military leader whom Philip II, king of Spain, often relied upon. Philip's plan was to send the Spanish fleet to join the army under Parma's command in the Netherlands and invade England.
3. **my lieutenant general . . . stead:** Elizabeth refers to Robert Dudley, the earl of Leicester. He was a courtier who for a time was Elizabeth's favorite at court.
4. **concord** (kŏn'kôrd') *n.* friendly and peaceful relations; harmony; agreement

---

COMMON CORE L 5a

C PARADOX
A **paradox** is an apparent contradiction that is actually true. During the Renaissance, to be both female and the powerful ruler of a nation was a contradiction in terms. As the female ruler of England, Queen Elizabeth I was herself a paradox. Reread lines 10–11. How does this rhetorical device help Elizabeth present herself as a powerful female monarch? How does she expand on this paradox in the course of her speech to inspire her people?

D DRAW CONCLUSIONS
Reread lines 17–21. What conclusions can you draw about the kinds of feelings a ruler should inspire in times of war?

Comprehension

1. **Recall** According to Sir Thomas More, what should a king's labor and effort secure for his people?

2. **Recall** Why does More think it is in a king's interest to ensure the prosperity of his people?

3. **Summarize** What does Elizabeth I claim she will do if "any prince of Europe" dares to invade her realm?

Text Analysis

4. **Understand Persuasive Techniques** Persuasive techniques are the methods writers use to influence others to accept their views. How does More appeal to the values of kings to persuade them not to impoverish their subjects?

● 5. **Analyze Rhetorical Devices** Reread lines 6–10 in the selection from *Utopia*. What effect do these **rhetorical questions** produce? How do they help support More's argument? Reread lines 21–24. What does More emphasize through the use of an **analogy** in this sentence?

● 6. **Draw Conclusions** Review the notes you took as you read the two selections. What conclusions can you draw about what Elizabeth felt was the proper role of a ruler? Do you think More would have approved of her governing style? Explain your ideas using specific details.

7. **Compare Tone** The expression of a writer's attitude toward a subject is **tone.** For each selection, use a graphic organizer like the one shown to record words and details that convey the tone. What similarities in tone do you find in *Utopia* and Elizabeth's speech? In what ways do these texts differ in tone?

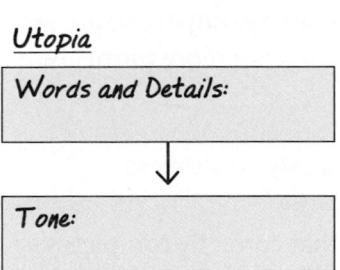

Text Criticism

8. **Social Context** Most women had little or no role outside the home in 16th-century England, yet Elizabeth I successfully ruled the country. What details in her speech suggest how she gained the respect of her subjects as a ruler who would fight to defend her country?

> *What should we expect from our* **LEADERS?**
>
> Under what circumstances may a leader benefit from revealing a personal flaw? Under what circumstances may it hurt a leader to do so?

COMMON CORE

RL 4 Determine the meaning of words and phrases as they are used in the text; analyze the impact of specific word choices on meaning and tone. **RI 2** Determine two or more central ideas of a text and analyze their development. **RI 9** Analyze foundational documents of historical and literary significance for their themes, purposes, and rhetorical features.

Vocabulary in Context

▲ **VOCABULARY PRACTICE**

Decide whether the boldfaced words make the statements true or false.

WORD LIST

indolence
lamentation
plundering
subjection

1. A slave is in a state of **subjection.**
2. A **lamentation** is made in a mournful tone.
3. An idle aristocrat typically displays **indolence.**
4. **Plundering** does not result in damage or loss.

ACADEMIC VOCABULARY IN WRITING

• attribute • feature • monitor • phase • primary

Queen Elizabeth marks an important **phase** in her rule when she presents herself to her subjects as a powerful warrior. Thomas More notes that a leader who lacks moral integrity could not lead effectively. Write a paragraph in which you discuss the **primary** characteristics you think make someone an ineffective leader. Use at least one of the Academic Vocabulary words in your response.

VOCABULARY STRATEGY: ANALOGIES AND CONNOTATIONS

An **analogy,** which compares two terms to clarify the meaning of the less familiar one, can illustrate the relationship between synonyms' connotations. For example, you could say *"Indolence* is to *laziness* as *urbanity* is to *politeness."* Just as *indolence* and *laziness* are synonyms, so are *urbanity* and *politeness.* However, like *indolence, urbanity* is a more formal term. A shorthand for this analogy is

INDOLENCE : LAZINESS :: urbanity : politeness

COMMON CORE

L 5 Demonstrate understanding of word relationships. **L 6** Acquire and use accurately general academic words.

PRACTICE Choose the item that correctly completes each analogy below. Use a dictionary if necessary.

1. STEALING : PLUNDERING :: criticizing : ____
   (a) pouting, (b) berating, (c) praising, (d) suggesting
2. LAMENTATIONS : WHIMPERS :: accolades : ____
   (a) sincerity, (b) attacks, (c) praise, (d) criticism
3. TYRANT : RULER :: hurricane : ____
   (a) tropics, (b) tranquility, (c) monsoon, (d) rainstorm
4. BEAUTIFUL : EXQUISITE :: surprising : ____
   (a) shocking, (b) amusing, (c) confirming, (d) numbing
5. STUPID : ASININE :: sad : ____
   (a) sorry, (b) relieved, (c) inconsolable, (d) agitated

Interactive Vocabulary THINK central

Go to **thinkcentral.com.**
KEYWORD: HML12-450

Language

◆ **GRAMMAR AND STYLE:** Use Effective Sentence Types

Review the **Grammar and Style** note on page 446. Notice that Sir Thomas More uses a series of **imperative sentences,** or sentences that express a command, to pronounce how a good king should behave. By using imperative sentences instead of less forceful declarative sentences, More emphasizes the urgency of his message.

Here is an example of one student's use of imperative sentences:

> *Follow my lead. Join me in the fight against hunger.*

Notice that imperative sentences begin with a verb in the active voice. The subject—*you*—is understood.

PRACTICE Rewrite the following paragraph, changing some sentences to make them imperative.

> You can make a difference in the lives of those less fortunate than you by giving a contribution today. You might consider donating canned goods to your local shelter. You could even surprise a needy family with the ingredients for a special meal. Together, we can defeat hunger.

READING-WRITING CONNECTION

YOUR TURN Expand your understanding of *Utopia* and "Speech Before the Spanish Armada Invasion" by responding to this prompt. Then use the **revising tips** to improve your editorial.

WRITING PROMPT

WRITE AN EDITORIAL In the selection from *Utopia*, Sir Thomas More explains how a good king should behave. Think of a few important leaders today. Choose one, and write a **three-to-five-paragraph editorial** in which you express your opinions about this leader. Consider both positive and negative aspects of the leader's performance. Be sure to provide instruction on how he or she could become a better leader.

REVISING TIPS

- Briefly define how you believe a good leader should behave to help establish your position.
- Briefly evaluate the leader's overall performance to give your readers a context for your opinions.
- Use specific details to describe how you think the leader's performance needs to improve.
- Use at least two imperative sentences in your editorial to urge the leader to change.

COMMON CORE

L 3 Apply knowledge of language to understand how language functions in different contexts. **W 1** Write arguments to support claims in an analysis of substantive topics or texts, using valid reasoning and relevant and sufficient evidence. **W 1a** Distinguish claims from alternate or opposing claims. **W 1b** Develop claims and counterclaims fairly and thoroughly. **W 4** Produce clear and coherent writing in which the style is appropriate to task, purpose, and audience.

◌ **COMMON CORE**

RI 4 Determine the meaning of words and phrases as they are used in a text, including figurative meanings; analyze how an author uses and refines the meaning of terms over the course of a text. **RI 6** Determine an author's point of view in a text in which the rhetoric is particularly effective, analyzing how style and content contribute to the power, persuasiveness, or beauty of the text. **L 5a** Interpret figures of speech in context and analyze their role in the text.

DID YOU KNOW?

Niccolò Machiavelli . . .

- always changed into his finest clothing before sitting down to write.
- dedicated *The Prince* to Lorenzo de' Medici, who probably never read it.
- enjoyed pranks and jokes.

Meet the Author

Niccolò Machiavelli 1469–1527

During the Renaisssance, Sir Thomas More and other scholars assumed that morality had a central role in politics. Italy's Niccolò Machiavelli broke with this tradition, arguing that rulers should ignore moral concerns that interfere with their ability to govern. Machiavelli's political treatise *The Prince* earned him such notoriety that the term *Machiavellian* was coined to refer to a ruthless drive for power. Today he is considered the founder of the modern field of political science.

Political Rise and Fall Niccolò Machiavelli was born into a prominent but impoverished family in Florence, Italy. In 1498, when he was only 29, Machiavelli landed an important job in the Florentine government that required considerable travel. His travels provided him with an insider's view of various rulers' strategies and policies.

In 1512, the republic of Florence fell, and the Medici, a wealthy family that had once ruled Florence, returned to power. Machiavelli attempted to curry favor with the Medici but was instead relieved of his post. In 1513, Machiavelli's political career effectively ended when he was accused of being an accomplice in a conspiracy against the Medici and was briefly imprisoned.

A Second Chance Although Machiavelli was eventually released from prison, there was no place for him in the Medici government. He spent much of his remaining years writing. During this period, he composed *The Prince,* detailing how a principality should be ruled, and a companion work, *Discourses on the First Ten Books of Livy,* focusing on how a republic should be ruled.

Machiavelli dedicated *The Prince* to Lorenzo de' Medici, hoping to regain political favor. Finally, in 1519, he succeeded in partly reconciling with the family when they appointed him Florence's official historian. He worked on a history of Florence and on several other commissions until he died.

The Power of *The Prince* Because *The Prince* was published in 1532, after Machiavelli's death, he never experienced the controversy surrounding his work. Most early readers of *The Prince* were scandalized by its message and by its disregard of morality and ethical rules. But over time, the treatise changed people's perception of government. For hundreds of years, leaders have used *The Prince* as a guide to wielding political power.

Author Online

Go to **thinkcentral.com**. KEYWORD: HML12-452

TEXT ANALYSIS: ARGUMENT

An **argument** is speech or writing that expresses a position on an issue or problem and supports it with reasons and evidence. In *The Prince*, Machiavelli presents his revolutionary argument on what it takes to be an effective ruler. Machiavelli uses these rhetorical elements to build his argument:

- **Irony:** a contrast between expectation and reality (*Therefore, it is necessary for a prince, who wishes to maintain himself, to learn how not to be good....*)

- **Paradox:** an apparent contradiction that is actually true (*[Is it] better to be loved more than feared or feared more than loved[?] The reply is one ought to be both feared and loved.*)

- **Subtlety:** making an argument using skillful distinctions (*... He must not deviate from what is good if possible, but be able to do evil if [forced].*)

READING SKILL: ANALYZE AUTHOR'S PERSPECTIVE

An **author's perspective** is the set of beliefs, values, and feelings through which a writer views a subject. Machiavelli's view of power was strongly influenced by his observations of politicians of his era. Unlike most political writers of his time, Machiavelli based his beliefs on first-hand knowledge rather than on ideas found in books. As you read, use a chart like the one below to identify how Machiavelli's perspective is revealed in his statements, tone, and descriptions.

Statement, Tone, or Description	What It Reveals About Author's Perspective
"He who abandons what is done for what ought to be done, will ... bring about his own ruin...."	Machiavelli believes a leader benefits from practical results, not ideals.

VOCABULARY IN CONTEXT

Machiavelli uses these words to help convey the qualities of an effective king. For each numbered item, choose a word from the list that has the same definition.

WORD LIST		
astute	laudable	venerated
constrain	pusillanimous	voluble
dissension	rapacious	

1. opposition
2. cowardly
3. shrewd
4. praiseworthy

Complete the activities in your **Reader/Writer Notebook**.

Would you rather be LOVED *or* RESPECTED?

Most people want to be loved as well as respected. But as Machiavelli points out in *The Prince*, these two needs sometimes come into conflict. If you were in a position of power, would you want people to consider you their best friend, or would you prefer them to admire you for your abilities—perhaps even feel intimidated by you?

DISCUSS With a partner, identify a position of authority, such as a sports coach. Then discuss whether love or respect would be more important for someone who holds that position.

THE PRINCE

Niccolò Machiavelli

> **BACKGROUND** In the 15th and 16th centuries, Italy was a collection of city-states. Some were republics, and some were principalities under the control of one person or family. During this period of political turmoil, Machiavelli wrote *The Prince*, a work in which he outlines the means by which a state can achieve peace and stability.

It now remains to be seen what are the methods and rules for a prince as regards his subjects and friends. And as I know that many have written of this, I fear that my writing about it may be deemed presumptuous, differing as I do, especially in this matter, from the opinions of others. But my intention being to write something of use to those who understand, it appears to me more proper to go to the real truth of the matter than to its imagination; and many have imagined republics and principalities[1] which have never been seen or known to exist in reality; for how we live is so far removed from how we ought to live, that he who abandons what is done for what ought to be done, will rather learn to bring about
10 his own ruin than his preservation.

A man who wishes to make a profession of goodness in everything must necessarily come to grief among so many who are not good. Therefore it is necessary for a prince, who wishes to maintain himself, to learn how not to be good, and to use this knowledge and not use it, according to the necessity of the case. **Ⓐ**

Leaving on one side, then, those things which concern only an imaginary prince, and speaking of those that are real, I state that all men, and especially princes, who are placed at a greater height, are reputed for certain qualities which bring them either praise or blame. Thus one is considered liberal, another . . . miserly; . . . one a free giver, another **rapacious;** one cruel, another merciful; one

Analyze Visuals ▶
What details in this painting help give the impression that the subject is a powerful person?

Ⓐ ARGUMENT
Why is the statement Machiavelli makes in lines 11-14 **ironic**? How does this help his argument?

rapacious (rə-pā'shəs) *adj.* greedy; grasping

---

1. **principalities** (prĭn'sə-păl'ĭ-tēz): monarchies. Throughout the treatise, Machiavelli uses *prince*—and related words—in a general sense, meaning any inherited ruler, not in the strict sense of ßthe son of a king.

Cosimo I Medici, Agnolo Bronzino. Galleria Sabauda, Turin, Italy. © Alinari/Art Resource, New York.

COSMVS MED FLOR ET SENARVM DVX II·

20 a breaker of his word, another trustworthy; one effeminate and **pusillanimous,**
another fierce and high-spirited; one humane, another haughty; one lascivious,
another chaste; one frank, another **astute;** one hard, another easy; one serious,
another frivolous; one religious, another an unbeliever, and so on. I know that
every one will admit that it would be highly praiseworthy in a prince to possess
all the above-named qualities that are reputed good, but as they cannot all be
possessed or observed, human conditions not permitting of it, it is necessary that
he should be prudent enough to avoid the scandal of those vices which would
lose him the state, and guard himself if possible against those which will not lose
it [for] him, but if not able to, he can indulge them with less scruple.[2] And yet
30 he must not mind incurring the scandal of those vices, without which it would
be difficult to save the state, for if one considers well, it will be found that some
things which seem virtues would, if followed, lead to one's ruin, and some others
which appear vices result in one's greater security and wellbeing. . . . **B**

    . . . I say that every prince must desire to be considered merciful and not cruel.
He must, however, take care not to misuse this mercifulness. Cesare Borgia was
considered cruel, but his cruelty had brought order to the Romagna,[3] united it,
and reduced it to peace and fealty. If this is considered well, it will be seen that
he was really much more merciful than the Florentine people, who, to avoid
the name of cruelty, allowed Pistoia to be destroyed.[4] A prince, therefore, must
40 not mind incurring the charge of cruelty for the purpose of keeping his subjects
united and faithful; for, with a very few examples, he will be more merciful than
those who, from excess of tenderness, allow disorders to arise, from whence spring
bloodshed and rapine; for these as a rule injure the whole community, while the
executions carried out by the prince injure only individuals. . . . **C**

    From this arises the question whether it is better to be loved more than feared,
or feared more than loved. The reply is, that one ought to be both feared and
loved, but as it is difficult for the two to go together, it is much safer to be feared
than loved, if one of the two has to be wanting. For it may be said of men in
general that they are ungrateful, **voluble,** dissemblers, anxious to avoid danger,
50 and covetous of gain; as long as you benefit them, they are entirely yours; they
offer you their blood, their goods, their life, and their children, as I have before
said, when the necessity is remote; but when it approaches, they revolt. And the
prince who has relied solely on their words, without making other preparations, is
ruined; for the friendship which is gained by purchase and not through grandeur
and nobility of spirit is bought but not secured, and at a pinch is not to be
expended in your service. And men have less scruple in offending one who makes

---

2. **with less scruple:** with less hesitancy about what is right or ethical.

3. **Cesare Borgia** (chā′zär-ā′ bôr′jə) . . . **Romagna** (rō-män′yə): The military leader Cesare Borgia (c. 1476–1507) temporarily made himself ruler of a region of north-central Italy known as Romagna and used cruelty and violence to bring the population into line.

4. **Florentine people . . . destroyed:** The small Italian city of Pistoia (pĭ-stoi′ə) was technically under the control of Florence when a small but violent civil war broke out there in 1501. Florentine authorities sent Machiavelli himself to investigate, but in the end those authorities feared intervening, and the two rival factions in Pistoia hacked one another to death.

---

pusillanimous
(pyōō′sə-lăn′ə-məs) *adj.*
timid; cowardly

astute (ə-stōōt′) *adj.*
having a clever or shrewd
mind; cunning; wily

B ARGUMENT
Reread lines 29–33. What
subtle distinctions
between vice and virtue
does Machiavelli make?

**C AUTHOR'S
PERSPECTIVE**
Reread lines 35–39.
What does Machiavelli's
comparison of Cesare
Borgia and the Florentines
reveal about his values?

voluble (vŏl′yə-bəl) *adj.*
talkative; glib

Language Coach

Cognates are words
from different languages
with similar origins and
spellings. *Remote* (line
52) is a cognate of the
Spanish *remoto.* Reread
lines 48–52. What does
the author describe as
remote in this passage?

himself loved than one who makes himself feared; for love is held by a chain of obligation which, men being selfish, is broken whenever it serves their purpose; but fear is maintained by a dread of punishment which never fails. **D**

60   Still, a prince should make himself feared in such a way that if he does not gain love, he at any rate avoids hatred; for fear and the absence of hatred may well go together, and will be always attained by one who abstains from interfering with the property of his citizens and subjects or with their women. And when he is obliged to take the life of any one, let him do so when there is a proper justification and manifest reason for it; but above all he must abstain from taking the property of others, for men forget more easily the death of their father than the loss of their patrimony. Then also pretexts for seizing property are never wanting, and one who begins to live by rapine will always find some reason for taking the goods of others, whereas causes for taking life are rarer and more fleeting.

70   But when the prince is with his army and has a large number of soldiers under his control, then it is extremely necessary that he should not mind being thought cruel; for without this reputation he could not keep an army united or disposed to any duty. Among the noteworthy actions of Hannibal is numbered this, that although he had an enormous army, composed of men of all nations and fighting in foreign countries, there never arose any **dissension** either among them or against the prince, either in good fortune or in bad. This could not be due to anything but his inhuman cruelty,[5] which together with his infinite other virtues, made him always **venerated** and terrible in the sight of his soldiers, and without it his other virtues would not have sufficed to produce that effect. Thoughtless
80 writers admire on the one hand his actions, and on the other blame the principal cause of them. . . .

    How **laudable** it is for a prince to keep good faith and live with integrity, and not with astuteness, every one knows. Still the experience of our times shows those princes to have done great things who have had little regard for good faith, and have been able by astuteness to confuse men's brains, and who have ultimately overcome those who have made loyalty their foundation. **E**

    You must know, then, that there are two methods of fighting, the one by law, the other by force: the first method is that of men, the second of beasts; but as the first method is often insufficient, one must have recourse to the second. It
90 is therefore necessary for a prince to know well how to use both the beast and the man. . . .

    A prince being thus obliged to know well how to act as a beast must imitate the fox and the lion, for the lion cannot protect himself from traps, and the fox cannot defend himself from wolves. One must therefore be a fox to recognize traps, and a lion to frighten wolves. Those that wish to be only lions do not understand this. Therefore, a prudent ruler ought not to keep faith when by so

---

D **GRAMMAR AND STYLE**
Machiavelli uses **formal language** suited to a serious argument. Notice, for example, the complex vocabulary and sentence structure in lines 48–52.

dissension (dĭ-sĕn'shən) *n.* disagreement; violent quarreling

venerated (vĕn'ər-ā'tĭd) *adj.* deeply respected; revered **venerate** *v.*

laudable (lô'də-bəl) *adj.* worthy of praise

E **ARGUMENT**
How is the prince's behavior **paradoxical**? Why does Machiavelli believe such behavior is necessary?

---

5. **Hannibal . . . inhuman cruelty:** Hannibal (247–183 B.C.) led the forces of the North African city-state of Carthage against Rome in the Second Punic War. A brilliant general whose military victories almost destroyed Roman power, Hannibal was criticized for his cruelty by the Roman historian Livy, whom Machiavelli had read.

doing it would be against his interest, and when the reasons which made him bind himself no longer exist. If men were all good, this precept would not be a good one; but as they are bad, and would not observe their faith with you, so you
100 are not bound to keep faith with them. Nor have legitimate grounds ever failed a prince who wished to show [plausible] excuse for the non-fulfilment of his promise. Of this one could furnish an infinite number of modern examples, and show how many times peace has been broken, and how many promises rendered worthless, by the faithlessness of princes, and those that have been best able to imitate the fox have succeeded best. But it is necessary to be able to disguise this character well, and to be a great feigner and dissembler; and men are so simple and so ready to obey present necessities, that one who deceives will always find those who allow themselves to be deceived. . . . **F**

. . . Thus it is well to seem merciful, faithful, humane, sincere, religious, and
110 also to be so; but you must have the mind so disposed that when it is needful to be otherwise you may be able to change to the opposite qualities. And it must be understood that a prince, and especially a new prince, cannot observe all those things which are considered good in men, being often obliged, in order to maintain the state, to act against faith, against charity, against humanity, and against religion. And, therefore, he must have a mind disposed to adapt itself according to the wind, and as the variations of fortune dictate, and, as I said before, not deviate from what is good, if possible, but be able to do evil if **constrained**.

A prince must take great care that nothing goes out of his mouth which is
120 not full of the above-named five qualities, and, to see and hear him, he should seem to be all mercy, faith, integrity, humanity, and religion. And nothing is more necessary than to seem to have this last quality, for men in general judge more by the eyes than by the hands, for every one can see, but very few have to feel. Everybody sees what you appear to be, few feel what you are, and those few will not dare to oppose themselves to the many, who have the majesty of the state to defend them; and in the actions of men, and especially of princes, from which there is no appeal, the end justifies the means. Let a prince therefore aim at conquering and maintaining the state, and the means will always be judged honorable and praised by every one, for the vulgar is always taken by appearances
130 and the issue of the event; and the world consists only of the vulgar, and the few who are not vulgar are isolated when the many have a rallying point in the prince. A certain prince of the present time, whom it is well not to name, never does anything but preach peace and good faith, but he is really a great enemy to both, and either of them, had he observed them, would have lost him state or reputation on many occasions. ꙮ **G**

F AUTHOR'S PERSPECTIVE
Read aloud lines 105–108. What does the **tone** of these lines suggest about Machiavelli's attitude toward human nature?

constrain (kən-strān′) *v.* to force; to compel

G ARGUMENT
Reread lines 124–131. In what way does the statement "The end justifies the means" support Machiavelli's claim about morality and power?

After Reading

Comprehension

1. **Recall** According to Machiavelli, how does his writing about the methods and rules for a prince differ from the writings of others?

2. **Clarify** What attitude does Machiavelli have toward Hannibal's cruelty?

3. **Summarize** What advice does Machiavelli give princes regarding religion?

Text Analysis

4. **Interpret a Statement** Reread lines 23–29. What is the main standard that Machiavelli uses to judge the personal behavior of a prince?

5. **Analyze Author's Perspective** Review the chart you created as you read. What beliefs and values influenced the author's perspective on what it takes to be an effective ruler?

6. **Evaluate an Argument** Do you think that Machiavelli presents a convincing argument? What evidence is most compelling? Decide what additional points, if any, might have strengthened his argument. Cite details in your answer.

7. **Compare Texts** Compare Machiavelli's ideas with those expressed by Sir Thomas More in *Utopia*. In what ways do their views of the relationship between rulers and subjects differ? What do these two writers have in common?

8. **Analyze Rhetorical Devices** Machiavelli uses **irony**, **paradox**, and **subtlety** to support his argument about how a prince can fortify his power. Why are these devices especially useful for Machiavelli's argument?

Text Criticism

9. **Critical Interpretations** Some critics have argued that Machiavelli intended *The Prince* as a work of satire. They believe that the author deliberately ridiculed the idea of cruel and ruthless rulers in his treatise for the purpose of exposing tyranny and promoting a republic. Do you agree or disagree with this opinion? Support your answer with evidence from the text.

Would you rather be **LOVED** *or* **RESPECTED?**

Machiavelli suggests that "love is held by a chain of obligation, which, men being selfish, is broken whenever it serves their purpose; but fear is maintained by a dread of punishment which never fails." What are some recent examples of "maintaining a dread of punishment" in order to control of a group of people? Do you think that using "dread of punishment" is an effective leadership strategy?

COMMON CORE

RI 4 Determine the meaning of words and phrases as they are used in a text, including figurative meanings; analyze how an author uses and refines the meaning of terms over the course of a text. **RI 6** Determine an author's point of view in a text in which the rhetoric is particularly effective, analyzing how style and content contribute to the power, persuasiveness, or beauty of the text. **L 5a** Interpret figures of speech in context and analyze their role in the text.

Vocabulary in Context

▲ **VOCABULARY PRACTICE**

Identify the antonym of each of the following words.

1. **voluble:** (a) outgoing, (b) tiny, (c) quiet
2. **laudable:** (a) noteworthy, (b) blameworthy, (c) silent
3. **astute:** (a) stupid, (b) practical, (c) scholarly
4. **pusillanimous:** (a) courageous, (b) fragrant, (c) shy
5. **rapacious:** (a) violent, (b) generous, (c) miserly
6. **constrained:** (a) untested, (b) unsupported, (c) unforced
7. **venerated:** (a) scorned, (b) cured, (c) donated
8. **dissension:** (a) conflict, (b) harmony, (c) adaptability

WORD LIST

astute

constrain

dissension

laudable

pusillanimous

rapacious

venerated

voluble

ACADEMIC VOCABULARY IN WRITING

> • attribute   • feature   • monitor   • phase   • primary

Machiavelli's *The Prince* advises rulers on how to **monitor** and maintain their political power by adopting ruthless **attributes,** including the belief that "the end justifies the means." Write a paragraph, using at least one of the Academic Vocabulary words, about why you do or do not believe this is the case.

VOCABULARY STRATEGY: USING CONTEXT CLUES

You can sometimes figure out the meaning of an unfamiliar word, including its nuances, or shades of meaning, by examining its **context**—the text surrounding it. Consider this example: "The king was an **astute** ruler. No <u>trick, it seemed, was too low</u> for him to achieve this end." The sentence "No trick, it seemed, was too low for him to achieve his end" gives you an important clue suggesting that *astute* means "cunning" and that the king is a clever, but disreputable, ruler.

PRACTICE Each boldfaced word in the following paragraph comes from *The Prince*. Use context to match each boldfaced word to a synonym below. Then tell what nuance, or shade of meaning, distinguishes each word from its synonym.

> • stingy   • cowardly   • greedy   • uneasiness   • disguising

The king of Wellandia was despised by his subjects. A **covetous** rogue, he took not only his share of his tenants' crops but the shares that were rightfully theirs. He put up a threadbare front for visiting royalty, but his subjects were not fooled by his **dissembling**. They knew his **miserly** strategy was meant to keep his fellow noblemen from asking him for loans. His **pusillanimous** behavior during an outbreak of plague shocked even his loyal subjects: While citizens within the city were dying, he fled without **scruple** to the safety of his country manor.

COMMON CORE

L 4a Use context as a clue to the meaning of a word or phrase. **L 5b** Analyze nuances in the meaning of words with similar denotations.

Interactive Vocabulary

Go to **thinkcentral.com.**
KEYWORD: HML12-460

Language

◆ **GRAMMAR AND STYLE:** Use Appropriate Language

Review the **Grammar and Style** note on page 457. To convey the serious nature of his topic, Machiavelli uses **formal language** to discuss strategies for maintaining power. Here is an example from the treatise:

> *Thus it is well to seem merciful, faithful, humane, sincere, religious, and also to be so; but you must have the mind so disposed that when it is needful to be otherwise you may be able to change to the opposite qualities.* (lines 109–111)

Notice that the passage contains key elements of formal language, including sophisticated vocabulary and complex sentence structure. Note that it does not contain slang or contractions.

PRACTICE Write down each of the following lines. Then rewrite the sentences using the kind of formal language Machiavelli might have used.

EXAMPLE

The outsiders who wanted to bring our nation to its knees won't be giving us any more trouble.

The infiltrators who threatened to bring this great nation to ruin have been vanquished.

---

1. We caught them red-handed—plotting with foreign powers who were just itching to invade and trash the countryside.

2. I didn't enjoy ordering those banishments, but I did it for the good of the nation.

3. Any other folks who are thinking about rebellion should know that we'll come down on them like a ton of bricks.

READING-WRITING CONNECTION

YOUR TURN Expand your understanding of *The Prince* by responding to this prompt. Then, use the **revising tips** to improve the speech you write.

WRITING PROMPT	**REVISING TIPS**
WRITE A SPEECH Are Machiavelli's ideas immoral or simply realistic? Write a **one-page speech** in which you take a position in response to this question and defend it. You will present your speech to your classmates and teacher.	• Briefly address the opposing point of view. • Present your position concisely and clearly. • Use formal language appropriate to a speech.

COMMON CORE

L 3 Apply knowledge of language to understand how language functions in different contexts to make effective choices for meaning or style, and to comprehend more fully when reading. **W 1a** Introduce precise, knowledgeable claims. **W 1d** Establish and maintain a formal style. **W 4** Produce clear and coherent writing in which the style is appropriate to task, purpose, and audience.

Interactive Revision **THINK** central

Go to **thinkcentral.com**.
KEYWORD: HML12-461

from Essays

Essays by Sir Francis Bacon

COMMON CORE

RI 5 Analyze and evaluate the effectiveness of the structure an author uses in his or her exposition, including whether the structure makes points clear, convincing, and engaging. **RI 6** Determine an author's point of view or purpose in a text.

Meet the Author

Sir Francis Bacon 1561–1626

A true Renaissance man, Sir Francis Bacon had interests extending from law and public service to philosophy and science. As a literary figure, he is perhaps most famous as the father of the English essay. His edition of ten essays, published in 1597, contained the first examples of that literary form to gain popularity in England. Thomas Jefferson was profoundly influenced by Bacon's writings; he called Bacon one of the three greatest men the world has ever known.

Little Lord Bacon Francis Bacon was born into a wealthy and powerful family. His father served as Elizabeth I's Lord Keeper of the Great Seal, and his mother's relatives had powerful connections within the court as well. As a boy, Bacon often crossed paths with the queen, who greeted him fondly as "my little Lord Keeper."

Bacon studied at Cambridge University for two years but suffered from poor health while there. He began to pursue a diplomatic career in France, but he had to return home in 1579 after the sudden death of his father, who left him little money.

Rise and Fall Although Bacon would have preferred a quiet life, concentrating on his interest in natural philosophy, his financial situation forced him to become a lawyer and a public servant. He rose steadily in royal service, acting as legal counsel to both Elizabeth I and James I. Bacon was eventually knighted, and in 1618 he was appointed to the highest judicial position in England.

Three years later, however, his career ended in scandal when he was charged with accepting bribes. He freely admitted to the charges, convinced that the bribes had never influenced his legal judgments. Bacon's accusers did not accept his defense, and he was forced to resign his post.

A Deadly Experiment Banished from public service, Bacon directed his energies to study and writing, expanding his edition of essays to a total of 58 on a variety of subjects, such as love, friendship, beauty, superstition, death, and revenge.

In addition to his essays, Bacon wrote many philosophical and scientific treatises. Unfortunately, his avid interest in science ultimately led to his death. One wintry day in March, it occurred to him that snow might slow the process of decomposition. Bacon obtained a dead chicken and carefully packed it with snow. Chilled by the experiment, he developed bronchitis and died a week later at the age of 65.

DID YOU KNOW?

Sir Francis Bacon . . .

- enrolled in Cambridge University at the age of 12.
- was once imprisoned in the Tower of London.
- is believed by some to be the real author of Shakespeare's plays.

Background: Tower of London

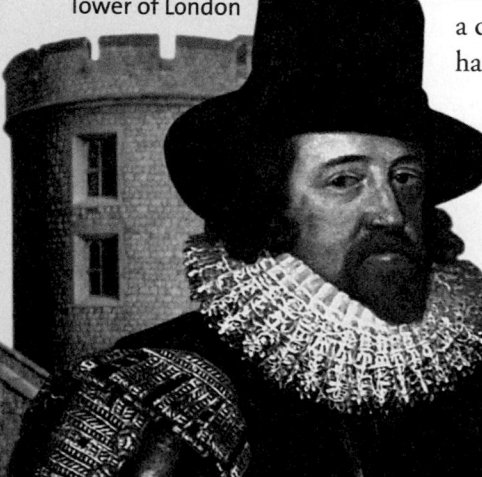

Author Online

Go to thinkcentral.com. KEYWORD: HML12-462

THiNK central

TEXT ANALYSIS: ESSAY

An **essay** is a relatively brief work of nonfiction that offers an opinion on a subject. The purpose of an essay may be to express ideas and feelings, to inform, to entertain, or to persuade. Sir Francis Bacon wrote essays to persuade the reader to accept his opinions. Bacon's essays are **formal;** that is, they are highly structured and written in a serious, impersonal style using formal language. To get across his points, however, Bacon sprinkles his essays with **aphorisms,** brief statements that express general observations about life in a witty, pointed way that makes them memorable for his reader. In the following aphorism from "Of Studies," for example, Bacon comments on the value of learning:

Natural abilities are like natural plants, that need pruning by study. . . .

As you read Bacon's essays, notice the aphorisms and the characteristics of a formal essay that the essays contain.

Review: **Rhetorical Devices**

READING SKILL: EVALUATE OPINIONS

Bacon's essays are filled with opinions based on his experiences and observations. When you read the essays, it is important to **evaluate** these opinions, determining whether you agree or disagree with them and the assumptions upon which they are based. Make a chart like the one shown for each of Bacon's essays. As you read each essay, look for statements of opinion. Write each statement in your chart, and give a brief explanation of why you agree or disagree with it.

"Of Studies"		
Opinion	Agree	Disagree
"Some books are to be tasted, others to be swallowed. . . ."	Not all books demand equal attention.	

 Complete the activities in your **Reader/Writer Notebook**.

What's the best ADVICE *you ever got?*

Francis Bacon wrote his essays to help guide young men who were ambitious to succeed. Like Bacon, many people love to dispense advice and share their knowledge and experience. You've probably received advice from your family and friends on everything from how to manage your homework to what clothes to wear. What advice has made a real difference in your life?

QUICKWRITE Think of some advice that you have found especially helpful. Craft the advice into an aphorism—a brief statement that expresses the advice.

DON'T SWEAT THE SMALL STUFF.

Of Studies

Sir Francis Bacon

Studies serve for delight, for ornament, and for ability. Their chief use for delight is in privateness and retiring; for ornament, is in discourse;[1] and for ability, is in the judgment and disposition of business. For expert men can execute, and perhaps judge of particulars, one by one; but the general counsels, and the plots and marshaling of affairs, come best from those that are learned. To spend too much time in studies is sloth; to use them too much for ornament is affectation; to make judgment wholly by their rules is the humor[2] of a scholar. They perfect Ⓐ nature, and are perfected by experience; for natural abilities are like natural plants, that need pruning by study; and studies themselves do give forth directions too
10 much at large, except they be bounded in by experience. Crafty men contemn[3] studies, simple men admire them, and wise men use them, for they teach not their own use; but that is a wisdom without them, and above them, won by observation. Read not to contradict and confute,[4] nor to believe and take for granted, nor to

Ⓐ **EVALUATE OPINIONS**
Reread lines 5–7. Explain why you agree or disagree with Bacon's opinions on the use of study.

Analyze Visuals ▶
Consider Bacon's discussion of the uses of studies. What might the pear in this image **symbolize?**

---

1. **discourse:** conversation.
2. **humor:** eccentricity; peculiar whim.
3. **Crafty men contemn:** practical men view with contempt.
4. **confute:** prove wrong.

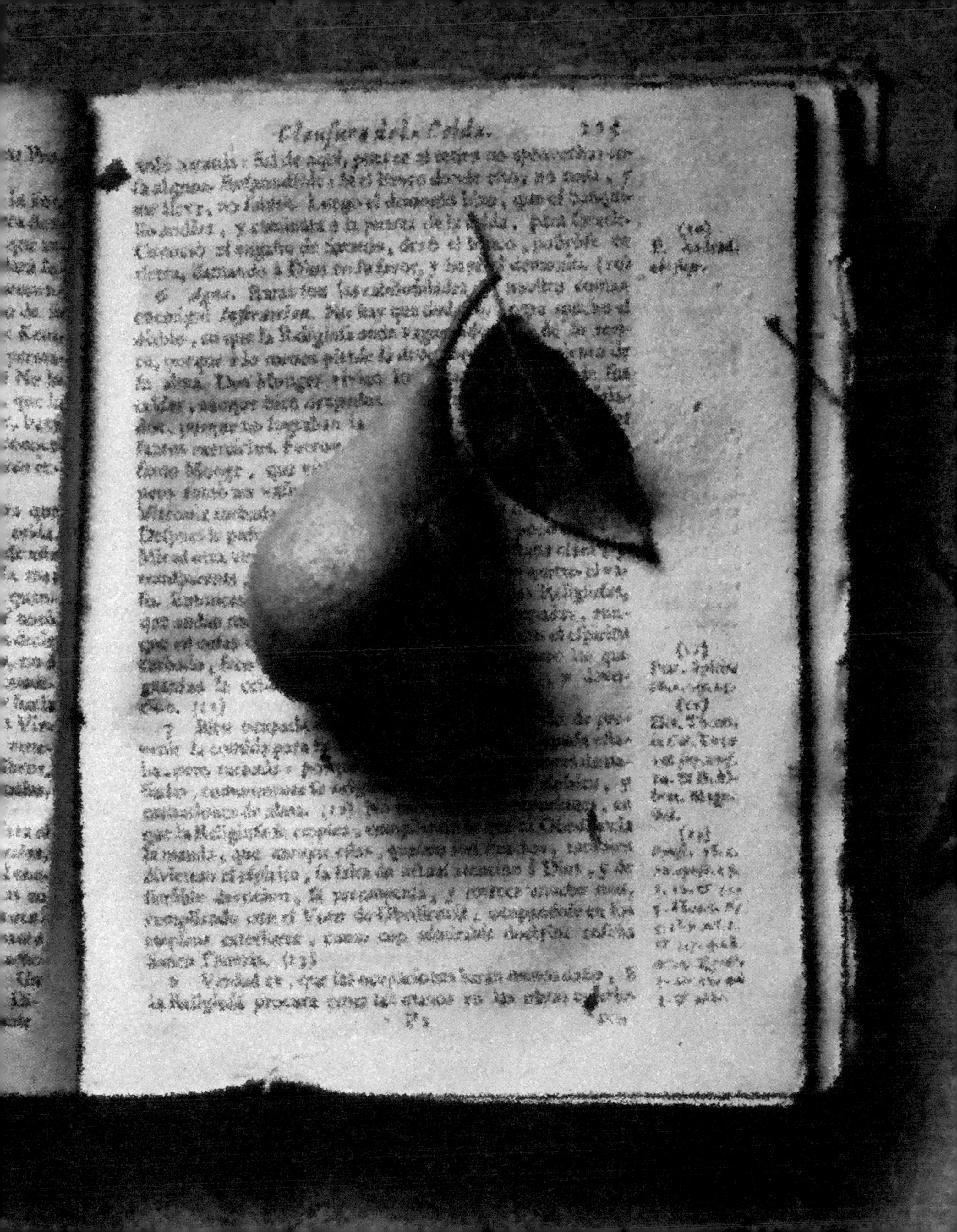

find talk and discourse, but to weigh and consider. Some books are to be tasted, others to be swallowed, and some few to be chewed and digested; that is, some books are to be read only in parts; others to be read, but not curiously;[5] and some few to be read wholly, and with diligence and attention. Some books also may be read by deputy and extracts made of them by others, but that would be only in the less important arguments and the meaner sort of books; else distilled books

20 are like common distilled waters, flashy things.[6] Reading maketh a full man, conference a ready man, and writing an exact man. And therefore, if a man write little, he had need have a great memory; if he confer little, he had need have a present wit; and if he read little, he had need have much cunning, to seem to know that he doth not. Histories make men wise; poets, witty; the mathematics, subtle; natural philosophy, deep; moral, grave; logic and rhetoric, able to contend. **B** *Abeunt studia in mores.*[7] Nay, there is no stond[8] or impediment in the wit but may be wrought out by fit studies, like as diseases of the body may have appropriate exercises. Bowling is good for the stone and reins,[9] shooting for the lungs and breast, gentle walking for the stomach, riding for the head, and the like. So if a

30 man's wit be wandering, let him study the mathematics; for in demonstrations, if his wit be called away never so little, he must begin again. If his wit be not apt to distinguish or find differences, let him study the schoolmen,[10] for they are *cymini sectores.*[11] If he be not apt to beat over matters and to call up one thing to prove and illustrate another, let him study the lawyers' cases. So every defect of the mind may have a special receipt.[12] ∽

B SUBTLETY
Bacon is a master of using **subtlety,** or fine distinctions, to build his argument. He frequently defines and then elaborates upon an idea by dividing it into distinct parts. For example, in lines 10-12 Bacon provides three distinct opinions about the value of studies: "crafty men contemn studies, simple men admire them, and wise men use them...." In lines 20-25, note the **aphorism** and its elaboration. What subtle distinctions does Bacon make between the acts of reading, of conversing, and of writing? What are the benefits of each? What do these subtle distinctions add to Bacon's argument about the purpose of studies?

---

5. **curiously:** carefully; thoroughly.

6. **else distilled books ... flashy things:** in other respects, abridged books are like herbal home remedies, flat, tasteless things.

7. *Abeunt studia in mores* (ä′bĕ-ŏŏnt stōō′dē-ä ĭn mō′rāz) *Latin:* Studies show themselves in behavior.

8. **stond:** obstacle.

9. **stone and reins:** gall bladder and kidneys.

10. **schoolmen:** medieval scholars.

11. *cymini sectores* (kē′mĭ-nē sĕk-tō′rāz) *Latin:* cutters of herbs—that is, people who make extremely fine distinctions; hairsplitters.

12. **receipt:** prescription; remedy.

Of Marriage and Single Life

Sir Francis Bacon

He that hath wife and children hath given hostages to fortune; for they are impediments to great enterprises, either of virtue or mischief. Certainly the best works, and of greatest merit for the public, have proceeded from the unmarried or childless men, which both in affection and means have married and endowed the public. Yet it were great reason that those that have children should have greatest **C** care of future times, unto which they know they must transmit their dearest pledges. Some there are who, though they lead a single life, yet their thoughts do end with themselves, and account future times impertinences.[1] Nay, there are some other that account wife and children but as bills of charges. Nay more, there are some foolish

10 rich covetous men that take a pride in having no children, because they may be thought so much the richer. For perhaps they have heard some talk, "Such an one is a great rich man," and another except to it, "Yea, but he hath a great charge of

C **EVALUATE OPINIONS**
Reread the opinion expressed in lines 2–5. Do you agree or disagree with this opinion? Explain.

---

1. **account future times impertinences** (ĭm-pûr′tn əns-ĕz): consider future times to be matters of no concern.

children"; as if it were an abatement to his riches. But the most ordinary cause of a single life is liberty, especially in certain self-pleasing and humorous minds, which are so sensible of every restraint, as they will go near to think their girdles and garters to be bonds and shackles. Unmarried men are best friends, best masters, best servants, but not always best subjects, for they are light to run **D** away, and almost all fugitives are of that condition. A single life doth well with churchmen, for charity will hardly water the ground where it must first fill a pool.

20 It is indifferent for judges and magistrates, for if they be facile[2] and corrupt, you shall have a servant five times worse than a wife. For soldiers, I find the generals commonly in their hortatives[3] put men in mind of their wives and children; and I think the despising of marriage amongst the Turks maketh the vulgar soldier more base. Certainly wife and children are a kind of discipline of humanity; and single men, though they be many times more charitable, because their means are less exhaust, yet, on the other side, they are more cruel and hard-hearted (good to make severe inquisitors), because their tenderness is not so oft called upon. Grave natures, led by custom, and therefore constant, are commonly loving husbands, as was said of Ulysses, *Vetulam suam praetulit immortalitati*.[4] Chaste women are often proud **E**

30 and froward,[5] as presuming upon the merit of their chastity. It is one of the best bonds, both of chastity and obedience, in the wife if she think her husband wise, which she will never do if she find him jealous. Wives are young men's mistresses, companions for middle age, and old men's nurses, so as a man may have a quarrel[6] to marry when he will. But yet he was reputed one of the wise men that made answer to the question when a man should marry: "A young man not yet, an elder man not at all."[7] It is often seen that bad husbands have very good wives; whether it be that it raiseth the price of their husbands' kindness when it comes, or that the wives take a pride in their patience. But this never fails, if the bad husbands were of their own choosing, against their friends' consent; for then they will be sure to

40 make good their own folly. ❧

D RHETORICAL DEVICES
Notice the **repetition** of the word *best* in lines 16–17. What effects does Bacon achieve by repeating this word?

E ESSAY
What characteristics of a formal essay do you observe in lines 27–29?

Language Coach

Commonly Confused Words Some words that look similar are easy to confuse. *Elder* and *older* have similar meanings, but *elder* is now mostly used to describe a senior member of a family or group. Does Bacon use *elder* (line 35) the way we do today?

2. **facile** (făs′əl): easily influenced or persuaded; pliable.

3. **hortatives** (hôr′tə-tĭvz): speeches to encourage troops before battle.

4. ***Vetulam suam praetulit immortalitati*** (vě′tŏŏ-läm sōō′äm prī′tŏŏ-lĭt ĭm-môr-tä′lē-tä′tē) *Latin:* He preferred his aged wife to immortality.

5. **froward** (frō-wərd): stubborn.

6. **quarrel:** excuse; reason.

7. **he was reputed . . . not at all:** a quote from the ancient Greek philosopher Thales (thā′lēz), who lived in the sixth century B.C.

Comprehension

1. **Recall** According to "Of Studies," why should people avoid studying too much or relying too much on their studies?

2. **Paraphrase** Reread lines 13–14 in "Of Studies." How would you paraphrase Bacon's advice on the purpose of reading?

3. **Recall** According to "Of Marriage and Single Life," why are single men more charitable than married ones?

4. **Clarify** What is the point of the quotation Bacon offers in lines 34–36 in "Of Marriage and Single Life"?

Text Analysis

5. **Identify Author's Purpose** Reread lines 14–17 in "Of Studies." Why might Bacon have chosen to give this advice to his young readers?

6. **Make Inferences** Think about the aspects of marriage that Bacon describes in "Of Marriage and Single Life." Why might he have chosen not to discuss romantic love in his essay?

7. **Draw Conclusions** After reading the two essays, what conclusions can you draw about Bacon's views on the following subjects? Cite evidence to support your conclusions.

   - the importance of reading to a person's development
   - the influence of marriage on a man's temperament
   - the role of women in society

8. **Analyze Essays** What advantages did Bacon gain by presenting his advice and opinions in formal essays? What might have been the disadvantages in writing this type of essay?

9. **Evaluate Opinions** Review the opinion charts you created as you read the essays. Which opinions do you consider most useful for people living today? Which ones have become most outdated? Explain.

> *What's the best* **ADVICE** *you ever got?*
>
> What is the least useful advice someone has given you? Why? What advice would have been more useful?

COMMON CORE

RI 5 Analyze and evaluate the effectiveness of the structure an author uses in his or her exposition, including whether the structure makes points clear, convincing, and engaging. **RI 6** Determine an author's point of view or purpose in a text.

Female Orations

Debate by Margaret Cavendish, Duchess of Newcastle

DID YOU KNOW?

Margaret Cavendish ...

- wrote what has been described as the first science fiction novel.
- thought it was against nature for a woman to spell correctly.
- used her own remedies to treat her illnesses, a course of action that probably hastened her death.

(background)
Rocky coast
near Newcastle

Meet the Author

Margaret Cavendish, Duchess of Newcastle 1623?–1674

Margaret Cavendish was probably the first Englishwoman who wrote with the intent of being published. She desired fame, but she gained notoriety. Her many critics called her "mad, conceited, and ridiculous." They attacked her writing style as well as the outlandish clothes she wore. Today, however, Cavendish is appreciated for her originality and for what Virginia Woolf called her "vein of authentic fire."

Loyal Royalists Born Margaret Lucas around 1623, Margaret was two years old when her father died. Her mother, who assumed control of the family's extensive estate, proved to be a shrewd businesswoman and as a result was not well liked by the locals. The Lucases further alienated their neighbors by allying themselves with the monarchy during the political and religious conflicts between Charles I and Parliament.

When civil war broke out in England in 1642, the Lucas family fled to Oxford, where the royal court was in exile. Margaret became an attendant to Queen Henrietta Maria and traveled with her to Paris in 1645. There, Margaret met and married William Cavendish, the duke of Newcastle, a man 30 years her senior.

A Writer Is Born William Cavendish had commanded an army for Charles I and was known to his enemies as "the greatest traitor in England." As a result, the Cavendishes were forced to live in France and later Belgium after the king was overthrown. During their exile, Cavendish completed her first book, *Poems and Fancies*.

When the monarchy was restored in 1660, Cavendish and her husband returned to England, where she began to pursue a literary career in earnest. Cavendish wrote about science, mathematics, and philosophy—subjects considered beyond the capacities of women in the 17th century—and produced numerous works of poetry, prose, and drama.

Mad Madge Cavendish's bold writings and strange manner earned her the nickname Mad Madge of Newcastle. In spite of her reputation, she became the first woman to attend the Royal Society of London, a scientific academy founded in 1660. Cavendish also enjoyed the love and support of her husband throughout their marriage. At her death, he wrote that "This duchess was a wise, witty and learned lady, which her many books do well testify."

Author Online

Go to **thinkcentral.com**. KEYWORD: HML12-470

THINK central

TEXT ANALYSIS: HISTORICAL CONTEXT

The **historical context** of a work consists of the events and social conditions that inspired or influenced its creation. In 17th-century England, society placed severe limitations on women. For the most part, women were confined to the home and family. Margaret Cavendish responded to these limitations by writing sentences such as the following in "Female Orations":

Alas! men, that are not only our tyrants but our devils, keep us in the hell of subjection, from whence I cannot perceive any redemption or getting out....

As you read, look for sentences that refer to the condition of Englishwomen in the 17th century.

READING STRATEGY: READING A DEBATE

A **debate** is an organized exchange of opinions on an issue. In academic settings, *debate* refers to a formal oral contest in which two opposing teams defend and attack a proposition. Cavendish loosely uses the debate form in "Female Orations" to express seven different views on the role of women in society. Determine two or more **claims**, or central ideas, that each speaker uses, and note how the speaker defends this claim. In addition, look for the following in each oration:

- **Counterarguments**, the arguments the speaker makes to oppose another speaker's claim

- **Support**, such as reasons, evidence, or appeals to the audience's values, that helps the speaker prove a claim

- **Assumptions**, the beliefs that are taken for granted by the speaker as the basis for a claim

As you read each oration, record the speaker's counterargument to the previous argument and her own claim in a chart like the one shown.

Speaker	Counterargument to Previous Argument	Speaker's Own Claim
I	no previous argument	Women should unite to free themselves from the control of men.

 Complete the activities in your **Reader/Writer Notebook**.

Does GENDER impose limits?

From birth, you are identified by your gender. In every society, certain traits and behaviors are considered typically masculine or feminine; for example, some of the speakers in "Female Orations" believe that women should be submissive toward men and strive only to become good housewives. Of course, attitudes toward women have changed greatly since the Renaissance, but many people feel that gender still influences how we see ourselves and how others see us.

DISCUSS With a partner of the same gender, discuss whether you feel that your gender has limited choices or opportunities. Share your conclusions with a pair of the opposite gender.

Female *Orations*

Margaret Cavendish, Duchess of Newcastle

> **BACKGROUND** In 17th-century England, women could not own property or vote, and most received little formal education. Their lives generally revolved around family, religion, and the responsibilities of keeping a household. Margaret Cavendish addresses some of these limitations in "Female Orations."

I

Ladies, gentlewomen, and other inferior women, but not less worthy: I have been industrious to assemble you together, and wish I were so fortunate as to persuade you to make frequent assemblies, associations, and combinations amongst our sex, that we may unite in prudent counsels, to make ourselves as free, happy, and famous as men; whereas now we live and die as if we were produced from beasts, rather than from men; for men are happy, and we women are miserable; they possess all the ease, rest, pleasure, wealth, power, and fame; whereas women are restless with labor, easeless with pain, melancholy for want of pleasures, helpless for want of power, and die in oblivion, for want of fame.
10 Nevertheless, men are so unconscionable and cruel against us that they endeavor to bar us of all sorts of liberty, and will not suffer us freely to associate amongst our own sex; but would fain[1] bury us in their houses or beds, as in a grave. The truth is, we live like bats or owls, labor like beasts, and die like worms. **Ⓐ**

II

Ladies, gentlewomen, and other inferior women: The lady that spoke to you hath spoken wisely and eloquently, in expressing our unhappiness; but she hath not declared a remedy, or showed us a way to come out of our miseries; but, if she could or would be our guide, to lead us out of the labyrinth men have put us into, we should not only praise and admire her, but adore and worship her as our goddess: but alas! men, that are not only our tyrants but our devils, keep us in

---

Ⓐ ANALYZE DEBATE
Reread lines 12–13, in which the speaker compares the condition of women to that of lowly animals. Why might Cavendish have chosen to have the first speaker use these **similes** as **support** for her position?

---

1. **fain:** gladly.

Conversation of Women During the Absence of Their Husbands, Abraham Bosse. ECL 846. Oil on wood. Photo by
Gérard Blot. Musée de la Renaissance, Ecouen, France. © Réunion des Musées Nationaux/Art Resource, New York.

◄ Analyze Visuals
How well does this
painting match the **mood**
of the selection? Explain.

20 the hell of subjection, from whence I cannot perceive any redemption or getting
out; we may complain and bewail our condition, yet that will not free us; we may
murmur and rail[2] against men, yet they regard not what we say. In short, our words
to men are as empty sounds; our sighs, as puffs of winds; and our tears, as fruitless
showers; and our power is so inconsiderable, that men laugh at our weakness. **B**

B HISTORICAL CONTEXT
What 17th-century social
conditions help explain
the sense of hopelessness
expressed in lines 21–24?

III

Ladies, gentlewomen, and other inferior women: The former orations were
exclamations against men, repining at their condition and mourning for our own;
but we have no reason to speak against men, who are our admirers and lovers; they
are our protectors, defenders, and maintainers; they admire our beauties, and love
our persons; they protect us from injuries, defend us from dangers, are industrious

---

2. **rail:** complain violently or speak bitterly about.

30 for our subsistence, and provide for our children; they swim great voyages by sea, travel long journeys by land, to get us rarities and curiosities; they dig to the center of the earth for gold for us; they dive to the bottom of the sea for jewels for us: they build to the skies houses for us: they hunt, fowl, fish, plant, and reap for food for us. All which, we could not do ourselves; and yet we complain of men, as if they were our enemies, whenas[3] we could not possibly live without them, which shows we are as ungrateful as inconstant. But we have more reason to murmur against Nature, than against men, who hath made men more ingenious, witty, and wise than women; more strong, industrious, and laborious than women; for women are witless and strengthless, and unprofitable creatures, did they not bear children. 40 Wherefore, let us love men, praise men, and pray for men; for without men, we should be the most miserable creatures that Nature hath made or could make. **C**

Noble ladies, gentlewomen, and other inferior women: The former oratoress says we are witless and strengthless; if so, it is that we neglect the one and make no use of the other, for strength is increased by exercise, and wit is lost for want of conversation. But to show men we are not so weak and foolish as the former **D** oratoress doth express us to be, let us hawk, hunt, race, and do the like exercises that men have; and let us converse in camps,[4] courts, and cities; in schools, colleges, and courts of judicature; in taverns, brothels, and gaming houses; all of which will make our strength and wit known, both to men and to our own selves, 50 for we are as ignorant of ourselves as men are of us. And how should we know ourselves, when we never made a trial of ourselves? Or how should men know us, when they never put us to the proof? Wherefore my advice is, we should imitate men; so will our bodies and minds appear more masculine, and our power will increase by our actions.

Noble, honorable, and virtuous women: The former oration was to persuade us to change the custom of our sex, which is a strange and unwise persuasion, since we cannot change the nature of our sex, nor make ourselves men; and to have female bodies, and yet to act masculine parts, will be very preposterous and unnatural. In truth, we shall make ourselves like the defects of Nature, and be 60 hermaphroditical,[5] neither perfect women, nor perfect men, but corrupt and imperfect creatures. Wherefore let me persuade you, since we cannot alter the nature of our persons, not to alter the course of our lives; but to rule so our lives and behaviors that we be acceptable and pleasing to God and men; which is, to be modest, chaste, temperate, humble, patient, and pious; also, be housewifely, cleanly, and of few words. All which will gain us praise from men and blessing from Heaven; love in this world and glory in the next. **E**

---

3. **whenas:** when in fact.

4. **camps:** military encampments.

5. **hermaphroditical** (hər-măf′rə-dĭt′-ĭ-kəl): having both male and female characteristics in one body.

C ANALYZE DEBATE
Reread lines 34–39. What objection does the third speaker make to the positions of the first two speakers? What is her **counterargument**?

D HISTORICAL CONTEXT
Reread lines 45–50. Judging from the background information you have read, how would most readers in 17th-century England have responded to the fourth speaker's suggestions?

E CONTRADICTION
As the debate progresses, each speaker begins by **contradicting**, or opposing, the **claims** of the previous speaker about the role of women in society. By disputing the previous speaker's claims, the fifth speaker attempts to strengthen her own position about the issue. Which of the previous speaker's claims does the speaker in this paragraph contradict?

VI

Worthy women: The former oratoress's oration endeavored to persuade us that it would not only be a reproach and disgrace, but unnatural, for women in their actions and behavior to imitate men: we may as well say it will be a reproach,
70　disgrace, and unnatural to imitate the gods, which imitation we are commanded both by the gods and their ministers; and shall we neglect the imitation of men, which is more easy and natural than the imitation of the gods? For how can terrestrial creatures imitate celestial deities?[6] Yet one terrestrial may imitate another, although in different sorts of creatures. Wherefore, since all terrestrial imitations ought to ascend to the better and not to descend to the worse, women ought to imitate men, as being a degree in nature more perfect than they themselves; and all masculine women ought to be as much praised as effeminate men to be dispraised; for the one advances to perfection, the other sinks to imperfection; that so, by our industry, we may come, at last, to equal men, both in perfection and power. **F**

VII

80　**Noble ladies, honorable gentlewomen, and worthy female-commoners:** The former oratoress's speech was to persuade us out of ourselves and to be that which Nature never intended us to be, to wit, masculine. But why should we desire to be masculine, since our own sex and condition is far the better? For if men have more courage, they have more danger; and if men have more strength, they have more labor than women have; if men are more eloquent in speech, women are more harmonious in voice; if men be more active, women are more graceful; if men have more liberty, women have more safety; for we never fight duels nor battles; nor do we go long travels or dangerous voyages; we labor not in building nor digging in mines, quarries, or pits, for metal, stone, or coals; neither do we waste
90　or shorten our lives with university or scholastical studies, questions, and disputes; we burn not our faces with smiths' forges or chemists' furnaces;[7] and hundreds of other actions which men are employed in; for they would not only fade the fresh beauty, spoil the lovely features, and decay the youth of women, causing them to appear old, when they are young; but would break their small limbs, and destroy their tender lives. Wherefore women have no reason to complain against Nature **G** or the god of Nature, for although the gifts are not the same as they have given to men, yet those gifts they have given to women are much better; for we women are much more favored by Nature than men, in giving us such beauties, features, shapes, graceful demeanor, and such insinuating and enticing attractives, that
100　men are forced to admire us, love us, and be desirous of us; insomuch that rather than not have and enjoy us, they will deliver to our disposals their power, persons, and lives, enslaving themselves to our will and pleasures; also, we are their saints, whom they adore and worship; and what can we desire more than to be men's tyrants, destinies, and goddesses? ✺

6.　**terrestrial creatures . . . celestial deities:** earthly creatures and heavenly gods.

7.　**smiths' forges or chemists' furnaces:** furnaces used by blacksmiths to heat metal or those used by alchemists to heat chemical substances.

F　ANALYZE DEBATE
What flaw does the sixth speaker point out in the fifth speaker's **claims**?

> **Language Coach**
>
> **Fixed Expressions** As a verb, *wit* ("to know") is now only used in the fixed expression *to wit*, meaning "that is; namely" (line 82). Rephrase lines 81–82 in your own words.

G　ANALYZE DEBATE
Speaker VII makes several **assumptions** about how men live. How do these assumptions **support** her **claim** that women should not "desire to be masculine"?

from
Eve's Apology
in Defense *of* Women

Amelia Lanier

> **BACKGROUND** In the biblical Book of Genesis, Eve is tempted by a serpent
> to eat the fruit of the forbidden tree of knowledge, and she in turn offers it
> to Adam. As a result of their disobedience, God expels them from the Garden
> of Eden, taking away the gift of human immortality. These stanzas are from
> Amelia Lanier's defense of Eve, in which the poet (1570?–1640?) adopts a
> position that was quite radical at the time.

But surely Adam cannot be excused;
Her fault though great, yet he was most to blame.
What weakness offered, strength might have refused;
Being lord of all, the greater was his shame;
5 Although the serpent's craft had her abused,
God's holy word ought all his actions frame;
　　For he was lord and king of all the earth,
　　Before poor Eve had either life or breath,

Who being framed by God's eternal hand
10 The perfectest man that ever breathed on earth,
And from God's mouth received that strait command,
The breach whereof he knew was present death;
Yea, having power to rule both sea and land,
Yet with one apple won to lose that breath
15　　Which God had breathéd in his beauteous face,
　　Bringing us all in danger and disgrace;

Detail of *Explusion from Paradise*
(1500s). Flemish tapestry from
Brussels. Accademia, Florence.
© Scala/Art Resource, New York.

And then to lay the fault on patience's back,
That we (poor women) must endure it all;
We know right well he did discretion lack,
20 Being not persuaded thereunto at all.
If Eve did err, it was for knowledge sake;
The fruit being fair persuaded him to fall.
   No subtle serpent's falsehood did betray him;
   If he would eat it, who had power to stay him?

25 Not Eve, whose fault was only too much love,
Which made her give this present to her dear,
That what she tasted he likewise might prove,
Whereby his knowledge might become more clear;
He never sought her weakness to reprove
30 With those sharp words which he of God did hear;
   Yet men will boast of knowledge, which he took
   From Eve's fair hand, as from a learned book.

Language Coach

Mutliple Meanings The
word *endure* has more
than one meaning. It can
mean "bear," "tolerate,"
or "last." What does it
mean in line 18? What
does in it mean in this
sentence? *Scruffy is gone
but his memory will
endure.*

Comprehension

1. **Recall** Why does the second speaker doubt that women will free themselves of male domination?

2. **Clarify** Why does the fourth speaker suggest that women should hunt, gamble, and engage in other typically male activities?

3. **Summarize** How would you summarize the seventh speaker's view of limitations placed on women?

Text Analysis

4. **Make Inferences** Reread the sixth speaker's oration. What can you infer about the speaker's values?

5. **Analyze a Debate** Review the chart you created as you read the speeches in "Female Orations." Why do you think Cavendish chose to present her discussion of women's issues in the form of a debate?

6. **Analyze Historical Context** In what ways does "Female Orations" reflect or challenge social conditions experienced by women in the 17th century?

7. **Compare Texts** Consider the view of the relationship between men and women expressed in "Eve's Apology in Defense of Women" (page 476). How is it similar to or different from the view of one or more of the speakers in "Female Orations"? Use details from the poem and from the orations to support your ideas.

8. **Evaluate an Argument** Choose one of the orations, and evaluate the argument that the speaker presents. Discuss how well the speaker uses **reasons** and **evidence** to support her **claims**.

Text Criticism

9. **Different Perspectives** In what ways do the views expressed about gender in "Female Orations" differ from commonly accepted views in our society today? Support your response with evidence from the text.

> *Does* **GENDER** *impose limits?*
>
> What are activities today that we still consider more appropriate for men than for women, or for women more than men? Why do you think this is the case?

COMMON CORE

RI 2 Determine two or more central ideas of a text and analyze their development over the course of the text, including how they interact and build on one another. **RI 3** Analyze a complex set of ideas and explain how specific ideas interact and develop over the course of the text. **RI 9** Analyze documents of historical and literary significance.

Persuasive Techniques in Humanist Literature

Writer John Milton once said, "Where there is much desire to learn, there of necessity will be much arguing, much writing, many opinions; for opinion in good men is but knowledge in the making." The writers in this section (pages 444–478) certainly have strong opinions, and they use a variety of persuasive techniques to convince their audiences to adopt those opinions, including incorporating rhetorical devices such as

- analogies
- repetition
- rhetorical questions
- antithesis

- aphorisms
- irony
- subtlety
- counterarguments

Writing to Evaluate

Write an evaluation of the persuasive techniques used by two of the writers whose work you have read in this section by focusing on the rhetorical devices they use to make their arguments. Be sure to cite specific passages to support your evaluation. Completing a chart like the one below will help you organize your thoughts. In the conclusion of your evaluation, explain which writer you think is most persuasive and why. Include specific references to rhetorical devices used by that author.

Title of Selection	Persuasive Techniques Used	Examples
from _Utopia_		
"Speech Before the Spanish Armada Invasion"		

Extension

SPEAKING & LISTENING

With a partner, choose one of the selections from this section and stage a point/counterpoint debate. One partner will argue the writer's position, while the other will offer counterarguments. Present your debate to the class.

COMMON CORE

W 1a Create an organization that logically sequences claims, counterclaims, reasons, and evidence. **SL 1c** Ensure a hearing for a full range of positions on a topic. **SL 3** Evaluate a speaker's point of view, reasoning, and use of evidence and rhetoric.

Selections from the King James Bible

COMMON CORE

RI 1 Cite strong and thorough textual evidence to support inferences drawn from the text. **RI 9** Analyze foundational documents of historical and literary significance for their themes, purposes, and rhetorical features.

Meet the Author

The King James Bible

In 1603, when James I, the successor of Elizabeth I, became king of England, Puritan leaders petitioned him to support a new translation of the Bible. Although James bore no great love for the Puritans, he agreed that English worshipers needed a better translation of the Bible than the ones that were currently popular.

A Massive Undertaking In 1604, the king appointed 54 distinguished scholars and clergymen to create a new version. (In the end, not all of them actively participated in the translation.) Their goal was to create a Bible that would be more accurate than previous English versions and more beautiful in its use of the English language. The scholars split into groups and translated the Bible piecemeal. To ensure consistency and impartiality of the new translation, they all followed a strict set of rules.

To make their translation as accurate as possible, they worked from original Greek and Hebrew texts. They also consulted previous English translations. In the preface to the new translation, they praised earlier translations and noted their indebtedness to them: "We never thought, from the beginning that we should need to make a new translation, nor yet to make of a bad one a good one; . . . but to make a good one better, or out of many good ones, one principal good one." The final result of their endeavors was the King James Bible, which was to remain the main English version of the Protestant Bible for some 300 years.

A Popular Classic Although the language of the King James Bible is elegant, it is also simple and straightforward. It was not intended solely for the educated elite. Clergymen throughout England read from it at services, making its message available to the most humble parishioners. The translation also had a tremendous impact on the authors of the time, including John Milton and John Bunyan, whom the 19th-century clergyman C. H. Spurgeon claimed was so "saturated with scripture" that he was "a living Bible." Centuries later, authors such as William Wordsworth, Herman Melville, Walt Whitman, and T. S. Eliot continued to find inspiration in the themes, imagery, and language of the King James Bible. Even today, although many other translations are available, it remains the most influential of all versions.

DID YOU KNOW?

The King James Bible . . .

- contains more than 12,000 different English words.

- is the source of many common expressions, such as "the apple of his eye" and "at their wits' end."

- is one of the most published books in history, with more than one billion copies printed.

Author Online

Go to thinkcentral.com. KEYWORD: HML12-480

THINK central

TEXT ANALYSIS: SCRIPTURAL WRITING

Scriptural writing, or sacred text, conveys the traditions and beliefs of particular religions. Such texts are often used in rituals of worship and may be considered divinely inspired. The King James Bible is an example of Christian scripture, notable for its lyrical language. It contains the following literary forms.

A **maxim** is a brief and memorable statement of general truth, one that often imparts guidance or advice. Such writing is common in the Book of Ecclesiastes, a work that stems from the wisdom movement of the early Hebrews.

A **psalm** is a sacred song or lyric poem. Most psalms were originally set to music and performed during worship services in the temples of ancient Israel. The Book of Psalms preserves 150 hymns.

A **parable** is a short story that is meant to teach a lesson or illustrate a moral truth. The characters and events of a parable are usually **allegorical**—that is, they stand for abstract ideas and principles, such as love and forgiveness. Among the best-known parables are those attributed to Jesus and presented in the Gospels of the New Testament.

As you read the selections, look for details that are characteristic of each literary form.

READING SKILL: MAKE INFERENCES

Many passages in the King James Bible are explicit and easy to grasp. However, certain parts—such as maxims, psalms, and parables—often require readers to **make inferences,** or logical guesses, about the wisdom they convey. Sometimes called "reading between the lines," making inferences involves using your own knowledge and details from a text to figure out information not directly stated. As you read each selection, make inferences about the spiritual advice or lesson communicated. Record your inferences using a chart like the one shown.

Selection	Details from the Text	Inferences About Spiritual Advice or Lesson
Ecclesiates, Chapter 3		
Psalm 23		
Parable of the Prodigal Son		

 Complete the activities in your **Reader/Writer Notebook.**

Where do we find WISDOM?

If you have ever "burned the midnight oil" to finish a paper or "stuck your neck out" for a friend, you were using expressions derived from the King James Bible. The Bible is one of the world's most important works of literature and, for many people, a source of great wisdom. For example, Ecclesiastes is intended to help people find meaning in life. Psalm 23 offers spiritual guidance, and the Parable of the Prodigal Son imparts a moral lesson.

DISCUSS Working with two or three classmates, create a list of the people, books, and other resources you regularly turn to when you seek advice about life's problems—great and small. Discuss each response. Then circle the example of the resource that has been the most reliable and helpful. Compare the results of your discussion with those of other groups.

> **Where We Find Wisdom**
> 1. Grandparents
> 2. Advice columns
> 3.
> 4.
> 5.

from the King James Bible

Ecclesiastes,
CHAPTER 3

Analyze Visuals ▶
This image is from a 16th-century Christian prayer book. In what ways does the scene relate to events described in Ecclesiastes, Chapter 3?

1 To every thing there is a season, and a time to every purpose under the heaven:

2 A time to be born, and a time to die; a time to plant, and a time to pluck up that which is planted;

3 A time to kill, and a time to heal; a time to break down, and a time to build up;

4 A time to weep, and a time to laugh; a time to mourn, and a time to dance;

5 A time to cast away stones, and a time to gather stones together; a time to embrace, and a time to refrain from embracing;

6 A time to get, and a time to lose; a time to keep, and a time to cast away;

7 A time to rend, and a time to sew; a time to keep silence, and a time to speak;

8 A time to love, and a time to hate; a time of war, and a time of peace. **A**

A **CONTRADICTION**
Opposites, such as the verbs "to weep" and "to laugh" or "to love" and "to hate," **contradict**, or oppose, each other. Pairing contradictory elements in this way demonstrates the full spectrum, or range, of an idea, emotion, or situation, such as "a time to be born and a time to die" in verse 2. This selection includes contradictory pairs of verbs in almost every line. What message do they help convey?

Text Analysis

1. **Analyze Repetition** Repetition is a technique in which a word or group of words is repeated throughout a text. What effect does the extensive repetition in this selection help create?

2. **Make Judgments** Which lines do you think have special relevance to contemporary life?

The Month of October: Ploughing and Sowing, Simon Bening. Miniature from *The Book of Hours.* Bodycolor on vellum, 14 cm × 9.5 cm. © Victoria & Albert Museum, London/Art Resource, New York.

Psalm 23

1 The Lord is my shepherd; I shall not want.

2 He maketh me to lie down in green pastures: he leadeth me beside the still waters.

3 He restoreth my soul: he leadeth me in the paths of righteousness for his name's sake.

4 Yea, though I walk through the valley of the shadow of death, I will fear no evil: for thou art with me; thy rod and thy staff they comfort me.

5 Thou preparest a table before me in the presence of mine enemies: thou anointest my head with oil; my cup runneth over.

6 Surely goodness and mercy shall follow me all the days of my life: and I will dwell in the house of the Lord for ever. **Ⓑ**

Ⓑ SCRIPTURAL WRITING
Psalm 23 is part of a collection of psalms often called "songs of trust." Why might it be included in this group?

Text Analysis

1. **Identify Metaphor** A metaphor is a figure of speech that compares two things that are basically unlike but have something in common. What metaphor does the speaker use in verses 1–4 to describe his relationship with the Lord?

2. **Analyze Word Choice** In verses 1–3, the speaker refers to the Lord using the pronouns *he* and *his*. However, beginning in verse 4, the speaker switches to *thou* and *thy*. What does this shift seem to suggest about the relationship between the speaker and the Lord?

3. **Make Inferences** Why does the speaker expect goodness and mercy to follow him all the days of his life? Give details to support your response.

The Parable of the
Prodigal Son
from LUKE, CHAPTER 15

The Parable of the Prodigal Son, section from the Mompelgarter Altarpiece, Matthias Gerung. Oil on panel, 41 cm × 28 cm. Kunsthistorisches Museum, Vienna. © Bridgeman Art Library.

11 And he said, A certain man had two sons:

12 And the younger of them said to his father, Father, give me the portion of goods that falleth to me. And he divided unto them his living.

13 And not many days after the younger son gathered all together, and took his journey into a far country, and there wasted his substance with riotous living.

14 And when he had spent all, there arose a mighty famine in that land; and he began to be in want.

12 And he divided unto them his living: And the father divided his livelihood, or wealth, between the two sons.

13 substance: material possessions.

15 And he went and joined himself to a citizen of that country; and he sent him into his fields to feed swine.

16 And he would fain have filled his belly with the husks that the swine did eat: and no man gave unto him.

17 And when he came to himself, he said, How many hired servants of my father's have bread enough and to spare, and I perish with hunger!

18 I will arise and go to my father, and will say unto him, Father, I have sinned against heaven, and before thee,

19 And am no more worthy to be called thy son: make me as one of thy hired servants. **C**

20 And he arose, and came to his father. But when he was yet a great way off, his father saw him, and had compassion, and ran, and fell on his neck, and kissed him.

21 And the son said unto him, Father, I have sinned against heaven, and in thy sight, and am no more worthy to be called thy son.

22 But the father said to his servants, Bring forth the best robe, and put it on him; and put a ring on his hand, and shoes on his feet:

23 And bring hither the fatted calf, and kill it; and let us eat, and be merry:

24 For this my son was dead, and is alive again; he was lost, and is found. And they began to be merry.

25 Now his elder son was in the field: and as he came and drew nigh to the house, he heard musick and dancing.

26 And he called one of the servants, and asked what these things meant.

27 And he said unto him, Thy brother is come; and thy father hath killed the fatted calf, because he hath received him safe and sound.

28 And he was angry, and would not go in: therefore came his father out, and intreated him.

29 And he answering said to his father, Lo, these many years do I serve thee, neither transgressed I at any time thy commandment: and yet thou never gavest me a kid, that I might make merry with my friends:

30 But as soon as this thy son was come, which hath devoured thy living with harlots, thou hast killed for him the fatted calf.

31 And he said unto him, Son, thou art ever with me, and all that I have is thine.

32 It was meet that we should make merry, and be glad: for this thy brother was dead, and is alive again; and was lost, and is found.

---

15 he sent: the citizen sent.

16 fain: gladly.

C MAKE INFERENCES
Judging from the younger son's realization in verses 17–19, what values does the parable suggest are important?

Language Coach

Oral Fluency The word *nigh* (verse 25), meaning "near," is rarely used today, but it contains a spelling pattern and pronunciation found in many English words. Pronounce *nigh* and then think of two other words with the same pattern.

28 intreated: entreated; urged.

29 transgressed: violated; broke; **kid:** young goat.

30 which hath . . . harlots: who has wasted your wealth on prostitutes.

32 meet: fitting; proper.

Comprehension

1. **Clarify** Ecclesiastes, Chapter 3, begins: "To every thing there is a season, and a time to every purpose under the heaven." What is meant by this statement?

2. **Clarify** In Psalm 23, what kind of relationship does the speaker have with the Lord?

3. **Summarize** Review the Parable of the Prodigal Son. Describe the responses of the father and the elder son to the return of the Prodigal Son.

Text Analysis

4. **Interpret Imagery** The King James Bible is widely admired for the beauty of its imagery—words and phrases that create vivid sensory experiences. Explain how each of the following images from Psalm 23 appeals to your senses. Which example creates the most memorable mental picture?

   - "leadeth me beside the still waters" (verse 2)
   - "walk through the valley of the shadow of death" (verse 4)
   - "anointest my head with oil" (verse 5)

5. **Analyze Parable** Many characters in parables are **allegorical**—that is, they stand for abstract ideas and principles. Describe the main characters from the Parable of the Prodigal Son. What might each character symbolize?

6. **Make Inferences** Review the chart you made as you read. What **wisdom** or spiritual advice does each selection convey? Cite evidence in your answer.

7. **Synthesize Information** Each biblical selection dates back thousands of years and derives from the traditions of the ancient Hebrews. Using evidence from all three texts, what general statements can you make about the values and way of life of these people?

8. **Evaluate Scriptural Writing** The three selections in the lesson are among the Bible's most famous passages. Review the forms of scriptural writing on page 481. In what ways does each selection fit the pattern of its literary form? Cite specific evidence to support your answer.

Text Criticism

9. **Different Perspectives** How might readers of varying ages—for example, a young adult and an elderly person—differ in their reactions to the passage from Ecclesiastes, the psalm, or the parable? Use details from the text and your own knowledge to support your ideas.

Where do we find **WISDOM?**

What are some contemporary examples of parables in print or other media, such as movies and television? What moral lessons do they convey?

COMMON CORE

RI 1 Cite strong and thorough textual evidence to support inferences drawn from the text. **RI 9** Analyze foundational documents of historical and literary significance for their themes, purposes, and rhetorical features.

How Soon Hath Time
When I Consider How My Light Is Spent

Poetry by John Milton

COMMON CORE

RL 4 Determine the meaning of words and phrases as they are used in the text, including figurative meanings. L 3a Apply an understanding of syntax to the study of complex texts when reading.

DID YOU KNOW?

John Milton . . .

- coined the word *pandemonium*.
- loved the Arthurian legends and nearly based his great English epic on them.
- deeply influenced the writing of J. R. R. Tolkien, author of *The Lord of the Rings*.

Meet the Author

John Milton 1608–1674

John Milton decided early in life that he would become an important writer, a goal that he accomplished without question. Amid political upheavals and personal struggles, he produced work that places him in the company of England's most revered poets. His crowning achievement, *Paradise Lost,* is widely accepted as the finest epic poem in the English language.

Youthful Dreams As a youth, Milton applied himself eagerly to his studies, often reading by candlelight until the early hours of morning. In 1625, at the age of 16, he entered Christ's College at Cambridge University. Although he was critical of the school's rigid curriculum, he remained there for seven years, eventually earning a master's degree in 1632. After leaving Cambridge, he continued his education independently, reading history, literature, and philosophy and writing his first eight sonnets.

A Dedicated Puritan When civil war erupted in 1642, Milton, a critic of the monarchy, allied himself with the Puritan faction, the Roundheads, who supported Parliament over the king. During this time Milton produced very little poetry, instead writing various political tracts and pamphlets

in support of a republican government. Following the execution of Charles I in 1649, a republic was established under the Puritan leadership of Oliver Cromwell. Milton was appointed to a post as one of Cromwell's secretaries, with duties that included handling foreign correspondence and writing defenses of the actions of the Puritan leadership.

Blind Despair The year of 1652 was one of tragedy for Milton. His wife, Mary, died shortly after giving birth to their third daughter, Deborah. Weeks later, Milton suffered the death of his infant son, John. Compounding his misery, Milton's eyesight, weak since childhood, failed completely. It was a shattering year for a man who had dedicated his life to family, faith, and literature.

Crowning Achievement Around 1658, shortly before the restoration of the monarchy, Milton began work on a poem he had been planning since he was 19, a great Christian epic that would "justify the ways of God to men." Using the biblical account of the Fall of Man as his basic source, Milton dictated long sentences in rhythmic blank verse to his daughters and various assistants and friends. After five years, he completed his epic poem, Paradise Lost, achieving what many had considered utterly impossible.

Author Online

Go to **thinkcentral.com**. KEYWORD: HML12-488

THINK central

TEXT ANALYSIS: FIGURATIVE LANGUAGE

In "How Soon Hath Time" and "When I Consider How My Light Is Spent," Milton offers readers powerful glimpses into his Puritan beliefs and practices. In each sonnet he experiences a profound crisis in which he strongly questions his ability to serve God. Milton conveys the intensity of his emotions through his use of **figurative language**—words that communicate ideas beyond their literal meanings. As you read these works of personal meditation, pay close attention to the following types of figurative language:

- **Personification**—an expression in which human qualities are attributed to an object, an animal, or an idea. For example, Milton gives human qualities to time: *How soon hath Time, the subtle thief of youth. . . .*

- **Metaphor**—an expression that makes a comparison between two seemingly unlike things. For example, Milton compares his youth to a delayed spring: *My hasting days fly on with full career, / But my late spring no bud or blossom show'th.*

READING STRATEGY: CLARIFY MEANING

When reading works by Milton, it is important to stop and **clarify meaning** by rereading and restating difficult sentences. Be aware of the following as you read the selections:

- **Archaic language**—words that were once in common use but that are now considered old-fashioned or out-of-date

- **Inverted syntax**—sentence structure in which the expected order of words is reversed

As you read each sonnet, use a chart like the one shown to record and restate examples of archaic language and inverted syntax.

"How Soon Hath Time"	
Archaic Language	Inverted Syntax
"hath" (has) line 1	"That I to manhood am arrived so near" (That I am arrived so near to manhood) line 6

 Complete the activities in your **Reader/Writer Notebook**.

What are life's major DISAPPOINTMENTS?

John Milton, one of England's most distinguished poets, was a man of great ambition and talent, but he sometimes despaired of ever achieving his goals. Ironically, he composed some of his finest sonnets during such bouts of disappointment. "How Soon Hath Time" marks the occasion of his 23rd birthday and laments the meagerness of his creative output. "When I Consider How My Light Is Spent" is an exploration of his feelings about the loss of his eyesight at the age of 43.

QUICKWRITE Think of someone you know or have read about—such as a musician or an athlete—who has suffered disappointment in trying to reach a desired goal or to realize a dream. Describe how he or she reacted to disappointment.

HOW SOON HATH TIME

John Milton

How soon hath Time, the subtle thief of youth,
    Stoln on his wing my three and twentieth year!
    My hasting days fly on with full career,
    But my late spring no bud or blossom show'th.
5 Perhaps my semblance might deceive the truth,
    That I to manhood am arrived so near,
    And inward ripeness doth much less appear,
    That some more timely-happy spirits endu'th.
    Yet be it less or more, or soon or slow,
10   It shall be still in strictest measure even
    To that same lot, however mean or high,
Toward which Time leads me, and the will of Heaven;
    All is, if I have grace to use it so,
    As ever in my great Taskmaster's eye. **Ⓐ**

3 career: speed.

5 my semblance . . . truth: my youthful appearance might keep you from recognizing the truth.

8 that . . . endu'th: that endows some early achievers.

14 Taskmaster's eye: a reference to God as an authority that imposes and oversees work.

Ⓐ FIGURATIVE LANGUAGE
Reread the poem. Examine Milton's use of **personification** in lines 1–2 and 9–12. How does personifying Time as a thief contribute to the poem's theme?

Text Analysis

1. **Clarify Sentence Meaning** Restate lines 1–4 using conventional word order and modern words. What is Milton's complaint?

2. **Make Inferences** What conclusions does Milton reach by the poem's end?

Books of Account (1600s), Franco-Flemish School. Galerie Berko, Brussels. © Fine Art Photographic Library, London/Art Resource, New York.

WHEN I CONSIDER HOW MY LIGHT IS SPENT

John Milton

When I consider how my light is spent
   Ere half my days, in this dark world and wide,
   And that one talent which is death to hide,
   Lodged with me useless, though my soul more bent
5 To serve therewith my Maker, and present
   My true account, lest he returning chide;
   "Doth God exact day-labor, light denied?"
   I fondly ask; but Patience to prevent
That murmur, soon replies, "God doth not need
10   Either man's work or his own gifts; who best
   Bear his mild yoke, they serve him best. His state
Is kingly. Thousands at his bidding speed
   And post o'er land and ocean without rest:
   They also serve who only stand and wait." **B**

3 talent: a reference to the biblical parable of the talents (Matthew 25: 14–30), in which a servant is reprimanded for not putting his talent to good use.

8 fondly: foolishly.

12 thousands: thousands of angels.

13 post: hasten; travel quickly.

B **CLARIFY MEANING**
Use modern words to paraphrase lines 1–6 of this sonnet. In what way has blindness affected Milton?

Comprehension

1. **Recall** According to "When I Consider How My Light Is Spent," at what point in Milton's life does blindness begin to affect him and his work?

2. **Clarify** In "When I Consider How My Light Is Spent," what "talent" is Milton unable to use because of his loss of sight?

3. **Paraphrase** Restate lines 7–8 of "When I Consider How My Light Is Spent." What does Milton ask about God?

Text Analysis

4. **Interpret Diction and Tone** Reread lines 1–8 of "When I Consider How My Light Is Spent," reviewing Milton's **diction**, or choice of words. On the basis of phrases such as "light is spent" and "dark world and wide," describe Milton's **tone**, or attitude, toward his blindness.

5. **Examine Symbol** Poets typically communicate their messages using little space and few words. One literary technique they often rely on is **symbolism**— using a person, a place, or an object to represent something beyond itself. What symbolic meaning might "light" have in the second poem?

● 6. **Analyze Figurative Language** Review Milton's use of figurative language in both poems. Identify each of the following examples as either **personification** or **metaphor.** How does each help communicate Milton's intense emotions?

   • the description of his talent (lines 5–8 of the first poem)

   • the reference to patience (lines 8–14 of the second poem)

7. **Understand Poetic Form** A **Petrarchan,** or **Italian, sonnet** is a 14-line lyric poem divided into an **octave** of 8 lines and a **sestet** of 6. The octave has a rhyme scheme of *abbaabba* and raises a question or problem. The sestet has a variable rhyme scheme and resolves or comments on the problem. Choose either poem and explain how well it fits this pattern.

● 8. **Clarify Meaning** Review the strategies for clarifying sentence meaning listed on page 489. Which reading strategy did you find most useful in helping you understand the poems? Offer examples to support your answer.

Text Criticism

9. **Biographical Context** Compare Milton's spiritual crisis in "How Soon Hath Time" with that in "When I Consider How My Life Is Spent." What do these events reveal about Milton's personality? Cite details to support your ideas.

What are life's major **DISAPPOINTMENTS?**

Is it better to resist sadness caused by a major loss or to embrace it? Why?

COMMON CORE

RL 4 Determine the meaning of words and phrases as they are used in the text, including figurative meanings. **L 3a** Apply an understanding of syntax to the study of complex texts when reading.

from Paradise Lost

Video link at
thinkcentral.com

Epic Poem by John Milton

VIDEO TRAILER **THINK** central | KEYWORD: HML12-493

COMMON CORE

RL 4, RL 10, L 3a

● TEXT ANALYSIS: ALLUSION

An **allusion** is a brief reference to a fictional or historical person, place, or event, or to another literary work or passage. In ordinary conversation, we might allude to a literary character or historical figure by calling a miserly person a Scrooge or a treacherous person a Benedict Arnold. In literature, writers often use allusions as a type of shorthand language to add color and vigor to their works. Most of the allusions Milton includes in his great Christian epic come from biblical stories and classical literature, such as Greek and Roman mythology. For example, in line 34, Milton calls Satan "Th' infernal serpent," a reference to Satan's temptation of Eve in the Bible. As you read *Paradise Lost,* refer to the sidenotes to help you interpret the poem's many allusions.

● READING STRATEGY: READING DIFFICULT TEXTS

In writing his masterpiece, Milton employed a dramatic writing style, one that most readers find challenging. Here are a few strategies you can use to confront common difficulties in reading *Paradise Lost:*

- Simplify difficult **syntax** (word order) by paraphrasing. For a difficult line, first identify its subject and verb. Then sort out the meaning conveyed in extra phrases and clauses by rearranging them in conventional order.

- Use sidenotes to interpret **archaic expressions,** or words and phrases we no longer use.

- Avoid becoming overwhelmed by small details. Instead, focus on the thoughts, words, and actions of the main character.

As you read, use a chart like the one shown to take notes about the thoughts, words, and actions of Satan, the main character in this portion of the poem.

Satan		
Thoughts	Words	Actions

Complete the activities in your **Reader/Writer Notebook.**

What are the dangers of PRIDE?

You've probably been encouraged to take pride in your accomplishments or your heritage. Were John Milton alive today, he may not have approved. As a devout and learned Puritan, he knew that the Bible cautions that "pride goeth before destruction," a warning he illustrates brilliantly in *Paradise Lost.*

DISCUSS Does pride have a darker side? With a small group make a list like the one shown of the various ways pride can manifest itself. Discuss the pros and cons of each pride-related item on your list.

Pride Week at School

Pros: Gives us a chance to feel good about our school's achievements

Cons: Some people use it as an excuse to say bad things about rival schools.

PARADISE LOST

John Milton

> **BACKGROUND** In this excerpt—the opening of Book I of *Paradise Lost*—Milton begins his epic like the ancient epics that were his models, with an invocation of, or call upon, a Muse. The speaker asks for inspiration and sets forth the subject and themes of the poem. There follows a summary of how Satan, once among the most powerful of God's angels, was cast out of Heaven for leading a rebellion against God's rule. Awakening in Hell alongside Beëlzebub (bē-ĕl′zə-bŭb′), another fallen angel, Satan considers what he has lost and reaffirms his defiance of God.

Of man's first disobedience, and the fruit
Of that forbidden tree whose mortal taste
Brought death into the world, and all our woe,
With loss of Eden, till one greater Man
5   Restore us, and regain the blissful seat,
Sing, Heavenly Muse, that on the secret top
Of Oreb, or of Sinai, didst inspire
That shepherd who first taught the chosen seed
In the beginning how the heavens and earth
10 Rose out of Chaos: or, if Sion hill
Delight thee more, and Siloa's brook that flowed
Fast by the oracle of God, I thence
Invoke thy aid to my adventurous song,
That with no middle flight intends to soar
15 Above th' Aonian mount, while it pursues
Things unattempted yet in prose or rhyme. Ⓐ
And chiefly thou, O Spirit, that dost prefer
Before all temples th' upright heart and pure,
Instruct me, for thou know'st; thou from the first
20 Wast present, and with mighty wings outspread
Dovelike sat'st brooding on the vast abyss,

4 one greater Man: Jesus Christ.

6 Heavenly Muse: the source of Milton's inspiration—here identified with the Spirit of God that spoke to Moses.

7 Oreb . . . Sinai: Mounts Horeb and Sinai, on which Moses heard the voice of God.

8 shepherd: Moses; **the chosen seed:** the Jews.

10–11 Sion Hill . . . Siloa's brook: places in Jerusalem, the holy city of the Jews.

15 Aonian (ā-ō′nē-ən) **mount:** Mount Helicon in Greece, sacred to Muses.

Ⓐ **ALLUSION**
Reread lines 1–16, using the sidenotes to interpret the various allusions. What will be the subject of Milton's poem?

Fall of the Rebel Angels (1866), Gustave Doré. Engraving. © Chris Hellier/Corbis.

And mad'st it pregnant: what in me is dark
Illumine; what is low, raise and support;
That to the height of this great argument
25 I may assert Eternal Providence,
And justify the ways of God to men.
   Say first (for Heaven hides nothing from thy view,
Nor the deep tract of Hell), say first what cause
Moved our grand parents, in that happy state,
30 Favored of Heaven so highly, to fall off
From their Creator, and transgress his will
For one restraint, lords of the world besides?
Who first seduced them to that foul revolt?
   Th' infernal serpent; he it was, whose guile,
35 Stirred up with envy and revenge, deceived
The mother of mankind, what time his pride
Had cast him out from Heaven, with all his host
Of rebel angels, by whose aid aspiring
To set himself in glory above his peers,
40 He trusted to have equaled the Most High,
If he opposed; and with ambitious aim
Against the throne and monarchy of God
Raised impious war in Heaven and battle proud,
With vain attempt. Him the Almighty Power
45 Hurled headlong flaming from th' ethereal sky
With hideous ruin and combustion down
To bottomless perdition, there to dwell
In adamantine chains and penal fire,
Who durst defy th' Omnipotent to arms.
50   Nine times the space that measures day and night
To mortal men, he with his horrid crew
Lay vanquished, rolling in the fiery gulf
Confounded though immortal. But his doom
Reserved him to more wrath; for now the thought
55 Both of lost happiness and lasting pain
Torments him; round he throws his baleful eyes,
That witnessed huge affliction and dismay,
Mixed with obdùrate pride and steadfast hate.
At once, as far as angels ken, he views
60 The dismal situation waste and wild:
A dungeon horrible, on all sides round
As one great furnace flamed; yet from those flames
No light, but rather darkness visible
Served only to discover sights of woe,

24 argument: subject.

25 Providence: God's plan for the universe.

26 justify: show the justice of. Milton states his purpose in this line.

29 our grand parents: Adam and Eve.

31 transgress: sin against.

32 for one restraint: on account of the command not to eat of the tree of knowledge.

34 th' infernal serpent: Satan, who in the Bible takes the form of a serpent and tempts Eve to eat the fruit of the tree of knowledge.

34–44 These lines introduce the figure of Satan.

36 what time: when.

37 host: army.

44–49 Him the Almighty Power... arms: God hurls Satan from the ethereal (ĭ-thîr′ē-əl) sky, or heaven, to hell, a bottomless pit of perdition, or damnation, where he must live in unbreakable chains and punishing fire.

53–54 his doom... wrath: fate had more punishment in store for him.

58 obdurate (ŏb′dŏŏ-rĭt): stubborn.

59 ken: can see.

62–63 Milton conveys the desolation of hell through a horrifying paradox: flames that give no light, only "darkness visible."

65 Regions of sorrow, doleful shades, where peace
And rest can never dwell, hope never comes
That comes to all, but torture without end
Still urges, and a fiery deluge, fed
With ever-burning sulphur unconsumed:
70 Such place Eternal Justice had prepared
For those rebellious; here their prison ordained
In utter darkness and their portion set
As far removed from God and light of Heaven
As from the center thrice to th' utmost pole.
75 O how unlike the place from whence they fell!
There the companions of his fall, o'erwhelmed
With floods and whirlwinds of tempestuous fire,
He soon discerns; and, weltering by his side,
One next himself in power, and next in crime,
80 Long after known in Palestine, and named
Beëlzebub. To whom th' arch-enemy,
And thence in Heaven called Satan, with bold words
Breaking the horrid silence thus began:
    "If thou beest he—but O how fallen! how changed
85 From him who in the happy realms of light
Clothed with transcendent brightness didst outshine
Myriads, though bright! if he whom mutual league, **B**
United thoughts and counsels, equal hope
And hazard in the glorious enterprise,
90 Joined with me once, now misery hath joined
In equal ruin; into what pit thou seest
From what height fallen, so much the stronger proved
He with his thunder: and till then who knew
The force of those dire arms? Yet not for those,
95 Nor what the potent Victor in his rage
Can else inflict, do I repent or change,
Though changed in outward luster, that fixed mind
And high disdain, from sense of injured merit, **C**
That with the Mightiest raised me to contend,
100 And to the fierce contention brought along
Innumerable force of spirits armed,
That durst dislike his reign, and me preferring,
His utmost power with adverse power opposed
In dubious battle on the plains of Heaven,
105 And shook his throne. What though the field be lost?
All is not lost: the unconquerable will,
And study of revenge, immortal hate,

68 still urges: always presses; afflicts.

69 sulphur: Burning sulphur, called brimstone, is often associated with God's wrath.

73–74 as far removed . . . utmost pole: The image is probably drawn from Virgil's *Aeneid,* which situates Tartarus, or hell, as twice as far below the earth's surface as the heavens are above it.

78 weltering: writhing; thrashing about.

80–82 long after known . . . Satan: The ancient Phoenicians, whose land is here called Palestine (păl'ĭ-stīn'), worshipped the god Baal, also known as Beëlzebub in the Bible. The name Satan comes from the Hebrew word meaning "enemy."

B **DIFFICULT TEXTS**
Clarify the pronoun referents for the words *thou* and *he* in line 84. What character is Satan addressing in this speech? Explain Satan's impression of this character.

C **DIFFICULT TEXTS**
Reread lines 94–98. **Paraphrase** this passage to clarify its meaning. What is Satan's attitude toward his defeat?

107 study: pursuit.

And courage never to submit or yield:
And what is else not to be overcome?
110 That glory never shall his wrath or might
Extort from me. To bow and sue for grace
With suppliant knee, and deify his power
Who from the terror of this arm so late
Doubted his empire—that were low indeed;
115 That were an ignominy and shame beneath
This downfall; since, by fate, the strength of gods
And this empyreal substance cannot fail;
Since, through experience of this great event,
In arms not worse, in foresight much advanced,
120 We may with more successful hope resolve
To wage by force or guile eternal war,
Irreconcilable to our grand Foe,
Who now triùmphs, and in th' excess of joy
Sole reigning holds the tyranny of Heaven." **D**
125 So spake th' apostate angel, though in pain,
Vaunting aloud, but racked with deep despair;
And him thus answered soon his bold compeer:
"O prince, O chief of many thronèd powers,
That led th' embattled seraphim to war
130 Under thy conduct, and in dreadful deeds
Fearless, endangered Heaven's perpetual King,
And put to proof his high supremacy,
Whether upheld by strength, or chance, or fate!
Too well I see and rue the dire event
135 That with sad overthrow and foul defeat
Hath lost us Heaven, and all this mighty host
In horrible destruction laid thus low,
As far as gods and heavenly essences
Can perish: for the mind and spirit remains
140 Invincible, and vigor soon returns,
Though all our glory extinct, and happy state
Here swallowed up in endless misery.
But what if he our Conqueror (whom I now
Of force believe almighty, since no less
145 Than such could have o'erpowered such force as ours)
Have left us this our spirit and strength entire,
Strongly to suffer and support our pains,
That we may so suffice his vengeful ire,
Or do him mightier service as his thralls

Now Night her Course began..(1882), Gustave Doré. Plate no. 26, Book VI, line 406, © Central Saint Martin's College of Art and Design, London/Bridgeman Art Library.

150 By right of war, whate'er his business be,
Here in the heart of Hell to work in fire,
Or do his errands in the gloomy deep?
What can it then avail though yet we feel
Strength undiminished, or eternal being
155 To undergo eternal punishment?"
    Whereto with speedy words th' arch-fiend replied:
"Fallen cherub, to be weak is miserable,   **157 cherub:** angel.
Doing or suffering: but of this be sure,

To do aught good never will be our task,
160 But ever to do ill our sole delight,
As being the contrary to his high will
Whom we resist. If then his providence
Out of our evil seek to bring forth good,
Our labor must be to pervert that end,
165 And out of good still to find means of evil; **E**
Which ofttimes may succeed, so as perhaps
Shall grieve him, if I fail not, and disturb
His inmost counsels from their destined aim.
But see! the angry Victor hath recalled
170 His ministers of vengeance and pursuit
Back to the gates of Heaven; the sulphurous hail,
Shot after us in storm, o'erblown hath laid
The fiery surge that from the precipice
Of Heaven received us falling; and the thunder,
175 Winged with red lightning and impetuous rage,
Perhaps hath spent his shafts, and ceases now
To bellow through the vast and boundless deep.
Let us not slip th' occasion, whether scorn
Or satiate fury yield it from our Foe.
180 Seest thou yon dreary plain, forlorn and wild,
The seat of desolation, void of light,
Save what the glimmering of these livid flames
Casts pale and dreadful? Thither let us tend
From off the tossing of these fiery waves;
185 There rest, if any rest can harbor there;
And reassembling our afflicted powers,
Consult how we may henceforth most offend
Our enemy, our own loss how repair,
How overcome this dire calamity,
190 What reinforcement we may gain from hope,
If not, what resolution from despair."
    Thus Satan talking to his nearest mate
With head uplift above the wave, and eyes
That sparkling blazed; his other parts besides
195 Prone on the flood, extended long and large
Lay floating many a rood, in bulk as huge
As whom the fables name of monstrous size,
Titanian or Earth-born, that warred on Jove,
Briareos or Typhon, whom the den
200 By ancient Tarsus held, or that sea beast
Leviathan, which God of all his works

159 **aught:** at all.

E **DIFFICULT TEXTS**
Rewrite lines 159–165, reordering
the **syntax.** What does Satan set
out to accomplish?

172 **laid:** calmed.

175 **impetuous** (ĭm-pĕch′ōō-əs):
violently forceful.

178 **slip th' occasion:** miss the
chance.
179 **satiate** (sā′shē-ĭt): satisfied.

186 **afflicted powers:** stricken troops.

190 **reinforcement:** increase of
strength.

196 **rood:** a unit of measure,
between six and eight yards.
197–200 **as whom . . . Tarsus held:**
In Greek mythology, both the huge
Titans—of whom Briareos was one—
and the earth-born giant Typhon
battled unsuccessfully against Jove
(Zeus), just as Satan rebelled against
God. Zeus defeated Typhon in Asia
Minor, near the town of Tarsus.

201 **Leviathan** (lə-vī′ə-thən): a huge
sea beast mentioned in the Bible—
here identified with the whale by
Milton.

Created hugest that swim th' ocean-stream.
Him, haply, slumbering on the Norway foam,
The pilot of some small night-foundered skiff,
205 Deeming some island, oft, as seamen tell,
With fixèd anchor in his scaly rind
Moors by his side under the lee, while night
Invests the sea, and wishèd morn delays: **F**
So stretched out huge in length the arch-fiend lay,
210 Chained on the burning lake; nor ever thence
Had risen or heaved his head, but that the will
And high permission of all-ruling Heaven
Left him at large to his own dark designs,
That with reiterated crimes he might
215 Heap on himself damnation, while he sought
Evil to others, and enraged might see
How all his malice served but to bring forth
Infinite goodness, grace, and mercy shown
On man by him seduced, but on himself
220 Treble confusion, wrath, and vengeance poured. **G**
    Forthwith upright he rears from off the pool
His mighty stature; on each hand the flames
Driven backward slope their pointing spires, and rolled
In billows, leave i' th' midst a horrid vale.
225 Then with expanded wings he steers his flight
Aloft, incumbent on the dusky air,
That felt unusual weight; till on dry land
He lights, if it were land that ever burned
With solid, as the lake with liquid fire,
230 And such appeared in hue; as when the force
Of subterranean wind transports a hill
Torn from Pelorus or the shattered side
Of thundering Etna, whose combustible
And fuelèd entrails thence conceiving fire,
235 Sublimed with mineral fury, aid the winds,
And leave a singèd bottom all involved
With stench and smoke: such resting found the sole
Of unblest feet. Him followed his next mate,
Both glorying to have 'scaped the Stygian flood
240 As gods, and by their own recovered strength,
Not by the sufferance of supernal power.
    "Is this the region, this the soil, the clime,"
Said then the lost archangel, "this the seat
That we must change for Heaven? this mournful gloom

245 For that celestial light? Be it so, since he
Who now is sovereign can dispose and bid
What shall be right: farthest from him is best,
Whom reason hath equaled, force hath made supreme
Above his equals. Farewell, happy fields,
250 Where joy forever dwells! Hail, horrors! hail,
Infernal world! and thou, profoundest Hell,
Receive thy new possessor, one who brings
A mind not to be changed by place or time.
The mind is its own place, and in itself
255 Can make a Heaven of Hell, a Hell of Heaven.
What matter where, if I be still the same,
And what I should be, all but less than he
Whom thunder hath made greater? Here at least
We shall be free; th' Almighty hath not built
260 Here for his envy, will not drive us hence.
Here we may reign secure; and in my choice
To reign is worth ambition, though in Hell:
Better to reign in Hell than serve in Heaven.
But wherefore let we then our faithful friends,
265 Th' associates and copartners of our loss,
Lie thus astonished on th' oblivious pool,
And call them not to share with us their part
In this unhappy mansion, or once more
With rallied arms to try what may be yet
270 Regained in Heaven, or what more lost in Hell?"

Language Coach

Oral Fluency The word *sovereign* (line 246) has a silent *g*. What word used three times in lines 261–263 has a similar spelling pattern? How is each word pronounced? How are the words' meanings related?

257 all but less than: second only to.

264 wherefore: why.

266 astonished: stunned; **th' oblivious pool:** the river Lethe— in Greek mythology, a river of the underworld that causes forgetfulness.
268 mansion: dwelling place.

Comprehension

1. **Recall** Where do the fallen angels find themselves after their rebellion?

2. **Recall** Who is their leader?

3. **Summarize** In your own words, describe the connection between the rebellion of the fallen angels and "man's first disobedience."

Text Analysis

4. **Draw Conclusions About the Speaker** Reread the opening invocation, lines 1–26. Do you view the speaker as humble, ambitious, or some combination of these? Support your answer with specific references.

5. **Understand Imagery** Generations of readers have been captivated by Milton's description of hell in *Paradise Lost*. Reread lines 59–74, noting Milton's use of imagery, or words and phrases that appeal to the senses. Which image is the most vivid? Explain your response.

● 6. **Interpret Difficult Texts** Review the character chart you created as you read the selection. Summarize Satan's words, thoughts, and behavior in each of the following scenes.

  • his thoughts as he lies in the fiery water (lines 53–58)
  • his first speech to Beëlzebub (lines 106–124)
  • his final speech (lines 242–270)

7. **Compare and Contrast Characters** A **foil** is a character who provides a striking contrast to other characters. In what way does Beëlzebub serve as a foil to Satan? Cite details to support your response.

● 8. **Analyze Allusions** Review the mythological, biblical, and geographical allusions that Milton uses in lines 192–241. Why do you think Milton draws on so many different sources for his description of Satan?

Text Criticism

9. **Critical Interpretations** In an essay on Milton, the 19th-century historian and critic Thomas Babington Macauley observed, "Poetry which relates to the beings of another world ought to be at once mysterious and picturesque. That of Milton is so." Do you agree or disagree with this opinion? Provide evidence to support your view.

> *What are the dangers of* **PRIDE?**
>
> The 14th-century poet Dante defined pride as "love of self perverted to hatred and contempt for one's neighbor" and ranked it as the very worst of all sins. How does Milton's portrayal of pride differ from or resemble Dante's?

COMMON CORE

RL 4 Determine the meaning of words and phrases as they are used in the text, including figurative meanings. RL 10 Read and comprehend literature, including poems. L 3a Apply an understanding of syntax to the study of complex texts when reading.

from **The Pilgrim's Progress**

Allegory by John Bunyan

COMMON CORE

RL 5 Analyze how an author's choices concerning how to structure specific parts of a text contribute to its overall structure and meaning as well as its aesthetic impact. **L 4d** Verify the preliminary determination of the meaning of a word or phrase.

DID YOU KNOW?

John Bunyan . . .

- wrote much of *The Pilgrim's Progress* in jail, using paper covers from milk bottles.
- presided over a congregation of 3,000 to 4,000 people in his last years.
- inspired the name of a famous 19th-century English novel and a popular American magazine.

Meet the Author

John Bunyan 1628–1688

John Bunyan's Christian allegory, *The Pilgrim's Progress,* is one of the most famous and widely read books in English literature. Since its original publication in 1678, the work has been consistently in print. It has also been translated into more than 100 different languages.

An Uncommon Commoner John Bunyan was born in Elstow, Bedfordshire, England. He grew up poor and attended a local school, where he learned to read and write. When Bunyan came of age he joined his father in his tinkering trade and traveled the countryside repairing pots and pans. At 16, Bunyan joined Oliver Cromwell's Parliamentary army to fight against the Royalists in the English Civil War. It is likely that he received his first exposure to Puritan thought and teachings during his military service.

Tempted By Satan Following his discharge from the army, Bunyan married a devoutly religious woman and began taking a deeper interest in religion. He attended church regularly and spent long hours reading theological literature. Bunyan underwent a long spiritual struggle during which, according to his memoir, Satan continually tempted him to betray his Christian beliefs. Eventually, with the guidance of the charismatic

Calvinist preacher John Gifford, Bunyan "experienced God's light." Soon Bunyan himself took to the pulpit and began preaching as a nonconformist minister in various towns in Bedfordshire.

A Prisoner's Progress When the monarchy was restored in 1660, Charles II sought to suppress religious dissent. Bunyan was imprisoned for "pertinaciously abstaining" from attending Church of England services and for holding "unlawful meetings." He was jailed twice, for a total of nearly 12 years. While in prison, Bunyan wrote *The Pilgrim's Progress,* which recounts the allegorical journey to salvation of an ordinary man named Christian. The direct, vivid style and the sense of spiritual urgency made the work an instant success. It was so popular, in fact, that six years later Bunyan wrote a second part to *The Pilgrim's Progress* in which Christian's wife and children set out on a similar journey.

The First Bestseller *The Pilgrim's Progress* was truly the first bestselling fiction written in English. Printed on inexpensive paper, it was quite affordable, and 100,000 copies were sold before Bunyan's death. Even in homes where books were a luxury, a copy of *The Pilgrim's Progress* might be found alongside the Bible.

Author Online

Go to **thinkcentral.com**. KEYWORD: HML12-504

THINK central

TEXT ANALYSIS: ALLEGORY

You can enjoy John Bunyan's story for its adventure and you can also read it as an **allegory,** a story with two levels of meaning. The characters, settings, and events of an allegory stand not only for themselves but also for abstract qualities and ideas. Like parables and fables, most allegories convey a specific moral message in the form of a story. *The Pilgrim's Progress* is the best-known allegory in the English language. Christian, the hero, represents those who face moral dilemmas on their way to salvation when they are encouraged by others to embrace the temptations of worldly life and reject a virtuous path. Other allegorical characters include Mr. No-good and Faithful. As you read the selection, use the allegorical elements to help you understand the story's deeper, symbolic meaning.

READING SKILL: UNDERSTAND AUTHOR'S PURPOSE

An author creates a work to achieve a particular **purpose,** or goal. John Bunyan wrote *The Pilgrim's Progress* primarily to persuade readers to follow a Christian way of life. However, a complex work such as this one often fulfills more than one purpose. As you read the selection, fill in a questionnaire like the one shown. Identify passages from the story to support each of your responses.

Question	Answer and Supporting Passage
1. Does the story make you laugh?	
2. Does it contain a lesson about life?	
3. Does it convince you of a particular viewpoint?	
4. Does it move you emotionally?	

VOCABULARY IN CONTEXT

The following boldfaced words are critical to your understanding of *The Pilgrim's Progress.* Use context clues to help you understand the meaning of each term.

1. **enmity** toward an enemy
2. dressed in satin **raiment**
3. **implacable** rules
4. the **vanity** of earthly wishes
5. the **celestial** kingdom in the sky
6. an evil **heretic** of the church
7. a brief **respite** from travel
8. to **transfigure** into angels

 Complete the activities in your **Reader/Writer Notebook.**

How can we resist TEMPTATION?

Temptation comes in many forms: a free concert, a favorite television show, even a leftover piece of chocolate cake. Situations like these can lead us off course and away from our intended goals. So how can we resist indulging?

QUICKWRITE Think of a goal that you worked hard to achieve. What obstacles did you encounter along the way? Describe the steps you took to "keep your eyes on the prize."

THE
Pilgrim's Progress

John Bunyan

> **BACKGROUND** *The Pilgrim's Progress* is told as if it were a story dreamt by the narrator. The hero is a devout wanderer named Christian who has fled his home in the City of Destruction because of its corruption. He sets off on a pilgrimage to the Celestial City, where he hopes to receive God's eternal blessing. On his journey he encounters allegorical characters with names such as Hypocrisy and Mistrust, who personify obstacles to salvation. Christian must also negotiate places—such as the Slough of Despond and Difficulty Hill—that tempt him to abandon his quest. In the excerpt that follows, Christian and another pilgrim, Faithful, come upon Vanity Fair, a veritable marketplace of sin and depravity.

Analyze Visuals ▶
Examine the composition of this image. How does the arrangement of figures help convey a sense of danger?

Then I saw in my dream that when they were got out of the wilderness, they presently saw a town before them, and the name of that Town is **Vanity**; and at the town there is a fair kept called Vanity Fair. It is kept all the year long; it beareth the name of Vanity Fair, because the town where 'tis kept is lighter than vanity, and also because all that is there sold or that cometh thither is Vanity. As is the saying of the wise, "All that cometh is vanity."

This fair is no new erected business, but a thing of ancient standing; I will show you the original of it.

Almost five thousand years agone, there were pilgrims walking to the
10 **Celestial** City, as these two honest persons are; and Beelzebub, Apollyon, and Legion, with their companions, perceiving by the path that the pilgrims made that their way to the city lay through this town of Vanity, they contrived here to set up a fair, a fair wherein should be sold of all sorts of vanity and that it should last all the year long. Therefore at this fair are all such merchandise sold, as houses, lands, trades, places, honors, preferments, titles, countries, kingdoms, lusts, pleasures, and delights of all sorts, as whores, bawds, wives, husbands, children, masters, servants, lives, blood, bodies, souls, silver, gold, pearls, precious stones, and what not.

And, moreover, at this fair there is at all times to be seen jugglings, cheats,
20 games, plays, fools, apes, knaves, and rogues, and that of all sorts. **Ⓐ**

vanity (văn'ĭ-tē) *n.* that which is without meaning or value; emptiness; worthlessness

celestial (sə-lĕs'chəl) *adj.* heavenly; divine

10–11 Beelzebub (bē-ĕl'zə-bŭb') **...Legion:** devils or demons mentioned in the Bible.

15 preferments: appointments and promotions to political or church positions.

Ⓐ ALLEGORY
Reread lines 1–20. In a few words, describe the people and activities of Vanity Fair. What symbolic meaning might this place have?

Vanity Fair (1872), Arthur Hughes. Black ink and watercolor on board, 16.6 cm × 10.9 cm.
© Delaware Art Museum, Wilmington, Delaware/Bridgeman Art Library.

Here are to be seen, too, and that for nothing, thefts, murders, adulteries, false swearers, and that of a blood-red color.

And as in other fairs of less moment, there are the several rows and streets under their proper names, where such and such wares are vended. So here likewise, you have the proper places, rows, streets (*viz.* countries and kingdoms), where the wares of this fair are soonest to be found. Here is the Britain Row, the French Row, the Italian Row, the Spanish Row, the German Row, where several sorts of vanities are to be sold. But as in other fairs, some one commodity is as the chief of all the fair, so the ware of Rome and her 30 merchandise is greatly promoted in this fair. Only our English nation, with some others, have taken a dislike thereat. **B**

Now, as I said, the way to the Celestial City lies just through this town, where this lusty fair is kept, and he that will go to the city, and yet not go through this town, must needs "go out of the world." The Prince of Princes himself, when here, went through this town to his own country and that upon a fair day, too. Yea, and as I think it was Beelzebub, the chief lord of this fair, that invited him to buy of his vanities; yea, would have made him lord of the fair would he but have done him reverence as he went through the town. Yea, because he was such a person of honor, Beelzebub had him 40 from street to street and showed him all the kingdoms of the world in a little time that he might, if possible, allure that Blessed One to cheapen and buy some of his vanities. But he had no mind to the merchandise and therefore left the town, without laying out so much as one farthing upon these vanities. This fair therefore is an ancient thing, of long standing, and a very great fair.

Now these pilgrims, as I said, must needs go through this fair. Well, so they did, but behold, even as they entered into the fair, all the people in the fair were moved and the town itself as it were in a hubbub about them, and that for several reasons; for,

50 First, the pilgrims were clothed with such kind of **raiment** as was diverse from the raiment of any that traded in that fair. The people therefore of the fair made a great gazing upon them. Some said they were fools, some they were bedlams, and some they are outlandish men.

Secondly, and as they wondered at their apparel, so they did likewise at their speech, for few could understand what they said. They naturally spoke the language of Canaan, but they that kept the fair were the men of this world. So that from one end of the fair to the other, they seemed barbarians each to the other.

Thirdly, but that which did not a little amuse the merchandisers was that 60 these pilgrims set very light by all their wares; they cared not so much as to look upon them, and if they called upon them to buy, they would put their fingers in their ears and cry, "Turn away mine eyes from beholding vanity," and look upwards, signifying that their trade and traffic was in heaven.

One chanced mockingly, beholding the carriages of the men, to say unto them, "What will ye buy?" But they, looking gravely upon him, said, "We buy the truth." At that, there was an occasion taken to despise the men the

---

29 Rome: the Roman Catholic Church, which England has broken from and which Protestants like Bunyan viewed with contempt and suspicion in this era of religious warfare.

B **AUTHOR'S PURPOSE**
Reread lines 23–31, using the side note on the page. Whom or what is Bunyan poking fun at? Explain the purpose this criticism might serve.

41 cheapen: barter or trade for; ask the price of.

Language Coach
Roots and Affixes The word *vanities* (lines 37, 42, and 44) comes from the Latin *vanus* ("empty"). Can you guess *vanities'* meaning?

raiment (rā′mənt) *n.* clothing

52–53 some they were bedlams . . . men: Some said they were lunatics, and some said they were foreign. Bethlehem Hospital, shortened to *Bethlem* or *Bedlam,* was the London insane asylum.

56–57 language . . . barbarians (bär-bâr′ē-ənz): Christian and Faithful speak the language of the Bible, but those at the fair speak a variety of languages and are foreigners to each other.

64 carriages: the way the men carried themselves; the men's actions or behavior.

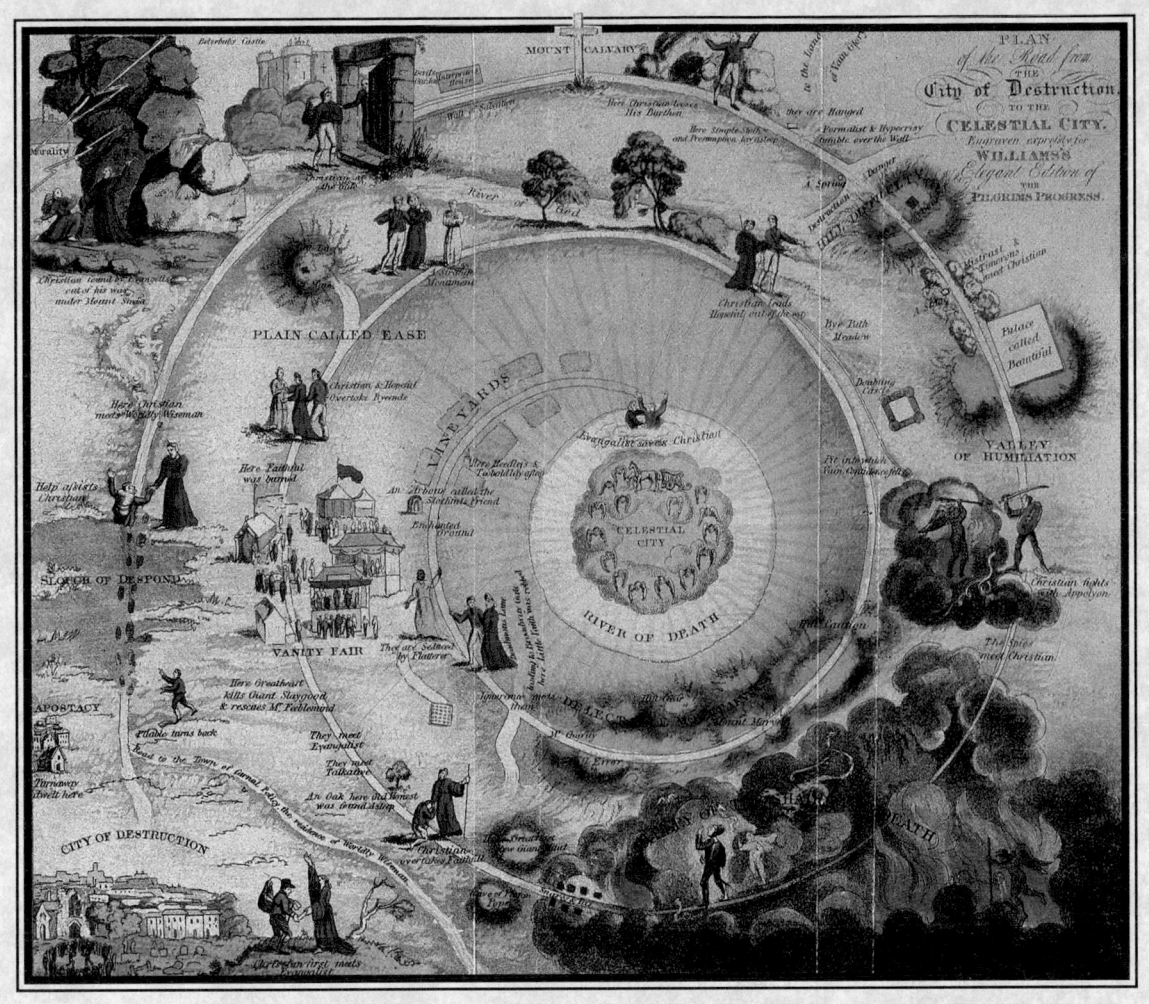

Plan of the road from the City of Destruction to the Celestial City (1800s). Engraved expressly for Williams's Elegant Edition of *The Pilgrim's Progress*. Private collection. © Bridgeman Art Library.

more; some mocking, some taunting, some speaking reproachfully, and some calling upon others to smite them. At last things came to an hubbub, and great stir in the fair, insomuch that all order was confounded. Now was word presently brought to the great one of the fair, who quickly came down and deputed some of his most trusty friends to take these men into examination, about whom the fair was almost overturned. . . . **C**

70

Suspicious of Christian and Faithful, the angry merchandisers at Vanity Fair arrest the pilgrims and bring them to trial. Three witnesses—Envy, Superstition, and Pick-thank—testify against Faithful. A jury of townspeople decides his fate.

Then went the jury out, whose names were Mr. Blind-man, Mr. No-good, Mr. Malice, Mr. Love-lust, Mr. Live-loose, Mr. Heady, Mr. High-mind, Mr. **Enmity,** Mr. Liar, Mr. Cruelty, Mr. Hate-light, and Mr. **Implacable,** who everyone gave in his private verdict against him among themselves, and afterwards unanimously concluded to bring him in guilty before the judge. And first Mr. Blind-man, the foreman, said, "I see clearly that this man is

C AUTHOR'S PURPOSE
Reread lines 46–72, and **summarize** the three reasons the merchandisers are surprised by Christian and Faithful. Does this episode make you laugh? Why, or why not?

enmity (ĕn′mĭ-tē) *n.* deep-seated hatred

implacable (ĭm-plăk′ə-bəl) *adj.* unable to be appeased or significantly changed; inflexible; relentless

an **heretic.**" Then said Mr. No-good, "Away with such a fellow from the
80 earth." "Ay," said Mr. Malice, "for I hate the very looks of him." Then said
Mr. Love-lust, "I could never endure him." "Nor I," said Mr. Live-loose,
"for he would always be condemning my way." "Hang him, hang him," said
Mr. Heady. "A sorry scrub," said Mr. High-mind. "My heart riseth against
him," said Mr. Enmity. "He is a rogue," said Mr. Liar. "Hanging is too
good for him," said Mr. Cruelty. "Let's dispatch him out of the way," said
Mr. Hate-light. Then said Mr. Implacable, "Might I have all the world given
me, I could not be reconciled to him; therefore let us forthwith bring him in
guilty of death." And so they did; therefore he was presently condemned, to
be had from the place where he was to the place from whence he came, and
90 there to be put to the most cruel death that could be invented. **D**

They therefore brought him out to do with him according to their law;
and first they scourged him, then they buffeted him, then they lanced his
flesh with knives; after that they stoned him with stones, then pricked him
with their swords, and last of all they burned him to ashes at the stake. Thus
came Faithful to his end. Now, I saw that there stood behind the multitude
a chariot and a couple of horses, waiting for Faithful, who (so soon as his
adversaries had dispatched him) was taken up into it, and straightway was
carried up through the clouds, with sound of trumpet, the nearest way to the
Celestial Gate. But as for Christian, he had some **respite,** and was remanded
100 back to prison; so he there remained for a space. But he that overrules all
things, having the power of their rage in his own hand, so wrought it about
that Christian for that time escaped them, and went his way. . . .

Christian continues on his journey and encounters another pilgrim, Hopeful.
After more difficulties, the two arrive at their long-awaited destination: the
Gates of the Celestial City.

Now I saw in my dream that these two men went in at the gate; and lo,
as they entered, they were **transfigured,** and they had raiment put on that
shone like gold. There was also that met them with harps and crowns and
gave them to them, the harp to praise withal and the crowns in token of
honor. Then I heard in my dream that all the bells in the city rang again
for joy, and that it was said unto them, "Enter ye into the joy of your Lord."
I also heard the men themselves that they sang with a loud voice, saying,
110 "Blessing, honor, glory, and power, be to Him that sitteth upon the throne,
and to the Lamb forever and ever."

Now just as the gates were opened to let in the men, I looked in after
them; and behold, the city shone like the sun, the streets also were paved
with gold, and in them walked many men, with crowns on their heads,
palms in their hands, and golden harps to sing praises withal.

There were also of them that had wings, and they answered one another
without intermission, saying, "Holy, Holy, Holy, is the Lord." And after
that, they shut up the gates. Which when I had seen, I wished myself
among them. **✑ E**

heretic (hĕr'ĭ-tĭk) *n.* someone
who expresses beliefs that
oppose church teachings or
established views

D ALLEGORY
Reread lines 73–90. Identify
several allegorical characters and
describe their attitude toward
Faithful.

**92 first they scourged . . . buffeted
him:** First they whipped him and
then they beat him.

respite (rĕs'pĭt) *n.* an interval
of temporary relief; a delay or
postponement

transfigure (trăns-fĭg'yər) *v.* to
transform, especially in a way
that exalts or glorifies

E AUTHOR'S PURPOSE
In lines 103–119, Bunyan presents
Christian and Hopeful reaching
their final destination, the
Celestial City. What emotional
effect, if any, does this episode
create?

Comprehension

1. **Recall** Why do the pilgrims have to pass through the town of Vanity?

2. **Recall** How do the merchandisers react to the pilgrims at the fair?

3. **Summarize** Describe what happens to Faithful after the jury reaches its verdict.

Text Analysis

4. **Understand Author's Purpose** Bunyan wrote *The Pilgrim's Progress* mainly to persuade readers to lead principled lives. Review the questionnaire you filled in as you read. In your opinion, what were Bunyan's other purposes in telling this story? Cite evidence to support your answer.

5. **Compare and Contrast Characters** What **character traits,** or consistent qualities, distinguish the pilgrims from the merchandisers?

6. **Examine Tone** In literature, **tone** is the attitude a writer takes toward a subject or character. What is Bunyan's tone in the scenes of Faithful's trial (lines 73–90) and the pilgrims' arrival at the Celestial City (lines 103–119)? Give specific words and phrases to support your answers.

7. **Draw Conclusions** Reread lines 91–102. Does Bunyan view Faithful's death as a loss or a victory? Support your conclusion with evidence from the text.

8. **Analyze Allegory** Using a chart like the one below, identify a possible symbolic meaning for each character or place. Include details from the story to support your interpretation. Based on your answers, what lesson about **temptation** does Bunyan's allegory convey?

	Possible Meaning	Supporting Details
Christian	all people	
Faithful		
Vanity Fair		
Jury Members		
Celestial City		

Text Criticism

9. **Social Context** What does *The Pilgrim's Progress* say about the way society treats the quest for virtue? Cite evidence to support your claim.

How can we resist **TEMPTATION?**

Advertisers often lure buyers by tempting them. What do advertisers do to make their products tempting?

COMMON CORE

RL 5 Analyze how an author's choices concerning how to structure specific parts of a text contribute to its overall structure and meaning as well as its aesthetic impact. **L 4d** Verify the preliminary determination of the meaning of a word or phrase.

Vocabulary in Context

▲ VOCABULARY PRACTICE

Choose the vocabulary word that best completes each sentence. Use the context clues in the sentence to help you decide.

1. We need a _____ from his constant complaining.

2. A new spiritual awareness may _____ a person.

3. Those attending the queen's court dressed in fine _____.

4. She was branded a _____ for stating controversial views.

5. The man's scowl and narrowed eyes revealed dark feelings of _____.

6. He was _____ in his resolve, refusing to change his mind even when the facts suggested that he should.

7. The Bible warns us against the _____ of worldly concerns.

8. Angels dwell in a _____ realm, far from earthly strife.

> **WORD LIST**
> celestial
> enmity
> heretic
> implacable
> raiment
> respite
> transfigure
> vanity

ACADEMIC VOCABULARY IN WRITING

> • attribute • feature • monitor • phase • primary

In a paragraph, describe the **primary features** of a contemporary open-air market or mall. How does a contemporary market or mall compare with Bunyan's Vanity Fair? Use at least one Academic Vocabulary word in your response.

VOCABULARY STRATEGY: THE LATIN PREFIX *trans-*

Many English words and word parts come from Latin. The Latin prefix *trans-*, for example, occurs in the word *transfigured* in *The Pilgrim's Progress* (page 510). *Trans–* can mean "over or across," "change," or "above and beyond." *Transfigure* means "change so as to exalt or glorify." Understanding the meaning of common Latin prefixes like *trans-* can help you figure out the meaning of words from many different disciplines, from biology and mathematics to psychology and geography.

PRACTICE Use context clues and your knowledge of word parts to explain the meaning of each boldfaced word. Then check your answers in the dictionary.

1. Upon its completion in 1869, the first **transcontinental** railway in the United States allowed passengers to travel from the eastern seaboard to California.

2. To develop **transference,** the psychologist encouraged her patient to think of her as a blank screen on which to project his feelings about his mother.

3. The choir conductor **transposed** the hymn into a higher key for the young singers.

4. Because of the extreme heat, the **transpiration** rate in the crops increased, requiring more irrigation.

COMMON CORE

L 4d Verify the preliminary determination of the meaning of a word or phrase. **L 6** Acquire and use accurately general academic words.

Interactive Vocabulary **THINK** central

Go to **thinkcentral.com**.
KEYWORD: HML12-512

Spiritual and Moral Beliefs

This period in British history was one of religious turmoil, beginning with Henry VIII's break from the Roman Catholic Church and subsequent formation of the Church of England, to his daughter "Bloody Mary's" persecution of Protestants, to Elizabeth I's execution of her Catholic cousin Mary, to the Puritan revolt against the monarchy. Yet amid all of this fighting, England remained a Christian nation whose people shared certain core beliefs.

Queen Elizabeth herself remarked upon the faith that united the people of England and Christian Europe despite the bitter conflicts between Catholics and Protestants.

> *"If there were two princes in Christendom who had good will and courage, it would be very easy to reconcile the religious difficulties; there is only one Jesus Christ and one faith, and all the rest is a dispute over trifles."*

Writing to Synthesize

Based on the spiritual and devotional writings you read on pages 482–510, identify some of the core beliefs shared by England's citizens. Review the selections and make a list of phrases or passages that impart spiritual beliefs or moral lessons. Use these quotations to write one to three paragraphs in which you synthesize the core beliefs that emerge from these works.

Consider

- moral lessons found in the biblical selections
- the meaning of the final sestet in each of Milton's sonnets
- themes of pride, free will, and responsibility in *Paradise Lost*
- allegorical characters and place names in *The Pilgrim's Progress*

Your paragraphs should be well organized and include a clear thesis statement that expresses your opinion. Be sure to include relevant evidence and well-chosen details from the text to support your synthesis.

Extension

VIEWING & REPRESENTING

Traditionally, the stained glass windows that were installed in many churches depicted saints or scenes from the Bible—a benefit for a mostly illiterate churchgoing population. Choose one of the selections from this section, and plan a **stained glass window** to illustrate it. Be sure to choose a particularly vivid image or scene to depict. Write a brief explanation of your plan, telling why you chose the scene you did.

COMMON CORE

W 2b Develop the topic thoroughly by selecting the most significant and relevant facts, quotations, or examples.

Metaphysical Poetry

Does logic apply to the emotions? Can you express deep feeling and spiritual devotion through the use of argument, rhetoric, and reasoning? In the 17th century, a small group of poets, who later became known as the metaphysical poets, attempted to do just that. Though criticized by generations of writers, their works ushered in a unique approach to the language of poetry.

COMMON CORE

Included in this workshop:
RL 4 Analyze the impact of specific word choices on meaning and tone, including words with multiple meanings or language that is particularly fresh, engaging, or beautiful. **L 5a** Interpret figures of speech in context and analyze their role in the text.

Transcending the Elizabethans

During the 1600s, a group of poets rejected the highly ornamented style of late-Elizabethan lyric poetry and began to write what became known as metaphysical poetry. The word *metaphysical* literally means "of or relating to the transcendent or to a reality beyond what is perceptible" and "abstract and theoretical reasoning." The term is appropriate because **metaphysical poetry** is primarily devotional and often mystical in content, even

Portrait of John Donne (1595), Anonymous. Private Collection. Photo © Bridgeman Art Library.

when dealing with subjects such as physical love and relationships. Typically, metaphysical poets used intellect, logic, and even argument to explore abstract concepts, such as love and the nature of death. The result is a poetry that is highly intellectual, slightly irreverent, and marked by unconventional imagery. John Donne is considered the movement's central figure. His innovative style led the way for other metaphysical poets, including Andrew Marvell, George Herbert, Richard Crashaw, and Henry Vaughan.

In the late 1700s, Samuel Johnson named the group "metaphysical poets," which he intended as a criticism, because he believed they used their poetry merely to show off their knowledge. Earlier, the writer John Dryden had made a similar criticism of Donne's poetry. Dryden wrote that Donne "affects the metaphysics . . . [even] in his amorous verse, where nature only should reign." Such criticism diminished the popularity of the metaphysical poets until the early 20th century, when poet and critic T. S. Eliot published a famous essay in which he praised them as having the ability to unify experience—in particular, to "feel their thought as immediately as the odor of a rose."

Experiments with Language

Metaphysical poetry can be difficult to understand, which is another chief complaint of its critics. The challenge of the poetry is mainly due to the poets' attempts at experimenting with language in order to explain and depict life's complexities in imaginative ways. Although each metaphysical poet had a unique style, their poetry tended to share several traits.

- simple, conversational **vocabulary**, but complex sentence patterns
- **metaphysical conceits,** a type of extended metaphor comparing very dissimilar things
- **paradoxes,** or statements that seem to contradict themselves
- disruptions of **poetic meter**
- witty and imaginative plays on words

The most distinguishing feature is the **metaphysical conceit,** an extended metaphor that makes a surprising connection between two quite dissimilar things. It is often used to persuade, or to bolster the "argument" of the speaker. An example is Donne's description of how his love for someone will outlast them both in "The Canonization."

> We can die by it, if not live by love;
>   And if unfit for tombs and hearse
> Our legend be, it will be fit for verse;
> And if no piece of chronicle we prove
>   We'll build in sonnets pretty rooms
>   **—John Donne, "The Canonization"**

Close Read

Paraphrase the argument being made in this passage.

Another important characteristic of metaphysical poetry is **paradox**—a statement that seems contradictory but nevertheless suggests a truth. The use of paradox forces the reader to think about an image or a subject from a new perspective. For this reason, it may strike some readers as irreverent.

> Oh do not die, for I shall hate
>   All women so when thou art gone,
> That thee I shall not celebrate
>   When I remember, thou wast one.
>   **—John Donne, "A Fever"**

Close Read

Identify the paradox in these lines. What feeling is the speaker attempting to express about his loved one?

One of the criticisms of metaphysical poetry concerned its disruption of poetic meter (the regular pattern of stressed and unstressed syllables). The metaphysical poets intentionally created "roughness," or a deliberate unevenness, in their meters. In the eyes of many critics, Donne used this poetic technique too often. Poet Ben Jonson, although a great admirer of Donne's, once declared that "Donne, for not keeping of accent, deserved hanging."

Selected Poetry and Nonfiction
by John Donne

VIDEO TRAILER **THiNK** central   KEYWORD: HML12-516A

Meet the Author

John Donne 1572–1631

Donne's life and his poetry contained startling contrasts. Donne was born and raised a Roman Catholic, but he became a popular Anglican priest whose powerful sermons drew overflowing crowds to St. Paul's Cathedral in London. In his youth, he was a ladies' man who later became a devoted husband and the father of 12 children. He was both worldly and spiritual, dramatic and introspective, a doubter and a believer, a sensualist and an intellectual.

The Price of Being Catholic Donne was born into a Roman Catholic family at a time when Protestants were the majority and had no tolerance for religious ideas outside their own. He studied at Oxford University and Cambridge University, but he never received a degree, because he was a Roman Catholic and would not take an oath of allegiance to the Protestant queen. In 1593, Donne's brother died in prison, where he was sent for sheltering a Jesuit priest. Donne began to question his faith; he later abandoned Catholicism and became an Anglican priest in 1615 at the urging of King James I.

Impoverished by Love Besides religion, marriage also strongly influenced Donne's fortunes in life. In 1597, at the age of 25, Donne became the personal secretary of Sir Thomas Egerton, an official of the royal court. Four years later, Donne secretly married Egerton's 17-year-old niece, Anne More, without seeking her father's permission. When the marriage was discovered, Donne lost his job and was briefly imprisoned. For more than ten years, he battled poverty as his family grew. Donne described the situation as "John Donne, Anne Donne, Undone."

Art Reflects Life Death was a prominent theme in Donne's writing. During the Renaissance, medical knowledge was limited. It was not unusual for people to die well before the age of 50. Donne's own wife died at age 33, shortly after giving birth to their 12th child. Two of his children were stillborn, and others died at the ages of 3, 7, and 19.

"Holy Sonnet 10" (page 521) reflects Donne's concerns about death and salvation. Donne wrote "Meditation 17" (page 522) in 1623 while recovering from a serious illness. He was inspired in part by hearing the ringing of church bells to announce a person's death. "A Valediction: Forbidding Mourning" (page 518) was written to console his wife, who was distressed over her husband's impending departure for France in 1611.

DID YOU KNOW?

John Donne . . .

- once sailed with Sir Walter Raleigh on a treasure-hunting expedition.

- had his portrait drawn while dressed in his burial shroud.

- wrote lines that inspired the titles of the novels *Death Be Not Proud* by John Gunther and *For Whom the Bell Tolls* by Ernest Hemingway.

Author Online

Go to **thinkcentral.com**. KEYWORD: HML12-516B   **THiNK** central

● TEXT ANALYSIS: METAPHYSICAL CONCEIT

A device that often appears in metaphysical poetry is the **metaphysical conceit,** a type of metaphor or simile in which the comparison is unusually striking, original, and elaborate. While all metaphors and similes show likeness in two unlike things, a conceit compares two unlike things that may at first seem to have no connection whatsoever. In "Meditation 17," for example, Donne compares humanity to a book in which each person makes up a chapter. As you read these selections, look for other examples of metaphysical conceits, and notice how Donne's elaboration and subtlety allows you to make sense of the unusual comparisons.

● READING SKILL: INTERPRET IDEAS

For centuries, Donne has been acclaimed for his ability to convey complex ideas in poetry and prose. Sometimes these ideas are expressed in the form of a **paradox**—a statement that seems to **contradict,** or oppose, itself but is actually true. To uncover Donne's ideas in this type of statement, you will need to **interpret,** or explain the meaning of, the paradox. Some paradoxes may be complex and not easily understood, so it is important to

- locate the apparent **contradictory,** or contrasting, elements in the paradox
- examine the surrounding words and phrases

As you read the selections, use a chart to record the paradoxes and your interpretations.

Selection	Paradox	Interpretation
"A Valediction"	"Our two souls therefore, which are one, / Though I must go, endure not yet / A breach, but an expansion"	Two people so closely connected cannot be separated when apart, only expanded.

 Complete the activities in your **Reader/Writer Notebook.**

What is the role of DEATH in LIFE?

Death is not something we only face at the end of our lives; it influences us when we lose loved ones or even when we contemplate our own mortality. John Donne, who experienced the early deaths of his wife and some of his children, struggled to understand the meaning of death. His thoughts about mortality inspired some of his greatest works.

QUICKWRITE How has the knowledge of death affected your life? Has it made you more cautious or more fearful for your personal safety? Does it influence your relationships with others? Does it affect your appreciation of life's pleasures? On a piece of paper, list three ways in which the knowledge of death influences you. Share your ideas with others.

A Valediction: Forbidding Mourning

John Donne

As virtuous men pass mildly away,
    And whisper to their souls to go,
Whilst some of their sad friends do say
    The breath goes now, and some say, No;

5 So let us melt, and make no noise,
    No tear-floods, nor sigh-tempests move,
'Twere profanation of our joys
    To tell the laity our love.

Moving of th' earth brings harms and fears,
10   Men reckon what it did and meant;
But trepidation of the spheres,
    Though greater far, is innocent.

Dull sublunary lovers' love
    (Whose soul is sense) cannot admit
15 Absence, because it doth remove
    Those things which elemented it.

But we by a love so much refined
    That our selves know not what it is,
Inter-assuréd of the mind,
20   Care less, eyes, lips, and hands to miss.

Analyze Visuals ▶

What do the gestures and facial expressions of the figures in this painting suggest about their relationship?

5 melt: part; dissolve our togetherness.

7 profanation (prŏf'ə-nā'shən): an act of contempt for what is sacred.

8 laity (lā'ĭ-tē): persons who do not understand the "religion" of love.

9 moving of th' earth: an earthquake.

11 trepidation of the spheres: apparently irregular movements of heavenly bodies.

12 innocent: harmless.

13 sublunary (sŭb'lōō-nĕr'ē) **lovers' love:** the love of earthly lovers, which, like all things beneath the moon, is subject to change and death.

14 soul . . . sense: essence is sensuality.

16 elemented: composed.

19 inter-assuréd of the mind: confident of each other's love.

Silent Persuasion (1860), Hugues Merle. Oil on canvas, 65.4 cm × 42.5 cm. © Sotheby's/akg-images.

Our two souls therefore, which are one,
 Though I must go, endure not yet
A breach, but an expansion,
 Like gold to airy thinness beat.

25 If they be two, they are two so
 As stiff twin compasses are two;
Thy soul, the fixed foot, makes no show
 To move, but doth, if th' other do.

And though it in the center sit,
30 Yet when the other far doth roam,
It leans and hearkens after it,
 And grows erect, as that comes home.

Such wilt thou be to me, who must
 Like th' other foot, obliquely run;
35 Thy firmness makes my circle just,
 And makes me end where I begun. Ⓐ

22 **endure not yet:** do not, nevertheless, suffer.

24 **like . . . beat:** Unlike less valuable metals, gold does not break when beaten thin.

26 **twin compasses:** the two legs of a compass used for drawing circles.

32 **as that comes home:** when the moving foot returns to the center as the compass is closed.

34 **obliquely** (ō-blēk'lē): not in a straight line.

35 **firmness:** constancy; **just:** perfect.

COMMON CORE RL 4

Ⓐ **METAPHYSICAL CONCEIT**
We know that a **metaphysical conceit** is a type of extended metaphor in which a poet makes an unusually striking, original, and elaborate comparison. A conceit often provides a key to the poem's theme. Reread lines 25–36. What is unusual about comparing two lovers to a compass? How does this comparison help express the speaker's love?

Text Analysis

1. **Clarify** Why is the speaker trying to console his wife?

2. **Analyze** Reread lines 13–20. How would you describe the relationship between the speaker and his wife? Cite details in the poem to support your answer.

Holy Sonnet 10

John Donne

Death, be not proud, though some have calléd thee
Mighty and dreadful, for thou art not so;
For those whom thou think'st thou dost overthrow
Die not, poor Death, nor yet canst thou kill me.
5 From rest and sleep, which but thy pictures be,
Much pleasure; then from thee much more must flow,
And soonest our best men with thee do go,
Rest of their bones, and soul's delivery.
Thou art slave to fate, chance, kings, and desperate men,
10 And dost with poison, war, and sickness dwell,
And poppy or charms can make us sleep as well
And better than thy stroke; why swell'st thou then?
One short sleep past, we wake eternally
And death shall be no more; Death, thou shalt die. **B**

5–6 From rest . . . flow: Since we derive pleasure from rest and sleep, which are only likenesses of death, we should derive much more from death itself.

8 soul's delivery: the freeing of the soul from the body.

11 poppy: opium, a narcotic drug made from the juice of the poppy plant.

12 swell'st: swell with pride.

B INTERPRET IDEAS
What wishful **paradox** does Donne include at the end of his poem? Why is this reference to death paradoxical?

Text Analysis

1. **Clarify** Why does the speaker state that death is not mighty or dreadful?

2. **Interpret** How do you interpret the statement "Death, thou shalt die"?

Meditation 17

John Donne

Perchance he for whom this bell tolls may be so ill as that he knows not it tolls for him; and perchance I may think myself so much better than I am, as that they who are about me and see my state may have caused it to toll for me, and I know not that. The church is catholic,[1] universal, so are all her actions; all that she does belongs to all. When she baptizes a child, that action concerns me; for that child is thereby connected to that body which is my head too, and ingrafted into that body whereof I am a member.[2] And when she buries a man, that action concerns me: all mankind is of one author and is one volume; when one man dies, one chapter is not torn out of the book, but translated into a better language; and
10 every chapter must be so translated. God employs several translators; some pieces are translated by age, some by sickness, some by war, some by justice; but God's hand is in every translation, and his hand shall bind up all our scattered leaves again for that library where every book shall lie open to one another. As therefore the bell **C** that rings to a sermon calls not upon the preacher only, but upon the congregation to come, so this bell calls us all; but how much more me, who am brought so near the door by this sickness. . . . Who casts not up his eye to the sun when it rises? but who takes off his eye from a comet when that breaks out? Who bends not his ear to any bell which upon any occasion rings? but who can remove it from that bell which is passing a piece of himself out of this world? No man is an island,
20 entire of itself; every man is a piece of the continent, a part of the main.[3] If a clod be washed away by the sea, Europe is the less, as well as if a promontory[4] were, as well as if a manor of thy friend's or of thine own were. Any man's death diminishes me because I am involved in mankind, and therefore never send to know for whom the bell tolls; it tolls for thee. ⌁ **D**

Language Coach

Multiple Meanings Lines 8 and 12 contain several words that have multiple meanings: *volume*, *bind*, and *leaves*. What does each word mean in this passage? How can you guess their meaning?

C **METAPHYSICAL CONCEIT**
Reread lines 8–13. What comparison is made in this conceit?

D **INTEPRET IDEAS**
What **paradox** do you find in lines 22–24? How would you interpret it?

---

1. **is catholic:** embraces all humankind.
2. **body which is my head . . . member:** Donne likens the church to the head, which controls every part of the body, and to the body itself, because it is made up of interconnected parts (the individuals who compose it).
3. **main:** mainland.
4. **promontory** (prŏm′ən-tôr′ē): a ridge of land jutting out into a body of water.

Comprehension

1. **Recall** What important church rituals does Donne describe in "Meditation 17"?

2. **Clarify** In "Meditation 17," what event does the tolling bell announce?

3. **Clarify** Why does Donne feel that the tolling bell calls more to him than to most people?

COMMON CORE

RL 4 Determine the meaning of words and phrases as they are used in the text, including figurative meanings. **L 5a** Interpret figures of speech in context and analyze their role in the text.

Text Analysis

4. **Analyze Simile** Reread lines 21–24 of "A Valediction: Forbidding Mourning." How will the speaker's marriage be similar to gold that has been beaten thin?

5. **Interpret Ideas** Review the chart you created as you read. Choose one **paradox** you identified, and explain how it connects to the **theme** of the work it appears in.

6. **Interpret Metaphysical Conceits** Explain the meaning of the conceits in the following passages:

   • "A Valediction: Forbidding Mourning," lines 1–6

   • "Meditation 17," lines 8–13

   • "Meditation 17," lines 19–22

7. **Draw Conclusions** Examine the ideas about mortality that Donne expresses in "Holy Sonnet 10" and "Meditation 17." Use a chart like the one shown to record your response, and then draw conclusions about Donne's view of mortality in general.

Selection	Ideas about Mortality
"Holy Sonnet 10"	
"Meditation 17"	

8. **Compare Texts** Compare Donne's depiction of love in "A Valediction: Forbidding Mourning" with Shakespeare's depiction of love in "Sonnet 116" on page 329. Do the two speakers appear to agree or disagree? Cite evidence to support your answer.

Text Criticism

9. **Critical Interpretations** Donne has been characterized as a writer who "married passion to reason." Reread "Holy Sonnet 10" and explain how this description does or does not apply to this poem. Consider Donne's ideas and the techniques he uses to present them. Support your answer with evidence from the text.

What is the role of DEATH in LIFE?

Humans by definition are mortal, susceptible to death. What characters in literature or films are portrayed as immortal? How would being immortal change the way you lived your life?

COMMON CORE

RL 4 Determine the meaning of words and phrases as they are used in the text, including figurative and connotative meanings; analyze the impact of specific word choices on meaning and tone, including words with multiple meanings or language that is particularly fresh, engaging, or beautiful.

On My First Son
Song: To Celia

Poetry by Ben Jonson

Meet the Author

Ben Jonson 1572–1637

In his day, Ben Johnson was a literary giant who knew most of London's important writers, including John Donne and William Shakespeare. In fact, Elizabethans considered him a more important literary figure than Shakespeare. But part of Jonson's fame resulted from his controversial life.

Stage Call Like Shakespeare, Jonson has been remembered chiefly as a great playwright. His route to the theater was indirect. Jonson's father, a minister, died about a month before Ben was born, and his mother then married a bricklayer. Although Jonson gained a strong early education, he did not have the money to attend college, so he joined his stepfather in bricklaying. Jonson hated the job, ran away to enlist in the British army, and fought in the Netherlands. After returning to London, he joined a group of touring actors and began to write plays. The production of his first play landed him in prison, because it offended government officials.

Success . . . and Near Death Jonson's second play, *Every Man in His Humor,* was a huge success. Shakespeare's company performed the comedy, and Shakespeare himself played one of the roles. The success was immediately followed by trouble,

however. The temperamental Jonson got into an argument with an actor in the company and killed him in a duel. Jonson escaped hanging by reading a passage from the Latin Bible, which allowed him to be tried by a church court rather than a harsher criminal court. At the time, knowledge of Latin was largely confined to clergymen. Jonson kept his life but was branded on the thumb as a convicted felon and had his property taken away.

A Literary Reformer Jonson considered himself a pioneer in drama, especially comedy, and set out to rid it of clichés, stale jokes, and improbable plots. He gained fame for his satiric comedies, which poked fun at the human vices and follies of his day. In 1616, he published a volume of his plays under the title *The Works of Ben Jonson.* At that time, scholars considered only such literary forms as poetry, historical writing, and sermons worthy of being called "works." Jonson challenged that notion, paving the way for the acceptance of plays as literature.

Jonson also wrote some of the finest poetry of his time. "On My First Son" is the poet's response to the death of his son, Benjamin. Like John Donne and other Elizabethans, Jonson experienced the anguish of the untimely death of a loved one more than once. Both of his children died at young ages, his son at the age of seven, a victim of the plague, and his daughter, Mary, in infancy.

DID YOU KNOW?

Ben Jonson . . .

• had a fan club of young writers called "the sons of Ben."

• converted to Catholicism while in prison for murder.

• continued to write plays from his bed after suffering a stroke.

Author Online

Go to **thinkcentral.com**. KEYWORD: HML12-524

THiNK central

POETIC FORM: EPITAPH

An **epitaph** is an inscription placed on a tomb or monument to honor the memory of the person buried there. The term *epitaph* has also been used more loosely to describe a poem, such as "On My First Son," which commemorates someone who has died. Notice the serious tone and somber mood of the following lines:

Farewell, thou child of my right hand, and joy;
My sin was too much hope of thee, loved boy

As you read "On My First Son," determine which lines are characteristic of an epitaph.

TEXT ANALYSIS: RHYME

The rhymes in Jonson's poems help give them a musical quality. **Rhyme** occurs when the sounds of the accented vowels in words and all the succeeding sounds in the words are identical. Rhyme at the end of verse lines is called **end rhyme** (*joy* and *boy* in the two lines above). The pattern of a poem's end rhymes is its **rhyme scheme.** There are two basic types of rhymes.

- An **exact rhyme** occurs when two words sound exactly alike except for their consonant sounds, as in *joy* and *boy*.
- A **slant rhyme,** or off rhyme, occurs when the rhyme is approximate, as in *come* and *doom*. Although rhymes normally fall on accented syllables, slant rhymes may pair an accented and an unaccented syllable, as in *though* and *fellow*.

As you read each poem, identify the rhyme scheme and notice where Jonson uses slant rhymes rather than exact ones.

READING SKILL: COMPARE SPEAKERS

Though a poet may speak with his or her own voice in a poem, the **speaker** is often a voice or character made up by the writer. Two poems by the same writer may therefore have very different speakers. As you read the following poems by Jonson, record the images and words that directly express or imply the speaker's feelings toward the poem's subject. Notice how these images and words allow Jonson to create distinct speakers in the poems.

"On My First Son"	"Song: To Celia"
"O could I lose all father now!"	

 Complete the activities in your **Reader/Writer Notebook**.

Is love a BLESSING or a CURSE?

There's no doubt that strong attachment—whether between lovers, family members, or friends—can bring both great pleasure and intense pain. Ben Jonson explored the different aspects of attachment in the selections that follow. Sometimes it's hard to know which feeling predominates.

DISCUSS How do you think most people would answer the question "Is love a blessing or a curse?" With a classmate, discuss the times when attachment to someone can be painful and when it brings joy.

On My First Son

Ben Jonson

Farewell, thou child of my right hand, and joy;
My sin was too much hope of thee, loved boy:
Seven years thou wert lent to me, and I thee pay,
Exacted by thy fate, on the just day.
5 O could I lose all father now! for why
Will man lament the state he should envy,
To have so soon 'scaped world's and flesh's rage,
And, if no other misery, yet age?
Rest in soft peace, and asked, say, "Here doth lie
10 Ben Jonson his best piece of poetry."
For whose sake henceforth all his vows be such
As what he loves may never like too much. **Ⓐ**

1 child of my right hand: Jonson's son was also named Benjamin, which literally means "son of my right hand" in Hebrew.

4 just: required; exact.

5 lose all father: lose all of the feeling or hope of being a father.

Ⓐ EPITAPH
What **mood** does Jonson convey in lines 11–12?

Analyze Visuals ▶
What elements of this painting help convey the subject's vulnerablity?

Text Analysis

1. **Clarify** Reread lines 1–2. What is the speaker's "sin"?

2. **Interpret** How do you interpret the statement in lines 9–10, "Here doth lie / Ben Jonson his best piece of poetry"?

Portrait of Master Bunbury (1780), Sir Joshua Reynolds. Oil on canvas, 30⅛″ × 25⅛″. The John Howard McFadden Collection, 1928. © The Philadelphia Museum of Art/Art Resource, New York.

Song: To Celia

Ben Jonson

Portrait of Lady Brownlow (1600s),
William Wissing. Oil on canvas, 127 cm × 103.2 cm.
Private collection. © Bridgeman Art Library.

Drink to me only with thine eyes,
    And I will pledge with mine;
Or leave a kiss but in the cup,
    And I'll not look for wine. **B**
5 The thirst that from the soul doth rise
    Doth ask a drink divine:
But might I of Jove's nectar sup,
    I would not change for thine.
I sent thee late a rosy wreath,
10   Not so much honoring thee,
As giving it a hope that there
    It could not withered be.
But thou thereon didst only breathe,
    And sent'st it back to me;
15 Since when it grows and smells, I swear,
    Not of itself, but thee. **C**

B COMPARE SPEAKERS
Reread lines 1–4. What emotion
does the speaker express?

7 **Jove's nectar:** the special drink of
the Greek and Roman gods. Jove is
another name for Jupiter, chief of
the Roman gods.

C RHYME
Which end rhyme in the poem
is an example of **slant rhyme?**

Comprehension

1. **Paraphrase** Restate in your own words lines 1–2 of "Song: To Celia."

2. **Clarify** In "Song: To Celia," what happens when the speaker sends a wreath to his beloved?

Text Analysis

● 3. **Examine Epitaph** Which lines from the poem "On My First Son" would be the best inscription on a gravestone for Jonson's son? Why?

4. **Interpret Theme** What is the speaker's message about loss in the following passages of "On My First Son"?

   • lines 1–2 ("Farewell, thou child . . . thee, loved boy")

   • lines 3–4 ("Seven years thou . . . on the just day.")

   • lines 11–12 ("For whose sake . . . never like too much.")

5. **Analyze Figurative Language** An **extended metaphor** compares two unlike things at length. Identify the extended metaphor in "Song: To Celia." What is its relevancy to the subject of the poem?

● 6. **Analyze Rhyme** Reread the two poems, noting Jonson's use of **exact** and **slant rhyme.** Study the following **rhyme schemes,** and decide which one matches each poem:

   • *aabbcdeecdff*

   • *abcbabcbdefedefe*

● 7. **Compare Speakers** Review the chart you filled in as you read the poems. How does each speaker feel about the person addressed in each poem? What is the main difference between the two speakers?

8. **Compare Author's Perspectives** Reread lines 5–8 of "On My First Son." Then compare Jonson's attitude toward death with that of John Donne in "Holy Sonnet 10" on page 521. Use evidence from the poems to explain the similarities and differences.

Text Criticism

9. **Different Perspectives** The English poet Alfred, Lord Tennyson, wrote, "'Tis better to have loved and lost / Than never to have loved at all." How might Jonson have responded to Tennyson's statement? Explain your answer.

> *Is love a* **BLESSING** *or a* **CURSE?**
>
> Sometimes attachment can be one-sided. Unrequited love is rarely considered a blessing, but are there any advantages to a painful or disappointing experience in love?

COMMON CORE

RL 4 Determine the meaning of words and phrases as they are used in the text, including figurative and connotative meanings; analyze the impact of specific word choices on meaning and tone, including words with multiple meanings or language that is particularly fresh, engaging, or beautiful.

To His Coy Mistress
Poem by Andrew Marvell

To the Virgins, to Make Much of Time
Poem by Robert Herrick

To Althea, from Prison
Poem by Richard Lovelace

COMMON CORE

RL 2 Determine themes or central ideas of a text and analyze their development. **L 5a** Interpret figures of speech in context and analyze their role in the text.

Meet the Authors

Andrew Marvell
1621–1678

Andrew Marvell is often grouped with Robert Herrick and Richard Lovelace as one of the Cavalier poets. They regarded Ben Jonson as their literary father, and like Jonson, they tried to imitate the grace and polish of classical Latin poetry. The Cavalier poets even referred to themselves as the "sons of Ben" or "tribe of Ben." Marvell combined the lighthearted and melodious style of Cavalier poetry with the intellectual depth and wit of metaphysical poetry.

During his lifetime, Marvell was known for his political activities rather than for his poetry. Unlike Herrick and Lovelace, he supported Parliament in the English Civil War of 1642–1651, and he served in Parliament from 1659 until his death. Marvell's poetry was published posthumously; his true worth as a poet was not fully recognized until the 20th century.

Robert Herrick
1591–1674

Robert Herrick was an Anglican priest and an ardent admirer of Ben Jonson. An active member of London society, he was disappointed when assigned to a rural church in Devonshire in 1629. However, in 1646, under a parliamentary government, he was deprived of this post due to his loyalty to the king.

In 1648, he published his only book of poems, *Hesperides*. At the time, the English were caught up in a civil war, and they showed little interest in Herrick's light, playful verse. In 1662, Herrick was able to return to Devonshire, where he again settled down as a country priest and enjoyed a quiet life, although he wrote no more poetry. Today, critics appreciate Herrick's poetry more; he has been called "the greatest songwriter ever born of English race."

Richard Lovelace
1618–1657

Richard Lovelace was a courtier, soldier, poet, and connoisseur of the arts. He was born into a distinguished military family, and from early on, he was associated with the extravagant court of Charles I. At age 15 he became a "Gentleman Wayter Extraordinary" to the king, and at 18, he received an honorary masters degree from Oxford University. When conflict erupted between Charles I and Parliament, Lovelace petitioned Parliament in the king's favor and was imprisoned. While in prison, he wrote one of his most famous poems, "To Althea, from Prison."

Authors Online
Go to **thinkcentral.com**. KEYWORD: HML12-530

THINK central

TEXT ANALYSIS: THEME

The **theme** of a poem is the central message the poet wishes to convey. The Cavalier poets were known for their themes about love, war, honor, and courtly behavior. They frequently advocated the philosophy of *carpe diem*, a Latin expression that means "seize the day," or live for the moment. A poem famous for its theme of *carpe diem* is "To His Coy Mistress," in which the speaker beseeches a young woman to be his love now because life is short. As you read each of the following poems, note the imagery, figurative language, and other descriptive details that help convey the poem's theme.

READING SKILL: INTERPRET FIGURATIVE LANGUAGE

Often in reading poetry, you will need to interpret **figurative language,** or language that communicates ideas beyond the literal meanings of the words. The words in a figurative expression suggest rather than state information, thus helping to create an impression in the reader's mind.

Metaphors, similes, and hyperbole are among the types of figurative language used in these poems. **Hyperbole** is any expression that greatly exaggerates facts or ideas for humorous effect or for emphasis. For example, in "To His Coy Mistress," the speaker says that he would spend a "hundred years" praising his beloved's eyes, which would be literally impossible, but figuratively it expresses the depth of his adoration.

Use the following strategies to interpret figurative meaning:

- Read each poem first to grasp its overall meaning.
- Then, ask questions about comparisons that are implied or directly stated. What is being compared, and how are these things alike?

As you read the poems, use a chart like the one shown to list examples of hyperbole, metaphor, and simile, and to record your interpretation of their meanings.

Poem	Figurative Language	Interpretation
"To His Coy Mistress"	Hyperbole: "My vegetable love should grow / Vaster than empires and more slow"	The speaker's love will not dissipate in the future but continue to grow.

 Complete the activities in your **Reader/Writer Notebook.**

Should we LIVE *for* TODAY?

The Latin phrase *carpe diem* means literally "seize the day." Many people subscribe to the idea that life is fleeting and that we should therefore focus on enjoyment of the present. But living for the moment can have its pitfalls too.

PRESENT Working with a partner, ask several friends and family members to identify the pros and cons of living for today. List all the responses you gather in a chart, and present your findings to your class. Which side seems to win out? What conclusion can you draw about people's attitudes?

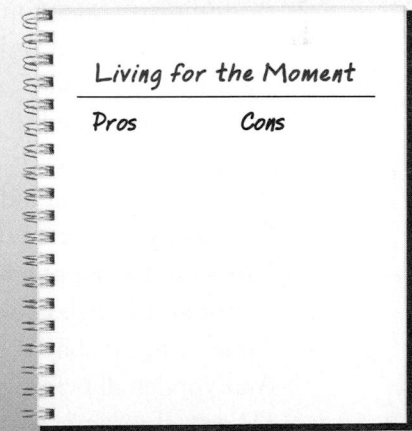

Living for the Moment

Pros	Cons

To His Coy Mistress

Andrew Marvell

Had we but world enough, and time,
This coyness, lady, were no crime.
We would sit down, and think which way
To walk, and pass our long love's day.
Thou by the Indian Ganges' side
Shouldst rubies find; I by the tide
Of Humber would complain. I would
Love you ten years before the flood,
And you should, if you please, refuse
10 Till the conversion of the Jews.
My vegetable love should grow
Vaster than empires and more slow;
An hundred years should go to praise
Thine eyes, and on thy forehead gaze;
15 Two hundred to adore each breast,
But thirty thousand to the rest;
An age at least to every part,
And the last age should show your heart.
For, lady, you deserve this state,
20 Nor would I love at lower rate.
    But at my back I always hear
Time's wingéd chariot hurrying near; **A**
And yonder all before us lie
Deserts of vast eternity.
25 Thy beauty shall no more be found,
Nor, in thy marble vault, shall sound
My echoing song; then worms shall try
That long-preserved virginity,
And your quaint honor turn to dust,
30 And into ashes all my lust: **B**
The grave's a fine and private place,
But none, I think, do there embrace.

5 **Ganges** (găn'jēz'): a great river of northern India.

7 **Humber:** a river of northern England, flowing through Marvell's hometown; **complain:** sing melancholy love songs.

8 **flood:** the biblical Flood.

10 **till . . . Jews:** In Marvell's day, Christians believed that all Jews would convert to Christianity just before the Last Judgment and the end of the world.

11 **vegetable love:** a love that grows like a plant (an oak tree, for example)—slowly but with the power to become very large.

19 **state:** dignity.

A THEME
Reread lines 21–22.
Explain how these lines help convey the theme of *carpe diem*.

B FIGURATIVE MEANING
In lines 29–30, the speaker refers metaphorically to honor and lust as physical objects. What idea does this figurative language emphasize?

Lovers in a Landscape, Peter Lely. Musée des Beaux-Arts, Valenciennes, France. © Erich Lessing/Art Resource, New York.

Now therefore, while the youthful hue
Sits on thy skin like morning dew,
35 And while thy willing soul transpires
At every pore with instant fires,
Now let us sport us while we may,
And now, like amorous birds of prey,
Rather at once our time devour
40 Than languish in his slow-chapped power.
Let us roll all our strength and all
Our sweetness up into one ball,
And tear our pleasures with rough strife
Thorough the iron gates of life:
45 Thus, though we cannot make our sun
Stand still, yet we will make him run.

35 transpires: breathes.

40 slow-chapped: slow-jawed.

44 thorough: through.

To the Virgins, to Make Much of Time

Robert Herrick

Gather ye rosebuds while ye may, **C**
    Old time is still a-flying;
And this same flower that smiles today
    Tomorrow will be dying.

5 The glorious lamp of heaven, the sun,
    The higher he's a-getting,
The sooner will his race be run,
    And nearer he's to setting.

That age is best which is the first,
10   When youth and blood are warmer;
But being spent, the worse, and worst
    Times still succeed the former.

Then be not coy, but use your time,
    And, while ye may, go marry;
15 For, having lost but once your prime,
    You may forever tarry.

C FIGURATIVE MEANING
Figuratively speaking, what might the rosebuds in line 1 be a reference to?

Language Coach

Word Definitions *Former* (line 12) means "previous or past." Paraphrase lines 11–12, starting with "and worst...."

13 coy: hesitant; modest.

16 tarry: wait.

Text Analysis

1. **Summarize** What argument does the speaker make in "To His Coy Mistress"?

2. **Clarify** In lines 9–12 of "To the Virgins, to Make Much of Time," what ideas does the speaker express about age?

3. **Compare Styles** In what ways are Marvell's poem and Herrick's poem similar in style? How do their styles differ?

To Althea, from Prison

Richard Lovelace

When Love with unconfinèd wings
    Hovers within my gates, **D**
And my divine Althea brings
    To whisper at the grates;
5 When I lie tangled in her hair
    And fettered to her eye,
The gods that wanton in the air
    Know no such liberty.

When flowing cups run swiftly round,
10   With no allaying Thames,
Our careless heads with roses bound,
    Our hearts with loyal flames;
When thirsty grief in wine we steep,
    When healths and draughts go free,
15 Fishes that tipple in the deep
    Know no such liberty.

When, like committed linnets, I
    With shriller throat shall sing
The sweetness, mercy, majesty,
20   And glories of my king;
When I shall voice aloud how good
    He is, how great should be,
Enlargèd winds, that curl the flood,
    Know no such liberty. **E**

25 Stone walls do not a prison make,
    Nor iron bars a cage;
Minds innocent and quiet take
    That for an hermitage.
If I have freedom in my love,
30   And in my soul am free,
Angels alone, that soar above,
    Enjoy such liberty.

D **FIGURATIVE MEANING**
What **metaphor** is introduced in lines 1 and 2?

7 **wanton:** sport; play.

10 **with no allaying Thames:** The Thames, a famous river running through London, is used here poetically to mean "water."

14 **healths and draughts:** toasts and drinks.

17 **committed linnets:** caged songbirds. A linnet is a type of finch.

E **THEME**
Note the last line of each stanza so far. What might this **repetition** suggest about the poem's theme?

Comprehension

COMMON CORE

RL 2 Determine themes or central ideas of a text and analyze their development. **L 5a** Interpret figures of speech in context and analyze their role in the text.

1. **Clarify** How does the speaker feel when Althea comes to visit him?

2. **Summarize** What activities in prison give the speaker a sense of liberty?

3. **Summarize** Reread the last stanza of "To Althea, from Prison." How does the speaker regard his imprisonment?

Text Analysis

4. **Interpret Figurative Language** Interpret and explain the following lines from the poems:

   - lines 38–40 from "To His Coy Mistress"
   - lines 3–4 from "To the Virgins, to Make Much of Time"
   - lines 25–26 from "To Althea, from Prison"

5. **Analyze Theme** In "To His Coy Mistress" and "To the Virgins, to Make Much of Time," which images of nature do the poets use to express the passing of time and the theme of *carpe diem?*

6. **Make Generalizations About Speakers** Think about the ways in which women are described in "To His Coy Mistress," "To the Virgins, to Make Much of Time," and "To Althea, from Prison." How would you characterize each speaker's attitude toward women? What generalizations can you make about this aspect of Cavalier poetry? Use a chart to make your responses.

Speaker's Attitude Toward Women	
First Poem:	
Second Poem:	
Third Poem:	

Generalizations:

7. **Compare Texts** In your opinion, what would each of the speakers of these poems think of the kind of love described in Donne's "A Valediction: Forbidding Mourning" (page 518)? Support your answer with evidence from the poems.

Text Criticism

8. **Different Perspectives** Some critics have stated that female and male readers are likely to respond differently to "To His Coy Mistress." Do you agree with this observation? Explain why, and cite evidence from the text to support your answer.

Should we LIVE for TODAY?

Because time is fleeting, Herrick and Marvell encourage us to seize the day, or live for the moment. What are some ways to actively do this?

Metaphysical Conceits

The metaphysical poets and, to a lesser extent, the Cavalier poets who followed them shared a love for elaborate conceits—extended metaphors that make a surprising connection between two very dissimilar things. John Donne was the master of this technique. Reread this example of one such conceit from Donne's "A Valediction: Forbidding Mourning."

> "If they be two, they are two so
>   As stiff twin compasses are two;
> Thy soul, the fixed foot, makes no show
>   To move, but doth, if th' other do."

Donne compares the souls of two separated lovers to the feet of a compass that turn in sync with one another; when one moves, so does the other, for they remain attached. Metaphysical conceits require imagination on the part of the reader, who must think carefully to understand the connection being made by the comparison.

Writing to Evaluate

The metaphysical poets' use of such fanciful and extended conceits led the writer and critic Samuel Johnson to complain about their "violent yoking together of heterogeneous ideas." What is your opinion of metaphysical conceits? Do you agree with Johnson that the comparisons are artificial and forced? Or do you find the comparisons add depth or complexity to your understanding? Cite specific lines from Donne's writing to support your argument.

Consider

- the nuances of each comparison

- the choice of words and images Donne uses in making each comparison

- whether, in your opinion, the conceits add to or detract from the work's overall theme

Extension Online

INQUIRY & RESEARCH

Samuel Johnson was only one of many literary critics who commented upon the work of John Donne and the metaphysical poets. Many critics did not care for the elaborate conceits and rough meter characteristic of metaphysical poetry, while others praised the poets' complexity of ideas. Search the Internet for literary criticism on the metaphysical poets. Then, with your classmates, create a classroom poster with the most intriguing critical comments, positive and negative.

COMMON CORE

W 7 Conduct short research projects to solve a problem. **W 9** Draw evidence from literary texts to support analysis.

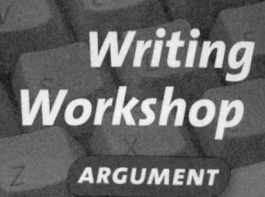

Writing Workshop

ARGUMENT

Critical Review

After seeing an adaptation of a play performed on screen or on stage, have you ever thought that the adaptation just didn't do the play justice? In this workshop, you will learn how to write a critical review of a film or theater adaptation of a key scene from a play. You will then support your claim, or position, with evidence from both the text and the movie or theater production.

 Complete the workshop activities in your **Reader/Writer Notebook**.

WRITE WITH A PURPOSE

WRITING TASK

Write a **critical review** of a key scene from a movie or theater adaptation of a play. Assert a claim that states whether the adaptation does justice to the source material—the original play.

Idea Starters

- a scene from *Macbeth,* such as Act One, Scene 3 (the witches' prophecies)
- a scene from *Pygmalion,* such as Act One, Scene 1 (introducing Eliza; see page 1227 of this book)
- a scene from *Waiting for Godot,* such as the argument in Act One on pages 1316–1317 of this book

THE ESSENTIALS

Here are some common purposes, audiences, and formats for writing a critical review.

PURPOSES	AUDIENCES	FORMATS
• to convince others to agree with your claim • to evaluate the success of the adaptation	• classmates and teacher • book or movie club members • Web users	• essay for class • review in the school newspaper • online movie or theater reviews • podcast

COMMON CORE TRAITS

1. DEVELOPMENT OF IDEAS

- includes a compelling **introduction** that states a **precise, knowledgeable claim**
- provides **valid reasons** and **relevant evidence** from both versions
- acknowledges **opposing claims** and refutes them fairly with **counterclaims**
- offers a **concluding section** that follows from and supports the argument presented

2. ORGANIZATION OF IDEAS

- **organizes** reasons and evidence in a **logical way**
- uses varied **transitions** to create cohesion and clarify the relationships among ideas

3. LANGUAGE FACILITY AND CONVENTIONS

- maintains a **formal style** and **objective tone**
- varies **syntax** for persuasive effect and cohesive flow
- employs correct **grammar, mechanics,** and **spelling**

Writing Online

THINK central

Go to **thinkcentral.com**.
KEYWORD: HML12N-538

Planning/Prewriting

COMMON CORE

W 1a–e Write arguments to support claims, using valid reasoning and relevant evidence. **W 5** Develop and strengthen writing by planning. **W 9a (RL 1, 7)** Draw evidence from literary texts; cite textual evidence; analyze multiple interpretations of a drama.

Getting Started

CHOOSE A SCENE

List movie or theater adaptations of a play you have seen. Consult the Idea Starters on page 538 for some sample plays and scenes. Choose a scene that is complex enough to be the subject of a **substantive,** or meaningful, argument. View the adaptation of the scene, jotting down notes about the ways in which it is the same as or different from the original. Also include ideas about the film techniques, the soundtrack, casting, and other elements.

► **ASK YOURSELF:**

- How does this scene from the film or theater adaptation compare to the original play?
- Are key parts of the play omitted from the adaptation?
- Does the director change elements of the play?
- If the adaptation is not successful, why?

THINK ABOUT AUDIENCE AND PURPOSE

To write an effective critical review, you must first identify your **purpose**—to convince your **audience** to accept your position as a valid opinion. To be successful, you need to consider what your audience may know about the scene and what opinions they might have about the source material or the adaptation. Then you can choose the reasons and evidence that will be most convincing to them.

► **ASK YOURSELF:**

- Who is my audience? What do I want them to believe about this adaptation?
- Do I expect my audience to have a bias for or against the adaptation? What evidence can I provide to change that bias?
- What background information about the scene will my audience need in order to understand my argument?

STATE YOUR CLAIM AND REASONS

Your argument should center on a **precise claim** in which you establish that you are knowledgeable about both the adaptation and original work. You will prove your claim with valid **reasons**—logical and insightful statements that support your claim. If you find that your claim can't be fully supported, revise it or try a new approach.

► **WHAT DOES IT LOOK LIKE?**

Claim: Orson Welles' film adaptation of Act One, Scene 3 of Macbeth makes Shakespeare's play come alive for modern viewers by intensifying the mood and pacing of the original.

Reason 1	Reason 2	Reason 3
Music, lighting, and camera shots create an eerie mood.	The addition of the clay figure enhances the supernatural element of the witches.	Shortened dialogue moves the plot along.

Planning/Prewriting *continued*

GATHER EVIDENCE

Strong reasons that clearly and directly support your claim are only the beginning of a convincing argument. Each reason must be supported by at least one of these kinds of **relevant,** or related, **evidence.**

- **expert opinions**—opinions or ideas from critics or other experts
- **examples and details**—specific instances that illustrate your ideas
- **quotations**—text from the play or adaptation that supports your ideas

▶ **WHAT DOES IT LOOK LIKE?**

> **Expert Opinion**
>
> As New York Times film critic Bosley Crowther said, "it has a great deal in its favor in the way of feudal spectacle and nightmare mood."

> **Quotation**
>
> The visual effects replace much of Shakespeare's descriptions, such as that of the witches: "so withered, and so wild in their attire."

PLAN COUNTERCLAIMS

Some readers may disagree with your claim. For your criticism to be convincing, you need to address any **alternative** or **opposing claims** and explain their limitations. For each opposing claim, list a **counterclaim,** a statement that refutes the opposition and explains why your viewpoint is more valid. Present information fairly and maintain an **objective,** or controlled, **tone.**

▶ **WHAT DOES IT LOOK LIKE?**

> **Opposing claim:** Doesn't the movie adaptation lose much of Shakespeare's original language in this scene?
>
> **Counterclaim:** Orson Welles replaces the language with eerie music, lighting, and close-up shots. These elements effectively express the mood of the play, even more powerfully than words could.

PLAN YOUR CONCLUDING SECTION

End your argument with an insightful, convincing concluding section. You should sum up your claim and your reasons. You might also present a thought-provoking quotation or an insight to keep your audience thinking about the ideas you have presented in your argument.

▶ **WHAT DOES IT LOOK LIKE?**

> **restatement of the claim:** Welles' depiction of Act One, Scene 3 creates a dark, eerie mood for viewers.
>
> **summary of reasons:** Welles' brilliant use of film techniques, added elements, and dialogue brings out the full impact of Shakespeare's words.
>
> **insight:** Welles' adaptation goes beyond the text to create a truly eerie, ominous mood, foreshadowing troubling events yet to come.

PEER REVIEW Describe to a peer your audience and purpose of your critical review. Then ask: Do my planned reasons and evidence effectively support my claim?

YOUR TURN In your *Reader/Writer Notebook,* choose a scene for evaluation. Decide whether that scene in a film or theater adaptation does justice to the original text. Use a chart or graphic organizer to list your reasons and evidence.

Drafting

The following chart shows how to organize your draft of a critical review.

COMMON
CORE

W 1c Use words, phrases, and clauses as well as varied syntax to link the major sections of the text, create cohesion, and clarify relationships. **W 4** Produce clear and coherent writing appropriate to task, purpose, and audience.

Organizing Your Critical Review

INTRODUCTION

- Grab the attention of the audience with a **challenging question, compelling quotation,** or **vivid description.**
- Introduce the **play, the author,** and the **director** of the film or theater adaptation. Provide any **background** information that your audience might need to understand your criticism.
- State your position in a **precise, knowledgeable claim.**

▼

BODY

- Present your reasons in **logical sequence,** such as by order of importance.
- Support each reason with the most **relevant evidence,** including quotations and examples.
- Acknowledge **opposing claims** fairly. Provide **counterclaims** to emphasize the strength of your claim.
- Maintain a **formal style** by using a confident voice and persuasive words. Use an **objective,** or controlled, **tone.** Vary your **syntax** by using different sentence structures and beginnings.

▼

CONCLUDING SECTION

- **Restate your claim** so that it follows from and supports your argument.
- Leave the reader with something to think about, such as a **thought-provoking question** or **insightful statement** about the play.

GRAMMAR IN CONTEXT: USE VARIED TRANSITIONS

A strong argument shows **cohesion**—clear connections and flow from one idea to the next. Use appropriate **transitions** to link the major sections of your essay, and clarify relationships between ideas. Be sure to vary your transitions to keep your argument clear and interesting.

Transitions that Create Cohesion

however
if . . . then
furthermore
first . . . next
consequently
for example

▶

Example

Although the dialogue and stage directions deviate from the original play, Welles enhances the dark mood with lighting and unusual camera angles. *For example,* flashes of lightning grab viewers' attention and emphasize the action; *in addition,* shadows add a level of mystery to the witches.

YOUR
TURN

Develop a draft of your essay, following the plan outlined in the chart above. Use appropriate and varied transitions to link your ideas, clarify relationships, and create a cohesive argument.

Revising

The revising stage gives you a chance to improve your draft. Verify that you address the writing task, achieve your purpose, and provide enough evidence to convince your audience of the validity of your argument. Use the chart shown to help you revise, rewrite, and try a new approach where necessary.

CRITICAL REVIEW

Ask Yourself	Tips	Revision Strategies
1. Do I capture the audience's attention in my opening lines?	**Bracket** interesting statements or thought-provoking ideas.	**Add** an attention-getting statement or quotation.
2. Does my introduction identify the title and author of the play, and the director of the film or theater adaptation? Do I state a precise, knowledgeable claim?	**Draw boxes** around the work's author, title, and director. **Underline** the claim.	**Add** information that identifies the play, author, and the director. **Revise** the claim to more precisely state your opinion.
3. Do at least two valid reasons support my claim? Do I provide the most relevant evidence to support each reason?	**Highlight** the reasons that support the claim. **Circle** the evidence that supports each reason. **Draw an arrow** from the evidence to the reason.	If necessary, **add** valid reasons to support the claim. **Add** examples, expert opinions, or quotations to bolster unsupported reasons. **Elaborate** on evidence by adding more details or explanation.
4. Do varied transitions clarify the relationships among my claim, counterclaim, reasons, and evidence?	**Draw a star** next to each transitional word or phrase.	**Check** your starred transitions and **add** variety if necessary. **Reread** the parts that lack stars. **Add** appropriate transitions to link ideas.
5. Do I acknowledge opposing claims and present counterclaims in an objective way?	**Draw a wavy line** under the opposing claims and your responses to them.	If necessary, **add** a counterclaim that points out the limitations of opposing claims and the strengths of your opinion.
6. Does the concluding section restate my claim and leave the reader with a significant insight into both works?	**Put a check mark** next to the restatement. **Underline** the sentence that states an important insight.	**Add** a restatement of the claim if it is missing. **Add** a thought-provoking question or insightful statement about both works.

 **YOUR TURN**

PEER REVIEW Working with a peer, review your drafts together. Answer each question in the chart to decide how to improve your drafts and where to try a new approach.

W 1b Develop claim(s) and counterclaims fairly, supplying relevant evidence for each. **W 5** Strengthen writing by revising, editing, rewriting, or trying a new approach.

COMMON CORE

ANALYZE A STUDENT DRAFT

Read this draft as a model for your own critical review.

Welles Shines an Eerie Light on *Macbeth*
by Tyler Higgins, Freemont High School

❶   If William Shakespeare had written Act One, Scene 3 of *Macbeth* centuries after his time, what would it be like? Would it remain dominated by dialogue, or would he have included more elaborate stage directions to take advantage of cutting-edge lighting, music, and other effects? In his film adaptation of *Macbeth,* director Orson Welles masterfully uses these effects in a way that probably would make Shakespeare himself proud. During the witches' prophecies in Act One, Scene 3, Welles uses film techniques, added elements, and shortened dialogue to intensify the mood and pacing, making the scene come alive for audiences.

❷   Shakespeare's stage directions setting the scene are minimal: "Thunder and lightning." Welles amplifies the ominous mood of the scene with creative lighting and spooky music. For example, the witches are cast in shadows throughout the scene. We see only their backs and hands, never their faces. The clay figure of Macbeth that they later raise in the air, however, is seen clearly with a flash of lightning. Since Shakespeare's plays were usually performed in the daylight, his special effects were probably very limited. Further emphasizing the clay figure is the dramatic chord the music strikes. Both of these elements work together to establish the dark and mysterious mood Shakespeare had intended for this scene.

> Tyler uses an **interesting question** to grab the attention of his audience.

> In his introduction, Tyler clearly states a **precise, knowledgeable claim.**

> Tyler does not supply the most relevant evidence in this paragraph.

LEARN HOW **Supply the Most Relevant Evidence** Tyler's sentence about the lack of special effects during Shakespeare's time does not directly relate to Welles' techniques. Tyler needs to replace this irrelevant fact with information that directly supports his claim and provides his readers with additional insight.

TYLER'S REVISION TO PARAGRAPH ❷

For example, the witches are cast in shadows throughout the scene. We see only their backs and hands, never their faces. The clay figure of Macbeth that they later raise in the air, however, is seen clearly with a flash of lightning. ~~Since Shakespeare's plays were usually performed in the daylight, his special effects were probably very limited.~~

As film critic Phil Hall states, "[They] are only seen in hideous silhouette against ashen white fog.... Long takes at distorted angles, framed in medium close-up, emphasized the psychological off-balance of this world."

❸   The clay figure itself is not in the original play. Welles' addition of it, however, enhances the supernatural element of the witches. When their hands remove the clay figure from the cauldron, for example, the witches are bringing their prophecies to life. Furthermore, the clay figure's resemblance to Macbeth has a chilling effect on the scene. It forces the audience to consider the powerful effect of the witches' prophecies on the development of Macbeth's character.

> Tyler uses **varied transitions** to clarify the relationships among his ideas for his audience.

❹   Some readers might view the shortening of the dialogue in this scene as an injustice to Shakespeare's play. However, the absence of lengthy lines helps to speed the plot along—and pacing is essential to a movie. Also, much of what is missing from the characters' dialogue is communicated through the visuals on screen. For example, Banquo uses nine lines in Shakespeare's play to decribe the witches in detail, but in Welles' version he simply says, "What are these, / That look not like th' inhabitants o' th' earth / And yet are on 't?" Welles' cinematic expertise frees him from the need to reproduce all of Shakespeare's words.

> Tyler addresses an **opposing claim** and offers a valid **counterclaim** in response.

❺   Though Orson Welles' adaptation of this scene from *Macbeth* is not a faithful retelling of Shakespeare's play, it fully captures the play's disturbing mood. The dialogue in Welles' film contains only the essential lines, allowing the music and film effects to create a powerful mood of mystery and gloom. There's no reason why anyone should think that Shakespeare's original play is better! This is hands-down my favorite scene ever.

> Tyler restates his claim in his conclusion, but he does not **maintain a formal and objective tone.**

LEARN HOW Maintain a Formal Style and Objective Tone   To be persuasive in your argument, adopt a **formal style** and an **objective,** or controlled, **tone.** Tyler decided to revise his conclusion to maintain a more formal style and controlled tone.

TYLER'S REVISION TO PARAGRAPH ❺

⋀ ~~There's no reason why anyone should think that Shakespeare's original play is better! This is hands-down my favorite scene ever.~~

If Shakespeare were able to rewrite this scene today, I believe he would make use of many of Orson Welles' techniques to convey the eerie setting and foreshadow the terrible events yet to come.

YOUR TURN   Use feedback from your peers and your teacher as well as the two "Learn How" lessons to revise your critical review.

Editing and Publishing

COMMON CORE · **W 1c, d** Use varied syntax to link the text; maintain a formal style and objective tone. **W 5** Strengthen writing by editing. **L 1** Demonstrate command of conventions. **L 2b** Spell correctly. **L 3a** Vary syntax for effect.

In the editing stage, you proofread your essay to make sure it is free of grammar, usage, and punctuation errors. You also should catch and correct any spelling errors. Misspellings can make your audience question your credibility, so check a dictionary to confirm the spelling of any word you are uncertain about.

GRAMMAR IN CONTEXT: VARY YOUR SYNTAX

The grammatical arrangement of words in a sentence is called **syntax.** You can vary your syntax, such as by using different sentence structures and beginnings. For ideas on how to vary your syntax, reread other selections in this unit.

When Tyler proofread his critical review, he noticed that several consecutive sentences all began with a transition followed by the subject of the sentence.

> However, the absence of lengthy lines helps to speed the plot along—and pacing is essential to a movie. ~~Also, much of what is missing from the characters' dialogue is communicated through the visuals on screen.~~ For example, Banquo uses nine lines in Shakespeare's play to describe the witches in detail, but in Welles' version he simply says, "What are these, / That look not like th' inhabitants o' th' earth / And yet are on 't?"
> Meaning, not lost with the dialogue, is instead conveyed through striking visuals.

PUBLISH YOUR WRITING

Share your critical review with an audience.
- Submit your work for publication in your school or local newspaper.
- Participate in an informal discussion in which you and a small group debate the success of the adaptation.
- Post your critical review on a blog and invite other classmates to post their viewpoints. Elicit others' opinions on the scene adaptation and your claim.

YOUR TURN Correct any errors in your review by carefully proofreading it. Vary your transitions and syntax for persuasive effect and cohesive flow. Then publish your writing where your audience is most likely to notice it.

Scoring Rubric

Use the rubric below to evaluate your critical review from the Writing Workshop or your response to the on-demand writing task on the next page.

CRITICAL REVIEW

SCORE	COMMON CORE TRAITS
6	• **Development** Confidently asserts a precise claim; supports the claim with valid reasons and the most relevant evidence; ably counters opposing claims with counterclaims; has a powerful concluding section • **Organization** Arranges reasons and evidence in a persuasive, logical way; effectively varies transitions and syntax to create cohesion • **Language** Consistently maintains a formal style and objective tone; shows a strong command of conventions
5	• **Development** States a precise claim; offers valid reasons and relevant evidence; counters opposing claims with counterclaims; has a strong concluding section • **Organization** Is logically organized; uses varied transitions and syntax to create cohesion • **Language** Maintains a formal style and objective tone; has a few errors in conventions
4	• **Development** States a claim; offers mostly valid support; needs to more thoroughly address opposing claims; has an adequate concluding section • **Organization** Reflects a logical organization, with one or two exceptions; could vary transitions and syntax more • **Language** Mostly maintains a formal style and tone; includes a few distracting errors in conventions
3	• **Development** States a claim that could be more precise; provides some relevant support, but not enough to be sufficient; unfairly dismisses other viewpoints; has a concluding section that repeats ideas • **Organization** Has some flaws in organization; needs more transitions and varied syntax to show how ideas relate • **Language** Often lapses into an informal style or inappropriate tone; has several errors in conventions
2	• **Development** Has a weak claim; offers some irrelevant reasons and insufficient evidence; fails to acknowledge other viewpoints; has a weak concluding section • **Organization** Has major organizational flaws; uses few transitions and rarely varies syntax • **Language** Uses an informal style and inappropriate tone; has many errors in conventions
1	• **Development** Lacks a claim; provides no support; ignores opposing claims; ends abruptly • **Organization** Lacks organization, transitions, and varied syntax • **Language** Uses an inappropriate style and tone; has major problems with grammar, mechanics, and spelling

Preparing for Timed Writing

COMMON CORE

W 10 Write routinely over shorter time frames for a range of tasks, purposes, and audiences.

1. ANALYZE THE TASK   5 MIN

Read the writing task carefully. Then read it again, underlining words that tell the topic, the audience, and the purpose. Circle the type of writing you are being asked to do.

> **WRITING TASK** *Audience*
>
> Your school newspaper has asked you to write about a movie you've seen recently that has been adapted from a story or novel you have read. Write a (critical review) in which you evaluate the movie in terms of how effectively it does justice to the original work.
>
> *Purpose*   *Type of Writing*

2. PLAN YOUR RESPONSE   10 MIN

First, jot down the **criteria,** or elements, of a successful movie adaptation. Ask yourself: How does the movie measure up to my criteria? Use a chart to list reasons and evidence from both the movie and original text. Note an opposing claim your readers might have. What counterclaim could you include to address their concerns?

Claim:	
Reason 1:	Evidence:
Reason 2:	Evidence:
Possible Opposing Claim: My Counterclaim:	

3. RESPOND TO THE TASK   20 MIN

Use your notes to draft your review. As you write, keep these guidelines in mind:
- In the introduction, grab your audience's attention, provide background information about the movie and original text, and state your claim precisely.
- In each body paragraph, provide a reason supported by relevant evidence.
- Acknowledge an opposing claim and refute it with an effective counterclaim. Remember to maintain an objective, or controlled, tone.
- Conclude by restating your claim and sharing a relevant observation or insight.

4. IMPROVE YOUR RESPONSE   5–10 MIN

Revising Check your draft against the writing task. Does your claim make your opinion clear? Do you include valid reasons, evidence, and a counterclaim?
Proofreading Neatly correct any errors in grammar, spelling, and mechanics.
Checking Your Final Copy Before you turn in your critical review, read it once more to correct any errors you may have missed.

Creating a Critics' Blog

Some critical reviews are written as blogs. Blogs (short for *Web logs*) are online journals that allow you to post information and let readers comment on it. Bloggers can write about anything, from daily activities to an analysis of a book or movie. Bloggers can even work with others to combine or link information on their pages.

 Complete the workshop activities in your **Reader/Writer Notebook**.

PRODUCE WITH A PURPOSE	COMMON CORE TRAITS
TASK Create a **critics' blog** to house all of your classmates' critical reviews of drama adaptations. Use the blog to discuss the various interpretations of scenes you and your classmates viewed.	**PARTICIPANTS IN AN EFFECTIVE BLOG . . .** • use technology to produce and publish their critical reviews • present information, findings, and supporting evidence clearly, concisely, and logically • respond thoughtfully to diverse perspectives and update their reviews to reflect any changes in their opinions or in response to reader feedback • evaluate each writer's point of view and reasoning, assessing any limitations in their claims, assumptions, points of emphasis, and tone

COMMON CORE

W 6 Use technology to produce shared writing in response to arguments. **SL 1a-d** Initiate and participate in a range of collaborative discussions. **SL 3** Evaluate a speaker's point of view, reasoning, and use of evidence and rhetoric. **SL 4** Present information and supporting evidence, conveying a clear and distinct perspective.

Planning and Producing the Blog

In your critics' blog, you will work with classmates to include all critical reviews from your class. Use the following list to help you plan and produce your blog.

- **Organize Critical Reviews** Collect electronic versions of your classmates' reviews and discuss how they will be organized on the blog, such as by adaptation. Because you may have different ideas about the clearest organization, you will need to reach a civil and democractic agreement.

- **Select a Blog Site** Many sites allow you to start a blog for free. With your classmates, select a teacher-approved blog site and follow the instructions for getting started.

- **Add Entries** Enter each critical review into the blog, either organized into groups or as separate entries. You might adapt the information in your essay to make it more appropriate for a blog posting. For example, consider bulleting or numbering your reasons to make your argument easier to read on screen.

- **Publish the Blog** Follow instructions on the site to publish the blog.

Media Tools

THINK central

Go to thinkcentral.com.
KEYWORD: HML12N-548

Using Your Blog Effectively

When you participate in a blog discussion, you have the chance to share your insights and respond to others' arguments by using the comments section of each blog entry. As you evaluate other bloggers' entries, remember to use a respectful tone and to be fair and objective in your evaluations.

GETTING STARTED

In a blog, you and your classmates have the chance to clarify, verify, and challenge each other's conclusions. Keep the following in mind:

Topic	What to Evaluate
Point of View	Does the blogger clearly state his or her viewpoint in a precise claim? Look for clue words that suggest the blogger is unclear or unsure of his or her claim, such as *might* or *maybe*.
Reasoning	How valid are the blogger's reasons? Think about whether the reasons make sense and support the claim.
Evidence and Rhetoric	Is any of the evidence that supports the blogger's reasons exaggerated or distorted? How well does the blogger use **rhetoric,** or persuasive language? Explain whether you are convinced to agree with the blogger's claim.
Other Perspectives	Do the diverse perspectives modify your own viewpoint? Be sure to update your own entries to reflect any changes in your opinion.

As you use the blog, remember to:

- **Identify and Support Your Claim** State whether you feel the adaptation does justice to the original play. Use reasons and evidence to support your claim.

- **Let Others Comment** Read what others post in the comments section of your entry. Determine whether their feedback changes or modifies your opinion. If so revise or rework your review, or add a new comment.

- **Evaluate Others** Evaluate the viewpoints, reasons, and evidence presented by other writers. Challenge or verify conclusions as needed in the comments section.

YOUR TURN

As a Blogger After publishing your critical review, read what your classmates post in the comments section. Respond to any opposing claims or adjust your claim accordingly.

As a Reader Evaluate how well the blogger presents and supports his or her claim. Post your evaluation in the comment section of the entry. Remember, to do so in a respectful and objective tone.

Assessment Practice

DIRECTIONS Read the following texts and then answer the questions.

Sonnet 97   *by William Shakespeare*

How like a winter hath my absence been
From thee, the pleasure of the fleeting year!
What freezings have I felt, what dark days seen!
What old December's bareness every where!
5 And yet this time remov'd was summer's time,
The teeming autumn, big¹ with rich increase,
Bearing the wanton burthen of the prime,²
Like widowed wombs after their lords' decease:
Yet this abundant issue seem'd to me
10 But hope of orphans and unfathered fruit,
For summer and his pleasures wait on thee,
And thou away, the very birds are mute;
    Or if they sing, 'tis with so dull a cheer
    That leaves look pale, dreading the winter's near.

---

1. **big:** pregnant.
2. **wanton burthen of the prime:** crops planted in the spring.

A Valediction: Of Weeping

by John Donne

Let me pour forth
My tears before thy face, whilst I stay here,
For thy face coins them,[1] and thy stamp they bear,
And by this mintage they are something worth,
5   For thus they be
     Pregnant of thee;
Fruits of much grief they are, emblems of more,
When a tear falls, that thou falls which it bore,[2]
So thou and I are nothing then, when on a divers shore.

10   On a round ball
A workman[3] that hath copies by, can lay
An Europe, Afric, and an Asia,
And quickly make that, which was nothing, all,
So doth each tear,
15   Which thee doth wear,
A globe, yea world by that impression grow,
Till thy tears mixed with mine do overflow
This world, by waters sent from thee, my heaven dissolved so.

O more than moon,
20 Draw not up seas to drown me in thy sphere,
Weep me not dead, in thine arms, but forbear
To teach the sea, what it may do too soon;
     Let not the wind
     Example find,
25 To do me more harm, than it purposeth;
Since thou and I sigh one another's breath,
Whoe'er sighs most, is cruellest, and hastes the other's death.

---

1. **coins them:** is reflected in them; also gives value to them.
2. **that thou falls which it bore:** The image of the beloved is lost with each falling tear.
3. **workman:** mapmaker, or artist.

Reading Comprehension

Use "Sonnet 97" (p. 550) to answer questions 1–9.

1. The rhyme scheme of this sonnet is —
   - **A.** *abab bcbc cdcd ee*
   - **B.** *aabb ccdd eeff gg*
   - **C.** *abab cdcd efef gg*
   - **D.** *abba cddc acca ee*

2. Which statement best summarizes the first quatrain?
   - **A.** An entire year has passed while two loved ones are separated.
   - **B.** The years go by quickly for two loved ones waiting to be reunited.
   - **C.** Remembering the summer is the best way to spend the lonely winter.
   - **D.** Being away from a loved one feels like a bleak winter.

3. By personifying "old December" in the first quatrain, the speaker conveys the feeling of —
   - **A.** anxiety
   - **B.** emptiness
   - **C.** pleasure
   - **D.** weariness

4. In the second quatrain the speaker reveals that —
   - **A.** the time is late summer or early autumn, when crops are ready for harvesting
   - **B.** although it is now almost autumn, the speaker still misses the loved one who is away
   - **C.** it is much easier to be apart during the summer when food and sun are plentiful
   - **D.** the loved ones' separation will end when summer arrives

5. Which season is personified as a mother ready to give birth?
   - **A.** Autumn
   - **B.** Spring
   - **C.** Summer
   - **D.** Winter

6. Which image in the poem conveys nature's bounty?
   - **A.** *From thee, the pleasure of the fleeting year*
   - **B.** *And yet this time remov'd was summer's time*
   - **C.** *The teeming autumn, big with rich increase*
   - **D.** *And thou away, the very birds are mute*

7. The image in lines 9–10 conveys the speaker's feelings of —
   - **A.** contentment
   - **B.** expectation
   - **C.** melancholy
   - **D.** shame

8. In the third quatrain, which idea is conveyed by the turn, or shift in thought?
   - **A.** The lovers' unhappy separation is reflected in the hot summer weather.
   - **B.** The speaker cannot experience summer until the lovers are reunited.
   - **C.** Signs of the changing seasons are visible everywhere to the speaker.
   - **D.** The season's harvest will benefit fatherless children.

9. In the couplet, Shakespeare evokes the sights and sounds of an approaching winter to emphasize the —
   - **A.** anticipation of unanswered love
   - **B.** chaos caused by the change of seasons
   - **C.** dismay over the loved one's absence
   - **D.** unpredictability of true love

Use "A Valediction: Of Weeping" (p. 551) to answer questions 10–16.

10. The rhyme scheme in this poem is —
    - **A.** *ababccded*
    - **B.** *aabbbbccc*
    - **C.** *abcbcdefe*
    - **D.** *abbaccddd*

11. In lines 1–9, the poet compares the speaker's tears to —

A. reflections of the loved one's face in water

B. coins minted with the loved one's image

C. fruits preserved as emblems of the summer

D. the distance that will separate the lovers

12. Which statement best summarizes lines 7–9?

A. The speaker dreads being separated from the lover.

B. Tears are meaningless to two people who are truly in love.

C. Distance will help the lovers overcome their unhappiness.

D. The lovers do not recognize the significance of their separation.

13. Which end rhyme is a slant rhyme?

A. Forth, worth

B. Be, thee

C. More, bore

D. Grow, so

14. In lines 10–16, the poet develops the metaphysical conceit by comparing a tear to a —

A. map worn by the beloved

B. workman's fine art

C. globe of the world

D. portrait of the beloved

15. In lines 19–22, the beloved's power to cause weeping is compared to the moon's power to —

A. illuminate the night sky

B. reflect off the surface of water

C. represent universal mystery

D. control the tides of the sea

16. In each stanza, Donne consistently uses exact rhymes in the —

A. first four lines

B. last three lines

C. fifth and sixth lines

D. first and third lines

Use both texts to answer question 17.

---

17. The pain of separation described in "A Valediction: Of Weeping" differs from that described in "Sonnet 97" in that it is —

A. anticipated rather than experienced

B. expected to last forever

C. brought on by astonishing events

D. emotional rather than analytical

SHORT CONSTRUCTED RESPONSE
Write three or four sentences to answer each question.

18. In the couplet of "Sonnet 97," what human emotion is attributed to the leaves? What does this image suggest about the speaker's feelings?

19. As he develops a metaphysical conceit in "A Valediction: Of Weeping," Donne likens tears to several physical objects. Name three of these objects and explain what quality they have in common.

Write two to three paragraphs to answer this question.

20. Compare both poets' use of nature imagery to express feelings about separation. In your answer, include two examples of nature imagery from each poem.

GO ON

Revising and Editing

DIRECTIONS **Read this passage and answer the questions that follow.**

(1) In there search for new symbolic representations, writers and artists often attach a lot of meaning to everyday objects. (2) For example, throughout the ages, flowers have come to represent certain human attributes. (3) In Chinese art and literature, flowers often signify feminine beauty. (4) Flowers frequently symbolize a multiplicity of emotions in Western culture. (5) Writers and artists can't seem to get enough of using flowers as a symbol of love, and the flower they're most taken with is the rose. (6) In his play *All's Well That Ends Well*, Shakespeare uses the rose to associate unrequited love with the pain of youth, saying, "This thorn / Doth to our rose of youth rightly belong." (7) Celebrating passionate love by writing, "O my Luve's like a red, red rose / That's newly sprung in June" in his poem "A Red, Red Rose," Robert Burns employs the rose.

(8) There are other, more sinister, meanings associated with flowers, however. (9) In Shakespeare's play *Hamlet*, Ophelia goes crazy after her father's death, handing out a bunch of flowers to the court. (10) Although she can't blame the king face-to-face for his silly errors, she deals with him instead by saying, "There's fennel for you and columbines." (11) Shakespeare's audience would have been well aware of the meaning of these two gifts. (12) The fennel plant stood for flattery. (13) Ingratitude was implied by the columbines.

1. What change, if any, should be made in sentence 1?
   A. Change *objects* to **stuff**
   B. Delete comma
   C. Change *there* to **their**
   D. Make no change

2. What is the most effective way to revise sentence 4 so that it is parallel in structure to sentence 3?
   A. Frequently symbolizing a multiplicity of emotions are flowers in Western culture.
   B. In Western culture, flowers frequently symbolize a multiplicity of emotions.
   C. Frequently, flowers symbolize a multiplicity of emotions in Western culture.
   D. Flowers in Western culture frequently symbolize a multiplicity of emotions.

3. What is the most effective way to revise sentence 5?

 A. Writers and artists traditionally associate flowers with love, and they find the rose to be the most illustrious flower to capture this emotion.

 B. Writers and artists like using flowers to stand for love, and, of all flowers, they're most likely to pick the rose.

 C. A lot of writers and artists use flowers to symbolize love, and they'll usually go for the rose over all the other flowers that they could choose.

 D. When they're looking for a flower that will best symbolize love, writers and artists most often pick the rose.

4. What change, if any, should be made in sentence 8?

 A. Delete comma after *sinister*

 B. Move *, however* after **are**

 C. Change *meanings* to **meaning**

 D. Make no change

5. What is the most effective way to revise sentence 9?

 A. In Shakespeare's play *Hamlet*, Ophelia acts out over her dad's death by giving flowers to the court.

 B. In that play about Hamlet, Ophelia gives out flowers to the court because she's feeling bad about her father's death.

 C. In Shakespeare's play *Hamlet*, Ophelia responds to the death of her father by bestowing flowers on members of the court.

 D. In Shakespeare's play about Hamlet, Ophelia reacts to her dad's death by supplying some flowers to the king's court.

6. What is the most effective way to revise sentence 13 so that it is parallel in structure to sentence 12?

 A. Columbines were the flowers that implied ingratitude.

 B. The columbines implied ingratitude.

 C. Implying gratitude were the columbines.

 D. It was ingratitude that the columbines implied.

STOP

Ideas for Independent Reading

Continue exploring the Questions of the Times on pages 292-293 with these additional works.

Should religion be tied to POLITICS?

The Children of Henry VIII
by Alison Weir

The 11 years between the death of King Henry VIII and the accession of his daughter Elizabeth were fraught with conspiracy, violence, and religious conflict. Those years began with the brief reign of Henry's son, Edward VI, followed by that of his cousin, Lady Jane Grey, who was forced at 15 to reign for nine days in a futile attempt to block the claims of Edward's Catholic half-sister, Mary. Queen Mary's persecutions of Protestants earned her the nickname Bloody Mary, while her successor, Elizabeth I, went on to reign successfully for 45 years. Capturing the drama of the Tudor court, Alison Weir brings the children of Henry VIII to life.

God's Secretaries: The Making of the King James Bible
by Adam Nicolson

How did a group of ordinary men—ambitious, obsequious, flawed—manage to create one of the most beautiful works of literature ever published in English? This account of the roughly 50 religious scholars whom James I charged with creating an English translation of the Bible explores the influences and beliefs that shaped these men and their work. It also considers the ambitions of the king: a man who hoped, with this translation, to unify his kingdom and act as God's emissary on earth.

Why is love so COMPLICATED?

Twelfth Night
by William Shakespeare

In one of Shakespeare's finest comedies, a series of mix-ups, misunderstandings, and mistaken identities impedes the course of true love. Yet by play's end, all the happy lovers have paired up. With silly characters and outrageous complications, Shakespeare pokes fun at the folly of lovers and our expectations of romantic love.

The Love Poems of John Donne
by John Donne, edited by Charles Fowkes

While John Donne may be better known for his religious poetry, his love poems are exceptionally beautiful. This collection includes sonnets, elegies, and wedding songs that explore the many facets of love: passion, grief, joy, jealousy, and even sadness.

The Cavalier Poets: An Anthology
edited by Thomas Crofts

This collection brings together more than 120 works by four poets associated with the court of Charles I: Robert Herrick, Thomas Carew, Sir John Suckling, and Richard Lovelace. Written to satisfy the sophisticated tastes of the court, the poems here—often focused on love in all its complexity—are characteristically witty and elegant.

COMMON CORE

RL 10 Read and comprehend literature. **RI 10** Read and comprehend literary nonfiction.

What is the IDEAL SOCIETY?

Three Early Modern Utopias
edited by Susan Bruce

This collection of early utopian writings contains the complete texts of *Utopia* by Sir Thomas More (1516), *New Atlantis* by Francis Bacon (1627), and *The Isle of Pines* by Henry Neville (1688). Together they highlight the shortcomings of English society as their authors saw them, the possibilities for alternative social structures and values, and the sheer diversity in utopian thought.

The Faerie Queene
by Edmund Spenser

This unfinished epic poem revolves around the court of Gloriana, the Faerie Queene—a symbol for England's Queen Elizabeth I. Gloriana's knights are endowed with specific virtues (Holiness, Temperance, Chastity, Friendship, Justice, and Courtesy) and go on epic quests, doing battle both with external enemies and with their own human weaknesses.

The Blazing World and Other Writings
by Margaret Cavendish

In the only known utopian fiction by a 17th-century woman writer, Margaret Cavendish asks, What would happen if women were given more power in the world? What, in fact, would happen if a woman was able to rise to absolute power? While *The Blazing World* could never be mistaken for a serious blueprint of an ideal society, it does a remarkable job of pointing out many shortcomings of the real world Cavendish inhabited.

Why do people seek POWER?

Doctor Faustus
by Christopher Marlowe

Dr. Faustus is perhaps Marlowe's most famous creation. A legendary scholar, Faustus is a gifted theologian who longs for the same sort of knowledge and power that God has. He sells his soul to the devil and spends the next 24 years indulging in riches and pleasures. In the end, Faustus realizes his experiences were not worth his soul, yet the devil's contract cannot be broken.

Queen Elizabeth I: Selected Works
by Elizabeth I, edited by Steven W. May

Elizabeth I may well have been one of the most compelling and powerful rulers in the world. This selection of her own writings—public speeches, poetry, essays, letters, prayers, and translations—gives readers a glimpse into the mind of this intriguing monarch, highlighting her political savvy as well as her literary talent.

Hamlet
by William Shakespeare

When *Hamlet* begins, the young prince is in deep mourning for his recently deceased father and in shock over his mother's quick remarriage to his Uncle Claudius. The ghost of his father appears to Hamlet, reveals that he was poisoned by Claudius, and asks Hamlet to avenge his death. For the remainder of the play, Hamlet becomes increasingly melancholy as he ponders what to do. A tragic ending leaves many ambiguities unresolved, forcing the audience to consider whether justice has indeed been served.

UNIT 3

Preview Unit Goals

TEXT ANALYSIS	• Understand the historical context of literature of the Restoration and the 18th century • Analyze nonfiction, including biographies, diaries, essays, and journals • Identify and analyze neoclassicism as a literary style • Identify, analyze, and interpret satire, including Horatian and Juvenalian, in poetry and prose • Distinguish what is directly stated from what is really meant in satire, sarcasm, irony, and overstatement • Analyze poetic forms, including elegy and mock epic • Analyze poetic structure, including heroic couplets • Analyze an argument, including claim, support, and counterargument
READING	• Identify and analyze author's purpose • Make inferences and draw conclusions
WRITING AND LANGUAGE	• Write a persuasive essay • Use subordinate clauses to add description • Use parallelism to add emphasis
SPEAKING AND LISTENING	• Present a persuasive speech
VOCABULARY	• Use analogies to determine relationships between words • Consult general and specialized reference materials to find the pronunciation of a word and determine or clarify its precise meaning • Resolve issues of complex usage, consulting references as needed • Use synonyms as context clues
ACADEMIC VOCABULARY	• affect • challenge • respond • consent • final
MEDIA AND VIEWING	• Analyze a film interpretation of a story, evaluating how it interprets the source text

Find It Online!

Go to **thinkcentral.com** for the interactive version of this unit.

The Restoration and the 18th Century

1660–1798

Mary
Wollstonecraft

TRADITION AND REASON

- Social Observers
- Satirical Voices
- The Age of Johnson
- The Rise of Women Writers

Media Smart DVD-ROM

Great Stories on Film

Discover how a movie captures the imagination
in a scene from *Gulliver's Travels*. Page 658

Questions of the Times

DISCUSS After reading the following questions and talking about them with a partner, discuss them with the class as a whole. Then read on to explore the ways in which writers of the Restoration period and the 18th century in England dealt with the same issues.

What can fix society's PROBLEMS?

Writers of the Restoration and 18th century often used satire to bring attention to the problems of the day. Appalled by their society's dark side, social critics castigated the aristocracy, educators, politicians, and any other persons who the writers believed had failed to exercise their innate sense of reason. Is satire an effective tool for changing society? Might it really make a difference?

Can SCIENCE *tell us how to live?*

Inspired by the many achievements in science, philosophers of this period hoped to apply the scientific method to human behavior, using reason to decide, for instance, what form of government would be best or how people ought to live their lives. What role should scientific reasoning play in society? Do you think logic and observation can tell us not just what is but what should be?

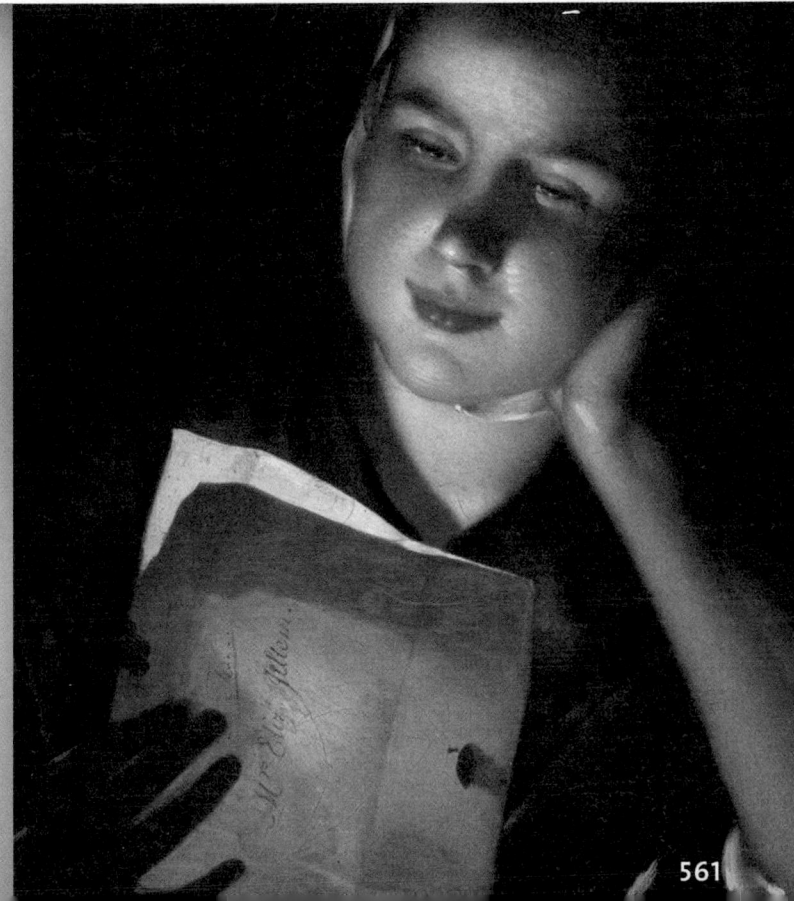

◌ COMMON CORE

RL 9 Demonstrate knowledge of foundational works of literature, including how two or more texts from the period treat similar themes or topics. **RI 9** Analyze documents of historical and literary significance for their themes, purposes, and rhetorical features.

What topics are
NEWSWORTHY?

Eighteenth-century writers Joseph Addison and Richard Steele changed the nature of news with their periodicals *The Tatler* and *The Spectator*. Often gossipy in character, the periodicals examined contemporary manners and customs as well as more serious subjects. Do you think news should focus only on serious subjects, or does the lighter side have a place as well?

What is a woman's
ROLE *in public life?*

Women of this period were as interested in new ideas as men were, but they were excluded from the public arenas where men enjoyed lively discussions. Undaunted, some women held salons, bringing intellectual life into their own homes; others, through their writing, broke into the public sphere. How are women today challenging their traditional roles and changing expectations?

NUMB. 1

The SPECTATOR.

*Non fumum ex fulgore, sed ex fumo dare lucem
Cogitat; ut speciosa dehinc miracula promat.* HOR.

To be Continued every Day.

Thursday, March 1. 1711.

ave observed, that a Reader seldom peruses Book with Pleasure 'till he knows whether e Writer of it be a black or a fair Man, of mild or cholerick Disposition, Married or a lor, with other Particulars of the like that conduce very much to the right Un-ding of an Author. To gratify this Curio-hich is so natural to a Reader, I design this and my next, as Prefatory Discourses to my ing Writings, and shall give some Account of the several Persons that are engaged in ork. As the chief Trouble of Compiling, ng and Correcting will fall to my Share, I o my self the Justice to open the Work y own History.

s born to a small Hereditary Estate, which by the Writings of the Family, was bounded same Hedges and Ditches in *William* the eror's Time that it is at present, and has elivered down from Father to Son whole tire, without the Loss or Acquisition of a Field or Meadow, during the Space of six

stinguished my self by a most profound Silence: For, during the Space of eight Years, excepting in the publick Exercises of the College, I scarce uttered the Quantity of an hundred Words; and indeed do not remember that I ever spoke three Sentences together in my whole Life. Whilst I was in this Learned Body I applied my self with so much Diligence to my Studies, that there are very few celebrated Books, either in the Learned or the Modern Tongues, which I am not acquainted with.

Upon the Death of my Father I was resolved to travel into Foreign Countries, and therefore left the University, with the Character of an odd unaccountable Fellow, that had a great deal of Learning, if I would but show it. An insatiable Thirst after Knowledge carried me into all the Countries of *Europe*, where there was any thing new or strange to be seen; nay, to such a Degree was my Curiosity raised, that having read the Controversies of some great Men concerning the Antiquities of *Egypt*, I made a Voyage to *Grand*

The Restoration and the 18th Century
1660–1798

Tradition and Reason

After years of tumult and upheaval, England settled happily into a time of peace, order, and prosperity. Behind the façade of tradition, however, was a radical new way of thinking— scientific, logical, "enlightened"—that would change the face of Britain. The monarchy had been restored, but in this era, reason ruled unchallenged.

The Restoration and the 18th Century: Historical Context

Writers of this era worked in a context of relative political stability and increasing rights under a more limited monarchy.

The Reign of Charles II

The coronation of Charles II in 1660 as he regained the throne was surely a sight to behold. **Samuel Pepys** recorded the event in his diary, describing the crowd of "10,000 people," who watched the king with "his scepter in his hand—under a canopy borne up by six silver staves, carried by Barons of the Cinque Ports—and little bells at every end." This grand celebration signaled the beginning of a new era in England: the **Restoration.**

SOPHISTICATED SOCIETY Turning its back on the grim era of Puritan rule, England entered a lively period in which the glittering Stuart court of Charles II set the tone for upper-class social and political life. Charles had spent much of his long exile in France, and upon his return, he tried to emulate the sophistication and splendor he'd observed at the court of Louis XIV. As a result, the lords and ladies of his court dressed in silks and lace, elaborate wigs and sparkling jewels. They held elegant balls and flocked to London's newly reopened theaters, where they proved their sophistication by attending **comedies of manners,** plays that poked fun at the glamorous but artificial society of the royal court.

Like Louis XIV, Charles was a patron of the arts and sciences, appointing **John Dryden** England's first official poet laureate and chartering the scientific organization known as the Royal Society. In addition, Charles re-established Anglicanism as England's state religion.

RESTORATION POLITICS With the restoration, however, came a realization that monarchs would have to share their authority with Parliament, whose influence had increased substantially. An astute politician, Charles at first won widespread support in Parliament, weathering a series of disasters that included the **Great Plague** of 1665 and the **Great Fire of London** a year later. Soon, however, old political rivalries resurfaced in two factions that became the nation's chief political parties: the **Tories** and the **Whigs.**

The Whigs, who wanted to limit royal authority, included wealthy merchants, financiers, and some nobles. They favored leniency toward Protestant dissenters and sought to curb French expansion in Europe and North America, which they saw as a threat to England's commercial interests. The Tories—supporters of royal authority—consisted mainly of land-owning aristocrats and conservative Anglicans, who had little tolerance for Protestant dissenters and no desire for war with France.

COMMON CORE

RL 9 Demonstrate knowledge of foundational works of literature, including how two or more texts from the period treat similar themes or topics. **RI 9** Analyze documents of historical and literary significance for their themes, purposes, and rhetorical features. **L 1a** Apply the understanding that usage is a matter of convention, can change over time, and is sometimes contested.

▶ **TAKING NOTES**

Outlining As you read this introduction, use an outline to record the main ideas about the history and literature of the period. You can use headings, boldfaced terms, and the information in these boxes as starting points. (See page R49 in the **Research Handbook** for more help with outlining.)

I. *Historical Context*
  A. *Charles II*
    1. *French sophistication*
    2. *Patron of arts & sciences*
    3. *Supported by Tories, limited by Whigs*
  B. *Royalty and the People*

Arthur Holdsworth Conversing with Thomas Taylor and Captain Stancombe by the River Dart (1757), Arthur Devis. Oil on canvas, 50¼" × 40¼". Paul Mellon Collection. © 2006 Board of Trustees, National Gallery of Art, Washington, D.C.

Royalty and the People

WILLIAM AND MARY Political conflict increased when Charles was succeeded in 1685 by his Catholic brother, James. A blundering, tactless statesman, James II was determined to restore Roman Catholicism as England's state religion. As a result, Parliament forced James to abdicate his throne. In 1688, James's Protestant daughter Mary and her husband, the Dutch nobleman William of Orange, took the throne peacefully in what came to be known as the **Glorious Revolution**—a triumph of parliamentary rule over the divine right of kings. The next year, Parliament passed the **English Bill of Rights,** which put specific limits on royal authority.

As a Dutchman and a Protestant, King William (who ruled alone after Mary died) was a natural enemy of Catholic France and its expansionist threats to Holland. From the first year of his reign, with Whig support, he took every opportunity to oppose the ambitions of Louis XIV with English military power, beginning a series of wars with France that some historians consider a second Hundred Years' War. A year before William's death, Parliament passed the Act of Settlement, which permanently barred Catholics from the throne. In 1702, therefore, the crown passed to Mary's Protestant sister, Anne, a somewhat stodgy but undemanding ruler who faithfully tended to her royal duties. During her reign, Scotland officially united with England to form **Great Britain.**

THE HOUSE OF HANOVER Outliving all 16 of her children, Anne was the last monarch in the house of Stuart. With her death in 1714, the crown passed to a distant cousin, the ruler of Hanover in Germany, who as George I became the first ruler of Britain's house of Hanover. The new king spoke no English and was viewed with contempt by many Tories, some of whom supported James II's Catholic son, James Edward Stuart. The Whigs, on the other hand, supported the new king and won his loyalty.

Because of the language barrier, George I relied heavily on his Whig ministers; and Robert Walpole, the head of the Whig party, emerged as the king's **prime minister** (the first official to be so called)—a position he continued to hold under George II, who succeeded his father in 1727. Toward the end of George II's reign, another able prime minister, **William Pitt,** arose on the political scene. Pitt led the nation to victory over France in the **Seven Years' War** (called the French and Indian War in America), which resulted in Britain's acquisition of French Canada.

▼ **Analyze Visuals**
Eighteenth-century artist James Gillray was known for his caricatures of political figures. In this cartoon, "Temperance enjoying a Frugal Meal" (1792), Gillray satirizes King George III and his wife, Charlotte, who were notorious for their miserliness—particularly when it came to food and drink. The king is shown dining on a boiled egg while the queen stuffs her large mouth with salad. Can you find another detail that points to the couple's frugality?

George II's grandson became the first British-born monarch of the house of Hanover. As George III, he sought a more active role in governing the country, but his highhanded ways antagonized many. Scornful of the Whigs, George had trouble working with nearly everyone, partly because he suffered from an illness that affected his mind and grew worse over the years. During his reign, he led Britain into a series of political blunders that ultimately resulted in the loss of the American colonies.

Ideas of the Age

This period became known as the Age of Reason, because people used reason, not faith, to make sense of the world.

The Age of Reason

The period including the late 1600s and the 1700s is called the **Enlightenment** or the **Age of Reason** because it was then that people began to use scientific reasoning to understand the world. Earlier, most people had regarded natural events such as comets and eclipses as warnings from God. The new, scientific way of understanding the world suggested that by applying reason, people could know the natural causes of such events.

THE SCIENTIFIC METHOD The British scientist **Sir Isaac Newton** set the tone for the era in his major work, *Mathematical Principles of Natural Philosophy* (1687), in which he laid out his newly formulated laws of gravity and motion and the methodology by which he arrived at his conclusions. Newton's **scientific method,** still employed today, consists of analyzing facts, developing a hypothesis, and testing that hypothesis with experimentation.

Newton's findings were enormously important because they suggested that the universe operated by logical principles that humans were capable of understanding. Inspired by Newton's example, scientists searched for these principles, making all kinds of discoveries along the way. Astronomers learned that stars were not fixed but moving and that the Milky Way was an immense collection of stars. Chemists isolated hydrogen, discovered carbon dioxide, and converted hydrogen and oxygen into water. Botanists and zoologists categorized literally millions of individual plants and animals, and in agriculture, breeding was improved, as were methods for cultivating and harvesting crops.

ENLIGHTENED PHILOSOPHIES The discoveries of Newton thrilled not only scientists but also philosophers. If nature operated by simple, orderly laws that could be worked out by logic, they asked, why not human nature as well? Why couldn't scientific methods be used to predict economic trends, for instance, or to figure out what form of government was best?

A replica of the first reflecting telescope, invented by Sir Isaac Newton and shown to the Royal Society in 1668

A Voice from the Times

Nature and Nature's laws lay hid in night:
God said, Let Newton be! and all was light.

—Alexander Pope

Believing that reasonable people could create a perfect society, philosophers such as **John Locke** encouraged people to use their intelligence to rid themselves of unjust authorities. Rejecting the "divine right" of kings, Locke provided a logical justification for the Glorious Revolution (and, later, the American Revolution) by asserting the right of citizens to revolt against an unfair government.

LIVING WELL The spirit of the Enlightenment led to many improvements in living conditions. Early in the century, for instance, writer **Lady Mary Wortley Montagu,** wife of a British ambassador, brought back from Turkey the idea of inoculation, and by the end of the 1700s, scientist Edward Jenner had developed an effective smallpox vaccination.

Many British citizens lived well during the 18th century, and a few lived sumptuously. Wealthy aristocrats built lavish country estates surrounded by beautifully tended lawns and gardens. When Parliament was in session, members relocated to their London townhouses on the spacious new streets and squares that had been laid out after the Great Fire. Writers, artists, politicians, and other members of society gathered daily in London's **coffeehouses** to exchange ideas, conduct business, and gossip. Educated women sometimes held **salons,** or private gatherings, where they, too, could participate in the nation's intellectual life. However, as the period drew to a close and the Industrial Revolution took hold, one writer noted, "No society can be flourishing and happy of which the far greater part of the members are poor and miserable."

Coffee House (1668), unknown artist. © Eileen Tweedy/British Museum/The Art Archive.

A view of London on the river Thames, 18th century

Literature of the Times

In this time of prosperity and relative stability, literature flourished, finding new audiences, new forms, and new voices.

Social Observers

Despite recurring warfare with France and the disaster of the American Revolution, the Restoration and the 18th century were a relatively stable time in Britain. The middle class grew and prospered, and ordinary men and women had more money, leisure, and education than ever before. For writers, that meant a broad new audience eager to read and willing to pay for literature. However, this audience did not have much taste for highbrow poetry full of sophisticated allusions to classics they had never read. Instead, they wanted writing that reflected their own concerns and experiences—working hard, doing right, gaining respectability—and they wanted it written in clear **prose** that they could understand.

One enormously popular form of "real-life" literature was **journalism.** Newspapers had been around since the early 1600s, but rigid censorship under both Charles I and Oliver Cromwell had discouraged their growth. As restrictions gradually eased, the press flourished. Daily newspapers appeared, and serials such as *The Tatler* and *The Spectator* published essays by **Joseph Addison** and **Richard Steele** that satisfied the middle-class appetite for instruction and amusement. Journalists did not simply report current events; they moralized, mocked, and gossiped, giving their opinions on everything from social manners to international politics.

▶ *For Your Outline*

SOCIAL OBSERVERS

- A growing middle class increased demand for middlebrow literature.
- Journalism became popular, providing opinions as well as facts.
- Novels were modeled on nonfiction forms.
- Pepys's diary captured Restoration period.

A Voice from the Times

The newspapers! Sir, they are the most villainous, licentious, abominable, infernal—Not that I ever read them! No, I make it a rule never to look into a newspaper.

—Richard Brinsley Sheridan

Journalist **Daniel Defoe** used his experience writing nonfiction when creating *Robinson Crusoe* (1719), considered by many to be England's first **novel.** As is typical of early novels, Defoe wrote in the familiar realistic style of a newspaper account, making it seem as if his tale of a shipwrecked man's survival on a desert island had really happened. Other writers followed with novels of their own, often modeled on nonfiction forms such as **letters**—for example, *Pamela* by **Samuel Richardson**—and **diaries.**

A real-life diary, although not intended for publication, provides modern readers with one of the best glimpses of life during these times. **Samuel Pepys,** a prosperous middle-class Londoner, began his diary in the first year of the Restoration and kept it for nine years. In it he tells of the major events of the day, including the coronation of Charles II and the Great London Fire.

Satirical Voices

While the realism of novels and newspapers pleased middle-class readers, another literary style—polished, witty, and formal—was aimed at the elite. This style was known as **neoclassicism** ("new classicism"). Neoclassical writers modeled their works on those of ancient Greece and Rome, emulating what they saw as the restraint, rationality, and dignity of classical writing. Indeed, the period in which these writers worked—the first half of the 18th century—is sometimes called the **Augustan Age,** so named because its writers likened their society to that of Rome in the prosperous, stable reign of the emperor Augustus, when the finest Roman literature was produced. Neoclassical writers stressed balance, order, logic, and emotional restraint, focusing on society and the human intellect and avoiding personal feelings.

Neoclassicists often used **satire,** or ridicule, to point out aspects of society that they felt needed to be changed. In this, too, they followed Roman models, choosing between the gentle, playful, and sympathetic approach of Horace (**Horatian satire**) and the darker, biting style of Juvenal (**Juvenalian satire**). Two outstanding writers of the period beautifully illustrate the two modes of satire.

One of the writers, **Alexander Pope,** wrote satiric poetry in the Horatian mode, poking fun at the dandies and ladies of high society and addressing moral, political, and philosophical issues in clever, elegant couplets. Pope's friend **Jonathan Swift,** on the other hand, wrote Juvenalian satire. Appalled by the hypocrisy and corruption he saw around him, Swift savagely attacked educators, politicians, churchmen, and any others he saw as corrupt. His masterpiece, *Gulliver's Travels,* is still a remarkably incisive commentary on human nature.

A CHANGING LANGUAGE

Standardizing the Language

During the Enlightenment, emphasis on reason and logic led to efforts to stabilize and systematize the English language. In 1693, the influential writer John Dryden complained, "We have yet no prosodia, not so much as a tolerable dictionary or grammar, so that our language is in a manner barbarous." Over the next several decades, scholars worked to remedy the situation.

The Dictionary One such scholar was Samuel Johnson, whose *Dictionary of the English Language* was published in 1755. Almost singlehandedly, Johnson created a work of gigantic proportions, consisting of 40,000 definitions and 110,000 quotations. Johnson recognized that language was always changing, but he also saw the value in having a standard for pronunciation, usage, and spelling. In his dictionary, he did not attempt to "fix the language"; he simply defined words as they had been used by the "best writers."

Grammar Seven years later, Robert Lowth published *A Short Introduction to English Grammar,* in which he attempted to establish a system of rules for judging correctness in matters under dispute. Since early grammarians like Lowth based their ideas on Latin, however, their rules often proved inappropriate for English. For example, they considered the infinitive form of an English verb to consist of two words ("to stun"); but because Latin infinitives are single words, they deemed it incorrect to "split" an English infinitive with an adverb ("to completely stun"), thus creating a puzzling "rule" that has frustrated generations of school children.

Gulliver Exhibited to the Brobdingnag Farmer, Richard Redgrave. Oil on canvas, 25″ × 30″. Victoria & Albert Museum, London. © Victoria & Albert Museum, London/Art Resource, New York.

England's newly reopened theaters provided another outlet for the period's most brilliant satirists. Influenced by the French comedies of manners, **John Dryden, William Congreve,** and other playwrights entertained audiences with **Restoration comedies** that satirized the artificial, sophisticated society centered in the Stuart court.

The Age of Johnson

The second half of the 18th century is sometimes affectionately referred to as the Age of Johnson—a tribute to **Samuel Johnson,** Britain's most influential man of letters of the day. Johnson, a poet, critic, journalist, essayist, scholar, and lexicographer, was also a talker, a brilliant conversationalist who enjoyed holding forth at coffeehouses, clubs, and parties. He was friends with many of the greatest literary and artistic talents of the time and stood at the center of a lively circle of intellectuals that included his biographer **James Boswell,** the historian **Edward Gibbon,** the novelist and diarist **Fanny Burney,** and the comic dramatist **Richard Brinsley Sheridan.**

▶ *For Your Outline*

SATIRICAL VOICES

- Neoclassicists emulated the rationality of ancient Greek and Roman writers.

- The early 1700s were called the Augustan Age, in reference to the times of Roman emperor Augustus.

- Satire pointed out society's problems; Horatian satire was gentle, Juvenalian was dark.

- Restoration comedies satirized the Stuart court.

The 18th-century concern with real life can be seen in the number, variety, and quality of nonfiction works published during the Age of Johnson. Works of biography, history, philosophy, politics, economics, literary criticism, aesthetics, and natural history all achieved the level of literature. Writers strove for a style not merely clear and accurate but also eloquent and persuasive. Edward Gibbon's *The History of the Decline and Fall of the Roman Empire* is a superb example of the heights achieved by nonfiction prose during these years. Also notable are the works of philosopher David Hume, the artist Sir Joshua Reynolds, and the economist Adam Smith—and, of course, Johnson himself, who described his notion of good style as "familiar but not coarse, and elegant but not ostentatious."

Johnson wrote *A Dictionary of the English Language,* a stupendous feat that won him an important place in literary history (see **A Changing Language,** page 568). His essays remain classic examples of the formal 18th-century prose of which he was the acknowledged master. He also wrote graceful biographies of poets, and critiques of poems and other literary works. Johnson was more than an accomplished writer; he was the literary dictator of London and the undisputed arbiter of taste for his time.

Though Johnson and most of his associates affirmed neoclassical ideals, during this time poetry entered a transitional stage in which poets began writing simpler, freer lyrics on subjects close to the human heart. The reflective poetry of **Oliver Goldsmith** and **Thomas Gray** and the lyrical songs of Scotland's **Robert Burns** anticipate the first stirrings of romanticism at the very end of the century.

▶ *For Your Outline*

THE AGE OF JOHNSON

- The late 1700s were called the Age of Johnson in tribute to Samuel Johnson, an influential writer.
- Nonfiction flourished.
- Poetry entered a transitional period.

WOMEN WRITERS

- Unable to participate in public intellectual life, women formed salons.
- Intellectual women were known as bluestockings.
- Women began publishing their work.
- Wollstonecraft called for women's rights.

Fanny Burney (1784), Edward Francis Burney. The Granger Collection, New York.

The Rise of Women Writers

Enlightenment ideals weren't the exclusive property of men; women—especially upper-class women—were equally interested in exercising their reason and learning about the world around them. However, the universities were closed to them, as were the nearly 3,000 coffeehouses that had sprung up in London. Denied access to these places, women missed out on many ideas being discussed by England's educated class—its writers, artists, politicians, and statesmen.

Unable to go out and participate in the intellectual life of the nation, several enterprising women in the mid-1700s decided to bring it into their own homes in the form of French-style private gatherings known as **salons.** Salons quickly became a popular form of evening entertainment, taking the place of card games, and were often attended by well-known writers and other public figures, such as Samuel Johnson and Horace Walpole. Because guests were invited to leave their silk stockings at home and come casually dressed in everyday blue worsted stockings (the 18th-century equivalent of wearing jeans to a party), the women who frequented salons—and intellectual women in general—became known as **bluestockings.**

Inspired by the example of pioneers such as **Aphra Behn,** the first woman in England to earn a living as a professional writer (indeed, she rivaled John Dryden as the most prolific playwright of the Restoration), many talented bluestockings began publishing their own works. For years, male writers had written novels aimed at female audiences, such as Samuel Richardson's *Pamela,* the story of a servant girl who resists her master's advances and ultimately wins an offer of marriage. Now, the men faced competition from women novelists such as **Charlotte Smith** and **Fanny Burney.**

Charlotte Smith wrote to support her family, beginning with poetry but soon turning to novels, which were more lucrative. Her work was similar to that of other women novelists of the day. It was quite radical, however, in its attitude toward morality and its examination of class equality.

Fanny Burney's novels, on the other hand, may seem overly sentimental and moralistic to modern readers. However, her understanding of women's concerns and her accurate portrayal of polite society won her a wide following in her day. Although Burney achieved immediate fame through her novels, readers today are more familiar with her diary, which she began when she was 15 and wrote in regularly for 70 years. Since Burney moved in high society, with Samuel Johnson and even the king and queen of England as acquaintances, her diary gives modern readers a fascinating glimpse into the lives of the upper class in the Age of Johnson.

While many women, such as Fanny Burney, defied the norms by educating themselves, engaging in salon discussions, and writing for publication (often under assumed names), **Mary Wollstonecraft** openly challenged the status quo. In *A Vindication of the Rights of Woman* (1792), she argued that women should be educated equally with men and allowed to join the professions so that the relationship between men and women could be one of "rational fellowship instead of slavish obedience." Her views were radical at a time when most women accepted their inferior status, or at least refrained from expressing their discontent. Although Wollstonecraft died shortly following the birth of her daughter Mary, she would surely have been proud to learn that the daughter, **Mary Wollstonecraft Shelley,** grew up to become one of the most enduring writers of the next period in England's literary history—the **romantic period.**

THE ARTISTS' GALLERY

Satire in Art

Satirizing everything from crooked elections to bad taste in opera, the paintings and engravings of **William Hogarth** (1697–1764) were received with great enthusiasm at all levels of mid-18th-century British society.

Mockery and Moralizing Hogarth was most famous for painting what he called "modern moral subjects"—series of lively, detailed scenes showing how bad behavior leads to ruin. While some of these series depicted the seamy side of London, others targeted the wealthier classes.

In the work shown in detail here (the second in a series called *Marriage à la Mode*), Hogarth depicts the downfall of a marriage based on greed and vanity. The wife appears exhausted from a card party held the night before, the house is in disarray, and the husband appears to have just returned from his own revels. The title of the series was taken from John Dryden's well-known comedy of manners; Hogarth's ideas of satire owed a great deal to the theater.

Artistic Independence Before Hogarth, artists had earned their living by painting flattering portraits of wealthy patrons. By turning his own popular paintings into engravings that could be printed and sold cheaply to ordinary people, Hogarth opened up new possibilities for artists. He also successfully lobbied Parliament for a copyright law that protected artists' rights by making it illegal for others to copy their work. The law's passage led to a dramatic growth in British printmaking.

Connecting Literature, History, and Culture

Use this timeline and the questions on the next page to learn more about the Restoration period and the 18th century. Consider to what extent British literature reflected the historical events of the day.

BRITISH LITERARY MILESTONES

1660

1660 Samuel Pepys begins his diary.

1668 John Dryden is named the first official poet laureate.

1671 John Milton's *Paradise Regained* is published.

1690 John Locke publishes his essay *Two Treatises on Government,* stating the natural rights of life, liberty, and property.

1695

1711 Addison and Steele begin periodical *The Spectator.*

1719 Daniel Defoe's *Robinson Crusoe,* considered by many to be the first novel in English, is published. ▶

1726 Jonathan Swift arranges for anonymous delivery of his manuscript of *Gulliver's Travels* to a London printer.

HISTORICAL CONTEXT

1660

1660 The monarchy is restored with the crowning of Charles II, who rules until 1685.

1665 The Great Plague of London kills thousands.

1666 The Great Fire of London destroys a large section of the city.

1687 Sir Isaac Newton publishes the law of gravity.

1695

1707 England, Wales, and Scotland unite as Great Britain.

1714 Reign of George I, the first Hanoverian monarch, begins (to 1727).

1718 Lady Mary Wortley Montagu introduces inoculation in England. ▶

1721 Robert Walpole, the first political leader to be called prime minister, takes office.

WORLD CULTURE AND EVENTS

1660

1661 Louis XIV begins building the grand palace at Versailles, near Paris. ▲

1684 China opens ports to foreign trade.

1695

1703 Peter the Great begins building the city of St. Petersburg.

1707 Mughal Empire in India breaks into a patchwork of independent states.

1717 French author Voltaire is imprisoned in the Bastille for nearly a year.

1721 Edo (Tokyo) becomes the world's largest city.

MAKING CONNECTIONS

- Were the early years of Charles II's reign a good time to live in London? Explain.
- Name three parts of the world held by the British Empire at this time.
- Name two scientific or medical advances that occurred during these years.
- What literary "first" occurred during this period?

COMMON CORE

RI 7 Integrate and evaluate multiple sources of information presented in different formats as well as in words in order to address a question or solve a problem.

1730

1740 Samuel Richardson's novel *Pamela* is published.

1746 Samuel Johnson signs a contract to write *A Dictionary of the English Language* (published 1755).

1763 James Boswell meets Samuel Johnson, beginning a 21-year friendship. ▶

1765

1768 The publication of *Encyclopaedia Britannica* begins in Scotland.

1784 William Blake creates illuminated printing, a technique for combining text and illustration.

1791 James Boswell issues the two-volume *Life of Samuel Johnson.*

1730

1732 A royal charter is granted for the founding of the American colony of Georgia; 114 passengers leave Gravesend, England, to settle there.

1757 British rule over India begins (to 1947).

1760 The reign of George III begins (to 1820).

1763 Britain defeats France in Seven Years' (French and Indian) War, acquiring French Canada.

1765

1775 War with colonies in North America begins (to 1783). ▶

1783 American independence is acknowledged in the Treaty of Paris.

1793 War with revolutionary France begins (to 1815).

DONT TREAD ON ME

1730

1740 Maria Theresa becomes queen of Austria, Bohemia, and Hungary (to 1780).

1756 Frederick the Great of Prussia starts the Seven Years' War, fought in Europe, North America, and India.

1762 Catherine the Great begins rule of Russia (to 1796). ▶

1765

1773 Phillis Wheatley becomes the first African American to publish a book of poetry.

1789 The French Revolution begins (to 1799).

1791 Austrian composer Wolfgang Amadeus Mozart dies at age 35. ▶

1793 French king Louis XVI is executed by guillotine.

The Legacy of the Era

Science and Society

The scientific method that was developed during the Age of Reason has given us everything from lifesaving heart transplants to potatoes bred to make the perfect French fry. However, despite the hopes of Enlightenment philosophers, science has failed to solve all our social problems; in fact, some scientific advances have created new problems.

DISCUSS With a small group, identify scientific advances that have truly benefited society. Then discuss any negatives—ethical, physical, ideological, or otherwise—associated with these advances.

COMMON CORE

W1 Write arguments to support claims in an analysis of substantive topics or texts. **W7** Conduct short research projects. **SL1** Initiate and participate effectively in a range of collaborative discussions.

A scientist pulls frozen cells from cryostorage.

Social Critics

Satire ruled in the 18th century—the age that brought us the wit and wisdom of Alexander Pope and Jonathan Swift and the artistry of William Hogarth. Today's newspaper columnists, cartoonists, comedians, and late-night TV show hosts also use humor to make serious points about contemporary political and social issues. Has social criticism changed to suit the issues of our modern world, or is satire, at its core, the same no matter what the era?

RESEARCH Find two examples of modern-day satire, one in the light Horatian style of Pope and one in the darker Juvenalian style of Swift. Share your examples with the class and discuss how they compare with the work of 18th-century satirists.

An example of modern satire in the Horatian mode

The Novel

Perhaps the most significant literary legacy of this period is the novel. From Daniel Defoe's *Robinson Crusoe* to today's bestsellers, the genre's popularity has never flagged.

QUICKWRITE Many pundits have predicted the demise of the novel, especially in its printed form, as other forms of literature and technology have gained popularity. Write several paragraphs to explain why you think the novel endures despite so many distractions.

Nonfiction in the 18th Century

We often refer to the current era as the information age, in which we have come to expect a steady stream of instant information through television, the Internet, radio, and print. England in the 18th century experienced a similar demand for information but was limited to one form of media—print.

COMMON CORE

Included in this workshop:
RI 10 Read and comprehend literary nonfiction.

A New World of Ideas

At the dawn of the 18th century in England, the movement known as the Enlightenment was ushered in by the writings of two major philosophical thinkers, John Locke and Thomas Hobbes. Their writings inspired the English people to rethink all aspects of society, question accepted beliefs, and explore new ideas. In this rich environment of ideas, **nonfiction** became a favored literary form. Though the aristocracy was the primary audience of the Enlightenment writers, the spread of education in the 17th century had caused the literacy rate in England to soar among the middle and lower classes. The newly literate public's appetite for information grew, and London became home to a number of periodicals. The practices of modern publishing, such as the use of copyright and royalty fees, began to emerge in London at this time.

The stereotype press, invented in 1805

The Development of the Essay

The contents of most 18th-century periodicals consisted of essays. An **essay** is a short work of nonfiction that offers a writer's opinion on a particular subject. The essay form became popular after the 16th-century French philosopher Michel de Montaigne published a collection of writings titled *Essais,* which means "attempts." In 1597, Francis Bacon became the first prominent English essayist when he published the first edition of his *Essays.* From then on, the essay became a popular means of expression—a way for English writers to air their views on public matters and to promote social reform. Works labeled "essays" were even written in verse, such as Alexander Pope's *An Essay on Criticism.*

Informal essays are essays in which writers express their opinions without adopting a completely serious or formal tone. Informal essays can include humor and may deal with unconventional topics, such as Joseph Addison's witty and entertaining commentaries on British morals and manners of the day, which appeared in the periodical *The Spectator* (page 602).

Formal essays explore topics in a more serious, thorough, and organized manner than informal essays. One example is Mary Wollstonecraft's argument against injustice in *A Vindication of the Rights of Woman* (page 720).

Other Forms of Nonfiction

Letters and **diaries** often provide personal details of everyday life at the time they were written. Most are private and not intended to be shared, but some are published because they are well written or concern famous historical or literary figures. *The Diary of Samuel Pepys* (page 580) is an important historical record of the Restoration in which Pepys observed life in its smallest details and then meditated on the meaning of what he had witnessed. Eighteenth-century examples include Fanny Burney's journal and collected letters (page 708).

Biography is nonfiction in which a writer recounts the events of another person's life. **Autobiographies** and **memoirs** are works in which people recall significant events in their own lives. James Boswell's *The Life of Samuel Johnson* (page 682) is an example of a biography about a great literary figure.

When you are reading nonfiction, use the following strategies:

- Take note of the **type of document** you are reading. Is it a formal essay, or is it an informal work with a loose structure?

- Draw conclusions about the **author's purpose.** Is the writer addressing a social problem? If so, what solutions does he or she suggest?

- Consider the **historical context** and the value of the work at the time it was written or published. Ask yourself if the work is still of value today.

- Summarize the **main ideas** of the work in your own words.

> Before marriage we cannot be too inquisitive and discerning in the faults of the person beloved, nor after it too dim-sighted and superficial.
>
> —Joseph Addison, *The Spectator*

Close Read

Do you find the ideas in this passage to be of value to today's audience? Explain.

THE RISE OF JOURNALISM

1650	1690	1700	1710
1650s Coffeehouses emerge as cultural and political discussion centers.	**1690s** Oral communication of the news decreases as printed news sources rapidly increase. **1694** Lifting of licensing act allows English newspapers to grow.	**1702** The *Daily Courant,* England's first daily newspaper, is established. **1709** *The Tatler* begins publication.	**1711** *The Spectator* is founded by Joseph Addison and Richard Steele.

from The Diary of Samuel Pepys

Diary by Samuel Pepys

COMMON CORE

RI 10 Read and comprehend literary nonfiction.

Meet the Author

Samuel Pepys 1633–1703

The Diary of Samuel Pepys contains firsthand accounts of some of the most important historical events of 17th-century England. Yet it is Pepys's candor in recording the minutiae of his private life—what he ate for dinner, a squabble with his wife, his childlike excitement over a new watch—that prompted his biographer Claire Tomalin to declare him "both the most ordinary and the most extraordinary writer you will ever meet."

An Insatiable Curiosity Pepys (pēps) had an insatiable curiosity and attempted to learn all that he could about every subject. It was undoubtedly this fascination with life that inspired him, at the age of 26, to begin keeping a diary in which he would eventually set down more than 1.2 million words. At the age of 35, he abandoned his diary, fearing it was straining his eyes so much that he might go blind.

"The Right Hand of the Navy" Shortly after starting his diary, Pepys became a clerk in the Royal Navy office and worked hard at rooting out corruption and streamlining management. Acknowledged as "the right hand of the Navy," in 1684 he was appointed the secretary of the

DID YOU KNOW?

Samuel Pepys...

- had 10 brothers and sisters.
- saved his house from the Great Fire of London, only to have it burn seven years later.
- kept his diary a secret— not even telling his wife about it.

Background: Diary entry written in Pepys's shorthand

admiralty. In that capacity, he doubled the number of battleships and restored the Royal Navy as a major sea power.

A Confidante of Kings During his years of public service, Pepys enjoyed a close relationship with King Charles II and his successor, James II. However, Pepys also made enemies in his rise to power. In 1678, some of his adversaries tried unsuccessfully to ruin his reputation, falsely accusing him of murder and treason. Although Pepys was imprisoned briefly, the intervention of Charles II kept him from further punishment.

A Scholarly Retirement Pepys lived in retirement for the last 14 years of his life. He spent his time amassing a large personal library, corresponding with various artists and scholars, and collecting material for a history of the navy, which he never completed. He bequeathed his large library, including his diary, to Cambridge University.

Postponed Publication Written in shorthand, the diary was not transcribed until the early 19th century. An abridged version—with his romantic dalliances and other details that "could not possibly be printed" removed—was published in 1825. The full, uncensored version did not appear until 1970.

Author Online
Go to thinkcentral.com. KEYWORD: HML12-578

THINK central

TEXT ANALYSIS: DIARY

A writer keeps a **diary** in order to make a daily account of his or her thoughts, experiences, and feelings. Diaries are **primary sources,** or materials created by people who were present at events either as participants or as observers. Most diaries are private and not intended to be shared. However, some have been published because, as primary documents, they provide valuable insights into historical events and eras. One example is *The Diary of Samuel Pepys,* which paints a fascinating portrait of English life in the early 1660s, the time of the Restoration. In the following passage, notice how Pepys conveys details about his household even as he reports on a major disaster of the period, the Great Fire of London:

Some of our maids sitting up late last night to get things ready against our feast today, Jane called us up, about 3 in the morning, to tell us of a great fire they saw in the city.

As you read the selection, pay attention to how Pepys discusses matters of both personal and public concern.

READING SKILL: CONNECT TO HISTORY

Eyewitness accounts like Pepys's diary often stir feelings of curiosity and excitement in readers. You may find yourself comparing the historical events retold in this selection to experiences you have read about, heard about, or known firsthand. You may even imagine yourself in Pepys's position, listening to the stories of Charles II or escaping the Great Fire. These responses are ways of **connecting** with what you are reading. As you read the selection, make connections between Pepys's world and your own by listing similarities between them. Record your observations in a chart like the one shown.

Pepys's World	My World
Great Fire of London	Hurricane Katrina

 Complete the activities in your **Reader/Writer Notebook**.

Why keep *a* DIARY?

Samuel Pepys had no aspirations for publication. In fact, he took great measures to ensure the secrecy of his diary, writing his entries in an encrypted shorthand. Today, diarykeeping remains a popular pastime. Yet with the advent of online journals and blogs, it seems to be evolving from a private to a more public activity.

QUICKWRITE Make a list of the reasons that might prompt you to keep a diary. If you already have a diary or a blog, record the reasons you started it. Consider your reasons and then write a paragraph describing whether you would prefer to keep a traditional diary—one you could keep hidden from prying eyes—or a public blog that has a potential readership of millions.

ONE-YEAR DIARY

THE DIARY OF
Samuel Pepys

Samuel Pepys

> **BACKGROUND** Few descriptions of daily life in any period of history are as vivid as those found in *The Diary of Samuel Pepys*—a rare firsthand account of events that occurred more than 300 years ago. As personal secretary to a British admiral, Pepys was aboard the ship on which King Charles II returned to England from exile in France. He also witnessed the Great Plague of 1665 and the Great Fire of London in 1666, which destroyed thousands of homes and most of London's government buildings.

The Restoration of Charles II   *1660*

MARCH 16. . . . To Westminster Hall, where I heard how the Parliament had this day dissolved themselves[1] and did pass very cheerfully through the Hall and the Speaker without his mace.[2] The whole Hall was joyful thereat, as well as themselves; and now they begin to talk loud of the King. . . .

MAY 22. . . . News brought that the two dukes are coming on board, which, by and by they did in a Dutch boat, the Duke of York in yellow trimming, the Duke of Gloucester[3] in gray and red. My Lord[4] went in a boat to meet them, the captain, myself, and others standing at the entering port. . . .

MAY 23. . . . All the afternoon the King walking here and there, up and down
10 (quite contrary to what I thought him to have been), very active and stirring. Upon the quarter-deck he fell in discourse of his escape from Worcester.[5] Where it made me ready to weep to hear the stories that he told of his difficulties that he had passed through. As his traveling four days and three nights on foot, every **Ⓐ**

---

1. **Parliament ... themselves:** This Parliament ended the government established by Oliver Cromwell and restored the monarchy under Charles II, who had been living in exile in France.
2. **Speaker ... mace:** a signal that Parliament is dissolved. The mace is the staff or stick used as a symbol of authority by the Speaker, or head, of Parliament's House of Commons.
3. **Duke of York ... Gloucester** (glŏs′tər): the younger brothers of Charles II.
4. **My Lord:** Sir Edward Montagu, Pepys's relative and employer, who commanded the fleet that brought Charles back to England.
5. **his escape from Worcester** (woŏs′tər): After the forces he led were defeated by Oliver Cromwell's troops at the Battle of Worcester in 1651, Charles went into hiding and managed to escape to continental Europe.

Analyze Visuals ▶
Pepys commissioned this portrait, choosing his costume and the music he holds. What image of himself do you think he was trying to convey?

Ⓐ DIARY
Reread lines 5–13. What details tell you that Pepys was an eyewitness to Charles II's return to England?

Samuel Pepys (1666), John Hayls. Oil on canvas. The Granger Collection, New York.

step up to his knees in dirt, with nothing but a green coat and a pair of country breeches on and a pair of country shoes, that made him so sore all over his feet that he could scarce stir. Yet he was forced to run away from a miller and other company that took them for rogues. His sitting at table at one place, where the master of the house, that had not seen him in eight years, did know him but kept it private; when at the same table there was one that had been of his own regiment
20 at Worcester, could not know him but made him drink the King's health and said that the King was at least four fingers higher than he. Another place, he was by some servants of the house made to drink, that they might know him not to be a Roundhead,[6] which they swore he was. In another place, at his inn, the master of the house, as the King was standing with his hands upon the back of a chair by the fire-side, he kneeled down and kissed his hand privately, saying that he would not ask him who he was, but bid God bless him whither that he was going. . . . **B**

The Coronation of the King *1661*

APRIL 23. . . . About 4 in the morning I rose. . . . And got to the Abbey,[7] . . . where with a great deal of patience I sat from past 4 till 11 before the King came in. And a pleasure it was to see the Abbey raised in the middle, all covered with red and
30 a throne (that is a chair) and footstool on the top of it. And all the officers of all kinds, so much as the very fiddlers, in red vests. At last comes in the dean and prebends of Westminster with the bishops (many of them in cloth-of-gold copes[8]); and after them the nobility all in their parliament-robes, which was a most magnificent sight. Then the duke and the King with a scepter (carried by my Lord of Sandwich) and sword and mond[9] before him, and the crown too.

The King in his robes, bare-headed, which was very fine. And after all had placed themselves—there was a sermon and the service. And then in the choir at the high altar he passed all the ceremonies of the coronation—which, to my very great grief, I and most in the Abbey could not see. The crown being put upon
40 his head, a great shout begun. And he came forth to the throne and there passed more ceremonies: as, taking the oath and having things read to him by the bishop, and his lords (who put on their caps as soon as the King put on his crown) and bishops came and kneeled before him. And three times the king-at-arms[10] went to the three open places on the scaffold and proclaimed that if any one could show any reason why Ch. Stuart[11] should not be King of England, that now he should come and speak. And a general pardon also was read by the Lord Chancellor; and

B IRONY
In **situational irony**, what happens is the opposite of what a character or the reader might expect. Authors often use situational irony to shock or surprise readers or to create a humorous situation. Reread the Diary entry for May 23rd. Which incidents in this passage might be considered ironic? How does Pepys feel about the events he relates?

---

6. **Roundhead:** a supporter of Cromwell's Puritan government, so called because of the close-cropped style of hair that Puritan men generally wore.

7. **Abbey:** Westminster Abbey, the London church where monarchs are traditionally crowned.

8. **copes:** long robes worn by church officials while performing services or rites.

9. **scepter** (sĕp′tər) . . . **mond:** symbols of royal authority. A scepter is a rod or staff held by a ruler; a mond is a sphere with a cross on top, used as a symbol of royal power and justice.

10. **king-at-arms:** one of the chief heralds assigned to make official proclamations.

11. **Ch. Stuart:** Charles Stuart, who will be crowned Charles II.

Detail of *Charles II's Cavalcade through the City of London, 22nd April, 1661* (1662), Dirck Stoop. Museum of London, London. © HIP/Art Resource, New York.

medals flung up and down by my Lord Cornwallis—of silver; but I could not come by any.

But so great a noise, that I could make but little of the music; and indeed,
50 it was lost to everybody. . . . I went out a little while before the King had done all his ceremonies and went round the Abbey to Westminster Hall, all the way within rails, and 10,000 people, with the ground covered with blue cloth—and scaffolds all the way. Into the hall I got—where it was very fine with hangings and scaffolds, one upon another, full of brave[12] ladies. And my wife in one little one on the right hand. Here I stayed walking up and down; and at last, upon one of the side-stalls, I stood and saw the King come in with all the persons (but the soldiers) that were yesterday in the cavalcade; and a most pleasant sight it was to see them in their several robes. And the King came in with his crown on and his scepter in his hand—under a canopy borne up by six silver staves, carried by barons of the
60 Cinque Ports[13]—and little bells at every end.

And after a long time he got up to the farther end, and all set themselves down at their several tables—and that was also a rare sight. And the King's first course carried up by the Knights of the Bath. And many fine ceremonies there was of the heralds

Language Coach

Oral Fluency Part of reading fluently is correct pronunciation. In most English words that begin with *sce* or *sci*, the *c* is silent. Thus, *scepter*—a rod used in ceremonies to symbolize power—is pronounced /sep t r/ (line 58). What other words are like *scepter*?

---

12. **brave:** having a fine appearance.
13. **Cinque** (sĭngk) **Ports:** a group of five seaports on England's southeastern coast that formed a defensive association.

leading up people before him and bowing; and my Lord of Albemarle going to the kitchen and ate a bit of the first dish that was to go to the Kings's table. . . . **C**

The Great London Fire   *1666*

SEPTEMBER 2. (Lord's day) Some of our maids sitting up late last night to get things ready against our feast today, Jane[14] called us up, about 3 in the morning, to tell us of a great fire they saw in the city. So I rose, and slipped on my nightgown and went to her window, and thought it to be on the back side of
70 Mark Lane at the furthest; but being unused to such fires as followed, I thought it far enough off, and so went to bed again and to sleep. About 7 rose again to dress myself, and there looked out at the window and saw the fire not so much as it was, and further off. So to my closet[15] to set things to rights after yesterday's cleaning. By and by Jane comes and tells me that she hears that above 300 houses have been burned down tonight by the fire we saw, and that it was now burning down all Fish Street by London Bridge. So I made myself ready presently, and walked to the Tower and there got up upon one of the high places, Sir J. Robinson's[16] little son going up with me; and there I did see the houses at that end of the bridge all on fire, and an infinite great fire on this and the other side
80 the end of the bridge—which, among other people, did trouble me for poor little Michell and our Sarah on the bridge.[17] So down, with my heart full of trouble, to the Lieutenant of the Tower, who tells me that it begun this morning in the King's baker's house in Pudding Lane, and that it hath burned down St. Magnus Church and most part of Fish Street already. So I down to the water-side and there got a boat and through bridge, and there saw a lamentable fire. Poor Michell's house, as far as the Old Swan, already burned that way and the fire running further, that in a very little time it got as far as the steelyard while I was there. Everybody endeavoring to remove their goods, and flinging into the river or bringing them into lighters[18] that lay off. Poor people staying in their houses as long as till the
90 very fire touched them, and then running into boats or clambering from one pair of stair by the water-side to another. And among other things, the poor pigeons I perceive were loath to leave their houses, but hovered about the windows and balconies till they were some of them burned, their wings, and fell down. **D**

. . . At last met my Lord Mayor in Canning Street, like a man spent, with a handkerchief about his neck. To the King's message,[19] he cried like a fainting woman, "Lord, what can I do? I am spent. People will not obey me. I have been pull[ing] down houses. But the fire overtakes us faster than we can do it." That

---

14. **Jane:** Jane Birch, Pepys's cook.

15. **closet:** private room.

16. **Tower . . . Sir J. Robinson's:** Sir John Robinson was Lieutenant of the Tower of London, built as a fortress and later used as a royal residence and a prison.

17. **on the bridge:** people living in one of the houses that lined Old London Bridge.

18. **lighters:** barges.

19. **the King's message:** The king has ordered Pepys to find the Lord Mayor of London and tell him to pull down all the houses in the path of the fire to keep it from spreading.

C **CONNECT TO HISTORY**
Reread lines 27–65. Compare the king's coronation to a modern event, such as a presidential inauguration. Would you have been as eager as Pepys to witness the ceremony? Explain your response.

D **GRAMMAR AND STYLE**
Reread lines 81–93. Note how Pepys's emotionally charged phrases, such as "heart full of trouble," and his use of **sentence fragments** reflect the intimacy and informality of a diary entry.

Great Fire of London, 1666 (1800s). Wood engraving. The Granger Collection, New York.

he needed no more soldiers; and that for himself, he must go and refresh himself, having been up all night. So he left me, and I him, and walked home—seeing
100 people all almost distracted and no manner of means used to quench the fire. The houses too, so very thick thereabouts, and full of matter for burning, as pitch and tar, in Thames Street[20]—and warehouses of oil and wines and brandy and other things. . . .

Having seen as much as I could now, I away to Whitehall[21] by appointment, and there walked to St. James's Park, and there met my wife and Creed and Wood and his wife and walked to my boat, and there upon the water again, and to the fire up and down, it still increasing and the wind great. So near the fire as we could for smoke; and all over the Thames, with one's face in the wind you were almost burned with a shower of firedrops—this is very true—so as houses were burned by
110 these drops and flakes of fire, three or four, nay five or six houses, one from another. When we could endure no more upon the water, we to a little alehouse on the bankside over against the Three Cranes, and there stayed till it was dark almost and saw the fire grow; and as it grew darker, appeared more and more, and in corners and upon steeples and between churches and houses, as far as we could see up the hill of the city, in a most horrid malicious bloody flame, not like the fine flame of an ordinary fire. Barbary and her husband away before us. We stayed till, it being darkish, we saw the fire as only one entire arch of fire from this to the other side the

> **Language Coach**
>
> **Meaning of Idioms** The word *away* usually appears after a verb and means "from that place" (*to go away*). Pepys often uses *away* without a verb but with the same meaning as the example above. How would you rephrase lines 104 and 116 in modern English?

---

20. **Thames** (tĕmz) **Street**: a street running along the Thames, the main river flowing through London.
21. **Whitehall**: a wide road in London, the location of many government offices.

bridge, and in a bow up the hill, for an arch of above a mile long. It made me weep to see it. The churches, houses, and all on fire and flaming at once, and a horrid noise the flames made, and the cracking of houses at their ruin. So home with a sad heart, and there find everybody discoursing and lamenting the fire. . . . **E**

SEPTEMBER 3. About 4 o'clock in the morning, my Lady Batten sent me a cart to carry away all my money and plate and best things to Sir W. Rider's at Bethnal Green; which I did, riding myself in my nightgown in the cart; and Lord, to see how the streets and the highways are crowded with people, running and riding and getting of carts at any rate to fetch away thing[s]. . . .

SEPTEMBER 8. . . . I met with many people undone, and more that have extraordinary great losses. People speaking their thoughts variously about the beginning of the fire and the rebuilding of the city. . . .

SEPTEMBER 20. . . . In the afternoon out by coach, my wife with me (which we have not done several weeks now), through all the ruins to show her them, which frets her much—and is a sad sight indeed. . . .

SEPTEMBER 25. . . . So home to bed—and all night still mightily troubled in my sleep with fire and houses pulling down.

Domestic Affairs *1663*

JANUARY 13. So my poor wife rose by 5 o'clock in the morning, before day, and went to market and bought fowl and many other things for dinner—with which I was highly pleased. And the chine of beef was down also before 6 o'clock, and my own jack,[22] of which I was doubtful, doth carry it very well. Things being put in order and the cook come, I went to the office, where we sat till noon; and then broke up and I home—whither by and by comes Dr. Clerke and his lady—his sister and a she-cousin, and Mr. Pierce and his wife, which was all my guest[s].

I had for them, after oysters—at first course, a hash of rabbits and lamb, and a rare chine of beef—next, a great dish of roasted fowl, cost me about 30s, and a tart; and then fruit and cheese. My dinner was noble and enough. I had my house mighty clean and neat, my room below with a good fire in it—my dining-room above, and my chamber being made a withdrawing-chamber, and my wife's a good fire also. I find my new table very proper, and will hold nine or ten people well, but eight with great room. After dinner, the women to cards in my wife's chamber and the doctor [and] Mr. Pierce in mine, because the dining-room smokes unless I keep a good charcoal fire, which I was not then provided with. . . .

OCTOBER 21. This evening after I came home, I begun to enter my wife in arithmetic, in order to her studying of the globes,[23] and she takes it very well—and I hope with great pleasure I shall bring her to understand many fine things. **F**

E CONNECT TO HISTORY
Reread Pepys's account of the Great Fire in lines 66–121. Think about your own reaction to an impending fire or another disaster. Would you have responded as Pepys did? Why or why not?

F DIARY
In lines 135–153, Pepys describes aspects of his home life. What roles and responsibilities do he and his wife each fulfill?

---

22. **chine of beef . . . jack:** a cut of meat containing part of the backbone, roasted on a device called a jack that rotates the meat.

23. **globes:** geography (the earthly globe) and astronomy (the heavenly globes).

1667

JANUARY 7. . . . To the duke's house and saw Macbeth;[24] which though I saw it lately, yet appears a most excellent play in all respects, but especially in divertisement,[25] though it be a deep tragedy; which is a strange perfection in a tragedy, it being most proper here and suitable. . . .

MAY 26. (Lord's day) . . . After dinner, I by water alone to Westminster . . . toward the parish church. . . . I did entertain myself with my perspective glass[26] up and
160 down the church, by which I had the great pleasure of seeing and gazing a great many very fine women; and what with that and sleeping, I passed away the time till sermon was done. . . .

MAY 27. . . . Stopped at the Bear Garden[27] stairs, there to see a prize fought; but the house so full, there was no getting in there; so forced to [go] through an alehouse into the pit where the bears are baited, and upon a stool did see them fight, which they did very furiously, a butcher and a waterman. The former had the better all along, till by and by the latter dropped his sword out of his hand, and the butcher, whether not seeing his sword dropped or I know not, but did give him a cut over the wrist, so as he was disabled to fight any longer. But Lord,
170 to see how in a minute the whole stage was full of watermen to revenge the foul play, and the butchers to defend their fellow, though most blamed him; and there they all fell to it, to knocking down and cutting many of each side. It was pleasant to see, but that I stood in the pit and feared that in the tumult I might get some hurt. At last the rabble broke up, and so I away. . . . **G**

1669

JANUARY 12. . . . This evening I observed my wife mighty dull; and I myself was not mighty fond, because of some hard words she did give me at noon, out of a jealousy at my being abroad this morning; when, God knows, it was upon the business of the office unexpectedly; but I to bed, not thinking but she would come after me; but waking by and by out of a slumber, which I usually fall into
180 presently after my coming into the bed, I found she did not prepare to come to bed, but got fresh candles and more wood for her fire, it being mighty cold too. At this being troubled, I after a while prayed her to come to bed, all my people being gone to bed; so after an hour or two, she silent, and I now and then praying her to come to bed, she fell out into a fury, that I was a rogue and false to her. . . . At last, about 1 o'clock, she came to my side of the bed and drew my curtain open, and with the tongs, red hot at the ends, made as if she did design to pinch me with them; at which in dismay I rose up, and with a few words she laid them down and did by little and little, very sillily, let all the discourse fall; and about 2, but with much seeming difficulty, came to bed and there lay well all night. . . . ∿

G DIARY
Reread lines 154–174. Which details suggest that Pepys led a privileged life during the Restoration?

---

24. **To the duke's house . . . Macbeth:** to the new Duke Theatre, to see a production of Shakespeare's *Macbeth*.

25. **divertisement** (də-vûr′tĭs-mənt): diversion; amusement.

26. **perspective glass:** small telescope.

27. **Bear Garden:** a London establishment used for the spectator sport of bearbaiting, in which a bear was chained to a post and tormented by dogs. The Bear Garden also held prizefights between men.

Comprehension

1. **Recall** What is Pepys's attitude toward the return of King Charles II?

2. **Clarify** What issue causes conflict between Pepys and his wife?

3. **Summarize** In your own words, describe Samuel Pepys's way of life.

COMMON CORE

RI 6 Determine an author's point of view or purpose in a text. RI 10 Read and comprehend literary nonfiction.

Text Analysis

4. **Make Inferences About the Author** Summarize Pepys's behavior. What can you infer about his **character traits,** or consistent qualities, from his diary?

5. **Interpret Diction and Tone** Reread lines 66–93 of the selection, noting Pepys's diction, or word choice. On the basis of phrases such as "my heart full of trouble" and "lamentable fire," describe Pepys's tone, or attitude toward his subject.

6. **Examine Author's Purpose** In general, an author writes to fulfill one or more of these purposes, or goals: to inform, to express thoughts or feelings, to persuade, or to entertain. What is Pepys's primary purpose in keeping his diary? Cite evidence from the text to support your conclusion.

7. **Analyze Diary** *The Diary of Samuel Pepys* not only records the drama of public events but also provides a rare glimpse into the author's views about social issues. What messages does Pepys communicate about the following?

   • the English monarchy (lines 36–60) • education (lines 151–153)

   • material wealth (lines 135–150) • marriage (lines 175–189)

8. **Connect to History** Review the chart you completed as you read the selection. What historical events presented in Pepys's diary did you find most compelling? Explain the connections you made between these events and your own life experiences.

Text Criticism

9. **Critical Interpretations** The author Virginia Woolf once said that the "chief delight" of Pepys's diary is its revelation of "those very weaknesses and idiosyncrasies that in our own case we would die rather than reveal." Do you agree or disagree with this opinion? Explain your answer.

Why keep a DIARY?

Why do you think so many people are compelled to record their thoughts and experiences in diaries? What advantages does a diary offer that other means of expression do not?

Language

◆ **GRAMMAR AND STYLE: Use Appropriate Language**

COMMON CORE

L 3a Vary syntax for effect.
W 3 Write narratives to develop real experiences. **W 3d** Use precise words and phrases to convey a vivid picture of the experiences.

Review the **Grammar and Style** note on page 584. Like most diarists, Samuel Pepys used his diary as a place to jot down the events of his life soon after they happened. Pepys dispenses with formal language in favor of an informal, conversational style peppered with **sentence fragments** and charged with raw emotion—a writing style that is appropriate for a diary. Here is an example:

> *Upon the quarter-deck he [Charles II] fell in discourse of his escape from Worcester. Where it made me ready to weep to hear the stories that he told of his difficulties that he had passed through.* (lines 11–13)

Pepys confesses that he had been "ready to weep," conveying a sense of how deeply the stories affected him. The sentence fragment gives the passage a sense of spontaneity—as if Pepys were transcribing an image from his memory directly to the pages of his diary.

PRACTICE Rewrite the following paragraph about the great Asian tsunami of 2004 as a diary entry, imitating Samuel Pepys's writing style. Make sure to incorporate emotionally charged words and sentence fragments to convey the difficult experiences of the time.

> On December 26, 2004, a massive undersea earthquake erupted in the waters off the western coast of the Indonesian island of Sumatra, setting off a tsunami, or giant shock wave, that was felt more than 3,000 miles away on the coast of East Africa. Survivors of the disaster described hearing a roar moments before seeing a wall of water rip through beaches and villages. Within minutes, the water swept trees, cars, buildings, and people hundreds of yards inland. The worst damage was in the Indonesian province of Ache, where at least 127,000 people died, another 30,000 were reported missing, and more than 500,000 were left homeless.

READING-WRITING CONNECTION

YOUR TURN Expand your understanding of *The Diary of Samuel Pepys* by responding to this prompt. Then, use the **revising tips** to improve your diary entry.

WRITING PROMPT	REVISING TIPS
WRITE A DIARY ENTRY What kind of information about life today could your diary provide to readers centuries from now? Write a **three-to-five-page diary entry** in which you describe how you spend a normal day.	• Describe your day in chronological order. • Make sure you include clear, detailed references to specific objects and activities.

Interactive Revision

THINK central

Go to <u>thinkcentral.com</u>.
KEYWORD: HML12-589

from **Robinson Crusoe**

Novel by Daniel Defoe

Daniel Defoe

BACKGROUND You are the sole survivor of a shipwreck. You are alive, but you are alone on a deserted island far from home. How can you survive, not just physically, but emotionally? What if you are never rescued? What if you never see another human being again? Robinson Crusoe must face this dilemma head-on. Published in 1719, *Robinson Crusoe* is often considered the first English novel. In writing this tale, Daniel Defoe could draw on his own experiences traveling. Before he became a writer, Defoe was a merchant who traveled widely in Europe. He never traveled as far as the New World, but he did read about—and possibly meet—Alexander Selkirk, a Scottish sailor who survived several years on an uninhabited island near Chile before returning to tell of his adventures. Drawing on Selkirk's experiences as well as on his own travels, Defoe produced *Robinson Crusoe,* a pioneering work of realistic fiction that continues to inspire tales of castaways, from the novel *The Swiss Family Robinson* to the television series *Survivor* and *Lost.*

TEXT ANALYSIS Defoe wanted to make Crusoe's story as realistic as possible. He could have used **third-person point of view,** in which a voice outside events narrates the story using pronouns like *he*, *she*, and *they*. Instead, the author uses the **first-person point of view,** in which Crusoe tells his story in his own words using the pronoun *I*. First-person narration emphasizes Crusoe's isolation: he has only his own thoughts to keep him company and must draw on his own mental resources to survive. First-person narration also allows us to experience what goes on in Crusoe's mind, as we follow the trials he undergoes. As he struggles to deal with his situation, we experience Crusoe's moments of desolation and triumph, such as Crusoe's conversation with himself about the positive, as well as negative, sides of his situation that he records in the following excerpt.

WRITE If *Robinson Crusoe* had been narrated from a third-person point of view instead of a first-person point of view, it would be a very different work. With a classmate, rewrite the excerpt from *Robinson Crusoe* from a third-person point of view, including Crusoe's list of the pros and cons of his situation. Discuss what kinds of changes you made and how you think your revision alters the effect of Crusoe's story on readers.

I now began to consider seriously my Condition, and the Circumstance I was reduc'd to, and I drew up the State of my Affairs in Writing, not so much to leave them to any that were to come after me, for I was like to have but few Heirs, as to deliver my Thoughts from daily poring upon them, and afflicting my Mind; and as my Reason began now to master my Despondency, I began to comfort my self as well as I could, and to set the good against the Evil, that I might have something to distinguish my Case from worse, and I stated it very impartially, like Debtor and Creditor, the Comforts I enjoy'd, against the Miseries I suffer'd, Thus,

Evil.	Good.
I am cast upon a horrible desolate Island, void of all hope of Recovery.	*But I am alive, and not drown'd as all my Ship's Company was.*
I am singl'd out and separated, as it were, from all the World to be miserable.	*But I am singl'd out too from all the Ship's Crew to be spar'd from Death; and he that miraculously sav'd me from Death, can deliver me from this Condition.*
I am divided from Mankind, a Solitaire, one banish'd from humane Society.	*But I am not starv'd and perishing on a barren Place, affording no Sustenance.*
I have not Clothes to cover me.	*But I am in a hot Climate, where if I had Clothes I could hardly wear them.*
I am without any Defence or Means to resist any Violence of Man or Beast.	*But I am cast on an Island, where I see no wild Beasts to hurt me, as I saw on the Coast of Africa: And what if I had been Shipwreck'd there?*
I have no Soul to speak to, or relieve me.	*But God wonderfully sent the Ship in near enough to the Shore, that I have gotten out so many necessary things as will either supply my Wants, or enable me to supply my self even as long as I live.*

from **A Journal of the Plague Year**
Fiction by Daniel Defoe

 Video link at
thinkcentral.com

DID YOU KNOW?

Daniel Defoe . . .

- was an undercover government spy.
- promoted several of his novels as memoirs.
- died while in hiding from creditors.

Meet the Author

Daniel Defoe 1660?–1731

Daniel Defoe has been hailed not only as a pioneer of modern journalism but also as the father of the English novel. Best known for *Robinson Crusoe* (page 590), the tale of a man's struggle for survival on a remote island, Defoe wrote more than 370 works, including novels, poems, histories, political and social commentaries, and essays, making him one of the most prolific writers of his day.

A Disastrous Childhood Defoe was born in London, probably in 1660, the year England reestablished itself as a monarchy. When Defoe was about five years old, bubonic plague broke out in London, taking the lives of thousands. A year later, a massive fire destroyed a considerable part of the city. Although Defoe and his family were spared, Defoe's childhood memories of how people coped with crisis and fear no doubt helped inform his writing.

A Daring Journalist Defoe began writing political essays in 1683, working at various times on behalf of both Tory and Whig causes. He contributed articles to more than 26 publications and started his own newspaper, the *Review,* writing nearly all the articles himself. He did not shy away from attacking government policies and was arrested more than once as a result of his inflammatory commentaries. In 1702, his writings landed him in the pillory, a wooden device with holes for the prisoner's head and hands. Prisoners in the pillory were usually pelted with rotten eggs and vegetables, but Defoe's views were so popular that people drank to his health and threw flowers instead.

Novel Approach Defoe did not write his first novel, *Robinson Crusoe* (1719), until he was nearly 60 years old. It was tremendously successful, and he quickly published two Crusoe sequels, following them with several other novels, including *Moll Flanders* (1722), *A Journal of the Plague Year* (1722), *Colonel Jack* (1722), and *Roxana* (1724).

Belated Approval During his lifetime, Defoe was not highly regarded by his literary contemporaries. Jonathan Swift, for example, stated witheringly, "There is no enduring him." By the mid-19th century, however, critics had come to appreciate Defoe's ability to plumb the depths of human emotion and to re-create in his fiction and nonfiction all the rich detail of real life.

THINK central

Author Online

Go to **thinkcentral.com**. KEYWORD: HML12-592

TEXT ANALYSIS: VERISIMILITUDE

Unlike the diary of Samuel Pepys, Daniel Defoe's *A Journal of the Plague Year* is a work of fiction. The novel portrays London during the summer of 1665, the darkest days of the city's bubonic plague epidemic. An innovative writer, Defoe incorporated details from mortality records, city maps, and other historical documents to help him achieve **verisimilitude**, or the appearance of reality. Presented as an eyewitness account, the novel purposefully blurs the line between fact and fiction. In this way, Defoe's writing anticipates the realism and psychological depth of modern novels. As you read, notice how the following conventions help make the selection seem like an authentic report of the tragedy:

- a first-person narrator
- numbers and statistics
- dates and references to time
- geographical names
- precise details

READING SKILL: DRAW CONCLUSIONS

As you read the selection, use your own reactions and text clues to help you make **inferences,** or logical guesses, about the effects of the plague on London society. For example, you can infer that the epidemic caused a collapse of social customs, such as public mourning, from the following lines:

London might well be said to be all in tears; the mourners did not go about the streets indeed, for nobody put on black or made a formal dress of mourning for their nearest friends. . . .

Record your inferences in a chart like the one shown. After reading the selection, you will use these notes to **draw conclusions,** or make general statements, about the tragedy.

Passages About London Society	My Reactions	My Inferences
"As near as I may judge, [the burial pit] was about forty feet in length, and about fifteen or sixteen feet broad, and ... about nine feet deep. . . ."	The burial pit was so large. What a terrible sight it must have been!	The plague caused Londoners to change their burial practices. Mass graves were created.

 Complete the activities in your **Reader/Writer Notebook**.

How can a PLAGUE affect society?

As Daniel Defoe emphasizes in his novel, a plague can strike indiscriminately and unpredictably. Even today, with advanced medicine, diseases capable of triggering epidemics remain terrible threats to society.

DISCUSS Imagine that you and a small group of classmates are public health officials. You have just discovered several cases of a highly infectious disease that you fear may develop into an epidemic. Discuss the ways that you might work with different sectors of society—such as the media, politicians, and the elderly—to limit the spread of disease. Compare your ideas with those of other groups.

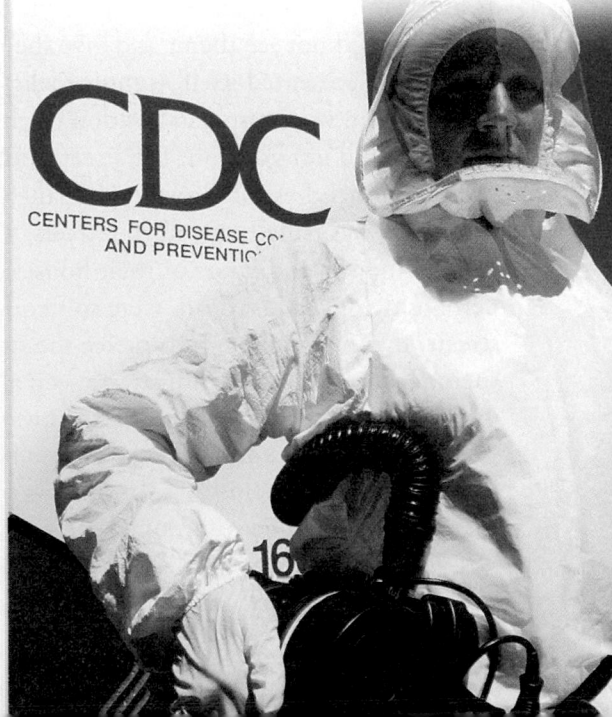

CDC

CENTERS FOR DISEASE CO
AND PREVENTIO

16

A JOURNAL of the PLAGUE YEAR

Daniel Defoe

> **BACKGROUND** In *A Journal of the Plague Year,* Defoe chronicles the epidemic through the eyes of his narrator, a saddle maker known only as H. F. Early in the novel, as many people are fleeing the city, H. F. agonizes over whether he too should leave London. After reading a passage in the Bible, he decides to stay and to do what he can for those in need, trusting that God will keep him from falling victim to "the noisome pestilence."

Analyze Visuals ▶
What details in the engraving reveal the terrible circumstances of the plague outbreak?

The face of London was now indeed strangely altered, I mean the whole mass of buildings, city, liberties, suburbs, Westminster, Southwark, and altogether; for as to the particular part called the city, or within the walls, that was not yet much infected. But in the whole the face of things, I say, was much altered; sorrow and sadness sat upon every face; and though some parts were not yet overwhelmed, yet all looked deeply concerned; and, as we saw it apparently coming on, so every one looked on himself and his family as in the utmost danger. Were it possible to represent those times exactly to those that did not see them, and give the reader due ideas of the horror that 10 everywhere presented itself, it must make just impressions upon their minds and fill them with surprise. London might well be said to be all in tears; the mourners did not go about the streets indeed, for nobody put on black or made a formal dress of mourning for their nearest friends; but the voice of mourning was truly heard in the streets. The shrieks of women and children at the windows and doors of their houses, where their dearest relations were perhaps dying, or just dead, were so frequent to be heard as we passed the streets, that it was enough to pierce the stoutest heart in the world to hear them. Tears and lamentations were seen almost in every house, especially in the first part of the visitation; for towards the latter end men's hearts 20 were hardened, and death was so always before their eyes, that they did not so much concern themselves for the loss of their friends, expecting that themselves should be summoned the next hour. . . . **A**

   I went all the first part of the time freely about the streets, though not so freely as to run myself into apparent danger, except when they dug the great

2 city: the portion of London once within the old city walls, with Westminster to the west and Southwark (sŭth′ərk) to the south; **liberties:** densely populated areas just outside the city walls.

A **DRAW CONCLUSIONS**
Reread lines 14–22. Which details suggest that the plague caused family relationships and friendships to fall apart?

The Great Pit in Aldgate (1865), Davenport after Cruikshank. © Science Museum Library/Science and Society Picture Library.

pit in the churchyard of our parish of Aldgate. A terrible pit it was, and I
could not resist my curiosity to go and see it. As near as I may judge, it was
about forty feet in length, and about fifteen or sixteen feet broad, and, at the
time I first looked at it, about nine feet deep; but it was said they dug it near
twenty feet deep afterwards in one part of it, till they could go no deeper
30 for the water; for they had, it seems, dug several large pits before this. For
though the plague was long a-coming to our parish, yet, when it did come,
there was no parish in or about London where it raged with such violence as
in the two parishes of Aldgate and Whitechapel. . . .

They had supposed this pit would have supplied them for a month or
more when they dug it, and some blamed the churchwardens for suffering
such a frightful thing, telling them they were making preparations to bury
the whole parish, and the like; but time made it appear the churchwardens
knew the condition of the parish better than they did, for the pit being
finished the 4th of September, I think, they began to bury in it the 6th,
40 and by the 20th, which was just two weeks, they had thrown into it 1,114
bodies when they were obliged to fill it up, the bodies being then come to
lie within six feet of the surface. . . .

It was about the 10th of September that my curiosity led, or rather drove,
me to go and see this pit again, when there had been near 400 people buried
in it; and I was not content to see it in the daytime, as I had done before, for
then there would have been nothing to have been seen but the loose earth;
for all the bodies that were thrown in were immediately covered with earth
by those they called the buriers, which at other times were called bearers; but
I resolved to go in the night and see some of them thrown in. **B**

50 There was a strict order to prevent people coming to those pits, and that
was only to prevent infection. But after some time that order was more
necessary, for people that were infected and near their end, and delirious
also, would run to those pits, wrapt in blankets or rugs, and throw
themselves in, and, as they said, bury themselves. I cannot say that the
officers suffered any willingly to lie there; but I have heard that in a great
pit in Finsbury, in the parish of Cripplegate, it lying open then to the fields,
for it was not then walled about, [some] came and threw themselves in,
and expired there, before they threw any earth upon them; and that when
they came to bury others and found them there, they were quite dead,
60 though not cold. **C**

This may serve a little to describe the dreadful condition of that day,
though it is impossible to say anything that is able to give a true idea of it to
those who did not see it, other than this, that it was indeed very, very, very
dreadful, and such as no tongue can express.

I got admittance into the churchyard by being acquainted with the
sexton who attended, who, though he did not refuse me at all, yet
earnestly persuaded me not to go, telling me very seriously, for he was a
good, religious, and sensible man, that it was indeed their business and
duty to venture, and to run all hazards, and that in it they might hope to
70 be preserved; but that I had no apparent call to it but my own curiosity,

25 **parish of Aldgate:** The street
and area known as Aldgate take
their name from the nearby old
gate, or Aldgate.

33 **Whitechapel:** an area just east of
Aldgate and the old city walls.

B VERISIMILITUDE
Review Defoe's use of **numbers,
dates,** and **statistics** in lines
25–49. Would the description
of the Aldgate burial pit be
as compelling without these
details? Explain your response.

C VERISIMILITUDE
The narrator recounts information
about Aldgate and Finsbury,
actual areas of London struck
by the epidemic. How might
Defoe's original audience have
reacted to reading these familiar
geographical names?

66 **sexton:** a church officer or
employee in charge of maintaining
church property.

which, he said, he believed I would not pretend was sufficient to justify my running that hazard. I told him I had been pressed in my mind to go, and that perhaps it might be an instructing sight, that might not be without its uses. "Nay," says the good man, "if you will venture upon that score, name of God go in; for, depend upon it, 't will be a sermon to you, it may be, the best that ever you heard in your life. 'T is a speaking sight," says he, "and has a voice with it, and a loud one, to call us all to repentance;" and with that he opened the door and said, "Go, if you will."

His discourse had shocked my resolution a little, and I stood wavering for
80 a good while, but just at that interval I saw two links come over from the end of the Minories, and heard the bellman, and then appeared a dead-cart, as they called it, coming over the streets; so I could no longer resist my desire of seeing it, and went in. There was nobody, as I could perceive at first, in the churchyard, or going into it, but the buriers and the fellow that drove the cart, or rather led the horse and cart; but when they came up to the pit they saw a man go to and again, muffled up in a brown cloak, and making motions with his hands under his cloak, as if he was in a great agony, and the buriers immediately gathered about him, supposing he was one of those poor delirious or desperate creatures that used to pretend, as I have said, to
90 bury themselves. He said nothing as he walked about, but two or three times groaned very deeply and loud, and sighed as he would break his heart.

When the buriers came up to him they soon found he was neither a person infected and desperate, as I have observed above, or a person distempered in mind, but one oppressed with a dreadful weight of grief indeed, having his wife and several of his children all in the cart that was just come in with him, and he followed in an agony and excess of sorrow. He mourned heartily, as it was easy to see, but with a kind of masculine grief that could not give itself vent by tears; and calmly defying the buriers to let him alone, said he would only see the bodies thrown in and go away,
100 so they left importuning him. But no sooner was the cart turned round and the bodies shot into the pit promiscuously, which was a surprise to him, for he at least expected they would have been decently laid in, though indeed he was afterwards convinced that was impracticable; I say, no sooner did he see the sight but he cried out aloud, unable to contain himself. I could not hear what he said, but he went backward two or three steps and fell down in a swoon. The buriers ran to him and took him up, and in a little while he came to himself, and they led him away to the Pie Tavern over against the end of Houndsditch, where, it seems, the man was known, and where they took care of him. He looked into the pit again as he went away, but the
110 buriers had covered the bodies so immediately with throwing in earth, that though there was light enough, for there were lanterns, and candles in them, placed all night round the sides of the pit, upon heaps of earth, seven or eight, or perhaps more, yet nothing could be seen. **D**

This was a mournful scene indeed, and affected me almost as much as the rest; but the other was awful and full of terror. The cart had in it sixteen or seventeen bodies; some were wrapt up in linen sheets, some in rags, some

74–75 if you will venture . . . go in: If you will go in for that reason, in the name of God, go in.

80 links: torches.

81–82 Minories: a street running from Aldgate to the Tower of London; **bellman . . . dead-cart:** In front of a cart bearing the dead away, a bellman walked ahead, ringing a bell and crying, "Bring out your dead!"

94 distempered: afflicted with distemper, or disorder, of the mind; deranged; mentally disturbed.

101 promiscuously (prə-mĭs′kyōō-əs-lē): without sorting or discrimination; without making distinctions.

108 Houndsditch: a street on the site of an old ditch running northwest along the city wall between Aldgate and Bishopsgate.

D DRAW CONCLUSIONS
Reread lines 79–113. Contrast the actions of the desperate man to those of the buriers. Whose response to the plague is more disturbing? Explain your thoughts.

little other than naked, or so loose that what covering they had fell from
them in the shooting out of the cart, and they fell quite naked among the
rest; but the matter was not much to them, or the indecency much to any
120 one else, seeing they were all dead, and were to be huddled together into
the common grave of mankind, as we may call it, for here was no difference
made, but poor and rich went together; there was no other way of burials,
neither was it possible there should, for coffins were not to be had for the
prodigious numbers that fell in such a calamity as this. . . .

I had some little obligations, indeed, upon me to go to my brother's
house, which was in Coleman Street parish, and which he had left to my
care, and I went at first every day, but afterwards only once or twice a week.

In these walks I had many dismal scenes before my eyes, as particularly of
persons falling dead in the streets, terrible shrieks and screechings of women,
130 who, in their agonies, would throw open their chamber windows and cry
out in a dismal, surprising manner. It is impossible to describe the variety of
postures in which the passions of the poor people would express themselves.
. . . People in the rage of the distemper, or in the torment of their swellings,
which was indeed intolerable, running out of their own government, raving
and distracted, and oftentimes laying violent hands upon themselves,
throwing themselves out at their windows, shooting themselves, etc.;
mothers murdering their own children in their lunacy, some dying of mere
grief as a passion, some of mere fright and surprise without any infection at
all, others frighted into idiotism and foolish distractions, some into despair
140 and lunacy, others into melancholy madness. . . . ⒠

I heard of one infected creature who, running out of his bed in his shirt
in the anguish and agony of his swellings, of which he had three upon
him, got his shoes on and went to put on his coat; but the nurse resisting,
and snatching the coat from him, he threw her down, ran over her, ran
downstairs and into the street, directly to the Thames in his shirt, the nurse
running after him, and calling to the watch to stop him; but the watchman,
frighted at the man, and afraid to touch him, let him go on; upon which he
ran down to the Stillyard stairs, threw away his shirt, and plunged into the
Thames, and, being a good swimmer, swam quite over the river; and the
150 tide being coming in, as they call it, that is, running westward, he reached
the land not till he came about the Falcon stairs, where landing, and finding
no people there, it being in the night, he ran about the streets there, naked
as he was, for a good while, when, it being by that time high water, he takes
the river again, and swam back to the Stillyard, landed, ran up the streets
again to his own house, knocking at the door, went up the stairs and into his
bed again; and that this terrible experiment cured him of the plague, that is
to say, that the violent motion of his arms and legs stretched the parts where
the swellings he had upon him were, that is to say, under his arms and his
groin, and caused them to ripen and break, and that the cold of the water
160 abated the fever in his blood. ❧

COMMON CORE RL 4

Language Coach

Denotations and Connotations
The feelings or images
connected to a word are the
word's **connotations**. How do
the connotations of *huddled*
(line 120) differ from those of its
synonyms *grouped* and *nestled*?

126 Coleman Street parish: an
area about half a mile west of the
narrator's parish.

133 swellings: Bubonic plague is
characterized by the painful swelling
of inflamed lymph glands, or buboes.

134 running . . . government: losing
the ability to control themselves.

ⓔ **VERISIMILITUDE**
In lines 128–140, the **first-person
narrator** describes the horrors
of London's infected parishes.
How might your sense of the
epidemic be different if a third-
person narrator described the
scene?

146 watch: the night watch, which
patrolled and guarded the city at
night.

Comprehension

1. **Recall** Why does the narrator want to visit the Aldgate burial pit at night?

2. **Clarify** Why does the sexton try to prevent the narrator from entering the burial grounds?

3. **Summarize** What horrors does the narrator witness during regular walks to his brother's house?

Text Analysis

4. **Make Inferences About the Narrator** Reread lines 23–49. Is the narrator compassionate, aggressive, or some combination of these? Support your answer with specific details.

5. **Interpret Imagery and Mood** Find several examples of sensory imagery—or words and phrases that appeal to the senses—in lines 1–22. What overall mood, or atmosphere, do these vivid images help create?

6. **Analyze Verisimilitude** Reread lines 79–124, about the narrator's encounter with the desperate man. What aspects of verisimilitude make the most impact in this scene? Review the list of conventions on page 593, if necessary.

7. **Draw Conclusions** Look over the **inferences** you recorded as you read the selection. Summarize the effects of the plague on various members of London society. What social customs and institutions did the epidemic of 1665 alter or destroy? Support your conclusion with evidence from the text.

8. **Compare Texts** Compare Defoe's work with *The Diary of Samuel Pepys* (page 580). Which author presents the more memorable account of London during the Restoration? Cite details from the texts to support your response.

Text Criticism

9. **Historical Context** In Defoe's day, any advice doctors might offer on what caused disease was based on suspicion and guesswork. How might modern society's response to a widespread outbreak of disease differ from the response Defoe describes in *A Journal of the Plague Year*?

How can a **PLAGUE** affect society?

Defoe published *A Journal of the Plague Year* in 1722, just decades after the actual epidemic struck London. Do you think Defoe wanted to create a moving, realistic portrayal of the suffering caused by the plague or did he want to exploit that suffering to provide readers with a sensational, shocking read? Explain your reasons.

COMMON CORE

RL 1 Cite textual evidence to support inferences drawn from the text. **RL 3** Analyze the impact of the author's choices regarding how to develop and relate elements of a story.

from The Spectator

Essays by Joseph Addison

COMMON CORE

RI 6 Determine an author's purpose in a text, analyzing how style contributes to the power, persuasiveness, or beauty of the text. **RI 10** Read and comprehend literary nonfiction.

Meet the Author

Joseph Addison 1672–1719

Together with his friend Richard Steele, Joseph Addison helped usher in a new age of journalism with the influential periodical *The Spectator,* which helped shape middle-class taste, manners, and morality during the 18th century.

From Poetry to Politics Addison attended Oxford University, where he distinguished himself as a master of Latin verse. In 1695, he wrote *A Poem to his Majesty* in praise of King William III. By dedicating the poem to John Somers, a prominent Whig politician, Addison won Somers's patronage and was given a grant to travel abroad in Europe on diplomatic missions. In 1705, he again used poetry to further his political career, penning *The Campaign,* which glorified John Churchill, the duke of Marlborough, for his role in the British conquest of the French during the War of the Spanish Succession. The poem helped secure his position in Whig political circles. He later served as a member of the British and Irish parliaments and eventually obtained several important government posts, including that of secretary of state.

A Friendship Rekindled When the Whigs lost power in 1710, Addison found himself without steady income. He reconnected with his old college friend Richard Steele, who had recently launched *The Tatler,* a journal that offered humorous pieces and political commentary with a decidedly Whig bias. Soon Addison began regularly contributing essays anonymously to *The Tatler.* They were so well received that the poet John Gay wondered why the author refused to sign "pieces which the greatest pens in England would be proud to own."

Manners, Morals, and the Middle Class *The Tatler* folded in January 1711, but two months later Steele and Addison inaugurated *The Spectator,* which, unlike their earlier venture, was nonpartisan. A masterful prose stylist, Addison was responsible for a considerable amount of the journal's content. Addison and Steele were successful in their attempt to bring philosophy "out of closets and libraries . . . and in[to] coffeehouses," partly because the light, humorous style of *The Spectator* made its moral content acceptable to its 18th-century audience. By praising marriage and honesty while ridiculing hypocrisy and pride, Addison sought to improve the morals and manners of the readers. His scenes of everyday life continue to provide readers valuable insights into how the emerging middle class of early 18th-century England lived.

DID YOU KNOW?

Joseph Addison . . .

- was shy around strangers.
- was nicknamed "the parson in a tie-wig" because of his intense moral convictions.
- was among England's first journalists to write for both men and women.

Author Online

Go to **thinkcentral.com**. KEYWORD: HML12-600

THINK central

TEXT ANALYSIS: NEOCLASSICISM

The literary style that prevailed in England from the Restoration to nearly the end of the 18th century is referred to as **neoclassicism,** or "new classicism." In this age, many writers intentionally modeled their works on classical Greek or Latin texts, which they had studied in school. Neoclassicists believed that such ancient works were valuable because they revealed universal and timeless truths about the human condition. These authors respected order, reason, and rules and viewed humans as essentially limited and imperfect. Their writing typically favors society, reason, and observable facts over individuality, emotions, and opinions. As you read, consider the ways in which Addison's essays embody the spirit and principles of the neoclassical movement.

READING SKILL: ANALYZE AUTHOR'S PURPOSE

Writers create their works to fulfill one or more of these general **purposes:** to express thoughts or feelings, to persuade, to inform, or to entertain. In the essay "Plan and Purpose," Addison states plainly:

I shall endeavor to enliven morality with wit, and to temper wit with morality, that my readers may, if possible, both ways find their account in the speculation of the day.

These works both inform and entertain, inspiring readers to acknowledge and change awkward or inappropriate behaviors. As you read Addison's essays, examine how he uses the following elements of style to achieve his dual purposes:

- amusing situations or **anecdotes**
- a gently mocking **tone,** or attitude toward his subject
- **overstatement**, or exaggeration

Record your observations in a chart like the one shown.

Essay	Details That Inform	Details That Entertain

 Complete the activities in your **Reader/Writer Notebook**.

Whose OPINIONS *matter?*

In the early 18th century, Joseph Addison wrote about matters that resonated with people of his class and background. His opinions helped people navigate their social sphere. Today, people still look to newspaper columnists, comedians, and other media personalities for advice on everything from how to vote to where to find the best pizza.

DISCUSS With a group of classmates, brainstorm a list of influential media figures. Discuss the way they present their opinions and the techniques of persuasion they use. Why do you think they are able to exercise influence over so many people?

Influential Media Figures

1. Anna Quindlen
2.
3.
4.

The SPECTATOR

Joseph Addison

> **BACKGROUND** In the late 1600s, certain writers began to offer moral instruction in periodicals, displaying a casual, good-natured approach to society's ills. Although hundreds of these periodicals were published before the 18th century, none enjoyed the popularity of those written by Joseph Addison and his friend Richard Steele in the early 1700s. Together, Addison and Steele created a form of writing that has remained popular for nearly three centuries—a predecessor of modern newspaper and magazine columns.

PLAN AND PURPOSE

It is with much satisfaction that I hear this great city inquiring day by day after these my papers, and receiving my morning lectures with a becoming seriousness and attention. My publisher tells me that there are already three thousand of them distributed every day. . . . Since I have raised to myself so great an audience, I shall spare no pains to make their instruction agreeable, and their diversion useful. For which reasons I shall endeavor to enliven morality with wit, and to temper wit with morality, that my readers may, if possible, both ways find their account in the speculation of the day. . . . The mind that lies fallow but a single day, sprouts up in follies that are only to be killed by a constant and assiduous culture.[1] It 10 was said of Socrates,[2] that he brought philosophy down from heaven to inhabit among men; and I shall be ambitious to have it said of me, that I have brought philosophy out of closets and libraries, schools and colleges, to dwell in clubs and assemblies, at tea tables and in coffeehouses. **A**

---

1. **The mind . . . culture:** The mind that is uncultivated for a single day sprouts up in foolishness that can be killed only by constant and careful cultivation. Addison is comparing an idle mind to an unsown field in which weeds sprout up.

2. **Socrates** (sŏk'rə-tēz'): an ancient Greek philosopher and teacher.

Analyze Visuals ▶
What sort of family is represented in the painting? Which details indicate the family's social class?

Ⓐ NEOCLASSICISM
Reread lines 1–13. What details suggest that Addison prefers public rather than private themes in his writing?

Detail of *The Strode Family at Tea* (1738), William Hogarth. Oil on canvas, 870 mm × 915 mm. Tate Gallery, London. © Tate Gallery, London/Art Resource, New York.

I would therefore in a very particular manner recommend these my speculations to all well-regulated families, that set apart an hour in every morning for tea and bread and butter; and would earnestly advise them for their good to order this paper to be punctually served up and to be looked upon as a part of the tea equipage.[3] . . .

COUNTRY MANNERS

The first and most obvious reflections which arise in a man who changes the city
20 for the country are upon the different manners of the people whom he meets with in those two different scenes of life. By manners I do not mean morals, but behavior and good breeding, as they show themselves in the town and in the country. . . .

Rural politeness is very troublesome to a man of my temper, who generally takes the chair that is next me and walks first or last, in the front or in the rear, as chance directs. I have known my friend Sir Roger's[4] dinner almost cold before the company could adjust the ceremonial and be prevailed upon to sit down. . . . Honest Will Wimble,[5] who I should have thought had been altogether uninfected with ceremony, gives me abundance of trouble in this particular. Though he has
30 been fishing all the morning, he will not help himself at dinner till I am served. When we are going out of the hall, he runs behind me; and last night, as we were walking in the fields, stopped short at a stile[6] till I came up to it, and upon my making signs to him to get over, told me, with a serious smile, that sure I believed they had no manners in the country. . . . **B**

ON COURTSHIP AND MARRIAGE

Before marriage we cannot be too inquisitive and discerning in the faults of the person beloved, nor after it too dim-sighted and superficial. However perfect and accomplished the person appears to you at a distance, you will find many blemishes and imperfections in her humor,[7] upon a more intimate acquaintance, which you never discovered or perhaps suspected. Here therefore discretion and
40 good nature are to show their strength; the first will hinder your thoughts from dwelling on what is disagreeable, the other will raise in you all the tenderness of compassion and humanity, and by degrees soften those very imperfections into beauties. . . . **C**

B AUTHOR'S PURPOSE
Reread lines 28–34. What is Addison's **tone** toward Honest Will Wimble? Cite specific words and phrases to support your answer.

C NEOCLASSICISM
In "On Courtship and Marriage," which details reflect the neoclassical idea that reason is more important than emotions?

---

3. **equipage** (ĕk'wə-pĭj): equipment.
4. **Sir Roger's:** referring to Sir Roger de Coverley, the central figure of a group of fictional characters that Addison sketches in his essays.
5. **Will Wimble:** another in the group of fictional characters that Addison portrays in his essays.
6. **stile:** a set of steps used to climb over a fence.
7. **humor:** disposition; temperament.

LUGUBRIOUS PEOPLE

There are many persons, who, by a natural uncheerfulness of heart, mistaken notions of piety, or weakness of understanding, love to indulge this uncomfortable way of life, and give up themselves a prey to grief and melancholy. Superstitious fears, and groundless scruples, cut them off from the pleasures of conversation, and all those social entertainments which are not only innocent but laudable; as if mirth was made for reprobates, and cheerfulness of heart denied those who are the only persons that have a proper title to it.

Sombrius[8] is one of these sons of sorrow. He thinks himself obliged in duty to be sad and disconsolate. He looks on a sudden fit of laughter, as a breach of his baptismal vow. An innocent jest startles him like blasphemy. Tell him of one who is advanced to a title of honor, he lifts up his hands and eyes; describe a public ceremony, he shakes his head. . . . All the little ornaments of life are pomps[9] and vanities. Mirth is wanton,[10] and wit profane. He is scandalized at youth for being lively, and at childhood for being playful. He sits at a Christening, or a marriage feast, as at a funeral; sighs at the conclusion of a merry story; and grows devout when the rest of the company grow pleasant. . . . **D**

ADVANTAGES OF MARRIAGE

There is another accidental advantage in marriage, which has likewise fallen to my share; I mean having a multitude of children. These I cannot but regard as very great blessings. When I see my little troop before me, I rejoice in the additions which I have made to my species, to my country, and to my religion, in having produced such a number of reasonable creatures, citizens, and Christians. I am pleased to see myself thus perpetuated, and as there is no production comparable to that of a human creature, I am more proud of having been the occasion of ten such glorious productions, than if I had built a hundred pyramids at my own expense, or published as many volumes of the finest wit and learning. . . . ❧

---

8. **Sombrius:** another fictional character that Addison sketches in his essays.

9. **pomps:** ostentatious or overly showy rituals or displays.

10. **wanton** (wŏn′ton): immoral or impure.

Comprehension

1. **Recall** What advice does Addison have for "well-regulated" families?

2. **Clarify** Why does Addison object to some practices stemming from "rural politeness"?

3. **Summarize** According to Addison, how should a person regard his or her beloved before marriage? after marriage?

Text Analysis

4. **Make Inferences About the Author** In his work, Addison comments on his own life, including his temperament (lines 24–27) and his children (lines 62–64). Summarize his statements and then explain what each reveals about his personality.

● 5. **Examine Neoclassicism** Reread "Plan and Purpose," lines 1–18. Explain how the selection exemplifies key aspects of neoclassical writing.

● 6. **Analyze Author's Purpose** Review the chart you completed as you read the essays. Among the purposes you identified, how important is the purpose of entertaining the reader? Cite examples or passages from the essays to support your opinion.

7. **Compare Texts** Compare and contrast the third and fifth excerpts from Addison's essays with Sir Francis Bacon's essay "Of Marriage and Single Life" (page 467). What differences in **subject matter** and **tone** do you notice? Use a chart like the one shown to help you organize your thoughts.

	Addison	Bacon
Subject Matter		
Tone		

Text Criticism

8. **Critical Interpretation** The author Samuel Johnson once described Addison's writing in the following way: "His prose is the model of the middle style; on grave subjects not formal, on light occasions not groveling." Cite specific examples and passages from the essays that support this opinion.

Whose **OPINIONS** matter?

What influential media figure's opinions do you consider overrated today and why? Which media figure do you think deserves a wider audience for his or her opinions? Why?

COMMON CORE

RI 6 Determine an author's purpose in a text, analyzing how style contributes to the power, persuasiveness, or beauty of the text. **RI 10** Read and comprehend literary nonfiction.

An Eye for Social Behavior

Everyone has something to say about society. Eavesdrop on almost any conversation and you're bound to hear comments about how people dress, how they treat their dogs, the latest election, or what's on television these days. The social observations of Samuel Pepys, Daniel Defoe, and Joseph Addison have held their place in literary history because of their keen insight and detailed description of English life during the Restoration and 18th century.

> *"May 23. . . . All the afternoon the King walking here and there, up and down (quite contrary to what I thought him to have been), very active and stirring. Upon the quarter-deck he fell in discourse of his escape from Worcester. Where it made me ready to weep to hear the stories that he told of his difficulties that he had passed through. As his traveling four days and three nights on foot, every step up to his knees in dirt, with nothing but a green coat and a pair of country breeches on and a pair of country shoes, that made him so sore all over his feet that he could scarce stir."*
>
> —*The Diary of Samuel Pepys*

Writing to Analyze

Covering both the mundane and the majestic, the writings of Pepys, Defoe, and Addison reveal a great deal about English society. What might these accounts have to offer that a history book would not? Write an essay in which you analyze the value of these writings as a window into a historical time.

Consider

- descriptive details provided by Pepys, Defoe, and Addison about historical events
- commentary by these writers about the events
- how a history book might cover these same events

Extension Online

INQUIRY & RESEARCH

Internet bloggers can be considered the modern-day heirs to the social observers of the 17th and 18th century. Search the Internet for personal weblogs offering social commentary, whether on high school life, national politics, the music business, or some other social arena. Choose two or three that in your opinion offer the most insightful observations. What, if anything, do these bloggers have in common with Pepys, Defoe, and Addison?

COMMON CORE

W 2 Write explanatory texts to examine and convey complex ideas. **W 2b** Develop the topic thoroughly by selecting concrete details or other information and examples. **W 7** Conduct short research projects to answer a question. **W 9** Draw evidence from literary or informational texts to support analysis.

Satire

Can humor make someone see the serious side of an issue? Since ancient times, writers have used satire to attack injustice, to highlight the absurd, and to show the brutal truth about one topic while seeming to write about another. In their works, satirists have employed every genre to surprise and delight readers with portraits of society that elicit an equal measure of amusement and shock.

COMMON CORE

Included in this workshop:
RL 6 Analyze a case in which grasping a point of view requires distinguishing what is directly stated in a text from what is really meant.

A History of Mockery

Satire is a literary technique in which behaviors or institutions are ridiculed for the purpose of improving society. What sets satire apart from other forms of social and political protest is humor. The use of satire began with the ancient Greeks but came into its own in ancient Rome, where the "fathers" of satire, Horace (1st century B.C.) and Juvenal (2nd century A.D.), were inspired by the decadence of the Roman Empire to write scathing critiques of their society.

This illustration lampoons women's fashions.

The next great flourishing of satire began in Europe in the second half of the 17th century and continued throughout the 18th century. In England, this "golden age" of satire encompassed the talents of the Restoration dramatists as well as John Dryden, Alexander Pope, Jonathan Swift, and Samuel Johnson. The 18th century was dominated by satiric poetry, prose, and drama. Satirists, as guardians of the culture, sought to protect their highly developed civilization from corruption by attacking hypocrisy, arrogance, greed, vanity, and stupidity. "The satirist is to be regarded as our physician, not our enemy," wrote 18th-century novelist Henry Fielding.

With a few notable exceptions—namely, the writings of Lord Byron, William Makepeace Thackeray, and Samuel Butler in England and Mark Twain in the United States—satirical writing faded in the 19th century. Literary satire in the 20th century has been somewhat scarce, but other forms of media, such as political cartoons and television shows, have shown a resurgence of satire.

Characteristics of Satire

For the most part, a satirist attempts to bring about change by exposing an oddity or a problem in an imaginative, often **humorous,** way. The target is often a social or political one. Typically, satirists use **irony** and **exaggeration** to poke fun at human faults and foolishness in order to correct human behavior. The two basic types of satire are named after the great Roman writers Horace and Juvenal, who perfected satire in different ways.

Horatian satire is playfully amusing and urbane. It seeks to correct vice or foolishness with gentle laughter and understanding. A famous example of Horatian satire is Alexander Pope's brilliant mock epic *The Rape of the Lock* (page 612). The poem, which satirizes the trivial pursuits of the idle wealthy, echoes the openings of ancient epics in its famous first lines.

> What dire offense from amorous causes springs,
> What mighty contests rise from trivial things,
> I sing— . . .
>
> —Alexander Pope, *The Rape of the Lock*

In the poem, a young lord is so smitten by a lady's beauty that he secretly cuts off a lock of her hair. The lady's offense at this violation takes on epic—or mock epic—proportions.

> Then flashed the living lightning from her eyes,
> And screams of horror rend the affrighted skies.
> Not louder shrieks to pitying heaven are cast,
> When husbands, or when lapdogs breathe their last;
>
> — Alexander Pope, *The Rape of the Lock*

Juvenalian satire provokes a darker kind of laughter. It is often bitter, or even angry, and criticizes corruption or incompetence with scorn and outrage. The most famous example of Juvenalian satire comes from Jonathan Swift, whose savage wit was unequaled among his 18th-century English contemporaries. Swift's fictional *Gulliver's Travels* (page 636) tended toward Juvenalian satire. But it was his famous essay, "A Modest Proposal" (page 622), that shocked and appalled readers. Notice the biting verbal irony in this passage from the essay, which describes certain abilities of young children.

> They can very seldom pick up a livelihood by stealing till they arrive at six years old, except where they are of towardly parts [have a promising talent]; although I confess they learn the rudiments much earlier . . .
>
> —Jonathan Swift, "A Modest Proposal"

STRATEGIES FOR READING SATIRE

Use the following strategies when reading a satirical work:

- Determine the object of the satire. The custom or character that provokes laughter is probably the undesirable part of society the writer is criticizing.
- Note what is criticized in order to infer what the satirist believes is right and proper.
- Watch for irony, which often points directly to the object of satire.
- Pay attention to anything that is exaggerated.
- Evaluate whether the satire is Horatian (playful and sympathetic) or Juvenalian (bitter and critical).

Close Read

What is exaggerated in this passage? What is ironic?

Close Read

What is humorous about this passage? What assumption is made that might shock readers?

from The Rape of the Lock

Poem by Alexander Pope

Meet the Author

DID YOU KNOW?

Alexander Pope . . .

- was run over by a wild cow when he was three years old.
- suffered from poor health and once said that his life had been a "long disease."
- wrote the first two cantos of *The Rape of the Lock* in less than two weeks.

Alexander Pope   1688–1744

As a poet and satirist, Alexander Pope was unrivaled during the early 18th century. Revered for his masterful use of the heroic couplet, Pope influenced the literature of the first half of the 18th century so undeniably that the time period is sometimes called the Age of Pope.

A Precocious Poet Pope was raised as a Roman Catholic during a period in England's history when only Protestants could obtain a university education or hold public office. For this reason, he was largely self-taught. Pope was an exceptional youth; by the time he was 17, his poems were being read and admired by many of England's best literary critics.

At the age of 12, Pope developed tuberculosis of the spine, possibly from drinking contaminated milk. The tuberculosis stunted his growth (he never grew taller than four feet six inches) and permanently deformed his spine. Pope's illness limited the amount of physical activity he could engage in, which may have contributed to his early devotion to reading and writing.

Fame and Fortune Pope's most celebrated work, *The Rape of the Lock,* appeared in 1712, when he was only 24. Poetry, however, did not pay the bills. Pope was a neoclassicist, modeling his writing on the works of ancient Greece and Rome, which stressed balance, order, rationality, and sophisticated wit. As a great admirer of classical poetry, he took on the task of translating Homer's *Iliad* and *Odyssey*. It was an enormous amount of work, but the money he made on the project made him financially independent—a luxury most poets of his day did not enjoy.

Good Friends and Cruel Enemies Pope was a member of the exclusive Scriblerus Club, a group of writers affiliated with the Tory political party who dedicated themselves to exposing the pretensions and affectations of literary society through satire. Other members of the club included his good friends John Gay and Jonathan Swift. Although Pope's poetry was widely admired, he was often the object of criticism from less talented writers who attacked his religion, politics, and, most cruelly, his physical appearance.

Pope's satire grew more biting as he aged, and he articulated his views on England's political and literary leaders in many of his later works. Pope died shortly after his 56th birthday and was buried near his parents in Twickenham, the rural town where he had spent the latter half of his life.

POETIC FORM: MOCK EPIC

A **mock epic** uses the lofty style and conventions of epic poetry to satirize a trivial subject. In *The Rape of the Lock,* Pope makes fun of a silly quarrel by narrating it in a grandiose manner. As you read, look for epic characteristics such as formal language, boasting speeches, supernatural intervention in human affairs, and elaborate descriptions of weapons and battles.

TEXT ANALYSIS: HEROIC COUPLET

A **heroic couplet** is a pair of rhymed lines written in **iambic pentameter,** a metrical pattern of five feet (units), each of which consists of two syllables, the first unstressed and the second stressed. Pope was a master of the heroic couplet, employing it for matters both witty and wise, as in the following example:

O thoughtless mortals! ever blind to fate,

Too soon dejected, and too soon elate:

As you read *The Rape of the Lock,* notice how Pope uses surprising rhymes to create humor.

READING SKILL: UNDERSTAND ELEVATED LANGUAGE

Pope often uses difficult words and unusual **syntax**, or word order, to mimic the style of epic poetry and to maintain the meter and rhyme scheme of heroic couplets. The following strategies can help you make sense of his elevated language:

- Use **sidenotes** to understand unfamiliar words and historical allusions in the text.
- Try to **visualize** the action and imagery in the poem.
- **Paraphrase** sentences, restating them in your own words. If sentences have unusual syntax, rearrange the words to form a more familiar sentence structure.

As you read, use a chart like the one shown to record and paraphrase examples of elevated language.

Example	Paraphrase
Hither the heroes and the nymphs resort . . .	The heroes and maidens often go to this place.

 Complete the activities in your **Reader/Writer Notebook.**

What are the signs of VANITY?

All of us are susceptible to occasional bouts of vanity. Some people find it difficult to resist a chance to gaze lovingly at themselves in a mirror or talk at length about their favorite subject—themselves. In *The Rape of the Lock,* Pope holds up a different kind of mirror, one that he hoped would prompt people to take a more critical look at themselves.

SURVEY How can you tell if someone is vain? Complete the following survey to help you distinguish between vanity and self-confidence. Then form a small group with three or four classmates and discuss how everyone answered each question.

1. You spend a lot of time choosing just the right outfit to wear.
   ☐ VAIN   ☐ SELF-CONFIDENT

2. You usually think you have the best solution to a problem.
   ☐ VAIN   ☐ SELF-CONFIDENT

3. You frequently check your appearance in mirrors, windows, etc.
   ☐ VAIN   ☐ SELF-CONFIDENT

4. What you have to say is almost always important.
   ☐ VAIN   ☐ SELF-CONFIDENT

5. People are sometimes envious of you.
   ☐ VAIN   ☐ SELF-CONFIDENT

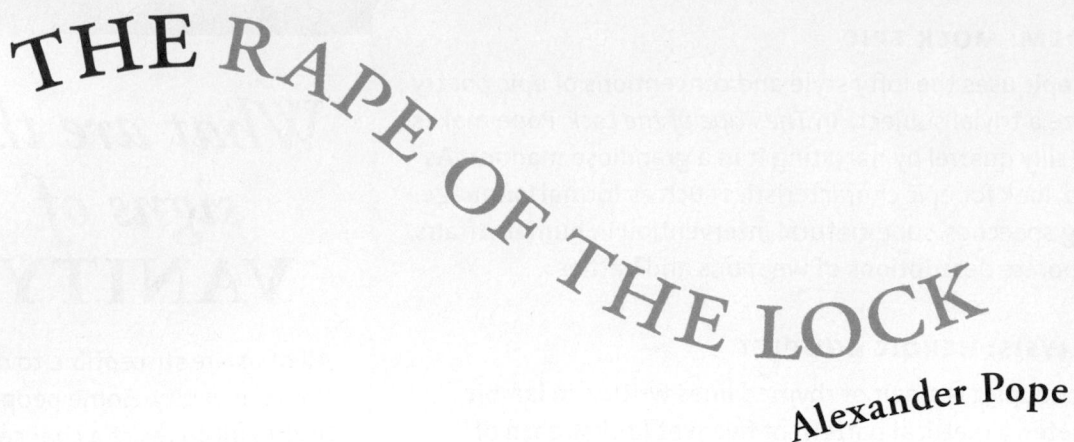

THE RAPE OF THE LOCK

Alexander Pope

> **BACKGROUND** *The Rape of the Lock* was based on a real-life quarrel between two affluent Roman Catholic families, the Fermors and the Petres. The feud began when young Lord Petre (the "Baron" in the poem) snipped a lock of hair from Arabella Fermor ("Belinda"). The dispute escalated out of all proportion, and a friend of Pope's asked him to intervene, hoping that he could "laugh them together again." Pope rose to the occasion, mocking the folly of the dispute by portraying it as if it were a battle of epic scale.

In the first of the poem's five cantos, a Muse is evoked for inspiration (a tradition in epic poetry) and Belinda is warned of impending danger by Ariel, a spirit sent to protect Belinda. In Canto 2, Belinda rides up the Thames River to a Hampton Court party and is noticed by the scheming Baron, who resolves to possess one of the two curly locks spiraling down Belinda's back.

from CANTO 3

Close by those meads, forever crowned with flowers,
Where Thames with pride surveys his rising towers,
There stands a structure of majestic frame,
Which from the neighboring Hampton takes its name.
5 Here Britain's statesmen oft the fall foredoom
Of foreign tyrants and of nymphs at home;
Here thou, great Anna! whom three realms obey,
Dost sometimes counsel take—and sometimes tea. **A**
　　Hither the heroes and the nymphs resort,
10 To taste awhile the pleasures of a court;
In various talk the instructive hours they passed,
Who gave the ball, or paid the visit last;
One speaks the glory of the British Queen,
And one describes a charming Indian screen;

1 meads: meadows.

2 Thames (tĕmz): a river that flows through southern England.

3–4 structure...name: the royal palace of Hampton Court, about 15 miles from London.

6 nymphs (nĭmfs): maidens; young women.

7 Anna...obey: Queen Anne, who rules over the three realms of England, Scotland, and Wales.

A HEROIC COUPLET
In Pope's time, *tea* was pronounced "tay." How does Pope use rhyme in lines 7–8 to mock pomposity?

The Toilet (1896), Aubrey Beardsley. Drawing for Alexander Pope's *The Rape of the Lock*. The Granger Collection.

15 A third interprets motions, looks, and eyes;
   At every word a reputation dies.
   Snuff, or the fan, supply each pause of chat,
   With singing, laughing, ogling, and all that.
          Meanwhile declining from the noon of day,
20 The sun obliquely shoots his burning ray;
   The hungry judges soon the sentence sign,
   And wretches hang that jurymen may dine;
   The merchant from the Exchange returns in peace,
   And the long labors of the toilet cease.
25 Belinda now, whom thirst of fame invites,
   Burns to encounter two adventurous knights,
   At ombre singly to decide their doom,
   And swells her breast with conquests yet to come. . . .
          The Baron now his Diamonds pours apace;
30 The embroidered King who shows but half his face,
   And his refulgent Queen, with powers combined,
   Of broken troops an easy conquest find.
   Clubs, Diamonds, Hearts, in wild disorder seen,
   With throngs promiscuous strew the level green.
35 Thus when dispersed a routed army runs,
   Of Asia's troops, and Afric's sable sons,
   With like confusion different nations fly,
   Of various habit, and of various dye,
   The pierced battalions disunited fall
40 In heaps on heaps; one fate o'erwhelms them all.
          The Knave of Diamonds tries his wily arts,
   And wins (oh, shameful chance!) the Queen of Hearts.
   At this, the blood the virgin's cheek forsook,
   A livid paleness spreads o'er all her look;
45 She sees, and trembles at the approaching ill,
   Just in the jaws of ruin, and Codille.
   And now (as oft in some distempered state)
   On one nice trick depends the general fate.
   An Ace of Hearts steps forth: The King unseen
50 Lurked in her hand, and mourned his captive Queen.
   He springs to vengeance with an eager pace,
   And falls like thunder on the prostrate Ace.
   The nymph exulting fills with shouts the sky,
   The walls, the woods, and long canals reply. **B**
55   O thoughtless mortals! ever blind to fate,
   Too soon dejected, and too soon elate:
   Sudden these honors shall be snatched away,
   And cursed forever this victorious day.
          For lo! the board with cups and spoons is crowned,
60 The berries crackle, and the mill turns round;

17 snuff: powdered tobacco that is inhaled.

24 toilet: the process of dressing, fixing one's hair, and otherwise grooming oneself.

27 ombre (ŏm'bər): a popular card game of the day, similar to bridge.

30 King . . . face: the king of diamonds, the only king shown in profile in a deck of cards.

31 refulgent (rĭ-fŏol'jənt) **Queen:** resplendent or shining queen of diamonds. The Baron is leading his highest diamonds in an effort to win.

34 promiscuous (prə-mĭs'kyŏo-əs): unsorted; **level green:** the green cloth-covered card table.

36 Afric's sable sons: Africa's black soldiers.

41 Knave: jack.

43 the virgin's: Belinda's.

46 Codille (kō-dēl'): a losing hand of cards in ombre.

47 distempered: disordered.

48 nice: delicate; subtle; **trick:** a single round of cards played and won.

B ELEVATED LANGUAGE
Reread lines 53–54, imagining the sounds that Pope describes. Write a **paraphrase** of this couplet.

60 berries: coffee beans.

On shining altars of Japan they raise
The silver lamp; the fiery spirits blaze:
From silver spouts the grateful liquors glide,
While China's earth receives the smoking tide.
65 At once they gratify their scent and taste,
And frequent cups prolong the rich repast.
Straight hover round the fair her airy band;
Some, as she sipped, the fuming liquor fanned,
Some o'er her lap their careful plumes displayed,
70 Trembling, and conscious of the rich brocade.
Coffee (which makes the politician wise,
And see through all things with his half-shut eyes)
Sent up in vapors to the Baron's brain
New stratagems, the radiant Lock to gain.
75 Ah, cease, rash youth! desist ere 'tis too late,
Fear the just Gods, and think of Scylla's fate!
Changed to a bird, and sent to flit in air,
She dearly pays for Nisus' injured hair!
　　　But when to mischief mortals bend their will,
80 How soon they find fit instruments of ill!
Just then, Clarissa drew with tempting grace
A two-edged weapon from her shining case:
So ladies in romance assist their knight,
Present the spear, and arm him for the fight.
85 He takes the gift with reverence, and extends
The little engine on his fingers' ends;
This just behind Belinda's neck he spread,
As o'er the fragrant steams she bends her head.
Swift to the Lock a thousand sprights repair,
90 A thousand wings, by turns, blow back the hair,
And thrice they twitched the diamond in her ear,
Thrice she looked back, and thrice the foe drew near.
Just in that instant, anxious Ariel sought
The close recesses of the virgin's thought;
95 As on the nosegay in her breast reclined,
He watched the ideas rising in her mind,
Sudden he viewed, in spite of all her art,
An earthly lover lurking at her heart.
Amazed, confused, he found his power expired,
100 Resigned to fate, and with a sigh retired.
　　　The Peer now spreads the glittering forfex wide,
To enclose the Lock; now joins it, to divide.
Even then, before the fatal engine closed,
A wretched Sylph too fondly interposed;
105 Fate urged the shears, and cut the Sylph in twain

61 shining altars of Japan: small lacquered tables. In mock-epic style, Pope elevates the tables to altars.

64 China's earth . . . tide: China cups receive the hot coffee.

66 repast (rĭ-păst′): meal.

67 the fair: Belinda; **her airy band:** the Sylphs (sĭlfs), supernatural creatures attending Belinda. Epic heroes and heroines are generally aided by higher powers.

74 new stratagems (străt′ə-jəmz) . . . **gain:** new schemes for acquiring a lock of Belinda's hair.

76–78 Scylla's (sĭl′əz) **fate . . . Nisus'** (nī′səs) **injured hair:** In ancient Greek legend, Scylla was turned into a bird because she betrayed her father, King Nisus, by giving his enemy the purple lock of his hair on which his safety depended.

89 sprights (sprīts): the Sylphs.

93 Ariel (âr′ē-əl): Belinda's special guardian among the Sylphs.

95 nosegay: a small bouquet of flowers.

101 the Peer: the Baron; **forfex:** a fancy term for scissors.

The Rape (1896), Aubrey Beardsley. From *The Rape of the Lock* by Alexander Pope. Line block print. CT46089. Victoria & Albert Museum, London. © Victoria & Albert Museum, London/Art Resource, New York.

(But airy substance soon unites again):
The meeting points the sacred hair dissever
From the fair head, forever and forever!
  Then flashed the living lightning from her eyes,
110 And screams of horror rend the affrighted skies. **C**
Not louder shrieks to pitying heaven are cast,
When husbands, or when lapdogs breathe their last;
Or when rich china vessels fallen from high,
In glittering dust and painted fragments lie!
115 "Let wreaths of triumph now my temples twine,"
The victor cried, "the glorious prize is mine!
While fish in streams, or birds delight in air,
Or in a coach and six the British fair,
As long as *Atalantis* shall be read,
120 Or the small pillow grace a lady's bed,
While visits shall be paid on solemn days,
When numerous wax-lights in bright order blaze,

C HEROIC COUPLET
Reread lines 107–110. Which details in these couplets highlight the contrast between the actual incident that occurs and Belinda's exaggerated reaction?

115 wreaths . . . twine: In epics, victors or champions traditionally wore laurel wreaths as a kind of crown.

118 coach and six: a coach drawn by six horses.

119 *Atalantis*: *The New Atalantis* by Mary Manley, a thinly disguised account of scandal among the rich.

While nymphs take treats, or assignations give,
So long my honor, name, and praise shall live!
125   "What time would spare, from steel receives its date,
And monuments, like men, submit to fate!
Steel could the labor of the Gods destroy,
And strike to dust the imperial towers of Troy;
Steel could the works of mortal pride confound,
130 And hew triumphal arches to the ground.
What wonder then, fair nymph! thy hairs should feel,
The conquering force of unresisted steel?" **D**

In Canto 4, following an epic tradition, a melancholy sprite descends to the Underworld—which Pope calls the "Cave of Spleen"—and returns to the party with a vial of grief and "flowing tears" and a bag of "sobs, sighs, and passions," which are emptied over Belinda's head, fanning her fury even further.

from **CANTO 5**

"To arms, to arms!" the fierce virago cries,
And swift as lightning to the combat flies.
135 All side in parties, and begin the attack;
Fans clap, silks rustle, and tough whalebones crack;
Heroes' and heroines' shouts confusedly rise,
And bass and treble voices strike the skies.
No common weapons in their hands are found,
140 Like Gods they fight, nor dread a mortal wound. . . . **E**
     See, fierce Belinda on the Baron flies,
With more than usual lightning in her eyes;
Nor feared the chief the unequal fight to try,
Who sought no more than on his foe to die.
145   But this bold lord with manly strength endued,
She with one finger and a thumb subdued:
Just where the breath of life his nostrils drew,
A charge of snuff the wily virgin threw;
The Gnomes direct, to every atom just,
150 The pungent grains of titillating dust.
Sudden, with starting tears each eye o'erflows,
And the high dome re-echoes to his nose.
     "Now meet thy fate," incensed Belinda cried,
And drew a deadly bodkin from her side.
155 (The same, his ancient personage to deck,
Her great-great-grandsire wore about his neck,
In three seal rings; which after, melted down,
Formed a vast buckle for his widow's gown:

125 date: end.

127–128 the labor of the Gods . . . towers of Troy: Troy, an ancient city famous for its towers, whose walls were said to have been built by the Greek gods Apollo and Poseidon.

D MOCK EPIC
In lines 125–132, what humorous effect does Pope create by using lofty language and allusions to Greek mythology?

133 virago (və-rä′gō): a woman who engages in warfare or other fighting. She has come to Belinda's aid at Ariel's request.

136 whalebones: elastic material from whales' mouths, used in corsets or support undergarments.

E MOCK EPIC
What characteristics of a mock epic do you find in lines 133–140?

145 endued (ĕn-dōōd′): endowed; provided with.

149 Gnomes (nōmz): supernatural creatures bent on causing mischief.

152 And the high . . . nose: In other words, he sneezes.

154 bodkin (bŏd′kĭn): a long, ornamental hairpin.

157 seal rings: signet rings bearing a person's family crest or initials.

Her infant grandame's whistle next it grew,
160 The bells she jingled, and the whistle blew;
Then in a bodkin graced her mother's hairs,
Which long she wore, and now Belinda wears.)
    "Boast not my fall," he cried, "insulting foe!
Thou by some other shalt be laid as low.
165 Nor think to die dejects my lofty mind:
All that I dread is leaving you behind!
Rather than so, ah, let me still survive,
And burn in Cupid's flames—but burn alive."
    "Restore the Lock!" she cries; and all around
170 "Restore the Lock!" the vaulted roofs rebound.
Not fierce Othello in so loud a strain
Roared for the handkerchief that caused his pain.
But see how oft ambitious aims are crossed,
And chiefs contend till all the prize is lost!
175 The lock, obtained with guilt, and kept with pain,
In every place is sought, but sought in vain:
With such a prize no mortal must be blessed,
So Heaven decrees! with Heaven who can contest?
    Some thought it mounted to the lunar sphere,
180 Since all things lost on earth are treasured there.
There heroes' wits are kept in ponderous vases,
And beaux' in snuffboxes and tweezer cases.
There broken vows and death-bed alms are found,
And lovers' hearts with ends of riband bound. . . .
185   But trust the Muse—she saw it upward rise,
Though marked by none but quick, poetic eyes. . . .
A sudden star, it shot through liquid air,
And drew behind a radiant trail of hair. . . .
    Then cease, bright nymph! to mourn thy ravished hair,
190 Which adds new glory to the shining sphere!
Not all the tresses that fair head can boast
Shall draw such envy as the Lock you lost.
For, after all the murders of your eye,
When, after millions slain, yourself shall die:
195 When those fair suns shall set, as set they must,
And all those tresses shall be laid in dust,
This Lock the Muse shall consecrate to fame,
And 'midst the stars inscribe Belinda's name. **F**

159 Her infant grandame's (grăn′dāmz) . . . **grew:** It was next melted down and turned into a whistle used by Belinda's grandmother as a child. Pope is here making fun of family heirlooms.

168 burn in Cupid's flames: burn with passion.

170 rebound: echo.

171–172 Othello . . . pain: In Shakespeare's *Othello,* the deeply jealous Othello demands the handkerchief that he believes is a sign of his wife's infidelity.

179 mounted to the lunar sphere: climbed up to the moon.

182 beaux' (bōz): the wits of fops.

184 riband (rĭb′ənd): ribbon.

185 Muse (myōōz): the goddess who inspires the writing of the poem. In typical epic fashion, the narrator opens the poem by addressing his Muse and continues to address her throughout the poem.

188 trail of hair: The word *comet* comes from a Greek word that means "long haired."

193 murders of your eye: men struck down by your glance.

F ELEVATED LANGUAGE
Reread lines 193–198 and the accompanying side note. **Paraphrase** what the narrator says to comfort Belinda about the loss of her lock.

Comprehension

1. **Summarize** What happens in the card game in lines 29–54?

2. **Recall** How does the Baron obtain the lock of Belinda's hair?

3. **Clarify** At the end of the poem, what happens to the lock of Belinda's hair?

Text Analysis

4. **Identify Irony** A contrast between expectations and actual outcomes is referred to as **situational irony.** Where is the irony in *The Rape of the Lock?*

5. **Interpret Satire** In addition to satirizing a quarrel, Pope used *The Rape of the Lock* to point out flaws in British society and upper-class behavior. For each of the following passages, describe the flaw that Pope is criticizing:

   • lines 15–16 ("A third interprets . . . dies.")

   • lines 21–22 ("The hungry judges . . . dine;")

   • lines 111–114 ("Not louder shrieks . . . lie!")

● 6. **Examine Heroic Couplet** One of the drawbacks of heroic couplets is that they can begin to sound monotonous in a long poem. Reread lines 167–168. How does Pope vary the rhythm in this couplet? What does the variation in the rhythm suggest about the Baron?

● 7. **Analyze Mock Epic** *The Rape of the Lock* parodies the epic form by treating a trivial subject in a grand, lofty style. Citing specific examples from the text, describe how Pope makes fun of these elements of traditional epic poetry:

   • elaborate descriptions of weapons and battles

   • plot affected by supernatural intervention

   • boasting speeches

● 8. **Draw Conclusions About Elevated Language** Review the chart you filled in as you read, comparing your paraphrases with the original lines. In what ways does Pope's use of elevated language enhance the poem?

Text Criticism

9. **Different Perspectives** Pope's friend Jonathan Swift once wrote, "Satire is a sort of glass, wherein beholders do generally discover everybody's face but their own." While the mock epic *The Rape of the Lock* was written nearly 300 years ago to poke fun at vanity, beauty, and pride, in what ways does the satire reflect today's society?

> *What are the signs of* **VANITY?**
>
> Judging from the excerpts you read from *The Rape of the Lock,* how do think Pope felt about vanity? Do you share his opinion?

COMMON CORE

RL 5 Analyze how an author's choices concerning how to structure specific parts of a text contribute to its aesthetic impact. **RL 6** Analyze a case in which grasping a point of view requires distinguishing what is directly stated in a text from what is really meant. **L 3a** Apply an understanding of syntax to the study of complex texts when reading.

A Modest Proposal
Essay by Jonathan Swift

VIDEO TRAILER THINKcentral KEYWORD: HML12-620A

COMMON CORE

RI 5 Analyze and evaluate the effectiveness of the structure an author uses in his or her argument. **RI 6** Determine an author's point of view or purpose in a text in which the rhetoric is particularly effective. **SL 1** Initiate and participate effectively in a range of collaborative discussions.

Meet the Author

Jonathan Swift 1667–1745

Jonathan Swift has been called the greatest satirist in the English language. His genuine outrage at man's inhumanity to man and his commitment to championing liberty found voice in his biting satire and unflinching criticism of his times. Few writers of the 18th century were as politically and socially influential as Swift.

A Priest with a Pen Jonathan Swift was born of Anglo-Irish parents in Dublin, Ireland. Though his family was not wealthy, Swift attended the prestigious Trinity College. After graduating, he moved to Surrey in England to accept a position as secretary to a retired diplomat. In 1695, Swift was ordained as an Anglican priest and became a full-fledged satirist, with two completed works ready for publication.

Swift was a clergyman and a political writer for the Whig party. His first two satires, *The Battle of the Books* and *A Tale of a Tub*, quickly established his acerbic style. Whether lampooning modern thinkers and scientists (John Locke and Sir Isaac Newton among them), religious abuses, or humanity at large, Swift raged at the arrogance, phoniness, and shallowness he saw infecting contemporary intellectual and moral life. Though his early publications were anonymous, people began to recognize his vicious and witty political writing through his contributions to London periodicals such as Richard Steele's and Joseph Addison's *The Spectator*.

When the Whigs lost power to the Tories in 1710, the Tories courted the conservative Swift to join their side. As a man of principle and a strict moralist, however, he ultimately became disenchanted with the compromises and manipulations of politics.

Irish Patriot In 1713, Swift was appointed dean of St. Patrick's Cathedral in Dublin. Though Swift at first felt exiled in Ireland, in time he regained his interest in politics. Angered by the way England tyrannized Ireland, Swift fought back in a series of publications called *The Drapier's Letters*, in which he wrote, "Am I a freeman in England, and do I become a slave in six hours by crossing the channel?" For Irish Catholics and Protestants alike, Swift became a hero. His last major work about Ireland, "A Modest Proposal," is one of the most famous satires ever written.

Gulliver's Success In 1726, Swift anonymously published the masterly satire *Gulliver's Travels*, in which he vents his fury at political corruption and his annoyance with the general worthlessness of human beings. Though Swift aroused controversy, *Gulliver's Travels* turned out to be surprisingly popular, and it remains a classic for readers of all ages.

DID YOU KNOW?

Jonathan Swift . . .

- had learned to read by the time he was three.
- coined the term *yahoo* to refer to a boorish and ignorant person.
- left much of his fortune to go toward the building of a mental hospital.

(background) St. Patrick's Cathedral, Dublin

Author Online

Go to **thinkcentral.com**. KEYWORD: HML12-620B

THINKcentral

While Alexander Pope is generally sympathetic to his satirical targets, Swift's work is darker and more biting. **Satire** is a literary technique in which people's behaviors or society's institutions are ridiculed for the purpose of bringing about social reform. Swift used satire to comment on specific political and cultural concerns that angered and offended him.

One of the satirist's most reliable tools is **verbal irony,** in which what is said is the opposite of what is meant. As you read "A Modest Proposal," notice how Swift uses verbal irony and **sarcasm,** the use of a mocking, ironic tone, to present his seemingly rational proposal.

● **READING SKILL: IDENTIFY PROPOSITION AND SUPPORT**

Although "A Modest Proposal" is a satire, it is written like a serious problem-solution essay. Specifically, it

- clearly identifies a **problem** and its causes
- proposes a **solution** to the problem—Swift's **proposition**—and explains how to implement it
- provides **support** for the proposed solution in the form of reasons and evidence
- notes **other possible solutions** and argues against them

As you read the essay, use a chart like the one shown to record Swift's proposition and the evidence he gives to support it.

Proposition:

Support:
- *"These children can help feed and clothe thousands."*
-

▲ **VOCABULARY IN CONTEXT**

Determine the meaning of each boldfaced word in context.

1. food needed for **sustenance**
2. a beginner just learning the **rudiments**
3. a **collateral** benefit in addition to the main one
4. politely show **deference** to others' views
5. an **expedient** that will make life easier
6. an **encumbrance** that will make life harder
7. **famine** caused by massive crop failures
8. **propagation** of the human race to increase population

Complete the activities in your **Reader/Writer Notebook**.

How can we fight INJUSTICE?

There's an old proverb that states, "The pen is mightier than the sword." Jonathan Swift wielded his pen like a rapier, using it to slash away at injustice. Though some may claim the power of the pen is greatly diminished these days, people still fight injustice with words—in speeches, in newspapers and magazines, and on the Internet.

DISCUSS With a small group, brainstorm a list of methods people use to fight injustice. Then think of a contemporary example of injustice. It may be a local, a national, or a global issue. With your group, discuss which method or methods would be most effective in publicizing, and possibly leading to a solution to, the problem.

A Modest Proposal

FOR PREVENTING THE CHILDREN OF POOR PEOPLE IN IRELAND FROM BEING A BURDEN TO THEIR PARENTS OR COUNTRY, AND FOR MAKING THEM BENEFICIAL TO THE PUBLIC

Jonathan Swift

BACKGROUND By 1700, Ireland was so completely dominated by England that it seemed like a conquered territory. The Catholic majority could not vote, hold public office, buy land, or receive an education. The repressive policies reduced many Irish people to poverty. When crops failed—as they did for several years during the 1720s—many faced starvation. Jonathan Swift, outraged by the injustice of England's treatment of Ireland, penned "A Modest Proposal," using ferocious satire to strike back at those who neglected Ireland's poor.

It is a melancholy object to those who walk through this great town[1] or travel in the country, when they see the streets, the roads, and cabin doors, crowded with beggars of the female sex, followed by three, four, or six children, all in rags and importuning every passenger for an alms.[2] These mothers, instead of being able to work for their honest livelihood, are forced to employ all their time in strolling to beg **sustenance** for their helpless infants, who, as they grow up, either turn thieves for want[3] of work, or leave their dear native country to fight for the Pretender[4] in Spain, or sell themselves to the Barbadoes.[5]

I think it is agreed by all parties that this prodigious number of children in
10 the arms, or on the backs, or at the heels of their mothers, and frequently of their fathers, is in the present deplorable state of the kingdom a very great additional grievance; and therefore whoever could find out a fair, cheap, and easy method of making these children sound, useful members of the commonwealth would deserve so well of the public as to have his statue set up for a preserver of the nation. **A**

Analyze Visuals ▶
What impression does the engraving convey about the lives of poor people in the 18th century? Cite details to support your answer.

sustenance (sŭs′tə-nəns) *n.* a means of support or nourishment

A PROPOSITION AND SUPPORT
What problem does Swift identify in lines 1–15?

---

1. **this great town:** Dublin, Ireland.
2. **importuning** (ĭm′pôr-tōōn′ĭng) . . . **alms** (ämz): begging from every passerby for a charitable handout.
3. **want:** lack; need.
4. **Pretender:** James Edward Stuart, who claimed the English throne, from which his now deceased father, James II, had been removed in 1688. Because James II and his son were Roman Catholic, the common people of Ireland were loyal to them.
5. **sell . . . Barbadoes:** To escape poverty, some Irish migrated to the West Indies, obtaining money for their passage by agreeing to work as slaves on plantations there for a set period.

Detail of *Gin Lane* (1700s), William Hogarth. Engraving. © Art Resource, New York.

But my intention is very far from being confined to provide only for the children of professed beggars; it is of a much greater extent, and shall take in the whole number of infants at a certain age who are born of parents in effect as little able to support them as those who demand our charity in the streets.

20   As to my own part, having turned my thoughts for many years upon this important subject, and maturely weighed the several schemes of other projectors,[6] I have always found them grossly mistaken in their computation. It is true, a child just dropped from its dam[7] may be supported by her milk for a solar year, with little other nourishment; at most not above the value of two shillings, which the mother may certainly get, or the value in scraps, by her lawful occupation of begging; and it is exactly at one year old that I propose to provide for them in such a manner as instead of being a charge upon their parents or the parish, or wanting food and raiment for the rest of their lives, they shall on the contrary contribute to the feeding, and partly to the clothing, of many thousands.

30   There is likewise another great advantage in my scheme, that it will prevent those voluntary abortions, and that horrid practice of women murdering their bastard children, alas, too frequent among us, sacrificing the poor innocent babes, I doubt,[8] more to avoid the expense than the shame, which would move tears and pity in the most savage and inhuman breast.

The number of souls in this kingdom being usually reckoned one million and a half, of these I calculate there may be about two hundred thousand couple whose wives are breeders; from which number I subtract thirty thousand couples who are able to maintain their own children, although I apprehend there cannot be so many under the present distresses of the kingdom; but this being granted, there will
40 remain an hundred and seventy thousand breeders. I again subtract fifty thousand for those women who miscarry, or whose children die by accident or disease within the year. There only remain an hundred and twenty thousand children of poor parents annually born. The question therefore is, how this number shall be reared and provided for, which, as I have already said, under the present situation of affairs, is utterly impossible by all the methods hitherto proposed. For we can neither employ them in handicraft or agriculture; we neither build houses (I mean in the country) nor cultivate land. They can very seldom pick up a livelihood by stealing till they arrive at six years old, except where they are of towardly parts;[9] although I confess they learn the **rudiments** much earlier, during which time
50 they can however be looked upon only as probationers, as I have been informed by a principal gentleman in the county of Cavan, who protested to me that he never knew above one or two instances under the age of six, even in a part of the kingdom so renowned for the quickest proficiency in that art. **B**

I am assured by our merchants that a boy or girl before twelve years old is no salable commodity; and even when they come to this age they will not yield above three pounds, or three pounds and half a crown at most on the Exchange; which

Language Coach

Synonyms Words with the same or almost the same meaning are **synonyms**. Which word in line 36 is a synonym for *reckon* (present tense of *reckoned*, line 35)?

rudiment (rōō′də-mənt) *n.* a basic principle or element

B SATIRE
Reread lines 43–53. What social problem does Swift blame for the widespread thievery in Ireland?

cannot turn to account[10] either to the parents or the kingdom, the charge of nutriment and rags having been at least four times that value.

I shall now therefore humbly propose my own thoughts, which I hope will not
60 be liable to the least objection.

I have been assured by a very knowing American of my acquaintance in London, that a young healthy child well nursed is at a year old a most delicious, nourishing, and wholesome food, whether stewed, roasted, baked, or boiled; and I make no doubt that it will equally serve in a fricassee or a ragout.[11]

I do therefore humbly offer it to public consideration that of the hundred and twenty thousand children, already computed, twenty thousand may be reserved for breed,[12] whereof only one fourth part to be males, which is more than we allow to sheep, black cattle, or swine; and my reason is that these children are seldom the fruits of marriage, a circumstance not much regarded by our savages, therefore
70 one male will be sufficient to serve four females. That the remaining hundred thousand may at a year old be offered in sale to the persons of quality and fortune through the kingdom, always advising the mother to let them suck plentifully in the last month, so as to render them plump and fat for a good table. A child will make two dishes at an entertainment for friends; and when the family dines alone, the fore or hind quarter will make a reasonable dish, and seasoned with a little pepper or salt will be very good boiled on the fourth day, especially in winter. **C**

I have reckoned upon a medium that a child just born will weigh twelve pounds, and in a solar year if tolerably nursed increaseth to twenty-eight pounds.

I grant this food will be somewhat dear, and therefore very proper for landlords,
80 who, as they have already devoured most of the parents, seem to have the best title to the children.

Infant's flesh will be in season throughout the year, but more plentiful in March, and a little before and after. For we are told by a grave author, an eminent French physician,[13] that fish being a prolific[14] diet, there are more children born in Roman Catholic countries about nine months after Lent[15] than at any other season; therefore, reckoning a year after Lent, the markets will be more glutted than usual, because the number of popish infants is at least three to one in this kingdom; and therefore it will have one other **collateral** advantage, by lessening the number of Papists[16] among us.
90 I have already computed the charge of nursing a beggar's child (in which list I reckon all cottagers, laborers, and four fifths of the farmers), to be about two shillings per annum, rags included; and I believe no gentleman would repine to give ten shillings for the carcass of a good fat child, which, as I have said, will

C PROPOSITION
AND SUPPORT
Reread lines 65–76. What is Swift's proposal?

collateral (kə-lăt′ər-əl) *adj.* accompanying as a parallel or subordinate factor; related

---

10. **turn to account:** earn a profit; benefit; prove useful.

11. **fricassee** (frĭk′ə-sē′) **...ragout** (ră-gōō′): types of meat stews.

12. **reserved for breed:** kept for breeding (instead of being slaughtered).

13. **grave ...physician:** François Rabelais (răb′ə-lā′), a 16th-century French satirist.

14. **prolific:** promoting fertility.

15. **Lent:** Catholics traditionally do not eat meat during Lent, the 40 days leading up to Easter, and instead eat a lot of fish.

16. **popish** (pō′pĭsh) **...Papists:** hostile or contemptuous terms referring to Roman Catholics.

make four dishes of excellent nutritive meat, when he hath only some particular friend or his own family to dine with him. Thus the squire will learn to be a good landlord, and grow popular among the tenants; the mother will have eight shillings net profit, and be fit for work till she produces another child.

Those who are more thrifty (as I must confess the times require) may flay the carcass; the skin of which artificially dressed will make admirable gloves for ladies, and summer boots for fine gentlemen. **D**

As to our city of Dublin, shambles[17] may be appointed for this purpose in the most convenient parts of it, and butchers we may be assured will not be wanting; although I rather recommend buying the children alive, and dressing them hot from the knife as we do roasting pigs.

A very worthy person, a true lover of his country, and whose virtues I highly esteem, was lately pleased in discoursing on this matter to offer a refinement upon my scheme. He said that many gentlemen of this kingdom, having of late destroyed their deer, he conceived that the want of venison might be well supplied by the bodies of young lads and maidens, not exceeding fourteen years of age nor under twelve, so great a number of both sexes in every county being now ready to starve for want of work and service; and these to be disposed of by their parents, if alive, or otherwise by their nearest relations. But with due **deference** to so excellent a friend and so deserving a patriot, I cannot be altogether in his sentiments; for as to the males, my American acquaintance assured me from

D SATIRE
Understatement is an ironic device that creates emphasis by saying less than is expected or appropriate. In what way are lines 98–100 an example of understatement?

deference (dĕf′ər-əns) *n.* a yielding or courteous regard toward the opinion, judgment, or wishes of others; respect

---

17. **shambles:** slaughterhouses.

The Idle 'Prentice Executed at Tyburn, William Hogarth. Plate XI of *Industry and Idleness,* 1833. Engraving. © Guildhall Library, City of London/Bridgeman Art Library.

frequent experience that their flesh was generally tough and lean, like that of our schoolboys, by continual exercise, and their taste disagreeable; and to fatten them would not answer the charge. Then as to the females, it would, I think with humble submission, be a loss to the public, because they soon would become breeders themselves; and besides, it is not improbable that some scrupulous people
120 might be apt to censure such a practice (although indeed very unjustly) as a little bordering upon cruelty; which, I confess, hath always been with me the strongest objection against any project, how well soever intended. **E**

But in order to justify my friend, he confessed that this **<u>expedient</u>** was put into his head by the famous Psalmanazar, a native of the island Formosa,[18] who came from thence to London above twenty years ago, and in conversation told my friend that in his country when any young person happened to be put to death, the executioner sold the carcass to persons of quality as a prime dainty; and that in his time the body of a plump girl of fifteen, who was crucified for an attempt to poison the emperor, was sold to his Imperial Majesty's prime minister of state,
130 and other great mandarins of the court, in joints from the gibbet,[19] at four hundred crowns. Neither indeed can I deny that if the same use were made of several plump young girls in this town, who without one single groat[20] to their fortunes cannot

E SATIRE
What is **ironic** about Swift's concern in lines 117–122 regarding what "some scrupulous people" might think?

expedient (ĭk-spē'dē-ənt) *n.* something useful in achieving the desired effect; a convenience; an advantage

---

18. **Psalmanazar** (săl'mə-năz'ər) **. . . Formosa** (fôr-mō'sə): a French imposter in London who called himself George Psalmanazar and pretended to be from Formosa (now Taiwan), where, he said, cannibalism was practiced.

19. **gibbet** (jĭb'ĭt): gallows.

20. **groat:** an old British coin worth four pennies.

stir abroad without a chair,[21] and appear at the playhouse and assemblies in foreign fineries which they never will pay for, the kingdom would not be the worse.

Some persons of a desponding spirit are in great concern about that vast number of poor people who are aged, diseased, or maimed, and I have been desired to employ my thoughts what course may be taken to ease the nation of so grievous an **encumbrance.** But I am not in the least pain upon that matter, because it is very well known that they are every day dying and rotting by cold and **famine,**
140 and filth and vermin, as fast as can be reasonably expected. And as to the younger laborers, they are now in almost as hopeful a condition. They cannot get work, and consequently pine away for want of nourishment to a degree that if at any time they are accidentally hired to common labor, they have not strength to perform it; and thus the country and themselves are happily delivered from the evils to come.

I have too long digressed, and therefore shall return to my subject. I think the advantages by the proposal which I have made are obvious and many, as well as of the highest importance.

For first, as I have already observed, it would greatly lessen the number of
150 Papists, with whom we are yearly overrun, being the principal breeders of the nation as well as our most dangerous enemies; and who stay at home on purpose to deliver the kingdom to the Pretender, hoping to take their advantage by the absence of so many good Protestants, who have chosen rather to leave their country than stay at home and pay tithes against their conscience to an Episcopal curate.[22]

Secondly, the poorer tenants will have something valuable of their own, which by law may be made liable to distress,[23] and help to pay their landlord's rent, their corn and cattle being already seized and money a thing unknown.

Thirdly, whereas the maintenance of an hundred thousand children, from two
160 years old and upwards, cannot be computed at less than ten shillings a piece per annum, the nation's stock will be thereby increased fifty thousand pounds per annum, besides the profit of a new dish introduced to the tables of all gentlemen of fortune in the kingdom who have any refinement in taste. And the money will circulate among ourselves, the goods being entirely of our own growth and manufacture. **F**

Fourthly, the constant breeders, besides the gain of eight shillings sterling per annum by the sale of their children, will be rid of the charge of maintaining them after the first year.

Fifthly, this food would likewise bring great custom to taverns, where the
170 vintners will certainly be so prudent as to procure the best receipts[24] for dressing it to perfection, and consequently have their houses frequented by all the fine gentlemen, who justly value themselves upon their knowledge in good eating; and

---

encumbrance
(ĕn-kŭm′brəns) *n.*
a burden

famine (făm′ĭn) *n.* a period in which there is a severe shortage of food

F **PROPOSITION AND SUPPORT**
Why does Swift supply these cost and profit calculations?

---

21. **cannot stir . . . chair:** cannot go outside without using an enclosed chair carried on poles by two men.

22. **Protestants . . . curate** (kyŏŏr′ĭt): Swift is criticizing absentee Anglo-Irish landowners who lived—and spent their income from their property—in England.

23. **distress:** seizure of a person's property for the payment of debts.

24. **receipts:** recipes.

a skillful cook, who understands how to oblige his guests, will contrive to make it as expensive as they please.

Sixthly, this would be a great inducement to marriage, which all wise nations have either encouraged by rewards or enforced by laws and penalties. It would increase the care and tenderness of mothers toward their children, when they were sure of a settlement for life to the poor babes, provided in some sort by the public, to their annual profit instead of expense. We should see an honest emulation among the married women, which of them could bring the fattest child to the market. Men would become as fond of their wives during the time of their pregnancy as they are now of their mares in foal, their cows in calf, or sows when they are ready to farrow; nor offer to beat or kick them (as is too frequent a practice) for fear of a miscarriage. **G**

Many other advantages might be enumerated. For instance, the addition of some thousand carcasses in our exportation of barreled beef, the **propagation** of swine's flesh, and improvement in the art of making good bacon, so much wanted among us by the great destruction of pigs, too frequent at our tables, which are no way comparable in taste or magnificence to a well-grown, fat, yearling child, which roasted whole will make a considerable figure at a lord mayor's feast or any other public entertainment. But this and many others I omit, being studious of brevity. **H**

Supposing that one thousand families in this city would be constant customers for infants' flesh, besides others who might have it at merry meetings, particularly weddings and christenings, I compute that Dublin would take off annually about twenty thousand carcasses, and the rest of the kingdom (where probably they will be sold somewhat cheaper) the remaining eighty thousand.

I can think of no one objection that will possibly be raised against this proposal, unless it should be urged that the number of people will be thereby much lessened in the kingdom. This I freely own, and it was indeed one principal design in offering it to the world. I desire the reader will observe, that I calculate my remedy for this one individual kingdom of Ireland and for no other that ever was, is, or I think ever can be upon earth. Therefore let no man talk to me of other expedients: of taxing our absentees at five shillings a pound: of using neither clothes nor household furniture except what is of our own growth and manufacture: of utterly rejecting the materials and instruments that promote foreign luxury: of curing the expensiveness of pride, vanity, idleness, and gaming in our women: of introducing a vein of parsimony,[25] prudence, and temperance: of learning to love our country, in the want of which we differ even from Laplanders and the inhabitants of Topinamboo:[26] of quitting our animosities and factions, nor acting any longer like the Jews, who were murdering one another at the very moment their city was taken:[27] of being a little cautious not to sell our country and conscience for nothing: of teaching landlords to have at least one degree of

---

G **PROPOSITION AND SUPPORT**
According to Swift in lines 175–184, how would his proposal improve family life?

propagation
(prŏp′ə-gā′shən) *n.* the act of reproducing, multiplying, or increasing

H **GRAMMAR AND STYLE**
Reread lines 185–191. Notice that Swift uses **nouns** such as *carcasses* and *flesh* to emphasize the dehumanization of the Irish by the English.

---

25. **parsimony** (pär′sə-mō′nē): frugality; thrift.

26. **Topinamboo** (tŏp′ĭ-năm′bōō): an area in Brazil supposedly inhabited by wild savages.

27. **Jews ... taken:** In A.D. 70, during a Jewish revolt against Roman rule, the inhabitants of Jerusalem, by fighting among themselves, made it easier for the Romans to capture the city.

Detail of *Gin Lane* (1700s), William Hogarth. Engraving. © Art Resource, New York.

mercy toward their tenants: lastly, of putting a spirit of honesty, industry, and skill into our shopkeepers; who, if a resolution could now be taken to buy only our native goods, would immediately unite to cheat and exact upon us in the price, the measure, and the goodness, nor could ever yet be brought to make one fair proposal of just dealing, though often and earnestly invited to it. ◗

Therefore I repeat, let no man talk to me of these and the like expedients,[28]
220 till he hath at least some glimpse of hope that there will ever be some hearty and sincere attempt to put them in practice.

But as to myself, having been wearied out for many years with offering vain, idle, visionary thoughts, and at length utterly despairing of success, I fortunately fell upon this proposal, which, as it is wholly new, so it hath something solid and real, of no expense and little trouble, full in our own power, and whereby

◗ **PROPOSITION AND SUPPORT**
Reread lines 198–203. What attitude toward the Irish does Swift reveal in refuting this **opposing view?**

28. **let no man ... expedients:** In his writings, Swift had suggested "other expedients" without success.

we can incur no danger in disobliging England. For this kind of commodity will not bear exportation, the flesh being of too tender a consistence to admit a long continuance in salt, although perhaps I could name a country which would be glad to eat up our whole nation without it.

230   After all, I am not so violently bent upon my own opinion as to reject any offer proposed by wise men, which shall be found equally innocent, cheap, easy, and effectual. But before something of that kind shall be advanced in contradiction to my scheme, and offering a better, I desire the author or authors will be pleased maturely to consider two points. First, as things now stand, how they will be able to find food and raiment for an hundred thousand useless mouths and backs. And secondly, there being a round million of creatures in human figure throughout this kingdom, whose sole subsistence put into a common stock[29] would leave them in debt two millions of pounds sterling, adding those who are beggars by profession to the bulk of farmers, cottagers, and laborers, with their wives
240 and children who are beggars in effect; I desire those politicians who dislike my overture, and may perhaps be so bold to attempt an answer, that they will first ask the parents of these mortals whether they would not at this day think it a great happiness to have been sold for food at a year old in the manner I prescribe, and thereby have avoided such a perpetual scene of misfortunes as they have since gone through by the oppression of landlords, the impossibility of paying rent without money or trade, the want of common sustenance, with neither house nor clothes to cover them from the inclemencies of the weather, and the most inevitable prospect of entailing the like or greater miseries upon their breed forever. **J**

    I profess, in the sincerity of my heart, that I have not the least personal interest
250 in endeavoring to promote this necessary work, having no other motive than the public good of my country, by advancing our trade, providing for infants, relieving the poor, and giving some pleasure to the rich. I have no children by which I can propose to get a single penny; the youngest being nine years old, and my wife past childbearing. ❧

Language Coach

Synonyms *Effectual* is a synonym of *effective* and *efficient*. All three mean "having an effect." *Effectual* applies to things and refers to hypothetical situations. *Effective* applies to actual results. *Efficient* implies minimum cost and effort. Could Swift's proposal be called *effective* or *efficient*?

J SATIRE

Swift employs biting **sarcasm**, or a mocking and ironic tone, in the final defense of his proposal. Sarcasm is a common feature in **Juvenalian satire** (page 609), which is noted for its harsh and unforgiving tone, and "A Modest Proposal" is a classic of this type of satire. What words sarcastically mock Swift's supposed critics? What do you think is Swift's real opinion of his critics?

---

29. **common stock:** ordinary stock in a company or business venture.

Comprehension

1. **Recall** What is Swift's proposal for easing poverty in Ireland?

2. **Recall** How will the proposal benefit Irish parents?

3. **Clarify** Reread lines 222–229. Why does Swift feel that his proposal is superior to others that have been put forward?

Text Analysis

4. **Examine Verbal Irony** What verbal irony does Swift use in each of the following parts of "A Modest Proposal"?

   - the title of the essay
   - lines 59–60 ("I shall now . . . least objection.")
   - lines 135–145 ("Some persons . . . evils to come.")

5. **Interpret Satire** Instead of directly attacking injustice and flawed behavior, Swift uses irony to convey his ideas indirectly. What conclusions would you draw about his attitude toward each of the following?

   - Irish landlords (lines 79–81)
   - the way most English and Irish Protestants view Irish Catholics (lines 82–89)
   - Irish Protestants living abroad (lines 149–155)

6. **Evaluate Proposition and Support** Review the chart you created as you read. Regardless of your emotional response to the essay, do you consider the proposal to be well supported? Explain why or why not.

7. **Compare Texts** Recall that on page 609, you learned the difference between **Horatian** and **Juvenalian satire.** Compare the tone of *The Rape of the Lock* with the tone of "A Modest Proposal." Why is Pope's poem considered Horatian and Swift's essay considered Juvenalian? Support your answer with examples from the texts.

Text Criticism

8. **Historical Context** The 18th century is often called the Age of Reason because advances in science and technology fueled belief that governments could apply rational thought to solve many social problems. Swift, a traditionalist, was often skeptical of new ideas. In what ways does "A Modest Proposal" reflect this attitude?

How can we fight **INJUSTICE?**

Based on "A Modest Proposal," Swift's satirical response to the problem of poverty in Ireland, do you think satire is an effective means of fighting injustice? Why or why not?

COMMON CORE

RI 5 Analyze and evaluate the effectiveness of the structure an author uses in his or her argument. **RI 6** Determine an author's point of view or purpose in a text in which the rhetoric is particularly effective.

Vocabulary in Context

▲ VOCABULARY PRACTICE

Indicate whether the words in each pair are synonyms or antonyms.

1. propagation/reduction
2. collateral/accompanying
3. famine/feast
4. deference/contempt

5. encumbrance/advantage
6. expedient/convenience
7. rudiment/foundation
8. sustenance/nourishment

WORD LIST

collateral
deference
encumbrance
expedient
famine
propagation
rudiment
sustenance

ACADEMIC VOCABULARY IN WRITING

> • affect • challenge • consent • final • respond

How might a food shortage **affect** our society today? How would we **respond** to such a disaster, and what kinds of cracks or divisions might it reveal in society? In your response, use at least two additional Academic Vocabulary words.

VOCABULARY STRATEGY: LANGUAGE REFERENCES

In addition to general dictionaries and thesauri, language references include the following types of books:

COMMON CORE

L 1b Resolve issues of complex or contested usage, consulting references. **L 6** Acquire and use accurately general academic words.

Type of Language Reference	Uses	Example
Usage dictionary	To understand the subtle differences in how similar words are used in actual language	Fowler's Dictionary of Modern English Usage
History of Language	To find detailed information about a word's origin	Concise Oxford Dictionary of English Etymology
	To learn about a word named after a person	New Dictionary of Eponyms
Other specialized dictionaries	To find the meaning of common English expressions	Oxford Dictionaries of Idioms
	To find a rhyme for a word	Oxford Dictionaries of Rhymes
	To understand the meaning of a foreign word or phrase in an English text	Oxford Essential Dictionary of Foreign Terms in English
Book of Quotations	To find a famous quotation that contains a certain word or is associated with a certain person	Bartlett's Familiar Quotations

PRACTICE Answer each question below based on the information in the chart above.

1. Where would you turn to find out how *bloomers* get their name?
2. Where could you find a word that rhymes with *aardvark*?
3. Where could you find out the difference between *regretful* and *regrettable*?

Interactive Vocabulary THINK central

Go to **thinkcentral.com**.
KEYWORD: HML12-633

Language

◆ **GRAMMAR AND STYLE: Choose Effective Words**

Review the **Grammar and Style** note on page 629. Swift underscores the shocking nature of his proposal by using disparaging **nouns** to describe the poor of Ireland, as shown in the passages below.

> *I am assured by our merchants that a boy or girl before twelve years old is no salable commodity;* (lines 54–55)

> *...these children are seldom the fruits of marriage, a circumstance not much regarded by our savages...* (lines 68–69)

Notice how Swift's carefully chosen nouns satirize the dismissive attitude that the wealthy Protestants had toward the Catholic poor, heightening the essay's effectiveness.

PRACTICE Copy the sentences below. Then rewrite them using nouns that will give the sentences a more satirical edge. An example sentence is provided.

> **EXAMPLE**
>
> Nine out of ten landlords overeat, and some weigh as much as 300 pounds.
>
> *Nine out of ten landlords are gluttons, and some weigh as much as a full-grown sow.*

1. Cars that use an excessive amount of gas make our oil-dependence problem worse.

2. Those who want to preserve the rain forests can be alarmists at times.

3. Companies that dump waste in our waterways are irresponsible corporate citizens.

READING-WRITING CONNECTION

YOUR TURN Expand your understanding of satire by responding to this prompt. Then use the **revising tips** to improve your proposal.

WRITING PROMPT	REVISING TIPS
WRITE A SATIRICAL PROPOSAL In the spirit of Swift's essay, write a **three-to-five-paragraph satirical proposal** on an issue you've heard or read about recently. The issue could relate to something at school, a problem in your town, or an issue that challenges the nation.	• Clearly identify the issue that your proposal will solve and choose something that you have strong opinions about. • Address possible opposing views. • Use carefully chosen nouns for satirical effect in your proposal.

◠ COMMON CORE

L 1 Demonstrate command of the conventions of standard English grammar when writing. **W 1** Write arguments to support claims in an analysis of substantive topics. **W 1a** Introduce precise, knowledgeable claim(s).

Interactive Revision **THINK** central

Go to **thinkcentral.com**.
KEYWORD: HML12-634

from Gulliver's Travels

Fiction by Jonathan Swift

COMMON CORE **RL 6**

● TEXT ANALYSIS: FANTASY

Fantasy is literature in which the limits of reality are purposely disregarded. The writer's aim may be pure entertainment or to convey a serious message. In *Gulliver's Travels,* the narrator visits four imaginary lands. These settings serve as ideal vehicles for Swift's **satire,** allowing him to criticize human nature and European society by comparing them with the strange beings and societies Gulliver observes in his travels. As you read *Gulliver's Travels,* notice how Swift's fantasy worlds parallel and comment on ours.

● READING SKILL: UNDERSTAND SATIRE IN HISTORICAL CONTEXT

You can clarify your understanding of a satire from an earlier period by focusing on the **historical context**—the conditions and events that inspired or influenced the work's creation. Swift participated on both sides in the struggle between England's two political parties, the Whigs and the Tories. As a clergyman, he was deeply concerned about religious differences that divided Europe. These conflicts inspired much of his satire in *Gulliver's Travels.* To familiarize yourself with the work's historical context, reread the author biography on page 620 and examine the background information on page 636. Then, as you read the selection, use footnotes to help you understand the specific context of Swift's satire.

▲ VOCABULARY IN CONTEXT

Use the following sentences to help you figure out the meanings of the boldfaced words.

1. The detective's accusation was pure **conjecture.**
2. The servant bowed in a **submissive** manner.
3. Her hands moved with **dexterity** across the keyboard.
4. The **diminutive** dog was smaller than the cat it chased.
5. Judging from its huge footprints, the beast is **prodigious.**
6. The **animosities** between the clans led to a bloody feud.
7. Her lies and deceit seemed designed to **foment** mistrust.
8. In 100 years, how will **posterity** judge today's leaders?

 Complete the activities in your **Reader/Writer Notebook**.

Can we trust our own PERCEPTIONS?

Have you ever misjudged a situation or a person? Sometimes our perceptions are not as keen as we'd like them to be. In *Gulliver's Travels,* Jonathan Swift creates fantastic encounters that challenge both his hero's and his readers' perceptions of the world.

QUICKWRITE With a group of classmates, look through your textbook and choose an interesting picture of two or more people. Have each member of your group write a paragraph about the picture, describing the people and their relationship to each other. Share your paragraphs with one another and discuss the ways in which your perceptions of the picture differ.

GULLIVER'S TRAVELS

JONATHAN SWIFT

> **BACKGROUND** In Swift's day, travel books, in which writers described their visits to foreign lands, had become a popular genre and a boon to the publishing business. Swift used the form for his four-part fantasy, which allowed him to comment freely on subjects like the 200-year-old religious divisions between Catholics and Protestants in England, as well as the rancorous political split between the Tories, who were obedient to the crown and the Church of England, and the Whigs, who wanted to limit the powers of both institutions.

PART 1. A VOYAGE TO LILLIPUT

The first part of Gulliver's Travels *describes Gulliver's adventures in Lilliput. After going to sea as a ship's doctor, Gulliver faces disaster as his ship breaks apart in a storm. He swims toward land, reaches shore, and falls exhausted on the ground.*

I lay down on the grass, which was very short and soft, where I slept sounder than ever I remember to have done in my life, and as I reckoned, above nine hours; for when I awaked, it was just daylight. I attempted to rise, but was not able to stir: for as I happened to lie on my back, I found my arms and legs were strongly fastened on each side to the ground; and my hair, which was long and thick, tied down in the same manner. I likewise felt several slender ligatures[1] across my body, from my armpits to my thighs. I could only look upwards; the sun began to grow hot, and the light offended my eyes. I heard a confused noise about me, but in the posture I lay, could see nothing except the sky. In a little time I felt
10 something alive moving on my left leg, which advancing gently forward over my

---

1. **ligatures** (lĭg′ə-chŏŏrz′): cords used to tie something up.

Analyze Visuals ▶
How well does this illustration correspond to Swift's description of Gulliver's captivity? Explain your answer.

breast, came almost up to my chin; when bending my eyes downwards as much as I could, I perceived it to be a human creature not six inches high, with a bow and arrow in his hands, and a quiver[2] at his back. In the meantime, I felt at least forty more of the same kind (as I **conjectured**) following the first. I was in the utmost astonishment, and roared so loud, that they all ran back in a fright; and some of them, as I was afterwards told, were hurt with the falls they got by leaping from my sides upon the ground. However, they soon returned; and one of them, who ventured so far as to get a full sight of my face, lifting up his hands and eyes by way of admiration, cried out in a shrill, but distinct voice, *Hekinah Degul:* the others
20 repeated the same words several times, but I then knew not what they meant.

    I lay all this while, as the reader may believe, in great uneasiness; at length, struggling to get loose, I had the fortune to break the strings, and wrench out the pegs that fastened my left arm to the ground; for, by lifting it up to my face, I discovered the methods they had taken to bind me; and, at the same time, with a violent pull, which gave me excessive pain, I a little loosened the strings that tied down my hair on the left side; so that I was just able to turn my head about two inches. But the creatures ran off a second time, before I could seize them; whereupon there was a great shout in a very shrill accent; and after it ceased, I heard one of them cry aloud, *Tolgo phonac;* when in an instant I felt above an
30 hundred arrows discharged on my left hand, which pricked me like so many needles; and besides they shot another flight into the air, as we do bombs in Europe, whereof many, I suppose, fell on my body (though I felt them not) and some on my face, which I immediately covered with my left hand. When this shower of arrows was over, I fell a groaning with grief and pain; and then striving again to get loose, they discharged another volley larger than the first, and some of them attempted with spears to stick me in the sides; but, by good luck, I had on me a buff jerkin,[3] which they could not pierce. I thought it the most prudent method to lie still; and my design was to continue so till night, when, my left hand being already loose, I could easily free myself: and as for the inhabitants, I
40 had reason to believe I might be a match for the greatest armies they could bring against me, if they were all of the same size with him that I saw. But fortune disposed otherwise of me. **Ⓐ**

    When the people observed I was quiet, they discharged no more arrows: but by the noise increasing, I knew their numbers were greater; and about four yards from me, over-against my right ear, I heard a knocking for above an hour, like people at work; when turning my head that way, as well as the pegs and strings would permit me, I saw a stage erected about a foot and a half from the ground, capable of holding four of the inhabitants, with two or three ladders to mount it: from whence one of them, who seemed to be a person of quality,[4] made me a long
50 speech, whereof I understood not one syllable. But I should have mentioned, that before the principal person began his oration, he cried out three times, *Langro Dehul san:* (these words and the former were afterwards repeated and explained

conjecture (kən-jĕk′chər) *v.* to infer based on incomplete evidence; guess

Ⓐ FANTASY
What details does Swift include in lines 21–42 to make this fantastic scene believable?

---

2. **quiver:** a case for carrying arrows.

3. **buff jerkin:** a jacket of brownish-yellow leather.

4. **person of quality:** a high-ranking person.

to me). Whereupon immediately about fifty of the inhabitants came, and cut the strings that fastened the left side of my head, which gave me the liberty of turning it to the right, and of observing the person and gesture of him who was to speak. He appeared to be of a middle age, and taller than any of the other three who attended him; whereof one was a page[5] who held up his train,[6] and seemed to be somewhat longer than my middle finger; the other two stood one on each side to support him. He acted every part of an orator, and I could observe many
60 periods of threatenings, and others of promises, pity and kindness. I answered in a few words, but in the most **submissive** manner, lifting up my left hand and both my eyes to the sun, as calling him for a witness; and being almost famished with hunger, having not eaten a morsel for some hours before I left the ship, I found the demands of nature so strong upon me, that I could not forbear showing my impatience (perhaps against the strict rules of decency) by putting my finger frequently on my mouth, to signify that I wanted food.

The *Hurgo* (for so they call a great lord, as I afterwards learned) understood me very well. He descended from the stage, and commanded that several ladders should be applied to my sides, on which above an hundred of the inhabitants
70 mounted, and walked towards my mouth, laden with baskets full of meat, which had been provided and sent thither by the King's orders upon the first intelligence[7] he received of me. I observed there was the flesh of several animals, but could not distinguish them by the taste. There were shoulders, legs, and loins shaped like those of mutton, and very well dressed, but smaller than the wings of a lark. I eat them by two or three at a mouthful, and took three loaves at a time, about the bigness of musket bullets. They supplied me as fast as they could, showing a thousand marks of wonder and astonishment at my bulk and appetite. I then made another sign that I wanted drink. They found by my eating that a small quantity would not suffice me; and being a most ingenious people,
80 they slung up with great **dexterity** one of their largest hogsheads;[8] then rolled it towards my hand, and beat out the top; I drank it off at a draft,[9] which I might well do, for it hardly held half a pint, and tasted like a small wine of Burgundy, but much more delicious. They brought me a second hogshead, which I drank in the same manner, and made signs for more, but they had none to give me. When I had performed these wonders, they shouted for joy, and danced upon my breast, repeating several times as they did at first, *Hekinah Degul.* They made me a sign that I should throw down the two hogsheads, but first warned the people below to stand out of the way, crying aloud, *Borach Mivola,* and when they saw the vessels in the air, there was an universal shout of *Hekinah Degul.* **B**
90 I confess I was often tempted, while they were passing backwards and forwards on my body, to seize forty or fifty of the first that came in my reach, and dash them against the ground. But the remembrance of what I had felt, which probably

---

5. **page:** a youth serving as a personal attendant.

6. **train:** the trailing section of a garment.

7. **intelligence:** news; information.

8. **hogsheads:** large barrels used to store liquids such as wine or ale.

9. **at a draft:** in one gulp.

submissive (səb-mĭs′ĭv) *adj.* tending to yield to the will of others; docile; meek

Language Coach

Etymology *Mutton* (line 74) is the word for the flesh, or meat, of a sheep. It comes from the French word for sheep. What do we call meat that comes from a pig or a cow? What does the word *veal* refer to?

dexterity (dĕk-stĕr′ĭ-tē) *n.* skill in manipulating one's hands or body

B **FANTASY**
What details in lines 67–89 help you **visualize** the difference in size between Gulliver and the Lilliputians?

might not be the worst they could do; and the promise of honor I made them, for so I interpreted my submissive behavior, soon drove out those imaginations. Besides, I now considered myself as bound by the laws of hospitality to a people who had treated me with so much expense and magnificence. However, in my thoughts I could not sufficiently wonder at the intrepidity[10] of these **diminutive** mortals, who durst[11] venture to mount and walk on my body, while one of my hands was at liberty, without trembling at the very sight of so **prodigious** a

100 creature as I must appear to them.

After some time, when they observed that I made no more demands for meat, there appeared before me a person of high rank from his Imperial Majesty. His Excellency, having mounted on the small of my right leg, advanced forwards up to my face, with about a dozen of his retinue. And producing his credentials under the Signet Royal,[12] which he applied close to my eyes, spoke about ten minutes, without any signs of anger, but with a kind of determinate resolution; often pointing forwards, which, as I afterwards found, was towards the capital city, about half a mile distant, whither it was agreed by his Majesty in council that I must be conveyed. I answered in a few words, but to no purpose, and made a

110 sign with my hand that was loose, putting it to the other (but over his Excellency's head, for fear of hurting him or his train) and then to my own head and body, to signify that I desired my liberty. It appeared that he understood me well enough; for he shook his head by way of disapprobation,[13] and held his hand in a posture to show that I must be carried as a prisoner. However, he made other signs to let me understand that I should have meat and drink enough, and very good treatment. Whereupon I once more thought of attempting to break my bonds; but again, when I felt the smart of their arrows upon my face and hands, which were all in blisters, and many of the darts still sticking in them; and observing likewise that the number of my enemies increased; I gave tokens to let them know

120 that they might do with me what they pleased. Upon this the *Hurgo* and his train withdrew, with much civility and cheerful countenances. Soon after I heard a general shout, with frequent repetitions of the words, *Peplom Selan,* and I felt great numbers of the people on my left side relaxing the cords to such a degree, that I was able to turn upon my right, and to ease myself. . . .

My gentleness and good behavior had gained so far on the Emperor and his court, and indeed upon the army and people in general, that I began to conceive hopes of getting my liberty in a short time. I took all possible methods to cultivate this favorable disposition. The natives came by degrees to be less apprehensive of any danger from me. I would sometimes lie down, and let five or six of them

130 dance on my hand. And at last the boys and girls would venture to come and play at hide-and-seek in my hair. I had now made a good progress in understanding and speaking their language. The Emperor had a mind one day to entertain me with several of the country shows; wherein they exceed all nations I have known,

diminutive
(dǐ-mǐn′yə-tǐv) *adj.* very small

prodigious (prə-dǐj′əs) *adj.* of great size or power; huge; impressive

---

10. **intrepidity** (ǐn′-trə-pǐd′ǐ-tē): boldness; courage.

11. **durst:** dared.

12. **Signet Royal:** the official seal of a king or a queen.

13. **disapprobation** (dǐs-ăp′rə-bā′shən): disapproval.

both for dexterity and magnificence. I was diverted with none so much as that of the rope-dancers,[14] performed upon a slender white thread, extended about two foot, and twelve inches from the ground. Upon which I shall desire liberty, with the reader's patience, to enlarge a little.

This diversion is only practiced by those persons who are candidates for great employments, and high favor, at court. They are trained in this art from their
140 youth, and are not always of noble birth, or liberal education. When a great office is vacant either by death or disgrace (which often happens) five or six of those candidates petition the Emperor to entertain his Majesty and the court with a dance on the rope; and whoever jumps the highest without falling, succeeds in the office. Very often the chief ministers themselves are commanded to show their skill, and to convince the Emperor that they have not lost their faculty. Flimnap, the Treasurer,[15] is allowed to cut a caper[16] on the strait rope, at least an inch higher than any other lord in the whole empire. I have seen him do the summerset several times together upon a trencher[17] fixed on the rope, which is no thicker than a common packthread[18] in England. My friend Reldresal, Principal Secretary
150 for Private Affairs, is, in my opinion, if I am not partial, the second after the Treasurer; the rest of the great officers are much upon a par. **C**

These diversions are often attended with fatal accidents, whereof great numbers are on record. I myself have seen two or three candidates break a limb. But the danger is much greater when the ministers themselves are commanded to show their dexterity; for, by contending to excel themselves and their fellows, they strain so far, that there is hardly one of them who hath not received a fall; and some of them two or three. I was assured, that a year or two before my arrival, Flimnap would have infallibly broke his neck, if one of the King's cushions, that accidentally lay on the ground, had not weakened the force of his fall.
160 There is likewise another diversion, which is only shown before the Emperor and Empress, and first minister, upon particular occasions. The Emperor lays on a table three fine silken threads of six inches long. One is blue, the other red, and the third green.[19] These threads are proposed as prizes for those persons whom the Emperor hath a mind to distinguish by a peculiar mark of his favor. The ceremony is performed in his Majesty's great chamber of state; where the candidates are to undergo a trial of dexterity very different from the former, and such as I have not observed the least resemblance of in any other country of the old or the new world. The Emperor holds a stick in his hands, both ends parallel to the horizon, while the candidates, advancing one by one, sometimes leap

C HISTORICAL CONTEXT
Reread lines 138–151 and the accompanying footnotes. What do you conclude is Swift's attitude toward the politicians he alludes to in this description? Explain.

---

14. **rope-dancers:** acrobats who perform on a tightrope. Here the rope-dancers represent Whig Party politicians at the court of George I, whose "acrobatics"—political maneuverings—were intended to increase their power. (Swift supported the opposing party, the Tories.)

15. **Flimnap, the Treasurer:** a character representing the Whig leader and statesman Sir Robert Walpole, who served as first lord of the Treasury from 1715 to 1717 and from 1721 to 1742.

16. **allowed . . . caper:** acknowledged to leap.

17. **summerset . . . trencher:** several somersaults on a wooden serving tray or platter.

18. **packthread:** a strong twine for tying packages.

19. **One is blue . . . green:** The threads represent the Order of the Garter, the Order of the Bath, and the Order of the Thistle, medieval orders of knighthood revived by Walpole as honors for the king to bestow.

170 over the stick, sometimes creep under it backwards and forwards several times, according as the stick is advanced or depressed. Sometimes the Emperor holds one end of the stick, and his first minister the other; sometimes the minister has it entirely to himself. Whoever performs his part with most agility, and holds out the longest in *leaping* and *creeping,* is rewarded with the blue-colored silk; the red is given to the next, and the green to the third, which they all wear girt[20] twice round about the middle; and you see few great persons about this court who are not adorned with one of these girdles. . . . **D**

I had sent so many memorials and petitions for my liberty, that his Majesty at length mentioned the matter first in the cabinet, and then in a full council;
180 where it was opposed by none, except Skyresh Bolgolam,[21] who was pleased, without any provocation, to be my mortal enemy. But it was carried against him by the whole board, and confirmed by the Emperor. That minister was *Galbet,* or Admiral of the Realm; very much in his master's confidence, and a person well versed in affairs, but of a morose and sour complexion. However, he was at length persuaded to comply; but prevailed that the articles and conditions upon which I should be set free, and to which I must swear, should be drawn up by himself. These articles were brought to me by Skyresh Bolgolam in person, attended by two under-secretaries, and several persons of distinction. After they were read, I was demanded to swear to the performance of them; first in the manner of my
190 own country, and afterwards in the method prescribed by their laws; which was to hold my right foot in my left hand, to place the middle finger of my right hand on the crown of my head, and my thumb on the tip of my right ear. But because the reader may perhaps be curious to have some idea of the style and manner of expression peculiar to that people, as well as to know the articles upon which I recovered my liberty, I have made a translation of the whole instrument, word for word, as near as I was able; which I here offer to the public. **E**

GOLBASTO MOMAREN EVLAME GURDILO SHEFIN MULLY ULLY GUE, most mighty Emperor of Lilliput, delight and terror of the universe, whose dominions extend five thousand blustrugs (about twelve miles in circumference) to the extremities
200 of the globe; Monarch of all Monarchs; taller than the sons of men; whose feet press down to the center, and whose head strikes against the sun; at whose nod the princes of the earth shake their knees; pleasant as the spring, comfortable as the summer, fruitful as autumn, dreadful as winter. His most sublime Majesty proposeth to the Man-Mountain, lately arrived at our celestial dominions, the following articles, which by a solemn oath he shall be obliged to perform. **F**

First, the Man-Mountain shall not depart from our dominions, without our license under our great seal.

Secondly, He shall not presume to come into our metropolis, without our express order; at which time the inhabitants shall have two hours warning, to keep
210 within their doors.

Thirdly, The said Man-Mountain shall confine his walks to our principal high roads; and not offer to walk or lie down in a meadow, or field of corn.

---

20. **girt:** wrapped.
21. **Skyresh Bolgolam:** probably the Earl of Nottingham, a Tory extremist who was an enemy of Swift's.

Fourthly, As he walks the said roads, he shall take the utmost care not to trample upon the bodies of any of our loving subjects, their horses, or carriages, nor take any of our said subjects into his hands, without their own consent.

Fifthly, If an express require extraordinary dispatch, the Man-Mountain shall be obliged to carry in his pocket the messenger and horse, a six days' journey once in every moon, and return the said messenger back (if so required) safe to our Imperial Presence.

220 Sixthly, He shall be our ally against our enemies in the island of Blefuscu,[22] and do his utmost to destroy their fleet, which is now preparing to invade us.

Seventhly, That the said Man-Mountain shall, at his times of leisure, be aiding and assisting to our workmen, in helping to raise certain great stones, towards covering the wall of the principal park, and other our royal buildings.

Eighthly, That the said Man-Mountain shall, in two moons' time, deliver in an exact survey of the circumference of our dominions by a computation of his own paces round the coast.

Lastly, That upon his solemn oath to observe all the above articles, the said Man-Mountain shall have a daily allowance of meat and drink sufficient for 230 the support of 1,728 of our subjects; with free access to our Royal Person, and other marks of our favor. Given at our palace at Belfaborac the twelfth day of the ninety-first moon of our reign.

I swore and subscribed to these articles with great cheerfulness and content . . . whereupon my chains were immediately unlocked, and I was at full liberty: the Emperor himself in person did me the honor to be by at the whole ceremony. I made my acknowledgements by prostrating myself at his Majesty's feet: but he commanded me to rise; and after many gracious expressions, which, to avoid the censure of vanity, I shall not repeat, he added, that he hoped I should prove a useful servant, and well deserve all the favors he had already conferred upon me, 240 or might do for the future.

The reader may please to observe, that in the last article for the recovery of my liberty, the Emperor stipulates to allow me a quantity of meat and drink, sufficient for the support of 1,728 Lilliputians. Some time after, asking a friend at court how they came to fix on that determinate number, he told me, that his Majesty's mathematicians, having taken the height of my body by the help of a quadrant,[23] and finding it to exceed theirs in the proportion of twelve to one, they concluded from the similarity of their bodies, that mine must contain at least 1,728 of theirs, and consequently would require as much food as was necessary to support that number of Lilliputians. By which, the reader may conceive an idea of the ingenuity 250 of that people, as well as the prudent and exact economy of so great a prince. **G**

One morning, about a fortnight after I had obtained my liberty, Reldresal, Principal Secretary (as they style him) of Private Affairs, came to my house, attended only by one servant. He ordered his coach to wait at a distance, and desired I would give him an hour's audience; which I readily consented to, on

G FANTASY
Reread lines 241–250. Why might Swift have included these exact calculations in his narrative?

---

22. **Blefuscu:** This imaginary country represents France, England's chief rival in Swift's day and a primarily Catholic country.

23. **quadrant** (kwŏd'rənt): an instrument for measuring altitude.

account of his quality, and personal merits, as well as of the many good offices he had done me during my solicitations at court.[24] I offered to lie down, that he might the more conveniently reach my ear; but he chose rather to let me hold him in my hand during our conversation. He began with compliments on my liberty, said he might pretend to[25] some merit in it; but, however, added, that if it had not been for the present situation of things at court, perhaps I might not have obtained it so soon. For, said he, as flourishing a condition as we appear to be in to foreigners, we labor under two mighty evils; a violent faction at home, and the danger of an invasion by a most potent enemy from abroad. As to the first, you are to understand, that for above seventy moons past, there have been two struggling parties in the empire, under the names of *Tramecksan,* and *Slamecksan,* from the high and low heels on their shoes,[26] by which they distinguish themselves.

It is alleged indeed, that the high heels are most agreeable to our ancient constitution: but however this be, his Majesty hath determined to make use of only low heels in the administration of the government and all offices in the gift of the crown; as you cannot but observe; and particularly, that his Majesty's imperial heels are lower at least by a *drurr* than any of his court; (*drurr* is a measure about the fourteenth part of an inch). The **animosities** between these two parties run so high, that they will neither eat nor drink, nor talk with each other. We compute the *Tramecksan,* or High-Heels, to exceed us in number, but the power is wholly on our side. We apprehend his Imperial Highness, the heir to the crown, to have some tendency towards the High-Heels; at least we can plainly discover one of his heels higher than the other, which gives him a hobble in his gait.[27] Now, in the midst of these intestine disquiets,[28] we are threatened with an invasion from the island of Blefuscu, which is the other great empire of the universe, almost as large and powerful as this of his Majesty. For as to what we have heard you affirm, that there are other kingdoms and states in the world, inhabited by human creatures as large as yourself, our philosophers are in much doubt; and would rather conjecture that you dropped from the moon, or one of the stars; because it is certain, that an hundred mortals of your bulk would, in a short time, destroy all the fruits and cattle of his Majesty's dominions. Besides, our histories of six thousand moons make no mention of any other regions, than the two great empires of Lilliput and Blefuscu. Which two mighty powers have, as I was going to tell you, been engaged in a most obstinate war[29] for six and thirty moons past. It began upon the following occasion. **H**

animosity (ăn′ə-mŏs′ĭ-tē) *n.* ill feeling; hostility

H **HISTORICAL CONTEXT**
Reread footnotes 26 and 27. How does the historical context help you understand the underlying meaning of Swift's description of the Lilliputian prince in lines 275–277?

---

24. **good offices . . . solicitations at court:** helpful services he had done for me during my pleadings or requests made at court.

25. **pretend to:** lay claim to.

26. **two struggling parties . . . shoes:** The "high heel" party corresponds to the Tories, who promoted the High Church (Catholic) aspects of the Church of England; the "low heel" party corresponds to the Whigs, who promoted the Low Church (Protestant) aspects. George I turned the Tories out when he came to the throne, since most of them had not supported his succession.

27. **his Imperial Highness . . . gait:** The Prince of Wales, who later reigned as George II, had both Tory and Whig friends.

28. **these intestine** (ĭn-tĕs′tĭn) **disquiets:** this internal unrest.

29. **most obstinate war:** The war corresponds to the War of the Spanish Succession (1702–1713), in which England and France were the chief opponents.

290　It is allowed on all hands, that the primitive way of breaking eggs before we eat them, was upon the larger end: but his present Majesty's grandfather, while he was a boy, going to eat an egg, and breaking it according to the ancient practice, happened to cut one of his fingers. Whereupon the Emperor his father published an edict, commanding all his subjects, upon great penalties, to break the smaller end of their eggs.[30] The people so highly resented this law, that our histories tell us there have been six rebellions raised on that account; wherein one emperor lost his life, and another his crown.[31] These civil commotions were constantly **fomented** by the monarchs of Blefuscu; and when they were quelled, the exiles always fled for refuge to that empire. It is computed, that eleven thousand persons have, at several

300　times, suffered death, rather than submit to break their eggs at the smaller end. Many hundred large volumes have been published upon this controversy: but the books of the Big-Endians have been long forbidden, and the whole party rendered incapable by law of holding employments.[32] During the course of these troubles, the emperors of Blefuscu did frequently expostulate by their ambassadors, accusing us of making a schism in religion, by offending against a fundamental doctrine of our great prophet Lustrog, in the fifty-fourth chapter of the *Brundecral* (which is their Alcoran). This, however, is thought to be a mere strain upon the text: for the words are these; *That all true believers shall break their eggs at the convenient end:* and which is the convenient end, seems, in my humble opinion, to be left to every man's

310　conscience, or at least in the power of the chief magistrate to determine. Now the Big-Endian exiles have found so much credit in the Emperor of Blefuscu's court, and so much private assistance and encouragement from their party here at home, that a bloody war hath been carried on between the two empires for six and thirty moons with various success; during which time we have lost forty capital ships, and a much greater number of smaller vessels, together with thirty thousand of our best seamen and soldiers; and the damage received by the enemy is reckoned to be somewhat greater than ours. However, they have now equipped a numerous fleet, and are just preparing to make a descent upon us; and his Imperial Majesty, placing great confidence in your valor and strength, hath commanded me to lay this account of

320　his affairs before you. **◆**

I desired the Secretary to present my humble duty to the Emperor, and to let him know, that I thought it would not become me, who was a foreigner, to interfere with parties;[33] but I was ready, with the hazard of my life, to defend his person and state against all invaders.

foment (fō-mĕnt′) *v.* to stir up trouble; to incite

◆ HISTORICAL CONTEXT
Reread lines 290–314 and the accompanying footnotes. What does Swift's account of Blefuscu suggest about France's role in England's religious conflicts?

---

30. **the Emperor his father . . . end of their eggs:** a reference to Henry VIII, who in 1533 split from the Roman Catholic Church (because it would not grant him a divorce from his wife) and founded the Church of England.

31. **six rebellions . . . his crown:** The dispute over egg breaking represents the conflict between Roman Catholics and Protestants in 17th-century England. The "emperor" who lost his life in the conflict was King Charles I; the one who lost his crown was King James II, who fled into exile.

32. **employments:** political offices.

33. **parties:** political parties; internal politics.

PART 2. A VOYAGE TO BROBDINGNAG

The second part of Gulliver's Travels *describes Gulliver's adventures in Brobdingnag. As the story opens, Gulliver has again gone to sea as a ship's doctor. The ship has been blown off course by a storm. When the ship comes in sight of land, the captain sends ashore a boatload of men (including Gulliver) to look for drinking water. While exploring the island, Gulliver is separated from the others, and when he returns to the boat he sees his shipmates rowing in a panic back to the ship, in flight from a huge monster who is chasing them. Gulliver turns back into the interior to hide from the giant.*

I fell into a highroad, for so I took it to be, although it served to the inhabitants only as a footpath through a field of barley. Here I walked on for some time, but could see little on either side, it being now near harvest, and the corn rising at least forty foot. I was an hour walking to the end of this field, which was fenced in with a hedge of at least one hundred and twenty foot high, and the trees so
330 lofty that I could make no computation of their altitude. There was a stile[34] to pass from this field into the next: it had four steps, and a stone to cross over when you came to the utmost. It was impossible for me to climb this stile, because every step was six foot high, and the upper stone above twenty. I was endeavoring to find some gap in the hedge when I discovered one of the inhabitants in the next field advancing towards the stile, of the same size with him whom I saw in the sea pursuing our boat. He appeared as tall as an ordinary spire-steeple, and took **J** about ten yards at every stride, as near as I could guess. I was struck with the utmost fear and astonishment, and ran to hide myself in the corn, from whence I saw him at the top of the stile, looking back into the next field on the right hand;
340 and heard him call in a voice many degrees louder than a speaking trumpet; but the noise was so high in the air that at first I certainly thought it was thunder. Whereupon seven monsters like himself came towards him with reaping hooks in their hands, each hook about the largeness of six scythes. These people were not so well clad as the first, whose servants or laborers they seemed to be. For, upon some words he spoke, they went to reap the corn in the field where I lay. I kept from them at as great a distance as I could, but was forced to move with extreme difficulty, for the stalks of the corn were sometimes not above a foot distant, so that I could hardly squeeze my body betwixt them. However, I made a shift to go forward till I came to a part of the field where the corn had been laid[35] by the
350 rain and wind; here it was impossible for me to advance a step, for the stalks were so interwoven that I could not creep through, and the beards of the fallen ears so strong and pointed that they pierced through my clothes into my flesh. At the same time I heard the reapers not above an hundred yards behind me. Being quite dispirited with toil, and wholly overcome by grief and despair, I lay down between two ridges and heartily wished I might there end my days. I bemoaned my

J GRAMMAR AND STYLE
Reread lines 332–336. Notice that Swift uses **subordinate clauses** beginning with *because, when,* and *whom* to convey specific details of the fantasy he is creating.

---

34. **stile:** a set of steps for climbing over a hedge or a fence.

35. **laid:** knocked down.

desolate widow and fatherless children; I lamented my own folly and willfulness in attempting a second voyage against the advice of all my friends and relations. In this terrible agitation of mind, I could not forbear thinking of Lilliput, whose inhabitants looked upon me as the greatest prodigy that ever appeared in the world; where I was able to draw an imperial fleet in my hand, and perform those other actions which will be recorded forever in the chronicles of that empire, while **posterity** shall hardly believe them, although attested by millions. I reflected what a mortification it must prove to me to appear as inconsiderable in this nation as one single Lilliputian would be among us. But this I conceived was to be the least of my misfortunes; for as human creatures are observed to be more savage and cruel in proportion to their bulk, what could I expect but to be a morsel in the mouth of the first among these enormous barbarians who should happen to seize me? Undoubtedly philosophers are in the right when they tell us that nothing is great or little otherwise than by comparison. It might have pleased fortune to let the Lilliputians find some nation where the people were as diminutive with respect to them as they were to me. And who knows but that even this prodigious race of mortals might be equally overmatched in some distant part of the world, whereof we have yet no discovery? **K**

    Scared and confounded as I was, I could not forbear going on with these reflections; when one of the reapers approaching within ten yards of the ridge where I lay, made me apprehend that with the next step I should be squashed to death under his foot, or cut in two with his reaping hook. And therefore when he was again about to move, I screamed as loud as fear could make me. Whereupon the huge creature trod short, and looking round about under him for some time, at last espied me as I lay on the ground. He considered a while with the caution of one who endeavors to lay hold on a small dangerous animal in such a manner that it shall not be able either to scratch or to bite him, as I myself have sometimes done with a weasel in England. At length he ventured to take me up behind by the middle between his forefinger and thumb, and brought me within three yards of his eyes, that he might behold my shape more perfectly. . . . Lifting up the lappet[36] of his coat, he put me gently into it, and immediately ran along with me to his master, who was a substantial farmer, and the same person I had first seen in the field.

    The farmer having (as I supposed by their talk) received such an account of me as his servant could give him, took a piece of a small straw about the size of a walking staff, and therewith lifted up the lappets of my coat, which it seems he thought to be some kind of covering that nature had given me. He blew my hairs aside to take a better view of my face. He called his hinds[37] about him, and asked them (as I afterwards learned) whether they had ever seen in the fields any little creature that resembled me. He then placed me softly on the ground upon all four; but I got immediately up, and walked slowly backwards and forwards, to let those people see I had no intent to run away. They all sat down in a circle

posterity (pŏ-stĕr'ĭ-tē) *n.* future generations

K FANTASY
Reread lines 358–373. What message about people and nations does Swift convey through the fantasy of the tiny Lilliputians and the giant Brobdingnagians?

---

36. **lappet:** flap or fold.

37. **hinds:** farm servants.

about me, the better to observe my motions. I pulled off my hat, and made a low bow towards the farmer; I fell on my knees, and lifted up my hands and eyes, and spoke several words as loud as I could; I took a purse of gold out of my pocket, and humbly presented it to him. . . .

The farmer by this time was convinced I must be a rational creature. He spoke often to me, but the sound of his voice pierced my ears like that of a water mill, yet his words were articulate enough. I answered as loud as I could in several languages, and he often laid his ear within two yards of me, but all in vain, for we were wholly unintelligible to each other. He then sent his servants to their work, and taking his handkerchief out of his pocket, he doubled and spread it on his hand, which he placed flat on the ground with the palm upwards, making me a sign to step into it, as I could easily do, for it was not above a foot in thickness. I thought it my part to obey, and for fear of falling, laid myself at full length upon the handkerchief, with the remainder of which he lapped me up to the head for further security, and in this manner carried me home to his house. . . .

Gulliver lives with the farmer and his family and grows especially close to the farmer's daughter, Glumdalclitch. After a number of adventures in the farmer's house, including an attack on Gulliver by two ferocious rats, he is taken to the metropolis where he is purchased from the farmer by the queen of Brobdingnag, who presents him to the king. Glumdalclitch remains with Gulliver at the royal court as his nurse and instructor. Gulliver becomes a favorite of the king and queen.

It is the custom that every Wednesday (which, as I have before observed, was their Sabbath) the King and Queen, with the royal issue of both sexes, dine together in the apartment of his Majesty, to whom I was now become a favorite; and at these times my little chair and table were placed at his left hand, before one of the salt-cellars. This prince took a pleasure in conversing with me, inquiring into the manners, religion, laws, government, and learning of Europe; wherein I gave him the best account I was able. His apprehension was so clear, and his judgment so exact, that he made very wise reflections and observations upon all I said. But I confess that after I had been a little too copious in talking of my own beloved country, of our trade and wars by sea and land, of our schisms in religion and parties in the state, the prejudices of his education prevailed so far that he could not forbear taking me up in his right hand, and stroking me gently with the other, after an hearty fit of laughing, asked me whether I were a Whig or a Tory. Then turning to his first minister, who waited behind him with a white staff, near as tall as the mainmast of the *Royal Sovereign,*[38] he observed how contemptible a thing was human grandeur, which could be mimicked by such diminutive insects as I: "and yet," said he, "I dare engage, these creatures have their titles and distinctions of honor; they contrive little nests and burrows, that they call houses and cities; they make a figure in dress and equipage; they love, they fight, they dispute, they cheat, they betray." And thus he continued on, while my color came and went

---

38. ***Royal Sovereign*** (sŏv′ər-ĭn): at the time, one of the largest ships in the British navy.

several times with indignation to hear our noble country, the mistress of arts and arms, the scourge of France, the arbitress of Europe, the seat of virtue, piety, honor, and truth, the pride and envy of the world, so contemptuously treated.

But as I was not in a condition to resent injuries, so, upon mature thoughts, I began to doubt whether I were injured or no. For, after having been accustomed several months to the sight and converse of this people, and observed every object upon which I cast my eyes to be of proportionable magnitude, the horror I had first
440 conceived from their bulk and aspect was so far worn off that if I had then beheld a company of English lords and ladies in their finery and birthday clothes,[39] acting their several parts in the most courtly manner of strutting and bowing and prating, to say the truth, I should have been strongly tempted to laugh as much at them as this King and his grandees did at me. Neither indeed could I forbear smiling at myself when the Queen used to place me upon her hand towards a looking glass, by which both our persons appeared before me in full view together; and there could be nothing more ridiculous than the comparison; so that I really began to imagine myself dwindled many degrees below my usual size. . . .

I was frequently rallied by the Queen upon account of my fearfulness, and she
450 used to ask me whether the people of my country were as great cowards as myself. The occasion was this. The kingdom is much pestered with flies in summer, and these odious insects, each of them as big as a Dunstable lark, hardly gave me any rest while I sat at dinner, with their continual humming and buzzing about my ears. They would sometimes alight upon my victuals, and leave their loathsome excrement or spawn behind, which to me was very visible, although not to the natives of that country, whose large optics[40] were not so acute as mine in viewing smaller objects. Sometimes they would fix upon my nose or forehead, where they stung me to the quick, smelling very offensively; and I could easily trace that viscous matter, which our naturalists tell us enables those creatures to walk with
460 their feet upwards upon a ceiling. I had much ado to defend myself against these detestable animals, and could not forbear starting when they came on my face. It was the common practice of the dwarf to catch a number of these insects in his hand, as schoolboys do among us, and let them out suddenly under my nose, on purpose to frighten me, and divert the Queen. My remedy was to cut them in pieces with my knife as they flew in the air, wherein my dexterity was much admired. **L**

I remember one morning when Glumdalclitch had set me in my box upon a window, as she usually did in fair days to give me air (for I durst not venture to let the box be hung on a nail out of the window, as we do with cages in England),
470 after I had lifted up one of my sashes, and sat down at my table to eat a piece of sweet cake for my breakfast, above twenty wasps, allured by the smell, came flying into the room, humming louder than the drones of as many bagpipes. Some of them seized my cake, and carried it piecemeal away; others flew about my head and face, confounding me with the noise, and putting me in the utmost terror of

L **FANTASY**
Reread lines 451–461. How do the details in this passage enhance the depiction of Gulliver's life in Brobdingnag?

---

39. **birthday clothes:** elaborate clothing worn at court on the monarch's birthday.
40. **optics:** eyes.

their stings. However, I had the courage to rise and draw my hanger,[41] and attack them in the air. I dispatched four of them, but the rest got away, and I presently shut my window. These insects were as large as partridges; I took out their stings, found them an inch and a half long, and as sharp as needles. I carefully preserved them all, and having since shown them with some other curiosities in several parts of Europe, upon my return to England I gave three of them to Gresham College,[42] and kept the fourth for myself. . . .

480   The King, who, as I before observed, was a prince of excellent understanding, would frequently order that I should be brought in my box and set upon the table in his closet. He would then command me to bring one of my chairs out of the box, and sit down within three yards distance upon the top of the cabinet, which brought me almost to a level with his face. In this manner I had several conversations with him. . . . He desired I would give him as exact an account of the government of England as I possibly could; because, as fond as princes commonly are of their

---

41. **hanger:** a small sword hanging from a person's belt.

42. **Gresham** (grĕsh′əm) **College:** a London school that was the meeting place of the Royal Society, the chief British scientific organization in Swift's day.

own customs (for so he conjectured of other monarchs, by my former discourses),
490 he should be glad to hear of anything that might deserve imitation. . . .

He wondered to hear me talk of such chargeable and extensive wars; that certainly we must be a quarrelsome people, or live among very bad neighbors, and that our generals must needs be richer than our kings.[43] He asked what business we had out of our own islands, unless upon the score of trade or treaty or to defend the coasts with our fleet. Above all, he was amazed to hear me talk of a mercenary standing army[44] in the midst of peace, and among a free people. He said if we were governed by our own consent in the persons of our representatives, he could not imagine of whom we were afraid, or against whom we were to fight; and would hear my opinion whether a private man's house might not better be defended
500 by himself, his children, and family, than by half a dozen rascals picked up at a venture[45] in the streets for small wages, who might get an hundred times more by cutting their throats. . . . **Ⓜ**

He was perfectly astonished with the historical account I gave him of our affairs during the last century, protesting it was only an heap of conspiracies, rebellions, murders, massacres, revolutions, banishments, the very worst effects that avarice, faction, hypocrisy, perfidiousness, cruelty, rage, madness, hatred, envy, lust, malice, or ambition could produce.

His Majesty in another audience was at the pains to recapitulate the sum of all I had spoken; compared the questions he made with the answers I had given;
510 then taking me into his hands, and stroking me gently, delivered himself in these words, which I shall never forget, nor the manner he spoke them in: "My little friend Grildrig, you have made a most admirable panegyric upon your country. You have clearly proved that ignorance, idleness, and vice are the proper ingredients for qualifying a legislator. That laws are best explained, interpreted, and applied by those whose interests and abilities lie in perverting, confounding, and eluding them. I observe among you some lines of an institution which in its original might have been tolerable; but these half erased, and the rest wholly blurred and blotted by corruptions. It doth not appear from all you have said how any one virtue is required towards the procurement of any one station among
520 you; much less that men are ennobled on account of their virtue, that priests are advanced for their piety or learning, soldiers for their conduct or valor, judges for their integrity, senators for the love of their country, or counselors for their wisdom. As for yourself," continued the King, "who have spent the greatest part of your life in traveling, I am well disposed to hope you may hitherto have escaped many vices of your country. But by what I have gathered from your own relation, and the answers I have with much pains wringed and extorted from you, I cannot but conclude the bulk of your natives to be the most pernicious race of little odious vermin that nature ever suffered to crawl upon the surface of the earth." ❧

Ⓜ HISTORICAL CONTEXT
Reread lines 491–502 and the accompanying footnotes. In what ways are Swift's own political views reflected in the questions and comments of the king?

---

43. **our generals . . . kings:** a reference to the great wealth of the Duke of Marlborough, a former general whom Swift detested and whose palace was larger than the king's.

44. **mercenary** (mûr′sə-nĕr′ē) **standing army:** an army of hired soldiers maintained on a permanent basis. In the English Bill of Rights of 1689, a standing army had been declared illegal, and Swift and the Tories remained strongly opposed to one.

45. **at a venture:** at random.

LETTER In this letter to his friend, Swift tells Pope some of the reasoning behind the writing of *Gulliver's Travels.* Swift also offers a friendly wager on whether Pope will agree with him or not.

Letter to Alexander Pope

September 29, 1725

Sir,

I am now returning to the noble scene of Dublin. . . . I have employed my time . . . in finishing correcting, amending, and transcribing my Travels, in four parts complete, newly augmented, and intended for the press when the world shall deserve them, or rather when a printer shall be found brave enough to venture his ears. I like your schemes of our meeting after distresses and dispersions; but the chief end I propose to myself in all my labors is to vex the world rather than divert it, and if I could compass that design without hurting my own person or fortune I would be the most indefatigable writer you have ever seen. . . . I have ever hated all nations, professions, and communities, and all my love is towards individuals; for instance, I hate the tribe of lawyers, but I love Counsellor Such-a-one, Judge Such-a-one: so with physicians—I will not speak of my own trade—soldiers, English, Scotch, French, and the rest. But principally I hate and detest that animal called man, although I heartily love John, Peter, Thomas, and so forth. This is the system upon which I have governed myself many years (but do not tell) and so I shall go on till I have done with them. . . . Upon this great foundation of misanthropy . . . the whole building of my Travels is erected; and I never will have peace of mind till all honest men are of my opinion. By consequence you are to embrace it immediately and procure that all who deserve my esteem may do so too. The matter is so clear that it will admit little dispute; nay I will hold a hundred pounds that you and I agree in the point.

J. S.

Comprehension

1. **Recall** How do the Lilliputians treat Gulliver when they first encounter him?

2. **Clarify** Why does Gulliver become important to the Lilliputians?

3. **Recall** What dangers does Gulliver face in Brobdingnag because of his size?

4. **Paraphrase** Based on Gulliver's descriptions, what does the king of Brobdingnag conclude about the English?

COMMON CORE

RL 6 Analyze a case in which grasping a point of view requires distinguishing what is directly stated in a text from what is really meant.

Text Analysis

5. **Analyze Fantasy** In order for a **fantasy** tale to succeed, the world that is created needs to be somewhat believable to the reader. How does Swift create a believable fantasy world in Lilliput? Cite examples from the text.

6. **Make Inferences** Reread lines 420–425. The king of Brobdingnag asks Gulliver if he is a Whig or a Tory. What does the king's laughter suggest about Swift's attitude toward political conflict in England?

7. **Interpret Satire in Historical Context** Swift's descriptions of people and events are intended to satirize specific individuals or aspects of English society and politics. Find examples of such descriptions from the selection, and interpret what Swift is satirizing.

8. **Compare Texts** In his letter to his friend Alexander Pope on page 654, Swift says that although he hates nations and communities, he reserves his love for individual people. Based on the excerpts you read from *Gulliver's Travels*, do you agree with Swift's self-assessment? Support your answer.

Text Criticism

9. **Different Perspectives** At the time Swift was writing his anonymously published satires, England had been entrenched in a long war with France, the British monarchy had undergone upheaval—King George I was unpopular yet very powerful—and the country was plagued by political scandals. *Gulliver's Travels* gave Swift the opportunity to express his anger and frustration with England's ruling class and monarchy. To what extent might Swift's satire be relevant today?

Can we trust our own **PERCEPTIONS?**

Gulliver's Travels is told from the first-person point of view, which means the reader is limited to Gulliver's perceptions—what he sees, hears, or experiences. What do Gulliver's reactions and thoughts tell us about his character?

Vocabulary in Context

▲ VOCABULARY PRACTICE

Show that you understand the meaning of each boldfaced vocabulary word by answering the question about it.

1. Who shows more **dexterity**, an acrobat or a clumsy oaf?
2. Would a sign of **animosity** be a kiss or a slap on the cheek?
3. Which is more **diminutive**, a whale or a goldfish?
4. When you **conjecture**, are you certain or are you just guessing?
5. Who **foments** trouble, a troublemaker or a peacemaker?
6. Is **posterity** a thing of the past or the future?
7. Does a **submissive** person usually obey or disobey orders?
8. Would a **prodigious** portion of food fill you up or leave you hungry?

WORD LIST

animosity

conjecture

dexterity

diminutive

foment

posterity

prodigious

submissive

ACADEMIC VOCABULARY IN WRITING

- affect   - challenge   - consent   - final   - respond

Imagine that you are visiting an inhabited planet that no one on Earth has ever visited before. Write a brief description of the people and their behavior. What **challenges** might you face? How might you **respond** to those challenges? Use at least one additional Academic Vocabulary word in your response.

VOCABULARY STRATEGY: ANALOGIES

Vocabulary **analogies** show similar relationships between pairs of words. You read the examples as "*Diminutive* **is to** *mouse* **as** *prodigious* **is to** *elephant*" and "*Submissive* **is to** *curtsy* **as** *aggressive* **is to** *punch*." In the first analogy, the pairs of words have a size relationship: just as a mouse is diminutive in size, an elephant is prodigious in size. In the second analogy, the relationship is one of example or illustration: just as a curtsy is an example of a submissive act, a punch is an example of an aggressive act.

COMMON CORE

L5 Demonstrate understanding of word relationships. **L6** Acquire and use accurately general academic words.

Analogy Examples

DIMINUTIVE : MOUSE :: prodigious : elephant

SUBMISSIVE : CURTSY :: aggressive : punch

PRACTICE Indicate which word makes the relationship of the second pair most like the relationship of the pair of words in capital letters. If you are unsure of the meaning of any word here, check a dictionary.

1. VILLAGE : METROPOLIS :: hill : (a) valley, (b) plain, (c) mountain, (d) forest
2. CIRCLE : CIRCUMFERENCE :: orange : (a) pit, (b) rind, (c) juice, (d) Florida
3. SPEAKER : ORATION :: singer : (a) concert, (b) rehearsal, (c) stage, (d) hoarse
4. KING : RETINUE :: train : (a) engine, (b) schedule, (c) station, (d) caboose
5. CLEVER : PRODIGY :: intelligent : (a) fool, (b) school, (c) small, (d) genius

Interactive Vocabulary   THINK central

Go to **thinkcentral.com**.
KEYWORD: HML12-656

Language

◆ **GRAMMAR AND STYLE: Add Descriptive Details**

Review the **Grammar and Style** note on page 647. Swift uses **subordinate clauses** to help readers visualize his fantastical lands. Subordinate clauses contain a subject and a verb but do not express a complete thought. They answer questions such as *where, when, how, what kind,* and *which one.* Notice Swift's description of Gulliver's arrival at Lilliput:

> *I lay down on the grass, which was very short and soft, where I slept sounder than ever I remember to have done in my life, and as I reckoned, above nine hours; for when I awaked, it was just daylight.* (lines 1–3)

Here, *which, where, than, as,* and *when* introduce the subordinate clauses. Words such as *after, that, while, who,* and *whose* can also signal subordinate clauses.

PRACTICE Mimic the following sentence by using the same signal words to form subordinate clauses. An example has been done for you.

EXAMPLE

I confess I was often tempted, while they were passing backwards and forwards on my body, to seize forty or fifty of the first that came in my reach, and dash them against the ground.

I was often amused, while reading Swift's satire, to learn that politicians in his time loved to hear themselves speak.

---

1. But the danger is much greater when the ministers themselves are commanded to show their dexterity; for, by contending to excel themselves and their fellows, they strain so far, that there is hardly one of them who hath not received a fall; and some of them two or three.

READING-WRITING CONNECTION

YOUR TURN Expand your understanding of these excerpts from *Gulliver's Travels* by responding to this prompt. Then use the **revising tips** to improve your analysis.

WRITING PROMPT

WRITE AN ANALYSIS Suppose that Gulliver could not return to England. Where do you think he would prefer to live out the rest of his life, in Lilliput or in Brobdingnag? Write a **one-page analysis** in which you determine which country he would choose as his home. Support your ideas with information from the text.

REVISING TIPS

- In your response, consider Gulliver's character traits.
- Describe living conditions and relationships in each country.

COMMON CORE

L1 Demonstrate command of the conventions of standard English grammar when writing. **W 2** Write explanatory texts to examine and convey complex ideas. **W 2b** Develop the topic thoroughly by selecting concrete details. **W 9** Draw evidence from literary texts to support analysis.

Interactive Revision   **THINK**central

Go to **thinkcentral.com**.
KEYWORD: HML12-657

from **Gulliver's Travels**

Film Clips on **Media◯Smart** DVD-ROM

From Page to Screen

In *Gulliver's Travels* Jonathan Swift achieved a rare feat—a novel that both entertains with its fantastic adventures and criticizes with its biting satire. In 1996 Charles Sturridge directed a TV miniseries version of Swift's popular novel. In this lesson, you'll view a clip from Gulliver's first voyage, to the island of Lilliput.

The Filmmakers' Challenge

Adapting *Gulliver's Travels* to film was an ambitious undertaking. The incredible characters and fantastic world that sprang from Swift's imagination almost 300 years ago had to be re-created believably for the screen. To achieve this goal, the filmmakers used a wide array of special effects, from **computer-generated imagery,** filmed images created from computer graphics, to

Gulliver meets the Lilliputian emperor.

models, scaled-down copies of settings, creatures, and objects. The scene you'll view was filmed using **bluescreen** effects. It was filmed on two locations. The actors portraying Lilliputians were in a real palace in Portugal, and the actor portraying Gulliver was in a studio with brightly lit blue walls, ceiling, and floor, speaking his dialogue to the air. The two scenes were then merged into one, using a computer editing system.

We know Lilliputians don't exist. However, if the elements of the scene—the acting, the real locations, the bluescreen effects—are combined just right, the viewer will be drawn into the story as though the six-inch people were real. "The word we used all the time," says Sturridge, "was 'unspecial' effects. We don't want the effects to look special. We want them to look invisible."

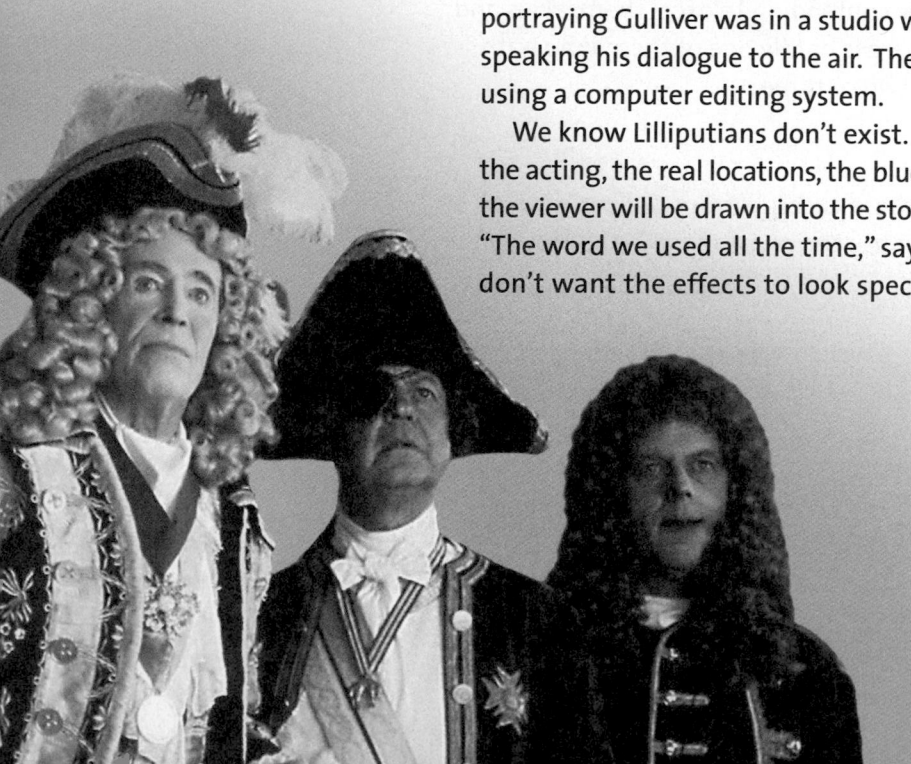

Comparing Texts: Suspension of Disbelief

In order to enjoy any work of fiction, a reader or viewer suspends disbelief to accept the unreal as possible. Suspension of disbelief is made possible through realistic details, through the characters' convincing reactions to the unbelievable events, and through the tone of the text or film. We know we're dealing with fiction—it's "just a movie," or "just a book"—but if the details are presented correctly, we experience the story as though it were real.

Read the following passage from *Gulliver's Travels*. Compare the treatment of the Lilliputians in the text with the film clip's special effects. Note the details that cause you to suspend your disbelief and accept these little people as real.

> In a little time I felt something alive moving on my left leg, which advancing gently forward over my breast, came almost up to my chin; when bending my eyes downwards as much as I could, I perceived it to be a human creature not six inches high, with a bow and arrow in his hands, and a quiver at his back.
> 5 In the meantime, I felt at least forty more of the same kind (*as I conjectured*) following the first. I was in the utmost astonishment, and roared so loud, that they all ran back in a fright; and some of them, as I was afterwards told, were hurt with the falls they got by leaping from my sides upon the ground.

Viewing Guide

Media ⦿ Smart DVD-ROM

- **Film:** *Gulliver's Travels*
- **Director:** Charles Sturridge
- **Genre:** Fantasy adventure
- **Running Time:** 5 minutes

In the clip from *Gulliver's Travels*, Gulliver has been captured by the Lilliputians. They bring him to the palace to present him to the emperor. To critically analyze the clip, you may want to view it more than once.

NOW VIEW

CLOSE VIEWING: Media Analysis

1. **Analyze Special Effects** Describe what you think the director meant by "unspecial," invisible effects. Do you think the filmmakers achieved their goal in this scene?

2. **Evaluate Actor's Performance** This scene was filmed with the actor playing Gulliver acting alone in a blue room. Was he successful in convincing you that he was truly a part of the scene's setting? Explain.

3. **Compare Suspension of Disbelief** Compare the ways in which Swift's text and the film version allow you to suspend disbelief and accept the fantastic elements of the story. Think about the following:
   - the tone of Swift's writing and its translation to film
   - Gulliver's reactions to the impossible events
   - the details included in the text and film

from **Candide**

Fiction by Voltaire

COMMON CORE

RL 3 Analyze the impact of the author's choices regarding how to develop and relate elements of a story. **RL 10** Read and comprehend literature, including stories.

Meet the Author

Voltaire 1694–1778

Voltaire (vōl-târ′), like his English counterparts Pope and Swift, used satire to rail against the oppression, prejudice, corruption, and religious intolerance he saw in France. During his lifetime, he was praised as a literary genius as well as condemned as a blasphemer. Today, he is acknowledged as one of the leading writers of his era and a champion of human rights.

Literature Trumps Law Voltaire, whose real name was François-Marie Arouet (är-wĕ′), was born into a middle-class Parisian family. At age 10, he began studies at the Jesuit Collège Louis-le-Grand, located in the heart of Paris, where he learned Latin and developed a love for classical literature, as well as a strong skepticism concerning established religions. Upon his graduation in 1711, his father expected him to pursue a law career, but Arouet rejected this plan. He wanted to become a writer.

Arouet had his first literary success at the age of 24 with the play *Oedipe,* which was produced in 1718. The tragedy was an enormous hit and prompted Arouet to choose the pen name Voltaire. Many theatrical successes followed.

A Very Enlightening Exile In 1726, Voltaire was forced to leave France after a feud with a young nobleman resulted in Voltaire's arrest. For nearly three years Voltaire lived in England, where he met fellow satirists Alexander Pope and Jonathan Swift. He came to look upon England as an enlightened society, with great tolerance for individual thought and expression.

After Voltaire returned to Paris in 1729, he wrote *Letters Concerning the English Nation,* a book that praised English traditions, institutions, and scholarship. The book was perceived as a criticism of the French government, and copies of it were ordered to be burned. Voltaire fled Paris once again. He made his home in the Lorraine region of France, where he produced copious political pamphlets on issues of the day and a series of *contes philosophiques,* or philosophical tales, the most famous of which is *Candide.*

A Warm Welcome in Paris Voltaire enjoyed worldwide fame. He returned to Paris for the last time early in February 1778 to oversee a production of his play *Irène.* On opening night, an actor stepped up to Voltaire's seat and placed a crown on the author's head as the audience applauded wildly. Soon after, the 83-year-old Voltaire's health failed, and he died in Paris on May 30, 1778.

DID YOU KNOW?

Voltaire . . .

- reportedly drank dozens of cups of coffee a day.
- spent 11 months in Bastille prison for writing poetry that offended the royal family.
- is sometimes credited with having written the first work of science fiction.

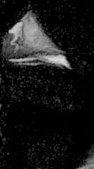

Author Online

Go to **thinkcentral.com**. KEYWORD: HML12-660

THINK central

● TEXT ANALYSIS: HUMOR

Voltaire conveys his satirical messages through **humor.** There are three basic types of humor.

- **Humor of situation** involves exaggerated plot structures or situational irony.

- **Humor of character** often involves exaggerated personality traits or characters who cannot recognize their own failings.

- **Humor of language** may involve devices such as verbal irony, puns, hyperbole, or absurd logic.

As you read, look for examples of these types of humor.

● READING SKILL: DRAW CONCLUSIONS ABOUT CHARACTERS

When you **draw conclusions** about a character in a literary work, you form opinions about his or her personality. You should base your conclusions on the character's words, thoughts, and behaviors as he or she faces various dilemmas, challenges, and obstacles. As you read, use a chart like the one below to record information about what each character says and does to better understand the meaning of Voltaire's satire.

Character	Speech	Actions	Descriptions
Candide			a most sweet disposition

▲ VOCABULARY IN CONTEXT

Knowing the following boldfaced words will help you understand this selection from *Candide.* To see how many words you know, substitute another word or phrase with the same meaning.

1. The **oracle** wisely predicted what would happen.

2. He believed her **implicitly** and asked no questions.

3. The teacher's **doctrine** included several new theories.

4. She was a creature of delicate **sensibility**.

5. The hurricane forecast brought great **consternation** to the community.

6. Was the monster a **terrestrial** creature, or did it come from outer space?

7. Behave with **civility,** not rudeness.

8. She tried in vain to **remonstrate** with the children.

 Complete the activities in your **Reader/Writer Notebook**.

Are you an OPTIMIST *or a* PESSIMIST?

It has been said that an optimist sees a doughnut and a pessimist sees the hole. This saying humorously captures the difference between the sunny attitude of the optimist and the bleak outlook of the pessimist. Believing that the world was filled with evils over which neither God nor humanity had any control, Voltaire wrote *Candide* in order to puncture the philosophy of optimism with his sharp satirical pen.

ROLE-PLAY With a partner, improvise a conversation between a pessimist and an optimist who are standing at a bus stop when it starts to rain. The optimist should try to persuade the pessimist that the rain is a good thing, while the pessimist should insist that it is bad.

CANDIDE

Voltaire

> **BACKGROUND** Voltaire wrote *Candide* partly in response to German philosopher Gottfried Leibniz, a proponent of the philosophy of optimism. According to Leibniz, God had created the "best of all possible worlds," and therefore people should accept evil because it is part of God's plan. Voltaire found such a philosophy both insufficient and appalling. In *Candide*, Voltaire exposes his innocent main character to a world of horrors and folly.

CHAPTER I
How Candide was brought up in a magnificent castle, and how he was driven from thence

In the country of Westphalia, in the castle of the most noble Baron of Thunder-ten-tronckh, lived a youth whom nature had endowed with a most sweet disposition. His face was the true index of his mind. He had a solid judgment joined to the most unaffected simplicity, and hence, I presume, he had his name of Candide.[1] The old servants of the house suspected him to have been the son of the Baron's sister, by a mighty good sort of a gentleman of the neighborhood, whom that young lady refused to marry because he could produce no more than threescore and eleven quarterings in his arms;[2] the rest of the genealogical tree belonging to the family having been lost through the injuries of time. **A**

10   The Baron was one of the most powerful lords in Westphalia, for his castle had not only a gate but even windows, and his great hall was hung with tapestry. He used to hunt with his mastiffs and spaniels instead of greyhounds; his groom served him for huntsman, and the parson of the parish officiated as grand almoner.[3] He was called "My Lord" by all his people, and he never told a story but everyone laughed at it.

---

1. **Candide** (kăn-dēd'): The name is a French word meaning "innocent" or "without guile."
2. **no more than . . . arms:** in his coat of arms, no more than 71 divisions indicating connections with other noble families. The number of quarterings is ridiculously large.
3. **grand almoner** (ăl'mə-nər): a person in charge of distributing charity to the poor.

Analyze Visuals ▶
Narrative painting is art that implies a story. Describe the story that Fragonard conveys in *The Stolen Kiss*.

A   DRAW CONCLUSIONS
Based on the description in lines 1–4, what is your initial impression of Candide?

The Stolen Kiss, Jean-Honoré Fragonard. The Hermitage, St. Petersburg, Russia. © Scala/Art Resource, New York.

My lady Baroness weighed three hundred and fifty pounds, consequently was a person of no small consideration; and then she did the honors of the house with a dignity that commanded universal respect. Her daughter Cunegund was about seventeen years of age, fresh colored, comely, plump, and desirable. The Baron's son seemed to be a youth in every respect worthy of his father. Pangloss the preceptor[4]
20 was the **oracle** of the family, and little Candide listened to his instructions with all the simplicity natural to his age and disposition.

Master Pangloss taught metaphysico-theologo-cosmolo-nigology.[5] He could prove admirably that there is no effect without a cause, and that, in this best of all possible worlds, the Baron's castle was the most magnificent of all castles and my lady the best of all possible baronesses.

"It is demonstrable," said he, "that things cannot be otherwise than they are; for as all things have been created for some end, they must necessarily be created for the best end. Observe, for instance, the nose is formed for spectacles, therefore we wear spectacles. The legs are visibly designed for stockings, accordingly we wear stockings.
30 Stones were made to be hewn, and to construct castles, therefore my lord has a magnificent castle; for the greatest baron in the province ought to be the best lodged. Swine were intended to be eaten; therefore we eat pork all the year round. And they who assert that everything is good do not express themselves correctly; they should say that everything is for the best." **B**

Candide listened attentively, and believed **implicitly;** for he thought Miss Cunegund excessively handsome, though he never had the courage to tell her so. He concluded that next to the happiness of being Baron of Thunder-ten-tronckh, the next was that of being Miss Cunegund, the next that of seeing her every day, and the last that of hearing the **doctrine** of Master Pangloss, the greatest philosopher of the
40 whole province, and consequently of the whole world.

One day, when Miss Cunegund went to take a walk in a little neighboring wood, which was called a park, . . . she happened to meet Candide; she blushed, he blushed also. She wished him a good morning in a faltering tone; he returned the salute, without knowing what he said. The next day, as they were rising from dinner, Cunegund and Candide slipped behind the screen. She dropped her handkerchief; the young man picked it up. She innocently took hold of his hand, and he as innocently kissed hers with a warmth, a **sensibility,** a grace—all very extraordinary—their lips met, their eyes sparkled, their knees trembled, their hands strayed. The Baron of Thunder-ten-tronckh chanced to come by; he beheld the cause and effect,
50 and, without hesitation, saluted Candide with some notable kicks on the breech and drove him out of doors. Miss Cunegund fainted away, and, as soon as she came to herself, the Baroness boxed her ears. Thus a general **consternation** was spread over this most magnificent and most agreeable of all possible castles.

---

4. **Pangloss the preceptor** (prĭ-sĕp′tər): Pangloss the teacher. The name of this know-it-all character is from the Greek for "all tongues" or "all languages."

5. **metaphysico-theologo-cosmolo-nigology:** Voltaire is satirizing the widely accepted optimistic philosophy of the day. In the pretentious yet nonsensical name that Voltaire gives the philosophy, the last part, *nigology*, is from the French word for "foolish."

oracle (ôr′ə-kəl) *n.* a wise person who foresees the future

B HUMOR
What examples of absurd logic can you find in lines 26–34?

implicitly (ĭm-plĭs′ĭt-lē) *adv.* without the need to hear spoken; without doubt or question

doctrine (dŏk′trĭn) *n.* teachings; theories

sensibility (sĕn′sə-bĭl′ĭ-tē) *n.* the ability to be affected emotionally; sensitivity

consternation (kŏn′stər-nā′shən) *n.* fear or shock that makes one feel bewildered or upset

CHAPTER II
What befell Candide among the Bulgarians

Candide, thus driven out of this **terrestrial** paradise, wandered a long time, without knowing where he went; sometimes he raised his eyes, all bedewed with tears, toward Heaven, and sometimes he cast a melancholy look toward the magnificent castle where dwelt the fairest of young baronesses. He laid himself down to sleep in a furrow, heartbroken and supperless. The snow fell in great flakes, and, in the morning when he awoke, he was almost frozen to death; however, he made shift to crawl to the
60 next town, which was called Waldberghoff-trarbk-dikdorff, without a penny in his pocket, and half dead with hunger and fatigue. He took up his stand at the door of an inn. He had not been long there before two men dressed in blue[6] fixed their eyes steadfastly upon him.

"Faith, comrade," said one of them to the other, "yonder is a well-made young fellow, and of the right size."

Thereupon they went up to Candide, and with the greatest **civility** and politeness invited him to dine with them.

"Gentlemen," replied Candide, with a most engaging modesty, "you do me much honor, but, upon my word, I have no money."

70 "Money, sir!" said one of the men in blue to him. "Young persons of your appearance and merit never pay anything. Why, are not you five feet five inches high?"[7]

"Yes, gentlemen, that is really my size," replied he with a low bow.

"Come then, sir, sit down along with us. We will not only pay your reckoning,[8] but will never suffer such a clever young fellow as you to want money. Mankind were born to assist one another."

"You are perfectly right, gentlemen," said Candide; "that is precisely the doctrine of Master Pangloss; and I am convinced that everything is for the best." **C**

His generous companions next entreated him to accept a few crowns, which he
80 readily complied with, at the same time offering them his note for the payment, which they refused, and sat down to table.

"Have you not a great affection for—"

"Oh, yes!" he replied. "I have a great affection for the lovely Miss Cunegund."

"Maybe so," replied one of the men, "but that is not the question! We are asking you whether you have not a great affection for the King of the Bulgarians?"

"For the King of the Bulgarians?" said Candide. "Not at all. Why, I never saw him in my life."

"Is it possible! Oh, he is a most charming king! Come, we must drink his health."

"With all my heart, gentlemen," Candide said, and he tossed off[9] his glass.

terrestrial (tə-rĕs′trē-əl)
adj. of the earth; earthly

civility (sĭ-vĭl′ĭ-tē) *n.* good manners; decent behavior

C DRAW CONCLUSIONS
What does Candide's reaction to the recruiting officers' kindness suggest about his character?

---

6. **dressed in blue:** Voltaire speaks of Bulgarians, but he is really satirizing the Prussian king Frederick the Great (1712–1786), whose recruiting officers wore blue uniforms.

7. **five feet five inches high:** Voltaire is poking fun at the Prussian king's height requirement for his soldiers.

8. **reckoning:** bill.

9. **tossed off:** drank down.

90 "Bravo!" cried the blues. "You are now the support, the defender, the hero of the Bulgarians; your fortune is made; you are on the high road to glory."

So saying, they put him in irons and carried him away to the regiment. There he was made to wheel about to the right, to the left, to draw his ramrod,[10] to return his ramrod, to present, to fire, to march, and they gave him thirty blows with a cane. The next day he performed his exercise a little better, and they gave him but twenty. The day following he came off with ten and was looked upon as a young fellow of surprising genius by all his comrades. **D**

Candide was struck with amazement and could not for the soul of him conceive how he came to be a hero. One fine spring morning, he took it into his head to take
100 a walk, and he marched straight forward, conceiving it to be a privilege of the human species, as well as of the brute creation, to make use of their legs how and when they pleased. He had not gone above two leagues[11] when he was overtaken by four other heroes, six feet high, who bound him neck and heels, and carried him to a dungeon. A court-martial sat upon him,[12] and he was asked which he liked best, either to run the gauntlet[13] six and thirty times through the whole regiment, or to have his brains blown out with a dozen musket balls. In vain did he **remonstrate** to them that the human will is free, and that he chose neither. They obliged him to make a choice, and he determined, in virtue of that divine gift called free will, to run the gauntlet six and thirty times. He had gone through his discipline twice, and the regiment being
110 composed of two thousand men, they composed for him exactly four thousand strokes, which laid bare all his muscles and nerves, from the nape of his neck to his rump. As they were preparing to make him set out the third time, our young hero, unable to support it any longer, begged as a favor they would be so obliging as to shoot him through the head. The favor being granted, a bandage was tied over his eyes, and he was made to kneel down. At that very instant, his Bulgarian Majesty, happening to pass by, inquired into the delinquent's crime, and being a prince of great penetration, he found, from what he heard of Candide, that he was a young metaphysician,[14] entirely ignorant of the world. And, therefore, out of his great clemency,[15] he condescended to pardon him, for which his name will be celebrated
120 in every journal, and in every age. A skillful surgeon made a cure of Candide in three weeks by means of emollient unguents prescribed by Dioscorides.[16] His sores were now skinned over, and he was able to march when the King of the Bulgarians gave battle to the King of the Abares. **E**

Translated by Tobias Smollett

D HUMOR
What **situational irony** does Voltaire develop in lines 90–97?

remonstrate
(rĭ-mŏn′strāt′) *v.* to say or plead in protest or complaint

E HUMOR
In lines 104–114, which types of humor does Voltaire employ?

---

10. **ramrod:** a rod used to ram gunpowder and bullets into a musket.

11. **two leagues:** about five or six miles.

12. **A court-martial . . . him:** He was put on trial at a military tribunal.

13. **run the gauntlet** (gônt′lĭt): submit to a form of military punishment in which the person being punished ran between two rows of soldiers, who struck him with clubs or other weapons.

14. **metaphysician** (mĕt′ə-fĭ-zĭsh′ən): someone skilled in metaphysics, the branch of philosophy that investigates the nature of reality.

15. **clemency** (klĕm′ən-sē): leniency or mercy toward offenders or enemies.

16. **emollient unguents** (ĭ-mŏl′yənt ŭng′gwənts) . . . **Dioscorides** (dī′ə-skôr′ĭ-dēz′): soothing ointments recommended by Dioscorides, a Greek physician of the first century A.D. whose influential book on the medicinal properties of plants was quite out-of-date even in Voltaire's day.

Comprehension

1. **Recall** Why does the Baron throw Candide out of the castle?

2. **Summarize** How does Candide become a soldier in the Bulgarian regiment?

Text Analysis

3. **Identify Humor** Voltaire employs different types of humor in *Candide*. For each basic type listed, find two examples in the selection.

   - humor of language   • humor of character   • humor of situation

4. **Make Inferences** The Baron houses the philosopher Pangloss, who teaches the Baron's children and Candide. Why might the Baron appreciate Pangloss's philosophy? Provide support from the text for your answer.

5. **Draw Conclusions About Character** Refer to the information you recorded in your chart as you read. What moral dilemmas do the Baron and Candide face? How do their actions reveal their character? Why do you think Voltaire chose to place his characters in such situations?

6. **Analyze Irony** Voltaire relies heavily on irony in *Candide*. **Verbal irony** occurs when a character says one thing but means something else, and **situational irony** occurs when a character expects one thing to happen but something else actually happens. For each example listed, determine what type of irony is employed and explain Voltaire's humorous intention.

   - lines 48–51 ("The Baron . . . out of doors.")
   - lines 90–92 ("'You are now . . . away to the regiment.")
   - lines 112–114 ("As they were preparing . . . shoot him through the head.")

7. **Compare Texts** Both Voltaire in *Candide* and Swift in *Gulliver's Travels* employ innocent or naive main characters for their tales. In your opinion, why would both authors have chosen this type of main character? Support your conclusion.

Text Criticism

8. **Critical Interpretations** Voltaire once said that he felt "satire is almost always unjust" because it presents only one side of an issue or argument—the author's. Do you agree, or does this kind of one-sided expression of ideas have any value in public discourse? Explain your opinion.

Are you an OPTIMIST or a PESSIMIST?

Based on what you've read of *Candide*, do you think that the main character's optimism will serve him well as the story unfolds? Or do you think Candide will become pessimistic? Explain your response.

COMMON CORE

RL 3 Analyze the impact of the author's choices regarding how to develop and relate elements of a story. RL 6 Analyze a case in which grasping point of view requires distinguishing what is directly stated in a text from what is really meant. RL 10 Read and comprehend literature, including stories.

Vocabulary in Context

▲ **VOCABULARY PRACTICE**

Choose the vocabulary word that best completes each sentence.

WORD LIST

civility

consternation

doctrine

implicitly

oracle

remonstrate

sensibility

terrestrial

1. The professor taught his _____ of universal truths.
2. The unexpected quiz caused great _____ in the class.
3. Laughing and weeping come easily to someone of such strong _____.
4. She felt no doubt but instead followed his instructions _____.
5. They lived in a _____ paradise, a heaven on earth.
6. The mother had to ___ with her noisy children, asking them to be quieter.
7. We asked the _____ to foretell the future.
8. She is never impolite but instead treats others with ____.

ACADEMIC VOCABULARY IN WRITING

> • affect   • challenge   • consent   • final   • respond

What do you learn about Candide based on how he **responds** to the obstacles that life throws in his path? Does misfortune **affect** his view of the world? Use at least one additional Academic Vocabulary word in your written response.

VOCABULARY STRATEGY: SYNONYMS AS CONTEXT CLUES

Often you can figure out the meaning of an unfamiliar word by examining its **context,** or surroundings. One type of context clue to look for is a **synonym,** or a word with a similar meaning. In the example from *Candide* that appears below, the context presents a synonym for the word *civility*, which means "politeness" or "good manners."

unfamiliar word

... they went up to Candide, and with the greatest (civility) and

synonym —(politeness) invited him to dine with them.

PRACTICE Study the context of each sentence, looking for a word that is a synonym for the boldfaced word. Then explain its meaning.

1. Candide had a sweet **disposition,** but the Baron's personality was not as sweet.
2. Candide was attracted to pretty girls, and Cunegund, who was especially **comely,** immediately caught his eye.
3. Stones were **hewn** to build the castle; trees were cut as well.
4. Feeling hesitant about approaching Candide, Cunegund spoke to him in a **faltering** tone.
5. Candide slept in a **furrow,** leaving the ditch in the morning.

COMMON CORE

L 4a Use context as a clue to the meaning of a word. **L 6** Acquire and use accurately general academic words.

Interactive Vocabulary
THINK central

Go to **thinkcentral.com.**
KEYWORD: HML12-668

The Golden Age of Satire

The rise of a literate middle class with an interest in social affairs was one reason for the tremendous popularity of satire in 18th-century England. Alexander Pope and Jonathan Swift are two of the most outstanding satirists from this period. In *The Rape of the Lock,* Pope elevates a minor insult—the theft of a lock of hair—to a level of epic grandeur.

> *"Just then, Clarissa drew with tempting grace*
> *A two-edged weapon from her shining case:*
> *So ladies in romance assist their knight,*
> *Present the spear, and arm him for the fight."*

In "A Modest Proposal," on the other hand, Jonathan Swift makes light of a horrible suggestion.

> *"A child will make two dishes at an entertainment for friends;*
> *and when the family dines alone, the fore or hind quarter will*
> *make a reasonable dish, and seasoned with a little pepper or*
> *salt will be very good boiled on the fourth day, especially in*
> *winter. . . . "*

Making liberal use of verbal irony, satirists often do not write literally about the targets of their scorn; instead, they create an imaginary scenario as a way to make an indirect point about a real-life problem.

Writing to Evaluate

Imagine that you are a member of the 18th-century English middle class, educated and concerned about the well-being of society. Consider the satires you have just read. Write a brief essay to explain which you find most compelling, and why.

Consider

- which piece you find the most clever or amusing
- how you feel about the social issues targeted by each piece
- which piece delivers the clearest social critique

Extension

VIEWING & REPRESENTING

The paintings and engravings of William Hogarth offered satirical commentary on 18th-century life that could be every bit as cutting and detailed as the works of Pope or Swift. In this painting, "The Bench," Hogarth caricatures a group of judges. Identify the qualities of the judges depicted. What satirical comment could Hogarth be making? Give a brief oral review, citing details from the image.

COMMON CORE

RL 9 Demonstrate knowledge of foundational works of literature. **W 1** Write arguments to support claims in an analysis of substantive topics or texts. **W 1a** Introduce precise, knowledgeable claim(s).

COMMON CORE

RI 6 Determine an author's purpose in a text. L 3a Apply an understanding of syntax to the study of complex texts when reading. L 5 Demonstrate understanding of nuances in word meanings.

from A Dictionary of the English Language

Nonfiction by Samuel Johnson

VIDEO TRAILER **THINK** central KEYWORD: HML12-670A

Meet the Author

Samuel Johnson 1709–1784

DID YOU KNOW?

Samuel Johnson . . .

- became known as "Dictionary Johnson" and "the Good Doctor."

- showed little sympathy for the American colonists who, he said, demanded liberty while keeping slaves.

- is second only to Shakespeare as the most frequently quoted English writer.

Samuel Johnson's wit and wisdom so dominated the English literary scene in the second half of the 18th century that historians have called the period the Age of Johnson. A consummate man of letters, Johnson wrote satires (in both poetry and prose), biographies, sermons, literary criticism, book reviews, and a multitude of essays, while also at various times working on Greek and Latin translations, editing magazines, and researching extensively for his ambitious dictionary and other scholarly works. His neoclassical literary style—highly intellectual and rational, with a sprinkling of dry wit and irony—greatly influenced the prose of the time. But as impressive as his literary credentials are, Johnson's reputation among modern readers rests primarily on his famous personality—at once cantankerous and lovable—and his dazzling conversation, which was recorded by his friend James Boswell in *The Life of Samuel Johnson* (page 682).

Years of Poverty and Obscurity Johnson's eminent reputation was a long time in the making. He was born the son of a poor small-town bookseller in the English Midlands. Several childhood illnesses left his hearing and vision impaired and his face disfigured by scars. Still, he grew into a tough, fiercely independent young man with a love of talk and scholarship. He was able to fulfill his dream of studying at Oxford University, but he had to leave after 13 months because he did not have the money to continue. After failing to make a career of teaching, he moved to London, where he earned a meager living publishing his poetry and prose, much of it in *The Gentleman's Magazine*.

Into the Limelight Until he published his long poem *The Vanity of Human Wishes* (1749), Johnson had never signed his name to his writing. But afterward, people took notice. Over the next decade, Johnson embarked on what he called the "anxious employment of a periodical writer." He wrote over 200 essays for his periodical, *The Rambler* (1750–1752). It was around this time that he was also working on *A Dictionary of the English Language* (1755), the two-volume masterpiece that would make him famous. In 1765, he was awarded an honorary doctorate of civil law, and in 1762 the British prime minister awarded him a pension for life to honor his literary contributions to date. Johnson never again had to worry about money.

Author Online

Go to thinkcentral.com. KEYWORD: HML12-670B

THINK central

TEXT ANALYSIS: VOICE

Samuel Johnson was known for being scholarly and witty yet personable, and the voice in his writing clearly reflects this reputation. **Voice** is the unique expression of a writer's personality on the page. To "hear" a writer's voice, examine **diction** (word choice and syntax), tone, and the ideas expressed by the writer. Note how these elements shape Johnson's distinctive voice in the following passage from the preface to *A Dictionary of the English Language:*

It is the fate of those who toil at the lower employments of life to be rather driven by the fear of evil than attracted by the prospect of good....

As you read, note Johnson's diction, tone, and ideas and how these reveal his voice.

READING SKILL: ANALYZE AUTHOR'S PURPOSE

Authors often have more than one purpose, or reason for writing a particular work. An author may wish to inform, entertain, or persuade readers about a controlling idea, or **main idea**. Johnson wrote his dictionary entries to inform his readers of the meanings and spellings of words, but he hoped to achieve something else with his preface. To determine Johnson's purposes for writing the preface, record examples of the following as you read:

- the main idea of each paragraph
- supporting details the author uses to develop his ideas
- descriptions that convey the author's opinions or feelings

▲ VOCABULARY IN CONTEXT

The boldfaced words in these sentences appear in Johnson's preface to the dictionary. Use the sentences to help you understand the words. Then try using the words in your own sentences.

1. Lois received strong **censure** for her bad conduct.
2. A volunteer works without expecting **recompense.**
3. We grow **copious** amounts of wheat—much, much more than we could ever eat.
4. Carla was so angry with Luis that she began **expunging** every mention of his name in her diary.
5. One sister died young, but the other had great **longevity.**
6. When the library is not open, you can drop your books in a **repository** outside the front door.

Complete the activities in your **Reader/Writer Notebook**.

What's in a WORD?

All languages change over time. Existing words take on new meanings, new words are coined, and others fall out of use. Lexicographers—those who, like Samuel Johnson, write dictionaries—attempt to establish standard definitions of words in hopes of maintaining common usage and understanding. Even so, word meanings are never static for very long.

QUICKWRITE Try your hand at defining a few words. On a piece of paper, write your own definitions for the following words: *artsy, blog, cool, flame, snail mail, text message.* Keep in mind how you and others use the words. Consider whether the words have more than one meaning. Share your definitions with your class.

A Dictionary of the English Language

Samuel Johnson

BACKGROUND By 1700, Italy and France both had national dictionaries that had taken their scholars decades to complete. The few English dictionaries of the time looked puny by comparison. So in 1746, Samuel Johnson—then a penniless, unknown writer—talked several booksellers into paying him to create a dictionary worthy of the English language. It took him nine years of painstaking work to define around 43,000 words, illustrated with some 114,000 quotations.

Analyze Visuals ▶

Examine the photograph of an 18th-century printing press. What **inferences** can you make about printing books in Johnson's time?

✚ FROM THE PREFACE ✚

It is the fate of those who toil at the lower employments of life to be rather driven by the fear of evil than attracted by the prospect of good; to be exposed to **censure** without hope of praise; to be disgraced by miscarriage, or punished for neglect, where success would have been without applause, and diligence without reward.

Among these unhappy mortals is the writer of dictionaries, whom mankind have considered not as the pupil, but the slave, of science, the pioneer of literature, doomed only to remove rubbish and clear obstructions from the paths through which learning and genius press forward to conquest and glory, without bestowing a smile on the humble drudge[1] that facilitates their progress. Every other author

10 may aspire to praise: the lexicographer[2] can only hope to escape reproach—and even this negative **recompense** has been yet granted to very few.

I have, notwithstanding this discouragement, attempted a dictionary of the English language, which, while it was employed in the cultivation of every species of literature, has itself been hitherto neglected, suffered to spread, under the direction of chance, into wild exuberance, resigned to the tyranny of time and fashion, and exposed to the corruptions of ignorance and caprices of innovation.

censure (sĕn′shər) *n.* criticism

recompense (rĕk′əm-pĕns′) *n.* payment or repayment; compensation

---

1. **drudge:** someone who labors at difficult, tedious work.
2. **lexicographer** (lĕk′sĭ-kŏg′rə-fər): someone who compiles a dictionary.

When I took the first survey of my undertaking, I found our speech **copious** without order, and energetic without rules: wherever I turned my view, there was perplexity to be disentangled and confusion to be regulated; choice was to 20 be made out of boundless variety, without any established principle of selection; adulterations were to be detected, without a settled test of purity; and modes of expression to be rejected or received, without the suffrages[3] of any writers of classical reputation or acknowledged authority. **Ⓐ**

Having therefore no assistance but from general grammar, I applied myself to the perusal of our writers; and noting whatever might be of use to ascertain or illustrate any word or phrase, accumulated in time the materials of a dictionary, which, by degrees, I reduced to method, establishing to myself, in the progress of the work, such rules as experience and analogy suggested to me—experience, which practice and observation were continually increasing, and analogy, which, 30 though in some words obscure, was evident in others. . . .

When first I collected these authorities I was desirous that every quotation should be useful to some other end than the illustration of a word; I therefore extracted from philosophers principles of science, from historians remarkable facts, from chemists complete processes, from divines[4] striking exhortations, and from poets beautiful descriptions. Such is design while it is yet at a distance from **Ⓑ** execution. When the time called upon me to range this accumulation of elegance and wisdom into an alphabetical series, I soon discovered that the bulk of my volumes would fright away the student, and was forced to depart from my scheme of including all that was pleasing or useful in English literature, and reduce 40 my transcripts very often to clusters of words in which scarcely any meaning is retained. Thus to the weariness of copying I was condemned to add the vexation of **expunging**. . . .

In hope of giving **longevity** to that which its own nature forbids to be immortal, I have devoted this book, the labor of years, to the honor of my country, that we may no longer yield the palm of philology,[5] without a contest, to the nations of the continent. The chief glory of every people arises from its authors. Whether I shall add anything by my own writings to the reputation of English literature must be left to time: much of my life has been lost under the pressures of disease, much has been trifled away, and much has always been 50 spent in provision for the day that was passing over me; but I shall not think my employment useless or ignoble if, by my assistance, foreign nations and distant ages gain access to the propagators of knowledge, and understand the teachers of

copious (kō′pē-əs) *adj.* plentiful; abundant

Ⓐ AUTHOR'S PURPOSE
Reread lines 17–23. What is the **controlling idea** of this paragraph? What might have motivated Johnson to make this point in his preface?

Ⓑ GRAMMAR AND STYLE
Reread lines 31–35. Notice how Johnson uses **parallelism**—listing a series of phrases beginning with *from*—to emphasize his careful research.

expunging (ĭk-spŭn′jĭng) *n.* erasing or removing completely **expunge** *v.*

longevity (lŏn-jĕv′ĭ-tē) *n.* endurance over a sizable span of time; long life

---

3. **suffrages** (sŭf′rĭ-jĭz): acts of support; assistance.

4. **divines:** religious leaders; members of the clergy.

5. **the palm of philology** (fĭ-lŏl′ə-jē): the symbol of triumph in the study of language and literature. Palm leaves were traditionally carried or worn as a symbol of victory.

truth, if my labors afford light to the **repositories** of science and add celebrity to Bacon, to Hooker, to Milton, and to Boyle.[6] . . . **C**

In this work, when it shall be found that much is omitted, let it not be forgotten that much likewise is performed; and, though no book was ever spared out of tenderness to the author, and the world is little solicitous[7] to know whence proceeded the faults of that which it condemns, yet it may gratify curiosity to inform it that the *English Dictionary* was written with little assistance of the
60 learned, and without any patronage of the great, not in the soft obscurities of retirement, or under the shelter of academic bowers,[8] but amid inconvenience and distraction, in sickness and in sorrow. It may repress the triumph of malignant criticism to observe that, if our language is not here fully displayed, I have only failed in an attempt which no human powers have hitherto completed. If the lexicons of ancient tongues, now immutably fixed,[9] and comprised in a few volumes, be yet, after the toil of successive ages, inadequate and delusive; if the aggregated knowledge and cooperating diligence of the Italian academicians did not secure them from the censure of
70 Beni;[10] if the embodied critics of France, when fifty years had been spent upon their work, were obliged to change its economy[11] and give their second edition another form, I may surely be contented without the praise of perfection, which, if I could obtain, in this gloom of solitude, what would it avail me? I have protracted my work till most of those whom I wished to please have sunk into the grave,
80 and success and miscarriage are empty sounds. I therefore dismiss it with frigid tranquility, having little to fear or hope from censure or from praise.

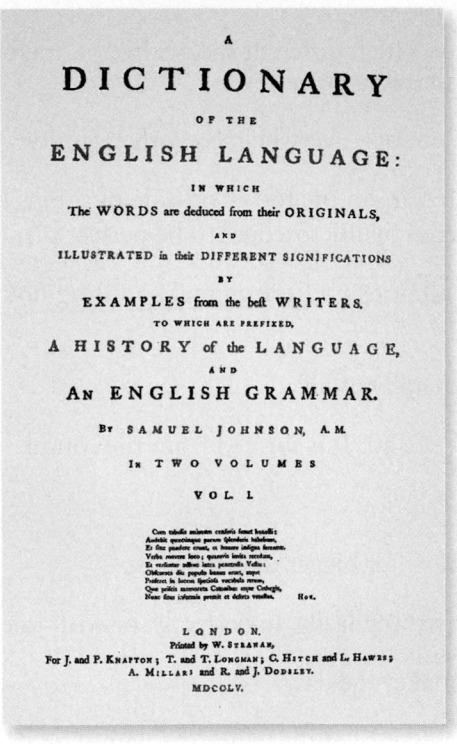

A

DICTIONARY

OF THE

ENGLISH LANGUAGE:

IN WHICH

The WORDS are deduced from their ORIGINALS,

AND

ILLUSTRATED in their DIFFERENT SIGNIFICATIONS

BY

EXAMPLES from the beſt WRITERS.

TO WHICH ARE PREFIXED,

A HISTORY of the LANGUAGE,

AND

AN ENGLISH GRAMMAR.

BY SAMUEL JOHNSON, A.M.

IN TWO VOLUMES

VOL. I.

LONDON.
Printed by W. STRAHAN,
For J. and P. KNAPTON; T. and T. LONGMAN; C. HITCH and L. HAWES;
A. MILLAR; and R. and J. DODSLEY.
MDCCLV.

repository (rĭ-pŏz'ĭ-tôr'ē) *n.* a place where information or physical items are stored

C **VOICE**
Reread lines 43–54. Identify the words and phrases that give this passage a scholarly **tone.**

6. **Bacon . . . Boyle:** English philosopher and essayist Francis Bacon (1561–1626), English clergyman and author Richard Hooker (1554–1600), English poet John Milton (1608–1674), and Irish-born scientist Robert Boyle (1627–1691), four authors whom Johnson quotes throughout his dictionary.

7. **little solicitous** (sə-lĭs'ĭ-təs): not very concerned.

8. **academic bowers** (bou'ərz): places of learning. Bowers are areas sheltered by overhanging trees, vine coverings like ivy, or other plants, as many traditional universities seem to be.

9. **lexicons** (lĕk'sĭ-kŏnz') . . . **immutably** (ĭ-myoo'tə-blē) **fixed:** dictionaries of ancient languages, now unchangeable.

10. **Beni:** Paolo Beni was a Renaissance thinker who strongly criticized the pioneering Italian dictionary put out by the Accademia della Crusca of Florence, Italy, in 1612. The dictionary nevertheless was an important milestone and served as a model for dictionaries in other languages.

11. **economy:** organization.

✥ SELECTED ENTRIES ✥

ADU´LT. A person above the age of infancy, or grown to some degree of strength; sometimes full grown: a word used chiefly by medicinal writers. **D**

TO A´MBLE. To move easily, without hard shocks, or shaking.

APE. A kind of monkey remarkable for imitating what he sees.

CORN. The seeds which grow in ears, not in pods; such as are made into bread.

90 **DULL.** Not exhilarating; not delightful; as, *to make dictionaries is* dull *work.*

FISH. An animal that inhabits the water.

TO HISS. To utter a noise like that of a serpent and some other animals. It is remarkable, that this word cannot be pronounced without making the noise which it signifies. **E**

LOUSE. A small animal, of which different species live on the bodies of men, beasts, and perhaps of all living creatures.

MI´SER. A wretched person; one overwhelmed with calamity.

MOULD. A kind of concretion on the top or outside of things kept, motionless and damp; now discovered by microscopes to be perfect plants.

100 **MOUSE.** The smallest of all beasts; a little animal haunting houses and corn fields, destroyed by cats.

NO´VEL. A small tale, generally of love.

POP. A small smart quick sound. It is formed from the sound.

RE´CIPE. A medical prescription.

RI´VER. A land current of water bigger than a brook.

TO SLU´BBER. To do any thing lazily, imperfectly, or with idle hurry.

SUN. The luminary that makes the day.

TE´MPEST. The utmost violence of the wind; the names by which the wind is called according to the gradual increase of its force seems to be,
110 a breeze; a gale; a gust; a storm; a tempest.

WA´RREN. A kind of park for rabbits. ❧

COMMON CORE L5

D SUBTLETY
Subtlety is a fine distinction in meaning based on small nuances of language. Why does Johnson use the subtle phrase "or grown to some degree of strength" here? How does this phrase help define *adult*?

E VOICE
Reread the entry for the verb *hiss.* Which words indicate Johnson's distinctive voice and would not likely be found in a more objective dictionary entry?

First Edition of Samuel Johnson's *A Dictionary of the English Language,* 1755. Courtesy of the Manhattan Rare Book Company.

Comprehension

1. **Recall** According to the preface, what is it like to be a lexicographer?

2. **Summarize** Describe Johnson's method of compiling information for his dictionary.

3. **Paraphrase** In your own words, restate Johnson's definition of the verb *slubber*.

Text Analysis

● 4. **Identify Author's Purpose** Based on his comments in the preface, what audience did Johnson have in mind when he compiled his dictionary? What was his purpose or purposes in writing the preface?

● 5. **Analyze Voice** Examine the stylistic elements that create Johnson's voice. Then, in your own words, describe his voice and provide examples from the text to support your response. Do you think Johnson's voice is appropriate and effective for a preface to a dictionary? Explain why or why not.

6. **Draw Conclusions** Find clues in the preface that express Johnson's deepest feelings about his great work. What conclusions about the **author's values** and **beliefs** can you draw from Johnson's remarks on the following topics?

   - the state of the English language (lines 12–23)
   - his explanation of the process for compiling the dictionary (lines 24–42)
   - his personal ambitions (lines 43–54)

7. **Evaluate a Primary Source** Examine the selected entries from Johnson's dictionary. Using a chart like the one shown, choose two or three words that have a substantially different meaning in our language today, and explain how their usage or meanings have changed. Considering these changes, what is the best use of Johnson's dictionary today?

Word	Johnson's Definition	Definition Today

Text Criticism

8. **Critical Interpretations** Critics have said that Johnson's writing is knowledgeable, honest, humane, and quick to seize the truth. On the basis of the preface and the entries from *A Dictionary of the English Language*, would you say that is an appropriate description of his writing? Cite evidence from the text.

What's in a **WORD?**

Which words do you know that have just entered the English language during your lifetime? Explain why you think this happened.

COMMON CORE

RI 6 Determine an author's purpose in a text. **L 1a** Apply the understanding that usage is a matter of convention, can change over time, and is sometimes contested. **L 3a** Apply an understanding of syntax to the study of complex texts when reading.

Vocabulary in Context

▲ VOCABULARY PRACTICE

Use your knowledge of the boldfaced vocabulary words to indicate whether each statement is true or false.

1. A person who lives to 100 has great **longevity.**
2. Someone with **copious** wealth is very poor.
3. There may be quite a few bottles in a bottle **repository.**
4. For **expunging** names on a list, you might use an eraser.
5. Most people welcome **censure** and desire more of it.
6. People who donate to charity always expect **recompense.**

WORD LIST

censure
copious
expunging
longevity
recompense
repository

ACADEMIC VOCABULARY IN WRITING

• affect • challenge • consent • final • respond

Samuel Johnson met the **challenge** of creating a dictionary of the English language, a task that took him years to complete. Johnson claims that one reason he wrote this dictonary was "to the honor of [his] country" (page 674). What do you think Johson means by this? Write a paragraph in which you use at least one of the Academic Vocabulary words in your **response.**

VOCABULARY STRATEGY: USING A DICTIONARY

Since Johnson's day, dictionaries have expanded to include a variety of information on a word. Study this sample dictionary entry for the word *censure:*

> PRONUNCIATION   ETYMOLOGY
> | |
> ENTRY WORD —— **cen•sure** (sĕn′shər) [L. *censura < censere,* to tax, value, judge]
> PART OF SPEECH —— ***n.* 1.** a condemnation as wrong; strong disapproval **2.** a judgment
> DEFINITION — condemning a person's misconduct—***vt.*** to express strong disapproval
> of. —***syn. criticize*** —**cen′sur•er** *n.*
> | |
>   SYNONYM   RELATED FORM

PRACTICE Use the information in the sample dictionary entry to help you answer these questions.

1. Where would you hyphenate *censure* if you had to type it on two lines?
2. Is the *s* in *censure* pronounced like the *s* in *sir* or the *s* in *sure?*
3. What is the meaning of the Latin word from which *censure* comes?
4. What synonym for *censure* does the entry provide?
5. The suffix *-er* often means "one who." What do you think the related form of *censurer* means?

⋯ **COMMON CORE**

L 2a Observe hyphenation conventions. **L 4c** Consult general and specialized reference materials to find the pronunciation of a word or determine or clarify its precise meaning, its part of speech, its etymology, or its standard usage. **L 6** Acquire and use accurately general academic words.

Interactive Vocabulary   **THINK** central

Go to **thinkcentral.com.**
KEYWORD: HML12-678

Language

♦ **GRAMMAR AND STYLE: Add Emphasis**

Review the **Grammar and Style** note on page 674. **Parallelism** is the use of similar grammatical structures to express related ideas. In this example, notice how Johnson repeats the infinitive *to be* to list his many tasks and the preposition *without* to detail the obstacles each task presented to him:

> . . . *choice was to be made out of boundless variety, without any established principle of selection; adulterations were to be detected, without a settled test of purity; and modes of expression to be rejected or received, without the suffrages of any writers of classical reputation or acknowledged authority.* (lines 19–23)

Such perfectly balanced syntax serves to emphasize the laborious—and lonely—effort of Johnson's undertaking.

PRACTICE Identify the parallel elements in each of the following sentences. Then write a sentence that contains similar parallel elements.

EXAMPLE

. . . Much of my life has been lost under the pressures of disease, much has been trifled away, and much has always been spent in provision for the day that was passing over me. . . .

Some of the summers are spent traveling to our cabin, some are spent hiking in the canyon, and some are spent at my grandparents' house on the lake.

---

1. It is the fate of those who toil at the lower employments of life to be rather driven by the fear of evil than attracted by the prospect of good; to be exposed to censure without hope of praise. . . .

2. . . . The *English Dictionary* was written with little assistance of the learned, and without any patronage of the great, not in the soft obscurities of retirement, or under the shelter of academic bowers, but amid inconvenience and distraction, in sickness and in sorrow.

READING-WRITING CONNECTION

YOUR TURN

Expand your understanding of Johnson by responding to this prompt. Then use the **revising tips** to improve your character analysis.

WRITING PROMPT	REVISING TIPS
WRITE A CHARACTER ANALYSIS Johnson states many opinions in his preface to the dictionary. Using what you learned about Johnson in the preface, write a **three-to-five-paragraph character analysis** describing the type of person you believe Johnson was.	• Cite specific examples that you think illustrate Johnson's character. • Use parallelism in at least one sentence.

Interactive Revision THINK central

Go to **thinkcentral.com**.
KEYWORD: HML12-679

COMMON CORE

L 1 Demonstrate command of the conventions of standard English grammar when writing. **W 2** Write explanatory texts. **W 2c** Use varied syntax to create cohesion. **W 9** Draw evidence from informational texts to support analysis.

from The Life of Samuel Johnson

Biography by James Boswell

COMMON CORE

RI 6 Determine an author's point of view in a text. **RI 10** Read and comprehend literary nonfiction. **SL 1** Initiate and participate effectively in a range of collaborative discussions.

Meet the Author

James Boswell 1740–1795

In 1763, James Boswell was a smart, fun-loving 22-year-old who had passed his law exams in his native Scotland and traveled to London to enjoy the many pleasures the city had to offer. He had also begun a journal where he recorded the drama of his unfolding life in minute detail. One dramatic moment occurred in a bookstore on May 16, when he met one of his heroes, the great Samuel Johnson. Although Johnson didn't at first like the brash young Scotsman, Boswell won him over in a matter of weeks. So began the famous 21-year friendship that produced one of the greatest biographies in Western literature.

An Odd Couple At first glance, the 53-year-old Dr. Johnson, a distinguished man of letters, and the rambunctious Boswell—a "bumbling egotist," according to one critic—made an odd pair. But Boswell was predisposed to latch onto the older man. His own father was a prestigious judge in Edinburgh with a 20,000-acre country estate. Stern and self-righteous, the senior Boswell had ambitions for his firstborn son that were constantly thwarted by James's promiscuous lifestyle. In a compromise with his father, Boswell became a lawyer in Edinburgh

but escaped to London for periodic visits. Boswell's relationship with Johnson not only provided the intellectual and social stimulation Boswell craved but also gave him the fatherly support he lacked. For his part, Johnson was genuinely charmed by Boswell, once describing his sociable friend as a man who "never left a house without leaving a wish for his return."

Personal Decline After Johnson's death in 1784, Boswell moved his wife and five children to London and spent the next seven years struggling to write *The Life of Samuel Johnson*. The book's instant success upon its publication in 1791 did not, however, halt Boswell's downward spiral into drink, dissolution, and debt. In the remaining few years of his life, he considered himself a failure. Later, in a nasty turn of events, the 19th-century essayist Thomas Macaulay wrote a withering critique of Boswell as "a man of the meanest and feeblest intellect," casting the talented biographer into the far reaches of Johnson's shadow for more than 100 years. Boswell's reputation didn't recover until his private papers were discovered in the 1920s and 1930s and were published to wide acclaim in the 1950s. Modern readers appreciated Boswell's particular genius at capturing life's imperfect moments in all their spontaneity and splendor.

DID YOU KNOW?

James Boswell . . .

- claimed to be distantly related to King George III.
- married his first cousin and had five children.
- was a lawyer for 17 years.

Author Online

Go to **thinkcentral.com**. KEYWORD: HML12-680

THINK central

● TEXT ANALYSIS: BIOGRAPHY

James Boswell's biography of Samuel Johnson is one of the most famous biographies in the English language. A **biography** is an account of a person's life written by another person, who may or may not be personally familiar with the subject. As a skilled biographer, Boswell synthesizes information from anecdotes, reconstructed dialogue, quotations, and interpretive passages and uses these various elements to form a full account of Dr. Johnson's life. As you read, notice how Boswell uses these various elements to depict Johnson.

● READING SKILL: ANALYZE AUTHOR'S PERSPECTIVE

The **author's perspective** is the unique combination of ideas, experiences, values, and beliefs that influence the writer's views about a subject. For 21 years, Boswell chronicled his conversations and experiences with Johnson, amassing numerous anecdotes and opinions about his subject. To determine Boswell's perspective, note these clues in the text:

- Boswell's personal observations
- anecdotes and dialogue that involve the biographer
- Boswell's tone and word choice

As you read, use a chart to record statements that reflect these clues. Note what these reveal about Boswell's perspective toward Johnson.

Statements from Biography	Boswell's Perspective
• "a masterly essay against gulosity" • •	• admires Johnson's writing • •

▲ VOCABULARY IN CONTEXT

Use these sentences to figure out the meanings of the boldfaced words, which all appear in the selection from *The Life of Samuel Johnson*.

1. She shook her head over and over in **vehement** refusal.
2. He was **abstemious,** refusing to indulge in any excess.
3. The climate is **temperate,** neither too hot nor too cold.
4. The **mason** worked on the stone exterior of the church.
5. Hawks often swoop down and **assail** small animals.
6. Tina held her ground with great **resolution.**

 Complete the activities in your **Reader/Writer Notebook.**

Why tell someone's LIFE STORY?

The lives of famous people have intrigued the public for centuries. Sometimes writers are inspired to write a biography because they know readers will be interested in the private details behind the public events of a famous person's life. Other biographers, such as Boswell, may have more personal reasons, such as the impact their subject had on them or their unique perspective on the subject.

DISCUSS Think of someone you know who leads an interesting life, is an unusual person, or is a hero to you in some way. He or she may be someone you know or someone famous. If you were to write a biography of this person, what kind of information would you include? What might you leave out, and why? With your classmates, discuss the information you think should be included in such a biography.

Biography

THE LIFE OF SAMUEL JOHNSON

James Boswell

ON EATING (1763)

At supper this night he talked of good eating with uncommon satisfaction. "Some people (said he,) have a foolish way of not minding, or pretending not to mind, what they eat. For my part, I mind my belly very studiously, and very carefully; for I look upon it, that he who does not mind his belly will hardly mind anything else."

He now appeared to me *Jean Bull philosophe,*[1] and he was, for the moment, not only serious but **vehement.** Yet I have heard him, upon other occasions, talk with great contempt of people who were anxious to gratify their palates; and the 206th number of his *Rambler* is a masterly essay against gulosity.[2] His practice, indeed, I must acknowledge, may be considered as casting the balance of his different opinions upon this subject; for I never knew any man who relished good eating more than he did. When at table, he was totally absorbed in the business of the moment; his looks seemed riveted to his plate; nor would he, unless when in very high company, say one word, or even pay the least attention to what was said by others, till he had satisfied his appetite, which was so fierce, and indulged with such intenseness, that while in the act of eating, the veins of his forehead swelled, and generally a strong perspiration was visible. To those whose sensations were delicate, this could not but be disgusting; and it was doubtless not very suitable to the character of a philosopher, who should be distinguished by self-command. **Ⓐ**

Analyze Visuals ▶

What personality traits come across in this portrait of Samuel Johnson?

vehement (vē′ə-mənt) *adj.* acting with or having great force; fervent

Ⓐ **AUTHOR'S PERSPECTIVE**
In your own words, describe Boswell's opinion of Johnson's eating habits. Do you think Boswell is objective in his view?

---

1. **Jean Bull philosophe** (zhäN bōōl fē′lô-zôf′): *French:* John Bull, philosopher. The name John Bull traditionally represents the typical Englishman, seen as honest, hearty, and gruff.

2. **206th number . . . gulosity** (gyōō-lŏs′ĭ-tē): In an issue of Johnson's *The Rambler, a* periodical published from 1750 to 1752, he wrote an essay criticizing excessive appetite, or gluttony.

Samuel Johnson (1775), Sir Joshua Reynolds. Canvas. The Granger Collection, New York.

But it must be owned,[3] that Johnson, though he could be rigidly **abstemious,** 20 was not a **temperate** man either in eating or drinking. He could refrain, but he could not use moderately. He told me, that he had fasted two days without inconvenience, and that he had never been hungry but once. They who beheld with wonder how much he ate upon all occasions when his dinner was to his taste, could not easily conceive what he must have meant by hunger; and not only was he remarkable for the extraordinary quantity which he ate, but he was, or affected to be, a man of very nice discernment in the science of cookery. He used to descant[4] critically on the dishes which had been at table where he had dined or supped, and to recollect very minutely what he had liked. . . .

When invited to dine, even with an intimate friend, he was not pleased if 30 something better than a plain dinner was not prepared for him. I have heard him say on such an occasion, "This was a good dinner enough, to be sure; but it was not a dinner to *ask* a man to." On the other hand, he was wont to express, with great glee, his satisfaction when he had been entertained quite to his mind.

ON EQUALITY OF THE SEXES (1778)

Mrs. Knowles[5] affected to complain that men had much more liberty allowed them than women.

JOHNSON. "Why, Madam, women have all the liberty they should wish to have. We have all the labor and the danger, and the women all the advantage. We go to sea, we build houses, we do everything, in short, to pay our court to the women."

MRS. KNOWLES. "The Doctor reasons very wittily, but not convincingly. Now, 40 take the instance of building; the **mason's** wife, if she is ever seen in liquor, is ruined; the mason may get himself drunk as often as he pleases, with little loss of character; nay, may let his wife and children starve."

JOHNSON. "Madam, you must consider, if the mason does get himself drunk, and let his wife and children starve, the parish will oblige him to find security for their maintenance. We have different modes of restraining evil. Stocks for the men, a ducking-stool for women, and a pound for beasts. If we require more perfection from women than from ourselves, it is doing them honor. And women have not the same temptations that we have: they may always live in virtuous company; men must mix in the world indiscriminately. If a woman has no 50 inclination to do what is wrong being secured from it is no restraint to her. I am at liberty to walk into the Thames;[6] but if I were to try it, my friends would restrain me in Bedlam,[7] and I should be obliged to them." **B**

MRS. KNOWLES. "Still, Doctor, I cannot help thinking it a hardship that more indulgence is allowed to men than to women. It gives a superiority to men, to which I do not see how they are entitled."

---

3. **owned:** admitted.

4. **descant** (dĕs′kănt′): speak at length.

5. **Mrs. Knowles:** Mary Knowles, a well-educated Quaker who challenged Johnson's opinions of women and gave her own account of their exchange in the *Gentleman's Magazine* of 1791.

6. **Thames** (tĕmz): the large river that flows through London.

7. **Bedlam:** a London institution for the mentally ill.

Sidebar:

abstemious (ăb-stē′mē-əs) *adj.* practicing abstinence; refraining from doing something

temperate (tĕm′pər-ĭt) *adj.* moderate

mason (mā′sən) *n.* someone whose work is to build walls, buildings, and other structures made of stone, brick, or concrete

B BIOGRAPHY
Reread lines 36–52. What do you learn about Johnson from this dialogue?

Mitre Tavern (1800s), unknown. Colored engraving. The Granger Collection, New York.

JOHNSON. "It is plain, Madam, one or other must have the superiority. As Shakespeare says, 'If two men ride on a horse, one must ride behind.'"

DILLY.[8] "I suppose, Sir, Mrs. Knowles would have them to ride in panniers,[9] one on each side."

60 JOHNSON. "Then, Sir, the horse would throw them both."

MRS. KNOWLES. "Well, I hope that in another world the sexes will be equal."

BOSWELL. "That is being too ambitious, Madam. *We* might as well desire to be equal with the angels. *We* shall all, I hope, be happy in a future state, but we must not expect to be all happy in the same degree. It is enough if we be happy according to our several capacities. A worthy carman[10] will get to heaven as well as Sir Isaac Newton.[11] Yet, though equally good, they will not have the same degrees of happiness."

JOHNSON. "Probably not." **C**

ON THE FEAR OF DEATH (1769)

I mentioned to him that I had seen the execution of several convicts at Tyburn,[12] 70 two days before, and that none of them seemed to be under any concern.

---

8. **Dilly:** Edward Dilly, a bookseller and publisher who was a friend of Johnson's.

9. **panniers** (păn'yərz): a pair of baskets hung across the back of a pack animal.

10. **carman:** carriage driver.

11. **Sir Isaac Newton:** a famous English mathematician and scientist who died in 1727.

12. **Tyburn** (tī'bûrn): a former site of public hangings in London.

JOHNSON. "Most of them, Sir, have never thought at all."

BOSWELL. "But is not the fear of death natural to man?"

JOHNSON. "So much so, Sir, that the whole of life is but keeping away the thoughts of it."

He then, in a low and earnest tone, talked of his meditating upon the awful hour of his own dissolution,[13] and in what manner he should conduct himself upon that occasion: "I know not (said he,) whether I should wish to have a friend by me, or have it all between God and myself." . . .

When we were alone, I introduced the subject of death, and endeavored to
80 maintain that the fear of it might be got over. I told him that David Hume[14] said to me, he was no more uneasy to think he should *not be* after this life, than that he *had not been* before he began to exist.

JOHNSON. "Sir, if he really thinks so, his perceptions are disturbed; he is mad: if he does not think so, he lies. He may tell you, he holds his finger in the flame of a candle, without feeling pain; would you believe him? When he dies, he at least gives up all he has."

BOSWELL. "Foote,[15] Sir, told me, that when he was very ill he was not afraid to die."

JOHNSON. "It is not true, Sir. Hold a pistol to Foote's breast, or to Hume's breast, and threaten to kill them, and you'll see how they behave."

90 BOSWELL. "But may we not fortify our minds for the approach of death?"

Here I am sensible[16] I was in the wrong, to bring before his view what he ever looked upon with horror; for although when in a celestial frame, in his "Vanity of Human Wishes,"[17] he has supposed death to be "kind Nature's signal for retreat," from this state of being to "a happier seat," his thoughts upon this awful change were in general full of dismal apprehensions. His mind resembled the vast amphitheater, the Colosseum at Rome. In the center stood his judgment, which, like a mighty gladiator, combated those apprehensions that, like the wild beasts of the *Arena,* were all around in cells, ready to be let out upon him. After a conflict, he drove them back into their dens; but not killing them, they were still
100 **assailing** him. To my question, whether we might not fortify our minds for the approach of death, he answered, in a passion, "No, Sir, let it alone. It matters not how a man dies, but how he lives. The act of dying is not of importance, it lasts so short a time." He added, (with an earnest look,) "A man knows it must be so, and submits. It will do him no good to whine."

I attempted to continue the conversation. He was so provoked, that he said, "Give us no more of this"; and was thrown into such a state of agitation, that he expressed himself in a way that alarmed and distressed me; showed an impatience that I should leave him, and when I was going away, called to me sternly, "Don't let us meet tomorrow." **D**

Language Coach

Cognates Cognates are words from different languages with a common origin. The word *fortify* (line 90) has cognates in French (*fortifier*), Spanish (*fortificar*), and Italian (*fortificare*). What does *fortify* mean in line 90?

assail (ə-sāl´) *v.* to attack

D AUTHOR'S PERSPECTIVE
Describe the relationship between Johnson and Boswell presented here. How might Boswell's view of Johnson have influenced his portrayal of this incident?

---

13. **awful . . . dissolution:** awe-inspiring hour of his own death.

14. **David Hume** (hyōōm): a Scottish philosopher and historian.

15. **Foote:** actor and playwright·Samuel Foote.

16. **sensible:** aware.

17. **"Vanity of Human Wishes":** a famous long poem by Johnson.

ON JOHNSON'S PHYSICAL COURAGE (1775)

110 . . . No man was ever more remarkable for personal courage. He had, indeed, an awful dread of death, or rather, "of something after death"; and what rational man, who seriously thinks of quitting all that he has ever known, and going into a new and unknown state of being, can be without that dread? But his fear was from reflection; his courage natural. His fear, in that one instance, was the result of philosophical and religious consideration. He feared death, but he feared nothing else, not even what might occasion death. Many instances of his **resolution** may be mentioned. One day, at Mr. Beauclerk's[18] house in the country, when two large dogs were fighting, he went up to them, and beat them till they separated; and at another time, when told of the danger there was that a gun might burst if charged
120 with many balls, he put in six or seven, and fired it off against a wall. Mr. Langton told me, that when they were swimming together near Oxford,[19] he cautioned Dr. Johnson against a pool, which was reckoned particularly dangerous; upon which Johnson directly swam into it. He told me himself that one night he was attacked in the street by four men, to whom he would not yield, but kept them all at bay, till the watch came up, and carried both him and them to the roundhouse.[20] In the playhouse at Lichfield, as Mr. Garrick[21] informed me, Johnson having for a moment quitted a chair which was placed for him between the side-scenes, a gentleman took possession of it, and when Johnson on his return civilly demanded his seat, rudely refused to give it up; upon which Johnson laid hold of it, and
130 tossed him and the chair into the pit. Foote, who so successfully revived the old comedy, by exhibiting living characters, had resolved to imitate Johnson on the stage, expecting great profits from his ridicule of so celebrated a man. Johnson being informed of his intention, and being at dinner at Mr. Thomas Davies's the bookseller, from whom I had the story, he asked Mr. Davies "what was the common price of an oak stick"; and being answered sixpence, "Why then, Sir, (said he,) give me leave to send your servant to purchase me a shilling one. I'll have a double quantity; for I am told Foote means to *take me off*,[22] as he calls it, and I am determined the fellow shall not do it with impunity." Davies took care to acquaint Foote of this, which effectually checked the wantonness of the mimic.
140 Mr. Macpherson's menaces[23] made Johnson provide himself with the same implement of defense; and had he been attacked, I have no doubt that, old as he was, he would have made his corporal prowess be felt as much as his intellectual. ❧ **Ⓔ**

---

resolution (rĕz′ə-lōō′shən) *n.* stubborn courage to face challenges; resolve

Ⓔ BIOGRAPHY
Reread lines 120-123. What do you think is Boswell's purpose in presenting this description of Johnson swimming in a dangerous pool?

---

18. **Mr. Beauclerk's** (bō′klər′): referring to Topham Beauclerk, a wealthy young man-about-town who became friendly with the older Johnson.

19. **Mr. Langton . . . Oxford:** Bennet Langton, a friend of Beauclerk's who attended Oxford with him, became friendly with Johnson and gave Boswell details for the biography.

20. **roundhouse:** jail.

21. **playhouse at Lichfield** (lĭch′fēld) . . . **Garrick:** David Garrick was the most famous actor of his day and a lifelong friend of Johnson's, as well as a former student of his at Lichfield.

22. *take me off:* do an imitation of me.

23. **Mr. Macpherson's menaces:** the threats of James Macpherson, a Scottish poet whose "translations" of supposed third-century poems had been exposed as frauds by Johnson.

Comprehension

1. **Recall** What were Johnson's eating habits?

2. **Clarify** Why did Johnson tell Boswell, "Don't let us meet tomorrow" after their discussion about the fear of death?

3. **Summarize** How did Johnson tend to behave in dangerous situations?

Text Analysis

4. **Interpret Text** In his biography, Boswell often presents dialogue to allow Johnson to voice his own opinions. Describe Johnson's opinions on the following issues:

    • the fear of death (lines 79–89)
    • an actor's imitation of him (lines 130–142)

5. **Draw Conclusions About the Biography** Compare the passages of reconstructed dialogue in Boswell's **biography** with the long passages in which he describes Johnson. Do you get a fuller sense of Johnson's personality from the dialogue or from the descriptive passages? Explain.

6. **Make Judgments** In your opinion, does revealing Johnson's faults and fears add to or detract from his image as a great man? Support your opinion with examples from the text.

7. **Evaluate Author's Perspective** Unlike many biographers, Boswell became intimately familiar with his subject over many years. Based on what you know about their long friendship, do you think Boswell is a **credible** biographer—one who is trustworthy and believable? Cite evidence in the text to support your opinion.

8. **Compare Texts** Compare Boswell's portrayal of Samuel Johnson with Johnson's references to himself in the preface to *A Dictionary of the English Language* on page 672. In what ways do your impressions of Johnson from these two sources differ? Support your conclusions with evidence from the texts.

Text Criticism

9. **Author's Style** Wit was highly prized in the 18th century, and both Boswell and Johnson famously practiced the art. Find two or three examples of **humor** in these excerpts to analyze. What purpose does humor serve in Boswell's biography?

> *Why tell someone's* **LIFE STORY?**
>
> When you read a biography of a person who deeply interests you, what information are you hoping to gain? What information would you prefer not to learn about that person? Why?

COMMON CORE

RI 6 Determine an author's point of view in a text. **RI 10** Read and comprehend literary nonfiction.

Vocabulary in Context

▲ VOCABULARY PRACTICE

Identify the word that is closest in meaning to the boldfaced vocabulary word.

1. **abstemious:** (a) wandering, (b) abstaining, (c) annoying
2. **assail:** (a) travel, (b) dominate, (c) assault
3. **mason:** (a) bricklayer, (b) carpenter, (c) lawyer
4. **resolution:** (a) initiation, (b) vagueness, (c) determination
5. **temperate:** (a) mild, (b) chilly, (c) argumentative
6. **vehement:** (a) intense, (b) unpleasant, (c) odorous

WORD LIST

abstemious
assail
mason
resolution
temperate
vehement

ACADEMIC VOCABULARY IN WRITING

> • affect   • challenge   • consent   • final   • respond

The subject of a biography may not **consent** to everything his or her biographer writes. Write a paragraph about how it might **affect** a biography if its subject had complete control of the information a biographer could use. Include at least one Academic Vocabulary word in your paragraph.

VOCABULARY STRATEGY: SPECIALIZED DICTIONARIES

Specialized dictionaries provide information on words related to particular subjects. In addition to language references, such as bilingual dictionaries, libraries may have dictionaries on subjects as diverse as business, food, and medicine. To illustrate the difference between a general and a specialized dictionary, consider *Mitre Tavern*, known as a *conversation piece*, on page 685.

> **EXAMPLE: GENERAL DICTIONARY (ONLINE)**
>
> **conversation piece,** *n.* **1.** a painting in which figures are posed in a domestic scene, popular in the 18th century. **2.** an object whose unusual quality makes it a topic of conversation.

> **EXAMPLE: DICTIONARY OF ART (ONLINE)**
>
> **conversation piece:** A portrait showing a group of full-length figures, often in a landscape or domestic setting, engaged in talk or other sedate social activity. Thomas <u>Gainsborough</u> and William <u>Hogarth</u> were famous practitioners. . . .

PRACTICE Using the examples above as needed, respond to the questions.

1. Which dictionary provides links, or cross-references, to related information?
2. Which dictionary provides more than one definition of *conversation piece*?
3. If you were reading a magazine article and were confused by the term *conversation piece*, which dictionary would be more useful? Why?

⸫ **COMMON CORE**

L 1b Resolve issues of complex usage, consulting references as needed.
L 6 Acquire and use accurately general academic words.

Interactive Vocabulary **THINK** central

Go to <u>thinkcentral.com</u>.
KEYWORD: HML12-689

Elegy Written in a Country Churchyard

Poem by Thomas Gray

COMMON CORE

RL 1 Cite textual evidence to support inferences drawn from the text. RL 10 Read and comprehend literature, including poems. SL 1c Propel conversations by posing and responding to questions that probe reasoning and evidence.

Meet the Author

Thomas Gray 1716–1771

In the boisterous Age of Johnson, Thomas Gray was something of an anomaly. He shunned lively public debate and the glare of intellectual celebrity for the gentler pursuit of private study and the company of an intimate circle of friends. The hustle and bustle of London held no attraction for him; he preferred the quiet confines of Cambridge University and solitary walks in the countryside. His medium was lyric poetry rather than satire. He was a shy, introverted, even secretive man who famously lacked ambition. After gaining national acclaim with the publication of "Elegy Written in a Country Churchyard" (1751), he adamantly refused the offered post of poet laureate and the publicity that came with it. His published body of work numbered less than 1,000 lines. And yet, his lyrical "Elegy" made him the dominant poet of his time and a precursor of the Romantic Age to come.

Surviving Childhood Gray was born in London, the only one of 12 brothers and sisters to survive to adulthood. His father, a "money-scrivener" (lender), was violent and abusive, while his long-suffering mother ran a small hat shop to help support the family. A frail but studious child, the young Gray escaped his frightening home life at age eight when his mother paid for him to attend boarding school at Eton College. Gray thrived at Eton and there developed the reclusive academic habits that remained with him for life.

"Far from the Madding Crowd" While at Eton, Gray met Horace Walpole, the son of the prime minister and a lifelong friend who would later encourage Gray to publish his poems. The young men traveled together on a grand tour of Europe, but their personal differences—Gray's love of museums and romantic scenery clashing with Walpole's social interests—led to a bitter falling out that lasted four years. By the time Gray settled in Cambridge in 1742, he had begun writing poetry. But that year his closest friend, Richard West, died at the tender age of 25, plunging Gray into a sadness that pervaded his next poems, especially his popular "Elegy." His later poems were not as well received by readers, who found them difficult to understand, and so Gray withdrew from his already minimal public life and even stopped writing poetry. A large inheritance ultimately allowed him to live out his remaining years doing what he liked best—reading in private, writing letters, exploring the English countryside, and spending tranquil hours with friends.

DID YOU KNOW?

Thomas Gray . . .

- hated math.
- may have had pyrophobia, or fear of fire.
- was buried in the cemetery described in his famous "Elegy."

(background) Eton College

Author Online

Go to thinkcentral.com. KEYWORD: HML12-690

THINK central

POETIC FORM: ELEGY

Gray's "Elegy Written in a Country Churchyard" is one of the most famous English elegies. An **elegy** is an extended meditative poem in which the speaker reflects on death—often in tribute to a person who has died recently—or on an equally serious subject. Most elegies are written in formal, dignified language and are serious in mood and tone. Consider these lines from Gray's poem, which describe a cemetery:

> *Beneath those rugged elms, that yew tree's shade,*
>   *Where heaves the turf in many a moldering heap,*
> *Each in his narrow cell forever laid,*
>   *The rude forefathers of the hamlet sleep.*

As you read this elegy, think about who the dead are, how the speaker pays tribute to them, and what observations are made about death.

READING SKILL: MAKE INFERENCES

To understand this poem you must **make inferences,** or logical guesses, about the dead who are described and about the speaker who describes them. Use details from the poem to infer ideas not stated outright. For example, what would you guess about the lives of the people portrayed in this stanza?

> *Oft did the harvest to their sickle yield,*
>   *Their furrow oft the stubborn glebe has broke;*
> *How jocund did they drive their team afield!*
>   *How bowed the woods beneath their sturdy stroke!*

From the words *harvest, sickle,* and *furrow,* you can infer that they were farmers. *Oft* ("often") suggests that they were hardworking; *jocund* ("merry") suggests that they were happy in their labor.

What would you guess are the speaker's feelings toward these people? Positive images of strength—a harvest yielding to the sickle, the woods bowing beneath an axe stroke—suggest that he admires them. As you read, record your inferences about the dead and the speaker, and clues that led to your inferences. Use a chart like the one shown.

Inferences About the Dead	Inferences About the Speaker	Clues

 Complete the activities in your **Reader/Writer Notebook.**

What are life's LIMITATIONS?

In our world of modern conveniences and endless possibilities, it's hard to think about limits. But for most people in the 18th century, life's limitations were readily apparent. From scarce resources and opportunities to dangerous health threats and premature death, ordinary people faced innumerable obstacles in their lives. Gray's "Elegy" addresses the limitations imposed upon ordinary people of his time.

SURVEY Ask your classmates: What is the biggest limitation faced by young people you know? Tally the different responses given and their frequency, and present your findings to the class. How do today's limitations compare with the limitations of the past?

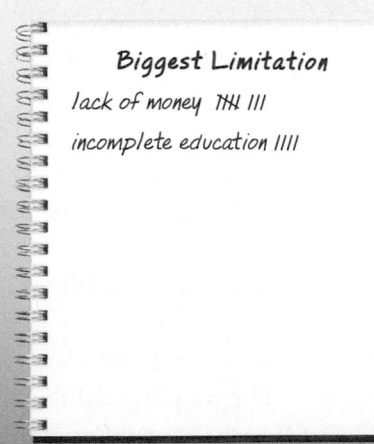

Biggest Limitation
lack of money 𝍖 III
incomplete education IIII

Elegy Written in A Country Churchyard

Thomas Gray

BACKGROUND Gray's "Elegy" is one of the most quoted poems in English literature. Gray worked eight years on it and never meant for it to be read by the public; he first published it reluctantly and anonymously. But the intense personal feelings the poem expresses gave it an immediate and universal appeal. The speaker is widely assumed to be the poet himself. He contemplates the deaths of those buried in the churchyard, then the deaths of all people, and then his own death.

The curfew tolls the knell of parting day,
    The lowing herd wind slowly o'er the lea,
The plowman homeward plods his weary way,
    And leaves the world to darkness and to me.

5 Now fades the glimmering landscape on the sight,
    And all the air a solemn stillness holds,
Save where the beetle wheels his droning flight,
    And drowsy tinklings lull the distant folds;

Save that from yonder ivy-mantled tower
10   The moping owl does to the moon complain
Of such, as wandering near her secret bower,
    Molest her ancient solitary reign. **Ⓐ**

Beneath those rugged elms, that yew tree's shade,
    Where heaves the turf in many a moldering heap,
15 Each in his narrow cell forever laid,
    The rude forefathers of the hamlet sleep.

2 lea (lē): meadow.

Analyze Visuals ▶
What ideas come to mind as you study this photo of an old country churchyard in England?

Ⓐ ELEGY
What **mood** is created by the images in the first three stanzas?

16 rude: unsophisticated; rustic.

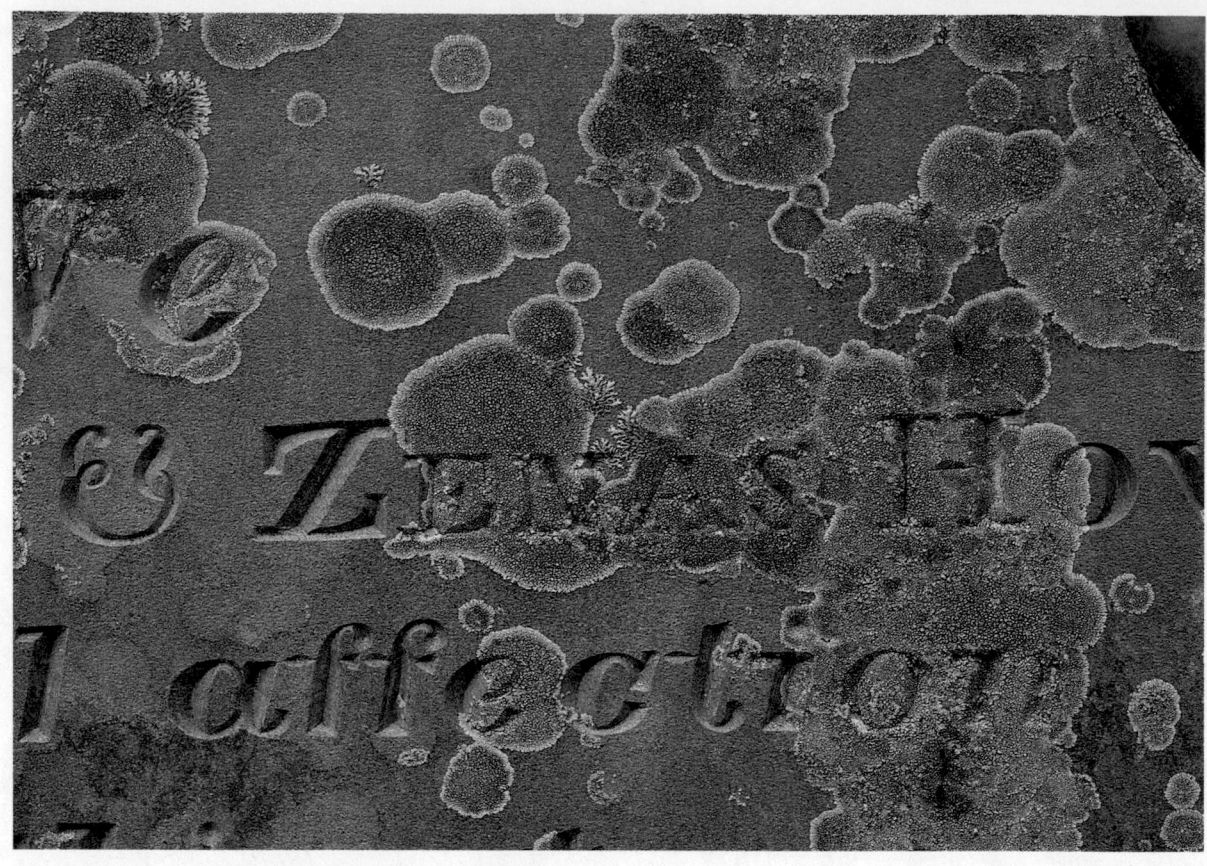

The breezy call of incense-breathing Morn,
    The swallow twittering from the straw-built shed,
The cock's shrill clarion, or the echoing horn,
20   No more shall rouse them from their lowly bed.

For them no more the blazing hearth shall burn,
    Or busy housewife ply her evening care;
No children run to lisp their sire's return,
    Or climb his knees the envied kiss to share. **B**

25 Oft did the harvest to their sickle yield,
    Their furrow oft the stubborn glebe has broke;
How jocund did they drive their team afield!
    How bowed the woods beneath their sturdy stroke!

Let not Ambition mock their useful toil,
30   Their homely joys, and destiny obscure;
Nor Grandeur hear with a disdainful smile
    The short and simple annals of the poor.

B **MAKE INFERENCES**
Reread lines 17–24. What do you infer about the lives and the values of those buried?

26 glebe: soil; earth.
27 jocund (jŏk′ənd): merry.

32 annals: descriptive records; history.

The boast of heraldry, the pomp of power,
  And all that beauty, all that wealth e'er gave,
35 Awaits alike the inevitable hour.
  The paths of glory lead but to the grave. **C**

Nor you, ye proud, impute to these the fault,
  If Memory o'er their tomb no trophies raise,
Where through the long-drawn aisle and fretted vault
40   The pealing anthem swells the note of praise.

Can storied urn or animated bust
  Back to its mansion call the fleeting breath?
Can Honor's voice provoke the silent dust,
  Or Flattery soothe the dull cold ear of Death?

45 Perhaps in this neglected spot is laid
  Some heart once pregnant with celestial fire;
Hands that the rod of empire might have swayed,
  Or waked to ecstasy the living lyre.

But Knowledge to their eyes her ample page
50   Rich with the spoils of time did ne'er unroll;
Chill Penury repressed their noble rage,
  And froze the genial current of the soul.

Full many a gem of purest ray serene,
  The dark unfathomed caves of ocean bear:
55 Full many a flower is born to blush unseen,
  And waste its sweetness on the desert air.

Some village Hampden, that with dauntless breast
  The little tyrant of his fields withstood;
Some mute inglorious Milton here may rest,
60   Some Cromwell guiltless of his country's blood.

The applause of listening senates to command,
  The threats of pain and ruin to despise,
To scatter plenty o'er a smiling land,
  And read their history in a nation's eyes,

65 Their lot forbade: nor circumscribed alone
  Their growing virtues, but their crimes confined;
Forbade to wade through slaughter to a throne,
  And shut the gates of mercy on mankind,

33 heraldry: noble birth.

C **ELEGY**
What observation about death is made in lines 33–36?

37 impute . . . fault: assign the blame to them.

38 trophies: sculptures depicting the achievements of the deceased.

39 fretted vault: space enclosed under a decorated arched ceiling.

41 storied . . . bust: an urn for the ashes of the deceased, decorated with scenes from the person's life, or a lifelike portrait sculpture.

43 provoke: call forth.

48 lyre: a small harplike musical instrument used in ancient Greece to accompany the singing of poetry, and therefore frequently used as a symbol of the poetic art.

51 penury (pĕn'yə-rē): extreme poverty.

52 genial current: warm, life-giving power.

57 Hampden: John Hampden, a 17th-century English politician who opposed the "tyrant" Charles I over unjust taxation.

60 Cromwell: Oliver Cromwell, leader of the Parliamentary forces in the English Civil War and head of the English government from 1653 to 1658.

65 circumscribed: limited; confined.

The struggling pangs of conscious truth to hide,
70   To quench the blushes of ingenuous shame,
Or heap the shrine of Luxury and Pride
     With incense kindled at the Muse's flame.

Far from the madding crowd's ignoble strife,
     Their sober wishes never learned to stray;
75 Along the cool sequestered vale of life
     They kept the noiseless tenor of their way.

Yet even these bones from insult to protect
     Some frail memorial still erected nigh,
With uncouth rhymes and shapeless sculpture decked,
80   Implores the passing tribute of a sigh.

Their name, their years, spelt by the unlettered Muse,
     The place of fame and elegy supply:
And many a holy text around she strews,
     That teach the rustic moralist to die.

85 For who to dumb Forgetfulness a prey,
     This pleasing anxious being e'er resigned,
Left the warm precincts of the cheerful day,
     Nor cast one longing lingering look behind?

On some fond breast the parting soul relies,
90   Some pious drops the closing eye requires;
Even from the tomb the voice of Nature cries,
     Even in our ashes live their wonted fires.

For thee, who mindful of the unhonored dead
     Dost in these lines their artless tale relate;
95 If chance, by lonely contemplation led,
     Some kindred spirit shall inquire thy fate,

Haply some hoary-headed swain may say,
     "Oft have we seen him at the peep of dawn
Brushing with hasty steps the dews away
100   To meet the sun upon the upland lawn.

"There at the foot of yonder nodding beech
     That wreathes its old fantastic roots so high,
His listless length at noontide would he stretch,
     And pore upon the brook that babbles by.

---

69 **conscious truth:** conscience.

72 **incense . . . flame:** poetic praise.

73 **madding:** wildly excited; disorderly.

75 **sequestered:** isolated; secluded.
76 **tenor:** unwavering course.

Language Coach

Multiple Meanings In Gray's day, *uncouth* could mean "awkward" (as it does today) or "unfamiliar." Which is meant in line 79?

81 **unlettered Muse:** the "inspiration" of the uneducated stonecutters who carved the inscriptions on the tombstones.

85–88 **For who . . . behind?:** For who has ever accepted that he will be forgotten, leaving the warmth of earthly life without any regret?

90 **drops:** tears.

92 **wonted** (wôn´tĭd): accustomed.

93 **thee:** that is, Gray himself.

97 **hoary-headed swain:** white-haired peasant.

104 **pore:** to gaze intently.

105 "Hard by yon wood, now smiling as in scorn,
        Muttering his wayward fancies he would rove,
   Now drooping, woeful wan, like one forlorn,
        Or crazed with care, or crossed in hopeless love. **D**

   "One morn I missed him on the customed hill,
110   Along the heath and near his favorite tree;
   Another came; nor yet beside the rill,
        Nor up the lawn, nor at the wood was he;

   "The next with dirges due in sad array
        Slow through the churchway path we saw him borne.
115 Approach and read (for thou canst read) the lay,
        Graved on the stone beneath yon aged thorn."

The Epitaph

Here rests his head upon the lap of Earth
        A youth to fortune and to Fame unknown.
Fair Science frowned not on his humble birth,
120   *And Melancholy marked him for her own.*

Large was his bounty, and his soul sincere,
        Heaven did a recompense as largely send:
He gave to Misery all he had, a tear,
        He gained from Heaven ('twas all he wished) a friend.

125 *No farther seek his merits to disclose,*
        Or draw his frailties from their dread abode
(There they alike in trembling hope repose),
        The bosom of his Father and his God. **E**

D MAKE INFERENCES
What can you infer about the speaker's life and values from the way he imagines himself described in lines 98–108?

111 **rill:** brook.

113 **dirges:** funeral hymns.

115 **lay:** poem.
116 **thorn:** hawthorn.

119 **science:** learning.

E ELEGY
In lines 117–128, the speaker imagines his own **epitaph,** an inscription on his tomb. How does he want to be viewed upon his death?

Comprehension

1. **Recall** At what time of day does the poem take place?

2. **Paraphrase** Relate the lives of the dead to lines 55–56: "Full many a flower is born to blush unseen, / And waste its sweetness on the desert air." Restate the meaning of these lines.

3. **Summarize** What do all the dead desire, according to the speaker?

Text Analysis

4. **Interpret Elegy** Explain the purpose of this elegy. Whom is the speaker praising, and why? What **themes** about death does he express? Cite lines to support your interpretation.

5. **Make Inferences About Characters** Review the chart of inferences you made about the dead villagers. Explain what you inferred about the following:

   • their values

   • the challenges they faced

   • the benefits of their lot

6. **Make Inferences About the Speaker** The speaker reveals almost as much about himself and his values as he does about the villagers. Infer his opinion on the following topics from the statements he makes:

   • the upper classes (lines 29–36)   • city life vs. country life (lines 73–76)

   • famous people (lines 67–72)   • himself (lines 105–108; 117–128)

7. **Compare and Contrast** How does the speaker's imagined gravesite with its moving epitaph fit in with the other graves in the churchyard? How does it stand out? Discuss what the comparison suggests about the speaker's relationship to the villagers.

8. **Analyze Influence of Author's Background** What in Thomas Gray's personality and experience might have led him to write a formal elegy about a rural cemetery? Review the biography on page 690 and the background on page 692, as well as details in the poem, for clues to his motivations.

Text Criticism

9. **Different Perspectives** In lines 65–76, Gray makes the point that the poor farmers were prevented from corruption as well as from achievement. Is it widely believed today that a rural existence is less corrupting than an urban one? Support your answer.

What are life's **LIMITATIONS?**

How might having limitations possibly increase, rather than limit, your sense of freedom?

COMMON CORE

RL 1 Cite textual evidence to support inferences drawn from the text. **RL 10** Read and comprehend literature, including poems.

A Man of Letters

James Boswell portrayed Samuel Johnson as a man larger than life—a man of great courage, greater appetites, strong principles, and an engaging personality. Johnson's own body of work suggests that Boswell was not far wrong; Johnson's extensive writings reveal a rigorous, insatiable mind and great wit. Rising to fame after the publication of his dictionary, Johnson was eventually rewarded by the king for his contribution to English letters and came to be seen as a great talent and a man of his age.

Writing to Analyze

Based on the Johnson selection you read, as well as the excerpts from his biography, what do you think are the qualities that made Johnson so widely revered? Additionally, what does his popularity tell you about the age in which he lived? Write an essay in which you present and explain your response, citing evidence from the selections.

Consider

- the way he organized his ideas
- his use of language
- his qualities as described by Boswell

Dr. Johnson in the Ante-Room of Lord Chesterfield Waiting for an Audience, 1748 (1845), Edward Matthew Ward. Tate Gallery, London. © Tate Gallery, London/Art Resource, New York.

Extension

SPEAKING & LISTENING With several classmates, stage a performance of the dialogue recorded by Boswell in the excerpts from *The Life of Samuel Johnson.* In preparation, review each section of dialogue. Discuss the traits of the people speaking as well as the ideas communicated by the dialogue, considering how to best convey both. After your performance, hold a wider discussion of the ideas that were presented. Do you agree with any of the speakers? Disagree? Why?

⸬ **COMMON CORE**

W 9 Draw evidence from informational texts to support analysis. **SL 1a** Draw on preparation by referring to evidence from texts.

On Her Loving Two Equally

Poem by Aphra Behn

Written at the Close of Spring

Poem by Charlotte Smith

COMMON CORE

RL 5 Analyze how an author's choices concerning how to structure specific parts of a text contribute to its overall structure and meaning as well as its aesthetic impact. **RL 10** Read and comprehend literature, including poems.

Meet the Authors

Aphra Behn 1640–1689

"All women together ought to let flowers fall upon the tomb of Aphra Behn . . . for it was she who earned them the right to speak their minds." So wrote Virginia Woolf in "A Room of One's Own" (1929) in tribute to England's first professional woman writer. Adventurous and talented, Aphra Behn turned to writing to support herself after a brief stint in prison for debt. She first became famous for her plays—comedies, mostly—rivaling John Dryden as the most prolific playwright of the Restoration. Modern critics have focused more on her poetry and innovative fiction.

Woman of Mystery Not much is known about Behn. She apparently achieved some renown in the court of Charles II, because after her husband's death the king sent her to the Netherlands to spy on his Dutch enemies. Agent 160, as Behn was called, returned about a year later, in debt and out of a job.

A Scandalous Freedom For the next 19 years, Behn enjoyed an extraordinary life as the only woman writer in theatrical and literary circles. Her lively personality won her many friends, even as her unusual independence and liberty created quite a scandal at the time.

Charlotte Smith 1749–1806

When Charlotte Smith attended a political dinner in Paris in 1792, 50 supporters of the French Revolution raised their glasses to honor her. It was a shining moment for the popular English writer, whose latest novel, *Desmond* (1792), brimmed with radical fervor. But soon the ideals of the revolution collapsed, bringing down the sales of Smith's novels along with them. Smith, who supported herself and her nine children by writing, was back at the brink of destitution.

From Riches to Rags Born into a wealthy family, Smith left home at age 16 for an arranged marriage. Her husband, besides being cruel and abusive, squandered their money until they both landed in debtor's prison. Smith used the time to write her first book of poems, *Elegiac Sonnets and Other Essays* (1784), and then paid their way out of prison with the profits.

From Poet to Novelist Although Smith's sonnets were highly respected at the time, fiction paid better. In 1788, she began writing the first of her 11 novels. Yet as her novels became increasingly radical, readers began to turn away. At the end of her life, Smith barely made ends meet by writing educational books.

Authors Online

Go to **thinkcentral.com**. KEYWORD: HML12-700

THINK central

TEXT ANALYSIS: SPEAKER

As you probably recall, the **speaker** in a poem is the voice that "talks" to the reader, like a narrator in a short story or novel. The two works you are about to read are **lyrics,** or short poems in which a single speaker conveys personal thoughts and feelings on a particular subject. Among England's first professional woman writers, Aphra Behn and Charlotte Smith helped change the nature of English lyric poetry. Unlike more conventional poems of the period, their works feature strong female speakers with complex emotions. In "On Her Loving Two Equally," for example, the speaker wonders

> *How strongly does my passion flow,*
> *Divided equally 'twixt two?*

As you read the poems, pay attention to the speakers and the feelings they convey.

READING SKILL: ANALYZE POETIC STRUCTURE

Written a century apart, the works of Behn and Smith reflect the beginning and the end of the neoclassical era. Although both poems celebrate similar values, they differ considerably in the way they are structured. In poetry, **structure** is the way words, images, and lines are arranged. Generally, a poem's structure and its content reinforce each other. The structure of "On Her Loving Two Equally" comprises three six-line stanzas. On the other hand, "Written at the Close of Spring" is a Shakespearean sonnet, with a fixed structure of three quatrains and a final, rhyming couplet. To help you understand how structure supports content in each poem, use the following strategies:

- Summarize each section to clarify the content. Identify the major events and emotions in the poem.

- Note where a **turn,** or shift in thought, occurs.

- Consider the overall effect this structure creates and how it might relate to the major events and emotions in the poem.

As you read each poem, use a chart like the one shown to record your observations.

Sections	Summaries	Turn

 Complete the activities in your **Reader/Writer Notebook**.

Why do we often WANT what we can't HAVE?

Because the majority of English writers during the 17th and 18th centuries were male, most poems expressed a man's point of view. In the works that follow, you will see desire expressed from another perspective—a woman's.

QUICKWRITE People often have yearnings that are difficult, if not impossible, to fulfill. Think of a character in a book, movie, or television show who suffers from a thwarted desire. Describe the character's predicament, and explain what advice you would offer him or her.

On Her Loving Two Equally

Aphra Behn

I

How strongly does my passion flow,
Divided equally 'twixt two?
Damon had ne'er subdued my heart
Had not Alexis took his part;
5 Nor could Alexis powerful prove,
Without my Damon's aid, to gain my love.

II

When my Alexis present is,
Then I for Damon sigh and mourn;
But when Alexis I do miss,
10 Damon gains nothing but my scorn.
But if it chance they both are by,
For both alike I languish, sigh, and die.

III

Cure then, thou mighty wingéd god,
This restless fever in my blood;
15 One golden-pointed dart take back:
But which, O Cupid, wilt thou take?
If Damon's, all my hopes are crossed;
Or that of my Alexis, I am lost. **A**

2 'twixt: between.

5 powerful prove: have shown himself to be powerful.

11 by: near.

13 wingéd god: Cupid, Roman god of love.

A POETIC STRUCTURE
Describe the **turn** that occurs in lines 13–18. Why might you expect this shift in thought to take place at the end of the poem?

Portrait Study, Sir Joshua Reynolds.
Kunsthistorisches Museum, Vienna, Austria.
© Nimatallah/Art Resource, New York.

Spring Flowers, Arthur Hacker. Fine Art of Oakham, Leicestershire, Great Britain. © Fine Art Photographic Library, London/Art Resource, New York.

Written at the Close of Spring

Charlotte Smith

The garlands fade that Spring so lately wove,
    Each simple flower, which she had nursed in dew,
Anemonies, that spangled every grove,
    The primrose wan, and hare-bell mildly blue.
5 No more shall violets linger in the dell,
    Or purple orchis variegate the plain,
Till Spring again shall call forth every bell,
    And dress with humid hands her wreaths again.—
Ah! poor humanity! so frail, so fair,
10   Are the fond visions of thy early day,
Till tyrant passion, and corrosive care,
    Bid all thy fairy colors fade away!
Another May new buds and flowers shall bring;
Ah! why has happiness—no second Spring? **B**

3 anemonies (ə-nĕm′ə-nēz): small woodland flowers that resemble poppies and bloom in early spring.

4 primrose: an early-blooming flower; **wan** (wŏn): pale.

5 dell: a small valley.

6 orchis (ôr′kĭs): the orchid, called here by its Latin name; **variegate** (vâr′ē-ĭ-gāt′): to make varied in color.

7 bell: bell-shaped flower, such as a harebell or a bluebell.

B SPEAKER
Reread lines 9–14. What emotions do "tyrant passion" and "corrosive care" help convey?

Comprehension

1. **Recall** What dilemma does the speaker face in Behn's poem?

2. **Clarify** What does the speaker ask of Cupid in lines 13–15?

3. **Recall** What transition is described in lines 1–8 of Smith's poem?

4. **Clarify** Why does the speaker feel that happiness is not possible for adults?

Text Analysis

● 5. **Make Inferences About Speaker** In lines 1–8 of "Written at the Close of Spring," the speaker refers to specific types of flowers and landscapes. What can you infer about the speaker's interests and personality based on these references?

● 6. **Draw Conclusions About Speaker** In "On Her Loving Two Equally," is the speaker really torn between two lovers, or does she simply enjoy the attention being paid to her?

● 7. **Analyze Poetic Structure** Review the notes you recorded in your charts. Identify the main idea of each section of the two poems. In what ways does the structure of each poem reinforce its meaning?

8. **Recognize Characteristics of Neoclassicism** The neoclassical writers of the 18th century developed a style that reflected these attributes:

   • order   • logic   • symmetry   • wit

   Examine each selection to identify characteristics of the neoclassical style. Which poem is more clearly neoclassical? Support your answer with details.

9. **Compare Sonnets** Although the English sonnet flourished during the Renaissance in the hands of William Shakespeare, the poetic form had fallen out of favor by the late 18th century, when Charlotte Smith published her sonnet collection. Compare and contrast Smith's "Written at the Close of Spring" with Shakespeare's "Sonnet 29" on page 328. In what way is the subject matter of Smith's sonnet different from that of Shakespeare's traditional love sonnet?

Text Criticism

10. **Critical Interpretations** William Wordsworth, a pioneer of English romantic poetry, once made the following observation about Smith's sonnets: "[They] appear to me the most exquisite, in which moral sentiments, affections, or feelings are deduced from, and associated with, the scenery of nature." In what way might this interpretation apply to "Written at the Close of Spring"?

> *Why do we often* **WANT** *what we can't* **HAVE?**
>
> Why do you think we hold on to some desires even when we know they cannot be fulfilled? Have you or someone you know ever done so? Why?

COMMON CORE

RL 5 Analyze how an author's choices concerning how to structure specific parts of a text contribute to its overall structure and meaning as well as its aesthetic impact. **RL 10** Read and comprehend literature, including poems.

COMMON CORE

RI 1 Cite textual evidence to support inferences drawn from the text. **RI 10** Read and comprehend literary nonfiction. **SL 1** Initiate and participate effectively in a range of collaborative discussions.

from The Journal and Letters of Fanny Burney
An Encounter with King George III
Diary by Fanny Burney

Meet the Author

Fanny Burney 1752–1840

In the robust world of the Age of Johnson, where novel writing was not considered a suitable occupation for a lady, Fanny Burney succeeded like no other woman. Small in stature, shy, and entirely self-educated, she had neither family money nor social status. Yet she carved out a respectable place for herself in society with her popular novels and secured her place in history with her richly detailed diary, first published a few years after her death. Critics today tend to view her as Jane Austen's predecessor and not exactly her literary equal, but Burney's novels outsold Austen's in their day, and Burney herself had a much more worldly and varied life. She counted Samuel Johnson and other members of his influential Literary Club among her friends. She also knew the king and queen of England personally, once chatted with the French king Louis XVIII, and even got a glimpse of Napoleon himself.

Out of Her Father's Shadow She was born Frances Burney, the middle child in a large, close family. Both of her parents were musicians, and her father had a doctorate in music from Oxford.

After the death of her mother, she devoted herself to her father's career, acting as his secretary and helping him write his ambitious history of music. Dr. Burney's growing reputation first brought her into contact with leading artists and intellectuals. With the spotlight on her father, Burney wrote for herself in secret and published all four of her novels anonymously. Even her father didn't know she was writing until after the runaway success of her first novel, *Evelina* (1778).

Literary Celebrity The popularity of Fanny Burney's novels didn't make her rich, but it did enhance her social standing. She became a fixture in literary circles and gained an appointment at the court of George III. In 1793, she met a group of liberal French émigrés, among them a handsome officer named D'Arblay (där′blā′) who won her heart. The couple had only a modest income, but the marriage was a happy one and produced a son. D'Arblay supported his wife's career by serving as her secretary, sometimes even copying manuscript pages for her. Burney lived 87 years, an unusually long life for the time. She survived cancer, exile in France during the Napoleonic Wars, and the deaths of both her husband and her son.

Author Online

Go to **thinkcentral.com**. KEYWORD: HML12-706

THINK central

TEXT ANALYSIS: DESCRIPTION IN NONFICTION

A keen observer of human nature, Fanny Burney kept a diary so she could record her descriptions of ordinary as well as famous people. Diaries such as Burney's provide a valuable record of life in previous eras. In the selection you are about to read, she offers an unusually candid portrait of George III. Although Burney writes about actual people, she relies on the same basic methods of description used in fiction to portray them vividly:

- describing a person's physical appearance
- quoting a person or describing his or her actions
- reporting what others say or think about a person
- including her own opinions about a person

As you read Burney's account, notice how she uses these different types of description to convey her impressions of the king.

READING SKILL: DRAW CONCLUSIONS

In her diary, Burney provides poignant revelations about George III and his illness and its effect on life at the royal court. As you read the selection, use text clues and your own knowledge to make **inferences,** or logical guesses, about the effects of the king's condition on those around him. For example, you can infer from the following lines that Burney avoids the king because his presence threatens her in some way:

This morning, when I received my intelligence of the king from Dr. John Willis, I begged to know where I might walk in safety? "In Kew gardens," he said, "as the king would be in Richmond."

Record your inferences in a chart like the one shown. After reading the selection, you will use these notes to **draw conclusions,** or make judgments, about the circumstances at court.

Passages About the King	My Inferences
"...I thought I saw the person of his majesty! Alarmed past all possible expression, I waited not to know more, but turning back, ran off with all my might." (lines 18–21)	Burney is terrified of the king. She may be afraid because she has broken the rules of the royal court.

 Complete the activities in your **Reader/Writer Notebook.**

What is your image of ROYALTY?

When you consider the lives of royals, you might focus on their glamour, power, and wealth. On the other hand, you may recall their frivolous scandals and squabbles. Whatever your image of royalty, the reality is probably a combination of pomp and pettiness. At least that's what Fanny Burney discovered when she spent five years at the court of George III in her official capacity as "second keeper of the Queen's robes."

DISCUSS With a small group of classmates, discuss how you imagine everyday life is for royals. In what ways might their lives be similar to those of ordinary people? In what ways might they be different?

AN ENCOUNTER WITH KING GEORGE III

Fanny Burney

BACKGROUND Fanny Burney's diaries chronicle the momentous events and outsized personalities of late 18th-century England and post-revolutionary France. What follows is her most famous account of George III during the period of his mental illness (1788–1789). By then, Burney's own health had begun to suffer after two unhappy years at court. Lonely and bored by her royal duties, she also chafed under the rule of her superior—referred to in this selection as "the coadjutrix"—a woman she found "gloomy, dark, suspicious, rude, reproachful."

Analyze Visuals ▶
What adjectives would you use to describe the architectural and landscaping styles shown in the photograph on the opposite page?

KEW PALACE, MONDAY FEBRUARY 2, 1789

What an adventure had I this morning! one that has occasioned me the severest personal terror I ever experienced in my life.

Sir Lucas Pepys[1] still persisting that exercise and air were absolutely necessary to save me from illness, I have continued my walks, varying my gardens from Richmond to Kew,[2] according to the accounts I received of the movements of the king. For this I had her majesty's permission, on the representation of Sir Lucas.

This morning, when I received my intelligence of the king from Dr. John Willis,[3] I begged to know where I might walk in safety? "In Kew gardens," he said, "as the king would be in Richmond." **A**

A DRAW CONCLUSIONS
What details suggest that the king's illness has forced Burney to change her personal habits?

---

1. **Sir Lucas Pepys** (pēps): a physician who was an old friend of the Burney family.
2. **gardens from Richmond to Kew:** the gardens at Richmond House and Kew House, two adjoining royal residences west of London that were often used by George III and his family.
3. **Dr. John Willis:** a clergyman and physician who attended George III during his illness. His son, John Willis, also a physician, assisted in treating the king.

10   "Should any unfortunate circumstance," I cried, "at any time, occasion my being seen by his majesty, do not mention my name, but let me run off without call or notice."

    This he promised. Everybody, indeed, is ordered to keep out of sight.

    Taking, therefore, the time I had most at command, I strolled into the gardens. I had proceeded, in my quick way, nearly half the round, when I suddenly perceived, through some trees, two or three figures. Relying on the instructions of Dr. John, I concluded them to be workmen and gardeners; yet tried to look sharp, and in so doing, as they were less shaded, I thought I saw the person of his majesty!

20   Alarmed past all possible expression, I waited not to know more, but turning back, ran off with all my might. But what was my terror to hear myself pursued!—to hear the voice of the king himself loudly and hoarsely calling after me, "Miss Burney! Miss Burney!"

    I protest I was ready to die. I knew not in what state he might be at the time; I only knew the orders to keep out of his way were universal; that the queen would highly disapprove any unauthorized meeting, and that the very action of my running away might deeply, in his present irritable state, offend him. Nevertheless, on I ran, too terrified to stop, and in search of some short passage, for the garden is full of little labyrinths, by which I might escape. **B**

30   The steps still pursued me, and still the poor hoarse and altered voice rang in my ears:—more and more footsteps resounded frightfully behind me,—the attendants all running, to catch their eager master, and the voices of the two Doctor Willises loudly exhorting him not to heat himself so unmercifully.

    Heavens, how I ran! I do not think I should have felt the hot lava from Vesuvius—at least not the hot cinders—had I so run during its eruption. My feet were not sensible that they even touched the ground.

    Soon after, I heard other voices, shriller, though less nervous, call out "Stop! stop! stop!"

    I could by no means consent; I knew not what was purposed, but I recollected
40 fully my agreement with Dr. John that very morning, that I should decamp if surprised, and not be named.

    My own fears and repugnance, also, after a flight and disobedience like this, were doubled in the thought of not escaping; I knew not to what I might be exposed, should the malady be then high,[4] and take the turn of resentment. Still, therefore, on I flew; and such was my speed, so almost incredible to relate or recollect, that I fairly believe no one of the whole party could have overtaken me, if these words, from one of the attendants, had not reached me: "Doctor Willis begs you to stop!" **C**

    "I cannot! I cannot!" I answered, still flying on, when he called out "You must,
50 ma'am; it hurts the king to run."

    Then, indeed, I stopped—in a state of fear really amounting to agony. I turned round, I saw the two doctors had got the king between them, and three attendants

B DRAW CONCLUSIONS
Reread lines 24–29. In what ways has the king's malady affected the activities of the royal court?

C DESCRIPTION
What do you learn about the king based on Burney's direct comments in lines 42–48?

---

4. **malady** (măl′ə-dē) **be then high:** illness then be greater, or worse, than usual.

of Dr. Willis's were hovering about. They all slackened their pace, as they saw me stand still; but such was the excess of my alarm, that I was wholly insensible[5] to the effects of a race which, at any other time, would have required an hour's recruit.[6]

As they approached, some little presence of mind happily came to my command; it occurred to me that, to appease the wrath of[7] my flight, I must now show some confidence. I therefore faced them as undauntedly as I was able, only charging the nearest of the attendants to stand by my side.

60 When they were within a few yards of me, the king called out, "Why did you run away?"

Shocked at a question impossible to answer, yet a little assured by the mild tone of his voice, I instantly forced myself forward, to meet him, though the internal sensation, which satisfied me this was a step the most proper to appease his suspicions and displeasure, was so violently combated by the tremor of my nerves, that I fairly think I may reckon it the greatest effort of personal courage I have ever made.

The effort answered:[8] I looked up, and met all his wonted benignity of countenance,[9] though something still of wildness in his eyes. Think, however, of 70 my surprise, to feel him put both his hands round my two shoulders, and then kiss my cheek!

I wonder I did not really sink, so exquisite was my affright when I saw him spread out his arms! Involuntarily, I concluded he meant to crush me; but the Willises, who have never seen him till this fatal illness, not knowing how very extraordinary an action this was from him, simply smiled and looked pleased, supposing, perhaps, it was his customary salutation! **D**

I believe, however, it was but the joy of a heart unbridled, now, by the forms and proprieties of established custom and sober reason. To see any of his household thus by accident, seemed such a near approach to liberty and recovery, 80 that who can wonder it should serve rather to elate than lessen what yet remains of his disorder!

He now spoke in such terms of his pleasure in seeing me, that I soon lost the whole of my terror; astonishment to find him so nearly well, and gratification to see him so pleased, removed every uneasy feeling, and the joy that succeeded, in my conviction of his recovery, made me ready to throw myself at his feet to express it.

What a conversation followed! When he saw me fearless, he grew more and more alive, and made me walk close by his side, away from the attendants, and even the Willises themselves, who, to indulge him, retreated. I own[10] myself not 90 completely composed, but alarm I could entertain no more.

D DESCRIPTION
Reread lines 68–76. What do the king's appearance and actions toward Burney reveal about him?

---

5. **wholly insensible:** completely unaware.

6. **recruit** (rĭ-krōōt'): recovery; renewal of strength.

7. **appease the wrath of:** make up for the fury of.

8. **answered:** met the situation; worked.

9. **his wonted benignity** (wôn'tĭd bĭ-nĭg'nĭ-tē) **of countenance** (koun'tə-nəns): the customary kindness of his facial expression.

10. **own:** admit.

King George III of England (1771), Johann Zoffany. Oil on canvas. The Granger Collection, New York.

Everything that came uppermost in his mind he mentioned; he seemed to have just such remains of his flightiness as heated his imagination without deranging his reason, and robbed him of all control over his speech, though nearly in his perfect state of mind as to his opinions.

What did he not say!—He opened his whole heart to me,—expounded all his sentiments, and acquainted me with all his intentions.

The heads of his discourse[11] I must give you briefly, as I am sure you will be highly curious to hear them, and as no accident can render of much consequence what a man says in such a state of physical intoxication. He assured me he was quite well—as well as he had ever been in his life; and then inquired how I did, and how I went on? and whether I was more comfortable? If these questions, in their implication, surprised me, imagine how that surprise must increase when he proceeded to explain them! He asked after the coadjutrix,[12] laughing, and saying "Never mind her!—don't be oppressed—I am your friend! don't let her cast you down!—I know you have a hard time of it—but don't mind her!"

Almost thunderstruck with astonishment, I merely curtsied to his kind "I am your friend," and said nothing.

Then presently he added, "Stick to your father—stick to your own family—let them be your objects."

How readily I assented!

Again he repeated all I have just written, nearly in the same words, but ended it more seriously: he suddenly stopped, and held me to stop too, and putting his hand on his breast, in the most solemn manner, he gravely and slowly said, "I will protect you!—I promise you that—and therefore depend upon me!"

I thanked him; and the Willises, thinking him rather too elevated,[13] came to propose my walking on. "No, no, no!" he cried, a hundred times in a breath; and their good humor prevailed, and they let him again walk on with his new companion.

He then gave me a history of his pages,[14] animating almost into a rage, as he related his subjects of displeasure with them, particularly with Mr. Ernst, who he told me had been brought up by himself. I hope his ideas upon these men are the result of the mistakes of his malady.

Then he asked me some questions that very greatly distressed me, relating to information given him in his illness, from various motives, but which he suspected to be false, and which I knew he had reason to suspect; yet was it most dangerous to set anything right, as I was not aware what might be the views of their having been stated wrong. I was as discreet as I knew how to be, and I hope I did no mischief; but this was the worst part of the dialogue.

◀ **Analyze Visuals**
Examine the portrait of George III on page 712. How does this image compare with the impression you get of him in Burney's diary?

---

11. **heads of his discourse:** main points of his conversation.

12. **coadjutrix** (kō-ə-jū'trĭks): Elizabeth Juliana Schwellenberg, First Keeper of the Robes to Queen Charlotte and Fanny's immediate superior. She was known to be bossy and difficult toward the rest of the royal household staff and gave Fanny a terrible time.

13. **elevated:** excited.

14. **pages:** young male servants attending a king or someone else of high rank.

He next talked to me a great deal of my dear father, and made a thousand
inquiries concerning his "History of Music."[15] This brought him to his favorite
theme, Handel;[16] and he told me innumerable anecdotes of him, and particularly
that celebrated tale of Handel's saying of himself, when a boy, "While that boy
lives, my music will never want a protector." And this, he said, I might relate to
my father. Then he ran over most of his oratorios, attempting to sing the subjects
of several airs and choruses,[17] but so dreadfully hoarse that the sound was terrible.

Dr. Willis, quite alarmed at this exertion, feared he would do himself harm,
and again proposed a separation. "No! no! no!" he exclaimed, "not yet; I have
something I must just mention first."

Dr. Willis, delighted to comply, even when uneasy at compliance, again gave
way. The good king then greatly affected me. He began upon my revered old
friend, Mrs. Delany;[18] and he spoke of her with such warmth—such kindness!
"She was my friend!" he cried, "and I loved her as a friend! I have made a
memorandum when I lost her—I will show it you."

He pulled out a pocketbook,[19] and rummaged some time, but to no purpose.
The tears stood in his eyes—he wiped them, and Dr. Willis again became very
anxious. "Come, sir," he cried, "now do you come in and let the lady go on
her walk,—come, now you have talked a long while,—so we'll go in,—if your
majesty pleases." **E**

"No, no!" he cried, "I want to ask her a few questions;—I have lived so long
out of the world, I know nothing!"

This touched me to the heart. . . . He then told me he was very much
dissatisfied with several of his state officers, and meant to form an entire new
establishment. He took a paper out of his pocketbook, and showed me his
new list.

This was the wildest thing that passed; and Dr. John Willis now seriously urged
our separating; but he would not consent; he had only three more words to say, he
declared, and again he conquered.

He now spoke of my father, with still more kindness, and told me he ought
to have had the post of master of the band, and not that little poor musician
Parsons,[20] who was not fit for it: "But Lord Salisbury,"[21] he cried, "used your

E DESCRIPTION
Examine the way Dr. Willis
responds to the king's
behavior in lines 136–148.
What do you learn about
the king's condition based
on Burney's description
of the doctor's reaction
to him?

---

15. **"History of Music":** Fanny's father, Dr. Charles Burney, was a music historian best known for his *General History of Music*, the third and fourth volumes of which were published in 1789, the same year in which the events in this selection occurred.

16. **Handel** (hăn'dl): George Frideric Handel (1685–1759), the great composer and a favorite of the king's father, George II.

17. **oratorios** (ôr'ə-tôr'ē-ōz) . . . **choruses:** long, dramatic musical compositions that contain arias (or "airs"), choruses, and other portions to be sung but that differ from operas in not being performed with stage action, scenery, and costumes.

18. **Mrs. Delany:** Mary Delany, an elderly friend of Fanny's who had recently died.

19. **pocketbook:** a case or folder for carrying money or papers in one's pocket.

20. **he ought . . . Parsons:** Dr. Burney applied for the position of Master of the King's Band when it became vacant, but the post was instead given to a William Parsons.

21. **Lord Salisbury** (sôlz'bĕr'ē): James Cecil, Marquess of Salisbury, who served as the royal household's Lord Chamberlain from 1783 to 1804, would have been involved in deciding who obtained the position of Master of the King's Band.

father very ill in that business, and so he did me! However, I have dashed out his name, and I shall put your father's in,—as soon as I get loose again!"

This again—how affecting was this!

"And what," cried he, "has your father got, at last? nothing but that poor thing at Chelsea?²² O fie! fie! fie! But never mind! I will take care of him! I will do it myself!" Then presently he added, "As to Lord Salisbury, he is out already, as this memorandum will show you, and so are many more. I shall be much better served; and when once I get away, I shall rule with a rod of iron!"

This was very unlike himself, and startled the two good doctors, who could not
170 bear to cross him, and were exulting at my seeing his great amendment,²³ but yet grew quite uneasy at his earnestness and volubility.

Finding we now must part, he stopped to take leave, and renewed again his charges about the coadjutrix. "Never mind her!" he cried, "depend upon me! I will be your friend as long as I live!—I here pledge myself to be your friend!" And then he saluted me again just as at the meeting, and suffered me to go on.

What a scene! how variously was I affected by it! but, upon the whole, how inexpressibly thankful to see him so nearly himself—so little removed from recovery! ∽

Language Coach

Frequently Misused Words The word *affect* is often confused with *effect*. As a verb, the first means "to have an influence on" and the second means "to cause." In line 163, *affecting* means "emotionally touching." Use *effecting* correctly in a sentence.

---

22. **that poor thing at Chelsea** (chĕl′sē): Instead of Master of the King's Band, Dr. Burney was made organist in the chapel on the grounds of Chelsea Hospital, a refuge for old and disabled soldiers located in London.

23. **amendment:** change for the better; improvement.

Comprehension

1. **Recall** Why was Burney surprised to run into the king on her walk?

2. **Clarify** Why was she so terrified of meeting him?

3. **Summarize** In the end, what is Burney's opinion of the king's mental health?

Text Analysis

4. **Analyze Description** Throughout the selection, Burney uses various methods of characterization to develop her portrait of George III. Identify one example of each method. Which method gives you the most vivid impression of the king's personality?

5. **Make Inferences About the Author** Summarize the events in each of the following scenes. To what extent is Burney's initial "terror" of the king justified?

   • her plans for a morning walk (lines 3–12)

   • her flight from the king (lines 20–29)

   • her "disobedience" (lines 37–48)

   • the king's treatment of her (lines 68–76)

6. **Make Judgments** Based on Burney's reaction to the king, what judgments can you make about how the king was expected to act?

7. **Draw Conclusions** Look over the **inferences** you recorded as you read the selection. What aspect of the king's illness do you think posed the most difficulty for those around him? Support your conclusion with evidence from the text.

8. **Synthesize Information** Using information from Burney's account and the newspaper article on page 717, what is your understanding of George III's condition? Cite specific details in your response.

Text Criticism

9. **Analyze Diary** Burney's diaries were first published in England in 1842. Diarists are often accused of invading the privacy of others because they record potentially embarrassing details about people's lives without their permission. Do you think this applies to this excerpt from Burney's diaries about King George III's mental illness? Why or why not?

What is your image of **ROYALTY?**

The royal family of England continues to fascinate people today. Why do you think this is the case? What symbolic roles does the royal family play for other people?

COMMON CORE

RI 1 Cite textual evidence to support inferences drawn from the text. **RI 10** Read and comprehend literary nonfiction.

NEWSPAPER ARTICLE In this recent article, Emma Ross offers a glimpse into the possible causes of George III's mental illness.

Madness of King George Tied to Arsenic EMMA ROSS

Scientists have found high levels of arsenic in the hair of King George III and say the deadly poison may be to blame for the bouts of apparent madness he suffered.

In 1969, researchers proposed that the strange behavior of the monarch who reigned during the American Revolution resulted from a rare hereditary blood disorder called porphyria.

However, a study published this week in the British medical journal the *Lancet* found high concentrations of arsenic in the king's hair and contends the severity and duration of his episodes of illness may have been caused by the toxic substance. . . .

While on the throne, George had five episodes of prolonged and profound mental derangement.

In 1969, psychiatrists investigating his documented symptoms such as lameness, acute abdominal pain, red urine, and temporary mental disturbance, proposed he suffered from porphyria. Subsequent studies that examined records of his ancestors, descendants, and other relatives refined the diagnosis to a certain type of porphyria.

However, the research did not explain the unusual persistence, severity, and late onset of attacks.

"People can have the faulty gene which makes them susceptible to attacks, but in about 80 percent of cases they never have any symptoms," said Martin Warren, a professor of biosciences at the University of Kent in England who led the latest study.

"If you are unfortunate enough to get them, porphyric attacks can be deadly, and some patients die from their first one," Warren

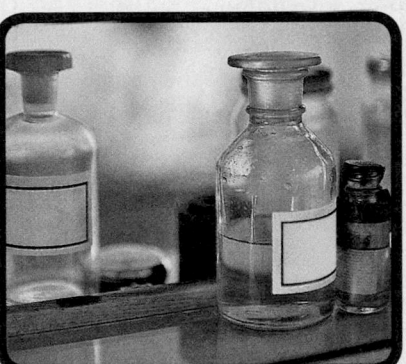

said. "But in many cases the attacks tend to be much less severe, and certainly not for the same duration that George III had."

Warren and his team set out to examine a sample of the king's hair on display at London's Science Museum for traces of mercury or lead, metals known to make porphyria worse.

"What surprised us was there were very high levels of arsenic. Arsenic is also known to push porphyric patients into a worse state," Warren said. The semimetallic element was found to be at 17 parts per million in the hair. Levels normally are found at less than one part per million.

Arsenic interferes with the production of heam, a key element of blood and the central problem of porphyria. The blood then gets toxic, which can cause mental disturbance and severe pain.

John Henry, a toxicologist at Imperial College in London, was cautious about interpreting the findings.

"He may have accumulated significant amounts in the last few months of his life, but that doesn't prove it caused his illness all his life," Henry said. "It's a nice theory, but it's just that—a theory." . . .

The king's medical records revealed he had consistently been given medicine containing antimony, a mineral often found in the ground with arsenic.

"The way antimony was extracted 200 years ago means that it was often quite contaminated with arsenic," Warren said. "The king was given large doses of antimony for his abdominal pains, and that was probably the

from A Vindication of the Rights of Woman

Essay by Mary Wollstonecraft

VIDEO TRAILER **THINK** central KEYWORD: HML12-718A

COMMON CORE

RI 5 Analyze and evaluate the effectiveness of the structure an author uses in his or her argument. RI 6 Determine an author's point of view or purpose in a text. RI 8 Delineate and evaluate the reasoning in seminal texts. RI 10 Read and comprehend literary nonfiction. SL 1 Initiate and participate effectively in a range of collaborative discussions.

Meet the Author

Mary Wollstonecraft 1759–1797

Passionate, outspoken, and bold—at times even reckless—Mary Wollstonecraft was the antithesis of the proper 18th-century English lady. Inflamed with the revolutionary ideas of the Enlightenment, she denounced not only monarchy and slavery but also the institution of marriage. Her embrace of natural rights included the rights of women, children, and even animals. While still an unknown book reviewer and translator, she took on the eminent conservative Edmund Burke, one of Samuel Johnson's inner circle, by responding to his criticism of the French Revolution with her own attack on class and privilege in *A Vindication of the Rights of Men* (1790). Two years later, she called for an end to the prevailing injustices against women in *A Vindication of the Rights of Woman.* Reviled by some at the time as a "hyena in petticoats," she was the mother of feminism as we know it today.

DID YOU KNOW?

Mary Wollstonecraft . . .

- inspired American women's rights pioneers Elizabeth Cady Stanton and Margaret Fuller.
- was the mother of Mary Shelley, author of *Frankenstein.*

Education of a Radical Wollstonecraft was the second of seven children born into a middle-class family spiraling into poverty. Wishing to escape hardship, the young Wollstonecraft supplemented her meager education with extensive reading on her own. When she came of age, she worked first as a lady's companion and later as a governess, two positions that showed her how the aristocracy lived while reinforcing her own servitude. For a while, she ran a school with her sisters in London, where she met a group of liberal reformers. These new friends gave the restless Wollstonecraft a larger, more political perspective from which to view her personal struggle for liberation.

A Life Cut Short By the time she turned 30, Wollstonecraft had written a pamphlet, *Thoughts on the Education of Daughters* (1787), as well as a novel. Her London publisher then hired her to write for his new journal and introduced her to reformist intellectuals such as the essayist Thomas Paine, the poet William Blake, and the political philosopher William Godwin. After writing her notorious book on women's rights, Wollstonecraft spent two years in Paris at the height of the bloody Reign of Terror, which sobered her on the French Revolution but not on its ideals. Back in London, she drew closer to William Godwin, finding in him a kindred spirit. Tragically, only a few months after marrying Godwin, she died from complications in giving birth to their only child, Mary.

Author Online

Go to thinkcentral.com. KEYWORD: HML12-718B

THINK central

TEXT ANALYSIS: COUNTERARGUMENTS

An **argument** is speech or writing that makes a major **claim**, or takes a position, about an issue and supports it with reasons and evidence. In *A Vindication of the Rights of Woman*, Mary Wollstonecraft's purpose is to convince her readers that there should be a change of policy about women's education to provide women with greater educational opportunities. Wollstonecraft uses persuasive techniques that appeal to reason rather than to emotion to support her claim. For example, she anticipates opposing viewpoints and responds with **counterarguments**. In other words, she foresees opposing arguments and responds logically to them using reasons and evidence to refute their claims and the assumptions upon which they are based. As you read, pay attention to the counterarguments Wollstonecraft presents in the selection.

READING SKILL: USE HISTORICAL CONTEXT

To best appreciate why Wollstonecraft wrote *A Vindication of the Rights of Woman,* you should have some sense of the essay's **historical context,** or the social conditions that inspired its creation. Although the essay might seem conservative by modern standards, its views were considered radical in 18th-century Britain, where few women publicly expressed discontent over their limited educational opportunities. To further your understanding of the historical context of Wollstonecraft's work, study the author biography on page 718, the background information on page 720, and the footnotes within the essay. Then, as you read, note statements that you are able to clarify by using this information.

Statement	Explanation
"[Women] spend many of the first years of their lives in acquiring a smattering of accomplishments." (lines 66–67)	In Wollstonecraft's era, girls were schooled primarily in domestic activities.

▲ VOCABULARY IN CONTEXT

The following boldfaced words are important to your understanding Wollstonecraft's controversial essay. Try to figure out the meaning of each word from the context.

1. **vindication** from blame or guilt
2. a **prerogative** of rank
3. **inculcate** the ideas through repetition
4. not long lasting but **evanescent**
5. **feign** illness when not really ill

 Complete the activities in your **Reader/Writer Notebook**.

What makes EQUALITY *elusive?*

Thomas Jefferson wrote that "all men are created equal," but he and the other Founding Fathers left out many men and all women when they first considered rights in the new United States. Writing 16 years after the Declaration of Independence, Mary Wollstonecraft was one of the first to confront the issue of equality for women, but even she confined her arguments to education.

DISCUSS Consider why equal rights have historically been so difficult to achieve. How does a country generally ensure that all of its citizens are treated equally and fairly? If you don't have these rights, how are you generally treated? Write down your thoughts on these issues and then discuss them with a small group of classmates.

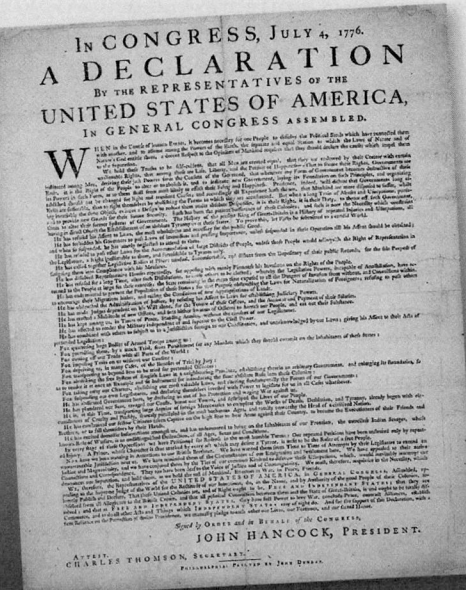

A VINDICATION
of the RIGHTS *of*
WOMAN

Mary Wollstonecraft

BACKGROUND In the late 18th century, daughters of English gentlemen were educated at home before being sent away to school for a few years. In addition to reading and studying foreign languages, girls learned how to play the piano, sing, draw, and do needlework. Young women were expected to marry, and those without independent wealth had few alternatives. Barred from any professional occupation, an unmarried woman could only support herself as a servant, a nurse, a governess, or some similar occupation.

FROM THE INTRODUCTION

After considering the historic page, and viewing the living world with anxious solicitude, the most melancholy emotions of sorrowful indignation have depressed my spirits, and I have sighed when obliged to confess, that either nature has made a great difference between man and man, or that the civilization which has hitherto taken place in the world has been very partial. I have turned over various books written on the subject of education, and patiently observed the conduct of parents and the management of schools; but what has been the result?—a profound conviction that the neglected education of my fellow-creatures is the grand source of the misery I deplore; and that women, in particular, are rendered

10 weak and wretched by a variety of concurring causes, originating from one hasty conclusion. The conduct and manners of women, in fact, evidently prove that their minds are not in a healthy state; for, like the flowers which are planted in too rich a soil, strength and usefulness are sacrificed to beauty; and the flaunting leaves, after having pleased a fastidious eye, fade, disregarded on the stalk, long before the season when they ought to have arrived at maturity. One cause of this barren blooming I attribute to a false system of education, gathered from the books written on this subject by men who, considering females rather as women

vindication
(vĭn'dĭ-kā'shən) *n.*
clearing from criticism, blame, guilt, or suspicion; justification

Analyze Visuals ▶

Describe the expressions on the faces of the two figures shown in the painting on the opposite page. What might the image suggest about relations between men and women in the 18th century?

A Girl Reading a Letter by Candlelight with a Young Man Peering over Her Shoulder (1760), Joseph Wright of Derby. Oil on canvas, 88.9 cm × 69.8 cm. Private collection. © Bridgeman Art Library.

than human creatures, have been more anxious to make them alluring mistresses than affectionate wives and rational mothers; and the understanding of the sex has been so bubbled by this specious homage,[1] that the civilized women of the present century, with a few exceptions, are only anxious to inspire love, when they ought to cherish a nobler ambition, and by their abilities and virtues exact respect. **A**

In a treatise,[2] therefore, on female rights and manners, the works which have been particularly written for their improvement must not be overlooked; especially when it is asserted, in direct terms, that the minds of women are enfeebled by false refinement; that the books of instruction, written by men of genius, have had the same tendency as more frivolous productions; and that . . . they are treated as a kind of subordinate beings, and not as a part of the human species, when improvable reason is allowed to be the dignified distinction which raises men above the brute creation, and puts a natural scepter in a feeble hand.

Yet, because I am a woman, I would not lead my readers to suppose that I mean violently to agitate the contested question respecting the quality or inferiority of the sex; but as the subject lies in my way, and I cannot pass it over without subjecting the main tendency of my reasoning to misconstruction, I shall stop a moment to deliver, in a few words, my opinion. In the government of the physical world it is observable that the female in point of strength is, in general, inferior to the male. This is the law of nature; and it does not appear to be suspended or abrogated in favor of woman. A degree of physical superiority cannot, therefore, be denied—and it is a noble **prerogative!** But not content with this natural pre-eminence, men endeavor to sink us still lower merely to render us alluring objects for a moment; and women, intoxicated by the adoration which men, under the influence of their senses, pay them, do not seek to obtain a durable interest in their hearts, or to become the friends of the fellow creatures who find amusement in their society. **B**

I am aware of an obvious inference: from every quarter have I heard exclamations against masculine women; but where are they to be found? If by this appellation men mean to inveigh against their ardor[3] in hunting, shooting, and gaming, I shall most cordially join in the cry; but if it be against the imitation of manly virtues, or, more properly speaking, the attainment of those talents and virtues, the exercise of which ennobles the human character, and which raise females in the scale of animal being, when they are comprehensively termed mankind; all those who view them with a philosophic eye must, I should think, wish with me, that they may every day grow more and more masculine. . . .

My own sex, I hope, will excuse me, if I treat them like rational creatures, instead of flattering their *fascinating* graces, and viewing them as if they were in a state of perpetual childhood, unable to stand alone. I earnestly wish to point out in what true dignity and human happiness consists—I wish to persuade women

A **HISTORICAL CONTEXT**
Reread the background information on page 720. Why might Wollstonecraft have considered women's education more appropriate for a mistress than for a wife and mother?

prerogative (prĭ-rŏg′ə-tĭv) *n.* a privilege or distinctive advantage

B **COUNTERARGUMENTS**
Reread lines 31–44. What is Wollstonecraft's counterargument to the **claim** that women are naturally inferior to men?

---

1. **bubbled by this specious homage** (spē′shəs hŏm′ĭj): deceived by this false honor.
2. **treatise:** a formal, detailed article or book on a particular subject.
3. **If by . . . inveigh** (ĭn-vā′) **against their ardor:** if by this term ("masculine women") men mean to condemn some women's enthusiasm.

to endeavor to acquire strength, both of mind and body, and to convince them that the soft phrases, susceptibility of heart, delicacy of sentiment, and refinement
60 of taste, are almost synonymous with epithets[4] of weakness, and that those beings who are only the objects of pity and that kind of love, which has been termed its sister, will soon become objects of contempt. . . . **C**

The education of women has, of late, been more attended to than formerly; yet they are still reckoned a frivolous sex, and ridiculed or pitied by the writers who endeavor by satire or instruction to improve them. It is acknowledged that they spend many of the first years of their lives in acquiring a smattering of accomplishments;[5] meanwhile strength of body and mind are sacrificed to libertine[6] notions of beauty, to the desire of establishing themselves—the only way women can rise in the world—by marriage. And this desire making mere animals
70 of them, when they marry they act as such children may be expected to act: they dress; they paint, and nickname God's creatures. Surely these weak beings are only fit for a seraglio![7] Can they be expected to govern a family with judgment, or take care of the poor babes whom they bring into the world?

If then it can be fairly deduced from the present conduct of the sex, from the prevalent fondness for pleasure which takes place of ambition and those nobler passions that open and enlarge the soul; that the instruction which women have hitherto received has only tended, with the constitution of civil society, to render them insignificant objects of desire—mere propagators of fools!—if it can be proved that in aiming to accomplish them, without cultivating their
80 understandings, they are taken out of their sphere of duties, and made ridiculous and useless when the short-lived bloom of beauty is over, I presume that *rational* men will excuse me for endeavoring to persuade them to become more masculine and respectable.

Indeed the word masculine is only a bugbear:[8] there is little reason to fear that women will acquire too much courage or fortitude; for their apparent inferiority with respect to bodily strength, must render them, in some degree, dependent on men in the various relations of life; but why should it be increased by prejudices that give a sex to virtue, and confound simple truths with sensual reveries?[9] **D**

FROM CHAPTER 2

Youth is the season for love in both sexes; but in those days of thoughtless
90 enjoyment provision should be made for the more important years of life, when reflection takes place of sensation. But Rousseau,[10] and most of the male writers

---

4. **epithets** (ĕp'ə-thĕts'): descriptive terms.

5. **accomplishments:** This term, when applied to women, designated only those achievements then considered suitable for middle- and upper-class women, such as painting, singing, playing a musical instrument, and embroidery.

6. **libertine** (lĭb'ər-tēn'): indecent or unseemly.

7. **seraglio** (sə-răl'yō): harem.

8. **bugbear:** an object of exaggerated fear.

9. **confound . . . reveries** (rĕv'ə-rēz): confuse simple truths with men's sexual daydreams.

10. **Rousseau** (rōō-sō'): The Swiss-born French philosopher Jean-Jacques Rousseau (1712–1778) presented a plan for female education in his famous 1762 novel *Émile.*

Language Coach

Roots and Affixes The English word *acquire* and the Spanish *adquirir* come from the same Latin root (*quaerere,* "to seek") and contain the same prefix, *ad-* ("to"). However, in English *ad-* becomes *ac-* before the letter *q.* What does *acquire* mean in line 58?

COMMON CORE RI 6

C SARCASM
Sarcasm is a mocking or joking tone. It may be used to emphasize a point by saying the opposite of what is meant. In line 54, Wollstonecraft asks other women to "excuse" her for "treat[ing] them as rational creatures." Wollstonecraft does not intend to apologize to women. On the contrary, she believes women are thoroughly rational and thus deserving of greater education. At whom does Wollstonecraft direct this sarcastic remark? Why does she do so?

D COUNTERARGUMENTS
Reread lines 63–88. What counterarguments does Wollstonecraft use to refute the **assumption** that improved education will make women too masculine?

who have followed his steps, have warmly **inculcated** that the whole tendency of female education ought to be directed to one point: to render them[11] pleasing.

Let me reason with the supporters of this opinion who have any knowledge of human nature, do they imagine that marriage can eradicate the habitude of life? The woman who has only been taught to please will soon find that her charms are oblique sunbeams, and that they cannot have much effect on her husband's heart when they are seen every day, when the summer is passed and gone. Will she then have sufficient native energy to look into herself for comfort, and cultivate her
100 dormant faculties? or, is it not more rational to expect that she will try to please other men; and, in the emotions raised by the expectation of new conquests, endeavor to forget the mortification her love or pride has received? When the husband ceases to be a lover—and the time will inevitably come, her desire of pleasing will then grow languid, or become a spring of bitterness; and love, perhaps, the most **evanescent** of all passions, gives place to jealousy or vanity.

I now speak of women who are restrained by principle or prejudice; such women, though they would shrink from an intrigue with real abhorrence, yet, nevertheless, wish to be convinced by the homage of gallantry that they are cruelly neglected by their husbands; or, days and weeks are spent in dreaming of the
110 happiness enjoyed by congenial souls till their health is undermined and their spirits broken by discontent. How then can the great art of pleasing be such a necessary study? it is only useful to a mistress; the chaste wife, and serious mother, should only consider her power to please as the polish of her virtues, and the affection of her husband as one of the comforts that render her talk less difficult and her life happier. But, whether she be loved or neglected, her first wish should be to make herself respectable, and not to rely for all her happiness on a being subject to like infirmities with herself. **E**

The worthy Dr. Gregory fell into a similar error. I respect his heart; but entirely disapprove of his celebrated Legacy to his Daughters.[12] . . .
120 He actually recommends dissimulation, and advises an innocent girl to give the lie to her feelings, and not dance with spirit, when gaiety of heart would make her feet eloquent without making her gestures immodest. In the name of truth and common sense, why should not one woman acknowledge that she can take more exercise than another? or, in other words, that she has a sound constitution; and why, to damp innocent vivacity, is she darkly to be told that men will draw conclusions which she little thinks of? Let the libertine draw what inference he pleases; but, I hope, that no sensible mother will restrain the natural frankness of youth by instilling such indecent cautions. Out of the abundance of the heart the mouth speaketh; and a wiser than Solomon[13] hath said, that the heart should be

inculcate (ĭn-kŭl′kāt′) *v.* to impress on the mind by frequent repetition; to teach; to instill

evanescent (ĕv′ə-nĕs′ənt) *adj.* quick to disappear

E HISTORICAL CONTEXT
Reread lines 89–117. In his writings, the French philosopher Jean-Jacques Rousseau placed a high value on liberty and equality. How does this information help you appreciate the radical nature of Wollstonecraft's argument?

---

11. **them:** that is, females.

12. **Dr. Gregory . . . Daughters:** In his 1774 work *A Father's Legacy for His Daughters,* John Gregory (1724–1773) offered a plan for female education that remained popular for decades.

13. **a wiser than Solomon:** King David, reputed author of many psalms in the Bible and the father of King Solomon, who was known for his wisdom. The words that follow draw on ideas in Psalm 24, which states that only those with "clean hands, and a pure heart" shall ascend into Heaven.

In the Artist's Studio (1800s), Thomas Myles. Oil on canvas, 39.4 cm × 29.2 cm. Private collection. © Bridgeman Art Library.

130 made clean, and not trivial ceremonies observed, which it is not very difficult to fulfil with scrupulous exactness when vice reigns in the heart.

Women ought to endeavor to purify their heart; but can they do so when their uncultivated understandings make them entirely dependent on their senses for employment and amusement, when no noble pursuit sets them above the little vanities of the day, or enables them to curb the wild emotions that agitate a reed over which every passing breeze has power? To gain the affections of a virtuous man, is affectation necessary? Nature has given woman a weaker frame than man; but, to ensure her husband's affections, must a wife, who by the exercise of her mind and body whilst she was discharging the duties of a daughter, wife, and

140 mother, has allowed her constitution to retain its natural strength, and her nerves a healthy tone, is she, I say, to condescend to use art and **feign** a sickly delicacy in order to secure her husband's affection? Weakness may excite tenderness, and gratify the arrogant pride of man; but the lordly caresses of a protector will not

feign (fān) *v.* to make a false show of; pretend

gratify a noble mind that pants for, and deserves to be respected. Fondness is a poor substitute for friendship! . . .

Besides, the woman who strengthens her body and exercises her mind will, by managing her family and practicing various virtues, become the friend, and not the humble dependent of her husband; and if she, by possessing such substantial qualities, merit his regard, she will not find it necessary to conceal her affection,
150 nor to pretend to an unnatural coldness of constitution to excite her husband's passions. . . . **F**

If all the faculties of woman's mind are only to be cultivated as they respect her dependence on man; if, when a husband be obtained, she have arrived at her goal, and meanly proud rests satisfied with such a paltry crown, let her grovel contentedly, scarcely raised by her employments above the animal kingdom; but, if, struggling for the prize of her high calling, she look beyond the present scene, let her cultivate her understanding without stopping to consider what character the husband may have whom she is destined to marry. Let her only determine, without being too anxious about present happiness, to acquire the qualities that
160 ennoble a rational being, and a rough inelegant husband may shock her taste without destroying her peace of mind. She will not model her soul to suit the frailties of her companion, but to bear with them: his character may be a trial, but not an impediment to virtue. . . . **G**

These may be termed Utopian dreams. Thanks to that Being who impressed them on my soul, and gave me sufficient strength of mind to dare to exert my own reason, till, becoming dependent only on him for the support of my virtue, I view, with indignation, the mistaken notions that enslave my sex.

I love man as my fellow; but his scepter, real, or usurped, extends not to me, unless the reason of an individual demands my homage; and even then the
170 submission is to reason, and not to man. In fact, the conduct of an accountable being must be regulated by the operations of its own reason; or on what foundation rests the throne of God?

It appears to me necessary to dwell on these obvious truths, because females have been insulated, as it were; and, while they have been stripped of the virtues that should clothe humanity, they have been decked with artificial graces that enable them to exercise a short-lived tyranny. Love, in their bosoms, taking place of every nobler passion, their sole ambition is to be fair, to raise emotion instead of inspiring respect; and this ignoble desire, like the servility in absolute monarchies, destroys all strength of character. Liberty is the mother of virtue, and
180 if women be, by their very constitution, slaves, and not allowed to breathe the sharp invigorating air of freedom, they must ever languish like exotics,[14] and be reckoned beautiful flaws in nature. ❧

F COUNTERARGUMENTS
Wollstonecraft suggests that a woman's marriage will actually improve if she "strengthens her body and exercises her mind" (line 146) instead of pretending "sickly delicacy" (line 141). According to Wollstonecraft, what kinds of improvements to the marriage will occur?

G HISTORICAL CONTEXT
Reread the information about Wollstonecraft's career on page 718. How might her experiences have influenced the views she expresses in lines 152–163?

---

14. **languish** (lăng'gwĭsh) **like exotics:** wilt like plants grown away from their natural environment.

Comprehension

1. **Recall** In what area does Wollstonecraft concede male superiority?

2. **Clarify** According to Wollstonecraft, why do most women go along with the "false system of education" that fails to develop their reason?

3. **Clarify** Why does she think women need strong minds and bodies?

Text Analysis

4. **Analyze Argument** What **claim,** or position on an issue, does Wollstonecraft make in her essay? Identify three examples of reasons or evidence that she offers to **support** her **claim.**

5. **Understand Historical Context** In the late 18th century, some writers were beginning to question traditional attitudes toward women, but most people would have found it hard to imagine the changes in gender roles that occurred over the next two centuries. Which of Wollstonecraft's statements anticipate modern ideas about women and their place in society? Which statements are more in line with 18th-century views? Cite examples from the text.

6. **Interpret Figurative Language** Wollstonecraft uses figurative language to appeal to her audience and enhance her argument. Explain the figurative language in the following passages:

   - flowers in too rich soil (lines 11–15)
   - tyranny and monarchy (lines 173–179)
   - liberty, virtue, and nature (lines 179–182)

7. **Evaluate Counterarguments** How well does Wollstonecraft use counter-arguments in developing her points? Analyze the following passages to arrive at your conclusion:

   - Rousseau's view on female education (lines 89–117)
   - Dr. Gregory's Legacy to his Daughters (lines 118–145)

Text Criticism

8. **Different Perspectives** What might Wollstonecraft say about the women in popular culture today? Name specific women that she would most likely admire and those she might criticize. Explain the reasons for your choices.

> *What makes* **EQUALITY** *elusive?*
>
> If Mary Wollstonecraft were alive today, what issues about women's lives do you think would concern her most? Why?

COMMON CORE

RI 5 Analyze and evaluate the effectiveness of the structure an author uses in his or her argument. **RI 8** Delineate and evaluate the reasoning in seminal texts. **RI 10** Read and comprehend literary nonfiction.

Vocabulary in Context

▲ VOCABULARY PRACTICE

Indicate which choice best completes each sentence.

WORD LIST
evanescent
feign
inculcate
prerogative
vindication

1. An **evanescent** image (a) vanishes, (b) reappears, (c) lingers.
2. Someone who **feigns** amnesia (a) has completely lost his or her memory,
   (b) has forgotten a few things, (c) is pretending.
3. To **inculcate** an idea, someone might (a) contradict it, (b) ask you to repeat it,
   (c) ask you to ignore it.
4. If someone accused of a crime gets **vindication** in court, he or she will likely
   (a) go to jail, (b) go free, (c) pay a large fine.
5. A **prerogative** is (a) a question to be asked, (b) a problem to be avoided,
   (c) a privilege to be enjoyed.

ACADEMIC VOCABULARY IN SPEAKING

• affect   • challenge   • consent   • final   • respond

What **challenges** do women face today? How might they **respond** to them?
Discuss this in a small group, using at least one additional Academic Vocabulary
word in your discussion.

VOCABULARY STRATEGY: ANALOGIES

An **analogy** compares two items that may have many points of similarity or
may be alike in only one way. Analyzing an analogy can help you clarify an idea.
Wollstonecraft draws an analogy between women's minds and plants grown in
over-fertilized soil in her discussion of women's education (lines 11–15):

*The conduct and manners of women, in fact, evidently prove that their minds
are not in a healthy state; for, like the flowers which are planted in too rich a soil,
strength and usefulness are sacrificed to beauty; and the flaunting leaves, after
having pleased a fastidious eye, fade, disregarded on the stalk, long before the
season when they ought to have arrived at maturity.*

You can use the relationship between words in an analogy to determine their
meanings or connotations. For example, Wollstonecraft believes too much
emphasis is placed on superficial qualities like beauty. Therefore, when she refers
to a plant's *flaunting* leaves, you can guess that *flaunting* is a negative word for
something attractive—that is, "showy or gaudy."

PRACTICE These questions refer to the analogy above. Answer each question.

1. Does a woman's *conduct* refer to her beliefs or her actions?
2. Is someone with a *fastidious* eye picky or penetrating?
3. If you *disregard* something do you pay more attention to it or less?

○ **COMMON CORE**

L 5 Demonstrate understanding
of word relationships. **L 6** Acquire
and use accurately general
academic words.

Interactive Vocabulary   **THINK** central

Go to thinkcentral.com.
KEYWORD: HML12-728

Differing Roles for Women

Literacy rates for both genders were on the rise in 18th-century England, but women were still excluded from universities and discouraged from pursuing careers. Instead, their lives were defined in advance for them: most women were destined solely for domestic roles as wives and mothers. Those who preferred to take a different path risked a serious social and financial backlash. In *A Vindication of the Rights of Woman*, Mary Wollstonecraft likened women's situation in her day to slavery:

> *Liberty is the mother of virtue, and if women be, by their very constitution, slaves, and not allowed to breathe the sharp invigorating air of freedom, they must ever languish like exotics, and be reckoned beautiful flaws in nature.*

The authors in this section write in a variety of genres. Examples in this section include Behn's and Smith's poems, Burney's personal diary, and Wollstonecraft's persuasive essay. Some of these authors write directly about their gender; others do not. What they all share, however, is the choice they made as women to become writers in the face of great cultural resistance.

Writing to Reflect

Choose two of the writers from this section. Why might the subjects they discuss have been controversial for a woman in 18th-century England to write about? What do you think these women may have gained from taking a risk and becoming writers rather than choosing not to do so?

Consider

- the subject each writer discusses
- how each writer portrays this subject
- what it might mean for an 18th-century female writer, rather than a male writer, to express her thoughts about this subject

Extension

SPEAKING & LISTENING

Develop an **oral response** to Mary Wollstonecraft's *A Vindication of the Rights of Woman*. You may wish to deliver a speech or team up with a partner and perform an imagined dialogue between Wollstonecraft and a modern-day reader.

⦂ COMMON CORE

W 2 Write explanatory texts to examine and convey complex ideas, concepts, and information. **SL 1a** Come to discussions prepared. **SL 1c** Challenge ideas and conclusions.

Writing Workshop

ARGUMENT

Persuasive Essay

In this unit, you have seen how writers use skilled arguments and persuasive techniques to change the way others think and feel. In this workshop, you will attempt to influence the attitudes or actions of a specific audience by writing a persuasive essay.

 Complete the workshop activities in your **Reader/Writer Notebook.**

WRITE WITH A PURPOSE

WRITING TASK

Write a **persuasive essay** that asserts a strong claim on an issue that is important to you. Support your claim with reasons and evidence that will convince a particular audience to adopt your position or take a specific action.

Idea Starters

- an important issue in your community, such as homelessness or disaster relief
- a national or international issue, such as pollution
- school policies, such as curriculum changes or the installation of surveillance cameras

THE ESSENTIALS

Here are some common purposes, audiences, and formats for persuasive writing.

PURPOSES	AUDIENCES	FORMATS
• to persuade people to agree with your claim • to motivate others to take a stand or take action	• classmates and teacher • parents • community members • city council members • blog readers	• essay for class • editorial • speech • blog • message board posting • letter to editor

COMMON CORE TRAITS

1. DEVELOPMENT OF IDEAS

- introduces a **precise, knowledgeable claim** and establishes its **significance**
- provides **valid reasons** and **relevant evidence** to support the claim
- acknowledges **opposing claims** and refutes them with **counterclaims**
- offers a **concluding section** that follows from and supports the claim

2. ORGANIZATION OF IDEAS

- **organizes** the claim, counterclaims, reasons, and evidence in a **logical sequence**
- uses **varied transitions** to create cohesion and clarify relationships among ideas

3. LANGUAGE FACILITY AND CONVENTIONS

- maintains a **formal style** and an **objective tone**
- uses **commas** correctly
- employs correct **grammar, mechanics,** and **spelling**

Writing Online

THINK central

Go to **thinkcentral.com**.
KEYWORD: HML12N-730

Planning/Prewriting

COMMON CORE   **W 1a–e** Write arguments to support claims, using valid reasoning and relevant and sufficient evidence. **W 5** Develop and strengthen writing by planning. **W 8** Gather relevant information from multiple sources.

Getting Started

CHOOSE A SUBSTANTIVE ISSUE

In your essay, discuss an issue—a topic about which reasonable people can disagree. Make sure you select a **substantive issue**—one you feel strongly about that is meaningful, not trivial. List several potential issues, and then evaluate each one to see if it is something an audience will feel strongly about as well. Also think about possible sources.

▶ **ASK YOURSELF:**

- Which issues do I care about the most?
- What reasons can I think of to support my viewpoint?
- What are some opinions that other people might have?
- What sources can I consult about this issue?

STATE YOUR CLAIM

Decide what you want to say about the issue you have chosen and adopt a **viewpoint,** or position, about it. This is your **claim.** State it precisely, so it makes a significant impression. Make sure that you can support your claim with valid reasons and evidence.

▶ **WHAT DOES IT LOOK LIKE?**

> _Topic_: drug and alcohol abuse in kids
>
> _Viewpoint_: mentoring can help prevent it
>
> _Claim_: We can combat the problem of addiction by building relationships that teach kids the harmful effects of drugs and alcohol.

THINK ABOUT AUDIENCE AND PURPOSE

As you consider your issue, keep in mind your **purpose**—to convince an audience that your claim has merit. In order to persuade your **audience,** you will need to anticipate what they already know about the issue and how they feel about it, including their concerns, values, and biases.

▶ **ASK YOURSELF:**

- Who is my audience? What do I want to convey to my audience?
- What do my audience members already know about the issue?
- Where do they stand on the issue? How can I change their minds?

SUPPORT YOUR CLAIM

Brainstorm solid **reasons** that explain why your readers should agree with your claim. Rely primarily on **logical appeals** that use facts and statistics to persuade. Logic will be most convincing to your audience. However, consider the sparing use of **emotional appeals,** which tap into readers' feelings, and **ethical appeals,** which focus on readers' sense of right and wrong. Such appeals can enhance an airtight argument and make it resonate with your audience.

▶ **WHAT DOES IT LOOK LIKE?**

> _Logical Appeal_: Addiction affects nine percent of the United States population.
>
> _Emotional Appeal_: Our country's children are suffering from a plague upon our land.
>
> _Ethical Appeal_: This epidemic must be addressed where it begins--with our young people.

Planning/Prewriting *continued*

Getting Started

GATHER SOLID EVIDENCE

You must support your reasons with **relevant evidence** that directly supports your points. Evidence can be:

- **Examples:** specific instances or illustrations of a general idea (**Case studies** are examples from scientific studies.)
- **Expert opinions:** statements made by authorities on the subject
- **Facts:** informational statements that can be proven true (**Statistics** are numerical facts that can be proven true.)

Evidence comes from the **primary and secondary sources** you consult to support your claim. A primary source is material written by someone who was an eyewitness to an event. A secondary source is an account written by someone who was not directly involved in or an eyewitness to an event. Either type of source must be evaluated for its **accuracy** (does it present correct information?) and its **credibility** (is it a trustworthy, authoritative source?).

▶ **WHAT DOES IT LOOK LIKE?**

Example: *The American Academy of Pediatrics states that parents are the most important influence on teens' decisions.*

Expert opinion: *According to Nora D. Volkow, the director of the National Institute on Drug Abuse, . . .*

Statistic: *. . . addiction affects nine percent of the United States population.*

CONSIDER OPPOSING CLAIMS

Readers might raise **opposing claims,** or viewpoints that differ from your own. Address their opposing claims with a **counterclaim**—a statement that describes the limitations of their claim and explains why yours is more valid. This is a good way to strengthen your claim.

▶ **WHAT DOES IT LOOK LIKE?**

Potential opposing claim: *Talking about addiction only encourages kids to try drugs.*

Counterclaim: *Studies show that kids are less likely to become addicted to drugs when adults are open and honest.*

PEER REVIEW Explain to a peer the claim you intend to assert and the evidence you will use as support. Then ask: What other sources could I consult to provide accurate and credible information? What new approach could I take to strengthen my claim?

 YOUR TURN In your *Reader/Writer Notebook,* develop your writing plan and a claim. Then, make lists of your reasons, evidence, and appeals. Consider the following tips as you gather evidence:

- Use reference books and articles as sources for evidence that supports your position.
- Use up-to-date and reliable Web sites to locate information on the issue, such as those ending in *.gov* or *.edu.*

Drafting

COMMON CORE **W 4** Produce clear and coherent writing appropriate to task, purpose, and audience. **L1** Demonstrate command of the conventions of English grammar and usage.

The following chart shows a structure for organizing an effective persuasive essay.

Organizing Your Persuasive Essay

INTRODUCTION
- Grab the audience's attention with an engaging **fact, statistic,** or **anecdote.**
- Identify the issue and state your position in a **precise claim.** Establish the **significance** of the claim—explain why it should matter to your audience.

▼

BODY
- Present your reasons in a **logical sequence,** such as order of importance.
- Support each reason with **relevant** and **sufficient evidence.**
- Fairly address **opposing claims** by acknowledging their strengths and limitations. Provide **well-supported counterclaims** in response.
- Use **transitions,** such as *because, furthermore,* and *consequently,* to create cohesion and link related ideas. **Vary your syntax** by using a mix of short and long, simple and complex sentences.
- Maintain a **formal style** and **objective,** or controlled, **tone.** Avoid language that sounds defensive or overly emotional.

▼

CONCLUDING SECTION
- Restate your **claim** and summarize your reasons and evidence.
- End with a **call to action**—tell readers to do something if they agree with your position.

GRAMMAR IN CONTEXT: CORRELATIVE CONJUNCTIONS

Parallel words or word groups are often joined by **correlative conjunctions** *(both . . . and; either . . . or; neither . . . nor; not only . . . but also; whether . . . or).* Correlative conjunctions help writers show relationships between ideas. When using them, make sure the verb agrees in number with the subject.

Correlative Conjunctions	Examples
neither . . . nor	▶ *Neither peer pressure **nor** popular culture has the good influence on kids that a positive adult role model has.*
both . . . and	▶ *Both parents **and** teachers are able to engage young adults on the issue of addiction.*
not only . . . but also	▶ *Young people look to adults **not only** for guidance **but also** for example.*

YOUR TURN Develop a first draft of your persuasive essay, following the structure outlined in the chart above. Be sure to include at least one claim, opposing claim, and counterclaim and one set of correlative conjunctions.

Revising

As you revise, evaluate the content, development, and style of your essay. Your goal is to determine if you have achieved your purpose and effectively communicated your ideas to your intended audience. The questions, tips, and strategies in the following chart will help you revise or rewrite where necessary.

PERSUASIVE ESSAY

Ask Yourself	Tips	Revision Strategies
1. Do I capture the audience's attention in my opening lines and introduce a precise claim?	**Bracket** interesting statements or thought-provoking questions. **Underline** the claim.	**Add** an attention-getting statement or quotation. **Add** your claim, or **rework** the claim to make it stronger.
2. Are there at least two valid reasons that support my claim? Is there evidence to support each reason?	**Highlight** the reasons that support the claim. **Draw** an arrow from the evidence to the reason.	**Add** valid reasons to support the claim. **Add** examples, facts, or quotations to bolster unsupported reasons.
3. Do I acknowledge opposing claims and present counterclaims?	**Draw a wavy line** under the opposing claims and your responses to them.	**Add** counterclaims stating the merits of your opinion and the limitations of opposing claims.
4. Are the counterclaims, reasons, and evidence in a logical sequence?	**Number** your reasons to reflect your ranking of their strength (1 = strongest, etc.).	If your strongest reason isn't last or first, **reorder** your reasons and evidence for emphasis.
5. Do transitions clarify relationships among my claim, counterclaim, reasons, and evidence?	**Draw a star** next to each transitional word or phrase.	**Add** a variety of appropriate transitions to link related ideas.
6. Does the concluding section restate my claim and give the reader something important to think about?	**Put a check mark** next to the restatement. **Underline** the sentence with an important insight or observation.	**Add** a restatement of the claim if it is missing. **Add** a thought-provoking question or statement about the issue.

YOUR TURN

PEER REVIEW Exchange your essay with a classmate. As you read and comment on your classmate's essay, make sure that you focus on its logic and organization. Discuss whether your classmate has convinced you of his or her position. Use the revision strategies in the chart to suggest improvements or a new approach.

 COMMON CORE

W 5 Develop and strengthen writing as needed by revising, editing, rewriting, or trying a new approach, focusing on how well purpose and audience have been addressed.

ANALYZE A STUDENT DRAFT

Read this student draft, and notice the comments on its strengths as well as the suggestions for improvement.

The Plague Upon the Land
by Stephen Laine, McCallum High School

❶   According to Nora D. Volkow, the director of the National Institute on Drug Abuse, addiction affects nine percent of the United States population. This epidemic must be addressed where it begins—with our young people. The effects are too widespread and too many people are susceptible to the black hole of drug and alcohol addiction for us to ignore the problem. We can combat America's addiction problem by building relationships that teach kids the harmful effects of drugs and alcohol.

❷   One way to create and nurture these relationships is through a mentoring program. Children who lack relationships with positive adult role models are more at risk to become drug and alcohol users. When kids connect with a responsible and caring mentor who engages them in productive and fun activities, they experience an alternative to drug use. A mentor can warn them about the power of peer pressure. Many kids who have avoided drinking and drugs will eventually try them. "It's just one sip; it can't hurt." Whether they know it or not that one sip can lead to one more, and then one more. A mentor can steer kids away from drugs, alcohol, and peer pressure.

> Stephen introduces his essay with a **statistic**, but a more relevant statistic would improve his logical appeal. Stephen states his **claim** at the end of the first paragraph.

> Stephen offers one **reason** that supports his opinion.

LEARN HOW   **Add Statistics**   You won't interest an audience in your issue if your introduction lacks appeal. To grab your readers' attention, add a relevant fact, statistic, quotation, or anecdote, or ask a rhetorical question. Stephen found additional statistics that emphasize the problem and draw readers into his essay.

STEPHEN'S REVISION TO PARAGRAPH ❶

In addition, the national PTA claims that every day about 4,700 American youth under the age of eighteen try marijuana for the first time. This equals the enrollment in six average-sized high schools.

This epidemic must be addressed where it begins—with our young people. The effects are too widespread and too many people are susceptible . . .

❸   Another way to combat drug use is to make a concerted effort in each household to teach kids that drugs and alcohol can ruin your life. The American Academy of Pediatrics states that parents or guardians are the most important influence in a teen's decisions about drug use. Children can be taught at an early age that drug use will lead to a life of destruction. Caring adults can teach children the facts: alcohol abuse will lead to liver failure and ultimately death, and drugs can decimate your body and mind. The government can create standardized teaching tools to address the dangers of addiction, but the most important tool is the parents' or guardians' interest, communication, and role as a model for their children. Communication in homes may be the best weapon we have to fight drug abuse in kids.

> Stephen cites an **example** to support the idea that mentoring works.

❹   We can take action against this epidemic of drug abuse and addiction. We can urge the community to teach schools, churches, clubs, and families how to approach the subject of drug and alcohol abuse. We can create meaningful relationships with children through effective mentoring programs.

> Stephen restates his **claim** in his concluding section, but he needs to give the reader something to think about in his **call to action**.

LEARN HOW **Create a Thought-Provoking Call to Action**   A good concluding section to a persuasive essay should restate the claim and provide a thought-provoking statement or question for the readers in the call to action. Stephen could rewrite his call to action to give his readers something that they should consider doing in support of his claim.

STEPHEN'S REVISION TO PARAGRAPH ❹

We can take action against this epidemic of drug abuse and addiction. We can urge the community to teach schools, churches, clubs, and families how to approach the subject of drug and alcohol abuse. We can create meaningful relationships with children through effective mentoring programs. *Our country's children are suffering from this plague upon our land. Our children are the future of our country. What are you willing to do to help educate them and protect their future—and ours?*

YOUR TURN   Use the feedback from your peers and teacher as well as the two "Learn How" lessons to revise your essay. Evaluate how thoroughly you have presented and supported your claim.

Editing and Publishing

COMMON CORE **W 5** Strengthen writing by revising, editing, rewriting, or trying a new approach. **L 2** Demonstrate command of the conventions of standard punctuation. **L 2b** Spell correctly.

In the editing stage, you review your essay to make sure it is free of grammar, spelling, and punctuation errors. Careless spelling mistakes make you sound less authoritative and can affect the credibilty of your argument. Read your essay carefully to correct any lingering misspelled words.

GRAMMAR IN CONTEXT: COMMAS AFTER INTRODUCTORY ELEMENTS

Writers use introductory phrases and clauses to help readers follow and understand their arguments. Such phrases and clauses also enliven writing by adding variety to sentence structures. When you use introductory phrases and clauses, be sure to separate them from the main clause of the sentence with a comma.

> *When kids connect with a responsible and caring mentor who engages them in productive and fun activities, they experience an alternative to drug use.*
>
> [A comma follows the **introductory clause.**]

As Stephen edited his essay, he noticed an incorrectly punctuated introductory phrase. A comma is necessary to set off the introductory phrase from the main clause.

> *Whether they know it or not, that one sip can lead to one more, and then one more.*

PUBLISH YOUR WRITING

To persuade people, first you have to reach them. Here are some ways you can share your essay with an audience.

- Submit your essay to the school or local newspaper.
- Present your essay as a speech during a meeting of your school's student council, your school district's board of education, or your local city council.
- Post your essay on a Web site that focuses on your issue.

YOUR TURN Correct any errors in your persuasive essay. Add a clear call to action to your concluding section. Edit carefully and check that you have placed commas after any introductory clauses or phrases. Then, publish your final essay where your audience is likely to see it.

Scoring Rubric

Use the rubric below to evaluate your persuasive essay from the Writing
Workshop or your response to the on-demand task on the next page.

PERSUASIVE ESSAY

SCORE	COMMON CORE TRAITS
6	• **Development** Asserts a precise, knowledgeable claim; supports the claim with valid reasons and relevant, sufficient evidence; fairly and thoroughly counters opposing claims with counterclaims; ends powerfully • **Organization** Has a logical, persuasive sequence; uses transitions to create cohesion and show the relationships among the claim, reasons, and evidence • **Language** Consistently maintains a formal style and objective tone; shows a strong command of conventions
5	• **Development** States a precise, knowledgeable claim; offers valid reasons and relevant evidence; fairly counters opposing claims with counterclaims; ends with a strong concluding section • **Organization** Is logically sequenced; uses transitions to show the relationships among the claim, reasons, and evidence • **Language** Uses a formal style and objective tone; has a few errors in conventions
4	• **Development** States a precise claim; offers mostly valid support; needs to more fairly address opposing claims; has an adequate concluding section • **Organization** Reflects a logical sequence, with one or two exceptions; could use a few more transitions • **Language** Mostly uses a formal style; sounds defensive or dismissive at times; includes a few distracting errors in conventions
3	• **Development** States a claim that could be more precise; provides little relevant support; unfairly dismisses other viewpoints; has a weak concluding section • **Organization** Has some flaws in organization; needs more transitions • **Language** Lapses into an informal style or indecisive tone; has errors in conventions
2	• **Development** Has an uninformed claim; offers irrelevant reasons and insufficient evidence; fails to acknowledge other viewpoints; has a weak concluding section • **Organization** Has major organizational flaws; lacks transitions throughout • **Language** Uses an informal style and indecisive tone; has many errors in conventions
1	• **Development** Lacks a claim; ignores opposing claims; ends abruptly • **Organization** Has no organization and no transitions • **Language** Uses an inappropriate style and tone; has major problems with grammar, mechanics, and spelling

Preparing for Timed Writing

COMMON CORE

W 10 Write routinely over shorter time frames for a range of tasks, purposes, and audiences.

1. ANALYZE THE TASK   5 MIN

Read the task carefully. Then, read it again, underlining the words that tell the audience, the topic, and the purpose.

> **WRITING TASK**
>
> *Topic* ↘
>
> Imagine that your school board is thinking of implementing <u>a graduation requirement mandating that students do part-time volunteer work.</u> Write a persuasive essay convincing (students) to support or oppose the requirement.
>
> *Purpose* ↗   ↖ *Audience*

2. PLAN YOUR RESPONSE   10 MIN

Think about the **reasons** for each side of the argument. Make a list of pros and cons for the volunteering requirement. Which side of the argument do you support? Which side can you defend with **reasons?** List at least two pieces of **evidence** (facts, statistics, anecdotes, examples) for each reason. Then decide on the position you will argue.

Reasons	Evidence

3. RESPOND TO THE TASK   20 MIN

Begin drafting your essay. You may want to start by simply stating your claim. As you write, keep the following points in mind:

- In the introduction, grab your readers' attention and state your claim.
- In each paragraph, provide a valid reason and relevant evidence that supports it.
- Acknowledge and counter opposing claims.
- Conclude by restating your claim and proposing some action that your audience should take.

4. IMPROVE YOUR RESPONSE   5–10 MIN

Revising Compare your draft with the task. Does your draft clearly state a claim? Does it provide relevant, sufficient evidence? Does it end with a persuasive concluding section and call to action?

Proofreading Find and correct any errors in grammar, usage, or mechanics. Make sure that your paper and any edits are neatly written and legible.

Checking Your Final Copy Before you submit your paper, examine it once more to catch any lingering errors and to make sure that you are presenting your best work.

Speaking & Listening Workshop

Giving a Persuasive Speech

Reach your audience in a new and effective way by presenting your persuasive essay as a speech. In presenting your ideas to listeners rather than readers, you can use your voice as well as your body language to make your point.

 Complete the workshop activities in your **Reader/Writer Notebook**.

SPEAK WITH A PURPOSE	COMMON CORE TRAITS
TASK Adapt your persuasive essay into a **formal persuasive speech.** Practice your speech, and then present it to your class.	**A STRONG PERSUASIVE SPEECH . . .** • asserts a distinct, precise claim • organizes reasons and supporting evidence in a logical order • addresses alternative or opposing claims and viewpoints

COMMON CORE

SL 3 Evaluate a speaker's point of view, reasoning, and use of evidence and rhetoric, assessing the premises and tone used.
SL 4 Present information, conveying a clear and distinct perspective, such that listeners can follow the line of reasoning.
L 3 Apply knowledge of language to understand how language functions in different contexts and to make effective choices for meaning or style.

Adapt Your Essay

Use these considerations to help you adapt your written essay into a powerful persuasive speech.

• **Type of Speech** Decide which type of persuasive speech you want to give.

Proposition of Fact	A speech that argues a claim as fact
Proposition of Policy	A speech that attempts to get an audience to support a particular plan of action by offering steps to follow
Proposition of Problem	A speech that tries to persuade an audience that a specific problem exists and requires solving
Proposition of Value	A speech that argues the relative merit of something

• **Audience** Know your audience members and use the appeal that suits them best.

• **Introduction** Grab listeners' attention by opening with a thought-provoking quotation, rhetorical question, or anecdote. Then state your claim clearly.

• **Reasons and Evidence** Evaluate your written essay for the strongest reasons and evidence. Present only reasons and evidence that will be most compelling.

• **Counterclaims** Acknowledge and counter opposing claims with strong evidence.

• **Language** Choose words carefully to make your meaning clear and to establish a style that is appropriate to your audience.

• **Concluding Section** Briefly summarize your claim and evidence. Include a statement that gives your audience something to consider.

Speaking & Listening Online

THINK central

Go to **thinkcentral.com**.
KEYWORD: HML12-740

Deliver Your Speech

USE VERBAL TECHNIQUES

How you use your voice is as important as what you say. Before you deliver your persuasive speech, practice your delivery techniques. Look at the list below for tips.

- **Volume** Speak forcefully but not too loudly—you don't want listeners to think that you are yelling at them.
- **Enunciation** Pronounce words, especially unfamiliar terms, clearly and precisely.
- **Pace** Speak at a reasonable rate and use a natural rhythm.
- **Tone** Use the same inflections and gestures you use when you share your opinion respectfully with adults, teachers, and other students. Maintain a formal style and an objective tone.

USE NONVERBAL TECHNIQUES

Facial expressions and gestures add meaning to your persuasive speech.

- Use gestures or body language to emphasize points in your argument and to underscore a particular rhythm or feeling.
- Make frequent eye contact with your audience.
- Employ facial expressions, such as smiling, frowning, or raising an eyebrow to add emphasis to your points. A frown, for example, conveys disapproval.

As a Speaker Before you present, create note cards that contain short words or phrases that remind you of important facts, statistics, quotations, or anecdotes that you want to include. By jotting down words and phrases, you will avoid sounding as if you are reading rather than speaking. Arrange the cards in the order in which you will present your ideas. As you give your presentation, use your notes to stay on track.

As a Listener Evaluate a classmate's delivery of his or her persuasive speech. Ask yourself the following questions to focus your evaluation:

- What claim does he or she assert? Do I agree with the claim? Why or why not?
- What, if any, flawed reasons or exaggerations do I detect?
- Is the evidence reliable? Does it support the speaker's claim?
- Does the speaker maintain a controlled tone through the speech, or does he or she sound defensive at times?

Assessment Practice

DIRECTIONS Read the following selection and then answer the questions.

from The Poor and Their Betters
by Henry Fielding

1   Of all the oppressions which the rich are guilty of, there seems to be none more impudent[1] and unjust than their endeavor to rob the poor of a title which is most clearly the property of the latter. Not contented with all the honorables, worshipfuls, reverends, and a thousand other proud epithets which they exact of the poor, and for which they give in return nothing but dirt, scrub, mob, and such like, they have laid violent hands on a word to which they have not the least pretense or shadow of any title.

2   The word I mean is the comparative of the adjective good, namely better, or as it is usually expressed in the plural number betters. An appellation which all the rich usurp[2] to themselves, and most shamefully use when they speak of, or to the poor: for do we not every day hear such phrases as these: Do not be saucy to your betters. Learn to behave yourself before your betters. Pray know your betters, etc.

3   It is possible that the rich have been so long in possession of this, that they now lay a kind of prescriptive claim to the property; but however that be, I doubt not but to make it appear, that if the word better is to be understood as the comparative of good, and is meant to convey an idea of superior goodness, it is with the highest impropriety applied to the rich, in comparison with the poor.

4   And this I the rather undertake, as the usurpation which I would obviate,[3] hath produced a very great mischief in society; for the poor having been deceived into an opinion (for monstrous as it is, such an opinion hath prevailed) that the rich are their betters, have been taught to honor, and of consequence to imitate the examples of those whom they ought to have despised; while the rich on the contrary are misled into a false contempt of what they ought to respect, and by this means lose all the advantage which they might draw from contemplating the exemplary lives of these their real betters.

5   First then let us imagine to ourselves, a person wallowing in wealth, and lolling in his chariot, his mind torn with ambition, avarice, envy, and every other bad passion, and his brain distracted with schemes to deceive and supplant some other man, to cheat his neighbor or perhaps the public, what a glorious use might

---

1. **impudent:** (ĭm′pyə-dənt) *adj.:* characterized by offensive boldness.
2. **usurp:** (yōō-sûrp′) *v.:* to seize by force.
3. **obviate:** (ŏb′vē-āt′) *v.:* to anticipate and prevent.

such a person derive to himself, as he is rolled through the outskirts of the town, by due meditations, on the lives of those who dwell in stalls and cellars! What a noble lesson of true Christian patience and contentment may such a person learn from his betters, who enjoy the highest cheerfulness in their poor condition; their minds being disturbed by no unruly passion, nor their heads by any racking cares!

6   Where again shall we look for an example of temperance? In the stinking kitchens of the rich, or under the humble roofs of the poor? Where for prudence but among those who have the fewest desires? Where for fortitude, but among those who have every natural evil to struggle with?

7   In modesty, I think, there will be little difficulty in knowing where we are to find our betters: for to this virtue there can be nothing more diametrically opposite than pride. Whenever therefore we observe persons stretching up their heads, and looking with an air of contempt on all around them, we may be well assured there is no modesty there. Indeed I never yet heard it enumerated among all the bad qualities of an oyster-woman or a cider-wench, that she had a great deal of pride, and consequently there is at least a possibility that such may have a great deal of modesty, whereas it is absolutely impossible that those to whom much pride belongs, should have any tincture[4] of its opposite virtue.

8   Nor are the pretensions of these same betters less strongly supported in that most exalted virtue of justice, witness the daily examples which they give of it in their own persons. When a man was punished for his crimes the Greeks said that he gave justice. Now this is a gift almost totally confined to the poor, and it is a gift which they very seldom fail of making as often as there is any very pressing occasion. Who can remember to have seen a rich man whipt at the cart's tail! And how seldom (I am sorry to say it) are such exalted to the pillory, or sentenced to transportation! And as for the most reputable, namely the capital punishments, how rarely do we see them executed on the rich! . . .

9   I do not pretend to say, that the mob have no faults; perhaps they have many. I assert no more than this, that they are in all laudable qualities very greatly superior to those who have hitherto, with much injustice, pretended to look down upon them.

10   In this attempt, I may perhaps have given offense to some of the inferior sort, but I am contented with the assurance of having espoused the cause of truth; and in so doing, I am well convinced I shall please all who are really my betters.

---

4. **tincture:** (tĭngk'chər) *n.*: slight trace, hint, or tint.

GO ON ➡️

Reading Comprehension

Use "The Poor and Their Betters" (pp. 742–743) to answer questions 1–17.

1. Fielding's main purpose in this essay is to —
   A. express his opinions about social class
   B. persuade lawmakers to implement reforms
   C. warn people of the danger of class warfare
   D. motivate readers to help poor people

2. Fielding achieves his purpose and reinforces his views by using —
   A. a satiric tone
   B. a humorous subject
   C. dramatic dialogue
   D. simple language

3. In his essay, Fielding identifies the problem of —
   A. the deterioration of the English language
   B. a lack of respect for poor people
   C. the government's indifference to people
   D. a breakdown of the accepted social order

4. What can you conclude about Fielding's attitude toward the poor?
   A. He hopes that poor people can learn to coexist with the rich.
   B. He wants the poor to be rewarded for their suffering.
   C. He predicts that one day the poor will rise up against the rich.
   D. He thinks that poor people are more virtuous than the rich.

5. Fielding probably titled his essay "The Poor and Their Betters" in order to —
   A. make poor people angry
   B. present an opinion he will refute
   C. justify economic and social inequality
   D. emphasize the problems of poverty

6. In paragraph 1, Fielding uses the phrase "dirt, scrub, mob, and such like" to support his claim that —
   A. although poor people can be rude and unruly, they deserve respect
   B. some people respond better to praise than to criticism
   C. rich people use many unflattering words to describe the poor
   D. name-calling is not a good way to solve social problems

7. Which statement summarizes the opposing viewpoint presented in paragraph 3?
   A. The wealth and privilege of the rich entitle them to a superior status.
   B. Only the rich understand the true meaning of the term *betters*.
   C. In calling themselves betters, the rich are upholding a long-standing custom.
   D. Poor people don't want to be placed above the rich.

8. Fielding counters the viewpoint expressed in paragraph 3 by arguing that —
   A. the poor have been tricked into thinking that they are not as good as the rich
   B. it is not fair to compare the rich and the poor because their lives and circumstances are different
   C. because *better* means "higher in quality," the term should not be used to compare the rich to the poor
   D. there is no evidence to prove that one social class is better or worse than another

9. You can conclude from the image in paragraph 5 that Fielding views wealthy people as —

A. hardworking **C.** intelligent

B. immoral **D.** passionate

10. To support his claim that poor people have great patience, Fielding notes in paragraph 5 that they —

A. are eager to learn from others

B. choose to live in harsh conditions

C. refuse to worry about anything important

D. accept their poverty with good spirits

11. In paragraph 6, Fielding contrasts "the stinking kitchens of the rich" with "the humble roofs of the poor" to support his claim that —

A. the rich live extravagantly, while the poor live simply

B. the rich are not good cooks, and the poor are not good builders

C. rich people and poor people both have problems

D. poor people are happier in life than rich people

12. When Fielding notes in paragraph 7 that the rich look on those around them "with an air of contempt," he is supporting the claim that —

A. poor people don't have pride

B. wealth is a sign of superiority

C. wealthy people are not modest

D. everyone deserves to live with dignity

13. What might you conclude about justice in 18th-century England from Fielding's discussion in paragraph 8?

A. The judicial system favored the rich.

B. Justice was valued more than other virtues.

C. Even minor crimes were punished harshly.

D. Laws were passed to protect the poor.

14. In paragraph 9, Fielding counters the view that poor people have flaws by arguing that —

A. society must learn to overlook the shortcomings of poor people

B. despite their flaws, the poor are more virtuous than the rich

C. if rich people were truly virtuous, they would treat poor people with respect

D. rich people should be punished severely for their crimes

15. In paragraph 10, Fielding thinks his essay will please —

A. inferior people

B. poor people

C. proud people

D. rich people

SHORT CONSTRUCTED RESPONSE
Write three or four sentences to answer this question.

16. List three moral failings that Fielding assigns to the wealthy class. Give one example of support that he offers to back up each claim.

Write two to three paragraphs to answer this question.

17. Discuss Fielding's claim in paragraph 3 that by using the term *betters* to describe themselves, rich people have produced "a very great mischief in society." Give examples of the support he offers for this claim.

GO ON ➡

745

Vocabulary

Use context clues and your knowledge of suffixes to answer the following questions.

1. The word *monster* means "a creature having a strange or hideous appearance." What is the most likely meaning of the word *monstrous* as it is used in paragraph 4?

A. Frightful

B. Lacking in variety

C. Massive in size

D. Unadorned

2. The word *exemplar* means "one that is a model; ideal." What is the most likely meaning of the word *exemplary* as it is used in paragraph 4?

A. Evenly balanced

B. Full of excitement

C. Meaningless

D. Worthy of imitation

3. The word *prudent* means "wise in handling practical matters." What is the most likely meaning of the word *prudence* as it is used in paragraph 6?

A. Conformity

B. Good judgment

C. Kindness

D. Laziness

4. The word *repute* means "the general estimation in which a person or thing is held by the public." What is the most likely meaning of the word *reputable* as it is used in paragraph 8?

A. Commonly used

B. Highly regarded

C. Physically brutal

D. Resistant to change

Use the dictionary entry to answer the following questions.

ex•act (ĭg-zăkt′) *adj.* **1.** Not having any mistakes. **2.** Characterized by precise measurements. **3.** Very strict. *tr. verb* **1.** To demand and obtain by force or authority. [Latin *exactus*, past participle of *exigere*, to weigh out, demand.] **Synonyms:** *verb*: claim, require, demand —**exactness** *n.*

5. Where would you hyphenate *exact* if you had to type it on two lines?

A. e-xact   C. exa-ct

B. ex-act   D. exac-t

6. Which meaning of the word *exact* is used in paragraph 1 of "The Poor and Their Betters"?

A. Adjective definition 1

B. Adjective definition 2

C. Adjective definition 3

D. Verb definition 1

7. The suffix *-ness* means "a condition or quality." The related word *exactness* in the dictionary entry means a quality of —

A. accuracy   C. measurement

B. forcefulness   D. authority

8. *Exact* comes from a Latin word that means to —

A. adhere   C. force

B. claim   D. weigh out

9. Which meaning of *exact* is used in the following sentence?

I didn't know the exact number of pages, so I gave an estimate.

A. Adjective definition 1

B. Adjective definition 2

C. Adjective definition 3

D. Verb definition 1

Revising and Editing

DIRECTIONS Read this passage and answer the questions that follow.

(1) Bartering the exchange of goods or services, predated the use of conventional money. (2) Around 9000 B.C., people began trading cattle and plant products with each other. (3) Several thousand years later, the Chinese started to use cowrie shells as currency. (4) These shells are still used in some areas. (5) Conventional money in China was not developed until about 1000 B.C. (6) The coins were made out of bronze or copper, and resembled cowrie shells. (7) The Chinese eventually changed the coins' shapes to resemble tools. (8) Turkey, Greece, Persia, and Rome eventually began to use coins, too.

1. What change, if any, should be made in sentence 1?
   A. Delete comma after *services*
   B. Change *Bartering* to **Barterring**
   C. Insert comma after *Bartering*
   D. Make no change

2. What is the most effective way to combine sentences 3 and 4?
   A. Several thousand years later, the Chinese started to use cowrie shells, which are still used in some areas, as currency.
   B. Several thousand years later, the Chinese started to use cowrie shells although they are still used in some areas.
   C. Several thousand years later, the Chinese started to use cowrie shells; therefore, these shells are still used in some areas.
   D. Several thousand years later, the Chinese started to use cowrie shells as a form of currency, which is still common in parts of China today.

3. What change, if any, should be made in sentence 6?
   A. Delete comma
   B. Insert a comma after *bronze*
   C. Change *resembled* to **resembling**
   D. Make no change

4. What is the most effective way to revise sentence 7 using a subordinate clause?
   A. The Chinese eventually changed the coins' shapes to resemble tools, such as knives and spades.
   B. The Chinese, who developed these coins, eventually changed the coins' shapes to resemble tools.
   C. The Chinese eventually changed the coins' shapes to resemble tools; they had at one time used tools as a form of money.
   D. The Chinese eventually changed the coins' shapes to resemble sharp, pointed tools.

5. What change, if any, should be made in sentence 8?
   A. Delete comma after *coins*
   B. Change *eventually* to **eventualy**
   C. Change *began* to **begins**
   D. Make no change

STOP

747

Ideas for Independent Reading

Continue exploring the Questions of the Times on pages 560–561 with these additional works.

What can fix society's PROBLEMS?

Gulliver's Travels
by Jonathan Swift

Gulliver's Travels is not only a comedy about an ordinary man's adventures in some extraordinary places but also a satire of English society in Swift's day and of humankind in general. A criticism of British colonialism, the work also satirizes political corruption, religious conflict, and the failings of human nature.

Selected Poetry
by Alexander Pope

This volume collects Pope's finest work, including his brilliant satirical poem *The Rape of the Lock*. Pope's insight into human nature, his powers of social observation, and his talent for satire have ensured his place as the most important poet of the early 18th century.

The History of Rasselas, Prince of Abissinia
by Samuel Johnson

Using a comic travelogue to analyze the world's persistent problems, *Rasselas* expresses Johnson's characteristic balance of optimism and stoicism. In the work, Prince Rasselas and his friends grow weary with happiness, and they forge out into the great world, finding much to discuss as they view scenes of misery, confusion, and random kindness.

Can SCIENCE tell us how to live?

Isaac Newton and the Scientific Revolution
by Gale E. Christianson

This compelling biography describes the genius of Isaac Newton and the central role he played in the history of science. It traces his development from a young, reclusive academic to a living legend—a quarrelsome and quirky man not unafraid to use his position to further his career. Yet the account never downplays Newton's legacy.

The Age of Reason Begins
by Will and Ariel Durant

This history of the Enlightenment begins with Queen Elizabeth I's ascension in 1558 and ends with the death of philosopher René Descartes in 1650. Along the way, it explores the politics, philosophy, literature, art, and science of the day, revealing the emergence of modern thinking.

Two Treatises of Government
by John Locke

More than three centuries after their writing, John Locke's political theories remain relevant today. In *Two Treatises,* Locke describes the natural laws and rights fundamental to all people, laws that can be used to distinguish legitimate governments from illegitimate ones. Locke's ideas scandalized traditionalists of his day, yet when Thomas Jefferson and other American patriots sought to justify their revolution, the ideas they seized upon were those of John Locke.

What topics are NEWSWORTHY?

The Great Fire of London
by Neil Hanson

This true story of the Great Fire of London makes for gripping reading. Over the course of four days in 1666, more than 13,000 homes, 80 churches, and most of London's government buildings were destroyed. As with all tragedies, the fire brought out the best and the worst in people. Yet in all, this account is a testament to the resiliency of a noble city and its people.

The Commerce of Everyday Life: Selections from *The Tatler* and *The Spectator*
edited by Erin Mackie

This volume gathers essays from *The Tatler* and *The Spectator* with excerpts from other 18th-century periodicals such as *The Guardian, The London Spy*, and *The Female Tatler*. Happily for today's readers, journalists in the days of Addison and Steele did more than just report on current events. They also gossiped and preached, giving their opinions on everything from marriage and manners to international relations.

The Great Plague
by A. Lloyd Moote and Dorothy C. Moote

In 1665, nearly 100,000 people died when the plague swept through London. This account of that terrible year describes the devastating effect the plague had on the city, using the words of real people who lived through the year, including the diarist Samuel Pepys, to bring immediacy and poignancy to the tale.

What is a woman's ROLE *in public life?*

Evelina
by Frances Burney

In *Evelina*, Fanny Burney's first and most popular novel, an innocent young woman plunges into the snobbish and sometimes cruel world of the fashionable set, where she learns to see through false values to find love and happiness. While shedding light on women's position in society in Burney's day, *Evelina* is at heart a love story.

Embassy to Constantinople: The Travels of Lady Mary Wortley Montagu
by Mary Wortley Montagu

Lady Mary Wortley Montagu traveled extensively and wrote extensively, publishing nearly 900 letters later in life. Some of the most celebrated of these were written from Constantinople, where she stayed with her husband, the ambassador to the sultan's court. An adventurous soul and a true traveler, Montagu's vivid and lively letters are eye opening.

Vindication: A Life of Mary Wollstonecraft
By Lyndall Gordon

Although a number of 18th-century writers discussed the role of women in society, none became as celebrated for their feminist views as Mary Wollstonecraft. This fascinating biography sheds light on the many influences that made Wollstonecraft the trailblazer she was. Her adventurous life is as interesting as her adventurous philosophies.

COMMON CORE

Preview Unit Goals

TEXT ANALYSIS	• Identify and analyze characteristics of romanticism • Understand the relationship between form and meaning in poetry • Determine the meaning of words and phrases as they are used in poetry, including figurative meanings • Identify and analyze rhythmic patterns and stanza structure in poetry • Identify and analyze sound devices in poetry • Identify and interpret imagery • Analyze literary criticism, including an author's position and support • Understand historical context
READING	• Visualize imagery in poetry • Paraphrase complex structures to enhance comprehension • Compare and contrast texts
WRITING AND LANGUAGE	• Write an online feature article • Observe hyphenation conventions • Use the Internet to produce, publish, and update writing products
VOCABULARY	• Understand the historical development of the English language
MEDIA AND VIEWING	• Analyze illustrations of poems, evaluating how they interpret the source texts • Analyze different techniques used in visual media

Find It Online!

Go to <u>thinkcentral.com</u> for the interactive version of this unit.

The Flowering of Romanticism

1798–1832

John Keats

EMOTION AND EXPERIMENTATION

- Revolt Against Neoclassicism
- The Lake Poets
- The Late Romantics

Media Smart DVD-ROM

The Art of William Blake

Examine art elements and techniques that have fueled the visions of artists for generations.
Page 778

Questions of the Times

DISCUSS In small groups or as a class, discuss the following questions. Then read on to learn how British writers grappled with these issues during the romantic period.

What can people learn from NATURE?

Romantic writers idealized nature and promoted the idea that human beings could learn a great deal from nature's simple truths. What do you think people can learn from interacting with the natural world? Can nature be a source of comfort? of inspiration? What might people learn from the harsher aspects of nature?

Is EMOTION *stronger than reason?*

In contrast to the writers of the Age of Reason, romantic writers saw emotions as the core of human experience and viewed literature as a means of expressing those emotions. Do you think that emotions trump reason when it comes to behavior? Do you think the best writing focuses on personal feelings, or do you prefer writing that examines less personal concerns?

COMMON CORE

RL 9 Demonstrate knowledge of foundational works of literature, including how two or more texts from the same period treat similar themes or topics. **RI 9** Analyze documents of historical and literary significance for their themes, purposes, and rhetorical features.

When is the ORDINARY *extraordinary?*

In their work, romantic writers celebrated the charm of everyday objects and experiences and the glory of commonplace people. They felt that even the most unnoticed of persons was deserving of respect and that ordinary interactions with nature were subjects worthy of poetry. What can you find that is special in the everyday?

How does **WAR** *change our values?*

Romantic writers lived in a time when Britain was growing more conservative because of the threat from revolutionary France and Napoleon. Most British romantics supported social reform, but reform faced an uphill battle in an era of government restrictions. Do freedom and social justice always suffer in a time of war? What is the proper balance between liberty and security?

753

The Flowering of Romanticism
1798–1832

Emotion and Experimentation

During this period, the noble promise of Enlightenment ideals gave way to grim reality—in France, a blood-soaked revolution; at home, industry's "dark Satanic mills." In turn, romantic writers searched for truth in its purest state: in nature, wild and majestic, and in their own passionate, untamed hearts.

Romanticism: Historical Context

The literary movement known as romanticism developed as
a reaction to many social influences: the unrest of the French
Revolution, the excesses of the Industrial Revolution, and the
widespread poverty and oppression of workers.

A Time of Revolution

"Liberty, equality, brotherhood"—the ideals that spurred the **French
Revolution** found an answering echo in the hearts of many of England's
finest romantic poets and novelists. In the heady early years of France's
revolution, writers such as **William Wordsworth, Samuel Taylor
Coleridge,** and **William Blake** saw it as a turning point in the history
of humankind, a move toward a more ideal and civilized society. William
Blake summed up his hopes for those struggling under oppression in
these lines from his poem "The French Revolution":

> Then the valleys of France shall cry to the soldier,
>   'Throw down thy sword and musket,
> And run and embrace the meek peasant.'
>   Her Nobles shall hear and shall weep, and put off
> The red robe of terror, the crown of oppression,
>   the shoes of contempt, and unbuckle
> The girdle of war from the desolate earth.

ENGLAND'S TIES TO REVOLUTION George III, later called by the poet
Percy Bysshe Shelley "an old, mad, blind, despised, and dying king," ruled
England during the years of the American and French revolutions. Many
blamed the loss of the American colonies chiefly on George's inflexible and
unsympathetic attitude toward the colonists.

George III was not a particularly capable king, and he was bewildered by
the unprecedented political events taking place in America and France. In
1788, the year before the French Revolution began, he suffered a major attack
of mental illnesss, and in 1811 he was declared permanently insane. His
son George ruled as prince regent until the king's death in 1820.

Initially, many English citizens felt sympathy for the French Revolution.
William Wordsworth, who had traveled to revolutionary France as a
young man, recalled those exciting times: "Bliss was it in that dawn to be
alive, / But to be young was very heaven!" However, when the moderate
revolutionary party lost power to a radical and violent faction, English
sympathy began to dissipate, and romantic writers turned elsewhere for
inspiration. During the **Reign of Terror,** radicals massacred and persecuted
thousands of French aristocrats and middle-class citizens, to the horror
of the English people who were all too aware of the restless laboring masses
in their own country and the social ills afflicting their own lower class.

COMMON CORE

RL 9 Demonstrate knowledge of
foundational works of literature,
including how two or more texts
from the same period treat similar
themes or topics. **RI 9** Analyze
documents of historical and
literary significance for their
themes, purposes, and rhetorical
features. **L 1a** Apply the
understanding that usage is a
matter of convention, can change
over time, and is sometimes
contested.

▶ **TAKING NOTES**

Outlining As you read
this introduction, use
an outline like the one
started here to record
the main ideas about the
history and literature of
the period. You can use
headings, boldfaced terms,
and the information in
these boxes as starting
points. (See page R49 in
the **Research Handbook** for
more help with outlining.)

I. Historical Context
  A. A Time of Revolution
    1. England's ties to
      revolution
    2. Resisting reform
  B. War with France

RESISTING REFORM At this time in England, there were indeed many social ills afflicting society. The new industrial centers in the north and west had no representation in Parliament, and archaic laws denied rights to many religious groups. The nation's growing cities suffered from crime and poor sanitation, among other problems. The criminal justice system offered harsh penalties—for example, people were hanged for theft and thrown into prison for debt. In addition, Britain's overseas empire faced a host of troubles, from corruption in India to the evils of the slave trade.

Yet for nearly 25 years, all efforts at reform were suppressed because of the fear that reform would lead to anarchy, as it had in France. Wary of revolution or a French invasion, Britain grew increasingly conservative, passing laws restricting the right to public assembly and outlawing writing or speech that was critical of the government.

War with France

FEAR OF INVASION When France invaded the Netherlands in 1793, Britain entered into a war with France that would ultimately last for more than 25 years. To complicate matters, near the end of the century rebellious Irishmen, encouraged by the promise of French assistance, rose up against their British-controlled rulers. Though this rebellion was quelled after poor weather prevented a major French landing, the threat of a French invasion of Britain by way of Ireland remained. Hoping to ease the situation, the Tory prime minister **William Pitt** (son of the William Pitt who had led Britain in the Seven Years' War) persuaded Parliament to pass the **Act of Union** in 1800. Ireland would be represented in the British Parliament, and all the British Isles would be joined as the **United Kingdom of Great Britain and Ireland.**

Napoleon on Horseback on the St. Bernard Pass (1801), Jacques-Louis David. © Archivo Iconografico, S.A./Corbis.

THE NAPOLEONIC WARS Meanwhile, the brilliant general **Napoleon Bonaparte** had taken over France's government. Abandoning democratic principles, he made himself emperor and, through clever military and political maneuvers, established control over much of continental Europe. Britain was continually threatened with invasion until the British fleet, under **Horatio Nelson,** destroyed the French navy at the **Battle of Trafalgar** in 1805. After that, Britain gradually liberated the Iberian peninsula (Portugal and Spain) from Napoleon's grip. In 1812, Napoleon overextended himself by invading Russia, where he lost many troops to the cold. Meanwhile, British forces were closing in on France from the south. After two more years of battles, Napoleon was finally captured and exiled to the island of Elba, and victorious diplomats met to decide Europe's fate at the **Congress of Vienna.** Napoleon escaped and returned to power, but shortly thereafter met final defeat at the **Battle of Waterloo** in 1815.

Nat-Y-Glo Ironworks, Wales (1788), George Robertson. The Granger Collection, New York.

Cultural Influences

Romantic writers reacted to the negative effects of industrialization— the poverty, appalling working conditions, and oppression of workers—by turning to nature for truth and beauty.

The Down Side of Industry

During this period, England was an industrial as well as an agricultural land. The **Industrial Revolution** and improvements in farming had brought increased prosperity to the middle and upper classes but degrading poverty to the families employed in the factories and mills. Living and working conditions for industrial laborers were generally appalling. Britain operated under the doctrine of **laissez faire** (lĕs′ā fâr′; French for "allow to do"), which argued that an economy works best without government intervention. No laws were passed to regulate factory safety, workers' hours, low wages, or child labor. The government also made no effort to control the economy's boom-and-bust fluctuations, which resulted in worker layoffs during frequent economic downturns.

THE LUDDITE RIOTS At the start of the Regency (the period in which George III's son ruled England in his father's place), an economic depression

> **A Voice from the Times**
>
> *Men of England, wherefore plough*
> *For the lords who lay ye low?*
> *Wherefore weave with toil and care*
> *The rich robes your tyrants wear?*
>
> —Percy Bysshe Shelley

brought the loss of many factory jobs. New equipment in textile mills added to the problem, as fewer workers were needed to perform certain tasks. In the ensuing **Luddite riots,** unemployed factory workers rioted in several counties, smashing the machinery they blamed for taking their jobs away. The violence was frightening to so many that Parliament passed a law making the breaking of factory machines an offense punishable by death. Yet those who understood the workers' grievances wondered why the government did nothing to try to solve the problem instead. In his first speech to the House of Lords (in which he was entitled by birth to belong), the poet **Lord Byron** spoke in sympathy with the Luddite rebels. However, he was only one of three members who voted against the new law.

POSTWAR PROBLEMS After the Battle of Waterloo, unemployment swelled as war veterans returned home. In addition, to keep cheap foreign grain from glutting the market, the Tory government passed a **Corn Law,** which taxed imported grain (in Britain, *corn* refers to any grain). These taxes protected the income of large landowners and small farmers, but they also devastated the poor and unemployed by keeping food prices high.

Given the trying times, factory workers wanted to join together to pool resources and fight for better work conditions. Labor unions were illegal, however, and when workers assembled in defiance of the law, government troops were called in to suppress their meetings. In one incident, 11 people were killed when troops were sent to break up a workers' gathering in St. Peter's Fields, Manchester. The incident was called the **Peterloo Massacre,** a bitter pun on the Battle of Waterloo.

▼ **Analyze Visuals**
Examine the cartoon on this page. Why might the artist have titled this work *Manchester Heroes*? What criticism is implied with the words, "None but the brave deserve the Fair"? Notice the scale in the upper-left corner that shows "Peculators" winning the balance over "Reformers." A peculator is a person who embezzles funds. Why might peculators have been against those trying to improve conditions for workers?

Manchester Heroes (1819). From *The Peterloo Massacres of 1819,* published by S.W. Forbes, London. British Museum, London. Photo © Bridgeman Art Library.

Romantic Literature

Romantic writers emphasized emotion over reason, nature over industry, and the individual over society.

The Revolt Against Neoclassicism

The word *romantic* was first used in Germany in 1798 by the critics Friedrich and August von Schlegel. In many ways romanticism as a literary style began in Germany, among such Sturm und Drang ("storm and stress") writers as Johann Wolfgang von Goethe and Johann Christoph Friedrich von Schiller.

A REVOLUTIONARY STYLE In England, the romantics were writers who revolted against the order, propriety, and traditionalism of the Age of Reason. Neoclassical writers had venerated the literary achievements of the ancient Greek and Roman writers; they had a great respect for rules, both in literature and in society, and they wrote about the human being as an integral part of an organized society, rather than as an individual.

The romantics, in contrast, were influenced by the same forces that gave rise to the American and French revolutions and by the agitation for political, social, and economic change taking place in their own country. As a result, they searched for freer artistic forms, outside the classical tradition. Romantic poets abandoned the measured, witty heroic couplet for the musical rhythms and richly evocative language of medieval and Renaissance poetry.

To the romantics, emotion became more important than reason, and the individual's relationship to nature was of primary concern. They found delight in the commonplace, celebrating ordinary things—a bird's song, a field of flowers—in their verse. Poetry became, in the words of William Wordsworth, "the spontaneous overflow of powerful feelings." The lyric poem, with its emphasis on subjective experiences, thoughts, feelings, and desires, was the most popular literary form among the romantic poets.

EARLY ROMANTIC POETRY Although the beginning of Britain's romantic period is traditionally assigned to the year 1798, aspects of romanticism are evident in earlier British literature. Poet **William Blake**, who began publishing in the 1780s, produced mystical verse expressing his own personal philosophy and illustrated it with his own engravings. A Londoner of humble origins, Blake saw poverty and suffering all around him and was an ardent supporter of the French Revolution in its early days. He could not accept the neoclassical idea of a stable, orderly hierarchy in the universe but instead viewed existence as a blending of opposite poles—goodness and evil, innocence and experience, heaven and hell. In his landmark *Songs of Innocence* and *Songs of Experience*, Blake included paired poems, one "innocent" and one "experienced," on similar topics.

▶ *For Your Outline*

THE REVOLT AGAINST NEOCLASSICISM

- English romantics revolted against the order and traditionalism of neoclassicism.
- They were influenced by revolutionary ideals and agitation for change.
- They valued emotion, nature, and the commonplace.
- They popularized lyric poems.
- William Blake and Robert Burns wrote poetry with romantic elements.
- Sir Walter Scott pioneered the historical novel.

A Voice from the Times

I must create a system, or be enslaved by another man's.
I will not reason and compare: my business is to create.

—William Blake

SCOTTISH PRIDE **Robert Burns,** who also published poetry in the 1780s, exercised his own brand of romanticism by drawing on earlier traditions, particularly the oral poetry of his native Scotland. The son of a farmer, Burns had great sympathy for the democratic vision of the American and French revolutions and tried to convey in his poetry the experiences of simple, everyday Scottish rural life. Hailed as **the Ploughman Poet,** he often wrote in the Lowland Scots dialect, using vocabulary and pronunciations unlike those of standard English. Burns did not break completely with neoclassical traditions; his witty mock epic *Tam o' Shanter,* for example, is reminiscent of Pope and Swift, but with a Scottish flavor. More in keeping with romantic attitudes are his well-known sentimental songs, such as "Flow Gently Sweet Afton," "My Love Is Like a Red, Red Rose," and the New Year's Eve favorite "Auld Lang Syne."

Another Scotsman who drew heavily on his heritage was **Sir Walter Scott.** Scott gathered traditional ballads and folk tales of his native land, collecting them in *Minstrelsy of the Scottish Border* and incorporating them into long narrative poems such as *The Lay of the Last Minstrel* and *The Lady of the Lake.* During the Regency, Scott became even more famous as a pioneer of the **historical novel,** reaching into Scotland's and England's legendary past for the plots and characters of *Waverley, Rob Roy, Ivanhoe,* and a string of other popular novels. In *Waverley,* for example, he focused on the romantic themes of revolution and rebellion but set the story in the early 1700s, the time of Britain's Jacobite rebellion.

▶ *For Your Outline*
ROMANTICISM EVOLVES

• *Lyrical Ballads* launched the romantic period.

• Romanticism valued the individual, emotion, nature, the commonplace, and the imagination.

• The Lake poets and personal essayists were romantics; Jane Austen wrote novels of manners.

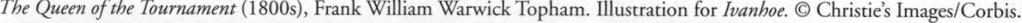

The Queen of the Tournament (1800s), Frank William Warwick Topham. Illustration for *Ivanhoe.* © Christie's Images/Corbis.

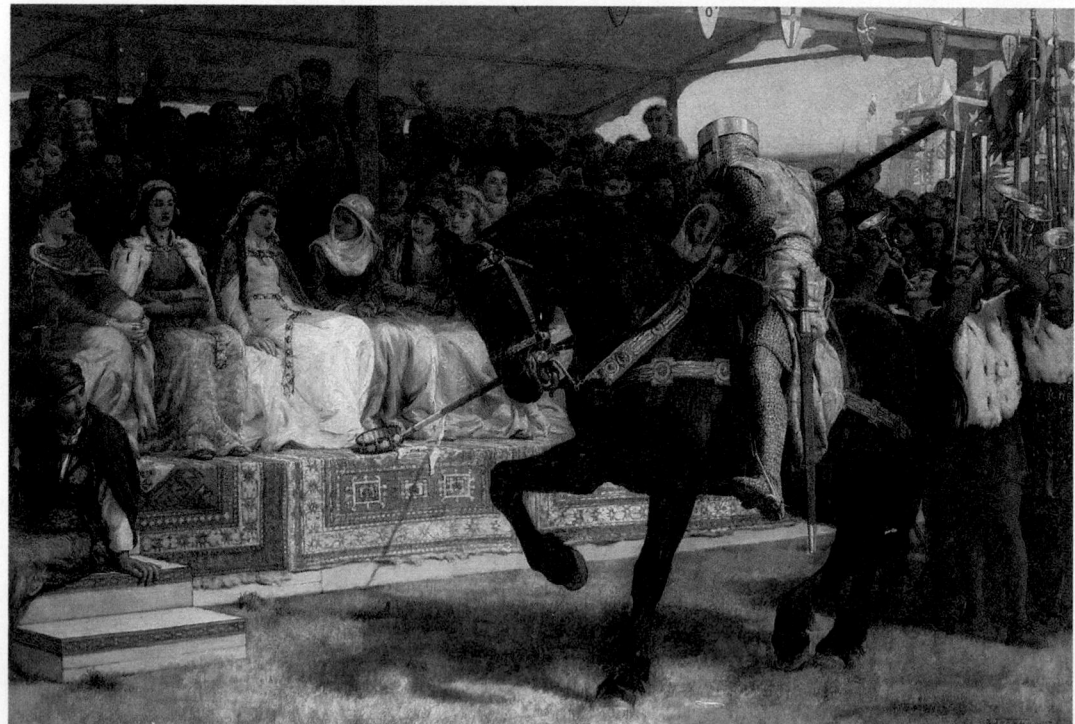

Romanticism Evolves

In 1798, **William Wordsworth** and **Samuel Taylor Coleridge** published their landmark poetry collaboration, *Lyrical Ballads, with a Few Other Poems.* It was with this publication that the **romantic period** is traditionally said to have begun.

The two poets, who had first met in 1795, were united by their shared desire to explore new modes of literary expression. Wordsworth had traveled extensively in both Germany and France, where he had become committed to the revolutionary cause. He developed into a poet of the common man, writing to capture everyday experiences in simple language, without concern for artificial rules or conventions. For both Wordsworth and Coleridge, nature and meditation were linked, with insight into the human experience flowing freely from communion with nature.

THE LAKE POETS Coleridge explained that the poems in *Lyrical Ballads* focused on two aspects of human experience, the natural and the supernatural. Wordsworth's nature poetry gave "the charm of novelty to things of every day," while Coleridge himself explored supernatural events that nevertheless had a "human interest" and "semblance of truth." In a preface to the work, Wordsworth would essentially define the features of English romanticism: an emphasis on the individual, a rejection of artificiality in favor of passion and emotion, a love of nature, a respect for the commonplace, and a freeing of the imagination (see page 796).

Lyrical Ballads was so different from the usual 18th-century neoclassical fare that romantic essayist **William Hazlitt** likened it to the French Revolution itself. Soon after its publication, Wordsworth, who had grown up in the beautiful Lake District of northwestern England, resettled there in the town of Grasmere, with Coleridge moving nearby. Along with their friend and fellow poet **Robert Southey,** they became known as the **Lake poets.** Also part of their circle was **Dorothy Wordsworth,** who lived with her brother in Grasmere and kept a keenly observed journal of their life.

ROMANTIC ESSAYISTS Another friend of Coleridge's, **Charles Lamb,** remained in London and won fame writing personal essays. Such essays—also called **familiar essays**—often appeared in leading journals of the day. They were a popular Romantic Age form because of their emphasis on personal experiences and feelings. Other romantic essayists of note were William Hazlitt and **Thomas De Quincey.**

Romanticism in British Art

During the romantic age, many artists turned to landscape painting, trying to capture the beauty and wonders of the natural world. Two of Britain's finest painters, **J. M. W. Turner** and **John Constable,** were products of this period.

The Painter of Light Joseph Mallord William Turner, whose work *Lake of Wyndermere* (1826) is shown here, was only 14 when he was accepted to study at Britain's prestigious Royal Academy of Art. Known for landscapes and seascapes in watercolors as well as oils (see page 754), Turner helped establish the use of watercolors as a popular medium. By using watercolor technique with oil paints, he achieved a new sense of light in his works, anticipating the experimentation with light that characterized impressionist art of the later 19th century.

A Late Bloomer Unlike Turner, John Constable was not made a member of the Royal Academy until he was more than 50 years old. A thoughtful observer of nature, he became famous for landscapes that focus on changes in light and weather. Constable generally based his final paintings on careful sketches he had made, sometimes years before. He painted many landscapes of the rural area in Suffolk, England, where he grew up—an area now known as Constable country.

AN ENGLISH ORIGINAL One talented prose writer of the era seems largely untouched by the romantic movement. Instead, **Jane Austen** remained in many ways a neoclassical writer. She confined her novels to the experiences of the intimate world she knew, the genteel society of England's rural villages. Her novels, often called **novels of manners,** include *Pride and Prejudice, Emma,* and *Sense and Sensibility.*

Austen's work does contain romantic elements, however: a focus on the details of daily life and a preoccupation with character and personality. Also, certain characters, such as the passionate Marianne of *Sense and Sensibility,* are imbued with the romantic spirit. However, Austen typically causes such characters to see the error of their ways and become more reserved by novel's end.

The Late Romantics

A NEW GENERATION During the Regency, a second generation of romantic poets came on the literary scene, the most prominent of whom was **George Gordon, Lord Byron.** The handsome aristocrat won instant fame with the 1812 publication of the first part of his long poem *Childe Harold's Pilgrimage,* whose darkly brooding romantic hero became associated with the poet himself.

For a time, Byron was the darling of fashionable London, but his radical politics and personal escapades soon made him the subject of scandal. In 1816 he abandoned Britain for a self-imposed exile on the European continent, where he died of a fever while helping the Greeks fight for independence. Throughout the 19th century, he remained the most famous of the romantic poets, known as much for his romantic life as his poetic talent. The **Byronic hero—** dark, handsome, restless, and a bit diabolical—became a staple of literary fiction that many younger poets and other artists tried to imitate.

Byron's friend **Percy Bysshe Shelley's** dismay at social injustice made him even more radical than Byron. An admirer of the philosopher **William Godwin,** Shelley scandalized London when he eloped to the continent with Godwin's 16-year-old daughter, Mary. He spent most of his remaining years abroad, writing the verse dramas *The Cenci* and *Prometheus Unbound* as well as beautiful lyric poetry that celebrates nature, freedom, artistic expression, and other values the romantics held dear. After Shelley died in a boating accident at age 29, his wife **Mary Shelley** returned to England, where she helped edit her husband's works for publication.

Mary Shelley was a talented writer who won fame in her own right for her gothic horror tale *Frankenstein.* Mary moved in intellectual circles and was familiar with the scientific theories

Actor Robert DeNiro as The Creature in the 1994 film *Frankenstein*

of her day. In her introduction to *Frankenstein,* she describes listening to conversations about "Dr. Darwin, . . . who preserved a piece of vermicelli in a glass case till by some extraordinary means it began to move with voluntary motion. Not thus, after all, would life be given. Perhaps a corpse would be reanimated; galvanism had given token of such things. . . ." Thus, Shelley's dark tale of a monster who destroys its maker can be read not only as a horror story, or a romantic meditation on passion versus reason, but as a warning against the dangers of science. Indeed, Frankenstein's monster can be seen as the embodiment and expression of Shelley's society's fears—fears of unchecked progress and of science and industry's negative effects on humanity.

Poet **John Keats** came from humbler origins than Byron and Shelley. He was acquainted with Shelley, however, through his friend **Leigh Hunt,** the publisher who encouraged his career and introduced him to leading artists of the day. Orphaned at 14, Keats spent much of his short life fighting the tuberculosis that killed his mother and brother and eventually claimed him as well. He produced most of his finest poetry in a feverish eight-month span—**sonnets, odes, ballads,** and other poetic forms, all handled with remarkable dexterity. Many of his poems use vivid images from nature as a starting point for philosophical meditation about joy, sorrow, love, death, art, and beauty. After Keats died, Shelley eulogized him in his famous elegy *Adonais:* "His fate and fame shall be / An echo and a light unto eternity!"

▶ *For Your Outline*

THE LATE ROMANTICS

• A new generation of romantic poets flourished during the Regency.

• The Byronic hero (dark, brooding, diabolical) became a literary staple.

• Percy B. Shelley wrote verse dramas and lyric poetry celebrating nature, freedom, and artistic expression.

• Mary Shelley's gothic tale *Frankenstein* expressed society's fears.

• John Keats wrote sonnets, odes, and ballads that used nature as a starting point for philosophical meditations.

Connecting Literature, History, and Culture

Use this timeline and the questions on the next page to gain insight into how Britain's romantic period reflected what was happening in other parts of the world.

BRITISH LITERARY MILESTONES

1790

1794 Robert Burns writes "An Ode to Liberty" and the song "My Love Is Like a Red, Red Rose"; William Blake publishes *Songs of Innocence and of Experience.* ▶

1798 William Wordsworth and Samuel Taylor Coleridge publish the first edition of *Lyrical Ballads.*

1800

1800 Dorothy Wordsworth begins keeping her *Grasmere Journal.*

1802 The influential literary magazine the *Edinburgh Review* begins publication.

1805 Sir Walter Scott wins fame with *Minstrelsy of the Scottish Border,* a long narrative poem based on a Scottish legend. ▶

HISTORICAL CONTEXT

1790

1792 Britain issues a proclamation against all seditious writings.

1793 War breaks out between Britain and revolutionary France.

1796 J. M. W. Turner exhibits his first oil painting; Edward Jenner develops a vaccine against smallpox.

1798 Rebellion fails to win Irish independence and is harshly suppressed.

1800

1800 The Act of Union creates the United Kingdom of Great Britain and Ireland.

1803 Richard Trevithick develops the first railway steam locomotive.

1805 The British fleet, under Horatio Nelson, defeats Napoleon's navy at the Battle of Trafalgar. ▶

1807 Britain abolishes the slave trade.

WORLD CULTURE AND EVENTS

1790

1793 The French Revolution moves into the Reign of Terror, in which many are killed.

1799 The Rosetta stone, which makes it possible to decipher Egyptian hieroglyphics, is discovered by Napoleon's army in Egypt; Napoleon takes the reins of power in France. ▶

1800

1803 The United States purchases the Louisiana Territory from Napoleonic France; German composer Ludwig van Beethoven composes his third symphony, known as the *Eroica.*

1804 Napoleon crowns himself emperor.

1808 German romantic author Johann Wolfgang von Goethe publishes the first part of his verse drama *Faust.*

MAKING CONNECTIONS

- What authors outside Britain were writing during the romantic period?
- Which incidents show Napoleon's influence on world events?
- Which developments show positive and negative effects of the Industrial Revolution?
- Which details suggest oppression in Britain, and which show eventual reform?

COMMON CORE

RI 7 Integrate and evaluate multiple sources of information presented in different media or formats as well as in words in order to address a question or solve a problem.

1810

1812 Lord Byron wins fame with his long poem *Childe Harold's Pilgrimage*.

1813 Jane Austen anonymously publishes her novel of manners *Pride and Prejudice*.

1818 Mary Shelley anonymously publishes her gothic novel *Frankenstein*.

1819 Percy Bysshe Shelley writes "Ode to the West Wind"; John Keats writes most of his greatest poems.

1820

1821 John Keats, age 25, dies of tuberculosis.

1822 Percy Bysshe Shelley, age 29, drowns off the coast of Italy.

1823 Lord Byron joins the Greek war of liberation from the Turks.

1824 Lord Byron, age 36, dies of a fever. ▶

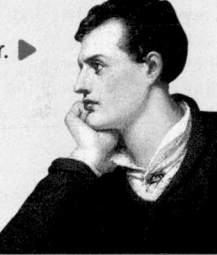

1810

1811 George III is declared insane; his son George is named regent, marking the start of the Regency; unemployed workers smash new machinery in the Luddite riots.

1815 The Duke of Wellington leads the final defeat of Napoleon at Waterloo.

1819 Eleven die in the Peterloo Massacre, in which troops break up a large workers' gathering. ▶

1820

1820 The Regency ends when George III dies and his son becomes George IV.

1821 John Constable paints *The Hay Wain*, considered one of his masterpieces.

1829 The Catholic Emancipation Act frees Catholics from many restrictions.

1832 The first Reform Bill extends voting rights to middle-class men but affects only 5 percent of the population.

1810

1810 Latin American nations begin declaring independence from Napoleonic Spain.

1812 Napoleon invades Russia; the brothers Grimm publish their first collection of German fairy tales. ▶

1819 The first steamship crosses the Atlantic Ocean.

1820

1820 Russian romantic poet Aleksandr Pushkin publishes the verse poem *Ruslan and Ludmila*.

1821 German Romantic poet Heinrich Heine publishes his first volume of poetry.

1826 Joseph-Nicéphore Niépce produces the first successful photograph.

1831 France's Victor Hugo publishes *The Hunchback of Notre Dame*. ▶

The Hunchback of Notre Dame
BY VICTOR HUGO

The Legacy of Romanticism

Fantasy, Horror, and Science Fiction

The romantic fascination with the supernatural is still thriving in today's books and movies. The laboratory-created monster in Mary Shelley's *Frankenstein*—sometimes called the world's first work of science fiction—is not so very different from the laboratory creations in the film *The Matrix,* and the eerie ghost-driven ship of Coleridge's *The Rime of the Ancient Mariner* is remarkably similar to the ship in *Pirates of the Caribbean.*

QUICKWRITE Jot down your own list of books, films, and TV shows in which the supernatural or paranormal is a strong element of the plot. Then consider the appeal of this kind of fiction and the reasons you think it remains so popular.

COMMON CORE

W 7 Conduct short research projects to answer a question; narrow the inquiry; synthesize multiple sources, demonstrating understanding of the subject.
W 8 Gather relevant information from multiple digital sources, using advanced searches effectively. **SL 1** Initiate and participate effectively in collaborative discussions, building on others' ideas and expressing their own clearly and persuasively.

Scene from *Pirates of the Caribbean: Dead Man's Chest* (2006)

Jane Austen Forever

They say that imitation is the sincerest form of flattery. If that's true, then Jane Austen would certainly be flattered by the many books and movies inspired by her work. Examples include *Bridget Jones's Diary*, a book and a movie about a modern Londoner looking for love that's based on *Pride and Prejudice;* the movie *Clueless,* about a high-school matchmaker who happens to be a lot like Austen's *Emma;* and several novels that imagine what happens to Austen's characters after her books have ended. And of course there are countless movie and TV adaptations of her original works.

CREATE With a small group, discuss any Austen-inspired books, TV shows, and movies that you know. Do a search on the Internet to find book covers and movie images, and create a collage or poster illustrating the breadth of Austen's influence.

Scene from *Bridget Jones: The Edge of Reason* (2004)

Respect for the Environment

A respect for nature, so evident in the poetry of Wordsworth, Keats, and Shelley, is evident in the environmental movement we know today. Like the romantic poets, today's environmentalists condemn the harm that urbanization and industrialization bring to the natural landscape. They educate people about environmental dangers and campaign to clean up pollution, save endangered species, and preserve natural wonders.

RESEARCH & DISCUSS As a class, consider recent issues involving the environment. You might bring in newspaper or magazine articles and summarize them for classmates. Then consider the degree to which love of nature motivates environmentalists. What are some of the other motives they may have for their efforts?

Volunteers rescuing birds harmed by an oil spill

Selected Poetry
by William Blake

VIDEO TRAILER KEYWORD: HML12-768A

COMMON CORE

RL 2 Determine two or more themes or central ideas of a text and analyze their development over the course of the text. **RL 4** Determine the meaning of words and phrases as they are used in the text; analyze the impact of specific word choices on meaning and tone, including words with multiple meanings or language that is particularly fresh, engaging, or beautiful. **L 4** Determine or clarify the meaning of multiple-meaning words.

DID YOU KNOW?

William Blake . . .

- met the radical American thinker Thomas Paine and supported the American and French revolutions.
- was charged with treason for cursing King George III but was later acquitted.
- championed racial and sexual equality.

Meet the Author

William Blake 1757–1827

In William Blake's own day, few saw or read any of his illustrated books, and those who did often dismissed them as the works of a madman. More than 100 years passed before people began to recognize Blake's stunning achievements as a poet and artist.

An Unusual Youth The son of a hosier, Blake spent nearly his entire life in London. As a schoolboy, he was precocious, reading the Bible and the works of John Milton at a young age, attending art school when he was only 10, and writing poetry by age 12. From early on in his life, Blake saw visions—first of angels and ghostly monks, and later of the Virgin Mary and various historical figures. He attributed these visions not to a supernatural source but to the interaction of his imagination with the world and with the infinite, or God. Blake believed that children's unfettered imagination was something of a state of grace. Though he was a Christian, he found church doctrine inadequate and thought it was used primarily as a form of social control.

Marriage and Art In 1782, Blake married Catherine Boucher, a poor, illiterate woman whom he taught to read and paint. The couple enjoyed a close, loving marriage, though Blake's mysticism sometimes exasperated his wife. "I have very little of Mr. Blake's company," she once quipped. "He is always in Paradise."

In 1784, Blake opened his own print shop, where he developed a technique called illuminated printing, which involved engraving a poem's text and illustration on the same plate. Blake's first illuminated book of poems, *Songs of Innocence,* appeared in 1789; in 1794, he added a group of contrasting poems called *Songs of Experience.* Blake indicated that his purpose in putting them together was to show "the two contrary states of the human soul."

A Modern Prophet Blake's later works were written on a grand scale, marked by prophetic and mythic visions. Imaginatively illustrated and difficult to understand, these complex works were almost totally ignored by his contemporaries. In his 60s, Blake at last found admirers among a group of younger artists. During this period he created some of his best designs, including illustrations for Dante's *Divine Comedy.* Blake died three months before his 70th birthday, "singing," a friend reported, "of the things he saw in heaven."

Author Online
Go to **thinkcentral.com**. KEYWORD: HML12-768B

TEXT ANALYSIS: SYMBOL

One of the most powerful tools a writer can use is symbolism. A **symbol** is a person, place, object, or action that represents an abstract idea or feeling. Symbols work by association, and they often have more than one meaning. For example, the subject of Blake's poem "The Lamb" symbolizes innocence and gentleness, but Blake also alludes to the lamb as a symbol for Jesus Christ in the New Testament. In addition to such common meanings, a symbol may take on a particular meaning from the context of the work in which it appears.

Although Blake's poems may seem simple and straight-forward, he uses symbols to convey important themes. As you read, analyze the subjects of his poems to determine their symbolic meaning.

READING SKILL: COMPARE AND CONTRAST POEMS

As stated in the biography on page 768, Blake wrote *Songs of Innocence* and *Songs of Experience* to explore "the two contrary states of the human soul." To further your understanding of his view of human nature, you can **compare and contrast** poems using the following criteria:

- **Word choice**—Look for descriptive words, and note how they are used to emphasize characteristics of the subject.
- **Ideas**—Identify common or contrasting ideas expressed in the poems.
- **Tone**—Notice the author's attitude toward the subject.

As you read, use a chart like the one shown to record similarities and differences for each pair of poems.

	"The Lamb"	"The Tyger"
Word Choice	little wooly bright tender voice	burning bright fire of thine eyes
Ideas		
Tone		

 Complete the activities in your **Reader/Writer Notebook**.

What is a VISIONARY?

Blake once wrote that "mental things are alone real," which is reflected in both his life and his work. Think about people you know or have read about who, like Blake, are visionary. It may be someone who claimed to see people and events in dreams, or someone who envisioned a better future. What kinds of visions—past, present, and future—have they had? What changes in their lives did their visions bring about?

DISCUSS With a small group, generate a list of people—living or dead—whom you consider to be visionaries. Note the qualities and traits that these individuals have in common. Then discuss the ways in which these individuals have made a difference in the world.

Visionaries

1. William Blake—poet, artist; wrote about the real world and visions that appeared to him.

2. Gandhi—political figure, spiritual leader; envisioned a better way for people to live.

3.

4.

5.

from SONGS OF INNOCENCE

THE LAMB

William Blake

Little Lamb, who made thee?
Dost thou know who made thee?
Gave thee life & bid thee feed,
By the stream & o'er the mead;

5 Gave thee clothing of delight,
Softest clothing wooly bright;
Gave thee such a tender voice,
Making all the vales rejoice!
　　Little Lamb who made thee?
10 　　Dost thou know who made thee?

　　Little Lamb I'll tell thee,
　　Little Lamb I'll tell thee!
He is callèd by thy name,
For he calls himself a Lamb:
15 He is meek & he is mild,
He became a little child:
I a child & thou a lamb,
We are callèd by his name. **Ⓐ**
　　Little Lamb God bless thee.
20 　　Little Lamb God bless thee.

4 mead: meadow.

8 vales: valleys.

13–14 He . . . Lamb: In the New Testament, Jesus is sometimes called the Lamb of God.

Ⓐ SYMBOL
In lines 13–18, Blake uses the symbol of the lamb to connect the poem's three characters. What is he suggesting about the relationship between them?

Analyze Visuals ▶
How does the style of this illustration reflect the **tone** of Blake's poem?

The Shepherd from *Songs of Innocence* (1789), William Blake. Color printed relief etching with water color on paper, 7.6 cm × 7 cm. © Yale Center for British Art, Paul Mellon Fund, United States of America/Bridgeman Art Library.

THE CHIMNEY SWEEPER

William Blake

When my mother died I was very young,
And my father sold me while yet my tongue
Could scarcely cry " 'weep! 'weep! 'weep! 'weep!"
So your chimneys I sweep & in soot I sleep.

5 There's little Tom Dacre, who cried when his head
That curl'd like a lamb's back, was shav'd, so I said,
"Hush, Tom! never mind it, for when your head's bare,
You know that the soot cannot spoil your white hair."

And so he was quiet, & that very night,
10 As Tom was a-sleeping he had such a sight!
That thousands of sweepers, Dick, Joe, Ned, & Jack,
Were all of them lock'd up in coffins of black;

And by came an Angel who had a bright key,
And he open'd the coffins & set them all free;
15 Then down a green plain, leaping, laughing they run,
And wash in a river and shine in the Sun.

Then naked & white, all their bags left behind,
They rise upon clouds, and sport in the wind.
And the Angel told Tom, if he'd be a good boy,
20 He'd have God for his father & never want joy.

And so Tom awoke; and we rose in the dark
And got with our bags & our brushes to work.
Tho' the morning was cold, Tom was happy & warm;
So if all do their duty, they need not fear harm. **B**

3 **'weep! 'weep!:** the child's attempt to say "Sweep! Sweep!"—a chimney sweeper's street cry.

COMMON CORE L 4

Language Coach

Etymology The origin of *cry* relates to the way it sounds: Its Latin ancestor, *quis,* imitates the squeal of a pig. *Cry* means one thing in line 3 and another, in the past tense, in line 5. How are the two meanings different?

18 **sport:** play or frolic.

20 **want:** lack.

B COMPARE AND CONTRAST
Reread lines 17–24. What view of meekness and gentleness is expressed in this passage and in "The Lamb"?

THE LITTLE BOY LOST

William Blake

"Father, father, where are you going?
O do not walk so fast.
Speak father, speak to your little boy,
Or else I shall be lost."

5 The night was dark, no father was there;
The child was wet with dew;
The mire was deep, & the child did weep,
And away the vapor flew.

7 mire: wet, swampy ground.

8 vapor: mist; fog.

THE LITTLE BOY FOUND

William Blake

The little boy lost in the lonely fen,
Led by the wand'ring light,
Began to cry, but God ever nigh,
Appear'd like his father in white.

5 He kissed the child & by the hand led
And to his mother brought,
Who in sorrow pale, thro' the lonely dale,
Her little boy weeping sought. **C**

1 fen: swamp; marsh.

3 nigh (nī): near.

7 thro': through; **dale:** valley.

C SYMBOL
What do the actions of being lost and found symbolize?

from SONGS OF EXPERIENCE
THE TYGER

William Blake

Tyger! Tyger! burning bright
In the forests of the night,
What immortal hand or eye
Could frame thy fearful symmetry?

5 In what distant deeps or skies
Burnt the fire of thine eyes?
On what wings dare he aspire?
What the hand dare seize the fire?

And what shoulder, & what art,
10 Could twist the sinews of thy heart?
And when thy heart began to beat,
What dread hand? & what dread feet?

What the hammer? what the chain?
In what furnace was thy brain?
15 What the anvil? what dread grasp
Dare its deadly terrors clasp?

When the stars threw down their spears
And watered heaven with their tears,
Did he smile his work to see?
20 Did he who made the Lamb make thee? **D**

Tyger! Tyger! burning bright
In the forests of the night,
What immortal hand or eye
Dare frame thy fearful symmetry?

4 symmetry (sĭm′ĭ-trē): balance or beauty of form.

7 he: the tiger's creator.

Language Coach

Roots A word's **root** may produce an image that helps you remember the word's meaning. The root of *aspire* (line 7) is *spirare*, "to breathe." What image helps you remember it means "reach toward a goal"?

15 anvil (ăn′vĭl): iron block on which metal objects are hammered into shape.

D COMPARE AND CONTRAST
How does Blake's **tone** in lines 17–20 differ from the tone used to discuss creation in "The Lamb"?

Analyze Visuals ▶

Note that in the reproduction of the original printing of "The Tyger," the hand-colored illustration is intertwined with the text. What does this composition suggest about Blake's attitude toward his work?

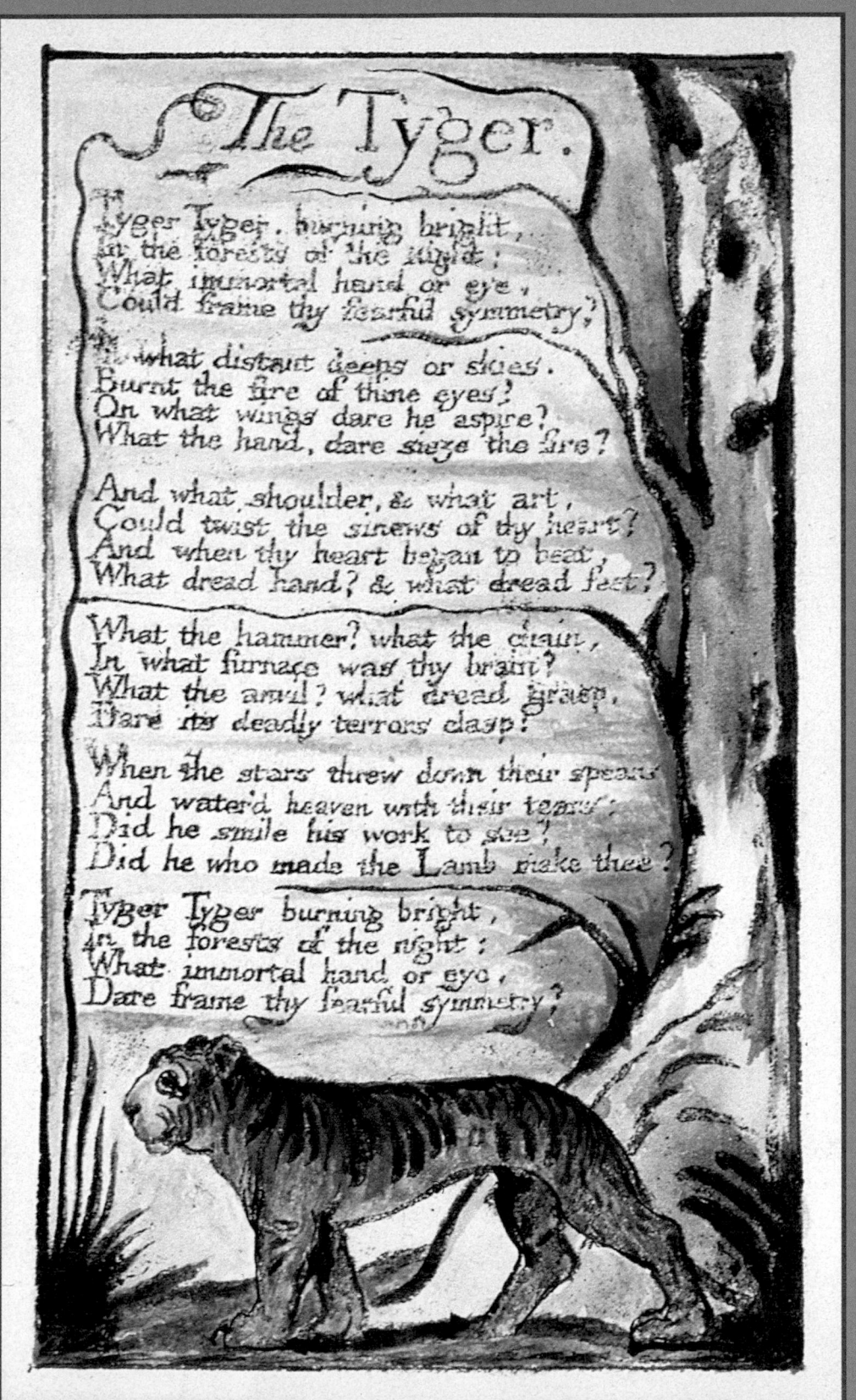

The Tyger: Plate 43 from *Songs of Innocence and of Experience* (1802–1808), William Blake. Copy R, page 124-1950. Etching, ink and water color. © Fitzwilliam Museum, University of Cambridge, United Kingdom/Bridgeman Art Library.

THE CHIMNEY SWEEPER

William Blake

A little black thing among the snow
Crying " 'weep, 'weep," in notes of woe!
"Where are thy father & mother? say?"
"They are both gone up to the church to pray.

5 "Because I was happy upon the heath,
And smil'd among the winter's snow;
They clothed me in the clothes of death,
And taught me to sing the notes of woe.

"And because I am happy, & dance & sing,
10 They think they have done me no injury,
And are gone to praise God & his Priest & King,
Who make up a heaven of our misery." **E**

2 'weep, 'weep: the child's attempt to say "Sweep, Sweep"—a chimney sweeper's street cry.

5 heath: a tract of open land that cannot be farmed.

E COMPARE AND CONTRAST
Reread lines 5–12. What words and phrases suggest that this speaker is less naive than the speaker of "The Chimney Sweeper" from *Songs of Innocence*?

THE SICK ROSE

William Blake

O Rose, thou art sick.
The invisible worm
That flies in the night
In the howling storm

5 Has found out thy bed
Of crimson joy,
And his dark secret love
Does thy life destroy. **F**

F SYMBOL
What does the rose's sickness symbolize?

Comprehension

1. **Recall** In "The Chimney Sweeper" from *Songs of Innocence*, why does Tom Dacre cry?

2. **Summarize** What happens to the boy in "The Little Boy Found"?

3. **Clarify** In "The Chimney Sweeper" from *Songs of Experience*, what does the speaker suggest with the phrase "make up a heaven of our misery"?

Text Analysis

4. **Examine Repetition** Reread "The Lamb" and "The Tyger," looking for repetition of phrases, lines, and stanzas. What does Blake emphasize through the use of repetition? Cite evidence to support your answer.

5. **Interpret Symbol** In "The Tyger," Blake uses the animal to symbolize his very complex view of creation—both heavenly and artistic. What troubling aspects of creation does the tiger represent? Cite details.

6. **Compare and Contrast Poems** In Blake's time, it was common practice in London to use small boys for cleaning chimneys, which was dangerous and often fatal work. Review the information you recorded in your chart relating to the "The Chimney Sweeper" poems. What difference do you see in the **word choice** and **tone** of these poems and in the **ideas** they convey?

7. **Analyze Imagery** In many of these poems, Blake uses words like *night* or *dark* and *light* or *bright* as a way to contrast ideas or characters. However, he doesn't always use the words to mean the same things in the poems. How does Blake employ the "night/light" contrast in the following?

   - "The Little Boy Lost" and "The Little Boy Found" pairing
   - "The Tyger"
   - "The Chimney Sweeper" from *Songs of Innocence*
   - "The Sick Rose"

Text Criticism

8. **Critical Interpretations** One critic has suggested that Blake pits himself against despotic authority, restrictive morality, and institutionalized religion: "His great insight is into the way these separate modes of control work together to squelch what is most holy in human beings." In your opinion, does this comment apply to the poems you read? Explain.

What is a **VISIONARY?**

The word *visionary* can be used to describe someone who is inspired by visions or who has great imagination and foresight. Based on the poems you have read, what do you think makes Blake a visionary?

COMMON CORE

RL 2 Determine two or more themes or central ideas of a text and analyze their development over the course of the text.
RL 4 Determine the meaning of words and phrases as they are used in the text; analyze the impact of specific word choices on meaning and tone, including words with multiple meanings or language that is particularly fresh, engaging, or beautiful.

The Art of William Blake

Image Collection on Media  **Smart** DVD-ROM

COMMON CORE

RL 7 Analyze multiple interpretations of a poem, evaluating how each version interprets the source text.

How can art ENHANCE *text?*

KEY IDEA William Blake was a printer and engraver by trade, and the **illumination** he provided for many of his poems was intended to be interpreted right along with the text. For Blake, the words and images were inseparable. In examining the elements of visual art found in Blake's illuminated poems, you'll see how he integrated the medium with the meaning of his words.

Background

Visionary Innovation From the time he was 15 years old until his death at age 69, William Blake supported himself as a tradesman. He apprenticed as an etcher and engraver for seven years before opening his own printing and publishing business with his friend James Parker. Blake briefly studied art at the Royal Academy but found the atmosphere uninspiring for the art he wanted to create. In the 1780s, the two predominant styles in the art world were the highly decorative rococo and the elegantly linear neoclassical. Blake's visual art didn't fall neatly into either category. He felt that line was superior to color, but the clash between the two elements—perhaps a reflection of both his writer and artist instincts—is readily apparent in his illuminated poems.

In 1788, Blake, inspired by a dream he had of his deceased younger brother, created a new art form he called "illuminated printing." Blake would etch images directly onto a printing plate by hand—including the text of the poems, which he would have to write backwards—then ink the plates and print the complete work with a rolling press. Later, he would paint each image by hand with watercolors. This new approach allowed Blake more control over the image because he could add new etched lines or change the color schemes whenever he wanted. Blake's illuminated printing method allowed him to fuse his visual and poetic visions.

Media Literacy: Illuminated Texts

Blake intended the poems from *Songs of Innocence and of Experience* to engage both the intellect and the imagination of his readers. He was working with the limited space that a 4½″ × 2½″ printing plate allowed, balancing the needs of the text with the visuals he'd imagined for the poem. Longer poems relied less on illustrative pictures and more on decoration; shorter poems often benefited from the additional image space.

Blake's decisions about the **color, line, shape,** and **texture** of each illustration were informed by the meaning he intended to convey. Consider the visual choices Blake made as you analyze the examples of his work.

STRATEGIES FOR ANALYZING ILLUSTRATIONS

- **Color,** or hue, can help create the mood of an image. Blake hand-colored his prints with watercolors, so the mood of a piece could well have depended on the materials he had available or on his feelings at the time. Think about what the color of this image suggests about the mood of the poem.

- Like many artists, Blake used **lines** to give an image expressive qualities. For example, the use of thick or jagged lines can suggest rigidity or harshness.

- **Shape** is the outline of the objects in an image. Depending on an artist's choices, shapes can be geometric, with distinct angles, or natural, to closely match objects found in nature. Note that much of the image area is white, so the shapes stand out in stark contrast.

- To give an image **texture,** an artist can mimic the surface quality or "feel" of a real object. For example, varying the colors of a tree's bark can simulate the bark's rough texture. Blake created texture by etching on the printing plates. Notice the difference in texture between the area behind the poem and the area around the chimney sweeper.

Viewing Guide for

The Art of William Blake

Access the full-sized illustrations on the DVD. Read each poem and examine the images closely, considering Blake's use of color, line, shape, and texture. Look for common visual elements among the prints: Does Blake frequently use a specific color to represent similar subject matter? Is his use of line clearly evident or subtle? How does his use of art elements reflect the meanings of the poems? Use these questions to help you analyze the images.

NOW VIEW

FIRST VIEWING: Comprehension

1. **Identify** Describe the setting of "The Chimney Sweeper" image.
2. **Identify** What is the girl in the background in "The Fly" doing?

CLOSE VIEWING: Media Literacy

3. **Analyze Shape** Based on your understanding of the poems, how well does each image reflect Blake's meaning?

4. **Compare Color and Line** Blake's use of color and line are vastly different in "The Chimney Sweeper" and "The Fly." Compare the choices Blake made about color and line in these images.

5. **Examine Art Elements** Reread "The Chimney Sweeper." In the poem, Blake is commenting on the horrible conditions many children were forced to endure in 18th-century England. Describe how Blake's use of any one of the art elements contributes to the meaning of the poem. Consider the following lines:

   - "A little black thing among the snow"
   - "Because I was happy upon the heath"
   - "And are gone to praise God & his Priest and King / Who make up a heaven of our misery."

Write or Discuss

Analyze Form Blake was highly creative as a child, attending art school at age 10 and writing poetry by age 12. His unique blending of visual art with poetry was a natural extension of his artistic nature, as was the development of his illuminated printing process. Based on the examples you've viewed, how successful do you think these poems are as both visual art and poetic expressions? Write your opinion in two paragraphs. Consider

- the relationship between the images and the poems' meanings
- the way Blake employs color, line, shape, and texture in the images
- the limitations of the printing plate and coloring method

Produce Your Own Media

Illustrate a Poem A visual accompaniment to a poem can simply reflect the theme or mood of the poem or bring additional meaning to both the image and the words. Blake was unique in that he did both simultaneously. Choose a poem—your own or one you've read—and create an **illustration** to accompany it. You can draw or paint an image, use a computer program to create an illustration, or try a mixed-media collage. The important thing is that your creation fit the theme or mood or main idea of the poem you've chosen. Be creative; your illustration doesn't have to be a literal depiction of your poem.

HERE'S HOW Keep the following in mind as you create your illustration:

- Decide if you want to closely tie your illustration to specifics in the poem or if you want to use the poem as inspiration for your own vision.
- Keep in mind the visual art elements of color, line, shape, and texture.
- Consider how someone viewing your illustration will understand the connection between the text and the images.

Further Exploration

A Question of Color Look at the multiple versions of Blake's "The Fly" on the DVD. Because he painted each individual poem print in watercolors by hand, the colors in each of these versions is different. Does the color variation affect the relationship between the words and the image?

An Artist's Interpretation Blake also did illustrations for other writers' works, including Dante's and Milton's. Find an image that Blake created for another writer's work and determine how Blake's interpretation illuminates the text.

COMMON CORE

RL 7 Analyze multiple interpretations of a poem, evaluating how each version interprets the source text. **W 1** Write arguments to support claims in an analysis of substantive topics or texts, using valid reasoning and relevant and sufficient evidence.

Media Tools **THINK** central

Go to **thinkcentral.com**. KEYWORD: HML12-781

Tech Tip

If available, use a design program to incorporate photographs, clip art, and image-manipulation tools.

To a Mouse
To a Louse

Poetry by Robert Burns

COMMON CORE

RL 2 Determine two or more themes or central ideas of a text and analyze their development over the course of the text. **RL 4** Determine the meaning of words and phrases as they are used in the text, including figurative and connotative meanings. **L 4a** Use context as a clue to the meaning of a word or phrase.

Meet the Author

Robert Burns 1759–1796

A handsome and charismatic figure, Robert Burns achieved considerable fame during his lifetime. After his death, he was elevated to the status of national hero. His unparalleled ability to speak for his people, along with the simple beauty of his verse, helped make him Scotland's "favorite son."

Childhood Hardship Born in the village of Alloway to an unsuccessful tenant farmer, Burns endured extreme poverty and hard labor as a child. This experience left him in poor health and fueled his hatred of Scotland's rigid class system. Though poor, Burns's father managed to provide his son with something of an education. Burns showed an early flair and passion for literature. One of the works that especially fired his imagination was the 15th-century Scottish poem "Wallace." The poem, Burns later wrote, "poured a Scottish prejudice into my veins, which will boil along there till the floodgates of life shut in natural rest." His discovery of this and other works written in a Scottish vernacular inspired Burns to use the Scots dialect, spoken primarily by the country's peasant class.

Charming Rebel After his father's death in 1784, Burns, along with his brother, struggled to farm independently. Burns became involved with a servant girl at the farm, the first of several liaisons that resulted in illegitimate offspring. In 1786, he fell in love with Jean Armour, but her father, disturbed by Burns's radical ideas and personal behavior, sent Armour away. Hurt and incensed, Burns resolved to emigrate to Jamaica. To raise the necessary money, he published *Poems, Chiefly in the Scottish Dialect* (1786), a collection that showed his love for Scottish peasant life. Its immense success induced Burns to move to Edinburgh, where he captivated the city's literary society with his keen wit, rough-hewn charm, and controversial views on class and religion.

Scotland's Greatest Songwriter In Edinburgh, Burns began to compile several volumes of Scottish folk songs. Collecting, adapting, and writing songs engaged him for the rest of his life. In his later years, Burns finally married Jean Armour and began working as a tax collector while still maintaining a farm. The arduous farm work undermined Burns's already weak constitution. At age 37, Burns contracted rheumatic fever and died soon after.

DID YOU KNOW?

Robert Burns . . .

- composed "Auld Lang Syne" to an old Scottish melody.
- alienated many by supporting the French Revolution.

Author Online

Go to **thinkcentral.com**. KEYWORD: HML12-782

THINK central

TEXT ANALYSIS: DIALECT

Dialect is the distinct form of a language spoken in one geographic area or by a particular group. Writers use dialect for specific reasons, such as establishing setting or providing local flavor. In reaction to many in Scottish society and letters who were beginning to favor standard, or British, English, Burns chose to write in Scots, a northern dialect of English spoken primarily by Scottish peasants. The following lines in the Scots dialect contain a few words foreign to most readers' ears, yet you can still discern Burns's general meaning:

I doubt na, whyles, but thou may thieve;
What then? poor beastie, thou maun live!

Inspired by earlier Scottish poets, Burns found that using dialect enabled him to convey both the speech and the spirit of those who made up much of Scotland's working class. This dedication to natural speech is one reason why Burns inspired later romantic poets such as William Wordsworth.

READING STRATEGY: CLARIFY MEANING

When reading a poem written in dialect, it is important to **clarify meaning** as you read. The following strategies can help you understand difficult passages in Burns's poems:

- Some words are completely unique to a dialect; use the **side notes** to learn their definitions.

- Use **context clues** to help you understand what the poet is saying or describing.

- Burns uses apostrophes to indicate the rhythm of spoken Scots; **reading the poem aloud** can help you better understand what Burns means.

Apply these strategies as you read the dialect in Burns's poems. Use a chart like the one shown to try to **paraphrase,** or restate in your own words, any difficult passages you encounter.

"To a Mouse"	
Excerpt	Paraphrase
"Thou need na start awa sae hasty, / Wi' bickering brattle!"	You don't need to run away with such a hurried scamper!

 Complete the activities in your **Reader/Writer Notebook**.

When do LITTLE THINGS mean a lot?

Too often we are so caught up in the bustle of our lives that we lose sight of what's important. The sensational and extraordinary can always grab our attention, but what about the more mundane things that make up most of our lives? In the poems that follow, Burns conveys the valuable insights he gained from examining the commonplace.

QUICKWRITE Think of an instance when you gained a new perspective on something or someone you encounter every day. Why did this ordinary subject appear different to you? What did you think at the time? Write a paragraph or two in which you describe this experience.

To a Mouse *On Turning Her up in Her Nest with the Plough, November, 1785*

Robert Burns

Wee, sleeket, cowran, tim'rous beastie,
O, what panic's in thy breastie!
Thou need na start awa sae hasty,
    Wi' bickering brattle!
5 I wad be laith to rin an' chase thee,
    Wi' murd'ring pattle! **Ⓐ**

I'm truly sorry Man's dominion
Has broken Nature's social union,
An' justifies that ill opinion,
10   Which makes thee startle,
At me, thy poor, earth-born companion,
    An' fellow-mortal!

I doubt na, whyles, but thou may thieve;
What then? poor beastie, thou maun live!
15 A daimen-icker in a thrave
    'S a sma' request:
I'll get a blessin wi' the lave,
    An' never miss 't!

Thy wee-bit housie, too, in ruin!
20 It's silly wa's the win's are strewin!
An' naething, now, to big a new ane,
    O' foggage green!
An' bleak December's winds ensuin,
    Baith snell an' keen!

1 **sleeket:** sleek; **cowran:** cowering.

4 **bickering brattle:** hurried scamper.

5 **laith:** loath; reluctant.

6 **pattle:** paddle-shaped staff used to scrape a plow.

Ⓐ DIALECT
Reread lines 1–6. What does the dialect in this stanza help to characterize about the speaker?

13 **whyles:** sometimes.

14 **maun:** must.

15 **daimen-icker in a thrave:** random ear in a bundle of corn.

17 **lave:** rest.

20 **silly wa's:** flimsy walls; **win's:** winds.

21 **big:** build; **ane:** one.

22 **foggage:** moss or coarse grass.

24 **Baith:** both; **snell:** bitter.

25 Thou saw the fields laid bare an' waste,
   An' weary Winter comin fast,
   An' cozie here, beneath the blast,
     Thou thought to dwell,
   Till crash! the cruel coulter past
30   Out thro' thy cell.

   That wee-bit heap o' leaves an' stibble,
   Has cost thee monie a weary nibble!
   Now thou 's turn'd out, for a' thy trouble,
     But house or hald,
35 To thole the Winter's sleety dribble,
     An' cranreuch cauld!

   But Mousie, thou are no thy-lane,
   In proving foresight may be vain:
   The best laid schemes o' Mice an' Men,
40   Gang aft agley,
   An' lea'e us nought but grief an' pain,
     For promis'd joy!

   Still, thou art blest, compar'd wi' me!
   The present only toucheth thee:
45 But Och! I backward cast my e'e,
     On prospects drear!
   An' forward, tho' I canna see,
     I guess an' fear!

© 1968 by Oxford University Press

29 coulter (kōl'tər): plow blade.

31 stibble: stubble.
32 monie: many.

34 But: without; **hald:** hold; property held.
35 thole: endure.
36 cranreuch (krôn'rōōкн): frost.

37 no thy-lane: not alone.

40 Gang aft agley (gông ôft ə-glē'): often go awry.

45 e'e: eye.

Language Coach

Multiple Meanings The word *prospects* can mean (1) apparent chances for success (2) broad views, or (3) searches for mineral deposits. Which meaning best fits in line 46? Explain.

TO A LOUSE *On Seeing One*
on a Lady's Bonnet at Church

Robert Burns

Ha! whare ye gaun, ye crowlan ferlie!
Your impudence protects you sairly:
I canna say but ye strunt rarely,
    Owre gawze and lace;
5 Tho' faith, I fear ye dine but sparely,
    On sic a place.

Ye ugly, creepan, blastet wonner,
Detested, shunn'd, by saunt an' sinner,
How daur ye set your fit upon her,
10   Sae fine a Lady!
Gae somewhere else and seek your dinner,
    On some poor body.

Swith, in some beggar's haffet squattle;
There ye may creep, and sprawl, and sprattle,
15 Wi' ither kindred, jumping cattle,
    In shoals and nations;
Whare horn nor bane ne'er daur unsettle,
    Your thick plantations.

1 crowlan ferlie: crawling wonder.

2 sairly: sorely; greatly.

3 strunt: strut.

4 Owre: over.

6 sic: such.

7 blastet: blasted; darned; **wonner:** wonder.

9 fit: foot.

11 Gae: go.

13 Swith: swift; **haffet:** locks of hair; **squattle:** squat; settle.

14 sprattle: struggle.

15 cattle: vermin.

16 shoals: large groups; crowds.

17 bane: bone (used to make combs).

Now haud you there, ye're out o' sight,
20 Below the fatt'rels, snug and tight,
Na faith ye yet! ye'll no be right,
    Till ye've got on it,
The vera tapmost, towrin height
      O' Miss's bonnet.

25 My sooth! right bauld ye set your nose out,
As plump an' grey as onie grozet:
O for some rank, mercurial rozet,
    Or fell, red smeddum,
I'd gie you sic a hearty dose o't,
30   Wad dress your droddum!

I wad na been surpriz'd to spy
You on an auld wife's flainen toy,
Or aiblins some bit duddie boy,
    On 's wylecoat;
35 But Miss's fine Lunardi, fye!
    How daur ye do 't?

O Jenny dinna toss your head,
An' set your beauties a' abread!
Ye little ken what cursed speed
40   The blastie's makin!
Thae winks and finger-ends, I dread,
    Are notice takin!

O wad some Pow'r the giftie gie us
To see oursels as others see us!
45 It wad frae monie a blunder free us
    An' foolish notion:
What airs in dress an' gait wad lea'e us,
    And ev'n Devotion! **B**

© 1968 by Oxford University Press

19 haud: hold.

20 fatt'rels: folderols—ribbon ends used as hair ornaments.

21 Na faith ye yet!: Confound you! Darn you!

25 My sooth!: indeed; **bauld:** bold.

26 onie grozet: any gooseberry.

27 rank . . . rozet: strong-smelling rosin used to get rid of lice.

28 fell: sharp; **smeddum:** powder.

29 gie: give; **o't:** of it.

30 dress your droddum: clean your bottom.

32 flainen toy: flannel cap.

33 aiblins: perhaps; **duddie:** ragged.

34 wylecoat: undershirt.

35 Lunardi: stylish balloon-shaped bonnet named after 1780s balloonist Vincenzo Lunardi.

37 dinna: do not.

38 a' abread: all abroad; in circulation.

39 ken: know.

40 blastie's: creature's.

41 Thae: those.

45 frae: from; **monie:** many.

B CLARIFY MEANING
Reread lines 43–48 aloud. Use context clues and the side notes to **paraphrase** this stanza.

Comprehension

1. **Recall** Why does the speaker in "To a Mouse" apologize to the mouse?

2. **Summarize** What does the speaker in "To a Mouse" conclude in lines 43–48?

3. **Summarize** In lines 13–18 of "To a Louse," where does the speaker suggest the louse go?

4. **Clarify** Why is the speaker surprised to see a louse on the lady's bonnet?

Text Analysis

5. **Clarify Meaning** Review the passages you **paraphrased** as you read the poems. Which passages did you find especially challenging? Give reasons for your choices.

6. **Identify Theme** Reread lines 37–42 of "To a Mouse." What observation about life does Burns convey in this stanza?

7. **Interpret Satire** "To a Louse" is a **satire,** a literary work in which people's behaviors or society's institutions are ridiculed for the purpose of bringing about reform. What is Burns satirizing about Scottish society in this poem? Provide support from the poem for your answer.

8. **Compare Speakers** The speakers in both poems have very different attitudes toward the creatures they encounter. How would you characterize the speakers' attitudes in "To a Mouse" and "To a Louse"?

9. **Draw Conclusions** In many of his poems, including "To a Mouse" and "To a Louse," Burns makes use of commonplace subjects to express larger statements about life. In your opinion, why might he have chosen to use commonplace subjects in his poems?

10. **Analyze Dialect** The Scots dialect Burns uses can be difficult to read at times, but he chose to employ it for specific effect. In what way does Burns's use of dialect contribute to the poems' setting, theme, and tone?

Text Criticism

11. **Biographical Context** When Robert Burns became famous after publishing his first volume of poetry, he did not object to those who considered him a "Heaven-taught plowman" who wrote spontaneously about his feelings for his native land. Yet Burns was an ambitious, well-read poet with radical political views for his time. Why might Burns have encouraged the public to think of him as a simple farmer instead of a sophisticated poet?

> *When do* **LITTLE THINGS** *mean a lot?*
>
> It is easy to take unremarkable everyday objects and events for granted. What can you gain from appreciating them rather than overlooking them?

COMMON CORE

RL 2 Determine two or more themes or central ideas of a text and analyze their development over the course of the text. RL 4 Determine the meaning of words and phrases as they are used in the text, including figurative and connotative meanings. RL 6 Analyze a case in which grasping point of view requires distinguishing what is directly stated in a text from what is really meant. L 4a Use context as a clue to the meaning of a word or phrase.

The Lorelei
Poem by Heinrich Heine

COMMON CORE

RL 4 Analyze the impact of specific word choices on meaning and tone, including language that is fresh, engaging, or beautiful. **RL 5** Analyze how an author's choices concerning how to structure specific parts of a text contribute to its overall structure and meaning as well as its aesthetic impact.

Meet the Author

Heinrich Heine 1797–1856

Although Heinrich Heine (hīn′rĭкн hī′nə) was a controversial figure in his native Germany, he was celebrated as one of Europe's most renowned love poets. Like Blake, Heine wrote in a simple, musical style. However, Heine's skepticism and emphasis on suffering and loneliness link him to late romantic poets such as Byron.

Changes in Direction Born to a Jewish textile merchant, Heine grew up in modest circumstances in the city of Düsseldorf (then part of Prussia). When his father's business failed, Heine was sent to Hamburg, where a wealthy uncle tried, unsuccessfully, to make a businessman of him. Heine eventually earned a law degree but showed more interest in writing poetry. He reluctantly converted to Protestantism because government jobs were closed to Jews at the time. However, he was never offered any of the jobs he desired.

Love's Pain Heine established his international reputation as a poet with the publication of *The Book of Poems* (1827). Containing love songs, ballads, and sonnets, the volume explored, among other subjects, Heine's unrequited and unhappy love for his cousin Amalie. Several poems in the collection, including "The Lorelei," also grew out of his interest in German

folklore. According to legend, a maiden who drowned herself after a lover's betrayal sits upon the Lorelei rock high above the Rhine River, combing her hair in the moonlight and singing a haunting song that lures boatmen to their death.

Critic of Society Although best known for his lyric poetry, Heine also wrote essays and verse attacking social injustice and government corruption in Germany. Throughout his life, he searched for solutions to these evils, exploring ideas ranging from various forms of socialism to the communism espoused by Karl Marx, an acquaintance of his. None of these models totally satisfied Heine, however, since he believed they would not lead to a more joyful human society.

Heine moved to Paris in 1831 and devoted his creative energy to writing essays criticizing the policies of the French monarchy and the militant nationalism he saw developing in Germany. These essays infuriated the German people, who considered them unpatriotic and dangerous. In 1835, the German government banned Heine's work.

When he was 51, a serious illness confined Heine to what he called "his mattress grave." Despite tremendous pain and the slow loss of his vision, he continued to write until his death.

DID YOU KNOW?

Heinrich Heine . . .

- first achieved fame for a series of travel books.
- inspired thousands of musical compositions through his verse.
- had his work banned by the German government for over 100 years.

Author Online

THINK central

Go to **thinkcentral.com**. KEYWORD: HML12-790

● TEXT ANALYSIS: LYRIC POETRY

A **lyric poem** is a short poem in which a single speaker expresses personal thoughts and feelings. Most poems other than dramatic and narrative poems are lyric poems. The term comes from the word *lyre*, a stringed instrument that ancient Greek poets used to accompany their singing. Lyric poems can be in a variety of forms and can cover many subjects, from love and death to everyday experiences. They usually have the following characteristics:

- Although lyric poems are no longer sung, they often have a melodic rhythm.
- The poems may describe an incident, but the focus is on conveying emotions and thoughts rather than on telling a story.
- Lyric poems contain elements such as imagery and figurative language, which create a strong, unified impression.

Many of Heine's poems have a songlike quality that made it easy for composers to set them to music after his death. As you read "The Lorelei," notice its melodic rhythm and other lyric characteristics.

● READING STRATEGY: VISUALIZE

The process of forming a mental picture from a written description is called **visualizing.** When reading poetry, it is important to try to "see" what the poet is describing through imagery and figurative language. Because lyric poets often use imagery to convey ideas, visualizing can also help you understand the meaning of a poem.

While reading Heine's "The Lorelei," look for

- **images** that elicit mental pictures
- language that suggests **spatial relationships,** such as *above, behind, here,* and *there,* which can help you picture the scene and its unfolding action

 Complete the activities in your **Reader/Writer Notebook.**

What makes people RECKLESS?

Though we try to act rationally in most situations, we all fall prey sometimes to recklessness—whether it's doing something without thinking or consciously deciding to act against our better judgment. In "The Lorelei," you will encounter a man who is haunted by a tale of recklessness.

DISCUSS What circumstances or emotions make us act recklessly? Record your ideas in a word web, with the word *recklessness* in the center. Then, with a partner, discuss some of the reasons people act this way. Come up with some solutions for how people can avoid making a reckless decision.

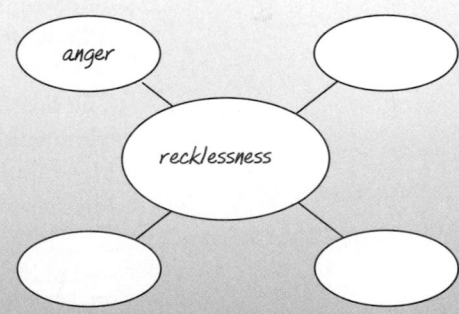

The Lorelei

Heinrich Heine

I cannot explain the sadness
That's fallen on my breast.
An old, old fable haunts me,
And will not let me rest. **A**

5 The air grows cool in the twilight,
And softly the Rhine flows on;
The peak of a mountain sparkles
Beneath the setting sun.

More lovely than a vision,
10 A girl sits high up there;
Her golden jewelry glistens,
She combs her golden hair. **B**

With a comb of gold she combs it,
And sings an evensong;
15 The wonderful melody reaches
A boat, as it sails along.

The boatman hears, with an anguish
More wild than was ever known;
He's blind to the rocks around him;
20 His eyes are for her alone.

—At last the waves devoured
The boat, and the boatman's cry;
And this she did with her singing,
The golden Lorelei.

Translated by Aaron Kramer

A **LYRIC POETRY**
What does the speaker convey about his thoughts and emotions in lines 1–4?

6 Rhine: a river that begins in Switzerland and flows through Germany and the Netherlands to the North Sea.

B **VISUALIZE**
Describe what you visualized as you read lines 9–12. Consider the **images** and **spatial relationship** Heine provides.

Language Coach

Connotations Look up *anguish* (line 17), *distress,* and *suffering* in a dictionary. Then place each synonym on a scale where 1 is "least intense" and 10 is "most intense." Explain your choices.

Analyze Visuals ▶

Which details in this painting suggest the otherworldly nature of the Lorelei?

Lorelei (1872), Ferdinand Marternsteig. St. Goarshausen, Germany. © SuperStock.

Comprehension

1. **Recall** What does the boatman encounter as he sails?

2. **Recall** What is the woman in the poem doing?

3. **Clarify** Why does the boatman crash into the rocks?

Text Analysis

4. **Make Inferences** Reread lines 1–4. Why might the speaker feel haunted by the legend of the Lorelei?

● 5. **Analyze Lyric Poetry** Review the description of lyric poetry on page 791. Then identify the characteristics of a lyric poem found in "The Lorelei."

● 6. **Visualize** Many of the images Heine uses elicit a visual picture when you read them. For the following examples from the poem, describe the mental picture you see when you read the lines:

   • "The peak of a mountain sparkles / Beneath the setting sun." (lines 7–8)
   • "With a comb of gold she combs it, / And sings an evensong;" (lines 13–14)
   • "He's blind to the rocks around him; / His eyes are for her alone." (lines 19–20)

7. **Make Judgments** What is more responsible for the boatman's death—the allure of the Lorelei's voice and beauty or the boatman's own recklessness? Explain your reasoning.

8. **Compare Texts** Compare Heine's "The Lorelei" with Blake's "The Tyger," noting similarities and differences you see in each of the following elements:

   • structure • imagery • mood

Text Criticism

9. **Critical Interpretations** Critic Lowell Bangerter wrote that Heine's "ability to convey, with penetrating exactitude, feelings, existential problems, and elements of the human condition ... enabled him to generate lyrics that belong more to the poetry of ideas than to the poetry of experience." Do you think this description applies to "The Lorelei"? Explain why or why not.

> *What makes people* **RECKLESS?**
>
> When people act without thinking, their impulsive decisions often have dire consequences. However, are there any times when recklessness might be necessary? Why might some people need to forgo thinking before they act?

COMMON CORE

RL 4 Analyze the impact of specific word choices on meaning and tone, including language that is fresh, engaging, or beautiful. **RL 5** Analyze how an author's choices concerning how to structure specific parts of a text contribute to its overall structure and meaning as well as its aesthetic impact.

Romantic Mavericks

Although they are often referred to as early romantics, William Blake and Robert Burns cannot be neatly classified with other romantic writers. It is true that like later romantics, they tended to emphasize emotion over reason and to feature both the everyday as well as the supernatural. But unlike the rich, majestic poems of the later romantics, Blake and Burns wrote gentle, rhyming verses that could almost masquerade as nursery rhymes.

However, these verses are not as simple as they seem. Hidden beneath the charming, playful images of lambs, children, and field mice lie startling truths and, sometimes, harsh commentary. Far from composers of light verse, Blake and Burns were serious, philosophical poets.

Writing to Evaluate

Reread the poems by Blake and Burns in this unit. Then, choosing the works of one of the poets, write about the contrast between the light tone and subject matter and the underlying truths conveyed. In your opinion, how does this contrast affect the impact? Cite specific examples from the text to support your views.

Consider

- what the poems seem to be about at first glance
- the underlying themes represented
- your own response to the poems after considering their deeper meanings

Extension Online

VIEWING & REPRESENTING
William Blake was a printmaker and poet; his technique of illuminated printing brought the two art forms together. Look at the illuminated print of "The Tyger," shown here and on page 775. In your opinion, how does the illustration emphasize or alter the poem's impact?

COMMON CORE

W 2 Write explanatory texts to convey complex ideas and information through the effective selection, organization, and analysis of content.

Romanticism

"There was a mighty ferment in the heads of statesmen and poets, kings, and people.... It was a time of promise, a renewal of the world," wrote essayist William Hazlitt in 1825 to describe the age of revolution that occurred at the turn of the 19th century. Born from this ferment was the literary movement known as romanticism.

Revolt Against Neoclassicism

COMMON CORE

Included in this workshop:
RL 5 Analyze how an author's choices concerning how to structure specific parts of a text contribute to its overall structure and meaning as well as its aesthetic impact. **RL 9** Demonstrate knowledge of eighteenth- and nineteenth-century foundational works of literature, including how two or more texts from the same period treat similar themes or topics.

In the British literary tradition, **romanticism** refers to a period dominated by William Wordsworth and four other poets: Samuel Taylor Coleridge, Lord Byron, Percy Bysshe Shelley, and John Keats. The movement in England is considered to have begun in 1798 with the publication of the poetry collection *Lyrical Ballads* by Wordsworth and Coleridge.

On the Minnow Stream, Dorking, Surrey, Charles Collins.

In his famous preface to *Lyrical Ballads,* Wordsworth declared the poems "experiments" in poetic language and subject matter. He deliberately chose language and subjects taken from common life instead of upper-class life. The second generation of romantic poets—Byron, Shelley, and Keats—added their unique voices and visions to Wordsworth's foundation, taking their poetry in slightly different directions. Despite their differences, the English romantics were united in rebellion against their Enlightenment forebears—John Dryden, Alexander Pope, and Samuel Johnson. In breaking from neoclassical conventions, the romantics expressed a new sensibility of freedom and self-expression. Where the neoclassical writers—also called the Augustans—admired and imitated classical forms, the romantics looked to nature for inspiration. Where the Augustans prized reason, the romantics celebrated strong emotions. Where the Augustans wrote witty satires ridiculing others, the romantics wrote serious lyric poems about their own experiences.

Romantic Poetry's Defining Features

Wordsworth essentially defined five features of English romanticism in his preface to *Lyrical Ballads.*

A New Concept in Poetry Wordsworth's emphasis on personal experience and the glorification of the individual are very different from earlier poets' emphasis on the greater world of human behavior. To some degree, all romantic poets wrote about the intricate workings of their own minds and emotions.

A New Spontaneity and Freedom Wordsworth described poetry as "the spontaneous overflow of powerful feelings." Critical of the artificiality they saw in much neoclassical literature, the romantics placed a high value on expressing strong emotion and the free play of imagination: "I fall upon the thorns of life! I bleed!" imparts Shelley in "Ode to the West Wind" (page 864).

Love of Nature Romantic poetry is often dubbed "nature poetry" because romantic poems often focus on aspects of the natural world. However, romantic poets did not simply describe natural settings and images; they used them as a catalyst to explore their own thoughts and feelings. For instance, "a beauteous evening" for Wordsworth is an occasion for spiritual contemplation.

The Importance of the Commonplace Wordsworth wanted to enlarge the province of poetry to include "incidents and situations from common life." Romantics often chose humble subjects, such as rustic life, and celebrated ordinary things, such as an early morning stroll or a field of daffodils.

> I wandered lonely as a cloud
> That floats on high o'er vales and hills,
> When all at once I saw a crowd,
> A host, of golden daffodils;
>
> **—William Wordsworth, "I Wandered Lonely as a Cloud"**

Fascination with the Supernatural and the Exotic While Wordsworth concentrated mostly on ordinary life, Coleridge introduced mystery and magic into English romantic poetry. From the wonderfully strange journey in "The Rime of the Ancient Mariner" (page 814) to the "stately pleasure dome" of "Kubla Khan" (page 841), Coleridge opened up to poetry the realm of the supernatural and the exotic.

The following chart lists the main differences between neoclassical and romantic writers.

Close Read

Which characteristics of romantic poetry does this passage contain? Explain.

NEOCLASSICAL WRITERS	ROMANTIC WRITERS
stressed reason and common sense	stressed emotion and imagination
wrote about objective issues that concerned society as a whole	wrote about subjective experiences of the individual
respected human institutions of church and state	exalted nature in all its creative and destructive forces
exercised controlled wit and urbanity	celebrated intense passion and vision
maintained traditional standards and believed in order	believed in experimentation and spontaneity of thought

Selected Poetry
by William Wordsworth

VIDEO TRAILER THINK central KEYWORD: HML12-798A

Meet the Author

DID YOU KNOW?

William Wordsworth . . .

- at first supported, but later denounced, the French Revolution.
- refused to publish his autobiographical masterpiece, *The Prelude,* during his lifetime.
- lost two of his five children to early deaths.

(background) Dove Cottage, Wordsworth's Lake District home

William Wordsworth 1770–1850

William Wordsworth, along with his friend Samuel Taylor Coleridge, helped launch the English romantic movement in literature. Rebelling against the formal diction and lofty subject matter favored by poets of the day, Wordsworth used simple language to celebrate subjects drawn mostly from nature and everyday life.

Childhood Turmoil As a child, Wordsworth spent many happy hours exploring the countryside in northwestern England's Lake District. This idyllic period lasted until he was seven, when his mother's death led to the breakup of the Wordsworth household. Unable to raise five children on his own, John Wordsworth sent young William away to school at Hawkshead, where he formed a passionate attachment to the surrounding countryside.

Love in a Time of War A walking tour through revolutionary France in the summer of 1790 was the high point of Wordsworth's college years. Excited by the changes he saw, Wordsworth returned to France in 1791 and soon fell in love with a young woman, Annette Vallon. Lacking money, Wordsworth returned to England in 1792. Almost immediately, war broke out between France and England, preventing Wordsworth from seeing Annette and the child she had recently borne

him. Distraught over his inability to help them and by the growing violence in France, Wordsworth fell into a deep depression.

Creative Partnership Wordsworth's bleak mood subsided in 1795 when he was reunited with his beloved sister Dorothy, from whom he had been separated since childhood. Resolving not to be parted again, he and Dorothy moved to Racedown, Dorset, where they met and grew close to Coleridge. Speaking later of this friendship, Wordsworth would say, "We were three persons with one soul." Working together, Wordsworth and Coleridge produced *Lyrical Ballads* (1798), the book that ushered in the English romantic movement.

Britain's Poet Laureate In 1799, Wordsworth and his sister resettled in the Lake District, with Coleridge residing nearby. Three years later, Wordsworth married a childhood friend, Mary Hutchinson. Over the next two decades, he struggled to find readers and critical acceptance for his work. In the 1820s, his reputation gradually improved, and by the 1830s, he was hugely popular. In 1843, his immense achievement as a poet was recognized with the poet laureateship.

Author Online
Go to thinkcentral.com. KEYWORD: HML12-798B

THINK central

TEXT ANALYSIS: ROMANTIC POETRY

In England, **romanticism** was a literary and artistic movement originating in the late 18th century and lasting until the early decades of the 19th century. Unlike their neoclassical predecessors, the romantic poets stressed the importance of the individual's subjective experiences rather than issues that concerned society as a whole. Their philosophy valued emotion, spontaneity, and imagination over reason and orderliness. Most significantly, they rejected the world of industry and science, turning instead to nature as a source of inspiration and solace. Other defining features of romantic poetry are as follows:

- an emphasis on the commonplace
- language resembling natural speech
- elements of the mysterious, exotic, and supernatural

As you read Wordsworth's innovative works, look for details that are characteristic of romantic poetry.

READING SKILL: ANALYZE STYLISTIC ELEMENTS

Wordsworth's poems contain distinctive **stylistic elements** such as the following:

- long, free-flowing sentences, often with phrases that interrupt main ideas
- **inverted syntax,** where the expected order of words is reversed
- unusual punctuation, such as dashes combined with other punctuation or exclamation points appearing within a sentence rather than at the end, and unusual capitalization

As you read each poem, be aware of these stylistic elements and note how they affect your impression of the speaker's thoughts.

 Complete the activities in your **Reader/Writer Notebook**.

Where do we find PEACE?

When filled with the stresses and strains of everyday life, people sometimes visit a particular place to regain a sense of peace. A person may, for example, spend time in a church or temple, while others may seek out the comfort of a grandparent's home. Still other individuals, like Wordsworth, find peace in nature.

DISCUSS Working with two or three classmates, create a list of the places you regularly turn to when you seek relief from life's problems. Discuss each place, then circle the one that seems the most satisfying. Compare the results of your discussion with those of other groups.

Lines Composed a Few Miles Above
Tintern Abbey

William Wordsworth

> **BACKGROUND** In many of his poems, Wordsworth describes a specific setting and conveys his thoughts and feelings about it. In "Tintern Abbey," he captures an outdoor scene in the Wye River valley, near the ruins of a Gothic abbey. "Composed upon Westminster Bridge" expresses his feelings on seeing the city of London early one morning from a bridge spanning the river Thames. In "I Wandered Lonely as a Cloud," Wordsworth describes the scenery of England's picturesque Lake District, near his home in Grasmere.

    Five years have passed; five summers, with the length
Of five long winters! and again I hear
These waters, rolling from their mountain-springs
With a soft inland murmur. Once again
5 Do I behold these steep and lofty cliffs,
That on a wild secluded scene impress
Thoughts of more deep seclusion; and connect
The landscape with the quiet of the sky.
The day is come when I again repose
10 Here, under this dark sycamore, and view
These plots of cottage ground, these orchard tufts,
Which at this season, with their unripe fruits,
Are clad in one green hue, and lose themselves
'Mid groves and copses. Once again I see
15 These hedgerows, hardly hedgerows, little lines
Of sportive wood run wild; these pastoral farms,
Green to the very door; and wreaths of smoke
Sent up, in silence, from among the trees!
With some uncertain notice, as might seem
20 Of vagrant dwellers in the houseless woods,
Or of some Hermit's cave, where by his fire
The Hermit sits alone. Ⓐ

Analyze Visuals ▶
What elements in this painting help give it a sense of grandeur?

9 repose: lie at rest.

14 copses (kŏp'sĭz): thickets of small trees.

16 pastoral (păs'tər-əl): rural and serene.

20 vagrant: wandering.

Ⓐ **POETRY**
What details in lines 14–22 suggest that Wordsworth preferred to celebrate the individual rather than society in his work?

Inside of Tintern Abbey, Monmouthshire (1794), Joseph Mallord William Turner. Pencil and water color on paper, 32.1 cm × 25.1 cm. © British Museum, London/Bridgeman Art Library.

These beauteous forms,
Through a long absence, have not been to me
As is a landscape to a blind man's eye;
25 But oft, in lonely rooms, and 'mid the din
Of towns and cities, I have owed to them,
In hours of weariness, sensations sweet,
Felt in the blood, and felt along the heart;
And passing even into my purer mind,
30 With tranquil restoration—feelings too
Of unremembered pleasure; such, perhaps,
As have no slight or trivial influence
On that best portion of a good man's life,
His little, nameless, unremembered, acts
35 Of kindness and of love. Nor less, I trust,
To them I may have owed another gift,
Of aspect more sublime; that blessed mood,
In which the burthen of the mystery,
In which the heavy and the weary weight
40 Of all this unintelligible world,
Is lightened—that serene and blessed mood,
In which the affections gently lead us on—
Until, the breath of this corporeal frame
And even the motion of our human blood
45 Almost suspended, we are laid asleep
In body, and become a living soul;
While with an eye made quiet by the power
Of harmony, and the deep power of joy,
We see into the life of things. **B**

If this
50 Be but a vain belief, yet, oh! how oft—
In darkness and amid the many shapes
Of joyless daylight; when the fretful stir
Unprofitable, and the fever of the world,
Have hung upon the beatings of my heart—
55 How oft, in spirit, have I turned to thee,
O sylvan Wye! thou wanderer through the woods,
How often has my spirit turned to thee! **C**

And now, with gleams of half-extinguished thought
With many recognitions dim and faint,
60 And somewhat of a sad perplexity,

38 burthen: burden.

43 corporeal (kôr-pôr′ē-əl): bodily.

B ROMANTIC POETRY
Reread lines 22–49. When he was living in towns and cities, in what ways was the speaker affected by his past experiences in the countryside near Tintern Abbey?

56 sylvan: located in a wood or forest; **Wye:** a river near Tintern Abbey.

C ROMANTIC POETRY
What feelings does the speaker express in lines 49–57 about his everyday life? Cite details.

The picture of the mind revives again;
While here I stand, not only with the sense
Of present pleasure, but with pleasing thoughts
That in this moment there is life and food
65 For future years. And so I dare to hope,
Though changed, no doubt, from what I was when first
I came among these hills; when like a roe
I bounded o'er the mountains, by the sides
Of the deep rivers, and the lonely streams,
70 Wherever nature led—more like a man
Flying from something that he dreads than one
Who sought the thing he loved. For nature then
(The coarser pleasures of my boyish days,
And their glad animal movements all gone by)
75 To me was all in all.—I cannot paint **D**
What then I was. The sounding cataract
Haunted me like a passion; the tall rock,
The mountain, and the deep and gloomy wood,
Their colors and their forms, were then to me
80 An appetite; a feeling and a love,
That had no need of a remoter charm,
By thought supplied, nor any interest
Unborrowed from the eye.—That time is past,
And all its aching joys are now no more,
85 And all its dizzy raptures. Not for this
Faint I, nor mourn nor murmur; other gifts
Have followed; for such loss, I would believe,
Abundant recompense. For I have learned
To look on nature, not as in the hour
90 Of thoughtless youth; but hearing oftentimes
The still, sad music of humanity,
Nor harsh nor grating, though of ample power
To chasten and subdue. And I have felt
A presence that disturbs me with the joy
95 Of elevated thoughts; a sense sublime
Of something far more deeply interfused,
Whose dwelling is the light of setting suns,
And the round ocean and the living air,
And the blue sky, and in the mind of man:
100 A motion and a spirit, that impels
All thinking things, all objects of all thought,
And rolls through all things. Therefore am I still
A lover of the meadows and the woods,

67 roe: deer.

D STYLISTIC ELEMENTS
Reread lines 72–75. Identify
the subject and the verb of
this sentence. What phrases
interrupt the main idea?
76 cataract (kăt'ə-răkt'): waterfall.

86 Faint I: I lose heart.

88 recompense (rĕk'əm-pĕns'):
compensation.

93 chasten (chā'sən): scold; make
modest.

Language Coach

Etymology A word's etymology
is its history. The word *impels*
(line 100) comes from the Latin
prefix *in-* ("on") and the root
pellere ("to push"). What do
you think *impels* means? What
other words contain this root?

Tintern Abbey (1800s), Frederick Waters Watts. Private collection. © Bridgeman Art Library.

And mountains; and of all that we behold
105 From this green earth; of all the mighty world
Of eye, and ear—both what they half create,
And what perceive; well pleased to recognize
In nature and the language of the sense
The anchor of my purest thoughts, the nurse,
110 The guide, the guardian of my heart, and soul
Of all my moral being.

                 Nor perchance,
If I were not thus taught, should I the more
Suffer my genial spirits to decay:
For thou art with me here upon the banks
115 Of this fair river; thou my dearest Friend,
My dear, dear Friend; and in thy voice I catch
The language of my former heart, and read
My former pleasures in the shooting lights
Of thy wild eyes. Oh! yet a little while
120 May I behold in thee what I was once,w
My dear, dear Sister! and this prayer I make,
Knowing that Nature never did betray **E**
The heart that loved her; 'tis her privilege,
Through all the years of this our life, to lead
125 From joy to joy: for she can so inform
The mind that is within us, so impress
With quietness and beauty, and so feed
With lofty thoughts, that neither evil tongues,

111 perchance: by chance; perhaps.

113 genial (jēn′yəl): relating to genius; creative.

115 thou my dearest Friend: Wordsworth's sister, Dorothy.

E STYLISTIC ELEMENTS
Wordsworth uses unusual capitalization and punctuation in his poems, employing typographic elements of text that draw his reader's attention to certain words or ideas. Why does he capitalize *Sister* in line 121 and *Nature* in line 122? Why does he include an exclamation point in line 119?

Rash judgments, nor the sneers of selfish men,
130 Nor greetings where no kindness is, nor all
The dreary intercourse of daily life,
Shall e'er prevail against us, or disturb
Our cheerful faith, that all which we behold
Is full of blessings. Therefore let the moon **F**
135 Shine on thee in thy solitary walk;
And let the misty mountain winds be free
To blow against thee: and, in after years,
When these wild ecstasies shall be matured
Into a sober pleasure; when thy mind
140 Shall be a mansion for all lovely forms,
Thy memory be as a dwelling place
For all sweet sounds and harmonies; oh! then,
If solitude, or fear, or pain, or grief
Should be thy portion, with what healing thoughts
145 Of tender joy wilt thou remember me,
And these my exhortations! Nor, perchance—
If I should be where I no more can hear
Thy voice, nor catch from thy wild eyes these gleams
Of past existence—wilt thou then forget
150 That on the banks of this delightful stream
We stood together; and that I, so long
A worshiper of Nature, hither came
Unwearied in that service; rather say
With warmer love—oh! with far deeper zeal
155 Of holier love. Nor wilt thou then forget,
That after many wanderings, many years
Of absence, these steep woods and lofty cliffs,
And this green pastoral landscape, were to me
More dear, both for themselves and for thy sake!

F STYLISTIC ELEMENTS
Paraphrase lines 119–134, breaking the information into two or more sentences. What does the speaker's "prayer" or hope for his sister reveal about him?

146 exhortations: words of encouraging advice.

149 past existence: the speaker's own past experience five years before (see lines 116–119).

Text Analysis

1. **Make Inferences** Compare the speaker's youthful experiences of the natural world with his present experiences. In what ways has his understanding of nature changed?

2. **Draw Conclusions** Describe the speaker's attitude in each of the following passages. Do you think that he regrets his loss of youth? Explain your response.

   • "The sounding cataract . . . dizzy raptures."
     (lines 76–85)

   • "Nor perchance. . . . Of thy wild eyes." (lines 111–119)

Composed upon Westminster Bridge, September 3, 1802

William Wordsworth

Earth has not anything to show more fair:
Dull would he be of soul who could pass by
A sight so touching in its majesty;  ⓖ
This City now doth, like a garment, wear
5 The beauty of the morning; silent, bare,
Ships, towers, domes, theaters, and temples lie
Open unto the fields, and to the sky;
All bright and glittering in the smokeless air.
Never did sun more beautifully steep
10 In his first splendor, valley, rock, or hill;
Ne'er saw I, never felt, a calm so deep!
The river glideth at his own sweet will:
Dear God! the very houses seem asleep;
And all that mighty heart is lying still!

ⓖ **STYLISTIC ELEMENTS**
Rewrite lines 1–3, reordering the **syntax.** What does this passage exaggerate?

9 steep: soak; saturate.

12 the river: the Thames (tĕmz)—the principal river in London.

13 houses: possibly a pun on the Houses of Parliament, near Westminster Bridge.

Text Analysis

1. **Examine Personification** Find three examples of personification, or figures of speech in which human qualities are attributed to an object, animal, or idea. In what ways do these examples enhance the description of the scene?

2. **Analyze Tone** What is Wordsworth's tone, or attitude, toward the scene? Cite specific words and phrases to support your response.

The World
Is Too Much with Us

William Wordsworth

The world is too much with us; late and soon,
Getting and spending, we lay waste our powers;
Little we see in Nature that is ours;
We have given our hearts away, a sordid boon!
5 This Sea that bares her bosom to the moon,
The winds that will be howling at all hours,
And are up-gathered now like sleeping flowers,
For this, for everything, we are out of tune;
It moves us not.—Great God! I'd rather be
10 A Pagan suckled in a creed outworn;
So might I, standing on this pleasant lea,
Have glimpses that would make me less forlorn;
Have sight of Proteus rising from the sea;
Or hear old Triton blow his wreathèd horn.

4 sordid boon: tarnished or selfish gift.

10 Pagan (pā′gən): someone who is not Christian, Jewish, or Muslim; **suckled in a creed outworn:** raised in an outdated faith or belief system.

11 lea: meadow.

13–14 Proteus (prō′tē-əs) **. . . Triton** (trīt′n): sea gods of Greek mythology.

Text Analysis

1. **Clarify Ideas** Reread lines 1–4. What do you think the speaker means by the phrase "The world is too much with us"?

2. **Make Inferences** Why would the speaker rather be a "Pagan" (line 10) than live in his present state? Support your response with details from the poem.

I Wandered
Lonely As a Cloud

William Wordsworth

Butterfly on Daffodils, Karen Armitage. Watercolor.
Private collection. © Bridgeman Art Library.

I wandered lonely as a cloud
That floats on high o'er vales and hills,
When all at once I saw a crowd,
A host, of golden daffodils;
5 Beside the lake, beneath the trees,
Fluttering and dancing in the breeze.

Continuous as the stars that shine
And twinkle on the milky way,
They stretched in never-ending line
10 Along the margin of a bay:
Ten thousand saw I at a glance,
Tossing their heads in sprightly dance.

The waves beside them danced; but they
Outdid the sparkling waves in glee;
15 A poet could not but be gay,
In such a jocund company;
I gazed—and gazed—but little thought
What wealth the show to me had brought:

For oft, when on my couch I lie
20 In vacant or in pensive mood,
They flash upon that inward eye
Which is the bliss of solitude;
And then my heart with pleasure fills,
And dances with the daffodils. **H**

2 vales: valleys.

COMMON CORE L 4b

Language Coach

Roots and Affixes The suffix *-ly* often signals an adverb, which modifies a verb, adjective, or other adverb; *-ly* can also form an adjective, which modifies a noun. Which type of word is *sprightly* (line 12)? How can you tell? What does *sprightly* mean?

16 jocund (jŏk'ənd): merry.

H ROMANTIC POETRY
According to lines 19–24, what has the speaker been able to accomplish by using his memory and imagination?

JOURNAL Many of Wordsworth's poems were inspired by his frequent walks with his sister Dorothy in the English countryside. This excerpt from Dorothy's journal records the same scene that inspired Wordworth's "I Wandered Lonely As a Cloud."

from the
Grasmere Journals
Dorothy Wordsworth

Apr. 15.

It was a threatening misty morning—but mild. We [Dorothy and William] set off after dinner from Eusemere.[1] Mrs. Clarkson went a short way with us but turned back. The wind was furious and we thought we must have returned. We first rested in the large Boat-house, then under a furze Bush opposite Mr. Clarkson's. Saw the plough going in the field. The wind seized our breath the Lake was rough. There was a Boat by itself floating in the middle of the Bay below Water Millock. We rested again in the Water Millock Lane. The hawthorns are black and green, the birches here and there greenish but there is yet more of purple to be seen on the Twigs. We got over into a field to avoid some cows—people working, a few primroses by the roadside, wood-sorrel flower, the anemone, scentless violets, strawberries, and that starry yellow flower which Mrs. C. calls pile wort. When we were in the woods beyond Gowbarrow park we saw a few daffodils close to the water side. We fancied that the lake had floated the seeds ashore and that the little colony had so sprung up. But as we went along there were more and yet more and at last under the boughs of the trees, we saw that there was a long belt of them along the shore, about the breadth of a country turnpike road.[2] I never saw daffodils so beautiful they grew among the mossy stones about and about them, some rested their heads upon these stones as on a pillow for weariness and the rest tossed and reeled and danced and seemed as if they verily laughed at the wind that blew upon them over the lake, they looked so gay ever glancing ever changing. This wind blew directly over the lake to them. There was here and there a little knot and a few stragglers a few yards higher up but they were so few as not to disturb the simplicity and unity and life of that one busy highway. We rested again and again. The Bays were stormy, and we heard the waves at different distances and in the middle of the water like the sea.

---

1. **Eusemere:** the home of Thomas and Catherine Clarkson, friends living near the Wordsworths on the banks of Lake Ullswater in the Lake District.

2. **breadth . . . road:** width of one of the narrow, centuries-old English roads that pedestrians once had to pay tolls to use.

Comprehension

1. **Clarify** The last poem begins: "I wandered lonely as a cloud / That floats on high o'er vales and hills." What is the meaning of this statement?

2. **Summarize** Reread lines 3–12 of the poem. In your own words, describe the scene the speaker encounters.

3. **Clarify** In line 21, what does the phrase "flash upon that inward eye" mean?

Text Analysis

4. **Make Inferences About Setting** In "Tintern Abbey," why do you think the speaker says so little about the ruined abbey named in the poem's title?

5. **Analyze Stylistic Elements** In his Preface to *Lyrical Ballads*, Wordsworth defines poetry as "the spontaneous overflow of powerful feelings." Review the list of Wordsworth's stylistic elements on page 799. How do the stylistic elements help him achieve this state in "Tintern Abbey"?

6. **Examine Romantic Poetry** Select one of the four poems in the lesson. For each convention of romantic poetry listed on page 799, provide an example from one of Wordsworth's poems. What overall effect do these conventions help create?

7. **Draw Conclusions** What connection does Wordsworth make between the speakers' memories of the past and their ability to experience peace in the present? Cite evidence from all four poems to support your response.

8. **Evaluate Sonnets** Both "Composed upon Westminster Bridge" and "The World Is Too Much with Us" are Petrarchan sonnets. For each poem, identify the speaker's situation or problem in the octave and his comments in the sestet. Which sonnet provides a more satisfying resolution?

9. **Compare Texts** Review "I Wandered Lonely As a Cloud" and Dorothy Wordsworth's journal entry on page 809. How does Dorothy's response to the daffodils compare with her brother's? Explain any similarities in the images and feelings expressed.

Text Criticism

10. **Critical Interpretations** Some critics have argued that Wordsworth presents an idealistic, and therefore unrealistic, portrait of childhood. Based on "Tintern Abbey," do you agree with this argument? Support your opinion with details from the poem.

Where do we find PEACE?

Why do we associate peace with the natural world? Are there times when nature is not serene or tranquil? Explain your response.

COMMON CORE

RL 5 Analyze how an author's choices concerning how to structure specific parts of a text contribute to its overall structure and meaning. **RL 9** Demonstrate knowledge of eighteenth- and nineteenth-century foundational works of literature. **L 3a** Apply an understanding of syntax to the study of complex texts when reading.

Language

COMMON CORE

L 2 Demonstrate command of the conventions of standard English punctuation when writing. **W 4** Produce clear and coherent writing in which the style is appropriate to task, purpose, and audience.

◆ **GRAMMAR AND STYLE: Add Emphasis**

One of the many delights of Wordsworth's style is his use of **repetition** and **exclamation points** to emphasize different thoughts and emotions. In "Tintern Abbey," for instance, he repeats phrases, such as "lofty cliffs" and "blessed mood," to underscore the feelings of joy that nature arouses in him. Notice how, in the excerpt below, Wordsworth repeats the adjective "dear" and uses exclamation points to express his affection for his sister Dorothy.

> *My dear, dear Friend; and in thy voice I catch*
> *The language of my former heart, and read*
> *My former pleasures in the shooting lights*
> *Of thy wild eyes. Oh! yet a little while*
> *May I behold in thee what I was once,*
> *My dear, dear Sister! . . .* (lines 116–121)

PRACTICE Write your own sentences about a topic you feel strongly about, imitating Wordsworth's use of repetition and exclamation points to create emphasis.

EXAMPLE

Five years have passed; five summers, with the length / Of five long winters!

One week has passed; seven slow days with seven slow nights! So many hours of waiting in the hospital to see if his condition had improved.

---

1. These hedgerows, hardly hedgerows, little lines / Of sportive wood run wild;

2. In hours of weariness, sensations sweet, / Felt in the blood, and felt along the heart;

3. How oft, in spirit, have I turned to thee, / O sylvan Wye! thou wanderer through the woods, / How often has my spirit turned to thee!

READING-WRITING CONNECTION

YOUR
TURN

Expand your understanding of imagery by responding to this prompt. Then, use the **revising tips** to improve your essay.

WRITING PROMPT

ANALYZE AUTHOR'S STYLE Wordsworth is widely praised for his use of **imagery,** or details that appeal to the senses. Identify several examples of visual and auditory imagery in "Lines Composed a Few Miles Above Tintern Abbey." Then write a **three-paragraph essay** in which you explain how this imagery enriches the poem.

REVISING TIPS

- Discuss what the poem would lose if the imagery were removed from it.

- Include direct quotations from the poem to show how imagery enriches its themes.

Interactive Revision

THINK central

Go to **thinkcentral.com.**
KEYWORD: HML12-811

The Rime of the Ancient Mariner
Poem by Samuel Taylor Coleridge

VIDEO TRAILER THINK central KEYWORD: HML12-812A

COMMON CORE

RL 3 Analyze the impact of the author's choices regarding how to develop and relate elements of a story. **RL 5** Analyze how an author's choices concerning how to structure specific parts of a text contribute to its overall structure and meaning as well as its aesthetic impact. **L 4** Determine or clarify the meaning of multiple-meaning words and phrases, choosing flexibly from a range of strategies.

DID YOU KNOW?

Samuel Taylor Coleridge . . .

- developed a fascination with the supernatural at age five.
- was known as a brilliant and captivating conversationalist.
- was the most influential literary critic of his day.
- liked to write poetry while walking.

Meet the Author

Samuel Taylor Coleridge 1772–1834

Samuel Taylor Coleridge is famous for composing "Kubla Khan" and "The Rime of the Ancient Mariner," considered two of the greatest English poems. As a critic and philosopher, he may have done more than any other writer to spread the ideas of the English romantic movement.

Precocious Reader The youngest of ten children, Coleridge grew up feeling rejected by his distant mother and bullied by his older brother Frank. These early experiences gave rise to feelings of insecurity and loneliness that plagued Coleridge throughout life. Despite his self-doubt, Coleridge was an exceptional student who impressed classmates with his eloquence, his knowledge of classical languages, and his flair for writing poetry.

Restless Youth At Cambridge University, Coleridge continued to read widely and hone his craft. Troubled by debt, though, he left Cambridge in 1793 and enlisted in the 15th Dragoons, a British army regiment, under the alias Silas Tomkyn Comberbache. After being rescued by his brothers, Coleridge returned to Cambridge, but he left again, in 1794, without having earned a degree. That year, Coleridge met the author Robert Southey, and together they dreamed about establishing a utopian community in the Pennsylvania wilderness of America. Southey, however, backed out of the project, and their dream was never realized.

Dream Poem In 1795, Coleridge developed a close friendship with the poet William Wordsworth. Inspired by the encouragement and intellectual stimulation he received from Wordsworth, Coleridge entered his most creative period. Over the next few years, he produced a series of extraordinary poems, four of which appeared along with poems by Wordsworth in *Lyrical Ballads* (1798). Coleridge said that when they had planned this landmark collection, "it was agreed that my endeavors should be directed to persons and characters supernatural, or at least romantic. . . ."

Lyrical Ballads opens with "The Rime of the Ancient Mariner." Coleridge got the idea for the poem from a friend who had dreamed about a skeleton ship. Before composing it, Coleridge discussed the poem extensively with Wordsworth, who contributed several plot ideas and even a few lines of verse.

Author Online

Go to **thinkcentral.com**. KEYWORD: HML12-812B

POETIC FORM: LITERARY BALLAD

"The Rime of the Ancient Mariner" is a celebrated **literary ballad,** or narrative poem written in deliberate imitation of the traditional **folk ballad** (see page 217). Like older ballads, Coleridge's masterpiece features sensational subject matter—the perilous journey of an old sailor. It also contains other conventional elements: dialogue, repetition of words and phrases, and strong patterns of rhyme and rhythm. However, there are aspects of the poem that reflect Coleridge's own romantic writing style: his emphasis on the supernatural, his sophisticated use of sound devices, and his use of archaic language. For example, notice his description of a mysterious ghost ship:

A speck, a mist, a shape, I wist!
And still it neared and neared:
As if it dodged a water-sprite,
It plunged, and tacked and veered.

As you read "The Rime of the Ancient Mariner," observe how Coleridge reworks the traditional ballad form and creates a poem of rare beauty and complexity.

READING STRATEGY: READING NARRATIVE POETRY

Like all ballads, "The Rime of the Ancient Mariner" is a **narrative poem**—a poem that tells a story. It has many of the basic elements of a prose story: setting, characters, point of view, plot, conflict, and theme. As you read the poem, use a chart like the one shown to take notes about each of these elements. Focus on the main story, not on the frame story. Additionally, use the red marginal notes, which were written by Coleridge, to help you clarify plot developments.

"The Rime of the Ancient Mariner"
Setting (Time/Place):
Characters:
Point of View:
Plot and Major Conflict:
Theme:

 Complete the activities in your **Reader/Writer Notebook**.

How can GUILT enslave us?

The famous expression "like an albatross around my neck" stems from Coleridge's "The Rime of the Ancient Mariner." It is often used to describe feelings of guilt that weigh heavily on a person. Have you ever felt burdened by guilt?

QUICKWRITE Think about a time when you felt ashamed about something you had done. For example, maybe you lost your brother's favorite CD or forgot your best friend's birthday. How did guilt affect you? Write a paragraph to describe the situation.

❧ THE RIME OF THE ❧
Ancient Mariner
Samuel Taylor Coleridge

Argument

How a Ship, having first sailed to the Equator, was driven by storms to the cold Country towards the South Pole; how the Ancient Mariner cruelly and in contempt of the laws of hospitality killed a Seabird and how he was followed by many strange Judgments; and in what manner he came back to his own Country.

PART I

It is an ancient Mariner,
And he stoppeth one of three.
"By thy long grey beard and glittering eye,
Now wherefore stopp'st thou me?

5 The Bridegroom's doors are opened wide,
And I am next of kin;
The guests are met, the feast is set:
May'st hear the merry din." **A**

He holds him with his skinny hand,
10 "There was a ship," quoth he.
"Hold off! unhand me, grey-beard loon!"
Eftsoons his hand dropped he.

He holds him with his glittering eye—
The Wedding-Guest stood still,
15 And listens like a three years' child:
The Mariner hath his will.

The Wedding-Guest sat on a stone:
He cannot choose but hear;
And thus spake on that ancient man,
20 The bright-eyed Mariner.

An ancient Mariner meeteth three Gallants bidden to a wedding feast, and detaineth one.

4 wherefore: why.

A **LITERARY BALLAD**
Based on lines 5–8, identify the length and rhyme scheme of a traditional ballad stanza.

12 eftsoons: quickly.

The Wedding-Guest is spellbound by the eye of the old seafaring man, and constrained to hear his tale.

Analyze Visuals ▶
Describe the mood conveyed by this engraving. What details contribute to this mood?

Engravings by Gustave F. Doré.

"The ship was cheered, the harbor cleared,
Merrily did we drop
Below the kirk, below the hill,
Below the lighthouse top.

25 The Sun came up upon the left,
Out of the sea came he!
And he shone bright, and on the right
Went down into the sea.

Higher and higher every day,
30 Till over the mast at noon—"
The Wedding-Guest here beat his breast,
For he heard the loud bassoon.

The bride hath paced into the hall,
Red as a rose is she;
35 Nodding their heads before her goes
The merry minstrelsy.

The Wedding-Guest he beat his breast,
Yet he cannot choose but hear;
And thus spake on that ancient man,
40 The bright-eyed Mariner.

"And now the Storm-blast came, and he
Was tyrannous and strong:
He struck with his o'ertaking wings,
And chased us south along.

45 With sloping masts and dipping prow,
As who pursued with yell and blow
Still treads the shadow of his foe,
And forward bends his head,
The ship drove fast, loud roared the blast,
50 And southward aye we fled. **B**

And now there came both mist and snow,
And it grew wondrous cold:
And ice, mast-high, came floating by,
As green as emerald.

55 And through the drifts the snowy clifts
Did send a dismal sheen:
Nor shapes of men nor beasts we ken—
The ice was all between.

23 kirk: church.

The Mariner tells how the ship sailed southward with a good wind and fair weather, till it reached the Line.

30 over . . . noon: The ship has reached the equator, or "Line."

The Wedding-Guest heareth the bridal music; but the Mariner continueth his tale.

36 minstrelsy: group of musicians.

The ship driven by a storm toward the South Pole.

B NARRATIVE POETRY
Compare the sailing conditions described in lines 21–28 and 41–50. In what way does the poem's **setting** change?

The land of ice, and of fearful sounds where no living thing was to be seen.

55 clifts: cliffs.

57 ken: perceive.

The ice was here, the ice was there,
60 The ice was all around:
It cracked and growled, and roared and howled,
Like noises in a swound!

At length did cross an Albatross,
Thorough the fog it came;
65 As if it had been a Christian soul,
We hailed it in God's name.

It ate the food it ne'er had eat,
And round and round it flew.
The ice did split with a thunder-fit;
70 The helmsman steered us through!

And a good south wind sprung up behind;
The Albatross did follow,
And every day, for food or play,
Came to the mariners' hollo!

75 In mist or cloud, on mast or shroud,
It perched for vespers nine;
Whiles all the night, through fog-smoke white,
Glimmered the white moonshine."

62 swound: swoon; fainting fit.

Till a great sea bird, called the Albatross, came through the snow-fog, and was received with great joy and hospitality.

63 Albatross (ăl'bə-trôs'): a large web-footed ocean bird common in the Southern Hemisphere.

And lo! the Albatross proveth a bird of good omen, and followeth the ship as it returned northward through fog and floating ice.

74 hollo (hä'lō): call.

75 shroud: one of the ropes that support a ship's mast.

76 vespers nine: nine evenings.

"God save thee, ancient Mariner,
80 From the fiends, that plague thee thus!—
Why look'st thou so?"—With my crossbow
I shot the Albatross. **C**

PART II

The Sun now rose upon the right:
Out of the sea came he,
85 Still hid in mist, and on the left
Went down into the sea.

And the good south wind still blew behind,
But no sweet bird did follow,
Nor any day for food or play
90 Came to the mariners' hollo!

And I had done a hellish thing,
And it would work'em woe:
For all averred I had killed the bird
That made the breeze to blow.
95 Ah wretch! said they, the bird to slay,
That made the breeze to blow!

Nor dim nor red, like God's own head,
The glorious Sun uprist:
Then all averred I had killed the bird
100 That brought the fog and mist.
'Twas right, said they, such birds to slay,
That bring the fog and mist.

The fair breeze blew, the white foam flew,
The furrow followed free;
105 We were the first that ever burst
Into that silent sea.

Down dropped the breeze, the sails dropped down,
'Twas sad as sad could be;
And we did speak only to break
110 The silence of the sea!

All in a hot and copper sky,
The bloody Sun, at noon,
Right up above the mast did stand,
No bigger than the Moon.

The ancient Mariner inhospitably killeth the pious bird of good omen.

C **NARRATIVE POETRY**
Summarize the **plot developments** of the poem to this point. What **conflicts** might arise because of the Mariner's action?

83 The Sun . . . right: The rising of the sun on the right indicates that the ship is now heading northward.

His shipmates cry out against the ancient Mariner, for killing the bird of good luck.

93 averred (ə-vûrd'): declared; asserted.

But when the fog cleared off, they justify the same, and thus make themselves accomplices in the crime.
98 uprist: rose.

The fair breeze continues; the ship enters the Pacific Ocean, and sails northward, even till it reaches the Line.

The ship hath been suddenly becalmed.

115 Day after day, day after day,
We stuck, nor breath nor motion;
As idle as a painted ship
Upon a painted ocean.

Water, water, everywhere,
120 And all the boards did shrink;
Water, water, everywhere
Nor any drop to drink.

The very deep did rot: O Christ!
That ever this should be!
125 Yea, slimy things did crawl with legs
Upon the slimy sea. **D**

About, about, in reel and rout
The death-fires danced at night;
The water, like a witch's oils,
130 Burnt green, and blue, and white.

And some in dreams assuréd were
Of the Spirit that plagued us so;
Nine fathom deep he had followed us
From the land of mist and snow.

135 And every tongue, through utter drought,
Was withered at the root;
We could not speak, no more than if
We had been choked with soot.

Ah! well a-day! what evil looks
140 Had I from old and young!
Instead of the cross, the Albatross
About my neck was hung.

PART III

There passed a weary time. Each throat
Was parched, and glazed each eye.
145 A weary time! a weary time!
How glazed each weary eye!
When, looking westward, I beheld
A something in the sky.

And the Albatross begins to be avenged.

D **LITERARY BALLAD**
Reread lines 123–126, identifying examples of **onomatopoeia,** or words whose sounds echo their meanings. In what way do these words contribute to the mood of the scene?

127 in reel and rout: with dizzying, unpredictable motion.

128 death-fires: dim flamelike lights reportedly seen above decomposing matter.

A Spirit had followed them; one of the invisible inhabitants of this planet, neither departed souls nor angels; concerning whom the learned Jew, Josephus, and the Platonic Constantinopolitan, Michael Psellus, may be consulted. They are very numerous, and there is no climate or element without one or more.

133 nine fathom: 54 feet.

The shipmates, in their sore distress, would fain throw the whole guilt on the ancient Mariner: in sign whereof they hang the dead sea bird round his neck.

The ancient Mariner beholdeth a sign in the element afar off.

At first it seemed a little speck,
150 And then it seemed a mist;
It moved and moved, and took at last
A certain shape, I wist.

A speck, a mist, a shape, I wist!
And still it neared and neared:
155 As if it dodged a water-sprite,
It plunged, and tacked and veered.

With throats unslaked, with black lips baked,
We could nor laugh nor wail;
Through utter drought all dumb we stood!
160 I bit my arm, I sucked the blood,
And cried, A sail! a sail!

With throats unslaked, with black lips baked,
Agape they heard me call:
Gramercy! they for joy did grin,
165 And all at once their breath drew in,
As they were drinking all.

See! see! (I cried) she tacks no more!
Hither to work us weal—
Without a breeze, without a tide,
170 She steadies with upright keel!

The western wave was all aflame,
The day was wellnigh done!
Almost upon the western wave
Rested the broad, bright Sun;
175 When that strange shape drove suddenly
Betwixt us and the Sun.

And straight the Sun was flecked with bars
(Heaven's Mother send us grace!),
As if through a dungeon-grate he peered
180 With broad and burning face.

Alas! (thought I, and my heart beat loud)
How fast she nears and nears!
Are those her sails that glance in the Sun,
Like restless gossameres?

152 wist: perceived; discerned.

155 water sprite: a mythical being living in water.

156 tacked and veered: zigzagged.

At its nearer approach, it seemeth him to be a ship; and at a dear ransom he freeth his speech from the bonds of thirst.

A flash of joy;

164 gramercy (grə-mûr′sē): an exclamation of gratitude.

And horror follows. For can it be a ship that comes onward without wind or tide?

168 hither to work us weal: in this direction to help us.

171 The western wave was all aflame: The water to the west was reflecting the light of the setting sun.

It seemeth him but the skeleton of a ship.

178 Heaven's Mother: the Virgin Mary.

184 gossameres (gŏs′ə-mērz′): cobwebs floating in the air.

185 Are those her ribs through which the Sun
      Did peer, as through a grate?
      And is that Woman all her crew?
      Is that a Death? and are there two?
      Is Death that Woman's mate?

190 Her lips were red, her looks were free,
      Her locks were yellow as gold:
      Her skin was as white as leprosy,
      The Nightmare Life-in-Death was she,
      Who thicks man's blood with cold.

195 The naked hulk alongside came,
      And the twain were casting dice;
      "The game is done! I've won! I've won!"
      Quoth she, and whistles thrice.

      The Sun's rim dips; the stars rush out:
200 At one stride comes the dark;
      With far-heard whisper, o'er the sea,
      Off shot the spectre-bark.

And its ribs are seen as bars on the face of the setting Sun. The Specter-Woman and her Deathmate, and no other on board the skeleton ship.

Like vessel, like crew!

192 leprosy (lĕp′rə-sē): a disease marked by spreading patches of discoloration on the skin and by deformities of the limbs and other parts of the body.

Death and Life-in-Death have diced for the ship's crew, and she (the latter) winneth the ancient Mariner.

No twilight within the courts of the Sun.

202 spectre-bark: ghost ship.

We listened and looked sideways up!
Fear at my heart, as at a cup,
205 My life-blood seemed to sip!
The stars were dim, and thick the night,
The steersman's face by his lamp gleamed white;
From the sails the dew did drip—
Till clomb above the eastern bar
210 The hornéd Moon, with one bright star
Within the nether tip.

One after one, by the star-dogged Moon,
Too quick for groan or sigh,
Each turned his face with a ghastly pang,
215 And cursed me with his eye.

Four times fifty living men
(And I heard nor sigh nor groan),
With heavy thump, a lifeless lump,
They dropped down one by one.

220 The souls did from their bodies fly—
They fled to bliss or woe!
And every soul, it passed me by
Like the whizz of my crossbow!

PART IV
"I fear thee, ancient Mariner!
225 I fear thy skinny hand!
And thou art long, and lank, and brown,
As is the ribbed sea-sand.

I fear thee and thy glittering eye,
And thy skinny hand so brown."—
230 Fear not, fear not, thou Wedding-Guest!
This body dropped not down.

Alone, alone, all, all alone
Alone on a wide, wide sea!
And never a saint took pity on
235 My soul in agony. **E**

The many men, so beautiful!
And they all dead did lie:
And a thousand thousand slimy things
Lived on; and so did I.

At the rising of the Moon,

209 **clomb** (klōm): climbed.
210 **hornéd Moon:** crescent moon.

One after another,

His shipmates drop down dead.

*But Life-in-Death begins her work
on the ancient Mariner.*

*The Wedding-Guest feareth that a
Spirit is talking to him;*

*But the ancient Mariner assureth him
of his bodily life, and proceedeth to
relate his horrible penance.*

E **LITERARY BALLAD**
Storytellers of traditional ballads
often repeated words to help
make their works memorable.
What ideas in lines 232–235 does
Coleridge want his readers to
remember?

*He despiseth the creatures of the
calm,*

240 I looked upon the rotting sea,
And drew my eyes away;
I looked upon the rotting deck,
And there the dead men lay.

I looked to heaven, and tried to pray;
245 But or ever a prayer had gushed,
A wicked whisper came, and made
My heart as dry as dust. **F**

I closed my lids, and kept them close,
And the balls like pulses beat;
250 But the sky and the sea, and the sea and the sky,
Lay like a load on my weary eye,
And the dead were at my feet.

The cold sweat melted from their limbs,
Nor rot nor reek did they:
255 The look with which they looked on me
Had never passed away.

An orphan's curse would drag to hell
A spirit from on high;
But oh! more horrible than that
260 Is the curse in a dead man's eye!
Seven days, seven nights, I saw that curse,
And yet I could not die.

The moving Moon went up the sky,
And nowhere did abide;
265 Softly she was going up,
And a star or two beside—

Her beams bemocked the sultry main,
Like April hoar-frost spread;
But where the ship's huge shadow lay,
270 The charmèd water burnt alway
A still and awful red.

Beyond the shadow of the ship,
I watched the water-snakes:
They moved in tracks of shining white,
275 And when they reared, the elfish light
Fell off in hoary flakes.

*And envieth that they should live, and
so many lie dead.*

F NARRATIVE POETRY
According to lines 244–247,
what is the Mariner unable to
do? Explain what this suggests
about his **character.**

249 balls: eyeballs.

*But the curse liveth for him in the eye
of the dead men.*

*In his loneliness and fixedness he
yearneth towards the journeying
Moon, and the stars that still
sojourn, yet still move onward; and
everywhere the blue sky belongs to
them, and is their appointed rest,
and their native country and their
own natural homes, which they
enter unannounced, as lords that
are certainly expected and yet there
is a silent joy at their arrival.*

267 bemocked . . . main: scornfully
defied the hot ocean (because the
moon's pale light made the sea
appear cool).
268 hoar-frost: frozen dew.

*By the light of the Moon he beholdeth
God's creatures of the great calm.*

276 fell off in hoary flakes: glittered
on water droplets falling from the
snakes.

Within the shadow of the ship
I watched their rich attire:
Blue, glossy green, and velvet black,
280 They coiled and swam; and every track
Was a flash of golden fire.

O happy living things! no tongue
Their beauty might declare:
A spring of love gushed from my heart,
285 And I blessed them unaware:
Sure my kind saint took pity on me,
And I blessed them unaware.

The selfsame moment I could pray;
And from my neck so free
290 The Albatross fell off, and sank
Like lead into the sea. **G**

PART V

O sleep! it is a gentle thing,
Beloved from pole to pole!
To Mary Queen the praise be given!
295 She sent the gentle sleep from Heaven,
That slid into my soul.

The silly buckets on the deck,
That had so long remained,
I dreamt that they were filled with dew;
300 And when I awoke, it rained.

My lips were wet, my throat was cold.
My garments all were dank;
Sure I had drunken in my dreams,
And still my body drank.

305 I moved, and could not feel my limbs:
I was so light—almost
I thought that I had died in sleep,
And was a blesséd ghost.

And soon I heard a roaring wind:
310 It did not come anear;
But with its sound it shook the sails,
That were so thin and sere.

Their beauty and their happiness.

He blesseth them in his heart.

The spell begins to break.

G **NARRATIVE POETRY**
Reread lines 272–291.
Explain why the spell begins to break at this point. What does this event suggest about the relationship between humans, nature, and the supernatural?

294 Mary Queen: the Virgin Mary.

By grace of the holy Mother, the ancient Mariner is refreshed with rain.

Language Coach

Synonyms Words with the same or nearly the same meaning are synonyms. Which word in line 302 is a synonym for *damp*? What word in line 300 gives you a clue?

He heareth sounds and seeth strange sights and commotions in the sky and the element.

312 sere (sîr): dry.

The upper air burst into life;
And a hundred fire-flags sheen;
315 To and fro they were hurried about!
And to and fro, and in and out,
The wan stars danced between.

And the coming wind did roar more loud,
And the sails did sigh like sedge;
320 And the rain poured down from one black cloud;
The Moon was at its edge.

The thick black cloud was cleft, and still
The Moon was at its side;
Like waters shot from some high crag,
325 The lightning fell with never a jag,
A river steep and wide.

The loud wind never reached the ship,
Yet now the ship moved on!
Beneath the lightning and the Moon
330 The dead men gave a groan.

They groaned, they stirred, they all uprose,
Nor spake, nor moved their eyes;
It had been strange, even in a dream,
To have seen those dead men rise.

335 The helmsman steered, the ship moved on;
Yet never a breeze up-blew;
The mariners all 'gan work the ropes,
Where they were wont to do;
They raised their limbs like lifeless tools—
340 We were a ghastly crew.

The body of my brother's son
Stood by me, knee to knee:
The body and I pulled at one rope,
But he said naught to me. **H**

345 "I fear thee, ancient Mariner!"
Be calm, thou Wedding-Guest:
'Twas not those souls that fled in pain,
Which to their corses came again,
But a troop of spirits blest:

---

314 fire-flags: probably the aurora australis, or southern lights—wavering bands of light in the night sky; **sheen:** bright.

317 wan: pale.

319 sedge: tall grasslike plants that make a rustling sound when blown by the wind.

The bodies of the ship's crew are inspirited, and the ship moves on;

338 wont: accustomed.

H NARRATIVE POETRY
In a narrative, the **climax** is the moment of greatest interest and intensity. What shocking discovery does the Mariner make in lines 331–344?

But not by the souls of the men, nor by demons of earth or middle air, but by a blessed troop of angelic spirits, sent down by the invocation of the guardian saint.

348 corses: bodies.

350 For when it dawned—they dropped their arms,
And clustered round the mast;
Sweet sounds rose slowly through their mouths,
And from their bodies passed.

Around, around, flew each sweet sound,
355 Then darted to the Sun;
Slowly the sounds came back again,
Now mixed, now one by one.

Sometimes a-dropping from the sky
I heard the skylark sing;
360 Sometimes all little birds that are,
How they seemed to fill the sea and air
With their sweet jargoning!

And now 'twas like all instruments,
Now like a lonely flute;
365 And now it is an angel's song,
That makes the Heavens be mute.

362 jargoning: warbling.

It ceased; yet still the sails made on
A pleasant noise till noon,
A noise like of a hidden brook
370 In the leafy month of June,
That to the sleeping woods all night
Singeth a quiet tune.

Till noon we quietly sailed on,
Yet never a breeze did breathe:
375 Slowly and smoothly went the ship,
Moved onward from beneath.

Under the keel nine fathom deep,
From the land of mist and snow,
The Spirit slid: and it was he
380 That made the ship to go.
The sails at noon left off their tune,
And the ship stood still also.

The Sun, right up above the mast,
Had fixed her to the ocean:
385 But in a minute she 'gan stir,
With a short uneasy motion—
Backwards and forwards half her length
With a short uneasy motion.

Then like a pawing horse let go,
390 She made a sudden bound:
It flung the blood into my head,
And I fell down in a swound. ❶

How long in that same fit I lay,
I have not to declare;
395 But ere my living life returned,
I heard, and in my soul discerned
Two voices in the air.

"Is it he?" quoth one, "is this the man?
By Him who died on cross,
400 With his cruel bow he laid full low
The harmless Albatross.

The Spirit who bideth by himself
In the land of mist and snow,
He loved the bird that loved the man
405 Who shot him with his bow."

The lonesome Spirit from the South Pole carries on the ship as far as the Line, in obedience to the angelic troop, but still requireth vengeance.

❶ **LITERARY BALLAD**
Reread lines 377–392. What **supernatural** element does Coleridge introduce to enhance the sensational nature of his tale?

394 have not: am not able.

The Polar Spirit's fellow demons, the invisible inhabitants of the element, take part in his wrong; and two of them relate, one to the other, that penance long and heavy for the ancient Mariner hath been accorded to the Polar Spirit, who returneth southward.

399 Him who died on cross: Jesus Christ.

The other was a softer voice,
As soft as honey-dew:
Quoth he, "The man hath penance done,
And penance more will do."

PART VI
First Voice:

410 "But tell me, tell me! speak again,
Thy soft response renewing—
What makes that ship drive on so fast?
What is the Ocean doing?"

Second Voice:

"Still as a slave before his lord,
415 The Ocean hath no blast;
His great bright eye most silently
Up to the Moon is cast—

If he may know which way to go;
For she guides him smooth or grim.
420 See, brother, see! how graciously
She looketh down on him."

First Voice:

"But why drives on that ship so fast,
Without or wave or wind?"

Second Voice:

"The air is cut away before,
425 And closes from behind.

Fly, brother, fly! more high, more high!
Or we shall be belated:
For slow and slow that ship will go,
When the Mariner's trance is abated." **J**

430 I woke, and we were sailing on
As in a gentle weather:
'Twas night, calm night, the Moon was high;
The dead men stood together.

All stood together on the deck,
435 For a charnel-dungeon fitter:
All fixed on me their stony eyes,
That in the Moon did glitter.

408 penance (pĕn´əns): suffering in repayment for a sin.

The Mariner hath been cast into a trance; for the angelic power causeth the vessel to drive northward faster than human life could endure.

J LITERARY BALLAD
Ballads often feature **dialogue,** which adds liveliness and conveys key information. In what ways does the dialogue in lines 410–429 conform to these conventions?

The supernatural motion is retarded; the Mariner awakes, and his penance begins anew.

435 For . . . fitter: more suitable for a burial vault.

The pang, the curse, with which they died,
Had never passed away:
440 I could not draw my eyes from theirs,
Nor turn them up to pray.

And now this spell was snapped: once more
I viewed the ocean green,
And looked far forth, yet little saw
445 Of what had else been seen—

Like one that on a lonesome road
Doth walk in fear and dread,
And having once turned round, walks on,
And turns no more his head;
450 Because he knows a frightful fiend
Doth close behind him tread.

But soon there breathed a wind on me,
Nor sound nor motion made:
Its path was not upon the sea,
455 In ripple or in shade.

It raised my hair, it fanned my cheek
Like a meadow-gale of spring—
It mingled strangely with my fears,
Yet it felt like a welcoming.

460 Swiftly, swiftly flew the ship,
Yet she sailed softly too:
Sweetly, sweetly blew the breeze—
On me alone it blew. **K**

O dream of joy! is this indeed
465 The lighthouse top I see?
Is this the hill? is this the kirk?
Is this mine own countree?

We drifted o'er the harbor-bar,
And I with sobs did pray—
470 O let me be awake, my God!
Or let me sleep alway.

The harbor-bay was clear as glass,
So smoothly it was strewn!
And on the bay the moonlight lay,
475 And the shadow of the Moon.

The curse is finally expiated.

450 fiend: demon.

K LITERARY BALLAD
Read aloud lines 460–463,
identifying examples of
alliteration, or the repetition
of consonant sounds at the
beginning of words. What effect
does this technique create?

*And the ancient Mariner beholdeth
his native country.*

The rock shone bright, the kirk no less
That stands above the rock:
The moonlight steeped in silentness
The steady weathercock.

479 **weathercock:** weathervane.

480 And the bay was white with silent light
Till rising from the same,
Full many shapes, that shadows were,
In crimson colors came.

The angelic spirits leave the dead bodies,

A little distance from the prow
485 Those crimson shadows were:
I turned my eyes upon the deck—
O Christ! what saw I there!

And appear in their own forms of light.

Each corse lay flat, lifeless and flat,
And, by the holy rood!
490 A man all light, a seraph-man,
On every corse there stood.

489 **the holy rood** (rōōd): the cross on which Christ was crucified.
490 **seraph** (sĕr'əf) **man:** angel.

This seraph-band, each waved his hand:
It was a heavenly sight!
They stood as signals to the land,
495 Each one a lovely light;

This seraph-band, each waved his hand,
No voice did they impart—
No voice; but O, the silence sank
Like music on my heart.

500 But soon I heard the dash of oars,
I heard the Pilot's cheer;
My head was turned perforce away,
And I saw a boat appear.

502 **perforce:** of necessity.

The Pilot and the Pilot's boy,
505 I heard them coming fast:
Dear Lord in Heaven! it was a joy
The dead men could not blast.

507 **blast:** destroy.

I saw a third—I heard his voice:
It is the Hermit good!
510 He singeth loud his godly hymns
That he makes in the wood.
He'll shrieve my soul, he'll wash away
The Albatross's blood.

PART VII

This hermit good lives in that wood
515 Which slopes down to the sea.
How loudly his sweet voice he rears!
He loves to talk with marineres
That come from a far countree.

He kneels at morn, and noon, and eve—
520 He hath a cushion plump.
It is the moss that wholly hides
The rotted old oak-stump.

The skiff-boat neared: I heard them talk,
"Why, this is strange, I trow!
525 Where are those lights so many and fair,
That signal made but now?"

"Strange, by my faith!" the Hermit said—
"And they answered not our cheer!
The planks look warped! and see those sails,
530 How thin they are and sere!
I never saw aught like to them,
Unless perchance it were
Brown skeletons of leaves that lag
My forest-brook along;
535 When the ivy-tod is heavy with snow,
And the owlet whoops to the wolf below,
That eats the she-wolf's young."

"Dear Lord! it hath a fiendish look—
(The Pilot made reply)
540 I am a-fear'd."—"Push on, push on!"
Said the Hermit cheerily.

512 shrieve (shrēv): absolve from sin; pardon.

The Hermit of the Wood

524 trow: believe.

Approacheth the ship with wonder.

535 tod: clump.

The boat came closer to the ship,
But I nor spake nor stirred;
The boat came close beneath the ship,
545 And straight a sound was heard.

Under the water it rumbled on   *The ship suddenly sinketh.*
Still louder and more dread:
It reached the ship, it split the bay;
The ship went down like lead.

550 Stunned by that loud and dreadful sound,
Which sky and ocean smote,   **551 smote:** struck.
Like one that hath been seven days drowned   *The ancient Mariner is saved*
My body lay afloat;   *in the Pilot's boat.*
But swift as dreams, myself I found
555 Within the Pilot's boat.
Upon the whirl, where sank the ship,
The boat spun round and round;
And all was still, save that the hill   **559 telling of:** echoing.
Was telling of the sound.

560 I moved my lips—the Pilot shrieked
And fell down in a fit;
The holy Hermit raised his eyes,
And prayed where he did sit.

I took the oars: the Pilot's boy,
565 Who now doth crazy go,
Laughed loud and long, and all the while
His eyes went to and fro.
"Ha! ha!" quoth he, "full plain I see
The Devil knows how to row."

570 And now, all in my own countree,
I stood on the firm land!
The Hermit stepped forth from the boat,
And scarcely he could stand. ⬤

"O shrieve me, shrieve me, holy man!"
575 The Hermit crossed his brow.
"Say quick," quoth he, "I bid thee say—
What manner of man art thou?"

Forthwith this frame of mine was wrenched
With a woeful agony,
580 Which forced me to begin my tale;
And then it left me free.

Since then, at an uncertain hour,
That agony returns:
And till my ghastly tale is told,
585 This heart within me burns.

I pass, like night, from land to land;
I have strange power of speech;
That moment that his face I see,
I know the man that must hear me:
590 To him my tale I teach.

What loud uproar bursts from that door!
The wedding-guests are there:
But in the garden-bower the bride
And bride-maids singing are:
595 And hark, the little vesper bell,
Which biddeth me to prayer!

ⓛ LITERARY BALLAD
Identify several examples
of **archaic language** in lines
564–573. What effect do
these antiquated expressions
help to create?

575 crossed his brow: made the sign
of the cross on his forehead.

*The ancient Mariner earnestly
entreateth the Hermit to shrieve him;
and the penance of life falls on him.*

*And ever and anon throughout his
future life an agony constraineth
him to travel from land to land;*

O Wedding-Guest! this soul hath been
Alone on a wide, wide sea:
So lonely 'twas, that God Himself
600 Scarce seeméd there to be.

O sweeter than the marriage-feast,
'Tis sweeter far to me,
To walk together to the kirk
With a goodly company!—

605 To walk together to the kirk,
And all together pray,
While each to his great Father bends,
Old men, and babes, and loving friends,
And youths and maidens gay!

610 Farewell, farewell! but this I tell
To thee, thou Wedding-Guest!
He prayeth well, who loveth well
Both man and bird and beast.

He prayeth best, who loveth best
615 All things both great and small;
For the dear God who loveth us,
He made and loveth all. Ⓜ

The Mariner, whose eye is bright,
Whose beard with age is hoar,
620 Is gone: and now the Wedding-Guest
Turned from the bridegroom's door.

He went like one that hath been stunned,
And is of sense forlorn:
A sadder and a wiser man
625 He rose the morrow morn.

Language Coach

Oral Fluency Coleridge sometimes uses contractions to make a line fit the ballad meter, or rhythm. Reread lines 597–600 aloud. In line 599, *it was* becomes *'twas*. How does he alter a word in line 600 to complete the meter of that line?

607 **his great Father:** God.

And to teach, by his own example, love and reverence to all things that God made and loveth.

Ⓜ **NARRATIVE POETRY**
Express in your own words the thematic statement in lines 612–617.

619 **hoar:** gray.

Comprehension

1. **Recall** In what ways does the albatross's arrival seem to affect the ship's voyage?

2. **Summarize** What happens to the rest of the crew after the Mariner kills the albatross?

3. **Clarify** Why does the albatross eventually fall from the Mariner's neck?

4. **Clarify** Why must the Mariner continue to tell his tale?

Text Analysis

5. **Understand Narrative Poetry** Like short stories and novels, **narrative poems** often focus on characters who undergo major changes. Identify the character traits the Mariner exhibits early on in the poem. In what ways does he grow and change as the plot unfolds? Review the chart you created as you read to help you respond.

6. **Make Inferences** What are the consequences of the Mariner's being won by Life-in-Death (lines 190–198) rather than by Death?

7. **Identify Symbol** In literature, a **symbol** is a person, place, object, or activity that represents something beyond itself. What symbolic meaning might the albatross have in the poem? Cite evidence to support your answer.

8. **Make Judgments** Do you think that the punishment the Mariner experiences fits his crime? Explain your thoughts.

9. **Interpret Theme** What overall message, or **theme**, about guilt does the poem convey? Offer evidence to support your ideas.

10. **Analyze Literary Ballad** Review the conventions of the ballad form listed on page 217. Identify the characteristics of the traditional ballad that are present in "The Rime of the Ancient Mariner." What qualities distinguish this poem from traditional ballads? Give examples to support your observations.

Text Criticism

11. **Critical Interpretations** Decades after the publication of "The Rime of the Ancient Mariner," Coleridge observed that it had "too much" of a moral for a work of "pure imagination." Do you agree or disagree with this view? Cite evidence from the poem to support your opinion.

How can **GUILT** *enslave us?*

Guilt is a feeling of self-reproach and self-condemnation that can dominate our thoughts. What are some ways people try to escape from guilt?

COMMON CORE

RL 3 Analyze the impact of the author's choices regarding how to develop and relate elements of a story. **RL 5** Analyze how an author's choices concerning how to structure specific parts of a text contribute to its overall structure and meaning as well as its aesthetic impact.

from Coleridge's Dreamscape: "The Rime of the Ancient Mariner"

Use with "The Rime of the Ancient Mariner," page 814.

COMMON CORE

RI 1 Cite strong and thorough textual evidence to support analysis of what the text says explicitly as well as inferences drawn from the text. **RI 5** Analyze and evaluate the effectiveness of the structure an author uses in his or her exposition or argument, including whether the structure makes points clear, convincing, and engaging.

Samuel Coleridge's "The Rime of the Ancient Mariner" is a tale of supernatural occurrences. Full of fantastic and dreamlike elements, it requires readers to suspend their ordinary disbelief of the otherworldly. Literary critic C. M. Bowra has praised Coleridge for his vivid and compelling rendition of events that might otherwise seem contrived and unbelievable.

Standards Focus: Analyze Literary Criticism

If you've ever read a book review, you've already read **literary criticism,** the category of writing that evaluates literary works, genres, and ideas. Text criticism, most often presented as a book review or an essay, strives to help readers better understand and appreciate literary works. Typically, it does this by providing the following:

- information about the work's historical or literary context
- a description of the text itself
- an evaluation of the work according to implicitly or explicitly stated criteria

A literary critic often writes persuasively, convincing readers that his or her position—a central **claim** or **argument** about the work—is worth taking seriously. The critic will present his or her **assumptions** and additional claims about the work and provide evidence to support them. As an engaged reader, you should identify the critic's position and evaluate the reasons and evidence given as support for it. Then you'll want to consider whether you agree or disagree with the critic's position. For help analyzing Bowra's essay, take notes on a chart such as the one shown here.

Author's Position:		
Claims	Evidence	My Thoughts and Reactions

Coleridge's Dreamscape:
"THE RIME OF THE ANCIENT MARINER"

BY C. M. BOWRA

The triumph of *The Ancient Mariner* is that it presents a series of incredible events through a method of narration which makes them not only convincing and exciting but in some sense a criticism of life. No other poet of the supernatural has quite done this, at least on such a scale and with such abundance of authentic poetry. In his conquest of the unknown, Coleridge went outside the commonplace thrills of horror. Of course, he evokes these, and his opening verses, in which the Mariner stays the Wedding-Guest, suggest that at first Coleridge followed familiar precedents in appealing to a kind of horrified fear. But as he worked at his poem, he widened its scope and created something much richer and more human. To be sure, he chose his
10 subject well. The weird adventures of his Mariner take place not in the trite Gothic setting of a medieval castle . . . but on a boundless sea with days of pitiless sun and soft nights lit by a moon and attendant stars. . . . The new setting and the new persons with which Coleridge shapes the supernatural give to it a new character. Instead of confining himself to an outworn dread of specters and phantoms, he moves over a wide range of emotions and touches equally on guilt and remorse, suffering and relief, hate and forgiveness, grief and joy. Nor has his creation the misty dimness commonly associated with the supernatural. What he imagines is indeed weird, but he sees it with so sharp a vision that it lives vividly before our eyes. At each point he anticipates the objection that his is an outmoded kind of composition, and
20 does the opposite of what his critics expect. **Ⓐ**

    The first problem for any poet of the supernatural is to relate it to familiar experience. So long as it was accepted as part of the scheme of things, there was no great difficulty in this. No doubt Homer's audience accepted the ghost of Odysseus' mother because they believed in ghosts and saw that they must be like this and behave in this way. But Coleridge could not rely on his readers' feeling at home with his unfamiliar theme. He must relate it to something which they knew and understood, something which touched their hearts and imaginations, and he did this by exploiting some of the characteristics of dream. Here was something which would appeal to them and through which they could be led to appreciate the remoter mysteries which
30 he keeps in reserve. . . . **Ⓑ**

    Dreams can have a curiously vivid quality which is often lacking in waking impressions. In them we have one experience at a time in a very concentrated form, and, since the critical self is not at work, the effect is more powerful and more haunting than most effects when we are awake. If we remember dreams at all, we remember them very clearly, even though by rational standards they are quite absurd and have no direct relation to our waking life. They have, too, a power of stirring elementary emotions, such as fear and desire, in a very direct way, though we do not

Ⓐ LITERARY CRITICISM
Reread this paragraph to identify Bowra's position on the poem. Then add a brief summary of his **claims** to your chart.

Ⓑ LITERARY CRITICISM
In this paragraph, what **assumptions** does Bowra make about how Coleridge wrote his poem?

at the time ask why this happens or understand it, but accept it without question as a fact. It is enough that the images of dreams are so penetrated with emotional 40 significance that they make a single and absorbing impression. Coleridge was much attracted by their strange power. . . . On the surface *The Ancient Mariner* shows many qualities of dream. It moves in abrupt stages, each of which has its own single, dominating character. Its visual impressions are remarkably brilliant and absorbing. Its emotional impacts change rapidly, but always come with an unusual force, as if the poet were haunted and obsessed by them. When it is all over, it clings to the memory with a peculiar tenacity, just as on waking it is difficult at first to disentangle ordinary experience from influences which still survive from sleep. **C**

In the criticism of *The Ancient Mariner* which Wordsworth added to the edition of *Lyrical Ballads* published in 1800, he complained that "the events, having no 50 necessary connection, do not produce each other." Now no one expects the events of dream to have the kind of necessary connection which we find in waking life, and Wordsworth's criticism is beside the mark. Indeed, he is less than fair to Coleridge, who gives to the world of his poem its own coherence and rules and logic. Things move indeed in a mysterious way, but not without some connecting relations which may reasonably be called causal. When in a fit of irritation or anger the Mariner shoots the albatross, he commits a hideous crime and is punished by the doom of "life-in-death," which means that, after being haunted by the presence of his dead comrades, he carries a gnawing memory to the end of his days. His shipmates, too, are the victims of the same laws when they are doomed to death as accomplices in his 60 crime for saying that he was right to kill the bird. In such a system it is no less appropriate that when the Mariner feels love gushing from his heart at the sight of the watersnakes, he begins to break the first horror of his spell, and the albatross falls from his neck. Once we accept the assumption that it is wrong to kill an albatross, the rest of the action follows. . . .

This imaginary world has its own rules, which are different from ours and yet touch some familiar chord in us. Nor, when we read the poem, do we really question their validity. Indeed, they are more convincing than most events in dreams, and we somehow admit that in such a world as Coleridge creates it is right that things should happen as they do. It is not too difficult to accept for the moment the ancient belief that spirits 70 watch over human actions, and, once we do this, we see that it is right for them to interfere with men and to do extraordinary things to them. Both the figures on the skeleton ship and the spirits who guide the Mariner on his northward voyage have sufficient reality for us to feel that their actions are appropriate to their characters and circumstances. Nor is it absurd that, when the ship at last comes home, it sinks; it has passed through adventures too unearthly for it to have a place in the world of common things. It and its stricken inmate bear the marks of their ordeal, and it is no wonder that the Pilot's boy goes mad at the sight or that the only person able to withstand their influence is the holy Hermit. Coleridge makes his events so coherent and so close to much that we know in ourselves that we accept them as valid in their own world, which 80 is not ultimately very dissimilar from ours. Because it has this inner coherence, *The Ancient Mariner* is not a phantasmagoria of unconnected events but a coherent whole which, by exploiting our acquaintance with dreams, has its own causal relations between events and lives in its own right as something intelligible and satisfying. **D**

C LITERARY CRITICISM
What **claim** does Bowra make in this paragraph? What observations does he offer to support this claim?

D LITERARY CRITICISM
Critics often respond to the positions of other critics who have written about their subject. What criticism of the poem does Bowra cite in lines 48–50? What **argument** does he provide in the subsequent lines to refute it?

Comprehension

1. **Recall** According to Bowra, what is new and remarkable about Coleridge's depiction of the supernatural? Be specific.

2. **Summarize** How, in Bowra's opinion, is Coleridge's poem like a dream?

Text Analysis

3. **Examine Literary Criticism** In what ways does Bowra establish the literary context for this poem? Consider what he suggests about other literature and other writers of the time as well as literature of previous eras. How is this context relevant to his **claims** about the poem?

4. **Synthesize** Based on your reading of this essay, what qualities would you say Bowra **assumes** are most valuable in a poem? Choose one other poem in this unit and explain whether you think he would like or dislike it.

◯ **COMMON CORE**

RI 1 Cite strong and thorough textual evidence to support analysis of what the text says explicitly as well as inferences drawn from the text. **RI 5** Analyze and evaluate the effectiveness of the structure an author uses in his or her exposition or argument, including whether the structure makes points clear, convincing, and engaging. **W 1** Write arguments to support claims in an analysis of substantive topics or texts, using valid reasoning and relevant and sufficient evidence.

Read for Information: Compare Your Reactions

WRITING PROMPT

How does C. M. Bowra's evaluation of "The Rime of the Ancient Mariner" compare with your own view of the poem? Consider whether you agree or disagree with his position.

To answer this prompt, follow these steps:

1. Consider the standards Bowra used to judge the poem. Would you use exactly the same standards? If not, identify the criteria by which you would judge the poem.

2. Evaluate the poem by your own standards, noting details from the text to support your position.

3. Compare your argument to Bowra's to identify the important points on which you agree or disagree.

4. Finally, write an essay in which you present your evaluation of "The Rime of the Ancient Mariner" by comparing and contrasting your claims with Bowra's.

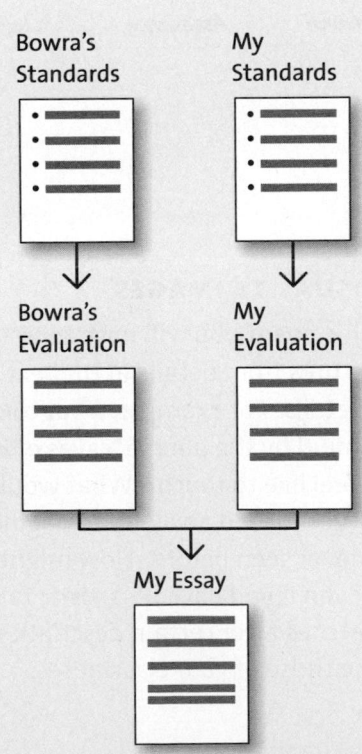

Bowra's Standards   My Standards

Bowra's Evaluation   My Evaluation

My Essay

Kubla Khan

Poem by Samuel Taylor Coleridge   COMMON CORE RL 4

● TEXT ANALYSIS: SOUND DEVICES

"Kubla Khan" is a poem that begs to be read aloud. The sounds of the words evoke almost as much as their meaning. Coleridge uses a variety of sound devices to unify his stanzas, create a mood, and delight the ear. These sound devices include

- **alliteration**—the repetition of consonant sounds at the beginning of words, as in _Kubla Khan_

- **consonance**—the repetition of consonant sounds in the middle and at the end of words, as in _As e'er beneath a waning moon was haunted_

- **assonance**—the repetition of a vowel sound in two or more stressed syllables that do not end with the same consonant, as in _ceaseless turmoil seething_

- **onomatopoeia**—the use of words whose sounds echo their meanings, such as _burst_

As you read the poem aloud, notice examples of these sound devices. On a second reading, record the examples and their location in a chart like the one shown.

Alliteration	Consonance	Assonance	Onomatopoeia
Kubla Khan (line 1)			

● READING STRATEGY: VISUALIZE IMAGES

To get the most from this poem, you will have to **visualize,** or construct mental pictures from details in the text. Most useful will be sensory details. For example, what colors and shapes are brought to mind by the phrase "caves of ice"? What would the caves feel like to touch? What would they smell like? Let yourself get carried away, and imagine the sight of things you've never seen before. How might a place called "Xanadu" look? Even if you have no artistic talent, it might help to make sketches after certain descriptions. See if your sketches look like those of your classmates.

 Complete the activities in your **Reader/Writer Notebook.**

Can DREAMS _reveal truths?_

In _Wuthering Heights,_ 19th-century novelist Emily Brontë wrote, "I've dreamt in my life dreams that have stayed with me ever after, and changed my ideas: they've gone through and through me, like wine through water, and altered the color of my mind." Artists and psychologists also have commented on the power of dreams to inspire and to reveal truths about the self and the world.

QUICKWRITE Describe, as fully as you can, an image or a sensation from a dream you once had. How easy is this to do? Also describe the emotions you associate with the dream. What meaning, if any, can you read into the dream? Read "Kubla Khan" to see how well it describes a dream and what truths it may hint at.

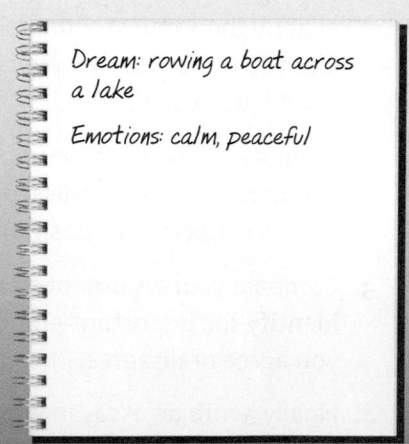

Dream: rowing a boat across a lake

Emotions: calm, peaceful

Kubla Khan
Samuel Taylor Coleridge

> **BACKGROUND** Coleridge wrote "Kubla Khan" in 1797 after taking opium prescribed to relieve pain. Affected by the powerful narcotic, he fell into a deep sleep while reading about the 13th-century Mongol emperor Kublai Khan. In his sleep, he composed 200 to 300 lines based on fantastic images that rose up as he dreamed. Awakening hours later, Coleridge began to write the poem down, but a visitor interrupted him, and later Coleridge could not recall the rest of the lines. He called the poem "a fragment" and "a vision in a dream."

In Xanadu did Kubla Khan
A stately pleasure dome decree:
Where Alph, the sacred river, ran
Through caverns measureless to man
5 Down to a sunless sea.
So twice five miles of fertile ground
With walls and towers were girdled round:
And there were gardens bright with sinuous rills,
Where blossomed many an incense-bearing tree;
10 And here were forests ancient as the hills,
Enfolding sunny spots of greenery. **A**

But oh! that deep romantic chasm which slanted
Down the green hill athwart a cedarn cover!
A savage place! as holy and enchanted
15 As e'er beneath a waning moon was haunted
By woman wailing for her demon lover!
And from this chasm, with ceaseless turmoil seething,
As if this earth in fast thick pants were breathing,
A mighty fountain momently was forced:
20 Amid whose swift half-intermitted burst
Huge fragments vaulted like rebounding hail,
Or chaffy grain beneath the thresher's flail:
And 'mid these dancing rocks at once and ever
It flung up momently the sacred river.

1 Xanadu (zăn′ə-dōō′): Shangdu, one of Kublai Khan's residences in what is now northern China.

8 sinuous rills: winding streams.

A SOUND DEVICES
Read lines 1–11 aloud. What sound devices do you notice, and what **mood** do they help create?

13 athwart a cedarn cover: across a grove of cedar trees.

19 momently: at every moment.
20 intermitted: interrupted.

22 chaffy . . . flail: grain being beaten to separate it from its husks, or chaff.

Peking Imperial Garden (1800s), Chinese artist. © Bibliotheque Nationale, Paris/The Art Archive.

25 Five miles meandering with a mazy motion
   Through wood and dale the sacred river ran,
   Then reached the caverns measureless to man,
   And sank in tumult to a lifeless ocean: **B**
   And 'mid this tumult Kubla heard from far
30 Ancestral voices prophesying war!
       The shadow of the dome of pleasure
       Floated midway on the waves;
       Where was heard the mingled measure
       From the fountain and the caves.
35 It was a miracle of rare device,
   A sunny pleasure dome with caves of ice!

       A damsel with a dulcimer
       In a vision once I saw:
       It was an Abyssinian maid,
40   And on her dulcimer she played,
       Singing of Mount Abora.
   Could I revive within me
   Her symphony and song,
   To such a deep delight 'twould win me,
45 That with music loud and long, **C**
   I would build that dome in air,
   That sunny dome! those caves of ice!
   And all who heard should see them there,
   And all should cry, Beware! Beware!
50 His flashing eyes, his floating hair!
   Weave a circle round him thrice,
   And close your eyes with holy dread,
   For he on honeydew hath fed,
   And drunk the milk of Paradise.

B VISUALIZE IMAGES
Sketch a map of the **setting** you visualize from the description in lines 12–28.

35 **device:** design.

37 **dulcimer:** a stringed musical instrument played with small hammers.

39 **Abyssinian:** from Abyssinia, now called Ethiopia.

41 **Mount Abora:** a legendary earthly paradise like Kubla Khan's.

C VISUALIZE IMAGES
From lines 45–54, create a mental picture of the speaker and his listeners. Why do the listeners cry "Beware"?

53 **honeydew:** an ideally sweet or luscious substance.

Comprehension

1. **Recall** What are some features of the site Kubla Khan chooses for his pleasure dome?

2. **Clarify** What does the speaker imagine would happen if he could again hear the "symphony and song" of the Abyssinian maid?

3. **Paraphrase** What does it mean to have fed on "honeydew" and "drunk the milk of Paradise"?

Text Analysis

4. **Visualize Images** Describe, in as much detail as you can, the images you visualized in lines 1–36. What qualities of nature are suggested through these images?

5. **Interpret Details** What do you predict about Kubla Khan and his pleasure dome from line 30—"Ancestral voices prophesying war"?

6. **Identify Sound Devices** Refer to the chart you created as you read, and identify examples of **alliteration, consonance, assonance,** and **onomatopoeia** in the poem. Which device does Coleridge use most often? Discuss instances in which sound supports mood or meaning.

7. **Analyze Form** How regular are the **rhyme scheme** and **meter** of the poem? At what specific points are the rhyme scheme and meter especially appropriate for the subject?

8. **Draw Conclusions About Theme** What ideas does the poem suggest about dreams and the act of creation? Comment on the following:

   • the circumstances of the poem's composition
   • Kubla Khan's construction of his pleasure dome
   • the speaker's vision of the Abyssinian maid

9. **Evaluate Structure** Recall that Coleridge said he was interrupted by a visitor as he wrote down this poem and later was unable to remember more lines. Does the poem seem complete or incomplete to you? Explain.

Text Criticism

10. **Author's Style** Coleridge's poetry demonstrates a romantic fascination with the supernatural and exotic. Name modern works of film or literature that conjure up a faraway, magical world. What do you think accounts for the continued appeal of the exotic?

Can **DREAMS** *reveal truths?*

What are other examples of imaginary dream worlds from film, television, or literature? Describe them. How do they resemble, or differ from, Xanadu?

COMMON CORE

RL 4 Determine the meaning of words and phrases as they are used in the text, including figurative and connotative meanings; analyze the impact of specific word choices on meaning and tone, including words with multiple meanings or language that is particularly fresh, engaging, or beautiful.

Two Faces of Romanticism

Samuel Taylor Coleridge and William Wordsworth were good friends who shared many conversations about the nature of poetry. In planning *Lyrical Ballads,* their joint book of verse, they agreed to write two different kinds of poems. Coleridge describes this agreement in his *Biographia Literaria.*

> *"In this idea originated the plan of the LYRICAL BALLADS; in which it was agreed, that my endeavours should be directed to persons and characters supernatural, or at least romantic; yet so as to transfer from our inward nature a human interest and a semblance of truth sufficient to procure... that willing suspension of disbelief for the moment, which constitutes poetic faith. Mr. Wordsworth, on the other hand, was... to give the charm of novelty to things of every day, and to excite a feeling analogous to the supernatural, by awakening the mind's attention to the lethargy of custom, and directing it to the loveliness and the wonders of the world before us...."*

In other words, Coleridge agreed to write about the supernatural in a way that was believable, while Wordsworth set out to awaken readers' senses to the magical wonder of everyday sights and sounds.

Writing to Analyze

Review the Coleridge and Wordsworth poems in this unit. Write an analysis of the poems, explaining how they illustrate the principles outlined in the excerpt from *Biographia Literaria.*

Consider

• the kinds of events and people depicted

• the portrayals of nature

• the attitudes of the speakers toward their subject matter

Extension Online

INQUIRY & RESEARCH Search the Internet for information about the Lake District, which was home to Coleridge and Wordsworth. What was the region like when they lived there? What is it like today? Choose two or three of the most interesting Web sites or articles on the subject and share them with your class.

COMMON CORE

W 7 Conduct short research projects to answer a question or solve a problem. **W 10** Write routinely over shorter time frames for a range of tasks, purposes, and audiences. **SL 4** Present information, findings, and supporting evidence, conveying a clear and distinct perspective, such that listeners can follow the line of reasoning.

Form and Meaning in Poetry

Poets from every era have experimented with poetic form and language to create unique expressions of meaning, and the romantic poets were no exception. For the romantic poets, meaning and poetic form were closely tied together.

Giving Shape to Ideas

COMMON CORE

Included in this workshop:
RL 5 Analyze how an author's choices concerning how to structure specific parts of a text contribute to its overall structure and meaning as well as its aesthetic impact.

Form in poetry refers to the principles of arrangement in a poem—the ways in which words and images are organized, including the length of lines, the placement of lines, and the grouping of lines. Some poems follow a **fixed form,** also known as **traditional,** which uses a conventional stanza pattern or a defined rhyme scheme. Other poems follow an **irregular form,** also known as **organic,** which is not defined by any traditional poetic structure. Samuel Taylor Coleridge wrote extensively about the relationship between content and form in his *Biographia Literaria* (1817).

Samuel Taylor Coleridge

He believed that a poem's form and content develop simultaneously, not independently. The romantics favored this organic form, which, as Coleridge explains, "is innate; it shapes, as it develops, itself from within." In other words, the poem's shape is tied to the poem's meaning.

The romantic poets experimented with a number of traditional lyric forms—including both Petrarchan and Shakespearean sonnets—and adapted them to suit the contemplative nature of their poetry. Wordsworth, Coleridge, Shelley, and Keats all used the ode form in some of their poems. Originally a choral Greek form that lent itself to dramatic poetry, an **ode** is an exalted, complex lyric that develops a dignified theme and may include an elaborate stanza pattern. In addition, the metrical pattern of an ode quickens and slows to match the emotional intensity of the idea being expressed. The romantic poets favored an irregular form of the ode, which allowed greater freedom of stanza pattern, rhyme scheme, and metrical movement.

Building Blocks of Poetry

In their experimentation with poetry, the romantic poets used the basic elements of line and stanza to create elaborate and complex poetic structures. The **line** is the most basic element of a poem. In **end-stopped lines,** the end of the line is the end of a thought, a clause, or a sentence, which is signaled by a period, hyphen, or semicolon. In **run-on lines,** the thought continues into the next line or farther.

> Heard melodies are sweet, but those unheard
>   Are sweeter; therefore, ye soft pipes, play on;
> Not to the sensual ear, but, more endear'd,
>
> **—John Keats, "Ode on a Grecian Urn"**

Close Read

Compare the end-stopped and run-on lines in this stanza. What is the effect of each?

A **stanza** is a grouping of lines that conveys a particular idea or set of related ideas. In traditional poetry, stanzas are often characterized by a set pattern of rhythm, rhyme, and number of lines. Some stanzas are named for the number of lines they contain, as shown in the following chart.

TYPES OF STANZAS	
Couplet—two lines	**Cinquain**—five lines
Tercet—three lines	**Sestet**—six lines
Quatrain—four lines	**Octave**—eight lines

The couplet, tercet, and quatrain are the three most commonly used stanzas in English poetry. The romantic poets experimented with various arrangements of these stanzas to group ideas concerning the poem's subject.

Some highly specialized stanzas have evolved from poets' experimenting with various combinations of line, rhyme scheme, and meter. For example, the **Spenserian stanza,** invented by Edmund Spenser for his poetic romance *The Faerie Queene*, is a nine-line stanza—eight lines of iambic pentameter and a ninth line of iambic hexameter, called an **alexandrine.** The rhyme scheme is *ababbcbcc.* Lord Byron used this type of stanza in *Childe Harold's Pilgrimage* (page 854). Other unique stanzas include the following:

- **Ottava rima**—an octave, or eight-line stanza, of iambic pentameter lines, usually rhyming *abababcc,* often used for a fast-paced narrative.

- **Terza rima**—a series of tercets, or three-line stanzas, that are rhyme-linked (e.g., *aba, bcb, cdc,* and so on). Shelley's "Ode to the West Wind" (page 864) is an example.

> O wild West Wind, thou breath of Autumn's being,
> Thou, from whose unseen presence the leaves dead
> Are driven, like ghosts from an enchanter fleeing,
>
> Yellow, and black, and pale, and hectic red,
> Pestilence-stricken multitudes: O thou,
> Who chariotest to their dark wintry bed
>
> **—Percy Bysshe Shelley, "Ode to the West Wind"**

Close Read

What is the rhyme scheme of these two tercets? What effect does the linking rhyme create?

Selected Poetry

by George Gordon, Lord Byron

DID YOU KNOW?

Lord Byron . . .

- kept wild and exotic animals as pets.
- made speeches in England's House of Lords in support of social reform.
- participated in the movement to free Italy from Austrian rule.

Meet the Author

George Gordon, Lord Byron 1788–1824

Like the celebrities of pop culture today, Lord Byron was a superstar personality in his own time. Daring, flirtatious, brooding, and strikingly handsome, Lord Byron was, as an acquaintance famously remarked, "mad, bad, and dangerous to know." His scorn for hypocrisy and repression and his enthusiasm for rebellion and great passion made him a symbol for the romantic spirit.

Changing Fortunes Born in London to a Scots heiress, Catherine Gordon of Gight, and her reckless husband, Captain John "Mad Jack" Byron, Byron endured a turbulent childhood. After squandering most of his wife's fortune, John Byron abandoned his family in 1789 and then died two years later. Mrs. Byron retreated with her three-year-old son to Aberdeen, Scotland, where they lived on a meager income until 1798, when Byron inherited the ancestral Byron estate from his great-uncle and with it the title of the sixth Baron Byron. In 1805, Byron entered Cambridge University, where he engaged in boxing, fencing, and swimming. Though Byron was born with a clubfoot that gave him a slight limp and was a source of misery for him, he enjoyed testing himself physically.

Outcast from Society Byron achieved literary renown with the publication in 1812 of the first two sections of his poetic travelogue *Childe Harold's Pilgrimage*. Inspired by a two-year adventure through Portugal, Spain, Malta, Greece, and Asia Minor, the book made Byron the darling of London society. With his subsequent publications, his literary reputation grew and he became known for the typical protagonist of his poems—the "Byronic hero," a restless, tortured soul who disdained conventional values. Unfortunately, the dashing poet's own reckless lifestyle often left him in debt and suffering from melancholy. Hoping to avoid scandal from his many romantic liaisons, he married in 1815, but his wife left him just one year later. The rumors circulated about his failed marriage caused Byron to flee from England in 1816, never to return. After living in Switzerland, where he grew close to the poet Percy Bysshe Shelley, Byron settled in Italy, where he wrote his greatest poem, *Don Juan.*

Greek National Hero Longing for adventure, Byron embarked on a mission in 1823 to help the Greek people in their war for independence from Turkish rule. While training soldiers, he contracted a fever and died shortly thereafter at age 36.

TEXT ANALYSIS: FIGURATIVE LANGUAGE

To express the intense emotions he wished to convey, Lord Byron frequently used **figurative language**—language that communicates meaning beyond the literal meaning of the words. Two types of figurative language are **metaphors** and **similes,** which make a comparison between two unlike things. A metaphor compares things directly; a simile uses the word *like* or *as.* Another type of figurative language used to express strong emotion is the **apostrophe.** With this figure of speech, an object, abstract quality, or absent or imaginary person is addressed directly, as if present and able to understand. *Childe Harold's Pilgrimage* contains an apostrophe to the ocean. As you read, be aware of these figures of speech and consider why Byron chose to use them.

READING SKILL: UNDERSTAND STANZA STRUCTURE

Poets often use a poem's **stanza structure** to reflect or emphasize the poem's main ideas. **Stanzas,** or groupings of lines, are used to group ideas. Byron often uses traditional stanza structures, in which all of the stanzas contain the same number of lines and often the same rhyme scheme and meter. Traditional stanza structures include

- the **quatrain,** consisting of four lines
- the **sestet,** consisting of six lines
- the **octave,** consisting of eight lines

A more unusual, but still traditional, type of stanza is the **Spenserian stanza,** named for the poet who created it, Edmund Spenser. In *Childe Harold's Pilgrimage,* Byron uses the Spenserian stanza, which consists of nine iambic lines rhyming in the pattern *ababbcbcc.* Each of the first eight lines contains five feet (pentameter), and the ninth, called an **alexandrine,** contains six (hexameter). The rhyming pattern of the stanza creates unity, and the six-foot line slows the rhythm of the stanza's ending, giving it a more dignified pace. As you read these poems, note the stanza structures for each poem and how they contribute to the poem's meaning. For each poem, record your observations in a chart.

"She Walks in Beauty"	
Type of Stanza	
Rhyme Scheme	
Effect Created	

 Complete the activities in your **Reader/Writer Notebook**.

What takes your BREATH away?

What sights and scenes fill you with emotion? What sorts of experiences trigger your imagination and take your breath away? During the romantic period, poets were often inspired by scenes in nature to write about their very intense responses to the world. They believed these experiences gave them a deeper understanding of life's spiritual dimensions.

QUICKWRITE With a small group, list sights or places in the natural world that have inspired powerful feelings in you. Then, choose one that had a particularly strong impact, and describe what you saw, how you felt, and what you learned.

She Walks in Beauty

George Gordon, Lord Byron

She walks in beauty, like the night
    Of cloudless climes and starry skies;
And all that's best of dark and bright
    Meet in her aspect and her eyes:
5 Thus mellowed to that tender light
    Which heaven to gaudy day denies.

One shade the more, one ray the less,
    Had half impaired the nameless grace
Which waves in every raven tress,
10   Or softly lightens o'er her face;
Where thoughts serenely sweet express
    How pure, how dear their dwelling place. **A**

And on that cheek, and o'er that brow,
    So soft, so calm, yet eloquent,
15 The smiles that win, the tints that glow,
    But tell of days in goodness spent,
A mind at peace with all below,
    A heart whose love is innocent!

2 climes: regions; climates.

4 aspect: appearance.

9 tress: lock of hair.

A **STANZA STRUCTURE**
What type of stanza is used in this poem so far? Do the lines follow a regular pattern of **rhythm?** Explain.

Text Analysis

1. **Clarify** Reread lines 3–4. What coexists, or "meets," within the woman?

2. **Interpret** What is the relationship between the woman's inner self and her appearance?

3. **Paraphrase** Reread lines 13–18, and restate the meaning of these lines in your own words.

The Lady Clare (1900), John William Waterhouse. Oil on canvas. Private collection. © Bridgeman Art Library.

When We Two Parted

George Gordon, Lord Byron

When we two parted
    In silence and tears,
Half broken-hearted
    To sever for years,
Pale grew thy cheek and cold,
    Colder thy kiss;
Truly that hour foretold
    Sorrow to this. **B**

The dew of the morning
    Sunk chill on my brow—
It felt like the warning
    Of what I feel now.
Thy vows are all broken,
    And light is thy fame;
I hear thy name spoken,
    And share in its shame.

They name thee before me,
    A knell to mine ear;
A shudder comes o'er me—
    Why wert thou so dear?
They know not I knew thee,
    Who knew thee too well—
Long, long shall I rue thee,
    Too deeply to tell.

Language Coach

Connotations *Part* (*parted,* line 1) and *sever* (line 4) are synonyms. How do the feelings connected with the words differ?

B FIGURATIVE LANGUAGE
The poet uses **apostrophe** in this poem. Who is the speaker addressing in the poem?

18 knell: the ringing of a bell to announce a death.

23 rue: remember with feelings of sorrow; regret.

The Confession, Sir Frank Dicksee. Roy Miles Fine Paintings. © Bridgeman Art Library.

25 In secret we met—
　　In silence I grieve,
That thy heart could forget,
　　Thy spirit deceive.
If I should meet thee
30　　After long years,
How should I greet thee?—
　　With silence and tears. **C**

C STANZA STRUCTURE
Reread lines 25–32. Identify the
type of stanza, and paraphrase
the ideas presented in it.

Text Analysis

1. **Clarify** Why does the speaker of "When We Two Parted"
   feel bitter toward his former lover?

2. **Interpret** In the poem's final line, Byron repeats the
   phrase from line 2 of "When We Two Parted." What
   idea is emphasized through this **repetition?**

3. **Compare Poems** Describe the emotions expressed by
   the speakers in "She Walks in Beauty" and "When We
   Two Parted." What similarities and differences are there?

from Childe Harold's Pilgrimage

George Gordon, Lord Byron

> **BACKGROUND** *Childe Harold's Pilgrimage* is considered a semiautobiographical account of Lord Byron's adventures on a European tour from 1809 to 1811. The complete poem contains four cantos. The publication of the first two cantos in 1812 propelled Byron to fame. *Childe* is an archaic term for a young nobleman awaiting knighthood.

Apostrophe to the Ocean

There is a pleasure in the pathless woods,
There is a rapture on the lonely shore,
There is society where none intrudes,
By the deep Sea, and music in its roar:
5   I love not Man the less, but Nature more,
From these our interviews, in which I steal
From all I may be or have been before,
To mingle with the Universe, and feel
What I can ne'er express, yet can not all conceal. **D**

10   Roll on, thou deep and dark blue Ocean, roll!
Ten thousand fleets sweep over thee in vain;
Man marks the earth with ruin, his control
Stops with the shore; upon the watery plain
The wrecks are all thy deed, nor doth remain
15   A shadow of man's ravage, save his own,
When, for a moment, like a drop of rain,
He sinks into thy depths with bubbling groan,
Without a grave, unknell'd, uncoffin'd, and unknown.

D **STANZA STRUCTURE**
Note the **rhythm** and **rhyme scheme** of this stanza. What idea is emphasized in the **alexandrine** line?

15 ravage: destruction.

18 unknell'd: with no announcement of his death.

Daybreak on the Goodwins, Thomas Rose Miles. Oil on canvas. Private collection. © Bridgeman Art Library.

His steps are not upon thy paths, thy fields
20 Are not a spoil for him,—thou dost arise
And shake him from thee; the vile strength he wields
For earth's destruction thou dost all despise,
Spurning him from thy bosom to the skies,
And send'st him, shivering in thy playful spray
25 And howling, to his Gods, where haply lies
His petty hope in some near port or bay,
And dashest him again to earth:—there let him lay. **E**

The armaments which thunderstrike the walls
Of rock-built cities, bidding nations quake
30 And monarchs tremble in their capitals,
The oak leviathans, whose huge ribs make
Their clay creator the vain title take
Of lord of thee and arbiter of war,—
These are thy toys, and, as the snowy flake,
35 They melt into thy yeast of waves, which mar
Alike the Armada's pride or spoils of Trafalgar.

Thy shores are empires, changed in all save thee—
Assyria, Greece, Rome, Carthage, what are they?
Thy waters wash'd them power while they were free,
40 And many a tyrant since; their shores obey
The stranger, slave, or savage; their decay
Has dried up realms to deserts:—not so thou,
Unchangeable save to thy wild waves' play;
Time writes no wrinkle on thine azure brow;
45 Such as creation's dawn beheld, thou rollest now.

Thou glorious mirror, where the Almighty's form
Glasses itself in tempests; in all time,
Calm or convulsed—in breeze, or gale, or storm,
Icing the pole, or in the torrid clime
50 Dark-heaving;—boundless, endless, and sublime—
The image of Eternity—the throne
Of the Invisible; even from out thy slime
The monsters of the deep are made; each zone
Obeys thee; thou goest forth, dread, fathomless, alone.

55 And I have loved thee, Ocean! and my joy
Of youthful sports was on thy breast to be
Borne, like thy bubbles, onward. From a boy
I wanton'd with thy breakers—they to me
Were a delight; and if the freshening sea
60 Made them a terror—'t was a pleasing fear,
For I was as it were a child of thee,
And trusted to thy billows far and near,
And laid my hand upon thy mane—as I do here. **F**

31 **oak leviathans:** large ships.

32 **their clay creator:** humankind.

33 **arbiter:** judge; decision-maker.

35 **yeast:** turbulent froth.

36 **Armada's . . . Trafalgar**
(trə-făl′gər): The British defeated
the mighty Spanish Armada in 1588;
Trafalgar is a Spanish cape, the site
of a great British naval victory over
the French and Spanish in 1805.

38 **Assyria . . . Carthage:** four
powerful ancient civilizations.

44 **azure** (ăzh′ər): sky blue.

47 **Glasses . . . tempests:** is reflected
in storms.

49 **torrid clime:** the intensely hot
regions near the equator.

53 **zone:** one of the five climatic
regions of the earth.

54 **fathomless:** too deep to measure;
beyond comprehension.

58 **wanton'd:** frolicked playfully;
breakers: large waves.

62 **billows:** swelling waters; waves.

F **FIGURATIVE LANGUAGE**
Identify the **metaphor** in the last
stanza, and explain what this
comparison indicates about the
speaker's relationship to the
ocean. Cite phrases that support
your opinion.

Comprehension

1. **Clarify** Why does the speaker in the excerpt from *Childe Harold's Pilgrimage* enjoy spending time by the "deep Sea"?

2. **Paraphrase** In your own words, restate the meaning of lines 46–50.

3. **Summarize** What aspects of the ocean does the speaker seem to admire most? Briefly explain.

Text Analysis

4. **Draw Conclusions** Although "She Walks in Beauty" contains the image of a woman walking, there are no descriptions of her legs or arms, only her face. Why do you think the poet chose to describe only her face?

5. **Examine Ideas** Reread lines 37–45 in the excerpt from *Childe Harold's Pilgrimage*. What is the speaker saying about the relationship between civilization and the ocean? Provide examples to support your interpretation.

6. **Analyze Figurative Language** Note **metaphors** and **similes** in the following passages. Explain the meaning of each comparison.

   • "She Walks in Beauty," lines 1–6
   • "When We Two Parted," lines 17–18
   • from *Childe Harold's Pilgrimage*, lines 34–35

7. **Compare Stanza Structure** Review the notes you recorded on stanza structure for "When We Two Parted" and the excerpt from *Childe Harold's Pilgrimage*. What similarities and differences are there in the structure of these two poems? How do the different stanza forms support the meaning of each poem?

8. **Evaluate Apostrophe** Is Byron's use of the apostrophe in *Childe Harold's Pilgrimage* an effective method for conveying strong emotion? Find two passages from the poem that you think serve as good illustrations, and explain why you chose them.

Text Criticism

9. **Critical Interpretations** The poet T. S. Eliot once remarked, "Of Byron one can say, as of no other English poet of his eminence, that he added nothing to the language, that he discovered nothing in the sounds, and developed nothing in the meaning, of individual words." Based on the poems you read, do you agree or disagree with Eliot's comment? Explain.

COMMON CORE

RL 4 Determine the meaning of words and phrases as they are used in the text, including figurative and connotative meanings. **RL 5** Analyze how an author's choices concerning how to structure specific parts of a text contribute to its overall structure and meaning as well as its aesthetic impact. **L 5** Demonstrate understanding of figurative language, word relationships, and nuances in word meanings.

What takes your **BREATH** *away?*

Standing on top of a mountain or seeing the ocean for the first time can inspire a strong reaction. Describe the intense emotions people feel when they are "at one" with nature. What do you think causes this reaction?

from **Frankenstein**

Video link at
thinkcentral.com

Novel by Mary Shelley

**Mary Wollstonecraft Shelley
1797–1851**

COMMON CORE

RL 4 Determine the meaning of words and phrases as they are used in the text, including figurative and connotative meanings. **SL 1** Initiate and participate effectively in a range of collaborative discussions.

BACKGROUND Mary Shelley was only eighteen when she wrote the novel *Frankenstein, or the Modern Prometheus.* Shelley claimed that, while on a visit to Lord Byron with her husband, Percy Bysshe Shelley, Byron suggested they hold a contest to write the best "ghost story." Even though she competed with two of the greatest poets of the day, it was Mary who produced the tale that would stand the test of time. Published anonymously in 1818, *Frankenstein* was an immediate popular success and one of the most effective gothic horror tales ever written. As a story of science gone awry, it warned against the dangers of the new industrial age and the desire to control nature; as the original source of all "mad scientist" stories, it is a pioneering work of science fiction and horror that has spawned countless film and stage adaptations.

The novel tells of obsessive Swiss scientist Victor Frankenstein, who uses an electrical charge to animate a lifeless body he has pieced together from human remains. He dreams of creating a perfect being; instead, he produces a miserable monster who causes harm and destruction wherever he goes as he faces rejection, rather than understanding, from those he encounters. The following excerpt is from the famous fifth chapter of the novel, in which Frankenstein describes his creature coming to life. When Frankenstein sees the result of his failed experiment, he rejects his creation in "horror and disgust."

TEXT ANALYSIS Frankenstein's monster is more than just a scientific experiment gone wrong. Monsters in literature are not just fantastic grotesques whose unusual appearance and behavior terrifies others. They act as mirrors, reflecting difficult truths about society and culture, such as the failure to treat with compassion those we do not understand.

The monster reflects the fears and flaws of his creator—aspects that Frankenstein cannot face about himself. In this excerpt, Shelley uses similar imagery and **diction,** or word choice, to describe both Frankenstein and his monster and show how closely the two are connected. In line 4, "a convulsive motion agitate[s]" the monster's limbs; in line 29, as Frankenstein awakens from his dream, his "every limb became convulsed." He sees the monster lurking at his bedside illuminated "by the dim and yellow light of the moon" that echoes the monster's own "dull yellow eye" in line 3. What other examples of imagery and diction linking the monster and his creator can you find in the following excerpt?

DISCUSS Create a list of contemporary examples of monsters from literature, film, or television. Compile a brief list of their physical and psychological characteristics. Why are they so frightening? What is human about them? What messages about the dark side of society do you think they convey?

It was already one in the morning; the rain pattered dismally against the panes, and my candle was nearly burnt out, when, by the glimmer of the half-extinguished light, I saw the dull yellow eye of the creature open; it breathed hard, and a convulsive motion agitated its limbs.

How can I describe my emotions at this catastrophe, or how delineate the wretch whom with such infinite pains and care I had endeavoured to form? His limbs were in proportion, and I had selected his features as beautiful. Beautiful! Great God! His yellow skin scarcely covered the work of muscles and arteries beneath; his hair was of a lustrous black, and flowing; his teeth of a pearly whiteness; but these luxuriances only formed a more horrid contrast with his watery eyes, that seemed almost of the same colour as the dun-white sockets in which they were set, his shrivelled complexion and straight black lips.

The different accidents of life are not so changeable as the feelings of human nature. I had worked hard for nearly two years, for the sole purpose of infusing life into an inanimate body. For this I had deprived myself of rest and health. I had desired it with an ardour that far exceeded moderation; but now that I had finished, the beauty of the dream vanished and breathless horror and disgust filled my heart. Unable to endure the aspect of the being I had created, I rushed out of the room and continued a long time traversing my bedchamber, unable to compose my mind to sleep. At length lassitude succeeded to the tumult I had before endured, and I threw myself on the bed in my clothes, endeavouring to seek a few moments of forgetfulness. But it was in vain; I slept, indeed, but I was disturbed by the wildest dreams. I thought I saw Elizabeth, in the bloom of health, walking in the streets of Ingolstadt. Delighted and surprised, I embraced her, but as I imprinted the first kiss on her lips, they became livid with the hue of death; her features appeared to change, and I thought that I held the corpse of my dead mother in my arms; a shroud enveloped her form, and I saw the grave-worms crawling in the folds of the flannel. I started from my sleep with horror; a cold dew covered my forehead, my teeth chattered, and every limb became convulsed; when, by the dim and yellow light of the moon, as it forced its way through the window shutters, I beheld the wretch—the miserable monster whom I had created. He held up the curtain of the bed; and his eyes, if eyes they may be called, were fixed on me. His jaws opened and he muttered some inarticulate sounds, while a grin wrinkled his cheeks. He might have spoken, but I did not hear; one hand was stretched out, seemingly to detain me, but I escaped and rushed downstairs.

Selected Poetry
by Percy Bysshe Shelley

Meet the Author

DID YOU KNOW?
Percy Bysshe Shelley . . .

- published two gothic novels while in his teens.
- wrote and circulated many controversial political pamphlets.
- supported vegetarianism.
- was not popular in his own day because of his radical views.

(background) Shelley's grave in Rome

Percy Bysshe Shelley 1792–1822

An idealist and a nonconformist, Percy Bysshe Shelley passionately opposed all injustice and dreamed of changing the world through poetry. He wrote with the fervent conviction that poetry nourishes the imagination, and the imagination—by enabling empathy for others—brings about social change.

Turbulent Early Years Born into an aristocratic family, Shelley enjoyed a happy early childhood. At school at Eton, however, the shy and eccentric adolescent suffered constant bullying, an experience that fueled a lifelong hatred of tyranny and conformity. Although Shelley enjoyed greater acceptance at Oxford University, he was soon expelled from the school for circulating an essay defending atheism. His refusal to renounce his views, coupled with his elopement in 1811 with the 16-year-old Harriet Westbrook, caused a permanent rupture with his conservative father.

Poet and Activist In 1812, Shelley moved to Dublin, where his work on behalf of Catholic emancipation and independence for Ireland brought him under the scrutiny of the British government. In his first major poem, *Queen Mab* (1813), he continued to attack social institutions such as marriage, the monarchy, and the church. In 1814, Shelley met and fell in love with another radical thinker, Mary Wollstonecraft Godwin, the daughter of the philosopher William Godwin and the feminist author Mary Wollstonecraft. Abandoning Harriet, who was then expecting their second child, Shelley eloped to France with Mary, returning to England several weeks later.

Social Outcast Shelley's scandalous behavior drew severe censure from British society, and he soon found himself an outcast. In 1816, Shelley fled with Mary to Geneva, Switzerland, where his stimulating conversations with the poet Lord Byron invigorated his thinking and writing. Two years later, following the suicide of Harriet, Shelley finally married Mary Godwin, and the couple settled permanently in Italy. In 1819, despite his grief over the recent deaths of his two infant children, Shelley produced many of his greatest poems, including "Ode to the West Wind" and the verse drama *Prometheus Unbound.*

A Tragic Death Between 1820 and 1822, Shelley enjoyed a period of relative stability in Pisa, during which he composed many fine lyrics, including *Adonais*, an elegy in memory of John Keats. On July 8, 1822, Shelley and a friend drowned when their boat capsized in a sudden storm. Shelley's ashes were buried in Rome, near the graves of John Keats and Shelley's son William.

TEXT ANALYSIS: RHYTHMIC PATTERNS

Shelley's poetry is admired for its musicality, among other qualities. One element that makes poetry musical is **meter,** the regular repetition of a rhythmic unit. Each unit of meter, known as a **foot,** consists of one stressed syllable (ˊ) and one or more unstressed syllables (˘). An **iamb** is a foot that contains an unstressed syllable followed by a stressed syllable: rĕgrét. A **trochee** is a foot that contains a stressed syllable followed by an unstressed syllable: sórrŏw. The first chart shows types of feet. Meter is also expressed in terms of the number of feet in a line, as shown in the second chart.

Type of Foot
iamb (˘ ˊ)
trochee (ˊ ˘)
anapest (˘ ˘ ˊ)
dactyl (ˊ ˘ ˘)

Number of Feet
monometer—one
dimeter—two
trimeter—three
tetrameter—four
pentameter—five
hexameter—six

Iambic pentameter, the most common meter in English, contains five sets of iambs:

˘ ˊ | ˘ ˊ | ˘ ˊ | ˘ ˊ | ˘ ˊ
I met|a trave|ler from|an an|tique land

As you read the following poems, identify the meter. Also notice departures from the regular meter and the effect they have.

Review: **Rhyme Scheme**

● READING SKILL: UNDERSTAND HISTORICAL CONTEXT

The **historical context** of a literary work refers to the social conditions that inspired or influenced its creation. Romanticism in 19th-century England developed in part as a reaction to the French Revolution, the rise and fall of Napoleon, the industrialization of the economy, and the poverty and oppression of workers. Shelley wrote "Ode to the West Wind" in 1819, the year of the Peterloo massacre, in which workers demonstrating for reform were killed by soldiers. Another poem, "Sonnet: England in 1819," explicitly condemns England's "leech-like" rulers, her army's "liberticide," and her "Christless" religion. As you read the following works by Shelley, written over a span of 2¹/₂ years, consider their historical context and that they are poems of protest.

 Complete the activities in your **Reader/Writer Notebook**.

What can NATURE *teach us?*

Romantic poets believed that profound lessons could be learned from observing nature. They believed that there was no greater beauty than that found in nature, and they saw higher truths reflected in natural scenes.

QUICKWRITE Visualize one of the following elements of nature—a sand dune, the wind, or a bird. Think deeply about it. What lesson about life could it suggest to you? Contemplating the wind, for example, might make you realize that any life circumstance can suddenly change, as the wind does. Jot down one possible lesson about life and discuss it in a small group. Then read Shelley's poems to find out what lessons he saw in sand, the west wind, and the song of a skylark.

Ozymandias

Percy Bysshe Shelley

I met a traveler from an antique land
Who said: Two vast and trunkless legs of stone
Stand in the desert . . . Near them, on the sand,
Half sunk, a shattered visage lies, whose frown,
5 And wrinkled lip, and sneer of cold command,
Tell that its sculptor well those passions read
Which yet survive, stamped on these lifeless things,
The hand that mocked them, and the heart that fed;
And on the pedestal these words appear:
10 "My name is Ozymandias, king of kings:
Look on my works, ye Mighty, and despair!"
Nothing beside remains. Round the decay **Ⓐ**
Of that colossal wreck, boundless and bare
The lone and level sands stretch far away.

2 trunkless legs: legs separated from the rest of the body.

4 visage (vĭz′ĭj): face.

6–8 The passions outlast the sculptor whose hand mocked those passions and the king whose heart fed those passions.

10 Ozymandias (ŏz′ĭ-măn′dē-əs): a Greek name for the Egyptian pharaoh Rameses II, who reigned from 1279 to 1213 B.C.

Ⓐ RHYTHMIC PATTERNS
What words in lines 12 and 13 are emphasized by their departure from the regular meter?

Text Analysis

1. **Clarify** What kind of man was Ozymandias?

2. **Identify Irony** What is ironic about the words on his pedestal?

3. **Understand Historical Context** What message is there in the poem for European kings or self-proclaimed emperors like Napoleon?

Head of Rameses II at Thebes, Egypt

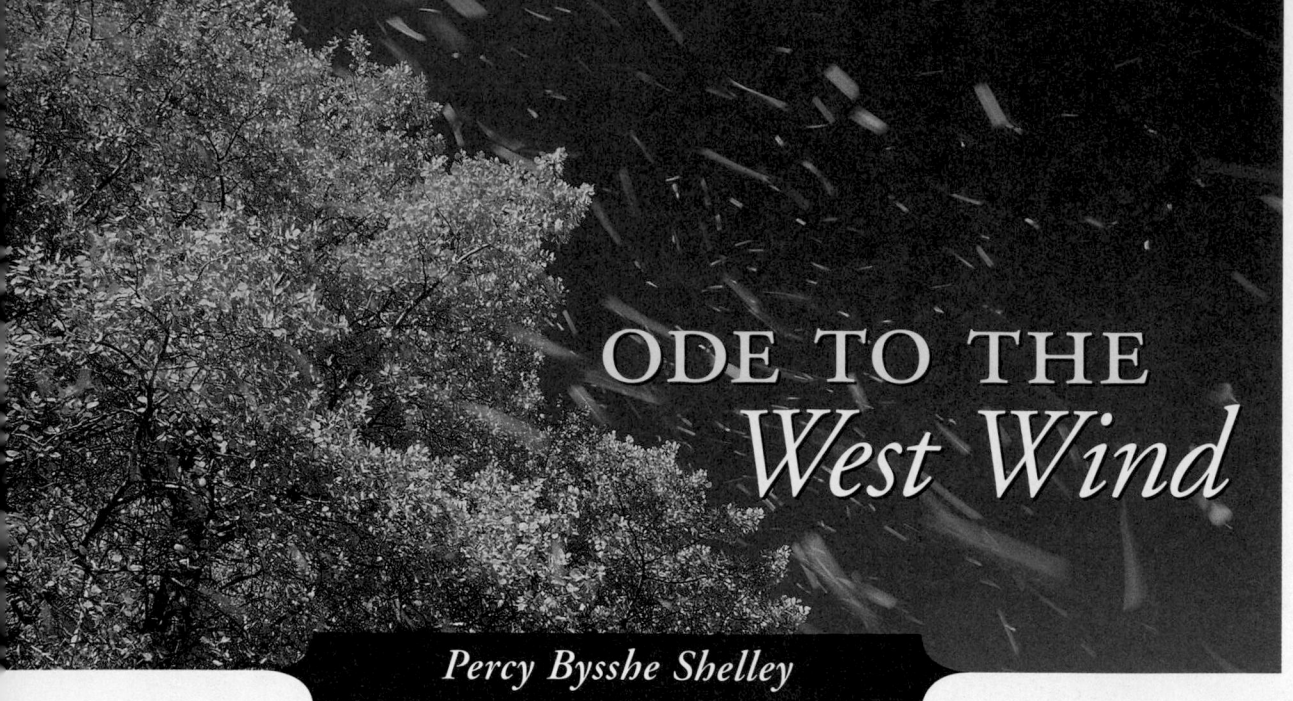

ODE TO THE *West Wind*

Percy Bysshe Shelley

I

O wild West Wind, thou breath of Autumn's being, **B**
Thou, from whose unseen presence the leaves dead
Are driven, like ghosts from an enchanter fleeing,

Yellow, and black, and pale, and hectic red,
5 Pestilence-stricken multitudes: O thou,
Who chariotest to their dark wintry bed

The wingéd seeds, where they lie cold and low,
Each like a corpse within its grave, until
Thine azure sister of the Spring shall blow

10 Her clarion o'er the dreaming earth, and fill
(Driving sweet buds like flocks to feed in air)
With living hues and odors plain and hill:

Wild Spirit, which art moving everywhere;
Destroyer and preserver; hear, oh, hear! **C**

II

15 Thou on whose stream, mid the steep sky's commotion,
Loose clouds like earth's decaying leaves are shed,
Shook from the tangled bough of Heaven and Ocean,

B RHYTHMIC PATTERNS
Read lines 1–9 aloud. What is the predominant **meter?**

4 **hectic:** feverish.

9 **sister . . . Spring:** the reviving south wind of spring.

10 **clarion:** a trumpet with a clear, ringing tone.

C RHYME SCHEME
Describe the interlocking pattern of rhyme, called **terza rima,** in the first four stanzas of section I. How does the fifth stanza bring the pattern to a close?

Angels of rain and lightning: there are spread
On the blue surface of thine aëry surge,
20 Like the bright hair uplifted from the head

Of some fierce Maenad, even from the dim verge
Of the horizon to the zenith's height,
The locks of the approaching storm. Thou dirge

Of the dying year, to which this closing night
25 Will be the dome of a vast sepulcher,
Vaulted with all thy congregated might

Of vapors, from whose solid atmosphere
Black rain, and fire, and hail will burst: oh, hear!

III

Thou who didst waken from his summer dreams
30 The blue Mediterranean, where he lay,
Lulled by the coil of his crystálline streams,

Beside a pumice isle in Baiae's bay,
And saw in sleep old palaces and towers
Quivering within the wave's intenser day,

35 All overgrown with azure moss and flowers
So sweet, the sense faints picturing them! Thou
For whose path the Atlantic's level powers

Cleave themselves into chasms, while far below
The sea-blooms and the oozy woods which wear
40 The sapless foliage of the ocean, know

Thy voice, and suddenly grow gray with fear,
And tremble and despoil themselves: oh, hear!

IV

If I were a dead leaf thou mightest bear;
If I were a swift cloud to fly with thee;
45 A wave to pant beneath thy power, and share

The impulse of thy strength, only less free
Than thou, O uncontrollable! If even
I were as in my boyhood, and could be

18 angels: messengers.

19 aëry: airy.

20–22 Like . . . height: The clouds lie in streaks from the horizon upward, looking like the streaming hair of a maenad (mē′năd′)—a wildly dancing female worshiper of Dionysus, the Greek god of wine.

23 dirge: funeral song.

25 sepulcher (sĕp′əl-kər): tomb.

31 crystálline (krĭs-tăl′ĭn) **streams:** the different-colored currents of the Mediterranean Sea.

32 pumice (pŭm′ĭs): a light volcanic rock; **Baiae's** (bī′ēz′) **bay:** the Bay of Naples, site of the ancient Roman resort of Baiae.

37 level powers: surface.

Language Coach

Formal Language Language that sounds formal may in fact be archaic, or out of date. In line 43, Shelley uses the archaic verb ending -est in mightest. What verbs in lines 6 and 29 have similar endings? Why does Shelley use this archaic form?

The comrade of thy wanderings over Heaven,
50 As then, when to outstrip thy skyey speed
Scarce seemed a vision; I would ne'er have striven

As thus with thee in prayer in my sore need.
Oh, lift me as a wave, a leaf, a cloud!
I fall upon the thorns of life! I bleed!

55 A heavy weight of hours has chained and bowed
One too like thee: tameless, and swift, and proud.

V

Make me thy lyre, even as the forest is:
What if my leaves are falling like its own!
The tumult of thy mighty harmonies

60 Will take from both a deep, autumnal tone,
Sweet though in sadness. Be thou, Spirit fierce,
My spirit! Be thou me, impetuous one!

Drive my dead thoughts over the universe
Like withered leaves to quicken a new birth!
65 And, by the incantation of this verse,

Scatter, as from an unextinguished hearth
Ashes and sparks, my words among mankind!
Be through my lips to unawakened earth

The trumpet of a prophecy! O Wind,
70 If Winter comes, can Spring be far behind? **D**

50 skyey (skī′ē) **speed:** the swiftness of clouds moving across the sky.

51 vision: something impossible to achieve.

57 lyre: a reference to the Aeolian harp, an instrument whose strings make musical sounds when the wind blows over them.

62 impetuous (ĭm-pĕch′ōō-əs): violently forceful; impulsive.

65 incantation: recitation, as of a magic spell.

D HISTORICAL CONTEXT
In lines 63–70, what does the poet imply is the state of the world? Relate these lines to the social conditions mentioned on pages 860 and 861.

Text Analysis

1. **Analyze the Ode** An **ode** is an exalted, complex lyric that develops a single, dignified theme. Many odes praise people or elements of nature. What qualities of the west wind are glorified in this ode?

2. **Make Inferences** What does the poet request of the west wind, and why?

3. **Interpret Metaphor** Give your interpretation of the last line. What might be meant by "Winter" and "Spring"?

TO A
Skylark

Percy Bysshe Shelley

Hail to thee, blithe Spirit!
　　Bird thou never wert,
That from Heaven, or near it,
　　Pourest thy full heart
5 In profuse strains of unpremeditated art.

　Higher still and higher
　　From the earth thou springest
Like a cloud of fire;
　　The blue deep thou wingest,
10 And singing still dost soar, and soaring ever singest. **E**

　In the golden lightning
　　Of the sunken sun,
O'er which clouds are bright'ning,
　　Thou dost float and run;
15 Like an unbodied joy whose race is just begun.

1 blithe (blīth): carefree.

5 unpremeditated (ŭn'prĭ- mĕd'ĭ-tā'tĭd): natural; not planned out ahead of time.

E **RHYTHMIC PATTERNS**
Describe the **meter** of the first stanza. Is the metrical pattern maintained in the second stanza? Explain.

The pale purple even
     Melts around thy flight;
Like a star of Heaven,
     In the broad daylight
20 Thou art unseen, but yet I hear thy shrill delight,

Keen as are the arrows
     Of that silver sphere,
Whose intense lamp narrows
     In the white dawn clear
25 Until we hardly see—we feel that it is there.

All the earth and air
     With thy voice is loud,
As, when night is bare,
     From one lonely cloud
30 The moon rains out her beams, and Heaven is overflowed.

What thou are we know not;
     What is most like thee?
From rainbow clouds there flow not
     Drops so bright to see
35 As from thy presence showers a rain of melody.

Like a Poet hidden
     In the light of thought,
Singing hymns unbidden,
     Till the world is wrought
40 To sympathy with hopes and fears it heeded not: **F**

Like a high-born maiden
     In a palace tower
Soothing her love-laden
     Soul in secret hour
45 With music sweet as love, which overflows her bower:

Like a glowworm golden
     In a dell of dew,
Scattering unbeholden
     Its aërial hue
50 Among the flowers and grass, which screen it from the view!

16 **even:** evening.

22 **silver sphere:** the planet Venus, called the morning star because it is visible in the east just before daybreak.

F **HISTORICAL CONTEXT**
Reread lines 36–40. Notice how Shelley views the poet's role. Use your background reading to speculate about the "hopes and fears" unheeded by the world.

45 **bower:** private room; boudoir or bedroom.

46 **glowworm:** wingless female firefly or firefly larva.

49 **aërial** (âr'ē-əl) **hue:** insubstantial glow.

Like a rose embowered
    In its own green leaves,
By warm winds deflowered,
    Till the scent it gives
55 Makes faint with too much sweet those heavy-wingéd thieves:

Sound of vernal showers
    On the twinkling grass,
Rain-awakened flowers,
    All that ever was
60 Joyous, and clear, and fresh, thy music doth surpass:

Teach us, Sprite or Bird,
    What sweet thoughts are thine:
I have never heard
    Praise of love or wine
65 That panted forth a flood of rapture so divine. **G**

Chorus Hymeneal,
    Or triumphal chant,
Matched with thine would be all
    But an empty vaunt,
70 A thing wherein we feel there is some hidden want.

What objects are the fountains
    Of thy happy strain?
What fields, or waves, or mountains?
    What shapes of sky or plain?
75 What love of thine own kind? what ignorance of pain?

With thy clear keen joyance
    Languor cannot be:
Shadow of annoyance
    Never came near thee:
80 Thou lovest—but ne'er knew love's sad satiety.

Waking or asleep,
    Thou of death must deem
Things more true and deep
    Than we mortals dream,
85 Or how could thy notes flow in such a crystal stream?

---

53 deflowered: fully opened.

55 thieves: the warm winds.

56 vernal: spring.

G FORM
Stanza form, line lengths, and unconventional use of punctuation are graphic elements that draw attention to the poem's appearance on the page. For example, Shelley capitalizes words that are not normally capitalized, such as *sprite* and *bird* in line 61. The poem's stanzas have a light and airy form, with a few short lines of varying lengths floating in the abundant white space of the page. How are Shelley's themes in the poem reflected by his use of these elements of form?

66 Chorus Hymeneal (hī'mə-nē'əl): a wedding song.
69 vaunt: boast.

71 fountains: sources.

77 languor (lăng'gər): lack of energy; listlessness.

80 satiety (sə-tī'ĭ-tē): fulfillment to excess.

82 deem: know.

We look before and after,
    And pine for what is not:
Our sincerest laughter
    With some pain is fraught;
90 Our sweetest songs are those that tell of saddest thought. **H**

Yet if we could scorn
    Hate, and pride, and fear;
If we were things born
    Not to shed a tear,
95 I know not how thy joy we ever should come near.

Better than all measures
    Of delightful sound,
Better than all treasures
    That in books are found,
100 Thy skill to poet were, thou scorner of the ground!

Teach me half the gladness
    That thy brain must know,
Such harmonious madness
    From my lips would flow
105 The world should listen then—as I am listening now. **I**

H RHYTHMIC PATTERNS
How is **rhythm** used to emphasize the last line of each stanza? Read line 90 aloud, considering what to stress and where to pause.

91 if: even if.

I HISTORICAL CONTEXT
Reread lines 101–105, considering the era in which Shelley was writing. What might he want the world to hear?

Text Analysis

1. **Recall** To what things does the speaker compare the skylark?

2. **Summarize** In the speaker's eyes, what makes the skylark different from humans and its song different from human songs?

3. **Clarify** In lines 101–105, what does the speaker want the skylark to teach him, and what would he do with this knowledge?

SONNET: *England in 1819*

Percy Bysshe Shelley

An old, mad, blind, despised, and dying king—
Princes, the dregs of their dull race, who flow
Through public scorn—mud from a muddy spring—
Rulers who neither see, nor feel, nor know,
5 But leechlike to their fainting country cling,
Till they drop, blind in blood, without a blow—
A people starved and stabbed in the untilled field—
An army, which liberticide and prey
Makes as a two-edged sword to all who wield—
10 Golden and sanguine laws which tempt and slay;
Religion Christless, Godless—a book sealed;
A Senate—Time's worst statute unrepealed,
Are graves, from which a glorious Phantom may
Burst, to illumine our tempestuous day. **J**

1. An old, mad ... king: King George III, who had ruled since 1760 and was declared incurably insane in 1811. He died in 1820.

8. liberticide: the killing of freedom.
10. Golden and sanguine laws: corrupt, unjust laws passed using bribery and resulting in bloodshed.
12. statute unrepealed: the law forbidding Catholics to hold office.

J **HISTORICAL CONTEXT**
Shelley strongly protests King George III's rule by building a dramatic list of the negative effects the king has had on England. How does the way Shelley constructs his poem as a list contribute to its power as a work of political protest?

Comprehension

1. **Recall** How does Shelley describe the king of England?

2. **Recall** According to the poem, what are the effects of the king's rule on England's people?

3. **Clarify** What does the "Phantom" at the end of the poem signify?

Text Analysis

4. **Compare Imagery** What are the most striking images in these four poems? Explain what makes this imagery effective.

5. **Interpret Symbols** In the poems, what larger ideas are symbolized by the following elements of **nature?**

   - the sands near the statue of Ozymandias
   - the skylark
   - the west wind
   - the muddy spring

6. **Examine Rhythmic Patterns** What is the **meter** of each poem? In which poem is the meter most regular? Discuss instances in which the rhythm of lines helps communicate ideas.

7. **Evaluate Sound Devices** How skillfully does Shelley use other sound devices besides meter? Support your opinion with examples.

8. **Analyze Form** Review page 311, and then explain how "Ozymandias" shows the characteristics of a **Petrarchan, or Italian, sonnet.** How closely do the numbered sections of "Ode to the West Wind" match the sonnet form?

9. **Apply Historical Context** Use your knowledge of Shelley's times and political views to interpret his four poems as protest poems. From the poems, what would you guess is his vision of an ideal society?

Text Criticism

10. **Critical Interpretations** In "A Defense of Poetry" (page 876), Shelley writes that "Poetry turns all things to loveliness; it exalts the beauty of that which is most beautiful, and it adds beauty to that which is most deformed." In what ways is this comment reflected in the poems you read? Explain.

> *What can* **NATURE** *teach us?*
>
> Name an animal that, to you, symbolizes an abstract concept, such as liberty or fear. Which characteristics of this animal symbolize the concept? Why?

COMMON CORE

RL 5 Analyze how an author's choices concerning how to structure specific parts of a text contribute to its overall structure and meaning as well as its aesthetic impact.
RL 9 Demonstrate knowledge of foundational works of literature, including how two or more texts from the same period treat similar themes or topics.

Language

◆ **GRAMMAR AND STYLE:** Create Effective Imagery

Shelley was an inventive poet who created striking and exquisite imagery through his use of personification. **Personification** is a figure of speech in which an object, animal, or idea is given human qualities. In the following passage from "Ode to the West Wind," Shelley personifies the sea life in the Mediterranean to show how powerfully the west wind affects it:

> *The sea-blooms and the oozy woods which wear*
> *The sapless foliage of the ocean, know*
>
> *Thy voice, and suddenly grow gray with fear,*
> *And tremble and despoil themselves: oh, hear!* (lines 39–42)

Notice how Shelley assigns characteristics to the natural world that would normally be attributed to humans, such as *fear* to the sea plants and a *voice* to the west wind. This use of personification enables readers to form a vivid mental picture of the wind and its power.

PRACTICE Copy each of the following lines from "Ode to the West Wind." Then compose your own lines about an element of nature, mimicking Shelley's use of personification in order to create effective imagery.

EXAMPLE

Wild Spirit, which art moving everywhere; / Destroyer and preserver; hear, oh, hear!

Lonely sky, which art weeping everywhere, / Mourner and rager; sleep, oh sleep!

---

1. . . . O thou, / Who chariotest to their dark wintry bed / The wingèd seeds, where they lie cold and low, . . .

2. Thine azure sister of the Spring shall blow / Her clarion o'er the dreaming earth, . . .

READING-WRITING CONNECTION

YOUR TURN

Expand your understanding of Shelley's poems by responding to this prompt. Then use the **revising tips** to improve your poem.

WRITING PROMPT	REVISING TIPS
WRITE A POEM Write a **poem** in which you attempt to capture the "sleeping beauty" of an element of nature, as Shelley does in "Ode to the West Wind" and "To a Skylark." Try to use **rhyme, meter,** and **personification** as Shelley does in his poems.	• Include rich imagery that appeals to the five senses. • Address your subject as if it were human to help personify it.

Interactive Revision THINK central

Go to **thinkcentral.com.**
KEYWORD: HML12-873

COMMON CORE

L 3 Apply knowledge of language to understand how language functions in different contexts.
W 4 Produce clear and coherent writing in which the style is appropriate to task, purpose, and audience.

Views on Poetry

- Book Preface, page 875
- Literary Essay, page 876

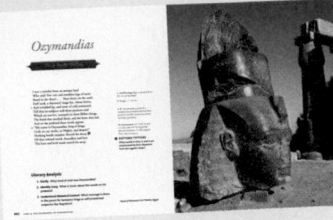

Use with Selected Poetry
by Percy Bysshe Shelley
page 860.

Many of the romantic poets knew each other personally, and many shared similar beliefs about art and politics. But, as individual artists, they disagreed with one another about the purpose and definition of poetry. Their differences in opinion were not dry or theoretical. They were vital differences that informed and animated their work, giving each poet a distinctive style and voice. For example, nature is a subject in the poetry of Wordsworth and Shelley, but it is impossible to confuse Wordsworth's elegant meditations on the English countryside with Shelley's soaring, ecstatic odes.

In the following selections—excerpts from Wordsworth's Preface to *Lyrical Ballads* and Shelley's *A Defense of Poetry*—we hear, directly from the poets, two different views on poetry. They tell us what poetry means to them, and what they think poetry can accomplish. As you read the excerpts, carefully consider the assumptions each poet makes about art and the world, paying special attention of their choice of words, or diction, and imagery.

COMMON CORE

RI 1 Cite strong and thorough textual evidence to support analysis of what the text says explicitly as well as inferences drawn from the text, including determining where the text leaves matters uncertain.
RI 4 Determine the meaning of words and phrases as they are used in a text; analyze how an author uses and refines the meaning of a key term or terms over the course of a text.

Standards Focus: Compare and Contrast

Comparing and contrasting two works often helps you understand them better than if you had read each work on its own. In order to identify similarities and differences between two works, focus on the key words and phrases each author uses to convey his or her ideas so you can identify each writer's main idea. Focusing on these key elements gives you the tools you need to make logical connections, or **inferences,** about each text. You can then use these inferences to synthesize, or combine, ideas from both texts to draw your own conclusions about them.

Use the chart below to keep track of the key words and phrases that each writer uses to define poetry and its purpose, including nouns, verbs, adjectives, and metaphors. First read each excerpt in its entirety. Then compare the excerpts side-by-side as you fill out the chart.

Words and Phrases about Poetry in Wordsworth	Words and Phrases about Poetry in Shelley
"...choose incidents and situations from common life..." (lines 1–2)	"Poetry is indeed something divine" (line 1)

Wordsworth included this preface, or introduction, to the 1802 edition of his and Coleridge's groundbreaking collection of poems, *Lyrical Ballads*. It describes what Wordsworth believed are the essential elements of poetry, many of which served as the foundation for romanticism.

from
Preface to *Lyrical Ballads, with Pastoral and Other Poems*

William Wordsworth

The principal object, then, which I proposed to myself in these Poems was to choose incidents and situations from common life, and to relate or describe them, throughout, as far as was possible, in a selection of language really used by men; and, at the same time, to throw over them a certain coloring of imagination, whereby ordinary things should be presented to the mind in an unusual way; and, further, and above all, to make these incidents and situations interesting by tracing in them, truly though not ostentatiously[1], the primary laws of our nature: chiefly, as far as regards the manner in which we associate ideas in a state of excitement. Low and rustic[2] life was generally **Ⓐ**
chosen, because in that condition, the essential passions of the heart find a better soil in
10 which they can attain their maturity, are less under restraint, and speak a plainer and more emphatic language; because in that condition of life our elementary feelings co-exist in a state of greater simplicity, and, consequently, may be more accurately contemplated, and more forcibly communicated; because the manners of rural life germinate[3] from those elementary feelings; and, from the necessary character of rural occupations, are more easily comprehended; and are more durable; and lastly, because in that condition the passions of men are incorporated with the beautiful and permanent forms of nature. The language, too, of these men is adopted (purified indeed from what **Ⓑ**
appear to be its real defects, from all lasting and rational causes of dislike or disgust) because such men hourly communicate with the best objects from which the best part of
20 language is originally derived; and because, from their rank in society and the sameness and narrow circle of their intercourse, being less under the influence of social vanity they convey their feelings and notions in simple and unelaborated expressions. Accordingly, **Ⓒ**
such a language, arising out of repeated experience and regular feelings, is a more permanent, and a far more philosophical language, than that which is frequently substituted for it by Poets, who think that they are conferring honor upon themselves and their art, in proportion as they separate themselves from the sympathies of men, and indulge in arbitrary and capricious[4] habits of expression, in order to furnish food for fickle tastes, and fickle appetites, of their own creation.[5]

Ⓐ COMPARE AND CONTRAST
In lines 8–17, what central features of romanticism does rural life represent?

Ⓑ COMPARE AND CONTRAST
Reread lines 17–22. What kind of language does Wordsworth think is best suited to poetry? Why?

Ⓒ COMPARE AND CONTRAST
To what kind of poetic language does Wordsworth object in lines 22–28? Why?

---

1. **ostentatiously** (ŏs-tĕn-tā´shəs lē): in a showy manner.
2. **rustic** (rŭs´tĭk): relating to country life.
3. **germinate** (jûr´mə-nāt): sprout or grow.
4. **capricious** (kə-prĭsh´əs): impulsive.
5. **[From Wordsworth's text]** It is worthwhile here to observe that the affecting parts of Chaucer are almost always expressed in language pure and universally intelligible even to this day.

Shelley wrote *A Defense of Poetry* in 1821 after reading a composition in which friend and fellow poet Thomas Love Peacock jokingly claimed that poetry no longer had a place in society. Because it seemed to Shelley that this view was in fact becoming widely held, he made a passionate argument for the value of poets and poetry.

from

A Defense of *Poetry*

Percy Bysshe Shelley

POETRY is indeed something divine. It is at once the center and circumference of knowledge; . . . Poetry is not like reasoning, a power to be exerted according to the determination of the will. A man cannot say, "I will compose poetry." The greatest poet even cannot say it; for the mind in creation is as a fading coal, which some invisible influence, like an inconstant wind, awakens to transitory brightness; this power arises from within, like the color of a flower which fades and changes as it is developed, and the conscious portions of our natures are
10 unprophetic either of its approach or its departure. . . **D**

Poetry turns all things to loveliness; it exalts the beauty of that which is most beautiful, and it adds beauty to that which is most deformed; it marries exultation and horror, grief and pleasure, eternity and change; it subdues to union under its light yoke all irreconcilable things. It transmutes all that it touches, and every form moving within the radiance of its presence is changed by wondrous sympathy to an incarnation[1] of the spirit which it breathes; its secret alchemy[2] turns to potable[3] gold the poisonous waters which flow from death through life; it strips the veil of
20 familiarity from the world, and lays bare the naked and sleeping beauty which is the spirit of its forms. **E**

---

1. **incarnation** (ĭn′kär-nā′shən): appearance in earthly form.
2. **alchemy** (ăl′kə-mē): chemical reaction.
3. **potable** (pō′tə-bəl): drinkable.

D COMPARE AND CONTRAST
How does Shelley define poetry in lines 1–2?

E COMPARE AND CONTRAST
What language does Shelley use in lines 18–21 to describe poetry's transformative power?

Comprehension

1. **Recall** According to Wordsworth, how does rural life influence poetry?

2. **Clarify** Why does Wordsworth favor "simple and unelaborated expressions" (lines 22–28)?

3. **Recall** How does Shelley define creativity in the first paragraph of *A Defense of Poetry*?

4. **Clarify** According to Shelley in lines 15–21, what is poetry's purpose?

Text Analysis

5. **Analyze Author's Message** What elements does Wordsworth consider essential to poetry? Why?

6. **Analyze Style** How does Shelley's diction, or choice of specific words, reflect his views about poetry?

COMMON CORE

RI 1 Cite strong and thorough textual evidence to support analysis of what the text says explicitly as well as inferences drawn from the text, including determining where the text leaves matters uncertain. **RI 4** Determine the meaning of words and phrases as they are used in a text; analyze how an author uses and refines the meaning of a key term or terms over the course of a text. **W 2b** Develop the topic thoroughly by selecting extended definitions appropriate to the audience's knowledge of the topic.

Reading for Information: Draw Conclusions

WRITING PROMPT

In an essay, compare how Wordsworth and Shelley define what poetry is and what it does. Highlight the most noticeable similarities and differences between these definitions. Then choose one poem by either Wordsworth (pages 800–808) or Shelley (pages 862–871). Discuss how specific features of the author's definition of poetry do or do not apply to one of his own poems. Support your opinion with direct quotations from the two excerpts and the poem.

To answer this prompt, follow these steps:

1. Review the chart you filled in as you compared and contrasted the excerpts. Look for the most noticeable similarities and differences you have listed. Where do Wordsworth and Shelley's definitions differ most? Develop a thesis statement based on your findings.

2. Incorporate examples, based on the key words and phrases from your chart, to support your thesis.

3. It is helpful to organize your essay by first discussing the excerpts' similarities, then their differences. Then, synthesize these ideas to determine how each author defines poetry. Apply your conclusions to one of the author's poems.

[Flow chart: Introduction → Similarities and Differences → Synthesize and Draw Conclusions → Apply Conclusions]

Selected Poetry

by John Keats

VIDEO TRAILER THINKcentral KEYWORD: HML12-878A

Meet the Author

John Keats 1795–1821

John Keats's life was tragically cut short by illness. Yet despite his early death at 25, he managed to compose some of the most evocative and exquisite poems in the English language.

Early Upheaval Born in 1795 to the manager of a livery stable, Keats spent his early years in a joyful household. These carefree times lasted until 1804, when his father died in a riding accident. In 1810, his mother died from tuberculosis. Despite this upheaval, Keats remained for a time at Enfield school, where a teacher, Charles Cowden Clarke, strongly encouraged his passion for reading and his literary ambitions.

A Passion for Poetry Shortly after the death of his mother, Keats was removed from school by his guardian and apprenticed to a surgeon. At the age of 18, he began writing poetry, which soon became the consuming passion of his life. After working as a wound dresser in a London hospital, Keats abandoned medicine for the less certain career of a poet. Initially, Keats experienced little success. His first book, *Poems* (1817), sold poorly, and critics savagely attacked his second book, *Endymion* (1818), a long narrative poem inspired by Greek legend. Although the critical reviews disappointed Keats, they spurred him on.

Triumph and Tragedy Beginning in 1818, Keats confronted a series of physical and emotional crises. Overexerting himself during a walking tour that summer, he fell seriously ill and soon showed early symptoms of tuberculosis. In the fall, he watched as his beloved brother Tom endured the final, terrible stages of that disease and died. Adding greatly to his distress during this period was his passionate love for the young Fanny Brawne, whom he had met prior to Tom's death. Although he became engaged to Fanny, he was prevented by poor health and poverty from marrying her, a situation that caused him severe anguish. Amazingly, in the midst of this misfortune, Keats produced his greatest works. Widely praised by critics, these poems conveyed Keats's intense longing for Fanny, for immortality, and for the beauty of the natural world.

An Early End In the fall of 1820, as his illness progressed, Keats followed the advice of friends and moved to Italy in search of a milder climate. He died less than six months later and was buried in Rome under an epitaph he had composed for himself: "Here lies one whose name was writ in water."

Author Online

Go to **thinkcentral.com**. KEYWORD: HML12-878B

THINKcentral

COMMON CORE

RL 4 Analyze the impact of specific word choices on meaning and tone, including words with multiple meanings or language that is particularly fresh, engaging, or beautiful. **RL 5** Analyze how an author's choices concerning how to structure specific parts of a text contribute to its overall structure and meaning as well as its aesthetic impact. **L 3a** Apply an understanding of syntax to the study of complex texts when reading.

DID YOU KNOW?

John Keats . . .

- was a passionate admirer of William Shakespeare.
- became engaged to, but never married, the love of his life.
- wrote all of his masterpieces in one year, at the age of 22.

(background) Interior of Keats's house in Hampstead

POETIC FORM: ODE

An **ode** is an exalted, complex lyric poem that develops a single, dignified theme. Typically, odes have a serious tone and appeal to both the imagination and the intellect. Many commemorate events or praise people or the beauty of nature. Though the ode had existed since ancient times, the romantic poets gave this poetic form new life. Keats's "Ode on a Grecian Urn," "To Autumn," and "Ode to a Nightingale" are examples of odes.

TEXT ANALYSIS: IMAGERY

Keats's poetry is known for being full of sounds, sights, smells, and warmth. He achieves these sensations through **imagery,** words and phrases that appeal to one or more of the five senses and create sensory experiences for the reader. Sometimes, a poet will create imagery in which one sensation is described in terms of another; this technique is called **synesthesia.** For example, in "Ode on a Grecian Urn," the phrase "Heard melodies are sweet" describes a sound in terms of a taste. As you read these poems, note the type of imagery Keats uses to vividly convey his ideas to the reader.

READING STRATEGY: PARAPHRASE

Keats's poetry can be challenging to read because of the **inverted syntax**—a change in word order that places the verb before the subject. Poets of his era often inverted word order to meet the demands of poetic meter and rhyme. To help you understand the complex phrasing and sentence structures within the poems, **paraphrase,** or restate in your own words, difficult or confusing passages. As you read the poems, use a chart like the one shown to record your paraphrases.

Poem	Keats's Phrase	Paraphrase
"To Autumn"	"...bless/With fruit the vines that round the thatch-eaves run"	Bless with fruit the vines that grow around the thatched roofs

 Complete the activities in your **Reader/Writer Notebook**.

What is BEAUTY?

Some people define beauty in physical terms, as in "That's a beautiful necklace." Others look at it in philosophical ways and try to equate beauty with another abstract idea, such as truth. John Keats saw beauty in both physical and philosophical terms. He also recognized beauty in things that you might not normally think of as beautiful. "I have loved the principle of beauty in all things," he once wrote.

QUICKWRITE Books of quotations, which can be found in library reference sections or online, can provide you with ideas about how famous writers over time have viewed important ideas and topics, such as the definition of *beauty*. Using a book of quotations, find some famous statements that deal with "beauty" or that define it in some way. Choose two that are quite dissimilar. In what ways do they differ? What do those differences reveal about each writer? Which do you think is more true?

When I Have Fears That I May Cease to Be

John Keats

When I have fears that I may cease to be
    Before my pen has glean'd my teeming brain,
Before high piled books, in charactry,
    Hold like rich garners the full ripen'd grain;
5 When I behold, upon the night's starr'd face,
    Huge cloudy symbols of a high romance,
And think that I may never live to trace
    Their shadows, with the magic hand of chance; **A**
And when I feel, fair creature of an hour,
10   That I shall never look upon thee more,
Never have relish in the fairy power
    Of unreflecting love;—then on the shore
Of the wide world I stand alone, and think
Till love and fame to nothingness do sink.

2 glean'd: collected all the bits from; examined bit by bit.

3 charactry: handwriting.

4 garners: storage bins.

A PARAPHRASE
In your own words, restate the meaning of lines 7–8.

Analyze Visuals ▶
Describe the artist's use of light and shadow in the painting. What thoughts or emotions are suggested by the lighting?

Text Analysis

1. **Clarify** What two things does the speaker sometimes fear?

2. **Interpret** In line 9, what does Keats mean by the phrase "fair creature of an hour"?

John Keats (1845), Joseph Severn. Oil. The Granger Collection, New York.

To Autumn   John Keats

Season of mists and mellow fruitfulness,
   Close bosom-friend of the maturing sun;
Conspiring with him how to load and bless
   With fruit the vines that round the thatch-eaves run;
5 To bend with apples the mossed cottage-trees,
   And fill all fruit with ripeness to the core;
     To swell the gourd, and plump the hazel shells
   With a sweet kernel; to set budding more,
And still more, later flowers for the bees,
10 Until they think warm days will never cease,
     For Summer has o'er-brimmed their clammy cells. **B**

Who hath not seen thee oft amid thy store?
   Sometimes whoever seeks abroad may find
Thee sitting careless on a granary floor,
15   Thy hair soft-lifted by the winnowing wind;
Or on a half-reaped furrow sound asleep,
   Drowsed with the fume of poppies, while thy hook
     Spares the next swath and all its twinéd flowers:
And sometimes like a gleaner thou dost keep
20   Steady thy laden head across a brook;
   Or by a cider-press, with patient look,
     Thou watchest the last oozings hours by hours. **C**

4 thatch-eaves: protruding edges of thatched roofs.

B IMAGERY
Reread lines 1–11. Point out words and phrases that suggest the abundance of the setting.

15 winnowing (wĭn'ō-ĭng): separating chaff from grain by blowing the chaff away.

17 hook: a scythe, or tool with a curved blade used for mowing and reaping.

18 swath: a row of grain to be cut.

C PARAPHRASE
Who is being addressed in lines 12–22? In your own words, restate the speaker's message.

Autumn Leaves (1856), Sir John Everett Millais. Oil on canvas, 104.3 cm × 74 cm.
© Manchester Art Gallery, United Kingdom/Bridgeman Art Library.

Where are the songs of Spring? Aye, where are they?
Think not of them, thou hast thy music too—
25 While barred clouds bloom the soft-dying day,
And touch the stubble-plains with rosy hue; **D**
Then in a wailful choir the small gnats mourn
Among the river sallows, borne aloft
Or sinking as the light wind lives or dies;
30 And full-grown lambs loud bleat from hilly bourn;
Hedge crickets sing; and now with treble soft
The redbreast whistles from a garden croft;
And gathering swallows twitter in the skies.

D **IMAGERY**
In line 26, Keats makes use of **synesthesia.** Identify the sensation that is used to describe another.

28 **sallows:** willow trees.

30 **bourn:** region.
31 **treble soft:** faint high pitch.
32 **croft:** a small enclosed field.

Ode on a Grecian Urn   John Keats

Thou still unravish'd bride of quietness,
    Thou foster-child of silence and slow time,
Sylvan historian, who canst thus express
    A flowery tale more sweetly than our rhyme:
5 What leaf-fring'd legend haunts about thy shape
    Of deities or mortals, or of both,
      In Tempe or the dales of Arcady?
    What men or gods are these? What maidens loath?
What mad pursuit? What struggle to escape?
10   What pipes and timbrels? What wild ecstasy?

Heard melodies are sweet, but those unheard
    Are sweeter; therefore, ye soft pipes, play on;
Not to the sensual ear, but, more endear'd,
    Pipe to the spirit ditties of no tone:
15 Fair youth, beneath the trees, thou canst not leave
    Thy song, nor ever can those trees be bare;
      Bold lover, never, never canst thou kiss,
Though winning near the goal—yet, do not grieve;
      She cannot fade, though thou hast not thy bliss,
20   For ever wilt thou love, and she be fair! **Ⓔ**

Ah, happy, happy boughs! that cannot shed
    Your leaves, nor ever bid the spring adieu;
And, happy melodist, unweariéd,
    For ever piping songs for ever new;
25   More happy love! more happy, happy love!
For ever warm and still to be enjoyed,
    For ever panting, and for ever young;
All breathing human passion far above,
    That leaves a heart high-sorrowful and cloy'd,
30   A burning forehead, and a parching tongue.

3 Sylvan: pertaining to trees or woods.

5 haunts about: surrounds.

7 Tempe (tĕm'pē') ... **Arcady** (är'kə-dē): two places in Greece that became traditional literary settings for an idealized rustic life. Tempe is a beautiful valley; Arcady (Arcadia) is a mountainous region.

8 loath: unwilling; reluctant.

10 timbrels: tambourines.

Language Coach

Misused Words Both *sensual* and *sensuous* originally meant "of the senses"—the meaning in line 13. One word now relates more to the pleasure of the senses. Find out which one by checking a dictionary.

Ⓔ ODE
Based on the imagery and ideas in the poem so far, what is being commemorated? Is it simply a Grecian urn? Explain.

29 cloy'd: having had too much of something; oversatisfied.

Who are these coming to the sacrifice?
　　To what green altar, O mysterious priest,
Lead'st thou that heifer lowing at the skies,
　　And all her silken flanks with garlands drest? **F**
35 What little town by river or sea shore,
　　Or mountain-built with peaceful citadel,
　　　Is emptied of this folk, this pious morn?
And, little town, thy streets for evermore
　　Will silent be; and not a soul to tell
40　　　Why thou art desolate, can e'er return.

O Attic shape! Fair attitude! with brede
　　Of marble men and maidens overwrought,
With forest branches and the trodden weed;
　　Thou, silent form, dost tease us out of thought
45 As doth eternity: Cold Pastoral!
　　When old age shall this generation waste,
　　　Thou shalt remain, in midst of other woe
Than ours, a friend to man, to whom thou say'st,
"Beauty is truth, truth beauty,"—that is all
50　　　Ye know on earth, and all ye need to know.

F PARAPHRASE
In your own words, describe the scene depicted in lines 32–34.

41 Attic: pure and classical; in the style of Attica, the part of Greece where Athens is located; **brede** (brēd): interwoven design.

45 Pastoral (păs'tər-əl): an artistic work that portrays rural life in an idealized way.

Text Analysis

1. **Clarify** In the first stanza of "Ode on a Grecian Urn," why is the urn referred to as a "sylvan historian"? What is the "flowery tale" it tells?

2. **Draw Conclusions** In "To Autumn," what impression of autumn emerges from the description given? What attitude toward spring is implied?

3. **Evaluate Poems** In both "To Autumn" and "Ode on a Grecian Urn," the speaker is directly addressing something as if it were present. This technique is known as **apostrophe.** Explain what or who is being addressed in each poem and whether or not this technique is effective in conveying the speaker's emotions toward the subject.

Ode to a Nightingale   John Keats

1

My heart aches, and a drowsy numbness pains
    My sense, as though of hemlock I had drunk,
Or emptied some dull opiate to the drains
    One minute past, and Lethe-wards had sunk:
5 'Tis not through envy of thy happy lot,
    But being too happy in thine happiness,—
        That thou, light-winged Dryad of the trees,
        In some melodious plot
    Of beechen green, and shadows numberless,
10   Singest of summer in full-throated ease.

2

O, for a draught of vintage! that hath been
    Cool'd a long age in the deep-delved earth,
Tasting of Flora and the country green,
    Dance, and Provençal song, and sunburnt mirth!
15 O for a beaker full of the warm South,
    Full of the true, the blushful Hippocrene,
        With beaded bubbles winking at the brim,
        And purple-stained mouth;
    That I might drink, and leave the world unseen,
20   And with thee fade away into the forest dim: **G**

3

Fade far away, dissolve, and quite forget
    What thou among the leaves hast never known,
The weariness, the fever, and the fret
    Here, where men sit and hear each other groan;
25 Where palsy shakes a few, sad, last grey hairs,
    Where youth grows pale, and spectre-thin, and dies;
        Where but to think is to be full of sorrow
        And leaden-eyed despairs,
    Where beauty cannot keep her lustrous eyes,
30   Or new Love pine at them beyond to-morrow.

2 hemlock: a poisonous plant.

4 Lethe-wards (lē′thē): into oblivion. The Lethe was a river in the underworld of Greek mythology; drinking its waters was said to bring forgetfulness.

7 Dryad (drī′əd): in Greek mythology, a nymph or god of the woods.

9 beechen: relating to beech trees.

11 draught (dräft) **of vintage:** drink of wine.

13 Flora: flowers. Flora was the Roman goddess of flowers.

14 Provençal (prō′vän-säl′) **song:** a song from the southern French area of Provence.

16 blushful Hippocrene (hĭp′ə-krēn′): Hippocrene was the fountain used by the Muses, the Greek goddesses said to inspire poetry and the other arts.

G IMAGERY
Reread lines 11–20 and identify examples of **synesthesia.**

25 palsy (pôl′zē): paralysis of the muscles, usually accompanied by tremors.

Sleeping Shepherd–Morning (1857), Samuel Palmer. © Fitzwilliam Museum, University of Cambridge, United Kingdom/Bridgeman Art Library.

4

Away! away! for I will fly to thee,
    Not charioted by Bacchus and his pards,
But on the viewless wings of Poesy,
    Though the dull brain perplexes and retards:
35 Already with thee! tender is the night,
    And haply the Queen-Moon is on her throne,
        Cluster'd around by all her starry Fays;
           But here there is no light,
    Save what from heaven is with the breezes blown
40   Through verdurous glooms and winding mossy ways.

32 Bacchus (băk′əs) **... pards:** the ancient Roman god and the leopards that drove his chariot.

33 viewless: invisible; **Poesy** (pō′ĭ-zē): poetry.

36 haply: perhaps.

37 Fays: fairies.

39 Save: except.

40 verdurous (vûr′jər-əs): green with plant life.

5

I cannot see what flowers are at my feet,
    Nor what soft incense hangs upon the boughs,
But, in embalmed darkness, guess each sweet
    Wherewith the seasonable month endows
45 The grass, the thicket, and the fruit-tree wild;
    White hawthorn, and the pastoral eglantine;
      Fast fading violets cover'd up in leaves;
        And mid-May's eldest child,
    The coming musk-rose, full of dewy wine,
50   The murmurous haunt of flies on summer eves.

43 embalmed (ĕm-bämd′): perfumed.

46 pastoral (păs′tər-əl): rural; **eglantine** (ĕg′lən-tīn′): honeysuckle or sweetbrier.

6

Darkling I listen; and, for many a time
    I have been half in love with easeful Death,
Call'd him soft names in many a mused rhyme,
    To take into the air my quiet breath;
55 Now more than ever seems it rich to die,
    To cease upon the midnight with no pain,
      While thou art pouring forth thy soul abroad
        In such an ecstasy!
    Still wouldst thou sing, and I have ears in vain—
60   To thy high requiem become a sod.

51 Darkling: in the dark.

53 mused: meditated; pondered.

60 requiem (rĕk′wē-əm): funeral mass; **sod:** a piece of earth.

7

Thou wast not born for death, immortal Bird!
    No hungry generations tread thee down;
The voice I hear this passing night was heard
    In ancient days by emperor and clown:
65 Perhaps the self-same song that found a path
    Through the sad heart of Ruth, when, sick for home,
      She stood in tears amid the alien corn;
        The same that oft-times hath
    Charm'd magic casements, opening on the foam
70   Of perilous seas, in faery lands forlorn.

64 clown: rustic; peasant.

66 Ruth: the biblical Ruth, who left her native land to live with her husband's people.

69 casements: hinged windows that open outward.

8

Forlorn! the very word is like a bell
    To toll me back from thee to my sole self!
Adieu! the fancy cannot cheat so well
    As she is fam'd to do, deceiving elf.
75 Adieu! adieu! thy plaintive anthem fades
    Past the near meadows, over the still stream,
      Up the hill-side; and now 'tis buried deep
        In the next valley-glades:
    Was it a vision, or a waking dream?
80   Fled is that music:—Do I wake or sleep? **Ⓗ**

73 fancy: the "viewless wings of Poesy" mentioned earlier.

Ⓗ ODE
Describe the **tone** of this poem. How is it characteristic of an ode?

LETTER John Keats wrote a number of poems for his fiancée, Fanny Brawne, and sent her dozens of letters. The following letter was written in February 1820, shortly after he became ill with the tuberculosis that would eventually take his life.

My dear Fanny,

Do not let your mother suppose that you hurt me by writing at night. For some reason or other your last night's note was not so treasurable as former ones. I would fain that you call me Love still. To see you happy and in high spirits is a great consolation to me—still let me believe that you are not half so happy as my restoration would make you. I am nervous, I own, and may think myself worse than I really am; if so you must indulge me, and pamper with that sort of tenderness you have manifested towards me in different Letters. My sweet creature when I look back upon the pains and torments I have suffered for you from the day I left you to go to the Isle of Wight; the ecstasies in which I have passed some days and the miseries in their turn, I wonder the more at the Beauty which has kept up the spell so fervently. When I send this round I shall be in the front parlor watching to see you show yourself for a minute in the garden. How illness stands as a barrier betwixt me and you! Even if I was well—I must make myself as good a Philosopher as possible. Now I have had opportunities of passing nights anxious and awake I have found other thoughts intrude upon me. "If I should die," said I to myself, "I have left no immortal work behind me—nothing to make my friends proud of my memory—but I have loved the principle of beauty in all things, and if I had had time I would have made myself remembered." Thoughts like these came very feebly whilst I was in health and every pulse beat for you—now you divide with this (may I say it?) "last infirmity of noble minds" all my reflection.

God bless you, Love.

J. Keats

Comprehension

1. **Recall** In "Ode to a Nightingale," what emotions does the speaker feel when he hears the bird's song?

2. **Clarify** Why does the speaker long to join the nightingale?

Text Analysis

3. **Paraphrase Quatrains** In each quatrain of the sonnet "When I Have Fears That I May Cease to Be," Keats examines an aspect of the fear of death. Paraphrase each quatrain, noting the parallel clauses at the beginning of each.

4. **Examine Personification** In "To Autumn," how is autumn personified, or given human attributes, in each of the stanzas? Cite examples from the poem to support your answer.

5. **Analyze Sound Devices** Find examples of these sound devices—**alliteration, assonance, consonance**—in "Ode to a Nightingale." How does each example contribute to the poem's effect?

6. **Interpret Imagery** Think about the imagery in lines 41–50 in "Ode to a Nightingale." In your own words, describe the scene the speaker conveys to the reader. Explain how these images are related to the nightingale and what they suggest about the nightingale's song.

7. **Intepret Ambiguity** Reread the final **couplet,** lines 49–50, of "Ode on a Grecian Urn." Explain what you think Keats meant to convey to his readers. Support your answer.

8. **Draw Conclusions About Odes** In "To Autumn," "Ode on a Grecian Urn," and "Ode to a Nightingale," Keats expresses a deep appreciation for the beauty of nature and of art. What value does he seem to ascribe to beauty?

9. **Compare Texts** Look again at "When I Have Fears That I May Cease to Be" and Keats's letter to Fanny Brawne (page 889). Note the poetic language—such as **poetic diction, imagery,** and **figurative language**—in the poem, and then look for similar examples in the letter. Explain your choices.

Text Criticism

10. **Biographical Context** Keats wrote the three odes you read following the death of his brother Tom and in the midst of his own worsening illness. In what ways are his experiences with illness and death reflected in the poems? Cite details to support your conclusions.

What is **BEAUTY?**

Keats claims that, "Beauty is truth, truth beauty." How may beauty conceal, rather than reveal, truth?

COMMON CORE

RL 4 Analyze the impact of specific word choices on meaning and tone, including words with multiple meanings or language that is particularly fresh, engaging, or beautiful. **RL 5** Analyze how an author's choices concerning how to structure specific parts of a text contribute to its overall structure and meaning as well as its aesthetic impact. **L 3a** Apply an understanding of syntax to the study of complex texts when reading.

Romantic Ideals

Byron, Shelley, and Keats were men of fervent ideals who lived radical lives and poured their feelings into passionate verse.

> *"She walks in beauty, like the night*
> *Of cloudless climes and starry skies;*
> *And all that's best of dark and bright*
> *Meet in her aspect and her eyes:"*
>
> **—George Gordon, Lord Byron**

Many of the ideas that the late romantics expressed have become intrinsic to Western culture, felt not only in art but in politics and even in the way people view themselves in relation to one another, to nature, and to the universe. In fact, these ideas are so pervasive in the modern world that some have gone so far as to say that the romantic era has yet to end.

Writing to Synthesize

Review the poems in this section (pages 848–890) and choose one from each poet. Look closely at the imagery and themes explored in the poems, and consider what they tell you about romantic ideas. Take notes in a chart like the one shown. Write a brief essay in which you discuss what the poems suggest about relationships, nature, or the human condition and how these ideas continue to be expressed in today's world.

	Poem #1	Poem #2	Poem #3
Imagery and Themes			
Ideas Conveyed			

Extension

SPEAKING & LISTENING Reread the excerpt from Shelley's *A Defense of Poetry* (page 876). Do you agree with his ideas about poetry's place in the world? Write a speech in which you pose your own defense of poetry and its role in today's world. Deliver the speech to your class.

⁙ **COMMON CORE**

W 9 Draw evidence from literary or informational texts to support analysis, reflection, and research. **SL 4** Present information, findings, and supporting evidence, conveying a clear and distinct perspective, such that listeners can follow the line of reasoning.

Writing Workshop

INFORMATIVE TEXT

Online Feature Article

The power of nature, the consequences of war, the price of technological progress—these are some of the ideas that writers of the romantic movement explored. To learn more about romanticism, you might turn to the World Wide Web to access a vast network of information. Now, you will contribute to this network by creating an **online feature article**—an informative piece of writing on an interesting topic or trend.

 Complete the workshop activities in your **Reader/Writer Notebook**.

WRITE WITH A PURPOSE

WRITING TASK

Write an **online feature article** about a topic, trend, person, or phenomenon that interests you.

Idea Starters
- the importance of nature as a retreat
- an environmental issue or solution
- a modern-day genre study of fantasy, science fiction, or horror
- Jane Austen's influence on modern pop culture

THE ESSENTIALS

Here are some common purposes, audiences, and formats for informative/explanatory online writing.

PURPOSES	AUDIENCES	FORMATS
• to learn more about a topic • to explain an unfamiliar topic to readers • to develop and maintain an online readership	• classmates and teacher • online groups with an interest in your subject • friends on a social networking site • organizations devoted to your subject	• wiki article • news report • magazine article • encyclopedia entry • podcast • how-to article

COMMON CORE TRAITS

1. DEVELOPMENT OF IDEAS
- provides a compelling **introduction** with a strong **controlling idea**
- develops the topic with **significant** and **relevant evidence**
- offers a **concluding section** that supports the information

2. ORGANIZATION OF IDEAS
- logically **organizes information** to create a unified whole
- effectively uses **formatting, links, graphics,** and **multimedia**
- uses varied **transitions** and **syntax** to create cohesion and connect ideas

3. LANGUAGE FACILITY AND CONVENTIONS
- uses **precise language, domain-specific vocabulary,** and **literary techniques**
- maintains a **formal style** and **objective tone**
- correctly hyphenates **compound adjectives**
- employs correct **grammar, mechanics,** and **spelling**

Writing Online THINK central

Go to **thinkcentral.com**.
KEYWORD: HML12N-892

Planning/Prewriting

COMMON CORE

W 2a–f Write informative/explanatory texts to convey complex information. **W 6** Use technology to produce writing products. **W 7** Conduct short research projects; synthesize multiple sources on the subject.

Getting Started

CHOOSE A TOPIC

To find inspiration for possible topics, browse newspapers or online news sites, consider your own interests, or brainstorm ideas with classmates. Then conduct a preliminary online search for information on the topic that most appeals to you. Skim books, articles, and Web sites to check the availability of sources and to narrow the scope of your article. Look for specific angles from which you might examine your subject. Finally, frame your topic as a **research question** to help guide a more extensive search for relevant information.

▶ **WHAT DOES IT LOOK LIKE?**

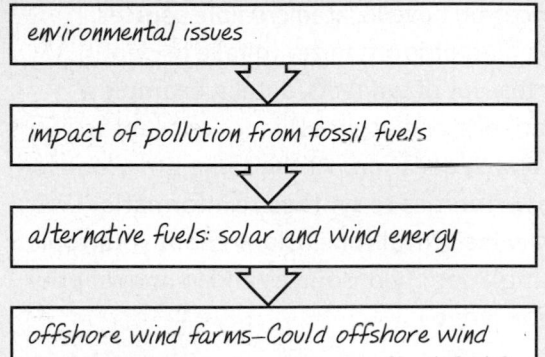

LOCATE SOURCES

Once you have narrowed your focus, you can begin to locate **authoritative print** and **digital sources.** Sites ending in *.gov, .edu,* or *.org* are usually worth investigating further. Look for resources with helpful information and **relevant** photos, videos, or audio clips that you might link to.

Keep track of each reliable source you find. Record the title, author, and page number of print sources, or the Web address (URL) for online sources. Briefly describe the information each source provides.

▶ **WHAT DOES IT LOOK LIKE?**

Sources	Description
Web site: "Offshore Wind Energy" ocsenergy.anl.gov	explains offshore wind technology
Book: <u>Cape Wind</u> by Wendy Williams and Robert Whitcomb	information on the wind farm project off Nantucket

THINK ABOUT AUDIENCE AND PURPOSE

Your **purpose** is to share your knowledge about a complex topic in a way that your **audience** can understand. Consider how much your audience may or may not know about the topic. This will determine the amount of background information you need to include as well as the way you approach your explanation.

▶ **TIPS**

As you survey your sources, look for:
- details that give general **background information** on your topic
- definitions or brief explanations of **domain-specific vocabulary** (specialized terms or jargon)
- ways to explain complex ideas through **metaphors, similes,** or **analogies**
- **graphics** and **multimedia** to illustrate complicated or essential ideas

Planning/Prewriting *continued*

Getting Started

GATHER EVIDENCE

Once you have located credible sources, use a graphic organizer to take in-depth notes. Jot down facts, details, examples, statistics, and other evidence relevant to your research question. At the same time, look for opportunities to **synthesize** information—to draw insightful conclusions about your topic using a variety of sources and your own prior knowledge.

▶ **WHAT DOES IT LOOK LIKE?**

Cape Wind, an offshore wind farm planned for the waters near Cape Cod, is still mired in controversy and lacks a working turbine after almost a decade. "Offshore Wind May Power the Future," <u>Scientific American</u>	European offshore wind farms are just a few miles off the coast. Those in the U.S. would be built farther out, requiring new technologies to ensure the operation of turbines in deeper and rougher waters. "Offshore Wind Energy"

Offshore wind farms in the United States have many obstacles to overcome; persistence and determination will be necessary for success.

DRAFT A CONTROLLING IDEA

Use your evidence to write a **controlling idea,** or thesis statement, that answers your research question. Your controlling idea should explain what you want your audience to know about your topic.

▶ **WHAT DOES IT LOOK LIKE?**

Dependency on fossil fuels is hurting us and our planet. We need to exploit wind energy, which is clean and renewable. Offshore wind farms are a viable solution, but only if obstacles currently preventing development of this technology are removed.

GENERATE A STORYBOARD

Create a storyboard to outline your information.

- Use **formatting,** such as headings, subheadings, bulleted lists, and links.
- Indicate where you will include **multimedia.**
- Open with a screen that includes a menu and background information.

▶ **WHAT DOES IT LOOK LIKE?**

Offshore Wind Farms

Sidebar <u>Contents</u> <u>Additional</u> <u>Resources</u>	Background Fossil fuel problems and overview of wind energy	Photo of an offshore wind farm

PEER REVIEW Exchange storyboards with a classmate. Discuss your controlling ideas and the evidence you plan to include. Then ask: What additional questions would you want my article to answer? Is my article easy to navigate?

YOUR TURN In your *Reader/Writer Notebook,* list topic ideas and choose one to write about. Phrase your topic in the form of a question. Then gather sources, draft your controlling idea, and create a storyboard.

Drafting

COMMON CORE

W 4 Produce clear and coherent writing appropriate to task, purpose, and audience. **W 8** Follow a standard format for citation. **W 9b (RI 1)** Draw evidence from informational texts; cite textual evidence. **L 2** Demonstrate command of standard English punctuation.

The following chart shows how to organize a coherent online feature article.

Organizing Your Online Feature Article

INTRODUCTION

- Grab the attention of the audience with a **challenging question, compelling quotation,** or **startling fact.**
- Provide enough **background information** for readers to understand the topic.
- Present a concise **controlling idea,** or thesis statement.
- Establish a **formal style,** using an **objective,** or controlled, **tone** and **precise language.**

▼

BODY

- State your **main ideas** clearly, so that each builds on the previous idea.
- Support your ideas with significant **facts, definitions, details, quotations,** and **multimedia.**
- Document the **source** of each idea that you did not originate, or create.
- Use **varied transitions** and **syntax** (sentence structures) to create cohesion and connect ideas.
- Include **text features,** such as heading and links, to facilitate navigation.

▼

CONCLUDING SECTION:

- Restate your **controlling idea,** and explain the **significance** of your topic.

GRAMMAR IN CONTEXT: INCORPORATING QUOTATIONS

Cite sources of direct quotations both in the text of your article and in your Works Cited section. Use these guidelines to help you.

- Place opening and closing quotation marks around someone else's direct words.
- Integrate short quotations into your own sentences.
- Use ellipses in place of words you want to omit from the quotation.
- Put the author's last name and the page number of the quotation in parentheses at the end of the sentence. If there is no author, include the title of the work. If you mention the author in your text, include only the page number in the citation.
- Link your in-text citation to your Works Cited section.

> The U.S. Department of Energy reports that offshore wind resources have the potential to provide "roughly four times the generating capacity currently carried on the U.S. electric grid" (Musial 4).

See pages 1438–1439 for Modern Language Association guidelines for creating a Works Cited list.

YOUR TURN Draft your article in a word-processing document. Integrate and punctuate your quotations. Using your storyboard as a guide, input text into the online forum you chose.

Revising

As you revise, make sure the development, organization, and style of your article supports your controlling idea and achieves your purpose. Rewrite parts to clarify important ideas for your audience. The following chart will help you revise and rewrite the parts of your draft that need reworking.

ONLINE FEATURE ARTICLE

Ask Yourself	Tips	Revision Strategies
1. Do I capture the audience's attention in my opening lines?	▶ **Bracket** the first sentences of your article.	▶ **Add** an attention-getting statement, quotation, or startling fact.
2. Is my controlling idea clear and appropriate to my audience and purpose?	▶ **Underline** the controlling idea.	▶ **Insert** a controlling idea if one is missing. **Rewrite** the existing one to more clearly state the main idea of your article.
3. Is my organization logical, effective, and easy to navigate?	▶ **Circle** headings, links, and menu options.	▶ **Group** related paragraphs under boldfaced headings. **Add** more links to your menu to allow users to jump to different sections of your article.
4. Do I include significant and relevant evidence to support my controlling idea?	▶ **Highlight** text or multimedia that appears unrelated to your controlling idea.	▶ **Delete** extraneous information. **Insert** concrete details, extended definitions, and quotations for ideas not supported.
5. Are all my sources documented correctly? See pages 1438–1439 for additional support.	▶ **Underline** each piece of evidence. **Draw a star** next to each corresponding citation and Works Cited entry.	▶ **Insert** in-text citations and/or Works Cited entries for evidence that lacks stars.
6. Does my concluding section follow from and support the information I presented?	▶ **Put check marks** next to the summary of what you learned and the statement of the topic's significance.	▶ **Add** a summary and/or explanation of the importance of the topic if needed.

YOUR TURN *PEER REVIEW* Have a peer use this chart to evaluate your article. Ask: How could I strengthen my controlling idea? What other evidence could I provide? Are my multimedia elements effective or distracting? Is my article easy to navigate?

ANALYZE A STUDENT DRAFT

As you read this student's draft, notice the comments on its strengths as well as suggestions for improvement.

 **COMMON CORE** **W 2a–b** Include formatting, graphics, and multimedia; develop the topic with relevant information. **W 5** Strengthen writing by revising, rewriting, or trying a new approach. **SL 5** Make strategic use of digital media.

Offshore Wind Farms
by Dimitri N.

Contents
- Background
- History of Wind Energy
- Pros and Cons
- Controversies
- Future of Offshore Wind Farms
- Glossary of Terms
- Works Cited

Additional Resources
- Schematics
- Images
- Video Clips
- Breaking News
- Discussion Board

Background

"Oh, lift me as a wave, a leaf, a cloud!" So pleads the speaker of Percy Bysshe Shelley's "Ode to the West Wind," celebrating the wind's powerful energy and the potential it holds to bring positive change. Although we might not talk about wind quite as passionately as Shelley, for us too, wind promises positive change. Wind energy, generated in offshore wind farms, is a viable alternative to fossil fuels, but only if current obstacles are removed.

We depend on coal-burning plants to generate most of the energy we consume. Inherent within this source of fuel are many problems. First, much of the energy from burning coal escapes because the process is inefficient. Second, these plants are major air polluters in the United States. One plant alone can empty close to 370 million tons of carbon dioxide into the air a year, equivalent to cutting down 161 million trees. In addition, that same plant annually emits tons of acid rain causing sulfur dioxide, ozone forming nitrogen oxide, carbon monoxide, mercury, and lead as well as other contaminants ("Coal Power").

While wind energy is not a solution for *all* the problems caused by fossil fuels, it offers a free, clean, and renewable alternative. Wind is created by heated air displacing cooler damper air. Over water, the speed of this exchange increases. As the wind speed increases, so does the amount of electricity that it can produce ("Wind Energy Basics"). Therefore, offshore would be a perfect location for wind farms.

A wind farm is a collection of wind turbines that form a single power plant. A wind turbine, a modern-day windmill, has blades that turn in the wind and spin a shaft, which, in turn, is connected to a generator to make electricity. The turbines used in offshore wind farms …

Next: Background, continued

> Dimitri opens with an **intriguing quotation from a poem.**

> The **sidebar** enables readers to easily **navigate** the article.

> Dimitri includes a **relevant statistic** to explain the dimensions of the problem.

> Dimitri could include **multimedia.** He is introducing important terms that are fundamental to his audience's understanding.

LEARN HOW Use Multimedia Effectively Dimitri uses technical terms and refers to ideas that his audience may not be familiar with. He can help readers understand his topic by linking to diagrams, definitions, and videos from reliable sources.

DIMITRI'S REVISION TO *BACKGROUND*

link to video of wind farm in operation   *link to a diagram of a wind turbine*

A <u>wind farm</u> is a collection of <u>wind turbines</u> that form a single power plant.

YOUR TURN Use feedback you received as well as the "Learn How" lesson to revise your article. Evaluate your use of multimedia elements and online text features. Consider a new approach if something is simply not working.

Editing and Publishing

COMMON CORE

W 5 Strengthen writing by editing. **L 1** Demonstrate command of the conventions of standard English grammar and usage. **L 2a** Observe hyphenation conventions.

In the editing stage, you proofread your article to make sure it is free of grammar, spelling, and punctuation errors. Mistakes can detract from your article and prevent your audience from understanding and appreciating your ideas. Also, be sure all your online features work correctly, including links and multimedia elements. Consider whether the fonts you have chosen are appropriate for your content and easy to read.

GRAMMAR IN CONTEXT: HYPHENS AND COMPOUND ADJECTIVES

A **hyphen** is a punctuation mark used to join compound adjectives that precede the nouns they modify. Often a hyphen is necessary to avoid ambiguous phrasing that might confuse readers. By placing hyphens in this sentence from his article, Dimitri improved the precision of his writing.

> In addition, that same plant may emit tons of acid-rain-causing sulfur dioxide, ozone-forming nitrogen oxide, carbon monoxide, mercury, and lead as well as other contaminants.

PUBLISH YOUR WRITING

After you have finished proofreading your article, you are ready to post it online. Consider these ideas:

- Embed links to your article on any social networking sites that you visit.
- Send e-mails to your contacts to let them know that your article is online and ready to view.
- Create a class menu of feature articles on the Web site that is hosting your work. Group related articles under descriptive boldfaced headings, and include links to everyone's article.

YOUR TURN Correct any errors in your article. Make sure to use correct hyphenation. After you've applied these finishing touches, publish your online feature article for your audience.

Scoring Rubric

Use this rubric to evaluate your online feature article.

ONLINE FEATURE ARTICLE

SCORE	COMMON CORE TRAITS
6	• **Development** Effectively introduces a well-researched topic and controlling idea; develops the topic with relevant evidence that builds to a unified whole; ends powerfully • **Organization** Logically organizes information; includes formatting and multimedia that enhances the information; uses varied transitions and syntax; correctly cites sources • **Language** Ably uses precise words; maintains a formal style and objective tone; shows a strong command of conventions
5	• **Development** Competently introduces a topic; states a controlling idea; offers relevant evidence that builds from point to point; has a strong concluding section • **Organization** Is logically organized; includes formatting and multimedia; often uses transitions and varies syntax; correctly cites sources • **Language** Uses precise words; generally maintains a formal style and neutral tone; has a few errors in conventions
4	• **Development** Sufficiently introduces a topic; states a controlling idea; offers mostly relevant evidence; has an adequate concluding section • **Organization** Is logically organized; could use more formatting and multimedia; uses transitions and varies syntax; correctly cites sources • **Language** Uses vague words in some places; mostly maintains a formal style and objective tone; includes a few distracting errors in conventions
3	• **Development** States a controlling idea, but the introduction could be more compelling; lacks sufficient evidence; has a somewhat weak concluding section • **Organization** Has some flaws in organization; doesn't include enough formatting and multimedia; uses some transitions and varied syntax; does not cite all sources • **Language** Needs more precise words; has frequent lapses in style and tone; has some critical errors in conventions
2	• **Development** Has a weak controlling idea; does not support most ideas; ends abruptly • **Organization** Has organizational flaws; lacks formatting and multimedia; lacks transitions and varied syntax; neglects to cite many sources • **Language** Lacks precise words or uses them incorrectly; uses an informal style and tone; has many distracting errors in conventions
1	• **Development** Lacks a controlling idea; offers little, if any, development; has no ending • **Organization** Has no organization, formatting, or multimedia; plagiarizes or does not credit sources • **Language** Uses vague words; has an inappropriate style and tone; has major problems in conventions

Technology Workshop

Updating an Online Feature Article

Once you have published your article online, it is important to keep it updated, revising or adding content to maintain its credibility. In this workshop, you will learn how to effectively update, improve, and enhance your online article.

 Complete the workshop activities in your **Reader/Writer Notebook**.

PRODUCE WITH A PURPOSE

TASK

Update your online feature article to provide new information on your topic, address issues of design and navigation, and replace dead (broken) links.

COMMON CORE TRAITS

A SUCCESSFUL UPDATE . . .

- removes obsolete information and dead links
- revises content to address new information about the topic
- responds promptly and respectfully to readers' questions and feedback
- modifies design or navigation when appropriate
- increases readership by seeking new audiences and drawing return visitors

COMMON CORE

W 6 Use technology to update writing products. **SL 1c–d** Propel conversations; respond thoughtfully to diverse perspectives. **SL 2** Integrate multiple sources of information presented in diverse media. **SL 5** Make strategic use of digital media.

Maintaining Your Article

After publishing your article online, visit the site frequently and spend a few minutes maintaining it. Use these guidelines to help you:

- **Update Your Links** The external Web sites you linked to may update the information and structure of their sites or even change their addresses. For this reason, you should check each link to make sure the Web address, or URL, you used is still functional and connects to the information you intended. Update dead or incorrect links to reflect the correct addresses, remove the links altogether, or replace them with new sites.

- **Respond to Comments** Make sure to read in a timely manner everything that's posted. Address any comments or requests for information with respectful responses. Remove inappropriate comments as quickly as possible.

- **Add a *Last Updated* Date** Include a line of text that provides the date you last updated your article. This lets your readers know how recent the information is and that you are committed to keeping it current.

Media Tools

Go to **thinkcentral.com**.
KEYWORD: HML12N-900

Modifying and Improving Your Article

Part of updating an online article is modifying or improving it as you receive feedback and learn more about your topic. Making improvements can add dimension to your article, attract new readers, and encourage readers to return. You might modify your article for a variety of reasons, such as:

- **To Add Content** If you have chosen a current topic for your online article, your original material may become outdated as new information becomes available. For example, the status of offshore wind farms in the United States could change quickly depending on decisions made by state and federal governments. Incorporate new content by revising the article or adding links to new sources of information from diverse media, including video news clips. Consider adding a Recent News or Updates section in which you link to other sites with new information.

- **To Address User Feedback** Readers may offer feedback about any aspect of your article, such as the accuracy of your facts, the design of your site, or the ease of using the navigational features you incorporate. Before making significant changes, synthesize the feedback you've received and decide what additional information or research is required. Be willing to revise your article, rework features, or even try a new approach to address valid feedback.

- **To Redesign Your Article** Periodically redesign your article to keep it looking current. Reorganize the menu or navigational features, add new images or multimedia, or try new fonts and backgrounds. Any changes you make should have a clear purpose—for example, to make your article look dynamic and engaging without detracting from what you want to communicate.

- **To Increase Your Readership** When you make changes to your article, consider posting a status update on your social networking site. Send e-mail updates to your target audience or post a link to your article on any related sites. That way, you can appeal to new readers and encourage previous readers to return.

> **Ancient Mariner** (reader) said...
>
> Certainly the construction of massive turbines will impact marine life. But have there been any studies on the possibility of creating artificial reefs with these foundations to balance this disruption?
>
> March 10, 3:30 p.m.
>
> **Dimitri** (Site Administrator) said...
>
> You've raised an interesting point. I'll have to research that. Do other readers have information on this concept?
>
> March 10, 7:15 p.m.

E-MAIL UPDATE

Dimitri: Check the new section I added to my feature article about ways to counteract the disruption of marine life in offshore wind farms. You can even view footage of thriving underwater colonies that have settled around the pilings of a Danish wind farm.

YOUR TURN   Visit your online article often. Check all links to make sure they work, replacing those that don't. Address any feedback promptly and respectfully. Keep your information current and try to engage your readers.

Assessment Practice

DIRECTIONS Read the following texts and then answer the questions.

from # The Prelude, Book VI
by William Wordsworth

           . . . The brook and road
      Were fellow-travellers in this gloomy Pass,
      And with them did we journey several hours
      At a slow step. The immeasurable height
5   Of woods decaying, never to be decayed,
      The stationary blasts of water-falls,
      And every where along the hollow rent
      Winds thwarting winds, bewildered and forlorn,
      The torrents shooting from the clear blue sky,
      The rocks that muttered close upon our ears,
10   Black drizzling crags that spake by the way-side
      As if a voice were in them, the sick sight
      And giddy prospect of the raving stream,
      The unfettered clouds and region of the heavens,
      Tumult and peace, the darkness and the light
15   Were all like workings of one mind, the features
      Of the same face, blossoms upon one tree,
      Characters of the great Apocalypse,
      The types and symbols of Eternity,
      Of first and last, and midst, and without end.
20

from Hymn to Intellectual[1] Beauty

by Percy Bysshe Shelley

1

The awful shadow of some unseen Power
    Floats though unseen amongst us,—visiting
    This various world with as inconstant wing
As summer winds that creep from flower to flower.—
5 Like moonbeams that behind some piny mountain shower,
    It visits with inconstant glance
    Each human heart and countenance;
Like hues and harmonies of evening,—
    Like clouds in starlight widely spread,—
10   Like memory of music fled,—
    Like aught that for its grace may be
Dear, and yet dearer for its mystery.

2

Spirit of BEAUTY, that dost consecrate
    With thine own hues all thou dost shine upon
    Of human thought or form,—where art thou gone?
15 Why dost thou pass away and leave our state,
This dim vast vale of tears, vacant and desolate?
    Ask why the sunlight not forever
    Weaves rainbows o'er yon mountain river,
20 Why aught should fail and fade that once is shewn,
    Why fear and dream and death and birth
    Cast on the daylight of this earth
    Such gloom,—why man has such a scope
For love and hate, despondency and hope?

---

1. **Intellectual:** not material.

GO ON

Reading Comprehension

Use "The Prelude" (p. 902) to answer questions 1–7.

1. The contradictory image of "woods decaying, never to be decayed" in line 5 suggests —
   A. harmony and discord
   B. perfection and imperfection
   C. change and permanence
   D. solitude and companionship

2. In lines 6–8, assonance and consonance help to convey the sounds of —
   A. water and wind
   B. birds and people
   C. hooves and people's feet
   D. echoes and whispers in the pass

3. Which phrase in the poem presents an image of freedom?
   A. *stationary blasts*
   B. *giddy prospect*
   C. *unfettered clouds*
   D. *blossoms upon one tree*

4. Which phrase presents an image of conflicting forces?
   A. *gloomy Pass*
   B. *immeasurable height*
   C. *Winds thwarting winds*
   D. *torrents shooting*

5. Wordsworth's use of personification and onomatopoeia in lines 10–11 helps to —
   A. create a humorous image
   B. convey a sense of harmony
   C. emphasize that nature is alive
   D. illustrate the beauty of nature

6. A characteristic of romanticism that is evident in lines 4–15 is the poet's use of —
   A. supernatural experiences to explain human feelings
   B. descriptions of common people and their daily lives
   C. natural phenomena to find solutions to society's problems
   D. images that exalt the creative and destructive forces of nature

7. The similes in lines 16–20 express the belief that —
   A. all of nature's variety stems from a single, timeless source
   B. nature is like the mind of a dangerous criminal
   C. ancient texts reveal the true meaning of the laws of nature
   D. the course of friendship is similar to a journey through the mountains

Use "Hymn to Intellectual Beauty" (p. 903) to answer questions 8–15.

8. Which image in the first stanza is a metaphor for the "intellectual beauty" of the title?
   A. *The awful shadow*
   B. *This various world*
   C. *summer winds*
   D. *piny mountain*

9. In lines 1–4 which quality is Shelley attributing to intellectual beauty in the simile "with as inconstant wing / As summer winds that creep from flower to flower"?
   A. Cheerfulness   C. Ordinariness
   B. Gentleness   D. Unpredictability

10. In line 8, the simile that compares the shadow to "hues and harmonies of evening" appeals to the senses of —

   A. sight and touch

   B. taste and smell

   C. hearing and taste

   D. sight and hearing

11. The alliteration in "Like memory of music fled" (line 10) mimics the quality of —

   A. speed, as when someone runs away

   B. loss, as when life changes over time

   C. a musical note, as when someone hums

   D. irony, as when something is appreciated only after it is gone

12. In the first stanza, the poet has created images and similes that describe —

   A. an idealized summer day in a "various world"

   B. the nature of the "shadow of some unseen Power"

   C. the troubles that he will suffer in his "human heart"

   D. how people respond to the "grace" and "mystery" of life

13. Which type of figurative language is used in lines 13–15 when the speaker mournfully questions the "Spirit of Beauty"?

   A. Apostrophe

   B. Metaphor

   C. Personification

   D. Simile

14. The alliteration in "This dim vast vale of tears, vacant and desolate" (line 17) helps convey an image of —

   A. a meaningless world

   B. overwhelming emptiness

   C. a severe rainstorm

   D. the darkness of winter

15. "Hymn to Intellectual Beauty" is characteristic of romantic poetry because Shelley —

   A. writes about subjective experiences of the individual

   B. stresses reason and common sense

   C. conveys a witty and refined view of his world

   D. comments on human interactions with institutions

Use both texts to answer question 16.

---

16. Which statement describes a characteristic of romanticism that is exhibited in both poems?

   A. The poets recount emotional responses to life in clear, simple language.

   B. All forces of nature are connected to the poets' religious beliefs.

   C. The celebration of love above all other emotions is central to the poem.

   D. Both poets draw extensively on nature and their imaginations to convey their ideas.

SHORT CONSTRUCTED RESPONSE
Write three or four sentences to answer this question.

17. In lines 1 and 2 of "The Prelude," the speaker calls the brook and the road "fellow-travellers." What does this metaphor suggest about the speaker's relationship to nature?

Write two to three paragraphs to answer this question.

18. What is the main idea that Wordsworth conveys in this stanza excerpted from "The Prelude"? Cite words and phrases from the poem to support your answer.

Revising and Editing

DIRECTIONS Read this passage and answer the questions that follow.

(1) In 1988, unrelenting fires burned about one-third of Yellowstone National Park's 2.2 million acres. (2) Lightning had struck several areas within the park, sparking small fires everywhere. (3) Under normal circumstances, the fires would have expired on their own, but that year the late spring and the summer were very dry. (4) Flames reached heights of up to 200 feet. (5) High afternoon winds blew flaming embers into the sky. (6) These embers, in turn, triggered even more fires. (7) The fires burned through June. (8) Tourists nonetheless continued to visit the park's star attraction the geyser known as Old Faithful. (9) It wasn't until the rain came in September though thousands of firefighters had been valiantly battling the fires since July that the flames finally began to die out. (10) And then the snow came. (11) In the spring the forest started to grow again; wildflowers and pine seedlings gradually sprouted up through the soil. (12) Yellowstone Park had begun its recovery.

1. What change, if any, should be made to sentence 1 to incorporate personification?

   A. Change *acres* to **expanse**

   B. Change *burned* to **devoured**

   C. Change *fires* to **flames**

   D. Make no change

2. Barbara wants to add this sentence.

   A national treasure was ablaze.

   Where is the best place to insert this sentence?

   A. At the beginning of the paragraph

   B. After sentence 2

   C. After sentence 3

   D. After sentence 4

3. What is the most effective way to combine sentences 5 and 6?

   A. High afternoon winds blew flaming embers into the sky, triggering even more fires.

   B. High afternoon winds blew flaming embers into the sky which, in turn, the embers triggered even more fires.

   C. High afternoon winds blew flaming embers into the sky; however, these embers, in turn, triggered even more fires.

   D. High afternoon winds blew flaming embers into the sky because the embers, in turn, triggered even more fires.

4. What change, if any, should be made to sentence 8?

   A. Insert comma after *nonetheless*

   B. Insert comma after *attraction*

   C. Change *continued* to **continuing**

   D. Make no change

5. What is the best way to revise sentence 9?

   A. It wasn't until the rain came in September; though thousands of firefighters had been valiantly battling the fires since July, that the flames finally began to die out.

   B. It wasn't until thousands of firefighters had been battling the fires since July that the rain came in September that the flames finally began to die out.

   C. Though thousands of firefighters had been valiantly battling the fires since July; it wasn't until the flames finally began to die out the rain came in September.

   D. Though thousands of firefighters had been valiantly battling the fires since July, it wasn't until the rain came in September that the flames finally began to die out.

6. Chris wants to add this sentence.

By early October, Yellowstone was blanketed with snow that later melted, sending water underground to nourish the remaining seeds and roots.

Where is the best place to insert this sentence?

   A. After sentence 9

   B. After sentence 10

   C. After sentence 11

   D. After sentence 12

STOP

Ideas for Independent Reading

Continue exploring the Questions of the Times on pages 752–753 with these additional works.

What can people learn from NATURE?

Songs of Innocence and of Experience
by William Blake

This Oxford University Press edition of William Blake's most well known and beloved poems, including "The Tyger" and "The Lamb," reproduces Blake's own brilliant and highly original illustrations. Readers can experience the poems exactly as Blake intended.

William Wordsworth: The Major Works
edited by Stephen Gill

More than any other early romantic poet, Wordsworth celebrated nature in all its diverse, majestic glory. This ample compilation includes his major poems, plus letters, prefaces, and essays on the subject of poetry.

A Literary Guide to the Lake District
by Grevel Lindop

Author Grevel Lindop richly describes pathways of the Lake District, invoking Wordsworth, Coleridge, and other literary giants who once trod the lakeside lanes. The tour is designed to be enjoyed by armchair readers as well as by travelers.

Is EMOTION *stronger than reason?*

Emma
by Jane Austen

Emma Woodhouse is a self-possessed young lady who finds an outlet for her considerable talents and energy in matchmaking among friends and acquaintances. However, she believes herself immune to the ups and downs of romantic passion. Readers for two centuries have delighted in Emma's comeuppance as her matchmaking schemes fall to pieces and her own heart becomes curiously vulnerable.

Lord Byron's Novel: The Evening Land
by John Crowley

What if Lord Byron had penned a gothic novel? John Crowley starts with this intriguing idea and weaves a literary fantasy in which Byron's lost novel is preserved and annotated by his daughter, Ada, Countess Lovelace, and is discovered in modern times by Web-site designer Alexandra Novak. The result is a novel within a novel within a novel.

Mary Shelley
by Miranda Seymour

British literary scholar Miranda Seymour presents Mary Shelley (1797–1851) as a multifaceted woman whose achievements far exceeded penning the famous gothic novel *Frankenstein* or preserving and promoting husband Percy Bysshe Shelley's poetic reputation. Shelley wrote at least five other novels, a travel book, journals, and letters, and edited her husband's works.

When is the ORDINARY *extraordinary?*

The New Penguin Book of Romantic Poetry
edited by Jonathan and Jessica Wordsworth

Romanticism was a celebration of the imagination and the spirit. Poets such as Wordsworth and Shelley found beauty and poetry in the commonplace objects and experiences of the natural world. This comprehensive collection features Lake poets Wordsworth and Coleridge as well as other such literary giants of the British romantic era as Blake, Keats, and Shelley.

John Keats: Selected Poems
edited by John Barnard

Keats immortalized a Grecian urn, a nightingale, and many other facets of commonplace experience. This collection features his classic poems with an introduction and commentary by the editor.

A Passionate Sisterhood: Women of the Wordsworth Circle
by Kathleen Jones

Lake poets William Wordsworth, Samuel Taylor Coleridge, and Robert Southey formed strong personal and professional bonds, but the women in their lives perpetuated the ties of friendship and kept daily life going. Kathleen Jones's book examines the lives of these extraordinary women—Sarah Coleridge, Dorothy Wordsworth, Edith Southey, and others—and narrates the mundane burdens of daily life among them.

How does WAR *change our values?*

Reflections on the Revolution in France
by Edmund Burke

The storming of the Bastille, the prison for the French king's political prisoners, was the first milestone of the French Revolution, an antifeudal upsurge that led to the beheading of the monarch and the foundation of the French republic. Across the English Channel, Edmund Burke viewed these developments with distaste and fear. Hoping to nip democracy in the bud, he argued in support of the church and royalty.

A Tale of Two Cities
by Charles Dickens

From the vantage point of 70 years later, Victorian novelist Charles Dickens tells his classic story of the French Revolution. The "two cities" of the title are Paris and London. The conflict focuses on Charles Darnay and the Manettes—people caught up in the tempest of the French Revolution—and on Sidney Carton, a British man who is given the chance to redeem his wasted life.

Lord Byron's Jackal: A Life of Edward John Trelawny
by David Crane

A familiar of poets Percy Bysshe Shelley and Lord Byron, Edward Trelawny (1792–1881) fancied himself a prototypical Byronic hero—accompanying Byron to fight for Greek independence—and became an accomplished author in his own right. Unlike Byron and Shelley, however, Trelawny lived a very long life, enabling him to write from the perspective of age and time.

Preview Unit Goals

TEXT ANALYSIS	• Understand the historical and cultural context of the Victorian era
	• Identify and analyze characteristics of realism and naturalism in fiction
	• Identify and analyze point of view and plot structure in fiction
	• Identify and analyze rhyme scheme and rhythm in poetry
	• Identify and analyze speaker, mood, and tone in poetry
	• Determine themes or central ideas of a text
	• Identify, analyze, and evaluate persuasive techniques

READING	• Make inferences and draw conclusions
	• Compare, contrast, and synthesize ideas

WRITING AND LANGUAGE	• Write an analytical essay
	• Add descriptive details, choose effective settings, and establish voice
	• Use rhetorical questions and interrogative sentences

VOCABULARY	• Use context clues and affixes to help determine the meaning of unfamiliar words
	• Consult general reference materials to find the pronunciation of a word or determine or clarify its precise meaning, its part of speech, its etymology, or its standard usage

ACADEMIC VOCABULARY	• analyze	• impact	• scheme
	• dominate	• resource	

MEDIA AND VIEWING	• Evaluate the presentation of social and cultural messages in media
	• Evaluate the interactions of different techniques used in multi-layered media
	• Evaluate how audience, bias, and purpose influence the representation of an issue or event, including changes in formality and tone
	• Create a power presentation

Find It Online!

Go to **thinkcentral.com** for the interactive version of this unit.

The Victorians

1832–1901

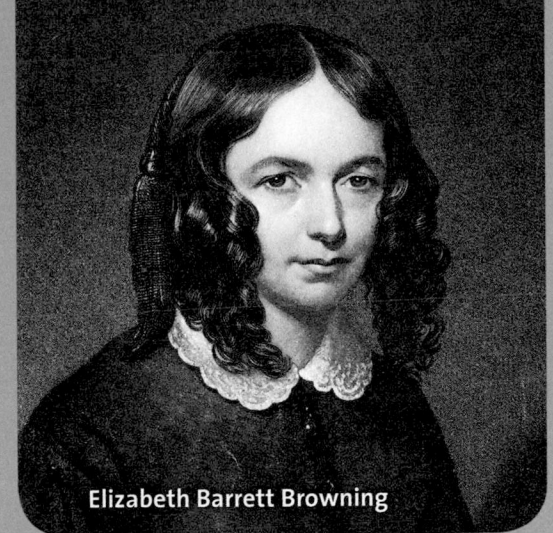

Elizabeth Barrett Browning

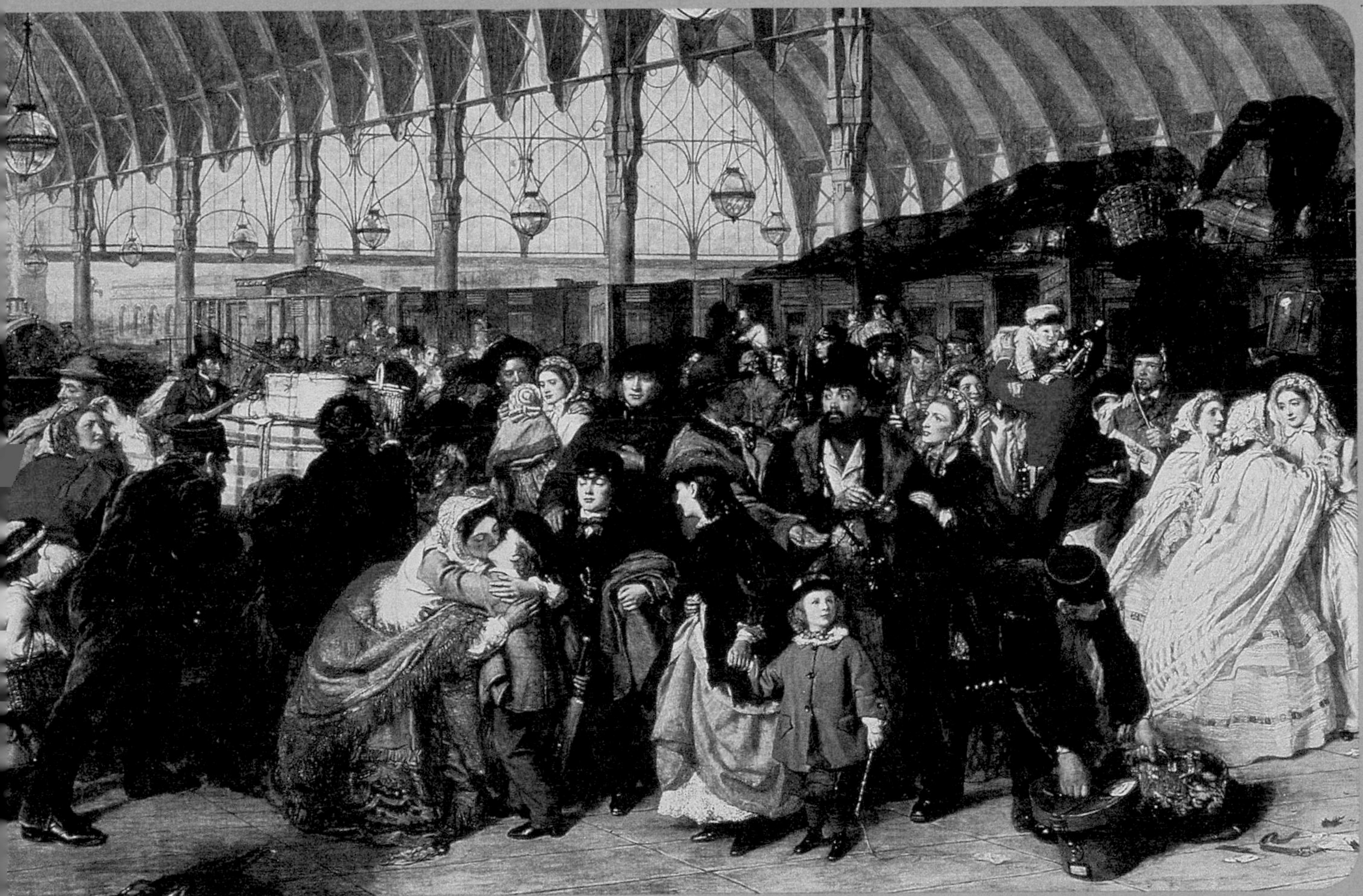

AN ERA OF RAPID CHANGE

- The Influence of Romanticism
- Realism in Fiction
- Victorian Viewpoints

Media Smart DVD-ROM

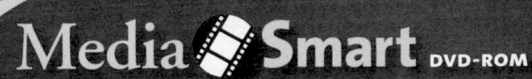

Great Stories on Film

Discover how visual and sound techniques combine to capture the driving motion of Britain's Industrial Revolution. Page 1050

Questions of the Times

DISCUSS After reading these questions and talking about them with a partner, discuss them with the class as a whole. Then read on to explore the ways in which writers of the Victorian period dealt with the same issues.

When is progress a PROBLEM?

England was the first nation to industrialize, and it made enormous strides during this period. Factories made more goods available to more people than ever before, and middle-class Victorians readily consumed these goods. At the same time, changes in working conditions and social structure led to a breakdown of communities, a rise in materialistic attitudes, and the creation of a class of poverty-stricken urban workers. Is progress always worth its price?

Can values be IMPOSED?

Many Victorians—among them the writer Rudyard Kipling and Queen Victoria herself—proudly supported imperialism, believing they were bringing the gift of English civilization to less civilized cultures. Bloody rebellions, however, proved that the colonized peoples did not share their view. Do you think a nation can or should impose its values on other people?

⋯○ **COMMON CORE**

RL 9 Demonstrate knowledge of foundational works of literature, including how two or more texts from the same period treat similar themes or topics. **RI 9** Analyze documents of historical and literary significance for their themes, purposes, and rhetorical features.

Is it better to escape or face REALITY?

Writers of this period were not unified in outlook. Early poets ignored the everyday realities of their society in favor of more poetic subjects. In contrast, many novelists and critics reflected and recorded their society as it was—warts and all. Yet by the end of the period, more and more readers turned to literature to escape from the problems of the day. Do you prefer literature that reflects your world or that takes you away from it all?

Why do people fear CHANGE?

The Victorian period was a time of rapid change—exciting yet troubling. Many Victorians felt as though the rug of their familiar world had been pulled out from under them. While some embraced change, others despaired for their society. Why do you think people resist change? What is the best way to live in a world where everything seems unpredictable?

The Victorians
1832–1901

An Era of Rapid Change

During Queen Victoria's reign, England went from horse-drawn carriages to motor cars, from rule by aristocrats to votes for every man, from a land of farmers to a land of factories. England also actively embraced imperialism as the country's destiny and duty to the world. Yet as their country changed in unexpected ways, the English moved from happy confidence in progress to increasing doubt. Some writers turned away from the new reality; others tackled it head-on.

The Victorians: Historical Context

Victorian writers responded to the economic, social, and political changes sweeping England during Victoria's reign.

A Time of Growth and Change

"The sun never sets on the British Empire," boasted the Victorians, and it was true: with holdings around the globe, from Africa to India, Ireland to New Zealand, and Hong Kong to Canada, it was always daytime in some part of the vast territory ruled by Britain. More than just a simple fact, however, this phrase captured the attitude of an era. During the reign of Queen Victoria, England was a nation in motion. "This is a world of action, and not for moping and droning in," said Victorian novelist **Charles Dickens,** and his contemporaries seemed to agree.

During this period, England was at the height of its power, both politically and economically. Abroad, Britain dominated world politics. At home, the Industrial Revolution was in full swing. With its new factories turning out goods of every kind at an unprecedented pace, England became known as "the workshop of the world." For those with wealth and influence—including the burgeoning middle class—it was an expansive time, a time of energy and vitality, a time of rapid and dramatic change. Yet large segments of the population suffered greatly during this period. Many writers decried the injustice, rapid pace, and materialism of the age—including poet **Matthew Arnold,** who referred to "[t]his strange disease of modern life, with its sick hurry, its divided aims."

Monarchy in the Modern Style

This period of change is named after the person who, more than any other, stood for the age: **Queen Victoria.** Just 18 years old when she was crowned in 1837, she went on to rule for 63 years, 7 months, and 2 days—the longest reign in English history. Victoria's devotion to hard work and duty, her insistence on proper behavior, and her unapologetic support of British imperialism became hallmarks of the Victorian period.

Victoria was well aware of how previous monarchs had clashed with Parliament and made themselves unpopular with their arrogant, inflexible attitudes. She realized that the role of royalty had to change. Pragmatically accepting the idea of a constitutional monarchy in which she gave advice rather than orders, Victoria yielded control of day-to-day governmental affairs to a series of very talented prime ministers: Lord Melbourne, Sir Robert Peel, Lord Palmerston, and the rival politicians Benjamin Disraeli and William E. Gladstone. The position of prime minister assumed even greater importance after the death of Victoria's beloved husband, Prince Albert, in 1861; grief-stricken, the queen withdrew from politics and spent the rest of her life in mourning.

Train at Shakespeare Cliff, Dover (1850), George Childs. Watercolor.
© NRM/Pictorial Collection/Science and Society Picture Library.

▶ **TAKING NOTES**

Outlining As you read this introduction, use an outline to record main ideas about the history and literature of this period. You can use headings, boldfaced terms, and the information in boxes like this one as starting points. (See page R49 in the **Research Handbook** for more help with outlining.)

I. Historical Context
 A. Growth and Change
  1. The British Empire expands.
  2. Britain dominates world politics.
  3. Industrial Revolution continues.
  4. Wealth and prosperity grow, but so does suffering.
 B. Monarchy

Progress, Problems, and Reform

The Industrial Revolution had already transformed England into a modern industrial state by the time Victoria took the throne. By 1850, England boasted 18,000 cotton mills and produced half the iron in the world.

MIDDLE-CLASS PROSPERITY The Industrial Revolution created vast new wealth for England's rapidly growing middle class. This material progress was celebrated in the Great Exhibition of 1851, the purpose of which was to display "the Works of Industry of All Nations." Housed in an enormous, glittering glass-and-steel building called the Crystal Palace, the Exhibition showcased every marvel of the age: indoor toilets, telegraphs, power looms, electric lights, even a full-size locomotive—17,000 exhibits in all.

For the middle class who ran the factories, all these inventions represented both a means of making money and a dazzling array of goods to spend it on. Middle-class Victorians enjoyed indulging themselves in displays of wealth, from top hats and ruffled dresses to large houses crammed with heavy, ornate furniture and fancy knickknacks. With the help of servants, hostesses vied to serve the most lavish feasts and—insecure in their new respectability—tried to outdo each other in displaying refined manners and behavior.

Some writers, such as **Thomas Babington Macaulay,** expressed enthusiasm for the material advantages afforded by the industrial age. Others, such as **Thomas Carlyle** and **William Morris,** were appalled by Victorian materialism, which they saw as tasteless, joyless, and destructive of community. Likewise, the virtuous airs adopted by the middle class, who often had trouble living up to their own uncompromising moral standards, led to angry charges of hypocrisy.

THE DOWNSIDE OF PROGRESS While the middle class was becoming more prosperous, conditions for the poor grew more intolerable. Factory workers spent 16-hour days toiling for low wages under harsh and dangerous conditions. Children, especially, suffered. Five-year-olds worked in the cotton mills as scavengers, crawling under the moving machinery to pick up bits of cotton from the floor, or in the coal mines, dragging heavy tubs of coal through narrow tunnels. Paid just a few cents a day, child workers endured empty bellies, frequent beatings, and air so filled with dust that they could hardly breathe.

To make matters worse, in the 1840s unemployment in England soared, leaving many families without a breadwinner. In addition, the potato blight and famine that devastated Ireland in 1845 forced 2 million starving people to emigrate. Many crowded into England's already squalid slums.

A CHANGING LANGUAGE

The Birth of Standard English

In Victorian times, as education spread and people entering the middle class tried to speak "proper" English, the English language became more homogeneous. Increased literacy also stabilized English, since the written language tends to change more slowly than the spoken. The period also saw the beginning of an effort to compile a definitive record of the histories, uses, and meanings of English words, resulting in the massive *Oxford English Dictionary,* the first volume of which was published in 1884. This landmark work, completed in 1928 and revised several times since, traces the changes in meaning of each entry word from its first recorded use to the present.

Jargon and Euphemisms Victorian advances in the natural and social sciences spurred the coinage of new words, such as *telephone, photography, psychiatrist,* and *feminist.* The new fields of study developed their own specialized and technical vocabulary, or jargon, which began to infiltrate everyday speech. Euphemisms—mild or vague terms substituted for words considered harsh or offensive—also grew more popular as Victorian propriety made certain words taboo. A chicken breast became "white meat"; the legs, "drumsticks." Even words such as *belly* and *stallion* were prudishly avoided.

Slang Although "proper" circles frowned on slang, it was widely used among the lower classes as a means of conversing safely in the presence of outsiders, including the police. The Cockneys of London's East End developed an elaborate system of rhyming slang in early Victorian times—using, for example, *loaf* to mean "head" because *loaf* is the first word in the expression *loaf of bread,* which rhymes with *head.* The expression "use your loaf" is still common in the East End today.

REFORM AND UNCERTAINTY Though Parliament enacted many important reforms during this period, change came slowly as the middle and upper classes came to realize that the poor were not to blame for their own plight. In 1833, Parliament abolished slavery in the British Empire and passed the first laws restricting child labor. It also ushered in free trade, repealing laws that kept out cheaper foreign grain. Slowly, more reforms followed. Gladstone and the new Liberal Party established public schools and mandated secret ballots for elections. Gladstone's rival, the Tory politician Disraeli, won passage of bills that improved housing and sanitation, legalized trade unions, eased harsh factory conditions, and, in 1867, gave the vote to working-class men.

Even for those who benefited most, though, progress could be painful. Despite their admiration for technology and their faith in human ingenuity, most Victorians were deeply religious, and some of the theories proposed by modern scientists threatened cherished beliefs. In 1830 the geologist Charles Lyell published evidence that the earth was formed not in 4004 B.C., as held by popular interpretations of the Bible, but millions of years earlier. Then, in 1859, Charles Darwin's *On the Origin of Species* introduced his theory that plant and animal species evolved through natural selection—an idea that prompted furious debate because it seemed to contradict the biblical account of creation. "There is not a creed which is not shaken," wrote poet and critic Matthew Arnold, "not an accredited dogma which is not shown to be questionable, not a received tradition which does not threaten to dissolve."

A Voice from the Times

Well: what we gain by science is, after all, sadness, as the Preacher saith. The more we know of the laws and nature of the Universe the more ghastly a business we perceive it all to be. . . .

—**Thomas Hardy**

Cultural Influences

Writers clashed over Britain's expanding imperialism.

British Imperialism

Though Disraeli and Gladstone worked in tandem for domestic reform, they bitterly opposed each other on the issue of British imperialism. Throughout Victoria's rule, the British Empire had been steadily expanding, starting with the annexation of New Zealand in 1840 and the acquisition of Hong Kong two years later. In 1858, after a rebellion in India by native troops called sepoys, Parliament took administrative control of the colony away from the British East India Company and put the colony under the direct administration of the British government.

Gladstone was a "Little Englander"—one who opposed further expansion; Disraeli, in contrast, saw imperialism as the key to Britain's prosperity and patriotic destiny. Victoria sided with Disraeli—in part because his flamboyant charm appealed to her, while she loathed the staid, self-righteous Gladstone—and she allowed him to pursue his ambitions. He bought England a large share in Egypt's newly completed Suez Canal, acquired the Mediterranean island of Cyprus, and annexed the Transvaal, a Dutch settlement in South Africa. Disraeli even persuaded the queen to accept the title "Empress of India."

Fascinated by the exploits of their explorers, missionaries, and empire builders in Africa and Asia, most British citizens—including certain writers—supported imperialism. **Rudyard Kipling,** for example, wrote short stories and poems glorifying the expansion of the British Empire. Indeed, it was Kipling who conveyed the idea that it was England's "burden," or duty, to bring civilization to the rest of the world. **William Morris** contradicted him, asking, "What is England's place? To carry civilization through the world? . . . [Civilization] cannot be worth much, when it is necessary to kill a man in order to make him accept it." As the years passed and colonial conflicts increased, British citizens began to agree with Morris, and support for imperialism waned.

▼ **Analyze Visuals**
This photograph (c. 1895) depicts an English lord and lady in India. What can you infer about the English couple's relationship with the Indians shown? What impression does the photograph give of English imperialism?

Victorian Literature

Victorian literature shifted gradually from romanticism to realism, with the change led by novelists, who enjoyed a golden age. Late Victorian writing moved into naturalism and escapist fiction.

The Influence of Romanticism

By the 1830s, romanticism was certainly past its height. Shelley, Keats, and Byron were dead, and Wordsworth was no longer a youthful revolutionary but a stuffy, elderly member of the establishment. Still, young up-and-coming poets such as **Robert Browning** and **Alfred, Lord Tennyson** had been raised on the romantics. Of course, they had their likes and dislikes: Tennyson said that Wordsworth at his best was "on the whole the greatest English poet since Milton," while Browning, who idolized Byron and Shelley, told fellow poet and future wife **Elizabeth Barrett** that he would travel to a distant city just to see a lock of Byron's hair but "could not get up enthusiasm enough to cross the room if at the other end of it all Wordsworth, Coleridge and Southey were condensed into the little china bottle yonder."

Overall, though, the romantic movement had an enormous influence on early Victorian poets—not so much on their style of writing, which was often brilliantly original, but on their ideas of what poetry should be. On the streets, they saw factories belching smoke and ragged, hungry children begging pennies. In their writing, though, they ignored this grim reality, focusing instead on more "poetic" subjects: ancient legends, exotic foreign lands, romantic love, and the awe-inspiring beauty of nature. **Matthew Arnold** argued that the poet could have no higher goal than "to delight himself with the contemplation of some noble action of a heroic time, and to enable others, through his representation of it, to delight in it also." Perhaps this approach was pure escapism, perhaps optimism; or perhaps—just as attitudes inherited from an earlier generation hindered social reform—literary ideals inherited from the romantics kept the first Victorian poets from redefining poetry for their own time.

Readers seemed to share this sense of dislocation. On the one hand, the Victorians revered their poets, seeing them as a higher order of human being—sensitive, intuitive, inspired—an image first popularized by the romantics, particularly Byron. On the other hand, many readers, especially among the middle class, increasingly viewed poetry as irrelevant to their

THE ARTISTS' GALLERY

The Pre-Raphaelites

In 1848, a group of art students at the Royal Academy in London banded together in a secret club, the Pre-Raphaelite Brotherhood. Tired of being told to imitate the techniques of great Renaissance painters such as Raphael— techniques they saw as stale and insincere— the group sought to return to an earlier time, when artists looked at nature with a fresh eye.

Dante Gabriel Rossetti Though the club itself lasted only a few years, it led to a larger pre-Raphaelite movement, spearheaded by one of the group's first members, poet and painter Dante Gabriel Rossetti, whose work *La Ghirlandata* (1873) is shown here. Rossetti's goal was to portray scenes as he imagined them, not as the rules of art dictated. He dreamed of painting like medieval artists—not in the same style, but with the same attitude of honesty, simplicity, and reverence.

Arts and Crafts Movement One of Rossetti's enthusiastic young followers was the writer, artist, and social reformer **William Morris.** Morris was appalled at the mountains of cheaply made, mass-produced goods churned out by factories to clutter Victorian homes. Urging a return to earlier standards of craftsmanship, he wrote, "We should have nothing in our homes that we do not know to be useful or believe to be beautiful." As the leader of the Arts and Crafts Movement, Morris himself designed wallpaper, pottery, fabrics, glass, and furniture.

own lives. While poet and painter **Dante Gabriel Rossetti** passionately insisted on "art for art's sake," the growing reading public turned to other forms of literature, particularly the novel.

Realism in Fiction

Looking at the range and quality of Victorian novelists—the humor, pathos, and unforgettable characters of **Charles Dickens,** the psychological depth of **George Eliot,** the dark passion of **Emily Brontë** and her sister **Charlotte Brontë**—it's hard to believe that at the time they wrote, fiction was widely considered to be simply light entertainment, not serious literature. To be fair, the vast majority of novels published weren't great books like *David Copperfield* and *Middlemarch.* The same mass production that filled Victorian homes with inexpensive bric-a-brac of doubtful taste also poured out cheap thrillers and maudlin, weepy tales known as "penny dreadfuls" and "shilling shockers," which the working classes in particular devoured.

Middle-class readers enjoyed a good cry, too, but they wanted more. They wanted to meet characters like themselves and the people they knew; they wanted to learn more about their rapidly changing world. In other words, they wanted **realism.** Realistic novels tried to capture everyday life as it was really lived. Rather than ignoring science and industry as romanticism did, realism focused on the effects of the Industrial Revolution on Great Britain. Keen-eyed and sharp-witted, realistic writers probed every corner of their society, from the drawing room to the slum, exposing problems and pretensions. Some openly crusaded for reform. Others were more restrained, considering their role to be, as George Eliot put it, "the rousing of the nobler emotions, which make mankind desire the social right, not the prescribing of special measures."

Romanticism didn't disappear entirely as soon as realism appeared; many of the best novelists combined elements of both and even borrowed reader-pleasing techniques from popular fiction. For instance, in *Jane Eyre,* Charlotte Brontë blended the spooky suspensefulness of the gothic novel with a realistic portrayal of the moral, social, and economic pressures faced by a Victorian woman. Charles Dickens filled his many novels with harshly realistic details drawn from his own experiences and observations, but he sweetened his social criticism with amusingly eccentric characters, engaging storytelling, and, often, sentimental endings. Other writers, such as **Anthony Trollope** and **William Makepeace Thackeray,** were known for a more straightforward realistic approach, faithfully depicting the manners and morals of the upper middle class to which they both belonged. **George Meredith** and George Eliot (the pen name of Mary Ann Evans) pioneered **psychological realism,** which focused less on external realities than on the inner realities of the mind, though still within the context of contemporary social changes.

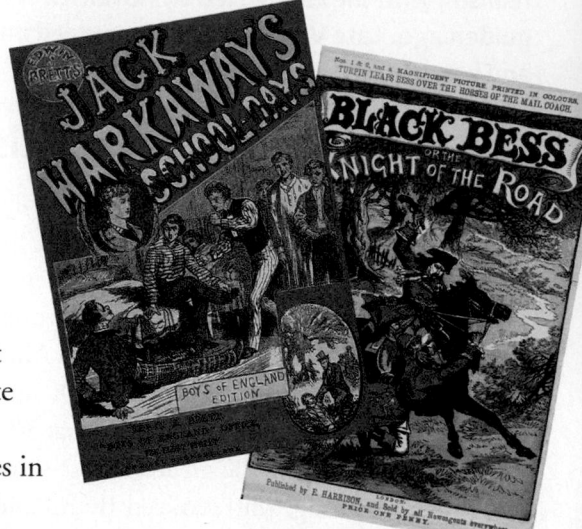

These "penny dreadfuls" focused on popular subjects—the adventures of boys at school and of highwaymen on the road.

▶ *For Your Outline*

ROMANTICISM

- Romantics influenced early Victorian writers.
- Early Victorian poets focused on "poetic" subjects.
- Readers turned to novels.

REALISM

- Fiction was considered light entertainment.
- Realism captured everyday life.
- Realist writers exposed social problems and pretensions.
- Psychological realism focused on internal realities.
- Novels were long and often published serially.

Victorian novels were weighty affairs, quite literally—so weighty that they typically had to be divided into three volumes, collectively known as a three-decker novel. Fortunately, readers had the time and the attention spans to appreciate these elaborately constructed fictional worlds, with their complex storylines and leisurely narrative pace. Families often spent the evening reading aloud to each other, laughing at the adventures of Dickens's Mr. Pickwick and his oddball friends or sighing over Heathcliff and Catherine's doomed romance in Emily Brontë's *Wuthering Heights*.

Many novels were first published in serial form in magazines and newspapers, that is, in monthly installments of several chapters each, meaning that readers might have to wait as long as two years to find out how a novel ended. Dickens was a master of this form. Hordes of fans—not just in England but around the world—rushed to snatch up each new installment of his 1841 novel *The Old Curiosity Shop*, especially as the beloved character Little Nell approached her tragic end. In fact, the suspense was so great that passengers aboard a British ship arriving in New York that year were met by crowds of anxious American readers who had not yet received the latest installment. They were shouting from the dock, "Is Little Nell dead?"

A poster from the 1939 film
Wuthering Heights

Victorian Viewpoints

Victorians' love of reading was by no means limited to fiction. The same periodicals that provided them with the most recent novel installment by Trollope, Thackeray, or Dickens also offered articles and essays on every imaginable subject, "from Arctic exploration to pinmaking," as one scholar put it. Victorians were generalists, curious about all aspects of their changing world, and they read for pleasure the sort of nonfiction that today might appeal only to specialists in a particular academic field.

A great deal of this nonfiction was not merely informational but conveyed strong opinions. In carefully worded prose that was at once impassioned and a model of restraint, England's greatest thinkers clashed over the issues of the day. While some, like **Thomas Babington Macaulay,** defended the status quo, most found much to criticize in Victorian society—though few went as far as **Thomas Carlyle,** who in his book *Past and Present* predicted bloody revolution as the inevitable result of the social breakdown caused by unregulated, profit-driven industry.

Whatever their viewpoint, these critics' authoritative tone must have been reassuring to a readership no longer sure what to think about anything. Could science and religious belief coexist, or would one destroy the other? Did British imperialism benefit both conqueror and conquered, or was it a disastrous mistake? Would the Industrial Revolution prove to be the dawning of a great new age or the end of civilization? Increasingly, the optimism of the early years of the era turned to uneasiness in the face of what **Tennyson** called "the thoughts that shake mankind."

This uneasiness permeated the literature written during the last years of Victoria's reign. Poets no longer contemplated life at a romantic distance

▶ *For Your Outline*

VICTORIAN VIEWPOINTS

- Periodicals offered nonfiction articles on all manner of subjects.
- England's thinkers clashed over issues of the day.
- Uncertainty permeated literature of the late Victorian period.
- Naturalist writers saw the universe as an uncaring force, indifferent to human suffering.
- Readers turned to escapist fare.

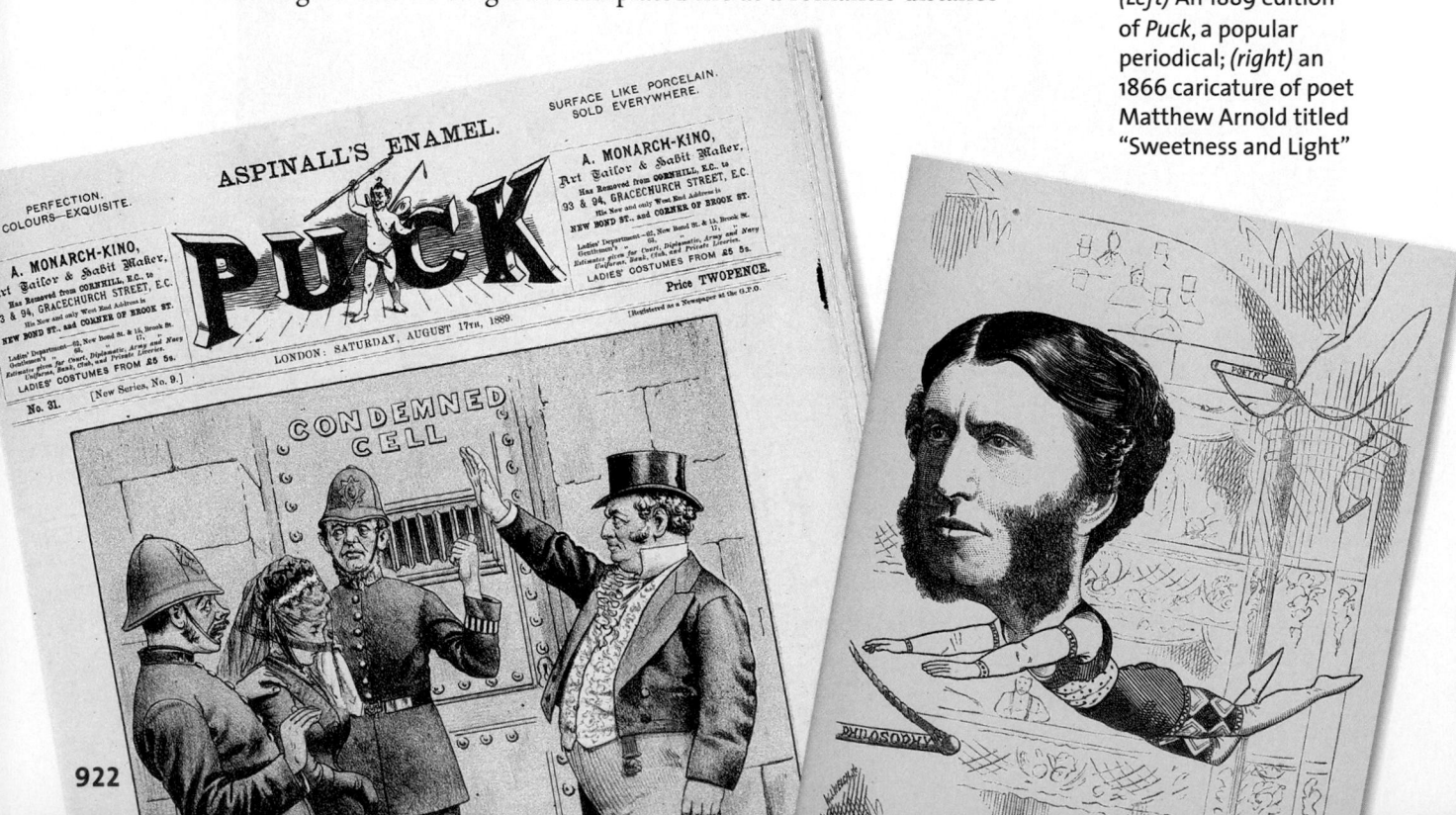

(Left) An 1889 edition of *Puck,* a popular periodical; *(right)* an 1866 caricature of poet Matthew Arnold titled "Sweetness and Light"

The Victorian period saw a boom in children's literature, including Robert Louis Stevenson's *Treasure Island*, illustrated in 1911 by N. C. Wyeth.

but instead expressed their sense of loss and pain at living in a world in which order had been replaced by chaos and confusion. In his poem "Dover Beach," **Matthew Arnold** describes a bright "sea of faith" retreating to the edges of the earth, leaving humanity stranded in darkness. Pessimistic themes also permeated the poetry and fiction of **Thomas Hardy,** who wrote in a new style called **naturalism.** An offshoot of realism, naturalism saw the universe as an uncaring force, indifferent to human suffering. Naturalist writers packed their novels with the harsh details of industrialized life, unrelieved by humor or a happy ending.

Not surprisingly, late Victorian readers began to avoid serious literature, finding it depressingly bleak. Instead, they turned to the adventure tales of **Rudyard Kipling,** who set his tales in India; the witty drawing-room comedies of **Oscar Wilde;** the science fiction of **H. G. Wells;** or the detective stories of **Arthur Conan Doyle,** whose Sherlock Holmes was England's first fictional detective. Along with children's literature that included **Lewis Carroll's** *Alice's Adventures in Wonderland* and **Robert Louis Stevenson's** *Treasure Island,* such wonderfully written escapist fare rounded out the great diversity of Victorian literary voices.

In the end, the pessimism of Hardy and Arnold came the closest to anticipating what lay just around the bend: the catastrophe of World War I. In the next century, modernist writers would pick up the torch from their Victorian predecessors and grapple with issues the Victorians could not have imagined.

A Voice from the Times

Pessimism is, in brief, playing the sure game. You cannot lose at it; you may gain. It is the only view of life in which you can never be disappointed. Having reckoned what to do in the worst possible circumstances, when better arise, as they may, life becomes child's play.

—Thomas Hardy

Connecting Literature, History, and Culture

Use this timeline and the questions on the next page to gain insight into developments during this period, both in Britain and in the world as a whole.

BRITISH LITERARY MILESTONES

1830

1833 Alfred, Lord Tennyson, begins writing his long poem *In Memoriam*.

1843 Charles Dickens publishes his short novel *A Christmas Carol.* ▼

1845

1846 Poets Robert Browning and Elizabeth Barrett elope and move to Italy.

1847 Charlotte Brontë publishes *Jane Eyre*; sister Emily publishes *Wuthering Heights*.

1850 Elizabeth Barrett Browning publishes love poems *Sonnets from the Portuguese*.

1860

1860 Dickens publishes first magazine installment of *Great Expectations*.

1861 George Eliot (pen name of Mary Ann Evans) publishes *Silas Marner*.

1865 Gerard Manley Hopkins enters Jesuit religious order and stops writing poetry.

HISTORICAL CONTEXT

1830

1833 Factory Act bans factory work for children under nine; slavery is abolished in British Empire.

1837 William IV dies and is succeeded by 18-year-old niece Victoria, ushering in Britain's age of greatest prosperity.

1842 The Opium War with China is settled, with Britain claiming Hong Kong.

1845

1845 The Irish potato famine begins, eventually killing more than a million people (to 1851).

1854 The Crimean War—in which Britain, Turkey, France, and Austria fight Russia—begins.

1859 Charles Darwin publishes *On the Origin of Species*.

1860

1861 Prince Albert dies. ▶

1867 Reform Bill doubles the number of voters by including working-class men.

1870 Local governments establish public schools; the Married Women's Act gives women economic rights.

WORLD CULTURE AND EVENTS

1830

1839 American Charles Goodyear invents process for making rubber strong and elastic.

1844 Samuel F. B. Morse sends the first long-distance telegraph message. ▼

1845

1848 Ethnic uprisings erupt throughout Europe; Karl Marx and Friedrich Engels publish *Communist Manifesto*.

1851 Widespread hunger and corruption lead to China's Taiping Rebellion (to 1864).

1853 U.S. Commodore Matthew Perry sails four ships into Tokyo harbor, ending Japan's self-imposed isolation.

1860

1861 Civil War erupts in the United States (to 1865); Alexander II frees serfs in Russia.

1869 The Suez Canal opens. ▼

1874 Alexander Graham Bell develops the telephone.

MAKING CONNECTIONS

- Which invention of the time do you think most changed people's lives?
- What events show Britain's commitment to imperialism?
- What evidence do you see of social progress and reform in Great Britain and elsewhere?
- What contributions did women make to British literature of the period?

COMMON CORE

RI 7 Integrate and evaluate multiple sources of information presented in different formats as well as in words in order to address a question or solve a problem.

1875

1875 Hopkins resumes writing.

1883 Robert Louis Stevenson publishes adventure novel *Treasure Island.*

1887 Sir Arthur Conan Doyle publishes *A Study in Scarlet,* introducing detective Sherlock Holmes.▲

1890

1891 Thomas Hardy publishes *Tess of the D'Urbervilles;* Oscar Wilde's novel *The Picture of Dorian Gray* shocks Victorian England with its theme of the corruption of wealth.

1895 H. G. Wells publishes the landmark science fiction novel *The Time Machine.*

1896 Reaction to Thomas Hardy's novel *Jude the Obscure* is so negative that thereafter he writes only poetry.

1900

1900 *Oxford Book of English Verse* is first published.

1901 Rudyard Kipling publishes his novel *Kim,* detailing life in India.

1875

1876 Disraeli secures the title "Empress of India" for Victoria; collective bargaining by trade unions is legalized.

1879 Ireland presses for home rule.

1884 Reform Bill gives vote to almost all adult males.

1890

1897 British-Sudanese War begins.

1899 The Boer War against Dutch South African settlers begins (to 1902). ▼

1900

1900 Nigeria becomes a British protectorate.

1901 Britain establishes the Commonwealth of Australia; Queen Victoria dies after nearly 64 years of rule.

1875

1876 Korea becomes an independent nation.

1879 Thomas Edison invents the first light bulb. ▶

1884 The Berlin Conference of 14 European nations sets rules for dividing Africa into colonies.

1890

1893 Henry Ford develops gasoline-powered automobile; New Zealand becomes the first country to grant women suffrage.

1895 Italian Guglielmo Marconi invents the first radio.

1896 The first modern Olympic Games are held in Athens, Greece.

1900

1900 Austrian psychiatrist Sigmund Freud publishes *The Interpretation of Dreams;* in China, the Boxer Rebellion against foreign influence breaks out.

1901 Theodore Roosevelt becomes president of the United States after William McKinley is assassinated.

The Legacy of the Era

COMMON CORE

W 1 Write arguments to support claims in an analysis of substantive topics or texts. **W 7** Conduct short research projects. **SL 5** Make strategic use of digital media in presentations.

Remnants of an Empire

The British Empire was the most extensive empire in world history. At the height of its power, it held sway over a quarter of the earth's people and land. Though it has since crumbled, the empire's influence remains strong. All over the world, British-style legal and governmental systems, economic practices, sports, and fashions— even the English language itself—are evidence of England's far-flung reach.

RESEARCH Choose one country in the Commonwealth of Nations (an association of 54 former British territories) and find out what aspects of British culture remain in that country today. Report your findings to the class, using visual aids to enhance your presentation.

The former British colony of Hong Kong continued its common law system after reverting to Chinese rule in 1997. Shown here are Supreme Court judges in 2002.

Made by Hand

Mass production is even more the norm today than it was in Victorian times. Despite the profusion of factory-produced goods, however, many people have come to appreciate handmade items, from quilts to furniture to cookies. These modern consumers value the same qualities once touted by William Morris and the Arts and Crafts Movement: fine craftsmanship that combines usefulness and aesthetic appeal with the personal touch.

DISCUSS Bring in something handmade by you or someone else and share it with the class. How is it different from a similar mass-produced item? Discuss the value of handmade items versus the value of inexpensive and accessible goods.

Glass blower at work

Truly Dickensian

The next time you hear someone referred to as a Scrooge, or a bleak situation described as Dickensian, you will know who to thank—Dickens himself. The influence of Dickens is widespread in today's world. There are Dickens societies and Dickens book clubs, Dickens museums and Dickens festivals, Dickens satires and even a Dickens theme park! In addition, there have been countless stage, film, and television versions of Dickens's works, including *A Tale of Two Cities, Oliver Twist, Great Expectations,* and *A Christmas Carol* (even Disney gave us Scrooge McDuck).

CREATE As a class, create a multimedia Dickens center to showcase Dickens's legacy. Include a variety of texts, visuals, film clips, and memorabilia related to Dickens in today's world.

A scene from the 2005 film *Oliver Twist,* directed by Roman Polanski

Selected Poetry
by Alfred, Lord Tennyson

VIDEO TRAILER **THINK** central | KEYWORD: HML12-928A

COMMON CORE

RL 1 Cite evidence to support inferences drawn from the text. **RL 4** Analyze the impact of specific word choices on meaning and tone, including language that is fresh, engaging, or beautiful. **RL 9** Demonstrate knowledge of foundational works of literature. **L 4b** Identify and correctly use patterns of word changes that indicate different meanings or parts of speech.

DID YOU KNOW?

Alfred, Lord Tennyson . . .

- was the most famous poet of his age.
- counted Queen Victoria as a close friend.
- wrote a book, *Idylls of the King,* inspired by King Arthur's legendary court.
- participated in an unsuccessful scheme to overthrow the Spanish king.

Meet the Author

Alfred, Lord Tennyson 1809–1892

In his own day, Alfred, Lord Tennyson, was considered the foremost spokesperson for the Victorian middle class. His poetry reflects many of the Victorians' concerns, especially their fear that new scientific theories and materialistic values were threatening accepted morality.

"Strangely Brought Up" The fourth son in a family of 12 children, Tennyson grew up in a turbulent household. His father, an educated but embittered clergyman, took out his frustrations on his wife and children and drank to relieve his melancholy. Over time, problems with addiction and mental illness plagued several of Tennyson's siblings. Before he died, Tennyson's father said of his children, "They are all strangely brought up."

Early Promise Depressed by his gloomy home life, Tennyson took refuge in poetry. By the age of 18, he was a published poet, and during his first year at Cambridge University, he won a poetry contest. The contest brought Tennyson into contact with Arthur Henry Hallam, a brilliant young man with whom Tennyson forged the deepest friendship of his life. The two friends joined the Apostles, a group of gifted undergraduates who offered Tennyson acceptance and encouragement. Unfortunately, lack of funds forced Tennyson to leave Cambridge in 1831 without earning a degree.

Bitter Times In the following years, Tennyson endured many difficulties, including financial problems, scathing reviews, and an engagement complicated by the disapproval of his future wife's father. Most wrenching of all was the sudden death of Hallam, who had recently become engaged to Tennyson's sister and was just 22 years old. Though Hallam's death grieved Tennyson deeply, it also inspired an outpouring of remarkable poems, including "Ulysses" and the lyrics contained in *In Memoriam.* Written over a period of 17 years, the 131-part *In Memoriam* mourns the early death of a greatly talented man.

Literary Legend The year 1850 marked a change in Tennyson's fortunes. In June, he published *In Memoriam,* and two weeks later he finally married Emily Sellwood. Later that year, Queen Victoria recognized Tennyson's poetic achievements by inviting him to succeed William Wordsworth as poet laureate. Decades later, he also accepted the rank of baron and, along with it, the title *Lord.*

Author Online

Go to thinkcentral.com. KEYWORD: HML12-928B

THINK central

TEXT ANALYSIS: MOOD

Mood is the feeling or atmosphere that a writer creates for a reader. Words that may describe mood are *mysterious, somber,* or *joyful,* for example. A poem's mood may change over the course of the work. Elements that help create the mood of a poem include diction, imagery, line structure, and sound devices such as repetition and rhyme. How would you describe the mood established in the first lines of "The Lady of Shalott"?

On either side the river lie
Long fields of barley and of rye,
That clothe the wold and meet the sky;
And through the field the road runs by
    To many-towered Camelot;

The meter, the unusual rhyme scheme, and the image of King Arthur's mythical realm Camelot help create a mood of tranquility and order. As you read the following poems by Tennyson, think about the mood each one creates and the particular elements that contribute to the mood.

READING SKILL: ANALYZE SPEAKER

The **speaker** in a poem is the voice that "talks" to the reader, much like the narrator in fiction. The choice of the speaker often contributes to the poem's mood. Sometimes the speaker can be identified with the poet; sometimes the speaker is an invented **persona,** or character. In many poems, the speaker is a distant observer; in others, the speaker is directly involved in the experience described, using the pronoun *I* and expressing personal feelings. Understanding the speaker is critical to understanding a poem.

The following four poems have a variety of speakers. As you read, identify the speaker in each poem. Notice the emotions each speaker reveals, if any, in response to characters and events in the poem. Then, list the clues from which you can infer these emotions, such as the speaker's choice of words. For each poem, fill in a diagram like the one shown. If you cannot infer the speaker's identity or emotions, write "unknown" on the appropriate line.

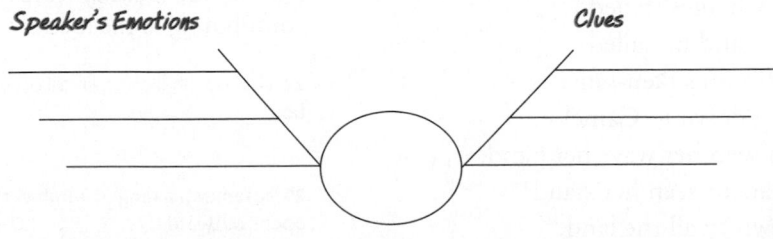

Speaker's Emotions   Clues

Speaker's Identity _____

 Complete the activities in your **Reader/Writer Notebook**.

How do you live LIFE to the FULLEST?

People who constantly seek out new experiences are said to be "living life to the fullest." Often, this phrase is used to describe adventurers, athletes, or connoisseurs. In your eyes, what experiences create a full life?

QUICKWRITE Think about either a person who lives life fully or a person whose life is lacking or incomplete. Based on your thoughts about this person, list five experiences you think are essential for a life lived to the fullest. Discuss your list with a small group of classmates. What are the benefits of having these experiences? Are there any downsides?

Experiences in a Full Life
1. Travel to foreign countries
2. Making many friends

THE *Lady* OF SHALOTT

Alfred, Lord Tennyson

Part I

On either side the river lie
Long fields of barley and of rye,
That clothe the wold and meet the sky;
And through the field the road runs by
5   To many-towered Camelot;
And up and down the people go,
Gazing where the lilies blow
Round an island there below,
     The island of Shalott.

10 Willows whiten, aspens quiver,
Little breezes dusk and shiver
Through the wave that runs forever
By the island in the river
     Flowing down to Camelot.
15 Four gray walls, and four gray towers,
Overlook a space of flowers,
And the silent isle imbowers
     The Lady of Shalott. **Ⓐ**

By the margin, willow-veiled,
20 Slide the heavy barges trailed
By slow horses; and unhailed
The shallop flitteth silken-sailed
     Skimming down to Camelot:
But who hath seen her wave her hand?
25 Or at the casement seen her stand?
Or is she known in all the land,
     The Lady of Shalott?

3 wold: rolling plain.

7 blow: bloom.

17 imbowers: encloses; surrounds.

Ⓐ MOOD
What mood is created by the description of the island in lines 10–18? Identify words contributing to the mood.

22 shallop (shăl′əp): a small open boat.

25 casement: a hinged window that opens outward.

'I am Half Sick of Shadows' Said the Lady of Shalott (1916),
John William Waterhouse. Oil on canvas, 100.3 cm × 73.7 cm.
© Art Gallery of Ontario, Toronto, Canada/Bridgeman Art Library.

Only reapers, reaping early
In among the bearded barley,
30 Hear a song that echoes cheerly
From the river winding clearly,
    Down to towered Camelot;
And by the moon the reaper weary,
Piling sheaves in uplands airy,
35 Listening, whispers "'Tis the fairy
    Lady of Shalott."

Part II

There she weaves by night and day
A magic web with colors gay.
She has heard a whisper say,
40 A curse is on her if she stay
    To look down to Camelot.
She knows not what the curse may be,
And so she weaveth steadily,
And little other care hath she,
45   The Lady of Shalott. **B**

And moving through a mirror clear
That hangs before her all the year,
Shadows of the world appear.
There she sees the highway near
50   Winding down to Camelot;
There the river eddy whirls,
And there the surly village churls,
And the red cloaks of market girls,
    Pass onward from Shalott.

55 Sometimes a troop of damsels glad,
An abbot on an ambling pad,
Sometimes a curly shepherd lad,
Or long-haired page in crimson clad,
    Goes by to towered Camelot;
60 And sometimes through the mirror blue
The knights come riding two and two:
She hath no loyal knight and true,
    The Lady of Shalott.

But in her web she still delights
65 To weave the mirror's magic sights,
For often through the silent nights
A funeral, with plumes and lights

COMMON CORE L 4b

Language Coach

Roots and Affixes Usually when adding the adverb-forming **suffix** *-ly* to an adjective ending in *-y*, the *y* changes to *i*. For example, *weary* becomes *wearily.* Reread line 30. How would you normally form an adverb from the adjective *cheery?*

B **SPEAKER**
How much have you learned about the speaker so far, and what has he or she told you about the Lady of Shalott?

46–48 Weavers often used mirrors while working from the back of a tapestry to view the tapestry's appearance, but this one is used to view the outside world.

52 surly village churls: rude members of the lower class in a village.

55 damsels: young, unmarried women.

56 abbot . . . pad: the head monk in a monastery on a slow-moving horse.

58 page: a boy in training to be a knight.

And music, went to Camelot;
Or when the moon was overhead,
70 Came two young lovers lately wed:
"I am half sick of shadows," said
⠀⠀⠀⠀The Lady of Shalott. **C**

Part III

A bowshot from her bower eaves,
He rode between the barley sheaves,
75 The sun came dazzling through the leaves,
And flamed upon the brazen greaves
⠀⠀⠀⠀Of bold Sir Lancelot.
A red-cross knight forever kneeled
To a lady in his shield,
80 That sparkled on the yellow field,
⠀⠀⠀⠀Beside remote Shalott.

The gemmy bridle glittered free,
Like to some branch of stars we see
Hung in the golden Galaxy.
85 The bridle bells rang merrily
⠀⠀⠀⠀As he rode down to Camelot;
And from his blazoned baldric slung
A mighty silver bugle hung,
And as he rode his armor rung,
90 ⠀⠀⠀⠀Beside remote Shalott.

All in the blue unclouded weather
Thick-jeweled shone the saddle leather,
The helmet and the helmet-feather
Burned like one burning flame together,
95 ⠀⠀⠀⠀As he rode down to Camelot;
As often through the purple night,
Below the starry clusters bright,
Some bearded meteor, trailing light,
⠀⠀⠀⠀Moves over still Shalott. **D**

100 His broad clear brow in sunlight glowed;
On burnished hooves his war horse trode;
From underneath his helmet flowed
His coal-black curls as on he rode,
⠀⠀⠀⠀As he rode down to Camelot.
105 From the bank and from the river
He flashed into the crystal mirror,

C MOOD
Describe the pattern of
repetition in the fifth and
ninth lines of each stanza.
How does the repetition
affect the mood?

73 bowshot: the distance an arrow
can be shot; **bower** (bou′ər) **eaves:**
the part of the roof that extends
above the lady's private room.

76 brazen greaves: metal armor
protecting the legs below the knees.

78–79 A red-cross ... shield: His
shield showed a knight wearing a
red cross and kneeling to honor a
lady. The red cross was a symbol
worn by knights who had fought in
the Crusades.

82 gemmy: studded with gems.

87 blazoned (blā′zənd) **baldric:** a
decorated leather belt, worn across
the chest to support a sword or, as
in this case, a bugle.

D MOOD
Reread lines 73–99, and
note all the **images** of light
associated with Sir Lancelot.
What mood do they create?

"Tirra lirra," by the river
　　Sang Sir Lancelot.

She left the web, she left the loom,
110 She made three paces through the room,
She saw the water lily bloom,
She saw the helmet and the plume,
　　She looked down to Camelot.
Out flew the web and floated wide;
115 The mirror cracked from side to side;
"The curse is come upon me," cried
　　The Lady of Shalott. **E**

Part IV

In the stormy east wind straining,
The pale yellow woods were waning,
120 The broad stream in his banks complaining,
Heavily the low sky raining
　　Over towered Camelot;
Down she came and found a boat
Beneath a willow left afloat,
125 And round about the prow she wrote
　　The Lady of Shalott.

And down the river's dim expanse
Like some bold seër in a trance,
Seeing all his own mischance—
130 With a glassy countenance
　　Did she look to Camelot.
And at the closing of the day
She loosed the chain, and down she lay;
The broad stream bore her far away,
135　　The Lady of Shalott.

Lying, robed in snowy white
That loosely flew to left and right—
The leaves upon her falling light—
Through the noises of the night
140　　She floated down to Camelot;
And as the boat-head wound along
The willowy hills and fields among,
They heard her singing her last song,
　　The Lady of Shalott.

E MOOD
How does the mood change
in lines 109–117?

128 seër (sē′ər): someone who can see
into the future; a prophet.

129 mischance: misfortune; bad luck.

Language Coach

Homographs Words that
have the same spelling
but different meanings or
pronunciations are **homographs.**
What is the meaning and
pronunciation of *wound* in
line 141? What is the other
pronunciation and meaning?

145 Heard a carol, mournful, holy,
 Chanted loudly, chanted lowly,
 Till her blood was frozen slowly,
 And her eyes were darkened wholly,
     Turned to towered Camelot.
150 For ere she reached upon the tide
 The first house by the waterside,
 Singing in her song she died,
     The Lady of Shalott. **F**

 Under tower and balcony,
155 By garden wall and gallery,
 A gleaming shape she floated by,
 Dead-pale between the houses high,
     Silent into Camelot.
 Out upon the wharfs they came,
160 Knight and burgher, lord and dame,
 And round the prow they read her name,
     The Lady of Shalott.

 Who is this? and what is here?
 And in the lighted palace near
165 Died the sound of royal cheer;
 And they crossed themselves for fear,
     All the knights at Camelot:
 But Lancelot mused a little space;
 He said, "She has a lovely face;
170 God in his mercy lend her grace,
     The Lady of Shalott."

150 **ere** (âr): before.

F MOOD
Reread lines 118–153. How do nature **imagery** and **sound devices** help create a tragic mood?

160 **burgher:** a middle-class citizen of a town.

Text Analysis

1. **Summarize** Briefly summarize the story told in this poem.

2. **Make Inferences** Why does the Lady of Shalott leave her tower?

3. **Make Judgments** What thoughts do you have about Lancelot's reaction in the last three lines?

4. **Analyze Sound Devices** What sound devices are predominant in the poem? Discuss the effects they create.

Detail of *The Blind Beggar and his Grand-daughter* (1700s), John Russell. Oil on canvas. © The Bowes Museum, Barnard Castle, County Durham, United Kingdom/ Bridgeman Art Library.

Ulysses
Alfred, Lord Tennyson

It little profits that an idle king,
By this still hearth, among these barren crags,
Match'd with an aged wife, I mete and dole
Unequal laws unto a savage race,
5 That hoard, and sleep, and feed, and know not me.
I cannot rest from travel: I will drink
Life to the lees: all times I have enjoy'd
Greatly, have suffer'd greatly, both with those
That loved me, and alone; on shore, and when
10 Thro' scudding drifts the rainy Hyades
Vext the dim sea: I am become a name;
For always roaming with a hungry heart
Much have I seen and known; cities of men
And manners, climates, councils, governments,
15 Myself not least, but honor'd of them all;
And drunk delight of battle with my peers,
Far on the ringing plains of windy Troy.
I am a part of all that I have met;
Yet all experience is an arch wherethro'
20 Gleams that untravell'd world, whose margin fades
For ever and for ever when I move. **G**
How dull it is to pause, to make an end,
To rust unburnish'd, not to shine in use!
As tho' to breathe were life. Life piled on life

3 mete (mēt) **and dole:** give and distribute.

7 to the lees: to the dregs or bottom of the cup; completely.

10 scudding drifts: windblown rainclouds; **Hyades:** a constellation whose rising was believed to signify the coming of rain.

17 Troy: the ancient city conquered by the Greeks in the Trojan War, in which Ulysses (Odysseus) was among the Greek leaders.

G SPEAKER
Who is the speaker, and how do you know?

25 Were all too little, and of one to me
   Little remains: but every hour is saved
   From that eternal silence, something more,
   A bringer of new things; and vile it were
   For some three suns to store and hoard myself,
30 And this gray spirit yearning in desire
   To follow knowledge like a sinking star,
   Beyond the utmost bound of human thought. ⓗ
   This is my son, mine own Telemachus,
   To whom I leave the sceptre and the isle—
35 Well-loved of me, discerning to fulfil
   This labor, by slow prudence to make mild
   A rugged people, and thro' soft degrees
   Subdue them to the useful and the good.
   Most blameless is he, centred in the sphere
40 Of common duties, decent not to fail
   In offices of tenderness, and pay
   Meet adoration to my household gods,
   When I am gone. He works his work, I mine.
       There lies the port; the vessel puffs her sail:
45 There gloom the dark broad seas. My mariners,
   Souls that have toil'd, and wrought, and thought with me—
   That ever with a frolic welcome took
   The thunder and the sunshine, and opposed
   Free hearts, free foreheads—you and I are old;
50 Old age hath yet his honor and his toil;
   Death closes all: but something ere the end,
   Some work of noble note, may yet be done,
   Not unbecoming men that strove with Gods.
   The lights begin to twinkle from the rocks;
55 The long day wanes; the slow moon climbs; the deep
   Moans round with many voices. Come, my friends,
   'Tis not too late to seek a newer world.
   Push off, and sitting well in order smite
   The sounding furrows; for my purpose holds
60 To sail beyond the sunset, and the baths
   Of all the western stars, until I die.
   It may be that the gulfs will wash us down:
   It may be we shall touch the Happy Isles,
   And see the great Achilles, whom we knew.
65 Tho' much is taken, much abides; and tho'
   We are not now that strength which in old days
   Moved earth and heaven; that which we are, we are;
   One equal temper of heroic hearts,
   Made weak by time and fate, but strong in will
70 To strive, to seek, to find, and not to yield. ⓘ

29 three suns: three years.

ⓗ **MOOD**
Describe the mood of lines 22–32.

33 Telemachus (tə-lĕm′ə-kəs).

34 sceptre (sĕp′tər): a staff held by a king or a queen as a symbol of royal authority.

42 meet: appropriate.

47 frolic: merry.

Language Coach

Oral Fluency Read lines 51–53 aloud. In line 51, *ere* (pronounced /er/) is a poetic word for *before*. Why is *ere* better than *before* in these lines?

58–59 smite . . . furrows: strike the waves with the boat's oars.

60–61 baths . . . stars: The ancient Greeks believed the earth was surrounded by an outer ocean or river, into which the stars descended.

63–64 Happy Isles . . . Achilles: the Islands of the Blessed, where the souls of heroes, like Achilles, dwelt after death.

ⓘ **SPEAKER**
How does the speaker characterize himself and his friends in lines 65–70?

from In *Memoriam*

Alfred, Lord Tennyson

27

I envy not in any moods
    The captive void of noble rage,
    The linnet born within the cage,
That never knew the summer woods;

5 I envy not the beast that takes
    His license in the field of time,
    Unfettered by the sense of crime,
To whom a conscience never wakes;

Nor, what may count itself as blest,
10   The heart that never plighted troth
    But stagnates in the weeds of sloth;
Nor any want-begotten rest.

I hold it true, whate'er befall;
    I feel it, when I sorrow most;
15   'Tis better to have loved and lost
Than never to have loved at all. **J**

54

O, yet we trust that somehow good
    Will be the final goal of ill,
    To pangs of nature, sins of will,
20 Defects of doubt, and taints of blood;

That nothing walks with aimless feet;
    That not one life shall be destroyed,
    Or cast as rubbish to the void,
When God hath made the pile complete;

2 void of: lacking in.

3 linnet: a kind of small songbird.

6 license: freedom of action; liberty.

7 unfettered: unrestricted.

9–12 nor, what . . . rest: nor do I envy the supposed peace of mind that arises from remaining sunk in inaction, never pledging one's love, or from any deficiency.

J SPEAKER
How closely can the speaker be identified with the poet, and what makes you think so?

19 pangs of nature: physical pain.

20 taints of blood: inherited faults.

23 void: empty space.

A Funeral Bearer (1830s). © Museum of London.

25 That not a worm is cloven in vain;
        That not a moth with vain desire
        Is shriveled in a fruitless fire,
    Or but subserves another's gain.

    Behold, we know not anything;
30   I can but trust that good shall fall
        At last—far off—at last, to all,
    And every winter change to spring.

    So runs my dream; but what am I?
        An infant crying in the night;
35   An infant crying for the light,
    And with no language but a cry. **K**

                130

    Thy voice is on the rolling air;
        I hear thee where the waters run;
        Thou standest in the rising sun,
40 And in the setting thou art fair.

    What are thou then? I cannot guess;
        But though I seem in star and flower
        To feel thee some diffusive power,
    I do not therefore love thee less.

45 My love involves the love before;
        My love is vaster passion now;
        Though mixed with God and Nature thou,
    I seem to love thee more and more.

    Far off thou art, but ever nigh;
50   I have thee still, and I rejoice;
        I prosper, circled with thy voice;
    I shall not lose thee though I die. **L**

25 cloven: split.

28 subserves: promotes or assists.

Language Coach

Formal Language The verb *behold* (line 29) is a somewhat formal verb for "to see" or "to look upon." How would you translate this line into everyday language?

K SPEAKER
Note how the speaker describes himself in lines 34–36. What emotion is he expressing?

43 diffusive: scattered about.

49 nigh: nearby.

L MOOD
What makes the mood of part 130 different from the mood of part 27?

Text Analysis

1. **Draw Conclusions** In "Ulysses," what situation is the speaker in, and how does he react to it?

2. **Paraphrase** Explain the meaning of these lines from part 27 of *In Memoriam*: "'Tis better to have loved and lost / Than never to have loved at all."

3. **Interpret Theme** In part 54 of *In Memoriam*, what does the speaker want to believe? Is he satisfied in this belief?

Lights in Harbour, John Atkinson Grimshaw. The Scarborough Art Gallery, Scarborough, United Kingdom.

CROSSING THE *Bar*

Alfred, Lord Tennyson

Sunset and evening star,
    And one clear call for me!
And may there be no moaning of the bar,
    When I put out to sea,

5 But such a tide as moving seems asleep,
    Too full for sound and foam,
When that which drew from out the boundless deep
    Turns again home.

Twilight and evening bell,
10   And after that the dark!
And may there be no sadness of farewell,
    When I embark;

For though from out our bourne of Time and Place
    The flood may bear me far,
15 I hope to see my Pilot face to face
    When I have crossed the bar. Ⓜ

3 moaning of the bar: the sound of the ocean waves pounding against a sandbar at the mouth of a harbor.

9 evening bell: a ship's bell rung to announce the changing of the watch.

13 from out ... Place: beyond the boundary of our lifetimes.

14 flood: ocean.

Ⓜ **MOOD**
Does the **parallelism** in lines 4, 12, and 16 make the mood lighter or more solemn?

Comprehension

1. **Clarify** In "Crossing the Bar," the sea voyage is a **metaphor** for what experience?

2. **Clarify** What might the Pilot represent?

3. **Paraphrase** Explain, in your own words, what the speaker desires.

Text Analysis

4. **Analyze Speakers** Look again at the diagrams you created as you read. Describe the speaker of each poem and the emotions the speaker expresses, if any. What are the advantages, in each poem, of Tennyson's choice of speaker?

5. **Analyze Mood** Describe the different moods Tennyson is able to create in these poems. Discuss what each of the following elements contributes to **mood**, giving examples:

   • diction   • imagery   • sound devices   • parallelism

6. **Contrast Texts** What different reactions to grief does the speaker express in the three lyrics from *In Memoriam*?

7. **Synthesize Author's Perspective** Judging from the four poems you have read, what seems to be Tennyson's conception of death? Support your answer with details from the poems.

8. **Evaluate Style** Tennyson is one of the most quoted English poets. Choose a passage that you recognize or admire, and explain what makes it memorable.

Text Criticism

9. **Critical Interpretations** An **allegory** is a story in which characters represent abstract ideas. Some critics have remarked that "The Lady of Shalott" is an allegory for the life of the artist. Think about the life the Lady leads as a weaver of webs, and think also about her relationship to the outside world. What might Tennyson be saying about the challenges of being an artist? Cite evidence from the poem to support your conclusions.

> *How do you live* **LIFE** *to the* **FULLEST?**
>
> What are some experiences you have had that made you feel you are living a full life? Do you think it's really possible to live life to the fullest? Explain.

COMMON CORE

RL 1 Cite evidence to support inferences drawn from the text. **RL 4** Analyze the impact of specific word choices on meaning and tone, including language that is fresh, engaging, or beautiful. **RL 9** Demonstrate knowledge of foundational works of literature.

Language

◆ GRAMMAR AND STYLE: Add Descriptive Details

Tennyson was a skilled craftsman who often used imagery based on the five senses to stunning effect. In the following passage, for instance, he uses **sensory details** to create an exquisite, dreamlike atmosphere:

> *And as the boat-head wound along*
> *The willowy hills and fields among,*
> *They heard her singing her last song,*
> *   The Lady of Shalott.*
>
> *Heard a carol, mournful, holy,*
> *Chanted loudly, chanted lowly,*
> *Till her blood was frozen slowly,*
> *And her eyes were darkened wholly,*
> *   Turned to towered Camelot.* (lines 141–149)

Notice how the highlighted **modifiers** *(willowy, mournful, loudly, lowly)* appeal to the reader's senses of sight, sound, and touch. These sensory details enable readers to fully imagine the Lady's song and appearance as she floats down the river toward Camelot.

PRACTICE Write a poem describing a natural scene, and model it on the following excerpt (you don't have to duplicate the rhyme scheme). Be sure to incorporate several modifiers that appeal to the senses.

> *In the stormy east wind straining,*
> *The pale yellow woods were waning,*
> *The broad stream in his banks complaining,*
> *Heavily the low sky raining*
> *   Over towered Camelot;*

COMMON CORE

L 3 Apply knowledge of language to make effective choices for style. **W 9** Draw evidence from literary or informational texts to support analysis.

READING-WRITING CONNECTION

YOUR TURN Expand your understanding of Tennyson's poem by responding to this prompt. Then, use the **revising tips** to improve your analysis of Tennyson's style.

WRITING PROMPT	REVISING TIPS
ANALYZE AUTHOR'S STYLE In "The Lady of Shalott," Tennyson employs the repetition of sounds, such as rhyme and alliteration, to weave the dark, dreamy tale of his doomed heroine. In a **three-to-five paragraph essay,** identify two specific examples of rhyme or alliteration in the poem and explain how these repetitions of sound enhance the poem's mood and themes.	• Include direct quotations from the poem to provide examples of Tennyson's use of the repetition of sounds. • Include line numbers for each quotation. • Make sure you have explained why your examples reflect the mood or themes of the poem.

Interactive Revision **THINK** central

Go to <u>thinkcentral.com</u>.
KEYWORD: HML12-943

COMMON CORE

RL 1 Cite strong and thorough textual evidence to support inferences drawn from the text. **RL 5** Analyze how an author's choices concerning how to structure specific parts of a text contribute to its overall structure and meaning as well as its aesthetic impact. **RL 10** Read and comprehend literature, including poems. **SL 1** Initiate and participate effectively in a range of collaborative discussions.

My Last Duchess
Porphyria's Lover

Poetry by Robert Browning

VIDEO TRAILER THINK central KEYWORD: HML12-944A

Meet the Author

Robert Browning 1812–1889

"A minute's success," remarked the poet Robert Browning, "pays for the failure of years." Browning spoke from experience: for years, critics either ignored or belittled his poetry. Then, when he was nearly 60, he became an object of near-worship.

Precocious Child An exceptionally bright child, Browning learned to read and write by the time he was 5 and composed his first, unpublished volume of poetry at 12. At the age of 21 he published his first book, *Pauline* (1833), to negative reviews. One critic, John Stuart Mill, wrote, "With considerable poetic powers the writer seems to me possessed with a more intense and morbid self-consciousness than I ever knew in any sane human being."

Poetic Pioneer Mill's remarks embarrassed Browning, who vowed to keep his writing free from personal information in the future. Over the next several years, he concentrated on writing verse dramas for the stage. Discovering that he had a talent for developing character through speech, he also began to write a type of poem called the **dramatic monologue.** In his monologues, he typically portrayed either a historical or an imaginary character in an emotionally charged situation. While critics attacked his early dramatic poems, finding them difficult to understand, Browning did not allow the reviews to keep him from continuing to develop this form.

Secret Love In 1845, Browning met the poet Elizabeth Barrett and began a famous romance that has been memorialized in both film and literature. Against the wishes of Barrett's overbearing father, the two poets married in secret in 1846 and eloped to Italy, where they lived happily for the next 15 years. Their joyful relationship inspired the book generally regarded as Browning's masterpiece, *Men and Women* (1855). Composed of 50 dramatic monologues, the collection reflects Browning's passion for his wife, as well as his interest in painters, poets, biblical figures, and madmen.

Literary Renown After his wife's death in 1861, Browning returned to England, where he concentrated on writing *The Ring and the Book,* a series of dramatic monologues based on the records of a 17th-century Roman murder trial. *The Ring and the Book* was published to impressive reviews, bringing Browning the recognition for which he had long waited.

DID YOU KNOW?

Robert Browning . . .

- became an ardent admirer of Percy Bysshe Shelley at age 12.
- achieved fluency in Latin, Greek, Italian, and French by age 14.
- wrote the children's poem "The Pied Piper of Hamelin."

(background) Marriage certificate of Robert and Elizabeth Barrett Browning

Author Online

Go to thinkcentral.com. KEYWORD: HML12-944B

● POETIC FORM: DRAMATIC MONOLOGUE

Critics praise Browning's mastery of the **dramatic monologue,** a poetic form in which a speaker addresses a silent or absent listener during a moment of high intensity or deep emotion. The speaker is usually a character distinct from the poet—for example, the Greek hero Ulysses in Tennyson's poem "Ulysses" (page 936). Browning's dramatic monologues require the reader to make many inferences: it is not always immediately clear who the speaker is, whom he is speaking to, and what setting they are in. "My Last Duchess" takes place in 16th-century Italy. The speaker is a duke who is negotiating with the agent of a powerful count to marry the count's daughter. What scene is created in your mind by the duke's first words?

> *That's my last Duchess painted on the wall,*
> *Looking as if she were alive. I call*
> *That piece a wonder, now: Frà Pandolf's hands*
> *Worked busily a day, and there she stands.*

As you read this poem and "Porphyria's Lover," continue to imagine the setting and action.

● READING SKILL: MAKE INFERENCES ABOUT SPEAKERS

Not only must readers make inferences about the setting and action in a dramatic monologue; they must **make inferences,** or logical assumptions based on evidence from the text, about the feelings, motives, and personality of the speaker. The speaker's words often reveal characteristics of which he or she is unaware. For example, what would be your thoughts about someone who told you, "I am the humblest man you'll ever meet. I'm much more humble than my older brother"? Would your image of him match his image of himself? For each of the following monologues, fill in a Venn diagram with your inferences about the speaker's self-image and true nature. In the space where the circles intersect, write self-perceptions of the speaker that appear actually true.

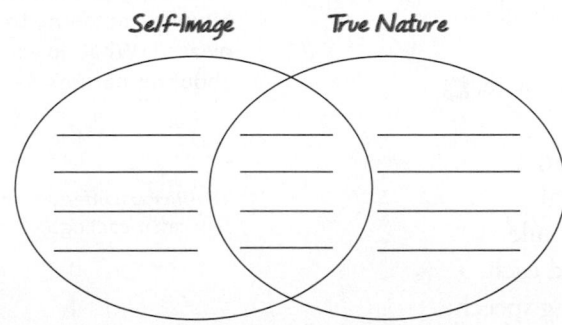

Self-Image   True Nature

 Complete the activities in your **Reader/Writer Notebook**.

What are the perils of JEALOUSY?

"Jealousy," notes one writer, "is a tiger that tears not only its prey but also its own raging heart." Think about whether this description is accurate. What happens when the "green-eyed monster" strikes a person? How can jealousy threaten a love relationship?

DISCUSS With a partner, discuss what the emotion of jealousy feels like. Talk about the causes of jealousy and the different ways people respond to having this feeling. Then identify some of the worst consequences of jealousy in a love relationship. You might draw on stories from the news or from literature and film.

MY LAST DUCHESS

Robert Browning

That's my last Duchess painted on the wall,
Looking as if she were alive. I call
That piece a wonder, now: Frà Pandolf's hands
Worked busily a day, and there she stands.
5 Will't please you sit and look at her? I said Ⓐ
"Frà Pandolf" by design, for never read
Strangers like you that pictured countenance,
The depth and passion of its earnest glance,
But to myself they turned (since none puts by
10 The curtain I have drawn for you, but I)
And seemed as they would ask me, if they durst,
How such a glance came there; so, not the first
Are you to turn and ask thus. Sir, 'twas not
Her husband's presence only, called that spot
15 Of joy into the Duchess' cheek: perhaps
Frà Pandolf chanced to say "Her mantle laps
Over my lady's wrist too much," or "Paint
Must never hope to reproduce the faint
Half-flush that dies along her throat": such stuff
20 Was courtesy, she thought, and cause enough
For calling up that spot of joy. She had
A heart—how shall I say?—too soon made glad,
Too easily impressed; she liked whate'er
She looked on, and her looks went everywhere. Ⓑ
25 Sir, 'twas all one! My favor at her breast,
The dropping of the daylight in the West,
The bough of cherries some officious fool
Broke in the orchard for her, the white mule
She rode with round the terrace—all and each
30 Would draw from her alike the approving speech,
Or blush, at least. She thanked men—good! but thanked

3 Frà Pandolf's: of Brother Pandolf, a fictitious friar-painter.

Ⓐ **DRAMATIC MONOLOGUE**
Read lines 5–13 aloud. What scene do you imagine?

11 durst: dared.

16 mantle: cloak.

Ⓑ **MAKE INFERENCES**
Note how the duke feels about his wife's tendency to be easily pleased. What do you infer about his nature?

27 officious: offering unwanted services; meddling.

Detail of *Choosing* (1864), George Frederic Watts. Oil on strawboard, 18⅝″ × 14″. © National Portrait Gallery, London.

Somehow—I know not how—as if she ranked
My gift of a nine-hundred-years-old name
With anybody's gift. Who'd stoop to blame
35 This sort of trifling? Even had you skill
In speech—(which I have not)—to make your will
Quite clear to such an one, and say, "Just this
Or that in you disgusts me; here you miss,
Or there exceed the mark"—and if she let
40 Herself be lessoned so, nor plainly set
Her wits to yours, forsooth, and made excuse
—E'en then would be some stooping; and I choose
Never to stoop. Oh sir, she smiled, no doubt, **C**
Whene'er I passed her; but who passed without
45 Much the same smile? This grew; I gave commands;
Then all smiles stopped together. There she stands
As if alive. Will't please you rise? We'll meet
The company below, then. I repeat,
The Count your master's known munificence
50 Is ample warrant that no just pretense
Of mine for dowry will be disallowed;
Though his fair daughter's self, as I avowed
At starting, is my object. Nay, we'll go
Together down, sir. Notice Neptune, though,
55 Taming a sea horse, thought a rarity,
Which Claus of Innsbruck cast in bronze for me! **D**

35 trifling: actions of little importance.

41 forsooth: in truth; indeed.

C MAKE INFERENCES
Reread lines 34–43. What ideas do you form about the duke from his insistence that he will never "stoop"?

49 munificence (myōō-nĭf'ĭ-səns): generosity.

50 just pretense: legitimate claim.

51 dowry (dou'rē): payment given to a groom by the bride's father.

54 Neptune: in Roman mythology, the god of the sea.

D DRAMATIC MONOLOGUE
What **tone** and actions are suggested in lines 47–56?

Text Analysis

1. **Make Inferences About Speakers** Describe the speaker's attitude toward his former wife, offering evidence from the poem.

2. **Draw Conclusions** What do you think happened to the duchess? Support your answer.

3. **Interpret Symbolism** What larger ideas are suggested by the description of the bronze sculpture of Neptune (lines 54–56)?

PORPHYRIA'S LOVER

Robert Browning

Mary Ann, Wife of Leonard Collman
(1854), Alfred Stevens.

The rain set early in tonight,
    The sullen wind was soon awake,
It tore the elm-tops down for spite,
    And did its worst to vex the lake:
5   I listened with heart fit to break.
When glided in Porphyria; straight
    She shut the cold out and the storm,
And kneeled and made the cheerless grate
    Blaze up, and all the cottage warm;
10   Which done, she rose, and from her form
Withdrew the dripping cloak and shawl,
    And laid her soiled gloves by, untied
Her hat and let the damp hair fall,
    And, last, she sat down by my side
15   And called me. When no voice replied, **E**
She put my arm about her waist,
    And made her smooth white shoulder bare,
And all her yellow hair displaced,

4 **vex:** to disturb; trouble the surface of.

6 **straight:** immediately.

8 **grate:** fireplace.

E **MAKE INFERENCES**
Why do you think the speaker does not reply to Porphyria?

And, stooping, made my cheek lie there,
20   And spread, o'er all, her yellow hair,
Murmuring how she loved me—she
        Too weak, for all her heart's endeavor,
To set its struggling passion free
        From pride, and vainer ties dissever,
25   And give herself to me forever. **F**
But passion sometimes would prevail,
        Nor could tonight's gay feast restrain
A sudden thought of one so pale
        For love of her, and all in vain:
30   So, she was come through wind and rain.
Be sure I looked up at her eyes
        Happy and proud; at last I knew
Porphyria worshiped me: surprise
        Made my heart swell, and still it grew
35   While I debated what to do.
That moment she was mine, mine, fair,
        Perfectly pure and good: I found
A thing to do, and all her hair
        In one long yellow string I wound
40   Three times her little throat around,
And strangled her. No pain felt she;
        I am quite sure she felt no pain. **G**
As a shut bud that holds a bee,
        I warily oped her lids: again
45   Laughed the blue eyes without a stain.
And I untightened next the tress
        About her neck; her cheek once more
Blushed bright beneath my burning kiss:
        I propped her head up as before,
50   Only, this time my shoulder bore
Her head, which droops upon it still:
        The smiling rosy little head,
So glad it has its utmost will,
        That all it scorned at once is fled,
55   And I, its love, am gained instead!
Porphyria's love: she guessed not how
        Her darling one wish would be heard.
And thus we sit together now,
        And all night long we have not stirred,
60   And yet God has not said a word! **H**

F **DRAMATIC MONOLOGUE**
Lines 22–25 refer to earlier events. What is Porphyria unable to do, and what might the "vainer ties" be?

G **MAKE INFERENCES**
What do you infer about the speaker from his thoughts and actions in lines 36–42?

Language Coach
Etymology A word's **etymology** is its history. The word *tress* may come from a Greek word meaning "threefold." How might this etymology help you understand the meaning of *tress* in line 46?

H **DRAMATIC MONOLOGUE**
Why might Browning have chosen not to suggest the presence of a listener in this poem, as he did in "My Last Duchess"?

Comprehension

1. **Recall** What is the setting of "Porphyria's Lover"?

2. **Summarize** Briefly recount the events in the poem.

Text Analysis

3. **Interpret Motives** What causes the speaker in "My Last Duchess" to distrust his wife? Is his reaction reasonable? Provide examples from the poem to support your interpretation.

4. **Draw Conclusions** Why does the speaker in "Porphyria's Lover" kill her? Do you think the speaker feels guilty about what he has done? Explain your reasoning.

5. **Make Inferences About Speakers** Describe the feelings, motives, and personality of the speakers in "My Last Duchess" and "Porphyria's Lover." How does each man's self-image differ from his true nature? Refer to the diagrams you completed as you read the poems.

6. **Analyze Dramatic Monologue** The speakers in these dramatic monologues are intensely involved in the events described. What would be the impact of each poem if Browning had chosen an outside observer as the speaker?

7. **Evaluate Style** In "My Last Duchess," how does the language create the sense that a person is speaking aloud to someone? What features remind you that the work is a poem, not an overheard conversation? Cite specific details.

8. **Synthesize Themes** How does the desire for possession of a woman motivate each of the speakers in these dramatic monologues? What does this desire reveal about each speaker?

Text Criticism

9. **Critical Interpretations** The critic Robert Langbaum has argued that a Browning dramatic monologue combines "sympathy" and "judgment." In your opinion, does Browning want the reader to feel sympathy and also judge the duke and Porphyria's lover? Explain.

> ## What are the perils of JEALOUSY?
>
> Jealousy appears to be inspired by love, but it often springs from other emotions. What are some of the hidden causes of jealousy?

COMMON CORE

RL 1 Cite strong and thorough textual evidence to support inferences drawn from the text. **RL 5** Analyze how an author's choices concerning how to structure specific parts of a text contribute to its overall structure and meaning as well as its aesthetic impact. **RL 10** Read and comprehend literature, including poems.

COMMON CORE

RL 2 Determine two or more themes or central ideas of a text. **RL 4** Determine the meaning of words and phrases as they are used in the text, including figurative meanings.

Sonnet 43
Poem by Elizabeth Barrett Browning

Remembrance
Poem by Emily Brontë

VIDEO TRAILER **THINK** central KEYWORD: HML12-952A

Meet the Authors

Elizabeth Barrett Browning
1806–1861

Born into a family involved in the Jamaican sugar trade, Elizabeth Barrett enjoyed a privileged childhood in Herefordshire, England. As a schoolgirl, she was precocious, reading several of Shakespeare's plays before she was 10 and publishing her first "epic" poem at 12. "I used to make up rhymes over my bread and milk when I was nearly a baby," she later recalled.

Kindred Spirits At 15, Barrett suffered an ailment that left her an invalid. Despite her condition, she continued to read voraciously and to write poetry, publishing three volumes between 1826 and 1844. Moved by a poem she wrote

praising his verse, Robert Browning initiated a correspondence with her that led to their falling in love. During their courtship, Barrett secretly wrote a group of sonnets, including "Sonnet 43," about her passionate love for Robert, but she did not show them to him until after they were married. Published as *Sonnets from the Portuguese* (1850), these lyrics are generally considered to be her finest work.

Active Years During the 15 years of her marriage, Barrett Browning gave birth to a son, wrote political poetry, and championed such causes as the abolition of slavery, the reform of child labor practices, and women's rights.

Emily Brontë
1818–1848

One of six children, Emily Brontë grew up on the wild, lonely moors of Yorkshire. She and her sisters Charlotte and Anne and her brother, Branwell, were inseparable companions. Often left to themselves, they began writing long, intricate stories about an imaginary world inhabited by heroic characters. Around 1833, Emily and Anne broke off from their siblings and invented their own kingdom, Gondal, the setting of many poems and stories of adventure.

First Book In 1845, Charlotte discovered a group of Emily's "Gondal poems." Stirred by their "wild, melancholy, and

elevating" music, she convinced Emily and Anne to combine their poems with hers in one volume. The book appeared under the pseudonyms Currer, Ellis, and Acton Bell and included "Remembrance," the Gondal heroine's elegy for the dead hero.

Romantic Genius In 1847, Emily published *Wuthering Heights,* a highly imaginative novel that disturbed and bewildered critics. This fierce, brooding story of star-crossed love and revenge eventually came to be considered one of England's finest novels.

Authors Online **THINK** central

Go to **thinkcentral.com.**
KEYWORD: HML12-952B

TEXT ANALYSIS: FIGURATIVE LANGUAGE

Much of the power of poetry comes from **figurative language**— language that communicates ideas beyond the literal meaning of the words. The most common figures of speech are **similes** (comparisons using *like* or *as,* such as *My love is like to ice*) and **metaphors** (direct comparisons that do not use *like* or *as,* such as *the flame of love*). Other figures of speech include

- **Personification**—the giving of human qualities to an object, animal, or idea (*Love's not Time's fool*)
- **Hyperbole**—exaggeration for emphasis or comic effect (*I prize thy love more than whole mines of gold*)

Figurative language allows a poet to describe abstract concepts or to present familiar things in a fresh way. In the preceding examples, the personification suggests that love does not change with the passage of time, and the hyperbole suggests the high value the speaker places on being loved. As you read the following two poems, notice different types of figurative language and the ideas about love communicated through this language.

READING SKILL: COMPARE THEMES

The **theme** of a poem is the underlying message about life or human nature that the writer wants readers to understand. The two poems you will read share a subject—love—but communicate different ideas about this subject. As you read each poem, examine direct statements and figurative language to determine the ideas about love that the poet conveys. Use a web diagram like the one shown for each poem.

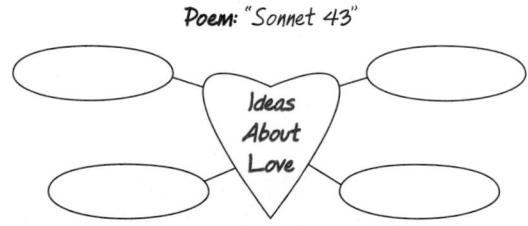

Poem: "Sonnet 43"

Ideas About Love

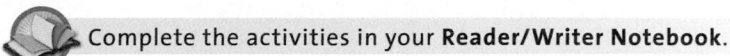

Complete the activities in your **Reader/Writer Notebook.**

Do you believe that LOVE *lasts forever?*

Do you believe in love everlasting, or that love must inevitably come to an end? What are some pressures of daily life that may pose challenges to the strength and permanence of romantic love? The poems that follow describe their speakers' conceptions about eternal love. Do you agree or disagree with each speaker's viewpoint about love that lasts forever?

REPRESENT To see how you feel about love, use the four scales below. Think about the kind of love relationship you desire or think is best to have. For each pair of opposite qualities, decide which point on the scale reflects your beliefs about what love should be. Be prepared to compare your own attitudes with those of the speakers in the poems.

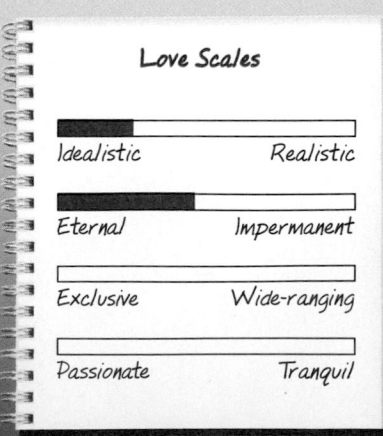

Love Scales

Idealistic — Realistic

Eternal — Impermanent

Exclusive — Wide-ranging

Passionate — Tranquil

SONNET 43

Elizabeth Barrett Browning

How do I love thee? Let me count the ways.
I love thee to the depth and breadth and height
My soul can reach, when feeling out of sight **Ⓐ**
For the ends of Being and ideal Grace.
5 I love thee to the level of everyday's
Most quiet need, by sun and candlelight.
I love thee freely, as men strive for Right;
I love thee purely, as they turn from Praise.
I love thee with the passion put to use
10 In my old griefs, and with my childhood's faith.
I love thee with a love I seemed to lose
With my lost saints,—I love thee with the breath,
Smiles, tears, of all my life!—and, if God choose,
I shall but love thee better after death. **Ⓑ**

Ⓐ FIGURATIVE LANGUAGE
Identify the type of figurative language used in lines 2–3. What idea about love does it communicate?

Ⓑ COMPARE THEMES
What belief about love is expressed in line 14?

Early, handmade Puzzle Purse Valentine (about 1790). © Christie's Images, Ltd.

"My dear the heart which you behold 1st"

Will break when you the same unfold 2nd

Even so my heart doth love dissemble 3rd

Sure wounded is such breaks in twain 4th

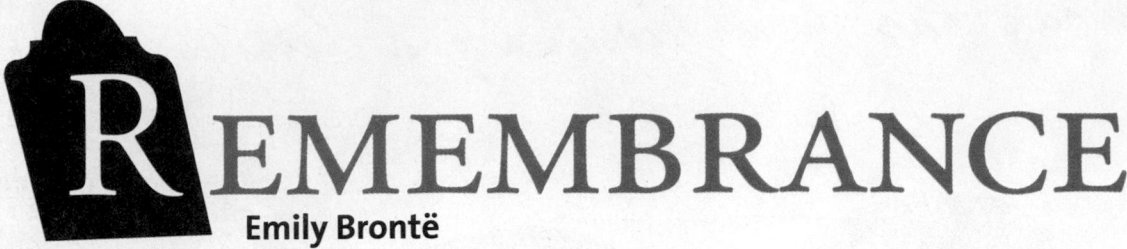

REMEMBRANCE

Emily Brontë

Cold in the earth, and the deep snow piled above thee!
Far, far removed, cold in the dreary grave!
Have I forgot, my Only Love, to love thee,
Severed at last by Time's all-wearing wave? **C**

5 Now, when alone, do my thoughts no longer hover
Over the mountains, on that northern shore;
Resting their wings where heath and fern-leaves cover
Thy noble heart for ever, ever more?

Cold in the earth, and fifteen wild Decembers
10 From those brown hills have melted into spring—
Faithful indeed is the spirit that remembers
After such years of change and suffering!

Sweet Love of youth, forgive if I forget thee
While the World's tide is bearing me along:
15 Other desires and other hopes beset me,
Hopes which obscure but cannot do thee wrong.

No later light has lightened up my heaven,
No second morn has ever shone for me:
All my life's bliss from thy dear life was given—
20 All my life's bliss is in the grave with thee. **D**

But when the days of golden dreams had perished
And even Despair was powerless to destroy,
Then did I learn how existence could be cherished,
Strengthened and fed without the aid of joy;

C FIGURATIVE LANGUAGE
State what time is compared to in the **metaphor** in line 4. According to the speaker, how does time affect love?

Language Coach

Roots and Affixes The **prefix** *be-* can mean "around" (*besiege*) or "make" (*belittle*), among other things. Which of these meanings makes more sense for *beset* (line 15)? What do you think *beset* means?

D COMPARE THEMES
Reread lines 13–20. Does the speaker love as intensely as the speaker in the previous poem?

25 Then did I check the tears of useless passion,
   Weaned my young soul from yearning after thine;
   Sternly denied its burning wish to hasten
   Down to that tomb already more than mine!

   And even yet, I dare not let it languish,
30 Dare not indulge in Memory's rapturous pain;
   Once drinking deep of that divinest anguish,
   How could I seek the empty world again? **E**

E **COMPARE THEMES**
What do lines 29–32 suggest about the speaker's feelings for her beloved?

LETTER Robert Browning wrote this letter to his future wife before he met her in person. He describes how reading her poetry affected him.

Letter to Elizabeth Barrett

January 10, 1845

I love your verses with all my heart, dear Miss Barrett—and this is no offhand complimentary letter that I shall write—whatever else, no prompt matter-of-course recognition of your genius, and there a graceful and natural end of the thing. Since the day last week when I first read your poems, I quite laugh to remember how I have been turning and turning again in my mind what I should be able to tell you of their effect upon me, for in the first flush of delight I thought I would this once get out of my habit of purely passive enjoyment, when I do really enjoy, and thoroughly justify my admiration—perhaps even, as a loyal fellow craftsman should, try and find fault and do you some little good to be proud of hereafter! But nothing comes of it all—so into me has it gone, and part of me has it become, this great living poetry of yours, not a flower of which but took root and grew—Oh, how different that is from lying to be dried and pressed flat, and prized highly, and put in a book with a proper account at top and bottom, and shut up and put away . . . and the book called a "Flora," besides! After all, I need not give up the thought of doing that, too, in time; because even now, talking with whoever is worthy, I can give a reason for my faith in one and another excellence, the fresh strange music, the affluent language, the exquisite pathos and true new brave thought; but in this addressing myself to you—your own self, and for the first time, my feeling rises altogether. I do, as I say, love these books with all my heart—and I love you too. Do you know I was once not very far from seeing—really seeing you? Mr. Kenyon said to me one morning "Would you like to see Miss Barrett?" then he went to announce me—then he returned . . . you were too unwell, and now it is years ago, and I feel as at some untoward passage in my travels, as if I had been close, so close, to some world's-wonder in chapel or crypt, only a screen to push and I might have entered, but there was some slight, so it now seems, slight and just sufficient bar to admission, and the half-opened door shut, and I went home my thousands of miles, and the sight was never to be?

Well, these poems were to be, and this true thankful joy and pride with which I feel myself,

Yours ever faithfully,
Robert Browning

Comprehension

1. **Recall** What question does the speaker of "Sonnet 43" pose and answer?

2. **Paraphrase** Describe three of the ways in which the speaker loves her husband in "Sonnet 43."

3. **Clarify** What question does the speaker of "Remembrance" ask in lines 1–8?

4. **Clarify** In lines 29–32, why does the speaker avoid remembering?

Text Analysis

5. **Analyze Figurative Language** Find one example each of **simile, metaphor, personification,** and **hyperbole** in these poems. What ideas are communicated through these figures of speech? Use the following chart to plan your answer.

Figurative Language	Example	Ideas Communicated
simile		
metaphor		
personification		
hyperbole		

6. **Compare Themes** Use the web diagrams you completed for the poems to compare their themes. What are the ideas about love conveyed in "Sonnet 43"? Are the same ideas conveyed in "Remembrance"? Support your response.

7. **Compare Texts** In "Letter to Elizabeth Barrett" (page 958), Robert Browning claims that her poetry "took root and grew" in him, and he praises "one and another excellence, the fresh strange music, the affluent language, the exquisite pathos and true new brave thought." Which of these qualities do you find in "Sonnet 43"? What other qualities do you find in the poem?

Text Criticism

8. **Different Perspectives** In writing about Elizabeth Barrett Browning's sonnets, the critic Beverly Taylor praised the poet for breaking "with the conventions of the Renaissance sonnet by making the speaker and lover a woman." Reread the sonnets by Shakespeare, Spenser, and Petrarch in Unit 2. In what other ways, stylistically and thematically, does "Sonnet 43" differ from these sonnets? Cite specific examples.

Do you believe that **LOVE** *lasts forever?*

Should people strive to love as the speakers in the poem do or not? What are the advantages and disadvantages of loving with such intensity?

COMMON CORE

RL 2 Determine two or more themes or central ideas of a text. **RL 4** Determine the meaning of words and phrases as they are used in the text, including figurative meanings.

from Jane Eyre

Novel by Charlotte Brontë

Charlotte Brontë
1816–1855

⋯ **COMMON CORE** ⋯

RL 3 Analyze the impact of the author's choices regarding how to develop and relate elements of a story.

BACKGROUND Jane Eyre, the narrator of Charlotte Brontë's novel of the same name, declares, "I am no bird; and no net ensnares me; I am a free human being with an independent will." This would be a strong statement coming from anyone, but it is extraordinary coming from her: Eyre is an orphan without means who must fend for herself in an unfriendly world. Her only relative, a heartless aunt, exiles her to a harsh boarding school for girls. Despite this and the many other cruelties that life in Victorian England held in store for a plain, penniless, and friendless young woman, Eyre develops an unwavering sense of self. She becomes a governess to a young girl, Adele, on a secluded country estate. Adele's guardian is the charismatic, but tortured, Mr. Rochester, and he and Eyre develop a deep attraction. The novel's basic plot—a poor young woman finds romance with her wealthy employer—crosses Gothic romance with the realistic struggles of a Victorian woman who insists on her right to self-determination whatever her circumstances. Since its publication in 1847, *Jane Eyre* has enjoyed enormous success with both literary critics and the general reading public. Along with her sister Emily, who penned the classic *Wuthering Heights*, Charlotte Brontë remains one of the most influential and best-known female writers of any literary period.

TEXT ANALYSIS Dialogue is more than a mere conversation between two or more characters—it can reveal the complexities of the relationship between them. Jane Eyre is from the lower classes: poor, orphaned, and female. Mr. Rochester is a wealthy, upper-class man who holds her financial fate in his hands. In the following excerpt, Eyre and Rochester may come from very different social classes, but their dialogue begins to erase the class boundaries between them. Eyre is startled to find herself in a conversation with her employer that bends social rules as Rochester encourages Jane to communicate her honest thoughts.

WRITE Eyre becomes concerned when she thinks she has inappropriately crossed a social boundary in her conversation with Mr. Rochester. Which elements in their dialogue are examples of the social boundaries that exist between Eyre and Mr. Rochester? Which words reinforce the social boundaries? Which words break them down? How does Eyre try to re-establish the social boundaries between herself and Mr. Rochester? How does Mr. Rochester try to erase those boundaries? Cite specific passages from the excerpt to support your response.

$\mathcal{M}$r. Rochester, as he sat in his damask-covered chair, looked different to what I had seen him look before; not quite so stern— much less gloomy. There was a smile on his lips, and his eyes sparked, whether with wine or not, I am not sure; but I think it very probable. He was, in short, in his after-dinner mood; more expanded and genial, and also more self-indulgent than the frigid and rigid temper of the morning: still he looked preciously grim, cushioning his massive head against the swelling back of his chair, and receiving the light of the fire on his granite-hewn features, and in his great,

10 dark eyes; for he had great, dark eyes, and very fine eyes, too—not without a certain change in their depths sometimes, which, if it was not softness, reminded you, at least, of that feeling.

He had been looking two minutes at the fire, and I had been looking the same length of time at him, when, turning suddenly, he caught my gaze fashioned on his physiognomy.

"You examine me, Miss Eyre," said he: "do you think me handsome?"

I should, if I had deliberated, have replied to this question by something conventionally vague and polite; but the answer somehow slipped from my tongue before I was aware:—"No, sir."

20 "Ah! By my word! there is something singular about you," said he: "you have the air of a little nonnette; quaint, quiet, grave, and simple, as you sit with your hands before you, and your eyes generally bent on the carpet (except, by-the-by, when they are directed piercingly to my face; as just now, for instance); and when one asks you a question, or makes a remark to which you are obliged to reply, you rap out a round rejoinder, which, if not blunt, is at least brusque. What do you mean by it?"

"Sir, I was too plain: I beg your pardon. I ought to have replied that it was not easy to give an impromptu answer to a question about appearances; that tastes differ; that beauty is of little consequence, or something of that sort."

"You ought to have replied no such thing. Beauty of little consequence, indeed!

30 And so, under pretence of softening the previous outrage, of stroking and soothing me into placidity, you stick a sly penknife under my ear! Go on: what fault do you find with me, pray? I suppose I have all my limbs and all my features like any other man?"

"Mr. Rochester, allow me to disown my first answer: I intended no pointed repartee: it was only a blunder."

Pied Beauty
Spring and Fall: To a Young Child
Poetry by Gerard Manley Hopkins

COMMON CORE

RL 1 Cite strong and thorough textual evidence to support inferences drawn from the text. **RL 4** Determine the meaning of words and phrases as they are used in the text, including figurative meanings. **RL 10** Read and comprehend literature, including poems.

DID YOU KNOW?

Gerard Manley Hopkins . . .

- considered becoming a professional artist.
- produced musical compositions.
- profoundly influenced T. S. Eliot, Dylan Thomas, W. H. Auden, and other 20th-century poets.

(background)
Jesus College, Oxford

Meet the Author

Gerard Manley Hopkins 1844–1889

Gerard Manley Hopkins was unknown as a poet during his lifetime. He had been dead for more than 25 years before a friend arranged the publication of his work, believing that the public was finally ready for Hopkins's daring innovations with language and rhythm. Not until the 1930s would Hopkins's unique verse achieve widespread acclaim.

Budding Talent Hopkins grew up in a family of writers and artists. Even as a youth, he demonstrated a talent for writing poetry. At the age of 15, he won his grammar school's poetry prize, and two years later, he was awarded the Governor's Medal for Latin Verse. At Oxford University, he continued to devote his energies to writing.

Religious Conversion At Oxford, Hopkins fell under the spell of the poet Christina Rossetti. Profoundly affected by her mystical verse, he experienced a growing interest in religious matters. In July of 1866, he "saw the impossibility of staying in the Church of England," and in October of that year, he converted to Catholicism. This action alienated him from his parents, who could never understand his decision. The rift widened in 1868 when Hopkins joined the Jesuit order.

Conflicting Commitments Preparing to enter the Society of Jesus, Hopkins burned his early poems, resolving "to write no more, as not belonging to my profession." For the next seven years, he composed no verse, although he did continue to write in his journal. In 1875, he finally broke his poetic silence after reading a newspaper article about a shipwreck involving five nuns. Deeply moved by their deaths, Hopkins wrote his most ambitious poem, "The Wreck of the Deutschland." From that moment on, he never stopped writing, though he continued to feel guilty about pursuing his art.

Bitter Ending While studying for his ordination in 1877, Hopkins produced a series of exquisite sonnets, including "Pied Beauty," which reflect his joy in God's creations. After being ordained a priest, Hopkins served in several parishes before becoming, in 1884, a professor of Greek at University College in Dublin. Hopkins did not care for Dublin, finding it a "joyless place." Isolated from friends and family and often in poor health, he fell into a deep depression. This psychological turmoil gave rise to his so-called "sonnets of desolation," which Hopkins composed up until his death in 1889.

THINK central

Author Online

Go to **thinkcentral.com**. KEYWORD: HML12-962

TEXT ANALYSIS: SPRUNG RHYTHM

In order to approximate the rhythms of natural speech in his poetry, Hopkins ignored traditional patterns of rhythm, instead using what he called **sprung rhythm.** The lines of a poem written in sprung rhythm usually have fixed numbers of stressed syllables but varying numbers of unstressed syllables. As in the following example, a line may contain several consecutive stressed syllables, or a stressed syllable may be followed by one, two, or even three unstressed syllables:

Lándscăpe plótted ănd piécĕd—fóld, fállŏw, ănd plóugh;

Ănd áll trádes, théir géar ănd táckle ănd trím.

Hopkins often included stress marks in his poems to indicate the rhythm he intended.

As you read the two poems, think about which lines come closest to reproducing the rhythms of natural speech.

READING SKILL: INFER MEANING

Hopkins's poems include difficult syntax and vocabulary words that may be unfamiliar to you. Even after slowly rereading the poems, you may still need to **infer,** or make an educated guess about, the meaning of difficult words and phrases. Your inferences should be based on **context clues,** or the nearby words and phrases that may shed some light on a difficult word or an obscure passage.

As you read and reread the poems, fill out a chart like the one below to help you interpret the meaning of any difficult phrases or complex **imagery**—words that appeal to one or more of the five senses.

Phrases or Imagery	Inferences
"rose-moles all in stipple upon trout that swim" (line 3)	The poet describes the fish as beautiful and vibrant.

 Complete the activities in your **Reader/Writer Notebook.**

How does nature affect your MOOD?

Think about a time when you closely examined a single leaf or a flower. What unique details do you recall observing? What mood did this natural object create for you? In the poems that follow, you will read about the mood-changing experiences of two individuals who encounter nature's rhythms and beauty.

QUICKWRITE Write a description of an object in nature without naming what it is. Include as much detail as possible, and try to capture the mood that the object conveys for you. Then, in a small group, take turns reading your descriptions aloud. Try to guess the identity of each other's object.

PIED BEAUTY

Gerard Manley Hopkins

Glory be to God for dappled things—
    For skies of couple-color as a brinded cow;
        For rose-moles all in stipple upon trout that swim;
Fresh-firecoal chestnut-falls; finches' wings;
5   Landscape plotted and pieced—fold, fallow, and plough;
        And all trades, their gear and tackle and trim.

All things counter, original, spare, strange;
    Whatever is fickle, freckled (who knows how?)
        With swift, slow; sweet, sour; adazzle, dim;
10 He fathers-forth whose beauty is past change: **A**
        Praise him.

1 dappled: spotted with color.

2 brinded: brindled—streaked or spotted with a darker color.

3 rose-moles . . . stipple: spots of pink in flecks or speckles.

4 fresh-firecoal: the color of glowing coals.

6 trim: equipment.

7 counter: opposing.

A INFER MEANING
What is Hopkins's attitude toward nature based on the imagery in this poem?

SPRING AND FALL:
TO A YOUNG CHILD

Gerard Manley Hopkins

Márgarét, are you grievíng **B**
Over Goldengrove unleaving?
Léaves, líke the things of man, you
With your fresh thoughts care for, can you?
5 Áh! ás the heart grows older
It will come to such sights colder
By and by, nor spare a sigh
Though worlds of wanwood leafmeal lie;
And yet you *will* weep and know why.
10 Now no matter, child, the name:
Sórrow's spríngs áre the same.
Nor mouth had, no nor mind, expressed
What heart heard of, ghost guessed:
It ís the blight man was born for,
15 It is Margaret you mourn for.

B **SPRUNG RHYTHM**
In line 1, what do the stressed syllables help Hopkins emphasize?

2 unleaving: losing its leaves.

3–4 Leaves . . . can you?: Do you in your innocence grieve about falling leaves as though they were equal to human loss?

8 wanwood: faded woodland; **leafmeal:** dry, ground-up leaves.

12 nor: neither.

13 ghost: spirit; soul.

14 blight: a condition that stops growth and brings withering and death.

Comprehension

1. **Paraphrase** Name the dappled things that Hopkins admires.

2. **Clarify** Why, in your opinion, does Hopkins include "all trades" with the details from nature?

3. **Recall** How does Margaret respond to the changing of the seasons?

4. **Clarify** How will she react in the future, according to the speaker?

Text Analysis

5. **Make Inferences About Theme** Reread "Pied Beauty," paying careful attention to the poem's rich **imagery.** What idea about God and his creations does Hopkins convey through his images of "dappled things"? Cite details.

6. **Interpret Ideas** Think about the meaning of the final line of "Spring and Fall." What is the real source of Margaret's grief, according to the speaker?

7. **Analyze Sprung Rhythm** Find instances of **sprung rhythm** in "Spring and Fall." What ideas does Hopkins emphasize through the use of this rhythmic technique?

8. **Infer Meaning** Review your list of imagery from each poem in your chart. How do these words and phrases help to convey the poet's view of the natural world in each poem? Cite specific examples to support your points.

9. **Compare Texts** As a schoolboy, Hopkins wrote verse in imitation of John Keats. Compare Hopkins's two poems with those of Keats on pages 880–888. What similarities and differences can you find in the two writers' poetic style and treatment of nature?

Text Criticism

10. **Critical Interpretations** Many poets have praised the beauty of nature. However, some scholars believe Hopkins goes one step further. One critic has observed that for Hopkins, "words are a means of possessing nature." On the basis of the two poems, decide if you agree. Cite evidence to support your opinion.

> *How does nature affect your* **MOOD?**
>
> What do you think is gained by a close examination of the natural world? What are the advantages and disadvantages of experiencing nature as Hopkins does?

COMMON CORE

RL 1 Cite strong and thorough textual evidence to support inferences drawn from the text. **RL 4** Determine the meaning of words and phrases as they are used in the text, including figurative meanings. **RL 9** Demonstrate knowledge of foundational works of literature, including how two or more texts treat similar themes or topics. **RL 10** Read and comprehend literature, including poems.

Romantic Influence

The emphasis on the importance of the individual and his or her emotions is one of the most significant legacies of romanticism and was a strong influence on early Victorian writers such as Alfred, Lord Tennyson and Emily Brontë. For the early Victorians, love, for example, often suggests a consuming passion whose joys may be surpassed only by its agonies. Consider the fate of Tennyson's Lady of Shalott once she is struck by the "curse" of love.

> "[She] Heard a carol, mournful, holy,
> Chanted loudly, chanted lowly,
> Till her blood was frozen slowly,
> And her eyes were darkened wholly,
>   Turned to towered Camelot.
> For ere she reached upon the tide
> The first house by the waterside,
> Singing in her song she died,
>   The Lady of Shalott."

Writing to Compare

Write an essay in which you reflect on the portrayals of love found in the poems by Tennyson, Robert Browning, Elizabeth Barrett Browning, and Emily Brontë. Look at the imagery and language of each poem. What do the poems have in common? Which do you find the most—or least—appealing?

Consider

- the imagery and descriptions of feelings about love
- the nature of the relationship between the lovers
- the outcome of the relationship

Extension

SPEAKING & LISTENING Find a contemporary love poem and read it aloud to your class. Then discuss with your classmates how this poem's portrayal of love is similar to or different from the notions of love found in the poems in this section.

⟨ COMMON CORE

W 2 Write explanatory texts to examine and convey complex ideas. **SL 1** Initiate and participate effectively in a range of collaborative discussions.

The Lady of Shalott (1888), John William Waterhouse. © Tate Gallery, London/ Art Resource, New York.

The Growth and Development of Fiction

It's hard to imagine a time when the novel, as we know it, was not a common literary form. However, in the long history of literature, the rise of fiction as a popular genre is a relatively recent phenomenon.

A Novel Idea

COMMON CORE

Included in this workshop:
RL 9 Demonstrate knowledge of foundational works of literature, including how two or more texts from the same period treat similar themes or topics. **RL 10** Read and comprehend literature, including stories.

The **novel** is an extended fictional narrative written in prose. Typically, the narrative depicts the development of a character and revolves around a plot and theme, which collectively act as its organizing principle. The novel as we think of it came into being after Daniel Defoe published *Robinson Crusoe* in 1719. During this time, the novel was viewed primarily as a form of entertainment. In the mid-18th century, the novels *Pamela* (1740) and *Clarissa* (1747–1748) by Samuel Richardson and *Tom Jones* (1749) by Henry Fielding advanced the development of plot and characterization. *The Life and Opinions of Tristram Shandy, Gentleman* (1760–1767), a highly original work by Laurence Sterne, focused on characters' conversations and remembrances instead of on action. These works inspired other writers to take the novel form in new directions.

The Novel Comes of Age

The Victorian period (1832–1901) is often called the age of the novel. The Victorian era ushered in the focus on realistic depictions of life that continues to this day. Victorian novels are known for their **realism**—the detailed presentation of everyday life. Through the novel, Victorian writers wanted to document the lives and the values of the English, including the lower classes. As the Victorian era continued, social concerns began playing a greater role in the general society, and the novel became a tool for exposing society's ills. No other writer used this tool as effectively as did Charles Dickens. His novels *Oliver Twist* (1837–1839), *A Christmas Carol* (1843), *David Copperfield* (1849–1850), and *Bleak House* (1852–1853) described in riveting detail the troubling state of England's lower classes. (See pages 1010–1011 for more on Dickens.)

Close Read

Based on this passage, describe the attitudes of the workhouse authorities and parish authorities toward Oliver. Do they seem indifferent? caring? cruel? Explain what led you to your conclusion.

> For the next eight or ten months, Oliver was the victim of a systematic course of treachery and deception. He was brought up by hand. The hungry and destitute situation of the infant orphan was duly reported by the workhouse authorities to the parish authorities. . . . The parish authorities magnanimously and humanely resolved, that Oliver should be "farmed," or, in other words, that he should be despatched to a branch-workhouse some three miles off, where twenty or thirty other juvenile offenders against the poor-laws, rolled about the floor all day, without the inconvenience of too much food or too much clothing. . . .
>
> —**Charles Dickens**, *Oliver Twist*

New Forms Emerge

In the 19th century, a remarkable variety of English novels were written, giving rise to several popular, new subgenres:

- **Historical novels**—In this type of novel, historical facts are combined with fictional elements to re-create the spirit of a past age. Charles Dickens based *A Tale of Two Cities* (1859) on historical accounts of the French Revolution.

- **Gothic novels**—Horror tales became extremely popular in England near the turn of the 19th century. *Frankenstein* (1818) by Mary Shelley is the best-known example of gothic fiction.

- **Detective novels**—Mystery is a major ingredient of detective fiction. Sir Arthur Conan Doyle mastered this form in the late 1800s and created Sherlock Holmes, still the world's most famous detective.

- **Newgate novels**—Stories focusing on criminals and their motives attracted a growing audience. Newgate fiction—named after a famous London prison—explored the nature of crime and violence. An example is Charles Dickens's *Barnaby Rudge* (1841), which looks at the effects of civil unrest and riot.

After 1880, realism spawned several other schools of literary writing, including psychological realism and naturalism. In France, **naturalism** promoted a grimmer, more "scientific" approach to fiction. Naturalistic writing was an attempt to depict the human condition as objectively as scientific writings depicted the processes of nature. An example is *Tess of the D'Urbervilles* (1891), in which Thomas Hardy portrayed a hostile world where only the "fittest" prospered.

WOMEN NOVELISTS

As the reading public became increasingly female and middle class, female writers emerged. Romantic writer Jane Austen led the way with novels of manners, works known for their focus on courtship, parental authority, and other domestic issues. However, Victorian women writers were determined to overcome the commonly accepted view that writing was a man's profession, and they extended the topics of many of their works far beyond the home.

Jane Austen
1775–1817

Sense and Sensibility
Pride and Prejudice
Emma

Elizabeth Cleghorn Gaskell
1810–1865

Mary Barton
Cranford
North and South

George Eliot (Mary Ann Evans)
1819–1880

The Mill on the Floss
Silas Marner
Middlemarch

Emily Brontë (Ellis Bell)
1818–1848

Wuthering Heights

Charlotte Brontë (Currer Bell)
1816–1855

Jane Eyre
The Professor
Shirley

Malachi's Cove

Short Story by Anthony Trollope

COMMON CORE

RL 3 Analyze the impact of the author's choices regarding how to develop and relate elements of a story. **RL 10** Read and comprehend literature, including stories.

Meet the Author

Anthony Trollope 1815–1882

Anthony Trollope was a highly successful English novelist and one of the most prolific writers of the Victorian era. Trollope's works are widely respected for their convincing dialogue, true-to-life characters, and astute analysis of class dynamics and social conflicts—all hallmarks of the burgeoning literary movement known as realism.

Great Expectations Trollope's sensitivity to social class was heightened by his childhood experiences. He was born into a well-to-do family whose financial situation declined. To keep up appearances, the family sent young Trollope to elite schools, where he was beaten and humiliated for his family's lack of wealth. Trollope, who aspired to a gentleman's life of leisure, found himself required to earn his living. He took a civil-service job in London's General Post Office, a low-paying but respectable position. Impractical and prone to mistakes, Trollope was an indifferent employee; he made little progress in his career until he was transferred to Ireland in 1841.

Life in Letters While in Ireland, Trollope established the writing discipline that he followed for the rest of his life, producing ten pages of fiction in three hours each and every day. In 1855, he published his first successful novel, *The Warden*, which was followed by his masterpiece *Barchester Towers* in 1857. Trollope's daily life left its mark on his work: many of his novels are set in Ireland, and letters, whether paraphrased, excerpted, or printed in full, frequently appear in his work. But before he retired in 1867, Trollope also left his mark on the British postal service: he was co-inventor of the now-famous red mailbox, which helped streamline mail delivery, especially in rural Britain.

Mixed Reviews During Trollope's lifetime, the novel became the most widely read literary form, and realism became the dominant style of writing. Like his contemporaries and fellow realists Charles Dickens and George Eliot, Trollope believed fiction had a moral purpose: a novel should teach readers how to behave, while offering them pleasant entertainment. However, after Trollope's death in 1882, literary trends changed, and realism fell out of favor. In this new context, Trollope's works appeared old-fashioned, and his inflexible work habits seemed to prove his lack of true artistry. After decades of neglect, readers and critics began to rediscover Trollope in the 1940s. Today, he continues to reach new audiences through television and radio adaptations of his work.

DID YOU KNOW?

Anthony Trollope . . .

- worked for the post office for over 25 years.
- published 47 novels in his lifetime.
- ran unsuccessfully for a seat in Parliament.

Author Online

Go to thinkcentral.com. KEYWORD: HML12-970

THINK central

● TEXT ANALYSIS: REALISM

Realism refers to writing that portrays everyday life in accurate detail. It also refers to a literary movement that developed in mid-19th century France and later spread to England. Devices of realism include

- **complex characters** portrayed in everyday circumstances, unlike the idealized romantic characters of earlier fiction
- carefully detailed **settings** drawn from real life
- **dialogue** that captures the sounds of everyday speech, including the use of dialects or idioms

As you read this story, notice how Trollope uses these elements to depict his characters' distinctive way of life.

● READING STRATEGY: PREDICT

Like any good storyteller, Trollope includes dramatic twists and turns in his plot. You can anticipate plot twists by using text clues to make **predictions,** reasonable guesses about what will happen next. To make good predictions,

- consider characters' words, thoughts, and actions as clues to how they will respond to a situation
- note passages that seem to hint at future plot events

As you read, use a chart like the one shown to note at least three predictions and the clues you used to make them.

Prediction	Support for Prediction

▲ VOCABULARY IN CONTEXT

Trollope uses the words in boldface below to portray life in Cornwall. Restate each phrase, using a different word or words for the boldface term.

1. awed by the **precipitous** cliffs
2. an **indefatigable** worker known for her diligence
3. an **interloper** on private property
4. **impede** the group's progress
5. fought to **garner** enough support
6. resolved to **desist** from bad habits
7. tossed by **eddying** stream currents
8. a large, mouthlike **orifice**

 Complete the activities in your **Reader/Writer Notebook**.

How do we learn to TRUST?

Babies learn to trust instinctively by responding to the adults who love and care for them. As we get older, trust becomes a trickier proposition, especially if experience has taught us to be wary of others. What enables us to overcome suspicion and reach out to other people?

QUICKWRITE Working in a small group, list five qualities that signal that a person is trustworthy and five qualities that tell you to be wary. Have someone from your group read your list to the class. Do others agree with your results?

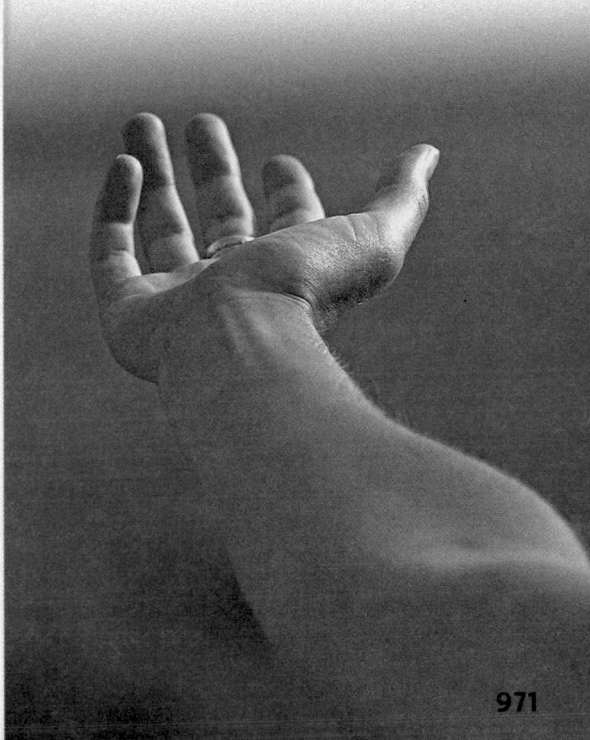

MALACHI'S COVE

Anthony Trollope

On the northern coast of Cornwall, between Tintagel and Bossiney,[1] down on the very margin of the sea, there lived not long since an old man who got his living by saving seaweed from the waves, and selling it for manure. The cliffs there are bold and fine, and the sea beats in upon them from the north with a grand violence. I doubt whether it be not the finest morsel of cliff scenery in England, though it is beaten by many portions of the west coast of Ireland, and perhaps also by spots in Wales and Scotland. Cliffs should be nearly **precipitous,** they should be broken in their outlines, and should barely admit here and there of an insecure passage from their summit to the sand at their feet. The sea should come, if not up to them, at

10 least very near to them, and then, above all things, the water below them should be blue, and not of that dead leaden color which is so familiar to us in England. At Tintagel all these requisites are there, except that bright blue color which is so lovely. But the cliffs themselves are bold and well broken, and the margin of sand at high water is very narrow—so narrow that at spring tides there is barely a footing there. **A**

Close upon this margin was the cottage or hovel of Malachi Trenglos,[2] the old man of whom I have spoken. But Malachi, or old Glos, as he was commonly called by the people around him, had not built his house absolutely upon the sand. There was a fissure in the rock so great that at the top it formed a narrow

20 ravine, and so complete from the summit to the base that it afforded an opening for a steep and rugged track from the top of the rock to the bottom. This fissure was so wide at the bottom that it had afforded space for Trenglos to fix his

---

1. **Cornwall . . . Tintagel** (tĭn-tăj´əl) **and Bossiney** (bôs´ĭ-nē): a remote peninsula on the southwestern tip of England that includes the picturesque village of Tintagel and an adjoining beach area called Bossiney.

2. **Malachi Trenglos** (măl´ə-kĭ´ trĕn´glôs): Many Cornish family names begin with *Tre*, which means "dwelling" in Cornish.

Analyze Visuals ▶

What details in this painting suggest the dangers of this **setting?**

precipitous (prĭ-sĭp´ĭ-təs) *adj.* nearly vertical; very steep

A REALISM
Reread lines 1–15. Which details in this passage help make Trollope's description seem realistic?

Ribbed and Paled in by Rocks Unscalable (1885), Peter Graham. Oil on paper and canvas, 158 cm long. Guildhall Art Gallery. © City of London.

habitation on a foundation of rock, and here he had lived for many years. It was told of him that in the early days of his trade he had always carried the weed in a basket on his back to the top, but latterly[3] he had been possessed of a donkey which had been trained to go up and down the steep track with a single pannier[4] over his loins, for the rocks would not admit of panniers hanging by his side; and for this assistant he had built a shed adjoining his own, and almost as large as that in which he himself resided.

30   But, as years went on, old Glos procured other assistance than that of the donkey, or, as I should rather say, Providence[5] supplied him with other help; and, indeed, had it not been so, the old man must have given up his cabin and his independence and gone into the workhouse at Camelford.[6] For rheumatism[7] had afflicted him, old age had bowed him till he was nearly double, and by degrees he became unable to attend the donkey on its upward passage to the world above, or even to assist in rescuing the coveted weed from the waves.

At the time to which our story refers Trenglos had not been up the cliff for twelve months, and for the last six months he had done nothing towards the furtherance of his trade, except to take the money and keep it, if any of it was 40 kept, and occasionally to shake down a bundle of fodder[8] for the donkey. The real work of the business was done altogether by Mahala Trenglos, his granddaughter.

Mally Trenglos was known to all the farmers round the coast, and to all the small tradespeople in Camelford. She was a wild-looking, almost unearthly creature, with wild-flowing, black, uncombed hair, small in stature, with small hands and bright black eyes; but people said that she was very strong, and the children around declared that she worked day and night and knew nothing of fatigue. As to her age there were many doubts. Some said she was ten, and others five-and-twenty, but the reader may be allowed to know that at this time she had in truth passed her twentieth birthday. The old people spoke well of Mally, 50 because she was so good to her grandfather; and it was said of her that though she carried to him a little gin and tobacco almost daily, she bought nothing for herself—and as to the gin, no one who looked at her would accuse her of meddling with that. But she had no friends and but few acquaintances among people of her own age. They said that she was fierce and ill-natured, that she had not a good word for anyone, and that she was, complete at all points, a thorough little vixen.[9] The young men did not care for her; for, as regarded dress, all days were alike with her. She never made herself smart on Sundays. She was generally without stockings, and seemed to care not at all to exercise any of those feminine

---

3. **latterly:** more recently.

4. **pannier** (păn'yər): one of a pair of baskets usually hung on either side of a pack animal to carry loads.

5. **Providence:** the helpful guidance or aid of God, fate, or nature.

6. **workhouse at Camelford:** the poorhouse at Camelford, a larger town near Tintagel. In Victorian times, poor people whose relatives could not support them were sent to workhouses; healthy residents were put to work.

7. **rheumatism** (rōō'mə-tĭz'əm): painful inflammation and stiffness of the joints and muscles.

8. **fodder:** coarse food for cattle and other farm animals.

9. **vixen** (vĭk'sən): a bad-tempered woman; a shrew.

attractions which might have been hers had she studied to attain them. All days
60 were the same to her in regard to dress; and, indeed, till lately, all days had, I fear,
been the same to her in other respects. Old Malachi had never been seen inside a
place of worship since he had taken to live under the cliff. **Ⓑ**

But within the last two years Mally had submitted herself to the teaching of the
clergyman at Tintagel, and had appeared at church on Sundays, if not absolutely
with punctuality, at any rate so often that no one who knew the peculiarity of
her residence was disposed to quarrel with her on that subject. But she made no
difference in her dress on these occasions. She took her place in a low stone seat
just inside the church door, clothed as usual in her thick red serge petticoat[10] and
loose brown serge jacket, such being the apparel which she had found to be best
70 adapted for her hard and perilous work among the waters. She had pleaded to
the clergyman when he attacked her on the subject of church attendance with
vigor that she had got no church-going clothes. He had explained to her that she
would be received there without distinction to her clothing. Mally had taken him
at his word, and had gone, with a courage which certainly deserved admiration,
though I doubt whether there was not mingled with it an obstinacy which was less
admirable.

For people said that old Glos was rich, and that Mally might have proper
clothes if she chose to buy them. Mr. Polwarth, the clergyman, who, as the old
man could not come to him, went down the rocks to the old man, did make some
80 hint on the matter in Mally's absence. But old Glos, who had been patient with
him on other matters, turned upon him so angrily when he made an allusion
to money, that Mr. Polwarth found himself obliged to give that matter up, and
Mally continued to sit upon the stone bench in her short serge petticoat, with her
long hair streaming down her face. She did so far sacrifice to decency as on such
occasions to tie up her black hair with an old shoestring. So tied it would remain
through the Monday and Tuesday, but by Wednesday afternoon Mally's hair had
generally managed to escape.

As to Mally's **indefatigable** industry there could be no manner of doubt, for
the quantity of seaweed which she and the donkey amassed between them was
90 very surprising. Old Glos, it was declared, had never collected half what Mally
gathered together; but then the article was becoming cheaper, and it was necessary
that the exertion should be greater. So Mally and the donkey toiled and toiled,
and the seaweed came up in heaps which surprised those who looked at her little
hands and light form. Was there not someone who helped her at nights, some
fairy, or demon, or the like? Mally was so snappish in her answers to people that
she had no right to be surprised if ill-natured things were said of her.

No one ever heard Mally Trenglos complain of her work, but about this time
she was heard to make great and loud complaints of the treatment she received
from some of her neighbors. It was known that she went with her plaints to Mr.
100 Polwarth; and when he could not help her, or did not give her such instant help

Ⓑ REALISM
Reread lines 42–62. In
what ways does this
description of Mally
differ from that of a
conventional romantic
heroine? Cite details in
your answer.

indefatigable
(ĭn'dĭ-făt'ĭ-gə-bəl) *adj.*
tireless

---

10. **serge petticoat:** a skirt made of a strong twilled woolen or silken fabric.

as she needed, she went—ah, so foolishly! to the office of a certain attorney at Camelford, who was not likely to prove himself a better friend than Mr. Polwarth.

Now the nature of her injury was as follows. The place in which she collected her seaweed was a little cove—the people had come to call it Malachi's Cove from the name of the old man who lived there—which was so formed that the margin of the sea therein could only be reached by the passage from the top down to Trenglos's hut. The breadth of the cove when the sea was out might perhaps be two hundred yards, and on each side the rocks ran out in such a way that both from north and south the domain of Trenglos was guarded from intruders. And
110 this locality had been well chosen for its intended purpose.

There was a rush of the sea into the cove, which carried there large, drifting masses of seaweed, leaving them among the rocks when the tide was out. During the equinoctial winds[11] of the spring and autumn the supply would never fail; and even when the sea was calm, the long, soft, salt-bedewed, trailing masses of the weed could be gathered there when they could not be found elsewhere for miles along the coast. The task of getting the weed from the breakers[12] was often difficult and dangerous—so difficult that much of it was left to be carried away by the next incoming tide.

Mally doubtless did not gather half the crop that was there at her feet. What
120 was taken by the returning waves she did not regret; but when **interlopers** came upon her cove, and gathered her wealth—her grandfather's wealth, beneath her eyes, then her heart was broken. It was this interloping, this intrusion, that drove poor Mally to the Camelford attorney. But, alas, though the Camelford attorney took Mally's money, he could do nothing for her, and her heart was broken!

She had an idea, in which no doubt her grandfather shared, that the path to the cove was, at any rate, their property. When she was told that the cove, and sea running into the cove, were not the freeholds[13] of her grandfather, she understood that the statement might be true. But what then as to the use of the path? Who had made the path what it was? Had she not painfully, wearily, with exceeding
130 toil, carried up bits of rock with her own little hands, that her grandfather's donkey might have footing for his feet? Had she not scraped together crumbs of earth along the face of the cliff that she might make easier to the animal the track of that rugged way? And now, when she saw big farmer's lads coming down with other donkeys—and, indeed, there was one who came with a pony; no boy, but a young man, old enough to know better than rob a poor old man and a young girl—she reviled the whole human race, and swore that the Camelford attorney was a fool.

Any attempt to explain to her that there was still weed enough for her was worse than useless. Was it not all hers and his, or, at any rate, was not the sole way
140 to it his and hers? And was not her trade stopped and **impeded**? Had she not been forced to back her laden donkey down, twenty yards she said, but it had, in truth,

interloper (ĭn′tər-lō′pər) *n.* intruder

impede (ĭm-pēd′) *v.* to hinder or obstruct

---

11. **equinoctial** (ē′kwə-nŏk′shəl) **winds:** strong winds around the time of the spring or autumn equinox, when day and night are of equal length.

12. **breakers:** waves that break into foam when they hit the shore.

13. **freeholds:** land that is inherited or held for life.

On the Shore, Paul Henry. Oil on canvas, 60.5 cm × 51 cm. T30352. © Phillips, The International Fine Art Auctioneers, United Kingdom. © Bonhams, London/Bridgeman Art Library.

◄ Analyze Visuals
How would you describe the **mood** of this painting? What details help convey the mood?

been five, because Farmer Gunliffe's son had been in the way with his thieving pony? Farmer Gunliffe had wanted to buy her weed at his own price, and because she had refused he had set on his thieving son to destroy her in this wicked way.

"I'll hamstring[14] the beast the next time as he's down here!" said Mally to old Glos, while the angry fire literally streamed from her eyes.

Farmer Gunliffe's small homestead—he held about fifty acres of land—was close by the village of Tintagel, and not a mile from the cliff. The sea-wrack, as they call it, was pretty well the only manure within his reach, and no doubt he

---

14. **hamstring:** to disable by cutting the hamstring, the large tendon found on the back of the leg in humans or on the hind leg in many quadrupeds.

150 thought it hard that he should be kept from using it by Mally Trenglos and her obstinacy.

"There's heaps of other coves, Barty," said Mally to Barty Gunliffe, the farmer's son.

"But none so nigh,[15] Mally, nor yet none that fills 'emselves as this place."

Then he explained to her that he would not take the weed that came up close to hand. He was bigger than she was, and stronger, and would get it from the outer rocks, with which she never meddled. Then, with scorn in her eye, she swore that she could get it where he durst[16] not venture, and repeated her threat of hamstringing the pony. Barty laughed at her wrath, jeered her because of her wild
160 hair, and called her a mermaid.

"I'll mermaid you!" she cried. "Mermaid, indeed! I wouldn't be a man to come and rob a poor girl and an old cripple. But you're no man, Barty Gunliffe! You're not half a man."

Nevertheless, Bartholomew Gunliffe was a very fine young fellow as far as the eye went. He was about five feet eight inches high, with strong arms and legs, with light curly brown hair and blue eyes. His father was but in a small way as a farmer, but, nevertheless, Barty Gunliffe was well thought of among the girls around. Everybody liked Barty—excepting only Mally Trenglos, and she hated him like poison. **C**

170 Barty, when he was asked why so good-natured a lad as he persecuted a poor girl and an old man, threw himself upon the justice of the thing. It wouldn't do at all, according to his view, that any single person should take upon himself to own that which God Almighty sent as the common property of all. He would do Mally no harm, and so he had told her. But Mally was a vixen—a wicked little vixen; and she must be taught to have a civil tongue in her head. When once Mally would speak him civil as he went for weed, he would get his father to pay the old man some sort of toll for the use of the path.

"Speak him civil?" said Mally. "Never; not while I have a tongue in my mouth!" And I fear old Glos encouraged her rather than otherwise in her view of the
180 matter.

But her grandfather did not encourage her to hamstring the pony. Hamstringing a pony would be a serious thing, and old Glos thought it might be very awkward for both of them if Mally were put into prison. He suggested, therefore, that all manner of impediments should be put in the way of the pony's feet, surmising that the well-trained donkey might be able to work in spite of them. And Barty Gunliffe, on his next descent, did find the passage very awkward when he came near to Malachi's hut, but he made his way down, and poor Mally saw the lumps of rock at which she had labored so hard pushed on one side or rolled out of the way with a steady persistency of injury towards herself that
190 almost drove her frantic.

C PREDICT
Based on what you know about Barty and Mally at this point in the story, what predictions would you make about their future interactions?

---

15. **nigh** (nī): near.

16. **durst**: dare.

"Well, Barty, you're a nice boy," said old Glos, sitting in the doorway of the hut, as he watched the intruder.

"I ain't a doing no harm to none as doesn't harm me," said Barty. "The sea's free to all, Malachi."

"And the sky's free to all, but I mustn't get up on the top of your big barn to look at it," said Mally, who was standing among the rocks with a long hook in her hand. The long hook was the tool with which she worked in dragging the weed from the waves. "But you ain't got no justice, nor yet no sperrit,[17] or you wouldn't come here to vex an old man like he."

200 "I didn't want to vex him, nor yet to vex you, Mally. You let me be for a while, and we'll be friends yet."

"Friends!" exclaimed Mally. "Who'd have the likes of you for a friend? What are you moving them stones for? Them stones belongs to grandfather." And in her wrath she made a movement as though she were going to fly at him.

"Let him be, Mally," said the old man; "let him be. He'll get his punishment. He'll come to be drowned some day if he comes down here when the wind is in shore."

"That he may be drowned then!" said Mally, in her anger. "If he was in the big hole there among the rocks, and the sea running in at half tide, I wouldn't lift a 210 hand to help him out."

"Yes, you would, Mally; you'd fish me up with your hook like a big stick of seaweed." **D**

She turned from him with scorn as he said this, and went into the hut. It was time for her to get ready for her work, and one of the great injuries done her lay in this—that such a one as Barty Gunliffe should come and look at her during her toil among the breakers.

It was an afternoon in April, and the hour was something after four o'clock. There had been a heavy wind from the northwest all the morning, with gusts of rain, and the seagulls had been in and out of the cove all the day, which was a sure 220 sign to Mally that the incoming tide would cover the rocks with weed.

The quick waves were now returning with wonderful celerity[18] over the low reefs, and the time had come at which the treasure must be seized, if it was to be **garnered** on that day. By seven o'clock it would be growing dark, at nine it would be high water, and before daylight the crop would be carried out again if not collected. All this Mally understood very well, and some of this Barty was beginning to understand also. **E**

As Mally came down with her bare feet, bearing her long hook in her hand, she saw Barty's pony standing patiently on the sand, and in her heart she longed to attack the brute. Barty at this moment, with a common three-pronged fork in his 230 hand, was standing down on a large rock, gazing forth towards the waters. He had declared that he would gather the weed only at places which were inaccessible to Mally, and he was looking out that he might settle where he would begin.

---

17. **sperrit:** dialect for *spirit,* here meaning "courage" or "character."

18. **celerity** (sə-lĕr′ĭ-tē): swiftness of action; speed.

D **PREDICT**
Reread lines 208–212. Which character's prediction seems more consistent with Mally's personality? Explain your answer.

garner (gär′nər) *v.* to gather up and store; to collect

E **REALISM**
Reread lines 217–226. What details of the setting help add realism to the story?

The Runaway, Henry Herbert La Thangue. Oil on canvas. Private collection.
© Bridgeman Art Library.

"Let 'un be, let 'un be," shouted the old man to Mally, as he saw her take a step towards the beast, which she hated almost as much as she hated the man.

Hearing her grandfather's voice through the wind, she **desisted** from her purpose, if any purpose she had had, and went forth to her work. As she passed down the cove, and scrambled in among the rocks, she saw Barty still standing on his perch; out beyond, the white-curling waves were cresting and breaking themselves with violence, and the wind was howling among the caverns and
240 abutments of the cliff.

Every now and then there came a squall[19] of rain, and though there was sufficient light, the heavens were black with clouds. A scene more beautiful might hardly be found by those who love the glories of the coast. The light for such objects was perfect. Nothing could exceed the grandeur of the colors—the blue of the open sea, the white of the breaking waves, the yellow sands, or the streaks of red and brown which gave such richness to the cliff.

But neither Mally nor Barty were thinking of such things as these. Indeed, they were hardly thinking of their trade after its ordinary forms. Barty was meditating how he might best accomplish his purpose of working beyond the reach of Mally's
250 feminine powers, and Mally was resolving that wherever Barty went she would go farther.

And, in many respects, Mally had the advantage. She knew every rock in the spot, and was sure of those which gave a good foothold, and sure also of those

desist (dĭ-sĭst′) *v.*
to cease or stop

19. **squall** (skwôl): a brief, violent windstorm, usually accompanied by rain or snow.

which did not. And then her activity had been made perfect by practice for the purpose to which it was to be devoted. Barty, no doubt, was stronger than she, and quite as active. But Barty could not jump among the waves from one stone to another as she could do, nor was he as yet able to get aid in his work from the very force of the water as she could get it. She had been hunting seaweed in that cove since she had been an urchin of six years old, and she knew every hole and corner and every spot of vantage.[20] The waves were her friends, and she could use them. She could measure their strength, and knew when and where it would cease.

Mally was great down in the salt pools of her own cove—great, and very fearless. As she watched Barty make his way forward from rock to rock, she told herself, gleefully, that he was going astray. The curl of the wind as it blew into the cove would not carry the weed up to the northern buttresses of the cove; and then there was the great hole just there—the great hole of which she had spoken when she wished him evil.

And now she went to work, hooking up the dishevelled hairs of the ocean, and landing many a cargo on the extreme margin of the sand, from whence she would be able in the evening to drag it back before the invading waters would return to reclaim the spoil.[21]

And on his side also Barty made his heap up against the northern buttresses of which I have spoken. Barty's heap became big and still bigger, so that he knew, let the pony work as he might, he could not take it all up that evening. But still it was not as large as Mally's heap. Mally's hook was better than his fork, and Mally's skill was better than his strength. And when he failed in some haul Mally would jeer him with a wild, weird laughter, and shriek to him through the wind that he was not half a man. At first he answered her with laughing words, but before long, as she boasted of her success and pointed to his failure, he became angry, and then he answered her no more. He became angry with himself, in that he missed so much of the plunder before him.

The broken sea was full of the long straggling growth which the waves had torn up from the bottom of the ocean, but the masses were carried past him, away from him—nay, once or twice over him; and then Mally's weird voice would sound in his ear, jeering him. The gloom among the rocks was now becoming thicker and thicker, the tide was beating in with increased strength, and the gusts of wind came with quicker and greater violence. But still he worked on. While Mally worked he would work, and he would work for some time after she was driven in. He would not be beaten by a girl. **F**

The great hole was now full of water, but of water which seemed to be boiling as though in a pot. And the pot was full of floating masses—large treasures of seaweed which were thrown to and fro upon its surface, but lying there so thick that one would seem almost able to rest upon it without sinking.

Language Coach

Word Definitions Some English words normally occur in combination with other specific words. In line 268, the word *dishevelled* (Americans spell it *disheveled*) means "untidy, rumpled," and it almost always describes hair or clothing. What do "the dishevelled hairs of the ocean" refer to?

F **GRAMMAR AND STYLE** Reread lines 282–287. Note how Trollope uses **prepositional phrases**, such as "among the rocks" and "with quicker and greater violence," to add details to his dramatic descriptions of the landscape.

---

20. **urchin** (ûr'chĭn) . . . **spot of vantage:** a mischievous youngster of six years old, who knew which places would give her the advantage (in her task).

21. **spoil:** treasure seized in battle; plunder or booty.

Mally knew well how useless it was to attempt to rescue aught[22] from the fury of that boiling caldron. The hole went in under the rocks, and the side of it towards the shore lay high, slippery, and steep. The hole, even at low water, was never empty; and Mally believed that there was no bottom to it. Fish thrown in there could escape out to the ocean, miles away—so Mally in her softer moods would tell the visitors to the cove. She knew the hole well. Poulnadioul[23] she was
300 accustomed to call it; which was supposed, when translated, to mean that this was the hole of the Evil One. Never did Mally attempt to make her own of weed which had found its way into that pot.

But Barty Gunliffe knew no better, and she watched him as he endeavoured to steady himself on the treacherously slippery edge of the pool. He fixed himself there and made a haul, with some small success. How he managed it she hardly knew, but she stood still for a while watching him anxiously, and then she saw him slip. He slipped, and recovered himself—slipped again, and again recovered himself.

"Barty, you fool!" she screamed, "if you get yourself pitched in there, you'll
310 never come out no more."

Whether she simply wished to frighten him, or whether her heart relented and she had thought of his danger with dismay, who shall say? She could not have told herself. She hated him as much as ever—but she could hardly have wished to see him drowned before her eyes.

"You go on, and don't mind me," said he, speaking in a hoarse, angry tone.

"Mind you—who minds you?" retorted the girl. And then she again prepared herself for her work.

But as she went down over the rocks with her long hook balanced in her hands, she suddenly heard a splash, and, turning quickly round, saw the body of her
320 enemy tumbling amidst the **eddying** waves in the pool. The tide had now come up so far that every succeeding wave washed into it and over it from the side nearest to the sea, and then ran down again back from the rocks, as the rolling wave receded, with a noise like the fall of a cataract.[24] And then, when the surplus water had retreated for a moment, the surface of the pool would be partly calm, though the fretting bubbles would still boil up and down, and there was ever a simmer on the surface, as though, in truth, the caldron were heated. But this time of comparative rest was but a moment, for the succeeding breaker would come up almost as soon as the foam of the preceding one had gone, and then again the waters would be dashed upon the rocks, and the sides would echo with the roar of
330 the angry wave.

Instantly Mally hurried across to the edge of the pool, crouching down upon her hands and knees for security as she did so. As a wave receded, Barty's head and face was carried round near to her, and she could see that his forehead was covered with blood. Whether he were alive or dead she did not know. She had seen nothing but his blood, and the light-colored hair of his head lying amidst the foam. Then his

eddying (ĕd′ē-ĭng) *adj.* moving in a whirlpool; swirling **eddy** *v.*

---

22. **aught** (ôt): anything.

23. **Poulnadioul** (pül′nä-jōōl′): Cornish for "pool of the devil."

24. **cataract** (kăt′ə-răkt′): waterfall.

body was drawn along by the suction of the retreating wave; but the mass of water that escaped was not on this occasion large enough to carry the man out with it.

Instantly Mally was at work with her hook, and getting it fixed into his coat, dragged him towards the spot on which she was kneeling. During the half minute of repose she got him so close that she could touch his shoulder. Straining herself down, laying herself over the long bending handle of the hook, she strove to grasp him with her right hand. But she could not do it; she could only touch him.

Then came the next breaker, forcing itself on with a roar, looking to Mally as though it must certainly knock her from her resting place and destroy them both. But she had nothing for it[25] but to kneel, and hold by her hook.

What prayer passed through her mind at that moment for herself or for him, or for that old man who was sitting unconsciously[26] up at the cabin, who can say? The great wave came and rushed over her as she lay almost prostrate, and when the water was gone from her eyes, and the tumult of the foam, and the violence of the roaring breaker had passed by her, she found herself at her length upon the rock, while his body had been lifted up, free from her hook, and was lying upon the slippery ledge, half in the water and half out of it. As she looked at him, in that instant, she could see that his eyes were open and that he was struggling with his hands.

"Hold by the hook, Barty," she cried, pushing the stick of it before him, while she seized the collar of his coat in her hands.

Had he been her brother, her lover, her father, she could not have clung to him with more of the energy of despair. He did contrive to hold by the stick which she had given him, and when the succeeding wave had passed by, he was still on the ledge. In the next moment she was seated a yard or two above the hole, in comparative safety, while Barty lay upon the rocks with his still bleeding head resting upon her lap.

What could she do now? She could not carry him; and in fifteen minutes the sea would be up where she was sitting. He was quite insensible and very pale, and the blood was coming slowly—very slowly—from the wound on his forehead. Ever so gently she put her hand upon his hair to move it back from his face; and then she bent over his mouth to see if he breathed, and as she looked at him she knew that he was beautiful. **G**

What would she not give that he might live? Nothing now was so precious to her as his life—as this life which she had so far rescued from the waters. But what could she do? Her grandfather could scarcely get himself down over the rocks, if indeed he could succeed in doing so much as that. Could she drag the wounded man backwards, if it were only a few feet, so that he might lie above the reach of the waves till further assistance could be procured?

She set herself to work and she moved him, almost lifting him. As she did so she wondered at her own strength, but she was very strong at that moment. Slowly, tenderly, falling on the rocks herself so that he might fall on her, she got

G REALISM
Reread lines 366–368. In what ways does this passage establish Mally as a **complex character?**

---

25. **had nothing for it:** had no alternative; could do nothing else.

26. **unconsciously:** unaware of what was happening to Mally and Barty.

Driftwood (1909), Winslow Homer. Oil on canvas, 24½″ × 28½″. Henry H. and Zoe Oliver Sherman Fund and other funds. 1993.564. © Museum of Fine Arts, Boston.

him back to the margin of the sand, to a spot which the waters would not reach for the next two hours.

380   Here her grandfather met them, having seen at last what had happened from the door.

"Dada," she said, "he fell into the pool yonder, and was battered against the rocks. See there at his forehead."

"Mally, I'm thinking that he's dead already," said old Glos, peering down over the body.

"No, dada; he is not dead; but mayhap²⁷ he's dying. But I'll go at once up to the farm."

"Mally," said the old man, "look at his head. They'll say we murdered him."

"Who'll say so? Who'll lie like that? Didn't I pull him out of the hole?"

390   "What matters that? His father'll say we killed him."

It was manifest to Mally that whatever anyone might say hereafter, her present course was plain before her. She must run up the path to Gunliffe's farm and get necessary assistance. If the world were as bad as her grandfather said, it would be

H PREDICT
Reread lines 388–390. In your opinion, has old Glos made a reasonable prediction? Why or why not?

---

27. **mayhap:** perhaps.

so bad that she would not care to live longer in it. But be that as it might, there was no doubt as to what she must do now.

So away she went as fast as her naked feet could carry her up the cliff. When at the top she looked round to see if any person might be within ken,[28] but she saw no one. So she ran with all her speed along the headland[29] of the cornfield which led in the direction of old Gunliffe's house, and as she drew near to the homestead she saw that Barty's mother was leaning on the gate. As she approached she attempted to call, but her breath failed her for any purpose of loud speech, so she ran on till she was able to grasp Mrs. Gunliffe by the arm.

"Where's himself?" she said, holding her hand upon her beating heart that she might husband her breath.

"Who is it you mean?" said Mrs. Gunliffe, who participated in the family feud against Trenglos and his granddaughter. "What does the girl clutch me for in that way?"

"He's dying then, that's all."

"Who is dying? Is it old Malachi? If the old man's bad, we'll send some one down."

"It ain't dada; it's Barty! Where's himself? where's the master?" But by this time Mrs. Gunliffe was in an agony of despair, and was calling out for assistance lustily. Happily Gunliffe, the father, was at hand, and with him a man from the neighboring village.

"Will you not send for the doctor?" said Mally. "Oh, man, you should send for the doctor!" ❶

Whether any orders were given for the doctor she did not know, but in a very few minutes she was hurrying across the field again towards the path to the cove, and Gunliffe with the other man and his wife were following her.

As Mally went along she recovered her voice, for their step was not so quick as hers, and that which to them was a hurried movement allowed her to get her breath again. And as she went she tried to explain to the father what had happened, saying but little, however, of her own doings in the matter. The wife hung behind listening, exclaiming every now and again that her boy was killed, and then asking wild questions as to his being yet alive. The father, as he went, said little. He was known as a silent, sober man, well spoken of for diligence and general conduct, but supposed to be stern and very hard when angered.

As they drew near to the top of the path the other man whispered something to him, and then he turned round upon Mally and stopped her.

"If he has come by his death between you, your blood shall be taken for his," said he.

Then the wife shrieked out that her child had been murdered, and Mally, looking round into the faces of the three, saw that her grandfather's words had come true. They suspected her of having taken the life, in saving which she had nearly lost her own.

❶ **REALISM**
Reread lines 403–416. What characteristics of the **dialogue** make this conversation seem true to life?

---

28. **within ken:** in view.

29. **headland:** a point of land extending out into a body of water.

She looked round at them with awe in her face, and then, without saying a word, preceded them down the path. What had she to answer when such a charge as that was made against her? If they chose to say that she pushed him into the pool and hit him with her hook as he lay amidst the waters, how could she show
440 that it was not so?

Poor Mally knew little of the law of evidence, and it seemed to her that she was in their hands. But as she went down the steep track with a hurried step—a step so quick that they could not keep up with her—her heart was very full—very full and very high. She had striven for the man's life as though he had been her brother. The blood was yet not dry on her own legs and arms, where she had torn them in his service. At one moment she had felt sure that she would die with him in that pool. And now they said that she had murdered him! It may be that he was not dead, and what would he say if ever he should speak again? Then she thought of that moment when his eyes had opened, and he had seemed to see her. She had
450 no fear for herself, for her heart was very high. But it was full also—full of scorn, disdain, and wrath.

When she had reached the bottom, she stood close to the door of the hut waiting for them, so that they might precede her to the other group, which was there in front of them, at a little distance on the sand.

"He is there, and dada is with him. Go and look at him," said Mally.

The father and mother ran on stumbling over the stones, but Mally remained behind by the door of the hut.

Barty Gunliffe was lying on the sand where Mally had left him, and old Malachi Trenglos was standing over him, resting himself with difficulty upon a stick.
460 "Not a move he's moved since she left him," said he, "not a move. I put his head on the old rug as you see, and I tried 'un with a drop of gin, but he wouldn't take it—he wouldn't take it."

"Oh, my boy! my boy!" said the mother, throwing herself beside her son upon the sand.

"Haud[30] your tongue, woman," said the father, kneeling down slowly by the lad's head, "whimpering that way will do 'un no good."

Then having gazed for a minute or two upon the pale face beneath him, he looked up sternly into that of Malachi Trenglos.

The old man hardly knew how to bear this terrible inquisition.
470 "He would come," said Malachi; "he brought it all upon hisself."

"Who was it struck him?" said the father.

"Sure he struck hisself, as he fell among the breakers."

"Liar!" said the father, looking up at the old man.

"They have murdered him—they have murdered him!" shrieked the mother.

"Haud your peace, woman!" said the husband again. "They shall give us blood for blood." **J**

Mally, leaning against the corner of the hovel, heard it all, but did not stir. They might say what they liked. They might make it out to be murder. They might

---

30. **haud:** hold.

J REALISM
Reread lines 471–476. In your opinion, are the characters' responses realistic? Explain.

drag her and her grandfather to Camelford gaol, and then to Bodmin,[31] and the
480 gallows; but they could not take from her the conscious feeling that was her own.
She had done her best to save him—her very best. And she had saved him!

She remembered her threat to him before they had gone down on the rocks
together, and her evil wish. Those words had been very wicked; but since that she
had risked her life to save his. They might say what they pleased of her, and do
what they pleased. She knew what she knew.

Then the father raised his son's head and shoulders in his arms, and called
on the others to assist him in carrying Barty towards the path. They raised him
between them carefully and tenderly, and lifted their burden on towards the spot
at which Mally was standing. She never moved, but watched them at their work;
490 and the old man followed them, hobbling after them with his crutch.

When they had reached the end of the hut she looked upon Barty's face, and
saw that it was very pale. There was no longer blood upon the forehead, but the
great gash was to be seen there plainly, with its jagged cut, and the skin livid and
blue round the **orifice.** His light brown hair was hanging back, as she had made it
to hang when she had gathered it with her hand after the big wave had passed over
them. Ah, how beautiful he was in Mally's eyes with that pale face, and the sad
scar upon his brow! She turned her face away, that they might not see her tears;
but she did not move, nor did she speak.

But now, when they had passed the end of the hut, shuffling along with their
500 burden, she heard a sound which stirred her. She roused herself quickly from her
leaning posture, and stretched forth her head as though to listen; then she moved
to follow them. Yes, they had stopped at the bottom of the path, and had again
laid the body on the rocks. She heard that sound again, as of a long, long sigh, and
then, regardless of any of them, she ran to the wounded man's head.

"He is not dead," she said. "There; he is not dead."

As she spoke Barty's eyes opened, and he looked about him.

"Barty, my boy, speak to me," said the mother.

Barty turned his face upon his mother, smiled, and then stared about him
wildly.

510 "How is it with thee, lad?" said his father. Then Barty turned his face again to
the latter voice, and as he did so his eyes fell upon Mally.

"Mally!" he said, "Mally!"

It could have wanted[32] nothing further to any of those present to teach them
that, according to Barty's own view of the case, Mally had not been his enemy;
and, in truth, Mally herself wanted no further triumph. That word had vindicated
her, and she withdrew back to the hut.

"Dada," she said, "Barty is not dead, and I'm thinking they won't say anything
more about our hurting him."

Old Glos shook his head. He was glad the lad hadn't met his death there; he
520 didn't want the young man's blood, but he knew what folk would say. The poorer

orifice (ôr′ə-fĭs) *n.* an
opening, especially to a
passage within the body

---

31. **to Camelford gaol** (jāl) . . . **Bodmin:** to Camelford jail and then to the county seat of Cornwall at Bodmin
      (for trial).

32. **wanted:** needed

he was the more sure the world would be to trample on him. Mally said what she could to comfort him, being full of comfort herself.

She would have crept up to the farm if she dared, to ask how Barty was. But her courage failed her when she thought of that, so she went to work again, dragging back the weed she had saved to the spot at which on the morrow she would load the donkey. As she did this she saw Barty's pony still standing patiently under the rock, so she got a lock of fodder and threw it down before the beast.

It had become dark down in the cove, but she was still dragging back the seaweed, when she saw the glimmer of a lantern coming down the pathway. It
530 was a most unusual sight, for lanterns were not common down in Malachi's Cove. Down came the lantern rather slowly—much more slowly than she was in the habit of descending, and then through the gloom she saw the figure of a man standing at the bottom of the path. She went up to him, and saw that it was Mr. Gunliffe, the father.

"Is that Mally?" said Gunliffe.

"Yes, it is Mally; and how is Barty, Mr. Gunliffe?"

"You must come to 'un yourself, now at once," said the farmer. "He won't sleep a wink till he's seed you. You must not say but you'll come."

"Sure I'll come if I'm wanted," said Mally.

540 Gunliffe waited a moment, thinking that Mally might have to prepare herself, but Mally needed no preparation. She was dripping with salt water from the weed which she had been dragging, and her elfin locks were streaming wildly from her head; but, such as she was, she was ready.

"Dada's in bed," she said, "and I can go now if you please."

Then Gunliffe turned round and followed her up the path, wondering at the life which this girl led so far away from all her sex. It was now dark night, and he had found her working at the very edge of the rolling waves by herself, in the darkness, while the only human being who might seem to be her protector had already gone to his bed.

550 When they were at the top of the cliff, Gunliffe took her by her hand and led her along. She did not comprehend this, but she made no attempt to take her hand from his. Something he said about falling on the cliffs, but it was muttered so lowly that Mally hardly understood him. But in truth the man knew that she had saved his boy's life, and that he had injured her instead of thanking her. He was now taking her to his heart, and as words were wanting to him, he was showing his love after this silent fashion. He held her by the hand as though she were a child, and Mally tripped along at his side asking him no questions.

When they were at the farmyard gate he stopped there for a moment.

"Mally, my girl," he said, "he'll not be content till he sees thee, but thou must
560 not stay long wi' him, lass. Doctor says he's weak like, and wants sleep badly."

Mally merely nodded her head, and then they entered the house. Mally had never been within it before, and looked about with wondering eyes at the furniture of the big kitchen. Did any idea of her future destiny flash upon her then, I wonder? But she did not pause here a moment, but was led up to the bedroom above stairs, where Barty was lying on his mother's bed. **K**

K PREDICT
Reread lines 563–564. What "future destiny" do you think the narrator is referring to? What clues support your guess?

"Is it Mally herself?" said the voice of the weak youth.

"It's Mally herself," said the mother, "so now you can say what you please."

"Mally," said he, "Mally, it's along of you[33] that I'm alive this moment."

"I'll not forget it on her," said the father, with his eyes turned away from her.
570 "I'll never forget it on her."

"We hadn't a one but only him," said the mother, with her apron up to her face.

"Mally, you'll be friends with me now?" said Barty.

To have been made lady of the manor of the cove for ever, Mally couldn't have spoken a word now. It was not only that the words and presence of the people there cowed her and made her speechless, but the big bed, and the looking-glass, and the unheard-of wonders of the chamber, made her feel her own insignificance. But she crept up to Barty's side, and put her hand upon his.

"I'll come and get the weed, Mally; but it shall all be for you," said Barty.

580 "Indeed, you won't then, Barty dear," said the mother; "you'll never go near the awesome place again. What would we do if you were took from us?"

"He mustn't go near the hole if he does," said Mally, speaking at last in a solemn voice, and imparting the knowledge which she had kept to herself while Barty was her enemy; "'specially not if the wind's any way from the nor'rard."

"She'd better go down now," said the father.

Barty kissed the hand which he held, and Mally, looking at him as he did so, thought that he was like an angel.

"You'll come and see us tomorrow, Mally?" said he.

To this she made no answer, but followed Mrs. Gunliffe out of the room. When
590 they were down in the kitchen the mother had tea for her, and thick milk, and a hot cake—all the delicacies which the farm could afford. I don't know that Mally cared much for the eating and drinking that night, but she began to think that the Gunliffes were good people—very good people. It was better thus, at any rate, than being accused of murder and carried off to Camelford prison.

"I'll never forget it on her—never," the father had said.

Those words stuck to her from that moment, and seemed to sound in her ears all the night. How glad she was that Barty had come down to the cove—oh, yes, how glad! There was no question of his dying now, and as for the blow on his forehead, what harm was that to a lad like him?

600 "But father shall go with you," said Mrs. Gunliffe, when Mally prepared to start for the cove by herself. Mally, however, would not hear of this. She could find her way to the cove whether it was light or dark.

"Mally, thou art my child now, and I shall think of thee so," said the mother, as the girl went off by herself.

Mally thought of this, too, as she walked home. How could she become Mrs. Gunliffe's child; ah, how?

I need not, I think, tell the tale any further. That Mally did become Mrs. Gunliffe's child, and how she became so the reader will understand; and in process

Language Coach

Meaning of Idioms
Idioms are groups of words that have a special meaning apart from the literal sense of the words. The idiom *unheard of* means "not previously seen or known" or "unacceptable." What does *unheard-of* mean in line 577? Explain.

---

33. **along of you:** because of you.

Tintagel (1887), Arthur Ackland Hunt. Watercolor with gouache on paper, 47.6 cm × 31.1 cm. Private collection. © The Maas Gallery, London/Bridgeman Art Library.

of time the big kitchen and all the wonders of the farmhouse were her own. The
610 people said that Barty Gunliffe had married a mermaid out of the sea; but when it
was said in Mally's hearing I doubt whether she liked it; and when Barty himself
would call her a mermaid she would frown at him, and throw about her black
hair, and pretend to cuff him with her little hand.

    Old Glos was brought up to the top of the cliff, and lived his few remaining
days under the roof of Mr. Gunliffe's house; and as for the cove and the right
of seaweed, from that time forth all that has been supposed to attach itself to
Gunliffe's farm, and I do not know that any of the neighbors are prepared to
dispute the right. ❧

Comprehension

1. **Recall** What conflict develops between the Trenglos family and the Gunliffes?

2. **Summarize** What events lead to Barty Gunliffe's accident?

3. **Clarify** What do the Gunliffes initially believe to be the cause of their son's accident?

Text Analysis

4. **Examine Predictions** Compare the predictions you recorded in your chart with the actual outcomes in the story. Which text clues proved to be the most reliable basis for your predictions?

5. **Analyze Realism** Choose three passages from the story that you feel best represent Trollope's realist style. What characteristics of realism does each passage illustrate?

6. **Interpret Mood** Describe the mood in each of the following passages. In what ways does Trollope use the **setting** to help create the mood?

   • the description of the cove (lines 235–240)

   • the description of the wind and the tide (lines 282–289)

   • the description of Barty's fall (lines 318–330)

7. **Draw Conclusions About Author's Purpose** What moral lesson might Trollope have intended this story to teach? Cite details to support your answer.

8. **Evaluate Plot** In your opinion, is the plot of "Malachi's Cove" believable? Why or why not?

Text Criticism

9. **Critical Interpretations** American writer and critic Henry James criticized Trollope's narrative voice for failing to maintain "the fiction of fiction," that is, for interrupting stories to remind the reader that the events portrayed are not real. Based on your reading, do you agree or disagree with James's criticism? Why might Trollope have chosen to use this narrative technique? Explain your answers.

How do we learn to TRUST?

Briefly describe a famous person who, in your estimation, appears trustworthy. What characteristics make him or her seem this way? What do you think is most important to look for when deciding if someone can be trusted?

COMMON CORE

RL 3 Analyze the impact of the author's choices regarding how to develop and relate elements of a story. RL 10 Read and comprehend literature, including stories.

Vocabulary in Context

▲ **VOCABULARY PRACTICE**

Decide whether the words in each pair are synonyms or antonyms.

1. precipitous/horizontal
2. indefatigable/lazy
3. interloper/trespasser
4. impede/ease

5. garner/distribute
6. desist/commence
7. eddying/whirling
8. orifice/cavity

WORD LIST

desist

eddying

garner

impede

indefatigable

interloper

orifice

precipitous

ACADEMIC VOCABULARY IN SPEAKING

- analyze   - dominate   - impact   - resource   - scheme

Analyze the **impact** of stories in literature, film, or television that are more realistic versus stories such as fairy tales or science fiction that are not realistic. Do you think realistic stories are more effective or engaging than fantasy or science fiction? Why? Use at least one additional Academic Vocabulary word in your discussion with a small group.

VOCABULARY STRATEGY: USING CONTEXT CLUES

A word's **context**—the words and sentences that surround it—often gives clues to the word's meaning. Considering the overall meaning of a passage often allows you to make logical guesses about the meaning of an unfamiliar word. A specific type of context clue is a contrast, within a sentence or within a paragraph, that hints at the unknown word's meaning. Another type of clue is an example. Study the following sentence.

> As fossil fuel sources <u>dwindle</u>, scientists are exploring the <u>biomass</u> energy potential of abundant "green" resources like corn, grasses, and seaweed.

The *dwindling* of fossil fuel contrasts with the *abundance* of "green" resources, so *dwindle* must mean "decrease." The examples of corn, grasses, and seaweed suggest that *biomass* refers to organic (including plant) matter.

PRACTICE On a separate sheet of paper, write the meaning of each underlined word below. Tell what clues, from a surrounding sentence or the passage as a whole, helped you figure out the word's meaning.

Seaweed is a promising source of energy for countries with <u>meager</u> arable land but substantial coastlines. Scottish scientists believe that biomass energy technology could <u>reinvigorate</u> the once-widespread practice of harvesting seaweed while also protecting the environment. Seaweed thrives on carbon dioxide, one of the pollutants responsible for global warming. Israeli scientists have developed a technology that funnels CO_2 <u>emissions</u> from a power plant into a pool of water that serves as both a coolant for the power plant and a <u>medium</u> for growing seaweed. Through this technology, seaweed grows at <u>concentrations</u> one million times the densities found in the nearby sea.

COMMON CORE

L 4a Use context as a clue to the meaning of a word.

Interactive Vocabulary **THINK** central

Go to **thinkcentral.com**.
KEYWORD: HML12-992

Language

◆ **GRAMMAR AND STYLE: Choose Effective Setting**

Review the **Grammar and Style** note on page 981. In his story, Trollope chooses a dramatic setting that reflects the volatility of his characters and their situation. He uses **prepositional phrases** to add details to his lavish descriptions of Malachi's cove and the churning sea, as in this example:

> *The tide had now come up so far that every succeeding wave washed into it and over it from the side nearest to the sea, and then ran down again back from the rocks, as the rolling wave receded, with a noise like the fall of a cataract.* (lines 320–323)

Common prepositions include *above, at, before, below, by, down, for, from, in, into, near, of, on, out, over, through, to, up, with,* and *without*. Prepositional phrases consist of a preposition, its object, and modifiers of the object. For clarity, these phrases should usually be placed near the word they modify.

PRACTICE Identify the prepositional phrases in each sentence from "Malachi's Cove." Then, write your own sentences, using prepositional phrases as Trollope does.

> **EXAMPLE**
>
> The cliffs there are bold and fine, and the sea beats in upon them from the north with a grand violence.
>
> *The plants there are delicate, and the sun shines down on them from the skylight with blazing heat.*

1. There was a rush of the sea into the cove, which carried there large, drifting masses of seaweed, leaving them among the rocks when the tide was out.

2. Nothing could exceed the grandeur of the colors—the blue of the open sea, the white of the breaking waves, the yellow sands, or the streaks of red and brown which gave such richness to the cliff.

READING-WRITING CONNECTION

YOUR TURN Expand your understanding of "Malachi's Cove" by responding to this prompt. Then, use the **revising tips** to improve your description of a scene.

WRITING PROMPT	REVISING TIPS
DESCRIBE A SCENE Descriptions can help convey both setting and mood. Visualize a scene that calls up a strong feeling in you. Write a **two-paragraph description** that not only describes the place or situation you picture in your mind but also gets across the way it makes you feel.	• Clearly establish the setting. • Include prepositional phrases to add details to your descriptions.

COMMON CORE

L 1 Demonstrate command of the conventions of standard English grammar when writing. **W 10** Write routinely over shorter time frames for a range of tasks.

Interactive Revision

THINK central

Go to **thinkcentral.com**.
KEYWORD: HML12-993

Christmas Storms and Sunshine

Short Story by Elizabeth Cleghorn Gaskell

COMMON CORE

RL 3 Analyze the impact of the author's choices regarding how to develop and relate elements of a story. **RL 4** Analyze the impact of specific word choices on meaning, including words with multiple meanings. **SL 1** Initiate and participate effectively in a range of collaborative discussions.

DID YOU KNOW?

Elizabeth Cleghorn Gaskell . . .

- was one of the most popular female novelists of her time.
- was close friends with fellow author Charlotte Brontë, whose biography she wrote.

Meet the Author

Elizabeth Cleghorn Gaskell 1810–1865

Elizabeth Cleghorn Gaskell was a literary trailblazer. She dared to examine illegitimacy, sexual exploitation, and oppression of the poor—risky topics for the Victorian era. Her stories and novels anticipated modern psychological fiction, delving into the daily lives and the emotional and intellectual growth of women. They also chronicled the social ills of the time. Gaskell was a careful observer who wrote about poverty and poor wages, unsafe working conditions, low life expectancy, and exploitation experienced by the lower classes.

Recreating Her Home Gaskell's life was shaped by the death of her mother when Elizabeth was an infant. Her father sent her to live with a maternal aunt in the Cheshire village of Knutsford; she was raised by that aunt, whom she called "my more than mother." In her popular novel *Cranford,* published in 1853, Gaskell recreated much of her life in Knutsford, with its leafy streets, gracious homes, and eccentric neighbors. Gaskell moved to the city of Manchester when she married William Gaskell in 1832. He was a Unitarian minister, an intellectual, and a community leader. Like Gaskell's Unitarian father, he influenced her

beliefs in tolerance, justice, and the equal worth of the rich and the poor.

Determined to Be Heard The Victorian era was a time of strict moral standards that were often applied hypocritically, with different expectations of men and women. Gaskell's 1853 novel *Ruth* shocked readers, because it dealt sympathetically with a young unwed mother. The author was well aware that her treatment of this issue would provoke attacks. "An unfit subject for fiction is the thing to say about it," she said, summing up her critics' objections. "I knew all this before, but I determined notwithstanding to speak my mind about it."

Victorian Crusader Throughout her career, Gaskell remained committed to raising the social awareness of her readers. The writer's era was rife with change, as the old English aristocracy declined and the roots of democracy began to take hold. Her novels *Mary Barton* and *North and South* both showed her support for Britain's liberal party, the Whigs. Her writings also demonstrated her support for legislation such as the Reform Bill of 1832, which granted voting rights to the middle class. Gaskell's last works, *Cousin Phillis* and *Wives and Daughters,* cemented her reputation as a novelist and social historian.

Author Online
Go to thinkcentral.com. KEYWORD: HML12-994

● TEXT ANALYSIS: OMNISCIENT POINT OF VIEW

A story told from the **third-person point of view** features a narrator who is not a character in the story but an outside observer. In contrast to other types of narrators, (see pages 183, 1127, and 1199) some third-person narrators are **omniscient**, or all-knowing, and can reveal the thoughts of multiple characters. The third-person omniscient point of view was popular with Victorian authors, who used it not only to reveal their characters' thoughts but also to express opinions on those characters and their dilemmas. As you read the following story, consider how the point of view affects both what you learn about the characters and how you react to their behavior.

● READING SKILL: IDENTIFY MOOD

The **mood** of a literary work is the feeling or atmosphere a writer creates for the reader. Fiction writers can create mood through imagery, descriptive details, word choice, and setting. For example, a story set during the last inning of a tied baseball game may have an exciting, suspenseful mood. Sometimes the mood of a story will change as the plot progresses. As you read, use a chart like the one shown to record the elements Gaskell uses to create mood in her story, and note any changes in the mood.

Literary Element	Examples	Mood Created
Imagery/Descriptive Details	It was the day before Christmas; such a cold east wind! such an inky sky! such blue-black looks on people's faces... (lines 47-49)	bleak, not festive
Word Choice		
Setting		

▲ VOCABULARY IN CONTEXT

Gaskell depicts a heated conflict using the following words. Choose the word that best completes each sentence.

WORD LIST	affronted	bigoted	propensity
	assent	penitence	upbraiding

1. A(n) _____ person fails to view others with an open mind.
2. Her _____ for singing led to a career in the spotlight.
3. The child received a harsh _____ for his bad behavior.
4. She calmly nodded her head in _____.

 Complete the activities in your **Reader/Writer Notebook**.

What can break down PREJUDICE?

Grim examples of prejudice are everywhere. People avoid neighborhoods where the residents are different from them. Kids make fun of other kids who aren't of the same race, religion, or social class. Obese or older people are often overlooked for job promotions, and men earn higher salaries than women. How can we overcome such unfair preconceived judgments?

DISCUSS With a partner, talk about examples of prejudice like the ones listed above. Then, choose one example and come up with specific tactics for overcoming it. Share your strategies in a class discussion.

CHRISTMAS STORMS AND SUNSHINE

Elizabeth Cleghorn Gaskell

BACKGROUND The early Victorian era was a time of political reform, as the old aristocracy reluctantly gave way to a more democratic system. The Tories, a conservative political party that represented the interests of wealthy landowners, opposed the democratic reforms. They scorned the Whig party for supporting measures that gradually allowed the middle class to become a major force in British politics. Gaskell chronicled the clashes between the parties, as well as the manners, morals, and living conditions of Victorian society.

Analyze Visuals ▶
Describe the time and place depicted in this etching. What details give you this sense?

In the town of—(no matter where) there circulated two local newspapers (no matter when). Now the *Flying Post* was long-established and respectable—alias **bigoted** and Tory;[1] the *Examiner* was spirited and intelligent—alias newfangled and democratic. Every week these newspapers contained articles abusing each other, as cross and peppery as articles could be, and evidently the production of irritated minds, although they seemed to have one stereotyped commencement[2]— "Though the article appearing in our last week's *Post* (or *Examiner*) is below contempt, yet we have been induced," &c.[3] &c.; and every Saturday the Radical[4] shopkeepers shook hands together, and agreed that the *Post* was done for by the
10 slashing, clever *Examiner;* while the more dignified Tories began by regretting that Johnson should think that low paper, only read by a few of the vulgar, worth wasting his wit upon; however, the *Examiner* was at its last gasp. **Ⓐ**

bigoted (bĭg′ə-tĭd) *adj.* prejudiced and narrow-minded; intolerant

Ⓐ POINT OF VIEW Consider what you learn about the two newspapers in lines 1–12. How do the narrator's comments affect your impression of the papers?

1. **Tory** (tôr′ē): referring to Britain's Conservative Party. Most British newspapers in Victorian times expressed the opinions of one political party or another.
2. **stereotyped commencement:** a beginning that was repeatedly used, without variation.
3. **&c.:** et cetera.
4. **Radical:** referring to members of Britain's Whig Party who were especially insistent in their desire for reform.

Newsboy with Papers from *Aunt Louisa's Welcome Gift* by H. W. Petherick, 1860. Mary Evans Picture Library.

It was not, though. It lived and flourished; at least it paid its way, as one of the heroes of my story could tell. He was chief compositor, or whatever title may be given to the headman of the mechanical part of a newspaper. He hardly confined himself to that department. Once or twice, unknown to the editor, when the manuscript had fallen short, he had filled up the vacant space by compositions of his own; announcements of a forthcoming crop of green peas in December; a grey thrush having been seen, or a white hare, or such interesting phenomena; invented
20 for the occasion, I must confess; but what of that? His wife always knew when to expect a little specimen of her husband's literary talent by a peculiar cough, which served as prelude; and, judging from this encouraging sign, and the high-pitched and emphatic voice in which he read them, she was inclined to think, that an "Ode to an Early Rosebud," in the corner devoted to original poetry, and a letter in the correspondence department, signed "Pro Bono Publico,"[5] were her husband's writing, and to hold up her head accordingly.

I never could find out what it was that occasioned the Hodgsons to lodge in the same house as the Jenkinses. Jenkins held the same office in the Tory Paper as Hodgson did in the *Examiner,* and, as I said before, I leave you to give it a name.
30 But Jenkins had a proper sense of his position, and a proper reverence for all in authority, from the king down to the editor and sub-editor. He would as soon have thought of borrowing the king's crown for a nightcap, or the king's scepter for a walking-stick as he would have thought of filling up any spare corner with any production of his own; and I think it would have even added to his contempt of Hodgson (if that were possible), had he known of the "productions of his brain," as the latter fondly alluded[6] to the paragraphs he inserted, when speaking to his wife. **B**

Jenkins had his wife too. Wives were wanting[7] to finish the completeness of the quarrel which existed one memorable Christmas week, some dozen years ago,
40 between the two neighbors, the two compositors. And with wives, it was a very pretty, a very complete quarrel. To make the opposing parties still more equal, still more well-matched, if the Hodgsons had a baby ("such a baby!—a poor, puny little thing"), Mrs. Jenkins had a cat ("such a cat! a great, nasty, miowling tom-cat, that was always stealing the milk put by for little Angel's supper"). And now, having matched Greek with Greek, I must proceed to the tug of war.[8] It was the day before Christmas; such a cold east wind! such an inky sky! such a blue-black look in people's faces, as they were driven out more than usual, to complete their purchases for the next day's festival. **C**

Before leaving home that morning, Jenkins had given some money to his wife
50 to buy the next day's dinner.

"My dear, I wish for turkey and sausages. It may be a weakness, but I own I am partial to sausages. My deceased mother was. Such tastes are hereditary. As to the sweets—whether plum-pudding or mince-pies—I leave such considerations to

---

5. **"Pro Bono Publico"** (prō bō′nō pŭb′lĭ-kō′): a Latin phrase meaning "for the public good."

6. **allude:** (E-ILdP) v. to refer to indirectly.

7. **wanting:** required; needed.

8. **having matched . . . tug of war:** a reference to the saying "When Greek meets Greek, then comes the tug of war," meaning that when evenly matched opponents fight, the battle will be fierce.

B POINT OF VIEW
Omniscient narrators of the Victorian era are often described as more "intrusive" than contemporary narrators. Reread lines 27–37. Why might the narrator of this story be described as intrusive?

C IDENTIFY MOOD
Reread lines 40–45. In setting up these two opposing families, what mood does Gaskell create? Cite **details** that help the author establish this mood.

you; I only beg you not to mind expense. Christmas comes but once a year."

And again he called out from the bottom of the first flight of stairs, just close to the Hodgsons' door ("such ostentatiousness," as Mrs. Hodgson observed), "You will not forget the sausages, my dear!"

"I should have liked to have had something above common, Mary," said Hodgson, as they too made their plans for the next day; "but I think roast beef
60 must do for us. You see, love, we've a family."

"Only one, Jem! I don't want more than roast beef, though, I'm sure. Before I went to service,[9] mother and me would have thought roast beef a very fine dinner."

"Well, let's settle it, then, roast beef and a plum-pudding; and now, good-bye. Mind and take care of little Tom. I thought he was a bit hoarse this morning."

And off he went to his work.

Now, it was a good while since Mrs. Jenkins and Mrs. Hodgson had spoken to each other, although they were quite as much in possession of the knowledge of events and opinions as though they did. Mary knew that Mrs. Jenkins despised
70 her for not having a real lace cap, which Mrs. Jenkins had; and for having been a servant, which Mrs. Jenkins had not; and the little occasional pinchings[10] which the Hodgsons were obliged to resort to, to make both ends meet, would have been very patiently endured by Mary, if she had not winced under Mrs. Jenkins's knowledge of such economy. But she had her revenge. She had a child, and Mrs. Jenkins had none. To have had a child, even such a puny baby as little Tom, Mrs. Jenkins would have worn commonest caps, and cleaned grates, and drudged her fingers to the bone. The great unspoken disappointment of her life soured her temper, and turned her thoughts inward, and made her morbid and selfish. **D**

"Hang that cat! he's been stealing again! he's gnawed the cold mutton in his
80 nasty mouth till it's not fit to set before a Christian; and I've nothing else for Jem's dinner. But I'll give it him now I've caught him, that I will!"

So saying, Mary Hodgson caught up her husband's Sunday cane, and despite pussy's cries and scratches, she gave him such a beating as she hoped might cure him of his thievish **propensities;** when, lo! and behold, Mrs. Jenkins stood at the door with a face of bitter wrath.

"Aren't you ashamed of yourself, ma'am, to abuse a poor dumb animal, ma'am, as knows no better than to take food when he sees it, ma'am? He only follows the nature which God has given, ma'am; and it's a pity your nature, ma'am, which I've heard is of the stingy saving species, does not make you shut your cupboard door a
90 little closer. There is such a thing as law for brute animals. I'll ask Mr. Jenkins, but I don't think them Radicals has done away with that law yet, for all their Reform Bill,[11] ma'am. My poor precious love of a Tommy, is he hurt? and is his leg broke for taking a mouthful of scraps, as most people would give away to a beggar—if

D POINT OF VIEW
Reread lines 67–78. What does the narrator reveal about the **motivation** of each of these characters? How might this passage be different if the narrator were not **omniscient**?

propensity (prə-pĕn′sĭ-tē) *n.* a likelihood to do or think something; tendency; inclination

---

9. **went to service:** took employment as a servant.

10. **pinchings:** cost-cutting measures.

11. **Reform Bill:** one of a series of bills in 19th-century England, generally supported by Whigs but not Tories, that extended voting rights to more men.

Cat Looks Out of Window from *Aunt Louisa's Welcome Gift* by H. W. Petherick, 1860. Mary Evans Picture Library.

he'd take 'em!" wound up Mrs. Jenkins, casting a contemptuous look on the remnant of a scrag end of mutton.

Mary felt very angry and very guilty. For she really pitied the poor limping animal as he crept up to his mistress, and there lay down to bemoan himself; she wished she had not beaten him so hard, for it certainly was her own careless way of never shutting the cupboard-door that had tempted him to his fault. But the
100 sneer at her little bit of mutton turned her **penitence** to fresh wrath, and she shut the door in Mrs. Jenkins's face, as she stood caressing her cat in the lobby, with such a bang, that it wakened little Tom, and he began to cry.

Everything was to go wrong with Mary today. Now baby was awake, who was to take her husband's dinner to the office? She took the child in her arms and tried to hush him off to sleep again, and as she sung she cried, she could hardly tell why,—a sort of reaction from her violent angry feelings. She wished she had never beaten the poor cat; she wondered if his leg was really broken. What would her mother say if she knew how cross and cruel her little Mary was getting? If she should live to beat her child in one of her angry fits?
110 It was of no use lullabying while she sobbed so; it must be given up, and she must just carry her baby in her arms, and take him with her to the office, for it was long past dinner-time. So she pared the mutton carefully, although by so

penitence (pĕn′ĭ-təns)
n. feeling regret for a wrongful act and wanting to atone for it

doing she reduced the meat to an infinitesimal [12] quantity, and taking the baked potatoes out of the oven, she popped them piping hot into her basket, with the etceteras of plate, butter, salt, and knife and fork.

It was, indeed, a bitter wind. She bent against it as she ran, and the flakes of snow were sharp and cutting as ice. Baby cried all the way, though she cuddled him up in her shawl. Then her husband had made his appetite up for a potato pie, and (literary man as he was) his body got so much the better of his mind, that he
120 looked rather black at the cold mutton. Mary had no appetite for her own dinner when she arrived at home again. So, after she had tried to feed baby, and he had fretfully refused to take his bread and milk, she laid him down as usual on his quilt, surrounded by playthings, while she sided away, and chopped suet for the next day's pudding. Early in the afternoon a parcel came, done up first in brown paper, then in such a white, grass-bleached, sweet-smelling towel, and a note from her dear, dear mother; in which quaint writing she endeavored to tell her daughter that she was not forgotten at Christmas time; but that, learning that Farmer Burton was killing his pig, she had made interest for some of his famous pork, out of which she had manufactured some sausages, and flavored them just as Mary
130 used to like when she lived at home.

"Dear, dear mother!" said Mary to herself. "There never was any one like her for remembering other folk. What rare sausages she used to make! Home things have a smack with 'em no bought things can ever have. Set them up with their sausages! I've a notion if Mrs. Jenkins had ever tasted mother's she'd have no fancy for them townmade things Fanny took in just now."

And so she went on thinking about home, till the smiles and the dimples came out again at the remembrance of that pretty cottage, which would look green even now in the depth of winter, with its pyracanthus,[13] and its holly-bushes, and the great Portugal laurel that was her mother's pride. And the back path through the
140 orchard to Farmer Burton's, how well she remembered it! The bushels of unripe apples she had picked up there and distributed among his pigs, till he had scolded her for giving them so much green trash!

She was interrupted—her baby (I call him a baby, because his father and mother did, and because he was so little of his age, but I rather think he was eighteen months old,) had fallen asleep some time before among his playthings; an uneasy, restless sleep; but of which Mary had been thankful, as his morning's nap had been too short, and as she was so busy. But now he began to make such a strange crowing noise, just like a chair drawn heavily and gratingly along a kitchen floor! His eyes were open, but expressive of nothing but pain.
150 "Mother's darling!" said Mary, in terror, lifting him up. "Baby, try not to make that noise. Hush, hush, darling; what hurts him?" But the noise came worse and worse.

"Fanny! Fanny!" Mary called in mortal fright, for her baby was almost black with his gasping breath, and she had no one to ask for aid or sympathy but her landlady's daughter, a little girl of twelve or thirteen, who attended to the house

COMMON CORE RL 4

Language Coach

Multiple Meanings
The word *fancy* can mean (1) decorated, not plain; (2) a liking or preference; (3) to like; or (4) to imagine. Meanings 2-4 are mainly British. What does *fancy* mean in line 134? Create a new sentence using *fancy* in a different way.

---

12. **infinitesimal:** (ĭn′fĭn-ĭ-tĕs′ə-məl) adj. extremely small; tiny

13. **pyracanthus** (pī′rə-kăn′thəs): a pyracantha—a thorny evergreen shrub.

in her mother's absence, as daily cook in gentlemen's families. Fanny was more especially considered the attendant of the upstairs lodgers (who paid for the use of the kitchen, "for Jenkins could not abide the smell of meat cooking"), but just now she was fortunately sitting at her afternoon's work of darning stockings, and hearing Mrs. Hodgson's cry of terror, she ran to her sitting-room, and understood the case at a glance.

"He's got the croup![14] O Mrs. Hodgson, he'll die as sure as fate. Little brother had it, and he died in no time. The doctor said he could do nothing for him—it had gone too far. He said if we'd put him in a warm bath at first, it might have saved him; but, bless you! he was never half so bad as your baby." Unconsciously there mingled in her statement some of a child's love of producing an effect; but the increasing danger was clear enough.

"Oh, my baby! my baby! Oh, love, love! don't look so ill! I cannot bear it. And my fire so low! There, I was thinking of home, and picking currants, and never minding the fire. O Fanny! what is the fire like in the kitchen? Speak."

"Mother told me to screw it up, and throw some slack[15] on as soon as Mrs. Jenkins had done with it, and so I did. It's very low and black. But, oh, Mrs. Hodgson! let me run for the doctor—I cannot abear to hear him, it's so like little brother."

Through her streaming tears Mary motioned her to go; and trembling, sinking, sick at heart, she laid her boy in his cradle, and ran to fill her kettle. **E**

Mrs. Jenkins, having cooked her husband's snug little dinner, to which he came home; having told him her story of pussy's beating, at which he was justly and dignifiedly (?) indignant, saying it was all of a piece with that abusive *Examiner;* having received the sausages, and turkey, and mince pies, which her husband had ordered; and cleaned up the room, and prepared everything for tea, and coaxed and duly bemoaned her cat (who had pretty nearly forgotten his beating, but very much enjoyed the petting); having done all these and many other things, Mrs. Jenkins sat down to get up the real lace cap. Every thread was pulled out separately, and carefully stretched: when—what was that? Outside, in the street, a chorus of piping children's voices sang the old carol she had heard a hundred times in the days of her youth—

As Joseph was a walking he heard an angel sing,
"This night shall be born our heavenly King.
He neither shall be born in housen nor in hall,
Nor in the place of Paradise, but in an ox's stall.
He neither shall be clothed in purple nor in pall,[16]
But all in fair linen, as were babies all:
He neither shall be rocked in silver nor in gold,
But in a wooden cradle that rocks on the mould," &c.[17]

E IDENTIFY MOOD
How would you describe the mood at this point in the story? Reread lines 150–176, identifying the descriptive **details** and **word choices** that allow Gaskell to build the mood to a crescendo.

---

14. **croup** (kro͞op): a respiratory disease in children, marked by difficulty in breathing and a sharp cough.

15. **slack:** fragments of coal.

16. **pall** (pôl): fine or rich cloth.

17. **mould:** soil; ground.

She got up and went to the window. There, below, stood the group of black little figures, relieved[18] against the snow, which now enveloped everything. "For old sake's sake," as she phrased it, she counted out a halfpenny apiece for the singers, out of the copper bag,[19] and threw them down below.

200 The room had become chilly while she had been counting out and throwing down her money, so she stirred her already glowing fire, and sat down right before it—but not to stretch her lace; like Mary Hodgson, she began to think over long past days, on softening remembrances of the dead and gone, on words long forgotten, on holy stories heard at her mother's knee.

"I cannot think what's come over me tonight," said she, half aloud, recovering herself by the sound of her own voice from her train of thought—"My head goes wandering on them old times. I'm sure more texts[20] have come into my head with thinking on my mother within this last half-hour, than I've thought on for years and years. I hope I'm not going to die. Folks says, thinking too much on the dead
210 betokens we're going to join 'em; I should be loth to go just yet—such a fine turkey as we've got for dinner tomorrow too!"

Knock, knock, knock, at the door, as fast as knuckles could go. And then, as if the comer could not wait, the door was opened, and Mary Hodgson stood there as white as death.

"Mrs. Jenkins!—oh, your kettle is boiling, thank God! Let me have the water for my baby, for the love of God! He's got croup, and is dying!"

Mrs. Jenkins turned on her chair with a wooden, inflexible look on her face, that (between ourselves) her husband knew and dreaded for all his pompous dignity.

220 "I'm sorry I can't oblige you, ma'am; my kettle is wanted for my husband's tea. Don't be afeared, Tommy, Mrs. Hodgson won't venture to intrude herself where she's not desired. You'd better send for the doctor, ma'am, instead of wasting your time in wringing your hands, ma'am—my kettle is engaged."

Mary clasped her hands together with passionate force, but spoke no word of entreaty to that wooden face—that sharp, determined voice; but, as she turned away, she prayed for strength to bear the coming trial, and strength to forgive Mrs. Jenkins.

Mrs. Jenkins watched her go away meekly, as one who has no hope, and then she turned upon herself as sharply as she ever did on any one else.

230 "What a brute I am, Lord forgive me! What's my husband's tea to a baby's life? In croup, too, where time is everything. You crabbed old vixen, you!—any one may know you never had a child!"

She was downstairs (kettle in hand) before she had finished her self-**upbraiding**; and when in Mrs. Hodgson's room, she rejected all thanks (Mary had not the voice for many words), saying, stiffly, "I do it for the poor baby's sake, ma'am, hoping he may live to have mercy to poor dumb beasts, if he does forget to lock his cupboards." **F**

Language Coach

Meaning of Idioms
Idioms are phrases that have a special meaning apart from the literal sense of the words. The phrase *train of thought* (line 206) is an example of an idiom. How do lines 202-204 help you understand its meaning?

upbraiding (ŭp-brād′ĭng) *n.* scolding **upbraid** *v.*

F **POINT OF VIEW**
What do lines 223–232 reveal about Mary and Mrs. Jenkins that they don't say directly to one another?

---

18. **relieved:** set off by contrast.

19. **copper bag:** a bag in which Mrs. Jenkins kept coins.

20. **texts:** passages from the Bible.

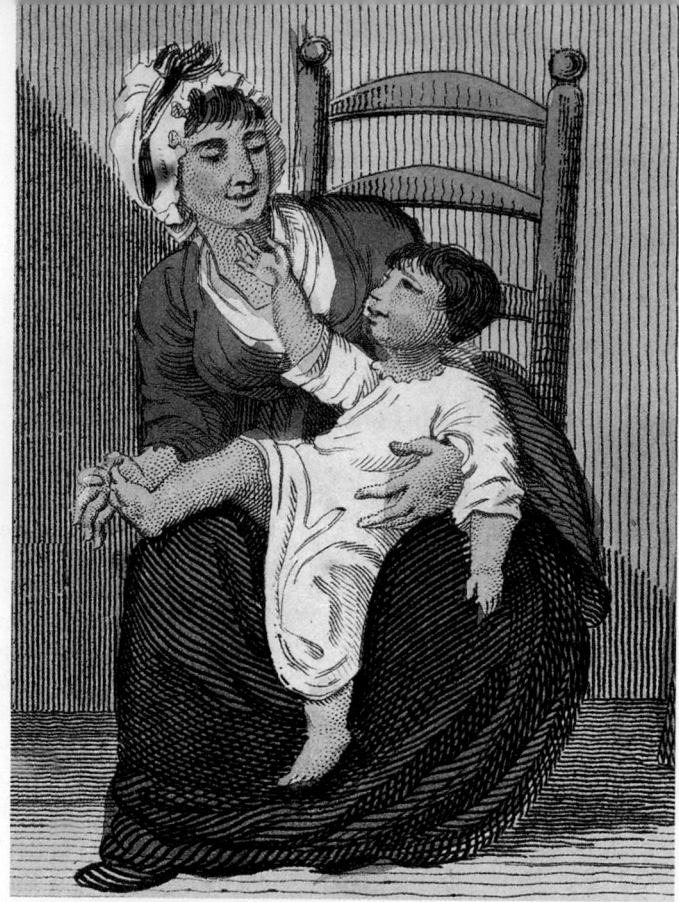

This Little Piggy Went from *Songs for the Nursery*, 1818. Mary Evans Picture Library.

But she did everything, and more than Mary, with her young inexperience, could have thought of. She prepared the warm bath, and tried it with her
240 husband's own thermometer (Mr. Jenkins was as punctual as clockwork in noting down the temperature of every day). She let his mother place her baby in the tub, still preserving the same rigid, **affronted** aspect, and then she went upstairs without a word. Mary longed to ask her to stay, but dared not; though, when she left the room, the tears chased each other down her cheeks faster than ever. Poor young mother! how she counted the minutes till the doctor should come. But, before he came, down again stalked Mrs. Jenkins, with something in her hand.

"I've seen many of these croup-fits, which, I take it, you've not, ma'am. Mustard plasters[21] is very sovereign,[22] put on the throat; I've been up and made one, ma'am, and, by your leave, I'll put it on the poor little fellow."
250 Mary could not speak, but she signed her grateful **assent.**

It began to smart while they still kept silence; and he looked up to his mother as if seeking courage from her looks to bear the stinging pain; but she was softly crying to see him suffer, and her want of courage reacted upon him, and he began to sob aloud. Instantly Mrs. Jenkins's apron was up, hiding her face: "Peep-bo, baby," said she, as merrily as she could. His little face brightened, and his mother having once got the cue, the two women kept the little fellow amused, until his plaster had taken effect.

---

21. **mustard plasters:** applications of a paste made of powdered mustard, water, and vinegar, used to relieve inflammation.

22. **sovereign** (sŏv′ər-ĭn): effective.

affronted (ə-frŭnt′ĭd)
adj. insulted; offended
affront *v.*

assent (ə-sĕnt′) *n.*
acceptance of an opinion or a proposal; agreement

"He's better—oh, Mrs. Jenkins, look at his eyes! how different! And he breathes quite softly"—

260 As Mary spoke thus, the doctor entered. He examined his patient. Baby was really better.

"It has been a sharp attack, but the remedies you have applied have been worth all the Pharmacopoeia[23] an hour later.—I shall send a powder," &c. &c.

Mrs. Jenkins stayed to hear this opinion; and (her heart wonderfully more easy) was going to leave the room, when Mary seized her hand and kissed it; she could not speak her gratitude.

Mrs. Jenkins looked affronted and awkward, and as if she must go upstairs and wash her hand directly.

But, in spite of these sour looks, she came softly down an hour or so afterwards
270 to see how baby was.

The little gentleman slept well after the fright he had given his friends; and on Christmas morning, when Mary awoke and looked at the sweet little pale face lying on her arm, she could hardly realize the danger he had been in.

When she came down (later than usual), she found the household in a commotion. What do you think had happened? Why, pussy had been traitor to his best friend, and eaten up some of Mr. Jenkins's own especial sausages; and gnawed and tumbled the rest so, that they were not fit to be eaten! There were no bounds to that cat's appetite! he would have eaten his own father if he had been tender enough. And now Mrs. Jenkins stormed and cried—"Hang the cat!" **G**

280 Christmas Day, too! and all the shops shut! "What was turkey without sausages?" gruffly asked Mr. Jenkins.

"O Jem!" whispered Mary, "hearken what a piece of work he's making about sausages—I should like to take Mrs. Jenkins up some of mother's; they're twice as good as bought sausages."

"I see no objection, my dear. Sausages do not involve intimacies, else his politics are what I can no ways respect."

"But, oh, Jem, if you had seen her last night about baby! I'm sure she may scold me forever, and I'll not answer. I'd even make her cat welcome to the sausages."
The tears gathered to Mary's eyes as she kissed her boy.

290 "Better take 'em upstairs, my dear, and give them to the cat's mistress." And Jem chuckled at his saying.

Mary put them on a plate, but still she loitered.

"What must I say, Jem? I never know."

"Say—I hope you'll accept of these sausages, as my mother—no, that's not grammar;—say what comes uppermost, Mary, it will be sure to be right."

So Mary carried them upstairs and knocked at the door; and when told to "come in," she looked very red, but went up to Mrs. Jenkins, saying, "Please take these. Mother made them." And was away before an answer could be given.

Just as Hodgson was ready to go to church, Mrs. Jenkins came downstairs, and
300 called Fanny. In a minute, the latter entered the Hodgsons' room, and delivered

---

23. **all the Pharmacopoeia** (fär′mə-kə-pē′ə): all the medicinal drugs listed in the standard reference work on the subject.

Mr. and Mrs. Jenkins's compliments, and they would be particular glad if Mr. and Mrs. Hodgson would eat their dinner with them.

"And carry baby upstairs in a shawl, be sure," added Mrs. Jenkins's voice in the passage, close to the door, whither she had followed her messenger. There was no discussing the matter, with the certainty of every word being overheard.

Mary looked anxiously at her husband. She remembered his saying he did not approve of Mr. Jenkins's politics.

"Do you think it would do for baby?" asked he.

"Oh, yes," answered she eagerly; "I would wrap him up so warm."

310 "And I've got our room up to sixty-five already, for all it's so frosty," added the voice outside.

Now, how do you think they settled the matter? The very best way in the world. Mr. and Mrs. Jenkins came down into the Hodgsons' room and dined there. Turkey at the top, roast beef at the bottom, sausages at one side, potatoes at the other. Second course, plum pudding at the top, and mince pies at the bottom.

And after dinner, Mrs. Jenkins would have baby on her knee, and he seemed quite to take to her; she declared he was admiring the real lace on her cap, but Mary thought (though she did not say so) that he was pleased by her kind looks and coaxing words. Then he was wrapped up and carried carefully upstairs to tea,

320 in Mrs. Jenkins's room. And after tea, Mrs. Jenkins, and Mary, and her husband, found out each other's mutual liking for music, and sat singing old glees and catches,[24] till I don't know what o'clock, without one word of politics or newspapers.

Before they parted, Mary had coaxed pussy on to her knee; for Mrs. Jenkins would not part with baby, who was sleeping on her lap.

"When you're busy bring him to me. Do, now, it will be a real favor. I know you must have a deal to do, with another coming; let him come up to me. I'll take the greatest of cares of him; pretty darling, how sweet he looks when he's asleep!" **H**

When the couples were once more alone, the husbands unburdened their minds to their wives.

330 Mr. Jenkins said to his— "Do you know, Burgess tried to make me believe Hodgson was such a fool as to put paragraphs into the *Examiner* now and then; but I see he knows his place, and has got too much sense to do any such thing."

Hodgson said— "Mary, love, I almost fancy from Jenkins's way of speaking (so much civiler than I expected), he guesses I wrote that 'Pro Bono' and the 'Rosebud,'—at any rate, I've no objection to your naming it, if the subject should come uppermost; I should like him to know I'm a literary man."

Well! I've ended my tale; I hope you don't think it too long; but, before I go, just let me say one thing.

If any of you have any quarrels, or misunderstandings, or coolnesses, or cold

340 shoulders, or shynesses, or tiffs, or miffs, or huffs, with anyone else, just make friends before Christmas,—you will be so much merrier if you do.

I ask it of you for the sake of that old angelic song, heard so many years ago by the shepherds, keeping watch by night, on Bethlehem Heights. [25] ∾

H IDENTIFY MOOD
Describe how the mood of this scene differs from the passages describing Mary's desperate attempts to save her baby. What literary elements work to achieve this mood?

---

24. **glees and catches:** unaccompanied part or round songs for several voices.

25. **the shepherds . . . Heights:** the shepherds who visited the baby Jesus in Bethlehem.

Comprehension

1. **Recall** What do Mr. Hodgson and Mr. Jenkins do for a living?

2. **Clarify** Why does Mary Hodgson beat Mrs. Jenkins's cat?

3. **Summarize** How does Mrs. Jenkins's attitude toward baby Tom change over the course of the story?

Text Analysis

4. **Draw Conclusions** Explain why the two families are antagonistic toward each other at the beginning of the story. What causes them to overcome their prejudice against each other? Support your conclusion with evidence.

5. **Make Predictions** In your opinion, is the truce between the two families likely to last? Explain why or why not, citing evidence from the story to support your answer.

6. **Identify Mood** Review the chart you filled in as you read. What shifts in mood occur as the story progresses? Citing specific examples, describe the literary elements Gaskell employs to create a distinct mood.

7. **Analyze Realism** Victorian literature is known for its realism—the careful and detailed presentation of everyday life. In addition to depicting reality, Victorian authors like Gaskell had another purpose: they used their writing to expose the problems plaguing their society. What aspects of Victorian society is Gaskell commenting on in this story? Support your answer with details, descriptions, and dialogue from the text.

8. **Evaluate Third-Person Omniscient Point of View** The word *omniscient* comes from the Latin words *omnis*, which means "all," and *scientia*, which means "knowledge." Identify at least two passages in the story that show that this narrator is omniscient. What insights provided by the narrator particularly affected you? Describe how the story might have been different if it had been told in the third-person limited point of view.

Text Criticism

9. **Critical Interpretations** Critics have praised Gaskell's "refusal to give easy answers to social and spiritual dilemmas." Do you think this comment applies to the problems Gaskell explores in this story? Cite evidence to support your opinion.

> *What can break down* **PREJUDICE?**
>
> How can focusing on similarities rather than differences help us overcome prejudices or other negative preconceptions we may have about others?

COMMON CORE

RL 3 Analyze the impact of the author's choices regarding how to develop and relate elements of a story.

Vocabulary in Context

▲ VOCABULARY PRACTICE

Use your knowledge of the boldface vocabulary words to indicate whether each statement is true or false.

1. A **bigoted** person often has a closed mind to new ideas.
2. A liar is someone with a **propensity** for honesty.
3. Prayer and good deeds are ways of showing **penitence.**
4. Most students welcome an **upbraiding** from the principal.
5. An **affronted** person usually smiles with joy.
6. *Yes* is a word of **assent.**

ACADEMIC VOCABULARY IN SPEAKING

> • analyze   • dominate   • impact   • resource   • scheme

Instead of trying to **scheme** against and **dominate** each other, the neighbors in Gaskell's story overcome their differences through compassion. In a small group, discuss situations in which you or someone you know made negative assumptions about another person, but came to see him or her in a more positive light. Use at least one additional Academic Vocabulary word in your discussion.

VOCABULARY STRATEGY: THE DEVELOPMENT OF ENGLISH

The English language has existed since Germanic tribes invaded the British Isles in the fifth century, and many factors have influenced its development. Many Old Norse words were absorbed into English as the Vikings began to invade in the eighth century. The Old Norse verb *hrópja,* meaning "to cry hoarsely," became *croup* in Scottish dialect. Along the way, a Scottish doctor coined the term *croup* as a noun to describe the childhood cough that afflicts many babies, including Mrs. Hodgson's. This is an example of how both **foreign languages** and **science and technology** have influenced the development of English. To learn more about the development of English, consult an online history of word origins or the etymology of words in a dictionary.

PRACTICE Each of the following quotations from Gaskell's story contains a boldface word. Use a reference source to decide whether we owe each word mainly to advances in science or technology or to the influence of immigration.

1. "He was chief **compositor**, or whatever title may be given to the headman of the mechanical part of a newspaper."
2. "His wife always knew when to expect a little **specimen** of her husband's literary talent . . ."
3. "'. . . take care of little Tom. I thought he was a bit **hoarse** this morning.'"
4. "'. . . he's gnawed the cold **mutton** in his nasty mouth . . . !'"
5. "She prepared the bath and tried it with her husband's own **thermometer.**"

COMMON CORE

L 1a Apply the understanding that usage can change over time.
L 6 Acquire and use accurately general academic and domain-specific words.

Interactive Vocabulary THINK central

Go to **thinkcentral.com.**
KEYWORD: HML12-1008

Language

◆ **GRAMMAR AND STYLE:** Establish Voice

Review the **Grammar and Style** note on page 1005. Part of what makes this story distinctive is Gaskell's **voice**—her unique style of expression that allows you to "hear" a human personality behind the words you read. Gaskell uses a conversational style that matches the gossipy nature of her characters. She establishes this voice through the narrator, who uses the **second-person pronoun** *you* to address the reader directly. The narrator also makes parenthetical asides to the reader that convey additional information and comment on the characters' behavior. Notice how, in this parenthetical aside, the narrator uses the phrase "between ourselves," addressing the reader directly as though speaking to a friend:

> *Mrs. Jenkins turned on her chair with a wooden, inflexible look on her face, that (between ourselves) her husband knew and dreaded for all his pompous dignity.* (lines 217–219)

PRACTICE The following paragraph is a sample response to the writing prompt. Rewrite the paragraph, adapting it to mimic Gaskell's voice. Be sure to add direct comments to the reader, as well as parenthetical asides that seem to convey inside information about the characters.

> *Jake's parents and Will's mother were best friends, and the boys had grown up together. They spent more time with one another than many siblings do, which only made them despise each other more. Forced by their parents to think of each other as "friends," the two boys had been fighting as long as they could remember.*

READING-WRITING CONNECTION

Expand your understanding of "Christmas Storms and Sunshine" by responding to this prompt. Then, use the **revising tips** to improve your story.

WRITING PROMPT

WRITE A STORY Omniscient narrators—particularly "intrusive" ones like that of "Christmas Storms and Sunshine"—were more common in the literature of the Victorian era than they are in contemporary writing. Conflicts between neighbors, however, are still at the heart of many modern stories. Using "Christmas Storms and Sunshine" as a model, write a **one- to three-page story** about modern neighbors wrapped in a compelling conflict. Use an intrusive third-person omniscient narrator similar to Gaskell's to tell your story.

REVISING TIPS

- Introduce dynamic characters, a vivid setting, and a fresh conflict to grab readers' attention.
- Employ a third-person omniscient narrator who reveals multiple characters' thoughts and who comments on the story's events.
- Have your narrator address the audience directly, using the second-person pronoun *you*.

Interactive Revision

THINKcentral

Go to thinkcentral.com.
KEYWORD: HML12-1009

COMMON CORE

L 1 Demonstrate command of the conventions of standard English grammar when writing. **W 3** Write narratives to develop real or imagined experiences or events.

from **Great Expectations**

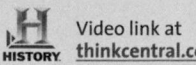

Video link at
thinkcentral.com

Novel by Charles Dickens

Charles Dickens

(COMMON CORE

RL 3 Analyze the impact of the author's choices regarding how to develop and relate elements of a story. **RL 10** Read and comprehend literature, including stories.

BACKGROUND Charles Dickens (1812–1870) brought to fiction a new degree of realism, yet his novels can also be powerfully moving, highly sentimental, and uproariously funny by turn. Never forgetting his own harsh adolescence, Dickens focused on problems of the poor or unfortunate in most of his work, often exposing social ills in the hope of reforming them. *Great Expectations*, one of Dickens's later novels, is the first-person story of Philip Pirrip, nicknamed Pip, an orphan who all his life is helped financially by a mysterious benefactor. In time he comes to believe that this benefactor is Miss Havisham, elderly guardian of Estella, the young woman with whom he falls in love. In the following scene, Pip meets both Miss Havisham and Estella for the first time.

TEXT ANALYSIS As you read, notice Dickens's use of **sensory details,** details that appeal to the five senses—sight, smell, hearing, taste, and touch. These details help reveal specific traits of the three characters. For example, the dialogue illustrates Estella's haughtiness as she ridicules Pip: "He calls the knaves, Jacks, this boy!" Pip's dialogue shows him as insecure and uneasy. When Miss Havisham asks Pip what he thinks of Estella, he hesitates before stammering, "I don't like to say." Details that describe Miss Havisham's appearance paint her as strange and "corpse-like," sitting in a "withered bridal dress" that looks like "grave-clothes." Even the details that describe the setting contribute to an understanding of Miss Havisham's eccentric nature. The stopped watch and clock, the return of a jewel to its exact location, and the yellow shoe atop the dressing table show how time has stopped for Miss Havisham.

WRITE After you read, write a brief paragraph describing an object, person, or place as it appeared in the past and as it appears in the present. Try to use sensory details that appeal to all five senses to describe how your subject has changed over time.

***FROM* GREAT EXPECTATIONS**

*M*iss Havisham beckoned [Estella] to come close, and took up a jewel from the table, and tried its effect upon her fair young bosom and against her pretty brown hair. "Your own one day, my dear, and you will use it well. Let me see you play cards with this boy."

"With this boy! Why, he is a common labouring-boy!"

I thought I overheard Miss Havisham answer—only it seemed so unlikely—"Well? You can break his heart."

"What do you play, boy?" asked Estella of myself, with the greatest disdain.

"Nothing but beggar my neighbour, Miss."

"Beggar him," said Miss Havisham to Estella. So we sat down to cards.

It was then I began to understand that everything in the room had stopped, like the watch and the clock a long time ago. I noticed that Miss Havisham put down the jewel exactly on the spot from which she had taken it up. As Estella dealt the cards, I glanced at the dressing-table again, and saw that the shoe upon it, once white, now yellow, had never been worn. I glanced down at the foot from which the shoe was absent, and saw that the silk stocking on it, once white, now yellow, had been trodden ragged. Without this arrest of everything, this standing still of all the pale decayed objects, not even the withered bridal dress on the collapsed form could have looked so like grave-clothes, or the long veil so like a shroud.

So she sat, corpse-like, as we played at cards; the frillings and trimmings on her bridal dress, looking like earthy paper. I knew nothing then of the discoveries that are occasionally made of bodies buried in ancient times, which fall to powder in the moment of being distinctly seen; but, I have often thought since, that she must have looked as if the admission of the natural light of day would have struck her to dust.

"He calls the knaves, Jacks, this boy!" said Estella with disdain before our first game was out. "And what coarse hands he has! And what thick boots!"

I had never thought of being ashamed of my hands before; but I began to consider them a very indifferent pair. Her contempt for me was so strong, that it became infectious, and I caught it.

She won the game, and I dealt. I misdealt as was only natural, when I knew she was lying in wait for me to do wrong; and she denounced me for a stupid, clumsy labouring-boy.

"You say nothing of her," remarked Miss Havisham to me, as she looked on. "She says many hard things of you, but you say nothing of her. What do you think of her?"

"I don't like to say," I stammered.

"Tell me in my ear," said Miss Havisham, bending down.

"I think she is very proud," I replied in a whisper.

"Anything else?"

"I think she is very pretty."

"Anything else?"

"I think she is very insulting." (She was looking at me then, with a look of supreme aversion.)

"Anything else?"

"I think I should like to go home."

from **Middlemarch**

Novel by George Eliot

George Eliot

COMMON CORE

RL 3 Analyze the impact of the author's choices regarding how to develop and relate elements of a story. **RL 10** Read and comprehend literature, including stories.

BACKGROUND The works of Mary Ann Evans, who adopted the pen name George Eliot, mark the high point in English realism. George Eliot (1819–1880) was a moralist, yet she also introduced skepticism and a desire for progress into her works. For example, in many of her novels, Eliot wrote about women whose need for education and useful employment went sadly unmet in a patriarchal society. Her novel *Middlemarch* focuses on one such woman, Dorothea Brooke. Dorothea marries elderly scholar Edward Casaubon but is unhappy from the start. She gets much sympathy from Casaubon's young cousin, Will Ladislaw, but Casaubon is jealous of their friendship. His dying wish is that Dorothea not take Will as her second husband, and his will stipulates that Dorothea can inherit his wealth only if she does not marry Will. Wanting not to fuel local gossip or ruin Dorothea's prospects, Will decides to leave Middlemarch. In the following scene, he and Dorothea are saying goodbye.

TEXT ANALYSIS An offshoot of **realism, psychological fiction** focuses on the inner workings of a character's mind in a realistic, or true-to-life, way. As people often do in real life, fictional characters face moral dilemmas that may not allow them to state directly to others what they feel. When this happens, readers often must rely on elements other than dialogue to identify what a character does not verbally express. Important details in the scene, such as body language, the setting, and comments by the narrator can all reveal a character's true state of mind. In *Middlemarch,* for example, the forbidden love between Dorothea and Will prevents them from expressing their true feelings. In the excerpt that follows, Will tells Dorothea, "What I care more for than I can ever care for anything else is absolutely forbidden to me," but he fails to tell her that he loves her, even though he may never see her again.

DISCUSS In a small group, choose two specific examples from the excerpt that illustrate the difference between what the characters say and what they really feel. How does each character's choice of words help conceal his or her true feelings? What clues about the characters' true feelings can you gather from the narrator's comments? What do these narrative techniques add to the realism of the scene? Do they make the scene more believable or true-to-life? Explain.

FROM MIDDLEMARCH

*T*hey were wasting these last moments together in wretched silence. What could he say, since what had gone obstinately uppermost in his mind was the passionate love for her which he forbade himself to utter? What could she say, since she might offer him no help, since she was forced to keep the money that ought to have been his, since today he seemed not to respond as he used to do to her thorough trust and liking?

But Will at last turned away from his portfolio and approached the window again.

"I must go," he said with that peculiar look of the eyes which sometimes
10 accompanies bitter feeling, as if they had been tired and burned with gazing too close at a light.

"What shall you do in life?" said Dorothea timidly. "Have your intentions remained just the same as when we said good-bye before?"

"Yes," said Will in a tone that seemed to waive the subject as uninteresting. "I shall work away at the first thing that offers. I suppose one gets a habit of doing without happiness or hope."

"Oh, what sad words!" said Dorothea with a dangerous tendency to sob. Then trying to smile, she added, "We used to argue that we were alike in speaking too strongly."

20 "I have not spoken too strongly now," said Will, leaning back against the angle of the wall. "There are certain things which a man can only go through once in his life, and he must know some time or other that the best is over with him. This experience has happened to me while I am very young—that is all. What I care more for than I can ever care for anything else is absolutely forbidden to me; I don't mean merely by being out of my reach, but forbidden me, even if it were within my reach, by my own pride and honour, by everything I respect myself for. Of course I shall go on living as a man might do who has seen heaven in a trance."

Will paused, imagining that it would be impossible for Dorothea to misunderstand this; indeed he felt that he was contradicting himself and offending
30 against his self-approval in speaking to her so plainly; but still—it could not be fairly called wooing a woman to tell her that he would never woo her. It must be admitted to be a ghostly kind of wooing.

But Dorothea's mind was rapidly going over the past with quite another vision than his. The thought that she herself might be what Will most cared for did throb through her an instant, but then came doubt.

The Darling

Short Story by Anton Chekhov

COMMON CORE

RL 3 Analyze the impact of the author's choices regarding how to develop and relate elements of a story. **RL 4** Determine the meaning of words as they are used in the text, including connotative meanings. **RL 5** Analyze how an author's choices concerning how to structure specific parts of a text contribute to its overall structure and meaning. **SL 1** Initiate and participate effectively in a range of collaborative discussions. **L 4b** Identify and correctly use patterns of word changes that indicate different parts of speech.

DID YOU KNOW?

Anton Chekhov . . .

- was a gossip columnist early in his career.
- traveled 6,000 miles across Siberia to study living conditions in a prison colony.
- wrote several thousand letters, notable for their lively humor.

Meet the Author

Anton Chekhov 1860–1904

Like British writers Anthony Trollope and Elizabeth Gaskell, Anton Chekhov (chĕk′ôf) focused on the lives of ordinary people. But while these realist predecessors used conventional plot devices to structure their fiction, Chekhov organized his stories around the unfolding of character. He pioneered a subtle, naturalistic style—unsentimental and deceptively simple—that marked a radical departure from the dominant literary styles of 19th-century Russia.

Accidental Humorist Chekhov began publishing as a freelance journalist and humorist when he was in his 20s. To support his parents and siblings after his father went bankrupt, he wrote brief comic sketches for several Russian newspapers—while juggling medical school and a thriving social life as well. Chekhov's comic work proved so popular that by his late 20s, his "lowbrow" works were already more numerous than all of his later works combined.

A Serious Turn Russian editors and readers accepted the lack of political or moral philosophy in Chekhov's comic sketches. However, as he began to publish more serious work, some critics denounced it as ambiguous

and "unprincipled" writing. Chekhov resented these attempts to force ideology into his work, insisting that the purpose of his writing was neither to entertain nor to philosophize, but to present life as honestly as possible. His short stories and plays, such as *Uncle Vanya, The Three Sisters,* and *The Cherry Orchard,* illustrate his commitment to this approach.

Lasting Influence Despite his apolitical stance, Chekhov was a deeply moral person, beloved by his friends for his humor and optimism. Colleagues were drawn to his earnest, down-to-earth personality, and he spent much of his time mentoring and encouraging other writers. In 1897, Chekhov learned that he had tuberculosis after he suffered a lung hemorrhage. Although he tried to conceal his illness, he was forced to adopt the lifestyle of a partial invalid, which limited his ability to participate in the intellectual culture he so enjoyed. Though critically ill, Chekhov fell in love with Olga Knipper, an actress appearing in his plays. They married in 1901, just a few years before his death. Today, he is considered one of the fathers of modern short fiction and drama, and his work remains a prime example of naturalism.

Author Online

Go to thinkcentral.com. KEYWORD: HML12-1014

THINK central

● TEXT ANALYSIS: NATURALISM

Naturalism, an offshoot of realism, emerged in Europe during the 1870s. Like the realists, naturalists depicted ordinary life, although usually from a more pessimistic viewpoint. Typical elements of naturalist fiction include

- detached, objective **narration** that conveys observations without moral judgments
- **characters** who are driven by forces they cannot control, such as instinct, personality, or environment
- skepticism about traditional ideals and values, such as faith, love, and progress
- avoidance of conventional **plot** devices

As you read this story, notice how Chekhov weaves these elements into his subtle, understated style.

● READING STRATEGY: ANALYZE PLOT STRUCTURE

To analyze a plot's **structure,** you examine how its content is organized. Chekhov organized "The Darling" as a series of **parallel episodes,** or a sequence of repeated actions. Parallel episodes are often found in folk tales, such as "The Three Little Pigs." In this story, Chekhov uses the repetitive structure to emphasize the main character's patterns of behavior. As you read, watch for patterns of repetition and consider what they reveal about Olga's character traits.

▲ VOCABULARY IN CONTEXT

Chekhov used these words to portray a woman in love. Complete each sentence with an appropriate word from the list.

WORD LIST	apathetically	naive	surmise
	capricious	ominous	unctuous
	inscrutable	prostrate	

1. A(n) _____ clap of thunder warned of the coming storm.
2. The _____ student was easily tricked.
3. It was easy to _____ what had happened.
4. No one could interpret her _____ smile.
5. He would _____ himself in an effort to appease her anger.

 Complete the activities in your **Reader/Writer Notebook**.

Can you be too AGREEABLE?

Most people enjoy being with someone who is agreeable and easy to get along with. Unfortunately, it's possible to get too much of a good thing. When does the desire to please others become a minus instead of a plus?

DISCUSS List three advantages of being agreeable and three ways this quality could work against you. Based on your answers, do you consider being agreeable to be more positive or negative as a character trait?

Pros	Cons
• attracts friends easily	• gets taken advantage of
•	•
•	•

The DARLING Anton Chekhov

Analyze Visuals ▶
What details in this portrait reflect traditional feminine characteristics?

Olga, the daughter of the retired middle-grade civil servant Plemyannikov,[1] was sitting on the steps of her house leading to the yard, lost in thought. It was a hot day. The flies were making an awful nuisance of themselves, and it was pleasant to think that evening was not far off. Dark rain clouds were gathering in the east, and from time to time there came a breath of moisture in the air from that direction.

Kukin,[2] manager and proprietor of the amusement park Tivoli, who lived in a wing of the house, was standing in the middle of it and looking at the sky.

"Again!" he cried in despair. "It's going to rain again! Every day it rains, every day, as though on purpose! It's the end! It's ruin! Terrible losses every day!"

10   He threw up his hands in despair, and turning to Olga he went on:

"That's what my life is like, my dear Olga. Enough to make you weep. You work, you do your best, you wear yourself out, you lie awake at night, always thinking how to improve things—and what happens? On the one hand, the public—ignorant savages. I give them the best musical comedies, dramatized fairy stories, first-class comics, but do you think they want it? Do they appreciate it? All they want is sideshows! All they ask for is vulgarity! On the other hand, look at the weather! Almost every day it rains. It started coming down in buckets on the tenth of May and it rained the whole of May and June. It's simply awful! No business, but I have to pay the rent just the same, haven't I? Paying the actors, aren't I?"

20   The next evening the clouds gathered again, and Kukin cried, laughing hysterically:

"Well, what do I care? Let it rain! Let it flood the park, damn me! Damn my luck in this world and the next! Let the actors sue me! I don't mind going to court. I don't mind going to prison! To Siberia![3] To the scaffold! Ha, ha, ha!"

The next day the same thing. . . . **Ⓐ**

Olga listened to Kukin in silence. She looked serious, and sometimes tears started in her eyes. In the end Kukin's misfortunes touched her and she fell in love with him. He was small and thin, with a yellow face, his curly hair combed back at the temples;

Ⓐ NATURALISM
Reread lines 6–24. Consider the techniques Chekhov uses to reveal Kukin's character traits. What details does the narrator state directly? What can you infer about Kukin from his dialogue?

---

1. **Plemyannikov** (plyĭm-yä′nĭ-kôf′).
2. **Kukin** (kü′kĭn).
3. **Siberia** (sī-bîr′ē-ə): a notoriously cold region in Russia, south of the Arctic Circle and stretching from the Ural Mountains to the Pacific Ocean, that was used as a place of exile for political prisoners.

An Auburn Beauty, Alexis Harlamoff.
© Christie's Images/Corbis.

he spoke in a thin falsetto,[4] and when he talked his mouth became twisted; his face always wore an expression of profound despair; and yet he aroused a deep and genuine feeling in her. She was always in love with someone and could not live without it. When she was a young girl she had loved her daddy, who now sat in a darkened room in an invalid chair, gasping for breath; she had loved her auntie, who sometimes used to come to visit them twice a year from Bryansk;[5] earlier still, as a schoolgirl, she had been in love with her French master.[6] She was a quiet, good-natured, compassionate girl, with gentle, soft eyes and excellent health. Looking at her full rosy cheeks, her soft white neck with a dark mole on it, her kind, **naive** smile, which came into her face when she listened to anything pleasant, men thought "Yes, you'll do!" and also smiled, while women visitors could not restrain themselves from catching hold of her hand suddenly in the middle of a conversation and declaring in a transport of delight: "Oh, you darling!" **B**

The house in which she had lived since she was born and which was left to her in her father's will was on the outskirts of the town in Gypsy Lane, not far from the Tivoli; in the evenings and at night she could hear the band playing in the park, the hissing and banging of the fireworks, and she could not help thinking that it was Kukin fighting with his fate and taking his chief enemy—the public—by storm; her heart thrilled at the thought, she did not feel like sleeping at all, and when he came back home early in the morning, she tapped softly at her bedroom window and, showing him only her face and one shoulder through the curtains, smiled tenderly at him. . . .

He proposed to her and they were married. And when he had had a good look at her neck and her robust, plump shoulders, he threw up his hands and said:

"Oh, you darling!"

He was happy, but as it never stopped raining on his wedding day and on his wedding night, the expression of despair never left his face.

They lived well after their wedding. She sat in the box office, saw that everything in the park was in excellent order, kept an account of the expenses, and paid the wages. Her rosy cheeks and her charming, naive, radiant smile could be seen now at the box-office window, now behind the scenes, now in the refreshment bar. And already she was telling her friends that the theater was the most remarkable, the most important, and the most necessary thing in the world, and that it was only in the theater that one could obtain true enjoyment and become truly educated and humane.

"But," she added, "do you think the public realizes this? All they want is a sideshow! Yesterday we gave *Faust Inside Out,* and almost all the boxes were empty. But if Vanya and I had put on some vulgar rubbish, then, I assure you, the theater would have been packed. Tomorrow Vanya and I are putting on *Orpheus in Hell.* Do come."

Whatever Kukin said about the theater and the actors she repeated. Like him, she despised the public for their ignorance and indifference to art, interfered at the rehearsals, corrected the actors, looked after the good behavior of the musicians; and when a bad notice appeared in the local paper, she cried and then went to the editorial office to demand an explanation.

The actors were fond of her and nicknamed her "Vanya and I" and "darling"; she was sorry for them, lent them small sums of money, and if they happened to deceive her she did not complain to her husband but only shed a few tears in secret.

naive (nī-ēv′) *adj.* simple; innocent or unworldly

B NATURALISM
Reread lines 31–34. What do these details reveal about Olga?

---

4. **falsetto** (fôl-sĕt′ō): a voice that sounds unnaturally high in pitch.

5. **Bryansk** (brē-änsk′): a city in western Russia, southwest of Moscow.

6. **master:** teacher.

In winter too they lived well. They rented the theater in the town for the winter season and let it for short periods to a Ukrainian company, to a conjurer, or to local amateurs. Olga was growing stouter and was always beaming with pleasure, while Kukin grew thinner and yellower and complained of their terrible losses, although they had not done at all badly all the winter. He coughed at night, and she made him drink hot raspberry tea and lime-flower water, rubbed him with eau de cologne and wrapped him in her soft shawls.

80 "Oh, my sweet," she used to say with complete sincerity, stroking his hair. "Oh, my handsome one!"

During Lent[7] he left for Moscow to engage actors, and she could not sleep without him. She sat at the window and gazed at the stars. All that time she compared herself to the hens who also cannot sleep at night and feel uneasy when the cock is not in the hen house. Kukin had to stay longer in Moscow; he wrote that he would be back at Easter and was already giving instructions in his letters about the Tivoli. But late at night on the Sunday before Easter there was an **ominous** knocking at the gate. Someone was hammering on the gate as though on a barrel: boom! boom! boom! The sleepy cook ran to open the gate, splashing through the puddles with her bare feet.

90 "Open up, please," someone was saying in a hollow voice. "There's a telegram for you."

Olga was used to getting telegrams from her husband, but this time for some reason she was paralyzed with fear. With shaking hands she opened the telegram, and read as follows: "Kukin died suddenly today stop metely awaiting instructions stop guneral tuesday."

That was how it was actually written in the telegram, "guneral,"[8] and some incomprehensible word, "metely." It was signed by the producer of the operetta company.

"Oh, my darling!" Olga sobbed. "My sweet little Vanya, my darling! Why did
100 I ever meet you? Why did I know you and love you? Who have you left your poor unhappy Olga to?"

Kukin was buried in Moscow on Tuesday. Olga returned home on Wednesday, and as soon as she got into her bedroom she flung herself on the bed and sobbed so loudly that it could be heard in the street and in the neighboring yards.

"The darling!" the neighbors said, crossing themselves. "Poor darling, how she does take on!"

Three months later Olga was returning home from mass, heartbroken and in deep mourning. It so happened that one of her neighbors, Vasily Andreyich Pustovalov, who was also returning home from church, walked beside her. Pustovalov, the
110 manager of the merchant Babakayev's[9] timber yard, who wore a straw hat, a white waistcoat, and a gold watch chain, looked more like a land owner than a business man.

"Everything," he said gravely, with a note of compassion in his voice, "happens according to the natural order of things. If any of your dear ones dies, it is because it is the will of God. In such a case we must be brave and bear our cross without a murmur."

---

ominous (ŏm'ə-nəs) *adj.* threatening

COMMON CORE RL 4

Language Coach

Word Definitions In line 94, *stop* means "period." Telegraphs use Morse code, a series of dots and dashes. To avoid confusion, a stop—which looks like a dot—is spelled out. How do the telegram's stops and strange words affect this scene's tone?

---

7. **Lent:** the 40 weekdays from Ash Wednesday until Easter, observed by Christians as a period of fasting and repentence.

8. **"guneral":** In the original Russian version of the story, the misprint for *funeral* looks like the Russian word meaning "to laugh."

9. **Vasily Andreyich Pustovalov** (vəs′yēl′yəĭ ən-dryā′yĭch′ püs-tō′vä-lôf′) . . . **Babakeyev's** (bä-bä′ kä-yĕfs′).

Portrait of Ilya Efimovich Repin (1876), Ivan Nikolaevich Kramskoy. Oil on canvas, 102 cm × 70 cm.
Tretyakov Gallery, Moscow. © Bridgeman Art Library.

After seeing Olga to her gate, he said goodbye and walked on. All day afterwards she could hear his grave voice and she had only to shut her eyes to see his dark beard. She liked him very much. And apparently she had made an impression on him too, for a few days later an elderly woman whom she did not know very well came to have a cup of coffee with her, and as soon as she sat down at the table she began talking about Pustovalov. According to her, he was a most excellent man, whom one could depend on and whom any girl would be glad to marry. Three days later Pustovalov paid her a visit himself. He did not stay long, about ten minutes, and did not say much, but Olga fell in love with him so passionately that she did not sleep a wink all night, tossing about as though in a fever; and in the morning she sent for the elderly woman. Soon they were engaged, and then came the wedding.

After their marriage Pustovalov and Olga lived happily together. He was usually at his office till dinner time, then he went out on business and his place at the office was taken by Olga, who was there till the evening, making out accounts and seeing to the delivery of the goods.

"The price of timber," she would say to her acquaintances and customers, "rises twenty per cent every year now. Why, we used to sell local timber, and now every year my Vasily has to go for timber to the Mogilyov province.[10] And the freight!" she cried, covering her cheeks with her hands in horror. "The freight!" **C**

It seemed to her that she had been in the timber business for years, and that the most important and necessary thing in life was timber; and there was something dearly familiar and touching to her in the sound of the words beam, block, board, balk, plank, slat, scantling, batten, slab.[11] . . . At night, when she was asleep, she
140 dreamt of mountains of planks and boards, long, endless strings of wagons carting timber somewhere far from the town; she dreamt of a whole regiment of six-inch beams, twenty-eight feet high, standing on end and marching on the timber yard; beams, logs, and boards knocking against each other with the resounding crash of dry wood, falling and getting up again and piling themselves on each other. Olga cried out in her sleep, and Pustovalov said to her tenderly:

"What's the matter, Olga darling? Cross yourself, my dear."

Her husband's ideas were her ideas. If he thought the room was too hot or business was slack, she thought the same. Her husband did not care for any diversions and spent the holidays at home. She did the same.
150 "Why are you always at home or at the office?" her friends asked her. "Why don't you go to the theater, darling, or to the circus?"

"Vasily and I have no time to go to the theater," she replied gravely. "We are working folk. We can't waste time on all sorts of nonsense. What's the good of theaters?" **D**

On Saturdays Pustovalov and Olga used to go to evening service, on holy days to early mass, and they walked side by side on the way back from church, an **unctuous** expression on their faces. There was a nice smell about both of them, and her silk dress rustled pleasantly. At home they drank tea with buns and various jams, and afterwards they ate pie. Every day at noon there was a lovely smell of beetroot soup and roast mutton or duck in the yard and in the street near the gate, and of fish on
160 fast days, and it was impossible to walk past the gate without feeling hungry. At the office the samovar[12] was always on the boil, and customers were treated to tea and ring-shaped rolls. Once a week husband and wife went to the baths and returned side by side, both red in the face.

"Oh, we're very happy, thank God," Olga used to say to her acquaintances. "God grant everyone such a life!" **E**

When Pustovalov was away buying timber in the Mogilyov province, Olga missed him very much and lay awake at night and cried. A young army veterinary surgeon called Smirnin, who rented the cottage in the yard, sometimes came to see her in the evenings. He used to tell her all sorts of stories and played cards with her, and this
170 used to divert her. His stories of his private life were particularly interesting; he was married and had a son, but was separated from his wife, who had been unfaithful to him, and now he hated her and sent her forty roubles[13] a month for the maintenance of their son. Hearing this, Olga sighed and shook her head. She was sorry for him.

---

10. **Mogilyov** (mə-gǐ-lyôf′) **province:** a part of the eastern European nation of Belarus that at the time of the story was controlled by Russia; often spelled *Mogilev*.

11. **beam . . . slab:** jargon associated with the wood or timber industry. A balk is a roughly cut piece of timber; a scantling is a small beam; a batten is a sawed strip of wood.

12. **samovar** (săm′ə-vär′): a metal urn with an inner tube for heating water, used in Russia to make tea.

13. **roubles** (rōō′bəlz): Russian money; usually spelled *rubles*.

C PLOT STRUCTURE
Compare lines 128–135 with lines 54–64. What pattern of repeated actions do these examples establish?

D PLOT STRUCTURE
Explain what is **ironic** about Olga's comment in lines 152–153. How does Chekhov's use of parallel episodes call attention to this irony?

unctuous
(ŭngk′chōō-əs) *adj.*
excessively or insincerely earnest; smug

E NATURALISM
Compare lines 154–165 with lines 49–53. In what ways do these descriptions differ from conventional portrayals of love?

"Well, God preserve you," she used to say, seeing him off to the stairs with a lighted candle. "Thank you for helping me to while away the time, and may the Lord and the Mother of God keep you in good health."

And she always expressed herself with the utmost gravity and soberness, in imitation of her husband. Before the veterinary surgeon disappeared downstairs behind the door, she used to say:

180 "I think you really ought to make it up with your wife, Mr. Smirnin. You ought to forgive her, if only for the sake of your son. I suppose the poor little boy understands everything."

When Pustovalov came back, she told him in a low voice all about the veterinary surgeon and his unhappy family life, and both of them, owing to some strange association of ideas, went down on their knees before the icons,[14] **prostrating** themselves and praying that God should give them children.

The Pustovalovs lived like that in peace and quiet, in love and complete concord, for six years. But one winter day, after drinking hot tea at the office, Vasily went out into the yard without his cap to see to the loading of some timber, caught a cold, and 190 was taken ill. He was attended by the best doctors, but his illness did not respond to treatment and he died after having been ill for four months. And Olga was once more a widow.

"Who have you left me to, my darling?" she sobbed, after burying her husband. "How can I live without you, unhappy wretch that I am! Take pity on me, good people, left with no one in the world to care for me!"

She went about in a black dress with long *pleureuses,*[15] and gave up wearing a hat and gloves for good. She seldom went out of the house, except to go to church or to pay a visit to her husband's grave, leading the secluded life of a nun. It was not till six months later that she took off the *pleureuses* and opened the shutters of the windows. 200 Sometimes she could even be seen in the morning, but how she lived and what went on in her house no one really knew. People did **surmise** something from the fact that they could see her, for instance, having tea in her garden with the veterinary surgeon, who read the newspaper to her, and also from the fact that on meeting a woman she knew at the post office she said:

"We haven't any proper veterinary inspection in our town, and that's why there are so many illnesses about. One is always hearing of people falling ill from drinking milk or catching some illness from horses and cows. One really ought to take as much care of the health of animals as of the health of people."

She was repeating the veterinary surgeon's ideas and now she was of the same 210 opinion as he about everything. It was clear that she could not live a single year without some attachment and that she had found new happiness in the wing of her own house. Anyone else would have been condemned for that, but no one could think ill of Olga, for everything about her was so natural. Neither she nor the veterinary surgeon said anything to anyone about the change in their relationship. They tried to conceal it, but without success, for Olga could not keep a secret. When she handed round tea or served supper to his visitors, fellow officers of his regiment, she would begin talking about foot-and-mouth disease or tuberculosis among the cattle, or about the municipal slaughter houses, while he looked terribly embarrassed; and after the visitors had gone he would seize her by the arm and hiss angrily:

prostrate (prŏs'trāt') *v.* to lie with the face down, as in prayer or submission

surmise (sər-mīz') *v.* to make a guess

---

14. **icons:** in the Eastern Orthodox Church, sacred pictures of Jesus, Mary, the saints, or other holy figures.

15. *pleureuses* (plœ-rœz') *French:* the white bands worn on the cuffs of mourning clothes.

220 "I've told you a hundred times not to talk about something you don't understand. When we vets are talking among ourselves, please don't interfere. Why, it's just silly!"

She would look at him with astonishment. "But what am I to talk about, darling?" she would ask him in dismay.

And she would embrace him with tears in her eyes, imploring him not to be angry with her, and they were both happy.

This happiness, however, did not last long. The veterinary surgeon left with his regiment, left for good, for the regiment had been transferred somewhere very far away, almost as far as Siberia; and poor Olga was left alone.

Now she was absolutely alone. Her father had long been dead, and his armchair lay
230 in the loft covered with dust and minus one leg. She grew thinner and not so good-looking, and people meeting her in the street no longer gazed at her as before and did not smile at her; her best years were apparently over, left behind her, and now a new kind of life was beginning, an **inscrutable** kind of life that did not bear thinking about. In the evening poor Olga sat on the front steps and she could hear the music in the Tivoli gardens and the banging of fireworks, but this no longer stirred up any thoughts in her mind. She gazed **apathetically** at her empty yard, thinking of nothing, desiring nothing, and afterwards, after nightfall, she went to bed and saw nothing but her empty yard in her dreams. She ate and drank as though against her will.

240 But the main thing, and what was worst of all, was that she had no opinions of any kind. She saw all sorts of things around her and she understood everything that was happening around, but she could form no opinions about anything and did not know what to talk about. Oh, how dreadful it is not to have any opinions! You see a bottle, for instance, or the rain, or a peasant, and you cannot say what they are there for, and you could not say it even for a thousand roubles. When married to Kukin or to Pustovalov, or when living with the vet, Olga could have explained everything and would have expressed an opinion about anything you like, but there was the same emptiness in her thoughts and in her heart as in her yard. And it was as frightening and as bitter as if she had supped on wormwood.[16]

250 The town was gradually spreading in all directions. Gypsy Lane was already called a street, and where the Tivoli and the timber yard had been there were houses and a whole row of side streets. How quickly time flies! Olga's house grew dingy, its roof got rusty, the shed rickety, and the whole yard was overgrown with weeds and stinging nettles. Olga herself had aged terribly and had lost her good looks; in summer she sat on the steps, and as before she felt empty and bored and there was a bitter taste in her mouth; and in winter she sat at the window and looked at the snow. When spring was in the air or when the sound of church bells came floating on the wind, she would be suddenly overwhelmed by memories of her past, a delightful thrill would shoot through her heart and a flood of tears gush out of her eyes; but
260 that lasted only for a short time, and then there was the same feeling of emptiness and again she wondered what she was living for. Her black cat Bryska rubbed against her, purring softly, but Olga remained unmoved by these feline caresses. It was something else she wanted. What she wanted was a love that would seize her whole being, her whole mind and soul, that would give her ideas, an aim in life, and would warm her aging blood. And she would shake the cat off her skirt and say with vexation:

"Go away, go away . . . I don't want you!"

---

inscrutable
(ĭn-skrōō'tə-bəl) *adj.*
difficult to understand

apathetically
(ăp'ə-thĕt'ĭk-lē) *adv.*
without interest or feeling; indifferently

COMMON CORE L 4b

Language Coach

Roots and Affixes An affix at the end of a word is a **suffix.** The suffix *-ation* added to a verb forms a noun. What word in line 265 is a form of *vex*? What does it mean?

---

16. **wormwood:** a plant that yields a bitter extract, sometimes used to flavor wine.

And so it went on, day after day, year after year—no joy of any kind and nothing to express an opinion about. Whatever her cook Mavra said was all right with her.

Late in the afternoon one hot July day, just as the herd of cattle was being driven along the street and the whole yard was full of dust, someone suddenly knocked at the gate. Olga went to open it herself, and she gazed thunderstruck at the visitor; it was Smirnin, the veterinary surgeon. His hair had gone quite grey and he wore civilian clothes. She suddenly remembered everything and, unable to restrain herself, burst into tears and put her head on his chest without uttering a word; and in her great excitement she never noticed how they both went into the house or how they sat down to tea.

"Oh, my dear," she murmured, trembling with joy, "what has brought you here?"

"I'd like to settle here for good," said the vet. "I've resigned from the army, and I've come to try my luck as my own master and open a practice of my own. Besides, it's time for my son to go to a secondary school. He's a big boy now. I've made it up with my wife, you know."

"Where is she?" asked Olga.

"She's at the hotel with our son. I'm looking for a flat."[17]

"But, good heavens, why not take my house? It's a good enough place to live in. I won't charge you any rent!" cried Olga excitedly and burst into tears again. "You can live here, the cottage will do nicely for me. Oh dear, I'm so happy!"

Next day the roof was already being painted and the walls whitewashed and Olga, arms akimbo, was walking about the yard giving orders. Her face lit up with her old smile, she brightened up and looked younger, as though she had awakened from a long sleep. The vet's wife arrived—a thin, plain woman with short hair and a **capricious** expression. With her was her little boy, Sasha, small for his age (he was nine years old), with bright blue eyes, chubby, and with dimples in his cheeks. As soon as the boy walked into the yard he ran after the cat, and immediately the place resounded with his gay, joyful laughter.

"Is that your cat, auntie?" he asked Olga. "When she has kittens, let's have one, please. Mummy is terribly afraid of mice."

Olga had a long talk with him, gave him tea, and her heart suddenly went out to him just as though he were her own son. And when he sat in the dining room in the evening doing his homework, she looked at him with great tenderness and pity and whispered:

"My darling, my pretty one. . . . Oh, my sweet child, so clever, and so fair . . ."

"An island," he read, "is a piece of land surrounded on all sides by water."

"An island is a piece of land . . ." she repeated, and this was the first opinion she had expressed with absolute conviction after so many years of silence and complete vacancy of mind.

She already had her own opinions and at supper she talked to Sasha's parents about how difficult children found it at secondary schools, but that a classical education was much better than a technical one for all that, for with a classical education all careers were open to you—you could be a doctor if you wished, or an engineer if you preferred it.

Sasha began going to school. His mother went on a visit to her sister in Kharkov[18] and did not return; his father went off every day somewhere to inspect cattle and

capricious (kə-prĭsh′əs) *adj.* impulsive or unpredictable

---

17. **flat:** an apartment.
18. **Kharkov** (kär′kôf′): a city in Ukraine.

Village Boy (1890), N. P. Bogdanov-Belsky. © akg-images.

was often away from home for three whole days. Olga could not help feeling that the poor boy had been completely abandoned, that no one cared for him, that he was dying of hunger, and so she took him to live with her in the cottage and made him comfortable there in a little room of his own.

For six months Sasha had been living with her in the cottage. Every morning she came into his room and found him fast asleep with his hand under his cheek, breathing inaudibly. She did not feel like waking him.

320   "Sasha dear," she would say sadly, "get up, darling. Time to go to school."

He got up, dressed, said a prayer, then sat down to breakfast, drinking three cups of tea and eating two large buns and half a buttered French loaf. He was only half awake and consequently in a bad mood.

"I don't think you really know your fable by heart, Sasha," said Olga, looking at him as though she were seeing him off on a long journey. "You're such a worry to me, dear. You must try and do your lessons well, darling. Obey your teachers."

"Oh, leave me alone," Sasha said.

Then he walked down the street to school, a little fellow but in a big cap and with a satchel on his back. Olga followed him noiselessly.

330 "Sa-a-sha!" she called after him.

He looked round, and she thrust a date or a caramel into his hand. When they turned into the street where his school was he would feel ashamed of being followed by a tall, stout woman.

"You'd better go home, auntie," he said. "I can go the rest of the way by myself."

She would stop and follow him with her unblinking eyes till he had disappeared in the entrance of the school. Oh, how she doted on him! Of all her former attachments not one had been so deep. Never before had her soul submitted so entirely, so selflessly, and with such delight as now, when her maternal instincts were getting a more and more powerful hold on her. For this little boy, to whom she was not related
340 in any way, for the dimples in his cheeks, for his school cap, she would have given her whole life, she would have given it gladly and with tears of tenderness. Why? Who can tell why? **F**

Having seen Sasha off to school, she would return home quietly, contented, at peace with herself, brimming over with love; her face, which had grown younger during the last six months, smiled and shone with pleasure. People who met her in the street could not help feeling pleased.

"Good morning, Olga darling! How are you, darling?"

"They make you work hard at school nowadays," she would tell them at the market. "It's no joke! They gave my boy, who is in the first form,[19] a fable to learn by heart, a
350 Latin translation, and a problem. How do they expect a little boy to do all that?"

And she would start talking about the teachers, the lessons, the school books, repeating what Sasha had said about them.

At three o'clock they had their dinner, in the evening they did his homework together and cried. When she put him to bed, she would make the sign of the cross over him for a long time and would whisper a prayer; then, when she went to bed herself, she would dream of the far away misty future when Sasha, having finished his studies, would become a doctor or an engineer, would have a big house of his own, horses, a carriage, would get married and have children. . . . She would fall asleep, thinking of the same things, and tears would run down her cheeks from her closed
360 eyes. Her black cat lay purring at her side: "Purr . . . purr . . . purr . . ."

Suddenly there would be a loud knock at the front gate. Olga would wake up, breathless with terror, her heart pounding violently. Half a minute later another knock.

"It's a telegram from Kharkov," she thought, beginning to tremble all over. "It must be Sasha's mother sending for him. Oh, dear!" She was in despair. Her head, feet, and hands would turn cold, and she could not help feeling that she was the most unhappy woman in the world. But a minute later she would hear voices: it was the veterinary surgeon coming home from the club.

"Well, thank God!" she would think. **G**

370 The weight was gradually lifted from her heart and she felt at ease again; she went back to bed, thinking of Sasha, who was sleeping soundly in the next room and crying out in his sleep from time to time:

"I'll give you one! Get out! Don't hit me!" ❧

Translated by David Magarshack

---

19. **first form:** the first grade of secondary school.

Comprehension

1. **Recall** Why does Olga's first marriage end?

2. **Summarize** What happens to Olga after the veterinary surgeon is transferred?

3. **Clarify** Why does Olga end up caring for Sasha?

Text Analysis

4. **Make Inferences** Reread lines 353–373. Describe Olga's and Sasha's state of mind in this concluding passage. Why might Chekhov have chosen to end the story on this note?

5. **Analyze Structure** Describe the pattern that characterizes Olga's relationships. What message about Olga's personality is illustrated through Chekhov's use of **parallel episodes?**

6. **Analyze Tone** Chekhov's tone, or his attitude toward his subject, varies throughout the story. Consider how he portrays Olga in each of the following passages. In each case, what attitude toward Olga does Chekhov convey?

   - description of Kukin (lines 25–30)
   - Pustovalov's courtship (lines 123–127)
   - description of Olga (lines 254–262)
   - Olga's feelings for Sasha (lines 335–342)

7. **Examine Naturalism** How does the plot structure and character-driven storytelling of Chekhov's story reflect the influence of naturalism? Explain your answers.

8. **Make Judgments** Consider what you learn about Olga's relationships and what motivates them. In your opinion, do her attachments qualify as true love? Explain your answer.

Text Criticism

9. **Critical Interpretations** Critic Robert Lynd described Chekhov as "something of a pessimist, but a pessimist who does not despair." Do you agree or disagree with this comment? Cite details from the story in your answer.

Can you be too AGREEABLE?

Olga is very agreeable, which seems to be a redeeming trait, but what kinds of problems does it create for her? What are other examples of traits that are usually deemed positive, but can become negative if taken to extremes?

COMMON CORE

RL1 Cite strong and thorough textual evidence to support inferences drawn from the text. RL3 Analyze the impact of the author's choices regarding how to develop and relate elements of a story. RL4 Analyze the impact of specific word choices on tone. RL5 Analyze how an author's choices concerning how to structure specific parts of a text contribute to its overall structure and meaning.

Vocabulary in Context

▲ VOCABULARY PRACTICE

Test your knowledge of the vocabulary words by answering these questions.

WORD LIST

apathetically

capricious

inscrutable

naive

ominous

prostrate

surmise

unctuous

1. Is a **capricious** person greedy or impulsive?
2. Which part of a movie is more **ominous,** closing credits or scary background music?
3. Is an **unctuous** person nervous or self-satisfied?
4. When you **surmise,** do you guess or wait to learn the facts?
5. Is an **inscrutable** facial expression clear or puzzling?
6. Would someone behaving **apathetically** yell or shrug?
7. Which is more **naive,** trusting a stranger or opening a bank account?
8. When you **prostrate** yourself, are you standing upright or lying down?

ACADEMIC VOCABULARY IN WRITING

> • analyze   • dominate   • impact   • resource   • scheme

Olga relies on her husbands and finally a small boy as the main **resources** she draws on to define herself. How do we rely on other people to define ourselves? Use two of the Academic Vocabulary words to respond to this question.

VOCABULARY STRATEGY: CONTRASTS AS CONTEXT CLUES

A **contrast,** or opposite, is a type of context clue. Terms like *but, however, unlike,* and *while* are clue words that point to a contrast. Other context clues may suggest the word's **nuance,** or shades of meaning.

> **EXAMPLE**
>
> Some students learned classical subjects, studying <u>literature, history, and Latin</u>, while others received <u>technical</u> training.

The clue word *while* points to a contrast. The underlined word, *technical,* is an **antonym,** or opposite, of *classical.* The double-underlined text supplies the nuance of *classical,* suggesting topics that would be part of a classical education.

PRACTICE Use context clues to determine the antonym of each boldface word below. Underline the clues in items 2 and 4 that tell you the word's nuance.

1. Weary of conflict, the former foes determined to achieve **concord,** putting aside all differences to find common ground.
2. The widow lived a **secluded** life, seldom taking part in public events.
3. Unlike Greta, whose **convictions** about the vote were firm, Jorge had doubts.
4. Rafi felt neglected even though his aunt **doted** on him, fulfilling every whim.

COMMON CORE

L 4a Use context as a clue to the meaning of a word.

Interactive Vocabulary **THINK** central

Go to **thinkcentral.com.**
KEYWORD: HML12-1028

Fiction as Social Teaching

Times of social upheaval invariably raise a great deal of concern about a society's moral health. As values and customs shift in response to changing times, some people see these shifts as cracks in the society's moral foundation. Changes cause many to reflect closely on social behavior and think seriously about what is right and what is wrong. The late 19th century in England was just such a time.

Realism in Victorian fiction developed very much in response to social and moral concerns. Novelists such as Charles Dickens and George Eliot exposed moral corruption and other social ills through elaborate tales and well-developed characters. Depicting everyday life in realistic detail, these and other authors devoted a great deal of attention to their characters' motivations and behaviors.

With the rise of a literate middle class came an audience hungry for such tales. Eager to read about middle-class characters struggling with everyday problems, these readers looked for opportunities to reflect on their own moral lives and decisions.

Writing to Reflect

George Eliot once wrote, "Our deeds determine us, as much as we determine our deeds." In light of this statement, consider the major characters in Anthony Trollope's "Malachi's Cove" and Elizabeth Cleghorn Gaskell's "Christmas Storms and Sunshine." Could it be said that their deeds determine who they are? Choose a major character from either story and write an essay in which you reflect on Eliot's statement as it relates to this character. As you write, think about the moral commentary delivered by the story.

Consider

- the moral dilemma faced by the character
- the character's final behavior
- the outcome of this behavior

Extension

VIEWING & REPRESENTING

It was not only literature that depicted the gritty, everyday realities of Victorian life. Photographers, too, turned their lenses to the street to document the lives of the working class in realistic detail. The photograph here shows female workers at an English factory, striking for the same wages as their male counterparts. What is the tone and message of this photograph? Write a brief analysis, citing details about the photograph's subject matter, light and shadow, and composition.

⌁ **COMMON CORE**

W 9 Draw evidence from literary or informational texts to support analysis and reflection.

Evidence of Progress
Critical Commentary by Thomas Babington Macaulay

The Condition of England
Critical Commentary by Thomas Carlyle

COMMON CORE **RI 1** Cite strong and thorough textual evidence to support analysis of what the text says explicitly as well as inferences drawn from the text, including determining where the text leaves matters uncertain. **RI 2** Determine two or more central ideas of a text. **RI 6** Determine an author's point of view or purpose in a text in which the rhetoric is particularly effective, analyzing how style and content contribute to the power, persuasiveness, or beauty of the text. **RI 9** Analyze documents of historical and literary significance for their themes, purposes, and rhetorical features. **SL 1c** Propel coversations by responding to questions that probe reasoning and evidence. **L 4b** Identify and correctly use patterns of word changes that indicate different parts of speech.

Meet the Authors

Thomas Babington Macaulay
1800–1859

Thomas Babington Macaulay read fluently at the age of three and wrote a complete history of the world at the age of seven. Yet, unlike many child prodigies, Macaulay was a happy, outgoing child. In keeping with his cheerful nature, the adult Macaulay adopted a rosy view of history in which social progress was an inevitable outcome.

Working for Reform Macaulay grew up in a suburb of London, where his father was a leader in the antislavery movement. After graduating from Cambridge University, Macaulay studied law and entered politics, winning his first seat in Parliament in 1830 and serving for four years on Britain's governing council in India. In 1857, to honor his years of service, Queen Victoria named him a baron.

Prolific Writer While in office, Macaulay published literary essays, biographical and historical sketches, and even a best-selling volume of poetry. Perhaps his best-known work is his *History of England.* Its precise, logical style set the standard for serious writing for decades after its publication.

Thomas Carlyle
1795–1881

Unlike Macaulay, Thomas Carlyle was a notorious pessimist who objected to Keats's poetry, democracy, and new technological developments in equal measure. He became one of the most prominent critics of the rampant materialism in Victorian society.

Rise to Fame As the son of a Scottish mason and poor farmer's daughter, Carlyle learned early in life to value thrift and hard work. After attending university in Edinburgh, he briefly taught mathematics while contributing articles to the *Edinburgh Encyclopaedia* and *London Magazine.* Soon he won fame with major works like the philosophical satire *Sartor Resartus* (The Tailor Retailored) and his *History of the French Revolution.*

A London Salon Carlyle married a charming, witty Scotswoman named Jane Welsh, and the couple moved to the Chelsea neighborhood of London. The Carlyle home on Cheyne Walk became a popular gathering place for leading writers and intellectuals of the day. Even Carlyle's critics read him thoroughly. "There is hardly a superior or active mind of this generation," said Victorian novelist George Eliot, "that has not been modified by Carlyle's writings."

TEXT ANALYSIS: PERSUASION

Writers use **persuasion** to convince readers about an issue. Common persuasive techniques include

- **logical appeals,** or arguments that use reasons and evidence to support a position
- **emotional appeals,** which create strong feelings, such as pity or fear, to influence readers' opinions
- **ethical appeals,** which invoke shared values and principles

As you read each essay, note which techniques lend more credibility to the authors' conclusions.

READING SKILL: RECOGNIZE IDEAS

Victorian writers used complex sentences filled with phrases, clauses, and modifiers. Use these strategies to sift through details and make subtle inferences about the important **ideas** in a sentence or paragraph:

- Clarify meaning by identifying the main subject and verb of a sentence. You may need to ignore some details.
- Watch for patterns in the text, such as repeated sentence structures, that the author uses to organize his thoughts.
- Once you identify the idea of a passage, reread it. Try to collect some of the details you initially overlooked.

As you read these essays, use a chart like the one shown to note the authors' key ideas and the details that support them.

Authors' Ideas	Supporting Details

▲ VOCABULARY IN CONTEXT

Restate each phrase, using a different word or phrase for the boldface term.

1. **debase** the currency until it is nearly worthless
2. to **prophesy** the final outcome
3. a **lucrative** business that provided good income
4. the angry frown that marked her **countenance**
5. to value **stoicism** rather than displays of emotion

 Complete the activities in your **Reader/Writer Notebook.**

How do we measure PROGRESS?

Think about how you would define social progress. For instance, does society improve through technological advances, by an increase in wealth, or by greater health and happiness among all people? Consider what social priorities each view of progress might suggest.

DEBATE As a class, think of different ways you might define progress. Then, break into small groups, with each group arguing for a different view. What are the pros and cons of each viewpoint?

EVIDENCE OF PROGRESS

Thomas Babington Macaulay

> **BACKGROUND** Industrialism brought sweeping changes to Victorian society. The invention of the steam engine in the 1780s helped create a new kind of workplace—the factory. The development of railways in the 1830s led to the growth of large industrial towns, where hundreds of thousands of workers migrated in search of work. Critics of industrialism focused on the plight of these workers. But other commentators celebrated the economic growth enabled by these technological advances. Macaulay, writing in 1830, found reasons for optimism in the midst of these rapid and unsettling changes.

History is full of the signs of [the] natural progress of society. We see in almost every part of the annals of mankind how the industry of individuals, struggling up against wars, taxes, famines, conflagrations, mischievous prohibitions, and more mischievous protections, creates faster than governments can squander, and repairs whatever invaders can destroy. We see the wealth of nations increasing, and all the arts of life approaching nearer and nearer to perfection, in spite of the grossest corruption and the wildest profusion on the part of rulers. **A**

The present moment is one of great distress. But how small will that distress appear when we think over the history of the last forty years; a war, compared with which all other wars sink into insignificance;[1] taxation, such as the most heavily taxed people of former times could not have conceived; a debt larger than all the public debts that ever existed in the world added together; the food of the people

Analyze Visuals ▶
In a caricature, exaggeration is used for comic or grotesque effect. What is comical or grotesque in this image of industrial progress?

A PERSUASION
Reread lines 1–7. Does Macaulay appeal more to **logic** or to **emotion** in this paragraph? Explain your answer.

---

1. **a war...insignificance:** the warfare with Revolutionary and Napoleonic France, which took place from 1792 to 1815.

Hyde Park As It Will Be (1840s), John Leech.
Hand-colored pen lithograph. Caricature. © NRM-Pictorial
Collection/Science and Society Picture Library.

studiously rendered dear; the currency imprudently **debased,** and imprudently restored. Yet is the country poorer than in 1790? We firmly believe that, in spite of all the misgovernment of her rulers, she has been almost constantly becoming richer and richer. Now and then there has been a stoppage, now and then a short retrogression; but as to the general tendency there can be no doubt. A single breaker may recede; but the tide is evidently coming in.

debase (dĭ-bās′) *v.* to lower in value, quality, or dignity; to cheapen

20   If we were to **prophesy** that in the year 1930 a population of fifty millions, better fed, clad, and lodged than the English of our time, will cover these islands, that Sussex and Huntingdonshire will be wealthier than the wealthiest parts of the West Riding of Yorkshire[2] now are, that cultivation, rich as that of a flower garden, will be carried up to the very tops of Ben Nevis and Helvellyn,[3] that machines constructed on principles yet undiscovered will be in every house, that there will be no highways but railroads, no traveling but by steam, that our debt, vast as it seems to us, will appear to our great-grandchildren a trifling encumbrance, which might easily be paid off in a year or two, many people would think us insane. We prophesy nothing; but this we say: If any person had told the Parliament which met in perplexity and terror after the crash in 1720[4] that

30 in 1830 the wealth of England would surpass all their wildest dreams, that the annual revenue would equal the principal of that debt which they considered as an intolerable burden, that for one man of ten thousand pounds then living there would be five men of fifty thousand pounds, that London would be twice as large and twice as populous, and that nevertheless the rate of mortality would have diminished to one-half of what it then was, that the post office would bring more into the exchequer than the excise and customs[5] had brought in together under Charles the Second,[6] that stage coaches would run from London to York in twenty-four hours, that men would be in the habit of sailing without wind, and would be beginning to ride without horses,[7] our ancestors would have given

40 as much credit to the prediction as they gave to *Gulliver's Travels.*[8] Yet the **B** prediction would have been true; and they would have perceived that it was not altogether absurd, if they had considered that the country was then raising every year a sum which would have purchased the fee-simple of the revenue of the Plantagenets,[9] ten times what supported the Government of Elizabeth, three times

prophesy (präf′ə-sī′) *v.* to predict (something) by or as if by divine guidance

B **RECOGNIZE IDEAS**
Reread lines 19–40. Notice how Macaulay creates **parallelism** by starting each subordinate clause with *that.* What two basic comparisons does Macaulay make in this passage?

---

2. **Sussex and Huntingdonshire ... West Riding of Yorkshire:** two former counties in southeastern England, and the western section of Yorkshire, a large county in northern England.

3. **Ben Nevis** (nĕ′vĭs) **and Helvellyn** (hĕl-vĕl′ən): mountains in Britain. Ben Nevis is located in Scotland; Helvellyn, in the Lake District of northwestern England.

4. **crash in 1720:** the financial crisis known as the South Sea Bubble, caused by the overvaluation of stock in the South Sea Company.

5. **more into the exchequer** (ĕks′chĕk′ər) **... customs:** more into the treasury than taxes on domestic and imported goods.

6. **Charles the Second:** king of England from 1660 to 1685.

7. **sailing without wind ... ride without horses:** traveling on steamships and beginning to travel on railroads.

8. *Gulliver's Travels:* the fanciful satire by Jonathan Swift, published in 1726.

9. **fee-simple ... Plantagenets** (plăn-tăj′ə-nĭts): complete ownership of the Plantagenet estates. The House of Plantagenet was the royal dynasty that ruled England from 1154 to 1399.

what, in the time of Cromwell,[10] had been thought intolerably oppressive. To almost all men the state of things under which they have been used to live seems to be the necessary state of things. We have heard it said that five per cent is the natural interest of money, that twelve is the natural number of a jury, that forty shillings is the natural qualification of a county voter.[11] Hence it is that, though in every age everybody knows that up to his own time progressive improvement has been taking place, nobody seems to reckon on any improvement during the next generation. We cannot absolutely prove that those are in error who tell us that society has reached a turning point, that we have seen our best days. But so said all who came before us, and with just as much apparent reason. "A million a year will beggar us," said the patriots of 1640. "Two millions a year will grind the country to powder," was the cry in 1660. "Six millions a year, and a debt of fifty millions!" exclaimed Swift, "the high allies have been the ruin of us." "A hundred and forty millions of debt!" said Junius; "well may we say that we owe Lord Chatham[12] more than we shall ever pay, if we owe him such a load as this." "Two hundred and forty millions of debt!" cried all the statesmen of 1783 in chorus; "what abilities, or what economy on the part of a minister, can save a country so burdened?" We know that if, since 1783, no fresh debt had been incurred, the increased resources of the country would have enabled us to defray that debt at which Pitt, Fox, and Burke[13] stood aghast, nay, to defray it over and over again, and that with much lighter taxation than what we have actually borne. On what principle is it that, when we see nothing but improvement behind us, we are to expect nothing but deterioration before us? **C**

It is . . . by the prudence and energy of the people that England has hitherto been carried forward in civilization; and it is to the same prudence and the same energy that we now look with comfort and good hope. Our rulers will best promote the improvement of the nation by strictly confining themselves to their own legitimate duties, by leaving capital to find its most **lucrative** course, commodities their fair price, industry and intelligence their natural reward, idleness and folly their natural punishment, by maintaining peace, by defending property, by diminishing the price of law, and by observing strict economy in every department of the State. Let the Government do this: the People will assuredly do the rest. ∾

COMMON CORE L 4b

Language Coach

Derivations Words formed from another word or base are derivations. When you learn a new word, try to learn its base and other derivations. What is the base of *intolerably*, ("unbearably" line 45)? What are other derivations of that base, and what do they mean?

C **RECOGNIZE IDEAS**
What idea is conveyed by the **rhetorical question** in lines 65–67? What details in the paragraph support this idea?

lucrative (loo′krə-tĭv) *adj.* producing wealth or profit

---

10. **Elizabeth . . . Cromwell:** Queen Elizabeth I, who ruled England from 1558 to 1603, and Oliver Cromwell, who ruled as Lord Protector from 1653 to 1658.

11. **forty shillings . . . voter:** In Macaulay's time, only males with a certain minimum income were able to vote in Britain. A shilling was a unit of currency equal to 1/20 of a pound.

12. **Junius . . . Lord Chatham:** William Pitt the Elder, the politician who led Britain into the costly Seven Years' War with France, was named Earl of Chatham in 1766. Junius was the pen name of a political commentator who usually supported Pitt.

13. **Pitt, Fox, and Burke:** William Pitt the Younger (second son of William Pitt the Elder), Charles James Fox, and Edmund Burke, British political leaders of the late 18th century.

THE CONDITION OF ENGLAND

Thomas Carlyle

> **BACKGROUND** Under the old Poor Law, each English parish gave the poor in its jurisdiction "outdoor relief" so that families could support themselves. In 1834, to reform abuses of this system, Parliament passed the Poor Law Amendment Act, which established a national system of workhouses for the poor. All able-bodied residents were required to work each day, often at useless tasks such as shredding rope, digging holes, or scrubbing already clean floors. Writing in 1843, Carlyle used life in the workhouse to illustrate the negative impact of industrialism on Britain.

The condition of England, on which many pamphlets are now in the course of publication, and many thoughts unpublished are going on in every reflective head, is justly regarded as one of the most ominous, and withal one of the strangest, ever seen in this world. England is full of wealth, of multifarious produce, supply for human want in every kind; yet England is dying of inanition.[1] With unabated bounty the land of England blooms and grows; waving with yellow harvests; thick-studded with workshops, industrial implements, with fifteen millions of workers, understood to be the strongest, the cunningest and the willingest our earth ever had; these men are here; the work they have done, the fruit they have
10 realized is here, abundant, exuberant on every hand of us: and behold, some baleful fiat[2] as of enchantment has gone forth, saying, "Touch it not, ye workers, ye master-workers, ye master-idlers;[3] none of you can touch it, no man of you shall be the better for it; this is enchanted fruit!" On the poor workers such fiat falls first, in its rudest shape; but on the rich master-workers too it falls; neither can the rich master-idlers, nor any richest or highest man escape, but all are like

Analyze Visuals ▶

What is your reaction to this image of an impoverished family? How might your response have been different if the image were a painting instead of a photograph?

---

1. **inanition** (ĭn´ə-nĭsh´ən): lack of spirit or vitality; loss or absence of social, moral, or intellectual vigor.

2. **baleful fiat** (bāl´fəl fē´ət): harmful decree or law.

3. **master-workers . . . master-idlers:** Carlyle's somewhat scornful terms for industrialists who employ other workers and for those wealthy enough, generally through inheritance, to live on rents, interest, and/or stock dividends without needing to work at all.

to be brought low with it, and made "poor" enough, in the money sense or a far fataler one. **D**

Of these successful skillful workers some two millions, it is now counted, sit in workhouses, poor-law prisons; or have "outdoor relief" flung over the wall to 20 them—the workhouse Bastille[4] being filled to bursting, and the strong poor law broken asunder by a stronger. They sit there, these many months now; their hope of deliverance as yet small. In workhouses, pleasantly so-named, because work cannot be done in them.[5] Twelve hundred thousand workers in England alone; their cunning right hand lamed, lying idle in their sorrowful bosom; their hopes, outlooks, share of this fair world, shut in by narrow walls. They sit there, pent up, as in a kind of horrid enchantment; glad to be imprisoned and enchanted, that they may not perish starved. The picturesque tourist, in a sunny autumn day, through this bounteous realm of England, descries the Union Workhouse on his path. "Passing by the Workhouse of St. Ives in Huntingdonshire, on a bright 30 day last autumn," says the picturesque tourist, "I saw sitting on wooden benches, in front of their Bastille and within their ring-wall and its railings, some half-hundred or more of these men. Tall robust figures, young mostly or of middle age; of honest **countenance**, many of them thoughtful and even intelligent-looking men. They sat there, near by one another; but in a kind of torpor, especially in a silence, which was very striking. In silence: for, alas, what word was to be said? An earth all lying round, crying, Come and till me, come and reap me—yet we here sit enchanted! In the eyes and brows of these men hung the gloomiest expression, not of anger, but of grief and shame and manifold inarticulate distress and weariness; they returned my glance with a glance that seemed to say 'Do not look 40 at us. We sit enchanted here, we know not why. The sun shines and the earth calls; and, by the governing powers and impotences[6] of this England, we are forbidden to obey. It is impossible, they tell us!' There was something that reminded me of Dante's hell[7] in the look of all this; and I rode swiftly away." **E**

So many hundred thousands sit in workhouses: and other hundred thousands have not yet got even workhouses; and in thrifty Scotland itself, in Glasgow or Edinburgh City,[8] in their dark lanes, hidden from all but the eye of God, and of rare benevolence the minister of God, there are scenes of woe and destitution and desolation, such as, one may hope, the sun never saw before in the most barbarous regions where men dwelt. Competent witnesses, the brave and humane 50 Dr. Alison,[9] who speaks what he knows, whose noble healing art in his charitable

D RECOGNIZE IDEAS
Reread lines 1–17, ignoring clauses and focusing on the main subject and verb of each sentence. What idea is Carlyle trying to get across?

countenance
(koun′tə-nəns) *n.* face; facial expression

E PERSUASION
Identify words and details in lines 18–43 that appeal to the reader's **emotions.** Does Carlyle state a logical argument in these lines? Explain your answer.

---

4. **Bastille** (bă-stēl′): prison. The Bastille was the famous royal prison destroyed by a mob at the start of the French Revolution in 1789.

5. **work cannot be done in them:** In this paragraph, Carlyle uses *work* to refer to gainful or useful employment.

6. **impotences** (ĭm′pə-təns-ĭz): weaknesses; inabilities.

7. **Dante's** (dän′tāz) **hell:** The Italian poet Dante Alighieri (1265–1321) gives a detailed account of hell, which he calls the Inferno, in the first book of his classic work *The Divine Comedy.*

8. **thrifty Scotland . . . Glasgow** (glăs′kō) **or Edinburgh** (ĕd′n-bûr′ə) **City:** The people of Scotland have a longstanding reputation for being thrifty. Glasgow and Edinburgh are Scotland's two largest cities.

9. **Dr. Alison:** Scottish physician William Pulteney Alison, author of *Observations on the Management of the Poor in Scotland* (1840).

hands becomes once more a truly sacred one, report these things for us: these things are not of this year, or of last year, have no reference to our present state of commercial stagnation, but only to the common state. Not in sharp fever-fits, but in chronic gangrene[10] of this kind is Scotland suffering. A poor law, any and every poor law, it may be observed, is but a temporary measure; an anodyne, not a remedy: rich and poor, when once the naked facts of their condition have come into collision, cannot long subsist together on a mere poor law. True enough—and yet, human beings cannot be left to die! Scotland too, till something better come, must have a poor law, if Scotland is not to be a byword[11] among the nations.

60   O, what a waste is there; of noble and thrice-noble national virtues; peasant **stoicisms,** heroisms; valiant manful habits, soul of a nation's worth—which all the metal of Potosi[12] cannot purchase back; to which the metal of Potosi, and all you can buy with *it,* is dross and dust! **F**

Why dwell on this aspect of the matter? It is too indisputable, not doubtful now to anyone. Descend where you will into the lower class, in town or country, by what avenue you will, by factory inquiries, agricultural inquiries, by revenue returns, by mining-laborer committees, by opening your own eyes and looking, the same sorrowful result discloses itself: you have to admit that the working body of this rich English nation has sunk or is fast sinking into a state, to which,

70   all sides of it considered, there was literally never any parallel. At Stockport Assizes[13]—and this too has no reference to the present state of trade, being of date prior to that—a mother and a father are arraigned and found guilty of poisoning three of their children, to defraud a "burial society" of some £3 8s.[14] due on the death of each child: they are arraigned, found guilty; and the official authorities, it is whispered, hint that perhaps the case is not solitary, that perhaps you had better not probe farther into that department of things. . . .

Nor are they of the St. Ives workhouses, of the Glasgow lanes, and Stockport cellars, the only unblessed among us. This successful industry of England, with its plethoric[15] wealth, has as yet made nobody rich; it is an enchanted wealth, and

80   belongs yet to nobody. We might ask, Which of us has it enriched? We can spend thousands where we once spent hundreds; but can purchase nothing good with them. In poor and rich, instead of noble thrift and plenty, there is idle luxury alternating with mean scarcity and inability. We have sumptuous garnitures[16] for our life, but have forgotten to *live* in the middle of them. It is an enchanted wealth; no man of us can yet touch it. The class of men who feel that they are truly better off by means of it, let them give us their name!

---

10. **Not in . . . gangrene** (găng′grēn′): not in occasional strong outbreaks but in a continual state of decay. Gangrene is the decay of tissue caused by the lack of blood flow to a particular part of the body.

11. **byword:** a topic of gossip.

12. **Potosi:** a South American city (now part of Bolivia) known for its large reserves of silver and other valuable resources.

13. **Stockport Assizes:** the superior court in the city of Stockport in northwestern England.

14. **£3 8s.:** an abbreviation meaning "three pounds, eight shillings"—about $16 in the exchange rate of the day.

15. **plethoric** (plĕ-thôr′ĭk): overabundant; excessive.

16. **garnitures** (gär′nĭ-chərz): furnishings; ornaments.

COMMON CORE RI 1

F VERBAL AMBIGUITY
Verbal ambiguity is a kind of word play in which a writer deliberately allows more than one meaning to be in play at the same time. It often centers on a word that has more than one meaning. Normally, good prose writers are careful to ensure that readers know exactly which meaning they intend to use for a given word. But, sometimes, the tension produced by ambiguity can help a writer communicate a deeper meaning. In lines 54–59, Carlyle repeats the phrase "poor law" four times. Which two meanings of *poor* are in play? What does the ambiguity of this phrase add to the writer's message?

Many men eat finer cookery, drink dearer liquors—with what advantage they can report, and their doctors can: but in the heart of them, if we go out of the dyspeptic stomach,[17] what increase of blessedness is there? Are they better, beautifuler, stonger, braver? Are they even what they call "happier"? Do they look with satisfaction on more things and human faces in this God's earth; do more things and human faces look with satisfaction on them? Not so. Human faces gloom discordantly, disloyally on one another. Things, if it be not mere cotton and iron things, are growing disobedient to man. The master-worker is enchanted, for the present, like his workhouse-workman; clamors, in vain hitherto, for a very simple sort of "liberty"; the liberty "to buy where he finds it cheapest, to sell where he finds it dearest." With guineas[18] jingling in every pocket, he was no whit[19] richer; but now, the very guineas threatening to vanish, he feels that he is poor indeed. Poor master-worker! And the master-unworker, is not he in a still fataler situation? Pausing amid his game preserves, with awful eye—as he well may! Coercing fifty-pound tenants;[20] coercing, bribing, cajoling; "doing what he likes with his own." His mouth full of loud futilities, and arguments to prove the excellence of his Corn Law;[21] and in his heart the blackest misgiving, a desperate half-consciousness that his excellent Corn Law is *in*defensible, that his loud arguments for it are of a kind to strike men too literally *dumb*. **G**

To whom, then, is this wealth of England wealth? Who is it that it blesses; makes happier, wiser, beautifuler, in any way better? Who has got hold of it, to make it fetch and carry for him, like a true servant, not like a false mock-servant; to do him any real service whatsoever? As yet no one. We have more riches than any nation ever had before; we have less good of them than any nation ever had before. Our successful industry is hitherto unsuccessful; a strange success, if we stop here! In the midst of plethoric plenty, the people perish; with gold walls, and full barns, no man feels himself safe or satisfied, Workers, master-workers, unworkers, all men, come to a pause; stand fixed, and cannot [go] farther. Fatal paralysis spreading inwards, from the extremities, in St. Ives workhouses, in Stockport cellars, through all limbs, as if towards the heart itself. Have we actually got enchanted, then; accursed by some God?

Midas longed for gold, and insulted the Olympians. He got gold, so that whatsoever he touched became gold—and he, with his long ears, was little the better for it. Midas had misjudged the celestial music tones; Midas had insulted Apollo and the gods: the gods gave him his wish, and a pair of long ears,[22] which also were a good appendage to it. What a truth in these old fables! 〰

G GRAMMAR AND STYLE
Reread lines 87–92. Note how Carlyle uses a series of **rhetorical questions** to get his message across.

---

17. **if we ... dyspeptic** (dĭs-pĕp′tĭk) **stomach**: if we move beyond the upset stomach.

18. **guineas** (gĭn′ēz): British gold coins worth 21 shillings (a pound and a shilling).

19. **no whit**: not a bit.

20. **fifty-pound tenants**: renters who paid 50 pounds a year to rent land from the wealthy landowner ("master-unworker").

21. **Corn Law**: The Corn Laws limited the import of cheaper foreign grain into Britain. By limiting food supplies and keeping grain prices artificially high, these laws increased poverty and hurt the poor.

22. **Midas ... long ears**: a reference to Midas of Greek mythology, who wished that everything he touched would turn to gold. He also insulted Apollo, god of music, by judging against him in a contest. As punishment, Apollo gave Midas the long ears of a donkey.

Comprehension

1. **Recall** To what does Macaulay attribute England's success?

2. **Paraphrase** In Carlyle's view, what problem does England currently face?

3. **Summarize** According to Carlyle, what is life like in the workhouses?

Text Analysis

4. **Make Inferences** Reread lines 28–40 of "Evidence of Progress." On the basis of this passage, what can you infer about Macaulay's social priorities?

5. **Interpret Allusion** Recall that an allusion is a reference to historical, literary, or cultural details outside of a literary work. Reread lines 118–122 of "The Condition of England." What point is Carlyle making with his allusion to Midas in these lines?

● 6. **Analyze Ideas** Review the chart you created as you read. Choose three ideas that best convey each author's overall message. What are the reasons for your choices?

7. **Interpret Extended Metaphor** Carlyle uses the metaphor of enchantment to convey his criticisms of British society. Paraphrase each of the following passages from his commentary. In each example, what characteristics of social life does this metaphor communicate?

   • on the condition of England (lines 5–13)
   • on life in the workhouse (lines 35–43)
   • on the limits of wealth (lines 77–86)

● 8. **Evaluate Persuasive Techniques** Complete a chart like the one shown for each selection. Then describe each author's use of persuasive techniques. Whose position did you find more credible, and why?

Logical	Emotional	Ethical

Text Criticism

9. **Different Perspectives** Which author's viewpoint would each of the following readers more likely agree with? Give reasons for your answer.

   • a wealthy industrialist   • Charles Dickens
   • a mill worker   • Anthony Trollope

How do we measure PROGRESS?

Explain the differences between Macaulay's view of society and Carlyle's. What indicators would each author consider to be a fair measure of progress? What do you consider social progress?

COMMON CORE

RI 1 Cite strong and thorough textual evidence to support analysis of what the text says explicitly as well as inferences drawn from the text, including determining where the text leaves matters uncertain. **RI 2** Determine two or more central ideas of a text. **RI 4** Determine the meaning of words and phrases as they are used in a text, Including figurative meanings. **RI 6** Determine an author's point of view or purpose in a text in which the rhetoric is particularly effective, analyzing how style and content contribute to the power, persuasiveness, or beauty of the text. **RI 9** Analyze documents of historical and literary significance for their themes, purposes, and rhetorical features.

Vocabulary in Context

▲ VOCABULARY PRACTICE

Choose the letter of the synonym for each boldface word.

1. **debase:** (a) debrief, (b) defy, (c) devalue
2. **prophesy:** (a) predict, (b) inform, (c) select
3. **lucrative:** (a) oily, (b) honorable, (c) profitable
4. **countenance:** (a) appearance, (b) amount, (c) nobility
5. **stoicism:** (a) belief, (b) activity, (c) indifference

WORD LIST
countenance
debase
lucrative
prophesy
stoicism

·ACADEMIC VOCABULARY IN WRITING

> • analyze   • dominate   • impact   • resource   • scheme

How do changes in the economy **impact** you or your community? What sectors of society suffer the most during hard economic times? Use at least two of the Academic Vocabulary words in your written response.

VOCABULARY STRATEGY: USING A DICTIONARY

As Macaulay was celebrating the fruits of human innovation, an American lexicographer named Noah Webster compiled a dictionary that promoted the innovation of English spelling. For example, in his *An American Dictionary of the English Language* (1828), Webster proposed the alteration of *musick* to *music* and *centre* to *center*. In some cases, the world followed Webster's advice; in others, only the U.S. went along. In the U.K., for example, *centre* persists. Study this entry from a general dictionary, based on Webster's.

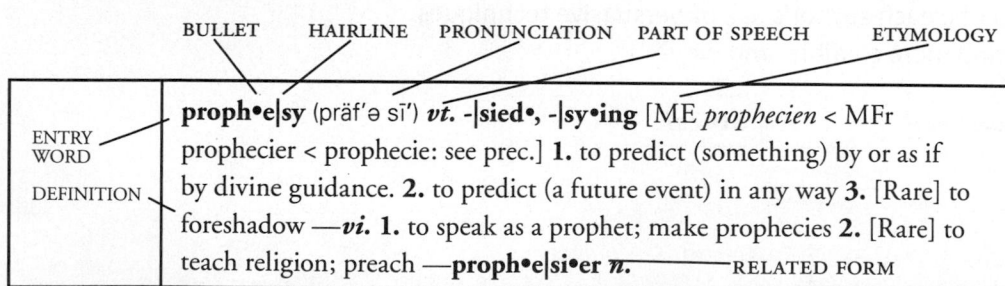

BULLET   HAIRLINE   PRONUNCIATION   PART OF SPEECH   ETYMOLOGY

ENTRY WORD / DEFINITION

proph•e|sy (präf′ə sī′) *vt.* -|sied•, -|sy•ing [ME *prophecien* < MFr *prophecier* < *prophecie*: see prec.] **1.** to predict (something) by or as if by divine guidance. **2.** to predict (a future event) in any way **3.** [Rare] to foreshadow —*vi.* **1.** to speak as a prophet; make prophecies **2.** [Rare] to teach religion; preach —**proph•e|si•er** *n.* ———RELATED FORM

PRACTICE Use the sample entry to answer these questions.

1. Where should you avoid hyphenating *prophesy*?
2. Which syllable in *prophesy* receives the most stress? Which receives least?
3. The abbreviation *vt.* means "verb, transitive"—that is, "carrying an object." Is *prophesy* a transitive verb in this sentence? *I prophesy disaster.*
4. Where would you find information about the etymology of *prophecie*?
5. Which meanings of *prophesy* would you be least likely to encounter or use?

COMMON CORE

L 2a Observe hyphenation conventions. **L 4c** Consult general reference materials to find the pronunciation of a word or determine or clarify its precise meaning, its part of speech, its etymology, or its standard usage.

Interactive Vocabulary   **THINK** central

Go to **thinkcentral.com**.
KEYWORD: HML12-1042

Language

COMMON CORE

L 3 Apply knowledge of language to understand how language functions in different contexts, to make effective choices for meaning or style, and to comprehend more fully when reading or listening. **W 1** Write arguments to support claims in an analysis of substantive topics.

◆ **GRAMMAR AND STYLE: Ask Rhetorical Questions**

Review the **Grammar and Style** note on page 1040. Writers often use **rhetorical questions**—questions asked only for effect—to drive home a point or evoke an emotional response. Carlyle uses these **interrogative sentences** throughout his essay, as in this example:

> To whom, then, is this wealth of England wealth? Who is it that it blesses; makes happier, wiser, beautifuler, in any way better? Who has got hold of it, to make it fetch and carry for him, like a true servant, not like a false mock-servant; to do him any real service whatsoever? (lines 106–109)

Notice how the questions express Carlyle's points in a more dynamic and compelling way than would be achieved had he merely stated his position.

PRACTICE Rewrite the following paragraph, changing at least two sentences into rhetorical questions to make the paragraph more persuasive. Then, add at least one additional rhetorical question.

> Carlyle complained about harsh conditions in workhouses and compared them to prisons like the Bastille. He believed that things were better for the poor in the centuries before his own. I do not think the good old days were really as good as he says. I wonder if wealthy aristocrats always met their responsibilities to the poor people living on their land. I do not know if poor peasants actually enjoyed having their lives almost completely controlled by others.

READING-WRITING CONNECTION

YOUR TURN

Expand your understanding of persuasion by responding to this prompt. Then use the **revising tips** to improve your letter.

WRITING PROMPT	REVISING TIPS
WRITE A LETTER TO THE EDITOR Newspapers provide a public forum for different opinions about social, political, and economic conditions. Write a **three-paragraph letter to the editor** of a local newspaper. In your letter, state a position on an issue that concerns you and then express your views in a way that will be persuasive to others.	• Make sure your position is clearly stated in the first paragraph. • Add other arguments in your second and third paragraphs. • If your arguments don't seem persuasive, use a different rhetorical device.

Interactive Revision

THiNK central

Go to **thinkcentral.com**.
KEYWORD: HML12-1043

Viewpoints on Globalization
Editorials

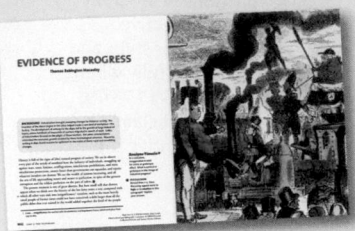

Use with "Evidence of Progress," page 1032, and "The Condition of England," page 1036.

COMMON CORE

RI 5 Analyze and evaluate the effectiveness of the structure an author uses in his or her exposition or argument including whether the structure makes points clear, convincing, and engaging. **RI 7** Integrate and evaluate multiple sources of information presented in different media or formats as well as in words in order to address a question or solve a problem. **RI 10** Read and comprehend literary nonfiction.

You have just read two writers' viewpoints on the effects of industrialization in Victorian England. Now read two other writers' contrasting views on the impact of another economic revolution, one occurring today.

Standards Focus: Distinguish Fact and Opinion

As a critical reader of an editorial, you have a twofold mission: to identify the writer's opinion and to determine whether this opinion is valid—that is, adequately supported by reasons, facts, and statistics. To do this, you need to distinguish facts from opinions.

When sorting facts from opinions, it's helpful to think of a fact as something that can be proved. An opinion, on the other hand, is an idea, belief, or outlook that can vary from one person to the next. Opinions can take various forms:

- **judgment statements,** or statements that express worth or value *(Globalization is good.)*

- **prediction statements** *(Globalization will destroy our economy.)*

- **policy or command statements** *(Americans should study economics. Study economics!)*

- **assumptions that cannot be proved** or that rely on unclear criteria *(People are suffering as never before.)*

- **opinions combined with facts** *(Worst of all, American jobs are being exported.)*

As you read the following editorials, keep track of the facts and opinions by completing a chart like the one shown here. This chart will also help you better understand the **organization,** or structure, of each author's argument.

	Facts	Opinions	Not sure
"Good News About Poverty"			
"The White-Collar Blues"			

The New York Times

SATURDAY, NOVEMBER 27, 2004　　**OP-ED**　　A25

Good News About Poverty

David Brooks

I hate to be the bearer of good news, because only pessimists are regarded as intellectually serious, but we're in the 11th month of the most prosperous year in human history. Last week, the World Bank released a report showing that global growth "accelerated sharply" this year to a rate of about 4 percent.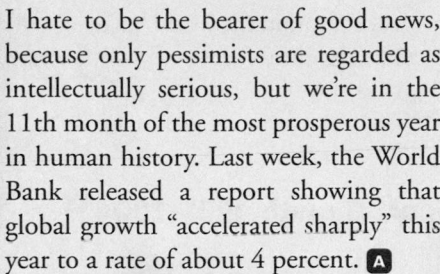

Best of all, the poorer nations are leading the way. Some rich countries, like the United States and Japan, are doing well, but the developing world is leading this economic surge. Developing countries are seeing their economies expand by 6.1 percent this year—an unprecedented rate—and, even if you take China, India, and Russia out of the equation, developing world growth is still around 5 percent. As even the cautious folks at the World Bank note, all developing regions are growing faster this decade than they did in the 1980s and 1990s.

This is having a wonderful effect on world poverty, because when regions grow, that growth is shared up and down the income ladder. In its report, the World Bank notes that economic growth is producing a "spectacular" decline in poverty in East and South Asia. In 1990, there were roughly 472 million people in the East Asia and Pacific region living on less than $1 a day. By 2001, there were 271 million living in extreme poverty, and by 2015, at current projections, there will only be 19 million people living under those conditions. Less dramatic declines in extreme poverty have been noted around the developing world, with the vital exception of sub-Saharan Africa. . . .

Economists have been arguing furiously about whether inequality is increasing or decreasing. But it now seems likely that while inequality has grown within particular nations, it is shrinking among individuals worldwide. . . .

What explains all this good news? The short answer is this thing we call globalization. Over the past decades, many nations have undertaken structural reforms to lower trade barriers, shore up property rights, and free economic activity. International trade is surging. The poor nations that opened themselves up to trade, investment, and those evil multinational corporations saw the sharpest poverty declines. Write this on your forehead: Free trade reduces world suffering.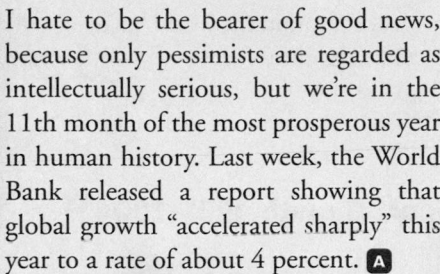

Of course, all the news is not good. Plagued by bad governments and AIDS,

---

A FACT AND OPINION
Reread the statement in lines 3–5. Is this a fact or an opinion? If it is a fact, how can it be verified?

B FACT AND OPINION
Reread lines 48–60. Identify each sentence in the paragraph as fact or opinion, explaining your decision in each case.

sub-Saharan Africa has not joined in the benefits of globalization. Big budget deficits in the United States and elsewhere threaten stable growth. High oil prices are a problem. Trade produces losers as well as winners, especially among less-skilled workers in the 70 developed world.

But especially around Thanksgiving, it's worth appreciating some of the things that have gone right, and not just sweeping reports like the one from the World Bank under the rug.

It's worth reminding ourselves that the key task ahead is spreading the benefits of globalization to Africa and the Middle East. It's worth noting this 80 perhaps not too surprising phenomenon: As free trade improves the lives of people in poor countries, it is viewed with suspicion by more people in rich countries. . . .

But if you really want to reduce world poverty, you should be cheering on those guys in pinstripe suits at the free-trade negotiations and those investors jetting around the world. Thanks, in part, to 90 them, we are making progress against poverty. Thanks, in part, to them, more people around the world have something to be thankful for.

COMMON CORE RI 7

C **UNDERSTAND CHARTS**
In a chart, the text that runs horizontally across the bottom is called the **x-axis**. The text that runs vertically along the side is called the **y-axis**. How does the scale of the numbers on the y-axis correspond to the dates on x-axis? What would the chart look like if the scale of the y-axis changed to include 0 to 100 percent? What conclusions about the Gross Domestic Product can you draw from this chart?

Gross Domestic Product Growth, 1961–2004 **C**

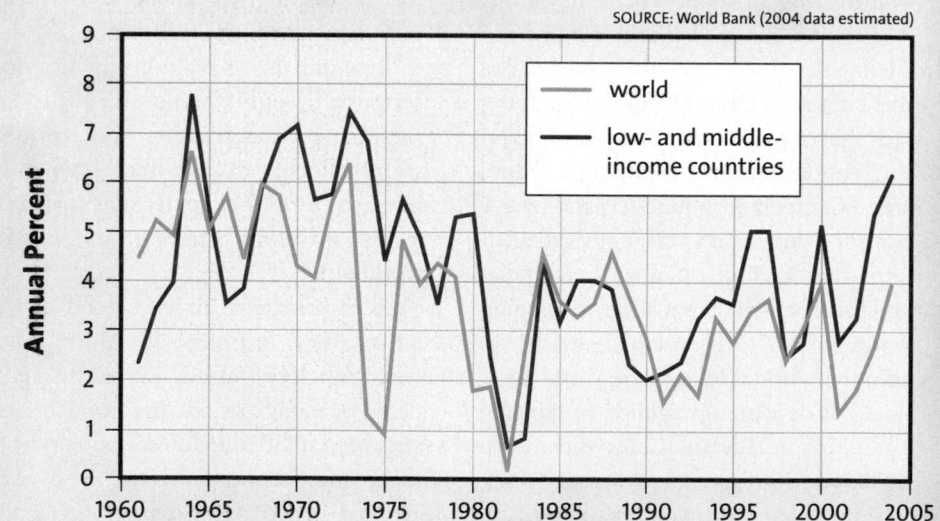

SOURCE: World Bank (2004 data estimated)

The New York Times

MONDAY, DECEMBER 29, 2003   **OP-ED**   *A27*

The White-Collar Blues

Bob Herbert

I am surprised at how passive American workers have become.

A couple of million factory positions have disappeared in the short time since we raised our glasses to toast the incoming century. And now the white-collar jobs are following the blue-collar jobs overseas.

Americans are working harder and have become ever more productive—astonishingly productive—but are not sharing in the benefits of their increased effort. If you think in terms of wages, benefits, and the creation of good jobs, the employment landscape is grim. **D**

The economy is going great guns, we're told, but nearly nine million Americans are officially unemployed, and the real tally of the jobless is much higher. . . . Lines at food banks and soup kitchens are lengthening. They're swollen in many cases by the children of men and women who are working but not making enough to house and feed their families.

IBM has crafted plans to send thousands of upscale jobs from the United States to lower-paid workers in China, India, and elsewhere. Anyone who doesn't believe this is the wave of the future should listen to comments made last spring by an IBM executive named Harry Newman:

"I think probably the biggest impact to employee relations and to the HR [human relations] field is this concept of globalization. It is rapidly accelerating, and it means shifting a lot of jobs, opening a lot of locations in places we had never dreamt of before, going where there's low-cost labor, low-cost competition, shifting jobs offshore."

An executive at Microsoft, the ultimate American success story, told his department heads last year to "Think India," and to "pick something to move offshore today."

These matters should be among the hottest topics of our national conversation. We've already witnessed the carnage in manufacturing jobs. Now, with white-collar jobs at stake, we've got executives at IBM and Microsoft exchanging high-fives at the prospect of getting "two heads for the price of one" in India.

It might be a good idea to throw a brighter spotlight on some of these trends and explore the implications for the long-term economy and the American standard of living. **E**

"If you take this to its logical extreme, the implications for the entire middle-

D **FACT AND OPINION**
Identify the facts in the first three paragraphs. How are they used in relation to the opinions in this passage?

E **FACT AND OPINION**
Review the types of opinions listed on page 1044. What type of opinion does Herbert state in lines 56–60?

Manufacturing Employment, 1960–2005

SOURCE: U. S. Department of Labor, Bureau of Labor Statistics

Language Coach

Roots and Affixes A word's root may contain its core meaning. The word *mitigated* comes from the Latin root *mitis,* meaning "soft." What do you think *mitigated* means in line 88?

F **FACT AND OPINION** Reread lines 76–84. What facts, according to Herbert, are indisputable? Do you agree? Explain.

class wage structure in the United States are terrifying," said Thea Lee, an economist with the AFL-CIO. "Now is the time to start thinking about policy solutions."

But that's exactly what we're not 70 thinking about. Government policy at the moment is focused primarily on what's best for the corporations. From that perspective, job destruction and wage compression are good things—as long as they don't get too much high-profile attention. . . .

Accurate data on the number of jobs already lost are all but impossible to come by. But there is no disputing the direction of the trend, or the fact that it 80 is accelerating. Allowing this movement to continue unchecked will eventually mean economic suicide for hundreds of thousands, if not millions, of American families. **F**

Globalization may be a fact of life. But that does not mean that its destructive impact on American families can't be mitigated. The best thing workers can do, including white-collar 90 and professional workers, is to organize. At the same time, the exportation of jobs and the effect that is having on the standard of living here should be relentlessly monitored by the government, the civic sector, and the media. The public has a right to know what's really going on.

Trade agreements and tax policies should be examined and updated to 100 encourage the creation of employment that enhances the quality of life here at home. Corporate leaders may not feel an obligation to contribute to the long-term well-being of local communities or the nation as a whole, but that shouldn't be the case with the rest of us.

Comprehension

1. **Summarize** What is David Brooks's opinion of globalization?

2. **Summarize** In lines 78–106 of "The White-Collar Blues," what does Bob Herbert conclude about globalization? What does he suggest doing about it?

Text Analysis

3. **Evaluate Fact and Opinion** Review the chart you filled in as you read. Look at the use of facts in relation to the use of opinions. In your view, is one type of statement more powerful than another? Explain whether you think each writer used fact and opinion in a way that was credible and compelling.

4. **Draw Conclusions** Based on the two editorials you have just read, what would you say about the effect of globalization on today's world? Be sure to consider both the economic effects of globalization and people's personal reactions to it.

COMMON CORE

RI 5 Analyze and evaluate the effectiveness of the structure an author uses in his or her exposition or argument including whether the structure makes points clear, convincing, and engaging. **RI 10** Read and comprehend literary nonfiction. **W 9** Draw evidence from informational texts to support analysis and reflection.

Read for Information: Synthesize and Compare

WRITING PROMPT

Review the two essays and the two editorials. In each case, synthesize what you have learned about the impact of dramatic economic change, first in Victorian England and then in today's world. Then, based on your syntheses, compare the role of industrialization in Victorian England with that of globalization in today's world. Use the facts and opinions expressed in the commentaries and editorials as the basis for your comparison.

To answer this prompt, follow these steps:

1. Reread Macaulay's and Carlyle's commentaries to remind yourself how industrialization affected people in Victorian England. Write a brief statement synthesizing your understanding.

2. Your answer to question 4 under Text Analysis should serve as a synthesis of your understanding about globalization today.

3. Reviewing your syntheses, identify the similarities between the two eras of economic change.

4. Write an essay in which you explain what you have learned about the two eras, and then compare them.

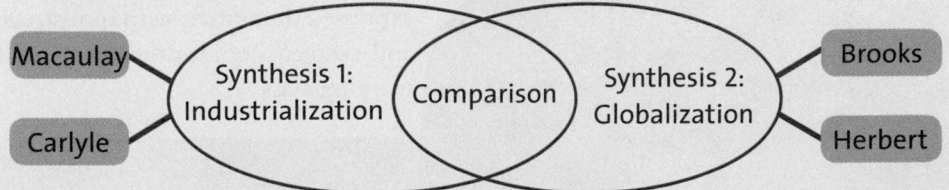

Macaulay — Synthesis 1: Industrialization — Comparison — Synthesis 2: Globalization — Brooks

Carlyle — Herbert

COMMON CORE

RI 7 Integrate and evaluate multiple sources of information presented in different media or formats as well as in words in order to address a question or solve a problem.

What brings HISTORY *to life?*

Judging only from the serene countenance displayed in Queen Victoria's portraits, one could characterize the Victorian age as a time of stability and high decorum. However, Victoria's image belied the supercharged reality of the Industrial Revolution, which by the latter years of her reign had irrevocably altered England's physical and social landscapes. In this lesson, you'll watch a documentary excerpt to examine how it depicts this complex period of **history.**

Background

Urban Sprawl By the mid-19th century, power-driven machines and factories had become widespread in England, leading to changes in social patterns. As the production of goods shifted from the countryside to the cities, people flocked there in search of factory work. The population of England's most important city, London, exploded, and many other cities doubled, tripled, and even quadrupled in population.

The city of Manchester became the leading example of the progress and price of industrialism. As French writer Alexis de Tocqueville described it, "From this filthy sewer pure gold flows." A leading manufacturer of textiles, Manchester generated fabulous profits. The factories required a large labor pool, but the housing and working conditions were abysmal. People crowded into tenements and row houses. Smoke belched from Manchester's factories and blackened its skies. Textile dyes and wastes polluted its nearby river.

The Industrial Revolution transformed not only Great Britain but the world. The results were so far-reaching that many of the period's technological innovations—factories, railway and canal systems, and shipping and steel industries—are global necessities in the 21st century.

A History of Britain is an acclaimed 15-part documentary that first aired on British television. It covers Britain's history from its earliest civilization to modern times. The clip you'll view is from the episode "Victoria and Her Sisters," which explores the impact of the Industrial Revolution and how writers of the day, such as Elizabeth Cleghorn Gaskell, expressed discontent with industrialism and deep concern for the downtrodden working class.

Media Literacy: Documentary

A **documentary** is a nonfiction film that is often about social, political, or historical subjects. In recent years, historical documentaries have changed as filmmakers have adopted a more cinematic style of storytelling. They now combine conventional documentary features with stylistic devices.

 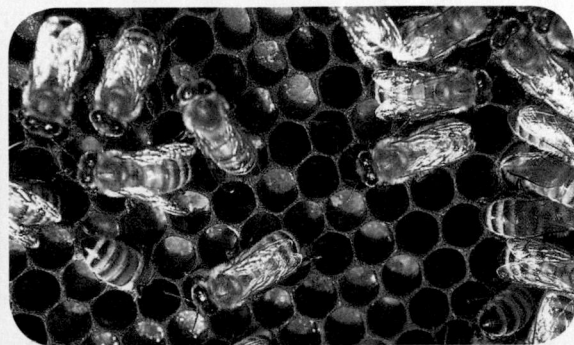

ELEMENTS OF DOCUMENTARIES

Conventional Features of Documentaries

Visual

- Filmmakers create **footage**—unedited material as recorded by the camera. The footage often includes representative pieces of a time period, such as paintings, photographs, and writings.

Sound

- **Voice-over narration,** or the voice of an unseen speaker, is heard as the footage plays.
- **Music** might be from, or in some way reflect, the time period of the subject.

Contemporary Features of Documentaries

Visual

- Filmmakers apply camera techniques to still images. Moving the camera to **pan** across the subject or to **zoom** in closer reveals details.
- A **reenactment** is the re-creation of key events or settings. Such scenes are used to portray a time and to highlight the filmmakers' themes.
- Documentary filmmakers might include images in symbolic ways, to comment on the times.

Sound

- In today's documentaries, one narrator might deliver facts while actors portray the people of a time, reading real-life letters, diary entries, and so on. Using the historical figures' own words gives the portrayals a human dimension.
- As with feature films, a **musical score** helps to set the overall mood and to add drama.

STRATEGIES FOR VIEWING

To better appreciate a historical documentary, think about how it is constructed.

- Be aware of the filmmakers' desired effect. Ask: How might the filmmakers want me to feel or react?
- Determine the filmmakers' perspective. Notice in particular the tone of the voice-over narration. Ask: What point of view or message is conveyed? What subject matter do the reenactments depict? How does this footage emphasize certain themes or ideas?
- Examine the content. Ask: What's the whole story? What might be missing?

Viewing Guide for

A History of Britain

The clip describes the factory system in Manchester, England, and the writings of Elizabeth Cleghorn Gaskell and Thomas Carlyle. As you watch, consider how the documentary is constructed both to deliver and to dramatize the information. To help you analyze the clip, refer to these questions.

NOW VIEW

FIRST VIEWING: Comprehension

1. **Recall** What images in the modern-day footage look as though they could have been recorded in late 1800s?

2. **Clarify** What different kinds of voice-over do you hear in the clip?

CLOSE VIEWING: Media Literacy

3. **Compare Sound Techniques** The beginning of the clip describes conditions in Manchester, and the end presents the views of Thomas Carlyle. Compare the **music** and **sound effects** you hear at the beginning of the clip with what you hear at the end.

4. **Analyze Visuals** At one point in the documentary, you see a section of magnified text from Elizabeth Cleghorn Gaskell's novel *Mary Barton* as the voice-over narrator talks about Gaskell's use of the word *clemmed*. What is the effect of presenting the writer's words in this way?

5. **Analyze Symbols** At certain points in the documentary, the modern-day footage shows a factory with broken glass and bees in a beehive. Interestingly, these images don't literally match the wording of the **voice-over narration.** What effect might the filmmakers be aiming for in using these images as **visual metaphors?**

6. **Analyze Reenactments** The filmmakers portray in reenactments certain descriptions from *Mary Barton*. Besides wanting to re-create moments from the past, why might the filmmakers be using these images?

7. **Evaluate Documentary** The makers of historical documentaries draw from an array of techniques to evoke a time period and to elicit certain emotions. Based on the clip, how effective a job does this documentary do of putting you in touch with a tumultuous time? Support your opinion.

Write or Discuss

Summarize Perspective This documentary clip comes from a 15-part series praised as a work that "re-animates familiar tales and illuminates overlooked aspects of England's past." For the excerpt you've viewed, consider what perspective the filmmakers were trying to convey. Briefly summarize that perspective. Think about

- the tone of the statements in the voice-over narration
- what the symbolic images represent
- other stylistic devices used to comment on the effects of the Industrial Revolution

Produce Your Own Media

Create a Voice-over Script Consider that many documentaries attempt to capture viewers' interest in the opening statements about what the documentary will cover. Choose a time period, from either the distant or recent past, that was marked by rapid and widespread change. In a page or two, create a **voice-over script** that introduces an imaginary documentary series.

HERE'S HOW Here are some suggestions for creating your script:

- Do research to characterize your time period accurately.
- Determine your perspective. Was the time period the best of times or the worst? Plan how to convey your views through the tone and pace of your delivery. Make sure to emphasize any dramatic details.
- Have a partner listen carefully as you read your voice-over script. Then have him or her summarize your information and comment on your delivery. If necessary, refine your tone or revise any part of the script that was difficult to follow.

Further Exploration

Explore Documentary Techniques The documentaries of Ken Burns are admired for their distinctive storytelling style. Burns is credited with reinventing the historical documentary. Such works as *The Civil War*, *Jazz*, and *Baseball* illustrate the signature techniques that have inspired a new generation of filmmakers. View these documentaries to find examples of the signature techniques—the distinctive camera techniques, the mixture of period and contemporary footage, and the emotionally effective voice-over and music.

COMMON CORE

RI 7 Integrate and evaluate multiple sources of information presented in different media or formats as well as in words in order to address a question or solve a problem. **W 10** Write routinely over shorter time frames for a range of tasks.

Media Tools

THINK central

Go to **thinkcentral.com**.
KEYWORD: HML12-1053

Tech Tip

If an audio recorder is available, record your voice-over.

COMMON CORE

RL 2 Determine themes or central ideas of a text. **RL 10** Read and comprehend literature, including poems.

Dover Beach
To Marguerite—Continued

Poetry by Matthew Arnold

VIDEO TRAILER **THINK** central KEYWORD: HML12-1054A

Meet the Author

Matthew Arnold 1822–1888

Matthew Arnold's poetry and prose made him a leading voice of the Victorian Age. Yet Arnold didn't earn his living as a writer. He worked for over 30 years as a school inspector, visiting schools all over Britain and traveling abroad to report on educational developments in other countries. His travels, both domestic and foreign, allowed him to study the culture and society of his day—and convinced him that he must speak out about the problems he perceived.

A Famous Father Arnold's career in education was not surprising, as he was the son of one of Victorian Britain's most famous educators. As headmaster of the Rugby School, Dr. Thomas Arnold initiated reforms that revolutionized British education of the day. Matthew Arnold was not a model student at his father's school— in fact, one biographer describes him as "a fanciful and relatively idle boy." Nevertheless, he managed to win a scholarship to Oxford University.

Mentors and Muses Arnold showed early promise as a poet, winning one prestigious poetry prize at Rugby and another at Oxford. His interest in verse was inspired in part by his family's friendship with William Wordsworth, who lived near the Arnolds' vacation home. It was also nurtured by future poet Arthur Hugh Clough, who became Arnold's critiquing partner at Oxford as well as his closest friend. When Arnold published his first book of poems in 1849, their sad and serious nature surprised many who knew him, since to the world he generally showed his charming, lighthearted side. But the young poet had certainly known sorrow—he lost his father to a heart attack while still at Oxford and suffered from unrequited love for a neighbor named Mary Claude, whom some biographers think is the Marguerite of his poetry.

A Part-Time Author In 1850, Arnold fell in love again, this time with the daughter of a prominent judge. In need of sufficient income to gain his future father-in-law's consent to the marriage, Arnold took the post of British schools inspector. For the rest of his life, he continued writing in his spare time. In addition to major literary criticism, Arnold produced several nonfiction works addressing the sense of isolation and loss that he expresses in his poetry. A passionate advocate of the arts, he stressed the value of culture in curbing modern feelings of alienation and in bringing direction to modern life.

DID YOU KNOW?

Matthew Arnold . . .

- spent more time socializing than studying while in college, and so barely passed his exams.

- may have written "Dover Beach" while on his honeymoon.

- published his first two books under the pen name "A."

Author Online

Go to thinkcentral.com. KEYWORD: HML12-1054B

THINK central

● TEXT ANALYSIS: THEME

You know that the **theme** of a poem is the central idea the poet wishes to convey. Matthew Arnold, a social critic as well as a poet, was disturbed by the massive shifts of the Victorian era—a time of rapid social, economic, and religious change. In his poetry, Arnold deals with the loneliness of humankind in an indifferent universe, bereft of old certainties. As you read "Dover Beach" and "To Marguerite—Continued," examine the literary elements that convey each poem's theme.

- **Mood**—Identify the atmosphere Arnold creates for the reader; determine whether the mood changes or remains consistent.

- **Imagery and figurative language**—Note the details that create a vivid mental picture of the scene described.

- **Allusions**—Note any indirect references to people, places, or literary works.

● READING SKILL: ANALYZE SPEAKER

One thing that will help you interpret the themes of Arnold's poems is a careful analysis of each **speaker**. As you read, ask yourself the following questions about the persona adopted in each poem. For each poem, use a chart like the one shown to record your thoughts, and be sure to note evidence from the text that supports your analysis.

Questions About the Speaker	My Thoughts	Evidence from the Text
Whom is he addressing?		
Where does he seem to be?		
What is his state of mind?		
Does his attitude change over the course of the poem? If so, how?		

 Complete the activities in your **Reader/Writer Notebook**.

Is the world INDIFFERENT to us?

In the Victorian era, new scientific theories challenged age-old beliefs about the world and our place within it. These developments stirred up feelings of doubt and isolation in many people, including Matthew Arnold, Unlike earlier poets, such as Wordsworth, who took comfort in nature, Arnold wrote about nature's indifference to the fate of humanity.

QUICKWRITE When you think about nature, do you feel a sense of belonging, or does the universe seem cold and indifferent to you? Respond to this question in one or two paragraphs.

Dover Beach

Matthew Arnold

The sea is calm tonight.
The tide is full, the moon lies fair
Upon the straits—on the French coast the light
Gleams and is gone; the cliffs of England stand,
5   Glimmering and vast, out in the tranquil bay.
Come to the window, sweet is the night air!
Only, from the long line of spray
Where the sea meets the moon-blanched land,
Listen! you hear the grating roar
10 Of pebbles which the waves draw back, and fling,
At their return, up the high strand,
Begin, and cease, and then again begin,
With tremulous cadence slow, and bring
The eternal note of sadness in.

15 Sophocles long ago
Heard it on the Aegean, and it brought
Into his mind the turbid ebb and flow
Of human misery; we
Find also in the sound a thought,
20 Hearing it by this distant northern sea.

The Sea of Faith
Was once, too, at the full, and round earth's shore
Lay like the folds of a bright girdle furled.
But now I only hear
25 Its melancholy, long, withdrawing roar,
Retreating, to the breath
Of the night wind, down the vast edges drear
And naked shingles of the world.

Ah, love, let us be true
30 To one another! for the world, which seems
To lie before us like a land of dreams,
So various, so beautiful, so new,
Hath really neither joy, nor love, nor light,
Nor certitude, nor peace, nor help for pain;
35 And we are here as on a darkling plain
Swept with confused alarms of struggle and flight,
Where ignorant armies clash by night. **Ⓐ**

---

3 straits: the Strait of Dover, a narrow channel separating England and France, located at the northern end of the English Channel.

8 moon-blanched: shining palely in the moonlight.

13 tremulous cadence (trĕm′yə-ləs kād′ns): trembling rhythm.

15 Sophocles (sŏf′ə-klēz′): an ancient Greek writer of tragic plays.

16 Aegean (ĭ-jē′ən): the Aegean Sea, the portion of the Mediterranean Sea between Greece and Turkey.

17 turbid: in a state of turmoil; muddled.

21 Sea of Faith: traditional religious beliefs about God and the world, long viewed as true and unshakable.

23 girdle: a belt or sash worn around the waist.

27 drear: dreary.
28 shingles: pebbly beaches.

Ⓐ ANALYZE SPEAKER
Whom is the speaker addressing, and why do you think the poem is addressed to this person? Explain what this indicates about the speaker's feelings regarding isolation.

Blue Moonlight over Yellow Sands (1824), Joseph Mallord William Turner. Watercolor on paper, 26.8 cm × 37.7 cm. Bequeathed by the artist, 1856. © Tate Gallery, London/Art Resource, New York.

To Marguerite —Continued

Matthew Arnold

Yes! in the sea of life enisled,
With echoing straits between us thrown,
Dotting the shoreless watery wild,
We mortal millions live alone.
5 The islands feel the enclasping flow,
And then their endless bounds they know.

But when the moon their hollows lights,
And they are swept by balms of spring,
And in their glens, on starry nights,
10 The nightingales divinely sing;
And lovely notes, from shore to shore,
Across the sounds and channels pour—

Oh! then a longing like despair
Is to their farthest caverns sent;
15 For surely once, they feel, we were
Parts of a single continent!
Now round us spreads the watery plain—
Oh might our marges meet again! **B**

Who ordered that their longing's fire
20 Should be, as soon as kindled, cooled?
Who renders vain their deep desire?—
A God, a God their severance ruled!
And bade betwixt their shores to be
The unplumbed, salt, estranging sea.

1 enisled (ĕn-īld′): separated, like islands.

6 bounds: limits or boundaries.

8 balms: soothing scents and airs.
9 glens: valleys.

12 sounds: long, wide bodies of water, larger than channels.

18 marges: margins.

B THEME
To what does Arnold compare mortals? What might this **metaphor** suggest about the poem's message?

22 severance: separation.

24 unplumbed: unmeasured; **estranging** (ĭ-strān′jĭng): alienating.

Comprehension

1. **Recall** In "Dover Beach," what emotion does the speaker associate with the sound of the tides?

2. **Summarize** Explain the request made by the speaker in the final stanza of "Dover Beach."

3. **Clarify** Who, according to the speaker of "To Marguerite—Continued," separates him from his love?

COMMON CORE

RL 2 Determine themes or central ideas of a text. **RL 10** Read and comprehend literature, including poems.

Text Analysis

4. **Identify Controlling Image** Poets often make use of a controlling image—a single image or comparison that extends throughout a literary work and shapes its meaning. Re-examine "To Marguerite—Continued." What controlling image shapes this poem? What yearning does this image convey?

5. **Analyze Speaker** Review the chart you filled in as you read. After reading these two poems, how would you describe each speaker? Citing evidence, explain

   - whom the speaker of each poem is addressing
   - each speaker's state of mind
   - the ideas each expresses about the possibilities or limitations of human love

6. **Interpret Allusion** "Dover Beach" contains an allusion to Sophocles, an ancient Greek playwright. Why do you think Arnold makes this reference?

7. **Examine Theme** What do these poems convey about mankind's sense of the universe's indifference? For each poem, write a sentence stating the theme. Reviewing the information on page 1055, explain which literary elements Arnold uses to convey each theme.

8. **Compare Texts** In his famous "Meditation 17" (page 522), John Donne writes, "No man is an island, entire of itself; every man is a piece of the continent, a part of the main." On the basis of these poems, how would you contrast Arnold's views with Donne's? Cite evidence from both writers' work to support your answer.

Text Criticism

9. **Different Perspectives** Comedic actress Lily Tomlin once advised, "Just remember, we're all in this alone." If Matthew Arnold were writing today, do you think he'd react to the modern world as he reacted to the world in his own time? Explain, citing examples from Arnold's work and aspects of modern life that shaped your opinion.

Is the world **INDIFFERENT** *to us?*

Is your view of nature like that of the Victorians or of the Lake Poets? Discuss a time when you found nature to be indifferent to your existence.

To an Athlete Dying Young
When I Was One-and-Twenty

Poetry by A. E. Housman

Meet the Author

COMMON CORE

RL1 Cite strong and thorough textual evidence to support inferences drawn from the text. **RL5** Analyze how an author's choices concerning how to structure specific parts of a text contribute to its aesthetic impact. **SL1** Initiate and participate effectively in a range of collaborative discussions.

DID YOU KNOW?

A. E. Housman . . .

- composed most of his poems while in his early 20s.

- had never actually been to Shropshire when he began writing *A Shropshire Lad,* his first and most popular collection of poems.

- turned down various awards and honors, including appointment as England's poet laureate.

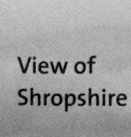

View of Shropshire

A. E. Housman 1859–1936

"In 1920, when I was about 17," author George Orwell once recalled, "I probably knew the whole of *A Shropshire Lad* by heart." Poems from *A Shropshire Lad* were carried into battle by British soldiers in World War I and set to music by some of the 20th century's greatest composers. Yet their author, A. E. Housman, published just one other poetry collection in his lifetime. Instead, he devoted himself to academic pursuits.

A Difficult Youth Alfred Edward Housman grew up in the English county of Worcestershire. From there, he could see the hills of neighboring Shropshire that appear so prominently in his verse. His childhood was made difficult by tensions with his father and the death of his mother when he was just 12. Slight and unathletic, he devoted himself to his studies, showing a brilliant mastery of classical Greek and Latin. Despite his talent, personal problems and anxiety soon took hold of the young scholar. He surprised everyone by failing his final tests at Oxford University. He left without a degree.

Perseverance Pays Off In 1882, Housman took a low-paying job in the patent office in London and shared lodgings with his close college friend Moses Jackson and Moses' brother Adalbert. Working there for ten long years, he pursued his classical studies on his own in the evening. When he began submitting papers to scholarly journals, his scholarship was so impressive that he eventually obtained a professorship at London's University College.

All this time, Housman had been composing poems that came to him when he was out walking. Some displayed a romantic love of nature, while others told dramatic tales of rural tragedy. Many expressed sorrow brought on by the deaths of his mother and father, the departure of Moses Jackson for India, and the death of Adalbert Jackson. When he decided to publish some of his verse, an old college friend suggested the title *A Shropshire Lad,* since many of the poems used Shropshire place names to represent rural life.

Later Years Housman devoted most of the rest of his life to Latin scholarship, moving from University College to Cambridge University in 1911. In 1922, he published a second volume of poetry from his notebooks, much of it written decades before. After his death, his brother Laurence found still more unpublished poetry in the notebooks; Housman's *Complete Poems* appeared in 1959.

Author Online

Go to **thinkcentral.com**. KEYWORD: HML12-1060

THINK central

● TEXT ANALYSIS: RHYME SCHEME

A poem's **rhyme scheme**—the pattern of end rhyme in a stanza or the entire work—can help make the poem memorable for readers. Rhyme is often used to emphasize important words, and it helps create a distinct rhythm. Consider these opening lines of "When I Was One-and-Twenty":

When I was one-and-twenty
I heard a wise man say,
"Give crowns and pounds and guineas
But not your heart away;

In these lines, the rhyme scheme is *abcb*. The first and third lines (*a* and *c*) do not rhyme, but the second and fourth lines (*b* and *b*) do. As you read Housman's poems, note the rhyme scheme of each. Think about the rhythm created by each pattern of rhyme. What overall effect does Housman achieve?

● READING SKILL: MAKE INFERENCES

Your experiences with poetry have probably taught you that when you read a poem, you usually need to **make inferences** to determine its meaning. An inference, or logical assumption, should be based on information in the text as well as your own knowledge and experience. The two poems you are about to read explore the advantages and disadvantages of youth and aging. As you read each poem, use a chart like the one shown to record the inferences you make about these topics. Be sure to note the textual information that allowed you to make each inference.

"To an Athlete Dying Young"	
Advantages	Disadvantages
Youth: • When you're young, you're often in good physical condition, like the triumphant athlete described in lines 1–4.	Youth:
Aging:	Aging:

 Complete the activities in your **Reader/Writer Notebook**.

What STAGE of LIFE *is best?*

The Irish playwright George Bernard Shaw once observed, "Youth is wasted on the young." Do you agree that young people fail to appreciate youth when they are living through it? Or do you think older people sometimes look back with nostalgia on earlier times, imagining them as better than they actually were?

DISCUSS Working with a partner, make a timeline charting the different stages of a typical person's life. For each stage, jot down the experiences and emotions, both positive and negative, that you associate with that stage of life. After completing your timeline, discuss which life stage you think is the most exciting or rewarding. Also consider how nostalgia may affect a person's view of earlier stages. For example, do you think you remember your early childhood accurately? Share your ideas with another group.

TO AN ATHLETE DYING YOUNG

A. E. Housman

The time you won your town the race
We chaired you through the market-place;
Man and boy stood cheering by,
And home we brought you shoulder-high.

5 Today, the road all runners come,
Shoulder-high we bring you home,
And set you at your threshold down,
Townsman of a stiller town.

Smart lad, to slip betimes away
10 From fields where glory does not stay
And early though the laurel grows
It withers quicker than the rose. **A**

Eyes the shady night has shut
Cannot see the record cut,
15 And silence sounds no worse than cheers
After earth has stopped the ears:

Now you will not swell the rout
Of lads that wore their honors out,
Runners whom renown outran
20 And the name died before the man.

So set, before its echoes fade,
The fleet foot on the sill of shade,
And hold to the low lintel up
The still-defended challenge-cup.

25 And round that early-laurelled head
Will flock to gaze the strengthless dead,
And find unwithered on its curls
The garland briefer than a girl's.

2 chaired: carried in public triumph on a chair or seat.

9 betimes: early.

11 laurel: Wreaths made of leaves of the laurel tree were worn by victorious athletes in ancient times as a token of honor and glory.

A **MAKE INFERENCES**
Reread lines 9–12 and consider the poem's title. Why does the speaker call the athlete a "smart lad"? Explain what he thinks the athlete has avoided, and how.

14 cut: broken.

17 rout (rout): crowd.

22 sill: threshold.
23 lintel: the beam across the top of a door frame.

28 garland: a wreath or woven chain of leaves or flowers.

WHEN I WAS
ONE-AND-TWENTY

A. E. Housman

When I was one-and-twenty
    I heard a wise man say,
"Give crowns and pounds and guineas
    But not your heart away;
5 Give pearls away and rubies
    But keep your fancy free."
But I was one-and-twenty,
    No use to talk to me.

When I was one-and-twenty
10   I heard him say again,
"The heart out of the bosom
    Was never given in vain;
'Tis paid with sighs a plenty
    And sold for endless rue."
15 And I am two-and-twenty,
    And oh, 'tis true, 'tis true. **Ⓑ**

3 crowns . . . guineas (gĭn'ēz): British units of money.

6 fancy: liking; affection.

14 rue: sorrow; regret.

Ⓑ RHYME SCHEME
Identify the rhyme scheme of each stanza. How would you describe the **rhythm** this pattern creates?

Comprehension

1. **Recall** In "To an Athlete Dying Young," why did the townspeople "chair" the athlete through the town?

2. **Clarify** What disappointment does the speaker say that the athlete will never know?

3. **Summarize** What advice does the "wise man" give the speaker of "When I Was One-and-Twenty"?

4. **Clarify** What has the speaker realized at the older and wiser age of 22?

Text Analysis

5. **Examine Imagery** In "To an Athlete Dying Young," compare the image in the second stanza with the image in the first stanza. What is the effect of repeating the image in this way?

6. **Analyze Figurative Language** Only in the title of "To an Athlete Dying Young" does Housman explicitly say that the young runner is dead. In light of this information, how would you interpret the following figurative phrases?

   • "the road all runners come" (line 5)
   • "a stiller town" (line 8)
   • "the shady night" (line 13)

7. **Analyze Speaker** Reread lines 9–16 of "When I Was One-and-Twenty." What might account for the change in the speaker's attitude? Give reasons for your answer.

8. **Draw Conclusions** Review the **inferences** you made as you read. On the basis of the details you recorded, what conclusions can you draw about Housman's view of youth and aging? Judging from these poems, what are the advantages and disadvantages of growing older? Explain your conclusions, citing evidence.

9. **Interpret Rhyme Scheme** Read aloud the first stanza of each poem. What musical quality does the rhyme scheme of each create? What relationship do you see between this musical quality and the subject of each poem?

Text Criticism

10. **Critical Interpretations** In 1936, the American poet Conrad Aiken commented that the thoughts expressed in Housman's poetry have an "adolescent note," or "boyishness." Do you think this characterization applies to these poems? Explain why or why not, citing evidence from both poems.

> *What* **STAGE** *of* **LIFE** *is best?*
>
> After reading Housman's biography on page 1060, which stage of his life sounds best to you? Why?

COMMON CORE

RL 1 Cite strong and thorough textual evidence to support inferences drawn from the text. **RL 4** Determine the meaning of words and phrases as they are used in the text, including figurative meanings. **RL 5** Analyze how an author's choices concerning how to structure specific parts of a text contribute to its aesthetic impact.

from The Importance of Being Earnest

Play by Oscar Wilde

Oscar Wilde
1854–1900

COMMON CORE

RL 3 Analyze the impact of the author's choices regarding how to develop and relate elements of a drama. **RL 10** Read and comprehend literature, including dramas.

BACKGROUND Oscar Wilde, one of the wittiest writers of the Victorian age, is famous for his brilliant conversation and flamboyant style. At Oxford University and later in London, he distinguished himself as a poet and scholar and became associated with the aesthetic movement, which stressed the importance of artistic expression for its beauty alone, or "art for art's sake." Although Wilde published poetry, fiction, and nonfiction, his clever conversational skills are most vividly evident in four comedies that he wrote for the London stage in the 1890s: *Lady Windermere's Fan, A Woman of No Importance, An Ideal Husband,* and *The Importance of Being Earnest.*

   The Importance of Being Earnest is one of the most frequently staged comedies in the English language. It is a hilarious romantic farce about two upper-class bachelors who each claim to be named Ernest but have trouble *being* earnest, or honest. Jack Worthing, country gentleman and guardian to a young lady named Cecily, escapes his responsibilities in the country by inventing a scandalous younger brother named Ernest to whose rescue he must often fly. This allows for frequent visits to London, where he takes on the role of Ernest, pursuing pleasure and courting the lovely Gwendolen. Meanwhile, his friend Algernon, Gwendolen's cousin, similarly escapes family duties in London by inventing a friend named Bunbury whose bad health demands frequent country visits. On discovering Jack's real identity and learning of the existence of Jack's ward, Algernon goes off on another country junket, this time posing as Jack's wicked brother Ernest in order to meet the mysterious—and hopefully beautiful—Cecily. In the following scene, Algernon, posing as Ernest, arrives at Jack's country estate and meets Jack's ward, Cecily, for the first time.

TEXT ANALYSIS Wilde is a master of using comedic language, specifically witty repartees and epigrams. In this excerpt, you see an example of an **epigram,** or clever contradictory statement, when Cecily says that she is afraid to meet a "wicked person," not because, as you might expect, she is terrified of someone who is bad, but because she is fearful that a bad person "will look just like every one else." The excerpt also contains an example of a repartee, an exchange of witty comments. Cecily and Algernon go back and forth about his wickedness. Cecily teases Algernon, telling him she hopes he is not "pretending to be wicked." He assures her that he has in fact been "rather reckless." Instead of scolding him for this behavior, she then retorts, "I am glad to hear it," and so it continues.

DISCUSS Read the excerpt through silently. Then, with two partners, assume the roles of Merriman, Cecily, and Algernon, and read the scene aloud. Discuss why you think audiences continue to respond with delight to such dialogue.

from **ACT TWO**

Merriman. Mr. Ernest Worthing has just driven over from the station. He has brought his luggage with him.

Cecily (*takes the card and reads it*). 'Mr. Ernest Worthing, B.4, The Albany, W.' Uncle Jack's brother! Did you tell him Mr. Worthing was in town?

Merriman. Yes, Miss. He seemed very much disappointed. I mentioned that you and Miss Prism were in the garden. He said he was anxious to speak to you privately for a moment.

Cecily. Ask Mr. Ernest Worthing to come here. I suppose you had better talk to the housekeeper about a room for him.

10 **Merriman.** Yes, Miss. (Merriman *goes off.*)

Cecily. I have never met any really wicked person before. I feel rather frightened. I am so afraid he will look just like every one else. (*Enter* Algernon, *very gay and debonair.*) He does!

Algernon (*raising his hat*). You are my little cousin Cecily, I'm sure.

Cecily. You are under some strange mistake. I am not little. In fact, I believe I am more than unusually tall for my age. (Algernon *is rather taken aback.*) But I am your cousin Cecily. You, I see from your card, are Uncle Jack's brother, my cousin Ernest, my wicked cousin Ernest.

Algernon. Oh! I am not really wicked at all, Cousin Cecily. You mustn't think that I 20 am wicked.

Cecily. If you are not, then you have certainly been deceiving us all in a very inexcusable manner. I hope you have not been leading a double life, pretending to be wicked and being really good all the time. That would be hypocrisy.

Algernon (*looks at her in amazement*). Oh! Of course I have been rather reckless.

Cecily. I am glad to hear it.

Algernon. In fact, now you mention the subject, I have been very bad in my own small way.

Cecily. I don't think you should be so proud of that, though I am sure it must have been very pleasant.

30 **Algernon.** It is much pleasanter being here with you.

Cecily. I can't understand how you are here at all. Uncle Jack won't be back till Monday afternoon.

Algernon. That is a great disappointment. I am obliged to go up by the first train on Monday morning. I have a business appointment that I am anxious . . . to miss!

Cecily. Couldn't you miss it anywhere but in London?

Algernon. No: the appointment is in London.

The Darkling Thrush
Ah, Are You Digging on My Grave?

Poetry by Thomas Hardy

COMMON CORE

RL 4 Analyze the impact of specific word choices on tone, including words with multiple meanings or language that is particularly fresh, engaging, or beautiful. RL 9 Demonstrate knowledge of how two or more texts from the same period treat similar themes or topics.

Meet the Author

Thomas Hardy 1840–1928

In the final years of Thomas Hardy's life, dozens of younger British writers made a pilgrimage to visit him at Max Gate, his home outside Dorchester, in southwest England. Virginia Woolf, Robert Graves, E. M. Forster—these and many other writers were paying homage to the novelist and poet whom British author D. H. Lawrence called "our last great writer."

Humble Roots Max Gate was not far from the humble cottage where Hardy grew up. The son of a stonemason, he was educated in Dorchester and later served as an apprentice to a local architect. In 1862, he left for London, where he worked for several years for an architecture firm that specialized in the building of churches. It was during these years that Hardy began writing poetry and fiction in his spare time; his first novel was published in 1871.

Fame for Wessex Success came three years later with *Far from the Madding Crowd,* the first of Hardy's novels to detail the landscape and people of "Wessex," his name for his native southwestern England. The novel's positive reception justified Hardy's decision to give up architecture entirely and devote his life to writing. Soon he had produced a string of successful novels, including *The Return of the Native* and *The Mayor of Casterbridge.*

Controversy and Change In 1891, Hardy's novel *Tess of the d'Urbervilles* provoked a storm of controversy because of its sympathetic treatment of what many viewed as immoral behavior. His next novel, *Jude the Obscure,* was also met with hostility. One critic called it *Jude the Obscene,* and it was banned by bookstores and libraries. Disgusted, Hardy abandoned the novel form and concentrated on his poetry. Gathering poems he had been writing since the 1860s, he revised and published them as *Wessex Poems.* He followed with more poetry collections, as well as *The Dynasts,* a verse drama.

Back to Wessex Like his fiction, Hardy's poems often delve into the ironies of life and explore the indifference of nature and society. Though his poetry, too, had its critics, Hardy was by now recognized as a lion of British literature. When he died, his ashes were interred in Poets' Corner at Westminster Abbey. His heart, however—removed at his request before cremation—was buried in his native "Wessex."

DID YOU KNOW?

Thomas Hardy . . .

- initially wanted to be an architect, not a writer.
- based his novel *A Pair of Blue Eyes* on his experiences courting his wife.
- published 14 novels, 3 volumes of short stories, and over 1,000 poems.

(background)
Hardy's home at Max Gate

Author Online

Go to thinkcentral.com. KEYWORD: HML12-1068

THINK central

TEXT ANALYSIS: TONE

Thomas Hardy is an author known for his **tone,** or attitude expressed toward his subject. In his work, he often focuses on the bitter ironies of life, causing his contemporaries to accuse him of being overly pessimistic—a charge Hardy hotly denied.

Sometimes you can detect a distinct tone in a poem's very first stanza. At other times, however, you must carefully read the whole poem to discern the poet's attitude. As you read "The Darkling Thrush" and "Ah, Are You Digging on My Grave?" consider Hardy's word choice and use of imagery. Think, too, about the mood created by each poem's setting. Exploring these elements will help you detect and analyze Hardy's tone.

READING SKILL: DRAW CONCLUSIONS ABOUT SOCIAL CONTEXT

The **social context** of a work refers to the social conditions that inspired or influenced its creation. Though some of his peers criticized Hardy's pessimistic outlook toward life, this outlook was becoming increasingly common as the Victorian era gave way to the 20th century. A time of transition, the late Victorian era was marked by an exodus to the city as millions of people deserted rural farms. Many social critics, Hardy among them, feared this mass move would mean the loss of old customs, traditions, and values. Also taking hold in this turbulent era was a strong feeling that both nature and society were indifferent to the suffering of the individual. As you read, use a chart to record lines from each poem that you think reveal something about the era in which they were written. After you read, you'll use your notes to **draw conclusions**—or make sound judgments based on evidence and experience—about the conditions to which Hardy is responding in these poems.

"The Darkling Thrush"	
Text Clues	Notes on Social Context
"The ancient pulse of germ and birth / Was shrunken hard and dry," ("The Darkling Thrush," lines 13–14)	These lines refer to the seeds of spring, usually a symbol of hope and rebirth, but here the speaker describes them as hard and lifeless. This might reflect the pessimism or unease about the future common in this era.

 Complete the activities in your **Reader/Writer Notebook**.

Would you rather keep your ILLUSIONS?

Thomas Hardy once remarked, "If way to the Better there be, it exacts a full look at the Worst." Do you agree that it is essential for people to face the truth, no matter how difficult, or is disillusionment just too painful?

DISCUSS With a group of classmates, discuss the definition of *disillusion.* Do you think that people must be free of their illusions in order to fully live? Are there some illusions you would rather hang on to, or is facing painful truths an important part of life? Describe the situations or examples—real or fictional—that influenced your answers.

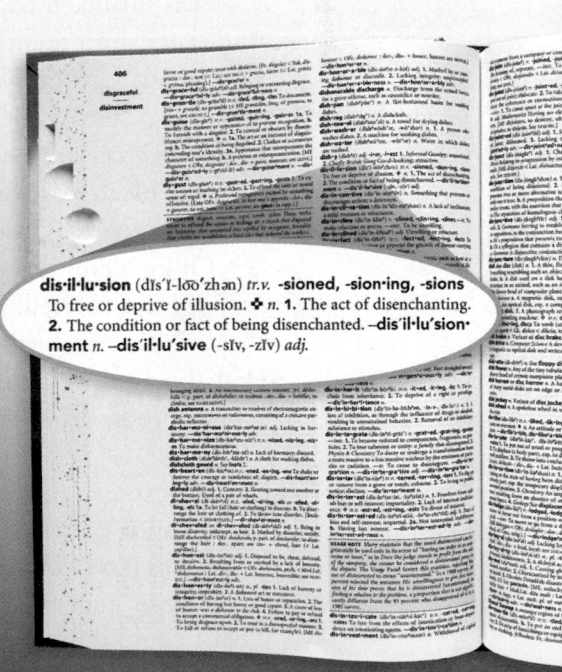

THE Darkling Thrush Thomas Hardy

> **BACKGROUND** This poem was first published in *Graphic* magazine a few days before the end of the 19th century. Its original title was "The Darkling Thrush: By the Century's Deathbed." The word *darkling* means "in the dark."

I leant upon a coppice gate
    When Frost was specter-gray,
And Winter's dregs made desolate
    The weakening eye of day.

5 The tangled bine-stems scored the sky
    Like strings of broken lyres,
And all mankind that haunted nigh
    Had sought their household fires.

The land's sharp features seemed to be
10   The Century's corpse outleant,
His crypt the cloudy canopy,
    The wind his death-lament.
The ancient pulse of germ and birth
    Was shrunken hard and dry,
15 And every spirit upon earth
    Seem'd fervorless as I. **Ⓐ**

At once a voice arose among
    The bleak twigs overhead
In a full-hearted evensong
20   Of joy illimited;
An aged thrush, frail, gaunt, and small,
    In blast-beruffled plume,
Had chosen thus to fling his soul
    Upon the growing gloom.

25 So little cause for carollings
    Of such ecstatic sound
Was written on terrestrial things
    Afar or nigh around,
That I could think there trembled through
30   His happy good-night air
Some blessed Hope, whereof he knew
    And I was unaware. **Ⓑ**

1 coppice (kŏp′ĭs) **gate:** a gate leading to a coppice, a small wood or thicket.

2 specter-gray: ghost-gray.

5 bine-stems scored: twining stems cut across.

6 lyres: harplike musical instruments.

7 nigh: near.

10 outleant: outstretched.

13 germ: seed; bud.

Ⓐ TONE
Consider the poem's **setting,** as well as Hardy's **personification** of the 19th century in line 10. Citing specific words and phrases, explain what tone is established by these literary elements.

19 evensong: evening song.
20 illimited: unlimited.
22 blast-beruffled plume: wind-ruffled feathers.

Ⓑ SOCIAL CONTEXT
Reread lines 25–28. Why does the speaker see "so little cause for carollings"? What aspect of late Victorian thought does this attitude seem to echo?

Song Thrush (1884), Harry Bright. Watercolor on paper. Private collection. © Bridgeman Art Library.

Ah, ARE YOU DIGGING ON MY GRAVE? Thomas Hardy

"Ah, are you digging on my grave,
    My loved one?—planting rue?"
—"No: yesterday he went to wed
One of the brightest wealth has bred.
5 'It cannot hurt her now,' he said,
    'That I should not be true.' "

"Then who is digging on my grave?
    My nearest dearest kin?"
—"Ah, no: they sit and think, 'What use!
10 What good will planting flowers produce?
No tendance of her mound can loose
    Her spirit from Death's gin.'"

"But someone digs upon my grave?
    My enemy?—prodding sly?"
15 —"Nay: when she heard you had passed the Gate
That shuts on all flesh soon or late,
She thought you no more worth her hate,
    And cares not where you lie." **C**

"Then, who is digging on my grave?
20   Say—since I have not guessed!"
—"O it is I, my mistress dear,
Your little dog, who still lives near,
And much I hope my movements here
    Have not disturbed your rest?"

2 rue: an herb associated with sorrow and regret because its name is identical to the word *rue*, meaning "sorrow and regret."

11 tendance: attendance; watchful care.

12 gin: a snare or trap.

C TONE
So far, how does Hardy's tone in this poem compare with the tone he takes in "The Darkling Thrush"? Explain, citing specific lines that influenced your answer.

Fox Terrier (1800s), Arthur Wardle. Oil on canvas. Private collection. © Bridgeman Art Library.

25 "Ah yes! *You* dig upon my grave . . .
        Why flashed it not on me
    That one true heart was left behind!
    What feeling do we ever find
    To equal among human kind
30   A dog's fidelity!"

    "Mistress, I dug upon your grave
        To bury a bone, in case
    I should be hungry near this spot
    When passing on my daily trot.
35 I am sorry, but I quite forgot
        It was your resting place." **D**

D **CONTEXT**
Do you see any connection between the way the woman's loved ones respond to her death and the late Victorian outlook described on page 1069? Explain what social conditions Hardy might be responding to in this poem.

Comprehension

1. **Summarize** What is the **setting** of "The Darkling Thrush"?

2. **Recall** Whose voice does the speaker of this poem hear, and how does he describe the sound?

3. **Clarify** Who are the two speakers conducting a dialogue in "Ah, Are You Digging on My Grave?"

Text Analysis

4. **Interpret Symbol** In "The Darkling Thrush," is the thrush's song hopeful or hopeless? Explain what you think the thrush symbolizes, making sure to address each of the following:

   • when and where the speaker sees the thrush

   • the thrush's appearance and what he has "chosen" to do

   • how the speaker feels about the thrush's song

5. **Identify Irony** Situational irony occurs when a character expects one thing to happen but something else happens instead. Re-examine "Ah, Are You Digging on My Grave?" What reactions to her death does the woman seem to expect? What is ironic about the revelation she receives? Cite evidence to support your answers.

6. **Analyze Satire** Satire is a literary technique in which ideas, customs, or behaviors are ridiculed in order to make a point or improve society. What is Hardy satirizing in "Ah, Are You Digging on My Grave?" Explain your answer.

● 7. **Compare Tone** How are these two poems similar or different in tone? In which poem does Hardy express a harsher or more biting attitude? Explain, citing examples from both poems to support your answers.

● 8. **Draw Conclusions About Social Context** Consider the social context that shaped Hardy's work. How does each of these poems reflect the sense of pessimism and disillusionment permeating the late Victorian era? How does each convey the anxiety about the indifference of nature and society? Cite the evidence you recorded from both poems to support your conclusions.

Text Criticism

9. **Author's Style** Though Hardy's poems reflect the concerns of his time, he is known for his eloquence in expressing **universal themes** as well. Identify the themes expressed in these works. In what way are they universal? Explain, citing evidence.

> *Would you rather keep your* **ILLUSIONS?**
>
> Would you describe Hardy as a realist or an idealist? Cite lines from the poems to defend your position.

COMMON CORE

RL 4 Analyze the impact of specific word choices on tone, including words with multiple meanings or language that is particularly fresh, engaging, or beautiful. **RL 6** Analyze a case in which grasping point of view requires distinguishing what is directly stated in a text from what is really meant. **RL 9** Demonstrate knowledge of how two or more texts from the same period treat similar themes or topics.

Changing Times, Changing Views

The Victorian age was a dynamic one, full of change, promise, and upheaval. Depending on one's perspective, the fast-paced change was either exciting or terrifying. Matthew Arnold's "Dover Beach" poignantly expresses sadness and alienation in response to the times; for this reason, it is viewed by many as the quintessential poem of the 19th century.

> "'Dover Beach' displays at its best Arnold's gift for expressing the feelings of the transitional times—the indecision, the confusion, the regret."
> —**Miriam Allott, *The Victorian Experience: The Poets***

> "'Dover Beach,' perhaps Matthew Arnold's best-known poem, . . . is the fullest expression of its author's religious doubt and a classic text of Victorian anxiety in the face of lost faith."
> —**Lance St. John Butler, "Dover Beach"**

> "'Dover Beach' has been called the first modern poem. If this is true, it is modern not so much in diction and technique . . . but in psychological orientation. Behind the troubled man standing at the lover's conventional moon-filled window looking on the sea, we sense . . . the shift in the human viewpoint from the Christian tradition to the impersonal world of Darwin and the 19th-century scientists."
> —**James Dickey, "Arnold: Dover Beach"**

Extension Online

INQUIRY & RESEARCH Like the Victorians, we live in an age of rapid change, hotly debated for its benefits and its costs. Choose one contemporary technological, intellectual, or cultural change and conduct online research about its advantages and disadvantages. Consult credible reference sites, news sources, and other informational sites for both facts and opinions on the topic. Share your findings with your classmates.

COMMON CORE

W 2 Write explanatory texts to examine and convey complex ideas, concepts, and information clearly and accurately. **W 7** Synthesize multiple sources on the subject, demonstrating understanding of the subject under investigation.

Writing to Synthesize

Matthew Arnold was not the only writer reflecting upon the turbulent changes of the day. In their respective essays "Evidence of Progress" and "The Condition of England," Thomas Macaulay and Thomas Carlyle wrote decisively about the virtues and evils of the age. Choose one of the two authors and write an essay in which you explain how he might have responded to Arnold's poem "Dover Beach." Do you think the essayist would have agreed that the poem expresses the essence of the Victorian age?

Consider

- what you know about the Victorian age as a whole
- the world view expressed by the essayist
- the world view suggested in "Dover Beach"

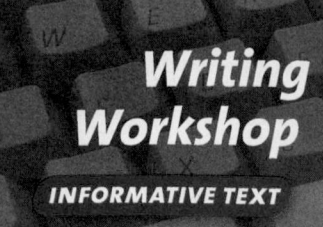

Writing Workshop
INFORMATIVE TEXT

Analysis of Literary Nonfiction

In this unit, you read several critical commentaries and opinion pieces that examine both the external world and the interior world of the mind. The essays represent the authors' efforts to understand the world and the different ways we think about it. In this workshop, you will learn how to write an analysis of literary nonfiction using a logical structure and textual evidence to support your controlling idea.

 Complete the workshop activities in your **Reader/Writer Notebook.**

WRITE WITH A PURPOSE

WRITING TASK

Write a **literary analysis** that focuses on a nonfiction text. Present a well-supported controlling idea and an analysis of the text's main idea and its validity. Your analysis should help the audience understand and appreciate the text.

Idea Starters
- nonfiction texts written by authors of fiction that you enjoy
- nonfiction texts written during a historical period that interests you
- nonfiction texts written about a topic or subject that interests you

THE ESSENTIALS

Here are some common purposes, audiences, and formats for a literary analysis.

PURPOSES	AUDIENCES	FORMATS
• to analyze a nonfiction text • to provide insight into an important subject or movement	• teacher and classmates • parents • literary club members • Web log readers	• essay for class • blog • message board posting • literary review in school newspaper

COMMON CORE TRAITS

1. DEVELOPMENT OF IDEAS
- presents an **engaging introduction**
- develops a **controlling idea** that offers an **analysis** of the author's main idea and its validity
- supports key points of analysis with **relevant examples**
- offers a **concluding section** that sums up the **key points**

2. ORGANIZATION OF IDEAS
- organizes **ideas** and **evidence** in a logical way
- uses appropriate, varied **transitions** to create **cohesion** and **connect ideas**

3. LANGUAGE FACILITY AND CONVENTIONS
- establishes and maintains a **formal style** and **objective**, neutral **tone**
- includes **precise language** and **domain-specific vocabulary**
- avoids **comma splices**
- employs correct **grammar, mechanics,** and **spelling**

Writing Online

THINK central

Go to **thinkcentral.com**.
KEYWORD: HML12N-1076

Planning/Prewriting

COMMON CORE

W 2a–f Write informative texts to examine and convey complex ideas clearly and accurately. **W 5** Develop and strengthen writing as needed by planning. **W 9b (RI 1, 4)** Cite textual evidence; determine meaning of words and phrases as used in a text.

Getting Started

CHOOSE A TEXT FOR ANALYSIS

Find a literary nonfiction text, such as an essay, speech, memoir, history, journal, or letter, about a subject that interests you. Identify the work's title, author, and topic.

▶ **ASK YOURSELF:**

- What subjects do I enjoy reading about?
- Which authors have written on the subject?
- What is the text's topic and the author's purpose for writing?

THINK ABOUT AUDIENCE AND PURPOSE

As you choose a text to analyze, keep in mind that your **purpose** is to develop and support your own analysis of the work. Your analysis should enhance your **audience's** understanding and appreciation of the text.

▶ **ASK YOURSELF:**

- Who is my audience?
- What do I want to convey about the text?
- How can I clearly and accurately explain my ideas?
- What information and **domain-specific vocabulary** will my audience need to know?

ANALYZE THE MAIN IDEA

Remember that nonfiction texts express an idea or insight. To determine the **main idea,** you will need to study the text carefully and then consider how relevant and valid that idea is.

▶ **ASK YOURSELF:**

- What does the author express directly?
- What does the author express indirectly?
- How do the writer's tone and word choice convey key ideas?

ANALYZE THE WRITER'S USE OF LANGUAGE

Pay attention to the writer's use of words and phrases to identify how they affect the writer's **tone,** or attitude toward the subject. Writers may choose specific words for their **connotative** meanings, the emotional response evoked by a word. They may create surprising comparisons by using **figurative** language, or figures of speech—language that communicates ideas beyond the literal meanings of words.

▶ **ASK YOURSELF:**

- What effect does the author's choice of words have on the reader?
- What things or ideas does the writer describe through figurative language?
- What things or ideas do the writer's words connote, or suggest?
- What is the writer's attitude toward the subject?

DEVELOP A CONTROLLING IDEA

Sum up the text's main idea and its validity in a sentence that will guide the rest of your literary analysis. The **controlling idea** should make a statement that you can support with textual evidence.

▶ **WHAT DOES IT LOOK LIKE?**

> In her essay "The Death of the Moth," Virginia Woolf effectively uses the existential struggle of an insect as an extended metaphor for all of human existence.

Planning/Prewriting *continued*

Getting Started

GATHER SUPPORT

Select two or more key points that support your controlling idea and give readers reason to accept the validity of your analysis. Use textual **evidence—significant and relevant facts, extended definitions, concrete details, quotations,** and **examples**—to support each key point. Your evidence must be **relevant**, or related, to your controlling idea and **thorough** enough to help your audience understand your analysis. **Elaborate** on each piece of evidence, providing information on other perspectives and analyzing views that contradict your controlling idea.

▶ **WHAT DOES IT LOOK LIKE?**

Key Point: The moth symbolizes life and energy.

Textual Evidence: Quotation: "The same energy . . . sent the moth fluttering . . ."

Elaboration: Woolf uses the word <u>energy</u> several times to make the connection clear.

ORGANIZE YOUR ANALYSIS

Your ideas and key points should build on one another in a logical and cohesive way. Organize your analysis—either **chronologically** or by **order of importance**. Create a plan to organize your thoughts. Use **syntax** (how words are arranged in a sentence) and **appropriate and varied transitions** to show relationships among ideas.

To show chronology, use words such as *after, before, during, then, next,* and *last.* To show order of importance, use words such as *most important, mainly,* and *first.* To connect ideas, use transition words such as *also, and, as well as,* and *like.*

▶ **WHAT DOES IT LOOK LIKE?**

<u>Title and Author:</u> "The Death of the Moth" by Virginia Woolf

<u>Organization:</u> Chronological order

* **Introduction:** Controlling idea--In her essay "The Death of the Moth," Virginia Woolf effectively uses the existential struggle of an insect as an extended metaphor for all of human existence.

* **Body:** Explain symbolism of moth; use evidence from essay; elaborate on details.

* **Concluding Section:** Restate controlling idea; provide insight with quote about life being strange.

PEER REVIEW Share your controlling idea with a peer. Ask: What evidence from the text will help support my analysis?

 YOUR TURN

In your *Reader/Writer Notebook,* develop your writing plan and controlling idea. Consider these tips as you gather evidence:

- Reread parts of the text that discuss important ideas.
- Write down textual evidence that supports your key points.
- Think about the relevance and validity of the ideas expressed in the text.

Drafting

 **COMMON CORE** **W 2c** Use appropriate and varied transitions. **W 4** Produce clear and coherent writing appropriate to task, purpose and audience.

The following chart shows a structure for organizing a clear and coherent literary analysis.

Organizing Your Literary Analysis

INTRODUCTION

- Begin with an engaging **question** or **statement,** and provide the text's **author** and **title.**
- Include a clear **controlling idea** about the text's main idea and its relevance or validity.
- Establish and maintain a **formal style** and **objective tone.**

▼

BODY

- Organize key points in a logical manner, such as **chronologically** or by **order of importance.**
- Include textual evidence—**relevant facts, extended definitions, concrete details, quotations,** or **examples—** to support your key points.
- Use **precise language** and define **domain-specific vocabulary** to convey ideas.

▼

CONCLUDING SECTION

- Restate your **controlling idea,** and summarize your **key points.**
- End your literary analysis with **a final thought** or **insight** for your audience to ponder.

GRAMMAR IN CONTEXT: TRANSITIONS

Writers use transitions to create cohesion and clarify relationships among ideas and concepts. Transitions can be used to show time, to compare and contrast, to show causation, to emphasize, and to show position, among other things.

Transitions

Time		The moth becomes temporarily still; **meanwhile,** she admits, "I forgot about him."
Compare/Contrast	▶	**However,** as the essay progresses, the inevitable occurs.
Causation	▶	She realizes her effort to help is fruitless. **Consequently,** she puts the pencil down.
Emphasis	▶	**Even** those who shrug at the death of a moth must consider that we all, as living, breathing creatures, face the same fate.
Position	▶	**Beyond** the moth, she sees a landscape through the window, full of energy and life.

YOUR TURN Develop a first draft of your literary analysis, following the structure outlined in the chart above. As you write, be sure to use varied and appropriate transitions to create cohesion and clarify relationships among ideas.

Revising

As you revise, evaluate the content, organization, and style of your essay. Your goal is to determine if you have achieved your purpose and effectively communicated your ideas to your intended audience. The questions, tips, and strategies in the following chart will help you revise or rework your analysis.

LITERARY ANALYSIS

Ask Yourself	Tips	Revision Strategies
1. **Does the essay have an engaging introduction? Does it include a clear controlling idea?**	▶ **Highlight** thought-provoking statements or questions. **Double underline** the controlling idea.	▶ **Add** an attention-getting statement or quotation. **Add** a controlling idea, or **replace** with a stronger, clearer one.
2. **Does the essay include key points that support the controlling idea? Is there relevant textual evidence to support each key point?**	▶ **Bracket** each key point. **Put a check mark** by each relevant piece of evidence—facts, definitions, details, quotes, or examples.	▶ **Add** key points that support the controlling idea. **Add** facts, definitions, details, quotes, or examples to bolster unsupported points.
3. **Do I maintain a formal style and objective tone throughout the analysis?**	▶ **Draw a wavy line** under contractions, slang, and subjective language or words.	▶ **Replace** informal language. **Make** subjective language more impartial.
4. **Are the key points and textual evidence presented in a logical sequence?**	▶ **Number** the points in the order in which they appear.	▶ **Reorder** the parts that feel out of place. Be sure to emphasize the most important points.
5. **Do I use appropriate and varied transitions to clarify the relationships among my key points and evidence?**	▶ **Draw a star** next to each transitional word or phrase.	▶ **Check** your starred transitions and **add** variety if necessary. **Reread** the parts that lack stars. **Add** appropriate transitions to link related ideas.
6. **Does the concluding section restate my controlling idea and explain its significance?**	▶ **Circle** the controlling idea. **Draw an arrow** to the statement about its signficance.	▶ **Restate** the controlling idea and **add** an insight about its significance.

 **YOUR TURN** **PEER REVIEW** Working with a classmate, review your drafts together. Discuss whether your classmate has provided clear reasons or key points and supported them with relevant textual evidence and elaboration. Using the revision strategies in the chart, give concrete suggestions on how to improve your drafts or where to try a new approach.

ANALYZE A STUDENT DRAFT

Read this student draft, and notice the comments on its strengths as well as suggestions for improvement.

COMMON CORE

W 2b Develop the topic by selecting the most significant and relevant quotations. **W 5** Develop and strengthen writing as needed by revising, editing, rewriting, or trying a new approach.

Life and Death
by Julia Morado, Donnellon High School

1   A close examination of a seemingly trivial event, a moth's death, can help us explore universal questions. In her essay "The Death of the Moth," Virginia Woolf effectively uses the existential struggle of an insect as an extended metaphor for all of human existence.

> Julia states the **title** and **author** and presents her **controlling idea.**

2   To Woolf, the moth symbolizes life and energy. She refers to the moth with the masculine pronouns "him" and "his." By doing so, she makes his struggle representative of all living things—including human beings. She explains, "The same energy which inspired the rooks, the ploughmen, the horses . . . sent the moth fluttering from side to side of his square window pane." She describes the moth by saying, "Watching him, it seemed as if a fibre, very thin but pure, of the enormous energy of the world had been thrust into his frail and diminutive body." Woolf contemplates that perhaps the moth's purpose was "to show us the true nature of life." The first part of the extended metaphor is clear as Woolf observes that the moth represents the essence of life.

> Her first **key point** is that the moth is a symbol of life and energy. Julia uses **direct quotations** from the text as supporting **evidence,** but she can better incorporate them into her analysis.

LEARN HOW Interweave Partial Quotations Julia can better incorporate quotations by using only the strongest part of the quoted material. Using strong verbs and direct objects is a good way to interweave quotations into your analysis.

JULIA'S REVISION TO PARAGRAPH **2**

reinforces this thought by saying it seemed as if some of that energy

She ~~describes the moth by saying, "Watching him, it seemed as if a fibre, very thin but pure, of the enormous energy of the world~~ had been thrust into his frail and diminutive body."

❸   Even when confronted with the representation of "something marvelous," Woolf confesses that she, like all human beings, "is apt to forget all about life." The moth becomes temporarily still; meanwhile, she admits, "I forgot about him." She forgets the moth—and the marvel of life it represents—in the course of her daily activities.

> Julia makes another **key point**—humans often take life for granted.

❹   However, as the essay progresses, the inevitable occurs. The moth begins to die, futilely struggling and fluttering to the bottom of the window, finally resting on his back on the windowsill. Seeing his vain efforts to recover, Woolf picks up a pencil to help the moth, but realizes the presence of death. Her effort to help is fruitless. As she observes the finally still moth, Woolf imagines him to say, "death is stronger than I am."

> Julia's analysis follows **chronological order** and uses **transitions** to show it. She quotes textual **evidence** but doesn't **connect it to her controlling idea.**

❺   Woolf uses the moth's struggle to contemplate life and death. "Just as life had been strange," she says, "death was now as strange." She explores the mysteries of both states through the extended metaphor of the moth's existential struggle. Human existence mirrors that of the insignificant moth, even those who shrug at the death of a moth must consider that we all, as living, breathing creatures, face the same fate.

> Her **concluding section** revisits the **controlling idea** and adds a final thought for readers to contemplate.

LEARN HOW   **Connect Supporting Evidence to the Controlling Idea**   Julia uses a quotation as evidence, but she does not connect it to her controlling idea. Julia revised paragraph 4 to connect textual evidence to her controlling idea.

JULIA'S REVISION TO PARAGRAPH ❹

As she observes the finally still moth, Woolf imagines him to say, "death is stronger than I am."

In the metaphor of the moth's death, Woolf's message is clear: All living things will inevitably succumb to death. In accepting that death is stronger than our will, we accept that there is a larger, more powerful force that controls our fate.

 **YOUR TURN**   Use the feedback from your peers and teacher as well as the two "Learn How" lessons to revise your literary analysis. Evaluate how thoroughly you have presented and supported your controlling idea. Also, consider how well you connected your evidence to your controlling idea.

W 5 Develop and strengthen writing as needed by revising, editing, rewriting, or trying a new approach. **L 2** Demonstrate command of the conventions of standard English capitalization, punctuation, and spelling.

COMMON
CORE

Editing and Publishing

In the editing stage, you review your essay to make sure that it is free of grammar, spelling, and punctuation errors. Read your essay slowly and carefully to catch any overlooked misspelled words. You don't want mistakes to distract your audience from focusing on your ideas.

GRAMMAR IN CONTEXT: COMMA SPLICES

A comma splice occurs when two complete thoughts are joined by only a comma. Also called a run-on sentence, a comma splice can be corrected in one of four ways: separate the comma splice into two sentences, change it to a compound sentence by adding a comma and coordinating conjunction, change it to a compound sentence by adding a semicolon, or change it to a compound sentence by adding a semicolon and conjunctive adverb.

As Julia edited her analysis, she realized she had incorrectly punctuated a sentence and created a comma splice. Julia corrected the comma splice by adding a semicolon and a conjunctive abverb.

> Human existence mirrors that of the insignificant moth ~~,~~ ; consequently, even those who shrug at the death of a moth must consider that we all, as living, breathing creatures, face the same fate.

PUBLISH YOUR WRITING

Share your literary analysis with an audience in one of the following ways:

- Submit or post your essay to a Web site devoted to the author of the text you analyzed.
- Create your own blog, and post your analysis on it. Add past and future writing assignments to your blog to create an online portfolio.
- Adapt your analysis into a power presentation, and present it to the class or make it available on the Web.

YOUR TURN

Correct any errors in your literary analysis. Make sure that you elaborate and connect your evidence—especially direct quotations—to your controlling idea. Edit carefully, ensuring that your analysis is free of comma splices. Then, publish your final analysis where your audience is likely to see it.

Scoring Rubric

Use the rubric below to evaluate your literary analysis from the Writing Workshop or your response to the on-demand task on the next page.

LITERARY ANALYSIS

SCORE	COMMON CORE TRAITS
6	• **Development** Has an engaging introduction; includes a controlling idea with an insightful analysis of the author's text; supports key points with relevant evidence; ends powerfully • **Organization** Arranges ideas in an effective, logical order; uses varied transitions to create cohesion and clarify relationships among ideas • **Language** Consistently maintains a formal style and objective tone; uses precise language; shows a strong command of conventions
5	• **Development** Has an effective introduction; provides a controlling idea that offers an original analysis of the author's text; supports key points with evidence; has a strong concluding section • **Organization** Arranges ideas logically; uses transitions to link ideas • **Language** Maintains a formal style and objective tone; uses precise language; has a few errors in conventions
4	• **Development** Has an introduction that could be more engaging; includes a controlling idea that states an analysis of the author's text; could use some more evidence; has an adequate concluding section • **Organization** Arranges ideas logically; could vary transitions more • **Language** Mostly maintains a formal style and objective tone; needs more precise language at times; has a few distracting errors in conventions
3	• **Development** Has an adequate introduction; has a controlling idea that makes an obvious statement about the author's text; lacks sufficient support; has a routine concluding section • **Organization** Reflects some flaws in organization; needs more transitions to link related ideas • **Language** Frequently lapses into an informal style and subjective tone; uses some vague word choices; has some significant errors in conventions
2	• **Development** Has a weak introduction and a controlling idea that does not relate to the writing task; lacks specific evidence; has a weak concluding section • **Organization** Has organizational flaws; lacks transitions throughout • **Language** Uses an informal style and vague language; has many distracting errors in conventions
1	• **Development** Has no introduction or controlling idea; offers unrelated points as evidence; ends abruptly • **Organization** Includes a string of disconnected ideas with no overall organization • **Language** Uses an inappropriate style and vague, tired language; has major problems with grammar, mechanics, and spelling

Preparing for Timed Writing

COMMON CORE

W 10 Write routinely over shorter time frames for a range of tasks, purposes, and audiences.

1. ANALYZE THE TASK   5 MIN

Read the task carefully. Then, read it again, underlining the words that identify the audience, the topic, and the purpose.

> **WRITING TASK**
>
> Works of literature are often associated with a literary movement, such as realism, regionalism, naturalism, or modernism. Choose a literary movement that you have *Topic →*
> studied. Write a literary analysis explaining to classmates how the movement affected literature of the period. *Purpose ↗*   *↖ Audience*

2. PLAN YOUR RESPONSE   10 MIN

Once you have decided on a literary movement, ask yourself some questions.
- What background information and domain-specific vocabulary will my readers need to understand?
- What literary texts or authors can I cite as examples of the movement?
- What effect did the movement have on literature?
- What contradictory views, if any, can I address about the movement?

3. RESPOND TO THE TASK   20 MIN

Start writing by introducing your controlling idea—a statement about the literary movement's effect on literature. Then, write down your key points. Organize your key points by order of importance, addressing the most important effect first. Then, do the following:
- Provide evidence—examples of authors or specific literary texts—to support your controlling idea.
- Elaborate on how each piece of evidence supports your controlling idea.
- Conclude your literary analysis with a restatement of your controlling idea and a summary of your key points.

4. IMPROVE YOUR RESPONSE   5–10 MIN

Revising Check your draft against the writing task. Does your draft clearly state a controlling idea about the literary movement's effect on literature? Does it provide relevant and sufficient supporting evidence? Do you end with an insight about the literary movement or its effect on society?

Proofreading Find and correct any errors in grammar, usage, spelling, or mechanics. Make sure that your paper and any edits are neatly written and legible.

Checking Your Final Copy Before you submit your paper, examine it once more to make sure that you are presenting your best work.

Technology Workshop

Creating a Power Presentation

You can reach an audience in a new and effective way by presenting your ideas in a power presentation. Modern computer software and other equipment can help you create a presentation that is informative, expressive, and interesting.

 Complete the workshop activities in your **Reader/Writer Notebook**.

PRODUCE WITH A PURPOSE	COMMON CORE TRAITS
TASK Adapt your literary analysis into a **power presentation** that conveys your controlling idea and supporting evidence in a clear and visually interesting way.	**A STRONG POWER PRESENTATION . . .** • integrates information and evidence from multiple sources • is clearly organized and includes at least one slide for each major idea or point in the analysis • makes strategic use of textual, graphical, audio, and visual elements to enhance understanding and add interest

COMMON CORE

SL 2 Integrate multiple sources of information presented in diverse formats and media. **SL 4** Present information and supporting evidence. **SL 5** Make strategic use of digital media in presentations.

Plan Your Presentation

As you adapt your literary analysis into a power presentation, use the following tips to help you present your information in a way that will engage your audience:

1. **Identify the Basics** First, identify the main elements of your presentation: your subject, purpose, controlling idea, and key points. Then review the evidence you used when developing your literary analysis. Identify any of that evidence that would lend itself to a power presentation. Be sure to integrate information and specific evidence, such as quotations or examples, from multiple sources on the topic to increase the credibility of your perspective.

2. **Plan Your Slides** Organize your presentation to include at least one slide for each of the following: your controlling idea, each key point, supporting evidence for each point, and your concluding statement. Be sure that your slides clearly present your perspective by including a headline and bullet points on each slide. Also, provide information on alternative or opposing perspectives.

3. **Use Appropriate Graphics and Design** Consider adding images that relate to your controlling idea and key points. Does the author use any imagery or figurative language that suggests an image you can incorporate into your presentation? Also, be sure to keep the style of your slides appropriate to your purpose and audience. For a formal style, use a simple font and subdued colors. Each headline should use the same font style, size, and color throughout the presentation. Likewise, present key points in the same font style, size, and color.

4. **Consider Adding Audio and Interactive Elements** Adding an audio element, such as music, or an interactive element, such as animation, is a great way to add interest to your presentation. Select elements that will best fit with the tone of your presentation and enhance the audience's understanding of the topic.

Media Tools

THINK central

Go to thinkcentral.com. KEYWORD: HML12-1086

Deliver Your Presentation

ENGAGE YOUR AUDIENCE

Don't simply read through each slide of your presentation. Explain and expand on each bullet point, making sure to clearly convey your information so that the listeners can follow your line of reasoning. When you are finished going through all the slides, ask listeners if they have any questions. Upon getting a question, thank the listener for the question and restate it so that the whole audience hears what has been asked. Then, as you answer each question, feel free to return to any slide(s) that might help clarify your response.

USE VERBAL TECHNIQUES

Be sure to consider how you will deliver your information. Your use of verbal techniques can be just as effective as the slides you are presenting. Although your presentation should be somewhat formal, try to speak in a relaxed manner. Speak loudly enough so that everyone can hear, but not so loudly that you are yelling. Use a slow, steady pace with a natural rhythm, and enunciate your words. State your ideas confidently rather than phrasing them like questions.

USE NONVERBAL TECHNIQUES

Just as verbal techniques can be used to complement your presentation, facial expressions and gestures can also make your presentation more effective. The following tips will help you make the most out of the facial expressions and gestures that you use:

- Make eye contact with your listeners as you explain the information contained in your slides.

- Use hand gestures to emphasize key points in your presentation.

- Adjust your facial expressions to match the content of your speech.

- Address all sections of the audience during your presentation by alternately facing people in different parts of the room as you speak.

YOUR TURN

As a Presenter Present your power presentation to a friend or family member. Ask for feedback on the organization and content of your slides as well as on your presentation techniques. Use the feedback to improve your slides and presentation skills.

As a Viewer/Listener Listen attentively to your classmates' presentations. Look at the presenters when they speak, and carefully consider the slides used in the presentation. Identify the controlling idea and key points of the analysis. If any points seem unclear, ask for clarification when the presentation is over. Pay attention to each presenter's use of digital media, and note the effectiveness of each element.

Assessment Practice

DIRECTIONS Read the following texts and then answer the questions.

Neutral Tones   *by Thomas Hardy*

We stood by a pond that winter day,
And the sun was white, as though chidden of God,[1]
And a few leaves lay on the starving sod;
    —They had fallen from an ash, and were gray.

5 Your eyes on me were as eyes that rove
Over tedious riddles of years ago;
And some words played between us to and fro
    On which lost the more by our love.

The smile on your mouth was the deadest thing
10 Alive enough to have strength to die;
And a grin of bitterness swept thereby
    Like an ominous bird a-wing. . . .

Since then, keen lessons that love deceives,
And wrings with wrong, have shaped to me
15 Your face, and the God-curst sun, and a tree,
    And a pond edged with grayish leaves.

---

1. **chidden of God:** scolded by God.

from Adam Bede *by George Eliot*

1   It was about three o'clock when Adam entered the farmyard and roused Alick and the dogs from their Sunday dozing. Alick said everybody was gone to church but "th' young missis"—so he called Dinah; but this did not disappoint Adam, although the "everybody" was so liberal as to include Nancy, the dairymaid, whose works of necessity were not unfrequently incompatible with church-going.

2   There was perfect stillness about the house: the doors were all closed, and the very stones and tubs seemed quieter than usual. Adam heard the water gently dripping from the pump—that was the only sound; and he knocked at the house door rather softly, as was suitable in that stillness.

3   The door opened and Dinah stood before him, coloring deeply with the great surprise of seeing Adam at this hour, when she knew it was his regular practice to be at church. Yesterday he would have said to her without any difficulty, "I came to see you, Dinah: I knew the rest were not at home." But today something prevented him from saying that, and he put out his hand to her in silence. Neither of them spoke, and yet both wished they could speak, as Adam entered, and they sat down. Dinah took the chair she had just left; it was at the corner of the table near the window, and there was a book lying on the table, but it was not open: she had been sitting perfectly still, looking at the small bit of clear fire in the bright grate. Adam sat down opposite her, in Mr Poyser's three-cornered chair.

4   "Your mother is not ill again, I hope, Adam," Dinah said, recovering herself. "Seth said she was well this morning."

5   "No, she's very hearty today," said Adam, happy in the signs of Dinah's feeling at the sight of him, but shy.

6   "There's nobody at home, you see," Dinah said; "but you'll wait. You've been hindered from going to church today, doubtless."

7   "Yes," Adam said, and then paused, before he added, "I was thinking about you: that was the reason."

8   This confession was very awkward and sudden, Adam felt; for he thought Dinah must understand all he meant. But the frankness of the words caused her immediately to interpret them into a renewal of his brotherly regrets that she was going away, and she answered calmly, "Do not be careful and troubled for me, Adam. I have all things and abound at Snowfield. And my mind is at rest, for I am not seeking my own will in going."

9   "But if things were different, Dinah," said Adam, hesitatingly—"if you knew things that perhaps you don't know now . . ."

10 Dinah looked at him inquiringly, but instead of going on, he reached a chair and brought it near the corner of the table where she was sitting. She wondered, and was afraid—and the next moment her thoughts flew to the past: was it something about those distant unhappy ones that she didn't know?

11 Adam looked at her: it was so sweet to look at her eyes, which had now a self-forgetful questioning in them,—for a moment he forgot that he wanted to say anything, or that it was necessary to tell her what he meant.

12 "Dinah," he said suddenly, taking both her hands between his, "I love you with my whole heart and soul."

Reading Comprehension

Use "Neutral Tones" (p. 1088) to answer questions 1–6.

1. Which word best describes the overall tone of this poem?
   A. Admiring   C. Indifferent
   B. Bleak   D. Sarcastic

2. Which words from the poem best convey its tone?
   A. Pond, leaves, winter
   B. Starving, gray, ominous
   C. Alive, keen, tedious
   D. Strength, wrong, white

3. In lines 5 and 15, the speaker in the poem is addressing a —
   A. deceased child
   B. new spouse
   C. former love
   D. younger self

4. The speaker of "Neutral Tones" is a —
   A. distant observer of events in the poem
   B. voice that talks to the reader
   C. symbol of the forces of nature
   D. person who is involved in the experience

5. The speaker is reflecting on —
   A. a failed relationship
   B. a newfound love
   C. childhood dreams
   D. the difficulties of marriage

6. You can infer from lines 13–16 that the speaker —
   A. believes that love is strengthened through separation
   B. has had other experiences that confirm a pessimistic view of love
   C. plans to reconcile with the beloved
   D. has found happiness in a current relationship

Use "Adam Bede" (p. 1089) to answer questions 7–13.

7. Paragraph 2 illustrates which characteristic of realism?
   A. A detailed setting that is drawn from real life
   B. The exposing of society's ills in order to help the oppressed
   C. A focus on characters' feelings rather than on action
   D. Dialogue that sounds like everyday speech

8. Adam and Dinah are realistic characters because they are —

A. certain of what the future holds for them

B. symbolic of popular ideas of the era

C. complex people shown in everyday circumstances

D. two young people who are deeply in love

9. In paragraphs 3–5 what can you infer about Adam's and Dinah's feelings from this encounter?

A. They are angry at each other.

B. They are attracted to each other.

C. They are confused about their plans.

D. They are happy about their upcoming marriage.

10. From the information the narrator reveals about Dinah, you can infer that she is —

A. arrogant

B. secretive

C. serious

D. unreasonable

11. Alick's expression "th' young missis" adds realism to the excerpt because it —

A. injects humor into a serious scene

B. deals with issues of youth and old age

C. reflects feelings of social discontent

D. captures the sound of everyday speech

12. You can tell that this excerpt is written from an omniscient point of view because the narrator is —

A. a main character who addresses the reader directly

B. an outside voice who reveals the thoughts and feelings of multiple characters

C. an observer who relays the emotions of just one character

D. a minor character who refers to himself or herself in the first person

13. The omniscient point of view helps the author create —

A. interesting and complex characters

B. a world of fantasy and reality

C. exciting and suspenseful action

D. sympathy for one character over another

> **Use both texts to answer question 14.**

14. Which statement accurately compares the themes presented in both selections?

A. "Neutral Tones" offers a lighthearted message about love, while *Adam Bede* suggests that love is a somber experience.

B. Both selections use nature imagery to convey a message about the fragile beauty of young love.

C. "Neutral Tones" contemplates a romantic breakup, while *Adam Bede* describes the hopeful beginning of a romance.

D. "Neutral Tones" implies that love grows over time, while *Adam Bede* implies that love fades over time.

SHORT CONSTRUCTED RESPONSE
Write three or four sentences to answer this question.

15. Omniscient narrators of the Victorian era are often described as "intrusive"; they frequently air their own opinions. Is the narrator of *Adam Bede* intrusive? Explain your answer.

Write two to three paragraphs to answer this question.

16. What words and images allow each writer's tone to emerge? Support your answer with examples from each selection.

GO ON ➡

Vocabulary

13. The penultimate point of

Use context clues to answer the following questions.

1. What is the most likely meaning of the word *ominous* as it is used in line 12 of "Neutral Tones"?

   A. Graceful

   B. Injured

   C. Predatory

   D. Threatening

2. What is the most likely meaning of the word *liberal* as it is used in paragraph 1 of the excerpt from *Adam Bede*?

   A. Broad

   B. Forceful

   C. Ironic

   D. Misunderstood

3. The word *abound* in paragraph 8 of the excerpt from *Adam Bede* means —

   A. well supplied

   B. tied with ropes

   C. living quietly

   D. eager to escape

4. What is the most likely meaning of the word *inquiringly* as it is used in paragraph 10 of the excerpt from *Adam Bede*?

   A. Without embarrassment

   B. With a suspicious mind

   C. In a questioning manner

   D. From a different perspective

Use context clues and the prefixes in the chart to answer the following questions.

Prefix	Meaning
dis-	not; absence of
in-	not
re-	again; in return
un-	not
trans-	across

5. What is the meaning of the word *unfrequently* as it is used in paragraph 1 of the excerpt from *Adam Bede*?

   A. Every Sunday

   B. Not very often

   C. Whenever possible

   D. A single time

6. What is the meaning of the word *incompatible* as it is used in paragraph 1 of the excerpt from *Adam Bede*?

   A. Not allowed

   B. Not needed

   C. Cannot occur at the same time

   D. Cannot happen in the same area

7. What is the meaning of the word *renewal* as it is used in paragraph 8 of the excerpt from *Adam Bede*?

   A. Refusal

   B. Relapse

   C. Remembrance

   D. Repetition

Revising and Editing

DIRECTIONS Read this passage and answer the questions that follow.

(1) At five A.M., Henry and Ann reluctantly awaken and breathing in the damp morning air. (2) The children look through the window of their family's flat. (3) The air looks gray and smoky. (4) The two get dressed and leave. (5) The cotton mill, where they will spend the next 12 hours, awaits. (6) The walk to work is unpleasant. (7) Once arrive at the mill, they will breathe in bad air. (8) The life of a Victorian child is not an easy one.

1. What change, if any, should be made in sentence 1?

  A. Insert a comma after *awaken*

  B. Change *reluctantly* to **reluctently**

  C. Change *breathing* to **breathe**

  D. Make no change

2. What is the most effective way to combine sentences 2 and 3?

  A. The children look through the window of their family's flat; the air looks gray and smoky.

  B. The children look through the window of their family's flat, but the air looks gray and smoky.

  C. The children look through the window of their family's flat; therefore, the air looks gray and smoky.

  D. The children look through the window of their family's flat which the air looks gray and smoky.

3. What is the most effective way to revise sentence 4 using a prepositional phrase?

  A. The two dress by candlelight and leave before sunrise.

  B. After they dress hurriedly, the two leave.

  C. The two dress blindly and leave just as morning breaks.

  D. Still half-asleep, the two dress and leave.

4. John wants to add this sentence to the paragraph.

They trudge through dank, filthy streets that are choked with garbage.

Where is the best place to insert this sentence?

  A. At the beginning of the paragraph

  B. After sentence 5

  C. After sentence 6

  D. After sentence 7

5. What change, if any, should be made in sentence 7?

  A. Change *breathe* to **breathed**

  B. Delete comma

  C. Insert *they* after **Once**

  D. Make no change

STOP

Ideas for Independent Reading

Continue exploring the Questions of the Times on pages 912–913 with these additional works.

When is progress a PROBLEM?

Hard Times
by Charles Dickens

This novel takes aim at the dark side of industrialization, focusing on its dehumanizing effects on workers and communities. Taking place in a fictional industrial center called Coketown, the story follows the Gradgrind family. Thomas Gradgrind teaches his children only the most factual, pragmatic information—leaving no room for culture or the imagination. He marries off his daughter to a ruthless manufacturer; his son grows up to be a callous and unscrupulous man. Only after a series of crises does Thomas understand that his pragmatic principles have corrupted his children's lives.

North and South
by Elizabeth Cleghorn Gaskell

North and South tells the story of Margaret Hale, a genteel woman from southern England who moves to the northern industrial town of Milton. Margaret sympathizes with the discontented millworkers she meets there, yet finds herself growing ever more attracted to the charismatic mill owner, John Thornton. A love story at heart, this novel contrasts the nostalgia Margaret feels for England's agrarian past with the disturbing yet exciting atmosphere of her present life.

Can values be IMPOSED?

Into Africa: The Epic Adventures of Stanley and Livingstone
by Martin Dugard

In the late 1860s, explorer and missionary David Livingstone journeyed far into the interior of Africa in search of the source of the river Nile. After several years with no word from Livingstone, members of the Royal Geographic Society feared he was dead. Sensing a good story, the owner of the *New York Herald* sent daredevil reporter Henry Morgan Stanley to find the lost explorer. This account of Stanley's successful journey vividly describes the astounding hardships—from malaria to monsoons to tribal wars—that Africa put in the way of the two men, while illuminating the activities of European imperialists in late-19th-century Africa.

Kim
by Rudyard Kipling

Rudyard Kipling was born in India and educated in England. He was an ardent imperialist whose work would come under attack by future generations for its sometimes chauvinistic attitude toward Britain's subjugated peoples. Yet no one disputes his talent for telling a story. *Kim* describes the rousing adventure of a young Irish orphan in India who becomes the disciple of a Tibetan monk while spying for the British secret service. In its telling, Kipling vividly and sympathetically describes the sights, sounds, and smells, the opulence and squalor, and the sheer complexity and diversity of India under British rule.

Is it better to escape or face REALITY?

Wuthering Heights
by Emily Brontë

After reading *Wuthering Heights,* Virginia Woolf wrote of Emily Brontë: "Hers . . . is the rarest of all powers. She could free life from its dependence on facts; with a few touches indicate the spirit of a face so that it needs no body; by speaking of the moor, make the wind blow and the thunder roar." Indeed, the epic love story of Catherine and Heathcliff—set in the wild, bleak Yorkshire moors—continues to transport readers more than a century later.

Tess of the D'Urbervilles
by Thomas Hardy

Thomas Hardy was not one to shy away from life's harsh realities. This novel of a young woman cruelly mistreated by both foe and friend is a perfect example of Hardy's genius. In the character of Tess Durbeyfield, innocent and powerless, Hardy illustrates his philosophy that human beings are incapable of controlling their destinies and instead are victims of an indifferent fate. After reading Tess's story, readers cannot help but feel sympathy for the character and outrage at the injustices of Victorian society.

Why do people fear CHANGE?

The Complete Short Stories of H. G. Wells
by H. G. Wells

H. G. Wells may be better known for his science fiction classics, such as *The Time Machine,* but it was through his short stories that Wells first explored the potential of the scientific discoveries of his day. The short stories in this collection—full of fantastic creatures and even more fantastic machines—probe what it means to live in an age of rapid scientific progress.

Victorian Poetry
edited by Valentine Cunningham and Duncan Wu

Victorian poets reacted in a variety of ways to their changing times. The early poets, such as Alfred, Lord Tennyson, turned away from the harsh realities of their day, while others, such as Matthew Arnold, meditated directly on their changing times. This collection brings together some of the most significant poetry of the period, including works by Tennyson and Arnold, as well as Elizabeth Barrett Browning, Christina Rossetti, Gerard Manley Hopkins, and others.

Gladstone: A Biography
by Roy Jenkins

William E. Gladstone (1809–1898) was four times prime minister of Great Britain, serving Queen Victoria at various intervals between 1868 and 1894. This biography probes the character of a man involved in all the major political travails of the Victorian age.

Preview Unit Goals

TEXT ANALYSIS	• Analyze the impact of specific word choices on meaning and tone • Analyze the impact of the author's choices regarding how to develop and relate elements of a story or drama • Analyze a case in which grasping a point of view requires distinguishing what is directly stated in a text from what is really meant • Analyze the development of themes or central ideas over the course of a text • Determine an author's point of view or purpose in a text
READING	• Develop strategies for reading modern verse • Make inferences and draw conclusions • Analyze cause-and-effect relationships
WRITING AND LANGUAGE	• Write a personal narrative • Use effective sentence types and structures • Use effective, realistic dialogue
SPEAKING AND LISTENING	• Learn job interview skills
VOCABULARY	• Demonstrate understanding of figurative language • Use knowledge of Latin and Greek roots and affixes to help determine word meaning • Use a thesarus, electronic resources, and specialized dictionaries
ACADEMIC VOCABULARY	• approach • assume • environment • method • strategy
MEDIA AND VIEWING	• Analyze how words, images, graphics, and sounds impact meaning • Evaluate how media messages reflect cultural views • Integrate and evaluate multiple sources of information presented in different media or formats

Find It Online!

Go to **thinkcentral.com** for the interactive version of this unit.

Modern and Contemporary Literature

1901–PRESENT

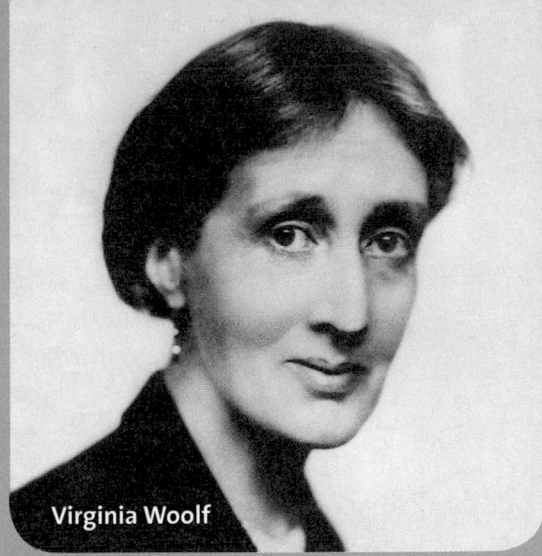

Virginia Woolf

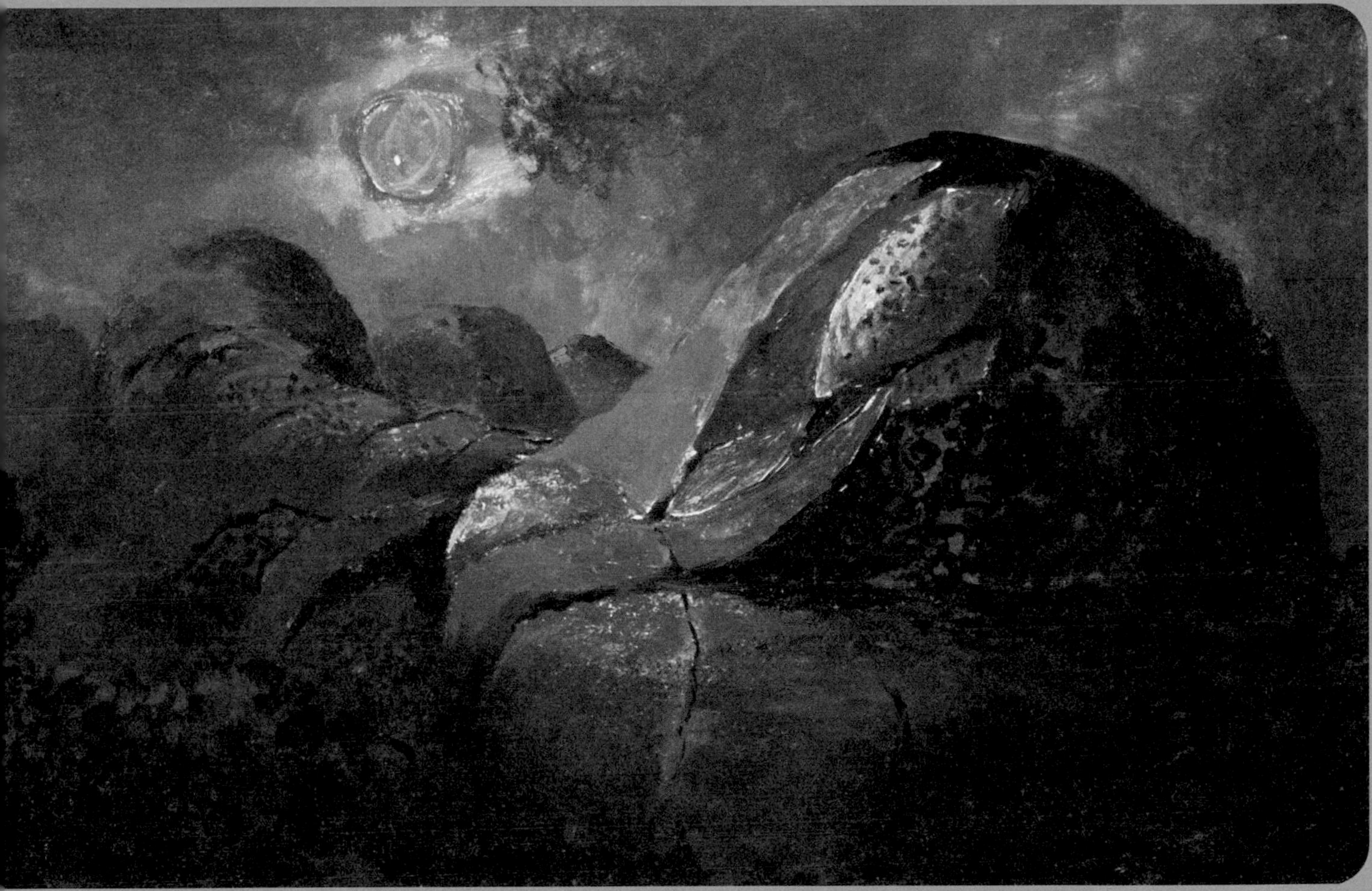

NEW IDEAS, NEW VOICES

- The Challenge of Modernism
- The Irish Literary Renaissance
- Responses to War and Colonialism
- Postwar Writers
- Legacy of Empire

MediaSmart DVD-ROM

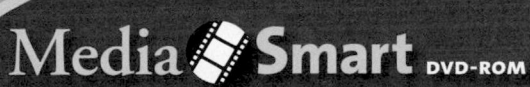

Wartime Propaganda

Dissect the messages, appeals, and symbols of propaganda posters to explore their persuasive power. Page 1298

Questions of the Times

DISCUSS After reading these questions and talking about them with a partner, discuss them with the class as a whole. Then read on to explore the ways in which writers of this era dealt with the same issues.

What does it mean to be MODERN?

In the 20th century, the British public was faced with a series of events that shook their view of the world. Two world wars, the crumbling of the British Empire, the loosening of the class system, and the advent of radical scientific theories caused writers, artists, and everyday people to move away from certain traditions of their past and embrace all things modern. What does *modern* mean to you? How do people today reinvent themselves?

Are we all ALONE?

During this era, the breakdown of old political and social systems left people feeling adrift and isolated. This feeling was intensified by groundbreaking theories in psychology, which suggested that each individual lived in a separate reality, calling into question whether genuine love and communication were possible. In today's society, isolation is even more prevalent. Do you think human beings are doomed to loneliness, or can we find a way to connect?

COMMON CORE

RL 9 Demonstrate knowledge of foundational works of literature, including how two or more texts from the same period treat similar themes or topics. **RI 9** Analyze documents of historical and literary significance for their themes, purposes, and rhetorical features.

How important is CULTURE?

Because of Britain's colonial past, many writers have had the advantage—and confusion—of a double heritage. Writers from Ireland, India, Africa, and other former British holdings all over the world have struggled to maintain a sense of their own culture and traditions after being engulfed in those of the British. How important is one's heritage? How do people assert their cultural identity?

Why is there always WAR?

Citizens living during World War I referred to it as the Great War, never dreaming there could be another. Yet World War II followed soon after, and this time fighting occurred not only on distant battlefields but right at home, with daily bombings of London. Sometimes it seems as if the history of humankind is one of continual battle, interrupted sparingly with moments of peace. Why is there so much war? What about human nature might cause unending conflict?

Modern and Contemporary Literature
1901–Present

New Ideas, New Voices

Responding to the devastation of two world wars and the loss of the once-powerful British Empire, British writers struggled to carve out a role for themselves in their new and different world. The old order had been shattered, and the familiar culture was dead. Out of the ashes, however, rose a new literature—exciting, experimental, and speaking with accents from every corner of the globe.

Modern and Contemporary Literature: Historical Context

British writers of this period experienced a crisis of identity as war and economic depression led to the end of the empire and of Britain's role as a major world power.

The Beginning of the End

At the turn of the 20th century, Great Britain was a nation at its peak—a peak it was about to topple from. Under the opulent reign of Victoria's successor, Edward VII, England was a land of prosperity, stability, and world dominance. Of course, no one could have known what the next hundred years would bring: the horrors of **World War I** trench warfare, the German bombing raids that would devastate British cities during **World War II,** and the end of the once-massive British Empire.

WORLD WAR I It all began with a single gunshot. In 1914, a Serbian nationalist assassinated Archduke Francis Ferdinand, heir to the throne of Austria-Hungary. Austria declared war on Serbia, and like a chain of dominoes, alliances fell into place: Austria and Germany on one side, Russia, France, and Britain on the other. Both sides dug in, locked together in bloody trench warfare—a chaos of mud, barbed wire, exploding shells and hand grenades, machine guns, tanks, and poison gas. The **Great War,** as World War I was then known, dragged on, devastating Europe, killing or wounding virtually an entire generation of young men, and bringing a profound sense of disillusionment to the people. **Siegfried Sassoon,** a poet and soldier, had this to say: "I have seen and endured the suffering of the troops, and I can no longer be a party to prolong these sufferings. . . ." In 1917, the United States entered the war, leading to Germany's capitulation the following year and to an uneasy peace.

BETWEEN THE WARS The war was finally over, but Europe now faced the consequences of four years of nonstop destruction. Britain had lost 750,000 men, and more than twice as many had been wounded; returning troops, promised a "land fit for heroes," instead came home to unemployment and economic depression. France was in a shambles, and Germany was crushed by the punishing terms of the treaty it had signed at Versailles. Russia was hard hit as well, rocked not just by war but also by a revolution, in 1917, in which the czar was overthrown and replaced by a Communist state.

Anxious to rebuild, war-torn European nations turned to the United States for loans. Then came the U.S. stock market crash of 1929, cutting off the flow of funds and causing a worldwide **depression.** Anger, fear, and uncertainty took hold, and in the chaos, dictators seized power: in Italy, **Benito Mussolini;** in Russia, **Joseph Stalin;** in Germany, the Nazi leader **Adolf Hitler.** At first, Britain stood back as Hitler forcibly annexed Austria

COMMON CORE

RL 9 Demonstrate knowledge of foundational works of literature, including how two or more works from the same period treat similar themes or topics. **RI 9** Analyze documents of historical and literary significance for their themes, purposes, and rhetorical features. **L 1a** Apply the understanding that usage is a matter of convention, can change over time, and is sometimes contested.

▶ **TAKING NOTES**

Outlining As you read this introduction, use an outline to record main ideas about the historical events and literature of this period. You can use headings, boldfaced terms, and the information in boxes like this one as starting points. (See page R49 in the **Research Handbook** for more help with outlining.)

I. *Historical Context*
  A. *Beginning of the End*
    1. WWI
    2. Between wars
    3. WWII
  B. *Britain in the Modern World*

Oxford Street, London (2000)

and marched into Czechoslovakia. Finally, in 1939, when Hitler invaded Poland, Britain and France declared war on Germany. Italy and Japan soon allied themselves with Hitler. World War II had begun.

WORLD WAR II Terrible as the Great War had been, for most British citizens it was a distant tragedy, played out on foreign battlefields. World War II was different. After the fall of France in 1940, German fighter planes crossed the English Channel and attacked Britain. As bombs rained down on London, the entire population mobilized to defend the home front. For one whole year, Britain held out alone against the Nazis. Then, in 1941, Germany invaded the Soviet Union and Japan attacked Pearl Harbor, bringing the United States into the war. Hitler was finally defeated in 1945.

After the war, Britain was financially drained, burdened by debt and the need to rebuild its cities. Everything, from butter to socks, was rationed. Determined to provide at least the basic necessities, the new Labor government transformed Britain with a new national health care system and public education. Liberal in outlook and concerned with pressing domestic issues, Labor leaders had little desire to cling to far-flung colonies eager for self-rule. Instead, they gave India its independence in 1947, continuing a trend begun in the 1920s of dissolving the British Empire into a loose **commonwealth** of independent nations.

British firefighters battle the results of a German air attack during the Battle of Britain.

Britain in the Modern World

When the British ruled much of the world, they had been famous for their provincialism—marching off into sweltering jungles, for example, wearing formal dress more suited to a London drawing-room. Ironically, as Britain let go of its colonies, it became a great deal more international. One reason was the influx of immigrants from former British holdings in the West Indies, Africa, and India. Another was the increasing power of the United States, whose policies Britain generally acceded to and whose culture had an overwhelming influence.

Britain's relationship with the rest of Europe changed as well, as the island nation forged strong links with its neighbors on the continent. In 1973, Great Britain entered the European Economic Community, and in 1992, the European Union; in 1994, it opened the Chunnel—a railway tunnel running underneath the English Channel, connecting Britain to France.

Cultural Influences

Great Britain had an uneasy, often violent relationship with Ireland throughout the 20th century.

The "Irish Question"

One issue that bedeviled Britain all through this period was that of independence for Ireland. The Irish had never accepted English rule and so were faced with a dilemma when Great Britain entered World War I: should they fight to defend an empire they hated? Many Irish did fight for that empire; others took the opportunity to rise up against England in a bid for independence known as the **Easter Rising** of 1916. Although planned to be a nationwide rebellion, a series of mishaps led it to be confined to Dublin with only about 1,700 men taking part. In fact, at the time only a small portion of the Irish public had supported the rebellion, yet the extreme harshness of the British response whipped up support for the Irish nationalist cause, represented by the political party **Sinn Fein** and the **Irish Republican Army.** In 1921, after a long struggle, the British split Ireland into two self-governing dominions: the Irish Free State (later renamed the Republic of Ireland) and Northern Ireland. Independence for all but Northern Ireland was achieved in 1949; reunification has never been achieved. Nor has lasting peace for Northern Ireland. At first sporadic, ongoing outbursts of violence between Protestant and Catholic factions in Northern Ireland escalated through the years until the 1990s, when paramilitary groups ordered a cease-fire. However, the peace process has been slow-moving and tensions continue today.

> **A Voice from the Times**
>
> *I know that I shall meet my fate*
> *Somewhere among the clouds*
>   *above;*
> *Those that I fight I do not hate,*
> *Those that I guard I do not love;*
>
> **—William Butler Yeats**
> *from* "An Irish Airman Foresees
> His Death"

An Irish protester throws stones at British soldiers (2000).

Ideas of the Age

A spirit of nationalism dominated the 20th century, leading to the dissolution of the British Empire.

Nationalism

The Irish were not alone in their nationalist fervor. Throughout Europe and the European colonial empires, nationalism was the dominating spirit of the 20th century. This nationalism took many forms, from the peaceful demands of activist Mahatma Gandhi, leader of India's independence movement, to the murderous ambitions of Hitler, who killed 11 million "racial undesirables," including 6 million Jews, in a quest to "purify" Germany. The English themselves were fiercely patriotic, yet perceptive writers began to see the ugly side of their own country's nationalism in such affairs as the Boer War, in which two independent South African republics were absorbed into the British Empire, mainly in order to acquire the area's newfound gold.

THE LOSS OF THE EMPIRE After World War I, Britain's grasp on its empire began to loosen as the spirit of nationalism increased in its far-flung holdings across the world. In turn, Britain granted ever greater degrees of self-determination to its subject lands. In 1926, British political leaders convened a conference at which Canada, South Africa, Australia, and New Zealand were made members of the British **Commonwealth of Nations.** In other words, these countries were now partners, not possessions, of Britain. In the decades after World War II, Britain yielded to nationalistic and economic pressures and relinquished control of most of its remaining colonies in Asia, Africa, and the West Indies. The last trace of the empire disappeared in 1997 when Hong Kong, which had been a British colony for 155 years, was returned to Chinese control.

▼ **Analyze Visuals**
According to the makers of this early-20th-century map, it "shows the world as it would appear from an aeroplane so high above London that the pilot saw the continents stretched out beneath him. He would thus be given a vivid idea of how the British Empire is scattered in relation to the home country." The red and shaded-red areas represent British territories. In what way does this map prove the old saying "The sun never sets on the British Empire"?

The Highways of Empire (early 1900s), L. M. Gill, for The Empire Marketing Board. E. 28-1928. © Victoria & Albert Museum, London/Art Resource, New York.

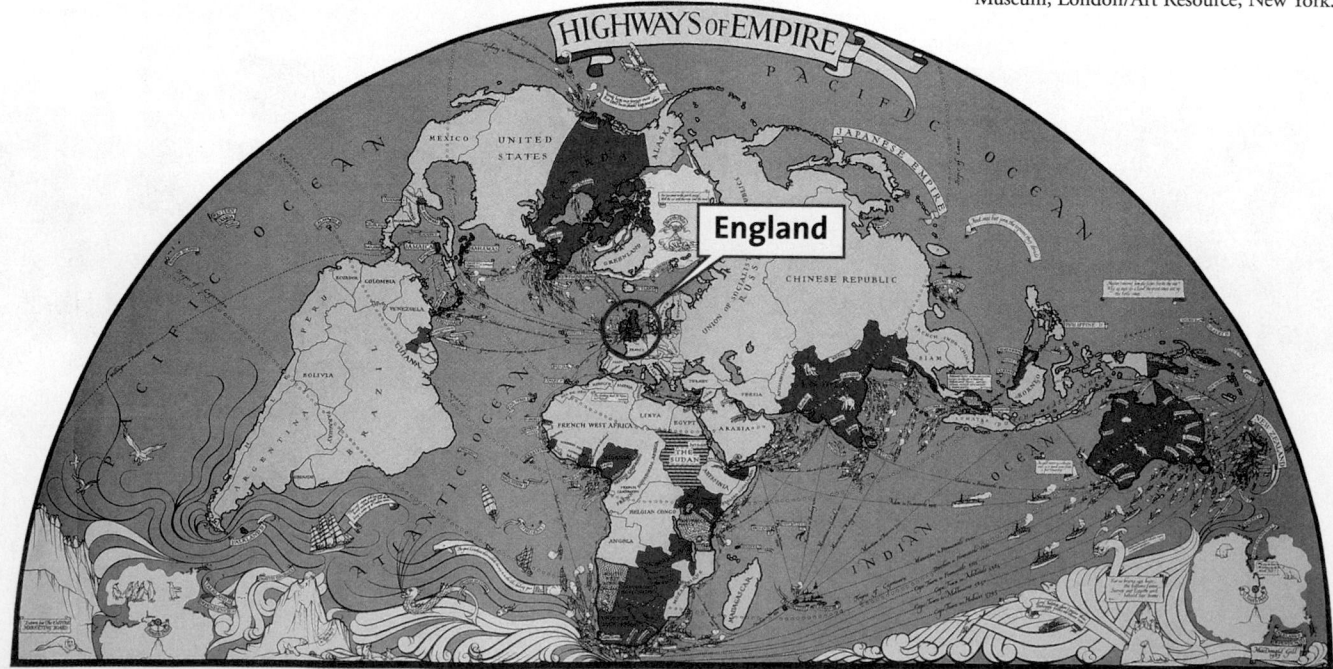

Literature of the Times

This literary period brought radical experimentation by modernists and postmodernists, while writers from Ireland and other parts of the British empire added fresh new voices and experiences.

The Challenge of Modernism

"Things fall apart; the center cannot hold; / Mere anarchy is loosed upon the world." These apocalyptic lines, written by poet **William Butler Yeats** in 1919, perfectly captured the uncertainty of the early 20th century. The old empires of Turkey and Austria-Hungary had fallen to pieces; Russia was in upheaval, Germany crushed. In England, a stable social order based on rigid class distinctions was giving way, and as cities continued to swell—London's population reached 5 million by 1910—a sense of community disappeared, replaced by the rootlessness and anonymity of urban life.

In the arts, modernism was a way of trying to make sense of this new, fragmented world. Before, the artist's task had been to represent a recognizable shared reality. Painters created portraits and landscapes; novelists took their heroes and villains through stories that had a beginning, a middle, and a satisfying end. These traditional forms, however, seemed inadequate as a response to modern life. A new kind of art was needed—one that would reject old versions of reality, create its own values rather than relying on any common assumptions, and somehow connect the disjointed pieces of human experience into a coherent, yet not false or artificial, whole.

This was a daunting task, but British writers were inspired by the bold innovations of modern artists such as **Henri Matisse** and **Pablo Picasso** and of composers such as **Igor Stravinsky.** Writers, however, faced unique challenges. Musicians still had notes, and painters still had line and color; but the basic materials of the narrative— character and plot—were being called into question.

During the 1920s, the works of psychoanalyst **Sigmund Freud** first appeared in English, published by novelist **Virginia Woolf** and her husband, Leonard. Freud showed that character could not be easily understood; people were complex, inconsistent, and unpredictable, driven by irrational urges that might be hidden even from themselves. Writers' past assumptions about plot—

20th-Century British Art

"The English are not gifted artistically," George Orwell commented in an essay in 1941. "Painting and sculpture have never flourished in England as they have in France." In the years following World War II, however, British artists proved Orwell wrong by embracing radical new approaches. By the 1980s, they had seized the international spotlight, and today British art is famous worldwide for its daring innovation.

David Hockney David Hockney (born 1937) is considered one of the most influential British artists of the 20th century. His work grew out of the modernist movement, which rejected the past, looked for new forms of art to capture the present, and was characterized by constant innovation. Witty and versatile (he dubbed a 1962 exhibit *Demonstrations of Versatility*), Hockney has worked in all kinds of media—oil and acrylic painting, lithography, photography, and stage design.

The work shown here, *Mr. and Mrs. Clark and Percy* (1970–71), depicts Hockney's friends, fashion designer Ossie Clark and textile designer Celia Birtwell. The painting was a challenge for Hockney technically. He wrote, "The figures are nearly life-size; it's difficult painting figures like that, and it was quite a struggle.... I probably painted [Ossie's] head alone twelve times." Clearly, his work was successful, however, as it was later voted the most popular modern painting in London's Tate Gallery.

that events should move in a straight line from here to there—were also being rethought. The French philosopher and writer Henri Bergson, for example, argued that time was like a stream in which past, present, and future all flowed together continuously.

Under the influence of these ideas, writers such as **James Joyce** and Virginia Woolf experimented with **stream of consciousness,** a technique in which the reader is inside the character's mind, hearing his or her thoughts just as they occur, in an apparently jumbled and random order. Because memories of the past, impressions of the present, and hopes and fears for the future are all mixed together in the character's consciousness, there is no need to follow the character through a series of important events; any ordinary day will do, and in fact, both Joyce and Woolf wrote novels taking place entirely in a single day. This approach, emphasizing depth rather than breadth and calling for a subtly perceptive use of detail and symbolism, led many writers to a fresh interest in the short story.

No longer able to assume that readers shared a common set of values, writers as diverse as Woolf, **Katherine Mansfield,** and **D. H. Lawrence** shifted concern to the human being in isolation, to human relationships, and to common human strengths and vulnerabilities. Yet the modernists did not all think or write alike; while they struggled with the same problems, they arrived at different solutions. What they shared, mainly, was a sense of alienation from their own society—many lived as expatriates—and especially from many readers and critics, whose reactions to their work ranged from bewilderment to fury.

As a result, their audience was limited at first to an elite minority known as the **avant-garde.** For example, **T. S. Eliot's** poetic masterpiece *The Waste Land* was first published in a tiny magazine with a circulation of only 600. It is no wonder that the work of modernist poets such as Eliot and Yeats took some time to catch on. They were writing an entirely new kind of poetry—intellectually challenging, ironic, and often disquieting.

The Bloomsbury group in a fake airplane. Tate Archives. Tate Modern, London. © Tate Gallery, London/Art Resource, New York.

Vanessa Bell *(third from left)* and other members of the Bloomsbury group

At the center of the avant-garde was a circle of friends known as the **Bloomsbury group,** which met at the homes of Virginia Woolf and her sister, the artist Vanessa Bell. The group included, among others, the novelist **E. M. Forster,** the art critic Roger Fry, and the economist John Maynard Keynes. Though novelist D. H. Lawrence ridiculed them as self-satisfied "black beetles," bustling around in their small circle, the Bloomsbury group was in fact quite influential.

The Irish Literary Renaissance

It was typical of this period that when one of the greatest modern writers—James Joyce—appeared on the scene, no one wanted to read his works, not even the avant-garde. Joyce struggled for nine years to get his first book, *Dubliners,* published. T. S. Eliot, who did appreciate Joyce's work, complained that it was "uphill and exasperating work trying to impose Joyce on such 'intellectual' people" as might be able to win him critical acceptance. Yet Joyce turned out to be tremendously important. His novels *A Portrait of the Artist as a Young Man* and *Ulysses* are not only among the most brilliant works in British literature but also the culmination of the **Irish Literary Renaissance.**

If the push for independence was the political side of Irish nationalism, the Irish Literary Renaissance (also called the Irish Revival) was the cultural side, led by writers determined to revive the rich traditional life that had fallen apart in the wake of the death and devastation caused by the potato famine of the previous century. At the center of the movement was the poet William Butler Yeats, a founder of both the Irish Literary Society and Dublin's Abbey Theatre. Other key figures included playwright **John Millington Synge,** playwright and director **Lady Isabella Augusta Gregory,** and **Douglas Hyde,** a poet and scholar who later became the first president of Ireland.

Yeats and his colleagues faced a dilemma. The true Irish language—the language of its history and folklore—was Gaelic. However, few people in Ireland actually spoke Gaelic anymore. If the writers wanted to be understood, they had to write in English; but English carried with it centuries of culture based in England, not Ireland. (Yeats himself was very much an heir to the English romantics.) In order to create an authentically Irish literature written in English, Irish writers turned to the legendary accounts of the Irish heroes Cuchulain and Finn MacCool for inspiration and to the colorful speech of the Irish peasants, who, to the writers, represented

W. B. Yeats and the Irish Theatre (1915), Edmund Dulac. Paint, watercolor, ink. Reproduced by permission of Hodder and Stoughton Limited. Photo courtesy of the National Gallery of Ireland, Dublin.

A Voice from the Times

Can we not build up . . . a national literature, which shall be none the less Irish in spirit from being English in language?

—William Butler Yeats

the truest link with Ireland's past. Though they succeeded magnificently, it would be Joyce who took the challenge one step further, making literature set in Ireland relevant to all, Irish or not.

Responses to War and Colonialism

When Yeats edited the *Oxford Book of Modern Verse* in 1936, he raised a furor by deliberately leaving out all the war poets, including **Wilfred Owen,** whom he later ridiculed as "unworthy of the poets' corner of a country newspaper." In truth, the poets of World War I were not wildly original when it came to form; they wrote in the same style as an earlier generation. However, what they had to say was radically new and powerfully influential.

Most of the war poets were soldiers themselves, and their early poems—such as those of **Rupert Brooke,** who was idolized for his handsome face and untimely death—reflected the enthusiastic patriotism of young men eager to win honor and glory by fighting for their country. Their idealism soon gave way to disillusionment and despair, however, as they realized with horror that the carnage was leading to no higher end. Owen, who died just a week before the armistice, conveyed a melancholy tone, while **Siegfried Sassoon's** poetry expressed his anger and frustration with those responsible for sending his friends to their deaths.

Soon, a new strain of pacifism and anti-imperialism entered British literature. Based on his own experiences as a police superintendent in Burma, **George Orwell** became increasingly disillusioned with British colonialism, sharing his thoughts in classic essays such as "A Hanging" and "Shooting an Elephant." He also made it his goal to expose and criticize totalitarianism in all forms. The "Ministry of Truth" in his novel *1984* was based on his own experiences writing wartime propaganda for the BBC during World War II. Similarly, **Graham Greene,** who looked with disdain on both the remains of the British Empire and the new influence of the United States, filled his novels with images of a sad, tawdry world stained by its colonial past.

Postwar Writers

The writers who emerged after World War II struggled to come to terms with their changing world. They responded in various ways: poet **Ted Hughes** with brutal imagery, novelist **Muriel Spark** with cool irony; and the **"angry young men"**—writers such as **John Osborne** and **Alan Sillitoe**—with anti-authoritarian rage and working-class resentment. In the words of a character from Osborne's *Look Back in Anger,* "There aren't any good brave causes left. If the big bang does come, and we all get killed off, it won't be in aid of the old-fashioned, grand design. It'll just be

George Orwell's *Animal Farm* uses the genre of fable to criticize the totalitarian nature of the Soviet Communist regime.

A scene from *Waiting for Godot*

for the Brave New nothing-very-much-thank-you. About as pointless and inglorious as stepping in front of a bus."

Most significant, however, was the shift to **postmodernism**, a style of writing that took modernism to a logical—though extreme—conclusion, dismantling literature entirely to examine its inner workings. The pioneer of British postmodernism was the playwright **Samuel Beckett,** whose first play, *Waiting for Godot,* stripped drama to its essence with minimal sets, darkly humorous circular dialogue, and—to the dismay of some audience members—absolutely no action at all.

The Legacy of Empire

England's relationship with its former colonies, including those still belonging to the British Commonwealth, has been complex. Writers from these areas have grappled with a range of issues stemming from their countries' colonial past, such as social problems or struggles for peace in their homelands, as well as the question of how to create authentic literature that draws on their dual heritage. In addition, writers who have immigrated to England often find themselves faced with the tensions of culture clash. In response, many write overtly political works, while others, such as **Nadine Gordimer,** focus more on the stories of their society. "I am not a preacher or a politician," she has said. "It is simply not the purpose of a novelist. . . . [M]y writing does not deal with my personal convictions; it deals with the society I live and write in." The multicultural perspective these writers bring has broadened the horizons of contemporary literature, as exciting new writers, including Kazuo Ishiguro, Margaret Atwood, Salman Rushdie, Derek Walcott, Yann Martel, and Arundhati Roy, push aside the dusty drawing-room drapes and step outside for a breath of fresh air.

▶ *For Your Outline*

WAR AND COLONIALISM

- WWI poets were unoriginal in form but radical in content.
- Orwell and Greene criticized colonialism.

POSTWAR WRITERS

- Writers responded to change in different ways.
- The "angry young men" championed the working class.
- Postmodernism dismantled literature to examine its inner workings.

LEGACY OF EMPIRE

- Writers from former colonies grapple with issues stemming from their countries' colonial pasts.
- Some of these writers are political, others not.
- Their multicultural perspective has broadened literature.

Connecting Literature, History, and Culture

Use this timeline and the questions on the next page to gain insight into developments during this period, both in Britain and in the world as a whole.

BRITISH LITERARY MILESTONES

1900

1902 Joseph Conrad's novel *Heart of Darkness* is published.

1913 George Bernard Shaw's play *Pygmalion* is produced.

1914 James Joyce begins writing his controversial novel *Ulysses* (to 1921).

1920

1921 T. S. Eliot writes his groundbreaking poem *The Waste Land*. ▶

1927 Yeats's "Sailing to Byzantium" is published.

1932 Aldous Huxley's novel *Brave New World* is published.

1940

1941 Depression and despair drive writer Virginia Woolf to suicide.

1949 George Orwell publishes *1984*, a nightmarish vision of a future totalitarian England.

1952 Samuel Beckett's play *Waiting for Godot* is published.

HISTORICAL CONTEXT

1900

1901 Queen Victoria dies and is succeeded by son Edward VII.

1910 Edward VII dies and is succeeded by son George V.

1914 Britain enters World War I after Germany invades Belgium. ▶

> BRITAIN IS FIGHTING FOR THE FREEDOM OF EUROPE AND TO DEFEND YOUR MOTHERS WIVES AND SISTERS FROM THE HORRORS OF WAR
>
> ENLIST NOW

1920

1921 Irish Free State is established; Northern Ireland remains part of Great Britain.

1932 At the depth of a global depression, the British unemployment rate is 23 percent.

1936 George V dies; son Edward VIII renounces throne; Edward's brother becomes King George VI.

1940

1945 At end of World War II, British military and civilian losses total 360,000.

1947 India and Pakistan are given independence. ▶

1952 George VI dies and is succeeded by his daughter, Elizabeth II.

WORLD CULTURE AND EVENTS

1900

1912 The last emperor of the Qing dynasty, which had ruled China since 1644, is overthrown.

1914 The assassination of Archduke Francis Ferdinand sparks World War I.

1917 V. I. Lenin leads the Bolshevik Revolution that topples the Russian monarchy.

1920

1920 Adolf Hitler takes control of new National Socialist German Workers' (Nazi) Party.

1939 Germany invades Poland and World War II begins. ▼

1940

1945 World War II ends; the United Nations is formed.

1946 Cold War between the United States and the Soviet Union begins (to 1991).

1949 Communists win civil war to gain control of China.

1957 Soviets launch *Sputnik I*, the first artificial space satellite.

MAKING CONNECTIONS

- What authors from former British holdings were writing during this period?
- What evidence do you see of changes in women's roles during this period?
- Name two world events that had an important impact on Great Britain.

◯ **COMMON CORE**

RI 7 Integrate and evaluate multiple sources of information presented in different formats as well as in words in order to address a question.

1960

1965 Doris Lessing's *African Stories* is published.

1975 Stevie Smith's illustrated *Collected Poems is* published. ▶

1980

1984 Ted Hughes, widower of American poet Sylvia Plath, is named poet laureate.

1991 South African Nadine Gordimer wins the Nobel Prize in literature.

1995 Irish poet Seamus Heaney wins the Nobel Prize in literature.

2000

2000 Zadie Smith publishes *White Teeth*, a novel about two London families, one Jamaican, one Bengali. ▲

2007 Salman Rushdie is awarded a knighthood by Queen Elizabeth II.

1960

1961 South Africa withdraws from the British Commonwealth.

1969 Violence erupts in Northern Ireland following an attempt to grant civil rights to the Catholic minority.

1970 The Equal Pay Act ensures that British women's wages will equal those of men with the same jobs.

1979 Margaret Thatcher becomes first female prime minister.

1980

1981 Charles, heir to British throne, marries Lady Diana Spencer. ▲

1997 Britain returns Hong Kong to China after 155 years of colonial rule; Princess Diana dies in Paris auto accident.

2000

2001 After several years of negotiation with the British, the Irish Republican Army begins disarmament.

2002 Queen Elizabeth II celebrates her 50th year of reign.

2005 Bombs explode on three London Underground trains and on a bus, killing 56.

2007 Gordon Brown replaces Tony Blair as Prime Minister of the United Kingdom.

1960

1962 Cuban missile crisis ends with removal of Soviet missiles from Cuba.

1969 U.S. author Kurt Vonnegut Jr. publishes *Slaughterhouse-Five*. ▲

1977 The first practical home computer, Apple II, hits the market.

1980

1985 Mikhail Gorbachev comes to power in Soviet Union and initiates reforms.

1989 The Berlin Wall falls; students demonstrating for Chinese democracy are killed in Beijing's Tiananmen Square.

1991 Iraq invades Kuwait, prompting Persian Gulf War.

2000

2001 Terrorist attacks in United States kill nearly 3,000 people.

2003 U.S.-led troops invade Iraq.

2004 Tsunami hits Asia; hundreds of thousands die.

2009 Barack Obama becomes first African-American President of the United States.

The Legacy of the Era

Big Brother Is Watching

COMMON CORE

W 7 Conduct short research projects to answer a question.
W 8 Gather relevant information from digital sources. **SL 1** Participate effectively in collaborative discussions.

The year 1984 has come and gone, but the legacy of George Orwell persists. In his apocalyptic book about a future totalitarian state, Orwell introduced countless ideas and phrases into our modern consciousness. He described a world in which "Big Brother" watches your every move, the "Thought Police" monitor your desires, "Newspeak" obliterates the very meaning of words, and war is never-ending.

DISCUSS Big Brother would have loved to get his hands on many of the surveillance methods we take for granted today, and modern governments use language and propaganda to mold public opinion as surely as they ever did. Discuss these "Orwellian" aspects of modern culture. What harm might arise from them?

The British Invasion

While the United States has had a major influence on Great Britain in the past century, the reverse has been true too. Americans have long swooned over British pop stars and sports stars, packed movie theaters to see adaptations of the English classics, and lined up to buy the latest installments of *Harry Potter*.

RESEARCH Search the Internet to find a British musician currently on America's hit music charts, a British athlete marketed in American sports stores, or a British actor currently headlining an American movie. Then, with your classmates, use your findings to create a display titled "The Modern British Invasion."

Children's Literature

A boy who refuses to grow up, a talking lion and a magical wardrobe, a woolly-headed bear named Pooh—these are just a few of the many memorable characters brought to life in British children's literature in the 20th century.

DISCUSS With a partner, choose *Peter Pan; The Lion, the Witch and the Wardrobe; Winnie-the-Pooh;* or another classic work of British children's literature written in the 20th or 21st century. Read, or reread, the story and discuss it with your partner. Why do you think the work became a classic? Is it enjoyable to read as a teenager? Are there elements in the story that you may have missed as a child?

A scene from the film *The Chronicles of Narnia: The Lion, the Witch and the Wardrobe*

Modernism

The British writer Virginia Woolf once declared that "on or about December, 1910, human character changed." Woolf picked that date to mark the enormous changes that occurred in her lifetime. Her bold statement sets the context for **modernism,** a literary and artistic movement that developed in the early decades of the 20th century.

Art for Art's Sake

In literature, **modernism** was a diverse movement that spanned Europe, the Americas, and even parts of Africa and Asia. In England, it took hold in the first decade of the 20th century. As the economic, political, and social structure of Britain began to crumble in those years, British writers began to experiment with ways that would question the basic elements of literature—whether it be the structure of a poem or the narrative elements of a fictional story. A key figure in the modernist movement was James Joyce, whose novels, short stories, and poetry were anything but traditional. The 1922 publication of his work *Ulysses* marked the peak of the modernist movement in fiction. In this work, Joyce used an array of modern writing styles in portraying the random thoughts of his main character, Leopold Bloom, as he wandered the streets of Dublin. Other modernist fiction writers besides Joyce and Woolf included D. H. Lawrence, Aldous Huxley, and Evelyn Waugh.

T. S. Eliot (1949), Patrick Heron. © 2007 Artists Rights Society (ARS), New York/DACS, London.

Breaking Form

Modernist poets typically broke new ground in style and form. T. S. Eliot and others abandoned traditional stanza forms and meter for the more natural flow of free verse and experimented with bold imagery and symbolism. Eliot also ushered in a new era in literary criticism. In his work as editor of the literary journal *The Criterion,* he argued for new standards of evaluation and re-examined the literary worth of past poets. While blasting the revered romantic and neoclassical poets, he resurrected the reputation of the metaphysical poets, who had been unpopular for at least a century.

The modernist period lasted through England's economic depression of the 1930s and the political turmoil of World War II in the 1940s. The period gave way in the early 1950s to **postmodernism,** which is characterized by experimentation with discontinuity, parody, popular culture, irony, and language.

Modernist Content and Techniques

While no two modernist writers employed the same style, their works do share some defining characteristics:

- a sense of alienation, loss, and despair

- rejection of traditional values and assumptions

- elevation of the individual

- emphasis on introspection and the depths of the human mind rather than on outward or social aspects

One narrative technique that allowed the modernist writer to fully reveal a character and to explore the depths of the human mind was **stream of consciousness,** in which the rapid and jumbled flow of a character's thoughts and feelings is presented as it occurs. Fiction writers Woolf and Joyce, along with poet T. S. Eliot, were known for using this technique.

For modernist writers, **irony** became something larger than a literary technique; it became an attitude that permeated the core of their writing. This new ironic attitude of the modernists is often described as detached and questioning. Modernists aimed for objectivity in presenting ideas and regarded such restraint as an appropriate response to the complexities of modern life. Recall that irony in literature is classified in three ways.

TYPES OF IRONY	
Verbal irony	Occurs when a writer says one thing but means another.
Situational irony	Occurs when a character or the reader expects one thing to happen but something entirely different happens.
Dramatic irony	Occurs when the audience or reader knows more than the character(s). Dramatic irony occurs in fiction when a character has a limited view or no view of events, but the reader is fully aware of what is going on.

In Katherine Mansfield's "A Cup of Tea" (page 1128), a young woman begging for a cup of tea is invited into the home of a wealthy woman named Rosemary, who wishes to act generously and help the poor woman. Note how the author describes Rosemary's thoughts as she helps the woman, who is nearly fainting from hunger, take off her coat:

> She [the poor woman] seemed to stagger like a child, and the thought came and went through Rosemary's mind, that if people wanted helping they must respond a little, just a little, otherwise it became very difficult indeed. And what was she to do with the coat now? She left it on the floor, and the hat too.
>
> **—Katherine Mansfield, "A Cup of Tea"**

Close Read

What is ironic about Rosemary's thoughts and actions in this scene? What type of irony is used in this passage?

Selected Poetry

by T. S. Eliot

COMMON CORE

RL 4 Determine the meaning of words and phrases as they are used in the text, including figurative and connotative meanings; analyze the impact of specific words choices on meaning and tone. **RL 7** Analyze multiple interpretations of a poem, evaluating how each version interprets the source text. **RL 10** Read and comprehend literature, including poems.

DID YOU KNOW?

T. S. Eliot . . .

- refused to publish his early work because he believed it mediocre.
- wrote the book that inspired the hit Broadway musical *Cats.*
- won the Nobel Prize in literature in 1948.

Meet the Author

T. S. Eliot 1888–1965

Claimed by his native America as well as his adopted homeland of Britain, T. S. Eliot was one of the giants of 20th-century literature. With friend and fellow American poet Ezra Pound, Eliot ushered in the modernist movement, transforming how poetry was written and understood.

Poet of Two Countries Thomas Stearns Eliot was born in St. Louis, Missouri, into a distinguished family with New England roots. Eliot's parents maintained close ties to New England, bringing their children each summer to Gloucester, Massachusetts. Later, Eliot remarked that as a child he did not feel as if he truly belonged in either New England or the Midwest.

After attending Harvard University, Eliot pursued graduate work in philosophy at the Sorbonne in Paris, at Harvard, and at Oxford University. However, he never earned his doctoral degree. In 1915, he fell in love with a vivacious English beauty named Vivien Haigh-Wood. He married Vivien just a few months later, much to the consternation of his parents, who were deeply troubled by her history of mental illness. Henceforth, Eliot would make his home in England.

Breaking with the Past A quiet, cultured man, Eliot supported himself and his wife by working successively as a teacher, a bank clerk, and an editor while trying to make a name for himself as a writer. In 1917, with Ezra Pound's support, Eliot published a collection of poems, *Prufrock and Other Observations,* which explored the alienating effects of modern life. Though now considered a cornerstone of the modernist movement, the volume received mixed reviews when it first appeared. Many critics were put off by Eliot's vivid depictions of the ugly realities of urban life and by his use of fragmentary images and colloquial language.

Modernist Master With the publication of *The Waste Land* in 1922, Eliot's reputation as a pre-eminent poet was solidified. Completed as his marriage was falling apart, the poem expresses the emotional pain and spiritual emptiness felt by the post–World War I generation and by Eliot himself. Yearning for spiritual comfort and meaning, Eliot joined the Church of England in 1927. In his later poems, such as "Ash Wednesday" (1930) and *Four Quartets* (1943), Eliot stressed the importance of religious belief to leading a purposeful life. When the legendary poet died in 1965, his friend and editor Robert Giroux wrote, "the world became a lesser place."

Credited with ushering in a new era of poetry, T. S. Eliot shattered the poetic conventions of his day. Eliot's revolutionary **style**—his individual way of communicating ideas—has inspired both praise and puzzlement for almost a century. Key elements of Eliot's poetic style include

- a frequent use of free verse, in which the rhythms fall into no fixed pattern
- the use of colloquial language, including slang and references to popular culture
- the conveying of ideas by complex figurative language, images, symbols, and allusions rather than by explicit statements

Eliot's tone is another important element of his style. Many of his poems have a tone of disillusionment or alienation, reflecting his despair at what he saw as the decline of Western civilization. "The Naming of Cats," written after Eliot came to terms with the modern age, shows the poet's witty, whimsical side.

As you read Eliot's poetry, notice examples of these stylistic elements.

● **READING STRATEGY: READING MODERN VERSE**

Eliot's modernist poetry, like much modern art, can be hard to understand at first. Eliot often presents a patchwork of images, symbols, and allusions; readers must supply the connections themselves. The following guidelines can help you interpret Eliot's poems:

- Read each poem aloud, pausing between sections and lingering over images you find particularly striking.
- Try paraphrasing lines you find puzzling.
- Use the sidenotes to decipher unfamiliar allusions.

For "Preludes" and "The Hollow Men," use a chart like the one shown to jot down the central image or idea conveyed in each stanza.

Poem / Stanza	Central Image or Idea
"Preludes," stanza 1	The speaker describes a lonely, rundown, working-class setting—this modern environment is terribly bleak

Complete the activities in your **Reader/Writer Notebook**.

Is the world FALLING APART?

Once in a while, an event takes place that makes people feel as if their world is in danger of disintegration. For T. S. Eliot and his contemporaries, World War I was an event of this kind. One of the bloodiest conflicts of all time, the war seemed to them a total breakdown of Western civilization. In two of the poems that follow, Eliot conveys the alienation and despair that people felt in the wake of this catastrophe.

QUICKWRITE Think about events—such as wars, terrorist attacks, or natural disasters—that have shaken entire nations. Choose one event and describe how it altered the lives of those affected. What changes in values or perceptions does such an act cause? How might it make people fear society's disintegration?

Preludes

T. S. Eliot

I

The winter evening settles down
With smell of steaks in passageways.
Six o'clock.
The burnt-out ends of smoky days.
5 And now a gusty shower wraps
The grimy scraps
Of withered leaves about your feet
And newspapers from vacant lots;
The showers beat
10 On broken blinds and chimney-pots,
And at the corner of the street
A lonely cab-horse steams and stamps.
And then the lighting of the lamps. **Ⓐ**

II

The morning comes to consciousness
15 Of faint stale smells of beer
From the sawdust-trampled street
With all its muddy feet that press
To early coffee-stands.
With the other masquerades
20 That time resumes,
One thinks of all the hands
That are raising dingy shades
In a thousand furnished rooms.

III

You tossed a blanket from the bed,
25 You lay upon your back, and waited;
You dozed, and watched the night revealing
The thousand sordid images
Of which your soul was constituted;
They flickered against the ceiling.

2 steaks: here, cheap cuts from low-grade beef, once a common working-class food.

Ⓐ READING MODERN VERSE
Which images in the first stanza create the most vivid impression? Explain why.

18 early coffee-stands: stands of vendors who cater to early-morning pedestrians.

23 furnished rooms: one-room apartments with furniture included, usually cheap and rundown.

30 And when all the world came back
And the light crept up between the shutters
And you heard the sparrows in the gutters,
You had such a vision of the street
As the street hardly understands;
35 Sitting along the bed's edge, where
You curled the papers from your hair,
Or clasped the yellow soles of feet
In the palms of both soiled hands.

36 curled . . . hair: removed the paper curlers around which hair was wound; suggests that the "you" being addressed is a woman.

IV

His soul stretched tight across the skies
40 That fade behind a city block,
Or trampled by insistent feet
At four and five and six o'clock;
And short square fingers stuffing pipes,
And evening newspapers, and eyes
45 Assured of certain certainties,
The conscience of a blackened street
Impatient to assume the world. **Ⓑ**

I am moved by fancies that are curled
Around these images, and cling:
50 The notion of some infinitely gentle
Infinitely suffering thing.

Wipe your hand across your mouth, and laugh;
The worlds revolve like ancient women
Gathering fuel in vacant lots.

Ⓑ STYLE
"His" in line 39 refers to the street. In lines 39–47, Eliot **personifies** the street, just as morning is personified in Section II. Why do you think Eliot employs this stylistic technique? Explain what you think it serves to convey or emphasize.

Text Analysis

1. **Summarize** Describe the poem's **setting**, citing specific lines or phrases that allow you to envision the place Eliot describes.

2. **Interpret** A prelude is a short musical piece based on a recurrent theme. Why do you think Eliot titled this poem "Preludes"? Does knowing the meaning of this word give you any new insights into the poem? Explain.

The Hollow Men

T. S. Eliot

Mistah Kurtz—he dead.
A penny for the Old Guy

I

We are the hollow men
We are the stuffed men
Leaning together
Headpiece filled with straw. Alas!
5 Our dried voices, when
We whisper together
Are quiet and meaningless
As wind in dry grass
Or rats' feet over broken glass
10 In our dry cellar

Shape without form, shade without colour,
Paralysed force, gesture without motion;

Those who have crossed
With direct eyes, to death's other Kingdom
15 Remember us—if at all—not as lost
Violent souls, but only
As the hollow men
The stuffed men. **C**

II

Eyes I dare not meet in dreams
20 In death's dream kingdom
These do not appear:
There, the eyes are
Sunlight on a broken column
There, is a tree swinging
25 And voices are
In the wind's singing
More distant and more solemn
Than a fading star.

[Epigraph] **Mistah . . . dead:** a quotation from Joseph Conrad's *Heart of Darkness,* in which Kurtz is a character whose descent into evil makes him like the "lost violent souls" in lines 15–16. **A penny . . . Guy:** a cry used by English children collecting money to buy fireworks for Guy Fawkes Day, a yearly celebration of the failure of Guy Fawkes and other conspirators to blow up Parliament in 1605. The celebration also traditionally includes the burning of straw effigies of Fawkes.

4 Headpiece . . . straw: The speaker likens himself and the other "hollow men" to the straw effigies burned on Guy Fawkes Day.

14 death's other Kingdom: perhaps heaven (as opposed to hell, where the "lost violent souls" go).

C STYLE
Recall that Eliot often conveys ideas through **symbols** and **allusions** instead of direct statements. Why does the speaker liken himself and his companions to straw effigies?

Let me be no nearer
30 In death's dream kingdom
Let me also wear
Such deliberate disguises
Rat's coat, crowskin, crossed staves
In a field
35 Behaving as the wind behaves
No nearer—

        Not that final meeting
In the twilight kingdom

III

This is the dead land
40 This is cactus land
Here the stone images
Are raised, here they receive
The supplication of a dead man's hand
Under the twinkle of a fading star.

45   Is it like this
In death's other kingdom
Waking alone
At the hour when we are
Trembling with tenderness
50 Lips that would kiss
Form prayers to broken stone. **D**

IV

The eyes are not here
There are no eyes here
In this valley of dying stars
55 In this hollow valley
This broken jaw of our lost kingdoms

        In this last of meeting places
We grope together
And avoid speech
60 Gathered on this beach of the tumid river

        Sightless, unless
The eyes reappear
As the perpetual star
Multifoliate rose
65 Of death's twilight kingdom
The hope only
Of empty men.

33 Rat's coat . . . field: a typical scarecrow with small animals attached. The staves are the poles that support it.

43 supplication (sŭp'lĭ-kā'shən): begging; plea.

D **READING MODERN VERSE**
Note the different **images** Eliot presents of the "dead land." What does each image convey? Together, what do they tell you about the hollow men's existence?

60 tumid (tōō'mĭd): swollen.

64 Multifoliate (mŭl'tə-fō'lē-āt') **rose:** an allusion to the many-petaled rose formed by the souls of the blessed in Dante's *Divine Comedy*.

V

Here we go round the prickly pear
Prickly pear prickly pear
70 Here we go round the prickly pear
At five o'clock in the morning.

Between the idea
And the reality
Between the motion
75 And the act
Falls the Shadow
                   For Thine is the Kingdom ⓔ
Between the conception
And the creation
80 Between the emotion
And the response
Falls the Shadow
                      Life is very long
Between the desire
85 And the spasm
Between the potency
And the existence
Between the essence
And the descent
90 Falls the Shadow ⓕ
                For Thine is the Kingdom
For Thine is
Life is
For Thine is the

95   This is the way the world ends
This is the way the world ends
This is the way the world ends
Not with a bang but a whimper.

68–71 *Here ... morning:* a variation of the children's rhyme "Here We Go 'Round the Mulberry Bush," replacing the mulberry bush with a prickly pear cactus, appropriate to the "cactus land" of line 40.

ⓔ **ALLUSION**
An **allusion** is an indirect reference to a person, place, event, or literary work with which the author believes the reader will be familiar. Here Eliot is quoting the beginning of a sentence added to the Lord's Prayer by many Christians. The "Kingdom" to which it refers is the kingdom of God. If this appears to be the speech of the Hollow Men, why might they repeat this line from the Lord's Prayer?

ⓕ **STYLE**
How do you interpret the "Shadow" mentioned here and in lines 76 and 82? Explain what you think it might **symbolize**.

COMMON CORE RL 7

READING MODERN VERSE
Eliot's style and tone invite a range of interpretations. Search an Internet video site using the terms "hollow men" and "eliot" to view more than one oral reading. How are they similar and different from one another and from your own interpretation of this poem?

Text Analysis

1. **Summarize** Describe the hollow men. What are their key **traits**, and what is their existence like?

2. **Analyze Imagery** What images are repeated in this poem? What ideas do these images convey? Cite evidence to support your answer.

from **The Book of Practical Cats**

The Naming of Cats

T. S. Eliot

The Naming of Cats is a difficult matter,
    It isn't just one of your holiday games;
You may think at first I'm as mad as a hatter
When I tell you, a cat must have THREE DIFFERENT NAMES.
5 First of all, there's the name that the family use daily,
    Such as Peter, Augustus, Alonzo or James,
Such as Victor or Jonathan, George or Bill Bailey—
    All of them sensible everyday names.
There are fancier names if you think they sound sweeter,
10   Some for the gentlemen, some for the dames:
Such as Plato, Admetus, Electra, Demeter—
    But all of them sensible everyday names.
But I tell you, a cat needs a name that's particular,
    A name that's peculiar, and more dignified,
15 Else how can he keep up his tail perpendicular,
    Or spread out his whiskers, or cherish his pride?
Of names of this kind, I can give you a quorum,
    Such as Munkustrap, Quaxo, or Coricopat,
Such as Bombalurina, or else Jellylorum—
20   Names that never belong to more than one cat.
But above and beyond there's still one name left over,
    And that is the name that you never will guess;
The name that no human research can discover—
    But the CAT HIMSELF KNOWS, and will never confess. **G**
25 When you notice a cat in profound meditation,
    The reason, I tell you, is always the same:
His mind is engaged in a rapt contemplation
    Of the thought, of the thought, of the thought of his name:
      His ineffable effable
30   Effanineffable
Deep and inscrutable singular Name.

11 Plato … Demeter: names from classical Greek and Roman times.

17 quorum (kwôr′əm): a select group or company.

G STYLE
How does this poem differ stylistically from the two preceding ones? Do you see any similarities? Explain, citing evidence.

29 ineffable (ĭn-ĕf′ə-bəl): too awesome or sacred to be spoken; **effable** (ĕf′ə-bəl): capable of being uttered.

Comprehension

1. **Recall** According to "The Naming of Cats," how many names must a cat have?

2. **Clarify** What are the different uses of the names?

Text Analysis

3. **Understand Modern Verse** Review the images and ideas you recorded as you read "Preludes." What view of modern urban life does Eliot convey through each of the following?

   - description of the storm (lines 5–13)
   - portrayal of morning (lines 14–23)
   - depiction of the street (lines 39–47)
   - final simile (lines 53–54)

4. **Draw Conclusions** How do you interpret Section V of "The Hollow Men"? What do you think keeps the hollow men from fulfillment? Support your conclusions with textual evidence.

5. **Analyze Sound Devices** Eliot often uses sound devices to connect his fragmentary images. Re-examine "The Hollow Men," noting examples of each sound device listed in the chart. Use your completed chart to describe the effect these sound devices have on the poem.

Sound Device	Example
rhyme	
alliteration	
consonance	

6. **Analyze Mood** The **imagery** in a poem usually contributes to its mood. How would you describe the mood of "Preludes" and that of "The Hollow Men"? How does the mood of "The Naming of Cats" differ?

7. **Examine Style** Re-examine "Preludes" and "The Hollow Men," noting examples of the stylistic elements discussed on page 1117. What relationship do you see between Eliot's style and his message? Do you think his style mirrors his ideas about the human condition? Cite evidence.

Text Criticism

8. **Critical Interpretations** Eliot has always been both praised and criticized. One of his detractors bemoaned the "sterility, inaction, detachment, and despair which dominate Eliot's poetry." Do you agree with this assessment of Eliot's work? Explain, citing evidence from the text.

Is the world FALLING APART?

"Preludes" and "The Hollow Men" are concerned with the disintegration of traditional values and beliefs in the modern world. What works of literature or films that you know of deal with this topic in today's culture?

COMMON CORE

RL 1 Cite evidence to support inferences drawn from the text. **RL 2** Determine two or more themes or central ideas of a text. **RL 4** Determine the meaning of words and phrases as they are used in the text, including figurative and connotative meanings; analyze the impact of specific word choices on meaning and tone. **RL 10** Read and comprehend literature, including poems.

Language

◆ **GRAMMAR AND STYLE: Choose Effective Words**

One of the striking aspects of Eliot's poetic style is his use of highly **effective words.** In "Preludes," for example, he uses fresh, evocative **adjectives** to create a disturbing image of an urban wasteland. Note how, in this passage, the adjectives work to create the atmosphere of desolation that Eliot wants to convey to the reader:

> *And now a gusty shower wraps*
> *The grimy scraps*
> *Of withered leaves about your feet*
> *And newspapers from vacant lots;* (lines 5–8)

PRACTICE Review the following stanza. Then, mimicking Eliot's poetic style, replace the adjectives in the stanza with more vivid ones that better convey an atmosphere of decay and destitution.

> The rain poured down
> On old gutters full of old leaves and faded trash
> And in the dark doorway of an unoccupied cafe
> A man clasped his thin knees
> To his skinny chest

READING-WRITING CONNECTION

Expand your understanding of Eliot's style by responding to this prompt. Then use the **revising tips** to improve your poem.

WRITING PROMPT	REVISING TIPS
COMPOSE A POEM Review lines 39–47 of "Preludes," carefully considering Eliot's personification of the street. Adopting the identity of the street itself, write a **three-to-five-stanza poem** that presents some of the images the street "sees" during the long night. Try to imitate Eliot's style by creating a patchwork of images, symbols, and allusions.	• Add more literary allusions or quotations if your poem does not seem to match Eliot's style. • Make sure your poem includes some examples of sound devices such as alliteration, consonance, or assonance (see page 840).

COMMON CORE

L 3 Apply knowledge of language to make effective choices for meaning and style. **W 3d** Use precise words and phrases to convey a vivid picture of the events, setting, and/or characters.

Interactive Revision | **THiNK** central

Go to **thinkcentral.com.**
KEYWORD: HML12-1125

A Cup of Tea

Short Story by Katherine Mansfield

COMMON CORE

RL 1 Cite evidence to support inferences drawn from the text. **RL 3** Analyze the impact of the author's choices regarding how to develop and relate elements of a story.

Meet the Author

Katherine Mansfield 1888–1923

"I want to be all that I am capable of becoming," Katherine Mansfield once declared. Although she lived to be only 34 years old, Mansfield made an enormous mark on the English short story. Striving to map her characters' inner lives, she pioneered a new style of writing characterized by mood and suggestion rather than by dramatic action. Her stories illuminate the subtle realities of personal relationships and class divisions.

Budding Writer Mansfield was born in Wellington, New Zealand, to Harold Beauchamp, a prosperous businessman, and his wife Annie, an ambitious social climber. Mansfield was close to her grandmother but had ambivalent feelings for her mother, who paid her shy, awkward daughter little attention. Katherine found an outlet for her feelings in fiction. "I imagine I was always writing," she later said. "Twaddle it was too. But better far [to] write twaddle . . . than nothing at all."

Rebellious Spirit In 1906, Mansfield returned to Wellington after three years at Queen's College in London, full of new ideas about personal fulfillment and women's rights. Finding her native country provincial, she begged her father to allow her to return to England. It took two years, but at last he agreed. Just weeks after her return, Mansfield

fell in love with violinist Garnet Trowell. When their relationship soured, she married musician G. C. Bowden, but left him the day after their wedding to return to Trowell. Despairing over her daughter's behavior, Mansfield's mother sent her to a health spa in Germany. Mansfield's observations there gave rise to her first short-story collection, *In a German Pension* (1911).

Symbol of Innovation Around 1912, Mansfield began a stormy relationship with English critic John Middleton Murray. Inspired by his call for a literature that was imbued with "guts and bloodiness," Mansfield began to write with brutal honesty about her own childhood. Mansfield and Murray finally married in 1919, but they spent all—save a few months—of their married life apart. Dogged by poor health, Mansfield traveled often in search of a more congenial climate. During her last years, she lived as an invalid, often alone, fighting a losing battle with tuberculosis. Amazingly, in the midst of these travails, she wrote many of her most powerful works, including *The Garden Party* (1922), recognized by many as her finest collection. Today, Mansfield is hailed, in the words of one critic, as "a symbol of liberation, innovation, and unconventionality."

DID YOU KNOW?

Katherine Mansfield . . .

- published her first story at the age of nine.
- inspired Virginia Woolf to comment, "I was jealous of her writing— the only writing I have ever been jealous of."
- was the model for a character in her good friend D. H. Lawrence's novel *Women in Love*.

Author Online

Go to **thinkcentral.com**. KEYWORD: HML12-1126

THINK central

TEXT ANALYSIS: THIRD-PERSON LIMITED POINT OF VIEW

Katherine Mansfield is renowned for depicting characters' subtle reactions to the seemingly trivial events of everyday life. In "A Cup of Tea," Mansfield accomplishes this in part through her use of the **third-person limited point of view.** The narrator is an outside voice that relates the thoughts, feelings, and observations of just one character. Readers may feel as if they are "looking over the shoulder" of the point-of-view character, getting emotionally involved in that character's experiences.

As you get to know this story's point-of-view character, a wealthy young woman named Rosemary, consider how the narrator reveals her thoughts and emotions. Think about how Rosemary perceives herself and others, and note how the story's point of view affects your impression of her.

READING SKILL: MAKE INFERENCES

You know from your experiences with fiction that writers don't explicitly state everything that goes through their characters' minds. Instead, they leave it up to the reader to **make inferences,** or logical assumptions, based on evidence and experience. One thing you'll often have to infer is a character's **motivation,** or the reasons driving his or her actions. As you read this story, think about what motivates Rosemary to act as she does. In a chart like the one shown, jot down notes about her actions. Consider evidence from the text as well as your own experiences, and then record what you can infer about Rosemary's motivation.

Action	Evidence or My Own Experience	Possible Motive
Rosemary, a woman who can shop anywhere she likes, particularly enjoys one little antique shop.	The owner of this shop is "ridiculously fond" of serving Rosemary and flatters her incessantly.	

 Complete the activities in your **Reader/Writer Notebook.**

What makes someone feel SUPERIOR?

How do people with a high status, or standing in society, perceive those who occupy lower positions? That's the question explored in "A Cup of Tea," the story of a remarkable encounter between two women, one poor and the other privileged.

DISCUSS With a group of classmates, generate a list of factors that determine a person's status in society. Then discuss how a person's standing in society can affect his or her self-image, perception of others, and outlook on life. How does society treat those with high status? How do those with high status treat the people around them? Share your observations with the members of another group.

A Cup of Tea

Katherine Mansfield

BACKGROUND In the early 1900s, when "A Cup of Tea" was written, class distinctions were quite evident in Britain. The best schools and neighborhoods were reserved for the rich, who tended to avoid contact with people of lower classes whenever possible. An upper-class wife never worked inside or outside the home. Instead, she spent her days shopping and entertaining. It was considered improper for her to associate with people of lower classes unless they were serving her in some way.

Rosemary Fell was not exactly beautiful. No, you couldn't have called her beautiful. Pretty? Well, if you took her to pieces . . . But why be so cruel as to take anyone to pieces? She was young, brilliant, extremely modern, exquisitely well dressed, amazingly well read in the newest of the new books, and her parties were the most delicious mixture of the really important people and . . . artists— quaint creatures, discoveries of hers, some of them too terrifying for words, but others quite presentable and amusing. **A**

Rosemary had been married two years. She had a duck[1] of a boy. No, not Peter—Michael. And her husband absolutely adored her. They were rich, really
10 rich, not just comfortably well off, which is odious and stuffy and sounds like one's grandparents. But if Rosemary wanted to shop she would go to Paris as you and I would go to Bond Street.[2] If she wanted to buy flowers, the car pulled up at that perfect shop in Regent Street, and Rosemary inside the shop just gazed in her

---

1. **duck:** a British expression for a darling person or thing.
2. **Bond Street:** a London street famous for its fashionable shops.

Analyze Visuals ▶

What personality traits are conveyed by this painting?

A **POINT OF VIEW**
In lines 1–7, Mansfield introduces the story's **third-person narrator** as well as the main character. How would you describe the narrator's **tone** in the description of Rosemary?

Girl with Mirror (1928), Walt Kuhn. Oil on canvas, 24″ × 20 ⅛″. Image courtesy of The Phillips Collection, Washington, D. C.

dazzled, rather exotic way, and said: "I want those and those and those. Give me four bunches of those. And that jar of roses. Yes, I'll have all the roses in the jar. No, no lilac. I hate lilac. It's got no shape." The attendant bowed and put the lilac out of sight, as though this was only too true; lilac was dreadfully shapeless. "Give me those stumpy little tulips. Those red and white ones." And she was followed to the car by a thin shopgirl staggering under an immense white paper armful that looked like a baby in long clothes. . . .

20

One winter afternoon she had been buying something in a little antique shop in Curzon Street. It was a shop she liked. For one thing, one usually had it to oneself. And then the man who kept it was ridiculously fond of serving her. He beamed whenever she came in. He clasped his hands; he was so gratified he could scarcely speak. Flattery, of course. All the same, there was something . . .

"You see, madam," he would explain in his low respectful tones, "I love my things. I would rather not part with them than sell them to someone who does not appreciate them, who has not that fine feeling which is so rare. . . ." And, breathing deeply, he unrolled a tiny square of blue velvet and pressed it on the glass counter with his pale fingertips.

30

Today it was a little box. He had been keeping it for her. He had shown it to nobody as yet. An exquisite little enamel box with a glaze so fine it looked as though it had been baked in cream. On the lid a minute creature stood under a flowery tree, and a more minute creature still had her arms around his neck. Her hat, really no bigger than a geranium petal, hung from a branch; it had green ribbons. And there was a pink cloud like a watchful cherub[3] floating above their heads. Rosemary took her hands out of her long gloves. She always took off her gloves to examine such things. Yes, she liked it very much. She loved it; it was a great duck. She must have it. And, turning the creamy box, opening and shutting it, she couldn't help noticing how charming her hands were against the blue velvet. The shopman, in some dim cavern of his mind, may have dared to think so too. For he took a pencil, leaned over the counter, and his pale bloodless fingers crept timidly towards those rosy, flashing ones, as he murmured gently: "If I may venture to point out to madam, the flowers on the little lady's bodice."[4] **B**

40

"Charming!" Rosemary admired the flowers. But what was the price? For a moment the shopman did not seem to hear. Then a murmur reached her. "Twenty-eight guineas,[5] madam."

"Twenty-eight guineas." Rosemary gave no sign. She laid the little box down; she buttoned her gloves again. Twenty-eight guineas. Even if one is rich . . .

50

She looked vague. She stared at a plump teakettle like a plump hen above the shopman's head, and her voice was dreamy as she answered: "Well, keep it for me—will you? I'll . . ."

But the shopman had already bowed as though keeping it for her was all any human being could ask. He would be willing, of course, to keep it for her forever.

B MAKE INFERENCES
Why does Rosemary enjoy patronizing this particular shop? Record your inferences about her **motivation** in your chart.

---

3. **cherub** (chĕr'əb): an angel depicted as a chubby child with wings.

4. **bodice** (bŏd'ĭs): the part of a dress above the waist.

5. **guineas** (gĭn'ēz): units of British money equal to one pound and one shilling, used mainly for pricing luxury items.

The discreet door shut with a click. She was outside on the step, gazing at the winter afternoon. Rain was falling, and with the rain it seemed the dark came too, spinning down like ashes. There was a cold bitter taste in the air, and the new-lighted lamps looked sad. Sad were the lights in the houses opposite. Dimly they burned as if regretting something. And people hurried by, hidden under
60 their hateful umbrellas. Rosemary felt a strange pang.[6] She pressed her muff to her breast; she wished she had the little box, too, to cling to. Of course, the car was there. She'd only to cross the pavement. But still she waited. There are moments, horrible moments in life, when one emerges from shelter and looks out, and it's awful. One oughtn't to give way to them. One ought to go home and have an extra-special tea. But at the very instant of thinking that, a young girl, thin, dark, shadowy—where had she come from?—was standing at Rosemary's elbow and a voice like a sigh, almost like a sob, breathed: "Madam, may I speak to you a moment?" **C**

"Speak to me?" Rosemary turned. She saw a little battered creature with
70 enormous eyes, someone quite young, no older than herself, who clutched at her coat-collar with reddened hands, and shivered as though she had just come out of the water.

"M-madam," stammered the voice. "Would you let me have the price of a cup of tea?"

"A cup of tea?" There was something simple, sincere in that voice; it wasn't in the least the voice of a beggar. "Then have you no money at all?" asked Rosemary.

"None, madam," came the answer.

"How extraordinary!" Rosemary peered through the dusk, and the girl gazed back at her. How more than extraordinary! And suddenly it seemed to Rosemary
80 such an adventure. It was like something out of a novel by Dostoyevsky,[7] this meeting in the dusk. Supposing she took the girl home? Supposing she did do one of those things she was always reading about or seeing on the stage, what would happen? It would be thrilling. And she heard herself saying afterwards to the amazement of her friends: "I simply took her home with me," as she stepped forward and said to that dim person beside her: "Come home to tea with me."

The girl drew back startled. She even stopped shivering for a moment. Rosemary put out a hand and touched her arm. "I mean it," she said, smiling. And she felt how simple and kind her smile was. "Why won't you? Do. Come home with me now in my car and have tea."

90 "You—you don't mean it, madam," said the girl, and there was pain in her voice.

"But I do," cried Rosemary. "I want you to. To please me. Come along."

The girl put her fingers to her lips and her eyes devoured Rosemary. "You're—you're not taking me to the police station?" she stammered.

"The police station!" Rosemary laughed out. "Why should I be so cruel? No, I only want to make you warm and to hear—anything you care to tell me." **D**

---

6. **pang** (păng): a sudden sharp pain or feeling.

7. **Dostoyevsky** (dŏs'tə-yĕf'skē): Feodor Dostoyevsky, a 19th-century Russian author who wrote a number of novels and stories dealing with the lives of the poor.

Language Coach

Homophones Words that sound alike but have different spellings are **homophones**. *Discreet* (line 55) means "keeping silent, preserving secrets." *Discrete* means "separate; made of distinct parts; discontinuous." How can a door be *discreet*? Could it also be *discrete*?

C POINT OF VIEW
In lines 55–65, Mansfield provides an intimate glimpse of the **point-of-view character's** thoughts and feelings as she pauses outside the shop. What impression of Rosemary do you get from this passage?

D MAKE INFERENCES
Think about how Rosemary feels as she leaves the shop, and consider her thoughts in lines 78–85. What is her **motivation** for inviting the girl to accompany her?

Hungry people are easily led. The footman[8] held the door of the car open, and a moment later they were skimming through the dusk.

"There!" said Rosemary. She had a feeling of triumph as she slipped her hand through the velvet strap. She could have said, "Now I've got you," as she gazed at the little captive she had netted. But of course she meant it kindly. Oh, more than kindly. She was going to prove to this girl that—wonderful things did happen in life, that—fairy godmothers were real, that—rich people had hearts, and that women *were* sisters. She turned impulsively, saying: "Don't be frightened. After all, why shouldn't you come back with me? We're both women. If I'm the more fortunate, you ought to expect . . ."

But happily at that moment, for she didn't know how the sentence was going to end, the car stopped. The bell was rung, the door opened, and with a charming, protecting, almost embracing movement, Rosemary drew the other into the hall. Warmth, softness, light, a sweet scent, all those things so familiar to her she never even thought about them, she watched that other receive. It was fascinating. She was like the little rich girl in her nursery with all the cupboards to open, all the boxes to unpack.

"Come, come upstairs," said Rosemary, longing to begin to be generous. "Come up to my room." And, besides, she wanted to spare this poor little thing from being stared at by the servants; she decided as they mounted the stairs she would not even ring for Jeanne, but take off her things by herself. The great thing was to be natural! **E**

And "There!" cried Rosemary again, as they reached her beautiful big bedroom with the curtains drawn, the fire leaping on her wonderful lacquer furniture, her gold cushions and the primrose and blue rugs.

The girl stood just inside the door; she seemed dazed. But Rosemary didn't mind that.

"Come and sit down," she cried, dragging her big chair up to the fire, "in this comfy chair. Come and get warm. You look so dreadfully cold."

"I daren't, madam," said the girl, and she edged backwards.

"Oh, please,"—Rosemary ran forward—"you mustn't be frightened, you mustn't, really. Sit down, and when I've taken off my things we shall go into the next room and have tea and be cozy. Why are you afraid?" And gently she half pushed the thin figure into its deep cradle.

But there was no answer. The girl stayed just as she had been put, with her hands by her sides and her mouth slightly open. To be quite sincere, she looked rather stupid. But Rosemary wouldn't acknowledge it. She leaned over her, saying: "Won't you take off your hat? Your pretty hair is all wet. And one is so much more comfortable without a hat, isn't one?"

There was a whisper that sounded like "Very good, madam," and the crushed hat was taken off.

"Let me help you off with your coat, too," said Rosemary.

E MAKE INFERENCES
Consider what you learn about Rosemary's **motivation** in line 113. Does she feel invested in the girl purely out of charity, or are there other reasons driving her to act as she does? Explain your answer.

---

8. **footman:** a household servant, here functioning as Rosemary's chauffeur.

The girl stood up. But she held on to the chair with one hand and let Rosemary pull. It was quite an effort. The other scarcely helped her at all. She seemed to
140 stagger like a child, and the thought came and went through Rosemary's mind, that if people wanted helping they must respond a little, just a little, otherwise it became very difficult indeed. And what was she to do with the coat now? She left it on the floor, and the hat too. She was just going to take a cigarette off the mantelpiece when the girl said quickly, but so lightly and strangely: "I'm very sorry, madam, but I'm going to faint. I shall go off, madam, if I don't have something." **F**

"Good heavens, how thoughtless I am!" Rosemary rushed to the bell.

"Tea! Tea at once! And some brandy immediately!"

The maid was gone again, but the girl almost cried out. "No, I don't want
150 no brandy. I never drink brandy. It's a cup of tea I want, madam." And she burst into tears.

It was a terrible and fascinating moment. Rosemary knelt beside her chair.

"Don't cry, poor little thing," she said. "Don't cry." And she gave the other her lace handkerchief. She really was touched beyond words. She put her arm round those thin, birdlike shoulders.

Now at last the other forgot to be shy, forgot everything except that they were both women, and gasped out: "I can't go on no longer like this. I can't bear it. I shall do away with myself. I can't bear no more."

F POINT OF VIEW
Notice that in lines 138–146, the narrator reveals only Rosemary's thoughts. How does Mansfield use the **third-person-limited point of view** to create irony?

160 "You shan't have to. I'll look after you. Don't cry anymore. Don't you see what a good thing it was that you met me? We'll have tea and you'll tell me everything. And I shall arrange something. I promise. *Do* stop crying. It's so exhausting. Please!"

The other did stop just in time for Rosemary to get up before the tea came. She had the table placed between them. She plied the poor little creature with everything, all the sandwiches, all the bread and butter, and every time her cup was empty she filled it with tea, cream and sugar. People always said sugar was so nourishing. As for herself she didn't eat; she smoked and looked away tactfully so that the other should not be shy.

And really the effect of that slight meal was marvelous. When the tea table was carried away a new being, a light, frail creature with tangled hair, dark lips, deep, 170 lighted eyes, lay back in the big chair in a kind of sweet languor,[9] looking at the blaze. Rosemary lit a fresh cigarette; it was time to begin.

"And when did you have your last meal?" she asked softly.

But at that moment the door-handle turned.

"Rosemary, may I come in?" It was Philip.

"Of course."

He came in. "Oh, I'm so sorry," he said, and stopped and stared.

"It's quite all right," said Rosemary smiling. "This is my friend, Miss—"

"Smith, madam," said the languid figure, who was strangely still and unafraid.

"Smith," said Rosemary. "We are going to have a little talk."

180 "Oh, yes," said Philip. "Quite," and his eye caught sight of the coat and hat on the floor. He came over to the fire and turned his back to it. "It's a beastly[10] afternoon," he said curiously, still looking at that listless figure, looking at its hands and boots, and then at Rosemary again.

"Yes, isn't it?" said Rosemary enthusiastically. "Vile."

Philip smiled his charming smile. "As a matter of fact," said he, "I wanted you to come into the library for a moment. Would you? Will Miss Smith excuse us?"

The big eyes were raised to him, but Rosemary answered for her. "Of course she will." And they went out of the room together.

"I say," said Philip, when they were alone. "Explain. Who is she? What does 190 it all mean?"

Rosemary, laughing, leaned against the door and said: "I picked her up in Curzon Street. Really. She's a real pick-up. She asked me for the price of a cup of tea, and I brought her home with me."

"But what on earth are you going to do with her?" cried Philip.

"Be nice to her," said Rosemary quickly. "Be frightfully nice to her. Look after her. I don't know how. We haven't talked yet. But show her—treat her—make her feel—"

"My darling girl," said Philip, "you're quite mad, you know. It simply can't be done."

200 "I knew you'd say that," retorted Rosemary. "Why not? I want to. Isn't that a reason? And besides, one's always reading about these things. I decided—"

---

9. **languor** (lăng′gər): a dreamy, lazy state.

10. **beastly**: awful; unpleasant.

Language Coach

Commonly Confused Words Traditionally, the words *shall* and *shan't*, used after *I*, expressed the future; after *you*, *he*, or *she*, they expressed a promise or determination. The reverse was true of *will/won't*. Today *shall* is generally used only in questions (*Shall we go?*). Modernize lines 159–161.

Analyze Visuals ▶
The background of this painting has been left relatively plain. Why do you think the artist chose this approach?

The Convalescent, Gwen John. Oil on canvas, 40.9 cm × 33 cm. PD.24-1951. © Fitzwilliam Museum, University of Cambridge, United Kingdom/Bridgeman Art Library. © 2007 Artists Rights Society (ARS), New York/DACS, London.

"But," said Philip slowly, and he cut the end of a cigar, "she's so astonishingly pretty."

"Pretty?" Rosemary was so surprised that she blushed. "Do you think so? I—I hadn't thought about it."

"Good Lord!" Philip struck a match. "She's absolutely lovely. Look again, my child. I was bowled over when I came into your room just now. However . . . I think you're making a ghastly mistake. Sorry, darling, if I'm crude and all that. But let me know if Miss Smith is going to dine with us in time for me to look
210 up *The Milliner's Gazette.*"[11] **G**

"You absurd creature!" said Rosemary, and she went out of the library, but not back to her bedroom. She went to her writing-room and sat down at her desk. Pretty! Absolutely lovely! Bowled over! Her heart beat like a heavy bell. Pretty! Lovely! She drew her checkbook towards her. But no, checks would be no use, of course. She opened a drawer and took out five pound notes, looked at them, put two back, and holding the three squeezed in her hand, she went back to her bedroom.

Half an hour later Philip was still in the library, when Rosemary came in.

"I only wanted to tell you," said she, and she leaned against the door again
220 and looked at him with her dazzled exotic gaze, "Miss Smith won't dine with us tonight."

Philip put down the paper. "Oh, what's happened? Previous engagement?"

Rosemary came over and sat down on his knee. "She insisted on going," said she, "so I gave the poor little thing a present of money. I couldn't keep her against her will, could I?" she added softly.

Rosemary had just done her hair, darkened her eyes a little, and put on her pearls. She put up her hands and touched Philip's cheeks.

"Do you like me?" said she, and her tone, sweet, husky, troubled him.

"I like you awfully," he said, and he held her tighter. "Kiss me."
230 There was a pause.

Then Rosemary said dreamily, "I saw a fascinating little box today. It cost twenty-eight guineas. May I have it?"

Philip jumped her on his knee. "You may, little wasteful one," said he.

But that was not really what Rosemary wanted to say.

"Philip," she whispered, and she pressed his head against her bosom, "am I *pretty?*" ❧

G **POINT OF VIEW**
Reread lines 202–207. In what way does the story's **limited point of view** enhance the impact of Philip's remark about the girl's appearance?

---

11. *The Milliner's Gazette:* an imaginary newsletter for working-class women. A milliner is a maker of women's hats.

Comprehension

1. **Recall** Where does Rosemary meet Miss Smith?

2. **Summarize** How does Philip react to Rosemary's guest?

3. **Clarify** How does Rosemary's gift to Miss Smith differ from her initial plan?

Text Analysis

4. **Identify Irony** In literature, **situational irony** is a contrast between what is expected to happen and what actually does happen. Consider how Rosemary feels when she first meets Miss Smith. How has Rosemary's perception of herself changed by the story's end? What is ironic about this change?

5. **Analyze Point of View** Employing the **third-person limited point of view** allows Mansfield to focus on the thoughts and feelings of just one character. How does this point of view affect your experience of the story and your judgment of Rosemary? How might the story have been different if the author had used the **omniscient point of view,** an all-seeing narrator who would relate the thoughts of all the characters, including Miss Smith?

6. **Make Inferences About Character Motivation** Examine the chart you filled in as you read. For each of the actions listed, explain what you inferred Rosemary's motivation to be. Be sure to discuss the textual evidence and any experiences from your own life that you used to make these inferences.

7. **Draw Conclusions About Social Context** Review the background information on page 1128. Through her depiction of Rosemary and Philip's marriage and of the status their upper-class lifestyle affords, what comments might Mansfield be making on the social conditions of her time? Support your answer with detailed examples from the text.

Text Criticism

8. **Critical Interpretations** In fiction, **realism** is a truthful, realistic presentation of life. John Middleton Murray, the critic who became Mansfield's husband, praised her work for its realism, recalling a printer who remarked after reading a manuscript of hers, "But these kids are real!" Based on this story, do you agree with this view of the realism in Mansfield's work? Find two or three passages from "A Cup of Tea" to support your answer.

What makes someone feel **SUPERIOR?**

Is status only determined by money? If everyone had the same amount of money, what other factors might society use to determine someone's status?

COMMON CORE

RL 1 Cite evidence to support inferences drawn from the text. **RL 3** Analyze the impact of the author's choices regarding how to develop and relate elements of a story. **RL 6** Analyze a case in which grasping point of view requires distinguishing what is directly stated in a text from what is really meant.

The Duchess and the Jeweller

Short Story by Virginia Woolf

COMMON CORE

RL 3 Determine the impact of the author's choices regarding how to develop and relate elements of a story. RL 4 Determine the meaning of words and phrases as they are used in the text, including connotative meanings; analyze the impact of specific word choices on meaning and tone.

Meet the Author

Virginia Woolf 1882–1941

Virginia Woolf was fascinated by the inner life: the interplay of memories, emotions, and sensations that occurs within each individual. To capture the fluid, random quality of human thoughts, Woolf began to experiment with stream of consciousness and other narrative techniques. Her groundbreaking novels, including *Mrs. Dalloway* (1925) and *To the Lighthouse* (1927), are considered masterpieces of modernist literature.

Early Influences Born Adeline Virginia Stephen, Woolf was raised in a cultured, upper-middle-class family whose friends included leading artists and thinkers of the day. Her vivacious mother died when Virginia was only 13, leaving her in the care of her remote, tyrannical father. Her mother's death, which Woolf called "the greatest disaster that could happen," also triggered the first of Woolf's several mental breakdowns.

Although Woolf's father encouraged her literary pursuits, he refused to send her to school. In keeping with Victorian custom, her brothers were sent to private schools and college, while Woolf and her sister were educated at home. Although she resented this injustice, she benefitted from exposure to her father's vast library, brilliant mind, and cultured friends. Later, she would credit him with teaching her how to write "in the fewest possible words, as clearly as possible, exactly what one meant."

The Bloomsbury Group After her father's death in 1904, Woolf and her siblings moved to the Bloomsbury district of London. There, they began to associate with a circle of artists and thinkers that became known as the Bloomsbury group. Gathering at Woolf's home, members debated current artistic, literary, and social issues and expressed their ardent support for artistic experimentation. Stimulated by the company of these free-thinking individuals, Woolf began work on her first novel, *The Voyage Out* (1912).

Pioneer of Modernism In 1912, Woolf married Bloomsbury member Leonard Woolf. In 1917, the couple established the Hogarth Press, which was dedicated to publishing groundbreaking literature. For the next 24 years, Woolf divided her time between running the press and writing a series of well-regarded novels. At the start of World War II, her despair over the bombing of her London home worsened her already deteriorating mental health. In 1941, deeply depressed and fearful that she was going insane, Woolf drowned herself in the river Ouse at the age of 59.

DID YOU KNOW?

Virginia Woolf . . .

- wrote a comic biography of a cocker spaniel.
- was nicknamed "Goat" by her family.
- was an outspoken pacifist during World War II.

Author Online
Go to thinkcentral.com. KEYWORD: HML12-1138

THINK central

TEXT ANALYSIS: PSYCHOLOGICAL FICTION

An offshoot of realism, **psychological fiction** largely ignores dramatic action to focus on the inner life of its characters. Psychological fiction emphasizes

- characters' thoughts, feelings, and impressions
- the hidden **motivations** for characters' actions
- the presence of **internal conflict**

A technique closely associated with this kind of fiction is **stream of consciousness,** which presents the random flow of thoughts and sensations in a character's mind. As you read this story, notice how Woolf uses these elements to portray the main character.

READING SKILL: ANALYZE DICTION

When you describe the language used in a work as formal or conversational, you are referring to the writer's **diction,** which includes word choice and syntax, or arrangement of words. Woolf chooses words that convey vivid impressions or strong sensations. She often uses complex sentences that cluster several strong words together in a series of short phrases, as in this example:

Then she loomed up, filling the door, filling the room with the aroma, the prestige, the arrogance, the pomp, the pride of all the Dukes and Duchesses swollen in one wave.

As you read, note when Woolf alters her sentence structure to heighten the impact of her carefully chosen words.

VOCABULARY IN CONTEXT

Woolf used these boldfaced words to portray one man's quest for social status. Use context clues to determine the meaning of each word.

1. **dismantle** the tent to put it away
2. bowed in **homage** to the queen
3. the glow of **burnished** steel
4. groveled **obsequiously**
5. moved with **lissome** grace
6. a ceremony full of **pomp**

 Complete the activities in your **Reader/Writer Notebook**.

What does it mean to have CLASS?

Some people think being rich is the key to having class. Others insist that class is an instinctive personal grace that can neither be bought nor taught. What are the essential qualities that determine whether a person truly has class?

DISCUSS Working with a partner, choose a fictional character or a real person whom you consider a model of class. Identify specific qualities and behaviors that make this person "classy." Based on the traits you identified, what relationship do you see between money and class? Explain your answer.

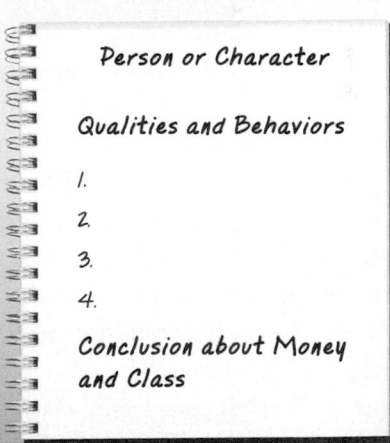

Person or Character

Qualities and Behaviors

1.
2.
3.
4.

Conclusion about Money and Class

The *Duchess* and the JEWELLER

Virginia Woolf

Oliver Bacon lived at the top of a house overlooking the Green Park.[1] He had a flat;[2] chairs jutted out at the right angles—chairs covered in hide. Sofas filled the bays[3] of the windows—sofas covered in tapestry. The windows, the three long windows, had the proper allowance of discreet net and figured satin.[4] The mahogany sideboard bulged discreetly with the right brandies, whiskeys and liqueurs. And from the middle window he looked down upon the glossy roofs of fashionable cars packed in the narrow straits of Piccadilly. A more central position could not be imagined. And at eight in the morning he would have his breakfast brought in on a tray by a manservant; the manservant would unfold his crimson
10 dressing gown; he would rip his letters open with his long pointed nails and would extract thick white cards of invitation upon which the engraving stood up roughly from duchesses, countesses, viscountesses[5] and Honorable Ladies. Then he would wash; then he would eat his toast; then he would read his paper by the bright burning fire of electric coals. **A**

Analyze Visuals ▶
What can you **infer** about the shop in this image?

A DICTION
Reread the description of Oliver's home in lines 1–7. Which of Woolf's **word choices** suggest Oliver is preoccupied with how others see him?

---

1. **Green Park:** a large park in London's fashionable West End, extending from just north of the royal residence of Buckingham Palace to Piccadilly (pĭk'dĭl'ē), a main London street.

2. **flat:** apartment.

3. **bays:** sections of wall that jut out from a building in which elegant windows are often placed.

4. **discreet . . . satin:** curtains made of lace that is not showy and satin with a woven design.

5. **viscountesses** (vī'koun'tĭs-ĭs): noblewomen ranking below duchesses and countesses but above baronesses.

JEWELLERY

5

All Repairs done on the Premises

JEWELLERY WATCHES & SILVER

Today's
LONDON
PRICES
PAID FOR
SCRAP

"Behold Oliver," he would say, addressing himself. "You who began life in a filthy little alley, you who . . ." and he would look down at his legs, so shapely in their perfect trousers; at his boots; at his spats. They were all shapely, shining; cut from the best cloth by the best scissors in Savile Row.[6] But he **dismantled** himself often and became again a little boy in a dark alley. He had once thought
20 that[7] the height of his ambition—selling stolen dogs to fashionable women in Whitechapel.[8] And once he had been done.[9] "Oh, Oliver," his mother had wailed. "Oh, Oliver! When will you have sense, my son?" . . . Then he had gone behind a counter; had sold cheap watches; then he had taken a wallet to Amsterdam.[10] . . . At that memory he would chuckle—the old Oliver remembering the young. Yes, he had done well with the three diamonds; also there was the commission on the emerald. After that he went into the private room behind the shop in Hatton Garden;[11] the room with the scales, the safe, the thick magnifying glasses. And then . . . and then . . . He chuckled. When he passed through the knots of jewellers in the hot evening who were discussing prices, gold mines, diamonds,
30 reports from South Africa, one of them would lay a finger to the side of his nose and murmur, "Hum–m–m," as he passed. It was no more than a murmur; no more than a nudge on the shoulder, a finger on the nose, a buzz that ran through the cluster of jewellers in Hatton Garden on a hot afternoon—oh, many years ago now! But still Oliver felt it purring down his spine, the nudge, the murmur that meant, "Look at him—young Oliver, the young jeweller—there he goes." Young he was then. And he dressed better and better; and had, first a hansom cab;[12] then a car; and first he went up to the dress circle, then down into the stalls.[13] And he had a villa at Richmond, overlooking the river, with trellises of red roses; and Mademoiselle used to pick one every morning and stick it in his buttonhole. **B**
40 "So," said Oliver Bacon, rising and stretching his legs. "So . . ."

And he stood beneath the picture of an old lady on the mantelpiece and raised his hands. "I have kept my word," he said, laying his hands together, palm to palm, as if he were doing **homage** to her. "I have won my bet." That was so; he was the richest jeweller in England; but his nose, which was long and flexible, like an elephant's trunk, seemed to say by its curious quiver at the nostrils (but it seemed as if the whole nose quivered, not only the nostrils) that he was not satisfied yet; still smelt something under the ground a little further off. Imagine

dismantle (dĭs-măn′tl) *v.* to take apart; to disassemble

B **PSYCHOLOGICAL FICTION**
Reread lines 15–24. Describe the differences between Oliver and his younger self. What is Oliver's attitude toward his past?

homage (hŏm′ĭj) *n.* an act showing great respect; tribute

---

6. **spats . . . Savile** (săv′əl) **Row:** cloth coverings for the top of the shoe and the ankle, worn by men as formal attire. Savile Row is a London street known for its exclusive men's clothing shops.

7. **that:** The word is used as a pronoun here, referring to the selling of stolen dogs mentioned later in the sentence.

8. **Whitechapel:** a working-class, inner-city neighborhood in London's East End, once notorious for its high crime rates and the poverty of its residents.

9. **done:** British slang for "arrested and charged with a crime."

10. **had taken a wallet to Amsterdam:** brought a package of uncut gems to the Dutch city of Amsterdam, a center of the diamond trade.

11. **Hatton Garden:** the center of London's jewelry trade.

12. **hansom cab:** a two-wheeled horse-drawn carriage.

13. **dress circle . . . stalls:** In British theaters or concert halls, the dress circle is the first balcony of seats, expensive but available to all. The stalls are seats near the stage, usually reserved for those of high rank.

a giant hog in a pasture rich with truffles;[14] after unearthing this truffle and that, still it smells a bigger, a blacker truffle under the ground further off. So Oliver
50 snuffed always in the rich earth of Mayfair[15] another truffle, a blacker, a bigger further off.

Now then he straightened the pearl in his tie, cased himself in his smart blue overcoat; took his yellow gloves and his cane; and swayed as he descended the stairs and half snuffed, half sighed through his long sharp nose as he passed out into Piccadilly. For was he not still a sad man, a dissatisfied man, a man who seeks something that is hidden, though he had won his bet?

He swayed slightly as he walked, as the camel at the zoo sways from side to side when it walks along the asphalt paths laden with grocers and their wives eating from paper bags and throwing little bits of silver paper crumpled up on to
60 the path. The camel despises the grocers; the camel is dissatisfied with its lot; the camel sees the blue lake and the fringe of palm trees in front of it. So the great jeweller, the greatest jeweller in the whole world, swung down Piccadilly, perfectly dressed, with his gloves, with his cane; but dissatisfied still, till he reached the dark little shop, that was famous in France, in Germany, in Austria, in Italy, and all over America—the dark little shop in the street off Bond Street.[16]

As usual he strode through the shop without speaking, though the four men, the two old men, Marshall and Spencer, and the two young men, Hammond and

---

14. **truffles:** edible fungi that grow underground, considered a rare delicacy. Hogs are often used to sniff them out.

15. **Mayfair:** a fashionable, mostly residential section of London's West End.

16. **Bond Street:** a main business street in Mayfair, known for its fashionable shops.

Wicks, stood straight behind the counter as he passed and looked at him, envying him. It was only with one finger of the amber-colored glove, waggling, that he acknowledged their presence. And he went in and shut the door of his private room behind him.

Then he unlocked the grating that barred the window. The cries of Bond Street came in; the purr of the distant traffic. The light from reflectors at the back of the shop struck upwards. One tree waved six green leaves, for it was June. But Mademoiselle had married Mr. Pedder of the local brewery—no one stuck roses in his buttonhole now. **C**

"So," he half sighed, half snorted, "so . . ."

Then he touched a spring in the wall and slowly the paneling slid open, and behind it were the steel safes, five, no, six of them, all of **burnished** steel. He twisted a key; unlocked one; then another. Each was lined with a pad of deep crimson velvet; in each lay jewels—bracelets, necklaces, rings, tiaras, ducal coronets;[17] loose stones in glass shells; rubies, emeralds, pearls, diamonds. All safe, shining, cool, yet burning, eternally, with their own compressed light.

"Tears!" said Oliver, looking at the pearls.

"Heart's blood!" he said, looking at the rubies.

"Gunpowder!" he continued, rattling the diamonds so that they flashed and blazed.

"Gunpowder enough to blow up Mayfair—sky high, high, high!" He threw his head back and made a sound like a horse neighing as he said it.

The telephone buzzed **obsequiously** in a low muted voice on his table. He shut the safe.

"In ten minutes," he said. "Not before." And he sat down at his desk and looked at the heads of the Roman emperors that were graved[18] on his sleeve links. And again he dismantled himself and became once more the little boy playing marbles in the alley where they sell stolen dogs on Sunday. He became that wily astute little boy, with lips like wet cherries. He dabbled his fingers in ropes of tripe;[19] he dipped them in pans of frying fish; he dodged in and out among the crowds. He was slim, **lissome,** with eyes like licked stones. And now—now—the hands of the clock ticked on. One, two, three, four . . . The Duchess of Lambourne waited his pleasure; the Duchess of Lambourne, daughter of a hundred Earls. She would wait for ten minutes on a chair at the counter. She would wait his pleasure. She would wait till he was ready to see her. He watched the clock in its shagreen[20] case. The hand moved on. With each tick the clock handed him—so it seemed—pâté de foie gras;[21] a glass of champagne; another of fine brandy; a cigar costing one guinea.[22] The clock laid them on the table beside

---

17. **ducal** (dōō'kəl) **coronets:** small crowns worn by dukes and duchesses.

18. **graved:** engraved.

19. **tripe:** the stomach lining of a cow or calf, used as food.

20. **shagreen** (shə-grēn'): untanned leather, often dyed green.

21. **pâté de foie gras** (pä-tā' də fwä grä'): a rich paste made from goose liver.

22. **guinea** (gĭn'ē): a unit of British money equal to one pound and one shilling, used mainly for pricing luxury items.

C **PSYCHOLOGICAL FICTION**
How would you explain the reference to Mademoiselle in lines 74–76? Based on this reference, what might be the cause of Oliver's dissatisfaction?

burnished (bûr'nĭsht) *adj.* polished until shiny **burnish** v.

obsequiously (ŏb-sē'kwē-əs-lē) *adv.* in an eagerly submissive way

lissome (lĭs'əm) *adj.* moving with graceful ease; limber

him, as the ten minutes passed. Then he heard soft slow footsteps approaching; a rustle in the corridor. The door opened. Mr. Hammond flattened himself against the wall. **D**

"Her Grace!"[23] he announced.

110 And he waited there, flattened against the wall.

And Oliver, rising, could hear the rustle of the dress of the Duchess as she came down the passage. Then she loomed up, filling the door, filling the room with the aroma, the prestige, the arrogance, the **pomp,** the pride of all the Dukes and Duchesses swollen in one wave. And as a wave breaks, she broke, as she sat down, spreading and splashing and falling over Oliver Bacon the great jeweller, covering him with sparkling bright colors, green, rose, violet; and odors; and iridescences; and rays shooting from fingers, nodding from plumes, flashing from silk; for she was very large, very fat, tightly girt[24] in pink taffeta, and past her prime. As a parasol with many flounces,[25] as a peacock with many feathers, shuts
120 its flounces, folds its feathers, so she subsided and shut herself as she sank down in the leather armchair. **E**

"Good morning, Mr. Bacon," said the Duchess. And she held out her hand which came through the slit of her white glove. And Oliver bent low as he shook it. And as their hands touched the link was forged between them once more. They were friends, yet enemies; he was master, she was mistress; each cheated the other, each needed the other, each feared the other, each felt this and knew this every time they touched hands thus in the little back room with the white light outside, and the tree with its six leaves, and the sound of the street in the distance and behind them the safes. **F**

130 "And today, Duchess—what can I do for you today?" said Oliver, very softly.

The Duchess opened; her heart, her private heart, gaped wide. And with a sigh, but no words, she took from her bag a long wash-leather pouch—it looked like a lean yellow ferret.[26] And from a slit in the ferret's belly she dropped pearls—ten pearls. They rolled from the slit in the ferret's belly—one, two, three, four—like the eggs of some heavenly bird.

"All that's left me, dear Mr. Bacon," she moaned. Five, six, seven—down they rolled, down the slopes of the vast mountainsides that fell between her knees into one narrow valley—the eighth, the ninth, and the tenth. There they lay in the glow of the peach-blossom taffeta. Ten pearls.

140 "From the Appleby cincture,"[27] she mourned. "The last . . . the last of them all."

Oliver stretched out and took one of the pearls between finger and thumb. It was round, it was lustrous. But real was it, or false? Was she lying again? Did she dare?

---

23. **Her Grace:** the appropriate way of referring to or directly addressing a duchess. A lower-ranking noblewoman (such as a countess or a baroness) would be referred to as *her ladyship* and directly addressed as *my lady.*

24. **girt:** wrapped; encircled.

25. **parasol** (păr′ə-sôl′) **. . . flounces:** a light umbrella with many ruffles.

26. **ferret:** a small animal similar to a weasel.

27. **cincture** (sĭngk′chər): an ornamental belt.

D PSYCHOLOGICAL FICTION
Reread lines 96–108. Note how Woolf uses **stream of consciousness** to convey Oliver's thoughts. What does this technique reveal about his motivation for making the Duchess wait?

pomp (pŏmp) *n.* vain display

E DICTION
What is unusual about the arrangement of phrases in lines 119–121?

F GRAMMAR AND STYLE
Note how Woolf uses long sentences layered with several phrases to imitate the flow of Oliver's thoughts.

She laid her plump padded finger across her lips. "If the Duke knew . . ." she whispered. "Dear Mr. Bacon, a bit of bad luck . . ."

Been gambling again, had she?

"That villain! That sharper!"[28] she hissed.

The man with the chipped cheek bone? A bad 'un. And the Duke was straight as a poker; with side whiskers; would cut her off, shut her up down there if he knew—what I know, thought Oliver, and glanced at the safe.

"Araminta, Daphne, Diana," she moaned. "It's for *them.*"

The Ladies Araminta, Daphne, Diana—her daughters. He knew them; adored them. But it was Diana he loved.

"You have all my secrets," she leered. Tears slid; tears fell; tears, like diamonds, collecting powder in the ruts of her cherry-blossom cheeks.

"Old friend," she murmured, "old friend."

"Old friend," he repeated, "old friend," as if he licked the words.

"How much?" he queried.

She covered the pearls with her hand.

"Twenty thousand," she whispered.

But was it real or false, the one he held in his hand? The Appleby cincture—hadn't she sold it already? He would ring for Spencer or Hammond. "Take it and test it," he would say. He stretched to the bell.

COMMON CORE RL 4

Language Coach

Denotations/Connotations
A word's **connotations** are its associated feelings and images. A *rut,* related to the word *route,* is a track worn in a dirt road. In lines 154–155, what is the effect of contrasting the duchess's rutted face with the images of diamonds and cherry blossoms?

---

28. **sharper:** a gambler who cheats.

"You will come down tomorrow?" she urged, she interrupted. "The Prime Minister—His Royal Highness . . ." She stopped. "And Diana," she added.

Oliver took his hand off the bell.

He looked past her, at the backs of the houses in Bond Street. But he saw, not the houses in Bond Street, but a dimpling river; and trout rising and salmon; and the Prime Minister; and himself too; in white waistcoats; and then, Diana. He looked down at the pearl in his hand. But how could he test it, in the light of the river, in the light of the eyes of Diana? But the eyes of the Duchess were on him. **G**

"Twenty thousand," she moaned. "My honor!"

The honor of the mother of Diana! He drew his checkbook towards him; he took out his pen.

"Twenty," he wrote. Then he stopped writing. The eyes of the old woman in the picture were on him—of the old woman, his mother.

"Oliver!" she warned him. "Have sense! Don't be a fool!"

"Oliver!" the Duchess entreated—it was "Oliver" now, not "Mr. Bacon." "You'll come for a long weekend?"

Alone in the woods with Diana! Riding alone in the woods with Diana!

"Thousand," he wrote, and signed it.

"Here you are," he said.

And there opened all the flounces of the parasol, all the plumes of the peacock, the radiance of the wave, the swords and spears of Agincourt,[29] as she rose from her chair. And the two old men and the two young men, Spencer and Marshall, Wicks and Hammond, flattened themselves behind the counter envying him as he led her through the shop to the door. And he waggled his yellow glove in their faces, and she held her honor—a check for twenty thousand pounds with his signature—quite firmly in her hands.

"Are they false or are they real?" asked Oliver, shutting his private door. There they were, ten pearls on the blotting paper on the table. He took them to the window. He held them under his lens to the light. . . . This, then, was the truffle he had routed out of the earth! Rotten at the center—rotten at the core!

"Forgive me, oh my mother!" he sighed, raising his hands as if he asked pardon of the old woman in the picture. And again he was a little boy in the alley where they sold dogs on Sunday.

"For," he murmured, laying the palms of his hands together, "it is to be a long weekend." ❧

G **PSYCHOLOGICAL FICTION**
Reread lines 166–171. What was Oliver about to do? What **internal conflict** causes him to hesitate?

---

29. **Agincourt** (ăj'ĭn-kôrt'): a French village where, in 1415, Henry V's English forces defeated a much larger French army in what is considered one of England's most glorious victories.

ESSAY E. M. Forster was, like Virginia Woolf, a member of the Bloomsbury group. He built his fame as a novelist and a writer of literary criticism. Shortly after Woolf died, Forster wrote a critical review of her work. In this excerpt he describes her process of writing.

from

Virginia Woolf

by E. M. Forster

She liked receiving sensations—sights, sounds, tastes—passing them through her mind, where they encountered theories and memories, and then bringing them out again, through a pen, on to a bit of paper. Now began the higher delights of authorship. For these pen-marks on paper were only the prelude to writing, little more than marks on a wall. They had to be combined, arranged, emphasized here, eliminated there, new relationships had to be generated, new pen-marks born, until out of the interactions, something, one thing, one, arose. This one thing, whether it was a novel or an essay or a short story or a biography or a private paper to be read to her friends, was, if it was successful, itself analogous to a sensation. Although it was so complex and intellectual, although it might be large and heavy with facts, it was akin to the very simple things which had started it off, to the sights, sounds, tastes. It could be best described as we describe them. For it was not about something. It was something. . . .

She liked writing with an intensity which few writers have attained, or even desired. Most of them write with half an eye on their royalties, half an eye on their critics, and a third half eye on improving the world, which leaves them with only half an eye for the task on which she concentrated her entire vision. She would not look elsewhere, and her circumstances combined with her temperament to focus her. Money she had not to consider, because she possessed a private income, and though financial independence is not always a safeguard against commercialism, it was in her case. Critics she never considered while she was writing, although she could be attentive to them and even humble afterwards. Improving the world she would not consider, on the ground that the world is man-made, and that she, a woman, had no responsibility for the mess. . . . Neither the desire for money nor the desire for reputation nor philanthropy could influence her. She had a singleness of purpose which will not recur in this country for many years, and writers who have liked writing as she liked it have not indeed been common in any age.

Comprehension

1. **Recall** What was Oliver's childhood like?

2. **Clarify** Who is the old woman in the picture?

3. **Clarify** Why does Oliver buy the pearls without having them tested?

4. **Recall** What does he discover about the pearls?

Text Analysis

5. **Examine Character** In what ways does Oliver's past life influence his present self? Identify specific experiences or memories that affect his behavior in the story.

6. **Analyze Poetic Language** Although Woolf wrote prose, she often chose words to create poetic effects. Reread the description of the Duchess in lines 112–121. Identify at least two examples of each of the following poetic devices from this description:

   - simile
   - alliteration
   - repetition
   - consonance

7. **Analyze Diction** Restate each of the following passages, using a more conventional sentence structure. What impressions or feelings are emphasized by Woolf's unique diction?

   - "He had a flat . . . in tapestry." (lines 1–3)
   - "And now—now . . . Earls." (lines 98–101)
   - "And from a slit . . . bird." (lines 133–135)
   - "And there opened . . . her chair." (lines 183–185)

8. **Draw Conclusions** Reread lines 124–129, which describe Oliver's relationship with the Duchess. Explain why the two characters need each other. What does their relationship suggest about the hypocrisy of class distinctions?

9. **Evaluate Psychological Fiction** In your opinion, does Woolf effectively capture the quality of a person's inner thoughts? What are some disadvantages of Woolf's experimental style? Support your answer with details from the story.

Text Criticism

10. **Social Context** Consider whether wealth and social status are as important now as they were in the Britain of Woolf's time. What observations from Woolf's story, if any, still seem relevant today? Explain your answer.

What does it mean to have **CLASS?**

Review the list of character traits you made earlier that identify a person as "classy." After reading this story, what new traits would you add? Which of these traits can be acquired and which are innate?

COMMON CORE

RL 1 Cite evidence to support inferences drawn from the text. **RL 3** Analyze the impact of the author's choices regarding how to develop and relate elements of a story. **RL 4** Determine the meaning of words and phrases as they are used in the text, including connotative meanings; analyze the impact of specific word choices on meaning and tone. **L 3a** Apply an understanding of syntax to the study of complex texts when reading.

Vocabulary in Context

▲ VOCABULARY PRACTICE

Test your knowledge of the vocabulary words by answering these questions.

1. To **dismantle** an engine, would you build it or take it apart?
2. Who usually receives **homage,** a powerful king or a lowly servant?
3. Is a **burnished** surface dull or shiny?
4. If Jonas behaves **obsequiously,** does he bow humbly or strut?
5. Who is more **lissome,** an athlete or someone with arthritis?
6. Would a celebration full of **pomp** tend to be casual or formal?

WORD LIST

burnished

dismantle

homage

lissome

obsequiously

pomp

ACADEMIC VOCABULARY IN WRITING

• approach • assume • environment • method • strategy

Does a person's **environment** determine his or her future? What **method** of upbringing is best for achieving high status? Using at least two of the Academic Vocabulary words, write a brief description of an encounter between people of high and low status.

VOCABULARY STRATEGY: FIGURATIVE LANGUAGE

Figurative language is not literal; it is used to create an image in a reader's mind. For example, the word *dismantled* literally means "took apart," with particular meaning (**nuance**) of "stripping something of its furnishings." When Woolf says Oliver "dismantled himself," she doesn't mean that he literally strips. Instead, he mentally removes his fine clothes—or what they stand for, his accomplishments—to reveal the story of his life. You can tell what Woolf means from **context,** the text surrounding the word. In the passage following "he dismantled himself often," Oliver fondly reminisces over his rise from a juvenile dog thief to the owner of an exclusive London jewel shop.

PRACTICE Explain how the figurative use of each boldfaced word or phrase differs from its literal meaning. Underline the context that points to the word's figurative meaning.

1. The wealthy residents stay on the west side of town; Holmes Avenue is a **strait** which few of them will cross.
2. An excellent shopper, she can enter a store and **sniff out a truffle** where no one else can find it.
3. As the angry crowd surged forward, **a wave** of contempt **broke over** the riot police.
4. Making the honor roll was another **plume** in her cap.
5. He used his wily charm to **snake** his way into her confidence.

COMMON CORE

L 5a Interpret figures of speech in context and analyze their role in the text. **L 6** Acquire and use accurately general academic words and phrases.

Interactive Vocabulary **THiNK** central

Go to **thinkcentral.com.**
KEYWORD: HML12-1150

Language

◆ **GRAMMAR AND STYLE: Craft Effective Sentences**

Review the **Grammar and Style** note on page 1145. In this story, Woolf imitates the flow of thoughts by using long sentences made up of several phrases and clauses. Instead of smooth transitions, she links seemingly unrelated phrases with commas and semicolons, as in this example:

> *But he saw, not the houses in Bond Street, but a dimpling river; and trout rising and salmon; and the Prime Minister; and himself too; in white waistcoats; and then, Diana.* (lines 167–169)

Notice how the layering of details in this sentence helps to evoke the random movements of Oliver's mind.

PRACTICE Using the following quotation as a model, write your own paragraph in the style of Woolf. Be sure your paragraph includes examples of Woolf's distinctive sentence structure.

> *And he dressed better and better; and had, first a hansom cab; then a car; and first he went up to the dress circle, then down into the stalls. And he had a villa at Richmond, overlooking the river, with trellises of red roses; and Mademoiselle used to pick one every morning and stick it in his buttonhole.*

COMMON CORE

L 2 Demonstrate command of the conventions of standard English punctuation when writing.
L 3 Apply knowledge of language to make effective choices for style. **W 3a–b, d–e** Introduce characters; use narrative techniques, such as description and reflection, to develop events and characters; use precise words and phrases and telling details to convey a vivid picture of the events, setting, and characters; provide a conclusion that reflects on what is experienced over the course of the narrative.

READING-WRITING CONNECTION

Expand your understanding of Virginia Woolf's story by responding to this prompt. Then use the **revising tips** to improve your descriptive narrative.

WRITING PROMPT	REVISING TIPS
WRITE A NARRATIVE What might have happened when Oliver visited the Duchess and her daughter Diana in the country? Use what you know about the personalities of Oliver and the Duchess to write a **three-to-five-paragraph descriptive narrative.** Conclude the narrative with a reflection on Oliver's experience.	• Add precise descriptive details about the setting. • Make sure your narrative includes clues to Oliver's personality. • Without using dialogue, try to show Oliver's emotional response to being with Diana.

Interactive Revision

Go to thinkcentral.com.
KEYWORD: HML12-1151

The Rocking-Horse Winner

Short Story by D. H. Lawrence

COMMON CORE

RL 1 Cite evidence to support inferences drawn from the text. **RL 2** Determine two or more themes or central ideas of a text and analyze their development over the course of the text, including how they interact and build on one anther to produce a complex account. **SL 1c–d** Pose and respond to questions that probe reasoning and evidence; ensure a hearing for a full range of positions on a topic or issue; clarify, verify, or challenge ideas and conclusions; synthesize comments, claims, and evidence made on all sides of an issue.

DID YOU KNOW?

D. H. Lawrence . . .

- was also an accomplished poet, painter, and playwright.
- lived in poverty for much of his life, as his censored books were deemed "unsellable."
- was buried first in France and then in New Mexico.

Meet the Author

D. H. Lawrence 1885–1930

Today, D. H. Lawrence is widely regarded as an imaginative genius. In his own time, however, his explicit depictions of male-female relationships and exploration of the dark sides of the human psyche garnered outrage and censorship. One of the most controversial writers of the early 20th century, Lawrence, whose racier works were banned for much of his lifetime, now occupies a prominent place in literary history.

A Miner's Son Lawrence spent his formative years in a Nottinghamshire coal-mining village. Growing up, he endured poverty, poor health, and constant strife between his mother—a former schoolteacher—and his father—an uneducated miner who drank. "Nothing," he later remarked, "depresses me more than to come home to the place where I was born, and where I lived my first 20 years." Despite this aversion, Lawrence returned to his hometown often in his fiction.

Birth of a Writer As a child, Lawrence formed a deep emotional bond with his mother. Wanting her son to be educated and refined, she encouraged him in school. Compelled by financial hardship to seek employment at age 16, Lawrence took a job in a surgical goods factory. In 1908, he earned a teaching certificate, but he abandoned his teaching career four years later when he became seriously ill in the wake of his mother's death. After his recovery, Lawrence was determined to try and make his living as a writer.

Groundbreaker According to his own account, Lawrence began writing on a "slightly self-conscious Sunday afternoon, when I was 19." By the time he was 26, he had published his first book, *The White Peacock* (1911). He then embarked on a series of novels reflecting his belief that industrialized society was damaging to the human psyche because it emphasized reason over emotion and intuition. These works not only fought against restrictive social and moral conventions but also broke many literary conventions of the day.

The "Here and Now" of Life Despite the censorship of his work, chronic poverty, and advancing tuberculosis, Lawrence continued to write prolifically until his death in 1930, completing masterpieces such as *Women in Love* (1920) and *Lady Chatterley's Lover* (1928). He and his wife, Frieda, lived all over the world. Later in his life, Lawrence wrote that "the magnificent here and now of life in the flesh is ours, and ours alone, and ours only for a time. We ought to dance with rapture that we should be alive."

Author Online

Go to thinkcentral.com. KEYWORD: HML12-1152

THINK central

TEXT ANALYSIS: THEME

The **theme** of a story—an underlying message about life or human nature that the writer wants readers to understand—is often what makes that story linger in your memory. In fiction, writers almost never directly state their themes. Instead, they develop them using literary elements. As you read, ask yourself the following questions. What theme or themes do your answers suggest?

- What ideas does the **title** highlight?
- What are the **characters'** dominant **traits?** What are their **motivations** for acting as they do?
- What is the main **conflict,** and how is it resolved?
- In what ways is the **setting** important to the story's action?

READING SKILL: DRAW CONCLUSIONS

In this story, luck plays a significant role in the characters' lives, though Lawrence does not always explicitly state that role. To **draw conclusions** about the role of luck, you must combine information stated in the text; your **inferences,** or logical guesses; and your own prior knowledge. As you read, use a chart to note information and your inferences about the three main characters. Consider what they indicate about each character's experiences with and conceptions of luck.

Character	Information	Inferences
Paul		
Paul's mother		
Oscar		

▲ VOCABULARY IN CONTEXT

Knowing the following boldfaced words will help you explore Lawrence's story of luck—and the lack thereof. Use context clues to determine the meaning of each word.

1. Sadly, the inheritance she expected did not **materialize.**
2. A frightened horse will often **career** wildly down the road.
3. He seated himself in the saddle and rode the **steed.**
4. Must I **reiterate** what I said before?
5. His resemblance to his sister is positively **uncanny.**

 Complete the activities in your **Reader/Writer Notebook**.

Can MONEY buy happiness?

It's easy to imagine that unlimited wealth would lead to almost perfect happiness. With all financial concerns swept away, what would be left to worry about? The story you're about to read explores the connection between money and happiness.

DEBATE With a small group, discuss whether money is the key to contentment. Are there other factors or achievements that are more important than wealth, or is it impossible to concentrate on anything else when money is a problem? Is it possible to be happy without money? After you have come to a consensus, square off against another group to debate whether money can buy happiness.

The Rocking-Horse Winner

D. H. Lawrence

> **BACKGROUND** Two of the five great annual horseraces in England are the St. Leger Stakes and the Derby. Other notable English races mentioned in this story are the Grand National, the Ascot Gold Cup, and the Lincolnshire. Large sums of money are bet on horseraces. The amount a bettor can win depends on the odds. The odds on each horse are expressed as a ratio—3 to 1, for example—and are determined by what proportion of the total amount bet on the race is bet on that horse. The more money bet on a horse, the lower the odds and the lower the payoff.

There was a woman who was beautiful, who started with all the advantages, yet she had no luck. She married for love, and the love turned to dust. She had bonny[1] children, yet she felt they had been thrust upon her, and she could not love them. They looked at her coldly, as if they were finding fault with her. And hurriedly she felt she must cover up some fault in herself. Yet what it was that she must cover up she never knew. Nevertheless, when her children were present, she always felt the center of her heart go hard. This troubled her, and in her manner she was all the more gentle and anxious for her children, as if she loved them very much. Only she herself knew that at the center of her heart was a hard little place

10 that could not feel love, no, not for anybody. Everybody else said of her: "She is such a good mother. She adores her children." Only she herself, and her children themselves, knew it was not so. They read it in each other's eyes.

There were a boy and two little girls. They lived in a pleasant house, with a garden, and they had discreet servants, and felt themselves superior to anyone in the neighborhood.

Although they lived in style, they felt always an anxiety in the house. There was never enough money. The mother had a small income, and the father had a small income, but not nearly enough for the social position which they had to keep up. The father went into town to some office. But though he had good

20 prospects, these prospects never **materialized**. There was always the grinding sense of the shortage of money, though the style was always kept up. **A**

At last the mother said: "I will see if *I* can't make something." But she did not know where to begin. She racked her brains, and tried this thing and the other,

---

1. **bonny:** pretty.

Analyze Visuals ▶
How would you describe the domestic scene depicted by this painting?

materialize (mə-tîr′ē-ə-līz) *v.* to take form; to appear; to become fact

A DRAW CONCLUSIONS
What information about the mother is explicitly stated in lines 1–21? What additional traits can you **infer** from these lines?

Mother and Child (1903), William Rothenstein. Oil on canvas, 969 cm × 765 cm. Purchased 1988. © Tate Gallery, London/Art Resource, New York. © Rothenstein Estate/Bridgeman Art Library, New York.

but could not find anything successful. The failure made deep lines come into her face. Her children were growing up, they would have to go to school. There must be more money, there must be more money. The father, who was always very handsome and expensive in his tastes, seemed as if he never *would* be able to do anything worth doing. And the mother, who had a great belief in herself, did not succeed any better, and her tastes were just as expensive.

30   And so the house came to be haunted by the unspoken phrase: *There must be more money! There must be more money!* The children could hear it all the time, though nobody said it aloud. They heard it at Christmas, when the expensive and splendid toys filled the nursery. Behind the shining modern rocking-horse, behind the smart doll's house, a voice would start whispering: "There *must* be more money! There *must* be more money!" And the children would stop playing, to listen for a moment. They would look into each other's eyes, to see if they had all heard. And each one saw in the eyes of the other two that they too had heard. "There *must* be more money! There *must* be more money!" **B**

    It came whispering from the springs of the still-swaying rocking-horse, and even
40 the horse, bending his wooden, champing head, heard it. The big doll, sitting so pink and smirking in her new pram,[2] could hear it quite plainly, and seemed to be smirking all the more self-consciously because of it. The foolish puppy, too, that took the place of the teddy bear, he was looking so extraordinarily foolish for no other reason but that he heard the secret whisper all over the house: "There *must* be more money!"

    Yet nobody ever said it aloud. The whisper was everywhere, and therefore no one spoke it. Just as no one ever says: "We are breathing!" in spite of the fact that breath is coming and going all the time. **C**

    "Mother," said the boy Paul one day, "why don't we keep a car of our own?
50 Why do we always use uncle's, or else a taxi?"

    "Because we're the poor members of the family," said the mother.

    "But why *are* we, mother?"

    "Well—I suppose," she said slowly and bitterly, "it's because your father has no luck."

    The boy was silent for some time.

    "Is luck money, mother?" he asked, rather timidly.

    "No, Paul. Not quite. It's what causes you to have money."

    "Oh!" said Paul vaguely. "I thought when Uncle Oscar said *filthy lucker*, it meant money."

60   "*Filthy lucre*[3] does mean money," said the mother. "But it's lucre, not luck."

    "Oh!" said the boy. "Then what *is* luck, mother?"

    "It's what causes you to have money. If you're lucky you have money. That's why it's better to be born lucky than rich. If you're rich, you may lose your money. But if you're lucky, you will always get more money."

2. **pram:** baby carriage (a shortened form of *perambulator*).

3. *filthy lucre* (lōō'kər): money, especially when obtained through fraud or greed. The term comes from the King James Bible (Titus 1:11) and has passed into familiar usage.

GRAMMAR AND STYLE
Reread lines 30–38. Lawrence creates suspense and foreshadows future events through his use of **effective sentence types** and **repetition** of key phrases. Note the repeated **exclamatory sentence** in these lines.

C THEME
Note details about the story's **setting** in lines 30–48. What ideas are suggested by the house's "whispers"?

"Oh! Will you? And is father not lucky?"

"Very unlucky, I should say," she said bitterly.

The boy watched her with unsure eyes.

"Why?" he asked.

"I don't know. Nobody ever knows why one person is lucky and another unlucky."

70 "Don't they? Nobody at all? Does *nobody* know?"

"Perhaps God. But He never tells."

"He ought to, then. And aren't you lucky either, mother?"

"I can't be, if I married an unlucky husband."

"But by yourself, aren't you?"

"I used to think I was, before I married. Now I think I am very unlucky indeed."

"Why?"

"Well—never mind! Perhaps I'm not really," she said.

The child looked at her to see if she meant it. But he saw, by the lines of her mouth, that she was only trying to hide something from him. **D**

80 "Well, anyhow," he said stoutly,[4] "I'm a lucky person."

"Why?" said his mother, with a sudden laugh.

He stared at her. He didn't even know why he had said it.

"God told me," he asserted, brazening it out.

"I hope He did, dear!" she said, again with a laugh, but rather bitter.

"He did, mother!"

"Excellent!" said the mother, using one of her husband's exclamations.

The boy saw she did not believe him; or rather, that she paid no attention to his assertion. This angered him somewhere, and made him want to compel her attention.

90 He went off by himself, vaguely, in a childish way, seeking for the clue to "luck." Absorbed, taking no heed of other people, he went about with a sort of stealth, seeking inwardly for luck. He wanted luck, he wanted it, he wanted it. When the two girls were playing dolls in the nursery, he would sit on his big rocking-horse, charging madly into space, with a frenzy that made the little girls peer at him uneasily. Wildly the horse **careered,** the waving dark hair of the boy tossed, his eyes had a strange glare in them. The little girls dared not speak to him.

When he had ridden to the end of his mad little journey, he climbed down and stood in front of his rocking-horse, staring fixedly into its lowered face. Its red mouth was slightly open, its big eye was wide and glassy-bright.

100 "Now!" he would silently command the snorting **steed.** "Now, take me to where there is luck! Now take me!"

And he would slash the horse on the neck with the little whip he had asked Uncle Oscar for. He *knew* the horse could take him to where there was luck, if only he forced it. So he would mount again and start on his furious ride, hoping at last to get there. He knew he could get there. **E**

"You'll break your horse, Paul!" said the nurse.

"He's always riding like that! I wish he'd leave off!" said his elder sister Joan.

---

4. **stoutly:** bravely; firmly.

D DRAW CONCLUSIONS Summarize Paul's mother's definition of *luck.* How does she characterize it, and why does she believe she's unlucky?

career (kə-rîr′) *v.* to move at full speed; to rush wildly

steed (stēd) *n.* a horse, especially a high-spirited riding horse

E THEME Why is Paul so furiously determined to find luck? Consider what message his **motivation** points toward.

But he only glared down on them in silence. Nurse gave him up. She could make nothing of him. Anyhow, he was growing beyond her.

One day his mother and his Uncle Oscar came in when he was on one of his furious rides. He did not speak to them.

"Hallo, you young jockey! Riding a winner?" said his uncle.

"Aren't you growing too big for a rocking-horse? You're not a very little boy any longer, you know," said his mother.

But Paul only gave a blue glare from his big, rather close-set eyes. He would speak to nobody when he was in full tilt.[5] His mother watched him with an anxious expression on her face.

At last he suddenly stopped forcing his horse into the mechanical gallop and slid down.

"Well, I got there!" he announced fiercely, his blue eyes still flaring, and his sturdy long legs straddling apart.

"Where did you get to?" asked his mother.

"Where I wanted to go," he flared back at her.

"That's right, son!" said Uncle Oscar. "Don't you stop till you get there. What's the horse's name?"

"He doesn't have a name," said the boy.

"Gets on without all right?" asked the uncle.

"Well, he has different names. He was called Sansovino last week."

"Sansovino, eh? Won the Ascot.[6] How did you know his name?"

"He always talks about horse races with Bassett," said Joan.

The uncle was delighted to find that his small nephew was posted with all the racing news. Bassett, the young gardener, who had been wounded in the left foot in the war and had got his present job through Oscar Cresswell, whose batman[7] he had been, was a perfect blade of the "turf."[8] He lived in the racing events, and the small boy lived with him. **F**

Oscar Cresswell got it all from Bassett.

"Master Paul comes and asks me, so I can't do more than tell him, sir," said Bassett, his face terribly serious, as if he were speaking of religious matters.

"And does he ever put anything on a horse he fancies?"

"Well—I don't want to give him away—he's a young sport,[9] a fine sport, sir. Would you mind asking him himself? He sort of takes a pleasure in it, and perhaps he'd feel I was giving him away, sir, if you don't mind."

Bassett was serious as a church.

The uncle went back to his nephew and took him off for a ride in the car.

"Say, Paul, old man, do you ever put anything on a horse?" the uncle asked.

The boy watched the handsome man closely.

F DRAW CONCLUSIONS
How does Oscar's attitude in lines 110–135 contrast with Paul's? What does this suggest about how important the races—and luck—are to each character?

---

5. **in full tilt:** moving at full speed.

6. **Won the Ascot:** won at the famous horse races held on Ascot Heath, a horsetrack southwest of London.

7. **batman:** in Britain, a soldier who acts as an officer's servant.

8. **blade of the "turf":** someone very knowledgeable about horseracing.

9. **sport:** good fellow.

Portrait of Caspar Goodrich (1887), John Singer Sargent. Oil on canvas. © Mr. and Mrs. C. Michael Kojaian. Image courtesy of Brooklyn Museum of Art.

"Why, do you think I oughtn't to?" he parried.

"Not a bit of it! I thought perhaps you might give me a tip for the Lincoln."

The car sped on into the country, going down to Uncle Oscar's place in
150 Hampshire.

"Honor bright?"[10] said the nephew.

"Honor bright, son!" said the uncle.

"Well, then, Daffodil."

"Daffodil! I doubt it, sonny. What about Mirza?"

"I only know the winner," said the boy. "That's Daffodil."

"Daffodil, eh?"

There was a pause. Daffodil was an obscure horse comparatively.

"Uncle!"

"Yes, son?"

160 "You won't let it go any further, will you? I promised Bassett."

"Bassett be damned, old man! What's he got to do with it?"

"We're partners. We've been partners from the first. Uncle, he lent me my first five shillings,[11] which I lost. I promised him, honor bright, it was only between me and him; only you gave me that ten-shilling note I started winning with, so I thought you were lucky. You won't let it go any further, will you?"

10. **Honor bright:** an expression meaning "on your (or my) honor."

11. **shillings:** former British coins worth 1/20 of a pound.

COMMON CORE L 4

Language Coach

Multiple Meanings The word *parried* literally means "turned aside a blow or thrust of a sword." What do you think it means in line 147?

The boy gazed at his uncle from those big, hot, blue eyes, set rather close together. The uncle stirred and laughed uneasily.

"Right you are, son! I'll keep your tip private. Daffodil, eh? How much are you putting on him?"

"All except twenty pounds,"[12] said the boy. "I keep that in reserve."

The uncle thought it a good joke.

"You keep twenty pounds in reserve, do you, you young romancer? What are you betting, then?"

"I'm betting three hundred," said the boy gravely. "But it's between you and me, Uncle Oscar! Honor bright?"

The uncle burst into a roar of laughter.

"It's between you and me all right, you young Nat Gould,"[13] he said, laughing. "But where's your three hundred?"

"Bassett keeps it for me. We're partners."

"You are, are you! And what is Bassett putting on Daffodil?"

"He won't go quite as high as I do, I expect. Perhaps he'll go a hundred and fifty."

"What, pennies?" laughed the uncle.

"Pounds," said the child, with a surprised look at his uncle. "Bassett keeps a bigger reserve than I do."

---

12. **twenty pounds:** the equivalent of about a thousand dollars in today's money. (In the mid-1920s, a pound was worth about five dollars, and the purchasing power of a dollar was about ten times what it is now.)

13. **Nat Gould:** a well-known British horseracing authority and writer.

Between wonder and amusement Uncle Oscar was silent. He pursued the matter no further, but he determined to take his nephew with him to the Lincoln races.

"Now, son," he said, "I'm putting twenty on Mirza, and I'll put five on for you on any horse you fancy. What's your pick?"

"Daffodil, uncle."

190   "No, not the fiver on Daffodil!"

"I should if it was my own fiver," said the child.

"Good! Good! Right you are! A fiver for me and a fiver for you on Daffodil."

The child had never been to a race-meeting before, and his eyes were blue fire. He pursed his mouth tight and watched. A Frenchman just in front had put his money on Lancelot. Wild with excitement, he flayed his arms up and down, yelling *"Lancelot! Lancelot!"* in his French accent.

Daffodil came in first, Lancelot second, Mirza third. The child, flushed and with eyes blazing, was curiously serene. His uncle brought him four five-pound notes, four to one.

200   "What am I to do with these?" he cried, waving them before the boy's eyes.

"I suppose we'll talk to Bassett," said the boy. "I expect I have fifteen hundred now; and twenty in reserve; and this twenty."

His uncle studied him for some moments.

"Look here, son!" he said. "You're not serious about Bassett and that fifteen hundred, are you?"

The Start, Alfred James Munnings. © Christie's Images/Corbis.

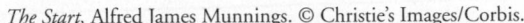

"Yes, I am. But it's between you and me, uncle. Honor bright?"

"Honor bright all right, son! But I must talk to Bassett."

"If you'd like to be a partner, uncle, with Bassett and me, we could all be partners. Only, you'd have to promise, honor bright, uncle, not to let it go beyond us three. Bassett and I are lucky, and you must be lucky, because it was your ten shillings I started winning with. . . ."

Uncle Oscar took both Bassett and Paul into Richmond Park for an afternoon, and there they talked.

"It's like this, you see, sir," Bassett said. "Master Paul would get me talking about racing events, spinning yarns, you know, sir. And he was always keen on knowing if I'd made or if I'd lost. It's about a year since, now, that I put five shillings on Blush of Dawn for him: and we lost. Then the luck turned, with that ten shillings he had from you: that we put on Singhalese. And since that time, it's been pretty steady, all things considering. What do you say, Master Paul?"

"We're all right when we're sure," said Paul. "It's when we're not quite sure that we go down."

"Oh, but we're careful then," said Bassett.

"But when are you *sure?*" smiled Uncle Oscar.

"It's Master Paul, sir," said Bassett in a secret, religious voice. "It's as if he had it from heaven. Like Daffodil, now, for the Lincoln. That was as sure as eggs."[14]

"Did you put anything on Daffodil?" asked Oscar Cresswell.

"Yes, sir. I made my bit."

"And my nephew?"

Bassett was obstinately silent, looking at Paul.

"I made twelve hundred, didn't I, Bassett? I told uncle I was putting three hundred on Daffodil."

"That's right," said Bassett, nodding.

"But where's the money?" asked the uncle.

"I keep it safe locked up, sir. Master Paul he can have it any minute he likes to ask for it."

"What, fifteen hundred pounds?"

"And twenty! And *forty,* that is, with the twenty he made on the course."

"It's amazing!" said the uncle.

"If Master Paul offers you to be partners, sir, I would, if I were you: if you'll excuse me," said Bassett.

Oscar Cresswell thought about it.

"I'll see the money," he said.

They drove home again, and, sure enough, Bassett came round to the garden-house with fifteen hundred pounds in notes. The twenty pounds reserve was left with Joe Glee, in the Turf Commission deposit.[15]

"You see, it's all right, uncle, when I'm *sure!* Then we go strong, for all we're worth. Don't we, Bassett?"

---

14. **as sure as eggs:** absolutely certain; shortened from the expression "as sure as eggs is eggs."

15. **Turf Commission deposit:** a bank in which bettors keep money for future bets.

"We do that, Master Paul."

"And when are you sure?" said the uncle, laughing.

250 "Oh, well, sometimes I'm *absolutely* sure, like about Daffodil," said the boy; "and sometimes I have an idea; and sometimes I haven't even an idea, have I, Bassett? Then we're careful, because we mostly go down."

"You do, do you! And when you're sure, like about Daffodil, what makes you sure, sonny?"

"Oh, well, I don't know," said the boy uneasily. "I'm sure, you know, uncle; that's all."

"It's as if he had it from heaven, sir," Bassett **reiterated.**

"I should say so!" said the uncle.

But he became a partner. And when the Leger was coming on Paul was "sure"
260 about Lively Spark, which was a quite inconsiderable horse. The boy insisted on putting a thousand on the horse, Bassett went for five hundred, and Oscar Cresswell two hundred. Lively Spark came in first, and the betting had been ten to one against him. Paul had made ten thousand.

"You see," he said, "I was absolutely sure of him."

Even Oscar Cresswell had cleared two thousand.

"Look here, son," he said, "this sort of thing makes me nervous."

"It needn't, uncle! Perhaps I shan't be sure again for a long time."

"But what are you going to do with your money?" asked the uncle.

"Of course," said the boy, "I started it for mother. She said she had no luck,
270 because father is unlucky, so I thought if I was lucky, it might stop whispering."

"What might stop whispering?"

"Our house. I *hate* our house for whispering."

"What does it whisper?"

"Why—why"—the boy fidgeted—"why, I don't know. But it's always short of money, you know, uncle."

"I know it, son, I know it."

"You know people send mother writs,[16] don't you, uncle?"

"I'm afraid I do," said the uncle.

"And then the house whispers, like people laughing at you behind your back.
280 It's awful, that is! I thought if I was lucky—"

"You might stop it," added the uncle. **G**

The boy watched him with big blue eyes, that had an **uncanny** cold fire in them, and he said never a word.

"Well, then!" said the uncle. "What are we doing?"

"I shouldn't like mother to know I was lucky," said the boy.

"Why not, son?"

"She'd stop me."

"I don't think she would."

"Oh!"—and the boy writhed in an odd way—"I *don't* want her to know, uncle."

290 "All right, son! We'll manage it without her knowing."

---

16. **writs:** legal documents, in this case demanding payment of debts.

reiterate (rē-ĭt′ə-rāt′)
v. to repeat

G DRAW CONCLUSIONS
Why do you think Oscar not only allows Paul to continue gambling but also becomes a partner in the venture, even though it makes him "nervous"? What does this decision reveal about his character?

uncanny (ŭn-kăn′ē) *adj.* strange or mysterious in a way that causes unease; eerie

They managed it very easily. Paul, at the other's suggestion, handed over five thousand pounds to his uncle, who deposited it with the family lawyer, who was then to inform Paul's mother that a relative had put five thousand pounds into his hands, which sum was to be paid out a thousand pounds at a time, on the mother's birthday, for the next five years.

"So she'll have a birthday present of a thousand pounds for five successive years," said Uncle Oscar. "I hope it won't make it all the harder for her later."

Paul's mother had her birthday in November. The house had been "whispering" worse than ever lately, and, even in spite of his luck, Paul could not bear up
300 against it. He was very anxious to see the effect of the birthday letter, telling his mother about the thousand pounds.

When there were no visitors, Paul now took his meals with his parents, as he was beyond the nursery control. His mother went into town nearly every day. She had discovered that she had an odd knack of sketching furs and dress materials, so she worked secretly in the studio of a friend who was the chief "artist" for the leading drapers.[17] She drew the figures of ladies in furs and ladies in silk and sequins for the newspaper advertisements. This young woman artist earned several thousand pounds a year, but Paul's mother only made several hundreds, and she was again dissatisfied. She so wanted to be first in something, and she did not
310 succeed, even in making sketches for drapery advertisements.

She was down to breakfast on the morning of her birthday. Paul watched her face as she read her letters. He knew the lawyer's letter. As his mother read it, her face hardened and became more expressionless. Then a cold, determined look came on her mouth. She hid the letter under the pile of others, and said not a word about it.

"Didn't you have anything nice in the post for your birthday, mother?" said Paul.

"Quite moderately nice," she said, her voice cold and absent.

She went away to town without saying more.

But in the afternoon Uncle Oscar appeared. He said Paul's mother had had
320 a long interview with the lawyer, asking if the whole five thousand could not be advanced at once, as she was in debt.

"What do you think, uncle?" said the boy.

"I leave it to you, son."

"Oh, let her have it, then! We can get some more with the other," said the boy.

"A bird in the hand is worth two in the bush, laddie!" said Uncle Oscar.

"But I'm sure to *know* for the Grand National; or the Lincolnshire; or else the Derby.[18] I'm sure to know for *one* of them," said Paul.

So Uncle Oscar signed the agreement, and Paul's mother touched[19] the whole five thousand. Then something very curious happened. The voices in the house
330 suddenly went mad, like a chorus of frogs on a spring evening. There were certain new furnishings, and Paul had a tutor. He was *really* going to Eton, his

---

17. **drapers:** British term for a dealer in cloth and dry goods.

18. **Grand National...Derby:** three major English horse races held annually. The Derby is England's best-known flat-track race.

19. **touched:** took.

father's school, in the following autumn. There were flowers in the winter, and a blossoming of the luxury Paul's mother had been used to. And yet the voices in the house, behind the sprays of mimosa and almond-blossom, and from under the piles of iridescent cushions, simply trilled and screamed in a sort of ecstasy: "There *must* be more money! Oh-h-h; there *must* be more money. Oh, now, now-w-w! Now-w-w—there *must* be more money!—more than ever! More than ever!" **H**

It frightened Paul terribly. He studied away at his Latin and Greek with his tutor. But his intense hours were spent with Bassett. The Grand National had 340 gone by: he had not "known," and had lost a hundred pounds. Summer was at hand. He was in agony for the Lincoln. But even for the Lincoln he didn't "know," and he lost fifty pounds. He became wild-eyed and strange, as if something were going to explode in him.

"Let it alone, son! Don't you bother about it!" urged Uncle Oscar. But it was as if the boy couldn't really hear what his uncle was saying.

"I've got to know for the Derby! I've got to know for the Derby!" the child reiterated, his big blue eyes blazing with a sort of madness.

His mother noticed how overwrought he was.

"You'd better go to the seaside. Wouldn't you like to go now to the seaside, 350 instead of waiting? I think you'd better," she said, looking down at him anxiously, her heart curiously heavy because of him.

But the child lifted his uncanny blue eyes.

"I couldn't possibly go before the Derby, mother!" he said. "I couldn't possibly!"

"Why not?" she said, her voice becoming heavy when she was opposed. "Why not? You can still go from the seaside to see the Derby with your Uncle Oscar, if that's what you wish. No need for you to wait here. Besides, I think you care too much about these races. It's a bad sign. My family has been a gambling family, and you won't know till you grow up how much damage it has done. But it has done damage. I shall have to send Bassett away, and ask Uncle Oscar not to talk 360 racing to you, unless you promise to be reasonable about it: go away to the seaside and forget it. You're all nerves!"

"I'll do what you like, mother, so long as you don't send me away till after the Derby," the boy said.

"Send you away from where? Just from this house?"

"Yes," he said, gazing at her.

"Why, you curious child, what makes you care about this house so much, suddenly? I never knew you loved it."

He gazed at her without speaking. He had a secret within a secret, something he had not divulged, even to Bassett or to his Uncle Oscar.

370 But his mother, after standing undecided and a little bit sullen for some moments, said:

"Very well, then! Don't go to the seaside till after the Derby, if you don't wish it. But promise me you won't let your nerves go to pieces. Promise you won't think so much about horse-racing and *events,* as you call them!"

H THEME
Why do you think the voices get louder after Paul's mother receives the 5,000 pounds? What point might Lawrence be making?

"Oh no," said the boy casually. "I won't think much about them, mother. You needn't worry. I wouldn't worry, mother, if I were you."

"If you were me and I were you," said his mother, "I wonder what we *should* do!"

"But you know you needn't worry, mother, don't you?" the boy repeated.

"I should be awfully glad to know it," she said wearily.

380 "Oh, well, you *can,* you know. I mean, you *ought* to know you needn't worry," he insisted.

"Ought I? Then I'll see about it," she said.

Paul's secret of secrets was his wooden horse, that which had no name. Since he was emancipated from a nurse and a nursery-governess, he had had his rocking-horse removed to his own bedroom at the top of the house.

"Surely you're too big for a rocking-horse!" his mother had remonstrated.

"Well, you see, mother, till I can have a *real* horse, I like to have *some* sort of animal about," had been his quaint answer.

"Do you feel he keeps you company?" she laughed.

390 "Oh yes! He's very good, he always keeps me company, when I'm there," said Paul.

So the horse, rather shabby, stood in an arrested prance in the boy's bedroom.

The Derby was drawing near, and the boy grew more and more tense. He hardly heard what was spoken to him, he was very frail, and his eyes were really uncanny. His mother had sudden strange seizures of uneasiness about him. Sometimes, for half an hour, she would feel a sudden anxiety about him that was almost anguish. She wanted to rush to him at once, and know he was safe.

Two nights before the Derby, she was at a big party in town, when one of her rushes of anxiety about her boy, her first-born, gripped her heart till she could 400 hardly speak. She fought with the feeling, might and main,[20] for she believed in common sense. But it was too strong. She had to leave the dance and go downstairs to telephone to the country. The children's nursery-governess was terribly surprised and startled at being rung up in the night.

"Are the children all right, Miss Wilmot?"

"Oh yes, they are quite all right."

"Master Paul? Is he all right?"

"He went to bed as right as a trivet.[21] Shall I run up and look at him?"

"No," said Paul's mother reluctantly. "No! Don't trouble. It's all right. Don't sit up. We shall be home fairly soon." She did not want her son's privacy intruded upon.

410 "Very good," said the governess.

It was about one o'clock when Paul's mother and father drove up to their house. All was still. Paul's mother went to her room and slipped off her white fur cloak. She had told her maid not to wait up for her. She heard her husband downstairs, mixing a whisky and soda.

And then, because of the strange anxiety at her heart, she stole upstairs to her son's room. Noiselessly she went along the upper corridor. Was there a faint noise? What was it?

---

20. **might and main:** with all her strength.

21. **as right as a trivet:** in fine condition.

Portrait of a Woman (1935), Gerald Leslie Brockhurst. Oil on canvas, 51 cm × 41 cm. © Southampton City Art Gallery, Hampshire, United Kingdom/Bridgeman Art Library.

◀ **Analyze Visuals**
In what respect does this portrait reflect the mother's emotional state at this point in the story?

She stood, with arrested muscles, outside his door, listening. There was a strange, heavy, and yet not loud noise. Her heart stood still. It was a soundless
420 noise, yet rushing and powerful. Something huge, in violent, hushed motion. What was it? What in God's name was it? She ought to know. She felt that she knew the noise. She knew what it was.

Yet she could not place it. She couldn't say what it was. And on and on it went, like a madness.

Softly, frozen with anxiety and fear, she turned the door handle.

The room was dark. Yet in the space near the window, she heard and saw something plunging to and fro. She gazed in fear and amazement.

Then suddenly she switched on the light, and saw her son, in his green pajamas, madly surging on the rocking-horse. The blaze of light suddenly lit
430 him up, as he urged the wooden horse, and lit her up, as she stood, blonde, in her dress of pale green and crystal, in the doorway.

"Paul!" she cried. "Whatever are you doing?"

"It's Malabar!" he screamed in a powerful, strange voice. "It's Malabar!"

His eyes blazed at her for one strange and senseless second, as he ceased urging his wooden horse. Then he fell with a crash to the ground, and she, all her tormented motherhood flooding upon her, rushed to gather him up.

But he was unconscious, and unconscious he remained, with some brain-fever. He talked and tossed, and his mother sat stonily by his side.

"Malabar! It's Malabar! Bassett, Bassett, I *know*! It's Malabar!"

440   So the child cried, trying to get up and urge the rocking-horse that gave him his inspiration.

"What does he mean by Malabar?" asked the heart-frozen mother.

"I don't know," said the father stonily.

"What does he mean by Malabar?" she asked her brother Oscar.

"It's one of the horses running for the Derby," was the answer.

And, in spite of himself, Oscar Cresswell spoke to Bassett, and himself put a thousand on Malabar: at fourteen to one.

The third day of the illness was critical: they were waiting for a change. The boy, with his rather long, curly hair, was tossing ceaselessly on the pillow. He

450   neither slept nor regained consciousness, and his eyes were like blue stones. His mother sat, feeling her heart had gone, turned actually into a stone.

In the evening, Oscar Cresswell did not come, but Bassett sent a message, saying could he come up for one moment, just one moment? Paul's mother was very angry at the intrusion, but on second thoughts she agreed. The boy was the same. Perhaps Bassett might bring him to consciousness.

The gardener, a shortish fellow with a little brown mustache and sharp little brown eyes, tiptoed into the room, touched his imaginary cap to Paul's mother, and stole to the bedside, staring with glittering, smallish eyes at the tossing, dying child.

460   "Master Paul!" he whispered. "Master Paul! Malabar came in first all right, a clean win. I did as you told me. You've made over seventy thousand pounds, you have; you've got over eighty thousand.²² Malabar came in all right, Master Paul."

"Malabar! Malabar! Did I say Malabar, mother? Did I say Malabar? Do you think I'm lucky, mother? I knew Malabar, didn't I? Over eighty thousand pounds! I call that lucky, don't you, mother? Over eighty thousand pounds! I knew, didn't I know I knew? Malabar came in all right. If I ride my horse till I'm sure, then I tell you, Bassett, you can go as high as you like. Did you go for all you were worth, Bassett?"

"I went a thousand on it, Master Paul."

"I never told you, mother, that if I can ride my horse, and *get there,* then I'm

470   absolutely sure—oh, absolutely! Mother, did I ever tell you? I *am* lucky!"

"No, you never did," said his mother. ▮

But the boy died in the night.

And even as he lay dead, his mother heard her brother's voice saying to her: "My God, Hester, you're eighty-odd thousand to the good, and a poor devil of a son to the bad. But, poor devil, poor devil, he's best gone out of a life where he rides his rocking-horse to find a winner." ☙

COMMON CORE L 4c, L 5b

Language Coach

Denotations/ Connotations The feelings and images associated with a word are its **connotations**. Several words meaning "unwanted entrance" have different levels of negativity: *infringement, interruption, invasion,* and *intrusion* (line 454). Use a dictionary to place these on a scale of 1–4 (1 being least negative).

▮ **DRAW CONCLUSIONS**
Recall that Paul did tell his mother that he was lucky at the beginning of the story (lines 80–89). Why do you think she answers as she does in line 471?

---

22. **eighty thousand:** the equivalent of about $4 million in today's dollars.

Comprehension

1. **Recall** What "secret whisper" does Paul keep hearing in his house?

2. **Clarify** What happens when Paul rides his rocking horse?

3. **Summarize** Describe Paul's final ride and the story's conclusion.

Text Analysis

4. **Analyze Character Reactions** In what way does Paul's relationship with his mother lead to his obsession with luck? Citing evidence from the story, describe each of the following:

   - Paul's mother's view of herself and her family
   - what she teaches her son about luck
   - what Paul longs to do for her

5. **Analyze Symbol** Consider what happens when Paul rides his rocking horse. What might riding the horse symbolize? Explain your answer.

6. **Draw Conclusions** Based on the information and **inferences** you recorded as you read, what conclusions can you draw about the role of luck in the lives of Paul, his mother, and Oscar? For each character, is luck a positive, a negative, or a neutral force? Support your conclusions with evidence from the story.

7. **Examine Imagery** A **controlling image** is a single image that extends throughout a literary work and shapes its meaning. Review the story, looking for lines in which Lawrence describes Paul's eyes. What does this repeated image draw attention to? Cite evidence.

8. **Interpret Theme** Consider what happens in this story because of the adults' desire for money. What theme about materialism is Lawrence communicating to the reader? What literary elements does he employ to convey this theme? Cite evidence.

Text Criticism

9. **Critical Interpretations** Several critics have argued that every adult in the story except for the nurse contributes to Paul's death. Do you agree with this interpretation? Explain why or why not, citing textual evidence to support your opinion.

> *Can* **MONEY** *buy happiness?*
>
> In what ways does money influence our emotions and actions? Why can't money buy happiness?

COMMON CORE

RL 1 Cite evidence to support inferences drawn from the text. **RL 2** Determine two or more themes or central ideas of a text and analyze their development over the course of the text, including how they interact and build on one another to produce a complex account.

Vocabulary in Context

▲ VOCABULARY PRACTICE

Indicate whether the words in each pair are synonyms or antonyms.

1. materialize/vanish
2. career/slacken
3. steed/stallion
4. reiterate/echo
5. uncanny/ordinary

WORD LIST

career

materialize

reiterate

steed

uncanny

ACADEMIC VOCABULARY IN WRITING

- approach   - assume   - environment   - method   - strategy

What can we **assume** about Paul's feeling toward his mother? How does Paul's mother **approach** his luck? Using at least two Academic Vocabulary words, write a paragraph describing one of the main characters in "The Rocking-Horse Winner."

VOCABULARY DEVELOPMENT: ANALOGIES

An **analogy** compares two things to clarify the less familiar one. Vocabulary analogies compare word pairs. The first example pair (below) reads, "*iridescent* is to *dull* as *uncanny* is to *familiar*." Even if you can't remember what *iridescent* means, you may remember that *uncanny* means "strange." Therefore, the second pair of words are opposites, or **antonyms**. That means the first pair are also opposites, and *iridescent* is an antonym of *dull*. The second analogy—"*career* is to *rush* as *overwrought* is to *nervous*" — shows two pairs of synonyms in which the first word in each pair has more extreme **connotations**. In other words, the emotion associated with the word is more intense.

> **ANALOGY EXAMPLES**
>
> *IRIDESCENT : DULL :: uncanny : familiar*
> *CAREER : RUSH :: overwrought : nervous*

PRACTICE Choose the word that makes the relationship in the second pair most like the relationship in the capitalized pair. Use a dictionary if needed.

1. TACTLESS:DISCREET::loud: (a) riotous (b) quiet (c) gossipy (d) audible
2. IMPRESSIVE:SPLENDID::hot: (a) scalding (b) warm (c) frigid (d) outstanding
3. COMPEL:ATTRACT:: condemn: (a) prosecute (b) defend (c) denounce (d) question
4. GRAVELY:JOKINGLY::frantically: (a) calmly (b) studiously (c) respectfully (d) hastily
5. OBSTINATELY:FIRMLY::icily: (a) warmly (b) coolly (c) stubbornly (d) angrily

Vocabulary Practice   THINK central

Go to **thinkcentral.com**.
KEYWORD: HML12-1170

Language

◆ **GRAMMAR AND STYLE:** Craft Effective Sentences

Review the **Grammar and Style** note on page 1156. Lawrence uses **repetition** of key phrases to create **suspense** in his writing. He heightens suspense through his use of effective **sentence types and structures** and **repetition** of key words and phrases. Lawrence frequently employs short interrogative and exclamatory sentences, such as the repeated exclamatory sentence "There *must* be more money!" which build suspense and foreshadow events to come. Consider how Lawrence's use of effective sentences builds suspense in this passage:

> *She stood, with arrested muscles, outside his door, listening. There was a strange, heavy, and yet not loud noise. Her heart stood still. It was a soundless noise, yet rushing and powerful. Something huge, in violent, hushed motion. What was it?* (lines 418–421)

Notice how the short sentences lend the passage a sense of urgency, while the interrogative sentence excites readers' curiosity and fear about what will happen next.

PRACTICE Write your own paragraph about a character on the brink of a shocking discovery. Mimic Lawrence's use of short sentences and effective sentence types. If possible, come up with a compelling word or phrase to repeat throughout your paragraph.

READING-WRITING CONNECTION

YOUR TURN Expand your understanding of "The Rocking-Horse Winner" by responding to this prompt. Then, use the **revising tips** to improve your analytical essay.

WRITING PROMPT	REVISING TIPS
WRITE AN ANALYSIS What could the adults in "The Rocking-Horse Winner" have done to prevent Paul's death? Write a **three-to-five-paragraph essay** analyzing the steps each adult could have taken to save Paul. Be sure to discuss specific scenes from the story and explain what each character could have done differently.	• Add more text evidence to demonstrate an understanding of the story's plot. • Make sure you offer insightful solutions to Paul's problem and outline the specific steps leading to those solutions. • Try to use different sentence types throughout your essay, and link the steps you note using appropriate transitions.

L 3a Vary syntax for effect.
W 2b–c Write informative/ explanatory texts to examine and convey complex ideas; develop the topic thoroughly by selecting concrete details, quotations, or other information and examples; use appropriate transitions to clarify the relationships among complex ideas.

COMMON CORE

Interactive Revision **THINK** central

Go to **thinkcentral.com**.
KEYWORD: HML12-1171

from **Heart of Darkness**

Novel by Joseph Conrad

Joseph Conrad
1857–1924

COMMON CORE

RL 9 Demonstrate knowledge of foundational works of literature. W 3 Write narratives to develop imagined events. W 3d Use precise words and phrases and telling details to convey a vivid picture of the setting.

BACKGROUND When he set foot in Britain for the first time in 1878, the 20-year-old Polish immigrant Józef Teodor Konrad Korzeniowski knew only a few words of English. Less than two decades later, he was writing books in English as Joseph Conrad, drawing on his seafaring experiences in the British merchant navy for the settings and themes of his fiction. First published in 1902, *Heart of Darkness* is a short novel based on Conrad's traumatic stint as a steamboat captain in the Congo, then a Belgian colony notorious for exploiting native Africans. Most of the novel is narrated by Charlie Marlow, a steamboat captain for a European company engaged in the African ivory trade. On the long, difficult journey up the Congo River to the company's Inner Station, Marlow is appalled by what he sees of colonial Africa. Several Europeans join Marlow on the trip, including a harsh, incompetent company manager and a group of prospective ivory traders, whom Marlow ironically calls "pilgrims." Most of the Europeans view the natives fearfully or with contempt, but Marlow hopes for better from Kurtz, a legendary figure who successfully runs the Inner Station and is reputed to be an educated man of great charisma.

TEXT ANALYSIS In the excerpt that follows, the details of the **setting** describe the time and place and contribute to the overall **mood** of the passage. In turn, the mood mirrors the mental state of the characters. The "choking, warm, [and] stifling" fog, which keeps the steamboat immobile; the jungle with its dense "river-side bushes" that conceal the people with "eyes that have seen"; and "unexpected, wild, and violent" cries all contribute to a mood of uncertainty and fear, which is exactly what the characters are feeling.

WRITE Using the excerpt as a model, write a scene in which the setting reflects the emotional frame of mind of a character or characters in an uncertain situation. Make sure to choose a setting that is different from the one Conrad describes and use precise details to create a vivid picture of it.

" '*I*t is very serious,' said the manager's voice behind me; 'I would be desolated if anything should happen to Mr. Kurtz before we came up.' I looked at him, and had not the slightest doubt that he was sincere. He was just the kind of man who would wish to preserve appearances. That was his restraint. But when he muttered something about going on at once, I did not even take the trouble to answer him. I knew, and he knew, that it was impossible. Were we to let go our hold of the bottom, we would be absolutely in the air—in space. We wouldn't be able to tell where we were going to—whether up or down stream, or across—till we fetched against one bank or the other,—and then we wouldn't know at first which it was.

10 Of course I made no move. I had no mind for a smash-up. You couldn't imagine a more deadly place for a shipwreck. Whether drowned at once or not, we were sure to perish speedily in one way or another. 'I authorize you to take all the risks,' he said, after a short silence. 'I refuse to take any,' I said, shortly; which was just the answer he expected, though its tone might have surprised him. 'Well, I must defer to your judgment. You are captain,' he said, with marked civility. I turned my shoulder to him in sign of my appreciation, and looked into the fog. How long would it last? It was the most hopeless look-out. The approach to this Kurtz grabbing for ivory in the wretched bush was beset by as many dangers as though he had been an enchanted princess sleeping in a fabulous castle. 'Will they attack, do you think?' asked the
20 manager, in a confidential tone.

"I did not think they would attack, for several obvious reasons. The thick fog was one. If they left the bank in their canoes they would get lost in it, as we would be if we attempted to move. Still, I had also judged the jungle of both banks quite impenetrable—and yet eyes were in it, eyes that had seen us. The river-side bushes were certainly very thick; but the undergrowth behind was evidently penetrable. However, during the short lift I had seen no canoes anywhere in the reach—certainly not abreast of the steamer. But what made the idea of attack inconceivable to me was the nature of the noise—of the cries we had heard. They had not the fierce character boding of immediate hostile intention. Unexpected, wild, and violent as
30 they had been, they had given me an irresistible impression of sorrow. The glimpse of the steamboat had for some reason filled those savages with unrestrained grief. The danger, if any, I expounded, was from our proximity to a great human passion let loose. Even extreme grief may ultimately vent itself in violence—but more generally takes the form of apathy. . . .

"You should have seen the pilgrims stare! They had no heart to grin, or even to revile me: but I believe they thought me gone mad—with fright, maybe. I delivered a regular lecture. My dear boys, it was no good bothering. Keep a lookout? Well, you may guess I watched the fog for signs of lifting as a cat watches a mouse; but for anything else our eyes were of no more use to us than if we had been buried miles
40 deep in a heap of cotton-wool. It felt like it, too—choking, warm, stifling. Besides, all I said, though it sounded extravagant, was absolutely true to fact. What we afterwards alluded to as an attack was really an attempt to repulse. The action was very far from being aggressive—it was not even defensive, in the usual sense: it was undertaken under the stress of desperation, and its essence was purely protective."

Musée des Beaux Arts
The Unknown Citizen

Poetry by W. H. Auden

COMMON CORE

RL 6 Analyze a case in which grasping point of view requires distinguishing what is directly stated in a text from what is really meant. **RL 10** Read and comprehend literature, including poems.

DID YOU KNOW?

W. H. Auden . . .

- was a stretcher-bearer during the Spanish Civil War.
- became a United States citizen in 1946.
- won a Pulitzer Prize for his book *The Age of Anxiety*.

Meet the Author

W. H. Auden 1907–1973

W. H. Auden brilliantly captured the turbulent climate of his era. In both lyrical and satirical poems, he communicated the anxieties and uncertainties people faced during the 1930s—the time of the Great Depression, the Spanish Civil War, and the outbreak of World War II.

Early Passions As a boy growing up in the British industrial city of Birmingham, Wystan Hugh Auden developed an interest in both urban landscapes and in urban social problems. Fascinated by science, he considered becoming a mining engineer. At the age of 15, however, he discovered his talent for writing poetry and grew determined to make writing his career. Nevertheless, his early interest in science didn't entirely leave him; references to scientific phenomena abound in his work.

Generation Auden While a student at Oxford University, Auden exerted a significant influence on a group of young, politically active writers who would become the literary leaders of the 1930s. Later known as the Auden Generation, this group included Louis MacNeice, Christopher Isherwood, and C. Day Lewis. Repulsed by the lingering horrors of World War I and by the deplorable living conditions endured by the growing ranks of England's unemployed, these writers lashed out against social and political injustices in their work.

New Home After graduating in 1928, Auden enjoyed the happiest period of his life. Beginning in 1930, he published several volumes of poetry to glowing reviews. In these works, he used a remarkable variety of poetic styles and forms to explore the problems afflicting modern society and the complexities of the human psyche. Seeking fresh inspiration, Auden moved to New York City in 1939. He maintained residence there until 1972, when his college at Oxford offered him a rent-free residence.

Eccentric Lifestyle Even after becoming a renowned literary figure who mingled with the rich and famous, Auden lived the life of an eccentric. He resided in messy, rundown apartments in New York's Greenwich Village; he dressed in shabby attire; and he frequently appeared in public wearing jeans and bedroom slippers. Although disorderly in his personal habits, Auden maintained a strict sense of order in his poetry and took delight in the beauty of words. "A poet," Auden explained, "is, before anything else, a person who is passionately in love with language."

Author Online

Go to **thinkcentral.com**. KEYWORD: HML12-1174

THINK central

● TEXT ANALYSIS: IRONY

W. H. Auden believed that his role as a poet was to present ordinary aspects of human existence, and to do so in a way that readers could understand and relate to their lives. To that end, he strove to write simply and avoid the finery of what he termed "grand poetry." The two poems you are about to read reveal Auden's knack for both simplicity of style and biting satire. One important component of Auden's satire is **irony**. Both "Musée des Beaux Arts" and "The Unknown Citizen" contain ironic elements. As you read, look for examples of the following types of irony:

- **situational irony,** a contrast between what is expected to happen and what actually happens

- **verbal irony,** in which a speaker or writer says one thing but means another

● READING SKILL: INTERPRET IDEAS

"Musée des Beaux Arts" was inspired by a trip to Brussels, where Auden viewed the paintings in the Royal Museum of Fine Arts, including several by the 16th-century artist Pieter Breughel. In "The Unknown Citizen," Auden explores the quality of life in the 20th century. As you read these poems, your goal should be to interpret the ideas Auden expresses about the human condition. For each poem, use a chart like the one shown to record specific phrases, images, or lines that convey Auden's ideas about human nature and life. Note what you think these examples reveal about Auden's ideas.

Phrases, Images, or Lines	My Interpretation
"… suffering … takes place/While someone else is eating or opening a window or just walking dully along …" ("Musée des Beaux Arts," lines 1–4)	

 Complete the activities in your **Reader/Writer Notebook**.

What makes you feel INVISIBLE?

In some situations, anonymity can feel good. Blending into a crowd on a bustling city street or losing yourself in a mass of fellow sports fans at a sold-out game can be exhilarating. But there are times when feeling exactly like everyone around you can make you feel invisible—unoriginal and not of much consequence.

QUICKWRITE Whether it's your first day at a new school or a frustrating night when your family seems to look right through you at the dinner table, some situations can cause a disconcerting sense that you're invisible. With a partner, list four or five such situations. Try to identify aspects of contemporary life that might contribute to this feeling. Then, on your own, choose one of the situations you listed and describe it in a paragraph or two. What emotions might this kind of situation trigger?

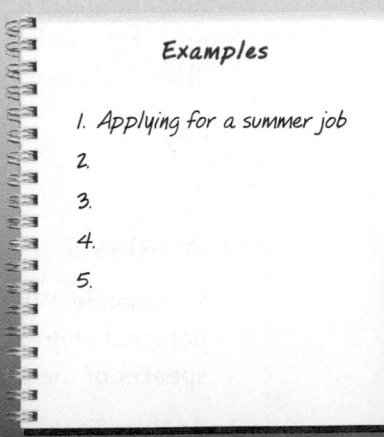

Examples

1. Applying for a summer job
2.
3.
4.
5.

MUSÉE DES BEAUX ARTS
W. H. AUDEN

About suffering they were never wrong,
The Old Masters: how well they understood
Its human position; how it takes place
While someone else is eating or opening a window or just
    walking dully along;
5 How, when the aged are reverently, passionately waiting
For the miraculous birth, there always must be
Children who did not specially want it to happen, skating
On a pond at the edge of the wood:
They never forgot
10 That even the dreadful martyrdom must run its course
Anyhow in a corner, some untidy spot
Where the dogs go on with their doggy life and the
    torturer's horse
Scratches its innocent behind on a tree. **A**

In Breughel's *Icarus,* for instance: how everything turns away
15 Quite leisurely from the disaster; the ploughman may
Have heard the splash, the forsaken cry,
But for him it was not an important failure; the sun shone
As it had to on the white legs disappearing into the green
Water; and the expensive delicate ship that must have seen
20 Something amazing, a boy falling out of the sky,
Had somewhere to get to and sailed calmly on.

[Title] Musée des Beaux Arts (myōō′zā dā bōz är): French for "Museum of Fine Arts." Auden saw the painting described in this poem in the Musée des Beaux Arts in Brussels, Belgium.

2 Old Masters: great European artists of the 16th–18th centuries.

A INTERPRET IDEAS
Reread lines 1–13. What is Auden saying about human suffering in these lines? Record your interpretation in your chart.

14 Breughel's Icarus (broi′gəlz ĭk′ər-əs): the painting *Landscape with the Fall of Icarus* by Pieter Breughel (also spelled *Bruegel* and *Brueghel*). In Greek mythology, Icarus and his father, Daedalus (dĕd′l-əs), escape imprisonment on wings crafted of wax and feathers. When Icarus flies too near the sun, the wax melts and he falls into the sea and drowns.

Text Analysis

1. **Summarize** What incident in the Icarus legend is depicted in Breughel's painting and **alluded** to by the speaker of the poem?

2. **Analyze Tone** Describe the tone of this poem. In what way is the tone at odds with the "miraculous" and "dreadful" events the speaker recounts?

Landscape with the Fall of Icarus, Pieter Breughel the Elder. Musée d'Art Ancien,
Musées Royaux des Beaux-Arts, Brussels, Belgium. © Scala/Art Resource, New York.

THE UNKNOWN CITIZEN
W. H. AUDEN

(To JS/07/M/378

This Marble Monument Is Erected by the State)

He was found by the Bureau of Statistics to be
One against whom there was no official complaint,
And all the reports on his conduct agree
That, in the modern sense of an old-fashioned word, he
    was a saint,
5 For in everything he did he served the Greater Community.
Except for the War till the day he retired
He worked in a factory and never got fired,
But satisfied his employers, Fudge Motors Inc.
Yet he wasn't a scab or odd in his views,
10 For his Union reports that he paid his dues,
(Our report on his Union shows it was sound)
And our Social Psychology workers found
That he was popular with his mates and liked a drink. **B**
The Press are convinced that he bought a paper every day
15 And that his reactions to advertisements were normal in
    every way.
Policies taken out in his name prove that he was fully
    insured,
And his Health-card shows he was once in hospital but
    left it cured.
Both Producers Research and High-Grade Living declare
He was fully sensible to the advantages of the Installment
    Plan
20 And had everything necessary to the Modern Man,
A phonograph, a radio, a car and a frigidaire.
Our researchers into Public Opinion are content
That he held the proper opinions for the time of year;
When there was peace, he was for peace; when there was
    war, he went.

Analyze Visuals ▶
What adjective seems most appropriate for describing the image on page 1179?

9 scab: a worker who refuses to support a union and crosses a picket line.

B IRONY
Consider what you learn about the poem's subject in lines 1–13. In light of this information, why is the poem's title ironic?

21 phonograph: a machine for playing music on vinyl records; **frigidaire** (frĭj′ĭ-dâr′): a refrigerator.

Portrait (1931–1932), Francis Bacon. © 2008 The Estate of Francis Bacon/Artists Rights Society (ARS), New York/DACS, London.

25 He was married and added five children to the
    population,
  Which our Eugenist says was the right number for a
    parent of his generation,
  And our teachers report that he never interfered with their
    education.
  Was he free? Was he happy? The question is absurd:
  Had anything been wrong, we should certainly have
    heard. **C**

26 Eugenist (yōō′jə-nĭst): a scientist who tries to improve the human race by controlling hereditary factors.

C IRONY
The speaker asserts in line 20 that the unknown citizen had "everything necessary to the Modern Man," and, in the poem's final lines, deems questions about happiness and freedom "absurd." What point is Auden making with these ironic statements? Explain.

Comprehension

1. **Recall** List three facts the speaker reveals about the subject in "The Unknown Citizen."

2. **Clarify** Why does the speaker refer to the unknown citizen as a "saint"? Explain why "no official complaint" could be brought against this citizen.

Text Analysis

3. **Examine Allusions** In "Musée des Beaux Arts," review the references to Christ's "miraculous birth" and "dreadful martyrdom," as well as the allusion to Icarus's "failure." Why might Auden have included these particular references, rather than less specific or less well-known images of suffering?

4. **Draw Conclusions** Look again at the reproduction of Breughel's painting *Landscape with the Fall of Icarus* on page 1177. Why do you think Auden chose this particular painting as the focus of "Musée des Beaux Arts"?

5. **Analyze Style** Review "The Unknown Citizen," noting Auden's unorthodox capitalization of words such as *Press, Union,* and *Public Opinion.* Why do you think Auden capitalizes these words?

6. **Analyze Speaker** In **satiric** poems, the poet often creates a specific "voice" in order to critique certain aspects of society. For "The Unknown Citizen," Auden created a speaker whose attitudes are quite different from his own. What do you think was Auden's purpose in speaking through this voice? Explain what using this voice helps him accomplish, citing specific lines from the poem.

7. **Interpret Ideas** Review the chart you filled in as you read. What ideas about the human condition does Auden convey in these poems? Citing evidence, explain how you interpret the poet's ideas regarding anonymity, history, and conformity.

8. **Evaluate Irony** Re-examine both poems, noting examples of **situational irony** in "Musée des Beaux Arts" and **verbal irony** in "The Unknown Citizen." In each poem, what ideas does Auden's use of irony help him convey? How might each have been less effective if Auden had stated his views more directly?

Text Criticism

9. **Historical Context** Auden wrote both of these poems around 1940, a time in which the world's attention was focused on World War II. The United States, Auden's adopted homeland, was following a policy of isolation, staying out of the war and other world affairs. What conclusions can you draw about how this context might have shaped Auden's work?

> *What makes you feel* **INVISIBLE?**
>
> What is the difference between being invisible and being ignored? Which gives you more control?

COMMON CORE

RL 1 Cite evidence to support inferences drawn from the text. **RL 6** Analyze a case in which grasping point of view requires distinguishing what is directly stated in a text from what is really meant. **RL 10** Read and comprehend literature, including poems.

Language

◆ **GRAMMAR AND STYLE: Choose Effective Words**

Auden, who wanted his poetry to reflect his concern for the common person, writes simply, avoiding flowery or figurative language. His use of plain images and uncomplicated diction makes his poetry widely accessible. For example, in the following description of Breughel's painting, notice how Auden employs **concrete nouns,** such as *water, ship,* and *boy,* and everyday adjectives and verbs:

> . . . *the sun shone*
> *As it had to on the white legs disappearing into the green*
> *Water; and the expensive delicate ship that must have seen*
> *Something amazing, a boy falling out of the sky,*
> *Had somewhere to get to and sailed calmly on.* (lines 17–21)

PRACTICE Rewrite the following stanza to better reflect Auden's style, replacing flowery language with simple, concrete words and images.

> The full moon, lustrous as a beacon, flooded the ocean
> With beams of lemon-colored light,
> Illuminating a diminutive, fragile vessel that bobbed
> On mammoth silver waves like a child's toy,
> As the despondent crew searched fruitlessly for a cove
> To shelter them in its arms from the tempestuous sea.

READING-WRITING CONNECTION

YOUR TURN Expand your understanding of Auden's "The Unknown Citizen" by responding to this prompt. Then use the **revising tips** to improve your analytical essay.

WRITING PROMPT	REVISING TIPS
WRITE AN ANALYSIS What developments in modern society is Auden warning readers against in "The Unknown Citizen"? In **three to five paragraphs,** analyze the flaws of the society he depicts and identify the changes he seems to be recommending.	• Identify the poem's theme in your opening paragraph. • Make sure you give specific examples of negative social tendencies explored in "The Unknown Citizen." • Try to use some of Auden's concrete nouns and other precise language.

COMMON CORE

L 3 Apply knowledge of language to make effective choices for style. **W 2** Write explanatory texts to examine and convey complex ideas. **W 2b, d** Develop the topic by selecting concrete details, quotations, or other information and examples; use precise language to manage the complexity of the topic.

Do Not Go Gentle into That Good Night
Fern Hill

Poetry by Dylan Thomas

VIDEO TRAILER **THiNK** central KEYWORD: HML12-1182A

DID YOU KNOW?

Dylan Thomas . . .

- left school at age 16 to take a job as a reporter.
- had produced half of his literary output by the time he was 20.
- also worked as an actor and a radio broadcaster.

Meet the Author

Dylan Thomas 1914–1953

During his life, Dylan Thomas became a mythical figure, both for the beauty of his work and for the outrageousness of his personality. Today, he is remembered for his poetry. Marked by depth of feeling, complexity of sound, and freshness of language, Thomas's verse is among the most original of the 20th century.

Welsh Roots Thomas's work is deeply rooted in the countryside and culture of his native Wales. He grew up in the industrial city of Swansea but spent his summers at his aunt's dairy farm in Carmarthenshire, the place that inspired his famous poem "Fern Hill." Though his father encouraged his interest in Welsh culture, he raised his son to speak English rather than Welsh. Despite never learning the language himself, Dylan Thomas would later capture its cadences and word sequences in his poetry.

Precocious Poet An unruly and sickly child, Thomas performed poorly in all subjects except for literature and dropped out of school at the age of 16. A few years later, he was a published poet. Thomas wrote about the things closest to his heart, calling his poetry, "the record of my individual struggle from darkness towards some measure of light." He focused on his own personal experiences rather than on social or political issues, writing about such topics as his childhood, the Welsh landscape, lost innocence, and death. He also experimented frequently with language, playing with sound devices and creating fresh imagery.

Financial Woes In the mid-1930s, Thomas moved to London and began writing fewer poems and more short stories, radio scripts, and screenplays. When he returned to Wales in 1938, he brought with him his new wife, Caitlin Macnamara. The marriage, volatile from the start, soured over time. Tired of living on the brink of poverty, Thomas and his wife took to begging money from friends as a source of income.

"Roaring Boy" In 1950, in an attempt to improve his finances, Thomas booked his first series of poetry readings in the United States. Wherever he went, Thomas enchanted audiences with charismatic performances. To his many fans, he personified the romantic image of the bohemian poet—reckless and flamboyant. Sadly, his charisma had a self-destructive edge. At the age of 39, in the midst of his fourth American tour, Thomas died in a hotel room from alcohol poisoning.

POETIC FORM: VILLANELLE

"Do Not Go Gentle into That Good Night" is an example of a **villanelle.** While this French verse form is designed to give the impression of simplicity, it is intricately patterned. A villanelle has 19 lines, composed of five tercets (three-line stanzas), followed by a quatrain (a four-line stanza). The poem's first line is repeated as a refrain at the end of the second and fourth stanzas. The last line of the first stanza is repeated at the end of the third and fifth stanzas. Both lines reappear as the final two lines of the poem. The rhyme scheme of a villanelle is *aba* for each tercet and then *abaa* for the quatrain.

TEXT ANALYSIS: CONSONANCE AND ASSONANCE

Dylan Thomas has been described as a poet in whose work "sound and sense are exquisitely blended." Consider this line from "Do Not Go Gentle into That Good Night":

Blind eyes could blaze like meteors and be gay . . .

The recurrence of the final *z* sound in *eyes, blaze,* and *meteors* is an example of **consonance,** the repetition of consonant sounds within and at the ends of words. The line also provides examples of **assonance,** a repetition of vowel sounds in words—the long *i* sound in *blind, eyes,* and *like* and the long *a* in *blaze* and *gay.* As you read each poem, look for other examples of these devices.

READING SKILL: ANALYZE IMAGERY

Thomas wrote "Do Not Go Gentle into That Good Night," which explores various ways to confront death, as a plea to his own dying father. "Fern Hill" recalls the idyllic childhood summers of his youth. In both poems, Thomas creates meaning and feeling in part through his use of **imagery,** words and phrases that recreate sensory experiences for the reader. As you read, note details that appeal to your senses. Jot down the thoughts and feelings engendered by each example of imagery you find.

Example of Imagery	Thoughts/Feelings Evoked
"Old age should burn . . ."	

 Complete the activities in your **Reader/Writer Notebook.**

When is LIFE *most precious?*

You wake up late and rush to get ready for school, cramming things into your backpack, hastily gulping down breakfast, and sprinting out the door. Your days are full of obligations—to your friends, family, teachers, sports team. When, in days already full to the brim, do you get a chance to ponder the precious, fleeting moments of life? The poems you are about to read will help you do just that.

QUICKWRITE "Fern Hill" captures the easy joy of childhood summers. "Do Not Go Gentle into That Good Night" explores how we should face the very end of our lives. When, in your opinion, is life most precious? Do you think people consciously realize they're happy when in a particularly satisfying period of their lives? Or is it only later that we know that period was a great one? Do you think life might seem more precious just as it's about to end? Explore these questions in a paragraph or two.

Do Not Go Gentle into That
GOOD NIGHT

Dylan Thomas

Do not go gentle into that good night,
Old age should burn and rave at close of day;
Rage, rage against the dying of the light.

Though wise men at their end know dark is right,
5 Because their words had forked no lightning they
Do not go gentle into that good night.

Good men, the last wave by, crying how bright
Their frail deeds might have danced in a green bay,
Rage, rage against the dying of the light.

10 Wild men who caught and sang the sun in flight,
And learn, too late, they grieved it on its way,
Do not go gentle into that good night. **A**

Grave men, near death, who see with blinding sight
Blind eyes could blaze like meteors and be gay,
15 Rage, rage against the dying of the light.

And you, my father, there on the sad height,
Curse, bless, me now with your fierce tears, I pray.
Do not go gentle into that good night.
Rage, rage against the dying of the light.

Analyze Visuals ▶
What effect does the sketchy quality of this image have on you as a viewer?

Language Coach

Word Definitions *Forked lightning* is a scientific term for lightning broken into branches, like a fork. What kinds of words would "[fork] no lightning" (line 5)?

A **VILLANELLE**
Reread lines 1–12. In what way is the poem's **rhyme scheme** built around the words that end the first two lines, *night* and *day*? What idea or feeling does this pattern help emphasize?

Text Analysis

1. **Draw Conclusions** How would you describe the speaker's attitude toward death? Support your answer with textual evidence.

2. **Interpret Figurative Language** Re-examine the poem, noting at least two examples of figurative language. Give your own interpretation of each example, explaining what feelings or ideas Thomas uses this language to convey.

Head of Seedo I, Leon Kossoff. Charcoal on paper, 78 cm × 56.5 cm. T33775. © Bridgeman Art Library.

FERN HILL

Dylan Thomas

Now as I was young and easy under the apple boughs
About the lilting house and happy as the grass was green,
  The night above the dingle starry,
   Time let me hail and climb
5 Golden in the heydays of his eyes,
And honored among wagons I was prince of the apple towns
And once below a time I lordly had the trees and leaves
   Trail with daisies and barley
  Down the rivers of the windfall light.

10 And as I was green and carefree, famous among the barns
About the happy yard and singing as the farm was home,
  In the sun that is young once only,
   Time let me play and be
  Golden in the mercy of his means,
15 And green and golden I was huntsman and herdsman, the calves
Sang to my horn, the foxes on the hills barked clear and cold,
   And the sabbath rang slowly
  In the pebbles of the holy streams.

All the sun long it was running, it was lovely, the hay
20 Fields high as the house, the tunes from the chimneys, it was air
  And playing, lovely and watery
   And fire green as grass. **B**
  And nightly under the simple stars
As I rode to sleep the owls were bearing the farm away,
25 All the moon long I heard, blessed among stables, the nightjars
  Flying with the ricks, and the horses
   Flashing into the dark.

[Title] Fern Hill: the name of Dylan Thomas's aunt's farm, which he visited in childhood.

3 dingle: a wooded valley.

B **ANALYZE IMAGERY**
In lines 1–22, Thomas presents the reader with a series of images meant to convey a certain **mood.** What kinds of **details** does the poet present, and what mood do they evoke?

25 nightjars: birds with harsh calls, active in evening and early night.

26 ricks: haystacks.

And then to awake, and the farm, like a wanderer white
With the dew, come back, the cock on his shoulder: it was all
30   Shining, it was Adam and maiden,
     The sky gathered again
   And the sun grew round that very day.
So it must have been after the birth of the simple light
In the first, spinning place, the spellbound horses walking warm
35   Out of the whinnying green stable
     On to the fields of praise. **C**

And honored among foxes and pheasants by the gay house
Under the new made clouds and happy as the heart was long,
   In the sun born over and over,
40   I ran my heedless ways,
     My wishes raced through the house high hay
And nothing I cared, at my sky blue trades, that time allows
In all his tuneful turning so few and such morning songs
   Before the children green and golden
45   Follow him out of grace,

Nothing I cared, in the lamb white days, that time would take me
Up to the swallow thronged loft by the shadow of my hand,
   In the moon that is always rising,
     Nor that riding to sleep
50   I should hear him fly with the high fields
And wake to the farm forever fled from the childless land.
Oh as I was young and easy in the mercy of his means,
     Time held me green and dying
   Though I sang in my chains like the sea.

30 Adam and maiden: A reference to the biblical story of Adam and Eve. Thomas is comparing the farm to the paradise of Eden.

C **CONSONANCE AND ASSONANCE**
Find at least one example of consonance and one of assonance in the poem thus far. What effect do these **sound devices** have on this joyous description of childhood?

(COMMON CORE L 5b

Language Coach

Synonyms Words with the same or nearly the same meaning are **synonyms.** The word *thronged* (line 47) is a synonym for *packed* or *crowded*. Why do you think Thomas chose *thronged* rather than *packed* in creating the image of a loft filled with swallows (a type of bird)?

Comprehension

1. **Recall** What is the setting of "Fern Hill"?

2. **Summarize** What kinds of experiences does the speaker of "Fern Hill" recount?

Text Analysis

3. **Examine Diction** Turn again to "Do Not Go Gentle into That Good Night." The intensity in this poem comes in part from words, particularly verbs, that themselves convey intensity. *Rage* is a good example. What other words in the poem have a similar effect? How do the connotations of the words you noted enrich the meaning of the poem?

4. **Understand Poetic Form** Review the characteristics of the **villanelle** form on page 1183. How closely does Thomas's poem follow this form? How effective is the form in conveying ideas and emotions? Explain, citing evidence.

5. **Analyze Personification** Re-examine "Fern Hill," identifying at least three examples of personification. Why do you think Thomas gives human attributes to animals, objects, and concepts in this poem? Describe the effect his use of this technique creates.

6. **Interpret Imagery** Review the chart you filled in as you read. In "Fern Hill," the speaker presents a series of images that let the reader know how the farm looked, sounded, and felt to the speaker when he was young. Contrast this imagery with that presented in lines 51–54. How does this change allow Thomas to convey the feelings of an adult looking back on his lost childhood?

7. **Analyze Sound Devices** In the art of poetry, sound devices like **consonance** and **assonance** are important ingredients. Examine the functions of sound devices listed here. Then review both poems, finding an example of how Thomas achieves each through his use of consonance and assonance.

   • to emphasize particular words
   • to create a specific mood
   • to add a musical quality

Text Criticism

8. **Critical Interpretations** One contemporary critic of Thomas's poetry has called it a "celebration of the wonder of growth and death." Based on these two poems, would you agree? Explain why or why not.

When is **LIFE** *most precious?*

Do you believe young people get more out of life than adults? Why or why not? Explain whether youth or old age offers a better perspective for contemplating mortality.

Modernist Detachment

Fresh on the heels of the social and economic changes wrought by industrialism, a new phase of upheaval rocked Britain in the early decades of the 20th century. As the British Empire began to crumble and the class system started to give way, England found itself in the bloody trenches of World War I. Back home, the population suffered from the personal losses and economic deprivations of war. As villages shrank and big cities grew, people felt a loss of community. In addition, radical ideas from such thinkers as Einstein and Freud caused a shift in long-held beliefs about the world and human nature.

Disillusioned by the loss of physical, economic, and moral security, people did not know quite where to turn. Modernist writers reflected this disillusionment by developing a sense of ironic detachment from reality.

> *"There was a woman who was beautiful, who started with all the advantages, yet she had no luck. She married for love, and the love turned to dust. She had bonny children, yet she felt they had been thrust upon her, and she could not love them."*
> —D. H. Lawrence, "The Rocking-Horse Winner"

Writing to Analyze

Review the stories and poems on pages 1118–1187 and choose one that conveys a strong sense of detachment. Analyze how the writer creates this sense of emotional distance and what ideas or values the piece seems to express, using examples from the text.

Consider

- the tone, or attitude of the writer toward his or her subject
- the author's use of verbal, situational, or dramatic irony
- the values embraced by the characters or expressed by the narrator or speaker
- the conflict described and its outcome

Extension

VIEWING & REPRESENTING

W. H. Auden was inspired by the painting *Landscape with the Fall of Icarus* by 16th-century artist Pieter Breughel (see page 1177). This Flemish master created bustling narrative panoramas. The broad chaos and sense of anonymity in these works have resonated greatly with modern viewers. Study this detail from Breughel's *Children's Games*. Use it as inspiration to write a brief narrative poem or story.

COMMON CORE

W 2 Write explanatory texts to examine and convey complex ideas. **W 2b** Develop the topic by selecting concrete details, quotations, or other examples.
W 3 Write narratives to develop imagined events.
W 9a (RL 2, RL 3, RL 6) Determine themes of a text; analyze the impact of an author's choices; analyze irony.

Selected Poetry

by William Butler Yeats

VIDEO TRAILER  KEYWORD: HML12-1190A

COMMON CORE

RL 2 Determine two or more themes or central ideas of a text and analyze their development over the course of the text.
RL 10 Read and comprehend literature, including poems.

Meet the Author

William Butler Yeats 1865–1939

William Butler Yeats is considered one of the finest poets of the English language. Already an important poet in his twenties, he changed his style as he matured, becoming that rare poet whose last poems include some of his best work. According to critic M. L. Rosenthal, Yeats "grew at last into the boldest, most vigorous voice of this [20th] century." In 1923, Yeats received the Nobel Prize for Literature.

Early Influences Born in Dublin, Ireland, Yeats was the eldest of four children born to Susan Pollexfen and John Butler Yeats. Although Yeats's family lived primarily in London and Dublin, they made frequent visits to Sligo, a rural area in western Ireland where his mother's parents lived. There, as a boy, Yeats became fascinated with local stories about Irish heroes, heroines, and magical creatures. Years later, he would draw on these experiences of Sligo and its rich folklore in both his poetry and drama.

Ireland as Inspiration Following the publication of his first volume of poetry in 1889, Yeats met and fell in love with the actress Maud Gonne, a fiery Irish patriot. Although Gonne refused to marry him, she inspired many of his finest lyrics and deepened his commitment to Irish nationalism. In 1899, Yeats, along with Lady Isabella Augusta Gregory and Edward Martyn, founded the Irish Literary Theatre (later the Abbey Theatre), which became the leading force in the Irish Literary Renaissance.

New Directions Throughout his life, Yeats had an intense interest in mysticism and the supernatural. This fascination grew stronger following his marriage in 1917 to Georgie Hyde-Lees, a spiritualist medium. In fact, Yeats created an entire system based on the metaphors and symbols revealed during his wife's séances. Many of his best works were produced in the following decade—including "Sailing to Byzantium" and "The Second Coming"— and reflect Yeats's new set of beliefs.

In later years, Yeats's poems often focused on themes of aging and mortality. In one of his last poems, he wrote lines that seemingly defied death and were to become his epitaph: "Cast a cold eye / On life, on death. / Horseman, pass by!" Yeats died in France in 1939; according to his wishes, his body was later reburied at Sligo.

DID YOU KNOW?

William Butler Yeats . . .

- performed poorly in high school because he daydreamed.
- studied magic as a member of a secret society.
- turned down the honor of knighthood.

Author Online

Go to thinkcentral.com. KEYWORD: HML12-1190B

● TEXT ANALYSIS: SYMBOL

A **symbol** is a person, place, object, or activity that represents something beyond itself. A flag, for example, often serves as a symbol of national heritage and patriotism. In literature, a symbol takes its meaning from its context. The symbols in Yeats's poetry often convey major ideas about life, death, and rebirth. One of his most important symbols involves Byzantium, an ancient Greek city. Yeats once commented, "Byzantium was the center of European civilization and the source of its spiritual philosophy, so I symbolize the search for spiritual life by a journey to that city." Other symbols that figure prominently in Yeats's writing include water, gold, birds, and beasts. As you read the following poems, consider what these and other symbols might represent and what themes they might support.

● READING SKILL: CLARIFY MEANING IN POETRY

When reading complex poems, you may encounter some unfamiliar ideas and images. If a poem's meaning seems obscure, reading several times may help clarify it. Use the following strategies for reading Yeats's works:

- On your first reading, refer to the explanations in the notes and think about the poem's **subject.**
- The next time you read the poem, note any **images** that stand out in your mind.
- On subsequent readings, spend time analyzing any **lines** that you think are especially difficult.

As you read each poem, use a chart like the one shown to describe the general subject of the poem. Then write down images and lines that you want to focus on.

Title of Poem:	
Subject:	
Images That Stand Out:	Difficult Lines:

 Complete the activities in your **Reader/Writer Notebook**.

Should we fear CHANGE?

You get up; you go to school; you come home; you do your homework; maybe you watch a little TV or surf the Internet. You may find such a familiar routine reassuring. Or perhaps you're just itching for something to happen that will shake everything up. In the three poems you are about to read, William Butler Yeats examines the thoughts and emotions stirred up by the prospect of change.

QUICKWRITE You've probably heard people say, "Change is good." Yet many people find change disorienting and frightening. Make a list of some changes in your life that you think may occur in the future. Choose one of the items on your list, and write a paragraph in which you examine your feelings regarding that change.

Sailing to Byzantium

William Butler Yeats

BACKGROUND William Butler Yeats developed his own set of beliefs to help him interpret the mysteries of life. According to his mystical faith, history occurs in 2,000-year cycles; as each era comes to an end, another era—its opposite—is ushered in by a momentous occurrence. Many of Yeats's poems, including "Sailing to Byzantium" and "The Second Coming," reflect this understanding of history.

I

That is no country for old men. The young
In one another's arms, birds in the trees
—Those dying generations—at their song,
The salmon-falls, the mackerel-crowded seas,
5 Fish, flesh, or fowl, commend all summer long
Whatever is begotten, born, and dies.
Caught in that sensual music all neglect
Monuments of unaging intellect. **A**

II

An aged man is but a paltry thing,
10 A tattered coat upon a stick, unless
Soul clap its hands and sing, and louder sing
For every tatter in its mortal dress,
Nor is there singing school but studying
Monuments of its own magnificence;
15 And therefore I have sailed the seas and come
To the holy city of Byzantium.

4 salmon-falls: the rapids in rivers that salmon swim up to spawn.

A SYMBOL
Reread lines 1–6. What might "salmon-falls" and "mackerel-crowded seas" symbolize in the poem?

13 but: except for.
14 its: the soul's.

16 Byzantium (bǐ-zǎn'shē-əm): a city of southeastern Europe (now Istanbul, Turkey) that was a center of European civilization, especially art and religion, in the Middle Ages.

Ships at Classis (early 500s). Copy of mosaic. Basilica of St. Apollinare Nuovo, Ravenna, Italy. The Granger Collection, New York.

III

O sages standing in God's holy fire
As in the gold mosaic of a wall,
Come from the holy fire, perne in a gyre,
20 And be the singing-masters of my soul.
Consume my heart away; sick with desire
And fastened to a dying animal
It knows not what it is; and gather me
Into the artifice of eternity.

IV

25 Once out of nature I shall never take
My bodily form from any natural thing,
But such a form as Grecian goldsmiths make
Of hammered gold and gold enameling
To keep a drowsy Emperor awake;
30 Or set upon a golden bough to sing
To lords and ladies of Byzantium
Of what is past, or passing, or to come.

17 sages: wise people; saints.

18 gold mosaic of a wall: artwork in an ancient church.

19 perne (pûrn) **in a gyre** (jīr): whirl in a spiral. (Yeats, however, pronounced this word with a hard *g* [gīr].)

23 it: the speaker's heart.

24 artifice: skilled craftsmanship.

29 Emperor: the ninth-century Byzantine emperor Theophilus, said to have possessed a golden sculpture of a tree with mechanical singing birds on its branches.

Text Analysis

1. **Make Inferences** Why does the speaker prefer the spiritual world of "unaging intellect" to the physical world of "fish, flesh, or fowl"?

2. **Clarify Ideas** Reread lines 20–24. To what "dying animal" is the speaker's heart fastened?

The Second Coming

William Butler Yeats

Turning and turning in the widening gyre
The falcon cannot hear the falconer;
Things fall apart; the center cannot hold;
Mere anarchy is loosed upon the world,
5 The blood-dimmed tide is loosed, and everywhere
The ceremony of innocence is drowned;
The best lack all conviction, while the worst
Are full of passionate intensity.

Surely some revelation is at hand;
10 Surely the Second Coming is at hand.
The Second Coming! Hardly are those words out
When a vast image out of *Spiritus Mundi*
Troubles my sight: somewhere in sands of the desert
A shape with lion body and the head of a man,
15 A gaze blank and pitiless as the sun,
Is moving its slow thighs, while all about it
Reel shadows of the indignant desert birds.
The darkness drops again; but now I know
That twenty centuries of stony sleep
20 Were vexed to nightmare by a rocking cradle,
And what rough beast, its hour come round at last,
Slouches towards Bethlehem to be born?

1 gyre (jīr): spiral.

2 falcon: a hawklike bird of prey;
falconer: a person who uses trained falcons to hunt small game.

6 ceremony of innocence: the rituals (such as the rites of baptism and marriage) that give order to life.

10 Second Coming: Christ's return to earth, predicted in the New Testament to be an event preceded by a time of terror and chaos.

12 *Spiritus Mundi* (spîr′ĭ-tōōs mōōn′dē) *Latin:* Spirit of the World. Yeats used this term to refer to the collective unconscious, a supposed source of images and memories that all human beings share.

14 This image suggests the Great Sphinx in Egypt, built more than 40 centuries ago.

20 rocking cradle: a reference to the birth of Christ.

Text Analysis

1. **Examine Diction and Tone** Review Yeats's diction, or choice of words, in the poem. Based on phrases such as "The blood-dimmed tide is loosed," describe Yeats's tone, or attitude, toward the Second Coming.

2. **Analyze Imagery** Describe the image that troubles the speaker. What details of the image are memorable?

3. **Evaluate Ideas** Paraphrase lines 18–22. Why might Yeats have ended the poem with a question?

When You Are Old

William Butler Yeats

When you are old and grey and full of sleep,
And nodding by the fire, take down this book,
And slowly read, and dream of the soft look
Your eyes had once, and of their shadows deep; **B**

5 How many loved your moments of glad grace,
And loved your beauty with love false or true,
But one man loved the pilgrim soul in you,
And loved the sorrows of your changing face;

And bending down beside the glowing bars,
10 Murmur, a little sadly, how Love fled
And paced upon the mountains overhead
And hid his face amid a crowd of stars.

B CLARIFY MEANING
What striking **image** is presented
in lines 1–4? Explain what you
learn about the poem's subject
matter based on this image.

Hommage (1999), Rowan Gillespie. Bronze, 150 cm.

Comprehension

1. **Recall** To whom does the speaker of "When You Are Old" address the poem?

2. **Clarify** Reread lines 5–8. What might the phrase "pilgrim soul" mean?

3. **Paraphrase** Restate lines 9–12 in your own words. In what way has the speaker's love changed?

Text Analysis

4. **Clarify Meaning in Poetry** Review the charts you completed as you read. Choose an image or a line that you think is particularly striking or important to the meaning of each poem. Explain your choice.

5. **Analyze Symbols** Using a chart like the one shown, select three symbols from the poems and write an explanation of what each represents. Be sure to consider what larger themes each symbol might reflect.

Title of Poem	Symbol	Explanation

6. **Draw Conclusions** "Sailing to Byzantium" is considered one of Yeats's most accomplished poems. What message does he communicate about each of the following subjects? Support your ideas with details from the poem.

   • youth   • immortality   • old age

7. **Understand Historical Context** Yeats wrote "The Second Coming" in January 1919, not long after the Russian Revolution of 1917 and the end of World War I in 1918. In what ways are these catastrophic events reflected in the poem? Cite details.

8. **Compare Poems** Compare and contrast the ways in which the speakers of the three poems view change. Do they share any attitudes or expectations? Support your response with specific references to the poems.

Text Criticism

9. **Author's Style** Yeats once wrote, "I tried to make the language of poetry coincide with that of passionate, normal speech." Keeping in mind the importance of both **word choice** and **rhythm,** select a poem and comment on how successful you think Yeats was in this endeavor.

Should we fear **CHANGE?**

What gives the word *change* negative or positive connotations? What situations make the idea of change seem either frightful or exciting?

COMMON CORE

RL1 Cite evidence to support inferences drawn from the text. **RL 2** Determine two or more themes or central ideas of a text and analyze their development over the course of the text. **RL 4** Analyze the impact of specific word choices on tone. **RL 10** Read and comprehend literature, including poems.

Araby

Short Story by James Joyce

VIDEO TRAILER **THINK** central KEYWORD: HML12-1198A

img_1

COMMON CORE

RL 3 Analyze the impact of an author's choices regarding how to develop and relate elements of a story. **RL 4** Analyze the impact of specific word choices on meaning and tone, including language that is fresh, engaging, or beautiful.

DID YOU KNOW?

James Joyce . . .

- had nine brothers and sisters.
- titled "Araby" after a real festival that came to Dublin in 1894.
- was initially offered only one pound each for the stories published in *Dubliners*.

Meet the Author

James Joyce 1882–1941

Often hailed as one of the greatest novelists of the 20th century, Irish novelist and short story writer James Joyce is noted for his experimental style and his facility with language. A highly influential writer, he popularized the stream-of-consciousness technique and pioneered a number of other literary innovations. Many critics consider his novel *Ulysses* (1922) to be the finest novel of the 20th century.

Down and Out in Dublin Joyce was born in Dublin in 1882. Financial problems forced the Joyce family to move frequently, each time to a poorer and shabbier section of the city. Joyce thus became acquainted with many facets of Dublin society. Despite the poverty he experienced, his mind was preoccupied with the people of Dublin, and the life of the city later became the focal point of all his fiction.

A Man of Many Interests In 1902, Joyce graduated from University College in Dublin, where he first began to write fiction. Writing, however, was not the only interest that he pursued. A fine singer, Joyce considered a musical career as a young man. During his lifetime, he tried his hand at various other jobs and enterprises, including teaching, banking, and the movie-theater business.

Moments of Truth In 1914, *Dubliners* was published, a volume of short stories based on his childhood experiences. A notable feature of the stories in the collection is what Joyce called an **epiphany**—an ordinary moment or situation in which an important truth about a character's life is suddenly revealed. "Araby" is among the collection's best-known stories. Two years after *Dubliners* appeared, Joyce published his first novel, *A Portrait of the Artist as a Young Man*.

Self-Imposed Exile In June 1904, Joyce met Nora Barnacle, a young woman from Galway; a few months later they left Ireland together. The couple lived in several European cities before settling in Paris after World War I. Throughout much of his adult life, Joyce coped with financial troubles as he continued to write. He also faced serious problems with his vision and suffered periods of temporary blindness. While working on his last novel, *Finnegans Wake* (1939), he was occasionally forced to write in crayon on large sheets of paper in order to see his own work.

Author Online

Go to **thinkcentral.com**. KEYWORD: HML12-1198B

THINK central

● TEXT ANALYSIS: FIRST-PERSON POINT OF VIEW

"Araby" is a celebrated coming-of-age story written from the **first-person point of view,** featuring a narrator who speaks directly to readers, using *I* and other first-person pronouns. In contrast with other narrative points of view (see pages 995 and 1127), a first-person story reveals everything through the narrator's eyes. The narrator and main character of "Araby" is an impressionable boy living in Dublin at the turn of the 20th century. His comments convey emotional intensity.

I could not call my wandering thoughts together. I had hardly any patience with the serious work of life....

At times, the boy does not fully understand what he sees or feels. Such a narrator is called a **naive narrator.** As you read "Araby," notice how Joyce's use of the first-person point of view affects what you learn about the story's characters, events, and setting.

● READING SKILL: ANALYZE DESCRIPTIVE DETAILS

Joyce uses a wealth of **descriptive details,** or colorful words and phrases, to help readers understand both the narrator's real circumstances and his imaginary experiences. For example, a visit to the market becomes a religious quest in the boy's mind.

We walked through the flaring streets, jostled by drunken men and bargaining women, amid the curses of laborers.... I imagined that I bore my chalice safely through a throng of foes.

As you read, use a chart like the one shown to note descriptive details and your assessment of them.

Descriptive Details	Real or Imaginary	My Analysis
"jostled by drunken men and bargaining women"	real	Unpleasant people surround the boy.

▲ VOCABULARY IN CONTEXT

The following boldfaced words are important in "Araby." Try to grasp the meaning of each word from the context.

1. He tried to upset her, but she remained **imperturbable.**
2. His **incessant** chatter gave me a headache.
3. I tried counting the stars, but they were **innumerable.**
4. The **garrulous** old man droned on and on.
5. Lovely fragrances **pervade** the flower-filled garden.

Complete the activities in your **Reader/Writer Notebook.**

How do you WIN someone's heart?

You spot your crush coming out of a nearby classroom. Your heart pounds and your stomach does a flip-flop. Should you risk smiling? Maybe it would be better to just duck out of sight. Such uncertainty and excitement are the hallmarks of infatuation. In "Araby," James Joyce examines with penetrating insight this inescapable and often painful aspect of adolescence.

QUICKWRITE Suppose you are an advice columnist and someone has written to you for advice on how to make a good impression on the person he or she has a crush on. Write a letter in which you offer advice to the person. To help organize your thoughts, start by making a list of do's and don'ts.

How to Win Someone's Heart	
Do	Don't
1. Be yourself.	1. Talk too much.
2.	2.
3.	3.
4.	4.
5.	5.

ARABY

James Joyce

North Richmond Street, being blind,[1] was a quiet street except at the hour when the Christian Brothers' School set the boys free. An uninhabited house of two stories stood at the blind end, detached from its neighbors in a square ground. The other houses of the street, conscious of decent lives within them, gazed at one another with brown **imperturbable** faces.

The former tenant of our house, a priest, had died in the back drawing-room. Air, musty from having been long enclosed, hung in all the rooms, and the waste room behind the kitchen was littered with old useless papers. Among these I found a few paper-covered books, the pages of which were curled and damp: *The Abbot,* by Walter Scott, *The Devout Communicant* and *The Memoirs of Vidocq.*[2] I liked the last best because its leaves were yellow. The wild garden behind the house contained a central apple-tree and a few straggling bushes under one of which I found the late tenant's rusty bicycle-pump. He had been a very charitable priest; in his will he had left all his money to institutions and the furniture of his house to his sister.

When the short days of winter came dusk fell before we had well eaten our dinners. When we met in the street the houses had grown somber. The space of sky above us was the color of ever-changing violet and towards it the lamps of the street lifted their feeble lanterns. The cold air stung us and we played till our bodies glowed. Our shouts echoed in the silent street. The career of our play brought us through the dark muddy lanes behind the houses where we ran the gantlet of the rough tribes from the cottages,[3] to the back doors of the dark dripping gardens where odors arose from the ashpits, to the dark odorous stables where a coachman smoothed and combed the horse or shook music from the buckled harness. When we returned to the street, light from the kitchen windows had filled the areas. **A**

---

1. **blind:** a dead end.

2. ***The Abbot . . . Vidocq*** (vē-dôk′): three widely different 19th-century works—the first a historical novel, the second a book of religious instruction, and the third an autobiography of a French police detective.

3. **ran the . . . cottages:** passed through an area of hostility or attack from the rough crowd living in the cottages.

Analyze Visuals ▶
How does the artist's use of color help evoke the setting?

imperturbable
(ĭm′-pər-tûr′bə-bəl) *adj.* not able to be excited or disturbed; impassive

A ANALYZE DETAILS
Reread lines 16–24. What **descriptive details** help you understand the circumstances of the narrator's life?

St. Patrick's Close, Dublin, Walter Osborne. Oil on canvas, 69 cm × 51 cm. © National Gallery of Ireland, Dublin.

If my uncle was seen turning the corner we hid in the shadow until we had seen him safely housed. Or if Mangan's sister came out on the doorstep to call her brother in to his tea we watched her from our shadow peer up and down the street. We waited to see whether she would remain or go in and, if she remained, we left our shadow and walked up to Mangan's steps resignedly. She was waiting for us, her figure defined by the light from the half-opened door. Her brother always teased her before he obeyed and I stood by the railings looking at her. Her dress swung as she moved her body and the soft rope of her hair tossed from side to side.

Every morning I lay on the floor in the front parlor watching her door. The blind was pulled down to within an inch of the sash so that I could not be seen. When she came out on the doorstep my heart leaped. I ran to the hall, seized my books and followed her. I kept her brown figure always in my eye and, when we came near the point at which our ways diverged, I quickened my pace and passed her. This happened morning after morning. I had never spoken to her, except for a few casual words, and yet her name was like a summons to all my foolish blood. **B**

Her image accompanied me even in places the most hostile to romance. On Saturday evenings when my aunt went marketing I had to go to carry some of the parcels. We walked through the flaring streets, jostled by drunken men and bargaining women, amid the curses of laborers, the shrill litanies of shopboys who stood on guard by the barrels of pigs' cheeks, the nasal chanting of street-singers, who sang a *come-all-you* about O'Donovan Rossa,[4] or a ballad about the troubles in our native land. These noises converged in a single sensation of life for me: I imagined that I bore my chalice[5] safely through a throng of foes. Her name sprang to my lips at moments in strange prayers and praises which I myself did not understand. My eyes were often full of tears (I could not tell why) and at times a flood from my heart seemed to pour itself out into my bosom. I thought little of the future. I did not know whether I would ever speak to her or not or, if I spoke to her, how I could tell her of my confused adoration. But my body was like a harp and her words and gestures were like fingers running upon the wires.

One evening I went into the back drawing-room in which the priest had died. It was a dark rainy evening and there was no sound in the house. Through one of the broken panes I heard the rain impinge[6] upon the earth, the fine **incessant** needles of water playing in the sodden beds. Some distant lamp or lighted window gleamed below me. I was thankful that I could see so little. All my senses seemed to desire to veil themselves and, feeling that I was about to slip from them, I pressed the palms of my hands together until they trembled, murmuring: *O love! O love!* many times.

At last she spoke to me. When she addressed the first words to me I was so confused that I did not know what to answer. She asked me was I going to *Araby.*

B POINT OF VIEW
The **first-person point of view** often allows readers to experience the immediacy of the narrator's feelings. What details in lines 35–41 help you identify with the narrator?

incessant (ĭn-sĕs′-ənt) *adj.* continuing or seeming to continue without stopping

---

4. *come-all-you . . .* **Rossa:** a ballad about Jeremiah O'Donovan Rossa, an Irish hero who fought against British rule in the 19th century.

5. **chalice** (chăl′ĭs): The communion chalice, or cup, commemorates the one used by Jesus Christ at the Last Supper, a chalice sometimes called the Holy Grail.

6. **impinge** (ĭm-pĭnj′): hit; strike.

Apple Blossom (1899), Sir George Clausen. Private collection. © Bridgeman Art Library.

I forgot whether I answered yes or no. It would be a splendid bazaar, she said; she would love to go.

—And why can't you? I asked.

While she spoke she turned a silver bracelet round and round her wrist. She
70 could not go, she said, because there would be a retreat that week in her convent. Her brother and two other boys were fighting for their caps and I was alone at the railings. She held one of the spikes, bowing her head towards me. The light from the lamp opposite our door caught the white curve of her neck, lit up her hair that rested there and, falling, lit up the hand upon the railing. It fell over one side of her dress and caught the white border of a petticoat, just visible as she stood at ease.

—It's well for you, she said.

—If I go, I said, I will bring you something. **C**

What **innumerable** follies laid waste my waking and sleeping thoughts after that evening! I wished to annihilate the tedious intervening days. I chafed against
80 the work of school. At night in my bedroom and by day in the classroom her image came between me and the page I strove to read. The syllables of the word

C POINT OF VIEW
Think about how the story's **first-person point of view** shapes your impression of Mangan's sister. What information about her might an omniscient, or all-knowing, narrator convey that the boy cannot?

innumerable
(ĭ-nōō′mər-ə-bəl) *adj.* too many to be counted

Araby were called to me through the silence in which my soul luxuriated, and cast an Eastern enchantment over me. I asked for leave to go to the bazaar on Saturday night. My aunt was surprised and hoped it was not some Freemason[7] affair. I answered few questions in class. I watched my master's face pass from amiability to sternness; he hoped I was not beginning to idle. I could not call my wandering thoughts together. I had hardly any patience with the serious work of life which, now that it stood between me and my desire, seemed to me child's play, ugly monotonous child's play. **D**

90   On Saturday morning I reminded my uncle that I wished to go to the bazaar in the evening. He was fussing at the hallstand, looking for the hat-brush, and answered me curtly:

—Yes, boy, I know.

As he was in the hall I could not go into the front parlor and lie at the window. I left the house in bad humor and walked slowly towards the school. The air was pitilessly raw and already my heart misgave[8] me.

When I came home to dinner my uncle had not yet been home. Still it was early. I sat staring at the clock for some time and, when its ticking began to irritate me, I left the room. I mounted the staircase and gained the upper part

100   of the house. The high cold empty gloomy rooms liberated me and I went from room to room singing. From the front window I saw my companions playing below in the street. Their cries reached me weakened and indistinct and, leaning my forehead against the cool glass, I looked over at the dark house where she lived. I may have stood there for an hour, seeing nothing but the brown-clad figure cast by my imagination, touched discreetly by the lamplight at the curved neck, at the hand upon the railings and at the border below the dress. **E**

When I came downstairs again I found Mrs. Mercer sitting at the fire. She was an old **garrulous** woman, a pawnbroker's widow, who collected used stamps for some pious purpose. I had to endure the gossip of the tea table. The meal was

110   prolonged beyond an hour and still my uncle did not come. Mrs. Mercer stood up to go: she was sorry she couldn't wait any longer, but it was after eight o'clock and she did not like to be out late, as the night air was bad for her. When she had gone I began to walk up and down the room, clenching my fists. My aunt said:

—I'm afraid you may put off your bazaar for this night of Our Lord.

At nine o'clock I heard my uncle's latchkey in the hall-door. I heard him talking to himself and heard the hall-stand rocking when it had received the weight of his overcoat. I could interpret these signs. When he was midway through his dinner I asked him to give me the money to go to the bazaar. He had forgotten.

—The people are in bed and after their first sleep now, he said.

120   I did not smile. My aunt said to him energetically:

—Can't you give him the money and let him go? You've kept him late enough as it is.

D POINT OF VIEW
Reread lines 81–84. In what way does the boy's description of Araby suggest that he is a **naive narrator**?

E ANALYZE DETAILS
What **descriptive details** about Mangan's sister recur in lines 97–106? Explain what these details reveal about the narrator's imagination and romantic longing.

garrulous (găr′ə-ləs) *adj.* talking a lot or too much, especially about unimportant things

---

7. **Freemason:** having to do with the Free and Accepted Masons, a worldwide charitable and social organization. In Ireland, its members were almost exclusively Protestant and were often hostile to Catholics (like the aunt).

8. **misgave:** caused to feel doubt or anxiety.

My uncle said he was very sorry he had forgotten. He said he believed in the old saying: *All work and no play makes Jack a dull boy.* He asked me where I was going and, when I had told him a second time he asked me did I know *The Arab's Farewell to His Steed.*[9] When I left the kitchen he was about to recite the opening lines of the piece to my aunt.

130 I held a florin[10] tightly in my hand as I strode down Buckingham Street towards the station. The sight of the streets thronged with buyers and glaring with gas[11] recalled to me the purpose of my journey. I took my seat in a third-class carriage of a deserted train. After an intolerable delay the train moved out of the station slowly. It crept onward among ruinous houses and over the twinkling river. At Westland Row Station a crowd of people pressed to the carriage doors; but the porters moved them back, saying that it was a special train for the bazaar. I remained alone in the bare carriage. In a few minutes the train drew up beside an improvised wooden platform. I passed out on to the road and saw by the lighted dial of a clock that it was ten minutes to ten. In front of me was a large building which displayed the magical name.

---

9. *The Arab's . . . Steed:* a popular 19th-century poem by Caroline Norton.

10. **florin:** a former British coin worth 2 shillings, or 24 pence.

11. **gas:** gaslight.

Hastings Railway Station (1889), Walter Osborne. Oil on canvas, 30.5 cm × 36.8 cm. The Taylor Gallery Ltd. © akg-images.

I could not find any sixpenny entrance and, fearing that the bazaar would be
140 closed, I passed in quickly through a turnstile, handing a shilling to a weary-
looking man. I found myself in a big hall girdled at half its height by a gallery.
Nearly all the stalls were closed and the greater part of the hall was in darkness.
I recognized a silence like that which **pervades** a church after a service. I walked
into the center of the bazaar timidly. A few people were gathered about the stalls
which were still open. Before a curtain, over which the words *Café Chantant*[12]
were written in colored lamps, two men were counting money on a salver.[13] I
listened to the fall of the coins.

Remembering with difficulty why I had come I went over to one of the stalls
and examined porcelain vases and flowered tea-sets. At the door of the stall a
150 young lady was talking and laughing with two young gentlemen. I remarked
their English accents and listened vaguely to their conversation.

—O, I never said such a thing!

—O, but you did!

—O, but I didn't!

—Didn't she say that?

—Yes. I heard her.

—O, there's a . . . fib!

Observing me the young lady came over and asked me did I wish to buy
anything. The tone of her voice was not encouraging; she seemed to have spoken
160 to me out of a sense of duty. I looked humbly at the great jars that stood like
eastern guards at either side of the dark entrance to the stall and murmured:

—No, thank you.

The young lady changed the position of one of the vases and went back to the
two young men. They began to talk of the same subject. Once or twice the young
lady glanced at me over her shoulder.

I lingered before her stall, though I knew my stay was useless, to make my
interest in her wares seem the more real. Then I turned away slowly and walked
down the middle of the bazaar. I allowed the two pennies to fall against the
sixpence in my pocket. I heard a voice call from one end of the gallery that the
170 light was out. The upper part of the hall was now completely dark.

Gazing up into the darkness I saw myself as a creature driven and derided by
vanity; and my eyes burned with anguish and anger. ॐ

pervade (pər-vād′) *v.* to be
prevalent throughout

Language Coach

Roots and Affixes A
word's **root** may contain
its core meaning. The
root of *derided* is the
Latin *ridere* meaning
"to laugh." What does
derided mean in line 171?
What other words share
the root *ridere*?

---

12. *Café Chantant* (kä-fä′ shäɴ-täɴ′) *French:* "singing café," a café providing musical entertainment.

13. **salver** (săl′vər): serving tray.

Comprehension

1. **Recall** What is Araby?

2. **Recall** Who suggests that the narrator go to Araby?

3. **Summarize** Describe the narrator's emotions in the days and hours leading up to his trip to Araby.

Text Analysis

4. **Interpret Symbol** What does Araby symbolize, or represent, to the narrator? Support your response with details from the story.

5. **Make Inferences About Character** What **epiphany,** or sudden awareness, does the narrator experience at the end of the story? Cite evidence.

6. **Analyze Descriptive Details** Look over the chart you completed as you read "Araby." What descriptive details most strongly convey the narrator's reality and his romantic vision?

7. **Examine Narrator** The story offers a **naive narrator**—a narrator who has limited knowledge and who does not fully understand what he or she sees or feels. Why did Joyce choose this kind of narrator for "Araby"?

8. **Evaluate Point of View** With a **first-person narrator,** the reader sees the story unfold through the eyes of one character. Consider how the boy views the story's characters and events. Would a **third-person-omniscient narrator**—one who sees into the minds of all characters—have presented a more engaging depiction of romantic infatuation? Explain why or why not.

9. **Compare Texts** James Joyce and D. H. Lawrence were both masters of **psychological fiction.** Compare Joyce's portrayal of the protagonist in "Araby" with Lawrence's portrayal of Paul in "The Rocking-Horse Winner" (page 1154). What techniques do they use to reveal the interior lives of these characters?

Text Criticism

10. **Critical Interpretations** According to American poet and critic Ezra Pound, one of Joyce's merits is that "he carefully avoids telling you a lot of what you don't want to know. He presents his people swiftly and vividly, he does not sentimentalize over them." In what way might these comments apply to "Araby"?

> *How do you* **WIN** *someone's heart?*
>
> Look back at the list of advice you created about how to make a good impression. What advice would you give to the narrator of "Araby"? How can he win over the object of his affection?

COMMON CORE

RL 1 Cite evidence to support inferences drawn from the text. **RL 3** Analyze the impact of an author's choices regarding how to develop and relate elements of a story. **RL 4** Analyze the impact of specific word choices on meaning and tone, including language that is fresh, engaging, or beautiful. **RL 9** Demonstrate knowledge of how two or more texts from the same period treat similar themes or topics.

Vocabulary in Context

▲ VOCABULARY PRACTICE

Identify the synonym of each boldfaced vocabulary word.

1. **imperturbable:** (a) nervous, (b) angry, (c) calm
2. **incessant:** (a) ceaseless, (b) useless, (c) humorless
3. **innumerable:** (a) speechless, (b) countless, (c) costly
4. **garrulous:** (a) shabby, (b) confined, (c) talkative
5. **pervade:** (a) witness, (b) permeate, (c) twist

WORD LIST

garrulous

imperturbable

incessant

innumerable

pervade

ACADEMIC VOCABULARY IN WRITING

• approach • assume • environment • method • strategy

Joyce's story culminates in the narrator's visit to Araby—a city bazaar. What **method** does Joyce use for describing the bazaar? Using at least two of the Academic Vocabulary words, describe the scene at a similar **environment**, such as an outdoor market or a shopping mall.

VOCABULARY STRATEGY: USING A THESAURUS

For the time-pressed writer, a **thesaurus** can be a lifesaver. For example, to describe a moving speech by a likable politician, the word *garrulous* may come to mind. But *garrulous* implies triviality, and the politician's speech is profound. The **main entry** for *garrulous* provides a definition, a list of synonyms, and a cross-reference to a larger **category entry,** WORDS. The thesaurus's category entries include a selection of broad concepts (BIG, FREE, WORDS, and so on). Within the category of WORDS, you will find a broad range of adjectives, each of which has a main entry like that for *garrulous*.

MAIN ENTRY — **garrulous** ADJECTIVE: Given to conversation: chatty, conversational, talkative, talky, voluble. *Slang:* gabby. *See* WORDS.

CATEGORY ENTRY — **words . . .** *Adjective* brief, conversational, descriptive, dumb, **eloquent, glib, gossipy, graphic, introductory, oral, oratorical, poetic, silent, sonorous, speechless, talkative, tautological, unspeakable, verbal, wordy**

The word *eloquent*, meaning "fluently persuasive and forceful," turns out to be the perfect word to describe the politician's speech. To determine precise meanings and connotations of thesaurus listings, you may need to refer to a general dictionary.

PRACTICE Use the thesaurus entries above to answer the following questions.

1. What are the synonyms for *garrulous*?
2. Why would it be inappropriate to use the word *gabby* in a critical essay?
3. How is the word *garrulous* related to the words following the entry for *words*?
4. How would you find out the different nuances of *garrulous, talkative,* and *voluble*?

○ **COMMON CORE**

L 4c Consult reference materials to determine or clarify a word's precise meaning. **L 5b** Analyze nuances in the meaning of words with similar denotations. **L 6** Acquire and use accurately general academic words and phrases.

Interactive Vocabulary **THINK** central

Go to **thinkcentral.com.**
KEYWORD: HML12-1208

Language

◆ **GRAMMAR AND STYLE:** Use Effective Dialogue

Review the **Grammar and Style** note on page 1205. James Joyce is famous for his use of **stream of consciousness**—a way of writing that presents a flow of images and ideas meant to represent the unfiltered thoughts of one or more characters. Although stream of consciousness does not figure prominently in "Araby," readers can see glimpses of this innovative technique in the story's **dialogue.** Instead of using conventional quotation marks, Joyce uses **dashes** or summarizes the exchange between two characters, as demonstrated in the following example.

> *She asked me was I going to* Araby. *I forgot whether I answered yes or no. It would be a splendid bazaar, she said; she would love to go.*
> —*And why can't you? I asked.* (lines 65–68)

In later works of fiction, such as *Ulysses* and *Finnegans Wake,* Joyce excludes quotation marks, hyphens in compound words, and chapter numbers and titles to better represent the continuous flow of characters' thoughts.

PRACTICE Rewrite the following dialogue, imitating Joyce's use of dashes and summarization.

"I can see you're a bookworm, like myself," said Mr. O'Malley, peering over the boy's shoulder. His clothes smelled of smoke and aftershave.

"Oh, hello, Mr. O'Malley," said the boy, quickly closing the book and putting a notebook on top of it.

"What is it then that you're reading?" asked Mr. O'Malley, attempting to push the notebook aside.

"Oh, nothing," said the boy, placing both hands on top of the notebook. "Just something we're supposed to read for school."

READING-WRITING CONNECTION

YOUR TURN Expand your understanding of "Araby" by responding to this prompt. Then use the **revising tips** to improve your scene.

WRITING PROMPT	**REVISING TIPS**
WRITE A DRAMATIC SCENE Write a **three-paragraph scene** describing the narrator's next encounter with Mangan's sister. The scene should include dialogue between the two characters. The scene should conclude in a way that follows logically from both the dialogue and the events of "Araby."	• Add more vivid descriptive details. • Check to see that you have maintained a consistent tone and point of view. • Try to reference some of the specific plot points in "Araby."

Interactive Revision

THINK central

Go to **thinkcentral.com**.
KEYWORD: HML12-1209

from **A Portrait of the Artist as a Young Man**

Novel by James Joyce

James Joyce
1882–1941

COMMON CORE

RL 9 Demonstrate knowledge of early-twentieth-century works of literature. **W 2** Write explanatory texts. **W 2b** Develop the topic by selecting quotations. **W 9a (RL 4)** Analyze the impact of specific word choices on meaning and tone, including language that is particularly fresh, engaging, or beautiful.

BACKGROUND James Joyce had something of a love-hate relationship with his native Ireland. On the one hand, he left Ireland as a young man, complaining of its provincialism. On the other hand, his greatest works are set in Ireland and vividly capture the Dublin of his boyhood. Joyce published three of his earliest stories (later collected in *Dubliners*) under the pen name of Stephen Dedalus, the same name he would use for the hero of his autobiographical novel *A Portrait of the Artist as a Young Man* and for a main character in a later novel, *Ulysses*.

Beginning with *A Portrait of the Artist as a Young Man,* Joyce revolutionized the English novel. The style of his third-person narration is remarkably fluid, reflecting the development of Stephen Dedalus's mind. Joyce also introduced the stream-of-consciousness technique that he used more extensively in his later works. The novel is divided into five chapters, each of which depicts an important phase in the protagonist's maturation. This passage is from Chapter 4, in which Stephen questions whether he should enter the priesthood. While walking along a beach, he has an epiphany—a sudden insight—as he watches a girl wade in the water. Stephen's reaction to her beauty makes him realize that he is destined to celebrate life through his writing.

TEXT ANALYSIS Pay attention to Joyce's choice of words and phrases in the following excerpt. His use of **imagery** creates sensory experiences for the reader that convey Stephen's joyful **epiphany**, or sudden revelation, that he has found his calling as an artist. The phrases "broken the holy silence of his ecstasy," "the earth that had borne him, that had taken him to her breast," and "wave of light by wave of light" not only appeal to the reader's senses of hearing, touch, and sight but also mirror Stephen's ecstatic transformation into an artist with imagery that evokes a beautiful landscape in a state of perpetual flux.

WRITE Stephen Dedalus undergoes an intense personal transformation in this excerpt. Identify specific examples of imagery representing at least two of the five senses. Write a three-to-five paragraph essay in which you analyze how this imagery helps convey the theme of personal transformation. Use specific quotations from the excerpt to support your observations.

*H*er image had passed into his soul for ever and no word had broken the holy silence of his ecstasy. Her eyes had called him and his soul had leaped at the call. To live, to err, to fall, to triumph, to recreate life out of life! A wild angel had appeared to him, the angel of mortal youth and beauty, an envoy from the fair courts of life, to throw open before him in an instant of ecstasy the gates of all the ways of error and glory. On and on and on and on!

He halted suddenly and heard his heart in the silence. How far had he walked? What hour was it?

There was no human figure near him nor any sound borne to him over the air.
10 But the tide was near the turn and already the day was on the wane. He turned landward and ran towards the shore and, running up the sloping beach, reckless of the sharp shingle, found a sandy nook amid a ring of tufted sandknolls and lay down there that the peace and silence of the evening might still the riot of his blood.

He felt above him the vast indifferent dome and the calm processes of the heavenly bodies; and the earth beneath him, the earth that had borne him, had taken him to her breast.

He closed his eyes in the languor of sleep. His eyelids trembled as if they felt the vast cyclic movement of the earth and her watchers, trembled as if they felt the
20 strange light of some new world. His soul was swooning into some new world, fantastic, dim, uncertain as under sea, traversed by cloudy shapes and beings. A world, a glimmer, or a flower? Glimmering and trembling, trembling and unfolding, a breaking light, an opening flower, it spread in endless succession to itself, breaking in full crimson and unfolding and fading to palest rose, leaf by leaf and wave of light by wave of light, flooding all the heavens with its soft flushes, every flush deeper than the other.

Evening had fallen when he woke and the sand and arid grasses of his bed glowed no longer. He rose slowly and, recalling the rapture of his sleep, sighed at its joy.

He climbed to the crest of the sandhill and gazed about him. Evening had fallen.
30 A rim of the young moon cleft the pale waste of sky like the rim of a silver hoop embedded in grey sand; and the tide was flowing in fast to the land with a low whisper of her waves, islanding a few last figures in distant pools.

Riders to the Sea

Drama by J. M. Synge

COMMON CORE

RL 3 Analyze the impact of the author's choices regarding how to develop and relate elements of a drama. **RL 10** Read and comprehend literature, including dramas. **L 1a** Apply the understanding that usage is a matter of convention.

Meet the Author

J. M. Synge 1871–1909

The leading playwright of the Irish Literary Renaissance, J. M. Synge was an astute and sometimes critical observer of Irish culture. In the seven plays Synge wrote during his short life, he forged a new style of drama that made use of the lyrical dialects and rich folk traditions of the Irish peasantry.

Love for the Irish Countryside Edmund John Millington Synge was born near Dublin into a once-prosperous Anglo-Irish family whose fortunes had begun to wane. While Synge was still an infant, his father died. Synge's mother came from a devout Protestant family, but Synge never shared her piety, preferring the wild beauty of the Irish countryside to the inside of a church.

A Scholar and Musician Synge graduated in 1892 from Trinity College, Dublin, where he won prizes for his academic achievements in Gaelic and Hebrew languages. Most of his energy, however, was put into musical studies. In 1893, he traveled to Germany to study music but eventually abandoned his dream because of an inability to conquer stage fright.

The Aran Islands From the mid-1890s to the early 1900s, Synge traveled Europe, often on foot, and began to write poetry and literary criticism. While in Paris, the poet

William Butler Yeats urged him to give up Paris literary life and visit the Aran Islands, off the western coast of Ireland. Synge made five trips to the islands between 1898 and 1902. He published his observations of peasant life and culture there in the book *The Aran Islands,* but his visits also deeply influenced most of his plays.

Scandal and Controversy In 1902, Synge wrote three plays, including *Riders to the Sea;* he quickly established himself as a promising, albeit provocative, playwright. Five years later, a major controversy erupted with the premiere of his comedy *The Playboy of the Western World.* Riots broke out on opening night, making it nearly impossible for the actors to deliver their lines. Considered scandalous, the play was condemned by many critics. A handful of influential figures including Yeats, however, championed the play. Today, it is generally considered Synge's masterpiece.

Unfinished Business In 1907, Synge's health, which had always been fragile, began to decline. Nevertheless, he began work on a new play, *Deirdre of the Sorrows.* The play remained unfinished at his death. Many critics believe, based on the promise shown in this work, that Synge would have gone on to even greater achievements had his life not been cut short.

DID YOU KNOW?

J. M. Synge . . .

• had an ear for languages and studied Gaelic, Hebrew, French, and Italian.

• revised his plays until the pages were "nearly unreadable."

• died shortly before his 38th birthday.

Author Online

Go to **thinkcentral.com.** KEYWORD: HML12-1212

THiNK central

TEXT ANALYSIS: DIALOGUE

Like most plays, J. M. Synge's *Riders to the Sea* tells its story almost exclusively through **dialogue**—conversation between two or more characters. In this one-act tragedy, dialogue advances the plot and establishes the overall mood. It also reveals the background and personalities of the play's characters—humble Aran Island fishermen and their families. Synge's dialogue features an unusual **dialect,** a nonstandard vocabulary, syntax, and grammar that reflects usage conventional to the play's remote Irish coastal **setting.** Dialect adds richness and authenticity to Synge's portrayals, as shown in this excerpt:

It's hard set I am to walk. . . . In the big world the old people do be leaving things after them for their sons and children, but in this place it is the young men do be leaving things behind for them that do be old.

As you read, note how Synge's dialogue helps to convey not only character but also the historical, social, and economic conditions of a particular time and place.

READING SKILL: UNDERSTAND CULTURAL CONTEXT

When you analyze the **cultural context** of a literary work, you consider the social or national traditions that influenced its creation. J. M. Synge was an important figure in the Irish Literary Renaissance, a movement that revived ancient Irish folklore and legends in literature. He was particularly inspired by the language and time-honored ways of the Aran Island people, who struggled to surivive on isloated islands in the bone-cold Atlantic Ocean. To fully appreciate the cultural context of *Riders to the Sea,* study the background information on page 1214 and the footnotes throughout the play. Then, as you read the play, note statements or references that you are able to clarify with this knowledge of cultural context.

Statement or Reference	Explanation
"[Bartley] won't go this day with the wind rising from the south and west." (lines 63–65)	The conditions of the sea were very important to the people of the Aran Islands. They couldn't travel to the mainland in bad weather.

 Complete the activities in your **Reader/Writer Notebook**.

How much GRIEF *can one endure?*

For most of us, the death of a loved one is a rare occurrence. After suffering such a loss, we have time to work through feelings of despair and anger and eventually accept the death. J. M. Synge's play *Riders to the Sea,* however, is set in a time and place where catastrophe strikes often and enduring grief is a part of daily life.

QUICKWRITE Think of a time in your life when you've felt grief—for example, after the death of a relative or a beloved pet. Write a journal entry to describe the strategies you used to come to terms with your loss.

RIDERS TO THE SEA

J. M. Synge

BACKGROUND *Riders to the Sea* is set in the stark, treeless landscape of the Aran Islands, off the western coast of Ireland. Isolated from the economic and cultural developments that were occurring elsewhere in Ireland and Europe at the turn of the 20th century, most Aran Islanders continued to rely on the sea for their livelihood, constantly subject to the fickle and dangerous weather of Galway Bay. Synge's play was strongly influenced by his visits to the Aran Islands. Details in the play—such as the practice of knitting garments with specific patterns—were drawn directly from the journals he kept while living there.

PERSONS IN THE PLAY

Maurya (môr′ə), an old woman

Bartley, her son

Cathleen, her daughter

Nora, a younger daughter

Men and **Women**

SCENE

An island off the West of Ireland

Cottage kitchen, with nets, oilskins, spinning-wheel, some new boards standing by the wall, etc. Cathleen, *a girl of about twenty, finishes kneading cake,[1] and puts it down in the pot-oven by the fire; then wipes her hands, and begins to spin at the wheel.* Nora, *a young girl, puts her head in at the door.*

Nora (*in a low voice*). Where is she?

Cathleen. She's lying down, God help her, and maybe sleeping, if she's able.

10 (Nora *comes in softly, and takes a bundle from under her shawl.*)

Cathleen (*spinning the wheel rapidly*). What is it you have?

Nora. The young priest is after bringing them. It's a shirt and a plain stocking were got off a drowned man in Donegal.[2]

(Cathleen *stops her wheel with a sudden movement, and leans out to listen.*)

Nora. We're to find out if it's Michael's they are,
20 some time herself will be down looking by the sea.

Cathleen. How would they be Michael's, Nora? How would he go the length of that way to the far north?

Nora. The young priest says he's known the like of it. "If it's Michael's they are," says he, "you can tell herself he's got a clean burial, by the grace of God; and if they're not his, let no one say a word about them, for she'll be getting her death," says he, "with crying and lamenting."

(*The door which* Nora *half closed is blown open by a*
30 *gust of wind.*)

Cathleen (*looking out anxiously*). Did you ask him would he stop Bartley going this day with the horses to the Galway fair?[3]

---

1. **cake:** Irish soda bread.
2. **Donegal** (dä′nĭ-gôl′): a seaport on the coast of the northwestern Irish county that is also called Donegal.
3. **the Galway** (gôl′wā′) **fair:** the closest market town, across the water on the mainland of County Galway.

Nora. "I won't stop him," says he; "but let you not be afraid. Herself does be saying prayers half through the night, and the Almighty God won't leave her destitute," says he, "with no son living."

Cathleen. Is the sea bad by the white rocks, Nora?

Nora. Middling bad, God help us. There's a great
40 roaring in the west, and it's worse it'll be getting when the tide's turned to the wind. (*She goes over to the table with the bundle.*) Shall I open it now?

Cathleen. Maybe she'd wake up on us, and come in before we'd done (*coming to the table*). It's a long time we'll be, and the two of us crying.

Nora (*goes to the inner door and listens*). She's moving about on the bed. She'll be coming in a minute.

Cathleen. Give me the ladder, and I'll put them up in the turf-loft,[4] the way she won't know of them at
50 all, and maybe when the tide turns she'll be going down to see would he be floating from the east.

(*They put the ladder against the gable of the chimney; Cathleen goes up a few steps and hides the bundle in the turf-loft. Maurya comes from the inner room.*)

Maurya (*looking up at Cathleen and speaking querulously*). Isn't it turf enough you have for this day and evening?

Cathleen. There's a cake baking at the fire for a short space (*throwing down the turf*), and Bartley will want
60 it when the tide turns if he goes to Connemara.[5]

(*Nora picks up the turf and puts it round the pot-oven.*)

Maurya (*sitting down on a stool at the fire*). He won't go this day with the wind rising from the south and west. He won't go this day, for the young priest will stop him surely.

Nora. He'll not stop him, mother; and I heard Eamon Simon and Stephen Pheety and Colum Shawn saying he would go.

70 **Maurya.** Where is he itself?

Nora. He went down to see would there be another boat sailing in the week, and I'm thinking it won't be long till he's here now, for the tide's turning at the green head,[6] and the hooker's tacking from the east.[7]

Cathleen. I hear some one passing the big stones.

Nora (*looking out*). He's coming now, and he in a hurry.

Bartley (*Comes in and looks round the room. Speaking sadly and quietly*). Where is the bit of new rope,
80 Cathleen, was bought in Connemara?

Cathleen (*coming down*). Give it to him, Nora; it's on a nail by the white boards. I hung it up this morning, for the pig with the black feet was eating it.

Nora (*giving him a rope*). Is that it, Bartley?

Maurya. You'd do right to leave that rope, Bartley, hanging by the boards. (Bartley *takes the rope.*) It will be wanting in this place, I'm telling you, if Michael is washed up tomorrow morning or the next morning, or any morning in the week; for it's
90 a deep grave we'll make him, by the grace of God.

Bartley (*beginning to work with the rope*). I've no halter[8] the way I can ride down on the mare, and I must go now quickly. This is the one boat going for two weeks or beyond it, and the fair will be a good fair for horses, I heard them saying below.

Maurya. It's a hard thing they'll be saying below if the body is washed up and there's no man in it to make the coffin, and I after giving a big price for the finest white boards you'd find in Connemara.
100 (*She looks round at the boards.*)

Bartley. How would it be washed up, and we after looking each day for nine days, and a strong wind blowing a while back from the west and south?

Maurya. If it wasn't found itself, that wind is raising the sea, and there was a star up against the moon,

---

4. **turf-loft:** the area for storing peat, partly decayed plant matter used as fuel.

5. **Connemara** (kŏn′ə-mär′ə): the southwestern part of County Galway, to which Bartley will travel by boat with the horses he is bringing to the Galway fair.

6. **green head:** a grassy section of land overlooking the sea.

7. **the hooker's . . . east:** The hooker—a small sailing ship—is changing course by turning across the wind from the east.

8. **I've no halter:** Bartley is commandeering the new rope to use as a halter for tying and leading the horses.

and it rising in the night. If it was a hundred horses, or a thousand horses, you had itself, what is the price of a thousand horses against a son where there is one son only?

Bartley (*working at the halter, to* Cathleen). Let you go down each day, and see the sheep aren't jumping in on the rye, and if the jobber[9] comes you can sell the pig with the black feet if there is a good price going.

Maurya. How would the like of her get a good price for a pig?

Bartley (*to* Cathleen). If the west wind holds with the last bit of the moon let you and Nora get up weed enough for another cock for the kelp.[10] It's hard set we'll be from this day with no one in it but one man to work.

Maurya. It's hard set we'll be surely the day you're drowned with the rest. What way will I live and the girls with me, and I an old woman looking for the grave?

(Bartley *lays down the halter, takes off his old coat, and puts on a newer one of the same flannel.*)

Bartley (*to* Nora). Is she[11] coming to the pier?

Nora (*looking out*). She's passing the green head and letting fall her sails.

Bartley (*getting his purse and tobacco*). I'll have half an hour to go down, and you'll see me coming again in two days, or in three days, or maybe in four days if the wind is bad.

Maurya (*turning round to the fire, and putting her shawl over her head*). Isn't it a hard and cruel man won't hear a word from an old woman, and she holding him from the sea?

Cathleen. It's the life of a young man to be going on the sea, and who would listen to an old woman with one thing and she saying it over?

Bartley (*taking the halter*). I must go now quickly. I'll ride down on the red mare, and the gray pony 'ill run behind me. . . . The blessing of God on you.

(*He goes out.*)

Maurya (*crying out as he is in the door*). He's gone now, God spare us, and we'll not see him again. He's gone now, and when the black night is falling I'll have no son left me in the world.

Cathleen. Why wouldn't you give him your blessing and he looking round in the door? Isn't it sorrow enough is on every one in this house without your sending him out with an unlucky word behind him, and a hard word in his ear?

(Maurya *takes up the tongs and begins raking the fire aimlessly without looking round.*)

Nora (*turning towards her*). You're taking away the turf from the cake.

Cathleen (*crying out*). The Son of God forgive us, Nora, we're after forgetting his bit of bread. (*She comes over to the fire.*)

Nora. And it's destroyed he'll be going till dark night, and he after eating nothing since the sun went up.

Cathleen (*turning the cake out of the oven*). It's destroyed he'll be, surely. There's no sense left on any person in a house where an old woman will be talking for ever.

(Maurya *sways herself on her stool.*)

Cathleen (*cutting off some of the bread and rolling it in a cloth; to* Maurya). Let you go down now to the spring well and give him this and he passing. You'll see him then and the dark word will be broken, and you can say "God speed you," the way he'll be easy in his mind.

Maurya (*taking the bread*). Will I be in it as soon as himself?

Cathleen. If you go now quickly.

Maurya (*standing up unsteadily*). It's hard set I am to walk.

Cathleen (*looking at her anxiously*). Give her the stick, Nora, or maybe she'll slip on the big stones.

Nora. What stick?

---

9. **jobber:** a traveling trader who buys goods to sell to others.

10. **cock for the kelp:** conical heaps of dried seaweed used for fertilizer.

11. **she:** Female pronouns are typically used to refer to boats and ships.

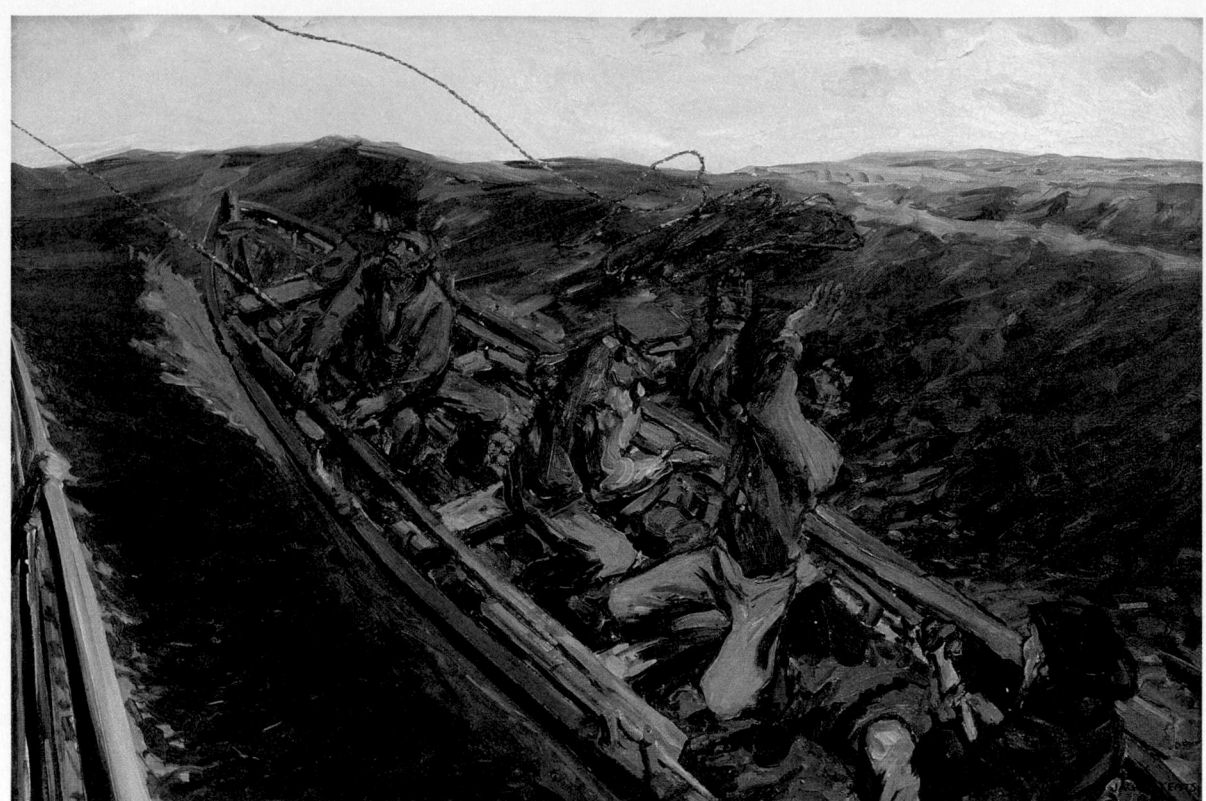

Off the Donegal Coast (1922), Jack Butler Yeats. Oil on canvas, 60.5 cm × 90.7 cm. © Crawford Municipal Art Gallery, Cork, Ireland/Bridgeman Art Library. © 2007 Artists Rights Society (ARS), New York/DACS, London.

Cathleen. The stick Michael brought from Connemara.

Maurya (*taking a stick* Nora *gives her*). In the big world the old people do be leaving things after them for their sons and children, but in this place it is the young men do be leaving things behind for them that do be old.

190 (*She goes out slowly.* Nora *goes over to the ladder.*)

Cathleen. Wait, Nora, maybe she'd turn back quickly. She's that sorry, God help her, you wouldn't know the thing she'd do.

Nora. Is she gone round by the bush?

Cathleen (*looking out*). She's gone now. Throw it down quickly, for the Lord knows when she'll be out of it again.

Nora (*getting the bundle from the loft*). The young priest said he'd be passing tomorrow, and we might 200 go down and speak to him below if it's Michael's they are surely.

Cathleen (*taking the bundle*). Did he say what way they were found?

Nora (*coming down*). "There were two men," says he, "and they rowing round with poteen[12] before the cocks crowed, and the oar of one of them caught the body, and they passing the black cliffs of the north."

Cathleen (*trying to open the bundle*). Give me a knife, Nora; the string's perished with the salt water, 210 and there's a black knot on it you wouldn't loosen in a week.

Nora (*giving her a knife*). I've heard tell it was a long way to Donegal.

Cathleen (*cutting the string*). It is surely. There was a man in here a while ago—the man sold us that knife—and he said if you set off walking from the rocks beyond, it would be in seven days you'd be in Donegal.

Nora. And what time would a man take, and he 220 floating?

---

12. **poteen** (pə-tēn′): illegally distilled whiskey; moonshine.

(Cathleen *opens the bundle and takes out a bit of a shirt and a stocking. They look at them eagerly.*)

Cathleen (*in a low voice*). The Lord spare us, Nora! isn't it a queer hard thing to say if it's his they are surely?

Nora. I'll get his shirt off the hook the way we can put the one flannel on the other. (*She looks through some clothes hanging in the corner.*) It's not with them, Cathleen, and where will it be?

230 **Cathleen.** I'm thinking Bartley put it on him in the morning, for his own shirt was heavy with the salt in it. (*pointing to the corner*) There's a bit of a sleeve was of the same stuff. Give me that and it will do.

(Nora *brings it to her and they compare the flannel.*)

Cathleen. It's the same stuff, Nora; but if it is itself, aren't there great rolls of it in the shops of Galway, and isn't it many another man may have a shirt of it as well as Michael himself?

Nora (*who has taken up the stocking and counted*
240 *the stitches, crying out*). It's Michael, Cathleen, it's Michael; God spare his soul, and what will herself say when she hears this story, and Bartley on the sea?

Cathleen (*taking the stocking*). It's a plain stocking.

Nora. It's the second one of the third pair I knitted, and I put up three-score[13] stitches, and I dropped four of them.

Cathleen (*counts the stitches*). It's that number is in it (*crying out*). Ah, Nora, isn't it a bitter thing to think of him floating that way to the far north, and
250 no one to keen[14] him but the black hags[15] that do be flying on the sea?

Nora (*swinging herself round, and throwing out her arms on the clothes*). And isn't it a pitiful thing when there is nothing left of a man who was a great rower and fisher but a bit of an old shirt and a plain stocking?

Cathleen (*after an instant*). Tell me is herself coming, Nora? I hear a little sound on the path.

Nora (*looking out*). She is, Cathleen. She's coming up to the door.

260 **Cathleen.** Put these things away before she'll come in. Maybe it's easier she'll be after giving her blessing to Bartley, and we won't let on we've heard anything the time he's on the sea.

Nora (*helping* Cathleen *to close the bundle*). We'll put them here in the corner.

(*They put them into a hole in the chimney corner.* Cathleen *goes back to the spinning-wheel.*)

Nora. Will she see it was crying I was?

Cathleen. Keep your back to the door the way the
270 light'll not be on you.

(Nora *sits down at the chimney corner, with her back to the door.* Maurya *comes in very slowly, without looking at the girls, and goes over to her stool at the other side of the fire. The cloth with the bread is still in her hand. The girls look at each other, and* Nora *points to the bundle of bread.*)

Cathleen (*after spinning for a moment*). You didn't give him his bit of bread?

(Maurya *begins to keen softly, without turning round.*)

280 **Cathleen.** Did you see him riding down?

(Maurya *goes on keening.*)

Cathleen (*a little impatiently*). God forgive you; isn't it a better thing to raise your voice and tell what you seen, than to be making lamentation for a thing that's done? Did you see Bartley, I'm saying to you?

Maurya (*with a weak voice*). My heart's broken from this day.

Cathleen (*as before*). Did you see Bartley?

Maurya. I seen the fearfulest thing.

290 **Cathleen** (*leaves her wheel and looks out*). God forgive you; he's riding the mare now over the green head, and the gray pony behind him.

Maurya (*Starts, so that her shawl falls back from her head and shows her white tossed hair. With a frightened voice*). The gray pony behind him. . . .

Cathleen (*coming to the fire*). What is it ails you at all?

---

13. **three-score:** 60. A score is 20.

14. **keen:** to wail over a dead body in mourning—a traditional Irish practice.

15. **black hags:** a literal translation of the Irish word for cormorants, dark sea birds that call out over the water.

Maurya (*speaking very slowly*). I've seen the fearfulest thing any person has seen since the day Bride Dara seen the dead man with the child in his arms.[16]

300 **Cathleen and Nora.** Uah.

(*They crouch down in front of the old woman at the fire.*)

Nora. Tell us what it is you seen.

Maurya. I went down to the spring well, and I stood there saying a prayer to myself. Then Bartley came along, and he riding on the red mare with the gray pony behind him. (*She puts up her hands, as if to hide something from her eyes.*) The Son of God spare us, Nora!

310 **Cathleen.** What is it you seen?

Maurya. I seen Michael himself.

Cathleen (*speaking softly*). You did not, mother. It wasn't Michael you seen, for his body is after being found in the far north, and he's got a clean burial, by the grace of God.

Maurya (*a little defiantly*). I'm after seeing him this day, and he riding and galloping. Bartley came first on the red mare, and I tried to say "God speed you," but something choked the words in my throat.

320 He went by quickly; and "the blessing of God on you," says he, and I could say nothing. I looked up then, and I crying, at the gray pony, and there was Michael upon it—with fine clothes on him, and new shoes on his feet.

Cathleen (*begins to keen*). It's destroyed we are from this day. It's destroyed, surely.

Nora. Didn't the young priest say the Almighty God won't leave her destitute with no son living?

Maurya (*in a low voice, but clearly*). It's little the
330 like of him knows of the sea. . . . Bartley will be lost now, and let you call in Eamon and make me a good coffin out of the white boards, for I won't live after them. I've had a husband, and a husband's father, and six sons in this house—six fine men,

though it was a hard birth I had with every one of them and they coming to the world—and some of them were found and some of them were not found, but they're gone now the lot of them. . . . There were Stephen and Shawn were lost in the great
340 wind, and found after in the Bay of Gregory of the Golden Mouth,[17] and carried up the two of them on one plank, and in by that door.

(*She pauses for a moment, the girls start as if they heard something through the door that is half open behind them.*)

Nora (*in a whisper*). Did you hear that, Cathleen? Did you hear a noise in the north-east?

Cathleen (*in a whisper*). There's someone after crying out by the seashore.

350 **Maurya** (*continues without hearing anything*). There was Sheamus and his father, and his own father again, were lost in a dark night, and not a stick or sign was seen of them when the sun went up. There was Patch after was drowned out of a curagh[18] that turned over. I was sitting here with Bartley, and he a baby lying on my two knees, and I seen two women, and three women, and four women coming in, and they crossing themselves and not saying a word. I looked out then, and there were men coming after
360 them, and they holding a thing in the half of a red sail, and water dripping out of it—it was a dry day, Nora—and leaving a track to the door.

(*She pauses again with her hand stretched out towards the door. It opens softly and old women begin to come in, crossing themselves on the threshold, and kneeling down in front of the stage with red petticoats over their heads.*[19])

Maurya (*half in a dream, to* Cathleen). Is it Patch, or Michael, or what is it at all?

370 **Cathleen.** Michael is after being found in the far north, and when he is found there how could he be here in this place?

---

16. **since the day Bride** (brī′dē) **. . . arms:** since Bride Dara saw a more frightening omen. *Bride,* often spelled *Bridie,* is a nickname for Bridget.

17. **Bay of . . . Mouth:** probably Gregory Sound, which separates the two larger Aran Islands.

18. **curagh** (cûr′ä): a small rowboat made of hides or canvas stretched over a wicker or wooden frame.

19. **red . . . heads:** Aran Island women traditionally wore red skirts; here, in their haste to reach the shore, the women had grabbed their skirts to use as shawls.

Maurya. There does be a power of young men floating round in the sea, and what way would they know if it was Michael they had, or another man like him, for when a man is nine days in the sea, and the wind blowing, it's hard set his own mother would be to say what man was in it.

Cathleen. It's Michael, God spare him, for they're
380 after sending us a bit of his clothes from the far north.

(*She reaches out and hands* Maurya *the clothes that belonged to Michael.* Maurya *stands up slowly, and takes them in her hands.* Nora *looks out.*)

Nora. They're carrying a thing among them, and there's water dripping out of it and leaving a track by the big stones.

Cathleen (*in a whisper to the women who have come in*). Is it Bartley it is?

390 **One of the Women.** It is, surely, God rest his soul.

(*Two younger women come in and pull out the table. Then men carry in the body of* Bartley, *laid on a plank, with a bit of a sail over it, and lay it on the table.*)

Cathleen (*to the women as they are doing so*). What way was he drowned?

One of the Women. The gray pony knocked him over into the sea, and he was washed out where there is a great surf on the white rocks.

400 (Maurya *has gone over and knelt down at the head of the table. The women are keening softly and swaying themselves with a slow movement.* Cathleen *and* Nora *kneel at the other end of the table. The men kneel near the door.*)

Maurya (*raising her head and speaking as if she did not see the people around her*). They're all gone now, and there isn't anything more the sea can do to me. . . . I'll have no call now to be up crying and praying when the wind breaks from the south, and
410 you can hear the surf is in the east, and the surf is in the west, making a great stir with the two noises, and they hitting one on the other. I'll have no call

Silent Man (1995), Andrew Gadd. Oil on canvas. Private collection.
© Bridgeman Art Library.

now to be going down and getting Holy Water[20] in the dark nights after Samhain,[21] and I won't care what way the sea is when the other women will be keening. (*to* Nora) Give me the Holy Water, Nora; there's a small sup still on the dresser.

(Nora *gives it to her.*)

420 **Maurya** (*drops Michael's clothes across* Bartley's *feet, and sprinkles the Holy Water over him*). It isn't that I haven't prayed for you, Bartley, to the Almighty God. It isn't that I haven't said prayers in the dark night till you wouldn't know what I'd be saying; but it's a great rest I'll have now, and it's time, surely. It's a great rest I'll have now, and great sleeping in the long nights after Samhain, if it's only a bit of wet flour we do have to eat, and maybe a fish that would be stinking.

(*She kneels down again, crossing herself, and saying* 430 *prayers under her breath.*)

Cathleen (*to an old man*). Maybe yourself and Eamon would make a coffin when the sun rises. We have fine white boards herself bought, God help her, thinking Michael would be found, and I have a new cake you can eat while you'll be working.

The Old Man (*looking at the boards*). Are there nails with them?

Cathleen. There are not, Colum; we didn't think of the nails.

440 **Another Man.** It's a great wonder she wouldn't think of the nails, and all the coffins she's seen made already.

Cathleen. It's getting old she is, and broken.

(Maurya *stands up again very slowly and spreads out the pieces of Michael's clothes beside the body, sprinkling them with the last of the Holy Water.*)

Nora (*in a whisper to* Cathleen). She's quiet now and easy; but the day Michael was drowned you could hear her crying out from this to the spring 450 well. It's fonder she was of Michael, and would any one have thought that?

Cathleen (*slowly and clearly*). An old woman will be soon tired with anything she will do, and isn't it nine days herself is after crying and keening, and making great sorrow in the house?

Maurya (*puts the empty cup mouth downwards on the table, and lays her hands together on* Bartley's *feet*). They're all together this time, and the end is come. May the Almighty God have mercy on Bartley's 460 soul, and on Michael's soul, and on the souls of Sheamus and Patch, and Stephen and Shawn (*bending her head*); and may He have mercy on my soul, Nora, and on the soul of every one is left living in the world.

(*She pauses, and the keen rises a little more loudly from the women, then sinks away.*)

Maurya (*continuing*). Michael has a clean burial in the far north, by the grace of the Almighty God. Bartley will have a fine coffin out of the white 470 boards, and a deep grave surely. What more can we want than that? No man at all can be living for ever, and we must be satisfied.

(*She kneels down again and the curtain falls slowly.*)

---

20. **Holy Water:** water blessed by a priest and used for religious purposes.

21. **Samhain** (sä-văn´): the Irish-language term for All Souls' Day or All Hallows' Day, a Christian holy day celebrated on November 1.

Comprehension

1. **Recall** What do Nora and Cathleen hope to find out from examining the clothes in the bundle?

2. **Clarify** Why does Maurya want to keep Bartley from going to the fair in Galway?

3. **Summarize** Describe the various mishaps Maurya and her family have experienced.

COMMON CORE

RL 3 Analyze the impact of the author's choices regarding how to develop and relate elements of a drama. **RL 10** Read and comprehend literature, including dramas. **L 1a** Apply the understanding that usage is a matter of convention.

Text Analysis

4. **Examine Dialogue** In his one-act play, Synge quickly establishes the main **characters** and the **conflict** they face. Reread the dialogue between Nora and Cathleen in lines 7–51. What important information do you learn about them and their difficulties in this exchange?

5. **Analyze Dialect** Consider how Synge's use of the Aran Island dialect contributes to his character portrayals. Would you have viewed Maurya and her family differently if they had spoken a more conventional form of English? Explain your answer.

6. **Interpret Mood** Review lines 146–154 and lines 289–324 in *Riders to the Sea*. What overall mood, or atmosphere, does the setting of the play help create?

7. **Understand Cultural Context** Look over the notes you recorded as you read the selection. In what ways was Synge influenced by each of the following aspects of Aran Island culture in his writing of *Riders to the Sea*? Cite details.

   • island setting   • religion   • fishing   • superstition

8. **Evaluate Dramatic Conventions** *Riders to the Sea* is a **tragedy**—a work that presents the downfall of a dignified character. In classical tragedies, the main character, or **hero,** has a **tragic flaw,** a quality that leads to his or her destruction. Often, other characters in the play will warn of the doom to come. To what extent does Synge's work conform to these conventions of tragedy?

9. **Compare Texts** Compare Synge's play with "For Men of Seaside Village, Lonely and Unfamiliar Roles" (page 1225). Is grief experienced similarly in the selections? Use details from both texts to support your response.

Text Criticism

10. **Social Context** What does Synge convey about the role of women in the society portrayed in *Riders to the Sea*? Provide examples from the play to support your response.

How much **GRIEF** *can one endure?*

People often have different reactions to the loss of a loved one. What are some ways to cope with the devastating loss of a sibling or close friend?

Language

◆ **GRAMMAR AND STYLE: Use Realistic Dialogue**

J. M. Synge strove to portray the characters in his plays as realistically as possible. One way he did this was to listen carefully to the lilting **dialect** of the Irish peasants he knew. He then reproduced their way of speaking in his plays to lend authenticity to the dialogue, as shown in this example:

> **Nora.** *Middling bad, God help us. There's a great roaring in the west, and it's worse it'll be getting when the tide's turned to the wind.* (She goes over to the table with the bundle.) *Shall I open it now?*

> **Cathleen.** *Maybe she'd wake up on us, and come in before we'd done* (coming to the table). *It's a long time we'll be, and the two of us crying.* (lines 39–45)

One feature of this particular Irish dialect is **inverted word order.** For example, notice how Nora says "it's worse it'll be getting" instead of "it'll be getting worse."

PRACTICE Review the way in which Synge constructs dialogue in *Riders to the Sea,* noting distinctive vocabulary, contractions, grammatical constructions, and word order that characterize the dialect used in the play. Then write six lines of dialogue that might have taken place between Nora and the young priest as he gave her the bundle of clothes. A sample has been done for you.

EXAMPLE

Priest: It's a drowned man in Donegal, the clothes were got off of. Find out if it's Michael's they are.

Nora: First, I'll have to see if herself is asleep. She's not slept much, God help her, for nine days.

READING-WRITING CONNECTION

YOUR TURN

Expand your understanding of dialogue by responding to this prompt. Then, use the **revising tips** to improve your dialogue.

WRITING PROMPT	**REVISING TIPS**
WRITE AN ALTERNATIVE ENDING Suppose that Bartley returns safely home, having gotten a good price for the horses. Write a **one-page dialogue** in which his mother and sisters welcome him home.	• Be sure to include some of the characteristic dialect used in the play. • Check to see that you have maintained a consistent tone and point of view. • Try to have the characters refer to some of the specific events or ideas in the play.

Interactive Revision **THINK** central

Go to **thinkcentral.com**.
KEYWORD: HML12-1224

COMMON CORE

L 3a Vary syntax for effect. **W 3a–c** Write narratives to develop imagined events; establish point of view; use narrative techniques, such as dialogue, to develop events and characters; build toward a particular tone.

NEWSPAPER ARTICLE This excerpt from a newspaper article describes the devastating effects of a tsunami that struck an Indonesian fishing village in 2004.

For Men of Seaside Village, Lonely and Unfamiliar Roles

ELLEN NAKASHIMA

LAMTEUNGOH, INDONESIA. Baharuddin, the head of this devastated Sumatran[1] fishing village, gently lifted the limp remains of his 11-year-old daughter, swaddled in a plaid sarong.[2]

"She was my youngest daughter," he said, gazing down mournfully and tenderly at the remains. "She was the most beautiful one."

He placed her in a communal grave not far from the sea, where a wall of black water crashed ashore last month and killed his wife and their five children. Baharuddin and two other villagers laid two other bodies in the grave and shoveled soil on top.

Then he and nine other men crouched under the searing sun, hands outstretched, palms turned up, and prayed.

When the tsunami[3] inundated the northern and western coasts of Indonesia's Aceh province, killing more than 100,000 people, most of the victims in seaside villages like this one were women and children. Three out of four of the survivors in relief camps are men or boys, according to United Nations officials.

Many in these coastal towns were fishermen who survived at sea or farmers in the hills above the high water line. But their wives and children were killed at home not far from the beach when the driving waves turned the village into ruins on December 26.

In Lamteungoh, there are 105 widowers and only 19 widows. These rugged men

Survivors pray for their loved ones.

are now grappling with unfamiliar roles, dependent on one another and uncertain about what comes next. With their families gone, some say their lives have lost purpose. They are caring for children in communal style and tending to the injured. They are struggling to move through their grief and reclaim their future.

"Life today has no meaning at all for me," said Baharuddin, 49, who has thinning hair, a furrowed brow, and a fisherman's lean, wiry body, tanned to a dark chocolate hue. "Now, suppose I find a job and make money. To whom can I distribute it?" he asked rhetorically, seated on a log in the rubble-strewn village and smoking a clove cigarette. "I have no wife anymore. No children anymore." . . .

---

1. **Sumatran** (sŏŏ-mä′trən): referring to the large Indonesian island of Sumatra.
2. **sarong** (sə-rông′): a long, often brightly colored strip of cloth worn draped over the hips like a skirt.
3. **tsunami** (tsŏŏ-nä′mē): a huge sea wave caused by a great disturbance under the ocean, such as an earthquake; sometimes called a tidal wave.

from Pygmalion

Video link at
thinkcentral.com

Drama by George Bernard Shaw

George Bernard Shaw
1856–1950

COMMON CORE

RL 10 Read and comprehend
literature, including dramas.
SL 1a Come to discussions
prepared, having read material
under study; explicitly draw on
that preparation by referring to
evidence from texts to stimulate
a thoughtful, well-reasoned
exchange of ideas.

BACKGROUND George Bernard Shaw might be described as a late bloomer. Born in Dublin, Ireland, in the early decades of the Victorian age, it was not until the dawn of the 20th century that he began to enjoy sustained success as a playwright, winning both critical and popular acclaim and the 1925 Nobel Prize in literature for plays such as *Major Barbara, Pygmalion, Saint Joan,* and many others.

Shaw's *Pygmalion,* his attack on the British class system, is considered one of his funniest plays; it is also one of his most popular. The play's title refers to the Pygmalion of Greek mythology, a sculptor who created a figure of a woman so beautiful that he fell in love with it. In Shaw's *Pygmalion,* a confirmed bachelor and professor of languages named Henry Higgins "shapes the clay" of a low-born young woman named Eliza Doolittle by teaching her proper English. In the following scene, Henry Higgins, known at first only as "The Note Taker," along with Colonel Pickering, "The Gentleman," meet flower-seller Eliza Doolittle among a crowd of people who have taken shelter from a downpour on the porch of a church near London's Covent Garden Theatre. Eliza complains when she realizes that Higgins has been taking notes about what she has been saying.

TEXT ANALYSIS The English language plays a key role in Shaw's *Pygmalion.* The characters' dialogue defines the broad social gap between them. Eliza speaks the Cockney dialect of London's East End, one of the city's poorest areas, occupied by immigrants and working-class British. Higgins and Pickering, one the other hand, use "Queen's English," speech associated with aristocracy and the educated. Dialogue is important, but **stage directions** also provide useful clues: Characters' facial expressions, tones of voice, and body language provide valuable insights into their social status and how they treat people from social classes different from their own. Notice how the stage directions tell us that Higgins speaks to Eliza "explosively," as if it is acceptable to speak rudely to a stranger if the stranger is of a lower social class. Notice, too, how Eliza responds. She attempts to defend herself, but she does so "with feeble defiance," as if she has no right to object to Higgins' treatment of her because of his superior social position.

DISCUSS After you have read the scene, discuss additional examples of stage directions, making specific reference to the text. What do these stage directions reveal about each character's personality? What do they reveal about the social differences between the characters and how they view one another?

The Note Taker (*explosively*). Woman: cease this detestable boohooing instantly; or else seek the shelter of some other place of worship.

The Flower Girl (*with feeble defiance*). I've a right to be here if I like, same as you.

The Note Taker. A woman who utters such depressing and disgusting sounds has no right to be anywhere—no right to live. Remember that you are a human being with a soul and the divine gift of articulate speech: that your native language is the language of Shakespeare and Milton and The Bible; and don't sit there crooning like a bilious pigeon.

10 **The Flower Girl** (*quite overwhelmed, looking up at him in mingled wonder and deprecation without daring to raise her head*). Ah-ah-ah-ow-ow-ow-oo!

The Note Taker (*whipping out his book*). Heavens! what a sound! (*He writes; then holds out the book and reads, reproducing her vowels exactly.*) Ah-ah-ah-ow-ow-ow-oo!

The Flower Girl (*tickled by the performance, and laughing in spite of herself*). Garn!

The Note Taker. You see this creature with her kerbstone English: the English that will keep her in the gutter to the end of her days. Well, sir, in three months I could pass that girl off as a duchess at an ambassador's garden party. I could even get her a place as lady's maid or shop assistant, which requires better English.

The Flower Girl. What's that you say?

20 **The Note Taker.** Yes, you squashed cabbage leaf, you disgrace of the noble architecture of these columns, you incarnate insult to the English language: I could pass you off as the Queen of Sheba. (*to the* Gentleman) Can you believe that?

The Gentleman. Of course I can. I am myself a student of Indian dialects; and—

The Note Taker (*eagerly*). Are you? Do you know Colonel Pickering, the author of Spoken Sanscrit?

The Gentleman. I am Colonel Pickering. Who are you?

The Note Taker. Henry Higgins, author of Higgins's Universal Alphabet.

Pickering (*with enthusiasm*). I came from India to meet you.

Higgins. I was going to India to meet you.

30 **Pickering.** Where do you live?

Higgins. 27A Wimpole Street. Come and see me tomorrow.

Pickering. I'm at the Carlton. Come with me now and let's have a jaw over some supper.

Higgins. Right you are.

The Demon Lover
Short Story by Elizabeth Bowen

DID YOU KNOW?

Elizabeth Bowen . . .

- served as an air-raid warden in London during World War II.
- counted writers Edith Sitwell, Aldous Huxley, and Virginia Woolf among her friends.

Meet the Author

Elizabeth Bowen 1899–1973

One of the 20th century's most important Anglo-Irish authors, Elizabeth Bowen published 10 novels and more than 70 short stories. Her fiction, which deals primarily with the upper middle class, is beautifully crafted, with finely drawn characters and detailed, evocative descriptions of setting.

Neither English Nor Irish Born in Dublin, Ireland, of Anglo-Irish parents, Bowen spent her early childhood at Bowen's Court, a large stately home that had been in the family since the 18th century. Although her family was well-to-do, her childhood was unsettled. When Bowen was seven, her father suffered a nervous breakdown, and Bowen was sent to England with her mother and a governess. Six years later, her mother died from cancer.

The death of her mother was one of the pivotal events of Bowen's life. The sense of abandonment she felt is evident in much of her fiction, which often explores the themes of grief, displacement, and lost innocence.

The Fulfillment of a Dream In 1923, Bowen married Alan Cameron, an educator. That year, she also published her first collection of stories, *Encounters;* the book was an immediate success, which Bowen found very encouraging. She had always dreamed of being a writer, once stating, "From the moment that my pen touched paper, I thought of nothing but writing, and since then I have thought of practically nothing else. . . .[W]hen I have nothing to write, I feel only half alive."

Life During Wartime In 1935, Bowen and Cameron moved to London. Many of her best works take place in wartime London, a setting she presents with realism and force. In fact, British novelist and critic Angus Wilson asserted that the short stories Bowen wrote during the war provide some of the best documentation— fact or fiction—of the psychological effects war had on Londoners. Her acclaimed novel *The Heat of the Day* (1949) also takes place in the battered city.

Diverse and Distinguished Bowen's literary career was diverse as well as distinguished. In addition to publishing a new book almost every year, she wrote essays and book reviews for prestigious journals such as the *Tatler,* the *Spectator,* and the *New York Times Magazine.* She also was appointed a Commander of the Order of the British Empire and was awarded honorary doctorates from Oxford University and Trinity College in Dublin.

THINKcentral

Author Online

Go to **thinkcentral.com**. KEYWORD: HML12-1228

● TEXT ANALYSIS: FORESHADOWING AND FLASHBACK

Authors of dark, spine-tingling tales like "The Demon Lover" often rely on the following narrative techniques to engage readers:

- **Foreshadowing**—a writer's use of hints and clues to indicate events that will occur later in the story. Writers often generate **suspense,** or excitement, through foreshadowing.

- **Flashback**—an episode that interrupts the action of the story's plot to show an experience that happened at an earlier time. Writers often provide important background information about characters in flashbacks.

As you read, notice how Bowen uses both foreshadowing and flashback to build your interest in the story.

● READING SKILL: ANALYZE AMBIGUITY

In fiction, **ambiguity** refers to the way in which a writer intentionally presents aspects of a story as confusing or open to interpretation. Writers often create ambiguity with words, phrases, and passages that have multiple meanings, as in the following lines from "The Demon Lover":

A cat wove itself in and out of railings, but no human eye watched Mrs. Drover's return.

The phrase "no human eye" could mean that nobody watched Mrs. Drover or something far more disturbing—that no *human* watched her. As you read the story, create a chart like the one shown to record and interpret examples of ambiguity.

Examples of Ambiguity	Possible Interpretations
the mysterious letter (lines 32–51)	The caretaker, Mr. Drover, or an unknown character left the letter.

▲ VOCABULARY IN CONTEXT

Use context clues to figure out the meanings of the boldfaced words.

1. Clearly he was no visionary, for his speech was **prosaic.**
2. The white moths had a **spectral** appearance in the night sky.
3. Never stingy, she gave without **stint** to many charities.
4. Official duties can **circumscribe** the life of a princess.
5. Brilliant ideas often **emanate** from creative discussions.

 Complete the activities in your **Reader/Writer Notebook.**

How can a PROMISE *haunt you?*

"The Demon Lover" is set in 1941 during the Blitz, the bombardment of London by the German air force. Against this dramatic backdrop, the story's main character, Mrs. Drover, recalls her romantic past, including a dreadful promise made to a soldier going off to battle.

DISCUSS With a partner, make a list of short stories, novels, and movies that feature a character making an important promise. Discuss the promise, the character, and the character's reasons for offering the promise. Explain whether the character keeps or breaks the promise by the end of the work.

The Demon Lover

Elizabeth Bowen

> **BACKGROUND** The onset of World War II placed a tremendous physical and psychological burden on Londoners. From September 1940 to May 1941, the German air force launched a series of bombing raids designed to obliterate London and force Great Britain to surrender. Many families evacuated the city and moved to country villages and towns. Those who could not leave took refuge in subway tunnels and air-raid shelters during the long nights of horror.

Towards the end of her day in London Mrs. Drover went round to her shut-up house to look for several things she wanted to take away. Some belonged to herself, some to her family, who were by now used to their country life. It was late August; it had been a steamy, showery day: at the moment the trees down the pavement glittered in an escape of humid yellow afternoon sun. Against the next batch of clouds, already piling up ink-dark, broken chimneys and parapets[1] stood out. In her once familiar street, as in any unused channel, an unfamiliar queerness had silted up;[2] a cat wove itself in and out of railings, but no human eye watched Mrs. Drover's return. Shifting some parcels under her arm, she slowly forced
10 round her latchkey in an unwilling lock, then gave the door, which had warped, a push with her knee. Dead air came out to meet her as she went in. **A**

The staircase window having been boarded up, no light came down into the hall. But one door, she could just see, stood ajar, so she went quickly through into the room and unshuttered the big window in there. Now the **prosaic** woman, looking about her, was more perplexed than she knew by everything that she saw, by traces of her long former habit of life—the yellow smoke stain up the white

Analyze Visuals ▶
Why do you think the photographer chose to tint and blur this image?

A FORESHADOWING
In lines 1–11, what details suggest that Mrs. Drover may be unsafe in her London home?

prosaic (prō-zā´ĭk) *adj.* not given to poetic flights of fancy; lacking imagination; dull

---

1. **parapets** (păr´ə-pĭts): low walls or railings, such as those on balconies.
2. **silted up:** piled up, like sediment deposited in a river.

marble mantelpiece, the ring left by a vase on the top of the escritoire;[3] the bruise in the wallpaper where, on the door being thrown open widely, the china handle had always hit the wall. The piano, having gone away to be stored, had left what

20 looked like claw marks on its part of the parquet.[4] Though not much dust had seeped in, each object wore a film of another kind; and, the only ventilation being the chimney, the whole drawing room smelled of the cold hearth. Mrs. Drover put down her parcels on the escritoire and left the room to proceed upstairs; the things she wanted were in a bedroom chest.

She had been anxious to see how the house was—the part-time caretaker she shared with some neighbors was away this week on his holiday, known to be not yet back. At the best of times he did not look in often, and she was never sure that she trusted him. There were some cracks in the structure, left by the last bombing, on which she was anxious to keep an eye. Not that one could do anything—

30 A shaft of refracted daylight now lay across the hall. She stopped dead and stared at the hall table—on this lay a letter addressed to her.

She thought first—then the caretaker *must* be back. All the same, who, seeing the house shuttered, would have dropped a letter in at the box? It was not a circular, it was not a bill. And the post office redirected, to the address in the country, everything for her that came through the post. The caretaker (even if he *were* back) did not know she was due in London today—her call here had been planned to be a surprise—so his negligence in the manner of this letter, leaving it to wait in the dusk and the dust, annoyed her. Annoyed, she picked up the letter, which bore no stamp. But it cannot be important, or they would know . . . She

40 took the letter rapidly upstairs with her, without a stop to look at the writing till she reached what had been her bedroom, where she let in light. The room looked over the garden and other gardens: the sun had gone in; as the clouds sharpened and lowered, the trees and rank[5] lawns seemed already to smoke with dark. Her reluctance to look again at the letter came from the fact that she felt intruded upon—and by someone contemptuous of her ways. However, in the tenseness preceding the fall of rain she read it: it was a few lines.

> *Dear Kathleen: You will not have forgotten that today is our anniversary, and the day we said. The years have gone by at once slowly and fast. In view of the fact that nothing has changed, I shall rely upon you to keep your promise. I was sorry to*
> 50 *see you leave London, but was satisfied that you would be back in time. You may expect me, therefore, at the hour arranged. Until then . . .*   K. **B**

Mrs. Drover looked for the date: it was today's. She dropped the letter onto the bedsprings, then picked it up to see the writing again—her lips, beneath the remains of lipstick, beginning to go white. She felt so much the change in her own face that she went to the mirror, polished a clear patch in it and looked at once urgently and stealthily in. She was confronted by a woman of forty-four,

B AMBIGUITY
Reread lines 47–51. Who is "K," the author of the mysterious letter? Offer two possible identifications for this ambiguous character.

---

3. **escritoire** (ĕs'krĭ-twär'): a writing desk or table.

4. **parquet** (pär-kā'): a wood floor made of small blocks laid in geometric patterns.

5. **rank:** growing vigorously and coarsely.

with eyes starting out under a hat brim that had been rather carelessly pulled down. She had not put on any more powder since she left the shop where she ate her solitary tea. The pearls her husband had given her on their marriage hung
60 loose round her now rather thinner throat, slipping in the V of the pink wool jumper[6] her sister knitted last autumn as they sat round the fire. Mrs. Drover's most normal expression was one of controlled worry, but of assent. Since the birth of the third of her little boys, attended by a quite serious illness, she had had an intermittent muscular flicker to the left of her mouth, but in spite of this she could always sustain a manner that was at once energetic and calm.

Turning from her own face as precipitately as she had gone to meet it, she went to the chest where the things were, unlocked it, threw up the lid and knelt to search. But as rain began to come crashing down she could not keep from looking over her shoulder at the stripped bed on which the letter lay. Behind the blanket
70 of rain the clock of the church that still stood struck six—with rapidly heightening apprehension she counted each of the slow strokes. "The hour arranged . . . My God," she said, "*what* hour? How should I . . . ? After twenty-five years . . ."

The young girl talking to the soldier in the garden had not ever completely seen his face. It was dark; they were saying goodbye under a tree. Now and then—for it felt, from not seeing him at this intense moment, as though she had never seen him at all—she verified his presence for these few moments longer by putting out a hand, which he each time pressed, without very much kindness, and painfully, onto one of the breast buttons of his uniform. That cut of the button on the palm of her hand was, principally, what she was to carry away. This was
80 so near the end of a leave from France that she could only wish him already gone. It was August 1916.[7] Being not kissed, being drawn away from and looked at, intimidated Kathleen till she imagined **spectral** glitters in the place of his eyes. Turning away and looking back up the lawn she saw, through branches of trees, the drawing-room window alight: she caught a breath for the moment when she could go running back there into the safe arms of her mother and sister, and cry: "What shall I do, what shall I do? He has gone."

Hearing her catch her breath, her fiancé said, without feeling: "Cold?"

"You're going away such a long way."

"Not so far as you think."
90 "I don't understand?"

"You don't have to," he said. "You will. You know what we said."

"But that was—suppose you—I mean, suppose."

"I shall be with you," he said, "sooner or later. You won't forget that. You need do nothing but wait."

Only a little more than a minute later she was free to run up the silent lawn. Looking in through the window at her mother and sister, who did not for the moment perceive her, she already felt that unnatural promise drive down between her and the rest of all humankind. No other way of having given herself could

COMMON CORE L 4b

Language Coach

Derivations Many different words are **derived**, or generated, from the same base word. A precipice, which comes from a Latin word meaning "headlong fall," is a steep cliff. How is *precipitately* (line 66), meaning "suddenly," related to *precipice*? What other word derivations are related to *precipice*?

spectral (spĕk′trəl) *adj.* ghostly

---

6. **jumper:** pullover sweater.
7. **leave . . . 1916:** The young man was on leave from the fighting in France during World War I.

have made her feel so apart, lost and foresworn.[8] She could not have plighted a
100 more sinister troth.[9] **C**

Kathleen behaved well when, some months later, her fiancé was reported
missing, presumed killed. Her family not only supported her but were able to
praise her courage without **stint** because they could not regret, as a husband for
her, the man they knew almost nothing about. They hoped she would, in a year
or two, console herself—and had it been only a question of consolation things
might have gone much straighter ahead. But her trouble, behind just a little grief,
was a complete dislocation from everything. She did not reject other lovers, for
these failed to appear: for years she failed to attract men—and with the approach
of her thirties she became natural enough to share her family's anxiousness on
110 this score. She began to put herself out, to wonder; and at thirty-two she was very
greatly relieved to find herself being courted by William Drover. She married
him, and the two of them settled down in this quiet, arboreal part of Kensington:[10]
in this house the years piled up, her children were born and they all lived till they
were driven out by the bombs of the next war. Her movements as Mrs. Drover
were **circumscribed,** and she dismissed any idea that they were still watched.

As things were—dead or living the letter-writer sent her only a threat. Unable,
for some minutes, to go on kneeling with her back exposed to the empty room,
Mrs. Drover rose from the chest to sit on an upright chair whose back was firmly
against the wall. The desuetude[11] of her former bedroom, her married London
120 home's whole air of being a cracked cup from which memory, with its reassuring
power, had either evaporated or leaked away, made a crisis—and at just this crisis
the letter-writer had, knowledgeably, struck. The hollowness of the house this
evening canceled years on years of voices, habits and steps. Through the shut
windows she only heard rain fall on the roofs around. To rally herself, she said she
was in a mood—and for two or three seconds shutting her eyes, told herself that
she had imagined the letter. But she opened them—there it lay on the bed.

On the supernatural side of the letter's entrance she was not permitting her
mind to dwell. Who, in London, knew she meant to call at the house today?
Evidently, however, this had been known. The caretaker, *had* he come back,
130 had had no cause to expect her: he would have taken the letter in his pocket, to
forward it, at his own time, through the post. There was no other sign that the
caretaker had been in—but, if not? Letters dropped in at doors of deserted houses
do not fly or walk to tables in halls. They do not sit on the dust of empty tables
with the air of certainty that they will be found. There is needed some human
hand—but nobody but the caretaker had a key. Under circumstances she did not
care to consider, a house can be entered without a key. It was possible that she
was not alone now. She might be being waited for, downstairs. Waited for—until
when? Until "the hour arranged." At least that was not six o'clock: six has struck.

She rose from the chair and went over and locked the door.

C **FLASHBACK**
Reread the flashback
in lines 73–100. What
important information
do you learn about Mrs.
Drover and the writer
of the letter in this
episode?

stint (stĭnt) *n.* limitation;
restriction

circumscribe
(sûr′kəm-skrīb′) *v.* to
restrict; to limit

---

8. **foresworn:** guilty of perjury.

9. **plighted . . . troth:** made a more ominous promise of marriage.

10. **arboreal** (är-bôr′ē-əl) **. . . Kensington:** woodsy part of Kensington, a residential London neighborhood.

11. **desuetude** (děs′wĭ-tōōd′): disuse.

Language Coach

Meanings of Idioms
Idioms are expressions that have a special meaning different from the dictionary meaning of the words. In some contexts, the expression *the thing* can mean "that which is important or essential." Paraphrase "The thing was, to get out" (line 140).

140　　The thing was, to get out. To fly? No, not that: she had to catch her train. As a woman whose utter dependability was the keystone of her family life she was not willing to return to the country, to her husband, her little boys and her sister, without the objects she had come up to fetch. Resuming work at the chest she set about making up a number of parcels in a rapid, fumbling-decisive way. These, with her shopping parcels, would be too much to carry; these meant a taxi—at the thought of the taxi her heart went up and her normal breathing resumed. I will ring up the taxi now; the taxi cannot come too soon: I shall hear the taxi out there running its engine, till I walk calmly down to it through the hall. I'll ring up—But no: the telephone is cut off . . . She tugged at a knot she had tied wrong.

150　　The idea of flight . . . He was never kind to me, not really. I don't remember him kind at all. Mother said he never considered me. He was set on me, that was what it was—not love. Not love, not meaning a person well. What did he do, to make me promise like that? I can't remember—But she found that she could.

　　She remembered with such dreadful acuteness that the twenty-five years since then dissolved like smoke and she instinctively looked for the weal[12] left by the button on the palm of her hand. She remembered not only all that he said and did but the complete suspension of *her* existence during that August week. I was not myself—they all told me so at the time. She remembered—but with one white burning blank as where acid has dropped on a photograph: *under no conditions*
160　　could she remember his face.

　　So, wherever he may be waiting, I shall not know him. You have no time to run from a face you do not expect.

　　The thing was to get to the taxi before any clock struck what could be the hour. She would slip down the street and round the side of the square to where the square gave on the main road. She would return in the taxi, safe, to her own door, and bring the solid driver into the house with her to pick up the parcels from room to room. The idea of the taxi driver made her decisive, bold: she unlocked her door, went to the top of the staircase and listened down.

　　She heard nothing—but while she was hearing nothing the *passé*[13] air of the
170　　staircase was disturbed by a draft that traveled up to her face. It **emanated** from the basement: down there a door or window was being opened by someone who chose this moment to leave the house.

　　The rain had stopped; the pavements steamily shone as Mrs. Drover let herself out by inches from her own front door into the empty street. The unoccupied houses opposite continued to meet her look with their damaged stare. Making towards the thoroughfare and the taxi, she tried not to keep looking behind. Indeed, the silence was so intense—one of those creeks of London silence exaggerated this summer by the damage of war—that no tread could have gained on hers unheard. Where her street debouched[14] on the square where people
180　　went on living, she grew conscious of, and checked, her unnatural pace. Across

emanate (ĕm′ə-nāt′) *v.* to issue forth

---

12. **weal:** a mark or ridge raised on the skin; a welt.

13. *passé* (pă-sā′) *French:* old; stale.

14. **debouched** (dĭ-bôcht′): emerged.

the open end of the square two buses impassively passed each other: women, a perambulator,[15] cyclists, a man wheeling a barrow signalized, once again, the ordinary flow of life. At the square's most populous corner should be—and was— the short taxi rank. This evening, only one taxi—but this, although it presented its blank rump, appeared already to be alertly waiting for her. Indeed, without looking round the driver started his engine as she panted up from behind and put her hand on the door. As she did so, the clock struck seven. The taxi faced the main road: to make the trip back to her house it would have to turn—she had settled back on the seat and the taxi *had* turned before she, surprised by its
190 knowing movement, recollected that she had not "said where." She leaned forward to scratch at the glass panel that divided the driver's head from her own.

The driver braked to what was almost a stop, turned round and slid the glass panel back: the jolt of this flung Mrs. Drover forward till her face was almost into the glass. Through the aperture[16] driver and passenger, not six inches between them, remained for an eternity eye to eye. Mrs. Drover's mouth hung open for some seconds before she could issue her first scream. After that she continued to scream freely and to beat with her gloved hands on the glass all round as the taxi, accelerating without mercy, made off with her into the hinterland[17] of deserted streets. ❧ **D**

> **D AMBIGUITY**
> Identify two possible interpretations of the story's conclusion. What effect does this ambiguous ending have on you as a reader?

---

15. **perambulator:** baby carriage.
16. **aperture** (ăp′ər-chər): opening.
17. **hinterland:** backcountry; wilderness.

Comprehension

1. **Recall** Why has the Drover family left their home in London?

2. **Recall** Why does Mrs. Drover return to the house?

3. **Summarize** Describe what happens after Mrs. Drover leaves the house.

Text Analysis

4. **Understand Setting and Mood** Review the description of the story's setting in lines 1–24. What mood, or atmosphere, does this passage establish? Cite specific words and phrases to support your answer.

5. **Examine Foreshadowing** Reread the following passages from "The Demon Lover." In what specific ways do they hint at important events presented later in the story?

   • "Her reluctance . . . of her ways." (lines 43–45)
   • "Only a little more . . . a more sinister troth." (lines 95–100)
   • "She heard nothing . . . leave the house." (lines 169–172)

6. **Draw Conclusions About Character** Describe the thoughts and behavior of Mrs. Drover in each of the following scenes. Do you think that she is a victim of her own troubled mind, some supernatural force, or a combination of these?

   • her reaction to the mysterious letter (lines 52–65)
   • her farewell meeting with her former fiancé (lines 73–100)
   • her memories as she packs (lines 150–160)

7. **Analyze Ambiguity** Review the chart in which you recorded different examples of ambiguity. Identify the ambiguous word, phrase, or passage that you found most intriguing or effective. In your opinion, what does this example contribute to the story?

8. **Evaluate Flashback** Reread the flashback in lines 73–100. Would the story be as powerful if the events had been told in chronological order without the use of flashback? Explain your thoughts.

Text Criticism

9. **Cultural Context** The title of Bowen's story derives from a figure in gothic literature, the demon lover—a man who abducts his sweetheart because she has broken her promise of faithfulness. The sweetheart happily follows her lover, only to discover too late that he is leading her toward death. In what ways does this information enhance your understanding of the story?

> *How can a* **PROMISE** *haunt you?*
>
> Do you think the protagonist of Bowen's story got what she deserved for breaking her promise? Why or why not?

COMMON CORE

RL 1 Cite evidence to support inferences drawn from the text, including determining where the text leaves matters uncertain.
RL 5 Analyze how an author's choices concerning how to structure specific parts of a text contribute to its overall structure and meaning as well as its aesthetic impact.

Vocabulary in Context

▲ VOCABULARY PRACTICE

Identify the antonym of each boldfaced vocabulary word.

1. **prosaic:** (a) prosperous, (b) everyday, (c) imaginative
2. **spectral:** (a) gloomy, (b) whimsical, (c) substantial
3. **stint:** (a) weakness, (b) generosity, (c) beginning
4. **circumscribe:** (a) control, (b) decide, (c) release
5. **emanate:** (a) influence, (b) absorb, (c) exude

ACADEMIC VOCABULARY IN SPEAKING

- approach • assume • environment • method • strategy

How do you **approach** the existence of the supernatural? Do you **assume** that ghosts and other supernatural figures may be real or do you think they are merely projections of the human mind? Discuss this question in a small group. Use at least two of the Academic Vocabulary words in your discussion.

⋯ **COMMON CORE**

L 6 Acquire and use accurately general academic and domain-specific words and phrases.

VOCABULARY STRATEGY: THE LATIN PREFIX *circum-*

The word *circumscribe* joins the prefix *circum-*, which means "around," to the root *scribe*, which comes from the Latin word for "to write." *Circumscribe* means "to write marks or a circle around someone or something," setting limits within which that person or thing can operate. *Circumscribe* also has a technical academic meaning: in geometry, it describes, for example, a circle surrounding and intersecting the corners of a square. Each word in the web diagram at right has a technical, academic usage. Some are also used in everyday speech.

circum**navigate**

circum**polar** — **circum-** — circum**stantial**

circum**ference**   circum**locution**

PRACTICE Use context clues and your knowledge of word parts to explain the meaning of each boldfaced word. Then, where possible, use the boldfaced word in an everyday sense. Note whether the common, everyday sense of the word is different from its technical meaning.

1. **Circumstantial** evidence—namely, motive and opportunity— pointed to the defendant's guilt; but no physical evidence linked her to the crime.
2. One form of euphemism, the substitution of mild or vague language for harsh, realistic terminology, is **circumlocution**.
3. The formula for the **circumference** of a circle is $2\pi r$.
4. Was Magellan the first explorer to **circumnavigate** the globe?
5. **Circumpolar** objects, such as stars, never sink below the horizon.

Interactive Vocabulary **THINK**central

Go to **thinkcentral.com**.
KEYWORD: HML12-1238

The Flowering of Irish Letters

For hundreds of years, Irish literature written in English did not have its own identity. However, in the 20th century, as Ireland undertook its quest for national independence and rebounded from the devastation of the potato famine, the Irish began to take stock of their own cultural heritage.

Led by William Butler Yeats, writers of the Irish literary revival vigorously explored Irish identity. Some wrote explicitly about such topics as Irish rural life, the effects of colonialism, and Irish folklore. Others wrote about classical topics or accounts of modern life, but always with an ear for the lyricism of Irish speech and a sensitivity toward common themes such as spirituality and repression, often tinged with fatalism. Also, modern Irish writers shared the clever and sometimes dark wit typical of their countrymen.

Writing to Compare

The Irish writers in this section explore different subject matter, but they share similarities in theme and tone. Choose two selections and write an essay comparing them, supporting your ideas with examples from both texts.

Consider

- each author's use of imagery and figurative language
- each author's tone, or attitude toward the subject
- the themes represented

Your two topics should be clearly organized and linked with transitions and sentence structures that make your comparison clear.

Extension Online

INQUIRY & RESEARCH Use the Internet to research the political and cultural conditions surrounding the Irish Literary Renaissance. What values were being expressed? How did the movement spread? How was this literature received by the public? Write a brief report to explain your findings.

COMMON CORE

W 2 Write explanatory texts to examine and convey complex ideas through the effective selection, organization, and analysis of content. **W 2b–c** Select quotations or other information and examples; use appropriate transitions and syntax to clarify the relationships among complex ideas and concepts. **W 7** Conduct short research projects to answer a question; synthesize multiple sources on the subject. **W 9a (RL 2, RL 4)** Determine themes of a text; determine figurative meanings; analyze the impact of word choices on meaning and tone.

Anglo-Irish writer Elizabeth Bowen at Bowen's Court, her ancestral home in County Cork, Ireland

Literature as Social Criticism

Can literature shape public opinion? When does a poem become a political statement, a story become a social force? In every society, there are writers who serve as witnesses to corruption and injustice. They create stories, poems, essays, and dramas to depict the problems they observe and to expose what they perceive to be moral or political failings. These literary works subsequently influence the way people think about the issues.

The Sharp Point of the Pen

Social criticism is a term used to distinguish literature that addresses specific political, social, economic, cultural, or religious issues. Throughout the history of English literature, writers have based their works on such issues. In the early 18th century, Jonathan Swift's fantasy *Gulliver's Travels* served as social criticism by satirizing political ideas and practices that Swift felt were either wrong or downright ridiculous. In the 19th century, Charles Dickens used his novels to expose the darker side of England's industrial development. Writers of the 20th century have often used literary works as commentary on the effects of war, the deplorable conditions of poverty, the results of oppression, and the fight for civil rights. For example, English poet Siegfried Sassoon wrote poems that graphically depicted the horrors of World War I in order to make a statement about the effects of war.

England has had complex relationships with its neighbors in the United Kingdom and with countries that were once British colonies. In the later decades of the 20th century, political conflicts and culture clashes inspired writers of the British Commonwealth to create fiction and poetry based on those conflicts and on the struggles for peace and justice. Writers Chinua Achebe, Wole Soyinka, Nadine Gordimer, and William Trevor are a few who have taken up the cause in their literary works.

Socially Active Ingredients

Typically, the writers whose works contain social criticism hope to do more than merely entertain readers. Although their reasons for addressing political and social problems may vary, most writers feel a responsibility to make readers aware of certain facts. Sometimes a writer's motives may be personal, based on direct experiences; in other instances, the writer may simply be presenting thoughts on a problem that has concerned him or her.

COMMON CORE

Included in this workshop:
RL 1 Cite evidence to support inferences drawn from the text.
RL 9 Demonstrate knowledge of works of literature, including how two or more texts from the same period treat similar themes or topics.

Fiction writers differ in the way they introduce social criticism into their works. One or more of the following elements may be evident in a single work.

Treatment of an Issue In some stories, a political or social issue may dominate the entire plot and become the central theme around which all actions revolve. In other stories, the social criticism is less direct, and the political or social issue serves as a backdrop for another situation. Often, the most striking examples of social criticism in fiction are those in which writers present the truth about situations without injecting their personal beliefs, thereby allowing readers to form their own opinions. In "The Distant Past" (page 1320), William Trevor illustrates how a large problem—the growing hostility between Protestants and Catholics in Northern Ireland—creates conflict between neighbors, but he does not directly pass judgment on the conflict.

Use of Tone Other writers convey their views through the use of tone. Nadine Gordimer, in her story "Six Feet of the Country" (page 1342), sharpens her social criticism with irony and casts a critical eye on her main character.

Focus on Individuals Typically, writers cast their characters as ordinary individuals caught up in the context of larger world issues. The reader then observes how the larger issues affect the motives, behaviors, and destinies of real people. Some writers simply dramatize a demeaning personal experience in order to shed light on a larger social problem; Wole Soyinka uses this approach in his poem "Telephone Conversation" (page 1334). Other poets, such as Siegfried Sassoon, paint a broad portrait and slowly pull the reader into the personal, as shown in this example.

TWO WRITERS' VIEWS OF SOCIAL CRITICISM

George Orwell

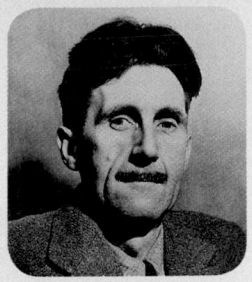

"When I sit down to write a book, I do not say to myself, 'I am going to produce a work of art.' I write it because there is some lie that I want to expose, some fact to which I want to draw attention, and my initial concern is to get a hearing."

Nadine Gordimer

"I am not a preacher or a politician. It is simply not the purpose of a novelist. I am totally opposed to apartheid and all the cruel and ugly things it stands for, and have been so all my life. But my writing does not deal with my personal convictions; it deals with the society I live and write in...."

Soldiers are citizens of death's gray land,
   Drawing no dividend from time's tomorrows.
In the great hour of destiny they stand,
   Each with his feuds, and jealousies, and sorrows.

          —**Siegfried Sassoon, *"Dreamers"***

Close Read

Explain how this passage represents a focus on the individual. Support your response with evidence from the passage.

An Irish Airman Foresees His Death
Poem by William Butler Yeats (See biography on page 1190.)

The Soldier
Poem by Rupert Brooke

Dreamers
Poem by Siegfried Sassoon

COMMON CORE

RL 1 Cite evidence to support inferences drawn from the text.
RL 4 Analyze the impact of specific word choices on meaning and tone. **SL 1a** Refer to evidence from texts and other research to stimulate a thoughtful exchange of ideas.

Meet the Authors

Rupert Brooke
1887–1915

A handsome, intelligent, and athletic young man, Rupert Brooke earned a reputation as one of Britain's most promising young poets after publishing a series of war sonnets that he wrote early in World War I. Tragically, Brooke's life was cut short: he died at the age of 27 while en route to battle.

The Poet-Soldier Brooke graduated in 1909 from Cambridge University, where he had begun to make a name for himself as a poet. Following graduation, he traveled to Germany, North America, and the South Pacific. Returning to England in 1914, Brooke joined the Royal Navy when World War I broke out and began combat training. During this time, he completed his most important literary work, a sequence of five war sonnets that includes "The Soldier."

Tragedy and Irony In February 1915, after participating in only one minor battle, Brooke sailed for Turkey, where he was to take part in a military campaign. During the voyage, he died from blood poisoning. He was buried on the Aegean island of Skíros. According to critic Doris L. Eder, "All England mourned the poet-soldier's death."

Siegfried Sassoon
1886–1967

Siegfried Sassoon wrote about the gruesome realities of trench warfare during World War I. Today, his verse is admired for the power with which it portrays the range of emotions experienced on the battlefield.

The Sporting Life Sassoon began writing poetry as a child, but he was more interested in sports than school. After dropping out of Cambridge University in 1907, he spent his time playing cricket, hunting foxes, and writing poetry. In 1914, he joined the army just days before England declared war on Germany.

From Idealism to Cynicism As an infantry officer in France, Sassoon was wounded several times and received the Military Cross for bravery. However, his wartime experiences affected him profoundly. In 1917, having become a pacifist, he wrote his commanding officer a letter protesting the war. The letter might have led to a court-martial, but Sassoon was instead briefly hospitalized for shell shock and then sent back to the battlefield. He continued to write about his wartime experiences long after the conflict ended.

Authors Online
Go to thinkcentral.com. KEYWORD: HML12-1242

THINK central

TEXT ANALYSIS: TONE

The **tone** of a literary work is an expression of the writer's attitude toward a subject. A poem's tone can usually be described in a single word, such as *solemn*, *joyous*, or *sarcastic*. Though sometimes subtle, tone plays a central role in conveying the poet's meaning. The three poems you are about to read all address warfare, but each has a distinctive tone. As you read, examine the following elements to help identify the tone of each poem:

- the **imagery** used to depict the subject or action
- the poet's **word choices**
- the **speaker's** feelings or thoughts

READING SKILL: MAKE INFERENCES IN POETRY

To better understand a poem's speaker, you can **make inferences**—or logical guesses—about the text based on evidence or clues you find in the poem and on your own experience. Making inferences is sometimes called "reading between the lines" because you come to an understanding of something that an author has not explicitly stated. For each poem, create a chart like the one shown. As you read, record your inferences and the details on which you based them.

"An Irish Airman Foresees His Death"	
Details from Text	Inferences
"meet my fate"	He's resigned to the possibility of dying.

 Complete the activities in your **Reader/Writer Notebook**.

Is PATRIOTISM *enough?*

Many soldiers enlist in the military out of a sense of patriotism—love for and dedication to one's country. It is difficult, however, for someone who has never experienced war to imagine the day-to-day realities of military life during war. In this selection, three poets with very different perspectives explore the effect of war on a soldier's psyche.

DISCUSS One way to learn more about others' ideas on a topic, such as patriotism or war, is to consult a book of quotations. These books contain well-known sayings on many different subjects. Use the Internet or your library to find a book of quotations and read what others have said about war. With a classmate, discuss which quotations help you understand more about patriotism and the effects of war.

An Irish Airman
Foresees His Death

William Butler Yeats

BACKGROUND Yeats wrote this poem to commemorate the death of Major Robert Gregory, who was killed during World War I. The young soldier was the son of Yeats's patron, Lady Gregory, a leading figure in the Irish Literary Renaissance.

I know that I shall meet my fate
Somewhere among the clouds above;
Those that I fight I do not hate,
Those that I guard I do not love;
5 My country is Kiltartan Cross,
My countrymen Kiltartan's poor,
No likely end could bring them loss
Or leave them happier than before.
Nor law, nor duty bade me fight,
10 Nor public men, nor cheering crowds.
A lonely impulse of delight
Drove to this tumult in the clouds;
I balanced all, brought all to mind,
The years to come seemed waste of breath,
15 A waste of breath the years behind
In balance with this life, this death. **A**

3–4 Those . . . love: Many of the Irish— even those who fought beside the English against the Germans in World War I—resented their English rulers.

5 Kiltartan Cross: crossroads in Kiltartan Parish in the west of Ireland. The Gregory estate, Coole Park, was located nearby.

A MAKE INFERENCES
Reread lines 13–16. What can you infer about the speaker's view of civilian life when he decided to become an airman?

Text Analysis

1. **Summarize** Reread lines 9–12. What reasons did *not* inspire the speaker to fight in World War I? What did inspire him?

2. **Analyze Historical Context** In the title, Yeats specifies that the speaker is Irish. Review the notes alongside the poem. How does the historical context help you understand the speaker's attitude toward World War I?

Lieutenant A. P. F. Rhys Davids, DSO, MC, Sir William Orpen. © Imperial War Museum, London, United Kingdom.

The Soldier

Rupert Brooke

If I should die, think only this of me,
    That there's some corner of a foreign field
That is forever England. There shall be
    In that rich earth a richer dust concealed,
5 A dust whom England bore, shaped, made aware,
    Gave, once, her flowers to love, her ways to roam,
A body of England's, breathing English air,
    Washed by the rivers, blest by suns of home. **Ⓑ**

And think, this heart, all evil shed away,
10   A pulse in the Eternal mind, no less
        Gives somewhere back the thoughts by England given,
Her sights and sounds; dreams happy as her day;
    And laughter, learnt of friends; and gentleness,
        In hearts at peace, under an English heaven.

Ⓑ TONE
Reread lines 1–8. What words and phrases help create a patriotic tone?

Text Analysis

1. **Paraphrase** What does the speaker say about the possibility of his death in lines 1–3?

2. **Analyze Speaker** Why might a young man going off to war think these thoughts?

Dreamers

Siegfried Sassoon

Soldiers are citizens of death's gray land,
    Drawing no dividend from time's tomorrows.  **C**
In the great hour of destiny they stand,
    Each with his feuds, and jealousies, and sorrows.
5 Soldiers are sworn to action; they must win
    Some flaming, fatal climax with their lives.
Soldiers are dreamers; when the guns begin
    They think of firelit homes, clean beds and wives.

I see them in foul dugouts, gnawed by rats,
10   And in the ruined trenches, lashed with rain,
Dreaming of things they did with balls and bats,
    And mocked by hopeless longing to regain
Bank holidays, and picture shows, and spats,
    And going to the office in the train.

C TONE
Reread lines 1–2. What tone is
established by the word choices
in these opening lines?

13 **bank holidays:** in Britain, a generic
term for holidays on which banks are
closed; **picture shows:** movies.

Over the Top, John Nash. © Imperial War Museum, London/Bridgeman Art Library.

Comprehension

1. **Recall** In "Dreamers," what do the soldiers dream of "when the guns begin"?

2. **Recall** What physical hardships does the speaker describe in "Dreamers"?

3. **Clarify** In "Dreamers," what fate does the speaker describe in lines 5–6?

Text Analysis

4. **Examine Structure** "Dreamers" is a sonnet consisting of an eight-line octave followed by a six-line sestet. What **turn,** or shift in thought, occurs between these two stanzas?

5. **Make Inferences in Poetry** There is a strong contrast between the feelings expressed in "The Soldier" and those expressed in "Dreamers." Review the chart you completed as you read. What inferences would help explain the difference in the speakers' feelings?

6. **Identify Tone** Describe the tone of each of the following passages. What imagery and phrases help create the tone of each passage?

   • lines 13–16 of "An Irish Airman Foresees his Death"

   • lines 12–14 of "The Soldier"

   • lines 9–14 of "Dreamers"

Text Criticism

7. **Different Perspectives** British philosopher John Stuart Mill said, "War is an ugly thing, but not the ugliest of things. . . . The person who has nothing for which he is willing to fight, nothing which is more important than his own personal safety, is a miserable creature and has no chance of being free unless made and kept so by the exertions of better men than himself." Consider the three poems you've just read. Which speaker or speakers do you think would agree with Mill, and why?

> *Is* **PATRIOTISM** *enough?*
>
> What message about war or patriotism is expressed in each of the three poems? Cite evidence from the poems to support your response.

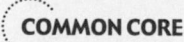

COMMON CORE

RL 1 Cite evidence to support inferences drawn from the text. **RL 4** Analyze the impact of specific word choices on meaning and tone. **RL 5** Analyze how an author's choices concerning how to structure specific parts of a text contribute to its overall structure and meaning as well as its aesthetic impact.

Language

◆ **GRAMMAR AND STYLE:** Add Emphasis and Rhythm

Throughout "An Irish Airman Foresees His Death," Yeats employs **repetition** and **parallelism,** the use of similar grammatical structures, to add emphasis and rhythm to his writing. Here is an example from the poem:

> Those that I fight I do not hate,
> Those that I guard I do not love;
> My country is Kiltartan Cross,
> My countrymen Kiltartan's poor, (lines 3–6)

In the first two lines, repetition and parallel structure lend balance and rhythm to the poem and emphasize the speaker's conflicted feelings about fighting. In the next two lines, repeated references to Kiltartan as well as *country* and *countrymen* emphasize the speaker's allegiance to his homeland of Ireland.

PRACTICE Rewrite the following paragraph, adding parallel elements or repetition.

> Anybody who had the good fortune to meet Jake Anderson knows what an optimist is. His great big smile had a way of brightening even the cloudiest of days. Jake was one of those rare people who always find a way to see the upside of everything. Even after his plane was shot down during battle last year, Jake wrote home to his parents and praised the training he'd received for just such an occurrence. Jake even praised the makers of the parachute that brought him safely to the ground. The glass was always half full for Jake.

READING-WRITING CONNECTION

Expand your understanding of these poems by responding to this prompt. Then, use the **revising tips** to improve your eulogy.

WRITING PROMPT	REVISING TIPS
COMPOSE A EULOGY Suppose that a military pilot has been recently shot down and killed during battle. In the spirit of Yeats's "An Irish Airman Foresees His Death," write a **two-paragraph eulogy** for him. Invent a history for the pilot and include details that convey his personality and outlook on life.	• Maintain a consistent and appropriate tone. • Use repetition and parallel structure to enhance the emotional effect of your words.

COMMON CORE

L 3 Apply knowledge of language to make effective choices for meaning or style. **W 4** Produce clear and coherent writing in which the development and style are appropriate to task and purpose.

Interactive Revision

Go to thinkcentral.com.
KEYWORD: HML12-1249

Shooting an Elephant
Essay by George Orwell

VIDEO TRAILER THINK central KEYWORD: HML12-1250A

DID YOU KNOW?

George Orwell . . .

- wrote his first poem when he was about five years old.
- never legally changed his name from Eric Blair to George Orwell.
- coined the terms "newspeak" and "Big Brother."

Meet the Author

George Orwell 1903–1950

Throughout his short life, George Orwell sympathized with the underdog and spoke out against social and political injustice. He is perhaps best known for his novel *1984,* which focused on the appalling possibilities of life in a totalitarian state.

An Uneasy Conscience Orwell was born in the Indian province of Bengal, where his father served in the Indian civil service. In 1922, Orwell joined the Indian Imperial Police and left for Burma, which at the time was ruled by Britain. When he discovered firsthand the oppression of British rule, however, he grew increasingly disenchanted with imperialist policies.

Voluntary Poverty and War In 1927, at the age of 25, Orwell resigned from the Imperial Police and decided to embark on a career as a writer. Turning his back on his middle-class upbringing, he moved to London and lived the destitute existence of the poor and downtrodden. Working as a dishwasher and a day laborer, he tramped through the countryside with the homeless. In 1928, he moved to Paris, where he continued to eke out a meager existence and wrote newspaper articles on unemployment, poverty, and social inequality. Out of these experiences came his first book, *Down and Out in Paris and London,* published in 1933.

In 1936, Orwell left England to fight with the antifascist forces in Spain's civil war. His experiences during the war helped solidify his political outlook, and he became a committed socialist (he rejected communism as it was practiced in the Soviet Union). The war also provided him with the material for his book *Homage to Catalonia* (1938), in which he articulated his conviction that totalitarianism was an imminent danger to Europe's future.

The Conscience of His Generation During World War II, Orwell became increasingly cynical about the way in which both the Allied forces and the Axis powers used propaganda. Near the end of World War II, he completed the first of his famous novels, *Animal Farm* (1945), a satiric fable about the dangers of dictatorships. The book established Orwell's literary reputation worldwide. In 1949, Orwell completed *1984* while battling tuberculosis. He died a year later at the peak of his career. In an obituary, author V. S. Pritchett called Orwell "the wintry conscience of his generation," a reference to Orwell's unrelenting—if at times somewhat despairing—campaign for honesty and intellectual freedom.

Author Online
Go to **thinkcentral.com**. KEYWORD: HML12-1250B

THINK central

● TEXT ANALYSIS: REFLECTIVE ESSAY

In a reflective essay, the writer makes a connection between a personal observation and a universal idea, such as love, honor, or freedom. In "Shooting an Elephant," Orwell reflects on a specific incident from his time as a young police officer in British-ruled Burma during the 1920s. Paradoxically, readers find Orwell—one of the 20th-century's most eloquent opponents of tyranny—as a representative of a sometimes-harsh colonial power. As you read, note the ambiguity of Orwell's situation, especially apparent in the tension between his role in the incident described and his role as the author.

■ READING SKILL: ANALYZE CAUSE-AND-EFFECT RELATIONSHIPS

The unfortunate climax of "Shooting an Elephant" develops from a series of related actions. In a **cause-and-effect relationship,** an event or action directly results in another event or action. Note that an effect can become the cause of a subsequent effect. As you read, use a chart like the one shown to trace the chain of cause-and-effect relationships that structures the essay.

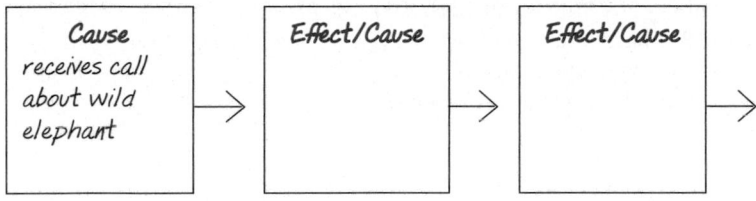

Cause
receives call about wild elephant
→
Effect/Cause
→
Effect/Cause
→

▲ VOCABULARY IN CONTEXT

Use the context of each sentence to help you determine the meaning of the boldface words.

1. Many natives resented British **imperialism.**
2. We are not a **cowed** people; we can still fight.
3. New rulers may **supplant** the old with little resistance.
4. The **prostrate** subjects cringed before their harsh king.
5. The **despotic** king rules with an iron fist.
6. The ancient town is a confusing **labyrinth** of streets.
7. Her costume was so **garish** that it hurt my eyes.
8. Is forgetfulness a sign of **senility** in older people?

 Complete the activities in your **Reader/Writer Notebook.**

How important is it to "SAVE FACE"?

George Orwell once said, "An autobiography is only to be trusted when it reveals something disgraceful." Most people have done things that they've regretted or about which they've later felt ashamed. Character flaws are difficult to admit, and people often go to great lengths—even compromising their values—to protect their reputation.

QUICKWRITE Recall a time or incident when you had to "save face." Try to remember why you reacted to the situation as you did. Write a short description of what happened, how you "saved face," and what you might do differently today in a similar situation.

Shooting an Elephant

George Orwell

> **BACKGROUND** Orwell's essay is set in Burma, a Southeast Asian country now known as Myanmar. In a series of wars in the 19th century, the British gained control of Burma and made it a province of British India. The Burmese resented British rule, under which they endured poverty and a lack of political and religious freedom. Like many of his fellow British officers, Orwell was inexperienced in police work when he arrived in Burma at age 19.

In Moulmein, in Lower Burma,[1] I was hated by large numbers of people—the only time in my life that I have been important enough for this to happen to me. I was subdivisional police officer of the town, and in an aimless, petty kind of way anti-European feeling was very bitter. No one had the guts to raise a riot, but if a European woman went through the bazaars alone somebody would probably spit betel juice[2] over her dress. As a police officer I was an obvious target and was baited whenever it seemed safe to do so. When a nimble Burman tripped me up on the football[3] field and the referee (another Burman) looked the other way, the crowd yelled with hideous laughter. This happened more than once. In the
10 end the sneering yellow faces of young men that met me everywhere, the insults hooted after me when I was at a safe distance, got badly on my nerves. The young Buddhist priests were the worst of all. There were several thousands of them in the town and none of them seemed to have anything to do except stand on street corners and jeer at Europeans. **Ⓐ**

---

1. **Moulmein** (mōōl-mān′), **in Lower Burma:** the main city of British-controlled Burma, now the independent Asian nation of Myanmar. Moulmein is now usually called Mawlamyine.
2. **betel** (bēt′l) **juice:** the saliva created when chewing a mixture of betel palm nuts, betel palm leaves, and lime.
3. **football:** soccer.

Analyze Visuals ▶
Draw as many conclusions as you can about this photograph.

Ⓐ REFLECTIVE ESSAY
Summarize the experiences Orwell describes in lines 1–14. What effect did these experiences have on him?

All this was perplexing and upsetting. For at that time I had already made up my mind that **imperialism** was an evil thing and the sooner I chucked up[4] my job and got out of it the better. Theoretically—and secretly, of course—I was all for the Burmese and all against their oppressors, the British. As for the job I was doing, I hated it more bitterly than I can perhaps make clear. In a job like
20 that you see the dirty work of Empire at close quarters. The wretched prisoners huddling in the stinking cages of the lock-ups, the gray, **cowed** faces of the long-term convicts, the scarred buttocks of the men who had been flogged with bamboos—all these oppressed me with an intolerable sense of guilt. But I could get nothing into perspective. I was young and ill-educated and I had had to think out my problems in the utter silence that is imposed on every Englishman in the East. I did not even know that the British Empire is dying, still less did I know that it is a great deal better than the younger empires that are going to **supplant** it. All I knew was that I was stuck between my hatred of the empire I served and my rage against the evil-spirited little beasts who tried to make my job impossible.
30 With one part of my mind I thought of the British Raj[5] as an unbreakable tyranny, as something clamped down, *in saecula saeculorum,*[6] upon the will of **prostrate** peoples; with another part I thought that the greatest joy in the world would be to drive a bayonet into a Buddhist priest's guts. Feelings like these are the normal by-products of imperialism; ask any Anglo-Indian official, if you can catch him off duty. **B**

One day something happened which in a roundabout way was enlightening. It was a tiny incident in itself, but it gave me a better glimpse than I had had before of the real nature of imperialism—the real motives for which **despotic** governments act. Early one morning the subinspector at a police station the
40 other end of the town rang me up on the phone and said that an elephant was ravaging the bazaar. Would I please come and do something about it? I did not know what I could do, but I wanted to see what was happening and I got on to a pony and started out. I took my rifle, an old .44 Winchester and much too small to kill an elephant, but I thought the noise might be useful *in terrorem.*[7] Various Burmans stopped me on the way and told me about the elephant's doings. It was not, of course, a wild elephant, but a tame one which had gone "must."[8] It had been chained up as tame elephants always are when their attack of "must" is due, but on the previous night it had broken its chain and escaped. Its mahout,[9] the only person who could manage it when it was in that state, had set out in pursuit,
50 but had taken the wrong direction and was now twelve hours' journey away, and in the morning the elephant had suddenly reappeared in the town. The Burmese population had no weapons and were quite helpless against it. It had already

---

imperialism (ĭm-pîr′ē-ə-lĭz′əm) *n.* the policy of forming and maintaining an empire, especially in the quest for raw materials and more markets

cowed (koud) *adj.* made timid and submissive through fear or awe **cow** *v.*

supplant (sə-plănt′) *v.* to take the place of

prostrate (prŏs′trāt′) *adj.* completely submissive

B REFLECTIVE ESSAY
What **internal conflict** does Orwell describe in lines 15–35?

despotic (dĭ-spŏt′ĭk) *adj.* ruling absolutely without allowing any dissent; tyrannical

---

4. **chucked up:** threw off; gave up.

5. **British Raj:** India and adjoining areas (such as Burma) controlled by Britain in the 19th and early 20th centuries. *Raj* is the word for "kingdom" or "rule" in Hindi, a chief language of India.

6. *in saecula saeculorum* (ĭn sĕk′yə-lə sĕk-yə-lôr′əm) *Latin:* forever and ever.

7. *in terrorem* (ĭn tĕ-rôr′əm) *Latin:* for terror.

8. **gone "must":** had an attack of must, a dangerous frenzy that periodically seizes male elephants.

9. **mahout** (mə-hout′): an elephant keeper.

George Orwell at the police training school in Burma, 1922.

destroyed somebody's bamboo hut, killed a cow and raided some fruit-stalls and devoured the stock; also it had met the municipal rubbish van, and, when the driver jumped out and took to his heels, had turned the van over and inflicted violences upon it.

The Burmese subinspector and some Indian constables[10] were waiting for me in the quarter where the elephant had been seen. It was a very poor quarter, a **labyrinth** of squalid bamboo huts, thatched with palm-leaf, winding all over a
60 steep hillside. I remember that it was a cloudy stuffy morning at the beginning of the rains. We began questioning the people as to where the elephant had gone, and, as usual, failed to get any definite information. That is invariably the case in the East; a story always sounds clear enough at a distance, but the nearer you get to the scene of events the vaguer it becomes. Some of the people said that the elephant had gone in one direction, some said that he had gone in another, some professed not even to have heard of any elephant. I had almost made up my mind that the whole story was a pack of lies, when we heard yells a little distance away. There was a loud, scandalized cry of "Go away, child! Go away this instant!" and an old woman with a switch in her hand came round the corner of a hut,
70 violently shooing away a crowd of naked children. Some more women followed, clicking their tongues and exclaiming; evidently there was something there that the children ought not to have seen. I rounded the hut and saw a man's dead body sprawling in the mud. He was an Indian, a black Dravidian coolie,[11] almost naked, and he could not have been dead many minutes. The people said that the

labyrinth (lăb′ə-rĭnth′) *n.* an intricate structure of winding passages; a maze

Language Coach

Commonly Confused Words Some words that sound or look similar are easy to confuse. Don't confuse *scandalized* and *scandalous*. One means "greatly offended" and the other means "causing a scandal (great offense)." Which is the meaning of *scandalized* in line 68?

---

10. **constables:** police officers.

11. **Dravidian** (drə-vĭd′ē-ən) **coolie:** a dark-skinned menial laborer from the south of India.

elephant had come suddenly upon him round the corner of the hut, caught him with its trunk, put its foot on his back and ground him into the earth. This was the rainy season and the ground was soft, and his face had scored a trench a foot deep and a couple of yards long. He was lying on his belly with arms crucified and head sharply twisted to one side. His face was coated with mud, the eyes wide open, the teeth bared and grinning with an expression of unendurable agony. (Never tell me, by the way, that the dead look peaceful. Most of the corpses I have seen looked devilish.) The friction of the great beast's foot had stripped the skin from his back as neatly as one skins a rabbit. As soon as I saw the dead man I sent an orderly[12] to a friend's house nearby to borrow an elephant rifle. I had already sent back the pony, not wanting it to go mad with fright and throw me if it smelled the elephant. **C**

The orderly came back in a few minutes with a rifle and five cartridges, and meanwhile some Burmans had arrived and told us that the elephant was in the paddy fields[13] below, only a few hundred yards away. As I started forward practically the whole population of the quarter flocked out of the houses and followed me. They had seen the rifle and were all shouting excitedly that I was going to shoot the elephant. They had not shown much interest in the elephant when he was merely ravaging their homes, but it was different now that he was going to be shot. It was a bit of fun to them, as it would be to an English crowd; besides, they wanted the meat. It made me vaguely uneasy. I had no intention of shooting the elephant—I had merely sent for the rifle to defend myself if necessary—and it is always unnerving to have a crowd following you. I marched down the hill, looking and feeling a fool, with the rifle over my shoulder and an ever-growing army of people jostling at my heels. At the bottom, when you got away from the huts, there was a metalled road and beyond that a miry waste of paddy fields a thousand yards across, not yet ploughed but soggy from the first rains and dotted with coarse grass. The elephant was standing eighty yards from the road, his left side towards us. He took not the slightest notice of the crowd's approach. He was tearing up bunches of grass, beating them against his knees to clean them and stuffing them into his mouth. **D**

I had halted on the road. As soon as I saw the elephant I knew with perfect certainty that I ought not to shoot him. It is a serious matter to shoot a working elephant—it is comparable to destroying a huge and costly piece of machinery— and obviously one ought not to do it if it can possibly be avoided. And at that distance, peacefully eating, the elephant looked no more dangerous than a cow. I thought then and I think now that his attack of "must" was already passing off; in which case he would merely wander harmlessly about until the mahout came back and caught him. Moreover, I did not in the least want to shoot him. I decided that I would watch him for a little while to make sure that he did not turn savage again, and then go home.

But at that moment I glanced round at the crowd that had followed me. It was an immense crowd, two thousand at the least and growing every minute. It blocked the road for a long distance on either side. I looked at the sea of yellow

C CAUSE
What causes the narrator to send the orderly for an elephant gun?

COMMON CORE RI 1

D AMBIGUITY
In this passage, Orwell hints at the uncertainty, or **ambiguity,** of the threat posed by the elephant. On the surface, the elephant is plainly quite peaceful at this point in the narrative. However, other details complicate the picture. As you finish reading the story, think about the following questions: Does Orwell ever really know that the elephant is a continuing threat? What replaces the threat of the elephant in the story?

---

12. **orderly:** a military aid.

13. **paddy fields:** rice fields.

faces above the **garish** clothes—faces all happy and excited over this bit of fun, all certain that the elephant was going to be shot. They were watching me as they
120 would watch a conjurer[14] about to perform a trick. They did not like me, but with the magical rifle in my hands I was momentarily worth watching. And suddenly I realized that I should have to shoot the elephant after all. The people expected it of me and I had got to do it; I could feel their two thousand wills pressing me forward, irresistibly. And it was at this moment, as I stood there with the rifle in my hands, that I first grasped the hollowness, the futility of the white man's dominion in the East. Here was I, the white man with his gun, standing in front of the unarmed native crowd—seemingly the leading actor of the piece; but in reality I was only an absurd puppet pushed to and fro by the will of those yellow faces behind. I perceived in this moment that when the white man turns tyrant it
130 is his own freedom that he destroys. He becomes a sort of hollow, posing dummy, the conventionalized figure of a sahib.[15] For it is the condition of his rule that he shall spend his life in trying to impress the "natives," and so in every crisis he has got to do what the "natives" expect of him. He wears a mask, and his face grows to fit it. I had got to shoot the elephant. I had committed myself to doing it when I sent for the rifle. A sahib has got to act like a sahib; he has got to appear resolute, to know his own mind and do definite things. To come all that way, rifle in hand, with two thousand people marching at my heels, and then to trail feebly away, having done nothing—no, that was impossible. The crowd would laugh at me. And my whole life, every white man's life in the East, was one long struggle
140 not to be laughed at. **E**

But I did not want to shoot the elephant. I watched him beating his bunch of grass against his knees, with that preoccupied grandmotherly air that elephants have. It seemed to me that it would be murder to shoot him. At that age I was not squeamish about killing animals, but I had never shot an elephant and never wanted to. (Somehow it always seems worse to kill a *large* animal.) Besides, there was the beast's owner to be considered. Alive, the elephant was worth at least a hundred pounds; dead, he would only be worth the value of his tusks—five pounds, possibly. But I had got to act quickly. I turned to some experienced-looking Burmans who had been there when we arrived, and asked them how the
150 elephant had been behaving. They all said the same thing: he took no notice of you if you left him alone, but he might charge if you went too close to him.

It was perfectly clear to me what I ought to do. I ought to walk up to within, say, twenty-five yards of the elephant and test his behavior. If he charged I could shoot, if he took no notice of me it would be safe to leave him until the mahout came back. But also I knew that I was going to do no such thing. I was a poor shot with a rifle and the ground was soft mud into which one would sink at every step. If the elephant charged and I missed him, I should have about as much chance as a toad under a steam-roller. But even then I was not thinking particularly of my own skin, only of the watchful yellow faces behind. For at that
160 moment, with the crowd watching me, I was not afraid in the ordinary sense,

---

14. **conjurer** (kŏn′jər-ər): magician.

15. **sahib** (sä′ĭb): a title of respect formerly used by native Indians to address a European gentleman.

garish (gâr′ĭsh) *adj.* too bright or showy; gaudy; glaring

as I would have been if I had been alone. A white man mustn't be frightened in front of "natives"; and so, in general, he isn't frightened. The sole thought in my mind was that if anything went wrong those two thousand Burmans would see me pursued, caught, trampled on and reduced to a grinning corpse like that Indian up the hill. And if that happened it was quite probable that some of them would laugh. That would never do. There was only one alternative. I shoved the cartridges into the magazine[16] and lay down on the road to get a better aim. **F**

The crowd grew very still, and a deep, low, happy sigh, as of people who see the theater curtain go up at last, breathed from innumerable throats. They were
170 going to have their bit of fun after all. The rifle was a beautiful German thing with cross-hair sights. I did not then know that in shooting an elephant one should shoot to cut an imaginary bar running from ear-hole to ear-hole. I ought, therefore, as the elephant was sideways on, to have aimed straight at his ear-hole; actually I aimed several inches in front of this, thinking the brain would be further forward.

When I pulled the trigger I did not hear the bang or feel the kick—one never does when a shot goes home—but I heard the devilish roar of glee that went up from the crowd. In that instant, in too short a time, one would have thought, even for the bullet to get there, a mysterious, terrible change had come over the elephant. He neither stirred nor fell, but every line of his body had altered. He
180 looked suddenly stricken, shrunken, immensely old, as though the frightful

F CAUSE AND EFFECT
What ultimately causes the narrator to shoot the elephant?

---

16. **magazine:** the compartment from which cartridges are fed into the rifle's firing chamber.

impact of the bullet had paralyzed him without knocking him down. At last, after what seemed a long time—it might have been five seconds, I dare say—he sagged flabbily to his knees. His mouth slobbered. An enormous **senility** seemed to have settled upon him. One could have imagined him thousands of years old. I fired again into the same spot. At the second shot he did not collapse but climbed with desperate slowness to his feet and stood weakly upright, with legs sagging and head drooping. I fired a third time. That was the shot that did for him. You could see the agony of it jolt his whole body and knock the last remnant of strength from his legs. But in falling he seemed for a moment to rise, for as his hind legs
190 collapsed beneath him he seemed to tower upwards like a huge rock toppling, his trunk reaching skyward like a tree. He trumpeted, for the first and only time. And then down he came, his belly towards me, with a crash that seemed to shake the ground even where I lay.

I got up. The Burmans were already racing past me across the mud. It was obvious that the elephant would never rise again, but he was not dead. He was breathing very rhythmically with long rattling gasps, his great mound of a side painfully rising and falling. His mouth was wide open—I could see far down into caverns of pale pink throat. I waited a long time for him to die, but his breathing did not weaken. Finally I fired my two remaining shots into the spot where I
200 thought his heart must be. The thick blood welled out of him like red velvet, but still he did not die. His body did not even jerk when the shots hit him, the tortured breathing continued without a pause. He was dying, very slowly and in great agony, but in some world remote from me where not even a bullet could damage him further. I felt that I had got to put an end to that dreadful noise. It seemed dreadful to see the great beast lying there, powerless to move and yet powerless to die, and not even to be able to finish him. I sent back for my small rifle and poured shot after shot into his heart and down his throat. They seemed to make no impression. The tortured gasps continued as steadily as the ticking of a clock.

In the end I could not stand it any longer and went away. I heard later that
210 it took him half an hour to die. Burmans were arriving with dahs[17] and baskets even before I left, and I was told they had stripped his body almost to the bones by the afternoon.

Afterwards, of course, there were endless discussions about the shooting of the elephant. The owner was furious, but he was only an Indian and could do nothing. Besides, legally I had done the right thing, for a mad elephant has to be killed, like a mad dog, if its owner fails to control it. Among the Europeans opinion was divided. The older men said I was right, the younger men said it was a damn shame to shoot an elephant for killing a coolie, because an elephant was worth more than any damn Coringhee[18] coolie. And afterwards I was very glad
220 that the coolie had been killed; it put me legally in the right and it gave me a sufficient pretext for shooting the elephant. I often wondered whether any of the others grasped that I had done it solely to avoid looking a fool. ∾ **G**

---

17. **dahs:** large knives.

18. **Coringhee:** coming from a port in southeastern India.

senility (sĭ-nĭl′ĭ-tē) *n.* the mental deterioration that sometimes comes with old age

Language Coach

Fixed Expressions The expression *have got to* can be used instead of *have to* for emphasis (*I have got to study!*). How would the narrator's feelings in line 204 seem different if he had said *had to* instead of *had got to*?

G **REFLECTIVE ESSAY**
What does the shooting of the elephant symbolize for Orwell?

Comprehension

1. **Recall** How was Orwell treated by the local Burmese?

2. **Recall** How does the Burmese crowd react when they see Orwell approach the elephant with his rifle?

3. **Summarize** What happens after Orwell starts firing at the elephant?

Text Analysis

4. **Identify Cause-and-Effect Relationships** Review the graphic organizer you created as you read the essay, paying special attention to the instances where an effect becomes the cause of a further effect. Which moments in the essay have the greatest influence on Orwell's actions? What makes this structure effective for the topic?

5. **Analyze a Reflective Essay** Orwell says that the incident with the elephant proved enlightening "in a roundabout way." What did he learn about himself and about imperialism through this incident?

6. **Analyze Conflict** Orwell depicts several conflicts that developed between British colonialists and native Burmese. Describe how each of the following conflicts is reflected in his essay, and explain Orwell's position on the conflict:

   • occupation vs. freedom

   • industrial society vs. pre-industrial society

   • tribal justice vs. legal justice

7. **Interpret Paradox** In lines 129–130, Orwell writes, "I perceived in this moment that when the white man turns tyrant it is his own freedom that he destroys." Why is this statement paradoxical? How does it reflect Orwell's point of view about British imperialism?

Text Criticism

8. The elephant is an important **symbol,** or a person, place, thing, or idea that stands for something beyond itself. What political idea or situation might the confused but violent elephant symbolize? Cite supporting details from the text to explain the elephant's symbolic importance.

How important is it to **"SAVE FACE"?**

A few times in the essay, Orwell talks about the need to "save face," or protect his reputation, as an agent of the British Empire. Why was this so important to him?

COMMON CORE

RI 2 Determine central ideas of a text and analyze their development. **RI 3** Analyze a sequence of events and explain how specific events interact and develop over the course of the text. **RI 5** Analyze and evaluate the effectiveness of the structure an author uses in his or her exposition, including whether the structure makes points clear and engaging. **RI 6** Determine an author's point of view or purpose in a text in which the rhetoric is particularly effective, analyzing how style and content contribute to the power of the text.

Vocabulary In Context

▲ VOCABULARY PRACTICE

Use your knowledge of the boldface vocabulary words to decide whether each statement is true or false.

1. Most small lands welcome the **imperialism** of larger nations.
2. A superhero is an easily **cowed** person.
3. The new president **supplants** the previous president.
4. A **prostrate** person always stands up for himself.
5. A **despotic** ruler allows little if any dissent.
6. It is easy for most people to get lost in a **labyrinth.**
7. Las Vegas singers may wear **garish** clothes when they perform.
8. People experiencing **senility** sometimes forget where they are.

> **WORD LIST**
>
> cowed
> despotic
> garish
> imperialism
> labyrinth
> prostrate
> senility
> supplant

ACADEMIC VOCABULARY IN WRITING

> • approach • assume • environment • method • strategy

Orwell discusses racism, oppression, and **environmental** rights. Write about one of these issues, using at least one additional Academic Vocabulary word.

VOCABULARY STRATEGY: USING ELECTRONIC RESOURCES

Electronic resources can expand your vocabulary by clarifying what a word means, how it is normally used, and how it functions in a sentence.

1. In your computer's word-processing program, you can type an unfamiliar word and right-click it for options such as LOOK UP and THESAURUS. The LOOK UP option lists references stored on your computer as well as Internet resources.
2. Other Internet resources include free dictionaries and encyclopedias. Be careful using "wiki" resources; they're "open-source" and may contain errors.
3. See if you are allowed to access your library's database through the Internet.

⋯ **COMMON CORE**

L 1b Consult usage references as needed. **L 3a** Consult syntax references for guidance as needed. **L 4c** Consult digital reference materials to clarify a word's precise meaning or its standard usage.

COMPUTER PROGRAM	INTERNET	LIBRARY DATABASES

—"look up" options
  —reference books
  —research sites
—thesaurus
—translations
	—online dictionaries
	—"wiki" resources
	—library Web sites
	—free encyclopedias
		—dictionaries & thesauri
		—online usage and syntax references

PRACTICE Answer the following questions about electronic resources.

1. How can you find a synonym for a word in a document you are writing?
2. What kind of vocabulary references may be available through a library database?
3. How can you find a translation for a word you know in Spanish but not English?

Interactive Vocabulary **THINK** central

Go to **thinkcentral.com**.
KEYWORD: HML12-1261

from 1984

Novel by George Orwell

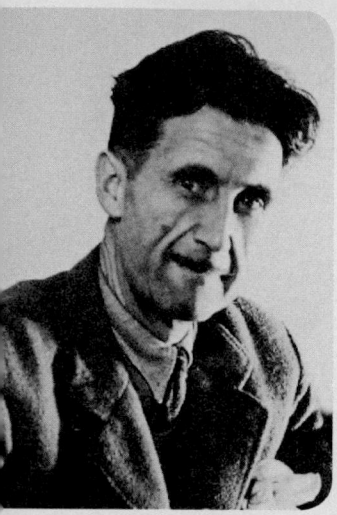

George Orwell
1903–1950

(background)
A scene from the movie *1984*.

BACKGROUND Born Eric Blair, the son of a minor official in British colonial India, Orwell was raised to be a supporter of the British Empire. He was sent to all the right schools in England and later took a post with the Imperial Police in British-controlled Burma. Yet he came to hate the job, which made him feel guilty for what he perceived to be colonial oppression of the Burmese people. He quit the job and left Burma, deciding to see how the "other half" lived. He wandered London's poorest sections, worked as a dishwasher in Paris, and lived among unemployed miners in northern England. Spurred by his loathing of totalitarian regimes, he produced two of the best known political novels of all time, *Animal Farm* and *1984*, before dying of tuberculosis at age 46.

The title *1984* refers to the year in which the novel takes place. Writing just after World War II, Orwell set his novel nearly 40 years into the future, imagining a world divided into three totalitarian superstates forever fighting one another. Britain, known in the novel as Airstrip One, has been absorbed by America into the superstate of Oceania. Society consists of proles (from *proletariat*) leading miserable lives and of members of the INGSOC (from *English Socialist*) Party, who have more privileges than proles do but are under constant surveillance by the Thought Police. In this nightmare world, Winston Smith labors as a minor bureaucrat whose job is to rewrite history. In secret, however, Smith is disgusted with his society and rebels by keeping a diary. The following passage, filled with "Newspeak," focuses on Winston Smith's perceptions of his society—and his dangerous plight.

TEXT ANALYSIS Orwell uses specific **details**, such as objects, places, and even language, to describe Oceania's society. For example, Winston's twenty-five-cent piece has a picture of Big Brother, the dictator of Oceania who may or may not really exist. Oceania has a Ministry of Truth that is housed in a building shaped like a pyramid. On the building are three slogans, examples of Newspeak, a language full of mindless slogans, simple ideas, and words designed to manipulate and mislead. These details help readers fully imagine Orwell's invented world.

WRITE After you have read the excerpt, write a scene in which you create your own futuristic society. Your society could be a miserable one like the one in *1984*, or it could be more hopeful. Use precise descriptions of objects and places to help readers envision your future world. In addition, use words, as Orwell does with Newspeak, to help readers understand the mood of the culture. To do that, consider writing a slogan that appears somewhere within your invented world.

"*O*ceania, 'tis for thee" gave way to lighter music. Winston walked over to the window, keeping his back to the telescreen. The day was still cold and clear. Somewhere far away a rocket bomb exploded with a dull, reverberating roar. About twenty or thirty of them a week were falling on London at present.

Down in the street the wind flapped the torn poster to and fro, and the word INGSOC fitfully appeared and vanished. Ingsoc. The sacred principles of Ingsoc. Newspeak, doublethink, the mutability of the past. He felt as though he were wandering in the forests of the sea bottom, lost in a monstrous
10 world where he himself was the monster. He was alone. The past was dead, the future was unimaginable. What certainty had he that a single human creature now living was on his side? And what way of knowing that the dominion of the Party would not endure *for ever?* Like an answer, the three slogans on the white face of the Ministry of Truth came back at him:

WAR IS PEACE

FREEDOM IS SLAVERY

IGNORANCE IS STRENGTH.

He took a twenty-five-cent piece out of his pocket. There, too, in tiny clear lettering, the same slogans were inscribed, and on the other face of the coin the head of
20 Big Brother. Even from the coin the eyes pursued you. On coins, on stamps, on the covers of books, on banners, on posters, and on the wrapping of a cigarette packet—everywhere. Always the eyes watching you and the voice enveloping you. Asleep or awake, working or eating, indoors or out of doors, in the bath or in bed—no escape. Nothing was your own except the few cubic centimeters inside your skull.

The sun had shifted round, and the myriad windows of the Ministry of Truth, with the light no longer shining on them, looked grim as the loopholes of a fortress. His heart quailed before the enormous pyramidal shape. It was too strong, it could not be stormed. A thousand rocket bombs would not batter it down. He wondered
30 again for whom he was writing the diary. For the future, for the past—for an age that might be imaginary. And in front of him there lay not death but annihilation. The diary would be reduced to ashes and himself to vapor. Only the Thought Police would read what he had written, before they wiped it out of existence and out of memory. How could you make an appeal to the future when not a trace of you, not even an anonymous word scribbled on a piece of paper, could physically survive?

a Novel

NINETEEN EIGHTY-FOUR

by George Orwell
AUTHOR OF *Animal Farm*

Words and Behavior

Essay by Aldous Huxley

DID YOU KNOW?

Aldous Huxley . . .

- was one of George Orwell's teachers.
- died on the same day President John F. Kennedy was assassinated.

Meet the Author

Aldous Huxley 1894–1963

In both his fiction and nonfiction, Aldous Huxley offered brilliant satiric commentary on political, social, and cultural trends. He is best known for his novel *Brave New World* (1932), a chilling work about a false utopia populated by mass-produced, genetically engineered people. The novel is considered a classic science fiction work of the 20th century.

Loss of Vision Aldous Huxley was born in Surrey, England, into a family of gifted intellectuals that included scientists, educators, and writers. As a student at Eton College, Huxley contracted keratitis, an eye disease that resulted in near blindness. He had intended to pursue a career in science or medicine, but he abandoned that ambition because of his illness. Learning Braille to continue his education, he studied English literature at Oxford University, where his sight showed signs of slight improvement. He was awarded an honors degree in 1916, the same year he published his first book, a collection of poetry.

Literary Rebel After working as a teacher and a journalist, Huxley concentrated on his own writing, moving away from poetry to fiction and essays. The witty skepticism of his first two novels, published in the 1920s, established his reputation and also brought him a certain popularity as a rebel. During the 1930s, Huxley's writing focused on political and cultural trends.

West Meets East In 1937, Huxley settled in southern California, where both the climate and new medical treatments improved his vision. About the time he emigrated, he became increasingly concerned with the lack of spiritual focus in contemporary life, noting, "For too long Europeans and Americans have believed in nothing but the values arising in a mechanized, commercialized, urbanized way of life." He began to study and write about Hinduism, Buddhism, and Christian mysticism.

Although Huxley had never intended to make the United States his permanent home, he remained there for the rest of his life, finding work in Hollywood as a screenwriter and continuing to produce novels, essays, literary criticism, and philosophical writings. Toward the end of his life, Huxley the social critic remarked, "It is a bit embarrassing to have been concerned with the human problem all one's life and find at the end that one has no more to offer by way of advice than 'Try to be a little kinder.'"

Author Online

Go to **thinkcentral.com**. KEYWORD: HML12-1264

THINK central

● TEXT ANALYSIS: DEDUCTIVE REASONING

Huxley's essay is a well-reasoned and well-supported argument that is based on deductive reasoning. When writers use **deductive reasoning,** they begin with a general principle, apply it to a specific situation, and then arrive at a logical conclusion. Here is Huxley's reasoning early in the essay:

- **General principle**—We use words to falsify facts because doing so benefits us in some way.
- **Specific situation**—war
- **Conclusion**—We create a verbal alternative to the reality of war to preserve our self-esteem.

As you read, notice how Huxley uses deductive reasoning at the beginning of the essay and toward the end.

Review: **Rhetorical Devices**

● READING SKILL: ANALYZE AN ARGUMENT

The cornerstone of every argument is its **claim,** the writer's position on an issue. In "Words and Behavior," Huxley's claim is the conclusion about war that he reaches via deductive reasoning. To convince readers that a claim is valid, a writer must provide **support,** which may consist of

- reasons that explain or justify an action, a belief, or a decision
- evidence in the form of facts, examples, statistics, or the views of experts

As you read, write down the reasons and evidence Huxley offers in support of his claim and consider his purpose for writing this essay.

▲ VOCABULARY IN CONTEXT

Huxley uses the following words to develop his argument. Complete each sentence with one of the words.

WORD LIST	abstraction	euphemism	propound
	balefully	iniquity	vitiate
	entity	intrinsically	

1. He used a(n) _____ to avoid offending his audience.
2. She _____ knew the story was fabricated.
3. Is the group an offshoot or an entirely new _____?
4. Will the senator_____ a new solution?

Complete the activities in your **Reader/Writer Notebook.**

How can WORDS *deceive?*

In "Words and Behavior," Aldous Huxley examines how words are used to mislead people and manipulate truth. Some say there's an art to such deception, which we can see in everything from pop-up ads on our computers to speeches given by world leaders. What motivates people to use deceptive language?

QUICKWRITE Suppose that you accidentally broke an expensive and beloved item in your house. Write a note to your parents explaining what happened. Before you write, consider how your choice of words will affect their impression of your behavior. Share your note with several classmates, and discuss the specific words you used to describe the accident.

WORDS
AND
BEHAVIOR

Aldous Huxley

Words form the thread on which we string our experiences. Without them we should live spasmodically and intermittently. Hatred itself is not so strong that animals will not forget it, if distracted, even in the presence of the enemy. Watch a pair of cats, crouching on the brink of a fight. **Balefully** the eyes glare; from far down in the throat of each come bursts of a strange, strangled noise of defiance; as though animated by a life of their own, the tails twitch and tremble. With aimed intensity of loathing! Another moment and surely there must be an explosion. But no; all of a sudden one of the two creatures turns away, hoists a hind leg in a more than fascist salute[1] and, with the same fixed and focused attention as it had

10　given a moment before to its enemy, begins to make a lingual toilet.[2] Animal **A** love is as much at the mercy of distractions as animal hatred. The dumb creation lives a life made up of discrete[3] and mutually irrelevant episodes. Such as it is, the consistency of human characters is due to the words upon which all human experiences are strung. We are purposeful because we can describe our feelings in remarkable words, can justify and rationalize our desires in terms of some kind of argument. Faced by an enemy we do not allow an itch to distract us from our emotions; the mere word "enemy" is enough to keep us reminded of our hatred,

---

1. **fascist** (făsh′ĭst) **salute:** a salute, used in Nazi Germany, in which the arm is rigidly extended forward, slightly above the horizontal.

2. **make a lingual toilet:** clean itself with its tongue, as cats commonly do.

3. **discrete:** separate; distinct.

balefully (bāl′fəl-ē) *adv.* in a manner that threatens evil or harm; ominously

A ANALYZE AN ARGUMENT
What contrast is Huxley drawing between humans and animals in this passage about the cats?

Analyze Visuals ▶
Summarize the message of this poster.

Together, World War II Poster. Color lithograph. Private collection. © Bridgeman Art Library.

TOGETHER

to convince us that we do well to be angry. Similarly the word "love" bridges for us those chasms of momentary indifference and boredom which gape from time to time between even the most ardent lovers. Feeling and desire provide us with our motive power; words give continuity to what we do and to a considerable extent determine our direction. Inappropriate and badly chosen words **vitiate** thought and lead to wrong or foolish conduct. Most ignorances are vincible,[4] and in the greater number of cases stupidity is what the Buddha pronounced it to be, a sin. For, consciously, or subconsciously, it is with deliberation that we do not know or fail to understand—because incomprehension allows us, with a good conscience, to evade unpleasant obligations and responsibilities, because ignorance is the best excuse for going on doing what one likes, but ought not, to do. Our egotisms are incessantly fighting to preserve themselves, not only from external enemies, but also from the assaults of the other and better self with which they are so uncomfortably associated. Ignorance is egotism's most effective defense against that Dr. Jekyll[5] in us who desires perfection; stupidity, its subtlest stratagem. If, as so often happens, we choose to give continuity to our experience by means of words which falsify the facts, this is because the falsification is somehow to our advantage as egotists. **B**

Consider, for example, the case of war. War is enormously discreditable to those who order it to be waged and even to those who merely tolerate its existence. Furthermore, to developed sensibilities the facts of war are revolting and horrifying. To falsify these facts, and by so doing to make war seem less evil than it really is, and our own responsibility in tolerating war less heavy, is doubly to our advantage. By suppressing and distorting the truth, we protect our sensibilities and preserve our self-esteem. Now, language is, among other things, a device which men use for suppressing and distorting the truth. Finding the reality of war too unpleasant to contemplate, we create a verbal alternative to that reality, parallel with it, but in quality quite different from it. That which we contemplate thenceforward is not that to which we react emotionally and upon which we pass our moral judgments, is not war as it is in fact, but the fiction of war as it exists in our pleasantly falsifying verbiage. Our stupidity in using inappropriate language turns out, on analysis, to be the most refined cunning. **C**

The most shocking fact about war is that its victims and its instruments are individual human beings, and that these individual human beings are condemned by the monstrous conventions of politics to murder or be murdered in quarrels not their own, to inflict upon the innocent and, innocent themselves of any crime against their enemies, to suffer cruelties of every kind.

The language of strategy and politics is designed, so far as it is possible, to conceal this fact, to make it appear as though wars were not fought by individuals drilled to murder one another in cold blood and without provocation, but either by impersonal and therefore wholly non-moral and impassible forces, or else by personified **abstractions.**

vitiate (vĭsh′ē-āt′) *v.* to corrupt or weaken

B DEDUCTIVE REASONING
In lines 1–35, Huxley develops his **general principle** from a series of ideas about language. Summarize the reasoning that leads to Huxley's general principle.

C DEDUCTIVE REASONING
Huxley states his **conclusion** in lines 43–48. Explain how he uses deductive reasoning to reach this conclusion.

abstraction (ăb-străk′shən) *n.* something that cannot be perceived by any of the five senses; an idea or a quality

---

4. **vincible** (vĭn′sə-bəl): capable of being overcome.

5. **Dr. Jekyll** (jĕk′əl): an idealistic medical researcher transformed by an experimental drug into the murderously evil Mr. Hyde in Robert Louis Stevenson's novel *The Strange Case of Dr. Jekyll and Mr. Hyde.*

60   Here are a few examples of the first kind of falsification. In place of "cavalrymen" or "foot soldiers" military writers like to speak of "sabers" and "rifles." Here is a sentence from a description of the Battle of Marengo:[6] "According to Victor's report, the French retreat was orderly; it is certain, at any rate, that the regiments held together, for the six thousand Austrian sabers found no opportunity to charge home." The battle is between sabers in line and muskets in échelon[7]—a mere clash of ironmongery.[8]

     On other occasions there is no question of anything so vulgarly material as ironmongery. The battles are between Platonic ideas,[9] between the abstractions of physics and mathematics. Forces interact; weights are flung into scales; masses
70 are set in motion. Or else it is all a matter of geometry. Lines swing and sweep; are protracted or curved; pivot on a fixed point. **D**

     Alternatively the combatants are personal, in the sense that they are personifications. There is "the enemy," in the singular, making "his" plans, striking "his" blows. The attribution of personal characteristics to collectivities,[10] to geographical expressions, to institutions, is a source, as we shall see, of endless confusions in political thought, of innumerable political mistakes and crimes. Personification in politics is an error which we make because it is to our advantage as egotists to be able to feel violently proud of our country and of ourselves as belonging to it, and to believe that all the misfortunes
80 due to our own mistakes are really the work of the Foreigner. It is easier to feel violently toward a person than toward an abstraction; hence our habit of making political personifications. In some cases military personifications are merely special instances of political personifications. A particular collectivity, the army or the warring nation, is given the name and, along with the name, the attributes of a single person, in order that we may be able to love or hate it more intensely than we could do if we thought of it as what it really is: a number of diverse individuals. In other cases personification is used for the purpose of concealing the fundamental absurdity and monstrosity of war. What is absurd and monstrous about war is that men who have no personal quarrel should be
90 trained to murder one another in cold blood. By personifying opposing armies or countries, we are able to think of war as a conflict between individuals. The same result is obtained by writing of war as though it were carried on exclusively by the generals in command and not by the private soldiers in their armies. ("Rennenkampf had pressed back von Schubert.") The implication in both cases is that war is indistinguishable from a bout of fisticuffs[11] in a bar room. Whereas in reality it is profoundly different. A scrap between two individuals is forgivable;

ANALYZE AN ARGUMENT
Reread lines 60–71. How do these examples of figurative language support Huxley's **claim**?

> **COMMON CORE** RI 4
> ## Language Coach
> **Roots and Affixes** A word's **root** may contain its core meaning. The root of *egotists* (line 78) is the Latin *ego* ("I"). An egotist is a self-centered person. Several other words come from *ego*. Identify some of these words and their **connotations** (associated feelings).

---

6. **Battle of Marengo:** a battle fought in 1800 in which French troops led by Napoleon Bonaparte defeated an Austrian army near the town of Marengo in northern Italy.

7. **échelon** (ĕsh′ə-lŏn′): an arrangement of groups of soldiers in a steplike formation.

8. **ironmongery** (ī′ərn-mŭng′gə-rē): ironware.

9. **Platonic** (plə-tŏn′ĭk) **ideas:** In the teachings of Plato, the fourth-century B.C. Greek philosopher, all things in the concrete world are actually mere copies of immaterial realities.

10. **collectivities:** groups of people.

11. **fisticuffs** (fĭs′tĭ-kŭfs′): fighting with the fists; bare-knuckle boxing.

mass murder, deliberately organized, is a monstrous **iniquity.** We still choose to use war as an instrument of policy; and to comprehend the full wickedness and absurdity of war would therefore be inconvenient. For, once we understood, we
100 should have to make some effort to get rid of the abominable thing. Accordingly, when we talk about war, we use a language which conceals or embellishes its reality. Ignoring the facts, so far as we possibly can, we imply that battles are not fought by soldiers, but by things, principles, allegories, personified collectivities, or (at the most human) by opposing commanders, pitched against one another in single combat. For the same reason, when we have to describe the processes and the results of war, we employ a rich variety of **euphemisms.** Even the most violently patriotic and militaristic are reluctant to call a spade by its own name. To conceal their intentions even from themselves, they make use of picturesque metaphors. We find them, for example, clamoring for war planes numerous
110 and powerful enough to go and "destroy the hornets in their nests"—in other words, to go and throw thermite,[12] high explosives and vesicants[13] upon the inhabitants of neighboring countries before they have time to come and do the same to us. And how reassuring is the language of historians and strategists! They write admiringly of those military geniuses who know "when to strike at the enemy's line" (a single combatant deranges the geometrical constructions of a personification); when to "turn his flank";[14] when to "execute an enveloping movement." As though they were engineers discussing the strength of materials and the distribution of stresses, they talk of abstract **entities** called "man power" and "fire power." They sum up the long-drawn sufferings and atrocities of trench
120 warfare in the phrase, "a war of attrition";[15] the massacre and mangling of human beings is assimilated to the grinding of a lens.[16]

A dangerously abstract word, which figures in all discussions about war, is "force." Those who believe in organizing collective security by means of military pacts against a possible aggressor are particularly fond of this word. "You cannot," they say, "have international justice unless you are prepared to impose it by force." "Peace-loving countries must unite to use force against aggressive dictatorships." "Democratic institutions must be protected, if need be, by force." And so on. **E**

Now, the word "force," when used in reference to human relations, has no
130 single, definite meaning. There is the "force" used by parents when, without resort to any kind of physical violence, they compel their children to act or refrain from acting in some particular way. There is the "force" used by attendants in an asylum when they try to prevent a maniac from hurting himself or others. There is the "force" used by the police when they control a crowd, and that other

iniquity (ĭ-nĭk′wĭ-tē) *n.* immorality; wickedness

euphemism (yōō′fə-mĭz′əm) *n.* a weaker word or phrase used in place of another in order to be less distasteful or offensive

entity (ĕn′tĭ-tē) *n.* something that has definitive existence; a creation

E ANALYZE AN ARGUMENT
Reread lines 106–127. What **evidence** does Huxley provide to support his idea that even supporters of war are uncomfortable with its reality?

---

12. **thermite:** a mixture of chemicals that burns very intensely, used in certain kinds of bombs.
13. **vesicants** (vĕs′ĭ-kənts): chemical agents, such as mustard gas, that cause inflammation and blistering of the skin and internal tissues.
14. **"turn his flank":** turn the right or left side of the enemy's attack force.
15. **attrition:** a gradual process of wearing down.
16. **assimilated . . . lens:** likened to the process by which glass is ground into lenses.

Come Lad, Slip Across and Help, World War I Poster. © Topham/The Image Works.

"force" which they use in a baton charge.[17] And finally there is the "force" used in war. This, of course, varies with the technological devices at the disposal of the belligerents, with the policies they are pursuing, and with the particular circumstances of the war in question. But in general it may be said that, in war, "force" connotes violence and fraud used to the limit of the combatants' capacity.

140   Variations in quantity, if sufficiently great, produce variations in quality. The "force" that is war, particularly modern war, is very different from the "force" that is police action, and the use of the same abstract word to describe the two dissimilar processes is profoundly misleading. (Still more misleading, of course, is the explicit assimilation of a war, waged by allied League-of-Nations powers[18] against an aggressor, to police action against a criminal. The first is the use of violence and fraud without limit against innocent and guilty alike; the second is the use of strictly limited violence and a minimum of fraud exclusively against the guilty.)

---

17. **baton charge:** the beating back of a mob by police officers wielding wooden clubs.

18. **League-of-Nations powers:** countries (including Britain) who joined the League of Nations, a former international association of nations organized after World War I with the stated purpose of promoting peace.

Reality is a succession of concrete and particular situations. When we think about such situations we should use the particular and concrete words which apply to them. If we use abstract words which apply equally well (and equally badly) to other, quite dissimilar situations, it is certain that we shall think incorrectly.

Let us take the sentences quoted above and translate the abstract word "force" into language that will render (however inadequately) the concrete and particular realities of contemporary warfare. **F**

"You cannot have international justice, unless you are prepared to impose it by force." Translated, this becomes: "You cannot have international justice unless you are prepared, with a view to imposing a just settlement, to drop thermite, high explosives and vesicants upon the inhabitants of foreign cities and to have thermite, high explosives and vesicants dropped in return upon the inhabitants of your cities." At the end of this proceeding, justice is to be imposed by the victorious party—that is, if there is a victorious party. It should be remarked that justice was to have been imposed by the victorious party at the end of the last war. But, unfortunately, after four years of fighting, the temper of the victors was such that they were quite incapable of making a just settlement. The Allies are reaping in Nazi Germany what they sowed at Versailles.[19] The victors of the next war will have undergone intensive bombardments with thermite, high explosives and vesicants. Will their temper be better than that of the Allies in 1918? Will they be in a fitter state to make a just settlement? The answer, quite obviously, is: No. It is psychologically all but impossible that justice should be secured by the methods of contemporary warfare. **G**

The next two sentences may be taken together. "Peace-loving countries must unite to use force against aggressive dictatorships. Democratic institutions must be protected, if need be, by force." Let us translate. "Peace-loving countries must unite to throw thermite, high explosives and vesicants on the inhabitants of countries ruled by aggressive dictators. They must do this, and of course abide the consequences, in order to preserve peace and democratic institutions." Two questions immediately **propound** themselves. First, is it likely that peace can be secured by a process calculated to reduce the orderly life of our complicated societies to chaos? And, second, is it likely that democratic institutions will flourish in a state of chaos? Again, the answers are pretty clearly in the negative.

By using the abstract word "force," instead of terms which at least attempt to describe the realities of war as it is today, the preachers of collective security through military collaboration disguise from themselves and from others, not only the contemporary facts, but also the probable consequences of their favorite policy. The attempt to secure justice, peace and democracy by "force" seems reasonable enough until we realize, first, that this noncommittal word stands, in the circumstances of our age, for activities which can hardly fail to result in social chaos; and second, that the consequences of social chaos are injustice,

COMMON CORE RI 4

F ANALYZE AN ARGUMENT
Think about how you would define the key term *force* in this context. How does Huxley refine the meaning of *force* over the course of this essay? What impact does this add to his argument?

G ANALYZE AN ARGUMENT
Compare the quoted statement with Huxley's translation in lines 156–161. How does his translation serve as **support** for his claim?

propound (prə-pound')
v. to put forward for consideration; propose

---

19. **The Allies . . . Versailles** (vər-sī): The peace treaty ending World War I, signed at the Palace of Versailles near Paris in 1919, imposed humiliating punishments on Germany, which led to the rise of German nationalism and Nazism in the 1920s and 1930s.

190 chronic warfare and tyranny. The moment we think in concrete and particular terms of the concrete and particular process called "modern war," we see that a policy which worked (or at least didn't result in complete disaster) in the past has no prospect whatever of working in the immediate future. The attempt to secure justice, peace and democracy by means of a "force," which means, at this particular moment of history, thermite, high explosives and vesicants, is about as reasonable as the attempt to put out a fire with a colorless liquid that happens to be, not water, but petrol.[20] **H**

What applies to the "force" that is war applies in large measure to the "force" that is revolution. It seems inherently very unlikely that social justice and social
200 peace can be secured by thermite, high explosives and vesicants. At first, it may be, the parties in a civil war would hesitate to use such instruments on their fellow-countrymen. But there can be little doubt that, if the conflict were prolonged (as it probably would be between the evenly balanced Right and Left of a highly industrialized society), the combatants would end by losing their scruples.

The alternatives confronting us seem to be plain enough. Either we invent and conscientiously employ a new technique for making revolutions and settling international disputes; or else we cling to the old technique and, using "force" (that is to say, thermite, high explosives and vesicants), destroy ourselves. Those who, for whatever motive, disguise the nature of the second alternative under
210 inappropriate language, render the world a grave disservice. They lead us into one of the temptations we find it hardest to resist—the temptation to run away from reality, to pretend that facts are not what they are. Like Shelley (but without Shelley's acute awareness of what he was doing) we are perpetually weaving

> *A shroud of talk to hide us from the sun*
> *Of this familiar life.*[21]

We protect our minds by an elaborate system of abstractions, ambiguities, metaphors and similes from the reality we do not wish to know too clearly; we lie to ourselves, in order that we may still have the excuse of ignorance, the alibi of stupidity and incomprehension, possessing which we can continue with a good
220 conscience to commit and tolerate the most monstrous crimes: **I**

> *The poor wretch who has learned his only prayers*
> *From curses, who knows scarcely words enough*
> *To ask a blessing from his Heavenly Father,*
> *Becomes a fluent phraseman, absolute*
> *And technical in victories and defeats,*
> *And all our dainty terms for fratricide;*[22]

---

20. **petrol** (pĕt'rəl): gasoline.

21. **Shelley . . . *familiar life:*** The romantic poet Percy Bysshe Shelley wrote these lines in his 1820 poem "Letter to Maria Gisborne."

22. **fratricide** (frăt'rĭ-sīd'): the killing of one's brother or sister.

H RHETORICAL DEVICES
What effect does Huxley create through **repetition** of the phrase "thermite, high explosives and vesicants"?

I AMBIGUITY
Ambiguity is a technique writers use in which a word, phrase, or event has more than one meaning or can be interpreted in more than one way. An ambiguous statement demonstrates an inexactness of meaning in language. In what way does Huxley believe ambiguity can protect our minds from monstrous crimes? As you read the poem that follows, watch for an example of this type of ambiguity.

Your Talk May Kill Your Comrades (1942), Abram Games. World War II Poster. The Granger Collection, New York.

Terms which we trundle smoothly o'er our tongues
Like mere abstractions, empty sounds to which
We join no meaning and attach no form!
230   *As if the soldier died without a wound:*
As if the fibers of this godlike frame
Were gored without a pang: as if the wretch
Who fell in battle, doing bloody deeds,
Passed off to Heaven translated and not killed;
As though he had no wife to pine for him,
No God to judge him.[23]

    The language we use about war is inappropriate, and its inappropriateness is designed to conceal a reality so odious that we do not wish to know it. The language we use about politics is also inappropriate; but here our mistake has a 240 different purpose. Our principal aim in this case is to arouse and, having aroused, to rationalize and justify such **intrinsically** agreeable sentiments as pride and hatred, self-esteem and contempt for others. To achieve this end we speak about the facts of politics in words which more or less completely misrepresent them. . . .

    The evil passions are further justified by another linguistic error—the error of speaking about certain categories of persons as though they were mere embodied abstractions. Foreigners and those who disagree with us are not thought of as men and women like ourselves and our fellow-countrymen; they are thought of as representatives and, so to say, symbols of a class. In so far as they have any personality at all, it is the personality we mistakenly attribute to their class—a 250 personality that is, by definition, intrinsically evil. We know that the harming or killing of men and women is wrong, and we are reluctant consciously to do what we know to be wrong. But when particular men and women are thought of merely as representatives of a class, which has previously been defined as evil and personified in the shape of a devil, then the reluctance to hurt or murder disappears. Brown, Jones and Robinson are no longer thought of as Brown, Jones and Robinson, but as heretics, gentiles, Yids, niggers, barbarians, Huns, communists, capitalists, fascists, liberals[24]—whichever the case may be. When they have been called such names and assimilated to the accursed class to which the names apply, Brown, Jones and Robinson cease to be conceived as 260 what they really are—human persons—and become for the users of this fatally inappropriate language mere vermin or, worse, demons whom it is right and proper to destroy as thoroughly and as painfully as possible. Wherever persons are present, questions of morality arise. Rulers of nations and leaders of parties find morality embarrassing. That is why they take such pains to depersonalize

COMMON CORE RI 4

Language Coach

Homographs The noun *gore* is unrelated to the verb. The noun, from Old English *gor* ("filth"), means "blood from a wound." The verb, from Old English *gar* ("spear"), means "stab." How does the noun affect the connotation of *gored* (line 232)?

intrinsically
(ĭn-trĭn′zĭ-klē) *adv.* in the manner of the true nature of a thing; inherently

---

23. ***The poor wretch . . . judge him:*** These lines are from "Fears in Solitude," a poem that romantic poet Samuel Taylor Coleridge wrote during what he called "the alarm of an invasion" of Britain by French forces near the start of the Napoleonic wars.

24. **heretics . . . liberals:** terms used to disparage groups of people. *Yids* is an offensive term for Jews, and *Huns* was a derogatory term for Germans during World War I.

their opponents. All propaganda directed against an opposing group has but one aim: to substitute diabolical abstractions for concrete persons. The propagandist's purpose is to make one set of people forget that certain other sets of people are human. By robbing them of their personality, he puts them outside the pale of moral obligation. Mere symbols can have no rights—particularly when that of
270 which they are symbolical is, by definition, evil. **J**

Politics can become moral only on one condition: that its problems shall be spoken of and thought about exclusively in terms of concrete reality; that is to say, of persons. To depersonify human beings and to personify abstractions are complementary errors which lead, by an inexorable[25] logic, to war between nations and to idolatrous worship of the State, with consequent governmental oppression. All current political thought is a mixture, in varying proportions, between thought in terms of concrete realities and thought in terms of depersonified symbols and personified abstractions. In the democratic countries the problems of internal politics are thought about mainly in terms of concrete
280 reality; those of external politics, mainly in terms of abstractions and symbols. In dictatorial countries the proportion of concrete to abstract and symbolic thought is lower than in democratic countries. Dictators talk little of persons, much of personified abstractions, such as the Nation, the State, the Party, and much of depersonified symbols, such as Yids, Bolshies,[26] Capitalists. The stupidity of politicians who talk about a world of persons as though it were not a world of persons is due in the main to self-interest. In a fictitious world of symbols and personified abstractions, rulers find that they can rule more effectively, and the ruled, that they can gratify instincts which the conventions of good manners and the imperatives of morality demand that they should repress. To think correctly **K**
290 is the condition of behaving well. It is also in itself a moral act; those who would think correctly must resist considerable temptations. ❧

J DEDUCTIVE REASONING
In lines 237–270, Huxley applies his general principle to politics. Summarize the deductive reasoning in this passage, and describe what Huxley offers as support for his claim.

K GRAMMAR AND STYLE
To convey his ideas about this serious topic, Huxley uses **formal language.** Notice the sophisticated vocabulary and complex sentence structure in lines 286–289.

---

25. **inexorable** (ĭn-ĕk′sər-ə-bəl): not able to be moved or influenced; unrelenting.

26. **Bolshies:** Communists. The word is shortened from *Bolsheviks,* members of the Russian Communist faction that came to power in the 1917 revolution.

Comprehension

1. **Recall** According to Huxley, what is the main reason why people use language inappropriately when discussing war?

2. **Recall** What does Huxley find "absurd and monstrous" about war?

3. **Clarify** According to Huxley in lines 237–243, why do politicians often use inappropriate language?

Text Analysis

4. **Examine Rhetorical Devices** Huxley uses **repetition** throughout his essay to emphasize ideas and refine the meaning of key terms. For each example that follows, explain how the repetition enhances his argument.

   - "ignorance" and "stupidity" (lines 23–49)
   - "force" (lines 129–139)
   - "Brown, Jones and Robinson" (lines 255–262)

5. **Analyze an Argument** Review your notes on the reasons and evidence that Huxley develops in the essay. What do you consider the strongest support for his claim that inappropriate use of language allows people to deceive themselves and others about the true nature of war? Explain your answer.

6. **Draw Conclusions About Deductive Reasoning** In his statement of the premise on which he bases his deductive reasoning, Huxley says that "words give continuity to what we do." Why might it be especially difficult for a nation's leaders to maintain such continuity in wartime?

7. **Evaluate the Essay** In your opinion, how well reasoned and persuasive is Huxley's argument? How does the structure of the essay support his argument? Does he achieve his purpose? Cite examples from the text to support your answer.

8. **Compare Texts** Reread the war poems by Yeats, Brooke, and Sassoon starting on page 1244. Which of these poems best captures the reality of war as described by Huxley? Explain your response.

Text Criticism

9. **Historical Context** Huxley wrote "Words and Behavior" in 1939 in reaction to developments in Nazi Germany and other nations. In his essay, he warns against the manipulation of language—both by political leaders and by ordinary citizens—to justify war. Are his observations true today? Explain.

How can **WORDS** deceive?

Think of some commonly used euphemisms. Choose one, and describe how it obscures the complexity of the real world.

COMMON CORE

RI 3 Analyze a complex set of ideas and explain how specific ideas develop over the course of the text. **RI 4** Analyze how an author uses and refines the meaning of key terms over the course of a text. **RI 5** Analyze and evaluate the effectiveness of the structure an author uses in his or her argument. **RI 6** Determine an author's purpose in a text in which the rhetoric is particularly effective.

Vocabulary in Context

▲ **VOCABULARY PRACTICE**

Answer the following questions based on your knowledge of the vocabulary words.

1. What kind of person is likely to stare **balefully?**
2. When factors **vitiate** a cause, what do they do?
3. What is an example of an **abstraction?**
4. What type of situation is clearly an **iniquity?**
5. What phrase is a **euphemism** for an old person?
6. What must an **entity** have?
7. If you **propound** an idea, what do you do?
8. What traits are **intrinsically** part of a person?

ACADEMIC VOCABULARY IN SPEAKING

- approach   - assume   - environment   - method   - strategy

Find an example of an editorial calling for a specific policy or supporting a particular position. Then, employ Huxley's **method** of analysis by closely examining the words that are used in the editorial. With a partner, analyze the author's use of language. Use an Academic Vocabulary word in your discussion.

VOCABULARY STRATEGY: USING CONTEXT CLUES TO FIND NUANCE

A word can have many shades of meaning, or **nuances.** Though the word *abstraction* generally denotes a removal from concrete reality, its **context**—the surrounding words—can express various nuances. For example, if you say a car that runs on water is a "mere *abstraction* because the technology is nonexistent," your use of *mere* and *nonexistent technology* suggests that the idea is unrealistic.

PRACTICE Use context to determine the nuance of *abstraction* in each sentence.

1. The film's vivid imagery makes poverty in Africa more than an **abstraction**.
2. In a state of **abstraction,** Amelia put on her slippers instead of her shoes.
3. The entire gallery was filled with **abstractions** in glass, plastic, and bronze.
4. Professor Ponce spoke in **abstractions,** making him difficult to understand.
5. The **abstraction** of key ideas from the articles required a critical editor.

COMMON CORE

L 5b Analyze nuances in the meaning of words with similar denotations. **L 6** Acquire and use accurately general academic words and phrases.

Interactive Vocabulary **THINK** central

Go to **thinkcentral.com.**
KEYWORD: HML12-1278

Language

◆ **GRAMMAR AND STYLE: Use Appropriate Language**

Review the **Grammar and Style** note on page 1276. Huxley uses **formal language** that is appropriate for the seriousness of his topic and the sophistication of his argument. Here is an example from his essay:

> *A particular collectivity, the army or the warring nation, is given the name and, along with the name, the attributes of a single person, in order that we may be able to love or hate it more intensely than we could do if we thought of it as what it really is: a number of diverse individuals.* (lines 83–87)

Notice that the passage contains key elements of formal language, including complex vocabulary and sentence structure and a lack of contractions.

PRACTICE Rewrite the following sentences using formal language. An example sentence has been done for you.

> Politicians can't always say the whole truth and nothing but the truth, especially if a war is going on.
>
> *Politicians cannot always speak with complete openness and honesty, especially during wartime.*

1. When a place is getting attacked by some bad guys, the government first of all has to protect its people.

2. After the war's over, educated types can get picky about the things their leaders said.

READING-WRITING CONNECTION

 YOUR TURN Expand your understanding of argument by responding to this prompt. Then, use the **revising tips** to improve your rebuttal.

WRITING PROMPT	REVISING TIPS
WRITE A REBUTTAL It's very clear in "Words and Behavior" how Huxley feels about language being manipulated to deceive. Write a **three- or four-paragraph rebuttal** to his essay in which you make the case for why language must sometimes be manipulated.	• Clearly state your opposing claim. • Provide a strong example to support your claim. • Use forceful and specific language, while maintaining a formal and respectful tone. • Wrap up your argument with a logical conclusion.

Interactive Revision

Go to **thinkcentral.com**.
KEYWORD: HML12-1279

 **COMMON CORE**

L 1 Demonstrate command of the conventions of standard English grammar and usage when writing. **W 1a–b, d–e** Introduce precise claim(s); develop claim(s) thoroughly, supplying relevant evidence; establish and maintain a formal style and tone; provide a concluding statement that follows from and supports the argument.

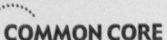

from **Night**

 Video link at thinkcentral.com

Memoir by Elie Wiesel

COMMON CORE

RI 1 Cite evidence to support inferences drawn from the text. RI 6 Determine an author's point of view in a text in which the rhetoric is particularly effective, analyzing how style and content contribute to the power, persuasiveness, or beauty of a text. L 5b Analyze nuances in the meaning of words with similar denotations.

Meet the Author

Elie Wiesel born 1928

British Prime Minister Winston Churchill described Nazi Germany as "the foulest and most soul-destroying tyranny which has ever darkened and stained the pages of history." Holocaust survivor Elie Wiesel's memoir *Night* provided the world with a harrowing firsthand account of the soul-destroying tactics used by the Nazis in their attempt to eradicate European Jews.

A Family Torn Apart Wiesel was born in Sighet (sē'gĕt), a town in the Romanian region of Transylvania. Raised as a devout Orthodox Jew, Wiesel was just 15 in the spring of 1944 when the Nazis ordered the deportation of Sighet's 15,000 Jews, shipping them out on a cattle train to the Auschwitz-Birkenau concentration camp in Poland. Wiesel's mother and one of his three sisters were murdered at Auschwitz. Separated from the women in the family, Wiesel and his father were eventually sent to the Buchenwald concentration camp in Germany, where Wiesel's father died of starvation and dysentery shortly before the camp was liberated in April 1945.

Bearing Witness After Wiesel was freed, he remained silent about the Holocaust for ten years, writing nothing about his experiences even

though he worked as a journalist and writer. "I didn't want to use the wrong words," he later explained. Wiesel's first attempt at writing about the Holocaust was an 800-page autobiographical account in Yiddish, the language of his childhood. He then wrote a French version of the account, condensed to just over 100 pages, which was published as *La Nuit* in 1958 and as *Night* in English two years later. Historian Daniel Stern described the book as "the single most powerful literary relic of the Holocaust." Wiesel has worked tirelessly to call attention to human rights violations around the world, winning the 1986 Nobel Peace Prize for his efforts.

Into the Night The excerpt that follows begins as the Jews of Sighet are huddled in a filthy cattle train bound for Auschwitz-Birkenau, where eventually some 2 million Jews would be killed in gas chambers or shot by firing squads. Others, who were forced to work as slaves, died of torture, starvation, exhaustion, and disease. Tragically, the Jews of Sighet had earlier been warned of Nazi atrocities by a man passing through the town who told them to run for their lives. They believed him to be mad, however, and did not heed his warning.

DID YOU KNOW?

Elie Wiesel . . .

- may have been the first person to use the word *Holocaust* to refer to the mass murder carried out by the Nazis.

- co-wrote a memoir with former French president François Mitterrand.

- is fluent in Yiddish, Hebrew, Hungarian, German, French, and English.

Author Online

Go to **thinkcentral.com**. KEYWORD: HML12-1280

● TEXT ANALYSIS: TONE

Tone is the expression of a writer's attitude, or point of view, toward a subject. The tone of nonfiction writing can vary widely; for example, an informational article may be detached and objective, while an opinion piece may be ardent and totally subjective. In this excerpt from *Night*, Wiesel's tone reflects his personal experience of horrific events. As you read, consider the following in determining the memoir's tone:

- the **descriptive details** the writer offers
- the **diction** the writer uses—that is, the **word choices** and **syntax,** or order of words in a sentence

● READING STRATEGY: READING A MEMOIR

A **memoir** is a form of autobiographical writing in which a writer shares his or her personal experiences and observations of significant events or people. Memoirs can provide a firsthand account of historical events, allowing us to generalize from an individual's experience to learn about history from a more personal perspective. In Wiesel's memoir *Night,* we view through his eyes the horrors that millions of European Jews experienced in Nazi concentration camps.

As you read Wiesel's memoir, think about which of his personal experiences would have been very similar for most Jews captured by the Nazis. Consider what you already know about the Holocaust and what you learn from Wiesel: are you able to make any generalizations about this historical event? Using a chart like the one shown, write down the specific details from Wiesel's personal experiences that help you arrive at historical generalizations.

Wiesel's Experience	Generalization
"If anyone goes missing, you will all be shot, like dogs."	Jewish prisoners were threatened and treated like animals.

 Complete the activities in your **Reader/Writer Notebook**.

Why must we never FORGET?

Elie Wiesel once said that the Holocaust is a tragedy "beyond words and beyond imagination, but not beyond memory." Because of the efforts of survivors like Wiesel and of other human rights activists, countless books, films, memorials, and museums have been created over the years to remember and honor the victims of the Holocaust and to serve as a reminder of one of the most shameful chapters in history.

DISCUSS With a small group of classmates, list a few major events from history, noting what we learned from each. Then, share your findings with other groups.

Historic Event	What We Learned
Civil War	A divided nation cannot survive; slavery is inhumane and unacceptable.

Night

Elie Wiesel

BACKGROUND Germany's invasion of Poland in 1939 marked the beginning of World War II. One of Adolf Hitler's goals was to eliminate the Jewish population (whom he blamed for every evil in the world). All across Europe, Jews were rounded up by Hitler's Nazi forces and sent—usually by train—to concentration camps, where many were killed in gas chambers, were executed by firing squads, or died of torture, starvation, or disease. The largest of these death camps was Auschwitz-Birkenau in Poland where, it is estimated, more than 2 million people were killed.

The train stopped in Kaschau, a small town on the Czechoslovakian border.[1] We realized then that we were not staying in Hungary. Our eyes opened. Too late.

The door of the car slid aside. A German officer stepped in accompanied by a Hungarian lieutenant, acting as his interpreter.

"From this moment on, you are under the authority of the German army. Anyone who still owns gold, silver, or watches must hand them over now. Anyone who will be found to have kept any of these will be shot on the spot. Secondly, anyone who is ill should report to the hospital car. That's all."

The Hungarian lieutenant went around with a basket and retrieved the last
10 possessions from those who chose not to go on tasting the bitterness of fear.

"There are eighty of you in the car," the German officer added. "If anyone goes missing, you will all be shot, like dogs." **A**

The two disappeared. The doors clanked shut. We had fallen into the trap, up to our necks. The doors were nailed, the way back irrevocably cut off. The world had become a hermetically[2] sealed cattle car.

Analyze Visuals ▶
How does the background information on this page affect how you think about this photograph?

A MEMOIR
What generalization can you make from Wiesel's experience in lines 9–12?

---

1. **Czechoslovakian** (chĕk'ə-slə-vä'kē-ən) **border:** the border of the former nation of Czechoslovakia (now the Czech Republic and Slovakia), occupied by Germany during World War II.
2. **hermetically** (hər-mĕt'ĭ-klē): in an airtight way; thoroughly.

Women and children arrive in freight trains at Auschwitz-Birkenau

There was a woman among us, a certain Mrs. Schächter. She was in her fifties and her ten-year-old son was with her, crouched in a corner. Her husband and two older sons had been deported with the first transport, by mistake. The separation had totally shattered her.

20 I knew her well. A quiet, tense woman with piercing eyes, she had been a frequent guest in our house. Her husband was a pious man who spent most of his days and nights in the house of study. It was she who supported the family.

Mrs. Schächter had lost her mind. On the first day of the journey, she had already begun to moan. She kept asking why she had been separated from her family. Later, her sobs and screams became hysterical.

On the third night, as we were sleeping, some of us sitting, huddled against each other, some of us standing, a piercing cry broke the silence:

"Fire! I see a fire! I see a fire!"

There was a moment of panic. Who had screamed? It was Mrs. Schächter.

30 Standing in the middle of the car, in the faint light filtering through the windows, she looked like a withered tree in a field of wheat. She was howling, pointing through the window: **B**

"Look! Look at this fire! This terrible fire! Have mercy on me!"

Some pressed against the bars to see. There was nothing. Only the darkness of night.

It took us a long time to recover from this harsh awakening. We were still trembling, and with every screech of the wheels, we felt the abyss opening beneath us. Unable to still our anguish, we tried to reassure each other:

"She is mad, poor woman . . ."

40 Someone had placed a damp rag on her forehead. But she nevertheless continued to scream:

"Fire! I see a fire!"

Her little boy was crying, clinging to her skirt, trying to hold her hand:

"It's nothing, Mother! There's nothing there . . . Please sit down . . ." He pained me even more than did his mother's cries.

Some of the women tried to calm her:

"You'll see, you'll find your husband and sons again . . . In a few days . . ."

She continued to scream and sob fitfully.

"Jews, listen to me," she cried. "I see a fire! I see flames, huge flames!"

50 It was as though she were possessed by some evil spirit.

We tried to reason with her, more to calm ourselves, to catch our breath, than to soothe her:

"She is hallucinating because she is thirsty, poor woman . . . That's why she speaks of flames devouring her . . ."

But it was all in vain. Our terror could no longer be contained. Our nerves had reached a breaking point. Our very skin was aching. It was as though madness had infected all of us. We gave up. A few young men forced her to sit down, then bound and gagged her. **C**

B TONE
Reread the description of Mrs. Schächter. How do Wiesel's word choices contribute to the general tone of the work?

C MEMOIR
Reread lines 36–58, focusing on the reactions of other passengers to Mrs. Schächter. How did the train ride to Auschwitz affect the prisoners?

Silence fell again. The small boy sat next to his mother, crying. I started to
60 breathe normally again as I listened to the rhythmic pounding of the wheels on
the tracks as the train raced through the night. We could begin to doze again,
to rest, to dream . . .

And so an hour or two passed. Another scream jolted us. The woman had
broken free of her bonds and was shouting louder than before:

"Look at the fire! Look at the flames! Flames everywhere . . ."

Once again, the young men bound and gagged her. When they actually struck
her, people shouted their approval:

"Keep her quiet! Make that madwoman shut up. She's not the only one here . . ."

She received several blows to the head, blows that could have been lethal. Her
70 son was clinging desperately to her, not uttering a word. He was no longer crying.

The night seemed endless. By daybreak, Mrs. Schächter had settled down.
Crouching in her corner, her blank gaze fixed on some faraway place, she no
longer saw us.

She remained like that all day, mute, absent, alone in the midst of us. Toward
evening she began to shout again:

"The fire, over there!"

She was pointing somewhere in the distance, always the same place. No one
felt like beating her anymore. The heat, the thirst, the stench, the lack of air, were
suffocating us. Yet all that was nothing compared to her screams, which tore us
80 apart. A few more days and all of us would have started to scream. **D**

But we were pulling into a station. Someone near a window read to us:
"Auschwitz."[3]

Nobody had ever heard that name.

The train did not move again. The afternoon went by slowly. Then the doors
of the wagon slid open. Two men were given permission to fetch water.

When they came back, they told us that they had learned, in exchange for a
gold watch, that this was the final destination. We were to leave the train here.
There was a labor camp on the site. The conditions were good. Families would
not be separated. Only the young would work in the factories. The old and the
90 sick would find work in the fields.

Confidence soared. Suddenly we felt free of the previous nights' terror. We
gave thanks to God.

Mrs. Schächter remained huddled in her corner, mute, untouched by the
optimism around her. Her little one was stroking her hand.

Dusk began to fill the wagon. We ate what was left of our food. At ten o'clock
in the evening, we were all trying to find a position for a quick nap and soon we
were dozing. Suddenly:

"Look at the fire! Look at the flames! Over there!"

---

3. **Auschwitz** (oush'vĭts'): a town in southern Poland near the site of the Auschwitz-Birkenau
extermination camp, where between 1 and 4 million people, mostly Jews from Germany and eastern
Europe, were systematically murdered by the Nazis between 1942 and 1945.

COMMON CORE L 5b

Language Coach

Synonyms Individual
synonyms have shades
of meaning, or **nuance**.
Lethal (line 69) and *fatal,*
for example, both mean
"deadly," but *lethal* implies
that death is possible, and
fatal means that death is
inevitable. Could *fatal* be
used in line 69?

D TONE
What words in lines
74–80 help convey the
passengers' emotional
state?

With a start, we awoke and rushed to the window yet again. We had believed
her, if only for an instant. But there was nothing outside but darkness. We
returned to our places, shame in our souls but fear gnawing at us nevertheless.
As she went on howling, she was struck again. Only with great difficulty did we
succeed in quieting her down.

The man in charge of our wagon called out to a German officer strolling down
the platform, asking him to have the sick woman moved to a hospital car.

"Patience," the German replied, "patience. She'll be taken there soon."

Around eleven o'clock, the train began to move again. We pressed against
the windows. The convoy was rolling slowly. A quarter of an hour later, it
began to slow down even more. Through the windows, we saw barbed wire; we
understood that this was the camp.

We had forgotten Mrs. Schächter's existence. Suddenly there was a terrible
scream:

"Jews, look! Look at the fire! Look at the flames!"

And as the train stopped, this time we saw flames rising from a tall chimney
into a black sky.

Mrs. Schächter had fallen silent on her own. Mute again, indifferent, absent,
she had returned to her corner.

We stared at the flames in the darkness. A wretched stench floated in the air.
Abruptly, our doors opened. Strange-looking creatures, dressed in striped jackets
and black pants, jumped into the wagon. Holding flashlights and sticks, they
began to strike at us left and right, shouting:

"Everybody get out! Leave everything inside. Hurry up!" **E**

We jumped out. I glanced at Mrs. Schächter. Her little boy was still holding
her hand.

In front of us, those flames. In the air, the smell of burning flesh. It must have
been around midnight. We had arrived. In Birkenau. ∾

Translated by Marion Wiesel

E MEMOIR
Lines 107–122 are
Wiesel's eyewitness
account of arriving
at Auschwitz. What
descriptive details convey
the terror that Jews felt
upon their arrival at the
concentration camps?

Comprehension

1. **Recall** What are the passengers forced to give up when the German army takes control of the train?

2. **Recall** What do the passengers see when they arrive at Birkenau?

3. **Clarify** What has led to Mrs. Schächter's mental breakdown?

Text Analysis

4. **Identify Irony** When a character expects one thing to happen but something else actually happens, it is referred to as **situational irony.** Identify an example of situational irony in this excerpt from *Night*.

5. **Analyze Tone** What tone does Wiesel use in his descriptions of Mrs. Schächter and her son? How does the way others interact with her contrast with that tone?

6. **Examine Writer's Style** Diction, or a writer's choice of words, is a significant component of style. Part of the power of this excerpt from *Night* is the way Wiesel conveys the emotional and psychological states of the passengers in the train car. For each of the following, identify the emotional state he describes and cite the words or phrases he uses to do so. Be sure to note the figurative language in these passages.

   • lines 13–15 ("The two disappeared ... cattle car.")

   • lines 55–57 ("But it was all ... We gave up.")

   • lines 87–92 ("We were to leave ... thanks to God.")

7. **Make Judgments About Memoir** Review the chart you completed as you read, and think about both the personal and historical insights Wiesel provides. In your opinion, what would be more valuable to a historian 100 years from now—Wiesel's memoir from his personal point of view or a more objective account of events surrounding the Holocaust? Explain.

Text Criticism

8. **Biographical Context** Elie Wiesel has stated, "I decided to devote my life to telling the story because I felt that having survived I owe something to the dead, and anyone who does not remember betrays them again." What might Wiesel "owe" to those who died in the Holocaust? Explain your response.

> *Why must we never* **FORGET?**
>
> What modern catastrophes can be considered important to remember? Try to think of at least two examples. What steps have survivors taken to memorialize those events? What important facts or details have they sought to remember?

COMMON CORE

RI 1 Cite evidence to support inferences drawn from the text. **RI 3** Explain how individuals interact over the course of a text. **RI 4** Determine the meaning of words and phrases as they are used in a text, including figurative meanings. **RI 6** Determine an author's point of view in a text in which the rhetoric is particularly effective, analyzing how style and content contribute to the power, persuasiveness, or beauty of a text.

from **The Speeches, May 19, 1940**

Speech by Winston Churchill

HISTORY. Video link at **thinkcentral.com**

VIDEO TRAILER **THINK** central KEYWORD: HML12-1288A

COMMON CORE

RI 2 Determine two or more central ideas of a text and analyze their development over the course of the text; provide an objective summary of the text. RI 8 Delineate and evaluate the reasoning in seminal texts. RI 9 Analyze foundational documents of historical significance for their themes, purposes, and rhetorical features. L 5a Interpret figures of speech in context and analyze their role in the text.

DID YOU KNOW?

Winston Churchill …

- prepared the speech you are about to read in only three hours?
- was 65 years old at the time he became prime minister and was active in politics until he was nearly 90?
- popularized the term "Iron Curtain"?

Meet the Author

Winston Churchill 1874–1965

It has been said that without Winston Churchill, the Allies might not have achieved victory in World War II. Churchill's heart-stirring speeches defied Hitler and inspired the British people to persevere. "His eloquence," wrote Churchill scholar Manfred Weidhorn, "rallied the free world in the face of mortal perils."

An Officer and a Journalist The son of a noble English father and an American mother, Churchill received a traditional English secondary education. Because of his poor performance at school, he attended the Royal Military College at Sandhurst instead of a university. However, he found his niche in the military, serving as both an officer and a war correspondent. In 1899, during the Boer War, he was captured by the Boers, but he made a daring escape.

A Checkered Career Churchill entered politics in 1900. His enthusiastic support for an ultimately disastrous naval attack on the Dardanelles during World War I and his switching of party affiliation from Conservative to Liberal and then back to Conservative caused many in England to distrust him. During the 1930s, Churchill warned of the potentially catastrophic consequences of Hitler's increasing power, but his concerns were largely ignored.

However, in 1940, following the resignation of Prime Minister Neville Chamberlain, Churchill became a compromise prime minister in a coalition government. His tenacious leadership and single-minded vision during World War II proved him to be one of England's greatest statesmen. Though his party was ousted from power after the war, he reclaimed his role as prime minister in 1951, at the age of 77, only to resign four years later because of poor health.

A Seasoned Historian During the war, Churchill assured Allied leaders President Franklin Roosevelt and Russian premier Joseph Stalin, "History will judge us kindly." When asked how he could be so sure, Churchill answered, "Because I shall write the history." And so he did, in his six-volume *The Second World War.* Throughout his political career, Churchill was a prolific writer, producing multivolume biographies, histories, and other works, all written in a forthright and energetic style. In 1953, he was awarded the Nobel Prize in literature "for his mastery of historical and biographical description as well as for brilliant oratory in defending exalted human values."

Author Online

Go to **thinkcentral.com**. KEYWORD: HML12-1288B

THINK central

● TEXT ANALYSIS: SPEECH

Although a **speech** is intended to be read aloud, the written texts of some speeches have become an important part of our literature. Winston Churchill was one of the finest speech writers of the 20th century. In the speech you will read, he uses a variety of techniques that make it effective oratory, including

- **Rhetorical devices**—such as repetition and parallelism (using similar grammatical constructions to express related ideas)
- **Persuasive techniques**—such as loaded language and emotional appeals
- **Clear narrative**—or a compelling and easy-to-follow "story"

As you read, look for examples of these techniques and notice how Churchill uses them to make his case for war.

● READING SKILL: IDENTIFY MAIN IDEAS

You know that the **main idea** of a paragraph is the basic point it makes. In a persuasive text, each main idea contributes to the writer's or speaker's reasoning. Winston Churchill delivered the following speech early in World War II, when the war was going badly for the Allies. In addition to describing recent developments in the war, he states his ideas about how Great Britain should respond to these events. As you read, summarize the main idea in each paragraph.

	Main Idea
Paragraph 1	
Paragraph 2	

▲ VOCABULARY IN CONTEXT

Restate each phrase, using a different word or words for the boldface term.

1. showed a **dogged** determination
2. ferocious opponent was **formidable**
3. his **invincible** armor
4. threats to **intimidate** the sheriff
5. inspiration to **animate** the troops
6. can't dampen her **indomitable** spirit

 Complete the activities in your **Reader/Writer Notebook**.

How can a crisis UNITE us?

When a crisis such as a war or a natural disaster occurs, people are often forced to re-evaluate their priorities. Everyday problems and differences of opinion are suddenly overshadowed by the greater public concern. When Winston Churchill took office, the German army threatened the whole of Europe. With his incomparable speaking abilities, Churchill was able to create unity among the British people—and ultimately the Allied forces—in the common goal of defeating the Nazis.

DISCUSS With a group of three or four classmates, make a list of some major crises that have occurred since the 21st century began. Then, discuss ways people pulled together to work toward a common goal or strategy for dealing with the crises. Consider the roles played by political leaders, the media, and private citizens.

The Speeches,
MAY 19, 1940

Winston Churchill

BACKGROUND World War II began in Europe two years before the United States became involved. Between September 1939 and May 1940, Nazi Germany—which had already annexed Austria and most of Czechoslovakia—conquered Poland, Denmark, and Norway. On May 10, 1940, the German army began sweeping through Holland and Belgium on its way to France. When Churchill broadcast this radio speech on May 19, the British troops fighting in western Europe were backed up against the ocean, ready to retreat to England.

I speak to you for the first time as Prime Minister in a solemn hour for the life of our country, of our Empire, of our Allies, and, above all, of the cause of Freedom. A tremendous battle is raging in France and Flanders.[1] The Germans, by a remarkable combination of air bombing and heavily armored tanks, have broken through the French defenses north of the Maginot Line,[2] and strong columns of their armored vehicles are ravaging the open country, which for the first day or two was without defenders. They have penetrated deeply and spread alarm and confusion in their track. Behind them there are now appearing infantry in lorries,[3] and behind them, again, the large masses are moving forward. The
10 regroupment of the French armies to make head against, and also to strike at, this intruding wedge has been proceeding for several days, largely assisted by the magnificent efforts of the Royal Air Force.[4] **Ⓐ**

Ⓐ SPEECH
Summarize the narrative Churchill presents in lines 1–12.

---

1. **Flanders:** western Belgium.
2. **Maginot** (măzh′ə-nō′) **Line:** a line of fortifications that the French built before World War II on their eastern border with Germany. The Maginot Line was thought to be impossible to penetrate.
3. **lorries** (lôr′ēz): the British term for trucks.
4. **Royal Air Force:** the British air force, offering aerial support to French forces on the ground.

Churchill inspects bombing damage to the Houses of Parliament

We must not allow ourselves to be **<u>intimidated</u>** by the presence of these armored vehicles in unexpected places behind our lines. If they are behind our Front, the French are also at many points fighting actively behind theirs. Both sides are therefore in an extremely dangerous position. And if the French Army, and our own Army, are well handled, as I believe they will be; if the French retain that genius for recovery and counterattack for which they have so long been famous; and if the British Army shows the **<u>dogged</u>** endurance and solid fighting
20 power of which there have been so many examples in the past—then a sudden transformation of the scene might spring into being. **B**

It would be foolish, however, to disguise the gravity of the hour. It would be still more foolish to lose heart and courage or to suppose that well-trained, well-equipped armies numbering three or four millions of men can be overcome in the space of a few weeks, or even months, by a scoop, or raid of mechanized vehicles, however **<u>formidable</u>.** We may look with confidence to the stabilization of the Front in France, and to the general engagement of the masses, which will enable the qualities of the French and British soldiers to be matched squarely against those of their adversaries. For myself, I have **<u>invincible</u>** confidence in the
30 French Army and its leaders. Only a very small part of that splendid army has yet been heavily engaged; and only a very small part of France has yet been invaded. There is good evidence to show that practically the whole of the specialized and mechanized forces of the enemy have been already thrown into the battle; and we know that very heavy losses have been inflicted upon them. No officer or man, no brigade or division, which grapples at close quarters with the enemy, wherever encountered, can fail to make a worthy contribution to the general result. The Armies must cast away the idea of resisting behind concrete lines or natural obstacles, and must realize that mastery can only be regained by furious and unrelenting assault. And this spirit must not only **<u>animate</u>** the High Command,
40 but must inspire every fighting man.

In the air—often at serious odds—often at odds hitherto thought overwhelming—we have been clawing down three or four to one of our enemies; and the relative balance of the British and German Air Forces is now considerably more favorable to us than at the beginning of the battle. In cutting down the German bombers, we are fighting our own battle as well as that of France. My confidence in our ability to fight it out to the finish with the German Air Force has been strengthened by the fierce encounters which have taken place and are taking place. At the same time, our heavy bombers are striking nightly at the taproot of German mechanized power, and have already inflicted serious damage upon the
50 oil refineries on which the Nazi effort to dominate the world directly depends. **C**

We must expect that as soon as stability is reached on the Western Front, the bulk of that hideous apparatus of aggression which gashed Holland into ruin and slavery in a few days, will be turned upon us. I am sure I speak for all when I say we are ready to face it; to endure it; and to retaliate against it—to any extent that

intimidate (ĭn-tĭm′ĭ-dāt′) *v.* to make timid or afraid

dogged (dô′gĭd) *adj.* not giving up; tenacious; stubborn

B   MAIN IDEAS
What is the main point Churchill makes in lines 13–21?

formidable (fôr′mĭ-də-bəl) *adj.* hard to handle or overcome

invincible (ĭn-vĭn′-sə-bel) *adj.* not able to be conquered

animate (ăn′ə-māt′) *v.* to stimulate to action or effort; inspire

C   MAIN IDEAS
What is the main idea in lines 41–50?

the unwritten laws of war permit. There will be many men, and many women, in this island who when the ordeal comes upon them, as come it will, will feel comfort, and even a pride—that they are sharing the perils of our lads at the Front—soldiers, sailors and airmen, God bless them—and are drawing away from them a part at least of the onslaught they have to bear. Is not this the appointed
60 time for all to make the utmost exertions in their power? If the battle is to be won, we must provide our men with ever-increasing quantities of the weapons and ammunition they need. We must have, and have quickly, more airplanes, more tanks, more shells, more guns. There is imperious[5] need for these vital munitions. They increase our strength against the powerfully armed enemy. They replace the wastage of the obstinate struggle; and the knowledge that wastage will speedily be replaced enables us to draw more readily upon our reserves and throw them in now that everything counts so much. **D**

Our task is not only to win the battle—but to win the War. After this battle in France abates its force, there will come the battle for our island—for all that
70 Britain is, and all that Britain means. That will be the struggle. In that supreme emergency we shall not hesitate to take every step, even the most drastic, to call

D SPEECH
Reread lines 59–67. Identify examples of **loaded language**—words and phrases with strong emotional content—that Churchill uses in this passage.

---

5. **imperious** (ĭm-pîr´ē-əs): urgent; pressing.

Churchill during one of his radio addresses

forth from our people the last ounce and the last inch of effort of which they are capable. The interests of property, the hours of labor, are nothing compared with the struggle for life and honor, for right and freedom, to which we have vowed ourselves.

I have received from the Chiefs of the French Republic, and in particular from its **indomitable** Prime Minister, M. Reynaud,[6] the most sacred pledges that whatever happens they will fight to the end, be it bitter or be it glorious. Nay, if we fight to the end, it can only be glorious.

80   Having received His Majesty's commission, I have found an administration of men and women of every party and of almost every point of view. We have differed and quarreled in the past; but now one bond unites us all—to wage war until victory is won, and never to surrender ourselves to servitude and shame, whatever the cost and the agony may be. This is one of the most awe-striking periods in the long history of France and Britain. It is also beyond doubt the most sublime. Side by side, unaided except by their kith and kin in the great Dominions[7] and by the wide Empires which rest beneath their shield—side by side, the British and French peoples have advanced to rescue not only Europe but mankind from the foulest and most soul-destroying tyranny which has ever

90   darkened and stained the pages of history. Behind them—behind us—behind the armies and fleets of Britain and France—gather a group of shattered States and bludgeoned races: the Czechs, the Poles, the Norwegians, the Danes, the Dutch, the Belgians—upon all of whom the long night of barbarism will descend, unbroken even by a star of hope, unless we conquer, as conquer we must; as conquer we shall. **E**

Today is Trinity Sunday.[8] Centuries ago words were written to be a call and a spur to the faithful servants of Truth and Justice: "Arm yourselves, and be ye men of valor, and be in readiness for the conflict; for it is better for us to perish in battle than to look upon the outrage of our nation and our altar. As the Will

100   of God is in Heaven, even so let it be."[9] ◞

indomitable
(ĭn-dŏm′ĭ-tə-bəl) *adj.*
not easily discouraged
or defeated

COMMON CORE L 5a

E OVERSTATEMENT
As a rhetorical technique, **overstatement** (also called hyperbole) is a deliberate exaggeration intended to influence one's audience. Political and military speeches often engage in some degree of exaggeration. Do you think Churchill is engaging in overstatement in this passage? What examples can you cite? Explain your answer.

---

6. **M. Reynaud** (rā-nō′): Paul Reynaud, who had long argued, like Churchill, for firmness toward Germany and for a close British-French alliance. (*M.* is an abbreviation for *Monsieur* [mə-syœ′], French for "Mister.")

7. **kith . . . Dominions:** friends and relatives in the self-governing nations of the British Commonwealth.

8. **Trinity Sunday:** the eighth Sunday after Easter, dedicated to Christianity's Holy Trinity (the Father, the Son, and the Holy Spirit).

9. **"Arm yourselves . . . let it be.":** a quotation from 1 Maccabees 3:58–60. The Book of Maccabees is part of the Apocrypha, found in only some versions of the Bible. It tells of the heroism of the Maccabees, a Jewish family who prevented the Syrians from destroying Judaism in the second century B.C.

Comprehension

1. **Recall** How did England come to the aid of France against Germany?

2. **Summarize** What strategy is Churchill asserting in lines 36–39?

3. **Clarify** What does Churchill expect to happen after the fighting in France subsides?

Text Analysis

● 4. **Identify Main Ideas** Look over the notes you kept while reading. Then, summarize the main ideas in Churchill's speech.

5. **Make Inferences** Reread lines 96–100 and the accompanying footnotes. Why might Churchill have thought this biblical quote would be an effective way to end his speech?

6. **Analyze Author's Attitude** How would you describe Churchill's attitude, or point of view, toward each of the following? Cite specific words and phrases to support your answers.

   • the French troops   • the British troops   • the German troops

● 7. **Evaluate a Speech** Churchill relies heavily on loaded language and emotional appeals in this speech. Which of these **persuasive techniques** did you find most effective in achieving his purpose? How do these techniques add to or detract from his reasoning? Cite specific examples to illustrate your answer.

8. **Compare Texts** Recall Aldous Huxley's discussion about how language is used in times of war in his essay "Words and Behavior." In this speech, Churchill warns his people about impending German attacks on Britain. To what extent does Huxley's criticism apply to Churchill's speech? Cite examples of what Huxley would consider "falsifying" language in your response. After reading Churchill's speech, and in light of its historical context, have your opinions about language manipulation changed to any degree? Explain.

Text Criticism

9. **Author's Style** American president John F. Kennedy, who fought with the Allied forces in World War II, said of Churchill that "he mobilized the English language and sent it into battle." How important is a political leader's speaking ability in motivating citizens in times of crisis?

How can a crisis **UNITE** *us?*

Based on this speech, how would you describe or characterize Churchill as a leader? How might this speech have united the British against their enemies?

COMMON CORE

RI 2 Determine two or more central ideas of a text and analyze their development over the course of the text; provide an objective summary of the text. **RI 6** Determine an author's point of view or purpose in a text in which the rhetoric is particularly effective. **RI 8** Delineate and evaluate the reasoning in seminal texts. **RI 9** Analyze foundational documents of historical significance for their themes, purposes, and rhetorical features.

Vocabulary in Context

▲ VOCABULARY PRACTICE

Look for context clues to help you decide which vocabulary word best completes each sentence. Use each word only once.

1. He displayed _____ persistence in clinging to his ideals.
2. A bully often tries to _____ smaller children.
3. Cataloguing all the books in the United States would be a(n) _____ task.
4. The team leader's enthusiasm helped _____ all the workers.
5. Our _____ captain never gives up, even against daunting odds.
6. The new weapons are so powerful that those who carry them feel _____.

ACADEMIC VOCABULARY IN WRITING

• approach   • assume   • environment   • method   • strategy

Effective persuasive speaking and writing often requires that the speaker or writer understand how to think from the perspective of his or her audience. What **methods** or techniques reveal Churchill's knowledge of how to **approach** his audience? Use at least one Academic Vocabulary word in your response.

VOCABULARY STRATEGY: IDIOMS

General dictionaries give the meanings of most common idioms; to find them, you have to look up the right key word (*raining cats and dogs*, for example, may be found under *rain*). A dictionary of idioms—a **specialized dictionary** that can be found in libraries— may cover even more idioms and also explain their origins. The entries in a dictionary of idioms are organized alphabetically by key word, and the dictionary is usually indexed. For example, *raining cats and dogs* would probably be covered under *rain*, but an index entry for *dogs* would guide you to the *rain* entry.

⸰⸰⸰ **COMMON CORE**

L 4c Consult specialized reference materials. **L 6** Acquire and use accurately general academic words and phrases.

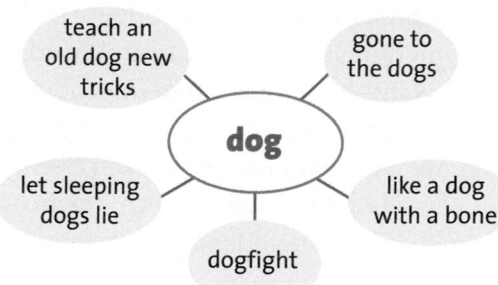

PRACTICE Complete each sentence with the idiom in the diagram that makes the most sense. Use your knowledge of dog behavior to help you choose the correct idiom. When you are done, try to define each idiom you used.

1. The possessive child clutched the toy _____.
2. I tried showing my grandfather how to use the computer, but you can't _____.
3. The combat flyer had a _____ with an enemy pilot.
4. Service was bad last time, but now it has really _____.
5. Stop raking up the past; it's better to _____.

Interactive Vocabulary **THINK**central

Go to <u>thinkcentral.com</u>.
KEYWORD: HML12-1296

Wartime Perspectives

England was at war for almost the entire first half of the 20th century. Although generally supportive, the British people did engage in critical discussion about how warfare is conducted, both in the trenches and in the political sphere. Aldous Huxley was one outspoken critic of the language used to justify war.

> *"We protect our minds by an elaborate system of abstractions, ambiguities, metaphors and similes from the reality we do not wish to know too clearly; we lie to ourselves, in order that we may still have the excuse of ignorance, the alibi of stupidity and incomprehension, possessing which we can continue with a good conscience to commit and tolerate the most monstrous crimes. . . ."*
>
> **—Aldous Huxley, "Words and Behavior"**

Winston Churchill broadcasting to the public

As prime minister during World War II, Winston Churchill used language to rally the British public to the cause.

> *"Side by side, the British and French peoples have advanced to rescue not only Europe but mankind from the foulest and most soul-destroying tyranny which has ever darkened and stained the pages of history. Behind them—behind us—behind the armies and fleets of Britain and France—gather a group of shattered States and bludgeoned races: the Czechs, the Poles, the Norwegians, the Danes, the Dutch, the Belgians—upon all of whom the long night of barbarism will descend, unbroken even by a star of hope, unless we conquer, as conquer we must; as conquer we shall."*
>
> **—Winston Churchill, The Speeches**

Extension Online

SPEAKING & LISTENING Go online or look in your library to find recordings of wartime speeches by Winston Churchill. Choose one speech that you find particularly vivid or compelling, and play it for your class. Discuss Churchill's purpose for the particular speech and whether you think it was well executed and convincing. How does the experience of listening to Churchill differ from reading his words on the page?

Writing to Persuade

Draft a letter that Churchill might have written to Huxley arguing that in a time of war, language must serve the greater good. Then draft Huxley's response. In both letters, support ideas with evidence that suits each reader's concerns.

Consider

- Churchill's reasons for using the language that he did
- how Churchill's language compares with that described by Huxley in "Words and Behavior"

COMMON CORE

W 1 Write arguments to support claims in an analysis of substantive topics or texts.
W 1b Develop claims and counterclaims fairly and thoroughly, supplying relevant evidence for each while anticipating the audience's concerns. **W 9b (RI 6)** Determine an author's point of view or purpose in a text in which the rhetoric is particularly effective, analyzing how style and content contribute to the power or persuasiveness of the text. **SL 3** Evaluate a speaker's use of rhetoric.

Wartime Propaganda
Image Collection on Media ● Smart DVD-ROM

What's the POWER of a poster?

KEY IDEA Think about what persuades you to act. Are you more likely to respond to cold, hard logic or to an emotional appeal? Creators of propaganda have long understood that targeting such human emotions as guilt, fear, and national pride can have potent effects. They attempt to tap into these emotions to convince large numbers of people to follow their agenda. In this lesson, you'll examine British and American propaganda posters from World War II. You'll analyze the persuasive techniques propagandists use to **influence** people's opinions and behavior.

Background

Pretty Persuasion The idea of propaganda often carries negative connotations, as it is thought of as a means of spreading false information. Technically, though, propaganda simply refers to any attempt to influence other people's beliefs or actions. Propaganda can be as innocuous as a magazine ad or as sinister as a Nazi war film.

No matter the form of government, leaders know that it is crucial to have the support of the people, especially during wartime. Effective propaganda can be used both at home and abroad to fuel support of the home country and its allies and to demoralize the enemy.

The United States and Britain used propaganda in World War II as a major weapon of war. For the British, the fighting was close to home, and its effects were apparent to the people. For Americans, however, the war was far away, so the average citizen could not see its effects firsthand. Much of the U.S. propaganda, therefore, attempted to convince Americans to contribute to the war effort with money and labor and to view the Germans and the Japanese as evil threats. The propaganda was meticulously designed and came in many forms, including films, radio broadcasts, leaflets, and posters such as the British one you see on this page.

Whether it's in the form of a political speech, a biased news report, or a television commercial, propaganda remains an important tool used to influence public opinion.

R.A.F. day raiders over Berlin's official quarter.

BACK THEM UP!

Media Literacy: Propaganda Posters

Artists during World War II designed propaganda posters to raise money, encourage productivity and conservation of resources, create negative images of the enemy, increase enlistment, and boost morale. Propaganda posters use the same design elements—**color, line, shape,** and **texture**—as other works of art to effectively convey their message. In addition, propagandists use some of the same **persuasive techniques** as advertisers to influence their audience.

STRATEGIES FOR ANALYZING PROPAGANDA POSTERS

- Identify the overall **message.** What action does the poster call for? What attitude or belief does it promote? Notice how the message is conveyed with a combination of words and visual images. Often, just a few carefully chosen words can drive home a powerful message.

- Recognize the **emotional appeals.** To persuade people to do something that doesn't directly benefit them, propaganda must hit at a deep emotional level. Watch for **appeals to fear,** messages that tap into people's fear of losing their safety or security, and **appeals to guilt,** which build support for an action or idea by tapping into the audience's conscience.

- Look for **symbols,** visual images that represent something beyond themselves. For example, the depiction of a country's flag, or even its leader, might come to symbolize the country as a whole. Think about how a given symbol might tap into very different sentiments for people on opposite sides of a conflict.

- Understand how the message is directed at the individual citizen. For propaganda to be successful, it must appeal to a large number of people on a personal level. Ask yourself: How does the poster address the average citizen as an individual?

When you ride ALONE you ride with Hitler!

Join a Car-Sharing Club TODAY!

Don't Let That Shadow Touch Them
Buy WAR BONDS

Viewing Guide for

Propaganda Posters

Use the DVD to examine these and other World War II propaganda posters more closely. As you study each, try to identify the persuasive techniques at work. Be aware of the feelings that are triggered by any symbols you see. Look for the ways each poster attempts to appeal to various emotions. Identify the poster's message, and think about how that message stands up without the poster's images. Consider these questions as you analyze each poster.

NOW VIEW

FIRST VIEWING: Comprehension

1. **Identify** In the "Don't Let That Shadow Touch Them" poster, what emotions do you see in the expressions on the children's faces?

2. **Clarify** According to the "When You Ride Alone You Ride with Hitler!" poster, what is the driver doing wrong?

CLOSE VIEWING: Media Literacy

3. **Interpret the Message** Look closely at the "Back Them Up!" poster on page 1298. What message do you think this poster is attempting to convey?

4. **Analyze Symbols** Identify any symbols you see in the "Don't Let That Shadow Touch Them" poster on this page. Explain what each symbol represents and the possible emotions it might have triggered in a citizen during World War II.

5. **Analyze a Poster** In your own words, describe how you think an American in 1943 would have reacted to the "When You Ride Alone You Ride with Hitler!" poster. Cite specific elements to support your analysis.

6. **Evaluate Persuasive Techniques** Choose one of the three posters and evaluate the effectiveness of its persuasive techniques. Think about
   - the use of symbols
   - the emotions the poster attempts to appeal to
   - how the poster is directed at its audience
   - the actions or beliefs the poster promotes

Write or Discuss

Compare Propaganda Posters The "Back Them Up!" poster on page 1298 is British. The other two posters in this lesson are American. Write a paragraph to compare the three posters. Examine the persuasive techniques used in each poster to influence the audience. How effective is each poster? Think about

- the message of each poster and how it's presented
- how emotional appeals and symbols are used
- the different ways that British and American citizens were affected by the war

Produce Your Own Media

Create a Propaganda Poster Choose an issue in the news today. Decide which side of the issue you support. Create your own propaganda poster to influence people's opinions or call them to action. Use the persuasive techniques you've learned in the lesson to create your poster.

HERE'S HOW Here are a few ideas to keep in mind as you design your poster:

- Think about symbols that are associated with the issue you've chosen. Consider the feelings these symbols might trigger and how you can use them to persuade your audience.
- Personalize your message. Remember, however, that you must appeal to a large number of people.
- Decide how you want to present your message. Propaganda posters can deliver their messages directly or indirectly. Use the method you find most effective.

Further Exploration

The Art of Persuasion Look at the additional propaganda posters included on the DVD. Consider the message of each and the persuasive techniques used to communicate it. Now think about the design elements—line, color, shape, and texture—in each poster. Discuss these elements and how they're used to convey the poster's message. Which posters do you think have the most effective design elements? Explain why you think so.

Propaganda vs. Advertising During World War I, the United States launched a massive propaganda campaign through the Committee on Public Information. Scholars, businesspeople, psychologists, and artists were hired to develop sophisticated techniques to generate public support for the war. Many of these techniques have since been put to use in the advertising world. Collect several print ads and compare them with the propaganda posters you've examined. What, if any, propaganda techniques do you see in the ads? How do the feelings the ads try to trigger compare with the emotions conveyed in the posters? Where does advertising end and propaganda begin?

Media Tools

THINK central

Go to **thinkcentral.com**.
KEYWORD: HML12-1301

Tech Tip

If available, use a design program to create your poster, using photographs, clip art, computer drawings, and text.

Digging
Poem by Seamus Heaney

The Horses
Poem by Ted Hughes

COMMON CORE **RL 4** Determine the meaning of words and phrases as they are used in the text, including connotative meanings; analyze the impact of specific word choices on meaning and tone, including language that is particularly fresh, engaging, or beautiful. **RL 10** Read and comprehend literature, including poems. **L 3** Apply knowledge of language to comprehend more fully when reading.

Meet the Authors

Seamus Heaney born 1939

Many critics consider Seamus Heaney (shā′məs hā′nē) the most important Irish poet since William Butler Yeats. Heaney's poems are characterized by themes and imagery taken from the natural world and rural life. In 1995, he won the Nobel Prize for Literature.

Farmboy Turned Poet Heaney was born to a Catholic farm family in Northern Ireland. In 1957, he won a scholarship to Queen's University in Belfast, where he became interested in the poetry of Robert Frost, Gerard Manley Hopkins, and Patrick Kavanagh, all of whom wrote about their local surroundings. These poets affirmed for Heaney the validity of his background, and after graduating, he too began writing poetry.

Famous Seamus In 1966, Heaney published his first book, *Death of a Naturalist,* a collection of poems about the experiences of his rural childhood. The book brought Heaney instant acclaim. It opens with "Digging," a poem whose "rhythms and noises" Heaney has said still please him.

Ted Hughes

1930–1998

When Ted Hughes was named England's poet laureate in 1984, it took many people by surprise. Hughes's verse often focused on the savage, predatory aspects of nature, an emphasis some people found disturbing. Although controversial, Hughes ranks as one of Britain's most influential 20th-century poets.

A Yorkshire Lad As a youth, Hughes loved to explore the bleak yet "exultant" moors (areas of high, open land) near his home in Yorkshire. In 1951 he went to Cambridge University, where he published his first poems. Five years later, he met and married the American poet Sylvia Plath.

Contest Winner Plath encouraged Hughes to enter some of his poetry in a contest. Hughes's manuscript was chosen out of 287 submissions and published in 1957 as *The Hawk in the Rain.* The collection immediately established his reputation as an important new poet. The poems in the book contain compelling descriptions of wild, natural settings and use animals to probe the instinctual, nonrational side of human life.

Tragedy and Recovery Hughes and Plath had a volatile marriage, and in 1962 they separated. In 1963 Plath committed suicide. For nearly three years, Hughes wrote no poetry at all. When he began writing again, however, he was prolific. During his life he published dozens of volumes of poetry and prose and received many literary honors.

Authors Online
Go to **thinkcentral.com**. KEYWORD: HML12-1302

● POETIC FORM: FREE VERSE

The following poems, like most contemporary poems, are written in **free verse,** without regular patterns of rhyme, rhythm, or meter. The lines are not random; they are just organized according to other principles chosen by the poet. Because free verse is unrhymed and unmetered, it can achieve a rhythm closer to that of everyday speech or unvoiced thoughts. In addition, the use of free verse affects the shape of a poem, allowing the poet to mix in shorter lines for effect.

● TEXT ANALYSIS: IMAGERY

Seamus Heaney and Ted Hughes are contemporary poets admired for the richness of their imagery. **Imagery,** as you recall, consists of words and phrases that re-create sensory experiences for the reader. Visual imagery appeals to the sense of sight; auditory imagery appeals to the sense of hearing; tactile, to the sense of touch; olfactory, to the sense of smell; and gustatory, to the sense of taste. A sixth kind of imagery, **kinesthetic,** re-creates the tension felt through muscles, tendons, and joints in the body. The first lines of Seamus Heaney's poem "Digging" contain kinesthetic imagery that describes the sensation of gripping a pen:

Between my finger and my thumb
The squat pen rests; snug as a gun.

Some imagery is uniquely mixed, appealing to one sense while describing another, as in "cold smell of potato mold." This blending is called **synesthesia.** Notice how the imagery in the poems conveys very specific memories.

● READING SKILL: ANALYZE WORD CHOICE

Word choice is important in poetry because the language is so compressed. Poets carefully choose words for their connotations—shades of meaning beyond the basic definitions of the words. For example, in "The Horses," Hughes uses the adjective *evil* to describe the early morning air. By choosing a word with such strong negative connotations, he captures the reader's attention and establishes an ominous mood. The sound of a word also influences a poet's choice, especially when the poet uses sound devices such as rhyme or alliteration. As you read each poem, note which words create the strongest impressions for you.

 Complete the activities in your **Reader/Writer Notebook.**

Why do MEMORIES *mean so much?*

As time passes, new experiences threaten to crowd out cherished memories. To preserve memories, some people take photographs or shoot video of experiences they don't want to forget. The poets Seamus Heaney and Ted Hughes, however, attempt to capture in words both the ordinary and the sublime moments of life.

QUICKWRITE Think about the kinds of experiences that have made a lasting impression on you. Did those experiences involve ordinary events or extraordinary moments? Jot down some of these experiences, and explain why they occupy a special place in your memory.

DIGGING *Seamus Heaney*

Between my finger and my thumb
The squat pen rests; snug as a gun.

Under my window, a clean rasping sound
When the spade sinks into gravelly ground:
5 My father, digging. I look down

Till his straining rump among the flowerbeds
Bends low, comes up twenty years away
Stooping in rhythm through potato drills
Where he was digging.

10 The coarse boot nestled on the lug, the shaft
Against the inside knee was levered firmly.
He rooted out tall tops, buried the bright edge deep
To scatter new potatoes that we picked
Loving their cool hardness in our hands. **A**

15 By God, the old man could handle a spade.
Just like his old man.

My grandfather cut more turf in a day
Than any other man on Toner's bog.
Once I carried him milk in a bottle
20 Corked sloppily with paper. He straightened up
To drink it, then fell to right away

Analyze Visuals ▶
What can you tell from the
photograph about the work
of digging peat?

8 **drills:** furrows for planting seeds.

10 **lug:** a widening at the top of a
shovel blade to support the foot.

A IMAGERY
Identify **kinesthetic imagery**
in lines 6–14.

17–22 Turf, or peat—partially
decayed matter found in wet areas
called bogs—was cut in blocks called
sods and used as fuel in Ireland.

Nicking and slicing neatly, heaving sods
Over his shoulder, going down and down
For the good turf. Digging.

25 The cold smell of potato mold, the squelch and slap
Of soggy peat, the curt cuts of an edge
Through living roots awaken in my head.
But I've no spade to follow men like them.

Between my finger and my thumb
30 The squat pen rests. **B**
I'll dig with it.

COMMON CORE L3

Language Coach

Word Definitions A word whose sound echoes its meaning is an example of **onomatopoeia.** Which words in line 25 are onomatopoeic? To what senses does the line appeal?

B **WORD CHOICE**
What connotations may have influenced Heaney to use the word *squat* to describe the pen in line 30? Explain.

Text Analysis

1. **Summarize** What **memories** does the speaker recall in this poem?

2. **Make Inferences** Describe the speaker's attitude toward his father and grandfather. How does he view himself in relation to them?

3. **Examine Sound Devices** Identify examples of **onomatopoeia** in the poem. How do the sounds of the words suggest the things or actions they describe?

THE HORSES *Ted Hughes*

I climbed through woods in the hour-before-dawn dark.
Evil air, a frost-making stillness,

Not a leaf, not a bird—
A world cast in frost. I came out above the wood

5 Where my breath left tortuous statues in the iron light.
But the valleys were draining the darkness

Till the moorline—blackening dregs of the brightening gray—
Halved the sky ahead. And I saw the horses:

Huge in the dense gray—ten together—
10 Megalith-still. They breathed, making no move,

5 tortuous: winding or twisting.

7 moorline: the horizon at the edge of a moor; **dregs:** small amounts left over.

10 megalith: a very large stone of the sort used in various prehistoric formations, such as Stonehenge.

With draped manes and tilted hind-hooves,
Making no sound.

I passed: not one snorted or jerked its head.
Gray silent fragments

15 Of a gray silent world. **C**

I listened in emptiness on the moor-ridge.
The curlew's tear turned its edge on the silence.

Slowly detail leafed from the darkness. Then the sun
Orange, red, red, erupted

20 Silently, and splitting to its core tore and flung cloud,
Shook the gulf open, showed blue,

And the big planets hanging. **D**
I turned,

Stumbling in the fever of a dream, down toward
25 The dark woods, from the kindling tops,

And came to the horses.
                              There, still they stood,
But now steaming and glistening under the flow of light,

Their draped stone manes, their tilted hind-hooves
30 Stirring under a thaw while all around them

The frost showed its fires. But still they made no sound.
Not one snorted or stamped,

Their hung heads patient as the horizons, **E**
High over valleys, in the red leveling rays—

35 In din of the crowded streets, going among the years, the faces,
May I still meet my memory in so lonely a place

Between the streams and the red clouds, hearing curlews,
Hearing the horizons endure.

C FREE VERSE
What effect does the
arrangement of lines have on
your reading of the poem?

17 curlew: a large, brownish, long-
legged shore bird with a long,
slender, downward-curving bill.

D IMAGERY
What examples of **synesthesia**
are there in lines 16–22?

E WORD CHOICE
Consider the connotations of
the word *horizons*. What effect
is achieved by calling the horses
"patient as the horizons" in
line 33?

Comprehension

1. **Recall** Where and at what time of day does the scene in "The Horses" take place?

2. **Clarify** How do the horses look to the speaker the first time he sees them? the second time?

3. **Paraphrase** Restate the meaning of the last line: "Hearing the horizons endure."

Text Analysis

4. **Make Inferences** What is the attitude of the speaker of "The Horses" toward the animals he encounters? What might they represent to him? Support your answer.

5. **Examine Imagery** In a chart like the one shown, identify the most powerful and immediate images in "Digging" and "The Horses." What senses do these images appeal to? Explain how the imagery affects the **mood** of each poem.

Poem:	
Image	Sense(s)

6. **Analyze Word Choice** For each poem, identify three words that seem particularly striking or unusual. What connotations or sounds may have influenced the poet to choose each of these words?

7. **Analyze Free Verse** How do the line length and the stanza structure affect the rhythm of each poem? Discuss how **repetition** of words is used to unify the poems.

8. **Evaluate Style** Which of the poems seems more "regional"—tied to a particular place? Give reasons for your choice.

Text Criticism

9. **Critical Interpretations** Heaney and Hughes were close friends, and at the memorial service for Hughes, Heaney said, "He was a born poet in as far as his first impulse was to give glory to creation." What evidence do you see of this in "The Horses"?

Why do **MEMORIES** *mean so much?*

What do these two poems suggest about the purpose and value of memories? Support your answer with details from the poems.

COMMON CORE

RL 1 Cite textual evidence to support inferences drawn from the text. **RL 4** Determine the meaning of words and phrases as they are used in the text, including connotative meanings; analyze the impact of specific word choices on meaning and tone, including language that is particularly fresh, engaging, or beautiful. **RL 10** Read and comprehend literature, including poems.

The Frog Prince
Not Waving but Drowning

Poetry by Stevie Smith

COMMON CORE

RL 2 Determine two or more themes or central ideas of a text. **RL 4** Analyze the impact of specific word choices on meaning and tone, including language that is particularly fresh, engaging, or beautiful. **RL 10** Read and comprehend literature, including poems.

DID YOU KNOW?

Stevie Smith . . .

- acquired the nickname "Stevie" after friends compared her to a famous jockey named Steve Donoghue.

- illustrated most of her poetry with little drawings she called "beastlies."

Meet the Author

Stevie Smith 1902–1971

The poetry of Stevie Smith is nothing like that of her contemporaries. Often taking inspiration from nursery rhymes and fairy tales, Smith's poetry at first glance seems simple and almost childlike. However, her supposedly "light" verse takes on such weighty topics as life and death, offering shrewd insights tinged with dark humor.

Family of Women Stevie Smith was born Florence Margaret Smith in Hull, Yorkshire. When she was three, her father abandoned the family. Smith, her mother, her sister, and a favorite aunt (whom Smith affectionately called the Lion Aunt) then moved to Palmers Green, a northern suburb of London. Smith and the Lion Aunt lived together in the house in Palmers Green until the aunt died at 96.

A Different Tune At school, Smith was an indifferent student in all subjects except music. She participated enthusiastically in sing-alongs, although she often sang a different tune from her classmates, exasperating her teachers. In 1917, Smith took a secretarial course and became a secretary for a large London publishing house. She found the job tedious, but it afforded her free time to write stories and poems.

From Rejection to Success In 1934, Smith submitted some of her poems to an agent who rejected them, claiming that they were "entirely incoherent." Later, a publisher suggested she write a novel. Typing on yellow scrap paper from her job, Smith wrote and published the autobiographical *Novel on Yellow Paper* (1936), which was an immediate success. Her first book of poetry followed in 1937. Although she kept her secretarial job, Smith enjoyed the admiration of London's literary world and was often invited to give readings.

Honored Eccentric As Smith became established as a writer, she gave free rein to her eccentricities, dressing as a schoolgirl in white stockings and a pinafore and frequently bursting into song at poetry readings. Despite her seemingly childlike gaiety and her success as an author, Smith suffered bouts of deep depression. In 1953, she slashed her wrists while at work and was forced to retire. However, she went on to greater fame as a writer with the publication of *Not Waving but Drowning* (1957). In 1969 Queen Elizabeth II presented Smith with the Queen's Gold Medal for Poetry. Less than two years later, Smith died of a brain tumor at the height of her popularity.

A REVIVED MODERN CLASSIC

STEVIE SMITH
NOVEL ON YELLOW PAPER

Author Online

Go to **thinkcentral.com**. KEYWORD: HML12-1310

THINK central

TEXT ANALYSIS: VOICE

Voice is that quality in writing that enables the reader to "hear" a personality behind the words. The term can refer to the poet's own voice or the voice of a **persona** (fictional character) created by the poet. Stevie Smith's poetry has a distinctive voice that has been called whimsical and darkly humorous. Read the first lines of "The Frog Prince."

I am a frog,
I live under a spell,
I live at the bottom
Of a green well.

Among the elements contributing to the voice are the childish diction, the short lines, the nursery-rhyme structure, and the fairy-tale subject. Later in the poem there is **irony** (the overturning of expectations) and **wordplay** (the intentional use of words with more than one meaning, or words that are **ambiguous**). As you read the following poems, notice what makes the voice so unusual.

READING SKILL: INTERPRET IDEAS IN POETRY

The diction in these poems is quite simple, but still the poems are not so easy to understand. The first time you read each poem, break the work into sections and summarize the major **ideas** presented in each section. The second time, read through a magnifying lens, so to speak, to discover the larger meaning. Imagine, for example, that the main character in the poem represents any person. What, then, does the situation suggest about human life? Take notes on a chart like the one shown. On your second reading, pay special attention to repeated words and words with double meanings.

"The Frog Prince"		
Lines	Ideas on 1st Reading (Literal)	Ideas on 2nd Reading (Metaphorical)
1–9	Speaker is a prince-turned-frog waiting for a princess to kiss him and break spell.	
10–29		
30–42		
43–48		

 Complete the activities in your **Reader/Writer Notebook**.

How do others SEE us?

Think back to your first day of high school. Surrounded by a sea of new faces, you probably formed first impressions about certain students based on their appearance or behavior. Perhaps you eventually got to know them and revised your initial impressions. "The Frog Prince" and "Not Waving but Drowning" are poems that question how reliable our impressions of others are.

QUIZ Create a quiz to find out how well someone *really* knows you. Write four true statements about yourself and one plausible but false statement. Then have a classmate take your quiz. Does he or she know you well enough to recognize the false statement? If not, what led to the faulty impression?

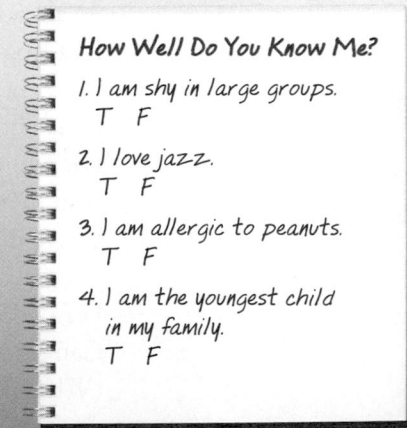

How Well Do You Know Me?

1. I am shy in large groups.
   T F

2. I love jazz.
   T F

3. I am allergic to peanuts.
   T F

4. I am the youngest child in my family.
   T F

The Frog Prince

Stevie Smith

I am a frog,
I live under a spell,
I live at the bottom
Of a green well.

5 And here I must wait
Until a maiden places me
On her royal pillow,
And kisses me,
In her father's palace.

10 The story is familiar,
Everybody knows it well,
But do other enchanted people feel as nervous
As I do? The stories do not tell,

Ask if they will be happier
15 When the changes come,
As already they are fairly happy
In a frog's doom? **Ⓐ**

I have been a frog now
For a hundred years
20 And in all this time
I have not shed many tears,

I am happy, I like the life,
Can swim for many a mile
(When I have hopped to the river)
25 And am for ever agile.

And the quietness,
Yes, I like to be quiet
I am habituated
To a quiet life, **Ⓑ**

Ⓐ VOICE
Describe the frog's personality. What is **ironic** about the questions he asks in lines 10–17?

Ⓑ IDEAS
How does the frog feel about his life? Think about people who feel similar to the frog.

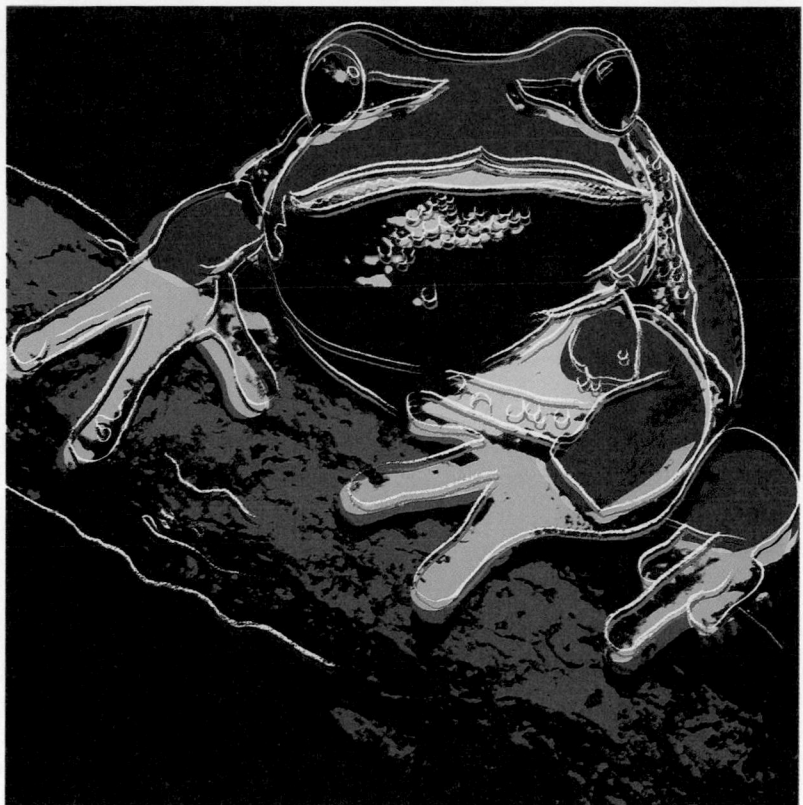

Pine Barrens Tree Frog from the *Endangered Species Series* (1983), Andy Warhol. Courtesy Ronald Feldman Fine Arts, New York. © 2007 Andy Warhol Foundation for the Visual Arts/Artists Rights Society (ARS), New York. Photo © Corbis.

30 But always when I think these thoughts
    As I sit in my well
    Another thought comes to me and says:
    It is part of the spell

    To be happy
35 To work up contentment
    To make much of being a frog
    To fear disenchantment

    Says, It will be *heavenly*
    To be set free,
40 Cries, *Heavenly* the girl who disenchants
    And the royal times, *heavenly,*
    And I think it will be. **C**

    Come, then, royal girl and royal times,
    Come quickly,
45 I can be happy until you come
    But I cannot be heavenly,
    Only disenchanted people
    Can be heavenly.

C VOICE
Notice the **wordplay** in lines 37–42. What are different meanings of *disenchantment* and *heavenly?*

Not Waving but Drowning

Stevie Smith

Nobody heard him, the dead man,
But still he lay moaning:
I was much further out than you thought
And not waving but drowning.

5 Poor chap, he always loved larking
And now he's dead
It must have been too cold for him his heart gave way, **D**
They said.

Oh, no no no, it was too cold always
10 (Still the dead one lay moaning)
I was much too far out all my life
And not waving but drowning. **E**

D VOICE
Who is speaking in lines 5–7? What emotion do you imagine behind the words?

E INTERPRET IDEAS
Line 12 repeats line 4 and the title. What does it mean in the context of swimming? in the context of living?

Bathers-Rescue (1975), Sir Sidney Nolan. Oil on board, 132 cm × 100 cm. Private collection. © Bridgeman Art Library.

Comprehension

1. **Recall** What is the frog in "The Frog Prince" waiting for?

2. **Clarify** What are his feelings as he waits?

3. **Clarify** Identify the different speakers in "Not Waving but Drowning" and the lines they speak.

4. **Paraphrase** What is meant by the statement "I was much too far out all my life"?

Text Analysis

5. **Examine Word Choice** In "The Frog Prince," what do the following words mean? Which words are cast as positive, and which are cast as negative?

   • "enchanted"   • "happy"
   • "disenchanted" • "heavenly"

6. **Examine Author's Perspective** Stevie Smith once commented that "The Frog Prince" was "a religious poem." What religious ideas could be read into it?

7. **Interpret Ideas in Poetry** Review your chart of major ideas in "Not Waving but Drowning." What situation is presented in the poem? How does this situation apply to human life in general? Discuss the following phrases:

   • "too far out"   • "his heart gave way"
   • "too cold"   • "not waving but drowning"

8. **Analyze Voice** In what way is the voice in these poems whimsical? In what way is it dark? Describe the effects of **irony** and **wordplay** on the voice. Be specific.

Text Criticism

9. **Biographical Context** Stevie Smith once said, "Being alive is like being in enemy territory." How is this belief reflected in these two poems?

How do others **SEE** *us?*

What do these two poems suggest about initial impressions? Support your answer with details from each poem.

COMMON CORE

RL 2 Determine two or more themes or central ideas of a text. **RL 4** Analyze the impact of specific word choices on meaning and tone, including language that is particularly fresh, engaging, or beautiful. **RL 10** Read and comprehend literature, including poems.

from Waiting for Godot

Drama by Samuel Beckett

Samuel Beckett
1906–1989

BACKGROUND Samuel Beckett led a rather unusual life. Irish by birth, Beckett settled in Paris. During World War II, he joined the French Resistance against the Nazis, who overran Paris. Eventually hiding out in the French countryside, he transmitted valuable information to the Allies and received two French medals for bravery when the war ended. Fame as a writer also came after the war, with plays such as *Waiting for Godot*. In 1969, Beckett won the Nobel Prize in literature.

   Waiting for Godot was inspired by Beckett's conversations with his wife while the two hid out during the long wait for World War II to end. The entire play takes place on a country road on which the only features are a low mound and a small tree. There, two somewhat clownish characters named Estragon and Vladimir wait on two consecutive evenings for the appearance of someone named Godot. Sometimes the two seem witty, sometimes witless; sometimes they talk philosophy, sometimes nonsense; and often they seem to forget why they are there and for whom they are waiting

TEXT ANALYSIS *Waiting for Godot* was a landmark work in a postwar movement called **theater of the absurd,** drama that suggests the absurdity of the human condition by abandoning realism. In the following passage, you'll notice that traditional elements of drama are missing. The plot, for example, seems stagnant. Estragon and Vladimir are waiting and waiting and waiting; no other action takes place. Also, the dialogue between them is unconventional.

DISCUSS Notice Beckett's use of **repetition** in this scene: words, phrases, and entire lines are repeated. Also, note the use of **wordplay,** or verbal ambiguity, where Beckett plays with the various meanings of words. With a partner, discuss how Beckett's use of these two literary elements creates an overall feeling of absurdity and irrationality. What can you infer about Beckett's view of human existence?

FROM ACT ONE

Estragon. Let's go.

Vladimir. We can't.

Estragon. Why not?

Vladimir. We're waiting for Godot.

Estragon (*despairingly*). Ah! (*pause*) You're sure it was here?

Vladimir. What?

Estragon. That we were to wait.

Vladimir. He said by the tree. (*They look at the tree.*) Do you see any others.

Estragon. What is it?

10 **Vladimir.** I don't know. A willow.

Estragon. Where are the leaves?

Vladimir. It must bc dead.

Estragon. No more weeping.

Vladimir. Or perhaps it's not the season.

Estragon. Looks to me more like a bush.

Vladimir. A shrub.

Estragon. A bush.

Vladimir. A—. What are you insinuating? That we've come to the wrong place?

Estragon. He should be here.

20 **Vladimir.** He didn't say for sure he'd come.

Estragon. And if he doesn't come?

Vladimir. We'll come back tomorrow.

Estragon. And then the day after tomorrow.

Vladimir. Possibly.

Estragon. And so on.

Vladimir. The point is—

Estragon. Until he comes.

Vladimir. You're merciless.

Estragon. We came here yesterday.

30 **Vladimir.** Ah no, there you're mistaken.

Estragon. What did we do yesterday?

Vladimir. What did we do yesterday?

Estragon. Yes.

Vladimir. Why . . . (*angrily*) Nothing is certain when you're about.

Estragon. In my opinion we were here.

The Distant Past

Short Story by William Trevor

Meet the Author

William Trevor born 1928

A masterful storyteller, William Trevor is admired both for his novels and for his short stories. Trevor often writes about ordinary people who fall victim to circumstance. He depicts their lives with compassion, subtle irony, and careful detail.

Middle-Class Gypsy Born in County Cork, Ireland, Trevor was raised as a Protestant. During his childhood, his family relocated often, moving from town to town throughout southern Ireland as his father pursued a career in banking. While leading the life of "a middle-class gypsy," as Trevor later termed it, there were times when he did not attend school at all as the family settled into a new home. Nevertheless, Trevor loved to read, devouring as many detective stories and crime novels as he could find. He also enjoyed going to the movies, even though they were often heavily censored in Ireland during this period.

Artist and Writer In 1950, Trevor graduated from Trinity College in Dublin. After teaching history for two years in Northern Ireland, he moved to England, where he taught art and began a career as a sculptor. He later took a job writing copy for a London advertising agency. With only four lines of copy to write in as many days, Trevor found himself with ample spare time. To supplement his income, he started writing fiction, publishing his first novel in 1958. It was largely ignored, but his second novel, *The Old Boys* (1964), won an important literary prize. His first book of short stories, *The Day We Got Drunk on Cake and Other Stories* (1967), cemented his reputation as a major new author.

Ireland's Troubles As a Protestant who grew up in the largely Catholic south of Ireland, Trevor has an unusual perspective on Anglo-Irish relations. He sets many of his stories in Ireland and frequently examines the ways in which people—both Protestant and Catholic—cope with Ireland's long history of violence and hatred. The conflict can be traced back to the 12th century, when England gained control of part of Ireland. The English later attempted to establish Protestantism as the sole religion in the predominately Catholic land. One way they tried to do this was by seizing land from Catholics and giving it to English and Scottish Protestant settlers. Over the centuries, Catholics suffered religious persecution and endured severe limitations on their rights to own land and participate in government, resulting in bitter anti-English sentiment among them.

DID YOU KNOW?

William Trevor . . .

- did not abandon his art career to write full-time until his mid-30s.
- gave up sculpting because his pieces became too abstract.
- enjoys Woody Allen and Marx Brothers movies.

● TEXT ANALYSIS: SETTING

Setting, as you recall, is the time and place of the action in a story. "The Distant Past" takes place in southern Ireland over a number of decades during the 20th century. In addition to time and place, setting encompasses culture and customs—the characters' way of life. Religion, historical events, economic conditions, popular attitudes, and leisure pastimes are all part of a story's setting. As you read this story, notice such aspects of the setting and how they affect the characters. Consider ways in which the setting contributes to the story's conflict.

● READING SKILL: ANALYZE CHARACTER RELATIONSHIPS

"The Distant Past" centers on the complex relationship between the main characters—the Middletons—and the townspeople who know them. Sometimes the narrator will state a relationship directly:

In the town they were regarded as harmlessly peculiar. Odd, people said, and in time the reference took on a burnish of affection.

At other times you must infer the relationship from clues such as laughter or kind actions. As you read, use a chart to make notes about the Middletons' relationship with the townspeople at different points in the story. Try to determine the reasons for their feelings toward each other.

Relationship	Evidence	Reasons

▲ VOCABULARY IN CONTEXT

Knowing the following boldfaced words will help you understand the story. Use context to help you figure out the meanings. Then provide your own definitions of the words.

1. The new **regime** began governing in October.
2. I enjoy the **convivial** spirit of small friendly gatherings.
3. No one else gave **credence** to the Gurneys' odd ideas.
4. They were an **anachronism,** out of touch with the times.
5. The comedy was so funny, it made us **guffaw.**
6. To persist in inappropriate behavior is sheer **perversity.**
7. The brutal invader committed a terrible **atrocity.**
8. "I see no happiness ahead," she sighed **disconsolately.**

 Complete the activities in your **Reader/Writer Notebook**.

When should we let go of the PAST?

There are many reasons why people, particularly older people, cling to the past. They may want to relive happy memories, nurse painful wounds, or avoid confronting present difficulties. Is it harmless to live in the past, or can it create problems? In the following story, William Trevor explores what can happen when people remain immersed in history.

DISCUSS Recall someone you know who likes to think and talk about events that happened long ago. Discuss this person with a small group of classmates. Why do you think he or she focuses on the past? How does this focus affect his or her life?

THE DISTANT PAST

William Trevor

BACKGROUND Catholics in Ireland demanded self-rule in the late 1800s, but Protestant settlers in the north opposed the plan. In 1920, following a violent rebellion, Britain divided Ireland into two self-governing entities: Northern Ireland and the mainly Catholic Southern Ireland, which a year later came to be called the Irish Free State. By 1949, the Irish Free State had severed all ties with Great Britain, becoming the independent Republic of Ireland. Meanwhile, bloody clashes between Protestants and Catholics in Northern Ireland increased. In the 1960s, the Irish Republican Army (IRA), an outlawed group of Catholic militants, launched terrorist attacks aimed at removing the British from Northern Ireland.

In the town and beyond it they were regarded as harmlessly peculiar. Odd, people said, and in time this reference took on a burnish[1] of affection.

They had always been thin, silent with one another, and similar in appearance: a brother and sister who shared a family face. It was a bony countenance, with pale blue eyes and a sharp, well-shaped nose and high cheek-bones. Their father had had it too, but unlike them their father had been an irresponsible and careless man, with red flecks in his cheeks that they didn't have at all. The Middletons of Carraveagh[2] the family had once been known as, but now the brother and sister were just the Middletons, for Carraveagh didn't count any more, except to them. **A**

10 They owned four Herefords,[3] a number of hens, and the house itself, three miles outside the town. It was a large house, built in the reign of George II,[4] a monument that reflected in its glory and later decay the fortunes of a family. As the brother and sister aged, its roof increasingly ceased to afford protection, rust ate at its gutters, grass thrived in two thick channels all along its avenue. Their father had mortgaged his inherited estate, so local rumor claimed, in order to keep a Catholic Dublin woman in brandy and jewels. When he died, in 1924, his two children discovered that they possessed

Analyze Visuals ▶
What **mood** do the painting's details help create? Explain.

A **ANALYZE RELATIONSHIPS**
Based on lines 1–9, what can you **infer** about the Middletons?

---

1. **burnish:** a smooth, polished finish.
2. **Carraveagh** (cär′ə-vā′)
3. **Herefords** (hûr′fərdz): cattle of a breed raised for beef.
4. **George II:** king of Great Britain, 1727–1760.

Back View of a Victorian House (1958), Ruskin Spear. Oil on canvas, 89 cm × 114.3 cm. Private collection. © Bridgeman Art Library.

only a dozen acres. It was locally said also that this adversity hardened their will and that because of it they came to love the remains of Carraveagh more than they could ever have loved a husband or a wife. They blamed for their ill-fortune the Catholic Dublin woman whom they'd never met and they blamed as well the new national **regime,** contriving in their eccentric way to relate the two. In the days of the Union Jack[5] such women would have known their place: wasn't it all part and parcel? **B**

Twice a week, on Fridays and Sundays, the Middletons journeyed into the town, first of all in a trap[6] and later in a Ford Anglia car. In the shops and elsewhere they made, quite gently, no secret of their continuing loyalty to the past. They attended on Sundays St. Patrick's Protestant Church, a place that matched their mood, for prayers were still said there for the King whose sovereignty their country had denied. The revolutionary regime would not last, they quietly informed the Reverend Packham: what sense was there in green-painted pillar-boxes[7] and a language that nobody understood?[8]

On Fridays, when they took seven or eight dozen eggs to the town, they dressed in pressed tweeds and were accompanied over the years by a series of red setters, the breed there had always been at Carraveagh. They sold the eggs in Keogh's grocery and then had a drink with Mrs. Keogh in the part of her shop that was devoted to the consumption of refreshment. Mr. Middleton had whisky and his sister Tio Pepe.[9] They enjoyed the occasion, for they liked Mrs. Keogh and were liked by her in return. Afterwards they shopped, chatting to the shopkeepers about whatever news there was, and then they went to Healy's Hotel for a few more drinks before driving home.

Drink was their pleasure and it was through it that they built up, in spite of their loyalty to the past, such **convivial** relationships with the people of the town. Fat Driscoll, who kept the butcher's shop, used even to joke about the past when he stood with them in Healy's Hotel or stood behind his own counter cutting their slender chops or thinly slicing their liver. "Will you ever forget it, Mr. Middleton? I'd ha' run like a rabbit if you'd lifted a finger at me." Fat Driscoll would laugh then, rocking back on his heels with a glass of stout[10] in his hand or banging their meat on to his weighing-scales. Mr. Middleton would smile. "There was alarm in your eyes, Mr. Driscoll," Miss Middleton would murmur, smiling also at the memory of the distant occasion.

Fat Driscoll, with a farmer called Maguire and another called Breen, had stood in the hall of Carraveagh, each of them in charge of a shotgun. The Middletons, children then, had been locked with their mother and father and an aunt into

regime (rā-zhēm′) *n.* a government in power

B SETTING
What do you learn about the setting from lines 10–22?

convivial (kən-vĭv′ē-əl) *adj.* characterized by friendly companionship; sociable

---

5. **days . . . Jack:** days when Ireland was part of the United Kingdom of Great Britain and Ireland. The Union Jack is the British flag.

6. **trap:** a light, two-wheeled, horse-drawn carriage.

7. **green-painted pillar-boxes:** mailboxes painted Irish green instead of the old red British mailboxes.

8. **a language nobody understood:** Irish is the traditional language of Ireland's Celtic inhabitants. By the 20th century, after centuries of English rule, it was spoken by a minority of Ireland's population. After independence, it became one of Ireland's official languages.

9. **Tio Pepe** (tē′ō pĕ′pĕ): a brand of Spanish sherry.

10. **stout:** a heavy, dark brown beer.

an upstairs room. Nothing else had happened: the expected British soldiers had not, after all, arrived and the men in the hall had eventually relaxed their vigil. "A massacre they wanted," the Middletons' father said after they'd gone. "Damn bloody ruffians." **C**

The Second World War took place. Two Germans, a man and his wife called Winkelmann who ran a glove factory in the town, were suspected by the Middletons of being spies for the Third Reich.[11] People laughed, for they knew
60 the Winkelmanns well and could lend no **credence** to the Middletons' latest fantasy: typical of them, they explained to the Winkelmanns, who had been worried. Soon after the War the Reverend Packham died and was replaced by the Reverend Bradshaw, a younger man who laughed also and regarded the Middletons as an **anachronism.** They protested when prayers were no longer said for the Royal Family in St. Patrick's, but the Reverend Bradshaw considered that their protests were as absurd as the prayers themselves had been. Why pray for the monarchy of a neighboring island when their own island had its chosen President now? The Middletons didn't reply to that argument. In the Reverend Bradshaw's presence they rose to their feet when the BBC played "God Save the King,"[12] and
70 on the day of the coronation of Queen Elizabeth II[13] they drove into the town with a small Union Jack propped up in the back window of their Ford Anglia. "Bedad, you're a holy terror, Mr. Middleton!" Fat Driscoll laughingly exclaimed, noticing the flag as he lifted a tray of pork-steaks from his display shelf. The Middletons smiled. It was a great day for the Commonwealth of Nations, they replied, a remark which further amused Fat Driscoll and which he later repeated in Phelan's public house. "Her Britannic Majesty," **guffawed** his friend Mr. Breen. **D**

Situated in a valley that was noted for its beauty and with convenient access to rich rivers and bogs over which game-birds flew, the town benefited from post-war tourism. Healy's Hotel changed its title and became, overnight, the New
80 Ormonde. Shopkeepers had their shop-fronts painted and Mr. Healy organized an annual Salmon Festival. Even Canon[14] Kelly, who had at first commented severely on the habits of the tourists, and in particular on the summertime dress of the women, was in the end obliged to confess that the morals of his flock remained unaffected. "God and good sense," he proclaimed, meaning God and his own teaching. In time he even derived pride from the fact that people with other values came briefly to the town and that the values esteemed by his parishioners were in no way diminished.

The town's grocers now stocked foreign cheeses, brie and camembert and Port Salut, and wines were available to go with them. The plush Cocktail Room of the
90 New Ormonde set a standard: the wife of a solicitor,[15] a Mrs. O'Brien, began to

C ANALYZE RELATIONSHIPS
From lines 31–56, what do you gather about the present and past relationships between the Middletons and the townspeople?

credence (krēd′ns) *n.* belief, especially in the ideas of another person

anachronism (ə-năk′rə-nĭz′əm) *n.* anything out of its proper time; someone or something that seems to belong to a former time but not the present

guffaw (gə-fô′) *v.* to laugh loudly

D ANALYZE RELATIONSHIPS
Reread lines 57–76. Why do the townspeople laugh at the Middletons?

---

11. **Third Reich** (rīk): Nazi-controlled Germany.

12. **when ... "God Save the King":** when the British Broadcasting Corporation played the British national anthem.

13. **the day ... Elizabeth II:** June 2, 1953, more than four years after Ireland withdrew from the British Commonwealth of Nations, severing all official ties with Britain and its monarch.

14. **Canon:** the title of certain Roman Catholic priests.

15. **solicitor:** a lawyer who represents clients in lower court cases and takes care of other legal matters.

give six o'clock parties once or twice a year, obliging her husband to mix gin and Martini[16] in glass jugs and herself handing round a selection of nuts and small Japanese crackers. Canon Kelly looked in as a rule and satisfied himself that all was above board. He rejected, though, the mixture in the jugs, retaining his taste for a glass of John Jameson.[17]

From the windows of their convent the Loretto nuns[18] observed the long, sleek cars with G.B. plates;[19] English and American accents drifted on the breeze to them. Mothers cleaned up their children and sent them to the Golf Club to seek employment as caddies. Sweet shops sold holiday mementoes. The brown, 100 soda and currant breads of Murphy-Flood's bakery were declared to be delicious. Mr. Healy doubled the number of local girls who served as waitresses in his dining-room, and in the winter of 1961 he had the builders in again, working on an extension for which the Munster and Leinster Bank had lent him twenty-two thousand pounds. **E**

But as the town increased its prosperity Carraveagh continued its decline. The Middletons were in their middle-sixties now and were reconciled to a life that became more uncomfortable with every passing year. Together they roved the vast lofts of their house, placing old paint tins and flowerpot saucers beneath the drips from the roof. At night they sat over their thin chops in a dining-room that 110 had once been gracious and which in a way was gracious still, except for the faded appearance of furniture that was dry from lack of polish and of a wallpaper that time had rendered colorless. In the hall their father gazed down at them, framed in ebony and gilt, in the uniform of the Irish Guards. He had conversed with Queen Victoria, and even in their middle-sixties they could still hear him saying that God and Empire and Queen formed a trinity unique in any worthy soldier's heart. In the hall hung the family crest, and on ancient Irish linen the Cross of St. George.[20] **F**

The dog that accompanied the Middletons now was called Turloch, an animal whose death they dreaded for they felt they couldn't manage the antics of another pup. Turloch, being thirteen, moved slowly and was blind and a little deaf. He 120 was a reminder to them of their own advancing years and of the effort it had become to tend the Herefords and collect the weekly eggs. More and more they looked forward to Fridays, to the warm companionship of Mrs. Keogh and Mr. Healy's chatter in the hotel. They stayed longer now with Mrs. Keogh and in the hotel, and idled longer in the shops, and drove home more slowly. Dimly, but with no less loyalty, they still recalled the distant past and were listened to without ill-feeling when they spoke of it and of Carraveagh as it had been, and of the Queen whose company their careless father had known.

E SETTING
In what ways does the town change, and why?

F SETTING
What does the Middletons' home convey about their status and political attitudes?

---

16. **Martini:** a brand of vermouth, often mixed with gin to create the cocktail that in America is called a martini.

17. **John Jameson:** a brand of Irish whiskey.

18. **Loretto nuns:** members of a Roman Catholic religious order founded near Dublin in 1822.

19. **G.B. plates:** British, instead of Irish, license plates. *G.B.* stands for *Great Britain*.

20. **Cross of St. George:** horizontal and vertical red bars crossing on a white background—an ancient flag of England.

The visitors who came to the town heard about the Middletons and were impressed. It was a

130 pleasant wonder, more than one of them remarked, that old wounds could heal so completely, that the Middletons continued in their loyalty to the past and that, in spite of it, they were respected in the town. When Miss Middleton had been ill with a form of pneumonia in 1958 Canon Kelly had driven out to Carraveagh twice a week with pullets and young ducks that his housekeeper had dressed. "An upright couple," was the Canon's public opinion of the Middletons, and he had been known to

140 add that eccentric views would hurt you less than malice. "We can disagree without guns in this town," Mr. Healy pronounced in his Cocktail Room, and his visitors usually replied that as far as they could see that was the result of living in a Christian country. That the Middletons bought their meat from a man who had once locked them into an upstairs room and had then waited to shoot soldiers in their hall was a fact that amazed the seasonal visitors. You lived and learned, they

150 remarked to Mr. Healy. **G**

One of the Regulars, Ruskin Spear. Oil on canvas. Private collection.
© Bridgeman Art Library.

G ANALYZE RELATIONSHIPS
What surprises visitors about the town's view of the Middletons?

perversity
(pər-vûr′sĭ-tē) *n.* a stubborn determination to act in an inappropriate or unexpected way

The Middletons, privately, often considered that they led a strange life. Alone in their two beds at night they now and again wondered why they hadn't just sold Carraveagh forty-eight years ago when their father had died: why had the tie been so strong and why had they in **perversity** encouraged it? They didn't fully know, nor did they attempt to discuss the matter in any way. Instinctively they had remained at Carraveagh, instinctively feeling that it would have been cowardly to go. Yet often it seemed to them now to be no more than a game they played, this worship of the distant past. And at other times it seemed as real and as important as the remaining acres of land, and the house itself.

160 "Isn't that shocking?" Mr. Healy said one day in 1967. "Did you hear about that, Mr. Middleton, blowing up them post offices in Belfast?"[21]

Mr. Healy, red-faced and short-haired, spoke casually in his Cocktail Room, making midday conversation. He had commented in much the same way at breakfast-time, looking up from the *Irish Independent.* Everyone in the town had said it too: that the blowing up of sub-post offices in Belfast was a shocking matter.

"A bad business," Fat Driscoll remarked, wrapping the Middletons' meat. "We don't want that old stuff all over again."

"We didn't want it in the first place," Miss Middleton reminded him. He laughed, and she laughed, and so did her brother. Yes, it was a game, she thought:

---

21. **blowing up ... Belfast:** In Northern Ireland, which remained part of the United Kingdom, some members of the Irish Republican Army (IRA) set off bombs in terrorist attacks aimed at ousting the British and winning independence. Belfast is the capital of Northern Ireland.

170 how could any of it be as real or as important as the afflictions and problems of the old butcher himself, his rheumatism and his reluctance to retire? Did her brother, she wondered, privately think so too?

"Come on, old Turloch," he said, stroking the flank of the red setter with the point of his shoe, and she reflected that you could never tell what he was thinking. Certainly it wasn't the kind of thing you wanted to talk about.

"I've put him in a bit of mince,"[22] Fat Driscoll said, which was something he often did these days, pretending the mince would otherwise be thrown away. There'd been a red setter about the place that night when he waited in the hall for the soldiers: Breen and Maguire had pushed it down into a cellar, frightened of it.

180 "There's a heart of gold in you, Mr. Driscoll," Miss Middleton murmured, nodding and smiling at him. He was the same age as she was, sixty-six: he should have shut up shop years ago. He would have, he'd once told them, if there'd been a son to leave the business to. As it was, he'd have to sell it and when it came to the point he found it hard to make the necessary arrangements. "Like us and Carraveagh," she'd said, even though on the face of it it didn't seem the same at all. **H**

Every evening they sat in the big old kitchen, hearing the news. It was only in Belfast and Derry,[23] the wireless[24] said; outside Belfast and Derry you wouldn't know anything was happening at all. On Fridays they listened to the talk in Mrs. Keogh's bar and in the hotel. "Well, thank God it has nothing to do with the

190 South," Mr. Healy said often, usually repeating the statement.

The first British soldiers landed in the North of Ireland, and soon people didn't so often say that outside Belfast and Derry you wouldn't know anything was happening. There were incidents in Fermanagh and Armagh,[25] in Border villages and towns. One Prime Minister resigned and then another one. The troops were unpopular, the newspapers said; internment[26] became part of the machinery of government. In the town, in St. Patrick's Protestant Church and in the Church of the Holy Assumption, prayers for peace were offered, but no peace came.

"We're hit, Mr. Middleton," Mr. Healy said one Friday morning. "If there's a dozen visitors this summer it'll be God's own stroke of luck for us."

200 "Luck?"

"Sure, who wants to come to a country with all that malarkey[27] in it?"

"But it's only in the North."

"Tell that to your tourists, Mr. Middleton."

The town's prosperity ebbed. The Border was more than sixty miles away, but over that distance had spread some wisps of the fog of war. As anger rose in the

H **ANALYZE RELATIONSHIPS**
What details in lines 168–185 reveal Miss Middleton's and Fat Driscoll's feelings toward each other?

Language Coach

Greek Roots The word *government* (line 196) comes from the Greek root *kubernan*, which means "to steer a ship." The idea is that a governor "steers the ship of state." Can you think of other words that come from this same Greek root?

---

22. **mince:** chopped meat.

23. **Derry:** another large city in Northern Ireland. The name *Derry,* which comes from the Irish name of the city, was expanded by the British to *Londonderry,* still the official city name.

24. **wireless:** radio.

25. **Fermanagh** (fər-mä'-nə) **and Armagh** (är-mä'): two districts in Northern Ireland, near its border with the independent Republic of Ireland.

26. **internment:** imprisonment of members of the Irish Republican Army suspected of plotting against the British government.

27. **malarkey** (mə-lär'kē): foolishness.

town at the loss of fortune so there rose also the kind of talk there had been in the distant past. There was talk of **atrocities** and counter-atrocities, and of guns and gelignite[28] and the rights of people. There was bitterness suddenly in Mrs. Keogh's bar because of the lack of trade, and in the empty hotel there was bitterness also. ⓘ

210   On Fridays, only sometimes at first, there was a silence when the Middletons appeared. It was as though, going back nearly twenty years, people remembered the Union Jack in the window of their car and saw it now in a different light. It wasn't something to laugh at any more, nor were certain words that the Middletons had gently spoken, nor were they themselves just an old, peculiar couple. Slowly the change crept about, all around them in the town, until Fat Driscoll didn't wish it to be remembered that he had ever given them mince for their dog. He had stood with a gun in the enemy's house, waiting for soldiers so that soldiers might be killed: it was better that people should remember that.

    One day Canon Kelly looked the other way when he saw the Middletons' car
220 coming and they noticed this movement of his head, although he hadn't wished them to. And on another day Mrs. O'Brien, who had always been keen to talk to them in the hotel, didn't reply when they addressed her. Ⓙ

---

28. **gelignite** (jĕl′ĭg-nīt′): a powerful explosive.

atrocity (ə-trŏs′ĭ-tē) *n.* a very cruel, brutal, or appalling act

ⓘ **SETTING**
Reread lines 186–209. How have conditions in Northern Ireland affected the town?

Ⓙ **ANALYZE RELATIONSHIPS**
Explain the change in the townspeople's view of the Middletons.

Last Self Portrait at Charleston (1960), Vanessa Bell. Oil on canvas. Private collection. Purchased with the assistance of The Art Fund and the V & A Purchase Grant Fund. © The Estate of Vanessa Bell courtesy of Henrietta Garnett. Photo © Bridgeman Art Library.

The Middletons naturally didn't discuss these rebuffs but they each of them privately knew that there was no conversation they could have at this time with the people of the town. The stand they had taken and kept to for so many years no longer seemed ridiculous in the town. Had they driven with a Union Jack now they would, astoundingly, have been shot.

"It will never cease." He spoke **disconsolately** one night, standing by the dresser where the wireless was.

230 She washed the dishes they'd eaten from, and the cutlery. "Not in our time," she said.

"It is worse than before."

"Yes, it is worse than before."

They took from the walls of the hall the portrait of their father in the uniform of the Irish Guards because it seemed wrong to them that at this time it should hang there. They took down also the crest of their family and the Cross of St. George, and from a vase on the drawing-room mantelpiece they removed the small Union Jack that had been there since the Coronation of Queen Elizabeth II. They did not remove these articles in fear but in mourning for the *modus*
240 *vivendi*[29] that had existed for so long between them and the people of the town. They had given their custom[30] to a butcher who had planned to shoot down soldiers in their hall and he, in turn, had given them mince for their dog. For fifty years they had experienced, after suspicion had seeped away, a tolerance that never again in the years that were left to them would they know.

One November night their dog died and he said to her after he had buried it that they must not be depressed by all that was happening. They would die themselves and the house would become a ruin because there was no one to inherit it, and the distant past would be set to rest. But she disagreed: the *modus vivendi* had been easy for them, she pointed out, because they hadn't really
250 minded the dwindling of their fortunes while the town prospered. It had given them a life, and a kind of dignity: you could take a pride out of living in peace.

He did not say anything and then, because of the emotion that both of them felt over the death of their dog, he said in a rushing way that they could no longer at their age hope to make a living out of the remains of Carraveagh. They must sell the hens and the four Herefords. As he spoke, he watched her nodding, agreeing with the sense of it. Now and again, he thought, he would drive slowly into the town, to buy groceries and meat with the money they had saved, and to face the silence that would sourly thicken as their own two deaths came closer and death increased in another part of their island. She felt him thinking that and she
260 knew that he was right. Because of the distant past they would die friendless. It was worse than being murdered in their beds. ✎ **K**

disconsolately
(dĭs-kŏn′sə-lĭt-lē) *adv.*
unhappily; inconsolably

> **Language Coach**
>
> **Cognates** Words from different languages that look and sound similar are **cognates**. *Coronation* (line 238) is cognate with the Spanish *coronación*. Both come from the Latin *corona*, which has a Spanish cognate. What is the English word (*not* a cognate) for *corona*? What does *coronation* mean?

K ANALYZE RELATIONSHIPS
How are the Middletons affected by the shift in attitude toward them?

---

29. ***modus vivendi*** (mō′dəs vĭ-vĕn′dē): Latin for "way of life."

30. **custom:** business; trade.

Comprehension

1. **Recall** Describe the Middletons' political loyalties.

2. **Recall** What do the Middletons do in town on Fridays?

3. **Clarify** Why do the town's fortunes rise and then decline?

4. **Paraphrase** What do the Middletons mean when they say, "It is worse than before"?

Text Analysis

5. **Contrast Characters** In what ways are the Middletons unlike the townspeople?

6. **Analyze Character Relationships** Review the chart you completed as you read. How does the relationship between the Middletons and the townspeople change over the years? Explain the reasons for the changes.

7. **Analyze Setting** What does this story reveal about Irish society in the 20th century? Consider the following aspects of setting:

   - economic conditions
   - social customs
   - religious values
   - political attitudes
   - the influence of history

8. **Make Judgments** How responsible are the Middletons for the townspeople's feelings toward them at the end of the story? Support your answer.

9. **Understand Irony** Trevor uses irony to illuminate truths about human nature. What examples of **situational irony** are there in the story? What **verbal irony** is there in the title "The Distant Past"?

Text Criticism

10. **Critical Interpretations** William Trevor's biographer, Dolores MacKenna, has observed that Trevor writes "with the objectivity of an outsider, but with a native's appreciation of [Ireland's] social and political complexities." Would you agree that in "The Distant Past" Trevor portrays both the townspeople and the Middletons with objectivity and empathy? Support your opinion with references to the story.

When should we let go of the **PAST?**

What historical or cultural events from the distant past have influenced how different groups of Americans presently view each other? Discuss specific examples.

COMMON CORE

RL 1 Cite textual evidence to support inferences drawn from the text. **RL 3** Analyze the impact of the author's choices regarding how to develop and relate elements of a story. **RL 6** Analyze a case in which grasping point of view requires distinguishing what is directly stated in a text from what is really meant.

Vocabulary in Context

▲ **VOCABULARY PRACTICE**

Use your knowledge of the boldfaced vocabulary words to indicate whether each statement is true or false.

1. An election may bring about a change in **regime.**
2. Partygoers enjoy **convivial** guests.
3. A suspicious person gives **credence** to nearly everything he or she is told.
4. In a movie set in ancient Rome, having the characters wear wristwatches would be an **anachronism.**
5. Only an unhappy person is likely to **guffaw.**
6. A constantly unruly child behaves with **perversity.**
7. Showing kindness is a common example of an **atrocity.**
8. A tragedy may cause someone to weep **disconsolately.**

WORD LIST

anachronism

atrocity

convivial

credence

disconsolately

guffaw

perversity

regime

ACADEMIC VOCABULARY IN WRITING

• approach   • assume   • environment   • method   • strategy

The **environment** one lives in can have a profound effect on one's happiness. Have you ever been in a situation where you were not entirely welcome? How did it affect you? Use at least one Academic Vocabulary word in your response.

COMMON CORE

L 4c Consult general reference materials. L 6 Acquire and use accurately general academic and domain-specific words.

VOCABULARY STRATEGY: GREEK ROOTS AND AFFIXES

The word *anachronism* contains the Greek root *chron,* which means "time," and the Greek affix *ana-,* which means "backwards." An *anachronism* is something out of its proper time. The Greek root *chron* appears in a large number of academic English words from a variety of different subject areas, as you can see from the word web to the right. The prefix *ana-,* however, is somewhat rare. (It appears, for example, in the words *anabolic* and *anagram.*)

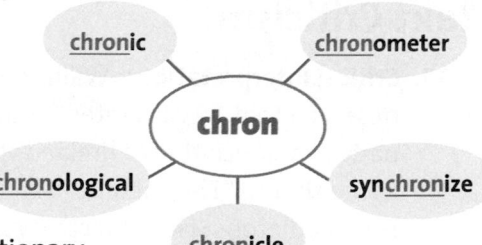

PRACTICE Below is a list of common Greek roots and affixes. Use a dictionary to find at least two English words that are formed from each root or affix. Make sure that at least one of the words for each item is related to science or technology.

1. The root *ortho-,* meaning "straight" or "right"
2. The root *bio-,* meaning "life"
3. The affix *a-* (or *an-*), meaning "not" or "without"
4. The affix *dia-,* meaning "through" or "apart"

Interactive Vocabulary
THINK central

Go to **thinkcentral.com.**
KEYWORD: HML12-1330

The Diversity of Postwar Writing

Writers working in the post–World War II era were a diverse group, whose work varied widely in subject matter, style, form, and theme. Yet all shared a sense of struggling with the realities of modern life.

Writing to Evaluate

Imagine Seamus Heaney, Ted Hughes, Stevie Smith, and William Trevor have been nominated for a prestigious literary award whose winner you will declare. Based on the selections you have just read, who should win? To help you consider carefully, use a chart like the one shown to organize your ideas about each piece; you can use the suggested criteria or develop your own. Then, write two or three formal paragraphs in which you explain the reasons for your choice, linking your ideas with appropriate transitions and concluding with the work's overall impact.

Selection:	
Criteria	Evaluation
Use of imagery and figurative language	
Musicality and lyricism	
Subject matter	
Emotional content	
Theme	
Overall impact	

Extension

SPEAKING & LISTENING Adapt your writing into a speech in which you attempt to persuade the other judges to vote for your candidate. In addition to pointing out the strengths of your chosen writer, it might be effective to compare his or her work with that of the other contenders. Be sure to use formal English.

○ **COMMON CORE**

W 1 Write arguments to support claims in an analysis of texts. **W 1b–e** Develop claims fairly and thoroughly, supplying relevant evidence; use words, phrases, and clauses to link the major sections of the text; establish and maintain a formal tone; provide a concluding statement. **SL 6** Adapt speech to a variety of contexts and tasks, demonstrating a command of formal English.

Seamus Heaney, Ted Hughes, Stevie Smith, and William Trevor

Telephone Conversation

Poem by Wole Soyinka

DID YOU KNOW?

Wole Soyinka ...

- was the first African to win the Nobel Prize in literature.
- is the cousin of Nigerian music star Fela Kuti.
- spent time working with inner-city kids in Jamaica.

Meet the Author

Wole Soyinka   born 1934

Although Wole Soyinka (wō′lĕ shô-yĭng′kə) may be best known for his challenging plays, he is also a distinguished poet and a passionate political activist. He has been arrested at least ten times for his outspoken criticism of government corruption in his native Nigeria. His activist impulses also inform his creative work, which often tackles difficult social issues through blistering satire. Soyinka's resolute advocacy, in art and in practical politics, has earned him the reputation as "the conscience of Nigeria."

Origins Soyinka grew up in an Anglican mission compound in western Nigeria, which was then under British colonial rule. He describes his childhood home as a place "where words were an integral part of culture." Soyinka's family were Yoruba, members of one of Nigeria's main ethnic or tribal groups. Soyinka's grandfather introduced him to Yoruban folklore, including legends of the god Ogun, who governed both the creative and destructive essence. Soyinka frequently invokes Ogun in his work and considers this figure to be his muse.

An African Abroad In late 1954, Soyinka left Nigeria for England, to study at the University of

Leeds. After graduating in 1957, he worked as a script reader, actor, and director for London's Royal Court Theater. He also began to write his first serious plays. *The Invention,* the first of Soyinka's plays to be produced, is a satire about the chaos that ensues when black South Africans lose their pigment and can no longer be distinguished from whites.

During his years in England, Soyinka had many personal encounters with the indignities of racism. He satirized one such encounter in his poem "Telephone Conversation," written in 1960. That same year, Nigeria gained its independence from Britain and Soyinka returned to his homeland to study West African drama at the University of Ibadan.

Hybrid Style As Soyinka matured, he became more aware of the tension between traditional African identity and Western-style modernization. He attempts to resolve this in his dramatic work by using a blend of traditional Yoruban folk-drama and European theatrical forms. His major works include *A Dance of the Forests* (1960) and *Death and the King's Horseman* (1976). He has described his writing as "preoccupied with the theme of the oppressive boot, the irrelevance of the color of the foot that wears it and the struggle for individuality."

Author Online

Go to **thinkcentral.com**. KEYWORD: HML12-1332

THiNK central

TEXT ANALYSIS: TONE IN SATIRE

As you've learned, **satire** is a literary form in which flaws in human behavior or social institutions are ridiculed in order to promote social change. Because the satirist relies on wit and humor to make a point, his or her **tone,** or attitude toward the subject, is a critical element in this kind of writing. Consider these lines from Soyinka's poem:

"ARE YOU DARK? OR VERY LIGHT?" Revelation came.
"You mean—like plain or milk chocolate?"

The comparison of skin color to varieties of chocolate highlights the absurdity of racial prejudice.

Writers choose words and details carefully to establish tone, which can range from light and humorous to sarcastic and bitter. In fact, the two main types of satire are defined primarily by differences in tone. In **Horatian satire,** the tone is playful and amusing, whereas in **Juvenalian satire,** the tone is biting and harsh. As you read Soyinka's poem, note how his tone helps to deliver his message.

READING SKILL: UNDERSTAND AUTHOR'S BACKGROUND

To understand why someone wrote a particular work, it can be helpful to examine the **author's background.** Background includes not only biographical details but also the values, traditions, and beliefs that have influenced the author's outlook. Before reading "Telephone Conversation," reread the biography of Soyinka on page 1332. Then, as you read the poem, consider how Soyinka's life experiences might have influenced his choice of subject.

 Complete the activities in your **Reader/Writer Notebook**.

What causes RACISM?

Most societies have had to confront the problem of racism. But how does racism develop? Are people born with an instinct for prejudice, or do they learn these attitudes from the world around them? What causes a person to feel contempt for another on the basis of race?

QUICKWRITE Consider several possible causes of racism, such as human instinct, fear, ignorance, or hatred. What do you think causes racism? Is it a problem that can be solved? Write a paragraph briefly explaining your position.

THE LONDO

APRIL 13, 1981

Riots Continue for Sec

Telephone Conversation

Wole Soyinka

The price seemed reasonable, location
Indifferent. The landlady swore she lived
Off premises. Nothing remained
But self-confession. "Madam," I warned,
5 "I hate a wasted journey—I am African." **A**
Silence. Silenced transmission of
Pressurized good-breeding. Voice, when it came,
Lipstick-coated, long gold-rolled
Cigarette-holder pipped. Caught I was, foully.

10 "HOW DARK?" . . . I had not misheard . . . "ARE YOU
      LIGHT
"OR VERY DARK?" Button B. Button A. Stench
Of rancid breath of public hide-and-speak.
Red booth. Red pillar-box. Red double-tiered
Omnibus squelching tar. It *was* real! Shamed
15 By ill-mannered silence, surrender
Pushed dumbfoundment to beg simplification.
Considerate she was, varying the emphasis—

A AUTHOR'S BACKGROUND
Reread lines 1–5. What aspects
of Soyinka's biography are
reflected in the speaker's
situation?

13 pillar-box: mailbox on a pillar.

Language Coach

Etymology Words formed
from another word or base are
derivations. Look up the word
dumbfoundment (line 16). What
words are at its base? What
does it mean? How can it "beg
simplification"?

Q.E.H. (1998), Anne Desmet. Wood engraving and linocut,
10.2 cm × 13.3 cm. Private collection. © Bridgeman Art Library.

"ARE YOU DARK? OR VERY LIGHT?" Revelation
    came.
"You mean—like plain or milk chocolate?"
20 Her assent was clinical, crushing in its light
Impersonality. Rapidly, wave-length adjusted,
I chose, "West African sepia"—and as an afterthought,
"Down in my passport." Silence for spectroscopic
Flight of fancy, till truthfulness clanged her accent
25 Hard on the mouthpiece "WHAT'S THAT?", conceding,
"DON'T KNOW WHAT THAT IS." "Like brunette."

"THAT'S DARK, ISN'T IT?" "Not altogether.
"Facially, I am brunette, but madam, you should see
"The rest of me. Palm of my hand, soles of my feet
30 "Are a peroxide blonde. Friction, caused—
"Foolishly, madam—by sitting down, has turned
"My bottom raven black.—One moment madam!"—
    sensing
Her receiver rearing on the thunder clap
About my ears—"Madam," I pleaded, "wouldn't you rather
35 "See for yourself?" **ⓑ**

22 sepia (sē′pē-ə): a dark yellow brown or olive brown.

23 spectroscopic: pertaining to the analysis of colors.

ⓑ TONE IN SATIRE
What is absurd about the conversation in this stanza? What in Soyinka's **word choice** helps convey this absurdity?

Comprehension

1. **Recall** What is the speaker's situation at the start of the poem?

2. **Clarify** Why does he reveal that he is African?

3. **Summarize** Reread lines 27–32. What is the speaker's response to the landlady's question?

Text Analysis

4. **Make Inferences About Speaker** Compare the speaker's emotional state at the beginning and the end of the poem. How has the conversation affected him?

5. **Examine Author's Background** What personal experiences, values, or beliefs seem to have inspired Soyinka to write this poem? Cite details from the author's biography and the poem in your answer.

6. **Identify Tone in Satire** Describe the tone of this poem. What specific word choices contribute to this tone? How does the tone affect the way you read the poem? Explain your answer.

7. **Analyze Irony** Satirists frequently use **verbal irony,** which occurs when what is said is the opposite of what is meant. Explain the verbal irony in each of the following passages:

   • the speaker's initial reaction (lines 14–16)
   • the landlady's second question (line 18)
   • the speaker's self-description (lines 30–32)

8. **Make Generalizations** Consider what the landlady's concern with the speaker's precise color suggests about the nature of her racism. What does her reaction tell you about how some people adopt and apply racist beliefs?

9. **Compare Texts** Compare Soyinka's poem with Jonathan Swift's "A Modest Proposal" on page 622. What do these two satires have in common? In what ways are they different? In your answer, compare the following elements:

   • tone   • author's style
   • type of satire   • the issue being satirized

Text Criticism

10. **Critical Interpretations** South African writer Nadine Gordimer has described Soyinka's work as "overly self-conscious." Based on the poem you read, do you agree or disagree? Explain, citing details to support your answer.

> *What causes* **RACISM?**
>
> What do you think Soyinka believes to be the cause of racism? Explain why you agree or disagree with him.

COMMON CORE

RL 1 Cite textual evidence to support inferences drawn from the text. **RL 4** Analyze the impact of specific word choices on meaning and tone. **RL 6** Analyze a case in which grasping point of view requires distinguishing what is directly stated in a text from what is really meant. **RL 10** Read and comprehend literature, including poems.

From Things Fall Apart

Novel by Chinua Achebe

Chinua Achebe
born 1930

⬤ **COMMON CORE**

RL 3 Analyze the impact of the author's choices regarding how to develop and relate elements of a story.

BACKGROUND Chinua Achebe (ä-chä′bä) grew up in Nigeria when it was still a colony of Britain. His parents, of Ibo background, largely accepted Western ways and even named him Albert to honor Queen Victoria's husband. By the time he reached college age, however, Achebe was tired of European authors who wrote about his homeland. Certain he could do better, he shortened his Ibo middle name and began writing as Chinua Achebe.

Like much of Achebe's fiction, *Things Fall Apart* deals with the cultural clashes brought about by European colonization of Africa and the tension between old ways and new. The central character, an Ibo villager named Okonkwo, is steeped in tradition and inflexible about change. He is also determined to live down his father's reputation for laziness and wastefulness. Working hard and faithfully following the old ways, he becomes an esteemed member of his village. Yet he also treats his wives and children with excessive harshness, and his fear of appearing weak like his father in fact proves to be a weakness of his own.

TEXT ANALYSIS In the excerpt that follows, notice how fear determines **character motivation** and behavior. Because Okonkwo is afraid to be like his father, who was gentle and idle, Okonkwo goes out of his way to be severe and stoic. His wives and children also live in fear, but they react with meekness, daring not to complain. When Ikemefuna arrives at Okonkwo's house, he demonstrates his fear through acceptance by not asking why he is taken from his family and by not crying.

DISCUSS In a small group, discuss how fear can influence the way one responds to the world and the choices one makes. Why is fear such a powerful motivator, and what are some of its both negative and positive consequences?

O konkwo ruled his household with a heavy hand. His wives, especially the youngest, lived in perpetual fear of his fiery temper, and so did his little children. Perhaps down in his heart Okonkwo was not a cruel man. But his whole life was dominated by fear, the fear of failure and of weakness. It was deeper and more intimate than the fear of evil and capricious gods and of magic, the fear of the forest, and of the forces of nature, malevolent, red in tooth and claw. Okonkwo's fear was greater than these. It was not external but lay deep within himself. It was the fear of himself, lest he should be found to resemble his father. Even as a little boy he had resented his father's failure and weakness, and even now he still

10 remembered how he had suffered when a playmate had told him that his father

was *agbala.* That was how Okonkwo first came to know that *agbala* was not only another name for a woman, it could also mean a man who had taken no title. And so Okonkwo was ruled by one passion—to hate everything that his father Unoka had loved. One of those things was gentleness and another was idleness.

During the planting season Okonkwo worked daily on his farms from cock-crow until the chickens went to roost. He was a very strong man and rarely felt fatigue. But his wives and young children were not as strong, and so they suffered. But they dared not complain openly. Okonkwo's first son, Nwoye,
20 was then twelve years old but was already causing his father great anxiety for his incipient laziness. At any rate, that was how it looked to his father, and he sought to correct him by constant nagging and beating. And so Nwoye was developing into a sad-faced youth.

Okonkwo's prosperity was visible in his household. He had a large compound enclosed by a thick wall of red earth. His own hut, or *obi,* stood immediately behind the only gate in the red walls. Each of his three wives had her own hut, which together formed a half moon behind the *obi.* The barn was built against one end of the red walls, and long stacks of yam stood out prosperously in it. At the opposite end of the compound was a shed for the goats, and each wife built a small attachment to
30 her hut for the hens. Near the barn was a small house, the "medicine house" or shrine where Okonkwo kept the wooden symbols of his personal god and of his ancestral spirits. He worshipped them with sacrifices of kola nut, food and palm-wine, and offered prayers to them on behalf of himself, his three wives and eight children.

So when the daughter of Umuofia was killed in Mbaino, Ikemefuna came into Okonkwo's household. When Okonkwo brought him home that day he called his most senior wife and handed him over to her.

"He belongs to the clan," he told her. "So look after him."

"Is he staying long with us?" she asked.

"Do what you are told, woman," Okonkwo thundered, and stammered. "When
40 did you become one of the *ndichie* of Umuofia?"

And so Nwoye's mother took Ikemefuna to her hut and asked no more questions.

As for the boy himself, he was terribly afraid. He could not understand what was happening to him or what he had done. How could he know that his father had taken a hand in killing a daughter of Umuofia? All he knew was that a few men had arrived at their house, conversing with his father in low tones, and at the end he had been taken out and handed over to a stranger. His mother had wept bitterly, but he had been too surprised to weep. And so the stranger had brought him, and a girl, a long, long way from home, through lonely forest paths. He did not know who the girl was, and he never saw her again.

Six Feet of the Country

Short Story by Nadine Gordimer

COMMON CORE

RL 3 Analyze the impact of the author's choices regarding how to develop and relate elements of a story. **RL 4** Determine the meaning of words and phrases as they are used in the text, including connotative meanings. **RL 10** Read and comprehend literature, including stories. **SL 1** Initiate and participate effectively in a range of collaborative discussions.

DID YOU KNOW?

Nadine Gordimer . . .

- published her first short story at the age of 15.
- was confined to her house from ages 10 to 16 with a heart condition.
- refused a literary award for which only women could be considered.

Meet the Author

Nadine Gordimer   born 1923

Nadine Gordimer credits her love of books with saving her from the belief that there was only one way to live. Born into a white, middle-class family in South Africa, Gordimer became an early critic of the racial segregation imposed by apartheid. In her novels and short stories, she explores the emotional and spiritual costs of living in a repressive, racist society. In precise, often ironic prose, Gordimer depicts the contradictions that result when ideology intersects with the daily life of individuals.

Duty of Writers Several of Gordimer's works were banned in South Africa because of their critical portrayal of apartheid. But she resists the label of "political author," and her complex, subtle fiction defies easy moral judgments. In Gordimer's view, a writer's true subject is "the consciousness of his own era." Her body of work chronicles the entire apartheid era, from its beginnings to the present-day effort to cope with its aftermath. But she focuses on the intersection of history and private lives, exploring her characters' experiences of shattered illusions, alienation, and fears of betrayal. Through these characters, usually middle-class whites, Gordimer tries to show "a terrified white consciousness in the midst of a mysterious and ominous sea of black humanity."

Her major works include the novels *A World of Strangers* (1958), *The Conservationist* (1974), and *A Sport of Nature* (1987). She has also published 11 volumes of short stories. In 1991, Gordimer received the Nobel Prize in literature.

Humanist, Not Feminist Gordimer sometimes draws parallels between women and black South Africans, portraying both as trapped in unequal relationships with white men. Yet she considers herself an advocate for human rights, not women's rights. She continues her commitment to the cause of freedom, dedicating her efforts to creating a postapartheid culture in the new South Africa. In 2004, Gordimer launched a fundraising effort to combat the HIV/AIDS epidemic in her homeland. She persuaded 21 of the world's most distinguished writers—including Chinua Achebe, Margaret Atwood, and Salman Rushdie—to contribute to a collection of short stories called *Telling Tales,* with the proceeds going to HIV/AIDS prevention and education programs in South Africa. Her high artistic standards and her strong sense of moral purpose make her an inspiring example for writers everywhere.

Author Online

Go to **thinkcentral.com**. KEYWORD: HML12-1340

THINK central

TEXT ANALYSIS: CULTURAL CONFLICT

You know that in literature, conflict is the struggle between opposing forces that moves the plot forward. This story centers on a **cultural conflict,** a clash between groups of people whose values, beliefs, and roles in society put them at odds with each other. The narrator of the story, a white South African, observes events from one side of this conflict. You'll need to question the narrator's statements carefully to get at the larger context. Pay special attention to

- details that describe the lives of whites and blacks
- the narrator's attitudes toward black South Africans
- causes of the tension between characters

As you read, watch for clues that reveal how living in a divided society has influenced the narrator's perceptions.

READING STRATEGY: PREDICT

To make a **prediction,** you use clues from the text to guess what will happen next. In the opening lines of this story, the narrator explains why he and his wife moved to the country.

We bought our place, ten miles out of Johannesburg on one of the main roads, to change something in ourselves....

As you read this story, try to anticipate what changes will occur in the lives of the main characters. Pay careful attention to the main characters' beliefs about themselves and their way of life, and consider how the events of the story might call these beliefs into question.

VOCABULARY IN CONTEXT

Use context clues to determine the meaning of each boldfaced word from "Six Feet of the Country."

1. tried to **imbue** us with team spirit
2. felt **extraneous** and unnecessary
3. not **enamored** of that sickening smell
4. went to the cemetery for the **interment**
5. began to **expostulate** with him to make him see reason
6. changed his hairstyle in **emulation** of his big brother
7. so **laconic** she barely says a word
8. the basketball player's long, **attenuated** body

 Complete the activities in your **Reader/Writer Notebook.**

Can you put a price on DIGNITY?

What helps a person hold on to self-respect? For a prisoner, perhaps it's being called by name instead of by number. For someone treated cruelly, it might be a smile or an offer of help. For people living under brutal and dehumanizing conditions, small gestures like these can become important affirmations of their human dignity.

DISCUSS What are some things that people do to preserve their sense of humanity, even in the face of inhumane circumstances? What do these responses tell you about the value people place on their dignity?

SIX FEET OF THE COUNTRY

Nadine Gordimer

> **BACKGROUND** In Afrikaans, the language of the Dutch settlers of South Africa, the term *apartheid* means "separateness." It refers to an official system of racial segregation that was in force from 1948 to 1991. This system restricted the education, housing, and voting rights of nonwhites; it also granted the state enhanced police powers to enforce its racial policies. In the 1970s and 1980s, after years of national and international protest, the government began to reform its apartheid policy. In 1991, the last of these discriminatory laws was finally repealed. Today, South Africa struggles with the lingering economic and social effects of the apartheid years. Gordimer wrote this story shortly after the apartheid system first went into effect.

My wife and I are not real farmers—not even Lerice, really. We bought our place, ten miles out of Johannesburg on one of the main roads, to change something in ourselves, I suppose; you seem to rattle about so much within a marriage like ours. You long to hear nothing but a deep, satisfying silence when you sound a marriage. The farm hasn't managed that for us, of course, but it has done other things, unexpected, illogical. Lerice, who I thought would retire there in Chekhovian sadness for a month or two, and then leave the place to the servants while she tried yet again to get a part she wanted and become the actress she would like to be, has sunk into the business of running the farm with all the
10 serious intensity with which she once **imbued** the shadows in a playwright's mind. I should have given it up long ago if it had not been for her. Her hands, once small and plain and well-kept—she was not the sort of actress who wears red paint and diamond rings—are hard as a dog's pads. **A**

I, of course, am there only in the evenings and at week-ends. I am a partner in a luxury-travel agency, which is flourishing—needs to be, as I tell Lerice, in order to carry on the farm. Still, though I know we can't afford it, and though the sweetish smell of the fowls Lerice breeds sickens me, so that I avoid going past their runs, the farm is beautiful in a way I had almost forgotten—especially on a Sunday morning when I get up and go out into the paddock and see not the palm
20 trees and fish pond and imitation-stone bird-bath of the suburbs but white ducks

Analyze Visuals ▶
What aspects of life does the artist choose to depict?

imbue (ĭm-byo͞o′) v. to fill, as with a quality; saturate

A **PREDICT**
Reread lines 1–11. Consider what the narrator reveals about his marriage. Do you expect his relationship to grow stronger or weaker over the course of the story? Explain.

Landscape, Jennifer Cross. Watercolor on paper, 387 cm × 306 cm.
© Nelson Mandela Metropolitan Art Museum, South Africa.

on the dam, the lucerne[1] field brilliant as window-dresser's grass, and the little, stocky, mean-eyed bull, lustful but bored, having his face tenderly licked by one of his ladies. Lerice comes out with her hair uncombed, in her hand a stick dripping with cattle-dip. She will stand and look dreamily for a moment, the way she would pretend to look sometimes in those plays. "They'll mate tomorrow," she will say. "This is their second day. Look how she loves him, my little Napoleon." So that when people come out to see us on Sunday afternoon, I am likely to hear myself saying, as I pour out the drinks, "When I drive back home from the city every day, past those rows of suburban houses, I wonder how the devil we ever did stand it. . . .

30 Would you care to look around?" And there I am, taking some pretty girl and her young husband stumbling down to our river-bank, the girl catching her stockings on the mealie-stooks[2] and stepping over cow-turds humming with jewel-green flies while she says, ". . . the *tensions* of the damned city. And you're near enough to get into town to a show, too! I think it's wonderful. Why, you've got it both ways!"

And for a moment I accept the triumph as if I *had* managed it—the impossibility that I've been trying for all my life—just as if the truth was that you could get it "both ways," instead of finding yourself with not even one way or the other but a third, one you had not provided for at all.

But even in our saner moments, when I find Lerice's earthy enthusiasms just as

40 irritating as I once found her histrionical[3] ones, and she finds what she calls my "jealousy" of her capacity for enthusiasm as big a proof of my inadequacy for her as a mate as ever it was, we do believe that we have at least honestly escaped those tensions peculiar to the city about which our visitors speak. When Johannesburg people speak of "tension" they don't mean hurrying people in crowded streets, the struggle for money, or the general competitive character of city life. They mean the guns under the white men's pillows and the burglar bars on the white men's windows. They mean those strange moments on city pavements when a black man won't stand aside for a white man. **B**

Out in the country, even ten miles out, life is better than that. In the country,

50 there is a lingering remnant of the pretransitional stage; our relationship with the blacks is almost feudal.[4] Wrong, I suppose, obsolete, but more comfortable all round. We have no burglar bars, no gun. Lerice's farm-boys have their wives and their piccanins[5] living with them on the land. They brew their sour beer without the fear of police raids. In fact, we've always rather prided ourselves that the poor devils have nothing much to fear, being with us; Lerice even keeps an eye on their children, with all the competence of a woman who has never had a child of her own, and she certainly doctors them all—children and adults—like babies whenever they happen to be sick. **C**

B PREDICT
Reread lines 39–48. Explain what the narrator believes he has achieved by moving to the country. Do you expect this belief to hold true over the course of the story or to be proved false? Explain.

C CULTURAL CONFLICT
Reread lines 49–58. Note the narrator's use of words and phrases like *farm-boys, piccanins,* and *poor devils.* What does this **word choice** suggest about the way he views black South Africans?

---

1. **lucerne** (lōō-sûrn'): a British and South African term for alfalfa, an herb grown as a pasture crop or to make hay.

2. **mealie-stooks:** a South African term for cornstalks.

3. **histrionical** (hĭs'trē-ŏn'ĭ-kəl): related to acting; excessively dramatic or emotional.

4. **feudal** (fyōōd'l): characteristic of feudalism, the medieval European economic, political, and social system in which serfs who worked the land were protected by their overlords, to whom they showed great deference.

5. **piccanins** (pĭk'ə-nĭnz'): a South African term (often considered derogatory) for native African children.

It was because of this that we were not particularly startled one night last winter
when the boy Albert came knocking at our window long after we had gone to bed. I
wasn't in our bed but sleeping in the little dressing-room-cum-linen room next door,
because Lerice had annoyed me, and I didn't want to find myself softening toward
her simply because of the sweet smell of the talcum powder on her flesh after her
bath. She came and woke me up. "Albert says one of the boys is very sick," she said. "I
think you'd better go down and see. He wouldn't get us up at this hour for nothing."

"What time is it?"

"What does it matter?" Lerice is maddeningly logical.

I got up awkwardly as she watched me—how is it I always feel a fool when I
have deserted her bed? After all, I know from the way she never looks at me when
she talks to me at breakfast the next day that she is hurt and humiliated at my not
wanting her—and I went out, clumsy with sleep. **D**

"Which of the boys is it?" I asked Albert as we followed the dance of my torch.

"He's too sick. Very sick, *Baas*,"[6] he said.

"But who? Franz?" I remembered Franz had had a bad cough for the past week.

Albert did not answer; he had given me the path, and was walking along beside
me in the tall dead grass. When the light of the torch[7] caught his face, I saw that
he looked acutely embarrassed. "What's this all about?" I said.

He lowered his head under the glance of the light. "It's not me, *Baas*. I don't
know. Petrus he send me."

Irritated, I hurried him along to the huts. And there, on Petrus's iron bedstead,
with its brick stilts, was a young man, dead. On his forehead there was still a
light, cold sweat; his body was warm. The boys stood around as they do in the
kitchen when it is discovered that someone has broken a dish—uncooperative,
silent. Somebody's wife hung about in the shadows, her hands wrung together
under her apron.

I had not seen a dead man since the war. This was very different. I felt like the
others—**extraneous,** useless.

"What was the matter?" I asked.

The woman patted at her chest and shook her head to indicate the painful
impossibility of breathing.

He must have died of pneumonia.

I turned to Petrus. "Who was this boy? What was he doing here?" The light of a
candle on the floor showed that Petrus was weeping. He followed me out the door.

When we were outside, in the dark, I waited for him to speak. But he didn't. "Now
come on, Petrus, you must tell me who this boy was. Was he a friend of yours?"

"He's my brother, *Baas*. He come from Rhodesia[8] to look for work."

The story startled Lerice and me a little. The young boy had walked down from
Rhodesia to look for work in Johannesburg, had caught a chill from sleeping out

D GRAMMAR AND STYLE
Reread lines 68–71.
Notice that Gordimer
uses dashes to set off the
first-person narrator's
thoughts about marriage,
which interrupt his
description of his actions.

extraneous
(ĭk-strā′nē-əs) *adj.*
irrelevant or inessential

---

6. *Baas* (bäs) *Afrikaans:* master; formerly used as a deferential term of address by black South Africans
   when speaking to a white man. The word's English counterpart, *boss*, is also of Dutch origin.

7. **torch:** the British and South African term for a flashlight.

8. **Rhodesia** (rō-dē′zhə): a British colony in south-central Africa, sometimes called Southern Rhodesia; now
   the independent nations of Zambia and Zimbabwe.

along the way, and had lain ill in his brother Petrus's hut since his arrival three
100 days before. Our boys had been frightened to ask us for help for him because we
had not been intended ever to know of his presence. Rhodesian natives are barred
from entering the Union[9] unless they have a permit; the young man was an illegal
immigrant. No doubt our boys had managed the whole thing successfully several
times before; a number of relatives must have walked the seven or eight hundred
miles from poverty to the paradise of zoot suits,[10] police raids, and black slum
townships that is their *Egoli*, City of Gold—the Bantu[11] name for Johannesburg.
It was merely a matter of getting such a man to lie low on our farm until a job
could be found with someone who would be glad to take the risk of prosecution
for employing an illegal immigrant in exchange for the services of someone as
110 yet untainted by the city.

Well, this was one who would never get up again.

"You would think they would have felt they could tell *us*," said Lerice next
morning. "Once the man was ill. You would have thought at least—" When she
is getting intense over something, she has a way of standing in the middle of a
room as people do when they are shortly to leave on a journey, looking searchingly
about her at the most familiar objects as if she had never seen them before. I had
noticed that in Petrus's presence in the kitchen, earlier, she had the air of being
almost offended with him, almost hurt.

In any case, I really haven't the time or inclination any more to go into
120 everything in our life that I know Lerice, from those alarmed and pressing eyes of
hers, would like us to go into. She is the kind of woman who doesn't mind if she
looks plain, or odd; I don't suppose she would even care if she knew how strange
she looks when her whole face is out of proportion with urgent uncertainty. I said,
"Now, I'm the one who'll have to do all the dirty work, I suppose."

She was still staring at me, trying me out with those eyes—wasting her time,
if she only knew.

"I'll have to notify the health authorities," I said calmly. "They can't just cart
him off and bury him. After all, we don't really know what he died of." **E**

She simply stood there, as if she had given up—simply ceased to see me at all.
130 I don't know when I've been so irritated. "It might have been something
contagious," I said. "God knows?" There was no answer.

I am not **enamored** of holding conversations with myself. I went out to shout
to one of the boys to open the garage and get the car ready for my morning drive
to town.

As I had expected, it turned out to be quite a business. I had to notify the police
as well as the health authorities, and answer a lot of tedious questions: How was it
I was ignorant of the boy's presence? If I did not supervise my native quarters, how
did I know that that sort of thing didn't go on all the time? Et cetera, et cetera. And

---

9. **Union:** the Union of South Africa, the official name of South Africa before the formation of the Republic of South Africa in 1961.

10. **zoot suits:** flashy men's suits with broad, padded shoulders and baggy trousers.

11. ***Egoli*** (ā-gō'lē) ... **Bantu** (băn'tōō): Bantu is a family of languages widely spoken in southern Africa. Zulu and Xhosa are part of the Bantu language family.

when I flared up and told them that so long as my natives did their work, I didn't
140 think it my right or concern to poke my nose into their private lives, I got from
the coarse, dull-witted police sergeant one of those looks that come not from any
thinking process going on in the brain but from that faculty common to all who are
possessed by the master-race theory—a look of insanely inane certainty. He grinned
at me with a mixture of scorn and delight at my stupidity.

Then I had to explain to Petrus why the health authorities had to take away
the body for a post-mortem[12]—and, in fact, what a post-mortem was. When I
telephoned the health department some days later to find out the result, I was
told the cause of death was, as we had thought, pneumonia, and that the body
had been suitably disposed of. I went out to where Petrus was mixing a mash for
150 the fowls and told him that it was all right, there would be no trouble; his brother
had died from that pain in his chest. Petrus put down the paraffin tin and said,
"When can we go to fetch him, *Baas?*"

"To fetch him?"

"Will the *Baas* please ask them when we must come?"

I went back inside and called Lerice, all over the house. She came down the
stairs from the spare bedrooms, and I said, "*Now* what am I going to do? When
I told Petrus, he just asked calmly when they could go and fetch the body. They
think they're going to bury him themselves."

"Well, go back and tell him," said Lerice. "You must tell him. Why didn't you
160 tell him then?"

---

12. **post-mortem:** an examination of a corpse to determine the cause of death.

▼ **Analyze Visuals**
Notice the artist's
technique of paint
application. What does
this help convey about
the couple's relationship?

Michael and Victoria Hastings (2005), Paul Richards. Oil on canvas, 10″ × 14″.
© Connaught Brown Gallery, London.

When I found Petrus again, he looked up politely. "Look, Petrus," I said. "You can't go to fetch your brother. They've done it already—they've *buried* him, you understand?"

"Where?" he said, slowly, dully, as if he thought that perhaps he was getting this wrong.

"You see, he was a stranger. They knew he wasn't from here, and they didn't know he had some of his people here, so they thought they must bury him." It was difficult to make a pauper's grave[13] sound like a privilege.

"Please, *Baas*, the *Baas* must ask them?" But he did not mean that he wanted to
170 know the burial-place. He simply ignored the incomprehensible machinery I told him had set to work on his dead brother; he wanted the brother back.

"But Petrus," I said, "how can I? Your brother is buried already. I can't ask them now."

"Oh *Baas!*" he said. He stood with his bran-smeared hands uncurled at his sides, one corner of his mouth twitching.

"Good God, Petrus, they won't listen to me! They can't, anyway. I'm sorry, but I can't do it. You understand?"

He just kept on looking at me, out of his knowledge that white men have everything, can do anything; if they don't, it is because they won't. **F**
180 And then, at dinner Lerice started. "You could at least phone," she said.

"*Christ*, what d'you think I am? Am I supposed to bring the dead back to life?"

But I could not exaggerate my way out of this ridiculous responsibility that had been thrust on me. "Phone them up," she went on. "And at least you'll be able to tell him you've done it and they've explained that it's impossible."

She disappeared somewhere into the kitchen quarters after coffee. A little later she came back to tell me, "The old father's coming down from Rhodesia to be at the funeral. He's got a permit and he's already on his way."

Unfortunately, it was not impossible to get the body back. The authorities said that it was somewhat irregular, but that since the hygiene conditions had been
190 fulfilled, they could not refuse permission for exhumation.[14] I found out that, with the undertaker's charges, it would cost twenty pounds. Ah, I thought, that settles it. On five pounds a month, Petrus won't have twenty pounds—and just as well, since it couldn't do the dead any good. Certainly I should not offer it to him myself. Twenty pounds—or anything else within reason, for that matter—I would have spent without grudging it on doctors or medicines that might have helped the boy when he was alive. Once he was dead, I had no intention of encouraging Petrus to throw away, on a gesture, more than he spent to clothe his whole family in a year.

When I told him, in the kitchen that night, he said, "Twenty pounds?"

I said, "Yes, that's right, twenty pounds."
200 For a moment, I had the feeling, from the look on his face, that he was calculating. But when he spoke again I thought I must have imagined it. "We must pay twenty pounds!" he said in the far-away voice in which a person speaks of something so unattainable that it does not bear thinking about.

F CULTURAL CONFLICT
Reread lines 169–179. What clash of values has put Petrus and the narrator in conflict with each other? What power does the narrator have in this situation that Petrus does not?

13. **pauper's grave:** an unmarked, often communal grave used for those unable to pay for private burial.

14. **exhumation** (ĕg′zyōō-mā′shən): the removal of a corpse from the grave.

"All right, Petrus," I said in dismissal, and went back to the living-room.

The next morning before I went to town, Petrus asked to see me. "Please *Baas*," he said, awkwardly handing me a bundle of notes. They're so seldom on the giving rather than the receiving side, poor devils, that they don't really know how to hand money to a white man. There it was, the twenty pounds, in ones and halves, some creased and folded until they were soft as dirty rags, others smooth and fairly new—Franz's money, I suppose, and Albert's, and Dora the cook's, and Jacob the gardener's, and God knows who else's besides, from all the farms and small holdings round about. I took it in irritation more than in astonishment, really—irritation at the waste, the uselessness of this sacrifice by people so poor. Just like the poor everywhere, I thought, who stint themselves the decencies of life in order to insure themselves the decencies of death. So incomprehensible to people like Lerice and me, who regard life as something to be spent extravagantly and, if we think about death at all, regard it as the final bankruptcy. **G**

The servants don't work on Saturday afternoon anyway, so it was a good day for the funeral. Petrus and his father had borrowed our donkey-cart to fetch the coffin from the city, where, Petrus told Lerice on their return, everything was "nice"—the coffin waiting for them, already sealed up to save them from what must have been a rather unpleasant sight after two weeks' **interment.** (It had taken all that time for the authorities and the undertaker to make the final arrangements for moving the body.) All morning, the coffin lay in Petrus's hut, awaiting the trip to the little old burial-ground, just outside the eastern boundary of our farm, that was a relic of the days when this was a real farming district rather than a fashionable rural estate. It was pure chance that I happened to be down there near the fence when the procession came past; once again Lerice had forgotten her promise to me and had made the house uninhabitable on a Saturday afternoon. I had come home and been infuriated to find her in a pair of filthy old slacks and with her hair uncombed since the night before, having all the varnish scraped off the living-room floor, if you please. So I had taken my No. 8 iron and gone off to practice my approach shots. In my annoyance I had forgotten about the funeral, and was reminded only when I saw the procession coming up the path along the outside of the fence toward me; from where I was standing, you can see the graves quite clearly, and that day the sun glinted on bits of broken pottery, a lopsided homemade cross, and jam-jars brown with rain-water and dead flowers. **H**

I felt a little awkward, and did not know whether to go on hitting my golf ball or stop at least until the whole gathering was decently past. The donkey-cart creaks and screeches with every revolution of the wheels and it came along in a slow, halting fashion somehow peculiarly suited to the two donkeys who drew it, their little potbellies rubbed and rough, their heads sunk between the shafts, and their ears flattened back with an air submissive and downcast; peculiarly suited, too, to the group of men and women who came along slowly behind. The patient ass. Watching, I thought, you can see now why the creature became a Biblical symbol.[15] Then the procession drew level with me and stopped, so I had to put

---

15. **creature . . . symbol:** In the Bible, the donkey, or ass, is sometimes presented as a symbol of patience, submission, and endurance.

G CULTURAL CONFLICT
Reread lines 205–217. Describe the narrator's response to the servants' sacrifice. What does he fail to understand about their motives?

interment (ĭn-tûr′mənt) *n.* burial

H PREDICT
Reread lines 218–237. What does the placement of the narrator at this scene lead you to expect?

Solomon (2005), Louise Ynclan. Oil on canvas, 90 cm × 90 cm.

down my club. The coffin was taken down off the cart—it was a shiny, yellow-varnished wood, like cheap furniture—and the donkeys twitched their ears against the flies. Petrus, Franz, Albert and the old father from Rhodesia hoisted
250 it on their shoulders and the procession moved on, on foot. It was really a very awkward moment. I stood there rather foolishly at the fence, quite still, and slowly they filed past, not looking up, the four men bent beneath the shiny wooden box, and the straggling troop of mourners. All of them were servants or neighbors' servants whom I knew as casual, easygoing gossipers about our lands or kitchen. I heard the old man's breathing.

I had just bent to pick up my club again when there was a sort of jar in the flowing solemnity of their processional mood; I felt it at once, like a wave of heat along the air, or one of those sudden currents of cold catching at your legs in a placid stream. The old man's voice was muttering something, and they bumped into one another,
260 some pressing to go on, others hissing at them to be still. I could see that they were embarrassed, but they could not ignore the voice; it was much the way that the mumblings of a prophet, though not clear at first, arrest the mind. The corner of the coffin the old man carried was sagging at an angle; he seemed to be trying to get out from under the weight of it. Now Petrus **expostulated** with him.

expostulate
(ĭk-spŏs′chə-lāt′) *v.* to reason with someone, in order to change his or her actions or plans

The little boy who had been left to watch the donkeys dropped the reins and ran to see. I don't know why—unless it was for the same reason people crowd round someone who has fainted in a cinema—but I parted the wires of the fence and went through, after him.

Petrus lifted his eyes to me—to anybody—with distress and horror. The old man from Rhodesia had let go of the coffin entirely, and the three others, unable to support it on their own, had laid it on the ground, in the pathway. Already there was a film of dust lightly wavering up its shiny sides. I did not understand what the old man was saying; I hesitated to interfere. But now the whole seething group turned on my silence. The old man himself came over to me, with his hands outspread and shaking, and spoke directly to me, saying something that I could tell from the tone, without understanding the words, was shocking and extraordinary.

"What is it, Petrus? What's wrong?" I appealed.

Petrus threw up his hands, bowed his head in a series of hysterical shakes, then thrust his face up at me suddenly.

"He says, 'My son was not so heavy.'"

Silence. I could hear the old man breathing; he kept his mouth a little open as old people do.

"My son was young and thin," he said, at last, in English.

Again silence. Then babble broke out. The old man thundered against everybody; his teeth were yellowed and few, and he had one of those fine, grizzled, sweeping moustaches that one doesn't often see nowadays, which must have been grown in **emulation** of early Empire builders.[16] It seemed to frame all his utterances with a special validity, perhaps merely because it was the symbol of the traditional wisdom of age—an idea so fearfully rooted that it carries still something awesome beyond reason. He shocked them; they thought he was mad, but they had to listen to him. With his own hands he began to prise the lid off the coffin and three of the men came forward to help him. Then he sat down on the ground; very old, very weak, and unable to speak, he merely lifted a trembling hand toward what was there. He abdicated, he handed it over to them; he was no good any more.

They crowded round to look (and so did I), and now they forgot the nature of this surprise and the occasion of grief to which it belonged, and for a few minutes were carried up in the astonishment of the surprise itself. They gasped and flared noisily with excitement. I even noticed the little boy who had held the donkeys jumping up and down, almost weeping with rage because the backs of the grown-ups crowded him out of his view.

In the coffin was someone no one had ever seen before: a heavily built, rather light-skinned native with a neatly stitched scar on his forehead—perhaps from a blow in a brawl that had also dealt him some other, slower-working injury which had killed him.

I wrangled with the authorities for a week over that body. I had the feeling that they were shocked, in a **laconic** fashion, by their own mistake, but that in the confusion of their anonymous dead they were helpless to put it right. They said

---

16. **Empire builders:** British colonizers.

COMMON CORE RL 4

Language Coach

Connotations/Denotations
One meaning of a word can affect the **connotations**—the connected feelings or images—of the other. *Seething* can mean either "bubbling and boiling" or "angry." How are the connotations of *seething* in line 273 more specific than those of *angry*?

emulation
(ĕm′yə-lā′shən)
n. imitation of an admired example

laconic (lə-kŏn′ĭk) *adj.*
using few words; concise

to me, "We are trying to find out," and "We are still making enquiries." It was as if at any moment they might conduct me into their mortuary[17] and say, "There! Lift
310 up the sheets; look for him—your poultry boy's brother. There are so many black faces—surely one will do?"

And every evening when I got home Petrus was waiting in the kitchen. "Well, they're trying. They're still looking. The *Baas* is seeing to it for you, Petrus," I would tell him. "God, half the time I should be in the office I'm driving around the back end of town chasing after this affair," I added aside, to Lerice, one night.

She and Petrus both kept their eyes turned on me as I spoke, and, oddly, for those moments they looked exactly alike, though it sounds impossible: my wife, with her high, white forehead and her **attenuated** Englishwoman's body, and the poultry boy, with his horny bare feet below khaki trousers tied at the knee with
320 string and the peculiar rankness of his nervous sweat coming from his skin.

"What makes you so indignant, so determined about this now?" said Lerice suddenly.

I stared at her. "It's a matter of principle. Why should they get away with a swindle? It's time these officials had a jolt from someone who'll bother to take the trouble."

She said, "Oh." And as Petrus slowly opened the kitchen door to leave, sensing that the talk had gone beyond him, she turned away too.

I continued to pass on assurances to Petrus every evening, but although what I said was the same, and the voice in which I said it was the same, every evening it
330 sounded weaker. At last, it became clear that we would never get Petrus's brother back, because nobody really knew where he was. Somewhere in a graveyard as uniform as a housing scheme, somewhere under a number that didn't belong to him, or in the medical school, perhaps, laboriously reduced to layers of muscles and strings of nerves? Goodness knows. He had no identity in this world anyway. ❶

It was only then, and in a voice of shame, that Petrus asked me to try and get the money back.

"From the way he asks, you'd think he was robbing his dead brother," I said to Lerice later. But as I've said, Lerice had got so intense about this business that she couldn't even appreciate a little ironic smile.
340 I tried to get the money; Lerice tried. We both telephoned and wrote and argued, but nothing came of it. It appeared that the main expense had been the undertaker, and, after all, he had done his job. So the whole thing was a complete waste, even more of a waste for the poor devils than I had thought it would be.

The old man from Rhodesia was about Lerice's father's size, so she gave him one of her father's old suits and he went back home rather better off, for the winter, than he had come. ❧

attenuated
(ə-tĕn′yōō-ā′tĭd) *adj.*
slender; thin **attenuate** *v.*

❶ **CULTURAL CONFLICT**
Reread lines 331–334. What does this passage convey about the value white society places on black South Africans?

---

17. **mortuary** (môr′chōō-ĕr′ē): a place where bodies of the dead are kept before burial or cremation; a funeral parlor.

Comprehension

1. **Recall** What happens to Petrus's brother?

2. **Recall** What does Petrus ask the narrator to do for him?

3. **Summarize** What disturbance occurs during the funeral procession?

Text Analysis

4. **Make Inferences About the Narrator** Reread the narrator's comment about Petrus's father in lines 344–346. Explain what it reveals about the narrator's understanding of what has occurred. What has the narrator learned by the end of the story?

5. **Examine Predictions** Recall your prediction about the narrator's relationship with his wife. Did the events of the story support your prediction? Cite details to support your answer.

6. **Analyze Cultural Conflict** In this story, Gordimer tries to show how interactions between individuals are distorted by the racial divisions of South African society. Consider the interactions described in each of the following passages. In each case, how does the racial divide aggravate the characters' misunderstandings and anxieties?

   • the report of the young man's death (lines 75–81)

   • Petrus's request for his brother's body (lines 145–160)

   • the funeral procession (lines 246–255)

7. **Interpret Title** Explain the meaning of the title "Six Feet of the Country." Based on your interpretation of the title, what do you consider to be the message of the story?

8. **Compare Characters' Perspectives** In what ways would the story change if it were told by Lerice? by Petrus? In your answer, mention specific scenes that would be told differently, as well as the types of details that would be included or excluded in the new version of the story.

Text Criticism

9. **Critical Interpretations** South African poet Dennis Brutus once called Nadine Gordimer "the living example of how dehumanized South African society has become." In his view, her work lacked warmth and feeling and her observations were so detached that they reflected "the coldness of a machine." Based on your reading of this story, do you agree with this view? Support your answer with details.

> *Can you put a price on* **DIGNITY?**
>
> Why is it so important to the servants to give Petrus's brother the dignity of a proper burial? Cite details from the story in your response.

COMMON CORE

RL 1 Cite textual evidence to support inferences drawn from the text. **RL 3** Analyze the impact of the author's choices regarding how to develop and relate elements of a story. **RL 10** Read and comprehend literature, including stories.

Vocabulary in Context

▲ VOCABULARY PRACTICE

Choose the word that is not related in meaning to the other words.

1. (a) imbue, (b) instill, (c) embarrass, (d) infuse
2. (a) extraneous, (b) necessary, (c) relevant, (d) germane
3. (a) enchanted, (b) enamored, (c) frustrated, (d) captivated
4. (a) interment, (b) burial, (c) visit, (d) sepulcher
5. (a) expostulate, (b) expose, (c) reveal, (d) divulge
6. (a) emulation, (b) scorn, (c) contempt, (d) disdain
7. (a) laconic, (b) silent, (c) smooth, (d) taciturn
8. (a) attenuated, (b) thick, (c) compact, (d) rotund

WORD LIST

attenuated

emulation

enamored

expostulate

extraneous

imbue

interment

laconic

ACADEMIC VOCABULARY IN SPEAKING

> • approach • assume • environment • method • strategy

What is the best **strategy** for avoiding misunderstandings? When can you **assume** that you are communicating clearly? Using at least two of the Academic Vocabulary words, describe to a partner a scene that involves a misunderstanding.

VOCABULARY STRATEGY: THE LATIN ROOT *terr*

The root *terr* comes from the Latin *terra,* meaning "earth" or "land." The root sometimes appears with only one *r,* as in the case of the word *interment,* which means "burial in the earth." The same root is found in a number of other English words from a variety of different subject areas, from science and biology to geography. To understand words with *terr,* use context clues as well as your knowledge of the root and affixes.

PRACTICE Choose the word from the word web that best completes each sentence. Consider what you know about the Latin root *terr* and other word parts shown. If necessary, consult a dictionary.

1. The pioneers struggled across the rugged _____ in a covered wagon.
2. In winter we grew plants in our glass _____.
3. After the funeral, the body was _____ in the cemetery.
4. Dogs can be very _____, trying to keep other animals or people away from the property where they live.
5. The science fiction novel told what happened when powerful _____ creatures visited our planet.

⋯ **COMMON CORE**

L 6 Acquire and use accurately general academic and domain-specific words.

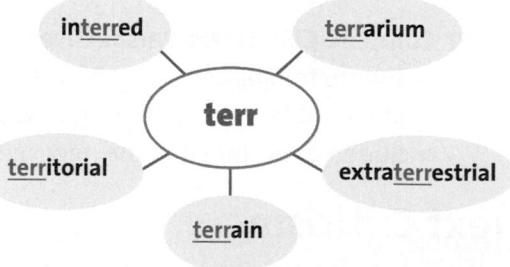

Interactive Vocabulary THINK central

Go to **thinkcentral.com.**
KEYWORD: HML12-1354

Language

◆ **GRAMMAR AND STYLE:** Choose Effective Point Of View

Review the **Grammar and Style** note on page 1345. By choosing to tell her story in the first person (using the **pronouns** *I* and *we*), Gordimer gives the reader an intimate view of the narrator's character. In doing so, she not only explores the complexity of his personal life but also reveals the prevailing attitudes of whites in South Africa during the apartheid era. Here is an example from the story:

> "...*And you're near enough to get into town to a show, too! I think it's wonderful. Why, you've got it both ways!*"
>
> *And for a moment I accept the triumph as if I had managed it—the impossibility that I've been trying for all my life—just as if the truth was that you could get it "both ways."*... (lines 33–37)

Notice how Gordimer uses **dashes** to signal an interruption of thought in which the narrator provides revealing commentary about himself.

PRACTICE Revise the following paragraph, writing it in the first person and adding details to create a greater sense of intimacy with the character. Use one or more dashes to indicate a shift in the character's thoughts or feelings.

> He turned off the highway and headed north on Second Avenue. Growing up, he often felt ashamed of his shabby neighborhood, but as he drove through it now he was comforted by the familiar sights he passed. There was the little grocery on Hawthorn Street, where he used to sit out front on the rickety bench trading baseball cards with his friends. He wondered where those friends were now and whether they would even recognize him.

> I turned off the highway—the same highway where I'd test-driven my first car—and headed north on Second Avenue.

READING-WRITING CONNECTION

Expand your understanding of "Six Feet of the Country" by responding to this prompt. Then use the **revising tips** to improve your journal entry.

WRITING PROMPT	REVISING TIPS
WRITE A JOURNAL ENTRY Although Lerice is an important character in "Six Feet of the Country," she is portrayed from her husband's perspective. By analyzing what she says and does, you can uncover clues about her feelings. Write a **three-to-five-paragraph journal entry** in which Lerice describes and reflects on one of the events in the story.	• Use dashes to indicate a change in the character's thoughts or feelings • Check to see that you are including only Lerice's point of view.

COMMON CORE

L 2 Demonstrate command of the conventions of standard English punctuation when writing. **W 3a–b** Engage and orient the reader by establishing one point of view; use narrative techniques, such as description and reflection, to develop events.

Interactive Revision

THINK central

Go to thinkcentral.com.
KEYWORD: HML12-1355

from No More Strangers Now: Young Voices from a New South Africa

Interviews

Use with "Six Feet of the Country," page 1342.

COMMON CORE

RI 6 Determine an author's point of view in a text.

Nadine Gordimer's "Six Feet of the Country" presents a white man's perspective on black South Africans during apartheid. Now you will read the perspectives of two teenage South Africans—one a black female and the other a white male—on what apartheid was like for their families and how South African culture has changed since apartheid was abolished. These interviews were published in 1998.

Standards Focus: Identify Perspectives

A person's **perspective**—that is, the way he or she views a subject—is shaped by his or her experiences, beliefs, and values. Consequently, people who have had different experiences or come from different cultural backgrounds often have very different perspectives on the same topic. As you read the two interviews that follow, identify each teenager's perspective on apartheid and apartheid-free South Africa by taking note of the following:

- what the teenagers tell you about their backgrounds and experiences
- any direct statements of their beliefs, opinions, feelings, or perceptions
- the reasons each gives to explain particular events, attitudes, and circumstances

Keep track of this information on a chart such as the one shown here.

	Information the Writer Provides	What This Reveals About His or Her Perspective
Mhlana		
Abrahamson		

After you have identified each teenager's perspective on apartheid, write a short summary of each viewpoint and explain why each teenager reached different conclusions on the topic.

No More Strangers Now:
Young Voices from a New South Africa

BREAKING THE CHAIN
Nomfundo Mhlana

I GREW UP on a white person's farm, where my father worked with the sheep in the fields and my mother cleaned the white person's house. My parents never even got a whole day off; they worked all 365 days of the year. **A**

When I was small, I saw the bad way the whites treated my parents. When the farmers went to work, for example, they wanted my mom to take care of their babies. My mother and the white babies began to love each other—when my mother was playing with the baby, the baby would laugh—but when the babies got older, their parents would tell them, "This is a black, and she is working for us. She is not like us." They didn't really see us as the same kind of human
10 beings. . . .

As a child I felt bad about being black. When I saw the way our parents worked for the whites, I thought the whites were superior to us and that their white skin made them rich. I would look at the color of my skin and then look at the whites' color, and I would think, I wish I was white.

Growing up on that farm, I didn't go to school until I was ten years old. The whites discouraged my brother and me from going to school because they were worried that we would get some knowledge and then want change. If I went to school, maybe I'd never come back and work in the farm kitchen. . . .

We lived far from where the whites lived because the whites didn't want the
20 noise from the black workers. I always wanted to go inside the "big house" because I could see outside there were grasses and flowers, so I thought that the inside of the house would be very interesting. But I was never allowed to go into the house because the whites thought that if I came in there, my shoes would make the house dirty or I would steal something. . . . **B**

A **IDENTIFY PERSPECTIVES**
In this first paragraph, what does Mhlana tell you about her background?

B **IDENTIFY PERSPECTIVES**
Reread lines 15–24. What events and circumstances does she explain here? What reasons does she give to explain them?

Now that Mandela is president, I think our society is more equal, but I also think whites still have apartheid in their hearts. They pay workers more because the democratic government says they must and because they're afraid of the law. But they still think they are better than us. We now live on a different farm than when I was a child, and my parents still have to call the whites **baas.** They still don't pay workers enough money. My parents have six children, and they would like to live in a nice house, but they only have enough money for food. C

But I do have hope that some whites are changing their minds. The whites on the farm now will come into our house and drink some tea with my mother. They also have a daughter who is nineteen, like me, and we are friends. . . . I'm now going to a school that was started by white farmers' wives, for children on the farms like me. The farmers at our place think it's okay that my brother and I are in this school, and they say that education is the best thing to have. In fact, they came to a party when the school first opened.

I will not work on the farm like my parents. They were illiterate and living in the times of apartheid, and working on the farm was all they could do. But my education will give me an advantage; it will help me get better jobs than they could. . . .

When I was small, I was jealous of whites; I wanted to be like them. But now I feel hope that I will have a bright future, and I am proud to be black. When I meet a white person who gives me respect and treats me like an equal, I treat him the way he treats me, but that does not mean I wish to be like him. I wish to be just like I am. D

Nomfundo Mhlana, center, helps her mother prepare a meal in their three-room house.

C IDENTIFY PERSPECTIVES
What beliefs does Mhlana state directly in this paragraph? What facts does she provide to support her opinions?

D IDENTIFY PERSPECTIVES
How does Mhlana feel about herself and her future now?

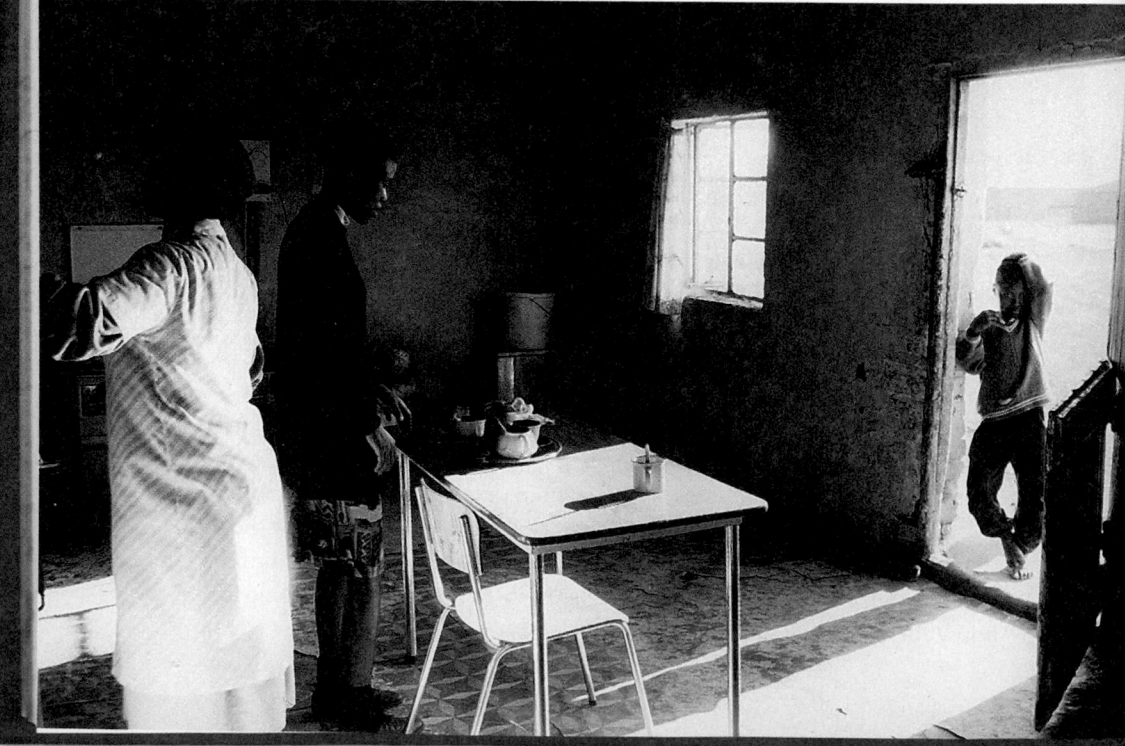

REDISCOVERING THE NATION

Mark Abrahamson

THE MAJORITY of South Africans were oppressed during the time of my upbringing, but I was in a very protected environment and was kept away from the violence and the atrocities that were being committed. I think a lot of people outside South Africa have this perception that it was so violent that someone was getting shot around every corner, but it wasn't like that in my area. I've never seen a man killed before, even though just twenty kilometers away in the townships, young kids were being subjected to some *oke* walking into their house and gunning their parents down. **E**

There were just such strong barriers between our two environments. As a kid
10 I remember being at parks in our area and thinking to myself, Now why is that black person there? He shouldn't be there. It wasn't because I had anything against that person; that was just the normal way it was. . . .

We weren't just sheltered; there was also an active hiding of the truth, propaganda, by the apartheid government. They knew that if we were able to analyze the true situation, sooner or later we would have come to the conclusion that it was wrong. The government controlled the television stations, for example, and the news became a joke after a while because it was so propagandist. If there was any violence in the townships, it was blamed on African forces fighting each other and not on white government intervention, which is what it was.

20 You also didn't really hear about the ANC. Whenever you did, it was through the news, "these people are messing up our land" kind of thing. And I hadn't seen pictures of Mandela, because you weren't allowed to have a picture of him anywhere around. He was made out to be a scary, violent character. "If he ever comes out," the government told us, "it will be the end of South Africa; we'll be thrown into civil war." I remember when I finally saw him released from prison on TV, it consciously came to mind: Why'd they put that funny old man in prison for so long? What could he have done? . . .

But things have changed. We weren't told the truth for so long, but now we're hearing it all. We're starting to hear about the brutal attacks on people, to see
30 pictures like the one of three policemen with their feet on a black man that they killed like it's a trophy. I've been shocked by what's come out, but I think it's necessary to hear it. What happened in our past is a wound. If we don't first put

E **IDENTIFY PERSPECTIVES**
What does Abrahamson tell you about his background in this paragraph?

Language Coach

Roots and Affixes An affix at the beginning of a word is a **prefix**. The prefix *inter–* means "between or among." The root *ven* means "to come." What do you think *white government intervention* (line 19) means?

antiseptic on the wound, if we don't dig up our skeletons, literally and figuratively, it's never going to heal properly.

There's an age of rediscovery in South Africa at the moment, of finding out what's really out there, of getting to know everyone who is living here and consciously trying to live in harmony. We're the generation that's the bridge from the previous South Africa to a new one. Therefore I think it's crucial to become involved in this transformation, so that you have the sense of actually making a
40 difference. . . .

There's a fear now, especially among the more paranoid whites, that we're moving from a white supremacy to a black one, that black people are going to come knocking on our door, saying, "We're gonna divide your house in two." But that isn't what's happening. It seems there's this incredible feeling of forgiveness on the part of black people. It's like, "You know these white people have been terrible to us, but we're just going to show them that we're not made of the same stuff." I think we must be quite thankful for this atmosphere because as far as I'm concerned, black people have every right to turn the whole thing around and say, "Three hundred years we've been under this oppression, now it's your turn for the
50 next three hundred." **F**

Some white people are leaving South Africa, but I have no intention of doing so. I think if I was to be scooped up and put in Europe or America, I would be able to survive, but I would be very homesick for South Africa. Not many people have the privilege to be living in a country that is changing so rapidly, and I feel quite proud of my land, and I know that I belong here. I see our future being a positive one. I would like to be able to look back on my youth and say to myself, I was, even in a small way, somehow part of this success.

Mark Abrahamson plays the piano for his parents in their living room.

Language Coach

Greek Affixes The suffix *-oid* comes to the English language from Greek and means "related to" or "having the appearance of." The word *paranoid* also has a Greek prefix: *para-,* meaning "beyond." The root *noos* means "mind." Based on this, what does *paranoid* mean? What other English words have the ending *-oid*?

F IDENTIFY PERSPECTIVES
What does Abrahamson believe is the prevailing attitude among black South Africans toward whites?

Comprehension

1. **Recall** Where did Nomfundo Mhlana grow up? In what kind of environment was Mark Abrahamson raised?

2. **Summarize** Abrahamson says that some white people are leaving South Africa. What does he say he plans to do, and why?

Text Analysis

3. **Analyze Perspective** As a young adult of 19, what is Nomfundo Mhlana's perspective on being black? How did she used to feel about being black? Aside from simply growing up, what events and interactions might have contributed to this change?

4. **Compare Perspectives** It is easy to see how Mhlana's and Abrahamson's perspectives differ. In what ways are their viewpoints similar? Explain your answer, citing evidence from the texts.

COMMON CORE

RI 6 Determine an author's point of view in a text. **W 1** Write arguments to support claims in an analysis of substantive topics or texts, using valid reasoning and relevant and sufficient evidence. **W 1a** Create an organization that logically sequences claims, reasons, and evidence. **W 9b (RI 1)** Cite evidence to support inferences drawn from the text.

Read for Information: Clarify and React to an Opinion

WRITING PROMPT

In "Breaking the Chain," Nomfundo Mhlana says that she believes "whites [in South Africa] still have apartheid in their hearts." Clarify what she means by this, reviewing what you've learned about apartheid from Gordimer's "Six Feet of the Country" as well as from the two interviews. Then tell whether you agree, disagree, or partially agree with her statement. Support your opinion with evidence from the interviews and your own reflections about human nature.

To answer this prompt, follow these steps.

1. Consider what you learned about white people's attitudes toward blacks during apartheid from "Six Feet of the Country" and from the two interviews. Use this information to clarify what Mhlana is saying.

2. Keeping in mind what you read in the two interviews, decide whether you agree, disagree, or partially agree with her statement.

3. Support your argument with details from the two interviews as well as comments about your own experiences and insights.

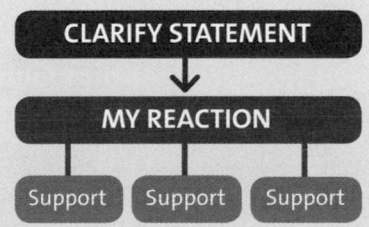

CLARIFY STATEMENT

↓

MY REACTION

Support   Support   Support

A Devoted Son

Short Story by Anita Desai

COMMON CORE

RL 1 Cite evidence to support inferences drawn from the text, including determining where the text leaves matters uncertain. **RL 6** Analyze a case in which grasping point of view requires distinguishing what is directly stated in a text from what is really meant. **L 4a** Use context as a clue to the meaning of a phrase. **L 4b** Identify and correctly use patterns of word changes that indicate different meanings or parts of speech. **L 5a** Interpret figures of speech (e.g., hyperbole) in context and analyze their role in the text.

DID YOU KNOW?

Anita Desai . . .

- had her first short story published when she was just nine years old.
- has a daughter who is also a novelist.
- has also written a highly praised children's book.

Meet the Author

Anita Desai   born 1937

Anita Desai (dā-sī′) has won critical praise for her ability to capture the sights and sounds of a changing India. In her work, she explores the often uneasy blend of traditional lifeways and modern attitudes, of colonial legacy and national pride, that characterizes life in postcolonial India.

Rich Heritage Born to a German mother and an Indian father, Anita Desai grew up in northern India, near the city of Delhi. Until she began school, she spoke German at home and Hindi to friends and neighbors. At school, classes were taught in English, which she came to think of as "the language of books." From these early years, Desai felt drawn to the "world of books" and went on to study English literature at the University of Delhi. She married in 1958 and shortly thereafter began her extraordinary writing career.

Competing Roles Desai took great care to separate her writing life from her role as a mother. She felt it frightened her children "to see their mother having a different life. . . . [They] think they know their mother . . . and then to discover her mind is actually elsewhere, it's not a comfortable feeling for them." She organized her writing time around the children's school schedule, carefully hiding her

work when they returned home. Desai recalls these years were often "very lonely" but notes that this time gave her the luxury to develop her craft at her own pace.

Much of Desai's fiction portrays the interior worlds of people torn by competing obligations to family, society, and religion. Her characters often seek release from the social demands that impede their search for self, especially the sometimes suffocating intimacy of the Indian family. Many of her novels focus on family dynamics, including *Voices in the City* (1965), *Clear Light of Day* (1980), and *Fasting, Feasting* (1999).

Reshaping Traditions While Desai is well respected in the West, she is not widely read in India, whose tradition of English-language fiction dates only from the 1930s. She explains, "At one time all literature was recited rather than read and that remains the tradition in India." To go out, buy a book, and then read it is "still a rather strange act . . . an unusual thing to do." Her writing also features perspectives often overlooked in Indian literature, such as those of women, children, and the elderly. Desai's sensitivity to the complexity of change and the challenges of identity give her an important place in postcolonial Indian literature.

Author Online

Go to **thinkcentral.com**. KEYWORD: HML12-1362

TEXT ANALYSIS: IRONY

All forms of **irony** consist of a contrast between expectation and reality. For example, **verbal irony** occurs when what is said is the opposite of what is really meant. This contrast between what the reader expects (the literal meaning) and the writer's true message can often go unnoticed. You'll need to pay careful attention to the writer's tone to catch these shifts in meaning. Desai typically uses irony to criticize her characters in a subtle, indirect way. In particular, her use of hyperbole, or exaggerated overstatement, is often meant ironically.

This story also features **situational irony,** a contrast between what a character or the reader expects and what actually happens. As you read the story, note the hopes and ambitions of the characters. Ask yourself whether success brings the rewards that the characters expected.

READING SKILL: EVALUATE CHARACTERS' ACTIONS

Writers often intentionally create **ambiguity** by leaving aspects of a story open to interpretation. In this story, Desai portrays a father-son relationship whose true nature is left ambiguous. To understand this relationship, you'll need to **evaluate,** or make judgments about, the characters' actions.

As you read, create a graphic for each significant action taken by the father or the son in the story. Then answer the three questions provided. On the basis of your responses, evaluate the action as positive or negative.

Action:

↓

Criteria for Evaluation:

• What motivations have prompted the action?

• What are its effects on other characters?

• Is it a reasonable response to the character's situation?

 Complete the activities in your **Reader/Writer Notebook**.

What do children OWE their parents?

It takes a lot of work and many sacrifices to raise a child. All that effort finally pays off when a child becomes an adult who is well prepared to lead an independent life. But what do children owe their parents for those long years of devotion and care? This story portrays one son's lifelong efforts to fulfill his obligations to his parents.

QUICKWRITE In your opinion, what obligations might a parent reasonably expect from a child? What expectations would you consider excessive? Express your thoughts in a short paragraph.

A Devoted Son

Anita Desai

> **BACKGROUND** Once a British colony, India became an independent nation in 1947. Some saw independence as an opportunity to return to authentically Indian ways of life. Others maintained that India would achieve greater success as a nation by adopting values and institutions from the West, a process known as modernization. Today, India is a society in transition, whose citizens confront startling gaps between rich and poor, old and new. The following story explores how the rush to adopt new, modern values changes one family in unexpected ways.

When the results appeared in the morning papers, Rakesh scanned them, barefoot and in his pajamas, at the garden gate, then went up the steps to the veranda[1] where his father sat sipping his morning tea and bowed down to touch his feet.[2]

"A first division, son?" his father asked, beaming, reaching for the papers.

"At the top of the list, Papa," Rakesh murmured, as if awed. "First in the country."

Bedlam broke loose then. The family whooped and danced. The whole day long visitors streamed into the small yellow house at the end of the road, to congratulate the parents of this *Wunderkind*,[3] to slap Rakesh on the back and fill the house and garden with the sounds and colors of a festival. There were garlands and *halwa*,[4]
10 party clothes and gifts (enough fountain pens to last years, even a watch or two), nerves and temper and joy, all in a multicolored whirl of pride and great shining vistas newly opened: Rakesh was the first son in the family to receive an education, so much had been sacrificed in order to send him to school and then medical college, and at last the fruits of their sacrifice had arrived, golden and glorious.

---

1. **veranda** (və-răn′də): a roofed, often partly enclosed porch or balcony extending along the outside of a building.

2. **touch his feet:** In India, the touching of the feet is a sign of respect given to an elder.

3. ***Wunderkind*** (vŏŏn′dər-kĭnd′) *German*: a child of remarkable talent or ability; a child prodigy.

4. ***halwa*** (häl′wä): a pudding made from almonds (*badam halwa*), carrots (*gajar halwa*), or semolina (*sooji halwa*) boiled in milk with sugar and cardamon.

Moods IV (2000), Meena Deva. Oil pastel. 15³/₄″ × 12¹/₂″. © 2000 Meena Deva.

To everyone who came to him to say, "*Mubarak*,[5] Varma-*ji*, your son has brought you glory," the father said, "Yes, and do you know what is the first thing he did when he saw the results this morning? He came and touched my feet. He bowed down and touched my feet." This moved many of the women in the crowd so much that they were seen to raise the ends of their saris[6] and dab at their tears
20 while the men reached out for the betel leaves and sweetmeats[7] that were offered around on trays and shook their heads in wonder and approval of such exemplary filial behavior. "One does not often see such behavior in sons any more," they all agreed, a little enviously perhaps. Leaving the house, some of the women said, sniffing, "At least on such an occasion they might have served pure *ghee*[8] sweets," and some of the men said, "Don't you think old Varma was giving himself airs? He needn't think we don't remember that he comes from the vegetable market himself, his father used to sell vegetables, and he has never seen the inside of a school." But there was more envy than rancor in their voices and it was, of course, inevitable— not every son in that shabby little colony at the edge of the city was destined to
30 shine as Rakesh shone, and who knew that better than the parents themselves?

And that was only the beginning, the first step in a great, sweeping ascent to the radiant heights of fame and fortune. The thesis he wrote for his M.D. brought Rakesh still greater glory, if only in select medical circles. He won a scholarship. He went to the U.S.A. (that was what his father learnt to call it and taught the whole family to say—not America, which was what the ignorant neighbors called it, but, with a grand familiarity, "the U.S.A.") where he pursued his career in the most prestigious of all hospitals and won encomiums[9] from his American colleagues which were relayed to his admiring and glowing family. What was more, he came *back,* he actually returned to that small yellow house in the once-
40 new but increasingly shabby colony, right at the end of the road where the rubbish vans tipped out their stinking contents for pigs to nose in and rag-pickers to build their shacks on, all steaming and smoking just outside the neat wire fences and well-tended gardens. To this Rakesh returned and the first thing he did on entering the house was to slip out of the embraces of his sisters and brothers and bow down and touch his father's feet. **Ⓐ**

As for his mother, she gloated chiefly over the strange fact that he had not married in America, had not brought home a foreign wife as all her neighbors had warned her he would, for wasn't that what all Indian boys went abroad for? Instead he agreed, almost without argument, to marry a girl she had picked
50 out for him in her own village, the daughter of a childhood friend, a plump and uneducated girl, it was true, but so old-fashioned, so placid, so complaisant

Ⓐ IRONY
Reread lines 31–38. Exaggerated overstatement, or **hyperbole,** is one device used to create **verbal irony.** What two examples of hyperbole can you find in these lines?

---

5. *Mubarak* (mōō-bär′ək) *Arabic:* "blessed." Many Arabic words are used in India, especially among Indian Muslims; Arabic is the language of the Muslim holy book, the Koran.

6. **saris** (sä′rēz): women's outer garments worn mainly in India and Pakistan. A sari is a length of cloth with one end draped over the shoulder or head and the other wrapped around the waist to form a skirt.

7. **betel** (bēt′l) **leaves and sweetmeats:** The leaves of the betel palm are commonly chewed in Asia as a digestive stimulant. Sweetmeats are sugared treats such as candy, sweetened nuts, or crystallized fruit.

8. *ghee* (gē): a clarified, semifluid butter widely used in Indian cooking.

9. **encomiums** (ĕn-kō′mē-əmz): glowing tributes; strong praise.

that she slipped into the household and settled in like a charm, seemingly too lazy and too good-natured to even try and make Rakesh leave home and set up independently, as any other girl might have done. What was more, she was pretty—really pretty, in a plump, pudding way that only gave way to fat—soft, spreading fat, like warm wax—after the birth of their first baby, a son, and then what did it matter? **B**

For some years Rakesh worked in the city hospital, quickly rising to the top of the administrative organization, and was made a director before he left to set up
60 his own clinic. He took his parents in his car—a new, sky-blue Ambassador[10] with a rear window full of stickers and charms revolving on strings—to see the clinic when it was built, and the large sign-board over the door on which his name was printed in letters of red, with a row of degrees and qualifications to follow it like so many little black slaves of the regent.[11] Thereafter his fame seemed to grow just a little dimmer—or maybe it was only that everyone in town had grown accustomed to it at last—but it was also the beginning of his fortune for he now became known not only as the best but also the richest doctor in town.

However, all this was not accomplished in the wink of an eye. Naturally not. It was the achievement of a lifetime and it took up Rakesh's whole life. At the
70 time he set up his clinic his father had grown into an old man and retired from his post at the kerosene dealer's depot at which he had worked for forty years, and his mother died soon after, giving up the ghost with a sigh that sounded positively happy, for it was her own son who ministered to her in her last illness and who sat pressing her feet at the last moment—such a son as few women had borne.

For it had to be admitted—and the most unsuccessful and most rancorous of neighbors eventually did so—that Rakesh was not only a devoted son and a miraculously good-natured man who contrived somehow to obey his parents and humor his wife and show concern equally for his children and his patients, but there was actually a brain inside this beautifully polished and formed body
80 of good manners and kind nature and, in between ministering to his family and playing host to many friends and coaxing them all into feeling happy and grateful and content, he had actually trained his hands as well and emerged an excellent doctor, a really fine surgeon. How one man—and a man born to illiterate parents, his father having worked for a kerosene dealer and his mother having spent her life in a kitchen—had achieved, combined and conducted such a medley of virtues, no one could fathom, but all acknowledged his talent and skill.

It was a strange fact, however, that talent and skill, if displayed for too long, cease to dazzle. It came to pass that the most admiring of all eyes eventually faded and no longer blinked at his glory. Having retired from work and having lost
90 his wife, the old father very quickly went to pieces, as they say. He developed so many complaints and fell ill so frequently and with such mysterious diseases that even his son could no longer make out when it was something of significance and

B EVALUATE ACTIONS
Reread lines 49–57. What seems to motivate Rakesh's choice in marriage?

COMMON CORE L 4a
Language Coach

Idioms An **idiom** is a phrase with a figurative, rather than literal, meaning. You can often figure out the meaning of an idiom through its **context**—the words, phrases, and sentences that surround it. What do you think *giving up the ghost* means in line 72? How can you tell?

---

10. **Ambassador:** the Hindustan Ambassador, the first car to be manufactured in India. The model was launched in 1948, a year after India achieved its independence from British rule.

11. **black slaves of the regent:** British colonial officers often referred to Indians as blacks, and considered them racially inferior. A regent is one who acts as a ruler or governor.

when it was merely a peevish whim. He sat huddled on his string bed most of the day and developed an exasperating habit of stretching out suddenly and lying absolutely still, allowing the whole family to fly around him in a flap, wailing and weeping, and then suddenly sitting up, stiff and gaunt, and spitting out a big gob of betel juice as if to mock their behavior.

He did this once too often: there had been a big party in the house, a birthday party for the youngest son, and the celebrations had to be suddenly hushed,
100 covered up and hustled out of the way when the daughter-in-law discovered, or thought she discovered, that the old man, stretched out from end to end of his string bed, had lost his pulse; the party broke up, dissolved, even turned into a band of mourners, when the old man sat up and the distraught daughter-in-law received a gob of red spittle right on the hem of her new organza[12] sari. After that no one much cared if he sat up cross-legged on his bed, hawking and spitting, or lay down flat and turned gray as a corpse. Except, of course, for that pearl amongst pearls, his son Rakesh. **C**

It was Rakesh who brought him his morning tea, not in one of the china cups from which the rest of the family drank, but in the old man's favorite brass
110 tumbler, and sat at the edge of his bed, comfortable and relaxed with the string of his pajamas dangling out from under his fine lawn night-shirt, and discussed or, rather, read out the morning news to his father. It made no difference to him that his father made no response apart from spitting. It was Rakesh, too, who, on

---

12. **organza:** a sheer, stiff fabric, often made from silk.

C EVALUATE ACTIONS
Reread lines 89–107. Describe the effect of the father's actions on the other characters. What changes might Varma be responding to?

Untitled, Chittaprosad Bhattacharya. Pastel on paper, 20.5″ × 30″. © Delhi Art Gallery, Pvt., Ltd., Delhi, India.

returning from the clinic in the evening, persuaded the old man to come out of his room, as bare and desolate as a cell, and take the evening air out in the garden, beautifully arranging the pillows and bolsters on the divan in the corner of the open veranda. On summer nights he saw to it that the servants carried out the old man's bed onto the lawn and himself helped his father down the steps and onto the bed, soothing him and settling him down for a night under the stars.

120   All this was very gratifying for the old man. What was not so gratifying was that he even undertook to supervise his father's diet. One day when the father was really sick, having ordered his daughter-in-law to make him a dish of *soojie halwa* and eaten it with a saucerful of cream, Rakesh marched into the room, not with his usual respectful step but with the confident and rather contemptuous stride of the famous doctor, and declared, "No more *halwa* for you, Papa. We must be sensible, at your age. If you must have something sweet, Veena will cook you a little *kheer*,[13] that's light, just a little rice and milk. But nothing fried, nothing rich. We can't have this happening again."

   The old man who had been lying stretched out on his bed, weak and feeble after
130 a day's illness, gave a start at the very sound, the tone of these words. He opened his eyes—rather, they fell open with shock—and he stared at his son with disbelief that darkened quickly to reproach. A son who actually refused his father the food he craved? No, it was unheard of, it was incredible. But Rakesh had turned his back to him and was cleaning up the litter of bottles and packets on the medicine shelf and did not notice while Veena slipped silently out of the room with a little smirk that only the old man saw, and hated.

   Halwa was only the first item to be crossed off the old man's diet. One delicacy after the other went—everything fried to begin with, then everything sweet, and eventually everything, everything that the old man enjoyed. The meals that
140 arrived for him on the shining stainless steel tray twice a day were frugal to say the least—dry bread, boiled lentils, boiled vegetables and, if there were a bit of chicken or fish, that was boiled too. If he called for another helping—in a cracked voice that quavered theatrically—Rakesh himself would come to the door, gaze at him sadly and shake his head, saying, "Now, Papa, we must be careful, we can't risk another illness, you know," and although the daughter-in-law kept tactfully out of the way, the old man could just see her smirk sliding merrily through the air. He tried to bribe his grandchildren into buying him sweets (and how he missed his wife now, that generous, indulgent and illiterate cook), whispering, "Here's fifty *paise*" as he stuffed the coins into a tight, hot fist. "Run down to
150 the shop at the crossroads and buy me thirty *paise* worth of *jalebis*,[14] and you can spend the remaining twenty *paise* on yourself. Eh? Understand? Will you do that?" He got away with it once or twice but then was found out, the conspirator was scolded by his father and smacked by his mother and Rakesh came storming into the room, almost tearing his hair as he shouted through compressed lips,

---

13. *kheer* (kîr): an Indian rice pudding usually spiced with cardamom.

14. *paise* (pī-sā´) . . . *jalebis* (jə-lā´bēz): *Paise* is the plural of *paisa*, a monetary unit of India and neighboring countries, equal to 1/100 of a rupee. *Jalebis* are Indian desserts made of coil-shaped, deep-fried batter.

"Now Papa, are you trying to turn my little son into a liar? Quite apart from spoiling your own stomach, you are spoiling him as well—you are encouraging him to lie to his own parents. You should have heard the lies he told his mother when she saw him bringing back those *jalebis* wrapped up in filthy newspaper. I don't allow anyone in my house to buy sweets in the bazaar, Papa, surely you know
160 that. There's cholera in the city, typhoid, gastro-enteritis[15]—I see these cases daily in the hospital, how can I allow my own family to run such risks?" The old man sighed and lay down in the corpse position. But that worried no one any longer. **D**

There was only one pleasure left the old man now (his son's early morning visits and readings from the newspaper could no longer be called that) and those were visits from elderly neighbors. These were not frequent as his contemporaries were mostly as decrepit and helpless as he and few could walk the length of the road to visit him any more. Old Bhatia, next door, however, who was still spry enough to refuse, adamantly, to bathe in the tiled bathroom indoors and to insist on carrying out his brass mug and towel, in all seasons and usually at impossible
170 hours, into the yard and bathe noisily under the garden tap, would look over the hedge to see if Varma were out on his veranda and would call to him and talk while he wrapped his *dhoti*[16] about him and dried the sparse hair on his head, shivering with enjoyable exaggeration. Of course these conversations, bawled across the hedge by two rather deaf old men conscious of having their entire households overhearing them, were not very satisfactory but Bhatia occasionally came out of his yard, walked down the bit of road and came in at Varma's gate to collapse onto the stone plinth built under the temple tree. If Rakesh were at home he would help his father down the steps into the garden and arrange him on his night bed under the tree and leave the two old men to chew betel leaves and
180 discuss the ills of their individual bodies with combined passion.

"At least you have a doctor in the house to look after you," sighed Bhatia, having vividly described his martyrdom to piles.[17]

"Look after me?" cried Varma, his voice cracking like an ancient clay jar. "He—he does not even give me enough to eat."

"What?" said Bhatia, the white hairs in his ears twitching. "Doesn't give you enough to eat? Your own son?"

"My own son. If I ask him for one more piece of bread, he says no, Papa, I weighed out the *ata*[18] myself and I can't allow you to have more than two hundred grams of cereal a day. He *weighs* the food he gives me, Bhatia—he has scales to
190 weigh it on. That is what it has come to."

"Never," murmured Bhatia in disbelief. "Is it possible, even in this evil age, for a son to refuse his father food?"

"Let me tell you," Varma whispered eagerly. "Today the family was having fried fish—I could smell it. I called to my daughter-in-law to bring me a piece. She came to the door and said No . . ."

D EVALUATE ACTIONS
Reread lines 137–162. Summarize the changes Rakesh makes in his father's life. Does Rakesh seem aware of how these changes affect his father? Explain.

---

15. **cholera** (kŏl'ər-ə) . . . **gastro-enteritis:** diseases that can be caused by contaminated food or water.

16. *dhoti* (dō'tē): a loincloth traditionally worn by Hindu men in India.

17. **piles:** hemorrhoids.

18. *ata* Hindi: grain or cereal. Hindi is one of the main languages of India.

Untitled, Tapan Ghosh. Mixed media on paper, 9.75″ × 9.75″. © Delhi Art Gallery, Pvt., Ltd., Delhi, India.

"Said No?" It was Bhatia's voice that cracked. A *drongo*[19] shot out of the tree and sped away. "*No?*"

"No, she said no, Rakesh has ordered her to give me nothing fried. No butter, he says, no oil—"

200 "No butter? No oil? How does he expect his father to *live?*"

Old Varma nodded with melancholy triumph. "That is how he treats me—after I have brought him up, given him an education, made him a great doctor. Great doctor! This is the way great doctors treat their fathers, Bhatia," for the son's sterling personality and character now underwent a curious sea change. Outwardly all might be the same but the interpretation had altered: his masterly efficiency was nothing but cold heartlessness, his authority was only tyranny in disguise. **E**

There was cold comfort in complaining to neighbors and, on such a miserable diet, Varma found himself slipping, weakening, and soon becoming a genuinely sick man. Powders and pills and mixtures were not only brought in when dealing with a

210 crisis like an upset stomach but became a regular part of his diet—became his diet,

E **EVALUATE ACTIONS**
Reread lines 201–206. Summarize Varma's understanding of Rakesh's actions. Is his interpretation reasonable? Explain.

---

19. *drongo*: a type of bird found in Asia, Africa, and Australia, usually black with a forked tail.

complained Varma, supplanting the natural foods he craved. There were pills to regulate his bowel movements, pills to bring down his blood pressure, pills to deal with his arthritis and, eventually, pills to keep his heart beating. In between there were panicky rushes to the hospital, some humiliating experiences with the stomach pump and enema, which left him frightened and helpless. He cried easily, shriveling up on his bed, but if he complained of a pain or even a vague, gray fear in the night, Rakesh would simply open another bottle of pills and force him to take one. "I have my duty to you, Papa," he said when his father begged to be let off. **F**

"Let me be," Varma begged, turning his face away from the pills on the
220 outstretched hand. "Let me die. It would be better. I do not want to live only to eat your medicines."

"Papa, be reasonable."

"I leave that to you," the father cried with sudden spirit. "Let me alone, let me die now, I cannot live like this."

"Lying all day on his pillows, fed every few hours by his daughter-in-law's own hands, visited by every member of his family daily—and then he says he does not want to live 'like this,'" Rakesh was heard to say, laughing, to someone outside the door.

"Deprived of food," screamed the old man on the bed, "his wishes ignored,
230 taunted by his daughter-in-law, laughed at by his grandchildren—*that* is how I live." But he was very old and weak and all anyone heard was an incoherent croak, some expressive grunts and cries of genuine pain. Only once, when old Bhatia had come to see him and they sat together under the temple tree, they heard him cry, "God is calling me—and they won't let me go."

The quantities of vitamins and tonics he was made to take were not altogether useless. They kept him alive and even gave him a kind of strength that made him hang on long after he ceased to wish to hang on. It was as though he were straining at a rope, trying to break it, and it would not break, it was still strong. He only hurt himself, trying.

240 In the evening, that summer, the servants would come into his cell, grip his bed, one at each end, and carry it out to the veranda, there setting it down with a thump that jarred every tooth in his head. In answer to his agonized complaints they said the Doctor Sahib[20] had told them he must take the evening air and the evening air they would make him take—thump. Then Veena, that smiling, hypocritical pudding in a rustling sari, would appear and pile up the pillows under his head till he was propped up stiffly into a sitting position that made his head swim and his back ache. "Let me lie down," he begged. "I can't sit up any more."

"Try, Papa, Rakesh said you can if you try," she said, and drifted away to the other end of the veranda where her transistor radio vibrated to the lovesick tunes
250 from the cinema that she listened to all day.

So there he sat, like some stiff corpse, terrified, gazing out on the lawn where his grandsons played cricket,[21] in danger of getting one of their hard-spun balls in

F IRONY
Recall Varma's ambitions for his son. What is ironic about his situation in lines 207–218?

COMMON CORE L 4b
Language Coach
Derivations Words derived from another word or base are derivations. *Incoherent* (line 231) is one of several words derived from *cohere,* which means "to stick together (either physically or logically)." List other derivations of *cohere* and their meanings. What does *incoherent* mean?

---

20. **Sahib** (sä′ĭb): a term of respect in India, the equivalent of *sir.*

21. **cricket:** a team sport played with bats and a ball, popular in Britain and India.

his eye, and at the gate that opened onto the dusty and rubbish-heaped lane but still bore, proudly, a newly touched-up signboard that bore his son's name and qualifications, his own name having vanished from the gate long ago.

At last the sky-blue Ambassador arrived, the cricket game broke up in haste, the car drove in smartly and the doctor, the great doctor, all in white, stepped out. Someone ran up to take his bag from him, others to escort him up the steps. "Will you have tea?" his wife called, turning down the transistor set, "or a Coca-Cola? Shall I fry you some *samosas*?"[22] But he did not reply or even glance in her direction. Ever a devoted son, he went first to the corner where his father sat gazing, stricken, at some undefined spot in the dusty yellow air that swam before him. He did not turn his head to look at his son. But he stopped gobbling air with his uncontrolled lips and set his jaw as hard as a sick and very old man could set it.

"Papa," his son said, tenderly, sitting down on the edge of the bed and reaching out to press his feet.

Old Varma tucked his feet under him, out of the way, and continued to gaze stubbornly into the yellow air of the summer evening.

"Papa, I'm home."

Varma's hand jerked suddenly, in a sharp, derisive movement, but he did not speak.

"How are you feeling, Papa?"

Then Varma turned and looked at his son. His face was so out of control and all in pieces, that the multitude of expressions that crossed it could not make up a whole and convey to the famous man exactly what his father thought of him, his skill, his art.

"I'm dying," he croaked. "Let me die, I tell you."

"Papa, you're joking," his son smiled at him, lovingly. "I've brought you a new tonic to make you feel better. You must take it, it will make you feel stronger again. Here it is. Promise me you will take it regularly, Papa."

Varma's mouth worked as hard as though he still had a gob of betel in it (his supply of betel had been cut off years ago). Then he spat out some words, as sharp and bitter as poison, into his son's face. "Keep your tonic—I want none—I want none—I won't take any more of—of your medicines. None. Never," and he swept the bottle out of his son's hand with a wave of his own, suddenly grand, suddenly effective. **G**

His son jumped, for the bottle was smashed and thick brown syrup had splashed up, staining his white trousers. His wife let out a cry and came running. All around the old man was hubbub once again, noise, attention.

He gave one push to the pillows at his back and dislodged them so he could sink down on his back, quite flat again. He closed his eyes and pointed his chin at the ceiling, like some dire prophet, groaning, "God is calling me—now let me go." ∾

G **EVALUATE ACTIONS**
In lines 285–286, the author describes Varma's action as "suddenly grand, suddenly effective." What message might Varma be trying to send his son by breaking the bottle?

---

22. *samosas* (sə-mō'səz): Indian turnovers consisting of fried dough filled with seasoned vegetables or meat.

Comprehension

1. **Recall** What is the first thing Rakesh does when he sees his exam results?

2. **Summarize** What disagreement causes Varma to change his feelings toward Rakesh?

3. **Clarify** Why are Varma and Bhatia so shocked when the daughter-in-law refuses Varma's request for fried fish?

Text Analysis

4. **Analyze Conflict** Rakesh becomes exposed to Western values while studying medicine in the United States. Do you think he would have remained on good terms with his father if he had never left India, or is the conflict that develops between them inevitable? Support your answer.

5. **Interpret Imagery** In her descriptions, Desai often juxtaposes images of traditional India with those suggesting modern attitudes and values. What contrasting images do you see in each of the following passages?

   - discussion of Rakesh's American education (lines 31–45)
   - account of Rakesh's medical career (lines 58–67)
   - description of Varma's healthy diet (lines 137–160)
   - the doctor's arrival at home (lines 256–260)

6. **Interpret Irony** Varma's expectations for his son are realized, but with consequences he did not anticipate. What message about ambition and the drive for modernization does Desai convey with this use of irony?

7. **Evaluate Characters' Actions** Review the graphics you created as you read to evaluate the ambiguous relationship between characters. Which character do you find more sympathetic, Rakesh or Varma? In your opinion, is Rakesh really a devoted son? Cite examples that support your answers.

Text Criticism

8. **Critical Interpretations** Critics have commented on Desai's use of imagery, calling it "a remarkable quality of her craft" and one of the most important literary devices in her work. Do you agree or disagree with this opinion? Support your answer with details from the story.

> *What do children* **OWE** *their parents?*
>
> According to Indian tradition, what obligations do children have toward their parents? In your own family, what obligations do you feel you owe to your parents?

COMMON CORE

RL 1 Cite evidence to support inferences drawn from the text, including determining where the text leaves matters uncertain. **RL 3** Analyze the impact of the author's choices regarding how to develop and relate elements of a story. **RL 6** Analyze a case in which grasping point of view requires distinguishing what is directly stated in a text from what is really meant.

Writing in the Wake of Colonialism

Writers from former British colonies have faced multiple challenges. Some, including Wole Soyinka and Nadine Gordimer, have encountered censorship; others have faced exile and even death threats in response to their provocative writings. Conversely, some have heard complaints that their work is not political enough, or—as in Gordimer's case—that they are not qualified to write on certain topics. And numerous critics have questioned the choice of many writers, such as Anita Desai, to write in English—the language of the colonizers. Yet a writer's job at heart is to speak the truth—to describe the world as he or she sees it.

> *"I happen to have lived in a politically charged atmosphere and milieu all my life; but I was writing long before I was aware of what politics was, so I don't really write out of motivation of politics. I began to write looking for explanations for life."*
>
> **—Nadine Gordimer**

The world known and described by postcolonial writers is a world in transition, and one of great political and social tension. Any truthful explanations of life in such a world are bound to be provocative.

Writing to Reflect

Review the selections by Soyinka, Gordimer, and Desai. Choose one piece and write an essay in which you reflect on the various responses it might have provoked when it was first published. Point to details from the text and explain how they might affect sympathetic or unsympathetic readers. Finally, conclude by explaining your own view of the piece, both as a work of literature and as a work of social commentary.

Consider

- the kinds of people represented in the selection
- what, if any, social critique is rendered by the author
- what you know about the selection's social and political context
- your impression of the author's purpose in writing the piece
- the piece's overall effectiveness

A South African farm, such as the one depicted in "Six Feet of the Country"

Extension Online

INQUIRY & RESEARCH For the selection you chose, do an online investigation to learn more about its social and political context. Find out what you can about the author's native (or chosen) country and the cultural and political developments there since the end of colonial rule. Also consider whether what you have learned changes your earlier reflections on the story or poem. Deliver a brief report on your findings.

COMMON CORE

W 2 Write explanatory texts to examine and convey complex ideas, concepts, and information. **W 2b, f** Develop the topic by selecting quotations or other examples; provide a concluding statement that follows from the information presented. **W 7** Conduct short research projects to answer a question.

COMMON CORE

RI 6 Determine an author's point of view in a text. **RI 7** Integrate and evaluate multiple sources of information presented in different media or formats as well as in words in order to address a question or solve a problem. **SL 2** Integrate multiple sources of information presented in diverse formats and media, evaluating the credibility and accuracy of each source and noting any discrepancies among the data.

How does the news COVER *history?*

Recall the last news report you saw or read about a major event that occurred someplace other than in the United States. Perhaps it was news about a natural disaster or a high-stakes election. How did the report portray the country or culture? In this lesson, you'll examine two examples of international **news coverage.** You'll consider how the images and words in the news can influence the public's perceptions.

Background

Unmade in Hong Kong On July 1 of 1997, Great Britain transferred the sovereignty of Hong Kong, the last major possession of the British Crown, to China.

Dignitaries from across the globe gathered in Hong Kong for formal ceremonies the night before the transfer. In his congratulatory speech, Prince Charles promised, "We shall not forget you, and we shall watch with the closest interest as you embark on this new era of your remarkable history."

Many Western nations—chief among them, the United States—regarded this transition with skepticism and uncertainty. The world wondered how Hong Kong, which for over a century had operated in a capitalist setting, would function under authoritarian Communist rule. It could mean that capitalist nations would lose a major force in the global economic landscape. The terms of the turnover included an agreement by China to observe a "one country, two systems" arrangement, under which Hong Kong would be allowed 50 years of relative autonomy. Tung Chee-hwa, the People's Republic of China's first chief executive of Hong Kong, had made assurances, stating, "Hong Kong's freedom of expression, movement, capital flow, information, is all guaranteed by the basic law, so Hong Kong will continue to be what it is today."

On any given day, complicated events like this one take the world stage through the media. American news sources covered Hong Kong's transition from countless angles or points of view. In this lesson, you'll watch a news clip from the nightly program "ABC World News Tonight" and read an article from the international section of the *New York Times*.

Media Literacy: International News

Our exposure to international news comes primarily through American news sources. The public's expectation is that the news is objective. Yet any coverage may reflect some bias or represent someone's interpretation of events. The **angle** of a report is the point of view from which it's written. Although an angle gives a story its focus, it might also impart certain values and influence perceptions. It therefore may have the effect of shaping public opinion.

ELEMENTS THAT INFLUENCE NEWS COVERAGE

TV News Report

- **Footage** is recorded material, including film and video. Carefully selected visuals convey what facts and statistics cannot. Footage can also set a mood or help convey a reporter's interpretation of events.

- The **tone** of the news anchor's introduction, or **lead-in,** can also convey general perceptions about an event or the people involved.

- A TV newscast depends on **sound bites**—brief quotations excerpted from taped interviews. Through careful editing, reporters choose sound bites that fit the story or impression they're trying to communicate.

- A TV newscast uses **voice-over narration,** the voice of an unseen speaker who is heard as the footage plays. As with sound bites, the voice-over can reflect the reporter's views.

Newspaper Article

- The **language** of an article, much like the language of an essay, can convey a certain **tone,** even though no opinions are explicitly stated.

- Major news organizations have foreign bureaus staffed with **correspondents** assigned to report from distant locations. In general, correspondents tend to interject their own opinions into reports.

- **Quotations** from an interview can offer revealing glimpses into an event or portray the reactions and emotions of those involved.

Chinese Count the Days to Hong Kong's Return

SHANGHAI All over China, schoolchildren call out the number in unison before classes begin each morning. Every major radio and television broadcast opens with the same count. And so Tiananmen

People in Hong Kong may be awaiting their return to Chinese rule with anxiety, but in Mainland China, the imminent handover is uniformly seen as one of the most glorious events in modern history. To recover Hong Kong, in the Chinese view, is to right one of the worst wrongs left over from an era of foreign domination in the 19th century.

Among ordinary people in China, Hong Kong's coming return evokes feelings of nationalist pride and historical justice along

STRATEGIES FOR VIEWING

- Consider the intended audience for the report and from what nation the news outlet originates. The perspective of the report may reflect the policies of that nation.

- Draw conclusions about who appears in the news story. Ask yourself: Who is interviewed? Why were they chosen? What association do they have with a particular party involved in the story?

- Compare the perspectives of more than one news source. Viewing coverage from several sources can not only highlight discrepancies but also help you integrate and evaluate the information to develop a thorough understanding.

Viewing Guide for

International News

You'll view an "ABC World News Tonight" network newscast that appeared three days before Hong Kong's transition to China. Then you'll read a *New York Times* newspaper article published about three weeks before the event by a journalist who worked and lived in China for over a decade. Consider the overall tone of these news stories and the predominant angles they present. Keep in mind the origins of these reports and their intended audiences. To help you analyze the news formats, refer to these questions.

NOW VIEW

FIRST VIEWING: Comprehension

1. **Recall** What nations other than Hong Kong and Great Britain are mentioned in the TV newscast?

2. **Clarify** According to the newspaper article, how does the mood of the Chinese at the time of the transition seem to differ from the mood of the residents of Hong Kong?

CLOSE VIEWING: Media Literacy

3. **Analyze Techniques** The TV newscast follows each **sound bite** with news **footage** related to the statements each individual makes. Why do you think the reporter included this footage?

4. **Analyze Target Audience** To what audience might the TV newscast be directing its message? Cite evidence from the report to support your answer.

5. **Compare Angles** The *New York Times* article runs for several paragraphs before even mentioning Britain. Describe the reporter's angle and how it differs from the angle of the TV newscast.

6. **Evaluate Language** Of the two news stories, which one seems to question the truthfulness of its statements? Consider:
   - the use of language in the TV news anchor's opening statements and in the correspondent's voice-over
   - words or phrases the newspaper correspondent uses to comment on the actions of officials

7. **Make Judgments** Despite the fact that these pieces primarily deal with Hong Kong, Britain, and China, the reporters themselves are American. In your opinion, are American values to any degree in evidence in these pieces? Explain your opinion.

Write or Discuss

Analyze Perceptions The American public relies on its major news organizations to be society's "window on the world," providing context for and insight into unfolding historical events while maintaining a level of objectivity. Choose one of the news reports in this lesson. Based only on this report, describe your perceptions of the parties involved, including the nations it focuses on, the reporter, and the news sources. Express your views in a brief written analysis. Think about

- the angle of each news story and its tone
- what, if any, viewpoints may have been missing that might have provided you a clearer understanding of the issues
- the impressions or effects the news reporter may have deliberately intended to create

Produce Your Own Media

Create a News Analysis With a partner, choose a recent event in the United States that had sufficient impact to warrant international coverage. Find news accounts from major news outlets that originate in the United States and in at least three other nations. Integrate information from these articles to create and present your own news analysis of worldwide news coverage.

HERE'S HOW Use these suggestions for your analysis:

- Research various news sources, including print and electronic reports.
- Be sure that your news sources are credible. Research will lead you to directories that list outlets by state, country, and continent. It's likely that these outlets will provide English translations for some of their stories.
- With a partner, determine the angles of these news stories and analyze their tone, use of sound bites or quotations, and political viewpoints. Compare the degrees to which these elements vary.
- Use a source card to summarize each news report.
- If possible, present representative clips from each report to support your findings and add interest to your presentation.

Further Exploration

Update Hong Kong's Transition How is Hong Kong faring over a decade after its return to China? Form small groups to research and write updated news stories from different angles, including a current look at Hong Kong's administration, economy, and culture, and at any lingering signs of Britain's colonial influence.

Media Tools THINK central

Go to **thinkcentral.com**.
KEYWORD: HML12-1379

Tech Tip

If available, use a graphics program to create a comparison chart of the news reports.

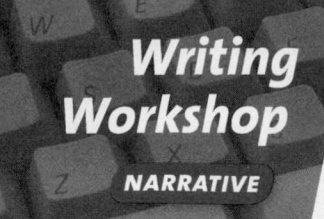

Writing Workshop
NARRATIVE

Personal Narrative

The writers in this unit transformed their personal experiences and observations about life into short stories, plays, and poems. Other writers choose the genre of personal narrative to record their experiences—for themselves, for publication, or for a college application. In this workshop, you will write a personal narrative focusing on a pivotal experience or event in your life.

 Complete the workshop activities in your **Reader/Writer Notebook.**

WRITE WITH A PURPOSE

WRITING TASK

Write a **personal narrative** in which you describe for a specific audience a meaningful experience in your life. Use narrative techniques such as dialogue, description, and reflection to explain the significance of your experience.

Idea Starters
- a hardship or obstacle that you overcame
- an experience that taught you a lesson
- an event that influenced the direction of your life

THE ESSENTIALS

Here are some common purposes, audiences, and formats for writing a personal narrative.

PURPOSES	AUDIENCES	FORMATS
• to record and reflect on an important experience in your life • to introduce yourself to someone who does not know you	• classmates and teacher • friends and family members • college officials or prospective employers • blog readers	• essay for class • college essay • employment application • blog posting • journal entry

COMMON CORE TRAITS

1. DEVELOPMENT OF IDEAS
- includes an engaging introduction that **sets up a situation** and establishes a **point of view**
- uses **dialogue, description,** and **reflection** to develop events
- provides a **conclusion** that reflects on the events

2. ORGANIZATION OF IDEAS
- **sequences** events clearly and effectively
- uses **transitions** to show the sequence of events

3. LANGUAGE FACILITY AND CONVENTIONS
- has a **tone** appropriate to the subject of the narrative
- uses **sensory language** and **telling details** to describe events and communicate the writer's personality
- employs correct **grammar, mechanics,** and **spelling**

Writing Online

THINKcentral

Go to **thinkcentral.com.**
KEYWORD: HML12N-1380

Planning/Prewriting

COMMON CORE

W 3a–e Write narratives to develop real experiences or events using effective technique, well-chosen details, and well-structured event sequences.
W 5 Develop and strengthen writing by planning.

Getting Started

CHOOSE AN EVENT

Generate a list of possible events or experiences for your personal narrative. For help, brainstorm with a group of friends, review the Idea Starters on page 1380, or browse through old photos and journal entries. Consider each topic on your list carefully before selecting the experience that has had the greatest impact on your behavior, attitudes, or beliefs.

▶ **ASK YOURSELF:**

- Which events have been turning points in my life?
- What challenges have I faced at school, at home, on the playing fields, or at work?
- What are my strengths? How did I discover them?
- What accomplishments am I proud of? Why?

CONSIDER YOUR AUDIENCE AND PURPOSE

Your **purpose** for writing a personal narrative is to share a significant experience in your life as well as your reflections on it. However, your essay needs to engage your audience and present insights they can relate to. Keeping both your purpose and audience in mind will guide your choice of details.

▶ **ASK YOURSELF:**

- Who is my audience? What do my readers already know about the event or experience I have chosen?
- Am I comfortable sharing this experience with my readers? If not, should I choose a different topic?
- How can I make the significance of this event relevant to my audience?

DEVELOP YOUR NARRATIVE

To help your readers feel as if they are sharing in your experience, develop the account of your incident with **well-chosen details.** Jot down **dialogue, descriptions, sensory details,** and even **interior monologues**—your unspoken comments—to bring your experience to life for your readers.

- **dialogue**—"Your time will come, Jen," Coach Stoddard counseled.
- **sensory details**—My sneakers squeaked on the shiny gym floor.
- **description**—I started finding myself in the right place at the right time, my arms and legs moving in sync.
- **interior monologue**—*Sure my time will come. When I'm a hundred!*

▶ **TIPS:**

- Decide on the **tone** that you want to communicate in your narrative. For example, your attitude toward your chosen experience might be humorous, ironic, or serious.
- Note that in a fictional narrative, you might experiment with multiple plot lines or points of view. For a narrative based on your life, however, you'll want to maintain a focus on the central incident and describe it from your distinctive first-person point of view.

Planning/Prewriting *continued*

Getting Started

REFLECT ON YOUR EXPERIENCE

Review your narrative details. In a list, write your thoughts, feelings, and observations about the experience. Prompt your reflection by considering why this experience has been important in your life. Then think about how it changed your attitudes or beliefs, what lessons you learned from it, or what others might gain from reading about your experience.

▶ WHAT DOES IT LOOK LIKE?

Narrative Details	Reflections
Coach Stoddard said, "Your time will come."	felt humiliated being so tall and yet the only one not playing
passed over for girls half my size	in retrospect, proud of myself for not giving up
sat on the bench for three years	
worked hard and became a starter in high school	reaped the reward of learning that challenges should be embraced not avoided

ORGANIZE YOUR NARRATIVE

Use an informal outline, flowchart, or list to map out the order in which you will present the events and details. Intersperse descriptions of your thoughts and feelings with the account of the experience.

As you organize your narrative, consider the **pacing** you will want to create. To ensure that you hold the interest of your audience, eliminate nonessential details that might stall the momentum of unfolding events.

▶ WHAT DOES IT LOOK LIKE?

A. Sitting the Bench
1. I was the tallest girl in my class.
2. I didn't play much in middle school.
3. Coach counseled me to be patient.

B. High School Breakthrough
1. I grew into my height.
2. Coach encouraged me to work hard.
3. I became a starter.

C. Effects of the Experience
1. I gained confidence.
2. I learned to embrace challenges.

PEER REVIEW Share with a peer the topic of your personal narrative. Describe the experience and its significance, as well as the details you intend to include. Ask: What additional details would help you envision the events more clearly?

 **YOUR TURN** In your *Reader/Writer Notebook*, brainstorm personal experiences and events that have had an impact on you. Then choose one incident to focus on. Using a graphic organizer, collect details that describe the incident as well as its importance in your life. If you have difficulty expressing its significance, try a new approach.

Drafting

COMMON CORE

W 4 Produce clear and coherent writing in which the development, organization, and style are appropriate to task, purpose, and audience. **L 3a** Vary syntax for effect.

The following chart shows how to organize your draft to create a well-structured and meaningful personal narrative.

Organizing Your Personal Narrative

INTRODUCTION

- Grab the audience's attention with a **quotation, dialogue,** or a **surprising statement.**
- Provide necessary **background** about the experience and its significance.

▼

BODY

- **Sequence** events to build logically to the outcome. Use **transitions,** such as *first, then, later,* and *in the end,* to clarify the order in which events unfold.
- Use techniques such as **dialogue** and **reflection** to describe the experience and reveal your personality.
- Keep the narrative progressing smoothly from start to finish. Don't include events or details that slow down the **pace.**
- Incorporate **telling details** and **sensory language** to convey a vivid picture of the settings, people, and events you describe.

▼

CONCLUDING SECTION

- Describe the **significance** of the experience or event.
- Show the **relevance** of the experience to readers' lives.

GRAMMAR IN CONTEXT: USING ITALICS FOR EFFECT

When writing a personal narrative, you can use **italics** to achieve specific stylistic effects. For instance, italics can help you grab readers' attention, emphasize ideas, or reveal your reactions, thoughts, and feelings.

In this example, the italics show the narrator's unspoken response to the coach's comment.

> The coach counseled me to be patient. "Your time will come, Jen," she said, when I found the courage to ask about playing the last quarter of the final game. "OK, Coach Stoddard," I meekly replied. *Sure, when I'm a hundred and too crippled to move.* Outwardly, I maintained my stoicism, reserving my tears for when I was home alone.

YOUR TURN Develop a draft of your personal narrative by following the plan outlined in the chart above. As you write, include italicized statements that express your unspoken thoughts and feelings.

Revising

As you revise, consider the organization, pacing, and development of your narrative. Determine whether you have achieved your purpose and communicated the experience and its significance to your intended audience. Use the chart shown to help you revise and rewrite where necessary.

PERSONAL NARRATIVE

Ask Yourself	Tips	Revision Strategies
1. Does my introduction engage my audience?	▶ **Bracket** interesting statements or thought-provoking questions.	▶ **Add** an attention-getting statement, question, or quotation.
2. Do I orient my readers with necessary background information about the experience?	▶ **Draw wavy lines** under details that set up the experience and its significance.	▶ **Add** sentences that explain the subject of your personal narrative.
3. Do I use dialogue and reflection to develop the events and reveal my personality?	▶ **Circle** lines of dialogue and reflections that help tell the story and communicate your personality.	▶ **Insert** reflection or dialogue to flesh out the development of events or reveal your character.
4. Do I use effective pacing?	▶ **Highlight** any sentences or phrases that slow down the momentum of your narrative.	▶ **Cross out** details that are not relevant or necessary.
5. Do I use sensory language and telling details to vividly describe settings, people, and events?	▶ **Draw an arrow** next to any details that appeal to readers' senses or that reveal a key insight.	▶ For parts of your narrative that lack arrows, **add** descriptive, precise language, including words that appeal to the senses.
6. Does my concluding section show the significance of the experience or event?	▶ **Read** your concluding section aloud to a peer. **Ask** him or her to restate the significance of your experience.	▶ **Insert** sentences explaining why the experience has resonated with you.

YOUR TURN   *PEER REVIEW*   Working with a peer, review your drafts together. Answer each question in the chart to identify which parts of your drafts need reworking or a new approach.

COMMON CORE

W 3a Engage and orient the reader by setting out a problem, situation, or observation and its significance.
W 5 Develop and strengthen writing by revising, editing, rewriting, or trying a new approach.

ANALYZE A STUDENT DRAFT

Read this student's draft and the comments about it as a model for revising your own personal narrative.

Head and Shoulders Above the Rest

by Jennifer Petlinski, Cumberland High School

❶   Being the tallest girl in my middle school and high school classes, I always felt that I needed to do things in a grander way. But my early experiences on a middle school basketball team made me feel insignificant. Although I practiced as hard, if not harder, than everyone else, I was not exactly the team's star. Whenever there was a crucial game, I commanded a special spot in the gym. For three long seasons, I developed an intimate bond with the bench. The only action I ever saw was during the warm-up exercises. Game after game, all 5′10″ of my long frame sat huddled in adolescent humiliation.

❷   My experience on this team was the first time in my life that I had ever felt completely defeated. At my age and height, it was devastating to occupy the designated spot at the left end of the bench. No matter how much I practiced, how much advice I sought, I still couldn't break through. The coach counseled me to be patient. "Your time will come, Jen," she said, when I found the courage to ask about playing the last quarter of the final game. "OK, Coach Stoddard," I meekly replied. *Sure, when I'm a hundred and too crippled to move.* Outwardly, I maintained my stoicism, reserving my tears for when I was home alone.

> Jennifer could more effectively **engage her readers** by opening with a thought-provoking quotation or surprising statement.

> To **orient** her audience, Jennifer provides a strong visual image that sets the stage for personal narrative.

> The **dialogue** Jennifer includes helps readers to understand her frustration.

> Jennifer's **unspoken comment** lets readers see a more private side of her thoughts.

LEARN HOW **Engage Readers** Jennifer's introduction includes some vivid images, but her opening line isn't likely to grab her audience's attention. When she revised her narrative, she added a thought-provoking and purposely misleading statement to compel her audience to read on.

JENNIFER'S REVISION TO PARAGRAPH ❶

I stand head and shoulders above the rest.

∧   Being the tallest girl in my middle school and high school classes, I always felt that I needed to do things in a grander way.

❸   Out of sheer stubbornness and love for the game, I stuck with basketball going into high school. At the start of my ninth-grade season, I began to notice a change. On the court, I started finding myself in the right place at the right time, my arms and legs moving in sync. The high school coach also noticed something in me worth training. Her encouragement inspired me to redouble my efforts. So I worked hard. As a result, I became one of the five starters on the team and eventually earned the honor of being captain of the varsity squad.

❹   None of this came easily. Raw talent has not been my ticket to success. The motivation to succeed, coupled with dependability, tenacity, and a good sense of humor, have served me well. I've discovered how to use my height to my advantage, and I know what it takes to lead a team.

❺   Basketball has taught me an important lesson in life. My perseverance in this sport extends beyond the court into my character and development as a person. The game that could have utterly destroyed my self-esteem, in the end, built my confidence. I have established a physical presence on the court, and off the court as well. No longer do I sit on a bench and watch the action pass. Instead, I stand tall and proud. To have learned this lesson from a sport I love, for what more could I ask?

> Jennifer uses **transitions** to show the passage of time, keeping her **pacing** quick and illustrating the **sequence** of events.

> Jennifer needs to show her readers her hard work by **using sensory language**.

> As Jennifer concludes her personal narrative, she **reflects** on the significance the experience holds in her life.

LEARN HOW **Use Sensory Language** Instead of telling readers about her experience, Jennifer should use sensory language to describe her sheer commitment to the game. When she rewrote this part of her narrative, she incorporated images that appeal to readers' senses of sight, hearing, and touch. In doing so, Jennifer transports readers to the empty gym, allowing them to see for themselves the results of her efforts.

JENNIFER'S REVISION TO PARAGRAPH ❸

I came in early; I stayed late. The empty gym echoed to the sound of my dribbling and the squeaking of my sneakers as I dodged and feinted past imaginary opponents. I practiced free throws until my arms felt like rubber clubs and sweat glued my hair to my scalp.

Her encouragement inspired me to redouble my efforts. ~~So I worked hard.~~ As a result, I became one of the five starters on the team and eventually earned the honor of being captain of the varsity squad.

YOUR TURN Use feedback from your peers and teacher as well as the two "Learn How" lessons to revise your personal narrative. Evaluate how well you communicate the significance of the experience.

Editing and Publishing

COMMON CORE W 3d Use precise words, telling details, and sensory language. W 5 Strengthen writing by editing. L 1a–b Apply understanding that usage is a matter of convention; resolve issues of contested usage.

In the editing stage, you proofread your personal narrative to make sure that it is free of any grammar, usage, and punctuation errors. Also read carefully to catch any spelling errors, even after doing a word-processing spell-check. These kinds of mistakes will distract your audience from focusing on your narrative.

GRAMMAR IN CONTEXT: PREPOSITIONS AND USAGE

Many writers agree that sentences should not end with prepositions. Others, however, believe that in certain cases, a preposition at the end of the sentence is acceptable since changing its position would make the writing sound stilted and unnatural. Generally, a good rule of thumb might be to avoid prepositions at the end of sentences in formal or official writing, but retain them in dialogue or less formal compositions.

In her rough draft, Jennifer deliberately avoided ending her final question with a preposition. However, as she edited her writing, she realized that by adhering to this grammatical rule, she weakened her concluding section. By revising the sentence as shown, she maintains the conversational tone and candid voice she established throughout the rest of her narrative.

To have learned this lesson from a sport I love, (for) what more could I ask?

PUBLISH YOUR WRITING

Share your personal narrative with an audience.

- Present your narrative, or parts of it, in a speech you might give to a prospective employer.
- Include your narrative as part of a college or job application.
- Post your personal narrative on your blog. Invite others to respond by sharing their experiences.

YOUR TURN Correct any errors in your narrative by carefully proofreading it. Check your placement of prepositions. Then publish your narrative where it is most likely to reach your intended audience.

Scoring Rubric

Use the rubric below to evaluate your personal narrative from the Writing Workshop or your response to the on-demand writing task on the next page.

PERSONAL NARRATIVE

SCORE	COMMON CORE TRAITS
6	• **Development** Has a memorable introduction; fully orients readers with details about the experience and its significance; skillfully uses dialogue, description, and other narrative techniques; has a powerful conclusion • **Organization** Creates coherence and unity by using transitions and structuring the narrative with a clear sequence of events; builds momentum through pacing • **Language** Uses vivid sensory language in unexpected ways; shows a strong command of conventions
5	• **Development** Presents an engaging introduction that provides details about the experience and its significance; uses dialogue, description, and other narrative techniques; has a strong conclusion • **Organization** Creates coherence by using transitions and a clear sequence of events; has effective pacing • **Language** Uses sensory language; has a few errors in conventions
4	• **Development** Has an introduction that offers some details about the experience and its significance; develops the narrative through some dialogue and description; has an adequate conclusion • **Organization** Needs a few more transitions to clarify the sequence of events; mostly maintains an appropriate pace • **Language** Uses some sensory language; includes a few distracting errors in conventions
3	• **Development** Includes an introduction that describes an experience but does not explain its significance; needs more dialogue and description; has a somewhat weak conclusion • **Organization** Sequences events with some transitions but needs more; has a lagging pace at times • **Language** Needs more sensory language in several parts; has several errors in conventions
2	• **Development** Does not adequately set up the experience or explain its significance; lacks dialogue and description throughout; has a weak conclusion • **Organization** Has a confusing sequence of events; needs more transitions; shows little awareness of pacing • **Language** Has very few examples of sensory language; has many errors in conventions
1	• **Development** Lacks an introduction; fails to describe and develop an important experience; has no conclusion • **Organization** Has no apparent sequence of events; shows no understanding of pacing • **Language** Fails to use sensory language; has major problems with grammar, mechanics, and spelling

Preparing for Timed Writing

COMMON CORE

W 10 Write routinely over shorter time frames for a range of tasks, purposes, and audiences.

1. ANALYZE THE TASK   5 MIN

Read the writing task carefully. Then read it again, underlining words that tell the topic, the audience, and the purpose. Circle the type of writing you are being asked to do.

> **WRITING TASK**
> *Type of Writing*
> *Audience*   *Purpose*
> Write a (personal narrative) for publication in a class journal that illustrates the truth of a
> *Topic* →
> well-known aphorism, such as "The early bird gets the worm" or "You can't judge a book
> by its cover." Develop your narrative with details from an incident or experience that
> supports your belief.

2. PLAN YOUR RESPONSE   10 MIN

Choose a saying that resonates with you. Jot it down and then brainstorm incidents or experiences in your life that relate to the saying's meaning. Record precise details that capture the incident or experience, including dialogue and sensory language. Then reflect on the incident you have chosen. In what way did the experience teach you the meaning of the saying? How have you applied the lesson at other times in your life?

Saying: "Don't put off until tomorrow what you can do today."	
Event: when I delayed starting my research project and then caught the flu	**Reflections/Significance**

3. RESPOND TO THE TASK   20 MIN

After identifying details that develop the event and its significance, draft your personal narrative. As you write, keep these guidelines in mind:

- In the introduction, provide details that set up the situation and its significance.
- In the body, develop the narrative, using dialogue and sensory language.
- Conclude by providing your reflections on the experience.

4. IMPROVE YOUR RESPONSE   5–10 MIN

Revising Review key aspects of your personal narrative. Do you open with an interesting quotation, question, or statement? Do you sequence events effectively? Do you reflect on why the experience matters to you?
Proofreading Neatly correct any errors in grammar, spelling, and mechanics.
Checking Your Final Copy Before you turn in your personal narrative, read it once more to catch any errors you may have missed and to apply any finishing touches.

Participating in Job Interviews

When you wrote your personal narrative, you shared experiences that have influenced who you are. In various situations in your life, you will be required to speak about these experiences and your skills. This workshop will help you to polish the speaking and listening skills demanded in formal interviews.

 Complete the workshop activities in your **Reader/Writer Notebook.**

SPEAK WITH A PURPOSE	COMMON CORE TRAITS
TASK	**A STRONG INTERVIEW . . .**
Prepare for an **interview** with a potential employer. Practice answering specific questions about yourself and your goals, and hold a mock interview with a friend or classmate.	• shows evidence of research and other preparation • maintains focus on relevant details and experiences • leads to a thoughtful exchange of ideas • uses effective verbal, nonverbal, and active listening skills • illustrates a strong command of formal English and its conventions

COMMON CORE

SL 1a Come to discussions prepared, having researched; draw on that preparation to stimulate exchange of ideas. **SL 6** Adapt speech to a variety of contexts and tasks, demonstrating a command of formal English. **L1** Demonstrate command of the conventions of standard English grammar and usage when speaking.

Prepare for Your Job Interview

A job interview is a formal meeting between you and a potential employer. It is usually held toward the end of the job application process, when the employer has narrowed the field of candidates. The steps below will help you prepare:

1. **Consider the purpose of the interview.** The interviewer wants to find out if you have the qualities and skills the job requires, while you want to know if the job is what you are looking for.

2. **Research your potential employer.** Research the company on the Internet. Talk to people who work there to find out what the expectations and priorities are. Consider how your skills and experiences might fit in.

3. **Know what you want to say.** A job interview is a great opportunity for you to share information about yourself—specifically your qualifications, goals, and interests. Even if an interviewer asks a question that can be answered "yes" or "no," elaborate on your skills and qualifications.

   Example interview question: Do you have any experience working with children?

   Possible answer: Yes, I worked at a day camp for kids with special needs. I learned a lot from the children's enthusiasm. If I felt tired, the kids would remind me that life is full of fun.

4. **Know what you want to ask.** Use what you have learned through your research to prepare some questions that you would like to ask about the company, their policies, their mission statement, or your possible role.

THINK central

Speaking & Listening Online

Go to thinkcentral.com.
KEYWORD: HML12N-1390

Practice for Your Interview

Think of a job interview as a formal speaking engagement. In the interview, you must be both informative and persuasive. How can you use your voice to achieve those purposes?

USE VERBAL TECHNIQUES

Use the tips in the chart below to practice answering these questions: Why do you want a job at this company? What is your strongest workplace skill?

Tips for Responding to Interview Questions	
Formal Language	Use formal English, avoiding slang and colloquial expressions. Follow the conventions of standard English grammar and usage throughout your interview, speaking in complete sentences. Address your potential employer respectfully.
Tone	Speak in a confident tone—even if you feel nervous.
Clarity	Enunciate your words clearly. Don't mumble. Don't fill your answers with "ums" and "uhs." Take a moment before you begin an answer to think about what you want to say.
Paraphrases	Paraphrase and repeat the interviewer's question if you need a moment to process the question and gather your thoughts.

USE NONVERBAL TECHNIQUES

In a face-to-face interview, your interviewer will "read" your body language. Your facial expressions and gestures should reflect your desire to impress and inform.

- **Appearance:** Make sure that you are neatly dressed and well groomed for your interview. First impressions are very important.
- **Poise:** Even if you feel nervous or excited, stay calm. Sit with your hands in your lap. Breathe normally. Maintain eye contact with your interviewer and smile politely. Nod to show your understanding. If you don't know how to answer, calmly ask the interviewer to rephrase the question.

USE ACTIVE LISTENING SKILLS

An interview is an opportunity to show that you are a good listener. Your interviewer will ask you specific questions. Pay attention to his or her questions, and never interrupt the interviewer. Use your listening skills to note key words and phrases and to identify the point of the question. If necessary, ask the interviewer for clarification.

YOUR TURN

As an Interviewee With a trusted friend, plan and participate in a mock interview. Make sure you use the speaking and listening techniques listed on this page. Also, use your listening skills to evaluate the questions. Ask your friend for feedback on your performance, and use it to improve your interviewing skills.

Assessment Practice

DIRECTIONS Read the two selections and the viewing and representing piece. Then answer the questions that follow.

from Testament of Youth *by Vera Brittain*

1   I saw the Sisters in their white overalls hurrying between the wards, the tired orderlies toiling along the paths with their loaded stretchers, the usual crowd of Red Cross ambulances outside the reception hut, and I recognised my world for a kingdom of death, in which the poor ghosts of the victims had no power to help their comrades by breaking nature's laws.

2   Angels of Mons still roaming about, I thought. Well, let them roam, if it cheers the men to believe in them! No doubt the Germans, too, had their Angels of Mons; I have often wondered what happened when the celestial backers of one Army encountered their angelic opponents in the nocturnal neutrality of No Man's Land. Michael's war in heaven was nothing, I feel certain, to what happened then.

3   Certainly no Angels of Mons were watching over Étaples, or they would not have allowed mutilated men and exhausted women to be further oppressed by the series of nocturnal air-raids which for over a month supplied the camps beside the railway with periodic intimations of the less pleasing characteristics of a front-line trench. The offensive seemed to have lasted since the beginning of creation, but must actually have been on for less than a fortnight, when the lights suddenly went out one evening as the day-staff was finishing its belated supper. Instead of the usual interval of silence followed by the return of the lights, an almost immediate series of crashes showed this alarm to be real.

4   After days of continuous heavy duty and scamped, inadequate meals, our nerves were none too reliable, and I don't suppose I was the only member of the staff whose teeth chattered with sheer terror as we groped our way to our individual huts in response to the order to scatter. Hope Milroy and I, thinking that we might as well be killed together, sat glassy-eyed in her small, pitch-black room. Suddenly, intermittent flashes half blinded us, and we listened frantically in the deafening din for the bugle-call which we knew would summon us to join the night-staff in the wards if bombs began to fall on the hospital.

5   One young Sister, who had previously been shelled at a Casualty Clearing Station, lost her nerve and rushed screaming through the Mess; two others seized her and forcibly put her to bed, holding her down while the raid lasted to prevent her from causing a panic. I knew that I was more frightened than I had ever been in my life, yet all the time a tense, triumphant pride that I was not revealing my fear to the others held me to the semblance of self-control.

Practice Test · THINK central
Take it at thinkcentral.com.
KEYWORD: HML12N-1392

1392 UNIT 6: MODERN AND CONTEMPORARY LITERATURE

from The Ghost Road   *by Pat Barker*

1 November, 1918

1   My turn to go out last night. One alarm post 'exterminated'. I hope it's the last. We crawled almost to the edge of the canal, and lay looking at it. There was just enough starlight to see by. A strong sense of the Germans on the other side, peering into the darkness as we were, silent, watchful. I had the sense that somewhere out there was a pair of eyes looking directly into mine.

2   The canal's raised about four feet above the surrounding fields, with drainage ditches on either side (the Germans have very sensibly flooded them). It's forty feet wide. Too wide to be easily bridged, too narrow from the point of view of a successful bombardment. There's no safety margin to allow for shells falling short, so men and equipment will have to be kept quite a long way back. Which means that when the barrage lifts, as it's supposed to do, and sweeps forward three hundred yards, there'll be about five minutes in which to get across the swampy fields, across the drainage ditches, and reach even our side of the canal. Plenty of time for them to get their breath and man the guns—though officially, of course, they'll all have been wiped out.

3   The field opposite's partially flooded already, and it's still raining. Not just rain, they've also flooded the drainage ditches on *their* side. From the canal the ground rises steeply to La Motte Farm, which is our objective in the attack. Uphill all the way. Not a scrap of cover. Machine-gunners behind every clump of grass.

4   Looking at the ground, even like that in semi-darkness, the problem became dreadfully apparent. Far clearer than it is on any of the maps, though we spend hours of every day bent over them. There are two possibilities. Either you bombard the opposite bank so heavily that no machine-gunner can possibly survive, in which case the ditches and quite possibly even the canal bank will burst, and the field on the other side will become a nightmare of weltering mud ten feet deep, as bad as anything at Passchendaele.[1] *Or* you keep the bombardment light, move it on quickly, and wait for the infantry to catch up. In that case you take the risk that unscathed machine-gunners will pop up all over the place, and settle down for a nice bit of concentrated target practice.

5   It's a choice between Passchendaele and the Somme.[2] Only a *miniature* version of each, but then that's not much consolation. It only takes one bullet per man.

---

1. **Passchendaele:** a village in Flanders where a British offensive was fought in fields of immobilizing mud.

2. **Somme:** battle in France that resulted in 1.2 million casualties but few strategic gains.

YOUR COUNTRY'S CALL

Isn't this worth fighting for?

ENLIST NOW

British recruitment poster for World War I.

Reading Comprehension

Use **"Testament of Youth" (p. 1392)** to answer questions 1–4.

1. Which descriptive details help you identify the setting of this excerpt?

   A. "the wards," "tired orderlies," "Red Cross ambulances," "reception hut"

   B. "series of crashes," "order to scatter," "intermittent flashes," "deafening din"

   C. "beside the railway," "less than a fortnight," "belated supper"

   D. "celestial backers," "war in heaven," "rushed screaming through the Mess"

2. During the air raid, the setting becomes —

   A. quiet and deserted

   B. hot and smoky

   C. dark and chaotic

   D. dirty and crowded

3. What does the author reveal about herself by using the first-person point of view?

   A. She keeps her fear to herself.

   B. She looks calm outwardly.

   C. Hope sat in her room in the dark.

   D. The raid has everyone frightened.

4. Which statement best expresses the theme of this excerpt?

   A. Working in a military hospital is more rewarding than fighting on the front lines.

   B. The experiences of war can push people to their limits, but can also draw out their unexpected strengths.

   C. In times of war, the common good is more important than the needs of the individual.

   D. During World War I, military hospitals were understaffed and not well protected.

Use **"The Ghost Road" (p. 1393)** to answer questions 5–8.

5. Which statement best describes the setting?

   A. On La Motte farm, above the camp of the German soldiers

   B. At an alarm post during a battle for the surrounding fields

   C. At the edge of a canal separating the German and Allied soldiers

   D. In muddy fields surrounding the Allied encampment at Passchendaele

6. From his reasoning in paragraph 4, you can conclude that the narrator views his situation —

A. idealistically   **C.** realistically

B. optimistically   **D.** sentimentally

7. Which statement best expresses the main theme of this excerpt from *The Ghost Road*?

A. In war, soldiers come face-to-face with the possibility of death.

B. Before committing to a specific battle plan, you need to study the land carefully.

C. War changes the rural landscape and affects farming practices.

D. During a war, soldiers' dangerous jobs lead them to question their abilities.

8. What can you conclude about the upcoming battle from the narrator's observations?

A. As long as the soldiers attack swiftly, the battle will be successful.

B. The attack will be a dangerous undertaking with an uncertain outcome for the soldiers.

C. The land and weather conditions will help the Allies accomplish their objective.

D. The surprise attack will most likely lead to a surrender by the German soldiers.

Use both selections to answer question 9.

---

9. *Testament of Youth* is an autobiographical memoir, and *The Ghost Road* is historical fiction. Both authors use the first-person point of view to emphasize —

A. an outside observer's understanding of how war affects the main characters

B. how the war affects entire groups of people

C. the immediacy of the narrators' observations, thoughts, and feelings

D. more than one person's perspective on the events described in the excerpts

---

Use the visual representation on page 1394 to answer questions 10–11.

---

10. Which qualities does the landscape represent?

A. Self-confidence and generosity

B. Endurance and humility

C. Peace and orderliness

D. Toughness and aggression

11. Which statement describes the overall message of this poster?

A. In order to bring modern factories to rural areas, the country needs more help.

B. Everyone should think about what makes going to war a worthwhile endeavor.

C. England's soldiers need the support of people who live in the country.

D. England needs more soldiers to protect the English way of life.

SHORT CONSTRUCTED RESPONSE
Write a short response to each question, using text evidence to support your answer.

12. Why does Brittain call her world "a kingdom of death" in *Testament of Youth*? Support your response with evidence from the selection.

13. In paragraph 5 of *The Ghost Road*, the narrator remarks that "It only takes one bullet per man." What does the narrator think of his situation? Support your response with evidence from the selection.

14. By relating her experiences from the first-person point of view, has Vera Brittain increased the suspense of her memoir? Explain why or why not and support your response with evidence from the selection.

Vocabulary

Use context clues and your knowledge of figurative and literal meanings of words to answer the following questions.

1. What is the figurative meaning of the expression underlined in paragraph 3 of the excerpt from *Testament of Youth*?

   "The offensive seemed to have lasted since the <u>beginning of creation</u>. . . ."
   - **A.** The first day of life on earth
   - **B.** A very long time
   - **C.** The start of the war
   - **D.** A specific time period

2. What is the figurative meaning of the expression underlined in paragraph 4 of the excerpt from *Testament of Youth*?

   "Hope Milroy and I, thinking that we might as well be killed together, sat <u>glassy-eyed</u> in her small, pitch-black room."
   - **A.** Vulnerable to criticism
   - **B.** Reflecting the surroundings
   - **C.** Fitted with artificial eyes
   - **D.** Without expression

3. What is the figurative meaning of the expression underlined in paragraph 4 of the excerpt from *The Ghost Road*?

   ". . . in which case the ditches and quite possibly even the canal bank will burst, and the field on the other side will become a <u>nightmare</u> of weltering mud ten feet deep. . . ."
   - **A.** A frightening dream
   - **B.** A late-night view
   - **C.** A very bad situation
   - **D.** An event that occurs at night

Use context clues and your knowledge of prefixes to answer the following questions.

4. The prefix *be-* means "to make; cause to become." What does the word *belated* mean in paragraph 3 of the excerpt from *Testament of Youth*?
   - **A.** Became insignificant
   - **B.** Made secure
   - **C.** Occurred after dusk
   - **D.** Was delayed

5. The prefix *in-* means "not." What does the word *inadequate* mean in paragraph 4 of the excerpt from *Testament of Youth*?
   - **A.** Without value
   - **B.** Not sufficient
   - **C.** Lacking flavor
   - **D.** Not expected

6. The prefix *inter-* means "between." What does the word *intermittent* mean in paragraph 4 of the excerpt from *Testament of Youth*?
   - **A.** Stopping and starting again from time to time
   - **B.** Occurring in a middle position or state of existence
   - **C.** Intervening during an episode or event
   - **D.** Pausing for a long time

7. The prefix *ex-* means "out of; away from." What does the word *exterminated* mean in paragraph 1 of the excerpt from *The Ghost Road*?
   - **A.** Far away
   - **B.** Totally inactive
   - **C.** Destroyed completely
   - **D.** Set free from danger

8. The prefix *un-* means "not." What does the word *unscathed* mean in paragraph 4 of the excerpt from *The Ghost Road*?
   - **A.** Disarmed
   - **B.** Not safe
   - **C.** Not injured
   - **D.** Never noticed

Revising and Editing

DIRECTIONS Read this passage and answer the questions that follow.

(1) The flashlight dimly flickers as we crept down the hallway. (2) "Can you hear that?" Dan asks. (3) At the entrance to the dining room, we stumble over boxes that line the walls. (4) "Which is the box that has all the candles?" he wonders. (5) We each take a side of the cavernous room and grope our way along the line of boxes, gently shaking each one, prying open the lids, and searching with our fingertips for the tell-tale smoothness of wax. (6) Something soft and sticky suddenly brushes up against my face. (7) A thunderous roar crashes overhead, and an explosion of light fills the room. (8) The shrouded furniture seems to shudder on the bright flash of light.

1. What change, if any, should be made in sentence 1?
   A. Change *dimly* to **dim**
   B. Insert a comma after *flickers*
   C. Change *crept* to **creep**
   D. Make no change

2. The writer wants to add this sentence to the paragraph.

   Strange scuttling sounds are coming from the ceiling!

   Where is the best place to insert this sentence?
   A. At the beginning of the paragraph
   B. After sentence 2
   C. After sentence 4
   D. After sentence 6

3. Which sentence could follow sentence 6 and build suspense?
   A. "Leave me alone," I say to whatever it is.
   B. What could it be?
   C. "Yikes!" I scream.
   D. I don't like this.

4. What change, if any, should be made in sentence 7?
   A. Delete the comma
   B. Change *thunderous* to **thunder**
   C. Change *and* to **because**
   D. Make no change

5. What change, if any, should be made in sentence 8?
   A. Change *shudder* to **shuddering**
   B. Change *on* to **in**
   C. Insert a comma after *shudder*
   D. Make no change

1397

Ideas for Independent Reading

Continue exploring the Questions of the Times on pages 1098–1099 with these additional works.

What does it mean to be MODERN?

Mrs. Dalloway
by Virginia Woolf

Many literary critics consider Virginia Woolf one of the most important novelists of the 20th century, and *Mrs. Dalloway* nicely illustrates her groundbreaking techniques of novel construction. With its stream-of-consciousness narration, a montage of thoughts and images helps paint a day in the life of Clarissa Dalloway, a middle-aged English society woman.

Collected Poems, 1909–1962
by T. S. Eliot

T. S. Eliot was a leader of the modernist movement in English poetry. He used interior monologue, images from the subconscious, and free verse to break free from the poetic conventions of the Victorian age. This collection includes "The Love Song of J. Alfred Prufrock," "Preludes," and Eliot's masterpiece, "The Waste Land."

The Penguin Book of Modern British Short Stories
edited by Malcolm Bradbury

These 34 representative British short stories of the postwar era convey the flavor of modern British culture. Writers include Samuel Beckett, Doris Lessing, and Ian McEwan.

Are we all ALONE?

Stories
by Katherine Mansfield

A master of the short story, Katherine Mansfield developed a distinct prose style characterized by mood and suggestion rather than dramatic action. Her characters—lonely, longing, complicated—suffer within a rigidly defined social setting. Virginia Woolf once described Mansfield as "of the cat kind, alien, composed, always solitary and observant." These qualities reverberate in the stories collected here.

Look Back in Anger
by John Osborne

Playwright John Osborne was once described in print as an "angry young man." The phrase perfectly captured the resentment of a whole generation of disaffected postwar writers—poets, dramatists, and novelists struggling to come to terms with their changing world. This play in three acts explored for the first time on stage the concerns of characters in their 20s and 30s: those who had not participated in World War II and found its aftermath lacking in possibilities.

Baumgartner's Bombay
by Anita Desai

This novel about a fugitive from the Nazi Holocaust offers a character who is truly "a man without a country." Baumgartner flees from Germany to India, only to be imprisoned as an alien. Later released, he lives on the margins of society, ever the outsider.

How important is CULTURE?

A Passage to India
by E. M. Forster

In this classic novel of colonial prejudice in the twilight of European imperialism, Forster explores the possibility of a new understanding between East and West. The character of Mrs. Moore, a British subject of unprejudiced mind who fully respects the dignity of the Indians whom she meets and the integrity of their culture, represents the future, postcolonial England that will come to recognize the limitations and evils of imperialism.

The Oxford Book of Irish Short Stories
edited by William Trevor

Storytelling flourished in the Irish oral tradition, and that tradition has carried over into the short story genre in the modern era. This collection features 45 stories exhibiting the literary talents of authors from Oscar Wilde to James Joyce to Edna O'Brien.

Nervous Conditions
by Tsitsi Dangarembga

In this novel, which takes place in the British colony of Rhodesia in the 1960s, a young girl must choose between her own African heritage and an education provided by the British. The oldest daughter of a native Shona family, Tambudzai is intent on getting an education and developing her independence. To do so, she must overcome the autocratic authority exercised by the men in her family and the racism and patriarchy of the colonial culture.

Why is there always WAR?

Testament of Youth
by Vera Brittain

Only 21 when World War I broke out, Vera Brittain volunteered for service as a nurse on the Western Front, where she witnessed the horrors of war firsthand. Losing her fiancé, brother, and close friends to the war, Brittain's gripping memoir echoes with poignancy the realities of this painful chapter of British history. It has been called "a moving elegy to a lost generation."

World War One British Poets
edited by Candace Ward

This collection of World War I poetry gives readers a good sense of the powerful sentiments of the day. Included are patriotic works, antiwar poems, male and female writers, writers who were soldiers, and writers who stayed home. Many of the best-known titles are here, including Wilfred Owen's "Anthem for a Doomed Youth" and Lt. Col. McCrae's "In Flanders Fields."

Winston Spencer Churchill: Alone, 1932–1940
by William Manchester

For a decade before World War II, Winston Churchill was "a voice in the wilderness"—almost the only public figure in Britain who recognized the enormous threat that Nazi Germany posed to the nations and civilization of Europe. The story of Churchill's lonely sojourn through the 1930s, as told by Manchester, becomes almost mythic and allegorical.

Preview Unit Goals

DEVELOPING RESEARCH SKILLS

- Select and shape a topic
- Plan research
- Identify relevant and credible sources
- Choose the best research tools, including primary and secondary sources and online resources
- Evaluate information and sources, including nonfiction books, newspapers, periodicals, and Web sites
- Make source lists and take notes
- Synthesize multiple sources
- Avoid plagiarism by quoting directly and crediting sources
- Verify information, detect bias, and develop a personal perspective

WRITING AND LANGUAGE

- Conduct sustained research projects
- Apply research skills
- Document sources
- Prepare Works Cited list
- Format your paper
- Use punctuation with parenthetical citations
- Use correct style for direct quotations

ACADEMIC VOCABULARY

- accurate
- hypothesis
- draft
- label
- goal

MEDIA AND VIEWING

- Create a Web site

Find It Online!

Go to **thinkcentral.com** for the interactive version of this unit.

THINK central

The Power of Research

INVESTIGATION AND DISCOVERY

- Research Strategies
- Writing Research Papers

Writing and Research in a Digital Age

THINK central

KEYWORD: HML12-1401

From online news feeds and electronic archives to podcasts and digital notebooks, technology tools can help you tackle any research project. Find out how.

What Is the Power of Research?

Throughout this book, you have explored the "big questions" of literature, history, and life. You can now take these questions to a new, more challenging level through formal research.

How much can ONE PERSON *change the world?*

How much influence can one person have on social, economic, or political events? You might explore this question by writing a **biographical research paper** that investigates the role of an individual in a war, a protest movement, or a medical breakthrough. Or, if you prefer, you could write a **historical research paper** that traces the effects of a particular event or discovery.

Are there PATTERNS *in history?*

When you read world history and literature, do you notice any situations or events that seem to recur over time? Ethnic and regional conflicts, reactions to disasters, political change, the power of music and art, the impulse to travel, and the importance of family seem universal. You might choose a pattern that interests you and make it the focus of a **multidisciplinary research paper** that explores findings from history and trends in literature.

How does SCIENCE *control our lives?*

Science and technology affect nearly every part of our lives. Does your breakfast cereal contain genetically modified grains? Will wearing a certain type of shoe make you a better athlete? Can eating specific combinations of foods make you smarter? In a **scientific research paper,** you collect data yourself, review and evaluate your findings and the findings of others, and present original conclusions.

When does LITERATURE *mirror real life?*

Novels, stories, plays, and poems can help you understand major and minor conflicts. Can they also provide guidance? One way to explore a work of literature is to write a **literary research paper** that shows how the work mirrors its own times or issues a warning about people and events. For example, you could focus on how the novels of Charles Dickens reflect the dark side of industrialization.

Developing Your Research Focus

An experienced researcher does more than just assemble and report the findings of others. He or she also develops original conclusions and insights by synthesizing information from a variety of reliable sources. Start your research by investigating which topic is right for you.

Choosing and Shaping a Topic

COMMON CORE

Included in this workshop:
RI 7 Evaluate multiple sources of information presented in different media or formats. **W 6** Use technology, including the Internet, to produce, publish, and update individual or shared writing. **W 7** Conduct sustained research projects to answer a question or solve a problem; narrow or broaden the inquiry when appropriate; synthesize multiple sources on the subject, demonstrating understanding of the subject under investigation. **W 8** Gather relevant information from multiple authoritative print and digital sources, using advanced searches effectively; assess the strengths and limitations of each source in terms of the task, purpose, and audience; integrate information into the text selectively to maintain the flow of ideas; avoid plagiarism and overreliance on any one source; follow a standard format for citation. **W 9** Draw evidence from literary or informational texts to support analysis, reflection, and research. **L 6** Acquire and use academic and domain-specific words and phrases.

When you are asked to write a research paper, you may need to develop your own topic or find your own unique approach to an assigned topic. For example, suppose your teacher asks you to write a research paper on a 20th-century novel. You are interested in George Orwell's depiction of totalitarianism in *1984,* but this topic is too broad for a research paper. How can you find a specific topic that will hold your interest as you research, write, and edit your paper?

EXPLORE TOPICS AND "LENSES"

You can narrow your topic and find a unique approach to it by viewing it through different "lenses," or perspectives. In other words, look at your topic as a historian, a psychologist, an artist, an economist, or another specialist might.

Psychological: How does a totalitarian society change the people who live in it?

Political: What ideas or events inspired Orwell to write the novel?

Topics Related to George Orwell's 1984

Multicultural: How have authors in other cultures depicted repressive societies?

Technological: How accurately does 1984 predict the loss of privacy in modern life?

As you brainstorm questions about different topics, you may want to consult with other students to get their feedback. Choose the major research question you find most interesting. Make sure that it is phrased as an open-ended question rather than one that can be answered "yes" or "no."

YES-OR-NO QUESTION: Did the Cold War inspire Orwell to write the novel?
OPEN-ENDED QUESTION: What ideas or events inspired Orwell to write the novel?

Eventually, you will develop your research question into a thesis. Your first goal, however, is to gather, evaluate, and synthesize information from a variety of sources.

Developing a Research Plan

Before you head to the library or search on the Internet, clarify your goal and your thinking by developing a research plan.

FORMULATE RESEARCH QUESTIONS

Take a few minutes to write down several open-ended research questions about your topic. Highlight **keywords**—terms, names, and phrases that are specific to your topic. Later, you will use these terms in search engines and look for them in library catalogs, tables of contents, and indexes.

> What threats to personal freedom existed in Britain after World War II?
> What was occurring in the Soviet Union at that time?
> I've read that Big Brother is supposed to resemble Stalin—what are the similarities between them?

IDENTIFY RELEVANT SOURCES

Now that you have formulated specific research questions, you are ready to start investigating sources. You should explore the full range of credible sources that are relevant to your topic and questions.

- **General encyclopedias** are often the best place to start. You can find an overview of your topic and identify additional keywords.

- **Almanacs and atlases** can give you quick access to geographical, political, and other data.

- **Specialized encyclopedias** can help give you important details about a topic.

- **Specialized dictionaries** give definitions of words and terms in a particular subject area, such as medicine, music, or literary criticism.

- **Newspapers and magazines** give you insight into history, values, popular culture, and events. Don't stop with the news articles; instead, delve into the variety of information available in these sources, ranging from advertisements and comics to obituaries and editorials. Older newspapers and magazines are often available on microfilm or microfiche or online in electronic files.

- **Documentaries** can help you understand eras, movements, inventions, trends, and individuals' lives.

- **Interviews and oral histories** present different perspectives on an era or event.

- **Original research**—such as questionnaires that you create and tabulate, experiments that you perform, or field research that you conduct—can provide valuable new information. For more about original research, see page R47.

- **Other sources** include photographs, maps, song lyrics, statistical abstracts, museum exhibits, databases, and government publications.

Ask a research librarian for help. He or she can help you find reliable information sources.

Find It Online!
THINK central

Go to <u>thinkcentral.com</u> for the interactive version of this unit.

Finding Relevant Sources

The more you know about the range of sources available to you, the more efficient and productive your search will be. As you search, you will expand your knowledge about what the different types of sources are and where you can find them.

Primary and Secondary Sources

Successful research papers often synthesize primary and secondary sources. Both types of sources can provide useful information, but each has its disadvantages as well.

TERMS FOR THE LIBRARY

You will use these terms when doing research in the library or media center:

- primary source
- secondary source
- database
- catalog
- abstract
- bibliography
- index
- appendix
- preface

PRIMARY SOURCES	SECONDARY SOURCES
Definition: materials written or created by people who took part in events or observed them	**Definition:** records created after events by people who were not directly involved
Examples: personal documents such as letters, diaries, autobiographies, speeches, e-mails, and Weblogs; first-person newspaper and magazine articles; public documents such as birth certificates, deeds, and wills	**Examples:** encyclopedias, textbooks, biographies, second-person newspaper and magazine articles, historical nonfiction books, and most documentaries
Advantages: supply firsthand information; usually provide insight into the attitudes and beliefs of the authors; can be very detailed and specific	**Advantages:** helpful for getting an overview of a topic; sometimes include excerpts from a variety of primary sources; often have a broad perspective and consider many viewpoints
Disadvantages: subjectivity and lack of broad perspective; may be biased; chance of inaccuracy	**Disadvantages:** only as reliable as the sources on which they are based; may be biased; can lack the interest provided by an individual voice

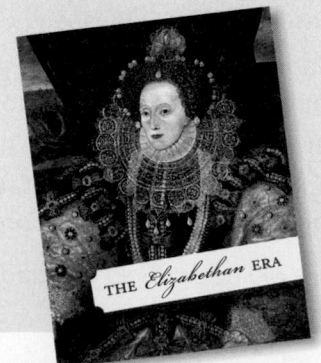

THE *Elizabethan* ERA

Resources for Searches

You can search for primary and secondary sources on the Internet or in a library catalog. To get useful results, you will need to have good search skills and choose the right resources for your search.

TERMS FOR THE INTERNET
You will use these terms when discussing the Internet:

- Web page
- Web site
- URL (uniform resource locator, also called Web address)
- search engine
- keyword search
- hyperlink
- menu

TYPES OF RESOURCES	EXAMPLES
LIBRARY CATALOGS Most library catalogs can now be accessed online through the library's Web site. A library catalog lets you create a customized database of materials related to your search terms. You can search by author, title, subject, or keyword. Results will provide you with bibliographic data and a call number to locate the material in the library.	http://catalog.loc.gov/ http://library.utah.gov http://libraries.vermont.gov/general
NEWSPAPER AND PERIODICAL INDEXES AND DATABASES Newspaper, magazine, and journal articles can be found by searching indexes and databases. Print indexes provide listings of articles by topic. Databases may provide bibliographic citations or access to full-text articles. Your library probably has both print indexes (for older publications) and electronic databases for newer and full-text versions.	*The New York Times Index* (available in both print and online) *Houston Chronicle* (Go to www.chron.com for free online access to full-text articles going back to 1985.) *Readers' Guide to Periodical Literature* (Available in print and online, this guide offers both full-text articles and indexing of over 400 periodicals.)
GENERAL AND SPECIALIZED DATABASES Libraries have access to many types of databases that provide full-text articles or bibliographic citations on a range of topics. These databases may be multidisciplinary (covering a multitude of subjects) or single-subject (specialized by particular subjects). Many databases include an abstract—a short content summary—for each article. A reference librarian can help you determine which databases might be the most helpful for the topic you are researching. You may also be able to access these databases through your library's Web site.	*InfoTrac* (general interest and business articles) *Academic Search Premier* (articles from all major fields of study) *MiddleSearch Plus* (full-text articles from middle-school magazines) *African American Experience* (articles and primary source documents on African American history)
OTHER ONLINE RESOURCES Some Web sites offer the full text of books online, including reference works and older literature that is no longer under copyright protection. In addition, you can view excerpts from many books on the Web sites of online booksellers and on specialized book-search engines.	*Bartleby.com* (offers free access to reference books and classic literature online) *books.google.com* (offers full text, previews, and reference information for books on a variety of subjects) *Amazon.com* (offers previews of books, including tables of contents, excerpts, and front and back covers)

ADVANTAGES OF DATABASES

"Why should I spend time figuring out how to use these databases?" you might ask. "I can just type my keywords into my favorite search engine." That's true—but when you're writing a research paper, specialized databases are often a better choice. Read on to find out why.

- Access to the "invisible Web"— Most databases are part of the "invisible Web" because they are available on the Internet only by subscription and not through search engines. Nevertheless, you can access many of these sites using a library card.

- Targeted information—Databases are usually limited to just one type of material.

- No advertisements—Unlike many search engines, most specialized databases do not have pop-up windows or sidebar advertisements to distract you.

- Abstracts—Many databases include an abstract, or short summary of an article's content, for each article. By reading abstracts, you can quickly decide whether the entire article is worth reading.

YOUR TURN

Examine Database Results

These results come from the InfoTrac database. Examine the results and think about whether this search is effective.

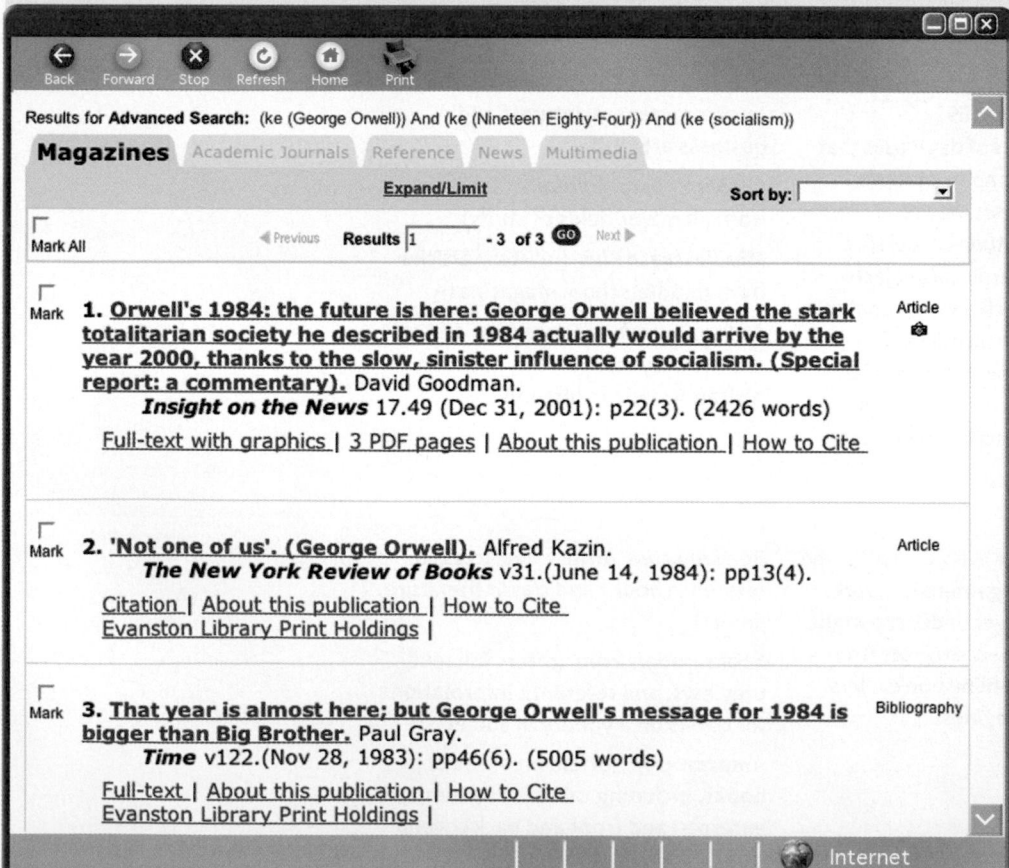

Close Read

1. Which three keywords did this researcher use? On this database, the abbreviation "ke" means keyword.

2. Which of these results could the user click on to get a complete article?

3. What other keywords might yield rich, full answers to the research questions on page 1405?

Using Search Engines

The key to finding the best online resources lies in knowing how to search. First, know your options. There isn't just one search engine; there are many, each of which will return different results. Follow these general rules for effective searching.

- **Use specific search terms.** Don't use *Smith* when you really want *Winston Smith*. Exact terms, such as *Soviet purges,* yield better results.

- **Use search limiters.** Enclose names, related words, and phrases in quotation marks—for instance, "Big Brother" or "Five-Year Plan." Some search engines allow you to combine search terms using AND or a plus sign, such as *Soviet AND totalitarian* or *+"Cold War" +"George Orwell."* To exclude unwanted results, use NOT or a minus sign: *"Cold War" NOT Truman* or *+Orwell –"Animal Farm."*

- **Assess results and select only the best.** Never just click on the first results. Instead, scan the first 10 to 15 descriptions the search engine provides and choose the ones most likely to be helpful in answering your research questions. Decide whether you need to add, delete, or revise keywords.

- For more effective results, click on the "advanced search" or "search tips" link of the search engine you are using.

YOUR TURN **Examine Search Engine Results**

Which of these results do you think would yield the most useful information?

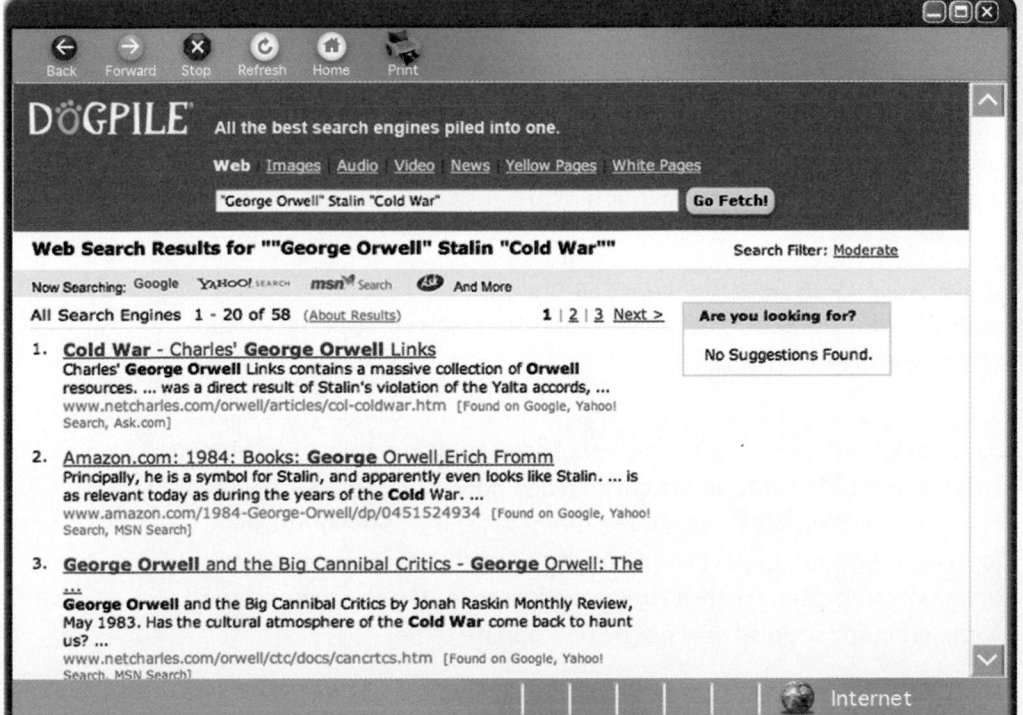

Close Read

1. Which terms did the researcher use? What are the advantages and disadvantages of doing such a specific search?

2. If the researcher changed the search terms to *"George Orwell" Stalin 1984,* how do you think the search results would change?

3. What are some differences between the information provided by this search engine and the information provided by the database on page 1408?

Evaluating and Choosing Sources

Always carefully evaluate sources before you decide to use them. The chart below shows the criteria you should use for evaluating each source.

GUIDELINES FOR EVALUATING SOURCES	
Relevance	If the source isn't related to your research goals and questions, then it won't improve your paper—no matter how interesting or unusual it is.
Timeliness/Currency	Topics in science, medicine, and sports often require recently updated information. Older sources can be valuable for historical or literary topics. For a print source, look at the last date listed on the copyright page. For a documentary, look for a copyright notice on the label. For online materials, check for a "last updated" notice.
Author's Purpose/ Publisher's Purpose	Was the source created to inform, entertain, persuade, or some combination of these? In general, informative pieces are researched more carefully than those designed to entertain or to sell. For information on bias, see page 1418.
Accuracy/ Verifiability	Most print encyclopedias, dictionaries, and almanacs are accurate because they are reviewed and edited carefully, and then updated regularly. Online reference works, as well as many databases, may be updated with even greater regularity. Nevertheless, even reliable sources can contain errors. To ensure accuracy, verify and clarify facts in more than one reputable source.
Author's Credentials	Look for an author who has written on the same topic before or who has a position or job title that qualifies him or her as an expert.
Publisher's Reputation	University presses tend to produce carefully researched and carefully edited books. Publications and Web sites that focus on celebrities, fads, and gossip are often unreliable.
Depth and Level of Coverage	For books, study the table of contents, index, and appendix to determine what aspects of your topic are covered and how much space is devoted to them. For Web sites, consult the site map for the same purpose. Try to gauge the source's level of difficulty as well. Don't use children's books or Web sites created for young learners. On the other hand, some scholarly sources may not be appropriate either.

Finding Credible Web Sites

Web sites vary widely in purpose, scope, and quality. Always evaluate sites thoroughly.

CLUES TO THE RELIABILITY OF A WEB SITE

- **Address/URL**—Remember that a commercial or personal site, whose address often contains *.com* or *.net,* could have been created by anyone for any purpose. On the other hand, an address that contains *.gov* was created by a state or by the U.S. government, so the information on the site is likely to be trustworthy. Similarly, addresses with *.org* are often reliable, as they represent nonprofit organizations and are usually the work of many people. The sites may, however, contain bias. For instance, many political groups create *.org* sites.

- **Purpose of site**—Click on "About Us" or a similar link that introduces you to the site's creators. You can also visit a domain lookup site, such as *www.whois .net.* Look for signs that the site was created carefully and honestly. Credited sources, explanatory notes, information about the author's credentials, and working links to reputable sites are all positive signs.

TIP When a personal name follows a tilde (~), a percent sign, or the words *users* or *members,* the site was created by an individual. Even though personal pages may be linked to an *.org* or *.edu* site, they probably have not been reviewed.

YOUR TURN

Evaluate a Web Site

Answer the questions about this British Broadcasting Corporation site.

Close Read

1. How could you learn more about this site's creators?

2. What part of the site is shown here, and what is its purpose?

3. What clues do you have to the accuracy and reliability of the information on this site?

Evaluating Newspapers and Periodicals

Newspapers, magazines, and journals vary greatly in quality. Remember, also, that even reliable publications may contain errors.

CRITERIA FOR EVALUATING NEWSPAPERS AND PERIODICALS

- **Publication reputation**—Many large-circulation newspapers and national magazines, such as the *Washington Post* and *Smithsonian,* have a reputation for excellence and can be trusted. These sources are considered trustworthy because they set careful editorial standards.

- **Author's credentials**—Many publications include information about their writers. Assume that staff writers are as reliable as the newspaper or periodical in which they appear.

- **Date**—Think about whether you need up-to-the-minute data or information from a specific era.

- **Verifiability**—Can you confirm the information in other sources?

- **Source**—If the article first appeared in another source, be sure the original source is reliable. Articles from AP (Associated Press) and the New York Times News Service are generally reliable.

YOUR TURN

Evaluate a Newspaper Article

Read and evaluate the beginning of this newspaper review of *1984*.

THE NEW YORK TIMES   *MONDAY, JUNE 13, 1949*

Books of the Times

BY ORVILLE PRESCOTT

Not so many years ago when authors wrote about life in the future they generally portrayed the world of their imagination as blissful indeed compared with the unhappy present. Utopia was just around the corner; if science couldn't solve all our problems political and social reorganization could. But that was in another century and, besides, such hopes are dead. . . . And the two things which frighten us most about the future are the two which so recently inspired hope—science and political, economic reorganization. A gruesome example of what the near future threatens to an informed and highly intelligent mind may be found in "Nineteen Eighty-Four," by George Orwell.

Mr. Orwell is the English critic and novelist whose rather elementary and superficial anti-Communist satire, "Animal Farm," was so over-praised three years ago. Compared with the present volume that political fairy tale for grown-ups seems like a bedtime story. "Nineteen Eighty-Four" is not impressive as a novel about particular human beings. Its account of life thirty-five years hence has little fanciful or gadgety interest. But as a prophecy and a warning it is superb. The ultimate degradation of a totalitarian state is here portrayed with repulsive power. . . .

Close Read

1. How would you summarize this review?

2. Is this review still useful even though it is so old? Explain your answer.

3. Which words from this review would you quote if you were writing a paper on *1984*? Give reasons for your answer.

Choosing Credible Books

Just as you write for different purposes and audiences, publishers put books on the market with different goals in mind. Some books are rushed to market and aimed at making money fast. Others are the result of years or even decades of work, including multiple revisions and comprehensive fact checking.

CRITERIA FOR EVALUATING NONFICTION BOOKS

- **Author's credentials**—Check for information on the book jacket and at the beginning and end of the book to determine whether the author is an expert on the topic.

- **Research-based findings**—To determine whether the book is based on research, check the back for a bibliography. Look for footnotes or endnotes in which the author credits his or her sources and provides additional insights or explanation. Check for an appendix that adds information such as maps, genealogical tables, or letters.

- **Author's purpose**—The author's purpose may be stated in a **preface,** a short introductory essay. The preface may also tell you more about the writer's background and research.

- **Copyright date**—This date will help you determine if the book is a primary or secondary source. For secondary sources, a series of updates and printings is a sign that the source has been highly regarded for many years.

 **YOUR TURN**

Evaluate a Nonfiction Book

Would these pages from a book called *Orwell: Rebel with Conflicting Causes* be useful to someone researching whether *1984* is a statement of protest?

Index (continued)

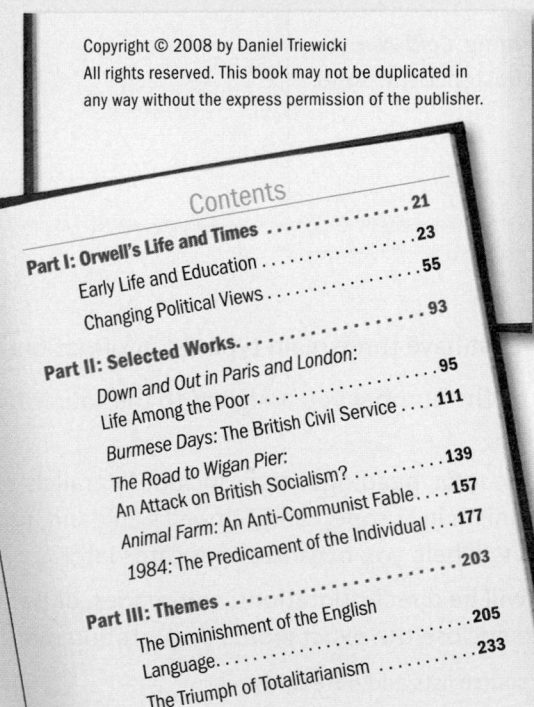

Contents

Close Read

1. How useful do you think this book would be to someone focusing on how *1984* reflected the events of the 1940s? Use details from the table of contents and the index to support your answer.

2. What chapters and/or page numbers might be most useful for the reader who wants to gain insights into *1984* as well as into Orwell's life and times?

Note Taking and Plagiarism

Plagiarism is taking someone else's words or ideas without properly crediting them. Because plagiarism is dishonest and sometimes even unlawful, it can have serious consequences, such as failing a class or losing a job.

Recording Information Accurately

Taking careful notes can help you avoid plagiarism. You can record notes using special note-taking software or any word-processing program, or you can simply write them down on index cards.

SOURCE LIST

Begin by listing your sources. If you are using index cards, make one source card for every source. Assign a number to each source and record the following information: the author or editor; the title of the work or Web page; and the date and medium of publication. For each of the following source types, add this information:

- **Web source**—date created or posted; date accessed
- **Book**—publishing information, including the name and location of the publisher; library call number; page numbers used
- **Encyclopedia**—name and year of encyclopedia; publishing information
- **Periodical article**—name of periodical; page numbers of article

Source Listing: Nonfiction Book

Source 2

Isaacs, Jeremy, and Taylor Downing. *Cold War: An Illustrated History, 1945–1991*. Boston: Little, 1998. Print.

909.82

I73

NOTES

Every note card you make must have three main types of information:

- **A number**—This should be the number you assigned to the source on the source list.
- **A heading**—For a paper on *1984,* headings might include "Parallels to the Soviet Union," "Totalitarianism in Europe," and "Orwell's England, 1946." Writing specific headings will help you organize your cards later.
- **Your notes**—Your notes will be direct quotations, summaries, or paraphrases. When quoting, be sure to enclose the exact words in quotation marks.

See page R48 for examples of source lists and note cards.

PARAPHRASES AND SUMMARIES

When you **paraphrase,** you restate someone else's ideas in your own words. When you **summarize,** you restate and condense someone else's ideas by including only the most important points. A paraphrase is about the same length as the original source; a summary is shorter than the original.

As these examples show, even though you are using your own words when you paraphrase or summarize, you must still credit your source.

Original Source

> The Soviet Union also basked in the glory of victory, since everywhere there was immense respect for the Red Army. From years of titanic struggle against the Wehrmacht, the Soviets were widely regarded as having borne the brunt of destroying Nazism. . . . In France the Communists were associated with the Maquis, resistance fighters during Nazi occupation.
>
> *Isaacs, Jeremy, and Taylor Downing. Cold War: An Illustrated History, 1945–1991.*

Responsible Paraphrase

Europeans' views of Communism	Source 2

Many people respected the Soviet Union's Red Army, which had fought mightily against the Nazis and had been largely responsible for their defeat. . . . French people linked the Communists with their own brave resistance fighters in France (24–25).

Accurately restates source; uses a source number; includes page numbers

Responsible Summary

Europeans' views of Communism	Source 2

Many Europeans (especially the French) respected the Communists, not only for helping to win World War II but also for resisting the Nazis (24–25).

Correctly condenses the source; uses a source number; includes page numbers

Plagiarized Paraphrase

Europeans' views of Communism

The Red Army basked in the glory of victory. After years of struggle against the Germans, the Soviets were widely regarded as having borne the brunt of destroying Nazism.

Uses the key phrases "basked in the glory of victory" and "borne the brunt of detroying Nazism" without attribution; omits source number and page numbers

Plagiarized Summary

Europeans' views of Communism

In Europe, many people felt immense respect for the Communists, who were widely regarded as having destroyed Nazism.

Uses the key phrases "immense respect" and "widely regarded" without credit or quotation marks; fails to include source number and page numbers

Avoiding Plagiarism

You can include others' words and ideas in your writing, but only if you give the proper credit. Follow these guidelines to make sure that you are not plagiarizing.

QUOTE RESPONSIBLY

Some ideas are so significant, original, or well stated that you want to include them exactly as you found them. Place quotation marks around everything that you have taken word for word from a source. If you change an entire sentence except for one key phrase, that key phrase still belongs to its author.

Original Source

> It is easy to tell which features of the party of *1984* satirize the British Labour Party rather than the Soviet Communist Party. Big Brother and his followers make no attempt to indoctrinate the working class, an omission Orwell would have been the last to ascribe to Stalinism.
>
> *Deutscher, Isaac. "'1984'—The Mysticism of Cruelty." Twentieth Century Interpretations of 1984.*

Plagiarized

English politics and *1984*	Source 6
Orwell was satirizing the English and not the Soviets because Big Brother and his followers make no attempt to indoctrinate the working class (35).	

Correctly restates most of source but does not enclose "Big Brother . . . working class" in quotation marks

Correctly Quoted

English politics and *1984*	Source 6
Orwell was satirizing the English and not the Soviets when he created a party that didn't try to "indoctrinate the working class" (35).	

Correctly restates source; includes quotation marks where needed

CREDIT INFORMATION AND IDEAS FROM OTHERS

Which facts and ideas need to be credited? Follow these rules:

- **Credit all facts except common knowledge.** There are some well-known facts that do not require credit. For example, almost everyone knows that the Nazis lost World War II, that water is made up of hydrogen and oxygen, and that many birds migrate south for the winter. Because these facts are common knowledge, they do not require documentation. However, if you are not sure whether a certain fact is common knowledge, cite a source or sources for it.

- **Credit ideas as well as facts.** If your paper includes an explanation, an inference, a conclusion, or even an insightful question that you did not arrive at yourself, you must credit the source. For example, if one of your sources states that *Animal Farm* was George Orwell's most influential novel, then you must credit the source of that insight.

Becoming a Critical Researcher

Critical researchers gather and assess information from different sources and then use that information to develop their own insights on a topic.

Evaluating Contradictory Sources

What happens if you find sources that seem to disagree with each other? A careful researcher takes responsibility for determining why differences exist. He or she then decides which sources are credible.

RECONCILE DIFFERENCES

Even reliable sources may use different methods of collecting or interpreting data. For instance, experts disagree on how many people "disappeared" during Stalin's rule of the Soviet Union. Use the criteria on page 1410 to determine whether the sources are credible. If all the sources appear to be reliable, you could state in your research paper that opinions vary, and then give the estimates presented by the different sources.

To determine accuracy, consult reputable print and online sources, such as most encyclopedias, almanacs, and library databases. The online sources below are also generally reliable.

FOR MORE INFORMATION . . .	GO ONLINE TO . . .
U.S. population, government, and history	www.census.gov (U.S. Bureau of the Census); www.whitehouse.gov; www.usa.gov (official U.S. government Web portal)
Your state's government and history	www.usa.gov (click on "Find Government Agencies")
Primary sources, maps, audio, and video related to American history	www.loc.gov (Library of Congress)
International data	europa.eu (European Union Online); www.un.org (United Nations)
Science, technology, and the environment	www.cnn.com/tech (CNN Technology News); www.epa.gov (Environmental Protection Agency); www.nasa.gov; www.noaa.gov (climate, weather and oceans)
Authors and works of literature	www.bartleby.com; www.ipl.org (the Internet Public Library)

Recognizing Bias

Bias is a preference or an attitude that can prevent a person from presenting information fairly and honestly. When an author presents personal opinions as fact, that is bias. Although bias is sometimes obvious, it can be very subtle.

CRITERIA FOR DETECTING BIAS

- **Intent**—Ask yourself why the author wrote the material. Someone who is trying to persuade you might not fully discuss the opposing point of view. For example, someone who disagreed with George Orwell's criticisms of British politics might leave out information about political unrest in Britain during the late 1940s.
- **Author's background**—Try to determine how an author's background or profession influences how that author interprets or presents facts.
- **Facts**—The author should present facts instead of just speculation.
- **Verifiable evidence**—Facts should be verifiable in reputable sources.
- **Balance**—All sides of an issue should be examined thoroughly and with equal regard and care.
- **Time period**—Think about how the time period when the author wrote may have influenced his or her views. For example, a person writing during the early Cold War might have been affected by the fear of Communism that was so pervasive during that time.
- **Loaded language**—Watch out for sources that use language with extremely positive or extremely negative connotations. "The self-absorbed nations of Western Europe did nothing as the Soviet menace gobbled up helpless Eastern European countries" is an example of loaded language.

Developing Your Thesis

Now that you have learned a great deal about your topic, it is time to decide what the main focus of your research paper will be. A high-quality, original thesis develops from careful analysis of multiple sources.

MAKE INFERENCES AND DRAW CONCLUSIONS

When you research, read between the lines to determine the author's implied meanings and attitudes. An **inference** is a logical assumption based on observations or information in a text in combination with your own knowledge and experience. This chart shows the inference that one student made.

What the Source Says	What I Already Know	My Inference
In *1984*, the Thought Police eliminate people who they think could be dangerous.	During Stalin's rule, millions of people "disappeared" because they were considered enemies of the state.	In *1984*, Orwell is referring to the constant policing and "disappearing" of individuals during Stalin's rule.

Making inferences is often called reading between the lines, but drawing conclusions could be called reading beyond the lines. A **conclusion** is a judgment or statement of belief based on evidence, experience, and reasoning. Making inferences is one of the steps you take toward drawing a conclusion, as you can see in this example.

What Sources Say	My Inferences	My Conclusion
Stalin's Five-Year Plans turned the Soviet Union from a farming nation into an industrial powerhouse. Orwell despised Stalin's brutal, repressive tactics.	Some Europeans probably thought that the Soviet model would be good for their countries, too. Orwell must have worried that Britain and other countries would end up with totalitarian governments like Stalin's.	Orwell wanted to warn people about the dangers of totalitarianism.

FORMULATE YOUR THESIS

As your knowledge of the topic increases, you will be able to make more inferences and draw more conclusions. Each of these will help you refine your goal statement into a sophisticated, intriguing thesis statement. This chart illustrates one method of drafting a thesis.

Facts from 1984 and My Research	My Conclusions	My Thesis
Orwell set 1984 in the future, but not in the distant future. Incidents in 1984 echo Stalin's policies: Thought Police, purges, surveillance, and disappearances. Some Europeans admired the Soviets and "Uncle Joe" Stalin. Orwell wrote that totalitarianism "could triumph anywhere."	The novel is not just science fiction from Orwell's imagination. It is based on real events that happened at the time he was writing. Britain or another Western country could have become a totalitarian state.	Orwell wrote 1984 as a protest of political events in his own time, the 1940s.

In the next section, you will see how one student incorporated research strategies into the writing process to produce a research paper.

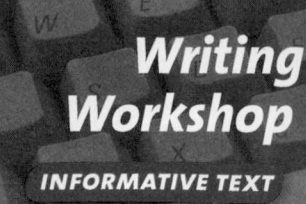

Writing Workshop

INFORMATIVE TEXT

Research Paper

A research paper is the result of a focused investigation and original thinking. It gives you the opportunity to develop and support personal opinions about a research topic by synthesizing information from multiple sources. In this workshop, you will identify a research topic, gather sources, synthesize information, and organize and write a research paper on a topic of your choice.

 Complete the workshop activities in your **Reader/Writer Notebook.**

WRITE WITH A PURPOSE

WRITING TASK

Write a **research paper** that thoroughly explores and answers a research question that interests you. Support original ideas and analysis with information from multiple relevant sources. Keep your audience in mind as you gather evidence and details to support your controlling idea.

Idea Starters
- how a famous historical figure reflects the values of a historical period
- how a novel serves as social or political protest
- the causes and effects of a historical event

THE ESSENTIALS

Here are some common purposes, audiences, and formats for research papers.

PURPOSES	AUDIENCES	FORMATS
• to explore a topic of interest	• classmates and teacher	• research paper for class
• to share information with others interested in the topic	• book club members	• blog
		• school newspaper
• to support personal opinions by synthesizing information from multiple sources	• blog readers	• school Web site

COMMON CORE TRAITS

1. DEVELOPMENT OF IDEAS
- introduces a clearly defined **topic** and supports a **controlling idea** with **evidence** drawn from multiple authoritative sources
- provides a **concluding section** that supports the information

2. ORGANIZATION OF IDEAS
- organizes ideas, information, and evidence in a **logical way**
- uses **appropriate transitions** to create cohesion and clarify relationships among ideas
- includes **formatting** and **graphics** when useful

3. LANGUAGE FACILITY AND CONVENTIONS
- maintains a **formal style** and **objective tone**
- effectively uses **precise language, domain-specific vocabulary,** and **literary techniques**
- uses **standard formatting** for quoting or citing sources
- uses **quotations** correctly
- demonstrates a command of **grammar, usage,** and **mechanics**

Writing Online

THINK central

Go to **thinkcentral.com**.
KEYWORD: HML12N-1420

Planning/Prewriting

COMMON CORE

W 2a–f Write informative texts to convey complex ideas through the effective selection, organization, and analysis of content. **W 5** Develop and strengthen writing by planning. **W 7** Conduct sustained research projects to answer a question.

Getting Started

ANALYZE THE TASK

Carefully reread the writing task. Place brackets around words that tell you *what* you have to produce, and underline the important details. Make notes on what you have to do and how you will do it. If you are unsure about any of the requirements, such as length, acceptable topics, or format, ask your teacher.

▶ WHAT DOES IT LOOK LIKE?

Analyzing the task:

Write a [research paper.]

This is the purpose and format for my writing.

. . . that thoroughly <u>explores and answers a research</u> question that interests you.

This is my starting point for exploring a topic.

. . . <u>Support original ideas and analysis with information from a variety of relevant sources.</u>

This is what will make my research paper successful.

CHOOSE A TOPIC

Explore a subject that interests you by brainstorming, asking questions, freewriting, or conferring with others. Try to settle on an engaging topic for which you will be able to find a variety of sources. Present original ideas rather than merely repeating existing information. Make sure your topic is narrow enough to be fully developed but not too narrow to support a full-length research paper.

▶ WHAT DOES IT LOOK LIKE?

<u>Questions:</u>

What were George Orwell's political beliefs? How did they affect his writing?

What was George Orwell's government like?

THINK ABOUT AUDIENCE AND PURPOSE

In selecting a topic and research question, keep in mind that your **purpose** is to find information, analyze it, and use it to support your own findings. Remember that when you share the information, you should avoid merely repeating facts. Instead, produce a paper that **synthesizes,** or combines, information from multiple authoritative sources. Your research paper should enhance your audience's understanding of a topic. In this case, your audience may include both teens and adults.

▶ ASK YOURSELF:

- What might my audience already know about the topic? What information might be new to them?
- What background information, extended definitions, or domain-specific vocabulary will I need to provide?
- Why should my audience care about my topic or my research question?

Planning/Prewriting *continued*

Getting Started

WRITE A RESEARCH QUESTION

Research encyclopedia articles, Web sites, or video documentaries about your topic. Review these sources to develop background knowledge. Then, use this information to write a research question that helps to focus your topic.

▶ **WHAT DOES IT LOOK LIKE?**

> Research Question
> How did George Orwell's view of totalitarianism affect his novel 1984?

IDENTIFY RELATED QUESTIONS

Develop a list of related research questions by using the **5W-How? method:** Answer the questions *Who? What? When? Where? Why?* and *How?* Developing this list of questions will help you identify if you need to broaden or narrow your research topic or question.

TIP Review your related questions, and consider whether you need to revise or rewrite your research question to refocus your research plan.

▶ **WHAT DOES IT LOOK LIKE?**

> * **Who** was George Orwell?
> * **What** is 1984?
> * **When** was 1984 written?
> * **Where** did Orwell live?
> * **Why** did he set the book in the future?
> * **How** did his readers respond?

MAKE A RESEARCH PLAN

Develop a research plan that outlines your purpose, audience, research question, and potential sources. Create a schedule that shows when your research, first draft, and final draft are due. Before you begin researching, you may consider asking your teacher to review your plan and to offer suggestions for improvement.

▶ **WHAT DOES IT LOOK LIKE?**

> **Name:** _____
> **Purpose:** _____
> **Audience:** _____
> **Research Question:** _____
> _____
> **Potential Sources:** _____
> _____

PEER REVIEW Discuss your topic and research question with a classmate. Ask: Will the topic interest other readers? What new or interesting point can I make about the topic? What sources could I use to develop the topic?

 YOUR TURN

Develop your research plan in your *Reader/Writer Notebook*. Consider these tips as you develop your plan:

* Choose a research topic and develop research questions to guide your investigation.
* Keep your audience and purpose in mind as you look for answers to your research questions.

Researching

**COMMON CORE** **W 8** Gather relevant information from multiple sources; assess the strength and limitations of each source; avoid plagiarism; follow a standard format for citation. **W 9** Draw evidence from informative texts to support research.

Following Your Research Plan

INVESTIGATE POSSIBLE SOURCES

After you have made a research plan, use a library catalog and several search engines to look for multiple sources from which to draw your information and evidence. Finding several sources will help you avoid relying too much on any one source, which would provide a very limited frame of reference for your research. Make use of both print and digital sources, and try to find both primary and secondary sources. **Primary sources** are firsthand, original information, and **secondary sources** include information derived from, or about, primary or other secondary sources.
List sources you find that appear to answer the questions you wrote in the planning stage. Write down the title of each source, the author's name (if available) and where you located the source. Comment on each source's potential relationship to your research question and general topic.

▶ WHAT DOES IT LOOK LIKE?

Sources	My Comments
World Wide Web "As I Please" www.netcharles.com	has Orwell's own essays and articles; these are primary sources
Public Library <u>Cold War: An Illustrated History, 1945–1991,</u> Isaacs and Downing (Ref 909.82 I73) "George Orwell and the Radical Eccentrics," <u>Journal of British Studies</u>	first part has information about Stalin and the beginning of the Cold War scholarly article that discusses Orwell and other writers and thinkers of his time

ASSESS YOUR SOURCES

Assess the strengths and limitations of each source before you use it by evaluating its relevance, credibility, and accuracy. A source is **relevant** if it relates to the topic you are researching and **credible** when the information it presents is reliable and well-documented. For **accuracy,** seek information published by major universities or established, credible publishing companies. Evaluate Internet sources by noting the creator of the site and the source of its information. Be careful using Web sites with *.com* or *.net* in their address.

When conducting research using digital sources or the Internet, make the most effective use of the advanced searches by filling in as many of the search parameters as you can. This will help filter out any unwanted sources or Web sites, narrowing down the number of sources you need to look through.

▶ ASK YOURSELF:

- How is the source relevant or directly related to my topic?
- What is the publication date of the source? Has it been updated recently?
- What type of documentation does the source include? Does the source contain a bibliography or citations of other credible sources?
- Who is the author of the source? Is it a scholar or a recognized, credible authority on the topic, rather than a student like me who also researched an aspect of this topic?
- Does the source present an unfounded theory, or does it provide a theory backed up with solid, or strong, evidence?
- What is the address of the Web site? Does it have *.org, .gov,* or *.edu* in the address, which indicates a Web site that is more reliable?

Researching *continued*

Following Your Research Plan

PREPARE A SOURCE LIST

Once you have identified the sources you want to use, you may want to create an electronic file of the complete list. **List** the sources alphabetically by author's last name—or by title if there is no author. (This list will be the basis of your Works Cited page, which must appear at the end of your research paper.) The list will help ensure that you have a variety of authoritative print and digital sources. It will also help you follow a standard format when you compile your Works Cited list.

For each source in your list, include the title, author, publisher, date and medium of publication, and other important information. Give each source a number. You will use that number later when you take notes.

If you are unable to create an electronic file, you can write the information for each source on a separate index card.

▶ WHAT DOES IT LOOK LIKE?

[Chapter in a book]

1) Deutscher, Isaac. "*1984*—The Mysticism of Cruelty." *Twentieth Century Interpretations of 1984.* Ed. Samuel Hynes. Englewood Cliffs: Prentice, 1971. 29–40. Print.

[Entry in a specialty encyclopedia]

2) Fisher, Christopher T. "Cold War." *Encyclopedia of Espionage, Intelligence, and Security.* Eds. K. Lee Lerner and Brenda Wilmoth Lerner. 3 vols. Detroit: Gale, 2004. Print.

[Book]

3) Orwell, George. *1984 and Related Readings.* 1949. Evanston: McDougal, 1998. Print.

[Newspaper article found online]

4) Orwell, George. "As I Please." *Tribune* 15 Nov. 1946. Web. 12 Apr. 2010.

TAKE NOTES

As you read through each source, look for information you may want to use in your research report. Record that information—**relevant facts or statistics, concrete details, quotations, examples,** paraphrases, or summaries—in a separate electronic file, on a separate index card, or with note-taking software. Make sure your notes identify the number that corresponds to the source in the list you created earlier.

At the top of each file or index card, write a heading that identifies what the notes are about. Also include the page number or section name from the source. Use the same heading in files or index cards with similar information. You will later use those headings to organize your paper.

▶ WHAT DOES IT LOOK LIKE?

European Attitudes About Communism   6

Some Europeans thought communism was a good thing. The French and Italians were grateful to the Communists for helping win World War II and for resisting the Fascists. (24–25)

Researching *continued*

Following Your Research Plan

DRAFT A CONTROLLING IDEA

Review your notes, and then write a **controlling idea,** or thesis statement, that states your topic and your research question. Remember, your controlling idea should pose an original research question that you will thoroughly explore in your paper. You may find that you will need to revise or rework your controlling idea when you draft your paper.

▶ ASK YOURSELF:

- What recurring ideas appear in the different sources?
- How does all the information I have collected fit together?
- What larger point, or general conclusion, does the information support?
- Are my original ideas about the topic supported or contradicted by the information I have collected?
- Does my controlling idea accurately reflect the information I have collected? If it does not accurately reflect the information, how should I rework it?

CREATE AN OUTLINE

After you finish taking notes and writing your controlling idea, organize your notes according to their headings. You may need to rework your subject headings in order to create groups of notes. Then, organize your groups so that each new main point builds on the one preceding it and creates a cohesive research report. There are three types of organization you might want to try:

- **chronological order:** the order in which events occur
- **logical order:** related ideas grouped together
- **order of importance:** most important ideas to least important or vice versa

You may organize your notes using just one organization type, but you will probably use a combination of all three patterns when you write your paper. After you organize your notes, create a basic **outline** for your paper.

▶ WHAT DOES IT LOOK LIKE?

I. *1984* and Orwell's 1940s
   A. Orwell's world
   B. The world of *1984*
II. Totalitarianism
   A. In *1984*
     1. Oceania
     2. "Big Brother" and Stalin
   B. Cold War and Soviet Union
     1. Stalin as enemy
     2. Meaning of "Cold War"
     3. Orwell's fear of constant war

YOUR TURN   Follow your research plan to create a source list for all the sources you will use. Skim your sources, and write relevant information on a note card or in an electronic file. Make sure your notes are labeled with numbers that correspond to the sources on your list. Then, write a controlling idea and an outline for your paper. If necessary, narrow or broaden your research question so that you can answer it thoroughly in your research paper.

Drafting

The following chart shows how to organize your draft to create an effective research paper.

Organizing Your Research Paper

INTRODUCTION

- Begin with an interesting and **relevant fact, detail,** or **quotation** to grab your readers' interest.
- Provide background information and a clear **controlling idea.**
- Establish and maintain a **formal style** and **objective tone.**

▼

BODY

- Use your outline as a guide to develop the body of your draft.
- Use **relevant facts, details, quotations,** and other evidence to support your main points.
- Use **precise language** and define any **domain-specific vocabulary**. Consider using a literary technique to describe an unfamiliar topic. For example, you could use a **metaphor, simile,** or **analogy** to compare abstract ideas with something the audience is familiar with.
- Use transitions throughout your draft to **clarify relationships** among ideas and create **cohesion. Vary your syntax** instead of relying on the same words, phrases, and clauses.
- Use **parenthetical citations** to document quotations, paraphrases, and summaries.

▼

CONCLUDING SECTION

- Restate your controlling idea and present your conclusion about the research question.
- Summarize the paper's main points and end with a **final insight** into your research.

▼

WORKS CITED LIST

- At the end of your paper, include a complete list of the works that you quoted or paraphrased in your paper.
- The Works Cited list usually begins on a separate page. It should follow the MLA (Modern Language Association) formatting rules, which include the following:
  - Works Cited pages usually begin on a separate page.
  - The words Works Cited are centered above the list of sources.
  - Each source entry begins on a separate line.
  - The first line of each entry is left aligned; additional lines have a hanging indent of a half-inch.
  - Sources are sorted alphabetically by authors' last names. Sources with no author are sorted by title.
  - If an author is cited for more than one source, his or her name appears only in the first entry. Additional entries use three hyphens (---) in place of the author's name.

Models of Works Cited entries appear at the end of this workshop.

COMMON CORE

W 4 Produce clear and coherent writing appropriate to task, purpose, and audience.
W 8 Integrate information to avoid plagiarism; follow a standard format for citation.
L 2 Demonstrate a command of standard English punctuation.

LEARN HOW Document Sources To avoid plagiarism, or copying someone else's work, you must correctly document your sources. Place **parenthetical citations** (source citations enclosed in parentheses) within the body of your paper as close as possible to the information they document. These citations direct readers to the Works Cited list at the end of your paper.

Guidelines for Parenthetical Documentation

TYPE OF SOURCE	CONTENT OF CITATION AND EXAMPLE
Sources with one author	▶ Author's last name and a page number, if any: (Orwell 23)
Sources with more than one author	▶ Authors' last names and page number, if any: (Isaacs and Downing 45) If more than three, use first author's last name and *et al.* (and others): (Anderson, et al. 313)
Same source, two citations	▶ Author's last name and page numbers, if any: (Orwell 23, 49)
Multivolume sources	▶ Author's last name, volume, and page number: (Smith 2: 214)
Sources with title only	▶ Title (often abbreviated) and page number: (*Lives* 38)
Indirect sources	▶ Abbreviation *qtd. in* (quoted in) before source: (qtd. in Orwell 38)

GRAMMAR IN CONTEXT: USING PARENTHETICAL CITATIONS

Here are some rules for adding parenthetical citations to your paper.
- Place citations **after** the closing quotation mark, if there is one.
- Place citations **before** the punctuation (such as periods) at the end of a sentence.

> The young Orwell believed they had "been swallowed up in one of the first great purges" (Orwell, *1984* 33).

Quotations that run more than four lines are indented and do not have quotation marks. When using block **quotations,** place all citations after the end punctuation.

> More and more obviously the surface of the earth is being parceled off into three great empires, each self-contained and cut off from contact with the outer world, and each ruled under one disguise or another, by a self-elected oligarchy.... ("Atom Bomb")

YOUR TURN Using your outline and organization chart, write a first draft of your research paper. Remember to document your sources correctly.

Revising

When you revise, you evaluate the content, organization, and style of your research paper. Your goal is to determine if you have achieved your purpose and effectively communicated your ideas to the intended audience. The questions, tips, and strategies in the following chart will help you revise or rewrite where necessary.

RESEARCH PAPER

Ask Yourself	Tips	Revision Strategies
1. Does the introduction engage the reader, provide background information, and clearly state my controlling idea?	► **Circle** the engaging introduction, **underline** the background information, and **bracket** the controlling idea.	► **Add** a quotation, interesting detail, or fact to hook readers. **Add** necessary background information. **Add** a controlling idea.
2. Is each main point supported with relevant facts, details, definitions, quotations, or examples?	► With a colored marker, **highlight** the main points. **Number** supporting evidence for each main point.	► **Delete** irrelevant points and evidence. **Add** evidence to support points with fewer than three supporting details.
3. Are sources credited appropriately? Are citations correctly placed and punctuated?	► **Place check marks** by material that requires documentation.	► **Add** parenthetical citations, if necessary. **Correct** placement and punctuation of citations where needed.
4. Do I maintain a formal style and objective tone throughout?	► **Draw a double line** under any contractions, slang, or informal or biased language.	► **Reword** text to avoid contractions or subjective statements. **Replace** any informal language.
5. Does the concluding section restate the controlling idea, summarize main points, and provide additional insight?	► **Bracket** the restatement of the controlling idea. **Draw a star** by the summary of the main points and a **wavy line** under the insight.	► **Add** a sentence or two restating the controlling idea. **Add** a summary of the main points. **Add** additional insight into the topic.
6. Is the Works Cited list complete? Does it follow a consistent format?	► **Compare** parenthetical citations with the entries in your Works Cited list.	► **Add** Works Cited entries if necessary, and **revise** incorrectly formatted entries.

YOUR TURN **PEER REVIEW** Exchange your draft with a classmate. Ask your partner to use the questions and tips in the chart above to evaluate your draft and suggest revisions. Make notes about your partner's observations and suggestions. If necessary, rework or try a new approach to further improve your paper.

COMMON CORE   **W 5** Strengthen writing by revising, editing, rewriting, or trying a new approach.

ANALYZE A STUDENT DRAFT

Read these excerpts from a student draft; notice the comments on its strengths as well as suggestions for improvement.

Santos 1

Christina Santos

Mr. McRae

English IV

April 17, 2010

1984: History and George Orwell's Fearful Vision of the Future

❶   The 1940s was a decade dominated by world war. Most of the world's countries participated in a six-year world war that pitted the political ideologies of totalitarianism and democracy against each other. The victory of the democratic Allied nations in 1945 would affect world politics for decades. In hindsight, the line between democracy and totalitarianism seems perfectly obvious. In George Orwell's lifetime, however, the lines were often blurred. Orwell believed that even after the end of an epic and devastating war, people could still be attracted to totalitarianism. His well-known novel *1984* explores a world in which the concept of individual liberty is unknown to characters who live under grim, totalitarian regimes.

> Christina uses her first paragraph to provide some historical background, but some essential information about Orwell and the concept of totalitarianism is missing. She needs to add some background information.

LEARN HOW Provide Background Information To make sure that readers can follow your research, provide background information about the topic. Christina added background information to help readers understand the period in history she is going to discuss.

CHRISTINA'S REVISION TO PARAGRAPH ❶

which spanned the first half of the twentieth   *, a journalist, essayist,*
century and was marked by two world wars,   *and novelist,*

In George Orwell's lifetime, ~~however,~~ the lines were often blurred. Orwell believed that even after the end of an epic and devastating war, people could still be attracted to totalitarianism.

, a form of government in which the state denies all personal freedoms and enforces the will of its leader.

2   Although *1984* is science fiction, it can also be interpreted as Orwell's urgent protest against political events of the 1940s. After witnessing the events leading up to and during the war, Orwell believed that if people did not defend the ideals of freedom and justice, any nation could become totalitarian. As Orwell explained after *1984* was published, "totalitarianism, if not fought against, could triumph anywhere" (Orwell and Angus 502). By examining events from the 1940s and his fiction, it is clear that Orwell was deeply concerned about the future of democracy in the Western world.

3   The main character of *1984,* Winston Smith, lives in a future that is both grim and frightening. His home is in London, a city in Oceania, a totalitarian state. Oceania is under the control of the Party and its mysterious leader, "Big Brother." In every home, a telescreen monitors peoples' actions and words. Winston's job at the Ministry of Truth is to falsify information. He has no memories of what life was like before the Party takeover, but he secretly obtains a diary and a pen and repeatedly writes "DOWN WITH BIG BROTHER" (21).

4   Critics and historians believe that the Big Brother character is a thinly disguised re-creation of Joseph Stalin, the Soviet Union's totalitarian dictator, who was once an ally of the Western powers but is now remembered for executing millions of his own people (Fears; Isaacs and Downing 6). Stalin's dedication to the spread of communism ended the alliance with the West. By 1946, the Soviet Union and the Western powers were already involved in what became a Cold War—a continuous state of military and political rivalry that could escalate into violence at any time (Fisher 233). Orwell echoes this in *1984* by creating an ongoing state of war with frequently shifting alliances (*1984* 38–39).

Christina waits until the second paragraph to introduce her **controlling idea.** Her paper will focus specifically on the novel *1984* and how it reflects Orwell's concerns about political developments in the 1940s.

Christina uses this paragraph to **summarize** the book *1984* for those who have not read it. To emphasize a key point in the book, she includes a **quotation** from the novel and cites it with a **parenthetical citation.**

This sentence clearly contains information that is not original to Christina. Instead of quoting directly from the source, she **paraphrases** the information. Christina correctly formats a parenthetical citation to identify the source.

Santos 3

5   Although Western governments greatly feared Stalin and communism, some Westerners admired them—a notion that Orwell found disturbing. Isaacs and Downing noted that many French and Italians respected the Communists for helping to win World War II and for resisting fascism (24–25). Furthermore, the Communist way of life appeared successful to many people in the West who believed that capitalism had failed during the Great Depression. During the same time, Stalin developed Five-Year Plans, which Orwell presents as "Three-Year Plan(s)" (*1984* 44). These plans helped to transform the Soviet Union, a farming nation, into an industrial powerhouse about which Isaacs and Downing said the following: "output doubled" (Isaacs and Downing 7). As a result of these factors and others, "'Uncle Joe' Stalin had become a popular figure in Europe and the United States" (Isaacs and Downing 25). However, Orwell felt nothing but disgust for "Uncle Joe," whose totalitarian methods he saw as threats to people's most basic freedoms (Orwell, "As I Please" Nov. 22; Orwell and Angus 175).

> Christina begins this paragraph with a **main point** that relates to her **controlling idea.** Then she gives **supporting details,** including **relevant evidence** from a specific source. She uses a **parenthetical citation** to credit the source.

> Christina's **introduction of a quotation** is awkward here. The reference to the authors interrupts the flow of the sentence. Since that information is included in the parenthetical citation, it is not needed in the sentence itself.

> Christina uses the **transition** word *however* to indicate a contrast between popular ideas and Orwell's personal opinion.

LEARN HOW   **Introduce Quotations**   Integrate quotations smoothly into your prose by using an introductory sentence followed by a colon, or weave them in, making them part of a sentence. Christina decided to weave the short quotation into her sentence and delete the unnecessary mention of the authors.

CHRISTINA'S REVISION TO PARAGRAPH 5

These plans helped to transform the Soviet Union, a farming nation, into an industrial powerhouse *where* ~~about which Isaacs and Downing said the following:~~ "output doubled" (Isaacs and Downing 7).

6   Orwell's fiction reflects real events from his world. He based the political purges and executions in *1984* on the purges that took place in the Soviet Union under Stalin (Pritchett 22). When Orwell refers to the actions of the Thought Police, "marking down and eliminating the few individuals who were judged capable of becoming dangerous" (*1984* 79), he is referring to the constant policing and "disappearing" of individuals during Stalin's rule. Winston's own mother, father, and sister become victims of the state. He vaguely remembers that they disappeared when he was ten or eleven and "must evidently have been swallowed up in one of the first great purges of the Fifties" (Orwell, *1984* 33). Horrific details such as these show how much Orwell feared a police state, which he felt could spread beyond the Soviet Union, maybe even to Britain.

7   Only a few years after the publication of *1984*, critic Isaac Deutscher suggested that Orwell was concerned about problems in Europe as well as in the Soviet Union (35). The novel's focus on bloodthirstiness and lies reflects Orwell's concern for his own country. In November 1946, in a weekly newspaper column he wrote, Orwell declared outrage over public executions that were occurring in Europe at the time. After he described how people liked to "gloat" over them, he concluded that this signaled a "downward spiral" of society ("As I Please" Nov. 15). Orwell echoes this feeling in *1984* when he refers to a hanging as a "popular spectacle" and notes, "Children always clamored to be taken to see it" (27).

8   Orwell also feared that British institutions, such as the press, were contributing to a mindset open to totalitarianism. For example, he believed that British newspapers routinely distorted the news to serve the government's purpose ("As I Please," Nov. 22). Similarly, distortion and

> Christina **reinforces her controlling idea** and creates **coherence** by repeatedly returning to Orwell's fear that totalitarian governments would take over the world.

> Christina cites two well-chosen examples of **significant and relevant evidence.** First, she cites a primary source, an article by Orwell from 1946. Then she uses gruesome details from his novel to reinforce the idea.

Santos 5

censorship appear throughout *1984.* The Party's slogans are carved into the Ministry of Truth: "WAR IS PEACE," "FREEDOM IS SLAVERY," and "IGNORANCE IS STRENGTH" (6). The absurdity of the slogans in the book seems to be Orwell's way of showing just how extreme the distortion of information could be. In *1984,* the state rewrites and redefines everything, including love, truth, language, history, and even thought. Facts are whatever the government says they are. Winston's job is to rewrite historical documents so that it seems as if things are always improving. He reflects, "It was merely the substitution of one piece of nonsense for another" (46).

❾ Orwell also feared superpowers, a new political reality that developed just before he began to write *1984.* In his novel, three superpowers exist: Eurasia, Oceania, and Eastasia. It was believed by Orwell that it was only a matter of time until there would be three superpowers in the world: the Soviet Union, the United States, and East Asia. Great Britain was not one of them.

> Christina **supports her assertion** about distortion and censorship with **evidence** from the novel. She also **interprets** the examples to show how they support her point.

> This passage is **wordy** and lacks unity. Use of passive voice at the beginning of the first sentence creates a wordy and awkward structure, and the second sentence is confusing.

LEARN HOW Avoid Wordiness   The best prose gets ideas across without using more words than necessary. Similarly, a unified paragraph contains only sentences that support its main idea. Effective writing also uses the active voice, rather than the passive voice, so that the subject of a sentence performs the action of the verb in the predicate. Notice how Christina revised to reduce wordiness, to eliminate the passive voice, and to eliminate an unnecessary sentence.

CHRISTINA'S REVISION TO PARAGRAPH ❾

Orwell believed that there soon would be three superpowers in the world: the Soviet Union, the United States, and East Asia.

~~It was believed by Orwell that it was only a matter of time until there would be three superpowers in the world: the Soviet Union, the United States, and East Asia. Great Britain was not one of them.~~

Here is how he explained this belief only a few months before he began writing 1984:

> More and more obviously the surface of the earth is being parceled off into three great empires, each self-contained and cut off from contact with the outer world, and each ruled under one disguise or another, by a self-elected oligarchy. . . . [T]he third of the three super-states—East Asia, dominated by China—is still potential rather than actual. But the general drift is unmistakable. ("Atom Bomb")

Orwell knew that the United States and the Soviet Union would dominate the world economically and politically for decades to come.

⑩ George Orwell's novel *1984* represents his protest against political events during the final years of his life. He feared that the Cold War was becoming the new "peace." He worried that freedom could be replaced with slavery in any society where people did not battle totalitarianism. He knew that in a totalitarian society, people could be kept ignorant of their rights and freedoms so that the state could stay strong. Orwell set his most famous novel not very far in the future because he feared that the world's democracies would not long resist the call to join totalitarian nations. The evidence presented in this paper suggests that for him, writing *1984* was a way of shaking people up and letting them know that they lived in a frightening world where no one was free and where even obvious facts—such as *two plus two equals four*—might soon be permanently distorted. Indeed, Orwell's worst nightmare was living in a world where everyone believed that two and two add up to five because that's what they were told to believe. Although the worst parts of Orwell's vision did not come true either on the scale or within the time frame he predicted, totalitarianism still thrives in the world, and the world's citizens are still suspicious and afraid of those on the other side. Perhaps we need a new Orwell to present an updated vision of the world—one in which sanity and democracy prevail.

Christina correctly uses an **introductory sentence followed by a colon** to lead into her **block quotation.** She indents the long quotation because it is more than four lines. Her **parenthetical citation** is also correctly set after the end punctuation.

Christina **restates her controlling idea** at the beginning of her **concluding section.**

Christina **summarizes main points** from the body of her paper.

Christina's concluding section includes a **closing insight** and suggests that Orwell's ideas are still meaningful and deserve further exploration.

Santos 7

Works Cited

Deutscher, Isaac. "*1984*—The Mysticism of Cruelty." *Twentieth Century Interpretations of 1984.* Ed. Samuel Hynes. Englewood Cliffs: Prentice, 1971. 29–40. Print.

Fears, J. Rufus. "George Orwell, *1984.*" *Books That Have Made History: Books That Can Change Your Life.* Part 2 of 3. Chantilly, VA: Teaching Company, 2005. CD.

Fisher, Christopher T. "Cold War." *Encyclopedia of Espionage, Intelligence, and Security.* Eds. K. Lee Lerner and Brenda Wilmoth Lerner. 3 vols. Detroit: Gale, 2004. *Print.*

Isaacs, Jeremy, and Taylor Downing. *Cold War: An Illustrated History, 1945–1991.* Boston: Little, 1998. Print.

Orwell, George. *1984 and Related Readings.* 1949. Evanston: McDougal, 1998. Print.

---. "As I Please." *Tribune* 15 Nov. 1946. Web. *12 Apr. 2010.*

---. "As I Please." *Tribune* 22 Nov. 1946. Web. 12 Apr. 2010.

---. "You and the Atom Bomb." *Tribune* 19 Oct. 1946. Web. 12 Apr. 2010.

Orwell, Sonia, and Ian Angus, eds. *George Orwell: The Collected Essays, Journalism, & Letters.* Vol. 4. 1968. Boston: Godine, 2000. Print.

Pritchett, V.S. "1984." *Twentieth Century Interpretations of 1984.* Ed. Samuel Hynes. Englewood Cliffs: Prentice, 1971. 20–23. *Print.*

YOUR TURN Use the feedback from your peers and teacher as well as the "Learn How" lessons to revise or rework your research paper. As you proofread your draft, check all of your quotations against the original text. Check your citations against the Works Cited list above to make sure you have used the correct format.

LEARN HOW Format a Works Cited List Correctly When you write a research paper, you need to be sure to cite all of your sources according to established guidelines. Christina forgot to adhere to the following formatting guidelines in a few of her entries:

- End each entry with a period.
- Include the date of access for online sources.
- Use quotation marks around the titles of articles found online or in periodicals.
- Add the medium of publication to each entry.

Notice Christina's revisions in blue. Check each entry of your Works Cited list against the guidelines to ensure that you follow the formatting guidelines consistently.

Editing and Publishing

COMMON CORE

W 5 Strengthen writing by editing.
L 2 Demonstrate command of the conventions of standard English capitalization, punctuation, and spelling.

In the editing stage, you proofread your research paper to make sure that it is free of grammar, usage, spelling, and punctuation errors. Careless spelling, capitalization, and punctuation mistakes distract your audience from focusing on your ideas. Read your paper carefully to correct any lingering mistakes. Be sure to format your paper according to the following guidelines:

- Double-space everything.
- Leave a one-inch margin at the left, right, top, and bottom of each page.
- At the top left of the first page, type your name, your teacher's name, the class, and the date. On the rest of the pages, type your last name and the page number in the upper right corner, half an inch from the top.
- Indent all paragraphs one-half inch (or five spaces) and indent quotations of four or more lines one inch (or ten spaces) from the left margin.

See the *MLA Handbook for Writers of Research Papers* for additional guidelines.

GRAMMAR IN CONTEXT: PUNCTUATING QUOTATIONS

When weaving a quotation into your text, you must sometimes add words or phrases to make the quotation fit your sentence. When you add words to a quotation, you must place your addition in brackets [ ]. At other times, you may want to omit part of a quotation. When you omit a word or phrase from a quotation, you use ellipses to show the omission (. . .).

As Christina proofread her paper, she realized that she had incorrectly punctuated a quotation, using parentheses instead of brackets to indicate added text. Note how she revised her paper to correct the error.

> During the same time, Stalin developed Five-Year Plans, which Orwell
> presents as "Three-Year ~~Plan(s)~~ Plan[s]" (*1984* 44).

PUBLISH YOUR WRITING

Here are some suggestions for sharing your research paper with an audience:

- Ask a school librarian to make your work available in the library or media center.
- Offer to present your paper to another class, such as an English class or a history class.
- Adapt your research report as the text of your own Web site. Add graphics and audiovisuals, and create hyperlinks that allow readers to view your Web sources.

YOUR TURN Correct any errors in your research paper. If you have altered quoted material, be sure that you have correctly used brackets and ellipses to show additions and omissions. Finally, publish your completed work.

Scoring Rubric

Use the rubric below to evaluate your research paper from the Writing Workshop.

RESEARCH PAPER

SCORE	COMMON CORE TRAITS
6	• **Development** Effectively introduces a topic; states an insightful, well-researched controlling idea; thoroughly supports the controlling idea with main points and relevant evidence; ends powerfully • **Organization** Logically organizes information; effectively uses varied, appropriate transitions and syntax; includes formatting and graphics to enhance the information • **Language** Ably uses precise words; consistently maintains a formal style and objective tone; shows a strong command of conventions; correctly cites all sources
5	• **Development** Competently introduces a topic; states a well-researched controlling idea; offers main points and relevant evidence; has a strong concluding section • **Organization** Is logically organized; effectively uses transitions; includes formatting and graphics • **Language** Uses a formal style and objective tone; has a few errors in conventions; correctly cites sources
4	• **Development** Sufficiently introduces a topic; states a clear controlling idea; offers mostly valid support; has an adequate concluding section • **Organization** Is mostly logically organized; needs more transitions; could use some formatting or graphics • **Language** Needs more precise words; has frequent lapses in style and tone; includes a few distracting errors in conventions; incorrectly formats a few source citations
3	• **Development** States a controlling idea, but the introduction could be more engaging; provides insufficient support; has a weak concluding section • **Organization** Has some flaws in organization; needs more transitions; doesn't include enough formatting or graphics • **Language** Lacks precise words; uses an informal style and subjective tone; has several errors in conventions; incorrectly formats some source citations
2	• **Development** Has an unclear controlling idea; does not support most ideas; ends abruptly • **Organization** Has organizational flaws; lacks transitions throughout; lacks formatting and graphics throughout • **Language** Lacks precise words; uses an informal style and subjective tone; has many errors in conventions; does not cite all sources and cites many incorrectly
1	• **Development** Lacks a controlling idea; fails to develop the topic; ends abruptly • **Organization** Has no organization, transitions, or formatting • **Language** Uses vague words; has an inappropriate style and tone; has major problems in conventions; plagiarizes or does not credit sources

MLA Citation Guidelines

You may be able to find free Web sites that help you create citations for research papers. While these sites may save time, you should always check your citations carefully before you turn in your paper. The MLA (Modern Language Association) has developed guidelines for documenting research. You can follow these examples to create the Works Cited list for your research paper.

BOOKS

One author
Orwell, George. *1984 and Related Readings.* 1949. Evanston: McDougal, 1998. Print.

Two authors or editors
Isaacs, Jeremy, and Taylor Downing. *Cold War: An Illustrated History, 1945–1991.* Boston: Little, 1998. Print.

Three authors or editors
Randolph, Carolyn, Catherine Coleman, and Thomas Mullens. *The Soviet Union During the Stalin Years.* Dallas: Strom, 2008. Print.

Four or more authors or editors
List only the first author followed by the abbreviation et al., *which means "and others."*
Reed, Nahid, et al. *Orwell the Satirist.* Milwaukee: Steuben, 2008. Print.

PARTS OF BOOKS

An introduction, a preface, a foreword, or an afterword written by someone other than the author or authors of a work
Symons, Julian. Introduction. *Nineteen Eighty-Four.* By George Orwell. New York: Knopf, 1992. ix–xiii. Print.

A poem, a short story, an essay, or a chapter in a collection of works
Pritchett, V.S. "1984." *Twentieth Century Interpretations of 1984.* Ed. Samuel Hynes. Englewood Cliffs: Prentice, 1971. 20–23. Print.

A poem, a short story, an essay, or a chapter in an anthology of works by several authors
Orwell, George. "Shooting an Elephant." *The Great English and American Essays.* Ed. Edmund Fuller. New York: Avon, 1964. Print.

A novel or play in a collection
Orwell, George. *Animal Farm. The Penguin Complete Novels of George Orwell.* Harmondsworth, Eng.: Penguin, 1983. Print.

 COMMON CORE

W 8 Gather relevant information from multiple print and digital sources; follow a standard format for citation.

MLA Citation Guidelines *continued*

MAGAZINES, NEWSPAPERS, AND ENCYCLOPEDIAS

An article in a newspaper
Vincent, Anne-Marie. "In the Land of Big Brother: Six Decades Later." *Fairview Press*
7 July 2008: B12. Print.

An article in a newspaper accessed from a database
Schorer, Mark. "An Indignant and Prophetic Novel." *New York Times* 12 June 1949: BR1.
ProQuest Historical Newspapers. Web. 9 Apr. 2010.

An article in a magazine or journal
Mayers, Oswald J. "The Road to 1984: George Orwell, the life that shaped the vision."
Library Journal 15 Nov. 1986: 68. Print.

An article in an encyclopedia
Fisher, Christopher T. "Cold War." *Encyclopedia of Espionage, Intelligence, and Security.*
Eds. K. Lee Lerner and Brenda Wilmoth Lerner. 3 vols. Detroit: Gale, 2004.

MISCELLANEOUS NONPRINT SOURCES

An interview
Delibes, Taisha. Personal interview. 19 Mar. 2011.

A video recording or film
Nineteen Eighty-Four. Dir. Michael Radford. Perf. John Hurt, Richard Burton, Suzanna
Hamilton, and Cyril Cusack. 1984. MGM, 2003. DVD.

A sound recording
Fears, J. Rufus. "George Orwell, *1984.*" *Books That Have Made History: Books That Can
Change Your Life.* Part 2 of 3. Chantilly, VA: Teaching Company, 2005. CD.

ELECTRONIC PUBLICATIONS

A document from an Internet site

Author or compiler | Title or description of document | Title of Internet site

Bixby, Ilana. | "George Orwell's London." | *George Orwell: Lone Crusader.*

Site sponsor | Date of Internet site | Medium of Publication | Date of access

Orwell Institute. | Jan. 2008. | Web. | 9 Apr. 2010.

An online book or e-book
Bloom, Harold. *George Orwell's Nineteen Eighty-Four.* New York: Chelsea, 1996. *Netlibrary.*
Web. 8 Apr. 2011.

A CD-ROM
"Stalin, Joseph." *Britannica Student Encyclopedia.* 2004 ed. Chicago: Encyclopaedia
Britannica, 2004. CD-ROM.

Creating a Web Site

Informational Web sites are similar to research papers. The people who create them look for the most relevant and current information and organize it in a logical way. Images, hyperlinks, and audio on Web sites heighten the viewer's learning experience.

 Complete the workshop activities in your **Reader/Writer Notebook.**

PRODUCE WITH A PURPOSE	COMMON CORE TRAITS
TASK Create and produce an informational **Web site** that incorporates text, graphics, audio, and visuals to present your research. Adapt your paper from the Writing Workshop.	**A STRONG WEB SITE . . .** • integrates information from multiple sources • makes strategic use of textual, graphical, audio, and visual elements to enhance understanding and add interest • employs an interesting and functional visual design • includes hyperlinks to source materials

COMMON CORE

W 6 Use technology to produce, publish, and update writing products. **SL 2** Integrate multiple sources of information presented in media. **SL 5** Make strategic use of digital media in presentations to enhance understanding and add interest.

Plan Your Web Site

Planning a Web site is similar to planning a research report. You must first identify your topic and gather the information you want to include. As you develop the Web site, make strategic use of the material and elements in order to enhance your audience's interest in and understanding of your topic.

1. **Identify Sources of Material.** Identify sources you used for your research paper that have information, graphics, or visual elements you can use on your Web site. Be sure to integrate material from multiple sources. Verify that they are credible, accurate, well-documented, and authoritative.

2. **Gather or Create Audiovisual Materials** Think about sights and sounds that relate to your topic. You can look for or create the following:
   • photographs, charts, diagrams, maps, timelines, fine art, and other graphics
   • audio clips of famous people or music associated with the time period or topic

3. **Create a Site Plan** Sketch a flow chart that plots out the pages and links on your Web site. Start with your homepage. Then, list other pages in categories or groups.

4. **Learn the Terms and Conditions of Use** Many audiovisuals and graphics may be copyrighted, requiring permission from the original creators before you can use them. Some sites allow students to use the elements in school projects. You must cite the source of any material you did not create and have a Works Cited list for your Web site, so keep track of all the sources you use.

5. **Plan the Pages' Content and Write the Text** Draw detailed sketches of how you want each page to look. Then, write the text, and create captions or titles for the visuals.

Media Tools **THINK** central

Go to **thinkcentral.com**.
KEYWORD: HML12-1440

Produce Your Web Site

CHOOSE AN AUTHORING PROGRAM AND IMPORT ELEMENTS

Find out what authoring programs your school has available, or download an authoring program from the Internet. Your school's computer specialist can advise you on this step and help you scan or download graphics and audio or visual clips. He or she can also help you save CD-ROM elements to your project file.

CREATE DESIGN ELEMENTS

Create uniform design elements, including the headings, text types or fonts, and graphics such as buttons and links. Follow the guidelines below.

Guidelines for Design Elements

Headings and Labels	• Create a title for every page using the same large, easily readable font. • Clearly label all buttons and links, and make sure your headings are clear and accurate.
Text Types (or Fonts)	• Use text types that are clear and easy to read at any size. • Avoid text types or fonts that are elaborate or difficult to read. • Use the same font for text that functions the same way on the page. All headings should be the same size and type, and all text should use the same size and type.
Color	• Use background colors that are pleasing to the eye, and make sure the text contrasts well with the background. • If you want to use an eye-catching patterned background, use it only on pages that have little text and few graphics.

TEST, REVISE, AND UPLOAD YOUR SITE

Proofread every screen. Check every link to make sure it connects to the right page. Then, get permission to upload your Web site to your school's server, or check with a parent or guardian about uploading your page directly to the Web.

As a Web Site Creator Ask a friend, family member, or classmate to test your site by visiting each page and trying out different buttons and links. Use the feedback to revise or rework your site.

As a Viewer Evaluate a classmate's Web site. Make sure all the links connect to the correct pages. Identify any confusing content or design problems. Determine whether the Web site's content, graphics, and audio are well suited to the topic, audience, and purpose.

Student Resource Bank

R1

Reading any text—short story, poem, magazine article, newspaper, Web page—requires the use of special strategies. For example, you might plot events in a short story on a diagram, while you may use text features to spot main ideas in a magazine article. You also need to identify patterns of organization in the text. Using such strategies can help you read different texts with ease and also help you understand what you're reading.

.... **COMMON CORE**

Included in this handbook:
RL 3, RL 5, RI 4, RI 6, RI 7, SL 2, SL 5

1 Reading Literary and Nonfiction Texts

Literary and nonfiction texts include short stories, novels, poems, dramas, biographies, autobiographies, and essays. To appreciate and analyze literary and nonfiction texts, you will need to understand the characteristics of each type of text.

1.1 READING A SHORT STORY
Strategies for Reading

- Read the title. As you read the story, you may notice that the title has a special meaning.

- Keep track of events as they happen. Plot the events on a diagram like this one.

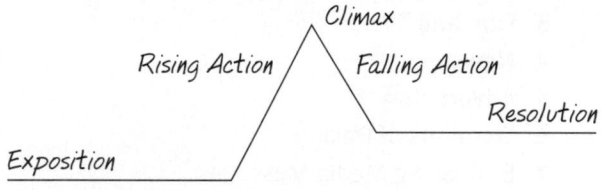

- From the details the writer provides, **visualize** the characters. **Predict** what they might do next.

- Look for specific adjectives that help you visualize the **setting**—the time and place in which events occur.

- Note **cause-and-effect relationships** and how these affect the **conflict**.

1.2 READING A POEM
Strategies for Reading

- Notice the **form** of the poem, or the arrangement of its lines and stanzas on the page.

- Read the poem aloud a few times. Listen for and note the **rhymes** and **rhythms.**

- **Visualize** the images and comparisons.

- **Connect** with the poem by asking yourself what message the poet is trying to send.

- Create a word web or another **graphic organizer** to record your reactions and questions.

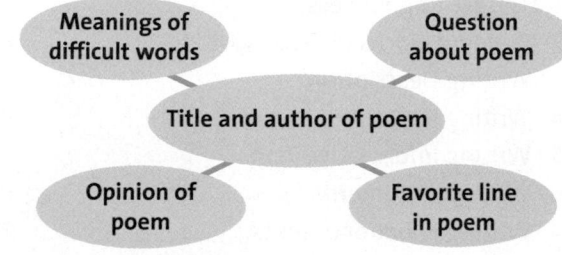

1.3 READING A PLAY
Strategies for Reading

- Read the stage directions to help you **visualize** the setting and characters.

- **Question** what the title means and why the playwright chose it.

- Identify the main conflict (struggle or problem) in the play. To **clarify** the conflict, make a chart that shows what the conflict is and how it is resolved.

- **Evaluate** the characters. What do they want? How do they change during the play? You may want to make a chart that lists each character's name, appearance, and traits.

1.4 READING NONFICTION
Strategies for Reading

- If you are reading a biography, an autobiography, or another type of biographical writing, such as a diary or memoir, use a family tree to keep track of the people mentioned.

- When reading an essay, **analyze** and **evaluate** the writer's ideas and reasoning. Does the writer present a thesis statement? use sound logic? adequately support opinions with facts and other evidence?

- For all types of nonfiction, be aware of the **author's purpose,** and note any personal **bias** of the writer that might influence the presentation of information.

❷ Reading Informational Texts: Text Features

An **informational text** is writing that provides factual information. Informational materials, such as chapters in textbooks and articles in magazines, encyclopedias, and newspapers, usually contain elements that help the reader recognize their purposes, organizations, and key ideas. These elements are known as **text features.**

2.1 UNDERSTANDING TEXT FEATURES

Text features are design elements of a text that indicate its organizational structure or otherwise make its key ideas and information understandable. Text features include titles, headings, subheadings, boldface type, bulleted and numbered lists, and graphic aids, such as charts, graphs, illustrations, art, and photographs. Notice how the text features help you find key information on the textbook page shown.

Ⓐ The **title** identifies the topic.

Ⓑ A **subheading** indicates the start of a new topic or section and identifies the focus of that section.

Ⓒ **Boldface type** is used to make key terms obvious.

Ⓓ A **bulleted list** shows items of equal importance.

Ⓔ **Graphic aids,** such as illustrations, art, photographs, charts, graphs, diagrams, maps, and timelines, often clarify ideas in the text.

PRACTICE AND APPLY

1. "The Romantic Movement" is a subheading under the title "Revolutions in the Arts." What does the heading suggest about the romantic movement?

2. What are two key terms associated with the romantic movement? How do you know?

3. What does the bulleted list explain? Is it an effective text organizer as used on this page? Explain why or why not.

Ⓐ Revolutions in the Arts

MAIN IDEA	WHY IT MATTERS NOW
Artistic and intellectual movements both reflected and fueled changes in Europe during the 1800s.	Romanticism and realism continue to dominate the novels, dramas, and films produced today.

SETTING THE STAGE European countries passed through severe political troubles during the 1800s. At the same time, two separate artistic and intellectual movements divided the century in half. Thinkers and artists focused on ideas of freedom, the rights of individuals, and an idealistic view of history during the first half of the century. After the great revolutions of 1848, political focus shifted to men who practiced realpolitik. Similarly, intellectuals and artists expressed a "realistic" view of the world. In their view of the world, the rich pursued their selfish interests while ordinary people struggled and suffered.

Ⓑ The Romantic Movement

Ⓒ At the beginning of the 19th century, the Enlightenment idea of reason gradually gave way to another major movement: romanticism. **Romanticism** was a movement in art and ideas. It showed deep interest both in nature and in the thoughts and feelings of the individual. In many ways, romantic thinkers and writers reacted against the ideals of the Enlightenment. Romantics rejected the rigidly ordered world of the middle-class. They turned from reason to emotion, from society to nature. **Nationalism** also fired the romantic imagination. For example, a fighter for freedom in Greece, Lord Byron also ranked as one of the leading romantic poets of the time.

The Ideas of Romanticism Emotion, sometimes wild emotion, was a key element of romanticism. Nevertheless, romanticism went beyond feelings. Romantics expressed a wide range of ideas and attitudes. In general, romantic thinkers and artists

Ⓓ
- emphasized inner feelings, emotions, imagination
- focused on the mysterious and the supernatural; also, on the odd, exotic, and grotesque or horrifying
- loved the beauties of untamed nature
- idealized the past as a simpler and nobler time
- glorified heroes and heroic actions
- cherished folk traditions, music, and stories
- valued the common people and the individual
- promoted radical change and democracy

Not all romantics gave the same emphasis to these features. The brothers Jakob and Wilhelm Grimm, for example, concentrated on history and the sense of national pride it fostered. During the first half of the 19th century, they collected German fairy tales. They also created a dictionary and grammar of the German language. Both the tales and the dictionary of the Grimm brothers celebrated the spirit of

Though created in the early 20th century, this watercolor of British artist Arthur Rackham is full of romantic fantasy. It illustrates the tale "The Old Woman in the Wood" by Jakob and Wilhelm Grimm.

THINK THROUGH HISTORY
A. Analyzing Causes Which ideas of romanticism would encourage nationalism?

Background
The Grimm brothers also collected tales from other countries: England, Scotland, Ireland, Spain, the Netherlands, Scandinavia, and Serbia.

Ⓔ

Nationalist Revolutions Sweep the West **619**

2.2 USING TEXT FEATURES

You can use text features to locate information, to help you understand it, and to categorize it. Just use the following strategies when you encounter informational text.

Strategies for Reading

- Scan the title, headings, and subheadings to get an idea of the main concepts and the way the text is organized.

- Before you begin reading the text more thoroughly, read any questions that appear at the end of a lesson or chapter. Doing this will help you set a purpose for your reading.

- Turn subheadings into questions. Then use the text below the subheadings to answer the questions. Your answers will be a summary of the text.

- Take notes by turning headings and subheadings into main ideas. You might use a chart like the following.

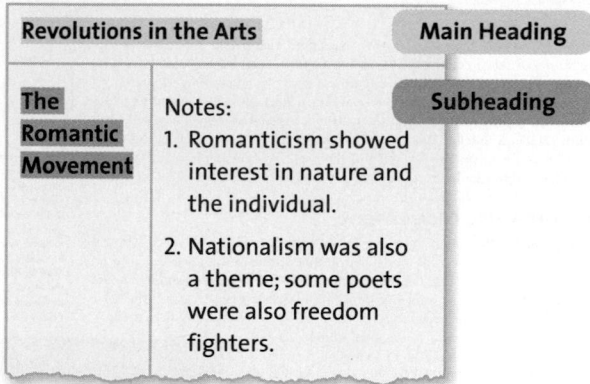

2.3 TURNING TEXT HEADINGS INTO OUTLINE ENTRIES

You can also use text features to take notes in outline form. The following outline shows how one student used text headings from the sample page on page R3. Study the outline and use the strategies that follow to create an outline based on text features.

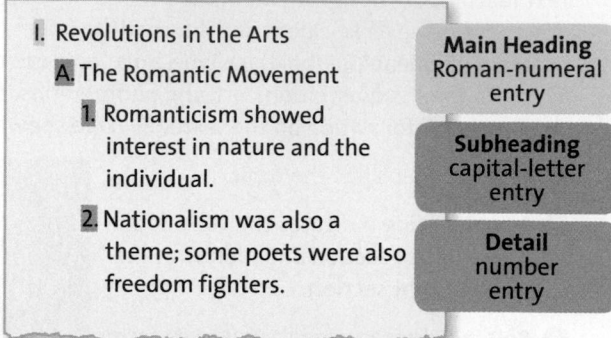

Strategies for Using Text Headings

- Preview the headings and subheadings in the text to get an idea of what different kinds there are and what their positions might be in an outline.

- Be consistent. Note that subheadings that are the same size and color should be used consistently in Roman-numeral or capital-letter entries in the outline. If you decide that a chapter heading should appear with a Roman numeral, then that's the level at which all other chapter headings should appear.

- Write the headings and subheadings that you will use as your Roman-numeral and capital-letter entries first. As you read, fill in numbered details from the text under the headings and subheadings in your outline.

PRACTICE AND APPLY

Find a suitable chapter in one of your textbooks, then, using its text features, take notes on the chapter in outline form.

Preview the subheadings in the text to get an idea of the different kinds. Write the headings and subheadings you are using as your Roman-numeral and capital-letter entries first. Then fill in the details.

2.4 GRAPHIC AIDS

Information is communicated not only with words but also with graphic aids. **Graphic aids** are visual representations of verbal statements. They can be charts, webs, diagrams, graphs, photographs, or other visual representations of information. Graphic aids usually make complex information easier to understand. For that reason, graphic aids are often used to organize, simplify, and summarize information for easy reference.

Graphs

Graphs are used to illustrate statistical information. A **graph** is a drawing that shows the relative values of numerical quantities. Different kinds of graphs are used to show different numerical relationships.

Strategies for Reading

Ⓐ Read the title.

Ⓑ Find out what is being represented or measured.

Ⓒ In a circle graph, compare the sizes of the parts.

Ⓓ In a line graph, study the slant of the line. The steeper the line, the faster the rate of change.

Ⓔ In a bar graph, compare the lengths of the bars.

A **circle graph,** or **pie graph,** shows the relationships of parts to a whole. The entire circle equals 100 percent. The parts of the circle represent percentages of the whole.

MODEL: CIRCLE GRAPH

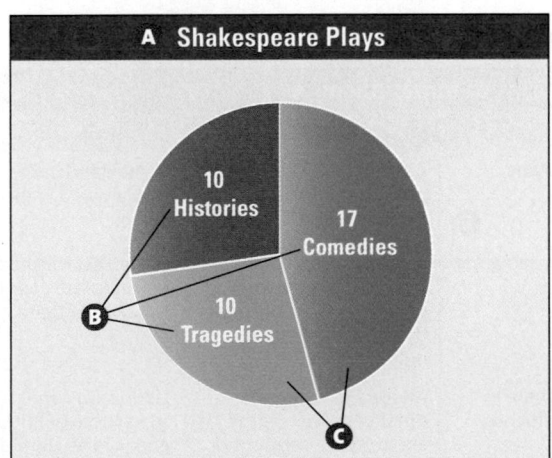

Line graphs show changes in numerical quantities over time and are effective in presenting trends, such as unemployment rates, production and consumption rates, and the like. A line graph is made on a grid. Here, the vertical axis indicates the amount of cotton consumption, and the horizontal axis shows years. Points on the graph indicate data. The lines that connect the points indicate the trends or patterns.

MODEL: LINE GRAPH

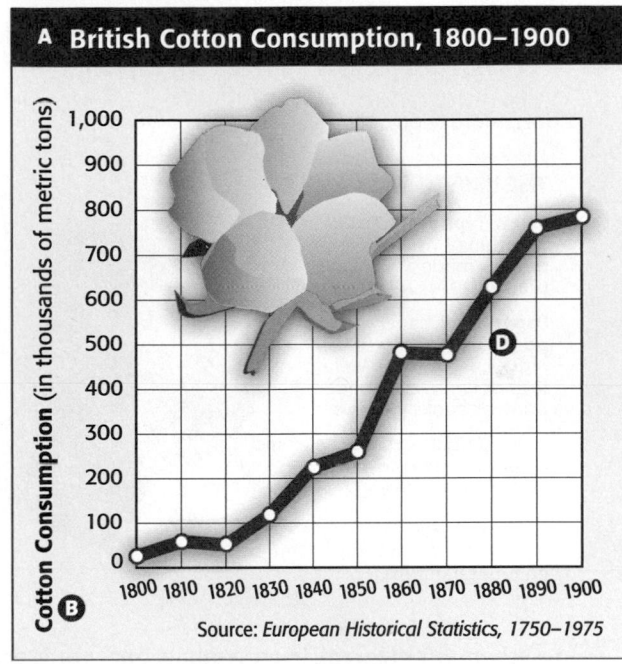

In a **bar graph,** vertical or horizontal bars are used to show or compare categories of information. The lengths of the bars typically correspond to quantities.

MODEL: BAR GRAPH

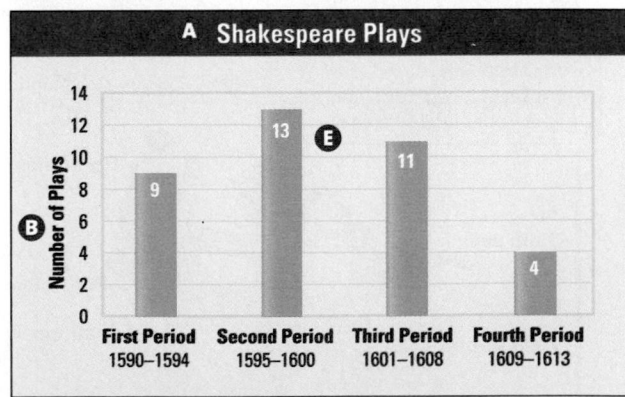

WATCH OUT! Evaluate carefully the information presented in graphs. For example, circle graphs show major factors and differences well but tend to minimize smaller factors and differences.

Diagrams

A **diagram** is a drawing that shows how something works or how its parts relate to one another.

A **picture diagram** is a picture or drawing of the subject being discussed.

Strategies for Reading

A Read the title.

B Read each label and look at the part it identifies.

C Follow any arrows or numbers that show the order of steps in a process, and read any captions.

MODEL: PICTURE DIAGRAM

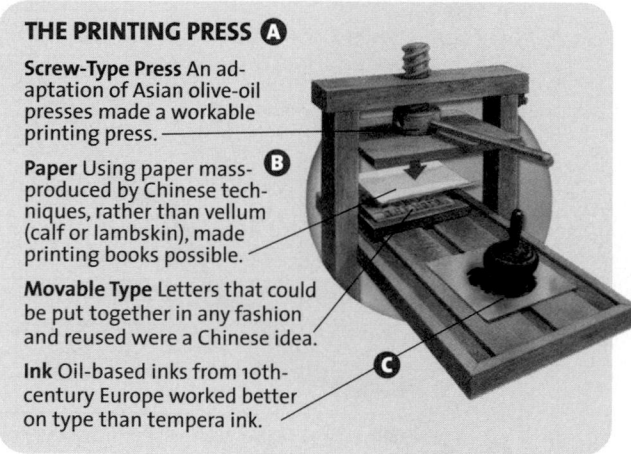

THE PRINTING PRESS **A**

Screw-Type Press An adaptation of Asian olive-oil presses made a workable printing press.

Paper **B** Using paper mass-produced by Chinese techniques, rather than vellum (calf or lambskin), made printing books possible.

Movable Type Letters that could be put together in any fashion and reused were a Chinese idea.

Ink Oil-based inks from 10th-century Europe worked better on type than tempera ink.

In a **schematic diagram,** lines, symbols, and words are used to help readers visualize processes or objects they wouldn't normally be able to see.

MODEL: SCHEMATIC DIAGRAM

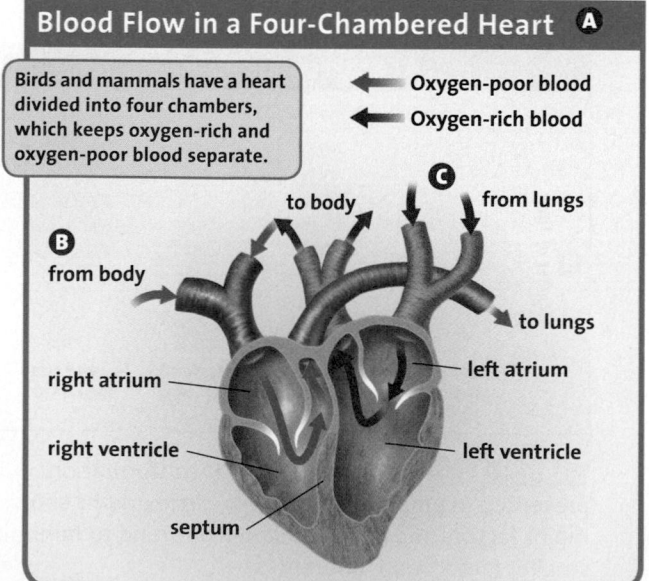

Blood Flow in a Four-Chambered Heart **A**

Birds and mammals have a heart divided into four chambers, which keeps oxygen-rich and oxygen-poor blood separate.

◀ Oxygen-poor blood
◀ Oxygen-rich blood

to body   **C**   from lungs

B from body

to lungs

right atrium   left atrium

right ventricle   left ventricle

septum

Charts and Tables

A **chart** presents information, shows a process, or makes comparisons, usually in rows or columns. A **table** is a specific type of chart that presents a collection of facts in rows and columns and shows how the facts relate to one another.

Strategies for Reading

A Read the title to learn what information the chart or table covers.

B Study column headings and row labels to determine the categories of information presented.

C Look down columns and across rows to find specific information.

MODEL: CHART

A The Development of England and France

England	France **B**
• William the Conqueror, duke of Normandy, invades England in 1066.	• Hugh Capet establishes Capetian Dynasty in 987, which rules until 1328.
• Henry II (ruled 1154–1189) introduces use of the jury in English courts.	• Philip II (ruled 1180–1223) increases the territory of France.
• Under pressure from his nobles, King John agrees to Magna Carta in 1215.	• Louis IX (ruled 1226–1270) strengthens France's central government.
• Edward I calls Model Parliament in 1295.	• Philip IV (ruled 1285–1314) adds Third Estate to Estates-General.

MODEL: TABLE

Forms of Imperialism **A**

Form	**B** Definition	Example
Colony	A country or a territory governed internally by a foreign power	Somaliland in East Africa was a French colony.
Protectorate	A country or a territory that has its own internal government but is under the control of an outside power	Britain established a protectorate over the Niger River delta.
Sphere of Influence	An area in which an outside power claims exclusive investment or trading privileges	Liberia was under the sphere of influence of the United States.
Economic Imperialism	The control of an independent but less-developed country by private business interests rather than other governments	The Dole Fruit company controlled the pineapple trade in Hawaii.

Maps

A **map** visually represents a geographic region, such as a state or a country. It provides information about areas through lines, colors, shapes, and symbols. There are different kinds of maps.

- **Political maps** show political features, such as national borders, states and capitols, and population demographics.
- **Physical maps** show the landforms in areas.
- **Road or travel maps** show streets, roads, and highways.
- **Thematic maps** show information on a specific topic, such as climate, natural resources, movements of people, or major battles in a war.

Strategies for Reading

Ⓐ Read the title to find out what kind of map it is.

Ⓑ Read the labels to get an overall sense of what the map shows.

Ⓒ Look at the **key** or **legend** to find out what the symbols and colors on the map stand for.

Ⓓ If there is a smaller **locator map**, or inset map that shows the geographic context of the main map, use it to understand the geographical relationship of the map's subject and the surrounding area.

MODEL: POLITICAL MAP

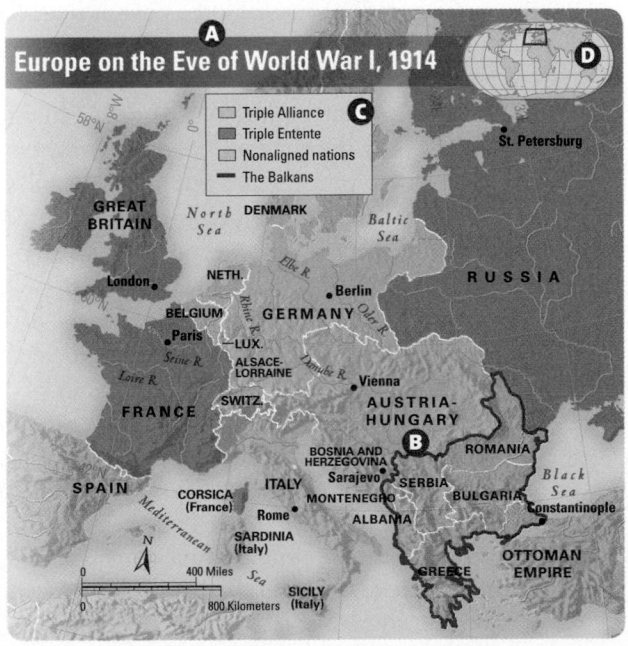

MODEL: THEMATIC MAP

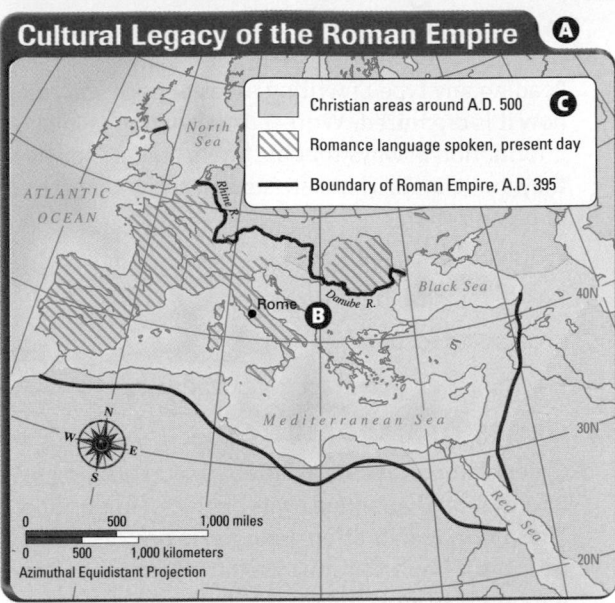

PRACTICE AND APPLY

Use the graphic aids on pages R5–R7 to answer the following questions:

1. According to the circle graph, in what genre did Shakespeare write most prolifically?

2. According to the line graph, how many metric tons of cotton were used in 1860?

3. According to the bar graph, in what artistic period was Shakespeare least prolific?

4. Where is the paper inserted in the printing press, according to the diagram?

5. According to the schematic diagram, blood from the lungs enters which chamber first? From which chamber does oxygen-rich blood exit to the body?

6. According to the chart, in what year and by whom was agreement reached on the Magna Carta?

7. Refer to the table to find the form of imperialism in which an interest is controlled by business rather than government.

8. Use the key with the political map to determine which countries were part of the Balkans in 1914.

9. According to the thematic map, did the Roman Empire extend north of the Rhine River in continental Europe?

3 Reading Informational Texts: Patterns of Organization

Reading any type of writing is easier once you recognize how it is organized. Writers usually arrange ideas and information in ways that best help readers see how they are related. There are several common patterns of organization:

- order of importance
- chronological order
- cause-effect organization
- compare-and-contrast organization

3.1 ORDER OF IMPORTANCE

Order of importance is a pattern of organization in which information is arranged by its degree of importance. The information is often arranged in one of two ways: from **most important to least important** or from **least important to most important.** In the first way, the most important quality, characteristic, or fact is presented at the beginning of the text, and the remaining details are presented in an order ending with the least significant. The second pattern is the reverse: the text builds from the less important elements to the most important one at the conclusion. Order of importance is frequently used in persuasive writing.

Strategies for Reading

- To identify order of importance in a piece of writing, skim the text to see if it moves from items of greater importance to items of lesser importance, or the reverse.

- Next, read the text carefully. Look for words and phrases such as *first, second, mainly, more important, less important, least important,* and *most important.* These indicate the relative importance of the ideas and information.

- Identify the topic of the text and what aspect of it is being discussed—its complexity, size, effectiveness, varieties, and so on. Note what the most important fact or idea seems to be.

- If you are having difficulty understanding the topic, try asking *who, what, when, where, why,* and *how* about the ideas or events.

Notice the order of importance of the ideas in the following model.

Subject	Words showing order of importance

MODEL

British Parliament has three divisions of responsibility—making laws, approving taxation, and monitoring actions of the government. Of the three, it is generally agreed that the first, making laws, is the most important.

The process of making laws begins with an idea in the form of a "bill." A bill is introduced to Parliament during the event of a *first reading.* Next, a *second reading* will be granted, after which members of Parliament vote to approve the bill "in principle," which means the bill will be *sent upstairs* to be reviewed by a smaller group of members called the "standing committee." Standing committee members regard the bill in detail, debating and amending as they see fit. Finally, the bill is returned to the floor for a final *third reading,* where it is usually not contested. This process must be completed in both houses of Parliament (House of Commons and House of Lords).

Also of high importance is the function of approving taxation. Parliament is charged with the onerous task of ensuring the government has adequate income. Proposing change in taxation law is the duty of one person—the Chancellor of the Exchequer. The process begins with a budget speech given by the chancellor, and ends when the Commons approves and publishes the bill's details in a finance bill, which is then instituted.

Lastly, the duty of monitoring the government, while a critical measure of checks and balances, is, if only subjectively, of slightly lesser importance than the functions of lawmaking and taxation. Yet, the first hour of each business day in the Commons is devoted to question time, in which members may question ministers on any matters relating to government or lawmaking.

Each of the three primary functions of Parliament relies on several factors. The process is complex, to say the least. Despite degree of importance, without each facet the government would not run smoothly as a whole.

Read each paragraph, and then do the following:

1. Identify whether the order is from most important to least important or from least important to most important.

2. Identify key words and phrases that helped you figure out the order.

3. What is the main idea of this passage? How does its organization help convey that idea?

3.2 CHRONOLOGICAL ORDER

Chronological order is the arrangement of events in their order of occurrence. This type of organization is used in fictional narratives, historical writing, biographies, and autobiographies. To indicate the order of events, writers use words such as *before, after, next,* and *later* and words and phrases that identify specific times of day, days of the week, and dates, such as *the next morning, Tuesday,* and *on July 4, 1776.*

Strategies for Reading

- Look in the text for headings and subheadings that may indicate a chronological pattern of organization. For example, subheadings such as "The Pretext for War" and "The Aftermath of the War" clearly suggest the text is arranged according to time periods.

- Look for words and phrases that identify times, such as *in a year, three hours earlier, in 1871,* and *the next day.*

- Look for words that signal order, such as *first, afterward, then, during,* and *finally,* to see how events or steps are related.

- Note that a paragraph or passage in which ideas and information are arranged chronologically will have several words or phrases that indicate time order, not just one.

- Ask yourself: Are the events in the paragraph or passage presented in time order?

Notice the words and phrases that signal time order in the following model.

MODEL

Henry VIII

Born in 1491, Henry VIII was crowned king of England when he was 18 years old. He was a devout Catholic, but his politics soon clashed with his religion.

Henry's father had become king after a long civil war. Henry was afraid that a similar war might start if he died without a son to take over the throne. The history of England during his reign became the bloody story of his need for a son.

Henry and his wife Catherine of Aragon had one living child—a daughter, Mary, born in 1516. However, a woman had never successfully claimed the English throne. By 1529, Catherine was 44 and Henry was convinced that she would have no more children. He wanted to divorce her and marry a younger woman, but Church law did not permit divorce. Henry asked the pope to annul his marriage—in other words, declare that it had never existed. The pope refused.

Henry then decided to take matters into his own hands. Later in 1529, he asked Parliament to pass laws to end the pope's power in England. Four years later, he secretly married Anne Boleyn, and Parliament voted to make his divorce from his first wife legal. But Henry was not satisfied and wanted to break completely with the pope. In 1534, Parliament passed the Act of Supremacy, which made the king the official head of the Church of England.

Although Henry had turned the country inside out in his attempt to have a son, Anne Boleyn gave birth to a daughter. Following the birth, Henry had Anne imprisoned in the Tower of London. In 1536, he had her beheaded.

Henry did not get his wish for a son until his third wife, Jane Seymour, gave birth to Edward. Jane died in childbirth. In 1540, Henry married his fourth wife but quickly divorced her to marry his fifth wife, Catherine Howard. However, the king soon found out that Catherine had had affairs before their marriage, and consequently, he had her beheaded in 1542. Henry's sixth wife survived her husband, who died in 1547 at the age of 56.

Event

Time phrases

Order words and phrases

Refer to the preceding model to do the following:

1. List at least six of the order and time words used in the model. Do not include those that have been identified for you.

2. Draw a timeline beginning with Henry's birth in 1491 and ending with his death in 1547. Include each event mentioned in the model.

3.3 CAUSE-EFFECT ORGANIZATION

Cause-effect organization is a pattern of organization that establishes causal relationships between events, ideas, and trends. Cause-effect relationships may be directly stated or merely implied by the order in which the information is presented. Writers often use the cause-effect pattern in historical and scientific writing. Cause-effect relationships may take several forms.

One cause with one effect

One cause with multiple effects

Multiple causes with a single effect

A chain of causes and effects

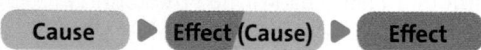

Strategies for Reading

- Look for headings and subheadings that indicate or suggest a cause-effect pattern of organization, such as "How the Printing Press Changed the World."
- To find the effect or effects, read to answer the question, What happened?
- To find the cause or causes, read to answer the question, Why did it happen?
- Look for words and phrases that help you identify specific relationships between events, such as *because, since, so, had the effect of, led to, as a result, resulted in, for that reason, due to, therefore, if . . . then,* and *consequently*.
- Evaluate each cause-effect relationship. Do not assume that because one event happened before another, the first event caused the second event.
- Use graphic organizers like the diagrams shown to record cause-effect relationships as you read.

Notice the words that signal causes and effects in the following model.

MODEL

A Turning Point in England's History

The Norman invasion of 1066 turned the tide of English history. In October of 1066, William the Conqueror, the duke of Normandy, successfully invaded England and defeated Harold—who had a claim to the throne—at the Battle of Hastings. Known as the Norman Conquest, William's sound defeat of the Anglo-Saxon forces ushered in the Anglo-Norman age and brought changes to England that altered its course forever.

One significant change occurred in the language. With the influx of the Norman people, the Latin-based Anglo-Norman language was introduced and began to replace the Germanic Anglo-Saxon speech of England. The language soon became dominant and remained so for nearly 300 years. Its influence is still felt today, as it is the basis of today's English language.

Another result of William's rule was the disappearance of English aristocracy. The ruling class was all but

Causes

Effect that in turn becomes a cause

Signal words and phrases

obliterated after Normans seized control of the Church of England. And, at the behest of William, formerly English-held lands were confiscated. As king, William was in the favorable position of having this lavish expanse of confiscated land, and he parceled it out generously to his supporters.

One thing the new "landowners" didn't alter, but instead dramatically improved upon, was the organizational system of territories. The Anglo-Saxons developed a centralized shire (or county) system in which small areas of land were run by "shire reeves," or sheriffs. The success of the system eventually led to the first organized census. Census taking soon resulted in the implementation of an effective system of taxation. And taxation, of course, led to growing revenue, power, and solvency for the kingdom.

In addition to affecting language and land ownership and introducing taxation, Norman rule also began a long-standing rivalry between France and England, of which there is still evidence today.

PRACTICE AND APPLY

Refer to the preceding model to do the following:

1. Create a graphic organizer using the "one cause with multiple effects" pattern on page R10 to list and illustrate the cause-and-effect relationships described in the model.

2. List the chain of causes and effects in the second to last paragraph.

3. List words and phrases the writer uses to signal cause and effect throughout the model.

3.4 COMPARE-AND-CONTRAST ORGANIZATION

Compare-and-contrast organization is a pattern of organization that serves as a framework for examining similarities and differences in two or more subjects. A writer may use this pattern of organization to analyze two or more subjects, such as characters or literary periods, in terms of their important points or characteristics. These points or characteristics are called points of comparison. The compare-and-contrast pattern of organization may be developed in either of two ways.

Point-by-point organization—The writer discusses one point of comparison for each subject, then goes on to the next point.

Subject-by-subject organization—The writer covers all points of comparison for one subject and then all points of comparison for the next subject.

Strategies for Reading

- Look in the text for headings, subheadings, and sentences that may suggest a compare-and-contrast pattern of organization, such as "*The Spectator* and *The Tatler:* Two Classic British Periodicals." These will help you identify where similarities and differences are addressed.

- To find similarities, look for words and phrases such as *like, similarly, both, also,* and *in the same way.*

- To find differences, look for words and phrases such as *unlike, but, on the other hand, in contrast,* and *however.*

- Use a graphic organizer, such as a Venn diagram or a compare-and-contrast chart, to record points of comparison and similarities and differences.

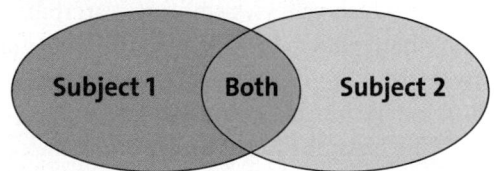

	Subject 1	Subject 2
Point 1		
Point 2		
Point 3		

Read the following models. As you read, use the signal words and phrases to identify the similarities and differences between the subjects and how the details

MODEL 1
Raleigh's Response to Marlowe

During the Renaissance, many poets expressed their thoughts and feelings in a type of poem called a pastoral. Pastorals paint a romantic picture of shepherds and their lives in the country. Many pastorals are about love.

One pastoral written by Christopher Marlowe, "The Passionate Shepherd to His Love," became very famous in 16th-century England. In fact, it became so famous that many poets wrote responses to it. One of these responses was Sir Walter Raleigh's pastoral "The Nymph's Reply to the Shepherd." These two poems have both similarities and differences.

Both poems are pastorals. They are set in the country and deal with love. They also have similar structures. Each has six stanzas with four lines. In each stanza, lines one and two rhyme, and lines three and four rhyme. The poems even repeat the same rhyming words—*move* and *love*.

However, the two poems evoke very different moods. "The Passionate Shepherd to His Love" creates a very romantic scene. The shepherd talks about the beauty of nature—lush valleys, tumbling waterfalls, and singing birds. He offers his love colorful, sweet-smelling flowers, soft wool dresses, and jewels. It's almost too good to be true.

"The Nymph's Reply to the Shepherd," however, is not at all romantic. The nymph doesn't focus on the beauty of the world, but rather on the passage of time, which destroys that beauty. She points out that "flowers do fade" and "rocks grow cold," and that love "is fancy's spring, but sorrow's fall." She mocks the love-struck shepherd in Marlowe's poem and concludes that love is more or less a silly waste of time.

Though the two poems are similar in form, they are very different in content.

Subjects

Comparison words

Contrast words and phrases

MODEL 2
Shelley and Heine: Contemporary Poets

The English romantic poet Percy Bysshe Shelley and the German romantic poet Heinrich Heine lived during the same age and were both passionate about social change. Yet no two people could have had more distinct beginnings.

Percy Bysshe Shelley (1792–1822) was born into an aristocratic and wealthy family in Sussex, England, and sent away to boarding school at the age of ten. As an adolescent, Shelley rejected the institutions of "normal" society. As a young man, he traveled to Scotland and Ireland, distributing pamphlets and raging against political injustice. When his scandalous writing and behavior drew criticism, he began to view himself as an outcast and left England for Italy, where he lived out his life. During his later years, he produced some of his best-known work.

In contrast to Shelley, German poet Heinrich Heine (1797–1856) was born to working-class Jewish parents. For financial reasons, he was sent to live with an uncle who eventually put Heinrich through university. Heine became concerned about political and social injustice and explored ideas ranging from forms of socialism to Marxist communism. Like Shelley, Heine endured political disgrace due to his liberal sympathies, and he fled to Paris. When he returned to Germany to spread his adopted French revolutionary ideas, German authorities permanently banned him and his written work from the country.

Though both Heine and Shelley came from very different social backgrounds, they shared a rebellious attitude toward society.

Subjects

Contrast words and phrases

Comparison words

PRACTICE AND APPLY

For each model presented here, create a compare-and-contrast chart. In your chart, list the points of comparison in each model, and identify the similarities or differences between each model's subjects.

❹ Reading Informational Texts: Formats

Magazines, newspapers, Web pages, and consumer, public, and workplace documents are all examples of informational materials. To understand and analyze informational texts, pay attention to text features and patterns of organization.

4.1 READING A MAGAZINE ARTICLE

Because people often skim magazines for topics of interest, magazine publishers use devices to attract attention to articles and to highlight key information.

Strategies for Reading

🅐 Read the **title** and other **headings** to find out more about the article's topic and organization.

🅑 Notice whether or not the article has a **byline,** a line naming the author, and make note of the date and source.

🅒 Examine **illustrations, photos,** or other **graphic aids** that visually convey or illustrate additional information, or information from the text.

🅓 Notice any **pull quotes,** or quotations that a publisher has pulled out of the text and displayed to get your attention.

PRACTICE AND APPLY

1. According to the title, what is the main topic of this article?

2. Why might this pull quote grab a reader's attention?

3. How does the picture help you understand the article?

4. Outline the main ideas of this article.

HISTORY

🅐 A Queen's Life

Royal Wives in Renaissance England

🅑 by Marianne Brown

Catherine of Aragon was the first wife of Henry VIII.

The wives of Renaissance kings enjoyed privileges that other women could only dream of. In addition to their more obvious perks—jewels and other luxuries, hundreds of servants—queens often wielded considerable power and influence at court. Yet they could not escape the prevailing view that women were inferior to men. Even a powerful queen was subordinate to her husband, who made all the important family decisions.

In royal households, marriage partners were chosen to increase the king's power at home or create alliances with foreign rulers. A wedding was not a private affair but a matter of great importance to the nation. Kings and queens were often betrothed to each other in childhood, and their marriage negotiations generally took years to complete. For example, Catherine of Aragon, the daughter of Spanish rulers Ferdinand II and Isabella I, was betrothed to Arthur, the son of Henry VII, when she was only three years old.

Most queens came from abroad, so marriage meant being separated forever from family and homeland. After a long and dangerous journey, the young woman would meet her spouse for the first time and be placed in the care of complete strangers. Catherine of Aragon traveled for more than three months before reaching England when she was almost 16. Six months after their wedding, her husband Arthur died, and soon after she was betrothed to his brother, the future Henry VIII. Catherine finally became Henry's wife and Queen of England when Henry took the throne in 1509, eight years after her departure from Spain.

A queen's most important responsibility was to bear male heirs. Failure to do so could have grave consequences for the royal family—and sometimes for the nation. Only one of Catherine's children lived past infancy, a daughter named Mary. Frustrated by his lack of a male heir, Henry eventually annulled his marriage, a decision that led to England's separation from the Roman Catholic Church.

🅓 **"Even a powerful queen was subordinate to her husband. "**

4.2 READING A PUBLIC DOCUMENT

Public documents are functional documents that are written for the public to provide information that is of public interest or concern. These documents are often free. They may be federal, state, or local government documents. They might be speeches or historical documents. They may even be laws, posted warnings, signs, or rules and regulations. The following is a public document that lists parking rules and regulations for a university.

Strategies for Reading

A Look at the **title** on the page to discover what the text is about.

B Note the **source** of the document.

C Sometimes, as in the model shown here, the majority of information is presented in a table. Carefully read the headings of **rows** or **columns** in the table, as well as the corresponding information.

D Pay attention to **notes** and to **asterisks** (*) and their accompanying footnotes. These will help clarify exceptions or exemptions to the rules, or add additional detail.

PRACTICE AND APPLY

Reread the parking policy document and answer the following questions:

1. Describe key points of the university's parking lottery.

2. Where must the sticker be displayed on the vehicle?

3. If students need to accommodate the parking needs of family or friends on the weekends, where should they go to make these arrangements?

4. What is the size of the scooters allowed to park on campus sidewalks?

5. What is the consequence for unpaid parking fines after 30 days?

RULES AND REGULATIONS

MOUNTAIN UNIVERSITY

A **Parking Policies, Procedures, and Guidelines**

All parking is general; there are no reserved or assigned spaces. Due to limited space in our lots, we regret we cannot provide general parking for every student's vehicle. Parking policies are as follows.

Parking Lottery **C**	An annual lottery is held by the Office of Public Safety to allocate 237 parking stickers. University seniors will enter first, followed by juniors, then sophomores. First-year students are not permitted to enter the lottery or have a vehicle on campus.
Sticker Display	All stickers and decals must be displayed in the rear window, lower right side. Vehicles without stickers will be ticketed.
Commuter Parking	Commuter students coming from Danton or beyond must purchase parking stickers ($5) and, with the sticker displayed, may park in the Greenwood lot, Field Study Garage, or Stadium lot. **D**
Weekend Guests	Unless special arrangements have been made,* family and other student guests may use yellow-lined parking spaces in all campus lots on weekends, from 5 P.M. Friday to 7 A.M. Monday.
Motorized Bike Parking	Motorized bikes or scooters under 50cc are allowed to park on campus sidewalks M–F from 7 A.M. to 9:00 P.M., and should be securely locked. Larger scooters and motorcycles must have a parking sticker and use designated lots.
Violations	Vehicles found in violation of these policies will be issued citations of $20, payable in the Student Union. After 30 days, unpaid parking tickets will result in revoked library privileges and the withholding of transcripts and final grades.

D * Special arrangements must be made in the Campus Building, where the student must obtain a temporary decal.

B

MOUNTAIN UNIVERSITY	511 University Circle	Range, CO 80695

4.3 READING A CONSUMER DOCUMENT

Consumer documents are functional documents that accompany goods and services. Consumer documents provide information about the use, care, and assembly of products, or contain key information used to evaluate the services of an institution, such as a school or travel service. Some common consumer documents are warranties, manuals, instructions, and guides to services, agencies, and institutions. The following is a page from a guide that features information on colleges across the United States.

Strategies for Reading

Ⓐ Read **title** and **headings** to identify the purpose of the document.

Ⓑ Find **name, address,** and **contact information** to ensure that you have the appropriate guide for your purposes.

Ⓒ Notice any **icons** or **symbols** and check the key for their meanings. These can relay important information about costs, locations, and services.

Ⓓ Study any **subheadings** and the **text** that follows them. This text will offer more in-depth consumer data to help in your evaluation.

PRACTICE AND APPLY

Refer to the college guide to answer the following questions:

1. According to the icon, what kind of campus does Mountain University have?

2. What does the computer icon indicate?

3. Does Mountain University welcome international students? Where is this information found?

4. What types of on-campus housing does Mountain University offer?

5. Is this document easy to read and understand? Explain why or why not.

GUIDE TO COLLEGES

COLORADO

CONTACT: **Ⓑ**
511 University Circle
Range, CO 80695
(303) 555-8179
www.mountainu.edu
or e-mail admission@mntu.edu

Ⓒ

Ⓐ

Mountain University Features & Facts	
• Public, four-year university	• 70% of applicants admitted
• 4,232 undergraduates	• Mid 50% SAT 1050; Mid 50% ACT 23
• 2,196 women, 2,036 men	• Financial aid available

Ⓓ
Mission Statement: The mission of Mountain University is to provide educational opportunities that assist students with clarification and pursuance of educational and professional goals. The university is committed to fostering a vital learning environment with equal opportunity for all students, regardless of race, political or religious affiliation, or country or state of origin.

Student Life: 67% of undergraduates are from Colorado. Others are from 34 states and 19 foreign countries. The average age of freshman is 18 and the average age of all undergraduates is 20. About 8% do not continue beyond their first year.

Housing: 60% of students can be accommodated in on-campus housing, which includes single-sex and coed dormitories. On-campus housing is guaranteed for all four years. 45% of students live on campus.

Ⓒ

KEY TO SYMBOLS

e-application available	⚑ surburban campus
⑤ inexpensive	⑪ urban campus
⑤⑤ moderately expensive	⚑ rural campus
⑤⑤⑤ very expensive	

4.4 READING AN APPLICATION

Applications are forms that are used to gather information from someone who is applying for a position, admission, services, a license, or membership. These functional documents often include a brief set of instructions such as mailing information, questions to be answered, and boxes or blanks to fill in with information you provide.

Strategies for Reading

Ⓐ Read the **title** of the form to make sure it is the correct form for you.

Ⓑ Look for boldfaced, italicized, and underlined words. These may signal important information such as due dates, required materials, or fees.

Ⓒ Some applications, such as a college application, require attachments. Be sure to submit any additional required materials, enclosing them with your application.

Ⓓ Note any **terms,** or conditions that you must agree to, and the place for your **signature,** usually located at the end of the application. In order for your application to be valid and complete, you will have to agree to the terms listed. Agreement is indicated by signing the document.

PRACTICE AND APPLY

Refer to the application to answer the following questions:

1. Can a student who is planning to enter Mountain University in the spring term use this form? Why or why not?

2. Describe what is required in applying for a scholarship.

3. What materials need to be submitted in addition to the fee and application?

4. According to the application, what could make you ineligible for admission to Mountain University?

5. Using the "Guide to Colleges" on page R15, verify that the address for Mountain University is accurate.

MOUNTAIN UNIVERSITY

Ⓐ APPLICATION FOR UNDERGRADUATE ADMISSION

APPLICATION INSTRUCTIONS   **Ⓑ**

This application is for students who will enter Mountain University in <u>the fall of the current year</u>. Send completed applications by regular or overnight mail to:

Mountain University Office of Undergraduate Admissions
511 University Circle
Range, CO 80695
(303) 555-8179

PLEASE NOTE: Your admissions application *must be received by April 1* if you wish to apply for the Mountain University merit scholarships. A separate scholarship application is also required.

Complete the Mountain University admissions application form (including your essay). There is a *$25 nonrefundable application fee* payable to Mountain University.

Arrange to have official transcripts sent to the Undergraduate Office. Your most recent high school transcript and your ACT or SAT test results are *required*.

Submit two letters of recommendation from an instructor or other individual who is qualified to comment on your college potential.

Please type the application or complete it in blue or black ink.

AUTOBIOGRAPHICAL INFORMATION

Social Security Number _____–_____–_____

Last Name _____ First Name _____

Mailing Address _____

City _____ State _____ Zip _____

Phone Number (____) _____

Date of Birth: Month _____ Day _____ Year _____

PERSONAL STATEMENT **Ⓒ**

Please submit an original personal statement of 1,500 words or less describing what your goals are in the coming year, the next five years, and the next ten years.

Ⓓ

I understand that providing false information may make me ineligible for admission to Mountain University. I agree to abide by the regulations of Mountain University as set forth in its current catalog and other official publications. I attest that all information I have supplied in this application and accompanying documentation is true and valid.

Applicant's Signature _____

Date Submitted _____

4.5 READING A WORKPLACE DOCUMENT

Workplace documents are materials that are produced or used within a workplace, usually to aid in the functioning of a business. These documents include meeting minutes, sales reports, company policy statements, organizational charts, and operating procedures. Workplace documents also include memos, business letters, job applications, and résumés.

Strategies for Reading

A Read a workplace document slowly and carefully, as it may contain **details** that should not be overlooked.

B Notice the contact information for the creator of the document. You will need this information to contact someone if you need to clear up anything that you don't understand.

C Note whether there are additional materials for you to consider and if a response is required.

PRACTICE AND APPLY

Refer to both workplace documents to answer the following questions:

1. Why is this letter from Tang Lao considered a workplace document?

2. According to the details in Tang Lao's letter, what action is he requesting of Dean Ripple?

3. What text features does the memo writer use to get his message across clearly?

4. What actions is Ms. Marion expected to take?

5. Verify that the university address is correct by comparing it to the address provided on the application on page R16.

BUSINESS LETTER

B Tang Lao
4311 North Central Place
Freehaven, CO 1234
(720) 555-1454

June 11, 2011 **A**

Dr. Harmon Ripple, Dean of the College of Sciences
Mountain University
511 University Circle
Range, CO 80695

Dear Dean Ripple,
In a recent conversation with your administrative assistant, Litha Marion, I was asked to contact you directly in pursuance of a faculty position with your university. I have recently moved to Colorado from Minnesota.

I am originally from Cambodia and was sponsored to come to Minnesota in 1976. I attended the University of Minnesota Twin Cities campus, and graduated with honors from the post-graduate program in the College of Biological Sciences.

I wish to share my knowledge and experience with students at your school. Attached, you will find my application and résumé of academic and teaching experience. Thank you for considering me for this position. **C**

Sincerely,
Tang Lao

MEMO

To: Litha Marion
From: Dean Ripple
Re: Hiring new faculty
Date: June 20, 2011

Litha, we have considered Tang Lao's application, résumé, and credentials, and are honored to welcome him to a faculty position at Mountain College. Please draft a letter of congratulations to inform him of our decision, and include the following:

B • welcome packet
 • invitation to new faculty meeting
 • university guidelines and policies manual
 • class schedule and descriptions

Thank you.

4.6 READING ELECTRONIC TEXT

Electronic text is any text that is in a form that a computer can store and display on a screen. Electronic text can be part of Web pages, CD-ROMs, search engines, and documents that you create with your computer software. Like books, Web pages often provide aids for finding information. However, each Web page is designed differently, and information is not in the same location on each page. It is important to know the functions of different parts of a Web page so that you can easily find the information you want.

Strategies for Reading

Ⓐ Look at the **title** of a page to determine what topics it covers.

Ⓑ For an online source, such as a Web page or a search engine, note the **Web address,** known as a **URL** (Uniform Resource Locator) in case you need to return to the page later or cite it as a source.

Ⓒ Look for the **menu options,** or navigation options that allow you to navigate through the site's main categories and pages. These options are **links** to other pages providing more in-depth information on the topic listed.

Ⓓ Read **introductory text** to get a sense of the site's subject matter and purpose.

Ⓔ Use **hyperlinks** to get to other pages. Hyperlinks may lead to pages listed in the menu options or to other Web sites related in subject matter. Hyperlinks are often highlighted or underlined in a contrasting color.

Ⓕ Look for **graphic aids,** such as photos, illustrations, or animation, that will provide you with more information about the site's topic(s).

WEB PAGE

PRACTICE AND APPLY

Refer to the Web page on this page to answer the following questions:

1. What is the topic of this site?

2. If you were looking for information on Mansfield's writing, which links or hyperlinks would you use?

3. Who has produced this Web site?

4. Verify the information on Katherine Mansfield presented on this Web page by consulting a reference source, such as an encyclopedia, or a government document.

5 Reading Persuasive Texts

5.1 ANALYZING AN ARGUMENT

An **argument** expresses a position on an issue or problem and supports it with reasons and evidence. Being able to analyze and evaluate arguments will help you distinguish between claims you should accept and those you should not. A sound argument should appeal strictly to reason. However, arguments are often used in texts that also contain other types of persuasive devices. An argument includes the following elements:

- A **claim** is the writer's position on an issue or problem.

- **Support** is any material that serves to prove a claim. In an argument, support usually consists of reasons and evidence.

- **Reasons** are declarations made to justify an action, decision, or belief—for example, "You should sleep on a good mattress in order *to avoid spinal problems.*"

- **Evidence** consists of the specific references, quotations, facts, examples, and opinions that support a claim. Evidence may also consist of statistics, reports of personal experience, or the views of experts.

- A **counterargument** is an argument made to oppose another argument. A good argument anticipates the opposition's objections and provides counterarguments to disprove or answer them.

Claim	Winston Churchill's contribution to victory in World War II was significant.
Reason	Churchill's strong leadership and persuasive rhetoric raised the morale of British citizens and soldiers.
Evidence	British citizens and soldiers never let London fall to the Germans, and British soldiers played a key role in the defeat of Germany.
Counterargument	His ideas seemed impractical and he was unpopular with much of England, but he succeeded in leading Britain to victory.

PRACTICE AND APPLY

Use a chart like the one shown to identify the claim, reasons, evidence, and counterargument in the following article.

Should Soft Drinks Be Banned from Schools?

A new substance has joined the list of those banned on school grounds: soft drinks. As the number of obese teenagers rises, there is a growing movement to limit the products of empty calories that are available in school vending machines. Los Angeles has banned the sale of soft drinks on the district's high school and elementary campuses. Other districts are debating whether to implement similar policies. Activists who favor the soda ban say schools must make a choice between student health and vending machine revenues.

Advocates of banning sodas point out that a typical can of soda has at least 10 teaspoons of sugar. Its 140 calories contain no vitamins, minerals, fiber, or other nutritional value. Poor eating habits contribute to teenage obesity. Dr. Jonathan E. Fielding, director of public health for Los Angeles County, describes obesity as a fast-growing, chronic disease that is "entirely preventable."

However, not everyone agrees that carbonated soft drinks are a hazard to students' health. A Georgetown University study found no link between obesity and the soda consumption of 12- to 16-year-olds. Surgeon General David Satcher, while concerned about unhealthy eating habits, considers lack of physical activity another important cause of excess weight.

Some schools are responding to the problem by expanding instead of restricting students' choices. A pilot program that offered Metro Detroit students a choice of pop or flavored milk was so successful that the district installed 80 more milk machines. . . . Other schools offer students a selection of juice-based drinks.

Stakes on both sides of the question are high: student health versus the $750 million that students put into school vending machines each year. The evidence currently available does not prove that the availability of soda pop in school vending machines causes obesity. Until that evidence is provided, I believe banning pop is an extreme solution. Instead, schools should keep both students and the budget healthy by offering both soft drinks and healthier alternatives.

5.2 RECOGNIZING PERSUASIVE TECHNIQUES

Persuasive texts typically rely on more than just the logical appeal of an argument to be convincing. They also rely on ethical and emotional appeals, as well as other **persuasive techniques**—devices that can sway you to adopt a position or take an action.

The chart shown here explains several of these techniques. Learn to recognize them, and you will be less likely to be influenced by them.

Persuasive Technique	Example
Appeals by Association	
Bandwagon Appeal Suggests that a person should believe or do something because "everyone else" does	Don't be the last person on earth to use High Speed TurboWhip for your Internet needs.
Testimonial Relies on endorsements from well-known people or satisfied customers	Seven top chefs from Sonoma County recommend Fivar Cutlery— why not feature it at your next dinner party?
Snob Appeal Taps into people's desire to be special or part of an elite group	Diamondshire Hotels provide luxurious accommodations in a premier setting.
Transfer Connnects a product, candidate, or cause with a positive emotion or idea	Volunteer with Elderly Help and go home happy— you've touched the life of someone special.
Appeal to Loyalty Relies on people's affiliation with a particular group	Buy a bumper sticker from the Skooner Seahawks today and show your true team spirit!
Emotional Appeals	
Appeals to Pity, Fear, or Vanity Use strong feelings, rather than facts, to persuade	Help! Bear Habitat needs refurbishing. Without your donation, polar bears at Cityside Zoo risk deadly heat stroke.
Word Choice	
Glittering Generality Makes a generalization that includes a word or phrase with positive connotations, such as *freedom* or *action-packed*, to promote a product or idea.	Elect E. Willmington and preserve dignity and honor.

PRACTICE AND APPLY

Identify the persuasive techniques used in the model.

Our city high schools are failing, and they need your help. Half of this city's freshmen drop out before their senior prom. Inner-city students need quality education and well-trained teachers. Your signature on our petition can make it happen and will show your loyalty to our city. Our petition demands re-evaluation of the city's fiscal priorities and a promise that more funds will be allocated for teachers next year. Sign our petition and you'll be in good company. Respected elected officials such as Alderman Donna Jones and County Clerk Tony Fitzharmon support this effort 100 percent. By signing, you will be on the frontline of a most important battle—the battle for the minds of our youth.

5.3 ANALYZING LOGIC AND REASONING

When you evaluate the credibility of an argument, you need to look closely at the writer's logic and reasoning. To do this, it is helpful to identify the type of reasoning the writer is using.

The Inductive Mode of Reasoning

When a writer leads from specific evidence to a general principle or generalization, that writer is using **inductive reasoning** to make **inferences**, or logical assumptions, and draw conclusions from them. Here is an example of inductive reasoning.

The Inductive Mode of Reasoning

SPECIFIC FACTS

Fact 1 *Oliver Twist* is about the hard life of a young orphan boy.

Fact 2 *Great Expectations* is about a poor young man who is given money to become a gentleman.

Fact 3 *David Copperfield* is about a young man's growth into adulthood.

GENERALIZATION

One of Charles Dickens's main themes is that of a young person matures, often under challenging circumstances, into adulthood.

Strategies for Determining the Soundness of Inductive Arguments

Ask yourself the following questions to evaluate an inductive argument:

- **Is the evidence valid and does it provide sufficient support for the conclusion?** Inaccurate facts lead to inaccurate conclusions. Make sure all facts are accurate.

- **Does the conclusion follow logically from the evidence?** Make sure the writer has used sound reasons—those that can be proved—as a basis for the conclusion and has avoided logical fallacies, such as circular reasoning and oversimplification.

- **Is the evidence drawn from a large enough sample?** Even though there are only three facts listed above, the sample is large enough to support the claim. By qualifying the generalization with words such as *sometimes*, *some*, or *many*, the writer indicates that the generalization is limited to a specific group.

The Deductive Mode of Reasoning

When a writer arrives at a conclusion by applying a general principle to a specific situation, the writer is using **deductive reasoning** to make inferences and draw conclusions. Here's an example.

Practices that harm others should be outlawed.	General principle or premise

Secondhand smoke has been proven to harm others.	Specific situation

Cigarette smoking in public should be outlawed.	Specific conclusion

Strategies for Determining the Soundness of Deductive Arguments

Ask yourself the following questions to evaluate a deductive argument:

- **Is the general principle stated, or is it implied?** Note that writers often use deductive reasoning in an argument without stating the general principle. They assume readers will understand the principle. You need to identify the writer's implicit assumptions.

- **Is the general principle sound?** Don't assume the general principle is sound. Ask yourself whether it is really true based on the evidence.

- **Is the conclusion valid?** To be valid, a conclusion in a deductive argument must follow logically from the general principle and the specific situation.

The following chart shows two conclusions drawn from the same general principle.

General Principle: All members of the soccer fan club wore red yesterday to support their team.	
Accurate Deduction	**Inaccurate Deduction**
Aida is a member of the soccer fan club; therefore, Aida wore red yesterday.	Clyde wore red yesterday; therefore Clyde is a member of the soccer fan club.

The inference that Clyde must be a member of the soccer fan club because he wore red lead to an inaccurate conclusion; Clyde may have chosen red for another reason.

PRACTICE AND APPLY

Identify the mode of reasoning used in this passage. Determine whether the argument is sound and valid.

Some literary critics believe that numerous works attributed to William Shakespeare may actually have been written by other authors of the time.

Edward de Vere was the 17th earl of Oxford and a contemporary of William Shakespeare's. He was a nobleman in Queen Elizabeth I's court, highly educated and very well traveled. Although de Vere was a writer in his early years, no literary manuscripts exist from later in his life. He seemed to have mysteriously stopped writing.

Sir Francis Bacon, also a contemporary of Shakespeare's, wrote prolifically throughout his life. Experts note that his correspondences, memoirs, and notebooks express "coincidences" and parallels with the life of the Bard.

Another writer close to Shakespeare was poet and dramatist Christopher Marlowe. He was allegedly stabbed to death in a bar fight in 1593, but many believe his death was faked and that he lived a long and secret life as a spy for the queen.

All of these three men had the occasion and the talent to have written a number of plays using the nom de plume of William Shakespeare. Therefore, Shakespeare was not the sole author of the works that bear his name.

Identifying Faulty Reasoning

Sometimes an argument at first appears to make sense, but as you take a closer look at the reasoning, you can see it isn't valid because it is based on a fallacy. A **fallacy** is an error in logic based on inaccurate inferences or invalid assumptions. Learn to recognize these common fallacies.

TYPE OF FALLACY	DEFINITION	EXAMPLE
Circular reasoning	Supporting a statement by simply repeating it in different words	That restaurant is popular **because more people go there than to any other restaurant in town.**
Either/or fallacy	A statement that suggests that there are only two choices available in a situation that really offers more than two options	**Either** you come pick me up **or** I will be stranded here forever.
Oversimplification	An explanation of a complex situation or problem as if it were much simpler than it is	If you make the manager laugh during the interview, **you will get the job.**
Overgeneralization	A generalization that is too broad. You can often recognize overgeneralizations by the use of words such as *all, everyone, every time, anything, no one,* and *none.*	**No one ever** wants to wear a bicycle helmet.
Stereotyping	A dangerous type of overgeneralization. Stereotypes are broad statements about people on the basis of their gender, ethnicity, race, or political, social, professional, or religious group.	**People from big cities** are unfriendly.
Attacking the person, or name-calling	An attempt to discredit an idea by attacking the person or group associated with it. Candidates often engage in name-calling during political campaigns.	The mayor's new program was developed by a **fool.**
Evading the issue	Refuting an objection with arguments and evidence that do not address its central point	Yes, I broke the window, **but then I mowed the lawn—doesn't the lawn look nice?**
Non sequitur	A conclusion that does not follow logically from the "proof" offered to support it. A non sequitur is sometimes used to win an argument by diverting the reader's attention to proof that can't be challenged.	I'm against building the new stadium **because I've lived in this town my whole life.**
False cause	The mistake of assuming that because one event occurred after another event, the first event caused the second one to occur	My brother sang in the shower this morning, **so when he auditioned for the spring musical this afternoon, he got the lead role.**
False analogy	A comparison that doesn't hold up because of a critical difference between the two subjects	If you are unable to understand T. S. Eliot, **you probably won't understand modernism.**
Hasty generalization	A conclusion drawn from too little evidence or from evidence that is biased	My job interview did not go well. **I'll never get a job.**

Look for examples of faulty reasoning in the following argument. Identify each one and explain why you identified it as such.

> Let's address the proposed expansion of our airport. Opponents claim that the land west of the airport is wetlands, and that we can't build on wetlands. Those people are dreamy-eyed do-gooders. Of course you can build on wetlands. Like my father said before me—hard work pays off and you get what you want. We are now competing internationally, so we need to expand in order to be competitive globally. If we expand runways, it will solve all our city's problems.

5.4 EVALUATING PERSUASIVE TEXTS

Learning how to evaluate the credibility of persuasive texts by identifying bias will help you become more selective when doing research and also help you improve your own reasoning and arguing skills. **Bias** is an inclination for or against a particular opinion or viewpoint. A writer may reveal a strongly positive or negative opinion on an issue by presenting only one way of looking at it or by heavily weighting the evidence on one side of the argument. Additionally, the presence of either of the following is often a sign of bias:

Loaded language consists of words with strongly positive or negative connotations that are intended to influence a reader's attitude.

EXAMPLE: *A vote for our candidate is a vote to secure your financial future, to ensure safe streets for your children, and to guarantee prosperity for people of all ages.* (*Secure future, safe for children,* and *guarantee prosperity* are phrases of loaded language with positive connotations.)

Propaganda is any form of communication that is so distorted that it conveys false or misleading information. Many logical fallacies, such as name-calling, the either/or fallacy, and false causes, are often used in propaganda. The following example shows an oversimplification. The writer uses one fact to support a particular point of view but does not reveal another fact that does not support that viewpoint.

EXAMPLE: *Since that new restaurant opened on our block, it is impossible to find a parking place on the street.* (The writer does not include the fact that two new apartment buildings recently opened, adding to the demand for street parking.)

*For more information, see **Identifying Faulty Reasoning**, page R22.*

Strategies for Evaluating Evidence

It is important to have a set of standards by which you can evaluate persuasive texts. Use the questions below to help you critically assess facts and opinions that are presented as evidence.

- **Are the facts presented verifiable?** Facts can be proved by eyewitness accounts, authoritative sources such as encyclopedias and almanacs, experts, or research.

- **Are the claims presented credible?** Any opinions offered should be supported by facts, research, eyewitness accounts, or the opinions of experts on the topic.

- **Is the evidence thorough?** Thorough evidence leaves no reasonable questions unanswered. If a choice is offered, background for making the choice should be provided. If taking a side is called for, all sides of the issue should be presented.

- **Is the evidence biased?** Be alert to evidence that contains loaded language and other signs of bias.

- **Is the evidence authoritative?** The people, groups, or organizations that provided the evidence should have credentials that verify their credibility.

- **Is it important that the evidence be current?** Where timeliness is crucial, as in the areas of medicine and technology, the evidence should reflect the latest developments in the areas.

Read the argument below. Identify the facts, opinions, and elements of bias.

> It is time to end the logging industry's destruction of the world's oldest and largest rain forests. Despite protests from environmentalists and conservationists, nature-hating, big-money interests still pay millions to have pristine forests mowed down, just to make roads! This is so their toxic, diesel-pumping logging trucks can haul cut-up pieces of the world's most precious woodlands to the mills. The worst part is that taxpayers fund the whole process—to the tune of $60 million a year. I don't know about you, but I'm going to make sure my hard-earned money isn't contributing to the destruction of the planet.

Strategies for Evaluating an Argument

Make sure that all or most of the following statements are true:

- The argument presents a claim or thesis.

- The claim is connected to its support by a **general principle**, or assumption, that most readers would readily agree with. Valid general principle: *It is the job of a corporation to provide adequate health benefits to full-time employees.* Invalid general principle: *It is the job of a corporation to ensure its employees are healthy and physically fit.*

- The reasons make sense.

- The reasons are presented in a logical and effective order.

- The claim and all reasons are adequately supported by sound, credible evidence.

- The evidence is adequate, accurate, and appropriate.

- The logic is sound. There are no instances of faulty reasoning.

- The argument adequately anticipates reader concerns and addresses them with counterarguments.

Use the preceding criteria to evaluate the strength of the following editorial.

> This city should submit a bid to host the summer Olympics. The building and development to plan such an event would take years, but it would also create jobs, lower unemployment, and boost the city's economy. We must face facts: either we submit a bid to host the games, or our city will never grow.
>
> Families citywide would be ecstatic to think that talented, famous people from all over the world would be invited to their lovely communities. There's no doubt families would open up their homes to guests from overseas, because they want our city to be considered the friendliest in the United States.
>
> Some people claim that being a host city is not as important as building new schools, so surplus money should go toward education. These antagonists have simply been too lazy to do proper research. Two other U.S. cities that have hosted the games profited immensely, which means our city could put millions of dollars toward education after the games. You wouldn't want to deprive your child the chance to see Olympic athletes in action, would you?
>
> We can't afford not to make the bid—and we can't afford not to win it! If the mayor decides not to put in a bid for our city, he'll be just like every other politician, always making wrong choices. So, write a letter to your alderman today, encouraging a vote for the summer games. Our city will be better for it.

6 Adjusting Reading Rate to Purpose

You may need to change the way you read certain texts in order to understand what you read. To properly adjust the way you read, you need to be aware of what you want to get out of the text you are reading. Once you know your purpose for reading, you can adjust the speed at which you read in response to your purpose and the difficulty of the material.

Determine Your Purpose for Reading

You read different types of materials for different purposes. You may read a novel for enjoyment. You may read a textbook unit to learn a new concept or to master the content for a test. When you read for enjoyment, you naturally read at a pace that is comfortable for you. When you read for information, you need to read material more slowly and thoroughly. When you are being tested on material, you may think you have to read fast, especially if the test is being timed. However, you can actually increase your understanding of the material if you slow down.

Determine Your Reading Rate

The rate at which you read most comfortably is called your **independent reading level.** It is the rate that you use to read materials that you enjoy. To learn to adjust your reading rate to read materials for other purposes, you need to be aware of your independent reading level. You can figure out your reading level by following these steps:

1. Select a passage from a book or story you enjoy.
2. Have a friend or classmate time you as you begin reading the passage silently.
3. Read at the rate that is most comfortable for you.
4. Stop when your friend or classmate tells you one minute has passed.
5. Determine the number of words you read in that minute and write down the number.
6. Repeat the process at least two more times, using different passages.
7. Add the numbers and divide the sum by the number of times your friend timed you. The number you end up with is the average number of words you read per minute—your independent reading rate.

Reading Techniques for Informational Material

Use the following techniques to adapt your reading for informational texts, to prepare for tests, and to better understand what you read:

- **Skimming** is reading quickly to get the general idea of a text. To skim, read the title, headings, graphic aids, highlighted words, and first sentence of each paragraph. In addition, read any introduction, conclusion, or summary. Skimming can be especially useful when taking a test. Before reading a passage, you can skim questions that follow it in order to find out what is expected and better focus on the important ideas in the text.

   When researching a topic, skimming can help you determine whether a source has information that is pertinent to your topic.

- **Scanning** is reading quickly to find a specific piece of information, such as a fact or a definition. When you scan, your eyes sweep across a page, looking for key words that may lead you to the information you want. Use scanning to review for tests and to find answers to questions.

- **Changing pace** is speeding up or slowing down the rate at which you read parts of a particular text. When you come across familiar concepts, you might be able to speed up without misunderstanding them. When you encounter unfamiliar concepts or material presented in an unpredictable way, however, you may need to slow down to process and absorb the information better.

WATCH OUT! Reading too slowly can affect your ability to comprehend what you read. Make sure you aren't just reading one word at a time.

PRACTICE AND APPLY

Find an article in a magazine or textbook. Skim the article. Then answer the following questions:

1. What did you notice about the organization of the article from skimming it?
2. What is the main idea of the article?

Writing is a process, a journey of discovery in which you can explore your thoughts, experiment with ideas, and search for connections. Through writing, you can explore and record your thoughts, feelings, and ideas for yourself alone, or you can communicate them to an audience.

COMMON CORE

Included in this handbook:
W 2, W 3, W 4, W 5, W 6

1 The Writing Process

The writing process consists of the following stages: prewriting, drafting, revising and editing, proofreading, and publishing. These are not stages that you must complete in a set order. Rather, you may return to an earlier stage at any time to improve your writing.

1.1 PREWRITING

In the prewriting stage, you explore what you want to write about, what your purpose for writing is, whom you are writing for, and what form you will use to express your ideas. Ask yourself the following questions to get started.

Topic	• Is my topic assigned, or can I choose it? • What am I interested in writing about?
Purpose	• Am I writing to entertain, to inform, or to persuade—or some combination of these? • What effect do I want to have on my readers?
Audience	• Who is the audience? • What might the audience members already know about my topic? • What about the topic might interest them?
Format	• Which format will work best? Essay? Poem? Speech? Short story? Article? Research paper?

Find Ideas for Writing

Here are some methods for generating topics.

- Browse through magazines, newspapers, and Web sites.

- Start a file of articles to save for future reference.

- With a group, brainstorm as many ideas as you can. Compile your ideas into a list.

- Interview an expert on a particular topic.

- Write down anything that comes into your head.

- Use a cluster map to explore subordinate ideas that relate to a general topic.

Organize Ideas

Once you've chosen a topic, you will need to compile and organize your ideas. If you are writing a description, you may need to gather sensory details. For an essay or a research paper, you may need to record information from different sources. To record notes from sources you read or view, use any or all of these methods:

- **Summarize**—Briefly retell the main ideas of a piece of writing in your own words.

- **Paraphrase**—Restate all or almost all of the information in your own words.

- **Quote**—Record the author's exact words.

Depending on what form your writing takes, you may also need to arrange your ideas in a certain pattern.

*For more information, see the **Writing Handbook,** pages R32–R39.*

1.2 DRAFTING

In the drafting stage, you put your ideas on paper and allow them to develop and change as you write. You don't need to worry about correct grammar and spelling at this stage. There are two ways that you can write a draft:

Discovery drafting is a good approach when you are not quite sure what you think about your subject. You just start writing and let your feelings and ideas lead you in developing the topic.

Planned drafting may work better if you know that your ideas have to be arranged in a certain way, as in a research paper. Try making a writing plan or an informal outline before you begin drafting.

1.3 REVISING AND EDITING

The revising and editing stage allows you to polish your draft and make changes in its content, organization, and style. Use the questions that follow to assess problems and determine what changes would improve your work.

- Does my writing have a **main idea** or central focus? Is my controlling idea clear?

- Have I used **precise** nouns, verbs, and modifiers?

- Have I incorporated **adequate detail** and **evidence?** Where might I include a telling detail, a revealing statistic, or a vivid example?

- Is my writing **unified?** Do all ideas and supporting details pertain to my main idea or advance my thesis?

- Is my writing clear and **coherent?** Is the flow of sentences and paragraphs smooth and logical?

- Have I used a consistent **point of view?**

- Do I need to add **transitional words, phrases,** or **sentences** to clarify relationships among ideas?

- Have I used a **variety of sentence types?** Are the sentences well constructed? What sentences might I combine to improve the rhythm of my writing?

- Have I used a **tone** appropriate for my audience and purpose?

1.4 PROOFREADING

When you are satisfied with your revision, proofread your paper for mistakes in grammar, usage, and mechanics. You may want to do this several times, looking for a different type of mistake each time. Use the following questions to help you correct errors:

- Have I corrected any errors in **subject-verb agreement** and **pronoun-antecedent agreement?**

- Have I double-checked for errors in **confusing word pairs,** such as *it's/its, than/then,* and *too/to?*

- Have I corrected any **run-on sentences** and **sentence fragments?**

- Have I followed rules for **correct capitalization?**

- Have I used **punctuation marks** correctly?

- Have I checked the **spellings of all unfamiliar words** in the dictionary?

TIP If possible, don't begin proofreading just after you've finished writing. Put your work away for at least a few hours. When you return to it, it will be easier for you to identify and correct mistakes.

For more information, see the **Grammar Handbook** *and the* **Vocabulary and Spelling Handbook,** *pages R50–R79.*

Use the proofreading symbols in the chart to mark changes on your draft.

Proofreading Symbols	
∧ Add letters or words.	/ Make a capital letter lowercase.
⊙ Add a period.	¶ Begin a new paragraph.
≡ Capitalize a letter.	↗ Delete letters or words.
⊂ Close up space.	∩ Switch the positions of letters or words.
∧ Add a comma.	

1.5 PUBLISHING AND REFLECTING

Always consider sharing your finished writing with a wider audience. Reflecting on your writing is another good way to finish a project.

Publishing Ideas

- Use a desktop-publishing software program to design and finalize your writing product.

- Post your writing on a Weblog.

- Create a multimedia presentation and share it with classmates.

- Publish your writing in a school newspaper, local newspaper, or literary magazine.

- Present your work orally in a report, speech, reading, or dramatic performance.

Reflecting on Your Writing

Think about your writing process and whether you would like to add what you have written to your writing portfolio. You might attach a note in which you answer questions like these:

- Which parts of the process did I find easiest? Which parts were more difficult?

- What was the biggest problem I faced during the writing process? How did I solve the problem?

- What changes have occurred in my writing style?

- Have I noticed any features in the writing of published authors or my peers that I can apply to my own work?

- What have I learned about the process of writing from this experience?

Writing Online

THINK central

Go to **thinkcentral.com.**
KEYWORD: HML12N-R27

1.6 PEER RESPONSE

Peer response consists of the suggestions and comments you make about the writing of your peers and also the comments and suggestions they make about your writing. You can ask a peer reader for help at any time in the writing process.

Using Peer Response as a Writer

- Indicate whether you are more interested in feedback about your ideas or about your presentation of them.

- Ask open-ended questions that will help you get specific information about your writing. Avoid questions that require yes-or-no answers.

- Encourage your readers to be honest.

Being a Peer Reader

- Respect the writer's feelings.

- Offer positive reactions first.

- Make sure you understand what kind of feedback the writer is looking for, and then respond accordingly.

For more information on the writing process , see the **Introductory Unit,** *pages 15–17.*

2 Building Blocks of Good Writing

Whatever your purpose in writing, you need to capture your reader's interest and organize your thoughts clearly.

2.1 INTRODUCTIONS

An introduction should capture your reader's attention and present a controlling idea.

Kinds of Introductions

There are a number of ways to begin an introduction. The one you choose depends on who the audience is and on your purpose for writing.

Make a Surprising Statement Beginning with a startling statement or an interesting fact can arouse your reader's curiosity about a subject, as in the following model.

> **MODEL**
>
> Since it was first published in 1883, Robert Louis Stevenson's *Treasure Island* has never been out of print, and it has been translated into languages as diverse as Welsh, Zulu, and Ukrainian. This unusual success attests to the universal appeal of Stevenson's storytelling skills.

Provide a Description A vivid description sets a mood and brings a scene to life for your reader. In the following model, details about visitors at Ellis Island set the tone for an essay about immigration to the United States.

> **MODEL**
>
> The visitors to the museum at Ellis Island wander almost reverently through rooms filled with photos and memorabilia. The walls seem to reverberate with countless stories—many long since forgotten—of immigrants who passed through this island.

Pose a Question Beginning with a question can make your reader want to read on to find out the answer. The following introduction asks a significant question about the careers of two women writers.

> **MODEL**
>
> George Eliot and George Sand were both successful writers in the 19th century; both were also women. At this time in history, why did they need to use male pen names?

Relate an Anecdote Beginning with an anecdote, or brief story, can hook your reader and help you make a point in a dramatic way. The following anecdote introduces an essay about gangsters in the 1920s.

> **MODEL**
>
> The man, in an immaculate suit with broad lapels, narrowed his eyes against the sun as he stepped from the shadowy doorway. Pulling his hat down, he tossed a dime to the dazed, grubby boy standing before him. "Go get me a coupla Cokes, willya? And step on it, kid!" So it was that my grandfather met Al Capone.

Address the Reader Speaking directly to your reader establishes a friendly, informal tone and involves the reader in your topic.

> **MODEL**
>
> If you are concerned about the appearance of our community, you should learn how you can participate in the Adopt-a-Street program that begins this April.

Begin with a Controlling Idea A controlling idea, or thesis statement, expressing a main idea may be woven into both the beginning and the end of a piece of nonfiction writing. The following is a controlling idea that introduces a literary analysis.

> **MODEL**
>
> In "Words and Behavior," Aldous Huxley argues that language must be used carefully. He shows that its misuse can establish and perpetuate great evil.

TIP To write a strong introduction, you may want to try more than one of the methods and then decide which is the most effective for your purpose and audience.

2.2 PARAGRAPHS

A paragraph is made up of sentences that work together to develop an idea or accomplish a purpose. Whether or not it contains a topic sentence stating the main idea, a good paragraph must have unity and coherence.

Unity

A paragraph has unity when all the sentences support and develop one stated or implied idea. Use the following techniques to create unity in your paragraphs:

Write a Topic Sentence A topic sentence states the main idea of the paragraph; all other sentences in the paragraph provide supporting details. A topic sentence is often the first sentence in a paragraph. However, it may also appear later in a paragraph or at the end, to summarize or reinforce the main idea, as shown in the model that follows.

> **MODEL**
>
> Magnesium is a mineral found in food sources such as beans, nuts, meats, and dairy products. This mineral is necessary for the breakdown of nutrients in cells and is important to the stimulation of muscles and nerves. A healthy body effectively conserves magnesium. Insufficient amounts of the mineral, however, are related to various health problems. Dietary magnesium is clearly vital to human health.

Relate All Sentences to an Implied Main Idea A paragraph can be unified without a topic sentence as long as every sentence supports an implied, or unstated, main idea. In the example, all the sentences work together to create a unified impression of an impending storm.

> **MODEL**
>
> All morning the wind had gently rustled the branches of trees and tossed back curtains from open windows. By early afternoon, however, it had picked up a force that tore green leaves from the trees and pushed thick and menacing clouds across the sky.

Coherence

A paragraph is coherent when all its sentences are related to one another and each flows logically to the next. The following techniques will help you achieve coherence in paragraphs:

- Present your ideas in the most logical order.
- Use pronouns, synonyms, and repeated words to connect ideas.
- Use transitional devices to show relationships among ideas.

In the model shown here, the writer used some of these techniques to create a unified paragraph.

> **MODEL**
>
> Most people know that the gravitational pull of the moon causes tides in the ocean. Are you aware, though, that the moon exerts the same pull on the solid part of the earth? Unlike ocean tides, however, earth tides are deformations of as much as a foot in the earth's surface. The extent to which its surface bulges is greatest during full moon and new moon, because the gravitational pull of the moon combines with that of the sun.

2.3 TRANSITIONS

Transitions are words and phrases that show connections between details. Clear transitions help show how your ideas relate to one another.

Kinds of Transitions

The types of transitions you choose depend on the ideas you want to convey.

Time or Sequence Some transitions help to clarify the sequence of events over time. When you are telling a story or describing a process, you can connect ideas with such transitional words as *first, second, always, then, next, later, soon, before, finally, after, earlier, afterward,* and *tomorrow.*

> **MODEL**
>
> Before a blood donation can be used, it must be processed carefully. First, a sample is tested for infectious diseases and identified by blood type. Next, preservatives are added. Finally, a blood cell separator breaks up the blood into its parts, such as red blood cells, platelets, and plasma.

Spatial Relationships Transitional words and phrases such as *in front, behind, next to, along, nearest, lowest, above, below, underneath, on the left,* and *in the middle* can help your reader visualize a scene.

> **MODEL**
>
> A theater-in-the-round stage is constructed in the middle of the theater space, with the audience sitting around the entire stage. To create a more intimate setting, the seats nearest the stage are often only a few feet away.

Degree of Importance Transitional words such as *mainly, strongest, weakest, first, second, most important, least important, worst,* and *best* may be used to rank ideas or to show degrees of importance.

> **MODEL**
>
> Cory made several New Year's resolutions. Most important, he decided to cut back on watching TV.

Compare and Contrast Words and phrases such as *similarly, likewise, also, like, as, neither . . . nor,* and *either . . . or* show similarity between details. *However, by contrast, yet, but, unlike, instead, whereas,* and *while* show difference. Note the use of both types of transitions in the model.

> **MODEL**
>
> Like running and bicycling, swimming helps you maintain aerobic fitness; however, swimming has the added benefit of exercising muscles throughout your body.

TIP Both *but* and *however* can be used to join two independent clauses. When *but* is used as a coordinating conjunction, it is preceded by a comma. When *however* is used as a conjunctive adverb, it is preceded by a semicolon and followed by a comma.

Cause and Effect When you are writing about a cause-effect relationship, use transitional words and phrases such as *since, because, thus, therefore, so, due to, for this reason,* and *as a result* to help clarify that relationship and make your writing coherent.

> **MODEL**
>
> Because the temperature dropped to 28 degrees after it rained for five hours, car door locks froze.

2.4 CONCLUSIONS

A conclusion should leave readers with a strong final impression.

Kinds of Conclusions

Good conclusions sum up ideas in a variety of ways. Here are some techniques you might try:

Restate Your Controlling Idea A good way to conclude an essay is by restating your controlling idea, or thesis, in different words. The following conclusion restates the controlling idea introduced on page R29.

> **MODEL**
>
> Aldous Huxley's "Words and Behavior" clearly warns of the danger of misusing language to manipulate and control. Unless we begin using concrete words and plain language, he maintains, we may ultimately destroy our civilization.

Ask a Question Try asking a question that sums up what you have said and gives your reader something new to think about. The following question concludes an appeal to halt funding for space exploration.

> **MODEL**
>
> Given all the evidence, can you imagine that continued investment in the space program will benefit future generations more than the same investment in the basic needs of those living now?

Make a Recommendation When you are persuading your audience to take a position on an issue, you can conclude by recommending a specific course of action.

> **MODEL**
>
> Voting is a vital way to influence your world. Add voter registration to your birthday plans.

Make a Prediction Readers are concerned about matters that may affect them and therefore are moved by a conclusion that predicts the future.

> **MODEL**
>
> If we continue to overuse antibiotics, we will speed the development of infections that resist treatment. Such infections will kill millions despite the best medical science.

Summarize Your Information Summarizing reinforces your main idea, leaving a strong, lasting impression. The model concludes with a statement that summarizes a book review.

> **MODEL**
>
> James Gurney's book *Dinotopia* appeals to adult readers, as well as to children, with its imaginative adventures, its fascinating drawings of dinosaurs, and its timeless theme of cooperation in a diverse community.

2.5 ELABORATION

Elaboration is the process of developing an idea by providing specific supporting details that are relevant and appropriate to the purpose and form of your writing. In some cases, you may want to present support with a visual aid.

Facts and Statistics A fact is a statement that can be verified, and a statistic is a fact expressed as a number. Make sure the facts and statistics you supply are from reliable, up-to-date sources, and support your statements, as in the following model.

MODEL

The decade from 1900 to 1910 saw 8,795,000 immigrants come to the United States. Then Congress passed the Emergency Quota Act of 1921. Between 1921 and 1930, only 4,107,000 immigrants entered the United States. The law had cut immigration by more than half.

Sensory Details Details that show how something looks, sounds, tastes, smells, or feels can enliven a description, making readers feel they are actually experiencing what you are describing.

MODEL

Gina wasn't sure she enjoyed her first hayride. As the wagon bumped along the furrows, she clumsily bounced between Marty and Deanna. She tried to imagine she was having fun as she shivered under the scratchy wool blankets that smelled of straw and dust.

Incidents From our earliest years, we are interested in stories. One way to illustrate a point is to relate an incident or tell a story, as shown in the example.

MODEL

Reforms often do not happen until a significant tragedy brings a problem to public attention. The deaths of 146 women workers in a fire at New York City's Triangle Shirtwaist factory in 1911 led to tougher protective labor laws in New York State and a national awareness of unsafe management practices.

Examples An example can help make an abstract idea concrete or can serve to clarify a complex point.

MODEL

There was a time when many of the foods eaten around the world today were found only in North, Central, and South America. For example, tomatoes, potatoes, beans, and corn all originated in the Americas.

Quotations Choose quotations that clearly support your points, and be sure that you copy each quotation word for word. Remember always to credit the source.

MODEL

Technological advances in the design of tennis rackets have changed the nature of the sport, but many players lament the passing of the wood racket. In his article "The Feel of Wood," Marshall Fisher states that after he switched to an aluminum racket in college competition, he concluded that the unavoidable "march of technology had degraded tennis."

3 Writing Description

Descriptive writing allows you to paint word pictures about anything, from events of global importance to the most personal feelings. It is an essential part of almost every piece of writing.

> **RUBRIC: Standards for Writing**
> **Successful descriptive writing should**
> - have a clear focus and sense of purpose
> - use sensory details and precise words to create a vivid image, establish a mood, or express emotion
> - present details in a logical order

3.1 KEY TECHNIQUES

Consider Your Goals What do you want to accomplish with your description? Do you want to show why something is important to you? Do you want to make a person or scene more memorable? Do you want to explain an event?

Identify Your Audience Who will read your description? How familiar are they with your subject? What background information will they need? Which details will they find most interesting?

Think Figuratively What figures of speech might help make your description vivid and interesting? What simile or metaphor comes to mind? What imaginative comparisons can you make? What living thing does an inanimate object remind you of?

Gather Sensory Details Which sights, smells, tastes, sounds, and textures make your subject come alive? Which details stick in your mind when you observe or recall your subject? Which sense does it most strongly affect?

You might want to use a chart like the one shown here to collect sensory details about your subject.

Sights	Sounds	Textures	Smells	Tastes

Create a Mood What feeling do you want to envoke in your readers? Do you want to soothe them with comforting images? Do you want to build tension with ominous details? Do you want to evoke sadness or joy?

3.2 OPTIONS FOR ORGANIZATION

Option 1: Spatial Order Choose one of these options to show the spatial order of elements in a scene you are describing.

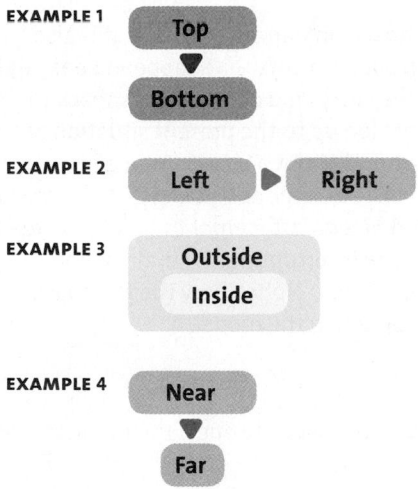

MODEL

Detective Malloy surveyed the scene. Just inside the ruined door, a torn letter lay on the floor. In the middle of the room stood a large oak desk, neatly organized except for a lamp that hung off the edge. Behind the desk, a chair lay against the far wall.

Option 2: Order of Impression Order of impression is the order in which you notice details.

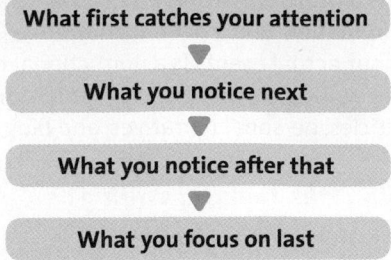

MODEL

First, we heard the screech of a car braking before our house. Next came the slam of a car door and then the staccato clicking of a woman's high heels as she ran up the cobblestone walk. It was already late in the evening, and we couldn't imagine who it could be.

TIP Use transitions that help readers understand the order of the impressions you are describing. Some useful transitions are *after, next, during, first, before, finally,* and *then.*

Option 3: Order of Importance You can use order of importance as the organizing structure for a description.

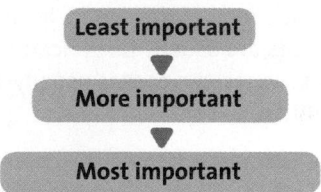

MODEL

All the Thanksgiving fixings were there: the perfectly browned, steaming turkey; the cranberry sauce glistening like rubies in the candlelight; the mounds of mashed potatoes like fluffy snowdrifts. The dining room resounded with chatter and laughter, but an emptiness clung to the corners and a silence cut through the conversation. Grandma wasn't with us.

*For more information, see **Transitions**, page R30.*

4 Writing Narratives

Narrative writing tells a story. If you write a story from your imagination, it is a fictional narrative. A true story about actual events is a nonfictional narrative. Narrative writing can be found in short stories, novels, news articles, personal narratives, and biographies.

> **RUBRIC: Standards for Writing**
>
> **A successful narrative should**
> - hook the reader's attention with a strong introduction
> - include descriptive details and dialogue to develop the characters, setting, and plot
> - have a clear beginning, middle, and end
> - have a logical organization, with clues and transitions that help the reader understand the order of events
> - maintain a consistent tone and point of view
> - use language that is appropriate to the audience
> - demonstrate the significance of events or ideas

4.1 KEY TECHNIQUES

Identify the Main Events What are the most important events in your narrative? Choose those that are most useful in creating an interesting plot. Develop each scene to fit the mood of the event. In comedy, for example, events are usually fast paced and funny. For more serious scenes, the pace is usually slower and more thoughtful.

Describe the Setting When do the events occur? Where do they take place? Create a setting that sets the stage for the characters and their actions and that builds mood. Use sensory details to describe the sights, smells, and sounds of the scenes.

Depict Characters Vividly What do your characters look like? What do they think and say? How do they act? To bring characters to life, describe their actions, movements, gestures, and feelings. Experiment with dialogue and other devices, such as interior monologues that reveal characters' thoughts and personalities.

TIP Dialogue is an effective means of developing both characters and plot. Choose words that express your characters' reactions to other characters and events. You can also shift perspectives to show how different characters feel about a conflict.

4.2 OPTIONS FOR ORGANIZATION

Option 1: Chronological Order One way to organize a piece of narrative writing is to arrange the events in chronological order, as shown in the following example.

> **EXAMPLE**
>
> The morning after my grandfather's funeral, I wake up early and walk to the cemetery.
>
> I stand by his grave and become angry and frustrated.
>
> I want to find someplace where I can remember my grandfather and all the good times we had together.
>
> On the beach, I sit on the huge piece of driftwood where my grandfather and I used to sit. The cool lake wind and the noise of the waves bring back my favorite memories of him.

Introduction
Characters and setting

Event 1

Event 2

End
Perhaps showing the significance of the events

Option 2: Flashback In narrative writing, it is also possible to introduce events that happened before the beginning of the story. You can use a flashback to show how past events led up to the present situation or to provide background about a character or event. Use clue words such as *last summer, as a young girl, the previous school year,* and *his earliest memories* to let your reader know that you are interrupting the main action to describe earlier events. Notice how the flashback interrupts the action in the model.

> **EXAMPLE**
>
> As the train barreled through the countryside, Isabelle stared at the passing farms and small towns with a sense of wonder. How could people live in such remote places? Then she recalled a visit to a cousin when she was young. "I would never live in the city," the cousin had said. "Everyone is so close together, and there's so much noise!" Isabelle had looked at her in surprise and responded, "But in the country everyone is so far apart, and it's so quiet!" Suddenly, the train whistle blew, and the thought vanished, and Isabelle began working on a puzzle to pass the time.

Option 3: Focus on Conflict When a fictional narrative focuses on a central conflict, the story's plot may be organized as shown in the following example.

EXAMPLE

Delores walked into the bank with the money that was about to change her life. For the past two years, she had worked two jobs and saved diligently so that she would have enough money to move out of her mother's home. Her mother had been supportive of her plans, and Delores resolved to buy her a gift to show her appreciation.

> **Describe main characters and setting.**
>
> ▼

Delores left the bank and walked down the street elated. She couldn't wait to share the news with her mother, but when she arrived home, Delores found her mother sitting in the kitchen looking distraught.

"What's happened?" asked Delores with a sense of alarm.

> **Present conflict.**
>
> ▼

"My car was hit while it was parked on the street today. The driver just drove off. It's completely destroyed," said her mother. "The insurance money won't be enough to buy a new car. I don't know how I'm going to get to work."

Delores's heart sank. In recent months, her mother had developed trouble walking, which would make it impossible for her to take the bus to work. As a result, she had come to depend upon the car.

> **Relate events that make conflict complex and cause characters to change.**

"I don't know what I'm going to do," said her tearful mother. Delores opened her purse and saw the bank deposit slip sticking out of her wallet. If she gave her mother her savings, Delores would not be able to move out. She knew that she didn't have to give her mother the money, but she also knew how much her mother had helped her.

> ▼

"Don't worry, Mom," Delores said. "I have enough in savings to help you out."

> **Present resolution or outcome of conflict.**

5 Writing Informative Texts

Expository writing informs and explains. You can use it to evaluate the effects of a new law, to compare two movies, to analyze a piece of literature, or to examine the problem of greenhouse gases in the atmosphere. There are many types of expository writing. Think about your topic and select the type that presents the information most clearly.

5.1 COMPARISON AND CONTRAST

Compare-and-contrast writing examines the similarities and differences between two or more subjects. You might, for example, compare and contrast two short stories, the main characters in a novel, or two movies.

> **RUBRIC: Standards for Writing**
>
> **Successful compare-and-contrast writing should**
>
> - hook the reader's attention with a strong introduction
> - clearly identify the subjects that are being compared and contrasted
> - include specific, relevant details
> - follow a clear plan of organization
> - use language and details appropriate to the audience
> - use transitional words and phrases to clarify similarities and differences

Options for Organization

Compare-and-contrast writing can be given a point-by-point organization or a subject-by-subject organization, as shown in these examples.

Option 1: Point-by-Point Organization

EXAMPLE

I. Noble qualities

> **Point 1**

  Subject A. Arthur: admires Launcelot as great knight, so is reluctant to fight him.

  Subject B. Launcelot: respects Arthur as his liege, so is reluctant to fight him.

II. Weaknesses

> **Point 2**

  Subject A. Arthur: trusts his knights' judgment over his own.

  Subject B. Launcelot: love for Arthur's wife stronger than respect for Arthur.

Option 2: Subject-by-Subject Organization

EXAMPLE

I. Arthur: **Subject A**

Point 1. Noble quality: admires Launcelot as great knight, so is reluctant to fight him.

Point 2. Weakness: trusts his knights' judgment over his own.

II. Launcelot: **Subject B**

Point 1. Noble quality: respects Arthur as his liege, so is reluctant to fight him.

Point 2. Weakness: love for Arthur's wife stronger than respect for Arthur.

For more information, see **Writing Workshop: Analysis of a Poem,** *pages 270–279;* **Writing Workshop: Analysis of Literary Nonfiction,** *pages 1076–1085;* **Research Paper,** *pages 1420–1441.*

5.2 CAUSE AND EFFECT

Cause-effect writing explains why something happened, why certain conditions exist, or what resulted from an action or a condition. You might use cause-effect writing to explain a character's actions, the progress of a disease, or the outcome of a war.

RUBRIC: Standards for Writing

Successful cause-effect writing should

- hook the reader's attention with a strong introduction
- clearly state the cause-and-effect relationship
- show clear connections between causes and effects
- present causes and effects in a logical order and use transitions effectively
- use facts, examples, and other details to illustrate each cause and effect
- use language and details appropriate to the audience

Options for Organization

Your organization will depend on your topic and your purpose for writing.

Option 1: Effect-to-Cause Organization If you want to explain the causes of an event, such as the closing of a factory, you might first state the effect and then examine its causes.

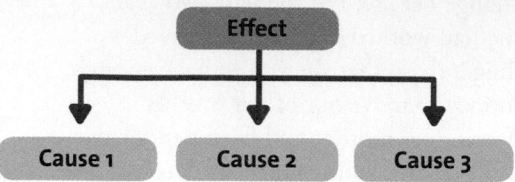

Option 2: Cause-to-Effect Organization If your focus is on explaining the effects of an event, such as the passage of a law, you might first state the cause and then explain the effects.

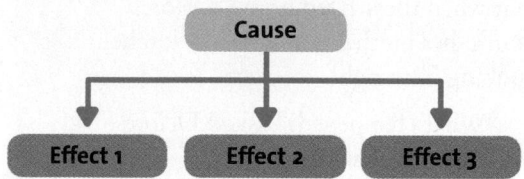

Option 3: Cause-Effect Chain Organization Sometimes you'll want to describe a chain of cause-effect relationships to explore a topic, such as the disappearance of tropical rain forests or the development of the Internet.

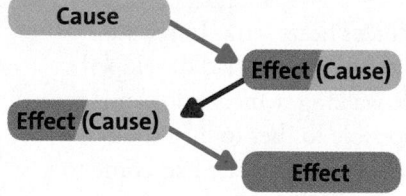

TIP Don't assume that a cause-effect relationship exists just because one event follows another. Look for evidence that the later event could not have happened if the first event had not caused it.

5.3 PROBLEM-SOLUTION

Problem-solution writing clearly states a problem, analyzes the problem, and proposes a solution to the problem. It can be used to identify and solve a conflict between characters, investigate global warming, or tell why the home team keeps losing.

RUBRIC: Standards for Writing

Successful problem-solution writing should

- hook the reader's attention with a strong introduction
- identify the problem and help the reader understand the issues involved
- analyze the causes and effects of the problem
- include quotations, facts, and statistics
- explore possible solutions to the problem and recommend the best one(s)
- use language, details, and a tone appropriate to the audience

Options for Organization

Your organization will depend on the goal of your problem-solution piece, your intended audience, and the specific problem you have chosen to address. The organizational methods that follow are effective for different kinds of problem-solution writing.

Option 1: Simple Problem-Solution

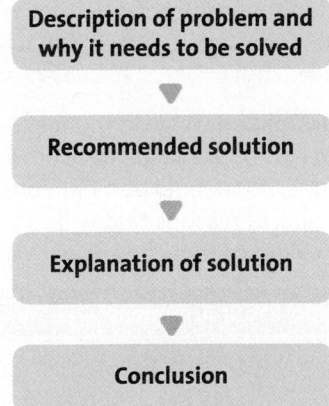

Option 2: Deciding Between Solutions

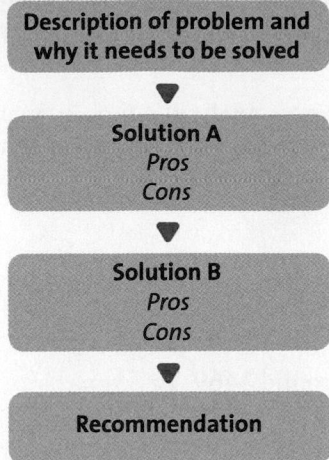

5.4 ANALYSIS

In writing an analysis, you explain how something works, how it is defined, or what its parts are. The details you include will depend upon the kind of analysis you write.

Process Analysis What are the major steps or stages in a process? What background information does the reader need to know—such as definitions of terms or a list of needed equipment—to understand the analysis? You might use process analysis to explain how to program a VCR or prepare for a test.

Definition What are the most important characteristics of a subject? You might use definition analysis to explain a quality, such as honor or loyalty, the characteristics of a sonnet, or the skills of a physicist.

Parts Analysis What are the parts, groups, or types that make up a subject? Parts analysis could be used to explain the makeup of King Arthur's army or the parts of the brain.

RUBRIC: Standards for Writing

A successful analysis should

- hook the reader's attention with a strong introduction
- clearly define the subject and its parts
- use a specific organizing structure to provide a logical flow of information
- show connections among facts and ideas through transitional words and phrases
- use language and details appropriate for the audience

Options for Organization

Organize your details in a logical order appropriate to the kind of analysis you're writing. Use one of the following options:

Option 1: Process Analysis A process analysis is usually organized chronologically, with steps or stages in the order in which they occur.

EXAMPLE

Arthurian legends reinterpreted	**Introduce process.**
British ruler in 500s	**Give background.**
Step 1: Around 1469, *Le Morte d'Arthur* is compiled.	**Explain steps.**
Step 2: Between 1842 and 1885, *Idylls of the King* is published.	
Step 3: In 1960, the musical *Camelot* opens.	

Option 2: Definition Analysis You can organize the details of a definition analysis in order of importance or impression.

EXAMPLE

Honor	**Introduce term.**
Honor defined as integrity, dignity, and pride.	**Give general definition.**
Quality 1: Integrity	**Explain features or qualities.**
Quality 2: Dignity	
Quality 3: Pride	

Option 3: Parts Analysis A parts analysis is organized by a listing of the subject's parts, with each explained.

EXAMPLE

Code of chivalry	**Introduce subject.**
Part 1: Devoted to Christianity	**Explain parts.**
Part 2: Protect the defenseless	
Part 3: Fight injustices, never surrender	

*For more information, see **Writing Workshop: Analysis of a Poem**, pages 270–279; **Writing Workshop: Analysis of Literary Nonfiction**, pages 1076–1085.*

6 Writing Arguments

Persuasive writing allows you to use the power of language to inform and influence others. It includes speeches, persuasive essays, newspaper editorials, advertisements, and critical reviews.

RUBRIC: Standards for Writing

Successful persuasive writing should

- hook the reader's attention with a strong introduction
- state the issue and the writer's position
- give claims and support them with facts or reasons
- have a reasonable and respectful tone
- answer opposing views
- use sound logic and effective language
- conclude by summing up reasons or calling for action

*For more information, see **Writing Workshop: Persuasive Essay**, pages 730–739.*

6.1 KEY TECHNIQUES

Clarify Your Claim What do you believe about the issue? Determine how you can express your opinion most clearly.

Know Your Audience Who will read your writing? Think about what your audience already knows and believes about the issue. Imagine any objections to your position that your audience might have. Determine additional information they will need. Decide on the tone and approach that will be most effective.

Support Your Opinion Why do you feel the way you do about the issue? Use facts, statistics, examples, quotations, anecdotes, or expert opinions to support your view. Think of reasons that will convince your readers and evidence that can answer their objections.

Ways to Support Your Argument	
Statistics	facts that are stated in numbers
Examples	specific instances that explain points
Observations	events or situations you yourself have seen
Anecdotes	brief stories that illustrate points
Quotations	direct statements from authorities

*For more information, see **Identifying Faulty Reasoning**, page R22.*

Begin and End with a Bang How can you hook your readers and make a lasting impression? Think of a quotation, an anecdote, or a statistic that will catch your reader's attention and remain memorable. Create a strong summary or call to action with which you can conclude.

MODEL

Beginning

Our forests are being cut down. The chip mill industry, which supplies the raw material for making so-called high-quality paper, has tripled in the southeastern United States in the last decade.

Conclusion

It's time to stop the rapid devastation of the forests. If it means less slick paper for magazines and computer printouts, so be it. Write the Conservation Department, the Forest Service, and especially your state's members of Congress.

6.2 OPTIONS FOR ORGANIZATION

In a two-sided persuasive essay, you want to show the weaknesses of other opinions as you explain the strengths of your own.

Option 1: Reasons for Your Opinion

Introduction states issue and your position on it.
▼
Reason 1 with evidence and support
▼
Reason 2 with evidence and support
▼
Reason 3 with evidence and support
▼
Objections to whole argument
▼
Response to objections
▼
Conclusion includes restatement of your position and recommended action.

Option 2: Point-by-Point Basis

Introduction states issue and your position on it.
▼
Reason 1 with evidence and support
▼
Objections and responses for reason 1
▼
Reason 2 with evidence and support
▼
Objections and responses for reason 2
▼
Reason 3 with evidence and support
▼
Objections and responses for reason 3
▼
Conclusion includes restatement of your position and recommended action.

7 Writing Functional Texts

Business writing is writing done in a workplace to support the work of a company or business. Several types of formats, such as memos, letters, e-mails, applications, and bylaws, have been developed to make communication easier.

> ## RUBRIC: Standards for Writing
> **Successful business writing should**
> - be courteous
> - use language that is geared to its audience
> - state the purpose clearly in the opening sentences or paragraph
> - have a formal tone and not contain slang, contractions, or sentence fragments
> - use precise words
> - present only essential information
> - present details in a logical order
> - conclude with a summary of important points

7.1 KEY TECHNIQUES

Think About Your Purpose Ask yourself why you are doing this writing. Do you want to promote yourself to a college admissions committee or a job interviewer? Do you want to order or complain about a product? Do you want to set up a meeting or respond to someone's ideas? Are you writing bylaws for an organization?

Identify Your Audience Determine who will read your writing. What background information will they need? What tone or language is appropriate?

Use a Pattern of Organization That Is Appropriate to the Content If you have to compare and contrast two products in a memo, for example, you can use the same compare-and-contrast organization that you would use in an essay.

Support Your Points What specific details might clarify your ideas? What reasons do you have for your statements?

Finish Strongly Determine the best way to sum up your statements. What is your main point? What action do you want the recipients to take?

Revise and Proofread Your Writing Just as you are graded on the quality of an essay you write for a class, you will be judged on the quality of your writing in the workplace.

7.2 MATCHING THE FORMAT TO THE OCCASION

E-mail messages, memos, and letters have similar purposes but are used in different situations. The chart shows how each format can be used.

Format	Occasion
Memo	Use to send correspondence **inside** the workplace only.
E-mail message	Use to send correspondence **inside or outside** the company.
Letter	Use to send correspondence **outside** the company.

TIP Memos are often sent as e-mail messages in the workplace. Remember that both require formal language and standard spelling, capitalization, and punctuation.

PRACTICE AND APPLY

Refer to the documents on page R41 to complete the following:

1. Draft a response to the letter. Then revise your letter as necessary according to the rubric at the beginning of this section. Make sure you have included the necessary information and have written in an appropriate tone. Proofread your letter for grammatical errors and spelling mistakes. Follow the format of the model and use appropriate spacing between elements.

2. Write a memo in response to the memo. Tell the recipient what actions you have taken. Follow the format of the model.

7.3 FORMATS

Business letters usually have a formal tone and a specific format as shown below. The key to writing a business letter is to get to the point as quickly as possible and to present your information clearly.

MODEL: BUSINESS LETTER

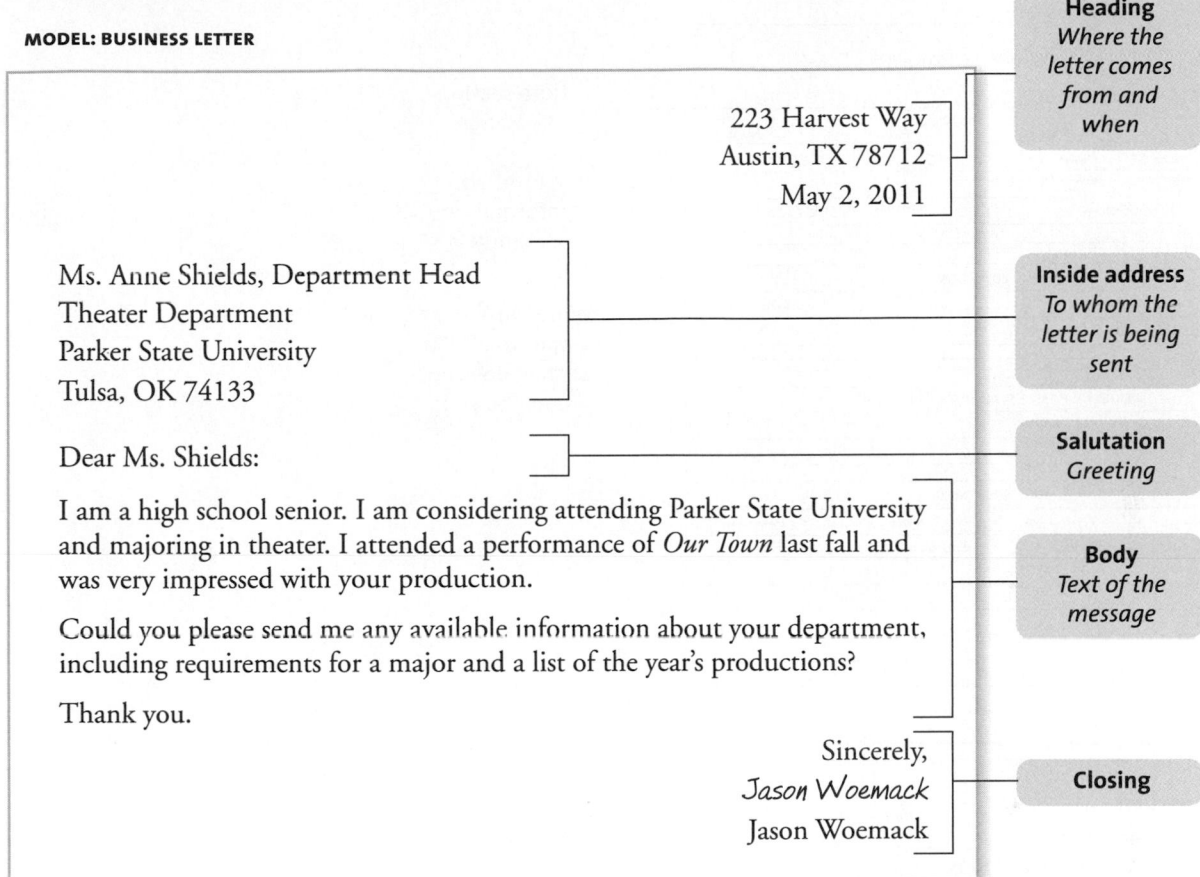

Heading
Where the letter comes from and when

223 Harvest Way
Austin, TX 78712
May 2, 2011

Inside address
To whom the letter is being sent

Ms. Anne Shields, Department Head
Theater Department
Parker State University
Tulsa, OK 74133

Salutation
Greeting

Dear Ms. Shields:

Body
Text of the message

I am a high school senior. I am considering attending Parker State University and majoring in theater. I attended a performance of *Our Town* last fall and was very impressed with your production.

Could you please send me any available information about your department, including requirements for a major and a list of the year's productions?

Thank you.

Sincerely,
Jason Woemack
Jason Woemack

Closing

Memos are often used in workplaces as a way of conveying information in a direct and concise manner. They can be used to announce or summarize meetings and to request actions or specific information.

MODEL: MEMO

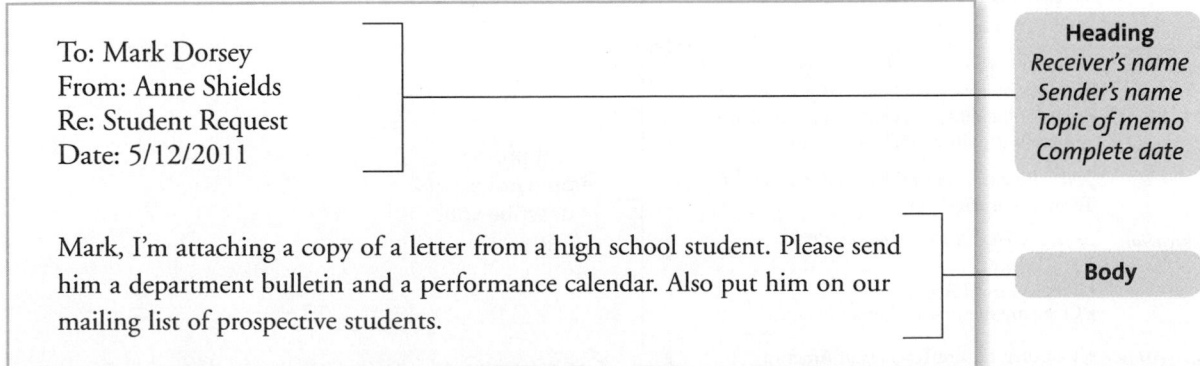

Heading
Receiver's name
Sender's name
Topic of memo
Complete date

To: Mark Dorsey
From: Anne Shields
Re: Student Request
Date: 5/12/2011

Body

Mark, I'm attaching a copy of a letter from a high school student. Please send him a department bulletin and a performance calendar. Also put him on our mailing list of prospective students.

TIP Don't forget to write the topic of your memo in the subject line. This will help the receiver determine the importance of your memo.

When you apply for a job, you may be asked to fill out an application form. Application forms vary, but most of them ask for similar kinds of information. If you are mailing your application, you may want to include a brief letter.

MODEL: JOB APPLICATION

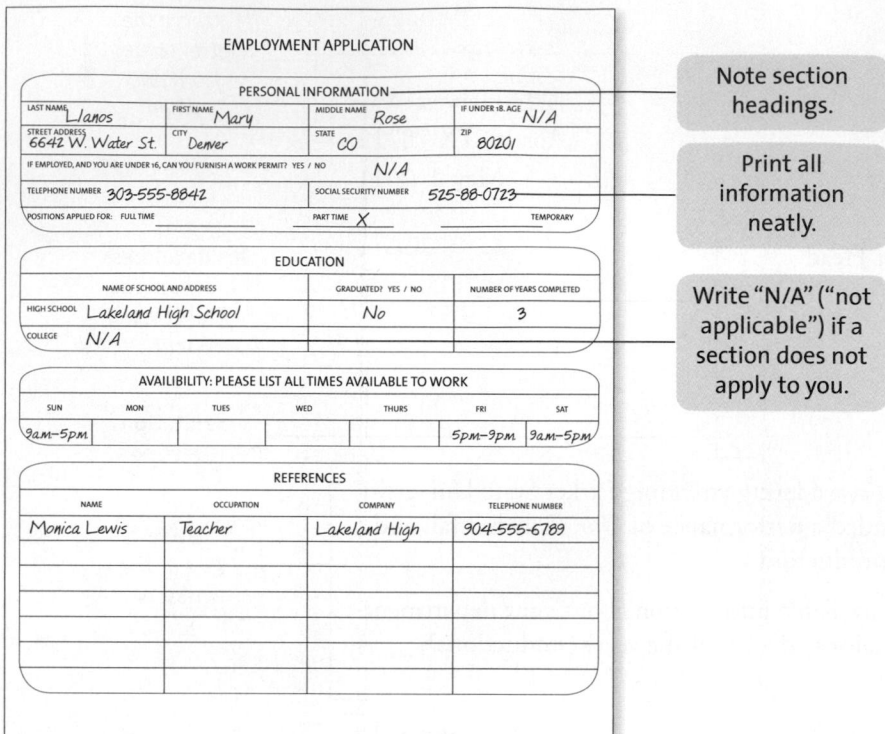

EMPLOYMENT APPLICATION

PERSONAL INFORMATION
LAST NAME *Llanos* | FIRST NAME *Mary* | MIDDLE NAME *Rose* | IF UNDER 18, AGE *N/A*
STREET ADDRESS *6642 W. Water St.* | CITY *Denver* | STATE *CO* | ZIP *80201*
IF EMPLOYED, AND YOU ARE UNDER 16, CAN YOU FURNISH A WORK PERMIT? YES / NO *N/A*
TELEPHONE NUMBER *303-555-8842* | SOCIAL SECURITY NUMBER *525-88-0723*
POSITIONS APPLIED FOR: FULL TIME _____ PART TIME *X* TEMPORARY _____

EDUCATION
NAME OF SCHOOL AND ADDRESS | GRADUATED? YES / NO | NUMBER OF YEARS COMPLETED
HIGH SCHOOL *Lakeland High School* | *No* | *3*
COLLEGE *N/A*

AVAILIBILITY: PLEASE LIST ALL TIMES AVAILABLE TO WORK
SUN | MON | TUES | WED | THURS | FRI | SAT
9am–5pm | | | | | *5pm–9pm* | *9am–5pm*

REFERENCES
NAME | OCCUPATION | COMPANY | TELEPHONE NUMBER
Monica Lewis | *Teacher* | *Lakeland High* | *904-555-6789*

Note section headings.

Print all information neatly.

Write "N/A" ("not applicable") if a section does not apply to you.

MODEL: RÉSUMÉ

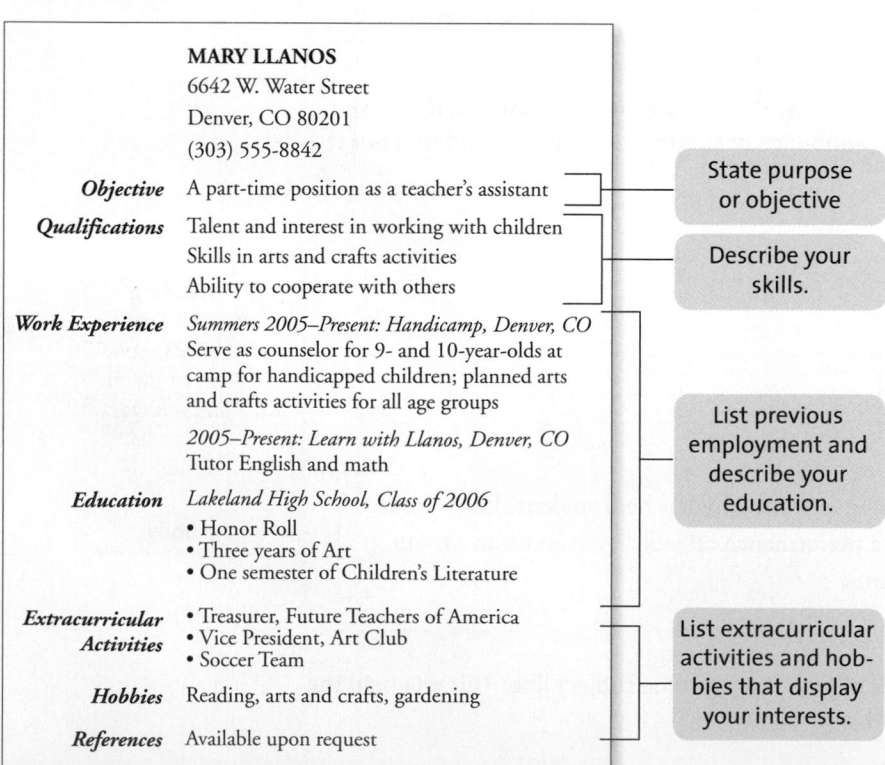

MARY LLANOS
6642 W. Water Street
Denver, CO 80201
(303) 555-8842

Objective — A part-time position as a teacher's assistant

Qualifications — Talent and interest in working with children
Skills in arts and crafts activities
Ability to cooperate with others

Work Experience — *Summers 2005–Present: Handicamp, Denver, CO* Serve as counselor for 9- and 10-year-olds at camp for handicapped children; planned arts and crafts activities for all age groups

2005–Present: Learn with Llanos, Denver, CO Tutor English and math

Education — *Lakeland High School, Class of 2006*
• Honor Roll
• Three years of Art
• One semester of Children's Literature

Extracurricular Activities — • Treasurer, Future Teachers of America
• Vice President, Art Club
• Soccer Team

Hobbies — Reading, arts and crafts, gardening

References — Available upon request

State purpose or objective

Describe your skills.

List previous employment and describe your education.

List extracurricular activities and hobbies that display your interests.

Technical writing is a type of writing used for detailed instructions or descriptions of procedures in a variety of fields, such as engineering, government, industry, and science. Types of technical writing include bylaws, science reports, and lists of procedures for conducting a meeting or assembling a product. The example below is a set of rules and regulations for dog owners in an apartment complex.

MODEL: RULES AND REGULATIONS

Paradise Heights Apartment Complex	BYLAWS page 218

Canine Control

Section 1. Dogs

No person shall own or keep any dog which by biting, barking, howling, or in any other manner disturbs the peace and quiet of any neighborhood, or endangers the safety of any person.

Section 2. Leashing of Dogs

A. Leash Required No person owning or keeping a dog in the Paradise Heights apartment complex shall permit such dog to be at large in the common areas unless accompanied by the owner or keeper, except if it be on the premises of another person with the knowledge and permission of such other person. Such owner or keeper of a dog, when it is not on the premises of the owner or upon the premises of another person with the knowledge and permission of such person, shall restrain such dog by a chain or leash not exceeding six feet in length.

B. Enforcement Any dog found to be at large in violation of this regulation shall be caught and confined by the building manager, who shall notify the licensed owner or keeper of said dog, giving the owner or keeper a period of ten days within which to recover the dog. The building manager shall enter and prosecute a complaint against the owner or keeper of any dog taken into his custody under this section. A building manager having custody of a dog confined under this regulation shall be allowed the sum of five dollars per day for each day of confinement for the care of such dog, payable by the owner or keeper thereof.

C. Fines Violations of Section 2 shall be punishable as follows:

> First offense: Warning
> Second offense: Fine of $50.00
> Third offense: Fine of $75.00
> Fourth and each subsequent offense: Fine of $100.00

D. Reporting Offenses Residents who wish to report problems with a dog, or who have questions about this ordinance, can contact Animal Control at 555-3380.

PRACTICE AND APPLY

Refer to the documents on pages R42 and R43 to complete the following:

1. Visit a business and request an employment application for a job you would like to have. Make sure you understand what each question is asking before you begin to write. Fill out the application as neatly and completely as possible.

2. Write a set of rules and regulations for a club or an organization that you already belong to or one that you would like to form. Follow the format of the document on page R43.

Good research involves using a variety of sources and materials. Knowing where to look for information, how to access it, and how to record your findings are important skills and strategies for managing the abundance of information at your fingertips.

COMMON CORE

Included in this handbook:
W 7, W 8, W 9

1 Finding Sources

The **library** or **media center** and the **Internet** are the places you will begin your research. Together, the library and the Internet offer a wealth of resources, including reference works, books, newspapers and periodicals, film, databases, catalogs, government publications, and other miscellaneous sources, such as music scores and maps.

1.1 REFERENCE WORKS

Reference works provide quick information that can help you refine or narrow your search. Reference works are roughly divided into two categories: general reference and specialized reference. Specialized reference works are focused on a particular field or area of study.

Reference Works	Examples
Encyclopedias—detailed information on nearly every subject, arranged alphabetically	*Encyclopaedia Britannica* *Encyclopedia.com* *Encyclopedia of Economics*
Dictionaries—word definitions, spellings, usage, pronunciations, and origins	*The American Heritage Dictionary* *Bartlett's Quotations*
Almanacs and Yearbooks—current facts and statistics	*World Almanac and Book of Facts*
Thesauri—lists of synonyms and antonyms	*Roget's International Thesaurus*
Biographical References—information on the lives of noteworthy people	*The Riverside Dictionary of Biography* *The International Who's Who*
Atlases—geographical and historical maps, charts, and graphics	*Rand McNally Atlas of the World*
Directories—names, addresses, and phone numbers of people and organizations	telephone books lists of business organizations, agencies, and publications
Indexes—alphabetical lists of newspaper and magazine articles	*Readers' Guide to Periodical Literature*

1.2 BOOKS

Nonfiction books provide in-depth information on specific topics. Your research may also require that you access fiction, poetry, or dramatic works. The following parts of a book will help you find information quickly and easily:

- **Title page**—a page that gives the book's name and the name of its author and publisher; usually the first full page of a book
- **Copyright page**—a page that gives the copyright date, or the date the book was published; usually located on the reverse side of the title page
- **Table of contents**—a list at the front of the book that gives the title of each chapter or section of the text and the page number on which it begins
- **Preface**—a short, preliminary section of a book in which the writer of the book briefly provides background information and, possibly, acknowledgments
- **Bibliography**—a list of related books and other materials used to write a text; usually placed at the end of the book
- **Glossary**—an alphabetized list of important and/or specialized words and their definitions; usually placed at the end of the book
- **Appendix**—a collection of additional materials that supply background or other related information on subject matter discussed in the main portion of the text; usually located at the end of the book
- **Index**—an alphabetized list of important topics, terms, and details covered in the book, together with the page numbers on which they can be found; located at the end of the book; useful for quickly finding specific information on a topic

For more information, see **Choosing Trustworthy Books,** *page 1413.*

Two basic systems are used to classify nonfiction books. Most high school and public libraries use the Dewey decimal system. University and research libraries generally use the Library of Congress system.

DEWEY DECIMAL SYSTEM

000–099	General works
100–199	Philosophy and psychology
200–299	Religion
300–399	Social science
400–499	Language
500–599	Natural sciences and mathematics
600–699	Technology (applied sciences)
700–799	Arts and recreation
800–899	Literature and rhetoric
900–999	Geography and history

LIBRARY OF CONGRESS SYSTEM

A	General works
B	Philosophy, psychology, religion
C	History
D	General history and history of Europe
E–F	American history
G	Geography, anthropology, recreation
H	Social sciences
J	Political science
K	Law
L	Education
M	Music
N	Fine arts
P	Language and literature
Q	Science
R	Medicine
S	Agriculture
T	Technology
U	Military science
V	Naval science
Z	Bibliography and library science

1.3 NEWSPAPERS AND PERIODICALS

Newspapers, magazines, and scholarly journals provide concise and current information on specific topics and the news of the day. Microforms are newspapers, periodicals, and reports stored on film (microfilm) or cards (microfiche) and viewable on special machines found at the library.

Types of Publications	Examples
Newspapers—published daily, weekly, or monthly; provide news reports, specialized features, and commentary; may be general or specialized	*New York Times* *Chicago Tribune* *Sacramento Bee*
Magazines—published monthly, quarterly, or at other intervals; provide news, articles on specific topics, and commentary; more in-depth than newspapers	*Newsweek* *Time* *Musician*
Journals—usually academic in scope; related to a specific field of study; highly specialized information	*Journal of Music Theory* *New England Journal of Medicine*

*For more information, see **Evaluating Newspapers and Periodicals**, page 1412.*

1.4 ELECTRONIC RESOURCES

Electronic resources include DVDs, videos, e-books, CD-ROMs, and audio resources. These resources may contain reference materials, movies, documentaries, television programs, books, music, speeches, textbooks, and a variety of resources. While most documentaries, movies, and interviews are available on DVDs or CDs, you may want to directly access a film version. To quickly determine whether the piece is useful for your research, check the following:

- **Description or summary** of the piece—Does it contain the information you need, or is it relevant to your topic? Is it nonfiction or fiction?
- **Copyright date**—How current is the documentary or interview?
- **Producer** of the piece and its **participants**—Is the producer or creator reputable? Who is interviewed or featured?

1.5 DATABASES AND ONLINE CATALOGS

The library and Internet also offer large databases that allow you to search for articles on any number of topics. Often the library will subscribe to a database service, such as InfoTrac, Newsbank, or SIRS Researcher. The information on these databases is updated regularly.

Electronic catalogs have mostly replaced the card catalog system of book listings, which were filed in labeled drawers in libraries, and can often be accessed from the library's Web site on the Internet.

1.6 OTHER RESOURCES

In addition to the library or media center and the Internet, the following sources can supply information: corporate and nonprofit publications, lectures, correspondence, career guides, recordings, and television programming.

PRACTICE AND APPLY

1. If you were looking through a nonfiction book on the romantic poets, which part(s) of the book would you search in order to find information on William Wordsworth, one of the romantic poets?

2. If you wanted the most current information on a given topic, which source(s) would you search first?

3. Describe a situation in which you might find it useful to search microfiche.

1.7 WEB SOURCES

Whole libraries are on the Internet, as are thousands of other reliable and comprehensive sources for research. To conduct a search efficiently and find the best information for your topic, familiarize yourself with the following terms and procedures.

The main search tools for finding information on the Web are search engines, metasearch tools, and directories. In addition, there are virtual libraries and a host of other sites, such as those of newspaper archives, news associations, encyclopedias, the Library of Congress, and specialized databases.

Search engines—A search engine is a Web site that allows you to look for information on the World Wide Web. Examples include Google, Yahoo!, and Bing.

Metasearch tools—A metasearch tool is similar to a search engine, except that it simultaneously searches multiple search engines for the keywords you request. Examples include Dogpile, SurfWax, and Metacrawler.

Directories—Directories arrange Internet resources into subject categories and are useful when you are researching a general topic. Examples include Lycos, Galaxy, Yahoo!, Web Directory, and About.com.

Keyword searches—In a keyword search, you access a search engine and type in a phrase or term related to your subject, which allows you to retrieve Web sites and documents that have those keywords in them. Here are some tips for doing a keyword search:

- In the search box, type in a specific word or two that clearly identify your subject.
- When you want to find an exact phrase, or words in a certain order, such as "romantic poet" (and not just "romantic" or just "poet"), use quotation marks around the entire phrase. For instance, "romantic poet" will provide results using those words in that order.
- If necessary, replace the end of a word with an asterisk. For example, the keyword *poet** leads to sites that contain *poet, poetry,* and *poetic.*

Boolean searches—A Boolean search lets you specify how the keywords in your search are related. This type of search allows you to refine, narrow, or expand your search so that your results are more focused on your topic needs. Use the following tips to conduct a Boolean search:

- For a search containing two or more words that do not need to be in a specific order, use the word AND between the words to indicate that the site or document should contain all the words specified. For example, *Wordsworth* AND *Keats* will produce results containing both those words, but not in any particular order. For some search engines, you can use a plus sign instead of AND.
- The word OR broadens the search to include all documents that contain either word (*Wordsworth* OR *Keats*).
- The word NOT—or, for some search engines, a minus sign—excludes unwanted terms from the search (*poetry* NOT *contemporary*).

Each Web site you encounter in your search will have a **URL** (uniform resource locator), which is its Web address. The abbreviation usually located at the end of the URL indicates the type and purpose of the Web site.

URL ABBREVIATIONS AND MEANINGS

.COM commercial—product information and sales; personal sites; some combinations of products and information, as at World Book Online

.EDU education—information about schools, courses, campus life, and research projects; students' and teachers' personal sites

.GOV United States government—official sites of the White House, NASA, the FBI, and other government agencies

.MIL United States military—official sites of the army, navy, air force, and marines, as well as the Department of Defense and related agencies

.NET network—product information and sales

.ORG organization—charities, libraries, and other nonprofits; political parties

1.8 YOUR OWN ORIGINAL DATA

Sometimes you will need information that you just can't find in books or online. A good way to get in-depth, first-hand information is by interviewing experts, conducting surveys, and recording data from your own observations, field work, or experiments.

Interviews with experts—Whatever the subject of your research, look for people who have knowledge or experience in that field. For example, if you were researching the *Titanic,* you might interview someone from the Titanic Historical Society. Use the following tips when conducting an interview:

1. Plan your questions and rehearse what you will say.
2. During the interview, listen carefully and take notes. Ask permission if you want to record the interview.
3. Request clarification and ask follow-up questions when necessary.
4. After the interview, review your notes and summarize the conversation. If you recorded the conversation, you might want to transcribe it.
5. Identify strong statements you might want to quote directly.
6. Send a thank-you note to the interviewee.

Oral histories—For some kinds of presentations and papers, you may want to include an **oral history,** or a story of a person's experiences told by that person in his or her own words. For example, if you were writing a paper on the London bombing in World War II, you might want to include an oral history of someone who experienced it firsthand. To conduct an oral history, follow all the tips for conducting an interview.

Surveys—Surveys allow you to gather information from a broad range of people through the use of a **questionnaire.** For example, you may want to gather and compare people's opinions, preferences, or beliefs about a current news topic. Use the following tips to conduct a survey or to distribute a questionnaire.

1. Plan the survey. Choose whether you want to use multiple-choice questions, yes/no questions, open-ended questions, true/false questions, or a rating scale. Write up your questionnaire.
2. Determine the sample population, or group of people, you want to survey.
3. Administer the survey the same way to each person. You may ask people to respond in person, on the phone, or by e-mail, but the method should be the same for each, with the questions asked in the same manner and order.
4. Once the questionnaires have been completed, compile the answers and interpret the responses. Was there a clear preference or opinion from the entire group? Do certain groups of people think one way while others think another? What conclusions can you draw from the results?
5. Summarize your results in writing; use charts or graphics to provide a visual representation of the data.

Independent observation and field research—Field research and independent observation include any purposeful observations you make at a site or event related to your topic. For example, if you were writing a report on how people behave at an art museum, you might spend a day at the museum, recording the activity you observe. For some research projects you may want to set up a **field study,** which is a systematic series of observations or a planned course of data collection. For some topics, you might conduct experiments, as for a report in a science class.

2 Collecting Information

Once you have your sources, you will need to sort through the information. To make the process useful and manageable, you will want to take detailed notes, arrange your information in a logical and organized manner, and make sure your sources are reliable and credible.

2.1 NOTE-TAKING

As you go through your sources, write down information that is relevant to your search.

Source list—You will need to document the sources where you find your information or evidence so that you can credit the sources in your work. Record all the information needed to identify each source you use in your research in the form or a list. Number each source card so that you can refer to it when you take notes and add documentation to your report, as in this example for a book.

> 1. Dickens, Charles. *Oliver Twist*. New York: Modern Library, 2001. Print.

HERE'S HOW

MAKING SOURCE LISTS

Follow these guidelines when you make source list:

- **Book** Write the author's or editor's complete name, the title, the location and name of the publisher, and the copyright date.
- **Magazine or Newspaper Article** Write the author's complete name (unless the article is unsigned), the title of the article, the name and date of the publication, and the page number(s) of the article.
- **Encyclopedia Article** Write the author's complete name (unless the article is unsigned), the title of the article, and the name and copyright date of the encyclopedia.
- **World Wide Web Site** Write the author's or editor's complete name (if available), the title of the document, publication information for any print version of it, the date of its electronic publication, the name of any institution or organization responsible for the site, and the date when you accessed the site.

Notes—As you read your sources, write down all relevant facts, quotations, statistics, anecdotes, and examples separately in your notes. When you're ready to draft your paper, you can choose the best method of organizing your information. Here is an example of a note featuring an exact quotation from the Charles Dickens novel.

> 1. "Oliver saw, but too plainly, that resistance would be of no avail. He held out his hand, which Nancy clasped tight in hers" (114).

HERE'S HOW

TAKING NOTES

Follow these guidelines as you take your notes:

- **Write a heading** indicating the subject of each note.
- **Write the number of the corresponding source** from your source list.
- **Put direct quotations in quotation marks.**
- **Record the number of the page** where you found the material.

When recording information in your notes, you can use the following forms of **restatement** to avoid **plagiarism,** or presenting someone else's work as your own:

Paraphrase—When you paraphrase, you restate the writer's idea in your own words. Be sure to enclose in quotation marks any of the author's exact words that you include in a paraphrase.

Summary—When you summarize, you restate the main idea of the original, including key facts and statistics, but in a shorter version, usually about one-third the length of the original. A summary omits unnecessary details.

Quotation—When you use a writer's exact statement, you will need to place quotation marks around it. Be sure to copy the words exactly as the writer wrote them, including all punctuation. Use quotations for

- extremely important ideas that might be misrepresented by paraphrases
- clear and concise explanations
- ideas presented in unusually lively or vivid language

2.2 OUTLINING

Once you've organized your notes in a way that is suitable for your topic, you can create a formal **outline** of how the information will be arranged in your report. An outline can be written in one of two ways: as a sentence outline or as a topic outline. The **sentence outline** contains entries written in sentence form; the **topic outline** contains only phrases or words that represent the ideas. With either choice, each main idea in the outline is designated by a Roman numeral. The subtopics that support the main ideas are designated with indented capital letters. The details that explain the subtopics are designated with indented numerals and lowercase letters.

MODEL: SENTENCE OUTLINE

> **Title:** The Two Worlds of Oliver Twist
>
> **Introduction:** Dickens blurs the distinction between good and evil.
>
> I. Dickens depicts the underworld of London by showing both evil criminal characters and those who commit crimes due to poverty or misfortune.
>
>   A. The criminal characters are cruel and brutal.
>
>   1. Sikes and Monks are characterized as men who will do anything to get what they want.
>
>   2. Fagin's amorality is shown in his manipulating children into committing crimes.
>
>   B. The good characters have believable human weaknesses and failings.
>
> II. The civilized world of London is populated with people who are far from perfect.

MODEL: TOPIC OUTLINE

> **Title: The Two Worlds of Oliver Twist**
>
> **Introduction:** Dickens blurs the distinction between good and evil.
>
> I. The underworld of London
>
>   A. The criminal characters
>
>   1. Sikes and Monks
>
>   2. Fagin
>
>   B. The good characters
>
> II. The civilized world of London

2.3 CHECKLIST FOR EVALUATING SOURCES

The information . . .

- ☑ is relevant to the topic you are researching
- ☑ is up-to-date (This point is especially important when researching time-sensitive topics, such as many related to science, medicine, and sports.)
- ☑ is from an author who is qualified to write about the topic
- ☑ is from a trusted source that is updated or reviewed regularly
- ☑ makes the author's or institution's purpose for writing clear
- ☑ is written at the right level for your needs (For example, a children's book is probably too simplistic, while a scientific paper may be too complex.)
- ☑ has the level of detail you need—neither too general nor too specific
- ☑ can be verified in more than one source

3 Sharing Your Research

At last you have established your research goals, located sources of information, evaluated the materials, and taken notes on what you learned. Now you have a chance to share the results with people in your world—and even beyond. Here are some options you may choose to present your work:

- Give a speech to your classmates or to people in your community.
- Create a power presentation using desktop publishing software and share it with classmates, friends, or family members.
- Describe your research findings on your own Web site.
- Summarize the information in a newsletter or brochure.
- Share the results of your research in a formal research paper. If appropriate, include graphics and spreadsheets as a way to present data.

Writing that has a lot of mistakes can confuse or even annoy a reader. A business letter with a punctuation error might lead to a miscommunication and delay a reply. A sentence fragment might lower your grade on an essay. Paying attention to grammar, punctuation, and capitalization rules can make your writing clearer and easier to read.

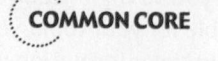

COMMON CORE

Included in this handbook:
L 1, L 2, L 2a, L 3a, L 4a, L 4b

Quick Reference: Parts of Speech

PART OF SPEECH	FUNCTION	EXAMPLES
Noun	names a person, a place, a thing, an idea, a quality, or an action	
Common	serves as a general name, or a name common to an entire group	king, monster, ship, ocean
Proper	names a specific, one-of-a-kind person, place, or thing	Chaucer, London, Thames River
Singular	refers to a single person, place, thing, or idea	woman, river, leaf, flame
Plural	refers to more than one person, place, thing, or idea	women, rivers, leaves, flames
Concrete	names something that can be perceived by the senses	rose, church, bell, sky
Abstract	names something that cannot be perceived by the senses	contentment, honor, faith, trust
Compound	expresses a single idea through a combination of two or more words	sunshine, middle class, mother-in-law
Collective	refers to a group of people or things	crop, crew, family
Possessive	shows who or what owns something	Burns's, mice's, nature's, fields'
Pronoun	takes the place of a noun or another pronoun	
Personal	refers to the person making a statement, the person(s) being addressed, or the person(s) or thing(s) the statement is about	I, me, my, mine, we, us, our, ours, you, your, yours, she, he, it, her, him, hers, his, its, they, them, their, theirs
Reflexive	follows a verb or preposition and refers to a preceding noun or pronoun	myself, yourself, herself, himself, itself, ourselves, yourselves, themselves
Intensive	emphasizes a noun or another pronoun	(same as reflexives)
Demonstrative	points to one or more specific persons or things	this, that, these, those
Interrogative	signals a question	who, whom, whose, which, what
Indefinite	refers to one or more persons or things not specifically mentioned	both, all, most, many, anyone, everybody, several, none, some
Relative	introduces an adjective clause by relating it to a word in the clause	who, whom, whose, which, that

PART OF SPEECH	FUNCTION	EXAMPLES
Verb	expresses an action, a condition, or a state of being	
Action	tells what the subject does or did, physically or mentally	run, reaches, listened, consider, decides, dreamed
Linking	connects the subject to something that identifies or describes it	am, is, are, was, were, sound, taste, appear, feel, become, remain, seem
Auxiliary	precedes the main verb in a verb phrase	be, have, do, can, could, will, would, may, might
Transitive	directs the action toward someone or something; always has an object	The wind **snapped** the young tree in half.
Intransitive	does not direct the action toward someone or something; does not have an object	The young tree **snapped.**
Adjective	modifies a noun or pronoun	**frightened** man, **two** epics, **enough** time
Adverb	modifies a verb, an adjective, or another adverb	walked **out, really** funny, **far** away
Preposition	relates one word to another word	at, by, for, from, in, of, on, to, with
Conjunction	joins words or word groups	
Coordinating	joins words or word groups used the same way	and, but, or, for, so, yet, nor
Correlative	used as a pair to join words or word groups used the same way	both . . . and, either . . . or, neither . . . nor
Subordinating	introduces a clause that cannot stand by itself as a complete sentence	although, after, as, before, because, when, if, unless
Interjection	expresses emotion	whew, yikes, uh-oh

Quick Reference: The Sentence and Its Parts

The diagrams that follow will give you a brief review of the essentials of a sentence and some of its parts.

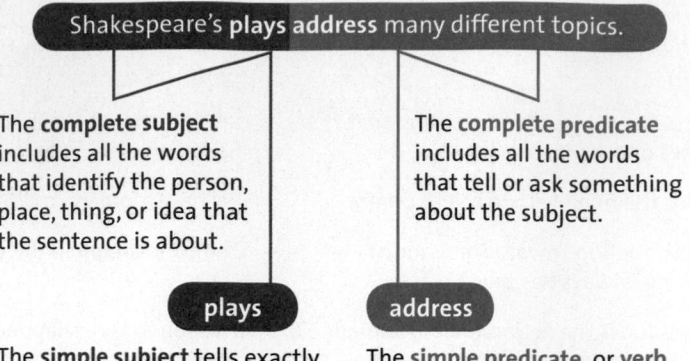

Shakespeare's **plays** **address** many different topics.

The **complete subject** includes all the words that identify the person, place, thing, or idea that the sentence is about.

plays

The **simple subject** tells exactly whom or what the sentence is about. It may be one word or a group of words, but it does not include modifiers.

The **complete predicate** includes all the words that tell or ask something about the subject.

address

The **simple predicate**, or **verb**, tells what the subject does or is. It may be one word or several, but it does not include modifiers.

Every word in a sentence is part of a complete subject or a complete predicate.

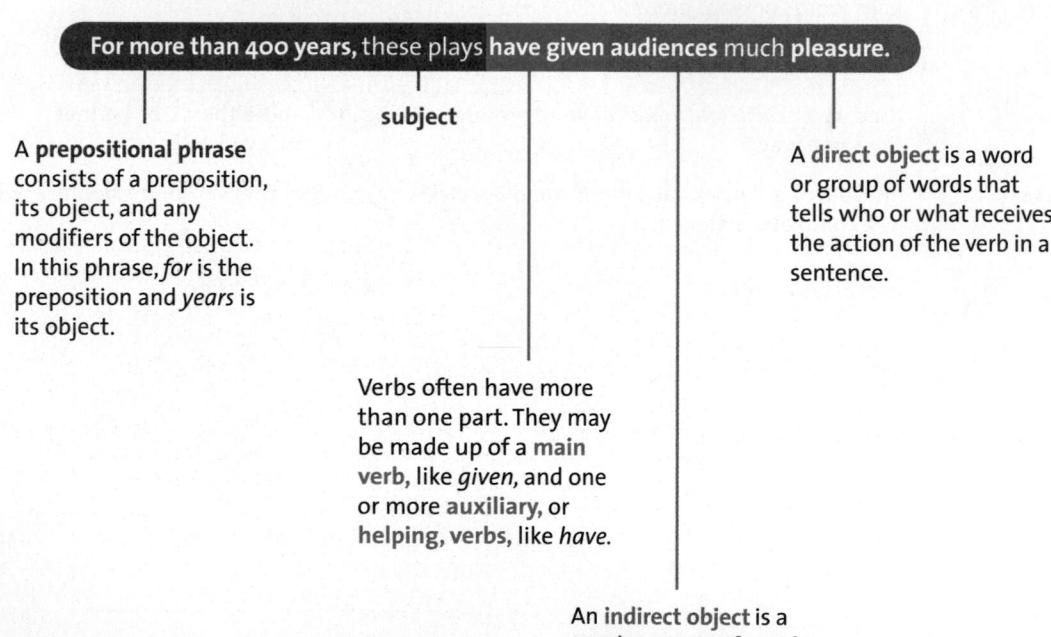

For more than 400 years, these plays **have given audiences** much **pleasure.**

subject

A **prepositional phrase** consists of a preposition, its object, and any modifiers of the object. In this phrase, *for* is the preposition and *years* is its object.

A **direct object** is a word or group of words that tells who or what receives the action of the verb in a sentence.

Verbs often have more than one part. They may be made up of a **main verb,** like *given,* and one or more **auxiliary,** or **helping, verbs,** like *have.*

An **indirect object** is a word or group of words that tells *to whom* or *for whom* or *to what* or *for what* about the verb. A sentence can have an indirect object only if it has a direct object. The indirect object always comes before the direct object in a sentence.

Quick Reference: Punctuation

MARK	FUNCTION	EXAMPLES
End Marks period, question mark, exclamation point	ends a sentence	The games begin today. Who is your favorite contestant? What a play Jamie made!
period	follows an initial or abbreviation **Exception:** postal abbreviations of states	Prof. Ted Bakerman, D. H. Lawrence, Houghton Mifflin Co., P.M., A.D., oz., ft., Blvd., St. NE (Nebraska), NV (Nevada)
period	follows a number or letter in an outline	I. Volcanoes A. Central-vent 1. Shield
Comma	separates parts of a compound sentence	I have never disliked poetry, but now I really love it.
	separates items in a series	She is brave, loyal, and kind.
	separates adjectives of equal rank that modify the same noun	The slow, easy route is best.
	sets off a term of address	O wind, if winter comes ... Come to the front, children.
	sets off a parenthetical expression	Hard workers, as you know, don't quit. I'm not a quitter, believe me.
	sets off an introductory word, phrase, or dependent clause	Yes, I forgot my key. At the beginning of the day, I feel fresh. While she was out, I was here. Having finished my chores, I went out.
	sets off a nonessential phrase or clause	Ed Pawn, the captain of the chess team, won. Ed Pawn, who is the captain, won. The two leading runners, sprinting toward the finish line, finished in a tie.
	sets off parts of dates and addresses	Send it by August 18, 2010, to Cherry Jubilee, Inc., 21 Vernona St., Oakland, Minnesota.
	follows the salutation and closing of a letter	Dear Jim, Sincerely yours,
	separates words to avoid confusion	By noon, time had run out. What the minister does, does matter. While cooking, Jim burned his hand.
Semicolon	separates items in a series if one or more items contain commas	We invited my sister, Jan; her friend, Don; my uncle Jack; and Mary Dodd.
	separates parts of a compound sentence that are not joined by a coordinating conjunction	The small books are on the top shelves; the large books are below. I dusted the books; however, I didn't wipe the shelves.
	separates parts of a compound sentence when the parts contain commas	After I ran out of money, I called my parents; but only my sister was home, unfortunately.

MARK	FUNCTION	EXAMPLES
Colon	introduces a list	Those we wrote were the following: Dana, John, and Will.
	introduces a long quotation	Mary Wollstonecraft wrote: "It appears to me necessary to dwell on these obvious truths, because females have been insulted...."
	follows the salutation of a business letter	Dear Ms. Williams: Dear Senator Wiley:
	separates certain numbers	1:28 P.M., Genesis 2:5
Dash	indicates an abrupt break in thought	I was thinking of my mother—who is arriving tomorrow—just as you walked in.
Parentheses	enclose less important material	Throughout her life (though some might think otherwise), she worked hard. The temperature on this July day (would you believe it?) is 65 degrees!
Hyphen	joins parts of a compound adjective before a noun	She lives in a first-floor apartment.
	joins part of a compound with *all-*, *ex-*, *self-*, or *-elect*	The president-elect is a well-respected woman.
	joins parts of a compound number (to ninety-nine)	Today, I turn twenty-one.
	joins parts of a fraction	My cup is one-third full.
	joins a prefix to a word beginning with a capital letter	The post-Victorian era was marked by great technological advancements.
	indicates that a word is divided at the end of a line	Yeats was a friend of Lady Gregory, an Irish gentle-woman.
Apostrophe	used with *s* to form the possessive of a noun or an indefinite pronoun	my friend's book, my friends' books, anyone's guess, somebody else's problem
	replaces one or more omitted letters in a contraction or numbers in a date	don't (omitted *o*), he'd (omitted *woul*), the class of '99 (omitted *19*)
	used with *s* to form the plural of a letter	I had two A's on my report card.
Quotation Marks	set off a speaker's exact words	Sara said, "I'm finally ready." "I'm ready," Sara said, "finally." Did Sara say, "I'm ready"? Sara said, "I'm ready!"
	set off the title of a story, an article, a short poem, an essay, a song, or a chapter	So far, we've read Swift's essay "A Modest Proposal," Eliot's poem "Preludes," and Joyce's short story "Araby."
Ellipses	replace material omitted from a quotation	"Candide listened attentively ... for he thought Miss Cunegund excessively handsome...."
Italics	indicate the title of a book, a play, a magazine, a long poem, an opera, a film, or a TV series, or the names of ships, trains, or spacecraft	*The Canterbury Tales, The Tragedy of Macbeth, Rolling Stone, Beowulf, Aida, Shakespeare in Love, The Office, Titanic*

Quick Reference: Capitalization

CATEGORY	EXAMPLES
People and Titles	
Names and initials of people	Samuel Johnson, E. M. Forster
Titles used before or in place of names	Professor Holmes, Senator Long
Deities and members of religious groups	Jesus, Allah, Buddha, Zeus, Baptists, Roman Catholics
Names of ethnic and national groups	Hispanics, Jews, African Americans
Geographical Names	
Cities, states, countries, continents	New York, Maine, Haiti, Africa
Regions, bodies of water, mountains	the South, Lake Erie, Mount Katahdin
Geographic features, parks	Continental Divide, Everglades, Yellowstone
Streets and roads, planets	55 East Ninety-fifth Street, Maple Lane, Venus, Jupiter
Organizations, Events, Etc.	
Companies, organizations, teams	General Motors, Lions Club, Utah Jazz
Buildings, bridges, monuments	the Alamo, Golden Gate Bridge, Lincoln Memorial
Documents, awards	the Constitution, World Cup
Special named events	Super Bowl, World Series
Government bodies, historical periods and events	the Supreme Court, the U.S. Senate, Harlem Renaissance, World War II
Days and months, holidays	Friday, May, Easter, Memorial Day
Specific cars, boats, trains, planes	Mustang, *Titanic*, *California Zephyr*
Proper Adjectives	
Adjectives formed from proper nouns	American League, French cooking, Dickensian period, Arctic waters
First Words and the Pronoun *I*	
First word in a sentence or quotation	This is it. He said, "Let's go."
First word of sentence in parentheses that is not within another sentence	The spelling rules are covered in another section. (Consult that section for more information.)
First words in the salutation and closing of a letter	Dear Madam, Very truly yours,
First word in each line of most poetry Personal pronoun *I*	Then am I A happy fly If I live Or if I die.
First word, last word, and all important words in a title	"A Vindication of the Rights of Woman," *Waiting for Godot*

1 Nouns

A **noun** is a word used to name a person, a place, a thing, an idea, a quality, or an action. Nouns can be classified in several ways.

For more information on different types of nouns, see **Quick Reference: Parts of Speech,** *page R50.*

1.1 COMMON NOUNS

Common nouns are general names, common to entire groups.

> **EXAMPLES:** *mountain, country, lake*

1.2 PROPER NOUNS

Proper nouns name specific, one-of-a-kind things.

Common	Proper
mountain, country, lake	Mt. Everest, Italy, Lake Michigan

For more information, see **Quick Reference: Capitalization,** *page R55.*

1.3 SINGULAR AND PLURAL NOUNS

A noun may take a singular or a plural form, depending on whether it names a single person, place, thing, or idea or more than one. Make sure you use appropriate spellings when forming plurals.

Singular	Plural
church, lily, wife	churches, lilies, wives

For more information, see **Forming Plural Nouns,** *page R78.*

1.4 COMPOUND AND COLLECTIVE NOUNS

Compound nouns are formed from two or more words but express a single idea. They are written as single words, as separate words, or with hyphens. Use a dictionary to check the correct spelling of a compound noun.

> **EXAMPLES:** *sunshine, middle class, mother-in-law*

Collective nouns are singular nouns that refer to groups of people or things.

> **EXAMPLES:** *army, flock, class, species*

1.5 POSSESSIVE NOUNS

A **possessive noun** shows who or what owns something.

> **EXAMPLES:** *Conrad's, jury's, children's*

For more information, see **Forming Possessives,** *page R78.*

2 Pronouns

A **pronoun** is a word that is used in place of a noun or another pronoun. The word or word group to which the pronoun refers is called its **antecedent.**

2.1 PERSONAL PRONOUNS

Personal pronouns change their form to express person, number, gender, and case. The forms of these pronouns are shown in the following chart.

	Nominative	Objective	Possessive
Singular			
First person	I	me	my, mine
Second person	you	you	your, yours
Third person	she, he, it	her, him, it	her, hers, his, its
Plural			
First person	we	us	our, ours
Second person	you	you	your, yours
Third person	they	them	their, theirs

2.2 AGREEMENT WITH ANTECEDENT

Pronouns should agree with their antecedents in number, gender, and person.

If an antecedent is singular, use a singular pronoun.

> **EXAMPLE:** ***Gulliver*** *reaches Lilliput after his ship breaks apart.*

If an antecedent is plural, use a plural pronoun.

> **EXAMPLES:**
> *The* **Lilliputians** *shoot their arrows into Gulliver. Gulliver cuts the* **flies** *into pieces as they fly through the air.*

The gender of a pronoun must be the same as the gender of its antecedent.

> **EXAMPLES:**
> *The* **king** *enjoys spending his time with Gulliver.*
> *The* **queen** *places Gulliver in her hand.*

The person of the pronoun must be the same as the person of its antecedent. As the chart in Section 2.1 shows, a pronoun can be in first-, second-, or third-person form.

> **EXAMPLE:**
> ***They*** *invite Gulliver into their home.*

Rewrite each sentence so that the underlined pronoun agrees with its antecedent.

1. The readers of *Gulliver's Travels* love the book as an adventure story, but <u>you</u> like the humor too.

2. In the book, Gulliver travels to strange lands that <u>she</u> never could have imagined.

3. You would be surprised, too, to find <u>their</u> arms and legs suddenly tied down.

4. At first, the Lilliputians fear for <u>its</u> lives.

2.3 PRONOUN CASE

Personal pronouns change form to show how they function in sentences. Different functions are shown by different **cases**. The three cases are **nominative, objective,** and **possessive**. For examples of these pronouns, see the chart in Section 2.1 on page R56.

A **nominative pronoun** is used as a subject or a predicate nominative in a sentence.

An **objective pronoun** is used as a direct object, an indirect object, or the object of a preposition.

SUBJECT   OBJECT   OBJECT OF PREPOSITION

He explained it to me.

A **possessive pronoun** shows ownership. The pronouns *mine, yours, hers, his, its, ours,* and *theirs* can be used in place of nouns.

> **EXAMPLE:** *These letters are yours.*

The pronouns *my, your, her, his, its, our,* and *their* are used before nouns.

> **EXAMPLE:** *These are your letters.*

WATCH OUT! Many spelling errors can be avoided if you watch out for *its* and *their*. Don't confuse the possessive pronoun *its* with the contraction *it's*, meaning "it is" or "it has." The homonyms *they're* (a contraction of *they are*) and *there* ("in that place") are often mistakenly used for *their*.

TIP To decide which pronoun to use in a comparison, such as "He tells better tales than (*I* or me)," fill in the missing word(s): *He tells better tales than I* **tell.**

Replace the underlined words in each sentence with an appropriate pronoun and identify the pronoun as a nominative, objective, or possessive pronoun.

1. <u>Percy Bysshe Shelley</u> was a romantic poet.

2. <u>Percy Bysshe Shelley's</u> friend Lord Byron was also a well-known poet.

3. The writer Mary Wollstonecraft Shelley was <u>Shelley's</u> wife.

4. Mary's novel *Frankenstein* has entertained <u>readers</u> for nearly 200 years.

5. Many film versions of <u>*Frankenstein*</u> exist.

2.4 REFLEXIVE AND INTENSIVE PRONOUNS

These pronouns are formed by adding -*self* or -*selves* to certain personal pronouns. Their forms are the same, and they differ only in how they are used.

A **reflexive pronoun** follows a verb or a preposition and reflects back on an earlier noun or pronoun.

> **EXAMPLES:**
> *He threw himself forward.*
> *Danielle mailed herself the package.*

Intensive pronouns intensify or emphasize the nouns or pronouns to which they refer.

> **EXAMPLES:**
> *The queen herself would have been amused.*
> *I saw it myself.*

WATCH OUT! Avoid using *hisself* or *theirselves*. Standard English does not include these forms.

> **NONSTANDARD:** *He had painted hisself into a corner.*

> **STANDARD:** *He had painted himself into a corner.*

2.5 DEMONSTRATIVE PRONOUNS

Demonstrative pronouns point out things and persons near and far.

	Singular	Plural
Near	this	these
Far	that	those

2.6 INDEFINITE PRONOUNS

Indefinite pronouns do not refer to specific persons or things and usually have no antecedents. The chart shows some commonly used indefinite pronouns.

Singular	Plural	Singular or Plural	
another	both	all	none
anybody	few	any	some
no one	many	more	most
neither	several		

TIP Indefinite pronouns that end in *one, body,* or *thing* are always singular.

INCORRECT: *Anyone who wants their research report can pick it up later today.*

CORRECT: *Anyone who wants his or her research report can pick it up later today.*

If the indefinite pronoun might refer to either a male or a female, *his or her* may be used to refer to it, or the sentence may be rewritten.

EXAMPLES: *Everybody wants his or her report back.*
All the students want their reports back.

2.7 INTERROGATIVE PRONOUNS

An **interrogative pronoun** is used to ask a question. The interrogative pronouns are *who, whom, whose, which,* and *what.*

EXAMPLES: *Who is going to the store?*
What time are we leaving?

TIP *Who* is used as a subject, *whom* as an object. To find out which pronoun you need to use in a question, change the question to a statement.

QUESTION: *(Who/Whom) did you meet there?*

STATEMENT: *You met (?) there.*

Since the verb has a subject (*you*), the needed word must be the object form, *whom.*

EXAMPLE: *Whom did you meet there?*

WATCH OUT! A special problem arises when you use an interrupter, such as *do you think,* within a question.

EXAMPLE: *(Who/Whom) do you believe is the more influential musician?*

If you eliminate the interrupter, it is clear that the word you need is *who.*

2.8 RELATIVE PRONOUNS

Relative pronouns relate, or connect, dependent (or subordinate) clauses to the words they modify in sentences. The relative pronouns are *that, what, whatever, which, whichever, who, whoever, whom, whomever,* and *whose.*

Sometimes short sentences with related ideas can be combined by using a relative pronoun.

SHORT SENTENCE: *William Blake was underappreciated by his contemporaries.*

RELATED SENTENCE: *William Blake was both an artist and a poet.*

COMBINED SENTENCE: *William Blake, who was both an artist and a poet, was underappreciated by his contemporaries.*

GRAMMAR PRACTICE

Choose the appropriate interrogative or relative pronoun from the words in parentheses.

1. William Blake wrote *Songs of Innocence,* (who, which) was a collection of poems.

2. (Who, Whom) or what was the inspiration for these poems?

3. Blake based the poems on street ballads and rhymes (that, what) children sang.

4. Blake was a visionary (whom, who) was ahead of his time.

2.9 PRONOUN REFERENCE PROBLEMS

The referent of a pronoun should always be clear.

An **indefinite reference** occurs when the pronoun *it, you,* or *they* does not clearly refer to a specific antecedent.

UNCLEAR: *When making bread, they must not overknead the dough.*

CLEAR: *When making bread, a baker must not overknead the dough.*

A **general reference** occurs when the pronoun *it, this, that, which,* or *such* is used to refer to a general idea rather than a specific antecedent.

UNCLEAR: *Jamie practices piano every day. This has made her an accomplished musician.*

CLEAR: *Jamie practices piano every day. Practicing has made her an accomplished musician.*

Ambiguous means "having more than one possible meaning." An **ambiguous reference** occurs when a pronoun could refer to two or more antecedents.

> UNCLEAR: *Sarah talked to Beth while she folded laundry.*

> CLEAR: *While Sarah folded laundry, she talked to Beth.*

GRAMMAR PRACTICE

Rewrite the following sentences to correct indefinite, ambiguous, and general pronoun references.

1. In "The Wife of Bath's Tale," it tells about a knight who is sent on a quest to find out what women most desire.

2. The knight is given the choice of either accepting the quest or being put to death. This makes him sorrowful.

3. An old woman provides the knight with the correct answer. This saves his life.

4. The queen agrees to the old woman's request that she marry the knight as a reward.

---

3 Verbs

A **verb** is a word that expresses an action, a condition, or a state of being.

*For more information, see **Quick Reference: Parts of Speech**, page R50.*

3.1 ACTION VERBS

Action verbs express mental or physical activity.

> EXAMPLE: *I walked to the store.*

3.2 LINKING VERBS

Linking verbs join subjects with words or phrases that rename or describe them.

> EXAMPLE: *You are my friend.*

3.3 PRINCIPAL PARTS

Action and linking verbs typically have four principal parts, which are used to form verb tenses. The principal parts are the **present,** the **present participle,** the **past,** and the **past participle.**

Action verbs and some linking verbs also fall into two categories: regular and irregular. A **regular verb** is a verb that forms its past and past participle by adding *-ed* or *-d* to the present form.

Present	Present Participle	Past	Past Participle
perform	(is) performing	performed	(has) performed
hope	(is) hoping	hoped	(has) hoped
stop	(is) stopping	stopped	(has) stopped
marry	(is) marrying	married	(has) married

An **irregular verb** is a verb that forms its past and past participle in some other way than by adding *-ed* or *-d* to the present form.

Present	Present Participle	Past	Past Participle
bring	(is) bringing	brought	(has) brought
swim	(is) swimming	swam	(has) swum
steal	(is) stealing	stole	(has) stolen
grow	(is) growing	grew	(has) grown

3.4 VERB TENSE

The **tense** of a verb indicates the time of the action or state of being. An action or state of being can occur in the present, the past, or the future. There are six tenses, each expressing a different range of time.

The **present tense** expresses an action or state that is happening at the present time, occurs regularly, or is constant or generally true. Use the present part.

> NOW: *That ballad sounds great.*

> REGULAR: *I read every day.*

> GENERAL: *The sun rises in the east.*

The **past tense** expresses an action that began and ended in the past. Use the past part.

> EXAMPLE: *The storyteller finished his tale.*

The **future tense** expresses an action or state that will occur. Use *shall* or *will* with the present part.

> EXAMPLE: *They will attend the next festival.*

The **present perfect tense** expresses an action or state that (1) was completed at an indefinite time in the past or (2) began in the past and continues into the present. Use *have* or *has* with the past participle.

> EXAMPLE: *Poetry has inspired readers throughout the ages.*

The **past perfect tense** expresses an action in the past that came before another action in the past. Use *had* with the past participle.

> **EXAMPLE:** *The messenger had traveled for days before he delivered his knight's response.*

The future perfect tense expresses an action in the future that will be completed before another action in the future. Use *shall have* or *will have* with the past participle.

> **EXAMPLE:** *They will have finished the novel before seeing the movie version of the tale.*

> **TIP** The past-tense form of an irregular verb is not paired with an auxiliary verb, but the past-perfect-tense form of an irregular verb is always paired with an auxiliary verb.
>
> **INCORRECT:** *I have went to that restaurant before.*
>
> **INCORRECT:** *I gone to that restaurant before.*
>
> **CORRECT:** *I have gone to that restaurant before.*

3.5 PROGRESSIVE FORMS

The progressive forms of the six tenses show ongoing actions. Use forms of *be* with the present participles of verbs.

> **PRESENT PROGRESSIVE:** *She is rehearsing her lines.*
>
> **PAST PROGRESSIVE:** *She was rehearsing her lines.*
>
> **FUTURE PROGRESSIVE:** *She will be rehearsing her lines.*
>
> **PRESENT PERFECT PROGRESSIVE:** *She has been rehearsing her lines.*
>
> **PAST PERFECT PROGRESSIVE:** *She had been rehearsing her lines.*
>
> **FUTURE PERFECT PROGRESSIVE:** *She will have been rehearsing her lines.*

> **WATCH OUT!** Do not shift from tense to tense needlessly. Watch out for these special cases:

- In most compound sentences and in sentences with compound predicates, keep the tenses the same.

  INCORRECT: *We work hard, and they paid us well.*

  CORRECT: *We work hard, and they pay us well.*

- If one past action happens before another, indicate this with a shift in tense.

  INCORRECT: *They wished they started earlier.*

  CORRECT: *They wished they had started earlier.*

GRAMMAR PRACTICE

Identify the tense of the verb(s) in each of the following sentences. If you find an unnecessary tense shift, correct it.

1. The tales of King Arthur and his knights were popular in the Middle Ages, and they continue to be popular today.

2. Gawain, Arthur's nephew, bravely accepts the Green Knight's challenge and will agree to the pact proposed by the Green Knight.

3. After Gawain cuts off the Green Knight's head, the Green Knight remained alive.

4. Gawain meets the Green Knight again, just as the Green Knight had instructed him to do the year before.

5. This time Gawain receives the blow of the Green Knight's ax, but he did not die.

3.6 ACTIVE AND PASSIVE VOICE

The voice of a verb tells whether its subject performs or receives the action expressed by the verb. When the subject performs the action, the verb is in the **active voice.** When the subject is the receiver of the action, the verb is in the **passive voice.**

Compare these two sentences:

> **ACTIVE:** *Gawain and the Green Knight make a pact with each other.*
>
> **PASSIVE:** *A pact is made between Gawain and the Green Knight.*

To form the passive voice, use a form of *be* with the past participle of the verb.

> **WATCH OUT!** Use the passive voice sparingly. It can make writing awkward and less direct.
>
> **AWKWARD:** *A meeting between the two knights is arranged.*
>
> **BETTER:** *The two knights arrange a meeting.*

There are occasions when you will choose to use the passive voice because

- you want to emphasize the receiver: *The king was shot.*
- the doer is unknown: *My books were stolen.*
- the doer is unimportant: *French is spoken here.*

For the four items below, identify the boldfaced verb phrase as active or passive.

1. King Arthur **was confronted** by the Green Knight.

2. The Green Knight **had been searching** for someone brave enough to meet his challenge.

3. Gawain **did** not **want** King Arthur to subject himself to the challenge.

4. The Green Knight **was struck** by the ax.

4 Modifiers

Modifiers are words or groups of words that change or limit the meanings of other words. Adjectives and adverbs are common modifiers.

4.1 ADJECTIVES

Adjectives modify nouns and pronouns by telling which one, what kind, how many, or how much.

WHICH ONE: *this, that, these, those*

EXAMPLE: *That girl used to live in my neighborhood.*

WHAT KIND: *large, unique, anxious, moldy*

EXAMPLE: *I bought a unique lamp at the yard sale.*

HOW MANY: *ten, many, several, every, each*

EXAMPLE: *I wake up at the same time every day.*

HOW MUCH: *more, less, little, barely*

EXAMPLE: *We bought more food than we could possibly eat.*

4.2 PREDICATE ADJECTIVES

Most adjectives come before the nouns they modify, as in the preview examples. A **predicate adjective,** however, follows a linking verb and describes the subject.

EXAMPLE: *My friends are very intelligent.*

Be especially careful to use adjectives (not adverbs) after such linking verbs as *look, feel, grow, taste,* and *smell.*

EXAMPLE: *The weather grows cold.*

4.3 ADVERBS

Adverbs modify verbs, adjectives, and other adverbs by telling where, when, how, or to what extent.

WHERE: *The children played outside.*

WHEN: *The author spoke yesterday.*

HOW: *We walked slowly behind the leader.*

TO WHAT EXTENT: *He worked very hard.*

Adverbs may occur in many places in sentences, both before and after the words they modify.

EXAMPLES: *Suddenly the wind shifted.*

The wind suddenly shifted.

The wind shifted suddenly.

4.4 ADJECTIVE OR ADVERB?

Many adverbs are formed by adding *-ly* to adjectives.

EXAMPLES: *sweet, sweetly; gentle, gently*

However, *-ly* added to a noun will usually yield an adjective.

EXAMPLES: *friend, friendly; woman, womanly*

4.5 COMPARISON OF MODIFIERS

Modifiers can be used to compare two or more things. The form of a modifier shows the degree of comparison. Both adjectives and adverbs have three forms: the **positive,** the **comparative,** and the **superlative.**

The **positive form** is used to describe individual things, groups, or actions.

EXAMPLES:

Jonathan Swift was a great satirist.

He had a savage wit.

The **comparative form** is used to compare two things, groups, or actions.

EXAMPLES:

I think Jonathan Swift was a greater satirist than Voltaire.

Swift had a more savage wit.

The **superlative form** is used to compare more than two things, groups, or actions.

EXAMPLES:

I think Jonathan Swift was the greatest satirist who ever lived.

Swift had the most savage wit of any writer.

4.6 REGULAR COMPARISONS

Most one-syllable and some two-syllable adjectives and adverbs have comparatives and superlatives formed by adding *-er* and *-est*. All three-syllable and most two-syllable modifiers have comparatives and superlatives formed with *more* or *most*.

Modifier	Comparative	Superlative
tall	taller	tallest
kind	kinder	kindest
droopy	droopier	droopiest
expensive	more expensive	most expensive
wasteful	more wasteful	most wasteful

WATCH OUT! Note that spelling changes must sometimes be made to form the comparatives and superlatives of modifiers.

> **EXAMPLES:**
>
> *friendly, friendlier* (Change *y* to *i* and add the ending.)
>
> *sad, sadder* (Double the final consonant and add the ending.)

4.7 IRREGULAR COMPARISONS

Some commonly used modifiers have irregular comparative and superlative forms. They are listed in the following chart.

Modifier	Comparative	Superlative
good	better	best
bad	worse	worst
far	farther *or* further	farthest *or* furthest
little	less *or* lesser	least
many	more	most
well	better	best
much	more	most

4.8 PROBLEMS WITH MODIFIERS

Study the tips that follow to avoid common mistakes:

Farther and Further Use *farther* for distances; use *further* for everything else.

Double Comparisons Make a comparison by using *-er/-est* or by using *more/most*. Using *-er* with *more* or using *-est* with *most* is incorrect.

> **INCORRECT:** *I like her more better than she likes me.*
>
> **CORRECT:** *I like her better than she likes me.*

Illogical Comparisons An illogical or confusing comparison results when two unrelated things are compared or when something is compared with itself. The word *other* or the word *else* should be used in a comparison of an individual member to the rest of a group.

> **ILLOGICAL:** *I think the orchid is more beautiful than any flower.* (implies that the orchid isn't a flower)
>
> **LOGICAL:** *I think the orchid is more beautiful than any other flower.* (identifies that the orchid is a flower)

Bad vs. Badly *Bad*, always an adjective, is used before a noun or after a linking verb. *Badly*, always an adverb, never modifies a noun. Be sure to use the right form after a linking verb.

> **INCORRECT:** *Ed felt badly after his team lost.*
>
> **CORRECT:** *Ed felt bad after his team lost.*

Good vs. Well *Good* is always an adjective. It is used before a noun or after a linking verb. *Well* is often an adverb meaning "expertly" or "properly." *Well* can also be used as an adjective after a linking verb when it means "in good health."

> **INCORRECT:** *Helen writes very good.*
>
> **CORRECT:** *Helen writes very well.*
>
> **CORRECT:** *Yesterday I felt bad; today I feel well.*

Double Negatives If you add a negative word to a sentence that is already negative, the result will be an error known as a double negative. When using *not* or *-n't* with a verb, use *any-* words, such as *anybody* or *anything*, rather than *no-* words, such as *nobody* or *nothing*, later in the sentence.

> **INCORRECT:** *I don't have no money.*
>
> **CORRECT:** *I don't have any money.*

Using *hardly*, *barely*, or *scarcely* after a negative word is also incorrect.

> **INCORRECT:** *They couldn't barely see two feet ahead.*
>
> **CORRECT:** *They could barely see two feet ahead.*

Misplaced Modifiers Sometimes a modifier is placed so far away from the word it modifies that the intended meaning of the sentence is unclear. Prepositional phrases and participial phrases are often misplaced. Place modifiers as close as possible to the words they modify.

> MISPLACED: *The ranger explained how to find ducks in her office.* (The ducks were not in the ranger's office.)

> CLEARER: *In her office, the ranger explained how to find ducks.*

Dangling Modifiers Sometimes a modifier doesn't appear to modify any word in a sentence. Most dangling modifiers are participial phrases or infinitive phrases.

> DANGLING: *Coming home with groceries, our parrot said, "Hello!"*

> CLEARER: *Coming home with groceries, we heard our parrot say, "Hello!"*

GRAMMAR PRACTICE

Choose the correct word or words from each pair in parentheses.

1. Sir Launcelot was King Arthur's (most favorite, favoritest) knight.

2. Launcelot, however, (wasn't, was) hardly loyal to Arthur.

3. He made the (most gravest, gravest) mistake when he fell in love with Gwynevere, the king's wife.

4. King Arthur felt (bad, badly) about their friendship coming to an end, but what could he do?

5. Launcelot tried to make peace with the king, but Sir Gawain, the king's nephew, didn't want (nothing, anything) to do with Launcelot.

6. Gawain challenged Launcelot to a battle, and Gawain initially fought very (good, well).

7. After three hours of battle, however, Launcelot became the (stronger, more strong) of the two men.

8. Though Gawain was injured in the battle, he wouldn't let (anything, nothing) stop him from fighting Launcelot again.

9. Launcelot felt (badly, bad) about having to fight Gawain once more, but he knew he had to do it.

10. Once again, Launcelot spared Gawain's life, proving himself to be the (nobler, noblest) of all knights.

5 Prepositions, Conjunctions, and Interjections

5.1 PREPOSITIONS

A preposition is a word used to show the relationship between a noun or a pronoun and another word in the sentence.

Commonly Used Prepositions			
above	down	near	through
at	for	of	to
before	from	on	up
below	in	out	with
by	into	over	without

A preposition is always followed by a word or group of words that serves as its object. The preposition, its object, and modifiers of the object are called the **prepositional phrase.** In each example below, the prepositional phrase is highlighted, and the object of the preposition is in boldface type.

> EXAMPLES
>
> *The future of the entire **kingdom** is uncertain.*
>
> *We searched through the deepest **woods.***

Prepositional phrases may be used as adjectives or as adverbs. The phrase in the first example is used as an adjective modifying the noun *future.* In the second example, the phrase is used as an adverb modifying the verb *searched.*

> *WATCH OUT!* Prepositional phrases must be as close as possible to the word they modify.

> MISPLACED: *We have clothes for leisurewear of many colors.*

> CLEARER: *We have clothes of many colors for leisurewear.*

5.2 CONJUNCTIONS

A conjunction is a word used to connect words, phrases, or sentences. There are three kinds of conjunctions: **coordinating conjunctions, correlative conjunctions,** and **subordinating conjunctions.**

Coordinating conjunctions connect words or word groups that have the same function in a sentence. Such conjunctions include *and, but, or, for, so, yet,* and *nor.*

Coordinating conjunctions can join nouns, pronouns, verbs, adjectives, adverbs, prepositional phrases, and clauses in a sentence.

These examples show coordinating conjunctions joining words that have the same function:

EXAMPLES

I have many friends but few enemies. (two noun objects)

We ran out the door and into the street. (two prepositional phrases)

They are pleasant yet seem aloof. (two predicates)

We have to go now, or we will be late. (two clauses)

Correlative conjunctions are similar to coordinating conjunctions. However, correlative conjunctions are always used in pairs.

Correlative Conjunctions		
both . . . and	neither . . . nor	whether . . . or
either . . . or	not only . . . but also	

Subordinating conjunctions introduce subordinate clauses—clauses that cannot stand by themselves as complete sentences. The subordinating conjunction shows how the subordinate clause relates to the rest of the sentence. The relationships include time, manner, place, cause, comparison, condition, and purpose.

Subordinating Conjunctions	
Time	after, as, as long as, as soon as, before, since, until, when, whenever, while
Manner	as, as if
Place	where, wherever
Cause	because, since
Comparison	as, as much as, than
Condition	although, as long as, even if, even though, if provided that, though, unless, while
Purpose	in order that, so that, that

In the example below, the boldface word is the subordinating conjunction, and the highlighted words are the subordinate clause:

EXAMPLE: **Though** *Grendel is a loathsome beast, Beowulf does not fear him.*

Beowulf does not fear him is an independent clause because it can stand alone as a complete sentence. *Though Grendel is a loathsome beast* cannot stand alone as a complete sentence; it is a subordinate clause.

Conjunctive adverbs are used to connect clauses that can stand by themselves as sentences. Conjunctive adverbs include *also, besides, finally, however, moreover, nevertheless, otherwise,* and *then.*

EXAMPLE: *She loved the fall; however, she also enjoyed winter.*

5.3 INTERJECTIONS

Interjections are words used to show strong emotion, such as *wow* and *cool.* Often followed by an exclamation point, they have no grammatical relationship to any other part of a sentence.

EXAMPLE: *Beowulf seizes Grendel, grasping the monster in his fists. Unbelievable!*

6 The Sentence and Its Parts

A **sentence** is a group of words used to express a complete thought. A complete sentence has a subject and a predicate.

For more information, see Quick Reference: The Sentence and Its Parts, page R52.

6.1 KINDS OF SENTENCES

There are four basic types of sentences.

Type	Definition	Example
Declarative	states a fact, wish, intent, or feeling	I just finished reading *Macbeth.*
Interrogative	asks a question	Have you ever read it?
Imperative	gives a command or direction	You must read it sometime.
Exclamatory	expresses strong feeling or excitement	It's so compelling!

6.2 COMPOUND SUBJECTS AND PREDICATES

A compound subject consists of two or more subjects that share the same verb. They are typically joined by the coordinating conjunction *and* or *or.*

EXAMPLE: *The knight and his horse rode into the forest.*

A compound predicate consists of two or more predicates that share the same subject. They too are typically joined by a coordinating conjunction, usually *and, but,* or *or.*

EXAMPLE: *Sir Gawain beheaded the Green Knight but did not kill him.*

6.3 COMPLEMENTS

A **complement** is a word or group of words that completes the meaning of the sentence. Some sentences contain only a subject and a verb. Most sentences, however, require additional words placed after the verb to complete the meaning of the sentence. There are three kinds of complements: direct objects, indirect objects, and subject complements.

Direct objects are words or word groups that receive the action of action verbs. A direct object answers the question *what* or *whom.*

> **EXAMPLES:**
>
> *The students asked many questions.* (Asked what?)
>
> *The teacher quickly answered the students.* (Answered whom?)

Indirect objects tell to whom or what or for whom or what the actions of verbs are performed. Indirect objects come before direct objects. In the examples that follow, the indirect objects are highlighted.

> **EXAMPLES:**
>
> My sister usually gave her *friends* good advice. (Gave to whom?)
>
> *Her brother sent the store a heavy package.* (Sent to what?)

Subject complements come after linking verbs and identify or describe the subjects. A subject complement that names or identifies a subject is called a **predicate nominative.** Predicate nominatives include **predicate nouns** and **predicate pronouns.**

> **EXAMPLES:**
>
> *My friends are very hard workers.*
>
> *The best writer in the class is she.*

A subject complement that describes a subject is called a **predicate adjective.**

> **EXAMPLE:** *The pianist appeared very energetic.*

7 Phrases

A **phrase** is a group of related words that does not contain a subject and a predicate but functions in a sentence as a single part of speech.

7.1 PREPOSITIONAL PHRASES

A **prepositional phrase** is a phrase that consists of a preposition, its object, and any modifiers of the object. Prepositional phrases that modify nouns or pronouns are called **adjective phrases.** Prepositional phrases that modify verbs, adjectives, or adverbs are **adverb phrases.**

> **ADJECTIVE PHRASE:** *The central character of the story is a villain.*
>
> **ADVERB PHRASE:** *He reveals his nature in the first scene.*

7.2 APPOSITIVES AND APPOSITIVE PHRASES

An **appositive** is a noun or pronoun that identifies or renames another noun or pronoun. An **appositive phrase** includes an appositive and modifiers of it.

An appositive can be either **essential** or **nonessential.** An **essential appositive** provides information that is needed to identify what is referred to by the preceding noun or pronoun.

> **EXAMPLE:** *The poet Percy Bysshe Shelley frequently used nature as the subject of his poems.*

A **nonessential appositive** adds extra information about a noun or pronoun whose meaning is already clear. Nonessential appositives and appositive phrases are set off with commas.

> **EXAMPLE:** *The skylark, a bird noted for its melodious song, is the subject of one of Shelley's poems.*

8 Verbals and Verbal Phrases

A **verbal** is a verb form that is used as a noun, an adjective, or an adverb. A **verbal phrase** consists of a verbal along with its modifiers and complements. There are three kinds of verbals: **infinitives, participles, and gerunds.**

8.1 INFINITIVES AND INFINITIVE PHRASES

An **infinitive** is a verb form that usually begins with *to* and functions as a noun, an adjective, or an adverb. An **infinitive phrase** consists of an infinitive plus its modifiers and complements. The examples that follow show several uses of infinitive phrases.

> **NOUN:** *To travel the world is my long-term plan.* (subject)
>
> *I'm trying to find a solution.* (direct object)
>
> *Her greatest wish was to return to her native country.* (predicate nominative)
>
> **ADJECTIVE:** *We supported his goal to become a pilot.* (adjective modifying *goal*)
>
> **ADVERB:** *To prepare for the marathon, Julie maintained a strict exercise regimen.* (adverb modifying *maintained*)

Because infinitives often begin with *to,* it is usually easy to recognize them. However, sometimes *to* may be omitted.

> **EXAMPLE:** *Should you dare [to] speak these forbidden words, a curse will fall upon you.*

8.2 PARTICIPLES AND PARTICIPIAL PHRASES

A **participle** is a verb form that functions as an adjective. Like adjectives, participles modify nouns and pronouns. Most participles are present-participle forms, ending in -*ing*, or past-participle forms ending in -*ed* or -*en*. In the examples that follow, the participles are highlighted.

> **MODIFYING A NOUN:** *The crying baby needed a nap.*
>
> **MODIFYING A PRONOUN:** *Scared, she decided not to walk home alone.*

Participial phrases are participles with all their modifiers and complements.

> **MODIFYING A NOUN:** *The light streaming in through the window woke up the boy.*
>
> **MODIFYING A PRONOUN:** *Walking across the field, she thought she saw a fox.*

8.3 DANGLING AND MISPLACED PARTICIPLES

A participle or participial phrase should be placed as close as possible to the word that it modifies. Otherwise the meaning of the sentence may not be clear.

> **MISPLACED:** *The boys were looking for squirrels searching the trees.*
>
> **CLEARER:** *The boys searching the trees were looking for squirrels.*

A participle or participial phrase that does not clearly modify anything in a sentence is called a **dangling participle.** A dangling participle causes confusion because it appears to modify a word that it cannot sensibly modify. Correct a dangling participle by providing a word for the participle to modify.

> **DANGLING:** *Running like the wind, my hat fell off.* (The hat wasn't running.)
>
> **CLEARER:** *Running like the wind, I lost my hat.*

8.4 GERUNDS AND GERUND PHRASES

A **gerund** is a verb form ending in -*ing* that functions as a noun. Gerunds may perform any function nouns perform.

> **SUBJECT:** *Running is my favorite pastime.*
>
> **DIRECT OBJECT:** *I truly love running.*
>
> **INDIRECT OBJECT:** *You should give running a try.*
>
> **SUBJECT COMPLEMENT:** *My deepest passion is running.*
>
> **OBJECT OF PREPOSITION:** *Her love of running keeps her strong.*

Gerund phrases are gerunds with all their modifiers and complements.

> **SUBJECT:** *Wishing on a star never got me far.*
>
> **OBJECT OF PREPOSITION:** *I will finish before leaving the office.*
>
> **APPOSITIVE:** *Her avocation, flying airplanes, finally led to full-time employment.*

GRAMMAR PRACTICE

Identify the underlined phrases as appositive phrases, infinitive phrases, participial phrases, or gerund phrases.

1. In D. H. Lawrence's story "The Rocking-Horse Winner," the protagonist becomes obsessed with <u>betting on horses</u>.

2. The protagonist, <u>a young boy</u>, starts to win a lot of money from the races.

3. <u>Feeling unbeatable</u>, the boy continues to bet more and more money.

4. He wants <u>to win as much as possible</u> but makes himself sick in the process.

5. After the boy dies of his illness, the mother discovers that <u>having a lot of money</u> isn't so important after all.

9 Clauses

A **clause** is a group of words that contains a subject and a verb. There are two kinds of clauses: independent clauses and subordinate clauses.

9.1 INDEPENDENT AND SUBORDINATE CLAUSES

An **independent clause** can stand alone as a sentence, as the word *independent* suggests.

> **INDEPENDENT CLAUSE:** *T. S. Eliot wrote a poem called "The Naming of Cats."*

A sentence may contain more than one independent clause.

> **EXAMPLE:** *T. S. Eliot wrote a poem called "The Naming of Cats," and he also wrote a poem called "The Hollow Men."*

In the preceding example, the coordinating conjunction *and* joins two independent clauses.

*For more information, see **Coordinating Conjunctions**, page R63.*

A **subordinate clause** cannot stand alone as a sentence. It is subordinate to, or dependent on, an independent clause.

> **EXAMPLE:** *Although Eliot was born in America, he later moved to England.*

The highlighted clause cannot stand by itself; it must be joined with an independent clause to form a complete sentence.

9.2 ADJECTIVE CLAUSES

An **adjective clause** is a subordinate clause used as an adjective. It usually follows the noun or pronoun it modifies. Adjective clauses are typically introduced by the relative pronoun *who, whom, whose, which,* or *that.*

> **EXAMPLES:** *"The Naming of Cats" is the poem that I like best.*
>
> *The poem, which is very humorous, discusses the difficulty of naming cats.*
>
> *I think the people who enjoy the poem most are cat lovers.*

*For more information, see **Relative Pronouns,** page R58.*

An adjective clause can be either essential or nonessential. An **essential adjective clause** provides information that is necessary to identify the preceding noun or pronoun.

> **EXAMPLE:** *Eliot was a poet who wrote about many different topics.*

A **nonessential adjective clause** adds additional information about a noun or pronoun whose meaning is already clear. Nonessential clauses are set off with commas.

> **EXAMPLE:** *Eliot, who was always fond of Lewis Carroll, decided to try his hand at humor.*

> **TIP** The relative pronouns *whom, which,* and *that* may sometimes be omitted when they are objects in adjective clauses.

> **EXAMPLE:** *The names [that] I like best are Augustus and Demeter.*

9.3 ADVERB CLAUSES

An **adverb clause** is a subordinate clause that is used to modify a verb, an adjective, or an adverb. It is introduced by a subordinating conjunction.

*For more information, see **Subordinating Conjunctions,** page R64.*

Adverb clauses typically occur at the beginning or end of sentences.

> **MODIFYING A VERB:** *When we need you, we will call.*
>
> **MODIFYING AN ADVERB:** *I'll stay here where there is shelter from the rain.*
>
> **MODIFYING AN ADJECTIVE:** *Roman felt as good as he had ever felt.*

9.4 NOUN CLAUSES

A **noun clause** is a subordinate clause that is used as a noun. A noun clause may be used as a subject, a direct object, an indirect object, a predicate nominative, or an object of a preposition. Noun clauses are introduced either by pronouns, such as *that, what, who, whoever, which,* and *whose,* or by subordinating conjunctions, such as *how, when, where, why,* and *whether.*

*For more information, see **Subordinating Conjunctions,** page R64.*

> **TIP** Because the same words may introduce adjective and noun clauses, you need to consider how a clause functions within its sentence. To determine if a clause is a noun clause, try substituting *something* or *someone* for the clause. If you can do it, it is probably a noun clause.

> **EXAMPLES:** *I asked her when I should leave.*
>
> ("I asked her *something*." The clause is a noun clause, direct object of the verb *asked.*)
>
> *Whoever decides to go can get a ride with me.*
>
> ("*Someone* can get a ride with me." The clause is a noun clause, functioning as the subject of the sentence.)

10 The Structure of Sentences

When classified by their structure, there are four kinds of sentences: simple, compound, complex, and compound-complex.

10.1 SIMPLE SENTENCES

A **simple sentence** is a sentence that has one independent clause and no subordinate clauses. Various parts of simple sentences may be compound, and simple sentences may contain grammatical structures such as appositive and verbal phrases.

> **EXAMPLES:**
>
> *William Blake, a rare talent, wrote poetry and created art.* (an appositive phrase and a compound predicate)
>
> *Inspired by both the human and the divine, Blake wanted to share his unique vision with the world.* (a participial phrase and an infinitive phrase)

10.2 COMPOUND SENTENCES

A **compound sentence** consists of two or more independent clauses. The clauses in compound sentences are joined with commas and coordinating conjunctions (*and, but, or, nor, yet, for, so*) or with semicolons. Like simple sentences, compound sentences do not contain any subordinate clauses.

> **EXAMPLES:**
>
> *I like to exercise, but it can be difficult to find the time. I went to the store first; then I went to the bank.*

> **WATCH OUT!** Do not confuse compound sentences with simple sentences that have compound parts.
>
> **EXAMPLE:** *He vacuumed the floor and shook out the rugs.* (Here *and* joins parts of a compound predicate, not a compound sentence.)

10.3 COMPLEX SENTENCES

A **complex sentence** consists of one independent clause and one or more subordinate clauses. Each subordinate clause can be used as a noun or as a modifier. If it is used as a modifier, a subordinate clause usually modifies a word in the independent clause, and the independent clause can stand alone. However, when a subordinate clause is a noun clause, it is a part of the independent clause; the two cannot be separated.

> **MODIFIER:** *As soon as I am finished with this, I will move on to the next project.*

> **NOUN CLAUSE:** *We're going to the park with whoever else wants to come along.* (The noun clause is the object of the preposition *with* and cannot be separated from the rest of the sentence.)

10.4 COMPOUND-COMPLEX SENTENCES

A **compound-complex sentence** contains two or more independent clauses and one or more subordinate clauses. Compound-complex sentences are, simply, both compound and complex. If you start with a compound sentence, all you need to do to form a compound-complex sentence is add a subordinate clause.

> **COMPOUND:** *We're going to the baseball game, and then we're going to get some ice cream.*

> **COMPOUND-COMPLEX:** *We're going to the baseball game that begins at six o'clock, and then we're going to get some ice cream.*

10.5 PARALLEL STRUCTURE

When you write sentences, make sure that coordinate parts are equivalent, or **parallel,** in structure.

> **NOT PARALLEL:** *I am going to hike and swimming.* (*To hike* is an infinitive; *swimming* is a gerund.)

> **PARALLEL:** *I am going hiking and swimming.* (*Hiking* and *swimming* are both gerunds.)

> **NOT PARALLEL:** *I like steak and to eat potatoes.* (*Steak* is a noun; *to eat potatoes* is a phrase.)

> **PARALLEL:** *I like steak and potatoes.* (*Steak* and *potatoes* are both nouns.)

11 Writing Complete Sentences

Remember, a sentence is a group of words that expresses a complete thought. In formal writing, try to avoid both sentence fragments and run-on sentences.

11.1 CORRECTING FRAGMENTS

A **sentence fragment** is a group of words that is only part of a sentence. It does not express a complete thought and may be confusing to a reader or listener. A sentence fragment may be lacking a subject, a predicate, or both.

> **FRAGMENT:** *Went for a boat ride.* (no subject)

> **CORRECTED:** *We went for a boat ride.*

> **FRAGMENT:** *People of all ages.* (no predicate)

> **CORRECTED:** *People of all ages tried to water ski.*

> **FRAGMENT:** *After the boat ride.* (neither subject nor predicate)

> **CORRECTED:** *We dried off by the fire after the boat ride.*

In your writing, fragments may be a result of haste or incorrect punctuation. Sometimes fixing a fragment will be a matter of attaching it to a preceding or following sentence.

> **FRAGMENT:** *We saw the two girls. Waiting for the bus to arrive.*

> **CORRECTED:** *We saw the two girls waiting for the bus to arrive.*

11.2 CORRECTING RUN-ON SENTENCES

A **run-on sentence** is made up of two or more sentences written as though they were one. Some run-ons have no punctuation within them. Others may have only commas where conjunctions or stronger punctuation marks are necessary. Use your judgment in correcting run-on sentences, as you have choices. You can make a run-on two sentences if the thoughts are not closely connected. If the thoughts are closely related, you can keep the run-on as one sentence by adding a semicolon or a conjunction.

RUN-ON: *We found a place for the picnic by a small pond it was three miles from the village.*

MAKE TWO SENTENCES: *We found a place for the picnic by a small pond. It was three miles from the village.*

RUN-ON: *We found a place for the picnic by a small pond it was perfect.*

USE A SEMICOLON: *We found a place for the picnic by a small pond; it was perfect.*

ADD A CONJUNCTION: *We found a place for the picnic by a small pond, and it was perfect.*

WATCH OUT! When you form compound sentences, make sure you use appropriate punctuation: a comma before a coordinating conjunction, a semicolon when there is no coordinating conjunction. A very common mistake is to use a comma alone instead of a comma and a conjunction. This error is called a **comma splice.**

INCORRECT: *He finished the apprenticeship, he left the village.*

CORRECT: *He finished the apprenticeship, and he left the village.*

GRAMMAR PRACTICE

Rewrite the following paragraph, correcting all fragments and run-ons.

The *Book of Margery Kempe* details the tremendous difficulties that Kempe experiences. After the birth of her first child. She sees demons and fears for her own life, her keepers restrain her so that she cannot do harm to herself. She says that one day she is visited by Jesus. And that, afterwards, she becomes calm and rational again. After this transformative experience, Kempe goes on to become a preacher. And a religious visionary.

12 Subject-Verb Agreement

The subject and verb in a clause must agree in number. Agreement means that if the subject is singular, the verb is also singular, and if the subject is plural, the verb is also plural.

12.1 BASIC AGREEMENT

Fortunately, agreement between subjects and verbs in English is simple. Most verbs show the difference between singular and plural only in the third person of the present tense. In the present tense, the third-person singular form ends in -s.

Present-Tense Verb Forms	
Singular	**Plural**
I eat	we eat
you eat	you eat
she, he, it eats	they eat

12.2 AGREEMENT WITH *BE*

The verb *be* presents special problems in agreement, because this verb does not follow the usual verb patterns.

Forms of *Be*			
Present Tense		**Past Tense**	
Singular	**Plural**	**Singular**	**Plural**
I am	we are	I was	we were
you are	you are	you were	you were
she, he, it is	they are	she, he, it was	they were

12.3 WORDS BETWEEN SUBJECT AND VERB

A verb agrees only with its subject. When words come between a subject and a verb, ignore them when considering proper agreement. Identify the subject and make sure the verb agrees with it.

EXAMPLES:

Several items in the storage unit need to be thrown out.

Many of the puppies in the litter are smaller than others.

12.4 AGREEMENT WITH COMPOUND SUBJECTS

Use plural verbs with most compound subjects joined by the word *and.*

EXAMPLE: *My mother and her sisters call each other every Sunday.*

To confirm that you need a plural verb, you could substitute the plural pronoun *they* for *my mother and her sisters.*

If a compound subject is thought of as a unit, use a singular verb. Test this by substituting the singular pronoun *it.*

EXAMPLE: *Liver and onions [it] is Robert's least favorite dish.*

Use a singular verb with a compound subject that is preceded by *each, every,* or *many a.*

> **EXAMPLE:** *Every man, woman, and child is being ordered off the ship.*

When the parts of a compound subject are joined by *or, nor,* or the correlative conjunctions *either ... or* or *neither ... nor,* make the verb agree with the noun or pronoun nearest the verb.

> **EXAMPLES:**
>
> *Cheddar or Swiss is my favorite cheese.*
>
> *Either my brother or my sisters are coming to pick me up.*
>
> *Neither I nor my two friends were here at the time of the accident.*

12.5 PERSONAL PRONOUNS AS SUBJECTS

When using a personal pronoun as a subject, make sure to match it with the correct form of the verb *be.* (See the chart in Section 12.2.) Note especially that the pronoun *you* takes the forms *are* and *were,* regardless of whether it is singular or plural.

> **WATCH OUT!** *You is* and *you was* are nonstandard forms and should be avoided in writing and speaking. *We was* and *they was* are also forms to be avoided.
>
> **INCORRECT:** *You is facing the wrong direction.*
>
> **CORRECT:** *You are facing the wrong direction.*
>
> **INCORRECT:** *We was telling ghost stories.*
>
> **CORRECT:** *We were telling ghost stories.*

12.6 INDEFINITE PRONOUNS AS SUBJECTS

Some indefinite pronouns are always singular; some are always plural.

Singular Indefinite Pronouns			
another	either	neither	one
anybody	everybody	nobody	somebody
anyone	everyone	no one	someone
anything	everything	nothing	something
each	much		

> **EXAMPLES:**
>
> *Each of the writers was given an award.*
>
> *Somebody in the room upstairs is sleeping.*

Plural Indefinite Pronouns			
both	few	many	several

> **EXAMPLES:**
>
> *Many of the books in our library are not in circulation.*
>
> *Few have been returned recently.*

Still other indefinite pronouns may be either singular or plural.

Singular or Plural Indefinite Pronouns		
all	more	none
any	most	some

The number of the indefinite pronoun *any* or *none* often depends on the intended meaning.

> **EXAMPLES:**
>
> *Any of these topics has potential for a good article.* (any one topic)
>
> *Any of these topics have potential for good articles.* (all of the many topics)

The indefinite pronouns *all, some, more, most,* and *none* are singular when they refer to quantities or parts of things. They are plural when they refer to numbers of individual things. Context will usually give a clue.

> **EXAMPLES:**
>
> *All of the flour is gone.* (referring to a quantity)
>
> *All of the flowers are gone.* (referring to individual items)

12.7 INVERTED SENTENCES

Problems in agreement often occur in inverted sentences beginning with *here* or *there;* in questions beginning with *how, when, why, where,* or *what;* and in inverted sentences beginning with phrases. Identify the subject—wherever it is—before deciding on the verb.

> **EXAMPLES:**
>
> *There clearly are far too many cooks in this kitchen.*
>
> *What is the correct ingredient for this stew?*
>
> *Far from the embroiled cooks stands the master chef.*

Locate the subject of each clause in the sentences below. Then choose the correct verb.

1. The work *A History of the English Church and People* (contain, contains) important historical information.

2. Few books (is, are) as valuable for researching early British history.

3. Many stories in the book (discuss, discusses) the spread of Christianity in England.

4. During the fifth century, both the pagan faith and the Christian faith (were, was) present in Britain.

5. Each of King Edwin's counselors (was, were) in agreement that the king should convert to Christianity.

6. Neither the counselors nor the king (were, was) convinced that he should continue to follow the pagan faith.

7. In the end, none of the pagan temples and altars (was, were) left standing.

12.8 SENTENCES WITH PREDICATE NOMINATIVES

When a predicate nominative serves as a complement in a sentence, use a verb that agrees with the subject, not the complement.

EXAMPLES:

The poems of John Keats are one component of this book. (The subject is the plural noun *poems*, not *component*, and it takes the plural verb *are*.)

One component of this book is the poems of John Keats. (The subject is the singular noun *component*, and it takes the singular verb *is*.)

12.9 *DON'T* AND *DOESN'T* AS AUXILIARY VERBS

The auxiliary verb *doesn't* is used with singular subjects and with the personal pronouns *she, he,* and *it*. The auxiliary verb *don't* is used with plural subjects and with the personal pronouns *I, we, you,* and *they*.

SINGULAR: *He doesn't have time to wait any longer.*

Doesn't Emily know where to meet us?

PLURAL: *We don't think we can make it to the party.*

The campers don't have enough wood to build a fire.

12.10 COLLECTIVE NOUNS AS SUBJECTS

Collective nouns are singular nouns that name groups of persons or things. *Family,* for example, is the collective name of a group of individuals. A collective noun takes a singular verb when the group acts as a single unit. It takes a plural verb when the members of the group act separately.

EXAMPLES:

Her family is moving to another state. (The family as a whole is moving.)

Her family are carrying furniture out to the truck. (The individual members are carrying furniture.)

12.11 RELATIVE PRONOUNS AS SUBJECTS

When the relative pronoun *who, which,* or *that* is used as a subject in an adjective clause, the verb in the clause must agree in number with the antecedent of the pronoun.

SINGULAR: *The scent that wafts through the air is jasmine.*

The antecedent of the relative pronoun *that* is the singular *scent*. Therefore, *that* is singular and must take the singular verb *wafts*.

PLURAL: *The muffins, which are an old family recipe, get eaten quickly.*

The antecedent of the relative pronoun *which* is the plural *muffins*. Therefore, *which* is plural, and it takes the plural verb *are*.

The key to becoming an independent reader is to develop a toolkit of vocabulary strategies. By learning and practicing the strategies, you'll know what to do when you encounter unfamiliar words while reading. You'll also know how to refine the words you use for different situations—personal, school, and work.

Being a good speller is important when communicating your ideas in writing. Learning basic spelling rules and checking your spelling in a dictionary will help you spell words that you may not use frequently.

COMMON CORE

Included in this handbook:
L 2b, L 4, L 4a–c, L 5, L 6

1 Using Context Clues

The context of a word is made up of the punctuation marks, words, sentences, and paragraphs that surround the word. A word's context can give you important clues about its meaning.

1.1 GENERAL CONTEXT

Sometimes you need to infer the meaning of an unfamiliar word by reading all the information in a passage.

Since he has received perfect scores on all of the tests, I'd say his forte is definitely history.

You can tell from the context that *forte* means "strength."

1.2 SPECIFIC CONTEXT CLUES

Sometimes writers help you understand the meanings of words by providing specific clues such as those shown in the chart.

1.3 IDIOMS, SLANG, AND FIGURATIVE LANGUAGE

Use context clues to figure out the meanings of idioms, figurative language, and slang.

An **idiom** is an expression whose overall meaning is different from the meaning of the individual words.

With only seconds left before the bell, Alison made it to class by the skin of her teeth. (By the skin of her teeth means "just in time.")

Figurative language is language that communicates meaning beyond the literal meaning of the words. Note this example from "A Sunrise on the Veld" by Doris Lessing:

Soon he could see them, small and wild-looking in a wild strange light, now that the bush stood trembling on the verge of color, waiting for the sun to paint earth and grass afresh. (Verge means "the point beyond which something is likely to occur.")

Slang is informal language composed of made-up words and ordinary words that are used to mean something different from their meanings in formal English.

We both thought the movie was really cool because of all the special effects. (Cool means "excellent.")

Specific Context Clues		
Type of Clue	**Key Words/ Phrases**	**Example**
Definition or restatement of the meaning of the word	or, which is, that is, in other words, also known as, also called	During the last week of the *dog days*—**that hot period of summer from July to early September**—our town was hit by a hurricane.
Example following an unfamiliar word	such as, like, as if, for example, especially, including	The hurricane wreaked *havoc*, **including downed power lines, toppled trees, and flooded roads.**
Comparison with a more familiar word or concept	as, like, also, similar to, in the same way, likewise	Ordinarily, the mayor is *loquacious*; **however, he hasn't said a word all day.**
Contrast with a familiar word or experience	unlike, but, however, although, on the other hand, on the contrary	The reporter was usually **focused,** but today he was *preoccupied*.
Synonym	An unfamiliar word is followed by a familiar word with a similar meaning	A reporter *impassively* relayed what happened in an equally **unemotional** account.

*For more information, see **Vocabulary Strategies** on pages 13, 264, 460, 668, 992, 1028, 1150, and 1278 and **Vocabulary Strategy: Idioms**, page 1296.*

2 Analyzing Word Structure

Many words can be broken into smaller parts, such as base words, roots, prefixes, and suffixes.

2.1 BASE WORDS

A **base word** is a word part that by itself is also a word. Other words or word parts can be added to base words to form new words.

2.2 ROOTS

A **root** is a word part that contains the core meaning of the word. Many English words contain roots that come from older languages such as Greek, Latin, Old English (Anglo-Saxon), and Norse. Knowing the meaning of a word's root can help you determine the word's meaning.

For more information, see **Vocabulary Strategies** *on pages 168, 198, 1330, and 1354.*

Root	Meaning	Example
log (Greek)	word; study	epilogue, ecology
card (Greek)	heart	cardiogram
stat (Greek)	standing	static
meter (Greek)	measure	thermometer
hydra / hydro (Greek)	water	hydraulics
cosm / cosmo (Greek)	world	cosmic
ped (Latin)	foot	pedestrian
pel / pul (Latin)	drive; thrust	repel, repulse
equ / equi (Latin)	equal	equitable

2.3 PREFIXES

A **prefix** is a word part attached to the beginning of a word. Most prefixes come from Greek, Latin, or Old English.

For more information, see **Vocabulary Strategies** *on pages 13, 182, 1238, and 1330.*

Prefix	Meaning	Example
di- / dia- (Greek)	through	disect
micro- (Greek)	small	microphone
a- (Anglo-Saxon)	in, on; away	asleep
quad- (Latin)	four	quadrangle
pro- (Latin)	forward	progress

2.4 SUFFIXES

A **suffix** is a word part that appears at the end of a root or base word to form a new word. Some suffixes do not change word meaning. These suffixes are

- added to nouns to change the number of persons or objects
- added to verbs to change the tense
- added to modifiers to change the degree of comparison

Suffix	Meaning	Example
-s, -es	to change the number of a noun	trunk + s = trunks
-d, -ed, -ing	to change verb tense	sprinkle + d = sprinkled
-er, -est	to change the degree of comparison in modifiers	cold + er = colder icy + est = iciest

Other suffixes can be added to a root or base to change the word's meaning. These suffixes can also determine a word's part of speech.

Suffix	Meaning	Example
-ence	state or condition of	independence
-ous	full of	furious
-ate	to make	activate
-ly, -ily	manner	quickly

For more information, see **Vocabulary Strategies** *on pages 13 and 72.*

Strategies for Understanding Unfamiliar Words

- Look for any prefixes or suffixes. Remove them to isolate the base word or the root.
- See if you recognize any elements—prefix, suffix, root, or base—of the word. You may be able to guess its meaning by analyzing one or two elements.
- Use the context in the sentence and the word parts to make a logical guess about the word's meaning.
- Consult a dictionary to see whether you are correct.

Interactive Vocabulary — THINK central

Go to **thinkcentral.com**.
KEYWORD: HML12-R73

Make inferences about the meanings of the following words from the fields of science and math. Consider what you have learned in this section about Greek, Latin, and Anglo-Saxon (Old English) word parts.

cardiology	hydrometer	perimeter
pathology	diameter	microcosm
diagram	hydrostatic	cosmology
electrocardiogram	quadruped	propulsion

3 Understanding Word Origins

3.1 ETYMOLOGIES

Etymologies show the origin and historical development of a word. When you study a word's history and origin, you can find out when, where, and how the word came to be. Histories of language and dictionaries are valuable tools for exploring how forms and meanings of words have changed through time:

boy•cott (boi′kŏt′) *tr.v.* **-cott•ed, -cott•ing, -cotts**
To abstain from or act together in abstaining from using, buying, or dealing with as an expression of protest or disfavor or as a means of coercion. See synonyms at **blackball.** *n.* The act or an instance of boycotting. [After Charles C. *Boycott* (1832–1897), English land agent in Ireland.] **—boy′-cott′er** *n.*

quo•rum (kwôr′əm, kwōr′-) *n.* **1.** The minimal number of officers and members of a committee or organization, usually a majority, who must be present for valid transaction of business. **2.** A select group. [Middle English, quorum of justices of the peace, from Latin *quōrum,* of whom (from the wording of a commission naming certain persons as members of a body), genitive pl. of *quī,* who.]

For more information, see **Vocabulary Strategy: Etymologies,** *page 94.*

Trace the etymology of the words below, often used in the fields of history and political science.

appropriate	filibuster	referendum
carpetbagger	immigrate	secession
caucus	impeach	tariff
communism	pacifism	veto
constitution	ratify	

3.2 WORD FAMILIES

Words that have the same root make up a word family and have related meanings. The chart shows a common Greek and a common Latin root. Notice how the meanings of the example words are related to the meanings of their roots.

Latin Root	*gen:* "race, kind"
English Words	**generalize** to reduce to a general form, class, law
	generation a stage in the life cycle
	regenerate to form or create anew
	engender to bring into existence
	generic relating to a group or class
Greek Root	*log:* "speech, word, reason"
English Words	**apology** an expression of regret
	epilogue a short poem or speech
	monologue a long speech made by one person
	syllogism reasoning from the general to the specific
	logic a system of reasoning

For more information, see **Vocabulary Strategies** *on pages 198, 1330, and 1354.*

3.3 WORDS FROM CLASSICAL MYTHOLOGY

The English language includes many words from classical mythology. You can use your knowledge of these myths to understand the origins and meanings of these words. For example, *herculean task* refers to the strongman Hercules. Thus, you can guess that *herculean task* means "a job that is large or difficult." The chart shows a few common words from mythology.

Greek	Roman	Norse
panic	cereal	Wednesday
atlas	mercurial	berserk
adonis	Saturday	gun
mentor	January	valkyrie

Look up the etymology of each word in the chart and locate the myth associated with it. Use the information from the myth to explain the origin and meaning of each word.

3.4 FOREIGN WORDS

The English language includes words from diverse languages, such as French, Dutch, Spanish, Italian, and Chinese. Many words stayed the way they were in their original language. Histories of the language trace how similar words become integrated into English.

French	Dutch	Spanish	Italian
entree	maelstrom	rodeo	pasta
nouveau riche	trek	salsa	opera
potpourri	cookie	bronco	vendetta
tête-à-tête	snoop	tornado	grotto

*For more information, see **Vocabulary Strategy: Words from French**, page 168.*

4 Synonyms and Antonyms

4.1 SYNONYMS

A **synonym** is a word with a meaning similar to that of another word. You can find synonyms in a thesaurus or a dictionary. In a dictionary, synonyms are often given as part of the definition of a word. The following word pairs are synonyms:

    dry/arid   enthralled/fascinated   gaunt/thin

*For more information, see **Vocabulary Strategy: Synonyms as Context Clues**, page 668.*

4.2 ANTONYMS

An **antonym** is a word with a meaning opposite that of another word. The following word pairs are antonyms:

    friend/enemy   absurd/logical
    courteous/rude   languid/energetic

5 Denotation and Connotation

5.1 DENOTATION

A word's dictionary meaning is called its **denotation.** For example, the denotation of the word *rascal* is "an unethical, dishonest person."

5.2 CONNOTATION

The images or feelings you connect to a word add a finer shade of meaning, called **connotation.** The connotation of a word goes beyond the word's basic dictionary definition. Writers use connotations of words to communicate positive or negative feelings.

Positive	Neutral	Negative
save	store	hoard
fragrance	smell	stench
display	show	flaunt

Make sure you understand the denotation and connotation of a word when you read it or use it in your writing.

*For more information, see **Vocabulary Strategy: Analogies and Connotations**, page 450.*

6 Analogies

An **analogy** is a comparison between two things that are similar in some way but are otherwise dissimilar. Analogies are sometimes used in writing when unfamiliar subjects or ideas are explained in terms of familiar ones. Analogies often appear on tests as well, usually in a format like this:

TERRIER : DOG ::   A) rat : fish
                   B) kitten : cat
                   C) trout : fish
                   D) fish : trout
                   E) poodle : collie

Follow these steps to determine the correct answer:

- Read the part in capital letters as "*terrier* is to *dog* as...."

- Read the answer choices as "*rat* is to *fish*," "*kitten* is to *cat*," and so on.

- Ask yourself how the words *terrier* and *dog* are related. (A terrier is a type of dog.)

- Ask yourself which of the choices shows the same relationship. (A kitten is a kind of cat, but not in the same way that a terrier is a kind of dog. A kitten is a baby cat. A trout, however, is a type of fish in the sense that a terrier is a type of dog. Therefore, the answer is C.)

*For more information, see **Vocabulary Strategy: Analogies and Connotations**, page 450 and **Vocabulary Strategy: Analogies**, pages 656, 728, and 1170.*

7 Homonyms and Homophones

7.1 HOMONYMS

Homonyms are words that have the same spelling and sound but have different origins and meanings.

I don't want to bore you with a story about how I had to bore through the living room wall.

Bore can mean "cause a person to lose interest," but an identically spelled word means "to drill a hole."

My dog likes to bark while it scratches the bark on the tree in the backyard.

Bark can refer to the sound made by a dog. However, another identically spelled word means "the outer covering of a tree." Each word has a different meaning and its own dictionary entry.

Sometimes only one of the meanings of two homonyms may be familiar to you. Use context clues to help you figure out the meaning of an unfamiliar word.

7.2 HOMOPHONES

Homophones are words that sound alike but have different meanings and spellings. The following homophones are frequently misused:

it's/its	they're/their/there
to/too/two	stationary/stationery

Many misused homophones are pronouns and contractions. Whenever you are unsure whether to write *your* or *you're* and *who's* or *whose*, ask yourself if you mean *you are* or *who is/has*. If you do, write the contraction. For other homophones, such as *scent* and *sent*, use the meaning of the word to help you decide which one to use.

8 Words with Multiple Meanings

Some words have acquired additional meanings over time that are based on the original meaning.

> **EXAMPLES:** *I was in a hurry so I jammed my clothes into the suitcase. Unfortunately, I jammed my finger in the process.*

These two uses of *jam* have different meanings, but both of them have the same origin. You will find all the meanings of *jam* listed in one entry in the dictionary.

9 Specialized Vocabulary

Specialized vocabulary is special terms belonging to a particular field of study or work. For example, science, mathematics, and history all have their own technical or specialized vocabularies. To figure out specialized terms, you can use context clues and reference sources, such as dictionaries on specific subjects, atlases, or manuals.

*For more information, see **Vocabulary Strategy: Specialized Dictionaries,** page 689.*

10 Using Reference Sources

10.1 DICTIONARIES

A **general dictionary** will tell you not only a word's definitions but also its pronunciation, its parts of speech, and its history and origin. A **specialized dictionary** focuses on terms related to a particular field of study or work. Use a dictionary to check the spelling of any word you are unsure of in your English class and other subjects as well.

*For more information, see **Vocabulary Strategy: Using a Dictionary,** page 678.*

10.2 THESAURI

A **thesaurus** (plural, thesauri) is a dictionary of synonyms. A thesaurus can be helpful when you find yourself using the same modifiers over and over again.

*For more information, see **Vocabulary Strategy: Using a Thesaurus,** page 1208.*

10.3 SYNONYM FINDERS

A **synonym finder** is often included in word-processing software. It enables you to highlight a word and be shown a display of its synonyms.

10.4 GLOSSARIES

A **glossary** is a list of specialized terms and their definitions. It is often found in the back of textbooks and sometimes includes pronunciations. In fact, this textbook has four glossaries: the **Glossary of Literary and Nonfiction Terms,** the **Glossary of Reading & Informational Terms,** the **Glossary of Academic Vocabulary in English & Spanish,** and the **Glossary of Vocabulary in English & Spanish.** Use these glossaries to help you understand how terms are used in this textbook.

11 Spelling Rules

Consult and employ the following English spelling rules as you write, achieving increasing accuracy.

11.1 WORDS ENDING IN A SILENT *E*

Before adding a suffix beginning with a vowel or *y* to a word ending in a silent *e*, drop the *e* (with some exceptions).

> **amaze + -ing = amazing**
> **love + -able = lovable**
> **create + -ed = created**
> **nerve + -ous = nervous**

Exceptions: *change + -able = changeable; courage + -ous = courageous.*

When adding a suffix beginning with a consonant to a word ending in a silent *e*, keep the *e* (with some exceptions).

late + -ly = lately
spite + -ful = spiteful
noise + -less = noiseless
state + -ment = statement

Exceptions: *truly, argument, ninth, wholly, awful,* and others.

When a suffix beginning with *a* or *o* is added to a word with a final silent *e*, the final *e* is usually retained if it is preceded by a soft *c* or a soft *g*.

bridge + -able = bridgeable
peace + -able = peaceable
outrage + -ous = outrageous
advantage + -ous = advantageous

When a suffix beginning with a vowel is added to words ending in *ee* or *oe,* the final, silent *e* is retained.

agree + -ing = agreeing   **free + -ing = freeing**
hoe + -ing = hoeing   **see + -ing = seeing**

11.2 WORDS ENDING IN *Y*

Before adding most suffixes to a word that ends in *y* preceded by a consonant, change the *y* to *i*.

easy + -est = easiest
crazy + -est = craziest
silly + -ness = silliness
marry + -age = marriage

Exceptions: *dryness, shyness,* and *slyness.*

However, when you add *-ing*, the *y* does not change.

empty + -ed = emptied   but
empty + -ing = emptying

When adding a suffix to a word that ends in *y* preceded by a vowel, the *y* usually does not change.

play + -er = player
employ + -ed = employed
coy + -ness = coyness
pay + -able = payable

11.3 WORDS ENDING IN A CONSONANT

In one-syllable words that end in one consonant preceded by one short vowel, double the final consonant before adding a suffix beginning with a vowel, such as *-ed* or *-ing.*

dip + -ed = dipped   **set + -ing = setting**
slim + -est = slimmest   **fit + -er = fitter**

The rule does not apply to words of one syllable that end in a consonant preceded by two vowels.

feel + -ing = feeling   **peel + -ed = peeled**
reap + -ed = reaped   **loot + -ed = looted**

In words of more than one syllable, double the final consonant when (1) the word ends with one consonant preceded by one vowel and (2) the word is accented on the last syllable.

be•gin´   per•mit´   re•fer´

In the following examples, note that in the new words formed with suffixes, the accent remains on the same syllable:

be•gin´ + -ing = be•gin´ning = beginning
per•mit´ + -ed = per•mit´ted = permitted

Exceptions: In some words with more than one syllable, though the accent remains on the same syllable when a suffix is added, the final consonant is nevertheless not doubled, as in the following examples:

tra´vel + -er = tra´vel•er = traveler
mar´ket + -er = mar´ket•er = marketer

In the following examples, the accent does not remain on the same syllable; thus, the final consonant is not doubled:

re•fer´ + -ence = ref´er•ence = reference
con•fer´ + -ence = con´fer•ence = conference

11.4 PREFIXES AND SUFFIXES

When adding a prefix to a word, do not change the spelling of the base word. When a prefix creates a double letter, keep both letters.

dis- + approve = disapprove
re- + build = rebuild
ir- + regular = irregular
mis- + spell = misspell
anti- + trust = antitrust
il- + logical = illogical

When adding *-ly* to a word ending in *l,* keep both *l*'s, and when adding *-ness* to a word ending in *n,* keep both *n*'s.

careful + -ly = carefully
sudden + -ness = suddenness
final + -ly = finally
thin + -ness = thinness

11.5 FORMING PLURAL NOUNS

To form the plural of most nouns, just add -s.

prizes   dreams   circles   stations

For most singular nouns ending in **o**, add -s.

solos   halos   studios   photos   pianos

For a few nouns ending in **o**, add -es.

heroes   tomatoes   potatoes   echoes

When the singular noun ends in **s, sh, ch, x,** or **z**, add -es.

**waitresses   brushes   ditches
axes   buzzes**

When a singular noun ends in **y** with a consonant before it, change the **y** to **i** and add -es.

**army—armies   candy—candies
baby—babies   diary—diaries
ferry—ferries   conspiracy—conspiracies**

When a vowel (**a, e, i, o, u**) comes before the **y**, just add -s.

**boy—boys   way—ways
array—arrays   alloy—alloys
weekday—weekdays   jockey—jockeys**

For most nouns ending in **f** or **fe**, change the **f** to **v** and add -es or -s.

**life—lives   calf—calves   knife—knives
thief—thieves   shelf—shelves   loaf—loaves**

For some nouns ending in **f**, add -s to make the plural.

roofs   chiefs   reefs   beliefs

Some nouns have the same form for both singular and plural.

deer   sheep   moose   salmon   trout

For some nouns, the plural is formed in a special way.

**man—men   goose—geese
ox—oxen   woman—women
mouse—mice   child—children**

For a compound noun written as one word, form the plural by changing the last word in the compound to its plural form.

stepchild—stepchildren   firefly—fireflies

If a compound noun is written as a hyphenated word or as two separate words, change the most important word to the plural form.

**brother-in-law—brothers-in-law
life jacket—life jackets**

11.6 FORMING POSSESSIVES

If a noun is singular, add **'s**.

mother—my mother's car   Ross—Ross's desk

Exception: The **s** after the apostrophe is dropped after *Jesus', Moses',* and certain names in classical mythology (*Zeus'*). These possessive forms can be pronounced easily.

If a noun is plural and ends with **s**, just add an apostrophe.

**parents—my parents' car
the Santinis—the Santinis' house**

If a noun is plural but does not end in **s**, add **'s**.

**people—the people's choice
women—the women's coats**

11.7 SPECIAL SPELLING PROBLEMS

Only one English word ends in -**sede:** *supersede.* Three words end in -**ceed:** *exceed, proceed,* and *succeed.* All other verbs ending in the sound "seed" are spelled with -**cede**.

concede   precede   recede   secede

In words with **ie** or **ei**, when the sound is long **e** (as in *she*), the word is spelled **ie** except after **c** (with some exceptions).

| *i* before *e* | thief | relieve | field |
| | piece | grieve | pier |

| except after *c* | conceit | perceive | ceiling |
| | receive | receipt | |

Exceptions: *either, neither, weird, leisure, seize.*

🕛 Commonly Confused Words

WORDS	DEFINITIONS	EXAMPLES
accept/except	The verb *accept* means "to receive" or "to believe"; *except* is usually a preposition meaning "excluding."	**Except** for some of the more extraordinary events, I can **accept** that the *Odyssey* recounts a real journey.
advice/advise	*Advise* is a verb; *advice* is a noun naming that which an *adviser* gives.	I **advise** you to take that job. Whom should I ask for **advice?**
affect/effect	As a verb, *affect* means "to influence." *Effect* as a verb means "to cause." If you want a noun, you will almost always want *effect*.	Did Circe's wine **affect** Odysseus' mind? It did **effect** a change in Odysseus' men. In fact, it had an **effect** on everyone else who drank it.
all ready/already	*All ready* is an adjective meaning "fully ready." *Already* is an adverb meaning "before" or "by this time."	He was **all ready** to go at noon. I have **already** seen that movie.
allusion/illusion	An *allusion* is an indirect reference to something. An *illusion* is a false picture or idea.	There are many **allusions** to the works of Homer in English literature. The world's apparent flatness is an **illusion.**
among/between	*Between* is used when you are speaking of only two things. *Among* is used for three or more.	**Between** *Hamlet* and *King Lear,* I prefer the latter. Emily Dickinson is **among** my favorite poets.
bring/take	*Bring* is used to denote motion toward a speaker or place. *Take* is used to denote motion away from such a person or place.	**Bring** the books over here, and I will **take** them to the library.
fewer/less	*Fewer* refers to the number of separate, countable units. *Less* refers to bulk quantity.	We have **less** literature and **fewer** selections in this year's curriculum.
leave/let	*Leave* means "to allow something to remain behind." *Let* means "to permit."	The librarian will **leave** some books on display but will not **let** us borrow any.
lie/lay	*Lie* means "to rest" or "to recline." It does not take an object. *Lay* always takes an object.	Rover loves to **lie** in the sun. We always **lay** some bones next to him.
loose/lose	*Loose* (lo͞os) means "free, not restrained"; *lose* (lo͞oz) means "to misplace" or "to fail to find."	Who turned the horses **loose**? I hope we won't **lose** any of them.
precede/proceed	*Precede* means "to go or come before." Use *proceed* for other meanings.	Emily Dickinson's poetry **precedes** that of Alice Walker. You may **proceed** to the next section of the test.
than/then	Use *than* in making comparisons; use *then* on all other occasions.	Who can say whether Amy Lowell is a better poet **than** Denise Levertov? I will read Lowell first, and **then** I will read Levertov.
their/there/they're	*Their* means "belonging to them." *There* means "in that place." *They're* is the contraction for "they are."	**There** is a movie playing at 9 P.M. **They're** going to see it with me. Sakara and Jessica drove away in **their** car after the movie.
two/too/to	*Two* is the number. *Too* is an adverb meaning "also" or "very." Use *to* before a verb or as a preposition.	Meg had **to** go **to** town, **too.** We had **too** much reading **to** do. **Two** chapters is **too** many.

Effective oral communication occurs when the audience understands a message the way the speaker intends it. Good speakers use specific techniques to present their ideas effectively, and good listeners are attentive and discriminating.

COMMON CORE

Included in this handbook:
SL 1, SL 1a–d, SL 2–SL 6

1 Speech

In school, in business, and in community life, a speech is one of the most effective means of communicating.

1.1 AUDIENCE, PURPOSE, AND OCCASION

When developing and delivering a speech, your goal is to deliver a focused, coherent presentation that conveys your ideas clearly and relates to the background of your audience. By understanding your audience, you can tailor your speech to them appropriately and effectively.

- **Know Your Audience** What kind of group are you presenting to? Fellow classmates? A group of teachers? What are their interests and backgrounds? Understanding their different points of view can help you organize the information so that they understand and are interested in it.

- **Understand Your Purpose** Keep in mind your purpose for speaking. Are you trying to persuade the audience to do something? Perhaps you simply want to entertain them by sharing a story or experience. Your reason for giving the speech will guide you in organizing your thoughts and deciding on how to deliver it.

- **Know the Occasion** Are you speaking at a special event? Is it formal? Will others be giving speeches besides you? Knowing the type of occasion will help you tailor the language and length of your speech for the event.

1.2 PREPARING YOUR SPEECH

There are several approaches to preparing a speech. Your teacher may tell you which one to use.

- **Manuscript** Prepare a complete script of the speech in advance and use it to deliver the speech. Use this approach for formal occasions, such as graduation speeches and political addresses, and to present technical or complicated information.

- **Memory** Prepare a written text in advance and then memorize it in order to deliver the speech word for word. This approach is suitable for short speeches, as when introducing another speaker or accepting an award.

- **Extemporaneous** Prepare the speech and deliver it using an outline or notes. Use this method for informal situations, for persuasive messages, and to make a more personal connection with the audience.

1.3 DRAFTING YOUR SPEECH

If you are writing your speech beforehand, rather than working from notes, use the following guidelines to help you:

- **Create a Unified Speech** Do this first by organizing your speech into paragraphs, each of which develops a single main idea. All the sentences in a paragraph should support the main idea of the paragraph, and all the paragraphs should support the main idea of the speech. Be sure that your speech has an introduction and a conclusion. Just as in a written product, use a pattern of organization that is appropriate to your subject and purpose.

- **Use Appropriate Language** The subject of your speech—and the way you choose to present it—should match your audience, your purpose, and the occasion. You can use informal language, such as slang, to share a story with your classmates. For a persuasive speech in front of a school assembly, use formal, standard American English. If you are giving an informative presentation, be sure to explain any terms that the audience may not be familiar with.

- **Provide Evidence** Include relevant facts, statistics, and incidents; quote experts to support your ideas and opinions. Elaborate—provide specific details, perhaps with visual or media displays—to clarify what you are saying.

- **Emphasize Important Points** To help your audience follow the main ideas and concepts of your speech, be sure to draw attention to important points. You can use rhyme, repetition, parallelism, and other rhetorical devices. You can also use figurative language for effect.

- **Use Precise Language** Use precise **diction**, or vocabulary and syntax, to convey your ideas, and vary the structure and length of your sentences. You can keep the audience's attention with a word that elicits strong emotion. You can use a question or an interjection to make a personal connection with the audience.

- **Start Strong, Finish Strong** As you begin your speech, consider using a "hook"—an interesting question or statement meant to capture your audience's attention. At the end of the speech, restate your main ideas simply and clearly. Perhaps conclude with a powerful example or anecdote to reinforce your message.

- **Revise Your Speech** After you write your speech, revise, edit, and proofread it as you would a written report. Use a variety of sentence structures to achieve a natural rhythm. Check for correct subject-verb agreement and consistent verb tense. Correct run-on sentences and sentence fragments. Use parallel structure to emphasize ideas. Make sure you use complete sentences and correct punctuation and capitalization, even if no one else will see it. Your written speech should be clear and error free.

1.4 DELIVERING YOUR SPEECH

Confidence is the key to a successful presentation. Use these techniques to help you prepare and present your speech:

Prepare

- **Review Your Information** Reread your notes and review any background research. You'll feel more confident during your speech.

- **Organize Your Notes** Some people prefer to include only key points. Others prefer the entire script. Write each main point, or each paragraph, of your speech on a separate numbered index card. Be sure to include your most important evidence and examples.

- **Plan Your Visual Aids and Sound Effects** If you are planning on using visual aids, such as slides, posters, charts, graphs, video clips, transparencies, or computer projections, now is the time to design your visual and sound elements and work them into your speech.

Practice

- **Rehearse** Rehearse your speech several times, possibly in front of a practice audience. Maintain good posture by standing with your shoulders back and your head up. If you are using visual aids, practice handling them. Adapt your rate of speaking, pitch, and tone of voice to your audience and setting. Glance at your notes to refresh your memory, but avoid reading them word for word. Your style of performance should express the purpose of your speech. Use the following chart to help you.

Purpose	Pace	Pitch	Tone
to persuade	fast but clear	even	urgent
to inform	using plenty of pauses	even	authoritative
to entertain	usually building to a "punch"	varied to create characters or drama	funny or dramatic

- **Use Audience Feedback** If you had a practice audience, ask them specific questions about your delivery: Did I use enough eye contact? Was my voice at the right volume? Did I stand straight, or did I slouch? Use the audience's comments to evaluate the effectiveness of your delivery and to set goals for future rehearsals.

- **Evaluate Your Performance** When you have finished each rehearsal, evaluate your performance. Did you pause to let an important point sink in, or use gestures for emphasis? Make a list of the aspects of your presentation that you will try to improve for your next rehearsal.

Present

- **Begin Your Speech** Try to look relaxed and smile.

- **Make Eye Contact** Try to make eye contact with as many audience members as possible. This will establish personal contact and help you determine if the audience understands your speech.

- **Remember to Pause** A slight pause after important points will provide emphasis and give your audience time to think about what you're saying.

- **Speak Clearly** Speak loud enough to be heard clearly, but not so loud that your voice is overwhelming. Use a conversational tone.

- **Maintain Good Posture** Stand up straight and avoid nervous movements that may distract the audience's attention from what you are saying.

- **Use Expressive Body Language** Use facial expressions to show your feelings toward your topic. Make purposeful gestures: Lean forward when you make an important point; move your hands and arms for emphasis. Use your body language to show your own style and reflect your personality.

- **Watch the Audience for Responses** If they start fidgeting or yawning, speak a little louder or get to your conclusion a little sooner. Use what you learn to decide what areas need improvement for future presentations.

- **Close Your Speech** As part of your closing remarks, be sure to thank your audience.

Respond to Questions

Depending on the content of your speech, your audience may have questions. Follow these steps to make sure that you answer questions in an appropriate manner:

- Think about what your audience may ask and prepare answers before your speech.

- Tell your audience at the beginning of your speech that you will take questions at the end. This helps avoid audience interruptions that may make your speech hard to follow.

- Call on audience members in the order in which they raise their hands.

- Repeat each question before you answer it to ensure that everyone has heard it. This step also gives you time to prepare your answer.

2 Different Types of Oral Presentations

2.1 INFORMATIVE SPEECH

When you deliver an informative speech, you give the audience new information, provide a better understanding of information, or enable the audience to use the information in a new way.

Use the following questions to evaluate your own presentation or that of a peer or a public figure.

Evaluate an Informative Speech

- Did the speaker have a specific, clearly focused position?
- Did the speaker take the audience's previous knowledge into consideration?
- Did the speaker cite sources for the information?
- Did the speaker communicate the information objectively?
- Did the speaker explain technical terms?
- Did the speaker use visual aids effectively?
- Did the speaker anticipate and address any audience concerns or misunderstandings?
- Is the speech informative and accurate?

2.2 PERSUASIVE SPEECH

When you deliver a persuasive speech, you offer a thesis or clear statement on a subject, you provide relevant evidence to support your position, and you attempt to convince the audience to accept your point of view.

For more information, see **Speaking and Listening: Giving a Persuasive Speech,** *page 740.*

Use the following questions to evaluate the presentation of a peer or a public figure, or your own presentation.

Evaluate a Persuasive Speech

- Did the speaker present a clear thesis or argument?
- Did the speaker anticipate and address audience concerns, biases, and counterclaims?
- Did the speaker use sound logic and reasoning in developing the argument?
- Did the speaker support the argument with valid evidence, examples, facts, expert opinions, and quotations?
- Did the speaker use precise, effective diction?
- Did the speaker use rhetorical devices, parallel structure, and persuasive techniques, such as emotional appeals?
- Were the speaker's voice, facial expressions, and gestures effective?
- Is your reaction to the speech similar to that of other audience members?
- Did you believe the speaker to be accurate, truthful, and ethical?

2.3 DEBATE

A debate is a balanced argument covering both sides of an issue. In a debate, two teams compete to win the support of the audience. In a formal debate, two teams, each with two members, present their arguments on a given proposition or policy statement. One team argues for the proposition or statement, and the other argues against it. Each debater must consider the proposition closely and must research both sides of it.

Preparing for the Debate

In preparing for a debate, the debaters prepare a **brief,** an outline of the debate, accounting for the evidence and arguments of both sides of the **proposition** (topic). Debaters also prepare a **rebuttal,** a follow-up speech to support their arguments and counter the opposition's. Propositions are usually one of four types:

- **Proposition of fact**—Debaters determine whether a statement is true or false. An example is "Deforestation is ruining the rain forest."

- **Proposition of value**—Debators determine the value of a person, place, or thing. An example is "Free trade will help small countries develop."

- **Proposition of problem**—Debators determine whether a problem exists and whether it requires action.

- **Proposition of policy**—Debators determine the action that will be taken. An example is "Students will provide tutoring services."

The two teams of debaters who argue a topic are called the **affirmative side** and the **negative side.** The affirmative side tries to convince the audience that the proposition should be accepted. The negative side argues against the proposition.

Use the following steps to prepare a brief:

- **Gather Information** Consult a variety of primary and secondary sources to gather the most reliable, up-to-date information about the proposition.

- **Identify Key Ideas** Sort out the important points and arrange them in order of importance.

- **List Arguments For and Against Each Key Idea** Look for strong arguments that support your side of the proposition, and also note those that support your opponents' side.

- **Support Your Arguments** Find facts, quotations, expert opinions, and examples that support your arguments and counter your opponents'.

- **Write the Brief** Begin your brief with a statement of the proposition. Then list the arguments and evidence that support both sides of the proposition.

Planning the Rebuttal

The rebuttal is the opportunity to rebuild your case. Use the following steps to build a strong rebuttal:

- Listen to your opponents respectfully. Note the points you wish to overturn.

- Defend what the opposition has challenged.

- Cite weaknesses in their arguments, such as points they overlooked.

- Present counterclaims and supporting evidence.

- Offer your summary arguments. Restate and solidify your stance.

Use the following questions to evaluate a debate.

Evaluate a Team in a Debate

- Did the team prove that a significant problem does or does not exist? How thorough was the team's analysis of the problem?

- How did the team convince you that the proposition is or is not the best solution to the problem?

- How effectively did the team present reasons and evidence supporting the case?

- How effectively did the team refute and rebut arguments made by the opposing team?

- Did the speakers maintain eye contact and speak at an appropriate rate and volume?

- Did the speakers observe proper debate etiquette?

PRACTICE AND APPLY

View a political debate for a local, state, or national election. Use the preceding criteria to evaluate it.

2.4 NARRATIVE SPEECH

When you deliver a narrative speech, you tell a story or present a subject using a story-type format. A good narrative keeps an audience informed and entertained. It also allows you to deliver a message in a creative way.

Use the following questions to evaluate a speaker or your own presentation.

Evaluate a Narrative Speech

- Did the speaker choose a context that makes sense and contributes to a believable narrative?

- Did the speaker locate scenes and incidents in specific places?

- Does the plot flow well?

- Did the speaker use words that convey the appropriate mood and tone?

- Did the speaker use sensory details that allow the audience to experience the sights, sounds, and smells of a scene and the specific actions, gestures, and thoughts of the characters?

- Did the speaker use a range of narrative devices to keep the audience interested?

- Is your reaction to the presentation similar to that of other audience members?

- Did the speaker use figurative language, irony, or other literary devices for an aesthetic effect?

2.5 REFLECTIVE SPEECH

In a reflective speech, you describe a personal experience and explore its significance. Use vivid description, visuals, and sound effects to re-create the experience for your audience and to convey meaning.

Use the following questions to evaluate a speaker or your own presentation.

Evaluate a Reflective Speech

- Did the speaker describe an important experience in his or her life?
- Did the speaker use figurative language, sensory details, or other devices to re-create the event for the audience?
- Did the speaker explain the significance of the event to the audience?
- Does the experience relate to a broader theme or a more general abstract idea about life?
- Did the speaker convey the message through one specific event or several related incidents?
- Did the speaker encourage the audience to think about the significance of the experience and apply it to their own lives?
- Was your reaction to the presentation similar to that of other audience members?

2.6 DESCRIPTIVE SPEECH

In a descriptive speech, you describe a subject with which you are personally familiar. A good description will enable your listeners to tell how you feel toward your subject.

Use the following questions to evaluate a speaker or your own presentation.

Evaluate a Descriptive Speech

- Did the speaker make clear his or her point of view toward the subject being described?
- Did the speaker use sensory details, figurative language, and factual details?
- Did the speaker use tone and pitch to emphasize important details?
- Did the speaker use facial expressions to emphasize his or her feelings toward the subject?
- Did the speaker change vantage points to help the audience see the subject from another position?
- Did the speaker change perspectives to show how someone else might feel toward the subject?

2.7 ORAL INTERPRETATION

When you perform an oral interpretation, you use appropriate vocal intonations, facial expressions, and gestures to bring a literature selection to life.

In an **oral reading,** you will present or read a poem, monologue, soliloquy, or passage from a literary selection, assuming the voice of a character, the narrator, or the speaker. An oral reading can also be a presentation of a dialogue between two or more characters, with you, as the sole performer, taking on all the roles.

Use the following techniques when giving an oral reading:

- **Speak Clearly** As you speak, pronounce your words clearly.
- **Control Your Volume** Make sure that you are loud enough to be heard, but do not shout.
- **Pace Yourself** Read at a moderate rate, but vary your pace if it seems appropriate to the emotions of the character or to the action you perform.
- **Vary Your Voice** Use a different voice for each character. Stress important words and phrases. Use your voice to express different emotions.

In a **dramatic reading,** several speakers participate in the reading of a play or some other work. Use the following techniques in your dramatic reading:

- **Prepare** Rehearse your material several times. Become familiar with the humorous and serious parts of the script. Develop a special voice that fits the personality of the character you portray.
- **Project** As you read your lines, aim your voice toward the back of the room to allow everyone to hear you.
- **Perform** React to the other characters as if you were hearing their lines for the first time. Deliver your own lines with the appropriate emotion. Use not only hand gestures and facial expressions but also other body movements to express your emotions.

*For more information, see **Speaking and Listening: Producing a Docudrama,** page 548.*

Use the following questions to evaluate an artistic performance by a peer or a public presenter, a media presentation, or your own performance.

Evaluate an Oral Interpretation

- Did the speaker speak clearly, enunciating each word carefully?
- Did the speaker maintain eye contact with the audience?
- Did the speaker control his or her volume, projecting without shouting?
- Did the speaker vary the rate of speech appropriately to express emotion, mood, and action?
- Did the speaker use a different voice for each character?
- Did the speaker stress important words or phrases?
- Did the speaker's presentation allow you to identify and appreciate elements of the text such as character development, rhyme, imagery, and language?

PRACTICE AND APPLY

Develop an oral reading and present it to your class. Evaluate the oral readings of your classmates, using the preceding criteria.

2.8 ORAL RESPONSE TO LITERATURE

An oral response to literature is a personal, analytical interpretation of a writer's story, novel, poem, or drama.

Use the following questions to evaluate a speaker or your own presentation.

Evaluate an Oral Response to Literature

- Did the speaker choose an interesting piece that he or she understands and feels strongly about?
- Did the speaker make a judgment that shows an understanding of significant ideas from the text?
- Did the speaker direct the audience to specific parts of the piece that support his or her ideas?
- Did the speaker identify and analyze the use of artistic elements such as imagery, figurative language, and character development?
- Did the speaker demonstrate an appreciation of the author's style?
- Did the speaker discuss any ambiguous or difficult passages and the impact of those passages on the audience?

PRACTICE AND APPLY

Listen as a classmate delivers an oral response to a selection you have read. Use the preceding criteria to evaluate the presentation.

3 Other Types of Communication

3.1 GROUP DISCUSSION

Successful groups assign a role to each member. These roles distribute responsibility among the members and help keep discussions focused.

Role	Responsibilities
Chairperson	- introduces topic - explains goal or purpose - participates in discussion and keeps it on track - helps resolves conflicts - helps group reach goal
Recorder	- takes notes on discussion - reports on suggestions and decisions - organizes and writes up notes - participates in discussion
Participants	- contribute relevant facts or ideas to discussion - respond constructively to one another's ideas - reach agreement or vote on final decision

3.2 INTERVIEWS

An **interview** is a formal type of conversation with a definite purpose and goal. To conduct a successful interview, use the following guidelines:

Prepare for the Interview

- Select your interviewee carefully. Identify who has the kind of knowledge and experience you are looking for.
- Set a time, a date, and a place. Ask permission to tape-record the interview.

- Learn all you can about the person you will interview or the topic you want information on.

- Prepare a list of questions. Create questions that encourage detailed responses instead of yes-or-no answers. Arrange your questions in order from most important to least important.

- Arrive on time with everything you need.

Conduct the Interview

- Ask your questions clearly and listen to the responses carefully. Give the person whom you are interviewing plenty of time to answer.

- Be flexible; follow up on any responses you find interesting.

- Avoid arguments; be tactful and polite.

- Even if you tape an interview, take notes on important points.

- Thank the person for the interview, and ask if you can call with any follow-up questions.

Follow Up on the Interview

- Summarize your notes or make a written copy of the tape recording as soon as possible.

- If any points are unclear or if information is missing, call and ask more questions while the person is still available.

- Select the most appropriate quotations to support your ideas.

- If possible, have the person you interviewed review your work to make sure you haven't misrepresented what he or she said.

- Send a thank-you note to the person in appreciation of his or her time and effort.

For more information, see **Speaking and Listening: Participating in Job Interviews,** *page 1390.*

Evaluate an Interview

You can determine how effective your interview was by asking yourself these questions:

- Did you get the type of information you were looking for?

- Were your most important questions answered to your satisfaction?

- Were you able to keep the interviewee focused on the subject?

Responding to a Job Interview

In a job interview, you will be the person being interviewed. The person asking you questions will have several objectives in mind, and you will need to be prepared to respond in a professional manner. Keep these strategies in mind when you are being interviewed for employment:

- Prior to the interview, prepare a short list of questions relevant to the position.

- Respond honestly and effectively to each question, and use language that conveys sensitivity, maturity, and respect.

- Give responses that demonstrate knowledge of the subject or organization.

- Use active listening skills, as outlined in the next section.

4 Active Listening

Active listening is the process of receiving, interpreting, evaluating, and responding to a message. Whether you listen to a class discussion or a formal speech, use the following strategies to get as much as you can from the message.

Before Listening

- Learn what the topic is beforehand. You may need to read background information about the topic or learn technical terms in order to understand the speaker's message.

- Think about what you know or want to know about the topic.

- Have a pen and paper or a laptop computer to take notes.

- Establish a purpose for listening.

While Listening

- Focus your attention on the speaker.

- Listen for the speaker's purpose (usually stated at the beginning), which alerts you to main ideas.

- Listen for words or phrases that signal important points, such as *to begin with, in addition, most important, finally,* and *in conclusion.*

- Listen carefully for explanations of technical terms.

- Listen for ideas that are repeated for emphasis.

- Take notes. Write down only the most important points. Use an outline or list format to organize main ideas and supporting points.

- Note comparisons and contrasts, causes and effects, or problems and solutions.

- Note how the speaker uses word choice, voice pitch, posture, and gestures to convey meaning.

After Listening

- Ask relevant questions to clarify anything that was unclear or confusing.

- Review your notes to make sure you understand what was said.

- Summarize and paraphrase the speaker's ideas.

- Reflect on the ideas presented and determine how the information is useful to you or how you might expand upon the ideas presented.

- You may also wish to compare your interpretation of the speech with the interpretations of others who listened to it.

4.1 CRITICAL LISTENING

Critical listening involves interpreting and analyzing a spoken message to judge its accuracy and reliability. Use these strategies as you listen to messages from advertisers, politicians, lecturers, and others:

- **Determine the Speaker's Purpose** Think about the background, viewpoint, and possible motives of the speaker. Separate facts from opinions. Listen carefully to details and evidence that a speaker uses to support the message.

- **Listen for the Main Idea** Figure out the speaker's main message before allowing yourself to be distracted by seemingly convincing facts and details.

- **Recognize the Use of Persuasive Techniques** Pay attention to a speaker's choice of words. Speakers may slant information to persuade you to buy a product or accept an idea. Persuasive devices such as inaccurate generalizations, either/or reasoning, and bandwagon or snob appeal may represent faulty reasoning and provide misleading information.

  *For more information, see **Recognizing Persuasive Techniques,** page R20.*

- **Observe Verbal and Nonverbal Messages** A speaker's gestures, facial expressions, and tone of voice should reinforce the message. If they don't, you should question the speaker's sincerity and the reliability of his or her message.

- **Give Appropriate Feedback** An effective speaker looks for verbal and nonverbal cues from you, the listener, to gauge how the message is being received. For example, if you understand or agree with the message, you might nod your head. If possible, during or after a presentation, ask questions to clarify understanding.

4.2 VERBAL FEEDBACK

At times you will be asked to give direct feedback to a speaker. You may be asked to evaluate the way the speaker delivers the presentation, as well as the content of the presentation.

Use the following questions to evaluate a speaker's delivery.

Evaluate Delivery

- Did the speaker articulate words clearly and distinctly?
- Did the speaker pronounce words correctly?
- Did the speaker vary his or her rate?
- Did the speaker's voice sound natural and not strained?
- Was the speaker's voice loud enough?

Use the following guidelines to give constructive suggestions for improvement on content.

Evaluate Content

Be Specific Don't make statements like "Your charts need work." Offer concrete suggestions, such as "Please make the type bigger so we can read the poster from the back of the room."

Discuss Only the Most Important Points Don't overload the speaker with too much feedback about too many details. Focus on important points, such as:

- Is the topic too advanced for the audience?
- Are the supporting details well organized?
- Is the conclusion weak?

Give Balanced Feedback Tell the speaker not only what didn't work but also what did work: "Consider dropping the last two slides, since you covered those points earlier. The first two slides got my attention."

Every day you are exposed to hundreds of images and messages from television, radio, movies, newspapers, and the Internet. What is the effect of all this media? What do you need to know to be a smart media consumer? Being media literate means that you have the ability to think critically about media messages. It means that you are able to analyze and evaluate media messages and how they influence you and your world. To become media literate, you'll need the tools to study media messages.

COMMON CORE

Included in this handbook:
RI 7, SL 2, SL 5

1 Five Core Concepts in Media Literacy

from The Center for Media Literacy

The five core concepts of media literacy provide you with the basic ideas you can consider when examining media messages.

All media messages are "constructed." All media messages are made by someone. In fact, they are carefully thought out and researched and have attitudes and values built into them. Much of the information that you use to make sense of the world comes from the media. Therefore, it is important to know how media are put together so you can better understand the message it conveys.

Media messages are constructed using a creative language with its own rules. Each means of communication—whether it is film, television, newspapers, magazines, radio, or the Internet—has its own language and design. Therefore, the content of a message must use the language and design of the medium that conveys the message. Thus, the medium actually shapes the message. For example, a horror film may use music to heighten suspense, or a newspaper may use a big headline to signal the significance of a story. Understanding the language of each medium can increase your enjoyment of it as well as alert you to obvious and subtle influences.

Different people experience the same media messages differently. Personal factors such as age, education, and experience will affect the way a person responds to a media message. How many times has your interpretation of a film or book differed from that of a friend? Everyone interprets media messages through their own personal lens.

Media have embedded values and points of view. Media messages carry underlying values, which are purposely built into them by the creators of the message. For example, a commercial's main purpose may be to persuade you to buy something, but it also conveys the value of a particular lifestyle. Understanding not only the core message but also the embedded points of view will help you decide whether to accept or reject the message.

Most media messages are organized to gain profit and/or power. The creators of media messages often provide a commodity, such as information or entertainment, in order to make money. The bigger the audience, the higher the cost of advertising. Consequently, media outlets want to build large audiences in order to bring in more revenue from advertising. For example, a television network creates programming that appeals to the largest audience possible, and then uses the viewer ratings to attract more advertising dollars.

2 Media Basics

2.1 MESSAGE

When a film or TV show is created, it becomes a media product. Each media product is created to send a **message,** or an expression of belief or opinion, that serves a specific purpose. In order to understand the message, you will need to deconstruct it.

Deconstruction is the process of analyzing a media presentation. To analyze a media presentation you will need to look at its content, its purpose, the audience it's aimed at, and the techniques and elements that are used to create certain effects.

2.2 AUDIENCE

A **target audience** is a specific group of people at whom a product or presentation is aimed. The members of a target audience usually share certain characteristics, such as age, gender, ethnic background, values, or lifestyle. For example, a target audience may be adults ages 40 to 60 who want to exercise and eat healthful foods.

Demographics are the characteristics of a population, including age, gender, profession, income, education, ethnicity, and geographic location. Media decision makers use demographics to shape their content to suit the needs and tastes of a target audience.

Nielsen ratings are the system used to track TV audiences and their viewing preferences. Nielsen Media Research, the company that provides this system, monitors TV viewing in a random sample of 5,000 U.S. households selected to represent the population as a whole.

2.3 PURPOSE

The **purpose,** or intent, of a media presentation is the reason it was made. Most media messages have more than one purpose, but each has a **core purpose.** To discover that purpose, think about why its creator paid for and produced the message. For example, an ad might entertain you with humor, but its core purpose is to persuade you to buy something.

2.4 TYPES AND GENRES OF MEDIA

The term *media* refers to television, newspapers, magazines, radio, movies, and the Internet. Each is a **medium,** or means for carrying information, entertainment, and advertisements to a large audience.

Each type of media has different characteristics, strengths, and weaknesses. Understanding how different types of media work and the role they play will help you become more informed about the choices you make in response to the media.

2.5 PRODUCERS AND CREATORS

People who control the media are known as **gatekeepers.** Gatekeepers decide what information to share with the public and the ways it will be presented. The following diagram gives some examples.

Who Controls the Media?

Media Owners
TV networks
Recording companies
Publishing companies

Media Products
Television
Radio
Magazines
Movies
Newspapers
Internet

Media Creators
Actors
Writers
Directors
Webmasters

Media Sponsors
Clothing manufacturers
Fast-food restaurants
Department stores

Some forms of media are independently owned, while others are part of a corporate family. Some corporate families might own several different kinds of media. For example, a company may own three radio stations, five newspapers, a publishing company, and a small television station. Often a corporate "parent" decides the content for all of its holdings.

2.6 LAWS GOVERNING MEDIA

Four main laws and policies affect the content, delivery, and use of mass media.

The First Amendment to the Constitution forbids Congress to limit speech or the press.

Copyright law protects the rights of authors and other media creators against the unauthorized publishing, reproduction, and selling of their works.

Laws prohibit **censorship,** any attempt to suppress or control people's access to media messages.

Laws prohibit **libel,** the publication of false statements that damage a person's reputation.

2.7 INFLUENCE OF MEDIA

By sheer volume alone, media influence our habits, values, opinions, and beliefs. Our environment is saturated with media messages from television, billboards, radio, newspapers, magazines, video games, and so on. Each of these media products is selling one message and conveying another—a message about values—in the subtext. For example, a car ad is meant to sell a car, but if you look closer, you will see that it is using a set of values, such as a luxurious lifestyle, to make the car attractive to the target audience. One message of the ad is that if you buy the car, you'll have the luxurious lifestyle. The other message is that the luxurious lifestyle is good and desirable. TV shows, movies, and news programs also convey subtexts of values and beliefs.

Media can also shape our opinions about the world. For example, news about crime shapes our understanding about how much and what type of crime is prevalent in the world around us. TV news items, talk show interviews, and commercials may shape our perception of a political candidate, a celebrity, an ethnic group, a country, or a region. As a consequence, our knowledge of a person or place may be completely based on the information we receive from the television or other media.

Media Tools

THiNK central

Go to thinkcentral.com.
KEYWORD: HML12-R89

3 Film and TV

Films and television programs come in a variety of types. Films include comedies, dramas, documentaries, and animated features. Televison programs cover an even wider array, including dramas, sitcoms, talk shows, reality shows, newscasts, and so on. Producers of films and producers of television programs rely on many of the same elements to convey their messages. Among these elements are scripts, visual and sound elements, special effects, and editing.

3.1 SCRIPT AND WRITTEN ELEMENTS

The writer and editor craft a story for television or film using a script and storyboard. A **script** is the text or words of a film or television show. A **storyboard** is a device often used to plan the shooting of a film and to help the director envision and convey what the finished product will look like. It consists of a sequence of sketches showing what will appear in the film's shots, often with explanatory notes and dialogue written beside or underneath them as shown in the example.

*For more information, see **Speaking and Listening: Producing a Docudrama**, page 548.*

Interviewer: Did you have any problems adjusting to life in an American high school?

Vi: (begins to answer question)

As Vi answers, pull back to mid-range shot to include both girls.

3.2 VISUAL ELEMENTS

Visual elements in film and television include camera shots, angles, and movements, as well as film components such as mise en scène, set design, props, and visual special effects.

A **camera shot** is a single, continuous view taken by a camera. **Camera angle** is the angle at which the camera is positioned during the recording of a shot or image. Each angle is carefully planned to create an effect. The following chart explains the different shots and angles.

Camera Shot/Angle	Effect
Establishing shot introduces viewers to the location of a scene, usually by presenting a wide view of an area	establishes the setting of a film or television show
Close-up shot shows a detailed view of a person or an object	helps to create emotion and make viewers feel as if they know the character
Medium shot shows a view wider than a close-up but narrower than an establishing or long shot	shows part of an object, or a character from the knees or waist up
Long shot is a wide view of a scene, showing the full figure(s) of a person or group and their surroundings	allows the viewer to see the "big picture" and shows the relationship between the subject and the environment
Reaction shot shows someone reacting to something that occurred in a previous shot	allows the viewer to see how the character feels in order to create empathy in the viewer
Low-angle shot looks up at an object or a person	makes a character, object, or scene appear more important or threatening
High-angle shot looks down on an object or a person	makes a character, object, or scene seem vulnerable or insignificant
Point-of-view (POV) shot shows a part of the story through a character's eyes	helps viewers identify with that character

Camera movement can create energy, reveal information, or establish a mood. The following chart shows some of the ways filmmakers move the camera to create an effect.

Camera Movement	Effect
Pan is a shot in which the camera scans a location from right to left or left to right	reveals information by showing a sweeping view of an area
Tracking shot is a shot in which the camera moves with the subject	establishes tension or creates a sense of drama
Zoom is the movement of the camera as it closes in on or moves farther away from the subject	captures action or draws the viewer's attention to detail

Mise en scène is a French term that refers to the arrangement of actors, props, and action on a film set. It is used to describe everything that can be seen in a frame, including the setting, lighting, visual composition, costumes, and action.

Framing is capturing people and objects within the "frame" of a screen or image. Framing is what the camera sees.

Composition is the arrangement of objects, characters, shapes, and colors within a frame and the relationship of the objects to one another.

3.3 SOUND ELEMENTS

Sound elements in film and television include music, voice-over, and sound effects.

Music may be used to set the mood and atmosphere in a scene. Music can have a powerful effect on the way viewers feel about a story. For example, fast-paced music helps viewers feel excited during an action scene.

Voice-over is the voice of the unseen commentator or narrator of a film, TV program, or commercial.

Sound effects are the sounds added to films, TV programs, and commercials during the editing process. Sound effects, such as laugh tracks or the sounds of punches in a fight scene, can create humor, emphasize a point, or contribute to the mood.

3.4 SPECIAL EFFECTS

Special effects include computer-generated animation, manipulated video images, and fast- or slow-motion sequences in films, TV programs, and commercials.

Animation on film involves the frame-by-frame photography of a series of drawings or objects. When these frames are projected—at a rate of 24 per second—the illusion of movement is achieved.

A **split screen** is a special-effects shot in which two or more separate images are shown in the same frame. One example is when two people, actually a distance apart, are shown talking to each other.

3.5 EDITING

Editing is the process of selecting and arranging shots in a sequence. The editor decides which scenes or shots to use, as well as the length of each shot, the number of shots, and their sequence. Editing establishes pace, mood, and a coherent story.

Cut is the transition from one shot to another. To create excitement, editors often use quick cuts, which are a series of short shots strung together.

Dissolve is a transitional device in which one scene fades into another.

Fade-in is a transitional device in which a white or black shot fades in to reveal the beginning of a new scene.

Fade-out is a transitional device in which a shot fades to darkness to end a scene.

Jump cut is an abrupt and jarring change from one shot to another. A jump cut shows a break in time or continuity.

Pace is determined by the length of time each shot stays on the screen and the rhythm that is created by the transitions between shots. Short, quick cuts create a fast pace in a story. Long cuts slow down a story.

Parallel editing is a technique that cuts from one shot to another so as to suggest simultaneous action—often in different locations.

4 News

The **news** is information on events, people, and places in your community, your region, the nation, and the world. The news can be categorized by type, as shown in the chart.

Type	Description	Examples
Hard News	fact-based accounts of current events	local newspapers, newscasts, online wire services
Soft News	human-interest stories and other accounts that are less current or urgent than hard news	magazines and tabloid TV shows such as *Sports Illustrated, Access Hollywood*
News Features	stories that elaborate on news reports	documentaries such as history reports on PBS
Commentary and Opinion	essays and perspectives by experts, professionals, and media personalities	editorial pages, personal Web pages

4.1 CHOOSING THE NEWS

Newsworthiness is the significance of an event or action that makes it worthy of media reporting. Journalists and their editors usually weigh the following criteria in determining which stories should make the news:

Timeliness is the quality of being very current. Timely events usually take priority over previously reported events. For example, a car accident with fatalities will be timely on the day it occurs. Because of its timeliness it may be on the front page of a newspaper or be the lead story on a newscast.

Widespread impact refers to the importance of an event and the number of people it could affect. The more widespread the impact of an event, the more likely it is to be newsworthy.

Proximity gauges the nearness of an event to a particular city, region, or country. People tend to be more interested in stories that take place locally and affect them directly.

Human interest is a quality of stories that cause readers or listeners to feel emotions such as happiness, anger, or sadness. People are interested in reading stories about other people.

Uniqueness refers to uncommon events or circumstances that are likely to be interesting to an audience.

Compelling video and **photographs** grab people's attention and stay in their minds.

4.2 REPORTING THE NEWS

When developing a news story, a journalist makes a variety of decisions about how to construct the story, such as what information to include and how to organize it. The following elements are commonly used in news stories:

5 *W*'s and *H* are the six questions reporters answer when writing news stories—*who, what, when, where, why,* and *how.* It is a journalist's job to answer these questions in any type of news report. These questions also serve as a structure for writing and editing a story.

Inverted pyramid is a means of organizing information according to importance. In the inverted pyramid diagram below, the most important information (the answers to the 5 *W*'s and *H*) appears at the top of the pyramid. The less important details appear at the bottom. Not all stories are reported using the inverted pyramid form. The style remains popular, however, because it enables a reader to get the essential information without reading the entire story. Consider the following example.

> A man and his daughters died in a boating accident off Montrose Beach in Chicago today.
>
> The boaters were fishing in the early morning hours when the boat apparently capsized.
>
> Officials say that weather was not a factor, and the accident's cause is still under investigation.

Angle or slant is the point of view from which a story is written. Even an objective report must have an angle.

Consider these two headlines that describe a marine accident.

The first headline alludes to other, possibly recent, cruise ship disasters and may be hinting that there is something wrong with the cruise ship industry. The second headline, however, suggests no such opinion and supplies only the most basic facts of the incident.

Standards for News Reporting

The ideal of journalism is to present news in a way that is objective, accurate, and thorough. The best news stories contain the following elements:

- **Objectivity** The story takes a balanced point of view toward the issues; it is not biased, nor does it reflect a specific attitude or opinion.

- **Accuracy** The story presents factual information that can be verified.

- **Thoroughness** The story presents all sides of an issue; it includes background information, telling *who, what, when, where, why,* and *how.*

Balanced Versus Biased Reporting

Objectivity in news reporting can be measured by how balanced or biased the story is.

Balanced reporting represents all sides of an issue equally and fairly.

A balanced news story

- represents people and subjects in a neutral light
- treats all sides of an issue equally
- does not include inappropriate questions
- does not show stereotypes or prejudice toward people of a particular race, gender, age, religion, or other group
- does not leave out important background information that is needed to establish a context or perspective

Biased reporting is reporting in which one side is favored over another or in which the subject is unfairly represented. Biased reporting may show an overly negative view of a subject, or it may encourage racial, gender, or other stereotypes and prejudices. Sometimes biased reporting is apparent in the journalist's choice of sources.

Sources are the people interviewed for the news report, and also any written materials and documents the journalist used for background information. From each source, the journalist gets a different point of view. To decide whether news reporting is balanced or biased, you will need to pay attention to the sources. For a news story on a new medicinal drug, for instance, if the journalist's only source is a representative from the company that made the drug, the report may be biased. But if the journalist also includes the perspective of someone neutral, such as a scientist who is objectively studying the effects of drugs, the report may be more balanced. It is important to evaluate the **credibility,** or believability and trustworthiness, of both a source and the report itself. The following chart shows which sources are credible.

Sources for News Stories	
Credible Sources	**Weak Sources**
• experts in a field or subject area • people directly affected by the reported event (eyewitnesses) • published reports that are specifically mentioned or shown	• unnamed or anonymous sources • people who are not involved in the reported event (for example, people who heard about a story from a friend) • research, data, or reports that are not specifically named or are referred to only in vague terms (for example, "Research shows that ...")

5 Advertising

Advertising is a sponsor's paid use of various media to promote products, services, or ideas. Some common forms of advertising are shown in the chart.

Type of Ad	Characteristics
Billboard	a large outdoor advertising sign
Print Ad	typically appears in magazines and newspapers; uses eye-catching graphics and persuasive copy
Flyer	a print ad that is circulated by hand or mail
Infomercial	an extended ad on TV that usually includes detailed product information, demonstrations, and testimonials
Public Service Announcement	a message aired on radio or TV to promote ideas that are considered to be in the public interest
Political Ad	broadcast on radio or TV to promote political candidates
Trailer	a short film promoting an upcoming movie, TV show, or video game

Marketing is the process of transferring products and services from producer to consumer. It involves determining the packaging and pricing of a product, how it will be promoted and advertised, and where it will be sold. One way companies market their products is by becoming media sponsors.

Sponsors pay for their products to be advertised. These companies hire advertising agencies to create and produce specific campaigns for their products. They then buy television or radio airtime or magazine, newspaper, or billboard space to feature ads where the target audience is sure to see them. Because selling time and space to advertisers generates much of the income the media need to function, the media need advertisers just as much as advertisers need the media.

Product placement is the intentional and identifiable featuring of brand-name products in movies, television shows, video games, and other media. The intention is to have viewers feel positive about a product because they see a favorite character using it. Another purpose may be to promote product recognition.

5.1 PERSUASIVE TECHNIQUES

Persuasive techniques are the methods used to convince an audience to buy a product or adopt an idea. Advertisers use a combination of visuals, sound, special effects, and words to persuade their target audience. Recognizing the following techniques can help you evaluate persuasive media messages and identify misleading information:

Emotional appeals use strong feelings rather than factual evidence to persuade consumers. Here is an example of an emotional appeal that targets people's pity: "Would you let a child go hungry? Give to St. Cecelia's Homeless and Hungry Program."

Bandwagon appeals use the argument that a person should believe or do something because "everyone else" does. These appeals take advantage of people's desire to be socially accepted. Purchasing a product seems less risky when many others also find it worthy to buy. An example of a bandwagon appeal is "Don't be the last to own a Little Jiffy digital camera."

Slogans are memorable phrases used in advertising campaigns. Slogans substitute catchy language for factual information.

Logical appeals rely on logic and facts, appealing to a consumer's reason and his or her respect for authority. Two examples of logical appeals are expert opinions and product comparisons.

Celebrity ads use one of the following two categories of spokesperson:

- **Celebrity authorities** are experts in a particular field. Advertisers hope that audiences will transfer the respect or admiration they have for the person to

the product. For example, a famous race car driver may endorse, or recommend, a particular car model. Associating the driver's expertise with the product, viewers assume it must be a high-performance car.

- **Celebrity spokespeople** are famous people who endorse a product. Advertisers hope that audiences will associate the product with the celebrity.

Product comparison involves comparing a product with its competition. The competing product is portrayed as inferior. The intended effect is for people to question the quality of the competing product and to believe the featured product is superior.

6 Elements of Design

The design of a media product is just as important as the words are in conveying the message. Like words, visual elements are used to persuade, inform, and entertain.

Graphics and images, such as charts, diagrams, maps, timelines, photographs, illustrations, cartoons, book covers, and symbols, present information that can be quickly and easily understood. The following basic elements are used to give meaning to visuals:

Color can be used to highlight important elements such as headlines and subheads. It can also create mood, because many colors have a strong emotional or psychological impact on the reader or viewer. For example, warm colors more readily draw the eye and are often associated with happiness and comfort. Cool colors are often associated with feelings of peace and contentment or sometimes sadness.

Lines—strokes or marks—can be thick or thin, long or short, and smooth or jagged. They can focus attention and create a feeling of depth. They can frame an object. They can also direct a viewer's eye or create a sense of motion.

Texture is the apparent surface quality of an object. For example, an object's texture can be glossy, rough, wet, or shiny. Texture can be used to create contrast. It can also be used to make an image look "real." For example, a pattern on wrapping paper can create a feeling of depth even though the texture is only visual and cannot be felt.

Shape is the external outline of an object. Shapes can be used to symbolize living things or geometric objects. They can emphasize visual elements and add interest. Shapes can also symbolize ideas.

Notice how this photograph uses these design elements to convey a message.

Live the life you want . . .
Drive the car you love . . .

In "reading" this visual image for its message, take note of the following:

- The **main image** in this photo is a sports car. The **lines** in this picture are intentionally blurred to suggest speed. Also, the primarily horizontal lines of the car and the background suggest motion and speed.

- The main **colors** in the photograph are red, orange, yellow, and black. The first three are warm colors, suggesting heat. The red also suggests speed, and the orange and yellow create a dazzling brilliance.

- The **shapes** in this photograph are rounded and slanted, conveying a sense of sleekness. The unclear edges lend a sense of mystery.

- The **texture** of the car appears shiny, due to the apparent shine on the hood and the side of the car. This texture suggests newness and sleekness.

Considering the design elements in this photograph, what message is it trying to convey about the car?

7 Evaluating Media Messages

Being able to respond critically to media images and messages will help you evaluate the reliability of the content and make informed decisions. Here are six questions to ask about any media message:

Who made—and who sponsored—this message, and for what purpose? The source of the message is a clue to its purpose. If the source of the message is a private company, that company may be trying to sell you a product. If the source is a government agency, that agency may be trying to promote a program or philosophy. To discover the purpose, think about why its creator paid for and produced the message.

Who is the target audience, and how is the message specifically tailored to it? Think about the age group, ethnic group, gender, and/or profession the message is targeting. Decide how it relates to you.

What are the different techniques used to inform, persuade, entertain, and attract attention? Analyze the elements—such as humor, music, special effects, and graphics—that have been used to create the message. Think about how visual and sound effects, such as symbols, color, photographs, words, and music, support the purpose behind the message.

What messages are communicated (and/or implied) about certain people, places, events, behaviors, lifestyles, and so forth? The media try to influence who we are, what we believe in, how we view things, and what values we hold. Look or listen closely to determine whether certain types of behavior are being depicted and if judgments or values are communicated through those behaviors. What are the biases in the message?

How current, accurate, and credible is the information in this message? Think about the reputation of the source. Note the broadcast or publication date of the message and whether the message might change quickly. If a report or account is not supported by facts, authoritative sources, or eyewitness accounts, you should question the credibility of the message.

What is left out of this message that might be important to know? Think about what the message is asking you to believe. Also think about what questions come to mind as you watch, read, or listen to the message.

Applying Strategies to the SAT* and ACT

The test items in this section are modeled after test formats that are used on the SAT and ACT. The strategies presented here will help you prepare for these tests and others. This section offers general test-taking strategies and tips for answering multiple-choice items in critical reading and writing, as well as samples for impromptu writing and essay writing. For each test, read the tips in the margin. Then apply the tips to the practice items. You can also apply the tips to Assessment Practice tests in this book.

1 General Test-Taking Strategies

- Arrive on time and be prepared. Be sure to bring either sharpened pencils with erasers or pens—whichever you are told to bring.
- If you have any questions, ask them before the test begins. Make sure you understand the test procedures, the timing, and the rules.
- Read the test directions carefully. Look at the passages and questions to get an overview of what is expected.
- Tackle the questions one at a time rather than thinking about the whole test.
- Refer back to the reading selections as needed. For example, if a question asks about an author's attitude, you might have to reread a passage for clues.
- If you are not sure of your answer, make a logical guess. You can often arrive at the correct answer by reasoning and eliminating wrong answers.
- As you fill in answers on your answer sheet, make sure you match the number of each test item to the numbered space on the answer sheet.
- Don't look for patterns in the positions of correct choices.
- Only change an answer if you are sure your original choice is incorrect. If you do change an answer, erase your original choice neatly and thoroughly.
- Look for main ideas as you read passages. They are often stated at the beginning or the end of a paragraph. Sometimes the main idea is implied.
- Check your answers and reread your essay.

* SAT is a registered trademark of the College Board, which was not involved in the production of, and does not endorse, this product.

2 Critical Reading

Most tests contain a critical reading section that measures your ability to read, understand, and interpret passages. The passages may be either fiction or nonfiction, and they can be 100 words or 500 to 850 words. They are drawn from literature, the humanities, social studies, and the natural sciences.

Directions: Read the following passage. Base your answers to questions 1 and 2 on what is stated or implied in the passage.

PASSAGE

Mathematics is a living plant which has flourished and languished with the rise and fall of civilizations. Created in some prehistoric period, it struggled for existence through centuries of prehistory and further centuries of recorded history. It finally secured a firm grip on life in the highly congenial soil of Greece and waxed strong for a brief period. In this period it produced one perfect flower, Euclidean geometry. The buds of other flowers opened slightly and with close inspection the outlines of trigonometry and algebra could be discerned; but these flowers withered with the decline of Greek civilization, and the plant remained dormant for one thousand years.

Such was the state of mathematics when the plant was transported to Europe proper and once more imbedded in fertile soil. By A.D. 1600 it had regained the vigor it had possessed at the very height of the Greek period and was prepared to break forth with unprecedented brilliance. If we may describe the mathematics known before 1600 as elementary mathematics, then we may state that elementary mathematics is infinitesimal compared to what has been created since. In fact, a person possessed of the knowledge Newton had at the height of his powers would not be considered a mathematician today for, contrary to popular belief, mathematics must now be said to begin with the calculus and not to end there.

—Morris Kline, *Mathematics in Western Culture*

---

① [stem]

1. Which statement expresses the (main) idea of the first paragraph in this passage? **②**

③ [choices]
   (A) Botany and mathematics both date back to prehistoric times.

   (B) Ancient Greeks saw a connection between numbers and plants.

   (C) Euclidian geometry is an advanced form of mathematical thinking.

   (D) New branches of mathematics developed over the centuries.

   (E) Mathematics thrived in some early civilizations but stagnated in others.

2. The comparison between mathematics and plants conveys the idea that **④**

   (A) both mathematics and plants need the right conditions to thrive

   (B) people who understand plants usually have strong mathematical skills

   (C) early civilizations believed that mathematics was a type of plant

   (D) mathematics and plants cannot be transported to new areas

   (E) mathematics and plants have both been useful to civilization **⑤**

Tips: Multiple Choice

A multiple-choice question consists of a stem and a set of choices. On some tests, there are four choices. On the SAT, there are five. The stem is usually in the form of a question or an incomplete sentence. One of the choices correctly answers the question or completes the sentence.

① Read the stem carefully and try to answer the question without looking at the choices.

② Pay attention to key words in the stem. They may direct you to the correct answer. Question 1 is looking for the *main* idea of a paragraph. There is no information in the paragraph to suggest choices (A) and (B). Choices (C) and (D) focus on minor points. Only choice (E) captures the main idea.

③ Read all the choices before deciding on the correct answer.

④ Some questions ask you to interpret a figure of speech. Question 2, for example, asks you to explain the meaning of a metaphor.

⑤ After reading all the choices, eliminate any that you know are incorrect. In question 2, all of the choices mention mathematics and plants, but only choice (A) expresses the correct relationship between the key words in the metaphor.

Answers: 1. (E), **2.** (A)

Directions: Base your answers to questions 1 and 2 on the two passages below.

Tips: Two Passages

PASSAGE 1

❷   ❸

I feel that writing is an act of hope, a sort of communion with our fellow men. The writer of good will carries a lamp to illuminate the dark corners. Only that, nothing more—a tiny beam of light to show some hidden aspect of reality, to help decipher and understand it and thus to initiate, if possible, a change in the conscience of some readers.

—Isabelle Allende, from "Writing as an Act of Hope"

PASSAGE 2

The most effective writer is not he who announces a particular discovery, who convinces men of a particular conclusion, who demonstrates that this measure is right and that measure wrong; but he who rouses in others the activities that must issue in discovery, who awakes men from their indifference to the right and the wrong, who nerves their energies to seek for the truth and live up to it at whatever cost. The influence of such a writer is dynamic. He does not teach men how to use sword and musket, but he inspires their souls with courage and sends a strong will into their muscles. He does not, perhaps, enrich your stock of data, but he clears away the film from your eyes that you may search for data to some purpose. He does not, perhaps, convince you, but he strikes you, undeceives you, animates you.

—George Eliot, from "Thomas Carlyle"

❷

❹

❶ 1. In passage 2, the phrase "the activities that must issue in discovery" refers to the

   (A) publication of scientific research

   (B) interpretation of hidden clues

   (C) pursuit of knowledge

   (D) development of an individual writing style

   (E) desire to discover the truth

2. To judge from these excerpts, the authors of these passages would most likely agree with which one of the following statements? ❺

   (A) A writer is effective when he or she has a social conscience.

   (B) Writers carry the burden of educating readers.

   (C) Writers are undervalued in some societies.

   (D) A writer can have a powerful effect on readers.

   (E) Writers have a rare talent that must not be wasted.

Tips: Two Passages

Questions are sometimes based on a pair of related passages, which may have completely different views or may simply describe different aspects of the same subject. The two passages here discuss the role of the writer.

❶ Before reading the passages, skim all the questions to see what information you will need.

❷ Find topic sentences and ask yourself whether the passages support or refute their topic sentences. In this case, both passages support their claims with examples and discussion.

❸ You can determine an author's attitude toward a subject by his or her choice of words. In passage 1, the words *hope* and *illuminate* convey the author's positive perspective.

❹ Analyze supporting details. The author of passage 2 uses examples to support the claim that an effective writer has a dynamic influence on readers.

❺ When working with two passages, look for related or contrasting ideas. To answer question 2, you have to find a common thread in the discussions on the role of the writer. Eliminate any answers that pertain to only one passage or to neither of the passages.

Answers: 1. (C), **2.** (D)

Directions: Read the following passage, taken from an early 20th-century short story. Based on what is stated or implied in the passage, answer questions 1 through 5, which appear on the next page.

PASSAGE

Mother called me to the house to bring cobs, and called me again to gather eggs in the middle of the afternoon. She called me a third time. Her face looked uncomfortable.

She said, "If the Slumps go by, do not ask them for any plums."

5   Mother knew I would not ask.

"If they offer any, do not take them."

"What shall I say?"

"Say we do not care for them."

"If they make me take them?"

10   "Refuse them."

When the Slumps came in sight the horses were walking. The Niniscaw was fifteen miles away and the team was tired. I thought I could talk to the children as the wagon passed, but just before it reached me, Mr. Slump hit the horses twice with a willow branch. They trotted, and the wagon rattled by.

15   The children on the last seat were facing toward me. They laughed and waved their arms. Clubby leaned backward and caught up a handful of plums. The wagon bed must have been half filled. He flung them toward me; and then another handful. They fell, scattering, in the thick dust, which curled around them in little eddies, almost hiding them before I could catch

20   them up.

The plums were small and red. They felt warm to my fingers. I wiped them on the front of my dress, and dropped them in my apron. I waited only for one secret rite, before I ran, heart pounding, to tell my mother what I had discovered.

25   She interrupted me, "Did they see you picking them up?"

I thought of myself standing like Clubby Slump, mouth open, without moving. I laughed till two plums rolled out of my apron. "Oh, yes! I had them picked up almost before the dust stopped wriggling. I called, 'Thank you.'"

30   Still mother was not pleased. "Throw them away," she said. "Surely you would not care to eat something flung to you in the road."

It was hard to speak. I moved close to her and whispered, "Can't I keep them?"

Mother left the room. It seemed long before she came back. She put

35   her arm around me and said, "Take them to the pump and wash them thoroughly. Eat them slowly, and do not swallow the skins. You will not want many of them, for you will find them bitter and not fit to eat."

I went out quietly, knowing I would never tell her that they were strange on my tongue as wild honey, holding the warmth of sand that sun had

40   fingered, and the mystery of water under leaning boughs.

For I had eaten one at the road.

—Grace Stone Coates, from "Wild Plums"

Tips: Reading Text

1 Notice the characters who are presented in a passage. Be alert to details about their appearance, personality, or behavior.

2 Identify the point of view from which the story is being told. In a first-person narrative, the narrator is a character in the story and uses the pronouns *I* and *me*. In a third-person narrative, the narrator is outside the story and uses the pronouns *he, she,* and *they.*

3 Try to visualize the setting as you read, filling in details as they are presented. In this passage, we see a young girl living on a farm. It is dry country, miles from water and covered with "thick dust."

4 Remember that a word can have several different meanings or subtle shades of meaning. The word *flung,* for example, expresses an attitude that a more neutral word could not convey.

5 Some test questions will ask you to interpret a figure of speech or an image. Try to understand why the author chose a particular image and what effect it achieves. The images in lines 38–40 capture the warmth and sweetness of the fresh plums.

Answers: 1. (A), **2.** (C), **3.** (D), **4.** (A), **5.** (E)

1. The dialogue between the girl and her mother in lines 4–10 helps to
   (A) reveal their personalities and suggest the conflict
   (B) foreshadow the Slumps' reaction to the girl
   (C) create sympathy for the girl
   (D) criticize the mother's bossiness
   (E) portray the Slumps in a negative light

2. The description in lines 11–14 suggests that Mr. Slump is
   (A) overbearing to people and cruel to animals
   (B) compassionate and well-disposed toward the girl
   (C) determined to avoid contact with the girl
   (D) picky and compulsively punctual
   (E) intimidated by the girl's mother

3. Later in the passage, readers learn that the "secret rite" referred to in lines 22–24 involves the girl's
   (A) thanking Clubby Slump for the plums
   (B) vowing to keep a secret from her mother
   (C) planting a plum seed beside the road
   (D) eating a plum before she gets home
   (E) getting revenge on Mr. Slump

4. The mother's use of the word *flung* in line 31 conveys an attitude of
   (A) disgust
   (B) indifference
   (C) joy
   (D) determination
   (E) graciousness

5. The simile "strange on my tongue as wild honey" suggests that the girl found the plums to be ❺
   (A) overly sweet
   (B) unpleasantly unfamiliar
   (C) hard to swallow
   (D) dangerously forbidden
   (E) deliciously exotic

The critical reading section may feature sentence completion questions that test your knowledge of vocabulary. They may also measure your ability to figure out how different parts of a sentence logically fit together.

Directions: Choose the word or set of words that, when inserted, best fits the meaning of the complete sentence.

1. In human relationships, making _____ about people's motivations often _____ misunderstandings and conflicts. ❶
   - (A) pronouncements . . diffuses
   - (B) assumptions . . creates
   - (C) jokes . . symbolizes
   - (D) comments . . contemplates ❷
   - (E) judgments . . explains

2. James Joyce _____ the traditional narrative structure of the novel by focusing on the stream of consciousness in the characters' minds rather than on the action in the _____ world. ❸
   - (A) debunked . . imaginary
   - (B) perpetuated . . multidimensional
   - (C) internalized . . unconscious
   - (D) redefined . . external
   - (E) explicated . . literary

3. The physical fit and similarities among fossils and rocks in widely separated land masses provided support for Alfred Wegener's theory of _____ drift. ❹
   - (A) continental
   - (B) galactic
   - (C) atmospheric
   - (D) oceanic
   - (E) ecological

4. ❺ Because the comatose patient was _____ to stimuli, the trauma physician ordered a complete panel of _____ and brain imaging studies.
   - (A) averse . . psychological
   - (B) overexposed . . personality
   - (C) unresponsive . . neurological ❻
   - (D) disinclined . . linguistic
   - (E) amenable . . computational

Tips: Sentence Completion

❶ When you are completing sentences with two words missing, think about which pair of suggested words fits both blanks.

❷ If one word in the answer choice is wrong, eliminate that choice from consideration. In sentence 1, *comments* makes sense, but *contemplates* does not.

❸ Look for key words or phrases that link the ideas in a sentence. The word *by* in sentence 2 introduces a phrase that explains how something was done—in this case, the way in which Joyce rejected traditional structure.

❹ If you don't know a word's meaning, look for context clues in the sentence. In sentence 3, for example, ask yourself: What sort of theory would deal with land masses?

❺ Identify relationships between ideas. In sentence 4, there is a cause-and-effect relationship, which is signaled by the word *because*.

❻ A prefix can help unlock the meaning of a word. The Greek prefix *neuro-* means "nerve." In this sentence, the doctor is concerned with the patient's neurological, or nervous, system.

Answers: **1.** (B), **2.** (D), **3.** (A), **4.** (C)

3 Writing

The writing section of standardized tests measures your ability to express ideas clearly and correctly. You will be asked to identify errors in grammar and usage and to improve sentences and paragraphs.

> **Directions:** The following sentence contains either a single error or no error. If it does contain an error, select the underlined part that must be changed to make the sentence correct. If the sentence is correct as written, select answer choice (E).

1. <u>Conscientious</u> people realize that <u>some of the responsibility</u> for carbon <u>dioxide</u>
   (A) ❸   ❷   (B)
   emissions <u>rest</u> with <u>their</u> personal consumption of energy. <u>No error</u> ❶
            (C)   (D)   (E)

> **Directions:** Determine if the underlined part of the following sentence needs improvement. If it does, select the best change presented. If the original phrasing is best, select answer (A).

2. Volunteering is a rewarding way of giving back to the community and <u>to develop</u> your own skills.
   (A) also develop ❹
   (B) a way to develop
   (C) development of
   (D) of developing ❺
   (E) developed

> **Directions:** Following is an early draft of an essay. Read it and answer the question.

The Grand Canyon: A Historical Lens

(1) The Grand Canyon offers a dramatic snapshot of natural history. (2) Caves in the cliffs hide many unique artifacts. (3) Archaeological evidence shows that hunter-gatherers inhabited the canyon for about 8,000 years. (4) The nomadic lifestyle of the region began to disappear around 1000 B.C. (5) At that time, villages appeared and introduced agriculture.

---

3. Which of the following sentences best combines sentences 4 and 5? ❻
   (A) The nomadic lifestyle of the region began to disappear around 1000 B.C., villages appeared and introduced agriculture.
   (B) The nomadic lifestyle of the region began to disappear around 1000 B.C., as villages appeared and introduced agriculture.
   (C) The nomadic lifestyle of the region began to disappear around 1000 B.C., being a time when agriculture was introduced and villages appeared.
   (D) The nomadic lifestyle of the region began to disappear around 1000 B.C., causing villages to appear, which introduced agriculture.
   (E) The nomadic lifestyle of the region began to disappear around 1000 B.C., introducing villages and agriculture.

Tips: Grammar and Style

❶ Read the entire sentence or passage to grasp its overall meaning. Pay particular attention to any underlined portions.

❷ Watch for subject-verb agreement when using an indefinite pronoun like *some*. If the word it refers to in the sentence is singular, the verb must also be singular; if the referent is plural, the verb must be plural.

❸ Use suffixes to uncover word meanings. Knowing that the suffix *–ous* means "full of" helps unlock the meaning of *conscientious*—"full of conscience."

❹ Read through all of the choices before deciding which revision is best. In this case, answer (A) is *not* correct, because it would create a sentence that did not have parallel structure.

❺ Be sure that words or phrases that serve similar grammatical functions in a sentence have parallel structures. In this case, gerund phrases should be used consistently.

❻ When combining sentences, think about how the ideas are related. Subordinating conjunctions such as *when, while,* and *before* express a relationship of time. Conjunctions that show the manner in which something occurs include *as* and *as if.*

Answers: 1. (C), **2.** (D), **3.** (B)

❹ Essay

To determine how well you can develop and express ideas, many tests ask you to write an essay in response to an assignment, or prompt. The essay will represent a first draft and be scored based on the following criteria:

- **Focus** Establish a point of view in the opening paragraph.
- **Organization** Maintain a logical progression of ideas.
- **Support for Ideas** Use details and examples to develop an argument.
- **Style/Word Choice** Use words accurately and vary your sentences.
- **Grammar** Use Standard English and proofread for errors.

Think carefully about the issue presented in this quotation and the assignment below.

> One of a community's most important assets is its land. There has been ongoing tension in many communities between those who favor using land for residential and commercial development and those who support preservation of natural habitats.

Assignment: If your community had proposed building a hospital on a tract of open prairie, would you support the project? Plan and write an essay in which you develop your opinion on this issue. Support your opinion with specific examples and reasons drawn from your reading and experience.

SAMPLE ESSAY

If my community proposed building a hospital on an expanse of prairie, I definitely would not support it. ❶

I know that community hospitals are important and that saving human lives should be a priority in civilized societies. The fact is, though, that a hospital can be built anywhere. There are also other ways of providing health care to community residents, including clinics and advanced transportation by ambulance and helicopter to fully equipped facilities. ❷

A prairie, on the other hand, is a delicate ecosystem that evolved naturally and can never be replaced. There would be no options available to the flora and fauna that have adapted to life in that specific habitat if we destroyed it. In demolishing a prairie, we would be dooming unique species of living things to extinction. ❸

As human beings, we wield an enormous amount of power. The mere fact that we can propose drastically changing our environment is an indication of that influence. But with power comes responsibility. It is essential that we transcend our individual points of view and consider the global impact of our actions.

We have an obligation to look out for the well-being not only of other human beings, but also of all the living things in our world. Building a hospital on our vanishing prairie is not the way to meet that obligation. ❹

Tips: Writing an Essay

The SAT allows only 25 minutes for you to write an essay. Before you begin writing, take a few minutes to jot down the main points you want to make. Allow time to reread and proofread your essay before you hand it in.

❶ When you're writing a persuasive essay, state your point of view in the introduction. Be sure to keep your purpose in mind as you write.

❷ Take the opposing point of view into consideration and respond to it.

❸ Include concrete examples in the body of your essay to clarify your points and strengthen your arguments.

❹ Make sure your essay has a conclusion, even if it is just a single sentence. A conclusion pulls your ideas together and lets the reader know that you have finished.

❺ There will not be time to recopy your essay, so if you have to make a correction, do so neatly and legibly.

❻ You don't have to write a long essay. Length is less important than clarity of thought and correctness of expression. Your essay could range from 200 to 400 words.

Act An act is a major unit of action in a play, similar to a chapter in a book. Depending on their lengths, plays can have as many as five acts.

See also **Drama; Scene.**

Alexandrine *See* **Spenserian Stanza.**

Allegory An allegory is a work with two levels of meaning, a literal one and a symbolic one. In such a work, most of the characters, objects, settings, and events represent abstract qualities. Personification is often used in traditional allegories. As in a fable or parable, the purpose of an allegory may be to convey truths about life, to teach religious or moral lessons, or to criticize social institutions.

Example: The best-known allegory in the English language is John Bunyan's *Pilgrim's Progress.* Christian, the hero of Bunyan's work, represents all people. Other allegorical characters include Mr. Worldly Wiseman, Faithful, and Hopeful. The allegory traces Christian's efforts to achieve a godly life.

See page 505.

Alliteration Alliteration is the repetition of consonant sounds at the beginnings of words. Poets use alliteration to impart a musical quality to their poems, to create mood, to reinforce meaning, to emphasize particular words, and to unify lines or stanzas. Note the examples of alliteration in the following lines:

> Out from the marsh, from the foot of misty
> Hills and bogs, bearing God's hatred,
> Grendel came . . .
>
> —*Beowulf*

See pages 41, 840.

Allusion An allusion is an indirect reference to a person, place, event, or literary work with which the author believes the reader will be familiar.

Example: In Thomas Gray's "Elegy Written in a Country Churchyard," the speaker alludes to Milton, the famous English poet, and Cromwell, the leader of the Puritan revolt in the 17th century. These allusions to two of the best-known figures in English life emphasize the poet's ideas about what the lives of the obscure people buried in the churchyard might have been like had they had different opportunities.

See page 493.

Ambiguity Ambiguity is a technique in which a word, phrase, or event has more than one meaning or can be interpreted in more than one way. Some writers deliberately create this effect to give richness and depth of meaning.

See page 1229.

Analogy An analogy is a point-by-point comparison between two things for the purpose of clarifying the less familiar of the two subjects.

Anapest *See* **Meter.**

Anecdote An anecdote is a brief story that focuses on a single episode or event in a person's life and that is used to illustrate a particular point.

Anglo-Saxon Poetry Anglo-Saxon poetry, which was written between the 7th and 12th centuries, is characterized by a strong rhythm, or cadence, that makes it easily chanted or sung. It was originally recited by **scops,** poet-singers who traveled from place to place. Lines of Anglo-Saxon poetry are unified through alliteration and through use of the same number of accented syllables in each line. Typically, a line is divided by a **caesura,** or pause, into two parts, with each part having two accented syllables. Usually, one or both of the accented syllables in the first part share a similar sound with an accented syllable in the second part. This passage illustrates some of these characteristics:

> He took what he wanted, // all the treasures
> That pleased his eye, // heavy plates
> And golden cups // and the glorious banner,
> Loaded his arms // with all they could hold.
>
> —*Beowulf*

Another characteristic of Anglo-Saxon poetry is the use of **kennings,** metaphorical compound words or phrases substituted for simple nouns.

Examples: Kennings from "The Seafarer" include "whales' home" for the sea and "givers of gold" for rulers or emperors. Examples from *Beowulf* include "shepherd of evil" for Grendel, and "folk-king" for Beowulf.

See pages 41, 103.

Antagonist An antagonist is usually the principal character in opposition to the **protagonist,** or hero of a narrative or drama. The antagonist can also be a force of nature.
See also **Character; Protagonist.**

Antithesis Antithesis is a figure of speech in which sharply contrasting words, phrases, clauses, or sentences are juxtaposed to emphasize a point. In a true antithesis, both the ideas and the grammatical structures are balanced.

Aphorism An aphorism is a brief statement that expresses a general observation about life in a witty, pointed way incorporating **subtlety,** or careful distinctions. Unlike proverbs, which may stem from oral folk tradition, aphorisms originate with specific authors. "Some books are to be tasted, others to be swallowed, and some few to be chewed and digested," from Francis Bacon's essay "Of Studies," is an example of an aphorism.
See page 463.

Apostrophe Apostrophe is a figure of speech in which an object, an abstract quality, or an absent or imaginary person is addressed directly, as if present and able to understand. Writers use apostrophe to express powerful emotions, as in this apostrophe to the ocean:

> Roll on, thou deep and dark blue Ocean, roll!
> Ten thousand fleets sweep over thee in vain;
> Man marks the earth with ruin, his control
> Stops with the shore; upon the watery plain
> The wrecks are all thy deed, nor doth remain
> A shadow of man's ravage, save his own,
> When, for a moment, like a drop of rain,
> He sinks into thy depths with bubbling groan,
> Without a grave, unknell'd, uncoffin'd, and
> unknown. . . .
>
> —George Gordon, Lord Byron,
> *Childe Harold's Pilgrimage*

See page 849.

Archetype An archetype is a pattern in literature that is found in a variety of works from different cultures throughout the ages. An archetype can be a plot, a character, an image, or a setting. For example, the association of death and rebirth with winter and spring is an archetype common to many cultures.

Aside In drama, an aside is a short speech directed to the audience, or another character, that is not heard by the other characters on stage.
See also **Soliloquy.**

Assonance Assonance is the repetition of a vowel sound in two or more stressed syllables that do not end with the same consonant. Poets use assonance to emphasize certain words, to impart a musical quality, to create a mood, or to unify a passage. An example of assonance is the repetition of the long *e* sound in the following lines. Note that the repeated sounds are not always spelled the same.

> When I have fears that I may cease to be
> Before my pen has glean'd my teeming brain
> —John Keats,
> "When I Have Fears That I May Cease to Be"

See pages 840, 1183.
See also **Alliteration; Consonance; Rhyme.**

Atmosphere *See* **Mood.**

Audience Audience is the person or persons who are intended to read or hear a piece of writing. The intended audience of a work determines its form, style, tone, and the details included.

Author's Purpose A writer usually writes for one or more of these purposes: to inform, to entertain, to express himself or herself, or to persuade readers to believe or do something. For example, the purpose of a news report is to inform; the purpose of an editorial is to persuade the readers or audience to do or believe something.
See pages 97, 505, 601, 671.

Author's Perspective An author's perspective is a unique combination of ideas, values, feelings, and beliefs that influences the way the writer looks at a topic. **Tone,** or attitude, often reveals an author's perspective. For example, in "An Encounter with King George III," Fanny Burney reveals her relationship with and sentiments toward the royal family, all of which feeds into the perspective she brings to her subject.
See pages 453, 681.
See also **Author's Purpose; Tone.**

Autobiographical Essay *See* **Essay.**

Autobiography An autobiography is a writer's account of his or her own life. Autobiographies often convey profound insights as writers recount past events from the perspective of greater understanding and distance. A formal autobiography involves a sustained, lengthy narrative of a person's history, but other autobiographical narratives may be less formal and briefer. Under the general category of autobiography fall such writings as diaries, journals, memoirs, and letters. Both formal and informal autobiographies provide revealing insights into the writer's character, attitudes, and motivations, as well as some understanding of the society in which the writer lived. *The Book of Margery Kempe* is an autobiography.

See page 117.

See also **Diary; Memoir.**

Ballad A ballad is a narrative poem that was originally intended to be sung. Traditional folk ballads, written by unknown authors and handed down orally, usually depict ordinary people in the midst of tragic events and adventures of love and bravery. They tend to begin abruptly, focus on a single incident, use dialogue and repetition, and suggest more than they actually state. They often contain supernatural elements.

Typically, a ballad consists of four-line stanzas, or quatrains, with the second and fourth lines of each stanza rhyming. Each stanza has a strong rhythmic pattern, usually with four stressed syllables in the first and third lines and three stressed syllables in the second and fourth lines. The rhyme scheme is usually *abcb* or *aabb*. "Barbara Allan," and "Get Up and Bar the Door" are ballads. Notice the rhythmic pattern in the following stanza:

> Ŏ slówlў, slówlў rasĕ shĕ úp,   *a*
>
> To thĕ plácĕ whĕre hĕ wăs lýin',   *b*
>
> And whĕn shĕ drĕw thĕ cúrtaĭn bў: *c*
>
> "Yŏung mán, Ĭ thínk yŏu're dýin'."   *b*
>
> —"Barbara Allan"

A **literary ballad** is a ballad with a single author. Modeled on the early English and Scottish folk ballads, literary ballads became popular during the romantic period. Samuel Taylor Coleridge's "The Rime of the Ancient Mariner" is a romantic literary ballad.

See pages 217, 813.

See also **Narrative Poem; Rhyme; Rhythm.**

Biography A biography is a type of nonfiction in which a writer gives a factual account of someone else's life. Written in the third person, a biography may cover a person's entire life or focus on only an important part of it. An outstanding example of a biography is James Boswell's *The Life of Samuel Johnson.* Modern biography includes a popular form called **fictionalized biography,** in which writers use their imaginations to re-create past conversations and to elaborate on some incidents.

Blank Verse Blank verse is unrhymed poetry written in iambic pentameter. Because iambic pentameter resembles the natural rhythm of spoken English, it has been considered the most suitable meter for dramatic verse in English. Shakespeare's plays are written largely in blank verse, as is Milton's epic *Paradise Lost.* Blank verse has also been used frequently for long poems, as in the following:

> Ănd nów, wĭth gléams ŏf hálf-ĕxtínguĭshĕd thóught
>
> Wĭth mánў rĕcógnĭtĭons dím ănd fáint,
>
> Ănd sómĕwhat ŏf ă sád pĕrpléxĭtў,
>
> Thĕ píctŭre ŏf thĕ mínd rĕvíves ăgáin;
>
> —**William Wordsworth,**
> **"Lines Composed a Few Miles Above Tintern Abbey"**

See pages 344, 347.

See also **Iambic Pentameter; Meter; Rhythm.**

Caesura A caesura is a pause or a break in a line of poetry. Poets use a caesura to emphasize the word or phrase that precedes it or to vary the rhythmical effects.

See also **Anglo-Saxon Poetry.**

Carpe Diem The term *carpe diem* is a Latin phrase meaning "seize the day." This "live for the moment" theme characterizes the work of the 17th-century Cavalier poets, including Andrew Marvell, Robert Herrick, and Richard Lovelace.

Cast of Characters The cast of characters is a list of all the characters in a play, usually in the order of appearance. This list is found at the beginning of a script.

Character Characters are the people, and sometimes animals or other beings, who take part in the action of a story or novel. Events center on the lives of one or more characters, referred to as **main characters.** The other characters, called **minor characters,** interact with the main characters and help move the story along.

Characters may also be classified as either static or dynamic. **Static characters** tend not to change much over the course of the story. They do not experience life-altering moments and seem to act the same, even though their situations may change. In contrast, **dynamic characters** evolve as individuals, learning from their experiences and growing emotionally.

See pages 77, 141, 143, 661, 945, 1127, 1319, 1363.

See also **Antagonist; Characterization; Foil; Motivation; Protagonist.**

Characterization   Characterization refers to the techniques that writers use to develop characters. There are four basic methods of characterization:

1. A writer may use physical description. In William Trevor's "The Distant Past," the narrator describes the Middletons. "They had always been thin, silent with one another, and similar in appearance: a brother and sister who shared a family face. It was a bony countenance, with pale blue eyes and a sharp, well-shaped nose and high cheekbones."

2. A character's nature may be revealed through his or her own speech, thoughts, feelings, or actions. In Trevor's story, the reader learns about the kind of life the Middletons lead: "Together they roved the vast lofts of their house, placing old paint tins and flowerpot saucers beneath the drips from the roof. At night they sat over their thin chops in a dining-room that had once been gracious. . . ."

3. The speech, thoughts, feelings, and actions of other characters can be used to develop a character. The attitudes of the townspeople to the Middletons help the reader understand the old couple better: "'An upright couple,' was the Canon's public opinion of the Middletons, and he had been known to add that eccentric views would hurt you less than malice."

4. The narrator can make direct comments about the character's nature. The narrator in Trevor's story comments, "The Middletons were in their middle-sixties now and were reconciled to a life that became more uncomfortable with every passing year."

See pages 141, 143, 1015, 1199, 1139, 1319, 1363.

See also **Character; Narrator.**

Chorus   In the theater of ancient Greece, the chorus was a group of actors who commented on the action of the play. Between scenes, the chorus sang and danced to musical accompaniment, giving insights into the message of the play. The chorus is often considered a kind of ideal spectator, representing the response of ordinary citizens to the tragic events that unfold. Certain dramatists have continued to employ this classical convention as a way of representing the views of the society being depicted.

See also **Drama.**

Cliché   A cliché is an overused expression that has lost its freshness, force, and appeal. The phrase "quiet as a mouse" is an example of a cliché.

Climax   In a plot structure, the climax, or turning point, is the moment when the reader's interest and emotional intensity reach a peak. The climax usually occurs toward the end of a story and often results in a change in the characters or a solution to the conflict.

See also **Plot; Resolution.**

Comedy   A comedy is a dramatic work that is light and often humorous in tone, usually ending happily with a peaceful resolution of the main conflict. A comedy differs from a **farce** by having a more believable plot, more realistic characters, and less boisterous behavior.

See also **Drama; Farce.**

Comic Relief   Comic relief consists of humorous scenes, incidents, or speeches that are included in a serious drama to provide a reduction in emotional intensity. Because it breaks the tension, comic relief allows an audience to prepare emotionally for events to come.

Example: Comic relief in *Macbeth* is provided by Macbeth's garrulous, vulgar porter at the beginning of Act II, Scene 3, just after Duncan's murder. This scene is needed to relax the tension built up in the preceding scenes.

Complication   A complication is an additional factor or problem introduced into the rising action of a story to make the conflict more difficult. In some cases, a plot complication presents a character with a moral dilemma or quandry that seems to make it harder or nearly impossible for a character to get what he or she wants.

Conceit   *See* **Extended Metaphor.**

Conflict   A conflict is a struggle between opposing forces that is the basis of a story's plot. An **external conflict** pits a character against nature, society, or another character. An **internal conflict** is a conflict between opposing forces within a character.

Example: In Elizabeth Gaskell's "Christmas Storms and Sunshine," Mrs. Hodgson is in a running conflict with Mrs. Jenkins.

See pages 247, 1341.

See also **Antagonist; Plot.**

Connotation Connotation is the emotional response evoked by a word, in contrast to its **denotation,** which is its literal meaning. *Kitten,* for example, is defined as "a young cat." However, the word also suggests, or connotes, images of softness, warmth, and playfulness.

Consonance Consonance is the repetition of consonant sounds within and at the ends of words, as in the following example:

> In Breughel's *Icarus,* for instance: how everything turns
> away
> Quite leisurely from the disaster; the ploughman may
> Have heard the splash, the forsaken cry,
> But for him it was not an important failure; . . .
> —W. H. Auden, "Musée des Beaux Arts"

See also **Alliteration; Assonance.**

Contradiction *See* **Paradox**

Controlling Image *See* **Extended Metaphor; Imagery.**

Couplet A couplet is a rhymed pair of lines. A simple couplet may be written in any rhythmic pattern. The following couplet is written in iambic tetrameter (lines of four iambs each):

> Had we but world enough, and time,
> This coyness, lady, were no crime.
> —Andrew Marvell, "To His Coy Mistress"

A **heroic couplet** consists of two rhyming lines written in iambic pentameter. The term *heroic* comes from the fact that English poems having heroic themes and elevated style have often been written in iambic pentameter. Alexander Pope's masterful use of the heroic couplet made it a popular verse form during the neoclassical period.

See page 611.

Creation Myth *See* **Myth.**

Critical Essay *See* **Essay.**

Dactyl *See* **Meter.**

Denotation *See* **Connotation.**

Dénouement *See* **Plot.**

Description Description is writing that helps a reader to picture scenes, events, and characters. It helps the reader understand exactly what someone or something is like. To create description, writers often use sensory images—words and phrases that enable the reader to see, hear, smell, taste, or feel the subject described—and figurative language. Effective description also relies on precise nouns, verbs, adjectives, and adverbs, as well as carefully selected details. The following passage contains clear details and images:

> Air, musty from having been long enclosed, hung in all the rooms, and the waste room behind the kitchen was littered with old useless papers. Among these I found a few paper-covered books, the pages of which were curled and damp. . . . The wild garden behind the house contained a central apple-tree and a few straggling bushes under one of which I found the late tenant's rusty bicycle-pump.
> —James Joyce, "Araby"

See page 1199.
See also **Diction; Figurative Language; Imagery.**

Dialect Dialect is a particular variety of language spoken in one place by a distinct group of people. A dialect reflects the colloquialisms, grammatical constructions, distinctive vocabulary, and pronunciations that are typical of a region. At times writers use dialect to establish or emphasize settings, as well as to develop characters.
See pages 217, 783, 1213.

Dialogue Dialogue is conversation between two or more characters in either fiction or nonfiction. In drama, the story is told almost exclusively through dialogue, which moves the plot forward and reveals characters' motives.
See page 1213.
See also **Drama.**

Diary A diary is a writer's personal day-to-day account of his or her experiences and impressions. Most diaries are private and not intended to be shared. Some, however, have been published because they are well written and provide useful perspectives on historical events or on the everyday life of particular eras. Samuel Pepys's diary is one of the most famous diaries in British literature.

Diction A writer's or speaker's choice of words is called diction. Diction includes both vocabulary (individual words) and syntax (the order or arrangement of words). Diction can be formal or informal, technical or common, abstract or concrete. In the following complex sentence, the diction is formal:

Examples: Much of the diction in Aldous Huxley's essay "Words and Behavior" is formal, which is appropriate to the seriousness of his subject. The lofty, elevated diction in John Milton's *Paradise Lost* befits the poem's exalted subject and themes. By contrast, the blandness of the diction in W. H. Auden's "The Unknown Citizen"—for example, the words *employers, advertisements, advantages,* and *population*—helps establish the detached, ironic tone of the poem.

See also **Connotation; Style.**

Drama Drama is literature in which plot and character are developed through dialogue and action; in other words, drama is literature in play form. It is performed on stage and radio and in films and television. Most plays are divided into acts, with each act having an emotional peak, or climax, of its own. The acts sometimes are divided into scenes; each scene is limited to a single time and place. Most contemporary plays have two or three acts, although some have only one act.

See pages 347, 1213

See also **Act; Dialogue; Scene; Stage Directions.**

Dramatic Irony *See* **Irony.**

Dramatic Monologue A dramatic monologue is a lyric poem in which a speaker addresses a silent or absent listener in a moment of high intensity or deep emotion, as if engaged in private conversation. The speaker proceeds without interruption or argument, and the effect on the reader is that of hearing just one side of a conversation. This technique allows the poet to focus on the feelings, personality, and motivations of the speaker.

See also **Lyric Poetry; Soliloquy.**

Dynamic Character *See* **Character.**

Elegy An elegy is an extended meditative poem in which the speaker reflects upon death—often in tribute to a person who has died recently—or on an equally serious subject. Most elegies are written in formal, dignified language and are serious in tone. Alfred, Lord Tennyson's *In Memoriam,* written in memory of his friend Arthur Henry Hallam, is a famous elegy.

Elizabethan (Shakespearean) Sonnet *See* **Sonnet.**

End Rhyme *See* **Rhyme.**

English (Shakespearean) Sonnet *See* **Sonnet.**

Epic Hero An epic hero is a larger-than-life figure who often embodies the ideals of a nation or race. Epic heroes take part in dangerous adventures and accomplish great deeds. Many undertake long, difficult journeys and display great courage and superhuman strength.

Epic Poem An epic is a long narrative poem on a serious subject presented in an elevated or formal style. An epic traces the adventures of a hero whose actions consist of courageous, even superhuman, deeds, which often represent the ideals and values of a nation or race. Epics typically address universal issues, such as good and evil, life and death, and sin and redemption. *Beowulf* is an enduring epic of the Anglo-Saxon period.

Epic Simile *See* **Simile.**

Epigram The epigram is a literary form that originated in ancient Greece. It developed from simple inscriptions on monuments into a literary genre—short poems or sayings characterized by conciseness, balance, clarity, and wit. A classic epigram is written in two parts, the first establishing the occasion or setting the tone and the second stating the main point. A few lines taken from a longer poem can also be an epigram. Epigrams are used for many purposes, including the expression of friendship, grief, criticism, praise, and philosophy.

Epitaph An epitaph is an inscription on a tomb or monument to honor the memory of a deceased person. The term *epitaph* is also used to describe any verse commemorating someone who has died. Although a few humorous epitaphs have been composed, most are serious in tone. Ben Jonson's "On My First Son" is sometimes called an epitaph.

See page 525.

Epithet An epithet is a brief phrase that points out traits associated with a particular person or thing. Homer's *Iliad* contains many examples of epithets, such as the references to Achilles as "the great runner" and to Hector as "killer of men."

Essay An essay is a brief work of nonfiction that offers an opinion on a subject. The purpose of an essay may be to express ideas and feelings, to analyze, to inform, to entertain, or to persuade. In a **persuasive essay,** a writer attempts to convince readers to adopt a particular opinion or to perform a certain action. Most persuasive essays present a series of facts, reasons, or examples in support of an opinion or proposal.

Essays can be formal or informal. A **formal essay** examines a topic in a thorough, serious, and highly organized manner. An **expository essay** is a formal essay that presents information or explains ideas. An **informal**

essay presents an opinion on a subject, but not in a completely serious or formal tone. Characteristics of this type of essay include humor, a personal or confidential approach, a loose and sometimes rambling style, and often a surprising or unconventional topic. Mary Wollstonecraft's *A Vindication of the Rights of Woman* is a formal essay, meant to analyze and persuade. Joseph Addison's essays from *The Spectator* are informal, meant to express observations, ideas, and feelings and to entertain with gentle humor and wit.

A **personal essay** is a type of informal essay. Personal essays allow writers to express their viewpoints on subjects by reflecting on events or incidents in their own lives. George Orwell's "Shooting an Elephant" is an example of a personal essay.

See pages 463, 719, 1251.

Exaggeration *See* **Hyperbole.**

Exemplum An exemplum is a short anecdote or story that helps illustrate a particular moral point. Developed in the Middle Ages, this form was widely used by Geoffrey Chaucer in *The Canterbury Tales.*

Exposition *See* **Plot.**

Expository Essay *See* **Essay.**

Extended Metaphor Like any metaphor, an extended metaphor is a comparison between two essentially unlike things that nevertheless have something in common. It does not contain the word *like* or *as.* In an extended metaphor, two things are compared at length and in various ways— perhaps throughout a stanza, a paragraph, or even an entire work. The likening of God to a shepherd in "Psalm 23" is an example of an extended metaphor.

Like an extended metaphor, a **conceit** parallels two essentially dissimilar things on several points. A conceit, though, is a more elaborate, formal, and ingenious comparison than the ordinary extended metaphor. Sometimes a conceit forms the framework of an entire poem, as in John Donne's "A Valediction: Forbidding Mourning," in which the poet describes his own and his lover's souls as the two legs of a mathematician's compass.

See page 517.
See also **Figurative Language; Metaphor; Simile.**

External Conflict *See* **Conflict.**

Falling Action *See* **Plot.**

Fantasy *Fantasy* is a term applied to works of fiction that display a disregard for the restraints of reality. The aim of a fantasy may be purely to delight or may be to make a serious comment. Some fantasies include extreme or grotesque

characters. Others portray realistic characters in a realistic world who only marginally overstep the bounds of reality.
Example: In *Gulliver's Travels,* Jonathan Swift creates imaginary worlds to present his satire of 18th-century England.
See page 635.

Farce A farce is a type of exaggerated comedy that features an absurd plot, ridiculous situations, and humorous dialogue. The main purpose of a farce is to keep an audience laughing. The characters are usually **stereotypes,** or simplified examples of different traits or qualities. Comic devices typically used in farces include mistaken identity, deception, wordplay—such as puns and double meanings—and exaggeration.
See also **Comedy; Stereotype.**

Fiction Fiction refers to works of prose that contain imaginary elements. Although fiction, like nonfiction, may be based on actual events and real people, it differs from nonfiction in that it is shaped primarily by the writer's imagination. The two major types of fiction are novels and short stories. The four basic elements of a work of fiction are **character, setting, plot,** and **theme.**
See also **Novel; Short Story.**

Figurative Language Figurative language is language that communicates ideas beyond the literal meaning of words. Figurative language can make descriptions and unfamiliar or difficult ideas easier to understand. Special types of figurative language, called **figures of speech,** include **simile, metaphor, personification, hyperbole,** and **apostrophe.**

Figures of Speech *See* **Figurative Language.**

First-Person Point of View *See* **Point of View.**

Flashback A flashback is a scene that interrupts the action of a narrative to describe events that took place at an earlier time. It provides background helpful in understanding a character's present situation.
Examples: The use of flashback in Virginia Woolf's "The Duchess and the Jeweller" helps to reveal the conflicting emotions and motivations of the jeweller. The use of flashback in William Trevor's "The Distant Past" provides important background for understanding the relationship of the Middletons to the townspeople.
See page 1229.

Foil A foil is a character whose traits contrast with those of another character. A writer might use a minor character as a foil to emphasize the positive traits of the main character.
See also **Character.**

Folk Ballad *See* **Ballad.**

Folk Tale A folk tale is a short, simple story that is handed down, usually by word of mouth, from generation to generation. Folk tales include legends, fairy tales, myths, and fables. Folk tales often teach family obligations or societal values.

See also **Legend; Myth; Fable.**

Foot *See* **Meter.**

Foreshadowing Foreshadowing is a writer's use of hints or clues to indicate events that will occur later in a story. Foreshadowing creates suspense and at the same time prepares the reader for what is to come.

Example: In "The Rocking-Horse Winner," the strange mad frenzy with which Paul rides his rocking horse early in the story foreshadows the tragedy of his final ride.

See pages 345, 1229.

Form At its simplest, form refers to the physical arrangement of words in a poem—the length and placement of the lines, the grouping of lines into stanzas, and any **graphical** element that enhances the poem's meaning. The term can also refer to other kinds of patterning in poetry—anything from rhythm and other sound patterns to the design of a traditional poetic type, such as a sonnet or dramatic monologue.

See also **Genre; Stanza.**

Frame Story A frame story exists when a story is told within a narrative setting or frame—hence creating a story within a story.

Examples: The collection of tales in Chaucer's *The Canterbury Tales,* including "The Pardoner's Tale" and "The Wife of Bath's Tale," are set within a frame story. The frame is introduced in "The Prologue," in which 30 characters on a pilgrimage to Canterbury agree to tell stories to pass the time. "Federigo's Falcon" and the other tales in Boccaccio's *Decameron* are set within a similar framework. The frame, or outer story, is about ten characters fleeing plague-ravaged Florence, Italy, who decide to amuse themselves by telling stories.

See page 183.

Free Verse Free verse is poetry that does not have regular patterns of rhyme and meter. The lines in free verse often flow more naturally than do rhymed, metrical lines and thus achieve a rhythm more like that of everyday human speech. Much 20th-century poetry, such as T. S. Eliot's "The Hollow Men," is written in free verse.

See pages 1117, 1303.

See also **Meter; Rhyme.**

Genre Genre refers to the distinct types into which literary works can be grouped. The four main literary genres are fiction, poetry, nonfiction, and drama.

Gothic Literature Gothic literature is characterized by grotesque characters, bizarre situations, and violent events. Mary Shelley's *Frankenstein* can be considered Gothic literature.

Graphics *See* **Form.**

Haiku Haiku is a form of Japanese poetry in which 17 syllables are arranged in three lines of 5, 7, and 5 syllables. The rules of haiku are strict. In addition to the syllabic count, the poet must create a clear picture that will evoke a strong emotional response in the reader. Nature is a particularly important source of inspiration for Japanese haiku poets, and details from nature are often the subjects of their poems.

Hero A hero, or **protagonist,** is a central character in a work of fiction, drama, or epic poetry. A traditional hero possesses good qualities that enable him or her to triumph over an antagonist who is bad or evil in some way.

The term *tragic hero,* first used by the Greek philosopher Aristotle, refers to a central character in a drama who is dignified or noble. According to Aristotle, a tragic hero possesses a defect, or tragic flaw, that brings about or contributes to his or her downfall. This flaw may be poor judgment, pride, weakness, or an excess of an admirable quality. The tragic hero, Aristotle noted, recognizes his or her flaw and its consequences, but only after it is too late to change the course of events. The characters Macbeth and Hamlet in Shakespeare's tragedies are tragic heroes.

A **cultural hero** is a hero who represents the values of his or her culture. Such a hero ranks somewhere between ordinary human beings and the gods. The role of a cultural hero is to provide a noble image that will inspire and guide the actions of mortals. Beowulf is a cultural hero.

In more recent literature, heroes do not necessarily command the attention and admiration of an entire culture. They tend to be individuals whose actions and decisions reflect personal courage. The conflicts they face are not on an epic scale but instead involve moral dilemmas presented in the course of living. Such heroes are often in a struggle with established authority because their actions challenge accepted beliefs.

See also **Epic; Protagonist; Tragedy.**

Heroic Couplet *See* **Couplet.**

Historical Context The historical context of a literary work refers to the social conditions that inspired or influenced its creation. To understand and appreciate some works, the reader must relate them to events in history.

See pages 471, 635, 719, 861.

Historical Writing Historical writing is the systematic telling, often in narrative form, of the past of a nation or group of people. Historical writing generally has the following characteristics: (1) it is concerned with real events; (2) it uses chronological order; and (3) it is usually an objective retelling of facts rather than a personal interpretation. The Venerable Bede's *A History of the English Church and People* is an example of historical writing.

See page 97.

See also **Primary Sources; Secondary Sources.**

Humor In literature there are three basic types of humor, all of which may involve exaggeration or irony. **Humor of situation** is derived from the plot of a work. It usually involves exaggerated events or situational irony, which occurs when something happens that is different from what was expected. **Humor of character** is often based on exaggerated personalities or on characters who fail to recognize their own flaws, a form of dramatic irony. **Humor of language** may include sarcasm, exaggeration, puns, or verbal irony, which occurs when what is said is not what is meant. In *Candide*, Voltaire uses all three kinds of humor, including absurd situations, ridiculous characters, and ironic descriptions.

See page 661.

See also **Comedy; Farce; Irony.**

Hyperbole Hyperbole is a figure of speech in which the truth is exaggerated for emphasis or for humorous effect. Notice the jarring effect created by this hyperbole:

> "Through the aperture driver and passenger, not six inches between them, remained for an eternity eye to eye."
> —Elizabeth Bowen, "The Demon Lover"

See also **Figurative Language; Understatement.**

Iamb *See* **Meter.**

Iambic Pentameter Iambic pentameter is a metrical pattern of five feet, or units, each of which is made up of two syllables, the first unstressed and the second stressed. Iambic pentameter is the most common meter used in English poetry; it is the meter used in blank verse and in the sonnet. The following line is an example of iambic pentameter:

> How soon hath Time, the subtle thief of youth
> —John Milton, "How Soon Hath Time"

See page 347, 611, 861.

See also **Blank Verse; Meter; Sonnet.**

Idiom An idiom is a common figure of speech whose meaning is different from the literal meaning of its words. For example, the phrase "raining cats and dogs" does not literally mean that cats and dogs are falling from the sky; the expression means "raining heavily."

Imagery The term *imagery* refers to words and phrases that create vivid sensory experiences for the reader. The majority of images are visual, but imagery may also appeal to the senses of smell, hearing, taste, and touch. In addition, images may re-create sensations of heat (thermal), movement (kinetic), or bodily tension (kinesthetic). Effective writers of both prose and poetry frequently use imagery that appeals to more than one sense simultaneously. For example, in John Keats's ode "To Autumn," the image "Thy hair soft-lifted by the winnowing wind" appeals to two senses—sight and touch.

When an image describes one sensation in terms of another, the technique is called **synesthesia.** For example, the phrase "cold smell of potato mold" from Seamus Heaney's poem "Digging" is an image appealing to smell described in terms of touch (temperature).

A poet may use a **controlling image** to convey thoughts or feelings. A controlling image is a single image or comparison that extends throughout a literary work and shapes its meaning. A controlling image is sometimes an **extended metaphor.** The image of the Greek vase in Keats's "Ode on a Grecian Urn" and the image of digging in Heaney's poem "Digging" are controlling images.

See pages 103, 325, 879, 1303.

See also **Description; Kinesthetic Imagery.**

Informal Essay *See* **Essay.**

Interior Monologue *See* **Monologue; Stream of Consciousness.**

Internal Conflict *See* **Conflict.**

Internal Rhyme *See* **Rhyme.**

Interview An interview is a conversation conducted by a writer or reporter in which facts or statements are elicited from another person, recorded, and then broadcast or published.

Irony Irony is a contrast between expectation and reality. This incongruity often has the effect of surprising the reader or viewer. The techniques of irony include hyperbole, understatement, and sarcasm. Irony is often subtle and easily overlooked or misinterpreted.

There are three main types of irony. **Situational irony** occurs when a character or the reader expects one thing to happen but something else actually happens. In Thomas Hardy's poem "Ah, Are You Digging on My Grave?" the speaker questions who is digging on her grave and why. The responses to her questions and the final revelation shock the speaker and create a shattering irony in the poem. **Verbal irony** occurs when a writer or character says one thing but means another. An example of verbal irony is the title of Jonathan Swift's essay "A Modest Proposal." The reader soon discovers that the narrator's proposal is outrageous rather than modest and unassuming. **Dramatic irony** occurs when the reader or viewer knows something that a character does not know. For example, in Act One of Shakespeare's *Macbeth*, the audience knows that Macbeth is thinking of killing Duncan, but Duncan does not.

See pages 453, 621, 1175, 1363.

Italian (Petrarchan) Sonnet *See* **Sonnet.**

Kenning *See* **Anglo-Saxon Poetry.**

Kinesthetic Imagery Kinesthetic imagery re-creates the tension felt through muscles, tendons, or joints in the body. In the following passage, Seamus Heaney uses kinesthetic imagery to describe his father's potato digging:

> . . . I look down
> Till his straining rump among the flowerbeds
> Bends low, comes up twenty years away
> Stooping in rhythm through potato drills
> Where he was digging.
> —Seamus Heaney, "Digging"

See page 1303.
See also **Imagery.**

Journal *See* **Diary.**

Legend A legend is a story passed down orally from generation to generation and popularly believed to have a historical basis. While some legends may be based on real people or situations, most of the events are either greatly exaggerated or fictitious. Like myths, legends may incorporate supernatural elements and magical deeds. But legends differ from myths in that they claim to be stories

about real human beings and are often set in a particular time and place.

Letters *Letters* refers to the written correspondence exchanged between acquaintances, friends, or family members. Most letters are private and not designed for publication. However, some are published and read by a wider audience because they are written by well-known public figures or provide important information about the period in which they were written.

Examples: The Paston Letters, the correspondence of a family in 15th-century England, is a famous collection of letters. John Keats's collected letters provide an excellent portrait of the poet's intellect, imagination, and relationships with others. *See page 127.*

Limited Point of View *See* **Point of View.**

Line The line is the core unit of a poem. In poetry, line length is an essential element of the poem's meaning and rhythm. There are a variety of terms to describe the way a line of poetry ends or is connected to the next line. Line breaks, where a line of poetry ends, may coincide with grammatical units. However, a line break may also occur in the middle of a grammatical or syntactical unit, creating a pause or emphasis. Poets use a variety of line breaks to play with meaning, thereby creating a wide range of effects.

Literary Ballad *See* **Ballad.**

Literary Criticism Literary criticism refers to writing that focuses on a literary work or a genre, describing some aspect of it, such as its origin, its characteristics, or its effects.

Literary Nonfiction Literary nonfiction is informational text that is recognized as being of artistic value or that is about literature. Autobiographies, biographies, essays, and eloquent speeches typically fall into this category.

Lyric A lyric is a short poem in which a single speaker expresses personal thoughts and feelings. Most poems other than dramatic and narrative poems are lyrics. In ancient Greece, lyrics were meant to be sung—the word *lyric* comes from the word *lyre,* the name of a musical instrument that was used to accompany songs. Modern lyrics are not usually intended for singing, but they are characterized by strong, melodic rhythms. Lyrics can be in a variety of forms and cover many subjects, from love and death to everyday experiences. They are marked by imagination and create for the reader a strong, unified impression. The following lines from John Keats's famous poem exemplify the emotional intensity of lyric poetry:

> When I have fears that I may cease to be
>   Before my pen has glean'd my teeming brain,
> Before high piled books, in charactry,
>   Hold like rich garners the full ripen'd grain;
>   —John Keats,
>   "When I Have Fears That I May Cease to Be"

See also **Poetry.**

Main Character *See* **Character.**

Major Character *See* **Character.**

Maxim A maxim is a brief and memorable statement of general truth, one that often imparts guidance or advice. This type of writing is common in the Book of Ecclesiastes of the Bible.

Memoir A memoir is a form of autobiographical writing in which a person recalls significant events and people in his or her life. Most memoirs share the following characteristics: (1) they usually are structured as narratives told by the writers themselves, using the first-person point of view; (2) although some names may be changed to protect privacy, memoirs are true accounts of actual events; (3) although basically personal, memoirs may deal with newsworthy events having a significance beyond the confines of the writer's life; (4) unlike strictly historical accounts, memoirs often include the writers' feelings and opinions about historical events, giving the reader insight into the impact of history on people's lives.

See also **Autobiography.**

Metaphor A metaphor is a figure of speech that compares two things that have something in common. Unlike similes, metaphors do not use the words *like* or *as,* but make comparisons directly. In the following poem, the phrase "Time's wingèd chariot" is a metaphor in which the swift passage of time is compared to a speeding chariot:

> But at my back I always hear
> Time's wingèd chariot hurrying near
>   —Andrew Marvell, "To His Coy Mistress"

See pages 335, 489, 849, 953.
See also **Extended Metaphor; Figurative Language; Simile.**

Metaphysical Poetry Metaphysical poetry is a style of poetry written by a group of 17th-century poets, of whom John Donne was the first. The metaphysical poets rejected the conventions of Elizabethan love poetry, with its musical quality and themes of courtly love. Instead, they approached subjects such as religion, death, and even love by analyzing them logically and philosophically. The metaphysical poets were intellectuals who, like the ideal Renaissance man, were well-read in a broad spectrum of subjects. The characteristics of metaphysical poetry include more than just an intellectual approach to subject matter, however. Instead of the lyrical style of most Elizabethan poetry, metaphysical poets used a more colloquial, or conversational, style. In spite of the simplicity of the words, the ideas may seem obscure or confusing at first, because metaphysical poets loved to play with language. Donne's writing is filled with surprising twists: unexpected images and comparisons, as well as the use of **paradox,** seemingly contradictory statements that in fact reveal some element of truth. Donne's poem "A Valediction: Forbidding Mourning" contains many characteristics of metaphysical poetry.

See page 514, 517.
See also **Paradox.**

Meter Meter is the repetition of a regular rhythmic unit in a line of poetry. Each unit, known as a **foot,** has one stressed syllable (indicated by a ˊ) and either one or two unstressed syllables (indicated by a ˘). The four basic types of metrical feet are the **iamb,** an unstressed syllable followed by a stressed syllable; the **trochee,** a stressed syllable followed by an unstressed syllable; the **anapest,** two unstressed syllables followed by a stressed syllable; and the **dactyl,** a stressed syllable followed by two unstressed syllables.

Two words are typically used to describe the meter of a line. The first word identifies the type of metrical foot—iambic, trochaic, anapestic, or dactylic—and the second word indicates the number of feet in a line: **monometer** (one foot); **dimeter** (two feet); **trimeter** (three feet); **tetrameter** (four feet); **pentameter** (five feet); **hexameter** (six feet); and so forth. The meter in this poem is iambic tetrameter:

> Ĭ hóld ĭt trúe, whăte'ér bĕfáll;
>   Ĭ féel ĭt, whĕn Ĭ sórrŏw móst;
>   'Tĭs bétter tŏ háve lóved ănd lóst
> Thăn néver tŏ háve lóved ăt áll.
>   —Alfred, Lord Tennyson, *In Memoriam*

See page 861.
See also **Free Verse; Iambic Pentameter; Rhythm; Scansion.**

Minor Character *See* **Character.**

Mise-en-Scène *Mise-en-scène* is a term from the French that refers to the various physical aspects of a dramatic presentation, such as lighting, costumes, scenery, makeup, and props.

Mock Epic A mock epic uses the lofty style and conventions of epic poetry to satirize a trivial subject. In *The Rape of the Lock,* Alexander Pope pokes fun of a silly quarrel by narrating it in a formal manner.
See page 611.

Modernism Modernism was a movement roughly spanning the time period between the two world wars, 1914–1945. Modernist writers departed from 19th century traditions, such as **realism,** preferring more flexible, experimental approaches emphasizing subjectivity and fragmentation, such as **stream-of-consciousness** and **free verse.** Modernist works often focus on the theme of the alienation of the individual. T. S. Eliot's poetry and Virginia Woolf's prose are examples of modernist literature.
See page 1114.

Monologue In a drama, the speech of a character who is alone on stage, voicing his or her thoughts, is known as a monologue. In a short story or a poem, the direct presentation of a character's unspoken thoughts is called an **interior monologue.** An interior monologue may jump back and forth between past and present, displaying thoughts, memories, and impressions just as they might occur in a person's mind.
See page 945.
See also **Stream of Consciousness; Dramatic Monologue.**

Mood Mood is the feeling or atmosphere that a writer creates for the reader. The writer's use of connotation, imagery, figurative language, sound and rhythm, and descriptive details all contribute to the mood. In his poem "Do Not Go Gentle into That Good Night," Dylan Thomas creates a solemn mood as he addresses his ailing father:

> Do not go gentle into that good night,
> Old age should burn and rave at close of day;
> Rage, rage against the dying of the light.
>
> —Dylan Thomas,
> "Do Not Go Gentle into That Good Night"

See pages 929, 995.
See also **Connotation; Description; Diction; Figurative Language; Imagery; Style; Tone.**

Motif A motif is a recurring word, phrase, image, object, idea, or action in a work of literature. Motifs function as unifying devices and often relate directly to one or more major themes. Motifs in "The Prologue" to *The Canterbury Tales,* for example, include images of earthly love along with images of spiritual devotion. In *Macbeth,* references to blood, sleep, and water form motifs in the play.

Motivation Motivation is the stated or implied reason behind a character's behavior. The grounds for a character's actions may not be obvious, but they should be comprehensible and consistent, in keeping with the character as developed by the writer.
See page 247, 1127.
See also **Character.**

Myth A myth is a traditional story, passed down through generations, that explains why the world is the way it is. Myths are essentially religious because they present supernatural events and beings and articulate the values and beliefs of a cultural group.

Narrative A narrative is any type of writing that is primarily concerned with relating an event or a series of events. A narrative can be imaginary, as is a short story or novel, or factual, as is a newspaper account or a work of history. The word *narration* can be used interchangeably with *narrative,* which comes from the Latin word meaning "tell."
See also **Fiction; Nonfiction; Novel; Plot; Short Story.**

Narrative Poem A narrative poem is a poem that tells a story using elements of character, setting, and plot to develop a theme. Epics, such as *Beowulf* and the *Iliad,* are narrative poems, as are ballads. Samuel Taylor Coleridge's *The Rime of the Ancient Mariner* is also a narrative poem.
See also **Ballad.**

Narrator The narrator of a story is the character or voice that relates the story's events to the reader.
Examples: In James Joyce's "Araby," the narrator participates in the incidents he recounts. The narrator of Elizabeth Gaskell's "Christmas Storms and Sunshine" is, on the other hand, observant but detached.
See pages 183, 995.

Naturalism An extreme form of realism, naturalism in fiction involves the depiction of life objectively and precisely, without idealizing. However, the naturalist creates characters who are victims of environmental forces and internal drives beyond their comprehension and control. Naturalistic fiction conveys the belief that universal forces result in an indifference to human suffering. Thomas Hardy's novel *Tess of the D'Urbervilles* is a famous example of British naturalism.

See page 1015.

See also **Realism.**

Neoclassicism *Neoclassicism* refers to the attitudes toward life and art that dominated English literature during the Restoration and the 18th century. Neoclassicists respected order, reason, and rules and viewed humans as limited and imperfect. To them, the intellect was more important than emotions, and society was more important than the individual. Imitating classical literature, neoclassical writers developed a style that was characterized by strict form, logic, symmetry, grace, good taste, restraint, clarity, and conciseness. Their works were meant not only to delight readers but also to instruct them in moral virtues and correct social behavior. Among the literary forms that flourished during the neoclassical period were the essay, the literary letter, and the epigram. The heroic couplet was the dominant verse form, and satire and parody prevailed in both prose and poetry. For examples of neoclassical works, see the selections by Alexander Pope, Jonathan Swift, and Samuel Johnson.

See page 601.

See also **Romanticism.**

Nonfiction Nonfiction, or informational text, is writing about real people, places, and events. Unlike fiction, nonfiction is largely concerned with factual information, although the writer shapes the information according to his or her purpose and viewpoint. Biography, autobiography, and newspaper articles are examples of nonfiction.

See also **Autobiography; Biography; Diary; Essay; Letters; Memoir.**

Novel A novel is an extended work of fiction. Like the short story, a novel is essentially the product of a writer's imagination. The most obvious difference between a novel and a short story is length. Because the novel is considerably longer, a novelist can develop a wider range of characters and a more complex plot.

Octave *See* **Sonnet.**

Ode An ode is a complex lyric poem that develops a serious and dignified theme. Odes appeal to both the imagination and the intellect, and many commemorate events or praise people or elements of nature. Examples of odes that celebrate an element of nature are Percy Bysshe Shelley's "Ode to the West Wind" and "To a Skylark."

Off Rhyme *See* **Rhyme.**

Omniscient Point of View *See* **Point of View.**

Onomatopoeia Onomatopoeia is the use of words whose sounds echo their meanings, such as *buzz, whisper, gargle,* and *murmur.* In the following lines, the poet uses onomatopoeia to help convey the images and meanings he wants to express:

> Four times fifty living men
> (And I heard nor <u>sigh</u> nor <u>groan</u>),
> With heavy <u>thump</u>, a lifeless lump,
> They dropped down one by one.
> —Samuel Taylor Coleridge,
> "The Rime of the Ancient Mariner"

See page 840.

Oral Literature Oral literature is literature that is passed from one generation to another by performance or word of mouth. Folk tales, fables, myths, chants, and legends are part of the oral tradition of cultures throughout the world.

See also **Fable; Folk Tale; Legend; Myth.**

Overstatement *See* **Understatement.**

Oxymoron *See* **Paradox.**

Parable A parable is a brief story that is meant to teach a lesson or illustrate a moral truth. A parable is more than a simple story, however. Each detail of the parable corresponds to some aspect of the problem or moral dilemma to which it is directed. The story of the prodigal son in the Bible is a classic parable.

Paradox A paradox is a statement that seems to **contradict,** or oppose, itself but, in fact, reveals some element of truth. Paradox is found frequently in the poetry of the 16th and 17th centuries. In Edmund Spenser's "Sonnet 30," he begins "My love is like to ice, and I to fire," and then continues to develop the paradox, asking why his "fire" does not melt and her "ice" and so on. A special kind of concise paradox is the **oxymoron,** which brings together two contradictory terms. Examples are "cruel kindness" and "brave fear."

See page 448, 453, 517.

See also **Metaphysical Poetry.**

Parallel Plot A parallel plot is a particular type of plot in which two stories of equal importance are told simultaneously. The story moves back and forth between the two plots.

Parallelism Parallelism is the use of similar grammatical constructions to express ideas that are related or equal in importance. The parallel elements may be words, phrases, sentences, or paragraphs. In the following excerpt from Seamus Heaney's poem "Digging," the repeating grammatical structure creates rhythm and emphasis:

> The cold smell of potato mold, the squelch and slap
> Of soggy peat, the curt cuts of an edge
> —Seamus Heaney, "Digging"

See also **Repetition.**

Parody Parody is writing that imitates either the style or the subject matter of a literary work for the purpose of criticism, humorous effect, or flattering tribute.

Pastoral A pastoral is a poem presenting shepherds in rural settings, usually in an idealized manner. The language and form of pastorals are artificial. The supposedly simple, rustic characters tend to use formal, courtly speech, and the meters and rhyme schemes are characteristic of formal poetry. Renaissance poets were drawn to the pastoral as a means of conveying their own emotions and ideas, particularly about love. Christopher Marlowe's "The Passionate Shepherd to His Love" is a pastoral.

See page 313.

Persona *See* **Speaker.**

Personal Essay *See* **Essay.**

Personification Personification is a figure of speech in which human qualities are attributed to an object, animal, or idea. Writers use personification to communicate feelings and images in a concise, concrete way. In line 117 of Thomas Gray's "Elegy Written in a Country Churchyard," for example, the earth is personified: "Here rests his head upon the lap of Earth." In the following lines, time is personified:

> Love's not Time's fool, though rosy lips and cheeks
> Within his bending sickle's compass come,
> —William Shakespeare, "Sonnet 116"

See pages 489, 953.
See also **Figurative Language; Metaphor; Simile.**

Persuasive Writing Persuasive writing is intended to convince a reader to adopt a particular opinion or to perform a certain action. Effective persuasion usually appeals to both the reason and the emotions of an audience.

Petrarchan Sonnet *See* **Sonnet.**

Plot The plot is the sequence of actions and events in a literary work. Generally, plots are built around a **conflict**—a problem or struggle between two or more opposing forces. Plots usually progress through stages: exposition, rising action, climax, and falling action.

The **exposition** provides important background information and introduces the setting, characters, and conflict. During the **rising action,** the conflict becomes more intense, and suspense builds as the main characters struggle to resolve their problem. The **climax** is the turning point in the plot when the outcome of the conflict becomes clear, usually resulting in a change in the characters or a solution to the conflict. After the climax, the **falling action** shows the effects of the climax. As the falling action begins, the suspense is over but the results of the decision or action that caused the climax are not yet fully worked out. The **resolution,** or **dénouement,** which often blends with the falling action, reveals the final outcome of events and ties up loose ends.

See pages 207, 247.
See also **Climax; Complication; Conflict.**

Poetry Poetry is language arranged in lines. Like other forms of literature, poetry attempts to re-create emotions and experiences. Poetry, however, is usually more condensed and suggestive than prose.

Poems often are divided into stanzas, or paragraph-like groups of lines. The stanzas in a poem may contain the same number of lines or may vary in length. Some poems have definite patterns of meter and rhyme. Others rely more on the sounds of words and less on fixed rhythms and rhyme schemes. The use of figurative language is also common in poetry.

The form and content of a poem combine to convey meaning. The way that a poem is arranged on the page, the impact of the images, the sounds of the words and phrases, and all the other details that make up a poem work together to help the reader grasp its central idea.

See also **Experimental Poetry; Form; Free Verse; Meter; Rhyme; Rhythm; Stanza.**

Point of View Point of view refers to the narrative perspective from which events in a story or novel are narrated.

In the **first-person point of view,** the narrator is a character in the work who tells everything in his or her own words and uses the pronouns *I, me,* and *my.* In the **third-person point of**

view, events are related by a voice outside the action, not by one of the characters. A third-person narrator uses pronouns like *he, she,* and *they.* In the **third-person omniscient point of view,** the narrator is an all-knowing, objective observer who stands outside the action and reports what different characters are thinking. In D. H. Lawrence's "The Rocking-Horse Winner," the use of a third-person omniscient narrator allows for psychological complexity and depth that would not be possible with a first-person narrator. In the **third-person limited point of view,** the narrator stands outside the action and focuses on one character's thoughts, observations, and feelings. Katherine Mansfield's "A Cup of Tea" is told primarily from the third-person limited point of view.

See pages 995, 1127, 1199.

See also **Narrator.**

Primary Sources Primary sources are accounts of events written by people who were directly involved in or witness to the events. Primary sources include materials such as diaries, letters, wills, and public documents. They also can include historical narratives in which the writer sets out to describe the specific experience of participating in or observing an event.

See also **Secondary Sources.**

Prologue A prologue is an introductory scene in a drama.

Prop Prop, an abbreviation of *property,* refers to a physical object that is used in a stage production.

Prose Generally, *prose* refers to all forms of written or spoken expression that are not in verse. The term, therefore, may be used to describe very different forms of writing—short stories as well as essays, for example.

Protagonist The protagonist is the main character in a work of literature, who is involved in the central conflict of the story. Usually, the protagonist changes after the central conflict reaches a climax. He or she may be a hero and is usually the one with whom the audience tends to identify. In Boccaccio's story "Federigo's Falcon," the protagonist is Federigo.

See also **Antagonist; Character; Tragic Hero.**

Psalm A psalm is a sacred song or lyric poem. Most psalms were originally set to music and performed during worship services in the temples of ancient Israel. In the Bible, the Book of Psalms contains 150 sacred psalms.

Psychological Fiction An offshoot of **realism,** psychological fiction focuses on the conflicts and motivations of its characters. In such literature, plot events are often less important than the inner workings of each character's mind. A technique closely associated with psychological fiction is **stream of consciousness,** which presents the random flow of

a character's thoughts. Though psychological fiction is often viewed as a 20th-century invention found in the writing of Virginia Woolf, James Joyce, and others, earlier writers—such as George Eliot, Elizabeth Gaskell, and Thomas Hardy—can be said to employ this technique in varying degrees.

See page 1139.

See also **Realism.**

Purpose *See* **Author's Purpose.**

Quatrain A quatrain is a four-line stanza, as in the following example:

> The story is familiar,
> Everybody knows it well,
> But do other enchanted people feel as nervous
> As I do? The stories do not tell,
> —Stevie Smith, "The Frog Prince"

See also **Poetry; Stanza.**

Realism As a general term, *realism* refers to any effort to offer an accurate and detailed portrayal of actual life. Thus, critics talk about Shakespeare's realistic portrayals of his characters and praise the medieval poet Chaucer for his realistic descriptions of people from different social classes.

More specifically, realism refers to a literary method developed in the 19th century. The realists based their writing on careful observations of ordinary life, often focusing on the middle or lower classes. They attempted to present life objectively and honestly, without the sentimentality or idealism that had colored earlier literature. Typically, realists developed their settings in great detail in an effort to re-create a specific time and place for the reader. Elements of realism can be found in the novels of Jane Austen and Charles Dickens, but it is not fully developed until the fiction of George Eliot. James Joyce's story "Araby" and Nadine Gordimer's "Six Feet of the Country" are examples of 20th-century realistic fiction.

See pages 968, 971.

See also **Naturalism.**

Recurring Theme *See* **Theme.**

Reflective Essay *See* **Essay.**

Refrain In poetry, a refrain is part of a stanza, consisting of one or more lines that are repeated regularly, sometimes with changes, often at the ends of succeeding stanzas.

Repetition Repetition is a technique in which a sound, word, phrase, or line is repeated for emphasis or unity. Repetition often helps to reinforce meaning and create an appealing rhythm. The term includes specific devices associated with both prose and poetry, such as **alliteration** and **parallelism**.

See also **Alliteration; Parallelism; Sound Devices.**

Resolution *See* **Plot.**

Rhetorical Devices *See* **Analogy; Repetition; Rhetorical Questions,** *Glossary of Reading and Informational Terms,* page R129.

Rhyme Words rhyme when the sounds of their accented vowels and all succeeding sounds are identical, as in *amuse* and *confuse.* For true rhyme, the consonants that precede the vowels must be different. Rhyme that occurs at the end of lines of poetry is called **end rhyme,** as in Thomas Hardy's rhyming of *face* and *place* in "The Man He Killed." End rhymes that are not exact but approximate are called **off rhyme,** or **slant rhyme,** as in the words *come* and *doom* in Stevie Smith's "The Frog Prince." Rhyme that occurs within a single line is called **internal rhyme:**

> Give cr<u>ow</u>ns and p<u>ou</u>nds and guineas
> —A. E. Housman, "When I Was One-and-Twenty"

Rhyme Scheme A rhyme scheme is the pattern of end rhyme in a poem. A rhyme scheme is charted by assigning a letter of the alphabet, beginning with *a,* to each line. Lines that rhyme are given the same letter. In the following stanza, for example, the rhyme scheme is *abab:*

> | Gather ye rosebuds while ye may, | *a* |
> | Old time is still a-flying; | *b* |
> | And this same flower that smiles today | *a* |
> | Tomorrow will be dying. | *b* |
> | —Robert Herrick, |
> | "To the Virgins, to Make Much of Time" |

See pages 525, 847, 1061.

See also **Ballad; Couplet; Quatrain; Rhyme; Sonnet; Spenserian Stanza; Villanelle.**

Rhythm Rhythm is a pattern of stressed and unstressed syllables in a line of poetry. Poets use rhythm to bring out the musical quality of language, to emphasize ideas, to create mood, to unify a work, and to heighten emotional response. Devices such as alliteration, rhyme, assonance, consonance, and parallelism often contribute to creating rhythm. The slow rhythms of the following lines help to convey the mysterious mood of the poem:

> Ĭ lĭstĕnĕd ĭn ĕmptĭnĕss ŏn thĕ moor-rĭdge.
> The curlew's tear turnĕd ĭts edge ŏn thĕ sĭlence.
> —Ted Hughes, "The Horses"

See page 861.

See also **Anglo-Saxon Poetry; Ballad; Meter; Spenserian Stanza; Sprung Rhythm.**

Rising Action *See* **Plot.**

Romance The romance has been a popular narrative form since the Middle Ages. Generally, the term refers to any imaginative adventure concerned with noble heroes, gallant love, a chivalric code of honor, daring deeds, and supernatural events. Romances usually have faraway settings, depict events unlike those of ordinary life, and idealize their heroes as well as the eras in which the heroes live. Medieval romances often are lighthearted in tone, consist of a number of episodes, and involve one or more characters in a quest.

Example: Thomas Malory's *Le Morte d'Arthur* is an example of a medieval romance. Its stories of kings, knights, and ladies relate many adventures, tales of love, superhuman feats, and quests for honor and virtue.

See pages 229, 247.

Romanticism *Romanticism* refers to a literary movement that flourished in Britain and Europe throughout much of the 19th century. Romantic writers looked to nature for their inspiration, idealized the distant past, and celebrated the individual. In reaction against neoclassicism, their treatment of subjects was emotional rather than rational, imaginative rather than analytical. The romantic period in English literature is generally viewed as beginning with the publication of *Lyrical Ballads,* poems by William Wordsworth and Samuel Taylor Coleridge.

See pages 796, 799.

See also **Neoclassicism.**

Sarcasm Sarcasm, a type of **verbal irony,** refers to a critical remark expressed in a mocking fashion. In some cases, a statement is sarcastic because its literal meaning is the opposite of its actual meaning.

See page 621.

See also **Irony.**

Satire Satire is a literary technique in which ideas, customs, behaviors, or institutions are ridiculed for the purpose of improving society. Satire may be gently witty, mildly abrasive, or bitterly critical, and it often uses exaggeration to force readers to see something in a more critical light.

Often, a satirist distances himself or herself from a subject by creating a fictional speaker—usually a calm and often naïve observer—who can address the topic without revealing the true emotions of the writer. The title character of Voltaire's *Candide* is an example of such an observer. Whether the object of a satiric work is an individual person or a group of people, the force of the satire will almost always cast light on foibles and failings that are universal to human experience.

There are two main types of satire, named for the Roman satirists Horace and Juvenal; they differ chiefly in tone. **Horatian satire** is playfully amusing and seeks to correct vice or foolishness with gentle laughter and sympathetic under-standing. Joseph Addison's essays are examples of Horatian satire. **Juvenalian satire** provokes a darker kind of laughter. It is biting and criticizes corruption or incompetence with scorn and outrage. Jonathan Swift's "A Modest Proposal" is an example of Juvenalian satire.

See pages 608, 621, 635, 1333.
See also **Irony.**

Scansion The process of determining meter is known as scansion. When you scan a line of poetry, you mark its stressed (´) and unstressed syllables (ˇ) in order to identify the rhythm.
See also **Meter.**

Scene In drama, a scene is a subdivision of an act. Each scene usually establishes a different time or place.
See also **Act; Drama.**

Scenery Scenery is a painted backdrop or other structures used to create the setting for a play.

Screenplay A screenplay is a play written for film.

Script The text of a play, film, or broadcast is called a script.

Scripture Scripture is literature that is considered sacred—that is, it is used in religious rituals of worship, initiation, celebration, and mourning. Such literature is usually preserved in what are considered holy books. The hymns, chants, prayers, myths, and other forms passed down through generations and combined as a body of scripture express the core beliefs of a group of people. The excerpts from the King James Bible are examples of scripture gathered from the Jewish and Christian traditions.

Secondary Sources Accounts written by people who were not directly involved in or witnesses to an event are called secondary sources. A history textbook is an example of a secondary source.
See also **Primary Sources.**

Sensory Details Sensory details are words and phrases that appeal to the reader's senses of sight, hearing, touch, taste, and smell. For example, the sensory detail "a fine film of rain" appeals to the senses of sight and touch. Sensory details stimulate the reader to create images in his or her mind.
See also **Imagery.**

Setting The setting of a literary work refers to the time and place in which the action occurs. A story can be set in an imaginary place, such as an enchanted castle, or a real place, such as London or Hampton Court. The time can be the past, the present, or the future. In addition to time and place, setting can include the larger historical and cultural contexts that form the background for a narrative. Setting is one of the main elements in fiction and often plays an important role in what happens and why.
See pages 971, 1213, 1319.

Sestet *See* **Sonnet.**

Shakespearean (English) Sonnet *See* **Sonnet.**

Short Story A short story is a work of fiction that centers on a single idea and can be read in one sitting. Generally, a short story has one main conflict that involves the characters, keeps the story moving, and stimulates readers' interest.
See also **Fiction.**

Simile A simile is a figure of speech that compares two things that have something in common, using a word such as *like* or *as*. Both poets and prose writers use similes to intensify emotional response, stimulate vibrant images, provide imaginative delight, and concentrate the expression of ideas. In her story "The Duchess and the Jeweller," Virginia Woolf uses similes to describe the duchess as she sits down:

> As a parasol with many flounces, as a peacock with many feathers, shuts its flounces, folds its feathers, so she subsided and shut herself as she sank down in the leather armchair.
>
> —Virginia Woolf, "The Duchess and the Jeweller"

An **epic simile** is a long comparison that often continues for a number of lines. It does not always contain the word *like* or *as*. Here is an example of an epic simile:

> Conspicuous as the evening star that comes, amid the first in heaven, at fall of night, and stands most lovely in the west, so shone in sunlight the fine-pointed spear Achilles poised in his right hand. . . .
>
> —Homer, the *Iliad*

See pages 77, 849, 953.
See also **Figurative Language; Metaphor.**

Situational Irony See Irony.

Slant Rhyme *See* Rhyme.

Soliloquy A soliloquy is a speech in a dramatic work in which a character speaks his or her thoughts aloud. Usually the character is on the stage alone, not speaking to other characters and perhaps not even consciously addressing the audience. (If there are other characters on stage, they are ignored temporarily.) The purpose of a soliloquy is to reveal a character's inner thoughts, feelings, and plans to the audience. Soliloquies are characteristic of Elizabethan drama; *Macbeth* has several soliloquies. Following is part of Macbeth's most famous soliloquy:

> Life's but a walking shadow, a poor player,
> That struts and frets his hour upon the stage
> And then is heard no more. It is a tale
> Told by an idiot, full of sound and fury,
> Signifying nothing.
> —William Shakespeare, *Macbeth*

See pages 344, 347.

Sonnet A sonnet is a lyric poem of 14 lines, commonly written in **iambic pentameter.** For centuries the sonnet has been a popular form because it is long enough to permit development of a complex idea, yet short and structured enough to challenge any poet's skills. Sonnets written in English usually follow one of two forms.

The **Petrarchan,** or **Italian, sonnet,** introduced into English by Sir Thomas Wyatt, is named after Petrarch, the 14th-century Italian poet. This type of sonnet consists of two parts, called the **octave** (the first eight lines) and the **sestet** (the last six lines). The usual rhyme scheme for the octave is *abbaabba.* The rhyme scheme for the sestet may be *cdecde, cdccdc,* or a similar variation. The octave generally presents a problem or raises a question, and the sestet resolves or comments on the problem. John Milton's sonnets are written in the Petrarchan form.

The **Shakespearean,** or **English, sonnet** is sometimes called the **Elizabethan sonnet.** It consists of three quatrains, or four-line units, and a final couplet. The typical rhyme scheme is *abab cdcd efef gg.* In the English sonnet, the rhymed couplet at the end of the sonnet provides a final commentary on the subject developed in the three quatrains. Shakespeare's sonnets are the finest examples of this type of sonnet.

A variation of the Shakespearean sonnet is the **Spenserian sonnet,** which has the same structure but uses the interlocking rhyme scheme *abab bcbc cdcd ee.* Edmund Spenser's "Sonnet 30" is an example.

Some poets have written a series of related sonnets that have the same subject. These are called **sonnet sequences,** or **sonnet cycles.** Toward the end of the 16th century, writing sonnet sequences became fashionable, with a common subject being love for a beautiful but unattainable woman. Francesco Petrarch, Edmund Spenser, and Elizabeth Barrett Browning wrote sonnet sequences.

See pages 310, 325, 335, 954.

See also **Iambic Pentameter; Lyric; Meter; Quatrain.**

Sound Devices *See* **Alliteration; Assonance; Consonance; Meter; Onomatopoeia; Repetition; Rhyme; Rhyme Scheme; Rhythm.**

Speaker The speaker of a poem, like the narrator of a story, is the voice that talks to the reader. In some poems, the speaker can be identified with the poet. In other poems, the poet invents a fictional character, or a persona, to play the role of the speaker. *Persona* is a Latin word meaning "actor's mask."

See pages 701, 929, 1055.

Speech A speech is a talk or public address. The purpose of a speech may be to entertain, to explain, to persuade, to inspire, or any combination of these aims.

Spenserian Stanza The **Spenserian stanza** (named for Edmund Spenser, who invented it for his romance *The Faerie Queene*) consists of nine iambic lines rhyming in the pattern *ababbcbcc.* Each of the first eight lines contains five feet, and the ninth contains six. The rhyming pattern helps to create unity, and the six-foot line, called an **alexandrine,** slows down the stanza and so gives dignity and allows for reflection on the ideas in the stanza. Byron used the Spenserian stanza in *Childe Harold's Pilgrimage.*

See also **Stanza.**

Sprung Rhythm In order to approximate the rhythms of natural speech in poetry, the poet Gerard Manley Hopkins developed what he called sprung rhythm. The lines of a poem written in sprung rhythm have fixed numbers of stressed syllables but varying numbers of unstressed syllables. A line may contain several consecutive stressed syllables, or a stressed syllable may be followed by one, two, or even three unstressed syllables. The following lines are written in sprung rhythm:

> Lándscape plottĕd ănd píecĕd—fóld, fállŏw, ănd plóugh;
>
> Ănd áll trádes, theĭr géar ănd tácklĕ ănd trím.
> —Gerard Manley Hopkins, "Pied Beauty"

See page 963.

Stage Directions *See* Drama.

Stanza A stanza is a group of lines that form a unit in a poem. A stanza is usually characterized by a common pattern of meter, rhyme, and number of lines. During the 20th century, poets experimented more freely with stanza form than did earlier poets, sometimes writing poems without any stanza breaks.
See page 847.

Static Character *See* Character.

Stereotype A stereotype is an oversimplified image of a person, group, or institution. Sweeping generalizations about "all English people" or "every used-car dealer" are stereotypes. Simplified or stock characters in literature are often called stereotypes. Such characters do not usually demonstrate the complexities of real people.

Stream of Consciousness Stream of consciousness is a technique that was developed by modernist writers to present the flow of a character's seemingly unconnected thoughts, responses, and sensations. A character's stream of consciousness is often expressed as an interior monologue, which may reveal the inner experience of the character on many levels of consciousness. Virginia Woolf and James Joyce make extensive use of stream of consciousness in their fiction.
See page 1139.
See also **Characterization; Modernism; Point of View; Psychological Fiction; Style.**

Structure The structure of a literary work is the way in which it is put together—the arrangement of its parts. In poetry, structure refers to the arrangement of words and lines to produce a desired effect. A common structural unit in poetry is the stanza, of which there are numerous types. In prose, structure is the arrangement of larger units or parts of a selection. Paragraphs, for example, are a basic unit in prose, as are chapters in novels and acts in plays. The structure of a poem, short story, novel, play, or nonfiction selection usually emphasizes certain important aspects of content.
See pages 183, 701, 1015.
See also **Form; Stanza.**

Style Style is the distinctive way in which a work of literature is written. Style refers not so much to what is said but how it is said. Word choice, sentence length, tone, imagery, and use of dialogue all contribute to a writer's style. A group of writers might exemplify common stylistic characteristics, as, for example, in the case of the 17th-century metaphysical poets, who employed complex meanings and unconventional rhythms and figurative language to achieve dramatic effect.
See pages 799, 1117.

Subtlety *See* Aphorism.

Supernatural Tale A supernatural tale is a story that goes beyond the bounds of reality, usually by involving supernatural elements—beings, powers, or events that are unexplainable by known forces or laws of nature. In Sir Thomas Malory's romance *Le Morte d'Arthur,* for example, Sir Launcelot uses supernatural powers in his battles against Sir Gawain.

In many supernatural tales, **foreshadowing**—hints or clues that point to later events—is used to encourage readers to anticipate the unthinkable. Sometimes readers are left wondering whether a supernatural event has really taken place or is the product of a character's imagination. In an effective supernatural tale, the writer manipulates readers' feelings of curiosity and fear to produce a mounting sense of excitement. Elizabeth Bowen's "The Demon Lover" is a supernatural tale.
See page 1229.

Surprise Ending A surprise ending is an unexpected plot twist at the end of a story.
Example: The final paragraph of "The Demon Lover," which sets off a new direction in the plot instead of bringing it to its expected conclusion, is an example of a surprise ending.
See also **Irony.**

Suspense Suspense is the excitement or tension that readers feel as they become involved in a story and eagerly await the outcome.
Example: Throughout D. H. Lawrence's "The Rocking-Horse Winner," suspense builds as Paul anxiously rides his rocking horse and wins money for the family, but then succumbs to the frenzy of his actions.
See also **Plot.**

Symbol A symbol is a person, place, or object that has a concrete meaning in itself and also stands for something beyond itself, such as an idea or feeling.
Examples: In Boccaccio's story "Federigo's Falcon," the falcon comes to symbolize the passionate and consuming love of Federigo for Monna Giovanna. Sometimes a literary symbol has more than one possible meaning. For example, the rose in William Blake's poem "The Sick Rose" might symbolize goodness, innocence, or all of humanity.
See pages 769, 1191.

Synesthesia *See* **Imagery.**

Terza Rima Terza rima is a three-line stanza form originating in Italy. Its rhyme scheme is *aba bcb cdc ded,* and so on. Terza rima was popular with many English poets, including Milton, Byron, and Shelley.

See page 847, 864.

Theme A theme is an underlying message that a writer wants the reader to understand. It is a perception about life or human nature that the writer shares with the reader. In most cases, themes are not stated directly but must be inferred. In addition, there may be more than one theme in a work of literature. In *Macbeth,* for example, the themes include the corrupting effect of unbridled ambition, the corrosiveness of guilt, the lure and power of inscrutable supernatural forces, and the tragedy of psychological disintegration. The theme of Coleridge's "The Rime of the Ancient Mariner" has been interpreted as the transformation of the human personality through a loss of innocence and youth; another interpretation of the theme concerns the effects of sin and spiritual redemption.

    Recurring themes are themes found in a variety of works. For example, authors from varying backgrounds might convey similar themes having to do with the importance of family values. **Universal themes** are themes that are found throughout the literature of all time periods.

See pages 531, 953, 1055, 1153.

Third-Person Point of View *See* **Point of View.**

Title The title of a literary work introduces readers to the piece and usually reveals something about its subject or theme. Although works are occasionally untitled or, in the case of some poems, merely identified by their first line, most literary works have been deliberately and carefully named. Some titles are straightforward, stating exactly what the reader can expect to discover in the work. Others hint at the subject and force the reader to search for interpretations.

Tone Tone is a writer's attitude toward his or her subject. A writer can communicate tone through diction, choice of details, and direct statements of his or her position. Unlike mood, which refers to the emotional response of the reader to a work, tone reflects the feelings of the writer. To identify the tone of a work of literature, you might find it helpful to read the work aloud, as if giving a dramatic reading before an audience. The emotions that you convey in an oral reading should give you hints as to the tone of the work.

Examples: The tone of Jonathan Swift's "A Modest Proposal" is searingly ironic; the tone of Katherine Mansfield's "A Cup of Tea" is amused and ironic. In "The Prologue" from *The Canterbury Tales,* Chaucer's jovial tone accounts for much of the work's humor.

See pages 1069, 1243, 1281, 1333.

See also **Connotation; Diction; Mood; Style.**

Tragedy A tragedy is a dramatic work that presents the downfall of a dignified character who is involved in historically, morally, or socially significant events. The main character, or **tragic hero,** has a **tragic flaw,** a quality that leads to his or her destruction. The events in a tragic plot are set in motion by a decision that is often an error in judgment caused by the tragic flaw. Succeeding events are linked in a cause-and-effect relationship and lead inevitably to a disastrous conclusion, usually death. Shakespeare's plays *Macbeth, Hamlet, Othello,* and *King Lear* are famous examples of tragedies.

See pages 342, 347.

Tragic Flaw *See* **Hero; Tragedy.**

Tragic Hero *See* **Hero; Tragedy.**

Traits *See* **Character.**

Trochee *See* **Meter.**

Turning Point *See* **Climax.**

Understatement Understatement is a technique of creating emphasis by saying less than is actually or literally true. It is the opposite of **overstatement,** a form of **hyperbole,** or exaggeration. One of the primary devices of **irony,** understatement can be used to develop a humorous effect, to create satire, or to achieve a restrained tone.

See also **Hyperbole; Irony.**

Universal Theme *See* **Theme.**

Verbal Irony *See* **Irony.**

Verisimilitude Verisimilitude refers to the appearance of truth and actuality. In *A Journal of the Plague Year,* a work of fiction, Daniel Defoe establishes a sense of verisimilitude through his use of precise details, statistics and dates, and geographical names as though the narrator were an eyewitness to the plague, which had actually preceded his time.

See page 593.

Villanelle The villanelle is an intricately patterned French verse form, planned to give the impression of simplicity. A villanelle has 19 lines, composed of 5 tercets, or 3-line stanzas, followed by a quatrain. The first line is repeated as a refrain at the end of the second and fourth stanzas. The last line of the first stanza is repeated at the end of the third and fifth stanzas. Both lines reappear as the final two lines of the poem. The rhyme scheme of a villanelle is *aba* for each tercet and then *abaa* for the quatrain. Dylan Thomas's "Do Not Go Gentle into That Good Night" is an example of a villanelle.

See page 1183.

See also **Quatrain; Stanza.**

Voice The term *voice* refers to a writer's unique use of language that allows a reader to "hear" a human personality in his or her writing. The elements of style that determine a writer's voice include sentence structure, diction, and tone. For example, some writers are noted for their reliance on short, simple sentences, while others make use of long, complicated ones. Certain writers use concrete words, such as *lake* or *cold*, which name things that you can see, hear, feel, taste, or smell. Others prefer abstract terms such as *memory,* which name things that cannot be perceived with the senses. A writer's tone also leaves its imprint on his or her personal voice. The term *voice* can be applied to the narrator of a selection, as well as to the writer.

See pages 671, 1311.

See also **Diction; Tone.**

Word Choice See **Diction.**

Wordplay Wordplay is the intentional use of more than one meaning of a word to express ambiguities, multiple interpretations, and irony.

Example: In Stevie Smith's poem "Not Waving but Drowning," the poet plays with the different meanings of *far out* and *cold* to give added meaning to her poem.

Almanac *See* **Reference Works.**

Analogy *See Glossary of Literary and Nonfiction Terms, page R104.*

Appeals by Association Appeals by association imply that one will gain acceptance or prestige by taking the writer's position.
See also **Recognizing Persuasive Techniques**—*Reading Handbook, page R20.*

Appeal to Authority An appeal to authority calls upon experts or others who warrant respect.
See also **Recognizing Persuasive Techniques**—*Reading Handbook, page R20.*

Appeal to Reason *See* **Logical Appeal.**

Argument An argument is speech or writing that expresses a position on an issue or problem and supports it with reasons and evidence. An argument often takes into account other points of view, anticipating and answering objections that opponents of the position might raise.
See also **Claim; Counterargument; Evidence; General Principle.**

Assumption An assumption is an opinion or belief that is taken for granted. It can be about a specific situation, a person, or the world in general. Assumptions are often unstated. *See also* **General Principle.**

Author's Message An author's message is the main idea or theme of a particular work.
See also **Main Idea; Theme,** *Glossary of Literary and Nonfiction Terms, page R123.*

Author's Perspective *See Glossary of Literary and Nonfiction Terms, page R105.*

Author's Position An author's position is his or her opinion on an issue or topic. *See also* **Claim.**

Author's Purpose *See Glossary of Literary and Nonfiction Terms, page R105.*

Autobiography *See Glossary of Literary and Nonfiction Terms, page R106.*

Bias Bias is an inclination toward a particular judgment on a topic or issue. A writer often reveals a strongly positive or strongly negative opinion by presenting only one way of looking at an issue or by heavily weighting the evidence. Words with intensely positive or negative connotations are often a signal of a writer's bias.

Bibliography A bibliography is a list of books and other materials related to the topic of a text. Bibliographies can be good sources of works for further study on a subject.
See also **Works Consulted.**

Biography *See Glossary of Literary and Nonfiction Terms, page R106.*

Business Correspondence Business correspondence includes all written business communications, such as business letters, e-mails, and memos. Business correspondence is to the point, clear, courteous, and professional.

Cause and Effect A **cause** is an event or action that directly results in another event or action. An **effect** is the direct or logical outcome of an event or action. Basic **cause-and-effect relationships** include a single cause with a single effect, one cause with multiple effects, multiple causes with a single effect, and a chain of causes and effects. The concept of cause and effect also provides a way of organizing a piece of writing. It helps a writer show the relationships between events or ideas.
See also **False Cause**—*Reading Handbook, page R22.*

Chronological Order Chronological order is the arrangement of events in their order of occurrence. This type of organization is used both in fictional narratives and in historical writing, biography, and autobiography.

Claim In an argument, a claim is the writer's position on an issue or problem. Although an argument focuses on supporting one claim, a writer may make more than one claim in a work.

Clarify Clarifying is a reading strategy that helps a reader to understand or make clear what he or she is reading. Readers usually clarify by rereading, reading aloud, or discussing.

Classification Classification is a pattern of organization in which objects, ideas, or information is presented in groups, or classes, based on common characteristics.

Cliché A cliché is an overused expression. "Better late than never" and "hard as nails" are common examples. Good writers generally avoid clichés unless they are using them in dialogue to indicate something about characters' personalities.

Compare and Contrast To compare and contrast is to identify similarities and differences in two or more subjects. Compare-and-contrast organization can be used to structure a piece of writing, serving as a framework for examining the similarities and differences in two or more subjects.

Conclusion A conclusion is a statement of belief based on evidence, experience, and reasoning. A **valid conclusion** is a conclusion that logically follows from the facts or statements upon which it is based. A **deductive conclusion** is one that follows from a particular generalization or premise. An **inductive conclusion** is a broad conclusion or generalization that is reached by arguing from specific facts and examples.

Connect Connecting is a reader's process of relating the content of a text to his or her own knowledge and experience.

Consumer Documents Consumer documents are printed materials that accompany products and services. They are intended for the buyers or users of the products or services and usually provide information about use, care, operation, or assembly. Some common consumer documents are applications, contracts, warranties, manuals, instructions, package inserts, labels, brochures, and schedules.

Context Clues When you encounter an unfamiliar word, you can often use context clues as aids for understanding. Context clues are the words and phrases surrounding the word that provide hints about the word's meaning.

Controlling Idea See **Thesis Statement.**

Counterargument A counterargument is an argument made to oppose another argument. A good argument anticipates opposing viewpoints and provides counterarguments to refute (disprove) or answer them.

Counterclaim See **Counterargument.**

Credibility *Credibility* refers to the believability or trustworthiness of a source and the information it contains.

Critical Review A critical review is an evaluation or critique by a reviewer or critic. Different types of reviews include film reviews, book reviews, music reviews, and art-show reviews.

Database A database is a collection of information that can be quickly and easily accessed and searched and from which information can be easily retrieved. It is frequently presented in an electronic format.

Debate A debate is an organized exchange of opinions on an issue. In academic settings, *debate* usually refers to a formal contest in which two opposing teams defend and attack a proposition.

See also **Argument; Debate**—*Speaking and Listening Handbook, pages R82–R83.*

Deductive Reasoning Deductive reasoning is a way of thinking that begins with a generalization, presents a specific situation, and then advances with facts and evidence to a logical conclusion. The following passage has a deductive argument imbedded in it: "All students in the drama class must attend the play on Thursday. Since Ava is in the class, she had better show up." This deductive argument can be broken down as follows: generalization— all students in the drama class must attend the play on Thursday; specific situation—Ava is a student in the drama class; conclusion—Ava must attend the play.

See also **Analyzing Logic and Reasoning**—*Reading Handbook, pages R20–R21.*

Dictionary *See* **Reference Works.**

Draw Conclusions To draw a conclusion is to make a judgment or arrive at a belief based on evidence, experience, and reasoning.

Editorial An editorial is an opinion piece that usually appears on the editorial page of a newspaper or as part of a news broadcast. The editorial section of a newspaper presents opinions rather than objective news reports.

See also **Op-Ed Piece.**

Either/Or Fallacy An either/or fallacy is a statement that suggests that there are only two possible ways to view a situation or only two options to choose from. In other words, it is a statement that falsely frames a dilemma, giving the impression that no options exist but the two presented— for example, "Either we stop the construction of a new airport, or the surrounding suburbs will become ghost towns."

See also **Identifying Faulty Reasoning**—*Reading Handbook, page R22.*

Emotional Appeals Emotional appeals are messages that evoke strong feelings—such as fear, pity, or vanity—in order to persuade instead of using facts and evidence to make a point. An **appeal to fear** is a message that taps into people's fear of losing their safety or security. An **appeal to pity** is a message that taps into people's sympathy and compassion for others to build support for an idea, a cause, or a proposed action. An **appeal to vanity** is a message that attempts to persuade by tapping into people's desire to feel good about themselves.

See also **Recognizing Persuasive Techniques**—*Reading Handbook, page R20.*

Encyclopedia *See* **Reference Works.**

Essay *See Glossary of Literary and Nonfiction Terms, page R109.*

Ethical Appeals Ethical appeals establish a writer's credibility and trustworthiness with an audience. When a writer links a claim to a widely accepted value, for example, the writer not only gains moral support for that claim but also establishes a connection with readers.
See also **Recognizing Persuasive Techniques**—*Reading Handbook, page R20.*

Evaluate To evaluate is to examine something carefully and judge its value or worth. Evaluating is an important skill for gaining insight into what you read. A reader can evaluate the actions of a particular character, for example, or can form an opinion about the value of an entire work.

Evidence Evidence is the specific pieces of information that support a claim. Evidence can take the form of facts, quotations, examples, statistics, or personal experiences.

Expository Essay *See* **Essay,** *Glossary of Literary and Nonfiction Terms, page R109.*

Fact versus Opinion A **fact** is a statement that can be proved or verified. An **opinion,** on the other hand, is a statement that cannot be proved because it expresses a person's beliefs, feelings, or thoughts.
See also **Inference; Generalization.**

Fallacy A fallacy is an error in reasoning. Typically, a fallacy is based on an incorrect inference or a misuse of evidence. Some common logical fallacies are **circular reasoning, either/or fallacy, oversimplification, overgeneralization,** and **stereotyping.**
See also **Either/Or Fallacy; Logical Appeal; Overgeneralization; Identifying Faulty Reasoning**—*Reading Handbook, page R22.*

Faulty Reasoning *See* **Fallacy.**

Feature Article A feature article is a main article in a newspaper or a cover story in a magazine. A feature article is focused more on entertaining than on informing. Features are lighter or more general than hard news and tend to be about human interest or lifestyles.

Functional Documents *See* **Consumer Documents; Workplace Documents.**

Generalization A generalization is a broad statement about a class or category of people, ideas, or things, based on a study of only some of its members.
See also **Overgeneralization.**

General Principle In an argument, a general principle is an assumption that links the support to the claim. If one does not accept the general principle as a truth, then the support is inadequate because it is beside the point.

Government Publications Government publications are documents produced by government organizations. Pamphlets, brochures, and reports are just some of the many forms these publications may take. Government publications can be good resources for a wide variety of topics.

Graphic Aid A graphic aid is a visual tool that is printed, handwritten, or drawn. Charts, diagrams, graphs, photographs, and maps can all be graphic aids.
See also **Graphic Aids**—*Reading Handbook, pages R5–R7.*

Graphic Organizer A graphic organizer is a visual illustration of a verbal statement that helps a reader understand a text. Charts, tables, webs, and diagrams can all be graphic organizers. Graphic organizers and graphic aids can look the same. However, graphic organizers and graphic aids do differ in how they are used. Graphic aids are the visual representations that people encounter when they read informational texts. Graphic organizers are visuals that people construct to help them understand texts or organize information.

Historical Documents Historical documents are writings that have played a significant role in human events or are themselves records of such events. The Declaration of Independence, for example, is a historical document.

How-To Book A how-to book is a book that is written to explain how to do something—usually an activity, a sport, or a household project.

Implied Main Idea *See* **Main Idea.**

Index The index of a book is an alphabetized list of important topics and details covered in the book and the page numbers on which they can be found. An index can be used to quickly find specific information about a topic.

Inductive Reasoning Inductive reasoning is the process of logical reasoning from observations, examples, and facts to a general conclusion or principle.
See also **Analyzing Logic and Reasoning**—*Reading Handbook, pages R20–R21.*

Inference An inference is a logical assumption that is based on observed facts and one's own knowledge and experience.

Informational Text Informational text is a category of writing that includes exposition, argument, and functional documents. These texts normally provide factual, historical, or technical information. However, the term also covers texts that make logical or emotional arguments in defense of a position. Examples include biographies, journalism, essays, narrative histories, instruction manuals, and speeches.

Internet The Internet is a global, interconnected system of computer networks that allows for communication through e-mail, listservers, and the World Wide Web.

Journal A journal is a periodical publication issued by a legal, medical, or other professional organization. Alternatively, the term may be used to refer to a diary or daily record.

Literary Criticism *See Glossary of Literary and Nonfiction Terms, page R113.*

Loaded Language Loaded language consists of words with strongly positive or negative connotations intended to influence a reader's or listener's attitude.

Logical Appeal A logical appeal relies on logic and facts, appealing to people's reasoning or intellect rather than to their values or emotions. Flawed logical appeals—that is, errors in reasoning—are considered logical fallacies. *See also* **Fallacy.**

Logical Argument A logical argument is an argument in which the logical relationship between the support and the claim is sound.

Main Idea A main idea is the central, controlling, or most important, idea about a topic that a writer or speaker conveys. It can be the central idea of an entire work or of just a paragraph. Often, the main idea of a paragraph is expressed in a topic sentence. However, a main idea may just be implied, or suggested, by details. A main idea and supporting details can serve as a basic pattern of organization in a piece of writing, with the central idea about a topic being supported by details.

Make Inferences *See* **Inference.**

Monitor Monitoring is the strategy of checking your comprehension as you are reading and modifying the strategies you are using to suit your needs. Monitoring may include some or all of the following strategies: **questioning, clarifying, visualizing, predicting, connecting,** and **rereading.**

News Article A news article is a piece of writing that reports on a recent event. In newspapers, news articles are usually written in a concise manner to report the latest news, presenting the most important facts first and then more detailed information. In magazines, news articles are usually more elaborate than those in newspapers because they are written to provide both information and analysis. Also, news articles in magazines do not necessarily present the most important facts first.

Nonfiction *See Glossary of Literary and Nonfiction Terms, page R116.*

Op-Ed Piece An op-ed piece is an opinion piece that usually appears opposite ("op") the editorial page of a newspaper. Unlike editorials, op-ed pieces are written and submitted by named writers.

Organization *See* **Pattern of Organization.**

Overgeneralization An overgeneralization is a generalization that is too broad. You can often recognize overgeneralizations by the appearance of words and phrases such as *all, everyone, every time, any, anything, no one,* and *none.* Consider, for example, this statement: "None of the sanitation workers in our city really care about keeping the environment clean." In all probability, there are many exceptions. The writer can't possibly know the feelings of every sanitation worker in the city. *See also* **Identifying Faulty Reasoning**—*Reading Handbook, page R22.*

Overview An overview is a short summary of a story, a speech, or an essay. It orients the reader by providing a preview of the text to come.

Paraphrase Paraphrasing is the restating of information in one's own words. *See also* **Summarize.**

Pattern of Organization A pattern of organization is a particular arrangement of ideas and information. Such a pattern may be used to organize an entire composition or a single paragraph within a longer work. The following are the most common patterns of organization: **cause-and-effect, chronological order, compare-and-contrast, classification, deductive, inductive, order of importance, problem-solution, sequential,** and **spatial.** *See also* **Cause and Effect; Chronological Order; Classification; Compare and Contrast; Problem-Solution Order; Sequential Order; Patterns of Organization**—*Reading Handbook, pages R8–R12.*

Periodical A periodical is a publication that is issued at regular intervals of more than one day. For example, a periodical may be a weekly, monthly, or quarterly journal or magazine. Newspapers and other daily publications generally are not classified as periodicals.

Personal Essay *See* **Essay,** *Glossary of Literary and Nonfiction Terms, page R109.*

Persuasion Persuasion is the art of swaying others' feelings, beliefs, or actions. Persuasion normally appeals to both the intellect and the emotions of readers. **Persuasive techniques** are the methods used to influence others to adopt certain opinions or beliefs or to act in certain ways. Types of persuasive techniques include emotional appeals, ethical appeals, logical appeals, and loaded language. When used properly, persuasive techniques can add depth to writing that's meant to persuade. Persuasive techniques can, however, be misused to cloud factual information, disguise poor reasoning, or unfairly exploit people's emotions in order to shape their opinions.

See also **Appeals by Association; Appeal to Authority; Emotional Appeals; Ethical Appeals; Loaded Language; Logical Appeal; Recognizing Persuasive Techniques—** *Reading Handbook, page R20.*

Predict Predicting is a reading strategy that involves using text clues to make a reasonable guess about what will happen next in a story.

Primary Source *See* **Sources.**

Prior Knowledge Prior knowledge is the knowledge a reader already possesses about a topic. This information might come from personal experiences, expert accounts, books, films, or other sources.

Problem-Solution Order Problem-solution order is a pattern of organization in which a problem is stated and analyzed and then one or more solutions are proposed and examined. Writers use words and phrases such as *propose, conclude, reason for, problem, answer,* and *solution* to connect ideas and details when writing about problems and solutions.

Propaganda Propaganda is a form of communication that may use distorted, false, or misleading information. It usually refers to manipulative political discourse.

Public Documents Public documents are documents that were written for the public to provide information that is of public interest or concern. They include government documents, speeches, signs, and rules and regulations. *See also* **Government Publications.**

Reference Works General reference works are sources that contain facts and background information on a wide range of subjects. More specific reference works contain in-depth information on a single subject. Most reference works are good sources of reliable information because they have been reviewed by experts. The following are some common reference works: **encyclopedias, dictionaries, thesauri, almanacs, atlases, chronologies, biographical dictionaries,** and **directories.**

Review *See* **Critical Review.**

Rhetorical Questions Rhetorical questions are those that do not require a reply. Writers use them to suggest that their arguments make the answer obvious or self-evident.

Scanning Scanning is the process of searching through writing for a particular fact or piece of information. When you scan, your eyes sweep across a page, looking for key words that may lead you to the information you want.

Secondary Source *See* **Sources.**

Sequential Order A pattern of organization that shows the order in which events or actions occur is called sequential order. Writers typically use this pattern of organization to explain steps or stages in a process.

Setting a Purpose The process of establishing specific reasons for reading a text is called setting a purpose.

Sidebar A sidebar is additional information set in a box alongside or within a news or feature article. Popular magazines often make use of sidebar information.

Signal Words Signal words are words and phrases that indicate what is to come in a text. Readers can use signal words to discover a text's pattern of organization and to analyze the relationships among the ideas in the text.

Sources A source is anything that supplies information. **Primary sources** are materials written or created by people who were present at events, either as participants or as observers. Letters, diaries, autobiographies, speeches, and photographs are primary sources. **Secondary sources** are records of events that were created sometime after the events occurred; the writers were not directly involved or were not present when the events took place. Encyclopedias, textbooks, biographies, most newspaper and magazine articles, and books and articles that interpret or review research are secondary sources.

Spatial Order Spatial order is a pattern of organization that highlights the physical positions or relationships of details or objects. This pattern of organization is typically found in descriptive writing. Writers use words and phrases such as *on the left, to the right, here, over there, above, below, beyond, nearby,* and *in the distance* to indicate the arrangement of details.

Speech *See Glossary of Literary and Nonfiction Terms, page R121.*

Stereotyping Stereotyping is a dangerous type of overgeneralization. Stereotypes are broad statements made about people on the basis of their gender, ethnicity, race, or political, social, professional, or religious group.

Summarize To summarize is to briefly retell, or encapsulate, the main ideas of a piece of writing in one's own words.
See also **Paraphrase.**

Support Support is any material that serves to prove a claim. In an argument, support typically consists of reasons and evidence. In persuasive texts and speeches, however, support may include appeals to the needs and values of the audience.
See also **General Principle.**

Supporting Detail *See* **Main Idea.**

Synthesize To synthesize information is to take individual pieces of information and combine them with other pieces of information and with prior knowledge or experience to gain a better understanding of a subject or to create a new product or idea.

Text Features Text features are design elements that indicate the organizational structure of a text and help make the key ideas and the supporting information understandable. Text features include headings, boldface

type, italic type, bulleted or numbered lists, sidebars, and graphic aids such as charts, tables, timelines, illustrations, and photographs.

Thesaurus *See* **Reference Works.**

Thesis Statement In an argument, a thesis statement, or controlling idea, is an expression of the claim that the writer or speaker is trying to support. In an essay, a thesis statement is an expression, in one or two sentences, of the main idea or purpose of the piece of writing.

Topic Sentence The topic sentence of a paragraph states the paragraph's main idea. All other sentences in the paragraph provide supporting details.

Transcript A transcript is a written record of words originally spoken aloud.

Visualize Visualizing is the process of forming a mental picture based on written or spoken information.

Web Site A Web site is a collection of "pages" on the World Wide Web that is usually devoted to one specific subject. Pages are linked together and are accessed by clicking hyperlinks or menus, which send the user from page to page within the site. Web sites are created by companies, organizations, educational institutions, branches of the government, the military, and individuals.

Workplace Documents Workplace documents are materials that are produced or used within a work setting, usually to aid in the functioning of the workplace. They include job applications, office memos, training manuals, job descriptions, and sales reports.

Works Cited A list of works cited lists names of all the works a writer has referred to in his or her text. This list often includes not only books and articles but also nonprint sources.

Works Consulted A list of works consulted names all the works a writer consulted in order to create his or her text. It is not limited just to those works cited in the text.
See also **Bibliography.**

The Glossary of Academic Vocabulary in this section is an alphabetical list of the Academic Vocabulary words found in this textbook. Use this glossary just as you would use a dictionary—to find out the meanings of words used in your literature class to talk about and to write about literary and informational texts and to talk about and to write about concepts and topics in your other academic classes.

For each word, the glossary includes the pronunciation, part of speech, and meaning in English and Spanish. For more information about the words in the Glossary of Academic Vocabulary, please consult a dictionary.

accurate (ăk′yər-ĭt) *adj.* exactly matching the facts
   preciso *adj.* que concuerda exactamente con los hechos

affect (ə-fĕkt′) *v.* to influence; *n.* (ăf′ekt′) feeling or emotions displayed in facial expression
   afectar *v.* influenciar; **afecto** *sust.* sentimiento o emoción que se manifiesta mediante expresiones faciales

analyze (ăn′ə-līz′) *v.* to examine something in detail to understand it better
   analizar *v.* examinar algo en detalle para comprenderlo mejor

approach (ə-prōch′) *v.* to come near; to begin to deal with or work on; *n.* a way of doing something
   enfocar *v.* acercarse; comenzar a tratar o trabajar en algo; **enfoque** *sust.* manera de hacer algo

assume (ə-sōōm′) *v.* to suppose or take for granted; to take on or put on
   asumir *v.* suponer o dar por sentado; aceptar o encargarse de algo

attribute (ə-trĭb′yōōt) *v.* regard as being caused by something; *n.* (ăt′rĭ-byōōt′) a characteristic
   atribuir *v.* considerar como causado por algo; **atributo** *sust.* característica

challenge (chăl′ənj) *v.* to call for a contest or fight; to dare; *n.* a call to fight; objection to something or someone
   desafiar *v.* invitar a competir o pelear; retar; **desafío** *sust.* invitación a pelear; objeción a algo o alguien

concept (kŏn′sĕpt′) *n.* general notion or idea about something
   concepto *sust.* noción o idea general sobre algo

consent (kən-sĕnt′) *v.* to agree to someone's proposal; *n.* approval or acceptance of someone's plan
   consentir *v.* aceptar la propuesta de una persona; **consentimiento** *sust.* aprobación o aceptación del plan de una persona

culture (kŭl′chər) *n.* all products of human work and thought, including behavioral patterns, arts, beliefs, and institutions; these products as an expression of a particular group, time, or place; a high degree of taste and refinement gained through education or other training
   cultura *sust.* todos los productos del trabajo y el pensamiento humanos, como los patrones de conducta, las artes, las creencias y las instituciones; estos productos como expresión de un grupo, momento o lugar en particular; nivel elevado de gusto y refinamiento adquirido por medio de la educación u otro tipo de capacitación

dominate (dŏm′ə-nāt′) *v.* to hold a commanding position
   dominar *v.* tener un puesto de autoridad

draft (drăft) *n.* any of the stages of development of a plan, document, or picture; *v.* to write or draw an early version of or plan for something
   boceto *sust.* cualquiera de las etapas de desarrollo de un plan, documento o pintura; **preparar un boceto** *loc. v.* escribir o dibujar una primera versión o un plan de algo

environment (ĕn-vī′rən-mənt) *n.* surroundings; the physical conditions that influence the growth and survival of organisms; the social circumstances that influence people
   ambiente *sust.* entorno; condiciones físicas que influencian el crecimiento y la subsistencia de los organismos; circunstancias sociales que influencian a las personas

feature (fē′chər) *n.* a prominent or distinctive characteristic; *v.* to give special attention to
   rasgo *sust.* característica prominente o distintiva; **poner de relieve** *loc. v.* destacar

final (fi′nəl) *adj.* last; ultimate; unalterable; *n.* the last in series of contests or exams
   final *adj.* último; definitivo; irrevocable; *sust.* el último en una serie de competencias o exámenes

goal (gōl) *n.* purpose or aim
   meta *sust.* propósito u objetivo

hypothesis (hī-pŏth′ĭ-sĭs) *n.* an assumption made in order to test its possible consequences
   hipótesis *sust.* suposición que se hace para evaluar sus posibles consecuencias

impact (ĭm′pakt′) *n.* the effect or impression of one thing on another; *v.* to have a direct effect on
   impacto *sust.* efecto o impresión de una cosa sobre otra; **impactar** *v.* tener un efecto directo sobre algo

label (lā′bəl) *n.* a descriptive term, often seen as limiting; *v.* to identify with a label
   rótulo *sust.* término descriptivo, a menudo considerado restrictivo; **rotular** *v.* identificar con un rótulo

method (mĕth′əd) *n.* a regular and systematic way of doing something
   método *sust.* manera habitual y sistemática de hacer algo

monitor (mŏn′ĭ-tər) *v.* to keep close watch over; supervise
   supervisar *v.* vigilar algo de cerca; controlar

parallel (păr′ə-lĕl′) *adj.* having comparable parts, aims, or grammatical structures; *n.* something that closely resembles something else
   paralelo *adj.* que tiene partes, objetivos o estructuras gramaticales comparables; *sust.* algo que se asemeja mucho a otra cosa

phase (fāz) *n.* a stage of development
   fase *sust.* etapa de desarrollo

primary (prī′mĕr′ē) *adj.* first (in sequence, rank, or importance); essential; immediate
   primario *adj.* primero (en secuencia, categoría o importancia); esencial; inmediato

resource (rē′sôrs′, rē-sôrs′) *n.* something that can be used for support or help; anything available for economic development, such as land, labor, or mineral deposits
   recurso *sust.* algo que se puede usar como apoyo o ayuda; cualquier medio disponible para el desarrollo económico, como la tierra, el trabajo o los yacimientos minerales

respond (rĭ-spŏnd′) *v.* to reply or react
   responder *v.* contestar o reaccionar

scheme (skēm) *n.* a secret plan; a plot; a chart, diagram, or outline of a system or object
   esquema *sust.* plan secreto; gráfico; tabla, diagrama o bosquejo de un sistema u objeto

section (sĕk′shən) *n.* part of a whole; a discussion group of students taking the same course in a college; *v.* to separate into parts
   sección *sust.* parte de un todo; grupo de debate formado por estudiantes que están en un mismo curso en la universidad; **seccionar** *v.* separar en partes

strategy (străt′ə-jē) *n.* a plan of action or policy intended to accomplish a specific goal
   estrategia *sust.* plan de acción o política dirigidos a alcanzar un objetivo específico

structure (strŭk′chər) *n.* arrangement or organization; something constructed, such as a building; *v.* to give form or order to
   estructura *sust.* disposición u organización; algo que se construye, como un edificio; **estructurar** *v.* dar forma u ordenar algo

The glossary that follows is an alphabetical list of words, found in the selections in this book. Use this glossary just as you would use a dictionary—to find out the meanings of unfamiliar words. (Some technical, foreign, and more obscure words in this book are not listed here but instead are defined for you in the footnotes that accompany many of the selections.)

Many words in the English language have more than one meaning. This glossary gives the meanings that apply to the words as they are used in the selections in this book. Words closely related in form and meaning are usually listed together in one entry (for instance, *cower* and *cowered*), and the definition is given for the first form.

The following abbreviations are used:

adj. adjective
adv. adverb
n. noun
v. verb

Each word's pronunciation is given in parentheses, followed by the word and definition in Spanish. For more information about the words in this glossary or for information about words not listed here, consult a dictionary.

abstain (ăb-stān′) *v.* to hold oneself back from doing something
abstenerse *v.* renunciar voluntariamente a hacer algo

abstemious (ăb-stē′mē-əs) *adj.* practicing abstinence; refraining from doing something
abstinente *adj.* que practica la abstinencia; que se priva de algo

abstraction (ăb-străk′shən) *n.* something that cannot be perceived by any of the five senses; an idea or a quality
abstracción *s.* algo que no se puede percibir por los cinco sentidos; idea o cualidad

accrue (ə-krōō′) *v.* to be added or gained; to accumulate
acumular *v.* añadir o ganar

affliction (ə-flĭk′shən) *n.* a force that oppresses or causes suffering
aflicción *s.* fuerza que oprime o causa sufrimiento

affronted (ə-frŭnt′ĭd) *adj.* insulted; offended **affront** *v.*
ofendido *adj.* insultado **ofender** *v.*

anachronism (ə-năk′rə-nĭz′əm) *n.* anything out of its proper time; someone or something that seems to belong to a former time but not the present
anacronismo *s.* lo que no corresponde a su época; alguien o algo que es propio de una época pasada

animate (ăn′ə-māt′) *v.* to stimulate to action or effort; inspire
animar *v.* estimular a la acción o al esfuerzo; inspirar

animosity (ăn′ə-mŏs′ĭ-tē) *n.* ill feeling; hostility
animosidad *s.* antipatía; hostilidad

apathetically (ăp′ə-thĕt′ĭk-lē) *adv.* without interest or feeling; indifferently
apáticamente *adv.* sin interés ni entusiasmo; indiferentemente

assail (ə-sāl′) *v.* to attack
asaltar *v.* atacar

assent (ə-sĕnt′) *n.* acceptance of an opinion or a proposal; agreement
asentimiento *s.* aceptación de una opinión o propuesta; acuerdo

astute (ə-stōōt′) *adj.* having a clever or shrewd mind; cunning; wily
astuto *adj.* sagaz; ingenioso; mañoso

atrocity (ə-trŏs′ĭ-tē) *n.* a very cruel, brutal, or appalling act
atrocidad *s.* acción muy cruel, brutal o chocante

attenuated (ə-tĕn′yōō-ā′tĭd) *adj.* slender; thin **attenuate** *v.*
adelgazado *adj.* esbelto; delgado **adelgazar** *v.*

avarice (ăv′ə-rĭs) *n.* greed
avaricia *s.* codicia

balefully (bāl′fəl-ē) *adv.* in a manner that threatens evil or harm; ominously
torvamente *adv.* funestamente; siniestramente

bequeath (bĭ-kwēth′) *v.* to leave in a will; to pass down as an inheritance

   legar *v.* heredar en un testamento; transmitir como herencia

bigoted (bĭg′ə-tĭd) *adj.* prejudiced and narrow-minded; intolerant

   intolerante *adj.* prejuiciado y cerrado

burnished (bûr′nĭsht) *adj.* polished until shiny **burnish** *v.*

   bruñido *adj.* que se le ha sacado brillo **bruñir** *v.*

capricious (kə-prĭsh′əs) *adj.* impulsive or unpredictable

   caprichoso *adj.* impulsivo o impredecible

career (kə-rîr′) *v.* to move at full speed; to rush wildly

   correr *v.* ir a toda velocidad

castigate (kăs′tĭ-gāt′) *v.* to criticize

   fustigar *v.* criticar

celestial (sə-lĕs′chəl) *adj.* heavenly; divine

   celestial *adj.* relativo al cielo; divino

censure (sĕn′shər) *n.* criticism

   censura *s.* crítica

circumscribe (sûr′kəm-skrīb′) *v.* to restrict; to limit

   circunscribir *v.* restringir; limitar

civility (sĭ-vĭl′ĭ-tē) *n.* good manners; decent behavior

   urbanidad *s.* educación; cortesía

collateral (kə-lăt′ər-əl) *adj.* accompanying as a parallel or subordinate factor; related

   colateral *adj.* paralelo o subordinado; relacionado

compel (kəm-pĕl′) *v.* to force or be forced to act in a certain way

   compeler *v.* obligar a actuar de determinada manera

conjecture (kən-jĕk′chər) *v.* to infer based on incomplete evidence; guess

   conjeturar *v.* inferir a partir de evidencia incompleta; suponer

consolation (kŏn′sə-lā′shən) *n.* something that makes someone feel less sad or disappointed; comfort

   consuelo *s.* lo que alivia la tristeza o la decepción

consternation (kŏn′stər-nā′shən) *n.* fear or shock that makes one feel bewildered or upset

   consternación *s.* alteración del ánimo o pérdida de la tranquilidad

constrain (kən-strān′) *v.* to force; to compel

   constreñir *v.* obligar; compeler

convivial (kən-vĭv′ē-əl) *adj.* characterized by friendly companionship; sociable

   sociable *adj.* cordial; simpático; expansivo

copious (kō′pē-əs) *adj.* plentiful; abundant

   copioso *adj.* abundante; numeroso

countenance (koun′tə-nəns) *n.* face; facial expression

   semblante *s.* expresión facial; rostro

courtliness (kôrt′lē-nĭs) *n.* polite, elegant manners; refined behavior

   cortesanía *s.* elegancia; refinamiento

cowed (koud) *adj.* made timid and submissive through fear or awe **cow** *v.*

   atemorizado *adj.* acobardado o intimidado por miedo o sobrecogimiento **atemorizar** *v.*

credence (krēd′ns) *n.* belief, especially in the ideas of another person

   crédito *s.* aceptación de algo como verdadero

crone (krōn) *n.* an ugly old woman

   bruja *s.* mujer vieja y fea

debase (dĭ-bās′) *v.* to lower in value, quality, or dignity; to cheapen

   degradar *v.* rebajar el valor, la cualidad o la dignidad; desvalorar

deference (dĕf′ər-əns) *n.* a yielding or courteous regard toward the opinion, judgment, or wishes of others; respect

   deferencia *s.* aceptación cortés de la opinión, juicio o deseos de otros; respeto

defile (dĭ-fīl′) *v.* to make filthy or impure; to violate the honor of

   manchar *v.* ensuciar o mancillar; violar el honor

deign (dān) *v.* to consider worthy of one's dignity; to condescend

   dignarse *v.* considerar digno de la dignidad de uno; condescender

desist (dĭ-sĭst′) *v.* to cease or stop

   desistir *v.* cesar o parar

despotic (dĭ-spŏt′ĭk) *adj.* ruling absolutely without allowing any dissent; tyrannical

   despótico *adj.* que gobierna sin tolerar disentimiento; tiránico

dexterity (děk-stěr′ĭ-tē) *n.* skill in manipulating one's hands or body
　　destreza *s.* agilidad para manipular las manos o el cuerpo

diminutive (dĭ-mĭn′yə-tĭv) *adj.* very small
　　diminutivo *adj.* muy pequeño

disconsolately (dĭs-kŏn′sə-lĭt-lē) *adv.* unhappily; inconsolably
　　desconsoladamente *adv.* abatidamente; inconsolablemente

discretion (dĭ-skrĕsh′ən) *n.* wise restraint; carefulness in one's actions and words
　　discreción *s.* tacto, moderación y sensatez para decir o hacer algo

dismantle (dĭs-măn′tl) *v.* to take apart; to disassemble
　　desmantelar *v.* desarmar; desmontar

dissension (dĭ-sĕn′shən) *n.* disagreement; violent quarreling
　　disensión *s.* desacuerdo; oposición violenta

doctrine (dŏk′trĭn) *n.* teachings; theories
　　doctrina *s.* enseñanzas; teorías

dogged (dô′gĭd) *adj.* not giving up; tenacious; stubborn
　　obstinado *adj.* tenaz; persistente; terco

dominion (də-mĭn′yən) *n.* rule or power to rule; mastery
　　dominio *s.* poder de gobernar; conocimiento profundo

eddying (ĕd′ē-ĭng) *adj.* moving in a whirlpool; swirling **eddy** *v.*
　　arremolinado *adj.* que se mueve en forma de remolino **arremolinar** *v.*

emanate (ĕm′ə-nāt′) *v.* to issue forth
　　emanar *v.* emitir; desprenderse

emulation (ĕm′yə-lā′shən) *n.* imitation of an admired example
　　emulación *s.* imitación de un ejemplo admirado

enamored (ĭ-năm′ərd) *adj.* infatuated; charmed
　　enamorado *adj.* que siente amor

encumbrance (ĕn-kŭm′brəns) *n.* a burden
　　traba *s.* carga; estorbo

enmity (ĕn′mĭ-tē) *n.* deep-seated hatred
　　enemistad *s.* odio profundo

entity (ĕn′tĭ-tē) *n.* something that has definitive existence; a creation
　　ente *s.* ser; lo que existe

entreaty (ĕn-trē′tē) *n.* a serious request or plea
　　súplica *s.* petición; ruego

euphemism (yōō′fə-mĭz′əm) *n.* a weaker word or phrase used in place of another in order to be less distasteful or offensive
　　eufemismo *s.* palabra o expresión suave con la que se sustituye otra que se considera grosera o malsonante

evanescent (ĕv′ə-nĕs′ənt) *adj.* quick to disappear
　　evanescente *adj.* que desaparece rápidamente

expedient (ĭk-spē′dē-ənt) *n.* something useful in achieving the desired effect; a convenience; an advantage
　　expediente *s.* medio o recurso que se emplea para resolver una dificultad

expostulate (ĭk-spŏs′chə-lāt′) *v.* to reason with someone, in order to change his or her actions or plans
　　objetar *v.* razonar con una persona a fin de hacerla cambiar de acción o de plan

expunging (ĭk-spŭn′jĭng) *n.* erasing or removing completely **expunge** *v.*
　　eliminación *s.* cancelación o supresión completa **eliminar** *v.*

extraneous (ĭk-strā′nē-əs) *adj.* irrelevant or inessential
　　accidental *adj.* irrelevante o superfluo

famine (făm′ĭn) *n.* a period in which there is a severe shortage of food
　　hambruna *s.* período de grave escasez de alimentos

feign (fān) *v.* to make a false show of; pretend
　　fingir *v.* simular; aparentar

felicity (fĭ-lĭs′ĭ-tē) *n.* happiness; good fortune
　　felicidad *s.* alegría; dicha

foment (fō-mĕnt′) *v.* to stir up trouble; to incite
　　fomentar *v.* promover; impulsar; incitar

formidable (fôr′mĭ-də-bəl) *adj.* hard to handle or overcome
　　formidable *adj.* muy temible; asombroso; extraordinario

garish (gâr′ĭsh) *adj.* too bright or showy; gaudy; glaring
　　chillón *adj.* muy llamativo; extravagante

garner (gär′nər) *v.* to gather up and store; to collect
almacenar *v.* reunir y guardar; acopiar

garrulous (găr′ə-ləs) *adj.* talking a lot or too much, especially about unimportant things
gárrulo *adj.* que habla demasiado, especialmente de cosas sin importancia

gorge (gôrj) *v.* to stuff with food; glut
hartarse *v.* llenarse de comida; engullir

guffaw (gə-fô′) *v.* to laugh loudly
carcajearse *v.* reírse a carcajadas

guile (gīl) *n.* clever trickery; deceit
maña *s.* engaño; ardid

havoc (hăv′ək) *n.* widespread destruction
estrago *s.* destrucción general

heretic (hĕr′ĭ-tĭk) *n.* someone who expresses beliefs that oppose church teachings or established views
hereje *s.* el que expresa creencias contrarias a la doctrina de la iglesia o a las ideas establecidas

homage (hŏm′ĭj) *n.* an act showing great respect; tribute
homenaje *s.* acto celebrado en honor de alguien; tributo

imbue (ĭm-byōō′) *v.* to fill, as with a quality; saturate
imbuir *v.* llenar de una cualidad; saturar

impede (ĭm-pēd′) *v.* to hinder or obstruct
impedir *v.* estorbar u obstruir

imperialism (ĭm-pîr′ē-ə-lĭz′əm) *n.* the policy of forming and maintaining an empire, especially in the quest for raw materials and more markets
imperialismo *s.* teoría política que defiende la formación de un imperio para obtener materias primas y mercados

imperturbable (ĭm′-pər-tûr′bə-bəl) *adj.* not able to be excited or disturbed; impassive
imperturbable *adj.* que no se deja excitar o molestar; impasivo

implacable (ĭm-plăk′ə-bəl) *adj.* unable to be appeased or significantly changed; inflexible; relentless
implacable *adj.* que no se puede aplacar o moderar; inflexible; inexorable

implicitly (ĭm-plĭs′ĭt-lē) *adv.* without the need to hear spoken; without doubt or question
implícitamente *adv.* sin necesidad de expresarlo; sin duda

implore (ĭm-plôr′) *v.* to plead; to beg
implorar *v.* rogar; pedir

incessant (ĭn-sĕs′-ənt) *adj.* continuing or seeming to continue without stopping
incesante *adj.* que no para

inculcate (ĭn-kŭl′kāt′) *v.* to impress on the mind by frequent repetition; to teach; to instill
inculcar *v.* fijar en la memoria por medio de la repetición frecuente; enseñar; infundir

incumbent (ĭn-kŭm′bənt) *adj.* required as a duty or an obligation
obligatorio *adj.* que se requiere como deber u obligación

indefatigable (ĭn′dĭ-făt′ĭ-gə-bəl) *adj.* tireless
infatigable *adj.* incansable

indolence (ĭn′də-ləns) *n.* the tendency to avoid work; laziness; idleness
indolencia *s.* tendencia a evitar el trabajo; pereza; ociosidad

indomitable (ĭn-dŏm′ĭ-tə-bəl) *adj.* not easily discouraged or defeated
indomable *adj.* invencible; insuperable

infamous (ĭn′fə-məs) *adj.* having a very bad reputation
infame *adj.* de pésima reputación

iniquity (ĭ-nĭk′wĭ-tē) *n.* immortality; wickedness
iniquidad *s.* inmoralidad; maldad

innumerable (ĭ-nōō′mər-ə-bəl) *adj.* too many to be counted
innumerable *adj.* imposible de contar

inscrutable (ĭn-skrōō′tə-bəl) *adj.* difficult to understand
inescrutable *adj.* difícil de entender

interloper (ĭn′tər-lō′pər) *n.* intruder
intruso *s.* entrometido

interment (ĭn-tûr′mənt) *n.* burial
enterramiento *s.* entierro

intimidate (ĭn-tĭm′ĭ-dāt′) *v.* to make timid or afraid
intimidar *v.* causar o infundir miedo

intrinsically (ĭn-trĭn′zĭ-klē) *adv.* in the manner of the true nature of a thing; inherently
intrínsecamente *adv.* de modo propio y característico de una cosa; inherentemente

invincible (ĭn-vĭn′-sə-bel) *adj.* not able to be conquered
invencible *adj.* que no se puede conquistar

labyrinth (lăb′ə-rĭnth′) *n.* an intricate structure of winding passages; a maze
laberinto *s.* estructura de pasajes cruzados en la que es difícil encontrar la salida

laconic (lə-kŏn′ĭk) *adj.* using few words; concise
lacónico *adj.* de pocas palabras; conciso

lair (lâr) *n.* the den or resting place of a wild animal
madriguera *s.* cueva en que vive un animal

lamentation (lăm′ən-tā′shən) *n.* an expression of sorrow or regret
lamentación *s.* expresión de tristeza o de dolor

laudable (lô′də-bəl) *adj.* worthy of praise
laudable *adj.* digno de alabanza

lissome (lĭs′əm) *adj.* moving with graceful ease; limber
flexible *adj.* ágil y elástico; ligero

livid (lĭv′ĭd) *adj.* discolored from being bruised
lívido *adj.* amoratado; ceniciento

loathsome (lōth′səm) *adj.* disgusting
repulsivo *adj.* repugnante

longevity (lŏn-jĕv′ĭ-tē) *n.* endurance over a sizable span of time; long life
longevidad *s.* larga duración de la vida

lucrative (lōō′krə-tĭv) *adj.* producing wealth or profit
lucrativo *adj.* que da riquezas o ganancias

malady (măl′ə-dē) *n.* a disease or disorder; an ailment
mal *s.* enfermedad o trastorno; dolencia

mason (mā′sən) *n.* someone whose work is to build walls, buildings, and other structures made of stone, brick, or concrete
albañil *s.* obrero que construye paredes, edificios y otras estructuras de piedra, ladrillo o concreto

materialize (mə-tîr′ē-ə-līz) *v.* to take form; to appear; to become fact
materializar *v.* realizar; hacer realidad; aparecer

naive (nī-ēv′) *adj.* simple; innocent or unworldly
ingenuo *adj.* simple; inocente o sencillo

obsequiously (ŏb-sē′kwē-əs-lē) *adv.* in an eagerly submissive way
obsequiosamente *adv.* servilmente

ominous (ŏm′ə-nəs) *adj.* threatening
ominoso *adj.* amenazante

oracle (ôr′ə-kəl) *n.* a wise person who foresees the future
oráculo *s.* persona sabia que prevé el futuro

orifice (ôr′ə-fĭs) *n.* an opening, especially to a passage within the body
orificio *s.* entrada, especialmente a una cavidad del cuerpo

parley (pär′lē) *n.* a discussion or a conference
parlamento *s.* plática o conferencia

penitence (pĕn′ĭ-təns) *n.* feeling regret for a wrongful act and wanting to atone for it
penitencia *s.* mortificación impuesta como castigo o reparación por un acto indebido

personable (pûr′sə-nə-bəl) *adj.* pleasing in behavior and appearance
agradable *adj.* de conducta y aspecto grato

pervade (pər-vād′) *v.* to be prevalent throughout
saturar *v.* llenar; penetrar

perversity (pər-vûr′sĭ-tē) *n.* a stubborn determination to act in an inappropriate or unexpected way
perversidad *s.* maldad muy grande e intencionada

plundering (plŭn′dər-ĭng) *n.* taking property by force plunder *v.*
saqueo *s.* pillaje saquear *v.*

pomp (pŏmp) *n.* vain display
pompa *s.* despliegue, grandeza o vanidad extraordinarios

ponderous (pŏn′dər-əs) *adj.* very heavy
ponderoso *adj.* muy pesado

posterity (pŏ-stĕr′ĭ-tē) *n.* future generations
posteridad *s.* generaciones futuras

precipitous (prĭ-sĭp′ĭ-təs) *adj.* nearly vertical; very steep
escarpado *adj.* casi vertical; muy inclinado

prerogative (prĭ-rŏg′ə-tĭv) *n.* a privilege or distinctive advantage
prerrogativa *s.* privilegio o ventaja

presumption (prĭ-zŭmp′shən) *n.* bold or outrageous behavior
   presunción *s.* engreimiento; atrevimiento; insolencia

prodigious (prə-dĭj′əs) *adj.* of great size or power; huge; impressive
   prodigioso *adj.* de gran tamaño o fuerza; enorme; impresionante

propagation (prŏp′ə-gā′shən) *n.* the act of reproducing, multiplying, or increasing
   propagación *s.* reproducción; multiplicación; aumento

propensity (prə-pĕn′sĭ-tē) *n.* a likelihood to do or think something; tendency; inclination
   propensión *s.* inclinación a hacer o pensar algo; tendencia

prophesy (prŏf′ĭ-sī) *v.* to predict something by, or as if by, devine guidance
   profetizar *v.* anunicar o predecir hechos futoros

propound (prə-pound′) *v.* to put forward for consideration; propose
   proponer *v.* plantear a consideración; exponer

prosaic (prō-zā′ĭk) *adj.* not given to poetic flights of fancy; lacking imagination; dull
   prosaico *adj.* falto de poesía; sin elevación, emoción o interés

prostrate (prŏs′trāt′) *adj.* completely submissive
   postrado *adj.* rendido

prostrate (prŏs′trāt′) *v.* to lie with the face down, as in prayer or submission
   postrar *v.* inclinarse al suelo en señal de respeto, de humildad o de ruego

purge (pûrj) *v.* to cleanse or rid of something undesirable
   purgar *v.* limpiar o purificar lo que se considera indeseable

pusillanimous (pyōō′sə-lăn′ə-məs) *adj.* timid; cowardly
   pusilánime *adj.* tímido; cobarde

raiment (rā′mənt) *n.* clothing
   vestimenta *s.* ropa

rancor (răng′kər) *n.* bitter, long-lasting anger; ill will
   rencor *s.* enojo duradero por algo pasado; animosidad

rapacious (rə-pā′shəs) *adj.* greedy; grasping
   rapaz *adj.* voraz; codicioso

rebuke (rĭ-byōōk′) *v.* to criticize
   reprender *v.* criticar

recompense (rĕk′əm-pĕns′) *n.* payment or repayment; compensation
   recompensa *s.* pago; compensación

redress (rĭ-drĕs′) *n.* repayment for a wrong or an injury
   remediar *v.* compensar por un daño o por una herida

regime (rā-zhēm′) *n.* a government in power
   régimen *s.* gobierno que detenta el poder

reiterate (rē-ĭt′ə-rāt′) *v.* to repeat
   reiterar *v.* repetir

remonstrate (rĭ-mŏn′strāt′) *v.* to say or plead in protest or complaint
   objetar *v.* protestar; reclamar

repository (rĭ-pŏz′ĭ-tôr′ē) *n.* a place where information or physical items are stored
   repositorio *s.* lugar donde se guarda información u objetos

resolution (rĕz′ə-lōō′shən) *n.* stubborn courage to face challenges; resolve
   resolución *s.* valor y energía ante un problema; tesón

respite (rĕs′pĭt) *n.* an interval of temporary relief; a delay or postponement
   respiro *s.* intervalo de alivio temporal; suspensión temporal

rudiment (rōō′də-mənt) *n.* a basic principle or element
   rudimento *s.* principio o elemento básico

scourge (skûrj) *n.* a source of great suffering or destruction
   flagelo *s.* fuente de gran sufrimiento y destrucción

sedately (sĭ-dāt′lē) *adv.* in a composed, dignified manner; calmly
   sosegadamente *adv.* de modo tranquilo y digno; calmadamente

senility (sĭ-nĭl′ĭ-tē) *n.* the mental deterioration that sometimes comes with old age
   senilidad *s.* deterioro mental que a veces acompaña la vejez

sensibility (sĕn′sə-bĭl′ĭ-tē) *n.* the ability to be affected emotionally; sensitivity
   sensibilidad *s.* facultad de sentir algo

sovereignty (sŏv′ər-ĭn-tē) *n.* rule; power
soberanía *s.* poder

spectral (spĕk′trəl) *adj.* ghostly
espectral *adj.* fantasmagórico

steed (stēd) *n.* a horse, especially a high-spirited riding horse
corcel *s.* caballo de gran alzada

stint (stĭnt) *n.* limitation; restriction
límite *s.* limitación; restricción

stoicism (stō′ĭ-sĭz′əm) *n.* indifference to pleasure or pain
estoicismo *s.* indiferencia al placer o al dolor

subjection (səb-jĕk′shən) *n.* the state of being under the authority or control of another
supeditación *s.* subyugación o dependencia

submissive (səb-mĭs′ĭv) *adj.* tending to yield to the will of others; docile; meek
sumiso *adj.* obediente; dócil; humilde

supplant (sə-plănt′) *v.* to take the place of
suplantar *v.* ocupar el lugar de otra persona

surmise (sər-mīz′) *v.* to jump to conclusions
suponer *v.* hacer una conjetura

sustenance (sŭs′tə-nəns) *n.* a means of support or nourishment
sustento *s.* alimento; sostenimiento

talon (tăl′ən) *n.* a claw
garra *s.* pata de animal con uñas fuertes

temperate (tĕm′pər-ĭt) *adj.* moderate
templado *adj.* moderado

temporal (tĕm′pər-əl) *adj.* of the material world; not eternal
temporal *adj.* del mundo material; que no es eterno

terrestrial (tə-rĕs′trē-əl) *adj.* of the earth; earthly
terrestre *adj.* de la tierra; terrenal

transfigure (trăns-fĭg′yər) *v.* to transform, especially in a way that exalts or glorifies
transfigurar *v.* transformar, especialmente para exaltar o glorificar

uncanny (ŭn-kăn′ē) *adj.* strange or mysterious in a way that causes unease; eerie
raro *adj.* extraño o misterioso de un modo que causa desasosiego; inquietante

unctuous (ŭngk′chōō-əs) *adj.* excessively or insincerely earnest; smug
untuoso *adj.* empalagoso o excesivamente amable; hipócrita

upbraiding (ŭp-brād′ĭng) *n.* scolding **upbraid** *v.*
reproche *s.* regaño **reprochar** *v.*

usurp (yōō-sûrp′) *v.* to seize unlawfully by force
usurpar *v.* apoderarse de algo ilegalmente por la fuerza

vanity (văn′ĭ-tē) *n.* that which is without meaning or value; emptiness; worthlessness
vanidad *s.* cosa vana, fútil o inútil; vacío; inutilidad

vehement (vē′ə-mənt) *adj.* acting with or having great force; fervent
vehemente *adj.* apasionado o lleno de ardor; ferviente

venerated (vĕn′ər-ā′tĭd) *adj.* deeply respected; revered **venerate** *v.*
venerado *adj.* que recibe profundo respeto y devoción **venerar** *v.*

vindication (vĭn′dĭ-kā′shən) *n.* clearing from criticism, blame, guilt, or suspicion; justification
vindicación *s.* rehabilitación tras crítica, culpa o sospecha; justificación

vitiate (vĭsh′ē-āt′) *v.* to corrupt or weaken
viciar *v.* corromper o debilitar

voluble (vŏl′yə-bəl) *adj.* talkative; glib
charlatán *adj.* hablador; suelto de lengua

vulnerable (vŭl′nər-ə-bəl) *adj.* open to attack; easily hurt
vulnerable *adj.* que puede ser atacado; fácil de herir

Pronunciation Key

Symbol	Examples	Symbol	Examples	Symbol	Examples
ă	at, gas	m	man, seem	v	van, save
ā	ape, day	n	night, mitten	w	web, twice
ä	father, barn	ng	sing, hanger	y	yard, lawyer
âr	fair, dare	ŏ	odd, not	z	zoo, reason
b	bell, table	ō	open, road, grow	zh	treasure, garage
ch	chin, lunch	ô	awful, bought, horse	ə	awake, even, pencil,
d	dig, bored	oi	coin, boy		pilot, focus
ĕ	egg, ten	ŏŏ	look, full	ər	perform, letter
ē	evil, see, meal	ōō	root, glue, through		
f	fall, laugh, phrase	ou	out, cow		
g	gold, big	p	pig, cap		
h	hit, inhale	r	rose, star		
hw	white, everywhere	s	sit, face		
ĭ	inch, fit	sh	she, mash		
ī	idle, my, tried	t	tap, hopped		
îr	dear, here	th	thing, with		
j	jar, gem, badge	*th*	then, other		
k	keep, cat, luck	ŭ	up, nut		
l	load, rattle	ûr	fur, earn, bird, worm		

Sounds in Foreign Words

Symbol	Examples
KH	*German* i**ch**, au**ch**; *Scottish* lo**ch**
N	*French* e**n**tre, bo**n**, fi**n**
œ	*French* f**eu**, c**œu**r; *German* sch**ö**n
ü	*French* **u**tile, r**u**e; *German* gr**ü**n

Stress Marks

' This mark indicates that the preceding syllable receives the primary stress. For example, in the word *language,* the first syllable is stressed: lăng′gwĭj.

' This mark is used only in words in which more than one syllable is stressed. It indicates that the preceding syllable is stressed, but somewhat more weakly than the syllable receiving the primary stress. In the word *literature,* for example, the first syllable receives the primary stress, and the last syllable receives a weaker stress: lĭt′ər-ə-chŏŏr′.

Adapted from *The American Heritage Dictionary of the English Language,* fourth edition. Copyright © 2006 by Houghton Mifflin Harcourt Publishing Company. Used with the permission of Houghton Mifflin Harcourt Publishing Company.

INDEX OF FINE ART

Index of Skills

A

Academic vocabulary, 10–13, 18, 72, 94, 168, 182, 198, 215, 264, 270, 272, 275, 290, 445, 450, 453, 460, 512, 558, 633, 656, 668, 678, 689, 728, 750, 892, 893, 910, 992, 1008, 1028, 1042, 1076, 1077, 1079, 1085, 1096, 1150, 1170, 1208, 1238, 1261, 1278, 1296, 1330, 1354, 1400, 1420, 1421, 1426. *See also* Specialized vocabulary.

Act (in a play), 344, R104

Active listening, R86–R87
 critical listening, R87
 verbal feedback, R87

Active voice, of verbs, R60–R61

Adjective clauses and phrases, R65, R67

Adjectives, R51, R61
 versus adverbs, R61
 comparative, R61
 irregular comparisons, R62
 predicate, R61
 regular comparisons, R62
 sensory, 323
 superlative, R61
 vivid, 54, 73, 1125

Advanced searches, 95, 1409, 1423

Adverb clauses and phrases, R65, R67

Adverbs, R51, R61
 versus adjectives, R61
 comparative, R61
 irregular comparisons, R62
 regular comparisons, R62
 superlative, R61

Advertising, R93–R94
 billboard, R93
 celebrities in, R94
 flyer, R93
 infomercial, R93
 marketing, R93
 persuasive techniques in, 1376–1379, R94
 political ad, R93
 print ad, R93
 product comparisons, R94
 product placement, R94
 public service announcement, R93
 sponsors, R94
 trailer, R93

Aesthetic impact, 183, R83

Aesthetics and literary criticism. *See* Text criticism.

Affixes. *See* Prefixes; Suffixes.

Agreement
 pronoun-antecedent, R56
 subject-verb, R69

Alexandrine. *See* Line, in poetry; Spenserian stanza.

Allegory, 124, 504, R104
 analysis of, 481, 505–511

Alliteration, 41, 237, 245, 840, R104

Allusion, 439, 493–503, 934, 1041, 1059, 1122, 1180, R104

Almanacs, R44. *See also* References.

Ambiguity, 890, 1039, 1122, 1250, 1256, 1264, 1273, 1277, 1361, R104
 in decision-making, 779, 1027, 1229–1237

Ambiguous pronoun references, R59

Analogies, 450, 656, 728, 1170, R75, R104. *See also* Rhetorical devices.

Analysis, writing, 73, 227, 443, 607, 657, 699, 781, 811, 845, 943, 1029, 1171, 1180, 1189
 options for organization, R38
 presenting an, 280–281
 rubric for, R37

Anglo-Saxon literature, 18–30, 40, 41–71, R104

Anglo-Saxon word parts, 72, R73–R74

Antagonist, 347, R105

Antecedent-pronoun agreement, R56

Antithesis, 445, R105

Antonyms, 376, R75

Aphorisms, 463, R105

Apostrophe (figure of speech), 849, 857, R105

Apostrophe (punctuation), R54

Appeals, R20. *See also* Argumentative techniques.
 by association, R20, R125
 to authority, R125
 bandwagon, R20, R94
 emotional, 731, 732, 1031–1041, 1289–1295, 1298–1301, R20, R94, R126
 ethical, 731, 732, 1031–1041, R127
 in propaganda, 1298–1301, 1376–1379
 logical, 479, 731, 732, 1031–1041, R94, R128. *See also* Arguments.
 to loyalty, R20
 to pity, fear, or vanity, 1031–1041, 1298–1301, R20, R94
 snob appeal, R20, R87
 testimonials, R20, R94
 transfer, R20

Appendix, R44

Application forms, R16, R42

Appositives and appositive phrases, R65

Approaches to literature. *See* Text criticism.

Archetype, R105

Arguments, R19–R24, R125. *See also* Appeals; Fallacies; Argumentative techniques.
 analysis of, 453–459, 727, 1265–1277, R19–R24
 assumption, 471, 836
 claims, 453–459, 538–547, 730–739, R19, R24, R125
 conclusions in, R20–R21, R126
 counterarguments, 453–459, 538–547, 730–739, 719–727, R19, R24, R126
 deductive, 1265–1277, R21, R126
 elements of, 453–459, R19

Bandwagon appeal, R20, R94

Base words. *See* Word parts; Word roots.

Bias, R2, R23, R93, R125. *See also* Media.

Bibliography, R44, R125. *See also* Works cited.

Biographical references, R44. *See also* References.

Biography, 577, 680, 681–688, 1280, R106

Blank verse, 344, 347, 354, 373, 375, 381, 396, 426, R106. *See also* Iambic pentameter; Meter; Rhythm.

Boldface type, as text feature, R16

Books
    nonfiction, as source, R44
    parts of, R44

Boolean searches, R46

Brainstorming, 601, 893

Business writing, R40–R43, R125. *See also* Workplace and technical writing.

C

Caesura, 41, R106

Call to action, 733, 736, 737

Camera shots and techniques, in film and video, 267, 441, 1051, R90

Capitalization, R55
    first words and pronoun, R55
    geographical names, R55
    organizations, events, R55
    proofreading for, R27
    proper adjectives, R55
    in quotations, R55
    as style element, 1180
    of titles, R55

Career-related writing. *See* Business writing.

Case, pronoun, R56, R57
    nominative, R56, R57
    objective, R56, R57
    possessive, R56, R57

Catastrophe, as element of tragedy, 347, 427, 432

Cause-and-effect organization, 207–214, 417, 1251–1259, R10, R36, R125. *See also* Patterns of organization.
    cause-effect chain, R36
    cause-to-effect, R36
    effect-to-cause, R36
    strategies for reading, R10

Cause-effect writing, R36
    options for organization, R36
    rubric for, R36

Central idea, 319–322, 343, 432, 471, 1055, 1117, R128

Chain of events. *See* Cause-and-effect organization.

Characterization, 141, R107
    in fiction, 1127–1137, 1139, 1153
    in narrative poetry, 143–167, 823, 834

Characters, R106–R107. *See also* Characterization; Character traits; Character types.
    analysis of, 77–93, 181, 214, 226, 244, 263, 367, 381, 399, 417, 503, 971, 983, 991, 1149, 1169, 1237, 1329, 1353, 1363–1374

motivation and behavior of, 41, 54, 127–138, 244, 399, 951, 1127–1137, 1153, R115
    relationships among, 1319–1329

Character traits, 41–71, 143–167, 1153

Character types, R106–R107
    antagonist, 347, 397, R105
    cultural hero, R111
    dynamic, R107
    epic hero, 41–71, 93, R109
    foil, 181, 503, R110
    hero, 41–71, 342–343, R111
    main, 342–343, 667, R106. *See also* Hero; Protagonist.
    minor, R106
    protagonist, 342–343, 848, R118
    static, R107
    tragic hero, 342–343, 347, 430, 432, R111, R123

Charts. *See* Graphic aids; Graphic organizers.

Choice of words. *See* Diction; Word choice.

Chronological order, 276, R9, R34, R125. *See also* Patterns of organization; Timelines.

Citations. *See* MLA citation guidelines; Works cited.
    parenthetical, 1427, 1430

Claims, 453–459, 538–547, 730–739, R19, R24, R125
    opposing, 730–739

Clarifying, 54, 61, 71, 101, 115, 122, 138, 181, 205, 214, 226, 244, 263, 317, 338, 367, 381, 399, 417, 432, 459, 469, 478, 492, 520, 521, 523, 529, 588, 599, 619, 632, 655, 688, 705, 777, 789, 794, 807, 810, 835, 844, 850, 853, 857, 862, 877, 880, 885, 890, 942, 959, 966, 991, 1007, 1027, 1059, 1065, 1074, 1124, 1137, 1149, 1169, 1180, 1223, 1248, 1277, 1287, 1295, 1309, 1315, 1329, 1337, 1374, R125. *See also* Monitoring.
    meaning, in poetry, 783–789, 1191–1197
    sentence meaning, 489–492

Clarity and coherence, maintaining, FM56–FM58

Clauses
    adjective, R67
    adverb, R67
    essential, R67
    independent (main), R66
    nonessential, R67
    noun, R67
    as style element, 1151
    subordinate (dependent), 121, 123, 647, 657, R67

Clear narrative, as oratorical technique, 1289

Cliché, R107, R125. *See also* Idioms.

Climax, 207, R107. *See also* Plot.

Cognates, 456, 686, 1328. *See also* Etymology.

Coherence, in writing, R29

Colons, R54

Combining sentences. *See* Conjunctions, coordinating.

Comedy, 342, R107. *See also* Drama; Farce.

Comic relief, 343, 374, 381, R107

Commas, R53
    in addresses, R53
    adjectives and, R53

Page numbers that appear in italics refer to biographical information.

ACKNOWLEDGMENTS

UNIT 1

Dutton Signet: Excerpt from *Beowulf* translated by Burton Raffel. Copyright © 1963, renewed © 1991 by Burton Raffel. Used by permission of Dutton Signet, a division of Penguin Group (USA) Inc.

New York Times: "Sweeping Aside 1,200 Years to Collaborate," by D. J. R. Bruckner from the *New York Times,* July 22, 1997. Copyright © 1997 The New York Times Co. All rights reserved. Used by permission and protected by the Copyright Laws of the United States. The printing, copying, redistribution, or retransmission of the Material without express written permission is prohibited.

Farrar, Straus & Giroux: Excerpt from "Book 18," "Book 22," and "Book 24" of *The Iliad,* translated by Robert Fitzgerald. Translation copyright © 1974 by Robert Fitzgerald. Reprinted by permission of Farrar, Straus and Giroux, LLC.

Penguin Group (UK): Excerpt from *A History of the English Church and People* by Bede, translated with an introduction by Leo Sherley-Price, revised by R. E. Latham. (Penguin Classics 1955, revised edition 1968). Copyright © 1955, 1968 by Leo Sherley-Price. Reprinted by permission of Penguin Group (UK).

Yale University Press: "The Seafarer" and "The Wanderer," from *Poems and Prose from the Old English,* translated by Burton Raffel. Copyright © 1997 by Yale University Press. Used by permission of Yale University Press.

Rosanna White Norton: "The Wife's Lament," from *The Women Poets in English,* edited by Ann Stanford. Used by permission of Rosanna White Norton, trustee.

Penguin Group (UK): Excerpt from *The Book of Margery Kempe,* translated by B. A. Windeatt (Penguin Classics, 1985). Copyright © 1985 by B. A. Windeatt. Used with permission of Penguin Group (UK).

Boydell & Brewer: Excerpts from *The Pastons: A Family in the Wars of the Roses,* edited by Richard Barber (The Folio Society 1981; Boydell Press [Woodbridge, UK, and Rochester, NY] 1993). Used by permission of Boydell & Brewer Ltd.

Curtis Brown Group Ltd.: Excerpts from "The Prologue," "The Pardoner's Prologue," "The Pardoner's Tale," "The Wife of Bath's Prologue," and "The Wife of Bath's Tale," from *The Canterbury Tales* by Geoffrey Chaucer, translated by Nevill Coghill. Copyright © 1952 by Nevill Coghill. Used by permission of Curtis Brown Group Ltd. On behalf of the Estate of Nevill Coghill.

Alfred A. Knopf and Russell & Volkening: Excerpt from *A Distant Mirror* by Barbara W. Tuchman. Text copyright © 1978 by Barbara W. Tuchman. Used by permission of Alfred A. Knopf, a division of Random House, Inc. and Russell & Volkening as agents for the author.

National Geographic Society: "In the Footsteps of the Faithful" by Taras Grescoe from *National Geographic Traveler,* October 2003. Copyright © 2003 by National Geographic Society. Used by permission of National Geographic Society.

W. W. Norton & Company: Excerpt from *The Decameron* by Giovanni Boccaccio, translated by Mark Musa and Peter Bondanella. Copyright © 1982 by Mark Musa and Peter Bondanella. Used by permission of W. W. Norton & Company.

University of Chicago Press: Excerpts from *Sir Gawain and the Green Knight,* translated by John Gardner. Copyright © 1965 by the University of Chicago. Reprinted by permission of the University of Chicago Press.

Dutton Signet: "The Siege of Benwick" and "The Day of Destiny" from *Le Morte d'Arthur* by Sir Thomas Malory, translated by Keith Baines. Copyright © 1962 by Keith Baines, renewed © 1990 by Francesca Evans. Used by permission of Dutton Signet, a division of Penguin Group (USA) Inc.

Boydell & Brewer: Excerpt from the preface by William Caxton from *Le Morte d'Arthur,* parts seven and eight by Sir Thomas Malory, edited by D. S. Brewer. Copyright © 1968 by D. S. Brewer. Used by permission of Boydell & Brewer Ltd.

UNIT 2

Penguin Group (UK): Sonnet 90 and Sonnet 292 from *Canzoniere: Selected Poems* by Petrarch, translated by Anthony Mortimer (Penguin Classics 2002). Translation copyright © 2002 by Anthony Mortimer. Used by permission of Penguin Group (UK).

Julie Traves: Excerpt from "Out, damn slander, out" by Julie Traves, from *The Globe and Mail,* May 7, 2005. Copyright © 2005 by Julie Traves. Used by permission of the author.

New Republic: Excerpt from "Bloody, Bold and Resolute" by Robert Hatch, from the *New Republic,* January 15, 1951. Copyright © 1951 by the New Republic. Used by permission of the New Republic.

Yale University Press: Excerpt from *Utopia* by St. Thomas More, edited with introduction and notes by Edward Surtz, S. J. Copyright © 1964 by Yale University Press. Used by permission of Yale University Press.

Oxford University Press: Excerpt from *The Prince* by Niccolo Machiavelli, translated by Luigi Ricci. Copyright © 2005 by Luigi Ricci. Used by Permission of Oxford University Press.

UNIT 3

University of California Press: Excerpts from *Diary of Samuel Pepys,* edited by Robert Latham and William Matthews. Copyright © 1972–1986 by The Master, Fellows and Scholars of Magdalen College, Cambridge, Robert Latham, and the Executors of William Matthews. Used by permission of the University of California Press, Berkeley, California.

The Associated Press: Excerpt from "Madness of King George Tied to Arsenic" by Emma Ross, from the *Associated Press,* November 3, 2006. Copyright © 2006 by the Associated Press. Used by permission of the Associated Press.

UNIT 4

Oxford University Press: "To a Mouse," and "To a Louse," from *The Poems and Songs of Robert Burns* by Robert Burns, edited by James Kinsley. Copyright © 1968 by Oxford University Press. Used by permission of Oxford University Press.

Citadel Press/Kensington Publishing Corp.: "The Lorelei" by Heinrich Heine, from *The Poetry and Prose of Heinrich Heine,* translated by Aaron Kramer. Copyright © 1948 by the Citadel Press. Used by permission of Citadel Press/Kensington Publishing Corp. (www. kensingtonbooks.com). All rights reserved.

Harvard University Press: Excerpt from "The Ancient Mariner," from *The Romantic Generation* by Cecil Maurice Bowra, published by Harvard University Press. Copyright © 1949 by the President and Fellows of Harvard College. Copyright © renewed by The Estates Bursar, the executor of Cecil Maurice Brown. Reprinted by permission of the publisher.

"Ode to a Nightingale," from *The Poems of John Keats,* edited by Jack Stillinger, pp. 279–281, Cambridge, Mass: The Belknap Press of Harvard University Press. Copyright © 1978, 1982 by the President and Fellows of Harvard College. Reprinted by permission of the publisher.

UNIT 5

Penguin Group (UK): "The Darling," from *Lady with Lapdog and Other Stories* by Anton Chekhov, translated by David Magarshack (Penguin Classics, 1964). Copyright © 1964 by David Magarshack. Reprinted by permission of Penguin Group (UK).

New York Times: "Good News About Poverty" by David Brooks, the *New York Times,* November 27, 2004. Copyright © 2004 by The New York Times Co. All rights reserved. Used by permission and protected by the Copyright Laws of the United States. The printing, copying, redistribution, or retransmission of the Material without express written permission is prohibited.

"White Collar Blues" by Bob Herbert from the *New York Times,* December 29, 2003. Copyright © 2003 by The New York Times Co. All rights reserved. Used by permission and protected by the Copyright Laws of the United States. The printing, copying, redistribution, or retransmission of the Material without express written permission is prohibited.

Henry Holt and Company: "To An Athlete Dying Young" and "When I Was One-and-Twenty," from *The Collected Poems of A. E. Housman* by A. E. Housman. Copyright © 1939, 1940 by Henry Holt and Co., Inc. Copyright © 1967 by Robert E. Symons. Reprinted by permission of Henry Holt and Company, LLC.

UNIT 6

Houghton Mifflin Harcourt and Faber and Faber Limited: "The Hollow Men" from *Collected Poems 1909–1962* by T. S. Eliot. Copyright © 1936 by Harcourt Brace & Company, copyright © 1964, 1963 by T. S. Eliot. Reprinted by permission of Houghton Mifflin Harcourt Publishing Company and Faber and Faber Limited.

"The Naming of Cats" from *Old Possum's Book of Practical Cats* by T. S. Eliot. Copyright © 1939 by T. S. Eliot and renewed 1967 © by Esme Valerie Eliot. Reprinted by permission of Houghton Mifflin Harcourt Publishing Company and Faber and Faber Limited.

Alfred A. Knopf: "A Cup of Tea," from *The Short Stories of Katherine Mansfield* by Katherine Mansfield. Copyright © 1937, renewed 1965 by Alfred A. Knopf, a division of Random House, Inc. Used by permission of Alfred A. Knopf, a division of Random House, Inc.

Houghton Mifflin Harcourt and Random House Group: "The Duchess and the Jeweller," by Virginia Woolf, from *The Complete Shorter Fiction of Virginia Woolf* by Susan Dick. Copyright © 1985 by Quentin Bell and Angelica Garnett. Reprinted by permission of Houghton Mifflin Harcourt Publishing Company and the Random House Group Ltd.

The Provost and Scholars of King's College, Cambridge and The Society of Authors: Excerpt from *Virginia Woolf* by E. M. Forster. Reprinted by permission of the Provost and Scholars of King's College, Cambridge and the Society of Authors as the Representatives of the Estate of E. M. Forster.

Pollinger Limited: "The Rocking-Horse Winner" from *The Complete Stories of D. H. Lawrence* by D. H. Lawrence. Copyright © 1933 by the Estate of D. H. Lawrence, renewed © 1961 by Angelo Ravagli and C. M. Weekley, Executors of the Estate of Frieda Lawrence Ravagli. Reproduced by permission of Pollinger Limited and the Estate of Frieda Lawrence Ravagli.

Random House and The Wylie Agency: "Musée des Beaux Arts" and "The Unknown Citizen," from *Collected Poems* by W. H. Auden. Copyright © 1940 and renewed © 1968 by W. H. Auden. Copyright © 1976, 1991 by the Estate of W. H. Auden. Used by permission of Random House, Inc. and The Wylie Agency.

New Directions Publishing Corporation and David Higham Associates: "Do Not Go Gentle into That Good Night" from *The Poems of Dylan Thomas* by Dylan Thomas. Copyright © 1952 by Dylan Thomas. Reprinted by permission of New Directions Publishing Corporation and David Higham Associates.

"Fern Hill," from *The Poems of Dylan Thomas* by Dylan Thomas. Copyright © 1945 by the Trustees for the Copyrights of Dylan Thomas. Reprinted by permission of New Directions Publishing Corporation and David Higham Associates.

Scribner: "Sailing to Byzantium" from *The Collected Works of W. B. Yeats, Volume 1: The Poems, Revised*, edited by Richard J. Finneran. Copyright © 1928 by The Macmillan Company, renewed © 1956 by Georgie Yeats. Reprinted with the permission of Scribner, a Division of Simon & Schuster, Inc. All rights reserved.

"The Second Coming" *The Collected Works of W. B. Yeats, Volume 1: The Poems, Revised*, edited by Richard J. Finneran. Copyright © 1924 by The Macmillan Company, renewed © 1952 by Bertha Georgie Yeats. Reprinted with the permission of Scribner, a Division of Simon & Schuster, Inc. All rights reserved.

Washington Post: "For Men of Seaside Village, Lonely and Unfamiliar Roles" by Ellen Nakashimai from the *Washington Post,* January 25, 2005. Copyright © 2005 by the Washington Post. Used with permission and protected by the Copyright Laws of the United States. The printing, copying, redistribution, or retransmission of the Material without express permission is prohibited.

Curtis Brown Group: "The Demon Lover" by Elizabeth Bowen from *The Collected Stories of Elizabeth Bowen*. Copyright © 1945 by Elizabeth Bowen. Reproduced with permission of Curtis Brown Group Ltd., London, on behalf of the Estate of Elizabeth Bowen.

Viking Penguin and Barbara Levy Literary Agency: "Dreamers," from *Collected Poems of Siegfried Sassoon* by Siegfried Sassoon. Copyright © 1918, 1920 by E. P. Dutton. Copyright © 1936, 1947, 1948 by Siegfried Sassoon. Used by permission of Viking Penguin, a division of Penguin Group (USA) Inc. and Barbara Levy Litereary Agency.

Houghton Mifflin Harcourt and the Estate of the Late Sonia Brownell Orwell and Secker & Warburg Ltd.: "Shooting an Elephant" from *Shooting an Elephant and Other Essays* by George Orwell. Copyright © 1950 by Sonia Brownell Orwell and renewed © 1978 by Sonia Pitt-Rivers. Reprinted by permission of Houghton Mifflin Harcourt Publishing Company and Bill Hamilton as the Literary Executor of the Estate of the Late Sonia Brownell Orwell and Secker & Warburg Ltd.

Excerpt from *1984* by George Orwell. Copyright © 1949 by George Orwell and renewed © 1977 by Sonia Brownell Orwell. Reprinted by permission of Houghton Mifflin Harcourt Publishing Company and Bill Hamilton as the Literary Executor of the Estate of the Late Sonia Brownell Orwell and Secker & Warburg Ltd.

Georges Borchardt: Excerpt from "Words and Behavior" from *Collected Essays* by Aldous Huxley. Copyright © 1923, 1925, 1926, 1928, 1929, 1930, 1931, 1934, 1937, 1941, 1946, 1949, 1950, 1951, 1952, 1953, 1954, 1955, 1956, 1957, 1958, 1959 by Aldous Huxley. Reprinted by permission of Georges Borchardt, Inc., for the Estate of Aldous Huxley.

Hill and Wang: Excerpt from *Night* by Elie Wiesel, translated by Marion Wiesel. Copyright © 2006 by Marion Wiesel. Reprinted by permission of Hill and Wang, a division of Farrar, Straus and Giroux, LLC.

Curtis Brown, London: "Be Ye Men of Valour," from *Blood, Toil, Tears and Sweat* by Winston Churchill. Copyright © the Estate of Sir Winston S. Churchill. Reproduced with permission of Curtis Brown Ltd., London, on behalf of the Estate of Sir Winston S. Churchill.

Farrar, Straus & Giroux and Faber and Faber Limited: "Digging," from *Poems 1965–1975* by Seamus Heaney. Copyright © 1980 by Seamus Heaney. Reprinted by permission of Farrar, Straus & Giroux, LLC, and Faber and Faber Limited.

"The Horses," from *The Hawk in the Rain* by Ted Hughes. Copyright © 1956, 1957 by Ted Hughes. Reprinted by permission of Farrar, Straus & Giroux, LLC, Faber and Faber Limited on behalf of the Estate of Ted Hughes.

New Directions Publishing Corporation and the Estate of James MacGibbon: "The Frog Prince" and "Not Waving but Drowning," from *Collected Poems of Stevie Smith* by Stevie Smith. Copyright © 1972 by Stevie Smith. Reprinted by permission of New Directions Publishing Corporation and the Estate of James MacGibbon.

Grove/Atlantic: Excerpt from *Waiting for Godot* by Samuel Beckett. Copyright © 1954 by Grove Press, Inc. renewed © 1982 by Samuel Beckett. Reprinted by permission of Grove/Atlantic, Inc.

Viking Penguin and Johnson & Alcock: "The Distant Past," from *Angels at the Ritz and Other Stories* by William Trevor. Copyright © 1975 by William Trevor. Spelling has been Americanized. Used by permission of Viking Penguin, a division of Penguin Group (USA) Inc. and Johnson & Alcock Ltd.

Melanie Jackson Agency: "Telephone Conversation," by Wole Soyinka. Copyright © 1962, 1990 by Wole Soyinka. Reprinted with permission of the Melanie Jackson Agency, LLC.

Pearson Education: Excerpt from *Things Fall Apart* by Chinua Achebe. Copyright © 1959 by Chinua Achebe. Reprinted with permission of Pearson Education.

Russell & Volkening: "Six Feet of the Country" by Nadine Gordimer from *Six Feet of the Country and Other Stories*. Copyright © 1952, 1956, 1957, 1959, 1960, 1961, 1964, 1965, 1968, 1969, 1971, 1975 by Nadine Gordimer. Reprinted by permission of Russell & Volkening as agents for the author.

DK Publishing: Excerpt from *No More Strangers Now: Young Voices from a New South Africa,* by Tim McKee. Text copyright © 1998 by Timothy Saunders McKee. All rights reserved. Reprinted by permission of DK Publishing.

Rogers, Coleridge and White Ltd.: "A Devoted Son" by Anita Desai from *Games at Twilight and Other Stories.* Copyright © 1978 by Anita Desai. Reproduced by permission of the author c/o Rogers, Coleridge and White Ltd.

The Vera Brittain Trust: Excerpt from *Testament of Youth* by Vera Brittain. Copyright © 1970. Reproduced by the permission of Mark Bostridge and Timothy Brittain-Catlin, literary executors of the Estate of Vera Brittain.

Dutton and Aitken Alexander Associates: Excerpt from *The Ghost Road* by Pat Barker. Copyright © 1995 by Pat Barker. Used by permission of Dutton, a division of Penguin Group (USA) Inc. and Aitken Alexander Associates Ltd.

UNIT 7

New York Times: Excerpt from "Book of the Times" by Orville Prescott from the *New York Times,* June 13, 1949. Copyright © 1949 The New York Times. All rights reserved. Used by permission and protected by the Copyright Laws of the United States. The printing, copying, redistribution, or retransmission of the Material without express written permission is prohibited.

STUDENT RESOURCE BOOK

Agencia Literaria Carmen Balcalles S.A.: Excerpt from "Writing as an Act of Hope" by Isabel Allende. Copyright © 1989 by Isabel Allende. Used by permission of Agencia Literaria Carmen Balcalles, S.A.

Dutton Signet: Excerpt from *Beowulf* translated by Burton Raffel. Copyright © 1963, renewed © 1991 by Burton Raffel. Used by permission of Dutton Signet, a division of Penguin Group (USA) Inc.

Random House and The Wylie Agency: "Musée des Beaux Arts" from *Collected Poems* by W. H. Auden. Copyright © 1940 and renewed © 1968 by W. H. Auden. Used by permission of Random House, Inc. and The Wylie Agency.

Curtis Brown Group: "The Demon Lover" by Elizabeth Bowen from *The Collected Stories of Elizabeth Bowen.* Copyright © 1945 by Elizabeth Bowen. Reproduced with permission of Curtis Brown Group Ltd., London, on behalf of the Estate of Elizabeth Bowen.

Farrar, Straus & Giroux and Faber and Faber Limited: "Digging," from *Poems 1965–1975* by Seamus Heaney. Copyright © 1980 by Seamus Heaney. Reprinted by permission of Farrar, Straus & Giroux, LLC, and Faber and Faber Limited.

New Directions Publishing Corporation and David Higham Associates: "Do Not Go Gentle into That Good Night" from *The Poems of Dylan Thomas* by Dylan Thomas. Copyright © 1952 by Dylan Thomas. Reprinted by permission of New Directions Publishing Corporation and David Higham Associates.

New Directions Publishing Corporation and the Estate of James MacGibbon: "The Frog Prince" from *Collected Poems of Stevie Smith* by Stevie Smith. Copyright © 1972 by Stevie Smith. Reprinted by permission of New Directions Publishing Corporation and the Estate of James MacGibbon.

Farrar, Straus & Giroux and Faber and Faber Limited: "The Horses," from *The Hawk in the Rain* by Ted Hughes. Copyright © 1956, 1957 by Ted Hughes. Reprinted by permission of Farrar, Staus, & Giroux and Faber and Faber Limited on behalf of the Estate of Ted Hughes.

Houghton Mifflin Harcourt and Random House Group: "The Duchess and the Jeweller," by Virginia Woolf, from *The Complete Shorter Fiction of Virginia Woolf* by Susan Dick. Copyright © 1985 by Quentin Bell and Angelica Garnett. Reprinted by permission of Houghton Mifflin Harcourt Publishing Company and the Random House Group Ltd.

CONSULTANTS

Janet Allen © Duane McCubrey; *Arthur Applebee* © Mark Schmidt; *Kylene Beers* © Sam Dudgeon/Houghton Mifflin Harcourt; *Jim Burke* © Bruce Forrester; *Douglas Carnine* © Houghton Mifflin Harcourt; *Carol Jago* © Maggie's Photography, Pacific Palisades, CA; *Yvette Jackson* © Howard Gollub; *Robert Jimenez* © Tamra Stallings; *Judith Langer* © Mark Schmidt; *Robert Marzano* © Robert J. Marzano; *Donna Ogle* © Houghton Mifflin Harcourt; *Carol Booth Olson* © Dawson & Associates Photography; *Carol Tomlinson* © Gitchell's Studio; *May Lou McClosky* © Michael Romeo; *Lydia Stack* © Monica Ani; *William McBride* © William McBride; *David Considine* © Bill Caldwell; *Larkin Pauluzzi* © Gabriel Pauluzzi; *Lisa Scheffler* © Steven Scheffler.

TABLE OF CONTENTS

FM9 © Getty Images; **FM12** *left* © Bettmann/Corbis; *right* © Hideo Kurihara/Alamy Images; **FM14** © PunchStock; **FM15** *left* The Granger Collection, New York; *right* Detail of *The Family of Henry VIII: An Allegory of the Tudor Succession* (1570–1575), Lucas de Heere. Oil on panel. © National Museum and Gallery of Wales, Cardiff/Bridgeman Art Library; **FM18** © PunchStock; **FM19** *left, Mary Godwin, née Wollstonecraft,* John Opie. Oil on canvas, 76.8 cm x 64.1 cm. Inv. 1237. Photo by Jochen Remmer. National Portrait Gallery, London. © Bildarchiv Preussischer Kulturbesitz/Art Resource, New York; *right* Detail of *The Restoration,1660 Charles II Lands at Dover* (1903), Charles M. Padday. From *The Boy's Own Paper.* © Mary Evans Picture Library; **FM21** © PunchStock; **FM22** *left, John Keats* (1845), Joseph Severn. The Granger Collection, New York; *right* The Granger Collection, New York; **FM24** © PunchStock; **FM25** *left* © Bettmann/Corbis; *right* Detail of *The Railway Station* (1862), William Powell Frith. Oil on canvas, 116.7 cm x 256.4 cm. © Royal Holloway and Bedford New College, Surrey, United Kingdom/Bridgeman Art Library; **FM27** © PunchStock; **FM28** *left* © Hulton Archive/Getty Images; *right* Detail of *Western Hills* (1938–1941), Graham Sutherland. Oil on canvas, 55.5 cm x 90.5 cm. Scottish National Gallery of Modern Art, Edinburgh. © The Estate of Graham Sutherland. Photo © Bridgeman Art Library; **FM31** © PunchStock; **FM32** *left* The Granger Collection, New York; *right* © Digital Vision Photography/Veer; *inset right* © Columbia/The Kobal Collection.

STUDENT GUIDE TO ACADEMIC SUCCESS

FM39 © Age Fotostock America, Inc.; **FM40** Maggie's Photography, Pacific Palisades, CA; **FM59** © Buena Vista Pictures/Photofest.

INTRODUCTORY UNIT

Verso *top* © Corbis; *center* © 2004 Pennsylvania Shakespeare Festival at DeSales University. Pictures: Carolyn Swift as Lady MacBeth and Anderson Matthews as Macbeth. Photo by Lee Butz; *bottom* The Granger Collection, New York; **1** *top left* Detail of *Choosing* (1864), George Frederic Watts. Oil on strawboard, 18 5/8" x 14". © National Portrait Gallery, London; *top right* Mandore. Signed and dated 1610. Pearwood. Height 42 cm. Paris. © Victoria & Albert Museum, London/Art Resource, New York; *top right background* © Randall Fung/Corbis; *bottom* © Patrick Sheandell/Getty Images; **2** *left* Detail of *Elizabeth I,* Armada portrait (1588), English school. Oil on panel, 110.5 cm x 127 cm.© Bridgeman Art Library; *right* Early, hand-made Puzzle

Purse Valentine (about 1790). © Christie's Images, Ltd.; **3** *left* Detail of *Portrait of William Shakespeare* (about 1610), John Taylor. Oil on canvas. National Portrait Gallery, London. © Bridgeman Art Library; *right* © Ace Stock Limited/Alamy Images; **4** *left* Text from *Beowulf* (1000). Page of manuscript in old English. British Museum, London. © HIP/Art Resource, New York; *center left* Detail of *Morte d'Arthur* (1862), John Mulcaster Carrick. Private collection. © Fine Art Photographic Library, London/Art Resource, New York; *center right* The Granger Collection, New York; *right* Detail of *The Great Pit in Aldgate* (1865), Davenport after Cruikshank. © Science Museum Library/Science and Society Picture Library; **5** *left* The Granger Collection, New York; *center left* Detail of *Choosing* (1864), George Frederic Watts. Oil on strawboard, 18 5/8" x 14". © National Portrait Gallery, London; *center right* Detail of *Back Them Up!* (1939–1945). World War II poster. National Archives, London. © HIP/Art Resource, New York; *right* Detail of *Michael and Victoria Hastings* (2005), Paul Richards. Oil on canvas, 10" x 14". © Connaught Brown Gallery, London; **6** *top* Public Domain; *2nd from top* © Getty Images; *3rd from top* © Hulton Archive/Getty Images; *bottom* The Granger Collection, New York; **8** © London Stereoscopic Company/Getty Images; **14** *left* © David Deas/DK Stock/Getty Images; *center* © Herb Watson/Corbis.

UNIT 1

19 *top* © Bettmann/Corbis; *bottom* © Hideo Kurihara/Alamy Images; **20** *left foreground* Iron helmet covered with decorative panels of tinned bronze (early 600s). Anglo-Saxon. From Mound 1, Sutton Hoo, Suffolk, England. © British Museum/Art Resource, New York; *left background* © Image100/Getty Images; *right* Detail of *Holy Grail appears to the knights of the Round Table* (1927–1932), Morris and Company. 250 cm x 530 cm. Merton Abbey Tapestry Works after design of 1891 by Edward Burne-Jones. Münchner Stadtmuseum. © akg-images; **21** *left foreground* Detail of *The Oseberg Ship* (850), Viking. Viking Ship Museum, Bygdoy, Norway. © Werner Forman/Art Resource, New York; *left background* © Harald Sund/Getty Images; *right* Detail of *La Belle Dame Sans Merci,* Walter Crane. Private collection. © Bridgeman Art Library; **22** © Bruce Coleman, Inc./Alamy Images; **24** Scale model of the Battle of Hastings, fought in 1066. Tower of London, London. © Erich Lessing/Art Resource, New York; **25** © GeoNova LLC; **26** *Beowulf* © 1999, 2000, 2007 by Gareth Hinds. Reproduced by permission of the publisher Candlewick Press, Inc., Cambridge, Massachusetts; **29** *View of London with London Bridge in far distance,* Royal Manuscript. From *The Poems of Charles, Duke of Orleans.* © British Museum/Harper Collins Publishers/ The Art Archive; **30** *La Belle Dame Sans Merci,* Walter Crane. Private collection. © Bridgeman Art Library; **31** *Lydgate and the Canterbury Pilgrims leaving Canterbury* (1520). From John Lydgate's *Troy Book and Story of Thebes.* (Roy.18.D.II. Folio No: 148). British Library, London. © HIP/Art Resource, New York; **33** *Morte d'Arthur* (1862), John Mulcaster Carrick. Private collection. © Fine Art Photographic Library, London/Art Resource, New York; **34** *top* © David Reed/Corbis; *center left, Bayeaux Tapestry. Harold reports his mission in Normandy to Edward the Confessor.* Musée de la Tapisserie, Bayeaux, France. © Erich Lessing/ Art Resource, New York; *center right, Relief depicting ritual navigation* (800s). Viking. Stone carving. From Gotland Island, Sweden. Statens Historiska Museet, Stockholm. © Giraudon/Art Resource, New York; *bottom left* © Bettmann/Corbis; *bottom right* © Gianni Dagli Orti/

© Touchstone Pictures/Jerry Bruckheimer Films/The Kobal Collection; **268** *top* Courtesy The Everett Collection; *bottom* © Touchstone Pictures/Jerry Bruckheimer Films/The Kobal Collection; *background* © Darama/Corbis; **270** © Craig Aurness/Corbis; **281** © Michael Newman/PhotoEdit; **288–289** © PunchStock.

UNIT 2

291 *top* The Granger Collection, New York; *bottom* Detail of *The Family of Henry VIII: An Allegory of the Tudor Succession* (1570–1575), Lucas de Heere. Oil on panel. © National Museum and Gallery of Wales, Cardiff/Bridgeman Art Library; **292** *left* Detail of *Henry VIII of England,* Hans Holbein the Younger. Oil on oak, 28 cm x 20 cm. Fundacion Coleccion Thyssen-Bornemisza, Madrid, Spain. Photo © Erich Lessing/Art Resource, New York; *right* © Bozena Cannizzaro/Getty Images; **293** *left* Detail of *The Island of Utopia.* Illustration from a contemporary edition of *Utopia* by Thomas More. Kunstbibliothek, Staatliche Museen zu Berlin, Berlin, Germany. Photo by Dietmas Katz. © Bildarchiv Preussischer Kulturbesitz/Art Resource, New York; *right* Detail of *Ellen Terry as Lady Macbeth* (1885–1886), John Singer Sargent. Oil on canvas, 221 cm x 114.3 cm. Tate Gallery, London. © Tate Gallery, London/Art Resource, New York; **294** *Queen Elizabeth watching* The Merry Wives of Windsor *at the Globe Theatre,* David Scott. Oil on canvas. © Victoria & Albert Museum, London/Art Resource, New York; **296** *Elizabeth I,* Armada portrait (1588), English school. Oil on panel, 110.5 cm x 127 cm. © Bridgeman Art Library; **297** *Self-portrait,* Nicholas Hilliard. Victoria & Albert Museum, London. © Victoria & Albert Museum, London/Art Resource, New York; **298** Telescope, triangle, magnet compass and pendulum clock belonging to Galileo Galilei. Museo della Scienza, Florence, Italy. Photo © Erich Lessing/Art Resource, New York; **299** *Young Man Leaning Against a Tree Among Roses,* Nicholas Hilliard. Miniature. Victoria & Albert Museum, London. © Victoria & Albert Museum, London/Art Resource, New York; **301** © Corbis Sygma; **302** *The Island of Utopia.* Illustration from a contemporary edition of *Utopia* by Thomas More. Kunstbibliothek, Staatliche Museen zu Berlin, Berlin, Germany. Photo by Dietmas Katz. © Bildarchiv Preussischer Kulturbesitz/Art Resource, New York; **303** *Princess Elizabeth, Later Queen of Bohemia* (1606), Robert Peake the Elder. Oil on canvas, 60 3/4" x 31 1/4". Gift of Kate T. Davison, in memory of her husband, Henry Pomeroy Davison, 1951 (51.194.1). © Metropolitan Museum of Art, New York; **304** *Demon Leaving Heaven,* from 1800s book illustration for *Paradise Lost* by John Milton. © Corbis; **305** *Andrew Marvell Visiting His Friend John Milton,* George Henry Boughton. Oil on canvas, 69.5 cm x 166 cm. Private collection. © Bridgeman Art Library; **306** *top, Henry VIII of England,* Hans Holbein the Younger. Oil on oak, 28 cm x 20 cm. Fundacion Coleccion Thyssen-Bornemisza, Madrid, Spain. Photo © Erich Lessing/Art Resource, New York; *bottom, Caravels of Columbus,* Rafael Monleon y Torres. Museo de la Torre del Oro, Seville, Spain. © Dagli Orti/The Art Archive; **307** *top, Sir Francis Bacon* (1700s), Louis-Francois Roubillac. Marble. © Collection of the Earl of Pembroke, Wilton House, Wiltshire/Bridgeman Art Library; *center, Pilgrims Set Sail on the Mayflower* (1600s), English School. Black and white woodcut. Private Collection. © Bridgeman Art Library; *bottom left* © Asian Art & Archaeology, Inc./Corbis; *bottom right, Equestrian Portrait of Louis XIV* (1688), Charles Le Brun. Oil on canvas. Musée de la Chartreuse, Douai, France. Photo © Bridgeman Art Library; **308** *left* © Time & Life Pictures/Getty Images; *center* © Getty Images; *right* © Gregory Heisler/Time Inc./Time & Life Pictures/Getty Images; **309** *top* © Herald Ace/Nippon Herald/Greenwich/The Kobal

Collection; *bottom left* © Warner Brothers/Photofest; *bottom right* © Jeffrey Zaruba/Getty Images; **310** *Henry Percy, 9th Earl of Northumberland* (1595), Nicholas Hilliard. Bodycolor on vellum stuck to a playing card. © Fitzwilliam Museum, University of Cambridge, United Kingdom/Bridgeman Art Library; **312** *top* The Granger Collection, New York; *bottom, Sir Walter Raleigh* (1600), Plate 4 from *Lives of Eminent and Illustrious Englishmen, from Alfred the Great to the Latest Times.* V. 2. Shelfmark ID: 613.i 5-8/ British Library, London. © HIP/Art Resource, New York; *background* © Bruce Burkhardt/Corbis; **313** © Tetra Images/Alamy Images; **315** *Working Wool* (1500). French tapestry from the series of *Noblemen in the Country,* 220 cm x 319 cm. Loire valley workshops. Inv.: OA 9408. Photo by Jean Schormans. Louvre, Paris. © Réunion des Musées Nationaux/Art Resource, New York; **318** *foreground* The Granger Collection, New York; *background* © David Noton Photography/Alamy Images; **320–321** © Piotr Powietrzynski/Alamy Images; **324** *foreground, Portrait of William Shakespeare* (about 1610), John Taylor. Oil on canvas. National Portrait Gallery, London. © Bridgeman Art Library; *background* © Chris Cole/Getty Images; **325** © Corbis; **327** *The Goddess Diana,* Isaac Oliver. © Victoria & Albert Museum, London/Art Resource, New York; *frame* © Image Farm, Inc.; *background* © Getty Images; **331** *Portrait of an Unknown Lady* (1646), Cornelius Johnson. Oil on canvas, 794 cm x 641 cm. Bequeathed by George Salting, 1910. © Tate Gallery, London/Art Resource, New York; **334** *top, Petrarch* (1500s), Anonymous. Painting on panel. Blickling Property, Norfolk, Great Britain. © National Trust/Art Resource, New York; *bottom* © Franz-Marc Frei/Corbis; **337** *Head of a Woman* (1472), Leonardo da Vinci. Inv.: 428E. Gabinetto dei Disegni e delle Stampe, Uffizi, Florence. © Scala/Art Resource, New York; **339** © Doug Menuez/Age Fotostock America, Inc.; **340** *top* © 2004 Pennsylvania Shakespeare Festival at DeSales University. Pictures: Carolyn Swift as Lady MacBeth and Anderson Matthews as Macbeth. Photo by Lee Butz; *bottom, Macbeth,* Oregon Shakespeare Festival, 2002. BW Gonzalez as Lady Macbeth. Photo by Andree Lanthier; **341** *left* © Time Life Pictures/Getty Images; *right* ©Adrian Dennis/AFP/Getty Images; **342** © Robbie Jack/Corbis; **343** *top, center, bottom, Macbeth* at Derby Playhouse, September 2005. A Derby Playhouse production directed by Karen Louise Hebden. Photography © Keith Pattison; **346** *foreground, Portrait of William Shakespeare* (about 1610), John Taylor. Oil on canvas. National Portrait Gallery, London. © Bridgeman Art Library; *background* © By permission of Shakespeare Birthplace Trust's Museums Department; **347** © Eureka/Alamy Images; **348–349** © Patrick Sheandell/Getty Images; **351** *Macbeth* at Derby Playhouse, September 2005. A Derby Playhouse production directed by Karen Louise Hebden. Photography © Keith Pattison; **359** *top* Out of Joint Theatre Company Production, London. Photo © 2005 by Alistair Muir/The Daily Telegraph; *center* © Queen's Theatre March, 1999 © ArenaPal/Topham/The Image Works, Inc.; *bottom* Albery Theatre Production, London, 2002. Sean Bean as Macbeth, Samantha Bond as Lady Macbeth. © Manuel Harlan Photography; **364, 369** *Macbeth* at Derby Playhouse, September 2005. A Derby Playhouse production directed by Karen Louise Hebden. Photography © Keith Pattison; **378** *top* Peter O'Toole as Macbeth. © UPPA/Topham/The Image Works, Inc.; *center* Albery Theatre Production, November, 2002. Sean Bean as Macbeth. © Manuel Harlan Photography; *bottom* Photo courtesy of Shakespeare & Company, Lenox, Massachusetts. Photo by Kevin Sprague; **383, 390** Macbeth at Derby Playhouse, September 2005. A Derby Playhouse production directed by Karen Louise Hebden. Photography © Keith Pattison; **395** *top* © Wictor Sadowski; *center* © Dalhousie University

Department of Theatre. Halifax, Nova Scotia; *bottom* The Large Group Production Company at The Maidment Theatre, Auckland City, New Zealand. Photograph © Patrick Reynolds; **401** *Macbeth* at Derby Playhouse, September 2005. A Derby Playhouse production directed by Karen Louise Hebden. Photography © Keith Pattison; **405** *top* © Joe Cocks Studio Collection/Shakespeare Birthplace Trust; *center* © Angus McBean/Royal Shakespeare Company; *bottom* © Photo by Robert Clayton/Used by permission of Pioneer Theatre Company, Salt Lake City, Utah; **409, 419** *Macbeth* at Derby Playhouse, September 2005. A Derby Playhouse production directed by Karen Louise Hebden. Photography © Keith Pattison; **425** *top* © Sara Krulwich/New York Times Photo; *center* © TOHO/The Kobal Collection; *bottom left* © Bob Hallinen/Anchorage Daily News; **437** © Time Life Pictures/Getty Images; **438** *Macbeth, Banquo and the Three Witches.* English School. Woodcut. Private collection. © Bridgeman Art Library; **440** *top* Photograph for Life by Allan Grant © Time Inc.; *bottom* © Corbis; **443** Detail of *Ellen Terry as Lady Macbeth* (1885–1886), John Singer Sargent. Oil on canvas, 221 cm x 114.3 cm. Tate Gallery, London. © Tate Gallery, London/Art Resource, New York; **444** *top, bottom* The Granger Collection, New York; *background, View of Hampton Court Palace* (1710), Jan the Elder Griffier. © Tate Gallery, London/Art Resource, New York; **447** *Bishop Sherbourne with Henry VIII* (1800s), Louise Barnard. Chichester Cathedral, Sussex, United Kingdom. © Bridgeman Art Library; **448** *Portrait of Elizabeth I, Queen of England* (1500s), Anonymous. Oil on wood, 65.4 cm x 48.3 cm. Inv. 200. Photo by Jochen Remmer. National Portrait Gallery, London. © Bildarchiv Preussischer Kulturbesitz/Art Resource, New York; **452** *foreground, Portrait of Niccolo Machiavelli,* Santi di Tito. Palazzo Vecchio, Florence, Italy. Photo © Scala/Art Resource, New York; *background* Machiavelli's writing desk while in exile in Sant'Andrea. Casa del Machiavelli, Sant'Andrea in Percussina, Italy. Photo © Erich Lessing/Art Resource, New York; **453** © Jacques M. Chenet/Corbis; **455** *Cosimo I Medici,* Agnolo Bronzino. Galleria Sabauda, Turin, Italy. © Alinari/Art Resource, New York; **462** *foreground* The Granger Collection, New York; *background* © Jonathan Blair/Corbis; **463** © Photodisc Photography/ Veer; **465** © Sean Kernan/Getty Images; **467** © Bozena Cannizzaro/ Getty Images; **470** *foreground* © Mary Evans Picture Library; *background* © Jason Friend/Alamy Images; **471** © Christopher Wilhelm/Getty Images; **473** *Conversation of Women During the Absence of Their Husbands,* Abraham Bosse. ECL 846. Oil on wood. Photo by Gérard Blot. Musée de la Renaissance, Ecouen, France. © Réunion des Musées Nationaux/Art Resource, New York; **477** *Expulsion from Paradise* (1500s). Flemish tapestry from Brussels. Accademia, Florence. © Scala/ Art Resource, New York; **479** © Stephen Johnson/Getty Images; **480** *top* The Granger Collection, New York; *bottom* © Superstock, Inc./ SuperStock; **483** *The Month of October: Ploughing and Sowing,* Simon Bening. Miniature from The Book of Hours. Bodycolor on vellum. 14 cm x 9.5 cm. © Victoria & Albert Museum, London/Art Resource, New York; **485** *The Parable of the Prodigal Son,* section from the Mompelgarter Altarpiece, Matthias Gerung. Oil on panel, 41 cm x 28 cm. Kunsthistorisches Museum, Vienna. © Bridgeman Art Library; **488** *foreground* The Granger Collection, New York; *background* © Bruce Burkhardt/Corbis; **489** © Tim De Waele/Isosport/Corbis; **491** *Books of Account* (1600s), Franco-Flemish School. Galerie Berko, Brussels. © Fine Art Photographic Library, London/Art Resource, New York; **495** *Fall of the Rebel Angels* (1866), Gustave Doré. Engraving. © Chris Hellier/ Corbis; **499** *Now Night Her Course began . . .* (1882), Gustave Doré. Engraved. Engraving by Ligny. Plate no. 26, Book VI, line 406. ©

Central Saint Martin's College of Art and Design, London/Bridgeman Art Library; **504** *foreground* The Granger Collection, New York; *background* © Macduff Everton/Corbis; **505** © Foodpix/Jupiter Images; **507** *Vanity Fair* (1872), Arthur Hughes. Black ink and watercolor on board, 16.6 cm x 10.9 cm. © Delaware Art Museum, Wilmington, Delaware/Bridgeman Art Library; *background* © Artbeats; **509** *Plan of the road from the City of Destruction to the Celestial City* (1800s). Engraved expressly for Williams's Elegant Edition of The Pilgrim's Progress. Private collection. © Bridgeman Art Library; **513** *A Sower* (1480–1500), from a series of labors of the month. English stained glass roundel. Norwich, England. Victoria & Albert Museum, London. © Victoria & Albert Museum, London/Art Resource, New York; **514** *Portrait of John Donne* (1595), Anonymous. Private collection. Photo © Bridgeman Art Library; **516** *foreground* The Granger Collection, New York; *background, St. Paul's, The Thames, The Bear Garden and The Globe Theatres.* Detail from *Londinium Florentissima Britanniae Urbs,* 1616, Claes Jansz Visscher. Engraving on paper. Private collection. © Snark/Art Resource, New York; **517** © John Kelly/Getty Images; **519** *Silent Persuasion* (1860), Hugues Merle. Oil on canvas, 65.4 cm x 42.5 cm. © Sotheby's/akg-images; **524** *foreground* © Time & Life Images/Getty Images; *background* © Image Farm/Jupiterimages Corporation/Royalty-Free; **525** © Kelly-Mooney Photography/Corbis; **527** *Portrait of Master Bunbury* (1780), Sir Joshua Reynolds. Oil on canvas, 30 1/8" x 25 1/8". The John Howard McFadden Collection, 1928. © The Philadelphia Museum of Art/Art Resource, New York; **528** *Portrait of Lady Brownlow* (1600s), William Wissing. Oil on canvas, 127 cm x 103.2 cm. Private collection. © Bridgeman Art Library; **530** *top, center, bottom* The Granger Collection, New York; *background* © Index Stock Imagery/ Jupiterimages Corporation; **533** *Lovers in a Landscape,* Peter Lely. Musée des Beaux-Arts, Valenciennes, France. © Erich Lessing/Art Resource, New York; **537** © Ryoichi Utsumi/Getty Images; **538** © Joseph Sohm/ ChromoSohm Inc./Corbis; **549** © Age Fotostock America, Inc.; **556–557** © PunchStock.

UNIT 3

559 *top, Mary Godwin, née Wollstonecraft,* John Opie. Oil on canvas, 76.8 cm x 64.1 cm. Inv. 1237. Photo by Jochen Remmer. National Portrait Gallery, London. © Bildarchiv Preussischer Kulturbesitz/Art Resource, New York; *bottom* Detail of *The Restoration, 1660 Charles II Lands at Dover* (1903), Charles M. Padday. From *The Boy's Own Paper.* © Mary Evans Picture Library; **560** *left* Detail of *Gin Lane* (1700s), William Hogarth. Engraving. © Art Resource, New York; *right* © Science Museum/Science and Society Picture Library; **561** *left* The Granger Collection, New York; *right* Detail of *A Girl Reading a Letter by Candlelight with a Young Man Peering over her Shoulder* (1760), Joseph Wright of Derby. Oil on canvas, 88.9 cm x 69.8 cm. Private collection. © Bridgeman Art Library; **562** *Arthur Holdsworth Conversing with Thomas Taylor and Captain Stancombe by the River Dart* (1757), Arthur Devis. Oil on canvas, 50 1/4" x 40 1/4". Paul Mellon Collection. © 2006 Board of Trustees, National Gallery of Art, Washington, D.C.; **564** The Granger Collection, New York; **565** © Science Museum/Science and Society Picture Library; **566** *Coffee House* (1668), unknown artist. © Eileen Tweedy/British Museum/The Art Archive; **567** © Historical Picture Archive/Corbis; **569** *Gulliver Exhibited to the Brobingnag Farmer,* Richard Redgrave. Oil on canvas, 25" x 30". Victoria & Albert Museum, London. © Victoria & Albert Museum, London/Art Resource, New York; **570** *Fanny Burney* (1784), Edward Francis Burney. The Granger Collection, New York; **571** *Shortly After the Wedding,* William Hogarth.

From *Marriage a la mode,* a series of six satyrical paintings. National Gallery, London. © Erich Lessing/Art Resource, New York; **572** *top* Cover of *Robinson Crusoe* by Daniel Defoe, published 1908 with illustration by John Hassall. 2527d.303. © Bodleian Library, Oxford/The Art Archive; *center* © Burstein Collection/Corbis; *bottom* © age fotostock/SuperStock; **573** *top, Boswell and Johnson* (1786), Thomas Rowlandson. Caricature etching. The Granger Collection, New York; *center right* The Granger Collection, New York; *bottom left, Equestrian Portrait of Catherine the Great,* Vigilius Erichsen. Musée des Beaux-Arts, Chartres, France. © Giraudon/Art Resource, New York; *bottom right* © Stock Montage/Getty Images; **574** © James King-Holmes/Photo Researchers, Inc.; **575** *top* © 2006 Tab. All rights reserved/Caglecartoons.com; *bottom* © Peter Holmes/Age Fotostock; **576** The Granger Collection, New York; **578** *foreground* The Granger Collection, New York; *background* Shorthand notes of Samuel Pepys (August 22, 1595). Add.39822/f.9 © The British Library Board. All rights reserved; **579** © David Young-Wolff/PhotoEdit; **581** *Samuel Pepys* (1666), John Hayls. Oil on canvas. The Granger Collection, New York; **583** Detail of *Charles II's Cavalcade through the City of London, 22nd April, 1661* (1662), Dirck Stoop. Museum of London, London. © HIP/Art Resource, New York; **585** *Great Fire of London, 1666* (1800s). Wood engraving. The Granger Collection, New York; **590–591** *bottom* © Don and Liysa King/Getty Images; **590** *Daniel Defoe* (1700s), Sir Godfrey Kneller. © National Maritime Museum, London; **591** *top* Public Domain; **592** *foreground, Daniel Defoe* (1706), after Michiel van der Gucht. The Granger Collection, New York; *background* The Granger Collection, New York; **593** © Shepard Sherbell/Corbis; **595** *The Great Pit in Aldgate* (1865), Davenport after Cruikshank. © Science Museum Library/Science and Society Picture Library; **600** *foreground, Joseph Addison,* Sir Godfrey Kneller. The Granger Collection, New York; *background, Masked Ball* (1700s), Georg Balthasar Probst. Engraving. © Münchner Stadtmuseum, Munich/akg-images; **603** Detail of *The Strode Family at Tea* (1738), William Hogarth. Oil on canvas, 87 cm x 91.5 cm. Tate Gallery, London. © Tate Gallery, London/Art Resource, New York; **607** The Granger Collection, New York; **608** *Bob Blunt in Amaze, or Female Fashionable Follies.* Courtesy of the Lewis Walpole Library, Yale University; **610** *foreground, Alexander Pope* (1740), William Hoare. The Granger Collection, New York; *background, View of Twickenham from the Lawn at Strawberry Hill* (1791), Joseph Charles Barrow. Watercolor, 24.6 cm x 37.9 cm. Courtesy of the Lewis Walpole Library, Yale University; **613** *The Toilet* (1896), Aubrey Beardsley. Drawing for Alexander Pope's *The Rape of the Lock.* The Granger Collection; **616** *The Rape* (1896), Aubrey Beardsley. From *The Rape of the Lock* by Alexander Pope. Line block print. CT46089. Victoria & Albert Museum, London. © Victoria & Albert Museum, London/Art Resource, New York; **620** *foreground* The Granger Collection, New York; *background* © Michael St. Maur Sheil/Corbis; **621** © Jim Ruymen/Reuters/Corbis; **623** Detail of *Gin Lane* (1700s), William Hogarth. Engraving. © Art Resource, New York; **626–627** *The Idle 'Prentice Executed at Tyburn,* William Hogarth. Plate XI of *Industry and Idleness,* 1833. Engraving. © Guildhall Library, City of London/Bridgeman Art Library; **630** Detail of *Gin Lane* (1700s), William Hogarth. Engraving. © Art Resource, New York; **635** © Ewing Galloway/Index Stock Imagery/Jupiter Images; **637** Illustration from *Gulliver's Travels* (1800s) by Jonathan Swift. The Granger Collection, New York; **643** *Gulliver in Lilliput* (1800s), Coppin. Lithograph. © Mary Evans Picture Library; **648** Illustration from *Gulliver's Travels* (1800s) by Jonathan Swift. The Granger Collection, New York; **652** Illustration from *Gulliver's Travels* (1800s) by Jonathan Swift. The

Granger Collection, New York; **658** *top* © NBC/Courtesy The Everett Collection; *bottom* © Bailey Alex/Corbis Sygma; **660** *top, Portrait of Voltaire at Age 23* (1718), Nicholas de Largilliere. Private collection. Paris. © Giraudon/Art Resource, New York; *bottom, Voltaire in His Nightshirt,* Jean Huber. Oil on paper glued on cardboard. Musée Voltaire, Fernet-Voltaire, France. © Erich Lessing/Art Resource, New York; **661** © Serge Kozak/Alamy Images; **663** *The Stolen Kiss,* Jean-Honoré Fragonard. Hermitage, St. Petersburg, Russia. © Scala/Art Resource, New York; **669** *The Bench* (1753), William Hogarth. Canvas backed onto panel, 14.8 cm x 18.2 cm. © Fitzwilliam Museum, University of Cambridge, United Kingdom/Bridgeman Art Library; **670** *foreground, Portrait of Dr. Samuel Johnson* (1783), John Opie. Oil on canvas, 76.2 cm x 63.5 cm. © Private collection. Photo © Philip Mould Ltd, London/Bridgeman Art Library; *background, George III and Queen Charlotte Driving Through Deptford* (1785), Thomas Rowlandson. Watercolor over pen, inks, and pencil on original wash line mount, 42 cm x 70 cm. © Sotheby's/akg-images; **671** © Janis Christie/Getty Images; **673** © Le Segretain Pascal/Corbis Sygma; **675** The Granger Collection, New York; **676** Courtesy of the Manhattan Rare Book Company; **680** *foreground, James Boswell* (1785), Sir Joshua Reynolds. The Granger Collection, New York; *background* © Roy Rainford/Robert Harding; **681** © Paul Doyle/Alamy Images; **683** *Samuel Johnson* (1775), Sir Joshua Reynolds. Canvas. The Granger Collection, New York; **685** *Mitre Tavern* (1800s), unknown. Colored engraving. The Granger Collection, New York; **690** *foreground, Thomas Gray* (1748), John Giles Eccardt. The Granger Collection, New York; *background* © Homer Sykes/Alamy Images; **693** © David Hiser/Getty Images; **694** © Sylvia Sharnoff/Getty Images; **699** *Dr. Johnson in the Ante-Room of Lord Chesterfield Waiting for an Audience* (1748), Edward Matthew Ward. Tate Gallery, London. © Tate Gallery, London/Art Resource, New York; **700** *top, Aphra Behn* (1716), Robert White, after John Riley. Line engraving, 5 1/8" x 3 3/8". © National Portrait Gallery, London; *bottom* © Mary Evans Picture Library; *background* © The Hoberman Collection/Alamy Images; **701** © Steve Cole/Getty Images; **703** *Portrait Study,* Sir Joshua Reynolds. Kunsthistorisches Museum, Vienna, Austria. © Nimatallah/Art Resource, New York; **704** *Spring Flowers,* Arthur Hacker. Fine Art of Oakham, Leicestershire, Great Britain. © Fine Art Photographic Library, London/Art Resource, New York; **706** *foreground, Fanny Burney* (1784), Edward Francis Burney. The Granger Collection, New York; *background* © Florian Monheim/Bildarchiv/akg-images; **707** AP/Wide World Photos; **709** © Philip Craven/Robert Harding; **712** *King George III of England* (1771), Johann Zoffany. Oil on canvas. The Granger Collection, New York; *frame* © Getty Images; **715** © Eric Crichton/Corbis; **717** © Digital Vision/Getty Images; **718** *foreground, Mary Wollstonecraft (Mrs. William Godwin)* (1790–1791), John Opie. Tate Gallery, London, Great Britain. Photo © Tate Gallery, London/Art Resource, New York; *background, The Storming of the Bastille* (1789). Musée Carnavalet. © akg-images; **719** Library of Congress; **721** *A Girl Reading a Letter by Candlelight with a Young Man Peering over her Shoulder* (1760), Joseph Wright of Derby. Oil on canvas, 88.9 cm x 69.8 cm. Private collection. © Bridgeman Art Library; **725** *In the Artist's Studio* (1800s), Thomas Myles. Oil on canvas, 39.4 cm x 29.2 cm. Private collection. © Bridgeman Art Library; **729** © Tom Le Goff/Getty Images; **730** © Daryl Benson/Masterfile; **741** *left* © David Young-Wolff/PhotoEdit; **748–749** © PunchStock.

UNIT 4

751 *top, bottom* The Granger Collection, New York; **752** *left, Daybreak*

on the Goodwins, Thomas Rose Miles. Oil on canvas. Private collection. © Bridgeman Art Library; **752** *right* Detail of *The Confession, Sir Frank Dicksee.* Roy Miles Fine Paintings. © Bridgeman Art Library; **753** *left* Detail of *Butterfly on Daffodils,* Karen Armitage. Watercolor. Private collection. © Bridgeman Art Library; *right* Detail of *The Peterloo Massacre* (1819), George Cruikshank. Published October 1, 1819 by Richard Carlile. © Manchester Art Gallery, United Kingdom/Bridgeman Art Library; **754** *A Storm (Shipwreck)* (1823), Joseph Mallord William Turner. Watercolor on paper, 43.4 cm x 63.2 cm. © The Trustees of the British Museum. All rights reserved; **756** *Napoleon on Horseback at the St. Bernard Pass* (1801), Jacques-Louis David. © Archivo Iconografico, S.A./Corbis; **757** *Nat-Y-Glo Ironworks, Wales* (1788), George Robertson. The Granger Collection, New York; **758** *Manchester Heroes* (1819). From *The Peterloo Massacres of 1819,* published by S.W. Forbes, London. British Museum, London. Photo © Bridgeman Art Library; **760** *left, The Queen of the Tournament* (1800s), Frank William Warwick Topham. Illustration for *Ivanhoe.* © Christie's Images/Corbis; **761** *Lake of Wyndermere* (1826), Joseph Mallord William Turner. From *Picturesque Views of England and Wales.* Color engraving. Private collection. © Bridgeman Art Library; **763** © American Zoetrope/TriStar Pictures. Photographer: Anne Marie Fox/Photofest; **764** *all* The Granger Collection, New York; **765** *top* The Granger Collection, New York; *center* Detail of *The Peterloo Massacre* (1819), George Cruikshank. Published October 1, 1819 by Richard Carlile. © Manchester Art Gallery, United Kingdom/Bridgeman Art Library; *bottom left, Hansel and Gretel in the Forest* (1880), Carl Offterdinger. Color lithograph. Private collection. © Bridgeman Art Library; *bottom right* Public Domain; **766** © Walt Disney/Courtesy The Everett Collection; **767** *top* © Miramax Films/Universal Pictures. Photographer: Laurie Sparham/Photofest; *bottom* AP/Wide World Photos; **768** *foreground, William Blake* (1807), Thomas Phillips. Oil on canvas. The Granger Collection, New York; *background, Infant Joy,* plate 23 from *Songs of Innocence and of Experience* (1789–1794), William Blake. Relief etching printed in dark brown with pen and ink and watercolor. © Yale Center for British Art, Paul Mellon Collection/Bridgeman Art Library; **771** *The Shepherd* from *Songs of Innocence* (1789), William Blake. Color printed relief etching with water color on paper, 7.6 cm x 7 cm. © Yale Center for British Art, Paul Mellon Fund, United States of America/Bridgeman Art Library; **775** *The Tyger:* plate 43 from *Songs of Innocence and of Experience* (1802–1808), William Blake. Copy R, page 124–1950. Etching, ink and water color. © Fitzwilliam Museum, University of Cambridge, United Kingdom/Bridgeman Art Library; **778** *inset, The Ancient of Days,* William Blake. Etching with pen and ink, watercolor and bodycolor on paper, 23.2 cm x 17 cm. © Whitworth Art Gallery, The University of Manchester, United Kingdom/Bridgeman Art Library; *background* © MedioImages/Getty Images; **779** *The Chimney Sweeper* (1815–1826), William Blake. Plate 37 from *Songs of Innocence and of Experience* (Copy AA). Etching, ink and watercolor. P.125–1950.pt37. © Fitzwilliam Museum, University of Cambridge, United Kingdom/Bridgeman Art Library; **780** *top, The Fly* (1815–1826), William Blake. Plate 40 from *Songs of Innocence and of Experience* (copyAA). Etching, ink and watercolor. P.125–1950. pt40. © Fitzwilliam Museum, University of Cambridge, United Kingdom/Bridgeman Art Library; *bottom* © Will Crocker/Getty Images; **782** *foreground* The Granger Collection, New York; *background* © Mary Evans Picture Library/Alamy Images; **783** © Hal Beral/Corbis; **785** © Bob Eisdale/Getty Images; **787** © Tim Graham/Corbis; **790** *foreground, Heinrich Heine* (1831), Moritz Daniel Oppenheim. Oil on paper, laid down on canvas, 43 cm x 34 cm. Photo by Elke

Walford. Hamburger Kunsthalle, Hamburg, Germany. © Bildarchiv Preussischer Kulturbesitz/Art Resource, New York; *background* © age fotostock/SuperStock; **793** *Lorelei* (1872), Ferdinand Marternsteig. St. Goarshausen, Germany. © SuperStock; **795** *The Tyger:* plate 43 from *Songs of Innocence and of Experience* (1802–1808), William Blake. Copy R, page 124–1950. Etching, ink and water color. © Fitzwilliam Museum, University of Cambridge, United Kingdom/Bridgeman Art Library; **796** *On the Minnow Stream, Dorking, Surrey,* Charles Collins. Sutcliffe Gallery, Harrogate, North Yorkshire, Great Britain. © Fine Art Photographic Library, London/Art Resource, New York; **798** *foreground* The Granger Collection, New York; *background* © Ben Ramos/Alamy Images; **799** © Peter Cade/Getty Images; **801** *Inside of Tintern Abbey, Monmouthshire* (1794), Joseph Mallord William Turner. Pencil and water color on paper, 32.1 cm. x 25.1 cm. © British Museum, London/Bridgeman Art Library; **804** *Tintern Abbey* (1800s), Frederick Waters Watts. Private collection. © Bridgeman Art Library; **808** *Butterfly on Daffodils,* Karen Armitage. Watercolor. Private collection. © Bridgeman Art Library; **809** © Getty Images; **812** *foreground* The Granger Collection, New York; *background* © Yannick Le Gal/Getty Images; **813** © Gary Rhijnsburger/Masterfile; **815, 817, 821, 826, 832** Public Domain; **842** *Peking Imperial Garden* (1800s), Chinese artist. © Bibliotheque Nationale, Paris/The Art Archive; **845** © Joe Cornish/Getty Images; **846** *inset-center* The Granger Collection, New York; *oval inset* © National Portrait Gallery, London/SuperStock; *frame* © Corbis; **848** *foreground* The Granger Collection, New York; *background* © Detail Nottingham/Alamy Images; **849** © Richard Nowitz/Getty Images; **851** *The Lady Clare* (1900), John William Waterhouse. Oil on canvas. Private collection. © Bridgeman Art Library; **853** *The Confession,* Sir Frank Dicksee. Roy Miles Fine Paintings. © Bridgeman Art Library; **855** *Daybreak on the Goodwins,* Thomas Rose Miles. Oil on canvas. Private collection. © Bridgeman Art Library; **858–859** *bottom* © Universal/The Kobal Collection; **858** *top left* The Granger Collection, New York; **860** *foreground* The Granger Collection, New York; *background* © Matthew Jackson/Alamy Images; **861** © Don Farrall/Getty Images; **863** © Roger Wood/Corbis; **864** © Daryl Benson/Masterfile; **867** © David Tipling/Jupiterimages Corporation; **871** © Michael Nicholson/Corbis; **878** *foreground* The Granger Collection, New York; *background* The Granger Collection, New York; **881** *John Keats* (1845), Joseph Severn. Oil. The Granger Collection, New York; **883** *Autumn Leaves* (1856), Sir John Everett Millais. Oil on canvas, 104.3 cm x 74 cm. © Manchester Art Gallery, United Kingdom/Bridgeman Art Library; **887** *Sleeping Shepherd Morning* (1857), Samuel Palmer. © Fitzwilliam Museum, University of Cambridge, United Kingdom/Bridgeman Art Library; **891** © Bryan Allen/Corbis; **892** © Richard Sisk/Jupiter Images; **897** © Jason Hawkes/Getty Images; **908–909** © PunchStock.

UNIT 5

911 *top* © Bettmann/Corbis; *bottom* Detail of *The Railway Station* (1862), William Powell Frith. Oil on canvas, 116.7 cm x 256.4 cm. © Royal Holloway and Bedford New College, Surrey, United Kingdom/Bridgeman Art Library; **912** *left* © Ann Ronan Picture Library/HIP/The Image Works, Inc.; *right* © NMPFT/Science and Society Picture Library; **913** *left* Detail of *An Auburn Beauty,* Alexis Harlamoff. © Christie's Images/Corbis; *right* © NRM-Pictorial Collection/Science and Society Picture Library; **914** *Train at Shakespeare Cliff, Dover* (1850), George Childs. Watercolor. © NRM/Pictorial Collection/Science and Society Picture Library; **917** © NMPFT/Hulton Getty/Science and Society Picture Library; **918** © NMPFT/Science and Society

Picture Library; **919** *La Ghirlandata* (1893), Dante Gabriel Rossetti. Guildhall Art Gallery, London. © Erich Lessing/Art Resource, New York; **920** *left, Jack Harkaway's Schooldays* (about 1880). Published by Edwin J. Brett. Illustrations by B. Hemyng. 26 x 18 cm. 11411.i.17 © The British Library Board. All rights reserved; *right, Black Bess; or, The Knight of the Road* (1861). Published by E. Harrison. Cover illustration by Edward Viles. 26 cm x 17 cm. C140.a.15. © The British Library Board. All rights reserved; **921** © The Everett Collection; **922** *left* 'John Bull (LOQ.): Hands off, men; let the woman go' by Tom Merry for *Puck*, August 17, 1889, issue. London. Colindale, front page. By permission of The British Library; *right* © The British Library/Mary Evans Picture Library/The Image Works, Inc.; **923** Illustration for *Treasure Island* (1911), N. C. Wyeth. The Granger Collection, New York; **924** *top* Courtesy of Glasgow University Library, Department of Special Collections; *center, bottom right* The Granger Collection, New York; *bottom left* © Bettmann/Corbis; **925** *top left* © Bettmann/Corbis; *center, The Jameson Raid, Johannesburg, Transvaal, 1896*. English school. Oil on canvas. Private collection. © Bridgeman Art Library; *bottom* The Granger Collection, New York; **926** © Reuters/Corbis; **927** *top* © Laurence Monneret/Getty Images; *bottom* © Columbia/Courtesy The Everett Collection; **928** *foreground* © Bettmann/Corbis; *background* © Val Corbett/National Trust Photographic Library/The Image Works, Inc.; **931** *'I am Half Sick of Shadows' Said the Lady of Shallott* (1915), John William Waterhouse. Oil on canvas, 100.3 x 73.7 cm. © Art Gallery of Ontario, Toronto, Canada/Bridgeman Art Library; **936** *The Blind Beggar and His Granddaughter* (1700s), John Russell. Oil on canvas. © The Bowes Museum, Barnard Castle, County Durham, United Kingdom/Bridgeman Art Library; **939** *A Funeral Bearer* (1830s). © Museum of London; **941** *Lights in Harbour,* John Atkinson Grimshaw. The Scarborough Art Gallery, Scarborough, United Kingdom; **944** *foreground* © Bettmann/Corbis; *background* © Getty Images; **945** © David Muir/Masterfile; **947** Detail of *Choosing* (1864), George Frederic Watts. Oil on strawboard, 18 5/8" x 14". © National Portrait Gallery, London; **949** *Mary Ann, Wife of Leonard Collman* (1854), Alfred Stevens. Oil on canvas, 70.5 cm x 55.2 cm. Purchased 1900. Tate Gallery, London. © Tate Gallery, London/Art Resource, New York; **952** *top* © Bettmann/Corbis; *bottom* © Jon Jones/Sygma/Corbis; *background* © Digital Vision/Robert Harding; **955** Early, hand-made Puzzle Purse Valentine (about 1790). © Christie's Images, Ltd.; **957** © Patrick Ward/Corbis; **960–961** *background* © Joe Cornish/National Trust Photographic Library; **960** *center* © Bettmann/Corbis; **962** *foreground* The Granger Collection, New York; *background* © Jon Davison/Lonely Planet Images; **963** © Niall Benvie/Corbis; **964** © Altrendo Nature/Getty Images; **965** © Darrell Gulin/Getty Images; **967** Detail of *The Lady of Shalott* (1888), John William Waterhouse. © Tate Gallery, London/Art Resource, New York; **969** *top, 2nd from top, 2nd from bottom* The Granger Collection, New York; *center, bottom* © Bettmann/Corbis; **970** *left* © Richard Kluna/Corbis; *center* The Granger Collection, New York; *background* © Ashley Cooper/Corbis; **971** © Raymond Forbes/Age Fotostock; **973** *Ribbed and Paled in by Rocks Unscaleable* (1885), Peter Graham. Oil on paper and canvas, 158 cm long. Guildhall Art Gallery. © City of London; **977** *On the Shore,* Paul Henry. Oil on canvas, 60.5 cm x 51 cm. T30352. © Phillips, The International Fine Art Auctioneers, United Kingdom. © Bonhams, London/Bridgeman Art Library; **980** *The Runaway,* Henry Herbert La Thangue. Oil on canvas. Private collection. © Bridgeman Art Library; **984** *Driftwood* (1909), Winslow Homer. Oil on canvas, 24 1/2" x 28 1/2". Henry H. and Zoe Oliver Sherman Fund and other funds. 1993.564. © Museum of Fine Arts, Boston; **990** *Tintagel*

(1887), Arthur Ackland Hunt. Watercolor with gouache on paper, 47.6 cm x 31.1 cm. Private collection. © The Maas Gallery, London/Bridgeman Art Library; **994** *foreground* The Granger Collection, New York; *background* © Andy Marshall/Alamy Images; **995** AP/Wide World Photos; **997** *Newsboy with Papers from Aunt Louisa's Welcome Gift* by H. W. Petherick, 1860. © Mary Evans Picture Library; **1000** *Cat Looks Out of Window* from *Aunt Louisa's Welcome Gift* by H. W. Petherick, 1860. © Mary Evans Picture Library; **1004** *This Little Piggy Went* from *Songs for the Nursery,* 1818. Mary Evans Picture Library; **1010–1011** *background* © Mary Evans Picture Library/The Image Works, Inc.; **1010** *top* © Hulton Archive/Getty Images; **1012–1013** *background* © Mary Evans Picture Library/The Image Works, Inc.; **1012** *top* © Bettmann/Corbis; **1014** *foreground* © Getty Images; *background* © Sarah Leen/National Geographic Image Collection; **1017** *An Auburn Beauty,* Alexis Harlamoff. © Christie's Images/Corbis; **1020** *Portrait of Ilya Efimovich Repin* (1876), Ivan Nikolaevich Kramskoy. Oil on canvas, 102 cm x 70 cm. Tretyakov Gallery, Moscow. © Bridgeman Art Library; **1025** *Village Boy* (1890), N.P. Bogdanov-Belsky. © akg-images; **1029** The Granger Collection, New York; **1030** *top, bottom* The Granger Collection, New York; *background* © Todd Gipstein/Corbis; **1031** © Steven May/Alamy Images; **1033** *Hyde Park as it Will Be* (1840s), John Leech. Hand colored pen lithograph. Caricature. © NRM-Pictorial Collection/Science and Society Picture Library; **1037** © Getty Images; **1045** © The New York Times/Redux; *masthead* The New York Times Company; **1046** *graph info* World Bank (2004 data estimated); *masthead* The New York Times Company; **1047** © Fred Conrad/New York Times/Redux; **1048** U.S. Department of Labor, Burueau of Statistics; *masthead* The New York Times Company; **1050** © Ann Ronan Picture Library/HIP/The Image Works, Inc.; **1051** *left* The Granger Collection, New York; *right* © Ladi Kirn/Alamy Images; **1052** *top* Interior and exterior of warehouse shot courtesy BBC Worldwide Americas Inc.; *bottom* The Granger Collection, New York; *background* Science Museum Library; **1054** *foreground* The Granger Collection, New York; *background* © Mary Evans Picture Library/The Image Works, Inc.; **1055** © Dean Conger/Corbis; **1057** *Blue Moonlight over Yellow Sands* (1824), Joseph Mallord William Turner. Watercolor on paper, 26.8 cm x 37.7 cm. Bequeathed by the artist, 1856. Tate Gallery, London. © Tate Gallery, London/Art Resource, New York; **1060** *foreground* © Hulton-Deutsch Collection/Corbis; *background* © Joe Cornish/National Trust Photographic Library; **1061** © Eli Reed/Magnum Photos; **1063** © Bettmann/Corbis; **1066–1067** *background, Tea at Parliament* (1907), Yoshio Markino. From *The Colour of London/*Mary Evans Picture Library; **1066** *top* © Bettmann/Corbis; **1067** © 1977 Playbill, Inc.; **1068** *foreground* © Bettmann/Corbis; *background* © Mary Evans Picture Library/The Image Works, Inc.; **1069** *dictionary* © Houghton Mifflin Company; *inset text* © Bill Gallery/Stock Boston LLC; Photograph by Sharon Hoogstraten; **1071** *Song Thrush* (1884), Harry Bright. Watercolor on paper. Private collection. © Bridgeman Art Library; **1073** *Fox Terrier* (1800s), Arthur Wardle. Oil on canvas. Private collection. © Bridgeman Art Library; **1075** © Image Source/Superstock; **1076** © Daryl Benson/Masterfile; **1087** © Justin Horrocks/istockphoto. com; **1094–1095** © PunchStock.

UNIT 6

1097 *top* © Hulton Archive/Getty Images; *bottom, Western Hills* (1938–1941), Graham Sutherland. Oil on canvas, 55.5 cm x 90.5 cm. Scottish National Gallery of Modern Art, Edinburgh. © The Estate of Graham

Sutherland. Photo © Bridgeman Art Library; **1098** *left* Detail of *Bathers-Rescue* (1975), Sir Sidney Nolan. Oil on board, 132 cm x 100 cm. Private collection. © Bridgeman Art Library; *right* Detail of *Portrait* (1932), Francis Bacon. © 2008 The Estate of Francis Bacon/Artists Rights Society (ARS), New York/DACS, London; **1099** *left* Detail of *Solomon* (2005), Louise Ynclan. Oil on canvas. 90 cm x 90 cm; *right* © Hulton-Deutsch Collection/Corbis; **1100** © Derek Cattani/Corbis; **1102** © Corbis; **1103** © Reuters/Corbis; **1104** *The Highways of Empire* (early 1900s), L.M. Gill, for The Empire Marketing Board. E. 28-1928. © Victoria & Albert Museum, London/Art Resource, New York; **1105** *Mr. and Mrs. Clark and Percy* (1970–1971), David Hockney. Acrylic on canvas, 84” x 120”. Photo © Tate Gallery, London/Art Resource, New York. © David Hockney/The David Hockney No. 1 U.S. Trust; **1106** The Bloomsbury Group in a fake airplane. Tate Archives. © Tate Gallery, London/Art Resource, New York; **1107** *W. B. Yeats and the Irish Theatre* (1915), Edmund Dulac. Paint, watercolor, ink. Reproduced by permission of Hodder and Stoughton Limited. Photo courtesy of the National Gallery of Ireland, Dublin; **1109** © Ivan Kyncl/ArenaPal/Topfoto/The Image Works, Inc.; **1110** *top, Caricature,* Butterfield in *Courier*/Mary Evans Picture Library; *center left* © Swim Ink 2, LLC/Corbis; *center right* © Jim Ballard/Getty Images; *bottom* © Hulton-Deutsch Collection/Corbis; **1111** *top left* Cover of *Collected Poems* by Stevie Smith. © 1937, 1938, 1950, 1957, 1966, 1971, 1972 Stevie Smith. Cover drawing by author. Reprinted by permission of New Directions Publishing Corporation, New York; *top right* © David Levenson/Getty Images; *center* © Corbis Sygma; *bottom left* AP/Wide World Photos; *bottom right* © Scott Barbour/Getty Images; **1112** *left* © Time Life Pictures/Getty Images; *right* © David Vintiner/zefa/Corbis; **1113** *top left* Mario Testino/*Vogue* © 2006 Conde Nast Publications; *top center* © Reuters/Corbis; *top left* © Time & Life Pictures/Getty Images; *bottom* © Walt Disney Pictures/Walden Media/The Kobal Collection; **1114** *T. S. Eliot* (1949), Patrick Heron. Oil on canvas. The Granger Collection, New York. © 2007 Artists Rights Society (ARS), New York/DACS, London; **1116** *left* © Bettmann/Corbis; *background* © Altrendo Panoramic/Getty Images; **1117** © Stephan Agostini/AFP/Getty Images; **1126** *left* The Granger Collection, New York; *background* © Doug Pearson/Alamy Images; **1127** © Guy Ryecart/Getty Images; **1129** *Girl with Mirror* (1928), Walt Kuhn. Oil on canvas, 24” x 20 1/8”. Image courtesy of The Phillips Collection, Washington, D. C.; **1133** © Images.com/Corbis; **1135** *The Convalescent,* Gwen John. Oil on canvas, 40.9 cm x 33 cm. PD.24-1951. © Fitzwilliam Museum, University of Cambridge, United Kingdom/Bridgeman Art Library. © 2007 Artists Rights Society (ARS), New York/DACS, London; **1138** *left* The Granger Collection, New York; *background* © Angelo Hornak/Corbis; **1141** © Paul Seheult/Eye Ubiquitous/Corbis; **1143** © Time Life Pictures/Getty Images; **1146** © Corbis; **1148** The Granger Collection, New York; **1152** *left* © Bettmann/Corbis; *background* © Mike Goldwater/Alamy Images; **1153** © Don Farrell/Getty Images; **1155** *Mother and Child* (1903), William Rothenstein. Oil on canvas, 969 cm x 765 cm. Purchased 1988. Photo © Tate Gallery, London/Art Resource, New York. © Rothenstein Estate/Bridgeman Art Library, New York; **1159** *Portrait of Caspar Goodrich* (1887), John Singer Sargent. Oil on canvas. © Mr. and Mrs. C. Michael Kojaian. Image courtesy of Brooklyn Museum of Art; **1160–1161** *The Start,* Alfred James Munnings. © Christie's Images/Corbis; **1167** *Portrait of a Woman* (1935), Gerald Leslie Brockhurst. Oil on canvas, 51 cm x 41 cm. © Southampton City Art Gallery, Hampshire, United Kingdom/Bridgeman Art Library; **1172–1173** © Macduff Everton/Getty Images; **1172** The Granger Collection, New York; **1174**

top © Corbis; *bottom* © Carolyn Schaefer/Getty Images; **1177** *Landscape with the Fall of Icarus,* Pieter Brueghel the Elder. Musée d'Art Ancien, Musées Royaux des Beaux-Arts, Brussels, Belgium. Photo © Scala/Art Resource, New York; **1179** *Portrait* (1932), Francis Bacon. © 2008 The Estate of Francis Bacon/Artists Rights Society (ARS), New York/DACS, London; **1182** *left* © Getty Images; *background* © The Photolibrary Wales/Alamy Images; **1183** © Dan Lepp/Etsa/Corbis; **1184** © Brand X Pictures; **1185** *Head of Seedo I,* Leon Kossoff. Charcoal on paper, 78 cm x 56.5 cm. T33775. © Bridgeman Art Library; *frame* © Getty Images; **1186** © Getty Images; **1189** *Children's Games* (1560), Pieter Brueghel the Elder. Oil on oakwood, 188 cm x 161 cm. Kunsthistorisches Museum, Vienna © Erich Lessing/Art Resource, New York; **1190** *left* The Granger Collection, New York; *background* © Gareth McCormack/Alamy Images; **1191** © Hill Street Studios/Getty Images; **1193** Ships at Classis (early 500s). Copy of mosaic. Basilica of St. Apollinare Nuovo, Ravenna, Italy. The Granger Collection, New York; **1196** *Hommage* (1999), Rowan Gillespie. Bronze, 150 cm; **1198** *left* © Corbis; *background* © Corbis Sygma; **1201** *St. Patrick's Close, Dublin,* Walter Osborne. Oil on canvas, 69 cm x 51 cm. © National Gallery of Ireland; **1203** *Apple Blossom* (1899), Sir. George Clausen. Private collection. © Bridgeman Art Library; **1205** *Hastings Railway Station* (1889), Walter Osborne. Oil on canvas, 30.5 cm x 36.8 cm. The Taylor Gallery Ltd. © akg-images; **1210–1211** Sackville Street and McConnell Bridge, Dublin. About 1900. Period color photograph. © Adoc-photos/Art Resource, New York; **1210** *Portrait of James Joyce.* Black and white photograph. Private Collection. © Bridgeman Art Library; **1212** *left* © Irish Picture Library; *background* © Jean Guichard/Corbis; **1213** © Russell Underwood/Corbis; **1215** © Stapleton Collection/Corbis; **1218** *Off the Donegal Coast* (1922), Jack Butler Yeats. Oil on canvas, 60.5 cm x 90.7 cm. © Crawford Municipal Art Gallery, Cork, Ireland/Bridgeman Art Library. © 2007 Artists Rights Society (ARS), New York/DACS, London; **1221** *Silent Man* (1995), Andrew Gadd. Oil on canvas. Private collection. © Bridgeman Art Library; **1225** © Michael Robinson-Chavez/The Washington Post; **1226–1227** © Art Kowalsky/Alamy Images; **1226** © Bettmann/Corbis; **1227** Cover Illustration by Mark Braught. © McDougal Littell; **1228** *top* © Hulton-Deutsch/Corbis; *bottom* © Bettmann/Corbis; **1229** © Newmann/zefa/Corbis; **1231** © Graphistock/Jupiterimages Corporation; **1236** © Ron Roytar/Getty Images; **1239** © Slim Aarons/Getty Images; **1240** © Peter Turnley/Corbis; **1241** *top* The Granger Collection, New York; *bottom* © Bassouls Sophie/Corbis Sygma; **1242** *top, bottom* The Granger Collection, New York; *background* © Deplix/Alamy Images; **1243** © Robin Adshead; **1245** *Lieutenant A. P. F. Rhys Davids, DSO, MC,* Sir William Orpen. © Imperial War Museum, London, United Kingdom; **1247** *Over the Top,* John Nash. © Imperial War Museum, London/Bridgeman Art Library; **1250** *foreground* The Granger Collection, New York; *background* © James Gritz/Alamy; **1251** © LWA-Dann Tardif/Corbis; **1253** © Bettmann/Corbis; **1255** © Orwell Archive/University College, London Library Services, Special Collections; **1258** © Michael Masian Historic Photographs/Corbis; **1262–1263** *background* © Atlantic Releasing Corp./Photofest; **1262, 1263** The Granger Collection, New York; **1264** *foreground* © Bettmann/Corbis; *background* © Digital Vision/Getty Images; **1265** © Ryan McVay/Getty Images; **1267** *Together,* WWII Poster. Color lithograph. Private collection. © Bridgeman Art Library; **1271** © Topham/The Image Works, Inc.; **1274** *Your Talk May Kill Your Comrades* (1942), Abram Games. WWII Poster. The Granger Collection, New York; **1280** *foreground* © Owen Franken/Corbis; *background* © Gianni Giansanti/Sygma/Corbis; **1283** © Bar Am Collection/Magnum